West's Law School
Advisory Board

CASES AND MATERIALS ON

LEGISLATION

STATUTES AND THE CREATION
OF PUBLIC POLICY

Fourth Edition

By

William N. Eskridge, Jr.
John A. Garver Professor of Jurisprudence
Yale University

Philip P. Frickey
Alexander F. & May T. Morrison Professor of Law
University of California at Berkeley

Elizabeth Garrett
Sydney M. Irmas Professor of Public Interest Law, Legal Ethics,
Political Science, and Policy, Planning, and Development
University of Southern California Gould School of Law

AMERICAN CASEBOOK SERIES®

THOMSON
™
WEST

Mat #40536015

American Casebook Series and West Group are trademarks registered in the U.S. Patent and Trademark Office.

COPYRIGHT © 1988, 1995 WEST PUBLISHING CO.
© West, a Thomson business, 2001
© 2007 Thomson/West
  610 Opperman Drive
  St. Paul, MN 55123
  1–800–313–9378

ISBN: 978–0–314–17256–3

 TEXT IS PRINTED ON 10% POST CONSUMER RECYCLED PAPER

To Elizabeth.

WNE, Jr.

To Mary Ann, Alex, and Beth.

PPF

To Andrei.

EG

Preface

In preparing the fourth edition of this casebook, we have benefitted from numerous suggestions and comments. Michael Bosworth, Peter Strauss, and David Super gave us special assistance regarding this edition. Many others have contributed to our thoughts on revising the earlier editions of the casebook. We would single out T. Alexander Aleinikoff, James Brudney, Jim Chen, Dan Farber, Christine Desan, Norman Dorsen, Alan Feld, Michael Froomkin, Rick Hasen, Bruce Hay, Daniel Farber, Daniel Lowenstein, Nelson Lund, Jerry Mashaw, Peter Menell, Nate Persily, Richard Posner, Daniel Rodriguez, Stephen Ross, Peter Shane, Michael Seidman, David Shapiro, Thomas Stoddard, Peter Swire, Mark Tushnet, and Adrian Vermeule for particularly helpful insights. We welcome your comments and suggestions about this edition; we find that letters and e-mails from people using the casebook are tremendously helpful as we work on supplements and new editions.

We could not have completed this edition without outstanding support from our institutions. We thank the deans of our law schools — Harold Koh at Yale, Christopher Edley at Berkeley, Robert Rasmussen at USC — for generous financial support for this project. We have been fortunate to have the assistance of several outstanding research assistants: Darsana Srinivasan (Yale Class of 2007), Baolu Lan (Yale Class of 2009), Diana Rusk (Yale Class of 2009), Lindsay Eyler (Yale Class of 2009), David Snyder (Boalt Class of 2008), Daniel Schwartz (USC Class of 2009), Derek Lazzaro (USC Class of 2009), Jenny Wiegley (USC Class of 2008), Meegan Maczek (USC Class of 2008), and Brent Tubbs (USC Class of 2007).

We reserve our deepest thanks for our families and friends. Successful completion of a project such as this requires encouragement and understanding from those who share our lives; all three of us are fortunate that our families and friends have unlimited quantities of patience and good humor. We continue to be eternally grateful for their support.

William N. Eskridge, Jr.
New Haven, Connecticut

Philip P. Frickey
Berkeley, California

Elizabeth Garrett
Los Angeles, California

September 2007

Summary of Contents

PREFACE v

TABLE OF CASES xxi

Chapter 1. An Introduction to Legislation 1
Section 1. The Story of the Civil Rights Act of 1964 and the
    Procedures of Statute-Creation 2
Section 2. Descriptive and Normative Theories of Legislation 47
Section 3. Title VII: Interpretive Issues and Political Theories 82

Chapter 2. Representational Structures 123
Section 1. Electoral Structures and Equality Values 125
Section 2. Eligibility To Serve in the Legislature 196
Section 3. Structures of Campaign Finance 235

Chapter 3. Structures of Legislative Deliberation 299
Section 1. Regulating "Corrupt" Deliberation 301
Section 2. Lobbying 318
Section 3. Rules Facilitating Legislative Deliberation 356

Chapter 4. Due Process of Lawmaking 409
Section 1. Structural Due Process 411
Section 2. The Federal Congressional Budget Process 446
Section 3. Other Congressional Structures 508

**Chapter 5. Direct Democracy as an Alternative
    to Republican Government** 523
Section 1. A Brief Overview of Direct Democracy 523
Section 2. Popular Lawmaking and the Constitution 535
Section 3. Recall 574

**Chapter 6. Statutes as a Source of Public Policy in the
    United States (Theories of Legisprudence)** 587
Section 1. Statutes as Principled Law (Legisprudence from
    Blackstone to Legal Process) 588
Section 2. Legisprudence and Statutory Doctrine: Vertical
    versus Horizontal Coherence in Statutory Law 630
Section 3. Retroactivity of Statutes 663

Chapter 7. Theories of Statutory Interpretation 689
Section 1. From Eclecticism to Systematic Theory, 1892–1938 691
Section 2. Legal Process Theories of Interpretation 712
Section 3. Current Debates in Statutory Interpretation 765

Chapter 8. Doctrines of Statutory Interpretation 847
Section 1. Rules, Presumptions, and Canons of Statutory Interpretation . . . 847
Section 2. Extrinsic Sources of Statutory Interpretation 955
Section 3. Interpretation of Statutes Created by Popular Initiatives 1101

Chapter 9. Implementation of Statutes 1117
Section 1. Law Implementation in the Administrative State 1118
Section 2. Congressional Control over Statutory Implementation 1139
Section 3. Judicial Deference to Agency Interpretations 1185

Appendices and Index

Appendix A. The Constitution of the United States . . . . [1]
Appendix B. The Rehnquist Court's Canons of Statutory Interpretation . . . [19]
Index . . . . [43]

Table of Contents

PREFACE V

TABLE OF CASES xxi

Chapter 1. An Introduction to Legislation 1

Section 1. The Story of the Civil Rights Act of 1964 and the
Procedures of Statute-Creation 2
Note on How a Bill Becomes a Federal Law 24
Title VII of the Civil Rights Act: An Introductory Problem 38
    Griggs v. Duke Power Company 42
        Questions about *Griggs* 47

Section 2. Descriptive and Normative Theories of Legislation 47
A. Pluralism and Interest Group Theories of Legislation 48
  1. *Pluralism: The Importance of Groups in Legislation* 48
  2. *Public Choice Theory: A Transactional View of the*
     Legislative Process 54
  3. *Criticisms of the Pluralist or Public Choice Vision* 60
B. Proceduralist Theories of Legislation 65
  1. *Vetogates: Procedural Doors that Bills Must Pass Through* 66
  2. *Liberal Theory: Statutes Should Be Hard To Enact* 68
  3. *Republican Theory: The Deliberative Value of Process* 69
C. Institutional Theories of Legislation 75
  1. *Introduction to the Institutional Perspective* 75
  2. *The Article I, § 7 Game* 77
  3. *The Statutory Implementation Game* 80

Section 3. Title VII: Interpretive Issues and Political Theories 82
A. The Supreme Court's Decision in *Griggs* 82
B. The Next Issue: Affirmative Action (*Weber*) 87
  United Steelworkers of America v. Weber 88
    Notes on *Weber* and Modes of Interpretation 100
  Johnson v. Transportation Agency 104
    Notes on *Johnson* 114
C. *Griggs* Revisited: Court versus Congress 115
  1. *Civil Rights in the Supreme Court's 1988 Term* 115
  2. *The Civil Rights Act of 1991* 118
  3. *A Transitional Note* 120

Chapter 2. Representational Structures 123

Section 1. Electoral Structures and Equality Values 125
  A. One Person, One Vote: Formal Equality in Representation 128
    1. *The House of Representatives* 130
    2. *State Legislatures* 132
    3. *Local Governments* 134
  B. Race and Electoral Structures 135
    1. *The Constitutionality of At-Large Electoral Schemes* 136
      City of Mobile v. Bolden 137
        Notes on *Bolden* and Constitutional
          Attacks on Minority Vote Dilution 146
    2. *The Voting Rights Act and Racial Vote Dilution* 148
      Thornburg v. Gingles 152
      A Voting Rights Act Problem 154
    3. *Redistricting Designed To Ensure Minority Representation* 155
      Shaw v. Reno 155
        Notes on *Shaw* and the Conundrum of Representation
          and Race 169
  C. Political Gerrymandering 174
      Davis v. Bandemer 175
      Vieth v. Jubelirer 177
        Notes on Judicial Review of Political Gerrymandering 191
        Notes on Alternative Voting Schemes 193

Section 2. Eligibility To Serve in the Legislature 196
  A. Congressionally Imposed Qualifications 196
    Powell v. McCormack 196
      Notes on *Powell* and the Legislature's
        Authority To Regulate Its Membership 205
    Problems of Congressional Exclusion and Expulsion 207
  B. Qualifications Imposed by States:
    Term Limitations for Federal Legislators 208
    U.S. Term Limits, Inc. v. Thornton 209
      Notes on *U.S. Term Limits* and Subsequent Developments 222
  C. Ballot Access Provisions 227
    Timmons v. Twin Cities Area New Party 228
      Notes on *Timmons* and the Idea of a Partisan Lockup 229
    Munro v. Socialist Workers Party 233
      Ballot Access Problems 234

Section 3. Structures of Campaign Finance 235
  A. The Constitutional Framework: *Buckley* v. *Valeo* 237
    Austin v. Michigan Chamber of Commerce 247
    Problem Relating to Campaign Finance Proposals 251
  B. The Bipartisan Campaign Reform Act and *McConnell*

v. Federal Election Commission 252
  1. *Federal Campaign Finance Reform Issues After* Buckley 252
  2. *The Bipartisan Campaign Reform Act of 2002* 258
    McConnell v. Federal Election Commission 261
      Notes on *McConnell v. FEC* 286
  3. *In the Wake of* McConnell*: Evolving Case Law and*
    the Influence of New Justices 290
    Randall v. Sorrell 290
    Federal Election Commission v. Wisconsin Right to Life 292
C. State Reforms and Public Financing 294

Chapter 3. Structures of Legislative Deliberation 299

Section 1. Regulating "Corrupt" Deliberation 301
  A. Bribery 302
    People ex rel. Dickinson v. Van de Carr 305
      Notes on Bribery Prosecutions and Theories of Representation ... 307
    A Bribery Problem 309
  B. Extortion 310
  C. Conflicts of Interest 311
    United States v. National Treasury Employees Union 314
    Conflict of Interest Problems 316

Section 2. Lobbying 318
  A. The Rise and Fall of the Federal Regulation of
    Lobbying Act of 1946 322
    Federal Regulation of Lobbying Act 324
    Lobbying Act Problems 326
    United States v. Harriss 327
      Notes on the Aftermath of *Harriss* 331
    *Post-*Harriss *Lobbying Act Problem* 333
  B. The Federal Lobbying Disclosure Act: Strengthening
    and Expanding Disclosure Requirements 333
    Lobbying Disclosure Act of 1995 335
      Notes on the Lobbying Disclosure Act 342
    Lobbying Disclosure Act Problems 347
  C. The Lawyer as Lobbyist and Ethical Questions
    Surrounding Lobbyists 348
    Note on Lobbying Regulation in the States 353

Section 3. Rules Facilitating Legislative Deliberation 356
  A. Substantive Limitations on the Legislative Process:
    Single Subject Rules and Generality Requirements 357
    Department of Education v. Lewis 360
      Notes on Enforcement of State Restrictions on
      Legislation and Legislative Procedures 362
  B. The Line Item Veto: A Rule To Enforce Budget Limitations 365

Rush v. Ray 367
   Notes on Different Approaches to the Item Veto 370
   Item Veto Problems 371
   Note on the Federal Line Item Veto Act 372
Clinton v. City of New York 373
   Notes on *Clinton v. City of New York* 385
C. Legislative Immunities 387
   1. *Federal Protection for Members of Congress (Speech or*
      Debate Clause) 387
   Gravel v. United States 388
      Notes on the Speech or Debate Clause After *Gravel* 393
      Speech or Debate Clause Problems 395
      Notes on Speech or Debate and Bribery Prosecutions 396
   United States v. Helstoski 397
      Note on Bribery Prosecutions After *Helstoski* 401
   2. *State Protection of State Legislators (Speech or Debate*
      Clauses in State Constitutions) 403
   3. *Federal Protection of State Legislators* 404
      Spallone v. United States 405
         Note on *Spallone* 407

Chapter 4. Due Process of Lawmaking 409

Section 1. Structural Due Process 411
A. Constitutional Requirements for the Procedures Followed
      in State and Federal Lawmaking 411
   Enrolled Bill Problem 415
   United States v. Munoz-Flores 416
   Origination Clause Problems 417
B. Requiring Lawmaking by the Most Institutionally
      Competent Branch of Government 420
   Hampton v. Mow Sun Wong 421
      Notes on *Mow Sun Wong* and Institutional Competence 424
   Paul Brest, *The Conscientious Legislator's Guide to*
      Constitutional Interpretation 428
      Notes on the "Conscientious Legislator" 430
C. Legislative Drafting and Due Process of Lawmaking 435

Section 2. The Federal Congressional Budget Process 446
A. The Development of the Modern Congressional Budget Process 447
   Train v. City of New York 455
B. The Budget Enforcement Act of 1990 and the Politics of Offsets 464
   Note on Lawsuits by Legislators 474
   Raines v. Byrd 475
   Congressional Standing Problems 476
   Budget Process Problems 484
C. A Case Study of the Budget Process: President Clinton's

Energy Tax Proposal 485
Omnibus Budget Reconciliation Act of 1993, Report of the
    Committee on the Budget, House of Representatives 494

Section 3. Other Congressional Structures 508
    A Final Due Process of Lawmaking Exercise 518

**Chapter 5. Direct Democracy as an Alternative
    to Republican Government** 523

Section 1. An Overview of Direct Democracy 523
    Buckley v. American Constitutional Law Foundation 528
    Introductory Problem on Direct Democracy 535

Section 2. Popular Lawmaking and the Constitution 535
    A. An Introduction to the Problem 535
    *St. Paul Citizens for Human Rights
        v. City Council of the City of St. Paul* 536
        Notes on *St. Paul Citizens* and the Fairness of Direct Democracy . 540
        Problems on Direct Democracy and the Single-Subject Rule 543
    B. Popular Lawmaking and the Equal Protection Clause 544
    Arthur v. City of Toledo 544
        Notes on *Arthur* and the Difficulty
            in Proving Equal Protection Violations 548
    Romer v. Evans 549
        Notes on *Romer* and Renewed Attention to the
            Constitutional Problems with Initiatives 556
    C. Popular Lawmaking and the Due Process Clause 559
    City of Eastlake v. Forest City Enterprises, Inc. 559
        Notes on *Eastlake* and "Due Process of Lawmaking" 566
    Philly's v. Byrne 568
        Note on *Philly's* and Due Process Principles 573

Section 3. Recall 574
    Chandler v. Otto 574
        Notes on Recall 581

**Chapter 6. Statutes as a Source of Public Policy in the
    United States (Theories of Legisprudence)** 587

Section 1. Statutes as Principled Law (Legisprudence from
    Blackstone to Legal Process) 588
    A. The Decline and Fall of Formalism, 1890–1940 588
    State v. Warshow 595
        Note on the Case of the Nuclear Protesters 598
    B. The Legal Process Era, 1940–1973 598
    Moragne v. States Marine Lines, Inc. 601
        Notes on Reasoning by Statutory Analogy and *Moragne* 609

Problems in the Wake of Moragne 613
More on the Interplay of Statutes and the Common Law:
Problems on the Employment-at-Will Doctrine 616
Guido Calabresi, *A Common Law for the Age of Statutes* 618
Notes on the Calabresi Proposal that Courts
Have the Power To Overrule Statutes 619
C. The Post-Legal Process Era, 1974–? 622
1. *Law and Economics Applied to Legislation* 623
2. *Critical Scholarship and Legislation* 625
3. *The New Legal Processes: Positivism, Pragmatism, Principles* .. 628

Section 2. Legisprudence and Statutory Doctrine: Vertical
versus Horizontal Coherence in Statutory Law 630
A. Introduction 630
B. Stare Decisis and Statutory Precedents 631
Flood v. Kuhn 632
Notes on *Flood* and the "Super-Strong" Presumption
Against Overruling Statutory Precedents 640
Patterson v. McLean Credit Union 646
Note on Abrogating Stare Decisis 648
Problem on Overruling Statutory Precedents 649
C. Prospective Judicial Decisions 649
James v. United States 650
Notes on the Rise and Decline of Judicial Prospectivity 651
James B. Beam Distilling Co. v. Georgia 655
Harper v. Virginia Department of Taxation 656
Problem on Prospective Judicial Decisions 662

Section 3. Retroactivity of Statutes 663
A. The Traditional Rule Against Statutory Retroactivity 663
Jawish v. Morlet 663
Notes on Constitutional Problems with Retroactive Statutes 665
Problems on Retroactivity of Change in Criminal Law 668
B. Constitutional Tolerance for Retroactive Statutes
in the Regulatory State 669
C. Presumptions Against Statutory Retroactivity 672
Landgraf v. USI Film Products 672
Rivers v. Roadway Express, Inc. 685
Notes on *Landgraf, Rivers*, and Statutory Retroactivity 686

Chapter 7. Theories of Statutory Interpretation 689

Section 1. From Eclecticism to Systematic Theory, 1892–1938 691
Henry M. Hart, Jr. & Albert M. Sacks, *The Legal Process:*
Basic Problems in the Making and Application of Law 693
Rector, Holy Trinity Church v. United States 695
Notes on *Holy Trinity* and Eclecticism in Statutory Interpretation ... 699

Caminetti v. United States 703
Roscoe Pound, *Spurious Interpretation* 704
   Notes on Interpretation as Intentionalism 706
   Fishgold v. Sullivan Drydock and Repair Corp. 707
Max Radin, *Statutory Interpretation* 708
   Notes on Early Critiques of Intentionalist Approaches 709
   Problems on Imaginative Reconstruction 712

Section 2. Legal Process Theories of Interpretation 712
  A. The Legal Process Classics, 1940s–50s 712
   Lon Fuller, *The Case Of the Speluncean Explorers* 712
   Henry M. Hart, Jr. and Albert M. Sacks, *The Legal Process:*
     Basic Problems in the Making and Application of Law 718
     Problems on Legal Process Approaches to Interpretation 721
  B. Implications of and Debates Within Legal Process
    Theory, 1950s–1980s 721
    1. *Correcting "Legislative Mistakes"?* 723
     Shine v. Shine 723
      Note on Judicial Correction of Legislative Mistakes 727
      United States v. Locke 728
    2. *Statutory Evolution in Light of Changed Circumstances* 729
     William Eskridge, Jr., *Dynamic Statutory Interpretation* 729
     In the Matter of Jacob 732
     Li v. Yellow Cab Co. of Calif. 737
     Notes on *Jacob, Li*, and Dynamic Readings of State Codes 739
    3. *Coherence with Public Norms* 743
     Public Citizen v. U.S. Department of Justice 743
     State of New Jersey v. 1979 Pontiac Trans Am 744
     Notes on *Public Citizen, Trans Am*, and Coherence-
      Based Justifications for "Judicial Surgery" 746
  C. Concerns about Legal Process Theory, 1970s–80s 749
   TVA v. Hill 752
   Griffin v. Oceanic Contractors, Inc. 755
    Notes on *Hill, Griffin*, and the Revival of the Plain Meaning Rule 763

Section 3. Current Debates in Statutory Interpretation 765
  A. The New Textualism 765
   Green v. Bock Laundry Machine Company 766
    Notes on *Bock Laundry* and Different Foundationalist
     Theories in Action 775
   Antonin Scalia, *A Matter of Interpretation* 778
   Problem Applying the New Textualism 781
   Chisom v. Roemer 781
    West Virginia University Hospitals v. Casey 790
    Notes on *Casey, Chisom*, and the New Textualism on the Court .. 791
    Zuni Public School Dist. No. 89 v. Department of Education 795
  B. Economic Theories of Statutory Interpretation 798

1. *Ex Ante Approaches to the Debate Between Textualists and Contextualists* 800
   United States v. Marshall 801
      Notes on the LSD Case and *Ex Ante* Thinking 810
      A New LSD Problem 812
2. *Advancing Public-Regarding Goals and Minimizing Rent-Seeking* 812
   Perez v. Wyeth Laboratories, Inc. 814
      Note on the Norplant Case and Narrow Interpretations
      of Rent-Seeking Statutes 818
3. *Institutional Cost-Benefit Analysis* 818
   FDA v. Brown & Williamson Tobacco Corp. 820
      Note on the FDA Tobacco Case and the Supreme
      Court as a Strategic Actor in Our Polity 828
C. Pragmatic and Critical Theories of Statutory Interpretation 830
  1. *Pragmatic Theories* 830
   William Eskridge, Jr. and Philip Frickey, *Statutory Interpretation as Practical Reasoning* 830
   Note on the Funnel of Abstraction 835
  2. *Critical Theories* 835
   The Case of the Speluncean Explorers: Contemporary Proceedings 838
   Note on Critical Race and Feminist Theories
   and Statutory Interpretation 842
  3. *Review of Various Theories of Statutory Interpretation* 842

Chapter 8. Doctrines of Statutory Interpretation 847

Section 1. Rules, Presumptions, and Canons of Statutory Interpretation ... 847
A. Textual Canons 849
  Introductory Problem: The No Vehicles in the Park Statute 849
  1. *Maxims of Word Meaning and Association* 849
  2. *Grammar Canons* 856
  3. *The Whole Act Rule* 862
   Babbitt v. Sweet Home Chapter of Communities for a Great Oregon 868
      Notes on *Sweet Home* and the Whole Act Rule 878
B. Substantive Canons 880
  1. *The Rule of Lenity in Criminal Cases* 884
   Muscarello v. United States 888
   McNally v. United States 898
      Notes on *Muscarello*, *McNally*, and the
      Supreme Court's Approach to Criminal Statutes 901
   People v. Davis 903
   Note on *Davis* and State Criminal Code Constructions 906
  2. *Interpretation to Avoid Constitutional Problems* 907
   United States v. Witkovich 907

National Labor Relations Board v. Catholic Bishop of Chicago .. 911
    Notes on the "Avoidance Canon" 917
    Department of Commerce v. U.S. House of Representatives 920
    Note on Severability 922
  3. *The New Federalism Canons* 922
   Gregory v. Ashcroft 923
    Notes on *Gregory* and Clear Statement Rules 933
   BFP v. Resolution Trust Corp. 936
    Notes on the *Gregory-BFP* Rule in Action and Criticisms
    of the New Federalism Canons 938
C. Debunking and Defending the Canons of Statutory Interpretation ... 941
  Karl Llewellyn, *Remarks on the Theory Of Appellate Decision and
  the Rules or Canons About How Statutes Are to Be Construed* ... 941
   Notes on the Intellectual Warfare over Canons
   of Statutory Interpretation 945
  James Brudney and Corey Ditslear, *Canons of Construction
  and the Elusive Quest for Neutral Reasoning* 950
  Problem for Applying the Textual and Substantive Canons 952
  Note on Interpretive Directions in Statutes 953

Section 2. Extrinsic Sources for Statutory Interpretation 955
A. The Common Law 956
  Introductory Problem on the Common Law as Extrinsic Evidence 957
  Smith v. Wade 959
   Notes on the Evolving Common Law as a
   Source for Construing Statutes 968
  Another Problem on the Common Law and Statutes 970
B. Legislative Background (History) 971
  1. *The Circumstances Surrounding the Introduction
  and Consideration of Legislation* 973
  Leo Sheep Co. v. United States 973
   Notes on *Leo Sheep* and Legislative Context 979
  2. *Committee Reports (and an Introduction to
  the Great Legislative History Debate)* 981
  Blanchard v. Bergeron 983
   Note on the New Textualist Critique of Committee Reports 987
  In re Sinclair 991
   Notes on *Sinclair* and the Search for Objectivity
   in Statutory Interpretation 995
  Perez v. Wyeth Laboratories, Inc. 998
   Note on the Norplant Case and State Court Reliance
   on Committee and Bill Reports 998
  3. *Statements by Sponsors or Drafters of Legislation* 1000
  Pepper v. Hart 1001
   Notes on *Pepper* and the Demise of the Exclusionary Rule ... 1001
  Kosak v. United States 1014
   Notes on *Kosak* and the Views of Nonlegislator Drafters 1018

   4. *Legislation Deliberation: Hearings, Floor Debate, Rejected*
      Proposals, and the Dogs that Didn't Bark   1020
      FDA v. Brown & Williamson Tobacco Co.   1022
         Rapanos v. United States   1022
         Note on Rejected Proposals   1026
      Montana Wilderness Ass'n v. United States Forest Service   1027
         Notes on the "Checkerboard Case" and Statements
            During Legislative Deliberation   1033
   5. *Post-Enactment Legislative History ("Subsequent Legislative*
      History")   1035
      Montana Wilderness Ass'n v. United States Forest Service   1036
         Notes on the Second Checkerboard Opinion
            and the Use of Post-Enactment Statements   1040
         Notes on Presidential Signing or Veto Statements   1043
         Problem on Presidential Signing Statements   1046
   6. *Legislative Inaction*   1047
      Bob Jones University v. United States   1050
         Notes on *Bob Jones* and the "Meaning"
            of Legislative Inaction   1061
         Note on Post-Enactment Acquiescence and "Law
            as Equilibrium"   1063
         Problems on the Use of Legislative History
            in Statutory Interpretation   1064
C. Interpretation in Light of Other Statutes   1066
   1. *Similar Statutes (the In Pari Materia Rule)*   1066
      Cartledge v. Miller   1066
      Lorillard v. Pons   1070
         Notes on *Cartledge*, *Lorillard*, and
            Reasoning from Statutes in Pari Materia   1073
   2. *The Modeled or Borrowed Statute Rule*   1073
      Zerbe v. State   1077
         Note on *Zerbe* and Interpretation of Borrowed Statutes   1081
   3. *Statutory Clashes — The Rule Against Implied Repeals*   1081
      Morton v. Mancari   1082
         Notes on *Mancari* and Interpretation
            in Light of Subsequent Statutes   1088
      Branch v. Smith   1089
         Notes on *Branch*   1098

Section 3. Interpretation of Statutes Created by Popular Initiatives   1101
      Evangelatos v. Superior Court   1103
      Problem Involving Popular Lawmaking   1104

Chapter 9. Implementation and Interpretation of Statutes
   in the Administrative State   1117

Section 1. Law Implementation in the Administrative State   1118

A. A Brief History of the Modern Administrative State 1119
    A Case Study: The National Traffic and Motor
        Vehicle Safety Act of 1966 1126
B. Private Causes of Action in the Bureaucratic State 1128
    Implied Right of Action Problem 1130
    Note on the Court's Post-*Borak* Practice: Shift from
        Legislative Purpose to Legislative Intent 1131
    Franklin v. Gwinnett County Public Schools 1133
    More Problems on Private Rights of Action 1135
C. The Nondelegation Doctrine in the Administrative State 1136

Section 2. Congressional Influence over Statutory Implementation 1139
    A. Legislative Oversight and Investigation 1142
    B. Congress' Budgetary and Appropriations Power 1146
    C. The Legislative Veto of Agency Rules 1148
        Immigration and Naturalization Service v. Chadha 1150
        Notes on Structural Separation of Powers 1154
    D. Legislative Control Through Power over Agency Officials
        and Their Tenure 1160
        Bowsher v. Synar 1161
        Notes on the Gramm-Rudman Case 1162
        Note on Presidential Review of Agency Rules 1163
    E. Congress' Policy Control Through Design of the Agency's
        Structure and Procedures 1166
    F. Judicial Review of Agency Rules and Orders 1168
        Problem on Judicial Review of Agency Action 1175
    Motor Vehicle Manufacturers Ass'n v.
        State Farm Mutual Automobile Ins. Co. 1176
        Notes on *State Farm* 1183

Section 3. Judicial Deference to Agency Interpretations 1185
    Problem on Executive Interpretation 1186
    A. The Basic Framework: *Skidmore* and *Chevron* 1194
        General Electric Co. v. Gilbert 1195
    Chevron, U.S.A., Inc. v. Natural Resources Defense Council 1197
        Notes on *Chevron* and Deference to Administrative
            Interpretations 1200
    MCI Telecommunications Corp. v. AT&T 1204
        Notes on *MCI*, the New Textualism, and Excessive
            Legislative Delegations to Agencies 1209
    United States v. Mead Corp. 1213
        Notes on *Mead* and Recent Reports of the "*Chevron*
            Revolution" 1223
    B. Important *Chevron* Issues 1227
        1. Is the Agency Operating Within Its Delegated Authority? 1227
            Gonzales v. Oregon 1228
            Notes on the Oregon Aid-in-Dying Case and Deference

for Issues of Agency Authority 1239
2. Does the Agency Have Broader Freedom To Interpret
Its Own Rules? 1242
Gonzales v. Oregon 1242
Notes on Agency Interpretations of Their Own Regulations 1244
3. Should Courts Defer When the Agency Interpretation
Presents Serious Constitutional Questions? 1245
*A Problem of Deference When There Are Constitutional
Issues* 1246
Palm Beach County Canvassing Board v. Harris 1247
Notes on *Palm Beach Canvassing Board* and the Role of
Canons in Judicial Evaluation of Agency Interpretations 1255
Note on Deference to Agencies in the State Courts 1258
4. Does Agency Deference Apply to Issues of Preemption? 1261
Geier v. Honda Motor Co. 1262
Notes on *Geier* and Federal Preemption of State Law 1266
5. Deference and *Stare Decisis* 1268
Neal v. United States 1268
Note on *Chevron* and Stare Decisis: The Case of the
Over-regulated Wetlands 1269
6. Deference in National Security and Foreign Affairs 1270
Hamdan v. Rumsfeld 1271
Note on *Curtiss-Wright* Deference 1275
C. Quo Vadis the "*Chevron* Revolution"? 1276
1. Sharpen *Chevron* and *Skidmore* Within the *Mead* Framework 1278
2. Reject *Mead* in Favor of Greater Deference to Agency
Interpretations 1280
3. Synthesize *Chevron* and *Skidmore* 1283

Appendices and Index
Appendix A. The Constitution of the United States .... [1]
Appendix B. The Supreme Court's Canons of Statutory Interpretation .... [19]
Index .... [43]

Table of Cases

The principal cases are in bold type. Cases cited or discussed in the text are in roman type. References are to pages. Cases cited in principal cases and within other quoted materials are not included.

1979 Pontiac Trans Am, State of New Jersey v. 744, 746-749, 818
A.L.A. Schechter Poultry Corp. v. United States 1121, 1136, 1137
Abate v. Mundt 150
Abbott Laboratories v. Gardner 883, 1169
Abrams v. Johnson 170
Adams Fruit Co. v. Barrett 952
Adkins v. Children's Hospital 665, 666
Advisory Opinion to the Attorney General — Restricts Laws Related to Discrimination, In re 543
Ahlborn, Commonwealth v. 999, 1000
Alaska, United States v. 865
Alaska Airlines v. Brock 922, 1157-1159
Albemarle Paper Co. v. Moody 87
Albrecht v. Herald Co. 646
Aldinger v. Howard 644
Alexander v. Choate 1074
Alexander v. Sandoval 1133
Allegheny Casualty Co., People v. 998
Allen v. Wright 1063
Allied Structural Steel Co. v. Spannaus 667
Almendarez-Torres v. United States 920
Amalgamated Meat Cutters and Butcher Workmen of North America v. Connolly 1136, 1138
Amalgamated Transit Union Local 1309 v. Laidlaw Transit Servs. 727, 728
American Dental Ass'n v. Martin 1172
Americans Disabled Accessible Public Transp. (ADAPT) v. Skywest Airlines 1135
American Red Cross v. S.G. 793
American Reserve Corp., In re 856
American Textile Mfrs. Inst., Inc. v. Donovan 1137
American Trucking Associations v. Smith 656
American Trucking Associations, United States v. 722

Anderson v. Celebrezze 231
Anderson v. Group Hospitalization, Inc. 663
Anderson v. Shook 857
Andrus v. Shell Oil Co. 1040
Angel Lace M., In re 740
Arangold Corp. v. Zehnder 363
Arizona Together v. Brewer 544
Arkansas Educational Television Commission v. Forbes 232
Arlington Cent. Sch. Dist. Bd. of Educ. v. Murphy 795, 800, 867, 941
Arthur v. City of Toledo 544, 548, 549, 557
Arthur Andersen LLP v. United States 902
Associated Commercial Protectors Ltd. v. Mason, In re 858
Association of Texas Prof. Educators v. Kirby 419
Astoria Federal Savings & Loan Assoc. v. Solimino 883
AT&T v. Iowa Utilities Bd. 853, 1210
Atascadero State Hospital v. Scanlon 922, 940
Atlantic City Transp. Co. v. Walsh 882
Attorney General v. Prince Ernest Augustus of Hanover 864
Auciello Iron Works v. NLRB 1224
Auer v. Robbins 1242, 1244, 1245
Austin v. Michigan Chamber of Commerce 247, 250
Avery v. Midland County 134, 135
B.L.V.B. and E.L.V.B., Adoptions of 740
Babbitt v. Sweet Home Chapter of Communities for a Great Oregon 779, 868, 878, 879, 881, 885, 989, 997, 1000, 1066, 1081, 1099, 1210, 1212, 1213, 1258, 1278
Baby Z, Adoption of 740
Bacchus Imports, Ltd. v. Dias 655, 656
Baker v. Carr 129, 131, 174
Ballin, United States v. 414
BankAmerica v. United States 1021, 1022

Bankers Life & Cas. Co. v. United States 1211

Barenblatt v. United States 1145

Barnhart v. Thomas 858

Barnhart v. Walton 1224, 1283

Barnsdall Refining Corp. v. Welsh 419

Bastien v. Office of Senator Ben Nighthorse Campbell 395

Bates v. Director of Campaign and Political Finance 296

Bates v. Jones 223, 1115

Batterton v. Francis 1203

Beazell v. Ohio 666

Becke v. Smith 860

Begier v. IRS 989

Bell v. Hood 1133

Bennis v. Michigan 746

Bernstein v. Comm'r of Public Safety 362

Beth Israel Hospital v. NLRB 1224, 1277, 1278

BFP v. Resolution Trust Corp. 779, 792, 936, 938, 939, 1025, 1098, 1269

Bi-Metallic Investment Co. v. State Board of Equalization 573

Biggs v. Vail 999

Bishop v. Linkway Stores, Inc. 764, 862

Bishop v. Montante 404

Blanchard v. Bergeron 793, **983**, 987, 998, 1001

Blanchette v. Connecticut General Ins. Corp. 1042

Blank v. Department of Corrections 1156

Board of Governors of the Federal Reserve System v. Dimension Financial Corp. 763

Board of Trustees v. Judge 858

Board of Trustees, Univ. of Ala. v. Garrett 410, 940

Bob Jones University v. United States 1050, 1061-1064, 12123

Boerne, City of v. Flores 150, 431

Bollman, Ex parte 692, 693, 917

Bond v. Floyd 206, 207

Borrell v. United States Int'l Communication Agency 1034

Boston Sand & Gravel Co. v. United States 710

Boston Housing Auth. v. Hemingway 613

Boutilier v. INS 1065

Bowen v. Georgetown University Hospital 672, 687, 1257

Bowers v. Hardwick 432

Bowles v. Seminole Rock & Sand Co. 1242, 1244, 1245, 1277, 1278

Bowsher v. Synar 452, 1159, 1161-1163

Bradley v. Fisher 957

Bradley v. School Board of City of Richmond 672, 687

Branch v. Smith 1089, 1098-1100

Brewster, United States v. 388, 394, 401

Brookpark Entertainment, Inc. v. Taft 574

Brown v. Board of Education 1, 2, 3, 621, 641

Brown v. Board of School Commissioners 148

Brown v. Hartlage 318

Brown v. Socialist Workers '74 Campaign Committee 257, 346

Brown, United States v. 666

Brown v. Thomson 134

Browning v. Clerk, U.S. House of Representatives 395

Bryan v. Itasca County 883

Buckley v. American Constitutional Law Foundation 528

Buckley v. Valeo 237-245, 247-249, 252, 255-257, 290, 346, 292, 622

Burdick v. Takushi 234

Burke v. Fleet Nat'l Bank 999

Burlington Indus., Inc. v. Ellerth 970

Burnet v. Coronado Oil and Gas Co. 641

Bush v. Gore 1256-1258

Bush v. Palm Beach County Canvassing Bd. 1255

Bush v. Vera 170, 172, 173

Califano v. Westcott 1158

California Democratic Party v. Jones 233

California Prolife Council Political Action Committee v. Scully 356

Caminetti v. United States 703, 704, 707, 711, 792

Campaign for Fiscal Equity v. New York 394

Campbell v. Clinton 477

Campbell, United States v. 304

Canada Sugar Refining Co. v. Regina 862

Cannon v. University of Chicago 1131, 1132, 1134, 1135

Carey v. Piphus 968

Carlton, United States v. 671

Carmell v. Texas 666

Cartmell's Estate, In re 860

Cartledge v. Miller 1066, 1073, 1075, 1076

Cathcart v. Meyer 225

Central Bank of Denver N.A. v. First Interstate Bank of Denver N.A. 1041, 1049, 1064

Chan v. Korean Air Lines 792, 855, 856

Chandler v. Otto 574, 582

Chapman v. United States 810, 812, 903, 1041, 1268, 1269

Chastain v. Sundquist 396

Cheek v. United States 886

Chevron Oil Co. v. Huson 651, 653, 655, 656

Chevron, U.S.A., Inc. v. Natural Resources Defense Council 1118, 1195, **1197**, 1200-1204, 1209-1213, 1223-1227, 1240-1242, 1244, 1245, 1257-1262, 1267-1271, 1276-1283

Chiarella v. United States 902

Chicago, City of v. Environmental Defense Fund 856, 1210, 1258, 1266

Chisom v. Roemer 779, **781**, 791-795, 811, 835, 843, 845, 858, 867, 934, 935, 1035

Christensen v. Harris County 855, 1203, 1270

Chrysler Corp. v. Department of Transportation 1171, 1172, 1184

CIO, United States v. 1046

Cipollone v. Liggett Group, Inc. 883, 938, 1262, 1266, 1267

Cipriano v. City of Houma 135

Circuit City Stores, Inc. v. Adams 854, 865, 866, 950, 951, 989, 998, 1019

Citizens Against Rent Control v. Berkeley 530

Citizens to Preserve Overton Park, Inc. v. Brinegar 1170

Citizens to Preserve Overton Park, Inc. v. Volpe 1169-1171

City of ____ v. ____. See name of city

Cleveland v. United States 643, 902

Clingman v. Beaver 231, 234

Clinkscales v. Carver 610

Clinton v. City of New York, 38, **373**, 385, 411, 425, 1159

Club Misty, Inc. v. Laski 574

Coalition for Political Honesty v. State Board of Elections 194

Coffman v. Colorado Common Cause 1260

Colautti v. Franklin 865

Colegrove v. Green 129, 135, 174

Colorado General Assembly v. Lamm 371

Colton v. Branstad 371

Commissioner v. ____. See name of other party

Committee for the Commonwealth of Canada v. Canada 863

Community for Creative Non-Violence v. Reid 852, 957

Conley v. Roman Catholic Archbishop of San Francisco 998

Connecticut State Medical Society v. Connecticut Board of Examiners in Podiatry 1259

Connell Construction Co. v. Plumbers & Steamfitters Local 100 1021

Connor v. Finch 134, 413

Conroy v. Aniskoff 862, 973, 989

Construction Indus. Force Account Coun. v. Amador Water Agency 999

Consumer Product Safety Comm'n v. GTE Sylvania 1040

Cook County v. United States 850

Cook v. Gralike 318

Cook v. United States 1089

Coons v. American Honda Motor Co. 652

Corsicana, City of v. Willman 858

Cort v. Ash 1131, 1132

Cottage Savs. Ass'n v. Commissioner 1225

County of ____ v. ____. See name of county

Cox v. Roth 881

CPSC v. GTE Sylvania 763

Crandon v. United States 793, 903

Crawford v. Board of Educ. of City of Los Angeles 557

Crockett v. Reagan 474

Crosby v. National Foreign Trade Council 989

Crowell v. Benson 917

Curtiss-Wright Export Co., United States v. 1270, 1271, 1275, 1277, 1278, 1280, 1283

Cuyahoga Met. Hous. Auth. v. City of Cleveland 999

D & W Auto Supply v. Dep't of Revenue 419

Daggett v. Comm'n on Governmental Ethics and Election Practices 295

Dague v. Piper Aircraft Corp. 362

Dames & Moore v. Regan 1281

Davis v. Bandemer 175-177, 193

Davis v. Monroe County Bd. of Educ. 1134, 1135

Davis, People v. 903, 906, 907

Delaware & Hudson Co., United States ex rel. Attorney General v. 917

Delaware Tribal Business Comm. v. Weeks 879

Dellmuth v. Muth 940, 941, 950

Democratic Party of Washington v. Reed 233

Demore v. Kim 883

Dennis v. Higgins 881

Department of Commerce v. U.S. House of Representatives 132, 920, 922, 949, 1245

Department of Education v. Lewis 360, 363, 364, 371

Department of the Navy v. Egan 884, 1270, 1271, 1275, 1276, 1283

Desist v. United States 651

Dewsnup v. Timm 866

Dickinson v. Fund for Support of Free Public Schools 1021

Dillehey v. State 1000

Dillon v. King 420

Director, Etc. v. Bethlehem Mines Corp. 855

Director, OWCP v. Greenwich Collieries 1013

Distribution of Liquid Assets, In re 1259

Dobbert v. Florida 666

Doe v. Chao 862, 1041

Doe v. McMillan 387

Dombrowski v. Pfister 387

Donato v. AT&T 1260

Dooley v. Korean Air Lines 614

Douglas v. Jeannette 644

Douglass v. Pike County 631, 652

Dr. Miles Medical Co. v. John D. Park & Sons Co. 646

Dunigan, People v. 419

Dunlop v. Bachowski 859, 883

Dunn v. Blumstein 127

Duplex Printing Press Co. v. Deering 707, 711

Easley v. Cromartie 173

Eastern Enterprises v. Apfel 671

Eastlake, City of v. Forest City Enterprises, Inc. 559, 566, 567, 573

Eastland v. United States' Servicemen's Fund 387, 393

Edward J. DeBartolo Corp. v. Florida Gulf Coast Building & Constr. Trades Council 918

EEOC v. Arabian American Oil Co. 884, 941, 950, 1203

Eichman, United States v. 431

El Paso, City of v. Simmons 671

Elizalde's Estate, In re 621

Employees v. Missouri Dep't of Public Health & Welfare 939

Energy Reserves Group, Inc. v. Kansas Power and Light Co. 671

Equality Foundation of Greater Cincinnati v. City of Cincinnati 557

Ernst & Ernst v. Hochfelder 1034

Escondido Mut. Water Co. v. LaJolla Indians 859

Ethyl Corp. v. EPA 1171

Euclid v. Ambler Realty Co. 567

Evangelatos v. Superior Court 1103

Evans v. United States 970, 971, 1048

Evans v. United States 311

Eyston v. Studd 707

Fair Political Practices Commission v. Superior Court 354

Far East Conf. v. United States 1128

Farragher v. City of Boca Raton 1049

FDA v. Brown & Williamson Tobacco Co. 820, 828-830, 835, 879, 991, 997, **1022**, 1026, 1042, 1049, 1064, 1099, 1138, 1210, 1213, 1240, 1278

FDIC v. Philadelphia Gear Corp. 763

Federal Baseball Club v. National League 640-642, 644, 651

Federal Election Commission v. Hall-Tyner Election Campaign Committee 257

Federal Election Comm. v. Massachusetts Citizens for Life, Inc 248, 256, 260

Federal Election Commission v. Wisconsin Right to Life, Inc. 292

Fiedler v. Marumsco Christian School 663

Fields v. Office of Eddie Bernice Johnson 395

Finley v. United States 792

Fior D'Italia, United States v. 882

First Nat'l Bank of Deerwood v. Gregg 999, 1021

Fisher, United States v. 862, 866

Fishgold v. Sullivan Drydock and Repair Corp. 707, 708

Fletcher v. Peck 147

Flood v. Kuhn 632, 640-646, 648, 651, 655, 1048

Florida East Coast Ry. Co., United States v. 573, 1122, 1174

Florida Lime & Avocado Growers, Inc. v. Paul 1261

Fogerty v. Fantasy, Inc. 1048

Foley Brothers v. Filardo 883, 884

Franklin v. Gwinnett County Public Schools 1042, 1133-1135

Franklin v. Massachusetts 131

Franks v. Bowman Transp. Co. 87

Fullilove v. Klutznick 409, 410

Fulton v. Lavallee 643

Fumo v. Pa. Public Utility Comm'n 419

Fyfe v. Barnett, People ex rel. 741

Garcia, People v. 906, 907

Garcia v. San Antonio Metropolitan Transit Authority 923, 934, 936, 938

Garcia v. United States 858

Garris v. Norfolk Shipbuilding & Drydock Corporation 613, 615

Gates v. Jensen 999

Gattis v. Chavez 855

Gebser v. Lago Vista 1134

Geier v. Honda Motor Co. 1262, 1266-1268, 1276

General Electric Co. v. Gilbert 87, 791, 1195, 1197, 1200, 1202, 1203, 1240

George Byers Sons, Inc. v. East Europe Import Export, Inc. 1135

Georgia v. Ashcroft 150

Gersman v. Group Health Association 688

Gibson v. Florida Legislative Investigation Commission 346

Gillock, United States v. 404

Goldblatt v. Hempstead 671

Golden v. Koch 1021

Gollust v. Mendell 1019

Gomez v. Toledo 881

Gomillion v. Lightfoot 135, 174

Gonzaga University v. Doe 1133

Gonzales v. Oregon 862, 938, 1212, 1223, **1228**, 1239-1245, 1268, 1276, 1278, 1279, 1283

Gonzales, United States v. 1045

Gore v. Harris 1256

Gossman v. Greatland Directional Drilling, Inc. 999

Gould v. Gould 882

Gozlon-Peretz v. United States 867, 903, 1042

Granholm v. Heald 1088

Gravel v. United States 388, 393, 394, 622

Great Northern Railway Co. v. Sunburst Oil and Refining Co. 654

Green v. Bock Laundry Machine Company 766, 775-777, 779, 793, 795, 835, 861, 933, 989, 1035

Greenshields v. Regina 862

Gregory v. Ashcroft 923, 933-936, 938-940, 950, 1102

Grey, In re 686

Griffin v. Oceanic Contractors, Inc. 755, 763, 765, 766, 781, 792, 798, 799, 830, 832-834

Griffith v. Kentucky 654, 655

Griffith v. Slinkard 959

Griggs v. Duke Power Company 42, 47, 67, 68, 81-87, 115-117

Groditsky v. Pinckney 582

Group Life & Health Inc. Co. v. Royal Drug Co. 1019

Grove City College v. Bell 791

Guardians Ass'n v. Civil Serv. Comm'n 1048

Gustafson v. Alloyd Co. 866, 1019, 1020

Gutierrez v. Ada 853, 865, 867

H.S.H.-K., In re Custody of 740

Hadley v. Junior College District 134

Hagen v. Utah 883

Haig v. Agee 884, 1061

Hallner, People v. 764

Hamdan v. Rumsfeld 688, 867, 883, 989, 1001, 1026, 1047, 1088, 1226, 1245, 1271-1276, 1279

Hamilton, United States v. 692

Hampton v. Mow Sun Wong 411, **421**, 424-428, 435-437, 566, 567, 1267

Handy v. General Motors Corp. 1130

Hankerson v. North Carolina 654

Harper v. Virginia Department of Taxation 127, **656**, 663, 668

Harris, Regina v. 886

Harrisburg, The 615, 621, 652

Harriss, United States v. 322, 327, 331, 332, 335, 346, 347, 355, 438

Harristown Development Corp. v. Commissioner 404

Hart, In re 740

Hayes v. Continental Ins. Co. 1019

Hays, United States v. 170

Heathman v. Giles 853

Hecht Co. v. Bowles 883

Heckler v. Chaney 1170

Heckler v. Day 1048

Heckler v. Mathews 1157

Hedman, United States v. 953

Helstoski, United States v. 397, 401, 622

Henning v. Industrial Welfare Comm'n 1261

Hentoff v. Ichord 394

Herman & MacLean v. Huddleston 855

Heydon's Case 693, 843, 1104

Higby v. Mahoney 643

Hill v. East and West India Dock Co. 694

Hill v. INS 1066

Hinck v. United States 856

Hines v. Davidowitz 1262

Hirschey v. FERC 987

Hishon v. King & Spalding 982

Hisquierdo v. Hisquierdo 1076

Ho King, In re 700

Hodgerney v. Baker 853

Hoffman v. Connecticut Dep't of Income Maintenance 940

Hoffman v. Jones 652

Hoffman, State v. 998

Holder v. Hall 154

Holy Trinity Church v. United States 444, 445, 693, **695**, 699-704, 711, 712, 727, 732, 743, 744, 747, 751, 778, 795, 798, 811, 814, 835-837, 842, 847, 850, 855, 863, 935, 997, 1012, 1013

Home Box Office, Inc. v. FCC 1173, 1175

Home Building and Loan Ass'n v. Blaisdell 670

House of Representatives of the United States, United States v. 1146

Howe v. Smith 1013

Hoyt v. Florida 742

Hughey v. United States 903

Humphrey's Executor v. United States 1160

Hunt v. Cromartie 173

Hunter v. Erickson 549, 557

Hutchinson v. Proxmire 396

ICC v. Louisville and Nashville Ry. Co. 1120

Illinois Brick Co. v. Illinois 643

Imbler v. Pachtman 959

Immigration & Naturalization Service v. Chadha 412, 1061, 1062, 1150, 1154-1156, 1158, 1159, 1161-1163

In re _____. See name of party in interest

Independent Community Bankers Ass'n v. South Dakota 419

Independent Federation of Flight Attendants v. Zipes 117

Industrial Union Dep't, AFL–CIO v. American Petroleum Institute 1137, 1138

INS v. Cardoza-Fonseca 1203, 1209

INS v. Phinpathya 791

INS v. St. Cyr 688, 918

Inst. of Governmental Advocates v. Fair Political Practices Comm'n 356

Insurance Co. v. New Orleans 644

International Harvester Co. v. Ruckelshaus 1174

International News Service v. Associated Press 591, 598

Isbrandtsen Co. v. Johnson 956

Ivy v. Security Barge Lines, Inc. 614, 615

J.I. Case Co. v. Borak 1129-1131, 1133

J.W. Hampton, Jr. & Co. v. United States 1136

Jackson v. Kansas City 1021

Jacob, In the Matter of 732, 739-742, 835

Jama v. Immigration & Customs Enforcement 857, 1048

James v. Board of Trustees of Public Employees' Retirement System 1259

James v. Valtierra 557

James v. Vernon Calhoun Packing Co. 643

James v. United States 650, 651, 655, 666, 854

James B. Beam Distilling Co. v. Georgia 655

Jane Doe, Adoption of 740

Jannotti, United States v. 953

Japan Whaling Ass'n v. American Cetacean Society 941

Jarecki v. G. D. Searle & Co. 852

Jawish v. Morlet 663, 665-667

Jefferson County Pharmaceutical Assoc. v. Abbott Labs 1019

Jepson v. Department of Labor and Indus. 643

Jodrey Estate v. Nova Scotia 852

Johnson v. De Grady 154

Johnson v. Edgar 362, 363

Johnson v. Southern Pacific Company 707

Johnson v. Transportation Agency, Santa Clara County 104, 114, 115, 622, 649, 781, 795, 799, 1048

Johnson, United States v. 387

Johnson v. Uncle Ben's, Inc. 688

K Mart Corp. v. Cartier, Inc. 1209, 1211

K.M. and D.M., Petition of 740

K.S.P., Adoption of 740

Kaiser Aluminum and Chemical Corp. v. Bonjorno 672

Kansas v. Neufeld 402

Karcher v. Daggett 130, 131, 133, 174, 175

Karr v. Robinson 612

Katz v. United States 1187

Katzenbach v. Morgan 150

Kaufman, State v. 419

Keene Corp. v. United States 867

Kennedy v. Mendoza-Martinez 1046

Kenosha, City of v. Bruno 644

Kent v. Dulles 426-428, 435-437

Keogh v. Chicago and N.W. Ry. 1129

Kern v. Blethen-Coluni 998

Key Tronic Corp. v. United States 856

Kilbourn v. Thompson 387, 393, 394

Kimel v. Florida Bd. of Regents 934, 938, 940

King v. St. Vincent's Hosp. 826, 881

Kirkpatrick v. Preisler 130

Kirksey v. Jackson 548, 549

Kokoszka v. Belford 862

Kolstad v. American Dental Ass'n 970

Kosak v. United States 1014, 1018-1020

Kungys v. United States 865

Kusper v. Pontikes 346

Laemoa, State v. 999

Lambert v. California 907

Lamie v. U.S. Trustee 861

Lamont, United States v. 1145

Land Comm'r v. Hutton 643

Landell v. Sorrell 247

Landgraf v. USI Film Products 672, 685-688, 793, 883, 998, 1001, 1046, 1047, 1074

Lanier, United States v. 886

Larios v. Cox 134, 192

Lassiter v. Northampton County Board of Elections 149

Lawrence v. Florida 867

Laws, United States v. 702

League of United Latin American Citizens v. Perry 154, 192

League of Women Voters of Pa. v. Commonwealth 419

Leake v. Long Island Jewish Medical Center 686

LeBlanc v. LeBlanc 864

Ledbetter v. Goodyear Tire & Rubber Co. 862, 1074, 1075

Ledbetter, State v. 999

Lee v. Keith 227

Lee v. Mitchell 999

Leegin Creative Leather Prods., Inc. v. PSKS, Inc. 646, 969

Legislature of the State of California v. Eu 223, 1115

Lehigh Valley Coal Co. v. Yensavage 707

Lehman v. Nakshian 1074

Lemon v. Kurtzman 652

Leo Sheep v. United States 882, 973, 979-981, 1014, 1033, 1034, 1041

Leonard v. Bothell 567

Li v. Yellow Cab of California 737, 739, 740, 742, 781, 835, 983

Libertarian Party of Ohio v. Blackwell 227

Liggetts-Findley Drug-Stores Ltd., Rex. v. 689

Lindahl v. Office of Personnel Management 1034

Lindh v. Murphy 688, 867

Linkletter v. Walker 651, 654

Linlee Enters., Inc. v. State 1021

Local 82, Furniture & Piano Moving Union v. Crowley 982

Local No. 93, Int'l Ass'n of Firefighters v. Cleveland 104

Local 189, United Papermakers v. United States 83

Local Union No. 1784 Firefighters v. Stotts 104

Lochner v. New York 434, 591, 592, 704

Locke, United States v. 728, 729, 842

Long Beach, City of v. Department of Industrial Relations 1261

Longstaff, In re 1066

Lopez v. Davis 860

Lopez v. Monterey County 150, 170

Lorance v. AT&T Technologies 117, 118

Lorillard v. Pons 1048, **1070**, 1073-1076

Lorillard Tobacco Co. v. Roth 1259

Louisiana, United States v. 149

Louisville Joint Stock Land Bank v. Radford 670

Lovett, United States v. 666

Lowe v. SEC 1020

Luciano, People v. 1021

Luke, Adoption of 740

Lundy, Commissioner v. 866

Lussier v. Dugger 686

Lynch v. United States 667

Mackey v. Lanier Collections Agency & Serv. 856, 1042

Mackey v. United States 651

Maikotter v. University of West Virginia Bd. of Trustees 1260

Majewski v. Broadalbin-Perth Cent. School Dist. 999

Management Council of the Wyoming Legislature v. Geringer 370

Mapp v. Ohio 657

Marbury v. Madison 656, 1202, 1280

Marrama v. Citizens Bank of Mass. 855

Marshall, United States v. **801**, 810-812, 835, 903, 989, 1041, 1268

Marshall Field & Co. v. Clark 414, 415, 701

Martin v. Hadix 688

Martin v. Herzog 610, 611

Martin v. OSHRC 1240

Martin v. Wilks 117, 118

Maryland v. Wirtz 922

Massachusetts v. EPA 1041, 1212

Maxwell, Commonwealth v. 741

May v. McNally 296

McBoyle v. United States 885, 886

McConnell v. Federal Election Commission 252, 260, **261**, 286, 287, 290, 292, 346

McCormick v. United States 311, 901

McCulloch v. Maryland 430, 882

McCulloch v. Sociedad Nacional de Marineros de Honduras 917

McDonald v. Santa Fe Trail Transp. Co. 87, 1046

MCI v. AT&T 792, 794, 1138, **1204**, 1209, 1212, 1213, 1227

McIntyre v. Ohio Elections Commission 257

McKeag v. Board of Pension Comm'rs of Los Angeles 764

McKnight v. General Motors Corp. 663

McNally v. United States 791, 898, 900-902, 947

Mead v. Arnell 1157

Mead Corp., United States v. **1213**, 1223-1227, 1240, 1278-1283

Mendoza, People v. 998

Meritor Sav. Bank FSB v. Vinson 1049

Merrell Dow Pharmaceuticals v. Thompson 1131

Merrill Lynch, Pierce, Fenner & Smith v. Curran 1132

Metzenbaum v. Federal Energy Regulatory Comm'n 471

Meyer v. Grant 527

Miah v. Ahmed 998

Midlantic Nat'l Bank v. New Jersey Dep't of Envir. Prot. 763, 1062

Miles v. Apex Marine Corp. 615

Miller v. Fenton 643

Miller v. Johnson 170-172

Miranda v. Arizona 651, 652, 654

Miranda, State v. 1021

Mississippi, United States v. 148, 149

Mississippi Band of Choctaw Indians v. Holyfield 856

Mississippi Power & Light v. Mississippi ex rel. Moore 1240

Mistretta v. United States 1137, 1138

Mobil Oil Corp. v. Federal Power Comm'n 1173, 1175

Mobil Oil Co. v. Higginbotham 614, 615

Mobile, City of v. Bolden 137, 146, 147, 151-153, 172, 193, 194

Monell v. Department of Social Servs. 643, 969

Monroe v. Pape 643-645

Monroe v. Standard Oil Co. 1019

Monsanto, United States v. 1042

Montana v. Blackfeet Tribe 883

Montana Wilderness Association v. United States Forest Service 1027, 1033-1035, **1036**, 1040-1042, 1066, 1081, 1099

Moor v. Alameda County 644

Moore v. United States House of Representatives 417

Moragne v. States Marine Lines, Inc. 601, 609, 610, 612-616, 621-623, 625, 628, 629, 641, 647, 648, 652, 688, 1062, 1074

Morrison v. Olson 1160

Morrison, United States. v. 410

Morton v. Mancari 1082, 1088, 1098

Moskal v. United States 971

Mossop, Canada (Attorney General) v. 850

Motor Vehicle Manufacturers Ass'n v. State Farm Mutual Automobile Ins. Co. 1176, 1183, 1184, 1202, 1267

Mountain States Tel. & Tel. v. Pueblo of Santa Ana 879

Moxley v. Roberts 968

Moynahan v. New York 860

Mrs. W. v. Tirozzi 686

Munoz-Flores, United States v. 416

Munro v. Socialist Workers Party 229, 233

Murphy v. Kenneth Cole Productions, Inc. 1000

Murray v. The Charming Betsy 883, 917

Murphy, United States v. 401

Muscarello v. United States 888, 898, 901-903, 947, 997

Myers, United States v. 401, 402

NAACP v. Alabama 240, 346

NAACP v. Allen 84

Nader v. Allegheny Airlines, Inc. 1129

National Ass'n of Securities Dealers, United States v. 1098

National Cable & Telecommunications Ass'n v. Brand X Internet Services 1223, 1268

National Credit Union Admin. v. First Nat'l Bank & Trust Co. 1258

National League of Cities v. Usery 922, 934, 936, 938

Natl. Lime & Stone Co., State ex rel. Celebrezze v. 1259

National Muffler Dealers v. United States 1224

National Petroleum Refiners Ass'n v. FTC 855

National Pride at Work, Inc. v. Governor 1011

National Railroad Passenger Corporation v. Boston & Maine Corp. 1210

National Treasury Employees Union, United States v. 314, 315

Neal v. United States 812, 1268, 1269

Negonsott v. Samuels 1019

Nevada Dep't Human Resources v. Hibbs 881

New Jersey Civ. Serv. Ass'n v. State 998

New York v. United States 819, 938

New York Times Co. v. Sullivan 236, 294

Newport News Shipbuilding & Dry Dock Co. v. EEOC 1197

Nix v. Hedden 851, 852

Nixon v. Administrator of General Servs. 666

Nixon v. Shrink Missouri Government PAC 243, 295

Nixon, United States v. 1146

NLRB v. Amax Coal Co. 852

NLRB v. Catholic Bishop of Chicago 911, 917-920, 934, 950, 1257

NLRB v. Fruit & Vegetable Packers 1021

NLRB v. Local 103, Int'l Ass'n of Bridge Workers 1021

NLRB v. Robbins Tire & Rubber Co. 1019

Nordic Village, United States v. 792, 940, 1020

Norfolk Southern Ry. v. Shankin 1270

Norfolk & Western Ry. Co. v. American Train Dispatchers Ass'n 853

North Colorado Medical Center, Inc. v. Committee on Anticompetitive Conduct 1260

Northern Pipeline Construction Co. v. Marathon Pipe Line Co. 653, 655, 663

O'Grady, United States v. 953

O'Malley Lumber Co. v. Riley 999

Oak Ridge, City of v. Roane County 999

Officers for Justice v. Civil Serv. Comm'n 649

Offshore Logistics v. Tallentire 615

Ohrenstein, People v. 404

Opinion of the Justices 1156

Osborn v. Bank of the United States 867

Paccar, Inc. v. NHTSA 1127

Pacific Bell v. California State and Consumer Services Agency 1021

Pacific States Tel. & Tel. Co. v. Oregon 525

Palm Beach County Canvassing Board v. Harris 1247, 1255, 1257, 1258

Papachristou v. Jacksonville 907

Pattern Makers' League of North Am. v. NLRB 1026

Patterson v. McLean Credit Union 117, 118, 646, 662, 663, 685-687, 791, 1061, 1269

Paul v. Virginia 644

Payne v. Tennessee 645

Pena, State v. 887

Penn Central Transp. Co. v. New York City 670

Pennhurst State School & Hospital v. Halderman 922, 941

Pennsylvania Coal Co. v. Mahon 667

People v. ___. See name of other party

People ex rel. ___. See name of other party

Pepper v. Hart 1001, 1011-1014, 1020, 1099

Perez v. Wyeth Laboratories, Inc. 814, 998, 818

Perlaza, United States v. 1045

Permanent Mission of India to the U.N. v. City of New York 969

Perry v. Jordan 541

Personnel Adm'r of Mass. v. Feeney 86, 87, 147

Petition For Authorization To Conduct A Referendum On Withdrawal Of North Haledon School Dist. From Passaic County Manchester Regional High School, In re 1259

Pharmacological Res. & Mfrs. v. Walsh 1267

Philly's v. Byrne 568, 573, 574

Phoenix, City of v. Kolodziejski 135

Picotte, State v. 669

Pierce v. Underwood 792, 866

Pierson v. Ray 958

Pinder, State v. 998

Pittston Coal Group v. Sebben 856

Platt v. Union Pac. R. 882

Plessy v. Ferguson 641

Porter v. Nussle 863

Powell v. McCormack 124, **196**, 205-207, 235, 387, 393, 431, 474, 622

Powerex Corp. v. Reliant Energy Servs., Inc. 866

Presley v. Etowah County Comm'n 150

Price Waterhouse v. Hopkins 117

Priestman, United States v. 862

Printz v. United States 515, 819, 938

Protective Life Ins. Co. v. Sullivan 1260

Public Citizen v. United States Department of Justice 743, 746-749, 933

Public Citizen v. United States District Court for the District of Columbia 415

Public Employees Retirement System of Ohio v. Betts 1042

Public Water Supply Co. v. DiPasquale 1261

Purvis v. Hubbell 652

Quarles v. Philip Morris, Inc. 83

Quelimane Co. v. Stewart Title Guar. Co. 1000

R.L.C., United States v. 793

Radzanower v. Touche Ross & Co. 1088

Raines v. Byrd 475, 477

Rake v. Wade 865

Raleigh & Galston R. Co. v. Reid 854

Randall v. Sorrell 247, 290, 294

Rapanos v. United States 938, 1022, 1026, 1035, 1041, 1043, 1064, 1210, 1269, 1270

Ratzlaf v. United States 886, 887, 901, 902

Rawluk v. Rawluk 864

Ray v. Atlantic Richfield Co. 883

Rayburn House Office Building, Room 2113, United States v. 403

Regan v. Wald 983, 1022

Regents of the University of California v. Bakke 426, 427

Regina (Jackson) v. Attorney General 1012

Reitman v. Mulkey 557

Reno v. Bossier Parish School Board 150

Republic of Austria v. Altmann 688

Reves v. Ernst & Young 954

Reynolds v. Sims 132-134, 174

Ricci v. Chicago Mercantile Exchange 1129

Rice v. Cayetano 135

Rice v. Santa Fe Elevator Corp. 1262

Richmond, City of v. J.A. Croson Co. 118

Ridgway v. Ridgway 1075

Riegle v. Federal Open Market Committee 474

Riggs v. Palmer 593

River Wear Comm'rs v. Adamson 693

Rivers v. Roadway Express, Inc. 685, 686

RLC, United States v. 902, 903

Robertson v. Seattle Audubon Society 1148

Robinson v. Secretary of State for Northern Ireland 1012

Robinson v. Shell Oil Co. 868

Roe v. Wade 668

Rogers v. Lodge 148, 151

Rogers v. Tennessee 669

Rome, City of v. United States 148, 150, 151

Romer v. Colorado General Assembly 404

Romer v. Evans 549, 556-558

Ron Pair Enterprises, Inc., United States v. 857

Rose v. Rose 938, 1076

Runyon v. McCrary 647, 648, 662, 663, 1049, 1061

Rush v. Ray 367, 370, 371, 386

Rush Prudential HMO v. Moran 883

Russello v. United States 954

Rust v. Sullivan 920, 1247

Rutkin v. United States 650

S/S Helena, In re 614

Sager v. McClenden 1021

Salorio v. Glaser 652

Salyer Land Co. v. Tulare Lake Basin Water Storage District 135

San Diego, County of v. Muniz 764

Scheidler v. NOW 852

Schmitz v. Younger 541

Schooner Peggy, United States v. 672

Schooner Paulina's Cargo v. United States 861

Schreiber v. Burlington Northern, Inc. 859

Schwegmann Bros. v. Calvert Distillers Corp. 722, 981

Sea-Land Services v. Gaudet 614, 615

Seatrain Shipbuilding Corp. v. Shell Oil Co. 1041

Sebastian v. Department of Labor and Industries 1260

Security Indus. Bank, United States v. 667

Seittelman v. Sabol 1259

Sharon S. v. Superior Court 740

Shaw v. Delta Airlines 1261

Shaw v. Hunt 170, 173

Shaw v. Railroad Co. 956

Shaw v. Reno 155, 169-174, 192

Shearer, United States v. 1081

Sheet Metal Workers v. EEOC 104

Sheldon G., In re 1021

Sheridan v. United States 1019

Shinault v. American Airlines, Inc. 1135

Shine v. Shine 723, 727, 728, 781, 845

Shroyer v. Harrison County Bd. of Educ. 1260

Sierra Club v. Costle 1173

Simpson v. Tobin 360

Sinclair, In re 989, 991, 995-997

Skaggs v. Carle 477

Skidmore v. Swift & Co. 1194, 1195, 1200, 1201, 1203, 1204, 1224-1226, 1240, 1244, 1245, 1262, 1267, 1268, 1276-1280, 1283

Smith v. Robinson 1088

Smith v. Turner 631

Smith, United States v. 856

Smith v. United States 903

Smith v. Wade 959, 968-970

Solid Waste Agency v. Army Corps of Eng'rs 856, 1026, 1041, 1042, 1048, 1049, 1061, 1064, 1210

Sorenson v. Secretary of the Treasury 879, 880

Sosa v. Alvarez-Machain 883

South Carolina v. Katzenbach 148, 150

South Carolina v. Regan 883, 1041

Southern Pacific Co. v. Jensen 589

Southland Corp. v. Keating 1019

Spallone v. United States 405-408

Spanel v. Mounds View School District No. 621 653

Speluncean Explorers, The Case of (Critical Scholars) 838, 842

Speluncean Explorers, The Case of (Fuller) 712, 721, 722, 751, 752, 811, 835, 838, 842

Spokane, City of v. State 1042

Square D Co. v. Niagara Frontier Tariff Bur., Inc. 643

St. Francis College v. Al-Khazraji 850

St. Martin Evangelical Lutheran Church v. South Dakota 1088

St. Paul Citizens for Human Rights v. City Council of the City of St. Paul 536, 540-542

Staples v. United States 886

State ex. rel. ___. See name of other party

State Farm Mutual Automobile Ins. Co. v. Dole 1184

State Oil Co. v. Khan 646. 969

Stinson v. United States 1241

Storer v. Brown 228, 231

Story, United States v. 1045

Stovall v. Denno 654

Sullivan v. Everhart 792

Sullivan v. Finkelstein 989, 1041

Sullivan v. Stroop 866

Sun-Diamond Growers of California, United States v. 308, 309

Superior Court, People ex rel. Lungren v. 1261

Suter v. Artist M 1132

Sutton v. United Airlines 864, 865, 1210, 1240

Syracuse Peace Council v. FCC 1172

Tallarico v. Trans World Airlines, Inc. 1135

Tammy, Adoption of 740

Tate v. Ogg 854

Taylor v. United States 436, 793

Tenney v. Brandhove 405

Terry v. Adams 127

Texas, United States v. 956

Texas and Pacific Ry. v. Rigsby 610, 611, 1129

Textile Workers Union v. Lincoln Mills 969

Thibodeau v. Design Group One Architects, LLC 616

Thomas Jefferson Univ. v. Shalala 1243, 1245

Thompson v. Thompson 1132, 1133

Thompson, State ex rel. Wisconsin Senate v. 370

Thompson/Center Arms Co., United States v. 989

Thornburg v. Gingles 152-154, 1042

Thorpe v. Housing Authority of City of Durham 672

Thunder Basin Coal Co. v. Reich 989

Thygesen v. Callahan 1137

Timmons v. Twin Cities Area New Party 228, 229, 231, 233

Toll v. Moreno 1062, 1262

Tool Sales & Service Co. v. Commonwealth 1260

Toolson v. New York Yankees 641, 642, 645, 646

Touche Ross & Co. v. Redington 1131, 1132

Train v. City of New York 455, 456, 1159

Transamerica Mortgage Advisors, Inc. (TAMA) v. Lewis 1132

Trbovich v. United Mine Workers of America 1020

TRW, Inc. v. Andrews 856

Turkette, United States v. 854

TWA v. Franklin Mint Corp. 1089

TVA v. Hill 364, **752**, 763, 765, 766, 781, 792, 1148

Tyrrell v. New York 857

Udall v. Tallman 1195

Union Bank v. Wolas 989

United Savings Ass'n of Texas v. Timbers of Inwood Forest Assocs. 862, 1066

United States v. ____. See name of other party

United States Department of Commerce v. Montana 131, 132

United States District Court, United States v. 1187

United States National Bank v. Independent Insurance Agents 857

U.S. Term Limits, Inc. v. Thornton 208, **209**, 222, 225, 226, 234, 235

United States Trust Co. v. New Jersey 667, 671

United Steelworkers v. Weber 1, 87, **88**, 100, 101, 102, 103, 104, 114, 115, 333, 622, 648, 649, 701, 703, 732, 747, 781, 795, 799, 814, 830, 831, 834, 836, 837, 842, 850, 935, 997, 1000, 1020, 1022, 1061, 1140, 1278

Usery v. Turner Elkhorn Mining Co. 670

Utah v. Andrus 980

Utah v. Evans 132

V.T., Regina v. 864

Vacher & Sons, Ltd. v. London Soc'y of Compositers 694

Valdes v. United States 304

Value Oil Co. v. Irvington 856

Van De Carr, People ex rel. Dickinson v. 305, 307, 308, 326, 396, 403

Van Sickle v. Shanahan 1157

Vander Jagt v. O'Neill 477

Vaughan v. Commonwealth 653

Vermont Yankee Nuclear Power Co. v. Natural Resources Defense Council, Inc. 1174, 1175

Vieth v. Jubelirer 177, 191, 193

Vincent v. Pabst Brewing Co. 653

Virginia Bankshares, Inc. v. Sandberg 1133

Vitex Mfg. Corp. v. Caribtex Corp. 611

Wabash, St. Louis and Pac. Ry. v. Illinois 1119

Wachovia Bank of N.C. v. Johnson 999

Wagner Electric Corp. v. Volpe 1127, 1176

Walgreen Co. v. Illinois Liquor Control Comm'n 573

Walker v. Jones 395

Wallace v. Kato 957

Walters v. Metropolitan Educ. Ents., Inc. 865

Wards Cove Packing Co. v. Atonio 115-120, 791

Warring v. Colpoys 667, 668

Warshow, State v. 595, 598, 622, 623, 626-629

Washington v. Davis 86, 146

Washington v. Glucksberg 1241, 1245

Washington v. Seattle Sch. Dist. No. 1 557

Washington State Motorcycle Dealers Ass'n v. State 370

Washington State Republican Party v. Washington 233

Waste Management of Seattle, Inc. v. Utilities and Transp. Comm'n 1260

Watkins v. United States 1145, 1146

Watt v. Alaska 1088

Webb v. Board of Ed. of Dyer County 1075

Wegematic Corp., United States v. 611

Weinberger v. Romero-Barcelo 883

Weinberger v. Rossi 883, 1061, 1089

Welosky, People v. 742

Wells v. Edwards 134

Wells, United States v. 852, 971

Welsh v. Branstad 371

Wesberry v. Sanders 130-134

West Bloomfield Hospital. v. Certificate of Need Bd. 1259

West Virginia University Hospitals v. Casey 779, 790-792, 794, 795, 799, 800, 811, 835, 843, 941, 970, 1066

Western Air Lines v. Board of Equalization 1042

Western Elec. Co., United States v. 1257

Western Pac. R. Co., United States v. 1128

Western Union Telegraph Co. v. Lenroot 865, 1021

Whirlpool Corp. v. Marshall 881

White v. Regester 134, 153

White v. State 998

White v. Weiser 130

Whiteley v. Chappell 721

Whitman v. American Trucking Ass'ns, Inc. 1136, 1138

Whitney v. Worcester 653

Wilcox, Commissioner v. 650, 651

Wilkins v. Gagliardi 404

Will v. Michigan Dep't of State Police 940
Williams v. Adams 968
Williams v. Crickman 643
Williams v. Ray 643
Williams v. Rhodes 227, 231
Williams, United States v. 401
Willing v. United States 860
Wiltberger, United States v. 887
Wingate v. Estate of Ryan 998
Winters, State ex rel. Heck's Discount Cen-
    ters v. 419, 420
Wisconsin v. City of New York 132
Wisconsin Public Intervenor v. Mortier 793,
    989, 990, 1210
Wiseman v. Keller 1021
Witkovich, United States v. 907, 917-920
Wolf v. Colorado 657
X-Citement Video, Inc., United States v. 886
Yakima, County of v. Confederated Tribes &
    Bands of Yakima Indian Nation 1088
Yakus v. United States 1136, 1138
Yale Express Sys., Inc., In re 611
Yamaha Motor Corp., U.S.A. v. Calhoun 615
Yermian, United States v. 1026, 1046
Young v. Kaye 999
Zadvydas v. Davis 918
Zemel v. Rusk 1137
Zerbe v. State 1077, 1081
Zimmerman, State ex rel. Martin v. 360
Zuni Public School District No. 89 v. Depart-
    ment of Education 795, 830, 852, 861,
    989, 1035, 1048

CASES AND MATERIALS ON

LEGISLATION

STATUTES AND THE CREATION OF PUBLIC POLICY

Fourth Edition

Chapter 1

AN INTRODUCTION TO LEGISLATION

We introduce this subject — legislation — through a statutory case study, followed by descriptions of several theoretical frameworks for understanding that story. Section 1 of this chapter tells the story of the Civil Rights Act of 1964, Pub. L. No. 88–352, 78 Stat. 241 (codified as amended in scattered sections of 42 U.S.C.). We have chosen this law, in part, because it is a dramatic example of how statutes can and do make a significant difference in our society and our lives. The principles set forth in *Brown v. Board of Education*, 347 U.S. 483 (1954), would have been left largely unfulfilled were it not for the statute, which amplified and implemented the principles in ways which the Court was not able, or willing, to do. Also, the story of the law's enactment is itself a case study of the legislative process and of the unpredictable path followed by the official as well as private implementers of the statute. In fairness, the path of the 1964 Civil Rights Act was and remains atypical of the federal legislative process, although, as we will discuss later in this chapter and in Chapter 4's study of the federal budget process, modern major legislation increasingly travels paths that diverge from the textbook descriptions of Congress.

The Civil Rights Act is also a useful starting point for a theoretical discussion of the legislative process in the United States. In Section 2, we offer three types of theories: pluralist theories, which focus on the role of interest groups in policymaking; proceduralist theories, which emphasize the many obstacles a bill must pass through before it becomes a law; and institutional theories, which approach statutes from the perspective of the various institutions charged with enacting, implementing, and overseeing them. Each theory has a descriptive feature (this is how the legislative process *does* work) and a normative dimension (this is how the legislative process *should* work).

In Section 3, we trace the dynamic interpretation of Title VII (the employment discrimination title) of the Civil Rights Act. We introduce you to theories of statutory interpretation through examination of an important case, *United Steelworkers v. Weber*, in which the Court interpreted the Act to allow voluntary affirmative action plans. We also consider the different interpretive methods used by the judges in light of the theories introduced in Section 2.

1

SECTION 1. THE STORY OF THE CIVIL RIGHTS ACT OF 1964 AND THE PROCEDURES OF STATUTE-CREATION[a]

Brown v. Board of Education declared a great principle — non-discrimination and racial equality — but the principle did little to change the day-to-day lives of most African Americans in the 1950s. *Brown* applied only to public institutions, leaving private hotels, restaurants, swimming pools, and employers free to continue racially discriminatory practices. Even public institutions (mainly schools) were only required to desegregate "with all deliberate speed." The pace of official desegregation was slothlike. In 1961, seven years after *Brown*, it required a bevy of federal marshals to escort James Meredith through the doors of the University of Mississippi as its first African-American student.

On February 2, 1960, four black students from North Carolina A & T University sat down to order at a "whites only" lunch counter at a Woolworth's store in Greensboro, North Carolina. The store's manager refused to serve them. They remained seated, silently demanding equal treatment. Hundreds of similar "sit-ins" followed in other Southern locales.

In April 1963, the Reverend Dr. Martin Luther King, Jr. launched a nonviolent offensive to protest and boycott the segregated shops, churches, and restaurants of Birmingham, Alabama. When Dr. King defied an injunction and led a protest march, the Birmingham Police Commissioner, T. Eugene "Bull" Connor, had him and 54 others arrested and jailed. In May 1963, Connor and his cohorts brutally attacked hundreds of black schoolchildren marching and singing the anthem "We Shall Overcome." Front-page photos of Connor's hounds attacking African-American youths, of fire hose water pressing back the waves of black bodies, and of burly policemen sitting on a prostrate woman aroused the national conscience (Harvey 55).

---

a. The authors gratefully acknowledge the critical assistance of John Rego, J.D., University of Virginia, 1986, in researching and writing this story. We relied on both primary and secondary sources for this account. The most informative source was Charles Whalen & Barbara Whalen, *The Longest Debate: A Legislative History of the 1964 Civil Rights Act* (1985) (cited in text as "Whalens," with page numbers). Not only does it provide valuable "inside" insights (Charles Whalen is a former Republican member of the House of Representatives), but its dramatic storytelling style inspired this short rendition. Quotations from *The Longest Debate* are reprinted with the permission of Charles Whalen, Barbara Whalen, and the publisher, Seven Locks Press, Inc., P.O. Box 27, Cabin John, Maryland 20818. Other useful sources were Carl Brauer, *John F. Kennedy and the Second Reconstruction* (1977) ("Brauer"); Hugh Davis Graham, *The Civil Rights Era: Origins and Development of National Policy, 1960–1972* (1990) ("Graham"); James Harvey, *Civil Rights During the Kennedy Administration* (1971) ("Harvey"); Hubert Humphrey, *Beyond Civil Rights: A New Day of Equality* (1968) ("Humphrey"); Neil MacNeil, *Dirksen: Portrait of a Public Man* (1970) ("MacNeil"); John Martin, *Civil Rights and the Crisis of Liberalism: The Democratic Party, 1945–76* (1979) ("Martin"); Merle Miller, *Lyndon: An Oral Biography* (1980) ("Miller"); Edward & Frederick Schapsmeier, *Dirksen of Illinois: Senatorial Statesman* (1985) ("Schapsmeier"); Bernard Schwartz, ed., *Statutory History of the United States: Civil Rights* (1970) ("Schwartz"); and Francis Vaas, *Title VII: Legislative History*, 7 B.C. Indus. & Com. L. Rev. 431 (1966) ("Vaas").

African-American leaders saw this as their historic moment. Dr. King wrote from his Birmingham jail cell:

> For years now I have heard the word "wait." It rings in the ear of every Negro with piercing familiarity. This "wait" has almost always meant "Never." * * * We have waited for more than 340 years for our constitutional and God-given rights. * * * [W]hen you take a cross-country drive and find it necessary to sleep night after night in the uncomfortable corners of your automobile because no motel will accept you; when you are humiliated day in and day out by nagging signs reading "white" and "colored"; when your first name becomes "nigger," your middle name becomes "boy" (however old you are) and your last name becomes "John," and your wife and mother are never given the respected title of "Mrs."; when you are harried by day and haunted by night by the fact that you are a Negro, living constantly at tiptoe stance, never quite knowing what to expect next, and plagued with inner fears and outer resentments; when you are forever fighting a degenerating sense of "no-bodiness" — then you will understand why we find it difficult to wait.

National media attention and outrage helped ensure the success of Dr. King's Birmingham campaign. On May 10, 1963, the city's businesses entered into a settlement in which the African-American community agreed to cease their boycott and the white-owned businesses agreed to hire blacks as clerks and salespeople, and to establish training programs in job categories previously closed to African Americans.

The Kennedy Administration was listening. Attorney General Robert Kennedy hailed the Birmingham settlement. On June 11, 1963, President John Kennedy addressed the country on national television and announced his intention to propose a comprehensive civil rights bill to the Congress:

> We are confronted primarily with a moral issue. It is as old as the Scriptures and it is as clear as the American Constitution. The heart of the question is whether all Americans are to be afforded equal rights and equal opportunities, whether we are going to treat our fellow Americans as we want to be treated. * * *

> One hundred years of delay have passed since President Lincoln freed the slaves, yet their heirs, their grandsons, are not fully free. They are not yet freed from the bonds of injustice. They are not yet freed from social and economic oppression. And this Nation, for all its hopes and all its boasts, will not be fully free until all its citizens are free.

> Now the time has come for this Nation to fulfill its promise.

OBSTACLES TO CIVIL RIGHTS LEGISLATION

The President's proposed legislation concentrated on four areas of concern: discrimination in public accommodations, desegregation of public schools, fair employment, and discrimination by recipients of federal funds. Title II of the bill, the public accommodations provision, would guarantee equal access to all hotels, restaurants, places of amusement, and retail establishments. Title III covered school desegregation. It would give the federal government, particularly the Attorney General, greater authority to implement the *Brown* decision. Employment discrimination was treated, though some thought half-heartedly, in Title V of the President's bill, which expanded the powers of the

Civil Rights Commission, and in Title VII, which would have established a Committee on Equal Employment to monitor the conduct of federal contractors. While not addressing private discrimination, the President reaffirmed his support for legislation addressing employment discrimination in the private sector. Finally, in Title VI, the President proposed that recipients of federal assistance be prohibited from discriminating on the basis of race.

The events of 1963 suggested the need for such legislation. But there was good reason to doubt that the President's bill would ever become law. The ambivalence of both political parties, the uncertain commitment of the President and Vice President, and significant unavoidable obstacles in the legislative process boded ill for the proposal.

1. *The Ambivalence of Both Political Parties.* On the issue of civil rights, the Democratic Party could be described as two parties. Throughout the century Southern Democrats normally controlled half or more of the party's votes in the Senate, and after the 1930s they systematically killed civil rights bills through parliamentary maneuvers (Martin 157). In 1948, the Democratic Party split when adoption of a civil rights plank at the national convention caused a walkout by segregationists. Efforts to heal those wounds led the Democrats to downplay civil rights in the 1952 and 1956 platforms. In contrast, the Republicans — the Party of Lincoln — showed renewed interest in civil rights. In 1957, President Eisenhower introduced a civil rights bill. The Republicans in the House of Representatives agreed to weaken the bill to enhance its chances for enactment. But a filibuster by Senate Democrats forced supporters to propose changes that made it an essentially toothless law. A similar presidential initiative in 1960 yielded a weak voting rights law, after Senate Democrats deleted school desegregation, employment, and housing discrimination provisions from the bill.

As the 1960 election approached, black leaders wondered which — if either — of the major parties was capable of delivering civil rights legislation. The Republicans had pushed for moderate civil rights laws in the 1950s but had been unable to deliver them. Democrats had both supported and torpedoed civil rights initiatives. The platforms of both parties called for civil rights legislation and prosecution of public segregation, but the support seemed increasingly rhetorical as the campaign wore on (Harvey 13). The Democrat (Kennedy) took stronger stands on the civil rights issue than did the Republican (Nixon), thereby winning the black vote. Indeed, his showing among African Americans and labor was the strongest since FDR (Martin 171) and was obviously crucial in that close election.

2. *The Uncertain Commitment of the President and Vice President.* Although President Kennedy opposed discrimination, he had no deep emotional concern for the issue. Kennedy saw his own family's Irish immigrant experience as proof that prejudice could be overcome without special assistance. Some have suggested that Kennedy was primarily concerned with foreign affairs and economic issues and thought of African Americans only in terms of votes (Harvey 19). As a senator in 1957, Kennedy had voted with the Democratic majority to weaken the Republicans' civil rights bill (Martin 167).

Thus it was hardly surprising that, after the 1960 election, President Kennedy disregarded his campaign rhetoric and decided not to seek legislation. He reasoned that such an effort would not only fail, but it would also delay enactment of important economic legislation (cf. Harvey 19–20). Kennedy did use his powers as chief executive to appoint African Americans to important positions and to establish equal opportunity in federal employment. But he demonstrated no sense of urgency. It was not until November 1962, for example, that he issued the order prohibiting racial discrimination in federally financed housing, the same order he had, as a candidate in 1960, chastised Eisenhower for not issuing with a "stroke of his pen" (Martin 177). And it was not until he was faced with blatant defiance by Governors Ross Barnett (D–Miss.) and George Wallace (D–Ala.) that Kennedy, as Commander-in-Chief, used federal troops to enforce judicial desegregation orders.

Nor had the President's 1960 running mate displayed much enthusiasm for civil rights as a pressing item on the national agenda. In his 1948 campaign for the Senate, Lyndon Johnson had called President Truman's civil rights program (repeal of the poll tax; anti-lynching law; nondiscrimination in employment) "a farce and a sham — an effort to set up a police state in the guise of liberty" (Miller 118). Through his friendship with powerful Senator Richard Russell (D–Ga.), Johnson became the Democrats' Senate leader in 1953. More ambitious and opportunistic than ideological, Johnson adapted his agenda to the political needs of the time. Although few in 1963 considered LBJ a racist, he was not considered a civil rights activist, either.

3. *Obstacles in Congress.* Over 90% of bills introduced in Congress die in the legislative labyrinth. Though a senator for eight years and representative for six years before that, Kennedy was not a skilled legislative strategist. It was unlikely that he could move a civil rights bill through Congress.

Virtually all bills introduced in Congress are referred initially to a committee for consideration and cannot be voted on until the committee has reported them out.[b] Because a committee's chair controls the committee's staff and agenda, he or she has the power to effectively kill a bill by preventing the committee from considering it. Committee chairmanships have generally been awarded on the basis of seniority, and at the time of the deliberations on the Civil Rights Act, many powerful chairs were held by senior congressmen from the "one-party" states of the South and Southwest (Harvey 16–17).

In the Senate, civil rights legislation fell under the jurisdiction of the Judiciary Committee. The chairman, Senator James Eastland (D–Miss.), was notorious for killing civil rights bills. The situation was little better in the House, where the Rules Committee — the committee through which almost

---

b. Current House Rule X, clause 1 and Senate Rule XXV, clause 1 identify the standing (permanent) committees in the two chambers and define the jurisdiction (area of exclusive authority) for each standing committee. House Rule XII, clause 2 and Senate Rule XVII, clause 3 govern referral to committees by the Speaker of the House and the Senate Majority Leader. (All citations to House and Senate Rules in this book are taken from *Standing Rules of the Senate*, in *Senate Manual*, S. Doc. No. 107–1 (2002), and *Rules of the House of Representatives*, 110th Congress, http://www.rules.house.gov/ruleprec/110th.pdf (May 24, 2007).)

every bill passes on its way to the floor — was headed by Howard W. "Judge" Smith (D–Va.), also a foe of civil rights laws. In 1957, Smith stalled consideration of the civil rights bill simply by leaving Washington; he claimed that he needed to attend to his barn in Virginia that had recently burned down. Speaker of the House Sam Rayburn (D–Tex.) replied that he knew Smith was opposed to civil rights, but he never suspected that the Chairman would resort to arson (Martin 166).

Even if the civil rights bill were to survive the committee process, it faced a certain *filibuster* on the floor of the Senate. Senate rules allow unlimited debate of a question before voting, and civil rights opponents had successfully used this tactic in 1957 and 1960 to prevent consideration of civil rights bills, allowing a vote only after they had exacted tremendous concessions from the bills' supporters. The only ways to break a filibuster are by permitting it to continue until the filibusterers are physically exhausted or by invoking *cloture* (a two-thirds vote to end discussion).[c] The former had been tried and had failed in 1957, while the latter had been successfully invoked only five times in the history of the Senate and never to end debate on a civil rights bill (Whalens 126).

PASSAGE IN THE HOUSE

The President's civil rights bill was introduced in both houses of Congress on June 19, 1963, but its supporters pushed for immediate consideration only in the House of Representatives. They believed that the obstacles would be less substantial in the House. If they could develop a strong record in support of the bill there, together with a large vote in favor of the bill, supporters hoped that political momentum would improve the bill's chances in the Senate.

1. *Writing a Bill the Hard Way — The Judiciary Committee.* House Speaker John McCormack (D–Mass.) referred H.R. 7152[d] to the House Judiciary Committee, which had jurisdiction over civil rights bills. Chairman Emanuel Celler (D–N.Y.) referred the bill to Subcommittee No. 5. The Chairman referred the bill to this subcommittee, which normally handled antitrust matters, because it was dominated by civil rights advocates: its Chairman was Celler himself, the ranking Republican was William McCulloch R–Ohio), and it had no senior Southern member (Harvey 60).

Chairman of the Judiciary Committee in 1949–53 and after 1955, Celler, a longtime representative from Brooklyn, had become one of Congress' leading civil rights advocates. Just after the 1960 election Celler introduced a civil rights bill based on Kennedy's platform. (The bill died when the President

---

c. Under current Senate Rule XXII, clause 2, cloture can be invoked in most cases by the vote of 60 of the 100 senators, but in 1963–64 the Rule provided for cloture of debate only by two-thirds of the senators voting on the question. Since important cloture votes could be expected to command all 100 senators, 67 votes were usually needed to close off debate. Even now, a two-thirds vote is required to end debate on any measure amending the Senate rules, including the rule governing cloture.

d. Bills introduced in the House and Senate are assigned identifying numbers — "H.R. ___" and "S. ___" — just as cases filed in U.S. courts are assigned a docket number.

failed to lend his support.) He was the House member chosen to sponsor President Kennedy's 1963 bill and was determined to see it become law. Bill McCulloch's district in rural Ohio was a universe away from Brooklyn. It was WASP and conservative, and it had an African-American population of only 2.7%. Although there was little interest in civil rights legislation at home, McCulloch's immense popularity allowed him latitude to pursue a personal legislative agenda. McCulloch was a man of firm principle, and a principle dear to him was antidiscrimination. McCulloch had worked hard to pass the Eisenhower civil rights bills in 1957 and 1960. In January 1963, he had introduced a civil rights bill of his own (Whalens 7–11). McCulloch's support, and the Republican votes he might bring with him, were essential to success in the House where, because of the split in the Democratic ranks, the Republicans held the balance of power (Harvey 59).

Celler scheduled subcommittee hearings to start before the Fourth of July recess. The free ride that the bill was expected to get through the subcommittee hit a snag with the first witness, Attorney General Robert Kennedy. The Attorney General was unaware of McCulloch's earlier bill, as well as a bill introduced by John Lindsay (R–N.Y.), and his failure to acknowledge Republican civil rights efforts was interpreted as a Democratic attempt to take partisan advantage of the civil rights issue. The Republican members of the subcommittee threatened to scuttle H.R. 7152 if it became a partisan measure. To repair the nascent bipartisan coalition, the Administration dispatched Assistant Attorney General Burke Marshall to negotiate a deal with McCulloch during the recess (Whalens 5–11).

Marshall found that the Ohio Congressman agreed with the President, but McCulloch was unwilling to allow the Democrats to hog the civil rights issue (particularly since the Democrats heading the Administration had undermined his efforts in 1957 and 1960). A compromise was reached under which McCulloch pledged his support in exchange for two promises. First, the Administration agreed not to allow the Senate to water down the bill, as it had done in 1957 when Vice President Johnson was Majority Leader. This meant that McCulloch would be consulted on all changes to H.R. 7152 that the Administration wanted to accept after the bill passed the House. Second, President Kennedy agreed to keep the issue a bipartisan effort by giving the Republicans equal credit when the bill was passed (Whalens 10–14).

As the congressional hearings progressed, the Administration engaged in a campaign to build public support for H.R. 7152, meeting with over 1,600 members of interest groups in June and July. Receiving special attention were representatives of labor, the clergy, and civil rights groups (Brauer 273–74). The President was especially interested in a vigorous clerical lobby because it provided a means of influencing legislators from states where the impact of blacks and labor was minimal (Brauer 275). On the other hand, the Administration cautioned against lobbying *too* vigorously. At the meeting with members of the Leadership Conference on Civil Rights — an alliance of 74 organizations lobbying for civil rights legislation — the President argued against overly ambitious demands. But civil rights leaders wanted the strongest possible bill (Brauer 282), and a parade of such advocates appeared before Subcommittee No. 5.

By August 2, the subcommittee had held 22 days of hearings on H.R. 7152 and was ready to *mark up* the bill. A mark-up is a committee's drafting session, where members consider amendments and rewrite bills. President Kennedy had asked Celler to stall final consideration on the bill until his tax reform proposal was voted out of the House Ways and Means Committee, where it had been languishing since January. The highly controversial tax cut was a cornerstone in the President's economic program, and Kennedy feared that Southerners on Ways and Means might use the bill as a target for retaliation if the civil rights bill cleared Subcommittee No. 5 first. Therefore, Celler delayed substantive mark-up of H.R. 7152 until September (Whalens 22–23). Meanwhile, public pressure for legislation mounted.[e]

On September 10, the Ways and Means Committee approved the tax bill, and Celler prepared for the mark-up of H.R. 7152. Deputy Attorney General Nicholas Katzenbach had written Celler a letter setting forth the "tactics" that the Administration expected him to follow, pursuant to its deal with McCulloch. But Celler chose to pursue a more aggressive approach. He remembered that the Senate had watered down the moderate civil rights bills passed by the House in 1957 and 1960. Why not start with a very strong bill this time, so that a compromise version would still be acceptable? Moreover, by publicly pushing a strong bill, Celler would be a hero to civil rights groups and would still be able to preserve his friendship with the conservatives by allowing them to score points with their constituents when the bill was inevitably weakened (Whalens 30–31).

Bill McCulloch watched in disbelief as Manny Celler and the liberal Democrats on the subcommittee proceeded to strengthen almost every title of the Administration bill, betraying the President's agreement with the Republican leadership in the process. Some of the changes were procedural. Byron Rogers (D–Colo.) offered a new Title III, which authorized the Attorney General to initiate or intervene in civil suits charging discrimination by state or local officials. Other changes were substantial and sweeping. Bob Kastenmeier (D–Wis.) offered an amendment to broaden Title II, the public accommodations provision, to include every private business — law firms, medical associations, and private schools — except rooming houses with five units or less (Whalens 34–35; Harvey 60). Finally, on September 25, the subcommittee

---

e. While the Administration put the civil rights bill on the back burner, civil rights groups continued to lobby for it. On August 28, 1963, as Congress prepared to adjourn for the Labor Day recess, almost a quarter of a million people converged on Washington, D.C., in a peaceful demonstration for equal rights — the March on Washington for Jobs and Freedom (Martin 176–77). In his address to the crowd that afternoon, Dr. King argued that, one hundred years after the Emancipation Proclamation, African Americans were still not free. "One hundred years later, the life of the Negro is still sadly crippled by the manacles and the chains of discrimination. * * * One hundred years later, the Negro is still languishing in the corners of American society and finds himself an exile in his own land." Dr. King concluded: "I have a dream today that my four little children will one day live in a nation where they will not be judged by the color of their skin but by the content of their character. I have a dream today" (see Whalens 26).

replaced H.R. 7152's weak equal employment provisions with a new title, embodied in a 30-page amendment offered by Peter Rodino (D–N.J.). The new title would create an Equal Employment Opportunity Commission (EEOC) with authority to investigate employment discrimination on account of race, religion, or national origin and to issue enforceable cease-and-desist orders (Vaas 435; Whalens 35).

On October 2, Subcommittee No. 5 reported the new H.R. 7152 to the full Judiciary Committee. Civil rights leaders, who had received virtually every provision they had lobbied for, called the bill a triumph. But McCulloch labeled the bill "a pail of garbage" with no chance of passage on the floor of the House (Whalens 38). The Southerners on the Judiciary Committee who hoped to derail the bill apparently agreed; they joined the liberals and voted H.R. 7152 as amended out of subcommittee (Harvey 60).

House Minority Leader Charles Halleck (R–Ind.) met with Katzenbach and Speaker McCormack on October 8 to tell them that the Republicans would allow the strengthened bill to go to the House floor, where it would probably die — unless the liberal Democrats themselves cooperated in weakening the bill. The Administration readily agreed to the Republicans' proposal and persuaded Celler to go along (Whalens 42–44). On October 15, the Attorney General testified before the Committee to recommend weakening changes (Brauer 304). On October 22, the amendments were to be offered, the first by Roland Libonati (D–Ill.). At the last moment Libonati backed out, leaving the Republicans feeling betrayed again. A Republican member moved to report the subcommittee bill to the full House. The motion would have easily passed had Celler not adjourned the Committee for the day. The situation was a mess.

Administration officials met with Halleck and McCulloch to work out a compromise bill that would satisfy the Republicans (Whalens 52–53). The President agreed to Republican demands that the bill should be revised. The new bill reconciled a Republican redraft and the original Administration bill. The President and Republican leadership agreed that the compromise bill would be offered as a substitute for the subcommittee bill (Harvey 61). All that remained was to defeat the motion to report out the unacceptable subcommittee version of H.R. 7152. Halleck and McCulloch agreed to provide seven Republican votes if the Democrats would provide ten votes. The President twisted arms and Celler invoked loyalty to party and the chairman to meet their quota (Whalens 59–64).

Now uneasy with Chairman Celler's ability to run the Judiciary Committee, the Administration prepared a "six-point script" for him to follow on October 29, describing precisely the manner in which to proceed. For once, events went as planned (Whalens 64–66). (1) A roll call vote was taken on the pending motion to report the subcommittee bill. Democratic members were called first, according to tradition, allowing Halleck and McCulloch to see if the Democrats could deliver their share of the votes to defeat the motion before having to commit themselves. Celler delivered ten Democratic votes, and Halleck provided nine Republicans (more than he had promised) to defeat the motion. (2) Celler moved to strike all but the first sentence of the subcommittee bill and to insert the compromise bill as an amendment. (3) Celler and McCulloch quickly explained the substitute, and Celler brushed aside a *point of order* challenge. (4) Once the compromise was read in its entirety, Representative Rodino moved the *previous question,* cutting off any debate on the proposed amendment. The Committee voted 20–12 in favor of the previous question. (5) The Judiciary Committee passed the compromise substitute by a vote of 20–14. (6) The Committee reported H.R. 7152 to the House.

Although civil rights leaders criticized the Administration for favoring cutbacks in the subcommittee substitute, the Committee version was decidedly stronger than the Administration's original bill. For example, Title II (public accommodations) broadly prohibited discrimination in places of lodging, sports stadiums and arenas, theaters, restaurants, cafeterias, lunch counters, and gas stations. Title VII (equal employment) retained the main features of Rodino's substitute for the Administration's weak monitoring provisions, though the EEOC's adjudicatory powers were limited. The President praised the bill as "comprehensive and fair," and the Administration evenly distributed credit among Democrats and Republicans (Whalens 66).

2. *Surviving the Rules Committee.* On November 21, H.R. 7152 and the Judiciary Committee's report were conveyed to the Clerk of the House and then to the Rules Committee. Each bill reported out of committee passes through the Rules Committee, where a resolution (the *rule*) governing floor debate is prepared.[f] In addition to providing that high priority bills receive expedited consideration, the Committee determines the amount of time to be allowed for debate, how the time for debate will be allocated, and the scope of permissible amendments.

The Rules Committee stage often constitutes a substantive consideration of the bill, and it presents an opportunity to derail a bill before the House itself has a chance to consider it. Unfortunately, the chairman of the Rules Committee, 80-year-old Judge Howard Smith, had spent 33 years in the House killing or eviscerating progressive legislation in the areas of labor, public housing, education, medical care and, of course, civil rights. His effectiveness had brought him a reputation as one of the most powerful members of the House[g] (Whalens 84, 90).

---

f. Current House Rule XIII, clause 2 provides that all committee reports, including the views of the minority, shall be delivered to the Clerk for printing and reference to the proper *calendar* (described *infra*, p. 31). Because House calendars contain many bills, and bills are to be considered in their order on the calendars, there is no assurance that the bill will be considered at all. The Rules Committee has the power to recommend a rule to expedite consideration of any bill — ahead of those previously placed on the calendars.

g. In an effort to curtail Smith's ability to bury the Administration's progressive legislative agenda, President Kennedy had worked prior to the 1961 session with then-Speaker of the House, Sam Rayburn, to enlarge the Rules Committee from ten to fifteen members (ten Democrats and five Republicans). The appointment of five new committee members allowed Rayburn and the Administration to create an 8–7 liberal majority on the Rules Committee and to increase the control of party leaders over it. While the enlargement improved prospects for the President's legislative agenda, highly controversial bills — like civil rights proposals — still faced unfavorable odds in Howard Smith's lair (Harvey 15–16).

President Kennedy's assassination on November 22 meant that the task of getting H.R. 7152 through the Rules Committee fell to Lyndon Johnson. In an effort to seize the moral leadership of the nation, President Johnson addressed a joint session of Congress soon after Kennedy's death:

> [N]o memorial oration or eulogy could more eloquently honor President Kennedy's memory than the earliest possible passage of the civil rights bill for which he fought so long. We have talked long enough in this country about equal rights. We have talked for one hundred years or more. It is time now to write the next chapter and to write it in the books of law.

As a posthumous tribute to their martyred President, the American people were coming to support the civil rights bill in growing numbers and with increasing ardor. But none of this sentiment moved Judge Smith, who had a firm grip on the fate of H.R. 7152. Following the Southern strategy of delay, he declined even to hold hearings on the bill.

There were three procedural options capable of dislodging Smith's stranglehold on H.R. 7152, and each was tried by the bill's supporters (Whalens 84–85). First, under House Rule XV, a petition signed by a majority of the House's members (218) can remove any bill from committee, including the Rules Committee, after it has been in committee for 30 days. On December 9, Manny Celler began circulating such a *discharge petition*, but McCulloch and Halleck refused to deliver the needed Republican signatures, on the ground that such a course was antithetical to the committee process (Whalens 84). (Of 563 discharge petitions initiated between 1931 and 2002, only 47 were successful in forcing floor consideration. Nineteen of the discharged bills passed the House, but only two became law, with another two resulting in changes in the House's rules. Richard Beth, Congressional Research Service Report for Congress, *The Discharge Rule in the House: Use in Historical Context* (April 17, 2003).)

On December 11, the Republicans announced their intent to use a second device, *Calendar Wednesday*, to call up H.R. 7152. House Rule XXV allows the Speaker on each Wednesday to call the standing committees in alphabetical order to inquire whether the chairman wishes the House to consider any bill previously reported out of that committee. But with 11 committees coming alphabetically before the Judiciary Committee, including six chaired by Southerners, the bill's opponents could easily defeat the tactic by calling up other bills to exhaust the available time. To prevent an embarrassing display of intraparty divisions, the Democratic leadership simply adjourned the House before the Calendar Wednesday maneuver could be tried (Whalens 85).

The third mechanism was to be the key. House Rule XI permits any three members of a committee to request the chairman to call a meeting to consider a bill; if the meeting is not scheduled within three days, a majority of the committee may schedule one. Liberal Democrats numbered five on the Rules Committee, so three Republican votes were needed. The pivotal votes were controlled by 70-year-old Clarence Brown (R–Ohio), the ranking minority member on the Rules Committee (Whalens 85). The conservative Brown shared the commitment to civil rights of his friend and neighboring Congressman, Bill McCulloch.[h] Brown informed his friend Judge Smith of his plans to lead a mutiny, so to head off a confrontation, Smith announced that hearings would begin on January 9, 1964 (Whalens 86).

Between January 9 and January 30, the House Rules Committee heard testimony from 40 different members of Congress (Vaas 438). No one expected the hearings to have any effect on the outcome, but they provided the Southern Democrats a forum for airing their opposition to the bill. On January 30, 1964, the Rules Committee approved House Resolution 616, governing debate on H.R. 7152, by a vote of 11–4 (Whalens 99). The bill had not only survived the Rules Committee, it had survived without a single amendment (Vaas 438).

3. *Bipartisan House Victory.* The House of Representatives follows a rather formal six-step process in considering a bill called up from the floor. First, the House debates and votes on the bill's rule. If the rule is accepted, the body will resolve into the *Committee of the Whole House on the State of the Union*, which is simply the full House following simplified procedures for purposes of debate. Next, pursuant to the rule, members offer amendments, which are debated and then accepted or rejected by unrecorded votes. The members will then resume sitting formally as the House and, if requested by one-fifth of the members, take recorded votes on any accepted amendments. A minority party member will be recognized to offer a motion to recommit the bill to committee. Finally, the House will vote on the bill, as amended by the Committee of the Whole (Whalens 101).

On January 3, 1964, Speaker John McCormack recognized a Rules Committee member to call up House Resolution 616 (the special rule) for immediate consideration. Under the rules of the House, debate on the resolution was limited to one hour, divided equally between each party. Clarence Brown spoke on behalf of the rule, and Rules Committee member William Colmer (D–Miss.) spoke against it. In a voice vote, the House ignored Colmer's plea not to succumb to the violent "blackmail" of civil rights activists, and approved the rule (Whalens 102–03). The House then resolved itself into the Committee of the Whole, and Speaker McCormack stepped down and handed the gavel to Eugene Keogh (D–N.Y.), who assumed his position as Chairman of the Committee of the Whole.

The rule approved for H.R. 7152 specified that general debate would be limited to ten hours, divided equally between the two parties (and further divided equally between North and South), after which amendments would be offered, title by title, in accordance with the *five minute rule.* Under this rule, all speakers — the amendment's sponsor, its proponents, and its opponents — were limited to five minutes of remarks each. Furthermore, in exchange for the bill's supporters' pledge not to limit debate on any amendment, the bill's

---

h. Two major black universities (Wilberforce and Central State) were situated in Brown's district. The town of Xenia in his district was one of the major links in the Underground Railway, used by slaves to escape to Canada in the nineteenth century (Whalens 86).

opponents agreed not to bog down the proceedings with redundant quorum calls. This was to be a battle, but it would be a genteel one (Whalens 108).

Celler and McCulloch delivered the opening statements. Manny Celler chose to describe the bill in broad dramatic terms:

> The legislation before you seeks only to honor the constitutional guarantees of equality under the law for all. It bestows no preferences on any one group; what it does is to place into balance the scales of justice so that the living force of our Constitution shall apply to all people, not only to those who by accident of birth were born with white skins.

Bill McCulloch discussed H.R. 7152 more simply, explaining the need for federal legislation and its validity under the Constitution. He argued that "this bill is comprehensive in scope, yet moderate in application."

Not surprisingly, the Southern Congressmen cast the bill in a very different light. Edwin Willis (D–La.), for example, characterized the bill as "the most drastic and far-reaching proposal and grab for power ever to be reported out of a committee of Congress in the history of our Republic." Congressman Thomas Abernethy (D–Miss.) went even further:

> If this bill is enacted, I predict it will precipitate upheaval that will make the sit-ins, kneel-ins, lie-ins, stand-ins, mass picketing, chanting, the march on Washington, and all the other elements of the so-called Negro revolution, all of these — I predict — will look like kindergarten play in comparison with the counter-revolution that is bound to arise and continue to grow and grow and grow.

After ten hours of such general debate, H.R. 7152 prepared to meet its ultimate test in the House — the amendment process on the floor.

McCulloch and Celler had prepared carefully for this stage of the process. Each manned a 20-foot-long table on their respective party's side of the chamber, on which they had assembled an impressive array of resources. There was a lengthy manual prepared by the Justice Department, containing a section-by-section defense of the bill and responding both to the opposing views expressed by the Southern Democratic minority in the Judiciary Committee's report and to expected amendments. The floor leaders had also assigned a member of the Judiciary Committee to each title with responsibility for becoming an expert on that particular area. Finally, there were eight Justice Department attorneys — one for each title of the bill — standing by for additional assistance (Whalens 103).

The major concern shared by Celler and McCulloch was their ability to keep sufficient members on the floor to defeat weakening amendments during the protracted debate. Because votes taken in the Committee of the Whole were unrecorded, constituents were not likely to find out how (or even if) their representatives had voted, and so marginally interested members often skipped those votes. Thus it was not unusual to find a determined minority passing substantial amendments to bills by simply waiting until enough of the bill's supporters left the floor. If such a situation arose, Celler and McCulloch planned to stall a final vote for ten minutes while they attempted to get their forces together. By objecting to the chair's call for a voice vote, they could force a standing vote. Then, with 20 members objecting to the standing vote, they could force a teller vote — a head count as the "yeas" and "nays" walked down the center aisle. During this delaying process, supporters could be rounded up.[i]

The amendment process began at noon on Monday, February 3, and continued, title-by-title and section-by-section, until 7:00 p.m. on February 10. Over the course of that week, 124 amendments were offered, debated, and voted on, but only 34 were accepted by the Committee of the Whole. Most were technical corrections, including 12 offered by Celler.

The most significant amendment expanded the scope of Title VII and was sponsored by none other than Judge Smith. He proposed the addition of the word "sex" to Title VII's list of impermissible bases for employment decisions. Smith hoped that by transforming the civil rights bill into a law guaranteeing women equal employment rights with men — thus drastically affecting virtually every employer, labor union, and governmental body in the country — the bill would become so controversial that it would fail, if not in the House, certainly in the Senate (Vaas 441–42; Whalens 115–16).

A shocked, flustered (and perhaps chauvinist) Manny Celler immediately rose to oppose the amendment. While McCulloch sat on the sidelines, many Democratic liberals joined Celler in speaking against the amendment. Then five Congresswomen — Frances Bolton (R–Ohio), Martha Griffiths (D–Mich.), Katherine St. George (R–N.Y.), Catherine May (R–Wash.), and Edna Kelly (D–N.Y.) — rose in support "of this little crumb of equality. The addition of the little, terrifying word 's-e-x' will not hurt this legislation in any way," argued St. George. With a coalition of Southerners and women supporting it and the rest of the House hopelessly divided on the apparent choice between equal rights for blacks and equal rights for women, the Smith amendment passed, 168–133 (Vaas 442).

At the close of amendments on February 10, the Committee of the Whole dissolved, John McCormack reclaimed the Speaker's chair, and the members resumed sitting as the House. Chairman Keogh reported H.R. 7152, as amended, back to the House, and the Speaker prepared to complete the final three steps in the process. It was 7:00 p.m., and few were interested in prolonging the affair. Attempts to obtain recorded votes on certain substantive amendments failed to receive sufficient support, and the motion to recommit the bill to the Judiciary Committee failed on a voice vote. Finally it was time

---

i. Celler and McCulloch relied on a three-level organization. First, 17 members of the Democratic Study Group, each with responsibility for six to eight colleagues, would be responsible for directly contacting their respective Congressmen whenever a vote was about to occur. Second, a group of 25 volunteers under the direction of labor lobbyist Jane O'Grady, known as O'Grady's Raiders, would patrol the halls of the Congressional Office Buildings, making sure that representatives knew when a vote was coming up. Finally, in an effort to coerce some public accountability, hundreds of volunteers from the Leadership Conference on Civil Rights in the House gallery watched who voted and how. Because writing is forbidden in the galleries, members had to memorize the face of a particular member and then remember how he or she voted (Whalens 108–09).

for the vote — up or down — on H.R. 7152. When the roll call was over, there were 152 Democratic votes and 138 Republican votes in favor, 96 Democratic votes and 34 Republican votes against. The civil rights bill passed overwhelmingly, 290–130 (Whalens 120–21). Now it was on to the Senate.

PASSAGE IN THE SENATE

The euphoria that accompanied passage in the House of Representatives was short-lived. H.R. 7152 next had to face the Senate, the body that had diluted civil rights bills in 1957 and 1960. Senator Eastland's Judiciary Committee had essentially ignored the Senate version of the Administration's bill (introduced in June 1963), holding only perfunctory hearings and calling only one witness: Attorney General Robert Kennedy.[j]

At that time, consideration of a typical bill in the Senate followed an eight-step process. First, the bill was read for the first time. If no objections were heard, the bill would immediately be read for the second time. After the second reading, the bill was generally referred to committee, unless a majority voted to place the bill directly on the Senate calendar. The fourth step was committee consideration where, as in the House, the bill could be amended or killed. If the bill survived committee action, it was placed on the Senate calendar. The sixth step was to call up the bill for consideration, and the seventh consisted of the actual debate of the bill under the Senate's unlimited debate rules. The final step was the third reading, followed by a vote on the bill, as amended by the committee and during floor debate (Whalens 131–32).

Majority Leader Mike Mansfield (D–Mont.) had a simple strategy. First, avoid referral of H.R. 7152 to Eastland's Judiciary Committee. Second, get the 67 votes needed to invoke cloture against the inevitable Southern filibuster.

1. *The Longest Debate Begins.* H.R. 7152 arrived in the Senate from the House on Monday, February 17, 1964. On Mike Mansfield's motion, the bill was read for the first time. However, Mansfield objected to a second reading of the bill because he wanted to delay a filibuster until the Senate had completed work on the tax bill. When the tax bill was completed on February 26, Mansfield called up the civil rights bill for its second reading. Mansfield then moved to have the bill placed directly on the Senate calendar, thereby bypassing the Judiciary Committee. Senator Richard Russell (D–Ga.), leader of the Southern bloc in the Senate, immediately objected and was joined by

---

j. The Attorney General had opened his testimony by quoting from a couple of tourist guidebooks covering the South. According to the guides, there was only one hotel serving African Americans in the city of Montgomery, Alabama and none in Danville, Virginia. However, a dog, if traveling with a white person, would have his choice of five places in Montgomery and four in Danville (Brauer 279). Kennedy spent a large portion of his time sparring with Senator Sam Ervin (D–N.C.), later to be Chair of the Watergate Committee, who claimed to oppose the bill because it was both unnecessary and unconstitutional. When Ervin claimed to have no personal knowledge of racial discrimination in Mississippi, the Attorney General quickly offered to arrange for a guided tour of the state, but the Senator declined, saying he was too busy fighting to "preserve constitutional principles and the individual freedoms of all citizens of the United States" (Brauer 280–81).

Minority Leader Everett Dirksen (R–Ill.) and others. Although Dirksen shared Mansfield's concern about referring a civil rights bill to Eastland's committee, he felt that a bill of this importance deserved the full legislative history that only committee consideration could provide. Mansfield persuaded 20 Republicans to join him and defeated Dirksen, 54–37, placing H.R. 7152 on the Senate calendar of pending bills (Whalens 132–35).

Mansfield delayed his next motion — to call up H.R. 7152 for debate — until after the Senate voted on a pending farm bill. This two-week hiatus provided an opportunity for the Senate leadership to organize for the coming battle. Although the chairman of the committee having jurisdiction over a bill is usually chosen to act as the primary floor leader during debate, Mansfield was not going to select Eastland. Instead he selected Hubert Horatio Humphrey (D–Minn.), the Democrats' Senate Whip. No one was more committed to civil rights legislation than Humphrey. In 1948, it was he who led the battle for a strong civil rights plank in the Democratic platform.[k] And the loquacious Humphrey had the energy and communication skills needed to organize the drive for 67 cloture votes.

The Republican floor manager was Thomas Kuchel (R–Cal.), that party's Senate Whip. Kuchel was a popular choice for the position because he was a progressive Republican who was still accepted in the conservative camp (Whalens 137–38). Dirksen appointed seven other Republicans to assist Kuchel, selecting representatives from each region of the country to ensure that he was kept informed of the movements in all parts of the Party (MacNeil 232). Senators Joseph Clark (D–Pa.) and Clifford Case (R–N.J.) were the senators responsible for handling issues involving Title VII, the equal employment title (Vaas 445).

One of Mansfield's and Johnson's chief concerns was the ability of the liberal supporters of the bill to maintain their discipline throughout the ordeal of getting H.R. 7152 through the Senate. The liberals' disorganization had contributed to the success of the last two civil rights filibusters. Johnson challenged Humphrey to keep the troops together this time. "You have this great opportunity now, Hubert, but you liberals will never deliver. You don't know the rules of the Senate, and your liberal friends will be off making speeches when they ought to be present. You've got a great opportunity here, but I'm afraid it's going to fall between the boards" (Miller 368). Humphrey accepted the challenge. He organized a daily bipartisan newsletter, designed to inform members of the status of the debate, to refute arguments made on the floor by the bill's opponents, and to maintain a united front (Humphrey 86–87). The Democratic floor leader also set up a "quorum duty" system to ensure that there would always be sufficient senators on the floor to prevent the Southern-

---

k. Hubert Humphrey's interest in the 1964 civil rights bill was not entirely philosophical; he was a politically ambitious man who correctly saw the bill as an opportunity to establish himself a leader in the Democratic Party. Lyndon Johnson was conceded the Party's presidential nomination in 1964, but Humphrey believed that if he could lead the Democrats to a solid legislative accomplishment on civil rights, he would solidify his position as front-runner for the vice presidency.

ers from adjourning the Senate. Finally, Humphrey scheduled regular strategy sessions with the bill's supporters (Humphrey 90).

By March 9, the Senate finished considering the farm bill, and Mike Mansfield moved to make H.R. 7152 the pending business of the Senate, a motion he knew would draw a filibuster by the Southern conservatives (Vaas 444).[l] For fourteen days the Senate debated this issue — not whether to pass H.R. 7152, but simply whether to consider the bill at all. Prior to moving for immediate consideration of the bill, Mansfield had met with the Southerners and had been assured that the filibuster on this preliminary issue would not last longer than four or five days. It became apparent, though, as debate dragged on, that the Southerners had merely been maneuvering to convince Mansfield not to call all-night sessions.[m] On March 23, Humphrey kept the Senate in session until 10:15 p.m. — not all night, but long enough to give the filibusterers a taste of what was to come. The next day, supporters announced that they would object to the holding of any committee hearings before the Senate had finished with the civil rights bill. The Southerners finally decided to allow a vote on Mansfield's motion. On March 26, 1964, the motion to take up H.R. 7152 passed 67–17, with only Southern Democrats opposing (Whalens 146–47).

On March 30, 1964, the Senate began debate on the merits of H.R. 7152. Hubert Humphrey delivered the opening statement. Knowing that with another filibuster around the corner there was no need to hurry (and never being the sort of speaker who strove for oratorical brevity), Humphrey treated the half-dozen Senators present to a 55-page, three and one-half hour speech. Tom Kuchel followed with an opening of a mere one and three-quarter hours (Whalens 150–51). Rather than let the Southerners monopolize debate, Humphrey decided to take the offensive early. His team held the floor for over 12 days, presenting a detailed, title-by-title defense of the bill. Senators were sent to appear on television and radio talk shows and were encouraged to send regular newsletters back to their constituents in an effort to maintain support for the bill in the press and public at large (Humphrey 89–90). Supporters of the civil rights bill emphasized the moral importance of the bill, attempting to

---

l. Unlike the House, the Senate does not have a Rules Committee which recommends to the full house a rule allowing expedited consideration of important bills. Instead, the Majority Leader normally expedites consideration by negotiating a *unanimous consent agreement*, in which all interested senators agree to consider the bill on a stated date, sometimes with limitations on debate and amendments (like a House rule). But if even a single senator objects to this arrangement, it is nullified. Obviously, the Southern senators in 1964 were not going to agree readily to expedited consideration of the civil rights bill.

m. Mansfield was not inclined to hold all-night sessions in any event. Round-the-clock sessions had not worked in 1960 or in 1957, when Strom Thurmond (D–S.C.) had set the all-time filibuster record of 24 hours and 18 minutes of uninterrupted talk. Mansfield thought the tactic was demeaning to the Senate. "This is not a circus or a sideshow. We are not operating in a pit with spectators coming into the galleries late at night to see senators of the republic come out in bedroom slippers without neckties, with their hair uncombed, and pajama tops sticking out of their necks." Also, Mansfield feared that some older senators would not survive the tactic (MacNeil 23).

elevate the issue above politics and appeal to a broad concept of justice (Humphrey 91–92).[n]

2. *Wooing the Wizard of Ooze.* The Southern filibusterers dominated debate after early April and seemed capable of talking the year away. Could Humphrey and Kuchel muster the 67 votes needed to invoke cloture? A block of about 20 Southern Democrats were certain to vote against cloture, and about 30 liberal Democrats, most representing the Northeast and Midwest, and 12 liberal Republicans were equally certain to vote for it. To reach the 67 votes needed for cloture, Humphrey and Kuchel needed to win the votes of 25 senators from two groups: 21 conservative Republicans and 17 moderate Democrats from Western and border states.

Invoking cloture would be tough. The crucial swing votes were expected to come from sparsely populated states in the West and Midwest (Schapsmeier 156–57), which had traditionally relied upon the filibuster to protect themselves from more populous states. These senators would be hesitant to cast a vote that might later weaken their ability to filibuster to protect their own interests (Miller 370). Other senators considered the filibuster to be an essential element of the Senate's legislative process and hence might refuse to vote for cloture as a matter of principle (Miller 368). There was also the force of tradition working against cloture: since 1917, when the procedure was formally codified in the Senate's standing rules, cloture had been invoked successfully only once (Vaas 446). Finally, although some conservative Republicans were willing to support cloture, the bill needed them to vote as a virtual block — which seemed unlikely unless the Minority Leader himself became an enthusiastic supporter of the bill.

Although he led the minority party, with only 33 of the 100 senators, Everett Dirksen ruled the Senate along with Majority Leader Mike Mansfield (MacNeil 230–31). Over a 29-year career, Dirksen had risen to his position of power on the strength of an oratorical prowess that combined flowery language with a throatily mellifluous voice, and an uncanny ability to turn the most difficult political situations into personal triumphs. The former earned him the sobriquet "Wizard of Ooze"; the latter, "Old Doctor Snake Oil" (Whalens 151).

Publicly, Dirksen struck a Delphic pose in his attitude toward the civil rights bill. When President Kennedy's bill was introduced in June 1963, Dirksen expressed doubts about either a public accommodations provision or a fair employment practices section (Humphrey 85), and as late as August he told representatives of the NAACP that a public accommodations title was not

---

n. As a consequence, Humphrey realized that among all the groups lobbying for passage, the religious lobby would be crucial. The support of this group was important for three reasons: (1) it reinforced the moral importance of the issue; (2) it provided a means of reaching senators not otherwise influenced by the labor and black lobbying efforts; and (3) it represented the form of lobbying least likely to alienate senators as unduly coercive. Therefore, Humphrey met with religious leaders and actively planned high-profile events to emphasize the interdenominational support for civil rights. Most successful of these efforts was a silent, 24-hour vigil maintained by Protestant, Catholic, and Jewish seminarians on the Capitol grounds throughout the Senate debate (Humphrey 93–94).

acceptable (MacNeil 223). The momentum created by House passage and increasing public support for the bill led him to soften his position. In early November he assured Katzenbach that a civil rights bill would make it to a vote in the Senate (Brauer 308). The bill's strong support from McCulloch and Halleck in the House put further pressure on Dirksen to play a leadership role — a role that Humphrey urged upon him. One of Humphrey's key strategies for collecting the support of GOP conservatives was to cast Dirksen in the starring role of this battle (Humphrey 85–86).

By the time the filibuster began in earnest, Dirksen was in all probability going to support some kind of strong civil rights bill. But his support carried a price tag — namely Dirksen's own conservative stamp on the final product (MacNeil 232–33). The day after the Senate took up consideration of the bill, Dirksen met with the Senate Republican Policy Committee to discuss the amendments he wanted to propose, and the next day he met with the Republican caucus. A week later he unveiled a package of 40 weakening amendments to Title VII. The amendments pleased conservative Republicans but created great concern among the party's influential liberals, including Senators George Aiken (Vt.), John Sherman Cooper (Ky.), Jacob Javits (NY), Tom Kuchel (Cal.), Leverett Saltonstall (Mass.), Hugh Scott (Pa.), and Margaret Chase Smith (Me.). The liberals' opposition forced Dirksen to trim the package to ten. On April 16, Dirksen publicly introduced his ten amendments, but did not seek a vote on the package (Whalens 159–64).

As April stretched on and Dirksen found himself unable to muster sufficient bipartisan support for his amendments, he decided to approach the President in an effort to bluff his way to a compromise. He met with Johnson on April 29 and offered to deliver 22 to 25 Republican votes for cloture if the Administration would go along with weakening the bill. By one account, Johnson and Humphrey refused to compromise, because they thought Dirksen had little choice but to support the civil rights bill (Whalens, 171–72). Another account, however, posits that Dirksen was in a much stronger bargaining position. When he met with Mansfield, Humphrey, and the Attorney General to hammer out a compromise on May 4, Dirksen achieved much of what he wanted to gain for the small businesses that were his primary concern. Thus, he procured the Administration's support for provisions in the jobs title limiting the authority of the EEOC, protecting employers against government-required quota programs, and expanding employer defenses.[o]

Dirksen spent the next week selling his deal to the Republican caucus. He presented his package — the most he thought he could get the Democrats to go along with — to the Republican senators (MacNeil 234–35). Just as his earlier amendments had been attacked by his party's liberals as going too far, Dirksen's latest proposal was attacked by some conservatives as not going nearly far enough. The Minority Leader's response was to go public, with a

---

o. Indispensable for understanding Dirksen's success is the politically sophisticated account in Daniel Rodriguez & Barry Weingast, *The Positive Political Theory of Legislative History: New Perspectives on the 1964 Civil Rights Act and Its Interpretation*, 151 U. Pa. L. Rev. 1417 (2003).

fait accompli challenging his Republicans to follow their Minority Leader. Following the caucus, Dirksen announced to stunned reporters that the time for action had arrived, that passage of the civil rights bill had become a moral imperative and that he was resolved to see it happen. Quoting Victor Hugo, Dirksen proclaimed, "No army is stronger than an idea whose time has come" (Whalens 185).

On May 26, Dirksen presented Amendment No. 656 to the Senate, an amendment in the nature of a substitute for H.R. 7152, known as the "Mansfield-Dirksen Amendment" (Vaas 445).[p] Although the Democrats and liberal Republicans were ultimately satisfied that the anti-discrimination goal of civil rights bill had not been significantly undermined (Whalens 188-89), the jobs title of the Mansfield-Dirksen substitute was in fact more business-friendly and less regulatory than the earlier version of the bill (Rodriguez & Weingast, 1487–96). Dirksen characteristically termed his bill "infinitely better than what came to us from the House" (Whalens 188), but Humphrey had little trouble concluding that he had kept his promise to Bill McCulloch not to support a weakened bill (Humphrey 85).

With cloture now a tangible possibility, the bill's supporters — the President, the Senate Democratic leaders, and the Senate Republican leaders — spent the next two weeks stumping for votes. President Johnson used a combination of arm-twisting and inducements to lobby Senate Democrats. He spoke with Howard Cannon (D–Nev.), whom Majority Leader Johnson had appointed to critical Senate committees, and J. Howard Edmondson (D–Okla.), whom Johnson had supported during the state's Democratic primary. While Johnson only stressed the principles in the bill, his personal involvement indicated that he was calling in markers (Whalens 187–88). Both senators would vote for cloture. A devastating earthquake had struck Alaska on March 27, and Johnson had responded promptly, making Air Force Two available to Senators Bartlett and Gruening (both D–Alas.) and moving to free up $77.5 million in relief for the state. Although both senators had been considered questionable votes for cloture, the President's timely political favor pulled them into line (Whalens 200).

Mansfield and Humphrey concentrated on Democratic senators from the key Western states, attempting to disrupt a traditional understanding between Southern and Western senators involving the exchange of Southern votes on water projects for Western votes against civil rights (Whalens 201). Meanwhile, Everett Dirksen worked to pull in the 11 or more conservative Republicans he would need for cloture. In shifting H.R. 7152's focus toward federal intervention as a secondary, rather than primary, enforcement alternative, Dirksen argued to conservative colleagues from states with anti-discrimination laws that the federal legislation would have only a small incremental effect in their states. He complemented this approach by pointing to the Republican Party's heritage as the "Party of Lincoln." Conservatives

---

p. An *amendment in the nature of a substitute* proposes a whole new bill to replace the bill under consideration. We will briefly discuss the various kinds of amendments in the "Note on How a Bill Becomes a Federal Law," *infra*.

were also influenced by the moral fervor of religious leaders who supported the bill. Finally, the effects of the filibuster itself were beginning to create pressure for cloture. The Senate had devoted 12 solid weeks to ducking the civil rights issue, and many senators were beginning to feel the embarrassment that came with public recognition of that fact (Whalens 202–03).

3. *Cloture and Victory in the Senate.* One by one the necessary commitments fell into place. On June 8, Mansfield and Dirksen moved for cloture: "We the undersigned Senators [27 Democrats, 11 Republicans], in accordance with the provisions of Rule XXII of the Standing Rules of the Senate, hereby move to bring to a close the debate on the bill * * *." After the required two-day wait, the time came to vote. Mansfield explained the importance of the cloture motion and then listened as a weary Richard Russell denounced the bill as contrary to both the spirit and the letter of the Constitution. After an uncharacteristically brief statement by Humphrey, Dirksen rose to make the final speech. He introduced Senate Amendment No. 1052, a second substitute for the entire bill to replace his earlier substitute amendment. Dirksen argued: "The time has come for equality of opportunity in sharing in government, in education, and in employment. It will not be stayed or denied."

The obligatory quorum call was a true formality on June 10: all 100 senators were present, including Clair Engle (D–Cal.), suffering from a brain tumor and unable to speak (Humphrey 91). The roll was called alphabetically by each senator's last name. Senator Engle cast his vote from his wheelchair by feebly lifting his left hand toward his eye. John Williams (R–Del.) cast the 67th vote for cloture. Hubert Humphrey raised his arms over his head in jubilation (Whalens 199). The final vote was 71–29, four votes more than required.

After over 534 hours of continuous debate, spanning 58 days, the longest filibuster in the history of the Senate had been broken — the first time ever that cloture had been achieved on a civil rights bill (Miller 368). The final breakdown was 44 Democrats and 27 Republicans in favor and 23 Democrats and 6 Republicans against. Johnson and Humphrey had succeeded in capturing the votes of 19 of the 21 Democrats from Western states, and Dirksen had convinced 16 of the 17 Republican senators from states with public accommodations and equal employment laws on the books (as well as eight of the ten senators from states with one or the other) to vote for cloture.

Even though cloture limited senators to sixty minutes of remarks — on both the bill and proposed amendments — the Southern opponents of H.R. 7152 continued to delay the bill's progress. They attempted to bog down the proceedings by calling up countless amendments, even though they knew their proposals had no chance of adoption. They slowed things down further by insisting on long roll-call votes (including a record 34 in one day) on virtually every question (Schwartz 1091).[q] But they succeeded only in delaying the

---

q. This phenomenon — the *post-cloture filibuster* — is made possible by the collegial Senate rules. During this period, absent a unanimous consent agreement, a Senator could propose any number of amendments, including those unrelated to the subject matter of the bill. (House Rule XVI, in contrast, limits amendments to those which are *germane* to the subject of

inevitable for another eight days (Vaas 446). In all, 115 different amendments were defeated, 106 on roll-call votes (Miller 371), with only two amendments of substance being accepted (Schwartz 1091).

On June 19, 1964 — one year after John Kennedy had sent his civil rights bill to Congress — the Senate finally voted on H.R. 7152, having accepted the second Mansfield-Dirksen substitute two days earlier by an overwhelming 76–18 margin. The bill was read for the third time and the Clerk called the roll (Vaas 446). At 7:40 p.m., to the applause of the observers in the gallery, the Clerk of the Senate announced the final vote: 73–27 in favor of H.R. 7152, as amended by the Mansfield-Dirksen substitute. The bill received the support of 46 Democrats and 27 Republicans, including four senators who had opposed cloture. Twenty-one Democrats and six Republicans voted nay (Whalens 215).

Most important, the bill approved by the Senate was in substance virtually identical to the bill approved by the House in February (Miller 371). For example, of the 24 amendments to Title VII that were offered from the floor, only five were accepted. Even considering Dirksen's important changes, the title was not significantly weaker than the version delivered from the House in February.[r]

THE BILL BECOMES LAW

A bill does not become a law unless both chambers of Congress agree to identical legislative language. Because the Senate had made a number of changes in H.R. 7152, it returned the bill to the House on June 27, 1964, together with a message asking for acquiescence in the Senate's changes. In a joint press release, Manny Celler and Bill McCulloch said that "none of the amendments do serious violence to the purpose of the bill. We are of a mind that a conference could fatally delay enactment of this measure" (Whalens 218). Celler and McCulloch knew that if the House refused to accept all of the Senate changes and a conference committee were called, the Senate conferees would be selected by Judiciary Chairman Eastland, guaranteeing further delay. Even if the conference committee did report out a bill, the Southerners would have another opportunity to filibuster in the Senate. On balance, the best strategy was simply to accept the Senate's changes (Whalens 218–19).

---

the bill.) Moreover, any Senator could demand roll-call votes, not only on the amendments, but also on the normally routine motion to reconsider, and could seek repeated quorum calls. In 1979, the Senate amended Rule XXII, clause 2 to limit each Senator to calling up two amendments and to impose an overall 100 hour limit on post-cloture consideration.

r. See Rodriguez & Weingast, *New Perspectives on the 1964 Civil Rights Act*, at 1487-96. A new provision specified that preferential hiring practices to correct racial imbalances in the workforce (*affirmative action*) would not be required. The authority of the EEOC to sue in court was eliminated and replaced with a provision authorizing the Commission, when conciliation efforts failed, to refer a case to the Attorney General for possible civil suit or to authorize private suit. However, the reduction in EEOC authority was agreed to only in exchange for the inclusion of provisions allowing the courts to appoint attorneys to represent private Title VII plaintiffs and providing for an award of attorney's fees to successful plaintiffs. The new version also allowed local authorities to retain jurisdiction over cases for a short time, to attempt conciliation, before the EEOC could step in (Vaas 447–56).

The revised H.R. 7152 returned to Judge Smith's Rules Committee. This time, with the national conventions of both parties approaching, supporters would tolerate no stalling by the Chairman. After a single day of hearings, the Rules Committee voted to report House Resolution 789, expressing the House's concurrence with the Senate's amendments to H.R. 7152. The Rules Committee also voted to limit debate to one hour prior to the final vote.

On July 2, the House took up consideration of House Resolution 789. Judge Smith spoke for 15 minutes, denouncing the Rules Committee's "exercise of raw, brutal power" in limiting debate to a single hour. But he conceded that "the bell has tolled. In a few minutes you will vote this monstrous instrument of oppression upon all of the American people." As he yielded the floor, Smith received applause from his Southern colleagues and a handshake from Manny Celler. Bill McCulloch, in his usual restrained manner, recommended approval of the Senate version of H.R. 7152 as a comprehensive, fair, and moderate statute. As he sat down, the House rose in a rare standing ovation. Finally, Manny Celler claimed the floor to use the remaining six minutes of the allotted hour. When he finished, the House rose once again in a standing ovation, this time led by the redoubtable Judge Smith (Whalens 224–26).

The House vote on House Resolution 789 was 289–126. After the House accepted the Senate bill, Speaker McCormack signed the official copy of H.R. 7152 and handed it to the House Clerk for return to the Senate. When the bill arrived in the other chamber, business was suspended so that Carl Hayden, the Senate's President pro tempore, could place his signature alongside McCormack's. H.R. 7152, as amended, was now ready to be signed into law by the President. At 6:00 that evening, July 2, 1964, members of Congress and civil rights leaders arrived at the White House and, after brief remarks by President Johnson, witnessed the presidential signing of H.R. 7152 into law. H.R. 7152 had finally become "The Civil Rights Act of 1964."

Within days, Lyndon Johnson met with Nicholas Katzenbach, the new Attorney General, to discuss the President's plans for the next civil rights bill: "I want you to write me the goddamndest, toughest voting rights act that you can devise." As he had told Hubert Humphrey during the battle for the 1964 Act, "Yes, yes, Hubert, I want all of those other things — buses, restaurants, all of that — but the right to vote with no ifs, ands, or buts, that's the key. When the Negroes get that, they'll have every politician, north and south, east and west, kissing their ass, begging for their support" (Miller 371).[s] Johnson may have been overly optimistic (and typically crude), but he was astute enough to realize that the Civil Rights Act of 1964 was merely a start toward true equality and the end of discrimination.

---

s. Johnson was successful. In 1965, Congress adopted a strong Voting Rights Act, which was reenacted in 1970, 1975, 1982, and 2006 and remains a major component of federal civil rights law. See Chapter 2, § 1.

NOTE ON HOW A BILL BECOMES A FEDERAL LAW

The Civil Rights Act illuminates the important features of the federal legislative process. The Constitution and its amendments set forth the basic structure: laws will be enacted by elected representatives, not by the people directly or by some authoritarian person or group. "All legislative powers herein granted shall be vested in a Congress of the United States, which shall consist of a Senate and House of Representatives." U.S. Const. art. I, § 1. House members are "chosen every second Year by the People of the several states," *id.* art. I, § 2, and each state has two Senators, "elected by the people thereof," *id.* amend. XVII. Laws must be approved by two legislative chambers (the *bicameralism* requirement) and the chief executive (the *presentment* requirement). If the President signs it, the "Bill" is "Law"; if he returns it without signature, it is not law unless two-thirds majorities of each chamber vote to override his *veto. Id.* art. I, § 7. If the President does not sign or return the bill within ten days and the Congress remains in session, the bill becomes law as though he had signed it. If Congress adjourns during the ten-day period, the bill does not become law, and the President has *pocket vetoed* the proposal.

Most of the procedures followed in Congress are the products of history and custom, rather than constitutional mandate.[a] It may be helpful to think about congressional rules as lying along a spectrum, with constitutional requirements such as bicameralism and presentment as the strongest and most durable. Each house also has a series of formal rules that bind it until they are changed by a vote of that house. As the Story of the Civil Rights Act demonstrates, there are many such rules affecting legislation, including committee consideration, scheduling procedures, and Senate rules allowing filibusters. All of these requirements are less durable than constitutional ones because, in most cases, they can be changed by a majority vote of the relevant house. Moreover, if the House or Senate violates the rules, there is often no effective enforcement mechanism to void the action. Courts have been reluctant to enforce congressional rules when they are ignored, holding instead that rulemaking and enforcement are committed by the Constitution to the discretion of each house. Finally, the least durable procedures are those that are matters of informal norms and practices, sometimes called the *folkways* of Congress. See Donald Matthews, *U.S. Senators and Their World* 151 (1960). One norm that played a role in the enactment of the Civil Rights Act was the seniority norm, which allocates power and position to members with long tenure and allows senior legislators and committee chairs to block bills they do not like even when a majority of the chamber or committee favors the legislation. The seniority norm is now weaker than it was at the time of our case study, perhaps because of higher turnover rates and an influx of junior members.

---

a. Among the best scholarly sources on legislative procedures are William Keefe & Morris Ogul, *The American Legislative Process: Congress and the States* (10th ed. 2001); Burdett Loomis & Wendy Schiller, *The Contemporary Congress* (5th ed. 2006); Walter Oleszek, *Congressional Procedures and the Policy Process* (7th ed. 2007); Steven Smith, Jason Roberts & Ryan Vander Wielen, *The American Congress* (4th ed. 2006).

Chart 1—1: How a Federal Bill Becomes a Law — Simplified Overview

HOUSE OF REPRESENTATIVES

Drafting of Bill or Resolution (e.g., by legislative staff, government agency, interest group, academic)

↓

Introduction of Bill by Member (revenue bills originate in House, see U.S. Const., art. I, § 7, cl. 1; customarily, appropriations bills do also)

↓

Referral to Standing Committee

↓

Committee Action
—can be referred to subcommittee
—hearings held on major bills
—committee resolution: take no action, defeat, accept or amend and report

↓

Major Calendars
—Union (appropriations and revenue)
—House (public)
—Discharge (extract bills from committee)

↓

Rules Committee (major bills) (closed rules possible but generally modified open or open rules)

↓

Floor Action (passage or defeat) ——

SENATE

Referred to standing committee

↓

Committee action (similar to House)

↓

Floor action (similar to House except that there is filibuster option in Senate; overriding filibuster requires 60 votes)

↓

CONFERENCE COMMITTEE (if House and Senate pass differing versions, a conference committee can be created with members from each house; each House must agree to the conference report)

↓

BILL SIGNED BY SPEAKER AND VICE PRESIDENT

↓

PRESENTMENT TO PRESIDENT (may sign, veto, or permit bill to become law without his/her signature; also possibility of "pocket veto" after adjournment)

The discussion that follows focuses on the traditional or "textbook" federal legislative process, which is presented in Chart 1-1. State legislatures usually follow similar procedures. In recent years, major federal legislation has often followed paths previously considered unorthodox. For example, Congress now enacts many major laws as part of complex omnibus legislation that is considered by several committees, may involve congressional party leaders and organizations in nontraditional ways, and provides challenges for congressional rules. Barbara Sinclair defines *omnibus legislation* as "[l]egislation that addresses numerous and not necessarily related subjects, issues, and programs, and therefore is usually highly complex and long." *Unorthodox Lawmaking: New Legislative Processes in the U.S. Congress* 71 (2d ed. 2000). In a few instances, party leaders appoint special task forces of sympathetic members to draft and negotiate important legislation, either bypassing committees entirely or reducing their role substantially. The Civil Rights Act is an early example of unorthodox lawmaking; as the case study reveals, party leaders were unusually influential in determining the path of enactment, and several strategies were used to bypass particular committees and undermine the power of senior lawmakers.

1. *Introduction of Bills.* More than 200,000 bills are introduced in the 50 state legislatures each biennium, and around 10,000 in each Congress. Only legislators can introduce bills, although in some states the governor is required to submit budget bills to the legislature. See, e.g., Ill. Const. art. VIII, § 2. The legislators themselves do not always come up with the ideas for major bills or draft them. The executive proposes or drafts much of the important legislation considered by the legislature.[b] Indeed, the President may be the country's chief law-initiator. For example, the Celler, Lindsay, and McCulloch civil rights bills went nowhere until President Kennedy publicized the issue; his Justice Department drafted the civil rights bill introduced in both the House and Senate in 1963. Private groups also present draft bills to members of the legislature or advise them about amendments to bills proposed by the executive. The NAACP, for example, probably helped draft liberalizing amendments to the Kennedy civil rights bill that were adopted by Subcommittee No. 5.

As the case study suggests, the President exerts substantial influence over the shape of the political agenda. John Kingdon defines *agenda* as "the list of subjects or problems to which governmental officials, and people outside of government closely associated with those officials, are paying some serious attention at any given time." *Agendas, Alternatives, and Public Policies* 3 (2d ed. 1995). Getting an issue on the agenda is a prerequisite to adopting a policy to address it. Kingdon identifies four aspects to policymaking: setting the agenda; specifying alternatives from which a policy choice is to be made; choosing among the alternatives; and implementing the decision. His work focuses on the first two processes and attempts to explain why some subjects and not others become salient to policymakers and the public, and why some alternatives receive serious consideration and others do not. With respect to the first, agenda setting, the President is the most influential political actor. "No other single actor in the political system has quite the capability of the president to set agendas in given policy areas for all who deal with those policies." *Id.* at 23. Interestingly, and consistent with the study of the Civil Rights Act, the President has substantially less control over which alternatives will then dominate the discussion concerning possible policies to deal with the salient issue. Thus, the President may be able to raise the issue of racial

---

b. See Paul Light, *The President's Agenda: Domestic Policy Choice from Kennedy to Clinton* (3rd ed. 1999); Vasan Kesavan & Gregory Sidak, *The Legislator-in-Chief*, 44 Wm. & Mary L. Rev. 1, 48–55 (2002).

equality and force others to propose and adopt solutions; he has less ability to dominate the debate over the appropriate response.

State legislators are often even more dependent upon the offices of state attorneys general and private groups to draft legislation than members of Congress because they do not have the staff support of federal lawmakers. The staff situation in state legislatures has improved somewhat in the last 20 years, however. Between 1979 and 2003, the size of state legislative staff grew by almost 30%. Many states provide personal staff to individual legislators, and most states have competent staff associated with legislative committees.

2. *Committee Consideration.* Bills are routinely referred to standing committees by the presiding officer of the legislative chamber. House Rule XII, clause 2 requires the Speaker to refer a bill to the committee(s) having jurisdiction over its subject matter. Clause 2 was amended in 1975 to give the Speaker the power to send parts of the same bill to more than one committee, to send the whole bill to more than one committee, and/or to create an "ad hoc committee" to consider a bill. In 1995, the House modified the process for referring legislation to committee by abolishing joint referrals and mandating instead that the Speaker designate a committee of "primary" jurisdiction upon initial referral. Senate Rule XVII and the rules in many state legislatures do not require referral of bills to the appropriate committees, but the practice is to do so.

Committee jurisdiction is akin to a property right over political issues, so lawmakers work hard to place important legislation within the jurisdiction of committees on which they serve. The parliamentarian, a relatively nonpartisan player, makes referral decisions using a "weight of the bill" test to assign a proposal to the committee or committees with the most compatible jurisdiction. In his study of changes in committee jurisdiction over time, David King argues that such change is incremental, resembling legal change in the courts.[c] Parliamentarians rely on congressional rules (a sort of *statutory jurisdiction*) and precedent (a sort of *common law jurisdiction*) to determine the appropriate referral. For example, congressional rules specify that tax legislation must be referred to the House Ways and Means and the Senate Finance Committees, but the rules provide only a partial list of all possible subject matter of federal legislation. When the rules are silent, the parliamentarian follows past practice to make the referral. This common law of jurisdiction is substantial; for example, King estimates that more than two-thirds of the House Commerce Committee's activity focuses on issues assigned to it through common law means. An ambitious politician works to frame bills so they fall within jurisdictionally ambiguous areas and then to convince the parliamentarian to assign them to a committee on which she has influence. Once a precedent is established, the same committee will prevail on referrals of bills in related areas through the common law reasoning so familiar to lawyers.

The emphasis on bill referrals underscores the importance of congressional committees. Perhaps the most important power of committees is the *power of*

---

c. See David King, *Turf Wars: How Congressional Committees Claim Jurisdiction* (1997).

negation; the vast majority of bills referred to committees never emerge for consideration by the full body. In a typical Congress, only around 14% of the bills introduced survive committee consideration and actually make it to the floor of either house.[d] The key player is the chair of the committee. If the chair refuses to schedule hearings for a bill or refer the bill to subcommittee, or refers the bill to a hostile subcommittee, the bill will usually die — even if most of the committee members favor the bill. House Rule XI and Senate Rule XXVI permit a majority of the committee to compel the chair to place a bill on the agenda, as Representative Brown threatened to do in the House Rules Committee's consideration of the civil rights bill. This is a maneuver rarely threatened and almost never attempted.

In addition, a majority of the House can bypass a committee by filing a *discharge petition* calling for a measure to be brought to the floor. When half of the House members have signed the petition, the bill is taken away from the committee and brought to the full House. Before 1993, the names of members signing a discharge petition were kept confidential until 218 people had signed. Now, the list of signers is public from the first signature, making it easier for supporters to pressure members to sign and to check if those who promised to sign actually have. Although the discharge petition route is seldom successful, Barbara Sinclair concludes that committees have been bypassed more frequently in recent Congresses than, for example, during the time of our case study, when the path of the Civil Rights Act was truly anomalous. See *Unorthodox Lawmaking, supra,* at 93–94. In the Senate, circumventing committees is easier because bills languishing in committees can be added as nongermane amendments to most bills as they are considered on the floor.

The committee process is also crucial for bills that have a good chance of being enacted. The committee can iron out difficulties and build a consensus in favor of the bill. The chair is again the critical person when a bill is actively considered. The committee or subcommittee chair schedules hearings, determines who will testify at the hearings, and asks most of the questions. Recall Representative Celler's power to manipulate both the committee and subcommittee consideration of the civil rights bill (although he did not always act very skillfully). The power of the committee chair has waned in recent years, as more power has been claimed by party organizations[e] and as recent Congresses have adopted rules diminishing the influence of chairs. For example, in 1995 as part of Republicans' "Contract with America," the House voted to limit the terms of committee chairs to six years and abolished several subcommittees, thereby reducing the power of these positions and some of the

---

    d. See Smith, Roberts & Vander Wielen, *supra,* at 99 (17% are reported to the House floor and 13% to the Senate floor).

    e. Since the mid-1990s, more legislative work has been done in informal task forces or leadership committees, entirely controlled by the majority party and often followed by perfunctory or no formal hearings. Because these are not governed by open meeting rules, lobbyists and interest groups can have substantial influence. See Roger Davidson, *Building the Republican Regime: Leaders and Committees,* in *New Majority or Old Minority? The Impact of Republicans on Congress* 69, 79–80 (Nicol Rae & Colton Campbell eds., 1999).

more senior members of the body. Even as power has changed hands in the House, term limits for committee chairs have stayed in effect.

In short, committees are congressional players with great influence over the agenda and legislative outcomes. Unlike some other constitutions, the U.S. Constitution does not require that Congress establish committees; instead, this organizational pattern is entirely a matter of lawmaker preference. The description of committee activities suggests several reasons legislators might prefer to do work through committees, even though such an organization transfers power from floor majorities to small groups of lawmakers and to committee chairs in particular.

First, committees allow members to specialize and accumulate expertise in a substantive area. Other members defer to the specialists, thereby avoiding the costly prospect of becoming experts in every matter raised for a vote. This *informational role* suggests that committees are part of an efficient congressional organization, particularly necessary in an increasingly complex world.[f] Members must monitor committees to ensure that they are faithful agents of the full body and that the information and recommendations they put forth are consistent with the wishes of the majority. As long as monitoring is less costly than developing expertise on all matters and allows members to detect divergence between committee activities and majority preferences, a committee structure is sensible.

Another theory of legislative organization, the *distributive theory*, describes committees as the engine of *rent-seeking*, or the distribution of unjustified benefits to interest groups. Members partly self-select their committee assignments, so they seek appointment to committees with jurisdiction over areas about which they and their constituents have particularly intense preferences. Accordingly, committees are typically composed of preference outliers.[g] In most cases, lawmakers specialize in areas that allow them to send benefits back to their constituents or to key special interests to improve their reelection chances. In other cases, they may seek committee assignments that allow them to capture personal benefits from interest groups (for example, the Senate Commerce Committee has wide jurisdiction over the telecommunications industry, full of wealthy interest groups willing to compensate its legislative friends) or that allow them to spend time on topics of interest to

---

f. See Keith Krehbiel, *Information and Legislative Organization* (1991); Arthur Lupia & Mathew McCubbins, *Who Controls? Information and the Structure of Legislative Decision Making*, 19 Legis. Studs. Q. 361 (1994).

g. See Glenn Parker, *Congress and the Rent-Seeking Society* 74–81 (1996); Barry Weingast & William Marshall, *The Industrial Organization of Congress; or, Why Legislatures, Like Firms, Are Not Organized as Markets*, 96 J. Pol. Econ. 132 (1988). See also Scott Adler, *Why Congressional Reforms Fail: Reelection and the House Committee System* (2002) (explaining the durability of committee structure and jurisdiction using the distributive theory).

them or provide them national prominence (for example, the House International Relations and Senate Foreign Affairs Committees).[h]

The two explanations for committees are not necessarily exclusive.[i] Members may be willing to invest time and resources in developing expertise and producing helpful information for the full body because they have special interest in the issues that fall within the jurisdiction of a particular committee. A member from a largely urban state may be unwilling to specialize in agriculture topics because she and her constituents have no special interest in farm policy, other than an attenuated desire that farm interests not receive a disproportionate share of the government's limited resources. Members from farm states, on the other hand, who want to channel public benefits to their farmer-constituents and may have extensive knowledge of agriculture before coming to the legislature, will actively seek membership on the Agriculture Committee. The more likely it is that committees consist of preference outliers, however, the more diligence is required of the other members to monitor committee activity and ensure that extreme policies are not enacted.

A third theory posits that committees are primarily the *tools of the majority party*.[j] Majority-party committee members exclude members of the other party from decisionmaking and cooperate among themselves to further the majority party's collective goals. Again, consider the Agriculture Committee. Although most members of the majority party are likely to support only modest agriculture subsidies, there are some members whose reelection prospects are substantially affected by enactment of generous subsidies. Committees provide a mechanism for members of the majority party to defer to the wishes of the few with intense preferences and to ensure that those lawmakers in turn defer in the future on other issues vital to the reelection of their colleagues. This process allows the majority party to remain in power by enhancing the reelection prospects of its members; party dominance is a goal shared by all party members who want to continue to receive the benefits of majority control.

Once a committee marks up the bill to its satisfaction and votes to send it to the full legislative chamber, the committee staff drafts a report on the bill that will be circulated to the other legislators. This is mandatory in both chambers of Congress (House Rule XIII; Senate Rule XXVI) and is the prevailing practice in state legislatures as well. Committee reports in Congress set forth the procedural and substantive background of the reported bill, the exact language of the bill, and a section-by-section analysis of the bill. Such reports in state legislatures are often shorter, more general descriptions of reported bills; thus, they are often less helpful to interpreters than the more extensive

---

h. See also Christopher Deering & Steven Smith, *Committees in Congress* 63–77 (3d ed. 1997) (discussing committees in terms of their primary benefits to lawmakers and providing tripartite classification: constituency, policy, and influence committees).

i. See Forrest Maltzman, *Competing Principals: Committees, Parties, and the Organization of Congress* (1997) (offering sophisticated theory of committee formation).

j. See Gary Cox & Mathew McCubbins, *Legislative Leviathan: Party Government in the House* (2d ed. 2007).

federal legislative history.[k] Committee reports, or distillations of them prepared by party organizations, are frequently the only documents that most legislators and their staffs read before a vote is taken on the bill. Reports are not only the principal means of communicating committee decisions to the chamber, but they are also persuasive briefs setting forth the factual and policy reasons justifying the proposed legislation. Committee members dissenting from all or part of the report are entitled to set forth their views as well. Finally, provisions in several laws require committees to include certain information about bills in committee reports. For example, the Unfunded Mandates Reform Act of 1995, Pub. L. No. 104–4, 109 Stat. 48 (codified in scattered sections of 2 U.S.C.), requires a committee to identify any substantial costs that a proposal would impose on state and local governments and Indian tribes.

3. *Scheduling Legislative Consideration.* Bills reported by committee are placed on a calendar of the legislative chamber. The U.S. House's calendar arrangement is especially complex. It has three primary calendars. The most important calendar is the *Union Calendar*, or the "Calendar of the Committee of the Whole House on the State of the Union." Virtually all bills are placed on this calendar. Second is the *House Calendar*, which now contains few bills, mostly special rules from the Rules Committee, changes in House rules, ethics resolutions, and some constitutional amendments. Third, private bills, such as those for the relief of individual aliens seeking to remain in the country, are placed on the *Private Calendar*. In addition, there are two calendars to which bills on the three main ones may move. The *Consent Calendar* consists of bills involving spending of less than $1 million on the Union or House Calendar that a member anticipates will be passed by unanimous consent. Minor bills on the Consent Calendar are considered by the House twice a month. The *Discharge Calendar* lists motions to discharge bills that are pending in committee.[l] Additionally, bills may be called up and considered by the House under a process called *suspension of the rules.* Suspension of the rules allows the House, with the consent of the Speaker, to consider a bill in an expedited fashion with no amendments or motions, but it requires that the bill be passed by a two-thirds vote. The U.S. Senate has only two calendars, the *Calendar of General Orders* and the *Executive Calendar* for treaties and executive nominations.

Simply being on the appropriate calendar does not, of course, assure that the chamber will consider the bill. Salient or time-sensitive bills usually will be considered before other bills ahead of them on the calendar. In the House, major legislation moves to the floor from committees in two ways. Budget and appropriations bills are privileged matters and can be brought to the floor at virtually any time. For other major bills, and often for budget and appropriations bills when supporters want to structure deliberation in a particular way,

---

k. See, e.g., Eric Lane, *How to Read a Statute in New York: A Response to Judge Kaye and Some More,* 28 Hofstra L. Rev. 85, 118–19 (1999) (describing committee reports in New York).

l. See Charles Tiefer, *Congressional Practice and Procedure: A Reference, Research, and Legislative Guide* 245–46 (1989).

the reporting committee will request a special order, or *rule*, from the Rules Committee to advance the bill for expedited floor consideration. The Rules Committee, which is essentially an arm of the majority party, then decides whether it will propose a rule for the bill (its refusal to grant a rule effectively kills the bill for that session); what kind of rule to grant (an *open rule* permitting amendments, a *closed rule* prohibiting all floor amendments, or a *modified closed rule* permitting specified floor amendments and structuring the order of their introduction); when a bill is to be considered; and how much time for debate. The full House votes on the proposed rule; such rules are almost always passed by party-line votes. Control of the legislative agenda, facilitated through the use of special rules, is a tactical advantage that accrues to the majority party; indeed, agenda control may well be the most significant power that the majority party wields.[m]

There is no Rules Committee in the Senate, and expedited consideration is usually accomplished by a *unanimous consent agreement* (Senate Rule V). Like a House rule, a unanimous consent agreement is a roadmap for the bill's consideration: when it may be brought up, what amendments may be proposed, and how much time may be spent on it. Unlike a House rule, a Senate unanimous consent agreement must be acceptable to all Senators; the objection of a single Senator kills it. Recall that the civil rights bill languished for weeks in a pre-consideration filibuster, during which Southern Senators objected to any expedition at all. Under current Senate rules, most bills are still susceptible to two filibuster threats: on the motion to proceed to consider the bill and on final passage.[n] Most filibusters now are virtual ones, which may explain the recent increase in threatened and actual filibusters. Members threaten to engage in extended debate, placing a *hold* on the bill until floor leaders can work out a compromise. For years, holds were largely anonymous, but their widespread use has prompted cries for reforms, and now the names of members blocking consideration of legislation or nominations are sometimes revealed.

Most state legislatures use only a single calendar on which they list all pending bills ready for floor action. As in Congress, the order of listing is not a reliable indication of when the bill will actually be considered; priority items of consequence are mixed with unimportant bills. Oversimplifying a little, one can say that the actual order of consideration is determined in one of two ways, parallel to the two methods used in Congress. State legislatures with strong party caucus systems tend to have their agendas set by the majority leader and/or the majority party caucus. State legislatures in which parties are weak typically vest agenda control in calendar committees, rules committees, or informal but less partisan mechanisms. In some states, the two methods

---

m. Gary Cox & Mathew McCubbins, *Setting the Agenda: Responsible Party Government in the U.S. House of Representatives* (2005).

n. As we will discuss in detail in Chapter 4, some forms of budget legislation cannot be filibustered because the Senate has adopted strict time limits on the consideration of these important legislative vehicles. See Sarah Binder & Steven Smith, *Politics or Principle? Filibustering in the United States Senate* 192–94 (1997) (contrasting budget rules from traditional rules allowing filibuster).

effectively merge. For instance, where the presiding officer of the legislative chamber is also the chair of the rules committee, there is little functional difference between the two methods.

4. *Floor Consideration: Debate, Amendment, Voting.* Once a bill has been placed on the agenda by the relevant committee and advanced for consideration by the full legislative chamber, the process is mostly automatic. Most legislators routinely vote "yes," and the bill is passed. In the Senate, for example, dozens of routine bills are adopted through unanimous consent agreements read quickly at the end of a day's session. Consistent with the informational theory of legislative organization, the chamber as a whole usually ratifies the decisions and compromises reached in the smaller, more expert groups (committees). Of course, much important legislation, such as the Civil Rights Act, is controversial and has to run the further gauntlet of floor consideration. Three important aspects of congressional decisionmaking occur during such floor consideration: debate, amendment, and vote.

In the U.S. House and most state chambers, debate is severely limited by general or special rules. (Indeed, because many state legislatures still only meet for several months each year, there is simply not enough time for extended public debate on more than a few issues.) Even where debate is not formally limited, as in the U.S. Senate, it normally consists of "set" speeches read by members to virtually empty chambers (although many staffers and some lawmakers will watch the floor proceedings on closed circuit television) or of *colloquies*, rehearsed questions posed to the bill's sponsor in order to build a legislative record on some issue. Frequently, members of Congress simply submit statements for printing in the *Congressional Record*, and the statements are never uttered on the floor. The *Record* identifies such a statement by either a "bullet" (●) preceding it or by a different typeface.

Few votes appear to be altered by floor debate; instead, debate is seen mainly in terms of its strategic value. Members may use it to demonstrate that they are competent in a certain field of policy; to gain publicity for their positions; and to attempt to pack the legislative history with remarks supporting an interpretation of the proposal that they favor. In the modern era of televised floor proceedings, members know that their constituents and lobbyists can easily monitor their activity and their positions. In addition, debate can be manipulated by organized minorities to delay passage of legislation that they oppose. For example, the filibuster used in the U.S. Senate enables a determined group of senators to kill a bill or force concessions from the majority by extended debate. Cloture (cutting off the debate) required a two-thirds vote of the Senators voting in 1964; under amended Senate Rule XXII, it now requires 60 votes except with respect to changes in the rules themselves.

More important than debate is amendment. Once they have been reported by committee, bills can be amended on "second reading," sometimes in the legislature sitting as a committee of the whole, or on "third reading" (just before the final up or down vote is taken on the bill). Amendment on third reading is rare and may require unanimous consent or some other special dispensation. Most legislative chambers do not follow the U.S. House practice of dissolving into a committee of the whole to consider amendments.

Major bills on controversial subjects will attract numerous proposed amendments. A first-degree amendment changing the text of the bill is a *perfecting amendment*, which can strike language, insert language, or do both. The reporting committee (through the chair or a sponsor) will sometimes propose perfecting amendments to correct minor problems with the bill or to attract more support for the bill. In the latter case, the amendment is often called a *saving amendment*. Perfecting amendments from the floor may include minor amendments addressed to a narrow problem with the bill; *riders*, or amendments seeking to add irrelevant matter to the bill (riders are prohibited by House Rule XVI and the rules of some state legislatures); and hostile amendments. Some floor amendments, called *killer amendments*, can be lethal to the bill's prospects. Killer amendments often appear friendly because they strengthen the bill, but they are designed to antagonize the bill's more moderate supporters. In the story of the Civil Rights Act, Judge Smith's amendment adding "sex" to the list of impermissible bases for employment decisions prompted the opposition of floor leaders worried that expanding the legislation would prove fatal. Amendments can be quite comprehensive; for example, *amendments in the nature of a substitute* seek to replace the entire bill, striking all after the enacting clause and inserting entirely new text. They can represent radically different approaches to the problem addressed by the bill, and adoption of such an amendment may spell the end of the bill either by ensuring its ultimate defeat or by impairing the operation of the bill, making passage useless. In other cases, the managers of the bill will propose an amendment in the nature of a substitute that reflects the results of negotiations on the proposal following committee action.

A different kind of amendment can be confused with amendments in the nature of a substitute because of its similar name. A *substitute amendment* is offered when another amendment is pending, and it changes part of the proposed amendment. This second-degree amendment can be minor — replacing only one word or phrase — or significant — proposing an entirely new text but in a way different from the pending amendment in the nature of a substitute. In the latter case, the amendment is both a substitute amendment and an amendment in the nature of a substitute. Both opponents and proponents of legislation use amendments strategically, seeking to fill up the complex *amendment tree* to foreclose other changes in the bill or to obtain a special rule in the House that favors a particular sequence of voting on amendments. In some cases, bill managers will accept floor amendments in order to move debate forward and ensure final passage, but they do not intend to support the amendment in the conference committee. Lawmakers often observe that amendments can be "lost" in the Capitol building when conferees walk across the Rotunda to the other chamber to begin negotiations on the final legislation.

The vote on an amendment or a bill may be taken in one of four ways: voice vote, division of the house, tellers, and roll calls (increasingly by use of electronic devices). The first three methods do not leave a record of how each member of the legislative chamber voted, but division (where the yeas and nays rise to be counted) and tellers (where the yeas pass down the aisle to be counted, then the nays) permit observers to record how each member voted.

The U.S. House of Representatives uses all four methods, and the Senate uses all but tellers. One-fifth of a quorum may demand a roll-call vote in either chamber, except when the House committee of the whole is in session. Moreover, congressional rules can often require roll call votes on particular matters; for example, House Rule XX requires roll call votes on all tax rate increases and appropriations bills.

The number of votes needed to adopt an amendment or pass a bill is normally a majority of those voting in each house of Congress, assuming a quorum is present. Some state legislatures, in contrast, require the votes of a majority of the members elected; thus, members not wanting to commit themselves against a measure may help defeat it simply by staying away when the vote is taken. Two-thirds supermajorities are needed for Congress to propose a constitutional amendment, to override a presidential veto, to expel a member, or for the Senate to concur in a treaty. In states, supermajorities can be required to override gubernatorial vetoes, to pass emergency legislation or special appropriation bills, or to enact new tax legislation.

5. *The Reconciliation Process: Conference Committee.* In the prevailing system of bicameral legislatures, there must be a "meeting of the minds" of the two legislative chambers to enact statutes. If the version passed by the U.S. House differs in any respect from that passed by the U.S. Senate, there is no enactment — unless one chamber recedes from its differences and joins the version of the other (as was the case for the Civil Rights Act). Sometimes the House and Senate send bills back and forth several times, acceding to part of the other chamber's alterations each time, in an effort to reconcile the two versions.

After both chambers have voted themselves into a state of disagreement, the last chamber to disagree may request a conference. The Speaker of the House and the Presiding Officer of the Senate formally appoint the conferees, but in practice the chair and ranking minority member of each relevant committee will submit a list of proposed conferees, who are then appointed. Note that this involvement in the final conference committee allows congressional committees influence over legislation both before and after the main floor consideration. Knowing that they will have this ex post influence will affect the interaction of committee leaders and floor managers with rank-and-file members. In both state and the federal legislatures, all the members of the reporting committees in each chamber are often appointed. There can be any number of conferees from either chamber, and modern conference committees vary in size from more than 200 members to only a handful of party leaders. Any compromise adopted in conference must be approved by a majority of the conferees from each chamber.

The objectives of the conferees are, first, to preserve the provisions most important to their respective chambers and, second, to achieve an overall result acceptable to a majority in each chamber. In Congress and most state legislatures, conferees are only authorized to consider matters about which the bills passed by the two chambers are in disagreement. Thus, they may not strike or amend any part of the bill that is identical in both versions, nor may they insert new matter not germane to the differences, nor may they expand any provision beyond that found in either version. In practice, because congressional conference committees do much of their work in private, it is difficult for other members, interest groups, and the public to monitor conferees' behavior. Lengthy omnibus bills that have been the product of long negotiations often emerge from conference with provisions never considered by either house or by any substantive committee. If the bill is nevertheless enacted, the rule against new provisions in conference is considered waived. When the conferees have reached agreement, they set forth their recommendations in a conference report, which will be printed in both chambers and will include a statement explaining the effect of the amendments or propositions agreed upon by the conferees on the measure.

In recent years, the legislative path of major legislation has become a bit more like that of the Civil Rights Act in the 1960s in that the textbook version of the process is seldom followed. In fact, Barbara Sinclair concludes that "the legislative process for major legislation is now less likely to conform to the textbook model than to unorthodox lawmaking," a term she uses to emphasize the extent of the change in congressional procedures. *Unorthodox Lawmaking, supra*, at xiv. Sinclair defines major legislation according to contemporary views of what bills were significant, so she studies the 45 to 55 proposals identified as major by the *Congressional Quarterly Weekly Report* (with some additions). A significant number of bills are referred to at least two House committees; in contrast, some major proposals bypass committees altogether. For example, in 1995, one in ten major measures bypassed committee in the House, and one in four avoided committee consideration in the Senate.[o] Although these rates may be unusually high, stronger party leaders, increased partisanship, and committee gridlock are factors that have encouraged lawmakers to use unorthodox lawmaking techniques for significant legislation. Through an increased use of amendments in the nature of a substitute, committee leaders and floor managers often make substantial changes in bills after they leave committee but before floor consideration. Interestingly, unlike most legislation, major legislation, which is more often subject to unorthodox lawmaking, has considerably better chances of enactment. Since the 1990s, nearly 60% of major legislation has been enacted, perhaps because the more complicated procedures allow advocates to form supporting coalitions and find consensus.

Another modern phenomenon is the use of summits between congressional leaders and the executive branch to work on compromise legislation concerning controversial topics. Since the mid-1980s, budget summits have become biennial affairs. We will discuss the role of budget summits in Chapter 4 when we study the federal budget process. Summits can occur in other contexts as well, and they disrupt the traditional legislative dynamics. For example, summits may not include committee leaders but instead involve only the top political leaders in the House and Senate. Although party leaders, who may better represent median as opposed to outlying preferences, can often reach

---

     o. See Sinclair, *supra,* at 15, 37. See also Oleszek, *supra,* at 107–09 (providing reasons for trend).

compromises more easily, and perhaps more legitimately, than committee chairs, they may lack the substantive expertise necessary to draft effective legislation. Summits also tend to take place in relative secrecy, allowing political actors to reach compromises without requiring that particular individuals take responsibility for advocating positions that their core constituencies view as "selling out."

John Gilmour argues that summitry is a response to a legislative situation where stalemate is unacceptable (which is one reason they occur so frequently in the budget context). *Strategic Disagreement: Stalemate in American Politics* (1995). In many cases, politics will lead to stalemate and inaction. "Politicians are never eager to make proposals that offend their supporters, but they are further deterred from submitting sensible, reasonable offers because of uncertainty about the response from the other side. Politicians who make 'reasonable' offers * * * can easily find themselves attacked by both their friends and enemies, and to avoid that unpleasant fate they propose [solutions] which have no chance of being adopted." *Id.* at 133. Occasionally, however, gridlock is disastrous, and lawmakers must find a way to reach a balanced compromise — one that imposes costs and benefits on all sides. Summit negotiations provide a nonpublic environment where compromise can occur in a way that will bind all the necessary parties in both branches of government to the agreement. Furthermore, the results of summits, which often come to the Congress as a legislative package not easily amended from the floor, present rank-and-file members with a palatable vote in a politically charged context. Much as with complex and large omnibus measures, a form many products of summits take, a lawmaker can explain to interest groups opposing particular provisions or compromises that she had no option other than to vote for the large negotiated deal. This explanation is more convincing when offered by House members, because special rules may foreclose amendments and changes to legislation on the floor, and less persuasive in the context of the Senate, where members can unravel deals by offering amendments and threatening filibusters.

In the normal course of events in which a bill goes to a conference committee rather than a summit, the chamber that did not request the conference acts first on the conference bill, because that chamber has the "papers" (the bill as originally introduced and the amendments to it). That chamber has three options — adopt the conference bill, reject it, or recommit it to conference (which is tantamount to killing the bill). If the first chamber adopts the conference bill, the conference committee is dissolved, and the other chamber is faced with a straight up-or-down vote on the bill. If the bill is agreed to by both chambers, a copy of the bill is enrolled for presentment to the President or the Governor for signature.

6. *Presentment for the Presidential or Gubernatorial Signature.* Under Article I, § 7 of the U.S. Constitution, once an enrolled bill is presented to the President, the Chief Executive has ten days (not including Sundays) to sign it or veto it. If the President vetoes the bill, it is returned to Congress, where the veto can be overridden by two-thirds of those voting in each chamber. If the veto is overridden, the bill then becomes law without the President's signature.

In most cases, if no action is taken within the constitutional ten-day period, the bill also becomes law without the President's signature. The exception to this last rule is that if Congress adjourns before the end of the ten-day period and the President fails to sign the bill, it is killed by a *pocket veto*. Many major bills are passed in the waning days of each Congress, and so the President often has ample discretion to kill legislation without immediate congressional override.

The U.S. President must accept or reject the entire bill; if there are several provisions the President dislikes in the bill, the only formal option is to veto (or pocket veto) the entire bill. State Governors typically have more options, because they can veto individual provisions called *items* in bills presented to them. Congress attempted to delegate a similar power to the President in the Line Item Veto Act of 1996, Pub. L. No. 104–130, 110 Stat. 1200, codified at 2 U.S.C. §§ 691–92, but the Supreme Court struck down the federal act in *Clinton v. City of New York*, 524 U.S. 417 (1998). We will discuss both the state line item veto power and the analogous federal statute in Chapter 3.

Title VII of the Civil Rights Act:
An Introductory Problem

The most complex, and most often litigated, portion of the Civil Rights Act has been Title VII, 78 Stat. 241, 253–66 (1964), codified as amended at 42 U.S.C. § 2000e *et seq.*, which prohibits job discrimination on the basis of race, sex, religion, or national origin. We shall now introduce you to the main provisions of the 1964 Act, before its amendments in 1972 and 1991. The prime directive of Title VII is found in § 703(a), 42 U.S.C. § 2000e–2(a):

> It shall be an unlawful employment practice for an employer —
>
> (1) to fail or refuse to hire or to discharge any individual, or otherwise to discriminate against any individual with respect to his compensation, terms, conditions, or privileges of employment, because of such individual's race, color, religion, sex, or national origin; or
>
> (2) to limit, segregate, or classify his employees or applicants for employment in any way which would deprive or tend to deprive any individual of employment opportunities or otherwise adversely affect his status as an employee, because of such individual's race, color, religion, sex, or national origin.

Section 703(b)–(c), *id.* § 2000e–2(b)–(c), sets forth similar prohibitions of "unlawful employment practices" by employment agencies and labor organizations (unions). Section 703(d), *id.* § 2000e–2(d), applies the antidiscrimination principle specifically to apprenticeship or training programs.

The exact scope of this anti-discrimination rule (i.e., how broadly does the rule apply?) is provided by § 701's definitions of key terms. Thus "employer" is defined in § 701(b), *id.* § 2000e(b):

> The term "employer" means a person engaged in an industry affecting commerce who has twenty-five or more employees for each working day in each of twenty or more calendar weeks in the current or preceding calendar year, and any agent of such a person, but such term does not include (1) the United States, a corporation wholly owned by the Government of the United States, an Indian tribe, or a State or political

subdivision thereof, (2) a bona fide private membership club (other than a labor organization) which is exempt from taxation under section 501(c) of the Internal Revenue Code of 1954 * * * .

Section 701(h), *id.* § 2000e(h), defines "an industry affecting commerce" as "any activity, business, or industry in commerce or in which a labor dispute would hinder or obstruct commerce or the free flow of commerce and includes any activity or industry 'affecting commerce' within the meaning of the Labor-Management Reporting and Disclosure Act of 1959, and further includes any governmental industry, business, or activity." Section 701(g), *id.* § 2000e(g), defines "commerce" as "trade, traffic, commerce, transportation, transmission, or communication among the several States; or between a State and any place outside thereof; or within the District of Columbia, or a possession of the United States; or between points in the same State but through a point outside thereof." Section 701(i), *id.* § 2000e(i), defines "State" to include "a State of the United States, the District of Columbia, Puerto Rico, the Virgin Islands, American Samoa, Guam, Wake Island, the Canal Zone, and Outer Continental Shelf lands defined in the Outer Continental Shelf Lands Act." Definitions for "employment agency" and "labor organization" are set forth in § 701(c)–(e), *id.* § 2000e(c)–(e). There is no definition of "discriminate" or "discrimination" in Title VII.

There are various "exemptions" or "defenses" to the charge of unlawful employment practices under Title VII. Section 702, *id.* § 2000e–1, for example, exempts employment of aliens outside any State or employment of persons by religious groups from Title VII's application. But the main defenses are those which qualify the meaning of "unlawful employment practice" in § 703. Section 703(e), *id.* § 2000e–2(e), presents a defense for practices based on bona fide occupational qualifications:

> Notwithstanding any other provision of this subchapter, (1) it shall not be an unlawful employment practice for an employer to hire and employ employees, for an employment agency to classify, or refer for employment any individual, for a labor organization to classify its membership or to classify or refer for employment any individual, or for an employer, labor organization, or joint labor-management committee controlling apprenticeship or other training or retraining programs to admit or employ any individual in any such program, on the basis of his religion, sex, or national origin in those certain instances where religion, sex, or national origin is a bona fide occupational qualification reasonably necessary to the normal operation of that particular business or enterprise, and (2) it shall not be an unlawful employment practice for a school, college, university, or other educational institution or institution of learning to hire and employ employees of a particular religion if such school, college, university, or other educational institution or institution of learning is, in whole or in substantial part, owned, supported, controlled, or managed by a particular religion or by a particular religious corporation, association, or society, or if the curriculum of such school, college, university, or other educational institution or institution of learning is directed toward the propagation of a particular religion.

Section 703(f)–(g), *id.* § 2000e–2(f)–(g), relates to employment decisions based upon Communist Party membership and national security reasons.

Section 703(h), *id.* § 2000e–2(h), protects employment decisions based upon bona fide seniority or merit systems:

> Notwithstanding any other provision of this subchapter, it shall not be an unlawful employment practice for an employer to apply different standards of compensation, or different terms, conditions, or privileges of employment pursuant to a bona fide seniority or merit system, or a system which measures earnings by quantity or quality of production or to employees who work in different locations, provided that such differences are not the result of an intention to discriminate because of race, color, religion, sex, or national origin, nor shall it be an unlawful employment practice for an employer to give and to act upon the results of any professionally developed ability test provided that such test, its administration or action upon the results is not designed, intended, or used to discriminate because of race, color, religion, sex or national origin. It shall not be an unlawful employment practice under this subchapter for any employer to differentiate upon the basis of sex in determining the amount of the wages or compensation paid or to be paid to employees of such employer if such differentiation is authorized by the provisions of [section 206(d) of title 29].

Section 703(i), *id.* § 2000e–2(i), stipulates Title VII's inapplicability "to any business or enterprise on or near an Indian reservation with respect to any publicly announced employment practice of such business or enterprise under which a preferential treatment is given to any individual because he is an Indian living on or near a reservation." Section 703(j), *id.* § 2000e–2(j), deals with affirmative action under Title VII:

> Nothing contained in this subchapter shall be interpreted to require any employer, employment agency, labor organization, or joint labor-management committee subject to this subchapter to grant preferential treatment to any individual or to any group because of the race, color, religion, sex, or national origin of such individual or group on account of an imbalance which may exist with respect to the total number or percentage of persons of any race, color, religion, sex, or national origin employed by any employer, referred or classified for employment by any employment agency or labor organization, admitted to membership or classified by any labor organization, or admitted to, or employed in, any apprenticeship or other training program, in comparison with the total number or percentage of persons of such race, color, religion, sex, or national origin in any community, State, section, or other area, or in the available work force in any community, State, section, or other area.

Section 713(b)(1), *id.* § 2000e–12(b)(1), provides a defense to a person charged with violating Title VII "if he pleads and proves that the act or omission complained of was in good faith, in conformity with, and in reliance on any written interpretation or opinion of the Commission."

A person "claiming to be aggrieved" may not file suit herself, but should file a "charge" with the EEOC asserting violation of the substantive norms of Title VII, pursuant to § 706(a), *id.* § 2000e–5(a). (Note that § 706(b), (d) sets forth time requirements within which the charge must be filed with the EEOC; the schedule depends in part on whether the state has a remedy for the violation.) Once the aggrieved person has filed a timely charge, the EEOC determines whether there is "reasonable cause to believe that the charge is true," and if so it will try to eliminate the unlawful practice informally through "conference, conciliation, and persuasion" (§ 706(a)). If the EEOC is unable to obtain voluntary compliance with Title VII, it notifies the aggrieved person and informs her that she may bring a lawsuit in federal court within thirty days (§ 706(e), *id.* § 2000e–5(e)). To remedy an unlawful employment practice, a court may enjoin the practice and order "such affirmative action as may be appropriate, which may include reinstatement or hiring of employees, with or without back pay" (§ 706(g), *id.* § 2000e– 5(g)).[p]

Consider the following problem that arose soon after the statute's enactment. The Duke Power Company's electrical generating plant at Dan River Stream Station in Draper, North Carolina had ninety-five employees in 1966, including fourteen African Americans. Employees were divided into five departments: (1) Operations (responsible for the day-to-day operation of the plant's generating equipment); (2) Maintenance (fixing and maintaining equipment); (3) Laboratory and Testing (analysis of water and coal used in the plant's operation); (4) Coal Handling (unloading and handling coal); and (5) Labor (janitorial services). The Labor Department was the lowest paid, with its maximum wage of $1.565 per hour being lower than the lowest wage of $1.705 per hour paid in other departments, and much lower than the maximum wages in other departments, which ran from $3.18 to $3.65 per hour.

In 1955 Duke Power began requiring that every employee, except those in the Labor Department, had to have a high school diploma. The company also made the diploma a prerequisite for promotion of workers from the Labor Department into any of the others. Before 1955 the company's policy was to limit African-American workers to the Labor Department. Under that policy, every African-American employee in the Dan River plant continued to work in Labor, and none was promoted. In 1965, when Title VII went into effect, the company instituted a new policy under which employees could be promoted out of Labor by passing one of two high school equivalency tests — either the Wonderlic general intelligence test or the Bennett Mechanical AA general mechanical test. Duke promoted Jesse Martin, a black man, from Labor to Coal Handling in 1966. Two other African-American workers were promoted in 1968. All had high school degrees.

---

p. This is the typical enforcement scenario, but there are two variations in which the aggrieved person plays less of a role. One is that the Commission itself can initiate an unfair employment practice investigation, resulting in voluntary compliance *or* notification to the individuals of their rights to sue *or* referral to the Attorney General for suit (§§ 705(a), 706(a), (e)). Another enforcement mechanism is a "pattern or practice" lawsuit that can be brought by the Attorney General under § 707, 42 U.S.C. § 2000e–6.

Like the enforcement program, the remedial program is bifurcated. If conciliation by the EEOC fails and the aggrieved person successfully sues for an unlawful employment practice, the federal court may enjoin the practice and "order such affirmative action as may be appropriate, which may include reinstatement or hiring of employees, with or without back pay" (§ 706(g)). Also the court may allow the prevailing private plaintiff a "reasonable attorney's fee" as part of the costs awarded (§ 706(k)). The main relief in Attorney General pattern or practice suits has been injunctive relief (§ 707(a)). Some court decrees have been broad, ordering the merger of unions, the creation of revised seniority systems, and affirmative action plans where there has been continued discrimination.

After exhausting their administrative remedies with the EEOC, 13 of the 14 African-American employees at Dan River sued Duke Power for job discrimination in violation of Title VII. Six of the plaintiffs had no high school diplomas and were hired in Labor before 1955 — when Duke had no high school diploma requirement for promotion but when it refused to promote African Americans as a matter of company policy. Four plaintiffs had no high school diplomas but were hired after the company instituted the diploma requirement. The plaintiffs sought an injunction requiring Duke to discontinue its diploma and testing requirements for promotion.

You are the General Counsel for Duke Power. The company wants to retain its diploma and testing requirements, and you believe that company policy is no longer to exclude African Americans from higher positions simply because of their race. What do you advise the company? Do the diploma and testing requirements violate Title VII? There is no precedent on this issue in the court system in early 1966, when the lawsuits are brought. You understand that the EEOC is going to issue guidelines on the subject of testing later in 1966. Can you predict what the EEOC guidelines will say? Take a few minutes, and jot down your thoughts. Then read the following opinion.

GRIGGS v. DUKE POWER COMPANY
United States Court of Appeals for the Fourth Circuit, 1970
420 F.2d 1225

BOREMAN, CIRCUIT JUDGE.

[Writing for the panel majority, Judge Boreman ruled that the claims of three plaintiffs were moot, because the plaintiffs had been promoted. Further, his opinion held that Duke's application of the diploma and testing requirement to the six pre-1955 employees violated Title VII because these employees were treated differently from white employees of the same period. Prior to 1955 whites were sometimes hired or promoted into the other departments without high school diplomas. But Judge Boreman rejected the claims of the four employees hired after 1955 and held that Duke's diploma and testing requirements were not discriminatory within the meaning of Title VII.]

Pointing out that it uses an intracompany promotion system to train its own employees for supervisory positions inside the company rather than hire supervisory personnel from outside, Duke claims that it initiated the high school education requirement, at least partially, so that it would have some reasonable assurance that its employees could advance into supervisory positions; further, that its educational and testing requirements are valid because they have a legitimate business purpose, and because the tests are professionally developed ability tests, as sanctioned under § 703(h) of the Act, 42 U.S.C. § 2000e–2(h).

* * * [I]t seems reasonably clear that this requirement did have a genuine business purpose and that the company initiated the policy with no intention to discriminate against Negro employees who might be hired after the adoption of the educational requirement. This conclusion would appear to be not merely supported, but actually compelled by the following facts:

(1) Duke had long ago established the practice of training its own employees for supervisory positions rather than bringing in supervisory personnel from outside.

(2) Duke instituted its educational requirement in 1955, nine years prior to the passage of the Civil Rights Act of 1964 and well before the civil rights movement had gathered enough momentum to indicate the inevitability of the passage of such an act.

(3) Duke has, by plaintiffs' own admission, discontinued the use of discriminatory tactics in employment, promotions and transfers.

(4) The company's expert witness, Dr. Moffie, testified that he had observed the Dan River operation * * * and he concluded that a high school education would provide the training, ability and judgment to perform the tasks in the higher skilled classifications. This testimony is uncontroverted in the record.

(5) When the educational requirement was adopted it adversely affected the advancement and transfer of white employees who were Watchmen [a miscellaneous category] or were in the Coal Handling Department as well as Negro employees in the Labor Department.

(6) Duke has a policy of paying the major portion of the expenses incurred by an employee who secures a high school education or its equivalent. In fact, one of the plaintiffs recently obtained such equivalent, the company paying seventy-five percent of the cost.

[Having found the diploma requirement acceptable under Title VII, the Court then examined the testing requirement, which Judge Boreman found to be "professionally developed" and presumptively acceptable under § 703(h).]

The plaintiffs claim that tests must be *job-related* in order to be valid under § 703(h). The Equal Employment Opportunity Commission * * * supports plaintiffs' view. The EEOC has ruled that tests are unlawful " * * * in the absence of evidence that the tests are properly related to specific jobs and have been properly validated * * *." Decision of EEOC, December 2, 1966, reprinted in CCH Employment Practices Guide, ¶ 17,304.53. * * *

[Judge Boreman conceded that courts should give "great weight" to agency interpretations of statutes they administer, citing *Udall v. Tallman*, 380 U.S. 1, 15 (1965). But such interpretations are not binding on courts.] We cannot agree with plaintiffs' contention that such an interpretation by [the] EEOC should be upheld where, as here, it is clearly contrary to compelling legislative history * * *.

The amendment which incorporated the testing provision of § 703(h) was proposed in modified form by Senator Tower, who was concerned about a then-recent finding by a hearing examiner for the Illinois Fair Employment Practices Commission in a case involving Motorola, Inc. The examiner had found that a pre-employment general intelligence test which Motorola had given to a Negro applicant for a job had denied the applicant an equal employment opportunity because Negroes were a culturally deprived or disadvantaged group. In proposing his original amendment, essentially the same as the version later unanimously accepted by the Senate, Senator Tower stated:

"It [the amendment which, in substance, became the ability testing provision of § 703(h)] is an effort to protect the system whereby employers give *general ability and intelligence tests to determine the trainability of prospective employees.* The amendment arises from my concern about what happened in the Motorola FEPC case * * *.

"*If we should fail to adopt language of this kind, there could be an Equal Employment Opportunity Commission ruling which would in effect invalidate tests of various kinds of employees by both private business and Government to determine the professional competence or ability or trainability or suitability of a person to do a job.*" (Emphasis added.) 110 Congressional Record 13492, June 11, 1964.

The discussion which ensued among members of the Senate reveals that proponents and opponents of the Act agreed that general intelligence and ability tests, if fairly administered and acted upon, were not invalidated by the Civil Rights Act of 1964. See 110 Congressional Record 13503–13505, June 11, 1964.

The "Clark-Case" interpretive memorandum pertaining to Title VII fortifies the conclusion that Congress did not intend to invalidate an employer's use of bona fide general intelligence and ability tests. It was stated in said memorandum:

"There is no requirement in Title VII that employers abandon bona fide qualification tests *where, because of differences in background and education, members of some groups are able to perform better on these tests than members of other groups.* An employer may set his qualifications as high as he likes, he may test to determine which applicants have these qualifications, and he may hire, assign, and promote on the basis of test performance." (Emphasis added.) 110 Congressional Record 7213, April 8, 1964.

[When the Tower amendment was called up for a vote, Senator Humphrey urged its adoption, and it passed without dissent.]

SOBELOFF, CIRCUIT JUDGE [concurring in granting injunctive relief to the six pre-1955 employees and dissenting in refusing relief to the four post-1955 employees].

The pattern of racial discrimination in employment parallels that which we have witnessed in other areas. Overt bias, when prohibited, has ofttimes been supplanted by more cunning devices designed to impart the appearance of neutrality, but to operate with the same invidious effect as before. Illustrative is the use of the Grandfather Clause in voter registration — a scheme that was condemned by the Supreme Court without dissent over a half century ago. *Guinn v. United States,* 238 U.S. 347 (1915). Another illustration is the resort to pupil transfer plans to nullify rezoning which would otherwise serve to desegregate school districts. Again, the illusory even-handedness did not shield the artifice from attack; the Supreme Court unanimously repudiated the plan. *Goss v. Bd. of Education,* 373 U.S. 683 (1963). It is long-recognized constitutional doctrine that "sophisticated as well as simple-minded modes of discrimination" are prohibited. *Lane v. Wilson,* 307 U.S. 268, 275 (1938)

(Frankfurter, J.). We should approach enforcement of the Civil Rights Act in much the same spirit. * * *

The statute is unambiguous. Overt racial discrimination in hiring and promotion is banned [by § 703(a)(1)]. So too, the statute [presumably § 703(a)(2)] interdicts practices that are fair in form but discriminatory in substance. Thus it has become well settled that "objective" or "neutral" standards that favor whites but do not serve business needs are indubitably unlawful employment practices. * * * For example, a requirement that all applicants for employment shall have attended a particular type of school would seem racially neutral. But what if it develops that the specified schools were open only to whites, and if, moreover, they taught nothing of particular significance to the employer's needs? No one can doubt that the requirement would be invalid. It is the position of the Equal Employment Opportunities Commission (EEOC) that educational or test requirements which are irrelevant to job qualifications and which put blacks at a disadvantage are similarly forbidden. * * *

Whites fare overwhelmingly better than blacks on all the criteria [imposed by Duke Power for promotion],[6] as evidenced by the relatively small promotion rate from the Labor Department since 1965. Therefore, the EEOC contends that use of the standards as condition for transfer, unless they have significant relation to performance on the job, is improper. The requirements, to withstand attack, must be shown to appraise accurately those characteristics (and only those) necessary for the job or jobs an employee will be expected to perform. In other words, the standards must be "job-related."

[Judge Sobeloff urged deference to the EEOC interpretation of § 703(h), as indeed other courts had done. He further maintained that the EEOC's interpretation was not only "not unreasonable, but it makes eminent common sense," especially compared with Duke Power's lenient approach, which only required tests to be "professionally developed" to assure protection under the statutory exemption.] But, what is professionally developed for one purpose is not necessarily so for another. * * * [A] test that is adequately designed to determine academic ability, such as a college entrance examination, may be grossly wide of the mark when used in hiring a machine operator. * * * [M]y brethren's resolution of the issue contains a built-in invitation to evade the mandate of the statute. To continue his discriminatory practices an employer need only choose any test that favors whites and is irrelevant to actual job qualifications. * * *

---

6. * * * *High School Education.* In North Carolina, census statistics show, as of 1960, while 34% of white males had completed high school, only 12% of Negro males had done so. On a gross level, then, use of the high school diploma requirement would favor whites by a ratio of approximately 3 to 1.

Standardized Tests. * * * Since for generations blacks have been afforded inadequate educational opportunities and have been culturally segregated from white society, it is no more surprising that their performance on "intelligence" tests is significantly different than whites' than it is that fewer blacks have high school diplomas. In one instance, for example, it was found that 58% of whites could pass a battery of standardized tests, as compared with only 6% of the blacks. Included among those tests were the Wonderlic and Bennett tests.

[Judge Soboloff then examined the legislative response to *Motorola*.] That case went to the extreme of suggesting that standardized tests on which whites performed better than Negroes could never be used. The decision was generally taken to mean that such tests could never be justified *even if the needs of the business required them.*

Understandably, there was an outcry in Congress that Title VII might produce a *Motorola* decision. [Judge Soboloff quoted the same language from the Clark-Case memorandum quoted above by Judge Boreman.] Read against the context of the *Motorola* controversy, the import of the Clark-Case statement plainly appears: employers were not to be prohibited from using tests to determine *qualifications*. "Qualification" implies qualification *for* something. A reasonable interpretation of what the Senators meant, in light of the events, was that nothing in the Act prevents employers from requiring that applicants be fit for the job. * * *

[Judge Soboloff quoted Senator Tower's amendment as targeted only to protect tests "designed to determine or predict whether such individual is suitable or trainable with respect to his employment in the particular business or enterprise involved." 110 Cong. Rec. 13492 (1964) (text of original Tower amendment). Senators Humphrey and Case opposed the amendment as redundant, and Senator Case feared it was too broad: "If this amendment were enacted, it * * * would give an absolute right to an employer to state as a fact that he had given a test to all applicants, whether it was a good test or not, so long as it was professionally designed." *Id.* at 13504. The original Tower amendment was then defeated. *Id.* at 13724. Tower revised his amendment to render it acceptable to Humphrey and Case, and as revised the amendment passed.]

[Judge Soboloff concluded that the EEOC interpretation, that employment tests must be job-related, was consistent with the legislative history. The District Court had found the tests not to be job-related, and Duke Power did not produce evidence showing in any way that a high school education was necessary for jobs such as coal handling. He rejected Duke's argument that the tests were designed to identify future prospects rather than immediate promotion. Judge Soboloff concluded his dissent with a separate, and broader, point.]

* * * [T]he Company's criteria unfairly apply only to outsiders seeking entrance to the inside departments. This policy disadvantages those who were not favored with the lax criteria used for whites before 1955. * * * [T]his when juxtaposed with the history of the Dan River plant, is itself sufficient to constitute a violation of Title VII. * * *

[While Duke's] practice does not constitute forthright racial discrimination, the policy disfavoring the outside employees has primary impact upon blacks. This effect is possible only because a history of overt bias caused the departments to become so imbalanced in the first place. The result is that in 1969, four years after the passage of Title VII, Dan River looks substantially like it did before 1965. The Labor Department is all black; the rest is virtually lily-white.

There no longer is room for doubt that a neutral superstructure built upon racial patterns that were discriminatorily erected in the past comes within the Title VII ban. * * *

A remedy for this kind of wrong is not without precedent. The "freezing" principle (more properly, the anti-freezing principle) developed by the Fifth Circuit in voting cases is analogous. In those cases a pattern or practice of discrimination excluded almost all eligible Negroes from the voting lists but enrolled the vast majority of whites. Faced with judicial attack, the authorities found that they could no longer avowedly employ discriminatory practices. They invented and put into effect instead new, unquestionably even-handed, but onerous voting requirements which had the effect of excluding new applicants of both races, but, as was to be expected, primarily affected Negroes, who in the main were the unlisted ones. [For this reason, the Fifth Circuit struck down the new rules, and the Supreme Court agreed. *Louisiana v. United States*, 380 U.S. 145 (1965).]

Title VII bars "freeze-outs" as well as pure discrimination, where the freeze is achieved by requirements that are arbitrary and have no real business justification. Thus Duke Power's discrimination against *all* those who did not benefit from the pre-1955 rule for whites operates as an illegal "freeze-out" of blacks from the inside departments.

QUESTIONS ABOUT *GRIGGS*

The NAACP Legal Defense & Education, Inc. Fund (the "Inc. Fund"), which represents the plaintiffs, appeals this decision's denial of relief for the post-1955 plaintiffs to the Supreme Court. Should defendant cross-appeal the Court's granting relief to the pre-1955 plaintiffs? Do you think the EEOC will join in plaintiffs' appeal? How will the Supreme Court rule on this issue?

As you ponder this last query, consider the issues that divide Judges Boreman and Sobeloff. Some are technical issues, such as how to read §§ 703(a), (h) and what to make of the legislative history of the Tower Amendment (§ 703(h)). But aren't there larger issues that separate the two opinions, including different visions of racial justice, different degrees of deference to the EEOC, and different visions of the role of courts in implementing Title VII? Relevant to all these differences are political theories of the statutory process — theories to which we now turn.

SECTION 2. DESCRIPTIVE AND NORMATIVE THEORIES OF LEGISLATION

Griggs is just the starting point for the fascinating story of Title VII's evolution. Congress launched the statute in 1964; in the following decades, the statute has evolved in ways scarcely imaginable to its enactors. To understand the statute's evolution (explored in Section 3), it is useful to consider both theories of how the legislative process actually works (*descriptive* theories) and of how it should work (*normative* theories). Examine the two opinions in *Griggs* again. Note, for example, the significance that the different judges attributed to the Clark-Case memorandum, to the Senate rejection of the original Tower Amendment and then its adoption of the revised version of it, to Senator Case's objection to the original Tower Amendment, and to the EEOC's position. The interpretation of these events varies depending upon the interpreter's descriptive and normative assumptions about the congressional process in 1964.

In this section, we explore insights provided by three theoretical approaches: *interest group theories*, which focus on the influence and behavior of organized groups in the political process (Part A); *proceduralist theories*, which focus on the procedures by which a bill becomes law (Part B); and *institutional theories*, which focus on broad governmental structures (Part C). Each theory attempts to describe the congressional process, and each one also contains explicit or implicit assumptions about how that process should function. No one theory fully describes the rich and complex world of legislatures, lawmakers, interest groups, and constituents. Scholars often draw insights from several of the perspectives; each highlights important aspects of the legislative process for students, judges, legislators, and lawyers seeking to influence Congress and state legislatures or to understand the legislative product.

A. PLURALISM AND INTEREST GROUP THEORIES OF LEGISLATION

1. *Pluralism: The Importance of Groups in Legislation*

Many modern theories of the legislative process claim their genesis in *The Federalist Papers*, more specifically, in the political thought of James Madison. All three of the theoretical approaches we discuss can be linked, more or less closely, to Madisonian principles. As he worked to construct institutions of governance, Madison started with the propensity of human society to contain "factions" of citizens "who are united and actuated by some common impulse or passion, or of interest, adverse to the rights of other citizens, or to the permanent and aggregate interests of the community." *Federalist* #10. Like the Anti-Federalists (who opposed adoption of the Constitution), Madison believed factions must be controlled. However, Madison rejected the Anti-Federalist view that government could educate people to avoid faction and petty self-interest. "The latent causes of faction are thus sown in the nature of man," and hence cannot be eliminated short of unacceptable limitations on liberty. Madison viewed institutions of government as ways to contain the effects of faction and to channel them in socially productive ways. We will talk about the proceduralist and institutional aspects of Madisonian thought, but for the moment, let us focus on the notion of faction.

Madison's definition of faction, or interest group, is not neutral; he wrote that factions are driven by common interests that are "adverse" to the public good. A group of modern American theorists of democratic institutions who have emphasized the role of organized interests have a more positive view of factions. These thinkers write in the *pluralist* tradition, exemplified by Robert Dahl, *A Preface to Democratic Theory* (1956). For them, an interest group is "any group that, on the basis of one or more shared attitudes, makes certain claims upon other groups in the society for the establishment, maintenance, or enhancement of forms of behavior that are implied by the shared attitudes." David Truman, *The Governmental Process* 33 (1951). Peter Schuck articulates an even broader definition: "special interests * * * include any group that pursues contested political or policy goals, and that is widely regarded by the public as being one contending interest among others." *Against (and For) Madison: An Essay in Praise of Factions*, 15 Yale Law & Pol'y Rev. 553, 558 (1997). Under some definitions, political parties would be interest groups; other theorists distinguish between the major political parties and other organized groups.

As we are using the term, pluralism entails a number of interrelated propositions and definitions. (1) *Citizens organize into groups for political action.* Citizens have different opinions and different economic interests, which leads to the formation of "interest groups." (2) *Interest group politics results in "pluralism" — the spreading of political power across many political actors.* "Actual authority tends to be dispersed and exercised not solely by governmental officials but also by private individuals and groups within the society. Moreover, the power structure tends to be segmented; authority over one question rests here and over another there. All this contrasts with the model of a clear and rigid hierarchical pattern of power." V.O. Key, *Politics, Parties, and Pressure Groups* 9 (1958). Strong interest groups, many of which are private or voluntary organizations, protect individuals against oppressive and tyrannical government. In a way, a decentralized pluralist system expands one of Madison's checks on self-serving factions, as the ambition of one group checks the ambition of others and of government actors. See *Federalist #10.* (3) *Politics can be conceptualized as the process by which conflicting interest-group desires are resolved.* Because the objectives of one interest group can often be obtained only at the expense of others, the groups will come into conflict. The state regulates that conflict, and indeed the political system might be seen as nothing more than the arena in which interest group conflict is played out.

This third assumption deserves special attention. The starkest models of pluralism assume that government officials simply enact into law whatever interest groups, on balance, want. Policymakers are little more than rubber stamps validating the deals struck by interest groups in private negotiation, or umpires enforcing the rules of the game but playing no role in its outcome. Optimistic pluralists are not concerned that the resulting policies will be ill-conceived or contrary to the public interest; instead, a political environment with many groups actively competing will tend to produce moderate and well-considered policies. In part, moderation results because of the connections among interest groups. All of us belong to many groups, and our overlapping memberships provide an effective restraint on the extremism of any one group. In addition, "[b]ecause constant negotiations among different centers of power are necessary in order to make decisions, citizens and leaders will perfect the precious art of dealing peacefully with their conflicts, and not merely to the benefit of one partisan but to the mutual benefit of all the parties to a conflict." Robert Dahl, *Pluralist Democracy in the United States: Conflict and Consent* 24 (1967).

Our pluralist system is a marketplace of ideas, where all perspectives are articulated forcefully and persuasively. The best ideas succeed, while the worst are discarded. Pluralists argue that groups have a degree of power proportionate to their numbers — the larger, more general interest will prevail over the smaller, special interest. In addition, they have a degree of power proportionate to the intensity with which they hold their views, a factor which can increase the influence of smaller groups. As Nathaniel Persily explains the pluralist vision: " '[I]nterests' are not all equal: some are intensely felt, others only weakly so. 'Democracy' is more than a math problem. The *number* of people favoring a particular candidate or proposition is only one factor for which [a governance] system needs to account. The intensity of preferences also must weigh in the balance." *Toward a Functional Defense of Political Party Autonomy*, 76 N.Y.U. L. Rev. 750 (2001).[a] In short, bargaining among interest groups allows the system to reach a long-term equilibrium providing many interest groups one or a few policy objectives they care deeply about because they are willing to give up on issues about which they care much less.

A crucial assumption underlying such optimistic visions of pluralism is that all views and interests are represented. One might view the policies that emerge from interest group conflict and interaction with concern, however, if some interests are systematically unrepresented, or if some groups cannot accurately communicate to policymakers the intensity with which they support particular perspectives. Even early critics of interest-group liberalism noted pervasive disparities of access to the political process. One prominent skeptic, Elmer Schattschneider, in *The Semisovereign People: A Realist's View of Democracy in America* (1960), argued that interest groups are not broad-based or representative of all societal interests. "The flaw in the pluralist heaven is that the heavenly chorus sings with a strong upper-class accent. Probably about 90 percent of the people cannot get into the pressure system. * * * Pressure politics is a selective process ill designed to serve diffuse interests," such as the interests of consumers and other ordinary people. *Id.* at 34–35.

Schattschneider based his observation in part on his study of the Smoot-Hawley Tariff, which he found to have been enacted as a result of deals struck by well-heeled special interest groups rather than any deliberative consideration of the public interest. See Elmer Schattschneider, *Politics, Pressures and the Tariff: A Study of Free Private Enterprise in Pressure Politics, as Shown in the 1929–1930 Revision of the Tariff* (1935). Kay Lehman Schlozman and John Tierney have provided a stronger empirical basis for this observation, which seems at least intuitively plausible to any observer of politics. They found that "the pressure community [in Washington] is heavily weighted in favor of business organizations: 70 percent of all organizations having a Washington presence and 52 percent of those having their own offices represent business. The overrepresentation of business interests takes place at the expense of two

---

a. See also Robert Dahl, *Democracy and Its Critics* 150 (1989) (arguing that our system is one of "minorities rule" rather than of "majority rule"); Sidney Verba, Kay Lehman Schlozman & Henry Brady, *Voice and Equality: Civic Voluntarism in American Politics* 179–82 (1995) (explaining the importance of intensity of preference for pluralist democratic theory).

other kinds of organizations: groups representing broad public interests and groups representing the less advantaged." *Organized Interests and American Democracy* 68 (1986). These numbers may somewhat overstate the business community's influence relative to citizen groups; although citizen groups may comprise less than the 7% of Washington representatives identified by Schlozman and Tierney, they represent nearly 32% of all congressional testimony. Jeffrey Berry, *The New Liberalism: The Rising Power of Citizen Groups* 21–22 (1999).

In *The Logic of Collective Action* (1965), Mancur Olson elaborated on Schattschneider's thesis and provided a theory to explain why some groups form and work to influence politics and why some do not. Legislation is a *public good*; once the state has decided to provide clean waterways or safe highways, for example, all in society will benefit. Yet any individual effort to pass such laws will have only an infinitesimal effect on the probability of its enactment. Therefore, a rational person will not participate in the political process at all, preferring instead to *free-ride* on the efforts of others. As long as the free-rider cannot be excluded from enjoying the public goods that legislation and the efforts of groups lobbying in favor of new laws provide, she will have no incentive to join the group or to expend time and resources. If all citizens follow this rational course, then none will work to influence her representative to pass legislation providing diffuse benefits to the public at large.

Olson's theory predicts, therefore, that groups will form most often when there are a few interested members. In that case, each member has a large enough stake in the sought-after law to justify its participation. Furthermore, in small groups, members can monitor the behavior of others, detect and punish shirking, and ensure collective action. In other cases, a group will form because one member will receive such a large fraction of the governmental benefit that it would work to obtain the legislation even if it had to internalize all the costs of political activity. Indeed, the interested party may expend significant resources forming an interest "group" as part of its political strategy. It may fare better in the political process if the policy it advocates appears to elicit broader support. For example, a great deal of modern grassroots activity is financed, and to some extent manufactured, by well-funded, relatively small groups that hope to lend populist credentials to their policy proposals.[b] Under both these scenarios of group formation, small groups have the advantage over larger ones, and they will work to obtain targeted benefits at the expense of the diffuse and unorganized public. As Olson concludes: "[T]here is a surprising tendency for the 'exploitation' of the great by the small." *The Logic of Collective Action, supra,* at 35 (emphasis omitted). Other groups form because they can successfully coerce members to participate. For example, some have argued labor unions' legislative and electoral clout results in part from their ability essentially to require workers to belong and to participate in their activities.

---

b. See Richard Davis, *The Web of Politics: The Internet's Impact on the American Political System* 81–83 (1999).

The work of Olson and Schattschneider is necessary to understand interest group activity in politics and the threat that minority interests pose to the public good. Their work points out a flaw in Madison's prediction of the threat of factions. In a democracy, Madison feared more the tyranny of majority factions that could adopt policies oppressing minorities. He blithely, and inaccurately, dismissed concerns about minority factions in *Federalist* #10: "If a faction consists of less than a majority, relief is supplied by the republican principle, which enables a majority to defeat its sinister views by regular vote." As we will discuss in our survey of proceduralist and institutional theories of the legislative process, not only do minority factions possess organizational advantages over majority factions, they may also be adept in using aspects of the political process to dominate the discussion of policy alternatives, the selection of a particular course of action, and the implementation of the policy.

Although in some ways he completes and improves Madison's view of factions, Olson himself did not put forth an entirely satisfying theory. Large groups do form and influence political outcomes. Under the logic of collective action, such groups should remain latent, quietly footing the bill for the self-serving legislation that small groups manage to enact. Olson explained large groups in two ways. First, some form for nonpolitical reasons and then turn to political activity as a *byproduct*. For these groups, the initial costs of organizing, often the greatest hurdle facing those who seek to influence governmental policies, have already been met. Notably, these existing groups tend to comprise more privileged people — such as cartels, unions, farmer cooperatives, monopolies, and oligopolies — and therefore fit comfortably into Schattschneider's elite chorus. In the story of the Civil Rights Act, however, religious groups participated in political activity as a byproduct of their other activities. Their involvement demonstrates that not all such groups consist of the wealthy or advantaged classes.

Large groups can also form if they offer desirable *selective benefits* only to their members. For example, groups may offer life insurance, discounts on travel, dinners and events, and other goodies only to their members. The AARP offers members discounts on drugs; the NRA offers members discounts on bullets. To explain large political groups on the basis of this sort of selective benefit seems rather unpersuasive, however. Why pay dues that fund the Sierra Club's political activity just to get the calendar when one can buy a nature calendar for much less money? The kind of selective benefit that prompts people to join large groups must relate to the political activity itself. Accordingly, some public choice theorists argue that participation in group activity provides members with purposive or solidary benefits that justify any costs they incur.[c] *Purposive benefits* accrue to members who seek ideological or issue-oriented goals and find pursuit of those objectives more meaningful as

---

c. See Paul Johnson, *Interest Group Recruiting: Finding Members and Keeping Them*, in *Interest Group Politics* 35 (Allan Cigler & Burdett Loomis eds., 5th ed. 1998).

part of an organized group.[d] *Solidary benefits* provide members social rewards, including the satisfaction of the desire to be politically motivated.

These sorts of benefits may explain the existence of groups representing the poor and powerless in society. People who do not vote or have economic resources to influence policymakers rely on others who receive purposive or solidary benefits from political activity on behalf of disempowered groups. In addition, such a group may be led by an activist who obtains nonpecuniary personal benefits, perhaps through publicity or by satisfying intense ideological preferences, and thus is willing to incur the costs of organizing and lobbying. Regardless of the existence of these altruistic groups, however, we might suspect that individuals who must rely on others to assert their interests face significant disadvantages in the political system and obtain fewer benefits than they would in an ideal world.

Olson's vision is also incomplete because legislators will sometimes pay attention to the concerns of the diffuse public even if no organized group works to place the concerns on the policy agenda. For example, Congress enacts environmental legislation with provisions that benefit the general public, and it would probably do so even if groups like the Sierra Club remained latent. And we all know that lawmakers work to avoid passing general tax rate increases even though taxpayers are largely unorganized and Congress could use the money to send targeted benefits to vocal and organized minority factions.

In *The Logic of Congressional Action* (1990), a book designed to expand on Olson's seminal work, R. Douglas Arnold explains why legislators respond to the general public, which he calls the *inattentive public*, and do not spend all their time legislating in favor of organized groups that comprise the *attentive public*. The simple explanation is the electoral connection between lawmakers and the public. Members of Congress want to be reelected, and they know that the inattentive public, many of whom will vote in the next election, can be roused into action on particular issues under certain conditions. To avoid reprisals at election time, legislators will consider the potential preferences of the inattentive public and the likelihood that voters will focus on these preferences at election time. Given their limited attention, however, the nonattentive public may be satisfied with legislation that is largely symbolic, effecting no real change in policy.

Again, the mechanism that Arnold describes does not ensure that lawmakers will take into account all public preferences or the intensity with which citizens hold them. Instead, lawmakers will pay attention to issues affecting the diffuse public when they believe the issues are likely to influence votes in the next election. Arnold identifies several factors that affect the likelihood that a citizen will care about a given issue when she enters the voting booth. The *magnitude* of the cost or benefit affects the probability that a citizen will

---

d. See Edward Rubin, *Getting Past Democracy*, 149 U. Pa. L. Rev. 711, 745–746 (2001) (describing social movement theorists and noting that "meaning, not self-interest, * * * motivated many citizens' participation.").

perceive it; and the *timing* of the cost or benefit is important because citizens can more easily trace the direct effects of a policy back to a legislative action than they can effects further down the causal chain. In addition, the *proximity* of a voter to others similarly affected will influence the probability that she will pay attention to the issue. Perhaps most importantly, the unorganized public is more likely to notice an issue when an *instigator* or *policy entrepreneur* brings the issue forcefully to its attention near election time. A policy entrepreneur is a person, sometimes but not necessarily a government official, who works to bring a particular issue to the forefront of the policy agenda and to mobilize public support for action.[e] Examples of policy entrepreneurs who can elevate an issue to the consciousness of the inattentive public are journalists or political opponents.

2. *Public Choice Theory: A Transactional View of the Legislative Process*

Based in part on the empirical work of scholars such as Schattschneider and on the theories of classical market economics, a group of pluralists called *public choice theorists* have developed a rich line of scholarship to explain the operation of the processes by which legislators are selected, take action and positions, and make collective decisions.[f] Public choice scholars apply economic models to political phenomena and decisionmaking. Politicians and voters are considered rational utility-maximizers operating in a competitive electoral market. One prominent aspect of public choice theory has been the creation of models treating the legislative process as a microeconomic system in which "actual political choices are determined by the efforts of individuals and groups to further their own interests." Gary Becker, *A Theory of Competition Among Pressure Groups for Political Influence*, 98 Q.J. Econ. 371, 371 (1983). "The basic assumption is that taxes, subsidies, regulations, and other political instruments are used to raise the welfare of more influential pressure groups." *Id.* at 373–74. Compared to the optimistic pluralists, who often adopt an avowedly normative position in their scholarship, public choice theorists claim to be less normative and more descriptive in their methods and objectives. They are not wholly descriptive, however; for example, they often criticize existing institutional arrangements and propose changes based on their assumptions about individual and group behavior.

True to their perspective as economists, public choice scholars model the legislative environment as a political market. Interest groups, and to a lesser extent the public, are the demanders of legislation. They send benefits to legislators, who can supply them with governmental largesse. Legislators can respond to demand by refusing to pass a bill, by avoiding a clear choice

---

e. See, e.g., Frank Baumgartner & Bryan Jones, *Agendas and Instability in American Politics* 6 (1993) (discussing the importance of policy entrepreneurs); Gregory Wawro, *Legislative Entrepreneurship in the U.S. House of Representatives* (2000) (studying entrepreneurial behavior in Congress).

f. In addition to Olson's book cited earlier, other prominent works of public choice theory include James Buchanan & Gordon Tullock, *The Calculus of Consent* (1962); Anthony Downs, *An Economic Theory of Democracy* (1957); William Riker, *Liberalism Against Populism* (1982).

through delegation of broad decisionmaking authority to an agency in the executive branch, or by explicitly allocating tangible benefits. Based on Olson's *Logic of Collective Action* and James Wilson's *Political Organizations* (1973), Michael Hayes posits a transactional theory of legislation in *Lobbyists and Legislators: A Theory of Political Markets* (1981). Inspired by the idea that political markets are analogous to economic markets, Hayes outlines the demand and supply patterns for several different categories of political issues.

a. *Demand Patterns in Political Markets.* On the demand side (what interest groups want out of the legislature), legislators are often faced with a myriad of interest groups on any given issue, and these groups may either agree (consensual pattern) or disagree (conflictual pattern) with each other. A consensual demand pattern is similar to a non-zero-sum situation, while a conflictual demand pattern is basically zero sum. If an issue is consensual, then everyone who is aware of and actively interested in the issue can come out a winner, while if it is conflictual, then the resolution of the conflict will necessarily result in immediately identifiable winners and losers. In a way, this dichotomy is unrealistic; in a world of limited resources, all policies are zero sum because someone, either now or later, has to pay for them. In the short run, however, government decisions can be relatively unconstrained by resource limitations if policymakers can push the costs onto an inattentive group or a group that does not vote in the next election. For example, government benefits funded through deficit financing places the costs on future generations of taxpayers, some of whom have not yet been born. See Daniel Shaviro, *Do Deficits Matter?* (1997). Living voters may be harmed by higher interest rates as the government competes for credit or by inflation if the government just prints more money, but those costs can be hard for citizens to trace back to particular legislative decisions. In these essentially consensual circumstances, interest groups may cooperate, making deals among themselves to obtain benefits at the expense of the general public. This type of interest group behavior is often called *logrolling* as minority interests work together to enact a bill, providing goodies to the organized constituents of a majority of lawmakers. Examples of these kinds of bills include tax bills that enact tax benefits for hundreds of interest groups, military construction bills that send money to projects in hundreds of congressional districts, or tariff bills like the Smoot-Hawley Act that Schattschneider studied.

The extent to which an interest group is formally organized is one key to its effectiveness in demanding legislation. Organized groups provide useful information to political actors and tend to frame the issues more clearly and precisely for legislators. And, as we have learned, certain kinds of groups are more likely to succeed in surmounting the hurdles to effective organization than others, potentially skewing the market for legislation.

Increasingly, the demand side of the market is characterized by interest groups working in coalitions in which several groups with shared interests work together typically for a limited time.[g] Some coalitions are relatively permanent, however; for example, the American Chamber of Commerce or the National Association of Manufacturers are really coalitions of smaller groups. Coordination among groups can reveal to lawmakers that a policy's advocates span numerous congressional districts, and coalitions are often nonpartisan, giving them the advantage of bipartisan support. Of course, coalitions are not invincible. The larger and broader a coalition, the more susceptible it may be to tactics that divide members and dissipate its strength. Those forming coalitions thus face a difficult tension. On the one hand, larger coalitions have more clout because they command more resources and they can maintain relationships with more lawmakers. On the other hand, large coalitions often comprise groups whose interests are aligned but not identical. Thus, a large coalition may face collective action problems or may begin to splinter when compromises are developed through the legislative process.

James Wilson maintains that the degree and nature of interest group organization is determined by the perceived incidence of costs and benefits from a specified policy. Similarly, Theodore Lowi argues that the political relationship among demanders of the legislative product is "determined by the type of policy at stake, so that for every type of policy there is likely to be a distinctive type of political relationship." *American Business, Public Policy, Case-Studies, and Political Theory*, 16 World Pol. 677, 688 (1964). Costs of a policy may be broadly *distributed*, such as a sales tax paid by all consumers, or may be *concentrated* on a small group, such as a license fee. Similarly, benefits may be widely distributed or shared by all, such as the benefits of national security, or they may be concentrated in the hands of a few, such as state subsidies to tobacco farmers. When Wilson's typology is combined with the insights of Olson's theory, a transactional theorist might surmise that because bills providing concentrated costs or benefits will affect smaller groups, they will *on average* stimulate more organizational activity than measures with distributed costs and benefits.[h] Table 1–1 sets forth this model.

Each of these quadrants produces a particular kind of political climate. Quadrant I is best described as *majoritarian politics*. Although there is little group activity on either side, some large groups of citizens will weigh in both in favor of distributed benefits (for example, environmental groups will favor clean air legislation) and against distributed costs (Citizens for a Sound Economy will oppose tax increases or the Concord Coalition will oppose deficit spending). Quadrant II fits the model of *entrepreneurial politics*.

---

g. See Kevin Hula, *Lobbying Together: Interest Group Coalitions in Legislative Politics* (2000).

h. Note the textual emphasis, *on average*; this is only a generalization, not an iron rule. Due to the free-rider problem, the formation of even small groups cannot be assumed. Extremely large groups sometimes organize. In addition, as our analysis of proceduralism will demonstrate, numerous advantages exist for groups in a defensive posture, which means that such groups are perhaps more likely to form. Also, an effective demand pattern is not limited to interest groups — the existence of an inattentive public can and does exert influence in certain situations. Finally, the work of interest groups can all be for naught due to the countervailing power of the latitude possessed by legislators.

Organized interests will form to derail the legislation; support is likely only if a policy entrepreneur is willing to push the proposal, rouse the inattentive public, and perhaps take the initiative in forming citizen groups offering purposive or solidary benefits to participants. *Client politics* describes the consensual interest group activity in Quadrant III, where logrolling dominates the essentially non-zero sum game that interest groups play. Finally, Quadrant IV is the area of conflictual *interest group politics* where the process produces identifiable and short-term winners and losers, and both sides are organized and active.

Table 1–1
Taxonomy of Demand for Legislation Based on Benefits/Costs

I *Distributed benefits/distributed costs*	**II** *Distributed benefits/concentrated costs*
A general benefit-general taxation case that usually involves public goods. Little group activity on either side of most cases.	A general benefit-specific taxation case in which the majority imposes its will on the minority up to the capacity of the minority to pay. Opposition will tend to be well organized.
III *Concentrated benefits/distributed costs*	**IV** *Concentrated benefits/concentrated costs*
Tends to have strong interest group support and weak, if any, organized opposition because of the free-rider problem. The benefit to an individual of having the policy changed is simply too immaterial.	Results in continuous organized conflict over payment of benefits and distribution of costs. A prime example is the NLRB and the conflicts between labor and management.

b. *Supply Patterns in Legislative Markets.* Public choice theorists tend to discount legislators' statements that they vote "for the public interest." Morris Fiorina, *Congress: Keystone of the Washington Establishment* (2d ed. 1989), and David Mayhew, *Congress: The Electoral Connection* (1974), posit that legislative behavior can best be explained by the assumption that the primary goal of legislators is to be reelected. Of course, regardless of the ultimate motivation for legislative behavior, the desire for reelection is a good focus of study because, as long as lawmakers do not face term limits, reelection is a prerequisite to achieving any other goals. To put it differently, legislators may ultimately want to enact particular policies that they believe benefit the country, or to receive benefits from interest groups, or to gain publicity because of their positions. But to achieve any of these goals, they must remain in office; thus, the electoral connection is a paramount concern.

A large majority of legislators respond to this electoral incentive effectively and are reelected time after time. Although the advantage of incumbency has declined slightly, it is still one of the strongest predictors of electoral success.[i]

---

i. See Bruce Cain, *The American Electoral System,* in *Developments in American Politics* 37, 43–46 (Gillian Peele, Christopher Bailey & Bruce Cain eds., 1992).

How can a politician ensure that she will remain undefeated if her elected position demands that she take public stands on controversial issues? Fiorina has suggested that *abstention* (the legislator does not take sides) or *casework* (the legislator dollops out individual, nonlegislative favors, such as intervention in agency decisionmaking, to the groups voted against) can ameliorate the harmful effects of conflicting constituent demands. Other transactional theorists argue that the most effective response is for the legislator to act so that each of the conflicting groups will believe it has won something. Thus, the legislator's best strategies for dealing with conflictual demand patterns are to persuade the conflicting groups to reach a compromise which the legislator will then support *or* to pass an ambiguous bill which delegates policy responsibility to an administrative agency which is even more prone to interest group manipulation. The capture theory has gained wide currency in administrative law: agencies charged with regulating an industry or making political value choices regarding a cluster of issues become tools of the interests they are supposed to be ruling.[j]

Again, Wilson's typology may be useful. If a policy imposes concentrated costs, legislators will want to avoid responsibility as much as possible, perhaps by delegating the cost-imposition to a regulatory agency, such as the Food and Drug Administration or the Environmental Protection Agency. The regulated interest may accept this outcome, hoping that its superior organization will allow it to capture the regulating agency and subvert the policy.[k] Even if the costs are distributed, such as in majoritarian politics, legislators may be wary of acting directly and decisively. Take, for example, the case of a clean air act funded through a general tax rate hike. The inattentive public is more likely to trace the immediate and somewhat costly increase in taxes back to lawmakers and vote against them than voters are apt to notice slight increases in air quality and to make the connection between cleaner air and a particular piece of legislation. In cases of concentrated benefits and distributed costs, however, legislators may risk the wrath of the electorate to gain the gratitude of the attentive and organized public, particularly if they believe that the cost-bearers will remain unaware of the costs or can be deceived by public-regarding half-truths about the statutory purposes. Thus, in the arena of client politics, legislators often reward friendly interest groups with self-regulation or distributive benefits.

Table 1–2 illustrates the transactional supply model. As you study the interest group dynamics in the various quadrants, ask yourself where the Civil Rights Act of 1964 fits. Businesses required to change their hiring and promotion practices may have believed they were subject to concentrated costs. On the other hand, businesses in the South that wanted to expand their client base or expand their pool of potential workers may have preferred legislation that would allow them to integrate without violating ingrained racist norms in

---

j. See, e.g., Thomas Merrill, *Capture Theory and the Courts: 1967–1983,* 72 Chi.-Kent L. Rev. 1039, 1050–52 (1997).

k. See Peter Aranson, Ernest Gellhorn, & Glen Robinson, *A Theory of Legislative Delegation,* 69 Cornell L. Rev. 1 (1982).

those regions.[1] What about the interest groups on the other side? As we have noted, the religious organizations favoring the bill were already organized; their political activity was a relatively cheap byproduct since the initial costs of organization had been defrayed and mechanisms of collecting financial support and harnessing human resources were well established. Policy entrepreneurs inside and outside of government abound, all with varying personal interests. And while blacks and other groups facing discrimination were relatively powerless in society, they had the potential to organize and affect electoral outcomes, particularly after President Johnson succeeded in meeting his subsequent objective of enacting strong voting rights laws.

Table 1–2
Taxonomy of Supply of Legislation Based on Benefits/Costs

I *Distributed benefits/distributed costs*

Because there is no strong pressure from organized interests, legislature will favor *no bill or symbolic action*. Sometimes delegation to agency regulation will occur.

II *Distributed benefits/concentrated costs*

Because the proposal will be opposed by organized interests, the best legislative solution is to draft an ambiguous bill and *delegate to agency regulation*, so all sides can claim victory. Regulatory capture can result.

III *Concentrated benefits/distributed costs*

Because the costs can be allocated to an uninformed public, legislature will follow a policy of *distribution* of subsidies and power to the organized beneficiaries. Often *self-regulation* is the chosen policy.

IV *Concentrated benefits/concentrated costs*

Because any policy choice will incur the wrath of opposing interest groups, legislators will favor *no bill* or delegation to *agency regulation*.

c. *The Implications of a Transactional Model of Legislation: Madison's Nightmare.* The transactional model developed in Tables 1–1 and 1–2 suggest considerable pessimism regarding the results of imperfect political markets. On the one hand, the public sector will tend to spend too much money on statutes that concentrate benefits on special interests while distributing their costs to the general, and often unsuspecting, public. There is an obvious tendency to logroll in a specific benefit-general taxation scheme such as ours, because legislators can please important groups with tax subsidies, while avoiding blame for the overspending that results.

On the other hand, the public sector will tend to supply too few statutes that are likely to be public-regarding, namely, statutes that distribute benefits broadly (e.g., infrastructure programs, commercial codes, effective criminal laws). Legislators often have little interest in such statutes, because they do not as reliably generate votes in the next election. And even if the populace were

---

1. But see Richard Epstein, *Forbidden Grounds: The Case Against Employment Discrimination Laws* 127–28 (1992) (contesting this prisoner's dilemma view and the conclusion that it justified regulation).

appreciative of these statutes, it is possible that in many cases Congress will be unaware of the demand, because the free-rider problem precludes effective organization. This problem is particularly acute in Quadrant II because a statute that provides distributed benefits through enacting concentrated costs will face strong and organized opposition that is likely to prevail over the shallow support that a policy entrepreneur can create. Some of these laws, notably federal criminal laws when violence and crime are salient for voters, may produce political payoffs attractive enough to encourage lawmakers to spend some time on these proposals and to pass legislation that is often primarily symbolic.

This taxonomy may suggest reforms that are likely to improve the legislative process because it helps to identify the equivalents of market failures. For example, if legislation in the majoritarian and entrepreneurial arenas tends to be more consistent with the public good but is underproduced because of interest group dynamics, reforms might emphasize empowering people whose interests are not well represented by organized groups. Alternatively, it might suggest that we should identify proxy groups with related interests that can serve as champions for the unorganized. Julie Roin argues, for example, that state and local governments' opposition to federal mandates that are not accompanied by federal funds to defray expenses protects the interests of the diffuse group of taxpayers who would pay for such mandates through higher state and local taxes or reduced services. *Reconceptualizing Unfunded Mandates and Other Regulations*, 93 Nw. U. L. Rev. 351, 375–80 (1999). Or, if we notice that inefficient, private-regarding legislation is less likely when interest group behavior is conflictual and not cooperative, we might seek to structure the legislative process to force interest groups to compete for limited resources. Structuring legislative processes so that losers are more clearly identified will make such legislation more difficult to pass.[m] It is also worth considering how changing technology may affect the dynamics of the transactional model. For example, as the Internet makes communication and organization less costly, will larger groups form and influence the political process? Or will these technologies work primarily to the advantage of the already powerful and organized interests? See Bruce Bimber, *Information and American Democracy: Technology in the Evolution of Power* (2003) (discussing effect of Internet and new communication technology on political organizations, citizens and government).

3. *Criticisms of the Pluralist or Public Choice Vision*

You might consider the transactional model suggested by public choice theory a distressing vision of our polity. In fact, the descriptive vision of public choice theory and the normative vision of pluralism are controversial.

Public choice models of the legislative process have come under increasing attack in the last decade for their oversimplification of the political process and

---

m. See Elizabeth Garrett, *Rethinking the Structures of Decisionmaking in the Federal Budget Process*, 35 Harv. J. Legis. 387 (1998).

their failure to recognize its institutional richness.[n] Even some scholars writing in the public choice tradition have criticized the transactional model because it treats legislators as ciphers, merely implementing the deals that interest groups reach. Perhaps the most interesting public-choice-inspired critique of this view of legislators' role has been offered by Fred McChesney. He notes that those who posit the economic theory of legislation and legal regulation largely ignore the ways in which politicians obtain benefits from their office other than by sending legislative goodies to interest groups. In *Money for Nothing: Politicians, Rent Extraction, and Political Extortion* 2–3 (1997), McChesney argues that

> payments to politicians [campaign contributions, gifts, post-tenure employment] often are made, not for particular political favors, but to avoid particular political disfavor, that is, as part of a system of political extortion or 'rent extraction.' * * * Because the state, quite legally, can (and does) take money and other forms of wealth from its citizens, politicians can extort from private parties payments *not* to expropriate private wealth. *** In that sense, rent extraction — receiving payments not to take or destroy private wealth — is "money for nothing" in the words of the song.

Rent extraction is theoretically possible in any field of legislation because lawmakers always have the capacity to repeal existing beneficial laws or to enact new taxes or fees burdening particular activities or industries. Practically, however, the threat to burden an interest group must be credible for successful rent extraction. In other words, the threatened group must believe that the chances are good that lawmakers will actually pass harmful legislation. One arena of particularly credible threats is the tax legislative arena because Congress frequently passes new tax laws decreasing some tax subsidies and increasing taxes on particular groups. This behavior produces enough uncertainty that current beneficiaries of tax subsidies are regularly worried that their provisions will be scaled back or modified and are willing to pay protection money to lawmakers.[o]

Rent extraction helps to fill out the complex and varied reality of the legislative process, but it is not completely satisfying. First, it accepts the inaccurate view of legislators as one-dimensional seekers of financial rewards from special interest groups. As we will discuss below, although reelection and

---

n. For commentary, see, e.g., Daniel Farber & Philip Frickey, *Law and Public Choice: A Critical Introduction* (1991); *The Rational Choice Controversy* (Jeffrey Friedman ed., 1996); Donald Green & Ian Shapiro, *Pathologies of Rational Choice Theory* (1994); Jerry Mashaw, *Greed, Chaos, and Governance: Using Public Choice To Improve Public Law* (1997); Maxwell Stearns, *Public Choice and Public Law: Readings and Commentary* (1997); Frank Cross, *The Judiciary and Public Choice*, 50 Hastings L. J. 355 (1999); Einer Elhauge, *Does Interest Group Theory Justify More Intensive Judicial Review?*, 101 Yale L.J. 31 (1991); Thomas Merrill, *Does Public Choice Justify Judicial Activism After All?*, 21 Harv. J. L. & Pub. Pol. 219 (1997); *Symposium: Getting Beyond Cynicism: New Theories of the Regulatory State*, 87 Cornell L. Rev. 267 (2002).

o. See, e.g., Richard Doernberg & Fred McChesney, *Doing Good or Doing Well?: Congress and the Tax Reform Act of 1986*, 62 N.Y.U. L. Rev. 891 (1987); Edward McCaffery & Linda Cohen, *Shakedown at Gucci Gulch: The New Logic of Collective Action*, 84 N.C. L. Rev. 1159 (2006).

interest group considerations are important to lawmakers, most are also pursuing other objectives, such as affecting policy in ways consistent with their ideological commitments. Second, the theory of rent extraction combined with the transactional model of legislation allows public choice scholars to explain every possible congressional decision in terms of the market model; it thereby loses a great deal of its explanatory and predictive force. If legislation is enacted, then the beneficiaries must have outbid their rivals; if legislation is not enacted, then the rivals clearly won. If a particular tax subsidy is repealed in order to pay for a new tax benefit for another group, then the holders of the repealed provision must not have paid enough to avoid the burden, perhaps erroneously believing that Congress was bluffing. If the repeal is proposed but not enacted, then the holders of the targeted provision must have met the extortionate demand in order to continue enjoying the federal largesse.

Empirical studies also provide a basis for a critique of public choice, revealing that money and organization do not always translate into clout. See Jeffrey Berry, *The Interest Group Society* 226–33 (3d ed. 1997). Instead, an interest group's influence depends upon the context. First, interest groups are more successful at blocking legislation than enacting a new policy. See Schlozman and Tierney, *supra*, at 314–15. Several factors make opposition an easier posture for interest groups. Groups defending the status quo need to prevail at only one stage in the convoluted legislative process. Proponents of new legislation must successfully navigate all of the procedural obstacles. In addition, cognitive psychology suggests that people work harder to preserve what they have than to gain a new benefit.[p] This finding is confirmed by leaders of interest groups who report it is easier to ward off an attack than to mount one. Second, interest groups succeed more frequently on issues that are not salient to the larger public and that are perceived as narrow, technical, nonpartisan issues. *Id.* at 314. Client politics is easier when it occurs outside the glare of publicity, and members are willing to trade support on minor issues in backroom deals. Finally, groups work to locate the decisionmaking in institutions that are sympathetic to their position or have procedures they can use to their advantage.[q]

Just as empirical studies have given us a different and more complex explanation than that provided by public choice theory for the demand side of legislation (interest group behavior), case studies of Congress by institutional political scientists have questioned the public choice explanation for the supply side (behavior of legislators). Richard Fenno's classic case study, *Congressmen in Committees* (1973), argues that legislators are interested in more than simply being reelected, contrary to the assumptions of public choice theory. While reelection is certainly a powerful motivating factor and a necessary intermediate goal, legislators also want to have "status" within government and to make some positive contribution to what they consider good public policy.

---

p. See Cass Sunstein, *Behavioral Analysis of Law*, 64 U. Chi. L. Rev. 1175, 1179–81 (1997).

q. See Neil Komesar, *Imperfect Alternatives: Choosing Institutions in Law, Economics, and Public Policy* (1994).

Especially when an issue involves moral questions and is publicly visible, the legislator's vote depends on something more than her calculations about reelection.[r] Recall the behavior of the legislators in our story of the Civil Rights Act; can it all be explained solely in terms of interest group influence, or were other factors at work?

Not only may public choice theory oversimplify legislator motivations, it may also misconceive the legislative process by viewing it statically and disregarding institutional changes that affect behavior. For example, centralized organizations like political parties have recently become stronger in the federal legislature, relative to committees and rank-and-file members, allowing lawmakers to coordinate their efforts more effectively and resist the urge to act in ways that benefit only narrow special interests or small constituencies. Lawmakers who serve in party leadership roles tend to come from relatively safe districts and therefore to be insulated from narrow constituent pressures. Thus, they can survive the electoral heat of authoring a compromise bill that offends the sensibilities of extremists or particular interest groups, and they may have more leeway in pursuing their vision of the public good without fearing electoral reprisals.[s] Counterbalancing this, however, is their desire to remain in the majority and an awareness that the reelection of some of their members may depend on legislation benefitting special interests.

Another institution that affects legislative behavior — the Presidency — was long slighted by traditional public choice theory. It is now receiving more attention.[t] The President may be the dominant influence in the national legislative process. As a unitary office backed by a more cohesive coalition than the multi-membered Congress, the Presidency is in a better position to develop coherent policies and, consequently, often initiates and propels controversial bills through the legislative labyrinth. As our nation's most visible public figure, the President is ideally situated to stimulate publicity about a public problem. As the chief of the executive branch, the President has access to an impressive brain trust (such as the Office of Management and Budget, the Treasury Department's Office of Tax Policy, and other prestigious executive branch entities), which can think creatively about a problem and draft proposed legislation. As the head of one of the political parties, representative of a uniquely national constituency, and someone who controls a number of desirable benefits, the President can be the best possible lobbyist a bill can have. Something as controversial as the Civil Rights Act (or the tax reform legislation in 1986 or the radical reform of federal welfare programs in the

---

r. See also Keith Poole & Howard Rosenthal, *Congress: A Political-Economic History of Roll Call Voting* (1997) (finding ideology was largest influence on roll call voting behavior).

s. See John Aldrich, *Why Parties? The Origin and Transformation of Political Parties in America* 205 (1995).

t. See, e.g., *The Presidency and the Political System* (Michael Nelson ed., 8th ed. 2006); Terry Moe & Scott Wilson, *Presidents and the Politics of Structure*, 57 Law & Contemp. Probs. 1 (Spring 1994).

1990s) would have likely been impossible without the President's active involvement.[u]

An increasing focus of institutional political science theory has been the dynamic nature of the legislative process. John Kingdon, in *Agenda, Alternatives, and Public Policies* (2d ed. 1995), has developed a dynamic model of the legislative process which synthesizes prior political science scholarship and presents an alternative to the static public choice model. Kingdon de-emphasizes the role of interest groups and argues that public officials (the President, the Cabinet appointed by the President, Congress, as well as leaders of political parties) play the key roles in setting the nation's political agenda. The role of interest groups is usually to formulate and debate policy alternatives, a role they share with other less visible (but perhaps more public-regarding) participants, such as civil servants, academics and experts, the media, and legislative staff.

Kingdon's model of the legislative process is drawn from the "garbage can model of organizational choice," described in Michael Cohen, James March & Johan Olsen, *A Garbage Can Model of Organizational Choice*, 17 Ad. L.Q. 1 (March 1972). Under this conceptualization, Congress operates through an "organized anarchy," in which there is no linear process for identifying a problem, defining alternative solutions, and reaching a decision. See also Charles Lindblom & Edward Woodhouse, *The Policy-Making Process* Chapters 1 & 2 (3d ed. 1993). Rather, salient problems, possible solutions, and choice opportunities will coexist as separate "streams" in the "garbage can" (the system). Sometimes problems are resolved; sometimes they go away; sometimes the system despairs of solving them. The outcome depends on the "coupling of the streams": A problem becomes salient at the same time a solution becomes well-regarded and participants favoring the solution can seize the legislative process for that end. To change policy, groups must have more than just political clout; they must draw attention to their proposal when the political environment is receptive to it. Activists need a focusing event, preferably after they have laid the groundwork necessary to increase the chances that the event will lead to movement in a direction they support. Sometimes streams connect and issues become prominent on the political agenda because of chance. Airline safety becomes a topic of national concern and attention after a tragic plane accident, for example. Political entrepreneurs, whether inside or out of government, need not leave matters completely to the vagaries of fate, however; they can manipulate the policy environment to increase receptivity to their objectives. When focusing events do not occur fortuitously, they can be created, much as Greenpeace has done in the environmental area when it confronts hunters and polluters on the high seas.

---

u. But see Benjamin Ginsberg, Walter Mebane & Martin Shefter, *The President and the "Interests": Why the White House Cannot Govern*, in *The Presidency and the Political System* 361 (Michael Nelson ed., 6th ed. 2000); Michael Fitts, *The Paradox of Power in the Modern State: Why a Unitary, Centralized Presidency May Not Exhibit Effective or Legitimate Leadership*, 144 U. Pa. L. Rev. 827 (1996).

Public choice suffers from another static perspective: most scholars assume that preferences are independent of and prior to political activity. To use economic terminology, pluralism, particularly public choice, tends to view preferences as *exogenous* rather than *endogenous*. This assumption is clearly unrealistic; we all know that participating in decisionmaking, whether in the political realm or elsewhere, significantly affects the way we think and feel about a particular issue.[v] As the members of Congress deliberated about the Civil Rights Act of 1964 and discussed their views with their colleagues and constituents, their conclusions about integration and racism surely developed and changed. As we turn to theories of the legislative process that focus on the procedures shaping it, we will consider how the structures of deliberation affect our preferences about outcomes.

One can reject the public choice description of the legislative process in favor of one of the institutional political descriptions, yet still believe that some form of pluralism is and should be characteristic of our political system. But this normative vision has also become controversial. Typically, defenders of pluralism will now concede that interest group government sacrifices elements of fairness, rational social choice, and/or other values but will argue that pluralism is justified by its facilitation of stability, moderation, and broad satisfaction with the political system. This may not be a persuasive justification for those who consider social justice more important than stability.[w] Furthermore, by defining "politics" as the relatively narrow conflict among professional groups, pluralism implicitly denies the existence or feasibility of other forms of political struggle to change existing institutions and to organize around broader lines of cleavage (such as class). Because most of the political activity under pluralism is by and among elites, pluralist democracy may tend to reinforce already-existing social and economic inequalities.[x]

B. PROCEDURALIST THEORIES OF LEGISLATION

Proceduralists also claim James Madison as their founding father, largely because his solution to the problem of faction lay in government design. Since the causes of faction cannot be eradicated except by destroying liberty or by somehow forcing all people to share identical opinions, interests, and passions, Madison reasoned the best strategy is to contain the effects of faction. Where the faction remains a minority, popular government is sufficient to contain it, because its views will not command the necessary majority. But, noted Madison, sometimes a faction will temporarily command majority support because of inflamed passions, deception, and so forth. In that circumstance, a direct democracy would be little protection against oppression. In contrast, a representative government has the structural ability "to refine and enlarge the public views, by passing them through the medium of a chosen body of

---

v. See Amartya Sen, *Behavior and the Concept of Preference*, 40 Economica 241 (1973); Cass Sunstein, *Preferences and Politics*, 20 Phil. & Pub. Aff. 3 (1991).

w. See, e.g., Stuart Hampshire *Justice in Conflict* (2000); Thomas Simon, *Democracy and Social Injustice: Law, Politics, and Philosophy* 151–71 (1995).

x. See C. Wright Mills, *The Power Elite* (1959).

citizens, whose wisdom may best discern the true interest of their country * * *. The public voice, pronounced by the representatives of the people, will be more consonant to the public good than if pronounced by the people themselves, convened for the purpose." *Federalist* #10. Madison admitted the possibility of corruption of representatives but argued that republics of great size (such as the United States) would have a large enough number of representatives and a broad enough constituency for each as to minimize the possibility of corruption of a majority of the elected representatives.

In *Federalist* #51, Madison explained another protective strategy, the theory of *checks and balances* among the departments of government. If ill-motivated officials control one or more of the branches of the government, they are countered by those officials in the other branches — even when they, too, are not public-spirited. "Ambition," said Madison, "must be made to counteract ambition." Bicameralism is particularly important, not only because it provides a double review of proposed legislation and essentially requires supermajority support for any legislative proposal, but also because the two chambers perform complementary tasks. With its representatives being from smaller districts and subject to electoral scrutiny every two years, the House of Representatives would have an "immediate dependence on, and an intimate sympathy with, the people." *Federalist* #52. The Senate, whose members were originally elected by state legislatures for six-year terms, would have a stabilizing influence. Its members would have greater leisure to acquaint themselves with the issues and to discuss the issues deliberatively. *Federalist* #62.

1. *Vetogates: Procedural Doors That Bills Must Pass Through*

The most obvious feature of the legislative process described in the "Note on How a Bill Becomes a Federal Law," *supra*, is that any legislative proposal has to surmount a series of hurdles before it becomes a law. Most basically, Article I, § 7 of the Constitution requires endorsement of the proposal in identical form by both the House and Senate and then presentment to the President. Hence any of these bodies, and not just the President, can "veto" a proposal. The congressional process itself creates most of the "gates" that a bill must pass through and where it can be killed rather than moved along to the next stage of the process. Because of the nature of each of these obstacles, scholars have coined the term *vetogates*[y] to apply to the choke points in the process, some with the durability of constitutional requirements, others matters of congressional rule or norm. Opponents of a bill have many vetogates to exploit: (1) kill the bill in committee; (2) if committee approval cannot be avoided, stop the bill before full chamber consideration; (3) if full chamber consideration occurs, kill the bill there by filibustering it in the Senate, by amending it to death, or by outright defeating it on the chamber floor; (4) if one chamber has approved the bill, exploit the veto opportunities in the other

---

y. See McNollgast (short for Mathew McCubbins, Roger Noll & Barry Weingast), *Legislative Intent: The Use of Positive Political Theory in Statutory Interpretation*, 57 Law & Contemp. Probs. 3 (1994).

chamber to prevent it from passing an identical measure; (5) if the other chamber produces a similar but not identical bill, amend or defeat it at the conference committee stage or in an interbranch summit; (6) if all else fails, persuade the President to veto it and then work against any congressional effort to override the veto.

Descriptively, the existence of vetogates means that determined minorities can often kill legislation or, in the alternative, maim legislation they cannot kill. Determined Southern opponents of civil rights legislation were able to stop or to dilute such bills until 1964 because they controlled pivotal vetogates (the House Rules Committee, the Senate Judiciary Committee). Rather than killing a measure, a minority controlling a vetogate may extract concessions from the enacting coalition by a threat to stall it or change it significantly. This was the approach taken by Senator Dirksen. Indeed, one way a small faction "exploits" majority factions, to use Mancur Olson's term, is the former's ability to influence those who control various vetogates. Interest groups spend time forming and maintaining connections with members of Congress and other participants in federal lawmaking. In this process, a group seeking to block legislation rather than to pass it has a tremendous advantage. Because legislation can be stopped at many points along the legislative path, groups need to secure the assistance of only one key player to succeed. The electoral strength of incumbents, combined with a strong seniority system that significantly influences committee assignments, gives organized groups great certainty about which legislator will occupy a strategic position in the system.

Normatively, the existence of vetogates may tell statutory interpreters (courts, administrative agencies, lawyers advising clients) to whom they should pay attention if they consult legislative history, as the Fourth Circuit judges did in *Griggs*. Legislative statements are most important when they reflect assurances by the enacting coalition — especially promises to or by gatekeepers — to enable the bill to pass through a vetogate. Thus committee reports are conventionally referred to, both because they reflect the understanding of the key gatekeepers (the committee), but also because they are important representations by the floor managers of the bill (usually members of the committee) to attract votes on the floor. Thus, they reflect the expertise of the specialists in the area who act as the agents of the full body. Moreover, their statements are credible; if non-committee members discover that committee reports contain inaccurate statements (perhaps because preference outliers dominate the drafting), then they will no longer trust the committee members' assurances and will be less likely to defer to them. To the extent that those who control vetogates are repeat players, they must maintain their reputations for honesty to assure their continuing influence.[z] Note, however, that the *Griggs* judges gave weight to statements by Senator Tower for a different reason.

---

z. See Daniel Rodriguez & Barry Weingast, *The Positive Political Theory of Legislative History: New Perspectives on the 1964 Civil Rights Act and its Interpretation*, 151 U. Pa. L. Rev. 1417, 1442–51 (2003) (applying similar approach to the 1964 Act); William Eskridge, Jr., Philip Frickey & Elizabeth Garrett, *Legislation and Statutory Interpretation* 76–79 (2d ed. 2006) (applying such an analysis to *Montana Wilderness Ass'n v. U.S. Forest Service*, Chapter 8, § 2B4).

Although he was not a supporter of the bill, his concerns were shared widely enough to assure the addition of the testing rule in § 703(h), his amendment. Representations made to him by Senator Humphrey were also considered because Humphrey was really speaking to all those Senators still on the fence and whose votes were needed to get the bill through its most difficult vetogate, the filibuster. It is not surprising, then, that all the judges in *Griggs* wanted their interpretation to be consistent with the assurances made to enable the bill to escape the filibuster.

2. *Liberal Theory: Statutes Should Be Hard to Enact*

The Framers believed that the Constitution's requirements of bicameral approval and presentment to the President (with the possibility of a veto) would assure that most social and economic problems would not generate legislation at all, because the two bodies would have different views about what should be done. *Federalist Papers* #73. Hamilton saw proceduralism as "an additional security against the [enactment] of improper laws." However, he admitted that "the power of preventing bad laws includes that of preventing good ones; and may be used to the one purpose as well as to the other. * * * The injury that may possibly be done by defeating a few good laws will be amply compensated by the advantage of preventing a few bad ones." As Nelson Polsby observes, we should not be surprised that periods of stalemate are longer than periods of innovation because collective action is difficult "when formal power and autonomy are as dispersed as they are in the United States and it is necessary legislatively to mobilize the consent of majorities over and over — successively first in subcommittees, then in committees, the on the floors of the two legislative chambers, and finally behind the occupant of the White House." *How Congress Evolves: Social Bases of Institutional Change* 147 (2004).

These consequences are consistent with some versions of *liberal theory*,[a] which favors private autonomy and free economic markets and thus generally disfavors government regulation. To what extent do these assumptions remain robust today? Perhaps they are outdated: the post-New Deal regulatory state may assume that governmental regulation is the norm and indeed is perhaps even essential for the proper functioning of the private market.[b] Common law ordering is not the natural order of things; instead, it is just another kind of regulatory regime. Thus, to the extent that proceduralism protects one vision of regulation — a particular liberal vision — and reduces the ability of lawmakers to adopt different regulatory systems, it must be defended on that basis. It is not a neutral decision.

---

a. Here the term "liberal" is being used in its classic sense, see, e.g., John Stuart Mill, *On Liberty* (1857), and not in the contemporary American sense in which it is associated with a wing of the Democratic Party. See Eskridge, Frickey & Garrett, *supra*, at 19–21 (discussing liberal theory).

b. See Cass Sunstein, *After the Rights Revolution: Reconceiving the Regulatory State* 19–20 (1990); Bruce Ackerman, *Constitutional Law/Constitutional Politics*, 99 Yale L.J. 453 (1989).

Moreover, the extreme liberal distaste for legislation may not be the political vision that the authors of *The Federalist Papers* subscribed to. They were not hostile to all legislative intrusions, and they did not believe that congressional enactments were inherently untrustworthy or harmful. Indeed, Madison and Hamilton expected that proceduralism would improve, not inevitably block, legislation designed to solve social or economic problems because the Article I, § 7 structure militates in favor of moderate rather than radical shifts from the status quo. See *Federalist* #63. But, some proposals are hastily conceived and unwise, incapable of being improved through delay, deliberation and compromise. Procedures serve to make their enactment difficult. Because we cannot require that enhanced procedures apply only to "unwise laws" and allow fewer procedures to stand in the way of "laws serving the public good," the protection we obtain from structural constraints is necessarily overinclusive. It will impede the passage of good laws as well as bad. This cost is one that we should not dismiss without some concern. For example, bicameralism and the Senate filibuster gutted civil rights bills in the 1950s, delaying such legislation for a decade. Hamilton argued that the loss of some good bills was a price worth paying. Is that right? What was the cost of delay in the civil rights context? Was that cost less than the cost of additional private-regarding laws that might have been passed in a world of more streamlined legislative procedures?

3. *Republican Theory: The Deliberative Value of Process*

Rather than blocking enactment of most legislation, procedures can be seen as the way to shape public deliberation on legislative proposals so that they better serve the public good. This view of proceduralism is consistent with *republican theory*, and such theorists also lay claim to *The Federalist Papers* as inspiration. Although the republican tradition was espoused by the Anti-Federalists, who opposed adoption of the Constitution, many political philosophers and historians now believe that the Federalists did not utterly reject republican concerns.[c] Under this view, Madison's *Federalist* #10 is, in fact, a redefinition of the republicans' concern about corruption of the common good (focusing on factions) and an argument that republican virtue might best be preserved through a national political structure with checks and balances than through local government.

In *Federalist* #39, James Madison defined the sort of government created by the Constitution as a *republic* — a "government which derives all its powers directly or indirectly from the great body of the people, and is administered by persons holding their offices during pleasure, for a limited period, or during good behavior." Less democratic forms, such as monarchy or oligarchy, would be inconsistent with the "genius of the people of America," Madison argued, invoking memories of "taxation without representation" that inspired the American Revolution. More democratic forms, such as direct democracy, in

---

c. See David Epstein, *The Political Theory of the Federalist* (1984); Edmund Morgan, *Madison's Theory of Representation in the Tenth Federalist*, 36 J. Pol. 852 (1974). See also Larry Kramer, *Madison's Audience*, 112 Harv. L. Rev. 611 (1999).

which important matters would be decided by an immediate vote of the people, were unacceptable as well because such structures would not restrain the tyranny of majority factions. A republican form of government, shaped by a variety of countermajoritarian or supermajoritarian procedures, would allow for deliberation among lawmakers, communication with constituents, and informed decisionmaking. For example, Madison justified the arguably duplicative role of the Senate as useful "to check the misguided career" of bills inspired by temporary passions or deception "and to suspend the blow mediated by the people against themselves, until reason, justice, and truth can regain their authority over the public mind." *Federalist #63*.

Many believe that the story of the Civil Rights Act of 1964 supports this optimism about the legislative process. Does a republican perspective also help resolve questions arising under the Act, such as in *Griggs*? Should the court decide open questions under the Act by interpreting it to promote the public interest in remedying racial injustice — or is that too one-sided a way to decide cases? Or is the more basic problem that this view of the legislative process is too optimistic?

Republican theorists, both past and current, emphasize the importance of deliberation to a normatively attractive legislative process. Deliberation shapes and changes public preferences on issues; it allows lawmakers to modify, amend, or discard proposals on the basis of new thinking and information; and it facilitates the development of civic virtue in citizens. Deliberation thus is an end in itself, and it serves the larger instrumental purpose of improving public policy. Madisonian deliberation remains a robust theory today as a justification for the procedurally complex legislative process. Henry Hart, Jr. and Albert Sacks, in their classic *legal process* materials, argued for the "vitally important relationship between procedure and substance. A procedure which is soundly adapted to the type of power to be exercised is conducive to well-informed and wise decisions. An unsound procedure invites ill-informed and unwise ones." Hart and Sacks reported a "general agreement" that "the best criterion of sound legislation is * * * whether it is the product of a sound process of enactment," namely, a process that is informed, deliberative, and efficient. Henry Hart, Jr. & Albert Sacks, *The Legal Process: Basic Problems in the Making and Application of Law* 154, 695 (William Eskridge, Jr. & Philip Frickey pub. eds., 1994) (from the 1958 "tentative edition").

Notice that this formulation attempts to defend the process of deliberation on the ground that it will improve the substance of legislation. Such a claim requires a metric to measure outcomes — what counts as "sound legislation" — and the metric is inevitably tied up with a normative vision of the public good. Joseph M. Bessette defines the special reasoning process of policy deliberation as "necessarily involv[ing] reasoning about the substantive benefits of public policy, reasoning about some *public* good — some good external to the decisionmakers themselves." *The Mild Voice of Reason: Deliberative Democracy and American National Government* 48 (1994).[d]

Many scholars educated under the aegis of the legal process materials emphasize deliberation as an achievable ideal in our representative democracy. Theories of "neo-republicanism" integrate earlier theories of politics with this legal process heritage.[e] Their essential point is that the legitimacy of government rests not just upon its democratic pedigree, but also upon the commitment of its officials to engage in a process of practical reasoning, deliberating for the common good.[f] The effect of proceduralism on deliberation and, in turn, the effect of deliberation on legislative outcomes are difficult to understand completely. Procedures cannot guarantee that deliberation will occur at all, or that any deliberation will be enlightened and positive. At the most, rules and structure provide an opportunity for deliberation and an environment conducive to public dialogue.

Ironically, some recent work of political scientists has found that the public holds Congress in very low esteem — lower than any other institution of government — in large part because of the ubiquity of vetogates and the delay that they and any resulting deliberation produce. John Hibbing and Elizabeth Theiss-Morse used a series of in-depth interviews with citizens and several focus groups to determine why the public is so dissatisfied with Congress as an institution. They summarize their findings: "Congress embodies practically everything Americans dislike about politics. It is large and ponderous; * * * it is open and therefore disputes are played out for all to see; it is based on compromise and therefore reminds people of the disturbing fact that most issues do not have right answers. * * * [T]he public does not like overly

---

d. See also Larry Alexander, *Are Procedural Rights Derivative of Substantive Rights?*, 17 Law & Phil. 19, 36–42 (1998). But see Mathew McCubbins & Daniel Rodriguez, *When Does Deliberating Improve Decisionmaking?*, 15 J. Contemp. Legal Iss. 9 (2006) (providing results from experiments suggesting that deliberation does not improve social welfare and "in all but rare circumstances, may decrease it").

e. For one of the leading republican statements, see Frank Michelman, *The Supreme Court, 1985 Term — Foreword: Traces of Self-Government*, 100 Harv. L. Rev. 4 (1986). Other important sources include Philip Petit, *Republicanism: A Theory of Freedom and Government* (1997); Michael Sandel, *Liberalism and the Limits of Justice* (2d ed. 1998); Marci Hamilton, *Discussion and Decisions: A Proposal to Replace the Myth of Self-Rule With an Attorneyship Model of Representation*, 69 N.Y.U. L. Rev. 477 (1994); Mark Seidenfeld, *A Civic Republican Justification for the Bureaucratic State*, 105 Harv. L. Rev. 1511 (1992); Suzanna Sherry, *Responsible Republicanism: Educating for Citizenship*, 62 U. Chi. L. Rev. 131 (1995); *Symposium: The Republican Civic Tradition*, 97 Yale L.J. 1043 (1988). The historical discussion in these legal materials should be supplemented by reference to the historiographical literature, especially Daniel Rodgers, *Republicanism: The Career of a Concept*, 79 J. Am. Hist. 11 (1992). For skeptical reactions to the neo-republicans, see Michael Fitts, *Can Ignorance Be Bliss? Imperfect Information as a Positive Influence in Political Institutions*, 88 Mich. L. Rev. 917 (1990); Jim Rossi, *Participation Run Amok: The Costs of Mass Participation for Deliberative Decisionmaking*, 92 Nw. L. Rev. 1 (1997).

f. See John Rawls, *Political Liberalism* 212–54 (1993) (classic statement of what constitutes acceptable public reason). See also Amy Gutmann & Dennis Thompson, *Democracy and Disagreement* (1996) (formulation of a principled framework for deliberation).

deliberative politics. They would like to see something done quickly when in fact legislatures * * * are not well-equipped for rapid action." *Congress as Public Enemy: Public Attitudes Toward American Political Institutions* 60–61 (1995).[g]

The answer to this dissatisfaction is not to dispense with proceduralism and to discourage deliberation; it lies instead in improving the conditions of deliberation and educating the public to appreciate the benefits of public consideration of alternatives by representatives. Sociologists have also found that some amount of public participation and deliberation in decisionmaking is necessary for citizens to view outcomes as legitimate and just.[h] As philosopher Jeremy Waldron has observed, at least part of law's legitimacy and authority comes from the fact that multi-member assemblies pass statutes through collective decisionmaking after some discussion that allows for an airing of diverse viewpoints. The "dignity of legislation" is a result of the ability of a legislature to act in concert in what Waldron terms "circumstances of politics"; such collective action in the face of disagreement is a significant achievement that deserves our respect. See *The Dignity of Legislation* 156–57 (1999). Importantly, the diversity of views represented in a deliberative body is related to the decisions that the group reaches. When people only hear "echoes of their own voices," the deliberating group may reach more extreme positions than its members' pre-deliberation tendencies suggested. See Cass Sunstein, *Deliberating Trouble? Why Groups Go to Extremes*, 110 Yale L.J. 71, 75–76 (2000). The conditions that shape deliberation, including the procedures governing it, play a role in whether group polarization develops, or more moderate compromise is reached.

Proceduralism is also important in a way that implicates both public choice and republican theories. It may provide an answer to a group of pessimistic public choice scholars who argue that the democratic process is inherently arbitrary and irrational. This set of theorists, often called social choice scholars, applies economic principles to political decisionmaking. Drawing from the work of Kenneth Arrow, they suggest that political outcomes under majority-voting schemes inevitably will be incoherent, will not necessarily reflect the preferences of the majority, and therefore will lack legitimacy. See Kenneth Arrow, *Social Choice and Individual Values* (2d ed. 1963). For example, *Arrow's Paradox*[i] asserts the irrationality of majority-voting systems, similar to those used to determine state and federal legislative outcomes. In

---

g. See also Carolyn Funk, *Process Performance: Public Reaction to Legislative Policy Debate,* in *What Is It About Government that Americans Dislike?* 193 (John Hibbing & Elizabeth Theiss-Morse eds., 2001).

h. See, e.g., Tom Tyler, *Why People Don't Obey the Law* (1990); Heather Smith & Tom Tyler, *Justice and Power: When Will Justice Concerns Encourage the Advantaged to Support Policies Which Redistribute Economic Resources and the Disadvantaged to Willingly Obey the Law?*, 26 Eur. J. Soc. Pscyh. 171 (1996).

i. The paradox is also closely associated with Duncan Black, *The Theory of Committees and Elections* (1958). The core idea was conceptualized in the later eighteenth century by the Marquis de Condorcet. See also Dennis Mueller, 2 *Public Choice* 384–99 (1989) (summarizing Arrow's Theorem and its proof).

some circumstances, majority rule may not resolve the choice among three or more mutually exclusive alternatives that are voted on in pairs. For a simple example, assume that three children — Alice, Bobby, and Cindy — have been pestering their parents for a pet. The parents agree that the children may vote on having a dog, a parrot, or a cat. Each child's order of pet preferences is as follows:

Alice: dog, parrot, cat

Bobby: parrot, cat, dog

Cindy: cat, dog, parrot.

If these are the voters' preferences and pairwise voting is required, then majority voting cannot resolve their dilemma. A majority (Alice and Cindy) will vote for a dog rather than a parrot; a majority (Alice and Bobby) will vote for a parrot rather than a cat; and a majority (Bobby and Cindy) will vote for a cat rather than a dog. Even if the children form coalitions to attempt to reach a lasting decision, each coalition will be unstable. For example if Alice and Cindy decide to vote for the dog to defeat Bobby's top choice of parrot, Bobby can convince Cindy to move to his camp if he promises to vote for the cat (a better outcome for him than dog).

The only way to stop this phenomenon of *majority cycling* is to intervene with some procedures to limit pure majority rule, such as allowing only one set of pairwise votes under a set agenda. For example, if the parents define the decisional agenda as (1) dog versus parrot [dog wins]; then (2) dog versus cat [cat wins], the children will have a cat. But note that if the parents structure the decisional agenda differently and still allow only one set of pairwise votes, a parrot can win ((1) cat versus dog [cat wins]; (2) cat versus parrot [parrot wins]) or a dog can win ((1) parrot versus cat [parrot wins]; (2) parrot versus dog [dog wins]). If, instead of three children, we hypothesize three legislative factions and, instead of three pets, we suppose three legislative alternatives, it is obvious that cycling can occur in a legislative setting. Legislative rules (for example, that allow a committee chair to structure a decisional agenda or that require the status quo to be included in the last pairwise vote) may result in the selection of one alternative by virtue of the order of voting, even though it has no more legitimate claim to majority support than the others.

In the simple example above we assumed that each child would vote sincerely in each pairwise contest. But one child with complete information can prevent the cycle — and substantially satisfy her desires — by *strategic* rather than *sincere* voting. For example, assume that Alice, who likes parrots almost as much as dogs but hates cats, has discovered the preferences of her siblings. If the first pairwise contest is dog versus parrot, sincere voting on her part will eventually lead to the selection of a cat. If she casts a strategic vote for a parrot rather than a dog, however, a parrot will win. Similar strategic behavior in a legislature — for example, sophisticated voting rules or amending, vote trading, and logrolling — obviously can affect legislative outcomes. What examples of strategic behavior occurred during the consideration of the Civil Rights Act of 1964? Do the incoherence and susceptibility to strategic behavior of majority voting schemes suggest that there may be no significant correlation between what laws a legislature passes (or fails to pass) and the preferences of the majority of legislators? Is our legislative process a "rational" way to decide issues of public policy?

The prevalence of strategic voting as a response to cycling has led some social choice scholars to be very pessimistic about democracy. William Riker, for example, concludes from Arrow's work that all methods of aggregating preferences are prone to irrationality and chaos, and therefore meaningless, or that they will be manipulated by those in power, and are therefore arbitrary and undemocratic. *Liberalism Against Populism: A Confrontation Between the Theory of Democracy and the Theory of Public Choice* 137 (1982). This conclusion is too pessimistic because it assumes that the procedures and decision rules chosen to avoid chaotic outcomes will be unfair and undemocratic. Certainly, that will not inevitably be the case, but the observation underscores the importance of designing rules and institutions that structure legislative choices in transparent and defensible ways.[j]

In short, one crucial consideration in political decisionmaking is to identify the mechanisms of stability, often found in institutional design. Thus, Arrow's work leads us to focus on institutions and proceduralism and what some political scientists term *structure-induced equilibrium.* See Kenneth Shepsle & Barry Weingast, *Positive Theories of Congressional Institutions* 8–9 (1995). Deliberation and the procedures that shape it may be structures that counteract cycling. Bernard Grofman identifies two norms of public discourse which enhance stability: the *idea of benefit of the doubt* means that voters will decide to shift from the status quo only when the alternative is clearly superior, and the *no-quibbling norm* means that voters disregard alternatives that are only trivially different from one another. *Public Choice, Civic Republicanism, and American Politics: Perspectives of a "Reasonable Choice" Modeler*, 71 Tex. L. Rev. 1541, 1563–64 (1993). Other scholars argue that stability comes not just from institutional arrangements, which themselves can be subject to instability if chosen by strategic players, but they also result from exogenous factors that are not easily manipulated. For example, an institution cannot cycle through alternatives without cost; thus, a group may meaningfully choose to stick with a policy and achieve stability.[k] Perhaps not surprisingly given these forces pushing toward stability in decisionmaking, Gerry Mackie's analysis of case studies of cycling calls into question virtually all "published and developed example[s] of cycling and manipulation," finding alternative explanations or consequences of "little practical importance." *Democracy Defended* 21 (2003).

---

j. See Jerry Mashaw, *Greed, Chaos, and Governance: Using Public Choice to Improve Public Law* 13 (1997); Saul Levmore, *Voting Paradoxes and Interest Groups*, 28 J. Legal Studs. 259 (1999); Richard Pildes & Elizabeth Anderson, *Slinging Arrows at Democracy: Social Choice Theory, Value Pluralism, and Democratic Politics*, 90 Colum. L. Rev. 2121, 2200 (1990).

k. See Arthur Lupia & Mathew McCubbins, *Lost in Translation: Social Choice Theory is Misapplied Against Legislative Intent*, 14 J. Contemp. Legal Iss. 585 (2005).

C. INSTITUTIONAL THEORIES OF LEGISLATION

1. *Introduction to the Institutional Perspective*

A body of political theory variously called the *new institutionalism* or *positive political theory* grows out of the public choice tradition and has been influenced by game theory developed by economists.[l] As with the other two groups, institutional theorists also claim the Madisonian tradition as their own. Like Madison, they emphasize the importance of institutional structures to constrain and shape behavior, and they characterize outcomes in terms of "balance" or "equilibrium." See, e.g., *The Federalist Papers and the New Institutionalism* (Bernard Grofman & Donald Wittman eds. 1989). Modern institutional theory is characterized by certain crucial assumptions.

The first and most important is that political outcomes are dependent on the actions of several decisionmakers, who sometimes act simultaneously and sometimes consecutively. Moreover, each decisionmaker is aware of this interdependence. Thus, it is not enough to say that Senators Dirksen and Mansfield entered into a deal which enabled the civil rights bill to escape the Senate filibuster. They entered into the deal, knowing that the House and President had to accept their compromise.[m] The formulation the Senate leaders devised not only reflected their own preferences but also took into account the reactions it would spark in other players in the legislative game and any continuing influence the Senate might have on subsequent developments. Relatedly, all the parties to the deal operate under assumptions about how the courts will interpret their bargain. They anticipate the judicial response as they draft and produce committee reports and floor debates. Depending on the issue, the federal actors may have to consider the response of state and local officials who may be required to implement some provisions of the legislation. Or, in some states, legislators are aware that the people can modify some laws through the referendum process, or they can enact their own through popular votes on initiatives. See Elisabeth Gerber, *The Populist Paradox* (1999). In other words, the representative institutions may have to take account of the reaction of constituents both at reelection time and through mechanisms of direct democracy.

This *anticipated response* feature of institutionalism is key. It requires us to think in a more complicated way about political actors. Dirksen chose the deal, not because the bill as modified reflected his own preferences, but because Dirksen believed that the other relevant actors (Senators, President, House Members) would otherwise make choices that had consequences he liked much less. Anticipating the responses of other players and calculating

---

l. See generally Douglas Baird, Robert Gertner & Randal Picker, *Game Theory and the Law* (1994); Peter Ordeshook, *A Political Theory Primer* (1992); Eric Posner, *Law and Social Norms* (2000); Kenneth Shepsle & Mark Bonchek, *Analyzing Politics: Rationality, Behavior, and Institutions* (1997); *Symposium on Positive Political Theory and Law*, 69 S. Cal. L. Rev. 1447 (1995).

m. See Rodriguez & Weingast, *supra*, at 1474–87 (using positive political theory to analyze the key role played by Dirksen and arguing that it should affect interpretation of the legislative history of the 1964 Act).

their consequences, Dirksen strategically "chose" the Dirksen-Mansfield substitute. This analysis implies another feature of institutionalism: political players are goal-oriented. Thus, when they anticipate the responses of other players, their preference for one scenario over others is determined by which scenario will ultimately achieve an outcome closest to their own preferred policies. Institutionalism does not assume that people's goals are economic or self-centered (though they often are). One goal that impelled Dirksen to support a compromise, for example, was his goal to position the Republican Party (of which he was a leader) advantageously on this issue.

One limitation of some of the institutional scholarship, however, is the simplifying view of preferences as stable and unchanging. Of course, preferences can be profoundly affected by deliberation and other aspects of the legislative process. Another unrealistic but simplifying assumption often used in the scholarship is that players have full information about the preferences of all the other players, even though we know that information is costly and therefore often incomplete and that players can make mistakes in their predictions of subsequent moves and reactions. For example, Manny Cellar decided to strengthen the committee version of the Civil Rights bill for strategic reasons, but he miscalculated and nearly scuttled the chances for success. Only the intervention of party leaders and the Administration assured that a palatable bill would emerge from committee. Using somewhat simplified models is justified, however, because it focuses attention on the interdependence of actions, the role of all players, including non-legislative ones, in the formation of policy, and the effect of anticipated responses. As we use this perspective, however, it is important to remember that it does not fully capture the complex and intricate world of the legislative process, and it should be used as a complement to the other theories to generate more accurate descriptions and predictions.

Finally, positive political theory emphasizes that institutions are the context in which political interdependence is shaped and people's goals are pursued. The structure of institutions makes a difference in the way people interact. Institutional theorists develop formal models which reveal regularities in such interaction. Just as the structures of institutions alter the ways in which players interact, players can also modify the contours of institutions in ways that allow them to reach their objectives with less difficulty. Institutions are seldom immutable; they can be reshaped, although the way that they have developed in the past may limit the possible range of alterations available to the players.[n]

Institutional models are often in the form of sequential anticipated response "games," in which each player's choice is determined not only by her own raw preferences about an issue, but also by her place in the decision process and her understanding of the preferences of players who follow her. Consider the following example of institutional game theory in the context of legislation.

---

n. See Sarah Binder, *Minority Rights, Majority Rule: Partisanship and the Development of Congress* 14 (1997) (arguing that policies and institutions are shaped both by participant preferences and by inherited rules, which can be changed but only in certain ways given the history of their development).

2. *The Article I, § 7 Game*

The procedural requirements of Article I, § 7 (bicameralism and present-ment) can be modeled as a sequential game, in which all players want to enact legislation reflecting their own preferences, but the players realize that their preferences may have to be compromised to guarantee the cooperation of other players as required by the constitutional structure. See William Eskridge, Jr. & John Ferejohn, *The Article I, Section 7 Game*, 80 Geo. L.J. 523 (1992).[o]

The game starts with the status quo, which prevails in the absence of legislation. Members of the House have preferences about policies that depart from the status quo, and committees help the chamber figure out the policy that will appeal to the preference of the *median legislator* (the one right in the middle of the 435 Representatives whose vote is needed to enact the legislation under majority-voting rules). See Duncan Black, *The Theory of Committees and Elections* (1958) (classic work on median voter theory, positing that policy equilibrium rests with the preference of the median voter if preferences over policies are single-peaked). In writing legislation, the committee will be aware that the Senate has to agree, too; hence, it might adjust the legislation to anticipate and head off problems in the Senate (as the House Judiciary Committee did in 1963). The same process will occur in the Senate if it acts on the legislation first. Sometimes, both houses consider companion legislation at the same time, and the proponents of the bill will watch the deliberation in the other chamber closely to learn as much as they can about the preferences of the other key player. Both the House and the Senate will consider the preferences of the President, who must sign the bill.[p] If the President is hostile to the legislation (not the case with the civil rights bill in 1963–64), the chambers usually will not go forward with a bill that does not have a chance of commanding the two-thirds majorities required to override a presidential veto. In a few cases, Congress will enact a bill that members know will be vetoed in order to gain partisan points in the next election.

Each participant in the game wants to impose its own policy preferences on federal statutory policy, but in most cases none will act in a way that subjects it to an immediate override. Each participant anticipates the moves that will be made by the next participants. The following notations describe the important points in this model:

SQ   =   Existing policy (status quo)

H and S   =   Preferences of the median legislator in the two chambers of the legislature

P   =   Preferences of the President

---

o. See also Eskridge, Frickey & Garrett, *supra*, at 106–16; John Ferejohn & Charles Shipan, *Congressional Influence on Bureaucracy*, 6 J.L. Econ. & Org. 1 (1990).

p. For a discussion of how the President's veto threat shapes legislative bargaining with recent examples, see Charles Cameron, *Veto Bargaining: Presidents and the Politics of Negative Power* (2000).

h and s   =   Pivotal voter in veto override in the two chambers of the bicameral legislature

x   =   Statutory policy resulting from model

Consider three scenarios:

Case 1: SQ > H, S > P. Start with a case in which the status quo is objectionable from the perspectives of both Congress and the President, and their preferences for changing the status quo run in the same direction, but the President would like to change the status quo more:

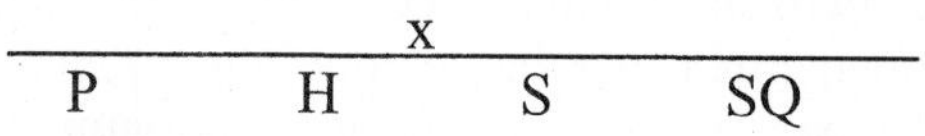

$$
\begin{array}{cccc}
& & x & \\
\hline
P & H & S & SQ
\end{array}
$$

Figure 1. Statutory policy H < x < S when P < H, S < SQ

In such a case, the House and the Senate will work out a compromise proposal, either through informal signals or a formal conference committee, because a majority of both chambers want to change the status quo and differ only as to how much to change it. The ultimate statutory policy (x) will fall somewhere between the preferences of the two legislative chambers (H and S). Note that in this scenario Congress does not have to accommodate the policy preferences of the President, because the latter cannot credibly threaten to veto the House-Senate compromise (x), which he prefers to the status quo (SQ).

Case 2: H < SQ < S. What if the actors' preferences for changing the status quo run in different directions? Figure 2 maps one illustration of such preferences:

$$
\begin{array}{cccc}
\hline
P & H & SQ & S
\end{array}
$$

Figure 2. No statute when H < SQ < S

If SQ is anywhere between H and S, Congress would be unable to agree on statutory policy, because the House would prefer the status quo to any point to the right of SQ, and the Senate would prefer the status quo to any point to the left of SQ. The requirement of bicameral approval prevents enactment of a statute, and as soon as this preference alignment becomes clear to the Members of Congress, they will abandon any effort to enact a statute until preferences change (which can occur after an election cycle, for example).

When the status quo (SQ) is located between h and H, the same result occurs, but because of the presentment requirement: Even though Congress would like to change that status quo, the President would be expected to veto any such legislation, and two-thirds of the House Members would not vote for an override. Because the congressional leadership knows it does not have the votes for an override, it will probably not even press the legislation to a vote, unless a vote-and-veto serves other political purposes (like embarrassing the President or his party or signaling important interest groups about their commitment to certain positions).

This example demonstrates the importance of the *pivotal voter* in determining legislative outcomes. Although the median voter's preference may exert a strong pull on the policy equilibrium, the existence of supermajoritarian procedures such as cloture rules and veto overrides allows pivotal voters to "dampen policy convergence to the median legislator's ideal point." Keith Krehbiel, *Pivotal Politics: A Theory of U.S. Lawmaking* 232 (1998). Krehbiel argues that the influence of the pivotal voter in Congress entrenches the status quo even further, leads to widespread gridlock, and explains why much major legislation is passed by relatively wide margins and with bipartisan support. In later chapters we will discuss other congressional procedures and institutional structures that allow different players or minority coalitions to block policies. All of these complicate the legislative game and move the point of policy equilibrium to different places along the spectrum of possibilities.

Case 3: SQ < h. The President's ability to block legislation ends when two-thirds of the legislators in each chamber disagree with the President about how the status quo should be changed:

$$\overline{} \overset{x}{} \overline{}$$

P	SQ	h	h(SQ)	s	H	S

Figure 3. Policy set at x = h(SQ) when SQ < h

Although the President does not have enough votes in Congress to sustain a veto, the threat of a veto significantly affects the location of statutory policy. The threat of a veto induces the median legislator in each chamber to offer a proposal to which the pivotal voter in a veto override vote (h) is indifferent relative to SQ. Knowing the preference of the pivotal voter, the enacting coalition will propose it as the statutory policy. Knowing that a veto will be overridden, the President will sign the bill unless a veto would serve some political purpose. Or, in the real world rather than in the artificial environment of our game where all players are omniscient, the President may be incompletely informed about members' preferences, or be overly optimistic about his ability to persuade lawmakers to support him, and thus he may veto the bill only to find that Congress can muster the two-thirds majority in both houses to override it.

Notice that this formal Article I, § 7 model makes more precise the Framers' intuitions about the constitutional structure for lawmaking: Many problems will not generate statutory solutions (Case 2), and the ones that do will generate statutes reflecting moderate rather than strong responses to the problem (see Cases 1 and 3). The model also demonstrates some of the ways in which the President's preferences affect statutory policy, and the circumstances under which they will do so. Most important, the model suggests that even when the political system does "nothing" (no bill is proposed or acted on), the system might actually be "working" (no bill is proposed because everyone realizes it would be a waste of time).

3. *The Statutory Implementation Game*

A further consequence of institutional game theory is that statute-making must consider statute-implementing. The players in the legislative process (Senators, House Members, the President) not only act in response to the anticipated preferences of one another, but they also anticipate and consider the preferences of subsequent implementers and interpreters of the statute. See Jonathan Macey, *Separated Powers and Positive Political Theory: The Tug of War Over Administrative Agencies*, 60 Geo. L.J. 671 (1992). That is, when Dirksen signed onto the Dirksen-Mansfield compromise, he was anticipating how that compromise would be implemented. Hence, he was acting in accord with theories he had about the administrative process (and the newly created EEOC) and the judicial process. For example, he thought that employers would be insulated from "overenforcement" of the statute by requiring complainants to exhaust lengthy administrative procedures before they could bring suit and by hamstringing the EEOC itself with limited powers.[q] Additionally, Dirksen assumed that the judiciary would enforce the deals which he insisted be encoded in the statutory text. An example of such a deal was § 703(j), which prevents the government from "requiring" companies to adopt affirmative action plans.

Let us now shift focus from the legislature to the agency and the courts. When the statute is enacted, the agency and the judiciary might be expected to follow the dictates of the enacting coalition, not only because these officials have internalized the norm of legislative supremacy, but also because their failure to do so would subject them to legislative override and perhaps some kind of discipline. In other words, agencies and courts, like Congress and the President, will consider the preferences and possible responses of other political actors before they choose a course of action. The EEOC, for example, would not have announced nonenforcement of a provision of the recently enacted statute because the President would have quashed any such revolt, and Congress would have punished the agency (perhaps by abolishing it, severely reducing its funding, or calling the agency head to testify and answer the questions of angry lawmakers). The game is further complicated by the seemingly entrenched phenomenon of divided government where the executive branch and at least one house of the legislature are consistently controlled by different parties.[r] In the current era of relatively polarized parties,[s] congressio-

---

q. See Mathew McCubbins, Roger Noll & Barry Weingast, *Administrative Procedures as Instruments of Political Control*, 3 J.L. Econ. & Org. 243 (1987) (this is a typical legislative strategy); Kathleen Bawn, *Political Control Versus Expertise: Congressional Choices About Administrative Procedures*, 89 Am. Pol. Sci. Rev. 62 (1995).

r. See Morris Fiorina, *Divided Government* (2d ed. 1996); David Mayhew, *Divided We Govern: Party Control, Lawmaking and Investigations, 1946–1990* (2d ed. 2005).

s. See *Polarized Politics: Congress and the President in a Partisan Era* (Jon Bond & Richard Fleisher eds., 2000).

nal and presidential preferences may be widely separated and make legislative action difficult.

In short, there is often no clear end to the legislative game. After Congress and the President enact a law, agencies, more or less under the control of the President, implement it. Judges oversee the implementation by requiring fidelity between execution and their interpretation of the statute's requirements.[t] Congress can usually modify a law to take account of judicial interpretation or agency action, and it can bring influence to bear on at least the executive branch and sometimes indirectly on courts themselves. After such a congressional reaction, the agencies and courts have their turn in implementing and interpreting the new policy. Institutional theorists have also turned their attention to courts, applying their tools to understanding and predicting to judicial actors.[u]

The situation of the Fourth Circuit in *Griggs* can also be analyzed as an anticipated response game, albeit one where the players had incomplete information. In deciding whether to sustain plaintiffs' claims, the judges would surely have considered the preferences of the Supreme Court, which had the formal power to reverse the Fourth Circuit. In figuring those preferences, the Fourth Circuit had little information because there was no Supreme Court decision interpreting the Civil Rights Act. Hence, the circuit judges looked to analogous Supreme Court decisions in the voting and school desegregation arenas, and to the kind of evidence (legislative history, such as the Tower colloquies) that the Supreme Court often invoked in construing statutes.

If the circuit judges were being particularly strategic, they would also have considered broader political currents that might, in turn, have influenced the Supreme Court's preferences. In 1969, Republican Richard Nixon had just been elected President, but his Administration fully accepted the Civil Rights Act as a good statute and his Department of Justice Civil Rights Division was headed by a liberal, Stanley Pottinger. The EEOC remained a hotbed of liberal sentiment. Several of the prominent congressional opponents of civil rights laws had been defeated (Judge Smith) or had died or retired from Congress (Senators Harry Byrd [D–Va.] and Spessard Holland [D–Fla.]), and the "new breed" of Southern Senators and Representatives were more moderate (e.g., Senators Charles Mathias [R–Md.], Howard Baker [R–Tenn.], Ernest Hollings [D–S.C.], Thomas Eagleton [D–Mo.], William Spong [D–Va.], all of whom came to the Senate by defeating segregationist Democrats in the elections of 1966 and 1968), perhaps reflecting the new voting clout of African Americans after enactment of the Voting Rights Act of 1965. We concede that "knowing" all this (and more) required a good deal of political sophistication, but note that

---

t. See William Landes & Richard Posner, *The Independent Judiciary in an Interest-Group Perspective*, 18 J.L. & Econ. 875 (1975).

u. See, e.g., Cornell Clayton & Howard Gillman, *Supreme Court Decision-Making: New Institutionalist Approaches* (1999); Maxwell Stearns, *Constitutional Process: A Social Choice Analysis of Supreme Court Decision Making* (2000); Lee Epstein, Jeffrey Segal & Jennifer Victor, *Dynamic Agenda-Setting on the United States Supreme Court: An Empirical Assessment*, 39 Harv. J. Legis. 395 (2002).

Judge Sobeloff was himself a Washington insider, having served as Eisenhower's Solicitor General in the early 1950s. Recall, too, that federal judgeships are not dolloped out to political naifs; most federal judges have extensive political experience and sophistication.

Given this political context, the NAACP Inc. Fund appealed the Fourth Circuit loss to the Supreme Court. If the Court were to take the case (which became highly probable when the Nixon Administration joined the Inc. Fund in petitioning the Court for review), what do you predict the Supreme Court would do with *Griggs*? Is this what the Court *should* do?

SECTION 3. TITLE VII: INTERPRETIVE ISSUES AND POLITICAL THEORIES

This section will introduce you to important themes of statutory implementation and will suggest that issues of legal theory and political theory are inextricably intertwined. We shall revisit the *Griggs* problem from Section 1 and provide a more detailed political account of the problem's resolution in the early 1970s (Part A). The Supreme Court's resolution of *Griggs* raised new problems, of course. The most notable is whether Title VII permits employers to engage in "affirmative action" to rectify underrepresentation of minority employees. That issue has been a vexing one (Part B) and impelled the Rehnquist Court to revisit *Griggs*, in a decision that triggered a firestorm of protest and a swift congressional override (Part C). In the course of our presentation, we shall draw on the descriptive theories developed in Section 2, but we shall leave to you the task of evaluating what we present along normative lines that are attractive to you.

A. THE SUPREME COURT'S DECISION IN *GRIGGS*

The *Griggs* problem analyzed in Section 1 is an example of a larger tension within Title VII: the statute that was enacted in 1964 focused on intentional discrimination (reread § 703) and set up a cumbersome administrative apparatus designed to minimize the role of the EEOC in the statute's development (see § 706). Both tradeoffs were necessary to pass the statute. The former ensured broad middle class support and an expansive coalition because it suggested that this would not be a redistributive statute. The latter was the price exacted by Senator Dirksen to get the bill through the filibuster vetogate. Yet Title VII's focus on intentional discrimination changed shortly after the statute went into force. The engine of this change was the declawed EEOC, as the activists who had worked to enact the statute — civil rights leaders and litigators, bureaucrats, law professors — turned to the task of making the statute work to implement President Johnson's goal of "not just equality as a right and a theory but equality as a fact and equality as a result."[a]

---

a. 2 *Public Papers: Lyndon B. Johnson, 1965*, at 636 (1966) (June 1965 speech by President Johnson at Howard University). The story that follows is drawn from the records in the main cases and from recent archival research set forth in Hugh Davis Graham, *The Civil Rights Era: Origins and Development of National Policy, 1962–1971* (1990), reviewed and

From its first year in operation, key players at all levels of the EEOC believed that racial inequality in employment was the result of structural factors, not just intentional discrimination, and that affirmative results were more important than formal requirements.[b] Based upon her labor law experience, EEOC staff member Sonia Pressman argued that it would be impractical to expect evidence of discriminatory intent in most cases. Just as litigants challenging racial discrimination in jury selection could rely on underrepresentation of minorities, Pressman urged that plaintiffs be permitted to make out a claim of employment discrimination based upon underrepresentation of minorities. Memorandum from Sonia Pressman to EEOC General Counsel Charles Duncan, 31 May 1966, described and quoted in Graham, *Civil Rights Era* 244–47. The EEOC legal staff were candid about the tension between their views and the apparent compromises adopted in the 1964 statute, but they urged their approach as the most practical way to enforce the statute. By the end of the Johnson Administration, the EEOC Commissioners publicly interpreted the statute to bar employer practices "which prove to have a demonstrable racial effect." EEOC Commissioner Samuel Jackson, *EEOC vs. Discrimination, Inc.*, The Crisis, Jan. 1968, 16–17.

The EEOC's rationale for an effects-based approach was that such an interpretation better served the statutory purpose. This position was shared by the Inc. Fund and other civil rights litigation groups. Directly encouraged by the EEOC, which filed helpful *amicus* briefs, civil rights litigation groups challenged employer testing and union seniority arrangements which had disproportionate and negative effects upon African Americans. These groups sometimes found a receptive audience in Eisenhower- and Johnson-appointed federal judges who were struggling with similar issues of racially discriminatory effects of arguably "neutral" state policies in the areas of education, voting, and jury selection. See, e.g., Judge Butzner's opinion in *Quarles v. Philip Morris, Inc.*, 279 F. Supp. 505 (E.D. Va. 1968), and Judge Wisdom's opinion in *Local 189, United Papermakers v. United States*, 416 F.2d 980 (5th Cir. 1969). Judge Sobeloff, dissenting in *Griggs*, relied on *Quarles* and *Local 189* to argue for a results-oriented rather than just intent-focused inquiry in Title VII.

The Inc. Fund appealed its loss in *Griggs*, with the support of the EEOC and the Nixon Administration's Solicitor General, Erwin Griswold. To the surprise of many pundits, the Supreme Court not only unanimously reversed in *Griggs v. Duke Power Co.*, 401 U.S. 424 (1971), but it expanded upon Sobeloff's opinion. The Supreme Court held that a facially neutral employment practice that was not demonstrably discriminatory in purpose was nonetheless unlawful

---

supplemented by Neal Devins, *The Civil Rights Hydra*, 89 Mich. L. Rev. 1723 (1991). See also Herman Belz, *Equality Transformed: A Quarter-Century of Affirmative Action* (1991).

b. See White House Conference on Equal Educational Opportunity (EEOC, 1965). Several key agency players published explanations and defenses of this ideology. See EEOC Executive Director Herman Edelsberg, *Title VII of the Civil Rights Act: The First Year*, 19 N.Y.U. Conf. on Labor 289–295 (1967), and EEOC staff member Alfred Blumrosen, *Black Employment and the Law* (1971).

if it had the effect of excluding a group on the basis of race and without a strict showing of business necessity. Although the Court reaffirmed the color-blindness of Title VII, its rationale stressed that "Congress directed the thrust of the Act to the *consequences* of employment practices." This appeared to be a recognition that while § 703(a) speaks in terms of individuals, the real problems addressed by Title VII are institutionalized societal practices that systematically exclude minority groups from employment opportunities. The lower courts, especially those in the South, viewed *Griggs* as a mandate to use Title VII to reform group employment practices in entire companies, based upon the disparate impact idea.[c]

Some commentators have denounced the Supreme Court's decision as inconsistent with the original "deal" encoded in Title VII. Assume that they are right. What, then, explains *Griggs*? Judge Sobeloff's opinion in the lower court suggests one way of explaining an effects-based inquiry: it is needed to fulfill the statute's purpose. Congress in 1964 did not focus on the possibility that pre-1964 discrimination would have continuing effects, but once that became clear to the EEOC and the courts, they had a responsibility to apply the statute to new circumstances in a way that carried out the original purpose. One way to think of this approach is as a *translation* of the statute, moving it away from its apparent textual mandates on the ground that new approaches are required to fulfill the objectives of the enactors. In other words, an interpretation that departs from the terms of the deal, as reflected in the text of the statute, is actually more faithful to legislative intent than a more literal interpretation. This sort of dynamic statutory interpretation is controversial because it places a great deal of discretionary power in the unelected judiciary. On the other hand, at least in theory, it requires judges to be the faithful and careful agents of the legislative drafters, modifying or enhancing statutory provisions only when necessary to avoid undermining legislative purpose and intent.

Another way of explaining *Griggs* is that the liberal EEOC and Supreme Court were moving statutory policy in a leftward direction away from legislative intent. This can be expressed in the game-theoretic terms familiar to us from our study of institutional theories of the legislative process. See Lee

---

c. Thus the Fifth Circuit sustained affirmative action remedies, finding that "[i]t is the collective interest, governmental as well as social, in effectively ending unconstitutional racial discrimination that justifies temporary, carefully circumscribed resort to racial criteria, whenever the chancellor determines that it represents the only rational, nonarbitrary means of eradicating past evils." *NAACP v. Allen*, 493 F.2d 614, 619 (5th Cir. 1974). "By reasonable affirmative action programs, courts can order employers to use ratios, percentages and quotas to ensure that members of minority groups traditionally discriminated against have reasonable opportunities to be hired." 2 Chester Antieau, *Federal Civil Rights Act: Civil Practice* § 528, at 237 (1980) (citing cases). Additional pressures for preferential hiring were generated by Executive Order 11,246, which required government contracts to include an affirmative action clause. 3 C.F.R. page 339 (1964–65). As elaborated in 1970, the Order required government contractors to establish "a set of specific and result-oriented procedures" to yield "equal employment opportunity." 35 Fed. Reg. 2586, 2587 (1970). For a discussion of the role of executive orders to expand civil rights, perhaps beyond what Congress would enact, see Kenneth Mayer, *With the Stroke of a Pen: Executive Orders and Presidential Power* Chapter 6 (2001).

Epstein & Jack Knight, *The Choices Justices Make* (1999) (applying positive political theory to judicial behavior). Remember that positive political theory underscores the importance of all the players in the policymaking game, including the executive branch agencies that will implement the statute and the judges who will interpret it. If their preferences diverge from the legislature's, they will try to move policy closer to their ideal point, realizing that the Congress will monitor them and try to avert any substantial change in the outcome. Consider the following diagram, similar to the earlier ones but with positions added to represent the EEOC (the agency, "A"), the Supreme Court (the judiciary, "J"), and other players we will identify shortly:

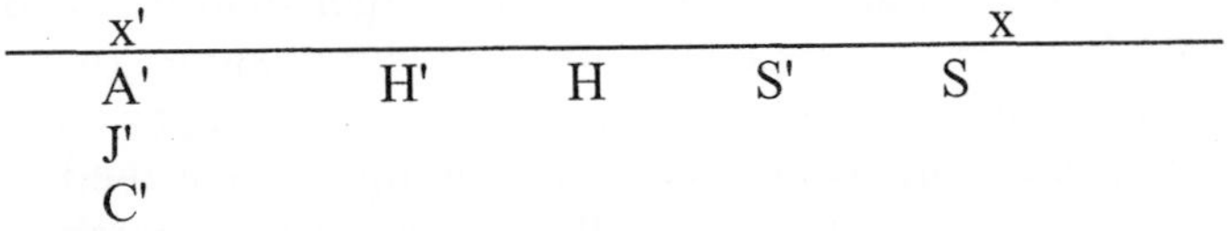

<pre>
x'   x
    A'   H'   H   S'   S
    J'
    C'
</pre>

Figure 4. The Griggs *Decision, 1971: Statutory policy shifts from S < x to x' = A' = C'*

Three different political dynamics enabled Title VII's policy to shift significantly to the left between 1964 and 1971. One dynamic was simply the internal politics of the EEOC and the Supreme Court, both of which were pressed from below by an academic and elite cultural consensus in favor of vigorous enforcement of Title VII. A second dynamic was some shift to the left in congressional preferences between 1964 (H and S) and 1971 (H' and S'), due at least in part to the increased electoral power of African Americans following enactment of the Voting Rights Act of 1965. When the preferences of Congress shift in the direction of the interpreter's (EEOC or the Court) preferences, then the interpreter has more freedom to interpret the statute dynamically, for the only Congress to which it is directly accountable is the current Congress. However, any shift in legislative preferences between 1964 and 1971 was modest[d] and does not explain how the EEOC and the Court could shift Title VII's policy so much further to the left.

Our judgment is that *Griggs* was a more liberal interpretation of Title VII than that which Congress (H' and S') would have wanted in 1971. Yet Congress did not override the decision, even though it amended Title VII in 1972 and even though the employer community wanted *Griggs* curtailed or overridden. The key to Congress' failure to override was the enthusiastic endorsement of *Griggs* in committee reports drafted in 1971 by the House and Senate labor committees (C'). See H.R. Rep. No. 238, 92d Cong., 1st Sess. 21–22 (1971), reprinted in 1972 U.S.C.C.A.N. 2137, 2156–57; Sen. Rep. No. 415, 92d Cong., 1st Sess. 14 (1971). Those reports may not have been representative of the views of the median member of Congress but instead reflective of preference outliers, consistent with the distributive theories of

---

d. See Barbara Sinclair, *Agenda, Policy, and Alignment Change from Coolidge to Reagan,* in *Congress Reconsidered* 291, 306–07 (Lawrence Dodd & Bruce Oppenheimer eds., 3d ed. 1985).

committee behavior we identified earlier. In the 1970s and 1980s, the House and Senate labor committees were dominated by representatives with preferences to the left of their chambers on issues of civil rights. And because those committees exercised gatekeeping power over issues on the legislative agenda, they had substantial ability to head off overrides of agency policies or judicial decisions, especially when they were supported by the majority party leadership, which was similarly liberal on civil rights issues and exerted great control over the congressional agenda and floor politics.

Under the foregoing analysis, the EEOC and the Supreme Court can set policy at the point reflecting the preferences of the median member of the House Committee on Education and Labor (x' = C'), rather than the median member of the House (x' = H'). This institutional dynamic alone gives the agency and the courts substantial discretion to move statutory policy away from the original equilibrium (x). Note that under the foregoing analysis the EEOC and the Court are more strongly influenced by the preferences of members of the *current* Congress than they are by the preferences of the *enacting* Congress. Thus, our study reveals that the notion of legislative intent has a temporal element. Although many think of courts and executive branch officials as the agents of the enacting Congress, current Congresses can exert substantial influence over policies because they control the budget and have close connections with agency personnel with day-to-day oversight of federal programs. Indeed, Einer Elhauge argues that the enacting legislators will rationally prefer interpreters to track current legislative preferences, which he calls "enactable preferences," because that allows them to influence not only the legislation they pass but all legislation being interpreted while they are in office. *Preference-Estimating Statutory Default Rules*, 102 Colum. L. Rev. 2027 (2002).

Under a game-theoretic analysis, *Griggs* itself might be subject to reinterpretation. After Justices Lewis Powell and William Rehnquist took their seats in 1972, the Burger Court became much more ambivalent about broadly defined antidiscrimination duties. In constitutional cases, where the Court is better protected against political overrides, the Burger Court rejected the *Griggs* approach and held that race-based or gender-based effects do not amount to unlawful discrimination. See *Washington v. Davis*, 426 U.S. 229 (1976); *Personnel Administrator of Massachusetts v. Feeney*, 442 U.S. 256 (1979); see also Jeffrey Segal & Albert Cover, *Ideological Values and the Votes of U.S. Supreme Court Justices*, 83 Am. Pol. Sci. Rev. 557, 560 (1989) (Table 1). The Burger Court narrowed *Griggs* itself only by tightening up proof burdens on plaintiffs but did not directly attack the decision.

The survival of *Griggs* through the 1970s is remarkable. Not only was the decision poorly reasoned and vulnerable to the charge that it was a significant leap from the expectations of the enacting Congress (x' is a long way down the line from x), but also a majority on the Court in the 1970s was not enthusiastic about outlawing discriminatory effects. We hypothesize that *Griggs* remained safe from being overruled in a period in which the Court was moving to the right because Congress moved further to the left on civil rights issues in the

1970s.[e] Thus the new policy (x' = A') was one that was acceptable to the median House member by the late 1970s. Any open retreat from *Griggs* would have generated immediate controversy because the civil rights community, the EEOC, and the gatekeeping (labor) committees would have mobilized for an override. In fact, this is precisely what happened when the Court retreated from *Griggs* by refusing to treat pregnancy discrimination as sex discrimination under Title VII: the Court suffered a firestorm of protest and was promptly overridden.[f]

B. THE NEXT ISSUE: AFFIRMATIVE ACTION (*WEBER*)

If you were counsel to a big company or a labor union in the 1970s, you would probably be very concerned about the representation of people of color in your company's workforce. Under *Griggs*, your company or union might be subject to a disparate impact lawsuit if bad numbers were not justified. And if your company did business with the federal government, the Johnson and Nixon Administrations had implemented a policy under which such companies had to improve their numbers or lose their lucrative contracts. In short, companies faced the loss of government contracts and judicially imposed back-pay awards and quota systems if their hiring efforts did not produce concrete results.

At the same time, consistent with *Griggs*, the Supreme Court encouraged companies to adopt their own plans. For example, in *Albemarle Paper Co. v. Moody*, 422 U.S. 405, 417–18 (1975), the Court approved broad EEOC guidelines out of an announced desire to provide the "spur or catalyst which causes employers and unions to self-examine and to self-evaluate their employment practices and to endeavor to eliminate, so far as possible, the last vestiges of an unfortunate and ignominious page in this country's history." See also *Franks v. Bowman Transp. Co.*, 424 U.S. 747, 778 (1976) (upholding retroactive award of seniority to African-American victims of discrimination and saying that "a collective bargaining agreement may go further, enhancing the seniority status of certain employees for purposes of furthering public policy interests beyond what is required by statute").

As a result of these developments, companies like Kaiser Aluminum and Chemical Corp. and labor unions like the United Steelworkers of America had incentives to adopt their own preferential hiring programs, with the hope that they could avoid having one thrust upon them by a court. In *McDonald v. Santa Fe Trail Transp. Co.*, 427 U.S. 273 (1976), however, the Court held that Title VII prohibits racial discrimination against whites as well as African Americans. The upshot of that case was that displaced white employees like Brian Weber had a colorable argument that voluntary affirmative action

---

e. Sinclair, *Agenda, Policy, and Alignment Change, supra*, at 307 (big jump in civil liberties scores for House members, 1973–1976).

f. The Pregnancy Discrimination Act of 1978, Pub. L. No. 95–555, 92 Stat. 2076 (1978), overriding *General Electric Co. v. Gilbert*, 429 U.S. 125 (1976); see William Eskridge, Jr., *Reneging on History? Playing the Court/Congress/President Civil Rights Game*, 79 Calif. L. Rev. 613 (1991).

programs were unlawfully discriminatory against them as well — and that they had a cause of action under Title VII. That clash of different statutory purposes, different legally protected civil rights, and different Supreme Court signals generated the following case.

UNITED STEELWORKERS OF AMERICA v. WEBER
Supreme Court of the United States, 1979
443 U.S. 193, 99 S.Ct. 2721, 61 L.Ed.2d 480

MR. JUSTICE BRENNAN delivered the opinion of the Court. * * *

In 1974, petitioner United Steelworkers of America (USWA) and petitioner Kaiser Aluminum & Chemical Corp. (Kaiser) entered into a master collective-bargaining agreement covering terms and conditions of employment at 15 Kaiser plants. The agreement contained, *inter alia*, an affirmative action plan designed to eliminate conspicuous racial imbalances in Kaiser's then almost exclusively white craft-work forces. Black craft-hiring goals were set for each Kaiser plant equal to the percentage of blacks in the respective local labor forces. To enable plants to meet these goals, on-the-job training programs were established to teach unskilled production workers — black and white — the skills necessary to become craftworkers. The plan reserved for black employees 50% of the openings in these newly created in-plant training programs.

This case arose from the operation of the plan at Kaiser's plant in Gramercy, La. Until 1974, Kaiser hired as craftworkers for that plant only persons who had had prior craft experience. Because blacks had long been excluded from craft unions, few were able to present such credentials. As a consequence, prior to 1974 only 1.83% (5 out of 273) of the skilled craftworkers at the Gramercy plant were black, even though the work force in the Gramercy area was approximately 39% black.

Pursuant to the national agreement Kaiser altered its craft-hiring practice in the Gramercy plant. Rather than hiring already trained outsiders, Kaiser established a training program to train its production workers to fill craft openings. Selection of craft trainees was made on the basis of seniority, with the proviso that at least 50% of the new trainees were to be black until the percentage of black skilled craftworkers in the Gramercy plant approximated the percentage of blacks in the local labor force.

During 1974, the first year of the operation of the Kaiser-USWA affirmative action plan, 13 craft trainees were selected from Gramercy's production work force. Of these, seven were black and six white. The most senior black selected into the program had less seniority than several white production workers whose bids for admission were rejected. Thereafter one of those white production workers, respondent Brian Weber (hereafter respondent), instituted this class action in the United States District Court for the Eastern District of Louisiana.

The complaint alleged that the filling of craft trainee positions at the Gramercy plant pursuant to the affirmative action program had resulted in junior black employees' receiving training in preference to senior white employees, thus discriminating against respondent and other similarly situated white employees in violation of §§ 703(a)[2] and (d)[3] of Title VII. The District Court held that the plan violated Title VII, entered a judgment in favor of the plaintiff class, and granted a permanent injunction prohibiting Kaiser and the USWA "from denying plaintiffs, Brian F. Weber and all other members of the class, access to on-the-job training programs on the basis of race." A divided panel of the Court of Appeals for the Fifth Circuit affirmed, holding that all employment preferences based upon race, including those preferences incidental to bona fide affirmative action plans, violated Title VII's prohibition against racial discrimination in employment. * * * We reverse.

We emphasize at the outset the narrowness of our inquiry. * * * [S]ince the Kaiser-USWA plan was adopted voluntarily, we are not concerned with what Title VII requires or with what a court might order to remedy a past proved violation of the Act. The only question before us is the narrow statutory issue of whether Title VII *forbids* private employers and unions from voluntarily agreeing upon bona fide affirmative action plans that accord racial preferences in the manner and for the purpose provided in the Kaiser-USWA plan. * * *

Respondent argues that Congress intended in Title VII to prohibit all race-conscious affirmative action plans. Respondent's argument rests upon a literal interpretation of §§ 703(a) and (d) of the Act. Those sections make it unlawful to "discriminate * * * because of * * * race" in hiring and in the selection of apprentices for training programs. Since, the argument runs, *McDonald v. Santa Fe Trail Transp. Co.,* [427 U.S. 273, 281 n.8 (1976)], settled that Title VII forbids discrimination against whites as well as blacks, and since the Kaiser-USWA affirmative action plan operates to discriminate against white employees solely because they are white, it follows that the Kaiser-USWA plan violates Title VII.

Respondent's argument is not without force. But it overlooks the significance of the fact that the Kaiser-USWA plan is an affirmative action plan voluntarily adopted by private parties to eliminate traditional patterns of racial segregation. In this context respondent's reliance upon a literal construction of §§ 703(a) and (d) and upon *McDonald* is misplaced. It is a "familiar rule,

---

2. Section 703(a), 78 Stat. 255, as amended, 86 Stat. 109, 42 U.S.C. § 2000e–2(a), provides:
"(a) * * * It shall be an unlawful employment practice for an employer —

(1) to fail or refuse to hire or to discharge any individual, or otherwise to discriminate against any individual with respect to his compensation, terms, conditions, or privileges of employment, because of such individual's race, color, religion, sex, or national origin; or

(2) to limit, segregate, or classify his employees or applicants for employment in any way which would deprive or tend to deprive any individual of employment opportunities or otherwise adversely affect his status as an employee, because of such individual's race, color, religion, sex, or national origin."

3. Section 703(d), 78 Stat. 256, 42 U.S.C. § 2000e–2(d), provides:
"It shall be an unlawful employment practice for any employer, labor organization, or joint labor-management committee controlling apprenticeship or other training or retraining, including on-the-job training programs to discriminate against any individual because of his race, color, religion, sex, or national origin in admission to, or employment in, any program established to provide apprenticeship or other training."

that a thing may be within the letter of the statute and yet not within the statute, because not within its spirit, nor within the intention of its makers." *Holy Trinity Church v. United States*, 143 U.S. 457, 459 (1892). The prohibition against racial discrimination in §§ 703(a) and (d) of Title VII must therefore be read against the background of the legislative history of Title VII and the historical context from which the Act arose. Examination of those sources makes clear that an interpretation of the sections that forbade all race-conscious affirmative action would "bring about an end completely at variance with the purpose of the statute" and must be rejected. *United States v. Public Utilities Comm'n*, 345 U.S. 295, 315 (1953).

Congress' primary concern in enacting the prohibition against racial discrimination in Title VII of the Civil Rights Act of 1964 was with "the plight of the Negro in our economy." 110 Cong. Rec. 6548 (1964) (remarks of Sen. Humphrey). Before 1964, blacks were largely relegated to "unskilled and semi-skilled jobs." *Ibid.* (remarks of Sen. Humphrey); *id.*, at 7204 (remarks of Sen. Clark); *id.*, at 7379–7380 (remarks of Sen. Kennedy). Because of automation the number of such jobs was rapidly decreasing. See *id.*, at 6548 (remarks of Sen. Humphrey); *id.*, at 7204 (remarks of Sen. Clark). As a consequence, "the relative position of the Negro worker [was] steadily worsening." * * *

Congress feared that the goals of the Civil Rights Act — the integration of blacks into the mainstream of American society — could not be achieved unless this trend were reversed. And Congress recognized that that would not be possible unless blacks were able to secure jobs "which have a future." *Id.*, at 7204 (remarks of Sen. Clark). See also *id.*, at 7379–7380 (remarks of Sen. Kennedy). As Senator Humphrey explained to the Senate:

> "What good does it do a Negro to be able to eat in a fine restaurant if he cannot afford to pay the bill? What good does it do him to be accepted in a hotel that is too expensive for his modest income? How can a Negro child be motivated to take full advantage of integrated educational facilities if he has no hope of getting a job where he can use that education?" *Id.*, at 6547. * * *

Accordingly, it was clear to Congress that "[t]he crux of the problem [was] to open employment opportunities for Negroes in occupations which have been traditionally closed to them," 110 Cong. Rec. 6548 (1964) (remarks of Sen. Humphrey), and it was to this problem that Title VII's prohibition against racial discrimination in employment was primarily addressed.

It plainly appears from the House Report accompanying the Civil Rights Act that Congress did not intend wholly to prohibit private and voluntary affirmative action efforts as one method of solving this problem. The Report provides:

> "No bill can or should lay claim to eliminating all of the causes and consequences of racial and other types of discrimination against minorities. There is reason to believe, however, that national leadership provided by the enactment of Federal legislation dealing with the most troublesome problems *will create an atmosphere conducive to voluntary or local resolution of other forms of discrimination.*" H.R. Rep. No. 914, 88th Cong., 1st Sess., pt. 1, p. 18 (1963). (Emphasis supplied.) * * *

Given this legislative history, we cannot agree with respondent that Congress intended to prohibit the private sector from taking effective steps to accomplish the goal that Congress designed Title VII to achieve. * * * It would be ironic indeed if a law triggered by a Nation's concern over centuries of racial injustice and intended to improve the lot of those who had "been excluded from the American dream for so long," 110 Cong. Rec. 6552 (1964) (remarks of Sen. Humphrey), constituted the first legislative prohibition of all voluntary, private, race-conscious efforts to abolish traditional patterns of racial segregation and hierarchy.

Our conclusion is further reinforced by examination of the language and legislative history of § 703(j) of Title VII.[5] Opponents of Title VII raised two related arguments against the bill. First, they argued that the Act would be interpreted to *require* employers with racially imbalanced work forces to grant preferential treatment to racial minorities in order to integrate. Second, they argued that employers with racially imbalanced work forces would grant preferential treatment to racial minorities, even if not required to do so by the Act. See 110 Cong. Rec. 8618–8619 (1964) (remarks of Sen. Sparkman). Had Congress meant to prohibit all race-conscious affirmative action, as respondent urges, it easily could have answered both objections by providing that Title VII would not require or *permit* racially preferential integration efforts. But Congress did not choose such a course. Rather, Congress added § 703(j) which addresses only the first objection. The section provides that nothing contained in Title VII "shall be interpreted to *require* any employer * * * to grant preferential treatment * * * to any group because of the race * * * of such * * * group on account of" a *de facto* racial imbalance in the employer's work force. The section does *not* state that "nothing in Title VII shall be interpreted to *permit*" voluntary affirmative efforts to correct racial imbalances. The natural inference is that Congress chose not to forbid all voluntary race-conscious affirmative action.

The reasons for this choice are evident from the legislative record. Title VII could not have been enacted into law without substantial support from legislators in both Houses who traditionally resisted federal regulation of private business. Those legislators demanded as a price for their support that

---

5. Section 703(j) of Title VII, 78 Stat. 257, 42 U.S.C. § 2000e–2(j), provides:

"Nothing contained in this title shall be interpreted to require any employer, employment agency, labor organization, or joint labor-management committee subject to this title to grant preferential treatment to any individual or to any group because of the race, color, religion, sex, or national origin of such individual or group on account of an imbalance which may exist with respect to the total number or percentage of persons of any race, color, religion, sex, or national origin employed by any employer, referred or classified for employment by any employment agency or labor organization, admitted to membership or classified by any labor organization, or admitted to, or employed in, any apprenticeship or other training program, in comparison with the total number or percentage of persons of such race, color, religion, sex, or national origin in any community, State, section, or other area, or in the available work force in any community, State, section, or other area."

Section 703(j) speaks to substantive liability under Title VII, but it does not preclude courts from considering racial imbalance as evidence of a Title VII violation. * * * Remedies for substantive violations are governed by § 706(g), 42 U.S.C. § 2000e–5(g).

"management prerogatives, and union freedoms * * * be left undisturbed to the greatest extent possible." H.R. Rep. No. 914, 88th Cong., 1st Sess., pt. 2, p. 29 (1963). Section 703(j) was proposed by Senator Dirksen to allay any fears that the Act might be interpreted in such a way as to upset this compromise. The section was designed to prevent § 703 of Title VII from being interpreted in such a way as to lead to undue "Federal Government interference with private businesses because of some Federal employee's ideas about racial balance or racial imbalance." 110 Cong. Rec. 14314 (1964) (remarks of Sen. Miller). See also id., at 9881 (remarks of Sen. Allott); id., at 10520 (remarks of Sen. Carlson); id., at 11471 (remarks of Sen. Javits); id., at 12817 (remarks of Sen. Dirksen). Clearly, a prohibition against all voluntary, race-conscious, affirmative action efforts would disserve these ends. Such a prohibition would augment the powers of the Federal Government and diminish traditional management prerogatives while at the same time impeding attainment of the ultimate statutory goals. In view of this legislative history and in view of Congress' desire to avoid undue federal regulation of private businesses, use of the word "require" rather than the phrase "require or permit" in § 703(j) fortifies the conclusion that Congress did not intend to limit traditional business freedom to such a degree as to prohibit all voluntary, race-conscious affirmative action.[7]

We therefore hold that Title VII's prohibition in §§ 703(a) and (d) against racial discrimination does not condemn all private, voluntary, race-conscious affirmative action plans. * * * [The Court held that the Kaiser plan was lawful under Title VII because both its purpose and effect were permissible: it was "designed to eliminate conspicuous racial imbalance in traditionally segregated job categories," and it "does not unnecessarily trammel the interests of white

---

7. Respondent argues that our construction of § 703 conflicts with various remarks in the legislative record. See, e.g., 110 Cong. Rec. 7213 (1964) (Sens. Clark and Case); id., at 7218 (Sens. Clark and Case); id., at 6549 (Sen. Humphrey); id., at 8921 (Sen. Williams). We do not agree. In Senator Humphrey's words, these comments were intended as assurances that Title VII would not allow establishment of systems "to *maintain* racial balance in employment." Id., at 11848 (emphasis added). They were not addressed to temporary, voluntary, affirmative action measures undertaken to eliminate manifest racial imbalance in traditionally segregated job categories. Moreover, the comments referred to by respondent all preceded the adoption of § 703(j), 42 U.S.C. § 2000e–2(j). After § 703(j) was adopted, congressional comments were all to the effect that employers would not be *required* to institute preferential quotas to avoid Title VII liability, see, e.g., 110 Cong. Rec. 12819 (1964) (remarks of Sen. Dirksen); id., at 13079–13080 (remarks of Sen. Clark); id., at 15876 (remarks of Rep. Lindsay). There was no suggestion after the adoption of § 703(j) that wholly voluntary, race-conscious, affirmative action efforts would in themselves constitute a violation of Title VII. On the contrary, as Representative MacGregor told the House shortly before the final vote on Title VII:

"Important as the scope and extent of this bill is, it is also vitally important that all Americans understand what this bill does not cover.

"Your mail and mine, your contacts and mine with our constituents, indicates a great degree of misunderstanding about this bill. People complain about * * * preferential treatment or quotas in employment. There is a mistaken belief that Congress is legislating in these areas in this bill. When we drafted this bill we excluded these issues largely because the problems raised by these controversial questions are more properly handled at a governmental level closer to the American people and by communities and individuals themselves." 110 Cong. Rec. 15893 (1964).

employees" because no white employees lost their jobs, half of those trained in the program will be white, and it was a temporary measure ending when "the percentage of black skilled craftworkers in the Gramercy plant approximates the percentage of blacks in the local labor force."]

MR. JUSTICE POWELL and MR. JUSTICE STEVENS took no part in the consideration or decision of these cases.

MR. JUSTICE BLACKMUN, concurring.

While I share some of the misgivings expressed in MR. JUSTICE REHNQUIST's dissent concerning the extent to which the legislative history of Title VII clearly supports the result the Court reaches today, I believe that additional considerations, practical and equitable, only partially perceived, if perceived at all, by the 88th Congress, support the conclusion reached by the Court today, and I therefore join its opinion as well as its judgment.

In his dissent from the decision of the United States Court of Appeals for the Fifth Circuit, Judge Wisdom pointed out that this litigation arises from a practical problem in the administration of Title VII. The broad prohibition against discrimination places the employer and the union on what he accurately described as a "high tightrope without a net beneath them." 563 F.2d 216, 230. If Title VII is read literally, on the one hand they face liability for past discrimination against blacks, and on the other they face liability to whites for any voluntary preferences adopted to mitigate the effects of prior discrimination against blacks.

In this litigation, Kaiser denies prior discrimination but concedes that its past hiring practices may be subject to question. Although the labor force in the Gramercy area was proximately 39% black, Kaiser's work force was less than 15% black, and its craftwork force was less than 2% black. Kaiser had made some effort to recruit black painters, carpenters, insulators, and other craftsmen, but it continued to insist that those hired have five years' prior industrial experience, a requirement that arguably was not sufficiently job related to justify under Title VII any discriminatory impact it may have had. * * * The parties dispute the extent to which black craftsmen were available in the local labor market. They agree, however, that after critical reviews from the Office of Federal Contract Compliance, Kaiser and the Steelworkers established the training program in question here and modeled it along the lines of a Title VII consent decree later entered for the steel industry. * * * Yet when they did this, respondent Weber sued, alleging that Title VII prohibited the program because it discriminated against him as a white person and it was not supported by a prior judicial finding of discrimination against blacks.

Respondent Weber's reading of Title VII, endorsed by the Court of Appeals, places voluntary compliance with Title VII in profound jeopardy. The only way for the employer and the union to keep their footing on the "tightrope" it creates would be to eschew all forms of voluntary affirmative action. Even a whisper of emphasis on minority recruiting would be forbidden. Because Congress intended to encourage private efforts to come into compliance with Title VII, see *Alexander v. Gardner-Denver Co.*, 415 U.S. 36, 44 (1974), Judge Wisdom concluded that employers and unions who had committed "arguable violations" of Title VII should be free to make reasonable responses without fear of liability to whites. Preferential hiring along the lines of the Kaiser program is a reasonable response for the employer, whether or not a court, on these facts, could order the same step as a remedy. The company is able to avoid identifying victims of past discrimination, and so avoids claims for backpay that would inevitably follow a response limited to such victims. If past victims should be benefited by the program, however, the company mitigates its liability to those persons. Also, to the extent that Title VII liability is predicated on the "disparate effect" of an employer's past hiring practices, the program makes it less likely that such an effect could be demonstrated. And the Court has recently held that work-force statistics resulting from private affirmative action were probative of benign intent in a "disparate treatment" case. *Furnco Construction Corp. v. Waters*, 438 U.S. 567 (1978).

The "arguable violation" theory has a number of advantages. It responds to a practical problem in the administration of Title VII not anticipated by Congress. It draws predictability from the outline of present law and closely effectuates the purpose of the Act. Both Kaiser and the United States urge its adoption here. Because I agree that it is the soundest way to approach this case, my preference would be to resolve this litigation by applying it and holding that Kaiser's craft training program meets the requirement that voluntary affirmative action be a reasonable response to an "arguable violation" of Title VII. * * *

MR. JUSTICE REHNQUIST, with whom THE CHIEF JUSTICE joins, dissenting.

In a very real sense, the Court's opinion is ahead of its time: it could more appropriately have been handed down five years from now, in 1984, a year coinciding with the title of a book from which the Court's opinion borrows, perhaps subconsciously, at least one idea. Orwell describes in his book a governmental official of Oceania, one of the three great world powers, denouncing the current enemy, Eurasia, to an assembled crowd:

> "It was almost impossible to listen to him without being first convinced and then maddened. * * * The speech had been proceeding for perhaps twenty minutes when a messenger hurried onto the platform and a scrap of paper was slipped into the speaker's hand. He unrolled and read it without pausing in his speech. Nothing altered in his voice or manner, or in the content of what he was saying, but suddenly the names were different. Without words said, a wave of understanding rippled through the crowd. Oceania was at war with Eastasia! * * * The banners and posters with which the square was decorated were all wrong! * * *
>
> "[T]he speaker had switched from one line to the other actually in mid-sentence, not only without a pause, but without even breaking the syntax." — G. Orwell, Nineteen Eighty-Four 181–182 (1949).

Today's decision represents an equally dramatic and equally unremarked switch in this Court's interpretation of Title VII. * * *

[II] Were Congress to act today specifically to prohibit the type of racial discrimination suffered by Weber, it would be hard pressed to draft language better tailored to the task than that found in § 703(d) of Title VII:

"It shall be an unlawful employment practice for any employer, labor organization, or joint labor-management committee controlling apprenticeship or other training or retraining, including on-the-job training programs to discriminate against any individual because of his race, color, religion, sex, or national origin in admission to, or employment in, any program established to provide apprenticeship or other training." 78 Stat. 256, 42 U.S.C. § 2000e–2(d).

Equally suited to the task would be § 703(a)(2), which makes it unlawful for an employer to classify his employees "in any way which would deprive or tend to deprive any individual of employment opportunities or otherwise adversely affect his status as an employee, because of such individual's race, color, religion, sex, or national origin." 78 Stat. 255, 42 U.S.C. § 2000e–2(a)(2).

Entirely consistent with these two express prohibitions is the language of § 703(j) of Title VII, which provides that the Act is not to be interpreted "to require any employer * * * to grant preferential treatment to any individual or to any group because of the race * * * of such individual or group" to correct a racial imbalance in the employer's work force. 42 U.S.C. § 2000e–2(j). Seizing on the word "require," the Court infers that Congress must have intended to "permit" this type of racial discrimination. Not only is this reading of § 703(j) outlandish in the light of the flat prohibitions of §§ 703(a) and (d), but also, as explained in Part III, it is totally belied by the Act's legislative history.

Quite simply, Kaiser's racially discriminatory admission quota is flatly prohibited by the plain language of Title VII. This normally dispositive fact, however, gives the Court only momentary pause. An "interpretation" of the statute upholding Weber's claim would, according to the Court, " 'bring about an end completely at variance with the purpose of the statute.' " To support this conclusion, the Court calls upon the "spirit" of the Act, which it divines from passages in Title VII's legislative history indicating that enactment of the statute was prompted by Congress' desire " 'to open employment opportunities for Negroes in occupations which [had] been traditionally closed to them.' " But the legislative history invoked by the Court to avoid the plain language of §§ 703(a) and (d) simply misses the point. To be sure, the reality of employment discrimination against Negroes provided the primary impetus for passage of Title VII. But this fact by no means supports the proposition that Congress intended to leave employers free to discriminate against white persons. In most cases, "[l]egislative history . . . is more vague than the statute we are called upon to interpret." [*United States v. Public Utilities Comm'n*, 345 U.S. 295, 320 (1953) (Jackson, J., concurring).] Here, however, the legislative history of Title VII is as clear as the language of §§ 703(a) and (d), and it irrefutably demonstrates that Congress meant precisely what it said in §§ 703(a) and (d) — that *no* racial discrimination in employment is permissible under Title VII, not even preferential treatment of minorities to correct racial imbalance.

[III] In undertaking to review the legislative history of Title VII, I am mindful that the topic hardly makes for light reading, but I am also fearful that nothing short of a thorough examination of the congressional debates will fully expose the magnitude of the Court's misinterpretation of Congress' intent.

[A] Introduced on the floor of the House of Representatives on June 20, 1963, the bill — H.R. 7152 — that ultimately became the Civil Rights Act of 1964 contained no compulsory provisions directed at private discrimination in employment. The bill was promptly referred to the Committee on the Judiciary, where it was amended to include Title VII. With two exceptions, the bill reported by the House Judiciary Committee contained §§ 703(a) and (d) as they were ultimately enacted. Amendments subsequently adopted on the House floor added § 703's prohibition against sex discrimination and § 703(d)'s coverage of "on-the-job training."

After noting that "[t]he purpose of [Title VII] is to eliminate * * * discrimination in employment based on race, color, religion, or national origin," the Judiciary Committee's Report simply paraphrased the provisions of Title VII without elaboration. H.R. Rep., pt. 1, p. 26. In a separate Minority Report, however, opponents of the measure on the Committee advanced a line of attack which was reiterated throughout the debates in both the House and Senate and which ultimately led to passage of § 703(j). Noting that the word "discrimination" was nowhere defined in H.R. 7152, the Minority Report charged that the absence from Title VII of any reference to "racial imbalance" was a "public relations" ruse and that "the administration intends to rely upon its own construction of 'discrimination' as including the lack of racial balance . . . ." H.R. Rep., pt. 1, pp. 67–68. To demonstrate how the bill would operate in practice, the Minority Report posited a number of hypothetical employment situations, concluding in each example that the employer *"may be forced to hire according to race*, to 'racially balance' those who work for him *in every job classification* or be in violation of Federal law." *Id.*, at 69 (emphasis in original).

When H.R. 7152 reached the House floor, the opening speech in support of its passage was delivered by Representative Celler, Chairman of the House Judiciary Committee and the Congressman responsible for introducing the legislation. A portion of that speech responded to criticism "seriously misrepresent[ing] what the bill would do and grossly distort[ing] its effects":

"[T]he charge has been made that the Equal Employment Opportunity Commission to be established by title VII of the bill would have the power to prevent a business from employing and promoting the people it wished, and that a 'Federal inspector' could then order the hiring and promotion only of employees of certain races or religious groups. This description of the bill is entirely wrong. * * *

"Even [a] court could not order that any preference be given to any particular race, religion or other group, but would be limited to ordering an end of discrimination. The statement that a Federal inspector could order the employment and promotion only of members of a specific racial or religious group is therefore patently erroneous. * * *

"* * * The Bill would do no more than prevent * * * employers from discriminating against *or in favor* of workers because of their race, religion, or national origin.

"It is likewise not true that the Equal Employment Opportunity Commission would have power to rectify existing 'racial or religious imbalance' in employment by requiring the hiring of certain people without regard to their qualifications simply because they are of a given race or religion. Only actual discrimination could be stopped." 110 Cong. Rec. 1518 (1964) (emphasis added).

Representative Celler's construction of Title VII was repeated by several other supporters during the House debate.

Thus, the battle lines were drawn early in the legislative struggle over Title VII, with opponents of the measure charging that agencies of the Federal Government such as the Equal Employment Opportunity Commission (EEOC), by interpreting the word "discrimination" to mean the existence of "racial imbalance," would "require" employers to grant preferential treatment to minorities, and supporters responding that the EEOC would be granted no such power and that, indeed, Title VII prohibits discrimination "in favor of workers because of their race." Supporters of H.R. 7152 in the House ultimately prevailed by a vote of 290 to 130, and the measure was sent to the Senate to begin what became the longest debate in that body's history.

[B] The Senate debate was broken into three phases: the debate on sending the bill to Committee, the general debate on the bill prior to invocation of cloture, and the debate following cloture. * * *

Formal debate on the merits of H.R. 7152 began on March 30, 1964. Supporters of the bill in the Senate had made elaborate preparations for this second round. Senator Humphrey, the majority whip, and Senator Kuchel, the minority whip, were selected as the bipartisan floor managers on the entire civil rights bill. Responsibility for explaining and defending each important title of the bill was placed on bipartisan "captains." Senators Clark and Case were selected as the bipartisan captains responsible for Title VII. Vaas, Title VII: Legislative History, 7 B.C. Ind. & Com. L. Rev. 431, 444–445 (1966) (hereinafter Title VII: Legislative History).

In the opening speech of the formal Senate debate on the bill, Senator Humphrey addressed the main concern of Title VII's opponents, advising that not only does Title VII not require use of racial quotas, *it does not permit* their use. "The truth," stated the floor leader of the bill, "is that this title forbids discriminating against anyone on account of race. This is the simple and complete truth about title VII." 110 Cong. Rec. 6549 (1964). Senator Humphrey continued:

"Contrary to the allegations of some opponents of this title, there is nothing in it that will give any power to the Commission or to any court to require hiring, firing, or promotion of employees in order to meet a racial 'quota' or to achieve a certain racial balance.

"That bugaboo has been brought up a dozen times; but it is nonexistent. In fact, *the very opposite is true. Title VII prohibits discrimination.* In effect, it says that race, religion and national origin are not to be used as the basis for hiring and firing. Title VII is designed to encourage hiring on the basis of ability and qualifications, not race or religion." *Ibid.* (emphasis added).

At the close of his speech, Senator Humphrey returned briefly to the subject of employment quotas: "It is claimed that the bill would require racial quotas for all hiring, when in fact it provides that race shall not be a basis for making personnel decisions." *Id.*, at 6553. * * *

A few days later the Senate's attention focused exclusively on Title VII, as Senators Clark and Case rose to discuss the title of H.R. 7152 on which they shared floor "captain" responsibilities. In an interpretative memorandum submitted jointly to the Senate, Senators Clark and Case took pains to refute the opposition's charge that Title VII would result in preferential treatment for minorities. * * * Of particular relevance to the instant litigation were their observations regarding seniority rights. As if directing their comments at Brian Weber, the Senators said:

> "Title VII would have no effect on established seniority rights. Its effect is prospective and not retrospective. Thus, for example, if a business has been discriminating in the past and as a result has an all-white working force, when the title comes into effect the employer's obligation would be simply to fill future vacancies on a nondiscriminatory basis. He would not be obliged – *or indeed permitted* – to fire whites in order to hire Negroes, *or to prefer Negroes for future vacancies, or, once Negroes are hired, to give them special seniority rights at the expense of the white workers hired earlier.*" *Id.*, at 7213 (emphasis added).

[In addition, Senator Kuchel made similar comments. Southern opponents to the bill were still not satisfied, though. Senator Robertson (D–Va.) argued that the bill would mandate quotas. Senator H. Williams (D–N.J.) responded:]

> "Those opposed to H.R. 7152 should realize that to hire a Negro solely because he is a Negro is racial discrimination, just as much as a 'white only' employment policy. Both forms of discrimination are prohibited by title VII of this bill. The language of that title simply states that race is not a qualification for employment. . . . Some people charge that H.R. 7152 favors the Negro, at the expense of the white majority. But how can the language of equality favor one race or one religion over another? Equality can have only one meaning, and that meaning is self-evident to reasonable men. Those who say that equality means favoritism do violence to common sense." *Id.*, at 8921. * * *

While the debate in the Senate raged, a bipartisan coalition under the leadership of Senators Dirksen, Mansfield, Humphrey, and Kuchel was working with House leaders and representatives of the Johnson administration on a number of amendments to H.R. 7152 designed to enhance its prospects of passage. The so-called "Dirksen-Mansfield" amendment was introduced on May 26 by Senator Dirksen as a substitute for the entire House-passed bill. The substitute bill, which ultimately became law, left unchanged the basic prohibitory language of §§ 703(a) and (d), as well as the remedial provisions in § 706(g). It added, however, several provisions defining and clarifying the scope of Title VII's substantive prohibitions. One of those clarifying amendments, § 703(j), was specifically directed at the opposition's concerns regarding racial balancing and preferential treatment of minorities, providing in pertinent part: "Nothing contained in [Title VII] shall be interpreted to require any employer . . . to grant preferential treatment to any individual or to any group because of the race . . . of such individual or group on account of" a racial imbalance in the employer's work force. 42 U.S.C. § 2000e–2(j). * * *

Contrary to the Court's analysis, the language of § 703(j) is precisely tailored to the objection voiced time and again by Title VII's opponents. Not once during the 83 days of debate in the Senate did a speaker, proponent or opponent, suggest that the bill would allow employers *voluntarily* to prefer racial minorities over white persons. In light of Title VII's flat prohibition on discrimination "against any individual . . . because of such individual's race," § 703(a), 42 U.S.C. § 2000e–2(a), such a contention would have been, in any event, too preposterous to warrant response. Indeed, speakers on both sides of the issue, as the legislative history makes clear, recognized that Title VII would tolerate no *voluntary* racial preference, whether in favor of blacks or whites. The complaint consistently voiced by the opponents was that Title VII, particularly the word "discrimination," would be *interpreted* by federal agencies such as the EEOC to *require* the correction of racial imbalance through the granting of preferential treatment to minorities. Verbal assurances that Title VII would not require — indeed, would not permit — preferential treatment of blacks having failed, supporters of H.R. 7152 responded by proposing an amendment carefully worded to meet, and put to rest, the opposition's charge. Indeed, unlike §§ 703(a) and (d), which are by their terms directed at entities — *e.g.*, employers, labor unions — whose actions are restricted by Title VII's prohibitions, the language of § 703(j) is specifically directed at entities — federal agencies and courts — charged with the responsibility of interpreting Title VII's provisions.

In light of the background and purpose of § 703(j), the irony of invoking the section to justify the result in this case is obvious. The Court's frequent references to the "voluntary" nature of Kaiser's racially discriminatory admission quota bear no relationship to the facts of this case. Kaiser and the Steelworkers acted under pressure from an agency of the Federal Government, the Office of Federal Contract Compliance, which found that minorities were being "underutilized" at Kaiser's plants. That is, Kaiser's work force was racially imbalanced. Bowing to that pressure, Kaiser instituted an admissions quota preferring blacks over whites, thus confirming that the fears of Title VII's opponents were well founded. Today, § 703(j), adopted to allay those fears, is invoked by the Court to uphold imposition of a racial quota under the very circumstances that the section was intended to prevent. * * *

[Justice Rehnquist also pointed to Senator Ervin's June 9 amendment to delete Title VII. Responding for the sponsors, Senator Clark emphasized that the bill "establishes no quotas." Senator Cotton (R–N.H.) offered an amendment to limit Title VII to firms having more than 100 employees. He opined that Title VII would forbid quotas. Although his amendment was defeated, Justice Rehnquist observed that the sponsors did not dispute the Cotton view.

[When cloture was invoked June 10, 1964, debate was limited, but several post-cloture statements by the bill's supporters reinforced the earlier view that Title VII imposed no quotas. The substitute bill was passed June 19. In final form, the bill was passed by the House on July 2 and signed by the President the same day.]

[V] Our task in this case, like any other case involving the construction of a statute, is to give effect to the intent of Congress. To divine that intent, we traditionally look first to the words of the statute and, if they are unclear, then to the statute's legislative history. Finding the desired result hopelessly foreclosed by these conventional sources, the Court turns to a third source — the "spirit" of the Act. But close examination of what the Court proffers as the spirit of the Act reveals it as the spirit animating the present majority, not the 88th Congress. For if the spirit of the Act eludes the cold words of the statute itself, it rings out with unmistakable clarity in the words of the elected representatives who made the Act law. It is *equality*. Senator Dirksen, I think, captured that spirit in a speech delivered on the floor of the Senate just moments before the bill was passed:

> " * * * [T]oday we come to grips finally with a bill that advances the enjoyment of living; but, more than that, it advances the equality of opportunity.

> "I do not emphasize the word 'equality' standing by itself. It means equality of opportunity in the field of education. It means equality of opportunity in the field of employment. It means equality of opportunity in the field of participation in the affairs of government * * *.

> "That is it.

> "Equality of opportunity, if we are going to talk about conscience, is the mass conscience of mankind that speaks in every generation, and it will continue to speak long after we are dead and gone." 110 Cong. Rec. 14510 (1964).

There is perhaps no device more destructive to the notion of equality than the *numerus clausus* — the quota. Whether described as "benign discrimination" or "affirmative action," the racial quota is nonetheless a creator of castes, a two-edged sword that must demean one in order to prefer another. In passing Title VII, Congress outlawed *all* racial discrimination, recognizing that no discrimination based on race is benign, that no action disadvantaging a person because of his color is affirmative. With today's holding, the Court introduces into Title VII a tolerance for the very evil that the law was intended to eradicate, without offering even a clue as to what the limits on that tolerance may be. We are told simply that Kaiser's racially discriminatory admission quota "falls on the permissible side of the line." By going not merely *beyond*, but directly *against* Title VII's language and legislative history, the Court has sown the wind. Later courts will face the impossible task of reaping the whirlwind.

NOTES ON *WEBER* AND MODES OF INTERPRETATION

We believe the three opinions in this case present strikingly different normative visions of the Court's role in statutory interpretation. See William Eskridge, Jr., *Dynamic Statutory Interpretation* 13–31, 35–44 (1994); Eskridge, Frickey & Garrett, *supra*, Chapter 6; Philip Frickey, *Wisdom on* Weber, 74 Tulane L. Rev. 1169 (2000). Each vision is beset with practical problems of evidence, however.

1. *Divining the "Intent" of Congress: Did the Court Invalidate the Original Legislative "Deal"?* One way to look at the role of the interpreter of a statute is to say that she is seeking the original intent of the author (the

enacting Congress).　Justices Brennan and Rehnquist both purport to be performing this interpretive role, with four Justices agreeing with Justice Brennan and only the Chief Justice agreeing with Justice Rehnquist.　But many of the commentators agree with Justice Rehnquist that the Court "changed" the meaning of the statute by judicial fiat, and "[t]hat change goes to the roots of the bargain struck by the 88th Congress, and the roots of our color-blind aspiration." Bernard Meltzer, *The* Weber *Case: The Judicial Abrogation of the Antidiscrimination Standard in Employment*, 47 U. Chi. L. Rev. 423, 456 (1980).[g] Do you agree?

Is Justice Rehnquist right in charging that Congress would have been "hard pressed" to have chosen language more clearly protecting Brian Weber than that of § 703(d), which makes it an unlawful practice for an employer "to discriminate against any individual because of his race * * * in admission to, or employment in, any program established to provide apprenticeship or other training"?　What about the following:

> It shall be an unlawful employment practice for the employer * * * not to include any individual in any program established to provide apprenticeship or other training as a result of prohibited criteria, namely race * * *.

Wouldn't that have been clearer?　Can we expect Congress, drafting statutory language in an environment of imperfect information and substantial time pressure, to anticipate specific questions that will arise under the law, or is it more realistic to expect general statements of policy that will require agencies and courts to use discretion in executing and interpreting the law?　And doesn't Justice Rehnquist overstate the clarity of § 703(d)?　The language enacted by Congress is amenable to another plausible interpretation supporting Justice Brennan's decision.　Justice Rehnquist's dissent assumed, as many dictionaries say, that an employer *discriminates* on the basis of race if it makes a race-based *differentiation*.　In a dictionary sense, it is a correct use of the term to say "I discriminate against peaches," if I prefer pears to peaches.　But that is not the way we usually use the word *discriminate*, which connotes an *invidious* differentiation.　Consider the definition of *discriminate* found in a desk dictionary published in 1968, just four years after Congress enacted Title VII.　In this dictionary, the "prejudice" meaning is the first definition given.　If one consults a newer desk dictionary, the "clear distinction" meaning is the first definition given.　Should the older dictionary be preferred, because it was essentially contemporaneous with the adoption of the statute?　Should the newer dictionary be preferred, because it might more accurately represent contemporary usage?　Should neither dictionary control because each acknowledges both dueling definitions?　How can the process be controlled so that advocates and judges don't merely cite the dictionary that supports them and ignore the others?

Perhaps it is not so clear that the "deal" described by Meltzer and Justice Rehnquist is inscribed in the language of the statute.　For that reason, statutory

---

g. See also Nelson Lund, *The Law of Affirmative Action In and After the Civil Rights Act of 1991: Congress Invites Judicial Reform*, 6 Geo. Mason L. Rev. 87, 90–101 (1997).

interpreters often look to the legislative history to elucidate the "intent" of Congress. As a rule, the most authoritative legislative history is the House and Senate committee reports, but Justice Rehnquist does not rely on them. Instead, like Justice Brennan, he relies on the colloquies between the bill's sponsors and the bill's opponents. Does this tell us anything about the "intent" of the 73 Senators and 290 Representatives who voted for the bill? Indeed, how can we know how many legislators actually heard the colloquies? Suppose Senator Humphrey was simply lying to the Southern opponents when he reassured them that the bill would not require preferential treatment — should his "lie" be binding not only on him, but also on his 72 colleagues who also voted for the bill? (There is no evidence that Senator Humphrey's statements "persuaded" any of the Southern senators to vote for the bill.) Did Senator Humphrey have an incentive to tell the truth to his colleagues, perhaps because as a leader in the Senate he was a repeat player who wanted to establish a reputation for truthfulness so he could make credible deals in future negotiations?

Suppose that the statements of the sponsors are binding on everyone. Does anyone say: "We never want preferences for whites or blacks. By that we mean either governmentally required preferences, or preferences voluntarily agreed to by an employer or union to redress past discrimination." Did Justice Rehnquist discover such a "smoking gun" in the Clark-Case memorandum's passage that he claimed spoke directly to Brian Weber's situation?

2. *Pitfalls of a Purpose-Oriented Interpretation.* Supporting the "spirit" approach taken by Justice Brennan, Professor Burt Neuborne (ACLU counsel in *Weber*) argues:

> At best, the concept of legislative intent is discernible primarily by the judges who claim to have deciphered it. The truth of the matter is that a legislature, especially in the civil rights area, generally enacts a statute aimed at a broad philosophical concept — in this case, equality in employment. It does not and cannot foresee, much less resolve, the myriad questions which must arise whenever a broad philosophical proposition is applied to the protean complexity of everyday life * * *.

Burt Neuborne, *Observations on* Weber, 54 N.Y.U. L. Rev. 546, 553 (1979). Is this a more realistic way of looking at the Civil Rights Act than Meltzer's specific bargain idea?

Is Justice Brennan right about the "spirit" of the Act? There is much to be said for Justice Rehnquist's position that when you read the committee report and the debate, you come away with the impression that the Act was mainly intended to eradicate racial criteria in hiring. Supporting Justice Brennan, Ronald Dworkin argues that the judge should interpret the statute to advance the policy that furnishes "the best political justification for the statute," because the "intent" of Congress on this issue is indeterminate. *How to Read the Civil Rights Act*, in *A Matter of Principle* 316, 327 (1985). Upon what model of the legislative process might this suggestion rest? Even if it is a valid approach, there seem to be two purposes in the Act — jobs for African Americans and creation of a color-blind society. How does the judge choose one politically coherent purpose over the other?

If we decide to interpret Title VII in light of its equal results spirit, will encouraging unions and companies to set up their own affirmative action programs (effectively shifting the costs of past discrimination from them onto "innocent" white employees) really contribute to this spirit? Consider some questions raised about *Weber*:

> In the longer run, the Court is taking frightful risks. (1) Can the Court insist on such intrusive use of racial classification without teaching the country that policies based on racial classification are legitimate? (2) Will those who are asked to step aside for the benefit of blacks not harbor ill will against them? Will this not be a particular problem for the young, who, having grown up on this side of the civil rights revolution, disassociate themselves from the racism of the old America, and may be surprised to learn that they are asked to pay for it? (3) Will the effect of pervasive affirmative action for blacks — combined with an equal pay principle — be to ensure that blacks are systematically promoted to the level just above their competence and cause affirmative action to become an engine of group defamation? * * * (5) Will affirmative action create incentives for employers to locate jobs away from black labor [so that they can avoid high black quotas]?

Edmund Kitch, *The Return of Color Consciousness to the Constitution*: Weber, Dayton, *and* Columbus, 1979 Sup. Ct. Rev. 1, 12–13. Indeed, in 1979 African-American unemployment was no less a problem than it had been in 1964 (in part because some companies did avoid African-American communities).

3. *Reading Statutes Dynamically.* Both Justices Brennan and Rehnquist purport to be interpreting the "will" of Congress on this issue as of 1964, when the statute was enacted. The implicit argument of each opinion is that on the day Title VII became law, this is the answer the interpreter (be it court or Congress) would have given to the *Weber* question. Does that make sense to you? For purposes of statutory interpretation, the *Weber* issue is so important because it represents a tension that did not really exist in the statute as enacted, as Justice Blackmun's concurring opinion suggests. In a functional sense, the Title VII of 1964 was not the same statute as the Title VII of 1979, not because the statute was formally amended (as it was in 1972), but because the ongoing process of interpretation and elaboration altered the statute in response to evolving circumstances — *Griggs* as well as other decisions changed not only the statute, but the society on which the statute operated. Justice Blackmun therefore urged that the interpretation of Title VII reflect the unanticipated tension created by the ongoing application and interpretation process and permit the affirmative action plan in *Weber*. Upon what model of legislation was Justice Blackmun operating?

Two of us have argued that the most persuasive approach to *Weber* is Justice Blackmun's pragmatic appeal to current problems of statutory fairness and workability, not just the historical choices allegedly made in 1964.[h] The argument is that statutes start with gaps and ambiguities (including the precise

---

h. See William Eskridge, Jr., *Dynamic Statutory Interpretation* 24–25 (1994); Philip Frickey, *From the Big Sleep to the Big Heat: The Revival of Theory in Statutory Interpretation*, 77 Minn. L. Rev. 241, 245–47, 259 (1992).

meaning of "discriminate," a term that is not self-defining), which the EEOC and the Court had to interpret in light of factual settings they faced, and their interpretations went "beyond" Congress' original expectations. The gaps and ambiguities proliferated as the world changed — often in response to the statute and its applications — and offered more radical variations, including repeated fact patterns like *Weber*, where past discrimination continued to have present effects. Moreover, Title VII changed, often "against" the original legislative expectations, because the EEOC and the Court had their own values and "spin" on the statute, because the Congress with power to discipline these interpreters was the current rather than the enacting Congress (and the latter had a different spin on the statute than the former), and because the legal and social context changed over time. This is offered as a description of what interpreters do with the statute. Do you find it normatively acceptable? In particular, is it appropriate for the judiciary to undertake this task of updating the statute and filling gaps with new policies, or should Congress have the sole responsibility for amending old statutes to account for new social and economic developments? Does the answer change when the new conditions have resulted in large part from prior judicial opinions interpreting the act in unexpected ways?

You should be aware that liberals have no monopoly on dynamic interpretation. The conservative Justices on the Burger Court had their own spin on affirmative action, and the cases after *Weber* were harder on affirmative action plans. See *Sheet Metal Workers v. EEOC*, 478 U.S. 421 (1986); *Local No. 93, Int'l Ass'n of Firefighters v. Cleveland*, 478 U.S. 501 (1986); *Local Union No. 1784 Firefighters v. Stotts*, 467 U.S. 561 (1984). When Justice Rehnquist became Chief Justice and yielded his seat to Judge Antonin Scalia, the new Court seemed poised to move Title VII policy in a more conservative direction. Yet consider the next case.

JOHNSON v. TRANSPORTATION AGENCY, SANTA CLARA COUNTY
Supreme Court of the United States, 1987
480 U.S. 616, 107 S.Ct. 1442, 94 L.Ed.2d 613

JUSTICE BRENNAN delivered the opinion of the Court.

[The Transportation Agency of Santa Clara County, California promulgated an Affirmative Action Plan to remedy historic patterns of discrimination against women and minorities in some job categories. The Plan provided that, in making promotions to positions within a traditionally segregated job classification in which women had been significantly underrepresented, the Agency was authorized to consider as one factor the sex of a qualified applicant. The Agency found women significantly underrepresented in its work force generally, and virtually unrepresented in the 238 Skilled Craft Worker positions. Pursuant to the Plan, the Agency promoted Diane Joyce to the position of road dispatcher in the Agency's Roads Division. Dispatchers assign road crews, equipment, and materials, and maintain records pertaining to road maintenance jobs. One of the applicants passed over was Paul Johnson, who had a slightly higher score than Joyce based upon his paper credentials and an oral interview.]

[Johnson filed a complaint with the EEOC, and subsequently a federal lawsuit. The district court granted Johnson relief, based upon its finding that Johnson was more qualified for the position than Joyce, and that sex was the "determining factor" in Joyce's selection. The Ninth Circuit reversed.]

[*Weber*] upheld the employer's decision to select less senior black applicants over the white respondent, for we found that taking race into account was consistent with Title VII's objective of "break[ing] down old patterns of racial segregation and hierarchy." As we stated:

> "It would be ironic indeed if a law triggered by a Nation's concern over centuries of racial injustice and intended to improve the lot of those who had 'been excluded from the American dream for so long' constituted the first legislative prohibition of all voluntary, private, race-conscious efforts to abolish traditional patterns of racial segregation and hierarchy." *Id.* (quoting remarks of Sen. Humphrey).[7]

* * * As JUSTICE BLACKMUN's concurrence made clear, *Weber* held that an employer seeking to justify the adoption of a plan need not point to its own prior discriminatory practices, nor even to evidence of an "arguable violation"

---

7. JUSTICE SCALIA's dissent maintains that *Weber*'s conclusion that Title VII does not prohibit voluntary affirmative action programs "rewrote the statute it purported to construe." *Weber*'s decisive rejection of the argument that the "plain language" of the statute prohibits affirmative action rested on (1) legislative history indicating Congress' clear intention that employers play a major role in eliminating the vestiges of discrimination, and (2) the language and legislative history of section 703(j) of the statute, which reflect a strong desire to preserve managerial prerogatives so that they might be utilized for this purpose. As JUSTICE BLACKMUN said in his concurrence in *Weber*, "[I]f the Court has misconceived the political will, it has the assurance that because the question is statutory Congress may set a different course if it so chooses." Congress has not amended the statute to reject our construction, nor have any such amendments even been proposed, and we therefore may assume that our interpretation was correct.

JUSTICE SCALIA's dissent faults the fact that we take note of the absence of Congressional efforts to amend the statute to nullify *Weber*. It suggests that Congressional inaction cannot be regarded as acquiescence under all circumstances, but then draws away from that unexceptional point the conclusion that *any* reliance on Congressional failure to act is necessarily a "canard." The fact that inaction may not always provide crystalline revelation, however, should not obscure the fact that it may be probative to varying degrees. *Weber*, for instance, was a widely-publicized decision that addressed a prominent issue of public debate. Legislative inattention thus is not a plausible explanation for Congressional inaction. Furthermore, Congress not only passed no contrary legislation in the wake of *Weber*, but not one legislator even proposed a bill to do so. The barriers of the legislative process therefore also seem a poor explanation for failure to act. By contrast, when Congress has been displeased with our interpretation of Title VII, it has not hesitated to amend the statute to tell us so. For instance, when Congress passed the Pregnancy Discrimination Act of 1978, 42 U.S.C. section 2000e(k), "it unambiguously expressed its disapproval of both the holding and the reasoning of the Court in [*General Electric v. Gilbert*, 429 U.S. 125 (1976)]." *Newport News Shipbuilding & Dry Dock v. EEOC*, 462 U.S. 669, 678 (1983). Surely, it is appropriate to find some probative value in such radically different Congressional reactions to this Court's interpretations of the same statute.

As one scholar has put it, "When a court says to a legislature: 'You (or your predecessor) meant X,' it almost invites the legislature to answer: 'We did not.'" G. Calabresi, A Common Law for the Age of Statutes 31–32 (1982). Any belief in the notion of a dialogue between the judiciary and the legislature must acknowledge that on occasion an invitation declined is as significant as one accepted.

on its part. Rather, it need point only to a "conspicuous . . . imbalance in traditionally segregated job categories." * * *

In reviewing the employment decision at issue in this case, we must first examine whether that decision was made pursuant to a plan prompted by concerns similar to those of the employer in *Weber*. Next, we must determine whether the effect of the plan on males and nonminorities is comparable to the effect of the plan in that case.

The first issue is therefore whether consideration of the sex of applicants for skilled craft jobs was justified by the existence of a "manifest imbalance" that reflected underrepresentation of women in "traditionally segregated job categories." In determining whether an imbalance exists that would justify taking sex or race into account, a comparison of the percentage of minorities or women in the employer's work force with the percentage in the area labor market or general population is appropriate in analyzing jobs that require no special expertise, or training programs designed to provide expertise. Where a job requires special training, however, the comparison should be with those in the labor force who possess the relevant qualifications. The requirement that the "manifest imbalance" relate to a "traditionally segregated job category" provides assurance both that sex or race will be taken into account in a manner consistent with Title VII's purpose of eliminating the effects of employment discrimination, and that the interests of those employees not benefitting from the plan will not be unduly infringed.

A manifest imbalance need not be such that it would support a prima facie case against the employer, as suggested in JUSTICE O'CONNOR's concurrence, since we do not regard as identical the constraints of Title VII and the Federal Constitution on voluntarily adopted affirmative action plans. Application of the "prima facie" standard in Title VII cases would be inconsistent with *Weber*'s focus on statistical imbalance, and could inappropriately create a significant disincentive for employers to adopt an affirmative action plan. A corporation concerned with maximizing return on investment, for instance, is hardly likely to adopt a plan if in order to do so it must compile evidence that could be used to subject it to a colorable Title VII suit.

It is clear that the decision to hire Joyce was made pursuant to an Agency plan that directed that sex or race be taken into account for the purpose of remedying underrepresentation. The Agency Plan acknowledged the "limited opportunities that have existed in the past" for women to find employment in certain job classifications "where women have not been traditionally employed in significant numbers." As a result, observed the Plan, women were concentrated in traditionally female jobs in the Agency, and represented a lower percentage in other job classifications than would be expected if such traditional segregation had not occurred. Specifically, 9 of the 10 Para-Professionals and 110 of the 145 Office and Clerical Workers were women. By contrast, women were only 2 of the 28 Officials and Administrators, 5 of the 58 Professionals, 12 of the 124 Technicians, none of the Skilled Craft Workers, and 1 — who was Joyce — of the 110 Road Maintenance Workers. The Plan sought to remedy these imbalances through "hiring, training and promotion of

. . . women throughout the Agency in all major job classifications where they are underrepresented." * * *

We next consider whether the Agency Plan unnecessarily trammeled the rights of male employees or created an absolute bar to their advancement. In contrast to the plan in *Weber*, which provided that 50% of the positions in the craft training program were exclusively for blacks, and to the consent decree upheld last term in *Firefighters v. Cleveland*, 478 U.S. 501 (1986), which required the promotion of specific numbers of minorities, the Plan sets aside no positions for women. The Plan expressly states that "[t]he 'goals' established for each Division should not be construed as 'quotas' that must be met." Rather, the Plan merely authorizes that consideration be given to affirmative action concerns when evaluating qualified applicants. As the Agency Director testified, the sex of Joyce was but one of numerous factors he took into account in arriving at his decision. The Plan thus resembles the "Harvard Plan" approvingly noted by JUSTICE POWELL in *University of California Regents v. Bakke*, 438 U.S. 265, 316–319 (1978), which considers race along with other criteria in determining admission to the college. As JUSTICE POWELL observed: "In such an admissions program, race or ethnic background may be deemed a 'plus' in a particular applicant's file, yet it does not insulate the individual from comparison with all other candidates for the available seats." Similarly, the Agency Plan requires women to compete with all other qualified applicants. No persons are automatically excluded from consideration; all are able to have their qualifications weighed against those of other applicants. * * *

We therefore hold that the Agency appropriately took into account as one factor the sex of Diane Joyce in determining that she should be promoted to the road dispatcher position. The decision to do so was made pursuant to an affirmative action plan that represents a moderate, flexible, case-by-case approach to effecting a gradual improvement in the representation of minorities and women in the Agency's work force. Such a plan is fully consistent with Title VII, for it embodies the contribution that voluntary employer action can make in eliminating the vestiges of discrimination in the workplace. Accordingly, the judgment of the Court of Appeals is

Affirmed.

JUSTICE STEVENS, concurring. * * *

Prior to 1978 the Court construed the Civil Rights Act of 1964 as an absolute blanket prohibition against discrimination which neither required nor permitted discriminatory preferences for any group, minority or majority. * * * As I explained in my separate opinion in *Bakke*, and as the Court forcefully stated in *McDonald v. Santa Fe Trail Transportation Co.*, Congress intended " 'to eliminate all practices which operate to disadvantage the employment opportunities of any group protected by Title VII including Caucasians.' " If the Court had adhered to that construction of the Act, petitioner would unquestionably prevail in this case. But it has not done so.

In the *Bakke* case in 1978 and again in *Weber*, a majority of the Court interpreted the antidiscriminatory strategy of the statute in a fundamentally different way. * * * [T]he only problem for me is whether to adhere to an authoritative construction of the Act that is at odds with my understanding of the actual intent of the authors of the legislation. I conclude without hesitation that I must answer that question in the affirmative[.]

Bakke and *Weber* have been decided and are now an important part of the fabric of our law. This consideration is sufficiently compelling for me to adhere to the basic construction of this legislation that the Court adopted in *Bakke* and in *Weber*. There is an undoubted public interest in "stability and orderly development of the law."

The logic of antidiscrimination legislation requires that judicial constructions of Title VII leave "breathing room" for employer initiatives to benefit members of minority groups. If Title VII had never been enacted, a private employer would be free to hire members of minority groups for any reason that might seem sensible from a business or a social point of view. The Court's opinion in *Weber* reflects the same approach; the opinion relied heavily on legislative history indicating that Congress intended that traditional management prerogatives be left undisturbed to the greatest extent possible. * * *

As construed in *Weber* * * * the statute does not absolutely prohibit preferential hiring in favor of minorities; it was merely intended to protect historically disadvantaged groups *against* discrimination and not to hamper managerial efforts to benefit members of disadvantaged groups that are consistent with that paramount purpose. The preference granted by respondent in this case does not violate the statute as so construed; the record amply supports the conclusion that the challenged employment decision served the legitimate purpose of creating diversity in a category of employment that had been almost an exclusive province of males in the past. Respondent's voluntary decision is surely not prohibited by Title VII as construed in *Weber*.

Whether a voluntary decision of the kind made by respondent would ever be prohibited by Title VII is a question we need not answer until it is squarely presented. Given the interpretation of the statute the Court adopted in *Weber*, I see no reason why the employer has any duty, prior to granting a preference to a qualified minority employee, to determine whether his past conduct might constitute an arguable violation of Title VII. Indeed, in some instances the employer may find it more helpful to focus on the future. Instead of retroactively scrutinizing his own or society's possible exclusions of minorities in the past to determine the outer limits of a valid affirmative-action program — or indeed, any particular affirmative-action decision — in many cases the employer will find it more appropriate to consider other legitimate reasons to give preferences to members of underrepresented groups. Statutes enacted for the benefit of minority groups should not block these forward-looking considerations. * * *

Justice O'Connor, concurring in the judgment. * * *

In my view, the proper initial inquiry in evaluating the legality of an affirmative action plan by a public employer under Title VII is no different from that required by the Equal Protection Clause. In either case, consistent with the congressional intent to provide some measure of protection to the interests of the employer's nonminority employees, the employer must have had a firm basis for believing that remedial action was required. An employer would have such a firm basis if it can point to a statistical disparity sufficient to support a prima facie claim under Title VII by the employee beneficiaries of the affirmative action plan of a pattern or practice claim of discrimination.

In *Weber*, this Court balanced two conflicting concerns in construing § 703(d): Congress' intent to root out invidious discrimination against *any* person on the basis of race or gender, and its goal of eliminating the lasting effects of discrimination against minorities. Given these conflicting concerns, the Court concluded that it would be inconsistent with the background and purpose of Title VII to prohibit affirmative action in all cases. As I read *Weber*, however, the Court also determined that Congress had balanced these two competing concerns by permitting affirmative action only as a remedial device to eliminate actual or apparent discrimination or the lingering effects of this discrimination. * * *

[Justice O'Connor argued that the constitutional standard for public employer affirmative action plans is consistent with the *Weber* standard for private employer affirmative action plans. In both cases, the Court has required that the employer have a "firm basis" for concluding that action be necessary to remedy past discrimination. In neither case has the Court required an employer to prove or admit that it "actually discriminated against women or minorities." Hence, evidence sufficient for a prima facie case under Title VII would justify an employer's adoption of voluntary affirmative action.]

In applying these principles to this case, it is important to pay close attention to both the affirmative action plan, and the manner in which that plan was applied to the specific promotion decision at issue in this case. * * * At the time the plan was adopted, not one woman was employed in respondents' 238 skilled craft positions, and the plan recognized that women "are not strongly motivated to seek employment in job classifications where they have not been traditionally employed because of the limited opportunities that have existed in the past for them to work in such classifications." Additionally, the plan stated that respondents "recognize[d] that mere prohibition of discriminatory practices is not enough to remedy the effects of past practices and to permit attainment of an equitable representation of minorities, women and handicapped persons," and that "the selection and appointment processes are areas where hidden discrimination frequently occurs." Thus, the respondents had the expectation that the plan "should result in improved personnel practices that will benefit all Agency employees who may have been subjected to discriminatory personnel practices in the past." * * *

[Justice O'Connor rejected Justice Scalia's characterization of the decision as resting upon a single factor, sex. She credited the Director's testimony that he looked at the "whole picture," and chose Joyce for a variety of reasons, one of which was her sex.] While I agree * * * that an affirmative action program that automatically and blindly promotes those marginally qualified candidates falling within a preferred race or gender category, or that can be equated with a permanent plan of "proportionate representation by race and sex," would violate Title VII, I cannot agree that this was such a case. Rather, as the Court demonstrates, Joyce's sex was simply used as a "plus" factor.

In this case, I am also satisfied that the respondent had a firm basis for adopting an affirmative action program. Although the District Court found no discrimination against women in fact, at the time the affirmative action plan was adopted, there were *no* women in its skilled craft positions. Petitioner concedes that women constituted approximately 5% of the local labor pool of skilled craft workers in 1970. Thus, when compared to the percentage of women in the qualified work force, the statistical disparity would have been sufficient for a prima facie Title VII case brought by unsuccessful women job applicants. * * *

[JUSTICE WHITE's dissenting opinion is omitted. Justice White indicated that he would overrule *Weber* (an opinion he joined in 1979), because the Court's reinterpretation of it was " a perversion of Title VII."]

JUSTICE SCALIA, with whom THE CHIEF JUSTICE [REHNQUIST] joins and with whom JUSTICE WHITE joins in Parts I and II, dissenting.

With a clarity which, had it not proven so unavailing, one might well recommend as a model of statutory draftsmanship, Title VII of the Civil Rights Act of 1964 declares:

> "It shall be an unlawful employment practice for an employer —
>
> "(1) to fail or refuse to hire or to discharge any individual, or otherwise to discriminate against any individual with respect to his compensation, terms, conditions, or privileges of employment, because of such individual's race, color, religion, sex, or national origin; or
>
> "(2) to limit, segregate, or classify his employees or applicants for employment in any way which would deprive or tend to deprive any individual of employment opportunities or otherwise adversely affect his status as an employee, because of such individual's race, color, religion, sex, or national origin."

The Court today completes the process of converting this from a guarantee that race or sex will *not* be the basis for employment determinations, to a guarantee that it often *will*. Ever so subtly, without even alluding to the last obstacles preserved by earlier opinions that we now push out of our path, we effectively replace the goal of a discrimination-free society with the quite incompatible goal of proportionate representation by race and by sex in the workplace. * * *

[In Part I of his dissent, Justice Scalia argued that the Court and Justice O'Connor wrongly ignored the District Court's finding of fact that "if the Affirmative Action Coordinator had not intervened, 'the decision as to whom to promote . . . would have been made by [the Road Operations Division Director],' who had recommended that Johnson be appointed to the position"; and the further findings of fact that Johnson was "more qualified for the position" and that Joyce's gender was "the determining factor" in her selection. Justice Scalia maintained in Part II that the Court's opinion basically sanctions affirmative action plans that remedy societal rather than employer discrimination, a holding flatly contrary to *Wygant* and in tension with the Court's holding in *Bakke*. Part III of his dissent follows.]

I have omitted from the foregoing discussion the most obvious respect in which today's decision o'erleaps, without analysis, a barrier that was thought still to be overcome. In *Weber*, this Court held that a private-sector affirmative-action training program that overtly discriminated against white applicants did not violate Title VII. However, although the majority does not advert to the fact, until today the applicability of *Weber* to public employers remained an open question. In *Weber* itself, and in later decisions, this Court has repeatedly emphasized that *Weber* involved only a private employer. This distinction between public and private employers has several possible justifications. *Weber* rested in part on the assertion that the 88th Congress did not wish to intrude too deeply into private employment decisions. Whatever validity that assertion may have with respect to private employers (and I think it negligible), it has none with respect to public employers or to the 92d Congress that brought them within Title VII. Another reason for limiting *Weber* to private employers is that state agencies, unlike private actors, are subject to the Fourteenth Amendment. As noted earlier, it would be strange to construe Title VII to permit discrimination by public actors that the Constitution forbids.

In truth, however, the language of 42 U.S.C. § 2000e–2 draws no distinction between private and public employers, and the only good reason for creating such a distinction would be to limit the damage of *Weber*. It would be better, in my view, to acknowledge that case as fully applicable precedent, and to use the Fourteenth Amendment ramifications — which *Weber* did not address and which are implicated for the first time here — as the occasion for reconsidering and overruling it. It is well to keep in mind just how thoroughly *Weber* rewrote the statute it purported to construe. The language of that statute, as quoted at the outset of this dissent, is unambiguous[.] *Weber* disregarded the text of the statute, invoking instead its " 'spirit,' " and "practical and equitable [consider-ations] only partially perceived, if perceived at all, by the 88th Congress" (Blackmun, J., concurring). It concluded, on the basis of these intangible guides, that Title VII's prohibition of intentional discrimination on the basis of race and sex does not prohibit intentional discrimination on the basis of race and sex, so long as it is "designed to break down old patterns of racial [or sexual] segregation and hierarchy," "does not unnecessarily trammel the interests of the white [or male] employees," "does not require the discharge of white [or male] workers and their replacement with new black [or female] hirees," "does [not] create an absolute bar to the advancement of white [or male] employees," and "is a temporary measure . . . not intended to maintain racial [or sexual] balance, but simply to eliminate a manifest racial [or sexual] imbalance." In effect, *Weber* held that the legality of intentional discrimination by private employers against certain disfavored groups or individuals is to be judged not by Title VII but by a judicially crafted code of conduct, the contours of which are determined by no discernible standard, aside from (as the dissent convincingly demonstrated) the divination of congressional "purposes" belied by the face of the statute and by its legislative history. We have been recasting that self-promulgated code of conduct ever since — and what it has led us to today adds to the reasons for abandoning it.

The majority's response to this criticism of *Weber* [see note 7 of the majority opinion] asserts that, since "Congress has not amended the statute to reject our construction, . . . we . . . may assume that our interpretation was correct." This assumption, which frequently haunts our opinions, should be put to rest. It is based, to begin with, on the patently false premise that the correctness of statutory construction is to be measured by what the current Congress desires, rather than by what the law as enacted meant. To make matters worse, it assays the current Congress' desires *with respect to the particular provision in isolation*, rather than (the way the provision was originally enacted) as part of a total legislative package containing many *quids pro quo*. Whereas the statute as originally proposed may have presented to the enacting Congress a question such as "Should hospitals be required to provide medical care for indigent patients, with federal subsidies to offset the cost?," the question theoretically asked of the later Congress, in order to establish the "correctness" of a judicial interpretation that the statute provides no subsidies, is simply "Should the medical care that hospitals are required to provide for indigent patients be federally subsidized?" Hardly the same question — and many of those legislators who accepted the subsidy provisions in order to gain the votes necessary for enactment of the care requirement would not vote for the subsidy in isolation, now that an unsubsidized care requirement is, thanks to the judicial opinion, safely on the books. But even accepting the flawed premise that the intent of the current Congress, with respect to the provision in isolation, is determinative, one must ignore rudimentary principles of political science to draw any conclusions regarding that intent from the *failure* to enact legislation. The "complicated check on legislation," The Federalist No. 62, p. 378 C. Rossiter ed. 1961), erected by our Constitution creates an inertia that makes it impossible to assert with any degree of assurance that congressional failure to act represents (1) approval of the status quo, as opposed to (2) inability to agree upon how to alter the status quo, (3) unawareness of the status quo, (4) indifference to the status quo, or even (5) political cowardice * * *. I think we should admit that vindication by congressional inaction is a canard.

JUSTICE STEVENS' concurring opinion emphasizes "the underlying public interest in 'stability and orderly development of the law' " that often requires adherence to an erroneous decision. As I have described above, however, today's decision is a demonstration not of stability and order but of the instability and unpredictable expansion which the substitution of judicial improvisation for statutory text has produced. For a number of reasons, *stare decisis* ought not to save *Weber*. First, this Court has applied the doctrine of stare decisis to civil rights statutes less rigorously than to other laws. See *Maine v. Thiboutot*, 448 U.S. 1, 33 (1980) (Powell, J., dissenting); *Monroe v. Pape*, [365 U.S. 167, 221–22 (1961)] (Frankfurter, J., dissenting in part). Second, * * * *Weber* was itself a dramatic departure from the Court's prior Title VII precedents, and can scarcely be said to be "so consistent with the warp and woof of civil rights law as to be beyond question." Third, *Weber* was decided a mere seven years ago, and has provided little guidance to persons seeking to conform their conduct to the law, beyond the proposition that Title VII does not mean what it says. Finally, "even under the most stringent test for the propriety of overruling a statutory decision . . . — 'that it appear beyond doubt . . . that [the decision] misapprehended the meaning of the controlling provision,' " *Weber* should be overruled.

In addition to complying with the commands of the statute, abandoning *Weber* would have the desirable side effect of eliminating the requirement of willing suspension of disbelief that is currently a credential for reading our opinions in the affirmative action field — from *Weber* itself, which demanded belief that the corporate employer adopted the affirmative action program "voluntarily," rather than under practical compulsion from government contracting agencies, to *Bakke*, a Title VI case cited as authority by the majority here, which demanded belief that the University of California took race into account as merely one of the many diversities to which it felt it was education-ally important to expose its medical students, to today's opinion, which — in the face of a plan obviously designed to force promoting officials to prefer candidates from the favored racial and sexual classes, warning them that their "personal commitment" will be determined by how successfully they "attain" certain numerical goals, and in the face of a particular promotion awarded to the less qualified applicant by an official who "did little or nothing" to inquire into sources "critical" to determining the final candidates' relative qualifica-tions other than their sex — in the face of all this, demands belief that we are dealing here with no more than a program that "merely authorizes that consideration be given to affirmative action concerns when evaluating qualified applicants." Any line of decisions rooted so firmly in naivete must be wrong.
* * *

Today's decision does more, however, than merely reaffirm *Weber*, and more than merely extend it to public actors. It is impossible not to be aware that the practical effect of our holding is to accomplish *de facto* what the law — in language even plainer than that ignored in *Weber*, see 42 U.S.C. § 2000e–2(j) — forbids anyone from accomplishing *de jure*: in many contexts it effectively *requires* employers, public as well as private, to engage in intentional discrimination on the basis of race or sex. This Court's prior interpretations of Title VII, especially *Griggs*, subject employers to a potential Title VII suit whenever there is a noticeable imbalance in the representation of minorities or women in the employer's work force. Even the employer who is confident of ultimately prevailing in such a suit must contemplate the expense and adverse publicity of a trial, because the extent of the imbalance, and the "job relatedness" of his selection criteria, are questions of fact to be explored through rebuttal and counterrebuttal of a "prima facie case" consisting of no more than the showing that the employer's selection process "selects those from the protected class at a 'significantly' lesser rate than their counterparts." B. Schlei & P. Grossman, Employment Discrimination Law 91 (2d ed. 1983). If, however, employers are free to discriminate through affirmative action, without fear of "reverse discrimination" suits by their nonminority or male victims, they are offered a threshold defense against Title VII liability premised on numerical disparities. Thus, after today's decision the *failure* to engage in reverse discrimination is economic folly, and arguably a breach of duty to shareholders or taxpayers, wherever the cost of anticipated Title VII litigation exceeds the cost of hiring less capable (though still minimally capable) workers. (This situation is more likely to obtain, of course, with respect to the least skilled jobs — perversely creating an incentive to discriminate against precisely those members of the nonfavored groups *least* likely to have profited from societal discrimination in the past.) It is predictable, moreover, that this incentive will be greatly magnified by economic pressures brought to bear by government contracting agencies upon employers who refuse to discriminate in the fashion we have now approved. A statute designed to establish a color-blind and gender-blind workplace has thus been converted into a powerful engine of racism and sexism, not merely *permitting* intentional race- and sex-based discrimination, but often making it, through operation of the legal system, practically compelled.

It is unlikely that today's result will be displeasing to politically elected officials, to whom it provides the means of quickly accommodating the demands of organized groups to achieve concrete, numerical improvement in the economic status of particular constituencies. Nor will it displease the world of corporate and governmental employers (many of whom have filed briefs as amici in the present case, all on the side of Santa Clara) for whom the cost of hiring less qualified workers is often substantially less — and infinitely more predictable — than the cost of litigating Title VII cases and of seeking to convince federal agencies by nonnumerical means that no discrimination exists. In fact, the only losers in the process are the Johnsons of the country, for whom Title VII has been not merely repealed but actually inverted. The irony is that these individuals — predominantly unknown, unaffluent, unorganized — suffer this injustice at the hands of a Court fond of thinking itself the champion of the politically impotent. I dissent.

NOTES ON *JOHNSON*

1. *What Happened to* Weber? The debate in *Weber* is hardly recognizable in *Johnson*, not only because there are two new players (O'Connor and Scalia), but also because the old players changed their positions. Most dramatic were Justice White's switch from part of the *Weber* majority to a vote for overruling the decision, Justice Stevens' switch from dissent from *Weber* (a case where he did not actually vote) to a more aggressive approval of affirmative action than Justice Brennan's opinion, and Justice Powell's unexplained decision to join the Brennan opinion (he, too, had not voted in *Weber*, but his opinion in *Regents of the University of California v. Bakke*, 438 U.S. 265 (1978), suggests a sympathy with the O'Connor position, and an internal memorandum written before his recusal in *Weber* states that he was on the fence in that case).

Almost as dramatic is Justice Brennan's new rationale for affirmative action. Recall that in *Weber* affirmative action was defended on the ground that it contributed to Title VII's main purpose, to get jobs for racial minorities (all of the evidence cited by Justice Brennan adverted to helping African Americans). In *Johnson*, affirmative action is extended to help women — but without any evidence from the legislative history that this was a primary purpose of the statute. Recall the humble origins of Title VII's prohibition of sex discrimination, namely, Judge Smith's killer amendment. Note, too, that the dissenting Justices (including Chief Justice Rehnquist) in *Johnson* pretty much ignore the legislative history of the 1964 statute, as well, although Justice Scalia's dissent incorporated Rehnquist's lengthy *Weber* dissent by reference.

2. *Congressional Acquiescence?* Footnote 7 of the Court's opinion is a classically dynamic move: Whatever the original validity of *Weber* as implementing the intent or purpose of the 1964 Congress, it should not be reconsidered because Congress in the 1980s approved of the decision. Justice Scalia considered this argument a "canard" (and study the perceptive political analysis he provides to support his charge), but the end of his opinion suggests that Justice Brennan may be right: The powerful political forces inside the Beltway — labor unions, civil rights groups, and the Chamber of Commerce — were all satisfied with *Weber*, because it allowed them to advance their own goals (such as avoiding *Griggs* lawsuits) rather costlessly, at least to them. The cost-payers were the diffuse group of blue-collar males like Paul Johnson and Brian Weber, unorganized and ill-represented on Capitol Hill. This point seems accurate, and it suggests that Congress in the 1980s was also happy with *Weber*. (By the way, and contrary to the Court's footnote 7, hearings were held in 1981 on a constitutional amendment introduced in Congress to override *Weber* and other affirmative action cases; none of the political powerhouses showed up, demonstrating the absence of interest among the powerful lobbies to override *Weber*.)

Justice Scalia's main point is a normative one, of course. He considers it objectionable for the Court to pay any attention to what goes on, or doesn't go on, in Congress short of formal bicameral approval mandated by Article I, § 7. And he also seems to have sympathy for the downtrodden, politically powerless, blue-collar white men who pay the price for affirmative action. Is this an appropriate factor to consider in statutory interpretation? Should statutory ambiguities be resolved *against* the more politically potent interests?

3. *The Court/Congress/President Civil Rights Game.* Recall that the blue-collar men whom Justice Scalia claims are politically "impotent" elected President Reagan twice, based upon a platform hostile to affirmative action — and Reagan delivered on his platform by appointing Rehnquist Chief Justice, elevating Scalia to the Court, and trying to elevate Judge Robert Bork to the Court (after *Johnson*). Although Bork was defeated, Reagan ended up appointing someone nearly as conservative, Judge Anthony Kennedy of the Ninth Circuit. Since Kennedy replaced Justice Powell — Brennan's critical fifth vote in *Johnson* — the Court in 1988 was poised to shift civil rights policy rightward: Four Justices (Rehnquist, White, Scalia, Kennedy) were openly opposed to affirmative action, and one (O'Connor) was skeptical. The Court had a great deal of room to maneuver, since a rightward shift in policy could be protected against congressional override by a presidential veto (by Reagan or his successor, George H.W. Bush). Consider the following discussion.

C. *GRIGGS* REVISITED: COURT VERSUS CONGRESS

1. Civil Rights in the Supreme Court's 1988 Term

The 1988 Term of the Court included several employment discrimination cases that bitterly divided the Court. For the *Weber* issue, the most important case was *Wards Cove Packing Co. v. Atonio*, 490 U.S. 642 (1989), which evaluated a Title VII claim against the operation of two salmon canneries in Alaska. Unskilled positions at the canneries were staffed almost entirely by

Pacific Americans (Filipinos and Native Alaskans) hired on the site of the canneries, while about half of the skilled office positions were filled by whites hired in the firm's Oregon and Washington offices, usually through word-of-mouth (and sometimes through nepotism). A cannery employee could not be promoted to an office position. The cannery jobs paid a lot less than the office jobs. Cannery employees ate and lived in separate areas from the office employees.

This arrangement may be viewed as a classic "plantation" set-up, and plaintiff cannery employees sued Wards Cove for discriminating against them in making its office hires. The Ninth Circuit (en banc) held that plaintiffs made out a prima facie case of disparate impact employment discrimination under *Griggs*. The Supreme Court reversed. The majority opinion was written by Justice White and was joined by Chief Justice Rehnquist and Justices O'Connor, Scalia, and Kennedy.

The Supreme Court majority held that the lower court's approach would impose excessive burdens on employers to get good numbers, and would encourage such employers to adopt quotas — which the Court found inconsistent with § 703(j). Thus, the Court held that a prima facie case of disparate impact discrimination is not made out unless the plaintiffs demonstrate that the bad numbers are out of line with the number of "qualified" minority applicants for the positions in question. "As long as there are no barriers or practices deterring qualified nonwhites from applying for noncannery positions, if the percentage of selected applicants who are nonwhite is not significantly less than the percentage of qualified applicants who are nonwhite, the employer's selection mechanism probably does not operate with a disparate impact upon minorities." The Court disapproved the Ninth Circuit's focus on the substantial disparity between the overwhelming minority composition of cannery workers and their trivial representation among office workers. To make out a prima facie case, the plaintiffs would have to show that the poor representation among office workers is disproportionate to the percentage of qualified minority applicants for those positions.

The Court remanded the case to the lower courts to reevaluate the disparate impact claim, but (in what may or may not be dicta) it also set forth some guidelines for the lower courts to follow: Plaintiffs' burden of proof in disparate impact cases includes the burden of identifying to the factfinder not only a statistical disparity (see the above discussion), but also the specific employment practice that caused the disparity. The *Wards Cove* plaintiffs argued that a congeries of practices contributed to the bad numbers — nepotism in hiring for office positions, the firm's refusal to advertise such positions locally, and the firm's failure to consider cannery employees for promotions. The Court admonished the plaintiffs "to demonstrate that the disparity they complain of is the result of one or more of the employment practices that they are attacking here, specifically showing that each challenged practice has a significantly disparate impact on employment opportunities for whites and nonwhites." In response to plaintiffs' argument that such a burden is unfair, the Court noted that "liberal civil discovery rules give plaintiffs access to employers' records in an effort to document their claims," and that most employers are required to keep impact-related employment records as a matter of federal law.

If plaintiffs were to succeed in establishing a prima facie disparate impact case, the Court further stated (again in what may be dicta) that the employer would have the burden of producing some evidence that the challenged practices were justified business practices. The Court carefully noted that the burden of persuasion would remain with the plaintiffs. Hence, plaintiffs would ultimately have to persuade the finder of fact (1) that there was a statistical disparity, (2) that the disparity can be linked to specific employment practices, and (3) that those practices do not have a substantial business justification.

Four Justices (Brennan, Marshall, Blackmun, and Stevens) dissented from the Court's opinion. The dissenting Justices argued that the Court's opinion, especially its dicta about plaintiffs' burden of persuasion on the business justification defense, represented a striking departure from existing law and a partial renunciation of *Griggs*.

At about the same time it was deciding *Wards Cove* (June 5, 1989), the Supreme Court handed down five other decisions that gave a narrow construction to Title VII and related statutes. In *Patterson v. McLean Credit Union*, 491 U.S. 164 (June 15, 1989), the Court (by the same five-to-four majority as in *Wards Cove*) interpreted 42 U.S.C. § 1981, protecting African Americans against discrimination in the making and enforcing of contracts, to be inapplicable to job discrimination during the course of their contracts (e.g., during the course of their employment under an employment contract). In *Martin v. Wilks*, 490 U.S. 755 (June 12, 1989), the same five-to-four majority held that white employees who were not parties to original job discrimination litigation could challenge court-approved consent decrees providing for affirmative action.

In *Lorance v. AT&T Technologies*, 490 U.S. 900 (June 12, 1989), the Court in a five-to-three vote held that Title VII's statute of limitations for challenging seniority plans begins to run when the plan is adopted, not when the plan is applied to specific individuals. In *Independent Federation of Flight Attendants v. Zipes*, 491 U.S. 754 (June 22, 1989), a five-to-two Court held that Title VII does not provide for the statutory award of counsel fees against intervening defendants unless the intervenors' action is frivolous. And in *Price Waterhouse v. Hopkins*, 490 U.S. 228 (May 1, 1989), a Court divided on other issues unanimously held that employment decisions motivated in part by prejudice do not violate Title VII if the employer can show after the fact that the same decision would have been made irrespective of the intentional discrimination.

These decisions created a number of practical difficulties for litigants challenging discriminatory employment practices. More generally, they signaled a determination by five Justices to close off the expansion of older civil rights statutes to help modern litigants (*Patterson*), to provide more procedural advantages for defendants in Title VII cases (*Wards Cove, Price Waterhouse, Lorance*), and, most important, to discourage employers from adopting affirmative action programs (*Wards Cove, Martin*). As to the last item, the Court earlier in the Term had struck down the Richmond municipal program for setting aside business for minority-owned enterprises in *City of Richmond v. J.A. Croson Co.*, 488 U.S. 469 (1989).

2. *The Civil Rights Act of 1991*

Coming within a few months of one another, these six statutory job-discrimination decisions produced a collective shock to the nation's civil rights community, which immediately sought to override them legislatively. On February 27, 1990, Senator Kennedy (D–Mass.) and 33 co-sponsors introduced S. 2104, the Civil Rights Act of 1990. A similar House bill, H.R. 4000, was introduced by Representative Augustus Hawkins (D–Cal.) at the same time. The bill's purpose was "to respond to the Supreme Court's recent decisions by restoring the civil rights protections that were dramatically limited by those decisions." The substantive sections of the bill then amended Title VII and § 1981 to override one or more of the offending Supreme Court cases. With complex transition rules, the bill would have overridden all six of the 1989 Supreme Court decisions, plus three earlier ones as well. The sponsors of the bill roundly condemned the Supreme Court's performance. "I believe the Supreme Court's recent rulings represent an effort to renege on history," said Senator Jeffords (R–Vt.). 136 Cong. Rec. S1022 (daily ed. Feb. 7, 1990).

The Bush Administration responded by agreeing that *Patterson* and *Lorance* should be overridden, but opposed the overrides of *Wards Cove* and *Martin v. Wilks* on the ground that the overrides as drafted encouraged employers to adopt racial quotas, in violation of § 703(j). See Letter from Attorney General Richard Thornburgh to Senator Kennedy, Apr. 3, 1990. The sponsors apparently believed (correctly) that they did not have enough votes in either chamber to override a presidential veto, and the result was a series of negotiations to work out a compromise bill. Between June and October 1990, rotating groups representing liberal Democrats, moderate Republicans, and the Administration engaged in such negotiations — which continued after the Senate passed a revised bill on July 18 (by a vote of 65–34) and the House passed its own bill on August 3 (by a vote of 272–154), and after the submission of conference reports on September 26 and October 12.

The final conference bill made a number of changes in the controversial *Wards Cove* provision in a final effort to appease the White House and/or to obtain Republican support for the bill. Specifically, the bill included a more liberal definition of the business necessity defense in disparate impact cases, required that plaintiffs prove which employer practices caused the disparate impact alleged, confirmed that bad numbers alone do not violate Title VII, and reiterated that Title VII does not require quotas. See 136 Cong. Rec. S15,327 (daily ed. Oct. 16, 1990) (statement of Sen. Kennedy). Nonetheless, the President vetoed the bill, *id*. at S16,562–63 (daily ed. Oct. 24, 1990), and the Senate failed to override the veto by one vote (66–34). *Id*. at S16,589.

The *Wards Cove* issue was a minor theme of the 1990 off-year elections, which yielded a net gain to the Democrats of one Senator (albeit by defeating a Republican who had voted to override the veto) and about a dozen House Members. On January 3, 1991, the bill that had come so close in 1990 was reintroduced as the Civil Rights and Women's Equity in Employment Act of

1991, H.R. 1, 102d Cong., 1st Sess. (1991). Hearings were held before the Education & Labor and the Judiciary Committees in February and March 1991, the Committees turned back Republican amendments and reported a very liberal bill, and the House passed H.R. 1 on June 5, 1991. See 137 Cong. Rec. H3924–25 (daily ed. June 5, 1991). It was a bill certain to be vetoed.

Again, once the bill reached the Senate floor, ongoing negotiations among liberal Democrats, moderate Republicans, and the Administration intensified. Negotiations yielded a new bipartisan compromise bill, the Danforth-Kennedy substitute, S. 1745, which significantly rewrote the House bill, just as the Senate had done in 1990. On the *Wards Cove* issues, S. 1745 simplified the burdens of proof in disparate impact cases (by adding new § 703(k)(1)(A)), generally required that plaintiffs link specific employer practices to their claimed disparate impact (see new § 703(k)(1)(B)), and abandoned prior efforts to define "business necessity" and left the definition to pre-*Wards Cove* caselaw (see § 3(2) of the Act).

Notwithstanding the freshly revised S. 1745, there was still substantial doubt whether there would be civil rights legislation in 1991, because the Administration remained publicly unpersuaded that it was not a "quota bill" and because it was not clear how many Republicans would support the bill (eleven GOP Senators voted to override the 1990 veto). According to some Inside-the-Beltway accounts, the key event was a meeting between President Bush and several GOP Senators in mid-October, in which the Senators suggested (perhaps with some emotion) that they wanted to vote for a civil rights bill and were inclined to vote to override a veto; the meeting included several GOP Senators who had voted to sustain the 1990 veto. After the meeting, the President dramatically changed his mind and announced he would sign the legislation, after a few more changes.

The final language of the bill was hammered out during the week of October 21. During the Senate's debate upon the compromise bill, between October 25 and 30, numerous amendments were accepted and rejected and — perhaps not surprisingly given the tools of interpretation used by the courts — a flurry of "interpretive statements" or "memoranda" were inserted into the Congressional Record to "explain" what the bill now "meant." Senator Danforth (R–Mo.), a key architect of the compromise, offered his own interpretive memorandum, as well as the following wisdom, in response to attempts to amend the bill to forbid courts from using legislative history to interpret provisions of the 1991 Act (137 Cong. Rec. S15325 (daily ed. Oct. 29, 1991)):

> It is very common for Members of the Senate to try to affect the way in which a court will interpret a statute by putting things into the Congressional Record. * * * [A] court would be well advised to take with a large grain of salt floor debate and statements placed into the Congressional Record which purport to create an interpretation for the legislation that is before us. * * * [A]ny judge who tries to make legislative history out of the free-for-all that takes place on the floor of the Senate is on very dangerous grounds.

The Senate passed S. 1745 on October 30, and the House passed it on November 7, 1991, in both cases by overwhelming margins (reflecting the new bipartisan consensus). The President signed the bill on November 21, 1991, as the "Civil Rights Act of 1991," Pub. L. No. 102–166, 105 Stat. 1071. See 1991 U.S. Code Cong. & Admin. News 768, for the President's signing statement.

3. A Transitional Note

This chapter introduced you to the legislative lawmaking process, warts and all. The empirical generalizations and models of the political process presented in this chapter are worth considering as you study the rest of this book. For example, Chapters 6 and 7 consider public law theory — the jurisprudence of the common law and constitutional law, which are both overtly made by judges, and the jurisprudence of statutory interpretation, where the judge's discretion in construing a statute requires theoretical underpinnings as well. The chapter you have just completed is important for your consideration of public law theory because that theory cannot be divorced from some conception of the legislative process.

For example, someone who empirically accepts the pluralist conception of the political process has several obvious choices about public law theory available. One would be to accept normatively what is assumed to happen empirically. Under this approach, there should be little outside (judicial) interference with the legislative process — let the market operate freely (even if squalidly). In contrast, theorists who accept the pluralist conception empirically but not normatively would probably adopt a different, interventionist, judicial strategy. They might seek to create constitutional rights protecting individuals from certain legislative intrusions and might attempt to break down barriers preventing politically powerless groups from bargaining effectively in the legislative arena. To some of these theorists, techniques of forcing legislative reconsideration of an issue or otherwise promoting legislative deliberation are of no utility, since the mechanistic process of legislation allows no thoughtful, independent deliberation to occur. A third approach emphasizes the importance of administrative procedures and argues that they work to ameliorate negative consequences of interest group behavior.[i] Administrative process, one focus of Chapter 9, may be the most pervasive framework affecting policy outcomes because agencies implement the laws enacted by Congress and many administrative decisions are never challenged in court.

Alternatively, those who believe that legislators can operate somewhat autonomously from private political interests have a different set of theoretical possibilities available. For those who find a common weal that is different from the equilibrium of interest group power either incapable of formulation or a tyrannical imposition upon those with dissenting views unless it is a result of some democratic process, the proper response might include techniques strengthening the electoral connection between average voters and their agents, the legislators. Those who have greater faith in the capacity of legislators to formulate and promote a beneficent public interest might urge restructuring of the processes of representation to encourage legislative insulation from

---

i. See, e.g., Steven Croley, *Public Interested Regulation*, 28 Fla. St. U. L. Rev. 7 (2000).

powerful private interests. Of course, it is sometimes difficult to determine which mechanisms facilitate which visions of the legislative process.

As you proceed through the rest of this book, ask yourself the following questions: (1) What assumptions about the political process are animating the judicial behavior under consideration? Are those conceptions realistic? How would public law theory change, in a given situation, if the judicial understanding of the political process were altered? Should judges modify public law theory in light of what social scientists or public choice theorists suggest about the nature of the political process? (2) What role, if any, should be played by the understandings of the constitutional framers? Should Madisonian theory be rejected in light of modern circumstances? Or should the courts attempt to develop public law theory that would encourage the representative process to act more in accord with Madison's vision? (3) In the modern world of interest group politics, is the legislature a truly legitimate entity to make important public policies largely unchallenged by judicial review? Conversely, in the modern world in which the meaning of the federal Constitution has strayed far from the original intent of the framers, does a court have a legitimate basis for interfering with legislative outcomes? Does democracy simply mean that voters have periodic opportunities to replace representatives, or should it mean more than that — and if so, do courts have any role in promoting enhanced democracy?

Modern American public law is the result of a complex, contentious lawmaking partnership among legislatures, administrative agencies, the courts, and the citizenry. The remainder of this book continues the inquiry about how this law is made.

Chapter 2

REPRESENTATIONAL STRUCTURES

Public policy, even in a modern democracy, is not created directly by the people, but by their representatives. Hanna Pitkin, in *The Concept of Representation* (1967), analyzes ways in which political theorists have conceptualized the ideal role of the representative. First, a representative may be viewed as *descriptive* of the larger group, a microcosm of the collective. John Adams, for example, argued that a representative legislature "should be an exact portrait, in miniature, of the people at large, as it should think, feel, reason and act like them." Letter to John Penn, in 4 *The Works of John Adams* 205 (1850). Descriptive theory retains a robust constituency today, particularly in thinking about the representation of minority groups.

Second, the representative may be viewed as the *agent* of the people who selected her. In most extreme form, the representative's every action must be explicitly authorized by her constituency, but a moderate position would urge the representative to act as she thinks her constituents would have her act if the constituency were in her position and knew all that she knows. Pluralist theories of democracy today tend to rely on a moderate version of such an agency theory.

Third, the representative may be viewed as the *trustee* of the interests of her constituents. She should exercise her own conscientious judgment on issues. As Madison put it, the role of representatives as trustees of the public good is to "refine and enlarge the public views" through the exercise of their wisdom which "may best discern the true interests of their country, and whose patriotism and love of justice will be least likely to sacrifice it to temporary or partial considerations." *The Federalist* #10. Republican theories of government usually envision legislators as trustees charged with deliberating among themselves for the common good.[a]

These three views of the representative are not mutually exclusive. Perhaps the ideal representative democracy would be one in which the legislative representatives broadly resemble the entire citizenry and thus naturally reflect the informed preferences of the majority, which happen to coincide with the

---

a. See *Symposium: The Republican Civic Tradition*, 97 Yale L.J. 1493–1723 (1988).

best course of action for the society as a whole. In practice, however, these visions of representation lead in different directions. In connection with the choice of representatives, descriptive theory would favor *proportionate representation*, in which each important segment of society is represented in the legislature; agency theory would favor frequent elections, so that the representative's votes could be periodically reviewed by her constituents; trusteeship theory would tend to eschew frequent elections and strict proportionality in favor of a system that would choose wise people and (perhaps) keep them in office for long periods of time. As we will see in our study of proposals to impose limitations on the terms of legislators, sometimes the various theories all lead adherents in one direction, albeit for different reasons. Some supporters of term limits hope they will allow principals-voters more ability to control agents-legislators; others more sympathetic to the republican vision argue that eliminating the possibility of reelection will free lawmakers to act more independently of the momentary passions of their constituents.[b]

Section 1 of this chapter explores the constitutional structures that shape the way we choose our legislative representatives. We outline the electoral structures laid out in the Constitution and then explore the further limitations that the Supreme Court has drawn from the constitutional norm of equal participation (a norm found in the Equal Protection Clause, the First Amendment, the Fifteenth Amendment, and elsewhere in the Constitution). Equality values include the principle of one person, one vote; a rule against racial vote dilution; and jurisprudence attempting to address *gerrymandering*, the political manipulation of district lines to produce a particular electoral result. As you read the materials, consider which theories influenced the specific constitutional choices and whether the choices are coherent or sensible ones.

In Section 2, we introduce you to several ways in which the eligibility to serve as a representative is restricted. The first vehicle for discussion is the famous case involving Representative Adam Clayton Powell, whom the people kept reelecting notwithstanding criminal and contempt charges against him. The Supreme Court in *Powell v. McCormack*, 385 U.S. 486 (1969), struck down the decision of the House of Representatives to exclude Powell. The Court's reasoning disallowing congressionally imposed qualifications in addition to those set forth in the Constitution served as the foundation for the Court's subsequent decision striking down state-imposed term limitations on federal lawmakers. We will discuss term limitations, which are a common feature of state legislatures and apply to most governors and to the President. Finally, we will focus on laws regulating candidate access to ballots because these laws significantly limit the choices voters can make on Election Day. Most ballot access laws have been adopted by incumbent legislators who are members of the two major political parties and who have tremendous incentives to entrench themselves in office by erecting formidable hurdles in the path of minor party candidates and challengers. However, the courts have

---

b. See Robert Kurfirst, *Term-Limit Logic: Paradigms and Paradoxes*, 29 Polity 119 (1996) (identifying four different philosophical positions that can lead to the support of term limits).

traditionally applied less rigorous scrutiny to ballot access regulations than to other rules restricting eligibility.

Section 3 examines problems of campaign financing. Money has always been the lifeblood of elections, and how a polity regulates the use of money speaks loudly about its political self-image. Is money in politics "corrupting," as republicans tend to think, or is it healthy, as pluralists often argue? Whatever the political theory of campaign finance, the First Amendment may be an impediment to extensive regulation of campaign finance, and this last part of the chapter introduces the debate within the First Amendment tradition.

SECTION 1. ELECTORAL STRUCTURES AND EQUALITY VALUES

The Constitution, in Article I, specifies the broad outlines of our national representative legislature, the Congress. "All legislative Powers herein granted shall be vested in a Congress of the United States, which shall consist of a Senate and House of Representatives." U.S. Const. art. I, § 1. From the outset, House members have been elected for two-year terms and apportioned among the states according to their population. *Id.* § 2, cl. 1 & 3. In 1911 Congress fixed House membership at 435. 37 Stat. 13, 14. The Constitution originally stated that each state would be represented by two senators elected to six-year terms by the state legislature. U.S. Const. art. I, § 3, cl. 1. The Seventeenth Amendment, ratified in 1913, now provides that senators are directly elected.

The Constitution also specifies the framework for congressional elections. "The Times, Places and Manner of holding Elections for Senators and Representatives, shall be prescribed in each State by the Legislature thereof; but the Congress may at any time by Law make or alter such Regulations." *Id.* art. I, § 4, cl. 1. Congress has exercised this authority in 2 U.S.C. §§ 1–9, providing, *inter alia*, for the date of each regular election; the number, apportionment, and reapportionment of representatives; and the manner in which to fill a vacancy. Persons qualified to vote for representatives "of the most numerous Branch of the State Legislature" are likewise qualified to vote for Representatives and Senators. U.S. Const. art. I, § 2, cl. 1; *id.* amend. XVII, cl. 1. Pursuant to the authority of "[e]ach House [to] * * * Judge * * * the Elections, Returns and Qualifications of its own Members," *id.* art. I, § 5, cl. 1, Congress has enacted a rather thorough code of provisions governing the resolution of contested elections. 2 U.S.C. §§ 381–396.

The "legislative power" of Congress is diffused through an intricate committee apparatus. Congress has standing committees, which are permanent entities provided for in the rules of each House, and select committees, which are created *ad hoc* to take on particular tasks. In addition, joint committees, which are composed of Members of each House, can be created by statute or resolution. Much committee business is handled through the numerous subcommittees. Indeed, by 2000 there were 140 subcommittees (compared to 36 standing committees). This figure is 25 percent lower than the number of subcommittees in the 1980's because the institutional reforms undertaken by the House Republicans in the 104th Congress included a reduction in the number of subcommittees.[a]

Committee assignments are made on a partisan basis, with either a committee of a party's membership in a House or the full membership of the party in that House serving as the final authority. In practice, seniority has been the primary criterion used to select the chair and ranking member of each committee or subcommittee. The seniority system is controversial largely because seniority does not ensure competence or the responsible exercise of power in a position that operates as a vetogate in the legislative process. In recent Congresses, particularly those characterized by significant turnover and thus relatively more junior members, the seniority norm has eroded slightly, and the selection of chairs has turned more on partisan concerns. Yet, because it both mediates a process of selection that might otherwise be anarchic and brings to the forefront the most experienced legislators, the seniority system is unlikely to wither away absent a shock to the legislative system such as the imposition of term limits.

Every state has a bicameral legislative system with competing political parties except Nebraska, which has a nonpartisan unicameral legislature. The size of the state legislatures varies greatly.[b] For example, the lower house of the New Hampshire legislature contains 400 members, almost seventeen times the number of its upper house. A member of the New Hampshire lower house represents around 3,000 people. In contrast, each of California's eighty members of its lower house represents a constituency about one-hundred-forty times larger. Alaska has the smallest lower house, with forty members. The number of members of the upper houses varies substantially as well, with Minnesota the largest with sixty-seven and Alaska the smallest with twenty.[c]

In most states, members of the upper house serve four-year terms; in the other states such officeholders serve two-year terms. Lower-house members generally serve two-year terms. As of 2007, 15 states limit the number of terms their state legislators can serve (see § 2B of this chapter). Most states have annual rather than biennial legislative sessions, but in a majority of states the length of the session is limited, often to no more than 60 or 90 calendar days. Only about one-half of the state legislatures are empowered to call special sessions. The committee structure and other features of state legislatures vary according to the type of careers that lawmakers pursue. In some states (e.g., New York), the norm of *professionalism* is quite strong, lawmakers

---

a. See William Keefe & Morris Ogul, *The American Legislative Process: Congress and the States* 204 (10th ed. 2001).

b. See National Conference of State Legislatures, *Constituents Per State Legislative District*, http://www.ncsl.org/programs/legismgt/elect/cnstprst.htm.

c. The size of the legislature is important for many reasons. It affects, among other things, the costs and difficulty of campaigning for office, the visibility and prestige of members, the difficulty of managing and administering the work of the legislature, and perhaps the degree to which a constituent feels "represented." Yet the great disparity in the legislative size among the states indicates that policymakers have given little attention to the relationship between state population and land area on the one hand and legislative size on the other.

serve for a long time, and the legislatures rely on committee structures similar to the federal Congress and organized according to the norm of seniority along with partisan considerations. Other state legislatures (e.g., California) tend to serve as *springboards* to other political careers, so that lawmakers are professional politicians but move from job to job fairly rapidly. Finally, even before the imposition of term limits, other state legislatures (e.g., Oklahoma) were characterized as *dead-end* because members served for only a few terms and then returned to their lives outside the political realm.[d] As nearly half the states, including those with professional legislatures, have felt the effect of term limits, their legislative organization and characteristics have changed, sometimes significantly. We will discuss these changes in greater detail in § 2 of this chapter.

Local government structure varies widely. Common forms include (1) the mayor-council format, in which the council and mayor share legislative and administrative functions; (2) the mayor-council format, in which the mayor's powers are predominant; and (3) the commission format, in which the legislative, executive, and administrative functions are performed by elected commissioners.[e] Many local governments are nonpartisan.

Each level of government has great freedom in determining whom or what group of people a member of the legislature represents, limited by historical curiosities found in national and state constitutions. In this century, however, the composition of state and local legislatures, as well as of Congress, has been subject to several kinds of constitutional challenges, and the so-called "right to vote" actually encompasses several different kinds of rights.[f]

Most basically, there is a right of *participation*. Outright exclusion from the vote — through such devices as the white primary, the poll tax, and durational residency requirements — is subject to searching judicial review.[g] Because the point of voting is to combine individual desires into a collective choice, however, the right to participate, standing alone, is insufficient. Therefore, a second conception of the right to vote involves a right to a fair rule of *aggregation*. At its simplest level, this right encompasses the notion that legislators should represent roughly an equal number of persons, the so-called "one person, one vote" requirement. More complex controversies involving aggregation include how to draw districts of equal population so that distinctive communities of interest are not split among different districts or otherwise have their political power submerged. As this chapter will explain,

---

d. See Peverill Squire, *Member Career Opportunities and the Internal Organization of Legislatures*, 50 J. of Pol. 726 (1988).

e. See generally Clayton Gillette & Lynn Baker, *Local Government Law* 46–52 (3d ed. 2004).

f. See Pamela Karlan, *The Rights to Vote: Some Pessimism About Formalism*, 71 Tex. L. Rev. 1705 (1993).

g. See, e.g., *Terry v. Adams*, 345 U.S. 461 (1953) (invalidating white primary as violating the Fifteenth Amendment); *Harper v. Virginia State Bd. of Elections*, 383 U.S. 663 (1966) (invalidating poll tax as violating Equal Protection Clause); *Dunn v. Blumstein*, 405 U.S. 330 (1972) (invalidating one-year residency requirement under Equal Protection Clause).

this problem of the *vote dilution* of distinctive communities — whether they are racial minorities or the minority political party — has generated complex litigation and confusing judicial responses.[h]

Constitutional constraints on aggregation frequently attack the practice of *gerrymandering*, the drawing of electoral district lines for political advantage. Consider the following gerrymandering techniques. *Cracking* occurs when a geographically concentrated political or racial group that is large enough to constitute a dominant force in a district is broken up by district lines and dispersed throughout two or more districts. *Stacking* occurs when a large political or racial group is not split up, but rather is combined with and dominated by a larger opposition group. A classic example of stacking in the context of racial politics would be creating one large multimember district for the state legislature by combining two majority-black counties with four majority-white counties. *Packing* occurs when the majority finds itself unable completely to deny representation to a minority, but minimizes minority representation by concentrating the minority into as few districts as possible — for example, creating one 97% black district rather than two 60% black districts.

Although political or racial gerrymandering would usually be easier to accomplish if population equality among districts were not required, a requirement of population equality will not prevent any of these tactics. Indeed, the use of multimember districting can sometimes be the "perfect gerrymander" because at-large elections involve perfect population equality and compactness of districts, but (as will be explained in Part B) can result in dilution of minority electoral influence. As you review the discussion that follows, consider whether the constitutional and statutory regulations of gerrymandering serve a coherent theory of representation, or perhaps policies associated with several theories.

A. ONE PERSON, ONE VOTE: FORMAL EQUALITY IN REPRESENTATION

Numerical equality in representation (one person, one vote) now seems fundamental to our polity. For most of this country's history this was only an aspirational goal, however, because the issue was considered "nonjusticiable," an essentially "political question" unsuited to federal adjudication under Article III of the Constitution, which limits the federal judicial power to resolving "cases" and "controversies." The federal judicial reluctance to intervene in state and local legislative apportionment stemmed in part from concerns about federalism, from the notion that other government institutions

---

h. Professor Karlan also posits a third conception of voting rights, as an integral part of *governance*. In this sense, voting involves not simply selecting the legislator of your choice, but being satisfied with the overall composition and operation of the legislative body in question. See Karlan, *supra*, at 1716–19. Her thesis is that the Supreme Court's decisions on voting rights are doctrinally incoherent because they fail to differentiate among the three interconnected features of a "right to vote."

were better suited to deal with essentially political issues, from the sense that no judicially administrable standard could be created to decide when there was too much population deviation across legislative districts, and from the concern that federal injunctions to remedy the problem would be too difficult to define and administer and would embroil the federal courts too much in local and state politics. The most famous catchphrase capturing these concerns is found in Justice Frankfurter's plurality opinion in *Colegrove v. Green*, 328 U.S. 549 (1946): "Courts ought not to enter this political thicket." But when demographic shifts after World War II exacerbated population disparities in local, state, and federal electoral districts, with booming urban and suburban areas greatly underrepresented and rural areas overrepresented, the Supreme Court changed direction (over the strident objection of Justice Frankfurter). *Baker v. Carr*, 369 U.S. 186 (1962), reversed the longstanding judicial avoidance and held that equal protection attacks on legislative apportionment are justiciable.

Baker is now the leading case setting out the political question doctrine. Justice Brennan's opinion for the Court reasoned that the doctrine stems from the separation of powers within the national government. The Court's survey of its precedents concluded that decisions finding nonjusticiable political questions did so for one or more of the following reasons:

> a textually demonstrable constitutional commitment of the issue to a coordinate political department; or a lack of judicially discoverable and manageable standards for resolving it; or the impossibility of deciding without an initial policy determination of a kind clearly for nonjudicial discretion; or the impossibility of a court's undertaking independent resolution without expressing lack of the respect due coordinate branches of government; or an unusual need for unquestioning adherence to a political decision already made; or the potentiality of embarrassment from multifarious pronouncements by various departments on one question.

Since *Baker*, the Court has developed equal representation rules for the U.S. House of Representatives,[i] the state legislatures, and local governments.

---

i. The national Senate flouts rules of formal equality, of course. The state with the smallest population has as many senators as the one with the largest population. And this inequality is particularly entrenched in the Constitution; Article V provides that no state can be deprived of its "equal Suffrage in the Senate" without its consent. In part this is the result of the historic compromise at the Convention of 1787: the small states, fearing domination by the large states, were given the Senate to make them more secure. See Gordon Wood, *The Creation of the American Republic, 1776–1787* (1969). In part, too, the Senate, with its six-year terms and larger geographic units of representation, reflects the Framers' desire that one body be insulated somewhat from "democratic" fluctuations, thus protecting "property" interests against "numbers." Under what theory of representation can this be justified? It has been suggested that the structure of the Senate systematically redistributes wealth from large population states to small ones and dilutes the influence of racial minorities in Congress. See Lynn Baker & Samuel Dinkin, *The Senate: An Institution Whose Time Has Gone?*, 13 J.L. & Pol. 21 (1997); Francis Lee & Bruce Oppenheimer, *Sizing Up the Senate: The Unequal Consequence of Equal Representation* (1999). For overviews of objections to Senate structure, see Scott Bowman, *Wild Political Dreaming: Constitutional Reformation of the United States Senate*, 72 Fordham L. Rev. 1017 (2004) (student note); Misha Tseytlin, *The United States Senate and the Problem of Equal State Suffrage*, 94 Geo. L.J. 859 (2006) (student note). We will return to this countermajoritarian function of the Senate and the supermajoritarian elements of bicameralism

1. *The House of Representatives*

Article I, § 2 of the Constitution requires that the members of the House of Representatives be "chosen every second Year by the People of the several States" and "apportioned among the several States * * * according to their respective Numbers." The task of drawing congressional district lines is left to the state legislatures. In *Wesberry v. Sanders*, 376 U.S. 1 (1964), the Court struck down a Georgia congressional districting scheme in which some districts had more than twice the population of others, and stated that Article I, § 2 requires that "as nearly as is practicable one [person's] vote in a congressional election is to be worth as much as another's." Does the text of § 2 support such a holding? Justice Harlan's dissent in *Wesberry* argued that before the Civil War the text of § 2 specifically mandated inequality, for it excluded "Indians not taxed" from those counted for districting purposes and included only "three-fifths of all other Persons," that is, slaves. Hence it was most improbable that this provision of the Constitution protects against disproportionate districts within a state, argued Harlan.

After *Wesberry*, the Court was faced with a series of cases in which it defined and applied the one person, one vote standard. In these cases, the Court first inquired whether there was a statistical disparity between the largest and smallest districts, and then it required the plaintiffs to show that disparities could have been reduced or eliminated by a "good faith effort to draw districts of equal population." If plaintiffs carried that burden of persuasion, then the state bore a burden of justifying the remediable disparities by reference to a "legitimate state goal." Under this approach, the Court struck down almost all the deviations that it examined.[j]

In *Karcher v. Daggett*, 462 U.S. 725 (1983), the Court struck down the New Jersey legislature's reapportionment of the state's congressional districts in response to the 1980 census, even though the population of the largest and smallest districts differed by 0.6984%. In a 5–4 vote, the Court rejected a *de minimis* exception to Article I, § 2 and swore fidelity to "absolute population equality" as "the paramount objective." Hence the Court applied the test described above. The New Jersey plan failed under the first requirement, the Court concluded, because the state could have achieved greater population equality "merely by shifting a handful of municipalities from one district to another." Nor did the State bear its burden of proving that the population variances were necessary to achieve some legitimate state objective such as making districts compact, respecting municipal boundaries, preserving the cores of prior districts, or avoiding contests between incumbent Representatives. The one justification presented by the State — the preservation of the voting strength of racial minority groups — was found to be factually unsupported.

---

in Chapter 4.

j. See, e.g., *Kirkpatrick v. Preisler*, 394 U.S. 526, 530–31 (1969) (striking down redistricting plan leaving deviation of 5.97% between most and least populous congressional districts); *White v. Weiser*, 412 U.S. 783 (1973) (striking down plan leaving deviation of 4.13%).

Writing for four dissenters, Justice White argued that the Court's precedents did not require strict scrutiny of a "minuscule" deviation, and that good policy did not require such mathematical exactitude. The critical fifth vote in the case was that of Justice Stevens, who rejected the formalist approach of the majority opinion of Justice Brennan and embraced a more functional approach. "In evaluating * * * challenges to districting plans * * * I would consider whether the plan has a significant adverse impact on an identifiable political group, whether the plan has objective indicia of irregularity, and then, whether the State is able to produce convincing evidence that the plan nevertheless serves neutral, legitimate interests of the community as a whole." (We shall return to Stevens' concurring opinion below, in Section 1(C).)

In response to Justices White and Stevens, Justice Brennan's opinion for the Court noted that exactitude in redistricting is now possible with the aid of computers, and that reality may explain why there was not a plethora of *Karcher* challenges after the 1990 and 2000 censuses.

Other issues have arisen, however. First, consider the obvious but difficult problem of allocating the seats in the House of Representatives. Allocating the 435 seats among fifty states of differing populations is made especially difficult because the Constitution guarantees each state at least one seat. The average size of a congressional district after the 1990 census was 572,466. The census found that Montana had 803,655 people, and under 2 U.S.C. § 2a(a), Montana was entitled to only one Representative (it had two before the 1990 census), because its population was less than 150% the size of the average district. Montana complained that this "method of equal proportions" violates Article I, § 2: If Montana had retained its two districts, each would have varied from the average congressional district by -170,638; with just one district, Montana varies from the average district by +231,189. The district court agreed that the principle of equal representation for equal numbers applied to intrastate districting in *Wesberry* should also be applied to interstate districting. Invoking *Baker v. Carr*, the Supreme Court rejected the government's argument on appeal that this is a nonjusticiable political question and reached the merits of Montana's claim. See *United States Department of Commerce v. Montana*, 503 U.S. 442 (1992). It unanimously upheld the apportionment, concluding that Congress had considered a variety of mathematical methods for House apportionment with the guidance of experts. Each method could be said to implement a norm of equal representation plausibly, but none could be said to be clearly superior based on simple equality principles. Thus, the mathematical precision required by *Wesberry* for intrastate congressional districts could not be required in making interstate comparisons.[k]

Second, the census method of asking persons to identify themselves and then having census counters attempt to enumerate any others obviously produces an undercount of the total number of persons. Racial minorities are

---

k. Cf. *Franklin v. Massachusetts*, 505 U.S. 788 (1992) (applying reasonableness standard rather than *Wesberry*'s stringent standards to method by which Secretary of Commerce allocates overseas federal employees among the states).

probably the group most prone to undercounting under the usual method.[1] By the use of statistical sampling, demographers can make a good-faith estimate of the undercount.   Is the Secretary of Commerce required by equality principles to revise the Census based on such statistical sampling? No, held the unanimous Court in *Wisconsin v. City of New York*, 517 U.S. 1 (1996). Under the Constitution, Congress is charged with implementing an "actual Enumeration . . . in such Manner as [it] shall by Law direct," U.S. Const., art. I, § 2, cl. 3, and has delegated the authority to do so to the Secretary of Commerce. The Secretary's exercise of discretion was not subject to heightened judicial scrutiny under either *Wesberry* (because, under *Montana*, it involved national rather than intrastate questions) or the Court's equal protection cases protecting racial minorities from discrimination (because the decision was not motivated by a desire to harm minorities). Applying a reasonableness standard, the Court deferred to the Secretary's decision to use traditional methods of census-taking.

Third, even if the Secretary is not required to use statistical sampling to modify the final census results, may the Secretary choose to do so if he or she wishes?   The Clinton Administration attempted to change policy on this question and factor in statistical sampling for the 2000 census. Here the Court's unanimity in Census disputes evaporated. In *Department of Commerce v. U.S. House of Representatives*, 525 U.S. 316 (1999) (excerpted in Chapter 8, § 1B2), by a 5–4 vote, the Court held that the Census Act did not authorize the Secretary to use statistical sampling to modify the count obtained through traditional means. Although the decision turns on an interpretation of the federal statutes, such that presumably Congress could amend them to authorize or require statistical sampling, Justice Scalia, writing separately, suggested that statistically rooted revisions might even be unconstitutional as inconsistent with the Constitution's text (requiring an "actual Enumeration") and our longstanding tradition of how to conduct the Census.[m]

2. *State Legislatures*

The Supreme Court in *Reynolds v. Sims*, 377 U.S. 533 (1964), held that apportionment in state legislatures must conform to the "one person, one vote" rule.   The Court thereby reached the issue not considered in *Wesberry v. Sanders* (whose holding rested upon Article I, § 2) and held that the Equal Protection Clause of the Fourteenth Amendment also ensures equality of representation. Chief Justice Warren's opinion for the Court reasoned:

---

l. See, e.g., Samuel Issacharoff & Allan Lichtman, *The Census Undercount and Minority Representation: The Constitutional Obligation of the States to Guarantee Equal Representa-tion*, 13 Rev. Litig. 1 (1993); Note, *Race, Rights, and Remedies: Census Sampling and the Voting Rights Act*, 114 Harv. L. Rev. 2502 (2001).

m. Cf. *Utah v. Evans*, 536 U.S. 452 (2002), in which the Court held that the census technique of "hot-deck imputation" — whereby a housing unit with unknown population characteristics is assumed to have the same characteristics as its closest neighbor of the same type — may be used for purposes of apportionment of the House of Representatives.   Justice O'Connor dissented on the ground that this technique was outlawed by the Census Act. Justice Thomas, joined by Justice Kennedy, dissented on constitutional grounds. Justice Scalia did not reach the merits, as he concluded that the appellants lacked standing.

Legislators represent people, not trees or acres. Legislators are elected by voters, not farms or cities or economic interests. As long as ours is a representative form of government, * * * the right to elect legislators in a free and unimpaired fashion is a bedrock of our political system. It could hardly be gainsaid that a constitutional claim had been asserted by an allegation that certain otherwise qualified voters had been entirely prohibited from voting for members of their state legislature. And, if a State should provide that the votes of citizens in one part of the State should be given two times, or five times, or 10 times the weight of votes of citizens in another part of the State, it could hardly be contended that the right to vote of those residing in the disfavored areas had not been effectively diluted. * * * Of course, the effect of state legislative districting schemes which give the same number of representatives to unequal numbers of constituents is identical. * * *

State legislatures are, historically, the fountainhead of representative government in this country. * * * Full and effective participation by all citizens in state government requires * * * that each citizen have an equally effective voice in the election of members of [that citizen's] state legislature. Modern and viable state government needs, and the Constitution demands, no less.

Logically, in a society ostensibly grounded on representative government, it would seem reasonable that a majority of the people of a State could elect a majority of that State's legislators. To conclude differently, and to sanction minority control of state legislative bodies, would appear to deny majority rights in a way that far surpasses any possible denial of minority rights that might otherwise be thought to result. * * *

Does this reasoning provide a better explanation for *Wesberry*? (Justice Clark's concurring opinion in *Wesberry* in fact relied on the Equal Protection Clause, as did Justice Stevens' concurring opinion in *Karcher*.) Under what theory of representation is this point of view operating?

The equal representation assured in state legislatures is both broader and narrower than that assured in the federal legislature. It is broader because the precept applies to both houses of bicameral state legislatures, and not just the lower house. Chief Justice Warren explained why the *Reynolds* Court found the analogy to the U.S. Senate (which flouts the equal representation precept) unpersuasive at the state level:

The system of representation in the two Houses of the Federal Congress is one ingrained in our Constitution, as part of the law of the land. It is one conceived out of compromise and concession indispensable to the establishment of our federal republic. Arising from unique historical circumstances, it is based on the consideration that in establishing our type of federalism a group of formerly independent States bound themselves together under one national government. * * *

* * * The right of a citizen to equal representation and to have [his or her] vote weighted equally with those of all other citizens in the election of members of one house of a bicameral state legislature would amount to little if States could effectively submerge the equal-population principle in the apportionment of seats in the other house. * * * Deadlock between the two bodies might result in compromise and concession on some issues. But in all too many cases the more probable result would be frustration of the majority will through minority veto in the house not apportioned on a population basis[.] * * *

Do you agree with this reasoning? Isn't the sort of "deadlock" suggested by the Chief Justice pretty much inherent in all the other blocking devices of legislatures, such as the committee system, expanded or unlimited debate, the amendment process, and so forth?

The equal representation guarantee for state legislatures is also narrower than that for the national legislature. Unlike apportionment of congressional districts under Article I, § 2, demonstrable population deviation among districts has been upheld in the context of state legislatures. For example, deviations under 10% have been routinely upheld.[n] Even an apportionment plan that contains a higher deviation may be upheld if it is deemed necessary to the achievement of legitimate state interests.[o] Why does the Court require perfection for U.S. House seat apportionment, while only general approximation for state legislatures?

3. *Local Governments*

In *Avery v. Midland County*, 390 U.S. 474 (1968), the Court held that the one person, one vote rule of *Reynolds v. Sims* applies to local governments. See also *Hadley v. Junior College District*, 397 U.S. 50 (1970). This was a logical extension, since the Equal Protection Clause invoked in *Reynolds* is applicable to all state action, including action through state agencies or subdivisions. "The actions of local governments *are* the actions of the State," the Court observed. "When the State apportions its legislature, it must have due regard for the Equal Protection Clause. Similarly, when the State delegates lawmaking power to local government and provides for the election of local officials from districts specified by statute, ordinance, or local charter, it must insure that those qualified to vote have the right to an equally effective voice in the electoral process."

More provocatively, the Court in *Avery* rejected the argument that the Midland County Commissioners Court should not be subject to one person, one vote on the grounds that its powers are not substantially "legislative" in nature. The Court found that because the Court had "authority to make a substantial number of decisions that affect all citizens," it must be formally accountable to all those citizens on an equal basis. This is a broader theory of representation than that needed in cases like *Wesberry* and *Reynolds*. What are its implications? Are elected judges "representatives" for one person, one vote purposes? See *Wells v. Edwards*, 347 F. Supp. 453 (M.D. La. 1972), *aff'd*, 409 U.S. 1095 (1973) (no). Why shouldn't they be?

---

n. See *Connor v. Finch*, 431 U.S. 407 (1977); *White v. Regester*, 412 U.S. 755 (1973). But cf. *Larios v. Cox*, 300 F. Supp. 2d 1320 (N.D. Ga.) (three-judge court), *aff'd*, 542 U.S. 947 (2004) (invalidating relatively small population deviation caused by political gerrymandering), discussed on pp. 192–93, *infra*.

o. See, e.g., *Brown v. Thomson*, 462 U.S. 835 (1983) (5–4 decision upholding reapportionment of Wyoming's lower house that included the allocation of one of its 64 seats to the state's least populous county, which created an average deviation from population equality of 16% and a maximum deviation of 89%).

In cases after *Avery*, the Court invalidated state laws limiting votes in municipal bond elections to taxpayers.[p] Later cases, however, saw the Court pull back when confronted with "special districts" created (for example) to aid agricultural development in sparsely populated areas. The Court has tended to treat these districts as private and proprietary rather than public and democratic and has therefore allowed landowning and other voting restrictions.[q] As with state legislatures, the Supreme Court has upheld apportionment of local legislatures despite some deviation in population.[r]

B.   RACE AND ELECTORAL STRUCTURES

Even under the regime of *Colegrove v. Green* (p. 129, *supra*), when the Supreme Court, led by Justice Frankfurter, generally refused to entertain claims concerning the distribution of political power, Frankfurter himself sometimes led the way in addressing claims that electoral structures were tainted by racial discrimination. *Gomillion v. Lightfoot*, 364 U.S. 339 (1960), involved an Alabama statute that allegedly altered the boundaries of the City of Tuskegee from the shape of a square to an irregular 28-sided figure, thereby removing from the city all but a few of its 400 African American voters while not removing a single white voter or resident. Justice Frankfurter's unanimous opinion for the Court concluded that these allegations stated a Fifteenth Amendment claim. He explained:

> [*Colegrove*] involved a complaint of discriminatory apportionment of congressional districts. The appellants in *Colegrove* complained only of a dilution of the strength of their votes as a result of legislative inaction over a course of many years. The petitioners here complain that affirmative legislative action deprives them of their votes and the consequent advantages that the ballot affords. When a legislature thus singles out a readily isolated segment of a racial minority for special discriminatory treatment, it violates the Fifteenth Amendment. In no case involving unequal weight in voting distribution that has come before the Court did the decision sanction a differentiation on racial lines whereby approval was given to unequivocal withdrawal of the vote solely from colored citizens. Apart from all else, these considerations lift this controversy out of the so-called "political" arena and into the conventional sphere of constitutional litigation.

A separate problem from the formal equality of one person, one vote and from protection against intentional discrimination against racial minorities in

---

p. See *Cipriano v. City of Houma*, 395 U.S. 701 (1969); *City of Phoenix v. Kolodziejski*, 399 U.S. 204 (1970).

q. See e.g., *Salyer Land Co. v. Tulare Lake Basin Water Storage District*, 410 U.S. 719 (1973); Richard Briffault, *Who Rules at Home? One Person/One Vote and Local Government*, 60 U. Chi. L. Rev. 339 (1993). Cf. *Rice v. Cayetano*, 528 U.S. 495 (2000) (Hawaiian laws providing that only Hawaiian natives may vote in the election of officials of state agencies governing resources set aside for the benefit of Hawaiian natives violate Fifteenth Amendment prohibition on racial discrimination in voting; the agencies are not special-use districts somehow exempt from the Fifteenth Amendment).

r. See, e.g., *Abate v. Mundt*, 403 U.S. 182 (1971) (upholding plan with maximum deviation of 11.9%).

drawing district lines is the tendency of majoritarian elections in the United States, by their very nature, to deprive minorities of "effective" voting strength. Thus, African Americans have tended to be underrepresented in legislatures; even the most perfect numerical equality will often not yield districts where African Americans will have a good chance of election (especially if whites tend to vote *en bloc*). The winner-take-all character of Senate elections and the concentration of African-American voters in big states resulted in the election of only two African-American senators in the twentieth century. Moreover, the one person, one vote rule has arguably impeded minority representation by making gerrymandering easier (states no longer have to follow subunit borders) and by encouraging multimember districts and at-large elections.[s]

These concerns generated legal efforts to secure increased minority legislative representation.[t] The relevant constitutional provisions are the Equal Protection Clause of the Fourteenth Amendment and § 1 of the Fifteenth Amendment, which provides that "[t]he right of citizens of the United States to vote shall not be denied or abridged by the United States or by any State on account of race, color, or previous condition of servitude." The first cases we analyze in this part are constitutional cases. The protections against vote dilution in these cases have been supplemented by statutory protections in the Voting Rights Act of 1965. In more recent years, efforts to comply with the Voting Rights Act have sometimes produced a reverse dynamic, in which state legislatures have reapportioned seats with an eye toward ensuring minority representation through the use of "majority-minority" districts. The remainder of this part addresses these complex subjects.

1. *The Constitutionality of At-Large Electoral Schemes*

The Progressive or "Good Government" movement of the late nineteenth and early twentieth centuries sought to eliminate the corruption and inefficiency purportedly endemic in the mayor-council form of municipal government that was then commonplace. The Progressives were "structural" reformers: they believed that a different format of municipal government, rather than just better officeholders, was the appropriate solution. The movement reached its zenith with the development of the "Galveston-Des Moines Plan." This scheme scuttled the mayor-council structure, in which council members are elected on a district basis and the mayor has power over the city's administration, in favor of a city commission, in which legislative and executive functions are combined. Usual features included: (1) centralized authority and responsibility; (2) a small number of commissioners; (3) the election of commissioners from the city at-large and not by wards or districts; and (4) each commissioner serving as the head of a single executive and

---

s. See, e.g., Jon Low-Beer, *The Constitutional Imperative of Proportional Representation*, 94 Yale L.J. 163, 173–74 (1984) (student note).

t. See generally *Quiet Revolution in the South* (1994) (Chandler Davidson & Bernard Grofman eds., 1994); Peyton McCrary, *How the Voting Rights Act Works: Implementation of a Civil Rights Policy, 1965-2005*, 57 S.C. L. Rev. 785 (2006); Richard Pildes, *The Politics of Race*, 108 Harv. L. Rev. 1359 (1995) (reviewing Davidson & Grofman).

administrative department. By 1917, nearly 500 cities had adopted the commission system. By 1976, only 215 cities, including 163 (or 4%) of those with populations over 5,000, had retained the plan. Well over five million people reside in cities that retained the plan, however; and its direct historical successor, the council-manager system, was found in over 2,400 cities, including seventy that contained more than 100,000 population.[u]

The traditional view that the reforms resulting from the Progressive Movement were beneficial has been questioned by scholars asserting that " '[t]he movement for reform in municipal government * * * constituted an attempt by upper-class, advanced professional and large business groups to take formal political power from the previously dominant lower- and middle-class elements so that they might advance their own conceptions of desirable public policy.' "[v] Moreover, some of the "reforms" were part of a larger historical process by which state and local governments ensured that African Americans would not be well represented in their legislatures. To marginalize racial minorities, state and local governments imposed literacy tests and other exclusionary requirements, enforced those requirements in a discriminatory way, and gerrymandered electoral districts to ensure white-only representation. One way to gerrymander was to elect all representatives "at large." If whites held a voting majority (as sometimes ensured by the other tactics just noted) and voted as a bloc, people of color could be denied any representation in the legislature. Consider the legitimacy of such practices under the various theories of representation (descriptive, agency, trustee). Now consider their constitutional legality. The following case summarizes the ones that came before it and provides an important starting point for current regulation.

CITY OF MOBILE v. BOLDEN
Supreme Court of the United States, 1980
446 U.S. 55, 100 S.Ct. 1490, 64 L.Ed.2d 47

MR. JUSTICE STEWART announced the judgment of the Court and delivered an opinion, in which THE CHIEF JUSTICE [BURGER], MR. JUSTICE POWELL, and MR. JUSTICE REHNQUIST joined.

[African American citizens of Mobile, Alabama, challenged the constitutionality of at-large elections for the city commission. The at-large scheme had been adopted in 1911, when African Americans in Alabama were effectively disenfranchised by the state's 1901 constitution. Although African Americans made up about one-third of the city's population, no African American had ever been elected to the city commission. The lower courts invalidated the electoral scheme, but a plurality of the Supreme Court reversed, because the lower courts had not required a proper showing of discriminatory intent.]

---

u. See Bradley Rice, *Progressive Cities* xi–xiv, xviii–xix (1977).

v. *Id.* at xvi (quoting Samuel Hays, *The Politics of Reform in Municipal Government in the Progressive Era*, 55 Pac. Nw. Q. 157, 162 (1964)). See also Chandler Davidson & George Korbel, *At-Large Elections and Minority-Group Representation: A Reexamination of Historical and Contemporary Evidence*, 43 J. of Pol. 982 (1981).

Our decisions * * * have made clear that action by a State that is racially neutral on its face violates the Fifteenth Amendment only if motivated by a discriminatory purpose. In *Guinn v. United States*, 238 U.S. 347, this Court struck down a "grandfather" clause in a state constitution exempting from the requirement that voters be literate any person or the descendants of any person who had been entitled to vote before January 1, 1866. It was asserted by way of defense that the provision was immune from successful challenge, since a law could not be found unconstitutional either "by attributing to the legislative authority an occult motive," or "because of conclusions concerning its operation in practical execution and resulting discrimination arising * * * from inequalities naturally inhering in those who must come within the standard in order to enjoy the right to vote." Despite this argument, the Court did not hesitate to hold the grandfather clause unconstitutional, because it was not "possible to discover any basis in reason for the standard thus fixed other than the purpose" to circumvent the Fifteenth Amendment.

The Court's more recent decisions confirm the principle that racially discriminatory motivation is a necessary ingredient of a Fifteenth Amendment violation. In *Gomillion v. Lightfoot*, 364 U.S. 339, the Court held that allegations of a racially motivated gerrymander of municipal boundaries stated a claim under the Fifteenth Amendment. The constitutional infirmity of the state law in that case, according to the allegations of the complaint, was that in drawing the municipal boundaries the legislature was "solely concerned with segregating white and colored voters by fencing Negro citizens out of town so as to deprive them of their pre-existing municipal vote." The Court made clear that in the absence of such an invidious purpose, a State is constitutionally free to redraw political boundaries in any manner it chooses. * * *

[The Court next considered the plaintiffs' claim that the electoral scheme violated the Equal Protection Clause.] "Criticism [of multimember districts] is rooted in their winner-take-all aspects, their tendency to submerge minorities * * *, a general preference for legislatures reflecting community interests as closely as possible and disenchantment with political parties and elections as devices to settle policy differences between contending interests."

Despite repeated constitutional attacks upon multimember legislative districts, the Court has consistently held that they are not unconstitutional *per se, e.g., White v. Regester*, 412 U.S. 755.[12] We have recognized, however, that such legislative apportionments could violate the Fourteenth Amendment if their purpose were invidiously to minimize or cancel out the voting potential of racial or ethnic minorities. To prove such a purpose it is not enough to show that the group allegedly discriminated against has not elected representatives in proportion to its numbers. A plaintiff must prove that the disputed plan was "conceived or operated as [a] purposeful devic[e] to further racial * * * discrimination."

---

12. We have made clear, however, that a court in formulating an apportionment plan as an exercise of its equity powers should, as a general rule, not permit multimember legislative districts. * * *

This burden of proof is simply one aspect of the basic principle that only if there is purposeful discrimination can there be a violation of the Equal Protection Clause of the Fourteenth Amendment. See *Washington v. Davis*, 426 U.S. 229. * * * Although dicta may be drawn from a few of the Court's earlier opinions suggesting that disproportionate effects alone may establish a claim of unconstitutional racial voter dilution, the fact is that such a view is not supported by any decision of this Court. More importantly, such a view is not consistent with the meaning of the Equal Protection Clause as it has been understood in a variety of other contexts involving alleged racial discrimination. *Washington v. Davis, supra* (employment); *Arlington Heights v. Metropolitan Housing Corp.*, [429 U.S. 252] (zoning); *Keyes v. School District No. 1, Denver, Colo.*, 413 U.S. 189, 208 (public schools); *Akins v. Texas*, 325 U.S. 398, 403–404 (jury selection).

In only one case has the Court sustained a claim that multimember legislative districts unconstitutionally diluted the voting strength of a discrete group. That case was *White v. Regester*. There the Court upheld a constitutional challenge by Negroes and Mexican Americans to parts of a legislative reapportionment plan adopted by the State of Texas. The plaintiffs alleged that the multimember districts for the two counties in which they resided minimized the effect of their votes in violation of the Fourteenth Amendment, and the Court held that the plaintiffs had been able to "produce evidence to support findings that the political processes leading to nomination and election were not equally open to participation by the group[s] in question." In so holding, the Court relied upon evidence in the record that included a long history of official discrimination against minorities as well as indifference to their needs and interests on the part of white elected officials. The Court also found in each county additional factors that restricted the access of minority groups to the political process. In one county, Negroes effectively were excluded from the process of slating candidates for the Democratic Party, while the plaintiffs in the other county were Mexican-Americans who "suffer[ed] a cultural and language barrier" that made "participation in community processes extremely difficult, particularly * * * with respect to the political life" of the county.

White v. Regester is thus consistent with "the basic equal protection principle that the invidious quality of a law claimed to be racially discriminatory must ultimately be traced to a racially discriminatory purpose," *Washington v. Davis*. The Court stated the constitutional question in *White* to be whether the "multimember districts [were] *being used invidiously* to cancel out or minimize the voting strength of racial groups," strongly indicating that only a purposeful dilution of the plaintiffs' vote would offend the Equal Protection Clause. Moreover, much of the evidence on which the Court relied in that case was relevant only for the reason that "official action will not be held unconstitutional solely because it results in a racially disproportionate impact." Of course, "[t]he impact of the official action — whether it 'bears more heavily on one race than another' — may provide an important starting point." But where the character of a law is readily explainable on grounds apart from race, as would nearly always be true where, as here, an entire system of local governance is brought into question, disproportionate impact alone cannot be decisive, and courts must look to other evidence to support a finding of discriminatory purpose.

[Justice Stewart's plurality opinion concluded that, absent proof of discriminatory intent, it was error for the lower courts to have granted relief. Finally, the opinion responded to the argument raised by the dissenting opinion that political groups permanently in the minority have a constitutional right to some kind of judicial relief. "The Equal Protection Clause of the Fourteenth Amendment does not require proportional representation as an imperative of political organization."]

More than 100 years ago the Court unanimously held that "the Constitution of the United States does not confer the right of suffrage upon any one * * *." *Minor v. Happersett*, 21 Wall. 162, 178. It is for the States "to determine the conditions under which the right of suffrage may be exercised * * *, absent of course the discrimination which the Constitution condemns." It is true, as the dissenting opinion states, that the Equal Protection Clause confers a substantive right to participate in elections on an equal basis with other qualified voters. See *Dunn v. Blumstein*, 405 U.S. 330, 336; *Reynolds v. Sims*. But this right to equal participation in the electoral process does not protect any "political group," however defined, from electoral defeat.

The dissenting opinion erroneously discovers the asserted entitlement to group representation within the "one person-one vote" principle of *Reynolds v. Sims, supra*, and its progeny. Those cases established that the Equal Protection Clause guarantees the right of each voter to "have his vote weighted equally with those of all other citizens." The Court recognized that a voter's right to "have an equally effective voice" in the election of representatives is impaired where representation is not apportioned substantially on a population basis. In such cases, the votes of persons in more populous districts carry less weight than do those of persons in smaller districts. There can be, of course, no claim that the "one person, one vote" principle has been violated in this case, because the city of Mobile is a unitary electoral district and the Commission elections are conducted at large. It is therefore obvious that nobody's vote has been "diluted" in the sense in which that word was used in the *Reynolds* case.

The dissenting opinion places an extraordinary interpretation on these decisions, an interpretation not justified by *Reynolds v. Sims* itself or by any other decision of this Court. It is, of course, true that the right of a person to vote on an equal basis with other voters draws much of its significance from the political associations that its exercise reflects, but it is an altogether different matter to conclude that political groups themselves have an independent constitutional claim to representation.[26] * * *

---

26. It is difficult to perceive how the implications of the dissenting opinion's theory of group representation could rationally be cabined. Indeed, certain preliminary practical questions immediately come to mind: Can only members of a minority of the voting population in a particular municipality be members of a "political group"? How large must a "group" be to be a "political group"? Can any "group" call itself a "political group"? If not, who is to say

[The opinion of MR. JUSTICE BLACKMUN, concurring in the judgment, is omitted.]

MR. JUSTICE STEVENS, concurring in the judgment.

In my view, there is a fundamental distinction between state action that inhibits an individual's right to vote and state action that affects the political strength of various groups that compete for leadership in a democratically governed community. * * *

In the first category are practices such as poll taxes or literacy tests that deny individuals access to the ballot. Districting practices that make an individual's vote in a heavily populated district less significant than an individual's vote in a smaller district also belong in that category. See *Baker v. Carr*; *Reynolds v. Sims*. Such practices must be tested by the strictest of constitutional standards, whether challenged under the Fifteenth Amendment or under the Equal Protection Clause of the Fourteenth Amendment.

This case does not fit within the first category. The District Court found that black citizens in Mobile "register and vote without hindrance" and there is no claim that any individual's vote is worth less than any other's. Rather, this case draws into question a political structure that treats all individuals as equals but adversely affects the political strength of a racially identifiable group. * * *

Neither *Gomillion* nor any other case decided by this Court establishes a constitutional right to proportional representation for racial minorities. What *Gomillion* holds is that a sufficiently "uncouth" or irrational racial gerrymander violates the Fifteenth Amendment. As Mr. Justice Whittaker's concurrence in that case demonstrates, the same result is compelled by the Equal Protection Clause of the Fourteenth Amendment. The fact that the "gerrymander" condemned in *Gomillion* was equally vulnerable under both Amendments indicates that the essential holding of that case is applicable, not merely to gerrymanders directed against racial minorities, but to those aimed at religious, ethnic, economic, and political groups as well. Whatever the proper standard for identifying an unconstitutional gerrymander may be, I have long been persuaded that it must apply equally to all forms of political gerrymandering — not just to racial gerrymandering. See *Cousins v. City Council of Chicago*, 466 F.2d 830, 848–852 (CA7 1972) (Stevens, J., dissenting), *cert. denied*, 409 U.S. 893.

---

which "groups" are "political groups"? Can a qualified voter belong to more than one "political group"? Can there be more than one "political group" among white voters (*e.g.*, Irish-American, Italian-American, Polish-American, Jews, Catholics, Protestants)? Can there be more than one "political group" among nonwhite voters? Do the answers to any of these questions depend upon the particular demographic composition of a given city? Upon the total size of its voting population? Upon the size of its governing body? Upon its form of government? Upon its history? Its geographic location? The fact that even these preliminary questions may be largely unanswerable suggests some of the conceptual and practical fallacies in the constitutional theory espoused by the dissenting opinion, putting to one side the total absence of support for that theory in the Constitution itself.

This conclusion follows, I believe, from the very nature of a gerrymander. By definition, gerrymandering involves drawing district boundaries (or using multimember districts or at-large elections) in order to maximize the voting strength of those loyal to the dominant political faction and to minimize the strength of those opposed to it. In seeking the desired result, legislators necessarily make judgments about the probability that the members of certain identifiable groups, whether racial, ethnic, economic, or religious, will vote in the same way. The success of the gerrymander from the legislators' point of view, as well as its impact on the disadvantaged group, depends on the accuracy of those predictions.

A prediction based on a racial characteristic is not necessarily more reliable than a prediction based on some other group characteristic. Nor, since a legislator's ultimate purpose in making the prediction is political in character, is it necessarily more invidious or benign than a prediction based on other group characteristics. In the line-drawing process, racial, religious, ethnic, and economic gerrymanders are all species of political gerrymanders.

From the standpoint of the groups of voters that are affected by the line-drawing process, it is also important to recognize that it is the group's interest in gaining or maintaining political power that is at stake. The mere fact that a number of citizens share a common ethnic, racial, or religious background does not create the need for protection against gerrymandering. It is only when their common interests are strong enough to be manifested in political action that the need arises. For the political strength of a group is not a function of its ethnic, racial, or religious composition; rather, it is a function of numbers — specifically the number of persons who will vote in the same way. In the long run there is no more certainty that individual members of racial groups will vote alike than that members of other identifiable groups will do so. And surely there is no national interest in creating an incentive to define political groups by racial characteristics. But if the Constitution were interpreted to give more favorable treatment to a racial minority alleging an unconstitutional impairment of its political strength than it gives to other identifiable groups making the same claim such an incentive would inevitably result.

My conclusion that the same standard should be applied to racial groups as is applied to other groups leads me also to conclude that the standard cannot condemn every adverse impact on one or more political groups without spawning more dilution litigation than the judiciary can manage. Difficult as the issues engendered by *Baker v. Carr* may have been, nothing comparable to the mathematical yardstick used in apportionment cases is available to identify the difference between permissible and impermissible adverse impacts on the voting strength of political groups. * * *

In my view, the proper standard is suggested by three characteristics of the gerrymander condemned in *Gomillion:* (1) the 28-sided configuration was, in the Court's word, "uncouth," that is to say, it was manifestly not the product of a routine or a traditional political decision; (2) it had a significant adverse impact on a minority group; and (3) it was unsupported by any neutral justification and thus was either totally irrational or entirely motivated by a desire to curtail the political strength of the minority. These characteristics suggest that a proper test should focus on the objective effects of the political decision rather than the subjective motivation of the decisionmaker. In this case, if the commission form of government in Mobile were extraordinary, or if it were nothing more than a vestige of history, with no greater justification than the grotesque figure in *Gomillion*, it would surely violate the Constitution. That conclusion would follow simply from its adverse impact on black voters plus the absence of any legitimate justification for the system, without reference to the subjective intent of the political body that has refused to alter it.

Conversely, I am also persuaded that a political decision that affects group voting rights may be valid even if it can be proved that irrational or invidious factors have played some part in its enactment or retention. The standard for testing the acceptability of such a decision must take into account the fact that the responsibility for drawing political boundaries is generally committed to the legislative process and that the process inevitably involves a series of compromises among different group interests. If the process is to work it must reflect an awareness of group interests and it must tolerate some attempts to advantage or to disadvantage particular segments of the voting populace. Indeed, the same "group interest" may simultaneously support and oppose a particular boundary change. The standard cannot, therefore, be so strict that any evidence of a purpose to disadvantage a bloc of voters will justify a finding of "invidious discrimination"; otherwise, the facts of political life would deny legislatures the right to perform the districting function. Accordingly, a political decision that is supported by valid and articulable justifications cannot be invalid simply because some participants in the decisionmaking process were motivated by a purpose to disadvantage a minority group.

The decision to retain the commission form of government in Mobile, Ala., is such a decision. I am persuaded that some support for its retention comes, directly or indirectly, from members of the white majority who are motivated by a desire to make it more difficult for members of the black minority to serve in positions of responsibility in city government. I deplore that motivation and wish that neither it nor any other irrational prejudice played any part in our political processes. But I do not believe otherwise legitimate political choices can be invalidated simply because an irrational or invidious purpose played some part in the decisionmaking process.

[The dissenting opinions of MR. JUSTICE WHITE and of MR. JUSTICE BRENNAN are omitted.]

MR. JUSTICE MARSHALL, dissenting.

The Court does not dispute the proposition that multimember districting can have the effect of submerging electoral minorities and overrepresenting electoral majorities.[3] * * * Although we have held that multimember districts

---

3. The Court does not quarrel with the generalization that in many instances an electoral minority will fare worse under multimember districting than under single-member districting. Multimember districting greatly enhances the opportunity of the majority political faction to elect all representatives of the district. In contrast, if the multimember district is divided into

are not unconstitutional *per se*, there is simply no basis for the plurality's conclusion that under our prior cases proof of discriminatory intent is a necessary condition for the invalidation of multimember districting.

[Justice Marshall contended that prior decisions had established that proof of discriminatory intent was unnecessary to establish a violation of the Equal Protection Clause when districting operated "to minimize or cancel out the voting strength" of a minority. He then turned to a comparison of this line of cases and *Reynolds*.]

Nearly a century ago, the Court recognized the elementary proposition upon which our structure of civil rights is based: "[T]he political franchise of voting is * * * a fundamental political right, because preservative of all rights." *Yick Wo v. Hopkins*, 118 U.S. 356 (1886). We reiterated that theme in our landmark decision in *Reynolds v. Sims* and stated that, because "the right of suffrage is a fundamental matter in a free and democratic society[,] * * * any alleged infringement of the right of citizens to vote must be carefully and meticulously scrutinized." We realized that "the right of suffrage can be denied by a debasement or dilution of the weight of a citizen's vote just as effectively as by wholly prohibiting the free exercise of the franchise." Accordingly, we recognized that the Equal Protection Clause protects "[t]he right of a citizen to equal representation and to have his vote weighted equally with those of all other citizens."

Reynolds v. Sims and its progeny focused solely on the discriminatory *effects* of malapportionment. They recognize that, when population figures for the representational districts of a legislature are not similar, the votes of citizens in larger districts do not carry as much weight in the legislature as do votes cast by citizens in smaller districts. The equal protection problem attacked by the "one person, one vote" principle is, then, one of vote dilution: under *Reynolds*, each citizen must have an "equally effective voice" in the election of representatives. In the present cases, the alleged vote dilution, though caused by the combined effects of the electoral structure and social and

---

several single-member districts, an electoral minority will have a better chance to elect a candidate of its choice, or at least to exert greater political influence. It is obvious that the greater the degree to which the electoral minority is homogeneous and insular and the greater the degree that bloc voting occurs along majority-minority lines, the greater will be the extent to which the minority's voting power is diluted by multimember districting. * * *

The electoral schemes in these cases involve majority-vote, numbered-post, and staggered-term requirements. These electoral rules exacerbate the vote-dilutive effects of multimember districting. A requirement that a candidate must win by a majority of the vote forces a minority candidate who wins a plurality of votes in the general election to engage in a run- off election with his nearest competitor. If the competitor is a member of the dominant political faction, the minority candidate stands little chance of winning in the second election. A requirement that each candidate must run for a particular "place" or "post" creates head-to-head contests that minority candidates cannot survive. When a number of positions on a governmental body are to be chosen in the same election, members of a minority will increase the likelihood of election of a favorite candidate by voting only for him. If the remainder of the electorate splits its votes among the other candidates, the minority's candidate might well be elected by the minority's "single-shot voting." If the terms of officeholders are staggered, the opportunity for single-shot voting is decreased.

historical factors rather than by unequal population distribution, is analytically the same concept: the unjustified abridgment of a fundamental right. * * *

* * * I explicitly reject the notion that the Constitution contains any [requirement of proportional representation.] The constitutional protection against vote dilution found in our prior cases does not extend to those situations in which a group has merely failed to elect representatives in proportion to its share of the population. To prove unconstitutional vote dilution, the group is also required to carry the far more onerous burden of demonstrating that it has been effectively fenced out of the political process. * * * The vote-dilution doctrine can logically apply only to groups whose electoral discreteness and insularity allow dominant political factions to ignore them. * * *

[The plaintiffs] proved that no Negro had ever been elected to the Mobile City Commission, despite the fact that Negroes constitute about one-third of the electorate, and that the persistence of severe racial bloc voting made it highly unlikely that any Negro could be elected at large in the foreseeable future. Contrary to the plurality's contention, however, I do not find unconstitutional vote dilution in this case simply because of that showing. The plaintiffs convinced the District Court that Mobile Negroes were unable to use alternative avenues of political influence. They showed that Mobile Negroes still suffered pervasive present effects of massive historical, official and private discrimination, and that the City Commission had been quite unresponsive to the needs of the minority community. The City of Mobile has been guilty of such pervasive racial discrimination in hiring employees that extensive intervention by the Federal District Court has been required. Negroes are grossly underrepresented on city boards and committees. The city's distribution of public services is racially discriminatory. City officials and police were largely unmoved by Negro complaints about police brutality and a "mock lynching." The District Court concluded that "[t]his sluggish and timid response is another manifestation of the low priority given to the needs of the black citizens and of the [commissioners'] political fear of a white backlash vote when black citizens' needs are at stake."

A requirement of proportional representation would indeed transform this Court into a "super-legislature," and would create the risk that some groups would receive an undeserved windfall of political influence. In contrast, the protection against vote dilution recognized by our prior cases serves as a minimally intrusive guarantee of political survival for a discrete political minority that is effectively locked out of governmental decisionmaking processes. * * *

[The requirement of purposeful discrimination for equal protection claims] was designed largely because [the Court] feared that a standard based solely on disproportionate impact would unduly interfere with the far ranging governmental distribution of constitutional gratuities. Underlying [*Washington v. Davis*] was a determination that, since the Constitution does not entitle any person to such governmental benefits, courts should accord discretion to those officials who decide how the government shall allocate its scarce resources. If the plaintiff proved only that governmental distribution of constitutional gratuities had a disproportionate effect on a racial minority, the Court was willing to presume that the officials who approved the allocation scheme either had made an honest error or had foreseen that the decision would have a discriminatory impact and had found persuasive, legitimate reasons for imposing it nonetheless. These assumptions about the good faith of officials allowed the Court to conclude that, standing alone, a showing that a governmental policy had a racially discriminatory impact did not indicate that the affected minority had suffered the stigma, frustration, and unjust treatment prohibited under * * * our equal protection jurisprudence.

Such judicial deference to official decisionmaking has no place under the Fifteenth Amendment. Section 1 of that Amendment differs from the Fourteenth Amendment's prohibition on racial discrimination in two crucial respects: it explicitly recognizes the right to vote free of hindrances related to race, and it sweeps no further. In my view, these distinctions justify the conclusion that proof of racially discriminatory impact should be sufficient to support a claim under the Fifteenth Amendment. The right to vote is of such fundamental importance in the constitutional scheme that the Fifteenth Amendment's command that it shall not be "abridged" on account of race must be interpreted as providing that the votes of citizens of all races shall be of substantially equal weight. Furthermore, a disproportionate-impact test under the Fifteenth Amendment would not lead to constant judicial intrusion into the process of official decisionmaking. Rather, the standard would reach only those decisions having a discriminatory effect upon the minority's vote. The Fifteenth Amendment cannot tolerate that kind of decision, even if made in good faith, because the Amendment grants racial minorities the full enjoyment of the right to vote, not simply protection against the unfairness of intentional vote dilution along racial lines.

In addition, it is beyond dispute that a standard based solely upon the motives of official decisionmakers creates significant problems of proof for plaintiffs and forces the inquiring court to undertake an unguided, tortuous look into the minds of officials in the hope of guessing why certain policies were adopted and others rejected. An approach based on motivation creates the risk that officials will be able to adopt policies that are the products of discriminatory intent so long as they sufficiently mask their motives through the use of subtlety and illusion. *Washington v. Davis* is premised on the notion that this risk is insufficient to overcome the deference the judiciary must accord to governmental decisions about the distribution of constitutional gratuities. That risk becomes intolerable, however, when the precious right to vote protected by the Fifteenth Amendment is concerned. * * *

NOTES ON *BOLDEN* AND CONSTITUTIONAL ATTACKS ON MINORITY VOTE DILUTION

1. *Discriminatory Intent. Bolden* says that legislative discrimination under the Fifteenth Amendment does not exist without proof of "intent" to discriminate. As the Court notes, a similar requirement of intentional legislative action was established for Fourteenth Amendment cases such as *Washington v. Davis*, 426 U.S. 229 (1976). These cases contemplate adjudication of legislative

motivations. But consider the cautionary words of Chief Justice John Marshall in *Fletcher v. Peck*, 10 U.S. (6 Cranch) 87 (1810):

> That * * * impure motives should contribute to the passage of a law * * * [is a circumstance] most deeply to be deplored. * * * [Nonetheless, it] may well be doubted how far the validity of a law depends upon the motives of its framers * * *. If the principle be conceded, that an act of the supreme sovereign power may be declared null by a court, in consequence of the means which procured it, still would there be much difficulty in saying to what extent those means must be applied to produce this effect. Must the vitiating cause operate on a majority, or on what number of its members? Would the act be null, whatever might be the wish of the nation, or would its * * * nullity depend upon the public sentiment?
>
> If the majority of the legislature be corrupted, it may well be doubted, whether it be within the province of the judiciary to control their conduct, and, if less than a majority act from impure motives, the principle by which judicial interference would be regulated, is not clearly discerned.

Why has the Court rejected the reasoning of Chief Justice Marshall?

2. *Proving Discriminatory Intent (Fourteenth Amendment). Personnel Administrator of Massachusetts v. Feeney*, 442 U.S. 256 (1979), upheld a state statute granting veterans a preference in being hired for state civil service positions. Although the obvious effect of the law was to discriminate against women, the Court rejected the Fourteenth Amendment challenge because there was no proof of discriminatory intent. In footnote 25, the Court stated:

> This is not to say that the inevitability or foreseeability of consequences of a neutral rule has no bearing upon the existence of discriminatory intent. Certainly, when the adverse consequences of a law upon an identifiable group are [plainly] inevitable * * *, a strong inference that the adverse effects were desired can reasonably be drawn. But in this inquiry * * * an inference is a working tool, not a synonym for proof. When * * * the impact is essentially an unavoidable consequence of legislative policy that has in itself always been deemed to be legitimate, and when * * * the statutory history and all of the available evidence effectively demonstrate the opposite, the inference simply fails to ripen into proof.

Would creating a rebuttable presumption that the decisionmaker intended the natural and foreseeable consequences of her act (a common concept in tort law) be a good idea because the decisionmaker has far better access to the true reasons for a decision and should be required to articulate a credible explanation? How about making that the Fifteenth Amendment standard?

3. *Proof of Discriminatory Intent (Fifteenth Amendment): The Subsequent History of* Bolden. In 1982, the federal district court on remand in *Bolden* held that the city's form of government had been adopted in 1911 for discriminatory purposes, even though blacks were already disenfranchised at the time by the Alabama Constitution of 1901, because the 1911 scheme was "adopted in substantial part to reinforce the 1901 Constitution as a buttress against the possibility of black office holding." 542 F. Supp. 1050, 1075 (S.D. Ala. 1982). The parties settled the case soon after this decision. In a companion case involving the School Commission of Mobile County, the district court also

found that the adoption in 1876 of an at-large election plan for the school board was motivated by discriminatory animus. See *Brown v. Board of School Commissioners*, 542 F. Supp. 1078 (S.D. Ala. 1982).

While *Brown* was pending on appeal to the Eleventh Circuit, the Supreme Court in *Rogers v. Lodge*, 458 U.S. 613 (1982), upheld a lower court's finding that the system of at-large election of county commissioners of Burke County, Georgia had been maintained for racially discriminatory purposes. Justice Powell, joined by Justice Rehnquist, protested in dissent that the evidence relied upon by the district court — the presence of racial bloc voting, the failure of any African American to be elected despite the fact that African Americans made up a majority of the county's citizens, the present impact upon Burke County blacks of past racial discrimination, and the county elected officials' unresponsiveness and insensitivity to the needs of African Americans — was no different in any relevant respect from that presented in *Bolden*, which in Justice Powell's view held that "this *kind* of evidence was not enough." Following *Rogers v. Lodge*, the Eleventh Circuit affirmed *Brown* in all respects, 706 F.2d 1103 (1983), and the Supreme Court summarily affirmed, 464 U.S. 1005 (1983). Do *Rogers* and *Brown* effectively nullify the thrust of *Bolden*?

2. *The Voting Rights Act and Racial Vote Dilution*

(a) *Section 5 Preclearance.* Although the Fifteenth Amendment was adopted in 1870 and provides Congress the "power to enforce this article by appropriate legislation" (§ 2), it was not until 1965 that "Congress found that racial discrimination in voting was an 'insidious and pervasive evil which had been perpetuated in certain parts of our country through unremitting and ingenious defiance of the Constitution.'" *City of Rome v. United States*, 446 U.S. 156, 182 (1980) (quoting *South Carolina v. Katzenbach*, 383 U.S. 301, 309 (1966)). Congress found that case-by-case litigation had failed to enforce compliance with the Amendment because it had proved to be too slow, too expensive, and too cumbersome and because a decree outlawing a discriminatory device could easily be circumvented simply by adopting a different method of discrimination. Consider, for example, the sequence of events alleged in *United States v. Mississippi*, 380 U.S. 128 (1965):

1. In 1890, a majority of qualified voters in Mississippi were African American. A new state constitution adopted in that year required that persons otherwise qualified to vote be able to read any section of the Mississippi Constitution, *or* understand the same when read to them, *or* "give a reasonable interpretation thereof." This requirement, coupled with the fact that until about 1952 African Americans could not vote in the Democratic primary (victory in which was tantamount to election because the Republican Party was virtually nonexistent), decreased the percentage of African-American registered voters to 9% in 1899 and 5% in 1954.

2. By the 1950s the white primary was unlawful and African-American literacy had improved. In response, the state constitution was amended to require prospective voters to be able to read and copy in writing any section of the Mississippi Constitution, *and* give a reasonable interpretation of it, *and*

demonstrate "a reasonable understanding of the duties and obligations of citizenship under a constitutional form of government." These provisions lent themselves to even greater discriminatory application in the hands of voting registrars.[w]

3.   In 1960 the state constitution was amended to add a new voting qualification of "good moral character." Moreover, in 1962 the state adopted laws requiring that application forms be filled out "properly and responsively" without any assistance.   Both of these devices were obviously subject to discriminatory application.

Congress' response to this pattern of voting discrimination was to adopt the Voting Rights Act of 1965, 42 U.S.C. § 1971 *et seq.* The Act outlawed "tests and devices" prerequisite to registering to vote, such as literacy tests, which had earlier been found constitutional in *Lassiter v. Northampton County Board of Elections*, 360 U.S. 45 (1959). To prevent circumvention of the Act by the adoption of other discriminatory methods, § 5 of the Act required that no change in voting qualifications or procedures may be implemented without the prior determination of either the Attorney General or the United States District Court for the District of Columbia that the change "does not have the purpose and will not have the effect of denying or abridging the right to vote on account of race or color." 42 U.S.C. § 1973c. The 1965 Act did not apply nationwide: it reached only those jurisdictions that on November 1, 1964, (1) maintained any "test or device" and (2) had less than 50% of the voting-age population registered or in which less than 50% of such persons voted in the presidential election of 1964. Although the coverage formula was written in these neutral terms, the Act was designed to have, and has had, the effect of bringing the Deep South within its coverage.

The 1965 Act provided that its preclearance requirement would lapse in five years. In 1970, the Act was renewed for another five years, and in 1975 the Act was renewed for another seven years. In 1982, the Act was renewed again, but this time it was extensively amended to terminate the Act's coverage in twenty-five years and to allow covered jurisdictions more opportunity

---

w. A vivid example of discriminatory application of a "read and understand" requirement is given in *United States v. Louisiana*, 225 F. Supp. 353, 384 (E.D. La. 1963) (3-judge court), affirmed, 380 U.S. 145 (1965):

Registrars were easily satisfied with answers from white voters.   In one instance "FRDUM FOOF SPETGH" was an acceptable response to the request to interpret Article I, § 3 of the Louisiana Constitution.

On the other hand, the record shows that Negroes whose application forms and answers indicate that they are highly qualified by literacy standards and have a high degree of intelligence have been turned down although they had given a reasonable interpretation of fairly technical clauses of the constitution. For example, the Louisiana Constitution, Article X, § 16 provides: "Rolling stock operated in this State, the owners of which have no domicile therein, shall be assessed by the Louisiana Tax Commission, and shall be taxed for State purposes only, at a rate not to exceed forty mills on the dollar assessed value." The rejected interpretation was: "My understanding is that it means if the owner of which does not have residence within the State, his rolling stock shall be taxed not to exceed forty mills on the dollar."

eventually to bail out of its coverage. Most recently, in 2006 the Act was extended yet again for another twenty-five years.[x] The Voting Rights Act has been successful in increasing minority registration, voting, and officeholding in the covered jurisdictions.[y] It has also been controversial because it singles out one region of the country, all but labels it as discriminatory, and requires the local and state governments covered by the Act to obtain federal approval before making even the simplest changes in voting procedures (e.g., moving a polling place).[z]

The Supreme Court in *South Carolina v. Katzenbach, supra*, upheld the 1965 Act's prohibition of literacy tests as a constitutional exercise of Congress' authority to enforce the Fifteenth Amendment, notwithstanding the Court's unwillingness to strike down literacy tests in *Lassiter*. In *Katzenbach v. Morgan*, 384 U.S. 641 (1966), the Court upheld § 4(e) of the Act, which provided that no person who had completed the sixth grade of school in Puerto Rico could be denied the right to vote on account of inability to read or write English. Even though the statutory right went well beyond what the Court would have enforced under the Fourteenth or Fifteenth Amendments, *Morgan* held that Congress' authority under § 5 of the Fourteenth Amendment gave it discretion to expand upon (but not to abridge) the rights created under the Amendment. In *Rome v. United States, supra*, the Court upheld the preclearance requirement, based upon the two earlier precedents. Justices Stewart, Powell, and Rehnquist dissented.[a]

---

x. Although the 2006 legislation passed by votes of 98-0 in the Senate and 390-33 in the House, there was considerable backroom grumbling from Southern legislators chafing at its continuation of regional preclearance coverage and from a spectrum of legislators concerning the requirement of bilingual ballots. On the conflictual legislative history behind the seeming consensus, see Nathaniel Persily, *The Promise and Pitfalls of the New Voting Rights Act*, 117 Yale L.J. ___ (2007) (forthcoming); James Tucker, *The Politics of Persuasion: Passage of the Voting Rights Act Reauthorization Act of 2006*, 33 J. Leg. 205 (2007). In addition, see generally *The Future of the Voting Rights Act* (David Epstein, Richard Pildes, Rodolfo de la Garza & Sharyn O'Halloran eds., 2006); *Voting Rights Act Reauthorization of 2006: Perspectives on Democracy, Participation, and Power* (Ana Henderson ed., 2006).

y. See Davidson & Grofman, *supra*; Pildes, *supra*; and the newer sources cited above concerning the legislative history of the 2006 extension.

z. The technicalities of § 5 are beyond our scope. For relatively recent decisions involving the application of § 5, see, e.g., *Georgia v. Ashcroft*, 539 U.S. 461 (2003) (concerning tradeoff of majority-minority districts, coalition districts, and minority-influence districts); *Reno v. Bossier Parish School Board*, 528 U.S. 320 (2000) (electoral change that does not dilute minority voting strength below preexisting threshold must be precleared even if the choice of the plan was tainted by discriminatory purpose); *Lopez v. Monterey County*, 525 U.S. 255 (1999) (county covered by the Act must preclear electoral changes mandated by changes in state law, even if the state itself is not a covered jurisdiction); *Presley v. Etowah County Comm'n*, 502 U.S. 491 (1992) (decision to shift power from individual commissioners to commission as a whole not covered by § 5).

a. *City of Boerne v. Flores*, 521 U.S. 507 (1997), which struck down the Religious Freedom Restoration Act as beyond Congress' authority and repudiated any broad understanding of *Katzenbach v. Morgan*, nonetheless contained language reaffirming the outcomes in the Voting Rights Act cases. See also *Lopez v. Monterey County*, 525 U.S. 255 (1999) (reaffirming constitutionality of § 5). On the constitutionality of the 2006 extension of the Act, see, e.g.,

Rome and *Bolden* were decided on the same day in 1980. Three Justices (Burger, Blackmun, and Stevens) were in the majority for both cases, and their votes sent the following message: The Court was unwilling to strike down electoral arrangements unless challengers could show that they were motivated by racially discriminatory animus. But the Court was willing to uphold at least some congressional legislation that attacked practices even when there was not such a showing, so long as Congress had a factual basis for believing that certain practices required stronger remedies than those the Court was willing to impose. This may have been a signal by the Court that Congress could feel free to override *Bolden* with a broader statutory protection against racial vote dilution — which, as explained next, Congress promptly proceeded to do.

(b) *Section 2 Protection Against Racial Vote Dilution.* African-American plaintiffs prevailed in *Rogers* and in *Bolden* on remand by satisfactorily proving that the at-large electoral schemes at issue in those cases had been adopted or maintained for discriminatory purposes. In the ordinary case, however, this burden of proof is hard to surmount: proof of discriminatory reasons for the adoption of an electoral scheme many years ago is usually unavailable because of the passage of time, and discriminatory maintenance of such a scheme cannot be shown without either overtly discriminatory actions or overwhelming circumstantial evidence. Moreover, to some extent the *Bolden* approach asks the wrong question, for it is the present discriminatory impact of the electoral scheme, and not the motivations of present or past officials, that unfairly skews the political process.

The *Bolden* result in the Supreme Court triggered a firestorm of protest from civil rights advocates and Members of Congress. A bipartisan coalition voted to amend the Voting Rights Act in 1982 to override the *Bolden* decision. The operative provision is revised § 2 of the Act, 42 U.S.C. § 1973, which provides a permanent, nationwide ban on electoral procedures with discriminatory "results":

(a) No voting qualification or prerequisite to voting or standard, practice, or procedure shall be imposed or applied by any State or political subdivision in a manner which results in a denial or abridgement of the right of any citizen of the United States to vote on account of race or color, or in contravention of the guarantees set forth in section 1973b(f)(2) of this title [dealing with language minority groups], as provided in subsection (b) of this section.

(b) A violation of subsection (a) of this section is established if, based on the totality of circumstances, it is shown that the political processes leading to nomination or election in the State or political subdivision are not equally open to participation by members of a class of citizens protected by subsection (a) of this section in that its

Luis Fuentes-Rohwer, *Legislative Findings, Congressional Powers, and the Future of the Voting Rights Act*, 82 Ind. L.J. 99 (2007); Richard Hasen, *Congressional Power to Renew the Preclearance Provisions of the Voting Rights Act After* Tennessee v. Lane, 66 Ohio St. L.J. 177 (2005); Pamela Karlan, *Section 5 Squared: Congressional Power to Extend and Amend the Voting Rights Act*, 44 Houston L. Rev. 1 (2007); Ellen Katz, *Congressional Power to Extend Preclearance: a Response to Professor Karlan*, 44 Houston L. Rev. 33 (2007); Persily, *supra.*

members have less opportunity than other members of the electorate to participate in the political process and to elect representatives of their choice. The extent to which members of a protected class have been elected to office in the State or political subdivision is one circumstance which may be considered: *Provided*, That nothing in this section establishes a right to have members of a protected class elected in numbers equal to their proportion in the population.

The Senate committee report explaining § 2 (S. Rep. 97–417, 97th Cong., 2d Sess. 28–29, reprinted in 1982 U.S. Code Cong. & Admin. News 206–07) cited these "typical factors," gleaned from pre-*Bolden* cases, as illustrative of the vote dilution Congress intended to outlaw by amending the statute:

1. the extent of any history of official discrimination in the state or political subdivision that touched the right of the members of the minority group to register, to vote, or otherwise to participate in the democratic process;

2. the extent to which voting in the elections of the state or political subdivision is racially polarized;

3. the extent to which the state or political subdivision has used unusually large election districts, majority vote requirements, anti-single shot provisions, or other voting practices or procedures that may enhance the opportunity for discrimination against the minority group;

4. if there is a candidate slating process, whether the members of the minority group have been denied access to that process;

5. the extent to which members of the minority group in the state or political subdivision bear the effects of discrimination in such areas as education, employment and health, which hinder their ability to participate effectively in the political process;

6. whether political campaigns have been characterized by overt or subtle racial appeals;

7. the extent to which members of the minority group have been elected to public office in the jurisdiction.

Other factors mentioned in the Senate report were:

whether there is a significant lack of responsiveness on the part of elected officials to the particularized needs of the members of the minority group.

whether the policy underlying the state or political subdivision's use of such voting qualification, prerequisite to voting, or standard, practice or procedure is tenuous.

————

THORNBURG v. GINGLES, 478 U.S. 30 (1986). In this case, the Supreme Court construed the "totality of the circumstances" test of new § 2. **Justice Brennan's** opinion for a five-Justice Court concluded that the factors identified in the Senate report were probative, but neither comprehensive nor exclusive. For multimember districting to violate § 2, the Court held, three elements must be shown: (1) "The minority group must be able to demonstrate that it is sufficiently large and geographically compact to constitute a majority in a single-member district." (2) "[T]he minority group must be able to show that it is politically cohesive." (3) "[T]he minority must be able to demonstrate that the white majority votes sufficiently as a bloc to enable it — in the absence of special circumstances, such as the minority candidate running unopposed * * * — usually to defeat the minority's preferred candidate."

The Court "observe[d] that the usual predictability of the majority's success distinguishes structural dilution from the mere loss of an occasional election." Thus, "a pattern of racial bloc voting that extends over a period of time is more probative of a claim that a district experiences legally significant polarization than are the results of a single election." Moreover, "in a district where elections are shown usually to be polarized, the fact that racially polarized voting is not present in one or a few individual elections [or] the success of a minority candidate in a particular election does not necessarily prove" that § 2 has not been violated. The district court's ultimate finding of the presence or absence of vote dilution is subject only to the clearly erroneous test in appellate review. The Court majority held that the occasional election of minority candidates does not, by itself, defeat a § 2 claim, but two Justices (**Brennan** and **White**) concluded that "persistent proportional representation" will do so unless the plaintiffs can show that this "sustained success does not accurately reflect the minority group's ability to elect its preferred representatives."

Justice O'Connor (writing also for **Chief Justice Burger** and **Justices Powell** and **Rehnquist**) concurred only in the judgment. Her opinion conceded that the 1982 Act overrode *Bolden*'s "intent" test and adopted the "results" test of *White v. Regester*, but she also noted that § 2 "unequivocally disclaims the creation of a right of proportional representation. This disclaimer was essential to the compromise that resulted in passage of the amendment," she argued, citing the views of Senator Dole in the Senate committee report. Note that in 1982 Dole was the Senate Majority Leader, and no bill opposed by the Republicans could have been enacted, either because they controlled the Senate or (most likely, given liberal Republican defections) because their opposition could trigger a presidential veto.

In *Gingles*, Justice O'Connor argued that the Court's approach would press enforcement of the Voting Rights Act toward proportional representation. Consider her hypothetical: A 1,000 person town has an African-American population of 30%, concentrated in one section of town. If the town council has four members, the configuration of districts could determine the number of African-American councilmembers (assuming racial bloc voting). Single-member districts could yield results ranging from two African-American representatives (if two of the districts had 60% African Americans in each, while the other two districts had none) to none (if the 30% African-American vote were evenly distributed through all four districts). At-large elections would likely yield no minority representation. Justice O'Connor agreed that the last two options might be challenged under the 1982 Act but posed the question: If the Act prohibits minority "vote dilution," what would an "undiluted" minority representation look like? Would it be proportional representation, as the Court suggested? Or a variety of results, including an all-white council whose members competed for the African-American vote and catered to minority group desires? Justice O'Connor argued for a more variegated approach than the relatively more bright-line approach adopted by the Court majority. She would have disallowed claims in three districts where African Americans had enjoyed some electoral success since the 1970s and would have reversed the trial court as to those three districts.[b]

A Voting Rights Act Problem

Problem 2–1. After the 1990 census, the state of North Carolina gained an additional seat in the House of Representatives (up from 11 to 12). The racial composition of the state is 78% white, 20% black, 1% Indian, and 1% predominantly Asian. The African-American population is relatively dispersed through the state, constituting a majority of only five of the state's 100 counties (all located in the Coastal Plain in the eastern part of the state). As of 1992, no African American had been elected to the House from North Carolina in this century.

(a) Assume that North Carolina redistricts after the 1990 census by creating a new Republican district and strengthening incumbents in surrounding districts. (Even though Democrats control the legislature, there was a Republican governor, and population growth had been in Republican areas.) Under this configuration, 12 whites will be elected in 1992. What are the odds that North Carolina could be successfully sued for violating § 2 of the Voting Rights Act, as amended in 1982 and as interpreted in *Gingles*?

(b) Assume that North Carolina redistricts after the 1990 census by creating a new "majority-minority" district (namely, a district where a majority of the population consists of racial minorities) in the Coastal Plain. If there were racial bloc voting, an African American would probably be elected in 1992, the first in that century. African-American plaintiffs challenge the plan under § 2, nonetheless. Their argument is that there should have been two rather than one majority-minority district and that a second district could have been created in the central part of the state by using boundary lines no more irregular than those found elsewhere. Does this lawsuit have a chance under § 2?

(c) North Carolina has 40 counties covered by § 5 of the Voting Rights Act, and any redistricting must be "precleared" by the Justice Department or approved by the D.C. Circuit. Assume that the Justice Department insists on two rather than one majority-minority district, for the reasons suggested in part

---

b. In *Holder v. Hall*, 512 U.S. 874 (1994), the Court held that § 2 provides no basis for a claim of racial vote dilution based on the size of a legislative body (for example, have a commission made up of a single member rather than of several members). In a companion case, *Johnson v. De Grady*, 512 U.S. 997 (1994), the Court applied *Gingles* and found no violation of § 2 in Florida's state legislative reapportionment plan. Justice Thomas, joined by Justice Scalia, concurred in the judgment in *Holder* and launched a full-scale attack upon *Gingles*, arguing that its test is inconsistent with the text of § 2 and encourages racial gerrymandering. Justices Thomas and Scalia would have overruled *Gingles* and held that § 2 applies only to claims of discriminatory denial of the ballot or discriminatory processing of ballots, and not to vote dilution claims. More recently, in *League of United Latin American Citizens v. Perry*, 126 S.Ct. 2594 (2006), a fractured Court concluded that at least one redrawn Texas congressional district violated § 2 by diluting the voting power of the Latino community.

(b) of this problem. The North Carolina General Assembly goes along with the suggestion and creates two such districts. The majority-minority districts are Districts 1 and 12. To create the second district (#12), the legislature snaked the district lines along Interstate 85; the district passes through 10 counties, cutting most of them in half, as it also does many towns and cities. It is contiguous but only barely so. In the 1992 elections, eight Democrats and four Republicans are elected, with the Democrats picking up the extra seat. Two of the eight Democrats are African American — from districts 1 and 12.

Republicans challenge this plan on the ground that it is a partisan gerrymander designed to minimize their representation. Population growth occurred in GOP areas, yet the Democratic legislature copped the extra seat for themselves. In another lawsuit, white voters in the odd-shaped District 12 challenge the plan because it "dilutes" their votes on racial grounds. Should either of these lawsuits succeed? Write down your answers, and then read on.

3. *Redistricting Designed To Ensure Minority Representation*

SHAW v. RENO
United States Supreme Court, 1993
509 U.S. 630, 113 S.Ct. 2816, 125 L.Ed.2d 511

Justice O'Connor delivered the opinion of the Court.

[The North Carolina General Assembly's reapportionment of the state's twelve seats in the federal House of Representatives based on the 1990 census included one majority-black congressional district. After the federal Attorney General objected to the plan pursuant to § 5 of the Voting Rights Act, the General Assembly revised the plan and created a second majority-black district. The facts of this case are those of Problem 2–1(c) above, which you should now review, especially the information concerning the shapes of the districts in question. Plaintiffs challenged the revised plan as involving an unconstitutional racial gerrymander.]

[Part I of the opinion began by describing North Carolina's original districting (with one majority-minority district (#1), the Justice Department's objections, and North Carolina's redistricting to satisfy the Justice Department by creating two majority-minority districts (##1, 12). See Problem 2–1(c).]

The first of the two majority-black districts contained in the revised plan, District 1, is somewhat hook shaped. Centered in the northeast portion of the State, it moves southward until it tapers to a narrow band; then, with finger-like extensions, it reaches far into the southern-most part of the State near the South Carolina border. District 1 has been compared to a "Rorschach ink-blot test" and a "bug splattered on a windshield."

The second majority-black district, District 12, is even more unusually shaped. It is approximately 160 miles long and, for much of its length, no wider than the I-85 corridor. It winds in snake-like fashion through tobacco country, financial centers, and manufacturing areas "until it gobbles in enough enclaves of black neighborhoods." Northbound and southbound drivers on I-85 sometimes find themselves in separate districts in one county, only to "trade" districts when they enter the next county. Of the 10 counties through which District 12 passes, five are cut into three different districts; even towns are divided. At one point the district remains contiguous only because it intersects at a single point with two other districts before crossing over them. * * *

[Appellants, five residents of Durham County, two of whom live in District 12 and three of whom in neighboring District 2,] alleged that the General Assembly deliberately "create[d] two Congressional Districts in which a majority of black voters was concentrated arbitrarily — without regard to any other considerations, such as compactness, contiguousness, geographical boundaries, or political subdivisions" with the purpose "to create Congressional Districts along racial lines" and to assure the election of two black representatives to Congress. [The lower courts denied relief.]

[IIA] [After the adoption of the Fifteenth Amendment, many states circumvented its " 'prohibition through the use of both subtle and blunt instruments, perpetuating ugly patterns of pervasive racial discrimination.' " In addition to such "ostensibly race-neutral devices" as literacy tests with "grandfather clauses" and "good character" provisos, states used "the racial gerrymander — 'the deliberate and arbitrary distortion of district boundaries * * * for (racial) purposes.' "] In the 1870's, for example, opponents of Reconstruction in Mississippi "concentrated the bulk of the black population in a 'shoestring' Congressional district running the length of the Mississippi River, leaving five others with white majorities." Some 90 years later, Alabama redefined the boundaries of the city of Tuskegee "from a square to an uncouth twenty-eight-sided figure" in a manner that was alleged to exclude black voters, and only black voters, from the city limits. *Gomillion v. Lightfoot*.

* * * [N]early a century after ratification of the Fifteenth Amendment[, in] some States, registration of eligible black voters ran 50% behind that of whites. Congress enacted the Voting Rights Act of 1965 as a dramatic and severe response to the situation. The Act proved immediately successful in ensuring racial minorities access to the voting booth; by the early 1970's, the spread between black and white registration in several of the targeted Southern States had fallen to well below 10%.

But it soon became apparent that guaranteeing equal access to the polls would not suffice to root out other racially discriminatory voting practices. Drawing on the "one person, one vote" principle, this Court recognized that "[t]he right to vote can be affected by a *dilution* of voting power as well as by an absolute prohibition on casting a ballot." Where members of a racial minority group vote as a cohesive unit, practices such as multimember or at-large electoral systems can reduce or nullify minority voters' ability, as a group, "to elect the candidate of their choice." Accordingly, the Court held that such schemes violate the Fourteenth Amendment when they are adopted with a discriminatory purpose and have the effect of diluting minority voting strength. See, e.g., *Rogers v. Lodge*; *White v. Regester*. Congress, too, responded to the problem of vote dilution. In 1982, it amended § 2 of the Voting Rights Act to prohibit legislation that *results* in the dilution of a minority group's voting strength, regardless of the legislature's intent.

[IIB] * * * [A]ppellants' claim that the State engaged in unconstitutional racial gerrymandering * * * strikes a powerful historical chord: It is unsettling how closely the North Carolina plan resembles the most egregious racial gerrymanders of the past. [Plaintiffs' complaint alleging that gerrymandering voters into districts that are "so extremely irregular" that they can only be understood as "an effort to segregate the races for purposes of voting" presents a claim for which relief can be granted under the Equal Protection Clause.]

[IIIA] * * * The * * * central purpose [of the Equal Protection Clause] is to prevent the States from purposefully discriminating between individuals on the basis of race. *Washington v. Davis.* Laws that explicitly distinguish between individuals on racial grounds fall within the core of that prohibition.

No inquiry into legislative purpose is necessary when the racial classification appears on the face of the statute. Express racial classifications are immediately suspect because, "[a]bsent searching judicial inquiry . . . , there is simply no way of determining what classifications are 'benign' or 'remedial' and what classifications are in fact motivated by illegitimate notions of racial inferiority or simple racial politics." *Richmond v. J.A. Croson Co.*, 488 U.S. 469 (1989) (plurality opinion); *id.* (Scalia, J., concurring in the judgment).

Classifications of citizens solely on the basis of race "are by their very nature odious to a free people whose institutions are founded upon the doctrine of equality." *Hirabayashi v. United States*, 320 U.S. 81, 100 (1943). They threaten to stigmatize individuals by reason of their membership in a racial group and to incite racial hostility. *Croson.* Accordingly, we have held that the Fourteenth Amendment requires state legislation that expressly distinguishes among citizens because of their race to be narrowly tailored to further a compelling governmental interest.

These principles apply not only to legislation that contains explicit racial distinctions, but also to those "rare" statutes that, although race-neutral, are, on their face, "unexplainable on grounds other than race." As we explained in *Personnel Administrator v. Feeney*, 442 U.S. 256 (1979):

> "A racial classification, regardless of purported motivation, is presumptively invalid and can be upheld only upon an extraordinary justification. This rule applies as well to a classification that is ostensibly neutral but is an obvious pretext for racial discrimination."

[IIIB] Appellants contend that redistricting legislation that is so bizarre on its face that it is "unexplainable on grounds other than race" demands the same close scrutiny that we give other state laws that classify citizens by race. Our voting rights precedents support that conclusion.

[In *Guinn v. United States*, 238 U. S. 347 (1915), the Court found a Fifteenth Amendment violation when a state adopted a literacy requirement with a " 'grandfather clause' applicable to individuals and their lineal descendants" entitled to vote on January 1, 1866. Although facially neutral, the Court concluded that the law "was invalid because, on its face, it could not be explained on grounds other than race."]

The Court applied the same reasoning to the "uncouth twenty-eight-sided" municipal boundary line at issue in *Gomillion*. Although the statute that redrew the city limits of Tuskegee was race-neutral on its face, plaintiffs alleged that its effect was impermissibly to remove from the city virtually all black voters and no white voters. The Court reasoned:

> "If these allegations upon a trial remained uncontradicted or unqualified, the conclusion would be irresistible, tantamount for all practical purposes to a mathematical demonstration, that the legislation is solely concerned with segregating white and colored voters by fencing Negro citizens out of town so as to deprive them of their pre-existing municipal vote." * * *

The Court extended the reasoning of *Gomillion* to congressional districting in *Wright v. Rockefeller*, 376 U.S. 52 (1964). At issue in *Wright* were four districts contained in a New York apportionment statute. The plaintiffs alleged that the statute excluded nonwhites from one district and concentrated them in the other three. Every member of the Court assumed that the plaintiffs' allegation that the statute "segregate[d] eligible voters by race and place of origin" stated a constitutional claim. The Justices disagreed only as to whether the plaintiffs had carried their burden of proof at trial. The dissenters thought the unusual shape of the district lines could "be explained only in racial terms." The majority, however, accepted the District Court's finding that the plaintiffs had failed to establish that the districts were in fact drawn on racial lines. Although the boundary lines were somewhat irregular, the majority reasoned, they were not so bizarre as to permit of no other conclusion. Indeed, because most of the nonwhite voters lived together in one area, it would have been difficult to construct voting districts without concentrations of nonwhite voters.

Wright illustrates the difficulty of determining from the face of a single-member districting plan that it purposefully distinguishes between voters on the basis of race. A reapportionment statute typically does not classify persons at all; it classifies tracts of land, or addresses. Moreover, redistricting differs from other kinds of state decisionmaking in that the legislature always is *aware* of race when it draws district lines, just as it is aware of age, economic status, religious and political persuasion, and a variety of other demographic factors. That sort of race consciousness does not lead inevitably to impermissible race discrimination. As *Wright* demonstrates, when members of a racial group live together in one community, a reapportionment plan that concentrates members of the group in one district and excludes them from others may reflect wholly legitimate purposes. The district lines may be drawn, for example, to provide for compact districts of contiguous territory, or to maintain the integrity of political subdivisions.

The difficulty of proof, of course, does not mean that a racial gerrymander, once established, should receive less scrutiny under the Equal Protection Clause than other state legislation classifying citizens by race. * * * In some exceptional cases, a reapportionment plan may be so highly irregular that, on its face, it rationally cannot be understood as anything other than an effort to "segregat[e] . . . voters" on the basis of race. *Gomillion*. *Gomillion*, in which a tortured municipal boundary line was drawn to exclude black voters, was such a case. So, too, would be a case in which a State concentrated a dispersed minority population in a single district by disregarding traditional districting principles such as compactness, contiguity, and respect for political subdivisions. We emphasize that these criteria are important not because they are constitutionally required — they are not — but because they are objective factors that may serve to defeat a claim that a district has been gerrymandered on racial lines.

Put differently, we believe that reapportionment is one area in which appearances do matter. A reapportionment plan that includes in one district individuals who belong to the same race, but who are otherwise widely separated by geographical and political boundaries, and who may have little in common with one another but the color of their skin, bears an uncomfortable resemblance to political apartheid. It reinforces the perception that members of the same racial group — regardless of their age, education, economic status, or the community in which they live — think alike, share the same political interests, and will prefer the same candidates at the polls. We have rejected such perceptions elsewhere as impermissible racial stereotypes. See, e.g., *Holland v. Illinois*, 493 U. S. 474 (1990) ("[A] prosecutor's assumption that a black juror may be presumed to be partial simply because he is black . . . violates the Equal Protection Clause")[.] By perpetuating such notions, a racial gerrymander may exacerbate the very patterns of racial bloc voting that majority-minority districting is sometimes said to counteract.

The message that such districting sends to elected representatives is equally pernicious. When a district obviously is created solely to effectuate the perceived common interests of one racial group, elected officials are more likely to believe that their primary obligation is to represent only the members of that group, rather than their constituency as a whole. This is altogether antithetical to our system of representative democracy. * * *

For these reasons, we conclude that a plaintiff challenging a reapportionment statute under the Equal Protection Clause may state a claim by alleging that the legislation, though race-neutral on its face, rationally cannot be understood as anything other than an effort to separate voters into different districts on the basis of race, and that the separation lacks sufficient justification. It is unnecessary for us to decide whether or how a reapportionment plan that, on its face, can be explained in nonracial terms successfully could be challenged. Thus, we express no view as to whether "the intentional creation of majority-minority districts, without more" always gives rise to an equal protection claim. * * *

[IIIC] The dissenters consider the circumstances of this case "functionally indistinguishable" from multimember districting and at-large voting systems, which are loosely described as "other varieties of gerrymandering." We have considered the constitutionality of these practices in other Fourteenth Amendment cases and have required plaintiffs to demonstrate that the challenged practice has the purpose and effect of diluting a racial group's voting strength. At-large and multimember schemes, however, do not classify voters on the basis of race. Classifying citizens by race, as we have said, threatens special harms that are not present in our vote-dilution cases.. It therefore warrants different analysis. * * *

The dissenters make two * * * arguments that cannot be reconciled with our precedents. First, they suggest that a racial gerrymander of the sort alleged here is functionally equivalent to gerrymanders for nonracial purposes, such as political gerrymanders. * * * But nothing in our case law compels the conclusion that racial and political gerrymanders are subject to precisely the same constitutional scrutiny. In fact, our country's long and persistent history of racial discrimination in voting — as well as our Fourteenth Amendment jurisprudence, which always has reserved the strictest scrutiny for discrimination on the basis of race — would seem to compel the opposite conclusion.

Second, JUSTICE STEVENS argues that racial gerrymandering poses no constitutional difficulties when district lines are drawn to favor the minority, rather than the majority. We have made clear, however, that equal protection analysis "is not dependent on the race of those burdened or benefited by a particular classification." *Croson.* * * *

[Here, Justice O'Connor distinguished *United Jewish Organizations v. Carey*, 430 U.S. 144 (1977). In that case plaintiffs, members of a Hasidic Jewish community split between two districts under New York's reapportionment, complained that the plan unduly diluted their voting strength. They did not allege that the plan "on its face was so highly irregular that it rationally could be understood only as an effort to segregate voters by race," nor would such a claim have been valid because New York had adhered to "traditional districting principles" such as compactness. In *UJO* the Court, with no majority opinion, denied relief, concluding that plaintiffs had failed to show that their voting strength had been cancelled out.] *UJO* set forth a standard under which white voters can establish unconstitutional vote dilution. * * * Nothing in the decision precludes white voters (or voters of any other race) from bringing the analytically distinct claim that a reapportionment plan rationally cannot be understood as anything other than an effort to segregate citizens into separate voting districts on the basis of race without sufficient justification.

[IV] JUSTICE SOUTER contends that exacting scrutiny of racial gerrymanders under the Fourteenth Amendment is inappropriate because reapportionment "nearly always require[s] some consideration of race for legitimate reasons." "As long as members of racial groups have [a] commonality of interest" and "racial bloc voting takes place," he argues, "legislators will have to take race into account" in order to comply with the Voting Rights Act. JUSTICE SOUTER's reasoning is flawed.

* * * That racial bloc voting or minority political cohesion may be found to exist in *some* cases, of course, is no reason to treat *all* racial gerrymanders differently from other kinds of racial classification. JUSTICE SOUTER apparently views racial gerrymandering of the type presented here as a special category of "benign" racial discrimination that should be subject to relaxed judicial review. As we have said, however, the very reason that the Equal Protection Clause demands strict scrutiny of all racial classifications is because without it, a court cannot determine whether or not the discrimination truly is "benign." Thus, if appellants' allegations of a racial gerrymander are not contradicted on remand, the District Court must determine whether the General

Assembly's reapportionment plan satisfies strict scrutiny. We therefore consider what that level of scrutiny requires in the reapportionment context.

The state appellees suggest that a covered jurisdiction may have a compelling interest in creating majority-minority districts in order to comply with the Voting Rights Act. * * *

For example, on remand North Carolina might claim that it adopted the revised plan in order to comply with the § 5 "nonretrogression" principle. Under that principle, a proposed voting change cannot be precleared if it will lead to "a retrogression in the position of racial minorities with respect to their effective exercise of the electoral franchise." * * *

* * * [W]e do not read [our] § 5 cases to give covered jurisdictions *carte blanche* to engage in racial gerrymandering in the name of nonretrogression. A reapportionment plan would not be narrowly tailored to the goal of avoiding retrogression if the State went beyond what was reasonably necessary to avoid retrogression. * * *

Before us, the state appellees contend that the General Assembly's revised plan was necessary not to prevent retrogression, but to avoid dilution of black voting strength in violation of § 2, as construed in *Thornburg v. Gingles*. In *Gingles* the Court considered a multimember redistricting plan for the North Carolina State Legislature. The Court held that members of a racial minority group claiming § 2 vote dilution through the use of multimember districts must prove three threshold conditions: that the minority group "is sufficiently large and geographically compact to constitute a majority in a single-member district," that the minority group is "politically cohesive," and that "the white majority votes sufficiently as a bloc to enable it . . . usually to defeat the minority's preferred candidate." We have indicated that similar preconditions apply in § 2 challenges to single-member districts.

Appellants maintain that the General Assembly's revised plan could not have been required by § 2. They contend that the State's black population is too dispersed to support two geographically compact majority-black districts, as the bizarre shape of District 12 demonstrates, and that there is no evidence of black political cohesion. They also contend that recent black electoral successes demonstrate the willingness of white voters in North Carolina to vote for black candidates. Appellants point out that blacks currently hold the positions of State Auditor, Speaker of the North Carolina House of Representatives, and chair of the North Carolina State Board of Elections. They also point out that in 1990 a black candidate defeated a white opponent in the Democratic Party run-off for a United States Senate seat before being defeated narrowly by the Republican incumbent in the general election. Appellants further argue that if § 2 did require adoption of North Carolina's revised plan, § 2 is to that extent unconstitutional. These arguments were not developed below, and the issues remain open for consideration on remand.

The state appellees alternatively argue that the General Assembly's plan advanced a compelling interest entirely distinct from the Voting Rights Act. We previously have recognized a significant state interest in eradicating the effects of past racial discrimination. But the State must have a " 'strong basis in evidence for [concluding] that remedial action [is] necessary.' " *Croson*.

The state appellees submit that two pieces of evidence gave the General Assembly a strong basis for believing that remedial action was warranted here: the Attorney General's imposition of the § 5 preclearance requirement on 40 North Carolina counties, and the *Gingles* District Court's findings of a long history of official racial discrimination in North Carolina's political system and of pervasive racial bloc voting. The state appellees assert that the deliberate creation of majority-minority districts is the most precise way — indeed the only effective way — to overcome the effects of racially polarized voting. This question also need not be decided at this stage of the litigation. We note, however, that only three Justices in *UJO* were prepared to say that States have a significant interest in minimizing the consequences of racial bloc voting apart from the requirements of the Voting Rights Act. And those three Justices specifically concluded that race-based districting, as a response to racially polarized voting, is constitutionally permissible only when the State "employ[s] sound districting principles," and only when the affected racial group's "residential patterns afford the opportunity of creating districts in which they will be in the majority." *UJO* (opinion of White, J., joined by Stevens and Rehnquist, JJ.).

[V] Racial classifications of any sort pose the risk of lasting harm to our society. They reinforce the belief, held by too many for too much of our history, that individuals should be judged by the color of their skin. Racial classifications with respect to voting carry particular dangers. Racial gerrymandering, even for remedial purposes, may balkanize us into competing racial factions; it threatens to carry us further from the goal of a political system in which race no longer matters — a goal that the Fourteenth and Fifteenth Amendments embody, and to which the Nation continues to aspire. It is for these reasons that race-based districting by our state legislatures demands close judicial scrutiny.

In this case, the Attorney General suggested that North Carolina could have created a reasonably compact second majority-minority district in the south-central to southeastern part of the State. We express no view as to whether appellants successfully could have challenged such a district under the Fourteenth Amendment. * * * Today we hold only that appellants have stated a claim under the Equal Protection Clause by alleging that the North Carolina General Assembly adopted a reapportionment scheme so irrational on its face that it can be understood only as an effort to segregate voters into separate voting districts because of their race, and that the separation lacks sufficient justification. If the allegation of racial gerrymandering remains uncontradicted, the District Court further must determine whether the North Carolina plan is narrowly tailored to further a compelling governmental interest. * * *

JUSTICE WHITE, with whom JUSTICE BLACKMUN and JUSTICE STEVENS join, dissenting.

The grounds for my disagreement with the majority are simply stated: Appellants have not presented a cognizable claim, because they have not alleged a cognizable injury. [Justice White asserted that in no prior voting case alleging unfair districting had relief been granted without a showing that the state action in question had both been intended to dilute the complaining group's power and had such a substantial discriminatory effect that the group was essentially "shut out of the political process." This requirement of substantial discriminatory impact was justified by "the nature of the redistricting process," which is inherently partisan and in which politically salient factors such as race are inevitably taken into account.]

[Justice White contended that this case is very similar to *UJO*.] As was the case in New York [in *UJO*], a number of North Carolina's political subdivisions have interfered with black citizens' meaningful exercise of the franchise, and are therefore subject to §§ 4 and 5 of the Voting Rights Act. * * * Like New York, North Carolina failed to prove to the Attorney General's satisfaction that its proposed redistricting had neither the purpose nor the effect of abridging the right to vote on account of race or color. The Attorney General's interposition of a § 5 objection "properly is viewed" as "an administrative finding of discrimination" against a racial minority. Finally, like New York, North Carolina reacted by modifying its plan and creating additional majority-minority districts.

In light of this background, it strains credulity to suggest that North Carolina's purpose in creating a second majority-minority district was to discriminate against members of the majority group by "impair[ing] or burden[ing their] opportunity . . . to participate in the political process." The State has made no mystery of its intent, which was to respond to the Attorney General's objections by improving the minority group's prospects of electing a candidate of its choice. I doubt that this constitutes a discriminatory purpose as defined in the Court's equal protection cases — i.e., an intent to aggravate "the unequal distribution of electoral power." But even assuming that it does, there is no question that appellants have not alleged the requisite discriminatory effects. Whites constitute roughly 76 percent of the total population and 79 percent of the voting age population in North Carolina. Yet, under the State's plan, they still constitute a voting majority in 10 (or 83 percent) of the 12 congressional districts. Though they might be dissatisfied at the prospect of casting a vote for a losing candidate — a lot shared by many, including a disproportionate number of minority voters — surely they cannot complain of discriminatory treatment.

* * * As I understand the [majority's theory], a redistricting plan that uses race to "segregate" voters by drawing "uncouth" lines is harmful in a way that a plan that uses race to distribute voters differently is not, for the former "bears an uncomfortable resemblance to political apartheid." The distinction is untenable.

Racial gerrymanders come in various shades: At-large voting schemes; the fragmentation of a minority group among various districts "so that it is a majority in none," otherwise known as "cracking"; the "stacking" of "a large minority population concentration . . . with a larger white population"; and, finally, the "concentration of [minority voters] into districts where they constitute an excessive majority," also called "packing." In each instance, race is consciously utilized by the legislature for electoral purposes; in each instance, we have put the plaintiff challenging the district lines to the burden of demonstrating that the plan was meant to, and did in fact, exclude an identifiable racial group from participation in the political process.

Not so, apparently, when the districting "segregates" by drawing odd-shaped lines.[7] In that case, we are told, such proof no longer is needed. Instead, it is the *State* that must rebut the allegation that race was taken into account, a fact that, together with the legislators' consideration of ethnic, religious, and other group characteristics, I had thought we practically took for granted. Part of the explanation for the majority's approach has to do, perhaps, with the emotions stirred by words such as "segregation" and "political apartheid." But their loose and imprecise use by today's majority has, I fear, led it astray. The consideration of race in "segregation" cases is no different than in other race-conscious districting; from the standpoint of the affected groups, moreover, the line-drawings all act in similar fashion. A plan that "segregates" being functionally indistinguishable from any of the other varieties of gerrymandering, we should be consistent in what we require from a claimant: Proof of discriminatory purpose and effect.

The other part of the majority's explanation of its holding is related to its simultaneous discomfort and fascination with irregularly shaped districts. * * *

[While] district irregularities may provide strong indicia of a potential gerrymander, they do no more than that. * * * Given two districts drawn on similar, race-based grounds, the one does not become more injurious than the other simply by virtue of being snake-like * * *. The majority's contrary view is perplexing in light of its concession that "compactness or attractiveness has never been held to constitute an independent federal constitutional requirement for state legislative districts." It is shortsighted as well, for a regularly shaped district can just as effectively effectuate racially discriminatory gerrymandering as an odd-shaped one. * * *

Limited by its own terms to cases involving unusually-shaped districts, the Court's approach nonetheless will unnecessarily hinder to some extent a State's voluntary effort to ensure a modicum of minority representation. This will be true in areas where the minority population is geographically dispersed. It also will be true where the minority population is not scattered but, for reasons unrelated to race — for example, incumbency protection — the State would

---

7. I borrow the term "segregate" from the majority, but, given its historical connotation, believe that its use is ill-advised. Nor is it a particularly accurate description of what has occurred. The majority-minority district that is at the center of the controversy is, according to the State, 54.71% African-American. Even if racial distribution was a factor, no racial group can be said to have been "segregated" — i.e., "set apart" or "isolate[d]." Webster's Collegiate Dictionary 1063 (9th ed. 1983).

rather not create the majority-minority district in its most "obvious" location.[8]
* * *

* * * [T]he Court's discussion of the level of scrutiny it requires warrants a few comments. I have no doubt that a State's compliance with the Voting Rights Act clearly constitutes a compelling interest. Here, the Attorney General objected to the State's plan on the ground that it failed to draw a second majority-minority district for what appeared to be pretextual reasons. Rather than challenge this conclusion, North Carolina chose to draw the second district. * * *

The Court * * * warns that the State's redistricting effort must be "narrowly tailored" to further its interest in complying with the law. It is evident to me, however, that what North Carolina did was precisely tailored to meet the objection of the Attorney General to its prior plan. Hence, I see no need for a remand at all, even accepting the majority's basic approach to this case.

Furthermore, how it intends to manage this standard, I do not know. Is it more "narrowly tailored" to create an irregular majority-minority district as opposed to one that is compact but harms other State interests such as incumbency protection or the representation of rural interests? Of the following two options — creation of two minority influence districts or of a single majority-minority district — is one "narrowly tailored" and the other not? Once the Attorney General has found that a proposed redistricting change violates § 5's nonretrogression principle in that it will abridge a racial minority's right to vote, does "narrow tailoring" mean that the most the State can do is preserve the *status quo*? Or can it maintain that change, while attempting to enhance minority voting power in some other manner? This small sample only begins to scratch the surface of the problems raised by the majority's test. But it suffices to illustrate the unworkability of a standard that is divorced from any measure of constitutional harm. In that, State efforts to remedy minority vote dilution are wholly unlike what typically has been labeled "affirmative action." To the extent that no other racial group is injured, remedying a Voting Rights Act violation does not involve preferential treatment. It involves, instead, an attempt to *equalize* treatment, and to provide minority voters with an effective voice in the political process. * * *

---

8. This appears to be what has occurred in this instance. In providing the reasons for the objection, the Attorney General noted that "[f]or the south-central to southeast area, there were several plans drawn providing for a second majority-minority congressional district" and that such a district would have been no more irregular than others in the State's plan. North Carolina's decision to create a majority-minority district can be explained as an attempt to meet this objection. Its decision not to create the more compact southern majority-minority district that was suggested, on the other hand, was more likely a result of partisan considerations. Indeed, in a suit brought prior to this one, different plaintiffs charged that District 12 was "grossly contorted" and had "no logical explanation other than incumbency protection and the enhancement of Democratic partisan interests. . . . The plan . . . ignores the directive of the [Department of Justice] to create a minority district in the southeastern portion of North Carolina since any such district would jeopardize the reelection of . . . the Democratic incumbent." Complaint in *Pope v. Blue*, No. 3:92CV71-P (WDNC). * * *

JUSTICE BLACKMUN, dissenting.

* * * It is particularly ironic that the case in which today's majority chooses to abandon settled law and to recognize for the first time this "analytically distinct" constitutional claim is a challenge by white voters to the plan under which North Carolina has sent black representatives to Congress for the first time since Reconstruction. * * *

JUSTICE STEVENS, dissenting.

* * * [T]wo critical facts in this case are undisputed: first, the shape of District 12 is so bizarre that it must have been drawn for the purpose of either advantaging or disadvantaging a cognizable group of voters; and, second, regardless of that shape, it *was* drawn for the purpose of facilitating the election of a second black representative from North Carolina.

These unarguable facts, which the Court devotes most of its opinion to proving, give rise to three constitutional questions: Does the Constitution impose a requirement of contiguity or compactness on how the States may draw their electoral districts? Does the Equal Protection Clause prevent a State from drawing district boundaries for the purpose of facilitating the election of a member of an identifiable group of voters? And, finally, if the answer to the second question is generally "No," should it be different when the favored group is defined by race? * * *

The first question is easy. There is no independent constitutional requirement of compactness or contiguity, and the Court's opinion (despite its many references to the shape of District 12) does not suggest otherwise. The existence of bizarre and uncouth district boundaries is powerful evidence of an ulterior purpose behind the shaping of those boundaries — usually a purpose to advantage the political party in control of the districting process. Such evidence will always be useful in cases that lack other evidence of invidious intent. In this case, however, we know what the legislators' purpose was: The North Carolina Legislature drew District 12 to include a majority of African-American voters. Evidence of the district's shape is therefore convincing, but it is also cumulative, and, for our purposes, irrelevant.

As for the second question, I believe that the Equal Protection Clause is violated when the State creates * * * uncouth district boundaries * * * for the sole purpose of making it more difficult for members of a minority group to win an election. The duty to govern impartially is abused when a group with power over the electoral process defines electoral boundaries solely to enhance its own political strength at the expense of any weaker group. That duty, however, is not violated when the majority acts to facilitate the election of a member of a group that lacks such power because it remains underrepresented in the state legislature — whether that group is defined by political affiliation, by common economic interests, or by religious, ethnic, or racial characteristics. The difference between constitutional and unconstitutional gerrymanders has nothing to do with whether they are based on assumptions about the groups they affect, but whether their purpose is to enhance the power of the group in control of the districting process at the expense of any minority group, and thereby to strengthen the unequal distribution of electoral power. When an assumption that people in a particular minority group (whether they are defined by the political party, religion, ethnic group, or race to which they belong) will vote in a particular way is used to benefit that group, no constitutional violation occurs. Politicians have always relied on assumptions that people in particular groups are likely to vote in a particular way when they draw new district lines, and I cannot believe that anything in today's opinion will stop them from doing so in the future.[3]

Finally, we must ask whether otherwise permissible redistricting to benefit an underrepresented minority group becomes impermissible when the minority group is defined by its race. The Court today answers this question in the affirmative, and its answer is wrong. If it is permissible to draw boundaries to provide adequate representation for rural voters, for union members, for Hasidic Jews, for Polish Americans, or for Republicans, it necessarily follows that it is permissible to do the same thing for members of the very minority group whose history in the United States gave birth to the Equal Protection Clause. A contrary conclusion could only be described as perverse.

JUSTICE SOUTER, dissenting.

* * * Unlike other contexts in which we have addressed the State's conscious use of race, see, e.g., *Croson* (city contracting), electoral districting calls for decisions that nearly always require some consideration of race for legitimate reasons where there is a racially mixed population. As long as members of racial groups have the commonality of interest implicit in our ability to talk about concepts like "minority voting strength," and "dilution of minority votes," cf. *Thornburg v. Gingles*, and as long as racial bloc voting takes place, legislators will have to take race into account in order to avoid dilution of minority voting strength in the districting plans they adopt.[2] One need look no further than the Voting Rights Act to understand that this may be required * * * .

A second distinction between districting and most other governmental decisions in which race has figured is that those other decisions using racial criteria characteristically occur in circumstances in which the use of race to the advantage of one person is necessarily at the obvious expense of a member of

---

3. The majority does not acknowledge that we require such a showing from plaintiffs who bring a vote dilution claim under § 2 of the Voting Rights Act. Under the three-part test established by *Thornburg v. Gingles*, a minority group must show that it could constitute the majority in a single-member district, "that it is politically cohesive," and "that the white majority votes sufficiently as a bloc to enable it . . . usually to defeat the minority's preferred candidate." At least the latter two of these three conditions depend on proving that what the Court today brands as "impermissible racial stereotypes" are true. Because *Gingles* involved North Carolina, which the Court admits has earlier established the existence of "pervasive racial bloc voting," its citizens and legislators — as well as those from other states — will no doubt be confused by the Court's requirement of evidence in one type of case that the Constitution now prevents reliance on in another. The Court offers them no explanation of this paradox.

2. Recognition of actual commonality of interest and racially-polarized bloc voting cannot be equated with the " 'invocation of race stereotypes' " described by the Court * * * and forbidden by our case law.

a different race. Thus, for example, awarding government contracts on a racial basis excludes certain firms from competition on racial grounds. See *Croson.* * * *

In districting, by contrast, the mere placement of an individual in one district instead of another denies no one a right or benefit provided to others.[4] All citizens may register, vote, and be represented. In whatever district, the individual voter has a right to vote in each election, and the election will result in the voter's representation. As we have held, one's constitutional rights are not violated merely because the candidate one supports loses the election or because a group (including a racial group) to which one belongs winds up with a representative from outside that group. It is true, of course, that one's vote may be more or less effective depending on the interests of the other individuals who are in one's district, and our cases recognize the reality that members of the same race often have shared interests. "Dilution" thus refers to the effects of districting decisions not on an individual's political power viewed in isolation, but on the political power of a group. This is the reason that the placement of given voters in a given district, even on the basis of race, does not, without more, diminish the effectiveness of the individual as a voter.

Our different approaches to equal protection in electoral districting and nondistricting cases reflect these differences. There is a characteristic coincidence of disadvantageous effect and illegitimate purpose associated with the State's use of race in those situations in which it has immediately triggered at least heightened scrutiny (which every Member of the Court to address the issue has agreed must be applied even to race-based classifications designed to serve some permissible state interest). Presumably because the legitimate consideration of race in a districting decision is usually inevitable under the Voting Rights Act when communities are racially mixed, however, and because, without more, it does not result in diminished political effectiveness for anyone, we have not taken the approach of applying the usual standard of such heightened "scrutiny" to race-based districting decisions. * * *

The Court offers no adequate justification for treating the narrow category of bizarrely shaped district claims differently from other districting claims.[5]

---

4. The majority's use of "segregation" to describe the effect of districting here may suggest that it carries effects comparable to school segregation making it subject to like scrutiny. But a principal consequence of school segregation was inequality in educational opportunity provided, whereas use of race (or any other group characteristic) in districting does not without more deny equality of political participation. * * *

5. The Court says its new cause of action is justified by what I understand to be some ingredients of stigmatic harm and by a "threa[t] . . . to our system of representative democracy," both caused by the mere adoption of a districting plan with the elements I have described in the text. To begin with, the complaint nowhere alleges any type of stigmatic harm. Putting that to one side, it seems utterly implausible to me to presume, as the Court does, that North Carolina's creation of this strangely-shaped majority-minority district "generates" within the white plaintiffs here anything comparable to "a feeling of inferiority as to their status in the community that may affect their hearts and minds in a way unlikely ever to be undone." *Brown.* As for representative democracy, I have difficulty seeing how it is threatened (indeed why it is not, rather, enhanced) by districts that are not even alleged to dilute anyone's vote.

The only justification I can imagine would be the preservation of "sound districting principles" such as compactness and contiguity. But * * * as the Court acknowledges, we have held that such principles are not constitutionally required, with the consequence that their absence cannot justify the distinct constitutional regime put in place by the Court today. * * * I would not respond to the seeming egregiousness of the redistricting now before us by untethering the concept of racial gerrymander in such a case from the concept of harm exemplified by dilution. * * *

NOTES ON *SHAW* AND THE
CONUNDRUM OF REPRESENTATION AND RACE

1. *What, Exactly, Did North Carolina Do Wrong?* Justice O'Connor creates a new cause of action: even if there is no dilution of the vote of a group nor any exclusion from the ballot, the Equal Protection Clause is violated if district lines are drawn with *too much* consideration of race and *not enough* consideration of traditional line-drawing practices. The opinion takes a sort of "Goldilocks" approach to the districting porridge — not too hot, not too cold, just right — that has bedeviled commentators and lower courts in trying to figure out how to apply it.[c] Her opinion is made all the more opaque by her apparent rejection of more judicially administrable approaches to intent (such as forbidding all consideration of race or allowing the consideration of race consistent with the purposes of the Voting Rights Act) or to traditional districting practices (note that she does not hold that such practices as maintaining contiguity and compactness are constitutionally required).

Suggesting that only majority-majority districts with uncouth lines and excessive considerations of race are vulnerable begs a number of questions. Surely the intentions of the redistricting would be just as clear to white voters in a nice square-shaped district drawn to be majority-minority as it was to the plaintiffs in *Shaw*. If the basis of *Shaw* is stigmatization and dignitary harm, are not the white voters in the square district injured in precisely the same way as the plaintiffs in *Shaw*? If the basis of *Shaw* is the pernicious effects upon the political process of the elected representative being beholden to a racial group, aren't those effects the same regardless of whether the district's shape is couth or uncouth?

Writing in the wake of *Shaw*, Richard Pildes and Richard Niemi stated: "In resisting the use of race in this specific way, *Shaw* requires that redistricting continue to be understood — and, perhaps more important, perceived — as

---

c. Scholarship analyzing *Shaw* and its aftermath has become its own cottage industry. For a small sampling of some of the more recent literature, see, in addition to other sources cited in these notes, J. Morgan Kousser, *Colorblind Injustice: Minority Voting Rights and the Undoing of the Second Reconstruction* 366–455 (1999); W. Mark Crain, *The Constitutionality of Race-Conscious Redistricting: An Empirical Analysis*, 30 J. Leg. Stud. 193 (2001); Heather Gerken, *Understanding the Right to an Undiluted Vote*, 114 Harv. L. Rev. 1663 (2001); Grant Hayden, *Resolving the Dilemma of Minority Representation*, 92 Cal. L. Rev. 1589 (2004); Daniel Lowenstein, *You Don't Have To Be a Liberal To Hate the Racial Gerrymandering Cases*, 50 Stan. L. Rev. 779 (1998); Melissa Lamb Saunders, *Reconsidering* Shaw: *The* Miranda *of Race-Conscious Districting*, 109 Yale L.J. 1603 (2000).

implicating multiple values. Public officials must maintain this commitment to value pluralism, even when they legitimately and intentionally take race into account."[d] If that is so, however, why does the Court emphasize "couthness"? Isn't that a pretty crude marker for value pluralism? Also, it appears that the "uncouthness" of District 12 was the result not only of the state's effort to create a majority-minority district, but also the Democrats' desire to protect their incumbents. In that event, it appears that race did not completely dominate the redistricting process. Pildes and Niemi draw from Niemi's earlier work quantifying criteria to determine relative compactness of districts (considering their geographic dispersion, perimeter, and population distribution). One finding of their study is that on a quantitative compactness scale, North Carolina's District 12 was the least compact district in the country. Would it have been preferable for the Court to adopt some statistical requirements for compactness, contiguity, and other factors, much like how it has used the one person, one vote principle to implement geographical redistricting?

2. *Questions Left Open by* Shaw. *Miller v. Johnson*, 515 U.S. 900 (1995), and *United States v. Hays*, 515 U.S. 737 (1995), resolved some of the issues opened up in *Shaw*, as to a lesser extent did *Bush v. Vera*, 517 U.S. 952 (1996), and *Shaw v. Hunt*, 517 U.S. 899 (1996).

(a) *Who may challenge majority-minority districting?* In *Hays*, the Court held that white Louisianans who did not live in the challenged majority-minority Louisiana district lacked "standing" to bring the case because they had not shown that they had been subjected to a racial classification.

(b) *What is the nature of the harm involved?* Justice O'Connor, in her plurality opinion in *Bush v. Vera*, wrote that some majority-minority districts "cause constitutional harm insofar as they convey the message that political identity is, or should be, predominantly racial." She labeled this an "expressive harm," which Justice Souter, in dissent, defined as "one that 'results from the idea or attitudes expressed through a governmental action, rather than from the more tangible or material consequences the action brings about' " (quoting Pildes & Niemi, *supra*.) Why is expressive harm, rather than more concrete harm, sufficient in this context to constitute a constitutional claim?

(c) *To be subject to challenge, must the challenged majority-minority district have a bizarre shape?* In *Miller*, Justice Kennedy's majority opinion for a Court that remained closely divided[e] answered this question in the

---

d. Richard Pildes & Richard Niemi, *Expressive Harms, "Bizarre Districts," and Voting Rights: Evaluating Election-District Appearances After* Shaw v. Reno, 92 Mich. L. Rev. 483, 501 (1993).

e. The same Justices who formed the majority in *Shaw* constituted the majority in *Miller*. Justices Ginsburg and Breyer, who joined the Court after *Shaw* was decided, dissented, as did Justices Stevens and Souter. In *Miller*, the Court affirmed the federal district court's holding that a Georgia majority-minority congressional district had been drawn unconstitutionally. On remand, the district court found that yet another Georgia majority-minority congressional district was unconstitutional as well. When the state legislature could not agree on redistricting, the district court imposed its own districting scheme, which contained only one majority-minority district. In *Abrams v. Johnson*, 521 U.S. 74 (1997), the same five-member majority

negative: "Shape is relevant not because bizarreness is a necessary element of the constitutional wrong or a threshold requirement of proof, but because it may be persuasive circumstantial evidence that race for its own sake, and not other districting principles, was the legislature's dominant and controlling rationale in drawing its district lines. The logical implication * * * is that parties may rely on evidence other than bizarreness to establish race-based districting."

(d) *If bizarre shape is not a requirement, what identifies presumptively unconstitutional majority-minority districts?* Recall the debate in *Shaw* about how the consideration of demographics, including race, is an inherent part of the redistricting process. If, as *Miller* held, there is no threshold requirement of bizarre configuration, what stops the *Shaw* cause of action from invalidating not only all majority-minority districts, but any district (regardless of demographics) that was designed in part because of racial considerations? *Miller* announced a potentially important qualification:

Federal court review of districting legislation represents a serious intrusion on the most vital of local functions. It is well settled that "reapportionment is primarily the duty and responsibility of the State." Electoral districting is a most difficult subject for legislatures, and so the States must have discretion to exercise the political judgment necessary to balance competing interests. Although race-based decisionmaking is inherently suspect, until a claimant makes a showing sufficient to support that allegation the good faith of a state legislature must be presumed. The courts, in assessing the sufficiency of a challenge to a districting plan, must be sensitive to the complex interplay of forces that enter a legislature's redistricting calculus. Redistricting legislatures will, for example, almost always be aware of racial demographics; but it does not follow that race predominates in the redistricting process. *Shaw*; see *Personnel Administrator v. Feeney* [p. 147, *supra*] (" '[D]iscriminatory purpose' . . . implies more than intent as volition or intent as awareness of consequences. It implies that the decisionmaker . . . selected or reaffirmed a particular course of action at least in part 'because of,' not merely 'in spite of,' its adverse effects"). The distinction between being aware of racial considerations and being motivated by them may be difficult to make. This evidentiary difficulty, together with the sensitive nature of redistricting and the presumption of good faith that must be accorded legislative enactments, requires courts to exercise extraordinary caution in adjudicating claims that a state has drawn district lines on the basis of race. The plaintiff's burden is to show, either through circumstantial evidence of a district's shape and demographics or more direct evidence going to legislative purpose, that race was the predominant factor motivating the legislature's decision to place a significant number of voters within or without a particular district. To make this showing, a plaintiff must prove that the legislature subordinated traditional race-neutral districting principles, including but not limited to compactness, contiguity, respect for political subdivisions or communities defined by actual shared interests, to racial considerations. Where these or other race-neutral considerations are the basis for redistricting legislation, and

that decided *Miller* upheld the district court's redistricting.

are not subordinated to race, a state can "defeat a claim that a district has been gerrymandered on racial lines." *Shaw.*[f]

Is this consistent with the Court's general approach to proving discriminatory intent under the Equal Protection Clause (see notes following *Mobile v. Bolden, supra*)? Will it not require intensive case-by-case review of every majority-minority district? If, as is commonly asserted, redistricting involves a host of complex and interactive questions, including potentially hundreds of small decisions about precisely where to draw each little segment of the lines, is it likely that one "predominant" motive can be isolated after the fact? Moreover, if the harm in these cases concerns social messages and perceptions arising from redistricting lines, shouldn't liability turn on the public processes and outcomes (*i.e.*, maps) of redistricting rather than whether, at the end of litigation some years later, a judge decides race was, or was not, the predominant motive? Consider Richard Pildes, *Principled Limitations on Racial and Partisan Redistricting*, 106 Yale L.J. 2505, 2540 (1997): "Judicial opinions in these cases, as well as editorial pages, reprint maps of the districts, not transcripts of political processes, for a reason. Social perceptions about the 'excessive' role of race are more likely attuned to objective characteristics of districts, such as their shapes, rather than the mysteries of intent."

(e) *What constitutes a compelling governmental interest sufficient to save majority-minority districting that would otherwise be unconstitutional? Miller* interpreted the Voting Rights Act narrowly to avoid any conflict between the statute and the equal-protection principle announced in *Shaw*. In *Miller*, Georgia had adopted the challenged majority-minority district after pressure from the federal Justice Department, which had refused to "preclear" earlier Georgia reapportionment plans under the Act. Justice Kennedy's opinion interpreted the Voting Rights Act as authorizing the Department of Justice to withhold preclearance only when a redistricting plan constitutes a "retrogression" in minority voting power. Thus, because earlier Georgia redistricting plans following the 1990 census had increased minority voting power over the scheme used to elect Georgia Congressmembers in the 1980s, the Department had wrongly withheld preclearance, and compliance with the Department's demands could not be justified as being required to comply with federal law.

---

f. In *Bush v. Vera*, Justice O'Connor's plurality opinion stated:

Strict scrutiny does not apply merely because redistricting is performed with consciousness of race. Nor does it apply to all cases of intentional creation of majority-minority districts. Electoral district lines are "facially race neutral," so a more searching inquiry is necessary before strict scrutiny can be found applicable in redistricting cases than in cases of "classifications based explicitly on race." For strict scrutiny to apply, the plaintiffs must prove that other, legitimate districting principles were "subordinated" to race. *Miller*. By that, we mean that race must be "*the predominant* factor motivating the legislature's [redistricting] decision." *Ibid.* (emphasis added). We thus differ from Justice Thomas [concurring in the judgment, joined by Justice Scalia], who would apparently hold that it suffices that racial considerations be *a* motivation for the drawing of a majority-minority district.

Only Chief Justice Rehnquist and Justice Kennedy joined this opinion, and Justice Kennedy wrote a short concurring opinion expressing reservations about the conclusion that the creation of a majority-minority district might not always trigger strict scrutiny.

Justice Kennedy then suggested that, had the Department been correct in its interpretation of the Voting Rights Act, the Act might have been unconstitutional.[g] In *Bush v. Vera* and *Shaw v. Hunt*, which also both struck down majority-minority congressional districting, the Court again did not resolve whether compliance with the Act would constitute a compelling governmental interest.[h]

---

g. Justice Kennedy stated:

* * * In *South Carolina v. Katzenbach*, we upheld § 5 [the preclearance provision of the Act] as a necessary and constitutional response to some states' "extraordinary stratagem[s] of contriving new rules of various kinds for the sole purpose of perpetuating voting discrimination in the face of adverse federal court decrees." But our belief in *Katzenbach* that the federalism costs exacted by § 5 preclearance could be justified by those extraordinary circumstances does not mean they can be justified in the circumstances of this case. And the Justice Department's implicit command that States engage in presumptively unconstitutional race-based districting brings the Voting Rights Act, once upheld as a proper exercise of Congress' authority under § 2 of the Fifteenth Amendment, into tension with the Fourteenth Amendment. As we recalled in *Katzenbach* itself, Congress' exercise of its Fifteenth Amendment authority even when otherwise proper still must " 'consist with the letter and spirit of the Constitution.' " We need not, however, resolve these troubling and difficult constitutional questions today. There is no indication Congress intended such a far-reaching application of § 5, so we reject the Justice Department's interpretation of the statute and avoid the constitutional problems that interpretation raises.

h. *Shaw v. Hunt* was the next round of Supreme Court review of the North Carolina congressional districting. On remand from *Shaw v. Reno*, the district court had concluded that racial considerations had been the predominant reason for the districting, but upheld it on the ground that it was necessary to further the state's compelling interest in complying with the Voting Rights Act. In an opinion by Chief Justice Rehnquist, joined by Justices O'Connor, Scalia, Kennedy, and Thomas, the Court reversed, concluding that the districting was not necessary to remedy any violation of the Act and refusing to reach the question whether compliance with the Act could be a compelling state interest. In yet another round of the controversy, the district court entered a summary judgment of unconstitutionality on the ground that the evidence plainly showed that the legislature had engaged in race-driven redistricting. In *Hunt v. Cromartie*, 526 U.S. 541 (1999), the Court, per Justice Thomas, reversed and remanded for a trial, concluding that expert testimony had demonstrated that it was a legitimately disputed question of fact whether creating a Democratic district was a stronger motive than racial concerns. After the district court again set aside the districting, the Supreme Court again reversed, this time per Justice Breyer, holding 5-4 that politics rather than race had been the predominant factor. See *Easley v. Cromartie*, 532 U.S. 234 (2001).

Bush v. Vera struck down majority-minority congressional districting in Texas. Justice O'Connor's plurality opinion, joined by Chief Justice Rehnquist and Justice Kennedy, upheld the district court's findings that racial considerations had been the predominant motive for the districting. Applying strict scrutiny, the plurality concluded that the districting could not be considered narrowly tailored to remedy (1) identified present or past racial discrimination or (2) any potential violation of the Voting Rights Act, because it failed to adhere to traditional districting principles such as compactness. (Thus, bizarre district shape is relevant not only to impermissible motive, but also to the inquiry about narrow tailoring.) As did the majority in *Shaw v. Hunt*, the plurality in *Bush* avoided addressing whether compliance with the statute would be a compelling government interest. In a highly unusual move, however, Justice O'Connor filed a separate concurring opinion to her own plurality opinion, in which she stated that compliance with the Act should amount to a compelling government interest. Justice Thomas, joined by Justice Scalia, concurred in the judgment.

Justice Stevens and Justice Souter both filed dissenting opinions in *Shaw v. Hunt* and in *Bush v. Vera*. Justices Ginsburg and Breyer joined Justice Souter's dissent and most portions

It seems that the issue here is not so much whether compliance with the Act constitutes a compelling governmental interest — the Justices seem to assume that it does — as it is what the Act in fact requires of the states. If the Act broadly requires race-conscious districting, then the Act itself may well be unconstitutional. If the Act is considerably narrower, than compliance with it presumably should suffice as a compelling governmental interest.

(f) *Nonjusticiability redux.* Recall that under the regime of *Colegrove v. Green*, federal courts were generally to stay out of "political thickets" involving state legislative apportionment — with an exception for cases involving intentional discrimination against racial minorities, who could invoke the specific protections of the Fifteenth Amendment (rather than merely the general protection of the Equal Protection Clause of the Fourteenth Amendment) and, at least in some cases, could plausibly claim they have been singled out as identified individuals, not simply as members of a group (*Gomillion*). *Baker v. Carr* and *Reynolds v. Sims* changed all that — or did they? Could *Baker* and *Reynolds* simply be understood as allowing federal courts to hear state apportionment cases invoking equal protection only in the context where a simple, administrable standard — one person, one vote — was available? Contrast *Shaw v. Reno*'s allowance of race to be taken into account in ensuring minority representation so long as it is not taken into account too much, which is surely a thicker political thicket, so to speak.[i] Should the Supreme Court's willingness to consider open-ended equality claims to state apportionment decisions be limited to unequal population claims (*Reynolds*) and race claims (*Gomillion* and *Shaw*)? What about apportionment designed to ensure the continued success of the political party currently in power, an even thicker political thicket? Consider the next part.

C. POLITICAL GERRYMANDERING

In *Karcher v. Daggett*, 462 U.S. 725 (1983) (discussed above in Section 1(A)(1)), the plaintiffs asserting that the New Jersey congressional districting was unconstitutional included all the Republican members of the House from New Jersey. They argued that "the bizarre configuration of New Jersey's congressional districts is sufficient to demonstrate that the plan was not adopted in 'good faith.' This argument * * * is a claim that the district boundaries are unconstitutional because they are the product of political gerrymandering." *Id.* (Stevens, J., concurring). Invoking the Equal Protection Clause, Justice Stevens, in his concurring opinion, was willing to strike down the redistricting based solely upon the taking of partisan advantage and to consider the noncompact shape of district configurations and "extensive deviation from established political boundaries" as evidence of illicit political gerrymandering. (Justice Powell voiced similar concerns in a separate opinion in *Karcher*.) Justice Stevens also stated:

---

of Justice Stevens' dissent.

i. With apologies to Peter Schuck, *The Thickest Thicket: Partisan Gerrymandering and Judicial Regulation of Politics*, 87 Colum. L. Rev. 1325 (1987).

A procedural standard * * * may also be enlightening. If the process for formulating and adopting a plan excluded divergent viewpoints, openly reflected the use of partisan criteria, and provided no explanation of the reasons for selecting one plan over another, it would seem appropriate to conclude that an adversely affected plaintiff group is entitled to have the majority explain its action. On the other hand, if neutral decisionmakers developed the plan on the basis of neutral criteria, if there was an adequate opportunity for the presentation and consideration of differing points of view, and if the guidelines used in selecting a plan were explained, a strong presumption of validity should attach to whatever plan such a process produced. * * *

A glance at the [districting] map * * * shows district configurations well deserving the kind of descriptive adjectives — "uncouth" and "bizarre" — that have traditionally been used to describe acknowledged gerrymanders. * * * In addition [to] disregarding geographical compactness, the redistricting scheme wantonly disregards county boundaries. For example, in the words of a commentator, "In a flight of cartographic fancy, the Legislature packed New Jersey Republicans into a new district many call 'the Swan.' Its long neck and twisted body stretch from the New York suburbs to the rural upper reaches of the Delaware River." That district, the Fifth, contains segments of at least seven counties. The same commentator described the Seventh District, comprised of parts of five counties, as tracing "a curving partisan path through industrial Elizabeth, liberal academic Princeton and largely Jewish Marlboro in Monmouth County. The resulting monstrosity was called 'the Fishhook' by detractors."

Such a map prompts an inquiry into the process that led to its adoption. The plan was sponsored by the leadership in the Democratic Party, which controlled both houses of the state legislature as well as the Governor's office, and was signed into law the day before the inauguration of a Republican Governor. The legislators never formally explained the guidelines used in formulating their plan or in selecting it over other available plans. Several [other plans] contained districts that were more nearly equal in population, more compact, and more consistent with subdivision boundaries[.] * * * [T]he record indicates that the decisionmaking process leading to adoption of the challenged plan was far from neutral. It was designed to increase the number of Democrats, and to decrease the number of Republicans, that New Jersey's voters would send to Congress in future years. * * *

Consider the full Court's various responses to political gerrymandering in the cases following *Karcher*.

––––––––

DAVIS v. BANDEMER, 478 U.S. 109 (1986). Democrats challenged the reapportionment of the Indiana legislature done in response to the 1980 census by the Republican majorities in both legislative houses and approved by the Republican governor. The three-judge district court invalidated the reapportionment on equal protection grounds, and the state appealed. The plurality opinion of **Justice White**, joined by **Justices Brennan**, **Marshall**, and **Blackmun**, first rejected the contention that the issue was a nonjusticiable political question. Justice White noted that, since *Baker v. Carr*, the Court has adjudicated claims based on population inequality among districts, racial gerrymandering, and racial vote dilution allegedly resulting from multi-member districting. The opinion found that none of *Baker*'s five "identifying characteristics" of a political question were present in this case, just as they had not been present in *Baker, Reynolds*, and other reapportionment cases. The plurality then endorsed a narrow cause of action under the Equal Protection Clause, by analogy to the approach taken in *Bolden*. "[U]nconstitutional discrimination occurs only when the electoral system is arranged in a manner that will consistently degrade a voter's or a group of voters' influence on the political process as a whole. * * * [T]he question is whether a particular group has been unconstitutionally denied its chance to effectively influence the political process. * * * Statewide, * * * the inquiry centers on the voters' direct or indirect influence on the elections of the state legislature as a whole." Thus, "[r]elying on a single election to prove unconstitutional discrimination is unsatisfactory." Because the district court's findings did not satisfy this test, the Court reversed.

Justice O'Connor, joined by **Chief Justice Burger** and **Justice Rehnquist**, concurred in the judgment of reversal, but on the ground that political gerrymandering raises only a nonjusticiable political question. The issue was certainly "political" in the classic sense of the term. In her view, legislatively controlled reapportionment was a "critical and traditional part of politics in the United States" that was generally self-correcting over time. Political (as opposed to racial) groups should have no constitutional protection against losses in the political process. The plurality's test for an equal protection violation provided no judicially manageable standard. "[T]his standard will over time either prove unmanageable and arbitrary or else evolve towards some loose form of proportionality."

Justice Powell, joined by **Justice Stevens**, dissented. They agreed with the plurality that the issue was justiciable but strongly disagreed with the plurality's constitutional test. Starting with the precept that "[t]he Equal Protection Clause guarantees citizens that their State will govern them impartially," Justice Powell drew two further precepts from the Court's prior cases on voting rights. First, those cases recognize that "equal protection encompasses a guarantee of equal *representation*, requiring a State to seek to achieve through redistricting 'fair and effective representation of all citizens.' " (Quoting *Reynolds*.) Second, those cases recognized that "redistricting should be based on a number of neutral criteria, of which districts of equal population was only one." In light of these precepts, the plurality opinion was "seriously flawed" by its formalistic, and unrealistic, focus on mathematical standards of representation and by its failure to announce any workable standard for review.

Relying upon Justice Stevens's concurring opinion in *Karcher*, Justice Powell proposed that judicial review should investigate such neutral criteria as "the shapes of voting districts and adherence to established political subdivision boundaries. Other relevant considerations include the nature of the legislative procedures by which the apportionment law was adopted and legislative history reflecting contemporaneous legislative goals. To make out a case of unconstitutional partisan gerrymandering, the plaintiff should be required to offer proof concerning these factors, which bear directly on the fairness of a redistricting plan, as well as evidence concerning population disparities and statistics tending to show vote dilution. No one factor should be dispositive." Tracing the history of the Indiana reapportionment, Justice Powell concluded that "[t]he legislative process consisted of nothing more than the majority party's private application of computer technology to map-making." The maps ignored traditional political subdivisions and communities of interest and appeared rooted solely in partisan considerations. He concluded that appellants "failed to justify the discriminatory impact of the plan by showing that the plan had a rational basis in permissible neutral criteria." For the plurality, **Justice White** argued in response that the Powell-Stevens approach was inconsistent with *Bolden* and would tend to promote judicially imposed proportional representation.

By finding political gerrymandering a justiciable issue, *Bandemer* fostered litigation in the lower courts. But because the plurality defined the cause of action so narrowly (as well as so vaguely), virtually no redress for political gerrymandering resulted. When given an opportunity to reconsider *Bandemer* in the following case, however, the Court could reach no definitive conclusion.

VIETH v. JUBELIRER
Supreme Court of the United States, 2004
541 U.S. 267, 124 S.Ct. 1769, 158 L.Ed.2d 546

JUSTICE SCALIA announced the judgment of the Court and delivered an opinion, in which THE CHIEF JUSTICE [REHNQUIST], JUSTICE O'CONNOR, and JUSTICE THOMAS join.

[I] The facts, as alleged by the plaintiffs, are as follows. The population figures derived from the 2000 census showed that Pennsylvania was entitled to only 19 Representatives in [the United States] Congress, a decrease in 2 from the Commonwealth's previous delegation. Pennsylvania's General Assembly took up the task of drawing a new districting map. At the time, the Republican Party controlled a majority of both state Houses and held the Governor's office. Prominent national figures in the Republican Party pressured the General Assembly to adopt a partisan redistricting plan as a punitive measure against Democrats for having enacted pro-Democrat redistricting plans elsewhere. The Republican members of Pennsylvania's House and Senate worked together on such a plan. On January 3, 2002, the General Assembly passed its plan, which was signed into law by Governor Schweiker * * *.

[The lawsuit filed by registered Democrats who vote in Pennsylvania alleged that the legislation created malapportioned districts, in violation of the one-person, one-vote requirement. Moreover, the plaintiffs argued that the redistricting plan constituted a political gerrymander, because the districts were "meandering and irregular" and "ignor[ed] all traditional redistricting criteria, including the preservation of local government boundaries, solely for the sake of partisan advantage." The plaintiffs initially won before a three-judge district court panel, Pennsylvania passed a remedial plan to cure the apportionment problems identified by the court, and the district court panel denied plaintiffs' claim that the remedial proposal was also an impermissible political gerrymander.]

[II] Political gerrymanders are not new to the American scene. One scholar traces them back to the Colony of Pennsylvania at the beginning of the 18th century, where several counties conspired to minimize the political power of the city of Philadelphia by refusing to allow it to merge or expand into surrounding jurisdictions, and denying it additional representatives. See E. Griffith, *The Rise and Development of the Gerrymander* 26–28 (1974). * * * The political gerrymander remained alive and well (though not yet known by that name) at the time of the framing. There were allegations that Patrick Henry attempted (unsuccessfully) to gerrymander James Madison out of the First Congress. * * * "By 1840 the gerrymander was a recognized force in party politics and was generally attempted in all legislation enacted for the formation of election districts. It was generally conceded that each party would attempt to gain power which was not proportionate to its numerical strength." Griffith, [p.] 123.

It is significant that the Framers provided a remedy for such practices in the Constitution. Article 1, § 4, while leaving in state legislatures the initial power to draw districts for federal elections, permitted Congress to "make or alter" those districts if it wished. Many objected to the congressional oversight established by this provision. In the course of the debates in the Constitutional Convention, Charles Pinkney and John Rutledge moved to strike the relevant language. James Madison responded in defense of the provision that Congress must be given the power to check partisan manipulation of the election process by the States. * * * Although the motion of Pinkney and Rutledge failed, opposition to the "make or alter" provision of Article I, § 4 — and the defense that it was needed to prevent political gerrymandering — continued to be voiced in the state ratifying debates. * * *

The power bestowed on Congress to regulate elections, and in particular to restrain the practice of political gerrymandering, has not lain dormant. In the Apportionment Act of 1842, Congress provided that Representatives must be elected from single-member districts "composed of contiguous territory." * * * Recent history [also] attests to Congress's awareness of the sort of districting practices appellants protest, and of its power under Article I, § 4 to control them. Since 1980, no fewer than five bills have been introduced to regulate gerrymandering in congressional districting. * * *

[III] [The plurality provided the *Baker v. Carr* tests for the existence of a political question (p. 129, *supra*). It stated that "there is no doubt" of the applicability of the second test to this case: the lack of "judicially discoverable and manageable standards" to resolve the claim.]

Over the dissent of three Justices, the Court held in *Davis v. Bandemer* that, since it was "not persuaded that there are no judicially discernible and manageable standards by which political gerrymander cases are to be decided," such cases *were* justiciable. The clumsy shifting of the burden of proof for the premise (the Court was "not persuaded" that standards do not exist, rather than "persuaded" that they do) was necessitated by the uncomfortable fact that the six-Justice majority could not discern what the judicially discernable standards might be. * * * The lower courts have lived with that assurance of a standard (or more precisely, lack of assurance that there is no standard), coupled with that inability to specify a standard, for the past 18 years. In that time, they have considered numerous political gerrymandering claims; this Court has never revisited the unanswered question of what standard governs.

[T]he lower courts have [not], over 18 years, succeeded in shaping the standard that this Court was initially unable to enunciate. They have simply applied the standard set forth in *Bandemer*'s four-Justice plurality opinion. This might be thought to prove that the four-Justice plurality standard has met the test of time — but for the fact that its application has almost invariably produced the same result (except for the incurring of attorney's fees) as would have obtained if the question were nonjusticiable: judicial intervention has been refused. As one commentary has put it, "[t]hroughout its subsequent history, *Bandemer* has served almost exclusively as an invitation to litigation without much prospect of redress." S. Issacharoff, P. Karlan, & R. Pildes, *The Law of Democracy* 886 (rev. 2d ed. 2002). * * *

Eighteen years of judicial effort with virtually nothing to show for it justify us in revisiting the question whether the standard promised by *Bandemer* exists. As the following discussion reveals, no judicially discernible and manageable standards for adjudicating political gerrymandering claims have emerged. Lacking them, we must conclude that political gerrymandering claims are nonjusticiable and that *Bandemer* was wrongly decided.

[IIIA] We begin our review of possible standards with that proposed by Justice White's plurality opinion in *Bandemer* because, as the narrowest ground for our decision in that case, it has been the standard employed by the lower courts. [The *Vieth* plurality argued that the *Bandemer* test had led only to "puzzlement and consternation" in the lower courts and to criticism by academic commentators.] Because this standard was misguided when proposed, has not been improved in subsequent application, and is not even defended before us today by the appellants, we decline to affirm it as a constitutional requirement.

[IIIB] Appellants take a run at enunciating their own workable standard based on Article I, § 2, and the Equal Protection Clause. We consider it at length not only because it reflects the litigant's view as to the best that can be derived from 18 years of experience, but also because it shares many features with other proposed standards, so that what is said of it may be said of them as well. Appellants' proposed standard retains the two-pronged framework of the *Bandemer* plurality — intent plus effect — but modifies the type of showing sufficient to satisfy each.

To satisfy appellants' intent standard, a plaintiff must "show that the mapmakers acted with a *predominant intent* to achieve partisan advantage," which can be shown "by direct evidence or by circumstantial evidence that other neutral and legitimate redistricting criteria were subordinated to the goal of achieving partisan advantage." (emphasis added). As compared with the *Bandemer* plurality's test of mere intent to disadvantage the plaintiff's group, this proposal seemingly makes the standard more difficult to meet — but only at the expense of making the standard more indeterminate.

"Predominant intent" to disadvantage the plaintiff political group refers to the relative importance of that goal as compared with all the other goals that the map seeks to pursue — contiguity of districts, compactness of districts, observance of the lines of political subdivision, protection of incumbents of all parties, cohesion of natural racial and ethnic neighborhoods, compliance with requirements of the Voting Rights Act of 1965 regarding racial distribution, etc. Appellants contend that their intent test *must* be discernible and manageable because it has been borrowed from our racial gerrymandering cases. To begin with, in a very important respect that is not so. In the racial gerrymandering context, the predominant intent test has been applied to the challenged district in which the plaintiffs voted. Here, however, appellants do not assert that an apportionment fails their intent test if any single district does so. Since "it would be quixotic to attempt to bar state legislatures from considering politics as they redraw district lines," appellants propose a test that is satisfied only when "partisan advantage was the predominant motivation *behind the entire statewide plan.*" (emphasis added). Vague as the "predominant motivation" test might be when used to evaluate single districts, it all but evaporates when applied statewide. Does it mean, for instance, that partisan intent must outweigh all other goals — contiguity, compactness, preservation of neighborhoods, etc. — *statewide*? And how is the statewide "outweighing" to be determined? If three-fifths of the map's districts forgo the pursuit of partisan ends in favor of strictly observing political-subdivision lines, and only two-fifths ignore those lines to disadvantage the plaintiffs, is the observance of political subdivisions the "predominant" goal between those two? We are sure appellants do not think so.

Even within the narrower compass of challenges to a single district, applying a "predominant intent" test to *racial* gerrymandering is easier and less disruptive. The Constitution clearly contemplates districting by political entities, and unsurprisingly that turns out to be root-and-branch a matter of politics. By contrast, the purpose of segregating voters on the basis of race is not a lawful one, and is much more rarely encountered. Determining whether the shape of a particular district is so substantially affected by the presence of a rare and constitutionally suspect motive as to invalidate it is quite different from determining whether it is so substantially affected by the excess of an ordinary and lawful motive as to invalidate it. Moreover, the fact that partisan districting is a lawful and common practice means that there is almost *always* room for an election-impeding lawsuit contending that partisan advantage was the predominant motivation; not so for claims of racial gerrymandering. Finally, courts might be justified in accepting a modest degree of unmanageability to enforce a constitutional command which (like the Fourteenth Amendment obligation to refrain from racial discrimination) is clear; whereas they are not justified in inferring a judicially enforceable constitutional obligation (the obligation not to apply *too much* partisanship in districting) which is both dubious and severely unmanageable. For these reasons, to the extent that our racial gerrymandering cases represent a model of discernible and manageable standards, they provide no comfort here.

The effects prong of appellants' proposal replaces the *Bandemer* plurality's vague test of "denied its chance to effectively influence the political process" with criteria that are seemingly more specific. The requisite effect is established when "(1) the plaintiffs show that the districts systematically 'pack' and 'crack' the rival party's voters,[7] *and* (2) the court's examination of the 'totality of circumstances' confirms that the map can thwart the plaintiffs' ability to translate a majority of votes into a majority of seats." (Emphasis and footnote added.) This test is loosely based on our cases applying § 2 of the Voting Rights Act to discrimination by race. But a person's politics is rarely as readily discernible — and *never* as permanently discernible — as a person's race. Political affiliation is not an immutable characteristic, but may shift from one election to the next; and even within a given election, not all voters follow the party line. We dare say (and hope) that the political party which puts forward an utterly incompetent candidate will lose even in its registration stronghold. These facts make it impossible to assess the effects of partisan gerrymandering, to fashion a standard for evaluating a violation, and finally to craft a remedy.

Assuming, however, that the effects of partisan gerrymandering can be determined, appellants' test would invalidate the districting only when it prevents a majority of the electorate from electing a majority of representatives. Before considering whether this particular standard is judicially manageable we question whether it is judicially discernible in the sense of being relevant to some constitutional violation. Deny it as appellants may (and do), this standard rests upon the principle that groups (or at least political-action groups) have a right to proportional representation. But the Constitution contains no such principle. It guarantees equal protection of the law to persons, not equal representation in government to equivalently sized groups. It nowhere says that farmers or urban dwellers, Christian fundamentalists or Jews, Republicans or Democrats, must be accorded political strength proportionate to their numbers.

Even if the standard were relevant, however, it is not judicially manageable. To begin with, how is a party's majority status to be established? Appellants propose using the results of statewide races as the benchmark of party support. But as their own complaint describes, in the 2000 Pennsylvania statewide elections some Republicans won and some Democrats won. Moreover, to think that majority status in statewide races establishes majority status for district contests, one would have to believe that the only factor determining voting behavior at all levels is political affiliation. That is assuredly not true. * * *

But if we could identify a majority party, we would find it impossible to assure that that party wins a majority of seats — unless we radically revise the States' traditional structure for elections. In any winner-take-all district system, there can be no guarantee, no matter how the district lines are drawn, that a majority of party votes statewide will produce a majority of seats for that party. * * * Consider, for example, a legislature that draws district lines with

---

7. "Packing" refers to the practice of filling a district with a supermajority of a given group or party. "Cracking" involves the splitting of a group or party among several districts to deny that group or party a majority in any of those districts.

no objectives in mind except compactness and respect for the lines of political subdivisions. Under that system, political groups that tend to cluster (as is the case with Democratic voters in cities) would be systematically affected by what might be called a "natural" packing effect.

Our one-person, one-vote cases, see *Reynolds v. Sims* [and] *Wesberry v. Sanders*, have no bearing upon this question, neither in principle nor in practicality. Not in principle, because to say that each individual must have an equal say in the selection of representatives, and hence that a majority of individuals must have a majority say, is not at all to say that each discernable group, whether farmers or urban dwellers or political parties, must have representation equivalent to its numbers. And not in practicality, because the easily administrable standard of population equality adopted by *Wesberry* and *Reynolds* enables judges to decide whether a violation has occurred (and to remedy it) essentially on the basis of three readily determined factors — where the plaintiff lives, how many voters are in his district, and how many voters are in other districts; whereas requiring judges to decide whether a districting system will produce a statewide majority for a majority party casts them forth upon a sea of imponderables, and asks them to make determinations that not even election experts can agree upon.

[The plurality also dismissed the standard proposed by Justice Powell in *Bandemer* as an unmanageable "totality-of-the-circumstances" test. In Part IV, the plurality responded to the contentions of the separate opinions; this discussion is summarized in the Notes following the case.]

JUSTICE KENNEDY, concurring in the judgment.

* * * When presented with a claim of injury from partisan gerrymandering, courts confront two obstacles. First is the lack of comprehensive and neutral principles for drawing electoral boundaries. No substantive definition of fairness in districting seems to command general assent. Second is the absence of rules to limit and confine judicial intervention. * * *

There are, then, weighty arguments for holding cases like these to be nonjusticiable; and those arguments may prevail in the long run. In my view, however, the arguments are not so compelling that they require us now to bar all future claims of injury from a partisan gerrymander. It is not in our tradition to foreclose the judicial process from the attempt to define standards and remedies where it is alleged that a constitutional right is burdened or denied. * * *

Our willingness to enter the political thicket of the apportionment process with respect to one-person, one-vote claims makes it particularly difficult to justify a categorical refusal to entertain claims against this other type of gerrymandering. The plurality's conclusion that absent an "easily administrable standard," the appellants' claim must be nonjusticiable contrasts starkly with the more patient approach of *Baker v. Carr*, not to mention the controlling precedent on the question of justiciability of *Davis v. Bandemer*, the case the plurality would overrule. * * *

That no [judicially manageable] standard [for partisan gerrymandering claims] has emerged in this case should not be taken to prove that none will emerge in the future. Where important rights are involved, the impossibility of full analytical satisfaction is reason to err on the side of caution. * * *

* * * [T]he rapid evolution of technologies in the apportionment field suggests yet unexplored possibilities. Computer assisted districting has become so routine and sophisticated that legislatures, experts, and courts can use databases to map electoral districts in a matter of hours, not months. Technology is both a threat and a promise. On the one hand, if courts refuse to entertain any claims of partisan gerrymandering, the temptation to use partisan favoritism in districting in an unconstitutional manner will grow. On the other hand, these new technologies may produce new methods of analysis that make more evident the precise nature of the burdens gerrymanders impose on the representational rights of voters and parties. That would facilitate court efforts to identify and remedy the burdens, with judicial intervention limited by the derived standards. * * *

Though * * * the appellants relied on the Equal Protection Clause as the source of their substantive right and as the basis for relief, I note that the complaint in this case also alleged a violation of First Amendment rights. The First Amendment may be the more relevant constitutional provision in future cases that allege unconstitutional partisan gerrymandering. After all, these allegations involve the First Amendment interest of not burdening or penalizing citizens because of their participation in the electoral process, their voting history, their association with a political party, or their expression of political views. Under general First Amendment principles those burdens in other contexts are unconstitutional absent a compelling government interest. * * * First Amendment concerns arise where a State enacts a law that has the purpose and effect of subjecting a group of voters or their party to disfavored treatment by reason of their views. In the context of partisan gerrymandering, that means that First Amendment concerns arise where an apportionment has the purpose and effect of burdening a group of voters' representational rights. * * *

Where it is alleged that a gerrymander had the purpose and effect of imposing burdens on a disfavored party and its voters, the First Amendment may offer a sounder and more prudential basis for intervention than does the Equal Protection Clause. The equal protection analysis puts its emphasis on the permissibility of an enactment's classifications. This works where race is involved since classifying by race is almost never permissible. It presents a more complicated question when the inquiry is whether a generally permissible classification has been used for an impermissible purpose. That question can only be answered in the affirmative by the subsidiary showing that the classification as applied imposes unlawful burdens. The First Amendment analysis concentrates on whether the legislation burdens the representational rights of the complaining party's voters for reasons of ideology, beliefs, or political association. The analysis allows a pragmatic or functional assessment that accords some latitude to the States.

Finally, I do not understand the plurality to conclude that partisan gerrymandering that disfavors one party is permissible. Indeed, the Court seems to acknowledge it is not. This is all the more reason to admit the possibility of later suits, while holding just that the parties have failed to prove, under our "well developed and familiar" standard, that these legislative classifications "reflec[t] *no* policy, but simply arbitrary and capricious action." That said, courts must be cautious about adopting a standard that turns on whether the partisan interests in the redistricting process were excessive. Excessiveness is not easily determined. * * *

JUSTICE STEVENS, dissenting.

* * * [W]hile political considerations may properly influence the decisions of our elected officials, when such decisions disadvantage members of a minority group — whether the minority is defined by its members' race, religion, or political affiliation — they must rest on a neutral predicate. * * * [T]he Equal Protection Clause implements a duty to govern impartially that requires, at the very least, that every decision by the sovereign serve some nonpartisan public purpose.

In evaluating a claim that a governmental decision violates the Equal Protection Clause, we have long required a showing of discriminatory purpose. That requirement applies with full force to districting decisions. The line that divides a racial or ethnic minority unevenly between school districts can be entirely legitimate if chosen on the basis of neutral factors — county lines, for example, or a natural boundary such as a river or major thoroughfare. But if the district lines were chosen for the purpose of limiting the number of minority students in the school, or the number of families holding unpopular religious or political views, that invidious purpose surely would invalidate the district.

Consistent with that principle, our recent racial gerrymandering cases have examined the shape of the district and the purpose of the districting body to determine whether race, above all other criteria, predominated in the line-drawing process. [Justice Stevens summarized *Shaw v. Reno* and its progeny.] Under the *Shaw* cases, * * * the use of race as a criterion in redistricting is not *per se* impermissible, but when race is elevated to paramount status — when it is the be-all and end-all of the redistricting process — the legislature has gone too far. * * *

Just as irrational shape can serve as an objective indicator of an impermissible legislative purpose, other objective features of a districting map can save the plan from invalidation. We have explained that "traditional districting principles," which include "compactness, contiguity, and respect for political subdivisions," are "important not because they are constitutionally required . . . but because they are objective factors that may serve to defeat a claim that a district has been gerrymandered on racial lines." * * *

In my view, the same standards should apply to claims of political gerrymandering, for the essence of a gerrymander is the same regardless of whether the group is identified as political or racial. Gerrymandering always involves the drawing of district boundaries to maximize the voting strength of the dominant political faction and to minimize the strength of one or more groups of opponents. In seeking the desired result, legislators necessarily make judgments about the probability that the members of identifiable groups — whether economic, religious, ethnic, or racial — will vote in a certain way. The overriding purpose of those predictions is political. It follows that the standards that enable courts to identify and redress a racial gerrymander could also perform the same function for other species of gerrymanders.

The racial gerrymandering cases therefore supply a judicially manageable standard for determining when partisanship, like race, has played too great of a role in the districting process. Just as race can be a factor in, but cannot dictate the outcome of, the districting process, so too can partisanship be a permissible consideration in drawing district lines, so long as it does not predominate. * * *

The plurality reasons that the standards for evaluating racial gerrymanders are not workable in cases such as this because partisan considerations, unlike racial ones, are perfectly legitimate. Until today, however, there has not been the slightest intimation in any opinion written by any Member of this Court that a naked purpose to disadvantage a political minority would provide a rational basis for drawing a district line. On the contrary, our opinions referring to political gerrymanders have consistently assumed that they were at least undesirable, and we always have indicated that political considerations are among those factors that may not dominate districting decisions. Purely partisan motives are "rational" in a literal sense, but there must be a limiting principle. * * * A legislature controlled by one party could not, for instance, impose special taxes on members of the minority party, or use tax revenues to pay the majority party's campaign expenses. The rational basis for government decisions must satisfy a standard of legitimacy and neutrality; an acceptable rational basis can be neither purely personal nor purely partisan. * * *

In sum, in evaluating a challenge to a specific district, I would apply the standard set forth in the [racial gerrymandering] cases and ask whether the legislature allowed partisan considerations to dominate and control the lines drawn, forsaking all neutral principles. Under my analysis, if no neutral criterion can be identified to justify the lines drawn, and if the only possible explanation for a district's bizarre shape is a naked desire to increase partisan strength, then no rational basis exists to save the district from an equal protection challenge. Such a narrow test would cover only a few meritorious claims, but it would preclude extreme abuses, * * * and it would perhaps shorten the time period in which the pernicious effects of such a gerrymander are felt. * * *

[JUSTICE SOUTER'S dissent, joined by JUSTICE GINSBURG, set out a five-part test. A plaintiff would be required to show (1) that he is a member of a "cohesive political group"; (2) that the district he lived in paid no or little attention to traditional districting principles; (3) that there were "specific correlations between the district's deviations from traditional districting principles and the distribution of the population of his group"; (4) that a hypothetical district exists which includes the plaintiff's residence, remedies the packing or cracking of the plaintiff's group, and deviates less from traditional districting principles; and (5) that "the defendants acted intention-ally to manipulate the shape of the district in order to pack or crack his group." When a plaintiff made such showings, the burden would shift to the defendants to justify the district by reference to goals other than "naked partisan advan-tage."]

[In response to the plurality's argument that his test was unworkable, he wrote: "It is common sense * * * to break down a large and intractable issue into discrete fragments as a way to get a handle on the larger one, and the elements I propose are not only tractable in theory, but the very subjects that judges already deal with in practice. The plurality asks, for example, '[w]hat . . . a lower court [is] to do when, as will often be the case, the district adheres to some traditional criteria but not others?' This question already arises in cases under § 2 of the Voting Rights Act of 1965, and the district courts have not had the same sort of difficulty answering it as they have in applying the *Davis v. Bandemer* plurality. The enquiries I am proposing are not, to be sure, as hard-edged as I wish they could be, but neither do they have a degree of subjectivity inconsistent with the judicial function."]

[Justice Souter also addressed the argument that he had not specified the target of judicial intervention. He likened partisan gerrymandering to "a species of vote dilution: the point of the gerrymander is to capture seats by manipulating district lines to diminish the weight of the other party's votes in elections. To devise a judicial remedy for that harm, however, it is not necessary to adopt a full-blown theory of fairness, furnishing a precise measure of harm caused by divergence from the ideal in each case. It is sufficient instead to agree that gerrymandering is, indeed, unfair, as the plurality does not dispute; to observe the traditional methods of the gerrymanderer, * * * and to adopt a test aimed at detecting and preventing the use of those methods, which, I think, mine is. * * * My test would no doubt leave substantial room for a party in power to seek advantage through its control of the districting process; the only way to prevent all opportunism would be to remove districting wholly from legislative control, which I am not prepared to say the Constitution requires. But that does not make it impossible for courts to identify at least the worst cases of gerrymandering, and to provide a remedy. The most the plurality can show is that my approach would not catch them all. Cf. Scalia, *The Rule of Law as a Law of Rules*, 56 U. Chi. L. Rev. 1175, 1178 (1989) ("To achieve what is, from the standpoint of the substantive policies involved, the 'perfect' answer is nice — but it is just one of a number of competing values")."]

JUSTICE BREYER, dissenting.

The use of purely political considerations in drawing district boundaries is not a "necessary evil" that, for lack of judicially manageable standards, the Constitution inevitably must tolerate. Rather, pure politics often helps to secure constitutionally important democratic objectives. But sometimes it does not. Sometimes purely political "gerrymandering" will fail to advance any plausible democratic objective while simultaneously threatening serious democratic harm. And sometimes when that is so, courts can identify an equal protection violation and provide a remedy. Because the plaintiffs could claim (but have not yet proved) that such circumstances exist here, I would reverse the District Court's dismissal of their complaint. * * *

[I] * * * [T]he workable democracy that the Constitution foresees must mean more than a guaranteed opportunity to elect legislators representing equally populous electoral districts. There must also be a method for transforming the will of the majority into effective government.

This Court has explained that political parties play a necessary role in that transformation. At a minimum, they help voters assign responsibility for current circumstances, thereby enabling those voters, through their votes for individual candidates, to express satisfaction or dissatisfaction with the political status quo. Those voters can either vote to support that status quo or vote to "throw the rascals out." A party-based political system that satisfies this minimal condition encourages democratic responsibility. It facilitates the transformation of the voters' will into a government that reflects that will.

Why do I refer to these elementary constitutional principles? Because I believe they can help courts identify at least one abuse at issue in this case. To understand how that is so, one should begin by asking why single-member electoral districts are the norm, why the Constitution does not insist that the membership of legislatures better reflect different political views held by different groups of voters. History, of course, is part of the answer, but it does not tell the entire story. The answer also lies in the fact that a single-member-district system helps to assure certain democratic objectives better than many "more representative" (i.e., proportional) electoral systems. Of course, single-member districts mean that only parties with candidates who finish "first past the post" will elect legislators. That fact means in turn that a party with a bare majority of votes or even a plurality of votes will often obtain a large legislative majority, perhaps freezing out smaller parties. But single-member districts thereby diminish the need for coalition governments. And that fact makes it easier for voters to identify which party is responsible for government decisionmaking (and which rascals to throw out), while simultaneously providing greater legislative stability. This is not to say that single-member districts are preferable; it is simply to say that single-member-district systems and more-directly-representational systems reflect different conclusions about the proper balance of different elements of a workable democratic government.

If single-member districts are the norm, however, then political considerations will likely play an important, and proper, role in the drawing of district boundaries. In part, that is because politicians, unlike nonpartisan observers, normally understand how "the location and shape of districts" determine "the political complexion of the area." It is precisely *because* politicians are best able to predict the effects of boundary changes that the districts they design usually make some political sense.

More important for present purposes, the role of political considerations reflects a surprising mathematical fact. Given a fairly large state population with a fairly large congressional delegation, districts assigned so as to be perfectly random in respect to politics would translate a small shift in political sentiment, say a shift from 51% Republican to 49% Republican, into a seismic shift in the makeup of the legislative delegation, say from 100% Republican to 100% Democrat. Any such exaggeration of tiny electoral changes — virtually wiping out legislative representation of the minority party — would itself seem highly undemocratic.

Given the resulting need for single-member districts with nonrandom boundaries, it is not surprising that "traditional" districting principles have rarely, if ever, been politically neutral. Rather, because, in recent political memory, Democrats have often been concentrated in cities while Republicans have often been concentrated in suburbs and sometimes rural areas, geographically drawn boundaries have tended to "pac[k]" the former. Neighborhood or community-based boundaries, seeking to group Irish, Jewish, or African-American voters, often did the same. All this is well known to politicians, who use their knowledge about the effects of the "neutral" criteria to partisan advantage when drawing electoral maps. And were it not so, the iron laws of mathematics would have worked their extraordinary volatility-enhancing will. * * *

* * * [R]eference back to these underlying considerations helps to explain why the legislature's use of political boundary drawing considerations ordinarily does *not* violate the Constitution's Equal Protection Clause. The reason lies not simply in the difficulty of identifying abuse or finding an appropriate judicial remedy. The reason is more fundamental: Ordinarily, there simply is no abuse. The use of purely political boundary-drawing factors, even where harmful to the members of one party, will often nonetheless find justification in other desirable democratic ends, such as maintaining relatively stable legislatures in which a minority party retains significant representation.

[II] At the same time, these considerations can help identify at least one circumstance where use of purely political boundary-drawing factors can amount to a serious, and remediable, abuse, namely the *unjustified* use of political factors to entrench a minority in power. By entrenchment I mean a situation in which a party that enjoys only minority support among the populace has nonetheless contrived to take, and hold, legislative power. By *unjustified* entrenchment I mean that the minority's hold on power is purely the result of partisan manipulation and not other factors. These "other" factors that could lead to "justified" (albeit temporary) minority entrenchment include sheer happenstance, the existence of more than two major parties, the unique constitutional requirements of certain representational bodies such as the Senate, or reliance on traditional (geographic, communities of interest, etc.) districting criteria. * * *

[III] Courts need not intervene often to prevent the kind of abuse I have described, because those harmed constitute a political majority, and a majority normally can work its political will. Where a State has improperly gerrymandered legislative or congressional districts to the majority's disadvantage, the majority should be able to elect officials in statewide races — particularly the Governor — who may help to undo the harm that districting has caused the majority's party, in the next round of districting if not sooner. And where a State has improperly gerrymandered congressional districts, Congress retains the power to revise the State's districting determinations.

Moreover, voters in some States, perhaps tiring of the political boundary-drawing rivalry, have found a procedural solution, confiding the task to a commission that is limited in the extent to which it may base districts on partisan concerns. According to the National Conference of State Legislatures, 12 States currently give "first and final authority for [state] legislative redistricting to a group other than the legislature." A number of States use a commission for congressional redistricting: Arizona, Hawaii, Idaho, Montana, New Jersey, and Washington, with Indiana using a commission if the legislature cannot pass a plan and Iowa requiring the district-drawing body not to consider political data. Indeed, where state governments have been unwilling or unable to act, "an informed, civically militant electorate" has occasionally taken matters into its own hands, through ballot initiatives or referendums. Arizona voters, for example, passed Proposition 106, which amended the State's Constitution and created an independent redistricting commission to draw legislative and congressional districts. * * *

But we cannot always count on a severely gerrymandered legislature itself to find and implement a remedy. The party that controls the process has no incentive to change it. And the political advantages of a gerrymander may become ever greater in the future. The availability of enhanced computer technology allows the parties to redraw boundaries in ways that target individual neighborhoods and homes, carving out safe but slim victory margins in the maximum number of districts, with little risk of cutting their margins too thin. By redrawing districts every 2 years, rather than every 10 years, a party might preserve its political advantages notwithstanding population shifts in the State. The combination of increasingly precise map-drawing technology and increasingly frequent map drawing means that a party may be able to bring about a gerrymander that is not only precise, but virtually impossible to dislodge. Thus, court action may prove necessary. * * *

[IV] I do not claim that the problem of identification and separation is easily solved, even in extreme instances. But courts can identify a number of strong indicia of abuse. The presence of actual entrenchment, while not always unjustified (being perhaps a chance occurrence), is such a sign, particularly when accompanied by the use of partisan boundary drawing criteria * * * that both departs from traditional criteria and cannot be explained other than by efforts to achieve partisan advantage. Below, I set forth several sets of circumstances that lay out the indicia of abuse I have in mind. The scenarios fall along a continuum: The more permanently entrenched the minority's hold on power becomes, the less evidence courts will need that the minority engaged in gerrymandering to achieve the desired result.

Consider, for example, the following sets of circumstances. First, suppose that the legislature has proceeded to redraw boundaries in what seem to be ordinary ways, but the entrenchment harm has become obvious. E.g., (a) the legislature has not redrawn district boundaries more than once within the traditional 10-year period; and (b) no radical departure from traditional districting criteria is alleged; but (c) a majority party (as measured by the votes actually cast for all candidates who identify themselves as members of that party in the relevant set of elections; i.e., in congressional elections if a congressional map is being challenged) has *twice* failed to obtain a majority of the relevant legislative seats in elections; and (d) the failure cannot be explained by the existence of multiple parties or in other neutral ways. In my view, these circumstances would be sufficient to support a claim of unconstitutional entrenchment.

Second, suppose that plaintiffs could point to more serious departures from redistricting norms. E.g., (a) the legislature has not redrawn district boundaries more than once within the traditional 10-year period; but (b) the boundary-drawing criteria depart radically from previous or traditional criteria; (c) the departure cannot be justified or explained other than by reference to an effort to obtain partisan political advantage; and (d) a majority party (as defined above) has once failed to obtain a majority of the relevant seats in election using the challenged map (which fact cannot be explained by the existence of multiple parties or in other neutral ways). These circumstances could also add up to unconstitutional gerrymandering.

Third, suppose that the legislature clearly departs from ordinary districting norms, but the entrenchment harm, while seriously threatened, has not yet occurred. E.g., (a) the legislature has redrawn district boundaries more than once within the traditional 10-year census-related period — either, as here, at the behest of a court that struck down an initial plan as unlawful, or of its own accord; (b) the boundary-drawing criteria depart radically from previous traditional boundary-drawing criteria; (c) strong, objective, unrefuted statistical evidence demonstrates that a party with a minority of the popular vote within the State in all likelihood will obtain a majority of the seats in the relevant representative delegation; and (d) the jettisoning of traditional districting criteria cannot be justified or explained other than by reference to an effort to obtain partisan political advantage. To my mind, such circumstances could also support a claim, because the presence of midcycle redistricting, for any reason, raises a fair inference that partisan machinations played a major role in the map-drawing process. Where such an inference is accompanied by statistical evidence that entrenchment will be the likely result, a court may conclude that the map crosses the constitutional line we are describing.

The presence of these, or similar, circumstances — where the risk of entrenchment is demonstrated, where partisan considerations render the traditional district-drawing compromises irrelevant, where no justification other than party advantage can be found — seem to me extreme enough to set off a constitutional alarm. The risk of harm to basic democratic principle is serious; identification is possible; and remedies can be found. * * *

[T]he plurality makes one criticism [of my approach] that warrants a * * * response. It observes "that the mere fact that these four dissenters come up with three different standards — all of them different from the two proposed in *Bandemer* and the one proposed here by appellants — goes a long way to establishing that there is no constitutionally discernible standard."

Does it? The dissenting opinions recommend sets of standards that differ in certain respects. Members of a majority might well seek to reconcile such differences. But dissenters might instead believe that the more thorough, specific reasoning that accompanies separate statements will stimulate further discussion. And that discussion could lead to change in the law, where, as here, one member of the majority, disagreeing with the plurality as to justiciability, remains in search of appropriate standards.

NOTES ON JUDICIAL REVIEW
OF POLITICAL GERRYMANDERING

1. *The Plurality's Response to the Separate Opinions in* Vieth. Justice Scalia responded:

(a) Justice Stevens's approach failed to appreciate the differences between the racial gerrymandering cases and the political gerrymandering cases.

(b) Justice Souter's five-part test was unworkable because it provided no guidance on "[*h*]*ow much* disregard of traditional districting principles? *How many* correlations between deviations and distribution? *How much* remedying of packing or cracking by the hypothetical district? *How many legislators* must have had the intent to pack and crack — and *how efficacious* must that intent have been (must it have been, for example, a *sine qua non* cause of the districting, or a *predominant* cause)? * * * The central problem is determining when political gerrymandering has gone too far. It does not solve that problem to break down the original unanswerable question (How much political motivation and effect is too much?) into four more discrete but equally unanswerable questions."

(c) Justice Breyer's opinion similarly lacked specification of what constitutes a constitutional violation and also failed to appreciate the costs of interposing judicial review (uncertainty, delay, expense) when the benefits seem minimal ("[h]e gives no instance (and we know none) of permanent frustration of majority will" through political gerrymandering).

(d) Justice Kennedy's preferred approach — to continue to allow litigation so that a justiciable standard might emerge — "is not legally available. The District Court in this case considered the plaintiffs' claims *justiciable* but dismissed them because the standard for unconstitutionality had not been met. It is logically impossible to affirm that dismissal without either (1) finding that the unconstitutional-districting standard applied by the District Court, or some other standard that it *should* have applied, has not been met, or (2) finding (as we have) that the claim is nonjusticiable. JUSTICE KENNEDY seeks to affirm '[b]ecause, in the case before us, we have no standard.' But it is *our* job, not the plaintiffs', to explicate the standard that makes the facts alleged by the plaintiffs adequate or inadequate to state a claim. We cannot nonsuit *them* for our failure to do so. * * * Reduced to its essence, JUSTICE KENNEDY's opinion boils down to this: 'As presently advised, I know of no discernible and manageable standard that can render this claim justiciable. I am unhappy about that, and hope that I will be able to change my opinion in the future.' What are the lower courts to make of this pronouncement? We suggest that they must treat it as a reluctant fifth vote against justiciability at district and statewide levels — a vote that may change in some future case but that holds, for the time being, that this matter is nonjusticiable."

2. *Another Case, Another Indeterminacy.* Two years after *Vieth*, in *League of United Latin American Citizens v. Perry*, 126 S.Ct. 2594 (2006), the Court considered a challenge, on gerrymandering and Voting Rights Act grounds, to the Texas Legislature's mid-decade redistricting of the Texas congressional seats. Although the Court granted relief on a Voting Rights Act claim, it denied the political gerrymandering contention. Justice Scalia, joined by Justice Thomas, reiterated that such claims should be nonjusticiable. The other Justices left for another day the final resolution of that issue. Justice Kennedy again concluded that appellants had not proffered a workable approach to political gerrymandering claims in this case; the two new Justices, Chief Justice Roberts and Justice Alito, agreed. Justice Souter, joined by Justice Ginsburg, treated the political gerrymandering claim as one that the Court had, for all practical purposes, ducked, as if it had determined that certiorari had been improvidently granted. Justice Stevens, joined by Justice Breyer, argued that the political gerrymandering was unconstitutional.

3. *Coherence Across the Cases?* Precisely why is it that a majority of Justices are confident they can hear *Shaw v. Reno* sorts of cases, but not political gerrymandering cases? How persuasive is it to say that the difference is that race, unlike politics, is a constitutionally forbidden factor — when *Shaw* itself says that race may be taken into account in ensuring minority representation, so long as it is not taken into account too much? Why not say, similarly, that entrenching the current political majority may be taken into account, but not too much? Could it be the case that courts are better at figuring out when racial considerations have gone too far than when political considerations have? Or perhaps there is a stronger dignitary harm in the former situation — though that still begs the question how the courts draw the line. Is a more salient difference that the Voting Rights Act requires state legislatures to consider race?

What of the possibility that, even if political gerrymandering claims will be largely immune to judicial review in and of themselves, cases that involve egregious political gerrymandering will provoke especially vigorous judicial enforcement of claims that are justiciable, such as one person, one vote? Consider *Larios v. Cox*, 300 F. Supp. 2d 1320 (N.D. Ga. 2004) (three-judge court), which dismissed a political gerrymandering claim but nonetheless invalidated the Georgia state legislative apportionment scheme on one person, one vote grounds. It was not lost on the district judges that the deviations from population equality were the result of partisan considerations. Fascinatingly, the Supreme Court summarily affirmed. *Cox v. Larios*, 542 U.S. 947 (2004). Only Justice Scalia noted a dissent. Justice Stevens, joined by Justice Breyer, wrote a short concurring statement squarely indicating that deviations from one person, one vote should be allowed to stand only if they are motivated by a neutral justification — even if the deviations are not substantial. Unsurprisingly, Justice Stevens left no doubt that, in his view, political entrenchment was not a sufficient justification. See *id.* (Stevens J., joined by Breyer, J., concurring). Note that three of the Justices who in *Vieth* would have held political gerrymandering nonjusticiable (Chief Justice Rehnquist and Justices O'Connor and Thomas) voted to affirm in the *Cox* litigation.[j]

Other troubling issues are raised by comparing the political vote dilution cases with the racial vote dilution ones. In cities such as Mobile, Alabama, a single-member districting system may well benefit racial or political minorities, as the *Bolden* litigation suggests. But just as multimember district, at-large election schemes may dilute the vote of a minority community, so too may single-member districting dilute the vote of minority interests, as the *Bandemer* and *Vieth* cases suggest. Obviously, even where there are only two political parties or factions involved, the proportion of seats gained by one may be greater or smaller than the proportion of votes cast for it in the election. If more than two parties or factions are in competition, the disparity between the percentage of votes received and the percentage of total offices held is likely to be substantial. This situation is problematic under at least some theories of representation (descriptive theories certainly, and agency theories to some degree). Are there ways to ameliorate this dilemma? Consider the following Note.

NOTE ON ALTERNATIVE VOTING SCHEMES

A number of countries — particularly those that have a more heterogeneous political environment than the United States — use systems of *proportional representation* (PR). "Most nations that use PR are divided into a number of multimember electoral districts with each district selecting a specified number of representatives by pure PR."[k] Consider the following argument:

> The constitutional values at stake [in the reapportionment and racial gerrymandering cases] can be fully guaranteed *only* by PR[,] * * * the only electoral system that can give equal representation to all groups. Proportional representation also achieves majority rule. It is the only system that can simultaneously guarantee the individual and group right to both an equally weighted vote and an equally meaningful vote. * * *

> In PR, the tension between majority and minorities, instead of being accommodated by reapportionment commissions, is transposed to another level: the legislature itself. This transposition allows full realization of the two fundamental values present in the Court's interpretation of the equal protection clause because the legislature becomes

---

j. On the political gerrymandering debate, see, e.g., Guy-Uriel Charles, *Democracy and Distortion*, 92 Cornell L. Rev. 601 (2007); Bernard Grofman & Gary King, *The Future of Partisan Symmetry as a Judicial Test for Partisan Gerrymandering after* LULAC v. Perry, 6 Election L.J. 1 (2007). For commentary seeking to place the partisan gerrymandering cases into this broader context of the judicial regulation of politics (e.g., one person, one vote; judicial regulation of political parties; campaign finance), see, e.g., Richard Hasen, *No Exit? The Roberts Court and the Future of Election Law*, 57 S.C. L. Rev. 669 (2006); Samuel Issacharoff & Pamela Karlan, *Where To Draw the Line?: Judicial Review of Political Gerrymanders*, 153 U. Pa. L. Rev. 541 (2004).

k. Michael Balinski & H. Peyton Young, *Fair Representation* 88 (1982).

a more true reflection of the polity; the tension is resolved in the legislative process rather than suppressed by the electoral machinery.[l]

Persuasive? PR has been tried in a number of U.S. cities, but largely abandoned. So far as we know, the only municipality using PR today is Cambridge, Massachusetts. In New York City, PR was discontinued because Tammany Hall complained that it led to the election of two Communists and several Republicans to the City Council.[m] Other reasons for discontinuance of PR experiments in U.S. cities included the increase of factionalism and voter confusion.

Another method to enhance minority representation is *cumulative voting*.[n] Recall Justice Marshall's description, in footnote 3 of his dissent in *Bolden*, of the discriminatory effects of "anti-single-shot" voting provisions, which in a multimember district election require a voter to cast votes equal to the number of offices to be filled in order for any of her votes to count. If the voter may engage in "single-shot voting," she will be allowed to vote for the candidate(s) of her choice in a multimember election without being forced to cast additional votes for candidates she does not prefer — additional votes that could mean the election of the latter candidates rather than the former. A cumulative scheme takes the principle of concentrated support at the heart of single-shot voting and multiplies its effectiveness. Under such a plan, for example, a voter casting a ballot in an election to choose four council members from nine candidates would be allowed to cast votes up to the number of offices to be filled — here, four — for any candidate or candidates she chooses: she may cast four votes for candidate A, or three for A and one for D, etc. Cumulative voting was used in the election of the lower house of the Illinois Legislature, see Ill. Const. of 1970, art. IV, § 2(b), until it was repealed by a 1980 initiative.[o]

Theorists have proposed numerous other electoral schemes that are alleged to produce superior fit between voter preferences and candidates elected. Consider two such alternatives. In *approval voting*, a voter faced with the choice of several candidates seeking a single office can vote for — that is, "approve of" — as many of the candidates as she wishes. The candidate with the most votes wins. In *preferential voting*, the voter in the above situation would be allowed to rank the candidates from best to worst. If a candidate receives a majority of first-place votes, she wins; otherwise, the candidate with

---

l. Jon Low-Beer, *The Constitutional Imperative of Proportional Representation*, 94 Yale L.J. 163, 182 (1984) (student note) (emphasis added).

m. See id. at 186 n.103.

n. For a list of state and local institutions that are reported as using proportional voting, cumulative voting, or other similar approaches, see *Communities in America Currently Using Proportional Voting*, http://www.fairvote.org/?page=243. For a case study of how cumulative voting worked in Chilton County, Alabama, after a federal judge approved a settlement of a voting rights case there on those terms, see Richard Pildes & Kristen Donoghue, *Cumulative Voting in the United States*, 1995 U. Chi. Legal F. 241.

o. See *Coalition for Political Honesty v. State Board of Elections*, 415 N.E.2d 368 (Ill. 1980).

the fewest first-place votes is eliminated and the second-place vote cast by each of her supporters is then tallied to whichever of the remaining candidates received it. This process of elimination continues until one candidate receives a majority. Preferential voting has been used in elections in Cambridge, Massachusetts.[p]

If it were proved that any of these alternatives produced electoral outcomes fairer to minorities, should a court require a local or state government to adopt it? Or consider it as a possible remedy if the current electoral scheme has been found to be tainted by discriminatory purpose?[q]

Public debate about alternative voting schemes became more widespread in the 1990s by virtue of the work of Professor Lani Guinier. In a series of law review articles and then in her 1994 book, *The Tyranny of the Majority*,[r] Professor Guinier argued that in some circumstances the disadvantages racial minorities face from winner-take-all elections justify a switch to cumulative voting. When President Clinton nominated her to head the Civil Rights Division of the Department of Justice, her views received widespread attention and were castigated by many political figures. In response, President Clinton withdrew her nomination.

What's so scary about cumulative voting? The scheme can benefit any minority interest and can encourage inter-group coalitions: it might be that poor persons regardless of race would coalesce to support a candidate, for example. It allows existing multimember districts to remain intact rather than undergoing the controversial splitting into multiple smaller single-member districts that has often been adopted as a remedy for minority vote dilution and that can only be done based on controversial, balkanizing, and perhaps self-fulfilling assumptions that blacks and whites bloc vote on racial grounds. It limits gerrymandering for the simple reason that drawing a smaller number of multimember districts reduces the opportunities for shenanigans in line-drawing. Would it be too confusing? Render representatives too beholden to narrowly defined interests?[s]

---

p. See generally Steven Brams & Peter Fishburn, *Approval Voting* (1983).

q. See Steven Mulroy, *Electoral Systems as Voting Rights Act Remedies*, 77 N.C. L. Rev. 1867 (1999).

r. For a sampling of the many extensive reviews of the book, see, e.g., Richard Briffault, *Lani Guinier and the Dilemmas of American Democracy*, 95 Colum. L. Rev. 418 (1995); Pamela Karlan, *Democracy and Dis-Appointment*, 93 Mich. L. Rev. 1273 (1995). See also James Gardner, *Madison's Hope: Virtue, Self-Interest, and the Design of Electoral Systems*, 86 Iowa L. Rev. 87 (2000); Mark Graber, *Conflicting Representations: Lani Guinier and James Madison on Electoral Systems*, 13 Const. Commentary 291 (1996).

s. For a wide-ranging analysis linking together the topics in this Section, see Richard Pildes, *The Supreme Court, 2003 Term — Foreword: The Constitutionalization of Democratic Politics*, 118 Harv. L. Rev. 28 (2004).

SECTION 2. ELIGIBILITY TO SERVE IN THE LEGISLATURE

Shift your attention from the process of voting for legislators to the process of serving in the legislature. Theoretically, most people are eligible to serve in the legislature because state and federal laws place few substantive restrictions on service. Article I, § 2 only requires that Members of the U.S. House of Representatives be at least 25 years of age, U.S. citizens for seven years or more, and inhabitants of the states from which they are elected. Article I, § 3 requires that Members of the U.S. Senate be at least 30 years of age, U.S. citizens for nine years or more, and inhabitants of the states from which they are elected. What theory or concept of representation inspires these particular limitations? State constitutions often have more elaborate eligibility requirements for state lawmakers. What requirements would you impose, based upon your preferred theory of representation?

Some extra-constitutional limitations on eligibility to serve in Congress have given rise to interesting constitutional litigation. We will first consider the case of Representative Adam Clayton Powell, in which Congress attempted to add to the constitutional qualifications and to exclude Powell from the federal legislature notwithstanding his election to the position. We will then turn to the effort through popular initiatives to impose term limitations on federal lawmakers, an effort that was halted abruptly when the Supreme Court ruled such limitations unconstitutional. We will conclude with a less obvious way of restricting eligibility to serve in public office: state laws regulating access to the ballot. These laws, which are routinely upheld by courts, present the biggest hurdles to election. After all, we may all be eligible to serve in Congress, but our chances of election are nonexistent if our names never appear on the ballot.

A. CONGRESSIONALLY IMPOSED QUALIFICATIONS

POWELL v. McCORMACK
Supreme Court of the United States, 1969
395 U.S. 486, 89 S.Ct. 1944, 23 L.Ed.2d 491

MR. CHIEF JUSTICE WARREN delivered the opinion of the Court.

In November 1966, petitioner Adam Clayton Powell, Jr., was duly elected from the 18th Congressional District of New York to serve in the United States House of Representatives for the 90th Congress. However, pursuant to a House resolution, he was not permitted to take his seat. Powell (and some of the voters of his district) then filed suit in Federal District Court, claiming that the House could exclude him only if it found he failed to meet the standing requirements of age, citizenship, and residence contained in Art. I, § 2, of the Constitution — requirements the House specifically found Powell met — and thus had excluded him unconstitutionally. The District Court dismissed petitioners' complaint "for want of jurisdiction of the subject matter." A panel of the Court of Appeals affirmed the dismissal, although on somewhat different grounds, each judge filing a separate opinion. We have determined that it was error to dismiss the complaint and that petitioner Powell is entitled to a declaratory judgment that he was unlawfully excluded from the 90th Congress.

[I. *Facts*] During the 89th Congress, a Special Subcommittee on Contracts of the Committee on House Administration conducted an investigation into the expenditures of the Committee on Education and Labor, of which petitioner Adam Clayton Powell, Jr., was chairman. The Special Subcommittee issued a report concluding that Powell and certain staff employees had deceived the House authorities as to travel expenses. The report also indicated there was strong evidence that certain illegal salary payments had been made to Powell's wife at his direction. No formal action was taken during the 89th Congress. However, prior to the organization of the 90th Congress, the Democratic members-elect met in caucus and voted to remove Powell as chairman of the Committee on Education and Labor.

When the 90th Congress met to organize in January 1967, Powell was asked to step aside while the oath was administered to the other members-elect. Following the administration of the oath to the remaining members, the House discussed the procedure to be followed in determining whether Powell was eligible to take his seat. After some debate, by a vote of 363 to 65 the House adopted House Resolution No. 1, which provided that the Speaker appoint a Select Committee to determine Powell's eligibility. Although the resolution prohibited Powell from taking his seat until the House acted on the Select Committee's report, it did provide that he should receive all the pay and allowances due a member during the period.

The Select Committee, composed of nine lawyer-members, issued an invitation to Powell to testify before the Committee. The invitation letter stated that the scope of the testimony and investigation would include Powell's qualifications as to age, citizenship, and residency; his involvement in a civil suit (in which he had been held in contempt); and "[m]atters of * * * alleged official misconduct since January 3, 1961." Powell appeared at the Committee hearing held on February 8, 1967. After the Committee denied in part Powell's request that certain adversary-type procedures be followed, Powell testified. He would, however, give information relating only to his age, citizenship, and residency; upon the advice of counsel, he refused to answer other questions.

On February 10, 1967, the Select Committee issued another invitation to Powell. In the letter, the Select Committee informed Powell that its responsibility under the House Resolution extended to determining not only whether he met the standing qualifications of Art. I, § 2, but also to "inquir[ing] into the question of whether you should be punished or expelled pursuant to the powers granted * * * the House under Article I, § 5, * * * of the Constitution. In other words, the Select Committee is of the opinion that at the conclusion of the present inquiry, it has authority to report back to the House recommendations with respect to * * * seating, expulsion or other punishment." Powell did not appear at the next hearing, held February 14, 1967. However, his attorneys were present, and they informed the Committee that Powell would not testify about matters other than his eligibility under the standing qualifications of Art. I, § 2. Powell's attorneys reasserted Powell's contention that the standing qualifications were the exclusive requirements for membership, and they further urged that punishment or expulsion was not possible until a member had been seated.

The Committee held one further hearing at which neither Powell nor his attorneys were present. Then, on February 23, 1967, the Committee issued its report, finding that Powell met the standing qualifications of Art. I, § 2. However, the Committee further reported that Powell had asserted an unwarranted privilege and immunity from the processes of the courts of New York; that he had wrongfully diverted House funds for the use of others and himself; and that he had made false reports on expenditures of foreign currency to the Committee on House Administration. The Committee recommended that Powell be sworn and seated as a member of the 90th Congress but that he be censured by the House, fined $40,000 and be deprived of his seniority.

The report was presented to the House on March 1, 1967, and the House debated the Select Committee's proposed resolution. At the conclusion of the debate, by a vote of 222 to 202 the House rejected a motion to bring the resolution to a vote. An amendment to the resolution was then offered; it called for the exclusion of Powell and a declaration that his seat was vacant. The Speaker ruled that a majority vote of the House would be sufficient to pass the resolution if it were so amended. 113 Cong. Rec. 5020. After further debate, the amendment was adopted by a vote of 248 to 176. Then the House adopted by a vote of 307 to 116 House Resolution No. 278 in its amended form, thereby excluding Powell and directing that the Speaker notify the Governor of New York that the seat was vacant.

[Powell and 13 voters in his district brought suit against five Members of the House seeking a declaratory judgment that he had been improperly excluded. Chief Justice Warren first decided that the controversy was not mooted by the seating of Powell by the 91st Congress and then held that the Speech or Debate Clause (examined in Chapter 3) did not bar the lawsuit.]

[IV. *Exclusion or Expulsion*] The resolution excluding petitioner Powell was adopted by a vote in excess of two-thirds of the 434 Members of Congress — 307 to 116. Article I, § 5, grants the House authority to expel a member "with the Concurrence of two thirds."[27] Respondents assert that the House may expel a member for any reason whatsoever and that, since a two-thirds vote was obtained, the procedure by which Powell was denied his seat in the 90th Congress should be regarded as an expulsion, not an exclusion. Cautioning us not to exalt form over substance, respondents quote from the concurring opinion of Judge McGowan in the court below:

"Appellant Powell's cause of action for a judicially compelled seating thus boils down, in my view, to the narrow issue of whether a member found by his colleagues

---

27. Powell was "excluded" from the 90th Congress, *i.e.*, he was not administered the oath of office and was prevented from taking his seat. If he had been allowed to take the oath and subsequently had been required to surrender his seat, the House's action would have constituted an "expulsion." Since we conclude that Powell was excluded from the 90th Congress, we express no view on what limitations may exist on Congress' power to expel or otherwise punish a member once he has been seated.

* * * to have engaged in official misconduct must, because of the accidents of timing, be formally admitted before he can be either investigated or expelled. The sponsor of the motion to exclude stated on the floor that he was proceeding on the theory that the power to expel included the power to exclude, provided a 2/3 vote was forthcoming. It was. Therefore, success for Mr. Powell on the merits would mean that the District Court must admonish the House that it is form, not substance, that should govern in great affairs, and accordingly command the House members to act out a charade."

Although respondents repeatedly urge this Court not to speculate as to the reasons for Powell's exclusion, their attempt to equate exclusion with expulsion would require a similar speculation that the House would have voted to expel Powell had it been faced with that question. Powell had not been seated at the time House Resolution No. 278 was debated and passed. After a motion to bring the Select Committee's proposed resolution to an immediate vote had been defeated, an amendment was offered which mandated Powell's exclusion. Mr. Celler, chairman of the Select Committee, then posed a parliamentary inquiry to determine whether a two-thirds vote was necessary to pass the resolution if so amended "in the sense that it might amount to an expulsion." The Speaker replied that "action by a majority vote would be in accordance with the rules." Had the amendment been regarded as an attempt to expel Powell, a two-thirds vote would have been constitutionally required. The Speaker ruled that the House was voting to exclude Powell, and we will not speculate what the result might have been if Powell had been seated and expulsion proceedings subsequently instituted.

Nor is the distinction between exclusion and expulsion merely one of form. The misconduct for which Powell was charged occurred prior to the convening of the 90th Congress. On several occasions the House has debated whether a member can be expelled for actions taken during a prior Congress and the House's own manual of procedure applicable in the 90th Congress states that "both Houses have distrusted their power to punish in such cases." * * * Members of the House having expressed a belief that such strictures apply to its own power to expel, we will not assume that two-thirds of its members would have expelled Powell for his prior conduct had the Speaker announced that House Resolution No. 278 was for expulsion rather than exclusion.[30]

Finally, the proceedings which culminated in Powell's exclusion cast considerable doubt upon respondents' assumption that the two-thirds vote necessary to expel would have been mustered. These proceedings have been succinctly described by Congressman Eckhardt:

---

30. We express no view as to whether such a ruling would have been proper. A further distinction between expulsion and exclusion inheres in the fact that a member whose expulsion is contemplated may as a matter of right address the House and participate fully in debate while a member-elect apparently does not have a similar right. In prior cases the member whose expulsion was under debate has been allowed to make a long and often impassioned defense. On at least one occasion the member has been allowed to cross-examine other members during the expulsion debate.

"The House voted 202 votes for the previous question leading toward the adoption of the [Select] Committee report. It voted 222 votes against the previous question, opening the floor for the Curtis Amendment which ultimately excluded Powell.

"Upon adoption of the Curtis Amendment, the vote again fell short of two-thirds, being 248 yeas to 176 nays. Only on the final vote, adopting the Resolution as amended, was more than a two-thirds vote obtained, the vote being 307 yeas to 116 nays. On this last vote, as a practical matter, members who would not have denied Powell a seat if they were given the choice to punish him had to cast an aye vote or else record themselves as opposed to the only punishment that was likely to come before the House. Had the matter come up through the processes of expulsion, it appears that the two-thirds vote would have failed, and then members would have been able to apply a lesser penalty."[32]

We need express no opinion as to the accuracy of Congressman Eckhardt's prediction that expulsion proceedings would have produced a different result. However, the House's own views of the extent of its power to expel combined with the Congressman's analysis counsel that exclusion and expulsion are not fungible proceedings. The Speaker ruled that House Resolution No. 278 contemplated an exclusion proceeding. We must reject respondents' suggestion that we overrule the Speaker and hold that, although the House manifested an intent to exclude Powell, its action should be tested by whatever standards may govern an expulsion.

[Part V of the opinion for the Court held that the federal courts had subject matter jurisdiction over the controversy.]

[VI. *Justiciability*.] [Justiciability implicates two determinations: (1) whether the claims presented and the relief sought are of the type which admit of judicial resolution, and (2) whether the structure of the federal government renders the issue a "political question" which is not justiciable because of the separation of powers provided by the Constitution. The Court found that the claims and relief did admit of judicial resolution and then turned to the second issue.]

---

32. Eckhardt, The Adam Clayton Powell Case, 45 Texas L. Rev. 1205, 1209 (1967). The views of Congressman Eckhardt were echoed during the exclusion proceedings. Congressman Cleveland stated that, although he voted in favor of and supported the Select Committee's recommendation, if the exclusion amendment received a favorable vote on the motion for the previous question, then he would support the amendment "on final passage." Congressman Gubser was even more explicit:

"I shall vote against the previous question on the Curtis amendment simply because I believe future and perfecting amendments should be allowed. But if the previous question is ordered, then I will be placed on the horns of an impossible dilemma.

"Mr. Speaker, I want to expel Adam Clayton Powell, by seating him first, but that will not be my choice when the Curtis amendment is before us. I will be forced to vote for exclusion, about which I have great constitutional doubts, or to vote for no punishment at all. Given this raw and isolated issue, the only alternative I can follow is to vote for the Curtis amendment. I shall do so, Mr. Speaker, with great reservation."

[*VIB. Political Question Doctrine — 1. Textually Demonstrable Constitutional Commitment*]. [The opinion quoted the criteria for political question cases found in *Baker v. Carr*.]

Respondents' first contention is that this case presents a political question because under Art. I, § 5, there has been a "textually demonstrable constitutional commitment" to the House of the "adjudicatory power" to determine Powell's qualifications. Thus it is argued that the House, and the House alone, has power to determine who is qualified to be a member.

In order to determine whether there has been a textual commitment to a coordinate department of the Government, we must interpret the Constitution. In other words, we must first determine what power the Constitution confers upon the House through Art. I, § 5, before we can determine to what extent, if any, the exercise of that power is subject to judicial review. Respondents maintain that the House has broad power under § 5, and, they argue, the House may determine which are the qualifications necessary for membership. On the other hand, petitioners allege that the Constitution provides that an elected representative may be denied his seat only if the House finds he does not meet one of the standing qualifications expressly prescribed by the Constitution.

If examination of § 5 disclosed that the Constitution gives the House judicially unreviewable power to set qualifications for membership and to judge whether prospective members meet those qualifications, further review of the House determination might well be barred by the political question doctrine. On the other hand, if the Constitution gives the House power to judge only whether elected members possess the three standing qualifications set forth in the Constitution, further consideration would be necessary to determine whether any of the other formulations of the political question doctrine are "inextricable from the case at bar." *Baker v. Carr*.

In other words, whether there is a "textually demonstrable constitutional commitment of the issue to a coordinate political department" of government and what is the scope of such commitment are questions we must resolve for the first time in this case. For, as we pointed out in *Baker v. Carr*, "[d]eciding whether a matter has in any measure been committed by the Constitution to another branch of government, or whether the action of that branch exceeds whatever authority has been committed, is itself a delicate exercise in constitutional interpretation, and is a responsibility of this Court as ultimate interpreter of the Constitution."

In order to determine the scope of any "textual commitment" under Art. I, § 5, we necessarily must determine the meaning of the phrase to "be the Judge of the Qualifications of its own Members." Petitioners argue that the records of the debates during the Constitutional Convention; available commentary from the post-Convention, pre-ratification period; and early congressional applications of Art. I, § 5, support their construction of the section. Respondents insist, however, that a careful examination of the pre-Convention practices of the English Parliament and American colonial assemblies demonstrates that by 1787, a legislature's power to judge the qualifications of its members was generally understood to encompass exclusion or expulsion on the ground that an individual's character or past conduct rendered him unfit to serve. When the Constitution and the debates over its adoption are thus viewed in historical perspective, argue respondents, it becomes clear that the "qualifications" expressly set forth in the Constitution were not meant to limit the long-recognized legislative power to exclude or expel at will, but merely to establish "standing incapacities," which could be altered only by a constitutional amendment. Our examination of the relevant historical materials leads us to the conclusion that petitioners are correct and that the Constitution leaves the House without authority to *exclude* any person, duly elected by his constituents, who meets all the requirements for membership expressly prescribed in the Constitution.

[*a.   The Pre-Convention Precedents*]   [The Court's opinion examined historical evidence of exclusion of Members from the English Parliament. The English Parliament in the eighteenth century had excluded Members, most notoriously Robert Walpole in 1712 and John Wilkes in the 1760s and 1770s. Wilkes was elected and reelected to Parliament several times during that period, and repeatedly excluded because of his 1763 published attack on the Treaty of Paris ending the Seven Years' War (the French and Indian War in the colonies). This repeated exclusion generated popular outrage in both England and the colonies, because it denied the voters their elected representative. The House of Commons in 1782 expunged from the record Wilkes' prior exclusions and a resolution declaring him incapable of reelection; the 1782 resolution found the earlier actions "subversive of the rights of the whole body of electors of this kingdom." The 1782 resolution was important, because it repudiated prior practice, and it was this resolution rather than the prior English practice which was celebrated in the colonies on the eve of their revolt.]

[*b. Convention Debates*]   The Convention opened in late May 1787. By the end of July, the delegates adopted, with a minimum of debate, age requirements for membership in both the Senate and the House. The Convention then appointed a Committee of Detail to draft a constitution incorporating these and other resolutions adopted during the preceding months. Two days after the Committee was appointed, George Mason, of Virginia, moved that the Committee consider a clause " 'requiring certain qualifications of landed property & citizenship' "   and disqualifying from membership in Congress persons who had unsettled accounts or who were indebted to the United States. A vigorous debate ensued.   * * * John Dickinson, of Delaware, opposed the inclusion of any statement of qualifications in the Constitution. He argued that it would be "impossible to make a compleat one, and a partial one would by implication tie up the hands of the Legislature from supplying the omissions." Dickinson's argument was rejected; and, after eliminating the disqualification of debtors and the limitation to "landed" property, the Convention adopted Mason's proposal to instruct the Committee of Detail to draft a property qualification.

The Committee reported in early August, proposing no change in the age requirement; however, it did recommend adding citizenship and residency requirements for membership. After first debating what the precise requirements should be, on August 8, 1787, the delegates unanimously adopted the three qualifications embodied in Art. I, § 2.

On August 10, the Convention considered the Committee of Detail's proposal that the "Legislature of the United States shall have authority to establish such uniform qualifications of the members of each House, with regard to property, as to the said Legislature shall seem expedient." * * * James Madison urged its rejection, stating that the proposal would vest

> "an improper & dangerous power in the Legislature. The qualifications of electors and elected were fundamental articles in a Republican Govt. and ought to be fixed by the Constitution. If the Legislature could regulate those of either, it can by degrees subvert the Constitution. A Republic can be converted into an aristocracy or oligarchy as well by limiting the number of capable of being elected, as the number authorized to elect. * * * It was a power also, which might be made subservient to the views of one faction agst. another. Qualifications founded on artificial distinctions may be devised, by the stronger in order to keep out partizans of [a weaker] faction." * * *

In view of what followed Madison's speech, it appears that on this critical day the Framers were facing and then rejecting the possibility that the legislature would have the power to usurp the "indisputable right [of the people] to return whom they thought proper" to the legislature. Oliver Ellsworth, of Connecticut, noted that a legislative power to establish property qualifications was exceptional and "dangerous because it would be much more liable to abuse." Gouverneur Morris then moved to strike "with regard to property" from the Committee's proposal. His intention was "to leave the Legislature entirely at large." * * * Madison then referred to the British Parliament's assumption of the power to regulate the qualifications of both electors and the elected and noted that "the abuse they had made of it was a lesson worthy of our attention. They had made the changes in both cases subservient to their own views, or to the views of political or Religious parties." Shortly thereafter, the Convention rejected both Gouverneur Morris' motion and the Committee's proposal. Later the same day, the Convention adopted without debate the provision authorizing each House to be "the judge of the * * * qualifications of its own members."

[On the same day, the Convention considered the Committee of Detail's provision empowering each house to expel members and adopted Madison's amendment that expulsion could only be accomplished "with the concurrence of two-thirds" of the chamber.] Thus, the Convention's decision to increase the vote required to expel, because that power was "too important to be exercised by a bare majority," while at the same time not restricting the power to judge qualifications, is compelling evidence that they considered the latter already limited to the standing qualifications previously adopted.

[The opinion then cited and quoted observations from the ratification debates.] Before the New York convention, for example, Hamilton emphasized: "[T]he true principle of a republic is, that the people should choose whom they please to govern them. Representation is imperfect in proportion as the current of popular favor is checked. The great source of free government, popular election, should be perfectly pure, and the most unbounded liberty allowed." * * *

[*c. Post-Ratification*] [The opinion emphasized that, until the Civil War, Congress was unwilling to exclude duly elected members. In 1807 the House agreed to seat William McCreery. Its Committee on Elections found that he met the constitutional requirements, and operated under the assumption that "neither the State nor the Federal Legislatures are vested with authority to add to those qualifications, so as to change them." In 1868, the House did exclude two members on the ground that they gave aid and comfort to the Confederacy during the Civil War. The last person to be excluded from the House before Powell was Victor Berger, a Socialist who was excluded after World War I for giving aid and comfort to the enemy in that war. The Court concluded that Congress' early understanding was the correct one, and that these subsequent exclusions had not changed the proper constitutional rule.]

[*d. Conclusion*] Had the intent of the Framers emerged from these materials with less clarity, we would nevertheless have been compelled to resolve any ambiguity in favor of a narrow construction of the scope of Congress' power to exclude members-elect. A fundamental principle of our representative democracy is, in Hamilton's words, "that the people should choose whom they please to govern them." As Madison pointed out at the Convention, this principle is undermined as much by limiting whom the people can select as by limiting the franchise itself. In apparent agreement with this basic philosophy, the Convention adopted his suggestion limiting the power to expel. To allow essentially that same power to be exercised under the guise of judging qualifications, would be to ignore Madison's warning, borne out in the Wilkes case and some of Congress' own post-Civil War exclusion cases, against "vesting an improper & dangerous power in the Legislature." Moreover, it would effectively nullify the Convention's decision to require a two-thirds vote for expulsion. Unquestionably, Congress has an interest in preserving its institutional integrity, but in most cases that interest can be sufficiently safeguarded by the exercise of its power to punish its members for disorderly behavior and, in extreme cases, to expel a member with the concurrence of two-thirds. In short, both the intention of the Framers, to the extent it can be determined, and an examination of the basic principles of our democratic system persuade us that the Constitution does not vest in the Congress a discretionary power to deny membership by a majority vote.

For these reasons, we have concluded that Art. I, § 5, is at most a "textually demonstrable commitment" to Congress to judge only the qualifications expressly set forth in the Constitution. Therefore, the "textual commitment" formulation of the political question doctrine does not bar federal courts from adjudicating petitioners' claims.

[*2. Other Considerations*] Respondents' alternate contention is that the case presents a political question because judicial resolution of petitioners' claim would produce a "potentially embarrassing confrontation between coordinate branches" of the Federal Government. But, as our interpretation of Art. I, § 5, discloses, a determination of petitioner Powell's right to sit would require no more than an interpretation of the Constitution. Such a determination falls within the traditional role accorded courts to interpret the law, and does not involve a "lack of the respect due [a] coordinate [branch] of government," nor does it involve an "initial policy determination of a kind clearly for nonjudicial discretion." *Baker*. Our system of government requires that federal courts on occasion interpret the Constitution in a manner at variance with the construction given the document by another branch. The alleged conflict that such an adjudication may cause cannot justify the courts' avoiding their constitutional responsibility.

Nor are any of the other formulations of a political question "inextricable from the case at bar." *Baker*. Petitioners seek a determination that the House was without power to exclude Powell from the 90th Congress, which, we have seen, requires an interpretation of the Constitution — a determination for which clearly there are "judicially * * * manageable standards." Finally, a judicial resolution of petitioners' claim will not result in "multifarious pronouncements by various departments on one question." For, as we noted in *Baker*, it is the responsibility of this Court to act as the ultimate interpreter of the Constitution. *Marbury v. Madison*. Thus, we conclude that petitioners' claim is not barred by the political question doctrine, and, having determined that the claim is otherwise generally justiciable, we hold that the case is justiciable.

[VII. *Conclusion*] To summarize, we have determined the following: (1) This case has not been mooted by Powell's seating in the 91st Congress. (2) Although this action should be dismissed against respondent Congressmen, it may be sustained against their agents. (3) The 90th Congress' denial of membership to Powell cannot be treated as an expulsion. (4) We have jurisdiction over the subject matter of this controversy. (5) The case is justiciable.

Further, analysis of the "textual commitment" under Art. I, § 5 (see Part VI, B(1)), has demonstrated that in judging the qualifications of its members Congress is limited to the standing qualifications prescribed in the Constitution. Respondents concede that Powell met these. Thus, there is no need to remand this case to determine whether he was entitled to be seated in the 90th Congress. Therefore, we hold that, since Adam Clayton Powell, Jr., was duly elected by the voters of the 18th Congressional District of New York and was not ineligible to serve under any provision of the Constitution, the House was without power to exclude him from its membership.

[The concurring opinion of JUSTICE DOUGLAS and the dissenting opinion of JUSTICE STEWART have been omitted.]

NOTES ON *POWELL* AND THE LEGISLATURE'S AUTHORITY TO REGULATE ITS MEMBERSHIP

1. *Rationale for* Powell. The general rule before *Powell* was that Congress and state legislatures have unreviewable authority to determine the qualifications of their members. Why was that rule not followed in *Powell*? Justice Douglas's concurring opinion asserts that the root concern in *Powell* "is the basic integrity of the electoral process. Today we proclaim the constitutional

principle of 'one [person], one vote.' When the principle is followed and the electors choose a person who is repulsive to the Establishment in Congress, by what constitutional authority can that group of electors be disenfranchised?" What view or theory of representation does this embody? Does it reflect the approach of the Court's opinion? Justice Douglas admits that the House could have expelled Powell, probably for the same reasons it excluded him. Is there a policy supporting the exclusion–expulsion distinction?

The institutional theories we discussed in Chapter 1, § 2C, provide support for the Court's refusal to equate a two-thirds vote to exclude Powell with a two-thirds vote to expel him. Understanding the order of voting illuminates the decision. The Committee that investigated the allegations against Powell recommended that he be seated and censured. After debate, the House rejected a motion that would have forced an immediate vote on the recommendation, thereby signaling that the Committee's proposal was in trouble. The resolution was then amended so that it required exclusion; that amendment passed by a simple majority of 248 to 176. In a pivotal ruling, the Chair determined that the final vote required to exclude Powell was also a simple majority; only expulsion required a two-thirds majority under the Constitution. Why was this ruling so important to the final vote margin? Think about the 59 members who changed their votes to support passage of the amended resolution even though they had opposed the amendment. Had they been convinced to change their positions because of persuasive debate by their colleagues? Probably not. These members voted strategically. They realized that the resolution of exclusion was going to pass because a simple majority had already voted in favor of it. Perhaps they changed their votes because they thought some punishment appropriate and this resolution was the only option, or perhaps they did not want their votes to become controversial issues in their next reelection campaigns. The Supreme Court was entirely right, under this analysis, to refuse to equate the exclusion motion with a decision to expel, given the difference in the voting rule applied to each.

2. *Exclusion and the First Amendment.* In *Bond v. Floyd*, 385 U.S. 116 (1966), the Supreme Court held that the Georgia House of Representatives had violated Julian Bond's First Amendment rights (as secured by the Due Process Clause of the Fourteenth Amendment) when it excluded him from membership, though he had been duly elected, because of his criticism of the Vietnam War and of the federal draft laws. Georgia argued that (1) the exclusion was proper because the Georgia Constitution requires representatives to take an oath pledging to support the constitutions of Georgia and the United States; (2) this requirement is clearly constitutional because the United States Constitution itself (Article VI, cl. 3) requires members of state legislatures to take an oath to support the federal Constitution; and (3) the state legislature has the power to determine whether a given representative can take the oath with sincerity. Georgia conceded that Bond stood ready to take the oath, but insisted on its legislature's right to withhold office because Bond's criticism of federal policy showed that he could not take the oath with sincerity.

The Court agreed that the Georgia oath requirement was constitutional, but held that neither Article VI, cl. 3 on its own force, nor the Georgia oath requirement in light of the First Amendment, can "authorize a majority of state legislators to test the sincerity with which another duly elected legislator can swear to uphold the Constitution. * * * [W]hile the State has an interest in requiring its legislators to swear to a belief in constitutional processes of government, surely the oath gives it no interest in limiting its legislators' capacity to discuss their views of local or national policy. The manifest function of the First Amendment in a representative government requires that legislators be given the widest latitude to express their views on issues of policy."

3. *Exclusion and Race.* Julian Bond was an African-American representative; Powell was a black Congressman from Harlem, one of the few African Americans then in the U.S. House. Justice Douglas adverted to the "racist overtones" of Powell's exclusion. During the debate on the exclusion, members who opposed the exclusion as unconstitutional noted that Congress had excluded members on the grounds of extra-constitutional qualifications only three times before "in rare instances of extreme political tension. * * * These deviations occurred in three categories of cases reflecting anti-Mormon[,] anti-Confederate[,] and antiradical [] feeling." 113 Cong. Rec. 5023 (Mar. 1, 1967) (statement of Rep. Celler). Should these factors have led the Court to investigate the motives of the Georgia legislature in Bond's case or of Congress in Powell's? If so, what records should the Court have used to determine the legislature's motivation — only public records of deliberations or also affidavits from legislators detailing private conversations or internal reasoning? What about evidence of constituent communications and views which might have influenced the outcome?

Some state constitutions use an additional method to guard against self-interested or improper expulsion from the legislature. They allow a state house to expel a member "only once for the same offense." See, e.g., Ill. Const. Art. IV, § 6(d); see also Conn. Const. III, § 13. Adrian Vermeule explains the advantages of this sort of protection. Not only does it allow the voters to override the legislature's decision by reelecting a member who has been expelled, but it provides "outside review [that] is, as a matter of institutional design, superior to any of the alternatives, either the supermajority requirement or the hypothetical alternatives that would vest review of expulsion decisions in the other house or in the president." *The Constitutional Law of Congressional Procedure*, 71 U. Chi. L. Rev. 361, 396 (2004).

Problems of Congressional Exclusion and Expulsion

Problem 2–2. Representative Powell was reelected and seated before the Supreme Court's decision, and he was not later excluded from Congress. But assume that after Powell's next reelection, the House voted by a two-thirds majority to expel him. Powell sues on the ground that his expulsion was racially motivated. Is that controversy justiciable? Has Powell stated a claim for which relief can be granted, if he can prove racially discriminatory intent? If Congress does not expel him but continues to deny him seniority, can he return to court to obtain an injunction restoring his status and placing him at the head of a subcommittee on which he is the most senior member? Or do matters of seniority and committee assignments present political questions that the courts should avoid? What if Powell sues for any backpay that was withheld during his unlawful exclusion?

Problem 2–3. The Senate last excluded an elected Senator in 1929, but it considered excluding Senator Theodore Bilbo (D-Miss.) in the late 1930s. The charges were that Bilbo had accepted bribes from war contractors and that his partisans had intimidated African-American voters during the Democratic primary. The Senator died before the charges could be investigated, but assume that both charges were well-founded. Can the Senate exclude a member for corrupting the electoral process? By what vote and with what procedures? Can the Senate expel him on this ground?

B. QUALIFICATIONS IMPOSED BY STATES: TERM LIMITATIONS FOR FEDERAL LEGISLATORS

By the end of the 1994 elections, 22 states had amended their constitutions or passed legislation limiting the terms of office of their U.S. Representatives and Senators. Fourteen of these provisions, including the Arkansas limitation at issue in *U.S. Term Limits, Inc. v. Thornton*, were designed as ballot access measures, allowing long-term incumbents to run but only as write-in candidates. We will discuss ballot access regulations, and the willingness of the courts to tolerate such restrictions, in Part C of this Section. Term-limits advocates hope to rid Congress of professional politicians because they believe that such lawmakers inevitably act in ways that are contrary to the public interest. They seek to replace the professionals with amateurs who, like the legendary Cincinnatus,[a] have little experience in politics but a great deal of experience as ordinary citizens. They believe that this reform will weaken the power of special interests and eliminate unseemly, close relationships between elected officials and lobbyists.[b]

Others, including many political scientists, have remained skeptical of term limits.[c] Some dispute that term limits will usher in the era of the citizen-legislator, noting that political careers remain possible with term limits, although a careerist will be forced to adopt a strategy of *progressive* political

---

a. In 458 B.C., Cincinnatus was appointed dictator of Rome in order to rescue a besieged army. At the time of his appointment, he was a farmer; after defeating the enemy, he is said to have resigned and returned to his plow.

b. See, e.g., George Will, *Restoration: Congress, Term Limits, and the Recovery of Deliberative Democracy* (1992) (arguing that term limits would enhance deliberation and representative democracy).

c. See *Legislative Term Limits: Public Choice Perspectives* (Bernard Grofman ed., 1996) (containing views of scholars on both sides of the debate); Thad Kousser, *Term Limits and the Dismantling of State Legislative Professionalism* (2005); Peter Schrag, *Paradise Lost: California's Experience, America's Future* (2004) (blaming term limits as well as direct democracy for California's political problems); Nelson Polsby, *Restoration Comedy*, 102 Yale L.J. 1515 (1993) (scathing review of Will's book).

ambition by moving periodically to a new office or political job.[d] Many object to term limits because they will deprive legislatures of their most experienced members, thereby reducing the ability of Congress to pass legislation to deal with controversial or difficult problems, without corresponding advantages in deliberativeness or public spiritedness. Reduced legislator effectiveness also may shift the balance of power between the branches of government. Long-time federal bureaucrats will represent a source of expertise for congressional amateurs, a situation that will strengthen the President and executive branch relative to Congress. Similarly, term-limited politicians may rely more heavily on unelected professional congressional staff or on lobbyists with congressional experience. Finally, some opponents argue that interest groups will continue to influence representatives disproportionately by giving campaign money either to them or to political parties. Moreover, term limits will provide special interests with an even more powerful tool for influence: post-service jobs for term-limited representatives.

As the debate about the effect of state-imposed term limitations on federal legislators heated up, the Supreme Court considered the constitutionality of such measures in the following case.

U.S. TERM LIMITS, INC. v. THORNTON
Supreme Court of the United States, 1995
514 U.S. 779, 115 S.Ct. 1842, 131 L.Ed.2d 881

JUSTICE STEVENS delivered the opinion of the Court.

* * * Today's cases present a challenge to an amendment to the Arkansas State Constitution that prohibits the name of an otherwise-eligible candidate for Congress from appearing on the general election ballot if that candidate has already served three terms in the House of Representatives or two terms in the Senate. The Arkansas Supreme Court held that the amendment violates the Federal Constitution. We agree with that holding. Such a state-imposed restriction is contrary to the "fundamental principle of our representative democracy," embodied in the Constitution, that "the people should choose whom they please to govern them." *Powell v. McCormack.* Allowing individual States to adopt their own qualifications for congressional service would be inconsistent with the Framers' vision of a uniform National Legislature representing the people of the United States. If the qualifications set forth in the text of the Constitution are to be changed, that text must be amended.

[I] At the general election on November 3, 1992, the voters of Arkansas adopted Amendment 73 to their State Constitution. Proposed as a "Term Limitation Amendment," its preamble stated:

"The people of Arkansas find and declare that elected officials who remain in office too long become preoccupied with reelection and ignore their duties as representatives of the people. Entrenched incumbency has reduced voter participation and has led to

---

d. See Elizabeth Garrett, *Term Limitations and the Myth of the Citizen-Legislator*, 81 Cornell L. Rev. 623 (1996).

an electoral system that is less free, less competitive, and less representative than the system established by the Founding Fathers. Therefore, the people of Arkansas, exercising their reserved powers, herein limit the terms of the elected officials."

[Section 3 prohibited any person who had served for three or more terms in the House of Representatives from appearing on the ballot. A similar restriction applied to persons who had served in the Senate for two or more terms. Bobbie Hill, a voter and citizen of Arkansas, brought suit in state court for a declaratory judgment that § 3 was unconstitutional. The Arkansas Supreme Court held the provision violated the federal Constitution because a state has no authority to change the qualifications for congressional office enumerated in Article I, § 5.]

[II] As the opinions of the Arkansas Supreme Court suggest, the constitutionality of Amendment 73 depends critically on the resolution of two distinct issues. The first is whether the Constitution forbids States to add or alter the qualifications specifically enumerated in the Constitution. The second is, if the Constitution does so forbid, whether the fact that Amendment 73 is formulated as a ballot access restriction rather than as an outright disqualification is of constitutional significance. Our resolution of these issues draws upon our prior resolution of a related but distinct issue: whether Congress has the power to add to or alter the qualifications of its Members. [Based on *Powell*, Justice Stevens then "reaffirm[ed] that the qualifications for service in Congress set forth in the text of the Constitution are 'fixed,' at least in the sense that they may not be supplemented by Congress."]

[III] Our reaffirmation of *Powell* does not necessarily resolve the specific questions presented in these cases. For petitioners argue that whatever the constitutionality of additional qualifications for membership imposed by Congress, the historical and textual materials discussed in *Powell* do not support the conclusion that the Constitution prohibits additional qualifications imposed by States. In the absence of such a constitutional prohibition, petitioners argue, the Tenth Amendment and the principle of reserved powers require that States be allowed to add such qualifications.

* * * We disagree for two independent reasons. First, we conclude that the power to add qualifications is not within the "original powers" of the States, and thus is not reserved to the States by the Tenth Amendment. Second, even if States possessed some original power in this area, we conclude that the Framers intended the Constitution to be the exclusive source of qualifications for members of Congress, and that the Framers thereby "divested" States of any power to add qualifications.

[Relying heavily on Justice Story's treatise on constitutional law, the Court determined that the only powers reserved to the states under the Tenth Amendment were those that they had possessed before the Constitution was ratified and that had not been transferred to the national government. The states did not have an "original power" to appoint a national official; thus, the power to set qualifications for such offices cannot be a reserved power.]

In short, as the Framers recognized, electing representatives to the National Legislature was a new right, arising from the Constitution itself. The Tenth

Amendment thus provides no basis for concluding that the States possess reserved power to add qualifications to those that are fixed in the Constitution. Instead, any state power to set the qualifications for membership in Congress must derive not from the reserved powers of state sovereignty, but rather from the delegated powers of national sovereignty. * * *

Even if we believed that States possessed as part of their original powers some control over congressional qualifications, the text and structure of the Constitution, the relevant historical materials, and, most importantly, the "basic principles of our democratic system" all demonstrate that the Qualifications Clauses were intended to preclude the States from exercising any such power and to fix as exclusive the qualifications in the Constitution.

[The Court began its analysis by reviewing the historical evidence that the Constitution did not delegate to the States the power to add qualifications. Constitutional provisions that minimize the possibility of state interference in national elections[e] and the ratification debates reveal the Framers' fear that the states would undermine the national legislature. For example, the Framers did not leave to the states the determination of congressional salaries because of fears of "improper dependence."]

The dissent nevertheless contends that the Framers' distrust of the States with respect to elections does not preclude the people of the States from adopting eligibility requirements to help narrow their own choices. As the dissent concedes, however, the Framers were unquestionably concerned that the States would simply not hold elections for federal officers, and therefore the Framers gave Congress the power to "make or alter" state election regulations. Yet under the dissent's approach, the States could achieve exactly the same result by simply setting qualifications for federal office sufficiently high that no one could meet those qualifications. In our view, it is inconceivable that the Framers would provide a specific constitutional provision to ensure that federal elections would be held while at the same time allowing States to render those elections meaningless by simply ensuring that no candidate could be qualified for office. * * *

We also find compelling the complete absence in the ratification debates of any assertion that States had the power to add qualifications. In those debates, the question whether to require term limits, or "rotation," was a major source of controversy. The draft of the Constitution that was submitted for ratification contained no provision for rotation. In arguments that echo in the preamble to Arkansas' Amendment 73, opponents of ratification condemned the absence of a rotation requirement, noting that "there is no doubt that senators will hold their office perpetually; and in this situation, they must of necessity lose their

---

e. *Editors' note*: Justice Stevens referred to Art. I, § 2, cl. 1 (qualifications for federal electors to be same as those for state electors); Art. I, § 4, cl. 1 (giving States the freedom to regulate the "Times, Places and Manner of holding Elections," but giving Congress the power "by Law [to] make or alter such Regulations"); Art I, § 6 (Congress sets its own compensation); Art. I, § 5, cl. 1 ("Each House shall be the Judge of the Elections, Returns and Qualifications of its own Members").

dependence, and their attachments to the people." Even proponents of ratification expressed concern about the "abandonment in every instance of the necessity of rotation in office." At several ratification conventions, participants proposed amendments that would have required rotation.

The Federalists' responses to those criticisms and proposals addressed the merits of the issue, arguing that rotation was incompatible with the people's right to choose. * * * Robert Livingston argued:

> "The people are the best judges who ought to represent them. To dictate and control them, to tell them whom they shall not elect, is to abridge their natural rights. This rotation is an absurd species of ostracism."

Similarly, Hamilton argued that the representatives' need for reelection rather than mandatory rotation was the more effective way to keep representatives responsive to the people, because "[w]hen a man knows he must quit his station, let his merit be what it may, he will turn his attention chiefly to his own emolument."

Regardless of which side has the better of the debate over rotation, it is most striking that nowhere in the extensive ratification debates have we found any statement by either a proponent or an opponent of rotation that the draft constitution would permit States to require rotation for the representatives of their own citizens. If the participants in the debate had believed that the States retained the authority to impose term limits, it is inconceivable that the Federalists would not have made this obvious response to the arguments of the pro-rotation forces. The absence in an otherwise freewheeling debate of any suggestion that States had the power to impose additional qualifications unquestionably reflects the Framers' common understanding that States lacked that power.

[The Court then reviewed the somewhat "erratic" congressional experience that might shed light on the states' power to add qualifications. It discussed the 1807 case of William McCreery, who was challenged as not meeting a residency requirement imposed by Maryland. The House Committee on Elections noted that the Constitution sets qualifications "without reserving any authority to the State Legislatures to change, add to, or diminish those qualifications." Although a minority on the Committee advocated the right of states to add qualifications, most contemporary observers viewed the McCreery decision as "confirmation of the States' lack of power to add qualifications." In 1887, the Senate seated Charles Faulkner, notwithstanding a state provision that seemed to render him ineligible. The relevant Senate committee concluded that "no State can prescribe any qualification to the office of United States Senator in addition to those declared in the Constitution of the United States."]

Our conclusion that States lack the power to impose qualifications vindicates the same "fundamental principle of our representative democracy" that we recognized in *Powell*, namely, that "the people should choose whom they please to govern them."

[The Court noted that *Powell*'s fundamental principle included two ideas. First, *Powell* "emphasized the egalitarian concept that the opportunity to be elected was open to all." Second, the Court recognized that "sovereignty confers on the people the right to choose freely their representatives to the National Government." State-imposed qualifications, the Court argued, are inconsistent with both these concepts; "the source of the qualification is of little moment in assessing the qualification's restrictive impact."]

Finally, state-imposed restrictions, unlike the congressionally imposed restrictions at issue in *Powell*, violate a third idea central to this basic principle: that the right to choose representatives belongs not to the States, but to the people. From the start, the Framers recognized that the "great and radical vice" of the Articles of Confederation was "the principle of LEGISLATION for STATES or GOVERNMENTS, in their CORPORATE or COLLECTIVE CAPACITIES, and as contradistinguished from the INDIVIDUALS of whom they consist." [The Federalist No. 15 (Hamilton).] Thus the Framers, in perhaps their most important contribution, conceived of a Federal Government directly responsible to the people, possessed of direct power over the people, and chosen directly, not by States, but by the people. * * * As Chief Justice John Marshall observed: "The government of the union, then, . . . is, emphatically, and truly, a government of the people. In form and in substance it emanates from them. Its powers are granted by them, and are to be exercised directly on them, and for their benefit." *McCulloch v. Maryland*, 4 Wheat. [316,] 404-405 [1819]. * * *

Consistent with these views, the constitutional structure provides for a uniform salary to be paid from the national treasury, allows the States but a limited role in federal elections, and maintains strict checks on state interference with the federal election process. The Constitution also provides that the qualifications of the representatives of each State will be judged by the representatives of the entire Nation. The Constitution thus creates a uniform national body representing the interests of a single people.

Permitting individual States to formulate diverse qualifications for their representatives would result in a patchwork of state qualifications, undermining the uniformity and the national character that the Framers envisioned and sought to ensure. Such a patchwork would also sever the direct link that the Framers found so critical between the National Government and the people of the United States.[32] * * *

[IV] Petitioners argue that, even if States may not add qualifications, Amendment 73 is constitutional because it is not such a qualification, and because Amendment 73 is a permissible exercise of state power to regulate the "Times, Places and Manner of Holding Elections." We reject these contentions.

---

32. There is little significance to the fact that Amendment 73 was adopted by a popular vote, rather than as an act of the state legislature. In fact, none of the petitioners argues that the constitutionality of a state law would depend on the method of its adoption. This is proper, because the voters of Arkansas, in adopting Amendment 73, were acting as citizens of the State of Arkansas, and not as citizens of the National Government. The people of the State of Arkansas have no more power than does the Arkansas Legislature to supplement the qualifications for service in Congress. * * *

* * * [Section 3 of Amendment 73] provides that certain Senators and Representatives shall not be certified as candidates and shall not have their names appear on the ballot. They may run as write-in candidates and, if elected, they may serve. Petitioners contend that only a legal bar to service creates an impermissible qualification, and that Amendment 73 is therefore consistent with the Constitution.

Petitioners support their restrictive definition of qualifications with language from *Storer v. Brown*, 415 U.S. 724 (1974), in which we faced a constitutional challenge to provisions of the California Elections Code that regulated the procedures by which both independent candidates and candidates affiliated with qualified political parties could obtain ballot position in general elections. The Code required candidates affiliated with a qualified party to win a primary election, and required independents to make timely filing of nomination papers signed by at least 5% of the entire vote cast in the last general election. The Code also denied ballot position to independents who had voted in the most recent primary election or who had registered their affiliation with a qualified party during the previous year.

In *Storer*, we rejected the argument that the challenged procedures created additional qualifications as "wholly without merit." We noted that petitioners "would not have been disqualified had they been nominated at a party primary or by an adequately supported independent petition and then elected at the general election." We concluded that the California Code "no more establishes an additional requirement for the office of Representative than the requirement that the candidate win the primary to secure a place on the general ballot or otherwise demonstrate substantial community support." Petitioners maintain that, under *Storer*, Amendment 73 is not a qualification.

We need not decide whether petitioners' narrow understanding of qualifications is correct because, even if it is, Amendment 73 may not stand. * * * In our view, Amendment 73 is an indirect attempt to accomplish what the Constitution prohibits Arkansas from accomplishing directly. As the plurality opinion of the Arkansas Supreme Court recognized, Amendment 73 is an "effort to dress eligibility to stand for Congress in ballot access clothing," because the "intent and the effect of Amendment 73 are to disqualify congressional incumbents from further service." We must, of course, accept the State Court's view of the purpose of its own law: we are thus authoritatively informed that the sole purpose of § 3 of Amendment 73 was to attempt to achieve a result that is forbidden by the Federal Constitution. Indeed, it cannot be seriously contended that the intent behind Amendment 73 is other than to prevent the election of incumbents. The preamble of Amendment 73 states explicitly: "[T]he people of Arkansas . . . herein limit the terms of elected officials." * * *

* * * In our view, an amendment with the avowed purpose and obvious effect of evading the requirements of the Qualifications Clauses by handicapping a class of candidates cannot stand. To argue otherwise is to suggest that the Framers spent significant time and energy in debating and crafting Clauses that could be easily evaded. More importantly, allowing States to evade the Qualifications Clauses by "dress[ing] eligibility to stand for Congress in ballot

access clothing" trivializes the basic principles of our democracy that underlie those Clauses. Petitioners' argument treats the Qualifications Clauses not as the embodiment of a grand principle, but rather as empty formalism. * * *

Petitioners make the related argument that Amendment 73 merely regulates the "Manner" of elections, and that the Amendment is therefore a permissible exercise of state power under Article I, § 4, cl. 1 (the Elections Clause), to regulate the "Times, Places and Manner" of elections. We cannot agree. * * * The Framers intended the Elections Clause to grant States authority to create procedural regulations, not to provide States with license to exclude classes of candidates from federal office. * * *

The provisions at issue in *Storer* and our other Elections Clause cases were thus constitutional because they regulated election *procedures* and did not even arguably impose any substantive qualification rendering a class of potential candidates ineligible for ballot position. They served the state interest in protecting the integrity and regularity of the election process, an interest independent of any attempt to evade the constitutional prohibition against the imposition of additional qualifications for service in Congress. And they did not involve measures that exclude candidates from the ballot without reference to the candidates' support in the electoral process. Our cases upholding state regulations of election procedures thus provide little support for the contention that a state-imposed ballot access restriction is constitutional when it is undertaken for the twin goals of disadvantaging a particular class of candidates and evading the dictates of the Qualifications Clauses.

[V] The merits of term limits, or "rotation," have been the subject of debate since the formation of our Constitution, when the Framers unanimously rejected a proposal to add such limits to the Constitution. The cogent arguments on both sides of the question that were articulated during the process of ratification largely retain their force today. Over half the States have adopted measures that impose such limits on some offices either directly or indirectly, and the Nation as a whole, notably by constitutional amendment, has imposed a limit on the number of terms that the President may serve. Term limits, like any other qualification for office, unquestionably restrict the ability of voters to vote for whom they wish. On the other hand, such limits may provide for the infusion of fresh ideas and new perspectives, and may decrease the likelihood that representatives will lose touch with their constituents. It is not our province to resolve this longstanding debate.

We are, however, firmly convinced that allowing the several States to adopt term limits for congressional service would effect a fundamental change in the constitutional framework. Any such change must come not by legislation adopted either by Congress or by an individual State, but rather — as have other important changes in the electoral process — through the Amendment procedures set forth in Article V. The Framers decided that the qualifications for service in the Congress of the United States be fixed in the Constitution and be uniform throughout the Nation. * * * In the absence of a properly passed constitutional amendment, allowing individual States to craft their own qualifications for Congress would thus erode the structure envisioned by the

Framers, a structure that was designed, in the words of the Preamble to our Constitution, to form a "more perfect Union."

[JUSTICE KENNEDY concurred in the opinion for the Court and wrote a separate opinion responding to Justice Thomas' theory of federal/state sovereignty. "Federalism was our Nation's own discovery. The Framers split the atom of sovereignty. It was the genius of their idea that our citizens would have two political capacities, one state and one federal, each protected from incursion by the other. The resulting Constitution created a legal system unprecedented in form and design, establishing two orders of government, each with its own direct relationship, its own privity, its own set of mutual rights and obligations to the people who sustain it and are governed by it." *McCulloch*. Because the Arkansas amendment directly affected the unique federal right to vote, a right also implicating the First Amendment, Justice Kennedy believed it crossed the line. But his concurring opinion emphasized that the states must be equally well protected against federal incursions.]

JUSTICE THOMAS, with whom THE CHIEF JUSTICE [REHNQUIST], JUSTICE O'CONNOR, and JUSTICE SCALIA join, dissenting.

It is ironic that the Court bases today's decision on the right of the people to "choose whom they please to govern them." Under our Constitution, there is only one State whose people have the right to "choose whom they please" to represent Arkansas in Congress. The Court holds, however, that neither the elected legislature of that State nor the people themselves (acting by ballot initiative) may prescribe any qualifications for those representatives. The majority therefore defends the right of the people of Arkansas to "choose whom they please to govern them" by invalidating a provision that won nearly 60% of the votes cast in a direct election and that carried every congressional district in the State.

I dissent. Nothing in the Constitution deprives the people of each State of the power to prescribe eligibility requirements for the candidates who seek to represent them in Congress. The Constitution is simply silent on this question. And where the Constitution is silent, it raises no bar to action by the States or the people.

[Justice Thomas first discussed the idea of "reserved powers" in the federal system. He argued that the States "can exercise all powers that the Constitution does not withhold from them." Whether the states enjoyed those powers before the adoption of the Constitution is not relevant.]

The majority's essential logic is that the state governments could not "reserve" any powers that they did not control at the time the Constitution was drafted. * * * The Tenth Amendment's use of the word "reserved" does not help the majority's position. If someone says that the power to use a particular facility is reserved to some group, he is not saying anything about whether that group has previously used the facility. He is merely saying that the people who control the facility have designated that group as the entity with authority to use it. The Tenth Amendment is similar: The people of the States, from whom all governmental powers stem, have specified that all powers not prohibited to the States by the Federal Constitution are reserved "to the States respectively, or to the people." * * *

In a final effort to deny that the people of the States enjoy "reserved" powers over the selection of their representatives in Congress, the majority suggests that the Constitution expressly delegates to the States certain powers over congressional elections. Such delegations of power, the majority argues, would be superfluous if the people of the States enjoyed reserved powers in this area.

Only one constitutional provision — the Times, Places and Manner Clause of Article I, § 4 — even arguably supports the majority's suggestion. * * * Contrary to the majority's assumption, however, this Clause does not delegate any authority to the States. Instead, it simply imposes a duty upon them. * * * This command meshes with one of the principal purposes of Congress' "make or alter" power: to ensure that the States hold congressional elections in the first place, so that Congress continues to exist. * * *

I take it to be established, then, that the people of Arkansas do enjoy "reserved" powers over the selection of their representatives in Congress. Purporting to exercise those reserved powers, they have agreed among themselves that the candidates covered by § 3 of Amendment 73 — those whom they have already elected to three or more terms in the House of Representatives or to two or more terms in the Senate — should not be eligible to appear on the ballot for reelection, but should nonetheless be returned to Congress if enough voters are sufficiently enthusiastic about their candidacy to write in their names. Whatever one might think of the wisdom of this arrangement, we may not override the decision of the people of Arkansas unless something in the Federal Constitution deprives them of the power to enact such measures. * * *

The people of other States could legitimately complain if the people of Arkansas decide, in a particular election, to send a 6-year-old to Congress. But the Constitution gives the people of other States no basis to complain if the people of Arkansas elect a freshman representative in preference to a long-term incumbent. That being the case, it is hard to see why the rights of the people of other States have been violated when the people of Arkansas decide to enact a more general disqualification of long-term incumbents. * * *

The majority responds that "a patchwork of state qualifications" would "undermin[e] the uniformity and the national character that the Framers envisioned and sought to ensure." Yet the Framers thought it perfectly consistent with the "national character" of Congress for the Senators and Representatives from each State to be chosen by the legislature or the people of that State. The majority never explains why Congress' fundamental character permits this state-centered system, but nonetheless prohibits the people of the States and their state legislatures from setting any eligibility requirements for the candidates who seek to represent them. * * *

Although the Qualifications Clauses neither state nor imply the prohibition that it finds in them, the majority infers from the Framers' "democratic principles" that the Clauses must have been generally understood to preclude the people of the States and their state legislatures from prescribing any additional qualifications for their representatives in Congress. * * * The logical conclusion [from the analysis in *Powell*, however,] is simply that the Framers did not want the people of the States and their state legislatures to be constrained by too many qualifications imposed at the national level. * * *

The fact that the Framers did not grant a qualification-setting power to Congress does not imply that they wanted to bar its exercise at the state level. One reason why the Framers decided not to let Congress prescribe the qualifications of its own members was that incumbents could have used this power to perpetuate themselves or their ilk in office. As Madison pointed out at the Philadelphia Convention, Members of Congress would have an obvious conflict of interest if they could determine who may run against them. But neither the people of the States nor the state legislatures would labor under the same conflict of interest when prescribing qualifications for Members of Congress, and so the Framers would have had to use a different calculus in determining whether to deprive them of this power.

* * * There is a world of difference between a self-imposed constraint and a constraint imposed from above. * * * Congressional power over qualifications would have enabled the representatives from some States, acting collectively in the National Legislature, to prevent the people of another State from electing their preferred candidates. * * *

* * * The majority never identifies the democratic principles that would have been violated if a state legislature, in the days before the Constitution was amended to provide for the direct election of Senators, had imposed some limits of its own on the field of candidates that it would consider for appointment. Likewise, the majority does not explain why democratic principles forbid the people of a State from adopting additional eligibility requirements to help narrow their choices among candidates seeking to represent them in the House of Representatives. Indeed, the invocation of democratic principles to invalidate Amendment 73 seems particularly difficult in the present case, because Amendment 73 remains fully within the control of the people of Arkansas. If they wanted to repeal it (despite the 20-point margin by which they enacted it less than three years ago), they could do so by a simple majority vote.

The majority appears to believe that restrictions on eligibility for office are inherently undemocratic. But the Qualifications Clauses themselves prove that the Framers did not share this view; eligibility requirements to which the people of the States consent are perfectly consistent with the Framers' scheme. In fact, we have described "the authority of the people of the States to determine the qualifications of their most important government officials" as "an authority that lies at the heart of representative government." *Gregory v. Ashcroft*, 501 U.S. 452, 463 (1991) [Chapter 8, § 1B3] (refusing to read federal law to preclude States from imposing a mandatory retirement age on state judges who are subject to periodic retention elections). When the people of a State themselves decide to restrict the field of candidates whom they are willing to send to Washington as their representatives, they simply have not violated the principle that "the people should choose whom they please to govern them." * * *

In fact, the authority to narrow the field of candidates in this way may be part and parcel of the right to elect Members of Congress. That is, the right to choose may include the right to winnow.

To appreciate this point, it is useful to consider the Constitution as it existed before the Seventeenth Amendment was adopted in 1913. The Framers' scheme called for the legislature of each State to choose the Senators from that State. The majority offers no reason to believe that state legislatures could not adopt prospective rules to guide themselves in carrying out this responsibility; not only is there no express language in the Constitution barring legislatures from passing laws to narrow their choices, but there also is absolutely no basis for inferring such a prohibition. Imagine the worst-case scenario: a state legislature, wishing to punish one of the Senators from its State for his vote on some bill, enacts a qualifications law that the Senator does not satisfy. The Senator would still be able to serve out his term; the Constitution provides for senators to be chosen for 6-year terms, and a person who has been seated in Congress can be removed only if two-thirds of the Members of his House vote to expel him. While the Senator would be disqualified from seeking reappointment, under the Framers' Constitution the state legislature already enjoyed unfettered discretion to deny him reappointment anyway. Instead of passing a qualifications law, the legislature could simply have passed a resolution declaring its intention to appoint someone else the next time around. Thus, the legislature's power to adopt laws to narrow its own choices added nothing to its general appointment power.

* * * Amendment 73 is not the act of a state legislature; it is the act of the people of Arkansas, adopted at a direct election and inserted into the state constitution. The majority never explains why giving effect to the people's decision would violate the "democratic principles" that undergird the Constitution. Instead, the majority's discussion of democratic principles is directed entirely to attacking eligibility requirements imposed on the people of a State by an entity other than themselves.

The majority protests that any distinction between the people of the States and the state legislatures is "untenable" and "astonishing." * * * In the context of congressional election, [however,] the framers obviously saw a meaningful difference between direct action by the people of each State [who elected U.S. Representatives] and action by their state legislatures [with the power to choose Senators].

[Justice Thomas exhaustively analyzed the historical evidence of the Framers' intentions, the ratification debates, state practice around the time the Constitution was adopted, and the congressional practice as revealed by the McCreery case. He concluded that "the historical evidence is simply inadequate to warrant the majority's conclusion that the Qualifications Clauses mean anything more than what they say."]

It is radical enough for the majority to hold that the Constitution implicitly precludes the people of the States from prescribing any eligibility requirements for the congressional candidates who seek their votes. This holding, after all, does not stop with negating the term limits that many States have seen fit to impose on their Senators and Representatives. Today's decision also means that no State may disqualify congressional candidates whom a court has found to be mentally incompetent, who are currently in prison, or who have past vote-fraud convictions. * * *

In order to invalidate § 3 of Amendment 73, however, the majority must go farther. * * * Amendment 73 does not actually create this kind of disqualification. It does not say that covered candidates may not serve any more terms in Congress if reelected, and it does not indirectly achieve the same result by barring those candidates from seeking reelection. It says only that if they are to win reelection, they must do so by write-in votes.

* * * The majority suggests that this does not matter, because Amendment 73 itself says that it has the purpose of "evading the requirements of the Qualifications Clauses." The majority bases this assertion on the Amendment's preamble, which speaks of "limit[ing] the terms of elected officials." [But this statement may] simply reflect the limiting effects that the drafters of the preamble expected to flow from what they perceived as the restoration of electoral competition to congressional races. In any event, inquiries into legislative intent are even more difficult than usual when the legislative body whose unified intent must be determined consists of 825,162 Arkansas voters. * * * One of petitioners' central arguments is that congressionally conferred advantages have artificially inflated the pre-existing electoral chances of the covered candidates, and that Amendment 73 is merely designed to level the playing field on which challengers compete with them.

To understand this argument requires some background. Current federal law (enacted, of course, by congressional incumbents) confers numerous advantages on incumbents, and these advantages are widely thought to make it "significantly more difficult" for challengers to defeat them. For instance, federal law gives incumbents enormous advantages in building name recognition and good will in their home districts. See, e.g., 39 U.S.C. § 3210 (permitting Members of Congress to send "franked" mail free of charge); 2 U.S.C. §§ 61-1, 72a, 332 (permitting Members to have sizable taxpayer-funded staffs); 2 U.S.C. § 123b (establishing the House Recording Studio and the Senate Recording and Photographic Studios). At the same time that incumbent Members of Congress enjoy these in-kind benefits, Congress imposes spending and contribution limits in congressional campaigns that "can prevent challengers from spending more . . . to overcome their disadvantage in name recognition." Many observers believe that the campaign-finance laws also give incumbents an "enormous fund-raising edge" over their challengers by giving a large financing role to entities with incentives to curry favor with incumbents. In addition, the internal rules of Congress put a substantial premium on seniority, with the result that each Member's already plentiful opportunities to distribute benefits to his constituents increase with the length of his tenure. In this manner, Congress effectively "fines" the electorate for voting against incumbents. * * *

At the same time that incumbents enjoy the electoral advantages that they have conferred upon themselves, they also enjoy astonishingly high reelection rates. * * * Even in the November 1994 elections, which are widely considered to have effected the most sweeping change in Congress in recent memory, 90% of the incumbents who sought reelection to the House were successful, and nearly half of the losers were completing only their first terms. Only 2 of the 26 Senate incumbents seeking reelection were defeated, and one of them had been elected for the first time in a special election only a few years earlier.

The voters of Arkansas evidently believe that incumbents would not enjoy such overwhelming success if electoral contests were truly fair — that is, if the government did not put its thumb on either side of the scale. The majority offers no reason to question the accuracy of this belief.

To be sure, the offset is only rough and approximate; no one knows exactly how large an electoral benefit comes with having been a long-term Member of Congress, and no one knows exactly how large an electoral disadvantage comes from forcing a well-funded candidate with high name recognition to run a write-in campaign. But the majority does not base its holding on the premise that Arkansas has struck the wrong balance. Instead, the majority holds that the Qualifications Clauses preclude Arkansas from trying to strike any balance at all; the majority simply says that "an amendment with the avowed purpose and obvious effect of evading the requirements of the Qualifications Clauses by handicapping a class of candidates cannot stand." Thus, the majority apparently would reach the same result even if one could demonstrate at trial that the electoral advantage conferred by Amendment 73 upon challengers precisely counterbalances the electoral advantages conferred by federal law upon long-term Members of Congress.

For me, this suggests only two possibilities. Either the majority's holding is wrong and Amendment 73 does not violate the Qualifications Clauses, or (assuming the accuracy of petitioners' factual claims) the electoral system that exists without Amendment 73 is no less unconstitutional than the electoral system that exists with Amendment 73.

* * * [L]aws that allegedly have the purpose and effect of handicapping a particular class of candidates traditionally are reviewed under the First and Fourteenth Amendments rather than the Qualifications Clauses. [See] *Storer.* * * * To analyze such laws under the Qualifications Clauses may open up whole new vistas for courts. If it is true that "the current congressional campaign finance system . . . has created an electoral system so stacked against challengers that in many elections voters have no real choices," are the Federal Election Campaign Act Amendments of 1974 unconstitutional under (of all things) the Qualifications Clauses? Cf. *Buckley v. Valeo* [*infra*] (upholding the current system against First Amendment challenge). If it can be shown that nonminorities are at a significant disadvantage when they seek election in districts dominated by minority voters, would the intentional creation of "majority-minority districts" violate the Qualifications Clauses even if it were to survive scrutiny under the Fourteenth Amendment? Cf. *Shaw v. Reno* [*supra*] ("we express no view as to whether [the intentional creation of such districts] always gives rise to an equal protection claim"). * * *

The majority's opinion may not go so far, although it does not itself suggest any principled stopping point. No matter how narrowly construed, however, today's decision reads the Qualifications Clauses to impose substantial implicit prohibitions on the States and the people of the States. I would not draw such an expansive negative inference from the fact that the Constitution requires Members of Congress to be a certain age, to be inhabitants of the States that they represent, and to have been United States citizens for a specified period. Rather, I would read the Qualifications Clauses to do no more than what they say. I respectfully dissent.

NOTES ON *U.S. TERM LIMITS* AND SUBSEQUENT DEVELOPMENTS

1. *Were the Voters Irrational?* At the same time that voters passed ballot initiatives imposing term limits on federal legislators, they also voted in most cases to return their senior incumbents to office. How can these seemingly inconsistent choices be reconciled? Einer Elhauge argues that this paradox disappears when we understand the collective-action problems that faced voters. "Incumbents by definition have more seniority than challengers, and this seniority gives them more legislative clout. Any individual district that ousts its incumbent is thus penalized by a smaller share of legislative power and governmental benefits unless the other districts also oust their incumbents."[f] Elhauge argues that voters might prefer less senior representatives with ideological views closer to theirs, but they will continue to vote for the incumbent who has more power in an institution like Congress that is largely organized according to seniority. On balance, voters will prefer a more influential representative, who can send her constituency a greater share of governmental benefits, to a junior member whose ideology may be more compatible. If, however, voters can be sure that no district can vote for a more senior lawmaker because of term limits, they reduce the penalty for electing a challenger. In addition, term limits allow voters to get rid of the senior representatives from other districts, a result that cannot be obtained through regular voting. In some cases, the benefits of removing these lawmakers from office may exceed any costs to voters of losing the ability to elect their own incumbent to an unlimited number of terms.

Elhauge's explanation suggests why rational voters might simultaneously support term limits for all federal lawmakers and yet still vote for their own incumbents in the absence of such restrictions. It does not explain, however, why voters in a particular state would limit the terms of their representatives without an assurance that other states would also adopt term limitations. Again, however, voters may have been wiser than they appear at first glance. It is no coincidence that groups of states adopted term limits at the same time through a coordinated national effort led by a few organized interest groups. For example, thirteen states adopted term limits in 1992. Some of the state

---

f. *Are Term Limits Undemocratic?*, 64 U. Chi. L. Rev. 83, 85 (1997). See also Edward Lopez, *Term Limits: Causes and Consequences,* 114 Pub. Choice 1 (2003) (discussing puzzle of why states would self-impose term limits).

constitutional amendments specified that the limitation would not go into effect until 21 or more states had also adopted limitations on terms of federal lawmakers. Moreover, many of the provisions had delayed effective dates, allowing time for the states that moved quickly to repeal term limits if voters from other states declined to follow their lead.[g] Once a critical mass of states had adopted federal term limits, their representatives would command the votes to change congressional rules to weaken the power of the seniority system and reduce the relative advantage of long-time incumbents over junior members.

2. *Limitations on State Officials.* Term limitations are common in state and local government. Fifteen states place term limits on state legislators, 37 states limit the number of terms their governors can serve, and many local officials face term limits after a few years of public service.[h] Although term limits on state legislators have been challenged as violating both state and federal constitutional requirements, they have generally been upheld. The leading case is *Legislature of the State of California v. Eu*, 816 P.2d 1309 (Cal. 1991), *cert. denied*, 503 U.S. 919 (1992), which balanced the interest of incumbents in retaining office and the interest of voters in having the choice of reelecting them against the state's interest in unclogging the political system and ending the "incumbent's advantage" in elections. The court found that no fundamental rights had been critically burdened (voters have no "right" to vote for a particular candidate) and the state's interest was considerable.[i]

In some states, term limits have had very little effect on political dynamics because legislators did not tend to serve for long periods of time even when their terms were unlimited. In states like California, however, where legislatures were full of career politicians, term limits have caused significant, and sometimes complete, turnover, helped bring to power new leaders, and may have decreased the ability of legislators to pass controversial or significant laws. Term limits appear also to have caused a change in the demographics of legislatures. In 2000, one of four lawmakers was a woman, up from 17% ten years before, and Hispanics held 19% of the seats, up from 6%. In a study of the California legislature under term limits, Bruce Cain and Thad Kousser find that limitations sped up the gender and racial diversification of the legislature that was already underway because of demographic and other changes. *Adapting to Term Limits: Recent Experiences and New Directions* (2004).

No longer assured of long careers in one elected position, incumbents have begun to leave office early to run for other attractive seats, perhaps in the federal legislature, in the upper house, or sometimes in local positions (a phenomenon once dismissed as *regressive ambition*). Thus, elections have

---

g. See John Carey, *Term Limits and Legislative Representation* 12–13 (1996) (detailing provisions of the state amendments).

h. For a discussion about the effects of term limits on local officials, see Eric Lane, *The Impact of Term Limits on Lawmaking in the City of New York*, 3 Election L.J. 670 (2004).

i. See also *Bates v. Jones*, 131 F.3d 843 (9th Cir. 1997) (en banc), *cert. denied*, 523 U.S. 1021 (1998) (holding that voters could constitutionally adopt lifetime bans on incumbents after a limited period of service "as a means to promote democracy by opening up the political process and restoring competitive elections").

become more competitive as incumbents face more challenging races against seasoned politicians. In these ways, term limits may not have ushered in the era of the citizen-legislator, but they have changed the profile of the professional politician. See John Carey, Richard Niemi & Lynda Powell, *Term Limits in the State Legislatures* 123–29 (2000) (finding little demographic change resulting from term limits other than more women lawmakers, and finding more focus on statewide issues, perhaps as part of a strategy to move up the political opportunity structure).

Carey, Niemi, and Powell find that term limits' most significant effects are institutional ones. Term limits appear to weaken legislative party leaders and to strengthen the influence of governors, who, even though term-limited themselves, have access to professional staff, substantial information, and seasoned political advisers. In several state legislatures, term limits have weakened the seniority norm and increased the involvement of junior members in key decisions. Although some opponents of term limits predicted they would increase the influence of lobbyists, some commentators have observed that lobbyists find the change a "mixed bag," as they have to establish relationships with new people and educate them about their issues.[j]

As you consider the effects of term limits in state legislatures, think about what steps lawmakers might take to develop expertise and regain power relative to the executive branch and lobbyists. Kousser describes several strategies used by term-limited state legislators to adapt, including expanded orientations for new members; more sophisticated databases and computerized information; growing reliance on professional staff in centralized, nonpartisan organizations within the legislature; different committee structures; and more attention to the "letter of the law" rather than norms and traditions. See *Term Limits and the Dismantling of State Legislative Professionalism* 214–20 (2005).

Recently, some states with term limitations on state legislators have witnessed efforts to roll back or repeal the limits. In February 2002, the Idaho legislature became the first to repeal term limits, a reform that had been enacted nearly eight years earlier through a ballot initiative. The governor vetoed the legislation, on the ground that the "will of the voters * * * must be protected," but the legislature overrode his veto with a two-thirds vote in both houses. A study of the vote to overturn term limits reveals that support came primarily from Republican legislators, who wanted to retain their party's control over the legislature, and from representatives of rural areas.[k] Legislators from rural districts argued that term limits would deprive their constituents in sparsely populated areas of experienced leaders, particularly in local offices that are traditionally hard to fill. The reaction following the legislature's decision was swift but not extraordinary. A few incumbents were defeated in the 2002 primary elections, but it appears that other issues played a large role in those

---

j. Alan Greenblatt, *The Truth About Term Limits,* Governing Mag., Jan. 2006, at 2.

k. See Daniel Smith, *Overturning Term Limits: The Legislature's Own Private Idaho?,* 36 PS 215 (2003).

elections. A popular referendum to "repeal the repeal" and reinstate term limits ended in a narrow victory for anti-term-limits forces.

Only a few states with term limitations passed them in legislative form that would allow state legislators to repeal or modify them; in the other states, a popular vote would be required to repeal provisions in state constitutions imposing term limits on legislators. So far voters have been unwilling to retreat from their decision to adopt legislative term limits, although they do not usually punish lawmakers who break their voluntary pledges to abide by term limits. Legislators have been more successful challenging term limits through litigation. Term limits adopted in 1992 in Wyoming were overturned in May 2004 by the state supreme court, which ruled in *Cathcart v. Meyer*, 88 P.3d 1050 (Wyo. 2004), that they should have been enacted as a constitutional amendment, not through a statutory ballot initiative. This holding substantially increased the obstacles for term limits supporters in Wyoming because constitutional amendments must be first approved by two-thirds of each legislative house before they can be placed on the ballot.

3. *Developments in Congress since* U.S. Term Limits. The majority in *U.S. Term Limits* made clear that the adoption of federal term limits requires a constitutional amendment. Shortly after the decision, Congress considered such an amendment to impose twelve-year limits on service in each house. Although the proposal received majority support, it lacked the two-thirds vote required for a constitutional amendment. (The Senate did not actually vote on the amendment because supporters lacked two votes to invoke cloture and cut off a filibuster.) In 1995, as part of the Republican "Contract with America," the House of Representatives limited committee chairmanships to six years. The effect of the rule was significant. Four senior Republican members, including the Chair of the powerful Ways and Means Committee, retired in 2000 because they could not retain their powerful positions. Members hoping to succeed retiring chairs worked to influence votes by raising campaign funds for other lawmakers; with seniority no longer the overriding criterion for selection to leadership positions, fundraising prowess became a greater factor.[1] In January 2002, the House eliminated the eight-year limit on holding the position as Speaker. House Democrats retained term limits committee chairs when they took power in 2007. Critics argue that these term limits make it more difficult for Congress to oversee the executive branch effectively, although defenders maintain that any loss is balanced by an increase in innovative ideas.

4. *Distinguishing Between Indirect Qualifications and Legitimate Ballot Access Provisions.* Remember that the Arkansas provision in *U.S. Term Limits* was phrased as a ballot access provision, denying a place on the ballot to lawmakers who had served a certain period of time in the House or Senate. The Court rejected the argument that the Arkansas amendment merely restricted incumbents' access to the ballot and found that it imposed an

---

1. See Karen Foerstel, *Chairmen's Term Limits Already Shaking Up House*, Cong. Q. Weekly, Mar. 25, 2000, at 628.

additional qualification on federal legislative offices. The Court looked to both the effect and the intent of the provision in reaching the conclusion that the state was trying to do indirectly what it was prohibited from doing directly. Although the Court indicated that empirical evidence was not required to determine the likely effect of a provision, it believed that the ballot restriction "will make it significantly more difficult for the barred candidate to win the election." It supported this conclusion with the following evidence: "[I]n over 1,300 Senate elections since the passage of the Seventeenth Amendment in 1913, only one has been won by a write-in candidate. In over 20,000 House elections since the turn of the century, only five have been won by write-in candidates." Justice Thomas responded that this empirical data would not describe the state of affairs in a world with term limits. He argued that most write-in candidates in the past had been fringe candidates with virtually no name recognition or financial backing, while write-in candidates under the Arkansas amendment would be well-known incumbents. In the past, only twice had *incumbent* Congressmembers sought reelection as write-in candidates; one of them won with 83% of the vote, and the other managed a respectable showing of 23% support. Which prediction is likely to have been more accurate? Should the determination of the effect of such an amendment rest on this kind of empirical analysis?

In the *U.S. Term Limits* case, the Court relied on the state supreme court's finding that the intent of the amendment was to impose term limits on federal lawmakers. The opinion, therefore, says little about how a court is to discern the intent behind such a provision, particularly one that was enacted by hundreds of thousands of voters. The majority mentioned the initiative's preamble, which stated explicitly that "the people of Arkansas * * * herein limit the terms of elected officials." Also, the name of the primary group supporting the amendment and participating in the lawsuit — U.S. Term Limits, Inc. — led one judge on the state supreme court to conclude that the ballot access provision was actually a qualification. Are these legitimate ways to discern the intent of those enacting this provision? As the dissent noted, the preamble also evidenced a concern with entrenched incumbency that results in a system offering voters very little real choice among candidates. Given the electoral advantages that Justice Thomas lists in his dissent, term limits may provide challengers — who lack the same access to the media, lists of donors and volunteers, and the ability to correspond with constituents using franked mail — a fair chance to unseat the incumbent. Would an intent to level the political playing field be acceptable under the majority's test, allowing a court to uphold a provision similar to the Arkansas amendment as a permissible ballot access regulation?

Determining whether a law imposes qualifications on candidates or only restricts their access to the ballot is more than merely a matter of semantics. As we will see in the next section, the Court tends to apply less exacting constitutional tests to ballot access regulations, even though *U.S. Term Limits* suggests that imposing explicit qualifications on candidates for the federal legislature may not be relevantly different from restricting access to the ballot for certain categories of people.

C. BALLOT ACCESS PROVISIONS

Article I, § 4 of the Constitution, the Elections Clause, allows the States to regulate the "Times, Places and Manner of holding Elections for Senators and Representatives," although Congress can pass legislation to make or alter state electoral regulations. Before 1900, concerns about ballot access restrictions were nonexistent. There were no official ballots; instead, political parties provided voters with ballots listing only their candidates for offices. Because party ballots were printed in distinctive colors, keeping one's vote secret was difficult, and voters were often bribed or intimidated into voting in a particular way. Only with the adoption of the secret, uniform, and government-printed ballot did the question of ballot access become important for policymakers and the courts.[m] Ballot access implicates the interests of many players in the political system: voters, who realistically can only elect candidates who appear on the ballot; candidates; and political parties, the groups that largely determine who will be listed on the ballot.

Although states have the constitutional power to regulate elections, their authority is limited because restrictions implicate constitutional guarantees. Most obviously, ballot access laws affect the right to vote. In addition, laws that impair the right of minor-party or independent candidates to obtain a spot on the ballot undermine the right to associate for political purposes. Balanced against these constitutional concerns in the Court's flexible test to assess ballot access laws is the states' legitimate interest in regulating elections to reduce voter confusion, disorder, and fraud. The Court has applied a sliding scale approach, calibrating the level of scrutiny to the burden imposed by the ballot access provision. In *Williams v. Rhodes*, 393 U.S. 23 (1968), the Court struck down a law requiring new political parties to obtain signatures equal to 15% of the ballots cast in the last election and to file the petitions long before the election. It required that regulations imposing serious burdens on rights, in this case, essentially making it impossible for new parties to obtain ballot access, be narrowly tailored to achieve a compelling state interest. Laws that do not operate as prohibitions on access trigger less exacting scrutiny, allowing legitimate state regulatory interests to support reasonable and nondiscriminatory burdens. The choice of the standard of review — strict scrutiny versus some lesser scrutiny — often determines the outcome of the judicial analysis. See, e.g., *Lee v. Keith*, 463 F.3d 763 (7th Cir. 2006) (applying strict scrutiny to Illinois requirements that independent candidates file 323 days before the general election, the earliest filing deadline in the country, as well as meet stringent petition requirements, and holding statute unconstitutional); *Libertarian Party of Ohio v. Blackwell*, 462 F.3d 579 (6th Cir. 2006) (using strict scrutiny, invalidating Ohio deadlines for minor parties that required filing petitions more than a year before the general election).

Permissible state interests are linked to the Court's belief that "there must be a substantial regulation of elections if they are to be fair and honest and if some sort of order, rather than chaos, is to accompany the democratic

---

m. See Marjorie Hershey, *Party Politics in America* 196 (12th ed. 2006).

processes." *Storer v. Brown*, 415 U.S. 724, 730 (1974). Consider the state interests identified in the following decision upholding a law that prohibits a candidate from appearing on the ballot as a candidate of more than one party. Such multiparty candidacies are called *fusion candidacies*. Is a ban on fusion candidacies designed to reduce voter confusion and protect the integrity of the electoral process, or is it a technique adopted by the two major parties to eliminate any threat from emerging political parties?

TIMMONS v. TWIN CITIES AREA NEW PARTY, 520 U.S. 351 (1997). State Representative Andy Dawkins was running unopposed in the Democratic-Farmer-Labor (DFL) Party's primary. The Minnesota chapter of the national New Party also chose him as their candidate for the state legislature. Because Dawkins had already filed as a candidate for the DFL's nomination, local election officials refused to accept the New Party's nominating petition, citing state laws that prohibit fusion candidacies. The New Party sued, contending that the laws violate their members' associational rights under the federal Constitution. Although noting that the First Amendment "protects the right of citizens to associate and to form political parties for the advancement of common political goals and ideas," **Chief Justice Rehnquist** for the six-Justice majority held that the antifusion law is a reasonable regulation of parties, elections, and ballots designed to reduce "election- and campaign-related disorder."

The Court reasoned that this burden on the New Party is a minor one. Although it cannot nominate the candidates of other parties, a political party "remains free to endorse whom it likes, to ally itself with others, to nominate candidates for office, and to spread its message to all who will listen." The state prohibition closes off one avenue of communication with the voters (i.e., the ballot), but "[b]allots serve primarily to elect candidates, not as forums for political expression." Because the burden on the New Party is slight, the state's interest in avoiding voter confusion and political chaos is sufficient to justify the law. As in previous ballot access cases, the majority did not require any empirical proof of voter confusion. Instead, it used the following worst-case scenario to support its conclusion that voters might be misled: "[M]embers of a major party could decide that a powerful way of 'sending a message' via the ballot would be for various factions of that party to nominate the major party's candidate as the candidate for the newly-formed 'No New Taxes,' 'Conserve Our Environment,' and 'Stop Crime Now' parties." Such tactics would transform the ballot "from a means of choosing candidates to a billboard for political advertising." This hypothetical implicated a second legitimate state interest: protecting the integrity of the electoral process and thus avoiding increased voter alienation and dissatisfaction.

Dissenting **Justice Stevens**, joined by **Justice Ginsburg**, thought fusion candidacies are "the best marriage of the virtues of minor party challenge to entrenched viewpoints and the political stability that the two-party system provides. * * * [They provide] a means by which voters with viewpoints not adequately represented by platforms of the two major parties can indicate to a particular candidate that — in addition to his support for the major party views

— he should be responsive to the views of the minor party whose support for him was demonstrated where political parties demonstrate support — on the ballot." The majority, however, dismissed the argument that without fusion-based alliances, minor parties will be unable to thrive, reasoning that the existence of benefits for minor parties does not mean that the state must permit fusion candidacies. "Many features of our political system — e.g., single-member districts, 'first past the post' elections, and the high costs of campaigning — make it difficult for third parties to succeed in American politics. But the Constitution does not require States to permit fusion any more than it requires them to move to proportional-representation elections or public financing of campaigns."

Justice Stevens' dissent took particular issue with the majority's suggestion that the interest in maintaining a stable two-party system might be an acceptable state concern to justify ballot restrictions. First, he noted that this interest was not one advanced by Minnesota and thus could not properly be considered by the majority. Second, "[i]n most States, perhaps in all, there are two and only two major political parties. It is not surprising, therefore, that most States have enacted election laws that impose burdens on the development and growth of third parties. * * * The fact that the law was both intended to disadvantage minor parties and has had that effect is a matter that should weigh against, rather than in favor of, its constitutionality." He concluded: "It demeans the strength of the two-party system to assume that the major parties need to rely on laws that discriminate against independent voters and minor parties in order to preserve their positions of power. Indeed, it is a central theme of our jurisprudence that the entire electorate, which necessarily includes the members of major parties, will benefit from robust competition in ideas and governmental policies * * * ."

NOTES ON *TIMMONS*
AND THE IDEA OF A PARTISAN LOCKUP

1. *Voter Confusion.* As in previous cases, the *Timmons* Court deferred to the state's allegation of voter confusion without requiring empirical proof. In *Munro v. Socialist Workers Party*, 479 U.S. 189, 195–96 (1986), the Court stated: "To require States to prove actual voter confusion, ballot overcrowding, or the presence of frivolous candidacies as a predicate to the imposition of reasonable ballot access restrictions would invariably lead to endless court battles over the sufficiency of the 'evidence' marshaled by a State to prove the predicate. Such a requirement would necessitate that a State's political system sustain some level of damage before the legislature could take corrective action. Legislatures, we think, should be permitted to respond to potential deficiencies in the electoral process with foresight rather than reactively, provided that the response is reasonable and does not significantly impinge on constitutionally protected rights." Criticizing this kind of approach, Justice Stevens noted in *Timmons* that the only empirical data from a state with vibrant fusion politics, New York, revealed that the majority's "parade of horribles is fantastical."

Should courts require some showing that long ballots, fusion candidates, or multi-candidate races actually confuse voters rather than provide them information or allow them more choices? With respect to fusion candidacies, is it not at least theoretically possible that the additional ballot information improves voters' ability to vote competently? Few voters are willing to invest significant time and energy to find and understand information about candidates for public office. Given their limited attention to political matters, most people vote on the basis of voting cues or shortcuts, like party affiliation, that will allow them to vote in the same way that they would if they had full information about the candidates and their positions. Helpful voting cues allow them to vote competently even with limited information.[n] The strongest voting cues—party affiliation and incumbency—are usually apparent from the ballot; indeed, party affiliation is provided for most elections.

But the major party cue may not sufficiently allow voters to distinguish among candidates. One result of a two-party system combined with single-member electoral districts is a convergence of the parties with respect to their positions on the issues.[o] Third-party endorsements, however, can provide a more particularized cue about a candidate's positions on the issues. Third parties that endorse candidates of major parties tend to be issue-oriented or ideologically driven; for example, knowing that the Republican candidate is supported by the Right-to-Life Party or the Libertarian Party reveals more completely her ideology than the Republican nomination alone. Can you make an argument that fusion candidacies actually help voters cast their ballots more competently, rather than add to their confusion?

Our discussion of ballot access rules demonstrates the profound importance of political parties in the organization of our electoral system. Political parties are challenging entities for the state to regulate. In a sense they organize government, and thus they are both the regulated and the regulators. They are fairly fragmented organizations,[p] with local, state and national organizations and with arms in the government and outside it.[q]

---

n. See Elisabeth Gerber & Arthur Lupia, *Voter Competence in Direct Legislation Elections*, in *Citizen Competence and Democratic Institutions* 147 (Stephen Elkin & Karol Soltan eds., 1999).

o. See Jeffrey Berry, *The Interest Group Society* 46–47 (3d ed. 1997); Anthony Downs, *An Economic Theory of Democracy* 136 (1957). But see John Aldrich, *Why Parties? The Origin and Transformation of Political Parties in America* 169–74 (1995) (providing data to suggest that the public perceives parties as distinct and arguing that the "perception has a plausible basis"); Morris Fiorina, *Divided Government* 121–22 (2d ed. 1996) (suggesting that the two major parties are further apart ideologically than in the past, largely because of internal party politics).

p. See V.O. Key, *Politics, Parties, and Pressure Groups* 163–65 (5th ed. 1964) (differentiating among the party-in-government, the party-organization, and the party-in-the-electorate).

q. For additional analysis of the regulation of political parties, see Samuel Issacharoff, Pamela Karlan & Richard Pildes, *The Law of Democracy: Legal Structure of the Political Process* chap. 4 (2d rev. ed. 2002); David K. Ryden, *Representation in Crisis: The Constitution, Interest Groups, and Political Parties* (1996); Daryl Levinson & Richard Pildes,

2. *The State Interest in Protecting the Two-Party System.* In some ballot access cases, the Court has accepted state claims that regulation was required to promote political stability, to avoid splintered parties, and to restrain factionalism.[r] This interest may be merely an interest in avoiding intraparty disputes by, for example, limiting the ability of people who have previously run in party primaries to appear on the ballot as independent candidates. See *Storer v. Brown, supra.* Framed in this manner, the interest is not sufficient to support restrictions that are applied to independent candidates not recently associated with political parties. See *Anderson v. Celebrezze,* 460 U.S. 780 (1983). In *Clingman v. Beaver,* 544 U.S. 581 (2005), the Court upheld Oklahoma's law limiting participation in party primaries to only that party's members and independents, thereby forbidding, for example, a Republican from voting in the Libertarian Party's primary even if the Libertarian Party wished to open its primary fully. One of the state interests accepted to justify this law was the goal of preserving political parties as clearly identifiable groups with particular ideologies, and therefore ensuring that party affiliation sends a meaningful signal to voters who rely on party cue in casting ballots.

Increasingly, courts such as *Timmons* are also willing to consider the state's interest in maintaining a stable, two-party electoral system. Even though he dissented in *Timmons,* Justice Souter agreed with the majority that "[i]f it could be shown that the disappearance of the two-party system would undermine" the state's interest in preserving a political system capable of governing effectively, it might justify certain restrictions. Unlike state interests tied to intraparty tension, this state interest can support broader ballot access regulations affecting independents, write-in candidates, and minor parties. In contrast, Stevens' dissent draws on *Williams v. Rhodes, supra,* where the Court seemed dubious about the legitimacy of a state interest to protect the two-party system. Very clearly, the Court in *Williams* rejected the notion that laws could favor two particular parties, giving them a duopoly over ballot access. Instead, "[c]ompetition in ideas and governmental policies is at the core of our electoral process and of the First Amendment freedoms."

Several scholars have been sympathetic to Justice Stevens' concern in *Timmons* and have argued that courts should not apply such deferential review to ballot access provisions. Instead, they argue that the Court should be particularly aggressive in its review of such laws because they are enacted by incumbents who are members of established political parties and who are hostile to strong minor parties or independent candidacies.[s] Michael Klarman,

---

Separation of Parties, Not Powers, 119 Harv. L. Rev. 2311 (2006); Daniel Lowenstein, *Associational Rights of Major Political Parties: A Skeptical Inquiry,* 71 Tex. L. Rev. 1741 (1993); Symposium, *Law and Political Parties,* 100 Colum. L. Rev. 593–899 (2000).

r. See generally Bradley Smith, *Judicial Protection of Ballot-Access Rights: Third Parties Need Not Apply,* 28 Harv. J. on Legis. 167 (1991).

s. See, e.g., Richard Hasen, *Entrenching the Duopoly: Why the Supreme Court Should Not Allow the States to Protect the Democrats and Republicans from Political Competition,* 1997 Sup. Ct. Rev. 331; Samuel Issacharoff & Richard Pildes, *Politics as Markets: Partisan Lockups of the Democratic Process,* 50 Stan. L. Rev. 643 (1998).

for example, cites ballot access laws as examples of *legislative entrenchment* that foreclose for voters the option of expressing discontent with the two major parties. Incumbents have little to lose by passing restrictive ballot access laws because the laws themselves operate to keep candidates who might change the system off the ballot.[t] These scholars not only do not accept protection of the current two-party system as a legitimate state interest, they argue that it should serve as a red flag to courts to view ballot access restrictions with great skepticism.[u]

Under the partisan lockup theory, are many well-established features of our electoral system subject to constitutional attack? Many features of our electoral system, including single-member districts and a simple plurality system, work to favor the development and entrenchment of two major parties.[v] For example, apply the partisan lockup perspective in the following section of this chapter as we discuss the way in which minor parties are treated differently from major parties in the public financing system in presidential elections.[w] Where should we draw the line between rigorous judicial scrutiny of laws that entrench the current political duopoly and more deferential review of choices made by the political branches? Are courts institutionally suited to draw such a line or to determine which laws fall on either side?

3. *The Other Side of the Balance: The First Amendment Rights Infringed by Ballot Access Restrictions.* Not only are courts willing to accept a variety of rationales as legitimate state interests justifying regulation, but they also tend to discount some of the interests of voters and political groups that are burdened by the restrictions. For example, the right to vote is viewed by the Court purely in instrumental terms.[x] Similarly, as *Timmons* and the following case suggest, the Court has viewed the role of minor parties in our political

---

t. *Majoritarian Judicial Review: The Entrenchment Problem*, 85 Geo. L.J. 491 (1997).

u. But see David Dulio & James Thurber, *America's Two-Party System: Friend or Foe?*, 52 Admin. L. Rev. 769 (2000) (defending the two-party system as "the natural and most effective system for the United States' government"); Nathaniel Persily & Bruce Cain, *The Legal Status of Political Parties: A Reassessment of Competing Paradigms*, 100 Colum. L. Rev. 775, 799–808 (2000) (providing five principles to guide decisions in ballot access cases from the perspective of "firm believers in the utility and value of the two-party system for American politics").

v. See Maurice Duverger, *Political Parties: Their Organization and Activity in the Modern State* (1954) (classic formulation of this "true sociological law"); Gary Cox, *Making Votes Count: Strategic Coordination in the World's Electoral Systems* (1997) (evaluating Duverger's law).

w. See also *Arkansas Educational Television Comm'n v. Forbes*, 523 U.S. 666 (1998) (allowing public television stations discretion to exclude minor party candidates from televised debates); Alan Schroeder, *Presidential Debates: Forty Years of High-Risk TV* (2000) (discussing role of debates in elections); Jamin Raskin, *The Debate Gerrymander*, 77 Tex. L. Rev. 1943 (1999) (criticizing the *Forbes* opinion).

x. See Adam Winkler, *Expressive Voting*, 68 N.Y.U. L. Rev. 330 (1993) (arguing that voting should be valued for its expressive qualities in addition to its instrumental values).

system as a narrow one: to elect their own candidates. Is this an accurate vision of the influence of third parties?[y]

MUNRO v. SOCIALIST WORKERS PARTY, 479 U.S. 189 (1986). The state of Washington used a blanket primary to select candidates for the general election.[z] There are three types of primaries: *closed*, in which only a voter who has declared her party affiliation can vote in the party's primary; *open*, in which a voter can participate in any party's primary, regardless of her partisan affiliation, but can vote in only one party's primary; and *blanket*, in which a voter not only does not declare a party affiliation, but may also vote in the primary of more than one party. In a blanket primary, for example, a voter can choose among Democrats for Governor and then among Republicans for Lieutenant Governor. In Washington's system, minor party candidates could appear on the ballot for general election only if they had been nominated at their parties' conventions and they had received at least 1 percent of all the votes cast in the primary election. Before the ballot access law was adopted in 1977, minor party candidates regularly appeared on the ballot (12 appeared in 1976); after the law was passed, only 1 in 12 minor-party candidates had qualified for the ballot for statewide office.

Dean Peoples was the nominee of the Socialist Workers Party, but he received only nine one-hundredths of one percent of the total votes cast in the blanket primary. Accordingly, his name did not appear on the general ballot. Peoples, the party and two voters argued that the ballot access law violated their rights under the First and Fourteenth Amendments. **Justice White** accepted as legitimate the state's interest in reducing ballot overcrowding and adopting reasonable regulations to ensure that candidates on the ballot had sufficient community support. Such regulations reduce voter confusion, avoid deception, and mitigate frustration of the democratic process. "We think that the State can properly reserve the general election ballot 'for major struggles,' " the Court wrote, citing *Storer*. The Court acknowledged that the restriction substantially burdened minor-party candidates and was a relatively greater burden than a requirement to gather signatures on a petition prior to the election, an alternative way of ensuring a modicum of support before a candidate appeared on the ballot. It noted, however, that in a blanket primary, minor-party candidates can campaign among the entire pool of electorates to garner their 1 percent.

---

y. See Steven Rosenstone, Roy Behr & Edward Lazarus, *Third Parties in America: Citizen Response to Major Party Failure* (2d ed. 1996).

z. Washington's blanket primary has since been ruled unconstitutional. *Democratic Party of Washington v. Reed*, 343 F.3d 1198 (9th Cir. 2003) (relying on *California Democratic Party v. Jones*, 530 U.S. 567 (2000), which struck down a California law enacted by popular vote to require blanket primaries on the ground that it interfered with the associational rights of political parties that had internal rules limiting participation in their primaries to members), *cert. denied*, 540 U.S. 1213 (2004). The constitutionality of the nonpartisan primary that Washington voters adopted in 2004 in the wake of that decision will be heard by the Supreme Court. *Washington State Republican Party v. Washington*, 460 F.3d 1108 (9th Cir. 2006) (ruling the modified primary unconstitutional), *cert. granted*, 127 S.Ct. 1373 (2007).

Although the majority realized that many minor parties only use a campaign as a platform to discuss issues, "[i]t can hardly be said that Washington's voters are denied freedom of association because they must channel their expressive activity into a campaign at the primary as opposed to the general election." Quoting *Storer*, the majority held that the foremost goal of the electoral process is "to winnow out and finally reject all but the chosen candidates." In dissent, **Justice Marshall** took vigorous exception to this cursory treatment of the associational rights of members of minor parties. "The minor party's often unconventional positions broaden political debate, expand the range of issues with which the electorate is concerned, and influence the positions of the majority, in some instances ultimately becoming majority positions. And its very existence provides an outlet for voters to express dissatisfaction with the candidates or platforms of the major parties." Marshall emphasized that minor parties' primary role is to affect political debate, not to elect their own candidates. To play a meaningful role in the process, minor-party candidates need to be included in the phase of the electoral process where voters are most seriously considering their choices — the general election.

Ballot Access Problems

Problem 2-4: Hawaii's election law requires a candidate to participate in a new-party, established party, or nonpartisan primary election to obtain a position on the general election ballot. Primaries in Hawaii are open. The State does not allow write-in voting, and a voter who notified state officials that he intended to vote for a write-in candidate in the Democratic primary was told that such a vote would be ignored. The voter files suit, claiming that the ban on write-in voting violates his freedom of expression and association under the First Amendment. How should this claim be analyzed? Remember the statistics marshaled by the majority and dissent in *U.S. Term Limits* about the success (or, more accurately, the lack of success) of write-in candidates for major offices. Also consider these facts about Hawaii's electoral system: Its election laws date to the 1890s when Hawaii was still a monarchy. Hawaii is for all practical purposes a one-party Democratic state, so that the winner of the Democratic primary invariably wins the general election. The rules for new-party primaries and partisan primaries discourage independent voters or candidates from using these avenues to challenge the established political structure. A new political party can be organized through a petition drive to obtain signatures of 1 percent of registered voters; independents can run in a nonpartisan primary, but to advance to the general election, they need 10 percent of the total primary vote or votes equal to the minimum number required to nominate a partisan candidate to the general election ballot. The real disincentive to serious rivals to the Democratic candidates is the price voters pay for voting in a primary other than the Democratic. Since the Democratic primary essentially determines the winner, a voter who chooses to vote in another primary will have no effect on the outcome. As Issacharoff and Pildes conclude: "[T]he cumulative structure of Hawaii's laws eviscerates any nascent resistance to the Democratic monopoly." Issacharoff & Pildes, *supra*, at 671. After thinking about this problem, look at *Burdick v. Takushi*, 504 U.S. 428 (1992), for the Supreme Court's approach. See also *Clingman v. Beaver*,

544 U.S. at 607 (O'Connor, concurring in part and concurring in the judgment) (expressing concern that the statutory framework governing elections, particularly provisions affecting party registration and affiliation, as a whole might impermissibly burden voters, but noting that the question of the "*cumulative* burdens imposed by the *overall* scheme of electoral regulation upon the rights of voters and parties to associate" had not been properly raised).

Problem 2-5: As more people have become convinced that ballot access laws restrict the electoral choice presented to voters, perhaps more fundamentally than do explicit qualifications like those at issue in *Powell v. McCormack* and *U.S. Term Limits*, there have been several reform proposals.[a] The main problem identified by partisan lockup theorists is that, in the realm of election law, there is an inherent conflict of interest. This conflict leads to ballot access provisions favoring major parties and penalizing minor parties and independent candidates, to partisan gerrymandering, and, as we will see, to certain kinds of campaign finance and other ethics laws. Are courts the only way to guard against the self-interest of politicians in this arena? Some countries, including Australia, Canada, and the United Kingdom, rely on nonpartisan electoral administration entities to take the lead in regulating campaigns and elections. For example, the U.K.'s Electoral Commission supervises elections and oversees the regulatory structure, and it also provides reports and recommendations to Parliament on issues affecting campaign finance laws, districting, and political advertising. See Christopher Elmendorf, *Representation Reinforcement through Advisory Commissions: The Case of Election Law*, 80 N.Y.U. L. Rev. 1366 (2005) (describing these entities and proposing such a commission for the U.S.); Heather Gerken, *The Double-Edged Sword of Independence: Inoculating Electoral Reform Commissions Against Everyday Politics*, 6 Election L.J. 184 (2007) (discussing weaknesses of entirely independent commissions). Could a nonpartisan, independent election commission work in the United States at the federal or state level? What are the constitutional, political, and logistical challenges for such a reform? How successful have nonpartisan redistricting commissions been in drawing legislative district boundaries without undue political influence? What other solutions to partisan lockup, besides aggressive judicial review, are possible? See, e.g., Dennis Thompson, *Just Elections* 156–57 (2002) (discussing the appropriate role for direct democracy in decisions affecting the design of democratic institutions).

SECTION 3. STRUCTURES OF CAMPAIGN FINANCE

Because of the variety of expenses associated with winning elections — the salaries of campaign workers and political consultants, sophisticated polling techniques, political advertising in the print, electronic and Internet media — the candidate who wants to be elected must raise a lot of money. In 2003–04,

---

a. See The Appleseed Center for Electoral Reform, *A Model Act for the Democratization of Ballot Access*, 36 Harv. J. on Legis. 451 (1999); Mark Brown, *Popularizing Ballot Access: The Front Door to Election Reform*, 58 Ohio St. L.J. 1281 (1997).

campaign expenditures for races for the U.S. House and Senate totaled over $697 million and $488.5 million, respectively. The 2004 Presidential campaign set new records: President George W. Bush spent over $345 million on his campaign, while Massachusetts Senator John Kerry spent over $309 million, including private contributions and public funds. . The congressional races in 2006 were also expensive, in part because control of the House and Senate turned on the results. Campaign expenditures for all House and Senate candidates totaled nearly $1.43 billion. These figures do not include independent expenditures made by groups other than the candidates and not (in theory) coordinated with their campaigns.

Concerns about the influence of money in electoral outcomes are not new, and they have led to a century of federal regulation. The Tillman Act of 1907, 34 Stat. 864 (1907), prohibited all corporations and national banks from making "money contribution[s]" in connection with federal elections. The prohibition was extended to *all* contributions by the Corrupt Practices Act of 1925, 43 Stat. 1074 (1925), codified (and later repealed) at 18 U.S.C. § 610. The Smith-Connally Act, 57 Stat. 167 (1943) (expired 1945), and then the Taft-Hartley Act, 61 Stat. 159 (1947), prohibited unions from making contributions in connection with federal elections. Because of the vagueness of these early laws, unions and corporations were able to make contributions virtually at will. The Federal Election Campaign Act of 1971, Pub. L. No. 92–225, 86 Stat. 3, created a new loophole by amending § 610 to give explicit approval to "the establishment, administration, and solicitation of contributions to a separate segregated fund to be utilized for political purposes by a corporation or labor organization." Comprehensive reform was triggered by concern over the $60 million raised by President Nixon's 1972 campaign for reelection. When it was discovered that some of this money was illegally diverted to finance the Watergate break-in, concern stimulated a change in the law. The Federal Election Campaign Act Amendments of 1974, Pub. L. No. 93–443, 88 Stat. 1263, codified at 2 U.S.C. § 431 *et seq.,* set limits on campaign contributions and expenditures in presidential and congressional election campaigns and established the Federal Election Commission (FEC) to administer and enforce the law. Many states enacted similar laws.

Pluralist thinkers might object to regulating campaign finance. First, they might argue that such regulation is counterproductive, because money can be used to express political views that need to be heard and reflected by the representative. Indeed, the amount of the contribution can signal the intensity of those political views. Second, they might argue that most regulation of money in politics is inconsistent with the Constitution. Whatever the outer limits of the sphere of the Free Speech Clause of the First Amendment, it is clear that at its core it protects "political speech." The Supreme Court has recognized "a profound national commitment to the principle that debate on public issues should be uninhibited, robust, and wide-open." *New York Times Co. v. Sullivan,* 376 U.S. 254 (1964). Is political speech involved when someone contributes money to a candidate? The contribution helps the candidate spread her message, and thus perhaps amounts to "indirect speech," or speech by proxy. Is this indistinguishable from the situation in which someone uses her money to engage in direct political speech independent of the candidate — for example, by directly purchasing an advertisement supporting the candidate or attacking her opponent? Which kind of expenditure poses the greater threat to corrupt the representational process? Does the answer to this question depend upon how "corruption" is defined?

Republican and critical theorists, however, consider the political advantages of wealth in an unregulated political system to be as corrupting as bribery. "The American system is rooted in the assumption of political equality: 'one person, one vote.' But money, which candidates need to harvest votes, is not distributed equally. The substantial inequities of campaign financing have hindered the quest for political equality and have worried concerned Americans since the beginning of the twentieth century."[a] More skeptical observers of electoral politics respond to those who advocate far-reaching regulation with a pragmatic argument. They point to developments since 1974 that suggest that regulations and limitations merely change the form of the expenditure, diverting the money into unregulated channels and rendering campaign finance laws largely futile.[b] We will return to these arguments and examine the theories that can justify particular kinds of campaign finance regulation after we first look at the two major cases setting out the constitutional framework in which such laws operate and the problems that reformers have identified in the current legal structure. We note that this is a shifting landscape, as different majorities on the Supreme Court have resolved these thorny questions differently.

A. THE CONSTITUTIONAL FRAMEWORK: *BUCKLEY v. VALEO*

In *Buckley v. Valeo*, 424 U.S. 1 (1976) (per curiam), the Supreme Court addressed the constitutionality of the Federal Election Campaign Act (FECA) as amended in 1974 and Subtitle H of the Internal Revenue Code, which provides for the public financing of presidential elections. The Act was challenged primarily under the Speech Clause of the First Amendment. The per curiam opinion set forth the Court's traditional understanding of the purpose of the First Amendment:

> Discussion of public issues and debate on the qualifications of candidates are integral to the operation of the system of government established by our Constitution. The First Amendment affords the broadest protection to such political expression in order "to assure [the] unfettered interchange of ideas for the bringing about of political and social changes desired by the people." * * *

> The First Amendment protects political association as well as political expression. The constitutional right of association explicated in *NAACP v. Alabama*, 357 U.S. 449, 460 (1958), stemmed from the Court's recognition that "[e]ffective advocacy of both

---

a. Herbert Alexander, *Financing Politics: Money, Elections, and Political Reform* 3 (4th ed. 1992).

b. See, e.g., Samuel Issacharoff & Pamela Karlan, *The Hydraulics of Campaign Finance Reform*, 77 Tex. L. Rev. 1705 (1999).

public and private points of view, particularly controversial ones, is undeniably enhanced by group association." * * *

The Court has never afforded these fundamental rights absolute protection but, under traditional First Amendment jurisprudence, has required the government to show a "compelling state interest" narrowly tailored to the regulation of political speech. *Buckley* remains an important part of the constitutional jurisprudence affecting campaign finance laws, as well as other regulation of political speech and activity. Thus, analyzing the Court's approach to the various provisions of FECA provides the initial step in understanding the current state of the evolving case law.

Limitations on political contributions. FECA, as amended in 1974, prohibited individuals and most groups from contributing more than $1,000 per candidate for each primary election, and more than $1,000 per candidate for each runoff or general election. In addition, individuals could not contribute more than a total of $25,000 per year. Certain "political committees" — those registered as political committees with the FEC for not less than six months that have received contributions from more than 50 persons and, except for state political party organizations, have contributed to five or more candidates for federal office — could contribute up to $5,000 to any candidate for federal office. The Court in *Buckley* upheld these provisions. Although the Court stated that contribution limitations significantly interfered with the First Amendment right of political association, the Court found that these provisions passed constitutional muster. Their purpose of limiting "the actuality and appearance of corruption resulting from large * * * financial contributions" was a sufficiently important government interest:

> To the extent that large contributions are given to secure a political *quid pro quo* from current and potential office holders, the integrity of our system of representative democracy is undermined. Although the scope of such pernicious practices can never be reliably ascertained, the deeply disturbing examples surfacing after the 1972 election demonstrate that the problem is not an illusory one.

> Of almost equal concern as the danger of actual *quid pro quo* arrangements is the impact of the appearance of corruption stemming from public awareness of the opportunities for abuse inherent in a regime of large individual financial contributions. * * *

Limitations on political expenditures. The Act (a) limited expenditures by individuals and groups "relative to a clearly identified candidate during a calendar year" to $1,000. Other provisions (b) limited spending by candidates from their personal or family funds and (c) limited overall expenditures by candidates to differing amounts depending upon the federal office sought. The Court in *Buckley* struck down these provisions. The Court first held that they operated as a substantial restriction on First Amendment freedoms because "[a] restriction on the amount of money a person or group can spend on political communication during a campaign necessarily reduces the quantity of expression by restricting the number of issues discussed, the depth of their exploration and the size of the audience reached."

The Court determined that these restrictions were more severe than the limitations on contributions because "[a] contribution serves as a general expression of support for the candidate and his views, but does not communicate the underlying basis for the support. The quantity of communication by the contributor does not increase perceptibly with the size of his contribution, since the expression rests solely on the undifferentiated, symbolic act of contributing." In contrast, the Court said, "a primary effect of these expenditure limitations is to restrict the quantity of campaign speech by individuals, groups and candidates. The restrictions, while neutral as to the ideas expressed, limit political expression 'at the core of our electoral process and of the First Amendment freedoms.'" Accordingly, their "constitutionality * * * turns on whether the governmental interests advanced in [their] support satisfy the exacting scrutiny applicable to limitations on core First Amendment rights of political expression."

The limitations on individual and group expenditures independent of a particular candidate did not survive this exacting scrutiny because, the Court held, they did not substantially serve the governmental interest in stemming actual or apparent corruption. Such expenditures are made independent of any candidates, alleviating the danger that expenditures will be given as a *quid pro quo* for improper commitments from the candidate. Furthermore, in response to the argument that the expenditure limitations serve a government interest "in equalizing the relative ability of individuals and groups to influence the outcome of elections," the Court stated:

> [T]he concept that government may restrict the speech of some elements of our society in order to enhance the relative voice of others is wholly foreign to the First Amendment, which was designed "to secure 'the widest possible dissemination of information from diverse and antagonistic sources,'" and "to assure unfettered interchange of ideas for the bringing about of political and social changes desired by the people." The First Amendment's protection against governmental abridgement of free expression cannot properly be made to depend on a person's financial ability to engage in public discussion.

The limitations on expenditures from the funds of the candidate and the candidate's family were also inconsistent with the First Amendment:

> The * * * interest in equalizing the relative financial resources of candidates competing for elective office * * * provides the sole relevant rationale for [this] expenditure ceiling. That interest is clearly not sufficient to justify the provision's infringement of fundamental First Amendment rights. First, the limitation may fail to promote financial equality among candidates. A candidate who spends less of his personal resources on his campaign may nonetheless outspend his rival as a result of more successful fundraising efforts. Indeed, a candidate's personal wealth may impede his efforts to persuade others that he needs their financial contributions or volunteer efforts to conduct an effective campaign. Second, and more fundamentally, the First Amendment simply cannot tolerate [this] restriction upon the freedom of a candidate to speak without legislative limit on behalf of his own candidacy. * * *

Assuming that the only legitimate government purpose can be prevention of *quid pro quo* corruption or the appearance of corruption, is the Court's rationale persuasive? Isn't it more realistic to assume that candidates will be aware of independent expenditures and be grateful if they play a role in their electoral success? Certainly, in a world where direct contributions are limited but independent expenditures are not, wouldn't we expect groups wanting to influence lawmakers to take advantage of the unregulated route in order to circumvent the statute's limitations?

Even if you agree with the Court that independent expenditures pose no threat of *quid pro quo* corruption, is prevention of corruption the only legitimate goal? Consider the goal of ensuring that the legislature mirrors (to some extent) the body politic. Under descriptive theory, a legislature that is a microcosm of America would contain mainly middle-income Americans. But, by striking down the limits on total expenditures and on the amount of permissible self-financing, the Court invites the election of millionaires, especially in races for offices that require expensive campaigns.

Reporting and disclosure requirements. FECA required political commit-tees to keep records of contributions and expenditures, including the names and addresses of contributors who gave them more than $10. Such committees were required to disclose to the FEC the source of every contribution over $100 and the payee and purpose of every expenditure over $100. (The current threshold for reporting is set at more than $200.) Moreover, the Act also mandated that individuals and groups, other than candidates and political committees, making contributions or expenditures exceeding $100 (now $250) "other than by contribution to a political committee or candidate" file reports with the Commission.

The Court in *Buckley* upheld these provisions. It noted that compelled disclosure, in itself, can seriously infringe on privacy of association and belief guaranteed by the First Amendment, but held that the governmental interests sought to be advanced by the required disclosures were sufficiently important to outweigh the possibility of infringement of First Amendment rights. The Court identified these governmental interests:

> First, disclosure provides the electorate with information "as to where political campaign money comes from and how it is spent by the candidate" in order to aid the voters in evaluating those who seek federal office. * * *

> Second, disclosure requirements deter actual corruption and avoid the appearance of corruption by exposing large contributions and expenditures to the light of publicity. * * *

> Third, * * * recordkeeping, reporting, and disclosure requirements are an essential means of gathering the data necessary to detect violations of the contribution limitations described above.

In response to the contention that disclosure would infringe upon the First Amendment rights of contributors to minor parties and independent candidates, see *NAACP v. Alabama*, 357 U.S. 449 (1958) (disclosure required by state law of NAACP members unconstitutional if it exposed those persons to physical or economic retaliation), the Court stated:

* * * [T]he damage done by disclosure to the associational interests of the minor parties and their members and to supporters of independents could be significant. These movements are less likely to have a sound financial base and thus are more vulnerable to falloffs in contributions. In some instances fears of reprisal may deter contributions to the point where the movement cannot survive. The public interest also suffers if that result comes to pass, for there is a consequent reduction in the free circulation of ideas both within and without the political arena.

There could well be a case * * * where the threat to the exercise of First Amendment rights is so serious and the state interest furthered by disclosure so insubstantial that the Act's requirements cannot be constitutionally applied. But no appellant in this case has tendered record evidence of the sort proffered in *NAACP v. Alabama*. Instead, appellants primarily rely on "the clearly articulated fears of individuals, well experienced in the political process." At best they offer the testimony of several minor-party officials that one or two persons refused to make contributions because of the possibility of disclosure. On this record, the substantial public interest in disclosure identified by the legislative history of this Act outweighs the harm generally alleged.

Turning to the requirement of disclosure by every person and group (other than a political committee or candidate) making contributions or expenditures aggregating over $100 in a year "other than by contribution to a political committee or candidate," the Court stated:

[This requirement] is part of Congress' effort to achieve "total disclosure" by reaching "every kind of political activity" in order to insure that the voters are fully informed and to achieve through publicity the maximum deterrence to corruption and undue influence possible. The provision is responsive to the legitimate fear that efforts would be made, as they had been in the past, to avoid the disclosure requirements by routing financial support of candidates through avenues not explicitly covered by the general provisions of the Act. * * *

* * * [This requirement, as we construe it,] imposes independent reporting requirements on individuals and groups that are not candidates or political committees only in the following circumstances: (1) when they make contributions earmarked for political purposes or authorized or requested by a candidate or his agent, to some person other than a candidate or political committee, and (2) when they make expenditures for communications that expressly advocate the election or defeat of a clearly identified candidate.

* * * As narrowed, [this requirement] does not reach all partisan discussion for it only requires disclosure of those expenditures that expressly advocate a particular election result. * * * [This requirement] goes beyond the general disclosure requirements to shed the light of publicity on spending that is unambiguously campaign related but would not otherwise be reported. * * *

Public financing of presidential election campaigns. At the time of *Buckley*, Subtitle H of the Internal Revenue Code provided that taxpayers could authorize payment to a Presidential Election Campaign Fund for one dollar of their tax liability in the case of an individual return and of two dollars in the case of a joint return. The Fund provides money to finance party nominating conventions, primary campaigns, and general election campaigns. In 1993,

Congress raised the tax checkoff amount to three dollars for single returns and six dollars for joint returns.

With respect to the financing of party nominating conventions, Subtitle H distinguishes among *major parties* (parties whose candidates for President in the most recent election received 25% or more of the popular vote), *minor parties* (parties whose candidates received at least 5% but less than 25% of the vote in the most recent election), and *new parties* (all others). Major parties are entitled to $2,000,000, adjusted for inflation, to defray the expenses incurred by their national committees in conducting presidential nominating conventions. In 2004, the Republicans and Democrats each received over $15 million for their conventions, although they also raised substantial additional amounts through business and civic organizations, arguably undermining the objectives of public financing. A minor party receives a percentage of the amount given to major parties, based on the ratio of the votes received by the minor party's candidate in the last election to the average of the votes received by the candidates of the major parties. New parties receive no financing.

The distinctions among major parties, minor parties, and new parties also govern financing for expenses of general election campaigns. Each major-party candidate is entitled to $20,000,000, adjusted for inflation, and is required to pledge not to incur expenses in excess of this amount and not to accept private contributions except to the extent that the public fund is insufficient to provide the full amount to which the candidate is entitled. In 2004, the major-party candidates each qualified for over $74.6 million in federal funds. Minor-party candidates, if they meet certain prerequisites, are entitled to a percentage of the amount available to major-party candidates; new-party candidates receive nothing. In 2000, for example, the Reform Party candidate was eligible for $12.6 million in federal funds because of the party's strong showing in 1992 and 1996.

Subtitle H also created the Presidential Primary Matching Payment Account, which provides funds to candidates running in presidential primary elections who, *inter alia*, raise at least $5,000 in each of 20 states. Funds are provided through a matching formula based on the amount of private contributions received by the candidate. In return for federal money during the primaries, candidates must agree to abide by limitations applied to aggregate and state-by-state expenditures. In recent years, this public financing system has been under substantial stress because major candidates have opted out during the campaign primaries in order to avoid expenditure limits. In 2000 and 2004, George W. Bush did not accept public funds during the primaries because he knew he could raise sufficient funds for a competitive campaign and he wanted the flexibility to spend large amounts of money in early races to lock in the nomination quickly. John Kerry also declined public funds during the 2004 primaries; future candidates confident of their ability to amass campaign war chests will no doubt follow Bush and Kerry's lead. Ironically, only because major candidates have opted out has the Presidential Election Campaign Fund managed to avoid insolvency, as the number of taxpayers participating in the check-off has declined.[c]

The Supreme Court in *Buckley* upheld the constitutionality of this system of partial public financing. The Court generally held that the important public interest in limiting "the improper influence of large private contributions" outweighed any First Amendment concerns, and that the distinctions among major parties, minor parties, and new parties did not violate the equal protection component of the Due Process Clause of the Fifth Amendment. Doesn't the Act, and the Supreme Court's decision upholding it, tend to ossify American politics by presumptively reinforcing the status quo? If the Court is correct that the First Amendment generally favors *more* variety, how could the Court justify such a heavy financial benefit to already-established political parties? Is this yet another instance of partisan lockup that we discussed in the context of ballot access laws?

As this description of *Buckley* reveals, the traditional justification for campaign finance regulation is connected to notions of corruption of the political system. Corruption, however, is an ambiguous term; it means different things to different theorists. Moreover, the extent and shape of regulation that one finds acceptable depends on one's vision of corruption that must be addressed. Before turning to the cases following *Buckley,* it is important to think about various kinds of corruption that may occur in the election process and determine whether regulation should target each of them — and whether regulation can effectively control them.

Quid pro quo *Corruption.* The traditional justification for campaign finance regulation provided by the Court in *Buckley* is to combat *quid pro quo* corruption or the appearance of such arrangements. A system dominated by large contributions from wealthy individuals and interest groups clearly seeking influence, access, and favorable legislation appears to be corrupt to ordinary voters. This notion of corruption can be a rather limited one, focused on activity that appears virtually indistinguishable from bribery, or a more expansive vision of corruption. In *Nixon v. Shrink Missouri Government PAC,* 528 U.S. 377, 389 (2000), the Court rejected an especially narrow notion. "In speaking [in *Buckley*] of 'improper influence' and 'opportunities for abuse' in addition to '*quid pro quo* arrangements,' we recognized a concern not confined to bribery of public officials, but extending to the broader threat from politicians too compliant with the wishes of large contributors." The Court worried that the "cynical assumption that large donors call the tune" jeopardizes public faith in the democratic system.

---

c. For discussion of the challenges facing the presidential system of public financing, see Task Force on Presidential Nomination Finance, Campaign Finance Institute, *Participation, Competition, Engagement: Reviving and Improving Public Funding for Presidential Nomination Politics* (2003), http://www.cfinst.org/president/participation.aspx. For a discussion of possible reforms, see John Green & Anthony Corrado, *The Impact of BCRA on Presidential Campaign Finance,* in *Life After Reform: When the Bipartisan Campaign Reform Act Meets Politics* 175, 180–86 (Michael Malbin ed., 2003).

Are the parameters of this more expansive notion of corruption clear? When is a lawmaker *too* compliant with the wishes of large donors, and when is the lawmaker merely representing constituents who supported her? Perhaps large contributions provide accurate signals of the intensity with which some constituents hold particular views. In a system where votes are equalized, campaign contributions and other electoral support can provide valuable information about the strength of voter preferences, certainly relevant information as lawmakers compromise and create policy. Theorists from a liberal tradition might be wary of the Court's apparent willingness to broaden its definition of *quid pro quo* corruption.

Bradley Smith attacks the *Buckley* formulation of political corruption on two grounds.[d] First, he points to empirical studies suggesting that money seldom buys votes or particular outcomes. Rather, "the dominant forces in legislative voting [are] personal ideology, party affiliation and agenda, and constituency views." To the extent that money influences politics, it affects the legislative agenda, the timing and subjects of lawmakers' speeches, and legislative drafting in the early stages. Second, Smith argues that "there are intuitive and logical reasons to believe that the problem [of *quid pro quo* corruption] is not as serious as it is made out to be. Most obviously, people who are attracted to electoral politics tend to have strong views on issues. Party support can be just as important to re-election efforts, if not more important, than private contributions. * * * And, of course, elected officials ultimately need votes, not cash." Are Smith's arguments persuasive? At the least, are they sufficient to encourage courts to demand persuasive empirical proof of the existence of *quid pro quo* corruption more subtle than outright bribery? Or does Smith ignore the corruption inherent in a system in which large donors can set the political agenda for the rest of us?

Increasing Voter Competence. A political system is corrupt if it systematically undermines voters' ability to vote competently. A competent voter is one who votes on the basis of the limited information available to her as she would have voted if she had complete information about candidates and their proposals.[e] Voters rely on numerous cues to improve their competence, including party affiliation and incumbency. Knowing who supports the candidate and with how much enthusiasm can also improve voter competence. Moreover, allowing all candidates — challengers and incumbents — the resources to participate in vigorous political debate may enrich the political environment for voters. An outsider watching our campaigns and listening to our political debates is unlikely to conclude that we have too much meaningful political dialogue, but rather that our political debate is often repetitive and devoid of substance.

---

d. Bradley Smith, *Money Talks: Speech, Corruption, Equality, and Campaign Finance*, 86 Geo. L.J. 45, 58–59 (1997).

e. See Elisabeth Gerber & Arthur Lupia, *Voter Competence in Direct Legislation Elections*, in *Citizen Competence and Democratic Institutions* 147 (Stephen Elkin & Karol Soltan eds., 1999) (providing definition of voter competence).

Does this idea of corruption support regulation broader than disclosure? The *Buckley* Court identified such an interest as an important justification for FECA's disclosure system. It might be the most significant interest supporting disclosure in campaigns on ballot initiatives where the threat of *quid pro quo* corruption is reduced. The kinds of regulation that would promote voter competence may turn on one's notion of what can realistically be expected of voters. Daniel Ortiz identifies two groups of voters: engaged citizens and civic slackers.[f] He argues that most democratic theory assumes that citizens are "engaged, informed voters who carefully reason through political arguments." Much of campaign finance reform, however, implicitly questions voters' ability or interest in spending the time required to develop civic virtue. Instead, most of us focus our attention on other aspects of life — our families, jobs or leisure activities — and thus are susceptible to manipulation by slick advertisements funded by well-heeled interests and overflowing political coffers. To be successful, campaign finance reform efforts should be directed toward helping people make political decisions in light of their limited attention and scanty information. "[I]f reformers are to make their case, they must force us to recognize our civic failings. For only by recognizing our failings can we ever hope to grapple with and perhaps eventually overcome them." What kind of information should be provided to civic slackers to improve their competence? What is the role of regulation in this process?

Protecting Legislator Time. Vincent Blasi has argued that a substantial government interest which might justify some sorts of campaign finance regulation is the need to ensure that lawmakers have sufficient time to deliberate, negotiate and enact good policies.[g] Any system that requires legislators to spend much of their time raising money is a corrupt one. "Whatever it is that representatives are supposed to represent, whether parochial interests, the public good of the nation as a whole, or something in between, they cannot discharge that representational function well if their schedules are consumed by the need to spend endless hours raising money and attending to time demands of those who give it." Lawmakers freely admit to spending too much time raising money for the next election. Senator Robert Byrd (D-W.Va.) claims that he and other senators have become "full-time fundraisers and part-time legislators."[h]

What reforms respond to this interest? Can it justify a system of public financing for campaigns? Perhaps one way to ameliorate Blasi's concern is to eliminate any restrictions on campaign contributions. After all, if a candidate could go to one wealthy individual, say, Bill Gates, and obtain all the money she needs for her campaign, she would have plenty of time to deliberate and draft legislation. As long as her benefactor is disclosed, her constituents could scour her record to determine if she has favored Microsoft or any other interest

---

f. See *The Democratic Paradox of Campaign Finance Reform*, 50 Stan. L. Rev. 893 (1998).

g. See *Free Speech and the Widening Gyre of Fund-Raising: Why Campaign Spending Limits May Not Violate the First Amendment After All*, 94 Colum. L. Rev. 1281 (1994).

h. See Steven Gillon, *"That's Not What We Meant to Do": Reform and Its Unintended Consequences in Twentieth-Century America* 200 (2000).

of Gates. Perhaps one advantage of a system of contribution limitations is that it forces representatives to contact many citizens in the effort to amass funds through relatively small individual donations. The current restriction on contributions — $2,300 per election in 2007 — is a sum that is not out-of-reach for many Americans, thereby reducing some of the elitism of a system in which money is so important. Politicians do not only discuss money when they meet with potential donors; they discover the concerns of their constituents and the policies that voters favor, and they must defend their votes and proposals in return. Is it accurate, then, to think of fundraising as an activity completely separate from the representational function of elected legislators?

Electoral Competitiveness. Richard Briffault has argued that the Court should consider another important state interest in assessing the constitutionality of campaign finance restrictions. He contends that "[f]air and vigorous competition among candidates and parties is critical for the legitimacy of our elections and of the government those elections produce. Campaign finance law, in turn, can have a direct effect on the competitiveness of elections. In constructing a new campaign finance doctrine — or in revamping current doctrine — the Court should give greater weight to the effect of campaign finance rules on electoral competition." Nixon v. Shrink Missouri Government PAC: *The Beginning of the End of the* Buckley *Era?*, 85 Minn. L. Rev. 1729, 1731–32 (2001). If competitiveness were a compelling interest, what sort of regulation of campaign finance spending is permissible under the Constitution? What reform is best suited to improve electoral competition? How should courts measure the level of competition and determine what features of the regulatory landscape are hindering more robust competition?[i] At least some studies suggest that spending by political parties is an important factor contributing to competitive races, both in the context of open seats and, more importantly, in the context of candidates challenging entrenched incumbents.[j] Should the Court be leery of further restrictions on expenditures by political parties? Or is it the province of the legislature to make the policy choices that will affect electoral competitiveness, at least in cases where reasonable people could disagree about the right answer? On the other hand, does the partisan lockup scholarship suggest that campaign finance regulation devised by incumbent politicians is more likely to work to their advantage than to herald the resurgence of competitiveness in legislative elections?

Equality Concerns and Corruption. Republican thinkers, along with many critical theorists, have argued that a system is corrupt if wealthy special interests and individuals have more political influence solely because of their

---

i. See Richard L. Hasen, *The Newer Incoherence: Competition, Social Science, and Balancing in Campaign Finance Law after* Randall v. Sorrell, 68 Ohio State L.J. 775 (2007).

j. See, e.g., Gary Jacobson, *The Politics of Congressional Elections* 71-77 (3d ed. 1992). See also Richard Briffault, *The Political Parties and Campaign Finance Reform*, 100 Colum. L. Rev. 620, 661 (2000) (although favoring more stringent regulation of party campaign expenditures, acknowledging that parties "are more likely to support promising challengers. * * * Thus, far more than PAC money or donations by wealthy individuals, party money promotes the value of electoral competition.").

wealth.[k] Equal opportunity to influence political outcomes is undermined if that opportunity is tied to wealth and if economic resources are not equally distributed. This situation is even more disturbing because there is no reason to believe that the distribution of economic resources is related in any way to people's ability or desire to participate in the political realm. In other words, a poor voter and a rich one may have very intensely held and important views, but only the latter will be able to affect the political agenda, participate in debate, and influence lawmakers. Such a system is corrupt if an important democratic ideal is political equality. Instead, there is a "donor class" of people wealthy enough to contribute money to candidates and parties and thus obtain special access to policy makers that ordinary Americans are denied.[l]

Buckley rejected egalitarian justifications for campaign finance reform, holding clearly that "the concept that government may restrict the speech of some elements of our society in order to enhance the relative voice of others is wholly foreign to the First Amendment, which was designed 'to secure "the widest possible dissemination of information from diverse and antagonistic sources,"' and 'to assure unfettered interchange of ideas for the bringing about of political and social changes desired by the people.'" 424 U.S. at 48–49. *Buckley* was thus consistent with a libertarian notion of the First Amendment, a view that the Amendment protects only *negative liberty* because it only prohibits government intervention. L. A. Powe, Jr., who popularized the term "enhancement theory" in *Mass Speech and the Newer First Amendment*, 1982 Sup. Ct. Rev. 243, maintains that the libertarian approach is consistent with traditional Supreme Court case law. Others, such as Judge Guido Calabresi, argue that the Supreme Court's jurisprudence is "impoverished" because it does not deal explicitly with egalitarian concerns which are "at least as important as [*quid pro quo* corruption], and, perhaps, at the very heart of the problem."[m] Does the following case provide some indication that the Court might be willing to accept some equality-based notion of corruption?

AUSTIN v. MICHIGAN CHAMBER OF COMMERCE, 494 U.S. 652 (1990). The Michigan Campaign Finance Act prohibited corporations from making contributions or independent expenditures in connection with state candidate elections. Corporations could use segregated funds to spend money in candidate elections; money for the segregated funds was solicited explicitly for political purposes. The Michigan Chamber of Commerce was a nonprofit

---

k. See Symposium: *Money, Politics, and Equality*, 77 Tex. L. Rev. 1603–2021 (1999); John Rawls, *The Idea of Public Reason Revisited*, 64 U. Chi. L. Rev. 765 (1997); David Strauss, *Corruption, Equality, and Campaign Finance Reform*, 94 Colum. L. Rev. 1369 (1994).

l. Spencer Overton, *The Donor Class: Campaign Finance, Democracy, and Participation*, 153 U. Pa. L. Rev. 73 (2004).

m. *Landell v. Sorrell*, 406 F.3d 159, 163 (2d Cir. 2005) (Calabresi, J., concurring in the denial of rehearing en banc), *rev'd sub nom., Randall v. Sorrell*, 126 S.Ct. 2479 (2006). See also Ronald Dworkin, *The Curse of American Politics*, N.Y. Rev. of Books, Oct. 17, 1996, at 19, 21 ("It is another premise of democracy that citizens must be able, as individuals, to participate on equal terms in both formal politics and in the informal cultural life that creates the moral environment of the community.").

corporation with 8,000 members, three-quarters of which were for-profit corporations. It used its general treasury funds to place an advertisement in a local paper supporting a particular candidate. Because such an expenditure was punishable as a felony, the Chamber brought suit for injunctive relief, arguing that the restriction on independent expenditures was unconstitutional. The Court upheld the statute.

Justice Marshall, writing for the majority, applied strict scrutiny to the regulation as required by *Buckley* for regulation of independent expenditures. The Court acknowledged that, although corporations could spend money from special segregated funds, the prohibition on the use of general treasury funds and the requirements surrounding the segregated funds were burdens on political speech. The Court then looked for a compelling state interest to justify the burden. "State law grants corporations special advantages — such as limited liability, perpetual life, and favorable treatment of the accumulation and distribution of assets — that enhance their ability to attract capital and to deploy their resources in ways that maximize the return on their shareholders' investments. These state-created advantages not only allow corporations to play a dominant role in the Nation's economy, but also permit them to use 'resources amassed in the economic marketplace' to obtain 'an unfair advantage in the political marketplace.' *FEC v. Massachusetts Citizens for Life*, 479 U.S. 238, 257 (1986) (*MCFL*). As the Court explained in *MCFL*, the political advantage of corporations is unfair because '[t]he resources in the treasury of a business corporation . . . are not an indication of popular support for the corporation's political ideas. They reflect instead the economically motivated decisions of investors and customers. The availability of these resources may make a corporation a formidable political presence, even though the power of the corporation may be no reflection of the power of its ideas.' "

The Court differentiated the corruption that justified the Michigan statute from the *quid pro quo* corruption in *Buckley* that justified limitations on contributions. "Michigan's regulation aims at a different type of corruption in the political arena: the corrosive and distorting effects of immense aggregations of wealth that are accumulated with the help of the corporate form and that have little or no correlation to the public's support for the corporation's political ideas. The Act does not attempt 'to equalize the relative influence of speakers on elections'; rather, it ensures that expenditures reflect actual public support for the political ideas espoused by corporations. We emphasize that the mere fact that corporations may accumulate large amounts of wealth is not the justification for [the Michigan statute]; rather, the unique state-conferred corporate structure that facilitates the amassing of large treasuries warrants the limit on independent expenditures. Corporate wealth can unfairly influence elections when it is deployed in the form of independent expenditures, just as it can when it assumes the guise of political contributions."

The Court also rejected the argument that the restriction could not be constitutionally applied to a nonprofit corporation like the Chamber of Commerce. In a previous case concerning the Massachusetts Citizens for Life, the Court had struck down similar restrictions on independent expenditures. Justice Marshall found that the Chamber of Commerce was more like a traditional corporation than an ideological one, such as the right-to-life group. The Chamber was primarily engaged in nonpolitical activities; its members might be reluctant to resign even if they disagreed with the Chamber's political stands because they wished to benefit from the Chamber's nonpolitical programs; and the Chamber could easily serve as a conduit for corporate independent expenditures, allowing circumvention of the Act. Accordingly, the restrictions could be applied to the Chamber of Commerce in the same way they applied to for-profit corporations.

Justice Scalia's dissent attacked the majority as engaged in "Orwellian" censorship on the "principle that too much speech is an evil that the democratic majority can proscribe." He challenged the majority's argument that limits on political speech can be justified because corporations have special advantages under state law and can amass great wealth. He pointed out that many individuals and private associations, not just corporations, receive special breaks under state law, and that in any event the government cannot condition the receipt of these benefits on the waiver of First Amendment rights. Great wealth alone does not render anyone or anything susceptible to lesser First Amendment rights, and Justice Scalia argued that the majority provided no reason to assume that corporate expenditures promoting candidates pose any substantial risk of corruption. (Indeed, *Buckley* struck down limits on independent expenditures by individuals as inconsistent with the First Amendment.)

Justice Scalia also pointed out that, even accepting the majority's assumptions, the Michigan statute was subject to attack because it was not narrowly tailored to reach only wealthy corporations. Justice Scalia further suggested that the majority's theory — that "too much speech" can come from powerful corporations — is especially true of media corporations, and thus the Michigan exception for them was at war with the statute's apparent fundamental objectives. The majority, however, had determined that the statute's media exception did not render it impermissibly under-inclusive. "Although all corporations enjoy the same state-conferred benefits inherent in the corporate form, media corporations differ significantly from other corporations in that their resources are devoted to the collection of information and its dissemination to the public. We have consistently recognized the unique role that the press plays in 'informing and educating the public, offering criticism, and providing a forum for discussion and debate.' The Act's definition of 'expenditure' conceivably could be interpreted to encompass election-related news stories and editorials. The Act's restriction on independent expenditures therefore might discourage incorporated news broadcasters or publishers from serving their crucial societal role. The media exception ensures that the Act does not hinder or prevent the institutional press from reporting on, and publishing editorials about, newsworthy events."

Justice Kennedy's dissent complained of two censorships of speech: first, a "content-based law which decrees it a crime for a nonprofit corporate speaker to endorse or oppose candidates for [office]"; and, second, a censorship scheme created by the Court "that permits some nonprofit corporate groups but not others to engage in political speech. After failing to disguise its animosity and distrust for a particular kind of political speech here at issue — the qualifications of a candidate to understand economic matters — the Court adopts a rule that allows Michigan to stifle the voices of some of the most respected groups in public life, on subjects central to the integrity of our democratic system." Essentially, Justice Kennedy returned to *Buckley*'s distinction between contributions and expenditures as the definitional line for "corruption." The majority's notion that the state may combat the "corrosive and distorting effects of immense aggregations of wealth" accumulated in corporate form deals not with fighting corruption, but with "altering political debate by muting the impact of certain speakers." Even if the majority's justification might support restricting political speech of for-profit corporations, Justice Kennedy continued, it cannot support interfering with expression from non-profit corporations like the Michigan Chamber of Commerce. Justice Kennedy concluded that "it is now a felony in Michigan for the Sierra Club, or the American Civil Liberties Union" to make independent expenditures. In his concurrence, **Justice Brennan** responded that "the dissent has overlooked the central lesson of *MCFL* that the First Amendment may require exemptions, on an as-applied basis, from expenditure restrictions. If a nonprofit corporation is formed with the express purpose of promoting political ideas, is not composed of members who face an economic incentive for disassociating with it, and does not accept contributions from business corporations or labor unions, then it would be governed by the *MCFL* holding."

Austin prompted a great deal of scholarly debate, in part because it appeared to resurrect an egalitarian justification for campaign finance regulations, although perhaps only in the case of corporations.[n] Arguably, the equality concern sounded in *Austin* is relatively narrow and limited to the distortion of the political environment when money raised for business purposes has been spent for political expression. The segregated fund mechanism matches fundraising with the genuine enthusiasm for the political ideas supported by the money.[o] The rationale in *Austin* may be related to an interest in democratizing the political process and increasing public participation in campaigns. Justice Breyer has articulated a First Amendment principle of participatory self-government that could be seen as a way to include some element of equality concerns into the campaign finance jurisprudence without expressly overruling *Buckley*. See Stephen Breyer, *Active Liberty: Interpreting our Democratic Constitution* 43–50 (2005).

Are contribution and expenditure limitations the best way to ensure political equality in a world where financial resources are distributed unevenly? Even

---

n. See, e.g., Gerald Ashdown, *Controlling Campaign Spending and the "New Corruption": Waiting for the Court*, 44 Vand. L. Rev. 767 (1991); Julian Eule, *Promoting Speaker Diversity: Austin and Metro Broadcasting*, 1990 Sup. Ct. Rev. 105; Adam Winkler, *The Corporation in Election Law*, 32 Loy. L.A. L. Rev. 1243 (1999).

o. See Kathleen Sullivan, *Political Money and Freedom of Speech*, *supra*, at 675–78 (describing this notion and suggesting problems with it, including the absence of a baseline against which to measure distortion).

if they successfully reduce the amount of political spending by the wealthy, how can such regulations provide resources to the poor who wish to be politically active? Some theorists have suggested a more radical egalitarian reform: allowing people to spend only special money, "red-white-and-blue" dollars in Bruce Ackerman's proposal, for election-related activities. All citizens would receive an equal amount of this special money; it could not be sold for green-money, but it could be contributed to candidate campaigns, used to fund independent advertisements, or accumulated by PACs to signal the support of a group of voters for an idea or candidate.[p] These proposals advocate a sort of public financing system, albeit a decentralized one where the voters determine how to channel the money. They are also consistent with the egalitarian arguments in voting rights cases. Just as all citizens have an equal number of votes, so would they all have equal amounts of political resources to deploy. Of course, these proposals do not claim to impose absolute equality among citizens; there would remain inequality of talents, ability to communicate persuasively, appearance, and access to people with free time to volunteer. Perhaps in a world where financial resources were equalized, the distribution of these other qualities would become more important. Or, perhaps, inequality along these dimensions is less pernicious.[q]

Problem Relating to Campaign Finance Proposals

Problem 2–6. Ian Ayres and Jeremy Bulow have argued that, instead of mandating disclosure of all campaign contributions, we should instead consider mandating that all contributions be anonymous.[r] Just as the secret ballot makes it more difficult for candidates to buy votes, requiring anonymity of contributors would make it more difficult for candidates to sell access or influence. Ayres and Bulow suggest setting up blind trusts that would receive all campaign contributions. This structure would eliminate *quid pro quo* corruption because candidates would not know who had wanted to pay the price for beneficial legislation or official actions. In a world of anonymous donors, anyone could claim to have contributed to the blind trust, just as anyone can claim to have voted for a certain candidate. Is such a proposal constitutional? Is it sensible policy? What are the likely effects of the proposal in the world of hydraulic political money?

---

p. See Bruce Ackerman, *Crediting the Voters: A New Beginning for Campaign Finance,* Am. Prospect 71 (1993). In addition, see Edward Foley, *Equal-Dollars-Per-Voter: A Constitutional Principle of Campaign Finance,* 94 Colum. L. Rev. 1204 (1994); Richard Hasen, *Clipping Coupons for Democracy: An Egalitarian/Public Choice Defense of Campaign Finance Vouchers,* 84 Cal. L. Rev. 1 (1996).

q. See Burt Neuborne, *Is Money Different?,* 77 Tex. L. Rev. 1609 (1999).

.**r.** See Ian Ayres & Jeremy Bulow, *The Donation Booth: Mandating Donor Anonymity to Disrupt the Market for Political Influence,* 50 Stan. L. Rev. 837 (1998). See also Bruce Ackerman & Ian Ayres, *Voting with Dollars: A New Paradigm for Campaign Finance* (2002) (combining Ackerman's public financing proposal with the anonymous donation booth).

B. THE BIPARTISAN CAMPAIGN REFORM ACT AND *McCONNELL v. FEDERAL ELECTION COMMISSION*

Decades of experience with FECA demonstrated that serious challenges remained to effective campaign finance regulation. We will first describe the problems that arose after *Buckley* — some caused by the Court's bifurcated approach to contributions and expenditures in campaigns. Then we will detail Congress' reaction to those problems with the passage of the Bipartisan Campaign Reform Act of 2002 ("BCRA"), which was largely upheld by the Court in *McConnell v. Federal Election Commission*, 540 U.S. 93 (2003). Finally we will discuss issues that have faced the Court since *McConnell*. Key changes in the Court's personnel, with Justices Roberts and Alito replacing Justices Rehnquist and O'Connor, likely mean that the equilibrium that *McConnell* seemed to put in place will be short-lived.

1. *Federal Campaign Finance Reform Issues After* Buckley

Political Action Committees. Political action committees are not creatures of the Federal Election Campaign Act. Instead, the first PAC was established in 1943 by a national labor union. Generally speaking, a PAC is a political committee, other than that of a political party, that receives contributions from more than 50 people and makes contributions to at least five candidates for federal office. (The term "political action committee" is not used in FECA. Our definition of a PAC is derived from the statute's definition of "multicandidate political committee.") PACs are required to register with and report information to the FEC. 1976 amendments to FECA limited PAC contributions to a candidate to $5,000 per election and limited PAC contributions to a national committee of a political party to $15,000. By creating limitations that were more generous than those applying to individuals at the time, FECA encouraged the formation and growth of PACs. In 1974, the number of registered PACs stood at 608; ten years later, 4,009 were registered; and in 2006 there were about 4,600 registered PACs, although all are not active in campaigns. The largest category of PACs consists of corporate PACs; in 2006, 1,712 registered PACs were characterized as corporate, and they donated more money in absolute terms to campaigns than labor or membership organizations.[s]

In the years immediately following *Buckley*, the issue of the influence of PACs, particularly corporate and business groups, on the electoral process was the primary focus for reformers. For example, Judge J. Skelly Wright of the D.C. Circuit, in *Money and the Pollution of Politics: Is the First Amendment an Obstacle to Political Equality?*, 82 Colum. L. Rev. 609, 616, 618–619 (1982), criticized the Supreme Court for all but proscribing federal limitations on PAC contributions, because he believed PACs have a malign effect on legislative policymaking: "When wealth of this magnitude is injected into the political bloodstream, the legislative process itself is affected. PAC contributions are given with a legislative purpose and it is a telling fact that they are

---

s. Federal Election Commission, *PAC Financial Activity Increases* (April 2006), http://www.fec.gov/press/press2006/20060828pac/20060830pac.html.

most numerous in the more highly regulated industries, such as oil, transportation, utilities, drugs, health care, and government contracting. * * * Whatever the cause and effect relationship, studies of issue after issue demonstrate that a much higher percentage of legislators who voted with a PAC's position received money from the PAC in the previous campaign than those who voted the other way, and among the beneficiaries of PAC money those supporting the PAC position had received a substantially higher average contribution." In the eighteen months before June 30, 2006, federal PACs raised over $773 million and contributed more than $248 million to federal candidates.

Empirical research, however, tends to show that PAC contributions are less important influences on legislative votes than are the legislator's personal philosophy, political party, and constituent views and interests.[t] Moreover, most of the money contributed to federal candidates comes from individuals, not PACs. One study of contributions to federal candidates in the 1999–2000 election cycle concluded that only around 22% of all money contributed to those campaigns could be considered special interest money (e.g., from corporations, unions, other associations, or PACs). Stephen Ansolabehere, John de Figueiredo & James Snyder, *Why Is There So Little Money in U.S. Politics?*, 17 J. Econ. Persp. 105 (2003). Critics of PACs reply that PACs overwhelmingly contribute to incumbents, thereby further entrenching the status quo.[u] In the 2003–04 election cycle, about 78% of PAC contributions to federal candidates went to incumbents.

Although they are often described as pernicious influences on the electoral process, PACs also empower individuals, who can increase their political influence by working collectively. One's view of PACs may depend significantly on the state and character of pluralism. If various and diverse interests use this type of political organization to wield electoral influence, then PACs can be seen as a positive political force. For example, EMILY's List contributes money to female candidates and promotes a moderately feminist agenda, a platform often supported by those who would eliminate or reduce the influence of PACs. Critics of PACs argue that EMILY's List is notable because it is so rare. They maintain that corporate and business PACs exert a disproportionate influence compared to labor PACs or public interest PACs. Opponents of further restrictions on PAC spending counter with a pragmatic argument, contending that any limitations will be easily circumvented. They point to the practice of *bundling*, in which individual contributions are presented as a group to a candidate in a way that makes it clear that the

---

t. See, e.g., Stephen Bronars & John Lott, Jr., *Do Campaign Contributions Alter How a Politician Votes?*, 40 J. Law & Econ. 317 (1997). See also David Austen-Smith, *Campaign Contributions and Access*, 89 Am. Pol. Sci. Rev. 566 (1995) (studying the relationship between PAC contributions and access to lawmakers); Jeffrey Milyo, David Primo & Timothy Groseclose, *Corporate PAC Campaign Contributions in Perspective*, 2 Bus. & Pol. 75 (2000) (arguing that corporate PAC contributions have little influence on policymakers and that other routes to influence, like lobbying and soft money contributions, are preferred by corporations).

u. See, e.g., William Cassie & Joel Thompson, *Patterns of PAC Contributions to State Legislative Candidates*, in *Campaign Finance in State Legislative Elections* 158 (Joel Thompson & Gary Moncrief eds., 1998).

contributions were organized through a collective effort.[v] Because the contributions are individual, the bundles of money do not count against the PAC contribution limit, although each check cannot exceed the ceiling for individual contributions. Until 2007, candidates were aware of the forces behind bundling and the interests that the contributions sought to advance, but they were not disclosed to the public unless the organizers voluntarily provided the information. As part of the Honest Leadership and Open Government Act of 2007, the 110th Congress required that federal candidates disclose the name of any lobbyist providing bundled contributions exceeding $15,000 in any six month period. Section 204, Pub. L. No. 110-81, 121 Stat. 735 (2007). The Act defines a bundled contribution as any contribution forwarded to the candidate by the person or any contribution "credited [by the candidate] to the person through records, designations, or other means of recognizing that a certain amount of money has been raised by the person."

Concerns about *stealth PACs* or *Section 527 Organizations* (named for the section of the tax code under which such groups were organized) prompted a congressional response a few years before passage of the more comprehensive BCRA. In the late 1990s, political entrepreneurs began to use tax-exempt entities to evade campaign finance disclosure laws and contributions limitations. Section 527 groups took advantage of a tax provision designed to protect most income of political parties from taxation. As is often the case in this area of unintended consequences, the drafters of Section 527 never envisioned its use as blueprint for stealth PACs.[w] The most visible stealth PAC in the late 1990s was the Republican Majority Issues Committee, headed by advisers of Representative Tom DeLay (R–Tex.), who later became House Majority Leader. They targeted donors interested in giving between $500,000 and $3 million in return for substantial access to congressional leaders, and they aimed to spend as much as $25 million in the 2000 election. They argued successfully that they did not have to comply with any federal campaign finance regulations, including disclosure laws and prohibitions on foreign contributors, as long as they confined their activities to grassroots political activities and issue advertisements that did not call specifically for the election or defeat of particular candidates. Moreover, at that time, the IRS did not require disclosure of donations, donors, or expenditures to these tax-exempt entities. In the summer of 2000, President Clinton signed a bill requiring Section 527 organizations to disclose their donors and their expenditures. Pub. L. No. 106–230, 114 Stat. 477 (2000). Within one month, nearly 5,000 organizations had filed disclosure forms with the IRS, which was then required to post the information on its website.

Soft money. Money spent in connection with federal candidates, and therefore regulated by the FECA, is hard money. *Soft money*, then, became the term used for any money left unregulated by FECA (although in 1990, the FEC

---

v. See John de Figueiredo & Elizabeth Garrett, *Paying for Politics*, 78 S. Cal. L. Rev. 591, 616–17 (2005).

w. See Donald Tobin, *Anonymous Speech and Section 527 of the Internal Revenue Code*, 37 Ga. L. Rev. 611, 623 (2003).

required limited disclosure of soft-money expenditures). Soft money is spent on activities to benefit state candidates, to build infrastructure, and to fund voter mobilization programs including direct mail campaigns. Political parties also use soft money to fund issue advertisements that do not expressly advocate the election or defeat of a particular candidate. Although soft money expenditures cannot be connected with a particular candidate, in fact they contribute significantly to the success of parties' nominees and are often intertwined with candidates' campaigns.

The use of soft money to evade federal restrictions, particularly in a presidential election where candidates must comply with expenditure limitations in order to qualify for federal matching funds, increased substantially in the 1990s. By the end of the 1995–96 election cycle, the two parties had raised $262 million in soft money. Federal candidates were also involved in soliciting this soft money to a greater extent than before. Videotapes of White House coffee meetings showed President Clinton asking supporters to contribute soft money in sums larger than allowed for direct contributions, so that the Democrats could buy television ads designed to aid his reelection bid. The campaign for his opponent, Robert Dole, similarly assisted the soft-money efforts of the Republican Party. Not only do these examples suggest that interest groups donated soft money to obtain access to important federal candidates, but they also undermine the claim that the use of soft money is meaningfully independent from candidates' campaigns.

The pace of soft money fundraising only escalated after 1996. A study of the 1998 congressional elections revealed that soft money spent by party committees and raised from a few large donors played an important role in competitive congressional elections.[x] Soft money expenditures in this midterm election were more than double the spending in 1994. From January 1999 through the end of November 2000, a time period that included a presidential campaign, the national party committees raised over $487 million in soft money. Not surprisingly given these figures, reformers argued that soft-money donations directly resulted in favorable legislation for the groups providing funds. For example, Common Cause published a report linking large soft money donations to particular tax breaks in the 1997 Budget Act.[y] Do such allegations provide support under any of the justification described previously for laws regulating soft money contributions?

Issue Advocacy. Adopting a narrow interpretation of FECA to avoid constitutional problems, the Court in *Buckley* upheld disclosure requirements only on independent expenditures that are used for communications which expressly advocate the election or defeat of a clearly identified federal candidate. In a footnote, the Court indicated that the following terms would meet the express advocacy test: "vote for," "elect," "support," "cast your ballot

x. See *Outside Money: Soft Money and Issue Ads in Competitive 1998 Congressional Elections* (David Magleby & Marianne Holt eds., 1999).

y. See Common Cause Corporate Welfare Project, *Return on Investment: The Hidden Story of Soft Money, Corporate Welfare and the 1997 Budget & Tax Deal* (1997).

for," "Smith for Congress," "vote against," "defeat," or "reject." *Buckley*, 424 U.S. at 44 n.52. Although the footnote does not state that using these words is the only way to meet the express advocacy test, they became known as the *magic words* distinguishing regulated communications from unregulated ones. See also *Federal Election Comm'n v. Massachusetts Citizens for Life, Inc.*, 479 U.S. 238 (1986) (indicating some flexibility in the "magic words" formulation by noting that a communication of support "marginally less direct than 'Vote for Smith' does not change its essential nature"). The Court in *Buckley* rejected any test for express advocacy that would depend on the speaker's purpose or the audience's understanding because such a subjective test would chill political speech.

The absence of federal regulation after *Buckley* resulted in an explosion in the use of issue advocacy — political speech that did not meet the test for express advocacy but that often mentioned specific candidates or political parties. The Annenberg Public Policy Center estimated that political parties and various interest groups spent between $135 million and $150 million for issue ads in the 1996 election cycle.[z] For example, the AFL-CIO announced a few months before the 1996 election its intention to spend $35 million in an issue-advocacy campaign. Unions were not alone; business groups and ideological groups also spent tens of millions of dollars to produce these unregulated but effective political ads. Although issue advertisements were supposedly designed only to further the discussion of particular issues, the Annenberg Center found that nearly 87% mentioned a candidate for office by name and 59% of them pictured a candidate. Furthermore, issue ads appeared to be more negative in tone than other political advertising, perhaps because candidates tried to avoid being associated in the voters' minds with negative campaigning but understand how effective such communication can be. Forty-one percent of the issue ads were purely negative in tone, whereas only 24% of the advertisements directly paid for by presidential candidates criticized their opponents.

A Brennan Center for Justice study of more than 2,100 separate commercials run over 300,000 times in the top 75 media markets in the 1998 elections provides additional information about issue advertisements.[a] Most (65%) issue ads were sponsored by political parties, rather than by interest groups, corporations or labor unions. Like the Annenberg study, these researchers found that issue ads tended to be more negative in tone than candidate ads: 60% of party issue advertisements attacked, while only 21% of candidate ads attacked opponents. Perhaps surprisingly, candidate ads, which can include express advocacy, seldom used the magic words. Only 9% of candidate ads in the final week of the campaign included any of the magic words. This conclusion casts doubt on the efficacy of the magic words test as a way to separate express advocacy from other political communication. While none of

z. See Deborah Beck, Paul Taylor, Jeffrey Stranger & Douglas Rivlin, *Issue Advocacy Advertising During the 1996 Campaign* (1997).

a. See Jonathan Krasno & Daniel Seltz, *Buying Time: Television Advertising in the 1998 Congressional Elections* (2000).

the issue ads contained the key phrases required by *Buckley*'s footnote, 87% of them urged viewers to take some concrete action like calling an elected official or candidate, although the ads rarely provided a phone number to assist motivated citizens. Only 15% of party-financed issue ads mentioned a political party by name, while 99% of them gave a candidate's name.

Disclosure Provisions. For many, disclosure appears to be the least problematic form of regulation and perhaps the only kind of law that is likely to work.[b] Not only does disclosure combat the concerns of corruption and undue influence, but it also provides helpful information to voters. By discovering what groups support a particular candidate, and the level of that support, voters can discover cues to the candidate's ideology and likely behavior once in office. Indeed, if limitations on contributions channel electoral spending into more covert forms, they may actually undermine voter competence and prevent dissemination of vital political information.

Far-reaching disclosure statutes will raise constitutional issues; ironically, the more a law succeeds in revealing the identities of supporters and opponents, the more serious the constitutional concern. Disclosure certainly chills some kinds of political speech, especially when it links the speaker to disfavored groups or ideas, and some individuals and organizations may be less likely to participate in political debate if their involvement will be publicized. In other contexts, the Court has held that the First Amendment protects anonymous political speech. See *McIntyre v. Ohio Elections Commission*, 514 U.S. 334 (1995) (protecting a person's decision to remain anonymous while distributing campaign literature for issue-based election). In *Buckley*, the Supreme Court held that the Act's provisions requiring the disclosure of contributors to a political group were constitutional on their face, but might conceivably be unconstitutional as applied to a given group. Given "the extensive body of state and federal legislation subjecting Communist Party members to civil disability and criminal liability, * * * the history of governmental surveillance and harassment of Communist Party members, and * * * the desire of contributors to the [Communist Party] to remain anonymous," are the Act's disclosure requirements invalid as applied to the Communist Party?[c]

Disclosure poses a practical problem as well. The more complex the reporting requirements, the more costly the burden placed on those who must provide information to the state. Moreover, this burden affects grassroots groups with few monetary resources and less access to consultants more

---

b. See, e.g., Elizabeth Garrett, *Voting with Cues*, 37 U. Rich. L. Rev. 1011 (2003) (noting nearly universal support among policymakers, scholars, and commentators for disclosure); Kathleen Sullivan, *Political Money and Freedom of Speech*, 30 U.C. Davis L. Rev. 663, 688–89 (1997) (arguing that aggressive disclosure is the only form of campaign finance regulation that will not prove futile or subject to the law of unintended consequences).

c. See *Federal Election Comm'n v. Hall-Tyner Election Campaign Committee*, 678 F.2d 416 (2d Cir. 1982), *cert. denied*, 459 U.S. 1145 (1983). See also *Brown v. Socialist Workers '74 Campaign Committee*, 459 U.S. 87 (1982), in which the Court struck down an Ohio statute requiring disclosure of contributors.

severely than it does well-funded groups and sophisticated political players.[d] Although exemptions or reduced reporting requirements for small groups or individuals spending little money can reduce some of the burden, exemptions also increase the complexity of the regulatory regime.[e]

2. *The Bipartisan Campaign Reform Act of 2002*

After decades of inaction on campaign finance reform, often because of successful filibusters in the Senate, in 2002 Congress passed sweeping amendments to the Federal Election Campaign Act. The Senate acted first, led by Senator John McCain (R–Ariz.) and Senator Russ Feingold (D–Wisc.). The effort stalled in the House, however, where Republican leaders were able to bottle up the legislation in committee for several months. But two events dislodged the bill from committee and moved it to the floor. First, supporters of campaign finance reform lobbied colleagues to sign a discharge petition, a process through which a majority of House members sign a petition to remove a bill from the committee and place it on the calendar for floor deliberation. A procedural reform adopted by the House in 1993 made the names on discharge petitions public, thereby allowing members using the tactic to monitor whether colleagues actually sign the petition and to target lobbying efforts accordingly. Second, the bankruptcy of Enron Corporation, an energy trading company, provided the momentum for reformers to get the last few signatures on the discharge petition. Enron and its officers had contributed millions of dollars in soft money, and thus its collapse made these contributions and the political clout they might have bought more salient to voters and lawmakers.

After two long days of floor debate, the House passed a version of reform virtually identical to the Senate-passed bill. House sponsors Christopher Shays (R–Conn.) and Martin Meehan (D–Mass.) were able to resist a number of killer amendments, although one change that was adopted postponed the effective date of the legislation until the day after the 2002 mid-term elections. Rather than send the bill to conference committee where Republican leaders might be able to kill it through delay, the House version was sent directly to the Senate floor for passage. Opponents there decided to forego a filibuster and instead to challenge the legislation in the courts; the act passed the Senate by a vote of 60 to 40. Although he had appeared to oppose certain provisions during the 2000 campaign, President Bush signed the Bipartisan Campaign Reform Act of 2002 ("BCRA") into law on March 27, 2002.

---

d. See Bradley Smith, *Faulty Assumptions and Undemocratic Consequences of Campaign Finance Reform*, 105 Yale L.J. 1049, 1082–83 (1996).

e. See also Robert Bauer, *Not Just a Private Matter: The Purposes of Disclosure in an Expanded Regulatory System*, 6 Election L.J. 38, 39 (2007) (arguing that disclosure now is often "the gateway to substantive regulation rather than merely the means of disseminating to voters useful information").

The key provisions of BCRA, Pub. L. No. 107-155, 116 Stat. 81,[f] include the following:

A Ban on Soft Money. The national committees of a political party can neither receive nor spend soft money. BCRA also prohibits federal-candidate-controlled PACs from raising or spending soft money. Local and state committees of political parties cannot spend soft money on federal election activities, although they can still spend such money solely to influence state or local races. "Federal election activity" is defined to include voter registration drives within 120 days of an election; get-out-the-vote drives conducted in connection with a federal election; any work by state or local campaign employees who spend more than 25% of their time on federal election activities; and advertisements specific to federal candidates. There is an exception to this ban that applies only to state and local party committees: they may use soft money to fund generic voter registration and get-out-the-vote drives that relate to federal elections, but they are limited to using contributions of no more than $10,000 per source.

A Ban on Candidate Solicitation of Soft Money. Federal office seekers and office holders and their agents can neither solicit nor spend soft money. They may engage in soft money fundraising efforts by nonprofit organizations for voter registration and get-out-the-vote drives, but they may only solicit up to $20,000 per individual and only from individuals.

Provisions Affecting Hard Money. The new law raises most of the hard money limits, and it indexes the limits on individuals' contributions to candidates and national parties for inflation. The aggregate limit for an individual's contributions to candidates is raised from $25,000 to $37,500 per election cycle. Individuals can contribute $25,000 per year per national party committee, with an aggregate contribution limit for donations to all national party committees of $20,000 to $57,500 per election cycle, depending on how much money the individual contributes to PACs. The limit on contributions that an individual can give to a federal candidate per election doubles to $2,000. This limit may be raised, as may the party-coordinated spending limits, for contributions to candidates facing self-financed opponents who spend substantial amounts of their own money in the campaign. This provision is known as the "millionaire opponent" provision.

---

f. For an excellent description and analysis of BCRA, see the Campaign Finance Institute's E-Guide on the Web: http://www.cfinst.org/eGuide/. The Campaign Legal Center's website, http://www.campaignlegalcenter.org/, provides helpful information, particularly about litigation and administrative proceedings related to BCRA implementation. Stanford Law School's library maintains a website with materials relating to BCRA and the judicial challenges. See http://www.law.stanford.edu/library/campaignfinance/. Other useful websites include http://www.publicintegrity.org (Center for Public Integrity); http://www.fec.gov (Federal Election Commission); http://www.jamesmadisoncenter.org (James Madison Center for Free Speech); http://www.citizen.org/congress/campaign/index.cfm (Public Citizen); and http://www.opensecrets.org (Center for Responsive Politics). Among the best books on BCRA are *The New Campaign Finance Sourcebook* (Anthony Corrado, Thomas Mann, Daniel Ortiz & Trevor Potter eds., 2005), and *The Election After Reform: Money, Politics, and the Bipartisan Campaign Reform Act* (Michael Malbin ed., 2006).

Limitation on Expenditures for Electioneering Communications. The Act defines "electioneering communication" to include broadcast, cable, or satellite advertisements that refer to a clearly identified candidate; that are run within 30 days of a primary election and 60 days of a general election; and that are "targeted" in that they can be received by 50,000 or more persons in the congressional district or state where the election is being held. Political parties and candidates may spend only hard money to fund such advertisements. Corporations and unions are prohibited from funding such communication directly; instead, they must fund these broadcast advertisements through political action committees that raise and use regulated hard money. Individuals and unincorporated entities can fund electioneering communication directly, but they must disclose within 24 hours the sources of contributions of $1,000 or more once an aggregate of $10,000 has been spent.

The new law appeared to require all nonprofit corporations to fund electioneering communication only through segregated accounts. The language is confusing because it is the product of a floor amendment offered in the Senate by Paul Wellstone (D–Minn.) and supported by opponents of the bill who considered the amendment unconstitutional. In *Federal Election Commission v. Massachusetts Citizens for Life*, 479 U.S. 238 (1986), the Court struck down a similar requirement as applied to a nonprofit that did not take donations from corporations and was organized to serve purely ideological purposes. Such nonprofits are commonly referred to as *MCFL*-exempt organizations. Whether and to what extent BCRA's electioneering communication regulations would be applied to nonprofit corporations was unclear until the Supreme Court's decision in *McConnell v. Federal Election Commission*, 540 U.S. 93 (2003). The Court interpreted the segregated funds provisions not to apply to *MCFL*-exempt nonprofits because the majority presumed "that the legislators who drafted [the provision] were fully aware that the provision could not validly apply to *MCFL*-type entities." *Id.* at 211. All other corporations, including other nonprofits, are required to comply with BCRA.

Within hours of its passage, opponents of the law filed suit, led by Senator Mitch McConnell (R–Ky.) and the National Rifle Association. Ultimately, the case consolidated the challenges of nearly 80 plaintiffs and generated 100,000 pages of evidence and testimony from more than 200 witnesses. A special district court panel of three judges first heard the case. Although BCRA required expedited review, the panel took five months to rule. The judges issued four separate opinions totaling over 1,600 typewritten pages which struck down parts of BCRA, upheld others, and even rewrote a few. *McConnell v. Federal Election Commission*, 251 F. Supp. 2d 176 (D.D.C. 2003) (three judge panel). This holding never went into effect; in another split decision the three-judge panel granted a stay of its ruling, citing its "desire to prevent the litigants from facing potentially three different regulatory regimes in a very short time span" and "the divisions among the panel about the constitutionality of the challenged provisions of BCRA." *McConnell v. Federal Election Commission*, 253 F. Supp. 2d 18, 21 (D.D.C. 2003).

BCRA required the Supreme Court to review the case following a decision by the special panel, so the case immediately went to the Supreme Court, which expedited the process and held oral arguments in September before the regular term began. With the campaigns for the 2004 federal elections well underway, the Supreme Court issued its opinion on the constitutionality of BCRA, upholding virtually all of it and certainly all of its key provisions.

McCONNELL v. FEDERAL ELECTION COMMISSION
Supreme Court of the United States, 2003
540 U.S. 93, 124 S.Ct. 619, 157 L.Ed.2d 491

JUSTICE STEVENS and JUSTICE O'CONNOR delivered the opinion of the Court with respect to BCRA Titles I [ban on soft money] and II [regulation of electioneering communications]. [This opinion was joined by JUSTICES SOUTER, GINSBURG, and BREYER.]

* * * Three important developments in the years after our decision in *Buckley* persuaded Congress that further legislation was necessary to regulate the role that corporations, unions, and wealthy contributors play in the electoral process. As a preface to our discussion of the specific provisions of BCRA, we comment briefly on the increased importance of "soft money," the proliferation of "issue ads," and the disturbing findings of a Senate investigation into campaign practices related to the 1996 federal elections.

Soft Money * * *

Many contributions of soft money were dramatically larger than the contributions of hard money permitted by FECA. For example, in 1996 the top five corporate soft-money donors gave, in total, more than $9 million in non-federal funds to the two national party committees. In the most recent election cycle the political parties raised almost $300 million — 60% of their total soft-money fund-raising — from just 800 donors, each of which contributed a minimum of $120,000. * * *

Not only were such soft-money contributions often designed to gain access to federal candidates, but they were in many cases solicited by the candidates themselves. Candidates often directed potential donors to party committees and tax-exempt organizations that could legally accept soft money. For example, a federal legislator running for reelection solicited soft money from a supporter by advising him that even though he had already "contributed the legal maximum" to the campaign committee, he could still make an additional contribution to a joint program supporting federal, state, and local candidates of his party. Such solicitations were not uncommon.

The solicitation, transfer, and use of soft money thus enabled parties and candidates to circumvent FECA's limitations on the source and amount of contributions in connection with federal elections.

Issue Advertising

[The Court described the "magic words" test that evolved after *Buckley* to differentiate express advocacy, which could be regulated, from issue advertisements, which were not regulated and thus could be financed with soft money and aired without disclosing the identity of, or any other information about, their sponsors.]

While the distinction between "issue" and express advocacy seemed neat in theory, the two categories of advertisements proved functionally identical in important respects. Both were used to advocate the election or defeat of clearly identified federal candidates, even though the so-called issue ads eschewed the use of magic words. Little difference existed, for example, between an ad that urged viewers to "vote against Jane Doe" and one that condemned Jane Doe's record on a particular issue before exhorting viewers to "call Jane Doe and tell her what you think." Indeed, campaign professionals testified that the most effective campaign ads, like the most effective commercials for products such as Coca-Cola, should, and did, avoid the use of the magic words. Moreover, the conclusion that such ads were specifically intended to affect election results was confirmed by the fact that almost all of them aired in the 60 days immediately preceding a federal election. Corporations and unions spent hundreds of millions of dollars of their general funds to pay for these ads, and those expenditures, like soft-money donations to the political parties, were unregulated under FECA. Indeed, the ads were attractive to organizations and candidates precisely because they were beyond FECA's reach, enabling candidates and their parties to work closely with friendly interest groups to sponsor so-called issue ads when the candidates themselves were running out of money.

Because FECA's disclosure requirements did not apply to so-called issue ads, sponsors of such ads often used misleading names to conceal their identity. "Citizens for Better Medicare," for instance, was not a grassroots organization of citizens, as its name might suggest, but was instead a platform for an association of drug manufacturers. And "Republicans for Clean Air," which ran ads in the 2000 Republican Presidential primary, was actually an organization consisting of just two individuals — brothers who together spent $25 million on ads supporting their favored candidate.

While the public may not have been fully informed about the sponsorship of so-called issue ads, the record indicates that candidates and officeholders often were. * * * As with soft-money contributions, political parties and candidates used the availability of so-called issue ads to circumvent FECA's limitations, asking donors who contributed their permitted quota of hard money to give money to nonprofit corporations to spend on "issue" advocacy.

Senate Committee Investigation

In 1998 the Senate Committee on Governmental Affairs issued a six-volume report summarizing the results of an extensive investigation into the campaign practices in the 1996 federal elections. The report gave particular attention to the effect of soft money on the American political system, including elected officials' practice of granting special access in return for political contributions. * * *

The report was critical of both parties' methods of raising soft money, as well as their use of those funds. It concluded that both parties promised and provided special access to candidates and senior Government officials in exchange for large soft-money contributions. The Committee majority described the White House coffees that rewarded major donors with access to

President Clinton, and the courtesies extended to an international businessman named Roger Tamraz, who candidly acknowledged that his donations of about $300,000 to the DNC and to state parties were motivated by his interest in gaining the Federal Government's support for an oil-line project in the Caucasus. The minority described the promotional materials used by the RNC's two principal donor programs, "Team 100" and the "Republican Eagles," which promised "special access to high-ranking Republican elected officials, including governors, senators, and representatives." * * * [The Court also noted that the Senate report discussed the role of state and local parties in this system of soft money and political influence.]

[III] The cornerstone of [the soft money provisions] is new FECA § 323(a), which prohibits national party committees and their agents from soliciting, receiving, directing, or spending any soft money. In short, § 323(a) takes national parties out of the soft-money business.

The remaining provisions of new FECA § 323 largely reinforce the restrictions in § 323(a). New FECA § 323(b) prevents the wholesale shift of soft-money influence from national to state party committees by prohibiting state and local party committees from using such funds for activities that affect federal elections. * * * [The term "Federal election activity" encompasses four distinct categories of electioneering: (1) voter registration activity during the 120 days preceding a regularly scheduled federal election; (2) voter identification, get-out-the-vote (GOTV), and generic campaign activity that is "conducted in connection with an election in which a candidate for Federal office appears on the ballot"; (3) any "public communication" that "refers to a clearly identified candidate for Federal office" and "promotes," "supports," "attacks," or "opposes" a candidate for that office; and (4) the services provided by a state committee employee who dedicates more than 25% of his or her time to "activities in connection with a Federal election."] New FECA § 323(d) reinforces these soft-money restrictions by prohibiting political parties from soliciting and donating funds to tax-exempt organizations that engage in electioneering activities. New FECA § 323(e) restricts federal candidates and officeholders from receiving, spending, or soliciting soft money in connection with federal elections and limits their ability to do so in connection with state and local elections. Finally, new FECA § 323(f) prevents circumvention of the restrictions on national, state, and local party committees by prohibiting state and local candidates from raising and spending soft money to fund advertisements and other public communications that promote or attack federal candidates.

[A] [The Court turned first to the First Amendment challenge to these provisions.] In *Buckley* and subsequent cases, we have subjected restrictions on campaign expenditures to closer scrutiny than limits on campaign contributions. [The Court reviewed the case law and held that a contribution limit involving even significant interference with First Amendment rights is constitutional if it satisfies the "lesser demand" of being "closely drawn" to match a "sufficiently important interest."]

Our treatment of contribution restrictions reflects more than the limited burdens they impose on First Amendment freedoms. It also reflects the importance of the interests that underlie contribution limits — interests in preventing "both the actual corruption threatened by large financial contributions and the eroding of public confidence in the electoral process through the appearance of corruption." * * * Because the electoral process is the very "means through which a free society democratically translates political speech into concrete governmental action," contribution limits, like other measures aimed at protecting the integrity of the process, tangibly benefit public participation in political debate. For that reason, when reviewing Congress' decision to enact contribution limits, "there is no place for a strong presumption against constitutionality, of the sort often thought to accompany the words 'strict scrutiny.' " The less rigorous standard of review we have applied to contribution limits (*Buckley*'s "closely drawn" scrutiny) shows proper deference to Congress' ability to weigh competing constitutional interests in an area in which it enjoys particular expertise. It also provides Congress with sufficient room to anticipate and respond to concerns about circumvention of regulations designed to protect the integrity of the political process.

* * * We are also mindful of the fact that in its lengthy deliberations leading to the enactment of BCRA, Congress properly relied on the recognition of its authority contained in *Buckley* and its progeny. Considerations of *stare decisis*, buttressed by the respect that the Legislative and Judicial Branches owe to one another, provide additional powerful reasons for adhering to the analysis of contribution limits that the Court has consistently followed since *Buckley* was decided. * * *

Section 323 * * * shows "due regard for the reality that solicitation is characteristically intertwined with informative and perhaps persuasive speech seeking support for particular causes or for particular views." The fact that party committees and federal candidates and officeholders must now ask only for limited dollar amounts or request that a corporation or union contribute money through its PAC in no way alters or impairs the political message "intertwined" with the solicitation. And rather than chill such solicitations, * * * the restriction here tends to increase the dissemination of information by forcing parties, candidates, and officeholders to solicit from a wider array of potential donors. * * *

With these principles in mind, we apply the less rigorous scrutiny applicable to contribution limits to evaluate the constitutionality of new FECA § 323. * * * We are mindful, however, that Congress enacted § 323 as an integrated whole to vindicate the Government's important interest in preventing corruption and the appearance of corruption.

New FECA § 323(a)'s Restrictions on National Party Committees

[The Court discussed first the provision prohibiting national political parties from raising soft money.] The main goal of § 323(a) is modest. In large part, it simply effects a return to the scheme that was approved in *Buckley* and that was subverted by the creation of the FEC's [allocation regulations], which permitted the political parties to fund federal electioneering efforts with a combination of hard and soft money. * * *

1. *Governmental Interests Underlying New FECA § 323(a)*

The Government defends § 323(a)'s ban on national parties' involvement with soft money as necessary to prevent the actual and apparent corruption of federal candidates and officeholders. Our cases have made clear that the prevention of corruption or its appearance constitutes a sufficiently important interest to justify political contribution limits. We have not limited that interest to the elimination of cash-for-votes exchanges. * * *

Take away Congress' authority to regulate the appearance of undue influence [by large campaign contributions] and "the cynical assumption that large donors call the tune could jeopardize the willingness of voters to take part in democratic governance." And because the First Amendment does not require Congress to ignore the fact that "candidates, donors, and parties test the limits of the current law," these interests have been sufficient to justify not only contribution limits themselves, but laws preventing the circumvention of such limits. * * *

The evidence in the record shows that candidates and donors alike have in fact exploited the soft-money loophole, the former to increase their prospects of election and the latter to create debt on the part of officeholders, with the national parties serving as willing intermediaries. * * * Parties kept tallies of the amounts of soft money raised by each officeholder, and "the amount of money a Member of Congress raise[d] for the national political committees often affect[ed] the amount the committees g[a]ve to assist the Member's campaign." Donors often asked that their contributions be credited to particular candidates, and the parties obliged, irrespective of whether the funds were hard or soft. National party committees often teamed with individual candidates' campaign committees to create joint fundraising committees, which enabled the candidates to take advantage of the party's higher contribution limits while still allowing donors to give to their preferred candidate. Even when not participating directly in the fundraising, federal officeholders were well aware of the identities of the donors: National party committees would distribute lists of potential or actual donors, or donors themselves would report their generosity to officeholders.

For their part, lobbyists, CEOs, and wealthy individuals alike all have candidly admitted donating substantial sums of soft money to national committees not on ideological grounds, but for the express purpose of securing influence over federal officials. * * * Particularly telling is the fact that, in 1996 and 2000, more than half of the top 50 soft-money donors gave substantial sums to *both* major national parties, leaving room for no other conclusion but that these donors were seeking influence, or avoiding retaliation, rather than promoting any particular ideology. * * *

Plaintiffs argue that without concrete evidence of an instance in which a federal officeholder has actually switched a vote (or, presumably, evidence of a specific instance where the public believes a vote was switched), Congress has not shown that there exists real or apparent corruption. But the record is to the contrary. The evidence connects soft money to manipulations of the legislative calendar, leading to Congress' failure to enact, among other things, generic drug legislation, tort reform, and tobacco legislation. To claim that such actions do not change legislative outcomes surely misunderstands the legislative process.

More importantly, plaintiffs conceive of corruption too narrowly. * * * Many of the "deeply disturbing examples" of corruption cited by this Court in *Buckley* to justify FECA's contribution limits were not episodes of vote buying, but evidence that various corporate interests had given substantial donations to gain access to high-level government officials. Even if that access did not secure actual influence, it certainly gave the "appearance of such influence."

The record in the present case is replete with similar examples of national party committees peddling access to federal candidates and officeholders in exchange for large soft-money donations. * * * So pervasive is this practice that the six national party committees actually furnish their own menus of opportunities for access to would-be soft-money donors, with increased prices reflecting an increased level of access. For example, the DCCC offers a range of donor options, starting with the $10,000-per-year Business Forum program, and going up to the $100,000-per-year National Finance Board program. The latter entitles the donor to bimonthly conference calls with the Democratic House leadership and chair of the DCCC, complimentary invitations to all DCCC fundraising events, two private dinners with the Democratic House leadership and ranking members, and two retreats with the Democratic House leader and DCCC chair in Telluride, Colorado, and Hyannisport, Massachusetts. * * *

[The Court held that it did not matter to the constitutional analysis that some of the contributions to national political parties now regulated by BCRA might be spent for activities related to state or local elections. The regulations were triggered because the Act regulates contributions, not activities funded by contributions. The Court also permitted these soft money provisions to be applied to minor parties because "the relevance of the interest in avoiding actual or apparent corruption is not a function of the number of legislators a given party manages to elect." It noted that minor parties could mount as-applied challenges if the soft money provisions prevented them from "amassing the resources necessary for effective advocacy." The Court then turned to the soft money provisions that restricted fundraising by state and local parties.]

New FECA § 323(b)'s Restrictions on State and Local Party Committees

In constructing a coherent scheme of campaign finance regulation, Congress recognized that, given the close ties between federal candidates and state party committees, BCRA's restrictions on national committee activity would rapidly become ineffective if state and local committees remained available as a conduit for soft-money donations. Section 323(b) is designed to foreclose wholesale evasion of § 323(a)'s anticorruption measures by sharply curbing state committees' ability to use large soft-money contributions to influence federal elections. * * *

1. *Governmental Interests Underlying New FECA § 323(b)*

We begin by noting that, in addressing the problem of soft-money contributions to state committees, Congress both drew a conclusion and made a prediction. Its conclusion, based on the evidence before it, was that the corrupting influence of soft money does not insinuate itself into the political process solely through national party committees. Rather, state committees function as an alternate avenue for precisely the same corrupting forces. * * *

Congress also made a prediction. Having been taught the hard lesson of circumvention by the entire history of campaign finance regulation, Congress knew that soft-money donors would react to § 323(a) by scrambling to find another way to purchase influence. It was "neither novel nor implausible" for Congress to conclude that political parties would react to § 323(a) by directing soft-money contributors to the state committees, and that federal candidates would be just as indebted to these contributors as they had been to those who had formerly contributed to the national parties. We "must accord substantial deference to the predictive judgments of Congress," particularly when, as here, those predictions are so firmly rooted in relevant history and common sense. * * *

2. *New FECA § 323(b)'s Tailoring*

Plaintiffs argue that even if some legitimate interest might be served by § 323(b), the provision's restrictions are unjustifiably burdensome and therefore cannot be considered "closely drawn" to match the Government's objectives. [One argument that the plaintiffs advanced was that BCRA regulated state-focused electioneering that could not corrupt or appear to corrupt federal officeholders and thus went beyond the permissible congressional focus on the federal level.]

Like the rest of Title I, § 323(b) is premised on Congress' judgment that if a large donation is capable of putting a federal candidate in the debt of the contributor, it poses a threat of corruption or the appearance of corruption. * * * [Section] 323(b) is narrowly focused on regulating contributions that pose the greatest risk of this kind of corruption: those contributions to state and local parties that can be used to benefit federal candidates directly. * * *

Because voter registration, voter identification, GOTV, and generic campaign activity all confer substantial benefits on federal candidates, the funding of such activities creates a significant risk of actual and apparent corruption. Section 323(b) is a reasonable response to that risk. Its contribution limitations are focused on the subset of voter registration activity that is most likely to affect the election prospects of federal candidates: activity that occurs within 120 days before a federal election. * * *

"Public communications" that promote or attack a candidate for federal office — the third category of "Federal election activity" — also undoubtedly have a dramatic effect on federal elections. * * * The record on this score could scarcely be more abundant. Given the overwhelming tendency of public communications, as carefully defined in [the Act], to benefit directly federal candidates, we hold that application of § 323(b)'s contribution caps to such communications is also closely drawn to the anticorruption interest it is intended to address.[64]

As for the final category of "Federal election activity," we find that Congress' interest in preventing circumvention of § 323(b)'s other restrictions justifies the requirement that state and local parties spend federal funds to pay the salary of any employee spending more than 25% of his or her compensated time on activities in connection with a federal election. In the absence of this provision, a party might use soft money to pay for the equivalent of a full-time employee engaged in federal electioneering, by the simple expedient of dividing the federal workload among multiple employees. Plaintiffs have suggested no reason for us to strike down this provision. Accordingly, we give "deference to [the] congressional determination of the need for [this] prophylactic rule."

*New FECA § 323(d)'s Restrictions on Parties' Solicitations for, and Donations to, Tax-Exempt Organizations * * ***

1. *New FECA § 323(d)'s Regulation of Solicitations*

The Government defends § 323(d)'s ban on [political parties'] solicitations to tax-exempt organizations engaged in political activity as preventing circumvention of Title I's limits on contributions of soft money to national, state, and local party committees. That justification is entirely reasonable. The history of Congress' efforts at campaign finance reform well demonstrates that "candidates, donors, and parties test the limits of the current law." Absent the solicitation provision, national, state, and local party committees would have significant incentives to mobilize their formidable fundraising apparatuses, including the peddling of access to federal officeholders, into the service of like-minded tax-exempt organizations that conduct activities benefiting their candidates. All of the corruption and appearance of corruption attendant on the operation of those fundraising apparatuses would follow. * * *

Experience under the current law demonstrates that Congress' concerns about circumvention are not merely hypothetical. Even without the added incentives created by [BCRA's soft money provisions], national, state, and local parties already solicit unregulated soft-money donations to tax-exempt organizations for the purpose of supporting federal electioneering activity.

---

64. We likewise reject the argument that [the provision] is unconstitutionally vague. The words "promote," "oppose," "attack," and "support" clearly set forth the confines within which potential party speakers must act in order to avoid triggering the provision. These words "provide explicit standards for those who apply them" and "give the person of ordinary intelligence a reasonable opportunity to know what is prohibited." This is particularly the case here, since actions taken by political parties are presumed to be in connection with election campaigns. See *Buckley* (noting that a general requirement that political committees disclose their expenditures raised no vagueness problems because the term "political committee" "need only encompass organizations that are under the control of a candidate or the major purpose of which is the nomination or election of a candidate" and thus a political committee's expenditures "are, by definition, campaign related"). Furthermore, should plaintiffs feel that they need further guidance, they are able to seek advisory opinions for clarification, and thereby "remove any doubt there may be as to the meaning of the law."

* * * Given BCRA's tighter restrictions on the raising and spending of soft money, the incentives for parties to exploit such organizations will only increase.

Section 323(d)'s solicitation restriction is closely drawn to prevent political parties from using tax-exempt organizations as soft-money surrogates. Though phrased as an absolute prohibition, the restriction does nothing more than subject contributions solicited by parties to FECA's regulatory regime, leaving open substantial opportunities for solicitation and other expressive activity in support of these organizations. * * *

New FECA § 323(e)'s Restrictions on Federal Candidates and Officeholders

New FECA § 323(e) regulates the raising and soliciting of soft money by federal candidates and officeholders. It prohibits federal candidates and officeholders from "solicit[ing], receiv[ing], direct[ing], transfer[ing], or spend[ing]" any soft money in connection with federal elections. * * *

No party seriously questions the constitutionality of § 323(e)'s general ban on donations of soft money made directly to federal candidates and officeholders, their agents, or entities established or controlled by them. Even on the narrowest reading of *Buckley*, a regulation restricting donations to a federal candidate, regardless of the ends to which those funds are ultimately put, qualifies as a contribution limit subject to less rigorous scrutiny. Such donations have only marginal speech and associational value, but at the same time pose a substantial threat of corruption. By severing the most direct link between the soft-money donor and the federal candidate, § 323(e)'s ban on donations of soft money is closely drawn to prevent the corruption or the appearance of corruption of federal candidates and officeholders. * * *

[IV] * * *

BCRA § 201's Definition of "Electioneering Communication"

* * * The major premise of plaintiffs' challenge to BCRA's use of the term "electioneering communication" is that *Buckley* drew a constitutionally mandated line between express advocacy and so-called issue advocacy, and that speakers possess an inviolable First Amendment right to engage in the latter category of speech. * * *

[A] plain reading of *Buckley* makes clear that the express advocacy limitation, in both the expenditure and the disclosure contexts, was the product of statutory interpretation rather than a constitutional command. In narrowly reading the FECA provisions in *Buckley* to avoid problems of vagueness and overbreadth, we nowhere suggested that a statute that was neither vague nor overbroad would be required to toe the same express advocacy line. * * * In short, the concept of express advocacy and the concomitant class of magic words were born of an effort to avoid constitutional infirmities. * * *

Nor are we persuaded, independent of our precedents, that the First Amendment erects a rigid barrier between express advocacy and so-called issue advocacy. That notion cannot be squared with our longstanding recognition that the presence or absence of magic words cannot meaningfully distinguish electioneering speech from a true issue ad. Indeed, the unmistakable lesson from the record in this litigation, as all three judges on the District Court agreed, is that *Buckley*'s magic-words requirement is functionally meaningless. Not only can advertisers easily evade the line by eschewing the use of magic words, but they would seldom choose to use such words even if permitted. And although the resulting advertisements do not urge the viewer to vote for or against a candidate in so many words, they are no less clearly intended to influence the election. *Buckley*'s express advocacy line, in short, has not aided the legislative effort to combat real or apparent corruption, and Congress enacted BCRA to correct the flaws it found in the existing system.

Finally we observe that [BCRA's] definition of "electioneering communication" raises none of the vagueness concerns that drove our analysis in *Buckley*. The term "electioneering communication" applies only (1) to a broadcast (2) clearly identifying a candidate for federal office, (3) aired within a specific time period, and (4) targeted to an identified audience of at least 50,000 viewers or listeners. These components are both easily understood and objectively determinable. Thus, the constitutional objection that persuaded the Court in *Buckley* to limit FECA's reach to express advocacy is simply inapposite here.

BCRA § 201's Disclosure Requirements

* * * Under [the disclosure] provisions, whenever any person makes disbursements totaling more than $10,000 during any calendar year for the direct costs of producing and airing electioneering communications, he must file a statement with the FEC identifying the pertinent elections and all persons sharing the costs of the disbursements. * * * [The Court upheld all the disclosure provisions, including those requiring that executory contracts to make a future expenditure for an electioneering communication be disclosed.]

We agree with the District Court that the important state interests that prompted the *Buckley* Court to uphold FECA's disclosure requirements — providing the electorate with information, deterring actual corruption and avoiding any appearance thereof, and gathering the data necessary to enforce more substantive electioneering restrictions — apply in full to BCRA. Accordingly, *Buckley* amply supports application of FECA § 304's disclosure requirements to the entire range of "electioneering communications." [The Court was particularly concerned, as was the District Court, with the evidence that showed groups and individuals running ads while "hiding behind dubious and misleading names." The Court worried that public debate was significantly harmed when organizations producing political communications could avoid the scrutiny of voters. Although the Court rejected the facial attack in this lawsuit, it allowed for the possibility of future lawsuits brought by organizations with credible evidence that their members had been exposed to "economic reprisals or physical threats as a result of the compelled disclosures."]

BCRA § 203's Prohibition of Corporate and Labor Disbursements for Electioneering Communications

Since our decision in *Buckley*, Congress' power to prohibit corporations and unions from using funds in their treasuries to finance advertisements expressly advocating the election or defeat of candidates in federal elections has been firmly embedded in our law. The ability to form and administer separate segregated funds * * * has provided corporations and unions with a constitutionally sufficient opportunity to engage in express advocacy. That has been this Court's unanimous view, and it is not challenged in this litigation.

[BCRA extends this segregated fund requirement to include all electioneering communication.] Thus, under BCRA, corporations and unions may not use their general treasury funds to finance electioneering communications, but they remain free to organize and administer segregated funds, or PACs, for that purpose. Because corporations can still fund electioneering communications with PAC money, it is "simply wrong" to view the provision as a "complete ban" on expression rather than a regulation. [Here, the Court cited *Austin v. Michigan Chamber of Commerce* (§ 3A of this chapter, *supra.*]

Rather than arguing that the prohibition on the use of general treasury funds is a complete ban that operates as a prior restraint, plaintiffs instead challenge the expanded regulation on the grounds that it is both overbroad and underinclusive. Our consideration of plaintiffs' challenge is informed by our earlier conclusion that the distinction between express advocacy and so-called issue advocacy is not constitutionally compelled. In that light, we must examine the degree to which BCRA burdens First Amendment expression and evaluate whether a compelling governmental interest justifies that burden. The latter question — whether the state interest is compelling — is easily answered by our prior decisions regarding campaign finance regulation, which "represent respect for the 'legislative judgment that the special characteristics of the corporate structure require particularly careful regulation.' " We have repeatedly sustained legislation aimed at "the corrosive and distorting effects of immense aggregations of wealth that are accumulated with the help of the corporate form and that have little or no correlation to the public's support for the corporation's political ideas." *Austin.* Moreover, recent cases have recognized that certain restrictions on corporate electoral involvement permissibly hedge against " 'circumvention of [valid] contribution limits.' " * * *

[The plaintiffs'] argument [that the justifications supporting regulation of express advocacy cannot be used to support regulation of electioneering communication] fails to the extent that the issue ads broadcast during the 30- and 60-day periods preceding federal primary and general elections are the functional equivalent of express advocacy. The justifications for the regulation of express advocacy apply equally to ads aired during those periods if the ads are intended to influence the voters' decisions and have that effect. The precise percentage of issue ads that clearly identified a candidate and were aired during those relatively brief preelection time spans but had no electioneering purpose is a matter of dispute between the parties and among the judges on the District Court. Nevertheless, the vast majority of ads clearly had such a purpose. Moreover, whatever the precise percentage may have been in the past, in the future corporations and unions may finance genuine issue ads during those time frames by simply avoiding any specific reference to federal candidates, or in doubtful cases by paying for the ad from a segregated fund. * * *

Plaintiffs also argue that [BCRA's] segregated-fund requirement for electioneering communications is underinclusive because it does not apply to advertising in the print media or on the Internet. The records developed in this litigation and by the Senate Committee adequately explain the reasons for this legislative choice. Congress found that corporations and unions used soft money to finance a virtual torrent of televised election-related ads during the periods immediately preceding federal elections, and that remedial legislation was needed to stanch that flow of money. As we held in *Buckley,* "reform may take one step at a time, addressing itself to the phase of the problem which seems most acute to the legislative mind." One might just as well argue that the electioneering communication definition is underinclusive because it leaves advertising 61 days in advance of an election entirely unregulated. The record amply justifies Congress' line drawing.

In addition to arguing that [the] segregated-fund requirement is underinclusive, some plaintiffs contend that it unconstitutionally discriminates in favor of media companies. [BCRA] excludes from the definition of electioneering communications any "communication appearing in a news story, commentary, or editorial distributed through the facilities of any broadcasting station, unless such facilities are owned or controlled by any political party, political committee, or candidate." Plaintiffs argue this provision gives free rein to media companies to engage in speech without resort to PAC money. [The effect of this exemption], however, is much narrower than plaintiffs suggest. The provision excepts news items and commentary only; it does not afford *carte blanche* to media companies generally to ignore FECA's provisions. The statute's narrow exception is wholly consistent with First Amendment principles. "A valid distinction . . . exists between corporations that are part of the media industry and other corporations that are not involved in the regular business of imparting news to the public." *Austin.* * * *

BCRA § 204's Application to Nonprofit Corporations

[The Court summarized the holding in *FEC v. Massachusetts Citizens for Life,* 479 U.S. 238 (1986), where it struck down a segregated fund requirement applied to nonprofit organizations that do not take donations from corporations and that are organized to serve purely ideological goals.] That [BCRA] does not, on its face, exempt *MCFL* organizations from its prohibition is not a sufficient reason to invalidate the entire section. If a reasonable limiting construction "has been or could be placed on the challenged statute" to avoid constitutional concerns, we should embrace it. Because our decision in the *MCFL* case was on the books for many years before BCRA was enacted, we presume that the legislators who drafted [the provision] were fully aware that the provision could not validly apply to *MCFL*-type entities. * * *

BCRA § 213's Requirement that Political Parties Choose Between Coordinated and Independent Expenditures After Nominating a Candidate

Section 213 of BCRA * * * impose[s] certain limits on party spending during the postnomination, preelection period. At first blush, the text of [this provision] appears to require political parties to make a straightforward choice between using limited coordinated expenditures or unlimited independent expenditures to support their nominees. [The Court agreed with the District Court panel that this provision is unconstitutional. It first noted that *Colorado Republican Federal Campaign Committee v. Federal Election Commission,* 518 U.S. 604 (1996), held that parties have a constitutional right to make independent expenditures.]

[The choice that BCRA requires of a political party is not as simple as the District Court's opinion suggested, the Court concluded after a close reading of BCRA, although it still found that requiring the party to make a choice is unconstitutional.] A party that wishes to spend more than $5,000 in coordination with its nominee is forced to forgo only the narrow category of independent expenditures that make use of magic words. But while the category of burdened speech is relatively small, it plainly is entitled to First Amendment protection. [A] political party's exercise of its constitutionally protected right to engage in "core First Amendment expression" results in the loss of a valuable statutory benefit that has been available to parties for many years. To survive constitutional scrutiny, a provision that has such consequences must be supported by a meaningful governmental interest.

* * * Any claim that a restriction on independent express advocacy serves a strong Government interest is belied by the overwhelming evidence that the line between express advocacy and other types of election-influencing expression is, for Congress' purposes, functionally meaningless. * * *

The Government argues that [the BCRA provision] nevertheless is constitutional because it is not an outright ban (or cap) on independent expenditures, but rather offers parties a voluntary choice between a constitutional right and a statutory benefit. Whatever merit that argument might have in the abstract, it fails to account for [the way BCRA implements the choice. It is not left up to each party committee to choose whether to make coordinated or independent expenditures. Instead, once *any* party committee — local, state, or national — makes an independent expenditure for express advocacy, then all other party committees are limited to no more than $5,000 in coordinated expenditures.]

Given that provision, it simply is not the case that each party committee can make a voluntary and independent choice between exercising its right to engage in independent advocacy and taking advantage of the increased limits on coordinated spending * * *. Instead, the decision resides solely in the hands of the first mover, such that a local party committee can bind both the state and national parties to its chosen spending option. It is one thing to say that Congress may require a party committee to give up its right to make independent expenditures if it believes that it can accomplish more with coordinated expenditures. It is quite another thing, however, to say that the RNC must limit itself to $5,000 in coordinated expenditures in support of its presidential nominee if any state or local committee first makes an independent expenditure for an ad that uses magic words. That odd result undermines any claim that [the new BCRA provision] can withstand constitutional scrutiny simply because it is cast as a voluntary choice rather than an outright prohibition on independent expenditures.

[The Court upheld BCRA's treatment of the definition of "coordinated" that is used in determining if an expenditure by a noncandidate is "controlled or coordinated" with the candidate's campaign and thus should be considered an indirect contribution. BCRA directs the Federal Election Commission to promulgate new regulations defining "coordinated" and mandates that the regulations "shall not require agreement or formal collaboration to establish coordination." The Court agreed that the presence of a formal agreement need not be the dividing line between expenditures that are the functional equivalent of contributions and expenditures that are truly independent.] [E]xpenditures made after a "wink or nod" often will be "as useful to the candidate as cash." For that reason, Congress has always treated expenditures made "at the request or suggestion of" a candidate as coordinated. * * *

[V] Many years ago we observed that "[t]o say that Congress is without power to pass appropriate legislation to safeguard . . . an election from the improper use of money to influence the result is to deny to the nation in a vital particular the power of self protection." We abide by that conviction in considering Congress' most recent effort to confine the ill effects of aggregated wealth on our political system. We are under no illusion that BCRA will be the last congressional statement on the matter. Money, like water, will always find an outlet. What problems will arise, and how Congress will respond, are concerns for another day. In the main we uphold BCRA's two principal, complementary features: the control of soft money and the regulation of electioneering communications. * * *

[The opinion for the Court of CHIEF JUSTICE REHNQUIST is omitted. In this opinion, the Court held the challenge to the increased contribution limits, such as the increase from $1,000 to $2,000 in the amount that individuals can contribute to candidates per election cycle, to be nonjusticiable because the plaintiffs lacked standing to bring such a challenge. It similarly held the challenge to the "millionaire opponent" provision nonjusticiable. The Court struck down as unconstitutional the provision that prohibited minors from making contributions to candidates or political parties because it violates their First Amendment rights. In addition, the opinion for the Court by JUSTICE BREYER is omitted. In this opinion, the Court upheld provisions requiring broadcasters to keep publicly available records of certain broadcasting requests relating to campaign and other political advertisements.]

JUSTICE SCALIA, concurring with respect to the Chief Justice's majority opinion, dissenting with respect to the soft money provisions, and concurring in the judgment in part and dissenting in part with respect to the electioneering communication provisions.

* * * This is a sad day for the freedom of speech. Who could have imagined that the same Court which, within the past four years, has sternly disapproved of restrictions upon such inconsequential forms of expression as virtual child pornography, tobacco advertising, dissemination of illegally intercepted communications, and sexually explicit cable programming, would smile with favor upon a law that cuts to the heart of what the First Amendment is meant to protect: the right to criticize the government. For that is what the most offensive provisions of this legislation are all about. We are governed by

Congress, and this legislation prohibits the criticism of Members of Congress by those entities most capable of giving such criticism loud voice: national political parties and corporations, both of the commercial and the not-for-profit sort. It forbids pre-election criticism of incumbents by corporations, even not-for-profit corporations, by use of their general funds; and forbids national-party use of "soft" money to fund "issue ads" that incumbents find so offensive.

To be sure, the legislation is evenhanded: It similarly prohibits criticism of the candidates who oppose Members of Congress in their reelection bids. But as everyone knows, this is an area in which evenhandedness is not fairness. If *all* electioneering were evenhandedly prohibited, incumbents would have an enormous advantage. Likewise, if incumbents and challengers are limited to the same quantity of electioneering, incumbents are favored. In other words, *any* restriction upon a type of campaign speech that is equally available to challengers and incumbents tends to favor incumbents.

Beyond that, however, the present legislation *targets* for prohibition certain categories of campaign speech that are particularly harmful to incumbents. Is it accidental, do you think, that incumbents raise about three times as much "hard money" — the sort of funding generally *not* restricted by this legislation — as do their challengers? Or that lobbyists (who seek the favor of incumbents) give 92 percent of their money in "hard" contributions? Is it an oversight, do you suppose, that the so-called "millionaire provisions" raise the contribution limit for a candidate running against an individual who devotes to the campaign (as challengers often do) great personal wealth, but do not raise the limit for a candidate running against an individual who devotes to the campaign (as incumbents often do) a massive election "war chest"? And is it mere happenstance, do you estimate, that national-party funding, which is severely limited by the Act, is more likely to assist cash-strapped challengers than flush-with-hard-money incumbents? Was it unintended, by any chance, that incumbents are free personally to receive some soft money and even to solicit it for other organizations, while national parties are not?

I wish to address three fallacious propositions that might be thought to justify some or all of the provisions of this legislation — only the last of which is explicitly embraced by the principal opinion for the Court, but all of which underlie, I think, its approach to these cases.

(a) Money is Not Speech

It was said by congressional proponents of this legislation * * * that since this legislation regulates nothing but the expenditure of money for speech, as opposed to speech itself, the burden it imposes is not subject to full First Amendment scrutiny; the government may regulate the raising and spending of campaign funds just as it regulates other forms of conduct, such as burning draft cards, * * *or camping out on the National Mall. * * * Until today, however, that view has been categorically rejected by our jurisprudence. * * *

Our traditional view was correct, and today's cavalier attitude toward regulating the financing of speech (the "exacting scrutiny" test of *Buckley* is not uttered in any majority opinion, and is not observed in the ones from which I dissent) frustrates the fundamental purpose of the First Amendment. In any economy operated on even the most rudimentary principles of division of labor, effective public communication requires the speaker to make use of the services of others. An author may write a novel, but he will seldom publish and distribute it himself. A freelance reporter may write a story, but he will rarely edit, print, and deliver it to subscribers. To a government bent on suppressing speech, this mode of organization presents opportunities: Control any cog in the machine, and you can halt the whole apparatus. License printers, and it matters little whether authors are still free to write. Restrict the sale of books, and it matters little who prints them. Predictably, repressive regimes have exploited these principles by attacking all levels of the production and dissemination of ideas. In response to this threat, we have interpreted the First Amendment broadly. * * *

(b) Pooling Money is Not Speech

Another proposition that could explain at least some of the results of today's opinion is that the First Amendment right to spend money for speech does not include the right to combine with others in spending money for speech. Such a proposition fits uncomfortably with the concluding words of our Declaration of Independence: "And for the support of this Declaration, . . . we mutually pledge to each other our Lives, *our Fortunes* and our sacred Honor." (Emphasis added.) The freedom to associate with others for the dissemination of ideas — not just by singing or speaking in unison, but by pooling financial resources for expressive purposes — is part of the freedom of speech. * * *

If it were otherwise, Congress would be empowered to enact legislation requiring newspapers to be sole proprietorships, banning their use of partnership or corporate form. That sort of restriction would be an obvious violation of the First Amendment, and it is incomprehensible why the conclusion should change when what is at issue is the pooling of funds for the most important (and most perennially threatened) category of speech: electoral speech. The principle that such financial association does not enjoy full First Amendment protection threatens the existence of all political parties.

(c) Speech by Corporations Can Be Abridged

The last proposition that might explain at least some of today's casual abridgment of free-speech rights is this: that the particular form of association known as a corporation does not enjoy full First Amendment protection. * * *

[Justice Scalia referred to several cases where corporations were allowed to assert First Amendment rights on their own behalf.] The Court changed course in *Austin v. Michigan Chamber of Commerce,* upholding a state prohibition of an independent corporate expenditure in support of a candidate for state office. I dissented in that case and remain of the view that it was error. In the modern world, giving the government power to exclude corporations from the political debate enables it effectively to muffle the voices that best represent the most significant segments of the economy and the most passionately held social and political views. People who associate — who pool their financial resources — for purposes of economic enterprise overwhelmingly do so in the corporate form; and with increasing frequency, incorporation is chosen by those who associate to defend and promote particular ideas — such as the American Civil

Liberties Union and the National Rifle Association, parties to these cases. Imagine, then, a government that wished to suppress nuclear power — or oil and gas exploration, or automobile manufacturing, or gun ownership, or civil liberties — and that had the power to prohibit corporate advertising against its proposals. To be sure, the individuals involved in, or benefited by, those industries, or interested in those causes, could (given enough time) form political action committees or other associations to make their case. But the organizational form in which those enterprises already *exist*, and in which they can most quickly and most effectively get their message across, is the corporate form. The First Amendment does not in my view permit the restriction of that political speech. And the same holds true for corporate electoral speech: A candidate should not be insulated from the most effective speech that the major participants in the economy and major incorporated interest groups can generate.

But what about the danger to the political system posed by "amassed wealth"? The most direct threat from that source comes in the form of undisclosed favors and payoffs to elected officials — which have already been criminalized, and will be rendered no more discoverable by the legislation at issue here. The use of corporate wealth (like individual wealth) to speak to the electorate is unlikely to "distort" elections — *especially* if disclosure requirements *tell* the people where the speech is coming from. The premise of the First Amendment is that the American people are neither sheep nor fools, and hence fully capable of considering both the substance of the speech presented to them and its proximate and ultimate source. If that premise is wrong, our democracy has a much greater problem to overcome than merely the influence of amassed wealth. Given the premises of democracy, there is no such thing as *too much* speech.

But, it is argued, quite apart from its effect upon the electorate, corporate speech in the form of contributions to the candidate's campaign, or even in the form of independent expenditures supporting the candidate, engenders an obligation which is later paid in the form of greater access to the officeholder, or indeed in the form of votes on particular bills. Any *quid-pro-quo* agreement for votes would of course violate criminal law, and actual payoff *votes* have not even been claimed by those favoring the restrictions on corporate speech. It cannot be denied, however, that corporate (like noncorporate) allies will have greater access to the officeholder, and that he will tend to favor the same causes as those who support him (which is usually *why* they supported him). That is the nature of politics — if not indeed human nature — and how this can properly be considered "corruption" (or "the appearance of corruption") with regard to corporate allies and not with regard to other allies is beyond me. If the Bill of Rights had intended an exception to the freedom of speech in order to combat this malign proclivity of the officeholder to agree with those who agree with him, and to speak more with his supporters than his opponents, it would surely have said so. It did not do so, I think, because the juice is not worth the squeeze. Evil corporate (and private affluent) influences are well enough checked (so long as adequate campaign-expenditure disclosure rules exist) by the politician's fear of being portrayed as "in the pocket" of so-called moneyed interests. * * *

But let us not be deceived. While the Government's briefs and arguments before this Court focused on the horrible "appearance of corruption," the most passionate floor statements during the debates on this legislation pertained to so-called attack ads, which the Constitution surely protects, but which Members of Congress analogized to "crack cocaine" (remarks of Sen. Daschle), "drive-by shooting[s]" (remarks of Sen. Durbin), and "air pollution" (remarks of Sen. Dorgan). There is good reason to believe that the ending of negative campaign ads was the principal attraction of the legislation. A Senate sponsor said, "I hope that we will not allow our attention to be distracted from the real issues at hand — how to raise the tenor of the debate in our elections and give people real choices. No one benefits from negative ads. They don't aid our Nation's political dialog." (Remarks of Sen. McCain). He assured the body that "[y]ou cut off the soft money, you are going to see a lot less of that [attack ads]. Prohibit unions and corporations, and you will see a lot less of that. If you demand full disclosure for those who pay for those ads, you are going to see a lot less of that . . . ."

* * * Perhaps voters do detest these 30-second spots — though I suspect they detest even more hour-long campaign-debate interruptions of their favorite entertainment programming. Evidently, however, these ads *do persuade* voters, or else they would not be so routinely used by sophisticated politicians of all parties. The point, in any event, is that it is not the proper role of those who govern us to judge which campaign speech has "substance" and "depth" (do you think it might be that which is least damaging to incumbents?) and to abridge the rest.

And what exactly are these outrageous sums [spent for broadcast advertising] frittered away in determining who will govern us? A report prepared for Congress concluded that the total amount, in hard and soft money, spent on the 2000 federal elections was between $2.4 and $2.5 billion. *All* campaign spending in the United States, including state elections, ballot initiatives, and judicial elections, has been estimated at $3.9 billion for 2000, which was a year that "shattered spending and contribution records." Even taking this last, larger figure as the benchmark, it means that Americans spent about half as much electing all their Nation's officials, state and federal, as they spent on movie tickets ($7.8 billion); about a fifth as much as they spent on cosmetics and perfume ($18.8 billion); and about a sixth as much as they spent on pork (the nongovernmental sort) ($22.8 billion). If our democracy is drowning from this much spending, it cannot swim.

* * * The most frightening passage in the lengthy floor debates on this legislation is the following assurance given by one of the cosponsoring Senators to his colleagues:

> "This is a modest step, it is a first step, it is an essential step, but it does not even begin to address, in some ways, the fundamental problems that exist with the hard money aspect of the system." (statement of Sen. Feingold).

The system indeed. The first instinct of power is the retention of power, and, under a Constitution that requires periodic elections, that is best achieved by the suppression of election-time speech. We have witnessed merely the second scene of Act I of what promises to be a lengthy tragedy. In scene 3 the Court, having abandoned most of the First Amendment weaponry that *Buckley* left intact, will be even less equipped to resist the incumbents' writing of the rules of political debate. The federal election campaign laws, which are already (as today's opinions show) so voluminous, so detailed, so complex, that no ordinary citizen dare run for office, or even contribute a significant sum, without hiring an expert advisor in the field, can be expected to grow more voluminous, more detailed, and more complex in the years to come — and always, always, with the objective of reducing the excessive amount of speech.

[The opinion of JUSTICE THOMAS, primarily dissenting in the case, is omitted. He argued that the appropriate standard of review is strict scrutiny, and that bribery laws and disclosure statutes would be less restrictive means of curtailing corruption. He also worried that the circumvention rationale used by the majority to uphold many of BCRA's main provisions would allow virtually any regulation of the campaign process. "Every law has limits, and there will always be behavior not covered by the law but at its edges; behavior easily characterized as 'circumventing' the law's prohibition." Unlike all the other Justices, Justice Thomas would have invalidated BCRA's disclosure requirements because they allowed "the established right to anonymous speech to be stripped away based on the flimsiest of justifications." He rejected the notion that the interest of voters in knowing the source of political speech could support disclosure statutes because this interest was outweighed by the First Amendment right to engage in anonymous political speech.]

[Finally, Justice Thomas argued that the logical end of the Court's ruling on electioneering communication is "outright regulation of the press" because such restrictions could be supported by all the state interests accepted by the majority. "Media companies can run procandidate editorials as easily as nonmedia corporations can pay for advertisements. Candidates can be just as grateful to media companies as they can be to corporations and unions. * * * Media corporations are influential. There is little doubt that the editorials and commentary they run can affect elections. Nor is there any doubt that media companies often wish to influence elections. * * * [W]hat is to stop a future Congress from concluding that the availability of unregulated media corporations creates a loophole that allows for easy 'circumvention' of the limitations of the current campaign finance laws?"]

JUSTICE KENNEDY, concurring in the judgment in part and dissenting in part with respect to [BCRA's soft money and electioneering communications provisions].

The First Amendment guarantees our citizens the right to judge for themselves the most effective means for the expression of political views and to decide for themselves which entities to trust as reliable speakers. * * * [BCRA's provisions] force speakers to abandon their own preference for speaking through parties and organizations. And they provide safe harbor to the mainstream press, suggesting that the corporate media alone suffice to alleviate the burdens the Act places on the rights and freedoms of ordinary citizens.

* * * BCRA escalates Congress' discrimination in favor of the speech rights of giant media corporations and against the speech rights of other corporations, both profit and nonprofit.

To the majority, all this is not only valid under the First Amendment but also is part of Congress' "steady improvement of the national election laws." We should make no mistake. It is neither. It is the codification of an assumption that the mainstream media alone can protect freedom of speech. It is an effort by Congress to ensure that civic discourse takes place only through the modes of its choosing. * * *

Until today's consolidated cases, the Court has accepted but two principles to use in determining the validity of campaign finance restrictions. First is the anticorruption rationale. The principal concern, of course, is the agreement for a *quid pro quo* between officeholders (or candidates) and those who would seek to influence them. The Court has said the interest in preventing corruption allows limitations on receipt of the *quid* by a candidate or officeholder, regardless of who gives it or of the intent of the donor or officeholder. Second, the Court has analyzed laws that classify on the basis of the speaker's corporate or union identity under the corporate speech rationale. The Court has said that the willing adoption of the entity form by corporations and unions justifies regulating them differently: Their ability to give candidates *quids* may be subject not only to limits but also to outright bans; their electoral speech may likewise be curtailed.

The majority today opens with rhetoric that suggests a conflation of the anticorruption rationale with the corporate speech rationale. The conflation appears designed to cast the speech regulated here as unseemly corporate speech. The effort, however, is unwarranted, and not just because money is not *per se* the evil the majority thinks. Most of the regulations at issue * * * do not draw distinctions based on corporate or union status. Referring to the corporate speech rationale as if it were the linchpin of the case, when corporate speech is not primarily at issue, adds no force to the Court's analysis. Instead, the focus must be on *Buckley*'s anticorruption rationale and the First Amendment rights of individual citizens. * * *

The Court ignores these constitutional bounds [that properly limit regulation to the *quid pro quo* corruption rationale] and in effect interprets the anticorruption rationale to allow regulation not just of "actual or apparent *quid pro quo* arrangements," but of any conduct that wins goodwill from or influences a Member of Congress. It is not that there is any quarrel between this opinion and the majority that the inquiry since *Buckley* has been whether certain conduct creates "undue influence." On that we agree. The very aim of *Buckley*'s standard, however, was to define undue influence by reference to the presence of *quid pro quo* involving the officeholder. The Court, in contrast, concludes that access, without more, proves influence is undue. Access, in the Court's view, has the same legal ramifications as actual or apparent corruption of officeholders. This new definition of corruption sweeps away all protections for speech that lie in its path. * * *

Access in itself, however, shows only that in a general sense an officeholder favors someone or that someone has influence on the officeholder. There is no basis, in law or in fact, to say favoritism or influence in general is the same as corrupt favoritism or influence in particular. * * *

The generic favoritism or influence theory articulated by the Court is at odds with standard First Amendment analyses because it is unbounded and susceptible to no limiting principle. Any given action might be favored by any given person, so by the Court's reasoning political loyalty of the purest sort can be prohibited. There is no remaining principled method for inquiring whether a campaign finance regulation does in fact regulate corruption in a serious and meaningful way. We are left to defer to a congressional conclusion that certain conduct creates favoritism or influence.

* * * Favoritism and influence are not, as the Government's theory suggests, avoidable in representative politics. It is in the nature of an elected representative to favor certain policies, and, by necessary corollary, to favor the voters and contributors who support those policies. It is well understood that a substantial and legitimate reason, if not the only reason, to cast a vote for, or to make a contribution to, one candidate over another is that the candidate will respond by producing those political outcomes the supporter favors. Democracy is premised on responsiveness. * * *

The piece of record evidence that the Government puts forward [to suggest that favoritism on the basis of soft money contributions changed voting behavior] comes by way of deposition testimony from former Senator Simon and Senator Feingold. Senator Simon reported an unidentified colleague indicated frustration with Simon's opposition to legislation that would benefit a party contributor on the grounds that " 'we've got to pay attention to who is buttering our bread' " and testified that he did not think there was any question " 'this' " (*i.e.*, "donors getting their way") was why the legislation passed. Senator Feingold, too, testified an unidentified colleague suggested he support the legislation because " ' they [*i.e.*, the donor] just gave us [*i.e.*, the party] $100,000.' "

That evidence in fact works against the Government. These two testifying Senators expressed disgust toward the favoring of a soft money giver, and not the good will one would have expected under the Government's theory. That necessarily undercuts the inference of corruption the Government would have us draw from the evidence.

Even more damaging to the Government's argument from the testimony is the absence of testimony that the Senator who allegedly succumbed to corrupt influence had himself solicited soft money from the donor in question. Equally, there is no indication he simply favored the company with his vote because it had, without any involvement from him, given funds to the party to which he belonged. This fact is crucial. If the Senator himself had been the solicitor of the soft money funds in question, the incident does nothing more than confirm that Congress' efforts at campaign finance reform ought to be directed to conduct that implicates *quid pro quo* relationships. Only if there was some evidence that the officeholder had not solicited funds from the donor could the

Court extrapolate from this episode that general party contributions function as *quids*, inspiring corrupt favoritism among party members. The episode is the single one of its type reported in the record and does not seem sufficient basis for major incursions into settled practice. Given the Government's claim that the corrupt favoritism problem is widespread, its inability to produce more than a single instance purporting to illustrate the point demonstrates the Government has not fairly characterized the general attitudes of Members towards soft money donors from whom they have not solicited. * * *

[Justice Kennedy turned to the Court's ruling upholding BCRA § 203, the segregated fund requirement imposed on corporations and unions that spend money on electioneering communication in the weeks before an election.] Instead of extending *Austin* to suppress new and vibrant voices, I would overrule it and return our campaign finance jurisprudence to principles consistent with the First Amendment.

The Government and the majority are right about one thing: The express-advocacy requirement, with its list of magic words, is easy to circumvent. The Government seizes on this observation to defend BCRA § 203, arguing it will prevent what it calls "sham issue ads" that are really to the same effect as their more express counterparts. What the Court and the Government call sham, however, are the ads speakers find most effective. Unlike express ads that leave nothing to the imagination, the record shows that issues ads are preferred by almost all candidates, even though politicians, unlike corporations, can lawfully broadcast express ads if they so choose. It is a measure of the Government's disdain for protected speech that it would label as a sham the mode of communication sophisticated speakers choose because it is the most powerful.

The Government's use of the pejorative label should not obscure § 203's practical effect: It prohibits a mass communication technique favored in the modern political process for the very reason that it is the most potent. That the Government would regulate it for this reason goes only to prove the illegitimacy of the Government's purpose. The majority's validation of it is not sustainable under accepted First Amendment principles. The problem is that the majority uses *Austin*, a decision itself unfaithful to our First Amendment precedents, to justify banning a far greater range of speech. This has it all backwards. If protected speech is being suppressed, that must be the end of the inquiry. * * *

Austin was based on a faulty assumption. Contrary to Justice Stevens' proposal [in *Austin*] that there is "vast difference between lobbying and debating public issues on the one hand, and political campaigns for election to public office on the other," there is a general recognition now that discussions of candidates and issues are quite often intertwined in practical terms. * * * Far from providing a rationale for expanding *Austin*, the evidence in these consolidated cases calls for its reexamination. Just as arguments about immense aggregations of corporate wealth and concerns about protecting shareholders and union members do not justify a ban on issue ads [in initiative campaigns, see *First National Bank of Boston v. Bellotti*, 435 U.S. 765 (1978)], they cannot sustain a ban on independent expenditures for express ads. In holding otherwise, *Austin* "forced a substantial amount of political speech underground" and created a species of covert speech incompatible with our free and open society. * * *

Continued adherence to *Austin*, of course, cannot be justified by the corporate identity of the speaker. Not only does this argument fail to account for *Bellotti*, but *Buckley* itself warned that "[t]he First Amendment's protection against governmental abridgment of free expression cannot properly be made to depend on a person's financial ability to engage in public discussion." The exemption for broadcast media companies, moreover, makes the First Amendment problems worse, not better. In the end the majority can supply no principled basis to reason away *Austin*'s anomaly. *Austin*'s errors stand exposed, and it is our duty to say so.

I surmise that even the majority, along with the Government, appreciates these problems with *Austin*. That is why it invents a new justification. We are now told that "the government also has a compelling interest in insulating federal elections from the type of corruption arising from the real or apparent creation of political debts." "[E]lectioneering communications paid for with the general treasury funds of labor unions and corporations," the Government warns, "endea[r] those entities to elected officials in a way that could be perceived by the public as corrupting."

This rationale has no limiting principle. Were we to accept it, Congress would have the authority to outlaw even pure issue ads, because they, too, could endear their sponsors to candidates who adopt the favored positions. Taken to its logical conclusion, the alleged Government interest "in insulating federal elections from . . . the real or apparent creation of political debts" also conflicts with *Buckley*. If a candidate feels grateful to a faceless, impersonal corporation for making independent expenditures, the gratitude cannot be any less when the money came from the CEO's own pocket. *Buckley*, however, struck down limitations on independent expenditures and rejected the Government's corruption argument absent evidence of coordination. The Government's position would eviscerate the line between expenditures and contributions and subject both to the same "complaisant review under the First Amendment." Complaisant or otherwise, we cannot cede authority to the Legislature to do with the First Amendment as it pleases. Since *Austin* is inconsistent with the First Amendment, its extension diminishes the First Amendment even further. For this reason § 203 [dealing with electioneering communication] should be held unconstitutional. * * *

These [segregated fund] regulations are more than minor clerical requirements. Rather, they create major disincentives for speech, with the effect falling most heavily on smaller entities that often have the most difficulty bearing the costs of compliance. Even worse, for an organization that has not yet set up a PAC, spontaneous speech that "refers to a clearly identified candidate for Federal office" becomes impossible, even if the group's vital interests are threatened by a piece of legislation pending before Congress on the eve of a federal election. Couple the litany of administrative burdens with the categorical restriction limiting PACs' solicitation activities to "members," and it is apparent that PACs are inadequate substitutes for corporations in their ability to engage in unfettered expression.

Even if the newly formed PACs manage to attract members and disseminate their messages against these heavy odds, they have been forced to assume a false identity while doing so. As the American Civil Liberties Union (ACLU) points out, political committees are regulated in minute detail because their primary purpose is to influence federal elections. [The ACLU goes on to argue:] "The ACLU and thousands of other organizations like it," however, "are not created for this purpose and therefore should not be required to operate as if they were." A requirement that coerces corporations to adopt alter egos in communicating with the public is, by itself, sufficient to make the PAC option a false choice for many civic organizations. [As I argued in *Austin*:] Forcing speech through an artificial "secondhand endorsement structure . . . debases the value of the voice of nonprofit corporate speakers . . . [because] PAC's are interim, ad hoc organizations with little continuity or responsibility." In contrast, their sponsoring organizations "have a continuity, a stability, and an influence" that allows "their members and the public at large to evaluate their . . . credibility."

The majority can articulate no compelling justification for imposing this scheme of compulsory ventriloquism. If the majority is concerned about corruption and distortion of the political process, it makes no sense to diffuse the corporate message and, under threat of criminal penalties, to compel the corporation to spread the blame to its ad hoc intermediary. * * *

[Justice Kennedy next addressed the definition of "electioneering communication."] The prohibition, with its crude temporal and geographic proxies, is a severe and unprecedented ban on protected speech. As discussed at the outset, suppose a few Senators want to show their constituents in the logging industry how much they care about working families and propose a law, 60 days before the election, that would harm the environment by allowing logging in national forests. Under [BCRA], a nonprofit environmental group would be unable to run an ad referring to these Senators in their districts. The suggestion that the group could form and fund a PAC in the short time required for effective participation in the political debate is fanciful. For reasons already discussed, moreover, an ad hoc PAC would not be as effective as the environmental group itself in gaining credibility with the public. Never before in our history has the Court upheld a law that suppresses speech to this extent.

The group would want to refer to these Senators, either by name or by photograph, not necessarily because an election is at stake. It might be supposed the hypothetical Senators have had an impeccable environmental record, so the environmental group might have no previous or present interest in expressing an opinion on their candidacies. Or, the election might not be hotly contested in some of the districts, so whatever the group says would have no practical effect on the electoral outcome. The ability to refer to candidates and officeholders is important because it allows the public to communicate with them on issues of common concern. [BCRA's] sweeping approach fails to take into account this significant free speech interest. Under any conventional definition of overbreadth, it fails to meet strict scrutiny standards. It forces electioneering communications sponsored by an environmental group to contend with faceless and nameless opponents and consign their broadcast, as the NRA well puts it, to a world where politicians who threaten the environment must be referred to as " 'He Whose Name Cannot Be Spoken.' "

In the example above, it makes no difference to § 203 or to the Court that the bill sponsors may have such well-known ideological biases that revealing their identity would provide essential instruction to citizens on whether the policy benefits them or their community. Nor does it make any difference that the names of the bill sponsors, perhaps through repetition in the news media, have become so synonymous with the proposal that referring to these politicians by name in an ad is the most effective way to communicate with the public. Section 203 is a comprehensive censor: On the pain of a felony offense, the ad must not refer to a candidate for federal office during the crucial weeks before an election.

We are supposed to find comfort in the knowledge that the ad is banned under § 203 only if it "is targeted to the relevant electorate," defined as communications that can be received by 50,000 or more persons in the candidate's district. This Orwellian criterion, however, is analogous to a law, unconstitutional under any known First Amendment theory, that would allow a speaker to say anything he chooses, so long as his intended audience could not hear him. A central purpose of issue ads is to urge the public to pay close attention to the candidate's platform on the featured issues. By banning broadcast in the very district where the candidate is standing for election, § 203 shields information at the heart of the First Amendment from precisely those citizens who most value the right to make a responsible judgment at the voting booth. * * *

The First Amendment commands that Congress "shall make no law . . . abridging the freedom of speech." The command cannot be read to allow Congress to provide for the imprisonment of those who attempt to establish new political parties and alter the civic discourse. Our pluralistic society is filled with voices expressing new and different viewpoints, speaking through modes and mechanisms that must be allowed to change in response to the demands of an interested public. As communities have grown and technology has evolved, concerted speech not only has become more effective than a single voice but also has become the natural preference and efficacious choice for many Americans. The Court, upholding multiple laws that suppress both spontaneous and concerted speech, leaves us less free than before. Today's decision breaks faith with our tradition of robust and unfettered debate. * * *

[The dissent of CHIEF JUSTICE REHNQUIST is omitted. He objected to BCRA's soft money restrictions because they regulate "*all donations* to national political committees, no matter the use to which the funds are put." He believed this broad restriction is not narrowly tailored to the concern that soft money contributions will inappropriately influence federal candidates and officeholders. "The Court fails to recognize that the national political parties are exemplars of political speech at all levels of government, in addition to effective fundraisers for federal candidates and officeholders. For sure, national political party committees exist in large part to elect federal candidates, but * * * they also promote coordinated political messages and participate in public policy debates unrelated to federal elections, promote, even in off-year elections, state and local candidates and seek to influence policy at those levels, and increase public participation in the electoral process. * * * As these activities illustrate, political parties often foster speech crucial to a healthy democracy, and fulfill the need for like-minded individuals to ban[d] together and promote a political philosophy. When political parties engage in pure political speech that has little or no potential to corrupt their federal candidates and officeholders, the government cannot constitutionally burden their speech any more than it could burden the speech of individuals engaging in these same activities."]

[Chief Justice Rehnquist also rejected the circumvention rationale used by the Court as partial justification for BCRA's provisions. "All political speech that is not sifted through federal regulation circumvents the regulatory scheme to some degree or another, and thus by the Court's standard would be a 'loophole' in the current system." In a footnote, he warned that the first loophole to BCRA was already developing. "Nonprofit organizations are currently able to accept, without disclosing, unlimited donations for voter registration, voter identification, and get-out-the-vote activities, and the record indicates that such organizations already receive large donations, sometimes in the millions of dollars, for these activities. * * * And who knows what the next 'loophole' will be."]

[The dissent by JUSTICE STEVENS is omitted. He dissented from the holding of nonjusticiability relating to the BCRA provisions requiring broadcasters charge candidates the "lowest unit charge" for advertisements aired within a certain period before an election and denying that favorable rate to candidates who do not promise to refrain from directly referring to other candidates unless such ads clearly identify the candidate paying for them. Justice Stevens would have found the challenge to be justiciable, and he would have upheld the provision on the merits.]

NOTES ON *McCONNELL v. FEC*

1. *Corruption and the Standard of Review. McConnell* clarifies that the standard of review for restrictions on campaign contributions is less rigorous than strict scrutiny, and it is less stringent than judicial review of expenditure limitations. In addition, the majority demonstrates a willingness to defer to Congress throughout its analysis. For example, it notes that Congress had enacted a comprehensive response to problems in the campaign fundraising system and thus judges should consider BCRA as an integrated approach to regulation. The implication of this language is that judges should be hesitant to strike down part of the statute and leave other parts in place because such a piecemeal approach could lead to unintended consequences. The majority ends the main opinion by underscoring the primary role Congress plays in designing campaign finance laws and predicting that it will need to formulate new approaches as money begins to find new outlets.

McConnell also continues to develop the notion of "corruption" by highlighting one aspect of corruption: the "special access" that large contributions appear to buy. As Richard Briffault writes: "Although the Court had previously made clear that corruption was not limited to outright vote-buying, the Court's language of undue influence had nonetheless focused on the effects of large contributions on government decision-making. By focusing on special access, *McConnell* reframed the corruption analysis from the consideration of the impact of contributions on formal decisions to their effect on the *opportunity to influence* government actions." McConnell v. FEC *and the Transformation of Campaign Finance Law*, 3 Election L.J. 147, 162–63 (2004). Much of Justice Kennedy's dissent argues against this expansion of the corruption rationale, contending that access to lawmakers is not inherently harmful but is instead an inevitable part of representative government. What do you think about this formulation of corruption? Does this state interest in preventing special access bought with large contributions, as the majority articulates it, have a limiting principle? What sorts of additional regulation of the electoral process would it support?

The Court is also willing in *McConnell* to accept restrictions justified by the need to prevent circumvention of other lawful restrictions. The judicial focus on plugging loopholes reflects decades of experience with campaign finance regulation and the substantial record in this case provided by politicians, political scientists, and others. Thus, *McConnell*'s tone differs from the tone of the opinion issued in *Buckley v. Valeo*, a case brought before much familiarity with the reactions of candidates, political parties, and donors to particular legal restrictions. Although the *McConnell* record included evidence of particular kinds of circumvention, primarily through soft money raised by national parties, the Court formulates the anti-circumvention rationale more broadly. For example, the majority defers to the congressional prediction that people would seek to evade BCRA's restrictions by using any loopholes in the coverage of state and local parties, which have not yet been used much to circumvent other restrictions. Thus, the Court upholds BCRA's provisions that limit the ability of state and local parties to raise soft money for federal election activities, a term that BCRA broadly defines.

2. *Fundraising for the 2004 Election*. The 2004 presidential and congressional campaigns were the first conducted under BCRA. Perhaps the biggest change was the increased importance of hard money both because of the BCRA's soft money restrictions and because of larger contribution limits for hard money. Thus, people who could bundle many $2,000 contributions from individuals were particularly important to candidates and political parties. President Bush formed donors' clubs to take advantage of bundling under the new hard money rules. Bush recognized those who raised over $100,000 for his 2004 presidential campaign as "Pioneers" and those who raised over $200,000 as "Rangers." The campaign laws do not require disclosure of fundraisers who solicit donations, although candidates keep careful track. Each Pioneer or Ranger was given a tracking number that had to appear on checks received by the campaign in order for the fundraiser to get credit. The *Washington Post* found that more than 40% of the Pioneers in the 2000 election received jobs in the Bush administration or on the transition team. One-fifth

of the Pioneers were lobbyists who participated, at least in part, to obtain access to the White House.[g]

Campaigns also worked to encourage more people to make contributions, whether at the $2,000 level or in smaller amounts. In the spring of 2004, President Bush announced that over 830,000 people had contributed to his campaign, compared to 345,000 in the 2000 election. The Republican National Committee received donations from more than one million first-time contributors during the first three years of Bush's term, with an average contribution of just under $30. 400,000 had donated to Democratic nominee John Kerry's campaign by March 2004. Fundraising over the Internet accounted for some of the increase in small, first-time donations. Democratic presidential candidates, especially Howard Dean, relied on their websites, emails and weblogs to encourage voters to use their credit cards to quickly and easily send contributions. By the spring, Kerry was raising approximately $1 million per day over the Internet.

Initially, the new emphasis on hard money was thought to provide a significant advantage to the Republican Party because it has a larger base of hard money donors, many of whom can give up to the new limits. Before enactment of BCRA, the two political parties were roughly equal in their ability to raise soft money, but the Republicans have always substantially outpaced the Democrats for hard money. In the 2002 election cycle, the GOP raised $289 million in hard money compared to the Democrats' $127 million, while it garnered $222 million in soft money compared to the Democrats' $200 million. As the 2004 election cycle developed, however, both parties were able to replace soft money with new hard money, and any Republican advantage was clearly not to be long-lived. Anthony Corrado found that "[b]y the end of the 2004 election, the national party committees had raised more money in hard dollars *alone* than they raised in hard and soft dollars *combined* in any previous election cycle." *Party Finance in the Wake of BCRA: An Overview,* in *The Election After Reform, supra,* at 19, 25. Although Bush and the Republican Party raised more hard money than Kerry and the Democrats, the playing field was evened by nonprofit organizations using a gap in BCRA's coverage to continue to raise soft money. These 527 organizations have become one of the next battlegrounds for reform.

3. *Regulating 527 Organizations.* With the closing of the soft money spigot for political parties, 527 organizations became increasingly crucial political players in the 2004 elections. Section 527 organizations are nonprofit groups organized for the "function of influencing or attempting to influence the selection, nomination, election, or appointment of any individual to any Federal, State, or local public office." Internal Revenue Code § 527(e)(2). Since 2000, 527 organizations have been required to disclose their donors, so they can no longer operate as "stealth PACs." These groups have argued that as long as they do not engage in express advocacy (as defined by the *Buckley*

---

g. Thomas Edsall, Sarah Cohen & James Grimaldi, *Pioneers Fill War Chest, Then Capitalize,* Wash. Post, May 16, 2004, at A1.

"magic words") and do not directly contribute to federal candidates' campaigns, they can raise unlimited amounts of soft money. Although all PACs are also 527 organizations, not all 527s involved in politics at the federal level were considered PACs before BCRA and *McConnell*. The organizers of 527s argue that BCRA did not change that aspect of the status quo.

Taking advantage of this loophole, federally active 527 groups spent approximately $424 million in the 2004 election cycle.[h] Over $169.5 million was contributed to these organizations in aggregate amounts of $250,000 or more, including more than $23 million contributed by liberal financier George Soros and over $22 million by liberal businessman Peter Lewis.[i] Although some of the top 527s, such as Progress for America, were politically conservative, most of the 527s with significant resources in 2004 — such as Americans Coming Together, supported by Soros, and the Media Fund, run by former Clinton aide Harold Ickes — supported Kerry and the Democrats. Many of the 527s worked informally with the political parties; leading political consultants affiliated with parties in the past helped them raise money, and party officials signaled their support for certain 527s. See Stephen Weissman & Ruth Hassan, *BCRA and the 527 Groups*, in *The Election After Reform, supra,* at 79.

527s continue to play a key role in federal campaigns. Expenditures by federally active 527 groups in the mid-term 2005–06 election cycle totaled more than $143 million, indicating that 527 groups continue to be effective means of influencing voters and conveying political or ideological messages. Although most of the major contributors to 527 groups gave less in the 2006 election cycle than during the 2004 cycle, conservative businessman Bob Perry's contributions increased. Perry, who previously was the largest single contributor to Swift Vets and POWs for Truth, the infamous 527 group that some credit for irreparably tarnishing Kerry's image as a Vietnam War hero, gave nearly $10 million to politically conservative 527 groups in the 2006 mid-term election. He also bank-rolled a new conservative 527 group, the Economic Freedom Fund, with a $5 million donation. With this single contribution, the Economic Freedom Fund instantly became one of the top ten federally active 527 groups in the 2006 election.[j]

The *McConnell* opinions note that evasion of BCRA is likely to center on the use of nonprofit organizations. Justice Rehnquist, in dissent, states that "[n]onprofit organizations are currently able to accept, without disclosing [in the case of nonprofits other than 527 organizations], unlimited donations for voter registration, voter identification, and get-out-the-vote activities, and the record indicates that such organizations already receive large donations,

---

h. Michael Malbin, *Assessing the Bipartisan Campaign Reform Act*, in *The Election After Reform, supra,* at 1, 11.

i. David Magleby, J. Quin Monson & Kelly Patterson, *Dancing Without Partners: How Candidates, Parties and Interest Groups Interact in the New Campaign Finance Environment* 14 (2005).

j. Stephen Weissman & Kara Ryan, *Soft Money in the 2006 Election and the Outlook for 2008: The Changing NonProfits Landscape* 21 (2007), http://www.cfinst.org/books_reports/pdf/NP_Softmoney_06-08.pdf.

sometimes in the millions of dollars, for these activities." The sponsors of BCRA, Senators McCain and Feingold, have both spoken out against the use of 527s as conduits of soft money, and bills to regulate 527s have been introduced in Congress. The Federal Election Commission declined to promulgate substantive regulations restricting the activities of 527s; thus, it appears that this issue, arguably the main loophole in BCRA, requires congressional action for any resolution. The holding in *McConnell*, particularly the broadening of permissible regulation to include electioneering communication and not just express advocacy using *Buckley*'s magic words, strongly suggests that further regulation would be constitutional if *McConnell* continues to represent the Court's view of campaign finance (a question we turn to below).[k]

3.　*In the Wake of* McConnell: *Evolving Case Law and the Influence of New Justices*

Although *McConnell* left some questions open, it initially appeared that the issues would be resolved within the *Buckley/McConnell* framework and that the courts would be relatively deferential to legislative decisions regarding the appropriate regulation of campaign contributions. However, two changes in Supreme Court personnel have unsettled the jurisprudential landscape again. Former District of Columbia circuit court judge John Roberts replaced Chief Justice Rehnquist, and, more crucially, federal appellate court judge Samuel Alito replaced retiring Justice Sandra Day O'Connor. In their rookie terms, these justices participated in an important campaign finance case that demonstrated the limits of judicial deference to legislative decisions in this realm.

————————

RANDALL v. SORRELL, 126 S.Ct. 2479 (2006). In 1997, Vermont enacted a very stringent campaign finance law, imposing expenditure limits on candidates for state office as well as strict contribution limits. For example, contributions during a two-year election cycle to candidates for statewide office were limited to $400; contributions to candidates for state senate were limited to $300; and donations to candidates for the state house to $200. These contribution limitations applied not only to individuals and political committees, but also to political parties that wished to support their candidates. The expenditure and contribution restrictions were challenged by former candidates for state office, Vermont voters, and political parties.

In his plurality opinion, **Justice Breyer** reaffirmed the vitality of *Buckley v. Valeo*; **Justice Alito** declined to join in this part of the opinion, noting that it was not necessary in this case to reach the issue of whether to overrule *Buckley*. Given the clear holding of *Buckley* that expenditure limits are subject to strict scrutiny and are unconstitutional, the plurality quickly struck down this aspect of Vermont's law. Breyer also held the contribution limits to be

————————

k.　See Miriam Galston, *Emerging Constitutional Paradigms and Justifications for Campaign Finance Regulation: The Case of 527 Groups*, 95 Geo. L.J. 1181 (2007) (discussing constitutional and other legal issues involved in extending regulation to 527s).

unconstitutional, a departure from previous cases where the Court had regularly deferred to legislative determinations of what constitutes a reasonable cap on campaign donations. "[W]e must recognize the existence of some lower bound [to contribution limits]. At some point the constitutional risks to the democratic electoral process become too great." The plurality explained that when a court discovers "danger signs" of risks to the fairness of the electoral process, it must "review the record independently and carefully with an eye toward assessing the statute's 'tailoring,' i.e., toward assessing the restrictions' proportionality."

Breyer identified several danger signs in the Vermont law that suggested it might "fall outside tolerable First Amendment limits." The Vermont law imposed contribution limits lower than any previously upheld by the Court and, considered as a whole, the limitations were the lowest in the U.S. For example, the law imposed one very low limit per election cycle, that is, for both the primary and general elections; it applied the same limitation to political parties as it did to individuals and political committees; and it did not index the thresholds for inflation.

Given these danger signs, the plurality then undertook an independent review of the record and found five factors that convinced it that "the Act is not closely drawn to meet its objectives." First, it found that the low contribution limits would restrict the funding available to challengers in competitive campaigns, which tend to be the most expensive races. The lower court had focused on funding in average campaigns, not competitive ones, and determined that the Vermont law would have only a minimal impact on challengers' ability to raise money. Second, the restriction on the ability of political parties to support their candidates "threatens harm to a particularly important political right, the right to associate in a political party." Third, the contribution limits counted the expenses incurred by campaign volunteers as well as direct financial contributions. Combined with very low limits, this aspect of the law would inhibit the activity of volunteers in state campaigns. Fourth, the failure to index the caps for inflation meant that they would become even lower over time. Fifth, the record did not include evidence that the political climate in Vermont warranted such a restrictive regulatory regime or that Vermont faced more intractable problems of corruption in political campaigns than other states with less severe regulatory regimes.

Can you link some of these arguments to the various notions of corruption described above? For example, how important is the value of electoral competition in the Court's independent assessment of the record? Can you discover arguments that seem inspired by Justice Breyer's vision of participatory democracy that is protected by the First Amendment? How deferential is this new test for assessing the constitutionality of contributions? Is it consistent with *McConnell*? Does the test provide clarity and certainty for a legislature seeking to impose stringent yet constitutional restrictions on contributions by individuals, political action committees and political parties?

Justice Kennedy's concurrence briefly noted his continuing dissatisfaction with the jurisprudence in this arena. "Viewed within the legal universe we have ratified and helped create, the result the plurality reaches is correct; given my own skepticism regarding that system and its operation, however, it seems to me appropriate to concur only in the judgment." **Justice Thomas** again sounded his opposition to *Buckley*, a decision he called "illegitimate." He agreed that the contribution limits here failed even the *Buckley* standard: "[I]t is almost impossible to imagine that any legislator would ever find his scruples overcome by a $201 donation." Moreover, he attacked the plurality's multifaceted test because it provides no guidance in drawing the line between permissible and impermissible restrictions, "and it is clear that no such line can be drawn rationally."

In dissent, **Justice Stevens** also concluded that *Buckley* should be overruled, but he would reject its holding with regard to expenditure limits and allow legislatures to place reasonable caps on campaign expenditures as well as contributions. Stevens refused to equate money and speech; rather, he considered expenditure limits as "time, place, and manner restrictions," not as limits on the content of speech. As long as regulation served "legitimate and sufficiently substantial" purposes, he would uphold the law. Here, Stevens accepted several purposes: to complement "corruption-reducing contribution limits," to protect "equal access to the political arena," and to "free candidates and their staffs from the interminable burden of fundraising." If one reads Alito and Kennedy as signaling serious doubts about *Buckley*, there are five justices sympathetic to overruling its framework, although one of those (Stevens) favors more regulation, not less. In contrast, **Justice Souter**'s dissent is based on deference to the legislative judgment and "our self-admonition against second-guessing legislative judgments about the risk of corruption to which contribution limits have to be fitted."

The following term, yet another important campaign finance case reached the Court, providing an opportunity for the new justices to participate in shaping First Amendment jurisprudence in the context of elections. As you read this case, ask yourself what this means for *McConnell* and perhaps even *Buckley*. One thing is clear: the jurisprudence of campaign finance law is far from settled.

FEDERAL ELECTION COMMISSION v. WISCONSIN RIGHT TO LIFE, INC., 127 S.Ct. 2652 (2007). Following the decision in *McConnell* upholding BCRA's restrictions on corporate funding for electioneering communications, Wisconsin Right to Life, Inc. (WRTL), a nonprofit ideological advocacy corporation, brought an as-applied challenge to § 203. During the thirty-day period before Wisconsin's 2004 primary election, WRTL planned to continue running several broadcast advertisements declaring that a group of senators was filibustering the consideration of certain conservative nominees for federal appellate judgeships and telling voters to contact Wisconsin Senators Feingold and Kohl to urge them to oppose the filibuster. Because WRTL accepts donations from for-profit corporations, it is not a *MCFL*-exempt organization. It admitted that the advertisements fit the language of § 203, and thus BCRA required that they be funded through a segregated fund, not WRTL's general treasury. However, it argued that applying the electioneering communication section to these ads violated the First Amendment.

Although five justices agreed with WRTL that § 203 could not be applied to these ads, there was no majority rationale. **Chief Justice Roberts**, writing for himself and **Justice Alito**, purported to apply *McConnell*, which had sustained § 203 to the extent that it covered issue ads broadcast during the 30-day period before a primary that are the *"functional equivalent"* of express advocacy. Because *McConnell* did not provide any standard to determine functional equivalence, Justice Roberts' opinion undertook that task. He first rejected any test that would turn on the "speaker's intent to affect an election" because that would "chill core political speech by opening the door to a trial on every ad within the terms of § 203, on the theory that the speaker actually intended to affect an election, no matter how compelling the indications that the ad concerned a pending legislative or policy issue." Instead, the opinion stated that "a court should find that an ad is the functional equivalent of express advocacy only if the ad is susceptible of no reasonable interpretation other than as an appeal to vote for or against a specific candidate." At several points in the opinion, the Chief Justice observed that the benefit of the doubt must always be provided to "protecting rather than stifling speech." "Where the First Amendment is implicated, the tie goes to the speaker, not the censor."

Using this standard, he found the WRTL ads to be "genuine" issue ads that could be funded directly by the nonprofit; § 203 could not be constitutionally applied in this instance. The opinion noted that strict scrutiny demands that a "compelling interest supports *each application* of a statute restricting speech." The governmental interest identified in *Buckley* and *McConnell* of preventing corruption and the appearance of corruption does not apply with respect to an ad that is not the functional equivalent of express advocacy. "Enough is enough. * * * To equate WRTL's ads with contributions is to ignore their value as political speech." In a separate concurrence, Justice Alito clarified that "[i]f it turns out that the implementation of the as-applied standard set out in the principal opinion impermissibly chills political speech, * * * we will presumably be asked in a future case to reconsider the holding in *McConnell* * * * that § 203 is facially constitutional."

Justice Scalia wrote for three justices who concurred in the judgment but would have reached the decision by overruling the part of *McConnell* that sustained § 203 against facial attack. He believed that none of the tests offered to separate "issue-speech from election-speech" was formulated with enough clarity to avoid unconstitutional vagueness. He argued that the Chief Justice's test opened to judicial judgment the determination of "reasonableness" that would necessarily rest "upon consideration of innumerable surrounding circumstances." In light of the uncertainty such a test would engender, political speech would be chilled. The only bright-line tests that Scalia could imagine are either unconstitutional (the objective test set forth in § 203 which would prohibit ads that are genuine issue ads) or incompatible with § 203 (*Buckley*'s magic-words test for express advocacy that Congress rejected in passing § 203). (Does the Roberts test for functional equivalence return us to the world of "magic words"?) In a footnote, Scalia excoriated the plurality for attempting to reconcile its holding with *McConnell*. He believed that seven justices "agree that the opinion effectively overrules *McConnell* without saying so. This faux judicial restraint is judicial obfuscation."

Justice Souter dissented on behalf of the remaining four justices. He also argued that the principal opinion essentially overruled *McConnell*'s holding with respect to the constitutionality of § 203 without admitting that it was doing so. He also noted that, ironically, the new test for functional equivalence is very close to the back-up definition of electioneering communication that Congress had passed in case the Court had rejected § 203. The back-up definition had identified as electioneering communication an ad that is "suggestive of no plausible meaning other than an exhortation to vote for or against a specific candidate." Because *McConnell* sustained Congress' preferred wording, this back-up never went into effect.

Souter provided evidence that the broadcast ads in question could be appropriately regulated by Congress as electioneering communication. WRTL runs a PAC that has made independent expenditures in federal campaigns including in two previous elections involving Senator Feingold. Throughout the 2004 campaign, it had opposed Feingold's reelection, frequently objecting to his support for the filibuster of the judicial nominees. At the conclusion of these broadcast ads (financed not through the PAC but WRTL's general treasury funds), viewers were encouraged to go to a website that clearly attacked both Senators for their position on the filibuster (even though the ad itself did not reveal the Senators' position). Moreover, the timing of the ads was related more to the election than to the Senate vote. Chief Justice Roberts had dismissed these contextual considerations and concluded that "contextual factors of [this] sort * * * should seldom play a significant role in the inquiry." In sum, Souter believed that Roberts got the test for electioneering communication precisely backwards: "[I]f an ad is reasonably understood as going beyond a discussion of issues (that is, if it can be understood as electoral advocacy), then by definition it is not 'genuine' or 'pure' " and thus can be regulated by § 203.

Souter's conclusion reinforces the sense that *McConnell* and even *Buckley* may be fragile precedents. "But the understanding of the voters and the Congress that this kind of corporate and union spending seriously jeopardizes the integrity of democratic government will remain. The facts are too powerful to be ignored, and further efforts at campaign finance reform will come. It is only the legal landscape that now is altered, and it may be that today's departure from precedent will drive further reexamination of the constitutional analysis: of the distinction between contributions and expenditures, or the relation between spending and speech, which have given structure to our thinking since *Buckley* itself was decided."

C. STATE REFORMS AND PUBLIC FINANCING

The past two decades have witnessed significant state activity regarding campaign finance. In 1980, twenty-nine states placed no limits on individual contributions to candidates running for the state legislature; by 2005, only thirteen had failed to adopt some sort of regulation. Several states have adopted sweeping campaign finance reforms, often through ballot initiatives. *Randall v. Sorrell* is an example of comprehensive reform focused on stringent individual contribution limits, as low as $200 per candidate in some state races.

The Vermont case is unusual, however, because the Court struck down the stringent regulation. Only six years before, the Court had accepted Missouri's campaign finance law imposing contribution limits as low as $250 in some state races, although this cap was indexed for inflation and applied per election, rather than per election cycle. *Nixon v. Shrink Missouri Government PAC*, 528 U.S. 377 (2000). Some empirical studies suggest that the state reforms may fall victim to the hydraulic quality of political money. Evidence from Oregon, for example, indicates that after the people passed a measure imposing a cap of $100 for contributions in statewide races, independent expenditures increased sharply in the next election.[l]

The other innovative state reform, largely a result of ballot initiatives, is public financing. Consistent with the presidential system upheld in *Buckley*, state public financing systems are voluntary, providing public money to candidates who agree either not to accept any private money, see Me. Rev. Stat. Ann. tit. 21-A, § 1121 *et seq.*, or to abide by strict spending limits, see Vt. Stat. Ann. tit. 17, § 2853 *et seq.* In Maine, candidates qualify for public funds by raising seed money from voters making small contributions; this threshold ensures that recipients demonstrate a level of popular support. Under some state systems, qualifying candidates receive additional funds if their competitors do not participate in the system and substantially outspend the publicly financed candidate.[m]

Is public financing a good idea? Is it constitutional?[n] What theories of democratic governance justify such a system? Does it increase electoral competition (perhaps too much if fringe candidates are encouraged to run, thereby wasting public resources), or does it operate as an incumbent protection system (perhaps if public subsidies are stingy and challengers cannot overcome the name recognition and other advantages of incumbency)?[o]

---

l. See Elizabeth Newlin Carney, *Taking on the Fat Cats*, Nat'l J., Jan. 18, 1997, at 110. Oregon's stringent limits were struck down by the state supreme court in 1997. *Vannatta v. Keisling*, 931 P.2d 770, 773–74 (Or. 1997). See also David Schultz, *Money, Politics, and Campaign Finance Reform Law in the States* 20–21 (2002) (finding rise in soft money and independent expenditures in some states with restrictions on individual contributions).

m. See Elizabeth Daniel, *Subsidizing Political Campaigns: The Varieties and Values of Public Financing* (2000) (a report of the Brennan Center for Justice describing the various kinds of public financing). See also *Dollars and Democracy: A Blueprint for Campaign Finance Reform* (2000) (proposal by the New York City Bar Association's Commission on Campaign Finance Reform to adopt a partial system of public funding on the national level).

n. See *Daggett v. Comm'n on Governmental Ethics and Election Practices*, 205 F.3d 445 (1st Cir. 2000) (sustaining the Maine statute against constitutional attack). See also Jason Frasco, *Full Public Funding: An Effective and Legally Viable Model for Campaign Finance Reform in the States*, 92 Cornell L. Rev. 733 (2007) (student note) (describing laws and judicial challenges).

o. See Michael Malbin & Thomas Gais, *The Day After Reform: Sobering Campaign Finance Lessons from the American States* Chap. 7 (1998) (finding that public financing is not a significant factor in making elections more competitive; instead, successful challengers are those with access to substantial amounts of money). Compare Richard Briffault, *Public Funding and Democratic Elections*, 148 U. Pa. L. Rev. 563 (1999) (supporting public financing as

Voters who enact public financing or other campaign finance reform through direct democracy often discover that entrenched interests in the legislature work to thwart the popular will by refusing to pass implementing legislation. In Massachusetts, a Clean Elections Law passed by a large margin in 1996, but the state legislature refused to enact appropriations laws to make the public financing system operative. In 2002, the Supreme Court of Massachusetts held that the initiative required the legislature either to repeal the law or to appropriate money to provide public funding for candidates, even though the state constitution excludes specific appropriations laws from the initiative process. *Bates v. Director of Campaign and Political Finance*, 763 N.E.2d 6 (Mass. 2002). Because the legislature had not yet directly repealed the Clean Elections Law, the state was under an obligation to provide funding to candidates who qualified for public money. The state supreme court therefore awarded damages of $811,050 to the plaintiff, a candidate who claimed he was owed money under the Clean Elections Law. Moreover, the court granted broad discretionary authority to one of the justices to settle other claims by qualifying candidates and to ensure that the state paid the damages awarded. Justice Cowin, in dissent, believed judicial intervention inappropriate, arguing that "[t]he plaintiffs' remedy, as it always is with political questions, is at the ballot box. If the public is truly concerned about this issue, it will retaliate in the next election against those they hold to be responsible for frustrating the public will."

After the ruling, thirteen cars owned by the Lottery Commission were sold to raise $177,000, and the Speaker of the Massachusetts House was forced to go to court to prevent his love seat, desk, and office chairs from being auctioned. In June 2003, the legislature repealed the Clean Elections Law, inserting an amendment to abolish the law into the proposed budget, chief features of which were Medicaid reform and a prescription drug program. On June 30, 2003, Governor Mitt Romney signed the bill, completing the repeal of the Clean Elections Law.

The Clean Elections Law in Arizona was unsuccessfully challenged on the ground that a 10% surcharge levied on criminal and civil fines and used for the Clean Elections fund violated the First Amendment because the money could be used to finance campaigns of candidates opposed by the person paying the fine. The Arizona Supreme Court upheld the financing mechanism because the public funding system enlarges and facilitates political discussion rather than restricts it. Furthermore, the Court held that the law is viewpoint neutral because "the Clean Elections Act allocates money to all qualifying candidates, regardless of party, position, or message, * * * and thus the surcharge payers are not linked to any specific message, position, or viewpoint." *May v. McNally*, 55 P.3d 768, 772 (Ariz. 2002), *cert. denied*, 538 U.S. 923 (2003).

---

preventing corruption and serving equality values) with Bradley Smith, *Some Problems with Taxpayer-Funded Political Campaigns*, 148 U. Pa. L. Rev. 591 (1999) (arguing that public financing serves neither goal and would be futile given the prevalence of soft money and issue advocacy).

Even with opposition from entrenched politicians and others, public financing has gone into effect in a few states and appears to be having some influence on campaigns. In 2000 and 2002, Maine and Arizona held the nation's first elections under public financing systems. In the 2002 election, 59% of Maine's and 36% of Arizona's current legislators successfully ran as publicly financed candidates. In Arizona, publicly financed candidates won seven of the nine available statewide offices, including Governor. The General Accounting Office study that provided these figures, *Campaign Finance Reform: Early Experiences of Two States that Offer Full Public Funding for Political Candidates* (May 2003), concludes that there is insufficient data to determine whether public funding can be linked to electoral outcomes, competitiveness in elections, interest group influence, voter turnout, or levels of campaign spending. In part, the inability to draw conclusions stems from the fact that other changes in the electoral environment, including term limits and redistricting, also affected these races. The study noted that average candidate spending decreased in Maine with the adoption of public funding, but such spending increased in Arizona in both 2000 and 2002. Furthermore, independent expenditures increased significantly in both states, and publicly funded candidates as well as candidates who declined public money expressed the opinion that independent expenditures will play an increasingly significant role in the future.

Chapter 3

STRUCTURES OF
LEGISLATIVE DELIBERATION

Chapter 2 discussed different theories of representation. Hanna Pitkin in *The Concept of Representation* (1967) posits that representatives can be viewed in three different ways: as a microcosm of the larger electorate, as agents of the voters who elect them, or as trustees for the public interest. We have explored the implications each theory might have for thinking about elections and legislator accountability. In this chapter we consider the implications each theory might have for thinking about what the legislator is supposed to be doing once elected. You might also review the materials in Chapter 1, § 2, especially those that contrast pluralist theories of government, which generally view legislators as agents of popular majorities or of interest group coalitions, with republican theories, which generally view legislators as trustees deliberating for the public good.[a]

In connection with the legislative deliberations of representatives, agency theory suggests that the representative should mirror the views of her constituents, while trusteeship theory suggests that the representative use her judgment to advance the common good. Pitkin argues that the tension between these two views is largely a false one. First, a representative necessarily acts in a dual capacity most of the time: she is acting for her constituents, but on matters about which they have given little informed thought. It is a false dichotomy, second, because what the representative thinks is right and what the people want "normally * * * will coincide, and * * * when they fail to coincide there is a reason." The duty is to do what serves the "objective interest" of the people — so when the representative acts against the apparent desires of the constituents, she must be able to justify that action in terms of the long-range interests of society. Overall, Pitkin argues, representative government is most legitimate when it both promotes the public interest and responds to the people's desires over time.

---

a. See also William Eskridge, Jr., Philip Frickey & Elizabeth Garrett, *Legislation and Statutory Interpretation* chap. 2 (2d ed. 2006) (discussing theories of representation and applying them to examples); Dennis Thompson, *Political Ethics and Public Office* 99–105 (1987) (applying various models of representation to the problem of political corruption).

Pitkin's general position that representative government should be broadly responsive to, but not specifically directed by, private preferences is widely accepted. Her more specific position, that representative government should sometimes seek to further the "public interest" and transform private preferences, is appealing to a republican vision of government. It seems consistent with, and surely is inspired by, Madison's argument in *Federalist #10* that "the public voice, pronounced by the representatives of the people, will be more consonant to the public good than if pronounced by the people themselves, convened for the purpose." Nonetheless, the Madison-Pitkin position is subject to a pluralist critique. Much pluralist political theory questions whether there is such a thing as the "public interest" (separate from aggregated private interests). Even if there is a public interest, how can it reliably be determined? When Congressman Howard Smith (D–Va.) opposed the Civil Rights Act in 1963–64, most of his constituents probably agreed with him. Was his vote in the public interest of Virginia? In retrospect, we think it was not, because over time the principles of that statute have made Virginia a "better" place. (Is our value judgment objectively supportable?) We believe, therefore, that Smith was a poor and shortsighted representative. He might have responded that a vote for the bill would have killed his reelection chances, denying him the opportunity to work for other policies and depriving Virginians of a senior and powerful representative.[b]

Both pluralist (agency) and republican (trusteeship) theories of representation emphasize the importance of legislative deliberation, although they view the process differently. Pluralism requires representatives to aggregate the preferences of various interests and work out compromises to satisfy as many interests as possible and, perhaps also, to satisfy the most intense preferences of each relevant group. To do this, the representatives must deliberate, both with their constituents and supporting groups, and with their colleagues in the legislature. As we discussed in Chapter 1, deliberation may help to solve some of the pathologies of majority rule (like cycling), thereby allowing legislatures to reach rational and relatively stable outcomes. Consistent with republican theory, deliberation seeks out useful information and points of view that advance our collective understanding of common goals and that perhaps also transform the preferences of political citizens.

Both pluralist and republican theorists consider legislative deliberation illegitimate if it is corrupt. The theorists differ, however, in their view of what unacceptably warps the deliberative process, as we saw in the discussion of corruption and campaign finance reform in the previous chapter. Virtually everyone agrees that a deliberative process is corrupt if it is tainted by monetary bribes, physical coercion or threats, or other cheating by forces outside the legislature.[c] Section 1 of this chapter explores issues associated

---

b. Smith was defeated in the Democratic primary in 1966, notwithstanding his opposition to civil rights.

c. But see Susan Rose-Ackerman, *Corruption and Government: Causes, Consequences, and Reform* chap. 6 (1999) (assessing cultural factors in the perception of bribery, patronage, and gift-giving in the political realm).

with a relatively straightforward conception of corruption in the legislative process, especially as it relates to laws governing bribery, extortion, and conflicts of interest. As we will see, even uncontroversial notions of corruption become fuzzy when we move away from the obvious examples of bribery and extortion.

Section 2 turns to lobbying, which is a liberty interest expressly protected by the First Amendment, but also a possible source of corruption in the legislative process, at least according to republican theory. We provide the current legal regime regulating lobbying contacts, a regime that was substantially altered in 1995 when Congress adopted The Lobbying Disclosure Act, Pub. L. 104–65, 109 Stat. 691 (codified at 2 U.S.C. §§ 1601–1607). In 2007, the LDA was strengthened as part of a larger ethics reform effort in the wake of several corruption scandals involving members of Congress and lobbyists. The analytical issues include whether this law is constitutional under the First Amendment and whether it is justifiable under any theory of representation. We will also mention other approaches to regulation that impose more burdens on First Amendment rights and thus are more problematic constitutionally.

Finally, Section 3 sets forth some of the constitutional provisions that have long shaped legislative deliberation in the states and the federal government. We will focus on substantive rules designed to decrease interest group pressure on lawmakers and to impede legislative deal-making that often leads to omnibus legislation full of provisions that individually could garner only minority support. We will discuss the item vetoes provided to governors in most states and assess a federal law that purported to give the same kind of power to the President. This section also suggests some tensions between legislative immunities which are designed to preserve the independence of lawmakers and the efforts described in Section 1 to keep the legislative process free from bribery, extortion and other forms of obvious and unhealthy corruption.

SECTION 1. REGULATING "CORRUPT" DELIBERATION

The Anglo-American tradition has a rich history of regulating corrupt legislators through laws regulating behavior falling into such categories as bribery, extortion, and conflicts of interest — all of which have received considerable elaboration in recent years. What is properly prohibited under these categories? Consider the following conduct:

- Senator Doris Soaper agrees to support a bill exempting labor unions from certain tax liabilities, in return for a promise by union leaders in her state that they will support her reelection bid.

- Senator Soaper and her husband attend a lavish cruise on the Potomac, hosted by the AFL–CIO. Pending labor legislation is discussed over drinks and a lobster dinner. The next day, Senator Soaper votes for a bill exempting labor unions from certain tax liabilities.

- Senator Soaper's law firm represents labor unions in matters before the National Labor Relations Board and derives substantial revenue from that activity. Senator Soaper introduces and supports a bill to exempt labor unions from certain tax liabilities.

- Senator Soaper has established a legal defense fund to raise money to pay lawyers representing her in an investigation of her legislative activities related to the AFL-CIO's agenda. All the high-ranking officials of that union contribute $50,000 each to her fund, which is run by a group of her supporters.

Should any of this conduct be regulated? Prohibited?

This section will briefly consider these broad questions. We shall proceed in three parts: Part A will examine laws prohibiting bribery and accepting gratuities. Part B will examine federal law prohibiting extortion, including the obtaining of property under color of official right. Part C will analyze ethical codes adopted by some American legislatures, including Congress, to minimize the appearance of biased deliberations by elected representatives. As you read these materials, consider whether it makes sense as a policy matter or as a constitutional matter to regulate political conduct as extensively as we do. Glenn Parker argues that the most effective mechanism to constrain corrupt behavior is a lawmaker's interest in maintaining a reputation for ethical behavior because, at least in the House, it increases the length of the lawmaker's career and enhances his chance for attractive post-elective employment. *Self-Policing in Politics: The Political Economy of Reputational Controls on Politicians* (2004). How do ethics codes benefit lawmakers who want to establish a reputation for trustworthiness? Are reputational controls sufficient given the temptations of elective office? Consider also what might be done to make existing regulations more meaningful (we give nothing away by telling you now that most of them are believed to be inefficacious).

A. BRIBERY

Anti-bribery statutes might serve three different purposes: (1) to protect the integrity of the public servant's decisionmaking process, so that decisions are made to advance the public interest and not the decisionmaker's private agenda; (2) to avoid the appearance of unfairness and abuse of office; (3) to assure equal access of all citizens to the services of public servants.[a] For such reasons, the United States and all the states have anti-bribery laws.

The federal bribery statute, 18 U.S.C. § 201(b)–(c) (as amended through 1998), provides in part:

(b) Whoever —

---

a. See John Noonan, Jr., *Bribes* 704 (1984); Beth Nolan, *Public Interest, Private Income: Conflicts and Control Limits on the Outside Income of Government Officials*, 87 Nw. U.L. Rev. 57, 71–80 (1992).

(1) directly or indirectly, corruptly gives, offers or promises anything of value to any public official or person who has been selected to be a public official, or offers or promises any public official or any person who has been selected to be a public official to give anything of value to any other person or entity, with intent —

(A) to influence any official act; or

(B) to influence such public official or person who has been selected to be a public official to commit or aid in committing, or collude in, or allow, any fraud, * * * on the United States; or

(C) to induce such public official or such person who has been selected to be a public official to do or omit to do any act in violation of the lawful duty of such official or person;

(2) being a public official or person selected to be a public official, directly or indirectly, corruptly demands, seeks, receives, accepts, or agrees to receive or accept anything of value personally or for any other person or entity, in return for:

(A) being influenced in the performance of any official act;

(B) being influenced to commit or aid in committing, or to collude in, or allow, any fraud, or make opportunity for the commission of any fraud, on the United States; or

(C) being induced to do or omit to do any act in violation of the official duty of such official or person;

[(3) and (4) regulate inducements by or to public officials to influence testimony under oath or affirmation at trials or hearings];

shall be fined under this title or not more than three times the monetary equivalent of the thing of value, whichever is greater, or imprisoned for not more than fifteen years, or both, and may be disqualified from holding any office of honor, trust, or profit under the United States.

(c) Whoever —

(1) otherwise than as provided by law for the proper discharge of official duty —

(A) directly or indirectly, gives, offers, or promises anything of value to any public official, former public official, or person selected to be a public official, for or because of any official act performed or to be performed by such public official, former public official, or person selected to be a public official; or

(B) being a public official, former public official, or person selected to be a public official, otherwise than as provided by law for the proper discharge of official duty, directly or indirectly demands, seeks, receives, accepts, or agrees to receive or accept anything of value personally for or because of any official act performed or to be performed by such official or person;

[(2) and (3) regulate inducements by or to public officials to influence testimony under oath or affirmation at trials or hearings]

shall be fined under this title or imprisoned for not more than two years, or both.

"Public official" is defined in § 201(a)(1) as "Member of Congress, Delegate, or Resident Commissioner, either before or after such official has qualified, or an officer or employee or person acting for or on behalf of the United States, or any department, agency or branch of Government thereof, including the District of Columbia, in any official function, under or by authority of any such department, agency, or branch of Government, or a juror." Section 201(a)(3) defines "official act" as any "decision or action on any question, matter, cause, suit, proceeding or controversy, which may at any time be pending, or which may by law be brought before any public official, in such official's official capacity, or in such official's place of trust or profit."

This federal statute covers conduct that state statutes traditionally have divided into categories of "bribery" (§ 201(b)) and "unlawful gratuities" (§ 201(c)). Section 201(b) has been interpreted to impose requirements similar to those of most state bribery statutes, namely, that a public official (1) obtains anything of value (2) in return for performing an official act, committing fraud on the U.S., or violating a lawful duty, and (3) the defendant public official or private person acted with "corrupt intent." The last element is the primary distinction between bribery and unlawful gratuity offenses. Payments to a public official for acts that would have occurred in any event are in most circumstances probably unlawful gratuities and not bribes. See *United States v. Campbell*, 684 F.2d 141 (D.C. Cir. 1982). Another difference between bribery and unlawful gratuity offenses is that the latter cover only "official acts," whereas the bribery provisions have a broader scope including "the violation of the lawful duty" of the official. See *Valdes v. United States*, 475 F.3d 1319 (D.C. Cir. 2007) (*en banc*) (explaining difference in scope as a "balance" because bribery requires that payment actually influence the action, but unlawful gratuities do not require such a narrow "compensatory link").

Section 201 and analogous state laws are phrased generally and might be interpreted to reach far beyond the prototype of bribery (the selling of one's legislative influence for money or a valuable thing). How far should these statutes reach? Should they include Senator Soaper's agreement to support a bill exempting labor unions from certain tax liabilities, in return for a promise by union leaders in her state that they will support her reelection bid? Should they cover campaign contributions to the Senator's campaign, based upon the mutual expectation that Soaper will continue to support labor legislation?

Daniel Lowenstein, *Political Bribery and the Intermediate Theory of Politics*, 32 UCLA L. Rev. 784 (1985), argues that the answers to these questions typically depend upon one's definition of "corrupt intent," which in turn depends upon one's theory of politics. If you view a legislative representative as a trustee for the public good, as Pitkin does, you might be inclined to criminalize campaign contributions that carry a commitment by the legislator to vote in specified ways on future issues. On the other hand, if you view the legislator as nothing more than an agent for popular desires, you might want to limit bribery prosecutions to those cases where the representative benefits personally (she fattens her bank account or acquires a new yacht). You might not want to prosecute in those cases where the representative is merely making political tradeoffs resulting in legislation that, on balance, serves the interests of her constituents. Obviously, most cases fall somewhere along the spectrum between clearly legitimate arrangements and patently corrupt deals — but where?

In light of this background, consider the following case, notes, and problem.

PEOPLE EX REL. DICKINSON v. VAN DE CARR
Supreme Court of New York, Appellate Division, First Department, 1903
87 App. Div. 386, 84 N.Y.S. 461

LAUGHLIN, J.

The relator is an alderman of the city of New York. He has been held to bail, and to appear at the Court of General Sessions, upon a charge of violating section 72 of the Penal Code, which relates to bribery, by Justice Wyatt, of the Court of Special Sessions, sitting as magistrate. The warden returned the commitment of the magistrate under which he held the relator. It is in due form, and appears to be valid. The relator traversed the return, claiming that the evidence upon which commitment was based does not show that any crime has been committed; and he annexed to his traverse the exhibits and testimony, which were conceded to be correct. The testimony showed that John McGaw Woodbury, the commissioner of street cleaning of the city of New York, wrote a letter to the relator on the 23d day of September, 1902, saying:

> "In reply to your letter of September 20th, I would say that the Department is so short of horses, particularly in the Borough of Brooklyn, that we have been very strict with the drivers during the warm weather to prevent any possibility of over-heating or damaging the stock. We are many behind our complement. Should, however, the Honorable Board grant me the moneys for new stock and plant, this would give employment to more drivers, and as the heavy season comes on, having made a note of your favorable recommendation, the case of Covino will be reconsidered."

— That on the 30th day of the same month the relator wrote and mailed a letter to Commissioner Woodbury in reply, saying:

> "If you will reinstate Antonio Covino, who I think was too severely punished by being dismissed from your Department, I will vote and otherwise help you to obtain the money needed for a new plant in Brooklyn."

And at this time there was pending in the board of aldermen a bill to authorize an issue of corporate stock "for new stock or plant for the department of street cleaning, Borough of Brooklyn."

There is no question but that the magistrate has jurisdiction to inquire into a violation of section 72 of the Penal Code, and thereafter, upon proper proof, to hold a person to answer for the crime. The relator has not been convicted. He has been merely held to answer. We are therefore not concerned with the weight of evidence. Our inquiry is limited to whether there was any evidence tending to show his guilt. This is the single question presented by the appeal. Section 72 of the Penal Code provides as follows:

> "Officer Accepting Bribe. A judicial officer, a person who executes any of the functions of a judicial office not designated in titles VI and VII of this Code, or a person employed by or acting for the state, or for any public officer in the business of

the state, who asks, receives, or agrees to receive a bribe, or any money, property, or value of any kind, or any promise or agreement therefor, upon any agreement or understanding that his vote, opinion, judgment, action, decision, judgment or any other official proceeding, shall be influenced thereby, or that he will do or omit any act or proceeding, or in any way neglect or violate any official duty, is punishable by imprisonment for not more than ten years, or by a fine of not more than five thousand dollars, or both. A conviction also forfeits any office held by the offender, and forever disqualifies him from holding any public office under the state."

It will be observed that the clause, "asks, receives or agrees to receive a bribe, or any money, property, or value of any kind, or any promise or agreement therefor," is disjunctive. It first specifically includes certain officers who ask, receive, or agree to receive a bribe. In the absence of any statute defining a bribe, we must have recourse to the decisions and text-writers to determine what was embraced in that term at common law. Bribery was an indictable offense at common law, and, although in the early days it was limited to judicial officers and those engaged in the administration of justice, it was later extended to all public officers. It was variously defined as taking or offering an "undue reward" or a "reward" to influence official action. Bribery is defined in 4 Am. & Eng. Enc. of Law, p. 908, to be "the giving, offering, or receiving of anything of value, or any valuable service, intended to influence one in the discharge of legal duty." The cases of bribery that have been before the courts of this state, so far as brought to our attention, have related to the offering or giving of property or something of intrinsic value. The relator claims that, as no money or property was asked or agreed to be received by him to influence the official action of the street commissioner, he has not violated this statute. In view of the circumstances disclosed, his letter is open to the inference that he desired to obtain a political or other personal advantage from or by securing Covino's reinstatement in the public service, and that he took advantage of the known desire on the part of the street commissioner to obtain this appropriation of public moneys to improperly influence the action of the street commissioner on the application of Covino for reinstatement, by offering, in case that were done, to vote for and further the desired appropriation, and impliedly threatening in case of refusal to withhold his support therefrom. The interests of the public service require that public officers shall act honestly and fairly upon propositions laid before them for consideration, and shall neither be influenced by, nor receive pecuniary benefit from, their official acts, or enter into bargains with their fellow legislators or officers or with others for the giving or withholding of their votes, conditioned upon their receiving any valuable favor, political or otherwise, for themselves or for others. It was the duty of the relator to act fairly and honestly and according to his judgment upon the proposition of the street commissioner. It does not appear to have been the mandatory duty of the board of aldermen to favor the recommendation of Commissioner Woodbury. In these circumstances, it was the duty of the relator to favor or oppose the recommendation according to its merits or demerits. If, in his judgment, it should have been disapproved, he should have opposed it, and he should not bargain to vote for it upon obtaining an agreement from the street commissioner to reinstate Covino. It is quite as demoralizing to the public service, and as much against the spirit and intent of the statute, for a legislator or other public official to bargain to sell his vote or official action for a political or other favor or reward as for money. Either is a bribe, and they only differ in degree. Nor should he, by holding out this inducement, have tempted the commissioner to act favorably upon Covino's application for reinstatement. This was undue influence, and would be detrimental to the public service. In addition to the word "bribe" in this section of the Code, other words are employed sufficiently broad to reach this case. It is a violation of the statute for a public officer to ask, receive, or agree to receive "property or value of any kind, or any promise or agreement therefor," upon any agreement or understanding that his vote or official action shall be influenced thereby. It is clear that words "value of any kind," as here used, are more comprehensive than "property." The benefit which the relator expected to receive from the reinstatement of his constituent would, we think, be embraced in the meaning of this clause, and would also constitute a bribe. We are therefore of the opinion that the facts tend to show that the relator has offended against the provisions of section 72 of the Penal Code, and that he was properly held to answer upon the charge.

It follows that the order should be affirmed. All concur.

NOTES ON BRIBERY PROSECUTIONS AND THEORIES OF REPRESENTATION

1. *Is this Prosecution Supportable by any Theory?* Wisconsin explicitly prohibits logrolling by legislators in a statute that dates back to the Progressive Era. Section 13.05 makes it a felony for a legislator to give, offer or promise his vote on a bill "in consideration or upon condition that any other person elected to the same legislature will give or will promise or agree to give his or her vote or influence in favor of or against any other measure or proposition" in the legislature. Similarly, a lawmaker cannot promise to vote in a particular way on a bill in return for a promise by the governor to sign, veto or line item veto any other legislation. Wisc. Stat, § 13.06. Wisconsin statutes further specify that these provisions shall not "be construed as prohibiting free discussion and deliberation upon any question pending before the legislature by members thereof, privately or publicly, nor as prohibiting agreements by members to support any single measure pending, on condition that certain changes be made in such measure, nor as prohibiting agreements to compromise conflicting provisions of different measures." Wisc. Stat, § 13.07.

Consider *Van de Carr* and the Wisconsin statutes in light of the different theories of representation developed in this and the preceding chapter. They might be consistent with a theory that considers the representative to be a trustee for the people, using her independent judgment to figure out what is best for the people. But even under a republican or trusteeship approach, shouldn't the representative be able to make deals with other officials, to ensure that her constituents receive needed services? Would *Van de Carr* and Wisconsin law outlaw most forms of cooperative behavior to construct majority support for bills? Does the rationale of *Van de Carr* criminalize any voting or legislative action for strategic reasons and require that the representative always sincerely believe in the merits of the positions she takes? Can a legislature effectively work under such constraints?   See also Dennis Thompson, *Ethics in Congress: From Individual to Institutional Corruption* (1995) (arguing that a concern of modern ethics rules should be institutional corruption, where the gains are political rather than personal, the service offered by the lawmaker is procedurally improper, and the connection between gain and service damages either the legislature or the democratic process).

2. *The Sweep of* Van de Carr. This case may be a product of its times. It was written during a period in New York politics where reformers in and out of government were working to eliminate rampant corruption and to break the power of party bosses.   Leaders like Theodore Roosevelt came to national attention because of their efforts to clean up the sewers of local politics. Thus, Judge Laughlin may well have known about aspects of this case which made the political deal more dubious than it appears from the facts he gives, or he may have been a reform-minded judge hoping his opinion would get the attention of graft-addicted politicos.[b]

If the *Van de Carr* facts had occurred in the District of Columbia today, would § 201 apply? Recall that § 201(b) and (c) use the same "anything of value" language that the New York bribery statute did, and that most bribery laws use. Would knowing the background of § 201 help you answer the question? If yes, read on.

Section 201 was enacted in 1962, Pub. L. No. 87–849, 76 Stat. 1119, and was revised in 1986, Pub. L. No. 99–646, § 46(1), 100 Stat. 779. The 1962 law replaced a section that had remained unchanged since its original enactment in 1862. Ch. 180, 12 Stat. 577. See Rev. Stat. § 1781; 18 U.S.C. § 205 (1958 ed.). The debates on the 1862 Act reveal no discussion of the precise issue. See, e.g., Cong. Globe, 37th Cong., 2d Sess. 3260 (1862). As explained in the House Report accompanying the 1962 Act, the purpose of the Act was "to render uniform the law describing a bribe and prescribing the intent or purpose which makes its transfer unlawful." H. R. Rep. No. 748, 87th Cong., 1st Sess. 15 (1961). The Senate Report expanded the explanation and said that a purpose of the Act was the "substitution of a single comprehensive section of the Criminal Code for a number of existing statutes concerned with bribery. This consolidation would make no significant changes of substance and, more particularly, would not restrict the broad scope of the present bribery statutes as construed by the courts." S. Rep. No. 2213, 87th Cong., 2d Sess., 4 (1962), reprinted in 1962 U.S. Code Cong. & Admin. News 3852, 3853. Is any of this relevant?

3. *The Connection between an Unlawful Gratuity and the Official's Position.* The Supreme Court construed the unlawful gratuities portion of § 201 in a case that grew out of an independent prosecutor's investigation of President Bill Clinton's Secretary of Agriculture Mike Espy. *United States v. Sun-Diamond Growers of California*, 526 U.S. 398 (1999). Sun-Diamond

---

b. For discussion of this era in New York and reform efforts, see Louis Eisenstein & Elliot Rosenberg, *A Stripe of Tammany's Tiger* (1966); Jerome Mushkat, *Tammany: The Evolution of a Political Machine, 1789–1865* (1971).

Growers was a trade association for businesses that grew raisins, figs, walnuts, prunes and hazelnuts. The independent prosecutor alleged that the association had given Espy tickets to the U.S. Open, luggage, meals and a crystal bowl, which had a total value of less than $6,000. The trade organization had several matters before the Secretary. For example, it wanted to be designated as a representative of "small-sized entities" so that it would continue to receive federal funds for overseas marketing plans for its members' commodities. It also wanted the Department of Agriculture to oppose plans by the Environmental Protection Agency to ban a particular kind of pesticide. The indictment of Sun-Diamond Growers described these matters, but it did not allege a direct nexus between them and the gratuities conferred on Espy. The Government argued that it need not show a link to a particular official act, but only that the gratuity was motivated more generally by "the recipient's capacity to exercise governmental power or influence in the donor's favor." Justice Scalia's opinion for the Court rejected that interpretation, arguing that § 201(c)(1)(A)'s explicit provision that the gift be made "for or because of any official act" requires that some official act be identified and proved. Thus, the unlawful gratuity statute does not criminalize gifts given merely because the recipient holds a powerful office; instead, laws and ethics rules prohibiting or limiting gift giving to officials are designed to cover such situations. Scalia's opinion underscores the relationship among the laws regulating corruption: "[T]his regulation, and the numerous other regulations and statutes littering this field, demonstrate that this is an area where precisely targeted prohibitions are commonplace, and where more general prohibitions have been qualified by numerous exceptions. Given that reality, a statute in this field that can linguistically be interpreted to be either a meat axe or a scalpel should reasonably be taken to be the latter."

A Bribery Problem

Problem 3–1. Robert McCormick is a member of the West Virginia House of Delegates in 1984, representing a district with a severe shortage of doctors. McCormick supports a state program that allows nonlicensed doctors, often from overseas, to practice in the state. During his campaign for reelection in 1984, McCormick informs the lobbyist for the foreign doctors association that his campaign is short of money and "we haven't heard anything from your association this year." The lobbyist gives McCormick $2,000 in cash, which McCormick pockets. McCormick wins reelection and subsequently sponsors legislation permitting experienced doctors to be licensed in West Virginia without passing the state licensing exams. Two weeks after the bill is enacted, McCormick receives more cash from the foreign doctors association. Consider the following. Decide your answer to each question before moving on to the next:

(a) Can McCormick be convicted of violating 18 U.S.C. § 201?

(b) Can McCormick be convicted of violating a West Virginia analogue to § 201?

(c) Would your answer to (a) or (b) change if McCormick had not pocketed the money but, instead, treated it as a campaign contribution reported under state law?

B. EXTORTION

Another type of public crime is *extortion*, which at common law consisted of a public official's use of official position to exact money or other benefits from private persons. 4 William Blackstone, *Commentaries* 141, defined extortion as "an abuse of public justice, which consists in an officer's unlawfully taking, by colour of his office, from any one, any money or thing of value, that is not due to him, or more than is due, or before it is due." Common law extortion was, apparently, very similar to modern bribery.[c] Why have two crimes that overlap so much?

The federal Hobbs Act, 18 U.S.C. § 1951, criminalizes extortion:

(a) Whoever in any way or degree obstructs, delays, or affects commerce or the movement of any article or commodity in commerce, by robbery or extortion or attempts or conspires so to do, or commits or threatens physical violence to any person or property in furtherance of a plan or purpose to do anything in violation of this section shall be fined under this title or imprisoned not more than twenty years, or both.

(b) As used in this section — * * *

(2) The term "extortion" means the obtaining of property from another, with his consent, induced by wrongful use of actual or threatened force, violence, or fear, or under color of official right.

Note that, unlike § 201, which criminalizes bribery and unlawful gratuities by federal "public officials," the federal Hobbs Act might apply to official misconduct at either the federal or state level.[d]

Would the Hobbs Act cover the conduct of McCormick described in Problem 3-1? A line of lower court cases decided in the 1970s and 1980s held that the Hobbs Act can be applied to public officials who receive a stream of benefits from people under their jurisdiction.[e] But the Supreme Court interpreted the Hobbs Act to require a "quid pro quo" by a public official who receives money from someone under his jurisdiction; a politician cannot be

---

c. See James Lindgren, *The Elusive Distinction Between Bribery and Extortion: From the Common Law to the Hobbs Act*, 35 UCLA L. Rev. 815 (1988).

d. There are a number of other federal criminal statutes which might be used against official legislative misconduct at either the federal or state level, including the Travel Act, 18 U.S.C. § 1952; the mail fraud statute, *id.* § 1341; and the wire fraud statute, *id.* § 1343. See Chapter 8, § 1B1 (rule of lenity case involving application of mail fraud statute to state officials and political bosses).

e. See Herbert Stern, *Prosecutions of Local Political Corruption Under the Hobbs Act: The Unnecessary Distinction Between Bribery and Extortion*, 3 Seton Hall L. Rev. 1 (1971) (important article by former U.S. Attorney for New Jersey, who pressed for this use of the Hobbs Act).

convicted of Hobbs Act extortion unless there is an explicit exchange of money for an official act. *McCormick v. United States*, 500 U.S. 257 (1991); see also *Evans v. United States*, 504 U.S. 255 (1992).[f]

C. CONFLICTS OF INTEREST

The criminal sanctions found in laws prohibiting bribery, unlawful gratuities, and extortion have inspired less than complete confidence in politicians and the government in the wake of Watergate; ethics scandals that dogged the Clinton administration; the successful prosecution of lobbyist Jack Abramoff for influence-peddling, including bribing Rep. Bob Ney (R–Ohio); the resignation of House Majority Leader Tom DeLay (R–Tex.) in 2006 amid allegations of corruption; and other infamous episodes. As a result of this enhanced concern for at least the appearance of integrity, both state and federal legislatures have enacted statutes or adopted new procedural rules to get at problems that we shall lump together as *conflicts of interest*, namely, any financial incentive the legislator might have that would affect her deliberations. As you review the various prescriptions and proscriptions, ask: Do the rules address important conflicts which would impair members' judgment or their ability to deliberate about the public good? Do the rules go further than necessary? Which rules could be most usefully pruned?

The responses to the overall problem of conflicted interest have been twofold: the disinfectant of full disclosure of financial interests and the adoption of prophylactic rules to prevent even the potential for certain types of financial incentives to slant public deliberations. At the national level, Title I of the Ethics in Government Act of 1978, Pub. L. No. 95–521, 92 Stat. 1824 (codified as amended at 5 U.S.C. App. § 101 (2000 & Supp. 2004)), sets forth comprehensive "Financial Disclosure Requirements of Federal Personnel." The requirements apply to Congressmembers, designated officers and employees of the legislative branch, and candidates seeking to become Congressmembers (§ 101(c)). Members of Congress, as well as the designated officers and employees, must file on or before May 15 of each year "full and complete statements" of income, gifts, honoraria, interest in property, liabilities owed to creditors, sales or exchanges of property or stocks, officership on corporate boards, and so forth (§ 102(a)).[g]

---

f. For helpful discussions, see Steven Yarbrough, *The Hobbs Act in the Nineties: Confusion or Clarification of the Quid Pro Quo Standard in Extortion Cases Involving Public Officials*, 31 Tulsa L.J. 781 (1996); Meredith Lee Hager, Note, *The Hobbs Act: Maintaining the Distinction between a Gift and a Bribe*, 83 Ky. L.J. 197 (1995).

g. Candidates seeking to become members of Congress must file a similar report (with fewer disclosures) within 30 days of becoming a candidate or by May 15 of that year (whichever is later) and in every successive year until the election (§§ 101(d), 102(b)). The reports filed pursuant to the Act must include similar information for the spouse and dependent children of the regulated individual (§ 102(e)). An exception from the reporting requirements is created in the Act for holdings of or the source of income from any holdings in "qualified blind trusts" and trusts not created by the regulated individual or the individual's spouse or dependent child (§ 102(f)). "Political campaign funds, including campaign receipts and expenditures, need not be included in any report filed pursuant to this title" (§ 102(g)).

In addition to these disclosure requirements are the various substantive prophylactic rules that have been adopted by Congress to head off even potential conflicts of interest. The relevant provisions are a rich array of statutory and legislative rules, which the following exposition introduces by describing the main regulatory developments. The rules governing members of Congress regulate the following:

1. *Gifts are severely limited.* The Ethics Reform Act of 1989, Pub. L. 101–194, 103 Stat. 1716, substantially amended federal law pertaining to gifts, bribes, honoraria, and other activities presenting potential conflicts of interest. In particular, it prohibits members of Congress from seeking or accepting "anything of value" from any person "whose interests may be substantially affected by the performance or nonperformance of the individual's official duties." 5 U.S.C. § 7353(a). The ethics offices of the House and Senate are empowered to devise reasonable exemptions to this rule. *Id.* § 7353 (b). Senate Rule XXXV and House Rule XXV, clause 5, set forth the gift rules of the respective chambers, which add further limitations on the receipt of gifts by members. These rules were substantially strengthened in 2007, largely as a response to corruption scandals involving high-profile lawmakers.

No member, employee, or officer of the House of Representatives or the Senate may accept gifts or meals from lobbyists unless they fit into certain exceptions, such as food, other than a meal that is served at a reception (sometimes called "the toothpick rule") or at a "widely attended" event on a particular issue that attracts many people other than just congressional aides. Furthermore, both chambers have adopted stringent restrictions on the kinds of travel for which members and their staff can be reimbursed by private parties. Because Congress has now prohibited much of the travel, entertainment and gifts previously allowed, the major arena excepted from regulation through ethics rules — campaign fundraisers in Washington and a lawmaker's state or district — will become increasingly important venues for lobbyists to interact with legislators and their aides. In the past, congressional gift and travel rules were regularly evaded as lawmakers took advantage of loopholes; it remains to be seen whether more stringent rules will allow similar circumvention.

One major change in the congressional gift rules occurred in 2007 when Congress amended the Lobbying Disclosure Act to require that lobbyists certify twice a year that no one covered in their disclosure filings (which may include other employees of the firm who engage in lobbying activities) has provided gifts or offered travel to senators or representatives that would violate the rules. Section 203 of the Honest Leadership and Open Government Act of 2007, Pub. L. No. 110–81, 121 Stat. 735 (2007). Violations of this provision can be punished by up to $200,000 in fines and, for knowing and corrupt

---

See also Thomas Little & David Ogle, *The Legislative Branch of State Government* (2006) (providing overview of ethics and conflict of interest rules (pp. 113–14) and state-by-state descriptions); Alan Rosenthal, *The Decline of Representative Democracy: Process, Participation, and Power in State Legislatures* 94–100 (1998) (detailing ethics laws and codes in various states).

violations, up to five years in prison. Before this, House and Senate rules could only be enforced against members and staff, although gifts that were part of a scheme to bribe legislators could always form the basis of a criminal prosecution.

2. *Outside earned income is limited.* The Ethics Reform Act, as amended in 1990, provides that Congressmembers can have "outside earned income" no greater than 15% of level II of the executive pay schedule under 5 U.S.C. § 5313 for each calendar year. 5 U.S.C. App. § 501(a)(1) (2000). Members may not serve in firms providing professional services with a fiduciary duty, receive compensation for practicing such a profession, serve on corporate boards of directors, or be paid for teaching (without the consent of the ethics body). *Id.* § 502(a).

3. *Post-employment lobbying is restricted.* The number of former members who become highly compensated lobbyists continues to rankle the public,[h] and there have been calls for reform to address the *revolving door* between government service and lobbying. As revised by the Ethics Reform Act, 18 U.S.C. § 207(e)(1) prohibits members of the House of Representatives, within a year of leaving office, from lobbying current members or employees of either House. The Honest Leadership and Open Government Act of 2007 extended the ban on lobbying that applies to former senators to two years. Unlike some of the other prohibitions, this one is found in the Criminal Code and is enforceable through criminal sanctions. Opponents of longer waiting periods argue that they make public service less attractive. It is too much, they contend, to ask that public servants not only forego large salaries while they work for Congress or the executive branch but then also to expect them to refrain from using their expertise and skills for a substantial time after they leave government. Lawmakers also enjoy perks that provide them special access to current legislators, including the use of the members' dining rooms and floor privileges. In the ethics reform bill that Congress enacted in 2007, these privileges were curtailed or eliminated for lawmakers-turned-lobbyists. For example, the Senate denied floor privileges, special parking spaces, and access to the Senate athletic facilities to former members who are now registered lobbyists. Senate Rule XXIII.

4. *No activity inconsistent with representational duties can be conducted.* Senate Rule XXXVII(2) provides: "No Member * * * shall engage in any outside business or professional activity or employment for compensation which is inconsistent or in conflict with the conscientious performance of official duties." House Rule XXV(2) provides: "A Member * * * may not receive compensation for affiliating with or being employed by a firm, partnership, association, corporation, or other entity that provides professional services involving a fiduciary relationship except for the practice of medicine." These rules go beyond the statutory requirements and are enforceable by the

---

h. See, e.g., Susan Crabtree, *Public Servants or Profiteers?*, Insight Mag., Oct. 30, 1995, at 8; Alan Ota, *Top-Tier Lobbyists: Ex-Members' Special Access Becomes an Issue*, CQ Weekly, Feb. 16, 2002, at 455 (including list of 149 former members of Congress who have registered as lobbyists).

chambers themselves. Unlike the House, the Senate does not have an exception to the rule that would allow senators to practice medicine while in office. As a Congressman, Senator Coburn (R–Okla.) continued his obstetrics practice on a nonprofit basis, but upon his election to the Senate, the Senate Ethics Committee declined to create a similar exception, and he is officially prohibited from practicing medicine.

5. *Honoraria are banned.* The Ethics Reform Act of 1989, as amended at 5 U.S.C. App. §§ 501, 505, prohibits members of Congress from receiving honoraria. The scope of this law was the subject of the following case:

UNITED STATES v. NATIONAL TREASURY EMPLOYEES UNION, 513 U.S. 454 (1995). The honoraria ban applied not only to members of Congress and top-level executive branch officials; it also broadly prohibited federal employees from accepting any compensation for making speeches or writing articles. This class action brought on behalf of executive branch employees below grade GS-16 (employees with salaries between $11,903 and $86,589, with a mean salary between $28,000 and $36,000) challenged the prohibition on First Amendment grounds. A mail handler employed by the Postal Service in Arlington, Virginia, had given lectures on the Quaker religion for which he received small payments that were "not much, but enough to supplement my income in a way that makes a difference." An aerospace engineer employed at the Goddard Space Flight Center in Greenbelt, Maryland, had lectured on black history for a fee of $100 per lecture. A microbiologist at the Food and Drug Administration had earned almost $3,000 per year writing articles and making radio and television appearances reviewing dance performances. A tax examiner employed by the Internal Revenue Service in Ogden, Utah, had received comparable pay for articles about the environment. The Act defined "honorarium" to mean "a payment of money or any thing of value for an appearance, speech or article (including a series of appearances, speeches, or articles if the subject matter is directly related to the individual's status with the Government)." Thus, the ban applied even without a nexus between the employee's work for the government and her speech, article or appearance. The text of the statute added the nexus requirement only in relation to a series of activities. Accordingly, all the individual plaintiffs had violated the Ethics in Government law.

Justice Stevens, writing for the majority, held that the law as applied to the class of lower-level federal employees was unconstitutional. Although the Court's jurisprudence allows Congress to impose restraints on the job-related speech of public employees that would be unconstitutional if applied to the public at large, see *Pickering v. Board of Educ.*, 391 U.S. 563 (1968), the government does not have unfettered discretion. The Court balances the interests of the employee in commenting on matters of public concern with the interests of the state, as an employer, in promoting efficiency of the public services it performs. Stevens noted that the broad sweep of the law worked a substantial burden on the expressive rights of federal employees. Several of the federal workers testified that the inability to receive compensation for their activities meant that they would no longer engage in them.

The Government's interest was "that federal officers not misuse or appear to misuse power by accepting compensation for their unofficial and nonpolitical writing and speaking activities." Stevens acknowledged that this interest is a powerful one, but he noted that there was no evidence that employees below grade GS-16 were engaged in this sort of misconduct. Indeed, the report of a special Commission on Executive, Legislative and Judicial Salaries that was the catalyst for the enactment of the law talked only about the honoraria practices of top government officials. The law that enacted the ban did so in part as a tradeoff for higher salaries for members of Congress, federal judges and executive branch employees above the GS-15 level. "[T]he Government has based its defense of the ban on abuses of honoraria by members of Congress. Congress reasonably could assume that payments of honoraria to judges or high-ranking officials in the Executive Branch might generate a similar appearance of improper influence. Congress could not, however, reasonably extend that assumption to all federal employees below Grade GS-16, an immense class of workers with negligible power to confer favors on those who might pay to hear them speak or to read their articles. A federal employee, such as a supervisor of mechanics at the mint, might impair efficiency and morale by using political criteria to judge the performance of his or her staff. But one can envision scant harm, or appearance of harm, resulting from the same employee's accepting pay to lecture on the Quaker religion or to write dance reviews."

Stevens also rejected the Government's argument that a wholesale prophylactic rule, rather than a rule that banned only activities with a nexus to the employee's work for the government, was justified on ease of administration grounds. "The nexus limitation for series, however, unambiguously reflects a congressional judgment that agency ethics officials and the [Office of Government Ethics] can enforce the statute when it includes a nexus test. A blanket burden on the speech of nearly 1.7 million federal employees requires a much stronger justification than the Government's dubious claim of administrative convenience."

Justice O'Connor agreed that the law violated the First Amendment, but she proposed remedying the violation by interpreting the statute to require a nexus not only for a series of speeches but also for single appearances. She argued that the statute could be easily fixed by moving the end of the parentheses forward several words in the definition of "honorarium." The majority rejected this approach. "We cannot be sure that our attempt to redraft the statute to limit its coverage to cases involving an undesirable nexus between the speaker's official duties and either the subject matter of the speaker's expression or the identity of the payor would correctly identify the nexus Congress would have adopted in a more limited honoraria ban. We cannot know whether Congress accurately reflected its sense of an appropriate nexus in the terse, 33-word parenthetical statement with which it exempted series of speeches and articles from the definition of honoraria in the 1992 amendment; in an elaborate, nearly 600-word provision with which it later exempted Department of Defense military school faculty and students from the ban; or in neither."

Finally, **Chief Justice Rehnquist** dissented. "The Court concedes that in light of the abuses of honoraria by its Members, Congress could reasonably assume that 'payments of honoraria to judges or high-ranking officials in the Executive Branch might generate a similar appearance of improper influence,' but it concludes that Congress could not extend this presumption to federal employees below grade GS-16. The theory underlying the Court's distinction — that federal employees below grade GS-16 have negligible power to confer favors on those who might pay to hear them speak or to read their articles — is seriously flawed. Tax examiners, bank examiners, enforcement officials, or any number of federal employees have substantial power to confer favors even though their compensation level is below Grade GS-16."

The honoraria ban for higher-level executive branch officials, members of Congress and federal judges is controversial.[i] In the Fiscal Year 2001 appropriations process, Senator McConnell (R-Ky.) inserted a provision into the appropriations bill for the Justice Department lifting the ban as it applies to federal judges. Following the advice of Chief Justice Rehnquist, he argued that federal judges now make less than first-year associates in major law firms so that more liberal rules for outside income are necessary to attract the best lawyers to the federal bench. The provision would have also required the Judicial Conference to promulgate regulations to avoid conflicts and impropriety before the ban was lifted. After the proposal received substantial negative publicity, the appropriations rider was dropped and not enacted.

Conflict of Interest Problems

Problem 3–2. Consider the following findings of the Senate Ethics Committee: From April 1987 to April 1989, Senator Alan Cranston (D–Cal.) personally or through his staff contacted the Federal Home Loan Bank Board on behalf of Lincoln Savings & Loan, during a period when Cranston was soliciting and accepting large campaign contributions from Charles Keating, who ran Lincoln. On at least four occasions, these contacts were made in close connection with the solicitation or receipt of contributions. For example, in January 1988 Keating offered to make an additional contribution and also asked Cranston to set up a meeting for him with Danny Wall, the Chair of the FHLBB. Cranston did so on January 20; Wall and Keating met eight days later. On February 10, Cranston personally collected checks from Keating for $500,000 for voter registration groups. (If not reported, does this violate federal campaign finance law, as described in Chapter 2, § 3?)

Joy Jacobson, Cranston's chief fundraiser and not a member of his Senate staff, sometimes solicited contributions from Keating for Cranston. She repeatedly scheduled meetings between the Senator and contributors (espe-

---

i. See also George Brown, *Putting Watergate Behind Us* — Salinas, Sun-Diamond, *and Two Views of the Anticorruption Model*, 74 Tul. L. Rev. 747 (2000) (analyzing the honoraria case as well as others discussed previously to discern Supreme Court's view of corruption); Daniel Koffsky, *Coming to Terms with Bureaucratic Ethics*, 11 J.L. & Pol. 235 (1995) (discussing ethics bureaucracies established to deal with conflict of interest problems and how consultation with these entities affects the judicial approach).

cially Keating) where regulatory issues were discussed. She was often the intermediary whom Keating or his assistant called when they could not reach the Senator or his legislative aides. Jacobson wrote memoranda to the Senator indicating her belief that contributors were entitled to special attention and special services. Cranston never told her that this was incorrect.

Lincoln went bankrupt; cleaning up the insolvent thrift cost taxpayers around $2 billion. The committee found no evidence that Cranston's interventions directly contributed to regulatory lapses that cost the taxpayers this money. Has Cranston behaved "unethically," in your view? Has he violated any of the laws or rules noted above? See Dennis Thompson, *Mediated Corruption: The Case of the Keating Five*, 87 Am. Pol. Sci. Rev. 369 (1993) (arguing that this case is an example of "mediated corruption" which is the use of public office for private purposes in a way that subverts the democratic process; the public official's contribution to "the corruption is filtered through various practices that are otherwise legitimate and may even be duties of office. As a result, both the official and citizens are less likely to recognize that the official has done anything wrong.").[j]

Problem 3–3. Jack Abramoff was a registered lobbyist whose clients included numerous Indian tribes and Foxcom, an Israeli start-up telecommunications firm. He formed an unofficial business partnership with Michael Scanlon, who ran a lobbying and grassroots public relations firm. Among his many dubious business practices, Abramoff would refer clients to Scanlon's firm for grassroots and public relations services without revealing that he received 50% of the profits from these deals. Abramoff also requested that some clients pay a nonprofit he set up, the Capital Athletic Foundation, rather than his law firm, and then used the money from the nonprofit to underwrite golfing trips for himself and members of Congress. Abramoff had a particularly close relationship with Rep. Bob Ney (R–Ohio), in part because a former Ney staffer joined Abramoff's firm after he left government employment. Neil Volz, Ney's former chief of staff, acted as an intermediary between the lobbyist and the Congressman beginning just months after he left the Hill.

Among the items of value given to Rep. Ney were all-expense paid trips to the Super Bowl in Florida and golf courses in Scotland, numerous tickets to concerts and sporting events (including tickets to classical and rock concerts worth more than $1,100), tens of thousands of dollars of campaign contributions, and regular meals and drinks at Abramoff's restaurant, Signatures. In return, Ney agreed to enter certain statements into the *Congressional Record* supporting Abramoff's clients or their positions; to endorse as Chair of the House Administration Committee Foxcom's bid to provide wireless telephone service to the House; and to work as the Co-Chair of the relevant conference committee to enact gaming legislation that would benefit Abramoff's tribal clients and to ensure that the government transferred property to a religious school founded by Abramoff. Ney also met with several of Abramoff's clients

---

j. See also Ronald Levin, *Congressional Ethics and Constituent Advocacy in an Age of Mistrust*, 95 Mich. L. Rev. 1 (1996) (discussing this example and other examples of allegations of corruption in the context of casework).

and promised them his help on matters or indicated to them that Abramoff was an effective lobbyist. Finally, Ney contacted executive branch officials to influence decisions in ways that benefited Abramoff's clients.

What laws or ethical rules have each of these four men violated? Which particular acts violated which law or rule? Would Abramoff's payment for travel and gifts to Ney be treated differently than the campaign contributions that he provided the Representative? Should there be different treatment? How would each violation be punished? As you read through the Lobbying Disclosure Act, amended in the wake of the Abramoff scandal and discussed in Section 2, consider how it might apply to these interactions and what it would require to be disclosed.

Problem 3–4. Is it corrupt for a politician to break a promise she made during the campaign? Take, for example, Representative Marty Meehan (D–Mass.) who in 1995 filed a letter with the clerk of the House of Representatives stating: "Should I be elected to serve more than two additional terms of office in the U.S. House of Representatives following the 104th Congress, by this letter I hereby resign and direct you to remove my name permanently from the Roll of Members." When Meehan announced that he was running for the 107th Congress (an election he ultimately won), the Massachusetts Republican Party began to investigate legal remedies to enforce the resignation letter. Are there other ways to ensure that candidates tell the truth during campaigns?[k] Is this sort of corruption policed effectively by requiring members of Congress to stand for frequent reelection, thereby holding members accountable for their promises? Or is the electoral tie insufficient in a world where incumbents are usually reelected despite disappointing records on campaign promises? Is it even corrupt to break a campaign promise when everyone understands that campaign themes are often aspirational (or pandering), rather than realistic? For a case concerning whether a campaign promise made generally to all voters could itself be corrupt, see *Brown v. Hartlage*, 456 U.S. 45 (1982) (candidate who promised to accept a lower salary, a promise that violated state law, prosecuted under state corrupt practices act as the equivalent of a bribe; prosecution held unconstitutional under the First Amendment).

SECTION 2. LOBBYING

The First Amendment to the U.S. Constitution provides that "Congress shall make no law * * * abridging the freedom of speech, or of the press; or the right of the people peaceably to assemble, and to petition the Government for a redress of grievances." The *Speech Clause* recognizes the general precept that speech, especially about political matters, presumptively cannot be limited by the government. The *Petition Clause* recognizes the general precept that

---

k. See Elizabeth Garrett, *The Law and Economics of "Informed Voter" Ballot Notations*, 85 Va. L. Rev. 1533 (1999) (discussing ballot notations that were used to punish federal lawmakers who failed to abide by term limits pledges; the notations were ruled unconstitutional in *Cook v. Gralike*, 531 U.S. 510 (2001)); Saul Levmore, *Precommitment Politics*, 82 Va. L. Rev. 567 (1996) (presenting creative approaches to this question).

legislative representatives in a democracy should be open to the viewpoints of their constituents, and the latter in turn should be encouraged to present their proposals and ideas to their representatives. But should "the people" be free to use any means to persuade their representatives to press their views in the legislature? Should lobbying efforts be regulated through reporting and disclosure requirements, or through more stringent regulations?

There is a stench often associated with the concept of "lobbying" legislative representatives. In the nineteenth century, lobbying was often thinly disguised bribery. Even in current times, everyday lobbying methods are termed "pressure tactics." But, in fact, most lobbying is, at least formally, a rather ordinary affair. Almost all organized lobbying before Congress is aimed at getting the group's point of view across to the legislators and influencing legislative decisions.[a] According to H.R. Mahood, *Interest Groups in American National Politics: An Overview* 54 (2000), methods of lobbying fall into two main categories:

- *Direct Lobbying* is the direct presentation of a group's point of view to the legislator or the staff. The most common means of direct lobbying are testimony at legislative hearings, calling up legislators or writing them directly, presenting research results, submitting drafts of proposed legislation, and making contributions to legislators' reelection campaigns. The most effective form of direct lobbying is member-to-member lobbying. If a group has a legislative insider as an ally, the insider can do a particularly effective job of selling the group's views to colleagues. Increasingly, interest groups focus not only on the legislature but also on the executive branch, seeking to influence agency outcomes, the position the executive branch takes on legislation, and other decisions of implementation or agenda setting. Direct lobbying also includes *social lobbying*, a less substantive method of influence. Social lobbying lays the groundwork for the future when the lobbyists and the interests they represent will seek access to the legislator and to influence policy outcomes. Much social lobbying occurs at glitzy Georgetown parties, where light social chatter paves the way for future substantive conversations, or at late night poker games in a senator's Capitol hide-away office. Another variation of social lobbying is to offer legislators gifts, trips, or fees for speaking engagements (this practice is stringently limited at the federal level by ethics rules described above). Finally, one can consider the involvement of lobbyists in raising campaign funds a form of social lobbying when it is not accompanied by any substantive discussion of the issues. Generally, social lobbying is on the decline, in part because of the new gift, travel, and other conflict of interest rules discussed in the previous section.

- *Indirect Lobbying* is a more circuitous way of influencing lawmakers and involves efforts by interest groups and their lobbyists to stir up outside forces, primarily constituents, to bring pressure to bear. Increasingly, interest groups are using indirect methods, including "stealth campaigns

---

a. See John Wright, *Interest Groups and Congress: Lobbying, Contributions, and Influence* chap. 4 (1996).

with other organizations, alliances under positive-sounding names such as Citizens for Reform, or sponsorship of research studies or public opinion polls through independent organizations such as think tanks."[b] The most important kind of indirect lobbying is *grassroots lobbying* or "any type of action that attempts to influence inside-the-beltway inhabitants by influencing the attitudes or behavior of outside-the-beltway inhabitants."[c] An interest group stimulates constituent interest by mobilizing its own members, talking with media representatives to ensure that the its point of view is presented favorably, conducting a public-relations campaign to inspire letter writing, phone calls, and emails by constituents, and publicizing the legislator's voting record or "scorecard" on relevant votes.[d] Although there is concern that some of this activity produces "astroturf" lobbying based on false information or misrepresenting the breadth of public support, grassroots lobbying generally communicates "real content" about public opinion to policymakers and represents one of the most vibrant forms of mass political participation. Ken Kollman, *Outside Lobbying: Public Opinion and Interest Group Strategies* (1998).

William Keefe & Morris Ogul, *The American Legislative Process: Congress and the States* 366–70 (10th ed. 2001), observe that interest groups and their lobbying techniques vary greatly as to effectiveness. Access (presenting the group's point of view) does not ensure success, and organization is not necessarily synonymous with clout. In fact, the term *access* can encompass a variety of concepts: "(1) convincing a policy maker to listen to arguments; (2) establishing a 'regular relationship' with a policy maker for the exchange of information; (3) becoming 'institutionalized' into the policy process, for example, acquiring formal representation on governing boards of agencies; and (4) gaining influence."[e] The most effective groups are those that have large, cohesive, and dispersed memberships, are considered prestigious, have skillful leaders who seem to have the support of the group's members and can rally them on an issue, and have a lot of money to spend. We would add other factors, such as the ability of the groups to form alliances and the value of the group in supplying information (and any monopoly it might have on information).[f]

---

b. Darrell West & Burdett Loomis, *The Sound of Money: How Political Interests Get What They Want* 207 (1999). See also Mark Smith, *American Business and Political Power: Public Opinion, Elections, and Democracy* (2000).

c. Kenneth Goldstein, *Interest Groups, Lobbying, and Participation in America* 3 (1999).

d. See William Browne, *Lobbying the Public: All-Directional Advocacy*, in *Interest Group Politics* 343 (Allan Cigler & Burdett Loomis eds., 5th ed. 1998). See also Richard Davis, *The Web of Politics: The Internet's Impact on the American Political System* chap. 3 (1999) (analyzing electronic methods of grassroots lobbying and arguing that the new technology merely reinforces past patterns).

e. Wright, *supra,* at 77 (citing S.J. Makielski, *Pressure Politics in America* (1980)).

f. On forming alliances, see Kevin Hula, *Lobbying Together: Interest Group Coalitions in Legislative Politics* (1999). For one of the most influential and comprehensive studies of lobbying activity, see Kay Schlozman & John Tierney, *Organized Interests and American Democracy* (1986).

Lobbyists can play a positive role in the legislative process by supplying information to elected officials, who then can focus their energies, and those of their staff, on assessing the credibility of the information and on producing data about aspects of policy that may have escaped the notice of interest groups. Critics of interest groups tend to overlook their beneficial effects on politics, including this information production role. Lobbyists produce three different but related kinds of information: information about the status and prospects of pending legislation; information about the electoral ramifications of the legislator's position on proposals; and analyses of the economic, social and other substantive consequences of bills.[g] Although an interest group and its lobbyists will usually present arguments in a light most favorable to its position, lobbyists suffer reputational sanctions for lying, and competing interest groups have an incentive to point out the flaws in arguments or any inaccuracies. See Bruce Wolpe & Bertram Levine, *Lobbying Congress: How the System Works* 13–19 (2d ed. 1996) (including in the "Five Commandments" of lobbying "Tell the Truth" and "Spring No Surprises"). Thus, the information can be accurate and useful, and the government benefits because it has externalized some of its information costs. We will return to this aspect of lobbying in Chapter 4, § 2, when we describe how interest groups provide important information in the congressional budget process.

Most lobbying activity consists of speech and written communications that are protected by the First Amendment. Very little lobbying involves clearly corrupt activity, and that sort of lobbying (or *influence-peddling*) can probably be prosecuted under state or federal bribery, extortion, or gratuity statutes. Think back to the broad wording of § 201, the federal law criminalizing bribery and extortion. What sorts of lobbying activity fall within the plain meaning of those provisions? How should courts distinguish corrupt attempts to influence legislators from ordinary politics? Is more regulation needed of behavior that is not quite corrupt but disturbing nonetheless? Some pluralist theorists might oppose any additional regulation. Viewing government officials, and especially legislators, as the accommodators of interest group pressures, who register the strength of the conflicting pressures and reach an appropriate middle position, pluralists might consider lobbying as simply part of the process itself.[h] This would suggest a relatively *laissez-faire* approach to the political process, though even some pluralist thinkers recoil from such an extreme position. David Truman, for example, did not view legislators as utterly passive objects of interest group pressures, and he argued that there were certain basic "rules of the game" (mainly, to avoid the appearance of corruption that would undermine confidence in the legislature) which must be obeyed.[i]

---

g. See Wright, *supra*, at 88.

h. See Earl Latham, *The Group Basis of Politics* 35–36 (1952); Nelson Polsby, *Money Gains Access. So What?*, N.Y. Times, April 13, 1997, at A23.

i. David Truman, *The Governmental Process: Political Interests and Public Opinion* 114–15, 159, 512 (1951).

However, Truman and other pluralist thinkers were skeptical of moral outrage against lobbying solely on the ground that it served the interests of narrow organized interest groups. Their rules of the game primarily involved disclosure of lobbying activities because secrecy can allow corruption that the light of public scrutiny can destroy. Their point of view was influential in post-World War II thought about regulating lobbying in the United States. The Federal Regulation of Lobbying Act, enacted in 1946, and its primary Supreme Court interpretation, *United States v. Harriss*, 347 U.S. 612 (1954), are both reprinted below and represent a relatively limited approach to the regulation of lobbying. Consistent with the pluralist vision, the statute prohibited nothing; it required only registration and disclosure of lobbying expenditures in the specified circumstances. Nonetheless, concern about the disproportionate influence of special interests continued to grow, reaching a crescendo in the 1980s and 1990s. Increased public demand for more effective regulation of lobbying resulted in the passage of the Lobbying Disclosure Act of 1995 ("LDA"). Several high-profile corruption scandals a decade after the enactment of the LDA resulted in proposals to amend the Act. Again, however, the current federal lobbying law, as well as the proposed amendments receiving the most attention, primarily requires extensive disclosure of lobbying activity, except for grassroots lobbying, and more widespread and immediate dissemination of the information.

A. THE RISE AND FALL OF THE FEDERAL REGULATION OF LOBBYING ACT OF 1946

As American government became increasingly activist after the Civil War, citizen dismay about certain kinds of lobbying became more pronounced. In Georgia, for example, the post-Reconstruction Constitution of 1877 prohibited lobbying altogether. More typical was the Massachusetts response in 1890, which required lobbyists to register and disclose the "expenses paid and incurred" by the lobbyist. 1890 Mass. Acts ch. 456 (repealed 1973).[j]

The Progressive Era included several serious federal investigations into lobbying "abuses," particularly hearings in 1913 by a House select committee. The committee found evidence that representatives of the National Association of Manufacturers controlled some committee appointments, paid the chief page of the House to report conversations on the House floor and in its cloakroom, and enjoyed its own office in the Capitol. H.R. Rep. No. 113, 63d Cong., 2d Sess. 30, 41, 71 (1913). The committee's report created a flurry of bills to regulate lobbying. From 1914 onwards, Congress followed this pattern: Newspapers, select committees, or standing committees would report on some "abuse" of lobbying; bills would be introduced to do something about lobbying "abuse"; and the bills would be politely ignored by the House or Senate Judiciary Committees or gatekeepers of chamber floor debate. Do the theories

---

j. See generally Note, *Control of Lobbying*, 45 Harv. L. Rev. 1241 (1932); Elisabeth Clemens, *The People's Lobby: Organizational Innovation and the Rise of Interest Group Politics in the United States, 1890–1925* (1997).

of legislatures outlined in Chapter 1, § 2 suggest some reasons why lobbying reform should have been so difficult to achieve?

In academic circles, one of the most influential works implicating lobbying was Elmer Schattschneider's *Politics, Pressures and the Tariff: A Study of Free Private Enterprise in Pressure Politics, as Shown in the 1929–1930 Revision of the Tariff* (1935). The study focused on the 1929 House and Senate hearings that crafted what was to become the notorious Smoot-Hawley Tariff of 1930. Schattschneider found that the deliberative process was essentially controlled by lobbyists for American businesses (every business facing actual or potential foreign competition was represented in Washington during these hearings). "Indeed, the language of the hearings often was not what one might expect to find in communications between a sovereign state and its citizens, nor was it, in many instances, that of an inquiry by a governmental body into the merits of a public policy. It was, rather, in the style and manner of equals engaged in negotiation." *Id.* at 43–44. The most striking consequences were that Congress acted with skewed and often inaccurate information, and that overall policy was dramatically tilted. Schattschneider also found that "insider" lobbyists (such as former members of Congress) had special access to the deliberative process and, correspondingly, significant advantages in representing their clients' interests.

At the same time Schattschneider's book was published, Senate hearings revealed similar patterns of conduct (misleading information, pressure, "inside" access) by public utility lobbyists. Responding to the Senate hearings, Senator Hugo Black championed lobbying reform in the mid-1930s. He introduced a bill to require registration of all persons seeking to influence any government official and requiring disclosure of the interests represented, activities undertaken, and expenses incurred in lobbying. S. 2512, 74th Cong., 1st Sess. (1935). The Black bill was passed by the Senate, 79 Cong. Rec. 8306 (1935), but ran into trouble in the House Judiciary Committee, which reported its own bill. 80 Cong. Rec. 4541 (1936). Like the Senate (Black) bill, the House Judiciary Committee bill, which was passed by the full body, required registration of lobbyists and disclosure of their employers. Unlike the Senate bill, however, the House bill did not require all persons expending money and receiving contributions to register and did not cover executive branch lobbying.

A House-Senate Conference reported a compromise. H.R. Conf. Rep. No. 2925, 74th Cong., 2d Sess. (1936), reprinted in 80 Cong. Rec. 9430–34 (1936). The Conference bill applied to individuals or organizations that sought (1) to enact or defeat legislation in Congress, (2) to influence the election of any candidate for federal office, or (3) to influence any federal agency or official. Lobbyists before Congress would be required to register with the Clerk of the House and/or Secretary of the Senate; the registration would disclose, *inter alia*, the interests represented, the compensation, and the expenses that would be met by the principal. Registered lobbyists would also be required to file monthly reports naming their contributors and amounts received, the recipients of their expenditures, and the total contributions received and expenditures paid out in the calendar year. The House rejected this Conference bill by a three-to-one majority. Lobbying reform was a dead issue in Congress for the next ten years, although Congress did enact the Foreign Agents Registration Act (FARA) in 1938, in order to expose Nazi propaganda efforts. The FARA, as amended in 1966 and 1995, imposes substantial registration and disclosure obligations on representatives of a "foreign principal" before Congress, agencies, and the executive. 22 U.S.C. § 611 et seq. (1994 & Supp. 2000).

The Joint Committee on the Organization of Congress proposed the Legislative Reorganization Act of 1946, which included a lobbying reform title as a minor part of its overall package of reforms. Title III was essentially the 1936 Conference bill (but without any provision for executive branch lobbying and with some new terminology). Congressional consideration of Title III was perfunctory, confused, and skeptical — but the whole package passed intact.[k] Below are the primary provisions of Title III, as they stood before the Act was repealed in 1995 as part of the passage of a more comprehensive regulatory regime. Although the 1946 Act is no longer effective, the gaps in its coverage that resulted from sloppy drafting and judicial interpretations greatly influenced the structure of the current Act. Only by comparing the two statutes can you develop a full sense of the modern framework. This section also provides you a chance to read and interpret statutory language directly — and to compare your approach with that of the Supreme Court.

FEDERAL REGULATION OF LOBBYING ACT
§§ 302–305, 307–308 & 310, 60 Stat. 839
Codified at 2 U.S.C. §§ 261–264, 266–267 & 269 (1988)

Definitions

SEC. 302. When used in this title —

(a) The term "contribution" includes a gift, subscription, loan, advance, or deposit of money or anything of value and includes a contract, promise, or agreement, whether or not legally enforceable, to make a contribution.

(b) The term "expenditure" includes a payment, distribution, loan, advance, deposit, or gift of money or anything of value, and includes a contract, promise, or agreement, whether or not legally enforceable, to make an expenditure.

(c) The term "person" includes an individual, partnership, committee, association, corporation, and any other organization or group of persons. * * *

(e) The term "legislation" means bills, resolutions, amendments, nominations, and other matters pending or proposed in either House of Congress, and includes any other matter which may be the subject of action by either House.

Detailed Accounts of Contributions * * *

SEC. 303. (a) It shall be the duty of every person who shall in any manner solicit or receive a contribution to any organization or fund for the purposes hereinafter designated to keep a detailed and exact account of —

(1) all contributions of any amount or of any value whatsoever;

---

k. See Belle Zeller, *American Government and Politics: The Federal Regulation of Lobbying Act*, 42 Am. Pol. Sci. Rev. 239 (1948) (providing detailed legislative history of Act).

(2) the name and address of every person making any such contribution of $500 or more and the date thereof;

(3) all expenditures made by or on behalf of such organization or fund; and

(4) the name and address of every person to whom any such expenditure is made and the date thereof.

Receipts for Contributions

SEC. 304. Every individual who receives a contribution of $500 or more for any of the purposes hereinafter designated shall within five days after receipt thereof rendered [*sic*] to the person or organization for which such contribution was received a detailed account thereof, including the name and address of the person making such contribution and the date on which received.

Statements of Accounts Filed With Clerk of House

SEC. 305. (a) Every person receiving any contributions or expending any money for the purposes designated in subparagraph (a) or (b) of section 307 shall file with the Clerk between the first and tenth day of each calendar quarter, a statement containing complete as of the day next preceding the date of filing—

(1) the name and address of each person who has made a contribution of $500 or more not mentioned in the preceding report; * * *

(4) the name and address of each person to whom an expenditure in one or more items of the aggregate amount or value, within the calendar year, of $10 or more has been made by or on behalf of such person, and the amount, date, and purpose of such expenditure; * * *

Persons to Whom Applicable

SEC. 307. The provisions of this title shall apply to any person (except a political committee as defined in the Federal Corrupt Practices Act, and duly organized State or local committees of a political party), who by himself, or through any agent or employee or other persons in any manner whatsoever, directly or indirectly, solicits, collects, or receives money or any other thing of value to be used principally to aid, or the principal purpose of which person is to aid, in the accomplishment of any of the following purposes:

(a) The passage or defeat of any legislation by the Congress of the United States.

(b) To influence, directly or indirectly, the passage or defeat of any legislation by the Congress of the United States.

Registration of Lobbyists With Secretary of the Senate and Clerk of the House
* * *

SEC. 308. (a) Any person who shall engage himself for pay or for any consideration for the purpose of attempting to influence the passage or defeat of any legislation by the Congress of the United States shall, before doing anything in furtherance of such object, register with the Clerk of the House of

Representatives and the Secretary of the Senate and shall give to those officers in writing and under oath, his name and business address, the name and address of the person by whom he is employed, and in whose interest he appears or works, the duration of such employment, how much he is paid and is to receive, by whom he is paid or is to be paid, how much he is to be paid for expenses, and what expenses are to be included. Each such person so registering shall, between the first and tenth day of each calendar quarter, so long as his activity continues, file with the Clerk and Secretary a detailed report under oath of all money received and expended by him during the preceding calendar quarter in carrying on his work; to whom paid; for what purposes; and the names of any papers, periodicals, magazines, or other publications in which he has caused to be published any articles or editorials; and the proposed legislation he is employed to support or oppose. The provisions of this section shall not apply to any person who merely appears before a committee of the Congress of the United States in support of or opposition to legislation; nor to any public official acting in his official capacity; nor in the case of any newspaper or other regularly published periodical (including any individual who owns, publishes, or is employed by any such newspaper or periodical) which in the ordinary course of business publishes news items, editorials, or other comments, or paid advertisements, which directly or indirectly urge the passage or defeat of legislation, if such newspaper, periodical, or individual, engages in no further or other activities in connection with the passage or defeat of such legislation, other than to appear before a committee of the Congress of the United States in support of or in opposition to such legislation.

(b) All information required to be filed under the provisions of this section with the Clerk of the House of Representatives and the Secretary of the Senate shall be compiled by said Clerk and Secretary, acting jointly, as soon as practicable after the close of the calendar quarter with respect to which such information is filed and shall be printed in the Congressional Record. * * *

Penalties

SEC. 310. (a) Any person who violates any of the provisions of this title, shall, upon conviction, be guilty of a misdemeanor, and shall be punished by a fine of not more than $5,000 or imprisonment for not more than twelve months, or by both such fine and imprisonment.

Lobbying Act Problems

Problem 3–5. Schattschneider's account of the tariff lobbying found that some industry representatives were allowed to attend executive (i.e., closed to the public) sessions of committee or subcommittee meetings and even the House-Senate Conference, received inside tips from congressional staff and from lawmakers themselves, and brokered deals between members of Congress (i.e., the member from a glass-works district would support higher tariffs for lumber, in return for the vote of the member from a lumber district for higher glass tariffs). Would any of this conduct violate the FRLA? Which of the conduct is problematic in our democratic system and which represents acceptable negotiation to construct a bill that will receive majority support? How would the judge in *Van de Carr* have answered that question?

Problem 3–6. Consider the following application of the FRLA to Robert Harriss, a commodity broker; Tom Linder, Commissioner of Agriculture for the State of Georgia; Ralph Moore, a trader of commodity futures; and the National Farm Committee (NFC), of which Harriss, Linder, and Moore were directors. Harriss funneled money to Moore ($50,000 in the last three months of 1946 alone), who would host dinners for Members of Congress in the name of NFC and other farmer groups. It is not clear what subjects were discussed at these social gatherings. None of the individuals, nor the NFC, registered or delivered reports under the FRLA. The Justice Department secured indictments against Harriss for failure to report expenditure of his own monies to influence legislation; Linder and Moore for seeking to influence Congress for pay without registering; and the NFC for failing to report the solicitation and receipt of contributions to influence the enactment of legislation. How would you defend each of these parties under the statute? In *United States v. Harriss*, 109 F. Supp. 641 (D.D.C. 1953), Judge Alexander Holtzoff dismissed the indictment against Harriss, Linder, Moore, and the NFC, on the ground that the FRLA as enacted was unconstitutional. This decision was appealed to the Supreme Court, with the following consequences.

UNITED STATES v. HARRISS
Supreme Court of the United States, 1954
347 U.S. 612, 74 S.Ct. 808, 98 L.Ed.2d 989

CHIEF JUSTICE WARREN delivered the opinion of the Court.

[I] The constitutional requirement of definiteness is violated by a criminal statute that fails to give a person of ordinary intelligence fair notice that his contemplated conduct is forbidden by the statute. The underlying principle is that no man shall be held criminally responsible for conduct which he could not reasonably understand to be proscribed. * * *

* * * The key section of the Lobbying Act is § 307, entitled "Persons to Whom Applicable." This section modifies the substantive provisions of the Act, including § 305 and § 308. In other words, unless a "person" falls within the category established by § 307, the disclosure requirements of § 305 and § 308 are inapplicable. Thus coverage under the Act is limited to those persons (except for the specified political committees) who solicit, collect, or receive contributions of money or other thing of value, and then only if "the principal purpose" of either the persons or the contributions is to aid in the accomplishment of the aims set forth in § 307(a) and (b). In any event, the solicitation, collection, or receipt of money or other thing of value is a prerequisite to coverage under the Act.

The Government urges a much broader construction — namely, that under § 305 a person must report his expenditures to influence legislation even though he does not solicit, collect, or receive contributions as provided in § 307.[8] Such a construction, we believe, would do violence to the title and

---

8. The Government's view is based on a variance between the language of § 307 and the language of § 305. Section 307 refers to any person who "solicits, collects, or receives" contributions; § 305, however, refers not only to "receiving any contributions" but also to

language of § 307 as well as its legislative history. If the construction urged by the Government is to become law, that is for Congress to accomplish by further legislation.

We now turn to the alleged vagueness of the purposes set forth in § 307(a) and (b). As in *United States v. Rumely*, 345 U.S. 41 (1953), which involved the interpretation of similar language, we believe this language should be construed to refer only to "lobbying in its commonly accepted sense" — to direct communication with members of Congress on pending or proposed federal legislation. The legislative history of the Act makes clear that, at the very least, Congress sought disclosure of such direct pressures, exerted by the lobbyists themselves or through their hirelings or through an artificially stimulated letter campaign.[10] It is likewise clear that Congress would have intended the Act to operate on this narrower basis, even if a broader application to organizations seeking to propagandize the general public were not permissible.

There remains for our consideration the meaning of "the principal purpose" and "to be used principally to aid." The legislative history of the Act indicates that the term "principal" was adopted merely to exclude from the scope of § 307 those contributions and persons having only an "incidental" purpose of influencing legislation. Conversely, the "principal purpose" requirement does

---

"expending any money." It is apparently the Government's contention that § 307 — since it makes no reference to expenditures — is inapplicable to the expenditure provisions of § 305. Section 307, however, limits the application of § 305 as a whole, not merely a part of it.

10. The Lobbying Act was enacted as Title III of the Legislative Reorganization Act of 1946, which was reported to Congress by the Joint Committee on the Organization of Congress. The Senate and House reports accompanying the bill were identical with respect to Title III. Both declared that the Lobbying Act applies "chiefly to three distinct classes of so-called lobbyists:

"First. Those who do not visit the Capitol but initiate propaganda from all over the country in the form of letters and telegrams, many of which have been based entirely upon misinformation as to facts. This class of persons and organizations will be required under the title, not to cease or curtail their activities in any respect, but merely to disclose the sources of their collections and the methods in which they are disbursed.

"Second. The second class of lobbyists are those who are employed to come to the Capitol under the false impression that they exert some powerful influence over Members of Congress. These individuals spend their time in Washington presumably exerting some mysterious influence with respect to the legislation in which their employers are interested, but carefully conceal from Members of Congress whom they happen to contact the purpose of their presence. The title in no wise prohibits or curtails their activities. It merely requires that they shall register and disclose the sources and purposes of their employment and the amount of their compensation.

"Third. There is a third class of entirely honest and respectable representatives of business, professional, and philanthropic organizations who come to Washington openly and frankly to express their views for or against legislation, many of whom serve a useful and perfectly legitimate purpose in expressing the views and interpretations of their employers with respect to legislation which concerns them. They will likewise be required to register and state their compensation and the sources of their employment."

S. Rep. No. 1400, 79th Cong., 2d Sess., p. 27; Committee Print, July 22, 1946, statement by Representative Monroney on Legislative Reorganization Act of 1946, 79th Cong., 2d Sess., pp. 32–33. See also the statement in the Senate by Senator La Follette, who was Chairman of the Joint Committee, at 92 Cong. Rec. 6367–6368.

not exclude a contribution which in substantial part is to be used to influence legislation through direct communication with Congress or a person whose activities in substantial part are directed to influencing legislation through direct communication with Congress.[13] If it were otherwise — if an organization, for example, were exempted because lobbying was only one of its main activities — the Act would in large measure be reduced to a mere exhortation against abuse of the legislative process. In construing the Act narrowly to avoid constitutional doubts, we must also avoid a construction that would seriously impair the effectiveness of the Act in coping with the problem it was designed to alleviate.

To summarize, therefore, there are three prerequisites to coverage under § 307: (1) the "person" must have solicited, collected, or received contributions; (2) one of the main purposes of such "person," or one of the main purposes of such contributions, must have been to influence the passage or defeat of legislation by Congress; (3) the intended method of accomplishing this purpose must have been through direct communication with members of Congress. And since § 307 modifies the substantive provisions of the Act, our construction of § 307 will of necessity also narrow the scope of § 305 and § 308, the substantive provisions underlying the information in this case. Thus § 305 is limited to those persons who are covered by § 307; and when so covered, they must report all contributions and expenditures having the purpose of attempting to influence legislation through direct communication with Congress. Similarly, § 308 is limited to those persons (with the stated exceptions) who are covered by § 307 and who, in addition, engage themselves for pay or for any other valuable consideration for the purpose of attempting to influence legislation through direct communication with Congress. Construed in this way, the Lobbying Act meets the constitutional requirement of definiteness.

[II] Thus construed, §§ 305 and 308 also do not violate the freedoms guaranteed by the First Amendment — freedom to speak, publish, and petition the Government.

Present-day legislative complexities are such that individual members of Congress cannot be expected to explore the myriad pressures to which they are regularly subjected. Yet full realization of the American ideal of government by elected representatives depends to no small extent on their ability to properly evaluate such pressures. Otherwise the voice of the people may all too easily be drowned out by the voice of special interest groups seeking favored treatment while masquerading as proponents of the public weal. This is the evil which the Lobbying Act was designed to help prevent.

Toward that end, Congress has not sought to prohibit these pressures. It has merely provided for a modicum of information from those who for hire attempt

---

13. Such a criterion is not novel in federal law. See Int. Rev. Code, § 23(*o*)(2) (income tax), § 812(d) (estate tax), and § 1004(a)(2)(B) (gift tax), providing tax exemption for contributions to charitable and educational organizations "no substantial part of the activities of which is carrying on propaganda, or otherwise attempting, to influence legislation." * * *

to influence legislation or who collect or spend funds for that purpose. It wants only to know who is being hired, who is putting up the money, and how much.
* * *

The judgment below is reversed and the cause is remanded to the District Court for further proceedings not inconsistent with this opinion.

MR. JUSTICE DOUGLAS, with whom MR. JUSTICE BLACK concurs, dissenting. * * *

I am now convinced that the formula adopted to save this Act is too dangerous for use. It can easily ensnare people who have done no more than exercise their constitutional rights of speech, assembly, and press. * * *

It is contended that the Act plainly applies:

— to persons who pay others to present views to Congress either in committee hearings or by letters or other communications to Congress or Congressmen and

— to persons who spend money to induce others to communicate with Congress.

The Court adopts that view, with one minor limitation which the Court places on the Act — that only persons who solicit, collect, or receive money are included.

The difficulty is that the Act has to be rewritten and words actually added and subtracted to produce that result. * * *

What contributions might be used "principally to aid" in influencing "directly or indirectly, the passage or defeat" of any such measure by Congress? When is one retained for the purpose of influencing the "passage or defeat of any legislation"?

(1) One who addresses a trade union for repeal of a labor law certainly hopes to influence legislation.

(2) So does a manufacturers' association which runs ads in newspapers for a sales tax.

(3) So does a farm group which undertakes to raise money for an educational program to be conducted in newspapers, magazines, and on radio and television, showing the need for revision of our attitude on world trade.

(4) So does a group of oil companies which puts agents in the Nation's capital to sound the alarm at hostile legislation, to exert influence on Congressmen to defeat it, to work on the Hill for the passage of laws favorable to the oil interests.

(5) So does a business, labor, farm, religious, social, racial, or other group which raises money to contact people with the request that they write their Congressman to get a law repealed or modified, to get a proposed law passed, or themselves to propose a law.

Are all of these activities covered by the Act? If one is included why are not the others? The Court apparently excludes the kind of activities listed in categories (1), (2), and (3) and includes part of the activities in (4) and (5) — those which entail contacts with the Congress.

There is, however, difficulty in that course, a difficulty which seems to me to be insuperable. I find no warrant in the Act for drawing the line, as the Court does, between "direct communication with Congress" and other pressures on Congress. The Act is as much concerned with one as with the other.

The words "direct communication with Congress" are not in the Act. Congress was concerned with the raising of money to aid in the passage or defeat of legislation, whatever tactics were used. But the Court not only strikes out one whole group of activities — to influence "indirectly" — but substitutes a new concept for the remaining group — to influence "directly." To influence "directly" the passage or defeat of legislation includes any number of methods — for example, nationwide radio, television or advertising programs promoting a particular measure, as well as the "buttonholing" of Congressmen. To include the latter while excluding the former is to rewrite the Act. * * *

[We have omitted the dissenting opinion of JUSTICE JACKSON, who believed that the FRLA infringed on the Petition Clause of the First Amendment. "[O]ur constitutional system is to allow the greatest freedom of access to Congress, so that the people may press for their selfish interests, with Congress acting as arbiter of their demands and conflicts."]

NOTES ON THE AFTERMATH OF *HARRISS*

1. *The Court's Analysis.* There are several ironies in the Court's debate. The most obvious is that Justice Black, the primary author of the 1935–36 proposals which were the basis for the FRLA, voted to strike down the statute altogether. Senator Black had said, "There is no constitutional right to lobby. There is no right on the part of greedy and predatory interests to use money taken from the pockets of the citizen to mislead him."[1]

Another irony is that the Court did essentially rewrite the statute (judicial activism) in order to save its constitutionality (judicial restraint). Was the Court on firm ground in reading § 307's "principal purpose" requirement into §§ 305 and 308? Where does the Court find the "direct communication" requirement? In its desire to trim back a "vague" statute, has the Court created a confusing one, instead?

Finally, consider whether the Court was doing the statute a "favor" by rewriting rather than just invalidating it. Justice Jackson thought not. Instead,

---

1. *Hearings Before a Special Comm. to Investigate Lobbying Activities*, 74th Cong., 1st Sess. (1935), quoted in William Gregory & Rennard Strickland, *Hugo Black's Congressional Investigations of Lobbying and the Public Utilities Holding Company Act: A Historical View of the Power Trust, New Deal Politics, and Regulatory Propaganda*, 29 Okla. L. Rev. 534, 551 (1976).

he made an institutional argument for striking down the law, rather than redrafting it. "Congress has power to regulate lobbying for hire as a business or profession and to require such agents to disclose their principals, their activities, and their receipts. However, to reach the real evils of lobbying without cutting into the constitutional right of petition is a difficult and delicate task for which the Court's action today gives little guidance. I am in doubt whether the Act as construed does not permit applications which would abridge the right of petition, for which clear, safe and workable channels must be maintained. I think we should point out the defects and limitations which condemn this Act so clearly that the Court cannot sustain it as written, and leave its rewriting to Congress. After all, it is Congress that should know from experience both the good in the right of petition and the evils of professional lobbying." Is he right? Think about his observation again after you read about the aftermath of *Harriss*.

2. *The Impact of* Harriss. The Supreme Court's decision remanded *Harriss* to Judge Holtzoff for further proceedings. The Justice Department not only abandoned the Harriss prosecutions (the last indictment, against Moore, was dropped on November 2, 1955), but essentially also abandoned any serious effort to enforce the statute, after having been fairly active between 1947 and 1954. Less than a handful of indictments were returned under the Act after 1955, and the Justice Department testified in 1979 that the statute was a dead letter.

Congress itself expressed dissatisfaction with the statute, as reconstructed. In the wake of the Watergate scandal and with a heightened sensitivity to ethics issues, the Senate Committee on Government Operations reported the following defects:

- Groups that used their own funds in an attempt to influence legislation were not required to register unless they solicited, collected, or received funds from others for that purpose.

- The FRLA did not apply to organizations or individuals unless lobbying was their principal purpose. Due to the vagueness of the definition, many organizations did not register at all, concluding that lobbying was not their "principal purpose."

- The FRLA did not clearly cover efforts by a lobbyist that did not involve direct contact with Congress. Thus, lobbyists who attempted to influence Congress by soliciting others to communicate with Congress did not report these grassroots lobbying efforts.

- The FRLA did not clearly include lobbying communications with staff employees of congressmembers.

- The FRLA's reporting requirements were so vague and ambiguous that the lobbyists who did report often filed incomplete information or interpreted the requirements differently. Some groups considered more kinds of expenses to be related to lobbying than others. As a result, it was difficult to make a meaningful comparison between the reports filed by any two lobbyists.

See Senate Report No. 94–763 on S. 2477, 94th Cong., 2d Sess. (1976).

*Post-*Harriss *Lobbying Act Problem*

Problem 3–7. You are a practitioner at a Washington, D.C. law firm in 1990. The following clients come to you for advice about their compliance with the FRLA in connection with activity concerning a proposed amendment to Title VII of the Civil Rights Act of 1964, the purpose of which would be to overturn the Supreme Court's decision in *United Steelworkers v. Weber* (found in Chapter 1, § 3):

(a) Jeff Martin is the general counsel of Kaiser Aluminum, one of the defendants in the *Weber* case (and delighted that it won the case). He spends three days in D.C., in which he speaks with several Members of Congress; Martin then returns home and never makes a subsequent appearance before Congress. Must he register under § 308 of the Lobbying Act? Must he file reports under § 305 of the Act?

(b) Kaiser Aluminum itself has a permanent office in D.C., and for several months in 1980 the office staff spends virtually all of its time working to defeat the proposed legislation. Its activities include consultations with legislative staff, writing articles for newspapers throughout the country defending the *Weber* decision, and direct contact with Members of Congress. Does Kaiser have to register under § 308 of the Lobbying Act? Must it file reports under § 305 of the Act? If so, what should the reports cover?

(c) The United Steelworkers hires Nancy Shea to be a full-time lobbyist on this issue, and she spends several months contacting members of Congress and legislative staff to arouse them to oppose the proposed legislation. The United Steelworkers assesses a special fee of $5 per member from each local union so it can pay Shea for her efforts. Does either Shea or the United Steelworkers have to register under § 308 of the Lobbying Act? Must either of them file reports under § 305 of the Act?

B. THE FEDERAL LOBBYING DISCLOSURE ACT: STRENGTHENING AND EXPANDING DISCLOSURE REQUIREMENTS

The concerns voiced in the 1970s did not abate but became louder and more insistent. Examples of unseemly interest group activity received a great deal of press scrutiny, and the people's distrust of and alienation from their representatives grew more acute. A number of influential popular books fueled the growing public dissatisfaction and public alienation. For example, Jonathan Rausch warned of the debilitating effects of *demosclerosis*:

> By definition, the government's power to solve problems comes from its ability to reassign resources, whether by taxing, spending, regulating, or simply passing laws. But that very ability energizes countless investors and entrepreneurs and ordinary Americans to go digging for gold by lobbying government. In time, a whole industry — large, sophisticated, professionalized, and to a considerable extent self-serving — emerges and then assumes a life of its own. This industry is a drain on the productive economy, and there appears to be no natural limit to its growth. As

it grows, the steady accumulation of subsidies and benefits, each defended in perpetuity by a professional interest group, calcifies government.[m]

Congress became serious about revising the laws regulating lobbying when Senator Carl Levin (D–Mich.) held hearings on the topic in 1991 in the Senate Governmental Affairs Subcommittee on Oversight of Government Management. In the 103rd Congress, the bill passed the Senate by a vote of 95–2; the House of Representatives also passed a version of a comprehensive lobbying disclosure bill in 1993. The conference committee managed to draft a compromise proposal, but opposition to the proposal had developed since floor consideration.

Most significantly, a coalition of interests had come together to oppose disclosure of grassroots lobbying. This coalition included a number of unusual political bedfellows, including the Christian Coalition and the American Civil Liberties Union. They argued that the reform proposal would violate the First Amendment by requiring them to open their membership lists to public scrutiny. Although the conference report passed the House, it was killed in the Senate by a filibuster led by the perennial opponent of campaign finance reform laws as well as this particular lobbying reform bill, Mitch McConnell (R–Ky.). In the next Congress, proponents dropped this controversial provision and made other concessions, and the Lobbying Disclosure Act of 1995 passed unanimously.

Lobbying and ethics reform became a salient issue again in the 110th Congress in the wake of several scandals involving lobbyists and members of Congress. For example, as part of the scandal involving lobbyist Jack Abramoff (detailed in Problem 3–3, *supra*), Representative Bob Ney (R–Ohio) pled guilty to conspiracy to commit, among other things, defrauding his constituents of their right to his honest service and making false statements about the items he received from Abramoff and others. Representative Randall "Duke" Cunningham (R–Calif.) pled guilty in 2005 to various charges stemming from his accepting at least $2.4 million in bribes. Cunningham, a member of the Defense Appropriations Subcommittee, provided a "menu" to defense contractors from which the contractor could determine how many millions of dollars in defense and intelligence contracts would be awarded to the contractor based upon the value of the bribe. Cunningham's dealings were more closely scrutinized, and eventually led to his arrest, when he sold his house to a defense contractor for substantially more than market value. Other bribes he admitted receiving included a used Rolls Royce, antique furniture, jewelry, and money for his daughter's graduation party. In Problem 3–15, *infra*, we will turn to another recent congressional scandal involving Representative William Jefferson (D–La.). During this investigation, law enforcement officers found wads of cash hidden in his freezer, and one of his former staffers pled guilty to bribing the congressman.

As with the 1995 Lobbying Disclosure Act, original ethics reform proposals were more far-reaching than the bill that ultimately passed in 2007. Again, for

---

m. Jonathan Rausch, *Demosclerosis: The Silent Killer of American Government* 17 (1994)

example, attempts to extend the Act's provisions to some grassroots lobbying were quickly abandoned after facing stiff opposition from many groups active in the legislative realm. Moreover, to enact the Honest Leadership and Open Government Act of 2007, Pub. L. No. 110–81, 121 Stat. 735 (2007), the Democratic leadership of both houses had to craft a compromise bill in secret negotiations, despite their promises at the beginning of Congress to be more open. The compromise they reached was passed overwhelmingly by both houses (411–8 in the House, and 83–14 in the Senate) in identical form to avoid a conference committee, and the act was sent to the President just days before Congress left on its August break. With two former lawmakers serving prison time, others in trouble, and campaign promises of cleaning up Congress' act in danger of remaining unfulfilled, legislators did not want to return to their districts and states without having taken action on anti-corruption legislation.

As you read the following excerpts from the Lobbying Disclosure Act, as amended in 2007, determine whether it remedies the defects in the old law identified in Senate Committee Report No. 94–763, *supra*. Also note the ways in which it adopts a different approach from the FRLA, as interpreted by *Harriss*. Will this new framework be more successful than the old law?

LOBBYING DISCLOSURE ACT OF 1995
Pub. L. 104–65, 109 Stat. 691; codified as amended at 2 U.S.C.A. §§ 1601–1607

* * *

SEC. 2. FINDINGS.

The Congress finds that —

(1) responsible representative Government requires public awareness of the efforts of paid lobbyists to influence the public decisionmaking process in both the legislative and executive branches of the Federal Government;

(2) existing lobbying disclosure statutes have been ineffective because of unclear statutory language, weak administrative and enforcement provisions, and an absence of clear guidance as to who is required to register and what they are required to disclose; and

(3) the effective public disclosure of the identity and extent of the efforts of paid lobbyists to influence Federal officials in the conduct of Government actions will increase public confidence in the integrity of Government.

SEC. 3. DEFINITIONS. * * *

(2) CLIENT. — The term "client" means any person or entity that employs or retains another person for financial or other compensation to conduct lobbying activities on behalf of that person or entity. A person or entity whose employees act as lobbyists on its own behalf is both a client and an employer of such employees. In the case of a coalition or association that employs or retains other persons to conduct lobbying activities, the client is the coalition or association and not its individual members.

(3) COVERED EXECUTIVE BRANCH OFFICIAL. — The term "covered executive branch official" means —

(A) the President;

(B) the Vice President;

(C) any officer or employee, or any other individual functioning in the capacity of such an officer or employee, in the Executive Office of the President;

(D) any officer or employee serving in a [senior position in the executive branch.] * * *

(4) COVERED LEGISLATIVE BRANCH OFFICIAL. — The term "covered legislative branch official" means —

(A) a Member of Congress;

(B) an elected officer of either House of Congress;

(C) any employee of, or any other individual functioning in the capacity of an employee of — (i) a Member of Congress; (ii) a committee of either House of Congress; (iii) the leadership staff of the House of Representatives or the leadership staff of the Senate; (iv) a joint committee of Congress; and (v) a working group or caucus organized to provide legislative services or other assistance to Members of Congress[.] * * *

(5) EMPLOYEE. — The term "employee" means any individual who is an officer, employee, partner, director, or proprietor of a person or entity, but does not include [independent contractors or volunteers]. * * *

(7) LOBBYING ACTIVITIES. — The term "lobbying activities" means lobbying contacts and efforts in support of such contacts, including preparation and planning activities, research and other background work that is intended, at the time it is performed, for use in contacts, and coordination with the lobbying activities of others.

(8) LOBBYING CONTACT. —

(A) DEFINITION. — The term "lobbying contact" means any oral or written communication (including an electronic communication) to a covered executive branch official or a covered legislative branch official that is made on behalf of a client with regard to —

(i) the formulation, modification, or adoption of Federal legislation (including legislative proposals);

(ii) the formulation, modification, or adoption of a Federal rule, regulation, Executive order, or any other program, policy, or position of the United States Government;

(iii) the administration or execution of a Federal program or policy (including the negotiation, award, or administration of a Federal contract, grant, loan, permit, or license); or

(iv) the nomination or confirmation of a person for a position subject to confirmation by the Senate.

(B) EXCEPTIONS. — The term "lobbying contact" does not include a communication that is —

(i) made by a public official acting in the public official's official capacity; * * *

(iii) made in a speech, article, publication or other material that is distributed and made available to the public, or through radio, television, cable television, or other medium of mass communication;

(iv) made on behalf of a government of a foreign country or a foreign political party and disclosed under the Foreign Agents Registration Act of 1938 (22 U.S.C. 611 et seq.);

(v) a request for a meeting, a request for the status of an action, or any other similar administrative request, if the request does not include an attempt to influence a covered executive branch official or a covered legislative branch official; * * *

(vii) testimony given before a committee, subcommittee, or task force of the Congress, or submitted for inclusion in the public record of a hearing conducted by such committee, subcommittee, or task force; * * *

(ix) required by subpoena, civil investigative demand, or otherwise compelled by statute, regulation, or other action of the Congress or an agency * * *;

(x) made in response to a notice in the Federal Register, Commerce Business Daily, or other similar publication soliciting communications from the public and directed to the agency official specifically designated in the notice to receive such communications;

(xi) not possible to report without disclosing information, the unauthorized disclosure of which is prohibited by law;

(xii) made to an official in an agency with regard to — (I) a judicial proceeding or a criminal or civil law enforcement inquiry, investigation, or proceeding; or (II) a filing or proceeding that the Government is specifically required by statute or regulation to maintain or conduct on a confidential basis, if that agency is charged with responsibility for such proceeding, inquiry, investigation, or filing; * * *

(xiv) a written comment filed in the course of a public proceeding or any other communication that is made on the record in a public proceeding;

(xv) a petition for agency action made in writing and required to be a matter of public record pursuant to established agency procedures;

(xvi) made on behalf of an individual with regard to that individual's benefits, employment, or other personal matters involving only that individual, except that this clause does not apply to any communication with — (I) a covered executive branch official, or (II) a covered legislative branch official (other than the individual's elected Members of Congress or employees who work under such Members' direct supervision), with respect to the formulation, modification, or adoption of private legislation for the relief of that individual;

(xvii) a disclosure by an individual that is protected under the amendments made by the Whistleblower Protection Act of 1989 [5 U.S.C. § 1211 et seq.], under the Inspector General Act of 1978 [5 U.S.C. app.] or under another provision of law;

(xviii) made by [a church, an association of churches, or a religious order]. * * *

(9) LOBBYING FIRM. — The term "lobbying firm" means a person or entity that has 1 or more employees who are lobbyists on behalf of a client other than that person or entity. The term also includes a self-employed individual who is a lobbyist.

(10) LOBBYIST. — The term "lobbyist" means any individual who is employed or retained by a client for financial or other compensation for services that include more than one lobbying contact, other than an individual whose lobbying activities constitute less than 20 percent of the time engaged in the services provided by such individual to that client over a 3-month period. * * *

(13) ORGANIZATION. — The term "organization" means a person or entity other than an individual.

(14) PERSON OR ENTITY. — The term "person or entity" means any individual, corporation, company, foundation, association, labor organization, firm, partnership, society, joint stock company, group of organizations, or State or local government. * * *

SEC. 4. REGISTRATION OF LOBBYISTS.

(a) REGISTRATION. —

(1) GENERAL RULE. — No later than 45 days after a lobbyist first makes a lobbying contact or is employed or retained to make a lobbying contact, whichever is earlier, * * * such lobbyist (or, as provided under paragraph (2), the organization employing such lobbyist), shall register with the Secretary of the Senate and the Clerk of the House of Representatives.

(2) EMPLOYER FILING. — Any organization that has 1 or more employees who are lobbyists shall file a single registration under this section on behalf of such employees for each client on whose behalf the employees act as lobbyists.

(3) EXEMPTION. — * * * Notwithstanding paragraphs (1) and (2), a person or entity whose —

(i) total income for matters related to lobbying activities on behalf of a particular client (in the case of a lobbying firm) does not exceed and is not expected to exceed $2,500 [adjusted for inflation]; or

(ii) total expenses in connection with lobbying activities (in the case of an organization whose employees engage in lobbying activities on its own behalf) do not exceed or are not expected to exceed $10,000 [adjusted for inflation],

(as estimated under section 5 of this title) in the quarterly period described in section 5(a) of this title during which the registration would be made is not required to register under this subsection with respect to such client.
* * *

(b) CONTENTS OF REGISTRATION. — Each registration * * * shall contain—

(1) the name, address, business telephone number, and principal place of business of the registrant, and a general description of its business or activities;

(2) the name, address, and principal place of business of the registrant's client, and a general description of its business or activities (if different from paragraph (1));

(3) the name, address, and principal place of business of any organization, other than the client, that —

(A) contributes more than $5,000 to the registrant or the client in the quarterly period to fund the lobbying activities of the registrant; and

(B) actively participates in the planning, supervision, or control of such lobbying activities * * * .

(5) a statement of —

(A) the general issue areas in which the registrant expects to engage in lobbying activities on behalf of the client; and

(B) to the extent practicable, specific issues that have (as of the date of the registration) already been addressed or are likely to be addressed in lobbying activities; and

(6) the name of each employee of the registrant who has acted or whom the registrant expects to act as a lobbyist on behalf of the client and, if any such employee has served as a covered executive branch official or a covered legislative branch official in the 20 years before the date on which the employee first acted. * * *

No disclosure is required under paragraph (3)(B) if the organization that would be identified as affiliated with the client is listed on the client's publicly accessible Internet website as being a member of or contributor to the client, unless the organization in whole or in major part plans, supervises, or controls such lobbying activities. If a registrant relies upon the preceding sentence, the registrant must disclose the specific Internet address of the web page containing the information relied upon. Nothing in paragraph (3)(B) shall be construed to require the disclosure of any information about individuals who are members of, or donors to, an entity treated as a client by this Act or an organization identified under that paragraph.

SEC. 5. REPORTS BY REGISTERED LOBBYISTS.

(a) QUARTERLY REPORT. — No later than 20 days after the end of the quarterly period beginning on the first day of January, April, July, and October of each year in which a registrant is registered under section 4, * * * each registrant shall file a report with the Secretary of the Senate and the Clerk of the House of Representatives on its lobbying activities during such quarterly period. A separate report shall be filed for each client of the registrant.

(b) CONTENTS OF REPORT. — Each quarterly report filed under subsection (a) of this section shall contain —

(1) the name of the registrant, the name of the client, and any changes or updates to the information provided in the initial registration * * *;

(2) for each general issue area in which the registrant engaged in lobbying activities on behalf of the client during the quarterly period —

(A) a list of the specific issues upon which a lobbyist employed by the registrant engaged in lobbying activities, including, to the maximum extent practicable, a list of bill numbers and references to specific executive branch actions;

(B) a statement of the Houses of Congress and the Federal agencies contacted by lobbyists employed by the registrant on behalf of the client; [and]

(C) a list of the employees of the registrant who acted as lobbyists on behalf of the client * * * [.]

(3) in the case of a lobbying firm, a good faith estimate of the total amount of all income from the client (including any payments to the registrant by any other person for lobbying activities on behalf of the client) during the quarterly period, other than income for matters that are unrelated to lobbying activities;

(4) in the case of a registrant engaged in lobbying activities on its own behalf, a good faith estimate of the total expenses that the registrant and its employees incurred in connection with lobbying activities during the quarterly period * * *.

(c) ESTIMATES OF INCOME OR EXPENSES. — For purposes of this section, estimates of income or expenses shall be made as follows:

(1) Estimates of amounts in excess of $5,000 shall be rounded to the nearest $10,000.

(2) In the event income or expenses do not exceed $5,000, the registrant shall include a statement that income or expenses totaled less than $5,000 for the reporting period. * * *

(e) ELECTRONIC FILING REQUIRED. — A report required to be filed under this section shall be filed in electronic form, in addition to any other form that the Secretary of the Senate or the Clerk of the House of Representatives may require or allow. * * *

SEC. 6. DISCLOSURE AND ENFORCEMENT.

(a) IN GENERAL. — The Secretary of the Senate and the Clerk of the House of Representatives shall

(1) provide guidance and assistance on the registration and reporting requirements of this chapter and develop common standards, rules, and procedures for compliance with this chapter;

(2) review, and, where necessary, verify and inquire to ensure the accuracy, completeness, and timeliness of registration and reports;

(3) develop filing, coding, and cross-indexing systems to carry out the purpose of this chapter, including —

(A) a publicly available list of all registered lobbyists, lobbying firms, and their clients; and

(B) computerized systems designed to minimize the burden of filing and maximize public access to materials filed under this chapter;

(4) make available for public inspection and copying at reasonable times the registrations and reports filed under this chapter and, in the case of a report filed in electronic form under section 5(e), make such report available for public inspection over the Internet as soon as technically practicable after the report is so filed; * * *

(7) notify any lobbyist or lobbying firm in writing that may be in noncompliance with this chapter;

(8) notify the United States Attorney for the District of Columbia that a lobbyist or lobbying firm may be in noncompliance with this chapter, if the registrant has been notified in writing and has failed to provide an appropriate response within 60 days after notice was given under paragraph (7); and

(9) maintain all registrations and reports filed under this Act, and make them available to the public over the Internet, without a fee or other access charge, in a searchable, sortable, and downloadable manner, to the extent technically practicable, that —

(A) includes the information contained in the registration and reports;

(B) is searchable and sortable to the maximum extent practicable, including searchable and sortable by each of the categories of information described in section 4(b) or 5(b); and

(C) provides electronic links or other appropriate mechanisms to allow users to obtain relevant information in the database of the Federal Election Commission * * *.

SEC. 7. PENALTIES.

(a) CIVIL PENALTY. — Whoever knowingly fails to

(1) remedy a defective filing within 60 days after notice of such a defect by the Secretary of the Senate or the Clerk of the House of Representatives; or

(2) comply with any other provision of this chapter;

shall, upon proof of such knowing violation by a preponderance of the evidence, be subject to a civil fine of not more than $200,000, depending on the extent and gravity of the violation.

(b) CRIMINAL PENALTY. — Whoever knowingly and corruptly fails to comply with any provision of this Act shall be imprisoned for not more than 5 years or fined under title 18, United States Code, or both.

SEC. 8. RULES OF CONSTRUCTION.

(a) CONSTITUTIONAL RIGHTS. — Nothing in this Act shall be construed to prohibit or interfere with — (1) the right to petition the government for the redress of grievances; (2) the right to express a personal opinion; or (3) the right of association, protected by the first amendment to the Constitution. * * *

NOTES ON THE LOBBYING DISCLOSURE ACT[n]

1. *Lobbying Contacts and Lobbying Activities.* The Act distinguishes between *lobbying contacts* and *lobbying activities*. The Act's requirements are triggered when an individual makes a lobbying contact, which is a certain kind of communication to a covered official. Once such a contact has occurred, the individual must report on all her lobbying activities, which, among other things, include planning and preparing for the contact. An individual who makes such a contact is considered a lobbyist unless her lobbying activities constitute less than 20% of the services she provides a client during a three-month period. As you can see, the definitions of *lobbying contact, lobbying activities,* and *lobbyist* work together to determine when the Act's registration and disclosure provisions are triggered. In addition, it is clear that the definitions of these terms were drafted to address some of the problems in the FRLA. For example, the 20% threshold provides a concrete way to determine whether someone's activities before the government are significant enough to make her a lobbyist. Furthermore, a communication need merely relate to legislation, executive branch rules, federal policies, nominations and the like; it need not be intended to influence the passage or defeat of legislation.

Interestingly, the definition of *lobbying contact* depends in large part on a series of exceptions. Perhaps drafters believed it was easier to state what kinds of communication are *not* lobbying and thus sought to define the term accordingly. The exceptions fall into four general categories: (1) ministerial or de minimis activities (e.g., a request for a meeting as long as there is no attempt to influence a covered official); (2) information that other laws require

---

n. For a comprehensive explanation and analysis of the LDA, before the 2007 amendments, see William Luneberg & Thomas Susman (eds.), *The Lobbying Manual: A Complete Guide to Federal Law Governing Lawyers and Lobbyists* (3d. ed. 2005).

people to disclose (e.g., disclosure pursuant to the Foreign Agents Registration Act of 1938) or that is otherwise a part of the public record (e.g., contacts made in response to a notice in the Federal Register soliciting public communications); (3) contacts that are required by other laws or court order (e.g., disclosure compelled by a subpoena); and (4) hardship cases (e.g., disclosure protected under the Whistleblower Protection Act and, perhaps, disclosure by churches).[o] Certainly, the definition in the Lobbying Disclosure Act provides more guidance about the precise activity that Congress wants to regulate than did the previous definition. Is it specific enough to withstand constitutional challenge? A court considering a challenge to the Act would apply strict scrutiny to this law that burdens fundamental political rights such as the right to petition the federal government and the right of free speech.

2. *Effects of the LDA.* The Lobbying Disclosure Act has been in effect since January 1, 1996. Significantly more information about lobbying at the federal level is available to the press and the public. For example, more people and organizations are registering. Before 1996, the General Accounting Office found that only 6,000 individuals and organizations had registered with Congress. As of 2007, the number of lobbyists registered with the Senate stood at 35,884, with 6,554 lobbying organizations filing. (Remember that a lobbying firm can file one registration listing all its employees.)

Lobbying the federal government is now an over two-billion-dollar-a-year industry. In the first half of 2006, $1.263 billion was spent on federal lobbying, with four organizations (USTelecom Association, the U.S. Chamber of Commerce, the American Association of Retired Persons ("AARP"), and the National Association of Realtors) spending more than $10 million each.[p] The Chamber of Commerce is a very active lobbying force, spending money at the federal and state level and as a member of active coalitions. In 2005, it spent nearly $40 million on lobbying. Like most other corporate interests,[q] the Chamber spends substantially more money to influence politics through lobbying than through campaign contributions. Six lobbying firms received over $10 million in the first half of 2006 from their clients, including $17.38 million paid to the firm of Patton Boggs by clients such as Mars, Inc. and the Association of Trial Lawyers of America. Spending on lobbying is connected, not surprisingly, to the legislation receiving serious consideration by Congress at any particular time. For example, in the first half of 2005, AARP spent more than $27.8 million on lobbying activities, primarily to oppose President Bush's proposed overhaul of Social Security. As Senator John McCain (R–Ariz.) observed: "This [sort of spending] indicates that either somebody is wasting

---

o. See also General Accounting Office, *Federal Lobbying: Differences in Lobbying Definitions and Their Impact* (1999) (discussing differences in definition of lobbying in the Act and in the Internal Revenue Code and implications for comprehensive regulation).

p. CQ's PoliticalMoneyLine, *Money in Politics Databases: 2006 Lobby Reports Covering 1/1/06–6/30/06*, http://www.politicalmoneyline.com.

q. See Jeffrey Milyo, David Primo & Timothy Groseclose, *Corporate PAC Campaign Contributions in Perspective*, 2 Bus. & Pol. 75, 83 (2000).

a lot of their money or there are some very strong influences around this town."[r]

3. *Limitations in the Information Disclosed.* The information provided by the registration and disclosure forms has been made publicly available by a number of news organizations. The *Legal Times* publishes "Influence," an annual report released in the spring on the lobbying activities of D.C. law firms and lobbying organizations. Congressional Quarterly's *www.politicalmoneyline.com* publishes mid-year and year-end reports on lobbying disclosures, updates a database of lobbyist registrations, and maintains a directory of lobbyists, firms and organizations. The Center for Public Integrity[s] publishes lobbying information organized by lobbying firms and by companies and organizations. Both House and Senate offices now have registration reports available on their respective websites, although it is ironic that the Government was slow to take advantage of electronic communication while lobbyists quickly adopted (and embraced as an integral part of their lobbying activities) blackberry cell phones. The 2007 amendments required Congress to make the information disclosed by lobbyists available on the Internet in a searchable, sortable and downloadable format, and to link the information to related information provided by the Federal Election Commission.

The Honest Leadership and Open Government Act of 2007 closed or reduced some of the loopholes in the LDA's coverage, but did not eliminate all the gaps. A crucial improvement made in 2007 was to lower the LDA's thresholds for reporting and to require quarterly, rather than semiannual reports, on lobbying activities. Now lobbyists must disclose income from each client in increments of $10,000 (rather than $20,000 as required by the 1995 Act). In addition, the thresholds that allow a lobbyist to be exempt from reporting were cut in half by the 2007 reform act. It is not clear how much these lower thresholds will affect reporting, however, because spending is now measured quarterly and not semiannually. Another major change in 2007, in provisions not included above, is the requirement that persons covered by the LDA file semiannual reports detailing their campaign contributions exceeding $200. Although this information has been available through Federal Election Commission filings, the new semiannual reports will bring more transparency to the campaign activities of lobbyists. The reports should make it easier for the media, political entrepreneurs and voters to trace campaign contributions to legislative activity. The 2007 provision requires that Congress work to move to quarterly reports of lobbyist campaign contributions as soon as "practicably feasible."

Nonetheless, significant gaps in coverage remain. First, the Act still does not require disclosure concerning expenditures for grassroots lobbying efforts. As we discussed above, this change from the legislation proposed in the 103rd

---

r. T.R. Goldman, *How Influence Pays: Lobby Fees Flow Freely*, Legal Times, Dec. 9, 1996, at S28.

s. See http://www.publicintegrity.org/lobby.

Congress was necessary to gain the votes to pass the 1995 law and the 2007 amendments. Second, the reports do not include much detail about the lobbyists' contacts. The reports indicate which house of Congress and which executive branch agencies were the objects of activities, but they do not reveal the names of specific legislators or staff members who met with the lobbyists.[t]

Why would lobbyists work to avoid disclosing some of the fees paid to them relating to their lobbying activities? Many of the press reports have focused on the fees paid by high-profile clients, such as the tobacco industry or defense contractors. For example, Philip Morris spent $11.3 million to lobby in Washington in the first six months covered by the Act. Even those figures (which include money spent by its in-house lobbyists and fees paid to outside consultants) may be understated because they do not include fees paid by coalitions of which Philip Morris was a member. Before the 2007 amendments, the Lobbying Disclosure Act did not require that lobbyists reveal all the members of coalitions that hired them; only the names of organizational members that contributed more than $10,000 in a six-month period and that planned, supervised, or controlled, *in whole or in major part*, lobbying activities had to be listed in registration forms. (Emphasis added.) Because interest groups work increasingly through coalitions, to increase their clout and broaden their base of support, this gap in the disclosure law was a target of reformers. The new law increases the disclosure relating to coalitions to include any organization that contributes more than $5,000 in any quarter and that "actively participates" in the planning, supervision or control of lobbying activities. In other words, the organization need not be the major force behind the coalition; it will be disclosed as long as it is actively participating in the group. Balancing this more aggressive disclosure is new language that protects individuals from disclosure and that allows a coalition to meet some of the disclosure requirements by posting information on its web site.

4. *Enforcing the LDA.* Another significant change made by the Act was the reformulation of the penalty section. Before the 2007 amendments, the LDA was enforced only through civil fines that could be calibrated up to $50,000 to reflect the "extent and gravity of the violation." In the hearings on the 2007 Act, a House committee noted that there was substantial noncompliance with the LDA's disclosure provisions, with over 2,000 late submissions, failure to file certain forms by virtually all the top lobbying firms, and "almost 300 individuals, companies or associates have lobbied without being registered." H.R. Rep. No. 110–161, 110th Cong., 1st Sess., at 10 (2007) (citing study by the Center for Public Integrity of activity since 1998). Firms realized that they could understate their expenses or fail to report certain lobbying contacts without much risk of a sanction. By 2005, the Department of Justice had pursued only thirteen cases of the possible LDA violations referred to it by Congress. Six cases had been resolved; three resulted in total fines of

---

t. See Anita Krishnakumar, *Towards a Madisonian, Interest-Group-Based Approach to Lobbying Regulation*, 58 Ala. L. Rev. 513 (2007) (proposing changes to the federal lobbying law so that disclosure obligations rested more on elected officials than lobbyists).

$47,000.[u] Accordingly, the Honest Leadership and Open Government Act of 2007 increased the possible civil fines to $200,000 and authorized criminal prosecutions for knowing and corrupt violations of the Act. In criminal cases, offenders can be sentenced to up to five years in prison, as well as fined. In addition, the Attorney General is required to submit semiannual reports on the aggregate number of enforcement actions and the sentences imposed. Should we expect enforcement to be more vigorous after the increase of the penalties? Why was disclosure up so significantly after passage of the 1995 Act, notwithstanding the absence of aggressive enforcement? What changes in behavior on the part of lobbyists and lawmakers are likely given the expansion of enforcement options?

5. *Constitutional Objections to the Lobbying Disclosure Act.* The Court in *Harriss* was unclear about how it would evaluate state justifications for burdening the right to petition, beyond some vague balancing of private rights and state interest. The standard First Amendment test is as follows: When disclosure requirements are so intrusive as to be a "substantial burden" on First Amendment rights of association, speech, or petition, they are permissible only if the government can "convincingly show a substantial relation between the information sought and a subject of overriding and compelling state interest." *Gibson v. Florida Legislative Investigation Commission,* 372 U.S. 539 (1963). Moreover, "a State may not choose means that unnecessarily restrict constitutionally protected liberty. * * * If the State has open to it a less drastic way of satisfying its legitimate interests, it may not choose a legislative scheme that broadly stifles the exercise of fundamental constitutional liberties." *Kusper v. Pontikes,* 414 U.S. 51 (1973).

The compelling state interest test is a steep one but not impossible to pass, particularly in the context of disclosure requirements. Thus, the Court in *Buckley v. Valeo,* 424 U.S. 1 (1976) (per curiam) (Chapter 2, § 3A) upheld the Federal Election Campaign Act's requirement that people making independent expenditures on behalf of a candidate disclose their identity and their expenditures. What the Court identified as "sufficiently important to outweigh the possibility of infringement" of associational privacy rights was the state interest in providing information about candidates and interests to which they are likely to be responsive. This holding was reaffirmed in *McConnell v. Federal Election Comm'n,* 540 U.S. 93 (2003), when the Court upheld even more sweeping disclosure provisions in the Bipartisan Campaign Reform Act of 2002 (Chapter 2, § 3).

In other cases, disclosure provisions can run afoul of the constitutional test. In *NAACP v. Alabama,* 357 U.S. 449 (1958), the Supreme Court invalidated a state's effort to obtain the NAACP's membership lists, on the ground that disclosure would invade and chill the members' freedom of association, a privacy-based right derived from the First Amendment. In *Brown v. Socialist Workers '74 Campaign Committee (Ohio),* 459 U.S. 87 (1982), the Court extended *NAACP v. Alabama* to hold that the disclosures of contributors

---

u. Kenneth Doyle, *Love It or Hate It, Lobbying, Ethics Bill Seen as Sea Change for Industry,* BNA Money & Politics Report (Aug. 20, 2007).

required by Ohio's election finance law could not be constitutionally applied to people contributing to the Socialist Workers party, which had shown a "reasonable probability" that disclosure would lead to harassment of its members. Both *Brown* and *NAACP v. Alabama* relied on the chilling effect that such disclosures might have on a group's associational activity, especially where the group espouses dissident views. How would the Court assess a constitutional challenge to the registration system put in place by the Lobbying Disclosure Act of 1995? How would you frame the compelling state interests?[v]

Lobbying Disclosure Act Problems

Problem 3-8. How would the Lobbying Disclosure Act affect Robert Harriss, Tom Linder, and Ralph Moore, the people involved in the *Harriss* case? Who would be required to register under the Act, and what information would they be required to disclose? Does it matter if the conversations at the dinners with the members of Congress focused on a possible nominee for the Secretary of Agriculture, whose name had not yet been sent to the Senate for its advice and consent? What if those attending the dinners talked only generally about the country's agricultural policy, including the future of price supports? Would your answer change if the people that Linder and Moore entertained were congressional staff working on the House Appropriations Committee? What if they were high-level appointees in the Department of Commerce?

Problem 3-9. Okarche Corporation is very concerned with a proposal in Congress to repeal the tax provision allowing small businesses to deduct immediately ("expense") their purchases of some capital equipment. The proposal would require them to depreciate the cost of business assets, i.e., deduct only part of the purchase price each year, over a five-year period. Sarah Gruntmeir, the President of Okarche, asks her assistant to call their Representative to discover the status of the proposal, the date and time of the committee hearings on it, and the timetable for consideration by Congress. Sarah discovers that the proposal has been included in a major tax proposal that seems to be on a fast track for enactment. She then schedules meetings with her Representative and Senator and their staffs; she flies to Washington for these discussions. Her Senator is too busy to see her, but she spends an hour with his legislative assistant who is responsible for tax matters.

While she is in Washington, she hires Robert Williams, a self-employed consultant specializing in federal tax and budget legislation. Robert accompanies Sarah on the visits to the Hill. He also arranges for Sarah to meet tax lawyers in the Department of Treasury who support this proposal. Finally, he convinces Okarche Corp. to join the Coalition to Preserve Small Businesses in America, which is coordinating a nationwide effort to oppose this legislation. Following Robert's advice, Sarah includes a note (that Robert has written) in Okarche's monthly bills explaining the reasons to oppose this tax proposal and urging Okarche's customers to write or call their federal representative.

---

v. See generally Elizabeth Garrett, Ronald Levin & Theodore Ruger, *Constitutional Issues Raised by the 1995 Lobbying Disclosure Act*, in *The Lobbying Manual, supra,* at 143.

In the end, Sarah spends about 10% of her time for three months working to oppose the tax proposal. Her company spends approximately $30,000, most of which is paid to Robert for his help. Sarah also pays $3,000 in dues to the Coalition to Preserve Small Business. (The Coalition pays Robert over $80,000 for his work as its leader.) Two months after the tax proposal is defeated (in small part due to Sarah's crusade), she puts Robert on a $20,000 annual retainer to keep Okarche informed about developments in Washington relating to small business and to advise her of strategies that Okarche can adopt to influence such matters. Under the Lobbying Disclosure Act, as amended in 2007, must either Sarah or Robert register with the Senate and the House? What information must be disclosed in any registration?

Now, suppose Okarche Corporation is a large multistate corporation lobbying in favor of the enactment of an investment tax credit. Sarah follows a similar strategy to the one described above (except this time, she follows Robert's advice and joins the Invest in America Coalition, a group of large corporations hoping to benefit from a new investment tax credit). Although she spends only 10 percent of her time on the matter, her vice-president for legislative affairs, Samantha Alexander, devotes nearly all her time to this matter during a three-month period. Okarche pays Robert about $40,000, spends $5,000 in dues to the coalition, and spends almost $25,000 on its in-house effort, including the letters to its customers. Who must register with the Senate and House? What information must be disclosed?

C. THE LAWYER AS LOBBYIST AND ETHICAL QUESTIONS SURROUNDING LOBBYISTS

Lawyers typically perform three roles in lobbying campaigns — as lobbyists, as analysts of the meaning and ramifications of proposed statutory language, and as drafters. The first role (lobbyist) calls upon lawyers to deal directly with staff members and legislators. Attorneys regularly mastermind legislative deals, later embodied in tax legislation, environmental statutes, or trade proposals. The second role (analyst) requires lawyers to predict the probable effect of proposed statutory language on their clients' interests and, often, to suggest changes that would negate or ameliorate bad effects. This is the area of strategic counseling, but it is also a routine matter of client counseling because many legal problems implicate statutes, regulations, or lawmaking. Third, lawyers are called upon to draft statutory language (the original bill or amendments), summaries and analyses of proposed legislation to be distributed to legislators and others, and testimony or other supporting documents presented at legislative hearings. Although the media has recently publicized "scandalous" examples of federal laws drafted by lobbyists and enacted without substantial change, this practice is a common one in Congress where members and their staff rely on lobbyists for expertise and information. Furthermore, lobbyists routinely draft statements or colloquies that are either delivered by the lawmakers or inserted into the *Record*. Staff or members may edit these statements somewhat, but time pressures often result in their being used unchanged. Accordingly, staffers and representatives learn to trust particular lobbyists and rely on them for information and assistance; reputable lobbyists know this and zealously guard their reputations for truthfulness and efficiency.

Although lobbying and legislative work is a common part of practice for many attorneys, especially those in Washington, D.C. or in state capitols, most rules of professional conduct do not provide much helpful guidance in this context. The restraints on a lawyer's conduct when representing a client in connection with proceedings involving legislation or proposed administrative regulations have never been clearly or fully stated.[w]

The current rules of professional conduct for lawyers provide some guidance to lawyers who lobby.[x] Generally, lawyer-lobbyists are governed by rules of professional responsibility, although under Model Rule 5.7(a)(2), a lawyer can opt out of the rules if she provides services through an entity distinct from one that provides legal services and she informs her client that her services are not legal in nature and that the traditional protections of the attorney-client relationship do not exist. Some lawyer-lobbyists may want to opt out of the coverage of the rules to avoid "the strict application of the conflict of interest rules to a lobbying practice; hav[e] fewer restrictions on soliciting and marketing; and [be] able to split fees with non-lawyers." Ronald Gifford, *The Ethical Responsibilities of a Lawyer-Lobbyist*, in *The Lobbying Manual, supra*, at 487.

The ABA Model Rules of Professional Conduct (2002) are not binding upon the various local bar associations which you will join, but most of those bar associations have adopted the Rules, or variations of the Rules, as their own. To complicate matters further, however, not all bar associations have adopted the most recent iteration of the rules and have instead continued to use the previous version formulated in 1983. We will focus primarily on the new rules in this discussion. The 2002 Model Rules provide:

Rule 3.9 *Advocate in Nonadjudicative Proceedings*

A lawyer representing a client before a legislative body or administrative agency in a nonadjudicative proceeding shall disclose that the appearance is in a representative capacity and shall conform to the provisions of rules 3.3(a) through (c), 3.4(a) through (c), and 3.5.

The relevant portions of Rules 3.3, 3.4, and 3.5 incorporated by reference in Rule 3.9 state:

Rule 3.3 *Candor Toward the Tribunal*

(a) A lawyer shall not knowingly:

---

w. See generally Charles Horsky, *The Washington Lawyer* (1952); Louis Brandeis, *The Opportunity in the Law*, 39 Am. L. Rev. 555 (1905); David A Marcello, *The Ethics and Politics of Legislative Drafting,* 70 Tulane L. Rev. 2437, 2457–63 (1996) (discussing the ethical guidelines and duty to a client a lawyer faces in helping to draft legislation).

x. For discussion of the relevant model rules and proposals for revisions, see Michelle Grant, *Legislative Lawyers and the Model Rules*, 14 Geo. J. Legal Ethics 823 (2001).

(1) make a false statement of material fact or law to a tribunal or fail to correct a false statement of material fact or law previously made to the tribunal by the lawyer;

(2) fail to disclose to the tribunal legal authority in the controlling jurisdiction known to the lawyer to be directly adverse to the position of the client and not disclosed by opposing counsel; or

(3) offer evidence that the lawyer knows to be false. If a lawyer, the lawyer's client, or a witness called by the lawyer, has offered material evidence and the lawyer comes to know of its falsity, the lawyer shall take reasonable remedial measures, including, if necessary, disclosure to the tribunal. A lawyer may refuse to offer evidence, other than the testimony of a defendant in a criminal matter, that the lawyer reasonably believes is false.

(b) A lawyer who represents a client in an adjudicative proceeding and who knows that a person intends to engage, is engaging or has engaged in criminal or fraudulent conduct related to the proceeding shall take reasonable remedial measures, including, if necessary, disclosure to the tribunal.

(c) The duties stated in paragraphs (a) and (b) continue to the conclusion of the proceeding, and apply even if compliance requires disclosure of information otherwise protected by Rule 1.6.

Note that (d) in Model Rule 3.3 was not incorporated in Model Rule 3.9, suggesting that a lobbyist meeting privately with a lawmaker or aide does not have an obligation to disclose all material facts. The relevant rules continue:

Rule 3.4 *Fairness to Opposing Party and Counsel*

A lawyer shall not:

(a) unlawfully obstruct another party's access to evidence or unlawfully alter, destroy or conceal a document or other material having potential evidentiary value. A lawyer shall not counsel or assist another person to do any such act;

(b) falsify evidence, counsel or assist a witness to testify falsely, or offer an inducement to a witness that is prohibited by law;

(c) knowingly disobey an obligation under the rules of a tribunal except for an open refusal based on an assertion that no valid obligation exists; * * *

Rule 3.5 *Impartiality and Decorum of the Tribunal*

A lawyer shall not:

(a) seek to influence a judge, juror, prospective juror or other official by means prohibited by law;

(b) communicate ex parte with such a person during the proceeding unless authorized to do so by law or court order; * * *

(d) engage in conduct intended to disrupt a tribunal.

What does it mean to engage in "disruptive" conduct in the context of lobbying the legislative and executive branches? Would any of the techniques described in *Harriss* rise to the level of disruption? Could a lawyer violate this rule if she coordinated an aggressive grassroots campaign against certain members of

Congress? What if the campaign included personal attacks on the lawmakers? Or if it was more "astroturf" than genuine?

The Comment to Rule 3.9 addresses a number of the relevant ethical concerns:

> In representation before bodies such as legislatures, municipal councils, and executive and administrative agencies acting in a rule-making or policy-making capacity, lawyers present facts, formulate issues and advance argument in the matters under consideration. The decision-making body, like a court, should be able to rely on the integrity of the submissions made to it. A lawyer appearing before such a body must deal with it honestly and in conformity with applicable rules of procedure * * *.
>
> Lawyers have no exclusive right to appear before nonadjudicative bodies, as they do before a court. The requirements of this Rule therefore may subject lawyers to regulations inapplicable to advocates who are not lawyers. However, legislatures and administrative agencies have a right to expect lawyers to deal with them as they deal with courts.
>
> This Rule only applies when a lawyer represents a client in connection with an official hearing or meeting of a governmental agency or a legislative body to which the lawyer or the lawyer's client is presenting evidence or argument. It does not apply to representation of a client in a negotiation or other bilateral transaction with a governmental agency or in connection with an application for a license or other privilege or the client's compliance with generally applicable reporting requirements, such as the filing of income-tax returns. Nor does it apply to the representation of a client in connection with an investigation or examination of the client's affairs conducted by government investigators or examiners. Representation in such matters is governed by Rules 4.1 through 4.4.

Rule 1.11 addresses the revolving door that circulates lawyer-lobbyists from government to private practice:

Rule 1.11 *Successive Government and Private Employment*

(a) Except as law may otherwise expressly permit, a lawyer who has formerly served as a public officer or employee of the government:

(1) is subject to Rule 1.9(c) [mandating confidentiality with respect to former clients]; and

(2) shall not otherwise represent a client in connection with a matter in which the lawyer participated personally and substantially as a public officer or employee, unless the appropriate government agency gives its informed consent, confirmed in writing, to the representation. * * *.

Most lawyers who appear before congressional committees and administrative agencies are members of the District of Columbia Bar. The D.C. Bar has not adopted the Model Rules verbatim. The differences are important for lawyers practicing in D.C. to keep in mind.

One significant difference is D.C.'s Rule 3.3(a)(2):

A lawyer shall not knowingly * * * [c]ounsel or assist a client to engage in conduct that the lawyer knows is criminal or fraudulent, but a lawyer may discuss the legal consequences of any proposed course of conduct with a client and may counsel or assist a client to make a good-faith effort to determine the validity, scope, meaning, or application of the law. * * *

The ABA Rule (quoted above) merely states that a lawyer has to disclose facts to the tribunal when it is necessary to prevent a criminal or fraudulent act by the client. The D.C. Rule is more open-ended; it says that a lawyer may not assist or engage in criminal or fraudulent conduct, but it appears to allow the lawyer to help the client develop a good story as long as the lawyer does not know for certain that it is untrue. D.C. Rule 3.3 also has a telling comment: "[A]n advocate does not vouch for the evidence submitted in a cause; the tribunal is responsible for assessing its probative value." The ABA's Rules do not appear to make this distinction.

The D.C. Rules have a stricter revolving door canon than the ABA's Model Rules. A comment to the D.C. Rule 1.11 best describes the D.C. Rule and its differences:

> [The D.C. Rule 1.11] flatly forbids a lawyer to accept other employment in a matter in which the lawyer participated personally and substantially as a public officer or employee. * * * There is no provision for waiver of the individual lawyer's disqualification.

The ABA Rule allows the government to waive Rule 1.11; D.C. does not. And D.C. more broadly defines the matters on which former government lawyers are restricted from working in private practice. In addition, the comment to D.C. Rule 1.11 makes the point that Rule 1.11 also applies to judges' law clerks. These rules work in tandem with the restrictions of federal law included in the Ethics in Government Act, discussed in Section 1 of this chapter. These rules are subset of the more extensive conflict of interest provisions found in the rules of professional responsibility. Although a lawyer-lobbyist bound by the rules is also bound by the conflict of interest provisions, they were not written with lobbying in mind and can present challenges in application.[y]

We have focused on the ethical obligations of the private attorney who appears on behalf of a client in front of a legislator or legislative committee. Congress itself is also full of lawyers, working for lawmakers in their personal offices, working as part of a committee staff or for party leadership entities, or working in the more technical organs of Congress like the Joint Tax Committee or the Congressional Research Service. They also face difficult ethical questions. For example, who is the client of a legislative aide working on a senator's personal staff? The senator? The Senate? The constituents? The public good (and whose conception)?[z]

---

y. See Gifford, *supra*, at 499–511; Kenneth Button, *The District of Columbia Conflict of Interest Rules and Lawyer–Lobbyists: A Troubled Marriage*, 8 Geo. J. Legal Ethics 961 (1995).

z. See generally Kathleen Clark, *Government Lawyering: The Ethics of Representing Elected Representatives*, 61 Law & Contemp. Probs. 31, 37–38 (1998) (claiming that political lawyers do not see their role as promoting the public interest, and arguing that client is not the committee, legislative branch, or the Senate, but rather the specific Senator or Congressman who is chair of the committee); Charles Tiefer, *The Senate and House Counsel Offices: Dilemmas*

NOTE ON LOBBYING REGULATION IN THE STATES

The great diversity of state laws regulating lobbying makes it impossible to provide a generalized understanding of state regulation in the space available. All states have enacted statutes requiring lobbying disclosure (with Pennsylvania's new law becoming effective on January 1, 2007), and the Center for Public Integrity found 47 states to have more effective lobbying regulation laws than did the federal government.[a] Six states have a two-year waiting period affecting lawmakers who become lobbyists, and 19 states have a one-year ban to combat the problem of the revolving door. Twenty-seven states have independent agencies to oversee lobbying disclosure, with 18 states delegating that authority to the secretary of state. Thirty-seven states, like the federal government, include lobbying of the executive branch within the scope of their regulatory structure. As one example of a comprehensive state regulatory scheme, we invite you to consider the approach taken in California, which has one of the most ambitious regulatory schemes that has developed over several decades, largely as a result of initiatives and judicial decisions.

The Political Reform Act of 1974 was approved by California voters as an initiative measure. It was codified, as amended, as West's Ann. Cal. Gov't Code § 81000 *et seq.* (West 1976).[b] The Act created a Fair Political Practices Commission to administer, implement, and enforce the law. The Act defined lobbyist as "any person who receives two thousand dollars or more in economic consideration in a calendar month, other than reimbursement for reasonable travel expenses, or whose principal duties as an employee are, to communicate directly or through his agents with any elective state official, agency official or legislative official for the purpose of influencing legislative or administrative action." *Id.* § 82039. Lobbyists were required to register with the Secretary of State "before doing anything to influence legislative or administrative action." *Id.* § 86100. When registering, lobbyists had to disclose their principals and list each state agency (which is defined to include the Legislature) that they "will attempt to influence as a substantial or regular portion of [their] activities as [lobbyists]." *Id.* § 86101.

Lobbyists were required to create separate accounts for the deposit of payments received for the purpose of paying lobbying expenses. *Id.* § 86105. Lobbyists were also required to file periodic reports disclosing, *inter alia*, (1) the sources and amounts of all payments "received in consideration for or directly or indirectly in support of or in connection with influencing legislative or administrative action"; (2) the deposits to and expenditures from each

---

of Representing in Court the Institutional Congressional Client, 61 Law & Contemp. Probs. 47 (1998) (discussing ethical issues facing the House and Senate Legal Counsels, the lawyers who represent Congress in court).

a. Leah Rush & David Jimenez, *States Outpace Congress in Upgrading Lobbying Laws*, The Center for Public Integrity, March 1, 2006, available at www.publicintegrity.com (analysis does not include new Pennsylvania law, 65 Pa.C.S. § 1301-A et seq.).

b. Citations to sections of the California code refer to sections of the 1974 Act and thus may now be different given the many changes to this section of the Government Code by law and popular initiative.

account controlled by the lobbyists, including descriptions of any considerations received in return for expenditures and the beneficiary of an expenditure if the beneficiary is someone other than the payee; and (3) the legislative or administrative action that the lobbyist has influenced or attempted to influence. *Id.* § 86107. In general, principals of lobbyists and "any person who directly or indirectly makes payments to influence legislative or administrative action of [$2,500] or more in value in any calendar quarter" also had to file periodic reports. *Id.* §§ 86107–09.

These disclosure and reporting requirements were upheld as constitutional in *Fair Political Practices Commission v. Superior Court*, 599 P.2d 46 (Cal. 1979), *cert. denied*, 444 U.S. 1049 (1980). But the Supreme Court of California held that the disclosure requirements found in § 86107(d)–(e) and § 86109(d)–(e) violated the First Amendment. Section 86107(d) required a lobbyist to disclose the names of any officials or candidates, and the names of each member of the immediate family of any such person, "with whom the lobbyist has engaged in an exchange of money, goods, services or anything of value and the nature and date of each such exchange and the monetary value exchanged." Section 86107(e) required disclosure of "the name and address of any business entity in which the lobbyist knows or has reason to know" that an official or candidate "is the proprietor, partner, director, officer, or manager, or has more than a fifty percent ownership interest, with whom the lobbyist has engaged in an exchange of money, goods, services, or anything of value and the nature and date of each exchange and the monetary value exchanged, if the total value of such exchanges is [$500] or more in a calendar year." In striking down these provisions, the court stated (559 P.2d at 54–55):

> * * * [T]he transaction reporting requirements will often be so onerous as to constitute a significant interference with the fundamental right to petition. The extent of reporting required is not directly related to the extent of lobbying activities but is determined mainly by lobbyist and employer transactions with others, which may be entirely unrelated to lobbyist activities. For example, the reporting requirement as to business transactions applies to transactions with a business entity where any state candidate, or legislative, agency, or elective state official is a director. (§ 86109, subd. (e).) Accordingly, if a director of the Bank of America is also an agency official — perhaps a Regent of the University of California — a lobbyist and any person who employs a lobbyist or spends more than $250 in a single month to influence legislative or administrative action must disclose transactions above the statutory amount with the Bank of America. The requirement applies even though the lobbying activities have nothing to do with the university or banks. * * *

> Because the transaction reporting requirements will often constitute a significant interference with the fundamental right to petition, the strict scrutiny doctrine is applicable. * * *

> * * * We are satisfied that the right to petition for redress of grievances similarly may not be conditioned upon disclosure of irrelevant private financial matters unrelated to the petition activity. Because the transaction reporting requirements apply to transactions having no relation to the lobbying activities, they are not "closely tailored" to any legitimate state interest in the regulation of lobbying but constitute an unnecessary curtailment of the right to petition.

Do you agree that the transaction reporting requirements "apply to transactions having no relation to the lobbying activities"? Why didn't the California court take the approach of the Supreme Court in *Harriss* and interpret the state statute in a relatively narrow way that avoided constitutional problems while still allowing some regulation? How would the California court's constitutional analysis apply to the Lobbying Disclosure Act?

The legislature responded by repealing much of the 1974 Act and replacing it with a new lobbying regulation law in September 1985. See Stats. 1985, ch. 1183, codified at West's Ann. Cal. Gov't Code § 81000 *et al.* The 1985 Act required lobbyists to be certified, and "lobbying firms" and designated "lobbyist employers" to register with the Secretary of State. *Id.* § 86100. Lobbying firms were required to file periodic reports which included (*inter alia*) those persons who contracted with the firm for lobbying services and the details of those contracts; detailed accounting of all contributions at or above $100 to state officials or candidates (or their committees); and identification of any firm partner, owner, officer or employee who engaged in at least five separate communications with state officials. *Id.* § 86114. Lobbyist employers who were required to file reports must include (*inter alia*) total payments made to lobbyists and lobbying firms; detailed accounting of all contributions at or above $100 to state officials or candidates (or their committees); and total payments made to influence legislative or administrative action. *Id.* § 86116. Do these provisions pass constitutional muster?

In addition to these registration, reporting, and disclosure provisions, the California Lobbying Act prohibits gifts aggregating more than $10 per month from lobbyists to any state official. *Id.* §§ 86203–86204. Section 86205 provides:

No lobbyist shall:

(a) Do anything with the purpose of placing any elected state officer, legislative official, agency official, or state candidate under personal obligation to him or his employer.

(b) Deceive or attempt to deceive any elected state officer, legislative official, or state candidate with regard to any material fact pertinent to any pending or proposed legislative or administrative action.

(c) Cause or influence the introduction of any bill or amendment thereto for the purpose of thereafter being employed to secure its passage or defeat.

(d) Attempt to create a fictitious appearance of public favor or disfavor of any proposed legislative or administrative action to cause any communication to be sent to any elected state officer, legislative official, agency official, or state candidate in the name of any fictitious person or in the name of any real person, except with the consent of such real person.

(e) Represent falsely either directly or indirectly, that he can control the official action of any elected state officer, legislative official, or agency official.

(f) Accept or agree to accept any payment in any way contingent upon the defeat, enactment or outcome of any proposed legislative or administrative action.

These are substantive limits on what lobbyists can say and do. Are they constitutional?

Two recent initiatives in California have further restricted the campaign activities of lobbyists. In 1996, voters approved the California Political Reform Act, Proposition 208, which is primarily a set of relatively restrictive campaign finance regulations. In § 85704, Proposition 208 prohibited candidates from soliciting or accepting a campaign contribution "from, through, or arranged by a registered state or local lobbyist if that lobbyist finances, engages, or is authorized to engage in lobbying the governmental agency for which the candidate is seeking election." After its enactment, Proposition 208 was preliminarily enjoined by a federal district court judge who found that its contribution and expenditure limits violated the Constitution. See *California Prolife Council Political Action Committee v. Scully*, 989 F. Supp. 1282 (E.D. Cal. 1998), *aff'd*, 164 F.3d 1189 (9th Cir. 1999). The district court judge singled out the provisions affecting contributions by lobbyists as "broader and more onerous" than the other restrictions.

As the proceedings surrounding the preliminary injunction dragged on, Californians passed another initiative, Proposition 34, that repealed Proposition 208 and put in its place a less draconian set of campaign finance regulations, effective in 2001. Section 85702 prohibits candidates for state offices from accepting contributions from lobbyists and prohibits lobbyists from making such contributions. Again, in order to be subject to the prohibition, the lobbyist must be registered to lobby the particular government agency for which the candidate is seeking election. Proposition 34 defines a lobbyist as someone who receives $2,000 or more in a month to communicate directly with a state official for the purpose of influencing legislative or administrative action, or someone whose principal duties are such activities. § 82039. Will Proposition 34's restrictions on lobbyists' campaign activities pass constitutional challenge? See *Inst. of Governmental Advocates v. Fair Political Practices Comm'n*, 164 F. Supp. 2d 1183 (E.D. Cal. 2001). Are they justified by corruption in the state legislative process? California is not the only state to prohibit campaign contributions by lobbyists; some like Kentucky and South Carolina prohibit contributions entirely, Alaska prohibits lobbyist contributions except to candidates in the district where the lobbyist votes, and other states prohibit any contributions while the legislature is in session (e.g., Arizona, Colorado, Connecticut, Louisiana, Maine and Maryland).

SECTION 3. RULES FACILITATING LEGISLATIVE DELIBERATION

At both the state and federal level there are rules that structure and facilitate deliberation in the legislature. These rules are found in state and federal constitutions, in statutes, at common law, and in customs and regulations of specific legislative chambers. For analytical convenience, we shall organize our discussion around three different kinds of rules: (A) substantive constitutional requirements affecting deliberation, primarily at the state level, including the single-subject rule and generality requirements; (B) line item veto provisions; and (C) legislative immunities. As we offer the different rules, you might consider, first, whether the vision of the legislative process that emerges from these rules is a coherent or desirable vision; and, second, whether specific rules are supported by one of the theories of legislatures. In this chapter we are focusing primarily on constitutional structures that operate in a relatively piecemeal fashion; in Chapter 4 we will expand our discussion to comprehensive procedural frameworks in the modern federal Congress that shape deliberation.

A. SUBSTANTIVE LIMITATIONS ON THE LEGISLATIVE PROCESS: SINGLE SUBJECT RULES AND GENERALITY REQUIREMENTS

The federal and state constitutions frequently contain a variety of limitations on legislation and the legislative process. Some are substantive limits on the nature of legislation.[a] One might generally say that the substantive constitutional protections found at the state level are aimed at various forms of rent-seeking by private groups at the public's expense. You might wonder why state constitutions seem more concerned about this problem than the U.S. Constitution seems to be. Perhaps part of the answer lies in the smaller geographic areas of the states relative to the entire United States. James Madison in *Federalist #10* argued that a benefit of a large country was the reduced likelihood that government would be captured by one faction. "[I]t is this circumstance [the greater extent of territory permitted by a representative government] principally which renders factious combinations less to be dreaded * * * Extend the sphere [of territory] and you take in a greater variety of parties and interests; you make it less probable that a majority of the whole will have a common motive to invade the rights of other citizens; or if such a common motive exists, it will be more difficult for all who feel it to discover their own strength and act in unison with each other." Is Madison's argument persuasive? Can you think of other reasons why state constitutions might be more concerned with rent-seeking?

Interestingly, there have been proposals to import some of the state limitations into the federal sphere,[b] if not by constitutional amendment then by congressional rule. For example, the tax-writing committees in Congress adopted a policy in the late 1980s against *rifleshot provisions* or tax provisions such as the transition rules in the Tax Reform Act of 1986 that benefit only one or a very few taxpayers. This was a self-imposed generality requirement of sorts.

Generality Requirements. Most state constitutions have provisions regulating the tendency of government to distribute benefits to special interests or private parties, at the state's expense. See Adrian Vermeule, *Veil of Ignorance Rules in Constitutional Law,* 111 Yale L.J. 399, 411–15 (2001)

---

a. For a good analysis, see Robert Williams, *State Constitutional Limits on Legislative Procedure: Legislative Compliance and Judicial Enforcement,* 48 U. Pitt. L. Rev. 797 (1987).

b. See Brannon Denning & Books Smith, *Uneasy Riders: The Case for a Truth-in-Legislation Amendment,* 1999 Utah L. Rev. 957; Nancy Townsend, *Single Subject Restriction as an Alternative to the Line-Item Veto,* 1 Notre Dame J. L. Ethics & Pub. Pol'y 227 (1985) (both arguing for a single-subject requirement on the federal level).

(describing how constitutional provisions requiring generality adopted behind a "partial veil of ignorance" can dampen self-interested behavior). Such "anti-rent-seeking" provisions include the following:

1. *Public Purpose Requirements.* Most state constitutions have general clauses requiring legislation (especially appropriations) to serve public rather than private purposes, and some state codes include general admonitions for courts to interpret statutes as though they were adopted for public rather than private purposes.[c] Theoretically (but usually not in practice) such requirements would require courts to invalidate or to construe rent-seeking legislation narrowly.[d]

2. *Rules Against Special Legislation.* Some state constitutions prohibit *special legislation*, others list subjects on which such legislation is not permitted, while others forbid special statutes when more general ones exist or might be drafted instead. Article 3, § 32 of the Pennsylvania Constitution combines these approaches, prohibiting special laws relating to specific subjects (remission of fines, property tax exemptions, labor regulations, for examples) or displacing general laws. Other state constitutions prohibit the government from making gifts, subsidies, or grants to private individuals.[e] For example, Article IV, § 13 of the Illinois Constitution states: "The General Assembly shall pass no special or local law when a general law is or can be made applicable. Whether a general law is or can be made applicable shall be a matter for judicial determination." Courts have not often found that targeted

---

c. See Donald Kochan, *"Public Use" and the Independent Judiciary: Condemnation in an Interest-Group Perspective*, 3 Tex. Rev. L. & Pol. 49 (1998) (noting that all states except North Carolina require that any takings of property by the government be only for public use); compare U.S. Const. Amend. V (takings of property must be for a "public use").

d. In addition to the specific limitations upon legislation, state constitutions routinely include general proscriptions, such as a due process, takings, or equal protection clause, that state courts may use to attack rent-seeking legislation. Despite its demise at the federal level, *substantive due process* and allied approaches to reviewing economic regulation rigorously are alive and well in many state supreme courts under their own state constitutions. A state supreme court is, of course, the ultimate expositor of what the state constitution means. See Daniel Rodriguez, *State Constitutional Theory and its Prospects*, 28 N.M. L. Rev. 271 (1998) (arguing that state constitutional theory should be developed as "an independent discourse" because of the "distinct roles of state constitutions in a federal system").

e. The U.S. Constitution has no general prohibition or limitation on special legislation. During each Congress various *private bills* are enacted; one common type consists of a waiver of immigration requirements for particular individuals, and another common type allows compensation to persons whose claims against the federal government fall outside the scope of the Federal Torts Claims Act and other claims statutes. Although, theoretically, federal legislation that is special in character might violate the equal protection component of the Due Process Clause of the Fifth Amendment, we know of no case so holding. See generally Note, *Private Bills in Congress*, 79 Harv. L. Rev. 1684 (1966). See also Bernadette Maguire, *Immigration: Public Legislation and Private Bills* (1997) (studying private bills in the immigration context through a series of case studies).

laws are so narrow as to violate the constitutional prohibition against special legislation.[f]

3. *Uniformity*. Many state constitutions require that laws (especially tax laws) be uniform. Compare U.S. Const. Art. I, § 8, cl. 1 (federal "Taxes, Duties, Imposts and Excises * * * shall be uniform throughout the United States") with *id.* Amend. XVI (allowing federal income tax without apportionment among the several states, overruling Supreme Court's interpretation of § 8, clause 1). State constitutions often require that state laws apply generally and uniformly across the state — an effort to prevent the legislature from providing special benefits to one region or locality. See, e.g., Wis. Const. art. VIII, § 1 (amended 1974) ("The rule of taxation shall be uniform but the legislature may empower cities, villages or towns to collect and return taxes on real estate located therein by optional methods."); N.J. Const. art. VIII, § 1 ("Property shall be assessed for taxation under general laws and by uniform rules."); Pa. Const. art. VIII, § 1 ("All taxes shall be uniform, upon the same class of subjects, within the territorial limits of the authority of levying the tax, and shall be levied and collected under general law.").[g]

Tax legislation is also increasingly the subject of state constitutional amendments, not all of which are substantive. For example, according to the Americans for Tax Reform, 16 states now require supermajority votes to pass certain kinds of tax rate increases. Six states have either a legislative or constitutional tax limitation provision that requires the state to return to the taxpayers amounts of tax collected that exceed a certain threshold (often determined by whether growth in tax collection exceeds growth in personal income).[h] All these provisions are designed to make it harder for legislators and organized interests to construct special interest tax breaks paid for by general tax revenues.

The Single-Subject Rule. Forty-two state constitutions have requirements that limit bills to one subject.[i] Under the majority of these provisions, the single subject of the bill must be expressed in its title. The requirement that the title explain what is in the bill historically predates the single-subject

---

f. See, e.g., *Cutinello v. Whitley*, 641 N.E.2d 360 (Ill. 1994) (statute allowing specified counties to impose tax on individuals who sell fuel at retail in respective counties does not violate special legislation provision of state constitution); *Village of Schaumburg v. Doyle*, 661 N.E.2d 496 (Ill. App. 1996) (amendment to Pesticide Act prohibiting regulation of pesticides by any political subdivisions except for counties and municipalities with populations over 2 million does not violate the state constitution's special legislation provision). See also Thomas Palisi, Comment, Town of Secaucus v. Hudson County Board of Taxation: *An Analysis of the Special Legislation and Tax Uniformity Clauses of the New Jersey Constitution*, 47 Rutgers L. Rev. 1229 (1995).

g. See also J. Anthony Coughlan, *Land Value Taxation and Constitutional Uniformity*, 7 Geo. Mason L. Rev. 261 (1999); Jack Stark, *The Uniformity Clause of the Wisconsin Constitution*, 76 Marq. L. Rev. 577 (1993).

h. Alison McCarthy & Elaine Maag, *Limits on State Revenue* 443 (July 2006), http://taxpolicycenter.org/UploadedPDF/1001018_Tax_Fact_07-31-06.pdf.

i. See Denning & Smith, *supra*, at 1005. For a classic study, see Millard Ruud, "*No Law Shall Embrace More than One Subject*," 42 Minn. L. Rev. 389 (1958).

requirement; it apparently resulted from the notorious Yazoo Act of the Georgia Legislature in 1795.[j]

The major purpose of single-subject provisions is to minimize logrolling, derogatorily described by one court as the "practice of jumbling together in one act inconsistent subjects in order to force passage by uniting minorities with different interests when the particular provisions could not pass on their own separate merits."[k] The fear is the following: Proposals A, B, and C are bad measures, each benefitting a special interest and each favored by only a minority of legislators. Thus, none could be enacted as a stand-alone bill. But if the three factions can assemble a "Christmas tree" bill — i.e., a bill that, like a Christmas tree, is available for hanging each legislator's pet "ornament" on — containing A, B, and C, a majority may well adopt the bill. This runs the risk of creating bad public policy and — if A, B, and C are spending proposals — state overspending.

Several states have single-subject and title requirements for popular initiatives.[l] These provisions are justified not only on the ground that they reduce logrolling, but also that they reduce voter confusion that might arise with complicated and intricate legislative proposals. We will return to the single-subject requirement in the context of direct democracy in Chapter 5, § 2.

Consider the following case concerning the single-subject requirement for law passed by a state legislature.

DEPARTMENT OF EDUCATION v. LEWIS
Supreme Court of Florida, 1982
416 So.2d 455

BOYD, JUSTICE.

House Bill No. 30–B was the general appropriations bill adopted by the 1981 Legislature[.] The appropriations for the Department of Education and the Commissioner of Education was prefaced by the following proviso:

> No funds appropriated herein shall be used to finance any state-supported public or private postsecondary educational institution that charters or gives official recognition or knowingly gives assistance to or provides meeting facilities for any group or

---

j. The Yazoo Act was entitled "An act supplementary to an act for appropriating part of the unlocated territory of this state, for the payment of the late state troops, and for other purposes therein mentioned, and declaring the right of this state to the unappropriated territory thereof, for the protection and support of the frontiers of this state, and for other purposes." In fact, the Act ordered the sale of a considerable portion of state land to certain companies. Later, in 1796, the Georgia legislature passed a statute declaring the Yazoo Act null and void because of undue influence and fraud in its enactment. In *Fletcher v. Peck*, 10 U.S. (6 Cranch.) 87 (1810), the Supreme Court held that the 1796 Act could not divest title to land sold to an innocent purchaser under the earlier Act.

k. *State ex rel. Martin v. Zimmerman*, 289 N.W. 662, 664 (Wis. 1940); see *Simpson v. Tobin*, 367 N.W.2d 757, 767 (S.D. 1985).

l. See Daniel Lowenstein, *California Initiatives and the Single-Subject Rule*, 30 UCLA L. Rev. 936 (1983).

organization that recommends or advocates sexual relations between persons not married to each other.

Sexual relations means contact with sexual organs of one person by the body of another person for sexual gratification. Any postsecondary educational institution found in violation of this provision shall have all state funds withheld until that institution is again in compliance with the law.

No state financial aid shall be given to students enrolled at any postsecondary educational institution located in Florida which is in violation of this provision.

Article III, section 12, Florida Constitution, provides:

Laws making appropriations for salaries of public officers and other current expenses of the state shall contain provisions on no other subject.

This provision is a corollary of Article III, section 6, which requires that all laws be limited to a single subject and matters properly related to that subject. An extensive body of constitutional law teaches that the purpose of article III, section 6 is to ensure that every proposed enactment is considered with deliberation and on its own merits. A lawmaker must not be placed in the position of having to accept a repugnant provision in order to achieve adoption of a desired one.

Through a number of cases decided over many years this Court has attempted to make clear to the Legislature that under our constitutional plan for the lawful exercise of governmental powers an appropriations act is not the proper place for the enactment of general public policies on matters other than appropriations. In *Brown v. Firestone*, [382 So.2d 654 (Fla. 1980)], the Court said:

* * * Provisions on substantive topics should not be ensconced in an appropriations bill in order to logroll or to circumvent the legislative process normally applicable to such action. Similarly, general appropriations bills should not be cluttered with extraneous matters which might cloud the legislative mind when it should be focused solely upon appropriations matters.

* * * [*Brown*] establish[ed] two principles[.] * * * First, if a provision in an appropriations bill changes existing law on any subject other than appropriations, it is invalid. Second, a qualification or restriction must directly and rationally relate to the purpose of the appropriation to which it applies. * * *

* * * The proviso [in question] attempts to make substantive policy on the governance of postsecondary educational institutions. Thus it amends a whole host of statutes pertaining to the operation of public colleges and universities and the regulation of private colleges and universities, [thereby failing the first test of *Brown*].

* * * The proviso is not directly and rationally related to the appropriation of state funds to postsecondary institutions and students. It is, rather, designed to further a legislative objective unrelated to such funding [and thereby fails the second test as well].

NOTES ON ENFORCEMENT OF STATE RESTRICTIONS ON LEGISLATION AND LEGISLATIVE PROCEDURES

1. *Enforcing the Single-Subject Rule.* State constitutions do not define what they mean by a "single subject" and "strict adherence to [the rule's] letter would seriously interfere with the practical business of legislation."[m] Thus, many state courts have articulated liberal tests that are easy for legislatures to meet. "[I]f, from the standpoint of legislative treatment, there is any reasonable basis for the grouping together in one 'act' of various matters, this court cannot say that such matters constitute more than one subject."[n] The remedy for a violation of the single-subject varies among the states. Some state constitutions explicitly provide the remedy; in Iowa, for example, the Constitution states that any provision that is not consistent with the subject of an Act may be severed and declared void, while the rest of the provisions remain in effect. Iowa Const. art III, § 29. Where constitutions are silent, courts must determine whether to sever the offending provisions or to strike down the entire law because the unconstitutional procedure of enactment tainted the entire bill. See Martha Dragich, *State Constitutional Restrictions on Legislative Procedure: Rethinking the Analysis of Original Purpose, Single Subject, and Clear Title Challenges*, 38 Harv. J. Legis. 103, 154–62 (2001) (arguing that severance tends to be the better remedy and providing severance analysis).

Illinois has more aggressively enforced the single-subject requirement than have most other states, and in some instances, it has used the rule to throw out entire statutes, not just the offending provisions. In *Johnson v. Edgar*, No. 95 CH 12004 (Ill. Circ. Ct. May 7, 1996), *aff'd*, 680 N.E.2d 1372 (Ill. 1997), the Illinois Circuit Court was faced with a challenge to a crime bill. The bill had begun its legislative life as "An act in relation to prisoners' reimbursement to the Department of Corrections for the expenses incurred by their incarcerations," but by the end of House consideration it was known merely as "An act in relation to crime" because so many provisions had been added. These amendments included provisions dealing with pupil expulsion for bringing a weapon to school, competitive selection procedures on contracts in the State Public Defender's office, and permission for the Attorney General to bring a civil action against organizations engaging in international terrorism. By the end of the second conference committee, the proposal was "An act in relation to public safety" because it now included provisions dealing with fees for motor fuels, regulations for underground storage tanks, and exemptions for businesses from the wiretapping statute. (The judicial challenge to the bill was brought by opponents of this last provision.) The bill had grown from 8 pages to 243 pages. In striking the entire law down, the judge described some of the rationales justifying the constitutional rule: "The Act is a textbook case of the type of situation that Article IV of the Illinois Constitution was enacted to prevent — attaching an unpopular bill to a popular one to circumvent legislative input or scrutiny. Imagine the public rebuke that would be directed at a legislator who did not vote for a bill that sought to protect children from

---

m. *Bernstein v. Comm'r of Public Safety*, 351 N.W.2d 24, 25 (Minn. App. 1984).

n. *Dague v. Piper Aircraft Corp.*, 418 N.E.2d 207, 214–15 (Ind. 1981).

the horrid abuses at the hand of sex offenders [one of the many provisions in the Act]. At the same time these legislators are drafting in a measure in the very same Act that would allow employers to, in effect, eavesdrop on their own workforce. It is a reprehensible measure to ride a potentially unpassable piece of legislation on the backs of abused children." The court objected not only to the violation of the single-subject requirement, but also to the extensive revisions made by a conference committee without public hearings or deliberation.

The Illinois courts will sometimes pull back, however, when the effect of invalidating a statute seems particularly disruptive. In *Arangold Corp. v. Zehnder*, 718 N.E.2d 191 (Ill. 1999), the Illinois Supreme Court found that an act implementing the fiscal year 1996 budget, and including provisions that began their legislative life as the Tobacco Products Tax Act, did not violate the single-subject rule. The supreme court held that all the provisions of the budget act, which amended over 20 other laws, related to the implementation of the state's budget. Unlike *Johnson*, where the court rejected the legislature's attempt to unite disparate provisions under the rubric of "public safety," the challenged legislation included "all the means reasonably necessary to accomplish" the purpose of implementing the state budget and thus covered only a single subject. The court held that all the provisions need not be related to each other, but only to the single subject identified by the legislature. Perhaps the law at issue in *Arangold Corp.* was different from the previous act in relation to public safety. Or, perhaps the court shied away from striking down the act that implemented Illinois' budget for an entire fiscal year. If the court had been able merely to invalidate the challenged portion of the bill, here the provisions taxing tobacco products, do you think the outcome would have been different?

2. *Public Choice Arguments*. The insights of public choice theory suggest that more rigorous enforcement of the single-subject rule might well limit logrolling and help foster legislative deliberation. For example, consider how the proviso held unconstitutional in *Lewis* might have been attached to the appropriations bill. What group was the likely target of the proviso in question? Are there not scenarios in which a conscientious legislator could get trapped into voting for the bill, proviso and all?

But public choice theory also might suggest the following normative argument for a narrow view of the single-subject rule: The overall political satisfaction of groups with their political system might be enhanced if each group receives the legislation that it most intensely desires. Hence, even though proposals A, B, and C reflect minority preferences, the groups favoring them might have very strong preferences for those policies (e.g., anti-smoking regulations, anti-discrimination protections, and stricter penalties for drunk driving). In a simple majority-vote model, these groups could not satisfy their strongest preferences. With logrolling, the groups can express the intensity of their preferences by their willingness to trade votes for their favored proposals, in return for supporting proposals they would otherwise oppose.[o] Furthermore, logrolling allows legislatures to assemble majority support for proposals and provides the necessary lubrication to allow multi-member bodies to overcome collective action problems and enact laws.

Michael Gilbert adopts this approach — arguing that logrolling is often beneficial and a court cannot easily distinguish a "bad" logroll from a "good" one — to provide a procedurally-based definition of "subject" for enforcement of the requirement. *Single Subject Rules and the Legislative Process*, 67 U. Pitt. L. Rev. 803 (2006). He contends that the more troublesome legislative phenomenon is the addition of riders, or unpopular substantive provisions attached to otherwise popular bills. Whereas logrolling leaves a majority of legislators better off through exchange, riders are a product of "manipulation of legislative procedures. Well-placed legislators can attach self-serving measures to otherwise popular bills, and they need not offer anything to the measures' opponents." Courts should therefore enforce the single-subject rule against riders but not against the product of legislative logrolls. How can a court distinguish one from the other? Gilbert suggests that any provisions added on the floor of the legislature are more likely to be logrolls; whereas, provisions attached in committee are often riders. Courts should be less deferential when a bill is considered under a relatively closed rule on the floor, and "[i]n general, more floor debate should correspond to less judicial scrutiny." He advises courts to look carefully at legislative history, "voting records, political affiliation, and even poll data to hypothesize how legislators would vote on a truncated bill." Is this test realistic? Can courts differentiate between logrolls that should be encouraged and riders which reflect manipulation of the political process? Isn't this analysis especially challenging in the context of state legislatures which produce less legislative history than the federal House or Senate? Is Gilbert's approach an improvement over the *Lewis* court's analysis?

3. *Substantive Legislation Through Riders to Appropriations Legislation.* As *Lewis* demonstrates, appropriations bills are a popular target for riders. Appropriations riders short-circuit the ordinary committee process because they emerge from a committee without primary jurisdiction over the legislative proposal, thereby depriving the legislature of the value of expert committee deliberation. However, many states exempt appropriations measures from their single-subject rule, presumably so that omnibus budgets can be enacted. For jurisdictions having no single-subject rule for appropriations measures, courts can protect deliberative processes by relying on devices like the canon of statutory interpretation that presumes against legislative amendment of substantive law through appropriations measures. The leading federal case is *TVA v. Hill*, 437 U.S. 153 (1978), Chapter 7, § 2C (Endangered Species Act of 1973 required halting $100+ million dam whose construction threatened endangered snail darter, notwithstanding continued post-1973 congressional appropriations for the dam and evidence that appropriations committees knew

---

o. See James Buchanan & Gordon Tullock, *The Calculus of Consent, Logical Foundations of Constitutional Democracy* 131–45 (1962).

of the Act and believed it inapplicable). The federal House and Senate also usually have in effect internal rules that prohibit members from adding riders to appropriations bills, although these rules can be waived or ignored without substantial political cost.[p] We will consider whether courts should be more aggressive in enforcing internal legislative rules, and whether the rules themselves can be strengthened, in Chapter 4's discussion of the due process of lawmaking.

B. THE LINE ITEM VETO: A RULE TO ENFORCE BUDGET LIMITATIONS

Extensive logrolling in budgetary measures yields a deeper problem than just biased law; it also produces budget deficits that might be debilitating to government. Unlike the U.S. Constitution, three-fourths of the state constitutions require state budgets to be balanced every year. All but one state, Vermont, have either constitutional or statutory balanced budget requirements.[q] Forty-three states also provide that the state governor may veto "items" in appropriations bills; a few of those states extend the power to all bills.[r] In such states, the line item veto is often a complement to single-subject rules which may not apply to appropriations bills. In other words, the traditional veto coupled with a single-subject rule protects the governor from take-it-or-leave-it proposals in most contexts, and the line item veto empowers him to unravel such deals with respect to omnibus appropriations laws. For 38 states with item vetoes, the veto can be overridden only by supermajority votes (two-thirds of legislators present, two-thirds of legislators elected, or three-fifths of legislators elected); for five states, an override requires only simple majorities in each legislative chamber.

The main purpose of the item veto is to supplement state balanced budgets, but the broader purpose of both the item veto and balanced budget requirements is to ameliorate logrolling. In that regard, the item veto may be more effective than the single-subject rule because it is focused on the most serious logrolling problem (spending money) and because it is vested in the governor, who bears responsibility for balancing the budget.[s] Some scholars have argued that spending constraints like balanced budget rules will be ineffective in changing legislative behavior without the threat of third-party enforcement, a

---

p. See Sandra Beth Zellmer, *Sacrificing Legislative Integrity at the Altar of Appropriations Riders: A Constitutional Crisis*, 21 Harv. Envtl. L. Rev. 457 (1997); Max Reynolds, Note, *The Impact of Congressional Rules on Appropriations Law*, 12 J. L. & Pol. 481 (1996).

q. See Richard Briffault, *Balancing Acts: The Reality Behind State Balanced Budget Amendments* (1996) (in-depth study of balanced budget requirements that describes them and identifies the ways states tend to get around the rules).

r. The only states without any line item veto provisions are Indiana, Maine, Nevada, New Hampshire, North Carolina, Rhode Island, and Vermont.

s. See Richard Briffault, *The Item Veto in State Courts*, 66 Temple L. Rev. 1171, 1178–79 (1993) (excellent article on item veto generally).

threat provided by an item veto.[t] In fact, most studies of the state item veto find that its availability does not push spending levels downward, although it does allow the executive more influence over budgetary decisions. In other words, the final budget will reflect more of the governor's preferences if she wields the item veto weapon; thus, the tool affects the mix of spending programs rather than the level of spending. Not surprisingly, the item veto plays a greater role in budget decisions when the two branches are controlled by different political parties.[u]

The empirical studies therefore suggest that the item veto also adds new dimensions to the legislature-executive-judiciary game outlined in Chapter 1, § 2C, allowing different bargains to be reached. The item veto gives the governor more options when responding to legislation because she has a scalpel-like tool that can carve out particular provisions while allowing her to enact the majority of an appropriations law. It provides the executive a more credible way to threaten to unravel deals struck in the legislature compared to the rather blunt threat provided by a veto such as that allowed in the federal Constitution.[v] Legislators will attempt to protect legislation from the governor's item veto through sophisticated drafting techniques and by reaching bargains with the governor. The latter strategy may actually increase the amount of spending if the price for the governor's forbearance is enactment of programs that she favors along with the legislative spending items.

Maxwell Stearns argues that the item veto will necessarily change the kind of deals legislators reach and the bargaining dynamics.[w] With respect to riders or what Stearns calls *length bargains*, relatively unrelated legislation added to proposals to attract majority support, a line item veto does not eliminate these deals; instead, it merely requires the executive's approval to assure bargainers that the item veto will not be used to eliminate goodies. In contrast, legislators can work unimpeded by the threat of an item veto to assemble majority support for bills by negotiating *substantive bargains* or substantive modifications in provisions to reduce any adverse effect on minority interests. Such changes do

---

t. See, e.g., Lawrence Lessig, *Lessons from a Line Item Veto Law*, 47 Case W. Res. L. Rev. 1659 (1997).

u. For some of the best studies of the line item veto power in the states, see George Abney & Thomas Lauth, *The Line-Item Veto in the States: An Instrument for Fiscal Restraint or Partnership?*, 45 Pub. Admin. Rev. 372 (1985); James Dearden & Thomas Husted, *Do Governors Get What They Want?: An Alternative Examination of the Line-Item Veto*, 77 Pub. Choice 707 (1993); Rui de Figueiredo, Jr., *Budget Institutions and Political Insulation: Why States Adopt the Item Veto*, 87 J. Pub. Econ. 2677 (2003); Douglas Holtz-Eakin, *The Line Item Veto and Public Sector Budgets: Evidence from the States*, 36 J. Pub. Econ. 269 (1988). For an article modeling the likely effect at the federal level, see Nolan McCarty, *Presidential Pork: Executive Veto Power and Distributive Politics*, 94 Am. Pol. Sci. Rev. 117 (2000).

v. See Daniel Shaviro, *Do Deficits Matter?* 291 (1997) (noting that the executive is a player in the legislative game who can affect the substance of deals); Glen Robinson, *Public Choice Speculations on the Item Veto*, 74 Va. L. Rev. 403 (1988) (arguing that item veto reduces decision costs of executive and describing likely dynamics of bargaining).

w. See *The Public Choice Case Against the Item Veto*, in Maxwell Stearns, *Public Choice and Public Law: Reading and Commentary* 77 (1997).

not produce new items and so are immune from the governor's item veto. Finally, legislative resistance to the item veto often kicks the issues into the courts, whose resolution will then affect subsequent interactions between the governor and the legislature in the veto game.

RUSH v. RAY
Supreme Court of Iowa, 1985
362 N.W.2d 479

SCHULTZ, JUSTICE.

[The Iowa General Assembly enacted five separate appropriation bills, each of which contained a provision that either provided "notwithstanding section eight point thirty-nine (8.39) of the Code, funds appropriated by this Act shall not be subject to transfer or expenditure for any purpose other than the purposes specified" or recited a phrase similar in language and content. Governor Robert D. Ray exercised his item veto power to excise the quoted and similar phrases from each act. The issue was whether use of the governor's item veto power to eliminate a provision in an appropriation bill which prohibits the expenditure or transfer of appropriated funds from one department of state government to another is proper.]

The constitutional provision which gives the governor item veto authority provides in pertinent part:

> The governor may approve appropriation bills in whole or in part and may disapprove any item of an appropriation bill; and the part approved shall become a law. Any item of an appropriation bill disapproved by the governor shall be returned, . . . Any such item of an appropriation bill may be enacted into law notwithstanding the governor's objections, in the same manner as provided for other bills.

Iowa Const. art. III, § 16 (1857, amended 1968).

Appellant [State Senator Robert Rush] asserts that the vetoed portions of these five acts are provisos or limitations, not items; thus, they were not subject to the governor's item veto power. On the other hand, the Governor asserts that the language stricken from the five appropriation bills constituted distinct, severable "items" within the meaning of article III, section 16 of the Iowa Constitution, that could be removed from the appropriation bills by the use of the item veto.

We have twice passed on the legality of the governor's exercise of the item veto power. * * * *Welden v. Ray*, 229 N.W.2d 710 (Iowa 1975); *State ex rel. Turner v. Iowa State Highway Commission*, 186 N.W.2d 141 (Iowa 1971). * * *

The problem presented in *Turner* arose when the legislature appropriated funds to the primary road fund, and the governor vetoed a portion of the bill that additionally prohibited removing certain established offices from their present location. When this item veto was challenged, we upheld the veto. We established certain principles to be used in interpreting the term "item" and distinguished items, which are subject to veto, from provisos or conditions inseparably connected to an appropriation, which are not subject to veto. We approved another court's statement that an "item" is "something that may be taken out of a bill without affecting its other purposes and provisions. It is something that can be lifted bodily from it rather than cut out. No damage can be done to the surrounding legislative tissue, nor should any scar tissue result therefrom." * * * While we surmised that the legislature may have intended to make the challenged language a limitation or proviso on the expenditure of funds, we held the act as drawn and enacted did not restrict the use of the appropriated funds for the purposes and uses referred to in the deleted language. We held the deleted language was an item rather than a qualification.

When the governor's authority to exercise his item veto power was challenged in *Welden*, we reached a different result than in *Turner*, holding that the attempted vetoes by the governor were beyond the scope of his constitutional power. The vetoed items in the appropriation bills provided limitations on how the money appropriated for each department was to be spent. Specifically, these provisions included limitations on the number of employees in a department, limitations on the percent of the appropriation that could be used for salaries, prohibition against construction of buildings, prohibition against spending beyond budget, and elimination of matching fund grants if the federal funds were discontinued — with the further provision that unused state matching funds would revert to the general fund. We held that these clauses were lawful qualifications upon the respective appropriations rather than separate, severable provisions.

In *Welden* we * * * quoted a New Mexico ruling that stated:

> The power of partial veto is the power to disapprove. This is a negative power, or a power to delete or destroy a part or item, and is not a positive power, or a power to alter, enlarge or increase the effect of the remaining parts or items. . . . Thus, a partial veto must be so exercised that it eliminates or destroys the whole of an item or part and does not distort the legislative intent, and in effect create legislation inconsistent with that enacted by the Legislature, by the careful striking of words, phrases, clauses or sentences.

Id. (quoting *State ex rel. Sego v. Kirkpatrick*, 86 N.M. 359, 524 P.2d 975 (1974)). * * * The message of these cases and others reviewed in *Welden* is that the governor's power is a negative one that does not allow him to legislate by striking qualifications in a manner which distorts legislative intent. Thus, he cannot strike a provision that would divert money appropriated by the legislature for one purpose so that it may be used for another. Finally, we held in *Welden* that the governor's veto of a legislatively-imposed qualification upon an appropriation must also include a veto of the appropriation.

In the present case the trial court determined that the vetoed portion of each appropriation bill did not change the basic purpose of the legislation; thus, the provision is properly considered a severable item rather than a legislatively-imposed condition. We agree with appellant's contention that "the effect of this veto was to make money from the treasury available for purposes not authorized by the legislation as it was originally written, contrary to the clear intent of the legislature." The Governor has used the item veto power affirmatively to create funds not authorized by the legislature. The vetoed language created conditions, restricting use of the money to the stated purpose. It is not severable, because upon excision of this language, the rest of the legislation is affected. The appropriated money is no longer required to be used only for the stated purpose; it could be used for other purposes. Thus, these are not items which are subject to veto.

This case is unlike *Turner* in which the deletion of directions concerning office changes had no effect on the appropriation of funds. We find it closer akin to *Welden* in which the governor had deleted provisions which dictated how and for what purposes the appropriated funds were to be expended. In the present case the legislature clearly limited the expenditure of the appropriated funds to specified purposes. The veto distorted the obvious legislative intent that the funds only be spent for the appropriated purposes and created additional ways the funds might be spent. This was use of the veto power to create rather than negate. We hold that the language vetoed constituted qualifications on the appropriations rather than separate items subject to veto.
* * *

All Justices concur except REYNOLDSON, C.J., and HARRIS and McGIVERIN, JJ., who dissent.

HARRIS, JUSTICE (dissenting [for all three dissenting Justices]).

The experience in other states shows that, at best, there tends to be a blurred line between an "item" (which can be vetoed from an appropriation bill) and a proviso or condition on how the funds are to be spent (which cannot). It does however seem clear that the line, no matter how blurred, is crossed when legislation (even if labeled a proviso or condition) is appended to an appropriation bill in violation of the single subject provision of a state constitution.

The cases recognize a difficulty faced by governors when presented with appropriation bills which have been infused with legislation, going beyond the appropriation, which impacts either on existing statutes or upon purely executive functions. Some governors are unprotected even by a single-subject constitutional provision. It is quite common to find provisions such as Art III, § 29 of the Iowa Constitution which provide that "every act shall embrace but one subject . . .." Single subject provisions offer some protection but it is limited. If a provision is attached to an appropriation bill in violation of the single-subject provision the whole act could be challenged as void. But a governor is usually in a poor position to ask for an appropriation bill to be declared void. This would be the case when the government could not continue to function without the funds from the appropriation. Legislation attached by means of proviso or condition labels to crucial appropriation bills might thus become impervious to veto. The upshot was a liberal definition of an item, mentioned by the majority, which we adopted in *Turner*. We said: ". . . should the . . . [l]egislature attempt to coerce the [g]overnor into approving a lump sum appropriation by combining purposes and amount the court [will] interpret the term 'item' liberally to preserve the purpose of the item veto amendment."

[Both *Turner* and *Welden* applied the "scar tissue" test, treating as vetoable "something that may be taken out of a bill without affecting its other purposes and provisions. It is something which can be lifted bodily from it rather than cut out. No damage can be done to the surrounding legislative tissue, nor should any scar tissue result therefrom." Senator Rush and the other plaintiffs object to that test.] But courts elsewhere commonly apply it. [Justice Harris cited decisions from nine other states.]

The majority recites, and seems to acknowledge the validity of, the "scar-tissue test", but does not follow it. Under the test the provisions in question here were proper subjects of item vetoes. Each appropriation was earmarked to a department of government which could use the funds only for the purpose specified by the legislature. The vetoes here in no way modified the legislative plan of how the department could use the funds. The vetoed provisions related only to funds which might remain unused. The power of the governor to transfer unused funds under section 8.39, acting after notice to and "review and comment by" appropriate legislative chairpersons, has been statutorily provided for more than forty years. All branches of Iowa government have become quite used to it. It is, to put it in simple terms, the way our state government works.

If the legislature were to pass an act calling for the repeal or suspension of section 8.39 the act would be subject to an executive veto. Under the scar tissue rule the governor should not be robbed of this veto power by the simple process of attaching the repeal or suspension of this existing statute to an appropriation bill. This is a textbook example of why we and states elsewhere adopted the scar tissue rule. The trial court should be affirmed.

NOTES ON DIFFERENT APPROACHES TO THE ITEM VETO

1. *Situating the Iowa Approach.* We have chosen this Iowa case in part because item vetoes have been rather frequently litigated in Iowa (see the next note) and in part because this approach is a fairly moderate one. Some state courts basically let the legislature define a vetoable "item," e.g., *Washington State Motorcycle Dealers Ass'n v. State*, 763 P.2d 442 (Wash. 1988). In his article *The Item Veto in State Court, supra,* Richard Briffault argues that these courts enable the legislature to evade the purposes of the item veto by clever drafting. See also Abney & Lauth, *supra,* at 373 (almost half of the states surveyed reported that legislatures drafted bills strategically to evade item vetoes). On the other hand, Wisconsin courts have very expansively inter-preted that state's item veto, to allow the governor to veto words and phrases even when the veto completely changes the meaning of the statute. In *State ex rel. Wisconsin Senate v. Thompson*, 424 N.W.2d 385 (Wis. 1988), a divided court allowed the governor to veto word fragments, individual letters from words, and even individual digits from numbers as long as the resulting law made grammatical sense.[x] The reaction to this "Vanna White veto" was swift, with the voters in 1990 prohibiting the governor from deleting individual letters or numerical characters to change the intent of the legislature. See also *Management Council of Wyoming Legislature v. Geringer*, 953 P.2d 839 (Wyo.

---

x. See Mary Burke, *The Wisconsin Partial Veto: Past, Present and Future*, 1989 Wis. L. Rev. 1395; Winston Holliday, Jr., Comment, *Tipping the Balance of Power: A Critical Survey of the Gubernatorial Line Item Veto*, 50 S.C. L. Rev. 503 (1999) (focusing on Wisconsin, Iowa, and Virginia).

1998) (sustaining an expansive interpretation of the term "item," thus providing the governor with broad authority to veto any portion of any bill making appropriations).

The Iowa approach is an effort to find a middle way between approaches too deferential to the legislature and those too empowering of the governor. This approach seeks to limit item vetoes in a way that will not negate them altogether. It originates in the old "affirmative-negative" test that prevents the governor from creating "affirmative" or new legislation, e.g., *Colorado General Assembly v. Lamm*, 704 P.2d 1371, 1382–83 (Colo. 1985), but then elaborates upon that test. Does *Rush* create an appropriate balance (as the court thought), or does it open up the item veto to evasion (as the dissenters thought)?

2. *Subsequent Iowa Cases.* In *Colton v. Branstad*, 372 N.W.2d 184 (Iowa 1985), the court upheld an item veto of a condition attached to an appropriations bill that the court characterized as a *rider*, a non-germane attachment to the bill. What the court saw as a rider was language in the appropriation for the State Department of Health that directed the Department to relinquish authority over certain grants to the State Family Planning Council. "The Governor's constitutional power to veto bills of general legislation cannot be abridged by the careful placement of such measures in a general appropriation bill, thereby forcing the Governor to choose between approving unacceptable substantive legislation or vetoing 'items' of expenditure essential to the operation of government." Isn't this more in the spirit of the *Rush* dissent than of the majority opinion?

You might wonder, what is a *rider*? What is *non-germane* to an appropriations bill? Recall *Lewis*, the Florida single-subject case, which involved a "substantive" provision added onto an appropriations measure, and the distinction between logrolls and riders for a procedural perspective; one of our notes to the case described a widely accepted policy of preventing substantive legislation through the appropriations process, presumably because riders of this sort do not receive the deliberative scrutiny of committees expert on the matter and often "slip by" the legislature without careful debate or focus.

Item Veto Problems

Problem 3–10. The Governor of Iowa vetoes language attached to an appropriation for tourism and export trade promotion which provided "as a condition, limitation, and qualification, any official Iowa trade delegation led by the governor which receives financial or other support from the appropriation in this subsection shall be represented by a bipartisan delegation." Under the Iowa precedents, could the governor veto this "condition"? Or was it really a "rider"? See *Welsh v. Branstad*, 470 N.W.2d 644 (Iowa 1991).

Problem 3–11. The legislature enacts a statewide sales tax of six percent. A clause in the bill sets a ceiling of $500 on the amount of tax that can be charged per product or service. The legislature apparently is concerned that the sales tax might discourage purchases of "big ticket" items, like cars, boats, and appliances. The governor uses the item veto to delete the $500 ceiling, arguing that the state needs the revenue and that the exemption favors the wealthy who purchase luxury goods. How would this exercise of the item veto be analyzed under the tests discussed above? How could the legislature draft the sales tax provision to insulate the ceiling from the item veto? See Antony Petrilla, *The Role of the Line-Item Veto in the Federal Balance of Power*, 31 Harv. J. Legis. 469 (1994) (providing this example and analyzing under various tests).

NOTE ON THE FEDERAL LINE ITEM VETO ACT

In 1996, Congress passed the Line Item Veto Act, Pub. L. 104–130, 110 Stat. 1200, which granted the President the power to cancel certain spending programs. Despite its name, the Act did not give the President the same kind of power enjoyed by governors. Governors can veto particular items in legislation while enacting only the rest of the bill into law; the vetoed items are never enacted. In contrast, before the President could exercise his power under the federal act, he was required to sign, and thereby enact, the entirety of the bill that contained provisions subject to the cancellation authority.[y] The President's cancellation power was also broader than that of most governors. Although he was limited to canceling spending items in their entirety (like most governors, he could not reduce spending for a program), he could use his power to eliminate certain tax provisions (those that provided benefits to 100 or fewer entities). In this way, the drafters of the Act recognized that spending programs can be found in the tax code as well as in appropriations bills. For example, Congress can subsidize homeowners through grants of federal money or through tax provisions allowing deductions for the payment of mortgage interest or eliminating tax on gains from the sales of homes. These sorts of tax provisions are often called *tax expenditures* because of their similarity to other kinds of government expenditures.

In the first year the Act was effective, President Clinton canceled 82 items in 11 laws. Congress reinstated 38 of the provisions over the President's veto, and a court case challenging another cancellation resulted in a settlement that required the executive branch to spend the funds. In the end, the savings to the federal government amounted to less than $600 million over five years. Notwithstanding the relatively trivial amounts involved, the Act provoked several constitutional challenges. Although the Supreme Court dismissed on standing grounds a challenge brought by legislators, see *Raines v. Byrd* (Chapter 4, § 2), the Court reached the merits of the constitutional challenge in the summer of 1998.

---

y. See Michael Rappaport, *Veto Burdens and the Line Item Veto Act*, 91 Nw. U. L. Rev. 771 (1997) (arguing that this requirement unconstitutionally burdened the President's power to veto entire acts).

CLINTON v. CITY OF NEW YORK
Supreme Court of the United States, 1998
524 U.S. 417, 118 S.Ct. 2091, 141 L.Ed.2d 393

JUSTICE STEVENS delivered the opinion of the Court.

[In the district court, the appellees had challenged two of the President's exercises of the cancellation power under the Line Item Veto Act. First, he canceled a provision in the Balanced Budget Act of 1997 that gave New York preferential treatment under the Medicaid law; no other state would have received such treatment. The federal government claimed that New York had inappropriately characterized taxes it had collected from Medicaid providers; unless granted a waiver, the state would owe the federal government as much as $2.6 billion. The canceled provision deemed the state's actions permissible and thereby waived the federal government's right to recoupment. New York City, a hospital and other related parties challenged the constitutionality of this cancellation. Second, President Clinton canceled a tax provision in the Taxpayer Relief Act of 1997 that allowed owners of certain food refiners and processors to defer paying tax on the gain from the sale of their stock if they sold to eligible farmers' cooperatives. Because very few taxpayers could take advantage of the tax expenditure, it was a limited tax benefit eligible for cancellation. An Idaho farmers' cooperative and an individual farmer, Mike Cranney, challenged this second cancellation.]

[The Court found that the appellees had standing because they each had a personal stake in having an actual injury redressed by the Court. They did not suffer the kind of abstract and widely dispersed institutional injury allegedly suffered by the members of Congress who were plaintiffs in *Raines v. Byrd,* Chapter 4, § 2.]

[IV] The Line Item Veto Act gives the President the power to "cancel in whole" three types of provisions that have been signed into law: "(1) any dollar amount of discretionary budget authority [*i.e.*, funds allocated by Congress during the annual appropriations process]; (2) any item of new direct spending [largely, entitlement programs like Medicaid]; or (3) any limited tax benefit [certain tax expenditures]." It is undisputed that the New York case involves an "item of new direct spending" and that the Snake River case involves a "limited tax benefit" as those terms are defined in the Act. It is also undisputed that each of those provisions had been signed into law pursuant to Article I, § 7, of the Constitution before it was canceled.

The Act requires the President to adhere to precise procedures whenever he exercises his cancellation authority. In identifying items for cancellation he must consider the legislative history, the purposes, and other relevant information about the items. He must determine, with respect to each cancellation, that it will "(i) reduce the Federal budget deficit; (ii) not impair any essential Government functions; and (iii) not harm the national interest." Moreover, he must transmit a special message to Congress notifying it of each cancellation within five calendar days (excluding Sundays) after the enactment of the canceled provision. It is undisputed that the President meticulously followed these procedures in these cases. * * *

The effect of a cancellation is plainly stated in § 691e, which defines the principal terms used in the Act. With respect to both an item of new direct spending and a limited tax benefit, the cancellation prevents the item "from having legal force or effect."[26] Thus, under the plain text of the statute, the two actions of the President that are challenged in these cases prevented one section of the Balanced Budget Act of 1997 and one section of the Taxpayer Relief Act of 1997 "from having legal force or effect." The remaining provisions of those statutes * * * continue to have the same force and effect as they had when signed into law.

In both legal and practical effect, the President has amended two Acts of Congress by repealing a portion of each. * * * There is no provision in the Constitution that authorizes the President to enact, to amend, or to repeal statutes. Both Article I and Article II assign responsibilities to the President that directly relate to the lawmaking process, but neither addresses the issue presented by these cases. * * * [A]fter a bill has passed both Houses of Congress, but "before it become[s] a Law," it must be presented to the President. If he approves it, "he shall sign it, but if not he shall return it, with his Objections to that House in which it shall have originated, who shall enter the Objections at large on their Journal, and proceed to reconsider it." Art. I, § 7, cl. 2. His "return" of a bill, which is usually described as a "veto," is subject to being overridden by a two-thirds vote in each House.

There are important differences between the President's "return" of a bill pursuant to Article I, § 7, and the exercise of the President's cancellation authority pursuant to the Line Item Veto Act. The constitutional return takes place *before* the bill becomes law; the statutory cancellation occurs *after* the bill becomes law. The constitutional return is of the entire bill; the statutory cancellation is of only a part. Although the Constitution expressly authorizes the President to play a role in the process of enacting statutes, it is silent on the subject of unilateral Presidential action that either repeals or amends parts of duly enacted statutes.

There are powerful reasons for construing constitutional silence on this profoundly important issue as equivalent to an express prohibition. The procedures governing the enactment of statutes set forth in the text of Article I were the product of the great debates and compromises that produced the Constitution itself. Familiar historical materials provide abundant support for the conclusion that the power to enact statutes may only "be exercised in accord with a single, finely wrought and exhaustively considered, procedure." * * * What has emerged in these cases from the President's exercise of his statutory cancellation powers, however, are truncated versions of two bills that passed both Houses of Congress. They are not the product of the "finely wrought" procedure that the Framers designed. * * *

[V] The Government advances two related arguments to support its position that despite the unambiguous provisions of the Act, cancellations do not amend

---

26. The term "cancel," used in connection with any dollar amount of discretionary budget authority, means "to rescind." * * *

or repeal properly enacted statutes in violation of the Presentment Clause. First, relying primarily on *Field v. Clark*, 143 U.S. 649 (1892), the Government contends that the cancellations were merely exercises of discretionary authority granted to the President by the Balanced Budget Act and the Taxpayer Relief Act read in light of the previously enacted Line Item Veto Act. Second, the Government submits that the substance of the authority to cancel tax and spending items "is, in practical effect, no more and no less than the power to 'decline to spend' specified sums of money, or to 'decline to implement' specified tax measures." Neither argument is persuasive.

[In *Field v. Clark*, the Court upheld the constitutionality of the Tariff Act of 1890, which allowed the President to suspend the exemption from import duties on certain products "whenever and so often" as he should be satisfied that any country producing and exporting those products imposed duties on the agricultural products of the United States that he deemed to be "reciprocally unequal and unreasonable." The Court upheld this provision as a constitutional delegation of power to the President because "[n]othing involving the expediency or the just operation of such legislation was left to the determination of the President. . . . [W]hen he ascertained the fact that duties and exactions reciprocally unequal and unreasonable were imposed upon the agricultural or other products of the United States by a country producing and exporting sugar, molasses, coffee, tea, or hides, it became his duty to issue a proclamation declaring the suspension, as to that country, which Congress had determined should occur."]

This passage identifies three critical differences between the power to suspend the exemption from import duties and the power to cancel portions of a duly enacted statute. First, the exercise of the suspension power was contingent upon a condition that did not exist when the Tariff Act was passed: the imposition of "reciprocally unequal and unreasonable" import duties by other countries. In contrast, the exercise of the cancellation power within five days after the enactment of the Balanced Budget and Tax Reform Acts necessarily was based on the same conditions that Congress evaluated when it passed those statutes. Second, under the Tariff Act, when the President determined that the contingency had arisen, he had a duty to suspend; in contrast, while it is true that the President was required by the Act to make three determinations before he canceled a provision, those determinations did not qualify his discretion to cancel or not to cancel. Finally, whenever the President suspended an exemption under the Tariff Act, he was executing the policy that Congress had embodied in the statute. In contrast, whenever the President cancels an item of new direct spending or a limited tax benefit he is rejecting the policy judgment made by Congress and relying on his own policy judgment. * * *

Neither are we persuaded by the Government's contention that the President's authority to cancel new direct spending and tax benefit items is no greater than his traditional authority to decline to spend appropriated funds. The Government has reviewed in some detail the series of statutes in which Congress has given the Executive broad discretion over the expenditure of appropriated funds. For example, the First Congress appropriated "sum[s] not exceeding" specified amounts to be spent on various Government operations. In those statutes, as in later years, the President was given wide discretion with respect to both the amounts to be spent and how the money would be allocated among different functions. It is argued that the Line Item Veto Act merely confers comparable discretionary authority over the expenditure of appropriated funds. The critical difference between this statute and all of its predecessors, however, is that unlike any of them, this Act gives the President the unilateral power to change the text of duly enacted statutes. None of the Act's predecessors could even arguably have been construed to authorize such a change.

[VI] Although they are implicit in what we have already written, the profound importance of these cases makes it appropriate to emphasize [several] points.

First, we express no opinion about the wisdom of the procedures authorized by the Line Item Veto Act. Many members of both major political parties who have served in the Legislative and the Executive Branches have long advocated the enactment of such procedures for the purpose of "ensur[ing] greater fiscal accountability in Washington." The text of the Act was itself the product of much debate and deliberation in both Houses of Congress and that precise text was signed into law by the President. We do not lightly conclude that their action was unauthorized by the Constitution. * * *

Second, although appellees challenge the validity of the Act on alternative grounds, the only issue we address concerns the "finely wrought" procedure commanded by the Constitution. We have been favored with extensive debate about the scope of Congress' power to delegate law-making authority, or its functional equivalent, to the President. The excellent briefs filed by the parties and their *amici curiae* have provided us with valuable historical information that illuminates the delegation issue but does not really bear on the narrow issue that is dispositive of these cases. Thus, because we conclude that the Act's cancellation provisions violate Article I, § 7, of the Constitution, we find it unnecessary to consider the District Court's alternative holding that the Act "impermissibly disrupts the balance of powers among the three branches of government."[43] * * *

If there is to be a new procedure in which the President will play a different role in determining the final text of what may "become a law," such change must come not by legislation but through the amendment procedures set forth in Article V of the Constitution. *Cf. U.S. Term Limits, Inc. v. Thornton* [Chapter 2, § 2B].

[JUSTICE KENNEDY's concurring opinion is omitted.]

---

43. We also find it unnecessary to consider whether the provisions of the Act relating to discretionary budget authority are severable from the Act's tax benefit and direct spending provisions. We note, however, that the Act contains no severability clause; a severability provision that had appeared in the Senate bill was dropped in conference without explanation.

JUSTICE SCALIA, with whom JUSTICE O'CONNOR joins, and with whom JUSTICE BREYER joins as to Part III, concurring in part and dissenting in part.

[III] * * * There is no question that enactment of the Balanced Budget Act complied with these requirements [of the Presentment Clause]: the House and Senate passed the bill, and the President signed it into law. It was only *after* the requirements of the Presentment Clause had been satisfied that the President exercised his authority under the Line Item Veto Act to cancel the spending item. Thus, the Court's problem with the Act is not that it authorizes the President to veto parts of a bill and sign others into law, but rather that it authorizes him to "cancel" — prevent from "having legal force or effect" — certain parts of duly enacted statutes.

* * * As much as the Court goes on about Art. I, § 7, therefore, that provision does not demand the result the Court reaches. It no more categorically prohibits the Executive *reduction* of congressional dispositions in the course of implementing statutes that authorize such reduction, than it categorically prohibits the Executive *augmentation* of congressional dispositions in the course of implementing statutes that authorize such augmentation — generally known as substantive rulemaking. There are, to be sure, limits upon the former just as there are limits upon the latter — and I am prepared to acknowledge that the limits upon the former may be much more severe. Those limits are established, however, not by some categorical prohibition of Art. I, § 7, which our cases conclusively disprove, but by what has come to be known as the doctrine of unconstitutional delegation of legislative authority: When authorized Executive reduction or augmentation is allowed to go too far, it usurps the nondelegable function of Congress and violates the separation of powers. * * *

Insofar as the degree of political, "law-making" power conferred upon the Executive is concerned, there is not a dime's worth of difference between Congress's authorizing the President to *cancel* a spending item, and Congress's authorizing money to be spent on a particular item at the President's discretion. And the latter has been done since the Founding of the Nation. From 1789–1791, the First Congress made lump-sum appropriations for the entire Government — "sum[s] not exceeding" specified amounts for broad purposes. From a very early date Congress also made permissive individual appropriations, leaving the decision whether to spend the money to the President's unfettered discretion. * * * The constitutionality of such appropriations has never seriously been questioned. * * *

The short of the matter is this: Had the Line Item Veto Act authorized the President to "decline to spend" any item of spending contained in the Balanced Budget Act of 1997, there is not the slightest doubt that authorization would have been constitutional. What the Line Item Veto Act does instead — authorizing the President to "cancel" an item of spending — is technically different. But the technical difference does *not* relate to the technicalities of the Presentment Clause, which have been fully complied with; and the doctrine of unconstitutional delegation, which *is* at issue here, is preeminently *not* a doctrine of technicalities. The title of the Line Item Veto Act, which was perhaps designed to simplify for public comprehension, or perhaps merely to comply with the terms of a campaign pledge, has succeeded in faking out the Supreme Court. The President's action it authorizes in fact is not a line-item veto and thus does not offend Art. I, § 7; and insofar as the substance of that action is concerned, it is no different from what Congress has permitted the President to do since the formation of the Union. * * *

JUSTICE BREYER, with whom JUSTICE O'CONNOR and JUSTICE SCALIA join as to Part III, dissenting.

[I] * * * In my view the Line Item Veto Act does not violate any specific textual constitutional command, nor does it violate any implicit Separation of Powers principle. Consequently, I believe that the Act is constitutional.

[II] I approach the constitutional question before us with three general considerations in mind. *First*, the Act represents a legislative effort to provide the President with the power to give effect to some, but not to all, of the expenditure and revenue-diminishing provisions contained in a single massive appropriations bill. And this objective is constitutionally proper.

When our Nation was founded, Congress could easily have provided the President with this kind of power. In that time period, our population was less than four million, federal employees numbered fewer than 5,000, annual federal budget outlays totaled approximately $4 million, and the entire operative text of Congress's first general appropriations law read as follows:

> Be it enacted . . . [t]hat there be appropriated for the service of the present year, to be paid out of the monies which arise, either from the requisitions heretofore made upon the several states, or from the duties on import and tonnage, the following sums, viz. A sum not exceeding two hundred and sixteen thousand dollars for defraying the expenses of the civil list, under the late and present government; a sum not exceeding one hundred and thirty-seven thousand dollars for defraying the expenses of the department of war; a sum not exceeding one hundred and ninety thousand dollars for discharging the warrants issued by the late board of treasury, and remaining unsatisfied; and a sum not exceeding ninety-six thousand dollars for paying the pensions to invalids.

At that time, a Congress, wishing to give a President the power to select among appropriations, could simply have embodied each appropriation in a separate bill, each bill subject to a separate Presidential veto.

Today, however, our population is about 250 million, the Federal Government employs more than four million people, the annual federal budget is $1.5 trillion, and a typical budget appropriations bill may have a dozen titles, hundreds of sections, and spread across more than 500 pages of the Statutes at Large. See, *e.g.,* Balanced Budget Act of 1997. Congress cannot divide such a bill into thousands, or tens of thousands, of separate appropriations bills, each one of which the President would have to sign, or to veto, separately. Thus, the question is whether the Constitution permits Congress to choose a particular novel *means* to achieve this same, constitutionally legitimate, *end*.

Second, the case in part requires us to focus upon the Constitution's generally phrased structural provisions, provisions that delegate all "legislative" power to Congress and vest all "executive" power in the President. The

Court, when applying these provisions, has interpreted them generously in terms of the institutional arrangements that they permit. * * *

Third, we need not here referee a dispute among the other two branches. And, as the majority points out,

> When this Court is asked to invalidate a statutory provision that has been approved by both Houses of the Congress and signed by the President, particularly an Act of Congress that confronts a deeply vexing national problem, it should only do so for the most compelling constitutional reasons.

These three background circumstances mean that, when one measures the *literal* words of the Act against the Constitution's *literal* commands, the fact that the Act may closely resemble a different, literally unconstitutional, arrangement is beside the point. To drive exactly 65 miles per hour on an interstate highway closely resembles an act that violates the speed limit. But it does not violate that limit, for small differences matter when the question is one of literal violation of law. No more does this Act literally violate the Constitution's words. * * *

[III]   The Court believes that the Act violates the literal text of the Constitution. A simple syllogism captures its basic reasoning:

> Major Premise: The Constitution sets forth an exclusive method for enacting, repealing, or amending laws.

> Minor Premise: The Act authorizes the President to "repea[l] or amen[d]" laws in a different way, namely by announcing a cancellation of a portion of a previously enacted law.

> Conclusion: The Act is inconsistent with the Constitution.

I find this syllogism unconvincing, however, because its Minor Premise is faulty. When the President "canceled" the two appropriation measures now before us, he did not *repeal* any law nor did he *amend* any law. He simply *followed* the law, leaving the statutes, as they are literally written, intact.

To understand why one cannot say, *literally speaking*, that the President has repealed or amended any law, imagine how the provisions of law before us might have been, but were not, written. Imagine that the canceled New York [Medicaid] provision at issue here had instead said the following:

> Section One. Taxes . . . that were collected by the State of New York from a health care provider before June 1, 1997 and for which a waiver of provisions [requiring payment] have been sought . . . are deemed to be permissible health care related taxes . . . *provided however that the President may prevent the just-mentioned provision from having legal force or effect if he determines x, y and z.* (Assume x, y and z to be the same determinations required by the Line Item Veto Act).

Whatever a person might say, or think, about the constitutionality of this imaginary law, there is one thing the English language would prevent one from saying. One could not say that a President who "prevent[s]" the deeming language from "having legal force or effect" has either *repealed* or *amended* this particular hypothetical statute. Rather, the President has *followed* that law to the letter. He has exercised the power it explicitly delegates to him. He has executed the law, not repealed it.

It could make no significant difference to this linguistic point were the italicized proviso to appear, not as part of what I have called Section One, but, instead, at the bottom of the statute page, say referenced by an asterisk, with a statement that it applies to every spending provision in the act next to which a similar asterisk appears. And that being so, it could make no difference if that proviso appeared, instead, in a different, earlier-enacted law, along with legal language that makes it applicable to every future spending provision picked out according to a specified formula.

But, of course, this last-mentioned possibility is this very case. The earlier law, namely, the Line Item Veto Act, says that "the President may . . . prevent such [future] budget authority from having legal force or effect." * * * For that reason, one cannot dispose of this case through a purely literal analysis as the majority does. Literally speaking, the President has not "repealed" or "amended" anything. He has simply *executed* a power conferred upon him by Congress, which power is contained in laws that were enacted in compliance with the exclusive method set forth in the Constitution.

Nor can one dismiss this literal compliance as some kind of formal quibble, as if it were somehow "obvious" that what the President has done "amounts to," "comes close to," or is "analogous to" the repeal or amendment of a previously enacted law. That is because the power the Act grants the President (to render designated appropriations items without "legal force or effect") also "amounts to," "comes close to," or is "analogous to" a different legal animal, the delegation of a power to choose one legal path as opposed to another * * *.

[IV] Because I disagree with the Court's holding of literal violation, I must consider whether the Act nonetheless violates Separation of Powers principles — principles that arise out of the Constitution's vesting of the "executive Power" in "a President," U.S. Const., Art. II, § 1, and "[a]ll legislative Powers" in "a Congress," Art. I, § 1. There are three relevant Separation of Powers questions here: (1) Has Congress given the President the wrong kind of power, *i.e.*, "non-Executive" power? (2) Has Congress given the President the power to "encroach" upon Congress' own constitutionally reserved territory? (3) Has Congress given the President too much power, violating the doctrine of "nondelegation?" * * * [W]ith respect to *this* Act, the answer to all these questions is "no."

[A] Viewed conceptually, the power the Act conveys is the right kind of power. It is "executive." As explained above, an exercise of that power "executes" the Act. Conceptually speaking, it closely resembles the kind of delegated authority — to spend or not to spend appropriations, to change or not to change tariff rates — that Congress has frequently granted the President, any differences being differences in degree, not kind. * * *

[B] The Act does not undermine what this Court has often described as the principal function of the Separation of Powers, which is to maintain the tripartite structure of the Federal Government — and thereby protect individual liberty — by providing a "safeguard against the encroachment or aggrandizement of one branch at the expense of the other." *Buckley v. Valeo* [discussed in Chapter 2, § 3].

[O]ne cannot say that the Act "encroaches" upon Congress' power, when Congress retained the power to insert, by simple majority, into any future appropriations bill, into any section of any such bill, or into any phrase of any section, a provision that says the Act will not apply. Congress also retained the power to "disapprov[e]," and thereby reinstate, any of the President's cancellations. And it is Congress that drafts and enacts the appropriations statutes that are subject to the Act in the first place — and thereby defines the outer limits of the President's cancellation authority. * * * Indeed, the President acts only in response to, and on the terms set by, the Congress.

* * * And, if an individual Member of Congress, who say, favors aid to Country A but not to Country B, objects to the Act on the ground that the President may "rewrite" an appropriations law to do the opposite, one can respond, "But a majority of Congress voted that he have that power; you may vote to exempt the relevant appropriations provision from the Act; and if you command a majority, your appropriation is safe." Where the burden of overcoming legislative inertia lies is within the power of Congress to determine by rule. Where is the encroachment? * * *

[C] The "nondelegation" doctrine represents an added constitutional check upon Congress' authority to delegate power to the Executive Branch. And it raises a more serious constitutional obstacle here. The Constitution permits Congress to "see[k] assistance from another branch" of Government, the "extent and character" of that assistance to be fixed "according to common sense and the inherent necessities of the governmental co-ordination." *J. W. Hampton, Jr., & Co. v. United States,* 276 U.S. [394,] 406 [(1928)]. But there are limits on the way in which Congress can obtain such assistance; it "cannot delegate any part of its legislative power except under the limitation of a prescribed standard." Or, in Chief Justice Taft's more familiar words, the Constitution permits only those delegations where Congress "shall lay down by legislative act an *intelligible principle* to which the person or body authorized to [act] is directed to conform." *J. W. Hampton* (emphasis added).

The Act before us seeks to create such a principle in three ways. The first is procedural. The Act tells the President that, in "identifying dollar amounts [or] . . . items . . . for cancellation" (which I take to refer to his selection of the amounts or items he will "prevent from having legal force or effect"), he is to "consider," among other things,

> the legislative history, construction, and purposes of the law which contains [those amounts or items, and] . . . any specific sources of information referenced in such law or . . . the best available information . . . .

The second is purposive. The clear purpose behind the Act, confirmed by its legislative history, is to promote "greater fiscal accountability" and to "eliminate wasteful federal spending and . . . special tax breaks."

The third is substantive. The President must determine that, to "prevent" the item or amount "from having legal force or effect" will "reduce the Federal budget deficit; . . . not impair any essential Government functions; and . . . not harm the national interest."

The resulting standards are broad. But this Court has upheld standards that are equally broad, or broader. See, *e.g.*, *National Broadcasting Co. v. United States,* 319 U.S. 190, 225–226 (1943) (upholding delegation to Federal Communications Commission to regulate broadcast licensing as "public interest, convenience, or necessity" require); *FPC v. Hope Natural Gas Co.,* 320 U.S. 591, 600–603 (1944) (upholding delegation to Federal Power Commission to determine "just and reasonable" rates).

* * * [The delegation under the Line Item Veto Act] is limited to one area of government, the budget, and it seeks to give the President the power, in one portion of that budget, to tailor spending and special tax relief to what he concludes are the demands of fiscal responsibility. Nor is the standard that governs his judgment, though broad, any broader than the standard that currently governs the award of television licenses, namely "public convenience, interest, *or* necessity." To the contrary, (a) the broadly phrased limitations in the Act, together with (b) its evident deficit reduction purpose, and (c) a procedure that guarantees Presidential awareness of the reasons for including a particular provision in a budget bill, taken together, guide the President's exercise of his discretionary powers.

[C1] The relevant similarities and differences among and between this case and other "nondelegation" cases can be listed more systematically as follows: First, as I have just said, like statutes delegating power to award broadcast television licenses, or to regulate the securities industry, or to develop and enforce workplace safety rules, the Act is aimed at a discrete problem: namely, a particular set of expenditures within the federal budget. * * * Within the budget it applies only to *discretionary* budget authority and *new* direct spending items, that together amount to approximately a third of the current annual budget outlays, and to "limited tax benefits" that (because each can affect no more than 100 people), amount to a tiny fraction of federal revenues and appropriations.

Second, * * * the particular problem involved — determining whether or not a particular amount of money should be spent or whether a particular dispensation from tax law should be granted a few individuals — does not readily lend itself to a significantly more specific standard. The Act makes clear that the President should consider the reasons for the expenditure, measure those reasons against the desirability of avoiding a deficit (or building a surplus) and make up his mind about the comparative weight of these conflicting goals. Congress might have expressed this matter in other language, but could it have done so in a *significantly* more specific way? The statute's language, I believe, is sufficient to provide the President, and the public, with a fairly clear idea as to what Congress had in mind. And the public can judge the merits of the President's choices accordingly.

Third, in insofar as monetary expenditure (but not "tax expenditure") is at issue, the President acts in an area where history helps to justify the discretionary power that Congress has delegated, and where history may inform his exercise of the Act's delegated authority. Congress has frequently delegated the President the authority to spend, or not to spend, particular sums of money. * * *

On the other hand, I must recognize that there are important differences between the delegation before us and other broad, constitutionally-acceptable delegations to Executive Branch agencies — differences that argue against my conclusion. In particular, a broad delegation of authority to an administrative agency differs from the delegation at issue here in that agencies often develop subsidiary rules under the statute, rules that explain the general "public interest" language. Doing so diminishes the risk that the agency will use the breadth of a grant of authority as a cloak for unreasonable or unfair implementation. Moreover, agencies are typically subject to judicial review, which review provides an additional check against arbitrary implementation. The President has not so narrowed his discretionary power through rule, nor is his implementation subject to judicial review under the terms of the Administrative Procedure Act.

While I believe that these last-mentioned considerations are important, they are not determinative. The President, unlike most agency decisionmakers, is an elected official. He is responsible to the voters, who, in principle, will judge the manner in which he exercises his delegated authority. Whether the President's expenditure decisions, for example, are arbitrary is a matter that in the past has been left primarily to those voters to consider. And this Court has made clear that judicial review is less appropriate when the President's own discretion, rather than that of an agency, is at stake. * * *

[C2] Most, but not all, of the considerations mentioned in the previous subsection apply to the Act's delegation to the President of the authority to prevent "from having legal force or effect" a "limited tax benefit," which term the Act defines in terms of special tax relief for fewer than 100 (or in some instances 10) beneficiaries, which tax relief is not available to others who are somewhat similarly situated. There are, however, two related significant differences between the "limited tax benefit" and the spending items considered above, which make the "limited tax benefit" question more difficult. First, the history is different. The history of Presidential authority to pick and to choose is less voluminous. Second, the subject matter (increasing or decreasing an individual's taxes) makes the considerations discussed at the end of the last section (*i.e.*, the danger of an arbitrary exercise of delegated power) of greater concern. But these differences, in my view, are not sufficient to change the "nondelegation" result.

For one thing, this Court has made clear that the standard we must use to judge whether a law violates the "nondelegation" doctrine is the same in the tax area as in any other. * * *

For another thing, this Court has upheld tax statutes that delegate to the President the power to change taxes under very broad standards. In 1890, for example, Congress authorized the President to "suspend" the provisions of the tariff statute, thereby raising tariff rates, if the President determined that other nations were imposing "reciprocally unequal and unreasonable" tariff rates on specialized commodities. And the Court upheld the statute against constitutional attack. *Field v. Clark.* * * *

[This delegation resembles] today's Act more closely than one might at first suspect. [It involved] a duty on imports, which is a tax. That tax in the last century was as important then as the income tax is now, for it provided most of the Federal Government's revenues. And the delegation then thus affected a far higher percentage of federal revenues than the tax-related delegation over extremely "limited" tax benefits here. * * *

Nor can I accept the majority's effort to distinguish [the tariff example]. * * * [The majority] tries to distinguish [tariffs] on the ground that the President there executed congressional policy while here he rejects that policy. The President here, however, in exercising his delegated authority does not *reject* congressional policy. Rather, he *executes* a law in which Congress has specified its desire that the President have the very authority he has exercised. * * *

Finally, the tax-related delegation is limited in ways that tend to diminish any widespread risk of arbitrary Presidential decisionmaking:

(1) The Act does not give the President authority to change general tax policy. That is because the limited tax benefits are defined in terms of deviations from tax policy, *i.e.*, special benefits to fewer than 100 individuals.

(2) The Act requires the President to make the same kind of policy judgment with respect to these special benefits as with respect to items of spending. He is to consider the budget as a whole, he is to consider the particular history of the tax benefit provision, and he is to consider whether the provision is worth the loss of revenue it causes in the same way that he must decide whether a particular expenditure item is worth the added revenue that it requires. * * *

(4) The "limited tax benefit" provisions involve only a small part of the federal budget, probably less than one percent of total annual outlays and revenues. * * *

[V] In sum, I recognize that the Act before us is novel. In a sense, it skirts a constitutional edge. But that edge has to do with means, not ends. The means chosen do not amount literally to the enactment, repeal, or amendment of a law. Nor, for that matter, do they amount literally to the "line item veto" that the Act's title announces. Those means do not violate any basic Separation of Powers principle. They do not improperly shift the constitutionally foreseen balance of power from Congress to the President. Nor, since they comply with Separation of Powers principles, do they threaten the liberties of individual citizens. They represent an experiment that may, or may not, help representative government work better. The Constitution, in my view, authorizes Congress and the President to try novel methods in this way. Consequently, with respect, I dissent.

NOTES ON *CLINTON v. CITY OF NEW YORK*

1. *Is the Line Item Veto Act Dead?* The cancellations before the Court concerned a tax provision and a provision affecting an entitlement program, Medicaid. As the dissents noted, presidents have long used a power functionally indistinguishable from cancellation — the impoundment authority — to withhold funds that Congress had allocated to government programs in the annual appropriations process. The aggressive use of impoundment by President Nixon, in the face of express congressional decisions to deny him that power, precipitated a crisis in the 1970s. See Chapter 4, § 2 (discussing the impoundment controversy and its role in the development of the modern congressional budget process). However, Presidents have long considered congressional appropriations to be permissive, allowing them to spend up to the amount appropriated but not requiring them to spend all the money. Congress has frequently given the President the power to decline to spend federal funds, sometimes in cases where congressional objectives can be met with fewer resources and sometimes as a tool to enforce spending ceilings and deficit targets. Indeed, even the majority in *Clinton v. City of New York* distinguished the cancellations before it from the President's "traditional authority to decline to spend appropriated funds."

Is the cancellation power relating to discretionary spending, which consists of appropriated funds that have been the traditional target of presidential impoundments, unconstitutional after this case? Seventy-nine of the 82 cancellations related to this kind of spending; the President canceled only two tax provisions and one entitlement provision. Notice that the definition of *cancel* is different in the context of discretionary spending. Rather than rendering a provision of law without "legal force and effect," the President "rescinds" an item of discretionary spending when he cancels it. In budget parlance, a rescission is a congressionally authorized impoundment. Since 1974, federal law has allowed the President to propose to rescind federal spending, but his proposal would not go into effect unless approved by Congress within 45 days. One way to view the Line Item Veto Act's provisions affecting appropriated money is as merely a change in the way Congress authorizes rescissions. Rather than requiring ex post congressional approval, the Line Item Veto Act delegates a continuing power to rescind spending, as long as the President complies with the standards set forth in the Act. In short, the Act amended the portion of the budget law relating to rescissions by changing the effect of congressional inaction — now Congress' failure to act after an impoundment means that the money will not be spent.

2. *The Congressional Reaction.* On the day that the Court decided *Clinton v. City of New York*, members of Congress announced plans to re-establish the President's power in a constitutional form. Although some are working to draft and ratify a constitutional amendment giving the President a true line item veto, others in Congress hope to find a less difficult path to success. The majority's formalist approach suggests that clever drafters may be able to construct an impoundment power that will meet the constitutional test.

One option is called *separate enrollment*. Using this procedure, Congress would divide an omnibus spending bill, formally enrolling each provision allocating funds to particular programs as a separate bill. The group of bills would be passed by Congress (probably using a procedure that would require only one vote to enact the bundle of bills). The President would then have the ability to use his constitutional veto to cancel as many of the programs as he wishes; Congress would have the opportunity to override any veto with a supermajority vote. For example, rather than one bill with 950 sections, Congress would pass 950 bills, and the President would sign only the bills that provided money to programs he supported. Justice Breyer appears to believe that separate enrollment is too unwieldy a procedure to work in the modern era; however, during the negotiations that led to the passage of the Line Item Veto Act, the Senate proposed separate enrollment as the best way to adopt a cancellation process that would survive constitutional review. Do you agree with the Senate's assessment? Are the political dynamics of separate enrollment different from those that resulted from the Line Item Veto Act? Would you expect members of Congress to be willing to pass as separate bills provisions that they had been willing to support as parts of one large bill? Does the state experience illustrated by *Rush v. Ray* suggest that Congress will divide omnibus bills in a way to minimize the effect of the President's veto?

In his 2006 State of the Union address, President Bush asked Congress to enact a new line item veto, but his proposal was different from the 1996 Act. He proposed an *expedited rescission* process whereby he would send cancellations to Congress, and Congress would be required, through internal rules, to consider his recommendations quickly and vote on them as a package without further amendment. In addition, the Senate would not be allowed to filibuster. This approach was considered by Congress in 1996, and it is generally considered to be constitutional because the decision not to spend money or enforce tax provisions is left to the Congress, albeit under stream-lined procedures.[z] How effective would expedited rescission be in reducing federal spending? Should Congress avoid using the words "line item veto" in the name of any bill it enacts? How binding are internal congressional procedures that purport to restrain congressional power to amend the President's proposal?

3. *How Significant Was the Cancellation Power?* Does it surprise you that President Clinton used this new power so infrequently and only to cancel relatively small projects? For example, he canceled $3.5 million allocated to dredge Lake George in Indiana, contending that "[s]ince the primary purpose of this project is to enhance local recreation opportunities in a non-Federal Lake, it should be undertaken by local interests." One explanation for the infrequent use of cancellation is that the effect of the new power occurred primarily during negotiations as Congress drafted and considered spending bills. Indeed, except for some symbolic uses of cancellation to score political

---

z. See Elizabeth Garrett, *The Story of* Clinton v. City of New York: *Congress Can Take Care of Itself,* in *Administrative Law Stories* 47 (Peter Strauss ed., 2005) (providing legislative history of 1996 Act); Aaron-Andrew Bruhl, *The New Line Item Veto Proposal: This Time It's Constitutional (Mostly),* 116 Yale L.J. Pocket Part 84 (2006) (discussing constitutionality of expedited rescission).

points with voters, the President might never actually have to impound funds, having reached agreements with members of Congress before the bill reaches his desk. Think about the empirical studies of governors' use of item vetoes and the effect on spending, as well as the theoretical arguments made by Stearns and others. Is the experience with the federal line item veto act consistent?[a]

The Court's decision has sparked substantial commentary about the majority's formalistic approach to separation of powers and the dissenters' more pragmatic analysis using nondelegation doctrine principles. We discuss other separation of powers issues in Chapter 9.[b]

C. LEGISLATIVE IMMUNITIES

1. *Federal Protection for Members of Congress (Speech or Debate Clause)*

Article I, § 6, clause 1 of the U.S. Constitution provides that "for any Speech or Debate in either House, [Members of Congress] shall not be questioned in any other place." The purpose of the clause was "to prevent intimidation [of legislators] by the executive and accountability before a possibly hostile judiciary." *United States v. Johnson*, 383 U.S. 169 (1966); see also *Kilbourn v. Thompson*, 103 U.S. 168 (1881) (the germinal case). "It insures that legislators are free to represent the interests of their constituents without fear that they will be later called to task in the courts for that representation." *Powell v. McCormack*, 395 U.S. 486 (1969). The clause encompasses speeches on the floor of Congress, voting on bills, conduct at committee hearings, preparation of committee reports, authorization of committee publications and their internal distribution, circulation of information to other members, and participation in committee investigations. *Eastland v. United States' Servicemen's Fund*, 421 U.S. 491 (1975); *Doe v. McMillan*, 412 U.S. 306 (1973); *Dombrowski v. Pfister*, 387 U.S. 82 (1967) (per curiam).

The Speech or Debate Clause is rooted in English history. In the sixteenth and seventeenth centuries, when Parliament was slowly wresting power from the Crown, the Tudor and Stuart monarchs would arrest Members of Parliament and question them about their legislative activities and try to coerce them into changing their policies. The framers of the Constitution, therefore, felt it important to insulate Members of Congress from such harassment. Without the

---

a. See Neal Devins, *In Search of the Lost Chord: Reflections on the 1996 Item Veto Act*, 47 Case W. Res. L. Rev. 1605 (1997) (arguing that the cancellation power was not likely to cause significant changes in the balance of power between Congress and the President).

b. For additional constitutional analysis of the Line Item Veto Act, see Bernard Bell, *Dead Again: The Nondelegation Doctrine, the Rules/Standards Dilemma and the Line Item Veto*, 44 Villanova L. Rev. 189 (1999); Steven Huefner, *The Supreme Court's Avoidance of the Nondelegation Doctrine in* Clinton v. City of New York: *More than "A Dime's Worth of Difference,"* 49 Cath. U. L. Rev. 337 (2000); Matthew Kline, *The Line Item Veto Case and the Separation of Powers*, 88 Calif. L. Rev. 181 (2000); Saikrishna Prakash, *Deviant Executive Lawmaking*, 67 Geo. Wash. L. Rev. 1 (1998).

Speech or Debate Clause, Members of Congress could be vulnerable to persecution from one of the other branches. The clause is a cornerstone of the separation of powers.

There is a tension in the Speech or Debate Clause between the desire to protect the independence of the legislative process and the desire not to create congressional "super-citizens." *United States v. Brewster*, 408 U.S. 501, 516 (1972). Thus, defining the scope of the clause is crucial and subject to much discussion in the case law. The next case implicates at least two questions relevant to scope. First, what activities fall under the protection of the speech or debate clause? The Court in *Brewster* distinguishes between acts that involve the legislative process per se and acts that are mere "legislative errands" such as constituent services and newsletters. Is this distinction realistic? Second, who besides members of Congress should receive the protection? Are legislative aides immunized, and if so, is the immunity co-extensive with that accorded to legislators?

GRAVEL v. UNITED STATES
Supreme Court of the United States, 1972
408 U.S. 606, 92 S.Ct. 2614, 33 L.Ed.2d 583

Opinion of the Court by MR. JUSTICE WHITE, announced by MR. JUSTICE BLACKMUN.

These cases arise out of the investigation by a federal grand jury into possible criminal conduct with respect to the release and publication of a classified Defense Department study entitled History of the United States Decision-Making Process on Viet Nam Policy. This document, popularly known as the Pentagon Papers, bore a Defense security classification of Top Secret-Sensitive. The crimes being investigated included the retention of public property or records with intent to convert (18 U.S.C. § 641), the gathering and transmitting of national defense information (18 U.S.C. § 793), the concealment or removal of public records or documents (18 U.S.C. § 2071), and conspiracy to commit such offenses and to defraud the United States (18 U.S.C. § 371).

Among the witnesses subpoenaed were Leonard S. Rodberg, an assistant to Senator Mike Gravel of Alaska and a resident fellow at the Institute of Policy Studies, and Howard Webber, Director of M.I.T. Press. Senator Gravel, as intervenor, filed motions to quash the subpoenas and to require the Government to specify the particular questions to be addressed to Rodberg. He asserted that requiring these witnesses to appear and testify would violate his privilege under the Speech or Debate Clause of the United States Constitution, Art. I, § 6, cl. 1.

It appeared that on the night of June 29, 1971, Senator Gravel, as Chairman of the Subcommittee on Buildings and Grounds of the Senate Public Works Committee, convened a meeting of the subcommittee and there read extensively from a copy of the Pentagon Papers. He then placed the entire 47 volumes of the study in the public record. Rodberg had been added to the Senator's staff earlier in the day and assisted Gravel in preparing for and conducting the hearing. Some weeks later there were press reports that Gravel had arranged for the papers to be published by Beacon Press, and that members of Gravel's staff had talked with Webber as editor of M.I.T. Press.

[The District Court overruled the motions to quash but prohibited the asking of certain questions. The Court of Appeals held that (a) neither the Senator nor his aide could be questioned about the episode on the Senate floor because of the Speech or Debate Clause, (b) third parties could be questioned about the episode, and (c) republication with Beacon Press was protected by a common law immunity but not by the Speech or Debate Clause. Although agreeing with much of its analysis, the Supreme Court vacated the Court of Appeals opinion.]

[I] * * * [T]he United States strongly urges that because the Speech or Debate Clause confers a privilege only upon "Senators and Representatives," Rodberg himself has no valid claim to constitutional immunity from grand jury inquiry. * * * We agree with the Court of Appeals that for the purpose of construing the privilege a Member and his aide are to be "treated as one," or, as the District Court put it: the "Speech or Debate Clause prohibits inquiry into things done by Dr. Rodberg as the Senator's agent or assistant which would have been legislative acts, and therefore privileged, if performed by the Senator personally." Both courts recognized what the Senate of the United States urgently presses here: that it is literally impossible, in view of the complexities of the modern legislative process, with Congress almost constantly in session and matters of legislative concern constantly proliferating, for Members of Congress to perform their legislative tasks without the help of aides and assistants; that the day-to-day work of such aides is so critical to the Members' performance that they must be treated as the latter's alter egos; and that if they are not so recognized, the central role of the Speech or Debate Clause — to prevent intimidation of legislators by the Executive and accountability before a possibly hostile judiciary — will inevitably be diminished and frustrated. * * *

It is true that the Clause itself mentions only "Senators and Representatives," but prior cases have plainly not taken a literalistic approach in applying the privilege. The Clause also speaks only of "Speech or Debate," but the Court's consistent approach has been that to confine the protection of the Speech or Debate Clause to words spoken in debate would be an unacceptably narrow view. Committee reports, resolutions, and the act of voting are equally covered; "[i]n short, . . . things generally done in a session of the House by one of its members in relation to the business before it." *Kilbourn*. Rather than giving the clause a cramped construction, the Court has sought to implement its fundamental purpose of freeing the legislator from executive and judicial oversight that realistically threatens to control his conduct as a legislator. We have little doubt that we are neither exceeding our judicial powers nor mistakenly construing the Constitution by holding that the Speech or Debate Clause applies not only to a Member but also to his aides insofar as the conduct of the latter would be a protected legislative act if performed by the Member himself.

Nor can we agree with the United States that our conclusion is foreclosed by *Kilbourn*, *Dombrowski*, and *Powell*, where the speech or debate privilege was held unavailable to certain House and committee employees. Those cases do not hold that persons other than Members of Congress are beyond the protection of the Clause when they perform or aid in the performance of legislative acts. In *Kilbourn*, the Speech or Debate Clause protected House Members who had adopted a resolution authorizing Kilbourn's arrest; that act was clearly legislative in nature. But the resolution was subject to judicial review insofar as its execution impinged on a citizen's rights as it did there. That the House could with impunity order an unconstitutional arrest afforded no protection for those who made the arrest. * * *

Dombrowski v. Eastland is little different in principle. The Speech or Debate Clause there protected a Senator, who was also a subcommittee chairman, but not the subcommittee counsel. The record contained no evidence of the Senator's involvement in any activity that could result in liability, whereas the committee counsel was charged with conspiring with state officials to carry out an illegal seizure of records that the committee sought for its own proceedings. The committee counsel was deemed protected to some extent by legislative privilege, but it did not shield him from answering as yet unproved charges of conspiring to violate the constitutional rights of private parties. Unlawful conduct of this kind the Speech or Debate Clause simply did not immunize.

Powell v. McCormack reasserted judicial power to determine the validity of legislative actions impinging on individual rights — there the illegal exclusion of a representative-elect — and to afford relief against House aides seeking to implement the invalid resolutions. The Members themselves were dismissed from the case because shielded by the Speech or Debate Clause both from liability for their illegal legislative act and from having to defend themselves with respect to it. * * *

* * * The three cases reflect a decidedly jaundiced view towards extending the Clause so as to privilege illegal or unconstitutional conduct beyond that essential to foreclose executive control of legislative speech or debate and associated matters such as voting and committee reports and proceedings. In *Kilbourn*, the Sergeant-at-Arms was executing a legislative order, the issuance of which fell within the Speech or Debate Clause; in *Eastland*, the committee counsel was gathering information for a hearing; and in *Powell*, the Clerk and Doorkeeper were merely carrying out directions that were protected by the Speech or Debate Clause. In each case, protecting the rights of others may have to some extent frustrated a planned or completed legislative act; but relief could be afforded without proof of a legislative act or the motives or purposes underlying such an act. No threat to legislative independence was posed, and Speech or Debate Clause protection did not attach.

None of this, as we see it, involves distinguishing between a Senator and his personal aides with respect to legislative immunity. In *Kilbourn*-type situations, both aide and Member should be immune with respect to committee and House action leading to the illegal resolution. So, too, in *Eastland*, as in this litigation, senatorial aides should enjoy immunity for helping a Member conduct committee hearings. On the other hand, no prior case has held that Members of Congress would be immune if they executed an invalid resolution by themselves carrying out an illegal arrest, or if, in order to secure information for a hearing, themselves seized the property or invaded the privacy of a citizen. Neither they nor their aides should be immune from liability or questioning in such circumstances. * * *

[II] We are convinced also that the Court of Appeals correctly determined that Senator Gravel's alleged arrangement with Beacon Press to publish the Pentagon Papers was not protected speech or debate within the meaning of Art. I, § 6, cl. 1, of the Constitution.

Historically, the English legislative privilege was not viewed as protecting republication of an otherwise immune libel on the floor of the House. *Stockdale v. Hansard*, 9 Ad. & E., at 114, 112 Eng. Rep., at 1156 (1839), recognized that "[f]or speeches made in Parliament by a member to the prejudice of any other person, or hazardous to the public peace, that member enjoys complete impunity." But it was clearly stated that "if the calumnious or inflammatory speeches should be reported and published, the law will attach responsibility on the publisher." This was accepted in *Kilbourn v. Thompson* as a "sound statement of the legal effect of the Bill of Rights and of the parliamentary law of England" and as a reasonable basis for inferring "that the framers of the Constitution meant the same thing by the use of language borrowed from that source."

Prior cases have read the Speech or Debate Clause "broadly to effectuate its purposes," *Johnson*, and have included within its reach anything "generally done in a session of the House by one of its members in relation to the business before it." *Kilbourn*. Thus, voting by Members and committee reports are protected; and we recognize today * * * that a Member's conduct at legislative committee hearings, although subject to judicial review in various circumstances, as is legislation itself, may not be made the basis for a civil or criminal judgment against a Member because that conduct is within the "sphere of legitimate legislative activity."

But the Clause has not been extended beyond the legislative sphere. That Senators generally perform certain acts in their official capacity as Senators does not necessarily make all such acts legislative in nature. Members of Congress are constantly in touch with the Executive Branch of the Government and with administrative agencies — they may cajole, and exhort with respect to the administration of a federal statute — but such conduct, though generally done, is not protected legislative activity. *United States v. Johnson* decided at least this much. "No argument is made, nor do we think that it could be successfully contended, that the Speech or Debate Clause reaches conduct, such as was involved in the attempt to influence the Department of Justice, that is in no wise related to the due functioning of the legislative process."

Legislative acts are not all-encompassing. The heart of the Clause is speech or debate in either House. Insofar as the Clause is construed to reach other matters, they must be an integral part of the deliberative and communicative processes by which Members participate in committee and House proceedings with respect to the consideration and passage or rejection of proposed legislation or with respect to other matters which the Constitution places within the jurisdiction of either House. As the Court of Appeals put it, the courts have extended the privilege to matters beyond pure speech or debate in either House, but "only when necessary to prevent indirect impairment of such deliberations."

Here, private publication by Senator Gravel through the cooperation of Beacon Press was in no way essential to the deliberations of the Senate; nor does questioning as to private publication threaten the integrity or independence of the Senate by impermissibly exposing its deliberations to executive influence. The Senator had conducted his hearings; the record and any report that was forthcoming were available both to his committee and the Senate. Insofar as we are advised, neither Congress nor the full committee ordered or authorized the publication. We cannot but conclude that the Senator's arrangements with Beacon Press were not part and parcel of the legislative process. * * *

[III] Similar considerations lead us to disagree with the Court of Appeals insofar as it fashioned, tentatively at least, a nonconstitutional testimonial privilege protecting Rodberg from any questioning by the grand jury concerning the matter of republication of the Pentagon Papers. This privilege, thought to be similar to that protecting executive officials from liability for libel, see *Barr v. Matteo*, 360 U.S. 564 (1959), was considered advisable "[t]o the extent that a congressman has responsibility to inform his constituents . . . ." But we cannot carry a judicially fashioned privilege so far as to immunize criminal conduct proscribed by an Act of Congress or to frustrate the grand jury's inquiry into whether publication of these classified documents violated a federal criminal statute. The so-called executive privilege has never been applied to shield executive officers from prosecution for crime, the Court of Appeals was quite sure that third parties were neither immune from liability nor from testifying about the republication matter, and we perceive no basis for conferring a testimonial privilege on Rodberg as the Court of Appeals seemed to do.

[Part IV of the Court's opinion defined the appropriate remedial order in the case to allow the grand jury to interrogate Rodberg about the arrangements for republication of the papers and about "the source of obviously highly classified documents that came into the Senator's possession and are the basic subject matter of inquiry in this case, as long as no legislative act is implicated by the questions." The Court prohibited questions "(1) concerning the Senator's conduct, or the conduct of his aides, at the June 29, 1971, meeting of the subcommittee; (2) concerning the motives and purposes behind the Senator's conduct, or that of his aides, at that meeting; (3) concerning communications between the Senator and his aides during the term of their employment and related to said meeting or any other legislative act of the Senator; (4) except as it proves relevant to investigating possible third-party crime, concerning any act, in itself not criminal, performed by the Senator, or by his aides in the course of their employment, in preparation for the subcommittee hearing."]

MR. JUSTICE DOUGLAS, dissenting.

I would construe the Speech or Debate Clause to insulate Senator Gravel and his aides from inquiry concerning the Pentagon Papers, and Beacon Press from inquiry concerning publication of them, for that publication was but another way of informing the public as to what had gone on in the privacy of the Executive Branch concerning the conception and pursuit of the so-called "war" in Vietnam. Alternatively, I would hold that Beacon Press is protected by the First Amendment from prosecution or investigations for publishing or undertaking to publish the Pentagon Papers. * * *

As to Senator Gravel's efforts to publish the Subcommittee record's contents, wide dissemination of this material as an educational service is as much a part of the Speech or Debate Clause philosophy as mailing under a frank a Senator's or a Congressman's speech across the Nation. * * * "[I]t is the proper duty of a representative body to look diligently into every affair of government and to talk much about what it sees. . . . The informing function of Congress should be preferred even to its legislative function." W. Wilson, *Congressional Government* 303 (1885). "From the earliest times in its history, the Congress has assiduously performed an 'informing function.' " *Watkins v. United States*, 354 U.S. 178, 200 n.3. "Legislators have an obligation to take positions on controversial political questions so that their constituents can be fully informed by them." *Bond v. Floyd*, 356 U.S. 116, 136.

We said in *Johnson* that the Speech or Debate Clause established a "legislative privilege" that protected a member of Congress against prosecution "by an unfriendly executive and conviction by a hostile judiciary" in order, as Mr. Justice Harlan put it, to ensure "the independence of the legislature." That hostility emanates from every stage of the present proceedings. It emphasizes the need to construe the Speech or Debate Clause generously, not niggardly. If republication of a Senator's speech in a newspaper carries the privilege, as it doubtless does, then republication of the exhibits introduced at a hearing before Congress must also do so. That means that republication by Beacon Press is within the ambit of the Speech or Debate Clause and that the confidences of the Senator in arranging it are not subject to inquiry "in any other Place" than the Congress.

[We have omitted the dissenting opinion of MR. JUSTICE BRENNAN, with whom MR. JUSTICE DOUGLAS and MR. JUSTICE MARSHALL joined. These Justices agreed that the Speech and Debate Clause protects legislative aides but dissented from the Court's refusal to protect republication.]

NOTES ON THE SPEECH OR DEBATE CLAUSE AFTER *GRAVEL*

1. *Analytical Conundrums Presented by the Court's Decision.* Why should the Speech or Debate Clause be construed very liberally to include staff, but then narrowly to exclude republication? The Court distinguishes *Kilbourn, Eastland,* and *Powell* because the officials in those cases committed illegal acts, but wasn't Rodberg's alleged conspiracy to disclose classified documents equally illegal? And what about Gravel: Could he be prosecuted for participating in a breach of national secrecy?

In *Kilbourn,* an 1881 case, the Supreme Court held that Thompson, the Sergeant-at-Arms of the House, was liable for his wrongful arrest of Kilbourn, who had refused to comply with a House subpoena *duces tecum.* Thompson made the arrest pursuant to the order of a House committee which was investigating Kilbourn's bankrupt company. The Court held that the members of the committee were protected by the Speech or Debate Clause for their actions and deliberation, but that the Sergeant-at-Arms was not for his actions. After *Gravel*, would the House Sergeant-at-Arms (a House staff member) still be liable? How can *Gravel* be reconciled with *Kilbourn*? And would the result in *Kilbourn* have been different if the wrongful arrest had been carried out by a member of Congress?

Gravel holds that the Speech or Debate Clause applies to Members of Congress and their aides who are their "alter egos." Is that a qualification of the Court's holding? If so, which staff qualify? All of them? The Sergeant-at-Arms in *Kilbourn*? How about the staff of the General Accounting Office, who work for the Congress but are not the aides of any one member? Should they have the same immunity as someone on a member's personal staff? See *Campaign for Fiscal Equity v. New York*, 687 N.Y.S. 2d 227 (NY. Sup. Ct), *aff'd* 265 A.D. 2d 277 (N.Y. App. 1999) (interpreting parallel state constitutional provision as extending speech or debate clause protection to employee of the State Education Department who assisted legislators in analyzing budget legislation).

2. *Whistleblowing versus Blacklisting.* The dissenters appeal to the value of whistleblowing: Members of Congress ought to be able to "blow the whistle" on government skullduggery by exposing documents that reveal valuable information to the American people. Leaking classified documents has become a widely imitated practice on Capitol Hill, and in many instances the public finds the ventilation of state secrets informative and useful. On the other hand, republication of legislative reports may also chill freedom. During the Cold War, members of Congress sometimes made lavish allegations about the loyalty of Americans who criticized our government, and their accusations would be republished, often to the ruin of those accused. Judge Gerhard Gesell enjoined the publication of a report of the Committee on Internal Security of the House of Representatives, on the ground that it served no "legitimate" public purpose and was little more than an effort to "blacklist" and smear people who held different points of view from the conservative House Committee. *Hentoff v. Ichord*, 318 F. Supp. 1175 (D.D.C. 1970). In 1970, he drew the same conclusion from the Court's precedents that Justice White drew in 1972: The Speech or Debate Clause does not protect republication.

3. *Balancing Legislative Independence Against Individual Rights.* Sometimes, as in *Hentoff*, recognizing legislative immunity would mean denial of rights to citizens that otherwise would be enforced in a court of law. Chief Justice Burger forcefully described this difficulty: "The immunities of the Speech or Debate Clause were not written into the Constitution simply for the personal or private benefit of Members of Congress, but to protect the integrity of the legislative process by insuring the independence of individual legislators." *Brewster*, 408 U.S. at 507. The tension is presented by cases where congressional staff seek to sue members of Congress for some form of employment discrimination. The Court of Appeals for the D.C. Circuit wrestled with this issue in several cases, and it initially ruled that members

were insulated from liability only with respect to employees whose duties were integral to the legislative process. *Browning v. Clerk, U.S. House of Representatives*, 789 F.2d 923 (D.C. Cir.), *cert. denied*, 479 U.S. 996 (1986). Thus, a female manager of the House of Representatives' restaurant could sue representatives who oversaw food services in the House on the ground that she was fired because she was female. *Walker v. Jones*, 733 F.2d 923 (D.C. Cir.), *cert. denied*, 469 U.S. 1036 (1984). In *Fields v. Office of Eddie Bernice Johnson*, 459 F.3d 1 (D.C. Cir. 2006) (en banc), *cert. denied,* 127 S.Ct. 2018 (2007), the D.C. Circuit rejected a broad reading of *Browning* and barred review only when the claim "question[s] the conduct of official Senate legislative business." *Id.* at 8 (relying on *Bastien v. Office of Senator Ben Nighthorse Campbell*, 390 F.3d 1301 (10th Cir. 2004), *cert. denied,* 126 S.Ct. 396 (2005)). Therefore, the plaintiffs, one of whom was fired after telling a senator he needed heart surgery and the other after objecting to a hiring decision, could maintain their suits, although they might be hindered in presenting arguments that turned on the motivation behind any legislative acts.

The Congressional Accountability Act of 1995, P.L. 104–1, 109 Stat. 3, *codified at* 2 U.S.C. § 1301 *et seq.*, adds a new wrinkle to this aspect of Speech or Debate Clause jurisprudence. The Act allows congressional employees to sue their employing office for wrongful discharge, but it also states that the Act is not a waiver of the Speech or Debate Clause privileges of any member. Members of Congress are not personally liable under the act for damages; instead, awards are paid by a contingent fund of the United States.[c]

Speech or Debate Clause Problems

Problem 3–12. Senator William Proxmire (D-Wis.) in the 1970s started a practice of awarding a "Golden Fleece of the Month Award" for egregiously wasteful governmental spending. The award went to federal agencies that funded projects that Proxmire felt accomplished little for their cost. The second such award, made in April 1975, went to the National Science Foundation and NASA for spending almost $500,000 to fund research by Ronald Hutchinson, a behavioral scientist who studied tension and aggressive behavior under conditions of stress. He studied the behavior of animals, focusing on their clenching of teeth when they were exposed to stressful stimuli.

Senator Proxmire found this wasteful and made the award to Hutchinson in a speech on the floor of the Senate, preceded by a press release to 275 members of the news media. The speech and newsletter said:

> The funding of this nonsense makes me almost angry enough to scream and kick or even clench my jaws. It seems to me it is outrageous.

---

c. See Christina Deneka, *Congressional Accountability and the Separation of Powers: A Survey of the Congressional Accountability Act's Problems*, 52 Rutgers L. Rev. 855 (2000) (discussing structural concerns with the Act); David Frederick, *Commentary on the Congressional Accountability Act of 1995: A Section-by-Section Analysis*, in *Lobbying the New Congress* (Thomas Susman & Barbara Timmer eds., 1995).

Dr. Hutchinson's studies should make the taxpayers as well as his monkeys grind their teeth. In fact, the good doctor has made a fortune from his monkeys and in the process made a monkey out of the American taxpayer.

In May 1975 Proxmire referred to this Fleece Award and quoted the above language from his speech in a newsletter to approximately 100,000 constituents. Later in 1975 Proxmire appeared on a television interview program and repeated the charge of waste.

Hutchinson sues Proxmire and Morton Schwartz (the aide who researched the matter and worked on the speech) for defamation. Assuming that he has made out a claim under state law (and a claim that is permissible under the First Amendment), should the court accept Proxmire's defense under the Speech or Debate Clause to immunize him from liability for his speech on the Senate floor? What about his press release? Is the republication in the constituent newsletter immunized? If there is a difference in treatment, what is the justification? Does Schwartz have a good defense? See *Hutchinson v. Proxmire*, 443 U.S. 111 (1979). Assume that Schwartz called the agency after the award had been given to discover if it had changed its decision or altered the way it dispensed federal money. During those phone calls with the National Science Foundation staff, Schwartz made allegedly defamatory remarks about Dr. Hutchinson. Can he be sued, or is he protected under the Speech or Debate Clause? What if his calls had been prompted initially by a constituent concerned about the way the agencies awarded federal money? See *Chastain v. Sundquist*, 833 F.2d 311 (D.C. Cir. 1987), *cert. denied*, 487 U.S. 120 (1988) (allowing defamation suit against congressman relating to casework concerning the activities of attorneys in the Memphis Area Legal Services office).

Problem 3–13. A member of the House of Representatives announces that she is a lesbian during debate on a bill extending the employment discrimination laws to gay men and women. The representative is also a member of the Army Reserve. Based solely on her statements on the floor of Congress, the only place she has discussed her sexual orientation, the Army began an investigation to discharge her under its "Don't Ask, Don't Tell" policy. Before her statement, she was being considered for a promotion on the basis of her outstanding performance in the armed services. Is the investigation barred by the Speech or Debate Clause? What if she repeats her statements in a subsequent interview on Larry King Live?

NOTES ON SPEECH OR DEBATE AND BRIBERY PROSECUTIONS

Do prosecutions for corruption, like that in *Van de Carr* (Section 1A of this chapter) undermine the independence of the legislature? If so, the decision might trigger concern under the speech or debate provision of the applicable constitution. The 1938 New York Constitution (Art. III, § 11) provided: "for any speech or debate in either house of the legislature, the members shall not be questioned in any other place." Would this change the result in *Van de Carr* if the defendant had been a state legislator? Would the federal Speech or Debate Clause preclude such a prosecution under the federal bribery statute, 18 U.S.C. § 201? Consider the following case.

UNITED STATES v. HELSTOSKI

Supreme Court of the United States, 1979
442 U.S. 477, 99 S.Ct. 2432, 61 L.Ed.2d 12

MR. CHIEF JUSTICE BURGER delivered the opinion of the Court.

[Henry Helstoski, a former Member of the House of Representatives from New Jersey, was indicted under § 201 for receiving money from noncitizens in return for introducing private bills in Congress that would suspend the application of U.S. immigration laws so that they could remain in the United States. The lower courts ruled that the Government could not introduce "evidence of the performance of a past legislative act on the part of the defendant * * * derived from any source and for any purpose." The Government appealed this ruling, arguing that it was not required by the Speech or Debate Clause.]

The Court's holdings in *United States v. Johnson*, 383 U.S. 169 (1966), and *United States v. Brewster*, 408 U.S. 501 (1972), leave no doubt that evidence of a legislative act of a Member may not be introduced by the Government in a prosecution under § 201. In *Johnson* there had been extensive questioning of both Johnson, a former Congressman, and others about a speech which Johnson had delivered in the House of Representatives and the motive for the speech. The Court's conclusion was unequivocal:

> "We see no escape from the conclusion that such an intensive judicial inquiry, made in the course of a prosecution by the Executive Branch under a general conspiracy statute, violates the express language of the Constitution and the policies which underlie it."

In *Brewster*, we explained the holding of *Johnson* in this way:

> "*Johnson* thus stands as a unanimous holding that a Member of Congress may be prosecuted under a criminal statute provided that the Government's case does not rely on legislative acts or the motivation for legislative acts. A legislative act has consistently been defined as an act generally done in Congress in relation to the business before it. In sum, the Speech or Debate Clause prohibits inquiry only into those things generally said or done in the House or the Senate in the performance of official duties and into the motivation for those acts."

The Government, however, argues that exclusion of references to past legislative acts will make prosecutions more difficult because such references are essential to show the motive for taking money. In addition, the Government argues that the exclusion of references to past acts is not logically consistent. In its view, if jurors are told of promises to perform legislative acts they will infer that the acts were performed, thereby calling the acts themselves into question.

We do not accept the Government's arguments; without doubt the exclusion of such evidence will make prosecutions more difficult. Indeed, the Speech or Debate Clause was designed to preclude prosecution of Members for legislative acts. The Clause protects "against inquiry into acts that occur in the regular course of the legislative process and into the motivation for those acts." It "precludes any showing of how [a legislator] acted, voted, or decided."

Brewster. Promises by a Member to perform an act in the future are not legislative acts. *Brewster* makes clear that the "compact" may be shown without impinging on the legislative function.

We therefore agree with the Court of Appeals that references to past legislative acts of a Member cannot be admitted without undermining the values protected by the Clause. We implied as much in *Brewster* when we explained: "To make a prima facie case under [the] indictment, the Government need not show any act of [Brewster] *subsequent* to the corrupt promise for payment, for it is taking the bribe, not performance of the illicit compact, that is a criminal act." A similar inference is appropriate from *Johnson* where we held that the Clause was violated by questions about motive addressed to others than Johnson himself. That holding would have been unnecessary if the Clause did not afford protection beyond legislative acts themselves.

MR. JUSTICE STEVENS misconstrues our holdings on the Speech or Debate Clause in urging: "The admissibility line should be based on the purpose of the offer rather than the specificity of the reference." The Speech or Debate Clause does not refer to the prosecutor's purpose in offering evidence. The Clause does not simply state, "No proof of a legislative act shall be offered"; the prohibition of the Clause is far broader. It provides that Members "shall not be questioned in any other Place." Indeed, as MR. JUSTICE STEVENS recognizes, the admission of evidence of legislative acts "may reveal [to the jury] some information about the performance of legislative acts and the legislator's motivation in conducting official duties." Revealing information as to a legislative act — speaking or debating — to a jury would subject a Member to being "questioned" in a place other than the House or Senate, thereby violating the explicit prohibition of the Speech or Debate Clause.

As to what restrictions the Clause places on the admission of evidence, our concern is not with the "specificity" of the reference. Instead, our concern is whether there is mention of a legislative act. To effectuate the intent of the Clause, the Court has construed it to protect other "legislative acts" such as utterances in committee hearings and reports. E.g., *Doe v. McMillan*, 412 U.S. 306 (1973). But it is clear from the language of the Clause that protection extends only to an act that has already been performed. A promise to deliver a speech, to vote, or to solicit other votes at some future date is not "speech or debate." Likewise, a promise to introduce a bill is not a legislative act. Thus, in light of the strictures of *Johnson* and *Brewster*, the District Court order prohibiting the introduction of evidence "of the performance of a past legislative act" was redundant.

[The Government also argued that the Speech or Debate Clause had been waived, either by (a) Helstoski's testimony before the grand jury in which he produced documentary evidence of his legislative acts or (b) the enactment of § 201 by Congress. The Court did not decide whether waiver was ever possible by the defendant, but held that any possible waiver would have to be an "explicit and unequivocal renunciation of the protection," which Helstoski's actions were not.]

The Speech or Debate Clause was designed neither to assure fair trials nor to avoid coercion. Rather, its purpose was to preserve the constitutional structure of separate, coequal, and independent branches of government. The English and American history of the privilege suggests that any lesser standard would risk intrusion by the Executive and the Judiciary into the sphere of protected legislative activities. The importance of the principle was recognized as early as 1808 in *Coffin v. Coffin*, 4 Mass. 1, 27, where the court said that the purpose of the principle was to secure to every member "*exemption* from prosecution, for every thing said or done by him, as a representative, in the exercise of the functions of that office."

This Court has reiterated the central importance of the Clause for preventing intrusion by Executive and Judiciary into the legislative sphere.

[I]t is apparent from the history of the clause that the privilege was not born primarily of a desire to avoid private suits . . . but rather to prevent intimidation by the executive and accountability before a possibly hostile judiciary. * * *

There is little doubt that the instigation of criminal charges against critical or disfavored legislators by the executive in a judicial forum was the chief fear prompting the long struggle for parliamentary privilege in England and, in the context of the American system of separation of powers, is the predominate thrust of the Speech or Debate Clause. *Johnson*. * * *

We recognize that an argument can be made from precedent and history that Congress, as a body, should not be free to strip individual Members of the protection guaranteed by the Clause from being "questioned" by the Executive in the courts. The controversy over the Alien and Sedition Acts reminds us how one political party in control of both the Legislative and the Executive Branches sought to use the courts to destroy political opponents.

The Supreme Judicial Court of Massachusetts noted in *Coffin* that "the privilege secured . . . is not so much the privilege of the house as an organized body, as of each individual member composing it, who is entitled to this privilege, *even against the declared will of the house*." In a similar vein in *Brewster* we stated:

"The immunities of the Speech or Debate Clause were not written into the Constitution simply for the personal or private benefit of Members of Congress, but to protect the integrity of the legislative process *by insuring the independence of individual legislators*."

We perceive no reason to undertake, in this case, consideration of the Clause in terms of separating the Members' rights from the rights of the body.

[*Affirmed.*]

MR. JUSTICE POWELL took no part in the consideration or decision of this case.

MR. JUSTICE STEVENS, with whom MR. JUSTICE STEWART joins, concurring in part and dissenting in part.

In *Johnson*, the Court held that a Member of Congress could not be prosecuted for conspiracy against the United States based on his preparation and delivery of an improperly motivated speech in the House of Representatives. After noting that the attention given to the speech was not merely "an incidental part of the Government's case," but rather was "an intensive judicial inquiry" into the speech's substance and motivation, the Court held that the prosecution violated the express language of the Speech or Debate Clause and the policies that underlie it. The Court carefully emphasized, however, that its decision was limited to a case of that character and "does not touch a prosecution which . . . does not draw in question the legislative acts of the defendant member of Congress or his motives for performing them."

In *Brewster*, the Court held that the Speech or Debate Clause did not bar prosecution of a former Senator for receiving money in return for being influenced in the performance of a legislative act. The Court read *Johnson* as allowing a prosecution of a Member of Congress so long as the Government's case does not rely on legislative acts or the motivation for such acts. It reasoned that Brewster was not being prosecuted for the performance of a legislative act, but rather for soliciting or agreeing to take money with knowledge that the donor intended to compensate him for an official act. Whether the Senator ever performed the official act was irrelevant.

As a practical matter, of course, it is clear that evidence relating to a legislator's motivation for accepting a bribe will also be probative of his intent in committing the official act for which the bribe was solicited or paid. Nonetheless, the Court made clear in *Brewster* that inquiries into the legislator's motivation in accepting payment are not barred by *Johnson*'s proscription against inquiry into legislative motivation. "[A]n inquiry into the purpose of a bribe," the *Brewster* Court held, " 'does not draw in question the legislative acts of the defendant member of Congress or his motives for performing them.' " Thus, so long as the Government's case does not depend upon the legislator's motivation in committing an official act, inquiries into his motivation in accepting a bribe — which obviously may be revealing as to both the existence of legislative acts and the motivation for them — are permissible under the Speech or Debate Clause, as interpreted in *Brewster*.

* * * Here, the Government is seeking to introduce written and testimonial evidence as to Helstoski's motivation in soliciting and accepting bribes. Some of this evidence makes reference to past or future legislative acts for which payment is being sought or given. Obviously, this evidence, to the extent it is probative of Helstoski's intent in accepting payment, is an important and legitimate part of the Government's case against the former Congressman. Whether or not he ever committed the legislative acts is wholly irrelevant to the Government's proof, and inquiry into that subject is prohibited by *Johnson* and *Brewster*. But the mere fact that legislative acts are mentioned does not, in my view, require that otherwise relevant and admissible evidence be excluded. * * * The admissibility line should be based on the purpose of the offer rather than the specificity of the reference. So long as the jury is instructed that it

should not consider the references as proof of legislative acts, and so long as no inquiry is made with respect to the motivations for such acts, *Brewster* does not bar the introduction of evidence simply because reference is made to legislative acts.

Indeed, I think it important to emphasize that the majority today does not read *Brewster* to foreclose the introduction of any evidence making reference to legislative acts. The Court holds that evidence referring only to acts to be performed in the future may be admitted into evidence. The Court explains this holding by noting that a promise to perform a legislative act in the future is not itself a legislative act. But it is equally true that the solicitation of a bribe which contains a self-laudatory reference to past performance is not itself a legislative act. Whether the legislator refers to past or to future performance, his statement will be probative of his intent in accepting payment and, in either event, may incidentally shed light on the performance and motivation of legislative acts. The proper remedy, in my judgment, is not automatic inadmissibility for past references and automatic admissibility for future references. Rather, drawing on the language of the Constitution itself, the test should require the trial court to analyze the purpose of the prosecutor's questioning. If the evidentiary references to legislative acts are merely incidental to a proper purpose, the judge should admit the evidence and instruct the jury as to its limited relevance. The Constitution mandates that legislative acts "shall not be questioned"; it does not say they shall not be mentioned.

[The dissenting opinion of MR. JUSTICE BRENNAN has been omitted. The dissent argued that the indictment should have been dismissed. "'[P]roof of an agreement to be 'influenced' in the performance of legislative acts is by definition an inquiry into their motives, whether or not the acts themselves or the circumstances surrounding them are questioned at trial.' " Quoting *Brewster*, 408 U.S. at 536 (Brennan, J., dissenting).]

NOTE ON BRIBERY PROSECUTIONS AFTER *HELSTOSKI*

In *United States v. Myers*, 635 F.2d 932 (2d Cir.), cert. denied, 449 U.S. 956 (1980), former Congressman Myers (D-Pa.) argued that his indictment for bribery in violation of § 201 as part of the Abscam investigation was subject to dismissal under the Speech or Debate Clause because it required or contemplated that the prosecutor present evidence protected by the Clause. In rejecting this argument, the Second Circuit noted that the indictment alleged a *promise* to perform a legislative act (introduction of a private bill to allow foreign businessmen to remain in the United States), not the performance of the act. See also *United States v. Murphy*, 642 F.2d 699 (2d Cir. 1980), where the court stated that, under *Brewster*, acceptance of bribes in return for corrupt promises to take official action is not protected by the Clause.

In *United States v. Williams*, 644 F.2d 950 (2d Cir. 1981), the court held that the Speech or Debate Clause was not violated when the indicting grand jury was shown a videotape of defendant, former Senator Harrison Williams (D-N.J.), discussing a proposed immigration bill, because this discussion involved only possible future performance of legislative functions. And in *United States v. Myers, supra*, the Second Circuit rejected the contention of a co-defendant, former Congressman Frank Thompson (D-N.J.), that the trial court had erred in allowing into evidence proof of his private conversations on the floor of the House of Representatives in which he invited a second Congressman to join the ranks of those accepting bribes. The court said that "[o]ne would think that a Congressman, even when grasping for objections to a criminal conviction, would understand that the Speech or Debate Clause accords immunity to what is said on the House floor in the course of the legislative process, * * * not to whispered solicitations to commit a crime."

These cases reflect the difficulty of applying the Court's test for Speech or Debate Clause immunity to instances of allegedly corrupt behavior. Inquiry into the lawmaker's decision to accept a bribe, which seems to be allowed, may well shed light on the motives in performing any subsequent related legislative act. And how should courts treat self-laudatory references to past legislative acts designed to convince listeners to participate in the corrupt scheme? Under the Court's jurisprudence, these statements would probably be excluded from the courtroom, even though the accuracy of the statements is arguably not relevant to the prosecution. Should we worry that the clause is too expansive in its coverage, immunizing from prosecution corrupt politicians who should be held to answer for their perfidy? See also *Kansas v. Neufeld*, 926 P.2d 1325 (Kan. 1996) (using state speech or debate provision to exclude evidence of a particularly squalid blackmail threat from one lawmaker to another on the floor of the legislature to coerce a vote, a result in tension with *Myers*, above). Remember that the Clause protects a member only from questioning "in any other Place," thereby allowing the legislature the power to investigate and discipline its members.

———

Problem 3–14. The House of Representatives was nearing a vote on the President's health reform proposal. The vote was going to be close, and the Republican Party leadership wanted to maintain party discipline to ensure passage. Representative Alex Noah, a Republican on the committee with jurisdiction over the bill, opposed the bill and announced his intention to vote no on the floor. A week before, Noah had announced that he was retiring from Congress, and his daughter Samantha had declared that she would run for her father's now-open seat in the next election.

On the floor of the House, during the voting period on the health care bill, the Speaker of the House told Noah that "a yes vote on this bill will help you and help your daughter because it will be a popular vote with the President and your Party." Minutes later, Noah was called off the floor into the cloak room (a room right off the House floor where only representatives can enter and that has phones and comfortable chairs) to take a phone call from the Secretary of Health and Human Services. The Secretary told Noah that it was important that he end his distinguished career on a high note of support for the President. The Secretary added that he was sure Noah's expertise would be crucial to several blue ribbon panels being established to study the challenges facing the health care system, and that he hoped the President would be in a position to nominate Noah for such positions after he retired. When Noah returned to the floor, the Republican Majority Leader told him that the state's Chamber of Commerce had decided to raise $100,000 for Samantha's campaign, but that a no vote would likely discourage the Chamber from helping Samantha's election effort. Representative Jane Skye, another Republican from Noah's state, told Noah on his way up to vote that if he voted no, she and other Republicans would make sure Samantha never came to Congress and that Samantha would be political "dead meat."

Noah voted no. Noah is willing to testify about the events in any criminal prosecutions that may be brought or in any other forum. What crimes may have been committed? What obstacles would stand in the way of any prosecutions? What arguments would you expect to be made by possible defendants? Are avenues available for an investigation into the events that Representative Noah has described other than criminal prosecutions in court?

Problem 3–15. In 2006, the FBI conducted an investigation of bribery and other allegations concerning Rep. William Jefferson (D–La.). It was alleged that Jefferson used his position to influence some African nations to buy telecommunications equipment and services from a Louisiana-based firm in return for substantial cash and stock. One of his former staffers and the president of the firm pleaded guilty to bribing and conspiring to bribe the Congressman. Pursuant to a search warrant but without alerting congressional leadership, the FBI searched Jefferson's congressional office in Washington, D.C. — apparently the first time that federal law enforcement officials had searched the office of a representative or senator. The FBI seized computer hard drives and boxes of paper records, which it agreed to review using a "Filter Team" to remove any irrelevant documents or any material protected by the Speech or Debate clause or any other privilege. (The FBI also searched Jefferson's home, where agents found $90,000 wrapped in aluminum foil and hidden in the freezer.) Lawmakers from both parties objected to the search as a violation of legislative privilege. Can congressional offices be searched consistent with the Speech or Debate Clause? Can law enforcement use the documents agents find there? How would the case against Representative Jefferson be affected by the constitutional privilege and the cases interpreting it? See *United States v. Rayburn House Office Building, Room 2113,* 2007 WL 2275237 (D.C. Cir. 2007) (holding that the execution of the search warrant violated the Speech or Debate Clause, that all privileged documents (originals and copies) must be returned, that the FBI officers who participated in the search cannot reveal contents of privileged documents or be involved in pending prosecution, but that non-privileged documents need not be returned). (As you consider this case, are you surprised that Jefferson was reelected after the raid of his home and office but before he was indicted for racketeering, soliciting bribes and money-laundering?)

2. *State Protection of State Legislators (Speech or Debate Clauses in State Constitutions)*

Just as New York did at the time of the *Van de Carr* prosecution (a provision that remains unchanged today), 43 state constitutions contain clauses similar to the U.S. Constitution's Speech or Debate Clause. State courts often interpret these clauses as having a similar meaning to the federal clause.[d] Some state constitutional provisions are much more narrowly phrased, however. Article 4, § 11 of the Michigan Constitution protects state legislators "from civil arrest and civil process during sessions of the legislature and for five days next before the commencement and after the termination thereof." The scope of these provisions is usually interpreted to be equivalent to the federal protection, notwithstanding the difference in formulation.

Thus, the Michigan provision immunizes lawmakers in their legislative activities, but it does not extend to casework or informing activities. See, e.g., *Wilkins v. Gagliardi*, 556 N.W.2d 171 (Mich. App. 1996). Michigan courts have had to determine the scope of the time period in which legislators are protected by the state immunity. In *Bishop v. Montante*, 237 N.W. 2d 465 (Mich. 1976), the Michigan Supreme Court was asked to interpret the word "sessions" in its state speech or debate clause. It found that the immunity continued even during a legislative recess, when the legislature was formally in session because it had not adjourned. The court reasoned that legislators continue to perform legislative business such as "[c]onstituent contact, research, [and] committee assignments" even when the body is not sitting. Is this expansive view of the constitutional protection consistent with courts' understanding of the scope of the clause to cover only legislative activities, and not casework, newsletters, or other interactions with constituents? For a comprehensive examination of state privileges and a list of all the provisions, see Steven Huefner, *The Neglected Value of the Legislative Privilege in State Legislatures*, 45 Wm. & Mary L. Rev. 221 (2003).

3. *Federal Protection of State Legislators*

The Court addressed whether the policies of the Speech or Debate Clause protected state legislators in *United States v. Gillock*, 445 U.S. 360 (1980). In that case a Tennessee state legislator was indicted on federal charges stemming from allegations that he had accepted money in return for using his office to block extradition of criminal defendants and for introducing legislation that would have enabled four persons to obtain electrician's licenses they had been unable to obtain by way of examination. The district court had granted Gillock's motion to suppress all evidence relating to his legislative activities, on the ground that the Federal Rules of Evidence should recognize a privilege to protect the integrity of the state legislative process. After the Court of Appeals affirmed, the Supreme Court reversed. The Court noted that the Speech or Debate Clause technically protects only federal legislators and rejected arguments that the policy considerations underlying the Speech or Debate Clause counsel recognition of a comparable evidentiary privilege for state legislators in federal prosecutions. The Court stated:

---

d. See, e.g., *Romer v. Colorado General Assembly*, 810 P.2d 215 (Colo. 1991); *People v. Ohrenstein*, 565 N.E.2d 493, 501 (N.Y. 1990); *Harristown Development Corp. v. Commissioner*, 580 A.2d 1174 (Pa. 1990).

Two interrelated rationales underlie the Speech or Debate Clause: first, the need to avoid intrusion by the Executive or Judiciary into the affairs of a coequal branch, and second, the desire to protect legislative independence. * * *

The first rationale, resting solely on the separation of powers doctrine, gives no support to the grant of a privilege to state legislators in federal criminal prosecutions. * * * [I]n those areas where the Constitution grants the Federal Government the power to act, the Supremacy Clause dictates that federal enactments will prevail over competing state exercises of power. * * *

[As to the second rationale,] we believe that recognition of an evidentiary privilege for state legislators for their legislative acts would impair the legitimate interest of the Federal Government in enforcing its criminal statutes with only speculative benefit to the state legislative process.

Compare *Tenney v. Brandhove*, 341 U.S. 367 (1951) (recognizing a federal common law immunity for state legislators against civil lawsuits brought under § 1983 for violations of federal constitutional or statutory rights).

Even more important immunity issues are raised by judicial sanctions that might be useful in enforcing constitutional remedial decrees. Consider the following note case, which presents a tension between the court's remedial powers and the federal common law of immunity.

SPALLONE v. UNITED STATES, 493 U.S. 265 (1990). District Judge Leonard Sand found that the city of Yonkers, New York had over a period of three decades gerrymandered sites for subsidized public housing in order to perpetuate residential racial segregation. Thus, 97% of the public housing projects were in southwest Yonkers (populated mainly by African Americans and Latinos). Since most of the public housing occupants were racial minorities, this systematic channeling exacerbated patterns of housing segregation in Yonkers, leaving east and northwest Yonkers completely white. Also, the city deliberately manipulated the public school system — altering attendance zone boundaries, opening and closing schools, assigning faculty — to maintain racially segregated schools, with minority population schools demonstrably inferior.

Judge Sand issued an extensive remedial order that directed the city to cease and desist its discriminatory practices, to build new public housing in east Yonkers, and to develop a long-term plan for the dispersal of public housing. The city complied with none of the affirmative obligations of Judge Sand's order, but after the order was affirmed on appeal the city entered into a consent decree. Then, on 14 June 1988, the council voted a moratorium on all public housing construction, in violation of the consent decree.

When further negotiations among plaintiffs, the city, and Judge Sand yielded no resolution, Judge Sand on 26 July issued a contempt order, to take effect if the council did not take satisfactory action by 1 August 1988. On 1 August, the council by a 4–3 vote (Spallone et al. in the majority) defeated a proposed resolution that would have taken action to reduce patterns of housing segregation, and Judge Sand held the city and each of the four majority councilmembers in civil contempt. The fines were $100 against the city for the first day of noncompliance, to be doubled for each consecutive day of noncompliance, and $500 per day for members of the city council. The Court of Appeals affirmed the contempt order but limited the fines against the city to $1 million per day. The Supreme Court granted certiorari on the council members' objection to the fines against them but refused to hear the city's objections. Hence the city's fines were left in place, and on 9 September 1988 the council adopted a housing plan.

Chief Justice Rehnquist delivered the majority opinion affirming the Court of Appeals. First, he acknowledged the broad inherent power of the judiciary to enforce compliance with judicial orders through civil contempt. In the context of orders to remedy past discrimination, the judicial power is even broader. But, Rehnquist observed, it is not unlimited. Courts must account for the interests of local authorities in managing their own governmental affairs, and judges must carefully calibrate the extent of the power that they use with their objectives. Rehnquist found it reasonable for the district court to use contempt sanctions against the city because the city had entered into a consent agreement that committed it to implement certain parts of the arrangement through legislation. The difficulty arose with respect to the contempt sanctions imposed on the individual councilmembers.

Rehnquist surveyed the caselaw dealing with immunity for state legislators, including *Tenney v. Brandhove, supra,* which held that state legislators were absolutely privileged in their legislative acts in an action against them for damages. Although the holding in such cases "do not control the question whether local legislators such as petitioners should be immune from contempt sanctions imposed for failure to vote in favor of a particular legislative bill. But some of the same considerations on which the immunity doctrine is based must inform the District Court's exercise of its discretion in a case such as this."

The majority found the sanctions directed toward the individuals problematic in a way that the sanctions directed against the city for failure to take actions required by the consent decree were not, even though both coerced the city councilmembers to vote in a certain way. "The imposition of sanctions on individual legislators is designed to cause them to vote, not with a view to the interest of their constituents or of the city, but with a view solely to their own personal interests. * * * This sort of individual sanction effects a much greater perversion of the normal legislative process than does the imposition of sanctions on the city for the failure of these same legislators to enact an ordinance. In that case, the legislator is only encouraged to vote in favor of an ordinance that he would not otherwise favor by reason of the adverse sanctions imposed on the city. A councilman who felt that his constituents would rather have the city enact the Affordable Housing Ordinance than pay a 'bankrupting fine' would be motivated to vote in favor of such an ordinance because the sanctions were a threat to the fiscal solvency of the city for whose welfare he was in part responsible. This is the sort of calculus in which legislators engage regularly." At the least, Rehnquist argued, the District Court should have first seen if the contempt sanctions against the city alone worked before imposing the extraordinary penalty on the councilmembers.

Justice Brennan, writing for himself and **Justices Marshall, Blackmun** and **Stevens,** angrily dissented because he believed the majority ignored the compelling evidence of bad faith on the part of individual councilmembers. "As the events leading up to the Contempt Order make clear, the recalcitrant councilmembers were extremely responsive to the strong segments of their constituencies that were vociferously opposed to racial residential integration. Councilmember Fagan, for example, explained that his vote against the Housing Ordinance required by the Consent Decree 'was an act of defiance. The people clearly wanted me to say no to the judge.' Councilmember Spallone declared openly that 'I will be taking on the judge all the way down the line. I made a commitment to my people and that commitment remains.' Moreover, once Yonkers had gained national attention over its refusal to integrate, many residents made it clear to their representatives on the council that they preferred bankrupt martyrdom to integration." Brennan observed that the councilmembers were playing a game of chicken, with each hoping another would capitulate and suffer the wrath of his constituents in order to avoid municipal bankruptcy. The District Court's order was a reasonable attempt to solve the collective action problem and account for the unacceptably racist behavior of the individuals.

Brennan distinguished this case from the usual one involving the doctrine of legislative immunity. "[O]nce a federal court has issued a valid order to remedy the effects of a prior, specific constitutional violation, the representatives are no longer 'acting in a field where legislators traditionally have power to act.' *Tenney*. At this point, the Constitution itself imposes an overriding definition of the 'public good,' and a court's valid command to obey constitutional dictates is not subject to override by any countervailing preferences of the polity, no matter how widely and ardently shared. * * * [L]egislators certainly may not defy court-ordered remedies for racial discrimination merely because their constituents prefer to maintain segregation[.] Defiance at this stage results, in essence, in a perpetuation of the very constitutional violation at which the remedy is aimed."

NOTE ON *SPALLONE*

The discrimination case which led to *Spallone* was brought by the Carter Administration Department of Justice against the city. The Department alleged, and successfully established, that the Yonkers' schools were segregated because the city strategically excluded public housing units from white neighborhoods. Judge Sand's opinion holding the city liable was "the first time a court provided both housing relief and school desegregation relief in the same law suit." Feron, *Confronting the Excavation*, N.Y. Times, Apr. 21, 1991, at § 12WC, p. 1.

The Council's defiance of Judge Sand's remedial order led to the contempt citations. Council Member Henry J. Spallone was able to parlay his defiance of Judge Sand into a winning mayoral campaign. In 1991, however, Spallone lost the Republican mayoral primary, in part because he was not able to resist Judge Sand's decree. See Feron, *Yonkers Result Could Affect Desegregation Case*, N.Y. Times, Sept. 14, 1991, at § 1, 22. Spallone's crusade cost the city

$12 million in legal fees and $450,000 in contempt fines. Feron, *Housing Construction Starts Without Fanfare in Yonkers*, N.Y. Times, Apr. 13, 1991, at § 1, 25.

In April 1991, the construction of the public housing ordered by Judge Sand started. The city avoided the high-rise public housing units of past decades and built seven clusters of two-story three bedroom homes in East Yonkers, which had traditionally been the white section of the city. Judge Sand's order called for two hundred "remedial" units and eight hundred units of affordable housing. One site was to be several blocks from Sarah Lawrence College. By the fall of 1991, most of the construction was complete. Foderaro, *Yonkers Public Housing Is Now a Cooler Issue,* N.Y. Times, Oct. 21, 1991, at § B, p. 1.

Particularly in the last section of this chapter, we have studied rules that shape legislative deliberation, in particular, those imposed by the federal or state constitutions and long a feature of legislative processes. Many other rules are a product of statute or internal decision. All of these rules strive to impose a "due process of lawmaking," to use the evocative phrase of Hans Linde in his important article, *Due Process of Lawmaking*, 55 Neb. L. Rev. 197 (1976). In the next chapter, we will draw on the insights of this chapter and focus directly on due process of lawmaking, expanding it to include several comprehensive legislative frameworks in the modern Congress such as the congressional budget process.

Chapter 4

DUE PROCESS OF LAWMAKING

In an article proposing an alternative method of judicial review to replace the deferential rational basis review accorded to many statutes, former Justice of the Oregon Supreme Court Hans Linde articulated a theory of *due process of lawmaking*. *Due Process of Lawmaking*, 55 Neb. L. Rev. 197 (1976). He argued that the due process clauses of the Constitution "instruct government itself to act by due process of law, not simply to legislate subject to later judicial second-guessing." *Id.* at 222. Legislative process should be designed, he argued, to produce "rational lawmaking," which he described: "It would oblige legislators to inform themselves in some fashion about the existing conditions on which the proposed law would operate, and about the likelihood that the proposal would in fact further the intended purpose. In order to weigh the anticipated benefits for some against the burdens the law would impose on others, legislators must inform themselves about those burdens. * * * The projections and assessments of conditions and consequences must presumably take some account of evidence, at least in committee sessions. * * * The committee must explain its factual and value premises to the full body. Surely there is no place for a vote on final passage by members who have never read even a summary of the bill, let alone a committee report or a resume of the factual documentation." *Id.* at 223–24.

Linde acknowledged that his description did not accurately depict reality, but he argued that courts should adopt methods of adjudication and statutory review designed to promote rational lawmaking by legislative bodies. Courts could work toward this objective by scrutinizing the rationale articulated by lawmakers to justify their choices of legislative ends and the means to reach those ends. Justices on the Supreme Court have only infrequently pursued this strategy of judicial review, however. One example is *Fullilove v. Klutznick*, 448 U.S. 448 (1980), a case in which the majority upheld a federal statute requiring that a certain percentage of federal contracting money go to minority business enterprises. Justice Stevens, in dissent, would have required a reasoned explanation for a congressional decision to provide preferential treatment for some racial and ethnic minorities.

More recently, the Supreme Court has adopted a similar technique in assessing the constitutionality of federal laws passed pursuant to Congress's interstate commerce authority and its authority to enforce the Reconstruction Amendments. In cases like *Board of Trustees of the University of Alabama v. Garrett*, 531 U.S. 356 (2001) (concerning the American with Disabilities Act) and *United States v. Morrison*, 529 U.S. 598 (2000) (concerning the Violence Against Women Act), the Court has reviewed the state of the legislative record to determine if the empirical basis on which Congress legislated was sufficient. Many commentators have criticized this new trend as an unacceptably intrusive encroachment on the prerogatives of the most politically accountable branch and as unsophisticated in its determination of what documents make up the legislative record. Ruth Colker and James Brudney, in their article *Dissing Congress*, argue that the Court "has treated the federal legislative process as akin to agency or lower court decisionmaking; in doing so, the Court has undermined Congress's ability to decide for itself how and whether to create a record in support of pending legislation." 100 Mich. L. Rev. 80, 83 (2001). Similarly, Philip Frickey and Steven Smith have suggested that the Court has placed unrealistic record-developing obligations upon Congress and failed to respect that, in circumstances of political conflict, legislatures decide by majority vote rather than by consensual deliberation. See *Judicial Review, the Congressional Process, and the Federalism Cases: An Interdisciplinary Critique*, 111 Yale L.J. 1707 (2002).[a]

In *Fullilove*, Stevens justified his departure from the norm because laws making distinctions on racial grounds are reviewed with strict scrutiny; it is unlikely he would be willing to require proof of rational lawmaking in cases challenging other kinds of laws. Linde was dubious about the merits of the more aggressive judicial approach. "Candor in giving reasons for a policy can be a mixed blessing. It may result in invalidating a policy for faulty premises even though it would be quite desirable if based on different reasons. * * * Pursued into the legislative process [past the context of administrative agencies], the hope for candor is more likely to produce hypocrisy. Recitals of findings and purposes are the task of anonymous draftsmen, committee staffs, and counsel for interested parties, not legislators." Linde, *supra*, at 230-31.

Accordingly, Linde focused on the process of lawmaking, its rules and structural arrangements that are designed to facilitate reasoned deliberation and rational decisionmaking. Lawmaking and legislative outcomes are shaped by a variety of requirements; in Chapters 2 and 3, we studied some of the constitutive and substantive rules that can have indirect effects on the process of lawmaking. The Constitution also spells out procedural requirements for lawmaking, notably the bicameralism and presentment requirements; statutes and congressional rules provide additional procedural constraints.[b] In Section 1 of this chapter, we will identify several constitutional rules that require particular processes be followed to enact laws. In a few cases, courts have

---

a. See also William Buzbee & Robert Schapiro, *Legislative Record Review*, 54 Stan. L. Rev. 87 (2001); Larry Kramer, *The Supreme Court, 2000 Term — Foreword: We the Court*, 115 Harv. L. Rev. 4, 137–53 (2001).

b. See Adrian Vermeule, *The Constitutional Law of Congressional Procedure*, 71 U. Chi. L. Rev. 361 (2004).

required that some decisions be made by Congress, rather than other governmental institutions, because its institutional features ensure the democratic pedigree of legislation. The concept of due process of lawmaking has relevance past the judicial arena, however. Legislatures have the ability to adopt rules and frameworks that add procedural requirements to the enactment of laws. In Section 2, we will describe the most important modern procedural framework that determines the fate of much of federal legislation — the congressional budget process. It has become such a ubiquitous and influential aspect of federal lawmaking that many scholars describe these rules, as well as those governing the executive branch's budgeting activities, as the *fiscal constitution*.[c] Finally, in Section 3, we will discuss some other rules and comprehensive procedural frameworks that Congress has adopted or has considered, many of which are based on the budget process.

SECTION 1. STRUCTURAL DUE PROCESS

Due process of lawmaking focuses in part on the "structures through which policies are both formed and applied." Laurence Tribe, *Structural Due Process*, 10 Harv. C.R.–C.L. L. Rev. 269, 269 (1975). This notion suggests that some kinds of actions should be taken only by entities with particular institutional features that enhance their special democratic legitimacy. After we assess requirements in the federal Constitution and in state constitutions setting forth procedural requirements for lawmaking, we will turn to *Hampton v. Mow Sun Wong*, 426 U.S. 88 (1976), where the Court adopted a due process of lawmaking approach. You should also review Chapter 3, § 3, which provides examples of substantive constitutional limitations on legislative deliberation. We conclude with a brief discussion of legislative drafting because one of the objectives of any lawmaking process is to produce well-written laws that can be understood and followed by citizens.

A. CONSTITUTIONAL REQUIREMENTS FOR THE PROCEDURES FOLLOWED IN STATE AND FEDERAL LAWMAKING

The Bicameralism and Presentment Requirements. Article I, § 7, clauses 2–3 of the U.S. Constitution provide that a bill becomes a law only if it is enacted in the same form by both the House and Senate, and then presented to the President. If the President vetoes the bill, the House and Senate can override the veto by a two-thirds vote in each chamber. State constitutions have similar provisions, with one exception (Nebraska only has one legislative chamber) and one interesting twist (most states allow their governors to veto specific items in some bills, discussed in Chapter 3, § 3B). The Court in *Clinton v. City of New York* (Chapter 3, § 3B) emphasized that bicameralism and presentment are mandatory requirements of the legislative process: "The procedures governing the enactment of statutes set forth in the text of Article I were the product of the great debates and compromises that produced the Constitution itself. Familiar historical materials provide abundant support for

---

c. See Kenneth Dam, *The American Fiscal Constitution*, 44 U. Chi. L. Rev. 271 (1977).

the conclusion that the power to enact statutes may only 'be exercised in accord with a single, finely wrought and exhaustively considered, procedure.' " 524 U.S. at 439–40 (quoting *INS v. Chadha*, Chapter 9, § 2C).

One justification for the bicameralism and presentment requirements is to ensure the sustained consideration of different points of view. In *Federalist* #51, James Madison defended the bicameralism requirement on the ground that it yields two bodies elected in different ways, representing different interests and electorates, and developing different internal customs. Moreover, requiring two heterogeneous bodies to agree on legislation ensures that factious and partial laws would not be adopted.[a] In *Federalist* #62, Madison argued that the Senate, with its longer terms and smaller membership, is a cooling-off chamber, preventing the enactment of hasty legislation. Alexander Hamilton argued in *Federalist* #73 that the executive veto is likewise "calculated to guard the community against the effects of faction, precipitancy, or of any impulse unfriendly to the public good, which may happen to influence a majority" of Congress.

Saul Levmore has offered a modern analysis of bicameralism in *Bicameralism: When Are Two Decisions Better than One?*, 12 Int'l Rev. L. & Econ. 145 (1992). He first considers the possibility that bicameralism reduces the "manipulative power of the agenda setter" because one cannot control outcomes as well in a bicameral system as in a unicameral process. Levmore concludes, however, that "only a very careful and difficult empirical inquiry would establish that a convener's power to influence committee and conference-committee membership does not offset the fact that bicameralism diminishes the convener's ability to manipulate the order in which alternative proposals are considered." *Id.* at 151. He acknowledges the Buchanan and Tullock argument that bicameralism protects the status quo by making it more difficult to enact legislation. Levmore argues that although supermajority voting requirements could achieve the same purpose, "supermajoritarianism [likely] encourages more wasteful rent-seeking and corruption than does bicameralism. The simple fact that in a bicameral system a proposal must be openly considered in two forums may work to expose misbehavior. And if the problems of corruption and inefficient rent-seeking are in-part functions of a legislator's ability to promise and deliver results, then it is surely the case that with supermajoritarianism a legislator, or small group of legislators, is more likely to be in a position to block legislation on behalf of some interest group than is a legislator likely to be able to block or promote legislation in a bicameral system with simple-majority voting." *Id.* at 155.

Bicameralism on the federal level requires that two legislative institutions that are constituted in very different ways each have a say in the enactment of laws. These differences were more pronounced before passage of the Seventeenth Amendment, which ended the practice of having state legislatures

---

a. For a formal proof of Madison's proposition, see James Buchanan & Gordon Tullock, *The Calculus of Consent* (1962).

select senators and required their direct election.[b] The most obvious remaining difference between the two institutions — the Senate's unique apportionment scheme in which each state is equally represented — has not received the scholarly attention that it deserves.[c] This feature of the Senate is almost certainly a permanent one; Article V of the Constitution provides that "no State, without its Consent, shall be deprived of its equal Suffrage in the Senate." In contrast, both houses of bicameral state legislatures are subject to the principle of one person, one vote, although courts may accept greater population deviations in state districting then in the context of districting for the House of Representatives. See, e.g., *Connor v. Finch*, 431 U.S. 407 (1977).[d]

Frances Lee and Bruce Oppenheimer have raised several fairness concerns in their study of the Senate, *Sizing Up the Senate: The Unequal Consequences of Equal Representation* (1999). They find first that state population "dramatically affects both the quantity of contact that constituents have with their senators and the perceived quality of those interactions." *Id.* at 12. Constituents from less populous states have more contact with their senators and are more likely to ask them for help with their problems, rather than just registering their opinion on some policy matter. This reality causes a disparity of access for both individuals and interest groups to influence members of Congress. Another troubling disparity that Lee and Oppenheimer link to the malapportionment of the Senate affects partisan control of the institution. "[E]qual representation of states often means that one political party wins Senate seats disproportionate to its share of the national popular vote, owing to its success in small-state elections." *Id.* at 226.[e] Small-state senators tend to spend more time pursuing particularized benefits for their constituents, whereas large-state senators spend relatively more time pursuing policy activism which appeals more to the media and thus furthers their reelection goal in states where personal campaigning is logistically impossible.

One way that small-state senators enhance their ability to obtain benefits for their constituents is that they often cast the decisive votes on closely fought legislation. "[C]oalition leaders tend to seek out senators from small states to find needed votes and * * * these senators — who know that their demands are less costly and thus more likely to be accommodated — delay committing

---

b. See Vikram Amar, *Indirect Effects of Direct Election: A Structural Examination of the Seventeenth Amendment*, 49 Vand. L. Rev. 1347 (1996); Jay Bybee, *Ulysses at the Mast: Democracy, Federalism, and the Sirens' Song of the Seventeenth Amendment*, 91 Nw. U. L. Rev. 500 (1997).

c. For an analysis of the behavior of representatives when two legislators share the same geographical constituency, see Wendy Schiller, *Partners and Rivals: Representation in U.S. Senate Delegations* (2000).

d. For a critique of the Senate as an institution that violates the one person, one vote principle, see William Eskridge, Jr., *The One Senator, One Vote Clause*, 12 Const. Comm. 159 (1995); Michael Lind, *75 Stars: How to Restore Democracy in the U.S. Senate (and End the Tyranny of Wyoming)*, Mother Jones, Jan.–Feb. 1998, at 44.

e. But see Franco Mattei, *Senate Apportionment and Partisan Advantage: A Second Look*, 26 Legis. Studs. Q. 391 (2001) (finding smaller apportionment bias than Lee & Oppenheimer).

themselves to a side, expecting to be courted by coalition leaders." *Id.* at 14. Not surprisingly given their disproportionate influence in the Senate, small-state senators are able to force the Senate to adopt funding formulas in government programs that systematically favor small states and distribute resources away from populous ones. Lee and Oppenheimer find that neither the House nor the President exerts "sufficient influence to counterbalance the effects of equal representation of states in the Senate in distributive policy-making." *Id.* at 14–15.[f]

An important issue is how one challenges a statute or provision of a statute on the ground that it has not been passed in the same form by both chambers of Congress or has not been presented properly to the President. The main check is institutional. The *enrolled bill* is signed by the presiding officers of the House and Senate; if it is then approved by the President, it is sent to the Secretary of State, who furnishes a correct copy to the Congressional Printer for publication in the Statutes at Large. What if a mistake is made? That was the argument in *Marshall Field & Co. v. Clark*, 143 U.S. 649 (1892). Because § 30 of the bill passed by both chambers of Congress was omitted from the enrolled bill, the appellants argued that the law was null and void. The Court agreed with the general proposition but still refused the relief requested; the Court refused to look at the extrinsic evidence offered by appellants to question the enrolled bill:

> It is said that * * * it becomes possible for the Speaker of the House of Representatives and the President of the Senate to impose upon the people as a law a bill that was never passed by Congress. But this possibility is too remote to be seriously considered in the present inquiry. It suggests a deliberate conspiracy to which the presiding officers, the committees on enrolled bills and the clerks of the two houses must necessarily be parties, all acting with a common purpose to defeat an expression of the popular will in the mode prescribed by the Constitution. Judicial action based upon such a suggestion is forbidden by the respect due to a coordinate branch of the government. The evils that may result from the recognition of the principle that an enrolled act, in the custody of the Secretary of State, attested by the signatures of the presiding officers of the two houses of Congress, and the approval of the President, is conclusive evidence that it was passed by Congress, according to the forms of the Constitution, would be far less than those that would certainly result from a rule making the validity of Congressional enactments depend upon the manner in which the journals of the respective houses are kept by the subordinate officers charged with the duty of keeping them.

Later that same year, however, in *United States v. Ballin*, 144 U.S. 1 (1892), the Court examined the Journal of the House of Representatives to conclude that a quorum had been present when a bill was passed.

---

f. See also Lynn Baker & Samuel Dinkin, *The Senate: An Institution Whose Time Has Gone?*, 13 J. L. & Pol. 21 (1997) (arguing that the unfairness that results from the malapportion-ment of the Senate (which includes, in addition to the arguments above, the underrepresentation of minority interests) justifies reform to allocate seats according to states' populations and to adopt a supermajority decision rule for passage of legislation).

Is the enrolled bill rule still a good one more than a century after *Field v. Clark*? Would differences in modern Congressional recordkeeping impact the viability of this rule? Think about this issue in connection with our discussion of the political question doctrine in Chapter 2, § 1. You might reconsider your answer after reading the discussion of the enrolled bill rule in state courts found later in this section.

Enrolled Bill Problem

Problem 4–1. The Deficit Reduction Act of 2005 ("DRA") contained ten titles and 181 pages dealing with subjects from deposit insurance for federal financial institutions, the allocation of the spectrum for commercial wireless users, student loans, filing fees in the federal courts, and assistance to people affected by Hurricane Katrina. It included provisions making substantial changes to the Medicare and Medicaid programs. The version of the DRA signed by the President provided that the duration of Medicare payments for certain medical equipment would be 13 months. That version passed the Senate (thanks to a tie-breaking vote by the Vice President), but, apparently because of an error by the Secretary of the Senate, the version of the DRA sent to the House, and voted on by that chamber, provided for a payment duration of 36 months. The enrolled bill, signed by the Speaker of the House and President pro tempore of the Senate, specified 13 months. Should *Field v. Clark* control the outcome, meaning that the court would not look past the enrolled bill to determine if the constitutional requirements for lawmaking were followed? Does it matter that the difference between the two versions of the bill is $2 billion in additional Medicare spending? If a court decides to look beyond the enrolled bill's language and determines that different versions of the bill passed the House and Senate, what is the appropriate remedy? Should the entire bill be void because of a failure to comply with bicameralism, or should the problematic provision be severed? See *Public Citizen v. United States District Court for the District of Columbia*, 486 F.3d 1342 (D.C. Cir. 2007) (applying the enrolled bill rule of *Field v. Clark* and dismissing challenge to DRA).

Special Procedures for Revenue Measures. Article I, § 7, clause 1 requires that "[a]ll Bills for raising Revenue shall originate in the House of Representatives." The purpose of this rule is to assure that the representatives "closest" to the people (House members, who are up for reelection every two years) bear responsibility for initiating measures (taxes) which have the greatest potential for oppressing the citizenry.[g] Some state constitutions have similar requirements.

The provision prompts several questions: When does a bill not "originate" in the House? If a bill does not so originate, but the House and Senate enact

---

g. See Michael Evans, *"A Source of Frequent and Obstinate Altercations": The History and Application of the Origination Clause*, Tax Notes, Nov. 29, 2004, at 1215; J. Michael Medina, *The Origination Clause in the American Constitution: A Comparative Survey*, 23 Tulsa L.J. 165 (1987).

the bill and the President signs it, do we have a "law" under Article I, § 7? Consider the following case.

UNITED STATES v. MUNOZ-FLORES, 495 U.S. 385 (1990). Munoz-Flores challenged his conviction and fines pursuant to 18 U.S.C. § 3013, on the ground that the statute is a revenue measure that had not originated in the House of Representatives. **Justice Marshall's** opinion for the Court first held that Origination Clause issues are justiciable under the standards set by *Baker v. Carr* (discussed and applied in Chapter 2, § 1).[h] Considering the merits, the Court held that § 3013 did not violate the Origination Clause. In *Twin City Bank v. Nebeker*, 167 U.S. 196, 202 (1897), the Court had earlier ruled that "revenue bills are those that levy taxes in the strict sense of the word, and are not bills for other purposes which may incidentally create revenue." The Victims of Crime Act of 1984 established a Crime Victims Fund, 42 U.S.C. § 10601(a) (as amended), as a federal source of funds for programs that compensate and assist crime victims. The scheme established by the Act included mechanisms to provide money for the Fund, including § 3013. Although the statute provided that if the total income to the Fund from all sources exceeded $100 million in any one year, the excess would be deposited in the general fund of the Treasury, that happened only once, in fiscal year 1989. Any revenue for the general Treasury generated by § 3013 was thus found to be "incidenta[l]" to the regulatory purposes of the statute. In footnote 7, the Court reserved judgment on whether it would apply the *Nebeker* rule to a funded program that was entirely unrelated to the persons paying for the program.

Justice Stevens (joined by **Justice O'Connor**), concurring in the judgment, argued from the structure of Article I, § 7 that improperly "originated" bills become "law" so long as they are passed by both the House and Senate and presented to the President. Read Article I, § 7, which says that "[e]very" bill passed by both Houses and presented to the President "shall become a Law." Also, compare the consequences of improper origination [no explicit consequence] with failure of bicameralism [no law] or presentment [also no law]. Justice Stevens agreed with the Court that the Origination Clause is an important means by which the most popularly accountable institution (the House) is to monitor efforts to tax the people, but Stevens argued that the House itself — rather than the Court — is in the best position to enforce and effectuate this goal.

---

h. Justice Marshall rejected the Government's contention that separation-of-powers issues are best left to enforcement by one of the political organs; he pointed to the Court's repeated adjudication of cases where the political branches were pitted against one another. E.g., *Mistretta v. United States*, 488 U.S. 361, 371–79 (1989) (holding that Sentencing Reform Act of 1984, 18 U.S.C. § 3551 et seq., and 28 U.S.C. § 991 et seq., did not result in Executive's wielding legislative powers, despite either House's power to block Act's passage); *Morrison v. Olson*, 487 U.S. 654, 685–96 (1988) (holding that independent counsel provision of Ethics in Government Act of 1978, 28 U.S.C. § 591 et seq., is not a congressional or judicial usurpation of executive functions, despite President's veto power); *INS v. Chadha*, 462 U.S. 919 (1983) (explicitly finding that separation-of-powers challenge to legislative veto presented no political question).

Justice Scalia concurred in the judgment as well. Relying on *Marshall Field & Co. v. Clark*, 143 U.S. 649 (1892), Justice Scalia argued that the Court cannot look behind the "enrolled bill" as it was presented to the President. The enrolled bill which became the Victims of Crime Act of 1984, 98 Stat. 2170, bore the indication "H.J. Res. 648." The designation "H.J. Res." ("House Joint Resolution") conclusively attested that the legislation originated in the House.

Origination Clause Problems

Problem 4–2. The Senate passes S. 93, which might fairly be characterized as a revenue bill. The House then passes a similar bill of its own, H.R. 617. The Senate requests a conference, and the bill that ultimately emerges is called H.R. 617, but its provisions are more like those in S. 93. The President signs the bill into law. Has the Origination Clause been violated? If so, what remedy (if any) is available?

Problem 4–3. One problem not present in *Munoz-Flores* is that of standing. The Supreme Court has disapproved of broad "taxpayer" standing. Assuming a general revenue measure, as in Problem 4–2, would Members of Congress have standing to bring suit for violation of the Origination Clause? For a pre-*Munoz-Flores* decision, see *Moore v. United States House of Representatives*, 733 F.2d 946 (D.C. Cir. 1984). What about nonjudicial ways to enforce the requirements of the Origination Clause? In the House of Representatives, members have the right to object to consideration of a bill because it violates the Origination Clause; a majority must vote against the constitutional point of order for deliberation to continue. The House also uses a "blue slip" procedure to notify the Senate when it believes that a Senate bill or amendment violates the Origination Clause. The blue slip informs the Senate that the House will not consider the proposal. Is this sufficient protection? We will return to the issue of the standing of members of Congress to bring lawsuits to enforce congressional rules in Section 2 of this chapter.

———

State Constitutional Requirements and the Enrolled Bill Rule. State constitutions often include more procedural requirements for the enactment of laws than the relatively spare federal Constitution. Many state constitutions, for example, require that a bill be read a certain number of times before it can be passed and set specific time limits for legislative sessions. However, a bill that has been passed without receiving the requisite number of readings will not reveal that defect on its face; the same is true if, as is sometimes done, a bill has been passed after the legislature was supposed to have adjourned, but the legislative clock had been covered before the time for adjournment and the legislature pretended that time was standing still. How could one prove such a defect or any other violation of constitutionally prescribed procedures?

In many states, the *enrolled bill rule* severely restricts judicial review of legislative procedural errors. Just as on the federal level, an enrolled bill is a bill that purports to have passed both houses of the legislature and that has been signed by the presiding officers of both houses. In some states, the process of enrollment also involves the signature of the governor and filing with the secretary of state. Courts following the enrolled bill rule conclusively presume that the enrolled bill was validly enacted according to the prescribed procedures and refuse to entertain evidence purporting to demonstrate the contrary. One commentator has noted that

> the rule has been supported by several theories. Traditionally the doctrine of separation of powers was the underlying support for the rule. Under this doctrine the courts are kept from being placed in the position of reviewing the work of a supposedly equal branch of government. Other practical considerations have been advanced in support of the rule. Certain defects are apparent on the face of the enrolled bill itself, but other judicial attacks on the status of legislation could undermine stability in the law and would confuse the trial of substantive issues. Often, such attacks would be totally out of proportion to any serious constitutional violations. Flagrant disregard for constitutional duties is better remedied by internal legislative procedures or by the electorate. The enrolled bill rule is further justified by the argument that legislative journals are subject to error and fraud, whereas enrollment includes "certification by the presiding officers * * * witnessed by other present members * * * [furnishing] adequate protection against the risk of error in the process of certification itself."

Allen Crigler, Comment, *Judicial Review of the Legislative Enactment Process: Louisiana's "Journal Entry" Rule*, 41 La. L. Rev. 1187, 1190 (1981). Are these arguments persuasive? Consider the responsive argument of Linde in *Due Process of Lawmaking, supra,* at 243:

> Neither [respect for a co-equal branch nor evidentiary difficulties] keeps courts from insisting on [adherence to procedural rules] by executive officers or by local lawmakers, and those who oppose judicial review of faulty lawmaking on evidentiary grounds will equally oppose it on uncontested pleadings or stipulations. Fear of legislative resentment at judicial interference is not borne out by experience where procedural review exists, any more than it was after the Supreme Court told Congress that it had used faulty procedure in unseating Representative Adam Clayton Powell. It is far more cause for resentment to invalidate the substance of a policy that the politically accountable branches and their constituents support than to invalidate a lawmaking procedure that can be repeated correctly, yet we take substantive judicial review for granted. Strikingly, the reverse view of propriety prevails in a number of nations where courts have never been empowered to set aside policies legitimately enacted into law but do have power to test the process of legislative enactment.

As Linde's analysis suggests, the enrolled bill rule has long been under sustained academic attack, and many state courts have responded favorably. See the useful discussion in Robert Williams, *State Constitutional Limits on Legislative Procedure: Legislative Compliance and Judicial Enforcement*, 48 U. Pitt. L. Rev. 797 (1987). Some courts have adopted special exceptions to the rule. In many cases, these exceptions are based on evidence found in the journals of legislative proceedings that all state constitutions require state legislatures to keep. (Article I, § 5 of the U.S. Constitution similarly requires that "[e]ach House shall keep a Journal of its Proceedings, and from time to time publish the same.") State constitutions differ on the timing and manner of publication, the number of members necessary to have roll call votes recorded in the journal, and whether dissenting comments or protests must be recorded. Courts seeking to modify the enrolled bill rule have often relied on information found in these official journals. As explained in Crigler's comment, *supra*, at 1191-92:

> [Two] general categories have been delineated: 1) the "pure" journal entry rule, a conclusive presumption that the enrolled bill is valid only if it is in accordance with procedures recorded in the journal and the constitution; 2) the "affirmative contradiction" rule, a determination that the enrolled bill is valid unless the journals affirmatively show a statement that there has not been compliance with constitutional requirements * * *.

South Dakota, for example, finds the enrolled bill conclusive evidence of proper enactment, except when the asserted impropriety concerns a provision for which the constitution requires a journal entry. *Barnsdall Refining Corp. v. Welsh*, 269 N.W. 853 (S.D. 1936); cf. *Independent Community Bankers Ass'n v. South Dakota*, 346 N.W.2d 737 (S.D. 1984) (reaffirming modified enrolled bill rule, over dissent arguing for abandonment of enrolled bill rule). For other examples of the journal entry rule, see *State v. Kaufman*, 430 So. 2d 904 (Fla. 1983); *People v. Dunigan*, 650 N.E.2d 1026 (Ill. 1995). See also *Fumo v. Pa. Public Utility Comm'n*, 719 A.2d 10 (Pa. Commw. Ct. 1998); *League of Women Voters of Pa. v. Commonwealth*, 692 A.2d 263 (Pa. Commw. Ct. 1996) (describing Pennsylvania's modified enrolled bill rule that allows courts some discretion when there is a clear violation of the state constitution).

Finally, some states follow an *extrinsic evidence rule*, in which they will entertain evidence beyond legislative journals. This rule was adopted in *D & W Auto Supply v. Dep't of Revenue*, 602 S.W.2d 420 (Ky. 1980), to invalidate a statute violating the constitution's requirement that appropriations measures be adopted by an absolute majority of the legislators in each chamber of the legislature. In contrast, see *Association of Texas Prof. Educators v. Kirby*, 788 S.W.2d 827 (Tex. 1990) (under enrolled bill rule, no extrinsic evidence may be considered to contradict enrolled version of bill). Even if commentators are generally right that extrinsic evidence should be considered, how far should courts carry that precept? Consider the problem of the legislature's "stopping the clock" and remaining in session past the time limit specified in the state constitution. In *State ex rel. Heck's Discount Centers v. Winters*, 132 S.E.2d 374 (W. Va. 1963), the Court concluded from the legislative journal and extrinsic evidence that the bill in question had been passed a few minutes into the early morning of March 10, 1963, when under the state constitution the legislative term had expired at midnight on March 9. The Court noted the common legislative practice of "staying the hands of the clock to enable the Legislature to effect an adjournment apparently within the time fixed by the Constitution for the expiration of the term," and it concluded that "[d]oubtless it is a fact that the legislature of this state is not unique in having indulged in that practice." Nonetheless, the Court held that when the legislative term expires the legislature "ceases to have the legislative power accorded to it while in lawful, constitutional session." Accordingly, it invalidated the legislation.

Consider the evidence in *Winters*. An affidavit by the clerk of the West Virginia House of Delegates stated that on March 9 "he was directed by the Speaker of the House of Delegates * * * to stop * * * the official clock of the

House of Delegates," and that the legislation in question "was passed when the official clock was stopped at 11:28 P.M., but that the actual time was 12:15 or 12:18 A.M. March 10, 1963." The journal of the House contained comments such as these:

> Mr. Nuzum. Mr. Watson, do you have a watch?
>
> Mr. Watson. Yes, sir.
>
> Mr. Nuzum. What time does your watch show?
>
> Mr. Watson. I've got nine after one. * * *
>
> Mr. Nuzum. Mr. Simonton, do you have a watch?
>
> Mr. Simonton. Yes, sir.
>
> Mr. Nuzum. What time does your watch show?
>
> Mr. Simonton. My watch shows six after one. * * *
>
> Mr. Nuzum. Mr. Myles, do you have a watch?
>
> Mr. Myles. Yes, sir.
>
> Mr. Nuzum. What time does your watch say?
>
> Mr. Myles. I can't see it but the clock on the wall says four minutes till twelve on March 9, 1963.
>
> Mr. Nuzum. You can't see your watch?
>
> Mr. Myles. No, sir. It's covered up with my shirt sleeve.

If you were on a state supreme court, how would you react to this evidence? Can the enrolled bill rule be defended in these circumstances? See *Dillon v. King*, 529 P.2d 745 (N. Mex. 1974), where the court held prospectively that the enrolled bill rule would no longer be applied to an allegation that the bill under review was adopted after the legislative term had expired.

B. REQUIRING LAWMAKING BY THE MOST INSTITUTIONALLY COMPETENT BRANCH OF GOVERNMENT

The structures of lawmaking put in place by constitutions, statutes and legislative rules are designed to ensure that legislatures discharge their responsibilities as the most democratically accountable governance entities in a rational and transparent way. Because of these features of institutional design, a due process of lawmaking perspective suggests that the legislature may be uniquely suited to make particular important decisions. Thus, perhaps some decisions made by administrative agencies should be subject to judicial invalidation and, in effect, remanded to the legislature (or perhaps the politically accountable chief executive) for reconsideration. Consider the following example of structural due process.

HAMPTON v. MOW SUN WONG
Supreme Court of the United States, 1976
426 U.S. 88, 96 S.Ct. 1895, 48 L.Ed.2d 495

JUSTICE STEVENS delivered the opinion of the Court.

[Respondents, five permanent resident aliens, had been denied employment by the General Services Administration, the Department of Health, Education and Welfare, and the Postal Department. They filed this action challenging a Civil Service Commission rule barring non-citizens, including lawfully admitted resident aliens, from employment in the federal civil service, on the ground that the rule violated the equal protection component of the Due Process Clause of the Fifth Amendment.

[Justice Stevens' opinion began with recognition of the "paramount federal power over immigration and naturalization," thereby distinguishing the case from *Sugarman v. Dougall*, 413 U.S. 634 (1973), in which the Court had invalidated a section of the New York civil service law providing that only U.S. citizens could hold permanent positions in the state's civil service. The opinion continued:]

When the Federal Government asserts an overriding national interest as justification for a discriminatory rule which would violate the Equal Protection Clause if adopted by a State, due process requires that there be a legitimate basis for presuming that the rule was actually intended to serve that interest. If the agency which promulgates the rule has direct responsibility for fostering or protecting that interest, it may reasonably be presumed that the asserted interest was the actual predicate for the rule. That presumption would, of course, be fortified by an appropriate statement of reasons identifying the relevant interest. Alternatively, if the rule were expressly mandated by the Congress or the President, we might presume that any interest which might rationally be served by the rule did in fact give rise to its adoption.

In this case the petitioners have identified several interests which the Congress or the President might deem sufficient to justify the exclusion of noncitizens from the federal service. They argue, for example, that the broad exclusion may facilitate the President's negotiation of treaties with foreign powers by enabling him to offer employment opportunities to citizens of a given foreign country in exchange for reciprocal concessions — an offer he could not make if those aliens were already eligible for federal jobs. Alternatively, the petitioners argue that reserving the federal service for citizens provides an appropriate incentive to aliens to qualify for naturalization and thereby to participate more effectively in our society. They also point out that the citizenship requirement has been imposed in the United States with substantial consistency for over 100 years and accords with international law and the practice of most foreign countries. Finally, they correctly state that the need for undivided loyalty in certain sensitive positions clearly justifies a citizenship requirement in at least some parts of the federal service, and that the broad exclusion serves the valid administrative purpose of avoiding the trouble and expense of classifying those positions which properly belong in executive or sensitive categories.

The difficulty with all of these arguments except the last is that they do not identify any interest which can reasonably be assumed to have influenced the Civil Service Commission, the Postal Service, the General Services Administration, or the Department of Health, Education, and Welfare in the administration of their respective responsibilities or, specifically, in the decision to deny employment to the respondents in this litigation. We may assume with the petitioners that if the Congress or the President had expressly imposed the citizenship requirement, it would be justified by the national interest in providing an incentive for aliens to become naturalized, or possibly even as providing the President with an expendable token for treaty negotiating purposes; but we are not willing to presume that the Chairman of the Civil Service Commission, or any of the other original defendants, was deliberately fostering an interest so far removed from his normal responsibilities. Consequently, before evaluating the sufficiency of the asserted justification for the rule, it is important to know whether we are reviewing a policy decision made by Congress and the President or a question of personnel administration determined by the Civil Service Commission.

It is perfectly clear that neither the Congress nor the President has ever *required* the Civil Service Commission to adopt the citizenship requirement as a condition to eligibility for employment in the federal civil service. On the other hand, in view of the fact that the policy has been in effect since the Commission was created in 1883, it is fair to infer that both the Legislature and the Executive have been aware of the policy and have acquiesced in it. In order to decide whether such acquiescence should give the Commission rule the same support as an express statutory or Presidential command, it is appropriate to review the extent to which the policy has been given consideration by Congress or the President, and the nature of the authority specifically delegated to the Commission. * * *

[The Court concluded that the Commission had the statutory authority to retain or modify the citizenship requirement without further authorization from Congress or the President. But "[e]ven if this conclusion were doubtful," the Court added in a footnote, "in view of the consequences of the rule it would be appropriate to require a much more explicit directive from either Congress or the President before accepting the conclusion that the political branches of Government would consciously adopt a policy raising the constitutional questions presented by this rule." The Court then turned to the question whether the rule was valid, assuming (without deciding) that Congress and the President have the constitutional power to impose the requirement that the Commission adopted.]

It is the business of the Civil Service Commission to adopt and enforce regulations which will best promote the efficiency of the federal civil service. That agency has no responsibility for foreign affairs, for treaty negotiations, for establishing immigration quotas or conditions of entry, or for naturalization policies. Indeed, it is not even within the responsibility of the Commission to be concerned with the economic consequences of permitting or prohibiting the participation by aliens in employment opportunities in different parts of the national market. On the contrary, the Commission performs a limited and specific function.

The only concern of the Civil Service Commission is the promotion of an efficient federal service. In general it is fair to assume that its goal would be best served by removing unnecessary restrictions on the eligibility of qualified applicants for employment. With only one exception, the interests which the petitioners have put forth as supporting the Commission regulation at issue in this case are not matters which are properly the business of the Commission. That one exception is the administrative desirability of having one simple rule excluding all noncitizens when it is manifest that citizenship is an appropriate and legitimate requirement for some important and sensitive positions. Arguably, therefore, administrative convenience may provide a rational basis for the general rule.

For several reasons that justification is unacceptable in this case. The Civil Service Commission, like other administrative agencies, has an obligation to perform its responsibilities with some degree of expertise, and to make known the reasons for its important decisions. There is nothing in the record before us, or in matter of which we may properly take judicial notice, to indicate that the Commission actually made any considered evaluation of the relative desirability of a simple exclusionary rule on the one hand, or the value to the service of enlarging the pool of eligible employees on the other. Nor can we reasonably infer that the administrative burden of establishing the job classifications for which citizenship is an appropriate requirement would be a particularly onerous task for an expert in personnel matters. * * * Of greater significance, however, is the quality of the interest at stake. Any fair balancing of the public interest in avoiding the wholesale deprivation of employment opportunities caused by the Commission's indiscriminate policy, as opposed to what may be nothing more than a hypothetical justification, requires rejection of the argument of administrative convenience in this case.

In sum, assuming without deciding that the national interests identified by the petitioners would adequately support an explicit determination by Congress or the President to exclude all noncitizens from the federal service, we conclude that those interests cannot provide an acceptable rationalization for such a determination by the Civil Service Commission. The impact of the rule on the millions of lawfully admitted resident aliens is precisely the same as the aggregate impact of comparable state rules which were invalidated by our decision in *Sugarman*. By broadly denying this class substantial opportunities for employment, the Civil Service Commission rule deprives its members of an aspect of liberty. Since these residents were admitted as a result of decisions made by the Congress and the President, implemented by the Immigration and Naturalization Service acting under the Attorney General of the United States, due process requires that the decision to impose that deprivation of an important liberty be made either at a comparable level of government or, if it is to be permitted to be made by the Civil Service Commission, that it be justified by reasons which are properly the concern of that agency. We hold that § 338.101(a) of the Civil Service Commission Regulations has deprived these respondents of liberty without due process of law and is therefore invalid.

JUSTICE BRENNAN, with whom JUSTICE MARSHALL joins, concurring.

I join the Court's opinion with the understanding that there are reserved the equal protection questions that would be raised by congressional or Presidential enactment of a bar on employment of aliens by the Federal Government.

[The dissenting opinion of JUSTICE REHNQUIST, joined by CHIEF JUSTICE BURGER and JUSTICES WHITE and BLACKMUN, is omitted.]

NOTES ON *MOW SUN WONG*
AND INSTITUTIONAL COMPETENCE

1. *Aftermath of* Mow Sun Wong. Three months after the Supreme Court decided *Mow Sun Wong*, President Ford issued Executive Order 11935, which barred almost all noncitizens from employment in the federal civil service. In a letter to the Speaker of the House and the President of the Senate, President Ford stated that it was in the national interest to preserve the long-standing policy of exclusion, at least pending thorough reconsideration of the matter. He also stated that "a recognition of the specific constitutional authority vested in the Congress prompts me to urge that the Congress promptly address these issues." See 41 Fed. Reg. 37,303–04 (1976). The lower courts upheld the constitutionality of the order. See *Mow Sun Wong v. Hampton*, 435 F. Supp. 37 (N.D. Cal. 1977), aff'd, 626 F.2d 739 (9th Cir. 1980), cert. denied, 450 U.S. 959 (1981) (Justices Brennan, White, and Marshall voted to grant certiorari). Congress has never modified President Ford's order.

Did President Ford's action demonstrate that the Court's decision in *Mow Sun Wong* was futile? Professor T. Alexander Aleinikoff has uncovered some internal government documents that shed light upon whether the Court's "remand for reconsideration" of the issue in *Mow Sun Wong* actually stimulated any thoughtful reconsideration. According to these documents, the impetus for President Ford's executive order came from the Civil Service Commission ("CSC"), which drafted the proposal to overturn the Court's decision. Several governmental departments, asked to comment on the proposal by the Office of Management and Budget ("OMB"), voiced support for the proposal without identifying any underlying reasons for their views; the U.S. Postal Service indicated that it had no difficulty with admitting resident aliens to nonsensitive and nonpolicymaking positions; the Department of Housing and Urban Development suggested a more narrowly drawn prohibition that would limit employment to resident aliens in nonpolicymaking positions; and the Department of State expressed doubts about the wisdom of a total prohibition. When the matter came before President Ford, accompanying it was a memorandum from the general counsel of the OMB that stated:

> * * * CSC suggested various reasons related to the national interest which might serve as justification for the issuance of [the] order. Agency comments, although generally favoring or having no objection to such an order, indicate that CSC's suggested justifications (*e.g.*, need for undivided loyalty; consistency with the practices of foreign states) are more apparent than real. Further, the Postal Service advises that its recent practice of employing aliens in nonsensitive and nonpolicymaking positions has not presented any policy difficulties. Nevertheless, there is a

widespread visceral feeling that Government jobs should be reserved for citizens, at least where there are qualified citizen-applicants.

The Department of Justice is of the opinion that the Congress, pursuant to its constitutional authority over immigration, has the authority to broadly prohibit aliens from employment in the competitive civil service. Although the Supreme Court left open the question whether the President could exclude aliens from the competitive service, there are Presidential concerns (*e.g.*, foreign policy) which would lend some support to Presidential order barring aliens from government employment. The Department of Justice concludes, based on the *Wong* decision, that an Executive order barring aliens would probably be upheld by a divided Supreme Court.[i]

What do you make of this? Consider this view (which was written without the benefit of the internal documents noted above):

If the Court's goal in *Mow Sun Wong* was * * * to force either the executive or legislative branch to face up to the underlying policy questions and accept political responsibility for the rule, the goal was plainly not achieved. * * * The whole point of [President Ford's] order, as his letter makes clear, was to preserve the status quo pending congressional rethinking of the problem. * * * But Congress may well prefer to stay clear of the issue and allow the present policy to remain in operation by default. * * * [W]e are left precisely where we were before the decision in *Mow Sun Wong*: Aliens are still barred from employment in the civil service, although neither of the political branches has taken clear responsibility for the formulation of the policy.[j]

As you consider the *Mow Sun Wong* approach, compare it to the cases raising the question of the constitutionality of a broad delegation by Congress to an executive agency (see Chapter 9, § 1) or to the President (see the dissents in *Clinton v. City of New York*, Chapter 3, § 3, assessing the Line Item Veto Act under the delegation doctrine).

2. *Precedential Value of* Mow Sun Wong. *Mow Sun Wong* and another case decided the same day were Justice Stevens' first opinions for the Supreme Court. It has been suggested that the other four Justices in the majority had voted to strike down the civil service regulation on the traditional equal protection ground that it discriminated against aliens, and that Stevens initially stood alone in proposing a due process of lawmaking solution to the case. The Chief Justice assigned the case to Justice Stevens, who wrote a proposed majority opinion in line with his personal views, and the other four Justices went along with it. See Bob Woodward & Scott Armstrong, *The Brethren* 402 (1979). We do not know if this is accurate, but assume for purposes of discussion that it is. Assume also that the other four Justices voted with Stevens at least in part to avoid friction over his first opinion (which is a plausible assumption, if the other assertions made above are accurate). Does this mean that *Mow Sun Wong* is of little precedential value? So far as we can

---

i. Memorandum from William N. Nichols, General Counsel, OMB, to Robert D. Linden, White House Chief Executive Clerk, Aug. 30, 1976 (on file in Gerald R. Ford Library, Ann Arbor, MI).

j. Gerald Rosberg, *The Protection of Aliens from Discriminatory Treatment by the National Government*, 1977 Sup. Ct. Rev. 275, 280–81.

ascertain, *Mow Sun Wong* has never directly controlled the result in any subsequent Supreme Court decision, although it has been cited a number of times.

3. *The Passport Case: A More Successful Suspensive Veto?* In *Kent v. Dulles*, 357 U.S. 116 (1958), the Secretary of State denied a passport to Kent because he was allegedly a Communist or Communist sympathizer. The Court avoided the question of the constitutionality of this decision by interpreting the relevant statutes narrowly: "Congress has made no such provision [of authority to the Secretary to withhold passports to citizens because of their beliefs or associations] in explicit terms; and absent one, the Secretary may not employ that standard to restrict the citizens' right of free movement." *Id.* at 130. Despite President Eisenhower's urgent message to Congress calling for legislative action, continued pressure from the White House, and strong support for it from many Members of Congress, Congress did not enact even a limited form of the legislation the President sought. Apparently the Senate leadership killed all such proposals.[k] At the least, this episode shows the potential impact of judicial decisions shifting the burden of inertia through a suspensive veto. But does it indicate that Congress "deliberated"? *Kent v. Dulles* and *Mow Sun Wong* demonstrate that many of the techniques of due process of lawmaking provide an opportunity for Congress to address particular issues with focused deliberation and thoughtful legislation, but they do not guarantee that Congress will take advantage of that opportunity.

4. *The* Bakke *Case.* In *Regents of the University of California v. Bakke*, 438 U.S. 265 (1978), the issue was whether a program under which a state medical school guaranteed admission to a specified number of students from certain minority groups violated the Equal Protection Clause on the theory that it discriminated against whites. Justice Powell, joined by no other Justice, set forth the judgment of the Court. He concluded that the affirmative action program was unconstitutional but that other, more carefully tailored, plans might be constitutional. Justice Powell relied in part on the absence of any judicial, legislative, or administrative findings of constitutional or statutory violation. "Without such findings of constitutional or statutory violations," he reasoned, "it cannot be said that the government has any greater interest in helping one individual than in refraining from harming another. Thus, the government has no compelling justification for inflicting such harm." *Id.* at 308–09. Citing *Mow Sun Wong*, Justice Powell concluded that the University of California was not the proper institution to determine that petitioner Bakke was to be harmed so that victims of "societal discrimination" might be helped, because "isolated segments of our vast governmental structures are not competent to make those decisions, at least in the absence of legislative mandates and legislatively determined criteria." *Id.* at 309.

---

k. See Daniel Farber, *National Security, The Right to Travel, and the Court*, 1981 Sup. Ct. Rev. 263, 278–81. See also Philip Frickey, *Getting from Joe to Gene (McCarthy): The Avoidance Canon, Legal Process Theory, and Narrowing Statutory Interpretation in the Early Warren Court*, 93 Cal. L. Rev. 397, 425–26 (2005) (assessing this "aggressive understanding of the passive virtues").

Is Justice Powell's position a persuasive one? A footnote in the joint opinion in *Bakke* of Justices Brennan, White, Marshall, and Blackmun responded as follows: (1) The manner in which the state wants to delegate governmental authority is left for it to decide. (2) The California Constitution has placed plenary authority over the University system with the Board of Regents, thereby vesting with them full legislative, judicial, and administrative power. (3) There is nothing in the Equal Protection Clause requiring the Court to limit the scope of the Regents' power more narrowly than the power that might be constitutionally exercised by the legislature. Is this a persuasive response to Justice Powell's position?

5. *Scholarly Interpretation.* Although it may not have influenced much jurisprudence, scholars have spent a great deal of time considering the ramifications of the Court's approach in *Mow Sun Wong.* First, consider Lawrence Sager, *Insular Majorities Unabated:* Warth v. Seldin *and* City of Eastlake v. Forest City Enterprises, Inc., 91 Harv. L. Rev. 1373, 1414, 1417 (1978):

> *Mow Sun Wong* posits a right to procedural due process which requires that some legislative actions be undertaken only by a governmental entity which is so structured and so charged as to make possible a reflective determination that the action contemplated is fair, reasonable, and not at odds with specific prohibitions in the Constitution. * * *

> * * * In *Mow Sun Wong* * * * the Court refused to consider two justifications offered for the policy of alien exclusion: the fact that the policy effected a reservation of a "token" for foreign affairs bargaining, and the fact that the exclusion operated to encourage aliens to become naturalized citizens. These interests can be viewed as beyond accurate judicial assessment for two reasons. First, consideration of their importance involves technical judgments informed by a range of material to which the judiciary does not have full access; and second, the interests, though potentially quite weighty, are discretionary in the sense that they depend for their importance on prior decisions of policy or strategy made by the President or Congress. These factors combine to result in a judiciary largely dependent upon the judgment of either the President or Congress as to whether there are "overriding national interests" which justify the exclusion policy; thus, when the judiciary is confronted with the enactment of such an exclusion by either of these two entities, it will defer broadly to the judgment thus manifested.

> In contrast, when a body — like the Civil Service Commission in *Mow Sun Wong* — which lacks the information, expertise, and discretion as to policy and strategy enacts such a rule, the courts face a dilemma. Either they sustain the enactment, thus endorsing a transgression of constitutional principles without any assurance that it is justified by weighty national interests; or they invalidate it and thus jeopardize what may indeed be weighty national interests. In such a circumstance, a decision like that in *Mow Sun Wong* seems entirely appropriate: it in effect constitutes a remand to the decisionmaking body able to make appropriate policy judgments for an initial assessment of the validity of the enactment.

6. *Judicial Minimalism.* Cass Sunstein has described *Mow Sun Wong* and *Kent v. Dulles* as examples of judicial minimalism that reinforces democratic

institutions. *One Case at a Time: Judicial Minimalism on the Supreme Court* (1999). He defines this "phenomenon of saying no more than necessary to justify an outcome, and leaving as much as possible undecided, as 'decisional minimalism.' Decisional minimalism has * * * attractive features. * * * [M]inimalism is likely to make judicial errors less frequent and (above all) less damaging. A court that leaves things open will not foreclose options in a way that may do a great deal of harm. * * * A court that decides relatively little will also reduce the risks that come from intervening in complex systems, where a single-shot intervention can have a range of unanticipated bad consequences. There is a relationship between judicial minimalism and democratic deliberation. Of course minimalist rulings increase the space for further reflection and debate at the local, state, and national levels, simply because they do not foreclose subsequent decisions." *Id.* at 3–4. Sunstein's work essentially updates the "passive virtues" philosophy of Alexander Bickel, most notably articulated in *The Least Dangerous Branch: The Supreme Court at the Bar of Politics* (1962). Sunstein argues that *Kent v. Dulles* and *Mow Sun Wong*, where the Court avoided deciding the constitutional issues presented, are "conspicuously" democracy-forcing because "in both cases the Court's judgment was expressly founded on the idea that publicly accountable bodes should make the decision that was challenged in the case." *One Case at a Time,* at 35. What do you think of this judicial strategy? Can we rely on legislators to take seriously an increased responsibility to consider constitutional issues? Consider the following discussion.

PAUL BREST, *THE CONSCIENTIOUS LEGISLATOR'S GUIDE TO CONSTITUTIONAL INTERPRETATION*
27 Stan. L. Rev. 585, 586–89 (1975)[*]

* * * Judicial restraint may be a matter of comity, reflecting respect for the decisions of a coordinate branch of the federal government or of a state's chief policymaking body. It may flow from the court's inability to separate constitutional questions from related empirical issues beyond its competence or from matters of policy within the legislature's domain. It may also reflect the court's inability to ascertain how the legislative process has actually worked in a particular case. None of these considerations suggests that the legislature should exercise restraint in assessing the constitutionality of its own product.

This Essay * * * assumes the perspective of a conscientious legislator, to inquire how he or she can assess the constitutionality of proposed legislation.

* * * Two [governing] assumptions should be made explicit. The first is that legislators are obligated to determine, as best they can, the constitutionality of proposed legislation. The second is that they should consider themselves bound by, or at least give great weight to, the Supreme Court's substantive constitutional holdings.

The first proposition may seem self-evident. It is worth discussion, however, because so many legislators have assumed the contrary — that their job is to make policy without regard to questions of constitutionality, which rest within the exclusive domain of the courts. Briefly, the following points support the proposition.

First, some provisions of the Constitution are explicitly addressed to legislators. [For example,] Article I, section 9 provides, "No Bill of Attainder or ex post facto law *shall be passed*." * * * Many other provisions are addressed to legislatures by clear implication. For example, it would seem odd if Congress were to legislate without inquiring whether article I or some other provision of the Constitution gave it the authority to do so.

Second, many of the framers of the Constitution and members of the early Congresses expressed and acted upon the belief that Congress should assess the constitutionality of pending legislation, whether or not it might later be subject to judicial review. Third, article VI requires that all legislators and officials "be bound by Oath or Affirmation to support this Constitution * * *." Although this does not entail that all constitutional questions are open to all institutions at all times, the most obvious way for a legislator to support the Constitution is to enact only legislation that is constitutional.

Fourth, Chief Justice Marshall's classic justification for judicial review in *Marbury v. Madison* was not premised on any special, let alone exclusive, constitutional function of the Court, but simply on its duty to decide the case before it in conformance with the superior law of the Constitution. Other arguments for judicial review have accorded the judiciary a special function, but none implies that its role as constitutional interpreter excludes that of other institutions. (There may, indeed, exist constitutional issues committed to the so-called "political branches" to the exclusion of the judiciary.)

Finally, courts often accord a challenged law a "presumption of constitutionality" based partly on the assumption that the legislature has previously passed upon the constitutional questions raised in litigation. Even where judicial deference is attenuated, the courts may lack the institutional capacity to review all aspects of legislative decisions, such as the subjective motivations of legislators. If the Constitution is to be applied at all in such cases, it must be applied by the lawmakers themselves.

The only plausible argument challenging legislative duty to consider constitutional questions is premised on institutional incompetence. Many legislators are not lawyers; the legislative process is not structured to allow constitutional questions to be examined systematically or dispassionately; and many constitutional problems arise only as legislation is implemented. Although these points may argue for judicial review, they do not argue against an initial legislative examination. The modern legislative committee, staffed by lawyers and others having expertise in particular areas of policy and law, is competent to consider the constitutional implications of pending measures. If many problems cannot be foreseen or adequately handled, that does not argue against confronting those that can. To be sure, legislatures will seldom engage in the disinterested and detailed analysis that we expect of courts. One can reasonably demand, however, that the lawmaking process take explicit account of constitutional values threatened by pending legislation.

I have deliberately hedged the second assumption. Whether or not one agrees with the Court's rather recent assertion that it is "the ultimate interpreter of the Constitution," the judiciary is its most skilled, disinterested, and articulate interpreter. For present purposes, therefore, one need not assume that a legislature is bound by judge-made constitutional doctrine. It is sufficient that such doctrine carry a strong presumption of correctness in the legislative chambers. * * *

If both assumptions are accepted, * * * the legislator must learn not only to interpret the Constitution, but also to interpret judicial decisions interpreting the Constitution. Decisions striking down laws are easy to understand: they mean that the laws are unconstitutional. Decisions *not* striking down laws do not always mean that the laws are constitutional, however, for a court's failure to invalidate may only reflect its institutional limitations.

NOTES ON THE "CONSCIENTIOUS LEGISLATOR"

1. *Antecedents to the "Conscientious Legislator."* Professor Brest's approach has its historical precedents. For example, in *McCulloch v. Maryland*, 17 U.S. (4 Wheat.) 316 (1819), the Supreme Court upheld the authority of Congress to create a Bank of the United States. Yet in 1832 President Jackson vetoed a bill to recharter the bank. He stated:

> It is maintained by the advocates of the bank that its constitutionality in all its features ought to be considered as settled by precedent and the decision of the Supreme Court [in *McCulloch*]. To this conclusion I cannot assent. * * *

> * * * The Congress, the Executive, and the Court must each for itself be guided by its own opinion of the Constitution. Each public officer who takes an oath to support the Constitution swears that he will support it as he understands it, and not as it is understood by others. It is as much the duty of the House of Representatives, of the Senate, and of the President to decide upon the constitutionality of any bill or resolution which may be presented to them for passage or approval as it is of the supreme judges when it may be brought before them for judicial decision. The opinion of the judges has no more authority over Congress than the opinion of Congress has over the judges, and on that point the President is independent of both. The authority of the Supreme Court must not, therefore, be permitted to control the Congress or the Executive when acting in their legislative capacities, but to have only such influence as the force of their reasoning may deserve.[1]

2. *More Recent Applications of the Brest Approach.* Both before and after Professor Brest's article, legislators have considered the constitutionality of

---

1. 2 *Messages and Papers of the Presidents* 576 (Richardson ed. 1897), quoted in Paul Brest & Sanford Levinson, *Processes of Constitutional Decisionmaking* 49–52 (3d ed. 1992). See also Louis Fisher, *One of the Guardians Some of the Time*, in *Is the Supreme Court the Guardian of the Constitution?* 82 (Robert Licht ed., 1993) (describing other historical examples).

bills during their deliberations. For example, much of the testimony in hearings in connection with the Civil Rights Act of 1964 and the Voting Rights Act of 1965 dealt with whether those proposed laws were within the constitutional power of Congress to enact. We also discussed some of the deliberation on the floor of the House about the constitutional ramifications of excluding, rather than expelling or censuring, Adam Clayton Powell. See Chapter 2, § 2A. More recently, Congress considered constitutional issues implicated by a law that would prohibit burning the American flag, the Flag Protection Act of 1989, Pub. L. No. 101–131, 103 Stat. 777 (codified at 18 U.S.C. § 700 (1994)) (later ruled unconstitutional in *United States v. Eichman*, 496 U.S. 310 (1990)), and the Religious Freedom Restoration Act of 1993, Pub. L. No. 103–141, 107 Stat. 1488 (codified at 42 U.S.C. § 2000bb to 2000bb–4 (1994)) (later ruled unconstitutional in *City of Boerne v. Flores*, 521 U.S. 507 (1997)).[m] In addition, much time was spent during the House impeachment and Senate trial of President Clinton on the constitutionality of the proceedings. None of these recent examples may prove that Congress does a good job in this arena. Both the laws were ruled unconstitutional by the Supreme Court (although in controversial decisions and by divided Courts), and many observers considered Clinton's impeachment more an exercise of raw partisan politics than an example of fine constitutional lawmaking.

One question in all these cases is whether Congress should engage in the same sort of constitutional analysis as the Supreme Court does, or if members of Congress should apply different standards and consider different arguments and evidence than judges might, perhaps because of the different features of the two institutions.[n] Consider the following episode from the "gays in the military" debate in the first year of Clinton's presidency. As you know from Chapter 2, § 1, a statute that is facially neutral but disproportionally disadvantages a suspect (i.e., racial minorities) or semi-suspect (e.g., women) class of persons violates the Equal Protection Clause only if it is motivated by animus against the disadvantaged class. In reaching this conclusion, the Supreme Court refused to adopt a "discriminatory effects" approach under which such legislation would be unconstitutional in some circumstances even if it were not improperly motivated. May a legislator adopt a "discriminatory effects" approach to her own review of pending legislation? If she does, is that decision motivated by what her views are likely to be as a matter of policy? And would that be inappropriate? Must a legislator vote against legislation that

---

m. For discussion of the constitutional deliberation with respect to the flag burning act, see Abner Mikva & Jeff Bleich, *When Congress Overrules the Court*, 79 Calif. L. Rev. 729 (1991), and with respect to the Religious Freedom Restoration Act, see Michael Bamberger, *Reckless Legislation: How Lawmakers Ignore the Constitution* 153–166 (2000); Michael McConnell, *Institutions and Interpretation: A Critique of City of* Boerne v. Flores, 111 Harv. L. Rev. 153, 160 (1997).

n. See Keith Whittington, *Constitutional Construction: Divided Powers and Constitutional Meaning* (1999) (describing "constitutional construction" as the "method of elaborating constitutional meaning in [the] political realm" and discussing Congress' role in the process); Neal Katyal, *Impeachment as Constitutional Interpretation*, 63 Law & Contemp. Probs. 169 (2000) (arguing that the style of constitutional interpretation used by the legislature should be different from the judicial approach).

she supports if she is aware that other legislators support it for discriminatory reasons? If that law is enacted due to the votes of illicitly motivated legislators, and if the conscientious legislator is aware of that, must she "blow the whistle" on that discriminatory intent in later litigation challenging the constitutionality of the law?[o]

Immediately after President Clinton announced his version of a "don't ask, don't tell" policy concerning lesbians, bisexuals, and gay men in the armed forces, a subcommittee of the House Armed Services Committee held hearings exploring the constitutionality of the new policy.[p] Three academics testified on this topic. Professor David Schleuter testified that on the whole the new policy probably passed constitutional muster for the same reasons (mainly deference to the military) the old policy did. Professor William Woodruff testified that the new policy raised additional constitutional problems because it seemed to penalize people simply because of what they said (the "don't tell" part of the new policy). Professor Cass Sunstein's written statement contained two different constitutional analyses. As a matter of predicting what the Supreme Court would do, Sunstein testified that invalidation of the new policy was "unlikely." Relying on *Bowers v. Hardwick*, 478 U.S. 186 (1986), he testified that the military's interest in morale would justify any discrimination against gay men, lesbians, and bisexuals and that its interest in suppressing sodomy would justify its penalization of speech (because the speech would be "evidence" of illegal conduct). At the end of his statement, Sunstein testified that Congress can make its own independent judgment of what is required by the Constitution. Specifically, he suggested that discrimination against "homosexuals" would require more justification if Congress concluded that sexual orientation were a suspect criterion or if Congress found such discrimination related to sex discrimination. Sunstein urged members to be conscientious (though he didn't use Brest's term) in making their own determination of what the Constitution requires.

There is no evidence from the transcript of the hearing that Sunstein's latter analysis was of controlling interest to any member of the Subcommittee. What did seem important to all concerned was simply whether Congress and the President could do what they wanted on the issue. If this abdication of the normative in favor of the predictive tends to happen in hearings generally, it would make many greatly more pessimistic that any but the most "conscientious" legislator will care much about what the Constitution might be read to mean.

3. *Criticisms of Congress' Performance on Constitutional Matters.* Perhaps because of these and other examples, some have expressed doubts that members of Congress can play a productive role in deliberating about constitutional issues. One problem is that in most instances constitutional

---

o. On these issues, see Stephen Ross, *Legislative Enforcement of Equal Protection*, 72 Minn. L. Rev. 311 (1987).

p. *Assessment of the Plan to Lift the Ban on Homosexuals in the Military: Hearings Before the Subcomm. on Military Forces and Personnel of the House Comm. on the Armed Services*, 103d Cong., 1st Sess. (July 21–22, 1993).

debate appears to change very few votes. Those opposed to proposed legislation on the merits tend also to be the ones who accept arguments that it would be unconstitutional. President Jackson, for example, vetoed the bank bill at least in part because he had a different political agenda and disliked the Bank of the United States as a relic of the dead Federalist era. Supporters of the Civil Rights Act of 1964 and the Voting Rights Act of 1965 worried about constitutionality because they wanted to pass a bill that would escape judicial invalidation. Professor Brest wants legislators to ask one question — "Is this bill really within the spirit of our Constitution?" — when they may be likely to ask a different and more practical one — "What will it take for this bill to get by judicial review?" or "Is there any legal argument against this bill that might help me kill it?"

Those who strategically raise constitutional arguments may spark serious deliberation of the issues, however, and at least the "civilizing force of hypocrisy"[q] in congressional debates may produce arguments that constrain what Congress can do without prompting public dismay. Elizabeth Garrett and Adrian Vermeule suggest: "Even a wholly self-interested legislator cannot afford to take positions in constitutional argument that are too transparently favorable to his own interests. So legislators who want to invest in credibility will have to adjust their positions to disfavor or disguise their own interests to some degree. Likewise, the pressure to maintain a reputation for consistency will, to some degree, cause even self-interested legislators to adhere to a constitutional position previously established when, in changed circumstances, that position works to a legislator's disadvantage."[r]

Former representative and federal judge Abner Mikva has been very critical of Congress' performance when considering constitutional issues. "Both institutionally and politically, Congress is designed to pass over the constitutional questions, leaving the hard decisions to the courts. * * * The paucity of constitutional dialogue in Congress is due to many factors. Structurally, both houses are large, making the process of engaging in complex arguments during a floor debate difficult. For the most part, the speeches made on the floor are designed to get a member's position on the record rather than to initiate a dialogue. Because of the volume of legislation, the time spent with constituents, and the technical knowledge required to understand the background of every piece of legislation, it is infrequent that a member considers the individual merits of a particular bill."[s]

Are Mikva's criticisms fair? As a former representative, he must be aware that most of Congress' work is done in committees, where specialized staff and more involved members consider issues and produce committee reports and

---

q. See Jon Elster, *Alchemies of the Mind: Transmutation and Misrepresentation*, 3 Legal Theory 133 (1997) (discussing the role of such "hypocrisy" in legitimate deliberation).

r. Elizabeth Garrett & Adrian Vermeule, *Institutional Design of a Thayerian Congress*, 50 Duke L.J. 1277, 1289 (2001).

s. *How Well Does Congress Support and Defend the Constitution?*, 61 N.C. L. Rev. 587, 609 (1983).

other documents to inform the body and enhance deliberation. Moreover, as Garrett and Vermeule argue, additional structures can be put in place to enhance congressional capacity in this area, providing more expertise to Congress, ensuring that focused deliberation on constitutional issues will occur in committee and on the floor, and providing information to interest groups so that they present arguments relevant to Congress' decisions.

4. *What Should Conscientious Legislators Do When They Disagree with the Supreme Court?* Brest admittedly hedges on a crucial question: What may legislators do if they think the Supreme Court has struck down legislation that should have been upheld? This issue arises frequently: two recent examples involve the efforts to get around the Supreme Court's abortion decisions and to convince the courts that pornography violates the civil rights of women and therefore ought not receive the protection the courts have provided it under the First Amendment.[t] Would not *Lochner v. New York* remain the law today unless the Congress and state legislators had enacted putatively unconstitutional legislation? Consider Bickel, *supra*, at 258:

> The Supreme Court's law * * * [cannot] in our system prevail * * * if it [runs] counter to deeply felt popular needs or convictions, or even if it [is] opposed by a determined and substantial minority and received with indifference by the rest of the country. This, in the end, is how and why judicial review is consistent with the theory and practice of political democracy. This is why the Supreme Court is a court of last resort presumptively only. No doubt in the vast majority of instances the Court prevails — not as a result of a sort of tacit referendum; rather, it just prevails, its authority is accepted more or less automatically, and no matter if grudgingly. It takes concerted effort at some risk, and hence not a little daring, to fight back, and then there is no guaranty of victory[.] * * * But given passion, vigor, and hard-headedness, it can be done and has been done. * * * Broad and sustained application of the court's law, when challenged, is a function of its rightness, not merely of its pronouncement.[u]

Larry Alexander and Frederick Schauer, *On Extrajudicial Constitutional Interpretation*, 110 Harv. L. Rev. 1359 (1997), defend the proposition that Congress should always accept the Constitution to mean whatever the Supreme Court says it means. Their view does not assert the relatively extreme position that the Constitution actually means whatever the Court says. Instead, the point is an institutional one. The primary criterion for good constitutional law, they argue, is that it should be clear and stable; clarity and stability require a single constitutional interpreter; and that interpreter should be the Court.[v] However,

---

t. On the abortion debate, see Neal Devins, *Shaping Constitutional Values: Elected Government, the Supreme Court, and the Abortion Debate* (1996); on pornography, see Andrea Dworkin & Catharine MacKinnon, *Pornography and Civil Rights: A New Day for Women's Equality* (1988).

u. See also Barry Friedman, *Dialogue and Judicial Review*, 91 Mich. L. Rev. 577 (1993) (arguing that all three branches participate in the process of constitutional interpretation by engaging in a sort of iterative dialogue).

v. But see Mark Tushnet, *Taking the Constitution Away from the Courts* (1999) (arguing that the single authority should be the political branches and that judicial review should be eliminated).

limitations on the judiciary's political reach and capacity create a broad area of constitutional determinations by Congress and the executive branch that go unreviewed. The Supreme Court speaks too infrequently to provide stability and clarity in many arenas of constitutional law. What, for example, should the Senate do when it must decide whether some presidential action amounts to a "high Crime or Misdemeanor"? One way to extend the judicial supremacy view into such a realm would be to say that Congress should decide constitutional questions by guessing how the Court would decide them. But this kind of imaginative reconstruction is often really substantive decisionmaking because the best way to determine what judges would do is to figure out what the best answer is.[w]

Congress's role in constitutional interpretation has been hotly contested at least since 1892, when James Bradley Thayer delivered his address, *The Origin and Scope of the American Doctrine of Constitutional Law,* at the Chicago World's Fair. Thayer argued that judges should employ a rational-basis standard for reviewing congressional determinations of constitutional questions, largely for two reasons. First, many constitutional questions raise significant issues of policy and politics that legislators are better suited to decide than judges. Second, more aggressive judicial review would encourage Congress to shift its constitutional responsibilities onto the courts, weakening representative democracy.[x] Even without changes in institutional arrangements and expectations, Congress will continue to play a role in constitutional interpretation because the courts do not decide every issue; thus, members will continue to consider how to fulfill their duties as conscientious legislators.

C. LEGISLATIVE DRAFTING AND DUE PROCESS OF LAWMAKING

How would a court determine whether legislators had addressed the constitutional issues in *Mow Sun Wong* or *Kent v. Dulles* that the Supreme Court remanded to Congress? What evidence would a judge look for in the records of committee hearings and floor debate to discover whether Congress had explicitly decided to exclude noncitizens from the federal Civil Service or to deny passports to Americans whose activities and speech were viewed as subversive? At the outset, a court would surely turn to the text of any legislation to see if Congress clearly made the particular policy determination. These cases appear to require a clear statement by Congress that it intends to pass a law that gets very close to, and perhaps steps across, the line separating constitutional from unconstitutional enactments. A clear statement, perhaps made in the text of the statute or in credible legislative history like a committee report, forces a court to decide the constitutional question directly rather than to adopt minimalistic techniques like the due process of lawmaking remands

---

w. See also Neal Devins & Louis Fisher, *Judicial Exclusivity and Political Instability*, 84 Va. L. Rev. 83 (1998) (critiquing the Alexander-Schauer approach).

x. For modern reactions to Thayer's influential work, see *Congress and the Constitution* (Neal Devins & Keith Whittington eds., 2005); *One Hundred Years of Judicial Review: The Thayer Centennial Symposium*, 88 Nw. U. L. Rev. 1–468 (1993).

in *Mow Sun Wong* and the passport case. We will discuss judicial clear statement requirements in the context of statutes that involve important constitutional values in Chapter 8, § 1B3.

Due process of lawmaking thus implicates legislative drafting in several ways. First, legislation can provide the most convincing evidence that the institutionally competent branch of government has considered and addressed a sensitive area that falls within its domain. Rather than parse the committee and floor debate to find a record of the relevant deliberations, courts can use a clear and specific textual statement as a signal that members were aware of the issue, considered it, and made a focused decision. In addition, judicial review that is inspired by due process of lawmaking theories often seeks to provide incentives to legislators to draft bills clearly and with specificity so that members will know what they are voting on and citizens will understand the rules they are to follow.[y]

Take, for example, the new textualism, an increasingly influential method of statutory interpretation that we discuss in Chapter 7, § 3A. Textualists claim to apply only the plain meaning of the statutory text, eschewing any resort to legislative history or other evidence of the subjective intent of the enactors. For the new textualists, the only legitimate sources for the interpretive inquiry are "text-based or -linked sources. Thus, the meaning an ordinary speaker of the English language would draw from the statutory text is the alpha and omega of [textualist] statutory interpretation."[z] We will spend a great deal of time in Chapters 7 and 8 discussing the justifications for and the critiques of textualism; here we want only to link it to due process of lawmaking.

Justice Scalia, the leading proponent of textualism in statutory interpretation, succinctly explains his view of the judiciary's role in encouraging lawmakers to improve the quality of decisionmaking and drafting: "I think we have an obligation to conduct our exegesis in a fashion which fosters that democratic process."[a] By placing so much interpretive emphasis on the text and refusing to look at supplemental legislative material to clarify vague or ambiguous language, textualists hope to provide strong incentives to lawmakers to draft carefully and with specificity and precision. Other legislators and competing interest groups will monitor the statute as it is drafted to ensure that its text reflects the legislative deal. They will be able to focus their attention on the statute itself, knowing that courts will not pay heed to agreements contained only in legislative materials like committee reports or floor debate.

---

y. See Jonathan Molot, *The Judicial Perspective in the Administrative State: Reconciling Modern Doctrines of Deference with the Judiciary's Structural Role*, 53 Stan. L. Rev. 1 (2000) (arguing that the framers saw judicial review as a way to exert a moderating influence on the legislative process and to provide incentives to lawmakers to internalize values of fairness and rationality and to engage to careful deliberation and drafting).

z. William Eskridge, Jr., Philip Frickey & Elizabeth Garrett, *Legislation and Statutory Interpretation* 236 (2d ed. 2006).

a. *United States v. Taylor*, 487 U.S. 326, 346 (1988) (Scalia, J., concurring in the judgment.) See also Antonin Scalia, *A Matter of Interpretation: Federal Courts and the Law* 16–17 (1997).

Thus, judicial requirements of clear textual statements and the interpretive technique of textualism are intended to change congressional behavior in the future as much as they are used to reach decisions about the meaning of a statute in the immediate case. Like Sunstein's characterization of *Mow Sun Wong* and *Kent v. Dulles*, they can be thought of as democracy-forcing or deliberation-forcing in their effect. Jane Schacter has characterized them in more pejorative terms; she calls such interpreters "disciplinarians" of the political process who hope to force Congress to pay close and sustained attention to statutory text and important constitutional and policy decisions before passing legislation.[b]

The notion of judges using incentives to improve democratic deliberation and legislative drafting may be normatively appealing, and certainly there is ample room for improvement in the federal and state legislative process. However, one suspects that those who adopt such strategies have unrealistically high hopes.[c] Think back to the discussion in Chapter 1 of how a bill becomes a federal law, and reflect on what you have seen watching C-SPAN or the nightly news of the rather chaotic and harried environment in which legislation is drafted. Do you expect that judicial strategies, applied in the few cases that are actually challenged in courts and applied only by some judges, will dramatically affect congressional behavior?

If the aspirations of due process of lawmaking techniques are unrealistic, the legitimacy of deliberation-forcing methods of adjudication is subject to serious question. Not only are they unlikely to achieve their objective of improving the legislative process, but in many cases their use will lead to statutory interpretation inconsistent with the intent of the legislators who passed the law.[d] Thus, in the guise of decisional minimalism, these techniques may actually mask an activist judicial stance. For example, a requirement for a clear statement on a particular issue may be impossible for Congress to meet given the realities of the messy legislative process, and thus the judicial strategy will deny Congress the ability to achieve the objective it desires because the statute will inevitably be phrased in relatively general or vague language. Such a denial may be justified on substantive grounds (perhaps congressional action in the area implicates important constitutional guarantees), but it cannot be accurately characterized as a humble procedural decision designed to improve the legislative process if empirical research demonstrates that such improvements are unlikely.

Is there any way to improve the communication between the judiciary and the legislative branch to ensure that particular interpretive strategies actually improve legislative drafting and deliberation? A study by the Governance Institute of the Brookings Institution found that congressional staff members

---

b. See *Metademocracy: The Changing Structure of Legitimacy in Statutory Interpretation*, 108 Harv. L. Rev. 593, 618–36 (1995).

c. See Elizabeth Garrett, *Legal Scholarship in the Age of Legislation*, 34 Tulsa L.J. 679 (1999) (discussing promise and limitations of such judicial approaches).

d. See Andrei Marmor, *The Immorality of Textualism*, 38 Loy. L.A. L. Rev. 2063 (2005).

were unaware of a majority of recent statutory cases that judges on the D.C. Circuit believed warranted congressional attention. To the extent they were aware of the cases, policymakers knew only of the results rather than of methodological techniques or other approaches used to influence their behavior.[e] Reacting to this study, the D.C. Circuit established a program to route certain statutory decisions to relevant congressional committees and to legislative counsel. Other circuits joined the project, which has the support of leaders in the legislative and judicial branches. Researchers at the Governance Institute, a Washington D.C. think tank concerned with interbranch relations, are monitoring the congressional reaction to the court decisions and sponsoring efforts to improve drafting, interpretation, and revision of statutes.

Others have suggested that the federal government consider reforms along the lines of state mechanisms that help legislators monitor court decisions and revise statutes accordingly. For example, in Illinois, the Legislative Reference Bureau produces an annual report of all federal and state appellate decisions that affect the interpretation of Illinois statutes, and the Bureau has the discretion to provide suggestions to the legislature for revisions. Other states have less formal mechanisms; Wisconsin has a Law Revision Committee, comprised of state legislators, which considers judicial decisions sent to it by the Revisor of Statutes.[f] Drawing on these examples, Ruth Bader Ginsburg and Peter Huber suggested that a "second look at laws" committee be created in Congress and that the professional drafters be explicitly charged with overseeing matters of statutory housekeeping.[g]

At the least, the increasingly popular judicial approaches like textualism and clear statement rules underscore the importance of legislative drafting. Well-drafted bills that accurately reflect the will of Congress will usually survive legal challenge, while poorly written statutes often become mired in controversy and may be interpreted in ways that undermine their purposes or at least do not allow the laws to fully meet those purposes. Consider the Federal Regulation of Lobbying Act that we discussed in Chapter 3, § 2, and the debilitating interpretation provided by the Supreme Court in *United States v. Harriss*, 347 U.S. 612 (1954). Adopting a strained and rather loony interpretation to avoid a possible constitutional problem with the 1946 FRLA, the Court emasculated the Act, leaving a toothless lobbying disclosure bill on the books for nearly fifty years.

In light of the importance of drafting generally and for due process of lawmaking theories in general, the remainder of this subsection will discuss techniques of legislative drafting. Legislative drafting is one of the most difficult legal writing skills, perhaps because statutes are a genre least like the essays and term papers that you have written before you entered law school.

---

e. See Robert Katzmann, *Courts and Congress* 73–76 (1997).

f. See Shirley Abrahamson & Robert Hughes, *Shall We Dance? Steps for Legislators and Judges in Statutory Interpretation*, 75 Minn. L. Rev. 1045, 1059–75 (1991) (detailing state mechanisms).

g. *The Intercircuit Committee*, 100 Harv. L. Rev. 1417, 1432 (1987).

This subsection will not teach you how to draft statutes proficiently. That skill can only be accomplished through practice, under expert guidance. Nor will this subsection give you a comprehensive analysis of statutory drafting techniques. For that, we refer you to Reed Dickerson's excellent treatise, *The Fundamentals of Legal Drafting* (2d ed. 1986), and classroom materials, *Materials on Legal Drafting* (1981).[h]

1. *A General Approach to Drafting a Statute.* Legislative drafting is a three-step process requiring distinct but related efforts. It is not a linear process, for a drafter will typically have to go back and rethink each step after completing the next one. And at each step in the process, it is critical to understand the existing statutory framework (as interpreted by courts and agencies) very carefully.

The first step is to determine what the proposed legislation is designed to do. This involves a determination of the ideal objective and, then, any amelioration of that objective to maximize the chance that the bill will receive the legislative attention its supporters desire. Most of the time, the objective of the drafting project will be given to the bill drafter by someone else — by a legislator to her personal or committee staff, usually aided by professional drafters called legislative counsels; by an agency or executive department official to agency or departmental lawyers; or by an organized lobbying group to its counsel or staff. However, the objective will usually be set forth in a general way allowing the drafter a great deal of discretion and responsibility. The first job of a thoughtful drafter, then, is to explore the objective more thoroughly on both a conceptual and a political level.

To the extent that the drafter is part of the process by which options are explored and narrowed, the drafter must be sensitive to what is politically possible. The drafter should consider the composition of the legislative committee to which such a bill would be referred under the jurisdictional rules of the legislative body. Not only can the committee effectively kill the bill by failing to report it, but also a severely divided committee is usually equally fatal (unless the President or one of the parties has made this a high priority item). Even if the drafter can envision a potential committee majority for the bill, she must also realize that if the bill is offensive to a major interest group, it will attract substantial adverse lobbying. A drafter must consider how to avoid potential interest group problems. With all this in mind, she will explore the various options with the person or group desiring this legislation. Would something largely symbolic be sufficient? If not, is there a compromise solution that will advance the lawmaker's goals a bit less, in return for the neutrality or even support of potentially opposed groups? How much is the lawmaker willing to compromise? And when? (A drafter may want to draft

---

h. Other helpful sources are Tobias Dorsey, *Legislative Drafter's Deskbook: A Practical Guide* (2006); Sandra Stokoff & Lawrence Filson, *The Legislative Drafter's Desk Reference* (2d ed. 2007, forthcoming) (both books written by the current or former House legislative counsels); Lance Rook, *Laying Down the Law: Canons for Drafting Complex Legislation*, 72 Ore. L. Rev. 663 (1993).

a very strong bill, with the expectation that it will be diluted as part of a compromise or logrolling process.)[i]

The second step is to determine the structure of the proposed legislation. Once the drafter and others have decided on the basic idea for the proposed legislation, the drafter must figure out what needs to be done to implement the idea. This is more than just devising a simple format for the bill. Because most proposed legislation operates in a framework created or molded by existing statutes, the drafter needs to decide how to fit her proposal into the code of laws. Is there any provision in existing law that should be repealed? What sections should be amended? How much should be accomplished by explicit statutory language, and how much by subsequent lawmaking by the administrative agencies or the courts? Below, we provide a more detailed analysis of the elements of a typical bill.

The third step is to draft the bill, so that the language and organization are no more complicated than necessary, serve the object of the legislation without creating unnecessary problems, and are internally coherent and consistent with usages in existing statutes. The hardest step in the drafting process is executing the concept and the organization developed in the first two steps. One of the cardinal rules for drafters is that the language chosen should be helpful to the reader. Statutes are meant to influence conduct, and the basic purpose of almost all statutes is, obviously, better served if the statute is clear, precise, and logically developed. If there is an overall purpose to the proposed statute, it should be announced simply. It is imperative that drafters provide definitions when common words are used in narrow or specialized ways. A drafter should organize the statute logically, perhaps including a table of contents in the first section of a lengthy bill. Titles or captions for sections and, sometimes, for subsections are often useful.

A drafter must also follow rules of consistency. She should not use different words to refer to the same thing. If the proposed legislation is to be integrated into an existing statutory scheme, word usage should be consistent with the usages adopted in the existing scheme. The best example of legislation that must be drafted with constant attention to the existing statutory structure is tax legislation; not surprisingly, Congress employs experts in drafting tax legislation to ensure that new proposals will fit harmoniously in the entirety of the Internal Revenue Code.[j] The drafting of federal tax legislation represents some of the best work of the professional drafting staff; nonetheless, the frequency of technical corrections proposals and clarifying administrative rulings demonstrates the challenge even to the most expert of drafters, particularly in the context of complex and technical statutory frameworks.

---

i. For further discussion of this information-gathering process, see David Marcello, *The Ethics and Politics of Legislative Drafting*, 70 Tul. L. Rev. 2437 (1996).

j. See Michael Livingston, *Congress, the Courts, and the Code: Legislative History and the Interpretation of Tax Statutes*, 69 Tex. L. Rev. 819 (1991) (discussing the tax legislative process and the role of expert staff).

2. *The Structure of a Bill.* The format for bills varies somewhat from jurisdiction to jurisdiction. Federal bills are subject to different constitutional, statutory, and practical requirements than state legislative bills, and states have different practices and requirements, many which are written into state constitutions. Nonetheless, the structural similarities far outweigh the differences. In this section, we introduce you to the format generally followed in the federal Congress and the Minnesota Legislature. Cross-references to Minnesota authority and practice will illustrate some of the differences in state legislative drafting.

The Long Title and the Enacting Clause. Statutes start with a *long title*, which generally describes the statute's nature and ambit. The formal beginning of the statute is the *enacting clause*, whose form is fixed at the federal level by 1 U.S.C. § 101 (1988). Only matter following the enacting clause is formally the law. The Lobbying Disclosure Act of 1995, *supra*, Chapter 3, § 2, began in the following way:

A BILL

To provide for the disclosure of lobbying activities to influence the Federal Government, and for other purposes.

Be it enacted by the Senate and the House of Representatives of the United States of America in Congress assembled,

The Minnesota Constitution provides that "no law shall embrace more than one subject which shall be expressed in its [long] title." See also Chapter 3, § 3, discussing the *single-subject rule.* The joint legislative rules further provide that the "title of each bill shall clearly state its subject and briefly state its purpose" and that "when a bill amends or repeals an existing act, the title shall refer to the chapter, section, or subdivision." Hence, the customary format for a long title in Minnesota (1) begins with opening boilerplate ("A bill for an Act"), followed by (2) the general subject (e.g., "relating to education"), (3) the object or specific subject (e.g., "authorizing school districts to provide teacherages"), (4) a statement where the bill would be codified, (5) a list of existing statutes that would be amended, and (6) a list of existing statutes that would be repealed. When pieced together, this long title would read:

A bill for an act

relating to education; authorizing school districts to provide teacherages; proposing new law coded in Minnesota Statutes, Chapter 122; amending Minnesota Statutes 1980, Section 122.12; repealing Minnesota Statutes 1980, Section 122.34, Subdivision 6.

The Minnesota Constitution requires that every bill have an enacting clause that says: "BE IT ENACTED BY THE LEGISLATURE OF THE STATE OF MINNESOTA:".

Introductory Clauses. Everything after the enacting clause is part of the statute. Where the substantive change in law is simple, it follows directly after the enacting clause. Where the statute makes more substantial changes in the law, there are frequently introductory clauses. For example, long statutes, especially those doing more than just amending existing law, often have a *short title* briefly describing the thrust of the statute. There may also be a table of contents to help the reader find provisions easily. Finally, statements of legislative findings and purpose are useful in conveying the overall policy of the statute. Both state and federal practice permits but does not require these sorts of introductory clauses. As you remember, such clauses in the Lobbying Disclosure Act took the following form:

> *Be it enacted by the Senate and House of Representatives of the United States of America in Congress assembled,*
>
> Section 1. This Act may be cited as the "Lobbying Disclosure Act of 1995."
>
> Section 2. The Congress finds that — [statement of findings].

Substantive Provisions. It is usually best to segregate different types of directives into different sections of the proposed statute and to order the sections logically. The typical sequence, which you can see in the Lobbying Disclosure Act, is the following:

- Definitions of unfamiliar words or phrases and terms of art;

- Substantive provisions setting forth rights and duties, together with defenses and exceptions;

- Administrative and procedural provisions, including identification of agencies or departments charged with enforcing or creating rules under the proposed statute;

- Sanctions and enforcement provisions;

- Miscellaneous provisions, such as those providing for transitional rules before the proposed legislation takes full effect, for rules of construction to guide courts, or for ongoing congressional oversight; and

- The effective date.

Provisions Amending or Repealing Existing Law. Even if the bill creates a new statutory scheme, a drafter may want to amend (or perhaps even repeal) existing provisions of related laws. With respect to the Lobbying Disclosure Act, the old lobbying law had to be repealed, and several other disclosure statutes, such as the Foreign Agents Registration Act of 1938, had to be amended. Interpreters presume that new statutes do not implicitly amend existing statutes, so it is very important to draft explicit amendments to existing provisions that ought to be changed. There are at least two different ways of doing this. One way is to *strike* specified language from the existing provision and *insert* new language. This technique can be quite cumbersome if the drafter is tinkering with several different features of the amended provision. In that event, the *full-restatement approach* is better. Drafters using this method identify the existing law that is being amended and then set forth the provision as amended in its entirety.

Both approaches are used in federal bills. The strike-and-insert approach is more appropriate when only one or two changes are being made to a long, complicated provision. The full-restatement approach is more appropriate when there are several changes to a short provision. The state legislative drafter often has just one option. Some state constitutions prohibit amendments to a law "by reference to its title only" and require that amended provisions be set forth fully in their amended form. The general practice in some states is to underline changes in the restated provision and to strike through language that is to be deleted.

A third approach to amendment is to repeal a provision and enact a replacement in its stead. Federal drafters typically will use this approach only when they want to delete more than just one section of existing law (e.g., a title or an entire act). When they want to delete part of a section, federal drafters will usually just amend the section to delete the specified portion. The use of repeals to amend small parts of statutes is more popular at the state level, especially in those states with constitutional requirements that amendments (but not necessarily repeals) must restate the entire provision as amended.[k]

Clauses at the End of the Bill. Several technical clauses may be used at the end of a bill. One is a *savings clause*, which preserves rights and duties that exist when the statute is passed:

> Section 17. This Act does not affect rights and duties that matured, penalties that were incurred, and proceedings that were begun, before its effective date.

Savings clauses are sometimes called *grandfather clauses*, after the post-Civil War practice in some states of extending the right to vote only to individuals whose grandfathers had been eligible to vote. Savings clauses are justified on fairness grounds because they do not unsettle arrangements that were designed in reliance on old laws. Although they have intuitive appeal, they have sparked an interesting scholarly debate about their effects and the wisdom of including them in most new laws.[l]

A second provision often found at the end of a bill is a *severability clause*, which seeks to preserve provisions of the proposed legislation if other provisions are invalidated:

> Section 18. If any provision of this Act is found to be invalid, all valid provisions that are severable from the invalid provision shall remain in effect. If a provision of this Act is invalid in one or more of its applications, the provision shall remain in effect for all valid applications that are severable from the invalid applications.

In some (relatively unusual) cases, enactors intend for the entire act to be nullified if one of the provisions is invalidated by a court. Then, an *inseverability clause* should be included.[m] In some cases, inseverability clauses are added to legislation as a way to kill the proposal; opponents will add clearly unconstitutional provisions along with an inseverability clause to increase the

---

k. See Lawrence Filson, *The Legislative Drafter's Desk Reference* Part V (1992) (discussing amendatory provisions).

l. For a recent comprehensive discussion of the scholarship, see Daniel Shaviro, *When Rules Change: An Economic and Political Analysis of Transition Rules and Retroactivity* (2000).

m. See Israel Friedman, Comment, *Inseverability Clauses in Statutes*, 64 U. Chi. L. Rev. 903 (1997).

chances that a court will strike down the entire law. During the Senate debate on comprehensive campaign finance reform in 2001 that led to enactment of the Bipartisan Campaign Reform Act, much discussion centered on whether an inseverability clause was warranted to preserve unchanged whatever compromise could be reached among the contending factions or whether it was a strategic move on the part of committed opponents. (In the end, no such clause was included.)

In most jurisdictions, there will be a statutory or constitutional provision establishing the effective date of any statute enacted. Unless it provides otherwise, a federal statute takes effect at the moment of enactment (i.e., when it is signed by the President). In many states, laws enacted in a session of the legislature do not normally become effective until a designated point in time after the session is over (either a specified future date in the same year or a specified number of days after adjournment). Subject to constitutional constraints, the date of effectiveness can be altered by a clause at the end of the statute. Because of judicial precedent which requires clear statements for legislation to be given retroactive effect, see Chapter 6, § 3C, drafters should be explicit about the temporal reach of legislation, providing clear effective dates and providing for retroactivity where it is intended.

3. *The Diseases of Legislative Language.* Reed Dickerson, in his books and articles, was our profession's champion of clear and precise statutory drafting, which is the drafter's paramount concern. The main purpose of statutes is to communicate directions to citizens, telling us what legal rights and duties we have in our polity. While the legislature may not always have clear goals and directives in mind when it passes a statute, it is certainly the job of the statutory drafter to communicate what directives there are with clarity and precision to the citizenry.

Dickerson, in *The Diseases of Legislative Language*, 1 Harv. J. Leg. 5 (1964), argues that many of the problems casually identified with unclear statutes actually flow from problematic word choice and sentence construction. His litany of the "major diseases" of language begins with *ambiguity.* *Semantic ambiguity* arises apart from context and describes uncertainty rooted in more than one dictionary definition of a word. For example, if you are asked to meet someone "by the bank," do you go to the Chicago River or to the Michigan Avenue office of Bank One? More important for drafting purposes is *syntactic ambiguity* caused by unclear modification or reference. For examples, Dickerson identifies *squinting modifiers*: If the statute says that "the trustee shall require him promptly to repay the loan," does "promptly" modify "require" or "repay"? And modifiers preceding or following a series can be troublesome: If the statute applies to "charitable corporations or institutions performing educational functions," does "charitable" modify "institutions," and does "performing educational functions" modify "corporations"? *Contextual ambiguity* is also common. Even when the words and syntax are clear, context may create ambiguity. In *Holy Trinity Church v. United States*, 143 U.S. 457 (1892) (Chapter 7, § 1), the Supreme Court applied a contextual gloss to seemingly clear and very broad statutory language in order to narrow the scope of the Act.

Vagueness is a very different problem from ambiguity. Ambiguity creates an "either/or" situation, while vagueness creates a variety of possible meanings. See Lawrence Solan, *The Language of Judges* 93–138 (1993). For example, the Sherman Act's prohibition of "contracts in restraint of trade" is vague. Its meaning cannot be narrowed to a choice between two propositions and is, instead, a range of possible meanings — from a prohibition of all contractual limitations on business freedom to a prohibition of only the most egregious or large-scale restraints. The Sherman Act is a case where vagueness may be desirable (in contrast to ambiguity, which should almost always be avoided). Congress did not attempt to define exactly what anticompetitive arrangements are unlawful and left the development of rules and standards to a common law process that has enabled the statute to respond to changing circumstances and theories of regulation.

A good deal of ambiguity and unintended vagueness may be eliminated by a working knowledge of the textual and substantive canons of statutory interpretation (discussed in Chapter 8, § 1, and listed in Appendix B). Although we believe that the canons do not always dictate judicial resolution of conflicting interpretations of a statute, they are useful guidelines for drafters. Similarly, many states have general construction statutes like the Model Statutory Construction Act, which establish rules of presumptive usage in statutes. The General Construction Law of New York's Code and Pennsylvania's Statutory Construction Act, 1 Pa. Consol. Stat. §§ 1921–1928, are examples of such statutes. Many of these canons and rules are simply precepts of language; if the drafter is aware that courts will generally interpret certain language constructs in a special way, then the drafter may avoid ambiguity.[n]

Another example of the drafting usefulness of the canons of interpretation is to avoid the sin of *overprecision*, or trying to cover all facets of a problem for which it is impossible to anticipate all facets. The statute in *Holy Trinity Church* prohibited any encouragement of alien migration to the United States but specifically excepted actors, lecturers, and singers from the prohibition. The drafters probably did not mean to include ministers in the general prohibition, but they created a problem when they failed to include "ministers" in the list of specific exceptions. The *expressio unius* canon posits that inclusion of one thing in a list implies the exclusion of all things not listed. Had the Supreme Court followed that canon, it would have invalidated the Church's arrangement in the case, under which it had hired a minister from England. By trying to be comprehensive, the drafter produced a statute that could yield unjust results and might not prove flexible enough to deal fairly with new occupational groups that might later want to migrate to the United States.[o]

---

n. For an influential analysis of how linguistics might be helpful to statutory drafters and interpreters, see Clark Cunningham, Judith Levi, Georgia Green & Jeffrey Kaplan, *Plain Meaning and Hard Cases*, 103 Yale L. J. 1561 (1994).

o. The Court in *Holy Trinity Church* declined to follow the *expressio unius* canon, but other courts in other cases have not been so generous to drafters, viewing the judicial role as implementing the "plain meaning" of statutory text as revealed through an application of

Generally, good rules of writing style are equally good rules of drafting style. One exception is *elegant variation* (of which Fowler but not other style authorities disapprove). While creative writers may like to use a variety of words to express the same thing, so as to avoid using the same word repetitiously, statutory drafters should generally use the same term with tedious regularity. Consistency rather than stylistic elegance is the overriding goal of the statutory drafter. Metaphors and similes are wonderful devices for creative writing yet are inappropriate for statutory writing, because the many layers of meaning and image they suggest — what makes them good literature — interfere with the main purpose of statutes — to communicate directives to citizens about their rights and duties under the law. For statutory writing, consistency serves this goal.

Finally, as in all other legal writing, a bill or statute cannot be written in one draft. The preliminary draft should be circulated to colleagues and, when appropriate, political actors in all branches of government who would be affected by it. Like the republican ideal of the political process we introduced in Chapter 1, the ideal drafting process is one that applies practical reason to solve problems through a deliberative process of discussion among public-spirited citizens. That is surely the ideal for which due process of lawmaking techniques are aiming; the practical question is whether the reality of the legislative process can ever live up to these hopes. How realistic is it to expect methodical drafting and insightful discussion of legislative language in the few days at the end of a legislative session when much law is amended and enacted? As they iron out last-minute compromises on the floor, how likely are lawmakers to consult the professional staffs provided to them by Congress and most state legislatures? If courts have only limited influence here, can legislatures themselves adopt rules to improve the process? In the remainder of this chapter, we will focus on the use of due process of lawmaking theories to analyze the internal rules of the legislative bodies.

SECTION 2. THE FEDERAL CONGRESSIONAL BUDGET PROCESS

Justice Linde observed that "the [legislative] process everywhere is governed by rules, * * * these rules are purposefully made and from time to time change, and * * * most of them are sufficiently concrete so that participants and observers alike will recognize when a legislative body is following the due process of lawmaking and when it is not." *Due Process of Lawmaking*, *supra*, at 242. Linde's primary focus was on rules set up by constitutions and the role of the judiciary in enforcing those rules, but he also acknowledged the importance of statutes and internal rules to the due process of lawmaking. The modern Congress is characterized by numerous procedural rules and formal institutions, all of which can change over time to accommodate changes in

---

established canons of interpretation even if implausible outcomes or hardship results. Drafters should never assume that statutory interpreters (judges, administrative officials, attorneys advising clients) will find some way to "fix" drafting mistakes.

membership and in society.[a] A comprehensive vision of due process of lawmaking includes an emphasis on procedural frameworks and rules that shape deliberation and that are largely enforced by members of Congress through the interplay of the political process. After all, if due process of lawmaking is intended to improve legislative decisionmaking, why should we rely solely or even primarily on the relatively indirect mechanism of judicial review? Why not approach the problems of congressional deliberation more directly through the use of internal legislative rules and procedures designed to foster full and transparent deliberation?

We will begin our study of procedural frameworks[b] that shape congressional deliberation with an extended analysis of the federal budget process. This framework is ubiquitous; indeed, one commentator has argued that the budget process has led to a "fiscalization" of federal policy because the budget rules significantly affect the scope and shape of most legislative enactments.[c] After providing the history of the development of the congressional rules and describing the current landscape, we will conclude with a case study of an energy tax provision included in the Omnibus Budget Reconciliation Act of 1993, Pub. L. No. 103–66, 107 Stat. 312 (codified as amended in scattered sections of U.S.C.), which will also provide you an opportunity to apply insights from the theories of the legislative process, set forth in Chapter 1, § 2. The case study will provide examples, including excerpts from legislative materials, that will make more concrete the description of the budget process.

A. THE DEVELOPMENT OF THE MODERN CONGRESSIONAL BUDGET PROCESS

The Constitution places the power of the purse in Congress' domain, specifying in Article I, § 9, cl. 7, that "No Money shall be drawn from the Treasury, but in Consequence of Appropriations made by Law." The founders thus placed the federal government's most important power in the most politically accountable branch. Kate Stith derives two principles from this constitutional directive: "first, a *Principle of the Public Fisc*, asserting that all monies received from whatever source by any part of the government are public funds, and second, a *Principle of Appropriations Control*, prohibiting expenditure of any public money without legislative authorization." *Congress' Power of the Purse*, 97 Yale L.J. 1343, 1345 (1988). In other words, Congress sets not only the amount of money appropriated to executive branch agencies or other projects, but it also directs how that total is to be spent by enacting instructions in appropriations bills. Stith observes that the power of the purse includes a correlative duty "to exercise legislative control over federal expenditures." Historically, however, Congress has not always discharged its budgetary obligations responsibly, occasionally abdicating its authority to the

---

a. For a classic work on the modern changes in Congress, see Nelson Polsby, *The Institutionalization of the U.S. House of Representatives*, 62 Am. Pol. Sci. Rev. 144 (1968).

b. For a discussion of framework laws, including the federal budget process, see Elizabeth Garrett, *The Purposes of Framework Legislation* 14 J. Contemp. Legal Iss. 717 (2005).

c. See Burdett Loomis, *The Contemporary Congress* 46 (2d ed. 1998).

executive branch. Shirking its constitutional role has substantial impact on congressional power generally because decisions about how to allocate limited resources lie at the heart of governance.

Before we begin to describe the procedural framework for congressional budgeting, a few definitions of key budget terms are in order.[d] Federal spending programs can take a variety of forms. When most people think of federal spending, they tend to think of programs funded through annual appropriations bills. This spending is called *discretionary spending*, because Congress exercises its discretion every year in deciding whether to continue funding. The key players in the appropriations process are the twelve subcommittees of each of the Senate and House Appropriations Committees. Perhaps surprisingly to many people, only about one-third of all federal spending is categorized as discretionary appropriations, which includes most defense spending and spending for many domestic programs like education, government operations, and law enforcement.

Before the appropriations subcommittees can appropriate money for a federal program, different committees must *authorize* the programs, or establish the programs in substantive legislation that enacts purposes, guidelines, and structures. Often, the authorization bill will set a limit on the appropriations, but the authorization itself does not provide any funding or allow the agency to spend funds. This requirement for dual legislation ensures that at least two committees will be involved in the creation and funding of discretionary programs, with the authorizing committees serving as the chief policymakers and the appropriators serving as the watchdogs who force officials to justify their funding requests each fiscal year. Of course, this process does not always work in practice as it is designed to operate; for example, sometimes appropriations bills establish programs as well as fund them, even though the congressional rules require separate legislation. See Congressional Budget Office, *Unauthorized Appropriations and Expiring Authorizations* 3 (Jan. 12, 2007) (noting that "[i]n recent years the total amount of unauthorized appropriations reported by the CBO has ranged between about $160 billion and $170 billion").

---

d. The best resource explaining the budget process, defining terminology, and providing examples of legislative language is Allen Schick, *The Federal Budget: Politics, Policy, Process* (rev. ed. 2000). The budget committees and other government entities produce explanations of the federal budget process. For example, the President's Budget, disseminated in February, has often included a separate document or section entitled *The Budget System and Concepts*. The Senate Budget Committee published *The Congressional Budget Process: An Explanation*, 105th Cong., 2d Sess. (Comm. Print 1998), and the House Budget Committee published *Compilation of Laws and Rules Relating to the Congressional Budget Process*, 106th Cong., 2d Sess. (Comm. Print 2000). A particularly clear compendium of definitions is found in Government Accountability Office, *A Glossary of Terms Used in the Federal Budget Process* (Sept. 2005). Our focus will be exclusively on the federal budget system; for some discussion of state procedures, see *Fiscal Challenges: An Interdisciplinary Approach to Budget Policy* (Elizabeth Garrett, Elizabeth Graddy & Howell Jackson eds., 2007, forthcoming); *Handbook of Government Budgeting* (Roy Meyers ed., 1999) (both also providing some comparative analysis to international budgeting).

One confusing aspect of the authorization-appropriations process stems from the similarity in terminology used in both kinds of legislation. When Congress appropriates money, it provides agencies *budget authority* to enter into obligations, a phrase also used in substantive authorization bills. An *obligation* occurs when the agency or department commits itself to spend money, for example, by signing a contract. An agency may have other *budget resources* available for obligation; some agencies collect fees that they can spend according to congressional directives, and others have been given multi-year appropriations, meaning that unobligated balances roll over into the new fiscal year rather than revert to the treasury. When obligated money is actually spent, it is called an *outlay*. Some outlays in a particular fiscal year correspond to budget authority appropriated in that fiscal year; other outlays relate to money obligated in previous years. *Spendout rates* for budget authority vary among programs. For example, outlays for salaries and other personnel costs often come from recent budget authority; outlays pursuant to long-term contracts to build military planes or government buildings often correspond to budget authority from past fiscal years.

A second type of spending is called *mandatory* or *direct spending*. Direct spending is spending pursuant to a binding legal obligation to pay, including, for example, interest on the national debt. The largest component of direct spending goes to entitlement programs, like Social Security, Medicare and Medicaid, veterans' pensions, and food stamps. Direct spending is not controlled by the annual appropriations process but is determined instead by legislation that establishes the rules for eligibility and the formulas for payment. Such legislation allows funding to continue as long as Congress has not repealed the law. Entitlement programs tend to fall within the jurisdiction of substantive committees rather than appropriations subcommittees; for example, Social Security and Medicare are overseen by the Senate Finance and House Ways and Means Committees, and the food stamps program falls within the purview of the House Agriculture Committee and the Senate Committee on Agriculture, Nutrition, and Forestry.

Finally, a federal program can be constructed as a *tax subsidy*. If a lawmaker wants to encourage home ownership, for example, she has several options. She can work to enact a program that gives people grants of federal money when they purchase a home; such a program can be one that receives annual appropriations or that is constructed as an entitlement program, automatically providing funds every year for qualifying purchasers. Or she can provide all taxpayers a deduction for the interest they pay on their mortgages. Indeed, estimated at over $75 billion in fiscal year 2007, the home mortgage interest tax deduction is one of the largest federal housing subsidies provided by the federal government, and one of the many tax provisions treating investments in residential housing favorably. Stanley Surrey worked to persuade policymakers to consider such tax provisions as *tax expenditures* in order to make explicit their relationship to other kinds of federal expenditures.

See Stanley Surrey, *Pathways to Tax Reform: The Concept of Tax Expenditures* (1973).[e]

A tax expenditure is a "revenue [loss] attributable to provisions of federal law that allow a special exclusion or deduction from income, or that provide a special credit, preferential tax rate, or deferral of tax liability. Tax expenditures entail no payment from the government. Rather, the Treasury foregoes some of the revenue it would otherwise have collected, and affected taxpayers pay lower taxes then they otherwise would have had to pay." Schick, *The Federal Budget: Politics, Policy, Process, supra*, at 296. Tax expenditures are part of the Internal Revenue Code, so they fall within the jurisdiction of the Senate Finance and House Ways and Means Committees. Thus, the same committees have jurisdiction over some of the largest spending programs — many entitlement programs and all tax expenditures — and over the Internal Revenue Code, the mechanism that raises most of the money to run the government. These committees also control the revenue sources for the Social Security and Medicare programs, primarily the money deducted from employee paychecks for and contributed by employers to the social insurance trust funds. In contrast, appropriators control only part of the spending side of the equation, either relying on other committees to raise money or depending on deficit spending to finance their programs.[f]

Finally, it is important to distinguish between the *federal budget deficit* and the *federal debt*.[g] When government outlays exceed receipts, the difference is a deficit. If receipts exceed outlays, then the government has a *surplus*. Both of these measures are cash-flow figures. Budget experts simply total everything that the government spends in twelve months and everything that it collects and then compare the two numbers. These figures do not take account of the need to fund obligations in the future even when those obligations are substantial, like the unfunded liabilities in the Social Security program and health entitlements. Moreover, although the Social Security program is supposed to be off-budget, and thus not to be counted in determining whether the government has a surplus or a deficit, most of the figures in the press refer to the *unified budget*, which includes receipts and outlays related to Social Security. Social Security is not like a private retirement system. The taxes collected from working Americans today are not invested for their retirement; instead, the money is paid directly to retired citizens in benefits. Currently, inclusion of Social Security provides a rosier financial picture of the federal government because the trust fund is collecting more in payroll taxes

---

e. See also Christopher Howard, *The Hidden Welfare State: Tax Expenditures and Social Policy in the United States* (1997); Stanley Surrey & Paul McDaniel, *Tax Expenditures* (1985); Nancy Staudt, *Redundant Tax and Spending Programs*, 100 Nw. U. L. Rev. 1197 (2006) (considering effect on policy of ability to use various methods and forms for federal programs).

f. See W. Mark Crain & Timothy Muris, *Legislative Organization of Fiscal Policy*, 38 J. L. & Econ. 311 (1995) (arguing that committee structure affects the level of revenue raised and spending allowed).

g. See Michael Boskin, *Perspectives on Federal Deficits and Debt*, in *Fiscal Challenges, supra*.

than it is paying out in benefits. But as the work force ages, the trust fund will need to find money in addition to current payroll taxes to pay beneficiaries, and including it in budget figures will no longer benefit politicians attempting to convince voters that the federal government has adopted prudent fiscal policies.

Figure 4–1

Fiscal Year 2006 Federal Government Outlays and Revenues (in Billions)
Deficit: $248 Billion

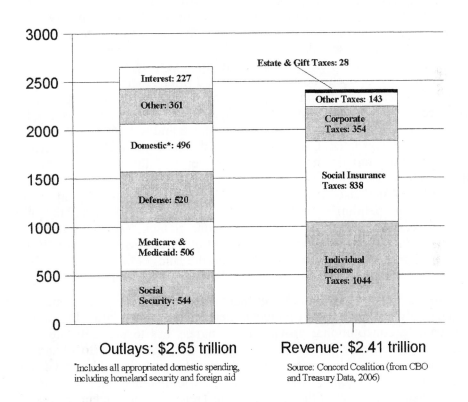

Outlays: $2.65 trillion   Revenue: $2.41 trillion

*Includes all appropriated domestic spending, including homeland security and foreign aid

Source: Concord Coalition (from CBO and Treasury Data, 2006)

When a government runs a deficit, it has to find money to pay its bills. The government finances deficits largely by borrowing money; it issues government bonds, it pays interest on the bonds, and ultimately it redeems the bonds. Congress controls the amount of debt that the government can issue by enacting a *debt ceiling*. The Congressional Budget Office's *The Budget and Economic Outlook: Fiscal Years 2008–2017* (2007) estimates that the debt held by the public will stand at just above $4.8 trillion by the end of 2006. The government must pay interest each year to service the debt, which is considered an item of direct spending. In fiscal year 2006, around nine cents of each federal dollar went to interest payments.

With these basic concepts in mind, we can now turn to a description of the events that led to the adoption of the current congressional budget framework:

1. *Executive Branch Budgeting and the Nixon Impoundments.* Early significant budget legislation was aimed at executive branch practices, rather than congressional budget procedures. Congress passed the Budget and Accounting Act of 1921, Pub. L. No. 67–13, 42 Stat. 20 (codified as amended in scattered sections of 31 U.S.C. (1994)), which, with some amendments, continues to govern the presidential budget process. The immediate impetus for the 1921 Act was a series of budget deficits and a sense that Congress could not restrain itself from profligate spending and thus needed stronger leadership from the President. The main drains on the federal budget were rivers and harbors bills and federal outlays for pension bills following the Civil War. In his first term, Grover Cleveland vetoed 304 bills, 241 of them private and general pension bills. Louis Fisher, *Presidential Spending Power* 25–26 (1975). Many of these bills dealt with claims rejected by the Pension Bureau because the disabilities existed prior to military service, were not incurred in the line of duty, or occurred after discharge. Fisher observes that Cleveland's vetoes "earned a reputation for their sarcastic quality. One claimant, who enrolled in the Army on March 25, 1865, entered a post hospital a week later with the measles. He returned to duty on May 8 and was mustered out of the service three days later. Cleveland observed that 15 years after this 'brilliant service and this terrific encounter with the measles,' the claimant discovered that the measles had somehow affected his eyes and spinal column." *Id.* at 26. World War I increased the demands on the federal treasury. From 1914 to 1919, federal spending soared from $726 million to $19 billion, and the public debt increased from $1 billion to $26 billion. Schick, *The Federal Budget: Politics, Policy, Process, supra,* at 14. At the urging of President Wilson, Congress appointed a Select Committee on the Budget to study the problem. Two years later, Warren Harding signed the 1921 Act into law.

The Budget Act of 1921 requires that the President develop and publish an annual budget. The executive budget is merely a recommendation to Congress; pursuant to constitutional provisions, Congress has to enact its provisions before it becomes effective, and Congress has the power to change the President's proposal however it pleases. But the presidential budget sets the agenda for congressional deliberation and decisionmaking. The 1921 Act also established the Bureau of the Budget in the Treasury Department, which later became the Office of Management and Budget (OMB) in the Executive Office of the President. In addition to its budget responsibilities, this office works to coordinate executive branch activities and to ensure that all the agents of the President work to further his agenda, rather than their own objectives.[h] Finally, the 1921 Act created the General Accounting Office, now known as the Government Accountability Office (GAO), as a congressional entity to review federal spending and programs. See *Bowsher v. Synar* (Chapter 9, § 2D) (discussing the relationship between Congress and the GAO).

---

h. See Larry Berman, *The Office of Management and Budget that Almost Wasn't,* 92 Pol. Sci. Q. 281 (1977); David Mowery, Mark Kamlet, & John Crecine, *Presidential Management of Budgetary and Fiscal Policymaking,* 95 Pol. Sci. Q. 395 (1980) (both tracing history of OMB and relationship to President's control of policy).

The Budget Act of 1921 is sometimes cited as the beginning of the modern, more powerful presidency. It "marked a sweeping change in the relations between the legislature and the executive branches. The new budget process gave the President enormous new powers by creating a unified presidential budget and strengthening the President's ability to oversee the agencies' execution of the budget. The President and his budget staff became the primary actors and Congress reacted to them. The act thus marks one of the most important changes in the balance of power between the branches of government in the nation's history."[i] In the following decades, the President continued to play the most important role in federal budgeting, as Congress with its fragmented organization of dozens of committees, all with some responsibility relating to its power of the purse, found that it could not develop rational spending and taxing policies on its own.

Relations between the two branches deteriorated so significantly beginning in the mid-1960s that Allen Schick terms the years between 1966 and 1973 as the "Seven-Year Budget War." *Congress and Money: Budgeting, Spending, and Taxing* chap. 2 (1980). He cites two primary reasons to explain why budget conflict escalated during this time. First, and in part as a result of the 1921 Act and congressional reactions to the new budget players, the budget process became characterized by "[m]ore varied participation, wider access to budgetary information, and relaxation of restrictive procedures [which] enlarged the circle of budget participants on Capitol Hill." *Id.* at 23. No longer was the budget a closed and obscure part of policymaking; instead, Congress and the executive branch produced better information, and nongovernmental organizations like the Brookings Institution began to produce independent and understandable analyses of the federal budget. The increase in participation in budget policy and the shift toward decentralized decisionmaking were part of a larger trend in Congress that dispersed power from a few autocratic barons to more of the members and that opened up the process to public scrutiny.[j]

Just as more interests were demanding their fair share of federal resources, fewer resources were available for them. Before this period, federal budgeting was a process of continuing to fund past programs with an established base of money and funding new or expanded programs with a yearly additional increment of revenues that was not already committed.[k] For *incrementalism* to work successfully, the base must remain stable and available for continuing commitments and a yearly increment must be found to satisfy new demands.

---

i. Donald Kettl, *Deficit Politics: Public Budgeting in Its Institutional and Historical Context* 128 (1992).

j. For a description of the larger institutional changes, see Joseph Schlesinger, *The New American Political Party*, 79 Am. Pol. Sci. Rev. 1152, 1163–64 (1985); Lawrence Dodd & Bruce Oppenheimer, *The House in Transition*, in *Congress Reconsidered* 21 (Lawrence Dodd & Bruce Oppenheimer eds., 1977); Norman Ornstein, Robert Peabody & David Rohde, *The Changing Senate: From the 1950s to the 1970s*, in *Congress Reconsidered, supra*, at 3.

k. See Aaron Wildavsky, *The Politics of the Budgetary Process* (1st ed. 1964) (the most influential work describing the budget strategy of incrementalism, with new editions published in 1974 and 1979, and, as incrementalism fell out of favor, ultimately reconceptualized in Aaron Wildavsky & Naomi Caiden, *The New Politics of the Budgetary Process* (3d ed. 1997)).

Without an increment, funding for new programs must come from the base, and this inevitably causes much wider conflict. To return to a theme from Chapter 1, § 2, the budget game during this period changed from a cooperative one among interest groups in which all demands could be met and logrolling predominated, to a conflictual, zero-sum game of clear winners and losers.

In part, the increment was lost to fund the Vietnam War, as President Johnson paid for the conflict through deficit financing, while also refusing to compromise the funding for his domestic priorities. Furthermore, the vast majority of any annual increment was already committed to fund growing entitlement programs like Social Security, public assistance, unemployment compensation, and military and civilian retirement programs. These programs, once enacted, are essentially on automatic pilot; they do not require annual appropriations to continue, and their expenditures increase automatically as more people qualify for benefits. In addition, many of these programs are now indexed so that the level of benefits automatically adjusts to account for changes in the cost of living. Some budget experts and politicians term these programs *uncontrollable spending*, although they are not technically uncontrollable because Congress can amend or repeal them to reduce the amount of expenditures they require. Politically, however, such entitlement programs tend to be uncontrollable because lawmakers have historically been unwilling to take the political heat that would inevitably follow any attempt to cut them back. During the Seven-Year Budget War, more than 90 percent of the increment (the increase in federal spending each year) went to uncontrollable spending, leaving very little money available for new programs or expansions in others. See Schick, *Congress and Money, supra,* at 27.

The interbranch battle escalated into open warfare with President Nixon's *policy impoundments.* Nixon, citing an inherent constitutional right, refused to spend billions of dollars that Congress had appropriated or otherwise provided for obligation. Such a refusal to spend appropriated funds is called an impoundment; we saw an example of a congressionally sanctioned impoundment authority in the study of the Line Item Veto Act's cancellation and rescission powers. See Chapter 3, § 3. Other Presidents had impounded funds, but the scale and severity of Nixon's impoundments were unprecedented. Fisher, *supra,* at 175–77.[1] Nixon's impoundments were not routine decisions to achieve congressional objectives more efficiently, nor were they limited to appropriations for defense or foreign affairs, areas where the President as Commander-in-Chief had always asserted substantial discretionary authority. Instead, Nixon used impoundments to change the domestic policy priorities of the Democratic Congress, refusing to spend money appropriated for agriculture, housing, environmental, and welfare programs. In some cases, he impounded money appropriated in bills enacted over his veto, ignoring a

---

[1]. See also Roderick Kiewiet & Mathew McCubbins, *The Logic of Delegation: Congressional Parties and the Appropriations Process* 217 (1991) (calling Nixon's constitutional assertions "radical, aggressive, and erroneous"); Richard Salomon, *The Case Against Impoundment,* 2 Hastings Const. L.Q. 277 (1975) (providing legal and constitutional arguments against Nixon's position).

clear legislative signal that Congress intended the programs to be fully funded. Schick reports that Nixon impounded over $18 billion, and that the "aim of impoundment was to change the mix, not merely the level, of expenditures." *Congress and Money, supra*, at 48. In essence, the President was using the impoundment authority as a *de facto* line item veto power, something not granted to him in the Constitution.

When the impoundments were challenged in court, the President usually lost.[m] One case concerning impoundments reached the Supreme Court, which avoided the constitutional question of reconciling any presidential power to withhold spending with the constitutional commitment of the power of the purse to Congress.

TRAIN v. CITY OF NEW YORK, 420 U.S. 35 (1975). The Federal Water Pollution Control Act Amendments of 1972 provided a comprehensive program for decreasing water pollution. The law made available federal money to offset some of the costs of municipal sewer and sewage treatment works. It directed that "[s]ums authorized to be appropriated" for fiscal year 1973 be allotted "not later than 30 days after October 18, 1972," and it authorized to be appropriated money "not to exceed" $5 billion. Similar provisions governed federal funding for the following two fiscal years. The program was structured like an entitlement program. "Under the * * * scheme before us now, there are authorizations for future appropriations but also initial and continuing authority in the Executive Branch contractually to commit funds of the United States up to the amount of the authorization. The expectation is that the appropriations will be automatically forthcoming to meet these contractual commitments. This mechanism considerably reduces whatever discretion Congress might have exercised in the course of making annual appropriations." The bill was vetoed by President Nixon, but Congress overrode the veto. Subsequently, President Nixon directed the Administrator of the Environmental Protection Agency to allot no more than $2 billion in fiscal year 1973. The City of New York sued to require the EPA to allot the full amount authorized by Congress.

Writing for a unanimous Court (although **Justice Douglas** concurred only in the result without explanation), **Justice White** held that the Act did not permit the President to impound money; rather, Congress required that all $5 billion be allotted. The Court viewed this case as an application of traditional principles of statutory interpretation. Earlier drafts of the legislation had required that the executive branch allot "all sums" authorized to be appropriated. The executive branch argued that the deletion of the word "all" and insertion of the phrase "not to exceed" before the specified sums demonstrated congressional intent to provide it discretion concerning how much of the funds to expend. The Court was unpersuaded after its review of the statutory language and the legislative history. "If the States failed to submit projects sufficient to require obligation, and hence the appropriation, of the entire amounts authorized, or if the Administrator, exercising whatever authority the

---

m. See Ralph Abascal & John Kramer, *Presidential Impoundment Part II: Judicial and Legislative Responses*, 63 Geo. L.J. 149 (1974).

Act might have given him to deny grants, refused to obligate these total amounts, [the provision] would obviously permit appropriation of the lesser amounts. But if, for example, the full amount provided for 1973 was obligated by the Administrator in the course of approving plans and making grants for municipal contracts, [the provision] plainly 'authorized' the appropriation of the entire [amount]."

The Supreme Court did not reach the executive branch's argument that the President had inherent powers under the Constitution to impound money appropriated by Congress. Since the inception of the Bureau of the Budget, the executive branch had maintained that congressional appropriations should generally be viewed as permissive, providing a ceiling on how much money could be spent, rather than as mandatory, requiring that the full amount appropriated be spent. The Court did not decide whether that position correctly stated the default rule with respect to appropriations. It held that, with regard to this particular statute, Congress intended the Administrator to allot the entirety of the amounts appropriated, as long as there were acceptable programs that qualified for financial assistance. If the President had some inherent power (a question left open by *Train*), Congress' clear directive that all the sums authorized for this water pollution program be spent overrode any such power. See also *Youngstown Sheet & Tube v. Sawyer*, 343 U.S. 579 (1952) (discussing the effect of a congressional prohibition on a presidential assertion of inherent power to seize steel mills threatened by a labor strike).

The outcome in *Train* was consistent with virtually all the cases challenging the Nixon impoundments, but the delay caused by litigation undermined congressional objectives nearly as seriously as the impoundments themselves. In *Train*, for example, the Court was considering appropriations for fiscal year 1973 nearly two years after the money should have been allotted. Congress realized that it had to fight the President's incursions on its power of the purse in a more effective way; accordingly, it passed the first significant congressional budget process law, the Congressional Budget and Impoundment Control Act of 1974. (Although effective at the time of *Train*, the Act included a provision clarifying that its terms did not affect pending impoundment litigation. Thus, the Court's ruling was unaffected by the new budget law.)

2. *The 1974 Budget Act.* The enactment of the Congressional Budget and Impoundment Control Act of 1974, Pub. L. No. 93–344, 88 Stat. 297 (codified as amended at 2 U.S.C. §§ 681–88 (1994)), took nearly two years. Although the impoundment controversy may have served as the main impetus for reform, members also wanted to construct a process that would allow coordination of the dozens of committees and subcommittees involved in spending or raising money. Coordination and control were seen as crucial objectives of the new budget process, particularly because of the public's concern with spiraling federal deficits and the President's charges that lawmakers lacked the discipline to formulate comprehensive and responsible fiscal policy.

Lawmakers who favored deficit reduction and spending discipline were particularly interested in coordinating mechanisms that would help Congress avoid a classic collective action problem.[n] Put simply, legislators who believe that the public interest is best served by reduced federal spending know that, in the absence of coordination, most of their colleagues will not resist the temptation to spend, nor would it be rational for them to do so. The cost of government programs is spread among millions of taxpayers, while the benefits of federal spending can be concentrated on a few who will reward their benefactors with votes and campaign contributions. The ability to pay for programs through government deficits further encourages spending, because the burden of government debt is even more diffuse than the tax burden — it extends across generations to the not-yet-born (and, more importantly, the not-yet-voting). This dynamic of dispersed costs to pay for targeted benefits often leads to grateful and energized beneficiaries without affecting those who foot the bill significantly enough to rouse them to political action. Even if taxpayers decide to exact an electoral price from politicians who impose costs on them, voters are likely to hold all lawmakers responsible for increased taxes or a higher deficit — not just the big spenders — because government programs are seldom linked closely to funding mechanisms. If that is the case, only a dupe of a legislator would abstain from pork barrel politics. She is going to suffer the consequences (if any) of her colleagues' actions so she might as well enjoy spending federal dollars on her constituents.

But, notwithstanding the awareness of this collective action problem, Congress did not achieve consensus in 1974 that deficit reduction should be the goal of the budget process. Instead, the Congressional Budget Act was designed to allow members more control, centralization, and coordination but in a way that was neutral with respect to outcomes. Of course, the process that it adopted would affect outcomes, but it was not designed at the outset to favor either reduced or increased spending. It was intended merely to provide a framework that would shape the political forces determining the scope and distribution of federal spending.[o]

Not surprisingly, given its genesis in the Nixon impoundment crisis, the Budget Act included provisions to formalize the impoundment process and to clarify that Congress retains a firm grasp on the power of the purse. Under its provisions. the President can propose to withhold spending (a *rescission*) or to delay spending (a *deferral*), although a deferral cannot serve policy reasons but can be used only to reflect efficiencies. Before a rescission can go into effect, both houses must approve it; a deferral can take effect without congressional action, but it cannot last longer than the end of the fiscal year. By requiring congressional approval for rescissions, the 1974 Act makes impoundments much less likely, and it largely ended this part of the interbranch budget war.

---

n. See John Cogan, *The Dispersion of Spending Authority and Federal Budget Deficits*, in *The Budget Puzzle: Understanding Federal Spending* 16, 26–27 (John Cogan, Timothy Muris & Allen Schick eds., 1994).

o. See Philip Joyce, *Congressional Budget Reform: The Unanticipated Implications for Federal Policy Making*, 56 Pub. Admin. Rev. 317, 318 (1996). But see Louis Fisher, *The Budget Act of 1974: A Further Loss of Spending Control*, in *Congressional Budgeting: Politics, Process, and Power* 170 (Thomas Wander, Ted Hebert & Gary Copeland eds., 1984) (arguing that the 1974 Act actually eroded budget discipline and increased federal spending).

Three other aspects of the 1974 Act are noteworthy: its emphasis on the development of information about the federal budget and creation of the Congressional Budget Office to produce that data; the establishment of two new budget committees; and the creation of a centralized budget process in Congress to increase accountability for spending and revenue decisions.

During the impoundment battles, Congress had been at a disadvantage because it lacked its own budget analysts and policy experts. The Congressional Budget Office (CBO) was created to provide Congress with objective and timely analyses needed for budget decisions and with the information and budget estimates required for the congressional budget process to function. CBO groups its current responsibilities, which have been expanded since 1974, into four categories: "helping Congress formulate a budget plan, helping it stay within that plan, helping it assess the impact of federal mandates, and helping it consider issues related to the budget and to economic policies."[p]

The CBO Director is appointed by the Speaker of the House and the President pro tempore of the Senate, with the input of the budget committees. The Director oversees a staff of over 230 full-time positions, 70% of whom are professionals with degrees in economics or public policy. One of the lasting effects of the 1974 Act has been the production and dissemination of a flood of budget information and a substantial improvement in the expertise available to lawmakers. Although budget estimates often prove to be erroneous because forecasting economic developments and budget trends is far from an exact science, CBO generally receives very high marks for its work.

Although CBO provides information and assistance to all legislators, it works most closely with the Senate and House budget committees, which are also creatures of the 1974 Act. The budget committees, which have their own specialized staffs, were layered on top of the existing committee structure; the tax-writing and appropriations committees were so jealous of their turfs that they would not willingly give up any of their power. Of course, the institutionalization of new congressional players inevitably affected the power of existing entities, but it was unclear in 1974 who would win and who would lose under the new arrangement, making adoption of the process politically possible. The House Budget Committee's composition reflects its uneasy relationship with the traditional power brokers of the budget process. The terms of members of this committee are limited, and the committee includes representatives from the Appropriations Committee and from Ways and Means.

At the outset, the budget committees' primary responsibility was drafting and managing the concurrent budget resolution, discussed below. Otherwise, they served mainly ministerial roles — collating other committees' submissions to create an omnibus budget reconciliation bill, for example — but over time

---

p. See the Congressional Budget Office web page at http://www.cbo.gov. See also Nancy Kates, Susan Irving, & James Verdier, *Starting from Scratch: Alice Rivlin and the Congressional Budget Office* (1989) (Harvard University's Kennedy School of Government Case Study C16–88–873) (a public policy school case study describing the first director of the CBO, Alice Rivlin, and her successful efforts to set up a relatively independent office).

they have received more substantive responsibilities. Furthermore, members now view these committees as important power bases with influence over a great deal of congressional business. Because of the circumstances surrounding their creation and because the longstanding norm of seniority was not firmly entrenched in these new committees, they are seen as more closely affiliated with party leaders, and their members behave more as partisans then do lawmakers on the other committees concerned with federal spending and revenue.[q]

Finally, the 1974 Act put into place a centralized process governing Congress' budget decisions for each fiscal year. This process was designed to ensure that important budget decisions are made by Congress through a transparent system that allows voters to hold their representatives accountable for the country's fiscal policies. Although there have been substantial changes over the nearly three decades since the 1974 Act's enactment, it established the basic features of the budget process. First, the 1974 Act set out a timetable to govern congressional budget decisionmakers, a timetable that begins with the submission of the President's budget early in the session (now the first Monday in February) and concludes with the passage of all the appropriations bills by the beginning of the fiscal year in October. The current budget timetable is set out in Figure 4–2.

Figure 4–2: Budget Calendar

The following timetable highlights the scheduled dates for significant budget events during the year.

Between the 1st Monday in January and
the 1st Monday in February .... President transmits the budget.

April 15 .... Action to be completed on congressional budget resolution.

May 15 .... House consideration of annual appropriations bills may begin.

June 15 .... Action to be completed on reconciliation.

June 30 .... Action on appropriations to be completed by House.

October 1 .... Fiscal year begins; All appropriations bill should be enacted.

15 days after the end of a
session of Congress .... OMB issues final sequestration report,
and the President issues a sequestration order, if necessary.

Source: *The Budget System and Concepts, Budget of the United States Government Fiscal Year 2001* 5 (2000)

In practice, Congress often misses the deadline to pass all appropriations bills and must keep the government running by passing a series of stopgap

---

q. See Lance LeLoup, *The Fiscal Congress: Legislative Control of the Budget* 57–105 (1980); Mathew McCubbins, *Note: Budget Policy-making and the Appearance of Power,* 6 J. L. Econ. & Org. 133, 140 (Special Issue, 1990).

continuing resolutions. These resolutions provide that funding for agencies and federal projects will continue until final appropriations bills are enacted; they usually provide the same funding level as the agencies were given in the previous fiscal year or some percentage of that amount. Continuing resolutions are temporary measures that typically expire in a few days or weeks, although they can control government spending for most or all of a fiscal year if Congress and the President cannot reach agreement on permanent bills.

Second, before any spending bills or revenue legislation can be considered, Congress must pass *a concurrent budget resolution* setting out the macro-budgetary goals for the next five fiscal years. John Gilmour explains the significance of the budget resolution: It is "a comprehensive statement of the general outlines of the budget; it is intended to be adopted early in the session, before floor consideration of actual spending and revenue legislation, and designed to structure subsequent legislative action." *Reconcilable Differences? Congress, the Budget Process, and the Deficit* 64 (1990). For example, the budget resolution sets spending limits for discretionary programs, determines the amount of revenue that should be raised in taxes every year, reveals congressional priorities by dividing resources among various budget functions (or major categories of governmental activities), and provides for the debt limit. The concurrent resolution does not require that any particular programmatic changes be made to achieve its broad objectives, although the budget committees often include nonbinding recommendations for specific changes. Filling in the details is left up to the appropriations subcommittees, the substantive committees with jurisdiction over entitlement programs, and the tax-writing committees. This fiscal blueprint is in the form of a concurrent resolution, so it is not law and is not signed by the President. Its aggregate totals are enforced only through parliamentary devices, discussed below.

Thus, the 1974 Act set the framework in place, but it provided only *process rules*, to govern how a decision is reached, and not *outcome-oriented rules*, which are explicitly designed to facilitate particular decisions.[r] An overlooked provision, the Act's elastic clause, was used by deficit hawks to begin the process of changing the congressional framework that was initially intended to be neutral in its effect on substantive budget outcomes into one designed to reduce federal deficits and federal spending. The final step in the development of the modern congressional budget process was the rise of the legislative vehicle of *reconciliation* and the enactment of the Balanced Budget and Emergency Deficit Control Act of 1985, Pub. L. No. 99–177, 99 Stat. 1037, better known as the Gramm-Rudman-Hollings Act.

3. *Gramm-Rudman-Hollings and the Preoccupation with the Federal Deficit.* The 1980s witnessed another series of budget conflicts, in this case driven by the country's preoccupation with budget deficits. In fiscal year 1982, the federal budget deficit was over $110 billion, and, by the middle of the decade, the federal deficit was well over $200 billion. During the mid-1980s, the federal deficit represented 5.5 percent of GNP, up significantly from 2

---

    r. See Eric Hanushek, *Formula Budgeting: The Economics and Analytics of Fiscal Policy under Rules,* 6 J. of Pol'y Analysis & Mgmt. 3 (1986) (drawing the distinction).

percent of GNP in the 1970s.[s] In response, Congress used an obscure part of the 1974 Act, reconciliation, to cut federal outlays. A brief history and description of reconciliation will clarify how it came to play such a vital role in the federal legislative process.

In addition to setting forth aggregate spending and revenue targets, concurrent budget resolutions often contain *reconciliation instructions*. These commands to other committees require them to report legislation to Congress bringing existing law into conformity with the macrobudgetary objectives of the resolution. Remember that the instructions do not mandate particular programmatic changes; they merely set forth the goals that each committee must reach through new laws. For example, the tax-writing committees might be instructed to raise an additional $50 billion in revenues or to find $50 billion in spending reductions in entitlement programs. Unlike the submission of the President's budget or the concurrent budget resolution, the reconciliation process is an optional part of the budget process and does not occur every year.

Reconciliation is now one of the most potent aspects of the congressional budget process, but it was not used at all in the first four years after the 1974 Act was adopted, in part because reconciliation was supposed to occur very late in the process.[t] Nevertheless, some budget experts understood that, if they reconfigured reconciliation, it could be among Congress' most powerful tools to control the budgeting process.[u] Not only does reconciliation centralize the process, but it also allows more opportunities for logrolling in order to form majority support. In a lengthy and complex bill like a reconciliation bill, many deals, some of them questionable, can often be hidden from public view, at least until after enactment. Moreover, opponents of such provisions may stifle their objections if the proposal contains enough other provisions that they support. Legislative commitments are more credible when they occur as part of one omnibus bill; for example, a lawmaker who will support cuts in Medicare only in return for significant tax breaks will prefer an arrangement that allows both parts of the deal to be enacted simultaneously. In addition, a reconciliation bill enjoys the benefit of a number of budget rules designed to ensure its smooth passage and to avoid delays. The time for consideration of the bill on the Senate floor is strictly limited; when twenty hours expire, the Senate must vote on all pending amendments and then on the underlying bill. In other words, a reconciliation bill cannot be debated to death in the Senate by a filibuster.

In 1981, the House Budget Committee solved the problems that had weakened reconciliation by aggressively interpreting the 1974 Act's *elastic clause*. A provision in the 1974 Budget Act allowed the budget committees to

---

s. See Allen Schick, *The Capacity to Budget* 70–75 (1990); Edward Gramlich, *U.S. Federal Budget Deficits and Gramm-Rudman-Hollings*, 80 Am. Econ. Rev. 75 (1990).

t. See Howard Shuman, *Politics and the Budget: The Struggle Between the President and Congress* 256 (3d ed. 1992).

u. See William Dauster, *The Congressional Budget Process*, in *Fiscal Challenges, supra*; Elizabeth Garrett, *The Congressional Budget Process: Strengthening the Party-in-Government*, 100 Colum. L. Rev. 702, 718–20 (2000).

implement "other procedures * * * as may be appropriate." Under the authority of this vague clause, the congressional rules were modified to coordinate reconciliation with the first budget resolution, typically passed in the spring. This change caused the second resolution to wither away. The following year, David Stockman, Reagan's first OMB Director, used the reconciliation process to enact unprecedented budget cuts, both in the entitlement arena and in appropriated discretionary spending. The Omnibus Budget Reconciliation Act passed in 1981 was projected to cut outlays by over $130 billion over three fiscal years.[v]

The use of reconciliation demonstrated that process rules could work to address the political problem of budget deficits, but it soon became apparent that the 1974 Act's framework was not sufficient to force change. After the congressional elections in 1982 increased the Democratic majority in the House and chastened the Republican majority in the Senate, reconciliation alone "no longer seemed a viable option to the [Reagan] administration," and it began to look for other tools. Wildavsky & Caiden, *The New Politics of the Budgetary Process, supra*, at 112. The pressure continued to build, and in 1985, Congress passed the Gramm-Rudman-Hollings Act (GRH), which was designed to force Congress to meet a series of deficit targets through draconian spending cuts so that the deficit would be eliminated in five years. If Congress did not adopt legislation implementing policy changes sufficient to meet deficit targets, then the Act required automatic and uniform reductions in government programs. This pro rata reduction in spending is a kind of impoundment called a *sequester*. In other words, GRH acted as a *precommitment device*, binding Congress in the future to reduce the federal deficit, either by rearranging priorities, trimming and eliminating some federal programs, and increasing government revenues; or by deploying an automatic process of sequester that would require deep and uniform cuts from all federal discretionary programs.[w]

This important change in the budget process — which made it explicitly outcome-oriented — was adopted without public hearings, without committee debate, and with virtually no debate on the floor. "Opinions understandably vary as to whether [GRH] was meant to be workable. If (as in the phrase Senator Rudman made famous, 'it's so bad, it's good') the idea was to scare lawmakers into reducing the deficit, the consequences would have to be horrendous. And, if it followed the full course, so they would be, wiping out half of general government. Anticipating this havoc, legislators might be motivated to settle on a more variegated and hence more sensible deficit-reduction package than across-the-board cuts. * * * In this game of budgetary chicken, one side assumed that as automatic cuts were triggered, the Republicans would blink by raising taxes while the other hoped that as meat-ax cuts in domestic spending drew near, Democrats would blink by making the policy decisions needed for domestic reductions. Each side hoped to prevail by

---

v. See Senator Howard Baker, *An Introduction to the Politics of Reconciliation*, 20 Harv. J. on Legis. 1, 2 (1983).

w. See Garrett, *The Purposes of Framework Laws, supra*, at 748–54 (discussing framework laws that facilitate precommitment).

making the budgetary process unworkable." Wildavsky & Caiden, *supra*, at 128. Most observers have concluded that the threat of sequestration never operated as anticipated; for example, negotiations to avoid a sequester in 1987 became serious only after a stock market crash convinced lawmakers that they needed to act responsibly to restore market confidence. Arguably, the distress in the market would have prompted spending changes without the GRH framework. See Gilmour, *Irreconcilable Differences, supra,* at 216–220.

GRH was both more and less draconian than it appears to be from this brief description. It was less draconian because nearly half of the federal budget, primarily entitlement spending, was exempted from any sequester. For example, Social Security and interest on the debt were fully exempted, and other entitlements like Medicare were partially exempted. In all, only fourteen percent of the domestic budget was threatened by a sequester.[x] Tax expenditures were also ignored by GRH. But this configuration of eligible and exempt programs also made GRH more draconian with respect to programs subject to sequestration, primarily discretionary spending for domestic and defense programs. GRH required these programs to share the pain in equal measure; half of all cuts were to come from domestic programs and half from defense. Because Congress found it could not accept the severe program cuts in domestic and defense that would have been required to meet GRH's deficit targets, it amended GRH in 1987, easing the targets and postponing the balanced budget to 1993.

Economic conditions only deteriorated after passage of GRH; the budget deficit was higher in the final year of GRH than it had been the year before the deficit reduction bill had been enacted. In 1990, the situation became intolerable. The GRH target allowed a deficit in fiscal year 1991 of only $64 billion, but budget forecasts indicated that the deficit might be as high as $230 billion, which would trigger a devastating sequester. President Bush had campaigned on a "read my lips" pledge not to raise taxes, so he found it politically difficult to accept a package of spending cuts and tax increases to avert the across-the-board cuts. Ultimately, congressional leaders and members of the executive branch retired to a *budget summit* to hammer out a compromise package of some tax increases and some reductions in both discretionary and entitlement spending. The package promised deficit reduction of $500 billion over five years, and it included an entirely new budget process that built on the past and provided the framework for the current budget process.

The 1990 budget summit is an example of a form of decisionmaking increasingly common in the modern legislative process, not only in the context of budget legislation.[y] Summits tend to occur when the normal legislative process has produced stalemate in an arena where gridlock is unacceptable. In

---

x. Kate Stith, *Rewriting the Fiscal Constitution: The Case of Gramm-Rudman-Hollings,* 76 Cal. L. Rev. 595, 655 (1988).

y. See Barbara Sinclair, *Unorthodox Lawmaking: New Legislative Processes in the U.S. Congress* 77–79 (2d ed. 2000) (discussing rise of summits as technique in budget and other contexts).

many cases, substantive divisions are simply not resolved. Gridlock continues until the next election allows different coalitions to form or brings new issues to the forefront of the political agenda. In contrast, budget stalemates can lead to temporary political disasters with parts of the government shutting down, but such a state of affairs cannot last indefinitely. In 1990, President Bush's "Read my lips, no new taxes" pledge seemed to rule out one way to deal with the substantial deficit. His political opponents in Congress were unwilling to sacrifice their own spending priorities to help him keep his word, and they hoped the pressure of the budget crisis would cause him to break his vow and significantly harm his chances for reelection. This incident demonstrates that reaching agreement can be stymied when compromise will diminish future electoral prospects by reducing issue advantages. Stalemate can also result from the unwillingness of any legislative player to be the first to propose the inevitable solution because of the political costs of such a reasonable offer. See John Gilmour, *Strategic Disagreement: Stalemate in American Politics* 39–41 (1995).

When continued inaction leads to calamitous outcomes such as a government shutdown, one solution is compromise through a summit. At a summit, where negotiations and compromise occur in private and cannot be traced to particular people or entities, participants can craft a proposal that allows a majority of lawmakers to vote for otherwise unacceptable legislation. In the budget context, the settlement is presented as a large omnibus proposal with palatable provisions balancing unpalatable ones, amendments are virtually impossible because of the rules of deliberation, and delay is unlikely. Usually, summit leaders have a sufficient feel for the positions of other lawmakers to draft a package with enough goodies to obtain majority support. Occasionally, the package remains too controversial to pass: The 1990 budget agreement, with its mix of entitlement cuts and tax increases, was first defeated in the House and was enacted only after the committees made changes in the provisions affecting Medicare spending. Congress finally passed the reconciliation bill, which included the Budget Enforcement Act of 1990 (BEA), Pub. L. No. 101–508, 104 Stat. 1388 (codified in scattered sections of 2 U.S.C.), the current framework for budget decisionmaking.

B. THE BUDGET ENFORCEMENT ACT OF 1990 AND THE POLITICS OF OFFSETS

Perhaps the BEA's most substantial change from Gramm-Rudman-Hollings is that deficit targets became much less important, and budgeting is now often controlled by a series of spending caps and offset requirements. Deficits and surpluses are the creatures of economic conditions outside Congress' control as much as they are the products of spending and revenue decisions. By allowing the spending and revenue decisions to control the process rather than the amount of the deficit, Congress adopted a more reasonable framework for federal budgeting and one that was more likely to be successful. It was also a less stringent system, giving some support to those who argue that Congress just changes the rules when they force difficult or unpopular decisions.[z] In fairness, however, while the BEA framework is a less onerous system, it is not an illusory one, and it included controls over tax expenditures and direct spending that GRH did not. Thus, Congress did not entirely give in to its desire to spend freely when it replaced Gramm-Rudman-Hollings with the BEA; it maintained some discipline that would influence fiscal decision-making.

The current process is divided into packages, or arenas of conflict.[a] Lawmakers set macrobudgetary spending or revenue goals for these packages and make tradeoffs among the programs within the budget packages. The budget is split into three arenas: 1) discretionary spending programs that receive periodic, usually annual, appropriations; 2) direct spending programs and revenue provisions that typically remain in effect until repealed; and 3) Social Security. We will focus on the first two packages in this chapter, although it is worth emphasizing the extraordinary protection accorded to Social Security by budget rules. The Social Security trust fund is theoretically *off-budget*, although it is shown as part of the unified budget, and lawmakers have relied on the surplus in the Social Security trust fund to reach overall balanced federal budgets. Social Security is protected by congressional rules so that changes reducing benefits or worsening the trust fund's actuarial condition are difficult to adopt. As we noted, Social Security has always been absolutely protected from sequesters. Of course, all this is in addition to the nearly invincible political protection the entitlement program enjoys.[b]

1. *Rules Affecting the Discretionary Spending Package.* Although a great deal of political rhetoric is lavished on Social Security reform, most of the action in Congress involves the two other packages. Until 2002, discretionary spending was controlled by statutory spending caps that were often decreased in real terms (and sometimes in nominal ones as well). For example, the balanced budget agreement reached in 1997 aimed to severely constrain discretionary spending; for example, the caps were not adjusted to increase with inflation. Figure 4–3 provides the caps set for budget authority by the 1997 budget act and also reveals the level of budget authority that Congress subsequently enacted so you can compare the targets to the spending that

---

z. For a balanced assessment of that argument, see James Thurber, *If the Game is Too Hard, Change the Rules: Congressional Budget Reforms in the 1990s*, in *Remaking Congress: Change and Stability in the 1990s* 130 (James Thurber & Roger Davidson eds., 1995).

a. See Naomi Caiden, *The New Rules of the Federal Budget Game*, 44 Pub. Admin. Rev., Mar.–Apr. 1984, at 109, 112–114.

b. See Committee for a Responsible Federal Budget, *Social Security Reform: Economic and Budget Concepts, Enforcement, and Scorekeeping Perspectives* (1998) (discussing the budget rules and their impact on various reform proposals). For discussion of the Social Security program, its history and reform proposals, see Michael Graetz & Jerry Mashaw, *True Security: Rethinking American Social Insurance* (1999); Eugene Steuerle & Jon Bakija, *Retooling Social Security for the 21st Century: Right and Wrong Approaches to Reform* (1994); *Framing the Social Security Debate: Values, Politics and Economics* (R. Douglas Arnold, Michael Graetz & Alicia Munnell eds., 1998); *Social Security: What Role for the Future?* (Peter Diamond, David Lindeman & Howard Young eds., 1996).

occurred. Why was there such divergence between the caps and actual experience? Read on for the description of how the BEA was supposed to work in theory and how it worked in practice.

Figure 4–3: Comparison of Discretionary Spending Caps & Actual Budget Authority (in billions)

	1998	1999	2000	2001
Discretionary Spending Caps set by 1997 Budget Act	527	533	537	542
Actual Budget Authority	534	583	587	635

Source: *A Blueprint for New Beginnings: A Responsible Budget for America's Priorities* 172 (2001).

If spending exceeded the statutory cap, the BEA required the President to enforce the cap by implementing a sequester to reduce funding for nonexempt programs in the package. In other words, excessive spending on discretionary programs should have resulted in a pro rata reduction in spending for discretionary programs. For example, as Figure 4–3 shows, discretionary spending for fiscal year 2001 — which was finalized only in a lame-duck congressional session after the passage of 21 stopgap continuing resolutions to keep the government running past the end of fiscal year 2000 — exceeded the original statutory cap by nearly $100 billion. Why didn't a sequester result? The spending that exceeded the statutory caps in fiscal year 2001 did not trigger sequestration because Congress had slipped into the Foreign Operations Appropriations Act a provision raising the statutory cap in an attempt to evade budget discipline without triggering public outcry.[c]

Is it a coincidence that there had been a $236 billion budget surplus in 2000 and projections indicated a sustained period of budget surpluses? We think not. Members of Congress were less eager to abide by fiscal constraints they had enacted in years of chronic deficits. Congress' decision to ignore stringent discretionary caps played a role in undermining the forecasts of large and sustained budget surpluses because those projections were based on the assumption that Congress would continue to restrain spending and forego large tax cuts. The combination of two substantial tax cuts enacted in 2001 and 2003, higher spending because of the terrorist attacks of September 11, 2001, a military action in Afghanistan and a war in Iraq, and a recession soon put the country back into cash-flow deficits. The Congressional Budget Office revealed that the fiscal year 2006 deficit was $248 billion. *The Budget and Economic Outlook: Fiscal Years 2008 to 2017, supra,* at XII. Although CBO projected deficits would grow smaller in subsequent years with a surplus by

---

c. See Daniel Parks, *Ballooning the Bottom Line: Blame Enough for Two Parties,* Cong. Q. Weekly Rep., Oct. 28, 2000, at 2529.

2012, this estimate depends on Congress and the President allowing some popular tax reductions to expire as scheduled over the next few years. If those cuts are made permanent, "total revenues would be almost $3 trillion lower over the next 10 years than CBO now projects."

With the return to chronic cash-flow deficits, how do you expect Congress and the President to respond? What changes, if any, should we anticipate in the federal budget process? Are procedural changes really necessary? For example, in 2003 President Bush originally proposed a tax cut of over $750 billion, but Republican moderates in the 108th Congress insisted that the ten-year cost of any tax cut be no more than $350 billion, and that some of the funds go to states to help them deal with their looming budget crises. Thus, the give-and-take of ordinary politics, even when the same party controlled both branches, apparently managed to reduce the cost of the tax bill by over half.

Will stringent budget rules really impose fiscal discipline? One way Congress met the demands of Senate moderates in 2003 was to phase out or sunset many of the tax reductions. For example, the provisions alleviating the tax burden on married couples expired at the end of 2004; the dividend tax relief provisions expired at the end of 2008; and the higher child credit expired at the end of 2004. (Many of the provisions were subsequently extended, although few were made permanent.) Using sunset provisions in this way kept the apparent cost of the tax bill within the bounds necessary to get 50 votes in the Senate for the reconciliation package, allowing Vice-President Cheney to break the tie. However, supporters of the cuts began working before the ink was dry on the reconciliation bill to extend them or make them permanent. Proponents had made it difficult for Congress to allow the provisions to expire by sunsetting them in election years when the failure to extend could be perceived by voters as a tax increase. Does this suggest that gimmicks allow legislators to evade fiscal discipline with little political cost?[d]

For congressional budgeting purposes, the discretionary package also has subdivisions that correspond to the jurisdiction of the twelve appropriations subcommittees. This system is separate from the statutory caps, and it shapes budgeting even in years where there are no spending caps in effect. Annual budget resolutions allocate discretionary funds to the House and Senate Appropriations Committees, which then make suballocations to their subcommittees. New programs can receive funding only if they can fit within the spending caps and within the suballocations; when the caps are not increasing each year, they can succeed legislatively only if some previously funded programs receive fewer funds or no money at all. These allocations are enforced through parliamentary rules, described below, not through the sequester process. Because of this de facto offset requirement, those seeking federal funds often must adopt the posture of funding predators searching for existing programs to target for elimination or reduction in order to make new funds available.

---

d. For a discussion of the various gimmicks in the 2003 tax bill and other revenue and budget laws, see Cheryl Block, *Budget Gimmicks*, in *Fiscal Challenges*, *supra*; Elizabeth Garrett, *Accounting for the Federal Budget and its Reform*, 41 Harv. J. on Legis. 187 (2004).

2. *The Package of Entitlements and Revenue Provisions.* The other large budget package consists of revenue provisions and direct spending programs. Most of the programs in this package fall within the jurisdiction of the tax-writing committees, although other committees have jurisdiction over some entitlement programs. Unlike discretionary funds which are typically subject to annual appropriations decisions, tax expenditures and direct spending programs usually remain in effect until repealed. Until 2002, decisions in the tax/direct spending package were enforced not through spending caps, but through an explicit offset requirement in the BEA called the pay-as-you-go (PAYGO) provision. Under PAYGO, "direct spending and revenue legislation that increases the deficit in any fiscal year * * * must be offset by legislation reducing spending or increasing revenues so that the net deficit is not increased."[e]

It was not the goal of PAYGO to reduce any deficit, to decrease spending for established entitlement programs, or to minimize revenue loss from existing tax expenditures. Rather, PAYGO aimed merely to ensure that new legislation would not increase the deficit or dissipate the surplus. In other words, if spending for an existing entitlement program increased because more persons qualified for it or because benefits were automatically adjusted to account for a higher cost of living, PAYGO was not triggered. Similarly, if revenue losses from previously enacted tax expenditures exceeded expectations because more taxpayers claimed them, PAYGO did not demand that Congress find an offset. However, if higher spending resulted from new entitlement programs, new tax expenditures, or new laws that expand existing programs, PAYGO applied. PAYGO was enforced through a sequester; if revenue losses were not fully offset, OMB was required to reduce outlays uniformly for certain direct spending programs. Just as with Gramm-Rudman-Hollings, however, most entitlement programs were exempt from a sequester, and tax expenditures were not subject to any pro rata reduction.

The short era of budget surpluses eroded much of the discipline provided by PAYGO, even before it expired in 2002. Throughout the 106th Congress, lawmakers enacted changes in revenues and direct spending that reduced the surplus by a net of $10.5 billion and would have triggered a PAYGO sequestration. In an omnibus Consolidated Appropriations Act for Fiscal Year 2001, Pub. L. No. 106–554, 114 Stat. 2763, however, Congress directed OMB scorekeepers to set the PAYGO scorecard (the mechanism that keeps track of changes and determines whether sequestration is necessary) to zero, thereby avoiding a sequester and allowing the next Congress a clean slate for the future. See Congressional Budget Office, *Final Sequestration Report for Fiscal Year 2001* 9–14 (2000). This technique of avoiding budget rules is called *directed scorekeeping*, because the legislators require the scorekeepers at OMB to act in particular ways to avoid negative budget outcomes like a sequester. Although the statutory PAYGO provisions expired in 2002, the Democratic Congress adopted PAYGO in 2007 as part of its internal rules.

---

e. Edward Davis, *"Pay-As-You-Go" Budget Enforcement Procedures in 1992* (Congressional Research Service document 1992).

Because this fiscal discipline was adopted as an internal rule in each house, and not as part of a statute, it is not enforced through sequester as the BEA's provisions were; rather, this form of PAYGO relies on parliamentary devices, discussed below, for its teeth.

While both sides of the budget were affected by offset requirements under the Budget Enforcement Act's structure, the nature of the competition engendered by the PAYGO requirement was different from the conflict that characterized the discretionary side of the budget. Caps on annually appropriated discretionary funds meant that advocates of new spending had to identify other spending programs that could be repealed or scaled back so that there was room under the cap. In most cases, the offset process occurred within the jurisdiction of the relevant appropriations subcommittee, which meant that the competition occurred within a subset of programs related loosely by subject matter. For example, the Appropriations Subcommittee on Agriculture and Rural Development oversees many, but not all, of the programs affecting agriculture (as well as some other unrelated programs). So a new program in the jurisdiction of that subcommittee mostly competed with other spending opportunities in agriculture.

In contrast, groups proposing a new tax subsidy were not limited to finding offsets in the universe of programs that largely serve the same governmental objective or benefit similar groups. Instead, proponents could meet PAYGO requirements by eliminating any current tax benefit or entitlement spending. For examples, advocates of a new tax deduction for farmers compete against all other beneficiaries of tax proposals and entitlements, not only against others seeking funds for agriculture initiatives. Presumably, then, the conflict that results from offset requirements look somewhat different in the two packages of discretionary spending and direct spending/tax subsidies. We will return to this dynamic caused by budget conflict when we discuss interest group behavior in the budget process.

3. *Enforcing the Budgetary Rules.* Statutory requirements like discretionary spending caps and PAYGO in the BEA (which expired in 2002) were enforced through sequesters implemented by the executive branch. But the budget process is also characterized by dozens of congressional rules that shape deliberation and decisionmaking and that are enforced through parliamentary devices called *points of order.* When legislation is considered on the floor of Congress and a member believes the proposal violates a budget rule or some aspect of the congressional budget resolution, the member may object that the bill is out of order. In the House, these points of order are often waived automatically in the special rule structuring the debate (see Chapter 1, § 1, discussing the role of rules in the House)); thus, House members cannot easily object to violations of congressional rules. In the Senate, however, any member can raise a point of order and force a vote of the body on whether to sustain the objection and derail the bill or to waive the objection and continue deliberation. In some cases, Senate rules require a supermajority vote of three-fifths of the senators to waive a point of order.

The 60-vote requirement in the Senate empowers the Senate Budget Committee relative to its House counterpart. If a deal proposed by the House during the conference committee stage threatens to require a supermajority vote in the Senate, Senate negotiators can usually successfully resist its inclusion into the final proposal. The supermajority requirement also mandates that both political parties in the Senate cooperate on budget matters, at least when a proposed course of action would violate certain budget rules and no party has a commanding majority of 60 or more senators. Actions that can prompt a 60-vote point of order include considering legislation that violates the suballocations of discretionary resources to appropriations subcommittees, considering an amendment to a reconciliation bill that is not revenue neutral, considering certain changes to the Social Security trust fund, and considering revenue or direct spending legislation that would increase the deficit during a ten-year window following enactment.

One of the budget rules that receive this extraordinary protection is the *Byrd Rule*, named after its author, the powerful Senator Byrd of West Virginia. The rule responds to concerns that senators would take advantage of the privileges accorded to a reconciliation bill — in particular, the protection from the filibuster, which virtually guarantees that a reconciliation proposal will pass Congress in some form — to attach as many provisions onto the omnibus bill as possible. A legislative vehicle that is virtually assured of enactment is too tempting for most senators to resist. Just as legislators adopt rules to discourage riders to appropriations bills because they are often the products of too little deliberation, members feared that floor amendments to reconciliation laws were more likely to be ill-conceived proposals that had escaped public scrutiny. Therefore, the Byrd Rule restricts the inclusion of *extraneous material* in a reconciliation bill, a change from the normal Senate practice of allowing nongermane provisions to be added to legislation without violating any rules. A provision is extraneous "if it does not change revenues or outlays, * * * is outside the jurisdiction of the committee that inserted the provision, has outlay or revenue provisions that are merely incidental to nonbudgetary items, or would increase future deficits. * * * Because of the rule's complexity, its application depends on parliamentary interpretation. The rule has blocked provisions that some may have deemed relevant to deficit reduction while permitting others that have had little impact on the deficit."[f]

These internal enforcement procedures, particularly the supermajority voting requirements, have sparked concern and criticism. First, what is the remedy if Congress passes a law in violation of a budget rule? For example, if a senator believes that a reconciliation law contains extraneous material, can he (or someone else) challenge that law in court because it violated the Byrd Rule? Does it make a difference whether he raised the objection in the Senate and lost? In Article I, § 5, cl. 2, the Constitution commits to each house the power to "determine the Rules of its Proceedings," and the courts have been unwilling to police congressional application of internal rules. Although most of the budget rules discussed in this Section are found in statutes enacted by both houses and signed by the President, the statutes always identify these sections as exercises of Congress' constitutional rulemaking authority and thus

---

f. Schick, *The Federal Budget: Politics, Policy, Process, supra*, at 128.

amenable to unilateral change without statutory amendment.[g] Again, courts have been willing to accept this argument and treat rules that appear in statutes just as they do rules enacted by the resolution of only one house. See, e.g., *Metzenbaum v. Federal Energy Regulatory Comm'n*, 675 F.2d 1282 (D.C. Cir. 1982) (describing such rules as "binding upon [the House] only by its own choice" and holding their enforcement to be nonjusticiable political questions).

Does a due process of lawmaking perspective suggest that courts should be more active in enforcing rules designed to promote deliberation and rational lawmaking? For example, if the Byrd Rule operates to prohibit the inclusion of provisions that have not received adequate committee consideration or that will be lost in a complex omnibus bill and thus allow representatives to escape accountability, should it be more aggressively enforced by an impartial judiciary?[h]

A second objection to the budget rules focuses on the supermajority requirements. For some time, there has been a concern that supermajority voting requirements entrench the policy preferences of one Congress with respect to future Congresses. In the budget context, the rules operate to privilege deficit reduction and spending control over increased federal spending, making it harder for current members of Congress to depart from the policies chosen by their predecessors. Under our system of democratic rule, the argument goes, current majorities ought to be able to determine policy without overcoming hurdles requiring supermajority votes.[i]

Critics of the supermajority requirements of budget rules have had to grapple with how their arguments affect the filibuster process in the Senate. As you remember from the Civil Rights Act case study in Chapter 1, Senate Rule XXII requires 60 senators to vote for cloture in order to bring debate to a close and end a filibuster. This rule is particularly problematic because it probably cannot be changed by a majority vote. First, any change to a Senate rule can be filibustered, and then a two-thirds vote is required for cloture. Moreover, Senate rules are difficult to change generally because they are perpetually in effect; budget rules expire occasionally and are the subject of frequent amendment. Unlike the House, which adopts its rules at the beginning of each session, a practice that allows for changes to be proposed as part of the new body of rules, the Senate is a continuing body because two-thirds of the membership remains the same after each election. Thus, "[t]he rules of the

---

g. See Aaron-Andrew Bruhl, *Using Statutes to Set Legislative Rules: Entrenchment, Separation of Powers, and the Rules of Proceedings Clause*, 19 J. L. & Pol. 345 (2003) (using the term "statutized rules").

h. For further discussion, see Michael Miller, *The Justiciability of Legislative Rules and the "Political" Political Question Doctrine*, 78 Cal. L. Rev. 1341 (1990).

i. See, e.g., Paul Kahn, *Gramm-Rudman and the Capacity of Congress To Control the Future*, 13 Hastings Const. L.Q. 185, 188 (1986) (arguing that "[t]he kind of control of the legislative function that [GRH] intends can only be accomplished constitutionally through the amendment process, not by statute"); Michael Klarman, *Majoritarian Judicial Review: The Entrenchment Problem*, 85 Geo. L.J. 491 (1997) (objecting to cross-temporal entrenchment that seeks to bind future majorities).

Senate shall continue from one Congress to the next Congress unless they are changed as provided in these rules." Senate Rule XXXII(2). Some have concluded that the combined force of these rules is to render the current filibuster system unconstitutional because it is virtually impossible to change them by simple majority vote.[j] In contrast, all budget rules, even those requiring supermajority votes, can be repealed or changed by a majority vote of the relevant house of Congress.

Some have argued that the need for 60 votes to invoke cloture could be avoided by the following parliamentary maneuver: A senator could raise a constitutional point of order suggesting that the filibuster is unconstitutional. The presiding officer of the Senate would agree, and through a series of procedural moves, the body would decide the constitutional point of order through a majority vote. Although this scenario is possible,[k] it has so far only been floated as a trial balloon. The threat of this so-called "nuclear option" in 2005 enabled a slim Republican majority in the Senate to ensure the confirmation of several conservative nominees to the federal courts of appeals, overcoming a filibuster by the Democratic minority. During the debate on these nominations, Majority Leader Bill First (R–Tenn.) also proposed to change the cloture rules with respect to judicial nominations so that the first attempt would still require 60 votes, but each successive attempt would require three fewer votes to pass until cloture could be invoked by a simple majority.[l]

Why would majority party leaders favor a change in the rules along the lines that Frist proposed? Do you expect the intensity of their support to change depending on whether they expect to remain in the majority for several years or whether they expect congressional control to see-saw between the parties? Which members of Congress would you expect to oppose such changes? Why hasn't the majority party been willing to force the larger issue of the filibuster's constitutionality and tried to change the filibuster through a tactic that requires only a majority vote? Do senators worry, as Ornstein argues, that "[a]ll hell would break loose" if they attempted the strategy? Or do they want to retain the filibuster for some matters?

The debate about the constitutionality of supermajority rules became particularly salient in 1995 when the Republican House of Representatives

---

j. See Julian Eule, *Temporal Limits on the Legislative Mandate: Entrenchment and Retroactivity*, 1987 Am. B. Found. Res. J. 379, 407–415 (1987); Catherine Fisk & Erwin Chemerinsky, *The Filibuster*, 49 Stan. L. Rev. 181, 245-52 (1997) (arguing that the problem with the current rule is that it cannot be changed by a simple majority and suggesting that supermajority voting requirements that are amenable to majority change may be acceptable). For a contrasting view, see Michael Gerhardt, *The Constitutionality of the Filibuster*, 21 Const. Comm. 445 (2004).

k. In the past, however, when the Senate has considered whether a simple majority could invoke cloture and stop a filibuster, a majority has rejected that position. See Bruhl, *supra,* at 379 (discussing votes in 1967, 1969, and 1975).

l. See Gregory Wawro & Eric Schickler, *Filibuster: Obstruction and Lawmaking in the U.S. Senate* 4–6, 269–76 (2006) (discussing this episode, the history of the filibuster, and the procedural moves necessary to eliminate the filibuster by majority vote).

adopted a new rule requiring a three-fifths vote to pass any legislation raising federal tax rates. See House Rule XXI(5)(b). In practice, the tax rule has not been particularly important in House deliberations because "tax rate increase" has been defined very narrowly. Furthermore, any objection that might be raised under Rule XXI(5) is usually waived, without a separate vote, by the special rule that structures the floor debate.

Nevertheless, reaction to the new rule was swift and largely negative. For example, a group of law professors argued that the supermajority requirement violated the Constitution and threatened to accelerate "the continuing erosion of our central constitutional commitments to majority rule and deliberative democracy." Bruce Ackerman, et al., *An Open Letter to Congressman Gingrich*, 104 Yale L.J. 1539 (1995). The signatories argued that the framers rejected supermajority rules for ordinary legislation, in part because the requirement in the Articles of Confederation for congressional supermajorities to raise and spend money had debilitated the federal government. The Constitution lists particular times when Congress must depart from majority rule, and the professors noted that even then the Constitution requires a two-thirds vote, not three-fifths support. John McGinnis and Michael Rappaport responded to the open letter and defended the House Rule, arguing that the Constitution's silence about whether majority rule was required to pass legislation signaled the framers' intent to "permit the houses of the legislature to decide the question." John McGinnis & Michael Rappaport, *The Constitutionality of Legislative Supermajority Requirements: A Defense*, 105 Yale L.J. 483, 484 (1995).

The opponents of House Rule XXI(5) tried to distinguish it from long-accepted supermajority requirements for procedural decisions, like the House rule requiring a two-thirds vote to suspend the rules for expeditious consideration of legislation. "This supermajority requirement [to suspend the rules] transparently serves the interest of efficient decision making. If it were too easy to suspend House rules, there would be undue disruption of the normal system of deliberation and decision; but if it were impossible, the House would be incapable of responding to emergencies. Hence, a two-thirds rule [to suspend the rules] is a perfectly appropriate way to exercise the House's power 'to determine the rules of its proceedings.' " Ackerman et al., *supra*, at 1541–42. Is this distinction between votes on passing substantive legislation and votes on procedural matters persuasive? If a majority of the Senate cannot muster 60 votes for cloture and a filibuster continues, hasn't the underlying legislation been defeated because of a supermajority requirement?[m]

---

m. See also Jed Rubenfeld, *Rights of Passage: Majority Rule in Congress*, 46 Duke L.J. 73 (1996) (arguing that inherent in the Constitution's use of the word "passed" is the assumption that majority rule will be the method of passing legislation); John McGinnis & Michael Rappaport, *The Rights of Legislators and the Wrongs of Interpretation: A Further Defense of the Constitutionality of Legislative Supermajority Rules*, 47 Duke L.J. 327 (1997) (responding to Rubenfeld).

Of course, this debate turns on whether supermajority requirements in congressional rules or statutes are constitutional. Constitutions can, and often do, require extraordinary votes before the legislature can take particular actions. The federal Constitution requires a two-thirds

One interesting question raised by the ongoing debate about the constitutionality of supermajority voting requirements, either for passage of a law or on procedural objections, is whether a member of Congress would be able to challenge such a provision in court. For example, if a bill is filibustered and only 54 senators vote to invoke cloture, can a senator go to court for an injunction arguing that the supermajority voting requirement is unconstitutional and demanding that the Senate stop debate and vote on the proposal? If a revenue bill raising tax rates received majority support in the House but was considered not to have passed because of House Rule XXI(5), could a representative sue to force the House to certify passage and send the bill to the Senate? Consider these questions as you read the following note.

NOTE ON LAWSUITS BY LEGISLATORS

After *Powell v. McCormack* (Chapter 2, § 2A), members of Congress increasingly turned to the courts to resolve policy disputes. Most of the cases were brought in the D.C. Circuit, which tended to find that the legislators had standing to bring suit but which then would dismiss the cases on other procedural grounds, such as lack of ripeness or the political question doctrine. One unusual approach to these cases was developed by Judge Carl McGowan, who argued that the use of standing and the other doctrines was not a good way to restrict legislator lawsuits. Instead, he proposed an independent doctrine of "equitable discretion," which he justified on separation-of-powers grounds. If the legislator could show injury in fact and the abridgement of a protected interest (the basic standing requirements generously applied), the legislator could bring a suit challenging a political policy. But the court could then decide to withhold relief, under its equitable discretion, if the relief would trench upon matters primarily reserved to the legislature or the executive. See *Congressmen in Court: The New Plaintiffs*, 15 Ga. L. Rev. 241 (1981).

The D.C. Circuit used this new doctrine in several cases, often over the vehement dissents of Judge Bork and then-Judge Scalia (who would have denied the lawmakers standing). See, e.g., *Riegle v. Federal Open Market Committee*, 656 F.2d 873 (D.C. Cir.), *cert. denied*, 454 U.S. 1082 (1981) (allowing lawmaker standing to challenge the presidential appointment of members of the Federal Open Market Committee without the advice and consent of the Senate, but declining to rule on the merits of the claim on the ground of equitable discretion); *Crockett v. Reagan*, 720 F.2d 1355 (D.C. Cir. 1983), *cert. denied*, 467 U.S. 1251 (1984) (treating similarly a challenge by 29 members of Congress to President Reagan's military assistance to El Salvador as inconsistent with the War Powers Resolution). By finding standing in these cases, the court kept open the possibility that it would reach the merits of such cases in the appropriate circumstances. Accordingly, disgruntled lawmakers

---

vote of a house to expel a member (Art. I, § 5, cl. 2) or to override a presidential veto (Art. I, § 7, cl. 3), and two-thirds of the Senate must vote to ratify treaties (Art. 2, § 2, cl. 2). Sixteen state constitutions either require supermajorities to pass tax bills, establish a cap on revenues that can be collected, or both. See Max Minzner, *Entrenching Interests: State Supermajority Requirements to Raise Taxes*, 14 Akron Tax J. 43 (1999).

regularly turned to the federal courts, using the initiation of their lawsuits as an opportunity to make speeches and gain publicity for their political causes. In turn, these cases allowed the D.C. Circuit to maintain its position as a player in Beltway politics.

After years of avoiding the issue, the Supreme Court considered the question of congressional standing in a challenge to the federal Line Item Veto Act. Among other things, the Act allowed the President to withhold money that Congress had appropriated for certain spending projects. (See Chapter 3, § 3, for a more detailed description of the Act and the Supreme Court decision holding it unconstitutional.) After the Act went into effect but before the President had exercised his new power, six members of Congress challenged the constitutionality of the Act on separation-of-powers grounds. The legislators claimed that the Act diminished their legislative powers, rendering their votes on appropriations and other spending bills less effective and changing the meaning of such votes. As you read the following case, think about the institutional reasons that Supreme Court Justices, unlike members of the D.C. Circuit, might be disinclined to entertain legislator lawsuits.[n]

RAINES v. BYRD, 521 U.S. 811 (1997). The Court, per **Chief Justice Rehnquist**, first reviewed the doctrine of standing generally, which is a component of Article III's requirement that federal courts hear only actual cases and controversies. A plaintiff must allege a concrete and particularized personal injury that is fairly traceable to the defendant's conduct and likely to be redressed by the requested relief. The majority emphasized that standing requirements are compelled by separation-of-powers concerns; thus, the inquiry is "especially rigorous" when the dispute involves deciding whether the action of another branch of the federal government is unconstitutional.

The majority found that the members of Congress did not have the kind of injury that meets constitutional requirements. They contrasted this vote-dilution case with two other kinds of cases brought by legislators in which the Court had found standing and resolved the merits. First, in *Powell v. McCormack* (Chapter 2, § 2A), Representative Powell alleged a personal injury, not an institutional one: He had been deprived of his seat and his salary as a result of the House's vote to exclude him. In *Coleman v. Miller*, 307 U.S. 433 (1939), state legislators brought suit to redress a concrete institutional injury. A vote on a proposed constitutional amendment had been deadlocked 20–20 in the Kansas Senate. The Lieutenant Governor, the presiding officer of the Senate, had cast his vote in favor of the amendment, which was deemed ratified. The 20 state senators who had voted against the amendment sued, claiming that their votes had been nullified by the Lieutenant Governor's action, which they alleged was improper. The Court in *Raines* interpreted *Coleman* as standing for "the proposition that legislators whose votes would have been sufficient to defeat (or enact) a specific legislative act have standing

---

n. See Neal Devins & Michael Fitts, *The Triumph of Timing: Raines v. Byrd and the Modern Supreme Court's Attempt to Control Constitutional Confrontations*, 86 Geo. L.J. 351 (1997).

to sue if that legislative action goes into effect (or does not go into effect), on the ground that their votes have been completely nullified." In their challenge to the Line Item Veto Act, the legislators were not alleging this sort of concrete injury. The Court explained: "There is a vast difference between the level of vote nullification at issue in *Coleman* and the abstract dilution of institutional legislative power that is alleged here." Moreover, a majority of Congress could repeal the Line Item Veto Act or exempt particular spending programs from its coverage, so the legislators had access to an adequate remedy without recourse to the courts.

Justices Souter and **Ginsburg** concurred in the judgment. Unlike the majority, they believed that the lawmakers' injury was relatively concrete. The legislators "allege that the Act deprives them of an element of their legislative power; as a factual matter they have a more direct and tangible interest in the preservation of that power than the general citizenry has." But the concurrence concluded that the standing question was at least a close call, so the Court should consider the important separation-of-powers questions raised by a lawmaker suit of this sort. "The counsel of restraint in this case begins with the fact that a dispute involving only officials, and the official interests of those, who serve in the branches of the National Government lies far from the model of the traditional common-law cause of action at the conceptual core of the case-or-controversy requirement. Although the contest here is not formally between the political branches (since Congress passed the bill augmenting Presidential power and the President signed it), it is in substance an interbranch controversy about calibrating the legislative and executive powers, as well as an intrabranch dispute between segments of Congress itself."

The concurrence also noted that a private party would certainly be able to bring suit challenging the Line Item Veto Act once the President exercised his power to withhold spending. Such a case would pose a "lesser risk" to the legitimacy of the judicial branch because it would raise "no specter of judicial readiness to enlist on one side of a political tug-of-war." Moreover, the possibility of suits by non-lawmakers meant that the Act was not insulated entirely from judicial review if the Court denied legislators standing in this challenge to the Line Item Veto Act. (Indeed, the Court faced such a challenge by parties related to disappointed beneficiaries of cancelled spending programs in the next Term.)

Justice Stevens, in dissent, argued that the lawmakers alleged a concrete and particularized injury because the Act altered the practical effect of their votes on bills that contained spending items subject to the President's power. He concluded that "the immediate, constant threat of the partial veto power has a palpable effect on their current legislative choices."

Congressional Standing Problems

Problem 4–4. The 107th Congress began with an evenly divided Senate. After much negotiation, the leaders of the two parties decided to split membership of each committee evenly and split committee resources among members evenly. Each committee would be chaired by a Republican, reflecting the ability of Vice-President Cheney to cast the deciding votes in ties. Assume that the Republicans had not been willing to share power in this way; instead, they had arranged committees so that Republicans had a one-vote advantage in each committee. Would Democratic leader Tom Daschle (D–S.D.) have standing to sue in the D.C. Circuit to force the Senate to organize its committees using equal ratios of members? Would it matter if Daschle and the Democrats had the ability to filibuster the resolution organizing Senate committees and either failed to do so or lost a cloture vote? See *Vander Jagt v. O'Neill*, 699 F.2d 1166 (D.C. Cir. 1982), *cert. denied*, 464 U.S. 823 (1983) (pre-*Raines v. Byrd* case refusing to decide a claim by 14 House Republicans that the Democratic leadership's method of dividing committee seats between the two parties was unconstitutional).

Problem 4–5. Representative Rob Gruntmeir believes that the House rule requiring a three-fifths majority to pass a tax rate hike is unconstitutional. He tried to strike the provision from the House resolution establishing the House rules, but his amendment was defeated. He also voted against the resolution, but the House rules, including the three-fifths requirement, passed by a majority vote. Does he have standing to bring suit? Does your answer change if he had proposed a bill raising tax rates that was considered not to have passed the House when 220 members voted in favor and 215 voted against? See *Skaggs v. Carle*, 110 F.3d 831 (D.C. Cir. 1997) (a case decided before *Raines v. Byrd*). See also *Campbell v. Clinton*, 203 F.3rd 19 (D.C. Cir.), *cert. denied*, 531 U.S. 815 (2000).(post-*Raines v. Byrd* challenge to President Clinton's use of the military in Kosovo under both the Constitution and the War Powers Act).

———

4. *Success (or Failure) of the Modern Budget Framework.* The budget process profoundly affects the legislative process. All bill drafters must take account of budget rules, particularly in the Senate where they might trigger supermajority votes. Again primarily in the Senate, the reconciliation vehicle has become an attractive vehicle for major policy change because these omnibus bills have privileged status, cannot be filibustered, and are likely to be signed by the President. Although the Byrd Rule and other requirements restrict senators' ability to load reconciliation acts with new programs and extraneous matters, modern Congresses have enacted many major policy changes through reconciliation acts, notably in the tax system (including the enactment of tax cuts) and in entitlement programs. The more difficult question is whether the budget process has achieved its objectives.

Many parts of the 1974 Act have been resounding successes. The information generated by the CBO and the staff of the budget committees has empowered lawmakers in the budget process. Relative to the executive branch, the legislative branch is still at a disadvantage because of Congress' collective nature, but the data that is generated and widely disseminated allows lawmakers to make better decisions and monitor the executive branch much more closely than they could before 1974. Not only has the process eliminated the monopoly on information enjoyed for decades by the executive branch, but the information it produces is used by private organizations, think tanks, the media, academics and others to hold policymakers more accountable for fiscal decisions.

Since Gramm-Rudman-Hollings, however, the budget process has been expressly designed to do more than produce information; the procedure has also been intended to reduce federal deficits and to restrain federal spending even in times of budgetary surplus. Some have argued that the process does little in this area, serving only as a symbolic gesture toward deficit reduction while leaving lawmakers free to reward special interest groups as lavishly as they did before. This position fails to recognize the real bite that the budget framework has, although it would be an exaggeration to attribute any improvement in the federal budget situation solely to the budget process. Spending caps and PAYGO exerted some fiscal discipline, but arguably the political environment would have dictated similar changes in budget decision-making without a structural framework. In addition, a strong and growing economy helps to improve the budget outlook.

A question raised by the experience with congressional budget frameworks is whether they facilitate difficult congressional decisions to cut spending, raise taxes, or both when the fiscal condition warrants such a course of action. The answer, we believe, is that the Budget Enforcement Act system did make enacting new programs or increasing spending for current programs more difficult than it would have been in the absence of the framework. Offset requirements forced those seeking federal benefits to undertake an additional, costly role; not only were they funding seekers, but they also became funding predators. One straightforward option to raise money — higher tax rates — was not an attractive option because lawmakers believed, with reason, that a decision to raise tax rates would hurt them at the polls. Because of the political taboo associated with tax increases, the budget process became characterized by an aggressive search for less obvious revenue offsets to pay for new spending programs and tax expenditures. To receive funding for any new program, groups had to also advocate eliminating or reducing an existing one. To see how this predatory system worked, let us focus on tax legislation and the effect of the PAYGO requirement.[o]

The search for offsetting revenue raised the cost of obtaining a tax benefit. Groups could have approached Congress to for tax subsidies without also presenting a way to pay for the new provisions, but success was more likely if they had a revenue neutral package. As one budget scholar put it: "Since the BEA was enacted, * * * explicit assumptions of deficit neutrality (PAYGO) ha[ve] made the question, 'How will you pay for it?' the first one asked of proponents of costly new spending." Philip Joyce, *Congressional Budget Reform: The Unanticipated Implications for Federal Policy Making*, 56 Pub. Admin. Rev. 317, 321 (1996). Advocates of new programs therefore invested resources in identifying a promising offset.

---

o. Much of this discussion is drawn from Elizabeth Garrett, *Harnessing Politics: The Dynamics of Offset Requirements in the Tax Legislative Process*, 65 U. Chi. L. Rev. 501 (1998).

Selecting an appropriate offset involved several determinations; one of the most important was whether other interest groups would defend the potential offset. Those seeking revenue used analysis much like that in Chapter 1, § 2 concerning interest group dynamics and the transactional model of legislation to predict whether repealing a particular existing tax subsidy was likely to elicit substantial and organized opposition. For example, one way to avoid vigorous opposition was to choose a provision that benefited the relatively needy, rather than an expenditure that benefited an organized and wealthy interest group. The former group is likely to be more dispersed and less able to organize, and thus likely to be more easily defeated in political battle. Of course, policy entrepreneurs in Congress and elsewhere work to protect the interests of the needy, and they were sometimes able to mount a successful defense of such tax provisions, using rhetoric that made opponents seem self-serving or careless of the public interest.

If political considerations largely ruled out increasing tax rates or reducing need-based tax expenditures, advocates of new provisions resorted to targeting other tax expenditures, which were often supported by organized groups. When conflict ensued, the group protecting the existing tax expenditure was likely to defeat the group proposing it as an offset, even if the latter had worked diligently to find a provision supported by a relatively less powerful or less well-organized group. We saw many of the reasons for this reality in the discussion of proceduralism and of interest group theories in Chapter 1, § 2. Groups defending the status quo are often in a better position to win than groups seeking change. In many cases, those advocating new benefits may be recently organized groups with less clout and experience than established players that have enjoyed benefits for years. As Robert Reischauer, former CBO Director, observed, "[E]xisting programs have much more political support than programs that promise something in the future. Proposed programs do not have interest groups and a whole set of beneficiaries out there salivating. Existing interest groups have offices on K Street [in Washington, D.C.] and executive directors, but it is hard to mobilize the future beneficiaries of a program to come and lobby you." *A Midcourse Review of the Budget Enforcement Act: Hearings Before the Task Force on Budget Process, Reconciliation, and Enforcement of the House Budget Committee*, 102d Cong. 19 (1991).

Also, as we know, it is generally easier to oppose legislative change than to enact it because of all the hurdles that stand in the way of passing a new law. Groups defending an existing federal program need to prevail only at one stage in the convoluted legislative process. Proponents of a new program, on the other hand, must successfully navigate all the obstacles. Knowing this, possible target groups in the PAYGO context focused their energies on establishing relationships with key players in congressional committees, the congressional leadership, or the administration. If target groups lost at one stage of the process, they knew they could continue to fight at the next stage. Winning might be difficult after an early loss, but it was still possible; in contrast, a predator seeking a change in the law had to win at each stage.

Any group that managed to obtain a tax benefit faced additional future costs because it had to protect its benefit from becoming an offset used by new predators. The costs of defending a tax subsidy comprised the *post-enactment costs* of PAYGO and similar offset rules. Tax provisions and other spending programs have always been at some risk of being repealed or scaled back, forcing beneficiaries to work to avoid losing valuable tax expenditures. However, offset requirements increased this risk because every new program had to be paid for by a change in existing programs. The increased uncertainty over the durability of benefits made them less attractive to interest groups and somewhat reduced the pressure on legislators to grant them in the first place.[p] An interest group had to consider post-enactment costs, as well as the up-front costs, when deciding whether the benefits of the federal program justified the effort necessary to obtain them. Although the future costs were discounted, they added to the burden imposed on those seeking new federal programs.

Those who decided that the benefits were worth the enactment and post-enactment costs had a variety of protective measures available to them. These strategies included both *monitoring* and *signaling* activities. First, monitoring costs were incurred as interest groups and their lobbyists tried to discover possible threats. In the tax arena, they watched anxiously to see if a powerful policymaker called their tax expenditure a "corrupt tax loophole" or an example of "insidious corporate welfare." Well-heeled tax lobbyists would attend committee mark-ups that could go late into the evening, or even longer, because these might result in the unveiling of carefully guarded offset proposals, sometimes to the surprise of unwitting targets.

Second, interest groups engaged in a process of signaling to indicate to predators that a particular offset proposal would generate substantial opposition. As we learned in our analysis of positive political theory in Chapter 1, § 2, a credible signal of vigorous opposition by those protecting the possible target could be enough to remove the provision from consideration. Interest groups built coalitions to demonstrate that supporters of a current federal program spanned numerous congressional districts and had connections to more members of Congress than one group alone could command. Another signaling tactic occurs when a group publicly communicates the strong support of pivotal lawmakers, perhaps those in the party leadership or serving in key positions on the tax-writing committees.

In short, then, offset requirements made it more difficult to enact new spending programs, and they reduced the value of any spending program because it was constantly susceptible to repeal in order to raise revenue. Therefore, at the same time the budget rules made new programs and tax subsidies more costly for interest groups to obtain, they also reduced the value of those programs by decreasing their durability. Why would members of Congress willingly adopt a budget process that made it more difficult to reward constituents with new spending programs and tax expenditures? Doesn't this legislative framework seem to undermine the public choice view of the

---

p. See Omri Ben-Shahar, *Legal Durability,* 1 Rev. Law & Econ. 15, 41–43 (2005).

lawmaker as single-minded in her desire to win reelection? Of course, some constituents might value a reduced deficit and lower federal spending more than the benefits of a particular program, but well-organized interest groups vital to the reelection prospects of lawmakers are unlikely to be keen on offset requirements. Does the fact that Congress adopted the federal budget process reinforce the more public-regarding theories of representative behavior? Or are there alternative explanations?

5. *Avoiding the Restrictions of the Budget Process.* An alternative explanation for the adoption of budget rules is that they are entirely symbolic, allowing interest groups to circumvent the rules entirely and obtain the benefits they want without too much additional cost. The unorganized and inattentive public is content with the symbolic legislation, never learning that interest groups and lawmakers continue to collaborate on enacting generous pork barrel programs. Accordingly, lawmakers have evaded the discipline of the budget process through gimmicks and loopholes.

Some of the favorite gimmicks of lawmakers and interest groups take advantage of the cash-flow nature of budgeting and the limited time period in which effects of new policies are measured. These timing gimmicks take many forms and are as venerable as the budget process itself. They are possible because of two features of the budget process. First, budget rules focus on the effects of any legislative change during a finite time period or *budget window.* For many years, the rules focused only on effects in the year following a policy change; the BEA extended the budget window to five years, and budget resolutions often expand the relevant budget window to ten years. Second, the cost of most federal programs is considered on a cash-flow, rather than a present-value, basis. Remember that the federal surplus or deficit is a cash-flow measure, revealing that in a particular fiscal year, the government took in more money than it paid out.

The truncated budget window and a cash-flow measure of spending allow wily drafters to game the system. Revenue-outflows beyond the budget window need not be offset — neither at the time of their enactment nor at the time the revenue losses occur. Perhaps the most egregious timing games were played in the years of Gramm-Rudman-Hollings when inflexible deficit targets put pressure on lawmakers and the budget window was only one year. For example, in 1987, Congress moved a pay date for some federal employees from the last day of 1987 to the first day of 1988, thereby shifting costs to the next fiscal year and "saving" money in the current year.[q] Similarly, $5.2 billion in outlays from 2006 were shifted to 2007 "by temporarily halting payments to Medicare providers for the last six business days of the 2006 fiscal year."[r]

Every tax bill passed since offset requirements became ubiquitous has contained such timing gimmicks. This reality might lead one to conclude that

---

q. See Timothy Muris, *The Uses and Abuses of Budget Baselines,* in *The Budget Puzzle: Understanding Federal Spending* 65–66 (John Cogan, Timothy Muris & Allen Schick eds., 1994).

r. See Block, *supra.*

PAYGO and offset requirements that use cash-flow measures have always been meaningless except to the extent that they distort and complicate federal programs. But timing gimmicks did not entirely eliminate the effect of PAYGO and related budget rules. Practical political considerations made it difficult to construct a tax provision with delayed benefits so large that they equaled (in present-value terms) benefits that could be enjoyed immediately. In short, interest groups worried that a backloaded tax benefit would not last long enough for them to enjoy it fully.

Before we conclude our assessment of the congressional budget rules with a case study from the 1993 Omnibus Budget Reconciliation Act, let us consider one final effect of offset requirements. The competition among interest groups that budget rules engender may result in the production of information about spending programs and tax policy that legislators can use to improve the law and to decide which programs to phase out and which to restructure.

6. *Using Budgetary Conflict to Generate Information about Federal Spending.* The offset process illustrates that procedures can be used to structure interest group conflict to generate better outcomes. Congressional decisionmaking can be enhanced if interest group activity can be harnessed so that groups actually do some of the work required in policymaking. For example, interest groups might be encouraged to produce valuable information that will reduce the cost to the government of producing its own data. This frees government analysts to assess the privately-generated information, as well as to produce analyses of spending in areas of little or no interest group activity. Interest groups, and the lobbyists they employ, are information specialists, particularly with regard to their own interests and related programs. If groups work in coalitions, they can coordinate with respect to the production and dissemination of information, reducing its cost and perhaps improving its quality.

Of course, interest groups have incentives to skew information in self-serving ways, but the system contains some checks on accuracy. The conflict caused by budget rules may act to keep groups relatively honest, because opponents will scrutinize their claims carefully, and government specialists can spend time assessing the merits of private studies and other information. Think tanks and academics may also present critical perspectives and question the methodologies employed by interested parties. Lobbyists are well aware that if lawmakers or staff catch them lying or misrepresenting facts, they may lose their credibility on the Hill and their access to key policymakers. This is a particularly potent enforcement mechanism to keep these repeat players in line because lobbyists value their reputations as among their most valuable assets.

The information provided by interest groups is likely to help lawmakers in their attempt to spend each federal dollar as effectively as possible. As part of this process, lawmakers will want to develop incentives to encourage beneficiaries to inform Congress of the most effective delivery system for the level of benefits accorded them. Consider the following hypothetical: The budget resolution allocates $20.3 billion in budgetary resources to agriculture, and this is the total amount of federal money, in any form, that will be spent on this governmental function. At this point, the affected interests have an incentive to choose programs that will produce the greatest benefits from that $20.3 billion investment, because the price of every new program will be a reduction or elimination of an alternative use of that money. The current system does not quite reflect this theoretical budget scheme because agriculture programs are divided between the discretionary spending side of the budget and the tax/direct spending side of the budget. So a tax subsidy for agriculture does not come at the cost of an appropriated program for farmers.

This vision of the positive effects of interest group activity is a bit too rosy, unfortunately. First, there is no guarantee that the process of deciding how to spend money for a particular government objective leads to the adoption of the most efficient delivery system instead of the enactment of programs that benefit clientele groups the most. In some cases, interest groups want only to maximize the returns that they receive and may care little if the program results in a lower return, or even a net loss, to society as a whole. So this competition may tell policymakers what the interest groups prefer, but legislators will still have to reach independent judgments, aided by specialized staff, about whether that result also accords with the best policy overall. Second, groups may claim to be paying for their own new benefit while really using an offset that benefits a different group, often one that is less well-organized. In 1993, the repeal of the luxury tax on boats was offset in part by a tax on diesel fuel used in noncommercial boats; supporters argued that they were paying for their own proposal and thereby signaling to lawmakers the best use of that money. This characterization, designed to reduce opposition to the offset, was misleading. The group benefiting from the luxury tax repeal (purchasers and manufacturers of expensive boats) was not entirely congruent with the group that paid for the new tax expenditure (all owners of noncommercial boats who now pay higher fuel prices).

Because it is likely that offsets usually come from groups other than the ones proposing the new benefit, the relevant question is whether this kind of wider interest group activity will produce helpful information for lawmakers. As predators seek offsets, they generate information not only about their own programs, but also about the programs they propose to repeal or scale back. Although they may target programs on the basis of interest group clout, choosing relatively weaker and unorganized beneficiary groups, they phrase their arguments differently in public. In public, they discuss the relative merits of the programs. In this way, conflict engendered by offset requirements produces information that lawmakers can use to make allocative decisions, along with information generated by government agencies and experts.

In the end, any evaluation of the budget process must account for all the effects of the process. Some of those effects concern the level of spending: Does the process reduce or increase the amount of federal spending? Is it neutral on that ground? Some concern the design of federal programs: Does the structure encourage interest groups to seek tax benefits rather than appropriated money, as Gramm-Rudman-Hollings did because it did not constrain the tax legislative process in any significant way? Should budget rules affect design issues, or should lawmakers be free to select the most efficient delivery system possible? And, finally, some of the effects are informational in nature, as we have just seen. Is the information produced by private interest groups credible and helpful? Do lawmakers consider the merits of the arguments when they make budget tradeoffs, or do they merely declare the most powerful interest group to be the winner?

Budget Process Problems

Problem 4–6. Imagine yourself as a lobbyist for a group seeking a federal benefit. What strategies would you pursue? Which kind of benefit would you seek — a discretionary program, a tax subsidy, or a direct spending program? What factors would play a role in your decision? How would you explain these budget rules to your clients? Do you think that lobbyists support procedural frameworks like the budget process even if they make it more difficult to obtain benefits? Certainly, there are advantages to lobbyists from such a system. The more complicated and arcane the rules of the legislative game, the more necessary are experts to help people navigate the complexity. Moreover, if federal programs, once enacted, are in constant danger of being repealed or scaled back because of offset requirements, then lobbyists will offer clients their skills in monitoring, building connections with lawmakers, and sending out credible signals of strength. Of course, these costs will be factored into the decision of an interest group to pursue a legislative benefit in the first place. At the least, this description suggests that the lobbyist's interests may not always align with those of her employer, which may explain in part why budget rules have continued in force over several decades. Those who deal with them every day — lawmakers, lobbyists, and executive branch officials — may receive benefits from them that constituents and interest groups do not.

Problem 4–7. Earmarks have received substantial scrutiny recently. Although the definition is disputed, an earmark is a targeted spending provision added by Congress during the appropriations process. Earmarks are often relatively small and are often slipped into legislation without much publicity or discussion. Allegations of corrupt lobbying added fuel to the fire surrounding earmarks because some of the improprieties concerned enactment of earmarks for certain interest groups, including Indian tribes and defense contractors. One watchdog group, Citizens Against Government Waste, claimed that earmarks had grown from 550 earmarks costing $3 billion in 1991 to nearly 14,000 earmarks costing $27 billion in 2005. Some commentators argued forcefully that earmark reform was a necessary component of meaningful lobbying and ethics reform. In 2007, Congress enacted rules aimed at earmarks. See House Rules XXI(9) & XXIII(16) & (17); Senate Rule XLIV. First, House committees, including conference committees, are required to publicize all earmarks, as well as tax subsidies affecting fewer than ten benefi-ciaries. In the Senate, the Majority Leader must certify with respect to all bills that "each congressionally direct spending item, limited tax benefit, and limited tariff benefit" has been identified, along with the senator who submitted it. This information must be publicly available on the Internet in a searchable format for two days before any vote on the legislation. Second, a member re-questing an earmark has to provide information about its purpose and beneficiaries, as well as certifying that neither she nor her family has a financial interest in the item (as recipients or lobbyists). Third, in the House, a member violates the rules if he conditions any vote on the inclusion of an earmark in legislation. Fourth, if a conference report contains a new earmark, a senator may raise a point of order, which can be waived only by a super-majority vote of 60 senators. Are these reforms likely to decrease the number of earmarks? Are they enforceable? Are there any other procedural reforms that might work? What is the best definition of an earmark, and why are earmarks problematic?

C. A CASE STUDY OF THE BUDGET PROCESS: PRESIDENT CLINTON'S ENERGY TAX PROPOSAL

THE PRESIDENT'S BUDGET

One of the tasks awaiting any newly elected President is to assemble his budget submission, due the first Monday in February. The President's budget is one of his first opportunities to demonstrate concretely the priorities of his administration and to provide assurances that he will follow up on some of his campaign promises. During Bill Clinton's campaign for the presidency, one of his central themes was a "new covenant" for economic change. See William Clinton & Albert Gore, *Putting People First: How We Can All Change America* 217 (1992). He promised to cut income taxes burdening the middle class, while raising taxes on the wealthy, whom he defined as those making over $200,000. His platform emphasized the middle-class tax cut, together with a number of new programs to "invest" in areas like health care, education, infrastructure, and job training. He also advocated that Congress quickly pass a large spending proposal to jump-start the sluggish economy.

Although much of the campaign focused on Clinton's proposals and President George Bush's record, including his decision to accept tax increases as part of the 1990 budget summit, a third party candidate shaped much of the political focus through his long infomercials, colorful pie charts, and folksy interjections in televised debates. H. Ross Perot, a wacky billionaire who formed his own political party, hammered on the economic threat posed by the substantial federal budget deficit. The deficit was projected to be over $300 billion in fiscal year 1993, and projected deficits of over $250 billion stretched on till the end of the century. Perot argued that the country ought be run just as a prudent citizen would run her life — by spending no more than she makes and by reducing her debt. See Ross Perot, *United We Stand: How We Can Take Back Our Country* (1992). In a world where most of us prudently go into debt to finance education and housing and where many have significant amounts of other consumer debt, this argument had more persuasive appeal than it had substantive merit. Nonetheless, Perot's unusual and often strange candidacy helped propel the budget deficit back into the consciousness of the American public, and his strong showing on Election Day convinced politicians that the deficit issue was one about which voters cared.

One other event after Clinton's election convinced the new President that he had to give some consideration to deficit reduction as he drafted his economic proposal. In December, Clinton met privately with Alan Greenspan, the powerful chairman of the Federal Reserve Board. Bob Woodward describes the meeting in *The Agenda: Inside the Clinton White House* 69–71 (1994). When President-elect Clinton complained that high interest rates harmed the middle class, Greenspan explained that the level of interest rates reflected that sophisticated players in the financial markets expected the budget deficit to continue its explosive growth for the foreseeable future. Their expectation meant that the long-term economic outlook for the country was unstable. The results of a Clinton policy to control the deficit and alter market expectations, according to Greenspan: lower interest rates which would cause economic growth; a shift of money from bonds to the stock market; and increased employment. The Fed Chairman told Clinton that a short-term economic stimulus proposal would have no effect on the economy, but it would harm the new administration's chance to signal credibly to the markets that it was serious about deficit reduction.

Even though the meeting with Greenspan caused Clinton to think more critically about his economic stimulus proposal, he had promised one to the voters in the first 100 days of his administration. Moreover, a number of his advisers remained committed to the proposal and to his platform of federal investment or spending in priority areas. Most notable in this group was Robert Reich, a liberal economist who had been a professor at Harvard's Kennedy School of Government before being named as Clinton's Secretary of Labor. The Clinton administration was already being pulled in two directions, one toward tax cuts for the middle class and greater federal spending on traditional Democratic programs and the other toward a package that would address the federal deficit. During the weeks of transition, Clinton's aides met frequently to determine how his campaign promises could fit together, how they could be translated into legislation and a budget proposal, and which of the promises had to give way to new priorities like deficit reduction. Robert Rubin, formerly the co-chairman of investment banking firm Goldman Sachs and now the head of Clinton's National Economic Council,[s] convened a series of meetings to discuss how to proceed. See Woodward, *supra*, at 81–89 (discussing the meetings, including the following one).

During these meetings, members of the President's economic team presented proposals to raise revenue to offset the middle-class tax cut and other tax initiatives. As deficit reduction became an overriding concern, some of the new taxes would also go to reduce the deficit by $500 billion over five years. The Secretary of the Treasury, Lloyd Bentsen, was the former Chair of the Senate Finance Committee, so he offered experience both in drafting revenue bills and in negotiating their progress through the Senate; the new Director of OMB, Leon Panetta, had been the Chair of the House Budget Committee. During one of the meetings, Vice President Al Gore suggested that the team consider a broad-based energy tax as a means to raise revenue. This proposal served two functions, Gore argued. Not only could it raise substantial amounts

---

s. Rubin ultimately became Clinton's Secretary of Treasury, where he developed a reputation for moderate economic policies that allowed the country's booming economic growth to continue unfettered.

of money to offset other revenue-losing proposals and reduce the deficit, but it would also allow tax policy to serve the objective of protecting the environment. If the tax were levied on the basis of British thermal units (BTUs), which was a basic measure of energy, it would be an efficient way to encourage more environmentally-friendly energy policies. A BTU tax would fall more heavily on the dirtiest fuel, coal, and relatively less heavily on oil and the cleanest fuel, natural gas. Even at these early meetings, participants discussed the political realities of the proposal; for example, a heavy tax on coal would be sure to anger West Virginia Senator Robert Byrd, the chair of the Senate Appropriations Committee and perhaps the most powerful senator in the budget realm because of his knowledge of Senate rules.

Meanwhile, time was slipping away. The President did propose an economic stimulus bill, but it fell prey to a filibuster in the Senate by Republicans and a few moderate Democrats who objected to the spending while the deficit was continuing to roar out of control. The President's budget did not come out on time, an error by the administration that caused it to lose some of the executive branch's advantage in controlling the agenda by staking out the first position. On February 17, 1993, Clinton finally released a small document previewing his budget. In *A Vision of Change for America*, Clinton proclaimed his hope that his administration "achieve the twin goals of economic growth and deficit reduction without asking those who were squeezed the hardest in the 1980s to contribute more." But he said that the magnitude of the deficit required all to share in the sacrifice. From the middle class, he asked for the sacrifice of about $10 more per month in a new broad-based energy tax, the BTU tax supported by Gore. In the brief description provided in *A Vision of Change for America*, the BTU tax was touted as reducing the deficit, decreasing dependence on foreign sources of oil by promoting conservation, and reducing environmental harm. Coal and natural gas were taxed at one rate, while oil was taxed at a slightly higher rate to reflect that it was more often imported into the country. In addition, the rate structure ended up taxing the cleanest fuel, natural gas, less heavily than the other sources.

Immediately, interest groups began to line up on either side of the BTU tax proposal. The day after the release of *A Vision of Change for America*, environmental groups pledged their full support for the BTU tax, as well as other environmental proposals in the President's budget. The political director of the Sierra Club urged members to "call and write members of Congress for support of the proposal, in order to 'fight back' against the oil, mining, timber, chemical, and ranching industries [that] will spend huge sums of money to kill the Clinton-Gore proposal."[t] This would be only one of many calls for grassroots activity; the energy tax saga is replete with examples of organized groups and Washington lobbyists working to deluge offices with letters and phone calls from citizens. At the same time as the White House was working to energize groups that would favor its proposal, it was also meeting with

---

t. *Environmental Groups Pledge Support for BTU Tax, Brace for Industry Opposition*, Daily Tax Rep. (BNA), Feb. 19, 1993, at G–11.

potential opponents to address their concerns and perhaps neutralize their opposition. Thus, on the day *A Vision of Change for America* was released, officials from the Departments of Energy and Treasury met with energy industry representatives. Nonetheless, most energy businesses staked out positions unfavorable to the BTU tax, with the President of the National Coal Association declaring that the BTU tax "is not good for America, the American economy, or the American worker." The energy industry is not monolithic, however, and the Administration quickly won the support of those representing renewable energy sources like wind and solar energy because they would become relatively more competitive under the proposal.

INITIAL CONGRESSIONAL DELIBERATION

Although the President's budget was still not out (and would not be released until early April), the congressional committees began their hearings on the sketchy proposal they had. Under the budget process timetable (*supra*, Figure 4–2), they could not wait for the official budget because the concurrent budget resolution was scheduled to be completed by early spring. No appropriations bills or other budget proposals could be considered until Congress had a resolution in place. The hearings in the tax-writing committees demonstrated the White House's advantage in setting and shaping the political agenda even without the timely release of important budget documents. In the Ways and Means Committee, the first witnesses were members of the Administration: Budget Director Panetta, the Chair of the Council of Economic Advisers Laura D'Andrea Tyson, and Secretary Bentsen. See *President Clinton's Proposals for Public Investment and Deficit Reduction: Hearings Before the House Committee on Ways & Means*, 103rd Cong. (1993). The list of other witnesses includes representatives from virtually every group interested in the tax proposals contained in the President's budget. Appearing before a congressional committee and offering testimony is a way for leaders of trade organizations to communicate to their members. Their testimony informs members of the group's position on a policy and signals that leaders are working diligently on behalf of their members. Hearings also operate to inform legislators of interest groups' positions, although private meetings with lawmakers and their staff are more effective ways to communicate this information, particularly because many committee hearings are sparsely attended by legislators.

Committee hearings contain another set of signals relevant to members of interest groups and to those concerned about the fate of legislative proposals. Lawmakers ask witnesses questions not only to discover new information, but also to publicize their own positions. Interest groups will send sympathetic legislators ideas for questions and statements, and lobbyists will often help harried staff members by writing questions or at least providing data that can serve as the basis for a member's inquiry. If a senator or representative asks a question that favors a particular interest group's position, this provides a strong signal that the lawmaker will work to protect this interest from harm in the legislative process. Thus, in the BTU tax context, where the energy industry was a potential offset to pay for other tax relief and deficit reduction, questions from key members of the tax-writing committees communicated that strong opposition should be expected. This signal was particularly important in the Senate Finance Committee, where the Democrats held only a one-vote advantage. If all the Republicans voted against the President's proposals, which appeared likely as the mood became increasingly partisan, then the defection of only one Democratic senator could defeat any administration proposal.

The Senate Finance Committee hearings on the tax proposals contain several instances of strategic questioning to stake out positions that would influence continuing negotiations. For example, Senator Boren (D–Okla.) asked questions that reflected the importance of the small independent oil and gas producer in his state. He noted that domestic oil production was down throughout the country, with a historically low rig count of 600. In Oklahoma, much of the production comes from *stripper wells*, which produce very little oil and often rely on expensive and energy-intensive methods to recover oil and natural gas. If production expenses increase, stripper wells become unprofitable, and many may be capped and their production lost. As Boren explained to Texan Lloyd Bentsen, "Most of this pumping [to recover oil from marginal wells] is done by electric motor as you know, Mr. Secretary. * * * I am very concerned that we are going to have the premature plugging of some of these marginal and stripper wells where the cost of electricity for pumping that oil is so high we are already right at the margin. They are barely breaking even. We lost 2,000 of those wells in Oklahoma in the last 2 years that were plugged because the lifting costs, primarily electric, finally exceeded the value that you could get from the well." *Administration's Energy Tax Proposals: Hearings before the Senate Committee on Finance*, 103rd Cong., at 25 (1993). Boren's question, full of statistics provided to his staff by the Independent Petroleum Association of America, was not designed merely to signal that he would protect their interests; his past record on the committee as one of the champions of tax incentives for the independent oil and gas industry was proof of that. His question mainly signaled that some sort of exemption for energy used to produce oil and gas from marginal wells or some other targeted tax subsidy for the industry might be a way to obtain its support, or at least mute its opposition.

In addition, Senator Conrad (D–N.D.) provided evidence of the Senate's traditional protection of farmers and rural interests, a role that senators play because of the composition of the Senate with every state equally represented. Traditionally, urban interests have done better in the Ways and Means Committee, and farmers and rural states rely on senators to protect their interests. Conrad arrived with charts and mountains of statistics about energy use in his state and in the country by farmers. One chart indicated that the BTU tax would decrease farm income by 6.7 percent, which he claimed was ten times the effect on income of the average regional impact around the country. "My point * * * is that agriculture is really taking a disproportionate hit. Let me just say that when one puts together the impact of the budget cuts, agriculture is tied for the highest percentage cut." One of the interesting aspects of this hearing before the Senate Finance Committee was Bentsen's interaction with his former colleagues. Had he still been Chair of the Committee and Senator from Texas, he would have been making many of the points that Boren and Conrad did in their questions to him. Thus, he responded sympathetically, noting that he had been a farmer all his life and that he had worked with Boren on a substantial tax expenditure for the independent oil and gas industry the previous year. His personal connection gave him credibility with the senators, and they knew that his own views might be more consistent with their proposals than with the BTU tax. This gave all parties hope that there would be room for compromise.

Hopes for compromise on the BTU tax were particularly high because the administration proposal had been changing between the time its general outline was released in February and the time the budget was finally submitted to Congress in April. By April 1993, a *Description of the Modified BTU Tax* released by the Treasury Department's Office of Tax Policy contained exemptions for nonfuel uses of fossil fuels (e.g., use for feedstocks); exported fuel and electricity; coal used for synthetic natural gas; natural gas used in enhanced oil recovery; and ethanol and methanol. In a concession to lawmakers from the cold Northeast, home heating oil was exempt from some parts of the BTU tax. However, the modified tax was still a significant part of the Administration's deficit reduction plan. The budget revealed that a "broad based energy tax" would raise over $50 billion in the next five years. *Budget of the United States Government Fiscal Year 1994* 12–13 (1993).

The BTU tax was increasingly problematic, however, because the Administration had made too many modifications and accepted too many exemptions. Over time, the tax began to resemble Swiss cheese as powerful lawmakers and interest groups were able to obtain special treatment for certain uses of energy or energy-intensive industries. In addition, the Administration often neglected to obtain a firm commitment of support once it accepted a modification. So groups would negotiate for exemptions or special provisions, get the Administration to agree, and then decline to support the resulting BTU tax proposal. Industry groups took full advantage of all the vetogates in the process to win as much as possible at each stage of legislative deliberation and then to come back for more at the next stage. In the House Ways and Means Committee, which was less friendly to rural and energy interests, the energy industry managed to add exemptions and modifications that made the tax less disastrous from their perspective. But, they continued to oppose the BTU tax absolutely in the Senate, where the makeup of the Finance Committee meant that the defection of one Democratic senator could derail the proposal.

One of the more interesting documents released along with the multi-volume President's budget was a paper with *Frequently Asked Questions Regarding the Administration's Proposed Modified BTU Tax*, Office of Tax Policy, Department of the Treasury (Apr. 9, 1993). This was a political document meant to provide friendly lawmakers and interest groups with answers for questions by constituents, other lawmakers, or the press and to convince undecided lawmakers to support the proposal. The answers were provided in easily understood bullets. So in answer to the question "Why did the Administration include an energy tax in the economic package?" the document provides three answers: It would "raise revenues to help reduce the deficit"; it would "reduce environmental damage, promote energy conservation, and reduce dependence on foreign sources of energy"; and it would "help move the U.S. economy from income-based to consumption-based taxation, with attendant benefits to saving and investment." The first and third justifications are not traditional Democratic themes, demonstrating President Clinton's background as a "New Democrat" and the importance of conservative and moderate Democrats to the success of the proposal.

Such political documents inundate a legislator's office during the consideration of controversial legislation such as the President's budget submission. They arrive from the administration, other lawmakers, party leaders, and interest groups. For example, Senator Boren's office received a study entitled *Impact of the Proposed BTU Tax on Oklahoma and Oklahomans.* The bottom line of the study was that the state would lose over 10,960 jobs, or nearly one percent of total employment if the BTU tax were enacted. The average Oklahoma household would face increased expenses of at least $180 per year. Thirty percent of Oklahoma's stripper wells would be abandoned prematurely. The parade of horribles continues for pages: "Oklahoma's approximately 3,600 churches, which not only provide a place for worship, but also day care centers and mothers' day out facilities will see their annual energy costs increase by an average of $403. Churches will not be exempt from this hidden tax." And the study ends with a warning: "The only ones that benefit from the BTU tax are our economic competitors — the Japanese and the Pacific Rim, as well as Germany and the European Economic Community." These studies are not only relevant to the legislator who is making up his mind how to vote, but they also provide him and his staff with statistics for speeches, letters to constituents, and floor statements. How should a staff member who receives such a study react? Can busy congressional aides be expected to check the accuracy of such a study and ensure that it is methodologically sound?

As hearings continued on the specific legislative proposals of the President, Congress was also working on the budget resolution and the other tasks assigned to it by the federal budget acts. By the end of March, the conference report on the concurrent budget resolution, H. Con. Res. 64, was completed. This resolution did not spell out program details or make decisions about whether the Congress would adopt a BTU tax or even a comprehensive energy tax. But it did contain *reconciliation instructions* to the Senate Finance Committee to "report changes in laws within its jurisdiction to increase revenues $27,293,000,000 in fiscal year 1994 and $272,105,000,000 for the period of fiscal years 1994 through 1998." The House Ways and Means Committee was instructed more generally to "report changes in laws within its jurisdiction sufficient to reduce the deficit, as follows: by $29,441,000,000 in fiscal year 1994, by $41,415,000,000 in fiscal year 1995, by $61,912,000,000 in fiscal year 1996, by $81,794,000,000 in fiscal year 1997, and by $85,209,000,000 in fiscal year 1998." In other words, the resolution technically allowed the Ways and Means Committee to meet its instructions through revenue increases; changes in direct spending programs like Medicare, Medicaid and welfare; or some combination. But, of course, any bill would have to be passed in the same form in both the Senate and the House so the two sets of instructions affected both committees. Although the budget committees that wrote the budget resolution assumed, for purposes of these figures, that the reconciliation bill would include a broad-based energy tax, the Finance and

Ways and Means Committees could meet the instructions in any way they wanted.

Because Democrats controlled both houses, the concurrent budget resolution contained figures generally consistent with the President's proposal. The situation is very different when government is divided. For example, subsequent Republican Congresses drafted budget resolutions that diverged substantially from Clinton's budget submissions. This can set up a substantial conflict when the appropriations bills and reconciliation bills implementing the congressional agenda reach the President for his signature.[u] Would it be better to require that the President sign the budget resolution (changing it from a concurrent resolution to a joint resolution that would have the force of law) and thus require interbranch agreement about macrobudgetary objectives early in the process? Or would that merely move the conflict too early in the process before compromises can be encouraged through trades involving particular programs in specific appropriations bills and other legislation? President George W. Bush has long supported using a joint resolution to set the framework for budgeting, arguing that it "would bring the President into the process at an early stage, encourage the President and the Congress to reach agreement on overall fiscal policy before individual tax and spending bills are considered, and give the budget resolution the force of law."[v] Is that a good idea? Remember that the concurrent budget resolution is not completely unenforceable; it is enforced through congressional procedures like points of order and supermajority voting requirements to waive the objections in the Senate.

The 1993 budget resolution also contained a series of provisions called *sense of the Senate provisions*. In one, the resolution announced that it was the sense of the Senate that "[t]he levels and amounts set forth in this resolution are based on the following assumptions [about revenues:] * * * (C) Consistent with the position of the Administration, the BTU tax will be imposed at the same rate on all fuels purchased by households for home heating purposes, and there the supplemental tax on oil will not be imposed on such fuels. (D) Any energy tax enacted during the One Hundred Third Congress should provide such relief to the agriculture industry as is necessary to ensure that the industry does not absorb a disproportionate impact of that tax." These provisions are signals of the positions of senators; most are enacted after a roll call vote on the floor and thus demonstrate concretely how many senators support the statements of principle and also which senators are supporters. The signal is not entirely credible, however. Although it puts senators on record through a vote that can be publicized, a sense of the Senate provision is not binding and can be disregarded by the substantive committees. The vote occurs months before the final bill will be considered by the Senate, so members can hope that

---

u. See, e.g., Anita Krishnakumar, Note, *Reconciliation and the Fiscal Constitution: The Anatomy of the 1995–96 Budget "Train Wreck,"* 35 Harv. J. Legis. 589 (1998) (describing the process that led to a government shutdown).

v. See *Analytical Perspectives, Fiscal Year 2008 Budget of the United States Government* 219 (2007).

any subsequent inconsistencies in voting will be overlooked. But an over-whelming vote on a sense of the Senate provision may well affect the deliberations of the committee with jurisdiction over the revenue or spending bill. These provisions communicate information from the body to committees and from individual members to interest groups and constituents.

HOUSE CONSIDERATION OF THE RECONCILIATION BILL

As the substantive committees considered and drafted revenue proposals to comply with their reconciliation instructions, interest group activity continued. On May 5, one of the most important players in the BTU tax story formed: the Affordable Energy Alliance, a coalition of 900 manufacturers, small busi-nesses, energy businesses, and other associations.[w] The coalition was a temporary one, formed to fight the broad-based energy tax, and it had a multipronged strategy. First, the members wanted to weaken the tax in the Ways and Means Committee, which would act first on any tax proposals, pursuant to the Constitution's provision requiring that revenue bills originate in the House. Second, the coalition would concentrate on pivotal lawmakers in states with many energy-intensive businesses: Louisiana, North Dakota, Texas, Indiana, and Arkansas. Third, the group would organize waves of grassroots opposition through letter-writing campaigns and phone banks. Today, a coalition like the Affordable Energy Alliance would also mount an e-mail campaign, but e-mail had not yet become a prevalent means of communi-cating with lawmakers in 1993. Fourth, the group began to commission and publicize studies of the economic effects of the BTU tax. It announced on May 5 that a study it had funded revealed that the BTU tax would cause the loss of over 600,000 jobs by 1998, and it would cost a middle-class family of four over $479 per year once it was implemented.

Ironically, at the same time the opposition was becoming more organized, some of the original supporters of the BTU tax were becoming increasingly unhappy with the modifications that the Administration had accepted. One of the tricky parts of legislative compromise is accepting deals that add support without either losing existing support or awakening new opposition. On May 17, the Friends of the Earth "expressed concern" about the change in the BTU tax that the Administration had accepted in order to ameliorate some of the objections of Democrats on the Ways and Means Committee.[x] The President of the organization wrote to President Clinton: "I am concerned that the erosion of crucial elements of the tax by special interests, combined with the quiet strategy being employed by your administration, will ruin the BTU tax's environmental benefits, and we will lose enthusiasm for it." Nonetheless, at the end of the month, the House Budget Committee reported out an Omnibus Budget Reconciliation Act, H.R. 2264, which contained revenue provisions,

---

w. *Energy-Intensive Business Form Coalition to Fight BTU Tax, NAM Announces*, Daily Tax Rep. (BNA), May 6, 1993, at G–7.

x. *Changes to Clinton Energy Tax Said to Undermine Environmental Benefits*, Daily Tax Rep. (BNA), May 18, 1993, at G–8.

drafted and passed by the Ways and Means Committee.[y] These tax provisions included a modified BTU tax.

The technical language of the modified BTU tax reads like any arcane tax bill, but the explanation of the committee in the report is more accessible to the layperson. The explanation reveals that the House committee had carved out a number of exemptions, some of which had been reflected in the April description of the tax. Remember that this excerpt from the committee report describes only a few of the exemptions that the House BTU tax included.

OMNIBUS BUDGET RECONCILIATION ACT OF 1993, REPORT OF THE COMMITTEE ON THE BUDGET, HOUSE OF REPRESENTATIVES, 103d Cong., 1st Sess., Rep. No. 103–111 (May 25, 1993).

Energy and Motor Fuels Tax Provisions

1. Btu energy tax (sec. 14241 of the bill and new secs. 4441–4442, 4444–4446, 4448, 4451–4454, 4456–4457, and 6714 of the [Internal Revenue] Code)

PRESENT LAW

No comprehensive Federal energy tax is imposed under present law. Specific Federal excise taxes are imposed on motor fuels (gasoline, special motor fuels, and diesel fuel) used for highway transportation, gasoline and special motor fuels used in motorboats, diesel fuel used in trains, fuels used in inland waterway transportation, and aviation fuels used in noncommercial aviation. Excise taxes also are imposed on coal from domestic mines and on crude oil received at domestic refineries and petroleum products entered into the United States. * * *

REASONS FOR CHANGE

The committee believes that imposition of a broad-based energy tax will help the United States achieve the important goals of deficit reduction and energy conservation. The monies the energy tax will raise are an integral part of the efforts of Congress and the President to reduce the Federal deficit.

In addition to deficit reduction, imposition of an energy tax will foster several worthwhile goals. First, the United States is one of the developed world's most intensive energy consumers. Most of the nation's energy is derived from non-renewable resources. Increasing the cost of non-renewable energy resources to individuals and businesses will provide an economic incentive to conserve these irreplaceable resources.

Second, the burning of fossil fuels contributes to atmospheric pollution and increases the potential for global warming. Consumers of fossil fuels do not directly bear the cost of the environmental damage pollution creates. Imposing

---

y. With respect to reconciliation bills, the Budget Committee's tasks are ministerial; the committee collates the legislation sent to it by the substantive committees, and it has no power to change the provisions as long as they are consistent with the aggregate figures in the concurrent budget resolution.

an energy tax on the consumer of fossil fuels will give consumers a financial incentive to reduce energy use. * * *

Third, the committee believes it is particularly important to reduce our nation's dependence on imported petroleum and that a higher tax on petroleum will help reduce that dependence.

The committee believes it is appropriate to impose a tax on imported high-energy products that is intended to equal the tax that would have been imposed if the product had been manufactured in the United States. * * *

EXPLANATION OF PROVISIONS

Overview

The bill imposes Federal excise taxes on fossil fuels (i.e., coal, natural gas, and petroleum products) (other than those used to generate electricity), alcohol fuels (i.e., ethanol and methanol and their ether derivatives), and electricity. * * *

Exemptions

     * * *

Electricity.—In certain cases, electricity may be utilized as a feedstock in a manner similar to fossil fuels. The bill includes an exemption * * * for this feedstock use. This exemption applies where electrolytic processes utilize electricity to provide a flow of electrons which bond with certain ions in the production process. The exemption is limited to electricity which acts as an electron donor. As with fossil fuels, to the extent the electricity is used as a source of heat, as a source of energy used in a chemical reaction, or is lost due to inefficiencies in conductors or other sources, no exemption is allowed. * * *

The committee expects that Treasury Department regulations will define the scope of the electricity feedstock exemption for products produced in other electrolytic processes in a manner analogous to that described for aluminum (with percentage exemptions determined by the energy embedded in the final product under the predominant electrolytic production process for that product used in the United States). * * *

Heating oil

Distillate fuel oil #2 (including such oil mixed with kerosene) used for space heating of buildings is exempt from the supplemental rate on petroleum products. * * *

Farm use

The bill exempts diesel fuel and gasoline used on farms for farming purposes * * * from the supplemental rate on refined petroleum products.

In the case of diesel fuel, this exemption will be accomplished by either (1) transfers without payment of tax if the dyeing requirements imposed under the bill are satisfied or (2) refunds to farmers in the case of tax-paid fuel used in a partially exempt use. The exemption for on-farm use of gasoline is accomplished by means of refunds to farmers. * * *

Tax on high-energy products

The bill imposes an imputed Btu tax on certain imported products that contain significant levels of direct energy inputs that would be taxable if the products were manufactured in the United States. This tax is intended to equal the tax that would be imposed on the energy inputs if the manufacturing had occurred in the United States.

The imputed Btu tax is imposed only on imported products which the Treasury Department lists as being "energy intensive." The tax is effective for all listed products that are imported after any product is listed.

This passage from the committee report demonstrates several aspects of legislative history. First, notice that some of the committee report language instructs the Treasury how to apply the electricity feedstock provision. Committee reports communicate to a variety of audiences: lawmakers off the committee, courts, interest groups, and, perhaps most importantly, administrative agencies that will implement the legislation. Every agency has books of detailed legislative history that they study when drafting regulations, and usually executive branch officials are involved in congressional drafting and deliberation so that they have a good feel for the intent of the legislative drafters. Agency officials have an incentive to be sensitive to congressional directives, even those that are not legally binding, because they are repeat players who want to maintain good relations with Congress and who rely on the legislature for funding in the future.

Second, the House version of the BTU tax was very much a work-in-progress. For example, the imputed tax on imported high-energy products was unworkable and may have constituted an illegal tax on imports under various international trade agreements. However, it was politically necessary to get the support of key Ways and Means members whose constituents included domestic industries that feared competition from overseas producers not subject to the BTU tax. So, in some sense, the imputed tax provision was a placeholder to signal that the Administration and party leaders were working to solve the concerns of the affected interest groups. If better language were worked out before the floor consideration, a new provision could be included in a large *managers' amendment* that would replace the unworkable language with a new provision and make other changes. The problem could also be solved in the Senate or, as a last resort, in the conference committee.

The next steps in our case study of the BTU tax occurred simultaneously: The Senate Finance Committee began to consider the revenue proposals, including the BTU tax, and the House floor took up the entire reconciliation package. Although these deliberations were separate, the various actors watched the other proceedings closely and calibrated their activities to account for developments on the other side of Capitol Hill. The main worry for House members from states with powerful constituents who opposed the BTU tax was that they would vote in favor of the omnibus bill that contained the tax, and then the Finance Committee would remove the provision. In that case, the House members would have cast a politically difficult vote for no good reason.

Understanding that, the Administration and party leaders worked first to keep the Democrats on the Finance Committee in line. In *The Agenda*, Bob Woodward describes several of those meetings, including an important meeting at the White House on May 6 between the President and all eleven of the Democrats on the Finance Committee. Remember that the Finance Committee's partisan composition of 11 Democrats and 9 Republicans meant that, as long as the Republicans voted in a block against the proposal, any one Democrat could defect and defeat the President's proposal in Committee.

The new Chairman of the Finance Committee, Senator Patrick Moynihan (D–N.Y.), did not have the close relationship with the moderate and conservative Democrats from energy-producing and rural states that his predecessor Bentsen had developed. Moreover, Moynihan had not been Chairman long enough to have done many favors for members that he could call in, but he did have the advantage of a Democratic President, the first in twelve years. "The important issue was to pass a budget of some form that could be called Clinton's plan. Although some of it was miserable and awful, Moynihan felt, details were almost irrelevant. Failure would mean the report would go out [to the country and the world:] The United States again doesn't have a government, another failed presidency." *The Agenda, supra,* at 179. During the meeting, which was also attended by the respected majority leader George Mitchell (D–Maine), Senator Conrad reiterated his concerns about the effect of the BTU tax on farmers. Senator Breaux (D–La.) "voiced reservations, especially about the BTU tax. It was a bad idea whose time has not come, he said, calling it downright 'goofy' and unworkably complicated. He would prefer some other kind of tax." *Id.* at 180. Senator Boren also indicated that he was uncertain whether he could support the BTU tax or the entire package, which was not aggressive enough on entitlement reform, a necessary component to any long-term effort to reduce the deficit. Boren was already talking with his friend and fellow moderate Senator John Danforth (R–Mo.) about an alternative budget proposal with more cuts in entitlements, a statutory cap on overall entitlement spending that would be enforced through a sequester, and without a BTU tax.

This meeting provided Moynihan and other leaders a sense of how difficult the path would be in the Senate for the President's proposal. House members knew of the dissatisfaction in the Finance Committee; their concerns became more serious when Senator Boren announced publicly before the Finance Committee deliberations that he would not support an energy tax.[z] To counter the effect of this announcement on the House vote, OMB Director Panetta categorically stated that the White House would retain the BTU tax, although it might be willing to accept modifications like those adopted in the Ways and Means Committee. Boren was also under a great deal of pressure not to derail the President's plan in committee; the two other waffling senators, Conrad and Breaux, ultimately announced that they would support the revenue bill even with a BTU tax. Most of these announcements and negotiations took place on

---

z. *House Democrats Plan to Move Forward on Budget Bill Despite Senate Challenge,* Daily Tax Rep. (BNA), May 25, 1993, at G–5.

the Sunday morning political talk shows like *Meet the Press,* with follow-up meetings in Senate hideaways and offices.

Against this backdrop, the House began its deliberations by passing a special rule that severely restricted members' ability to offer amendments. Remember that the House Rules Committee determines the structure for the consideration of legislation by the full House. Many special rules promulgated by the Rules Committee limit the time for debate and the number of amendments that can be offered, and they usually govern the order of amendments. In this case, the House rule waived all points of order that might be raised against the Omnibus Budget Reconciliation Bill, a common practice in the House. See 139 Cong. Rec. 11,596 (May 27, 1993) (House consideration of H. Res. 186, setting forth the rule). The debate was limited to two hours. The rule allowed only one amendment in the nature of a substitute to be offered by the ranking Republican member on the Budget Committee, Rep. Kasich (R–Ohio). The rule was vociferously opposed by the Republicans who called it a "gag rule permitting just one Republican substitute but no separate votes on * * * critical areas" like an amendment to strike the BTU tax. *Id.* at 11,599 (statement of Rep. Solomon (R–N.Y.)). The Republicans claimed that their amendment was revenue neutral (a requirement of the budget rules) because it would have replaced the BTU tax with spending cuts. In a vote that adhered fairly closely to party lines, however, the restrictive rule was adopted.

Note how this rule protected the Democrats from states with interest groups that opposed the BTU tax. These lawmakers were never forced to vote on an amendment to strike the tax and replace it with spending cuts that did not harm energy or related industries. Thus, they could tell constituents that they were forced to accept a package that contained some provisions they disliked in order to obtain favorable provisions, to implement the deficit reduction that the public wanted, and to support their President. The House rules allow party leadership to construct packages that protect members in this way, and omnibus proposals like the reconciliation bill allow majorities to be assembled by sweetening the medicine just enough to make it palatable.

Even with this protective structure, several House Democrats from energy-producing and farm states were increasingly nervous about voting for the reconciliation package, particularly if their Senate colleagues would ultimately manage to eliminate the BTU tax entirely. With a block of conservative Democrats from the South and West holding a balance of power, the Administration had to cultivate every vote. Bob Woodward continues the story by focusing on the pressure placed on Representative David McCurdy, a New Democrat from Oklahoma. McCurdy had already publicly announced that he believed the reconciliation package contained too many taxes and not enough spending cuts. His contact in the Administration was former oil and gas executive Mack McLarty, Clinton's Chief of Staff. On the day of the vote in the House, McCurdy told Clinton that he "could not see voting for it. The administration was assembling the wrong coalition, sending the wrong signals, and planning to set up an unwieldy new bureaucracy for the new BTU tax." *The Agenda, supra,* at 205. McCurdy wanted more spending cuts in the entitlement arena, and he didn't want to wait for Mrs. Clinton's health care reform package to get them.

An hour later, McCurdy met with about ten other Democrats who were experiencing similar anguish. They talked to Bentsen about their dislike of the BTU tax; they talked to Breaux who said that the Administration had promised him that they would dump the BTU tax. Although it was too late to implement this change in the House (given the restrictive special rule), Breaux promised that the Senate would work out the problems in the conference committee. "McCurdy said it was madness. The White House wanted the House members to walk the plank and vote for the unpopular BTU tax, only then to drop it in the Senate. The Senate would get credit for its elimination while House Democrats would be seen as energy-tax supporters. This last-minute panic was precisely the wrong way to change government." *Id.* at 206.

It was almost time for the House vote. McCurdy received one more call from McLarty. The White House Chief of Staff told the Oklahoman that if he didn't vote for this bill, he would kill the President's first major policy initiative. McCurdy had been a strong friend and supporter of the President. Moreover, McLarty assured him that the President finally understood that it was the moderate New Democrats who held the key to success, that he would consult with them more, and that he would guarantee that the BTU tax would be eliminated in the Senate. McCurdy related these promises to his colleagues and convinced enough to vote for the bill so that it passed by a vote of 219–213. *Id.* at 207-08. At least in McCurdy's case and probably in other instances as well, the vote cast was strategic; McCurdy did not sincerely support the proposal, but he believed continuing the process was a better result than delivering such a blow to his friend and the leader of his party, Bill Clinton. In the next election, McCurdy was defeated by a Republican who campaigned in large part on the issue of the BTU tax and the Clinton budget proposal.

SENATE CONSIDERATION OF THE RECONCILIATION BILL

At this point, all eyes were on the Senate Finance Committee. The support for the BTU tax had eroded as the exemptions had reduced its positive effect on the environment. Furthermore, the exemptions and other complications added to the design of the tax in order to gain votes had undermined any support that it had in the Clinton economic team. Many energy-intensive industries had received favorable treatment under the modified tax, decreasing the possibility that it would significantly reduce energy usage in the country and leading to fears that it would distort the economy. And, finally, the more exemptions added to the tax, the less money it would raise and the less substantial its effect on deficit reduction. The Wall Street Journal proclaimed, "If you don't have an exemption from the BTU tax yet, maybe you just aren't trying." Timothy Noah, *BTU Tax is Dying Death of a Thousand Cuts As Lobbyists Seem Able to Write Own Exemptions*, Wall St. J., June 8, 1993, at A18. Interest groups unable to win concessions in the design of the tax tried to obtain other tax benefits as a sort of payoff for their support. For example, the Wall Street Journal article reported that Senator Boren, still publicly stating that he would vote against the BTU tax in committee, was "holding out in part for a $1.7 billion tax credit for low-producing, or 'stripper,' wells, though an aide says that concession alone isn't likely to be enough to win him over." In fact, by this time in the process, nothing short of elimination of the BTU tax would be sufficient to placate Boren.

These negotiations reveal the two kinds of bargains available to legislators trying to forge a majority consensus. First, affected groups can work to evade any burden of the proposed legislation or at least to ameliorate any effects of the proposal. These substantive bargains require redrafting the proposal to change its scope. Second, groups can agree to accept the legislation that harms them in return for a benefit that they value more. These deals are more likely to be accepted when both parts of the bargain can be enacted at the same time. Otherwise, the group will fear that the distasteful legislation will be enacted, but that the benefit they want will somehow not manage to overcome all of the hurdles in the legislative process. Omnibus legislation thus facilitates the second kind of deal because it allows for simultaneous enactment of both parts of the bargain. The germaneness rule, the Byrd Rule, and other procedural budget rules limit the universe of possible provisions that can be included in one bill, but there remains a substantial amount of leeway to allow legislators to assemble the support they need to enact the law. For example, the tax credit for stripper wells to pay off the independent oil and gas producers could have been part of an omnibus budget reconciliation bill; the difficult part of the deal would have been finding the money to pay for a tax subsidy of that size. Remember that the reconciliation instructions required the Finance Committee's package to raise a sizable amount of revenue for deficit reduction, and PAYGO rules required at least revenue neutrality. The independent oil and gas industry had another problem as they worked to obtain a benefit in return for their support. They had just received a tax benefit of over $1 billion in the revenue title of the Energy Policy Act of 1992, Pub. L. No. 102–486, 106 Stat. 2776, and legislators from non-oil-producing states saw a further request as unacceptably greedy.

These bargains also demonstrate the difficulty of managing a coalition like the Affordable Energy Alliance with its over 900 members. One irony of coalitions of interest groups is that size is both an advantage and disadvantage. The size of the Affordable Energy Alliance made it a potent force with influence in every district and state. It was a force to be reckoned with, and it had resources sufficient to commission and publicize studies about the effects of the BTU tax. But the larger and broader the coalition, the more susceptible it may be to tactics that divide its members and dissipate its strength. Large coalitions often comprise groups whose interests are aligned but are not identical. Accordingly, the opponents of a coalition can modify a proposal to satisfy the concerns of some of the coalition members, as the House Ways and Means Committee did with the various exemptions and the imputed tax on imports.

Alternatively, bargainers can undermine the coalition by bribing some members with benefits and programs that they value greatly. In the case of the Affordable Energy Alliance, the Independent Petroleum Association of America refused to participate in the coalition from the outset because it wanted the freedom to negotiate its own deal and pursue its own interest without fear of a conflict with the coalition's objectives. The fragility of the coalition became apparent as members of the Senate Finance Committee worked to transform the unpopular and now unworkable BTU tax into something that would raise some money, allow the Administration to save face, and get the bill through Congress. Many members of the coalition would be relieved, but some might face an even greater burden than before.

On June 9, Senator Breaux's office issued a press release that revealed the details of a compromise on which he had been working for weeks. He announced a proposal to replace the BTU tax with $30 billion in spending cuts in the Medicare program and an energy tax on transportation fuels that would raise $40 billion. "My compromise proposal will cost consumers less, cut spending more, preserve jobs, and still reach President Clinton's overall goal of $500 billion deficit reduction over the next five years," Breaux said. The transportation tax would add 7.3 cents per gallon to all fuels used in transportation, including cars, trucks, boats, trains, and airplanes. It would not require a new bureaucracy for collection, as the BTU tax would have, but would be collected in the same way as existing taxes on transportation fuels.

Senator Breaux's transportation tax now became the focal point of negotiations. Although some Democrats in the White House and in the House of Representatives remained committed to the modified BTU tax, the changes already made in it had weakened its support. The tax on transportation fuels could be characterized as a "broad based energy tax" and thus could be sold as consistent with the President's objectives. The Administration was willing to forget Clinton's campaign promise, made in the primaries, not to impose a gas tax to raise revenue for deficit reduction or new spending programs. After all, the BTU tax would have indirectly raised the price of gasoline (by around 7.5 cents per gallon), so in a sense that campaign pledge had already been broken. Many of the producers of energy did not worry about the transportation tax, which was levied directly on consumers; the only energy-intensive industries affected were those that used disproportionate amounts of transportation services. In short, this proposal realigned most of the interests, seriously eroding the ability of coalitions like the Affordable Energy Alliance to remain intact and viable. Perhaps the more accurate description, however, is that the move from a BTU tax to a transportation fuels tax meant that the coalition had essentially won. Only a few of their members were worse off under the Breaux proposal; the majority were much better off. The predator in this offset battle had to a large extent been vanquished.

Opposition still existed, of course. There was opposition from groups ideologically opposed to any increased federal taxes. Certainly, it did not appear that any Republicans would agree to support the Breaux proposal. One conservative think tank, the Institute for Research on the Economics of Taxation (IRET), released an attack of the proposal on June 11; the document was entitled *The Breaux Budget Proposal: A Smaller Dose of Poison*. "[T]he Breaux proposal may be described as consisting of smaller tax increases and more spending cuts than the Clinton plan. In the sense that it is better to be shot four times in the foot than five times, the Breaux proposal is a marginal improvement." Relying on a previous study of the economic effects of a 10 cents per gallon tax, IRET projected that the Breaux tax would reduce GNP by $25–26 billion in the 1990s and cause the loss of 200,000 to 225,000 jobs. Groups that would be hard hit by the new tax, like the transportation industry, began to try to negotiate exemptions or special deals. One lobbyist for the American Association of Railroads signaled to lawmakers that his client would endorse the Breaux plan if another tax on railroad fuels was eliminated or allowed to expire in 1995.

Party leaders began meeting with Senator Boren to convince him to support a compromise proposal in the Senate Finance Committee. Because of their generally good relationship, Majority Leader Mitchell took the lead in these negotiations. At this point, Boren had joined with a group of Republicans and Democrats and released his own bipartisan budget proposal with substantial reductions in entitlement spending achieved through imposing a cap on entitlement spending enforced by a sequester. Not surprisingly, the bipartisan budget proposal also eliminated the BTU tax; perhaps largely for that reason, the other Democratic sponsor of the proposal was Senator Bennett Johnston from Louisiana. Thus, Boren's support now was not contingent only on the death of the BTU tax; he also demanded a greater level of spending cuts in entitlement programs than Clinton had proposed and than some liberal Democrats were willing to accept. After days of shuttle diplomacy between Democrats on the Senate Finance Committee, Mitchell got agreement on a package that included a $20 billion transportation tax of 4.3 cents per gallon and an additional $20 billion in reduced Medicare spending.

On June 16, all eleven Democrats voted for this package that was included in the Omnibus Budget Reconciliation Act sent to the floor by the Senate Budget Committee. In the committee report description of the modified tax on transportation fuels, the reasons for change were given:

> The committee believes that deficit reduction is critical to the nation's economic well-being and that responsible actions must be taken to address growing annual budget deficits and the increasing balance of federal government debt. It is the committee's view that the revenues raised by a broad-based transportation fuels excise tax will make an important contribution toward reducing the deficit.
>
> The committee also believes that a transportation fuels tax should further other important objectives. The committee understands that in 1992, approximately two-thirds of domestic consumption of petroleum was for transportation uses. By providing an incentive to reduce motor fuel consumption, this tax should tend to improve environmental problems that result from the transport, storage and burning of petroleum products to power motor vehicles, vessels, and aircraft. In addition, reduced consumption of petroleum products should decrease U.S. reliance on imported oil.[a]

---

a. Senate Committee on the Budget, 103rd. Cong., 1st Sess., *Reconciliation Submissions of the Instructed Committees Pursuant to the Concurrent Resolution on the Budget (H. Con. Res. 64)* 379 (Comm. Print 1993).

The committee proposal shows signs of the haste with which this agreement was forged. For example, the proposed tax applied to ethanol and methanol, fuels produced by an industry with strong supporters on the Senate Finance Committee. Remember that the Administration's April version of the BTU tax exempted these fuels from taxation, and several members in the Finance Committee were demanding their exemption from the transportation fuels tax. But there wasn't time during the committee deliberations to find the money to offset this exemption, and some in the Senate opposed special treatment for this industry, a result of the clout of farmers and corporate interests like Archer-Daniels-Midland. Thus the committee report includes the following language: "Ethanol, methanol, and their ether derivatives are fully taxable at the 4.3-cent rate. The committee recognizes, however, that the impact of the transportation tax on ethanol, methanol, and their derivative ethers, as well as on other alternative fuels, requires further analysis, and the committee intends that these matters be addressed in the conference on this legislation."

On June 23, the floor consideration of the reconciliation bill began in the Senate. Although budget rules restrict floor debate to twenty hours, the Senate does not structure those twenty hours through a rule promulgated by a committee like the House Rules Committee. Instead, the majority leader works to put together unanimous consent agreements about the length of debate and the order of amendments. Often, he can get agreement for only part of the debate; for example, on June 22, Mitchell propounded a unanimous consent agreement that the first four hours of debate be equally divided between the two parties. On the morning of June 23, he propounded a new unanimous consent agreement ordering that the first amendment be a Democratic one concerning small business and the second be a Republican one in the nature of a substitute.

Senator Bumpers (D–Ark.) offered the first amendment. It was a tax proposal to reduce the capital gains rate on the sale of stock in certain small venture capital businesses. The amendment had broad support on the merits, and it had been included in a tax bill the previous year that President Bush had vetoed. It had not been one of the lucky few, however, to make it into the Finance Committee mark in 1993. After the amendment was introduced, the ranking Republican member of the Senate Budget Committee, Senator Domenici (R–N.M.), raised a point of order against the amendment on the ground that it was not germane. Under the budget rules in the Senate, an amendment to a reconciliation bill must be germane, which means it can only strike a provision, change a number or date, restrict the scope of the bill without adding new subject matter, or add precatory language such as sense of the Senate provisions. See Section 305(b)(2) of the 1974 Budget Act, as amended. Like the Byrd Rule, this rule attempts to restrict logrolling opportunities by reducing the number of provisions that can be added to a reconciliation bill. It also reduces the power of individual senators and increases the power of committees relative to their power with respect to non-reconciliation bills, because legislators cannot add anything they want as an amendment on the floor. The germaneness requirement takes 60 votes in the Senate to waive.

Senator Bumpers' reaction to this point of order reflects the frustration felt by many senators when their substantive proposals run into the hurdle of a procedural requirement of the budget acts. "Mr. President," he remonstrated, "I never cease to be amazed in this body about how important issues can be made light of, how people can obfuscate the issue and distract people's attention from what we are trying to do here. * * * I have worked on this amendment for 4 years. It has passed the U.S. Senate twice. It was vetoed in [H.R.] 11 last year by President Bush, not because of this. He was for it. President Bush was for it. President Clinton was for it. President Clinton is for it. And, God knows, every small businessman in America is for it." 139 Cong. Rec. 13,788 (June 23, 1993). However, Senator Bumpers did not have 60 votes in the Senate for it this time; only 54 senators voted to waive the point of order, so the amendment was ruled not germane and disallowed.

What do you think of this supermajority voting requirement? Should the Senate have been allowed to amend the reconciliation bill if a majority supported the amendment? If Bumpers had 54 votes in favor, why didn't he first try to amend the germaneness rule, which would have required only a majority vote if done in a particular way, and then worked to pass his proposal? Would he have been able to obtain the same 54 votes to amend the rule?

Later that day, the Senate considered an amendment that House members had been denied the opportunity to consider. Senator Nickles (R–Okla.) moved to strike the tax on transportation fuels. In this way, he forced a more difficult vote politically for some Senate Democrats than their House counterparts had faced when voting for the entire package that contained the tax. Nickles worked to embarrass the Administration, noting that President Clinton had stated his opposition to a gas tax many times during the campaign. Nickles talked about the effect of the tax on Oklahoma, using figures provided to him by constituents like American Airlines. Senator Breaux rose to defend his transportation fuels tax, arguing that in real terms gasoline would be cheaper with the tax than it had been in 1985 or other points in our history. He contrasted the economic effects that Nickles cited with the effects of a continued high deficit, and he argued that other parts of the reconciliation act would reduce the tax burden on lower-income Americans. Finally, he assured members of his own party that the BTU tax, which remained a part of the House version and would be considered in the conference committee, was "dead, and I predict it is not going to come back, because people now realize it is a bad idea." 139 Cong. Rec. 13,999 (June 23, 1993). Although the Nickles amendment was susceptible to budget points of order, Senator Breaux moved to table it instead, a parliamentary tactic which has the effect of killing the amendment in the Senate. By a close vote of 50–48, the amendment was tabled; even Democratic senators like Boren and Johnston voted to table in part because the amendment did not offset the revenue lost by striking the transportation fuels tax. Nickles and his colleagues knew that the amendment would lose, but they insisted on the vote anyway for political reasons. They wanted a campaign issue in 1994 in close congressional races in states hard hit by any such tax.

Ultimately, the Senate was ready to vote. After a roll call on June 24, the Senate was tied, 49–49. The defecting Democrats were Senators Bryan (D–Nev.), DeConcini (D–Ariz.), Johnston, Lautenberg (D–N.J.), Nunn (D–Ga.), and Shelby (D–Ala.). The transportation tax was the key issue for Johnston only. For example, DeConcini, who represented a state with many elderly retirees, was upset primarily about a provision that would increase the tax on some income earned by relatively well-off Social Security recipients. Nunn announced that he would vote against the package because the proposal did not sufficiently address entitlement reform, a fundamental element of deficit reduction. Shelby became a Republican in the next Congress, so his vote was likely the result of his closer identification with the opposing party. Vice-President Gore knew that the vote was likely to be close, so he had presided over the Senate, and he cast the tie-breaking vote necessary to move the reconciliation bill into a conference committee of the Senate and the House.

CONFERENCE COMMITTEE CONSIDERATION

Although technically still alive, the BTU tax was doomed in the conference committee. Not only could it not pass the Senate, but the reconciliation bill had passed the House of Representatives only because members like McCurdy had been promised that the BTU tax would be killed in the Senate and never resurrected. Thus, attention was focused on the transportation fuels tax, a proposal that had been hurriedly drafted and enacted before many interest groups could gear up to oppose it or to lobby for special treatment. They were ready for the conference committee. On July 19, twenty-one Democratic senators sent a *Dear Colleague letter* to the Democratic members of the conference committee. A Dear Colleague letter is a way that members communicate with each other. They use such letters to alert staff and members about amendments or about their opposition to amendments; letters go around Capitol Hill to announce new legislation or seek cosponsors. This Dear Colleague letter concerned an amendment that had been adopted on the Senate floor to exempt aviation fuels from the transportation fuels tax. The letter noted that the tax would have cost the airline industry "$2.53 billion over the next five years, and resulted in an increased after-tax operating loss of over $75 million per year for the average major U.S. airline. [The decision to pass the exemption] was taken in direct response to the $10 billion loss the industry has experienced over the past three years, and the resulting elimination of over 100,000 aviation related jobs. * * * The financial recovery of this important segment of our economy will be greatly influenced by the decisions of the conference committee."

This was one of several such letters or communications designed to signal to the conference committee which proposals were likely to survive floor consideration and which were not. The difficult thing about such signals is determining how serious the signatories are. Would the 21 senators vote against the entire reconciliation bill if the conference committee applied the tax to aviation fuels? The letter also reflects the continuing concern of members about the fate of successful floor amendments. Sometimes the managers of legislation will accept amendments in order to ensure passage, but then they will not work actively in the conference committee to keep the amendments in the bill. They can always claim to concerned members that, while they fought valiantly to retain the amendment, the other house forced them to recede in order to reach a compromise. Because most negotiations between conference committee members take place in private between party leaders and committee chairs, rank-and-file members find it difficult to know whether such claims are accurate.

Finally, on August 4, the conference committee report was published. The Senate proposal had survived virtually intact. With respect to the issue of concern in the Dear Colleague letter, a compromise had been reached. Jet fuel used in noncommercial aviation would be taxed fully. Gasoline and jet fuel used in commercial aviation would be subject to the tax beginning on October 1, 1995, so the industry received a temporary exemption, which it could work to make permanent in the next session. On August 5, the House considered the reconciliation bill under a special rule that waived all points of order, allowed for six hours of equally divided debate, and allowed only a motion to recommit (a motion to reject the bill and send it back to the conference committee). After the debate, the reconciliation act passed by a narrow margin, 218–216. In the end, 41 Democrats, including Dave McCurdy, voted against the President's deficit reduction plan with its very scaled back transportation fuels tax. Nevertheless, it survived the House and moved on to the even more closely divided Senate.

Under budget rules, Senate debate on the reconciliation conference report is limited to ten hours. Democratic leaders and the Administration focused their efforts on a handful of Democrats who seemed to be wavering. The President has a remarkable number of goodies that he can trade for votes, and as the first Democrat in twelve years, he could make the strong argument that his copartisans owed him the chance to implement his vision. But his persuasive abilities, while impressive, were not always successful. For example, David Boren had already announced that he would not vote for the conference report even though he had voted for the bill in committee and in the Senate. In the end, he had decided that it was not sufficiently aggressive on deficit reduction and entitlement reform, and he preferred a bipartisan approach rather than a bill that won only with Democratic votes. See Woodward, *The Agenda, supra*, at 272–76 (describing the meetings between the White House and Boren). His defection no doubt influenced House Democrats in his state and other oil-producing states to vote against the bill since they would face harder questions from constituents who had evidence that some Democrats managed to resist the President's entreaties. Bryan, Nunn, Johnston, Lautenberg and Shelby remained opposed, but DeConcini decided, after intense lobbying by the President and Democratic leaders, to vote in favor of the conference report. Ultimately, the attention was focused on Bob Kerrey (D–Neb.), who had run against Clinton in the primaries and was known as an intelligent and sincere legislator, if a bit eccentric at times.

Republicans and Democrats worked to influence Kerrey. Clinton and Kerrey had a private meeting on the Truman balcony of the White House. According to Woodward, Kerrey told Clinton that he thought this deficit reduction plan was too modest. The country faced an impending disaster in the entitlement area as the country aged and demanded more health care and put great strain on the Social Security system. The reductions in entitlement spending in the reconciliation bill were insubstantial and did not fundamentally restructure the Medicare program as was required for long-term solvency. *The Agenda, supra,* at 303–305. When the White House later learned that Kerrey wanted to head a bipartisan commission to consider adopting spending cuts and restructuring entitlement programs, the Administration worked on a proposal to establish a presidential commission that Kerrey would find attractive. Finally, on August 6, Senator Kerrey had made up his mind and came to the floor to deliver a dramatic speech that had the attention of everyone in Washington, D.C.

"I have taken too long, I am afraid to reach this decision. My head, I confess, aches with all the thinking," Kerrey began. "But my heart aches with the conclusion that I will vote 'yes' for a bill which challenges America too little, because I do not trust what my colleagues on the other side of the aisle will do if I say no. * * * Collectively, [you, Republicans] have locked yourselves together into the idea of opposition; opposition, not to an idea, but to a man — a man who came to this town green and inexperienced in our ways, and who wants America to do better, to be better, and to continue to believe in the invincibility of ideas, of courage and action." He told the Republicans that he did not trust that they would work constructively with the President and Democrats to pass a different deficit reduction plan if this proposal were defeated. "So I vote yes, and we pass a bill that seems to follow a perverse interpretation of the Sermon on the Mount: The meek shall inherit the Earth."

Kerrey then spoke to the new President: "President Clinton, if you are watching now, as I suspect you are, I tell you this: I could not and should not cast a vote that brings down your Presidency." He urged the President to be bolder in his proposals to reduce the deficit and control entitlement spending. "On February 17 [in the State of the Union address] you told America the deficit reduction was a moral issue and that shared sacrifice was need to put it behind us. * * * But it is not shared sacrifice for us to brag that we are only raising taxes on those who earned over $180,000 a year. It is political revenge. * * * Our fiscal problems exist because of rapid, uncontrolled growth in programs that primarily benefit the middle class [like Social Security and Medicare]."

Kerrey also addressed the BTU tax: "You had the right idea, Mr. President, with the BTU tax. And when we came after you with both barrels blazing, threatening to walk if you did not yield, you should have let us walk. * * * Instead, we find ourselves with a bill that asks Americans to pay 4.3 cents a gallon more. If they notice, they will be surprised. And if they complain, I will be ashamed." He concluded, "I began by saying that I do not trust 44 Republicans enough to say no to this bill. I close by saying that I suspect the feeling is mutual. The challenge for us — and too much is at stake for us to even consider the possibility of failing — is for us to end this distrust and to put this too partisan debate behind us. For the sake of our place in history, rise to the high road that this occasion requires." 139 Cong. Rec. 19,813 (Aug. 6, 1993).

Floor deliberation continued after the speech, but the conclusion was inevitable given Gore's ability to break a tie. Finally, the Omnibus Budget Reconciliation Act of 1993 passed, with Al Gore casting the 51st vote in favor. Note how important the budget rules pertaining to a reconciliation bill were to the success of the proposal. The supporters of the President did not have the votes to invoke cloture. Had the rules not ruled out the possibility of a filibuster, the Democratic leaders and the Administration would have had to negotiate with the conservative Democrats and more liberal Republicans to construct an entirely different deal with fewer taxes, no energy tax, more spending cuts, and perhaps an entitlement cap or other more stringent budget procedures. The final version of a broad based energy tax, a 4.3 cents per gallon tax on transportation fuels, was estimated to raise about $25 billion over five years. The entire package was designed to reduce the deficit by $500 billion over five years. Before the end of the century, the budget was actually balanced because of a strong economy and higher-than-expected tax revenue collections. The 1993 bill had something to do with that success, as did further spending restraint adopted after the Republican Congress reached a series of budget deals with President Clinton.

Although Senator Kerrey, along with Senator Danforth, chaired a Bipartisan Commission on Entitlement and Tax Reform that presented several reports on ways to reform entitlement programs to ensure their long-term viability, no serious reforms effort ever received sustained attention from the Clinton administration after the defeat of its health care reform proposal. The exemption for aviation fuel used in the commercial airline industry expired in 1995. It was not extended, in part because of the difficulty of finding an acceptable offset for the revenue loss that an extension would produce. Finally, there were some half-hearted efforts by the Republican Congress to repeal the tax on transportation fuels, but again the PAYGO requirements meant that a substantial offset had to be found to replace the loss in revenue. Budget rules serve as additional procedures that protect the status quo by making changes, here revenue-losing proposals in the tax code, hard to accomplish.

SECTION 3. OTHER CONGRESSIONAL STRUCTURES

The congressional budget process is perhaps the most pervasive comprehensive structure to shape congressional decisionmaking in a particular arena. It is not, however, the only such framework. To conclude our analysis of due process of lawmaking, we will describe and assess the Unfunded Mandates Reform Act (UMRA), Pub. L. No. 104–4, 109 Stat. 48, and congressional structures relating to the oversight of regulations.

The Unfunded Mandates Reform Act. In the 1990s, the issue of unfunded federal mandates on state, local and tribal governments was placed on the national agenda. An unfunded mandate is an enforceable duty imposed on subnational governments by the federal government that is not accompanied by federal funding to defray the costs of compliance. So, for example, if Congress requires local sewage systems to adopt extensive improvements to meet environmental standards or requires all state and local agencies to pay workers no less than a set minimum wage and does not also send funds to the sub-national governments to pay the additional costs, then the federal government has imposed an unfunded mandate.

The campaign to eliminate or reduce unfunded mandates was led by the intergovernmental lobby. This group is a loosely-coordinated coalition of more than sixty organizations representing state and local public officials.[a] The most influential are "The Big Seven," comprising the Council of State Governments, International City Management Association, Nation's Association of Counties, National Conference of State Legislatures, National Governors' Association, National League of Cities, and the U.S. Conference of Mayors. These groups funded several studies about the impact of unfunded mandates on states and localities, and they organized high-profile protests at the U.S. Capitol to move the issue to the forefront of the national agenda. Perhaps the best known study estimated the costs of unfunded mandates on 314 cities surveyed to be $6.5 billion in 1993 and $54 billion in the following five years. Price Waterhouse, *Impact of Unfunded Federal Mandates on U.S. Cities: A 314–City Survey* (1993) (funded by the U.S. Conference of Mayors). Although the methodology of the study was attacked, it was influential in shaping the policy debate.

The rise to power of the intergovernmental lobby provides an interesting example of group formation, concretely illustrating some of the theoretical work we discussed in Chapter 1, § 2's analysis of pluralist theory. Most of these organizations were formed at the beginning of the century as part of the effort to professionalize government service. National politicians encouraged their growth to serve the politicians' own purposes. For example, Theodore Roosevelt called a conference of governors in 1908 to further his conservation efforts, and Franklin Roosevelt strengthened intergovernmental organizations that were advocates of his New Deal programs. At first, lobbying the national government was not among the top priorities of these fledgling organizations, and most moved their headquarters to Washington, D.C., only with the growth of federal grant programs in the 1960s and 1970s. Thus, the initial costs of organizing, often the greatest hurdle facing groups that seek to influence governmental policies, were already defrayed when the associations decided to turn some of their attention to lobbying the national government.

Unfunded mandates presented a difficult problem for state and local government officials. They worried that voters blamed them for increased taxes or reduced services that were required to meet the costs of complying with the federal mandates. State and local officials were not convinced that they could rely on federal lawmakers to sufficiently protect states' interests. Certainly, some members of Congress are sincerely concerned about the effects of unfunded mandates on state and local financial resources or are committed to a more robust federalism that would impose fewer obligations on sub-national governments. National lawmakers occasionally demonstrate concern for federalism, in part because a substantial majority has experience in state or local government. This experience, as well as the strong ties between national

---

a. See David Arnold & Jeremy Plant, *Public Official Associations and State and Local Government: A Bridge Across One Hundred Years* (1994).

lawmakers and state and local officials, increases the sensitivity of national lawmakers to arguments made by members of the intergovernmental lobby.[b] Even with such receptivity, state and local officials nonetheless feared that national lawmakers were systematically failing to enact the appropriate level of unfunded mandates for several reasons.

First, federal lawmakers might not have been aware that a bill included an unfunded mandate when they voted on it. As we saw in the study of the BTU tax, Congress does a significant portion of its work through large omnibus proposals that can include provisions that escape the notice of most lawmakers. Moreover, interest groups may find it more difficult to monitor the contents of complex and lengthy bills, particularly when they have to keep track of virtually every committee of Congress. Unfunded mandates can be parts of bills in the jurisdiction of any of the congressional committees, so even a strong and organized lobby with close ties to federal legislators like the intergovernmental group may find it nearly impossible to keep up with developments and inform lawmakers of troublesome provisions.

Any failure on the part of national lawmakers to act consistently with their views on unfunded mandates might have stemmed from more than mere ignorance, however. The process appeared to be plagued with the same sort of systematic collective action problem that we studied in the context of deficit spending.[c] Federal lawmakers who hope to be reelected — as most of them do — prefer to separate the act of establishing popular federal programs from that of raising the money to pay for them, and to avoid responsibility for the latter. They particularly wish to avoid raising taxes, a salient issue for taxpayers during an election. National lawmakers had discovered that unfunded mandates presented a very attractive financing option for new programs. Unfunded mandates forced other officials, those in the states and localities, to raise taxes or otherwise find the funding for programs. The ability to engage in liability shifting might have led members of Congress to impose more mandates on states and localities than they thought were consistent with a robust federal system.[d]

Some have contested the notion that unfunded mandates reduce the political accountability of federal lawmakers.[e] After all, the unfortunate state and local officials have every reason to inform voters that the real scoundrels behind

---

b. See *How Much Does Federalism Matter in the U.S. Senate?*, Intergovernmental Persp., Spr. 1990, at 35 (discussion with Senators Bond (R–Mo.) and Sarbanes (D–Md.) on effect of such experience on congressional deliberations).

c. See Jenna Bednar & William Eskridge, Jr., *Steadying the Court's "Unsteady Path": A Theory of Judicial Enforcement of Federalism*, 68 S. Cal. L. Rev. 1447, 1472–73 (1995); Edward Zelinsky, *Unfunded Mandates, Hidden Taxation, and the Tenth Amendment: On Public Choice, Public Interest, and Public Services*, 46 Vand. L. Rev. 1355 (1993).

d. See Evan Caminker, *State Sovereignty and Subordinacy: May Congress Commandeer State Officers to Implement Federal Law?*, 95 Colum. L. Rev. 1001, 1065 (1995) (discussing accountability concerns with federal mandates).

e. See, e.g., David Dana, *The Case for Unfunded Environmental Mandates*, 69 S. Cal. L. Rev. 1, 18–21 (1995).

higher taxes or reduced programs are in Washington. However, tracing a particular tax increase to the cost of several unfunded mandates is difficult and time-consuming, exceeding the abilities and attention spans of most voters. People are also apt to be cynical when they hear such explanations from state and local politicians, thinking that the lower-level officials are the ones engaged in liability-shifting. Thus, the suspicion that substantial liability shifting was occurring in Congress and harming state and local officials was not a fanciful one.

Responding to the political pressure brought to bear by the intergovernmental lobby, Congress enacted in 1995 the Unfunded Mandates Reform Act, Pub. L. No. 104–4, 109 Stat. 48 (codified in scattered sections of 2 U.S.C.).[f] The design of UMRA drew on the experience with the congressional budget process. According to its purpose section, UMRA was intended "to end the imposition, in the absence of full consideration by Congress, of Federal mandates on State, local, and tribal governments without adequate Federal funding, in a manner that may displace other essential State, local, and tribal government priorities." Not only does the Act require that the necessary information be generated, but it also "establish[es] a mechanism to bring such information to the attention of" Congress in a timely fashion. More generally, the changes in the legislative process will "promote informed and deliberate decisions by Congress on the appropriateness of Federal mandates in any particular instance."

UMRA's coverage is not complete, and the gaps undermine its effectiveness. A federal intergovernmental mandate regulated by the Act is a provision that "would impose an enforceable duty upon State, local, or tribal governments, *except a condition of Federal assistance*." § 658(5)(A) (emphasis added). The exception for conditions creates a significant hole in coverage because many federal requirements take this form. In the first year that UMRA was effective, CBO reviewed 75 bills that imposed costs on states and localities and that were not intergovernmental mandates; the vast majority of these provisions imposed conditions of assistance. An example of a condition is a requirement that states adopt laws prohibiting drunk driving or requiring helmets for motorcyclists as a condition of receiving federal highway funds. Those who study unfunded mandates debate whether conditions of assistance should be treated differently because states and localities technically can decline the federal money if they do not want to comply. Moreover, the conditions are connected with some federal funds, even if the money may not be sufficient to cover all the costs.[g] Whether justified or not, UMRA's definition results in a gap in its scope which is likely to become wider as legislators work to avoid UMRA and as more federal programs provide federal funds to states using block grants restricted by various conditions.

---

f. See Elizabeth Garrett, *Enhancing the Political Safeguards of Federalism? The Unfunded Mandates Reform Act of 1995*, 45 U. Kan. L. Rev. 1113 (1997) (discussing the Act's provisions, motivations, and effects).

g. See, e.g., Michael Fix & Daphne Kenyon, *Introduction*, in *Coping with Mandates: What are the Alternatives?* 3–4 (Michael Fix & Daphne Kenyon eds., 1990).

UMRA is limited in another, less obvious way. UMRA requires special procedures only when an intergovernmental mandate imposes "direct costs" greater than $50 million. A direct cost is the amount the state or local government is required to spend or is prohibited from raising in revenue in order to comply with a federal mandate. Thus, UMRA is not relevant to national laws that impose significant indirect costs on state and local budgets. To illustrate the difference between direct and indirect costs, take, for example, the Immigration Control and Financial Responsibility Act, S. 269, considered in 1996. As amended by a manager's amendment before floor consideration, the Act was estimated to impose direct costs of $10–20 million over six years because of provisions regulating driver's licenses. (Interestingly, the bill in committee had imposed direct costs of $80–200 million; the greater scrutiny required by UMRA and the threat of points of order prompted a compromise proposal reducing the direct costs to facilitate passage.) Senator Graham (D–Fla.) focused, however, on the bill's provisions which attributed to legal aliens the resources of their American sponsors when determining the aliens' eligibility for federal means-tested entitlement programs. These provisions rendered more legal aliens ineligible for federal benefits and would thereby place significant financial burdens on some states and localities because some state general assistance laws require local governments to provide at least basic subsistence-level benefits to all residents. Graham cited figures from the National Conference of State Legislatures showing that the states would have to shoulder additional costs of at least $744 million as a result of these provisions. Under UMRA's definition, however, this cost was not a direct one of the immigration reform act so the immigration act did not trigger UMRA's protections on the floor.

The major goals of UMRA are to produce more information about the direct costs of mandates and to ensure that the information plays a role in congressional decisionmaking. With regard to disclosure, authorizing committees must include reports on unfunded mandates with their committee reports. Most of this information is produced by the State and Local Government Cost Estimates Unit of CBO, to which committees submit all bills and resolutions. If the total direct costs of an intergovernmental mandate in such a proposal exceed $50 million in any of the first five years after the legislation becomes effective, CBO must provide an estimate of the budget authority necessary to defray the direct costs for up to ten years. The committee must also identify any increase in federal appropriations that has been provided to states and localities to meet the costs of the mandate. In addition, CBO produces other analyses of intergovernmental mandates, including a yearly report on the congressional experience with UMRA. See, e.g., CBO, *A Review of CBO's Activities in 2006 Under the Unfunded Mandates Reform Act* (2007).

UMRA has been successful in increasing the amount of information available to Congress. Between 1996 and 2004, CBO reviewed more than 4,700 bills and other legislative proposals to determine whether they contained federal mandates. 551 bills (12%) had intergovernmental mandates; 49 of those (9% of the bills with intergovernmental mandates) included mandates exceeding the $50 million threshold Only three of those bills became law.[h] Moreover, the intergovernmental lobby and other interest groups are consulted by CBO during the early stages of legislative drafting; they often provide information to the estimators about the costs of compliance. They find that UMRA has made their lobbying job easier in at least two ways. First, they know early in the process about the presence of unfunded mandates so they can develop a strategy with more chance of success. Second, because they now have one contact entity, a unit in CBO, they do not need to monitor every committee as closely to learn of laws with unfunded mandates. Of course, intergovernmental organizations still need supporters on the committees to advocate changes and block unfavorable legislation, but UMRA allows groups to use limited resources more effectively.

The information produced has also affected the deliberative process and altered the content of some legislation. CBO reports that its analysts meet frequently with congressional aides so that legislation is drafted to avoid running afoul of UMRA. Generally, observers believe that UMRA has the most influence before a bill reaches the floor as drafters work to avoid its provisions. Rules Committee Chairman Solomon (R–N.Y.) observed: "It has changed the way that prospective legislation is drafted. Anytime there is a markup, this always comes up."[i] For example, the Internet Tax Freedom Act (IFTA), Pub. L. No. 105–277, 112 Stat. 2681–719, considered in 1997, would have prohibited the states and localities from collecting some taxes for a period of time. Gullo, *supra*, at 567. This falls under UMRA's scope because direct costs include amounts that states and localities "would be prohibited from raising in revenues" as a consequence of a mandate. CBO originally estimated that the Act's direct costs would exceed the UMRA threshold. The cost statement was a significant factor in Congress' decision to amend IFTA so that it was "narrower in scope and specifically allowed states that were currently collecting a sales tax on Internet access to continue to do so." *Id*. at 568. The amended proposal's direct costs fell below the threshold; thus, the bill was not subject to a point of order when it was considered on the floor.

Like the congressional budget process, UMRA uses a variety of points of order to enforce its provisions. A point of order lies against any reported bill that contains a federal mandate and is not accompanied by a cost statement from the authorizing committee and CBO. That enforces the requirement of timely disclosure. In addition, any bill, joint resolution, amendment, motion, or conference report that includes an intergovernmental mandate costing more than $50 million in one fiscal year is out of order unless Congress has also provided the funding for that mandate. Until recently, UMRA points of order could be waived by either chamber with a simple majority vote. In fiscal year 2006, the Senate required 60 votes to waive an UMRA point of order; that supermajority requirement stays into effect through September 2010. Points

---

h. Theresa Gullo, *History and Evaluation of the Unfunded Mandates Reform Act,* 57 Nat'l Tax J. 559, 563 (2004).

i. Allan Freedman, *Unfunded Mandates Reform Act: A Partial "Contract" Success*, Cong. Q. Weekly, Sept. 5, 1998, at 2318 (providing other examples).

of order cannot be waived by a special rule in the House, so they provide more protection there than budget points of order. In fact, UMRA points of order arguably make the most difference in the House because of their immunity from special rules; in the Senate, one member could always force targeted discussion on an unfunded mandate through the amendment process. Perhaps not surprisingly, the point of order has been more frequently raised in the House than the Senate; from 1996 to 2005, "UMRA's explicit enforcement mechanism [was used] relatively infrequently (roughly two dozen times in the House and twice in the Senate)".[j] Both points of order in the Senate were raised after the adoption of the three-fifths vote for waiver, and both points of order were sustained, killing two amendments to an appropriations bill that dealt with the minimum wage.

This point-of-order enforcement scheme increases the chances that certain issues will be considered by Congress in a focused way and through a transparent process. Of course, the point of order allows only the *opportunity* for focused deliberation. Like many of the aspects of due process of lawmaking, it does not provide an *assurance* that such deliberation will occur. The opportunity for deliberation does not always come when the point of order is raised. The threat provided by the enforcement provisions affects the drafting, consideration by the committee, and the negotiations before the floor debate. Indeed, given accurate information on all sides, parties should often negotiate before floor deliberations to remove the threat of the point of order. We should not often see points of order raised — and we do not often see them in Congress — if parties make accommodations to avoid the problem.

Furthermore, the point of order may increase accountability and decrease members' ability to shift liability for tax increases to state and local officials. A vote requires members to take a clear stand on the mandate issue alone. Unlike other budget points of order, which can be arcane and confusing even to legislative experts, the meaning of a vote to waive an UMRA point of order is relatively straightforward. The member who votes to waive has voted to impose the costs of a federal program on states or localities. The point of order also reduces a national lawmaker's ability to disclaim full responsibility for a mandate because she can no longer assert that she had no choice but to vote for a repugnant mandate in order to pass a bill that was, on balance, a good one. Nor can she be certain that an unpopular unfunded mandate will slip through the cracks, unnoticed as one small part of a complex and impenetrable bill. The ability to use a point of order to disaggregate the parts of a large omnibus bill and force an unfunded mandate to survive a separate vote can be a significant weapon.

UMRA is generally seen as a qualified success; the success is only partial because the scope of UMRA is limited by its definitions. There do seem to be fewer unfunded mandates enacted since it became effective, although that could also reflect the partisan change in Congress that occurred in the late 1990s. Should the framework be extended or the gaps closed? We will return

---

j. CBO, *A Review of CBO's Activities Under the Unfunded Mandates Reform Act, 1996 to 2005* 5 (2006).

to this question in the problem at the end of this chapter when we provide a proposed Federalism Act. Do lawmakers continue to act as they wish, heedless of federalism concerns and accountability problems, despite laws like UMRA?

Opponents of UMRA argued that it was designed to undermine important national priorities, like the protection of the environment, at least as much as, if not more than, it was intended to protect the values of federalism. UMRA makes it more difficult to adopt proposals that impose national standards on certain behavior, arguably leading to balkanization and less uniformity. National action is required for effective regulation in some cases, for example, in many environmental contexts where pollution has negative effects beyond one state's borders. It was widely argued that many who supported UMRA, and who rely on federalism arguments generally in the legislative process, did not do so sincerely, but as part of an agenda to dismantle a great deal of national regulation. Environmentalists are particularly concerned about any framework that concentrates on the costs of regulation without balancing them against the benefits of proposed laws. Moreover, they worry that even a balancing may not give sufficient weight to the benefits of environmental regulation because they are often qualitative and difficult to quantify, unlike direct costs.[k] Although even strategic use of arguments like federalism may spark sincere and important debate on the matter, there is reason to be concerned about the effects of a procedural framework on Congress' ability to act decisively to solve national problems. One of the certain consequences of procedures that erect hurdles in the legislative process is that the inertia that characterizes the process will become further entrenched, making it more difficult to enact good laws, as well as bad laws.

UMRA presents a different case study than the budget process because federalism is an area where the courts have also been active. In Chapter 8, § 1B3, we will discuss some of the judicial strategies of statutory interpretation designed to protect principles of federalism and to encourage Congress to pay special attention to laws that seem to intrude improperly on state sovereignty. Which approach — the one reflected in UMRA or judicial review — is likely to have the most effect on Congress? Which is most appropriate? Should the two institutions try to calibrate their strategies, for example, with the courts paying closer attention to laws that fall into the gaps in UMRA's coverage? At least one justice has noted the passage of UMRA as relevant to constitutional analysis by courts. In *Printz v. United States*, 521 U.S. 898 (1997), Justice Stevens dissented from the Court's interpretation of the Tenth Amendment in part because passage of UMRA demonstrated that "the political safeguards protecting Our Federalism are effective. * * * Whatever the ultimate impact of [UMRA], its passage demonstrates that unelected judges are better off leaving the protection of federalism to the political process in all but the most extraordinary circumstances." *Id.* at 957–59 (Stevens, J., dissenting).

---

k. See Makram Jaber, *Unfunded Federal Mandates: An Issue of Federalism or a "Brilliant Sound Bite"?*, 45 Emory L.J. 281, 294–95 (1996).

UMRA also has a separate title dealing with regulatory accountability and reform. This second part of UMRA leads us to a discussion of regulatory reform statutes that are part of a due process of lawmaking structure.

Congressional Procedures Affecting the Oversight of Regulations. After the 1994 Republican takeover of Congress, proposals to reform the regulatory process received more serious consideration. Not only did Republicans push such reforms, but many moderate Democrats supported these proposals as ways to improve the administrative state. Some of these proposals aimed to change the regulatory process itself, for example, by requiring all regulations to meet some sort of cost-benefit analysis. None of the sweeping single-statute reform bills was enacted, however.[l] UMRA's regulatory provisions were also intended to implement direct, albeit less sweeping, changes in agency procedure, although they are procedural rather than substantive modifications. Before beginning the rulemaking process for a rule that might result in an intergovernmental mandate, the agency has to assess the costs and benefits of the mandate and describe the agency's "prior consultation with elected representatives" of state, local and tribal governments. Generally, the agency is directed to establish a process to allow subnational governmental officials to have access and input into the regulatory process. The agency must attempt to reduce the costs of a regulatory mandate on small governments, and with regard to all intergovernmental and private-sector mandates that cost $100 million or more, the agency must identify and consider the least burdensome regulatory alternatives. A Government Accountability Office report concludes that this portion of UMRA has been less successful than the provisions applying to Congress, in part because the regulatory provisions lack the point-of-order enforcement or similar disciplinary devices. *Unfunded Mandates: Views Vary About Reform Act's Strengths, Weaknesses, and Options for Improvement* 5 (Mar. 2005).

A due process of lawmaking perspective focuses our attention on the congressional process, and there was some action in this realm as well. Several changes in congressional oversight procedures have been suggested since the 104th Congress, and a few have been enacted. Many of these show the influence of the congressional budget process in their design. In 1996, Congress enacted the Congressional Review Act, Pub. L. No. 104–121, 110 Stat. 857, 868 (codified at 5 U.S.C. §§ 801–808).[m] The Act provides Congress a period of 60 days after promulgation of a final regulation during which expedited review procedures may be used to disapprove the regulation. Any resolution of disapproval introduced during this period enjoys procedural

---

l. For discussions of this legislation, see William Buzbee, *Regulatory Reform or Statutory Muddle: The "Legislative Mirage" of Single Statute Regulatory Reform*, 5 N.Y.U. Envtl. L.J. 298 (1996); Cass Sunstein, *Congress, Constitutional Moments, and the Cost-Benefit State*, 48 Stan. L. Rev. 247 (1996).

m. See Daniel Cohen & Peter Strauss, *Congressional Review of Agency Regulations*, 49 Admin. L. Rev. 95 (1997). For critiques of the Act, see Julie Parks, *Lessons in Politics: Initial Use of the Congressional Review Act*, 55 Admin. L. Rev. 187 (2003); Morton Rosenberg, *Whatever Happened to Congressional Review of Agency Rulemaking?: A Brief Overview, Assessment, and Proposal for Reform*, 51 Admin. L. Rev. 1051 (1999).

advantages during congressional deliberation. For example, a resolution of regulatory disapproval can be discharged from committee with the support of fewer members than is usually required; the resolution is protected from amendments; and floor debate is limited. As with similar budget process rules, many of these special procedures apply only in the Senate where debate is usually unlimited, filibusters are possible, and amendments difficult to bar. A regulation is prohibited from taking effect when a resolution is passed by both chambers and signed by the President (which is unlikely since he probably supports the regulation issued by his agency officials) or when the President's veto is overridden by Congress. In other words, a resolution of disapproval is a regular piece of legislation, but it is considered under expedited and protective procedures in Congress. Once a regulation has been disapproved, the agency can reissue it only if it is not in "substantially the same form," a controversial legislative directive that will doubtlessly give rise to litigation that will delay the implementation of any subsequently promulgated regulation.

In the first full Congress after the Act was passed, only four resolutions were introduced in the House, and two were introduced in the Senate. No resolution emerged from committee, and only one prompted a hearing.[n] During the controversy over sweeping regulations promulgated in the final days of the Clinton administration, however, the Congressional Review Act was a tool used by Republicans to overturn the regulations. For example, OSHA regulations dealing with ergonomics in the workplace, and estimated to cost business at least $4.5 billion and perhaps up to $90 billion annually, were attacked and ultimately overturned with a disapproval resolution in March 2001. Because of the protective rules governing floor debate, the Democrats in the Senate could not threaten to filibuster the resolution, as they could have a traditional bill overturning the regulations. Why have there been so few resolutions of disapproval? Would the process be more robust if the President's signature was not required for a disapproval resolution to take effect? Would that be constitutional? Does it surprise you that the Act became politically potent only after a Republican President signaled to a Republican Congress that he was willing to sign disapproval resolutions concerning his Democratic predecessor's regulations?

Is it accurate to view the Act as ineffective just because few resolutions have been introduced? Steven Balla provides an example of the Act's indirect influence. In 1998, the Health Care Financing Authority (HCFA) promulgated a regulation that would have required home health care agencies to post a substantial bond to protect against Medicare fraud. The industry protested the rule as economically ruinous to its members. Resolutions of disapproval were introduced in both the House and Senate, and they received dozens of cosponsors. Cosponsorship is a signal of support and demonstrates how many votes a proposal is likely to get once it reaches the floor. In light of this relatively credible signal, HCFA quickly suspended its rule and revised the

---

n. See Steven Balla, *Legislative Organization and Congressional Review of Agency Regulations*, 16 J.L., Econ. & Org. 424 (2000) (studying the Act and patterns of cosponsorship of resolutions).

regulations. The industry trade association believes that "it would have been much harder to get the agency to back down so quickly" without the pressure of the Act.[o]

A Final Due Process of Lawmaking Exercise

In the 106th Congress, several bills were introduced to enact a due process of lawmaking structure for all bills that implicate federalism concerns. The Federalism Act, H.R. 2245, was introduced by Rep. McIntosh (R–Ind.) and was designed "to ensure the liberties of the people by promoting federalism, to protect the reserved powers of the States, to impose accountability for Federal preemption of State and local laws." A similar bill was introduced in the Senate by two powerful legislators, Sen. Thompson (R–Tenn.) and Sen. Lieberman (D–Conn.). Interestingly, supporters justified the proposal as required in part because UMRA has made unfunded mandates more difficult to pass. They argued that people who favor national regulation that unduly trampled on states' rights have turned to other mechanisms to implement their programs, such as federal preemption of state laws. As you read through the provisions of H.R. 2245, ask yourself: Will this structure change deliberation and decisionmaking? How? What are the justifications for changing the normal rules of deliberation to give special protection to issues concerning federalism? Would you change the level of protection in any way? Finally, is the bill an example of good legislative drafting? What parts would you rewrite, and in what way?

H.R. 2245

IN THE HOUSE OF REPRESENTATIVES

June 16, 1999

A BILL

To ensure the liberties of the people by promoting federalism, to protect the reserved powers of the States, to impose accountability for Federal preemption of State and local laws, and for other purposes.

Be it enacted by the Senate and House of Representatives of the United States of America in Congress assembled,

SECTION 1. SHORT TITLE.

This Act may be cited as the "Federalism Act of 1999."

SEC. 2. FINDINGS.

The Congress finds the following:
    (1) The Constitution created a strong Federal system, reserving to the States all powers not expressly delegated to the Federal Government.

---

o. Allan Freedman, *GOP's Secret Weapon Against Regulations: Finesse,* Cong. Q. Weekly, Sept. 5, 1998, at 2314, 2320.

(2) Preemptive statutes and regulations have at times been an appropriate exercise of Federal powers, and at other times have been an inappropriate infringement on State and local government authority.

(3) On numerous occasions, the Congress has enacted statutes and Federal agencies have promulgated rules that expressly preempt State and local government authority and describe the scope of the preemption.

(4) In addition to statutes and rules that expressly preempt State and local government authority, many other statutes and rules that lack an express statement by the Congress or Federal agencies of their intent to preempt and a clear description of the scope of the preemption have been construed to preempt State and local government authority. * * *

(6) State and local governments are full partners in all Federal programs administered by those governments.

SEC. 3. PURPOSES.

The purposes of this Act are the following:

(1) To promote and preserve the integrity and effectiveness of our federalist system of government.

(2) To set forth principles governing the interpretation of congressional intent regarding preemption of State and local government authority by Federal laws and rules.

(3) To recognize the partnership between the Federal Government and State and local governments in the implementation of certain Federal programs.

(4) To establish a reporting requirement to monitor the incidence of Federal statutory, regulatory, and judicial preemption.

SEC. 4. DEFINITIONS.

In this Act:

(1) DEFINITIONS IN 5 U.S.C. 551 — The definitions under section 551 of title 5, United States Code, shall apply.

(2) BILL — The term "bill" includes a joint resolution.

(3) DIRECTOR — The term "Director" means the Director of the Congressional Budget Office.

(4) LOCAL GOVERNMENT — The term "local government" means a county, city, town, borough, township, village, school district, special district, or other political subdivision of a State.

(5) PUBLIC OFFICIALS — The term "public officials" —

(A) means elected officials of State and local governments; and

(B) includes the following national organizations that represent such officials:

(i) The National Governors' Association.

(ii) The National Conference of State Legislatures.

(iii) The Council of State Governments.

(iv) The United States Conference of Mayors.

(v) The National League of Cities.

(vi) The National Association of Counties.

(vii) The International City/County Management Association.

(6) STATE — The term "State" —

(A) means a State of the United States and an agency or instrumentality of a State;

(B) includes —

(i) the District of Columbia and any territory of the United States, and an agency or instrumentality of the District of Columbia or such territory; and

(ii) any tribal government and an agency or instrumentality of such government; and

(C) does not include a local government of a State. * * *

SEC. 8. LEGISLATIVE REQUIREMENTS.

(a) IN GENERAL — The report accompanying any bill of a public character reported from a committee of the Senate or House of Representatives, or the joint explanatory statement accompanying a conference report on any such bill, shall include a statement that —

(1) identifies each section of the bill or conference report that constitutes an express preemption of State or local government authority, or asserts that the bill does not contain any such section; and

(2) describes the constitutional basis for any such preemption;

(3) sets forth the reasons for each such preemption; and

(4) includes the federalism impact assessment by the Director under subsection (b).

(b) FEDERALISM IMPACT ASSESSMENT BY CONGRESSIONAL BUDGET OFFICE —

(1) PROVISION OF BILL OR CONFERENCE REPORT TO DIREC-TOR—When a committee of the Senate or the House of Representatives orders reported a bill of a public character, and before a conference committee files a conference report thereon, the committee or conference committee shall promptly provide the bill to the Director and shall identify to the Director each section of the bill that constitutes a preemption of State or local government authority.

(2) FEDERALISM IMPACT ASSESSMENT —

(A) For each bill of a public character reported by any committee of the Senate or the House of Representatives, and for each conference report thereon, the Director shall prepare and submit to the committee or conference committee a federalism impact assessment that describes the preemptive impact of the bill or conference report thereon on State and local governments, including the estimated costs that would be incurred by State and local governments as a result of its enactment.

(B) In the case of a bill or conference report that authorizes a Federal grant program, the federalism impact assessment shall also identify any provision that establishes a condition for receipt of funds under the program that is not related to the purposes of the program.

(c) ABSENCE OF COMMITTEE REPORT OR STATEMENT OF MANAGERS — In the absence of a committee report or joint explanatory statement in accordance with subsection (a) accompanying a bill or conference report thereon, respectively, the committee or conference committee shall report to the Senate and the House of Representatives a statement described in subsection (a) before consideration of the bill or conference report.

SEC. 9. RULES OF CONSTRUCTION RELATING TO PREEMPTION.

(a) STATUTES — No Federal statute enacted after the effective date of this Act shall preempt, in whole or in part, any State or local government law, ordinance, or regulation, unless the statute expressly states that such preemption is intended or unless there is a direct conflict between such statute and a State or local law, ordinance, or regulation so the two cannot be reconciled or consistently stand together. * * *

(c) FAVORABLE CONSTRUCTION — Any ambiguity in this Act, or in any other Federal rule issued or Federal statute enacted after the date of the enactment of this Act, shall be construed in favor of preserving the authority of State and local governments.

SEC. 10. REPORTS ON PREEMPTION.

* * *

(c) CONGRESSIONAL BUDGET OFFICE REPORT —
(1) IN GENERAL — Not later than the adjournment sine die of each Congress, the Director of the Congressional Budget Office shall submit to the Congress a report on the extent of preemption of State and local government authority —
(A) by Federal laws enacted during the previous session of Congress; and
(B) by judicial or agency interpretations of Federal statutes issued during such session, using —
(i) information regarding agency rules submitted by the Office of Management and Budget under subsection (a); and
(ii) information regarding Federal and State court decisions submitted by the Director of the Congressional Research Service under subsection (b).
(2) CONTENT — The report under paragraph (1) shall contain —
(A) a cumulative list of Federal statutes preempting, in whole or in part, State or local powers;
(B) a summary of legislation enacted during the previous session preempting, in whole or in part, State or local government authority;
(C) a summary of rules of agencies promulgated during the previous session of Congress preempting, in whole or in part, State or local government authority; and
(D) a summary of Federal and State court decisions issued during the previous session of Congress preempting, in whole or in part, State or local government authority.
(3) AVAILABILITY — The Director shall make the report under this subsection available to —
(A) each committee of the Congress;
(B) each Governor of a State;
(C) the presiding officer of each chamber of the legislature of each State; and

(D)   other public officials and the public through publication in the Congressional Record and on the Internet.

SEC. 11. LIMITATION ON APPLICATION WITH RESPECT TO PROHIBITIONS AGAINST DISCRIMINATION.

This Act shall not apply with respect to any section of a bill, or any provision of a Federal regulation or statute, that establishes or enforces any statutory prohibition against discrimination on the basis of race, color, religion, sex, national origin, age, handicap, or disability.

SEC. 12. EFFECTIVE DATE.

This Act shall take effect 90 days after the date of the enactment of this Act.

Chapter 5

DIRECT DEMOCRACY

Our focus thus far has involved lawmaking by elected representatives. We have examined a considerable variety of problems each of these representatives face in formulating public policy. Is governance improved by some sort of *hybrid democracy* where representative government operates alongside forms of popular lawmaking, rather than the relatively pure system of representative government that we have at the federal level? And, if so, what is the right mix of direct democracy and representative institutions?

SECTION 1. AN OVERVIEW OF DIRECT DEMOCRACY

Doubts about the capacity of legislatures to address social problems, as well as fears that legislatures were often captured by powerful business interests and were subject to corruption, led the Populists (circa 1890) and their political successors, the Progressives, to propose a "return of the government to the people." The two major methods of providing the people with lawmaking authority that resulted are the initiative and the referendum. In addition, a third device, recall, allows voters to remove elected officials from office before the expiration of their terms.

The *initiative* is a method whereby a certain percentage of the electorate may petition to have a proposed statute or amendment to the state constitution put on the ballot for a vote of the electorate. There are two common forms. The *direct initiative* refers to the method in which the issue goes on the ballot automatically after the requisite signatures of voters are collected. In contrast, under the format of the *indirect initiative*, upon the collection of the requisite signatures, the proposed statute is submitted to the legislature, which is given a period of time to approve or disapprove the measure. If the legislature fails to pass the proposal, or if it adopts a significantly amended version, the proposed statute in its original form is placed on the ballot, sometimes along with any legislatively approved variation.

The *referendum* is direct democracy from the other end of the telescope: it is a method whereby the electorate may approve or disapprove of a law proposed by or already enacted by the legislature. One form, called the *popular referendum,* provides that, upon the collection of the requisite signatures, a law already passed by the legislature is subject to approval or rejection by the electorate. Under the other form, referred to as the *legislative* or *submitted referendum,* the legislature places before the electorate a proposed law for approval or disapproval (a "binding legislative referendum") or for the electorate's advice (an "advisory legislative referendum").

Twenty-seven states provide for initiative, popular referendum or both. Eighteen of those states have a constitutional initiative process, through which the people can initiate constitutional change; 21 have some sort of statutory initiative process; and 24 allow for popular referendum.[a] From 1904, when the first statewide initiative appeared on Oregon's ballot, until 2006, there have been 2,231 statewide initiatives, with 909 (41%) of these being approved.[b] According to the *Initiative and Referendum Almanac,* "over 60% of all initiative activity has taken place in just six states — Arizona, California, Colorado, North Dakota, Oregon and Washington."[c] Legislative referendum, in which state legislatures or other government entities place questions on the ballot for popular vote, is generally required for constitutional amendments. Moreover, state or local law often requires that certain other questions — e.g., whether to issue bonds for construction of public facilities — must be submitted to referendum as well. In many states, the popular initiative and referendum exist at the local level, even if one or both are not statewide institutions. Over 70% of Americans have either state or local initiative available.[d]

The *recall* has a different relationship to representative government. Using this mechanism, a certain percentage of the electorate, by petition, may force the continued service of an elected official to be put to a vote. Fewer than one-third of the states have statewide recall provisions;[e] recall is more frequently used on the local level to target school board members, city councilmembers, and other local officials. Is recall a good way to "throw the bums out"? Or does it inhibit elected officials from adopting policies that are wise in the long run but painful in the short run? More generally, does the recall have an important impact upon the concept of representation?

---

a. See M. Dane Waters, *Initiative and Referendum Almanac* 12 (2003) (the most comprehensive guide to the initiative and referendum process in the United States). The Initiative and Referendum Institute (IRI) at the University of Southern California maintains a database of statewide initiatives and referendums and provides links to information provided by each state about its initiative process. See http://www.iandrinstitute.org/ballotwatch.htm (for the Ballotwatch database) and http://www.iandrinstitute.org/statewide_i&r.htm (for information on each state and links).

b. Initiative and Referendum Institute, *Overview of Initiative Use, 1904–2006* (Nov. 2006).

c. See Waters, *supra,* at 7. Oregon has had the most initiatives on the ballot, with 341 through 2006, and California is a close second with 315 during the same time period.

d. John Matsusaka, *Direct Democracy Works,* 19 J. Econ. Persp. 185, 185–86 (2005). For an analysis of the local initiative process in one key state, see Tracy Gordon, *The Local Initiative in California* (2004).

e. See Thomas Cronin, *Direct Democracy: The Politics of Initiative, Referendum, and Recall* 125–27 (1999).

The initiative and referendum have venerable historical roots. In Switzerland, for example, these practices date back to the Middle Ages, and since the middle of the nineteenth century, many major laws have been adopted through direct democracy.[f] Use of referendums is on the rise worldwide, with recent activity on every continent except Antarctica.[g] The United States is one of the few major democracies not to have held a national referendum. However, ballot propositions have grown in importance in the states and addressed such controversial subjects as tax or governmental spending limitations, same-sex marriage and civil unions, the death penalty, educational policy including charter schools and affirmative action, and a variety of contentious social issues. The 1990s saw the most initiatives on the ballot, with more than 375 proposed, and the first decade of the 21st Century appears to be on track to match or exceed that figure. Yet direct democracy may be in tension with the conception of representative government embraced by the Framers of the American Constitution. The contrast is evident in the writings of James Madison, who urged the adoption of a representational form of government rather than a more "democratic" form. Madison believed that a "republican" form of government was necessary to prevent a tyranny of the majority faction over the minority.[h]

The Framers included in the Constitution a provision requiring the United States to "guarantee to every State in this Union a Republican Form of Government." U.S. Const., art. IV, § 4. Challenges to direct democracy in the states on the theory that it is inconsistent with this provision have, however, been held to be nonjusticiable political questions.[i] Does it make a difference to the analysis that direct democracy always exists together with representative institutions? Does the Guarantee Clause suggest a constitutional reason to

---

f. For an overview, see Philip Dubois & Floyd Feeney, *Lawmaking by Initiative: Issues, Options and Comparisons* 46–62 (1998); Jean-Francois Aubert, *Switzerland*, in *Referendums: A Comparative Study of Practice and Theory* 39–66 (David Butler & Austin Ranney eds., 1978).

g. See K.K. DuVivier, *The United States as a Democratic Ideal? International Lessons in Referendum Democracy*, 79 Temple L. Rev. 821, 834–41 (2006).

h. See, e.g., Cronin, *supra*, at 7–37; Philip Frickey, *The Communion of Strangers: Representative Government, Direct Democracy, and the Privatization of the Public Sphere*, 34 Willamette L. Rev. 421, 423–427 (1998); Marci Hamilton, *The People: The Least Accountable Branch*, 4 U. Chi. L. Sch. Roundtable 1 (1997).

i. See *Pacific States Tel. & Tel. Co. v. Oregon*, 223 U.S. 118 (1912). On the Guarantee Clause generally, see James Fischer, *Plebiscites, the Guaranty Clause, and the Role of the Judiciary*, 41 Santa Clara L. Rev. 973 (2001). For the argument that state courts should enforce the Guarantee Clause in the context of direct democracy, see Hans Linde, *Who is Responsible for Republican Government?*, 65 U. Colo. L. Rev. 709 (1994) ("[T]he Guarantee Clause precludes misuse of initiatives for * * * measures of popular passion or self-interest * * * [and the use] of initiatives to enact ordinary laws * * * in the form of constitutional text so as to insulate a law from change by elected lawmakers as well as from review of its constitutionality"). For an attempt at resuscitating both legal republicanism and the Guarantee Clause, see Ethan Leib, *Redeeming the Welshed Guarantee: A Scheme for Achieving Justiciability*, 24 Whittier L. Rev. 143 (2002).

prefer methods of popular lawmaking that include some meaningful role for elected officials, such as the indirect initiative or the popular referendum?[j]

Think back to the discussion in Chapter 2, § 2C, about theories of partisan lockup: the concern that elected officials will not pass certain reforms of the electoral system that voters might prefer because the changes are not in the self-interest of lawmakers. Could that theory provide an argument that representative government might actually work better if some avenues of direct lawmaking are incorporated?[k] The early proponents of direct democracy saw it as a way to circumvent state legislators and political parties that would block governance reforms like the direct primary and anti-corruption laws. Many modern initiatives deal with electoral reforms such as changes in the primary system, lobbying and campaign finance laws, term limits for legislators, and less partisan redistricting commissions. The evidence that states with hybrid democracy design their representative institutions differently than states without any form of direct democracy, however, is mixed. States with vibrant initiative processes are more likely, Caroline Tolbert has found, to have legislative term limits, tax and expenditure limitations, and supermajority voting requirements for tax increases.[l] Although Nathaniel Persily and Melissa Anderson determined that only the enactment of term limits would be "unimaginable" without the outlet of direct democracy, the presence of the initiative process has also influenced the adoption of public financing for legislative elections and redistricting commissions.[m]

Is this too rosy of view of hybrid democracy? Critics argue that the ballot measures proposed and passed by the people tend to weaken representative institutions and undermine the ability of lawmakers to govern.[n] They point to term limits and tax limitations as examples. They contend that because people turn to initiatives out of frustration with their elected representatives, they will mostly enact legislation in the arena of electoral reform that reduces the power of elected officials. Certainly, there is some validity to this argument. Even the "good government" reforms such as campaign finance legislation and nonpartisan redistricting commissions work to reduce the discretion of elected

---

j. For a proposal to reform the direct initiative process to provide opportunities for legislative involvement and to allow flexibility to amend the language of proposals before they are placed on the ballot, see Elizabeth Garrett & Mathew McCubbins, *The Dual Path Initiative Framework*, 80 S. Cal. L. Rev. 299 (2007).

k. See Dennis Thompson, *The Role of Theorists and Citizens in* Just Elections: *A Response to Professors Cain, Garrett, and Sabl*, 4 Election L.J. 153, 158–60 (2005).

l. *Changing Rules for State Legislatures: Direct Democracy and Governance Policies*, in *Citizens as Legislators: Direct Democracy in the United States* 171 (Shaun Bowler, Todd Donovan & Caroline Tolbert eds., 1998).

m. *Regulating Democracy Through Democracy: The Use of Direct Legislation in Election Law Reform*, 78 S. Cal. L. Rev. 997 (2005). See also Michael Kang, *De-Rigging Elections: Direct Democracy and the Future of Redistricting Reform,* 84 U. Wash. L. Rev. 667 (2006) (proposing requirement that the people vote on all redistricting plans to "moderate partisan gerrymandering, induce the major parties to compete for public approval, and draw the public into a healthier political process").

n. See, e.g., Peter Schrag, *California: America's High-Stakes Experiment* (2006).

officials. The question is whether the policies adopted through popular means tend to reduce legislative discretion in ways that improve or harm representative institutions. This is a key question in the assessment of hybrid democracy because no matter how robust the initiative process becomes, the vast majority of decisions made by government will always be made by elected representatives and the officials they appoint.

The issues raised by the increasing use of the popular initiative and referendum are many. In this section, we will discuss three of the most important for assessing the initiative process and crafting reform: the role of money in ballot access and in outcomes of initiative elections; the ability of voters to make decisions competently when they go to the polls; and the effect of the initiative process on the legislative agenda. As you read through these materials, keep in mind that one must evaluate the mechanisms of direct democracy by comparing them realistically to representative institutions. For example, money plays a role in both issue and candidate campaigns, and voters are often not fully informed about all the candidates on the ballot.

The Importance of Money. The romantic vision of direct democracy is that it is a tool used by ordinary citizens to take control of government away from special interests. Although it is not clear whether that picture was ever entirely accurate,[o] the modern concern is that the initiative process is dominated by monied interests and is merely another avenue for the wealthy to unduly influence public policy. In 1998, $400 million was spent nationwide on ballot questions, compared to $326 million spent in the presidential campaign in 2000. "In 2004, gambling interests spent $90 million in California on two propositions alone, roughly a quarter of what George W. Bush and John Kerry each spent on their presidential campaigns."[p]

One substantial expense for initiative proponents is money spent to qualify a question for the ballot. It often requires hundreds of thousands of signatures to trigger a direct initiative or popular referendum. Well-heeled interests have a great advantage at this stage because states may not prohibit them from paying petition circulators.[q] In California, circulating petitions can cost $2–3 million per ballot proposition,[r] and some firms will offer money-back guarantees if they are paid enough. In short, money is a sufficient condition for ballot access. Even if the outcome of any vote on a ballot question mirrors the preference of the median voter, the dominance of money at the qualification stage means that groups with funds will determine which issues are placed before the people. As we discussed in Chapter 1, the control of the political agenda is a valuable asset.

---

o. See, e.g., Daniel Smith & Joseph Lubinski, *Direct Democracy During the Progressive Era: A Crack in the Populist Veneer?*, 14 J. Pol'y Hist. 4 (2002).

p. Matsusaka, *Direct Democracy Works, supra*, at 191.

q. See *Meyer v. Grant*, 486 U.S. 414 (1988) (First Amendment violation to prohibit paid petition circulators).

r. Andrew Gloger, *Initiative and Referendum Institute Report 2006–1: Paid Petitioners after* Prete 1 (May 2006).

Although the Supreme Court has ruled out laws prohibiting paid petition circulators, states continue to seek to regulate this process. The following case involves a challenge to Colorado's law. As you read this, ask whether the restrictions are apt to reduce the role of money in the initiative process while retaining an outlet for expression of the popular will, or whether the statute was mainly an attempt to muzzle direct democracy.

———

BUCKLEY v. AMERICAN CONSTITUTIONAL LAW FOUNDA-TION, 525 U.S. 182 (1999). Colorado's statute controlling the initiative petition process included three provisions at issue in this case: petition circulators were required to be registered voters; circulators were required to wear name badges; and initiative backers had to report the names and addresses of paid circulators and how much each was paid. **Justice Ginsburg** began with the proposition that petition circulation is "core political speech" that involves "interactive communication concerning political change"; therefore, First Amendment protection is "at its zenith." On the other hand, citing the ballot access cases (Chapter 2, § 2C), she noted that states can regulate elections to avoid chaos and to ensure fairness. The Court concluded that "the First Amendment requires us to be vigilant in making * * * judgments [about the constitutionality of electoral regulations], to guard against undue hindrances to political conversations and the exchange of ideas."

The Court struck down the requirement that circulators be registered voters, noting that it burdened political speech by reducing the number of potential speakers, i.e., the number of people who could engage in discourse about initiatives as they gathered signatures. **Justice Thomas**, concurring, noted the "anecdotal evidence" that petition circulators do not actually engage in much political speech, working to gather as many signatures as possible as quickly as possible because often their pay is tied to the number of signatures. He concluded, however, that "the level of scrutiny cannot turn on the content or sophistication of a political message."

The Court acknowledged the argument, made by **Justice O'Connor** in dissent, that it is relatively easy for a circulator to register to vote and that this law is not a severe burden on many. However, it contended that some who wished to circulate petitions did not register as a form of protest against the system or because they were alienated from the political process. The state's primary justification for the provision, to police illegal activity among circulators, was already served by the requirement that signature gatherers be residents of the state or could be better served by requiring that circulators be eligible to vote, rather than actually registered. **Chief Justice Rehnquist** was scornful in his dissent on this point, noting that the majority held that "a State is constitutionally required to instead allow those who make no effort to register to vote — political dropouts — and convicted drug dealers to engage in this electoral activity."

The majority also struck down the requirement that circulators wear name badges, which the state had justified as necessary to help it combat fraudulent practices by signature gatherers seeking to increase their compensation. (The Court did not address the related issue of whether a badge could identify a circulator as either PAID or VOLUNTEER. Is that provision constitutional? Is it good policy?) The Court worried that those circulating petitions on unpopular issues might face harassment in face-to-face conversations with passersby; requiring them to provide their names would chill political speech. Unlike the constitutional requirement that each petition submitted to the state include the circulator's name and address, the badge required identification "at the precise moment when the circulator's interest in anonymity is greatest." See also *McIntyre v. Ohio Elections Comm'n*, 514 U.S. 334 (1995) (protecting right of leafleteer to distribute campaign literature anonymously).

The Court also trimmed the disclosure provisions relating to the information provided by initiative proponents to the state. It struck down requirements that information specific to each circulator be provided (e.g., the name, address and total amount paid), but it left unchanged the requirement that proponents report how much they paid per signature, which effectively disclosed the entire amount spent in the petition drive. Justice Ginsburg was sympathetic to the notion that some disclosure was necessary as "a control or check on domination of the initiative process by affluent special interest groups" and to inform voters "of the source and amount of money spent" on ballot access. But the majority believed that the more targeted disclosure was unnecessary to achieve those objectives. It noted that, in contrast to candidate elections where the courts had allowed states to force substantial disclosure to discourage *quid pro quo* corruption, initiative campaigns did not involve candidates who might be susceptible to undue influence. See *First Nat'l Bank of Boston v. Bellotti*, 435 U.S. 765 (1978).

In dissent, Justice O'Connor was willing to be much more deferential to the state's determination of what information it needed to regulate the electoral process effectively, particularly with regard to information disclosed to a state official rather than information disclosed during the signature gathering stage to citizens in one-on-one discussions. She was not concerned that Colorado applied the more burdensome disclosure only to paid circulators because "the record suggests that paid circulators are more likely to commit fraud and gather false signatures than other circulators."

Money also plays a role in the outcomes of ballot contests, but the picture here is more complicated than the influence of wealth in ballot access.[s] Studies suggest that money spent to defeat initiatives and referendums is more effective than money spent to pass them. In an early influential study, Daniel Lowenstein found that between 1968 and 1980 in California, in elections where spending levels exceeded $250,000 and one side had a two-to-one spending advantage, opposition committees defeated 90% of the measures they opposed, and proponent committees won 64% of the time. *Campaign Spending and Ballot Propositions: Recent Experience, Public Choice Theory,*

---

s. For a discussion of the studies on the role of money in ballot campaigns, see Elizabeth Garrett & Elisabeth Gerber, *Money in the Initiative and Referendum Process: Evidence of its Effects and Prospects for Reform*, in *The Battle Over Citizen Lawmaking* 73 (M. Dane Waters ed., 2001).

and the First Amendment, 29 UCLA L. Rev. 505 (1982). Subsequent studies have similarly found that money has a greater effect when spent to defeat an initiative, although increasingly sophisticated analyses of ballot campaigns may begin to reveal the influence of well-funded advocacy campaigns.[t] For example, Elisabeth Gerber's work has assessed whether spending by certain groups is particularly influential, finding, for example, that contributions from citizen groups have greater success in passing initiatives than do contributions from economic groups.[u]

Unlike candidate elections where courts have allowed some restrictions on campaign contributions, the Supreme Court has consistently held that the First Amendment forbids states from limiting the amount of money spent in support of or in opposition to a ballot measure.[v] Just as in the candidate-election context, the Court has not been willing to accept egalitarian arguments to justify restrictions on spending in initiative contests. As more candidates take advantage of hybrid democracy and use initiatives to serve their own electoral and political goals, there are increasing attempts to limit contributions to campaign committees in initiative campaigns that are controlled by candidates or elected officials.[w] In these cases, the traditional *quid pro quo* argument could support contribution limits. Certainly the experience in California, where Governor Arnold Schwarzenegger has used popular initiatives to bargain with the legislature or to circumvent lawmakers when they refuse to compromise, suggests that politicians may be just as grateful for financial support for initiatives they favor as for contributions made directly to their campaigns.[x] If such restrictions are constitutional, are they desirable? Is it wise policy to restrict contributions to candidate-controlled ballot measure committees if the courts won't allow restrictions on contributions to more independent committees? How would you expect politicians to try to evade such regulations?

Voter Confusion and Voting Cues. Whatever one concludes about the wisdom of a system with elements of direct democracy, it seems likely that the initiative process will endure in states that have it because voters like popular lawmaking. When asked what they thought about the initiative process after a costly special election in 2005 in which voters had rejected every question on

---

t. For a recent study that finds both advocacy and opposition campaigns have statistically significant effects in campaigns and that opposition advertising may not have an advantage, see Thomas Stratmann, *The Effectiveness of Money in Ballot Measure Campaigns*, 78 S. Cal. L. Rev. 1041 (2005).

u. See *The Populist Paradox: Interest Group Influence and the Promise of Direct Legislation* 101–20 (1999).

v. See *Citizens Against Rent Control v. Berkeley*, 454 U.S. 290 (1981).

w. See Hank Dempsey, *The "Overlooked Hermaphrodite" of Campaign Finance: Candidate-Controlled Ballot Measure Committees in California Politics*, 95 Calif. L. Rev. 123 (2007) (student comment).

x. See Elizabeth Garrett, *Hybrid Democracy*, 73 Geo. Wash. L. Rev. 1096, 1105–10 (2005). See generally Richard Hasen, *Rethinking the Unconstitutionality of Contribution and Expenditures Limits in Ballot Measure Campaigns*, 78 S. Cal. L. Rev. 885 (2005).

the ballot, nearly half of Californians who voted said that the initiative process generated better public policy than representative institutions. Seventy-nine percent of those polled said that initiatives put important issues on the political agenda that would be otherwise ignored by elected officials.[y] One important question in assessing whether those opinions are accurate — that is, whether the policies adopted at the voting booth are actually better than those formulated by legislators — is whether voters are sufficiently informed about the issues they are asked to decide.

If decisionmaking at the polls required voters to be well-versed in all the issues surrounding every contest, then very few voters would be able to meet that standard. Of course, very few lawmakers casting their votes in a state legislature or Congress would meet that standard for more than a handful of crucial bills. A more reasonable standard is voter competence. Voters are competent "if they cast the same votes they would have cast had they possessed all available knowledge about the policy consequences of their decision."[z] They need not have encyclopedic knowledge about every choice, but they need to have reliable shortcuts — voting cues or heuristics — that can allow them to vote in the same way that they would have with more complete information. Thinking back to the theories of politics discussed in Chapter 1, how would republican thinkers react to this notion of voter competence? Is it consistent with the ideal of civic virtue?

Scholars continue to work to determine when cues are helpful to voters and how to structure disclosure of information so that it provides them the information they need at the time they can use it most effectively. In candidate elections, voters can use the strong voting cue of partisan affiliation, and they may also be able to use the cue of incumbency. But the information environment for ballot measures is much less rich; even though political parties and candidates now often associate themselves on one side or the other of an initiative, this information is not available on the ballot itself. Interestingly, the hybrid nature of democracy provides information to voters through the interaction of candidate and issue elections: candidates seek to use initiatives to demonstrate their commitment to certain issues, and the information environment surrounding ballot measures is enriched by the support or opposition of elected officials with a political brand name.

Another helpful cue in direct democracy is knowing the groups — economic and ideological — that support and oppose an initiative. For example, in a study of voting on insurance-related ballot initiatives, Arthur Lupia compared voters who knew nothing about the initiatives' details but

---

y. Mark Baldassare (Public Policy Institute of California), *Special Survey on Californians and the Initiative Process* 13 (Nov. 2005).

z. Elisabeth Gerber & Arthur Lupia, *Voter Competence in Direct Legislation Elections,* in *Citizen Competence and Democratic Institutions* 147, 149 (Stephen Elkin & Karol Soltan eds., 1999). See also Elizabeth Garrett & Daniel Smith, *Veiled Political Actors and Campaign Disclosure Laws in Direct Democracy*, 4 Election L.J. 295 (2005) (providing survey of literature, empirical study of how groups seek to cloak their involvement in issue campaigns, and a proposal for disclosure of key information).

knew the insurance industry's preference, with voters who were "model citizens" in that they consistently gave correct answers to detailed questions about ballot measures. His study also included a third group who knew nothing about the ballot measures or the insurance industry's views. The first two groups of voters voted similarly, while the third group had completely different voting patterns. *Shortcuts versus Encyclopedias: Information and Voting Behavior in California Insurance Reform Elections*, 88 Am. Pol. Sci. Rev. 63 (1994). This finding suggests that under certain circumstances, just knowing which group supports an initiative (or opposes it) may be enough to vote competently. Here, Californians could ascertain the economic interests of the insurance industry, determine if their interests differed from those companies, and vote accordingly. Of course, not all elections will provide voters with the amount of credible information that was available to them in the election studied by Lupia,[a] but often voters can glean trustworthy information from the behavior of well-known interest groups in issue campaigns.

What other information might provide voters shortcuts to enable them to vote competently? Knowing the amount of money that a group spends to support or oppose a ballot measure might give voters a sense of the intensity of the group's preferences. Knowing how much money out-of-state interests contributed to an issue committee might be important. Having a sense of the percentage of small donations to a campaign might allow a voter to determine if this issue elicits widespread grassroots appeal or is being bankrolled by only a few well-heeled individuals or groups. As you think about the kind of information most necessary for voter competence, consider also how to ensure that the information reaches citizens in a timely way and how to structure the information so that they can use it. Does this interest in voter competence justify fairly aggressive disclosure laws about campaign spending in direct elections? What groups would you expect to try to avoid disclosure, and how would they do so? Could laws be drafted to pierce through such veiled political actors to discern the true parties in interest?

Various features of the initiative process are designed to reduce voter confusion. For example, as we will discuss below in Section 2, initiatives are typically governed by a single-subject requirement, so that voters are presented with a proposal on a single subject that they can accept or reject.[b] States send voters pamphlets with explanations of each ballot measure and arguments submitted by proponents and opponents. Some states restrict the subject matter of initiatives; for example, several states do not allow revenue or appropriations measures to be proposed through the initiative process.[c] Voters also protect themselves when they are confused. The "defensive no" is the typical

---

a. For a discussion of the conditions necessary to provide voters with credible information, see Arthur Lupia & Mathew McCubbins, *The Democratic Dilemma: Can Citizens Learn What They Need to Know?* (1998).

b. For a description of why this binary form of decisionmaking can lead to sub-optimal policy decisions, see Thad Kousser & Mathew McCubbins, *Social Choice, Crypto-Initiatives, and Policymaking by Direct Democracy*, 78 S. Cal. L. Rev. 949 (2005).

c. See Waters, *supra*, at 18 (listing subject matter restrictions).

reaction by voters who are unsure about initiatives. See Shaun Bowler & Todd Donovan, *Demanding Choices: Opinion, Voting, and Direct Democracy* 47 (2000). Knowing that, opponents of an initiative sometimes qualify a competing initiative as a tactic to defeat the first; often, they are not particularly concerned whether their alternate proposition fails or passes. State law typically provides rules for how to deal with the situation when two dueling propositions both succeed. In most states, the proposition with the most votes goes into effect.

Effect on the Lawmaking Agenda. The term "hybrid democracy" makes salient the reality that the presence of a robust initiative process affects the legislative branch in several ways. First, the presence of an initiative on the ballot will affect turnout generally, which in turn influences the results of candidate elections. Daniel Smith and Caroline Tolbert found that, in presidential elections, each ballot measure boosts turnout by half a percentage, and in midterm elections, each ballot measure increases turnout by 1.2%.[d] Of course, turnout is not increased randomly; rather, the subject matter of the initiative motivates different groups of people to vote, and the shape of that turnout may determine who is elected to serve at the state and federal levels. The initiatives prohibiting same-sex marriage on the ballot in 11 states in 2004 certainly affected the outcome of Senate and other legislative races, and they may even have played a role in President Bush's reelection by encouraging the turnout of conservative voters in Ohio, the key state for his victory.

Perhaps one of the most interesting findings by political scientists who focus on the interaction between the two sides of hybrid democracy is that the mere possibility of an initiative influences the outcomes in the state legislature. Gerber describes the *indirect effect* of direct democracy, which she describes as political actors using initiatives to pressure state lawmakers to pass a new law. *The Populist Paradox: Interest Group Influence and the Promise of Direct Democracy* 23– 28 (1999). Sometimes the pressure can be overt. For example, in 1998, Silicon Valley entrepreneur Reed Hastings led a group frustrated by California Assembly's refusal to expand the charter school program. They believed that an entrenched special interest, the teachers' union, was blocking meaningful reform through the traditional legislative process. Accordingly, they spent $3.5 million to pay petition circulators and obtained 1.2 million signatures for a proposal to institute their vision of charter schools. This is twice the number of signatures required at the time, so the group provided a credible signal of their intention to spend money to enact their preferences. In addition, they threatened to spend another $12 million to pass the initiative. Hastings made it clear, however, that his group would halt the petition drive if representatives increased the number of charter schools and addressed other concerns. Within a short time, a compromise bill had passed the state legislature; once Governor Pete Wilson signed the bill, the initiative drive stopped.

---

d. *Educated by Initiative: The Effects of Direct Democracy on Citizens and Political Organizations in the American States* 42 (2004) (also finding that at a certain point, each additional measure does not further increase turnout).

Not all groups can enter into this sort of bargaining game with politicians. Under what conditions will such a threat be successful? Gerber identifies three conditions. First, "the group has sufficient resources to attract the legislature's attention." Second, "the group must have something legislators want," such as the ability to provide future campaign contributions. Third, "legislators must be electorally vulnerable." Often the indirect influence of direct democracy is not as overt as in the charter schools example in California. For example, political scientists have found that legislative outcomes in states with the possibility of initiatives are different in meaningful ways from the outcomes in states without robust popular democracy. In *For the Many or the Few* (2004), John Matsusaka focuses his attention on fiscal policies, and he finds that initiative states have lower overall spending by state and local governments; that spending in these states has shifted from the state to local governments; and that broad-based taxes in initiative states are cut and replaced with more user fees. Using opinion polls, he determines that a majority of voters in those states favor such fiscal policies, leading him to conclude that, at least in this realm, direct democracy favors the majority, rather than special interests. Importantly, these policies are not all adopted through the initiative; rather, it is the pressure of the possibility of direct democracy that may be responsible for these systematic differences.[e] The existence of the initiative process may empower the median voter in all legislative realms, under some conditions. Of course, this may lead to other concerns — of the tyranny of the majority undermining the rights of those in the minority — and we will turn to those issues in Section 2.

Another interaction between direct democracy and representative institutions occurs after an initiative is passed. Once enacted, many initiatives must be implemented by elected and appointed officials, people who often resisted the policy in the first place. After all, the people resort to enacting laws themselves when their representatives have been insufficiently attentive. This leads to the "implementation problem" in direct democracy. For example, a ballot measure might enact sweeping reform of the state's school system, which then must be implemented by the Department of Education, school administrators and unions. Or the initiative might enact public financing for campaigns, but the legislature has to appropriate the money. Of course, some initiatives are struck down by courts convinced that they are unconstitutional or legally flawed in some way. Here the people cannot get what they want because their preferences conflict with larger principles and values, such as the protection of individual rights guaranteed in the Constitution. But when state officials block initiatives by surreptitiously undermining them, they ignore the will of the majority in a way that reduces accountability.

---

e. See also Elisabeth Gerber, *Legislative Response to the Threat of Popular Initiatives*, 40 Am. J. Pol. Sci. 99 (1996) (finding that parental consent laws in initiative states are closer to the median voter's preference than such laws in states without the initiative process); John Matsusaka & Nolan McCarty, *Political Resource Allocation: Benefits and Costs of Voter Initiatives*, 17 J. Law, Econ. & Org. 413 (2001) (detailing conditions under which outcomes are closer to median voter's preference in initiative states).

In *Stealing the Initiative: How State Government Responds to Direct Democracy* (2001), Gerber, Lupia, McCubbins and Kiewiet identify several conditions that allow government officials to ignore or undermine initiatives more easily. First, substantial technical or political costs will lead to lower levels of compliance because the net value of implementation is reduced. Technical costs might include the effort involved in writing and adopting legislation or regulations to implement the initiative. Political costs might be incurred if legislators have to make promises to enact legislation or take steps that will be opposed by powerful organized interests. Or money to implement the initiative may reduce the resources available for other important legislative goals. Second, if implementers face significant sanctions for noncompliance, they are more likely to work to implement the initiative. Third, and related to the second factor, when it is easier for the public or others who support the initiative to observe compliance, it is more likely that officials will comply. Finally, the more people required for full compliance, the lower the chances of implementation.

Introductory Problem on Direct Democracy

Problem 5–1: Consider some of the policies we have already studied that have often been implemented as a result of direct democracy: term limits for legislators, public financing of campaigns, ethics rules, changes in party primaries, supermajority voting requirements for tax increases, and redistricting commissions. Why do groups resort to direct democracy to enact these policies? What hurdles will each face in the effort to gain ballot access? Which interest groups are likely to be active as proponents and opponents, and how successfully can they raise money? Are political candidates likely to align themselves with either side to increase their chances at the polls? Which face significant implementation problems? If you are a proponent of the initiative, how can you minimize the implementation problems when you draft the initiative? See Gerber, Lupia, McCubbins & Kiewiet, *supra* (providing case studies, including term limits and open primaries).

SECTION 2. POPULAR LAWMAKING AND THE CONSTITUTION

A. AN INTRODUCTION TO THE PROBLEM

According to one analyst, "A perennial fear about direct democracy has been that majorities at the ballot box might be less sensitive than state legislators to the rights of minorities — whether an ethnic, racial, or religious minority or perhaps a small ideological or partisan group. * * * Direct democracy measures in recent years have not generally had the effect of diminishing minority rights."[a] Is this correct?[b] Consider the following cases.

---

a. Cronin, *supra*, at 212.

b. The definitive study of the empirical evidence concerning the effect of direct democracy on minority rights remains to be done; current conclusions are mixed, although they suggest that fears of the tyranny of the majority may be overstated. Compare, e.g., Barbara Gamble, *Putting*

ST. PAUL CITIZENS FOR HUMAN RIGHTS
v. CITY COUNCIL OF THE CITY OF ST. PAUL

Supreme Court of Minnesota, 1979
289 N.W.2d 402

[The St. Paul City Charter provided:

Sec. 8.01. *Initiative, referendum and recall.* The people shall have the right to propose ordinances, to require ordinances to be submitted to a vote, and to recall officials by processes known as initiative, referendum, and recall.

Sec. 8.02. *Petition.* Initiative, referendum, or recall shall be initiated by a petition signed by registered voters of the city equal to eight per cent of those who voted for the office of mayor in the last preceding city election in the case of initiative or referendum, and twenty per cent in the case of recall. * * *

Sec. 8.04. *Initiative.* Any ordinance may be proposed by a petition which shall state at the head of each page or attached thereto the exact text of the ordinance sought to be proposed. If the council fails to enact the ordinance without change within sixty days after the filing of the petition with the city clerk, it shall be placed on the ballot at the next election occurring in the city. * * * If a majority of those voting on the ordinance vote in its favor, it shall become effective immediately.

Sec. 8.05. *Referendum.* Any ordinance * * * may be subjected to referendum by a petition filed within forty-five days after its publication. The petition shall state, at the head of each page or in an attached paper, a description of the ordinance * * * involved. Any ordinance * * * upon which a petition is filed, other than an emergency ordinance, shall be suspended in its operation as soon as the petition is found sufficient. If the ordinance * * * is not thereafter entirely repealed, it shall be placed on the ballot at the next election, or at a special election called for that purpose, as the council shall determine. The ordinance * * * shall not become operative until a majority of those voting on the ordinance * * * vote in its favor.

Sec. 8.06. *Repeal of ordinances * * * submitted to voters.* No ordinance adopted by the voters on initiative or ordinance * * * approved by referendum shall be repealed within one year after its approval.

[In April 1978 a majority of those voting in St. Paul voted "yes" on the following initiative question:

Civil Rights to a Popular Vote, 41 Am. J. Pol. Sci. 245 (1997) (from 1959–93, voters adopted 58% of ballot measures restricting civil rights, suggesting that direct democracy is especially dangerous to minority groups), with Todd Donovan & Shaun Bowler, *Reforming the Republic: Democratic Institutions For the New America* 140–42 (2004) (suggesting that concerns over the repressive nature of direct democracy are overstated since the pass rate for statewide initiatives targeting homosexuals is lower than the overall pass rate and courts have invalidated almost all anti-civil rights initiatives affecting any group that did pass); Zoltan Hajnal, Elisabeth Gerber & Hugh Louch, *Minorities and Direct Legislation: Evidence from California Ballot Proposition Elections,* 64 J. Pol. 154 (2002) (concluding that the detrimental effects of direct democracy on minorities have been overstated and, considering the outcome across all propositions, the majority of Latino, Asian American and African American voters were on the winning side of the vote).

Should Chapter 74 of the St. Paul Legislative Code which prohibits discrimination in employment, education, housing, public accommodations and public services based on race, creed, religion, sex, color, national origin or ancestry, affectional or sexual preference, age or disability be amended by removing "affectional or sexual preference" from the ordinance and should Section 74.04 which provides as follows:

"No person shall discriminate, on grounds of race, creed, religion, color, sex, national origin or ancestry, affectional or sexual preference, age or disability, with respect to access to, use of, or benefit from any institution of education or services and facilities rendered in connection therewith, except that a school operated by a religious denomination may require membership in such denomination as a condition of enrollment, provided such requirement is placed upon all applicants"

be further amended by removing "provided such requirement is placed upon all applicants"?]

TODD, JUSTICE.

* * * Plaintiffs contend that voters in St. Paul cannot use the initiative process to repeal an ordinance; they claim that council action or a referendum are the only means by which an ordinance can be repealed. Defendants argue that the power to legislate includes the power to repeal, that there are no restrictions on the power of initiative, and, thus, that an initiative can be used to repeal an existing ordinance. Whether or not voters have the power to repeal an existing ordinance by initiative is a question of first impression in Minnesota.

Municipal ordinances are enacted either by action of the city council or by the initiative process. 5 McQuillan, Municipal Corporations (3d ed. 1969 rev. vol.), § 16.01. The power to enact ordinances generally implies the power to repeal them. 6 McQuillan, Municipal Corporations, § 21.10. The city council repeals existing ordinances by enacting new ordinances. See, 6 McQuillan, Municipal Corporations, § 21.09. The voters of St. Paul are, therefore, also able to repeal existing ordinances by enacting new ordinances through the initiative process unless the grant of authority provides otherwise. See, 6 McQuillan, Municipal Corporations, § 21.11.

The St. Paul City Charter grants the people "the right to propose ordinances, to require ordinances to be submitted to a vote, and to recall elective officials by processes known respectively as initiative, referendum, and recall." St. Paul City Charter, § 8.01. It also provides that "[a]ny ordinance may be proposed by [initiative] petition * * *." St. Paul City Charter, § 8.04. These two provisions indicate that the city charter commission intended the voters to be able to repeal or amend existing ordinances by initiative.[3] See, *State v. City of*

---

3. The majority of courts that have faced this issue have held that municipal voters can repeal existing ordinances by initiative. See, *Duran v. Cassidy*, 28 Cal.App.3d 574 (1972); *State ex rel. Boyer v. Grady*, 269 N.W.2d 73 (Neb. 1978); *Smith v. Township of Livingston*, 256 A.2d 85, affirmed, 257 A.2d 698 (N.J. 1969); *State ex rel. Sharpe v. Hitt*, 99 N.E.2d 659 (Ohio 1951). But, see, *Batten v. Hambley*, 400 S.W.2d 683 (Ky.1966); *Wyatt v. Clark*, 299 P.2d 799 (Okl.1956); *Landt v. City of Wisconsin Dells*, 141 N.W.2d 245 (Wis. 1966).

Wheeling, 120 S.E.2d 389 (W. Va. 1961), in which the court emphasized that the term "any proposed ordinance" must include a repealing ordinance. * * *

3. Plaintiffs also claim that the ballot question repealing the St. Paul Gay Rights Ordinance was improperly drawn because it actually contained two questions. The first question dealt with deleting all reference to "affectional or sexual preference" from the St. Paul Human Rights Ordinance, and the second question dealt with deleting the clause "provided such requirement is placed upon all applicants" from the provision which permits a religious institution to require membership in its denomination as a condition of enrollment.

A municipal ordinance must contain only a single subject. See, St. Paul City Charter, § 6.04. An ordinance violates this proscription only when it contains subjects which are so dissimilar as to have no legitimate connection. See, *City of Duluth v. Cerveny,* 16 N.W.2d 779 (Minn. 1944), where we held that an ordinance providing for the forfeiture of intoxicating liquor did not violate the Duluth Charter provision that no law shall embrace more than one subject because the question of forfeiture had a logical and material connection to the subject of regulating the sale of intoxicating liquor. The purpose of such a charter provision is to avoid the possibility of logrolling, deceit, or voter confusion. See, *Bogen v. Sheedy,* 229 N.W.2d 19 (Minn. 1975), where we held that a referendum petition concerning two ordinances was valid despite the fact that it contained two questions, because the ordinances had been debated together, considered together, were passed at the same council meeting, and dealt with the same subject matter.

In the instant case, both questions concerned the same subject matter — the St. Paul Human Rights Ordinance. Given the public debate on the initiative, there was little possibility of deceit, voter confusion, or logrolling. Because the St. Paul City Council could have deleted all reference to "affectional or sexual preference" and the clause relating to religious institutions by enacting one ordinance, there is no reason that the voters could not do the same through the initiative process.

4. Plaintiffs argue that repealing the St. Paul Gay Rights Ordinance deprives them of due process and equal protection. These arguments were not presented to the trial court; thus, they will not be considered for the first time on appeal.

Affirmed.

WAHL, JUSTICE (dissenting).

I respectfully dissent from the majority holding that the voters of St. Paul can repeal an existing ordinance by the initiative process. Few courts have addressed this issue, and the case is one of the first impression in Minnesota. We must consider this decision in terms of its long-range implications and not on the basis of any one issue brought before the voters by the initiative process. Whether an existing ordinance can be repealed through the initiative process depends on the constitutional and/or statutory grant of authority. See, 6 McQuillan, Municipal Corporations (3d ed. 1969 rev. vol.) § 21.11.

Initiative and referendum provisions were introduced in this country early in this century by reformers who hoped that these processes would (1) increase voter involvement in the legislative process, (2) provide a check on the domination of legislatures by special interest groups, and (3) permit voters to act more objectively by considering issues rather than personalities so that there would be greater accuracy in expressing the public will. See, Note, 5 Fla. St. U.L. Rev. 925.

The experience with initiative and referendum provisions has indicated that these hopes have been frustrated. First, ordinances enacted through the initiative process may be poorly drafted because only one person or a small group drafts the ordinance to be placed on the initiative petition. There is no review to ensure that the ordinance is internally consistent, not in conflict with existing laws or policies, or based on inaccurate factual premises. Further, there is no critical evaluation, input, or feedback from those in society who may be affected by the legislation; nor is there the refining process that occurs in the legislature. Second, the fact that the issues may be very complex necessitates long, detailed explanations and perhaps specialized knowledge in order that voters may make an informed choice. An election campaign does not lend itself to such explanations but to simple fact statements or slogans. As a result voters may be confused and make decisions, not on a factual or philosophical basis, but for emotional or political reasons. Third, the initiative process does not necessarily avoid domination of the legislature or council by special interest groups, because small groups, e.g., only eight percent of the voters of the City of St. Paul, can place an initiative question on the ballot. Because of the small voter turnout, a well-organized minority can secure or block passage of an ordinance. Thus, the initiative process is not always the voice of the people.

Because of these grave problems, I believe that statutory and charter provisions providing for initiative and referendum must be narrowly construed. I am confirmed in this belief by the fact that neither the framers of the state constitution nor the legislature has seen fit to provide for initiative and referendum on a statewide level. In Minnesota, the powers of initiative and referendum are confined by statute to the municipal level of government. The statute provides that municipalities "may also provide for submitting ordinances to the council by petition of the electors of such city and for the repeal of ordinances in like manner." Minn. St. 410.20. Instead of using the statutory language, however, the St. Paul City Charter grants the people "the right to propose ordinances, to require ordinances to be submitted to a vote, and to recall elective officials by processes known respectively as initiative, referendum, and recall." St. Paul City Charter, § 8.01. The St. Paul City Charter permits voters to vote on emergency ordinances by referendum, and all ordinances submitted to the voters by initiative or referendum can be repealed in one year.

Although the repeal of an ordinance may be considered an act of proposing legislation in a broad sense, there is a recognized distinction between an initiative, which is designed to propose new legislation, and a referendum, which is designed to review existing legislation. See, *Landt v. City of Wisconsin Dells*, 141 N.W.2d 245 (Wis. 1966). Under Chapter 8 of the St.

Paul City Charter, the only distinction between the initiative and the referendum is the time limit in which a petition must be filed. To hold that the St. Paul voters can repeal an existing ordinance by initiative would be to render the referendum provision meaningless, because it would eliminate the need to file the referendum petition within 45 days. It is not reasonable to suppose that the St. Paul City Charter Commission intended such a result. On this ground I would reverse the decision of the trial court.

OTIS, JUSTICE (dissenting).

I join in the dissent of Justice Wahl for the reasons stated therein and for the further reason that the proposed ordinance embraces two unrelated subjects in violation of the city charter.

NOTES ON *ST. PAUL CITIZENS* AND THE FAIRNESS OF DIRECT DEMOCRACY

1. *Direct Democracy and Fair Treatment of Minorities.* The St. Paul case arose in an era in which ballot measures seemed increasingly hostile to minorities. In the most prominent legal scholarship at that time on this question, Derrick Bell maintained:

> * * * Supporters of minority rights must be concerned that both the initiative and the referendum often serve those opposed to reform. It is clear, for example, that direct legislation is used effectively by residents of homogeneous middle-class communities to prevent unwanted development — especially development that portends increased size or heterogeneity of population.
>
> Today, direct democracy is used comparatively infrequently to curb abuses in government or otherwise to control elected officials. Rather, intense interest is generated when the issues are seemingly clear-cut and often emotional matters such as liquor, gun control, pollution, pornography, or race. * * *
>
> The emotionally charged atmosphere often surrounding referenda and initiatives can easily reduce the care with which the voters consider the matters submitted to them. Tumultuous, media-oriented campaigns, such as the ones successfully used to repeal ordinances recognizing the rights of homosexuals in Dade County, Florida, St. Paul, Minnesota, and Eugene, Oregon, are not conducive to careful thinking and voting.[c]

How well can direct democracy handle such single-issue concerns?[d]

Nonetheless, it would be misleading to consider the direct democracy dispute as one between conservatives and liberals. Indeed, a national initiative proposal in the 1970s was supported by such liberals as Senator James

---

c. Derrick Bell, *The Referendum: Democracy's Barrier to Racial Equality*, 54 Wash. L. Rev. 1, 18 (1978).

d. For a communitarian critique of direct democracy, see Frickey, *Communion of Strangers, supra* (arguing that legislative processes force sensitive social issues into the public sphere, where conflicting interests may be required to interact and publicly elected officials who have taken an oath to uphold the Constitution are required to act and to be held accountable publicly, whereas direct democracy allows each citizen to follow her preconceptions anonymously and unaccountably in isolation from any interaction with others having different views).

Abourezk (D–S.D.) and Ralph Nader.　Consider this account of liberal outcomes of direct democracy:

> Right-to-work legislation, generally considered conservative, has been defeated by referendum in several states.　And Oregon led the way with progressive initiatives that abolished the poll tax and introduced female suffrage by popular ballot at the beginning of the century.　More recently Michigan and Maine banned disposable soft-drink containers by popular vote, Colorado voted down an Olympics proposal for the state that had been widely supported by business and political elites, New Jersey introduced casino gambling by referendum, and bond issues have continued to win popular support for selected projects despite the increasing fiscal conservatism of the electorate.[e]

2. *The Single Subject Rule and Direct Democracy.*　Recall the justifications for the single subject rule (Chapter 3, § 3A).　Does that rule have a role to play in direct democracy, or is it only directed to legislative lawmaking?　Is there any argument that it should be enforced more strictly in the context of direct democracy?　Reread the way the ballot issue was phrased in *St. Paul Citizens.*

The California Constitution has a single-subject rule specifically designed for direct democracy.　It provides: "An initiative measure embracing more than one subject may not be submitted to the electors or have any effect."　Cal. Const., art. II, § 8(d).　The California Supreme Court has construed it identically with the state constitution's single-subject rule regarding legislation,[f] applying to both a standard under which the rule is construed " 'liberally to uphold proper legislation, all parts of which are reasonably germane.' "　*Perry v. Jordan*, 207 P.2d 47 (Cal. 1949) (quoting *Evans v. Superior Court of Los Angeles County*, 8 P.2d 467 (Cal. 1932)).　Several justices have suggested, however, that a more stringent standard should apply in the context of direct democracy, under which the parts of an initiative must be "functionally related in furtherance of a common underlying purpose."　*Schmitz v. Younger*, 577 P.2d 652 (Cal. 1978) (Manuel, J., dissenting).　What policies support adoption of a stricter standard?　Compare Comment, *Putting the "Single" Back in the Single-Subject Rule: A Proposal for Initiative Reform in California*, 24 U.C. Davis L. Rev. 879 (1991) (proposing an amendment to encourage the court to engage in single-subject review), with Richard Hasen, *Ending Court Protection of Voters from the Initiative Process,* 116 Yale L.J. Pocket Part 117 (2006) (arguing that justifications for aggressive enforcement of the single-subject rule are unpersuasive and that the rule should be repealed).　Would adoption of the stricter approach interfere fundamentally with the people's right to use direct democracy?　See generally Daniel Lowenstein, *California Initiatives and the Single-Subject Rule*, 30 UCLA L. Rev. 936

---

　　e. Benjamin Barber, *Strong Democracy: Participatory Politics for a New Age* 284 (2003). Barber asserts that, "[w]hile Madisonian theorists have stood trembling at the prospects of a leviathan public running amok in schoolrooms filled with voting machines, students of the referendum's practical effects have been offering more soothing pictures." *Id.* at 282–83.

　　f. Cal. Const., art. IV, § 9: "A statute shall embrace but one subject, which shall be expressed in its title.　If a statute embraces a subject not expressed in its title, only the part not expressed is void * * *."

(1983). How would the ballot proposal in *St. Paul Citizens* fare under these alternative standards?

Perhaps an invigoration of the single-subject rule for ballot propositions is in the offing. Florida has had a reputation for applying the single-subject rule aggressively; interestingly, the state is a relative newcomer to the initiative process, adopting it in 1968 for constitutional changes. Although deferential until the mid-1980s, Florida courts began to wield the single-subject rule so enthusiastically to strike down initiatives or keep them off the ballot that a 1994 ballot measure exempted initiatives limiting government revenues from the single-subject requirement.[g] A recent study by Daniel Lowenstein reveals that Florida is no longer the only state with a judiciary willing to enforce the single-subject rule aggressively in the context of initiatives. *Initiatives and the New Single Subject Rule*, 1 Election L.J. 35 (2002). Between 1998 and 1999, the supreme courts of California, Oregon, and Montana applied the single-subject doctrine "with surprising strictness," and Oklahoma, Missouri, and Colorado have inconsistently adopted a strict approach. Lowenstein concludes: "Whether the decisions in [California, Oregon, and Montana] really set a new course or will turn out to be aberrations is impossible to say. * * * [But] even in states that have not so far been affected by the trend toward restrictive review, the developments in the states reviewed above may provide a strong temptation to supreme court justices who are personally hostile to an initiative that comes before them." *Id.* at 44.

3. *Other Constitutional Problems. St. Paul Citizens* suggests a number of important constitutional issues about direct democracy in addition to the single-subject rule question. Because direct democracy risks oppression of a minority by a majority, it obviously creates equal protection problems. Moreover, because the electorate may not seem to be the appropriate decisionmaker for certain kinds of public issues, direct democracy might violate latent norms of due process of lawmaking (see Chapter 4, § 1) other than those associated with the single subject rule.[h] The equal protection and due process inquiries will be considered throughout much of the remainder of this chapter.

As you begin this inquiry, note that measures adopted by direct democracy are peculiarly likely to be set aside by courts. Kenneth Miller found that 52% of initiatives adopted in California, Oregon, Colorado and Washington during the last four decades of the twentieth century were challenged in court, and in

---

g. See Dubois & Feeney, *supra,* at 136–38.

h. On these constitutional questions, see, e.g., William Adams, Jr., *Is It Animus or a Difference of Opinion? The Problems Caused by the Invidious Intent of Anti-Gay Ballot Measures*, 34 Willamette L. Rev. 449 (1998); Lynn Baker, *Direct Democracy and Discrimination: A Public Choice Perspective*, 67 Chi.-Kent L. Rev. 707 (1992); Robin Charlow, *Judicial Review, Equal Protection and the Problem with Plebiscites*, 79 Cornell L. Rev. 527 (1994); Julian Eule, *Judicial Review of Direct Democracy*, 99 Yale L.J. 1503 (1990); Philip Frickey, *Interpretation on the Borderline: Constitution, Canons, Direct Democracy*, 1996 NYU Ann. Surv. Am. L. 477.

54% of those cases, courts invalidated part or all of the challenged measure.[i] Does the presence of judicial review — and an apparent pattern of aggressive judicial second-guessing of direct democracy — help legitimate direct democracy by providing an important check upon its excesses? Or is it "one of the great ironies in this age of participatory democracy . . . that the least democratic branch has ended up with enhanced practical authority"?[j] Could the practice of vigorous judicial review allow supporters of controversial ballot propositions to urge that constitutional issues be disregarded by the voters because the courts will clean them up after the fact?

Problems on Direct Democracy and the Single-Subject Rule

Problem 5–2. Citizens in Florida petition to add the following to Article I, section 10 of the Florida Constitution:

> The state, political subdivisions of the state, municipalities or any other governmental entity shall not enact or adopt any law regarding discrimination against persons which creates, establishes or recognizes any right, privilege or protection for any person based upon any characteristic, trait, status, or condition other than race, color, sex, national origin, age, handicap, ethnic background, marital status, or familial status.
> * * *

As we noted in Chapter 3, § 3A, Florida has a single-subject rule: Any revision to the Florida Constitution by initiative "shall embrace but one subject and matter directly connected therewith." The Florida Supreme Court has stated that the rule is "designed to insulate Florida's organic law from precipitous and cataclysmic change."

As is often done now, groups opposing this initiative bring suit to knock it off the ballot. Should the Florida Supreme Court hear such preliminary challenges? If so, how should it rule? See *In re Advisory Opinion to the Attorney General — Restricts Laws Related to Discrimination,* 632 So. 2d 1018 (Fla. 1994).

Problem 5–3. A proposed amendment to the Arizona state constitution provides:

> To preserve and protect marriage in this state, only a union between one man and one woman shall be valid or recognized as a marriage by this state or its political subdivisions and no legal status for unmarried persons shall be created or recognized by this state or its political subdivisions that is similar to that of marriage.

Does this measure contain a single subject? Consider the formal argument that it (1) defines marriage, (2) prohibits same-sex marriages, (3) might prohibit

---

i. Kenneth Miller, *Courts as Watchdogs of the Washington State Initiative Process,* 24 Seattle U. L. Rev. 1053, 1085 n.12 (2001).

j. Frickey, *Communion of Strangers, supra,* at 438. Of course, if state courts are involved, elected judges are making these judgments. Some commentators have suggested that re-election desires make such judges wary of setting aside lawmaking by the voters. See, e.g., Julian Eule, *Crocodiles in the Bathtub: State Courts, Voter Initiatives and the Threat of Electoral Reprisal,* 65 U. Colo. L. Rev. 733 (1994).

civil unions and domestic partnerships, and (4) might even prohibit the state and its subdivisions from conferring any benefits upon persons in same-sex relationships, whether that status is recognized by law or not (e.g., it might prohibit the University of Arizona from extending health insurance coverage to partners of its employees). In addition, consider the functional argument that common sense and public opinion polls alike indicate that many voters who support (1) and (2) will not understand that (3) and (4) might also be involved — and at least a good number of them might oppose either or both (3) and (4) if they could vote separately on them. See *Arizona Together v. Brewer*, 214 Ariz. 118, 149 P.3d 742 (Ariz. 2007).

B. POPULAR LAWMAKING AND THE EQUAL PROTECTION CLAUSE

ARTHUR v. CITY OF TOLEDO
United States Court of Appeals, Sixth Circuit, 1986
782 F.2d 565

[Toledo's voters had repealed by referendum two city ordinances authorizing the local housing authority to construct sewer extensions to two proposed public housing sites outside the inner city. The city council had passed the ordinances by 5–4 votes, after the federal Department of Housing and Urban Development had threatened both not to recertify the city's housing plan and to withhold previously approved federal money on the ground that the city was not dispersing low and moderate income housing outside the inner city. The district court found that plaintiffs, a class of persons seeking low income housing and a subclass of that group consisting of racial minorities, had failed to prove either racial bias in the electorate or discriminatory intent connected with the referendum on the part of government officials.]

Before KENNEDY and KRUPANSKY, Circuit Judges, and BROWN, Senior Circuit Judge.

CORNELIA G. KENNEDY, CIRCUIT JUDGE.

Plaintiffs-appellants contend that the District Court's finding that racial discrimination was not a motivating factor in the referendums was clearly erroneous. In *Village of Arlington Heights v. Metropolitan Housing Development Corp.*, 429 U.S. 252, 265 (1977), the Supreme Court held that a plaintiff must present proof of a racially discriminatory intent or purpose to establish a violation of the equal protection clause. The District Court held that plaintiffs had not presented sufficient evidence to support the conclusion that racial discrimination motivated the City's electorate.

The Supreme Court has considered several cases involving referendums or initiatives and charges of racial discrimination. In *Hunter v. Erickson*, 393 U.S. 385 (1969), the Supreme Court held that an amendment to the Akron, Ohio city charter which prevented the city council from implementing any ordinance dealing with racial, religious, or ancestral discrimination in housing without the approval of the majority of the city's voters violated the equal protection clause. The petition of more than ten percent of the city's voters placed the proposal for the charter amendment on the ballot and a majority of the city's voters approved the amendment. The amendment not only suspended the operation of the existing city ordinance assuring "equal opportunity to all persons to live in decent housing facilities regardless of race, color, religion, ancestry or national origin," but also required the city's electorate to approve future racial, religious, or ancestral housing discrimination ordinances before the ordinance could take effect. Ordinances prohibiting other types of housing discrimination or otherwise regulating real estate did not require referendum approval. The Supreme Court concluded that an explicitly racial classification treated racial housing matters differently from other racial and housing matters. The Court decided that the amendment disadvantaged those groups who would have benefitted from laws barring racial, religious, or ancestral discrimination as against other groups who would bar other discriminations or who would otherwise regulate the real estate market in their favor by making enactment of ordinances prohibiting racial, religious, or ancestral discrimination in housing substantially more difficult. On their face, however, the referendums at issue in this case are racially neutral.

In *James v. Valtierra*, 402 U.S. 137 (1971), the Supreme Court upheld Article XXXIV of the California Constitution, which amended the California Constitution to bring public housing decisions under California's referendum provisions, against an equal protection challenge. Article XXXIV provided that a state public body could not develop, construct, or acquire in any manner a low-rent housing project until a majority of the voters at a community election approved the project. The Supreme Court specifically rejected the invitation to extend *Hunter v. Erickson, supra*. Since Article XXXIV did not rest on " ' distinctions based on race,' " *id.*, quoting *Hunter*, the Court concluded:

> The people of California have also decided by their own vote to require referendum approval of low-rent public housing projects. This procedure ensures that all the people of a community will have a voice in a decision which may lead to large expenditures of local governmental funds for increased public services and to lower tax revenues. It gives them a voice in decisions that will affect the future development of their own community. This procedure for democratic decisionmaking does not violate the constitutional command that no State shall deny to any person "the equal protection of the laws."

Defendants-appellees argue that this Court should uphold the referendums because the referendum power in this case has a broader application than the referendum power in *James v. Valtierra*, which dealt specifically and exclusively with public housing, because the City's electorate can approve or disapprove any legislative action.

More recently, in *Washington v. Seattle School District No. 1*, 458 U.S. 457 (1982), the Supreme Court held that Initiative 350, a statewide voter initiative designed to terminate the use of mandatory busing for purposes of racial integration in the public schools in the State of Washington, violated the equal protection clause. The Court decided that the initiative used the racial nature of an issue to define the governmental decisionmaking structure and therefore imposed substantial and unique burdens on racial minorities. The district court found that by carefully tailoring the initiative, the initiative permitted almost all of the busing previously taking place in Washington, except for desegregative busing. Although Initiative 350 was facially neutral because the initiative did not mention "race" or "integration," the Court did not doubt that the initiative organizers effectively drew the initiative for racial purposes. Next, the Court concluded that from a practical standpoint, the initiative reallocated "the authority to address a racial problem — and only a racial problem — from the existing decisionmaking body, in such a way as to burden minority interests." Since local school boards previously had the discretion to determine what program would most appropriately fill a school district's educational needs, the Court concluded that "Initiative 350 worked a major reordering of the State's educational decisionmaking process." The Court, however, recognized that:

> To be sure, "the simple repeal or modification of desegregation or antidiscrimination laws, without more, never has been viewed as embodying a presumptively invalid racial classification." As Justice Harlan noted in *Hunter*, the voters of the polity may express their displeasure through an established legislative or referendum procedure when particular legislation "arouses passionate opposition." Had Akron's fair housing ordinance been defeated at a referendum, for example, "Negroes would undoubtedly [have lost] an important political battle but they would not thereby [have been] denied equal protection."

Since Initiative 350 "burden[ed] all future attempts to integrate Washington schools in districts throughout the State, by lodging decisionmaking authority over the question at a new and remote level of government," the initiative "work[ed] something more than the 'mere repeal' of a desegregation law by the political entity that created it."

In this case, we conclude that the City did not reallocate "the authority to address a racial problem — and only a racial problem — from the existing decisionmaking body, in such a way as to burden minority interests." Rather, the City's electorate repealed ordinances authorizing sewer extensions to two, and only two, public housing projects. Nothing prevented low-income public housing in those neighborhoods or in other white neighborhoods. In fact, the City spent the money allocated to the two rejected projects on other similar projects in other white neighborhoods.

Plaintiffs-appellants contend that the District Court did not "make a sensitive inquiry as to whether race was a factor in the referendum election." While this Court recognizes that the City's "electorate as whole, whether by referendum or otherwise, could not order city action violative of the Equal Protection Clause . . . and the City may not avoid the strictures of that Clause by deferring to the wishes or objections of some fraction of the body politic," *City of Cleburne, Texas v. Cleburne Living Center*, 473 U.S. 432 (1985), neither the Supreme Court nor this Court has ever inquired into the motivation of voters in an equal protection clause challenge to a referendum election involving a facially neutral referendum unless racial discrimination was the only possible motivation behind the referendum results.[2]

Several important policy considerations limit a court's examination of the factors motivating the electorate in a referendum election. Initially, this country has traditionally protected the "secret ballot." *See, e.g., Kirksey v. City of Jackson, Mississippi*, 663 F.2d 659, 661–62 (5th Cir.1981), *reh'g denied*, 669 F.2d 316 (1982). *See also Washington v. Seattle School District No. 1*, *supra* ("The District Court acknowledged that it was impossible to determine whether the supporters of Initiative 350 'subjectively [had] a racially discriminatory intent or purpose,' because '[a]s to that subjective intent the secret ballot raises an impenetrable barrier.' [473 F. Supp.] at 1014.") (dicta). Since a court cannot ask voters how they voted or why they voted that way, a court has no way of ascertaining what motivated the electorate. Furthermore, the Supreme Court has recognized the value of referendum elections. *See, e.g., James v. Valtierra, supra* ("Provisions for referendums demonstrate devotion to democracy, not to bias, discrimination, or prejudice."). Consequently, this Court will not lightly set aside the results of voter referendums. Finally, in *Metropolitan Housing Development Corp. v. Village of Arlington Heights*, 558 F.2d 1283, 1292 (7th Cir.1977), *cert. denied*, 434 U.S. 1025 (1978) ("*Arlington II*"), the Seventh Circuit warned that the "bigoted comments of a few citizens, even those with power, should not invalidate action which in fact has a legitimate basis." Although the District Court found that "a few individuals made racial slurs in contacts and meetings leading to the Referendum of 1977," the District Court also found that "[a]bsent any facts to the contrary, the Court cannot infer racial bias in the total electorate." If courts could always inquire into the motivation of voters even when the electorate has an otherwise valid reason for its decision, a municipality could never reject a low-income public housing project because proponents of the project could always introduce race as an issue in the referendum election.

Plaintiffs-appellants cite *Village of Arlington Heights v. Metropolitan Housing Development Corp.*, 429 U.S. at 270 n.21 (proof that a racially discriminatory purpose motivated the Village's decision would have shifted the burden to the Village to establish that the Village would have reached the same decision absent the racially discriminatory purpose), and *Smith v. Town of Clarkton, North Carolina*, 682 F.2d 1055, 1066 (4th Cir.1982) (emphasis in original) ("It is not necessary, in proving a violation of the equal protection clause, to show that the challenged actions rested *solely* on a racially-discriminatory intent in order to demonstrate that the involved officials acted with an intent to illegally discriminate."), for the proposition that if discriminatory intent motivated the electorate, the District Court could not brush aside racial discrimination even if the District Court also found that other factors motivated

---

2. *Hunter v. Erickson, supra*, invalidated an amendment to the city charter which, on its face, mentioned racial discrimination. In *Washington v. Seattle School District No. 1, supra*, the Supreme Court concluded that since the initiative permitted almost all of the busing previously taking place in the state, except for desegregative busing, the initiative organizers effectively drew the initiative for racial purposes. * * *

the electorate. Carried to its logical extreme, plaintiffs-appellants could establish a violation of the equal protection clause if one voter testified that racial considerations motivated the voter's vote to repeal the sewer extension ordinances. Furthermore, we note that although courts have inquired into the votes of city council members, the policies underlying the "secret ballot" prevent courts from inquiring into the votes of the electorate. Fed.R.Evid. 606(b) prohibits federal courts from inquiring into the validity of a jury verdict. *See* Fed.R.Evid. 606(b) advisory committee note. Similar policy reasons prohibit courts from asking voters how they voted or why they voted as they did. Just as a juror cannot set aside a jury verdict, courts should not permit a member of the electorate or an expert witness to set aside an election or referendum. Accordingly, we conclude that we cannot apply the "motivating factor" test to equal protection clause challenges to referendum elections.

The equal protection clause, however, would require this Court to set aside a referendum if the referendum, although facially neutral, engendered discrimination based on an obvious racial classification. *See, e.g., Washington v. Seattle School District No. 1* ("despite its facial neutrality there is little doubt that the initiative was effectively drawn for racial purposes"). We hold that absent a referendum that facially discriminates racially, or one where although facially neutral, the only possible rationale is racially motivated, a district court cannot inquire into the electorate's motivations in an equal protection clause context. Furthermore, in this case, the City introduced evidence that concerns regarding the costs of the projects, flooding and sanitary sewer surcharges, and the general advisability of the projects influenced the electorate's decision. Accordingly, we hold that the District Court did not err in concluding that plaintiffs-appellants had not presented sufficient evidence to justify a finding that the referendum electorate intended to racially discriminate.

[The court also rejected a claim made under the Fair Housing Act of 1968.]

NOTES ON *ARTHUR* AND THE DIFFICULTY
IN PROVING EQUAL PROTECTION VIOLATIONS

Should it make any difference if plaintiffs in *Arthur* offer evidence that voters who supported an initiative or referendum did so for discriminatory reasons? Consider *Kirksey v. Jackson*, 506 F. Supp. 491 (S.D. Miss. 1981), *aff'd*, 663 F.2d 659 (5th Cir. 1981). The city council of Jackson, Mississippi had been elected at-large since 1912. No African American had ever been elected to the city council even though approximately 40% of the city's population was African American. In the 1970s, a local political coalition was able to place a ballot measure before the city's voters on whether to change to single-member districting. About 57% of those who voted favored retaining the at-large system. In subsequent litigation, African American plaintiffs presented statistical analyses that purported to show that 83.8% of the variance in the election was associated with the race of the voters, that 72.4% of white voters voted to retain the at-large system, and that 97.9% of the African American voters voted for the proposed single-member districts. The plaintiffs also tried to introduce a public opinion poll taken in October 1980 that stated that 61% of the voters who voted to retain the at-large system gave at least one racial reason for their vote and that 44% gave two or more racial reasons. This evidence was excluded by the district court on the grounds that plaintiffs had not given defendants fair warning prior to trial that they would use this evidence. On the evidence as a whole, the district court held, and the court of appeals agreed, that no sufficient showing of discriminatory intent had been made.

Both the district court and the court of appeals held that no inquiry could be made into the motivations of individual voters because the First Amendment assures every citizen the right to cast her ballot for whatever reason she pleases. For the court of appeals, "[s]tigmatized racial attitudes, neither socially admirable nor civically attuned, are not constitutionally proscribed." 663 F.2d at 662. On rehearing, 669 F.2d 316, 317 (5th Cir. 1982), the court of appeals stated:

> Our [earlier] opinion * * * holds that an individual voter may not be subjected to judicial examination concerning how he voted or why he personally voted in that fashion. We affirm that conclusion. However, we specifically note that our decision is not to be misunderstood as holding or suggesting that, in a proper case, the motivation of the electorate may not be examined by the introduction of either direct or circumstantial evidence. The latter inquiry may be a proper inquiry. The referendum process may not be used to legitimate an unconstitutional act. See [*Hunter*]. But the record in the case before us does not establish that type of abuse of the electoral process.

What does this mean? Is it consistent with *Arthur*? Can it be squared with language in *Hunter v. Erickson* (which is discussed in *Arthur*) stating that "[t]he sovereignty of the people is itself subject to those constitutional limitations which have been duly adopted and remain unrepealed"? Can it or *Arthur*'s approach be squared with the next case?

ROMER v. EVANS
Supreme Court of the United States, 1996
517 U.S. 620, 116 S.Ct. 1620, 134 L.Ed.2d 855

JUSTICE KENNEDY delivered the opinion of the Court.

One century ago, the first Justice Harlan admonished this Court that the Constitution "neither knows nor tolerates classes among citizens." *Plessy v. Ferguson*, 163 U.S. 537, 559 (1896) (dissenting opinion). Unheeded then, those words now are understood to state a commitment to the law's neutrality where the rights of persons are at stake. The Equal Protection Clause enforces this principle and today requires us to hold invalid a provision of Colorado's Constitution.

[Aspen, Boulder, and Denver, Colorado adopted ordinances prohibiting private as well as public workplace, housing, and public accommodations discrimination on the basis of sexual orientation. Responding to these ordinances, in 1992 Colorado voters adopted a ballot proposal adding an Amendment 2 to the state constitution, which read:

> Neither the State of Colorado, through any of its branches or departments, nor any of its agencies, political subdivisions, municipalities or school districts, shall enact, adopt

or enforce any statute, regulation, ordinance or policy whereby homosexual, lesbian or bisexual orientation, conduct, practices or relationships shall constitute or otherwise be the basis of or entitle any person or class of persons to have or claim any minority status, quota preferences, protected status or claim of discrimination.]

The State's principal argument in defense of Amendment 2 is that it puts gays and lesbians in the same position as all other persons. So, the State says, the measure does no more than deny homosexuals special rights. This reading of the amendment's language is implausible. [The Colorado Supreme Court interpreted the amendment as repealing local protections for gay people and preventing further protections from being adopted unless the state constitution was first amended.]

Sweeping and comprehensive is the change in legal status effected by this law. So much is evident from the ordinances the Colorado Supreme Court declared would be void by operation of Amendment 2. Homosexuals, by state decree, are put in a solitary class with respect to transactions and relations in both the private and governmental spheres. The amendment withdraws from homosexuals, but no others, specific legal protection from the injuries caused by discrimination, and it forbids reinstatement of these laws and policies.

The change that Amendment 2 works in the legal status of gays and lesbians in the private sphere is far-reaching, both on its own terms and when considered in light of the structure and operation of modern antidiscrimination laws. [Justice Kennedy explained that the common law afforded no protection against discrimination by public accommodations because of race, sex, etc. The common law also placed few, if any, restrictions on employment discrimination. The Aspen, Boulder, and Denver ordinances are typical of antidiscrimination regulations adopted in hundreds of jurisdictions filling this gap in the common law. Additionally, those regulations, like others, prohibit discrimination on the basis of criteria that have not triggered constitutional strict scrutiny, including age, military status, marital status, pregnancy, parenthood, custody of a minor child, political affiliation, physical or mental disability of an individual or of his or her associates, and sexual orientation. The effect of Amendment 2 was to deprive gay people of those protections in public accommodations, housing, sale of real estate, insurance, health and welfare services, private education, and employment.]

Amendment 2's reach may not be limited to specific laws passed for the benefit of gays and lesbians. It is a fair, if not necessary, inference from the broad language of the amendment that it deprives gays and lesbians even of the protection of general laws and policies that prohibit arbitrary discrimination in governmental and private settings. See, *e.g.*, Colo. Rev. Stat. § 24–4–106(7) (1988) (agency action subject to judicial review under arbitrary and capricious standard); § 18–8–405 (making it a criminal offense for a public servant knowingly, arbitrarily or capriciously to refrain from performing a duty imposed on him by law); * * * 4 Colo. Code of Regulations 801–1, Policy 11–1 (1983) (prohibiting discrimination in state employment on grounds of specified traits or "other non-merit factor"). At some point in the systematic administration of these laws, an official must determine whether homosexuality is an arbitrary and, thus, forbidden basis for decision. Yet a decision to that effect would itself amount to a policy prohibiting discrimination on the basis of homosexuality, and so would appear to be no more valid under Amendment 2 than the specific prohibitions against discrimination the state court held invalid.

If this consequence follows from Amendment 2, as its broad language suggests, it would compound the constitutional difficulties the law creates. [The Colorado Supreme Court made the limited observation that the amendment is not intended to affect many antidiscrimination laws protecting non-suspect classes, *Romer II*, 882 P.2d at 1346, n.9, but the state court's construction left open the possibility of broader application. Justice Kennedy specifically rejected the view that Amendment 2's prohibition on specific legal protections does no more than deprive homosexuals of special rights.] We find nothing special in the protections Amendment 2 withholds. These are protections taken for granted by most people either because they already have them or do not need them; these are protections against exclusion from an almost limitless number of transactions and endeavors that constitute ordinary civic life in a free society. * * *

Amendment 2 fails, indeed defies, [rational basis] inquiry. First, the amendment has the peculiar property of imposing a broad and undifferentiated disability on a single named group, an exceptional and, as we shall explain, invalid form of legislation. Second, its sheer breadth is so discontinuous with the reasons offered for it that the amendment seems inexplicable by anything but animus toward the class that it affects; it lacks a rational relationship to legitimate state interests.

Taking the first point, even in the ordinary equal protection case calling for the most deferential of standards, we insist on knowing the relation between the classification adopted and the object to be attained. The search for the link between classification and objective gives substance to the Equal Protection Clause; it provides guidance and discipline for the legislature, which is entitled to know what sorts of laws it can pass; and it marks the limits of our own authority. In the ordinary case, a law will be sustained if it can be said to advance a legitimate government interest, even if the law seems unwise or works to the disadvantage of a particular group, or if the rationale for it seems tenuous. * * * By requiring that the classification bear a rational relationship to an independent and legitimate legislative end, we ensure that classifications are not drawn for the purpose of disadvantaging the group burdened by the law.

Amendment 2 confounds this normal process of judicial review. It is at once too narrow and too broad. It identifies persons by a single trait and then denies them protection across the board. The resulting disqualification of a class of persons from the right to seek specific protection from the law is unprecedented in our jurisprudence. The absence of precedent for Amendment 2 is itself instructive; "[d]iscriminations of an unusual character especially suggest careful consideration to determine whether they are obnoxious to the constitutional provision."

It is not within our constitutional tradition to enact laws of this sort. Central both to the idea of the rule of law and to our own Constitution's guarantee of equal protection is the principle that government and each of its parts remain open on impartial terms to all who seek its assistance. " 'Equal protection of the laws is not achieved through indiscriminate imposition of inequalities.' " *Sweatt v. Painter*, 339 U.S. 629, 635 (1950) (quoting *Shelley v. Kraemer*, 334 U.S. 1, 22 (1948)). Respect for this principle explains why laws singling out a certain class of citizens for disfavored legal status or general hardships are rare. A law declaring that in general it shall be more difficult for one group of citizens than for all others to seek aid from the government is itself a denial of equal protection of the laws in the most literal sense. * * *

A second and related point is that laws of the kind now before us raise the inevitable inference that the disadvantage imposed is born of animosity toward the class of persons affected. "[I]f the constitutional conception of 'equal protection of the laws' means anything, it must at the very least mean that a bare . . . desire to harm a politically unpopular group cannot constitute a *legitimate* governmental interest." Even laws enacted for broad and ambitious purposes often can be explained by reference to legitimate public policies which justify the incidental disadvantages they impose on certain persons. Amendment 2, however, in making a general announcement that gays and lesbians shall not have any particular protections from the law, inflicts on them immediate, continuing, and real injuries that outrun and belie any legitimate justifications that may be claimed for it. We conclude that, in addition to the far-reaching deficiencies of Amendment 2 that we have noted, the principles it offends, in another sense, are conventional and venerable; a law must bear a rational relationship to a legitimate governmental purpose, and Amendment 2 does not.

The primary rationale the State offers for Amendment 2 is respect for other citizens' freedom of association, and in particular the liberties of landlords or employers who have personal or religious objections to homosexuality. Colorado also cites its interest in conserving resources to fight discrimination against other groups. The breadth of the Amendment is so far removed from these particular justifications that we find it impossible to credit them. We cannot say that Amendment 2 is directed to any identifiable legitimate purpose or discrete objective. It is a status-based enactment divorced from any factual context from which we could discern a relationship to legitimate state interests; it is a classification of persons undertaken for its own sake, something the Equal Protection Clause does not permit. "[C]lass legislation . . . [is] obnoxious to the prohibitions of the Fourteenth Amendment . . . . " * * *

JUSTICE SCALIA, with whom THE CHIEF JUSTICE [REHNQUIST] and JUSTICE THOMAS join, dissenting.

The Court has mistaken a Kulturkampf for a fit of spite. The constitutional amendment before us here is not the manifestation of a " 'bare . . . desire to harm' " homosexuals, but is rather a modest attempt by seemingly tolerant Coloradans to preserve traditional sexual mores against the efforts of a politically powerful minority to revise those mores through use of the laws. That objective, and the means chosen to achieve it, are not only unimpeachable under any constitutional doctrine hitherto pronounced (hence the opinion's heavy reliance upon principles of righteousness rather than judicial holdings);

they have been specifically approved by the Congress of the United States and by this Court. * * *

[Justice Scalia criticized the Court for suggesting that Amendment 2 had a potentially broad impact upon gay people, for the Colorado Supreme Court authoritatively construed Amendment 2 "only to prevent the adoption of antidiscrimination laws intended to protect gays, lesbians, and bisexuals."] The amendment prohibits *special treatment* of homosexuals, and nothing more. It would not affect, for example, a requirement of state law that pensions be paid to all retiring state employees with a certain length of service; homosexual employees, as well as others, would be entitled to that benefit. But it would prevent the State or any municipality from making death-benefit payments to the "life partner" of a homosexual when it does not make such payments to the long-time roommate of a nonhomosexual employee. Or again, it does not affect the requirement of the State's general insurance laws that customers be afforded coverage without discrimination unrelated to anticipated risk. Thus, homosexuals could not be denied coverage, or charged a greater premium, with respect to auto collision insurance; but neither the State nor any municipality could require that distinctive health insurance risks associated with homosexuality (if there are any) be ignored.

Despite all of its hand wringing about the potential effect of Amendment 2 on general antidiscrimination laws, the Court's opinion ultimately does not dispute all this, but assumes it to be true. The only denial of equal treatment it contends homosexuals have suffered is this: They may not obtain *preferential* treatment without amending the state constitution. That is to say, the principle underlying the Court's opinion is that one who is accorded equal treatment under the laws, but cannot as readily as others obtain *preferential* treatment under the laws, has been denied equal protection of the laws. If merely stating this alleged "equal protection" violation does not suffice to refute it, our constitutional jurisprudence has achieved terminal silliness. * * *

I turn next to whether there was a legitimate rational basis for the substance of the constitutional amendment — for the prohibition of special protection for homosexuals. It is unsurprising that the Court avoids discussion of this question, since the answer is so obviously yes. The case most relevant to the issue before us today is not even mentioned in the Court's opinion: In *Bowers v. Hardwick*, 478 U.S. 186 (1986), we held that the Constitution does not prohibit what virtually all States had done from the founding of the Republic until very recent years — making homosexual conduct a crime. That holding is unassailable, except by those who think that the Constitution changes to suit current fashions. But in any event it is a given in the present case: Respondents' briefs did not urge overruling *Bowers*, and at oral argument respondents' counsel expressly disavowed any intent to seek such overruling. If it is constitutionally permissible for a State to make homosexual conduct criminal, surely it is constitutionally permissible for a State to enact other laws merely *disfavoring* homosexual conduct. * * * And *a fortiori* it is constitutionally permissible for a State to adopt a provision *not even* disfavoring homosexual conduct, but merely prohibiting all levels of state government from bestowing *special protections* upon homosexual conduct. Respondents (who, unlike the

Court, cannot afford the luxury of ignoring inconvenient precedent) counter *Bowers* with the argument that a greater-includes-the-lesser rationale cannot justify Amendment 2's application to individuals who do not engage in homosexual acts, but are merely of homosexual "orientation." * * *

But assuming that, in Amendment 2, a person of homosexual "orientation" is someone who does not engage in homosexual conduct but merely has a tendency or desire to do so, *Bowers* still suffices to establish a rational basis for the provision. If it is rational to criminalize the conduct, surely it is rational to deny special favor and protection to those with a self-avowed tendency or desire to engage in the conduct. Indeed, where criminal sanctions are not involved, homosexual "orientation" is an acceptable stand-in for homosexual conduct. * * * Just as a policy barring the hiring of methadone users as transit employees does not violate equal protection simply because *some* methadone users pose no threat to passenger safety, see *New York City Transit Authority v. Beazer*, 440 U.S. 568 (1979), and just as a mandatory retirement age of 50 for police officers does not violate equal protection even though it prematurely ends the careers of many policemen over 50 who still have the capacity to do the job, see *Massachusetts Board of Retirement v. Murgia*, 427 U.S. 307 (1976), Amendment 2 is not constitutionally invalid simply because it could have been drawn more precisely so as to withdraw special antidiscrimination protections only from those of homosexual "orientation" who actually engage in homosexual conduct. * * *

* * * The Court's opinion contains grim, disapproving hints that Coloradans have been guilty of "animus" or "animosity" toward homosexuality, as though that has been established as un-American. Of course it is our moral heritage that one should not hate any human being or class of human beings. But I had thought that one could consider certain conduct reprehensible — murder, for example, or polygamy, or cruelty to animals — and could exhibit even "animus" toward such conduct. Surely that is the only sort of "animus" at issue here: moral disapproval of homosexual conduct, the same sort of moral disapproval that produced the centuries-old criminal laws that we held constitutional in *Bowers*. The Colorado amendment does not, to speak entirely precisely, prohibit giving favored status to people who are *homosexuals*; they can be favored for many reasons — for example, because they are senior citizens or members of racial minorities. But it prohibits giving them favored status *because of their homosexual conduct* — that is, it prohibits favored status *for homosexuality*.

[Justice Scalia maintained that Colorado had, in fact, engaged in a measured response to homosexuality. The state in 1971 repealed its law making consensual sodomy a crime, but that repeal was not intended to connote an approval of homosexuality.] The problem (a problem, that is, for those who wish to retain social disapprobation of homosexuality) is that, because those who engage in homosexual conduct tend to reside in disproportionate numbers in certain communities, see Record, Exh. MMM, have high disposable income, see *ibid.*; App. 254 (affidavit of Prof. James Hunter), and, of course, care about homosexual-rights issues much more ardently than the public at large, they possess political power much greater than their numbers, both locally and statewide. Quite understandably, they devote this political power to achieving not merely a grudging social toleration, but full social acceptance, of homosexuality. * * *

That is where Amendment 2 came in. It sought to counter both the geographic concentration and the disproportionate political power of homosexuals by (1) resolving the controversy at the statewide level, and (2) making the election a single-issue contest for both sides. It put directly, to all the citizens of the State, the question: Should homosexuality be given special protection? They answered no. The Court today asserts that this most democratic of procedures is unconstitutional. Lacking any cases to establish that facially absurd proposition, it simply asserts that it *must* be unconstitutional, because it has never happened before. [This is completely false, says Justice Scalia. In the late nineteenth century, the federal government enacted a series of statutes singling out polygamists for special criminal, civil, and juridical treatment; the Court upheld all the legal disabilities, including one that disenfranchised not only polygamists, but also people who taught or counseled polygamy. *Davis v. Beason*, 133 U.S. 333 (1890). Although abstract advocacy cannot today be punished, *Beason* remains good for the proposition that disapproved status can be the basis for civil penalty.] Has the Court concluded that the perceived social harm of polygamy is a "legitimate concern of government," and the perceived social harm of homosexuality is not? [Justice Scalia concluded his opinion:]

When the Court takes sides in the culture wars, it tends to be with the knights rather than the villeins — and more specifically with the Templars, reflecting the views and values of the lawyer class from which the Court's Members are drawn. How that class feels about homosexuality will be evident to anyone who wishes to interview job applicants at virtually any of the Nation's law schools. The interviewer may refuse to offer a job because the applicant is a Republican; because he is an adulterer; because he went to the wrong prep school or belongs to the wrong country club; because he eats snails; because he is a womanizer; because she wears real-animal fur; or even because he hates the Chicago Cubs. But if the interviewer should wish not to be an associate or partner of an applicant because he disapproves of the applicant's homosexuality, *then* he will have violated the pledge which the Association of American Law Schools requires all its member schools to exact from job interviewers: "assurance of the employer's willingness" to hire homosexuals. This law-school view of what "prejudices" must be stamped out may be contrasted with the more plebeian attitudes that apparently still prevail in the United States Congress, which has been unresponsive to repeated attempts to extend to homosexuals the protections of federal civil rights laws, see, *e.g.*, Employment Non-Discrimination Act of 1994, S. 2238, 103d Cong., 2d Sess. (1994); Civil Rights Amendments of 1975, H.R. 5452, 94th Cong., 1st Sess. (1975), and which took the pains to exclude them specifically from the Americans With Disabilities Act of 1990, see 42 U.S.C. § 12211(a) (1988 ed., Supp. V). * * *

NOTES ON *ROMER* AND RENEWED ATTENTION TO THE CONSTITUTIONAL PROBLEMS WITH INITIATIVES

1. *What Is the Holding of* Romer? What exactly was wrong with Amendment 2? Some possibilities:

(a) it deprived gay people of the right to participate equally in the political process;[k]

(b) the law was a denial of the "equal protection of the laws" in the most literal sense, as it closed off state process to one vulnerable group;[l]

(c) the law may not draw moral distinctions based upon sexual practices between consenting adults;[m]

(d) the state cannot, without justification, single out one social group for "pariah" status by creating a constitutional right to discriminate against that group,[n] or the state has an obligation to remedy pervasive discrimination against a vulnerable group similar to those the state does protect;[o]

(e) the law's goal — state action reflecting widespread animus against gay people — was impermissible;[p]

(f) the measure, unprecedented in its sweep, was way overbroad.[q]

Note that none of these interpretations depends upon the fact that Amendment 2 was enacted by the voters rather than the legislature. How did Justice (Anthony) Kennedy avoid the conundrums in applying the Equal Protection

---

k. This was the theory followed by the Colorado Supreme Court, *Evans v. Romer*, 854 P.2d 1270 (1993), and has been viewed by some commentators as essentially the U.S. Supreme Court's theory, notwithstanding the Court's refusal even to mention it. See Pamela Karlan, *Just Politics? Five Not So Easy Pieces of the 1995 Term*, 34 Hous. L. Rev. 289, 296 (1997); Nicholas Zeppos, *The Dynamics of Democracy: Travel, Premature Predation, and the Components of Political Identity*, 50 Vand. L. Rev. 445 (1997), as well as Caren Dubnoff, Romer v. Evans: *A Legal and Political Analysis*, 15 Law & Ineq. 275 (1997) (this is the theory the Court should have adopted).

l. Brief by Laurence Tribe et al., in *Romer*, the so-called "Scholars' Brief" filed in the case.

m. Robert Bork, *Slouching Towards Gomorrah* 112–14 (1996) (disapproving); Ronald Dworkin, *Sex, Death, and the Courts*, N.Y. Rev. Books, Aug. 8, 1996, at 44, 49 (approving); William Eskridge, Jr., *Gaylaw: Challenging the Apartheid of the Closet* 149–52, 205–18 (1999) (approving).

n. Daniel Farber & Suzanna Sherry, *The Pariah Principle*, 13 Const. Comment 257 (1996), as well as Akhil Amar, *Attainder and Amendment 2: * Romer's *Rightness*, 95 Mich. L. Rev. 203 (1996).

o. Louis Michael Seidman, Romer's *Radicalism: The Unexpected Revival of Warren Court Activism*, 1996 Sup. Ct. Rev. 67.

p. Andrew Koppelman, Romer v. Evans *and Invidious Intent*, 6 Wm. & Mary Bill Rts. J. 89 (1997).

q. Richard Duncan, *The Narrow and Shallow Bite of* Romer *and the Eminent Rationality of Dual-Gender Marriage: A (Partial) Response to Professor Koppelman*, 6 Wm. & Mary Bill Rts. J. 147 (1997).

Clause to initiatives that were faced by Judge (Cornelia) Kennedy in *Arthur*? In light of Justice Scalia's understanding of what motivated the Colorado voters who supported Amendment 2, how can Justice Kennedy be so certain that he correctly identified the purpose of the Amendment?

In a later case, the Supreme Court declined an opportunity to clarify the holding in *Romer*. The Court first vacated a Sixth Circuit decision upholding a similarly worded municipal initiative that repealed a Cincinnati gay rights ordinance and wrote the following into the municipal charter:

> The City of Cincinnati and its various Boards and Commissions may not enact, adopt, enforce or administer any ordinance, regulation, rule or policy which provides that homosexual, lesbian, or bisexual orientation, status, conduct, or relationship constitutes, entitles, or otherwise provides a person with the basis to have any claim of minority or protected status, quota preference or other preferential treatment. This provision of the City Charter shall in all respects be self-executing. Any ordinance, regulation, rule or policy enacted before this amendment is adopted that violates the foregoing prohibition shall be null and void and of no force or effect. * * *

Then, on remand in *Equality Foundation of Greater Cincinnati v. City of Cincinnati*, 128 F.3d 289 (6th Cir. 1997), the Sixth Circuit reaffirmed its previous disposition and distinguished *Romer*:

> Whereas Colorado Amendment 2 ominously threatened to reduce an entire segment of the state's population to the status of virtual non-citizens (or even non-persons) without legal rights under any and every type of state law, the Cincinnati Charter Amendment had no such sweeping and conscience-shocking effect, because (1) it applied only at the lowest (municipal) level of government and thus could not dispossess gay Cincinnatians of any rights derived from any higher level of state law and enforced by a superior apparatus of state government, and (2) its narrow, restrictive language could not be construed to deprive homosexuals of all legal protections even under municipal law, but instead eliminated only 'special class status' and 'preferential treatment' for gays as gays under Cincinnati ordinances and policies, leaving untouched the application, to gay citizens, of any and all legal rights generally accorded by the municipal government to all persons as persons.

The Supreme Court denied certiorari, 525 U.S. 943 (1998), with three Justices (Stevens, Souter, and Ginsburg) writing separately to explain that this was an inappropriate case for review, because the circuit court's second ground for distinction involved its interpretation of local law, which the Supreme Court is reluctant to second-guess.

    2. *Should Direct-Democracy Measures Be Treated Differently for Purposes of Judicial Review?* The Supreme Court has rarely reviewed the constitutionality of direct lawmaking, and until *Romer* its review had largely focused on initiatives having a race-based impact.[r] With a few dissenting voices, scholars

---

r. See *Reitman v. Mulkey*, 387 U.S. 369 (1967); *Hunter v. Erickson*, 393 U.S. 385 (1969); *James v. Valtierra*, 402 U.S. 137 (1971); *Washington v. Seattle Sch. Dist. No. 1*, 458 U.S. 457 (1982); *Crawford v. Board of Educ. of City of Los Angeles*, 458 U.S. 527 (1982). In all but *James* and *Crawford*, the Court invalidated the initiative because it impaired racial minority

have urged the Court to scrutinize popular initiatives for equal protection violations more vigorously than the Court reviews ordinary statutes adopted by legislatures, on the ground that ballot campaigns are more prone to abuse.[s] *Romer* might be an example of that realist argument.

Other scholars reject or caution against this academic conventional wisdom.[t] Initiatives are an intrinsically fair way for the voting population to focus on an issue that concerns them — and are often a better path to active citizen engagement in substantive issues. Public choice theory, for example, suggests that legislators have incentives not to confront or resolve conflictual issues, and this may have been the reason the Colorado legislature ducked the issue of sexual orientation protections at the local level. Moreover, the same kinds of questions raised against direct democracy — the inability of minorities to win, the lack of genuine deliberation, private interests winning over the common good — have been posed by public choice theorists criticizing representative democracy.

How does the Colorado experience bear on these arguments? Judge Hans Linde contends that the history of antigay initiatives supports the conventional academic wisdom and heightened judicial review under Article IV.[u] One argument is that, as soon as states and municipalities stopped discriminating against lesbian and gay employees and couples and started granting these citizens equal rights, antigay initiatives sought to overturn positive laws, in part by appeals to arguments that gay people are child molesters (the main argument in the 1970s) or that the community should not "promote the homosexual lifestyle" by providing "special rights" (the main argument in the 1990s).

3. *Statutory Interpretation Techniques as an Alternative.* As discussed in Chapter 8, § 3, and as *Romer* illustrates, the interpretation of ballot measures is often extremely difficult, in part because they are often worded vaguely and in part because the electorate's intent concerning their meaning is often quite speculative. For reasons similar to those supporting heightened constitutional scrutiny for ballot measures, should a statute adopted by the voters be subject

---

equality.

s. See, e.g., Eule, *Judicial Review of Direct Democracy, supra*; Sylvia Lazos Vargas, *Judicial Review of Initiatives and Referendums in which Majorities Vote on Minorities' Democratic Citizenship*, 60 Ohio St. L.J. 399 (1999); Lawrence Sager, *Insular Majorities Unabated:* Warth v. Seldin *and* City of Eastlake v. Forest City Enterprises, Inc., 91 Harv. L. Rev. 1373 (1978); Note, *Judicial Approaches to Direct Democracy*, 118 Harv. L. Rev. 2748 (2005).

t. See, e.g., Richard Briffault, *Distrust of Democracy*, 63 Tex. L. Rev. 1347 (1985); Clayton Gillette, *Is Direct Democracy Anti-Democractic?*, 34 Willamette L. Rev. 609 (1998); Ethan Leib, *Can Direct Democracy be Made Deliberative?*, 54 Buff. L. Rev. 903 (2006); Mark Tushnet, *Fear of Voting: Differential Standards of Judicial Review of Direct Legislation*, 1996 NYU Ann. Surv. Am. L. 373.

u. See Hans Linde, *When Initiative Lawmaking Is Not "Republican Government": The Campaign Against Homosexuality*, 72 Ore. L. Rev. 19 (1993). On the intellectual history of antigay initiatives, see William Eskridge, Jr., *Challenging the Apartheid of the Closet*, 25 Hofstra L. Rev. 817, 928–30 (1997); Jane Schacter, *The Gay Civil Rights Debate in the States: Decoding the Discourse of Equivalents*, 29 Harv. C.R.-C.L. L. Rev. 283 (1994).

to narrow interpretation, in order to preserve all prior legislatively created law not squarely displaced by it? Note that unclearly worded ballot proposals that are aimed at minorities create a dilemma for attorneys wishing to challenge them. The broader the measure is understood, the more likely it will be held unconstitutional, but the narrower it is understood, the less harm it does to minorities. (Consider how this dilemma plays out in *Romer*.) In the worst possible circumstance from this perspective, attorneys will argue for a broad construction, the court will accept it, but then hold that the measure so construed is constitutional.

C. POPULAR LAWMAKING AND THE DUE PROCESS CLAUSE

CITY OF EASTLAKE v. FOREST CITY ENTERPRISES, INC.
Supreme Court of the United States, 1976
426 U.S. 668, 96 S.Ct. 2358, 49 L.Ed.2d 132

MR. CHIEF JUSTICE BURGER delivered the opinion of the Court.

The question in this case is whether a city charter provision requiring proposed land use changes to be ratified by 55% of the votes cast violates the due process rights of a landowner who applies for a zoning change.

The city of Eastlake, Ohio, a suburb of Cleveland, has a comprehensive zoning plan codified in a municipal ordinance. Respondent, a real estate developer, acquired an eight-acre parcel of real estate in Eastlake zoned for "light industrial" uses at the time of purchase.

In May 1971, respondent applied to the City Planning Commission for a zoning change to permit construction of a multifamily, high-rise apartment building. The Planning Commission recommended the proposed change to the City Council, which under Eastlake's procedures could either accept or reject the Planning Commission's recommendation. Meanwhile, by popular vote, the voters of Eastlake amended the city charter to require that any changes in land use agreed to by the Council be approved by a 55% vote in a referendum. The City Council approved the Planning Commission's recommendation for reclassification of respondent's property to permit the proposed project. Respondent then applied to the Planning Commission for "parking and yard" approval for the proposed building. The Commission rejected the application, on the ground that the City Council's rezoning action had not yet been submitted to the voters for ratification.

Respondent then filed an action in state court, seeking a judgment declaring the charter provision invalid as an unconstitutional delegation of legislative power to the people. While the case was pending, the City Council's action was submitted to a referendum, but the proposed zoning change was not approved by the requisite 55% margin. Following the election, the Court of Common Pleas and the Ohio Court of Appeals sustained the charter provision.

The Ohio Supreme Court reversed. 324 N.E.2d 740 (1975). Concluding that enactment of zoning and rezoning provisions is a legislative function, the court held that a popular referendum requirement, lacking standards to guide the decision of the voters, permitted the police power to be exercised in a standardless, hence arbitrary and capricious manner. Relying on this Court's decisions in *Washington ex rel. Seattle Title Trust Co. v. Roberge*, 278 U.S. 116 (1928), *Thomas Cusack Co. v. Chicago*, 242 U.S. 526 (1917), and *Eubank v. Richmond*, 226 U.S. 137 (1912), but distinguishing *James v. Valtierra*, 402 U.S. 137 (1971), the court concluded that the referendum provision constituted an unlawful delegation of legislative power.

We reverse.

[In Part I, the Court concluded that the referendum did not constitute a delegation of legislative power. "In establishing legislative bodies, the people can reserve to themselves power to deal directly with matters which might otherwise be assigned to the legislature." Thus, the referendum was an exercise of the people's reserved powers, not a delegation from the legislature to the people of a legislative power.]

[II] The Ohio Supreme Court further concluded that the amendment to the city charter constituted a "delegation" of power violative of federal constitutional guarantees because the voters were given no standards to guide their decision. Under Eastlake's procedure, the Ohio Supreme Court reasoned, no mechanism existed, nor indeed could exist, to assure that the voters would act rationally in passing upon a proposed zoning change. This meant that "appropriate legislative action [would] be made dependent upon the potentially arbitrary and unreasonable whims of the voting public." 324 N.E.2d, at 746. The potential for arbitrariness in the process, the court concluded, violated due process.

Courts have frequently held in other contexts that a congressional delegation of power to a regulatory entity must be accompanied by discernible standards, so that the delegatee's action can be measured for its fidelity to the legislative will. See, *e.g., Yakus v. United States*, 321 U.S. 414 (1944); *Amalgamated Meat Cutters v. Connally*, 337 F.Supp. 737 (DC 1971). Assuming, *arguendo*, their relevance to state governmental functions, these cases involved a delegation of power by the legislature to regulatory bodies, which are not directly responsible to the people; this doctrine is inapplicable where, as here, rather than dealing with a delegation of power, we deal with a power reserved by the people to themselves.[10]

In basing its claim on federal due process requirements, respondent also invokes *Euclid v. Ambler Realty Co.*, 272 U.S. 365 (1926), but it does not rely

---

10. The Ohio Supreme Court's analysis of the requirements for standards flowing from the Fourteenth Amendment also sweeps too broadly. Except as a legislative history informs an analysis of legislative action, there is no more advance assurance that a legislative body will act by conscientiously applying consistent standards than there is with respect to voters. For example, there is no certainty that the City Council in this case would act on the basis of "standards" explicit or otherwise in Eastlake's comprehensive zoning ordinance. Nor is there any assurance that townspeople assembling in a town meeting, as the people of Eastlake could do, *Hunter v. Erickson*, 393 U.S. 385, 392 (1969), will act according to consistent standards. The critical constitutional inquiry, rather, is whether the zoning restriction produces arbitrary or capricious results.

on the direct teaching of that case. Under *Euclid*, a property owner can challenge a zoning restriction if the measure is "clearly arbitrary and unreasonable, having no substantial relation to the public health, safety, morals, or general welfare." If the substantive result of the referendum is arbitrary and capricious, bearing no relation to the police power, then the fact that the voters of Eastlake wish it so would not save the restriction. As this Court held in invalidating a charter amendment enacted by referendum:

> "The sovereignty of the people is itself subject to those constitutional limitations which have been duly adopted and remain unrepealed." *Hunter v. Erickson*, 393 U.S., at 392.
> * * *

But no challenge of the sort contemplated in *Euclid v. Ambler Realty* is before us. The Ohio Supreme Court did not hold, and respondent does not argue, that the present zoning classification under Eastlake's comprehensive ordinance violates the principles established in *Euclid v. Ambler Realty*. If respondent considers the referendum result itself to be unreasonable, the zoning restriction is open to challenge in state court, where the scope of the state remedy available to respondent would be determined as a matter of state law, as well as under Fourteenth Amendment standards. That being so, nothing more is required by the Constitution.

Nothing in our cases is inconsistent with this conclusion. Two decisions of this Court were relied on by the Ohio Supreme Court in invalidating Eastlake's procedure. The thread common to both decisions is the delegation of legislative power, originally given by the people to a legislative body, and in turn delegated by the legislature to a *narrow segment* of the community, not to the people at large. In *Eubank v. Richmond*, 226 U.S. 137 (1912), the Court invalidated a city ordinance which conferred the power to establish building setback lines upon the owners of two-thirds of the property abutting any street. Similarly, in *Washington ex rel. Seattle Title Trust Co. v. Roberge*, 278 U.S. 116 (1928), the Court struck down an ordinance which permitted the establishment of philanthropic homes for the aged in residential areas, but only upon the written consent of the owners of two-thirds of the property within 400 feet of the proposed facility.

Neither *Eubank* nor *Roberge* involved a referendum procedure such as we have in this case; the standardless delegation of power to a limited group of property owners condemned by the Court in *Eubank* and *Roberge* is not to be equated with decision-making by the people through the referendum process. The Court of Appeals for the Ninth Circuit put it this way:

> "A referendum, however, is far more than an expression of ambiguously founded neighborhood preference. It is the city itself legislating through its voters — an exercise by the voters of their traditional right through direct legislation to override the views of their elected representatives as to what serves the public interest." *Southern Alameda Spanish Speaking Organization v. Union City, California*, 424 F.2d 291, 294 (1970).

Our decision in *James v. Valtierra*, upholding California's mandatory referendum requirement, confirms this view. Mr. Justice Black, speaking for the Court in that case, said:

"This procedure ensures that *all the people* of a community will have a voice in a decision which may lead to large expenditures of local governmental funds for increased public services . . . ." 402 U.S., at 143 (emphasis added).

Mr. Justice Black went on to say that a referendum procedure, such as the one at issue here, is a classic demonstration of "devotion to democracy . . . ." As a basic instrument of democratic government, the referendum process does not, in itself, violate the Due Process Clause of the Fourteenth Amendment when applied to a rezoning ordinance.[13] Since the rezoning decision in this case was properly reserved to the People of Eastlake under the Ohio Constitution, the Ohio Supreme Court erred in holding invalid, on federal constitutional grounds, the charter amendment permitting the voters to decide whether the zoned use of respondent's property could be altered.

The judgment of the Ohio Supreme Court is reversed, and the case is remanded for further proceedings not inconsistent with this opinion.

MR. JUSTICE POWELL, dissenting.

There can be no doubt as to the propriety and legality of submitting generally applicable legislative questions, including zoning provisions, to a popular referendum. But here the only issue concerned the status of a single small parcel owned by a single "person." This procedure, affording no realistic opportunity for the affected person to be heard, even by the electorate, is fundamentally unfair. The "spot" referendum technique appears to open disquieting opportunities for local government bodies to bypass normal protective procedures for resolving issues affecting individual rights.

MR. JUSTICE STEVENS, with whom MR. JUSTICE BRENNAN joins, dissenting.

* * * When we examine a state procedure for the purpose of deciding whether it comports with the constitutional standard of due process, the fact that a State may give it a "legislative" label should not save an otherwise invalid procedure. We should, however, give some deference to the conclusion of the highest court of the State that the procedure represents an arbitrary and unreasonable way of handling a local problem.

---

13. The fears expressed in dissent rest on the proposition that the procedure at issue here is "fundamentally unfair" to landowners; this fails to take into account the mechanisms for relief potentially available to property owners whose desired land use changes are rejected by the voters. First, if hardship is occasioned by zoning restrictions, *administrative* relief is potentially available. Indeed, the very purpose of "variances" allowed by zoning officials is to avoid "practical difficulties and unnecessary hardship." 8 E. McQuillan, Municipal Corporations § 25.159, p. 511 (3d ed. 1965). As we noted, *supra*, remedies remain available under the Ohio Supreme Court's holding and provide a means to challenge unreasonable or arbitrary action. *Euclid v. Ambler Realty Co.*, 272 U.S. 365 (1926).

The situation presented in this case is not one of a zoning action denigrating the use or depreciating the value of land; instead, it involves an effort to *change* a reasonable zoning restriction. No existing rights are being impaired; new use rights are being sought from the City Council. Thus, this case involves an owner's seeking approval of a new use free from the restrictions attached to the land when it was acquired.

In this case, the Ohio courts arrived at the conclusion that Art. VIII, § 3, of the charter of the city of Eastlake, as amended on November 2, 1971, is wholly invalid in three stages.[8] At no stage of the case has there been any suggestion that respondent's proposed use of its property would be inconsistent with the city's basic zoning plan, or would have any impact on the municipal budget or adversely affect the city's potential economic development.

First, the requirement that the property owner pay the cost of the special election was invalidated in the trial court and in the Ohio Court of Appeals. Second, the Ohio Supreme Court held that the mandatory referendum was "clearly invalid" insofar as it purported to apply to a change in land use approved by the City Council "in an administrative capacity." Without explaining when the Council's action is properly characterized as legislative

---

8. This exceptional bit of legislation is worth reading in its entirety:

"SECTION 3. MANDATORY REFERRAL

"That any change to the existing land uses or any change whatsoever to any ordinance, or the enactment of any ordinance referring to other regulations controlling the development of land and the selling or leasing or rental of parkways, playgrounds, or other city lands or real property, or for the widening, narrowing, re-locating, vacating, or changing the use of any public street, avenue, boulevard, or alley cannot be approved unless and until it shall have been submitted to the Planning Commission, for approval or disapproval. That in the event the city council should approve any of the preceding changes, or enactments, whether * * * approved or disapproved by the Planning Commission it shall not be approved or passed by the declaration of an emergency, and it shall not be effective, but it shall be mandatory that the same be approved by a 55% favorable vote of all votes cast of the qualified electors of the City of Eastlake at the next regular municipal election, if one shall occur not less than sixty (60) or more than one hundred and twenty (120) days after its passage, otherwise at a special election falling on the generally established day of the primary election. Said issue shall be submitted to the electors of the City only after approval of a change of an existing land use by the Council for an applicant, and the applicant agrees to assume all costs of the election and post bond with the city Auditor in an amount estimated by the County Auditor or the Board of Elections proportionate with any other issues that may be on the ballot at the same time. The applicant shall further agree to authorize the City Auditor to advertise, and assume the obligations to pay, for a notice of the posted bond and the requested land use change in a newspaper of general circulation, whose circulation is either the largest, or second to the largest within the limits of the City for two consecutive times, with at least two weeks between notices and a third notice one week prior to the election. Should the land use request not be affirmed by a 55% favorable vote it cannot be presented again for one full year and a new request must be made at that time.

"It shall be the duty of any applicant for a land use change to obtain zoning codes, maps, thoroughfare and sewer plans or advice of the city council and officials and approving bodies for interpretation of this section as they are always available. If this section is violated and a building is under construction or completely constructed it shall be mandatory for the Mayor, Safety Director, Service Director and Building Inspector equally to have the building or structure removed completely within 60 days at the owner[']s expense as these officials are charged with the enforcement of this section. It shall be mandatory that the City Council charge and fund the Planning Commission to have on display at all times in the council chambers and available to the public a zone map, showing a legend and summary of zoning regulations by district, [m]ajor use, [m]inimum and maximum lot width and that each district, city park, playground and city lands be accurately located and identified with the date of adoption and the date of revisions to date. Any and all revisions will be posted to the zone map, within 90 days of their occurrence. Maps shall be available to each land owner of the city for a nominal cost not to exceed $2.50 each on demand. Maps shall be available within six months of this charter change."

instead of administrative, the court then held that even though its approval in this case was legislative, the entire referendum requirement was invalid. The court reasoned:

> "Due process of law requires that procedures for the exercise of municipal power be structured such that fundamental choices among competing municipal policies are resolved by a responsible organ of government. It also requires that a municipality protect individuals against the arbitrary exercise of municipal power, by assuring that fundamental policy choices underlying the exercise of that power are articulated by some responsible organ of municipal government. *McGautha v. California* (1971), 402 U.S. 183, 256, 270. The Eastlake charter provision ignored these concepts and blatantly delegated legislative authority, with no assurance that the result reached thereby would be reasonable or rational. For these reasons, the provision clearly violates the due process clause of the Fourteenth Amendment." 324 N.E.2d 740, 746 (Ohio 1975) (footnote omitted).

The concurring opinion expressed additional reasons for regarding the referendum requirement as arbitrary. Speaking for four members of the Ohio Supreme Court, Justice Stern stated:

> "There can be little doubt of the true purpose of Eastlake's charter provision — it is to obstruct change in land use, by rendering such change so burdensome as to be prohibitive. The charter provision was apparently adopted specifically to prevent multi-family housing, and indeed was adopted while Forest City's application for rezoning to permit a multi-family housing project was pending before the City Planning Commission and City Council. The restrictive purpose of the provision is crudely apparent on its face. Any zoning change, regardless of how minor, and regardless of its approval by the Planning Commission and the City Council, must be approved by a city-wide referendum. The proposed change must receive, rather than a simple majority, at least a 55 percent affirmative vote. Finally, the owner of the property affected is required to pay the cost of the election, although the provision gives no hint as to exactly which costs would be billed to a property owner.

> "There is no subtlety to this; it is simply an attempt to render change difficult and expensive under the guise of popular democracy.

> "Even stripped of its harsher provisions the charter provision poses serious problems. A mandatory, city-wide referendum which applies to any zoning change must, of necessity, submit decisions that affect one person's use of his property to thousands of voters with no interest whatever in that property. We need only imagine the adoption of this same provision in a city such as Cleveland. By such a provision, rezoning for a corner gasoline station would require the approval of hundreds of thousands of voters, most of them living miles away, and few of them with the slightest interest in the matter. This would be government by caprice, and would seriously dilute the right of private ownership of property. The law recognizes that the use a person makes of his property must inevitably affect his neighbors and, in some cases, the surrounding community. These real interests are entitled to be balanced against the rights of a property owner; but a law which requires a property owner, who proposes a wholly benign use of his property, to obtain the assent of thousands of persons with no such interest, goes beyond any reasonable public purpose." *Id.*, at 748–749.

As the Justices of the Ohio Supreme Court recognized, we are concerned with the fairness of a provision for determining the right to make a particular use of a particular parcel of land. In such cases, the state courts have frequently described the capricious character of a decision supported by majority sentiment rather than reference to articulable standards. Moreover, they have limited statutory referendum procedures to apply only to approvals of comprehensive zoning ordinances as opposed to amendments affecting specific parcels. This conclusion has been supported by characterizing particular amendments as "administrative" and revision of an entire plan as "legislative."

In this case the Ohio Supreme Court characterized the Council's approval of respondent's proposal as "legislative." I think many state courts would have characterized it as "administrative." The courts thus may well differ in their selection of the label to apply to this action, but I find substantial agreement among state tribunals on the proposition that requiring a citywide referendum for approval of a particular proposal like this is manifestly unreasonable. Surely that is my view.

The essence of fair procedure is that the interested parties be given a reasonable opportunity to have their dispute resolved on the merits by reference to articulable rules. If a dispute involves only the conflicting rights of private litigants, it is elementary that the decision-maker must be impartial and qualified to understand and to apply the controlling rules.

I have no doubt about the validity of the initiative or the referendum as an appropriate method of deciding questions of community policy.[15] I think it is equally clear that the popular vote is not an acceptable method of adjudicating the rights of individual litigants. The problem presented by this case is unique, because it may involve a three-sided controversy, in which there is at least potential conflict between the rights of the property owner and the rights of his neighbors, and also potential conflict with the public interest in preserving the city's basic zoning plan. If the latter aspect of the controversy were predominant, the referendum would be an acceptable procedure. On the other hand, when the record indicates without contradiction that there is no threat to the general public interest in preserving the city's plan — as it does in this case, since respondent's proposal was approved by both the Planning Commission and the City Council and there has been no allegation that the use of this eight-acre parcel for apartments rather than light industry would adversely affect the community or raise any policy issue of citywide concern — I think the case should be treated as one in which it is essential that the private property owner be given a fair opportunity to have his claim determined on its merits.

---

15. *James v. Valtierra*, 402 U.S. 137, sustained the "use of referendums to give citizens a voice on questions of public policy." The approval of a publicly financed housing project, which might "lead to large expenditures of local governmental funds for increased public services and to lower tax revenues," raises policy questions not involved in a zoning change for a private property owner. That case presented no due process or other procedural issue.

As Justice Stern points out in his concurring opinion, it would be absurd to use a referendum to decide whether a gasoline station could be operated on a particular corner in the city of Cleveland. The case before us is not that clear because we are told that there are only 20,000 people in the city of Eastlake. Conceivably, an eight-acre development could be sufficiently dramatic to arouse the legitimate interest of the entire community; it is also conceivable that most of the voters would be indifferent and uninformed about the wisdom of building apartments rather than a warehouse or factory on these eight acres. The record is silent on which of these alternatives is the more probable. Since the ordinance places a manifestly unreasonable obstacle in the path of every property owner seeking any zoning change, since it provides no standards or procedures for exempting particular parcels or claims from the referendum requirement, and since the record contains no justification for the use of the procedure in this case, I am persuaded that we should respect the state judiciary's appraisal of the fundamental fairness of this decisionmaking process in this case.

I therefore conclude that the Ohio Supreme Court correctly held that Art. VIII, § 3, of the Eastlake charter violates the Due Process Clause of the Fourteenth Amendment, and that its judgment should be affirmed.

NOTES ON *EASTLAKE* AND "DUE PROCESS OF LAWMAKING"

Lawrence Sager has suggested that *Eastlake* is inconsistent with the "due process of lawmaking" principles of *Hampton v. Mow Sun Wong*, 426 U.S. 88 (1976) (excerpted in Chapter 4, § 1B). Lawrence Sager, *Insular Majorities Unabated:* Warth v. Seldin *and* City of Eastlake v. Forest City Enterprises, Inc., 91 Harv. L. Rev. 1373, 1411–12, 1414–16, 1418–23 (1978). Sager objects to "the unreflective, nondeliberative aggregate will of the electorate as the basis for lot-by-lot determinations of zoning status" and "the shortcomings of the electorate as a decisionmaker on zoning issues." He continues:

> Our constitutional tradition — as it comprehends both state and federal constitutions — includes a large measure of deference by courts to the decisions of legislative and administrative bodies. Central to the justification for judicial deference is the proposition that the governmental body which has enacted a regulatory measure is best equipped to make judgments of policy and strategy, and further, that the body in question can and will measure its own conduct against constitutional requirements. Conversely, judicial departures from the tradition of deference are often justified by circumstances which impair or render suspect this process of legislative deliberation. Thus, while lauding elected bodies as capable of reflecting the public will, we have clearly charged them with the responsibility of mediating majority sentiment with judgments of reasonability and fairness. From this premise, there follows an argument of considerable force that, at least as regards some species of legislative decisions, it is constitutionally impermissible that they be confided to an electoral mechanism, where the public will cannot enjoy the requisite deliberative mediation. * * * *Mow Sun Wong* posits a right to procedural due process which requires that some legislative actions be undertaken only by a governmental entity which is so structured and so charged as to make possible a reflective determination that the action contemplated is

fair, reasonable, and not at odds with specific prohibitions in the Constitution. It is a right, to borrow Professor Linde's phrase, to a "due process of lawmaking."

The inconsistency of this premise with direct electoral legislation should be obvious. Legislation by plebiscite is not and cannot be a deliberative process. We expect and presumably derive from an initiative or referendum an expression of the aggregate will of the majority, or the majority of those who vote. But there is no genuine debate or discussion, no individual record or accountability, no occasion for individual commitment to a consistent or fair course of conduct. In those circumstances where a person who is adversely affected by a legislative determination is entitled to the due process right recognized in *Mow Sun Wong*, a plebiscitary process seems wholly improper.

Sager concedes that such a right to "initial legislative decisionmaking by an appropriate deliberative entity" should only be triggered "when two conditions are met: first, where substantial constitutional values are placed in jeopardy by the enactment at issue; and second, where *substantive* review of the enactment by the judiciary is largely unavailable and hence cannot secure these constitutional values." *Eastlake*, Sager contends, is a case where both conditions are triggered. Zoning is a governmental function which affects citizens deeply; for this reason, zoning changes have traditionally been brigaded with procedural protections ensuring deliberation discouraging precipitous action. Additionally, local zoning decisions do not receive any kind of meaningful constitutional review, under either the Due Process Clause, *Euclid v. Ambler Realty Co.*, 272 U.S. 365 (1926), or the Equal Protection Clause. Under these circumstances, and given the capacity of zoning decisions to perpetuate or create racial and other segregations, Sager maintains that the Court was wrong in closing off due process challenges in *Eastlake*.

Is Sager too pessimistic regarding the possibility of attacking initiatives and referenda on equal protection grounds? In addition to spot zoning, what other kinds of decisions raise due process of lawmaking concerns if made by the electorate? Are there any decisions that can be made by the electorate that do not raise such concerns?

The categorization of rezoning decisions as "legislative" or "administrative" is, of course, determined by state law. Some state courts have disagreed with the Ohio courts in *Eastlake* and have concluded that rezoning is an administrative act that cannot be accomplished by direct democracy, a legislative activity. Consider, for example, *Leonard v. Bothell*, 557 P.2d 1306 (Wash. 1976):

> Generally, when a municipality adopts a zoning code and a comprehensive plan, it acts in a legislative policy-making capacity. * * * Amendments of the zoning code, or rezones, usually are decisions by a municipal legislative body implementing the zoning code and a comprehensive plan. The legislative body essentially is then performing its administrative function. * * *

> [Here] [t]he ordinance merely rezoned the property and modified the language of the plan to reflect the anticipated land-use change. We do not view the ordinance as a legislative policy-making decision, and thus it is not subject to a referendum election. * * *

Amendments to the zoning code or rezone decisions require an informed and intelligent choice by individuals who possess the expertise to consider the total economic, social, and physical characteristics of the community. [The city's] planning commission and city council normally possess the necessary expertise to make these difficult decisions. * * *

In a referendum election, the voters may not have an adequate opportunity to read the environmental impact statement or any other relevant information concerning the proposed land-use change.[v]

PHILLY'S v. BYRNE
United States Court of Appeals for the Seventh Circuit, 1984
732 F.2d 87

[The Illinois local-option liquor law allows the voters of a precinct to vote the precinct "dry." Two Chicago restaurant owners brought this action, contending that they were deprived of property without due process of law when, in one instance, the owner lost a license as the result of such a referendum and, in the other instance, the owner was unable to obtain a license, which had been earlier approved, because of such a referendum.]

Before WOOD, ESCHBACH, and POSNER, Circuit Judges.

POSNER, CIRCUIT JUDGE.

* * * [Even] if there was a deprivation of property here, there was no denial of due process.

This may seem a startling conclusion. To make rights depend on the outcome of a popular election may seem the very opposite of due process of law. The Constitution would not have empowered judges insulated from the electoral process to protect the members of electoral minorities from certain consequences of majority rule unless the framers had to some extent distrusted popular elections. The Constitution's provisions for the indirect election of the President and (until the Seventeenth Amendment was adopted) the Senate as well are further evidence of this distrust. If there is cause to distrust majority rule even when mediated through legislative representatives, who exercise some independent judgment and are not merely transmission belts for their constituents' desires, there is greater cause to distrust lawmaking by referendum. Voters, even more obviously than legislators, are not judges, are guided by no standards, do not give reasons for their decisions, and are not subject to judicial review. To entrust rights to their discretion may therefore seem to eliminate the due process clause as a bulwark against the tyranny of majorities.

But to equate due process of law with a particular type of procedure, the adversary hearing modeled on the Anglo-American trial, and thus to create an unbridgeable chasm between democracy and due process, would take too

---

v. For more discussion, see David Callies, Nancy Neuffer & Carlito Caliboso, *Ballot Box Zoning: Initiative, Referendum, and the Law*, 39 Wash. U.J. Urb. & Contemp. Law 53 (1991); Aaron Reber & Karin Mika, *Democratic Excess in the Use of Zoning Referenda*, 29 Urb. Law. 277 (1997); Daniel Selmi, *Reconsidering the Use of Direct Democracy in Making Land Use Decisions*, 19 UCLA J. Envt'l L. & Pol'y 293 (2002).

narrow a view of due process. See *City of Eastlake v. Forest City Enterprises, Inc.*, 427 U.S. 668, 678–79 (1976). Whatever the original meaning of the term, a question on which much ink has been spilled, it has come to stand (quite independently of the concept of "substantive due process") for a general requirement of "a fair process of decision-making * * *." *Fuentes v. Shevin* [407 U.S. 67, 80 (1972)]. That is not the same thing as a uniform code of procedure. "The Fifth Amendment guarantees no particular form of procedure; it protects substantial rights." *NLRB v. Mackay Radio & Telegraph Co.*, 304 U.S. 333, 351 (1938). Of course we must not lean too heavily on general language; none of the cases from which we have just quoted dealt with the popular referendum as a method of decision-making. In many settings, for example that of proceedings to revoke a television broadcast license because of the licensee's misconduct, a referendum would be a highly questionable method of decision-making, to say the least. But used to decide whether liquor may be sold in a particular area it is a pragmatic as well as venerable response to the social problems created by the sale and consumption of liquor. As the bitter experience of Prohibition should remind us, no national or even regional consensus has emerged with respect to the morality and consequences of alcoholic beverages. It has seemed best in default of consensus to leave the matter to local preference as expressed in the voting booth. Illinois' local-option liquor law is just section 2 of the Twenty-First Amendment writ small. It is not obvious to us that the question whether to forbid the sale of liquor in a particular precinct in Chicago would be decided more wisely, more speedily, or more cheaply by an administrative agency subject to judicial review than by the precinct's voters. The issue is well within a layman's competence and the small size of the precinct electorate should foster a sense of civic responsibility, each voter knowing that his vote could be decisive.

Whether a particular procedure for deciding a question is "fair" depends on the nature of the abuse that the procedure is designed to prevent. Usually it is designed to prevent a mistaken application of law. See, e.g., *Mathews v. Eldridge*, 424 U.S. 319, 335 (1976). That is not the problem here. The concern is not that the voters of a precinct might make a mistake in deciding to ban the retail sale of liquor; when they vote on the question they are voting their personal values and there is no criterion by which a court or other outsider could judge their decision correct or incorrect. The concern is that the voters might "gang up" to drive out of business a seller of liquor whom they disliked for reasons unrelated to any plausible public interest. This is a distinct type of arbitrary action that the requirement of fair procedure is designed to prevent, or at least make less likely to occur. See Tribe, American Constitutional Law 503–04 (1978). It is therefore relevant to point out that the Illinois act does not permit the precinct's voters to single out a particular liquor seller to shut down. Compare *Larkin v. Grendel's Den, Inc.*, 454 U.S. 116 (1982). The precinct can choose only between allowing and not allowing the retail sale of alcoholic beverages. See Ill. Rev. Stat. 1981, ch. 43, ¶ 171. The voters must shut down all the retail liquor outlets in the precinct in order to shut down one and they must shut them down for four years because a new referendum cannot be held before that period has elapsed. *Id.*, ¶ 175. This means not only that the licensee who is disliked is protected to some extent by the licensee who is liked but also that the voters cannot impose costs on liquor sellers without imposing costs on themselves — the costs of not being able to buy liquor in the precinct.

The requirement that the precinct electorate act across the board shows that the judgment the voters are asked to make is legislative rather than adjudicative in character. (The Illinois courts have held that the local-option provision of the Liquor Control Act is not a delegation of legislative power, and no doubt for many purposes it is not; but for the purpose of deciding whether the procedural safeguards of the adjudicative process are required, it is.) And notice and opportunity for a hearing are not constitutionally required safe-guards of legislative action. *Bi-Metallic Investment Co. v. State Bd. of Equalization*, 239 U.S. 441, 445 (1915). The fact that a statute (or statute-like regulation) applies across the board provides a substitute safeguard. See *United States v. Florida East Coast Ry.*, 410 U.S. 224, 245–46 (1973). This safeguard is built into Illinois' local-option provision, and supplies a practical reason for classifying the referendum procedure as legislative for purposes of this case. And although the appellants did not have notice or an opportunity for a hearing in the sense familiar in adjudicative proceedings, they of course had ample notice of the forthcoming election and an opportunity to campaign against the proposition that the precinct should vote itself dry.

We do not submit gracefully to the tyranny of labels, and therefore do not hold that there is never any requirement of due process in the legislative process, cf. *Vermont Yankee Nuclear Power Corp. v. National Resources Defense Council, Inc.*, 435 U.S. 519, 524 (1978) (dictum), beyond what is implicit in the observation that the across-the-board character of legislation provides some protection against the use of the legislative process to single people out for adverse governmental action. See generally Linde, Due Process of Lawmaking, 55 Neb.L.Rev. 197, 238–51 (1976). More may be required especially in a case like this where the legislation affects only a tiny class of people — maybe a class with only one member. This is the concern that lies behind the prohibition (applicable to both the federal government and the states, see U.S. Const. art. I, §§ 9, 10) of the bill of attainder, "a law that legislatively determines guilt and inflicts punishment upon an identifiable individual without provision of the protections of a judicial trial." *Nixon v. Administrator of General Services*, 433 U.S. 425, 468 (1977). Of course the fact that the Constitution explicitly prohibits both bills of attainder and (in the same clauses) ex post facto laws, when combined with the extensive substantive limitations that the Constitution imposes on legislation (notably in the equal protection clause of the Fourteenth Amendment), could be used to support an argument that the courts have no authority to impose any other procedural requirements on the legislative process. But we are reluctant to go so far, at least in a case where the legislative process is as particularistic as it is here. There are almost 3,000 precincts in Chicago, each having between 350 and 850 registered voters. Most of the precincts are very small, and more than 20 consist of a single high-rise building. No doubt many precincts contain only one liquor store or bar. And because the precincts are so small, the inconvenience that the voters must visit on themselves to ban a particular vendor will often be slight. If the registered voters living in a precinct consisting of a single high-rise building decided to shut down a bar in the building not because they did not approve of liquor or of its being sold in their building but because they did not like the bar's owner, they could vote the precinct dry with little inconvenience to themselves; some of the surrounding precincts would be bound to be wet. And yet the fact that even slight inconvenience is a price that the voters must pay to get rid of a bar or a liquor store (unless a majority of the voters are teetotalers) makes this a more than usually responsible electoral process, for there is no general requirement that a legislative or popular majority place any burden on itself as a condition of being allowed to place a burden on others.

We conclude that although the small size of the Chicago precincts creates an opportunity for abuse, the danger is not so great as to make the local-option feature of Illinois' law unconstitutional. Cf. *City of Eastlake v. Forest City Enterprises, Inc., supra*, 426 U.S. at 679. If as we believe the basic principle of such laws is constitutional, that must be the end of the judicial inquiry. To redraw the precinct map of Chicago — or force the city or the state to do so — merely to assure that every precinct is large enough to make the voters in it think twice before voting the precinct dry would be a remedy disproportionate to the evil sought to be prevented. Although the Twenty-First Amendment did not repeal the Fourteenth Amendment, *Wisconsin v. Constantineau*, 400 U.S. 433, 436 (1971); *California v. La Rue*, 409 U.S. 109, 115 (1972), it provides additional support for upholding a state's local-option liquor law.

In holding that the referendum is a constitutionally permissible method of regulating the local sale of liquor, we assume that the referendum is conducted fairly and honestly. Although the plaintiffs question the adequacy of the statutory procedures for challenging fraud in the conduct of local-option referenda, we do not find any allegation of fraud in the complaint. The allegation was made for the first time in the petition for rehearing, and comes too late.

AFFIRMED.

HARLINGTON WOOD, JR., CIRCUIT JUDGE, concurring.

I join the result reached by the majority, but I believe there is a little more direct route to that result. I consider it unnecessary to reach and decide the question of whether in this situation the process that is due under the fourteenth amendment may consist of a popular election.

Appellants argue that the local option provision is an unconstitutional delegation of legislative authority to the voters, violating due process by depriving appellants of liquor licenses without notice or a hearing. District Judge Kocoras' analysis delivered from the bench provided an adequate and appropriate ground upon which to uphold the local option provision against due process challenge.

Appellants concede, as they must, that the Illinois General Assembly is empowered to prohibit or regulate the sale of alcoholic beverages in the state. The Liquor Control Act clearly reflects a legislative determination to discourage the use of alcohol through close regulation. The General Assembly, by enacting the local option provision, acted upon this determination to pass a valid prohibition on the sale of alcoholic beverages. The legislature, however, chose to suspend imposition of this prohibition pending the choice of local voters to make it operative in their village or precinct.

The legislature could have enacted a prohibition of alcoholic beverages effective without further action, and thus was within its authority to enact a prohibition effective only upon a local referendum. *See Rippey v. Texas*, 193 U.S. 504, 509–10 (1904). While Justice Holmes' assertion in *Rippey*, that the power to prohibit includes the power to prohibit conditionally, has proven overbroad in other contexts, the holding of the case remains in force in the context of a local option provision of an otherwise constitutional legislative enactment such as a prohibition on the sale of liquor under the unique aegis of the twenty-first amendment.

The local option referendum gives local voters no discretion other than the choice to put the legislative enactment and its underlying policy determination into effect in their community. *Cf. Larkin v. Grendel's Den, Inc.*, 459 U.S. 116 (1982) (standardless discretion given nearby churches to disapprove liquor licenses reflected entanglement in violation of Establishment Clause); *Washington ex rel. Seattle Title Trust Co. v. Roberge*, 278 U.S. 116, 121–22 (1928) (due process violation where legislature suggested approval of land use but left zoning decision to neighboring landowners). Illinois courts upholding the local option law against due process challenge have held that the legislative power indeed remained in the legislature. *See, e.g., Malito v. Marcin*, 303 N.E.2d 262, 264 (Ill. App. 1973), *appeal denied*, 55 Ill.2d 602, *appeal dismissed for lack of a substantial federal question*, 417 U.S. 963 (1974) (while the legislature may not delegate its function to private persons, it may enact a law which will become operative upon the affirmative vote of the people affected, provided the law contains an "entire and perfect declaration of the legislative will"); *see also Hoogasian v. Regional Transportation Authority*, 317 N.E.2d 534, 540–41, *appeal dismissed for lack of a substantial federal question*, 419 U.S. 988 (1974) (upholding against due process challenge the statutory creation of regional transportation authority upon voter approval by referendum).

We thus are left with a due process challenge to the legislative action itself. Legislative actions which are of general applicability are not subject to a due process requirement that affected persons be given notice and an opportunity to be heard; the process due is found in the electorate's power over its chosen representatives. *See Bi-Metallic Investment Co. v. State Board of Equalization of Colorado*, 239 U.S. 441, 445 (1915).

The venerable local option law is not an unconstitutional delegation of legislative authority in violation of the due process clause, but a complete legislative enactment which goes into effect contingent upon a future event. Appellants may seek relief from the local option law through legislative revision, a challenge of the procedures used in a particular referendum, or by launching a local campaign to pass a new referendum.

NOTE ON *PHILLY'S* AND DUE PROCESS PRINCIPLES

As Judge Posner noted, *Philly's* is one example of the "*Bi-Metallic* problem." In *Bi-Metallic Investment Co. v. State Board of Equalization*, 239 U.S. 441 (1915), Justice Holmes' opinion held that no hearing was required before a state agency increased the valuation of all taxable property in Denver. Justice Holmes stated: "When a rule of conduct applies to more than a few people it is impracticable that every one should have a direct voice in its adoption. The Constitution does not require all public acts to be done in a town meeting or an assembly of the whole." In *United States v. Florida East Coast Ry. Co.*, 410 U.S. 224 (1973), the Court interpreted *Bi-Metallic* and the cases following it as establishing "a recognized distinction in administrative law between proceedings for the purpose of promulgating policy-type rules or standards, on the one hand, and proceedings designed to adjudicate disputed facts in particular cases on the other."

Are you more inclined to find a substantial due process problem in *Philly's* or in *Eastlake*? If Judge Posner were unfettered by precedent, how do you think he would vote in a case like *Eastlake*?

Note Judge Posner's discussion of bills of attainder. Consider Professor Tribe's attempt to weave bill-of-attainder analysis into an assessment of *Eastlake*:

> * * * [I]n [*Eastlake*], the enterprise seeking the variance might have done better to argue not that the referendum requirement was an "unconstitutional delegation of legislative power to the people," but that the requirement operated much like a forbidden bill of attainder — particularly since it was enacted (1) while the respondent's application "for a zoning change to permit construction of a multifamily, highrise apartment building" was pending, and (2) in the face of the City Planning Commission's recommendation that the City Council approve the change. To be sure, no "existing rights [were] being impaired; new use rights [were] being sought from the City Council," and administrative as well as other forms of relief remained available if hardship could be shown. * * * [But] it is doubtful that either the character of the variance as a "privilege" or the availability of relief from demonstrated hardship could meet the less familiar but in some ways more basic objection that popular assemblies — and even more clearly, the populace itself — cannot constitutionally be empowered to dispose of important interests of identified individuals without some "realistic opportunity for the affected persons to be heard, even by the electorate."

Laurence Tribe, *American Constitutional Law* 658–59 (2d ed. 1988) (last quotation is from Justice Powell's dissent in *Eastlake*; other quotations are from the majority opinion in *Eastlake*).

Note that in *Philly's* Illinois law required that the local option liquor referendum petition contain the signatures of at least 25% of a precinct's registered voters. Under Illinois law, some referendum petitions needed the signatures of only 10% of registered voters. Does the increased signature requirement for the local option liquor law make sense? Does it ameliorate some of the due process of lawmaking problems identified by Judge Posner? In *Walgreen Co. v. Illinois Liquor Control Comm'n*, 488 N.E.2d 980 (Ill. 1986), the Supreme Court of Illinois rejected the argument that the 25%

requirement unduly burdened the right to vote. Concluding that voting in a referendum is not a fundamental right, the court applied "rational basis" scrutiny to the higher signature requirement for liquor referenda. The court stated that "[t]he State has a strong interest in maintaining the economic stability of a legally authorized industry and protecting the licensed purveyors of its products from irrational and capricious changes in the wet/dry status of their precincts every four years." 488 N.E.2d at 983.

Recall that Judge Posner in *Philly's* suggested that due process might be violated if voters could shut down a targeted establishment, rather than all establishments in a precinct. For later cases so holding, see *Club Misty, Inc. v. Laski*, 208 F.3d 615 (7th Cir.) (Posner, J.), *cert. denied*, 531 U.S. 1011 (2000); *Brookpark Entertainment, Inc. v. Taft*, 951 F.2d 710 (6th Cir.1991).

SECTION 3. RECALL

CHANDLER v. OTTO
Supreme Court of Washington, 1984
103 Wash.2d 268, 693 P.2d 71

[*Editors' note:* In considering this case, the reader may find useful the language of the Washington Constitution governing recall:

Recall of Elective Officers. Every elective public officer in the state of Washington except judges of courts of record is subject to recall and discharge by the legal voters of the state, or of the political subdivision of the state, from which he was elected whenever a petition demanding his recall, reciting that such officer has committed some act or acts of malfeasance or misfeasance while in office, or who has violated his oath of office, stating the matters complained of, signed by the percentages of the qualified electors thereof, hereinafter provided, the percentage required to be computed from the total number of votes cast for all candidates for his said office to which he was elected at the preceding election, is filed with the officer with whom a petition for nomination, or certificate for nomination, to such office must be filed under the laws of this state, and the same officer shall call a special election as provided by the general election laws of this state, and the result determined as therein provided. Wash. Const. Art. I, § 33 (amendment 8).

Same. The legislature shall pass the necessary laws to carry out the provisions of section thirty-three (33) of this article, and to facilitate its operation and effect without delay: Provided, That the authority hereby conferred upon the legislature shall not be construed to grant to the legislature any exclusive power of lawmaking nor in any way limit the initiative and referendum powers reserved by the people. The percentages required shall be, state officers, other than judges, senators and representatives, city officers of cities of the first class, school district boards in cities of the first class; county officers of counties of the first, second and third classes, twenty-five per cent. Officers of all other political subdivisions, cities, towns, townships, precincts and school districts not herein mentioned, and state senators and representatives, thirty-five percent. Wash. Const. Art. I, § 34 (also adopted as amendment 8).]

PEARSON, JUSTICE.

This case involves a recall petition filed against members of the Moses Lake City Council. The issue presented is whether the charges propounded in the petition allege sufficient grounds for recall. The trial court, pursuant to RCW 29.82.010, as amended by Laws of 1984, ch. 170, conducted a hearing to determine the sufficiency of the charges and adequacy of the ballot synopsis and concluded that the charges were sufficient. We hold that the recall charges were legally insufficient to serve as the basis for a recall election. Accordingly, we reverse the decision of the trial court.

The salient facts are as follows. In early 1984 the City of Moses Lake invited bids from interested persons desiring to contract with the City for the handling of the city's solid waste. The invitations for bids called for a bid opening on April 27, 1984. The bids were opened on that date and there were seven bidders. Superior Refuse Removal submitted the lowest bid. Shortly after the opening it was discovered that Superior's bid failed to fully comply with the invitation in that some of the pages were not signed as required. Similarly, the second lowest bidder, Western Refuse, had also failed to sign all the pages of its bid. The third lowest bidder was Lakeside Disposal. Lakeside had complied with the invitation and signed each proposal page.

At its regular meeting on May 22, 1984, the City Council considered the seven bids. After some discussion about whether the Council could waive the irregularities in the bids submitted by Superior Refuse and Western Refuse, the Council voted 4 to 3 not to waive the irregularities and awarded the contract to Lakeside Disposal as the lowest responsible bidder. Thereafter on July 12, 1984, a petition for recall was filed against each of the four councilmen who had voted to award the contract to Lakeside. The petition alleged the foregoing facts and contended that the actions of the councilmen were an abuse of discretion, done in contravention of the public interest, and would result in increased costs to the citizens of Moses Lake.

On July 24, 1984, a ballot synopsis was prepared by Paul A. Klasen, Jr., Grant County Prosecuting Attorney. On August 9, 1984, a hearing was held in the Superior Court for Grant County wherein the judge determined that the allegations contained in the recall petitions were sufficient to warrant proceeding with the recall election. The councilmen immediately appealed this decision.

Recall is the electoral process by which an elected officer is removed before the expiration of the term of office. Provisions for the recall of public officers did not appear in the Washington Constitution until 1912 when a constitutional recall referendum proposed by the State House of Representatives was passed by the voters. Laws of 1911, ch. 108, § 1, p. 504; Const. art. 1, §§ 33, 34 (amend. 8). This amendment is the only constitutional recall provision that requires a showing of cause before recall will be allowed. Cohen, *Recall in Washington: A Time for Reform*, 50 Wash.L.Rev. 29 (1974). In addition, Washington is one of only a few states that requires a recall petition to allege acts of malfeasance, misfeasance or a violation of the oath of office. See 4 E. McQuillin, *Municipal Corporations* § 12.251b, at 336 n. 12 (3d rev. ed. 1979).

These requirements indicate that the drafters of Washington's recall provision wanted to prevent recall elections from reflecting on the popularity of the political decisions made by elected officers. *See* 4 E. McQuillin, at 334.

In 1913 the Legislature passed the necessary laws to carry out the provisions of the new constitutional amendment. *See* RCW 29.82. The Legislature did not, however, define misfeasance, malfeasance, or violation of the oath of office. Nor did the Legislature suggest what might constitute cause. Because of this, interpretation of the unique requirements of Washington's recall provision has been the focus of over half the recall cases at the appellate level. These cases, in trying to interpret the right of recall, developed a narrow scope of review based on the court's traditional role of nonintervention in political controversies. *Cudihee v. Phelps*, 136 P. 367 (Wash. 1913); *McCormick v. Okanogan Cy.*, 578 P.2d 1303 (Wash. 1978). This scope of review has in most instances allowed the court to uphold nearly every recall petition. Such a narrow scope of review, however, disregards the apparent intent of the framers of the recall provision to limit the scope of the recall right to recall for cause. Furthermore, it has encouraged two abuses:

(1) The charges, though adequate on their face as cause for recall, may lack any factual basis whatsoever,

(2) The charge may be entirely unrelated to the dispute; the real political issue or dispute between the recall petitioners and the elective officer may be submerged beneath the rhetoric of the charge.

Cohen, 50 Wash.L.Rev. at 30.

The narrow scope of review dictated by the vagueness of the enabling legislation has until recently prevented the courts from dealing with these abuses. Recent amendments to RCW 29.82, however, indicate that the Legislature has finally followed the suggestions of members of this court and has provided safeguards to protect an elected official from being subjected to the financial and personal burden of a recall election grounded on false or frivolous charges. *Bocek v. Bayley*, 505 P.2d 814 (Wash. 1973) (Utter, J., concurring).

In 1976 the Legislature amended RCW 29.82. The statute was amended to require the state official with whom the charges were filed to serve the officer whose recall is demanded with a copy of the ballot synopsis. RCW 29.82.015. More importantly, the specificity requirements were changed by adding the portions italicized below.

> Whenever any legal voter . . . shall desire to demand the recall and discharge of any elective public officer * * * under the provisions of sections 33 and 34 of Article 1 of the Constitution, he . . . shall prepare a typewritten charge, reciting that such officer . . . has committed an act or acts of malfeasance, or an act or acts of misfeasance while in office, or has violated his oath of office * * * which charge shall state the act or acts complained of in concise language, *giving a detailed description including the approximate date, location, and nature of each act complained of* . . .

(Italics ours.) RCW 29.82.010 (as amended by Laws of 1975, 2d Ex.Sess., ch. 47, § 1, p. 199).

RCW 29.82 was amended for a second time in 1984. First, in addition to believing a charge to be true a petitioner must now *verify under oath that he or she has knowledge of the alleged facts upon which the stated grounds for recall are based.* (Italics ours.) Laws of 1984, ch. 170, § 1, p. 821. Second, the amendments codify the definitions of misfeasance, malfeasance, or violation of the oath of office in accordance with case law definitions:

(1) "Misfeasance" or "malfeasance" in office means any wrongful conduct that affects, interrupts, or interferes with the performance of official duty;

(a) Additionally, "misfeasance" in office means the performance of a duty in an improper manner, and

(b) Additionally, "malfeasance" in office means the commission of an unlawful act;

(2) "Violation of the oath of office" means the wilful neglect or failure by an elective public officer to perform faithfully a duty imposed by law.

Laws of 1984, ch. 170, § 1, p. 821. *See also Bocek v. Bayley, supra.* Third, a new section requires the recall petitioner to file the petition with a specified officer who will formulate a ballot synopsis. The preparer shall additionally certify and transmit the charges and the ballot synopsis to the superior court and shall petition the superior court to approve the synopsis and to determine the sufficiency of the charges. Hence, under the new statute the superior courts, rather than the prosecuting attorney, attorney general or Chief Justice of the Supreme Court, are entrusted with initially determining whether the charges are sufficient. Laws of 1984, ch. 170, § 3, p. 823. A fourth section outlines the duties of the superior court.

Within fifteen days after receiving the petition, the superior court shall have conducted a hearing on and shall have determined, without cost to any party, (1) whether or not the acts stated in the charge satisfy the criteria for which a recall petition may be filed, and (2) the adequacy of the ballot synopsis. The clerk of the superior court shall notify the person subject to recall and the person demanding recall of the hearing date. Both persons may appear with counsel. The court may hear arguments as to the sufficiency of the charges and the adequacy of the ballot synopsis. *The court shall not consider the truth of the charges, but only their sufficiency.* An appeal of a sufficiency decision shall be filed in the supreme court as specified by RCW 29.82.160. The superior court shall correct any ballot synopsis it deems inadequate. Any decision regarding the ballot synopsis by the superior court is final. The court shall certify and transmit the ballot synopsis to the officer subject to recall, the person demanding the recall, and either the secretary of state or the county auditor, as appropriate.

(Italics ours.) Laws of 1984, ch. 170, § 4, p. 823.

Our obligation in interpreting the foregoing amendments is to ascertain and give effect to the intent of the Legislature. The changes to RCW 29.82 are presumed to indicate a change in the legislative purpose behind recall petitions. We believe the changes indicate a legislative intent to place limits on the recall right, *i.e.* to allow recall for cause yet free public officials from the harassment of recall elections grounded on frivolous charges or mere insinuations. We perceive the legislative amendments to mean that a recall petition must be both legally and factually sufficient.

Factually sufficient means the petition must comply with the specificity requirements of RCW 29.82.010. As noted in *Herron*, "these statutory requirements ensure that both the public electorate and the challenged elective official will make informed decisions in the recall process." Factually sufficient indicates that although the charges may contain some conclusions, taken as a whole they do state sufficient facts to identify to the electors and to the official being recalled acts or failure to act which without justification would constitute a prima facie showing of misfeasance, malfeasance, or a violation of the oath of office. *See Amberg v. Welsh*, 8 N.W.2d 304 (Mich. 1949); and *Tolar v. Johns*, 147 So.2d 196 (Fla. Dist. Ct. App. 1962).

Legally sufficient means that an elected official cannot be recalled for appropriately exercising the discretion granted him or her by law. To be legally sufficient, the petition must state with specificity substantial conduct clearly amounting to misfeasance, malfeasance or violation of the oath of office. 4 E. McQuillin, *Municipal Corporations* § 12.251b, at 334 (3d rev. ed. 1979).

In analyzing the recall petition in the instant case, we conclude that it is not legally sufficient. Pursuant to RCW 35.23.352–.353, members of Moses Lake City Council have the authority to let contracts, such as the one in question here, to the "lowest responsible bidder". This authority is well analyzed in 10 E. McQuillin, *Municipal Corporations* § 29.73, at 398 (3d rev. ed. 1981):

> Concerning the inquiry, how the responsibility is to be determined, "the authorities speak with practically one voice," namely, that the officers in whom the power is vested "must determine the fact, and such determination cannot be set aside unless the action of the tribunal is arbitrary, oppressive or fraudulent. The determination of the question of who is the lowest responsible bidder does not rest in the exercise of an arbitrary and unlimited discretion, but upon a bona fide judgment, based upon facts tending to support the determination." This view has in general been supported by the authorities. The determination of the municipal officials concerning the lowest responsible bidder will not be disturbed by the courts, unless it is shown to have been influenced by fraud, or unless it is an arbitrary, unreasonable misuse of discretion. When the officers have exercised their discretion in the award of the contract, the presumption obtains that such action was regular and lawful, and such presumption can be overcome only by proof that the officers acted without justification or fraudulently.

(Footnotes omitted.)

Respondent's recall petition fails to allege any fraud or arbitrary, unreasonable misuse of discretion. There is no evidence that the appellants exercised their discretion inappropriately. The petition merely attacks the judgment of the councilmen. The exercise of judgment is not grounds for recall. Hence, the petition does not state with specificity substantial conduct clearly amounting to misfeasance, malfeasance, or violation of the oath of office.

Accordingly, we reverse the decision of the trial court and direct a dismissal of the recall charges.

WILLIAM H. WILLIAMS, C.J., and BRACHTENBACH, DOLLIVER and ANDERSEN, JJ., concur.

UTTER, J., concurs but adheres to his views in *Bocek v. Bayley*, 81 Wash.2d 831, 505 P.2d 814 (1973).

DORE, JUSTICE (dissenting).

The majority affirms the action of the Moses Lake City Council in refusing to award a 5-year garbage contract to the lowest bidder but instead awarded it to the third lowest bidder, at an additional cost to the Moses Lake taxpayers of $3,000 a month, or $180,000 over the life of the contract. It is undisputed that both are competent contractors. The majority affirms the holding that the Council properly exercised its discretion. I disagree and would hold that the Moses Lake Council's actions were a manifest abuse of discretion, and I believe the citizens of Moses Lake, who have to pay the bill, would agree with me.

From the time this court first decided a case dealing with the recall right promulgated in Const. art. 1, §§ 33 and 34, to as recently as last year, we have always interpreted the recall provision broadly so as to allow the people to exercise their right of self-governance.

Only last year, we reaffirmed the principle that

> our constitution establishes a very broad right of the electorate to recall elective public officials. * * * The rights of initiative, referendum, and recall form a weighty triumvirate intended to preserve the people's most basic right of self-governance and any interference with these rights requires strong justification.

Pederson v. Moser, [662 P.2d 866 (Wash. 1983)]. This broad right of recall has manifested itself by providing the foundation for many of the rules which protect this basic right:

> First, in determining the validity of recall charges, courts are limited to examination of the charges stated and cannot inquire into factual matters extraneous to the allegations. *E.g., State ex rel. LaMon v. Westport*, [438 P.2d 200 (Wash.)]. Second, courts must assume the truth of the charges in determining whether legally sufficient grounds for recall have been stated. *E.g., Skidmore v. Fuller*, [370 P.2d 975 (Wash. 1962)]. Third, just as there can be no inquiry into the truth or falsity of the charges, there can be no inquiry into the motives of those filing the charges. *Roberts v. Millikin*, [93 P.2d 393 (Wash. 1939)]. Fourth, recall charges are sufficiently specific if they are definite enough to allow the charged official to meet them before the tribunal of the people. *E.g., State ex rel. LaMon v. Westport, supra*. Finally, any one sufficient charge requires the holding of a recall election. *E.g., Morton v. McDonald*, [252 P.2d 577 (Wash. 1953)].

State ex rel. Citizens Against Mandatory Bussing v. Brooks, [492 P.2d 536 (Wash. 1972)]. The majority now restricts this fundamental right. The majority provides two arguments to justify narrowing the recall right. First, it cites our constitutional requirement that a recall petition allege an act of malfeasance, or a violation of the oath of office. Not once, however, in the past 72 years has this court ever interpreted these requirements to mean that the right of recall should be narrowly construed. Indeed, in the past 72 years this court has always held that the constitution establishes a very broad right of recall. [Citations omitted.] The majority fails to explain what prompted it to decide that over 70 years of case law interpreting the recall provision was wrong. Instead, it meekly states that our constitution requires that cause be shown for a recall election[3] and concludes, without providing any reasoning, that our right of recall has been construed too broadly in the past.

The second justification the majority narrates for its surprising interpretation of the recall provision is that the Legislature, in 1976 and 1984, amended the enabling legislation to the recall provision. The majority asserts that the amendments show that the Legislature intended to narrow the right of recall.[4] As to the 1976 amendment, the majority points to two changes that it asserts shows that the Legislature intended to narrow the right of recall. First, it points out that the statute was amended to require that the official who is the subject of the recall receive a copy of the ballot synopsis. RCW 29.82.015. This provision, however, can hardly be characterized as narrowing the recall right. Secondly, the statute was amended to require the petitioner to give a detailed description of the changes, including the approximate date, location and nature of each act complained of. RCW 29.82.010. This provision is a procedural clarification and does not restrict the electorate's right of recall. Instead, it merely ensures that both the public and the challenged official will make an informed decision in the recall process. *See Herron v. McClanahan*, 625 P.2d 707 (Wash. 1981).

Discussing the 1984 amendment, the majority points to four changes which it claims is evidence that the right of recall has been narrowed. The majority never explains how these changes have narrowed the recall right. Nor could it, since all the changes were either procedural in nature or incorporated this court's interpretation of the constitution's recall provision. Yet the majority

---

3. The majority erroneously asserts that our constitution is the only one in the nation that requires a showing of cause before recall will be allowed. That is simply untrue. West Virginia's constitution provides that

> All officers elected or appointed under this Constitution, may, unless in cases herein otherwise provided for, be removed from office for *official misconduct, incompetence, neglect of duty, or gross immorality, in such manner as may be prescribed by general laws, . . .*

(Italics mine.) W.Va. Const. art. 4, § 6. Moreover, while some state constitutions do not explicitly state that cause must be shown, their courts have construed their constitutional recall provisions to require that cause must be shown. *See, e.g., Amberg v. Welsh*, [38 N.W.2d 304 (Mich. 1949)]. Consequently, contrary to what the majority concludes, the drafters of our recall provision did not intend the recall right to be narrowly construed.

4. The Legislature's authority to enact enabling legislation is limited and cannot be used to change the scope of recall right.

> The legislature shall pass the necessary laws to carry out the provisions of section thirty-three (33) of this article, and to facilitate its operation and effect without delay: *Provided, That the authority hereby conferred upon the legislature shall not be construed to grant to the legislature any exclusive power of lawmaking nor in any way limit the initiative and referendum powers reserved by the people.*

(Italics mine.) Const. art. 1, § 34.

still concludes, without citing any legislative history, that the Legislature intended to narrow the recall right.

Consequently, it is clear that our recall provision should be judicially interpreted broadly as it has been for the last seven decades. Manifestly, the allegations in this recall provision are sufficient.

The majority asserts that there was no abuse of discretion when the Moses Lake City Council refused to accept the lowest bid and, instead, accepted the third lowest bid. The majority finds that this is not an abuse of discretion. It does not cite any cases to support its position; instead, it cites a treatise on municipal corporations which discusses *judicial review* of bid acceptances. The standard a court uses for reviewing an official's conduct is different from the standard the electorate uses for review. The majority may not feel that accepting a higher bid is an abuse of discretion but the voters of Moses Lake might find that the Council's award of a contract, for an additional windfall of $180,000 to the third bidder, was an abuse of discretion, especially when an equally competent contractor (low bidder) admittedly was available for $180,000 less.

The majority claims that the City Council's acceptance of the higher bid was permissible because the two lower bids were not signed on every page. However, it is undisputed that the City Council could have accepted the lowest bid even with the technical errors and still had a binding contract. The Council chose not to do so and should now be subject to the voters' approval or disapproval of its decision.

I believe that the average person in Moses Lake, if allowed to vote, would find that the Council members who voted for the garbage "windfall" abused their discretion. The majority, by depriving such person of his constitutional right to recall public officials, unfortunately prohibits this.

I would affirm the trial court.

NOTES ON RECALL

1. *The Value of Recall.* Consider R. Perry Sentell, Jr., *Remembering Recall in Local Government Law*, 10 Ga. L. Rev. 883, 886 (1976) (footnotes omitted):

> [The value of recall] to the science of local government has been long debated. On the one side, the arguments are that it provides unremitting popular control over persons in public office; it permits the lengthening of terms of elective local officials with the least possible risk; it encourages principles of both responsibility and responsiveness; and it maintains public interest and confidence in the process of government. Alternative contentions are that recall engenders political demoralization; that it can be invoked to displace conscientious officials and thus discourages their participation in government; and that its operation entails prohibitive public expense. That both perspectives are persuasive is manifested by the split of jurisdictions authorizing recall, as well as the varying extent of utilization even where it is authorized.

There is no recall procedure for members of Congress. Should there be? For a proposal, see Timothy Zick, *The Consent of The Governed: Recall of United States Senators*, 103 Dick. L. Rev. 567 (1999).

2. *Formal versus Informal Standards for Recall.* In some states, there are at least three methods available to evict state officials from office: (1) removal by impeachment, whereby certain high state officials may be impeached by a majority of the state house of representatives for misconduct, tried by the state senate, and convicted (that is, removed from office and disqualified from holding "any office of honor, trust or profit in the state") by a vote of a supermajority of the senators; (2) removal of officers not subject to impeachment (removal for misconduct through statutory procedures); and (3) recall. The Supreme Court of Colorado has explained that the first two methods of defrocking contemplate removal from office for cause, but that

> [r]ecall, on the other hand, may be used for a purely political reason. The purpose underlying recall of public officials for political reasons is to provide an effective and speedy remedy to remove an official who is unsatisfactory to the public and whom the electors do not want to remain in office, regardless of whether the person is discharging his or her duties consistent with his or her abilities and conscience.

Groditsky v. Pinckney, 661 P.2d 279, 283 (Colo. 1983). The court stated that "the power of recall is a fundamental constitutional right of Colorado citizens and the reservation of this power in the people must be liberally construed," *id.* at 281, and that "[i]t is not within the purview of courts to pass upon the sufficiency of the grounds in recall petitions." *Id.* at 284.

Is the Colorado approach superior to the judicialized and more limited Washington approach to recall discussed in *Chandler*? Would it matter to your answer what percentage of voters is required to initiate a recall election?

Do principles of due process of lawmaking have any role to play in the context of recall? Is the argument that courts should examine the motivations of voters as strong in the context of recall as it is in the context of initiative or referendum? Is a recall election "state action"?

Cronin, *Direct Democracy, supra,* at 245–46, suggests that the petition should contain the names of the persons or groups sponsoring the petition and state why the official should be recalled. Moreover, there should be a "high signature requirement" (perhaps 20–25% of those voting in the last gubernatorial election), to deter personal vendettas ending up imposing costly elections upon the public. Furthermore, elected officials should not be subject to recall during their first six months of office; again, this stops "sour grapes" attacks upon them through the recall process. Finally, if a recall election results in the retention of an official, that official should be immune from another recall effort for six months. Cronin also suggests that some neutral, public body conduct a hearing concerning the merits of the proposed recall.

3. *Reinvigorating Recall on the State Level: California's Gubernatorial Recall.* Historically low approval ratings (21%) and an historically high budget deficit (over $38 billion) led to the recall of California's Democratic governor Gray Davis in 2003. The recall was initially backed mostly by anti-tax crusaders who used talk radio and the Internet to make their case. Once the movement began to gain ground, a Republican member of the U.S. House of Representatives, Darrell Issa, decided to actively support the effort, raising over $1 million for the petition drive. Primarily using paid petition circulators, the

pro-recall forces submitted petitions with 1.36 million signatures, substantially more than the nearly 900,000 signatures required to trigger a recall election. Moreover, the use of paid signature gatherers allowed Davis' opponents to gather the signatures quickly enough to trigger a special election in the fall of 2003, rather than placing the recall on the ballot at the same time as the Democratic presidential primary in March 2004. Turnout in March probably would have included more Davis supporters, and recall advocates wanted to force a quick election to take advantage of voter dissatisfaction with the Governor.

The recall election in California was historic not only because it was the first gubernatorial recall in California to qualify for a vote but also because it was only the second time in U.S. history that a governor was successfully recalled.[a] The California recall election received a great deal of media attention throughout the country and the world because it was so unusual, and also because the main contender to succeed Davis was movie star Arnold Schwarzenegger. Under California state law, the names of Davis' potential successors appeared on the same ballot as the recall measure; thus, voters decided whether to recall Davis at the same time that they chose his replacement if the recall passed. Not all states with the recall process structure the election in this way. Some first hold the recall vote, and only if the recall succeeds is a subsequent election held to choose a new governor. Other states allow the target of the recall also to appear on the ballot as a candidate in the election for a successor, which can lead to the anomalous situation where the recall barely succeeds, but the recalled official is reelected by a plurality. In California, state law prohibited Davis from running to succeed himself, and, because of constitutional term limits on the governor, he cannot run again for the office.

The recall election was also noteworthy because 135 candidates appeared on the recall ballot in the election to succeed the governor. Poorly drafted state statutes provided no clear rules for ballot access, and the rules chosen by the Secretary of State in the exercise of his discretion as chief election officer posed only minor hurdles for hopefuls.[b] Candidates seeking ballot access needed to obtain only 65 signatures and pay $3,500 or to obtain 10,000 signatures. That opened the door for the multitude of candidates, the majority of whom ran for reasons other than winning. A few were concerned with

---

a. The other instance occurred in 1921, when North Dakota recalled Governor Lynn Frazier. Arizona Governor Evan Mecham probably would have been recalled in the late 1980s had he not been impeached and removed from office by the legislature, which was reacting to the recall effort.

b. In the early days of recall in California, potential candidates had to obtain signatures equal to one percent of those who voted in the last elections, which was about 4,000 signatures when the provision was adopted. This requirement was repealed in 1976 and replaced with directions to use "the manner prescribed for nominating a candidate to that office in a regular election." Cal. Elec. Code § 11381 (West 2004). However, the provision regulating ballot access for primary elections explicitly states that it does not apply to recalls. *Id.* at §§ 8000, 8062. In the face of this conflict, the Secretary of State applied the permissive primary election ballot access provision.

publicizing particular political issues or concerns. Some, like Gary Coleman, the former child actor, Mary Carey, a porn star, and Gallagher, the melon-smashing comedian, ran to enhance their visibility in other careers. More important for the result of the recall, the wide-open process for getting on the ballot allowed a candidate like Arnold Schwarzenegger, who is more liberal than many in his party on some issues, to bypass the usual route to a general election, the Republican Party's closed primary, and proceed directly to a final election.[c]

The two-part ballot and the 135 candidates not only had the potential for a great deal of voter confusion but also the possibility of a number of troubling election outcomes.[d] For example, because the successor to Davis needed only a plurality to win the office, there was a chance that the recall would barely succeed, and the next governor would be elected by a relatively small plurality. In such a case, there could be more "no" votes on the recall than votes for the governor-elect, a possibility which could undermine the legitimacy of the new administration. That scenario did not come to pass in California because Schwarzenegger won decisively with 48.6% of the votes, while only 44.6% of voters cast ballots against the recall.

In the immediate aftermath of the recall election, the specter of a governor without much of a voter mandate prompted proposals to modify California's recall process. In the end, no changes were made, but some reform is necessary. Most evidently, election laws need to be changed to make ballot access harder and to reduce the number of candidates. Others have suggested holding two elections, one on the recall and then another for governor, perhaps allowing the recalled candidate also to run in the second election.[e] Alternatively, the current format could be retained, but the laws could provide for a run-off between the two top candidates for governor if the recall succeeded. What reforms of the election process would you suggest? How would each affect the likelihood of the recall's success and the kind of candidate likely to appear on the ballot? For example, are voters more likely to vote for or against a recall when they know for certain who the candidates for successor are? Should they make those two decisions separately? Should the recalled official be able to succeed herself? The recall campaign period in California can be very short: the Constitution requires that a recall election usually be held

---

c. For a discussion of Schwarzenegger's rise to political power, see Joe Mathews, *The People's Machine: Arnold Schwarzenegger and the Rise of Blockbuster Democracy* (2006).

d. For a discussion of the voter confusion that did occur in this recall, see Michael Alvarez, Melanie Goodrich, Thad Hall, Roderick Kiewiet & Sarah Sled, *The Complexity of the California Recall Election*, PS, Jan. 2004, at 23. See also Michael Alvarez, Roderick Kiewiet & Betsy Sinclair, *Rational Voters and the Recall Election*, in *Clicker Politics* 87 (Shawn Bowler & Bruce Cain eds., 2006) (finding that "all but a small number of voters appear able to [make sense of the recall's two question structure], and that they appear to have cast their ballots in a manner that was consistent with their preferences").

e. Others, typically those hostile to any sort of recall, have proposed eliminating the election for successors and allowing the Lieutenant Governor to succeed a recalled Governor. See, e.g., Mark Ridley-Thomas & Erwin Chemerinsky, *Now That It's Finally Over, Let's Revamp the Recall*, L.A. Times, Oct. 29, 2003, at B15.

within 80 days of the certification of the recall petitions and under no circumstances can the election be delayed more than six months. How should the rules account for this relatively brief campaign period? Is a longer campaign necessary, or would it paralyze governance?

Another aspect of the California recall dramatically pointed out the consequences of the state's bifurcated campaign finance regime, where there are different rules for candidate elections and for direct democracy.[f] Campaign laws limited only those running for governor in the second part of the election from accepting contributions greater than $21,200 from each individual. Committees formed to campaign for or against the recall — even those controlled by candidates or Gray Davis — were not subject to contribution limits, although they were required to comply with disclosure rules. Instead, the recall was considered an issue campaign which was regulated only through disclosure and not through contribution limits. This bifurcation led to a variety of strategies by candidates to evade the effect of contribution limitations.

First, very wealthy candidates could spend as much of their own money as they wished because, as we saw in Chapter 2, Supreme Court jurisprudence has disallowed expenditure limits while upholding contribution limits. The largest single contributor in the election was Arnold Schwarzenegger, who spent over $10.5 million of his own money, mainly through his "Californians for Schwarzenegger" committee. The theme of his successful campaign was that he would stand for the people against special interests. As part of that strategy, he announced that he would spend his own money instead of taking money from special interests. He told voters that his own personal wealth made him beholden to no one. In the end, he did accept substantial campaign contributions from a variety of interests including real estate developers, car dealers, insurance interests, and financial institutions.[g] It turned out that his definition of "special interests" included mainly Indian tribes and labor unions — two of the most powerful special interests in California. But he also self-financed a great portion of his campaign, demonstrating the advantages for multi-millionaires willing to spend their own money in a campaign system where contributions from others are limited but overall expenditures are not.

A second method of evasion was possible because the election for governor was held at the same time as the recall. The target of the recall, Gray Davis, raised nearly $18.3 million through his anti-recall committee, "Californians Against the Costly Recall of the Governor," a sum made possible by the absence of contribution limitations in the recall campaign. The bifurcated campaign finance system also allowed candidates for governor to form separate pro-recall committees and raise unrestricted money for those efforts. For example, Schwarzenegger's "Total Recall" committee raised over $4.5 million, spent largely on advertisements supporting the recall. Unless a viewer noticed

---

f. For more extensive discussion of the bifurcated campaign rules and Schwarzenegger's use of direct democracy as a tool of governance, see Elizabeth Garrett, *Democracy in the Wake of the California Recall*, 153 U. Pa. L. Rev. 239 (2004).

    g. See Shaun Bowler & Bruce Cain, *Introduction — Recalling the Recall: Reflections on California's Recent Political Adventure*, PS, Jan. 2004, at 7, 8 (detailing these contributions).

the fine print identifying the sponsor of the ad, she would have been hard pressed to tell the difference between one funded by the Schwarzenegger campaign committee and one paid for by the "Total Recall" committee.

During the campaign, opponents argued that this election would usher in an era of frequent recalls throughout the nation, much as the success of Proposition 13 in California played a role in launching more frequent use of the initiative and referendum. Although a group in Nevada began a drive to recall that state's governor, the effort failed to qualify for the ballot.[h] It is unlikely that recall efforts in the other states that allow statewide recall will succeed as easily as did the movement to oust Davis. California's signature threshold of 12% of those who voted in the last gubernatorial election is among the lowest in the nation, where the norm is 25%. It is also important to keep in mind that recalls at the local level have always occurred more frequently than statewide efforts, so claims that recalls will paralyze government or enfeeble elected representatives must be assessed with the larger background in mind. Nearly three-fourths of recall elections in America are at the city council or school board level.[i]

Perhaps the most frequently suggested reform of the California recall system is to raise the signature threshold, but the likelihood of this change is small because it would require a constitutional amendment and a popular vote. Whether California's relatively low threshold for a gubernatorial recall is *too* low is unclear. After all, there has been only one effort that has qualified for the ballot in ninety years, and, for the past several decades, the initiative industry in California has surely been sophisticated enough to realize that a substantial war chest could qualify a recall just as it can an initiative. The success of the 2003 recall has made the process salient, however, so it is likely that there will be an increase in the attempts to qualify statewide recalls. While some increase in the signature threshold to align California with other states seems sensible, any substantial increase seems motivated more by a dislike of direct democracy than by a genuine desire to improve the process. In essence, such proposals reduce the number of recalls by raising the cost of petition drives. This sort of reform will ensure that recall is a tool only of well-funded interests that can afford to pay signature gatherers working for professional firms. This is not a new issue for direct democracy, where the use of paid petition circulators has transformed this grassroots process into a weapon in the arsenal of wealthy interests. It does, however, suggest that reform proposals should focus on ways to reorient direct democracy — whether initiative, referendum, or recall — to its historic roots.

---

h. The recall effort collected only 51,000 signatures, short of the more than 128,000 needed to qualify for the ballot. It used volunteers to gather signatures, not paid petition circulators. Brendan Riley, *Nevada Recall Drive Terminated*, Houston Chron., Nov. 25, 2003, at A9.

i. National Conference of State Legislatures, *Recall of State Officials* (Mar. 21, 2006), ttp://www.ncsl.org/programs/legman/elect/recallprovision.htm.

Chapter 6

STATUTES AS A SOURCE OF PUBLIC POLICY IN THE UNITED STATES (THEORIES OF LEGISPRUDENCE)

Chapters 1 through 4 introduced you to theories of "legislatures" (who is in them, how they are organized, what incentives legislators have), and Chapter 5 provided an overview of the other method of producing legislation, direct democracy. The remainder of this book focuses on theories of "legislation," the statutory product. How do statutes fit in with other sources of law (this chapter)? How should statutes be interpreted (Chapters 7 and 8)? What are the dynamics of statutory implementation over time (Chapter 9)?

Traditional American "legisprudence"[a] (especially during the "classical" period, around the turn of the twentieth century) was of two minds about statutes. As a formal matter, it treated statutes as a superior source of law. Our Constitution reflects this: Article I vests "[a]ll legislative Powers" in the Congress, Article II commands that the President and the executive branch "shall take Care that the Laws be faithfully executed," and Article III assures that the "judicial Power" shall be available to adjudicate cases and controversies. State constitutions either explicitly or implicitly set forth the same division. Clearly, the primary lawmaking power is vested in the legislature; the executive simply implements statutes, and courts exist to interpret and apply them in specific cases.

On the other hand, the formal superiority of statutes over executive and judicial decisions did not prevent traditional legisprudes from considering statutes functionally inferior to judicial decisions, which were treated as the primary source of legal reasoning and policy guidance. Several provisions of the Constitution (such as the Ex Post Facto, Bill of Attainder, and Contract Clauses) explicitly restrict the power of federal or state legislatures to enact statutes which operate retroactively, while there are no such restrictions on

---

a. This term describes the systematic analysis of statutes within the framework of jurisprudential philosophies about the role and nature of law. See Julius Cohen, *Towards Realism in Legisprudence*, 59 Yale L.J. 886 (1950).

judicial decisions. Many state constitutions simply prohibit any and all "retrospective" laws. The reason: Statutes are "political" intrusions into the body politic and create new and unexpected rights and duties, but judicial decisions merely "declare" what the "law" (whether common law or statutory law) already was. Of course, the power of judicial review threatens statutes with invalidation if their political will falls athwart the Constitution, as interpreted by courts. Even the separation of powers precept seems to work against the functional importance of statutes. Although the legislature has the power to enact statutes, it must rely on the executive and the judiciary to enforce and apply them.

The classical vision of the formal primacy but functional inferiority of statutes has become outdated in the past century, the "age of statutes." There was an intellectual shift in legisprudential emphasis systematized by "legal process" scholars and jurists after World War II. Legal process theory emphasizes the duty of government institutions to operate within their realm of "competence" but defines that realm quite flexibly; the purpose of all branches of government is to cooperate in the creation of *dynamic* and *rational* public policy. Under legal process precepts, statutes reflect the purposive and reason-centered goals of the state. Section 1 will offer a brief history of legisprudence, through the prism of a central issue: What is the relationship between statutes and the common law? We suggest different ways of examining this issue in theory, in examples from case law, and in a striking proposal made by then-Dean (now Judge) Calabresi.

Sections 2 and 3 explore the implications of legal process theory for important doctrinal issues about the American practice of *stare decisis* in statutory cases and the differences in retroactive effect given to judicial decisions and statutes. Legal process theory may have been the most sustained intellectual accomplishment in legal theory in the twentieth century, but (as suggested in Section 1 and developed in Sections 2 and 3) legal process theory has left an ambiguous heritage. In practice, its prescriptions have not been followed; the U.S. Supreme Court and most state courts continue to follow more purely formalistic modes of thought. In theory, legal process thought has been attacked from several directions, leaving its conceptual validity in dispute.

SECTION 1. STATUTES AS PRINCIPLED LAW (LEGISPRUDENCE FROM BLACKSTONE TO LEGAL PROCESS)

A. THE DECLINE AND FALL OF FORMALISM, 1890–1940[a]

Legisprudence in the common law era can be understood by examining 1 William Blackstone, *Commentaries on the Laws of England* 63–92 (1765). Judges, Blackstone's "depositories of law," must and do decide cases

---

a. This part is adapted from William Eskridge, Jr. & Philip Frickey, *Historical and Critical Introduction*, to Henry Hart and Albert Sacks, *The Legal Process* (1994 publication of 1958 tentative edition"), and has been much influenced by Neil Duxbury, *Faith in Reason: The Process Tradition in American Jurisprudence*, 15 Cardozo L. Rev. 601 (1993).

according to objective rules — that is, rules that are known to everyone beforehand and do not arbitrarily favor one person or group over another. Judges do not "make" law; they simply "declare" the existing objective law (whether it be written statute or prior decisions). Blackstone readily admitted the preeminence of legislation. Judges apply statutes, not because they reflect principles of natural order, but because they are dictates of sovereign will; as opposed to "reasoned" judicial decisions, statutes are intrusions into the organic law. (As James Landis later put it, they are "in" but not "of" the law.) They are political, not principled. Blackstone saw law as preserving order and the existing social fabric. Objective law better preserves order because it is stable, gives citizens advance notice of its application, and thus can be relied upon by private actors.

Blackstone's legisprudence contrasted reasoned, ordered, objective, eternal, principled *judicial decisions*, against willful, disorderly, subjective, contingent, changing, political *legislative decisions*. Central was the idea that statutes are formally but not functionally superior sources of law. A corollary to Blackstone's basic vision is that statutes should not be treated as sources for legal reasoning, while judicial decisions should be. Statutes are ad hoc, while judicial decisions are part of an historical pyramid, each decision building upon the others. Similarly, statutes are only effective after their enactment, while judicial decisions are effective retroactively, because they are thought to be just "statements" of pre-existing law. A final corollary (less important to Blackstone but critical in the late nineteenth century) is that statutes should be narrowly construed. Because it was assumed that no reasoning process was involved in formulating statutes, it fell to judges to squeeze the political aims of the legislature into the interstices of the organic law; relatedly, statutes in derogation of the common law were to be narrowly construed. The latter maxim neatly encapsulates the view of late nineteenth century "common law formalists" that judge-made law, which Justice Holmes sarcastically described as "a brooding omnipresence in the sky," *Southern Pacific Co. v. Jensen*, 244 U.S. 205, 222 (1917) (Holmes, J., dissenting), was a relatively closed, rational, objective system which brooked minimal interference from half-baked statutory trespassers.[b] This view of law came under sustained intellectual

---

b. See Grant Gilmore, *The Ages of American Law* 62–63 (1977). We use "formalism" to signify systematic deductive reasoning from pre-established principles. "Common law formalism" signifies systematic reasoning from axioms pre-established by judicial case law, to the virtual exclusion of statutes as a source of "principled" legal reasoning. An alternative vision of legisprudence was the civil law tradition on the European Continent. Like its common law counterpart, civil law formalism maintained that judges were passive figures who simply "found" the law. Civil law formalism, however, posited that the judge would find the law from statutory codes, not judicial precedents (which were not binding on civil law judges). Also, civil law judges did not approach statutes as ad hoc political reactions to localized problems (or acts of fiat); instead, they were carefully considered, systematic attempts to set forth in written form the organic law which common law formalism found in the corpus of judicial precedent. General principles of law, in fact, could be found in statutes and codes. Finally, civil law judges were encouraged to interpret statutes expansively, according to the Roman law concept of the "equity of the statute." Where a gap has been left by any statutory rule, it is filled by analogy to another rule in the same or related statute; the *ratio legis* of the latter is taken as a general

challenge in the twentieth century, as statutes have come to displace common law as the source of policy, law, and even principle.

1. *Law as Policy.* Justice Oliver Wendell Holmes, first of the Massachusetts and then of the United States Supreme Court, was the most perceptive critic of common law formalism.[c] Holmes' articles and opinions between 1894 and 1906 viewed law as the product of social struggle, a view in striking contrast to the formalists' claim that law was an apolitical, neutral set of rules. This was best illustrated in the labor cases of the period, in which courts relied on vested rights of property and freedom of contract to justify injunctions against labor activity and invalidation of labor-protective legislation. Holmes dissented from this judicial practice, positing that the cases submerged a conflict between two legally acknowledged "rights," the freedom of contract right (which courts recognized) and the right to free economic competition (equally supported by precedent but suppressed in the labor cases). Notwithstanding judges' characterization of these decisions as apolitical and predetermined by precedent, Holmes insisted that prior decisional law suggested no single answer, because the new labor controversies fit into more than one category. Hence, deductive reasoning could not resolve the labor cases. Holmes argued that they should be resolved through a process of policy balancing, his balance being to tolerate labor activities that were nonviolent and not animated by malice. In *The Path of the Law* (1899), Holmes argued that experience, and not logic, is the life of the law; the goal of law should be pragmatic and utilitarian rather than formal.

Holmes' analysis inspired anti-formalist legal scholars of all stripes for the next two generations. Harvard's Dean Roscoe Pound followed Holmes in denouncing common law formalism and founded a school of "sociological jurisprudence," advocating an era of policy science transformed into law through legislation and administration. Subsequently, the legal realists pursued both the deconstructive and constructive features of Holmes' critique of formalism.[d] Deconstructively, realists like Wesley Hohfeld, Felix Cohen, and Jerome Frank delighted in showing how there was no determinate way to move from the generalities of rules and precedents to one inevitable result in particular cases, and realists such as Robert Hale argued that the results in cases were more easily traceable to a commonly held judicial ideology than to any logical consistency. Constructively, some realists studied judicial behavior to ascertain consistent patterns, while others studied social phenomena as the best starting point for their regulation. Karl Llewellyn was exemplary of the latter; his work in sales law rested upon a deep understanding of custom and practice among businessmen.

---

rule of law applicable to all cases. See John Merryman, *The Civil Law Tradition* (1969).

     c. See Morton Horwitz, *The Transformation of American Law, 1870–1950*, at 129–43 (1992); G. Edward White, *Oliver Wendell Holmes* (1993); Thomas Grey, *Holmes and Legal Pragmatism*, 41 Stan. L. Rev. 787 (1989).

     d. See Horwitz, *Transformation, 1870–1950, supra*, at 193–212; Laura Kalman, *Legal Realism at Yale, 1927–1960* (1986); William Twining, *Karl Llewellyn and the Realist Movement* 2d ed. 1985); Gary Peller, *The Metaphysics of American Law*, 73 Calif. L. Rev. 1151 (1985).

By the 1930s the scholars actively writing in American public law agreed upon the proposition that law is the creation and elaboration of social policy. The policy theorists were also forming a tentative consensus around several corollaries to that axiom. One was that law itself has social purposes that must be understood and evaluated along criteria that are not exclusively legal. Whatever its source, law should be instrumental toward some social purpose. A further implication of the view that law is policy was that scholars questioned the juriscentric nature of Anglo-American law. Although some realists wrote mainly about common law policymaking, the sorry performance of the Supreme Court as a policymaking institution between 1894 and 1937 — the era of *Lochner* and the labor injunction — made this an unattractive aspiration for law. Pound argued that the Supreme Court's statutory and constitutional decisions were both illegitimate and stupid policymaking.[e] The Court's decisions were illegitimate, because they represented policy choices by unelected judges who refused to give full effect to the policy preferences of elected legislators. The Court's choices were stupid policy as well, because the complicated social problems of industrial America were beyond the ken of common law judges; legislative policy preferences on such issues were presumptively to be preferred. An implication of Pound's position, shared by other thinkers, was that the role of courts in a democratic society should be the elaboration and application of statutory policy, rather than the direct creation of public policy in the common law.

2. *Institutional Responsibilities in the Modern Regulatory State.* Common law formalism was further superseded by theories of the regulatory state. Here, there were two seminal figures: Louis Brandeis and Felix Frankfurter.[f] They developed affirmative theories of government, especially of the institutional architecture of the modern administrative state. Brandeis was probably the leading intellectual force behind Woodrow Wilson's New Freedom programs for policing market abuses, and Frankfurter and his students played a similar role during the New Deal. While both had substantive theories of regulation, it was their theories of institutional architecture and process that were the more important contribution to American public law.

The difference between Holmes's law-is-policy viewpoint and a Brandeis's law-is-policy-but-also-institutional-architecture viewpoint is illustrated in *International News Service v. Associated Press*, 248 U.S. 215 (1918). The issue was whether the Associated Press (AP) held a protected property interest in news stories it generated and was entitled to an injunction against theft of those stories by International News Service (INS), a rival news service. The opinion for the Court was a typical formalist one, deciding that AP was entitled to an injunction because its investment of time, effort, and resources in generating the news stories was analogous to other efforts treated as property.

---

e. See, e.g., *Mechanical Jurisprudence*, 8 Colum. L. Rev. (1908).

f. See Leonard Baker, *Brandeis and Frankfurter: A Dual Biography* (1984); Robert Burt, *Two Jewish Justices: Outcasts in the Promised Land* (1988); Thomas McCraw, *Prophets of Regulation: Charles Francis Adams, Louis D. Brandeis, James M. Landis, Alfred E. Kahn* (1984).

The Court's assumption of a preexisting concept of property was challenged in Holmes' concurring opinion, which argued that property is a consequence and not an antecedent of law. The issue for him was whether state policy would be advanced by recognizing rights in newsgathering; he decided that it was worth it, in order to encourage this socially productive activity.

Brandeis agreed with Holmes that there is no natural category, "property," and that the decision whether to characterize news stories in this way depends upon a balancing of the consequences of the different positions. But Brandeis dissented on the ground that the policy balancing required by Holmes was best done by the legislature and not the judiciary:

> [W]ith the increasing complexity of society * * * the problems presented by new demands for justice cease to be simple. Then the creation or recognition by courts of a new private right may work serious injury to the general public, unless the boundaries of the right are definitely established and wisely guarded. In order to reconcile the private right with the public interest, it may be necessary to prescribe limitations and rules for its enjoyment; and also to provide administrative machinery for enforcing the rules. It is largely for that reason that, in the effort to meet the many new demands for justice incident to a rapidly changing civilization, resort to legislation has latterly been had with increasing frequency. * * *

> Courts are ill-equipped to make the investigations which should precede a determination of the limitations which should be set upon any property right in news or of the circumstances under which news gathered by a private agency should be deemed affected with a public interest. Courts would be powerless to prescribe the detailed regulations essential to full enjoyment of the rights conferred or to introduce the machinery required for enforcement of such regulations. Considerations such as these should lead us to decline to establish a new rule of law in the effort to redress a newly-disclosed wrong, although the propriety of some remedy appears to be clear.

Thus Brandeis deepened Holmes' critique of the *Lochner* judiciary: Its decisions were not only analytically misleading, poor policy choices, and undemocratic, but reflected a power grabbiness that was beyond the competence of the judiciary and indeed dangerously debilitating to the entire system of government.

Professors Frankfurter and James Landis applied this idea of institutional specialization to develop a defense of the key feature of the modern regulatory state — lawmaking by agencies. Frankfurter argued in 1930 that government's aspiration to develop useful policies depended not only upon the enactment of good legislation and judicial deference to those legislative judgments (Holmesian points), but much more upon their elaboration and application by an expert administration. Neither the legislature nor the judiciary was competent to make all the technical, fact-bound judgments necessary for the regulatory process, tasks an agency filled with specially trained experts was particularly competent to fulfill. Expertise not only solved problems, but offered neutral criteria for the solution of problems, which obviated democratic theory concerns with broad legislative delegations to agencies. This is, of course, precisely what happened during the New Deal, which Brandeis defended within the Court, Frankfurter helped craft as an adviser to the President, and Landis (just after his appointment as Dean at Harvard) defended in Yale's 1938 Storrs Lectures on *The Administrative Process*.

3. *Statutes and Reason*. The implications of the New Deal were most profound for understanding the relationship between law and society. The New Deal was the death knell for the formalists' belief that law and society were separate and impermeable. Precisely the opposite was the case: The law structured the market and other private institutions, which could not operate at all, or at all well, without the coordinating function of law. In turn, the law depended upon the market, for successful regulation could not easily occur if it did not fit into established private institutions or meet the needs of private actors. Many of the realists, especially those who served in the New Deal, believed that law's legitimacy rested upon its instrumental value, its ability to deliver good policy. But there was another way of looking at law's legitimacy once one rejected formalism, and that other way was the rationalist tradition in American law.

Judge Benjamin Cardozo, in *The Nature of the Judicial Process* (1921), explicitly agreed with Holmes that judges create law but maintained that "some principle, however unavowed and inarticulate and subconscious, has regulated" such creation. The judge "is not free to innovate at pleasure. * * * He is to draw his inspiration from consecrated principles." Cardozo argued that principles emerge from the testing, retesting, and reformulation process of common law judging, in which an accepted principle "becomes a datum, a point of departure, from which new lines will be run, from which new courses will be measured" and "principles that have served their day expire, and new principles are born."

Cardozo provided a concrete illustration for the operation of principles in the law. In *Riggs v. Palmer*, 22 N.E.188 (N.Y. 1889), the New York Court of Appeals refused to construe the state's inheritance statutes to permit a killer to inherit from his victim's estate. Although the statutes, literally read, seemed to permit the inheritance, the Court held that "all laws . . . may be controlled in their operation and effect by general, fundamental maxims of the common law," such as the principle that no one shall profit by his own wrongdoing. Cardozo approved of the decision and its reasoning, even though the court could have chosen other principles, such as the maxim that the plain language of a statute should be followed. "In the end, the principle that was thought to be most fundamental, to represent the larger and deeper social interests, put its competitors to flight. . . . The murderer lost the legacy . . . because the social interest served by refusing to permit the criminal to profit by his crime is greater than that served by the preservation and enforcement of legal rights of ownership." Cardozo, *supra*, at 42–43.

Implicitly assuming that law's legitimacy is tied in some way to reason, Cardozo suggested that the effect of statutes will be tempered by principle. Roscoe Pound had earlier suggested another consequence: Statutes in turn could be a source of principle. He argued in *Common Law and Legislation*, 21 Harv. L. Rev. 383, 385–86 (1908):

Four ways may be conceived of in which courts in such a legal system as ours might deal with a legislative innovation. (1) They might receive it fully into the body of the law as affording not only a rule to be applied but a principle from which to reason, and hold it, as a later and more direct expression of the general will, of superior authority to judge-made rules on the same general subject; and so reason from it by analogy in preference to them. (2) They might receive it fully into the body of the law to be reasoned from by analogy the same as any other rule of law, regarding it, however, as of equal or co-ordinate authority in this respect with judge-made rules upon the same general subject. (3) They might refuse to receive it fully into the body of the law and give effect to it directly only; refusing to reason from it by analogy but giving it, nevertheless, a liberal interpretation to cover the whole field it was intended to cover. (4) They might not only refuse to reason from it by analogy and apply it directly only, but also give to it a strict and narrow interpretation, holding it down rigidly to those cases which it covers expressly. The fourth hypothesis represents the orthodox common law attitude toward legislative innovations. Probably the third hypothesis, however, represents more nearly the attitude toward which we are tending. The second and first hypotheses doubtless appeal to the common law lawyer as absurd. He can hardly conceive that a rule of statutory origin may be treated as a permanent part of the general body of the law. But it is submitted that the course of legal development upon which we have entered already must lead us to adopt the method of the second and eventually the method of the first hypothesis.

Justice Harlan Stone likewise argued that there is "no adequate reason for our failure to treat a statute much more as we treat a judicial precedent, as both a declaration and source of law, and as a premise for legal reasoning."[g]

While virtually all of the post-formalists accepted the proposition that law is policy creation, and most endorsed the new institutional relationships of the New Deal (Pound being the main exception), the role of principle was much contested in the 1930s. Many legal realists made sport of the role of principles, viewing them as simply a kind of formalism. Rationalists insisted that reason in law was what differentiated American law from, say, Nazi law (which like the realists' vision was policy-centered).[h]

Perhaps the most sophisticated attack was made in Lon Fuller's 1940 Rosenthal Lectures, published as *The Law in Quest of Itself.*[i] Fuller argued against the prevailing positivism of American law. Consistent with prior work of the new rationalists, Fuller argued that fact could not be separated from value, and law could not be separated from moral evaluation — "in the moving

---

g. Stone, *The Common Law in the United States*, 50 Harv. L. Rev. 4, 12–13 (1936). See also James Landis, *Statutes as the Sources of Law*, in *Harvard Legal Essays* 213 (1934) (urging revival of civil law concept, "equity of a statute").

h. See Edward Purcell, Jr., *The Crisis of Democratic Theory: Scientific Naturalism and the Problem of Value* (1973); David Bixby, *The Roosevelt Court, Democratic Ideology, and Minority Rights: Another Look at* United States v. Classic, 90 Yale L.J. 741 (1981).

i. See Robert Summers, *Professor Fuller's Jurisprudence and America's Dominant Philosophy of Law*, 92 Harv. L. Rev. 433 (1978); Martin Golding, *Jurisprudence and Legal Philosophy in 20th Century America: Major Themes and Developments*, 36 J. Leg. Ed. 441 (1986).

world of law, the *is* and the *ought* are inseparably linked." *Id*. at 64. What facts get noticed, how they are interpreted and assembled depends upon values and is useless without integration into a normative framework, Fuller claimed; conversely, the normative framework itself is influenced by what one perceives to be possible in the world and by a variety of facts that one has collected from experience. Fuller's analysis transformed the new rationalism into an organic theory of law as "purposive." Fuller argued that when law fails to fulfill worthy goals it falls short of being law, just as a steam engine that does not work might be junked.

The new rationalist writing also maintained that issues of law's relationship to democracy should be central. Again reflecting the views of his contemporaries, Fuller emphasized that a democracy had to be committed to organic principle. Indeed, what most distinguished democratic society from a totalitarian one is the former's commitment to free exchange of ideas. See *id*. at 122–23, 126. Fuller also suggested (more explicitly in his later work) that defining and implicitly valorizing law as nothing more than power (the realists' positivism) was corrupting of a polity, for it may induce people to behave in that way. Once a polity accepts a philosophy of "I'll obey the law only because I have to," it is encouraging its citizens to think, "I'll get away with what I can." In contrast, a polity based upon organic principle (Fuller's philosophy) vests the citizenry with responsibility for the law. That responsibility might induce the population to behave in a principled and cooperative way.

STATE v. WARSHOW
Supreme Court of Vermont, 1979
138 Vt. 22, 410 A.2d 1000

BARNEY, CHIEF JUSTICE.

[John Warshow and his fellow defendants traveled to Vernon, Vermont, to protest against alleged safety risks of nuclear power; the defendants engaged in a sit-in at the main gate of the Vermont Yankee nuclear plant. The plant had been shut down for repairs and refueling, and these protestors sought to prevent workers from gaining access to the plant and placing it on-line. They were arrested for criminal trespass, and they were convicted at trial after the court refused to permit the jury to hear their "necessity" defense. The Supreme Court of Vermont affirmed.]

* * * [I]f the qualifications for the defense of necessity are not closely delineated, the definition of criminal activity becomes uncertain and even whimsical. * * *

In the various definitions and examples recited as incorporating the concept of necessity, certain fundamental requirements stand out: (1) there must be a situation of emergency arising without fault on the part of the actor concerned; (2) this emergency must be so imminent and compelling as to raise a reasonable expectation of harm, either directly to the actor or upon those he was protecting; (3) this emergency must present no reasonable opportunity to avoid the injury without doing the criminal act; and (4) the injury impending from the emergency must be of sufficient seriousness to out measure the criminal wrong. * * *

There is no doubt that the defendants wished to call attention to the dangers of low-level radiation, nuclear waste, and nuclear accident. But low-level radiation and nuclear waste are not the types of imminent danger classified as an emergency sufficient to justify criminal activity. To be imminent, a danger must be, or must reasonably appear to be, threatening to occur immediately, near at hand, and impending. We do not understand the defendants to have taken the position in their offer of proof that the hazards of low-level radiation and nuclear waste buildup are immediate in nature. On the contrary, they cite long-range risks and dangers that do not presently threaten health and safety. Where the hazards are long term, the danger is not imminent, because the defendants have time to exercise options other than breaking the law. * * *

HILL, JUSTICE, concurring. * * *

The defense of necessity proceeds from the appreciation that, as a matter of public policy, there are circumstances where the value protected by the law is eclipsed by a superseding value, and that it would be inappropriate and unjust to apply the usual criminal rule. The balancing of competing values cannot, of course, be committed to the private judgment of the actor, but must, in most cases, be determined at trial with due regard being given for the crime charged and the higher value sought to be achieved.

Determination of the issue of competing values and, therefore, the availability of the defense of necessity is precluded, however, when there has been a deliberate legislative choice as to the values at issue. The common law defense of necessity deals with imminent dangers from obvious and generally recognized harms. It does not deal with non-imminent or debatable harms, nor does it deal with activities that the legislative branch has expressly sanctioned and found not to be harms.

Both the state of Vermont and the federal government have given their imprimatur to the development and normal operation of nuclear energy and have established mechanisms for the regulation of nuclear power. See, e. g., 18 V.S.A. §§ 1652–1658, 1700–1702; 3 V.S.A. §§ 3116a–3117; 10 V.S.A. §§ 6501–6504; 42 U.S.C. §§ 2011–2296, 5801–5891. Implicit within these statutory enactments is the policy choice that the benefits of nuclear energy outweigh its dangers.

If we were to allow defendants to present the necessity defense in this case we would, in effect, be allowing a jury to redetermine questions of policy already decided by the legislative branches of the federal and state governments. This is not how our system of government was meant to operate.

I express no opinion as to the relative merits or demerits of nuclear energy, nor do I question the sincerity of the defendants' beliefs. All that I would hold is that this Court is not the proper forum to grant defendants the relief they seek. Defendants still have the right to try to induce those forums that have made the policy choices at issue today to reconsider their decisions. But until that time I feel constrained to follow the law as it is, not as some would like it to be. * * *

BILLINGS, JUSTICE, dissenting.

The majority states that the danger of low-level radiation and nuclear waste, which the defendants offered to prove, are "not the types of imminent danger classified as an emergency sufficient to justify criminal activity." Furthermore, the majority dismisses those portions of the proof dealing with the threat of a nuclear accident by characterizing them as mere "speculative and uncertain dangers." In doing so the majority has decided to so read the evidence as to give credibility only to that evidence offered on the effects of low-level radiation. This approach is clearly inconsistent with the case of *State v. Fernie*, 285 A.2d at 727, in which then Justice Barney held that it is reversible prejudicial error for the trial court to exclude a whole line of material evidence tending to support a defense even though "[d]eficiencies in the admissibility of such evidence might . . . have later appeared." It is not for this Court to weigh the credibility of the evidence in this manner where there is evidence offered on the elements of the defense. * * * Where there is evidence offered which supports the elements of the defense, the questions of reasonableness and credibility are for the jury to decide. * * *

While the offer made by the defendants was laced with statements about the dangers they saw in nuclear power generally, it is clear that they offered to show that the Vermont Yankee facility at which they were arrested was an imminent danger to the community on the day of the arrests; that, if it commenced operation, there was a danger of meltdown and severe radiation damage to persons and property. In support of this contention, the defendants stated that they would call experts familiar with the Vermont Yankee facility and the dangerous manner of its construction, as well as other experts who would testify on the effects of meltdown and radiation leakage, on the results of governmental testing, and on the regulation of the Vermont Yankee facility. These witnesses were highly qualified to testify about the dangers at the Vermont Yankee facility based either on personal knowledge or on conditions the defendants offered to show existed at the time of the trespass.

Furthermore, the defendants offered to show that, in light of the imminent danger of an accident, they had exhausted all alternative means of preventing the start up of the plant and the immediate catastrophe it would bring. Under the circumstances of imminent danger arising from the start up of the plant, coupled with the resistance of Vermont Yankee and government officials, which the defendants offered to prove, nothing short of preventing the workers access to start up the plant would have averted the accident that the defendants expected. * * *

I would also dissent from the concurring opinion in so far as it attempts to hide behind inferences that the legislature precluded the courts from hearing the defense of necessity in the instant case * * * . Even assuming that such inferences can be drawn from the regulatory schemes cited, they have no bearing on this case. We were asked to infer under the facts, which the defendants offered to prove (that they were acting to avert an imminent nuclear disaster), that the legislative branch of government would not permit the courts of this state to entertain the defense of necessity because it had legislatively determined nuclear power to be safe. Were the defense raised without any offer to show an imminent danger of serious accident, it might fail both because defendants did not offer evidence on imminent danger and on the basis of legislative preclusion. But, where, as here, the defendants offer to prove an emergency which the regulatory scheme failed to avert, the inference of preclusion is unwarranted. The defendants are entitled to show that although there is a comprehensive regulatory scheme, it had failed to such an extent as to raise for them the choice between criminal trespass and the nuclear disaster which the regulatory scheme was created to prevent.

Moreover, statutory enactments in derogation of the common law are strictly construed. This Court has heretofore been of the opinion that with regard to the language of statutes, the "[r]ules of the common law are not to be changed by doubtful implication." The concurring opinion fails to indicate any basis for its implication, and I can find none that meets this test. In fact, the statutes to which the concurring opinion directs our attention make it the duty of the Nuclear Advisory Panel "[t]o develop awareness in the state . . . of the potential liabilities . . . of a fixed nuclear facility in this state," 18 V.S.A. § 1701(a)(5), and generally secure to the people, as individuals and through their local and state representatives, the right to evaluate the dangers of depositing, storing, or reprocessing high-level radioactive waste materials, 10 V.S.A. §§ 6501–6504. Moreover, the legislature has seen fit to recognize the right of individuals to sue for damages resulting from ionizing radiation. 12 V.S.A. § 518. It cannot be said categorically that "[i]mplicit within these statutory enactments is the policy choice that the benefits of nuclear energy outweigh its dangers," as the concurring opinion states.

NOTE ON THE CASE OF THE NUCLEAR PROTESTERS

We present this case as a concrete example of the abstract ideas presented above. Justice Barney's opinion is a simple example of common law formalism, applying traditional common law categories in a mechanical way, and not coincidentally in a way that protects traditional common law property (or, in other types of cases, contract) rights. Like Holmes, Justices Hill and Billings find the mechanical categories unhelpful, pointing out that Vermont precedents would just as well support the opposite result. Although both Justices approached Warshow's case from a policy angle, they (like Holmes and Brandeis in *Associated Press*) emphasized different policies: Hill emphasized the policy of institutional responsibility, while Billings emphasized the policy of law as reason. Both made explicit appeals to democratic values. How would you vote in this case? Write your answer in the margin, and revise it as you work through this Section.

B. THE LEGAL PROCESS ERA, 1940–1973

Holmes, Pound, Brandeis, Cardozo, Frankfurter, and Landis were all godparents to the approach to law that crystallized in the period just before World War II and dominated American law after the war. Many legal philosophers contributed to this school of thought, notably Lon Fuller, Willard Hurst, Louis Jaffe, and Herbert Wechsler. The most complete elaboration of its vision was in Henry Hart and Albert Sacks' teaching materials, *The Legal*

Process: Basic Problems in the Making and Application of Law, which took their final mimeographed form in 1958.[j] The Hart and Sacks synthesis sought the best of each pre-war tradition, without its drawbacks. Hart and Sacks' view of law as policy tried to avoid the realists' conclusion that law is nothing but politics and whimsy. They incorporated the idea of comparative institutional competence but eschewed a conception bereft of substantive evaluation. And the materials viewed law in terms of reasons, coherence, and rationality, without lapsing into natural law modes of thought.

    1.   *The Reasoned Elaboration of Purposive Law.*   Hart and Sacks posited a New Deal-inspired theory of society different from traditional liberal (social contract) theory. Central to society are people's recognition of "the fact of their interdependence with other human beings and the community of interest that grows out of it. So recognizing, people form themselves into groups for the protection and advancement of their common interests * * * ." *Id.* at 2. The state is one of several institutions thus formed, but it is also the "overriding general purpose group" which has the greatest power, and the greatest responsibility, for " 'establishing, maintaining and perfecting the conditions necessary for community life to perform its role in the complete development of man.' " *Id.* at 102. In accord with this activist view of the state, Hart and Sacks posited: "Law is a doing of something, a purposive activity, a continuous striving to solve the basic problems of social living." *Id.* at 148.

    Law's purposiveness generated Hart and Sacks' theory of "reasoned elaboration." *Id.* at 145–52. General directives often do not transparently tell officials and citizens what to do in specific situations, but Hart and Sacks sharply disputed the realist claim that this lack of easy transparency meant that the official simply imposed a political interpretation on the general directive. To the contrary, an official applying a "general directive arrangement" must "elaborate the arrangement in a way which is consistent with the other established applications of it" and "must do so in a way which best serves the principles and policies it expresses." *Id.* at 147. Hart and Sacks extended this idea to legal interpretation. A judge interpreting common law precedents has a responsibility to draw from those precedents some rule, principle, or standard, a responsibility that is only fulfilled if the judge reads the precedents, and the law generally, to figure out what purposes they serve. *Id.* at 397–403. A judge interpreting a statute must first identify the purpose of the statute, what policy or principle it embodies, and then reason toward the interpretation most consistent with that policy or principle. *Id.* at 148–50, 1149–71.

    2.   *Law as an Institutional System; Rules and Standards, Policies and Principles.*   As a purposive system, law contains a number of "substantive understandings or arrangements" to coordinate people's conduct. But Hart and

---

    j.   The materials were published as Henry Hart, Jr. & Albert Sacks, *The Legal Process: Basic Problems in the Making and Application of Law* (William Eskridge, Jr. & Philip Frickey eds. 1994), and all citations are to this edition. This part draws upon the *Historical and Critical Introduction* we wrote for that edition. Other useful sources are Duxbury, *Faith in Reason, supra*; Gary Peller, *Neutral Principles in the 1950's*, 21 U. Mich. J.L. Ref. 561 (1988); Jan Vetter, *Postwar Legal Scholarship on Judicial Decision Making*, 33 J. Legal Educ. 412 (1983).

Sacks emphasized the greater importance of the "constitutive or procedural understandings or arrangements" by which the substantive arrangements are applied, interpreted, and changed. *Id.* at 3. Broad dispersion of decision-making is the most practical way to proceed. Because of the "boundless and unpredictable variety" of our dynamic society, they asserted that "private ordering is the primary process of social adjustment." *Id.* at 161–63. To the extent that private ordering does not work, Hart and Sacks contemplated an interaction between private and public institutions — allocated according to their relative "competence" to handle the matter. For example, although they accepted the conventional view that the common law is the "initial resort" for problems not solved privately, Hart and Sacks were concerned "as much with the shortcomings of the common law as a form of law as with its merits" and sought "to lay a foundation for an understanding of the frequent need for one of the more sophisticated types of administered regulation or non-regulatory control." *Id.* at 342.

Hart and Sacks then explored the ways in which legislated policy choices and implementational discretion interact. One way is through the choice of rules versus standards. *Id.* at 138–41. If the legislature decides to deal with a social problem through specific rules, it is expressing its confidence that it has sufficient information to solve the social problem. If the legislature is unsure of how to proceed, it will adopt a standard, essentially delegating rulemaking responsibilities to courts, agencies, or private institutions. Even when a statute simply sets forth a policy or objective, official discretion is usually limited by more specific statements of a policy or by an underlying "principle," or a policy supported by reasons it will be good for society. If underlying statutory policy is ambiguous, "the official should interpret it in the way which best harmonizes with more basic principles and policies of law." *Id.* at 147. Thus, basic principles and policies form the basis for extending a rule or statute to a novel context, *id.* at 362–83; reformulating old rules or provisions, *id.* at 383–403; and even replacing prior rules or practices with new ones. *Id.* at 545–70.

3. *The Centrality of Process.* In a government of dispersed power and diverse views about substantive issues, frequently "the substance of decision cannot be planned in advance in the form of rules and standards," but "the procedure of decision commonly can be." *Id.* at 154. Procedure is practically important in three different ways. To begin, a procedure "which is soundly adapted to the type of power to be exercised is conducive to well-informed and wise decisions. An unsound procedure invites ill-informed and unwise ones." The procedures that facilitate good policy decisions by the legislature, for example, are (1) openness to the views of all affected persons and groups, (2) focus on factual information subjected to expert and critical scrutiny, and (3) public deliberation through which the pros and cons are thoroughly discussed. *Id.* at 694–95. The suggestion that "the best criterion of sound legislation is the test of whether it is the product of a sound process of enactment" epitomized the legal process philosophy. *Id.* at 695.

Additionally, procedure is the means by which the interconnected institutional system works together smoothly. Process also provides mechanisms for controlling discretion and for self-correction. For the administrative process, such safeguards include "the arrangements which prescribe the procedure to be followed in exercising . . . power; the information which must be secured; the people whose views must be listened to; the findings and justification of the decision which must be made; and the formal requisites of action which must be observed." *Id.* at 153–54. For the legislative process, the safeguards include the constitutional requirements of bicameralism and presentment, plus the rules and safeguards adopted voluntarily by Congress, and the "ultimate check" of the ballot box. *Id.* at 153–54, 157–58. For the judicial process, safeguards include the due process guarantees of notice, an impartial decisionmaker, and a right to appeal, as well as prudential limitations on the types of cases or controversies that courts will hear.

Last, process is critical to law's legitimacy. The "principle of institutional settlement" was, for Hart and Sacks, "the central idea of law" (*id.* at 4–5):

> The alternative to disintegrating resort to violence is the establishment of regularized and peaceable methods of decision. The principle of institutional settlement expresses the judgment that decisions which are the duly arrived at result of duly established procedures [for making decisions] of this kind ought to be accepted as binding upon the whole society unless and until they are changed. * * *

> * * * When the principle of institutional settlement is plainly applicable, we say that the law "is" thus and so, and brush aside further discussion of what it "ought" to be. Yet the "is" is not really an "is" but a special kind of "ought" — a statement that, for the reasons just reviewed, a decision which is the duly arrived at result of a duly established procedure for making decisions of that kind "ought" to be accepted as binding upon the whole society unless and until it has been duly changed.

Based upon this principle and their general framework, how would Hart and Sacks have analyzed our Case of the Nuclear Protesters? If they had joined any opinion, which one would they have joined? (Or perhaps parts of different opinions?)

The philosophy laid out in *The Legal Process* has been highly influential. Consider its application in the following opinion.

MORAGNE v. STATES MARINE LINES, INC.
Supreme Court of the United States, 1970
398 U.S. 375, 90 S.Ct. 1772, 26 L.Ed.2d 339

MR. JUSTICE HARLAN delivered the opinion of the Court.

[Edward Moragne, a longshoreman, was killed while working aboard the vessel *Palmetto State* in Florida's navigable waters. His surviving spouse sued the owner of the vessel for wrongful death, relying on theories of negligence and unseaworthiness. (Unseaworthiness is akin to strict liability: If the vessel is unseaworthy, the owner is liable even if it took reasonable precautions.)

[Plaintiff Moragne was unlucky. Under virtually any other circumstance, she would have had an unseaworthiness claim. If her husband had died a league or more from Florida's shores, her claim would have been covered by the Death on the High Seas Act, 46 U.S.C. §§ 761–768, which permitted claims based on unseaworthiness. If her husband had died within the state's territorial waters as a result of the owner's negligence, she would have had a state law negligence claim in all state jurisdictions. And in the overwhelming majority of states, the wrongful death laws were construed to include unseaworthiness claims. That was not the case in Florida, however; its Supreme Court held that its wrongful death statute, originally enacted in 1833, before the federal courts established the tort of unseaworthiness, encompassed only traditional common law torts requiring a showing of fault, and that it was up to the legislature to make the changes in Florida law required to expand the statute beyond that.

[Federal maritime law overlaps with state tort law in a good many instances. Thus it would be entirely appropriate to sue for state law negligence and federal law unseaworthiness. But the U.S. Supreme Court held in *The Harrisburg*, 119 U.S. 199 (1886), that federal maritime law does not afford a cause of action for wrongful death.]

[I] The Court's opinion in *The Harrisburg* acknowledged that the result reached had little justification except in primitive English legal history — a history far removed from the American law of remedies for maritime deaths. That case, like this, was a suit on behalf of the family of a maritime worker for his death on the navigable waters of a State. [The lower courts afforded damages relief.] This Court, in reversing, relied primarily on * * * *Insurance Co. v. Brame*, 95 U.S. 754 (1878), in which it had held that in American common law, as in English, "no civil action lies for an injury which results in * * * death." In *The Harrisburg*, as in *Brame*, the Court did not examine the justifications for this common-law rule; rather, it simply noted that "we know of no country that has adopted a different rule on this subject for the sea from that which it maintains on the land," and concluded, despite contrary decisions of the lower federal courts both before and after *Brame*, that the rule of *Brame* should apply equally to maritime deaths. * * *

One would expect, upon an inquiry into the sources of the common-law rule, to find a clear and compelling justification for what seems a striking departure from the result dictated by elementary principles in the law of remedies. Where existing law imposes a primary duty, violations of which are compensable if they cause injury, nothing in ordinary notions of justice suggests that a violation should be nonactionable simply because it was serious enough to cause death. On the contrary, that rule has been criticized ever since its inception, and described in such terms as "barbarous." *E.g., Osborn v. Gilliett*, L.R. 8 Ex. 88, 94 (1873) (Lord Bramwell, dissenting); F. Pollock, Law of Torts 55 (Landon ed. 1951); 3 W. Holdsworth, History of English Law 676–677 (3d ed. 1927). Because the primary duty already exists, the decision whether to allow recovery for violations causing death is entirely a remedial matter. * * * One expects, therefore, to find a persuasive, independent justification for this apparent legal anomaly.

Legal historians have concluded that the sole substantial basis for the rule at common law is a feature of the early English law that did not survive into this century — the felony-merger doctrine. According to this doctrine, the common law did not allow civil recovery for an act that constituted both a tort and a felony. The tort was treated as less important than the offense against the Crown, and was merged into, or pre-empted by, the felony. The doctrine found practical justification in the fact that the punishment for the felony was the death of the felon and the forfeiture of his property to the Crown; thus, after the crime had been punished, nothing remained of the felon or his property on which to base a civil action. Since all intentional or negligent homicide was felonious, there could be no civil suit for wrongful death.

The first explicit statement of the common-law rule against recovery for wrongful death came in the opinion of Lord Ellenborough, sitting at *nisi prius*, in *Baker v. Bolton*, 1 Camp. 493, 170 Eng.Rep. 1033 (1808). That opinion did not cite authority, or give supporting reasoning, or refer to the felony-merger doctrine in announcing that "[i]n a Civil court, the death of a human being could not be complained of as an injury." Nor had the felony-merger doctrine seemingly been cited as the basis for the denial of recovery in any of the other reported wrongful-death cases since the earliest ones, in the 17th century. However, it seems clear from those first cases that the rule of *Baker v. Bolton* did derive from the felony-merger doctrine, and that there was no other ground on which it might be supported even at the time of its inception. * * *

The historical justification marshaled for the rule in England never existed in this country. In limited instances American law did adopt a vestige of the felony-merger doctrine, to the effect that a civil action was delayed until after the criminal trial. However, in this country the felony punishment did not include forfeiture of property; therefore, there was nothing, even in those limited instances, to bar a subsequent civil suit. Nevertheless, * * * American courts generally adopted the English rule as the common law of this country as well. Throughout the period of this adoption, culminating in this Court's decision in *Brame*, the courts failed to produce any satisfactory justification for applying the rule in this country. * * *

The most likely reason that the English rule was adopted in this country without much question is simply that it had the blessing of age. That was the thrust of this Court's opinion in *Brame*, as well as many of the lower court opinions. Such nearly automatic adoption seems at odds with the general principle, widely accepted during the early years of our Nation, that while "[o]ur ancestors brought with them [the] general principles [of the common law] and claimed it as their birthright[,] * * * they brought with them and adopted only that portion which was applicable to their situation." *Van Ness v. Pacard*, 2 Pet. 137, 144 (1829) (Story, J.); *The Lottawanna*, 21 Wall. 558, 571–574 (1875); see R. Pound, The Formative Era of American Law 93–97 (1938); H. Hart & A. Sacks, The Legal Process 450 (tent. ed. 1958). The American courts never made the inquiry whether this particular English rule, bitterly criticized in England, "was applicable to their situation," and it is difficult to imagine on what basis they might have concluded that it was. * * *

[II] We need not, however, pronounce a verdict on whether *The Harrisburg*, when decided, was a correct extrapolation of the principles of decisional law then in existence. A development of major significance has intervened, making clear that the rule against recovery for wrongful death is sharply out of keeping with the policies of modern American maritime law. This development is the wholesale abandonment of the rule in most of the areas where it once held sway, quite evidently prompted by the same sense of the rule's injustice that generated so much criticism of its original promulgation. * * *

* * * The legislatures both here and in England began to evidence unanimous disapproval of the rule against recovery for wrongful death. The first statute partially abrogating the rule was Lord Campbell's Act, 9 & 10 Vict., c. 93 (1846), which granted recovery to the families of persons killed by tortious conduct, "although the Death shall have been caused under such Circumstances as amount in Law to Felony."

In the United States, every State today has enacted a wrongful-death statute. The Congress has created actions for wrongful deaths of railroad employees, Federal Employers' Liability Act, 45 U.S.C. §§ 51–59; of merchant seamen, Jones Act, 46 U.S.C. § 688; and of persons on the high seas, Death on the High Seas Act, 46 U.S.C. §§ 761, 762. Congress has also, in the Federal Tort Claims Act, 28 U.S.C. § 1346(b), made the United States subject to liability in certain circumstances for negligently caused wrongful death to the same extent as a private person.

These numerous and broadly applicable statutes, taken as a whole, make it clear that there is no present public policy against allowing recovery for wrongful death. The statutes evidence a wide rejection by the legislatures of whatever justifications may once have existed for a general refusal to allow such recovery. This legislative establishment of policy carries significance beyond the particular scope of each of the statutes involved. The policy thus established has become itself a part of our law, to be given its appropriate weight not only in matters of statutory construction but also in those of decisional law. See Landis, Statutes and the Sources of Law, in Harvard Legal Essays 213, 226–227 (1934). Mr. Justice Holmes, speaking also for Chief Justice Taft and Justices Brandeis and McKenna, stated on the very topic of remedies for wrongful death:

> "[I]t seems to me that courts in dealing with statutes sometimes have been too slow to recognize that statutes even when in terms covering only particular cases may imply a policy different from that of the common law, and therefore may exclude a reference to the common law for the purpose of limiting their scope. Without going into the reasons for the notion that an action (other than an appeal) does not lie for causing the death of a human being, it is enough to say that they have disappeared. The policy that forbade such an action, if it was more profound than the absence of a remedy when a man's body was hanged and his goods confiscated for the felony, has been shown not to be the policy of present law by statutes of the United States and of most if not all of the States." *Panama R. Co. v. Rock*, 266 U.S. 209, 216 (1924) (dissenting opinion).

Dean Pound subsequently echoed this observation, concluding that: "Today we should be thinking of the death statutes as part of the general law." Pound, Comment on State Death Statutes — Application to Death in Admiralty, 13 NACCA L.J. 188, 189 (1954).

This appreciation of the broader role played by legislation in the development of the law reflects the practices of common-law courts from the most ancient times. As Professor Landis has said, "much of what is ordinarily regarded as 'common law' finds its source in legislative enactment." Landis, *supra*. It has always been the duty of the common-law court to perceive the impact of major legislative innovations and to interweave the new legislative policies with the inherited body of common-law principles — many of them deriving from earlier legislative exertions.

The legislature does not, of course, merely enact general policies. By the terms of a statute, it also indicates its conception of the sphere within which the policy is to have effect. In many cases the scope of a statute may reflect nothing more than the dimensions of the particular problem that came to the attention of the legislature, inviting the conclusion that the legislative policy is equally applicable to other situations in which the mischief is identical. This conclusion is reinforced where there exists not one enactment but a course of legislation dealing with a series of situations, and where the generality of the underlying principle is attested by the legislation of other jurisdictions. On the other hand, the legislature may, in order to promote other, conflicting interests, prescribe with particularity the compass of the legislative aim, erecting a strong inference that territories beyond the boundaries so drawn are not to feel the impact of the new legislative dispensation. We must, therefore, analyze with care the congressional enactments that have abrogated the common-law rule in the maritime field, to determine the impact of the fact that none applies in terms to the situation of this case. See Part III, *infra*. However, it is sufficient at this point to conclude, as Mr. Justice Holmes did 45 years ago, that the work of the legislatures has made the allowance of recovery for wrongful death the general rule of American law, and its denial the exception. Where death is caused by the breach of a duty imposed by federal maritime law, Congress has established a policy favoring recovery in the absence of a legislative direction to except a particular class of cases.

[III] Our undertaking, therefore, is to determine whether Congress has given such a direction in its legislation granting remedies for wrongful deaths in portions of the maritime domain. We find that Congress has given no affirmative indication of an intent to preclude the judicial allowance of a remedy for wrongful death to persons in the situation of this petitioner.

From the date of *The Harrisburg* until 1920, there was no remedy for death on the high seas caused by breach of one of the duties imposed by federal maritime law. For deaths within state territorial waters, the federal law accommodated the humane policies of state wrongful-death statutes by allowing recovery whenever an applicable state statute favored such recovery. Congress acted in 1920 to furnish the remedy denied by the courts for deaths beyond the jurisdiction of any State, by passing two landmark statutes. The first of these was the Death on the High Seas Act, 41 Stat. 537, 46 U.S.C. § 761 *et seq.* Section 1 of that Act provides that:

> "Whenever the death of a person shall be caused by wrongful act, neglect, or default occurring on the high seas beyond a marine league from the shore of any State, * * * the personal representative of the decedent may maintain a suit for damages in the district courts of the United States, in admiralty, for the exclusive benefit of the decedent's wife, husband, parent, child or dependent relative against the vessel, person, or corporation which would have been liable if death had not ensued."

Section 7 of the Act further provides:

"The provisions of any State statute giving or regulating rights of action or remedies for death shall not be affected by this [Act]. Nor shall this [Act] apply to the Great Lakes or to any waters within the territorial limits of any State * * *."

The second statute was the Jones Act, 41 Stat. 1007, 46 U.S.C. § 688, which, by extending to seamen the protections of the Federal Employers' Liability Act, provided a right of recovery against their employers for negligence resulting in injury or death. This right follows from the seaman's employment status and is not limited to injury or death occurring on the high seas.

The United States, participating as *amicus curiae*, contended at oral argument that these statutes, if construed to forbid recognition of a general maritime remedy for wrongful death within territorial waters, would perpetuate three anomalies of present law. The first of these is simply the discrepancy produced whenever the rule of *The Harrisburg* holds sway: within territorial waters, identical conduct violating federal law (here the furnishing of an unseaworthy vessel) produces liability if the victim is merely injured, but frequently not if he is killed. As we have concluded, such a distinction is not compatible with the general policies of federal maritime law.

The second incongruity is that identical breaches of the duty to provide a seaworthy ship, resulting in death, produce liability outside the three-mile limit — since a claim under the Death on the High Seas Act may be founded on unseaworthiness, see *Kernan v. American Dredging Co.*, 355 U.S. 426, 430 n.4 (1958) — but not within the territorial waters of a State whose local statute excludes unseaworthiness claims. The United States argues that since the substantive duty is federal, and federal maritime jurisdiction covers navigable waters within and without the three-mile limit, no rational policy supports this distinction in the availability of a remedy.[12]

The third, and assertedly the "strangest" anomaly is that a true seaman — that is, a member of a ship's company, covered by the Jones Act — is provided no remedy for death caused by unseaworthiness within territorial waters, while a longshoreman, to whom the duty of seaworthiness was extended only because he performs work traditionally done by seamen, does have such a remedy when allowed by a state statute.

There is much force to the United States' argument that these distinctions are so lacking in any apparent justification that we should not, in the absence of compelling evidence, presume that Congress affirmatively intended to freeze them into maritime law. There should be no presumption that Congress has removed this Court's traditional responsibility to vindicate the policies of maritime law by ceding that function exclusively to the States. However,

---

12. [Here Justice Harlan explained that *Gillespie v. United States Steel Corp.*, 379 U.S. 148 (1964), had held that the Jones Act preempted *any* state remedy for wrongful death of a seaman in territorial waters, whether founded upon negligence (the cause of action the Jones Act provides) or otherwise.]

respondents argue that an intent to do just that is manifested by the portions of the Death on the High Seas Act quoted above.

The legislative history of the Act suggests that respondents misconceive the thrust of the congressional concern. Both the Senate and House Reports consist primarily of quoted remarks by supporters of the proposed Act. Those supporters stated that the rule of *The Harrisburg*, which had been rejected by "[e]very country of western Europe," was a "disgrace to a civilized people." "There is no reason why the admiralty law of the United States should longer depend on the statute laws of the States. * * * Congress can now bring our maritime law into line with the laws of those enlightened nations which confer a right of action for death at sea." The Act would accomplish that result "for deaths on the high seas, leaving unimpaired the rights under State statutes as to deaths on waters within the territorial jurisdiction of the States. * * * This is for the purpose of uniformity, as the States can not properly legislate for the high seas." S. Rep. No. 216, 66th Cong., 1st Sess., 3, 4, (1919); H.R. Rep. No. 674, 66th Cong., 2d Sess., 3, 4 (1920). The discussion of the bill on the floor of the House evidenced the same concern that a cause of action be provided "in cases where there is now no remedy," 59 Cong.Rec. 4486, and at the same time that "the power of the States to create actions for wrongful death in no way be affected by enactment of the federal law." *The Tungus v. Skovgaard*, 358 U.S., at 593.

Read in light of the state of maritime law in 1920, we believe this legislative history indicates that Congress intended to ensure the continued availability of a remedy, historically provided by the States, for deaths in territorial waters; its failure to extend the Act to cover such deaths primarily reflected the lack of necessity for coverage by a federal statute, rather than an affirmative desire to insulate such deaths from the benefits of any federal remedy that might be available independently of the Act. The void that existed in maritime law up until 1920 was the absence of any remedy for wrongful death on the high seas. Congress, in acting to fill that void, legislated only to the three-mile limit because that was the extent of the problem. The express provision that state remedies in territorial waters were not disturbed by the Act ensured that Congress' solution of one problem would not create another by inviting the courts to find that the Act pre-empted the entire field, destroying the state remedies that had previously existed. * * *

To put it another way, the message of the Act is that it does not by its own force abrogate available state remedies; no intention appears that the Act have the effect of foreclosing any nonstatutory federal remedies that might be found appropriate to effectuate the policies of general maritime law.

That our conclusion is wholly consistent with the congressional purpose is confirmed by the passage of the Jones Act almost simultaneously with the Death on the High Seas Act. As we observed in *Gillespie v. United States Steel Corp.*, 379 U.S. 148, 155 (1964), the Jones Act was intended to achieve "uniformity in the exercise of admiralty jurisdiction" by giving seamen a federal right to recover from their employers for negligence regardless of the location of the injury or death. That strong concern for uniformity is scarcely consistent with a conclusion that Congress intended to *require* the present nonuniformity in the effectuation of the duty to provide a seaworthy ship. Our recognition of a right to recover for wrongful death under general maritime law will assure uniform vindication of federal policies, removing the tensions and discrepancies that have resulted from the necessity to accommodate state remedial statutes to exclusively maritime substantive concepts. Such uniformity not only will further the concerns of both of the 1920 Acts but also will give effect to the constitutionally based principle that federal admiralty law should be "a system of law coextensive with, and operating uniformly in, the whole country." *The Lottawanna*, 21 Wall. 558, 575 (1875).

We conclude that the Death on the High Seas Act was not intended to preclude the availability of a remedy for wrongful death under general maritime law in situations not covered by the Act. Because the refusal of maritime law to provide such a remedy appears to be jurisprudentially unsound and to have produced serious confusion and hardship, that refusal should cease unless there are substantial countervailing factors that dictate adherence to *The Harrisburg* simply as a matter of *stare decisis*. We now turn to a consideration of those factors.

[IV] Very weighty considerations underlie the principle that courts should not lightly overrule past decisions. Among these are the desirability that the law furnish a clear guide for the conduct of individuals, to enable them to plan their affairs with assurance against untoward surprise; the importance of furthering fair and expeditious adjudication by eliminating the need to relitigate every relevant proposition in every case; and the necessity of maintaining public faith in the judiciary as a source of impersonal and reasoned judgments. The reasons for rejecting any established rule must always be weighed against these factors.

The first factor, often considered the mainstay of *stare decisis*, is singularly absent in this case. The confidence of people in their ability to predict the legal consequences of their actions is vitally necessary to facilitate the planning of primary activity and to encourage the settlement of disputes without resort to the courts. However, that confidence is threatened least by the announcement of a new remedial rule to effectuate well-established primary rules of behavior. There is no question in this case of any change in the duties owed by ship-owners to those who work aboard their vessels. Shipowners well understand that breach of the duty to provide a seaworthy ship may subject them to liability for injury regardless of where it occurs, and for death occurring on the high seas or in the territorial waters of most States. It can hardly be said that shipowners have molded their conduct around the possibility that in a few special circumstances they may escape liability for such a breach. Rather, the established expectations of both those who own ships and those who work on them are that there is a duty to make the ship seaworthy and that a breach of that federally imposed duty will generally provide a basis for recovery. It is the exceptional denial of recovery that disturbs these expectations. "If the new remedial doctrine serves simply to reenforce and make more effectual well-understood primary obligations, the net result of innovation may be to strengthen rather than to disturb the general sense of security." Hart & Sacks, *supra*, at 577; *id.*, at 485, 574–577, 585–595, 606–607; Pound, Some Thoughts About Stare Decisis, 13 NACCA L.J. 19 (1954).

Nor do either of the other relevant strands of *stare decisis* counsel persuasively against the overruling of *The Harrisburg*. Certainly the courts could not provide expeditious resolution of disputes if every rule were fair game for *de novo* reconsideration in every case. However, the situation we face is far removed from any such consequence as that. We do not regard the rule of *The Harrisburg* as a closely arguable proposition — it rested on a most dubious foundation when announced, has become an increasingly unjustifiable anomaly as the law over the years has left it behind, and, in conjunction with its corollary, *The Tungus*, has produced litigation-spawning confusion in an area that should be easily susceptible of more workable solutions. The rule has had a long opportunity to prove its acceptability, and instead has suffered universal criticism and wide repudiation. To supplant the present disarray in this area with a rule both simpler and more just will further, not impede, efficiency in adjudication. Finally, a judicious reconsideration of precedent cannot be as threatening to public faith in the judiciary as continued adherence to a rule unjustified in reason, which produces different results for breaches of duty in situations that cannot be differentiated in policy. Respect for the process of adjudication should be enhanced, not diminished, by our ruling today.

[V] Respondents argue that overruling *The Harrisburg* will necessitate a long course of decisions to spell out the elements of the new "cause of action." We believe these fears are exaggerated, because our decision does not require the fashioning of a whole new body of federal law, but merely removes a bar to access to the existing general maritime law. In most respects the law applied in personal-injury cases will answer all questions that arise in death cases. * * *

In sum, in contrast to the torrent of difficult litigation that has swirled about *The Harrisburg, The Tungus*, which followed upon it, and the problems of federal-state accommodation they occasioned, the recognition of a remedy for wrongful death under general maritime law can be expected to bring more placid waters. That prospect indeed makes for, and not against, the discarding of *The Harrisburg*.

We accordingly overrule *The Harrisburg*, and hold that an action does lie under general maritime law for death caused by violation of maritime duties. * * *

MR. JUSTICE BLACKMUN took no part in the consideration or decision of this case.

NOTES ON REASONING BY
STATUTORY ANALOGY AND *MORAGNE*

1. *Pre*-Moragne *Common Law Examples of Creating Norms by Analogy from Statutes.* Justice Harlan cites the Hart and Sacks materials, and their endorsement of the purposive, principled nature of statutes certainly anticipated *Moragne*. Other legal process scholars and jurists anticipated the *Moragne* approach in other contexts. Chief Justice Traynor of the California Supreme

Court suggested prior to *Moragne* that "it has long since been normal procedure for judges, even those who resist reading up on any law outside that inscribed in their own caves, to consult the richly worked relevant statutes when they come upon problems of the marketplace."[k] Consider the following pre-*Moragne* examples. Is Justice Harlan's use of statutes similar or different?

(a) *Criminal or Mandatory Statutes Creating Tort Standards.* Although criminal statutes do not usually stipulate civil liability, state common law courts have used such statutes (i) as setting forth a standard for negligence per se in tort actions, (ii) as a declaration of public policy justifying a judicial finding that a contract is void or unenforceable, and (iii) as a standard for a new cause of action for damages.[l] An early leading decision is *Martin v. Herzog*, 126 N.E. 814, 815 (N.Y. 1920), in which Judge Cardozo found contributory negligence as a matter of law in plaintiff's failure to have lights on his car, as required by New York's Highway Law. "We think the unexcused omission of the statutory signals is more than some evidence of negligence. It *is* negligence in itself. * * * By the very terms of the hypothesis, to omit, willfully or heedlessly, the safeguards prescribed by law for the benefit of another that he may be preserved in life or limb, is to fall short of the standard of diligence to which those who live in organized society are under a duty to conform."

In *Clinkscales v. Carver*, 136 P.2d 777 (Cal. 1943), defendant ran a stop sign and crashed into plaintiff. The defendant could not have been prosecuted criminally, because the stop sign had been set up under an ordinance which had never become effective since it was not properly published. Justice Traynor still upheld per se negligence. The significance of the statute lay, not in its legal force, but in its "formulation of a standard of conduct which the court adopts in the determination of [civil] liability. * * * When a legislative body has generalized a standard from the experience of the community and prohibits conduct that is likely to cause harm, the court accepts the formulated standards and applies them."

Federal courts generally do not create common law in the same way state courts do, but they have grappled with the question of creating standards of conduct from criminal or mandatory statutes. In *Texas and Pacific Ry. v. Rigsby*, 241 U.S. 33, 39 (1916), the Court held that an employee switchman could sue the defendant railroad for injuries sustained when he fell off a train due to defects in the "grab irons" (handholds) on the side of the train. Federal relief was based on the railroad's violation of the Safety Appliance Act of 1893, as amended in 1910. Although the Act itself did not provide the worker with a cause of action, the Court inferred one from the statutory purpose to promote the safety of employees. "A disregard of the command of the statute is a wrongful act, and where it results in damage to one of the class for whose

---

k. Traynor, *Statutes Revolving in Common-Law Orbits*, 17 Cath. U.L. Rev. 401, 421 (1968).

l. See Harvey Perlman, *Thoughts on the Role of Legislation in Tort Cases*, 36 Willamette L. Rev. 813 (2000); Robert Williams, *Statutes as Sources of Law Beyond Their Terms in Common-Law Cases*, 50 Geo. Wash. L. Rev. 554, 570–80 (1982); Note, *The Use of Criminal Statutes in the Creation of New Torts*, 48 Colum. L. Rev. 456 (1948).

especial benefit the statute was enacted, the right to recover damages from the party in default is implied," reasoned the Court. How is *Rigsby*'s treatment of the federal statute different from Judge Cardozo's treatment of the state statute in *Herzog*? For the development of the federal implied cause of action line of cases, see Chapter 9, § 1B.

(b) *The Uniform Commercial Code (UCC).* The UCC encourages decision-makers to apply its policies by analogy to unprovided for situations and to apply the Code liberally according to its rationale, see U.C.C. §§ 1–102, Comment 1; 2–313, Comment 2, and legal scholars have eagerly urged this civil law approach.[m] For example, the Third Circuit in *Vitex Mfg. Corp. v. Caribtex Corp.*, 377 F.2d 795, 799 (3d Cir. 1967), relied on the damages provisions of Article Two to set the recovery for breach of a service contract (not covered by the Code), "because it embodies the foremost modern legal thought concerning commercial transactions." The UCC expressly refuses to cover service contracts — should that be reason not to follow its principles in such cases? Consider Chief Justice Traynor's position that the Code's "authority" derives from its being "the culmination of years of scholarly work," drafted by impartial experts beholden to no one, criticized at open meetings of the ALI and elsewhere, and closely checked against existing law and commercial customs.[n]

The Code has had a particularly enthusiastic reception at the federal level, particularly in molding the law of government contracts, one aspect of federal common law. A leading opinion is that of Judge Friendly, in *United States v. Wegematic Corp.*, 360 F.2d 674, 676 (2d Cir. 1966), which applied § 2–615 (the impracticability section) to government contracts:

> We find persuasive the defendant's suggestion of looking to the Uniform Commercial Code as a source for the "federal" law of sales. The Code has been adopted by Congress for the District of Columbia, has been enacted in over forty states, and is thus well on its way to becoming a truly national law of commerce, which, as Judge L. Hand said of the Negotiable Instruments Law, is "more complete and more certain, than any other which can conceivably be drawn from those sources of 'general law' to which we were accustomed to resort in the days of *Swift v. Tyson.*" When the states have gone so far in achieving the desirable goal of a uniform law governing commercial transactions, it would be a distinct disservice to insist on a different one for the segment of commerce, important but still small in relation to the total, consisting of transactions with the United States.

See *In re Yale Express Sys., Inc.*, 370 F.2d 433, 437–38 (2d Cir. 1966) (applying UCC as a source for the formulation of analogous rules for federal bankruptcy law).

(c) *Property Matters.* "In matters involving property, statutory rules have been adopted by analogy as principles of common law and equity. Among

---

m. See, e.g., Mitchell Franklin, *On the Legal Method of the Uniform Commercial Code*, 16 Law & Contemp. Prob. 330 (1951); Note, *The Uniform Commercial Code as a Premise for Judicial Reasoning*, 65 Colum. L. Rev. 880 (1965).

n. Traynor, *supra*, at 424.

them are the adoption by analogy of statutes which apply to realty, in cases which involve personalty," and so forth.[o] One of the cases discussed is *Karr v. Robinson*, 173 A. 584 (Md. 1934), which involved a testator who failed to change his will after the birth of his child. Although Maryland made no provision for this situation, almost all other English-speaking jurisdictions provided for the child to inherit (either by treating the child's birth as a revocation of the will or by imputing new terms into the will). The Maryland Court of Appeals followed the principle underlying the legislation of the other states, and the child inherited. How is this case like *Moragne*? Consider the next note.

2. *Equal Protection Analysis Applied to* Moragne. Given Moragne's unique predicament — under almost any other circumstances and in any other state she would have had an unseaworthiness cause of action — would it have been an unconstitutional denial of equal protection if the law denied her a wrongful death recovery? Consider the following analysis:

> Under our traditional [equal protection] view, underinclusive legislation will be invalidated unless some reasonable justification can be perceived for the legislature's failure to extend the benefits or burdens of that legislation to others who would appear to be similarly situated with respect to the legislation's purpose. But under civil law methodology, the benefits or burdens of a particular piece or course of legislation will be extended to those similarly situated, unless it can be shown that there is no justification for analogous treatment because no sound analogy itself exists.[p]

This commentary argues that there is a difference of presumption: Common law courts will presume that the legislature excluded the class for a valid reason and the court will try to figure out a valid reason so that the exclusion can be upheld, whereas a civil law court will presume that the legislature intended all the logical consequences following from the specific legislative formulation.

Does equal protection analysis support the result in *Moragne*? If the decedent had been a truck driver, the surviving spouse would only have received worker's compensation damages (at most), since assumedly no one was negligent under the facts of the case. Viewed this way, isn't *Moragne* itself anachronistic in rendering maritime employers strictly liable for full wrongful death damages in situations where most employer liability would be defined by worker's compensation laws?[q]

Based on *Moragne* and similar cases, some states will look at statutes not only as specific mandates, but also as sources of policy which "carr[y] significance beyond the particular scope of each of the statutes involved."

---

o. William Page, *Statutes as Common Law Principles*, 1944 Wis. L. Rev. 175, 208.

p. Note, *The Legitimacy of Civil Law Reasoning in the Common Law: Justice Harlan's Contribution*, 82 Yale L.J. 258, 273 (1972).

q. See Richard Posner, *Legal Formalism, Legal Realism and the Interpretation of Statutes and the Constitution*, 37 Case W. Res. L. Rev. 179, 201–03 (1987).

Boston Housing Auth. v. Hemingway, 293 N.E.2d 831, 840 (Mass. 1973).[r] Other states, such as California, had already moved in this direction before *Moragne*. Nonetheless, we know of no flood of decisions following the methodology of *Moragne*. Are there good reasons to expect that in most instances a limited statutory ambit should preclude courts from applying the statute in analogous circumstances? Could it be that many attorneys miss the argument that statutes may be sources of principles beyond their terms?

3. *Stare de Statute.* In *Moragne*, the Supreme Court used statutory developments as authority for overruling a prior decision. Similarly, legislatures may use prior statutes as the basis for drafting new ones. Professor Frank Horack, *The Common Law of Legislation*, 23 Iowa L. Rev. 41, 41–43 (1937), describes this process as "Stare de Statute" and explains:

> The function of precedent in judge-made law has been discussed elaborately; its similar function in legislation has been ignored. Nevertheless, legislation, like judge-made law, follows precedent. * * *

> Statutory precedent grows as case-precedent grows. First, someone bolder than the rest marks a new course. If the course appears satisfactory, others follow. Legal science calls this doctrine *stare decisis*. Legislative process is similar. For example, the common-law rule prior to legislative change was that the operator of an automobile owed a duty to an invited guest to exercise due care to protect the guest from unreasonable danger of injury. A few states limited the operator's liability to "gross negligence." When this seemed to provide an undesirable stimulus to hitchhiking and to assist collusion between guest and host for the recovery of insurance, legislative change was thought to be desirable. Connecticut adopted a statute relieving the operator from liability to a guest, except for "wilful or wanton conduct." Twenty-three states followed that lead. Described in juristic language, the legislatures have followed the rules of precedent. In popular language, the statute has been copied. The result is the same.

Problems in the Wake of Moragne

"Over the past three decades, Justice Harlan's opinion in *Moragne* has come to occupy an important place within the Supreme Court's canon. Generations of law students have studied *Moragne* for its scholarly discussion of legal process and the role of precedent. But before those students reach these abstract questions, their professors have no doubt tormented them by asking a seemingly simple question that defies a simple answer: What, precisely, is the holding of *Moragne*?" *Garris* v. *Norfolk Shipbuilding & Drydock Corpora-*

---

r. Examples of post-*Moragne* modification of the common law in light of principles reflected in statutes include the decisions of state courts to abolish the common law cause of action for alienation of affections in light of the statutes in other states that have done away with the tort. See Eugene Volokh, *The Mechanisms of the Slippery Slope*, 116 Harv. L. Rev. 1026, 1083 & n. 167 (2003). For a discussion of recent developments in New Zealand common law using statutes as sources of principles, see Gehan Gunasekara & Alexandra Sims, *Statutory Trends and the 'Genetic Modification' of the Common Law: Company Law as a Paradigm*, 26 Statute L. Rev. 82 (2005).

tion, 210 F.3d 209, 222–23 (4th Cir. 2000) (Hall, J., concurring in the judgment), *aff'd*, 532 U.S. 811 (2001).

Problem 6–1. A longshoreman died as a result of injuries suffered while working aboard a vessel in state territorial waters. In a *Moragne* wrongful death action based on unseaworthiness, may decedent's dependents recover for their loss of society (that is, their loss of decedent's love, affection, companionship, etc.)? The Death on the High Seas Act (DOHSA) limits recovery to "a fair and just compensation for the *pecuniary* loss sustained by the persons for whose benefit the suit is brought," 46 U.S.C. § 762, and longstanding precedent has held that DOHSA does not allow recovery for loss of society. Should recovery in a *Moragne* action for unseaworthiness within the territorial waters be similarly limited? See *Sea-Land Services v. Gaudet*, 414 U.S. 573 (1974).

Problem 6–2. Assume that the Court in *Gaudet*, discussed in Problem 6–1, held that loss of society is recoverable because that element of damages was recoverable in the clear majority of the states and because recovery was favored by "the humanitarian policy of the maritime law." Assume that the Court refused to allow recovery for the dependents' mental grief or anguish, however. In an action brought for a wrongful death that occurred in territorial waters, may decedent's dependents recover for mental anguish and grief if the state wrongful death statute generally allows such recovery, or is the state statute preempted by the general federal law under *Moragne*, in which case under *Gaudet* there can be no recovery for mental anguish and grief? See *In re S/S Helena*, 529 F.2d 744 (5th Cir. 1976) (Wisdom, J.).

Problem 6–3. After *Gaudet*, assume that an action is brought for a wrongful death that occurred on the High Seas. Should the court conceptualize the wrongful death action as a *Moragne* action (and thus allow recovery for loss of society under *Gaudet*), or should it conceptualize it as a DOHSA action (and therefore deny recovery for loss of society)? See *Mobil Oil Co. v. Higginbotham*, 436 U.S. 618 (1978). Cf. *Dooley v. Korean Air Lines*, 524 U.S. 116 (1998) (concerning whether to create, under general maritime law, a survival action for pre-death pain and suffering of victims of airline tragedies or instead limit recovery to the terms of DOHSA).

Problem 6–4. Assume that the Court in *Higginbotham*, discussed in Problem 6–3, held that loss of society was not recoverable in that case. After this decision, in an action for wrongful death in the territorial waters resulting from negligence that is brought under the Jones Act, may decedent's dependents recover loss of society? Prior to *Moragne, Gaudet*, and *Higginbotham*, it was settled that only pecuniary loss was recoverable in a Jones Act death action. How should a lower court rule in this new case? See *Ivy v. Security Barge Lines, Inc.*, 606 F.2d 524 (5th Cir. 1979) (en banc) (Rubin, J.).

Problem 6–5. Assume that the Court in *Higginbotham*, discussed in Problem 6–3, held that loss of society was not recoverable. After this decision, in an action for wrongful death on the High Seas, may decedent's dependents bring their action under a state wrongful death statute that allows recovery for nonpecuniary loss, or are such state statutes preempted by DOHSA? In answering this question, note that § 7 of DOHSA provides that "[t]he provisions of any state statute giving or regulating rights of action or remedies for death shall not be affected by this chapter." See *Offshore Logistics v. Tallentire*, 477 U.S. 207 (1986), reversing 754 F.2d 1274 (5th Cir. 1985).

Problem 6–6. Assume that (a) the Court in *Higginbotham*, discussed in Problem 6–3, held that there was no *Moragne* cause of action for death on the high seas; (b) the court of appeals in *Ivy*, discussed in Problem 6–4, held that the survivors of a *seaman* who died within territorial waters do not have a *Moragne-Gaudet* cause of action for loss of society; and (c) Congress amends the Longshore and Harbor Workers' Compensation Act to bar any recovery from shipowners for the death or injury to a *longshore* or *harbor worker* resulting from breach of the duty of unseaworthiness (see 86 Stat. 1251, codified at 33 U.S.C. §§ 901–950). After all this occurs, the estate of a *seaman* killed within territorial waters brings a *Moragne-Gaudet* action for wrongful death due to breach of the duty of unseaworthiness and seeks recovery for loss of society. Will the Court allow this cause of action? If so, should damages for loss of society be recoverable? See *Miles v. Apex Marine Corp.*, 498 U.S. 19 (1990).

Problem 6–7. Assume that the Court in *Tallentire* and in *Miles* refused to allow the recovery of nonpecuniary loss, in part on the rationale that the common law recovery under *Moragne* should not exceed the amount of recovery that would be available under the express terms of DOHSA and the Jones Act if those statutes applied. Now suppose a *nonseaworker* is killed in state waters. In this case, a 12-year-old child was killed in a jet ski accident in state waters, and her family sued the manufacturer, seeking to apply state wrongful death and survival statutes. As *Moragne* indicated, historically the federal courts routinely applied these statutes to deaths in territorial waters to soften the harshness of *The Harrisburg* rule, and this approach worked fairly well until the creation of the of unseaworthiness, which some state courts (as the Florida courts did in *Moragne*) held were not within the scope of their wrongful death and survival statutes. The manufacturer argues that *Moragne* created a uniform federal approach to wrongful death on the waters that preempts the application of state law; thus, the family cannot recover nonpecuniary loss. What should the family argue? Who should win? See *Yamaha Motor Corp., U.S.A. v. Calhoun*, 516 U.S. 199 (1996).

Problem 6–8. A case arises with facts similar to *Moragne* except that the survivors of the person who died as the result of injuries in state territorial waters wish to state a claim in general federal maritime law for negligence, not unseaworthiness. (The decedent had been repairing a ship when injured, and thus was not a seaman (so the Jones Act did not apply).) Because this is not a hard problem, we will give you the answer: had the worker lived, he would have had a general maritime law cause of action for negligence; had he died, his survivors would have had a cause of action for unseaworthiness (*Moragne*), and so it only made sense to allow his survivors a cause of action for wrongful death negligence. See *Norfolk Shipbuilding & Drydock Corp. v. Garris*, 532 U.S. 811 (2001). We call it to your attention because the majority opinion states: "Because of Congress's extensive involvement in legislating causes of action for maritime personal injuries, it will be the better course, in many cases that assert new claims beyond what those statutes ... allow, to leave further development to Congress." Justice Ginsburg, joined by Justices Souter and Breyer, objected to this language on the ground that *Moragne*

> tugs in the opposite direction. Inspecting the relevant legislation, the Court in *Moragne* found no measures counseling against the judicial elaboration of general maritime law there advanced. See *Moragne* ("Where death is caused by the breach of a duty imposed by federal maritime law, Congress has established a policy favoring recovery in the absence of a legislative direction to except a particular class of cases."). In accord with *Moragne*, I see development of the law in admiralty as a shared venture in which "federal common lawmaking" does not stand still, but "harmonize[s] with the enactments of Congress in the field." (Quoting *Moragne*).

Is Justice Ginsburg correct in her sense of *Moragne*? Even if so, is the majority's language truer to the more recent cases cited in these Problems?

More on the Interplay of Statutes and the Common Law: Problems on the Employment-at-Will Doctrine

A fundamental principle of the common law provided that, unless there was a provision to the contrary in the employment contract, an employer could discharge an employee for any reason. This is called the "employment-at-will doctrine." Since World War II, numerous federal and state statutes have overridden this doctrine by providing employees with protections against discharge from employment on certain grounds, such as race or sex (Title VII of the 1964 Civil Rights Act being a prominent example, see Chapter 1). The dull-headed lawyer will assume that, unless these statutes squarely apply to a set of facts, the employment-at-will doctrine remains the rule. The clever lawyer will perceive that the method of *Moragne* provides an argument that, even where these statutes do not apply, they indicate a shift in public values that could — and perhaps should — inform common law evolution, making the employment-at-will doctrine no longer sacrosanct. The sophisticated lawyer will understand that the problem can involve a challenging question of assessing the appropriate lawmaking roles of the legislature and the courts. Consider the following examples, which hypothetically arise in the State of Edley, one of the states of the United States.

Problem 6–9. Small Architecture Firm (SAF) fired Susan Jones from her job as receptionist, secretary, and bookkeeper because she was pregnant. The Edley statute that is otherwise on point — the state Fair Employment Practices Act, which explicitly forbids discharge on account of pregnancy — also is explicit in stating that it applies only to employers with five or more employees, and SAF has always had only two employees (as well as three principals, the architects who are officers of the limited liability corporation). Title VII, which as amended by the federal Pregnancy Discrimination Act also forbids discharge on account of pregnancy, applies only to employers with fifteen or more employees. How should Jones's attorney make the case that the state courts should grant relief to her nonetheless? How should counsel for SAF respond? What should the Edley Supreme Court do? Compare *Thibodeau v. Design Group One Architects, LLC*, 260 Conn. 691, 802 A.2d 731 (2002) with *id.*, 802 A.2d at 747–53 (Vertefeuille, J., joined by Norcott, J., dissenting), and with the opinion that was reversed (64 Conn. App. 573, 781 A.2d 363 (2001)).

Problem 6–10. Small Firm (SF) declined to hire John Smith. Smith believes that it was because of his race. SF has only four employees. Would the arguments for and against creating a common law cause of action for Smith be different in any meaningful way from the arguments in Problem 6–9?

Problem 6–11. Title VII and many state fair employment practices statutes contain anti-retaliation provisions. For example, if an employee files a sex discrimination complaint with the state fair employment practices board against her employer and the employer retaliates by firing her, the firing is a violation of the Fair Employment Practices Act even if the underlying claim of sex discrimination turns out to be unfounded.

Frank Thomas works at Big Factory (BF), which employs several hundred persons. He believes that the working conditions are unsafe and in violation of the Edley Occupational Safety Act (OSA), which establishes workplace safety rules. Thomas files a complaint with the Edley Occupational Safety Commission, the agency that enforces the statute, alerting it to the perceived problems and requesting a safety inspection. In retaliation, BF fires him. OSA contains no provision making such a retaliatory discharge a violation of state law. Should the Edley Supreme Court follow the employment-at-will doctrine and uphold the discharge, or create a common law cause of action for retaliatory discharge even though the statute fails to do that?

Problems 6–3 and 6–4 deal with old statutes that are no longer consistent with the common law landscape (they provide recovery only for pecuniary loss resulting from wrongful death, while the common law now also recognizes recovery for such nonpecuniary matters as loss of society). When adopted, the statutes were progressive, providing rights beyond those found in the common law; now, after years of legislative failure to amend them in light of common law developments, the statutes are arguably obsolescent. In these Problems, the courts could have adopted a work-around by creating a common law remedy to supplement the statutory remedies, though that would have raised sensitive questions of the relationship of the judiciary and the legislature. But sometimes this work-around seems precluded by the general notion that statutes are superior to the common law. For example, suppose that a workers' compensation statute states that it provides the sole remedy for workplace injury (thereby expressly preempting the common law). Suppose further that the statutory schedule of recovery for workplace injury has not been updated for a long time and is completely out of whack with what a common law recovery would provide (e.g., if it provides that the loss of a limb is compensated by the payment of $10,000). Short of declaring the statute unconstitutional on some ground or another, it would seem that the courts have no option but to apply the statute as written. But consider the following proposal.

GUIDO CALABRESI
A COMMON LAW FOR THE AGE OF STATUTES
5–7, 82 (1982)[*]

This legal world has totally changed. The peculiarly American way of achieving continuity and change has fallen apart for reasons that are too long and complex to be discussed in detail now. In part they have to do with the perceived need for laws that are either more structured or more immediate than could be afforded by judicial decisions. The slow, unsystematic, and organic quality of common law change made it clearly unsuitable to many legal demands of the welfare state. At the same time, the speed with which perceived economic crises have followed upon economic crises has brought forth legislative responses even in areas where the common law might have been capable of making the necessary adjustments. Be that as it may, starting with the Progressive Era but with increasing rapidity since the New Deal, we have become a nation governed by written laws.

Moreover, unlike earlier codifications of law, which were so general that common law courts could continue to act pretty much as they always had, the new breed of statutes were specific, detailed, and "well drafted." Again, unlike the codes, which were compilations of the common law, the new statutes were frequently meant to be the primary source of law. Courts, limited to honest interpretations of these statutes and committed to legislative supremacy, soon enough began to give them the authority they claimed for themselves.

When these laws were new and functional, so that they represented in a sense the majority and its needs, the change presented few fundamental problems. Soon, however, these laws, like all laws, became middle-aged. They no longer served current needs or represented current majorities. Changed circumstances, or newer statutory and common law developments, rendered some statutes inconsistent with a new social or legal topography. Others were oddities when passed (in the throes of a crisis or, perhaps, in an experimental spirit that started no new trend in the law). Still others became increasingly inconsistent with new constitutional developments without, for all that, actually becoming unconstitutional. Despite this inconsistency with the legal landscape, however, such statutes remained effective and continued to govern important areas of social concern, because getting a statute enacted is much easier than getting it revised. They remained effective, even though some of them at least could not have been reenacted and thus could be said to lack current majoritarian support; checks and balances still worked, and interests served by these outdated laws could successfully block their amendment or repeal.

All this led to a peculiar dilemma for the common law courts. America's view of law is still founded on the traditional paradigm I have just described. Judges have been taught to honor legislative supremacy and to leave untouched all constitutionally valid statutes, but they have also been trained to think of the

---

*. Reprinted by permission of the publisher from A COMMON LAW FOR THE AGE OF STATUTES by Guido Calabresi, pp. 5-7, 82, Cambridge, Mass.: Harvard University Press, Copyright © 1982 by the President and Fellows of Harvard College.

law as functional, as responsive to current needs and current majorities, and as abhorring discriminations, special treatments, and inconsistencies not required by current majorities. They have been taught, and have come to believe, that they have a crucial role to play in keeping the law functional and that the persistence of outdated rules is, to some extent, their responsibility. The common law judicial-legislative balance permitted them to honor legislative supremacy and keep the law functional. Today doing both no longer seems possible.

Faced with this dilemma, it is little wonder that the least willful of judges have responded to their task with open aversion, but have enforced time-worn interpretations of even more time-worn laws. Other judges have acted more aggressively and have used the Constitution or farfetched interpretations to make obsolete laws functional. Not surprisingly, as more judges have taken this road, concern has increased. I would argue that much of the current criticism of judicial activism, and of our judicial system generally, can be traced to the rather desperate responses of our courts to a multitude of obsolete statutes in the face of the manifest incapacity of legislatures to keep those statutes up to date. * * *

A Hypothetical Doctrine

I will start out by suggesting what at first sounds like a new approach, but which in fact is not much different from what courts have been doing for years through various subterfuges. * * * My object throughout is to examine the possibility of defining a modern version of what can be described as the traditional legislative-judicial balance, on the assumption that the aim of such a balance is the thoughtful allocation of the burden of inertia in a system of checks and balances which seeks both continuity and change.

To state the approach in summary form is easy; to outline, let alone fill out, its workings is far more difficult. So I will state the approach as a hypothesis. Let us suppose that common law courts have the power to treat statutes in precisely the same way that they treat the common law. They can (without resort to constitutions or passive virtues or strained interpretations) alter a written law or some part of it in the same way (and with the same reluctance) in which they can modify or abandon a common law doctrine or even a whole complex set of interrelated doctrines. They can use this power either to make changes themselves or, by threatening to use the power, to induce legislatures to act. Let us not, for the moment, concern ourselves with the question of whether this authority has been given explicitly to the courts by the legislatures or has been asserted independently by the courts themselves, in a common law way. ("We have, in fact, been doing this indirectly, it is time we said what we were doing and, so to speak, gave a name and a legitimacy to what has simply grown to be the law.")

NOTES ON THE CALABRESI PROPOSAL THAT COURTS HAVE THE POWER TO OVERRULE STATUTES

1. *Details of the Calabresi Proposal.* Later in his book (pages 120–41), Calabresi lays out his proposed approach in greater detail. Courts should only

deal in areas of legislative inertia and should only overturn statutes which have clearly lost their original majoritarian support; a clear loss of support is correlated to whether the statute still "fits" into the legal landscape of statutes, judicial decisions, administrative rules and adjudications. Calabresi favors a "retentionist bias" in his test: The statute remains in force unless it is quite clear that it is out-of-sync with other sources of law. Questions relevant to that determination include the following:

* Has the common law surrounding the statute so changed that the statute no longer makes sense, or fits in? Has the constitutional terrain relevant to the statute changed?

* Have other statutes been passed within the state which indicate a shifting approach to the same, or a similar, problem? Within other states?

* Has there been a sufficient accretion of scholarly criticism of the bases of the rule? Empirical studies demonstrating the invalidity of its assumptions? Indications that the public values implicit in the statute have changed?

If the legal terrain has changed decisively and clearly, Calabresi then would decide whether the statute should be overturned. Some specific factors to be considered:

* *Age of the Statute.* Recent statutes deserve a presumption of majoritarian support. The older the statute, the less likely the continued support.

* *Specifically Oriented Laws.* If a statute was enacted in response to a crisis or some specific problem, it will age more rapidly. The retentionist bias applies less strongly here. On the other hand, a systematic codification or complex statutory scheme worked out over a period of years deserves greater deference.

* *Constitutional Doubts.* Constitutional doubts about the statute create a revisionist bias. To the extent that a law trenches on fundamental concerns and rights, there should be greater willingness to abandon it as its policies fade.

Other factors specific to certain types of laws might facilitate revision: Did the statute codify a common law rule that has changed? Has part of the statute's original uniformity already been lost? Has the original interest-group compromise that produced the statute been lost? Has a specific monetary figure been severely and unintentionally attenuated by inflation?

2. *The Legitimacy of the Proposal.* Calabresi recognizes that legitimacy is the obvious problem with his proposal. His main level of response is that judicial overruling of statutes is not significantly countermajoritarian. *Id.* at 91–119. The traditional explanation for judicial lawmaking is that courts are loyal to principles over politics (reasoned elaboration). Principles are found by judges in the legal landscape, and Calabresi argues that the legal terrain (statutes, cases, the Constitution, custom) is a good approximation of the "popular will." To the extent, therefore, that old statutes have fallen away from the shifting legal terrain, they no longer "represent" the popular will and, therefore, ought to be annulled. Outdated statutes are no more entitled to

deference than outdated judicial precedents, because "[i]t is the artesian source of the rule that entitles it to a long-run conservative bias in a democratic polity, rather than the immediate ground or institution from which it springs." *Id.* at 104. Should the legislature be the only institution capable of removing outdated authorities (case and statute law)? No, because that creates too much of a conservative bias in our government, and because courts are better equipped by training and temperament to make the judgments about "fit" into "legal landscapes" than legislatures are. In any event, the legislature remains "formally" supreme, as it can simply reenact the invalidated statute.

A more subtle level of response is Calabresi's claim that his proposal has well-entrenched "antecedents" — jurisprudential ancestors which are now accepted by most legal scholars. Consider whether these antecedents support Calabresi's approach, or suggest other ways of updating statutes:

a. *The Pomeroy Precept and the Restaters.* Professor Pomeroy's flexible approach to interpreting the California Civil Code has been summarized: "[E]xcept in those instances where [the Code's] language clearly and unequivocally discloses an intention to depart from, alter, or abrogate the common-law rule concerning a particular subject matter, a section of the Code purporting to embody such doctrine or rule will be construed in light of common-law decisions on the same subject." *In re Elizalde's Estate*, 188 P. 560 (Cal. 1920). Calabresi also relies on the American Law Institute's effort to "restate" the law to create integrated, rational policy. But in its constitution, the American Law Institute explicitly stated that "[w]here the change proposed in the restatement is a change in the present statute law, the mere adoption of the principles set forth in the restatement as a guide to courts would not warrant the courts disregarding the statute."[s]

b. *Equity of the Statute.* Calabresi's second antecedent is Dean Landis's revival of the civil law idea of "equity of the statute." Landis wanted to expand the force of statutes beyond their formal setting by treating them as precedential principles — but he never sought to deny the formal power of statutes.[t] Would Justice Harlan's *Moragne* approach be just as appropriate had *The Harrisburg* been a federal statute? See Problems 6–3 and 6–4, *supra*.

c. *The Legal Process School.* Calabresi claims that Hart and Sacks' "open recognition that courts not only make law but that they also do and should update statutes, broke down simplistic barriers between written law and judicial roles." Calabresi, *supra*, at 88. Alexander Bickel and Harry Wellington (students of Hart) argued for a "passive virtues" approach, in which courts ought not to go out of their way to create conflict with the other branches of government unless they absolutely have to (as in *Brown v. Board of Education*). Calabresi responds: Judicial manipulation through interpretation and strained constitutional doctrine is less desirable than more candid approaches because the former delays real and decisive change and creates

---

s. 1 ALI Procs. 1, 48–49 (1923).

t. Landis, *Statutes as Sources of Law*, in *Harvard Legal Essays* 213 (1934) (discussed *supra*).

precedents which can be misunderstood or overgeneralized by uncomprehending lower court judges. *Id.* at 178–80.

3. *Limits on the Application of the Calabresi Proposal.* In a book review, Archibald Cox notes that the approach seems to work best in "areas in which the law has long been predominantly judge-made and statutes, except for codifications, are pretty much interstitial."[u] In these traditionally judge-law areas, there is substantial "legal terrain" easily accessible to judges, because they created most of it. Moreover, while these areas involve just as many value choices as more novel public legislation, the legal and political community is more accustomed to judicial latitude there. But how, asks Professor Cox, would the proposal deal with elderly municipal rent-control laws?

> The court would be required first to compare current conditions in the housing market with conditions when the ordinance was adopted; then, if in the judges' opinion conditions had changed sufficiently, the court would determine whether the ordinance was so inconsistent with "the context of a predominantly 'free price' society" as to be nullified as obsolete. Is this the same kind of landscape as the court could examine in the contributory negligence case? A traditionalist would describe one as a body of law and the other as a body of economic data and policy.

C. THE POST-LEGAL PROCESS ERA, 1974–?

In addition to *Moragne*, legal process theory is strongly reflected in *Weber* and *Johnson* (Chapter 1), *Powell v. McCormack* and *Buckley v. Valeo* (Chapter 2), Speech and Debate Clause cases such as *Gravel* and *Helstoski* (Chapter 3), *Mow Sun Wong* (Chapter 4), and many cases excerpted later in the book (especially in the coverage of statutory interpretation in Chapters 7 and 8). Key to all these decisions are the legal process assumptions that law is purposive and should be applied to subserve its ultimate as well as particular purposes; the Court should be deferential to the political branches of our government and should be protective of their institutional autonomy; any branch of government is on weakest ground when it proceeds in ways that are procedurally irregular or inconsistent with fundamental principles and policies. Although legal process theory was the dominant mode of thinking about law from the 1940s to the 1960s, since the 1970s it has been challenged by law and economics and critical theory, both of which posit substantive rather than procedural visions for the polity. Legal process theory remains fundamentally important and perhaps even preeminent, but it has fragmented, partly in response to these new challenges. In this part we shall outline different visions of legisprudence that compete for attention in the post-legal process era.[v] We shall try to make the discussion more concrete by applying it to the Case of the Nuclear Protesters (*Warshow*), *Moragne*, and the Calabresi proposal.

---

u. Book Review, 70 Calif. L. Rev. 1463, 1467 (1982).

v. This account is derived from William Eskridge, Jr. & Philip Frickey, *Legislation Scholarship and Pedagogy in the Post-Legal Process Era*, 48 U. Pitt. L. Rev. 691 (1987).

1. *Law and Economics Applied to Legislation*

Starting with the typical economic assumption that people are rational self-maximizers, one can imagine the following outline of a law-and-economics legisprudence, one quite distinct from the legal process approach.[w] Rational people will form a social contract to avoid market failures (like feuds) occurring in the state of nature and to solve collective action problems. The latter simply means that certain projects, like building roads, cannot easily be done by individual action or even private contracting and therefore require state coordination. The goal of the state is, in short, to adopt measures that improve the overall efficiency of the body politick. State actions should be evaluated according to *ex ante* (rather than *ex post*) criteria: Does this rule interfere with (or create incentives that interfere with) the operation of the efficiently operating market?

An economics-oriented legisprudence would criticize *Moragne* for considering only issues of coherence (an *ex post* perspective) and slighting issues of efficiency (an *ex ante* perspective). There is room to doubt whether a new wrongful death action for the strict liability tort of unseaworthiness provides any useful incentive for the shipowner, who is liable for damages under unseaworthiness even if not negligent. Indeed, the new *Moragne* cause of action might be counterproductive, not only by raising shipowners' costs, but also by pressing owners to be more cautious than they should be because of the strict liability feature of the tort. The new action might be useful to provide relief for survivors, but law and economics suggests that the market might so provide, through insurance and the like. Is there any reason to believe that insurance does not cover this problem adequately?

Interestingly, law and economics would take a more liberal approach to the Case of the Nuclear Protesters. An economist would analyze Vermont Yankee's claims of private property trespass and Warshow's necessity defense functionally. From a utilitarian perspective, Vermont Yankee's property rights do not protect it against protests if

$$R \times C > I$$

where R = risk of disaster at the plant that is not caught by the regulators (probably small but not zero); C = cost of the disaster (extremely high for a nuclear one); and I = injury suffered by the plant and third parties on account of the protest. Thus a law and economics approach would reject the majority opinion in *Warshow* and would be open to the arguments of the dissent, though the economist would criticize Justice Billings for not thinking more clearly in cost-benefit terms and supporting his general point with some empirical evidence.

---

w. See James Buchanan & Gordon Tullock, *The Calculus of Consent* (1962); Dennis Mueller, *Public Choice II* (1991); Frank Easterbrook, *The Supreme Court, 1983 Term — Foreword: The Court and the Economic System*, 98 Harv. L. Rev. 4 (1984); Richard Posner, *Economics, Politics and the Reading of Statutes and the Constitution*, 49 U. Chi. L. Rev. 263 (1982); Richard Posner & David Landes, *The Independent Judiciary in an Interest Group Perspective*, 18 J.L. & Econ. 875 (1975).

Like legal process, law and economics would be interested in structuring the state to ensure that its policies would be efficient. Assuming that democracy is the preferred form of government for this purpose, rational people will not desire a direct democracy, where the people vote on all proposals. Problems with direct democracy include (1) high transactions costs of obtaining agreement of so many people; (2) failure to register voters' "intensity" of preference; and (3) the danger of bad decisions, because participants will generally be poorly informed and temporary and arbitrary majorities might assemble for "rent-seeking" policies (i.e., those distributing wealth to groups without any efficiency justification). The second and third problems can be alleviated by requiring unanimity or a supermajority to make policy, but that greatly increases the magnitude of the first problem.

A sizeable democracy will adopt a "representative" form of government as a partial solution to the problems of direct democracy. The problems of transactions costs, poor information, and intensity of preferences can be greatly ameliorated in the legislature by the use of specialized subgroups, primarily committees. In this construct, the operation of the legislature resembles a market, in which statutes are deals between buyers (interest groups) and sellers (legislators), along the lines suggested by public choice theory. Recall from our discussion of public choice theory in Chapter 1, § 2A2, that laws generally distributing costs and benefits, such as the UCC and criminal laws, do not often stimulate the creation of interest groups in favor of such legislation, because each beneficiary has only a small stake in the benefit. In contrast, the existence of concentrated benefits or costs — subsidies or taxes falling upon a smaller and well-defined group of actors — will tend to stimulate interest group activity, because each beneficiary or cost payer has a substantial stake in the outcome and has both incentive and opportunity to coordinate her efforts with those similarly situated.

The supply pattern in the market for legislation is determined by legislator motivation, which is assumed to be reelection. The legislator prefers "nonconflictual" demand patterns, in which there is substantial consensus among interested persons and groups. Thus, the legislator will want to do nothing if there is organized opposition to legislation (as in concentrated-cost laws) but will be willing to grant subsidies to organized groups paid out of general revenues (concentrated-benefit laws), so long as the general public is largely unaware of what is happening. Unhappily, the legislator cannot always avoid conflictual demand patterns, either because an issue is politically salient or organized groups are on both sides. In that event, the legislator has every incentive to work out some compromise statute that satisfies as many interest groups as possible, or even to delegate the sensitive decisions to agencies.

Under an economic theory, the danger of temporary majorities reemerges as a significant problem with decisionmaking by elected representatives: the polity might end up with too little efficient, public-regarding law, and much too much rent-seeking law. The latter might be reduced by establishing procedural hurdles to legislation, including requirements that two different legislative chambers and an executive officer approve a proposal before it becomes a law, that determined minorities can obstruct proposals that are very harmful to them (e.g., by filibusters or opposition in committee), and that an independent judiciary may strike down unconstitutional laws and mitigate harsh laws by interpreting them to render them less oppressive.

The last point would provide an economic rationale for the Calabresi proposal, which would vest judges with authority to update efficient laws to assure their continued efficacy and perhaps also with authority to weed out laws which turn out to be inefficient or which were rent-seeking all along. An economic response to this argument is that courts might be corrupted by rent-seeking just as legislatures are.[x] Also, once judges have this power to overrule statutes, or even the more limited power to expand statutes as the Court did in *Moragne*, the legislature might be more reluctant to enact statutes in the first place, for fear that a statute embodying a limited political compromise could be judicially transformed into something much broader.[y] This is an example of the "anticipated response" feature of positive political theory, also surveyed in Chapter 1, § 2C1.

2. *Critical Scholarship and Legislation*

The legal process vision of law as reasoned elaboration of legitimate legislative activity was persuasive in the 1950s in part because of society's consensus about what is "reasonable" and who is "legitimate." That consensus shattered in the 1960s, as it became clear that most Americans — women, people of color, gays and lesbians, people living in poverty, non-English-speaking citizens — had not been consulted as to what is reasonable and who is legitimate. When these were heard from in the 1960s, consensus died, and it remained dead for a generation of identity politics. Critical scholars have developed anti-legal process insights into public law out of this experience.[z]

---

x. The arguments in text are related to the old debate whether the common law is a more efficient policymaking mechanism than legislation. It appears not to be. See Gillian Hadfield, *Bias in the Evolution of Legal Rules*, 80 Geo. L.J. 583 (1992); Paul Rubin, *Common Law and Statute Law*, 11 J. Leg. Stud. 205 (1982).

y. For example, suppose a Senator proposes a new federal statute establishing a retirement fund for people who work predominantly on the "high seas." It is a statute much needed to prevent destitution in old age, according to extensive hearings. But the bill is opposed by another Senator, who makes the following argument: "Who knows how much this will cost — especially if courts expand the statute to cover people who work within the coastal waters! Look what the Court did in *Moragne*!" Congress' nervousness about an expansive interpretation of the proposal ultimately kills the bill. If Congress perceives the Court to be an expansive interpreter of good but limited legislation, Congress might be discouraged from enacting such laws altogether. In the long run the best is the enemy of the good.

z. See Catharine MacKinnon, *Feminism Unmodified* (1986); Roberto Unger, *Knowledge and Politics* (1975); Paul Brest, *Interpretation and Interest*, 34 Stan. L. Rev. 765 (1982); Duncan Kennedy, *Form and Substance in Private Law Adjudication*, 89 Harv. L. Rev. 1685 (1976); Richard Parker, *The Past of Constitutional Theory — And Its Future*, 42 Ohio St. L.J. 223, 239–46 (1981); Gary Peller, *The Metaphysics of American Law*, 73 Calif. L. Rev. 1152 (1985); Joseph Singer, *The Player and the Cards: Nihilism and Legal Theory*, 94 Yale L.J. 1 (1984); Mark Tushnet, *Darkness on the Edge of the Town: The Contributions of John Hart Ely to Constitutional Theory*, 89 Yale L.J. 1037 (1980).

Hart and Sacks implicitly claimed that all law, legislative as well as judicial, is (or can be) rational, objective, and neutral. Law and economics scholars assert a dichotomy between rational, objective, neutral efficiency and irrational, subjective, partisan rent-seeking. Critical scholars, in turn, claim that *all* law, legislative as well as judicial, is ultimately arational, subjective, and political; they further claim that the difference between efficient law and rent-seeking (the economists' lodestar) is hard to divine and impossible to apply. Critical scholars have dismissed the Calabresi thesis for this sort of reason. "It is as much a myth that courts can determine whether a statute fit when it was passed, or fits today, as it is a myth that prescient courts can use the perceived values of tomorrow's majority in a value-neutral way. As much as shaping the present by predicting the future, courts will shape the present by interpreting the past."[a]

A more general claim is that the whole "rule of law" idea is incoherent with liberal, pluralist society. In a pluralist society whose members have conflicting desires, a rule of law cannot really be neutral (i.e., avoid making substantive value choices), because then it could not resolve the conflicts among interests in society. Yet once it is admitted that the rule of law is not neutral, one admits that law subordinates the wills of some citizens to the wills of others — which is in tension with the liberal assumption that there is no way to evaluate and prefer the will of some over that of others. This is what was going on in the Case of the Nuclear Protesters: The state was "siding" with the power plant and the economic interests it represented, against the protesters. The legal reasoning was just window-dressing for the court's alignment of its authority with the position of those in power.

Critical scholars would be particularly scornful of Justice Hill's concurring opinion in *Warshow*, which deferred to the legislature's assessment of risks and benefits of nuclear power and used that deference to distance the judges from the power they were wielding. This standard legal process move is illegitimate, because there is not any neutral justification for deference to the legislature. The traditional justification for deference is that the elected legislature represents the majority will better than the nonelected judiciary, but is this factually true? Or normatively meaningful? The vast majority of the electorate is utterly passive and, to the extent they express political preferences, those preferences are so conditioned by their relative ignorance and inequality as to be meaningless. Once elected, legislators are excessively responsive to the monied and the well-organized, to the detriment of groups already disadvantaged in American society. Under these circumstances, what compelling reason is there for courts, or anybody, to defer to legislative policies?

Process theory, furthermore, is structurally biased: It fallaciously assumes that formal access to the political process usually entails meaningful access (which makes it wrong) and diverts attention away from malign power structures and inequality in society (which makes it evil). The mythology of

a. Allan Hutchinson & Derek Morgan, *Calabresian Sunset: Statutes in the Shade*, 82 Colum. L. Rev. 1752, 1772–73 (1982); see David Cole, *Agon at the Agora: Creative Misreadings in the First Amendment Tradition*, 95 Yale L.J. 857 (1986).

societal consent perpetuated by process theory obfuscates the urgency of law reform and pacifies the victims of oppression. As an example of the power of language to create a false consciousness, consider the principle of institutional settlement (explicitly echoed in the *Warshow* concurring opinion), the notion that in order to avoid "disintegrating resort to violence" there must be "regularized and peaceable methods of decision" which are scrupulously adhered to. This principle has traditionally been accepted as noncontroversial, because of its creation of two dichotomies — peace versus violence and order versus disorder — and its association of peace with order. The principle not only asks the reader to prefer peace to violence, the aspect of the principle which establishes its appeal, but further asks citizens to associate violence with disorder and peace with order, which is much more questionable. That is, there is no necessary connection between peace and order. Disorderly but nonviolent protests against the War in Vietnam subserved the cause of peace, while the orderly obedience of thousands of Americans to the morally bankrupt consequences of the legal process contributed to violence. Disorderly but nonviolent protests against racism contributed to the disruption of violent but orderly oppression of blacks in the South. John Warshow's "disorderly" protest was action against the potential "violence" of Vermont Yankee's risky operation, under critical theory.

Some critical scholars insist that traditional pluralism be more thoroughgoing. If legal standards are essentially subjective, political choices, it is important to focus on who makes the political decisions. Many of the inadequacies of the current legal order may be attributable to political decisionmaking by a very narrow elite group. For example, the many traditional restrictions on rape prosecutions (such as the noncriminality of marital rape and requirements of corroborating evidence) cannot be explained by reference to rational and objective criteria. They can best be explained as expressions of a male-oriented view of rape, not surprising since legal decisionmakers were traditionally male. Until recently, the rules of rape law were *not* the rules which would have been created by a community of women and men more sensitive to the degradation of the various forms of sexual oppression. Critical scholars urge rethinking of concepts of representation, perhaps reviving the descriptive theory, in which the legislature's composition mirrors that of society.

Other critical scholars reject the premises of pluralism — that government exists to ensure societal peace and stability, in large part by regulating the clashing interests of individuals and groups in society. Thus they reject the concept that "interests" are exogenous facts and claim that interests are socially constituted and subject to change through politics. Attitudes and values are, similarly, subject to change; and much of the critical agenda is a call to transform our society by alerting it to inhuman modes of oppression and anomie. Hence, some of the critical scholars who have set forth a positive vision of government have urged a redefinition of what "law" does. Law's agenda should not be determinacy, objectivity, or certainty (the legal process, pluralist hallmarks of statutory law), but rather "edification." The law is pulled toward formalism and its concomitant certainty, apparently because of fears that uncertainty about what exactly the law is will leave us without fair means of regulating private conflicts, or even of knowing how to behave, and will encourage predatory conduct by the government and private power centers. Some critical scholars contend that legal rules do not protect us against these horribles and that, in truth, the main value of legal rules is constitutive: The formulation of rules is how we create and express shared values.

3. *The New Legal Processes: Positivism, Pragmatism, Principles*

Legal process theory remains important in American law, but for recent generations of lawyers, process theory has taken on new meanings and nuances. Like Justice Hill in *Warshow*, one group (and by far the largest group among judges) emphasizes the positivist features of process theory: its commitment to neutrality and neutral principles, the principle of institutional settlement, and the importance of vertical continuity (precedent, tradition) in law. This group of thinkers is on the whole preservationist and formalist in its approach to law — seeking to preserve the New Deal regulatory status quo and protecting formal values through procedural requirements (standing, mootness, clear statement rules).[b] Process formalists may well be shocked by the Calabresi proposal, because it vests potentially enormous lawmaking power in courts and would permit the recasting of statutes outside the normal constitutional structure. And such thinkers would even be tempted to quarrel with *Moragne*, which after all did edit "High" out of the Death on the High Seas Act. (We make this point tentatively, since the *Moragne* opinion may be one that all process types would embrace.)

At the other extreme, but still within the legal process tradition, are the progressives, who emphasize law's purposivism, the fidelity owed by officials to reason, and the central role of principle.[c] Common themes tie together these process progressives. One is anti-pluralist: Legislation must be more than the accommodation of exogenously defined interests; lawmaking is a process of value creation that should be informed by theories of justice and fairness. Another theme is that legislation too often fails to achieve this aspiration and that creative lawmaking by courts and agencies is needed to ensure rationality and justice in law. A final theme is the importance of dialogue or conversation as the means by which innovative lawmaking can be validated in a democratic polity and by which the rule of law can best be defended against charges of unfairness or illegitimacy. Calabresi's proposal and Justice Billings' dissent in *Warshow* exemplify this new process tradition.

---

b. Exemplifying process formalism are Robert Bork, *The Tempting of America* (1989); Martin Redish, *The Federal Courts in the Political Order* (1991); Antonin Scalia, *The Rule of Law as a Law of Rules*, 56 U. Chi. L. Rev. 1775 (1989).

c. See Ronald Dworkin, *Law's Empire* (1986); Bruce Ackerman, *The Storrs Lectures: Discovering the Constitution*, 93 Yale L.J. 1013 (1984); Robert Cover, *The Supreme Court, 1982 Term — Foreword: Nomos and Narrative*, 97 Harv. L. Rev. 4 (1983); Owen Fiss, *The Supreme Court, 1978 Term — Foreword: The Forms of Justice*, 93 Harv. L. Rev. 1 (1978); Cass Sunstein, *Interest Groups in American Public Law*, 38 Stan. L. Rev. 29 (1985); Lawrence Tribe, *Constitutional Calculus: Equal Justice or Economic Efficiency?*, 98 Harv. L. Rev. 592, 617 (1985).

The distinction between formalist and progressive process theorists may be captured in Ronald Dworkin's distinction between a pluralist "rulebook community," in which citizens generally agree to obey rules created by the government, and a "community of principle," in which citizens see themselves governed by basic principles, not just political compromises. The latter is a worthier sense of community, Dworkin argues (and many new legal process thinkers would agree), and legislation as well as adjudication must be evaluated by its contribution to the principled integrity of the community. Thus, in Dworkin's ideal community of principle, "integrity in legislation" requires lawmakers to try to make the total set of laws morally coherent. Like justice and fairness, integrity in the law contributes to the sorority/fraternity of the body politick, the moral community that bonds the nation together. The role of courts is to interpret authoritative statements of law (the Constitution, statutes, common law precedents) in light of the underlying principles of the community. In the "hard cases" of statutory interpretation, for example, the best interpretation is the one that is most consonant with the underlying values of society and makes the statute the best statute it can be (within the limitations imposed by the statutory language). Calabresi's proposal is an alternative for enhancing the integrity of Dworkin's community of principle.

In between the process formalists and the progressives lies a centrist group, one which travels under the banner of "pragmatism."[d] These thinkers emphasize the eclectic and instrumental features of the process tradition: Legal reasoning is a grab bag of different techniques, including not just textual analysis, but also sophisticated appreciation of the goals underlying the legal text and the consequences of adopting different interpretations. Law involves a balance between form and substance, tradition and innovation, text and context. Pragmatists tend to agree with *Moragne* as sound and practical, while disagreeing with Calabresi as more clever than cogent. Centrists might be ambivalent about the Case of the Nuclear Protesters. On the one hand, the case should go to the jury, because the community at large should consider the tough issues discussed above. On the other hand, sending such cases to juries is too expensive and provides perverse incentives for future protesters: They get two media soapboxes (the protest plus the jury trial) for the price of one (the penalty for doing the protest).

---

d. Exemplars include Jerry Mashaw, *Bureaucratic Justice* (1983); Richard Posner, *Overcoming Law* (1995); William Eskridge, Jr. & Philip Frickey, *Statutory Interpretation as Practical Reasoning*, 42 Stan. L. Rev. 321 (1990); Martha Minow, *The Supreme Court, 1986 Term — Foreword: Justice Engendered*, 101 Harv. L. Rev. 10 (1987); Francis Mootz III, *The Ontological Basis of Legal Hermeneutics*, 68 B.U.L. Rev. 523 (1988); Margaret Jane Radin, *Reconsidering the Rule of Law*, 69 B.U.L. Rev. 781 (1989); Richard Stewart, *The Reformation of Administrative Law*, 88 Harv. L. Rev. 1669 (1975); Cass Sunstein, *Interpreting Statutes in the Regulatory State*, 103 Harv. L. Rev. 405 (1989).

SECTION 2. LEGISPRUDENCE AND STATUTORY DOCTRINE: VERTICAL VERSUS HORIZONTAL COHERENCE IN STATUTORY LAW

A. INTRODUCTION

Traditional American law emphasized vertical coherence in statutory interpretation. That is, the statutory interpreter demonstrates that her interpretation is coherent with authoritative sources situated in the past: the original intent of the enacting legislature, previous administrative or judicial precedents interpreting the statute, and traditional or customary norms. This was important to the formalism popular at the end of the nineteenth century, for which law's legitimacy rests upon consent, either express (original text and intent) or implied (acceptance over time). The formalists also valorized vertical coherence in order to assure predictability and stability in the law.

The legal realists debunked arguments based upon vertical coherence, arguing descriptively that there was no determinate "past" to which judges could link their current interpretations (vertical sources being manipulable) and then arguing prescriptively that law ought to be present-oriented rather than archaeological. Thus, the realists suggested that statutory interpretation depends more on horizontal coherence, or "consistency with the rest of the law" today.[a] The statutory interpreter demonstrates that her interpretation is coherent with authorities or norms located in the present: the statute's contemporary purposes, other statutes now in effect and their statutory policies, and current values, perhaps even the judge's personal values. Because the realists considered law's legitimacy to be grounded upon present policy needs, they were willing to throw over historical practice.

Although the realist critique revealed the importance of horizontal coherence for law's legitimacy, its cynical attitude was not welcome within the mainstream legal academy or the federal judiciary. Mainstream scholars pragmatically sought ways to reconcile the formal legitimacy and rule of law values subserved by vertical coherence, with the functional legitimacy and efficiency values subserved by horizontal coherence. Legal process thinkers sought to mediate the tension between vertical and horizontal coherence in statutory interpretation. Their challenge was to develop theories that paid due regard to vertical sources and tradition, while serving present needs in statutory interpretation. The key to the legal process resolution was, in our view, the concept of reliance on public law: The formalists were right that law should be predictable, and the citizenry ought to be able to rely on it, but the realists were right that the public interest could override private reliance on traditional rules. Legal process theory adds this to the mix: the public interest itself may involve a reliance upon those rules. During the legal process era, this idea accommodated realist policy thinking, but without requiring great shifts in public law.

---

a. Charles Curtis, *A Better Theory of Legal Interpretation*, 3 Vand. L. Rev. 407, 423 (1950).

Doctrinal debates about stare decisis for statutory precedents, the prospectivity of judicial decisions (both discussed in this Section), and the retroactivity of new statutes (Section 3, *infra*) were carried on within the legal process philosophy during the Warren and Burger Courts, with an emphasis on public reliance as a justification for preserving a status quo bias. Today the debates have moved away somewhat from the legal process synthesis.

B. STARE DECISIS AND STATUTORY PRECEDENTS

Under common law formalist theory, the role of courts is to declare the law and not to change it. The doctrine of stare decisis requires that a court treat prior decisions as presumptively correct. Nineteenth century liberal theory specifically held that private law precedents, involving "vested rights" of contract or property, should almost never be overruled, although the Court had greater discretion to rethink constitutional precedents. See *Smith v. Turner*, 48 U.S. 283, 470 (1849). The same virtually absolute stare decisis applied to decisions interpreting at least some statutes: "After a statute has been settled by judicial construction, the construction becomes, so far as contract rights acquired under it are concerned, as much a part of the statute as the text itself, and a change of decision is to all intents and purposes the same in its effect on contracts as an amendment of the law by means of a legislative enactment," *Douglass v. Pike County*, 101 U.S. 677, 687 (1879), and hence unavailable under traditional premises.

The legal realists argued that judges are not particularly constrained by precedent and that stare decisis should be more of a functional rule of thumb than a formal command. A court is not, and should not be, "inexorably bound by its own precedents, but, in the interest of uniformity of treatment to litigants, and of stability and certainty in the law * * * will follow the rule of law which it has established in earlier cases unless clearly convinced that the rule was originally erroneous or is no longer sound because of changed conditions and that more good than harm would come by departing from precedent."[b]

The realists' willingness to reexamine precedents freely made the mainstream legal community very nervous. Responsive to that nervousness, legal process judges of the 1930s and 1940s suggested functional reasons for something like the old liberal position. Justices Brandeis, Stone, and Frankfurter maintained (in different cases) that the Court's statutory decisions are entitled to extra stare decisis deference, because Congress and not the Court is more institutionally competent to change statutory meaning. Also important was Dean Edward Levi's argument that public as well as private decision-makers rely on statutory precedents, which set a direction for the statute that ought not be unraveled unless unconstitutional. A heightened adherence to stare decisis "marks an essential difference between statutory interpretation on

---

b. J.W. Moore & R.S. Oglebay, *The Supreme Court, Stare Decisis and Law of the Case*, 21 Tex. L. Rev. 514, 539–40 (1943); accord, Justice William Douglas, *Stare Decisis*, 49 Colum. L. Rev. 735 (1949).

the one hand and [common] law and constitutional interpretation on the other."[c] Consider the Brandeis-Levi rule as applied in the following case.

FLOOD v. KUHN
Supreme Court of the United States, 1972
407 U.S. 258, 92 S.Ct. 2099, 32 L.Ed.2d 728

MR. JUSTICE BLACKMUN delivered the opinion of the Court.

[I. *The Game*] It is a century and a quarter since the New York Nine defeated the Knickerbockers 23 to 1 on Hoboken's Elysian Fields June 19, 1846, with Alexander Jay Cartwright as the instigator and the umpire. The teams were amateur, but the contest marked a significant date in baseball's beginnings. That early game led ultimately to the development of professional baseball and its tightly organized structure.

The Cincinnati Red Stockings came into existence in 1869 upon an outpouring of local pride. With only one Cincinnatian on the payroll, this professional team traveled over 11,000 miles that summer, winning 56 games and tying one. Shortly thereafter, on St. Patrick's Day in 1871, the National Association of Professional Baseball Players was founded and the professional league was born.

The ensuing colorful days are well known. The ardent follower and the student of baseball know of General Abner Doubleday; the formation of the National League in 1876; Chicago's supremacy in the first year's competition under the leadership of Al Spalding and with Cap Anson at third base; the formation of the American Association and then of the Union Association in the 1880's; the introduction of Sunday baseball; interleague warfare with cut-rate admission prices and player raiding; the development of the reserve "clause"; the emergence in 1885 of the Brotherhood of Professional Ball Players, and in 1890 of the Players League; the appearance of the American League, or "junior circuit," in 1901, rising from the minor Western Association; the first World Series in 1903, disruption in 1904, and the Series' resumption in 1905; the short-lived Federal League on the majors' scene during World War I years; the troublesome and discouraging episode of the 1919 Series; the home run ball; the shifting of franchises; the expansion of the leagues; the installation in 1965 of the major league draft of potential new players; and the formation of the Major League Baseball Players Association in 1966.[2]

Then there are the many names, celebrated for one reason or another, that have sparked the diamond and its environs and that have provided tinder for recaptured thrills, for reminiscence and comparisons, and for conversation and anticipation in-season and off-season: Ty Cobb, Babe Ruth, Tris Speaker, Walter Johnson, Henry Chadwick, Eddie Collins, Lou Gehrig, Grover

---

c. Levi, *An Introduction to Legal Reasoning*, 15 U. Chi. L. Rev. 501, 540 (1948).

2. See generally The Baseball Encyclopedia (1969): L. Ritter, The Glory of Their Times (1966); 1 & 2 H. Seymour, Baseball (1960, 1971); 1 & 2 D. Voigt, American Baseball (1966, 1970).

Cleveland Alexander, Rogers Hornsby, Harry Hooper, Goose Goslin, Jackie Robinson, Honus Wagner, Joe McCarthy, John McGraw, Deacon Phillippe, Rube Marquard, Christy Mathewson, Tommy Leach, Big Ed Delahanty, Davy Jones, Germany Schaefer, King Kelly, Big Dan Brouthers, Wahoo Sam Crawford, Wee Willie Keeler, Big Ed Walsh, Jimmy Austin, Fred Snodgrass, Satchel Paige, Hugh Jennings, Fred Merkle, Iron Man McGinnity, Three-Finger Brown, Harry and Stan Coveleski, Connie Mack, Al Bridwell, Red Ruffing, Amos Rusie, Cy Young, Smokey Joe Wood, Chief Meyers, Chief Bender, Bill Klem, Hans Lobert, Johnny Evers, Joe Tinker, Roy Campanella, Miller Huggins, Rube Bressler, Dazzy Vance, Edd Roush, Bill Wambsganss, Clark Griffith, Branch Rickey, Frank Chance, Cap Anson, Nap Lajoie, Sad Sam Jones, Bob O'Farrell, Lefty O'Doul, Bobby Veach, Willie Kamm, Heinie Groh, Lloyd and Paul Waner, Stuffy McInnis, Charles Comiskey, Roger Bresnahan, Bill Dickey, Zack Wheat, George Sisler, Charlie Gehringer, Eppa Rixey, Harry Heilmann, Fred Clarke, Dizzy Dean, Hank Greenberg, Pie Traynor, Rube Waddell, Bill Terry, Carl Hubbell, Old Hoss Radbourne, Moe Berg, Rabbit Maranville, Jimmie Foxx, Lefty Grove.[3] The list seems endless.

And one recalls the appropriate reference to the "World Serious," attributed to Ring Lardner, Sr.; Ernest L. Thayer's "Casey at the Bat"[4]; the ring of "Tinker to Evers to Chance"; and all the other happenings, habits, and superstitions about and around baseball that made it the "national pastime" or, depending upon the point of view, "the great American tragedy."

[Curt Flood, the petitioner, was a star center fielder with the St. Louis Cardinals. Under the "reserve clause" in his contract he was required to play for the Cardinals, the Cardinals could unilaterally assign his contract to another team, and the Cardinals could annually renew that contract so long as the minimum salary was provided.

---

3. These are names only from earlier years. By mentioning some, one risks unintended omission of others equally celebrated.

4. Millions have known and enjoyed baseball. One writer knowledgeable in the field of sports almost assumed that everyone did until, one day, he discovered otherwise:

"I knew a cove who'd never heard of Washington and Lee,
Of Caesar and Napoleon from the ancient jamboree.
But, bli'me, there are queerer things than anything like that,
For here's a cove who never heard of 'Casey at the Bat'!
* * *
"Ten million never heard of Keats, or Shelley, Burns or Poe;
But they know 'the air was shattered by the force of Casey's blow';
They never heard of Shakespeare, nor of Dickens, like as not.
But they know the somber drama from old Mudville's haunted lot.

"He never heard of Casey! Am I dreaming? Is it true?
Is fame but windblown ashes when the summer day is through?
Does greatness fade so quickly and is grandeur doomed to die
That bloomed in early morning, ere the dusk rides down the sky?"

"He Never Heard of Casey" Grantland Rice, The Sportlight, New York Herald Tribune, June 1, 1926, p. 23.

[In October 1969, the Cards traded Flood to the Philadelphia Phillies. Flood refused to report to the Phillies and asked Bowie Kuhn, the Commissioner of Baseball, to be allowed to negotiate a contract with the team of his choice. Kuhn refused. Flood filed a lawsuit claiming, *inter alia*, that the reserve clause violated the antitrust laws because it prevented him from contracting with the team of his choice. Lower courts denied relief based on Supreme Court precedents holding baseball immune from the antitrust laws.]

[IVA. *The Legal Background*] *Federal Baseball Club v. National League*, 259 U.S. 200 (1922), was a suit for treble damages instituted by a member of the Federal League (Baltimore) against the National and American Leagues and others. The plaintiff obtained a verdict in the trial court, but the Court of Appeals reversed. The main brief filed by the plaintiff with this Court discloses that it was strenuously argued, among other things, that the business in which the defendants were engaged was interstate commerce; that the interstate relationship among the several clubs, located as they were in different States, was predominant; that organized baseball represented an investment of colossal wealth; that it was an engagement in moneymaking; that gate receipts were divided by agreement between the home club and the visiting club; and that the business of baseball was to be distinguished from the mere playing of the game as a sport for physical exercise and diversion.

Mr. Justice Holmes, in speaking succinctly for a unanimous Court, said:

"The business is giving exhibitions of base ball, which are purely state affairs. * * * But the fact that in order to give the exhibitions the Leagues must induce free persons to cross state lines and must arrange and pay for their doing so is not enough to change the character of the business. * * * [T]he transport is a mere incident, not the essential thing. That to which it is incident, the exhibition, although made, for money would not be called trade or commerce in the commonly accepted use of those words. As it is put by the defendant, personal effort, not related to production, is not a subject of commerce. That which in its consummation is not commerce does not become commerce among the States because the transportation that we have mentioned takes place. To repeat the illustrations given by the Court below, a firm of lawyers sending out a member to argue a case, or the Chautauqua lecture bureau sending out lecturers, does not engage in such commerce because the lawyer or lecturer goes to another State.

"If we are right the plaintiff's business is to be described in the same way and the restrictions by contract that prevented the plaintiff from getting players to break their bargains and the other conduct charged against the defendants were not an interference with commerce among the States." 259 U.S., at 208–209.[10] * * *

---

10. "What really saved baseball, legally at least, for the next half century was the protective canopy spread over it by the United States Supreme Court's decision in the Baltimore Federal League antitrust suit against Organized Baseball in 1922. In it Justice Holmes, speaking for a unanimous court, ruled that the business of giving baseball exhibitions for profit was not 'trade or commerce in the commonly-accepted use of those words' because 'personal effort, not related to production, is not a subject of commerce'; nor was it interstate, because the movement of ball clubs across state lines was merely 'incidental' to the business. It should be noted that, contrary to what many believe, Holmes did call baseball a business; time and again those who

In the years that followed, baseball continued to be subject to intermittent antitrust attack. The courts, however, rejected these challenges on the authority of *Federal Baseball*. In some cases stress was laid, although unsuccessfully, on new factors such as the development of radio and television with their substantial additional revenues to baseball. For the most part, however, the Holmes opinion was generally and necessarily accepted as controlling authority. And in the 1952 Report of the Subcommittee on Study of Monopoly Power of the House Committee on the Judiciary, H.R.Rep. No. 2002, 82d Cong., 2d Sess., 229, it was said, in conclusion:

> "On the other hand the overwhelming preponderance of the evidence established baseball's need for some sort of reserve clause. Baseball's history shows that chaotic conditions prevailed when there was no reserve clause. Experience points to no feasible substitute to protect the integrity of the game or to guarantee a comparatively even competitive struggle. The evidence adduced at the hearings would clearly not justify the enactment of legislation flatly condemning the reserve clause."

C. The Court granted certiorari in [*Toolson, Kowalski*, and *Corbett*], and, by a short per curiam (Warren, C.J., and Black, Frankfurter, Douglas, Jackson, Clark, and Minton, JJ.), affirmed the judgments of the respective courts of appeals in those three cases. *Toolson v. New York Yankees, Inc.*, 346 U.S. 356 (1953). *Federal Baseball* was cited as holding "that the business of providing public baseball games for profit between clubs of professional baseball players was not within the scope of the federal antitrust laws," and:

> "Congress has had the ruling under consideration but has not seen fit to bring such business under these laws by legislation having prospective effect. The business has thus been left for thirty years to develop, on the understanding that it was not subject to existing antitrust legislation. The present cases ask us to overrule the prior decision and, with retrospective effect, hold the legislation applicable. We think that if there are evils in this field which now warrant application to it of the antitrust laws it should be by legislation. Without re-examination of the underlying issues, the judgments below are affirmed on the authority of *Federal Baseball Club of Baltimore v. National League of Professional Baseball Clubs, supra*, so far as that decision determines that Congress had no intention of including the business of baseball within the scope of the federal antitrust laws."

This quotation reveals four reasons for the Court's affirmance of *Toolson* and its companion cases: (a) Congressional awareness for three decades of the Court's ruling in *Federal Baseball*, coupled with congressional inaction. (b) The fact that baseball was left alone to develop for that period upon the understanding that the reserve system was not subject to existing federal antitrust laws. (c) A reluctance to overrule *Federal Baseball* with consequent retroactive effect. (d) A professed desire that any needed remedy be provided by legislation rather than by court decree. The emphasis in *Toolson* was on the determination, attributed even to *Federal Baseball*, that Congress had no intention to include baseball within the reach of the federal antitrust laws. * * *

---

have not troubled to read the text of the decision have claimed incorrectly that the court said baseball was a sport and not a business." 2 H. Seymour, Baseball 420 (1971).

[Justice Blackmun recounts three subsequent opinions. In *United States v. Shubert*, 348 U.S. 222 (1955), the Court reversed a dismissal of an antitrust suit against defendants engaged in theatrical attractions across the country, indicating that *Federal Baseball* and *Toolson* gave no general antitrust exemption for businesses built around local exhibitions. Similarly, the Court in *United States v. International Boxing Club*, 348 U.S. 236 (1955), reversed a district court for dismissing the antitrust complaint; the Court denied that *Federal Baseball* gave sports other than baseball an exemption from the antitrust laws. Finally, in *Radovich v. National Football League*, 352 U.S. 445 (1957), the Supreme Court reversed the lower courts for dismissing another antitrust complaint against a football league. Justice Clark's opinion for the Court noted that *Toolson* upheld baseball's immunity, "because it was concluded that more harm would be done in overruling *Federal Base Ball* than in upholding a ruling which at best was of dubious validity." The opinion said:]

"All this, combined with the flood of litigation that would follow its repudiation, the harassment that would ensue, and the retroactive effect of such a decision, led the Court to the practical result that it should sustain the unequivocal line of authority reaching over many years.

"[S]ince *Toolson* and *Federal Base Ball* are still cited as controlling authority in antitrust actions involving other fields of business, we now specifically limit the rule there established to the facts there involved, *i.e.*, the business of organized professional baseball. As long as the Congress continues to acquiesce we should adhere to — but not extend — the interpretation of the Act made in those cases. * * *

"If this ruling is unrealistic, inconsistent, or illogical, it is sufficient to answer, aside from the distinctions between the businesses, that were we considering the question of baseball for the first time upon a clean slate we would have no doubts. But *Federal Base Ball* held the business of baseball outside the scope of the Act. No other business claiming the coverage of those cases has such an adjudication. We therefore, conclude that the orderly way to eliminate error or discrimination, if any there be, is by legislation and not by court decision. Congressional processes are more accommodative, affording the whole industry hearings and an opportunity to assist in the formulation of new legislation. The resulting product is therefore more likely to protect the industry and the public alike. The whole scope of congressional action would be known long in advance and effective dates for the legislation could be set in the future without the injustices of retroactivity and surprise which might follow court action."

Mr. Justice Frankfurter dissented essentially for the reasons stated in his dissent in *International Boxing*. Mr. Justice Harlan, joined by Mr. Justice Brennan, also dissented because he, too, was "unable to distinguish football from baseball." Here again the dissenting Justices did not call for the overruling of the baseball decisions. They merely could not distinguish the two sports and, out of respect for *stare decisis*, voted to affirm.

G. Finally, in *Haywood v. National Basketball Assn.*, 401 U.S. 1204 (1971), Mr. Justice Douglas, in his capacity as Circuit Justice, reinstated a District Court's injunction *pendente lite* in favor of a professional basketball player and said, "Basketball * * * does not enjoy exemption from the antitrust laws."

H. This series of decisions understandably spawned extensive commentary, some of it mildly critical and much of it not; nearly all of it looked to Congress for any remedy that might be deemed essential.

I. Legislative proposals have been numerous and persistent. Since *Toolson* more than 50 bills have been introduced in Congress relative to the applicability or nonapplicability of the antitrust laws to baseball. A few of these passed one house or the other. Those that did would have expanded, not restricted, the reserve system's exemption to other professional league sports. And the Act of Sept. 30, 1961, Pub.L. 87–331, 75 Stat. 732, and the merger addition thereto effected by the Act of Nov. 8, 1966, Pub.L. 89–800, § 6(b), 80 Stat. 1515, 15 U.S.C. §§ 1291–1295, were also expansive rather than restrictive as to antitrust exemption.

[V.] In view of all this, it seems appropriate now to say that:

1. Professional baseball is a business and it is engaged in interstate commerce.

2. With its reserve system enjoying exemption from the federal antitrust laws, baseball is, in a very distinct sense, an exception and an anomaly. *Federal Baseball* and *Toolson* have become an aberration confined to baseball.

3. Even though others might regard this as "unrealistic, inconsistent, or illogical," see *Radovich*, the aberration is an established one, and one that has been recognized not only in *Federal Baseball* and *Toolson*, but in *Shubert, International Boxing*, and *Radovich*, as well, a total of five consecutive cases in this Court. It is an aberration that has been with us now for half a century, one heretofore deemed fully entitled to the benefit of *stare decisis*, and one that has survived the Court's expanding concept of interstate commerce. It rests on a recognition and an acceptance of baseball's unique characteristics and needs.

4. Other professional sports operating interstate — football, boxing, basketball, and, presumably, hockey and golf — are not so exempt.

5. The advent of radio and television, with their consequent increased coverage and additional revenues, has not occasioned an overruling of *Federal Baseball* and *Toolson*.

6. The Court has emphasized that since 1922 baseball, with full and continuing congressional awareness, has been allowed to develop and to expand unhindered by federal legislative action. Remedial legislation has been introduced repeatedly in Congress but none has ever been enacted. The Court, accordingly, has concluded that Congress as yet has had no intention to subject baseball's reserve system to the reach of the antitrust statutes. This, obviously, has been deemed to be something other than mere congressional silence and passivity.

7. The Court has expressed concern about the confusion and the retroactivity problems that inevitably would result with a judicial overturning of *Federal Baseball*. It has voiced a preference that if any change is to be

made, it come by legislative action that, by its nature, is only prospective in operation.

8.   The Court noted in *Radovich* that the slate with respect to baseball is not clean. Indeed, it has not been clean for half a century.

This emphasis and this concern are still with us. We continue to be loath, 50 years after *Federal Baseball* and almost two decades after *Toolson*, to overturn those cases judicially when Congress, by its positive inaction, has allowed those decisions to stand for so long and, far beyond mere inference and implication, has clearly evinced a desire not to disapprove them legislatively.

Accordingly, we adhere once again to *Federal Baseball* and *Toolson* and to their application to professional baseball. We adhere also to *International Boxing* and *Radovich* and to their respective applications to professional boxing and professional football. If there is any inconsistency or illogic in all this, it is an inconsistency and illogic of long standing that is to be remedied by the Congress and not by this Court. If we were to act otherwise, we would be withdrawing from the conclusion as to congressional intent made in *Toolson* and from the concerns as to retrospectivity therein expressed. Under these circumstances, there is merit in consistency even though some might claim that beneath that consistency is a layer of inconsistency.

* * * [W]hat the Court said in *Federal Baseball* in 1922 and what it said in *Toolson* in 1953, we say again here in 1972: the remedy, if any is indicated, is for congressional, and not judicial, action.

MR. JUSTICE WHITE joins in the judgment of the Court, and in all but Part I of the Court's opinion.

MR. JUSTICE POWELL took no part in the consideration or decision of this case.

MR. CHIEF JUSTICE BURGER, concurring.

I concur in all but Part I of the Court's opinion but, like Mr. Justice Douglas, I have grave reservations as to the correctness of *Toolson*; as he notes in his dissent, he joined that holding but has "lived to regret it." The error, if such it be, is one on which the affairs of a great many people have rested for a long time. Courts are not the forum in which this tangled web ought to be unsnarled. I agree with Mr. Justice Douglas that congressional inaction is not a solid base, but the least undesirable course now is to let the matter rest with Congress; it is time the Congress acted to solve this problem.

MR. JUSTICE DOUGLAS, with whom MR. JUSTICE BRENNAN concurs, dissenting.

This Court's decision in *Federal Baseball Club*, made in 1922, is a derelict in the stream of the law that we, its creator, should remove. Only a romantic view[1] of a rather dismal business account over the last 50 years would keep that derelict in midstream.

In 1922 the Court had a narrow, parochial view of commerce. With the demise of the old landmarks of that era, the whole concept of commerce has changed.

Under the modern [commerce clause] decisions, the power of Congress was recognized as broad enough to reach all phases of the vast operations of our national industrial system. An industry so dependent on radio and television as is baseball and gleaning vast interstate revenues (see H.R.Rep. No. 2002, 82d Cong., 2d Sess., 4, 5 (1952)) would be hard put today to say with the Court in the *Federal Baseball Club* case that baseball was only a local exhibition, not trade or commerce.

Baseball is today big business that is packaged with beer, with broadcasting, and with other industries. The beneficiaries of the *Federal Baseball Club* decision are not the Babe Ruths, Ty Cobbs, and Lou Gehrigs.

The owners, whose records many say reveal a proclivity for predatory practices, do not come to us with equities. The equities are with the victims of the reserve clause. I use the word "victims" in the Sherman Act sense, since a contract which forbids anyone to practice his calling is commonly called an unreasonable restraint of trade.

If congressional inaction is our guide, we should rely upon the fact that Congress has refused to enact bills broadly exempting professional sports from antitrust regulation.[3] H.R.Rep. No. 2002, 82nd Cong., 2d Sess. (1952). The only statutory exemption granted by Congress to professional sports concerns broadcasting rights. 15 U.S.C. §§ 1291–1295. I would not ascribe a broader exemption through inaction than Congress has seen fit to grant explicitly.

There can be no doubt "that were we considering the question of baseball for the first time upon a clean slate" we would hold it to be subject to federal antitrust regulation. *Radovich.* The unbroken silence of Congress should not prevent us from correcting our own mistakes.

---

1. While I joined the Court's opinion in *Toolson*, I have lived to regret it; and I would now correct what I believe to be its fundamental error.

3. The Court's reliance upon congressional inaction disregards the wisdom of *Helvering v. Hallock*, 309 U.S. 106, 119–121, where we said:

"Nor does want of specific Congressional repudiations * * * serve as an implied instruction by Congress to us not to reconsider, in the light of new experience * * * those decisions * * *. It would require very persuasive circumstances enveloping Congressional silence to debar this Court from re-examining its own doctrines. * * * Various considerations of parliamentary tactics and strategy might be suggested as reasons for the inaction of * * * Congress, but they would only be sufficient to indicate that we walk on quicksand when we try to find in the absence of corrective legislation a controlling legal principle."

Mr. Justice Marshall, with whom Mr. Justice Brennan joins, dissenting.

This is a difficult case because we are torn between the principle of *stare decisis* and the knowledge that the decisions in *Federal Baseball Club* and *Toolson* are totally at odds with more recent and better reasoned cases. * * *

Has Congress acquiesced in our decisions in *Federal Baseball Club* and *Toolson*? I think not. Had the Court been consistent and treated all sports in the same way baseball was treated, Congress might have become concerned enough to take action. But, the Court was inconsistent, and baseball was isolated and distinguished from all other sports. In *Toolson* the Court refused to act because Congress had been silent. But the Court may have read too much into this legislative inaction.

Americans love baseball as they love all sports. Perhaps we become so enamored of athletics that we assume that they are foremost in the minds of legislators as well as fans. We must not forget, however, that there are only some 600 major league baseball players. Whatever muscle they might have been able to muster by combining forces with other athletes has been greatly impaired by the manner in which this Court has isolated them. It is this Court that has made them impotent, and this Court should correct its error.

We do not lightly overrule our prior constructions of federal statutes, but when our errors deny substantial federal rights, like the right to compete freely and effectively to the best of one's ability as guaranteed by the antitrust laws, we must admit our error and correct it. We have done so before and we should do so again here. See, *e.g.*, *Blonder-Tongue Laboratories, Inc. v. University of Illinois Foundation*, 402 U.S. 313 (1971); *Boys Markets, Inc. v. Retail Clerks Union*, 398 U.S. 235, 241 (1970).[4]

To the extent that there is concern over any reliance interests that club owners may assert, they can be satisfied by making our decision prospective only. Baseball should be covered by the antitrust laws beginning with this case and henceforth, unless Congress decides otherwise.[5]

NOTES ON *FLOOD* AND THE "SUPER-STRONG" PRESUMPTION AGAINST OVERRULING STATUTORY PRECEDENTS

1. *Is There a Rationale for* Flood? *What of Its Aftermath?* It appears that every member of the Court thought that *Federal Baseball* was wrongly decided, yet a majority nevertheless applied the wrongheaded precedent. Is there something to Justice Blackmun's view that this is "an inconsistency and

---

4. In the past this Court has not hesitated to change its view as to what constitutes interstate commerce. Compare *United States v. E. C. Knight Co.*, 156 U.S. 1 (1895), with *Mandeville Island Farms v. American Crystal Sugar Co.*, 334 U.S. 219 (1948), and *United States v. Darby*, 312 U.S. 100 (1941).

5. We said recently that "[i]n rare cases, decisions construing federal statutes might be denied full retroactive effect, as for instance where this Court overrules its own construction of a statute * * *." *United States v. Estate of Donnelly*, 397 U.S. 286, 295 (1970).

illogic of long standing" which might as well be perpetuated? One's initial reaction to Justice Blackmun's opinion might be that it is simply silly not to overrule discredited precedents. The same argument might have been made to the *Brown* Court not to overrule *Plessy v. Ferguson*, 163 U.S. 537 (1896). Justice Blackmun would respond that he would be more willing to overrule constitutional precedents:

> *Stare decisis* is usually the wise policy because in most matters it is more important that the applicable rule of law be settled than that it be settled right. * * * This is commonly true even where the error is a matter of serious concern, provided correction can be had by legislation. But in cases involving the Federal Constitution, where correction through legislative action is practically impossible, this Court has often overruled its earlier decisions.

Burnet v. Coronado Oil and Gas Co., 285 U.S. 393, 406–07 (1932) (Brandeis, J., dissenting). Is this reasoning persuasive? Contrast *Moragne*, in which the Court overruled a common law decision affecting a minuscule range of cases. Wouldn't the same reasons (decisive shift in the legal terrain) have justified overruling *Federal Baseball*? Does *Flood* present more compelling justifications for stare decisis?[d]

In strictly respecting stare decisis, the *Flood* Court notes "retrospectivity" problems that would inhere if it were to overturn *Toolson* and *Federal Baseball*, suggesting (we suppose) that the Court assumed that the industry had been relying on these precedents in conducting its affairs. Yet the testimony of post-*Toolson* purchasers of baseball teams indicated that they had been advised of the distinct possibility of changes in the antitrust exemption. *Flood v. Kuhn*, Brief for Petitioner, at 24. In any event, why couldn't the Court simply have overruled *Federal Baseball* prospectively, if it were concerned about the reliance interest?

Perhaps another rationale for the Court's decision is the Chief Justice's suggestion that "[c]ourts are not the forum in which this tangled web ought to be unsnarled." Let Congress make the change. Yet, given the past history of congressional involvement, recounted by the Court, was there any reason to believe that Congress would do anything? The reaction to *Flood* in Congress was, indeed, immediate: Two bills were introduced in the House of Representatives, H.R. 12401 and H.R. 14614, 92d Cong., 2d Sess. (1972), and a hearing was held by the appropriate subcommittee, but neither bill went anywhere. Is that because Congress "liked" the Court's decision? Or didn't "dislike" it enough to revoke it? Or was lobbied very hard by the baseball owners? Note that in the 1970s, various Members of Congress were actively promoting the return of major league baseball to the nation's capital, leading one commentator to opine: "It thus appears that there is more bicameral interest in where baseball will be played than in the legalities of the sport."[e]

---

d. See William Eskridge, Jr., *Overruling Statutory Precedents*, 76 Geo. L.J. 1361 (1988).

e. Philip Martin, *The Aftermath of* Flood v. Kuhn: *Professional Baseball's Exemption from Antitrust Regulation*, 3 West. St. U.L. Rev. 262, 280 (1976).

Could *Flood v. Kuhn* be an example of stare nostalgia? Consider Justice Blackmun's "Ode to Baseball" in Part I of the opinion. Was that an appropriate matter to be included in a judicial opinion? Even if not, were Chief Justice Burger and Justice White right in making a point of not joining Part I? (We think this is the only time in history that all of an opinion commanded a Court majority except for its statement of facts!)

The Court never returned to the *Flood* issue (maybe on the ground that, after *Federal Baseball, Toolson*, and *Flood*, three strikes and you're out?).[f] Thwarted on antitrust grounds, players used labor law to their advantage. They formed a union and agitated for change. Five years after *Flood*, an arbitrator awarded free-agent status to two players; the collective bargaining between owners and the players' union that followed, with impasses sometimes resulting in strikes, led to labor agreements that provided players with significant freedom. In the mid-1990s, following particularly acrimonious labor conflict, management agreed with the union to approach Congress jointly and request legislation effectively overriding *Flood*. Congress responded by enacting the Curt Flood Act of 1998, Pub. L. 105-297, 112 Stat. 2824. The statute subjects any business practices "directly relating to or affecting employment of major league baseball players * * * to the antitrust laws to the same extent such * * * practices * * * would be subject to the antitrust laws if engaged in by persons in any other professional sports business affecting interstate commerce." Drafted to avoid any application of the antitrust laws to such matters as franchise relocation and the treatment of minor-league players, it is not clear that the statute changed the law in general or, in particular, provides any rights to players that they had not already achieved through collective bargaining.[g]

Nonetheless, the statute was at least a symbolic victory. When Flood decided that he would not accept his trade, he wrote the baseball commissioner: "After 12 years in the Major Leagues, I do not feel I am a piece of property to be bought and sold irrespective of my wishes. I believe that any system which produces that result violates my basic rights as a citizen."[h] A year before Congress belatedly agreed, Flood died of cancer at age 59, an undaunted and proud man.[i]

2. *When Is It Appropriate To Overrule a Statutory Precedent?* As *Flood* suggests, the Supreme Court will not routinely overrule a prior interpretation

---

f. For the argument that *Flood* was ripe for overruling, see Stephen Ross, *Reconsidering Flood v. Kuhn*, 12 U. Miami Ent. & Sports L. Rev. 169 (1995).

g. See, e.g., Roger Abrams, *Before the Flood: The History of Baseball's Antitrust Exemption*, 9 Marq. Sports L.J. 307 (1999); J. Philip Calabrese, *Recent Legislation: Antitrust and Baseball*, 36 Harv. J. on Legis. 531 (1999); Edmund Edmonds, *The Curt Flood Act of 1998: A Hollow Gesture After All These Years?*, 9 Marq. Sports L.J. 315 (1999).

h. Quoted in Abrams, *Before the Flood, supra*, at 311.

i. See Edmonds, *supra*, at 315 & n.3.

of a statute.[j] Many state courts are even more emphatic that statutory precedents should rarely, or never (in some states), be overruled, since the legislature can change the statute.[k] Thus, even though the extra-strong presumption of stare decisis for statutory precedents may lack historical support in practices before the twentieth century,[l] it seems to be deeply rooted at the beginning of the twenty-first. Is it ever appropriate to overrule a statutory precedent?

In *Monell v. Department of Social Servs.*, 436 U.S. 658 (1978), the Supreme Court held that municipal corporations were "persons" subject to suit under § 1983 for depriving people of the "rights, privileges, or immunities secured by the Constitution and laws." The Court thereby overruled *Monroe v. Pape*, 365 U.S. 167 (1961), which had inferred that Congress meant to immunize municipalities when it rejected such a provision in the bill which became the Civil Rights Act of 1871. The proposed provision would have held a municipal corporation liable for damage done to its inhabitants by private persons "riotously and tumultuously assembled" and was rejected (apparently) because the House of Representatives doubted that Congress had the constitutional power to impose that obligation.

Justice Brennan's opinion in *Monell* explained that the objection to the proposed provision was not that it imposed liability on municipal corporations, but that it held them responsible for the actions of private citizens, which carried *respondeat superior* beyond the bounds of the Constitution. Justice Brennan then made his positive case for finding municipal corporations to be persons by citing to (1) statements of Representative Bingham (a sponsor of the Act) that the statute would effectively provide a remedy in cases of unlawful municipal actions, (2) cases decided before 1871 in which municipalities were held liable to private persons, and (3) the "Dictionary Act," which defined "persons" to include "bodies politic." Justice Brennan recognized the seriousness of overruling *Monroe* and sought to justify it, as did the concurring opinion of Justice Powell. Consider the following articulated grounds for softening stare decisis and overruling *Monroe*. Does any of them suggest that *Monell* presents a better-justified case for overruling prior judicial construction of statutes than *Flood*?

---

j. For examples of the Court's refusal to overrule arguably obsolete statutory precedents, see, e.g., *Square D Co. v. Niagara Frontier Tariff Bur., Inc.*, 476 U.S. 409 (1986) (Sherman Act); *Miller v. Fenton*, 474 U.S. 104 (1985) (habeas corpus statute); *Illinois Brick Co. v. Illinois*, 431 U.S. 720 (1977) (Sherman Act); *Cleveland v. United States*, 329 U.S. 14 (1945) (Mann Act).

k. Representative of this approach are *Williams v. Ray*, 246 S.E.2d 387 (Ga. App. 1978); *Williams v. Crickman*, 405 N.E.2d 799 (Ill. 1980); *Land Comm'r v. Hutton*, 307 So.2d 415 (Miss. 1974); *Higby v. Mahoney*, 396 N.E.2d 183 (N.Y. 1979); *Fulton v. Lavallee*, 265 A.2d 655 (R.I. 1970); *James v. Vernon Calhoun Packing Co.*, 498 S.W.2d 160 (Tex. 1973). But see, e.g., *Jepson v. Department of Labor and Indus.*, 573 P.2d 10 (Wash. 1977).

l. See Thomas Lee, *Stare Decisis in Historical Perspective: From the Founding Era to the Rehnquist Court*, 52 Vand. L. Rev. 647 (1999); Eskridge, *supra*.

(a) *Clearly Erroneous Precedent.* Justice Harlan in *Monroe* said that statutory decisions should only be overruled if "it appear[s] beyond doubt from the legislative history of the * * * statute that [the Court] misapprehended the meaning of the [provision]." 365 U.S. at 192. Justice Brennan claimed that his historical analysis met that stringent test, but Justice Rehnquist's dissent contended that the history is not so clear. The dissent posited that in 1871 municipal corporations were not "citizens" within the meaning of the Privileges and Immunities Clause, U.S. Const., art. IV, § 2; *Paul v. Virginia*, 75 U.S. (8 Wall.) 168, 177 (1868), and were neither a "citizen" nor a "person" within the Fourteenth Amendment. *Insurance Co. v. New Orleans*, 13 Fed.Cas. 67 (C.C.D. La. 1870) (No. 7052). Also, Justice Rehnquist objected to Justice Brennan's almost exclusive reliance on remarks by Congressman Bingham to divine legislative intent: Why should Congressman Bingham's opinions be given greater weight than those of any other?

(b) *Stare Decisis Cuts Both Ways.* Justices Brennan and Powell both thought that stare decisis was less of a problem because *Monroe*'s construction of § 1983 was inconsistent with other Supreme Court cases — earlier cases in which municipal corporations had been defendants, e.g., *Douglas v. Jeannette*, 319 U.S. 157 (1943), and post-*Monroe* cases in which school boards were found liable under § 1983. But Justice Rehnquist pointed out that three subsequent Supreme Court decisions — *Moor v. Alameda County*, 411 U.S. 693 (1973); *City of Kenosha v. Bruno*, 412 U.S. 507 (1973) (extending *Monroe* to suits for injunctive relief); *Aldinger v. Howard*, 427 U.S. 1 (1976) — had explicitly reaffirmed *Monroe*. Isn't this like *Flood*? Indeed, the Supreme Court's reaffirmance of *Monroe* had never been grudging, as its reaffirmance of the moribund *Federal Baseball* had been in the cases cited by Justice Blackmun in *Flood*.

(c) *Congressional Nonacquiescence.* Justice Brennan argued that Congress implicitly approved of § 1983 suits against school boards and other "local bodies" when it enacted the Civil Rights Attorney's Fees Awards Act of 1976, 90 Stat. 2641, codified at 42 U.S.C. § 1988 (1982); see S. Rep. No. 94–1011, 94th Cong., 2d Sess. 5 (1976) (noting that defendants in § 1983 cases "are often State or local bodies"). But Justice Rehnquist noted that there was nothing in the language of the Attorney's Fees Awards Act to suggest that municipal corporations were liable under § 1983, and the Senate Report cited by Justice Brennan states that liability may be imposed "whether or not the agency or government is a named party," which suggests that Congress did not view the Act as inconsistent with *Monroe*. More important, Justice Brennan's assertion of congressional nonacquiescence is inconsistent with 1978 Senate hearings on a bill to remove the municipal immunity imposed by *Monroe*.[m] Isn't that the very same argument that prevailed in *Flood*?

(d) *The Requirements of a Dynamic Statutory Scheme.* Justice Powell's concurrence quoted Holmes, *The Path of the Law*, 10 Harv. L. Rev. 457, 469 (1897): The law recognizes the necessity of change, lest rules "simply persis[t]

---

m. See *Civil Rights Improvements Act of 1977: Hearings on S. 35 Before the Subcomm. on the Constitution of the Senate Comm. on the Judiciary*, 95th Cong., 2d Sess. (1978).

from blind imitation of the past." Doesn't this suggest a decent reason to overrule *Monroe*'s holding that municipalities were not subject to § 1983 suits? *Monroe* ironically had breathed new life into § 1983 in the 1960s, but it became clear over time that violations of civil rights, especially rights to free speech and nondiscriminatory treatment, were systemic at the local level: They were caused by city or county policy, and not just by individual misconduct. Whether they were named defendants or not, municipal corporations were very often the "real" defendants (for example, they regularly provided attorneys for individual defendants and/or reimbursed them for awards rendered against them). By 1978, it was painfully clear — from many of the Court's own § 1983 cases, which were brought against local agencies — that it was blinking reality not to permit direct suit against municipal corporations. That § 1983 was one means by which constitutional rights were protected made an expansive construction of § 1983 liability all the more natural. Does this explain the Court's willingness, by a 7–2 vote, to overrule *Monroe*?[n]

3. *Reflections on Statutory Stare Decisis.* The debate over the super-strong presumption of correctness for statutory precedents has intensified in the last several years. Following Hart and Sacks, who strongly disapproved of *Toolson* for some of the reasons developed above, most legal process academics (whether of the formalist, centrist, or progressive flavors) have endorsed a relaxation of the super-strong presumption, so that statutory precedents would be treated more like other precedents.[o]

The Rehnquist Court may have been less committed to stare decisis than earlier Courts.[p] In *Payne v. Tennessee*, 501 U.S. 808 (1991) (a constitutional criminal procedure case), the Court held that it was not bound by precedents that are "unworkable or badly reasoned" and that stare decisis is most constraining "in cases involving property and contract rights, where reliance interests are involved," but "the opposite is true in cases * * * involving procedural and evidentiary rules" protecting constitutional and civil rights. This seems a more pragmatic approach to the topic than *Toolson* and *Flood*.

---

n. For other examples of the Supreme Court's willingness to overrule statutory precedents, see Eskridge, *Overruling Statutory Precedents, supra* (appendix of cases where the Court has overruled statutory precedents, 1961–86).

o. See, e.g., Reed Dickerson, *The Interpretation and Application of Statutes* 252–55 (1975); Frank Easterbrook, *Stability and Reliability in Judicial Decisions*, 73 Corn. L. Rev. 422 (1988); Eskridge, *Overruling Statutory Precedents, supra*; Earl Maltz, *The Nature of Precedent*, 66 N.C. L. Rev. 367 (1988); Caleb Nelson, *Stare Decisis and Demonstrably Erroneous Precedents*, 87 Va. L. Rev. 1 (2001). But see Lawrence Marshall, *"Let Congress Do It": The Case for an Absolute Rule of Statutory Stare Decisis*, 88 Mich. L. Rev. 177 (1989), who argues for an "absolute" rule of stare decisis in statutory cases: The Court should never overrule any of its interpretations of statutory precedents. See also Amy Coney Barrett, *Statutory Stare Decisis in the Courts of Appeals*, 73 Geo. Wash. L. Rev. 317 (2005) (federal courts of appeals wrongly apply the super-strong presumption in favor of statutory precedents to their own decisions).

p. The point is debated in Lee, *supra*. For a theoretical examination of stare decisis from the standpoint of decision theory that also examines the practices of the Rehnquist Court, see Rafael Gely, *Of Sinking And Escalating: A (Somewhat) New Look at Stare Decisis*, 60 U. Pitt. L. Rev. 89 (1998) (concluding, among other things, that statutory precedents should not be accorded stronger *stare decisis* force).

In the context of the antitrust laws, consider *State Oil Co. v. Khan*, 522 U.S. 3 (1997), in which the Court unanimously overruled *Albrecht v. Herald Co.*, 390 U.S. 145 (1968), which had considered vertical maximum price fixing a per se antitrust violation, and replaced that approach with the "rule of reason." The Court quickly dismissed any barrier created by *Toolson* and *Flood*, viewing those cases as having no import outside the peculiar context of baseball. That Congress had not reacted adversely to *Albrecht* "seems neither clearly to support nor to denounce" the holding of that case. The Court also concluded that stare decisis has somewhat less force in antitrust law because, "[i]n the area of antitrust law, there is a competing interest, well represented in this Court's decisions, in recognizing and adapting to changed circumstances and the lessons of accumulated experience. Thus, the general presumption that legislative changes should be left to Congress has less force with respect to the Sherman Act in light of the accepted view that Congress 'expected the courts to give shape to the statute's broad mandate by drawing on common-law tradition.' As we have explained, the term 'restraint of trade' * * * also 'invokes the common law itself, and not merely the static content that the common law had assigned to the term in 1890.' "[q] Compare the Rehnquist Court's performance in an earlier case.

PATTERSON v. McLEAN CREDIT UNION, 491 U.S. 164 (1989). Brenda Patterson brought a lawsuit against her former employer for workplace racial harassment. She based her claim on 42 U.S.C. § 1981, which prohibits discrimination on the basis of race in the making and enforcement of contracts.

---

q. Recently, the Roberts Court relied upon the analysis in *Khan* in overruling a century-old Sherman Act precedent. See *Leegin Creative Leather Products, Inc. v. PSKS, Inc.*, 127 S.Ct. 2705 (2007), overruling *Dr. Miles Medical Co. v. John D. Park & Sons Co.*, 220 U.S. 373 (1911), which had applied a per se rule forbidding vertical price restraints rather than the usual Sherman Act approach of the "rule of reason." But this time four Justices dissented. Justice Breyer's dissent, joined by Justices Stevens, Souter, and Ginsburg, stated that the arguments relied upon by the majority have been "well known in the antitrust literature for close to half a century," but "Congress has repeatedly found in these arguments insufficient grounds for overturning the per se rule" (citing congressional hearings). Moreover, "[w]e write, not on a blank slate, but on a slate that begins with *Dr. Miles* and goes on to list a century's worth of similar cases, massive amounts of advice that lawyers have provided their clients, and untold numbers of business decisions those clients have taken in reliance upon that advice. * * * I am not aware of any case in which this Court has overturned so well-established a statutory precedent." Justice Breyer contended that there had been no major changes in the economy or other evolutive reasons supporting the overruling. Further, he argued that every factor concerning stare decisis — the heightened precedential force of statutory stare decisis, the longstanding nature of the precedent, the practicability of implementing the precedent, the well-settledness of the precedent, the nature of the reliance interests surrounding the precedent (involving property rights and contract rights), and the embeddedness of the precedent in the web of antitrust law — disfavored overruling. He acknowledged that the Court treats Sherman Act precedents more flexibly that most other statutory precedents, but argued that overruling would be unjustified even under the more relaxed approach to common law precedents. The majority responded by stating that the scholarly literature condemning *Dr. Miles* was clearly persuasive (a matter disputed by Justice Breyer), the reliance interests were not strong, there were no significant signs of congressional acquiescence, and *Dr. Miles* was already in significant tension with later Supreme Court cases that had softened its rule.

Her complaint was dismissed by the lower courts on the ground that it did not state a claim for relief under § 1981. On its own motion after receiving briefs in the case, the Supreme Court requested the parties to brief the issue whether § 1981 affords a remedy against private, as opposed to public, employers. *Runyon v. McCrary*, 427 U.S. 160 (1976), had interpreted § 1981 to provide such a remedy against private schools excluding children on the basis of race, and so the Court invited the parties to address the question whether *Runyon* should be "reconsidered" (i.e., overruled). The Court's request stimulated a firestorm of protest from the civil rights community, the press, legal scholars, historians, and Members of Congress (who took the unusual step of submitting a brief on the issue). To some observers, the request raised the possibility that a new conservative majority on the Court would use a relaxed approach to stare decisis to overturn decades of Warren and Burger Court civil rights precedents.

In the end, the Court chose a somewhat more politique path. The opinion for the Court, written by **Justice Kennedy** and joined by the other four Justices (**Chief Justice Rehnquist** and **Justices White**, **Scalia**, and **O'Connor**) who had requested rehearing, declined to overrule *Runyon* but also declined to extend it to workplace harassment claims. The majority opinion essentially adopted the commentators' position that statutory precedents are subject to normal (not super-strong) stare decisis rules (although not the very lenient stare decisis of constitutional precedents). The Court's reason for preserving *Runyon* recalls the sort of analysis we saw in *Moragne*:

> We conclude * * * that no special justification has been shown for overruling *Runyon*. In cases where statutory precedents have been overruled, the primary reason for the Court's shift in position has been the intervening development of the law, through either the growth of judicial doctrine or further action taken by Congress. Where such changes have removed or weakened the conceptual underpinnings from the primary decision, or where the law has rendered the decision irreconcilable with competing legal doctrines or policies, the Court has not hesitated to overrule an earlier decision. Our decision in *Runyon* has not been undermined by subsequent changes or developments in the law.

> Another traditional justification for overruling a prior case is that a precedent may be a positive detriment to coherence and consistency in the law, either because of inherent confusion created by an unworkable decision, or because the decision poses a direct obstacle to the realization of important objectives embodied in other laws. In this regard, we do not find *Runyon* to be unworkable or confusing. * * *

> Finally, it has sometimes been said that a precedent becomes more vulnerable as it becomes outdated and after being " 'tested by experience, has been found to be inconsistent with the sense of justice or with the social welfare.' " *Runyon* (Stevens, J., concurring), quoting B. Cardozo, The Nature of the Judicial Process 149 (1921). Whatever the effect of this consideration may be in statutory cases, it offers no support for overruling *Runyon*. In recent decades, state and federal legislation has been enacted to prohibit private racial discrimination in many aspects of our society. Whether *Runyon*'s interpretation of section 1981 as prohibiting racial discrimination in the making and enforcement of private contracts is right or wrong as an original matter, it is certain that it is not inconsistent with the prevailing sense of justice in this country. To the contrary, *Runyon* is entirely consistent with our society's deep

commitment to the eradication of discrimination based on a person's race or the color of his or her skin.

Although the Court reaffirmed its prior interpretation applying § 1981 to prohibit racial discrimination in the "mak[ing] and enforce[ment]" of private contracts, the five-Justice majority declined to find that racial harassment on the job is actionable. The majority reasoned that racial harassment did not impair Patterson's ability to "make" or "enforce" the employment contract and, hence, did not fall under § 1981's plain language.

Justice Brennan wrote a separate opinion concurring in the judgment, joined by three other Justices (**Marshall**, **Blackmun**, and **Stevens**). They sharply disagreed with the majority on the *Runyon* issue in three different ways. First, they argued that *Runyon* was correctly decided as an initial matter (a proposition not squarely addressed by the majority). Second, they argued that Congress had "ratified" *Runyon* (a) by failing to overturn the precedent even while Congress was overturning a number of other civil rights precedents in the late 1970s and 1980s, (b) by rejecting an amendment to the Civil Rights Act of 1964 inconsistent with *Runyon*, and (c) by relying on *Runyon* when it enacted an attorney's fees statute in 1976, 42 U.S.C. § 1988. Third, these Justices argued that the Court's refusal to apply *Runyon* to the instant case was a failure to take the precedent's authority seriously. If the Court really believed in the current policy and other reasons for reaffirming *Runyon*, they argued, the Court would have applied the precedent to Patterson's claims of racial harassment on the job. The implications of the separate opinion are that the Court was giving lip service to stare decisis, while actually departing from the principles and policies it seemingly reaffirmed.

NOTE ON ABROGATING *STARE DECISIS*

The traditional view is that, although adhering to any given precedent is a matter of policy and is not compelled by an iron rule of law, the American practice of *stare decisis* is deeply rooted and may in some circumstances even be constitutionally compelled.[r] Could Congress by statute abrogate the practice of *stare decisis* in a given area (social conservatives might pick abortion rights, social liberals might pick affirmative action) and require the Supreme Court to overrule a constitutional precedent if the Court is persuaded that the prior case was incorrect on the merits?[s] Should it make any difference whether the area in question involves common law (e.g., *Moragne*), statutory interpretation (e.g., *Weber* or *Flood*), or constitutional interpretation?

---

r. See, e.g., Michael Dorf, *Dicta and Article III*, 142 U. Pa. L. Rev. 1997, 1997 (1994) ("[T]he precept that like cases should be treated alike [is] rooted . . . in Article III's invocation of the 'judicial Power.' "); Henry Monaghan, *Stare Decisis and Constitutional Adjudication*, 88 Colum. L. Rev. 723, 748 (1988) ("[p]recedent is, of course, part of our understanding of what law is").

s. See Michael Paulsen, *Abrogating Stare Decisis by Statute: May Congress Remove the Precedential Effect of* Roe *and* Casey?, 109 Yale L.J. 1535 (2000).

Problem on Overruling Statutory Precedents

Problem 6–12. Recall the *Weber* issue from Chapter 1. The Court has once reaffirmed *Weber*, over a strong dissent by Justice Scalia, in *Johnson v. Transportation Agency.* Assume you are Justice Scalia's law clerk. If another challenge to voluntary affirmative action in the workplace comes up, should he mount another attack on *Weber?* Consider the following new § 703(m), added by the Civil Rights Act of 1991 (described in Chapter 1, § 3):

> (m) Except as otherwise provided in this title, an unlawful employment practice is established when the complaining party demonstrates that race, color, religion, sex, or national origin was a motivating factor for any employment practice, even though other factors also motivated the practice.

Should *Weber* be overruled?[t]

C. PROSPECTIVE JUDICIAL DECISIONS

The Blackstonian view was that judicial decisions are always retroactive, and the common law formalists largely embraced that view. It came under sustained attack from the legal realists and other policy jurisprudes. The classic argument, by Chief Justice Roger Traynor in *Quo Vadis, Prospective Overruling: A Question of Judicial Responsibility,* 28 Hastings L.J. 533 (1977), advocated "occasional exceptions to the normally retroactive operation of judicial decisions." Traynor criticized Blackstone's "discovery theory" of law for inducing judges to apply as retroactive judicial "decisions that they would have invalidated in statutes as contrary to the ex post facto clause, the impairment of contracts clause, or the due process clause of the Constitution."[u]

Traynor continued: "It is my opinion that however sound this prevailing rule may be in the main, it can on occasion unduly restrict the development of the law. A court usually will not overrule a precedent even if it is convinced that the precedent is unsound, when the hardship caused by a retroactive change would not be offset by its benefits. The technique of prospective overruling enables courts to solve this dilemma by changing bad law without upsetting the reasonable expectations of those who relied on it. Only occasionally will there be cases that clearly demand this technique. In the hands of skilled judicial craftsmen, acting under well-reasoned guidelines, it can be an instrument of justice that fosters public respect for the law. Although the technique is frequently invoked in overruling precedents, it can serve in any case in which new rules are announced." Note the relationship between Traynor's endorsement of prospective overruling and Calabresi's proposal that courts overrule statutes; presumably, the latter would generally be prospective.

---

t. See *Officers for Justice v. Civil Serv. Comm'n,* 979 F.2d 721, 725 (9th Cir. 1992) (no); Michael Paulsen, *Reverse Discrimination and Law School Faculty Hiring: The Undiscovered Opinion,* 71 Tex. L. Rev. 993, 1005–06 (1993) (yes).

u. For other realist defenses of prospective overrulings, see Beryl Harold Levy, *Realist Jurisprudence and Prospective Overruling,* 109 U. Pa. L. Rev. 1, 17–25 (1960); Note, *Prospective Overruling and Retroactive Application in the Federal Courts,* 71 Yale L.J. 907, 945 (1962).

JAMES v. UNITED STATES, 366 U.S. 213 (1961). James was a union official who embezzled more than $738,000 between 1951 and 1954. He was convicted of willfully attempting to evade the federal income tax laws for that period and sentenced to three years in prison. He appealed his conviction on the ground that the Court in *Commissioner v. Wilcox*, 327 U.S. 404 (1946), had found embezzled money not to be income under the Internal Revenue Code. The Supreme Court overruled *Wilcox* but only prospectively; James' conviction was overturned.

Chief Justice Warren, joined by **Justices Brennan** and **Stewart**, wrote a plurality opinion and delivered the judgment of the Court. He was willing to overrule *Wilcox*, in part because the reasoning of that decision had been overtaken by the Court's decision in *Rutkin v. United States*, 343 U.S. 130 (1952), which held that extorted money is taxable income to the extortionist. The lower courts had strained to apply *Rutkin*, even in embezzlement situations, and were loathe to apply *Wilcox*. "Thus, we believe that we should now correct the error and the confusion resulting from [*Wilcox*], certainly if we do so in a manner that will not prejudice those who might have relied on it. * * * But, we are dealing here with a felony conviction under statutes which apply to any person who 'willfully' fails to account for his tax or who 'willfully' attempts to evade his obligation. * * * We believe that the criminal element of willfulness could not be proven in a criminal prosecution for failing to include embezzled funds in gross income for the year of misappropriation so long as the statute contained the gloss placed upon it by *Wilcox* at the time the alleged crime was committed."

Three Justices (**Black**, **Douglas**, **Whittaker**) believed that *Wilcox* should not have been overruled and voted to reverse James' conviction on the authority of that case. This gave the Chief Justice six votes to reverse the conviction. Justice Black's opinion (joined by Justice Douglas) objected to the "questionable formula, at least a new one in the annals of this Court" by which the Chief Justice overruled *Wilcox* but still gave the defendant the benefit of the precedent.

Two Justices (**Frankfurter** and **Harlan**) agreed with the Chief Justice that *Wilcox* should have been overruled but would have remanded for a new trial, where James could have argued that his reliance on *Wilcox* negated the wilfulness requirement; they believed that the overruling of *Wilcox* should have applied to James. Justice Harlan's opinion (joined by Justice Frankfurter) asserted that outright reversal was inconsistent with the Court's responsibilities under Article III to adjudicate "cases or controversies," which imply retroactive application rather than the prospective application concomitant to agency proceedings. "It is hard to see what further point is being made, once it is conceded that [James], if he is misled by decisions of this Court, is entitled to plead in defense that misconception. Only in the most metaphorical sense has the law changed: the decisions of this Court have changed, and the decisions of a court interpreting the acts of a legislature have never been subject to the same limitations which are imposed on legislatures themselves," giving as examples the prohibition of *ex post facto* laws and laws impairing the obligations of contracts. U.S. Const. Art. I, §§ 9–10.

One Justice (**Clark**) voted to overrule *Wilcox* and to affirm James' conviction (the only Justice voting to affirm). This gave the Chief Justice six votes to overrule *Wilcox*.

NOTES ON THE RISE AND DECLINE
OF JUDICIAL PROSPECTIVITY

1. *Prospective Overrulings in Statutory Cases*. On the one hand, *James* can be cited to support Traynor's proposition that overrulings in statutory cases can sometimes be prospective. On the other hand, note how little support *James* actually affords that proposal. No one on the Court actually endorsed prospective overruling: The Warren (plurality) Justices premised non-retroactive application on the special requirement of willfulness for criminal liability; three other Justices went along with reversal because they didn't think *Wilcox* should have been overruled, but they (including super-realist Justice Douglas, who favored relaxed stare decisis) specifically objected to prospective overruling; two other Justices favored retroactive application of the overruling and defended compulsory retroactivity on constitutional grounds. *James*, therefore, might be *sui generis*.

Recall that Justice Marshall in *Flood* argued that the Court might overrule *Federal Baseball Club* prospectively, so as to ameliorate reliance interests that might have built up around baseball's longstanding antitrust exemption. But only Justice Brennan joined that discussion, consistent with his position in *James*; the other dissenter, Justice Douglas, refused to do so, also consistent with his position in *James*. We are not aware of any statutory case in which the Supreme Court has, since *James*, applied its ruling prospectively.

2. *Prospective Overrulings in Constitutional Criminal Cases*. *James* was followed by a number of other Warren Court decisions applying the Court's new rules of criminal constitutional law prospectively. E.g., *Miranda v. Arizona*, 384 U.S. 436 (1966). The leading decision was *Linkletter v. Walker*, 381 U.S. 618 (1965), which declined to apply retroactively the Court's earlier extension of the Fourth Amendment exclusionary rule to the states. The decision was based on the purpose of the new constitutional rule, the reliance placed on the previous state of the law, and the practical effects on the administration of justice if the new rule were applied retroactively.

These decisions were immediately controversial within the Court. Consistent with his position in *James*, Justice Harlan objected that the prospectivity of these new rules made it too easy for the Court to slide from adjudicatory modes of thought into legislative ones. He objected that the Court's prospectivity jurisprudence was inconsistent with the traditions surrounding Article III. See *Mackey v. United States*, 401 U.S. 667, 675 (1971) (Harlan, J., concurring in the judgment); *Desist v. United States*, 394 U.S. 244, 256 (1969) (Harlan, J., dissenting).

3. *Prospective Overrulings in Constitutional Civil Cases*. In *Chevron Oil Co. v. Huson*, 404 U.S. 97, 106–07 (1971), the Supreme Court articulated three

factors to determine whether its overruling of prior precedents should only apply prospectively:

> First, the decision to be applied nonretroactively must establish a new principle of law, either by overruling clear past precedent on which litigants may have relied * * * or by deciding an issue of first impression whose resolution was not clearly foreshadowed * * *. Second, it has been stressed that "we must * * * weigh the merits and demerits in each case by looking to the prior history of the rule in question, its purpose and effect, and whether retrospective operation will further or retard its operation." * * * Finally, we have weighed the inequity imposed by retroactive application, for "[w]here a decision of this Court could produce substantial inequitable results if applied retroactively, there is ample basis in our cases for avoiding the 'injustice or hardship' by a holding of nonretroactivity."

See *Lemon v. Kurtzman*, 411 U.S. 192, 199 (1973), which stressed the importance of private reliance in announcing new judge-made rules prospectively, reasoning that "statutory or even judge-made rules of law are hard facts on which people must rely in making decisions and shaping their conduct."

In light of these tests, why was *Moragne* not a prospective overruling of *The Harrisburg*? Traynor suggested that prospective overruling should be used to "preclude undue hardship to a party that has justifiably relied on [the old rule]. Reliance plays its heaviest role in such areas as property, contracts, and taxation, where lawyers advise clients extensively in their planning on the basis of existing precedents." Traynor, *supra*, 28 Hastings L.J. at 543. For examples, see *Douglass v. Pike County*, 101 U.S. (11 Otto) 677 (1879) (municipal bonds); *Purvis v. Hubbell*, 620 S.W.2d 282 (Ark. 1981) (same); *Salorio v. Glaser*, 461 A.2d 1100 (N.J. 1983).

4. *Alternatives to Pure Retroactivity or Pure Prospectivity.* In certain cases, courts may want to depart from the rule of pure retroactivity but not give their new decision only prospective effect. There are several options available:

a. *Prospective Application, except as to the Prevailing Party.* The new rule on police interrogation set forth in *Miranda* was applied to Miranda and the defendants in three companion cases before the Court, but not to any other pending case — including the 129 other cases that were pending before the Supreme Court raising the same issue. This approach might be justified as a reward to the litigants who successfully espoused the new rule, but isn't that bizarre when there were 129 other litigants who were just as eager to espouse a new rule before the Court but who were unable to obtain certiorari? Compare *Coons v. American Honda Motor Co.*, 476 A.2d 763 (N.J. 1984) (declining to apply new statute of limitations rule, because prevailing parties were "institutional litigants" which would benefit from the new rule in other cases).

b. *Retroactivity Limited to Prevailing Party and Pending Cases.* Traynor advocated that in cases such as *Miranda* the new rule should be applied to all cases that have not reached final judgment. See *Hoffman v. Jones*, 280 So.2d 431 (Fla. 1973) (decision retroactive to litigating parties and to cases which had not reached final judgment in which the issue had been properly raised).

c. *Delayed Prospectivity.* In *Spanel v. Mounds View School District No. 621*, 118 N.W.2d 795, 796 (Minn. 1962), a tort action brought against a school district, the trial court granted a motion to dismiss on sovereign immunity grounds. The Supreme Court of Minnesota affirmed, sort of:

> We hold that the order of dismissal is affirmed with the caveat, however, that subject to the limitations we now discuss, the defense of sovereign immunity will no longer be available to school districts, municipal corporations, and other subdivisions of government on whom immunity has been conferred by judicial decision *with respect to torts which are committed after the adjournment of the next regular session of the Minnesota Legislature.* (Emphasis added.)

What is the justification for this "prospective prospective" overruling, effectively postponing the effect of the decision? Isn't it an essentially legislative act? An approach related to *Spanel* would be the "prospective retroactive" overruling of *Whitney v. Worcester*, 366 N.E.2d 1210 (Mass. 1977), in which the court delayed trial in the case until the state legislature acted on the immunity issue; if no action were taken by January 1978, the court indicated that it would abolish the immunity defense retroactively. Ironically, the legislature responded by abolishing governmental immunity only for causes of action that arose on or after the date of the *Whitney* decision. The court, noting that the legislature "has spoken explicitly on the issue of retroactivity," then refused to abolish the immunity more broadly. See *Vaughan v. Commonwealth*, 388 N.E.2d 694 (Mass. 1979).[v]

An example similar to "prospective prospective" overruling is *Northern Pipeline Construction Co. v. Marathon Pipe Line Co.*, 458 U.S. 50 (1982), holding that § 241(a) of the Bankruptcy Act of 1978 was unconstitutional because it conferred Article III judicial power on bankruptcy judges who lacked the Article III safeguards of life tenure and protection from salary diminution. Justice Brennan's plurality opinion applied the *Chevron* test and found retroactivity unjustified:

> * * * In the present case, all of these considerations militate against the retroactive application of our holding today. It is plain that Congress' broad grant of judicial power to non-Art. III bankruptcy judges presents an unprecedented question of interpretation of Art. III. It is equally plain that retroactive application would not further the operation of our holding, and would surely visit substantial injustice and hardship upon those litigants who relied upon the Act's vesting of jurisdiction in the bankruptcy courts. We hold therefore that our decision today shall apply only prospectively.

> The judgment of the District Court is affirmed. However, we stay our judgment until October 4, 1982. This limited stay will afford Congress an opportunity to reconstitute the bankruptcy courts or to adopt other valid means of adjudication, without impairing the interim administration of the bankruptcy laws.

---

v. See Note, *Prospective Retroactive Overruling: Remanding Cases Pending Legislative Determinations of Law*, 58 B.U. L. Rev. 818, 833–36 (1978). See also *Vincent v. Pabst Brewing Co.*, 177 N.W.2d 513 (Wis. 1970).

Congress failed to act by October 4, 1982, and on that date the Court extended the stay of judgment to December 24, 1982. 459 U.S. 813. Congress again did nothing, and on December 23, 1982, the Court refused further to extend the stay. 459 U.S. 1094. Congress finally acted in June 1984.

5. *Constitutional Considerations.* Is there any constitutional objection to partially prospective overruling? Consider Traynor's suggestion that applying the benefits of the *Miranda* holding to the four defendants before the Supreme Court, but not to the 129 others who raised the issue, might violate equal protection. But if, to the contrary, the Court *fails* to apply to the instant parties the effect of its overruling of precedent or its invalidation of a challenged statute, has the party denied the fruits of that decision been deprived of due process of law? See *Great Northern Railway Co. v. Sunburst Oil and Refining Co.*, 287 U.S. 358, 364–66 (1932), where the Court upheld such a denial:[w]

> A state in defining the limits of adherence to precedent may make a choice for itself between the principle of forward operation and that of relation backward * * *. [Here the Supreme Court of Montana ascribed to its decisions] a power to bind and loose that is unextinguished, for intermediate transactions, by a decision overruling them. As applied to such transactions we may say of the earlier decision that it has not been overruled at all. It has been translated into a judgment of affirmance and recognition of law anew. Accompanying the recognition is a prophecy, which may not be realized in conduct, that transactions arising in the future will be governed by a different rule.

Note that Article III of the U.S. Constitution has been interpreted to prohibit the giving of advisory opinions. Does this suggest that federal courts should not engage in prospective overruling? Or, in the very least, that the new rule adopted prospectively is mere dictum? See *Stovall v. Denno*, 388 U.S. 293, 301 (1967); cf. Traynor, *supra*, at 560. Another argument against prospective overruling is Justice Harlan's argument that Article III gives the Court no "lawmaking" authority. Since a hallmark of lawmaking is its shifting of legal rights/duties, and since such shifting has traditionally been done only prospectively, the Court's willingness to engage in prospective overrulings bears an important mark of lawmaking and tempts the Court in that direction.

6. *Later Developments in Prospective Overruling Jurisprudence.* The Harlan view continued to be sounded after Justice Harlan left the Court in 1971. See *Hankerson v. North Carolina*, 432 U.S. 233, 246 (1977) (Powell, J., concurring). The Court rethought its retroactivity jurisprudence in the 1980s, and in *Griffith v. Kentucky*, 479 U.S. 314 (1987), the Court announced that new rules of constitutional criminal procedure would be applied retroactively and would not be subject to the *Linkletter* balancing approach. The

---

w. Justice Cardozo wrote the opinion in *Sunburst* and had earlier written approvingly of prospective overruling as a technique to avoid the harshness that can result from retroactive application of changed rules. Cardozo, *The Nature of the Judicial Process* 147–49. According to one commentator, Cardozo's recurrent interest in this issue "may perhaps be explained * * * by the injustice he suffered while a student at the Columbia Law School. After he embarked upon his studies there in a prescribed two-year course, the faculty decided that the course requirements should be extended to three years. Cardozo would not submit — and never got his law degree!" Levy, *supra*, 109 U. Pa. L. Rev. at 10 n.31.

opinion was written by Justice Blackmun and was joined by Justices Brennan (a switch from his *James* position?), Marshall (a retreat from his *Flood* views?), Powell, Stevens, and Scalia. Chief Justice Rehnquist and Justices White and O'Connor dissented.

Blackmun's opinion relied on the Harlan arguments that selective application of new rules violates the principle of treating similarly situated defendants the same and violates the Article III limitation of the Court to adjudicating cases and controversies (and creating new rules only under the constraints of that limitation). The opinion left civil constitutional cases to be governed by *Chevron Oil* — until the next case, that is.

JAMES B. BEAM DISTILLING CO. v. GEORGIA, 501 U.S. 529 (1991). The Court applied a civil constitutional precedent, *Bacchus Imports, Ltd. v. Dias*, 468 U.S. 263 (1984) (state tax on alcohol sales that exempts local liquor violates dormant commerce clause and is not saved by twenty-first amendment) retroactively, but fractured as to rationale.

The judgment of the Court was delivered by **Justice Souter**, in an opinion joined only by **Justice Stevens**. Justice Souter started from the baseline that retroactivity of judicial decisions, including constitutional decisions, is "overwhelmingly the norm," because it "is in keeping with the traditional function of the courts to decide cases before them based upon their best current understanding of the law" and reflects "the declaratory theory of the law." "But in some circumstances," he continued, "retroactive application may prompt difficulties of a practical sort. However much it comports with our received notions of the judicial role, the practice has been attacked for its failure to take account of reliance on cases subsequently abandoned, a fact of life if not always one of jurisprudential recognition." For that reason, the Court in cases like *Chevron Oil* and *Marathon Pipe Line* has applied some constitutional decisions purely prospectively, applicable only to conduct and controversies arising after the date of the Court's decision. "But this equitable method has its own drawback: it tends to relax the force of precedent, by minimizing the costs of overruling, and thereby allows the courts to act with a freedom comparable to that of legislatures."

Justice Souter categorically rejected a third approach, selective prospectivity (retroactive as to the litigants and/or pending cases but prospective as to others similarly situated), because it "breaches the principle that litigants in similar situations should be treated the same, a fundamental component of *stare decisis* and the rule of law generally." Although selective prospectivity was used in some of the Court's criminal procedure precedents, the Court abandoned it for criminal cases in *Griffith*. Justice Souter rejected its application in civil constitutional cases. Since the Court in *Bacchus* applied its new rule to the litigants in that case, Justice Souter felt compelled to apply it to all similarly situated parties, including those in this case.

Justice White concurred in the judgment, generally agreeing with Justice Souter's opinion but relying more on the Court's prior opinions, which have upheld the use of pure prospectivity in civil cases that meet the *Chevron Oil* test but have never accepted selective prospectivity in civil cases (and have abandoned the rule in criminal cases).

Justice Scalia, writing also for **Justices Marshall** and **Blackmun**, concurred in the judgment upon a broader ground, that either pure or selective prospectivity in judicial decisions is unconstitutional, as a violation of Article III's vesting the "judicial Power" in the federal courts. "That is the power 'to say what the law is,' *Marbury v. Madison*, 1 Cranch 137, 177 (1803), not the power to change it. I am not so naive (nor do I think our forebears were) as to be unaware that judges in a real sense 'make' law. But they make it *as judges make it*, which is to say *as though* they were 'finding' it — discerning what the law *is*, rather than decreeing what it is today *changed to*, or what it will *tomorrow* be. Of course, this mode of action poses 'difficulties of a practical sort,' when courts decide to overrule prior precedent. But those difficulties are one of the understood checks upon judicial law making; to eliminate them is to render courts more substantially free to 'make new law,' and thus to alter in a fundamental way the assigned balance of responsibility and power among the three Branches."

Justice O'Connor, joined by **Chief Justice Rehnquist** and **Justice Kennedy**, dissented. She argued that *Chevron Oil* has long framed the Court's inquiry as to whether a constitutional ruling in a civil case should be prospective. See also *American Trucking Associations v. Smith*, 496 U.S. 167 (1990). Because *Bacchus* did not perform a *Chevron Oil* analysis in making its new rule applicable to its litigants, Justice O'Connor argued that the Court was free to make that determination afresh. "If retroactive application was inequitable in *Bacchus* itself, the Court only hinders the cause of fairness by repeating the mistake. Because I conclude that the *Chevron Oil* test dictates that *Bacchus* not be applied retroactively, I would decline the Court's invitation to impose liability on every jurisdiction in the Nation that reasonably relied on pre-*Bacchus* law."

Like Justice Souter, Justice O'Connor invoked precepts underlying stare decisis. "At its core, *stare decisis* allows those affected by the law to order their affairs without fear that the established law upon which they rely will suddenly be pulled out from under them. A decision *not* to apply a new rule retroactively is based upon principles of *stare decisis*. By not applying a law-changing decision retroactively, a court respects the settled expectations that have built up around the old law."

HARPER v. VIRGINIA DEPARTMENT OF TAXATION
Supreme Court of the United States, 1993
509 U.S. 86, 113 S.Ct. 2510, 125 L.Ed.2d 74

JUSTICE THOMAS delivered the opinion of the Court.

In *Davis v. Michigan Dept. of Treasury*, 489 U.S. 803 (1989), we held that a State violates the constitutional doctrine of intergovernmental tax immunity when it taxes retirement benefits paid by the Federal Government but exempts from taxation all retirement benefits paid by the State or its political subdivisions. Relying on the retroactivity analysis of *Chevron Oil Co. v. Huson*, 404 U.S. 97 (1971), the Supreme Court of Virginia twice refused to apply *Davis* to taxes imposed before *Davis* was decided. In accord with *Griffith v. Kentucky*, 479 U.S. 314 (1987), and *James B. Beam Distilling Co. v. Georgia*, 501 U.S. 529 (1991), we hold that this Court's application of a rule of federal law to the parties before the Court requires every court to give retroactive effect to that decision. We therefore reverse.

[Like Michigan in *Davis*, Virginia in this case taxed the retirement benefits of federal, but not state and local, employees. Relying upon the *Chevron Oil* case, the Virginia trial court refused to allow refunds for taxes paid by federal employees prior to *Davis* because "*Davis* decided an issue of first impression whose resolution was not clearly foreshadowed," "prospective application of *Davis* will not retard its operation," and "retroactive application would result in inequity, injustice and hardship." The Supreme Court of Virginia affirmed.]

"[B]oth the common law and our own decisions" have "recognized a general rule of retrospective effect for the constitutional decisions of this Court." Nothing in the Constitution alters the fundamental rule of "retrospective operation" that has governed "[j]udicial decisions . . . for near a thousand years." In *Linkletter v. Walker*, 381 U.S. 618 (1965), however, we developed a doctrine under which we could deny retroactive effect to a newly announced rule of criminal law. [*] Under *Linkletter*, a decision to confine a new rule to prospective application rested on the purpose of the new rule, the reliance placed upon the previous view of the law, and "the effect on the administration of justice of a retrospective application" of the new rule. In the civil context, we similarly permitted the denial of retroactive effect to "a new principle of law" if such a limitation would avoid " 'injustice or hardship' " without unduly undermining the "purpose and effect" of the new rule. *Chevron Oil Co. v. Huson.*

We subsequently overruled *Linkletter* in *Griffith v. Kentucky*, 479 U.S. 314 (1987), and eliminated limits on retroactivity in the criminal context by holding that all "newly declared . . . rule[s]" must be applied retroactively to all "criminal cases pending on direct review." This holding rested on two "basic norms of constitutional adjudication." First, we reasoned that "the nature of judicial review" strips us of the quintessentially "legislat[ive]" prerogative to make rules of law retroactive or prospective as we see fit. Second, we concluded that "selective application of new rules violates the principle of treating similarly situated [parties] the same."

Dicta in *Griffith*, however, stated that "civil retroactivity . . . continue[d] to be governed by the standard announced in *Chevron Oil*." We divided over the meaning of this dicta in *American Trucking Assns., Inc. v. Smith*, 496 U.S. 167 (1990). The four Justices in the plurality used "the *Chevron Oil* test" to consider whether to confine "the application of [*American Trucking Assns., Inc. v. Scheiner*, 483 U.S. 266 (1987)] to taxation of highway use prior to June 23, 1987, the date we decided *Scheiner*." *Id.* (opinion of O'Connor, J., joined

---

[*]   Editors' note: *Linkletter* denied retroactive effect to *Mapp v. Ohio*, 367 U.S. 643 (1961), which had overruled *Wolf v. Colorado*, 338 U.S. 25 (1949), and held that evidence illegally seized by the police was inadmissible in a criminal trial.

by Rehnquist, C.J., and White and Kennedy, JJ.). Four other Justices rejected the plurality's "anomalous approach" to retroactivity and declined to hold that "the law applicable to a particular case is the law which the parties believe in good faith to be applicable to the case." *Id.* (Stevens, J., dissenting, joined by Brennan, Marshall, and Blackmun, JJ.). Finally, despite concurring in the judgment, Justice Scalia "share[d]" the dissent's "perception that prospective decisionmaking is incompatible with the judicial role."

Griffith and *American Trucking* thus left unresolved the precise extent to which the presumptively retroactive effect of this Court's decisions may be altered in civil cases. But we have since adopted a rule requiring the retroactive application of a civil decision such as *Davis.* Although *James B. Beam Distilling Co.* did not produce a unified opinion for the Court, a majority of Justices agreed that a rule of federal law, once announced and applied to the parties to the controversy, must be given full retroactive effect by all courts adjudicating federal law. In announcing the judgment of the Court, Justice Souter laid down a rule for determining the retroactive effect of a civil decision: After the case announcing any rule of federal law has "appl[ied] that rule with respect to the litigants" before the court, no court may "refuse to apply [that] rule . . . retroactively." *Id.* (opinion of Souter, J., joined by Stevens, J.). Justice Souter's view of retroactivity superseded "any claim based on a *Chevron Oil* analysis." *Ibid.* Justice White likewise concluded that a decision "extending the benefit of the judgment" to the winning party "is to be applied to other litigants whose cases were not final at the time of the [first] decision." *Id.* (opinion concurring in judgment). Three other Justices agreed that "our judicial responsibility . . . requir[es] retroactive application of each . . . rule we announce." *Id.* (Blackmun, J., joined by Marshall and Scalia, JJ., concurring in judgment). See also *id.* (Scalia, J., joined by Marshall and Blackmun, JJ., concurring in judgment).

Beam controls this case, and we accordingly adopt a rule that fairly reflects the position of a majority of Justices in *Beam*: When this Court applies a rule of federal law to the parties before it, that rule is the controlling interpretation of federal law and must be given full retroactive effect in all cases still open on direct review and as to all events, regardless of whether such events predate or postdate our announcement of the rule. This rule extends *Griffith*'s ban against "selective application of new rules." Mindful of the "basic norms of constitutional adjudication" that animated our view of retroactivity in the criminal context, we now prohibit the erection of selective temporal barriers to the application of federal law in noncriminal cases. In both civil and criminal cases, we can scarcely permit "the substantive law [to] shift and spring" according to "the particular equities of [individual parties'] claims" of actual reliance on an old rule and of harm from a retroactive application of the new rule. *Beam* (opinion of Souter, J.). Our approach to retroactivity heeds the admonition that "[t]he Court has no more constitutional authority in civil cases than in criminal cases to disregard current law or to treat similarly situated litigants differently." *American Trucking* (Stevens, J., dissenting).

The Supreme Court of Virginia "appl[ied] the three-pronged *Chevron Oil* test in deciding the retroactivity issue" presented by this litigation. When this

Court does not "reserve the question whether its holding should be applied to the parties before it," however, an opinion announcing a rule of federal law "is properly understood to have followed the normal rule of retroactive application" and must be "read to hold . . . that its rule should apply retroactively to the litigants then before the Court." *Beam* (opinion of Souter, J.). *Accord, id.* (White, J., concurring in judgment); *id.* (O'Connor, J., dissenting). Furthermore, the legal imperative "to apply a rule of federal law retroactively after the case announcing the rule has already done so" must "prevai[l] over any claim based on a *Chevron Oil* analysis." *Id.* (opinion of Souter, J.).

In an effort to distinguish *Davis*, the Supreme Court of Virginia surmised that this Court had "made no . . . ruling" about the application of the rule announced in *Davis* "retroactively to the litigants in that case." "[B]ecause the retroactivity issue was not decided in *Davis*," the court believed that it was "not foreclosed by precedent from applying the three-pronged *Chevron Oil* test in deciding the retroactivity issue in the present case."

We disagree. *Davis* did not hold that preferential state tax treatment of state and local employee pensions, though constitutionally invalid in the future, should be upheld as to all events predating the announcement of *Davis*. The governmental appellee in *Davis* "conceded that a refund [would have been] appropriate" if we were to conclude that "the Michigan Income Tax Act violate[d] principles of intergovernmental tax immunity by favoring retired state and local governmental employees over retired federal employees." We stated that "to the extent appellant has paid taxes pursuant to this invalid tax scheme, he is entitled to a refund." Far from reserving the retroactivity question, our response to the appellee's concession constituted a retroactive application of the rule announced in *Davis* to the parties before the Court. Because a decision to accord solely prospective effect to *Davis* would have foreclosed any discussion of remedial issues, our "consideration of remedial issues" meant "necessarily" that we retroactively applied the rule we announced in Davis to the litigants before us. *Beam* (opinion of Souter, J.). Therefore, under *Griffith*, *Beam*, and the retroactivity approach we adopt today, the Supreme Court of Virginia must apply *Davis* in petitioners' refund action.

[Next, the Court concluded that, under the Supremacy Clause of the Constitution, federal law governs the retroactivity of decisions striking down a state law as inconsistent with the federal Constitution. "Whatever freedom state courts may enjoy to limit the retroactive operation of their own interpretations of state law, see *Great Northern R. Co. v. Sunburst Oil and Refining Co.*, 287 U.S. 358 (1932), cannot extend to their interpretations of federal law."]

JUSTICE SCALIA, concurring.

[Justice Scalia noted that Justice O'Connor, in dissent, complained that the majority was violating principles of *stare decisis* by abandoning *Chevron Oil*. Justice Scalia considered it ironic to invoke *stare decisis* in support of prospectivity.] Prospective decisionmaking is the handmaid of judicial activism, and the born enemy of *stare decisis*. It was formulated in the heyday of legal realism and promoted as a "techniqu[e] of judicial lawmaking" in general, and more specifically as a means of making it easier to overrule prior precedent. * * *

Justice O'Connor asserts that " '[w]hen the Court changes its mind, the law changes with it.' " That concept is quite foreign to the American legal and constitutional tradition. It would have struck John Marshall as an extraordinary assertion of raw power. The conception of the judicial role that he possessed, and that was shared by succeeding generations of American judges until very recent times, took it to be "the province and duty of the judicial department to say what the law *is*," *Marbury v. Madison* — not what the law shall be. That original and enduring American perception of the judicial role sprang not from the philosophy of Nietzsche but from the jurisprudence of Blackstone, which viewed retroactivity as an inherent characteristic of the judicial power, a power "not delegated to pronounce a new law, but to maintain and expound the old one." 1 W. Blackstone, Commentaries 69 (1765). Even when a "former determination is most evidently contrary to reason . . . [or] contrary to the divine law," a judge overruling that decision would "not pretend to make a new law, but to vindicate the old one from misrepresentation." "For if it be found that the former decision is manifestly absurd or unjust, it is declared, not that such a sentence was *bad law*, but that it was *not law*." *Id.* (emphases in original). Fully retroactive decisionmaking was considered a principal distinction between the judicial and the legislative power: "[I]t is said that that which distinguishes a judicial from a legislative act is, that the one is a determination of what the existing law is in relation to some existing thing already done or happened, while the other is a predetermination of what the law shall be for the regulation of all future cases." T. Cooley, Constitutional Limitations 91 (1868). The critics of the traditional rule of full retroactivity were well aware that it was grounded in what one of them contemptuously called "another fiction known as the Separation of powers." Kocourek, Retrospective Decisions and Stare Decisis and a Proposal, 17 A.B.A.J. 180, 181 (1931).

Prospective decisionmaking was known to foe and friend alike as a practical tool of judicial activism, born out of disregard for *stare decisis*. In the eyes of its enemies, the doctrine "smack[ed] of the legislative process," "encroach[ed] on the prerogatives of the legislative department of government," removed "one of the great inherent restraints upon this Court's depart[ing] from the field of interpretation to enter that of lawmaking," caused the Court's behavior to become "assimilated to that of a legislature," and tended "to cut [the courts] loose from the force of precedent, allowing [them] to restructure artificially those expectations legitimately created by extant law and thereby mitigate the practical force of stare decisis." All this was not denied by the doctrine's friends, who also viewed it as a device to "augmen[t] the power of the courts to contribute to the growth of the law in keeping with the demands of society," as "a deliberate and conscious technique of judicial lawmaking," as a means of "facilitating more effective and defensible judicial lawmaking."

Justice Harlan described this Court's embrace of the prospectivity principle as "the product of the Court's disquietude with the impacts of its fast-moving pace of constitutional innovation," [*Mackey v. United States*, 401 U.S. 667

(1971).] The Court itself, however, glowingly described the doctrine as the cause rather than the effect of innovation, extolling it as a "technique" providing the "impetus . . . for the implementation of long overdue reforms." *Jenkins v. Delaware*, 395 U.S. 213 (1969). Whether cause or effect, there is no doubt that the era which gave birth to the prospectivity principle was marked by a newfound disregard for *stare decisis*. As one commentator calculated, "[b]y 1959, the number of instances in which the Court had reversals involving constitutional issues had grown to sixty; in the two decades which followed, the Court overruled constitutional cases on no less than forty-seven occasions." It was an era when this Court cast overboard numerous settled decisions, and indeed even whole areas of law, with an unceremonious "heave-ho." [Citing examples of opinions overruling precedent.] To argue now that one of the jurisprudential tools of judicial activism from that period should be extended on grounds of *stare decisis* can only be described as paradoxical.

[JUSTICE KENNEDY, joined by JUSTICE WHITE, concurred in part and in the judgment. Justice Kennedy wished to continue to adhere to *Chevron Oil*. He joined the Court's judgment because he believed that, under the *Chevron Oil* analysis, *Davis* "must be given retroactive effect" because it was sufficiently foreshadowed in prior law.]

JUSTICE O'CONNOR, with whom THE CHIEF JUSTICE [REHNQUIST] joins, dissenting.

Today the Court applies a new rule of retroactivity to impose crushing and unnecessary liability on the States, precisely at a time when they can least afford it. Were the Court's decision the product of statutory or constitutional command, I would have no choice but to join it. But nothing in the Constitution or statute requires us to adopt the retroactivity rule the majority now applies. In fact, longstanding precedent requires the opposite result. * * * [Here Justice O'Connor argued that *Chevron Oil* should be followed as a matter of *stare decisis*.]

* * * In the usual case, of course, retroactivity is not an issue; the courts simply apply their best understanding of current law in resolving each case that comes before them. But where the law changes in some respect, the courts sometimes may elect not to apply the new law; instead, they apply the law that governed when the events giving rise to the suit took place, especially where the change in law is abrupt and the parties may have relied on the prior law. This can be done in one of two ways. First, a court may choose to make the decision purely prospective, refusing to apply it not only to the parties before the court but also to any case where the relevant facts predate the decision. Second, a court may apply the rule to some but not all cases where the operative events occurred before the court's decision, depending on the equities. The first option is called "pure prospectivity" and the second "selective prospectivity."

As the majority notes, six Justices in *Beam* expressed their disagreement with selective prospectivity. Thus, even though there was no majority opinion in that case, one can derive from that case the proposition the Court announces today: Once "this Court applies a rule of federal law to the parties before it, that rule . . . must be given full retroactive effect in all cases still open on direct review." But no decision of this Court forecloses the possibility of pure prospectivity — refusal to apply a new rule in the very case in which it is announced and every case thereafter. * * *

Rather than limiting its pronouncements to the question of selective prospectivity, the Court intimates that pure prospectivity may be prohibited as well. See *ante* (referring to our lack of " 'constitutional authority . . . to disregard current law' "). The intimation is incorrect. As I have explained before and will touch upon only briefly here:

> "[W]hen the Court changes its mind, the law changes with it. If the Court decides, in the context of a civil case or controversy, to change the law, it must make [a] determination whether the new law or the old is to apply to conduct occurring before the law-changing decision. *Chevron Oil* describes our long-established procedure for making this inquiry."

Beam (O'Connor, J., dissenting). Nor can the Court's suggestion be squared with our cases, which repeatedly have announced rules of purely prospective effect. [Citing examples.]

In any event, the question of pure prospectivity is not implicated here. The majority first holds that once a rule *has been* applied retroactively, the rule must be applied retroactively to all cases thereafter. Then it holds that *Davis* in fact retroactively applied the rule it announced. Under the majority's approach, that should end the matter: Because the Court applied the rule retroactively in *Davis*, it must do so here as well. Accordingly, there is no reason for the Court's careless dictum regarding pure prospectivity, much less dictum that is contrary to clear precedent.

Plainly enough, Justice Scalia would cast overboard our entire retroactivity doctrine with precisely the "unceremonious 'heave-ho' " he decries in his concurrence. Behind the undisguised hostility to an era whose jurisprudence he finds distasteful, Justice Scalia raises but two substantive arguments, both of which were raised in *Beam* (Scalia, J., concurring in judgment), and neither of which has been adopted by a majority of this Court. Justice White appropriately responded to those arguments then, see *id*. (White, J., concurring in judgment), and there is no reason to repeat the responses now. As Justice Frankfurter explained more than 35 years ago:

> "We should not indulge in the fiction that the law now announced has always been the law. . . . It is much more conducive to law's self-respect to recognize candidly the considerations that give prospective content to a new pronouncement of law."

Griffin v. Illinois, 351 U.S. 12 (1956) (opinion concurring in judgment). * * *

Problem on Prospective Judicial Decisions

Problem 6–13. Recall the Court's decision in *Patterson*, which held that § 1981's prohibition of race discrimination in the making and enforcement of contracts does not cover discriminatory job termination. Before *Patterson*, all the courts of appeals that considered the issue held or assumed that *Runyon* applied to racially discriminatory contract terminations. E.g., *Anderson v. Group Hospitalization, Inc.*, 820 F.2d 465 (D.C. Cir. 1987); *Fiedler v. Marumsco Christian School*, 631 F.2d 1144 (4th Cir. 1980). *Runyon* itself held that private schools could not refuse to admit children on the basis of race; that holding would have been meaningless if schools could have admitted black children, taken their parents' money, and then expelled the children for racist reasons. Judge Posner described *Patterson*'s interpretation of § 1981 as one that "could not reasonably have been anticipated" before 1989. *McKnight v. General Motors Corp.*, 908 F.2d 104, 108 (7th Cir. 1990). Few persons openly argued that *Patterson* was a good decision, and indeed even the Bush Administration called for its override. Congress did override the decision in the Civil Rights Act of 1991.

In light of all this evidence, why shouldn't *Patterson* have been a prospective judicial decision? Consider the possible ways to render *Patterson* prospective and evaluate which ones are foreclosed under the later decision in *Harper*. Should the Court have followed its *Marathon Oil* approach of prospective-prospective lawmaking: stay the effect of the decision for a year, so that Congress could override it if it desired?

SECTION 3. RETROACTIVITY OF STATUTES

A. THE TRADITIONAL RULE AGAINST STATUTORY RETROACTIVITY

Consistent with Blackstone, the traditional view in American law is that statutes apply prospectively.[a] Consider the following case and its notes as an indirect way of introducing you to this doctrine. On the surface, the case involves the effect of a *retroactive judicial decision* on a statute that has lain dormant. Beneath the surface, the case raises questions about whether a *statute*'s obligations could be *retroactively* applied to citizens.

JAWISH v. MORLET
Municipal Court of Appeals for the District of Columbia, 1952
86 A.2d 96

Before CAYTON, CHIEF JUDGE, and HOOD and QUINN, ASSOCIATE JUDGES.

HOOD, ASSOCIATE JUDGE.

In 1918 Congress enacted a law fixing minimum wages for women and children in the District of Columbia. In 1923 the Supreme Court, in *Adkins v. Children's Hospital*, 261 U.S. 525, held the law unconstitutional. In 1937 the Supreme Court, in *West Coast Hotel Co. v. Parrish*, 300 U.S. 379, held a similar law of the State of Washington to be constitutional and expressly overruled the *Adkins* case. President Roosevelt then requested the opinion of

---

a. See, e.g., Debra Bassett, *In the Wake of* Schooner Peggy: *Deconstructing Legislative Retroactivity Analysis*, 69 U. Cin. L. Rev. 453 (2001); Ann Woolhandler, *Public Rights, Private Rights, and Statutory Retroactivity*, 94 Geo. L.J. 1015 (2006); Elmer Smead, *The Rule Against Retroactive Legislation: A Basic Principle of Jurisprudence*, 20 Minn. L. Rev. 775 (1936).

the Attorney General as to the status of the District of Columbia law, and in reply the Attorney General stated:

> "The decisions are practically in accord in holding that the courts have no power to repeal or abolish a statute, and that notwithstanding a decision holding it unconstitutional a statute continues to remain on the statute books; and that if a statute be declared unconstitutional and the decision so declaring it be subsequently overruled the statute will then be held valid from the date it became effective.

> "It is, therefore, my opinion that the District of Columbia minimum wage law is now a valid act of the Congress and may be administered in accordance with its terms." 39 Op.Attys.Gen. 22.

Congress never re-enacted the law but did enact amendments to it in 1938, 1941 and 1944. The 1940 District of Columbia Code (unofficial) contains the law, § 36–401 et seq., with the following note of the annotator: "On the theory that the last-mentioned case (West Coast Hotel case) revitalized the District of Columbia Minimum Wage Law, it is incorporated in this Code." Enforcement of the law was resumed after the issuance of the opinion of the Attorney General and has continued to the present time.

This action was brought by a woman employee against her employer to recover the difference between the wages she had been paid and the minimum wages fixed under the minimum wage law for such employment. The only defense raised by the employer was that no minimum wage law exists in the District of Columbia. The trial court ruled against this contention and awarded judgment for the employee. The employer has appealed.

The contention of the employer is that the District of Columbia statute was held unconstitutional in the *Adkins* case, that the effect of that ruling was to make the statute null and void, that the *West Coast Hotel* case did not operate to revive the statute, and that without re-enactment by Congress no such statute today exists.

Since the days of *Marbury v. Madison*, 1 Cr. 137, 180, when Chief Justice Marshall, speaking for the Court, declared that "a law repugnant to the constitution is void," courts have frequently referred to unconstitutional laws as void, of no force and effect, and as inoperative as if never passed. "Yet a realistic approach is eroding this doctrine. * * * When a statute is declared unconstitutional it falls because it must yield to the basic, superior law. There is much more reason to argue that the unconstitutional statute never was the law. Yet today even such a statute is an operative fact and decisions made under its color have the blessing of res judicata." *Warring v. Colpoys*, 74 App. D.C. 303, 307, 122 F.2d 642, 646, certiorari denied, 314 U.S. 678, per Vinson, J., now Chief Justice of the United States.

There are comparatively few cases dealing squarely with the question before us, but they are unanimous in holding that a law once declared unconstitutional and later held to be constitutional does not require re-enactment by the legislature in order to restore its operative force. They proceed on the principle that a statute declared unconstitutional is void in the sense that it is inoperative or unenforceable, but not void in the sense that it is repealed or abolished; that so long as the decision stands the statute is dormant but not dead; and that if the decision is reversed the statute is valid from its first effective date. See *State ex rel. Badgett v. Lee*, 156 Fla. 291, 22 So.2d 804; *Pierce v. Pierce*, 46 Ind. 86; *McCollum v. McConaughy*, 141 Iowa 172, 119 N.W. 539; *Allison v. Corker*, 67 N.J.L. 596, 52 A. 362; *Shephard v. City of Wheeling*, 30 W.Va. 479, 4 S.E. 635.

This principle is in accord with the principle "that a decision of a court of appellate jurisdiction overruling a former decision is retrospective in its operation, and the effect is not that the former decision is bad law but that it never was the law." *Ruppert v. Ruppert*, 77 U.S.App.D.C. 65, 68, 134 F.2d 497, 500.

If the effect of the *West Coast Hotel* decision is that the decision in the *Adkins* case never was the law, it follows that the District of Columbia Minimum Wage law never was unconstitutional. And since the *Adkins* case never was the law, its only effect, to use the language of Justice Vinson in the *Warring* case, was "that just about everybody was fooled." Our conclusion is that the *Adkins* case did not repeal or abolish the District of Columbia Minimum Wage law and when the effect of the *Adkins* case was removed by the *West Coast Hotel* case, the law was effective without re-enactment by Congress.

Affirmed.

NOTES ON CONSTITUTIONAL PROBLEMS WITH RETROACTIVE STATUTES

1. *Statutory Repeals.* Consider some variations on the problem in *Jawish*. If statute A is repealed by statute B, which is enacted in its place, and then a court strikes down statute B, is statute A revived? If statute B provides that statute A shall not be revived in such circumstances, or if another statute announced, for example, that "[t]he repeal * * * of any provision of a statute, which repeals any provision of a prior statute, does not revive such prior provision," N.Y.–McKinney's Gen. Constr. Law § 90, then presumably the earlier statute is not revived. Otherwise, the common-law rule is that the earlier statute is revived and becomes operative again. See, e.g., 1A Sutherland, *Statutes and Statutory Construction* § 23.31 (6th ed. 2002). Similarly, the repeal or invalidation of a statute that overrode the common law rather than an earlier statute revives the common law. See *id.* § 41.02.

2. Jawish *and Constitutional Problems With Retroactive Statutes.* On one level, the analysis of *Jawish* makes sense: only the legislature can enact or repeal a statute. Accordingly, a judicial decision that the statute is unconstitutional does not tear it out of the statute books, it simply renders the statute inoperative.[b] But there are troubling implications of some of the reasoning in *Jawish* — that *Adkins* "never was the law" and "just about everybody was

---

b. See Richard Fallon, *If* Roe *Were Overruled: Abortion and the Constitution in a Post-*Roe *World*, 51 St. L.U. L. Rev. 611 (2007); William Michael Treanor & Gene Sperling, *Prospective Overruling and the Revival of "Unconstitutional" Statutes*, 93 Colum. L. Rev. 1902 (1993).

fooled." Consider the following hypothetical: Eva Rishious ran a sweat shop in D.C. from 1924 to 1938, paying women and children wages lower than those required by the law declared unconstitutional in *Adkins*. When the Supreme Court overruled *Adkins* in 1937, Eva Rishious complied with the law and ceased her prior practices (but went bankrupt doing so in 1938). She is federally prosecuted for violating the law before 1937. She claims she relied on the *Adkins* precedent. Ho ho, rejoins the prosecutor, that "never was the law." Once the decision was overruled, the statute was valid and effective from its first effective date! Although the defendant, like "everyone" else, "was fooled," she is liable for not following "the law." If you really believe everything in *Jawish*, is there any way around the prosecutor's argument? Yet isn't the argument ridiculous? Recall *James v. United States*.

Federal constitutional problems might attend the criminal or civil prosecution of Eva Rishious based upon either a retroactive statute or (as in *Jawish*) a statute that springs back retroactively.[c] There might be persuasive challenges pursuant to the state constitutions as well. Some state constitutions contain sweeping prohibitions on all retrospective lawmaking. On the other hand, Justice Harlan asserted in *James* that the following limitations on the legislature's enactment of statutes do not apply to the judiciary's vacillating interpretation of them. Is that too harsh a view?

a. *Ex Post Facto Laws and Bills of Attainder.* The Constitution prohibits both state and federal governments from enacting any "Bill of Attainder" or "ex post facto law." U.S. Const. art. I, §§ 9 (federal) & 10 (state). "[A]ny statute which punishes as a crime an act previously committed, which was innocent when done; which makes more burdensome the punishment for a crime, after its commission, or which deprives one charged with a crime of any defense available according to law at the time when the act was committed, is prohibited as *ex post facto.*" *Beazell v. Ohio*, 269 U.S. 167, 169–70 (1925) (Stone, J.), quoted in *Dobbert v. Florida*, 432 U.S. 282, 292 (1977). For a recent decision, see *Carmell v. Texas*, 529 U.S. 513 (2000) (laws that alter legal rules of evidence and require less evidence to obtain conviction than was required when the alleged criminal act took place are ex post facto laws). Prohibited bills of attainder are "legislative acts, no matter what their form," in other words, criminal as well as civil statutes, "that apply either to named individuals or to easily ascertainable members of a group in such a way as to inflict punishment on them without a judicial trial." *United States v. Lovett*, 328 U.S. 303, 315–16 (1946). Most cases overturning laws based upon the Bill of Attainder Clause have related to the classic situation in which certain Members of Congress hone in on persons or small groups whom they dislike, make findings that such persons have violated the law, and then penalize them. See *United States v. Brown*, 381 U.S. 437 (1965) (invalidating law making it a crime for members of the Communist Party to serve as union officers). Cf. *Nixon v. Administrator of General Servs.*, 433 U.S. 425, 475–76 (1977).

---

c. See Fallon, *supra*; Treanor & Sperling, *supra*.

b. *The Contract Clause.* The Contract Clause provides that "[n]o state shall * * * pass any * * * Law impairing the Obligation of Contracts." U.S. Const. art. I, § 10. It reflects the Framers' strong disapproval of widespread retroactive state laws altering private contracts during and after the Revolution and was intended as an "added * * * constitutional bulwark in favor of personal security and private rights." *The Federalist*, No. 44, at 301 (J. Cooke ed. 1961); see Benjamin Wright, *The Contract Clause of the Constitution* (1938). While the prohibition is not an absolute one, it does impose restraints on the authority of a State "to abridge existing contractual relationships, even in the exercise of its otherwise legitimate police power." *Allied Structural Steel Co. v. Spannaus*, 438 U.S. 234, 242 (1978). Where a state law has substantially impaired a preexisting contractual relationship and cannot justify the impairment as a reasonable means to address an important social problem, the statute might be invalidated. *United States Trust Co. v. New Jersey*, 431 U.S. 1 (1977) (striking down state alteration of the terms of its debt). It is doubtful that the Contract Clause would apply to the case of Eva Rishious, since it is by its terms only applicable to state laws.

c. *Takings and Due Process.* Just as the Contracts Clause urges special caution with regard to retroactive laws affecting contract rights, so the Takings Clause of the Fifth Amendment restricts retroactive laws unduly affecting property rights. See *United States v. Security Indus. Bank*, 459 U.S. 70 (1982); *Pennsylvania Coal Co. v. Mahon*, 260 U.S. 393 (1922) (Holmes, J.). A more general, somewhat catch-all, retroactivity limitation might be found in the Due Process Clauses of the Fifth and Fourteenth Amendments, which preclude federal and state governments from depriving persons of "life, liberty, or property, without due process of law." The Supreme Court has used the Fifth Amendment to extend Contract Clause precepts to federal legislation. E.g., *Lynch v. United States*, 292 U.S. 571 (1934). Thus Eva Rishious could use the Fifth Amendment to make her Contract Clause argument or to argue that the legislature's statute as applied by the courts cannot create new and unexpected duties for regulated persons, unless there is a compelling societal need or some other reason that ought to have put people on notice that their past activities were problematic.

3. *Retroactive Changes in Criminal Statutes.* The *Jawish* decision relied heavily on dicta in *Warring v. Colpoys*, where D.C. Associate Justice, later U.S. Chief Justice, Vinson refused a writ of habeas corpus to the appellant, who had been convicted under a broad interpretation of the D.C. criminal contempt statute that had been subsequently narrowed by the Supreme Court to exclude his conduct. Vinson stressed the trend in civil cases toward prospective application of new rules when there had been reliance on the old ones and noted that "[i]f instead of a court changing the construction of a statute, the legislature passed a new act which in effect repeals the old one, there would be little doubt that the old act was the law until the new one was enacted." This is surely correct when the change works against the defendant. But what about pro-defendant changes such as the one in *Warring*? Consider Traynor, *supra*, 28 Hastings L.J. at 553–54 n.54:

There may be a trend toward retroactivity of new rules that would beneficently affect a defendant. * * *

In the simplest example, when a court declares a criminal statute unconstitutional, the invariable rule is that all defendants previously convicted under that statute are entitled to release, whether their convictions are final or not. The rule is at least as old as an 1879 case in which the United States Supreme Court declared that a conviction under an unconstitutional statute is void and therefore subject to collateral attack. *See Ex Parte Siebold*, 100 U.S. 371, 376–77 (1879).

As for legislative repeal of a criminal statute, it was normally attended at common law by automatic abatement of all prosecutions under it, on the presumption that the legislation intended repeal to operate as a pardon for past acts. Abatement did not extend, however, to final convictions, probably because of the originally limited nature of habeas corpus and general unavailability of remedies via collateral attack in early Anglo-American law. * * *

Sometimes there are legislative changes in punishment. They are usually subject to a rule precluding retroactive application to defendants whose convictions have become final. Such a rule is of course inevitable as to increases in punishment, where retroactive application would not be constitutionally permissible under the usual ex post facto clause. As to statutes mitigating punishment, however, there is no constitutional barrier to retroactive application, and there are compelling arguments in its favor. Once the legislature adopts a lesser penalty as adequate, the retention of the harsher penalty no longer serves any legitimate penological goal. Hence we declared in California that when a criminal statute is amended to mitigate punishment after the prohibited act was committed, but before a final judgment of conviction is entered, the amended statute governs. *See In re Estrada*, 408 P.2d 948 (Cal. 1965).

Under this analysis, is *Warring* wrong?

Problems on Retroactivity of Change in Criminal Law

Problem 6–14. In *Roe v. Wade*, 410 U.S. 113 (1973), the Supreme Court held that in many circumstances a pregnant woman has a constitutional right to choose an abortion free of state regulation. In many states, pre-*Roe* statutes criminalizing abortion remain on the statute books. If the current Supreme Court overrules *Roe*, are these statutes revived? If so, could a prosecutor enforce the revived statute retroactively and bring charges against a doctor who performed an abortion before the Supreme Court's overruling decision? Could the Supreme Court avoid this possibility by making its overruling decision prospective, or does *Harper* forbid that? See Fallon, *supra* note b; Treanor & Sperling, *supra* note b.

Problem 6–15. At common law, the crime of murder required that the victim die within a year and a day of when the injury was inflicted. The common law doctrine was a conclusive presumption that, when death occurred after a year and a day, it was not caused by the initial injury. The states of the United States inherited this rule as part of their reception of the common law of England. In Wisconsin, for example, the state constitution has always provided: "*Common law continued in force.* Such parts of the common law as are now in force in the territory of Wisconsin, not inconsistent with this constitution, shall be and continue part of the law of this state until altered or suspended by the legislature." Wis. Const., Art. XIV, § 13. Thus, the Wisconsin courts always understood that a defendant charged with homicide (which of course has long been a statutory crime) had the defense of the year-and-a-day rule. But the Wisconsin courts also interpret the state constitution as providing that this rule is a common law rule, not a statutory or constitutional defense — that is, the legislature has never expressly or impliedly adopted the rule as a statutory defense, nor does the state constitution require that the rule remain Wisconsin law (it is just a common law rule subject to judicial reconsideration through the common law process). Assume that the state supreme court determines that the year-and-a-day rule serves no contemporary purpose (e.g., that advances in medical science make it quite possible to prove that a death resulted from an old injury) and ought to be abandoned by overruling the common law precedents recognizing it. Should the court make the overruling retroactive, prospective, or somewhere in between? See *State v. Picotte*, 261 Wis.2d 249, 661 N.W.2d 381 (2003) (Abrahamson, C.J.). Is this simply a question of common law policy analysis, or does the federal Constitution set limits upon common law overrulings in criminal cases that have the effect of expanding criminal liability? Note that, had the year-and-a-day rule been a statutory defense, the Constitution's Ex Post Facto Clause, Art. I, § 10, cl. 1, would forbid the state legislature from repealing the statute retroactively to reach acts done while the defense was in the statute. Should there be a similar per se prohibition on retroactive overruling of common law defenses, which in this example in effect upgrades the crime from attempted murder to murder? Or should merely a due process balancing test apply, taking into account the foreseeability of the overruling, whether reliance interests are involved, and so on? See *Rogers v. Tennessee*, 532 U.S. 451 (2001) (5–4 decision).

B. CONSTITUTIONAL TOLERANCE FOR RETROACTIVE STATUTES IN THE REGULATORY STATE

The overriding need for legislation to deal with social and economic problems since the New Deal, if not earlier, has stimulated academic and official rethinking of the general rule of statutory prospectivity. Consider Charles Hochman, *The Supreme Court and the Constitutionality of Retroactive Legislation*, 73 Harv. L. Rev. 692, 693 (1960):

> Perhaps the most fundamental reason why retroactive legislation is suspect stems from the principle that a person should be able to plan his [or her] conduct with reasonable certainty of the legal consequences. * * * Closely allied to this factor is the [person's] desire for stability with respect to past transactions. Moreover, to the extent that statutory law should serve as a guide to individual conduct, this purpose is thwarted by retroactive enactments. Still another reason underlying the hostility to retroactive legislation is that such a statute may be passed without an exact knowledge of who will benefit from it. * * *

> As is readily observable, these objections to retroactive statutes are neither totally absent from prospective legislation nor are they totally persuasive. A prospective statute may equally defeat reasonable expectations; moreover, many people do not

bother to ascertain the niceties of the law in planning their conduct. A retroactive statute, by remedying an unexpected judicial decision, may actually effectuate the intentions of the parties. And it is arguable that in many instances legislation passed with a knowledge of the transactions to which it will apply can be more responsive to the needs of a particular situation.

Since the New Deal, the constitutionality of retroactive legislation has been evaluated by balancing the public need against the private interest. Some of the factors which tend to support retroactivity are the following:

(a) *Emergency Situation.* Unforeseen, urgent, crisis situations often call forth decisive legislative responses. Wider constitutional latitude is given when the situation calls for strong measures. Thus in *Home Building and Loan Ass'n v. Blaisdell*, 290 U.S. 398 (1934), a leading Contract Clause case, the Court approved Depression measures creating a moratorium on mortgage foreclosures. But cf. *Louisville Joint Stock Land Bank v. Radford*, 295 U.S. 555 (1935) (striking down Frazier-Lemke Act suspending mortgage default proceedings for five years).

(b) *Strong Public Interest Requiring Retroactivity.* A related justification is that if retroactivity is necessary to the success of a statutory regime aimed at some important social policy, it will typically be accepted. The Court in *Usery v. Turner Elkhorn Mining Co.*, 428 U.S. 1, 14–20 (1976), upheld provisions in the Federal Coal Mine Health and Safety Act which required employers to compensate miners having black lung disease, even when their employment had terminated before the relevant provisions were enacted. The Court reasoned that the statute was a rational way to spread the costs of an important social problem — especially since mine operators had known about the effects of black lung disease for two decades and done nothing about it. Could the operators have been criminally punished retroactively?

(c) *Limited Abrogation of the Preenactment Right.* The more limited the legislative alteration of the legal incidents of a claim arising from a pre-enactment transaction, the stronger the case for the validity of the retroactive legislation. For example, the Court in *Penn Central Transp. Co. v. New York City*, 438 U.S. 104 (1978), upheld against a Takings Clause challenge New York's restrictions on the use that could be made of Grand Central Terminal because of its designation as a historic landmark. The Court reasoned that ownership of the landmark included a complex "bundle of rights," only some of which had been taken by the retroactive regulation. The Minnesota act in *Blaisdell*, extending the period for redemption of foreclosed mortgages and permitting the mortgagor to remain in control of the property also required the mortgagor to pay a reasonable rent on the property. And the statute stated that it would expire within two years, or whenever the emergency ended (whichever came first). Thus both the duration of the statutory impairment *and* the number of legal incidents taken away may be relevant to analysis of the validity of retroactive legislation.

(d) *Reasonable Expectation of Regulation.* Fairness concerns are greatly attenuated when the persons retroactively deprived of contractual or property rights had no reasonable expectation that they would be able to keep them. In other words, retroactivity can be justified to prevent "windfalls." Thus the Court in *Energy Reserves Group, Inc. v. Kansas Power and Light Co.*, 459 U.S. 400, 419–20 (1983), upheld a state law retroactively restricting price escalator clauses in contracts for the intrastate sale of natural gas. A critical reason for the retroactivity was that due to partial federal deregulation of interstate gas, intrastate gas prices had unexpectedly gone up, which would have given energy producers a $128 million windfall, to be borne by consumers (according to the legislature). Where a law only serves to restrict a party to those gains reasonably to be expected from the contract, *City of El Paso v. Simmons*, 379 U.S. 497, 515 (1965), its retroactive application will usually be upheld.

(e) *Lack of Process Corruption.* The Court may look askance at retroactive legislation when there is self-dealing. For example, when a state tries to void or substantially alter its own contractual obligations, the Court will apply a stricter standard of scrutiny and often invalidate the regulation. E.g., *United States Trust Co. v. New Jersey*, 431 U.S. 1 (1977). One consideration in Takings Clause cases is whether the burden of regulation is "disproportionately" concentrated on a few persons, suggesting process bias. See *Goldblatt v. Hempstead*, 369 U.S. 590, 594 (1962). See generally Note, *A Process-Oriented Approach to the Contract Clause*, 89 Yale L.J. 1623, 1638–39 (1980) (judicial review should require that the political process provide all groups interested in retroactive legislation with meaningful opportunity for their objections to be heard and considered).[d]

(f) *Revival of Constitutional Limits on Retroactivity?* Recently, the Supreme Court held that a statute regulating economic relations was impermissibly retroactive, but could not agree on why. *Eastern Enterprises v. Apfel*, 524 U.S. 498 (1998), involved a highly complicated setting in which, by virtue of a 1992 federal statute, a company that had left the coal mining industry in 1965 was required to assist in financing current health care costs for retired miners. The 1992 law, which required current contributions from companies that had participated in a 1950 benefit plan for miners, was sparked by a funding crisis relating to benefit plans for retired miners. Justice O'Connor, joined by Chief Justice Rehnquist and Justices Scalia and Thomas, labeled this a "taking" of the funds needed to comply with the statute. For them, when government action "singles out certain employers to bear a burden that is substantial in amount, based on the employer's conduct far in the past, and unrelated to any commitment that the employers made or to any injury they caused, the governmental action implicates fundamental principles of fairness underlying the Takings Clause." Justice Kennedy concurred in the judgment on the ground that the statute violated due process because it fell "far outside the bounds of retroactivity permissible under our law." He agreed with the dissenting Justices that the law did not effectuate a taking because no "specific property right or interest" was at stake. The dissenting Justices thought the

---

d. For a fairly recent decision in which these factors led the Court to uphold the retroactive application of an amendment to federal tax law even though a taxpayer had arguably relied to his detriment on prior law, see *United States v. Carlton*, 512 U.S. 26 (1994).

statute was not fundamentally unfair because it comported with long-term, if informal, expectations within the industry.

C. PRESUMPTIONS AGAINST STATUTORY RETROACTIVITY

Although the post-New Deal consensus is that the legislature can now make most statutory obligations retroactive to some extent, there remains substantial reluctance on the part of legislators to enact statutes that are retroactive on their face and on the part of judges to apply statutes retroactively where the statute is not clear. Hart and Sacks were amenable to this approach, for example, see *The Legal Process* at 618–30, and the Supreme Court has even in the post-New Deal era stated that "[r]etroactivity is not favored in the law. * * * Congressional enactments and administrative rules will not be construed to have retroactive effect unless their language requires this result." *Bowen v. Georgetown University Hospital*, 488 U.S. 204 (1988).

On the other hand are Supreme Court decisions that require application of a change in law — whether arising from a judicial decision or from enactment of a new statute — to all pending civil cases. The germinal case is *United States v. Schooner Peggy*, 5 U.S. (1 Cranch) 103 (1800), a decision by Chief Justice Marshall. More recent precedents are *Bradley v. School Board of City of Richmond*, 416 U.S. 696 (1974), and *Thorpe v. Housing Authority of City of Durham*, 393 U.S. 268 (1969). In *Bradley*, the Court held that a change in law should apply to pending civil cases so long as the legislature or the court making the change did not clearly intend to prohibit retroactive application and manifest injustice does not result.

The Supreme Court noted in *Kaiser Aluminum and Chemical Corp. v. Bonjorno*, 494 U.S. 827 (1990), that there is a tension between the *Bradley-Thorpe* line of cases and the *Bowen* line of cases but declined to resolve the matter, because a majority of the Court thought both lines required non-retroactivity of Congress' amendment of the postjudgment interest law, 28 U.S.C. § 1961. The Civil Rights Act of 1991 provided the Court the opportunity to resolve the tension between the competing lines of cases.

LANDGRAF v. USI FILM PRODUCTS
Supreme Court of the United States, 1994
511 U.S. 244, 114 S.Ct. 1483, 128 L.Ed.2d 229

JUSTICE STEVENS delivered the opinion of the Court.

[From September 4, 1984, through January 17, 1986, Barbara Landgraf was employed in the USI Film Products (USI) plant in Tyler, Texas. She worked the 11 p.m. to 7 a.m. shift operating a machine that produced plastic bags. A fellow employee named John Williams repeatedly harassed her with inappropriate remarks and physical contact. Petitioner's complaints to her immediate supervisor brought her no relief, but when she reported the incidents to the personnel manager, he conducted an investigation, reprimanded Williams, and transferred him to another department.

[Four days later Landgraf quit her job. She filed a complaint with the EEOC, which found that USI had created a "hostile work environment," in violation of Title VII, but also that the employer had adequately remedied the violation. Landgraf brought a lawsuit, which was dismissed. On November 21, 1991, while petitioner's appeal was pending, the President signed into law the Civil Rights Act of 1991. The Court of Appeals rejected Landgraf's argument that her case should be remanded for a jury trial on damages pursuant to the 1991 Act.]

[II] The Civil Rights Act of 1991 is in large part a response to a series of decisions of this Court interpreting the Civil Rights Acts of 1866 and 1964. Section 3(4) expressly identifies as one of the Act's purposes "to respond to recent decisions of the Supreme Court by expanding the scope of relevant civil rights statutes in order to provide adequate protection to victims of discrimination." That section, as well as a specific finding in § 2(2), identifies *Wards Cove Packing Co. v. Atonio*, 490 U.S. 642 (1989), as a decision that gave rise to special concerns. Section 105 of the Act, entitled "Burden of Proof in Disparate Impact Cases," is a direct response to *Wards Cove*.

Other sections of the Act were obviously drafted with "recent decisions of the Supreme Court" in mind. Thus, § 101 amended the 1866 Civil Rights Act's prohibition of racial discrimination in the "mak[ing] and enforce[ment] [of] contracts," 42 U.S.C. § 1981 (1988 ed., Supp. III), in response to *Patterson v. McLean Credit Union*, 491 U.S. 164 (1989); § 107 responds to *Price Waterhouse v. Hopkins*, 490 U.S. 228 (1989), by setting forth standards applicable in "mixed motive" cases; § 108 responds to *Martin v. Wilks*, 490 U.S. 755 (1989), by prohibiting certain challenges to employment practices implementing consent decrees; § 109 responds to *EEOC v. Arabian American Oil Co.*, 499 U.S. 244 (1991), by redefining the term "employee" as used in Title VII to include certain United States citizens working in foreign countries for United States employers; § 112 responds to *Lorance v. AT & T Technologies, Inc.*, 490 U.S. 900 (1989), by expanding employees' rights to challenge discriminatory seniority systems; § 113 responds to *West Virginia Univ. Hospitals, Inc. v. Casey*, 499 U.S. 83 (1991), by providing that an award of attorney's fees may include expert fees; and § 114 responds to *Library of Congress v. Shaw*, 478 U.S. 310 (1986), by allowing interest on judgments against the United States.

A number of important provisions in the Act, however, were not responses to Supreme Court decisions. * * * Among the provisions that did not directly respond to any Supreme Court decision is the one at issue in this case, § 102.

Entitled "Damages in Cases of Intentional Discrimination," § 102 provides in relevant part:

"(a) Right of Recovery. —

"(1) Civil Rights. — In an action brought by a complaining party under section 706 or 717 of the Civil Rights Act of 1964 (42 U.S.C. 2000e–5) against a respondent who engaged in unlawful intentional discrimination (not an employment practice that is unlawful because of its disparate impact) prohibited under section 703, 704, or 717 of the Act (42 U.S.C. 2000e–2 or 2000e–3), and provided that the complaining party cannot recover under section 1977 of the Revised Statutes (42 U.S.C. 1981), the complaining party may recover compensatory and punitive damages . . . in addition to any relief authorized by section 706(g) of the Civil Rights Act of 1964, from the respondent.

· · · · ·

"(c) Jury Trial. — If a complaining party seeks compensatory or punitive damages under this section —

"(1) any party may demand a trial by jury."

Before the enactment of the 1991 Act, Title VII afforded only "equitable" remedies. The primary form of monetary relief available was backpay. * * * [T]he new compensatory damages provision of the 1991 Act is "in addition to," and does not replace or duplicate, the backpay remedy allowed under prior law.[6] * * *

Section 102 also allows monetary relief for some forms of workplace discrimination that would not previously have justified *any* relief under Title VII. As this case illustrates, even if unlawful discrimination was proved, under prior law a Title VII plaintiff could not recover monetary relief unless the discrimination was also found to have some concrete effect on the plaintiff's employment status, such as a denied promotion, a differential in compensation, or termination. Section 102, however, allows a plaintiff to recover in circumstances in which there has been unlawful discrimination in the "terms, conditions, or privileges of employment," 42 U.S.C. § 2000e–2(a)(1), even though the discrimination did not involve a discharge or a loss of pay. * * *

In 1990, a comprehensive civil rights bill passed both Houses of Congress. Although similar to the 1991 Act in many other respects, the 1990 bill differed in that it contained language expressly calling for application of many of its provisions, including the section providing for damages in cases of intentional employment discrimination, to cases arising before its (expected) enactment.[8]

---

6. Section 102(b)(3) imposes limits, varying with the size of the employer, on the amount of compensatory and punitive damages that may be awarded to an individual plaintiff. Thus, the sum of such damages awarded a plaintiff may not exceed $50,000 for employers with between 14 and 100 employees; $100,000 for employers with between 101 and 200 employees; $200,000 for employers with between 200 and 500 employees; and $300,000 for employers with more than 500 employees.

8. The relevant section of the Civil Rights Act of 1990, S. 2104, 101st Cong., 1st Sess. (1990), provided:

"SEC. 15. APPLICATION OF AMENDMENTS AND TRANSITION RULES.

"(a) APPLICATION OF AMENDMENTS. — The amendments made by —

"(1) section 4 shall apply to all proceedings pending on or commenced after June 5, 1989 [the date of *Wards Cove Packing Co. v. Atonio*, 490 U.S. 642];

"(2) section 5 shall apply to all proceedings pending on or commenced after May 1, 1989 [the date of *Price Waterhouse v. Hopkins*, 490 U.S. 228];

"(3) section 6 shall apply to all proceedings pending on or commenced after June 12, 1989 [the date of *Martin v. Wilks*, 490 U.S. 755];

"(4) sections 7(a)(1), 7(a)(3) and 7(a)(4), 7(b), 8 [providing for compensatory and

The President vetoed the 1990 legislation, however, citing the bill's "unfair retroactivity rules" as one reason for his disapproval. Congress narrowly failed to override the veto. See 136 Cong.Rec. S16589 (Oct. 24, 1990) (66–34 Senate vote in favor of override). * * *

The omission of the elaborate retroactivity provision of the 1990 bill — which was by no means the only source of political controversy over that legislation — is not dispositive because it does not tell us precisely where the compromise was struck in the 1991 Act. The Legislature might, for example, have settled in 1991 on a less expansive form of retroactivity that, unlike the 1990 bill, did not reach cases already finally decided. See n. 8 *supra*. A decision to reach only cases still pending might explain Congress' failure to provide in the 1991 Act, as it had in 1990, that certain sections would apply to proceedings pending on specific preenactment dates. Our first question, then, is whether the statutory text on which petitioner relies manifests an intent that the 1991 Act should be applied to cases that arose and went to trial before its enactment.

[III] Petitioner's textual argument relies on three provisions of the 1991 Act: §§ 402(a), 402(b), and 109(c). Section 402(a), the only provision of the Act that speaks directly to the question before us, states:

> "Except as otherwise specifically provided, this Act and the amendments made by this Act shall take effect upon enactment."

That language does not, by itself, resolve the question before us. A statement that a statute will become effective on a certain date does not even arguably

---

punitive damages for intentional discrimination], 9, 10, and 11 shall apply to all proceedings pending on or commenced after the date of enactment of this Act;

"(5) section 7(a)(2) shall apply to all proceedings pending on or after June 12, 1989 [the date of *Lorance v. AT & T Technologies, Inc.*, 490 U.S. 900]; and

"(6) section 12 shall apply to all proceedings pending on or commenced after June 15, 1989 [the date of *Patterson v. McLean Credit Union*, 491 U.S. 164].

"(b) TRANSITION RULES. —

"(1) IN GENERAL. — Any orders entered by a court between the effective dates described in subsection (a) and the date of enactment of this Act that are inconsistent with the amendments made by sections 4, 5, 7(a)(2), or 12, shall be vacated if, not later than 1 year after such date of enactment, a request for such relief is made.

. . . . . .

"(3) FINAL JUDGMENTS. — Pursuant to paragraphs (1) and (2), any final judgment entered prior to the date of the enactment of this Act as to which the rights of any of the parties thereto have become fixed and vested, where the time for seeking further judicial review of such judgment has otherwise expired pursuant to title 28 of the United States Code, the Federal Rules of Civil Procedure, and the Federal Rules of Appellate Procedure, shall be vacated in whole or in part if justice requires pursuant to rule 60(b)(6) of the Federal Rules of Civil Procedure or other appropriate authority, and consistent with the constitutional requirements of due process of law."

suggest that it has any application to conduct that occurred at an earlier date.[10] Petitioner does not argue otherwise. Rather, she contends that the introductory clause of § 402(a) would be superfluous unless it refers to §§ 402(b) and 109(c), which provide for prospective application in limited contexts.

The parties agree that § 402(b) was intended to exempt a single disparate impact lawsuit against the Wards Cove Packing Company. Section 402(b) provides:

> "(b) CERTAIN DISPARATE IMPACT CASES. — Notwithstanding any other provision of this Act, nothing in this Act shall apply to any disparate impact case for which a complaint was filed before March 1, 1975, and for which an initial decision was rendered after October 30, 1983."

Section 109(c), part of the section extending Title VII to overseas employers, states:

> "(c) APPLICATION OF AMENDMENTS. — The amendments made by this section shall not apply with respect to conduct occurring before the date of the enactment of this Act."

According to petitioner, these two subsections are the "other provisions" contemplated in the first clause of § 402(a), and together create a strong negative inference that all sections of the Act not specifically declared prospective apply to pending cases that arose before November 21, 1991.

Before addressing the particulars of petitioner's argument, we observe that she places extraordinary weight on two comparatively minor and narrow provisions in a long and complex statute. Applying the entire Act to cases arising from preenactment conduct would have important consequences, including the possibility that trials completed before its enactment would need to be retried and the possibility that employers would be liable for punitive damages for conduct antedating the Act's enactment. Purely prospective application, on the other hand, would prolong the life of a remedial scheme, and of judicial constructions of civil rights statutes, that Congress obviously

---

10. The history of prior amendments to Title VII suggests that the "effective-upon-enactment" formula would have been an especially inapt way to reach pending cases. When it amended Title VII in the Equal Employment Opportunity Act of 1972, Congress explicitly provided:

> "The amendments made by this Act to section 706 of the Civil Rights Act of 1964 shall be applicable with respect to charges pending with the Commission on the date of enactment of this Act and all charges filed thereafter." Pub.L. 92–261, § 14, 86 Stat. 113.

In contrast, in amending Title VII to bar discrimination on the basis of pregnancy in 1978, Congress provided:

> "Except as provided in subsection (b), the amendment made by this Act shall be effective on the date of enactment." § 2(a), 92 Stat. 2076.

The only Courts of Appeals to consider whether the 1978 amendments applied to pending cases concluded that they did not. If we assume that Congress was familiar with those decisions, cf. *Cannon v. University of Chicago*, 441 U.S. 677, 698–699 (1979), its choice of language in § 402(a) would imply non-retroactivity.

found wanting. Given the high stakes of the retroactivity question, the broad coverage of the statute, and the prominent and specific retroactivity provisions in the 1990 bill, it would be surprising for Congress to have chosen to resolve that question through negative inferences drawn from two provisions of quite limited effect.

Petitioner, however, invokes the canon that a court should give effect to every provision of a statute and thus avoid redundancy among different provisions. Unless the word "otherwise" in § 402(a) refers to either § 402(b) or § 109(c), she contends, the first five words in § 402(a) are entirely superfluous. Moreover, relying on the canon "[e]xpressio unius est exclusio alterius," petitioner argues that because Congress provided specifically for prospectivity in two places (§§ 109(c) and 402(b)), we should infer that it intended the opposite for the remainder of the statute.

* * * Petitioner's argument has some force, but we find it most unlikely that Congress intended the introductory clause to carry the critically important meaning petitioner assigns it. Had Congress wished § 402(a) to have such a determinate meaning, it surely would have used language comparable to its reference to the predecessor Title VII damages provisions in the 1990 legislation: that the new provisions "shall apply to all proceedings pending on or commenced after the date of enactment of this Act." S. 2104, 101st Cong., 1st Sess. § 15(a)(4) (1990).

It is entirely possible that Congress inserted the "otherwise specifically provided" language not because it understood the "takes effect" clause to establish a rule of retroactivity to which only two "other specific provisions" would be exceptions, but instead to assure that any specific timing provisions in the Act would prevail over the general "take effect on enactment" command. The drafters of a complicated piece of legislation containing more than 50 separate sections may well have inserted the "except as otherwise provided" language merely to avoid the risk of an inadvertent conflict in the statute. If the introductory clause of § 402(a) was intended to refer specifically to §§ 402(b), 109(c), or both, it is difficult to understand why the drafters chose the word "otherwise" rather than either or both of the appropriate section numbers.

* * * It is entirely possible — indeed, highly probable — that, because it was unable to resolve the retroactivity issue with the clarity of the 1990 legislation, Congress viewed the matter as an open issue to be resolved by the courts. Our precedents on retroactivity left doubts about what default rule would apply in the absence of congressional guidance, and suggested that some provisions might apply to cases arising before enactment while others might not. Compare *Bowen v. Georgetown Univ. Hospital*, 488 U.S. 204 (1988) with *Bradley v. Richmond School Bd.*, 416 U.S. 696 (1974). The only matters Congress did *not* leave to the courts were set out with specificity in §§ 109(c) and 402(b). Congressional doubt concerning judicial retroactivity doctrine, coupled with the likelihood that the routine "take effect upon enactment" language would require courts to fall back upon that doctrine, provide a plausible explanation for both §§ 402(b) and 109(c) that makes neither provision redundant. * * *

The relevant legislative history of the 1991 Act reinforces our conclusion that §§ 402(a), 109(c) and 402(b) cannot bear the weight petitioner places upon them. The 1991 bill as originally introduced in the House contained explicit retroactivity provisions similar to those found in the 1990 bill. However, the Senate substitute that was agreed upon omitted those explicit retroactivity provisions.[14] The legislative history discloses some frankly partisan statements about the meaning of the final effective date language, but those statements cannot plausibly be read as reflecting any general agreement.[15] The history reveals no evidence that Members believed that an agreement had been tacitly struck on the controversial retroactivity issue, and little to suggest that *Congress* understood or intended the interplay of §§ 402(a), 402(b) and 109(c) to have the decisive effect petitioner assigns them. Instead, the history of the 1991 Act conveys the impression that legislators agreed to disagree about whether and to what extent the Act would apply to preenactment conduct.

Although the passage of the 1990 bill may indicate that a majority of the 1991 Congress also favored retroactive application, even the will of the majority does not become law unless it follows the path charted in Article I, § 7, cl. 2 of the Constitution. See *INS v. Chadha*, 462 U.S. 919, 946–951 (1983). In the absence of the kind of unambiguous directive found in § 15 of the 1990 bill, we must look elsewhere for guidance on whether § 102 applies to this case.

[IV] * * * [T]he presumption against retroactive legislation is deeply rooted in our jurisprudence, and embodies a legal doctrine centuries older than our Republic. Elementary considerations of fairness dictate that individuals should have an opportunity to know what the law is and to conform their conduct accordingly; settled expectations should not be lightly disrupted. For that reason, the "principle that the legal effect of conduct should ordinarily be assessed under the law that existed when the conduct took place has timeless and universal appeal." In a free, dynamic society, creativity in both commercial and artistic endeavors is fostered by a rule of law that gives people confidence about the legal consequences of their actions.

---

14. On the other hand, two proposals that would have provided explicitly for prospectivity also foundered. See 137 Cong. Rec. S3021, S3023 (Mar. 12, 1991); 137 Cong. Rec. H3898, H3908 (June 4, 1991).

15. For example, in an "interpretive memorandum" introduced on behalf of seven Republican sponsors of S. 1745, the bill that became the 1991 Act, Senator Danforth stated that "[t]he bill provides that, unless otherwise specified, the provisions of this legislation shall take effect upon enactment *and shall not apply retroactively.*" 137 Cong.Rec. S15485 (Oct. 30, 1991) (emphasis added). Senator Kennedy responded that it "will be up to the courts to determine the extent to which the bill will apply to cases and claims that were pending on the date of enactment." *Ibid.* (citing *Bradley*). The legislative history reveals other partisan statements on the proper meaning of the Act's "effective date" provisions. Senator Danforth observed that such statements carry little weight as legislative history. As he put it, "a court would be well advised to take with a large grain of salt floor debate and statements placed in the CONGRESSIONAL RECORD which purport to create an interpretation for the legislation that is before us." 137 Cong. Rec. S15325 (Oct. 29, 1991).

It is therefore not surprising that the antiretroactivity principle finds expression in several provisions of our Constitution. The *Ex Post Facto* Clause flatly prohibits retroactive application of penal legislation. Article I, § 10, cl. 1 prohibits States from passing another type of retroactive legislation, laws "impairing the Obligation of Contracts." The Fifth Amendment's Takings Clause prevents the Legislature (and other government actors) from depriving private persons of vested property rights except for a "public use" and upon payment of "just compensation." The prohibitions on "Bills of Attainder" in Art. I, §§ 9–10, prohibit legislatures from singling out disfavored persons and meting out summary punishment for past conduct. The Due Process Clause also protects the interests in fair notice and repose that may be compromised by retroactive legislation; a justification sufficient to validate a statute's prospective application under the Clause "may not suffice" to warrant its retroactive application.

These provisions demonstrate that retroactive statutes raise particular concerns. The Legislature's unmatched powers allow it to sweep away settled expectations suddenly and without individualized consideration. Its responsivity to political pressures poses a risk that it may be tempted to use retroactive legislation as a means of retribution against unpopular groups or individuals. As Justice Marshall observed in his opinion for the Court in *Weaver v. Graham*, 450 U.S. 24 (1981), the *Ex Post Facto* Clause not only ensures that individuals have "fair warning" about the effect of criminal statutes, but also "restricts governmental power by restraining arbitrary and potentially vindictive legislation."

The Constitution's restrictions, of course, are of limited scope. Absent a violation of one of those specific provisions, the potential unfairness of retroactive civil legislation is not a sufficient reason for a court to fail to give a statute its intended scope. Retroactivity provisions often serve entirely benign and legitimate purposes, whether to respond to emergencies, to correct mistakes, to prevent circumvention of a new statute in the interval immediately preceding its passage, or simply to give comprehensive effect to a new law Congress considers salutary. However, a requirement that Congress first make its intention clear helps ensure that Congress itself has determined that the benefits of retroactivity outweigh the potential for disruption or unfairness. * * *

A statute does not operate "retrospectively" merely because it is applied in a case arising from conduct antedating the statute's enactment, or upsets expectations based in prior law. Rather, the court must ask whether the new provision attaches new legal consequences to events completed before its enactment. The conclusion that a particular rule operates "retroactively" comes at the end of a process of judgment concerning the nature and extent of the change in the law and the degree of connection between the operation of the new rule and a relevant past event. Any test of retroactivity will leave room for disagreement in hard cases, and is unlikely to classify the enormous variety of legal changes with perfect philosophical clarity. However, retroactivity is a matter on which judges tend to have "sound . . . instinct[s]," and familiar considerations of fair notice, reasonable reliance, and settled expectations offer sound guidance.

Since the early days of this Court, we have declined to give retroactive effect to statutes burdening private rights unless Congress had made clear its intent. * * *

Our statement in *Bowen* that "congressional enactments and administrative rules will not be construed to have retroactive effect unless their language requires this result" was in step with this long line of cases. *Bowen* itself was a paradigmatic case of retroactivity in which a federal agency sought to recoup, under cost limit regulations issued in 1984, funds that had been paid to hospitals for services rendered earlier; our search for clear congressional intent authorizing retroactivity was consistent with the approach taken in decisions spanning two centuries.

* * * [W]hile the *constitutional* impediments to retroactive civil legislation are now modest, prospectivity remains the appropriate default rule. Because it accords with widely held intuitions about how statutes ordinarily operate, a presumption against retroactivity will generally coincide with legislative and public expectations. Requiring clear intent assures that Congress itself has affirmatively considered the potential unfairness of retroactive application and determined that it is an acceptable price to pay for the countervailing benefits. Such a requirement allocates to Congress responsibility for fundamental policy judgments concerning the proper temporal reach of statutes, and has the additional virtue of giving legislators a predictable background rule against which to legislate.

[B] Although we have long embraced a presumption against statutory retroactivity, for just as long we have recognized that, in many situations, a court should "apply the law in effect at the time it renders its decision," *Bradley*, even though that law was enacted after the events that gave rise to the suit. There is, of course, no conflict between that principle and a presumption against retroactivity when the statute in question is unambiguous. Chief Justice Marshall's opinion in *United States v. Schooner Peggy*, 1 Cranch 103 (1801), illustrates this point. Because a treaty signed on September 30, 1800, while the case was pending on appeal, unambiguously provided for the restoration of captured property "not yet *definitively* condemned," (emphasis in original), we reversed a decree entered on September 23, 1800, condemning a French vessel that had been seized in American waters. Our application of "the law in effect" at the time of our decision in *Schooner Peggy* was simply a response to the language of the statute.

Even absent specific legislative authorization, application of new statutes passed after the events in suit is unquestionably proper in many situations. When the intervening statute authorizes or affects the propriety of prospective relief, application of the new provision is not retroactive. Thus, in *American Steel Foundries v. Tri-City Central Trades Council*, 257 U.S. 184 (1921), we held that § 20 of the Clayton Act, enacted while the case was pending on appeal, governed the propriety of injunctive relief against labor picketing. * * *

Changes in procedural rules may often be applied in suits arising before their enactment without raising concerns about retroactivity. For example, in *Ex parte Collett*, 337 U.S. 55, 71 (1949), we held that 28 U.S.C. § 1404(a) governed the transfer of an action instituted prior to that statute's enactment. We noted the diminished reliance interests in matters of procedure. Because rules of procedure regulate secondary rather than primary conduct, the fact that a new procedural rule was instituted after the conduct giving rise to the suit does not make application of the rule at trial retroactive. * * *

Our holding in *Bradley* is * * * compatible with the line of decisions disfavoring "retroactive" application of statutes. In *Bradley*, the District Court had awarded attorney's fees and costs, upon general equitable principles, to parents who had prevailed in an action seeking to desegregate the public schools of Richmond, Virginia. While the case was pending before the Court of Appeals, Congress enacted § 718 of the Education Amendments of 1972, which authorized federal courts to award the prevailing parties in school desegregation cases a reasonable attorney's fee. The Court of Appeals held that the new fee provision did not authorize the award of fees for services rendered before the effective date of the amendments. This Court reversed. We concluded that the private parties could rely on § 718 to support their claim for attorney's fees, resting our decision "on the principle that a court is to apply the law in effect at the time it renders its decision, unless doing so would result in manifest injustice or there is statutory direction or legislative history to the contrary."

Although that language suggests a categorical presumption in favor of application of *all* new rules of law, we now make it clear that *Bradley* did not alter the well-settled presumption against application of the class of new statutes that would have genuinely "retroactive" effect. * * * [T]he attorney's fee provision at issue in *Bradley* did not resemble the cases in which we have invoked the presumption against statutory retroactivity. Attorney's fee determinations, we have observed, are "collateral to the main cause of action" and "uniquely separable from the cause of action to be proved at trial." Moreover, even before the enactment of § 718, federal courts had authority to award fees based upon equitable principles. As our opinion in *Bradley* made clear, it would be difficult to imagine a stronger equitable case for an attorney's fee award than a lawsuit in which the plaintiff parents would otherwise have to bear the costs of desegregating their children's public schools. * * *

[V] * * * The jury trial right set out in § 102(c)(1) is plainly a procedural change of the sort that would ordinarily govern in trials conducted after its effective date. If § 102 did no more than introduce a right to jury trial in Title VII cases, the provision would presumably apply to cases tried after November 21, 1991, regardless of when the underlying conduct occurred. However, because § 102(c) makes a jury trial available only "[i]f a complaining party seeks compensatory or punitive damages," the jury trial option must stand or fall with the attached damages provisions.

Section 102(b)(1) is clearly on the other side of the line. That subsection authorizes punitive damages if the plaintiff shows that the defendant "engaged in a discriminatory practice or discriminatory practices with malice or with reckless indifference to the federally protected rights of an aggrieved individual." The very labels given "punitive" or "exemplary" damages, as well as the rationales that support them, demonstrate that they share key characteristics of criminal sanctions. Retroactive imposition of punitive damages would raise a serious constitutional question. Before we entertained that question, we would have to be confronted with a statute that explicitly authorized punitive damages for preenactment conduct. The Civil Rights Act of 1991 contains no such explicit command.

The provision of § 102(a)(1) authorizing the recovery of compensatory damages is not easily classified. It does not make unlawful conduct that was lawful when it occurred; as we have noted, § 102 only reaches discriminatory conduct already prohibited by Title VII. Concerns about a lack of fair notice are further muted by the fact that such discrimination was in many cases (although not this one) already subject to monetary liability in the form of backpay. Nor could anyone seriously contend that the compensatory damages provisions smack of a "retributive" or other suspect legislative purpose. Section 102 reflects Congress' desire to afford victims of discrimination more complete redress for violations of rules established more than a generation ago in the Civil Rights Act of 1964. At least with respect to its compensatory damages provisions, then, § 102 is not in a category in which objections to retroactive application on grounds of fairness have their greatest force.

Nonetheless, the new compensatory damages provision would operate "retrospectively" if it were applied to conduct occurring before November 21, 1991. Unlike certain other forms of relief, compensatory damages are quintessentially backward-looking. Compensatory damages may be intended less to sanction wrongdoers than to make victims whole, but they do so by a mechanism that affects the liabilities of defendants. They do not "compensate" by distributing funds from the public coffers, but by requiring particular employers to pay for harms they caused. The introduction of a right to compensatory damages is also the type of legal change that would have an impact on private parties' planning. In this case, the event to which the new damages provision relates is the discriminatory conduct of respondents' agent John Williams; if applied here, that provision would attach an important new legal burden to that conduct. The new damages remedy in § 102, we conclude, is the kind of provision that does not apply to events antedating its enactment in the absence of clear congressional intent. * * *

JUSTICE BLACKMUN, dissenting. * * *

* * * The well-established presumption against retroactive legislation, which serves to protect settled expectations, is grounded in a respect for vested rights. See, e.g., Smead, *The Rule Against Retroactive Legislation: A Basic Principle of Jurisprudence*, 20 Minn. L. Rev. 774, 784 (1936) (retroactivity doctrine developed as an "inhibition against a construction which . . . would violate vested rights"). This presumption need not be applied to remedial legislation, such as § 102, that does not proscribe any conduct that was previously legal.

At no time within the last generation has an employer had a vested right to engage in or to permit sexual harassment; " 'there is no such thing as a vested right to do wrong.' " *Freeborn v. Smith*, 2 Wall. 160 (1865). Section 102 of the Act expands the remedies available for acts of intentional discrimination, but does not alter the scope of the employee's basic right to be free from discrimination or the employer's corresponding legal duty. There is nothing unjust about holding an employer responsible for injuries caused by conduct that has been illegal for almost 30 years.

JUSTICE SCALIA, with whom JUSTICE KENNEDY and JUSTICE THOMAS, join, concurring in the [judgment].

[Justice Scalia first objects to the Court's failure to announce a "clear statement rule" against statutory retroactivity, one that can only be rebutted by a clear statement in the statutory text. He then complains about the failure to overrule *Bradley* and *Thorpe*.]

My last, and most significant, disagreement with the Court's analysis of this case pertains to the meaning of retroactivity. The Court adopts as its own the definition crafted by Justice Story in a case involving a provision of the New Hampshire Constitution that prohibited "retrospective" laws: a law is retroactive only if it "takes away or impairs vested rights acquired under existing laws, or creates a new obligation, imposes a new duty, or attaches a new disability, in respect to transactions or considerations already past." *Society for Propagation of the Gospel v. Wheeler*, 22 F.Cas. 756, 767 (No. 13,516) (CCNH 1814) (Story, J.).

One might expect from this "vested rights" focus that the Court would hold all changes in rules of procedure (as opposed to matters of substance) to apply retroactively. And one would draw the same conclusion from the Court's formulation of the test as being "whether the new provision attaches new legal consequences to events completed before its enactment" — a test borrowed directly from our *ex post facto* Clause jurisprudence, see, e.g., *Miller v. Florida*, 482 U.S. 423, 430 (1987), where we have adopted a substantive-procedural line, see *id*. ("no *ex post facto* violation occurs if the change in law is merely procedural"). In fact, however, the Court shrinks from faithfully applying the test that it has announced. It first seemingly defends the procedural-substantive distinction that a "vested rights" theory entails ("[b]e-cause rules of procedure regulate secondary rather than primary conduct, the fact that a new procedural rule was instituted after the conduct giving rise to the suit does not make application of the rule at trial retroactive"). But it soon acknowledges a broad and ill defined (indeed, utterly undefined) exception: "Whether a new rule of trial procedure applies will generally depend upon the posture of the case in question." Under this exception, "a new rule concerning the filing of complaints would not govern an action in which the complaint had already been filed," and "the promulgation of a new jury trial rule would ordinarily not warrant retrial of cases that had previously been tried to a judge." It is hard to see how either of these refusals to allow retroactive application preserves any "vested right." " 'No one has a vested right in any given mode of procedure.' " *Ex parte Collett*, 337 U.S. 55, 71 (1949)[.]

The seemingly random exceptions to the Court's "vested rights" (substance-*vs.*-procedure) criterion must be made, I suggest, because that criterion is fundamentally wrong. It may well be that the upsetting of "vested substantive rights" was the proper touchstone for interpretation of New Hampshire's constitutional prohibition, as it is for interpretation of the United States Constitution's *ex post facto* Clauses. But I doubt that it has anything to do with the more mundane question before us here: absent clear statement to the contrary, what is the presumed temporal application of a statute? For purposes of *that* question, a *procedural* change should no more be presumed to be retroactive than a *substantive* one. The critical issue, I think, is not whether the rule affects "vested rights," or governs substance or procedure, but rather what is the relevant activity that the rule regulates. Absent clear statement otherwise, only such relevant activity which occurs *after* the effective date of the statute is covered. Most statutes are meant to regulate primary conduct, and hence will not be applied in trials involving conduct that occurred before their effective date. But other statutes have a different purpose and therefore a different relevant retroactivity event. A new rule of evidence governing expert testimony, for example, is aimed at regulating the conduct of trial, and the event relevant to retroactivity of the rule is introduction of the testimony. Even though it is a procedural rule, it would unquestionably not be applied to *testimony already taken* — reversing a case on appeal, for example, because the new rule had not been applied at a trial which antedated the statute.

The inadequacy of the Court's "vested rights" approach becomes apparent when a change in one of the incidents of trial alters substantive entitlements. The opinion classifies attorney's fees provisions as procedural and permits "retroactive" application (in the sense of application to cases involving pre-enactment conduct). It seems to me, however, that holding a person liable for attorney's fees affects a "substantive right" no less than holding him liable for compensatory or punitive damages, which the Court treats as affecting a vested right. If attorney's fees can be awarded in a suit involving conduct that antedated the fee-authorizing statute, it is because the purpose of the fee award is not to affect that conduct, but to encourage suit for the vindication of certain rights — so that the retroactivity event is the filing of suit, whereafter encouragement is no longer needed. Or perhaps because the purpose of the fee award is to *facilitate* suit — so that the retroactivity event is the termination of suit, whereafter facilitation can no longer be achieved. * * *

Finally, statutes eliminating previously available forms of prospective relief provide another challenge to the Court's approach. Courts traditionally withhold requested injunctions that are not authorized by then-current law, even if they were authorized at the time suit commenced and at the time the primary conduct sought to be enjoined was first engaged in. The reason, which has nothing to do with whether it is possible to have a vested right to prospective relief, is that "[o]bviously, this form of relief operates only *in futuro*." Since the purpose of prospective relief is to affect the future rather than remedy the past, the relevant time for judging its retroactivity is the very moment at which it is ordered.[3] * * *

RIVERS v. ROADWAY EXPRESS, INC., 511 U.S. 298 (1994). Section 101 of the Civil Rights Act of 1991, Pub. L. No. 102–166, 105 Stat. 1071, defines the term "make and enforce contracts" as used in § 1 of the Civil Rights Act of 1866, Rev. Stat. 1977, 42 U.S.C. § 1981, to include "the making, performance, modification, and termination of contracts, and the enjoyment of all benefits, privileges, terms, and conditions of the contractual relationship." Section 101 overrides *Patterson v. McLean Credit Union* (Section 2B above), which had held the 1866 Act inapplicable to discrimination during an employment contract period.

Justice Stevens' opinion for the Court applied the *Landgraf* presumption to hold § 101, like § 102, prospective only. The Court reasoned that "the presumption is even more clearly applicable to § 101 than to § 102. Section 102 altered the liabilities of employers under Title VII by subjecting them to expanded monetary liability, but it did not alter the normative scope of Title VII's prohibition on workplace discrimination. In contrast, because § 101 amended § 1981 to embrace all aspects of the contractual relationship, including contract terminations, it enlarged the category of conduct that is subject to § 1981 liability."

On the other hand, the plaintiff in this case had an argument that the plaintiff in *Landgraf* did not have, because § 101 was " 'restorative' of the understanding of § 1981 that prevailed before [the Court's] decision in *Patterson*." Justice Stevens observed that Congress often responds to, and overrides, judicial decisions. "A legislative response does not necessarily indicate that Congress viewed the judicial decision as 'wrongly decided' as an interpretive matter. Congress may view the judicial decision as an entirely correct reading of prior law — or it may be altogether indifferent to the decision's technical merits — but may nevertheless decide that the old law should be amended. * * * Because retroactivity raises special policy concerns, the choice to enact a statute that responds to a judicial decision is quite distinct from the choice to make the responding statute retroactive." Indeed, Justice Stevens noted, the 1991 statute not only dropped the specific retroactivity provision for applying § 101, but also dropped an explicit statutory statement that the statute was "restoring" pre-existing rights; § 3(4) of the 1991 Act states its goal as "expanding the scope of relevant civil rights statutes in order to provide adequate protection to victims of discrimination." Nor did the legislative history of the 1991 bill, as opposed to the 1990 bill, demonstrate

---

3. A focus on the relevant retroactivity event also explains why the presumption against retroactivity is not violated by interpreting a statute to alter the future legal effect of past transactions — so-called secondary retroactivity. A new ban on gambling applies to existing casinos and casinos under construction, even though it "attaches a new disability" to those past investments. The relevant retroactivity event is the primary activity of gambling, not the primary activity of constructing casinos.

that Congress saw § 101 as overriding a judicial error and "restoring" established prior law.

The plaintiff also argued against any presumption of prospectivity for restorative statutes, as they do not implicate fairness concerns relating to retroactivity at least when the new statute simply enacts a rule that the parties believed to be the law when they acted; indeed, fairness concerns favor retroactivity because *Patterson* cut off, after the fact, rights of action under § 1981 that had been recognized when the complained of conduct occurred. Justice Stevens found nothing in the Court's precedents to support such a presumption. The old nineteenth century cases relied on by plaintiff only stood for the proposition that Congress has the *constitutional authority* to make restorative statutes retroactive, not for the more ambitious proposition that such statutes should be *presumed* retroactive.

Justice Scalia (joined by **Justices Kennedy** and **Thomas**) concurred in the judgment, and **Justice Blackmun** dissented.

NOTES ON *LANDGRAF*, *RIVERS*, AND STATUTORY RETROACTIVITY

1. *Why Not Different Presumptions in* Landgraf *and* Rivers? Justice Stevens' opinions apply the same presumption against retroactivity in both cases, but why couldn't the Court carve out a separate rule for restoration statutes? Lower courts had held that "curative" legislation should be presumed applicable to pending litigation. For example, in *Lussier v. Dugger*, 904 F.2d 661, 688 (11th Cir. 1990), the court applied the Civil Rights Restoration Act of 1988 to a case pending on its date of enactment, because the statute "does not change prior legislation, but merely corrects prior judicial interpretations which the Congress believed 'unduly narrowed' * * * the civil rights laws." Accord, *Leake v. Long Island Jewish Medical Center*, 869 F.2d 130 (2d Cir. 1989). In *Mrs. W. v. Tirozzi*, 832 F.2d 748, 754–55 (2d Cir. 1987), the court applied a new statute to pending cases, because the "amendment in the present case simply codifies a congressional purpose long in place which Congress believed the Supreme Court had misinterpreted." Some courts interpreting state statutes have followed the same approach: "The general rule against retrospective application is inapplicable to curative statutes, which by their very nature are designed to affect the past." *In re Grey*, 29 B.R. 286, 289 (D. Kan. 1983). Does *Rivers* displace all these lower court cases?

Representative Edwards, a sponsor of the 1991 Act who favored retroactivity, provided a detailed practical justification for his position:

> To have limited this legislation to conduct occurring after the date of enactment would have led to an intolerable result: for the next two decades, the courts would be handing down two sets of contradictory decisions: one set of decisions to explicate the law as Congress has enacted it, and the other would further develop the fine points of the law under *Wards Cove, Patterson, Lorance, Price Waterhouse, etc.*, long after Congress has repudiated those decisions. * * * When Congress has determined that its legislation has been wrongly construed, the error must be brought to an end, not given artificial respiration for the foreseeable future.

137 Cong. Rec. H9530–31 (daily ed. Nov. 7, 1991). There were in 1994 literally hundreds, if not thousands, of *Patterson* cases already in the lower federal courts; the "clearing out" problem is not insubstantial. How would Justice Stevens respond to this concern? Do you find it persuasive?

2. *Why Should There Be a Presumption Against Retroactivity?* In the modern administrative state, with its ubiquitous regulation, the traditional presumption against retroactive legislation (*Bowen* and now *Landgraf*) may be no longer normatively supportable. Historically, it rests upon a common law conception of vested property and contract rights which arguably did not survive the New Deal. Since then, it has rested upon a realist or legal-process conception of private and public reliance on prior law, but that may no longer be a robust justification, either. See William Eskridge, Jr., *Dynamic Statutory Interpretation* ch. 8 (1994); Louis Kaplow, *An Economic Analysis of Legal Transitions*, 99 Harv. L. Rev. 509 (1986). It has long been recognized that reliance interests can be overborne when justice or social utility require retroactive rulemaking. It is also increasingly recognized that reliance interests themselves are contingent: expectations cannot be considered a legally cognizable reliance interest unless they are "reasonable," but is it reasonable to act as though government rules will not change? A realistic view of the modern state could support the *Bradley* formulation: A statute or administrative rule can be retroactive, but not if it results in "manifest injustice" by unsettling social practice without a sufficient policy justification.

The reasonableness of expectations depends ultimately upon an interplay between social and legal practice, under a pragmatic philosophy. Legal practice has progressively discouraged exclusionary employment policies and practices, especially those that directly or even indirectly prevent African Americans and other racial minorities from getting jobs and promotions. Social practice has substantially assimilated the prohibitions against facial discriminations on the basis of race and has been increasingly alert to policies having a discriminatory racial impact. The sort of openly harassing racial discrimination Brenda Patterson complained of has long been unlawful in our society, has since the 1970s been subject to multiple remedies, and is worth deterring under almost all of the respectable theories of racial justice and employment economics. The only legitimate objection is one of social cost: Does the extra amount of deterrence created by the additional remedy for black employees outweigh the administrative and other direct employer costs, as well as any intangible workplace costs? On that issue, Congress has said that the costs are worth it.

Are you persuaded by this argument? How would Justice Stevens respond? Justice Scalia?

3. *The Presumption Against Retroactivity After* Landgraf. Justice Stevens declines to adopt a presumption that each and every statute is presumed to be prospective only. What approach does he take for differentiating among statutes? One approach he flirts with is to distinguish statutes altering rules of "primary" behavior (presumptively nonretroactive) from statutes altering "remedies" (presumptively retroactive). This distinction is inspired by Hart and Sacks' legal process materials, and is exploited in Justice Harlan's

Moragne decision. It was applied to the 1991 Act in *Johnson v. Uncle Ben's, Inc.*, 965 F.2d 1363, 1374 (5th Cir. 1992); *Gersman v. Group Health Ass'n, Inc.*, 975 F.2d 886, 898-899 (D.C. Cir. 1992) (Wald, J., dissenting).

Where does § 101 fit in this typology? While § 101 expands § 1981's duty of nondiscrimination to include conduct during the contract period, which seems to affect primary behavior, in most employment cases (before the new remedies provisions in Title VII cases become applicable) § 1981 penalizes conduct already made illegal by Title VII, and in those cases § 101 merely expands the remedies (compensatory and punitive damages) available to a victim of racial discrimination in the workplace. Adding the damages relief of § 1981 to the backpay and injunctive relief of Title VII is in economic terms additional regulation of primary behavior. This sort of analysis can be applied to a whole range of changes in this law. Because of the substantive relationship between rules of behavior and penalties for noncompliance, the primary behavior/new remedy distinction may not be an analytically helpful one. Exactly how does Justice Stevens determine when the presumption fully applies?

Landgraf may have clarified the general federal judicial approach to questions of statutory retroactivity, but it has not led to consensus in later decisions.[e] The most interesting case, *Hamdan v. Rumsfeld*, 126 S.Ct. 2749 (2006) (5-3 decision), involved a statute that restricts federal habeas corpus jurisdiction over petitions by alleged foreign combatants incarcerated at Guantanamo Bay, Cuba. Even though *Landgraf* suggests that procedural and jurisdictional statutes routinely apply retroactively (or at least are not subject to the general presumption against retroactive application), the majority of the Justices refused to apply the statute to cases pending at the time of its enactment.[f] In part, the Court used the ordinary tools of statutory interpretation to conclude that the statute was not designed to apply to pending cases, but there is little doubt that the Justices sought to avoid the potentially serious constitutional questions surrounding the limits on congressional power to restrict the authority of the federal judiciary in habeas corpus cases.[g]

---

e. See, e.g., *Republic of Austria v. Altmann*, 541 U.S. 677 (2004) (6-3 decision) (Foreign Sovereign Immunities Act applies to conduct that occurred prior to its enactment); *Martin v. Hadix*, 527 U.S. 343 (1999) (7-2 decision) (statute restricting amount of attorney's fees for representing successful state prisoners challenging conditions of confinement applies to work done after the statute was enacted even in cases that were filed before the enactment date).

f. See also *Lindh v. Murphy*, 521 U.S. 320 (1997) (5-4 decision) (refusing to apply to pending cases a statute limiting the availability of habeas corpus relief to state prisoners).

g. Cf. *INS v. St. Cyr*, 533 U.S. 289 (2001) (interpreting statute to allow allegedly deportable alien to file habeas corpus petition and refusing to apply statutory repeal of Attorney General's discretion to provide relief from deportation retroactively to aliens who had pleaded guilty to crimes before the statutory repeal in reliance on the existence of that discretionary power).

On the canon counseling courts to read statutes in ways that avoid constitutional questions, see Chapter 8, § 1B2.

Chapter 7

THEORIES OF
STATUTORY INTERPRETATION

———

We suggested in Chapters 1 and 6 that statutes, rather than the common law or constitutional law, are the dominant source of modern American law. Notwithstanding the "statutorification" of American law (Grant Gilmore's phrase), courts retain a great role, because they apply and interpret statutes in the "hard cases" not clearly answered by the statutory language. Such hard cases are inevitable, partly because of the inherent imprecision of language and partly because of the inability of statute drafters to anticipate all problems or circumstances within the statute's ambit. Justice Felix Frankfurter, in *Some Reflections on the Reading of Statutes*, 47 Colum. L. Rev. 527, 528 (1947), expressed this problem in his own distinctive style:

> [U]nlike mathematical symbols, the phrasing of a document, especially a complicated enactment, seldom attains more than approximate precision. If individual words are inexact symbols, with shifting variables, their configuration can hardly achieve invariant meaning or assured definiteness. Apart from the ambiguity inherent in its symbols, a statute suffers from dubieties. It is not an equation or a formula representing a clearly marked process, nor is it an expression of individual thought to which is imparted the definiteness a single authorship can give. A statute is an instrument of government partaking of its practical purposes but also of its infirmities and limitations, of its awkward and groping efforts. * * *

Thus, while Frankfurter, as a professor at Harvard Law School, had developed "his threefold imperative to law students: (1) Read the statute; (2) read the statute; (3) read the statute," Henry Friendly, *Mr. Justice Frankfurter and the Reading of Statutes*, in Friendly, *Benchmarks* 202 (1967), he appreciated the difficulty of understanding a statute simply by parsing its language. The following example illustrates Frankfurter's point: A municipal ordinance provides that "all drug shops * * * shall be closed * * * at 10 p.m. on each and every day of the week." Does this require all such shops to remain open until 10 p.m., at which time they must be closed (i.e., is "closed" used as a verb or an adjective)? If a shop is closed at 10 p.m. may it lawfully open ten minutes later? In *Rex v. Liggetts-Findley Drug-Stores Ltd.*, [1919] 3 W.W.R. 1025, the Supreme Court of Alberta answered the latter of these questions in the negative. The judge delivering the judgment stated:

I think no one but a lawyer — I mean a person trained in legal technicalities such as a Judge or a lawyer — would ever think of imputing such a meaning to the [ordinance]. Everyone knows what is meant by closing a shop at 10 o'clock p.m. The meaning conveyed by the words used is too obvious for doubt. The rule, of course, is that the grammatical sense must in general be adhered to but with this limitation that if it leads to an absurdity or to something meaningless an effort must be made to give some sensible reading unless the language is absolutely intractable. * * * I think we should take the words to mean what they would quite clearly mean to the ordinary person and that is that shops should be closed not only at the moment of 10 o'clock but for the rest of that day.

Under this decision, could a store lawfully open at one minute after midnight?

Most statutes do not clearly answer all the questions that might arise, and over time the number of ambiguities or unanswered questions tends to increase. This gives rise to a predicament in our constitutional system. On the one hand, it is generally assumed that "any conflict between the legislative will and the judicial will must be resolved in favor of the former." Reed Dickerson, *The Interpretation and Application of Statutes* 8 (1975). Thus, statutory interpretation is not "an opportunity for a judge to use words as 'empty vessels into which he can pour anything he will' — his caprices, fixed notions, even statesmanlike beliefs in a particular policy." Frankfurter, *supra*, at 529. On the other hand, statutory interpretation cannot be appropriately undertaken by a mechanical application of rules or "unimaginative adherence to well-worn professional phrases." *Id.* The proper interplay among statutory language, legislative purposes, extrinsic material such as other statutes and legislative history, and the particular facts of the case at hand may not be discerned by any formula. As a consequence, statutory interpretation in the hard cases involves substantial judicial discretion and political judgment. See Richard Posner, *Legal Formalism, Legal Realism and the Interpretation of Statutes and the Constitution*, 37 Case W. Res. L. Rev. 179 (1987). It is very much an art and not a science.

Given the importance of statutory interpretation for students of legislation, we have divided the subject into two chapters. This chapter introduces you to the subject both theoretically and historically. Three different theoretical approaches have dominated the history of American judicial practice: *intentionalism*, in which the interpreter identifies and then follows the original intent of the statute's drafters; *purposivism*, in which the interpreter chooses the interpretation that best carries out the statute's purpose; and *textualism*, in which the interpreter follows the "plain meaning" of the statute's text. These different approaches rest upon different visions of the role of the interpreter and the nature of our constitutional system. Each is, of course, subject to critique.

We have organized this chapter around the following historical dynamic: For most of this country's history, both the theory and the practice of statutory interpretation have been "eclectic" rather than systematic — that is, more case-by-case and inductive than rule-oriented and deductive. After the turn of the twentieth century, judges and scholars began to formulate their thoughts more systematically. An initial impulse was to emphasize original legislative intent as the foundational enterprise in statutory cases. In turn, beginning in the 1930s an influential group of skeptics, the "legal realists," debunked original intent as an indeterminate and incoherent concept for statutory interpretation. During the New Deal, American public law turned toward purpose-based approaches as the foundation for statutory meaning. This purpose approach was reflected in the influential Hart and Sacks materials on "The Legal Process" and in opinions of both state and federal courts. Purposivism was in turn criticized for slighting traditional rule-of-law values (e.g., predictability of law, limiting judicial discretion) and for engaging courts in policy analysis for which they are ill-equipped. The "new textualism" that arose in the 1980s seeks to return statutory interpretation to textual analysis, though this approach has in turn been criticized as impractical and unrealistic.

Our goal in this theoretical and historical survey is to offer you different theories from which you can learn, even as you criticize each of them. We think you will find the history and the theory useful, both in developing your own analytical skills in interpreting statutes and in appreciating the doctrinal material presented in Chapter 8.

SECTION 1. FROM ECLECTICISM TO SYSTEMATIC THEORY, 1789–1938

The early history of statutory interpretation in the United States is a complicated one, with American courts employing a grab-bag variety of approaches. Following English rhetoric and practice,[a] American courts in the eighteenth and early nineteenth centuries generally proclaimed their fidelity to legislative "intent" but would consider as evidence of such intent the statute's text, canons of statutory construction, the common law, the circumstances of enactment, principles of equity, and so forth.[b] Indeed, the big debate at the time of the drafting of the Constitution was how much discretion a court's *equity* powers gave it to ameliorate or extend the letter of the statute.[c]

Chief Justice John Marshall was the first great American statutory interpreter, vigorously exercising equitable powers of construction in pursuit of his nationalist understanding of the Constitution, but under cover of rigorous

---

a. See Samuel Thorne, *A Discourse upon the Exposicion & Understanding of Statutes* (1942) (reprinting leading early modern English treatise developing intent as lodestar of statutory interpretation). See also Peter Tiersma, *A Message in a Bottle: Text, Autonomy, and Statutory Interpretation*, 76 Tul. L. Rev. 431 (2001) (medieval English law treated statutes as mere "evidence of law").

b. See Hans Baade, *"Original Intent" in Historical Perspective: Some Critical Glosses*, 69 Tex. L. Rev. 1001, 1062–1107 (1991), and *The Casus Omissus: A Pre-History of Statutory Analogy*, 20 Syr. J. Int'l L. 45 (1994). See also William Popkin, *Statutes in Court: The History and Theory of Statutory Interpretation* (1999); William Blatt, *The History of Statutory Interpretation: A Study in Form and Substance*, 6 Cardozo L. Rev. 799 (1985).

c. See William Eskridge, Jr., *All About Words: Early Understandings of the "Judicial Power" in Statutory Interpretation, 1776–1806*, 101 Colum. L. Rev. 990 (2001); John Manning, *Textualism and Equity of the Statute*, 101 Colum. L. Rev. 1 (2001).

and sometimes brilliant textual analysis.[d] For example, his opinion in *Ex parte Bollman*, 8 U.S. 75 (1807), remains a leading construction of the federal habeas corpus law. Section 14 of the Judiciary Act of 1789 provided, in its first sentence, that the Supreme Court and other federal courts "shall have power to issue writs of *scire facias*, *habeas corpus*, and all other writs not specially provided for by statute, which may be necessary for the exercise of their respective jurisdictions * * *." The second sentence provided that Supreme Court Justices and district judges, in their chambers, "shall have power to grant writs of *habeas corpus* for the purpose of an inquiry into the cause of commitment." The government maintained that the Supreme Court had no jurisdiction to inquire into the legality of Bollman's confinement, as that power was only given to individual judges.

This was a good plain meaning argument, yet not one the Court was prepared to accept. Marshall suggested there was a grammatical objection to this argument but declined to rest the decision on linguistic niceties.[e] Instead, "the sound construction, which the court thinks it safer to adopt," was the one consistent with a central goal of the Constitution — to assure "that the privilege of the writ of *Habeas Corpus* should not be suspended unless when in cases of rebellion or invasion the public safety might require it." *Id.* at 95. "Acting under the immediate influence of this injunction, they [Congress in 1789] must have felt, with peculiar force, the obligation of providing efficient means by which this great constitutional privilege should receive life and activity." *Id.* Given the centrality of this writ to the liberty assured by the Constitution as well as the common law, the Chief Justice reasoned "that congress could never intend to give a power of this kind, to one of the judges of this court which is refused to all of them when assembled. * * * This is not consistent with the genius of our legislation, nor with the course of our judicial proceedings." *Id.* at 96. To reconcile the first and second sentences of the confusing statute, Marshall concluded that "the first sentence vests this power in all courts of the United States; but as those courts are not always in session, the second sentence vests it in every justice or judge of the United States." *Id.* Marshall cemented his argument with precedent: the Court had implicitly resolved the issue of its habeas jurisdiction by granting the writ in the 1795 case of *United States v. Hamilton*, 3 U.S. 17 (1795).

---

d. See G. Edward White, *The Marshall Court and Cultural Change, 1815–1835* (1988) (vol. 3 of the Oliver Wendell Holmes Devise, History of the Supreme Court of the United States); Eskridge, *All About Words, supra*; John Yoo, Note, *Marshall's Plan: The Early Supreme Court and Statutory Interpretation*, 101 Yale L.J. 1607 (1991).

e. Marshall noted the rule of the last antecedent: because the limiting language of the first sentence followed "and all other writs etc.," it only modified that item in the list, and not the habeas corpus item. 8 U.S. at 95. As the Chief surely recognized, this was a weak argument, in part because a comma set off the qualifying phrase from the items in the list, see Lawrence Solan, *The Language of Judges* 29–38 (1993) (last antecedent rule — weak to begin with — does not apply when the modifying phrase is set off from the list by a comma), and in part because the point of the first sentence seems to be the qualification, with no apparent reason for limiting it only to the third catch-all item in the list.

Note the eclectic mode of argumentation in *Bollman*: Marshall's opinion considered the statutory text, its purpose in light of the constitutional background, and prior precedent. Such eclecticism was characteristic of American practice throughout the nineteenth century.

Treatise-writers sought to systematize Anglo-American practice by developing elaborate lists of "canons" of statutory interpretation — most of them borrowed or derived from English treatises.[f] By the end of the century, statutory interpretation was pretty settled in practice, but was theoretically chaotic. Consider the sampler of general theoretical approaches, which we have excerpted from the Hart and Sacks "Legal Process" materials, and then consider a leading case that unsettled practice — *Holy Trinity Church*.

HENRY M. HART, JR. and ALBERT M. SACKS, *THE LEGAL PROCESS: BASIC PROBLEMS IN THE MAKING AND APPLICATION OF LAW*
1111–15 (William Eskridge, Jr. & Philip Frickey eds. 1994)[*]

A.   *The Mischief Rule*

HEYDON'S CASE
Exchequer, 1584
30 Co. 7a, 76 Eng. Rep. 637

* * * And it was resolved by them, that for the sure and true interpretation of all statutes in general (be they penal or beneficial, restrictive or enlarging of the common law,) four things are to be discerned and considered:—

1st. What was the common law before the making of the Act.

2nd. What was the mischief and defect for which the common law did not provide.

3rd. What remedy the Parliament hath resolved and appointed to cure the disease of the commonwealth.

And, 4th. The true reason of the remedy; and then the office of all the Judges is always to make such construction as shall suppress the mischief, and advance the remedy, and to suppress subtle inventions and evasions for continuance of the mischief, and *pro privato commodo*, and to add force and life to the cure and remedy, according to the true intent of the makers of the Act, *pro bono publico*.

B.   *The "Golden" Rule*

Lord Blackburn, in *River Wear Comm'rs v. Adamson*, 2 App. Cas. 743, 764 (House of Lords, 1877):

---

f. See, e.g., Theodore Sedgwick, *A Treatise on the Rules Which Govern the Interpretation and Application of Statutory and Constitutional Law* (1857); J.G. Sutherland, *Statutes and Statutory Construction* (1st ed. 1891).

* * * But it is to be borne in mind that the office of the Judges is not to legislate, but to declare the expressed intention of the Legislature, even if that intention appears to the Court injudicious; and I believe that it is not disputed that what *Lord Wensleydale* used to call the golden rule is right, viz., that we are to take the whole statute together, and construe it all together, giving the words their ordinary signification, unless when so applied they produce an inconsistency, or an absurdity or inconvenience so great as to convince the Court that the intention could not have been to use them in their ordinary signification, and to justify the Court in putting on them some other signification, which, though less proper, is one which the Court thinks the words will bear.

C.   *The Literal Rule*

Lord Atkinson, in *Vacher & Sons, Ltd. v. London Soc'y of Compositers*, [1913] App. Cas. 107, 121–22 (House of Lords):

> If the language of a statute be plain, admitting of only one meaning, the Legislature must be taken to have meant and intended what it has plainly expressed, and whatever it has in clear terms enacted must be enforced though it should lead to absurd or mischievous results. If the language of this subsection be not controlled by some of the other provisions of the statute, it must, since its language is plain and unambiguous, be enforced, and your Lordships' House sitting judicially is not concerned with the question whether the policy it embodies is wise or unwise, or whether it leads to consequences just or unjust, beneficial or mischievous.

Lord Bramwell, in *Hill v. East and West India Dock Co.*, 9 App. Cas. 448, 464–65 (House of Lords, 1884):

> I should like to have a good definition of what is such an absurdity that you are to disregard the plain words of an Act of Parliament. It is to be remembered that what seems absurd to one man does not seem absurd to another. * * * I think it is infinitely better, although an absurdity or an injustice or other objectionable result may be evolved as the consequence of your construction, to adhere to the words of an Act of Parliament and leave the legislature to set it right than to alter those words according to one's notion of an absurdity.

* * *

F.   *A Second Breath of Fresh Air*

LIEBER, LEGAL AND POLITICAL HERMENEUTICS
(2d ed. St. Louis, 1880) pp. 17–20

IV. Let us take an instance of the simplest kind, to show in what degree we are continually obliged to resort to interpretation. By and by we shall find that the same rules which common sense teaches every one to use, in order to understand his neighbor in the most trivial intercourse, are necessary likewise, although not sufficient, for the interpretation of documents or texts of the highest importance, constitutions as well as treaties between the great nations.

Suppose a housekeeper says to a domestic: "fetch some soupmeat," accompanying the act with giving some money to the latter; he will be unable to execute the order without interpretation, however easy and, consequently, rapid the performance of the process may be. Common sense and good faith tell the domestic, that the housekeeper's meaning was this: 1. He should go immediately, or as soon as his other occupations are finished; or, if he be directed to do so in the evening, that he should go next day at the *usual* hour; 2. that the money handed him by the housekeeper is intended to pay for the meat thus ordered, and not as a present to him; 3. that he should buy such meat and of such part of the animal, as, to his knowledge, has commonly been used in the house he stays at, for making soups; 4. that he buy the best meat he can obtain, for a fair price; 5. that he go to that butcher who usually provides the family, with whom the domestic resides, with meat, or to some convenient stall, and not to any unnecessarily distant place; 6. that he return the rest of the money; 7. that he bring home the meat in good faith, neither adding anything disagreeable nor injurious; 8. that he fetch the meat for the use of the family and not for himself. Suppose, on the other hand, the housekeeper, afraid of being misunderstood, had mentioned these eight specifications, she would not have obtained her object, if it were to exclude all *possibility* of misunderstanding. For, the various specifications would have required new ones. Where would be the end? We are constrained then, always, to leave a considerable part of our meaning to be found out by interpretation, which, in many cases must necessarily cause greater or less obscurity with regard to the exact meaning, which our words were intended to convey.

Experience is a plant growing as slowly as confidence, which Chatham said increased so tardily. In fact, confidence grows slowly because it depends upon experience. The British spirit of civil liberty induced the English judges to adhere strictly to the law, to its exact expressions. This again induced the law-makers to be, in their phraseology, as explicit and minute as possible, which causes such a tautology and endless repetition in the statutes of that country that even so eminent a statesman as Sir Robert Peel declared, in parliament, that he "contemplates no task with so much distaste as the reading through an ordinary act of parliament." Men have at length found out that little or nothing is gained by attempting to speak with absolute clearness and endless specifications, but that human speech is the clearer, the less we endeavor to supply by words and specifications that interpretation which common sense must give to human words. However minutely we may define, somewhere we [must] trust at last to common sense and good faith. * * *

RECTOR, HOLY TRINITY CHURCH v. UNITED STATES
Supreme Court of the United States, 1892
143 U.S. 457, 12 S.Ct. 511, 36 L.Ed. 226

MR. JUSTICE BREWER delivered the opinion of the Court.

Plaintiff in error is a corporation, duly organized and incorporated as a religious society under the laws of the State of New York. E. Walpole Warren was, prior to September, 1887, an alien residing in England. In that month the plaintiff in error made a contract with him, by which he was to remove to the city of New York and enter into its service as rector and pastor; and in pursuance of such contract, Warren did so remove and enter upon such service. It is claimed by the United States that this contract on the part of the plaintiff in error was forbidden by the act of February 26, 1885, 23 Stat. 332, c. 164, and an action was commenced to recover the penalty prescribed by that act. The Circuit Court held that the contract was within the prohibition of the statute, and rendered judgment accordingly, and the single question presented for our determination is whether it erred in that conclusion.

The first section describes the act forbidden, and is in these words:

> "*Be it enacted by the Senate and House of Representatives of the United States of America in Congress assembled*, That from and after the passage of this act it shall be unlawful for any person, company, partnership, or corporation, in any manner whatsoever, to prepay the transportation, or in any way assist or encourage the importation or migration of any alien or aliens, any foreigner or foreigners, into the United States, its Territories, or the District of Columbia, under contract or agreement, parol or special, express or implied, made previous to the importation or migration of such alien or aliens, foreigner or foreigners, to perform labor or service of any kind in the United States, its Territories, or the District of Columbia."

It must be conceded that the act of the corporation is within the letter of this section, for the relation of rector to his church is one of service, and implies labor on the one side with compensation on the other. Not only are the general words labor and service both used, but also, as it were to guard against any narrow interpretation and emphasize a breadth of meaning, to them is added "of any kind;" and, further, as noticed by the Circuit Judge in his opinion, the fifth section, which makes specific exceptions, among them professional actors, artists, lecturers, singers and domestic servants, strengthens the idea that every other kind of labor and service was intended to be reached by the first section. While there is great force to this reasoning, we cannot think Congress intended to denounce with penalties a transaction like that in the present case. It is a familiar rule, that a thing may be within the letter of the statute and yet not within the statute, because not within its spirit, nor within the intention of its makers. This has been often asserted, and the reports are full of cases illustrating its application. This is not the substitution of the will of the judge for that of the legislator, for frequently words of general meaning are used in a statute, words broad enough to include an act in question, and yet a consideration of the whole legislation, or of the circumstances surrounding its enactment, or of the absurd results which follow from giving such broad meaning to the words, makes it unreasonable to believe that the legislator intended to include the particular act. As said in Plowden, 205: "From which cases, it appears that the sages of the law heretofore have construed statutes quite contrary to the letter in some appearance, and those statutes which comprehend all things in the letter they have expounded to extend to but some things, and those which generally prohibit all people from doing such an act they have interpreted to permit some people to do it, and those which include every person in the letter, they have adjudged to reach to some persons only, which expositions have always been founded upon the intent of the legislature, which they have collected sometimes by considering the cause and necessity of making the act, sometimes by comparing one part of the act with another, and sometimes by foreign circumstances." * * *

* * * [T]he title of this act is, "An act to prohibit the importation and migration of foreigners and aliens under contract or agreement to perform labor in the United States, its Territories and the District of Columbia." Obviously the thought expressed in this reaches only to the work of the manual laborer, as distinguished from that of the professional man. No one reading such a title would suppose that Congress had in its mind any purpose of staying the coming into this country of ministers of the gospel, or, indeed, of any class whose toil is that of the brain. The common understanding of the terms labor and laborers does not include preaching and preachers; and it is to be assumed that words and phrases are used in their ordinary meaning. So whatever of light is thrown upon the statute by the language of the title indicates an exclusion from its penal provisions of all contracts for the employment of ministers, rectors and pastors.

Again, another guide to the meaning of a statute is found in the evil which it is designed to remedy; and for this the court properly looks at contemporaneous events, the situation as it existed, and as it was pressed upon the attention of the legislative body. The situation which called for this statute was briefly but fully stated by Mr. Justice Brown when, as District Judge, he decided the case of *United States v. Craig*, 28 Fed.Rep. 795, 798: "The motives and history of the act are matters of common knowledge. It had become the practice for large capitalists in this country to contract with their agents abroad for the shipment of great numbers of an ignorant and servile class of foreign laborers, under contracts, by which the employer agreed, upon the one hand, to prepay their passage, while, upon the other hand, the laborers agreed to work after their arrival for a certain time at a low rate of wages. The effect of this was to break down the labor market, and to reduce other laborers engaged in like occupations to the level of the assisted immigrant. The evil finally became so flagrant that an appeal was made to Congress for relief by the passage of the act in question, the design of which was to raise the standard of foreign immigrants, and to discountenance the migration of those who had not sufficient means in their own hands, or those of their friends, to pay their passage."

It appears, also, from the petitions, and in the testimony presented before the committees of Congress, that it was this cheap unskilled labor which was making the trouble, and the influx of which Congress sought to prevent. It was never suggested that we had in this country a surplus of brain toilers, and, least of all, that the market for the services of Christian ministers was depressed by foreign competition. Those were matters to which the attention of Congress, or of the people, was not directed. So far, then, as the evil which was sought to be remedied interprets the statute, it also guides to an exclusion of this contract from the penalties of the act.

A singular circumstance, throwing light upon the intent of Congress, is found in this extract from the report of the Senate Committee on Education and Labor, recommending the passage of the bill: "The general facts and considerations which induce the committee to recommend the passage of this bill are set forth in the Report of the Committee of the House. The committee report the bill back without amendment, although there are certain features thereof which might well be changed or modified, in the hope that the bill may not fail of passage during the present session. Especially would the committee have otherwise recommended amendments, substituting for the expression 'labor and service,' whenever it occurs in the body of the bill, the words 'manual labor' or 'manual service,' as sufficiently broad to accomplish the purposes of the bill, and that such amendments would remove objections which a sharp and perhaps unfriendly criticism may urge to the proposed legislation. The committee, however, believing that the bill in its present form will be construed as including only those whose labor or service is manual in character, and being very desirous that the bill become a law before the adjournment, have reported the bill without change." [Page] 6059, Congressional Record, 48th Congress. And, referring back to the report of the Committee of the House, there appears this language: "It seeks to restrain and prohibit the immigration or importation of laborers who would have never seen our shores but for the inducements and allurements of men whose only object is to obtain labor at the lowest possible rate, regardless of the social and material well-being of our own citizens and regardless of the evil consequences which result to American laborers from such immigration. This class of immigrants care nothing about our institutions, and in many instances never even heard of them; they are men whose passage is paid by the importers; they come here under contract to labor for a certain number of years; they are ignorant of our social condition, and that they may remain so they are isolated and prevented from coming into contact with Americans. They are generally from the lowest social stratum, and live upon the coarsest food and in hovels of a character before unknown to American workmen. They, as a rule, do not become citizens, and are certainly not a desirable acquisition to the body politic. The inevitable tendency of their presence among us is to degrade American labor, and to reduce it to the level of the imported pauper labor." Page 5359, Congressional Record, 48th Congress.

We find, therefore, that the title of the act, the evil which was intended to be remedied, the circumstances surrounding the appeal to Congress, the reports of the committee of each house, all concur in affirming that the intent of Congress was simply to stay the influx of this cheap unskilled labor.

But beyond all these matters no purpose of action against religion can be imputed to any legislation, state or national, because this is a religious people. This is historically true. From the discovery of this continent to the present hour, there is a single voice making this affirmation. The commission to Christopher Columbus, prior to his sail westward, is from "Ferdinand and Isabella, by the grace of God, King and Queen of Castile," etc., and recites that "it is hoped that by God's assistance some of the continents and islands in the ocean will be discovered," etc. The first colonial grant, that made to Sir Walter Raleigh in 1584, was from "Elizabeth, by the grace of God, of England, Fraunce and Ireland, queene, defender of the faith," etc.; and the grant authorizing him to enact statutes for the government of the proposed colony provided that "they be not against the true Christian faith nowe professed in the Church of England." * * *

If we examine the constitutions of the various States we find in them a constant recognition of religious obligations. Every constitution of every one of the forty-four States contains language which either directly or by clear implication recognizes a profound reverence for religion and an assumption that its influence in all human affairs is essential to the well being of the community. This recognition may be in the preamble, such as is found in the constitution of Illinois, 1870; "We, the people of the State of Illinois, grateful to Almighty God for the civil, political and religious liberty which He hath so long permitted us to enjoy, and looking to Him for a blessing upon our endeavors to secure and transmit the same unimpaired to succeeding generations," etc. * * *

Even the Constitution of the United States, which is supposed to have little touch upon the private life of the individual, contains in the First Amendment a declaration common to the constitutions of all the States, as follows: "Congress shall make no law respecting an establishment of religion, or prohibiting the free exercise thereof," etc. And also provides in Article 1, section 7, (a provision common to many constitutions,) that the Executive shall have ten days (Sundays excepted) within which to determine whether he will approve or veto a bill. * * *

If we pass beyond these matters to a view of American life as expressed by its laws, its business, its customs and its society, we find everywhere a clear recognition of the same truth. Among other matters note the following: The form of oath universally prevailing, concluding with an appeal to the Almighty; the custom of opening sessions of all deliberative bodies and most conventions with prayer; the prefatory words of all wills, "In the name of God, amen;" the laws respecting the observance of the Sabbath, with the general cessation of all secular business, and the closing of courts, legislatures, and other similar public assemblies on that day; the churches and church organizations which abound in every city, town and hamlet; the multitude of charitable organizations existing everywhere under Christian auspices; the gigantic missionary associations, with general support, and aiming to establish Christian missions in every quarter of the globe. These, and many other matters which might be noticed, add a volume of unofficial declarations to the mass of organic utterances that this is a Christian nation. In the face of all these, shall it be believed that a Congress of the United States intended to make it a misdemeanor for a church of this country to contract for the services of a Christian minister residing in another nation?

NOTES ON *HOLY TRINITY* AND ECLECTICISM IN STATUTORY INTERPRETATION

1. *The Court's Eclectic Approach and the Text of the Statute.* Justice Brewer's opinion seems to follow all the theories introduced at the beginning of this Section — except that it seems to violate the "literal rule" of *Vacher & Sons*. Brewer concedes that his interpretation is not "within the letter of the statute." Was his concession too quickly made?

The first definition of the term "labor" listed in the 1879 and 1886 editions of *Webster's Dictionary* was "Physical toil or bodily exertion * * * hard muscular effort directed to some useful end, as agriculture, manufactures, and the like." The second (less authoritative) definition was "Intellectual exertion, mental effort." In the 1880s, judges interpreting the laws and treaties excluding Chinese "laborers" or persons brought over for "labor" held that the terms should be read in their primary popular senses, to mean "physical labor for another for wages," and therefore not to include actors, teachers, or merchants, for example. See, e.g., *In re Ho King*, 14 Fed. Rep. 724 (D. Or. 1883). *Webster's* (1879 and 1886) first, and only relevant, definition of "service" was this: "The act of serving; the occupation of a servant; the performance of labor for the benefit of another, or at another's command; the attendance of an inferior, or hired helper or slave, etc., on a superior employer, master, and the like." *Black's Law Dictionary* (1891) defined service as "being employed to serve another; duty or labor to be rendered by one person to another." Is it 100% clear that the letter of the law supported the prosecution?[g]

2. *The Structure of the Statute.* The prohibition is found in § 1 of the 1885 law. (Section 2 voids contracts made in violation of § 1, and § 3 provides for criminal penalties for such alien labor contracts.) Although ignored by the Court, also relevant is § 4, which holds criminally accountable the master of a ship "who shall knowingly bring within the United States * * * any alien *laborer, mechanic or artisan*" who had contracted to perform "labor or service in the United States." What light does § 4 shed on the meaning of "labor or service of any kind" in § 1? Should § 1 be read narrowly, to track the terms in § 4, or does the narrowness of § 4 confirm a broader reading for § 1? The marginal note (not part of the enacted law) describes § 4 as applying to the master of a vessel who knowingly brings "such emigrant laborer" to our shores. 23 Stat. 332 (1885).

Justice Brewer does mention § 5, a list of exemptions to the liabilities imposed by §§ 1-4. Section 5 exempts "professional actors, artists, lecturers, or singers" as well as "persons employed strictly as personal or domestic servants" from the "provisions of this act." Does the omission of ministers from § 5 confirm their inclusion in § 1? To § 4, which is also subject to the § 5 exclusions? Might a minister fall under one of the exemptions? Section 5 also provides that §§ 1-4 shall not be construed to bar "any individual from assisting any member of his family or any relative or personal friend" in migrating to the United States. If a member of the Church were a "personal friend" of Reverend Warren, would that defeat the prosecution?

3. *Legislative History as Evidence of Legislative "Intent."* To narrow what he views as the apparent plain meaning of the law, Brewer relies on the evil (or mischief) against which the Act was aimed and the inapplicability of a statute seeking to exclude "laborers" to a "brain toiler," as well as a "smoking gun" in the legislative history, specifically the Senate committee report saying that the bill was only intended to exclude people engaged in "manual labor" but that it was too late in the session to amend the statute to add that precise language. Note the two ways that Brewer deploys the idea of legislative intent: one looks

---

g. See William Eskridge, Jr., *Textualism, The Unknown Ideal?*, 96 Mich. L. Rev. 1509, 1517–19, 1533, 1539–40 (1998) (no).

to the general goal of the law and tailors the text to meet the goal ("general intent"), and the other asks what the legislators thought they were doing as to the particular issue ("specific intent"). Recall these two levels of intent at work in *Weber*, the affirmative action case in Chapter 1, § 3. Recall, too, that the *Weber* majority quoted and followed *Holy Trinity*.

The Supreme Court had essentially rewritten statutes in earlier cases, in order to avoid absurd consequences (the golden rule) or where required by common law or constitutional maxims, but both the Court and commentators followed a rule whereby legislative materials were inadmissible evidence to alter "plain" statutory meanings.[h] *Holy Trinity Church* seems to be the first case where the Supreme Court rewrote the statute based upon evidence from the legislative record. A revised edition of the leading treatise cited it repeatedly and endorsed its proposition that courts could consider legislative records to figure out what the intent of the legislature was on a particular issue.[i] The federal courts in the twentieth century cited an increasing amount and variety of legislative history, a trend that abated only in the late 1980s.

4. *Legislative History the Court Missed.* Independent examination by modern scholars suggests that Brewer was right about the general intent of Congress and the problem it was addressing,[j] but missed important evidence bearing on legislators' specific intent. Contrary to his opinion, the alien contract labor bill was not enacted in 1884, as the Senate committee had hoped, and was brought up in the 1885 session of the 48th Congress, just before the Cleveland Administration took office. The Senate had a lengthy debate about the bill, which was amended in minor ways. Among the amendments were those expanding the exempted classes, but no amendment was proposed to make clear that "labor" referred only to "manual labor." When pressed by an opponent of the bill, who argued that § 5 discriminated against "other classes of professional men" by granting exemptions to singers and lecturers and actors, Senator Blair, the floor manager, engaged in this exchange with the opponent:

> Mr. MORGAN: * * * [If the alien] happens to be a lawyer, an artist, a painter, an engraver, a sculptor, a great author, or what not, and he comes under employment to write for a newspaper, or to write books, or to paint pictures * * * he comes under the general provisions of the bill. * * *

---

h. Cf. *Marshall Field & Co. v. Clark*, 143 U.S. 649 (1892) (Court refused to examine legislative record to evaluate argument that enrolled bill was not same as bill that passed Congress).

i. See J.G. Sutherland, *Statutes and Statutory Construction* 879–83 (John Lewis ed., 2d ed. 1904). The first edition of the Sutherland treatise, published in 1891, followed the English practice of excluding extrinsic legislative materials from consideration in statutory cases.

j. See Carol Chomsky, *Unlocking the Mysteries of* Holy Trinity: *Spirit, Letter, and History in Statutory Interpretation*, 100 Colum. L. Rev. 901 (2000) (after a thorough investigation of the statute's legislative history, concluding that the Court correctly applied Congress's general purpose).

Mr. BLAIR: If that class of people are liable to become the subject-matter of such importation, then the bill applies to them. Perhaps the bill ought to be further amended.

Mr. MORGAN: * * * I shall propose when we get to it to put an amendment in there. I want to associate with the lecturers and singers and actors, painters, sculptors [etc.], or any person having special skill in any business, art, trade or profession. * * *

16 Cong. Rec. 1633 (Feb. 13, 1885) (emphasis added). The House floor manager, Representative Hopkins, responded to an inquiry regarding agricultural workers by saying that the bill "prohibits the importation under contract of all classes with the exceptions named in the bill [§ 5]." 16 Cong. Rec. 2032 (1885). Does this more complete record undermine Brewer's conclusion? [k]

There is more legislative history that both the Court and subsequent commentators also missed. What is the relationship between § 1, with seemingly broad application to "labor or service of any kind," and § 4, with narrower application only to "labor or service" by "any alien laborer, mechanic, or artisan"? Senator Blair repeatedly assured his colleagues that § 4 was aimed at "the man who knowingly brings an immigrant * * * who comes here under and by virtue of a contract such as is prohibited by [§ 1] of the bill." 16 Cong. Rec. 1630 (1885); accord, 779 (Senator Miller), 1626 (Blair), 1629 (Senator McPherson), 1785 (Blair). We are not aware of any on-the-record statement to the contrary. Should this evidence influence the Court's understanding of the relationship between §§ 1 and 4? [l]

5. *Subsequent Legislation.* After the federal circuit court in the Southern District of New York construed the statute to apply to Reverend Warren in the *Holy Trinity Church* litigation, Congress amended the alien contract labor law to exempt ministers and professionals generally. Reversing the lower court, the Supreme Court in *Holy Trinity* did not mention the 1891 statute, which by its terms did not apply to pending proceedings, Act of March 3, 1891, § 12, 26 Stat. 1084, 1086. Does this later statute vindicate, or undermine, the Court's holding? Cf. *United States v. Laws*, 163 U.S. 258, 265 (1896) (discussing the 1891 amendment).

6. *What About the "Christian Nation" Stuff?* We are not aware of any strong reaction in 1892, but current readers might be taken aback by *Holy Trinity*'s invocation of the "Christian nation" analysis to clinch the Court's argument. (Born of Christian missionaries in Asia Minor, Justice Brewer was something of an evangelical jurist.) Was this critical to the Court's opinion? Would Justice Brewer have exempted a doctor from the statute's exclusion, for example? Cf. *Laws* (determining whether the 1885 law covered chemists).

---

k. For a "yes", see Adrian Vermeule, *Judging Under Uncertainty* 86-117 (2006) (filling in many gaps in Brewer's deployment of legislative history and concluding that the judiciary is incompetent to evaluate legislative history then and now).

l. For another "yes", see William Eskridge, Jr., *No Frills Textualism*, 119 Harv. L. Rev. 2041, 2065-70 (2006).

Review the competing English approaches to statutory interpretation presented by Hart and Sacks. Note that *Holy Trinity Church* draws from two of them — the golden rule, under which statutory text need not be followed if it produces an absurd result; and the mischief rule, promoting statutory purpose as the touchstone of statutory meaning. Because the doctrine of precedent in the United States only counsels later courts to adhere to the holding of prior cases, not to the methodology used in those cases to reach the holding, however, *Holy Trinity Church* in no way conclusively resolved how federal courts would henceforth undertake the interpretation of statutes.[m] Indeed, although *Holy Trinity Church* gave barely a passing reference to the force of literalism in statutory interpretation, the other English approach identified by Hart and Sacks, some other Supreme Court cases around the turn of the twentieth century embraced literalism. These cases promoted the *plain meaning rule* — if the statutory text had a "plain meaning," that was the end of the interpretive enterprise (one did not go on to consult legislative history, statutory purpose, or other potential sources of meaning). The most famous of these cases follows.

CAMINETTI v. UNITED STATES, 242 U.S. 470 (1917). A federal statute criminalized the transportation of, or the inducement to travel of, "any woman or girl to go from one place to another in interstate or foreign commerce, or in any territory or the District of Columbia, for the purpose of prostitution or debauchery, or for any other immoral purpose * * * ." The case concerned a man who brought a woman from Sacramento, California, to Reno, Nevada, to "become his mistress and concubine." The Court, per **Justice Day**, stated that "it is elementary that the meaning of a statute must, in the first instance, be sought in the language in which the act is framed, and if that is plain, and if the law is within the constitutional authority of the lawmaking body which passed it, the sole function of the courts is to enforce it according to its terms." The majority found the statutory meaning plain — the conduct in question was for an "immoral purpose" — and held that Caminetti violated the statute. It refused to consider the title to the Act ("the White Slave Traffic

---

m. In other words, under *stare decisis*, the lower courts were bound to interpret the immigration statute at issue in *Holy Trinity Church* as authorizing the entry of "brain toilers" into the United States, but not strictly bound to follow the golden rule and mischief rule in determining the meaning of statutes. To take another example, consistent with *Weber* (Chapter 1, § 3), lower courts are required to interpret Title VII of the 1964 Civil Rights Act as not prohibiting certain kinds of affirmative action in employment — but not bound to use *Weber*'s strongly purposive, nonliteral, *Holy Trinity Church* approach to the interpretation of statutes in general. At most, under the idea of adhering to judicial tradition, *Weber* might most strongly influence the interpretive method taken to other sections of the Civil Rights Act, less so that taken to other civil rights statutes, and even less so that taken to different sorts of statutes (the judge who uses the *Weber* method outside the civil rights area is using the method because she finds it persuasive on its own terms, not because of any strong sense of obligation). For discussion of the difference between *stare decisis* as to holding and as to methodology used to reach the holding, see Sydney Foster, *The Case for Super-Strong Statutory Interpretation Doctrine Stare Decisis* (unpublished draft 2007); Philip Frickey, *Interpretive-Regime Change*, 38 Loy. L.A. L. Rev. 1971 (2005).

Act") or legislative history suggesting that the purpose of the statute was narrower than its plain meaning (to reach only "commercialized vice").

The majority did not cite *Holy Trinity Church*, but **Justice McKenna**, joined in dissent by two other Justices, relied on it for the proposition that "the words of the statute should be construed to execute [the statutory purpose], and they may be so construed even if their literal meaning be otherwise." The dissent also argued that the statutory text was not plain:"other immoral purpose" should not be read literally and in isolation, but in light of the limiting words preceding them. As illuminated by the legislative history and by the principle that statutes should be read with "common sense" to avoid absurd applications, the statute should not reach "the occasional immoralities of men and women," but rather the "systematized and mercenary immorality epitomized in the statute's graphic phrase 'white slave traffic.' "

Although the free-wheeling approach of *Holy Trinity Church* may seem worlds apart from the mechanical approach of *Caminetti*, one might worry that unarticulated judicial values played a heavy role in both cases. That is, the Court would stick with literalism (*Caminetti*), or trump literalism with the mischief approach and the golden rule (*Holy Trinity Church)*, to reach the interpretation that better matched its sensibilities. In *Caminetti*, for example, Justice McKenna's dissent stated that "[t]here is much in the present case to tempt to a violation of the [mischief] rule. Any measure that protects the purity of women from assault or enticement to degradation finds an instant advocate in our best emotions; but the judicial function cannot yield to emotion * * * ." Similarly, in *Holy Trinity Church* the Court's importation of "Christian nation" and other reasoning to rework the statute caused anxiety among progressive commentators, the same people who would later decry the Court's opinion in *Lochner v. New York*, 198 U.S. 45 (1905) (invalidating a state statute establishing the maximum hours per week certain employees could be required to work on the ground that the due process clause protects economic liberty against unjustified regulation). For progressives who favored aggressive legislation supplanting the common law, decisions like *Lochner* and *Holy Trinity Church* sent the same message of judicial reluctance to accept new statutes. Dean Roscoe Pound of Harvard, the founder of sociological jurisprudence, laid out the following theory of statutory interpretation, designed to cabin judicial wilfulness. Recall his argument that statutes should be a source of principles affecting the common law (Chapter 6, § 1).

ROSCOE POUND, *SPURIOUS INTERPRETATION*, 7 Colum. L. Rev. 379, 381 (1907). "The object of genuine interpretation is to discover the rule which the law-maker intended to establish; to discover the intention which the law-maker made the rule, or the sense which he attached to the words wherein the rule is expressed. Its object is to enable others to derive from the language used 'the same idea which the author intended to convey.'[2] Employed for these purposes, interpretation is purely judicial in character; and so long as the

---

2. Lieber, Legal and Political Hermeneutics, Chap. 1, § 8.

ordinary means of interpretation, namely the literal meaning of the language used and the context, are resorted to, there can be no question. But when, as often happens, these primary indices to the meaning and intention of the law-maker fail to lead to a satisfactory result, and recourse must be had to the reason and spirit of the rule, or to the intrinsic merit of the several possible interpretations, the line between a genuine ascertaining of the meaning of the law, and the making over of the law under guise of interpretation, becomes more difficult. Strictly, both are means of genuine interpretation. * * * The former means of interpretation tries to find out directly what the law-maker meant by assuming his position, in the surroundings in which he acted, and endeavoring to gather from the mischiefs he had to meet and the remedy by which he sought to meet them, his intention with respect to the particular point in controversy. The latter, if the former fails to yield sufficient light, seeks to reach the intent of the law-maker indirectly. It assumes that the law-maker thought as we do on general questions of morals and policy and fair dealing. Hence it assumes that of several possible interpretations the one which appeals most to our sense of right and justice for the time being is most likely to give the meaning of those who framed the rule. If resorted to in the first instance, or without regard to the other means of interpretation, this could not be regarded as a means of genuine interpretation. But inherent difficulties of expression and want of care in drafting require continual resort to this means of interpretation for the legitimate purpose of ascertaining what the law-maker in fact meant.

"On the other hand, the object of spurious interpretation is to make, unmake, or remake, and not merely to discover. It puts a meaning into the text as a juggler puts coins, or what not, into a dummy's hair, to be pulled forth presently with an air of discovery. It is essentially a legislative, not a judicial process, made necessary in formative periods by the paucity of principles, feebleness of legislation, and rigidity of rules characteristic of archaic law. * * *

"Spurious interpretation is an anachronism in an age of legislation. It is a fiction. * * *

"* * * Rigid constitutions, difficult of amendment, * * * are presenting to modern common-law courts the same problem which the rigid formalism of archaic procedure, and the terse obscurity of ancient codes, put before the jurists of antiquity. Cases must be decided, and they must be decided in the long run so as to accord with the moral sense of the community. This is the good side of spurious interpretation. It is this situation that provokes the general popular demand for judicial amendment of constitutions, state and federal, under the guise of interpretation.

"Looking at the matter purely from the standpoint of expediency, * * * the bad features of spurious interpretation, as applied to the modern state, may be said to be three: (1) That it tends to bring law into disrepute, (2) that it subjects the courts to political pressure, (3) that it reintroduces the personal element into judicial administration. * * * "

NOTES ON INTERPRETATION AS INTENTIONALISM

1. *"Genuine Interpretation" versus "Spurious Interpretation."* Dean Pound assumes that "genuine interpretation" means ascertaining the meaning a speaker intended to convey when uttering a statement. His approach may seem simple, but in fact it raises highly controversial questions at the core of statutory interpretation theory. On his understanding, textual meaning and authorial intent are not separable concepts: the text has no autonomous significance; it merely consists of signifiers encoding an intended message, however difficult it might be for the interpreter to decode that message. This understanding retains force for some students of interpretation today, both in law and other fields.[n]

Thus, one cannot speak about the "plain meaning" of statutory text in isolation and be engaged in "interpretation" at all. In this way, Pound denies that the "plain meaning" approach to statutory construction constitutes "interpretation" — unless the best textual meaning is simply used as good evidence of legislative intent, to be supplemented by any other evidence of legislative intent available. On this reading, his argument is a remarkable rejection of literalism in statutory interpretation. It also suggests that purposivism is "genuine interpretation," but only so long as the interpreter sticks as closely as possible to the probable purposes that animated the enacting legislature and avoids imposing her own views of appropriate public-policy purposes upon the statute.

What should we make of Pound's analysis? Is it merely a definitional fight, or is more at stake than that? For example, one might speculate that Pound wants interpreters who deviate from legislative intentions to call their approach something other than "interpretation" — that term sounds neutral and legitimate, and its usage may conceal the difficult normative questions that arise when, in a democracy such as ours, interpreters essentially revise statutes contrary to original legislative expectations, even if the revised understanding of the statute promotes justice or other laudable goals. Pound is not saying that what he calls "spurious interpretation" is always illegitimate; his point is that it should be called what it actually is — "revising to promote justice," or whatever — and debated on its own merits.

2. *Ascertaining Legislative Intent: Actual/Specific Intent versus Imaginative Reconstruction.* Pound proposes that interpreters follow legislative "intent," but admits that this method is frequently difficult to implement. Based on his excerpt, one might divide his vision of interpretation into two categories. First, and foremost, if the interpreter has clear evidence of the

---

n. Joseph Raz, *Intention in Interpretation*, in *The Autonomy of Law: Essays on Legal Positivism* 249, 258 (Robert George ed. 1996). See also Paul Campos, *That Obscure Object of Desire: Hermeneutics and the Autonomous Text*, 77 Minn. L. Rev. 1065 (1993); *Against Constitutional Theory*, 4 Yale J.L. & Human. 279 (1992); Caleb Nelson, *What Is Textualism?*, 91 Va. L. Rev. 347 (2005) (arguing that both textualists and legislative history readers are, at bottom, seeking evidence of "legislative intent"). Compare John Manning, *Textualism and Legislative Intent*, 91 Va. L. Rev. 419 (2005) (arguing that textualists are not fundamentally seeking to apply "intent," which they consider an unhelpful and misleading construct).

actual (specific) intent of the enacting legislature about what the statute should mean in the context under consideration, the interpreter should, of course, follow it. Second, because strong evidence of actual intent will often be absent, the interpreter usually must engage in a second-best inquiry, what we might call the *imaginative reconstruction of legislative intent*. This approach requires the interpreter to put herself in the position of the enacting legislature and, like a historian, examine the available historical evidence against a background of assumptions about the legislature (that it would prefer justice to injustice, for example) that are commonplace to our legal system, but can be rebutted by evidence that this enacting legislature had a different view (for example, that it defined "justice" and "injustice" differently than the interpreter would).[o] These remain the two fundamental inquiries of intentionalist interpretation today. Note that for both, the statutory text is important because it frequently will be the best evidence of legislative intent.

3. *Federal Court Reception of the Pound Approach.* The Supreme Court grew increasingly interested in what legislators actually expected out of their statutes, e.g., *Johnson v. Southern Pacific Company*, 196 U.S. 1 (1904), though the Court did not always follow legislative history (recall *Caminetti*). Consider *Duplex Printing Press Co. v. Deering*, 254 U.S. 443 (1921), which interpreted the Clayton Act to justify an injunction against a secondary boycott by print workers against an "unfair" employer. Although the Clayton Act contained two broad provisions exempting most labor activity from antitrust regulation, the Court held that it was not the actual intent of Congress to insulate labor boycotts from regulation. The Court relied on a statement by the Clayton Act's House floor manager that neither he nor any member of the reporting committee intended the bill to exempt boycotts from the regulation courts had imposed on them under the older Sherman Act. Justice Brandeis's dissenting opinion railed against this narrowing interpretation, also based upon the actual, subjective expectations of the enacting Congress. (Brandeis was a close adviser of President Wilson, who had proposed the Clayton Act, and hence had an "inside view" of the Act.)

The classic early practitioner of imaginative reconstruction was Judge Learned Hand of the Second Circuit, one of the judges reversed in *Duplex Printing*. See, e.g., *Lehigh Valley Coal Co. v. Yensavage*, 218 F. 547, 553 (2d Cir. 1914); Archibald Cox, *Judge Learned Hand and the Interpretation of Statutes*, 60 Harv. L. Rev. 370 (1947). Consider the following exemplar of Pound's theory.

FISHGOLD v. SULLIVAN DRYDOCK AND REPAIR CORP., 154 F.2d 785 (2d Cir. 1946), *aff'd*, 328 U.S. 275 (1946). Section 8(b)(B) of the Selective Training & Service Act of 1940, 49 Stat. 888, 890, as amended in

---

o. Pound's statement of imaginative reconstruction is taken from the commentary to *Eyston v. Studd*, 2 Plowden 459, 467, 75 Eng. Rep. 688, 699 (K.B. 1574), paraphrasing Aristotle, *The Nicomachean Ethics* bk 5, ch. 10 (W.D. Ross tr., rev. ed. J.O. Ormson 1984). For a modern exposition of this approach, see Richard Posner, *The Federal Courts: Crisis and Reform* 286–93 (1985).

1944, provided that the private employer of a person who had left employment for U.S. military service and then sought to return to the same position after discharge from the service "shall restore such person to such position or to a position of like seniority, status, and pay unless the employer's circumstances have so changed as to make it impossible or unreasonable to do so." Section 8(c) provided:

> Any person who is restored to a position in accordance with the provisions of paragraph (A) or (B) of subsection (b) shall be considered as having been on furlough or leave of absence during his period of training and service in the land or naval forces, shall be so restored without loss of seniority * * * and shall not be discharged from such position without cause within one year after such restoration.

Fishgold returned from service in the army during World War II and then was laid off within a year, while non-veteran employees who had more seniority were not laid off. Fishgold challenged the decision to lay him off, relying on § 8(c). **Judge Hand**'s opinion concluded that the layoff was legal. He avoided the thrust of § 8(c)'s protection against "discharge" by noting that its dictionary definition was a permanent termination of employment, rather than the temporary termination denoted by "layoff." (This reflects the traditional labor law distinction between being terminated or fired [the employment relationship is severed] and being laid off [the employee is not employed but might be recalled to employment]. Seniority typically affords virtually absolute protection against discharge or termination but only limited protection against layoffs.)

Judge Hand was also sensitive to the general policy preferences favoring veterans that were being considered and enacted after World War II, but dispatched the policy argument as follows:

> When we consider the situation at the time that the Act was passed — September, 1940 — it is extremely improbable that Congress should have meant to grant any broader privilege than as we are measuring it. * * * The original act limited service to one year, and it was most improbable that within that time we should be called upon to fight upon our own soil; as indeed the event proved, for we were still at peace in September, 1941. Congress was calling young men to the colors to give them an adequate preparation for our defence, but with no forecast of the appalling experiences which they were later to undergo. Against that background it is not likely that a proposal would then have been accepted which gave industrial priority, regardless of their length of employment, to unmarried men — for the most part under thirty — over men in the thirties, forties or fifties, who had wives and children dependent upon them. Today, in the light of what has happened, the privilege then granted may appear an altogether inadequate equivalent for their services; but we have not to decide what is now proper; we are to reconstruct, as best we may, what was the purpose of Congress when it used the words in which § 8(b) and § 8(c) were cast.

Judge Chase dissented, based upon a broader view of the statute's purpose.

———

MAX RADIN, STATUTORY INTERPRETATION, 43 Harv. L. Rev. 863, 870–71 (1930). "It has frequently been declared that the most approved method is to discover the intent of the legislator. * * * On this transparent and absurd fiction it ought not to be necessary to dwell. It is clearly enough an illegitimate transference to law of concepts proper enough in literature and theology. * * *

"That the intention of the legislature is undiscoverable in any real sense is almost an immediate inference from a statement of the proposition. The chances that of several hundred men each will have exactly the same determinate situations in mind as possible reductions of a given [statutory issue], are infinitesimally small. * * * In an extreme case, it might be that we could learn all that was in the mind of the draftsman, or of a committee of half a dozen men who completely approved of every word. But when this draft is submitted to the legislature and at once accepted without a dissentient voice and without debate, what have we then learned of the intentions of the four or five hundred approvers? Even if the contents of the minds of the legislature were uniform, we have no means of knowing that content except by the external utterances or behavior of these hundreds of men, and in almost every case the only external act is the extremely ambiguous one of acquiescence, which may be motivated in literally hundreds of ways, and which by itself indicates little or nothing of the pictures which the statutory descriptions imply. * * *

"And if [legislative intent] were discoverable, it would be powerless to bind us. What gives the intention of the legislature obligating force? * * * [I]n law, the specific individuals who make up the legislature are men to whom a specialized function has been temporarily assigned. That function is not to impose their will even within limits on their fellow citizens, but to 'pass statutes,' which is a fairly precise operation. That is, they make statements in general terms of undesirable and desirable situations, from which flow certain results. * * * When the legislature has uttered the words of a statute, it is *functus officio*, not because of the Montesquieuan separation of powers, but because that is what legislating means. The legislature might also be a court and an executive, but it can never be all three things simultaneously.

"And once the words are out, recorded, engrossed, registered, proclaimed, inscribed in bronze, they in turn become instrumentalities which administrators and courts must use in performing their own specialized functions. The principal use is that of 'interpretation.' Interpretation is an act which requires an existing determinate event — the issue to be litigated — and obviously that determinate event cannot exist until after the statute has come into force. To say that the intent of the legislature decides the interpretation is to say that the legislature interprets in advance * * * a situation which does not exist."

**NOTES ON EARLY CRITIQUES
OF INTENTIONALIST APPROACHES**

1. *The Narrow Role of Legislatures.* Radin's last point, that legislatures exist only to pass statutes and not to impose their will on the citizenry, echoed Oliver Wendell Holmes, who insisted that in a "government of laws, not men," legal standards must be external to the decisionmaker. Holmes, *The Common Law* 41, 44 (1881). "[W]e ask, not what this man meant, but what those words would mean in the mouth of a normal speaker of English, using them in the circumstances in which they were used. * * * [T]he normal speaker of English

is merely a special variety, a literary form, so to speak, of our old friend the prudent man. He is external to the particular writer, and a reference to him as the criterion is simply another instance of the externality of law. * * * We do not inquire what the legislature meant; we ask only what the statute means." Holmes, *The Theory of Legal Interpretation*, 12 Harv. L. Rev. 417, 417–18, 419 (1899).

But "what the statute means" is not always clear. If the law is ambiguous, should interpreters consider the expectations of the legislators who wrote the statute?[p] If a judge were interpreting a contract, would the judge prefer an interpretation that reconstructs the intent or expectations of the parties to one that the parties did not want? Shouldn't a court pay at least as much attention to the intent of Congress, not only because Congress drafts and enacts statutes, but also because Congress-acting-with-the-President (as required by Article I, § 7) is the "supreme" lawmaking authority in our constitutional democracy?[q]

2. *The Incoherence or Indeterminacy of Collective Intent.* Radin responds that legislative intent is incoherent or undiscoverable. It is incoherent to the extent that a collective body cannot easily be charged with having an "intent." As political scientist Kenneth Shepsle subsequently put it, "Congress is a They, not an It."[r] Intent is undiscoverable because too little evidence of collective understanding finds its way into the public record, and even when reported is hard to interpret. Also, how can the different "intents" of the House, Senate, and President be aggregated?

These are logical quarrels, but there is another way of looking at this matter. If the President or the Board of Directors of a company negotiates a contract with Joan Doe, the President's or Board's representations might be taken to be those of the company itself. As linguist and legal scholar Lawrence Solan has argued, both common sense and the law routinely attribute "intent" to collective bodies based upon the purposive declarations made by subgroups or agents publicly deputized to deliberate for the whole group.[s] Political scientists make the same point about committees and sponsors in Congress.[t] In the same manner, statements by sponsors and committees might reasonably be thought

---

p. See Frederick de Sloovère, *Textual Interpretation of Statutes*, 11 N.Y.U. L. Rev. 538 (1934); cf. *Boston Sand & Gravel Co. v. United States*, 278 U.S. 41, 48 (1928) (Holmes, J., consulting legislative history to figure out "what the statute means").

q. For elaboration, see Daniel Farber, *Statutory Interpretation and Legislative Supremacy*, 78 Geo. L.J. 281 (1989).

r. Kenneth Shepsle, *Congress Is a "They," Not an "It": Legislative Intent as Oxymoron*, 12 Int'l Rev. L. & Econ. 239 (1992). See also Frank Easterbrook, *Text, History, and Structure in Statutory Interpretation*, 17 Harv. J.L. & Pub. Pol'y 61 (1994).

s. Lawrence Solan, *Private Language, Public Laws: The Central Role of Legislative Intent in Statutory Interpretation*, 93 Geo. L.J. 427, 437–49 (2005). See also Margaret Gilbert, *Sociability and Responsibility: New Essays in Plural Subject Theory* (2000) (developing this idea along the lines of linguistic theory).

t. Daniel Rodriguez & Barry Weingast, *The Positive Political Theory of Legislative History: New Perspectives on the 1964 Civil Rights Act and Its Interpretation*, 151 U. Pa. L. Rev. 1417 (2003).

to represent congressional consensus unless denied by other Members. Arguably, this is an institutional convention that is reasonable, and which Congress can be expected to adjust to (through better monitoring) if it yields results that systematically fail to reflect legislative bargains or consensuses.[u]

3. *The Inevitability of Interpretive Discretion and Interstitial Lawmaking?* A further critique of imaginative reconstruction is that it is more "imaginative" than it is "reconstruction." Judges in the early twentieth century were considered hidebound and hostile to many legislative innovations (especially those protecting labor unions). The enthusiasm Pound and Hand felt for imaginative reconstruction was, in part, motivated by the need to tie judges more closely to progressive developments in the legislature. This was only partially achieved at the Supreme Court level, for imaginative reconstruction could also be utilized by conservatives bending statutes their way, as in *Duplex Printing* and *Holy Trinity Church*, and then ignoring legislative expectations in cases like *Caminetti.*

An underlying theme of Radin's article is that the nature of the judicial process — application of generally phrased statutes to unforeseen fact situations by an independent and co-equal branch of government — assures discretion. Cf. Benjamin Cardozo, *The Nature of the Judicial Process* 166 (1921) (judicial decisionmaking "in its highest reaches is not discovery but creation"). This suggested the possibility that often statutory interpretation might be "spurious," to use Pound's provocative label, or at least not an easy exercise in imaginative reconstruction.

The debates over statutory interpretation took several important turns in the 1930s.[v] The unprecedented degree of statute-making during the New Deal vindicated Pound's earlier arguments that the twentieth century would be the age of legislatures rather than courts, but this statutory binge also vindicated Radin's points that there was unlikely to be a clear legislative intent (reconstructed or otherwise) on any but a handful of issues and that interpretive discretion was required. During the New Deal and right before U.S. entry into World War II, an academic consensus found a way to accept both points of view. This approach, whose outlines were clear in the period 1938–41,[w]

---

u. See James Landis, *A Note on "Statutory Interpretation,"* 43 Harv. L. Rev. 886, 888–90 (1930) (responding to Radin's article); McNollgast, *Positive Canons: The Role of Legislative Bargains in Statutory Interpretation,* 80 Geo. L.J. 705 (1992).

v. See our "Historical and Critical Introduction," in Henry Hart, Jr. & Albert Sacks, *The Legal Process: Basic Problems in the Making and Application of Law* (William Eskridge, Jr. & Philip Frickey eds. 1994).

w. The leading precursors of the budding legal process theory were Lloyd Garrison & Willard Hurst, "Law in Society" (1940 & 1941) (teaching materials at Wisconsin); A.B. Feller, Walter Gellhorn & Henry Hart, Jr., "Materials on Legislation" (1st ed. 1941–42) (teaching materials at Columbia, Yale, Harvard); Lon Fuller, *The Law in Quest of Itself* (1940); Harry Willmer Jones, *Statutory Doubts and Legislative Intention,* 40 Colum. L. Rev. 957 (1940); Frederick de Sloovère, *Extrinsic Aids in the Interpretation of Statutes,* 88 U. Pa. L. Rev. 527 (1940).

bloomed into "legal process" theory after World War II, to which our next Section turns.

Problems on Imaginative Reconstruction

Problem 7–1. How would Judge Hand and Dean Pound have voted if they were presented with *Holy Trinity Church*? Professor Radin? Justice Holmes?

Problem 7–2. Williams tells her servant to "fetch me some soupmeat" from "Store X" (recall Lieber's hypothetical). The servant goes to Store X and discovers that the store only has one pound of soupmeat left, and it looks old and wormy. The servant knows that Store Y also carries soupmeat and, upon inspection, sees that Store Y's soupmeat looks pretty good. How would the following "servants" interpret the boss' command: Dean Pound? Judge Hand? Justice Holmes? What do you think the proper interpretation is? Is statutory interpretation similar to this example?

SECTION 2. LEGAL PROCESS THEORIES OF INTERPRETATION

A. THE LEGAL PROCESS CLASSICS, 1940s–50s

The consensus about public law issues reached by intellectuals between 1938 and 1941 was reflected, after World War II, in Supreme Court decisions, law review articles, and teaching materials dealing with statutory issues. This consensus gave rise to "legal process theory," the history of which was traced in Chapter 6, § 1. The following materials are the two legal process classics regarding issues of statutory interpretation.

LON FULLER, *THE CASE OF THE SPELUNCEAN EXPLORERS*
62 Harv. L. Rev. 616, 619–21, 623–26, 628–40 (1949)[*]

TRUEPENNY, C.J. [The members of the Speluncean Society were amateur cave explorers. In May 4299, several members, including Roger Whetmore, were trapped in a cave because of a rockslide. Rescue efforts were delayed for various reasons, such as fresh rockslides, and the explorers were not rescued until the 32d day of their ordeal. Communication with the explorers was established on day 20 of the ordeal, and the explorers learned that they would not likely be rescued for another ten days, that they would probably die if they did not have sustenance within that period, and that they would probably not die if they cannibalized one of their number; the last datum was reluctantly conveyed by a doctor in response to the explorers' specific inquiry. After assimilating the doctor's predictions, all of the explorers agreed that one of them must die, and they further agreed that the person to die would be chosen by lots (rolls of the dice). Whetmore agreed to both propositions and suggested the method of lots, but before the dice were rolled he declared his withdrawal from the plan. The other explorers proceeded with the agreement, and

---

Whetmore was the one chosen by lots. On the 23d day of their ordeal, the explorers killed and dined on Whetmore. After the surviving explorers were saved, they were indicted for the murder of Whetmore.]

[At trial, the foreman of the jury (a lawyer) asked the judge whether the jury could return a special verdict and leave it to the judge to determine guilt or innocence. With the agreement of the prosecutor and counsel for defendants, the judge agreed. The jury found the facts as related above. The trial judge ruled the defendants guilty based upon these facts and (according to the nondiscretionary requirement of the sentencing law) sentenced them to death by hanging. Both jury and judge issued communications to the Chief Executive seeking commutation of defendants' sentence to six months' imprisonment.]

* * * The language of our statute is well known: "Whoever shall willfully take the life of another shall be punished by death." N. C. S. A. (N. S.) § 12–A. This statute permits of no exception applicable to this case, however our sympathies may incline us to make allowance for the tragic situation in which these men found themselves.

In a case like this the principle of executive clemency seems admirably suited to mitigate the rigors of the law, and I propose to my colleagues that we follow the example of the jury and the trial judge by joining in the communications they have addressed to the Chief Executive. * * * I think we may therefore assume that some form of clemency will be extended to these defendants. If this is done, then justice will be accomplished without impairing either the letter or spirit of our statutes and without offering any encouragement for the disregard of law.

FOSTER, J. * * * If this Court declares that under our law these men have committed a crime, then our law is itself convicted in the tribunal of common sense * * *.

* * * I take the view that the enacted or positive law of this Commonwealth, including all of its statutes and precedents, is inapplicable to this case, and that the case is governed instead by what ancient writers in Europe and America called "the law of nature." [Judge Foster argued that once the reason for law disappears, so too does the law itself. As a matter of political morality, the defendants' conduct was justified by the agreement they entered into that ensured the survival of five at the expense of one.]

This concludes the exposition of the first ground of my decision. My second ground proceeds by rejecting hypothetically all the premises on which I have so far proceeded. I concede for purposes of argument that I am wrong in saying that the situation of these men removed them from the effect of our positive law, and I assume that the Consolidated Statutes have the power to penetrate five hundred feet of rock and to impose themselves upon these starving men huddled in their underground prison.

Now it is, of course, perfectly clear that these men did an act that violates the literal wording of the statute which declares that he who "shall willfully take the life of another" is a murderer. But one of the most ancient bits of legal wisdom is the saying that a man may break the letter of the law without breaking the law itself. Every proposition of positive law, whether contained in a statute or a judicial precedent, is to be interpreted reasonably, in the light of its evident purpose. * * *

The statute before us for interpretation has never been applied literally. Centuries ago it was established that a killing in self-defense is excused. There is nothing in the wording of the statute that suggests this exception. Various attempts have been made to reconcile the legal treatment of self-defense with the words of the statute, but in my opinion these are all merely ingenious sophistries. The truth is that the exception in favor of self-defense cannot be reconciled with the *words* of the statute, but only with its *purpose*.

The true reconciliation of the excuse of self-defense with the statute making it a crime to kill another is to be found in the following line of reasoning. One of the principal objects underlying any criminal legislation is that of deterring men from crime. Now it is apparent that if it were declared to be the law that a killing in self-defense is murder such a rule could not operate in a deterrent manner. A man whose life is threatened will repel his aggressor, whatever the law may say. Looking therefore to the broad purposes of criminal legislation, we may safely declare that this statute was not intended to apply to cases of self-defense. * * *

* * * [P]recisely the same reasoning is applicable to the case at bar. If in the future any group of men ever find themselves in the tragic predicament of these defendants, we may be sure that their decision whether to live or die will not be controlled by the contents of our criminal code. * * * The withdrawal of this situation from the effect of this statute is justified by precisely the same considerations that were applied by our predecessors in office centuries ago to the case of self-defense.

* * * The line of reasoning I have applied above raises no question of fidelity to enacted law, though it may possibly raise a question of the distinction between intelligent and unintelligent fidelity. No superior wants a servant who lacks the capacity to read between the lines. The stupidest housemaid knows that when she is told "to peel the soup and skim the potatoes" her mistress does not mean what she says. She also knows that when her master tells her to "drop everything and come running" he has overlooked the possibility that she is at the moment in the act of rescuing the baby from the rain barrel. Surely we have a right to expect the same modicum of intelligence from the judiciary. The correction of obvious legislative errors or oversights is not to supplant the legislative will, but to make that will effective. * * *

TATTING, J. [This jurist responds to both arguments raised by Judge Foster. At what point, exactly, did the explorers find themselves back in a state of nature? Even if they were in a state of nature, by what authority or right can the Court resolve itself into a "Court of Nature"? Isn't the propounded code of nature a "topsy-turvy and odious" one? "It is a code in which the law of contracts is more fundamental than the law of murder." Would Whetmore have had a defense if he had shot his assailants as they set upon him? For these reasons, Judge Tatting cannot join Judge Foster's first reason. Nor can he join the second.]

* * * It is true that a statute should be applied in the light of its purpose, and that *one* of the purposes of criminal legislation is recognized to be deterrence. The difficulty is that other purposes are also ascribed to the law of crimes. It has been said that one of its objects is to provide an orderly outlet for the instinctive human demand for retribution. It has also been said that its object is the rehabilitation of the wrongdoer. Other theories have been propounded. Assuming that we must interpret a statute in the light of its purpose, what are we to do when it has many purposes or when its purposes are disputed?

[These other purposes provide a different explanation for self-defense as outside the murder prohibition. The statute requires a "willful" act, but the person who acts to repel a threat to life is not acting "willfully," according to at least one precedent, *Commonwealth v. Parry*. This purpose of the statute provides no justification for the explorers, who acted willfully. Moreover, the Court's decision in *Commonwealth v. Valjean* upheld the larceny conviction of a man who stole bread to prevent his own starvation.] If hunger cannot justify the theft of wholesome and natural food, how can it justify the killing and eating of a man? Again, if we look at the thing in terms of deterrence, is it likely that a man will starve to death to avoid a jail sentence for the theft of a loaf of bread? My brother's demonstrations would compel us to overrule *Commonwealth v. Valjean* and many other precedents that have been built on that case. * * *

There is still a further difficulty in my brother Foster's proposal to read an exception into the statute to favor this case * * *. What shall be the scope of this exception? Here the men cast lots and the victim was himself originally a party to the agreement. What would we have to decide if Whetmore had refused from the beginning to participate in the plan? Would a majority be permitted to overrule him? Or, suppose that no plan were adopted at all and the others simply conspired to bring about Whetmore's death, justifying their act by saying that he was in the weakest condition. Or again, that a plan of selection was followed but one based on a different justification than the one adopted here, as if the others were atheists and insisted that Whetmore should die because he was the only one who believed in an afterlife. These illustrations could be multiplied, but enough have been suggested to reveal what a quagmire of hidden difficulties my brother's reasoning contains. * * *

Since I have been wholly unable to resolve the doubts that beset me about the law of this case, I am with regret announcing a step that is, I believe, unprecedented in the history of this tribunal. I declare my withdrawal from the decision of this case.

KEEN, J. [This jurist insists that the Court put aside the issue, raised by the Chief Justice, of whether the Chief Executive should grant clemency. This is a "confusion of government functions," and judges should not intrude into this realm of the executive.]

The second question that I wish to put to one side is that of deciding whether what these men did was "right" or "wrong," "wicked" or "good." That is also a question that is irrelevant to the discharge of my office as a judge sworn to apply, not my conceptions of morality, but the law of the land. * * *

Whence arise all the difficulties of the case, then, and the necessity for so many pages of discussion about what ought to be so obvious? The difficulties, in whatever tortured form they may present themselves, all trace back to a single source, and that is a failure to distinguish the legal from the moral aspects of this case. To put it bluntly, my brothers do not like the fact that the written law requires the conviction of these defendants. Neither do I, but unlike my brothers I respect the obligations of an office that requires me to put my personal predilections out of my mind when I come to interpret and apply the law of this Commonwealth. * * *

[After a period in which the Commonwealth's judiciary often freely interpreted statutes,] we now have a clear-cut principle, which is the supremacy of the legislative branch of our government. From that principle flows the obligation of the judiciary to enforce faithfully the written law, and to interpret that law in accordance with its plain meaning without reference to our personal desires or our individual conceptions of justice. I am not concerned with the question whether the principle that forbids the judicial revision of statutes is right or wrong, desirable or undesirable; I observe merely that this principle has become a tacit premise underlying the whole of the legal and governmental order I am sworn to administer. * * *

My brother Foster's penchant for finding holes in statutes reminds one of the story told by an ancient author about the man who ate a pair of shoes. Asked how he liked them, he replied that the part he liked best was the holes. That is the way my brother feels about statutes; the more holes they have in them the better he likes them. In short, he doesn't like statutes.

One could not wish for a better case to illustrate the specious nature of this gap-filling process than the one before us. My brother thinks he knows exactly what was sought when men made murder a crime, and that was something he calls "deterrence." My brother Tatting has already shown how much is passed over in that interpretation. But I think the trouble goes deeper. I doubt very much whether our statute making murder a crime really has a "purpose" in any ordinary sense of the term. Primarily, such a statute reflects a deeply-felt human conviction that murder is wrong and that something should be done to the man who commits it. * * *

Now I know that the line of reasoning I have developed in this opinion will not be acceptable to those who look only to the immediate effects of a decision and ignore the long-run implications of an assumption by the judiciary of a power of dispensation. A hard decision is never a popular decision. * * * Hard cases may even have a certain moral value by bringing home to the people their own responsibilities toward the law that is ultimately their creation, and by reminding them that there is no principle of personal grace that can relieve the mistakes of their representatives.

Indeed, I will go farther and say that not only are the principles I have been expounding those which are soundest for our present conditions, but that we would have inherited a better legal system from our forefathers if those principles had been observed from the beginning. For example, with respect to the excuse of self-defense, if our courts had stood steadfast on the language of the statute the result would undoubtedly have been a legislative revision of it. Such a revision would have drawn on the assistance of natural philosophers and psychologists, and the resulting regulation of the matter would have had an understandable and rational basis, instead of the hodgepodge of verbalisms and metaphysical distinctions that have emerged from the judicial and professional treatment.

HANDY, J. * * * I never cease to wonder at my colleagues' ability to throw an obscuring curtain of legalisms about every issue presented to them for decision. * * *

* * * The problem before us is what we, as officers of the government, ought to do with these defendants. That is a question of practical wisdom to be exercised in a context, not of abstract theory, but of human realities. When the case is approached in this light, it becomes, I think, one of the easiest to decide that has ever been argued before this Court. * * *

I have never been able to make my brothers see that government is a human affair, and that men are ruled, not by words on paper or by abstract theories, but by other men. They are ruled well when their rulers understand the feelings and conceptions of the masses. They are ruled badly when that understanding is lacking. * * *

* * * I believe that all government officials, including judges, will do their jobs best if they treat forms and abstract concepts as instruments. We should take as our model, I think, the good administrator, who accommodates procedures and principles to the case at hand, selecting from among the available forms those most suited to reach the proper result.

The most obvious advantage of this method of government is that it permits us to go about our daily tasks with efficiency and common sense. My adherence to this philosophy has, however, deeper roots. I believe that it is only with the insight this philosophy gives that we can preserve the flexibility essential if we are to keep our actions in reasonable accord with the sentiments of those subject to our rule. More governments have been wrecked, and more human misery caused, by the lack of this accord between ruler and ruled than by any other factor that can be discerned in history. Once drive a sufficient wedge between the mass of people and those who direct their legal, political, and economic life, and our society is ruined. Then neither Foster's law of nature nor Keen's fidelity to written law will avail us anything.

* * * One of the great newspaper chains made a poll of public opinion on the question, "What do you think the Supreme Court should do with the Speluncean explorers?" About ninety per cent expressed a belief that the defendants should be pardoned or let off with a kind of token punishment. It is perfectly clear, then, how the public feels about the case. We could have known this without the poll, of course, on the basis of common sense, or even by observing that on this Court there are apparently four-and-a-half men, or ninety per cent, who share the common opinion.

This makes it obvious, not only what we should do, but what we must do if we are to preserve between ourselves and public opinion a reasonable and decent accord. Declaring these men innocent need not involve us in any undignified quibble or trick. No principle of statutory construction is required that is not consistent with the past practices of this Court. Certainly no layman would think that in letting these men off we had stretched the statute any more than our ancestors did when they created the excuse of self-defense. If a more detailed demonstration of the method of reconciling our decision with the statute is required, I should be content to rest on the arguments developed in the second and less visionary part of my brother Foster's opinion.

HENRY M. HART, JR. AND ALBERT M. SACKS, *THE LEGAL PROCESS: BASIC PROBLEMS IN THE MAKING AND APPLICATION OF LAW*
pp. 1374–80 (William Eskridge, Jr. & Philip Frickey eds., 1994)[*]

NOTE ON THE RUDIMENTS OF STATUTORY INTERPRETATION

Consider the adequacy of the following summation:

A. The General Nature of the Task of Interpretation

The function of the court in interpreting a statute is to decide what meaning ought to be given to the directions of the statute in the respects relevant to the case before it. * * *

B. The Mood in Which the Task Should Be Done

In trying to discharge this function the court should:

1. Respect the position of the legislature as the chief policy-determining agency of the society, subject only to the limitations of the constitution under which it exercises its powers; * * *

5. Be mindful of the nature of law and of the fact that every statute is a part of the law and partakes of the qualities of law, and particularly of the quality of striving for even-handed justice.

C. A Concise Statement of the Task

In interpreting a statute a court should:

1. Decide what purpose ought to be attributed to the statute and to any subordinate provision of it which may be involved; and then

2. Interpret the words of the statute immediately in question so as to carry out the purpose as best it can, making sure, however, that it does not give the words either —

(a) a meaning they will not bear, or

(b) a meaning which would violate any established policy of clear statement.

D. The Double Role of the Words as Guides to Interpretation

* * * When the words fit with all the relevant elements of their context to convey a single meaning, as applied to the matter at hand, the mind of the interpreter moves to a confident conclusion almost instantaneously * * * .

Interpretation requires a conscious effort when the words do not fit with their context to convey any single meaning. It is in such case that the words will be seen to play a double part, first, as a factor together with relevant elements of the context in the formulation of hypotheses about possible purposes, and, second, as a separately limiting factor in checking the hypotheses.

E. The Meaning the Words Will Bear

* * * The words of the statute are what the legislature has enacted as law, and all that it has the power to enact. Unenacted intentions or wishes cannot be given effect as law.

In deciding whether words will bear a particular meaning, a court needs to be linguistically wise and not naive. It needs to understand, especially, that meaning depends upon context. But language is a social institution. Humpty Dumpty was wrong when he said that you can make words mean whatever you want them to mean.

The language belongs to the whole society and not to the legislature in office for the time being. Courts on occasion can correct mistakes, as by inserting or striking out a negative, when it is completely clear from the context that a mistake has been made. But they cannot permit the legislative process, and all the other processes which depend upon the integrity of language, to be subverted by the misuse of words. * * *

* * * [T]he proposition that words must not be given a meaning they will not bear operates almost wholly to *prevent* rather than to *compel* expansion of the scope of statutes. The meaning of words can almost always be narrowed if the context seems to call for narrowing.

F. Policies of Clear Statement

* * * Like the first requirement just considered that words must bear the meaning given them, these policies of clear statement may on occasion operate to defeat the actual, consciously held intention of particular legislators, or of the members of the legislature generally. * * * But the requirement should be thought of as constitutionally imposed. The policies have been judicially developed to promote objectives of the legal system which transcend the wishes of any particular session of the legislature. * * *

Two policies of clear statement call for particular mention.

The first of these * * * requires that words which mark the boundary between criminal and non-criminal conduct should speak with more than ordinary clearness. This policy has special force when the conduct on the safe side of the line is not, in the general understanding of the community, morally blameworthy.

The second forbids a court to understand the legislature as directing a departure from a generally prevailing principle or policy of the law unless it does so clearly. This policy has special force when the departure is so great as to raise a serious question of constitutional power. * * *

G. The Attribution of Purpose

[Hart and Sacks emphasize the complexity of the task. A statute may have several purposes, each one may be of differing degrees of definiteness, and purpose includes both the immediate policy objective as well as "a larger and subtler purpose as to how the particular statute is to be fitted into the legal system as a whole."]

In determining the more immediate purpose which ought to be attributed to a statute * * * a court should try to put itself in imagination in the position of the legislature which enacted the measure.

The court, however, should not do this in the mood of a cynical political observer, taking account of all the short-run currents of political expedience that swirl around any legislative session.

It should assume, unless the contrary unmistakably appears, that the legislature was made up of reasonable persons pursuing reasonable purposes reasonably. * * *

[The court should follow the approach of *Heydon's Case*.] Why would reasonable men, confronted with the law as it was, have enacted this new law to replace it? * * *

The most reliable guides to an answer will be found in the instances of unquestioned application of the statute. Even in the case of a new statute there almost invariably *are* such instances, in which, because of the perfect fit of words and context, the meaning seems unmistakable.

Once these points of reference are established, they throw a double light. The purposes necessarily implied in them illuminate facets of the general purpose. At the same time they provide a basis for reasoning by analogy to the disputed application in hand. * * * What is crucial here is the realization that law is being made, and that law is not supposed to be irrational. * * *

[Hart and Sacks urge that "the whole context of the statute" should be examined, including the "state of the law" both before and after enactment, "general public knowledge" of the mischief to be remedied, and published legislative history as it sheds light on the statute's general purpose.]

The judicial, administrative, and popular construction of a statute, subsequent to its enactment, are all relevant in attributing a purpose to it.

The court's own prior interpretations of a statute in related applications should be accepted, on the principle of *stare decisis*, unless they are manifestly out of accord with other indications of purpose. * * *

H. Interpreting the Words to Carry Out the Purpose

* * * The main burden of the [interpretive] task should be carried by the institution (court or administrative agency) which has the first-line responsibility for applying the statute authoritatively.

This agency should give sympathetic attention to indications in the legislative history of the lines of contemplated growth, if the history is available. It should give weight to popular construction of self-operating elements of the statute, if that is uniform. Primarily, it should strive to develop a coherent and reasoned pattern of applications intelligibly related to the general purpose. * * *

An interpretation by an administrative agency charged with first-line responsibility for the authoritative application of the statute should be accepted by the court as conclusive, if it is consistent with the purpose properly to be attributed to the statute, and if it has been arrived at with regard to the factors which should be taken into account in elaborating it.

————————

Problems on Legal Process Approaches to Interpretation

Problem 7–3. If they were to join one of the opinions in *Speluncean Explorers*, which ones would the following thinkers have joined, and why: (a) Justice Holmes; (b) Professor Radin; (c) Professors Hart and Sacks. See William Eskridge, Jr., The Case of the Speluncean Explorers: *Twentieth Century Statutory Interpretation in a Nutshell*, 61 Geo. Wash. L. Rev. 1731 (1993).

Problem 7–4. A British statute provides criminal penalties for a person who willfully, fraudulently, and with intent to affect the result in an election "personate[s] any person entitled to vote at such election." The defendant, Whiteley, is charged with having "personated" Marston, a person who had been entitled to vote at an election of guardians for the township of Bradford; Marston was a ratepayer listed in the proper book and was authorized to vote at the election. Marston had died before the election, and Whiteley delivered a vote ostensibly signed by Marston to the proper voting personnel. The dictionary defines "personate" as meaning "to act or play the part of a character in a drama or the like." There is no relevant legislative history.

How would Hart and Sacks decide such a case? Before you answer, try their suggestion of figuring out the statute's purpose by posing various situations, starting with the "core" of the statutory policy and radiating out with variations. Compare *The Legal Process* 1116–26 (1994 ed.), with *Whiteley v. Chappell,* 4 Q.B. 147 (1868).

B. IMPLICATIONS OF AND DEBATES WITHIN LEGAL PROCESS THEORY, 1950s–1980s

The legal process methodology was the dominant mode for thinking about statutes for a generation and, in fact, remains highly relevant to issues of statutory interpretation.[a] At the very same time Lon Fuller, Henry Hart, and other scholars were crystallizing their purposive theory, it was being written into the U.S. Reports. Consider the analysis of Justice Stanley Reed (President Franklin Roosevelt's Solicitor General) in *United States v. American Trucking Associations*, 310 U.S. 534, 543 (1940):

> There is, of course, no more persuasive evidence of the purpose of a statute than the words by which the legislature undertook to give expression to its wishes. Often these words are sufficient in and of themselves to determine the purpose of the legislation. In such cases we have followed their plain meaning. When that meaning has led to absurd or futile results, however, this Court has looked beyond the words to the purpose of the Act. Frequently, however, even when the plain meaning did not produce absurd results but merely an unreasonable one "plainly at variance with the policy of the legislation as a whole" this Court has followed that purpose, rather than the literal words. When aid to construction of the meaning of words, as used in the statute, is available, there certainly can be no "rule of law" which forbids its use, however clear the words may appear on "superficial examination."

The Supreme Court in the 1950s and 1960s generally followed this approach, but not without some debate as to how far to carry out purposive analysis. *Schwegmann Brothers v. Calvert Distillers Corp.*, 341 U.S. 384 (1951), for example, contained an excellent debate among the Justices as to whether the Court's responsibility to apply the statute's purpose (as Justice Douglas' plurality opinion did), could trump the original legislative expectations (Justice Frankfurter's dissenting opinion argued not). Justice Jackson's influential concurring opinion relied solely on the statutory text: because its meaning was plain, he did not care much about the original legislative intent.

As the debate in *Schwegmann* illustrated and the Speluncean Explorers essay anticipated, the two generations of judges and lawyers who have deployed legal process arguments have followed more than one path. Oversimplifying somewhat, one can identify two contesting strains within legal process thinking that have often diverged into competing schools of thought.[b] One strain, represented by Judge Foster in Speluncean Explorers, emphasizes statutory purposes and sees judges and agencies as helpful partners as well as normative updaters in the ongoing statutory enterprise. The other strain, represented by Judge Keen, emphasizes the rule-of-law virtues in following

---

a. On the robustness of legal process thought for current theorizing, see, e.g., Stephen Breyer, *Active Liberty: Interpreting Our Democratic Constitution* (2005); Daniel Rodriguez, *The Substance of the New Legal Process*, 77 Calif. L. Rev. 919 (1989) (book review); Edward Rubin, *Legal Reasoning, Legal Process and the Judiciary as an Institution*, 85 Calif. L. Rev. 265 (1997); Peter Strauss, *On Resegregating the Worlds of Statute and Common Law*, 1994 Sup. Ct. Rev. 429.

The "comeback" of legal process theory has not been hurt by the fact that a majority of the sitting Justices on the U.S. Supreme Court (Scalia, Kennedy, Souter, Ginsburg, Breyer) took the Legal Process course from Professors Hart and Sacks. See William Eskridge, Jr. & Philip Frickey, *The Supreme Court, 1993 Term — Foreword: Law as Equilibrium*, 108 Harv. L. Rev. 26, 27 (1994).

b. This is the argument of William Eskridge, Jr. & Gary Peller, *The New Public Law Movement: Moderation as a Postmodern Cultural Form*, 89 Mich. L. Rev. 707 (1991).

statutory plain meanings and the greater institutional competence of the legislature to make and update public policy. See how these legal process debates play out in three kinds of cases: When, if ever, should judges or agencies correct what they consider to be legislative "mistakes"? Can courts or agencies "update" statutes or read them "dynamically"? To what extent should judges "bend" statutes in light of larger public values?

1. *Correcting Legislative "Mistakes"?*

SHINE v. SHINE
United States Court of Appeals, First Circuit, 1986
802 F.2d 583

Before COFFIN, BOWNES and BREYER, Circuit Judges.

BOWNES, CIRCUIT JUDGE. * * *

The plaintiff, Marguerite Shine, and the defendant, Louis Shine, were married in the District of Columbia on September 20, 1969. They did not have any children and, on October 30, 1972, they divided their property and separated without making any agreement regarding support. In December of 1972, plaintiff commenced an action for separate maintenance from defendant in the Superior Court of the District of Columbia where defendant was a resident. The Superior Court issued an order requiring defendant to pay $250 per month to plaintiff beginning in April 1973. In 1975, plaintiff, then a resident of Virginia, was granted a decree of divorce from defendant by the Circuit Court of Fairfax County, Virginia. The decree made no provision for alimony and support. [Marguerite later secured a judgment requiring Louis to pay his support arrearage. Louis still did not pay, and Marguerite brought a second lawsuit, which was stayed when Louis filed for bankruptcy.]

Plaintiff then filed a complaint in the United States Bankruptcy Court for the District of New Hampshire seeking to have the support obligation declared nondischargeable under 11 U.S.C. § 523(a)(5) (1978). Section 523(a)(5) excepted from discharge any debt "to a spouse, former spouse, or child of the debtor, for alimony to, maintenance for, or support of such spouse or child, in connection with a separation agreement, divorce decree, or property settlement agreement * * *." The Bankruptcy Court initially held that the debt was not dischargeable because it "relates to the oral separation agreement between the parties." *In re Shine*, 43 B.R. 686, 688 (Bankr.D.N.H.1984). Upon motion for reconsideration, however, it held that the debt was dischargeable because it was not created by a "separation agreement *which itself* embodies an agreed arrangement between the parties for the obligation to make support payments." Upon appeal, the district court held that the debt was not dischargeable because "to allow the defendant's debt to be discharged would be contrary to Congressional intent and public policy." Defendant has appealed. [The courts are divided on the issue whether child or spousal support obligations ordered by a court independent of a divorce proceeding or formal agreement are dischargeable.]

These conflicting interpretations of the statute derive from the two established public policies in this area. The general bankruptcy rule of construing exceptions to discharge against the creditor and in favor of the debtor, *Gleason v. Thaw*, 236 U.S. 558, 562 (1915), supports a narrow construction of the statute. This general rule implements "[t]he overriding purpose of the bankruptcy laws * * * to provide the bankrupt with comprehensive, much needed relief from the burden of his indebtedness by releasing him from virtually all his debts." On the other hand, the long-standing policy of excepting spousal and child support from discharge in bankruptcy supports a more liberal construction:

> The bankruptcy law should receive such an interpretation as will effectuate its beneficent purposes and not make it an instrument to deprive dependent wife and children of the support and maintenance due them from the husband and father, which it has ever been the purpose of the law to enforce. * * * Unless positively required by direct enactment the courts should not presume a design upon the part of Congress in relieving the unfortunate debtor to make the law a means of avoiding enforcement of the obligation, moral and legal, devolved upon the husband to support his wife and to maintain and educate his children.

Wetmore v. Markoe, 196 U.S. 68, 77 (1904).

The exception from discharge for alimony and payments for maintenance and support has long been an accepted part of bankruptcy law. Even prior to the 1903 Amendment to § 17 of the 1898 Bankruptcy Act, which explicitly incorporated this exception, the majority of courts held that such payments constituted a nondischargeable "duty" rather than a provable "debt." In *Audubon v. Shufeldt*, 181 U.S. 575 (1901), the Supreme Court found this exception to be implied in the 1898 Act, which discharged all debts "founded * * * upon a contract, expressed or implied," Act of July 1, 1898, ch. 541, § 63(4), 30 Stat. 544, 563:

> Alimony does not arise from any business transaction but from the relation of marriage. It is not founded on a contract, express or implied, but on the natural and legal duty of the husband to support the wife. The general obligation to support is made specific by the decree of the Court of appropriate jurisdiction. * * * But its obligation in that respect does not affect its nature.

And in *Wetmore*, the Court found that the 1903 Amendment explicitly including the exception was "declaratory of the true meaning and sense of the statute," rather than indicating the exception's absence prior to 1903.

Litigation arose under amended § 17 concerning the definition of "alimony." Cases were decided on the basis of whether the payments in question constituted genuine "alimony" or, rather, dischargeable "property settlements." In making this determination courts looked at the substance, rather than the formal designation, of the payments. [Citing cases.]

Under the interpretation of the statute urged by the appellant, the 1978 Amendment would be viewed as reversing this long-standing differentiation between property settlements and alimony or payments for maintenance and support. Under appellant's interpretation, property settlements, traditionally dischargeable, would have become nondischargeable, while alimony and payments for maintenance and support, traditionally nondischargeable, would have been limited by a strictly construed "in connection" clause. We, therefore, examine the history of the 1978 Amendment to determine whether such a reversal was intended by Congress.

In 1970, the Commission on the Bankruptcy Laws of the United States was charged with recommending changes in the statute. Act of July 24, 1970, Pub.L. No. 91–354, 84 Stat. 468. The Commission proposed amending § 17(a)(7) to make nondischargeable "any liability to a spouse or child for maintenance or support, for alimony due or to become due, or under a property settlement in connection with a separation agreement or divorce decree." *Report of the Commission*, H.R. Doc. No. 93–137, 93d Cong., 1st Sess. (1973)[.] The Commission's proposal left untouched the existing broad exemption for *any* liability for maintenance or support. * * * The Commission intended to expand nondischargeable support debts beyond the support, maintenance and alimony obligations which had traditionally been nondischargeable. The proposal included property settlements in divorce or separation agreements which were in the nature of support but which did not take the form of periodic payments. The Commission did not intend to *limit* the nondischargeability of the traditionally protected categories. It sought, rather, to broaden the bankruptcy law's protection of the families of the bankrupt spouse in accordance with changing times.

The version of the Amendment that originally passed the House of Representatives, H.R. 8200, retained the traditional exception to dischargeability:

(a) A discharge * * * does not discharge an individual debtor from any debt —

* * *

(5) to a spouse, former spouse, or child of the debtor, for alimony to, maintenance for, or support of such spouse or child * * *.

H.R. 8200, § 523, 95th Cong., 1st Sess., U.S. Code Cong. & Admin. News 1978, p. 5787 (1977).

In the Senate, the original version of the Amendment substantially repeated the Commission's language, making nondischargeable "any liability to a spouse or child for maintenance or support, or for alimony due or to become due, or under a property settlement in connection with a separation agreement or divorce decree * * *." S. 2266, 95th Cong., 1st Sess. (1977). When it was reported out of committee, the Amendment read:

(a) A discharge * * * does not discharge an individual debtor from * * * —

* * *

(6) any liability to a spouse or child for maintenance or support, or for alimony due or to become due, in connection with a separation agreement or divorce decree.

S. 2266, § 523, 95th Cong., 2d Sess. (1978).

The final text of the bill was an amalgam of the Commission, House and Senate versions. The first part of the new § 523(a)(5) derived from the House language, while the "in connection" clause combines the wording of the House and Senate. The result, if construed narrowly, could convey a meaning not intended by anyone.

This final version, produced in the "harried and hurried atmosphere" in which the bill was finally enacted,[1] should not be read to effect a reversal of the long-standing principles governing this area. Such a reversal would surely have been noted in the congressional discussions. Yet, neither the House nor Senate Committee Reports accompanying the final version make any reference to a limitation upon support debts considered nondischargeable. The Senate Report does not even mention the "in connection" language in its discussion of the section nor does it suggest that any kind of new limitation had been imposed. S.Rep. No. 989, 95th Cong., 2d Sess. 79, *reprinted in* 1978 U.S. Code Cong. & Ad. News 5787, 5865. The House Report follows the Senate Report in its general discussion, H.R.Rep. No. 595, 95th Cong., 2d Sess. 364, *reprinted in* 1978 U.S. Code Cong. & Ad. News 5963, 6320. In its section-by-section discussion of § 523(a)(5), the House Report merely restates the "in connection" language without explaining any effect it might have on dischargeability. *Id.* at 6454.

In 1984, the statute was amended again, clearly making nondischargeable the kind of court-ordered debts involved in this case. Spousal or child support debts incurred "in connection with a separation agreement, divorce decree, or other order of a court of record or property settlement agreement" are now nondischargeable. 11 U.S.C. § 523(a)(5) (Supp. II) (as amended by the Bankruptcy Amendments and Federal Judgeship Act of 1984, Pub.L. 98–353, effective July 10, 1984).[2] This Amendment should not be read as proof of a contrary state of the law from 1978 through 1984. Rather, as the Supreme Court, in *Wetmore*, analogously noted in relation to the 1903 Amendment, it simply declares and clarifies the "true meaning and sense" of the law, allowing it to "effectuate its beneficent purposes."

After this examination of the legislative history of § 523, as well as of the established principles in this area, we cannot agree with the Bankruptcy Court's view of the requirements for nondischargeability under the 1978 statute. Congressional policy in this area has always been to ensure that genuine support obligations would not be discharged. Interpreting the statute to require the test proposed would violate the principle that in bankruptcy law, "substance will not give way to form * * * technical considerations will not prevent substantial justice from being done." *Pepper v. Litton*, 308 U.S. 295, 305 (1939). While the wording of the statute may have given rise to some confusion, "[t]he result of an obvious mistake should not be enforced, particularly when it 'overrides common sense and evident statutory purpose.'"

---

1. The final version of the new Bankruptcy law was arrived at in October, 1978 as the deadline for Congressional action drew near. If a final bill had not been approved by both houses prior to adjournment it would have been necessary to begin anew the following year. It was in this harried and hurried atmosphere that the Bankruptcy Reform Act as we now know it was produced in its final form.

2. This case was filed in 1982. Since the 1984 Amendment became effective for cases filed ninety days after its enactment, Pub.L. 98–353, § 552, it does not directly govern this case.

In re Adamo, 619 F.2d 216, 222 (2d Cir. 1980), *cert. denied*, 449 U.S. 843 (1980) (quoting *United States v. Brown*, 333 U.S. 18, 26 (1948)).

We hold, therefore, that this support obligation is not dischargeable in bankruptcy. * * *

NOTE ON JUDICIAL CORRECTION OF LEGISLATIVE MISTAKES

Hart and Sacks opined that "[c]ourts on occasion can correct mistakes, as by inserting or striking out a negative, when it is completely clear from the context that a mistake has been made. But they cannot permit the legislative process, and all the other processes which depend upon the integrity of language, to be subverted by the misuse of words." *The Legal Process* 1375 (1994 ed.). Is *Shine* correctly decided under this precept? There are cases in which courts have disregarded, eliminated, transposed, or inserted words in a statute when it is clear that a drafting error or other mistake was made, or where an absurd interpretation would otherwise result. See 2A Sutherland, *Statutes and Statutory Construction*, §§ 47.35–.38 (5th ed. 1992).[c] Is *Shine* really a "scrivener's error" case? Would the contrary result be "absurd"? (Hint: it appears that the statute contained a drafting mistake. See if you can figure out where that occurred.)

The new textualists have questioned this conventional wisdom. Consider this example. The district court entered an order denying remand back to state court of a lawsuit that had been removed by the defendant to federal court. 28 U.S.C. § 1453(c)(1) requires that any appeal from such an order must be made "not *less* than 7 days after entry of the order." Was there no time limit on appeals? The Ninth Circuit held this was a scrivener's error and interpreted the statute to require an appeal to be filed "not *more* than 7 days after entry of the order." *Amalgamated Transit Union Local 1309 v. Laidlaw Transit Servs., Inc.*, 435 F.3d 1140 (9th Cir. 2006). Dissenting from the full court's denial of en banc review, 448 F.3d 1092 (2006), Judge Bybee (joined by Judges Kozinski, O'Scannlain, Rymer, Callahan, and Bea) rejected the panel's rewrite of a statute. This kind of judging "is a trap for citizens (and their lawyers) who can no longer trust the statute as written to mean what it plainly says." Also, "[w]hen courts turn the meaning of statutes up-side-down, Congress must legislate defensively, not by enacting statutes in the plainest possible language, but by enacting statutes in the language that it predicts the courts will interpret to effectuate its intentions." 448 F.3d at 1100. For a response to these kinds of arguments, see Siegel, *Statutory Drafting Errors, supra*, at 333–44.

Shine noted that in 1984 Congress amended the statute *prospectively* to correct the problem in that case. (Recall the same phenomenon in *Holy Trinity*, though the Court did not note it.) Which way does that cut? Does it suggest

---

c. See also Michael Fried, *A Theory of Scrivener's Error*, 52 Rutgers L. Rev. 589 (2000) (Constitution allows courts to deviate from words enacted by legislature and signed by executive that are absurd and can be easily fixed); Jonathan Siegel, *What Statutory Drafting Errors Teach Us About Statutory Interpretation*, 69 Geo. Wash. L. Rev. 309 (2001) (arguing that statutory drafting errors, which show up with some frequency, create intractable problems for strict textualists and highlight some advantages for more contextualist approaches).

that Congress can fix its own mistakes or oversights, and thus that courts ought not roam freely about the United States Code correcting legislative imprudence? Had there been no 1984 amendment, would it be easier or harder for you to agree with *Shine*? The effect of *Shine* is to make the 1984 amendment retroactive. Should this be a concern?

If a client brought you the *Shine* problem, what would you have advised? Would you have looked just at the United States Code, and if so, would you have simply concluded that the support obligation was dischargeable? Might the "need" for legal certainty and for the availability of low-cost, accurate legal advice militate against the approach of *Shine*? (Recall the Bybee critique in *Laidlaw*.) Consider these and any other objections you might have to *Shine*'s implicit use of the "golden rule" (avoiding absurd results) in light of the following case.

———

UNITED STATES v. LOCKE, 471 U.S. 84 (1985). The Federal Land Policy and Management Act (FLPMA), Pub. L. 94–579, 90 Stat. 2743, codified at 43 U.S.C. §§ 1701–1784 (1982), provided that holders of certain mining claims to federal land must, "prior to December 31" of every year, file certain documents with state officials and the federal Bureau of Land Management (BLM) or lose their claims. *Id.* § 1744. Simply put, this is the quintessential trap for the unwary, since it seems wholly illogical to require someone to file something, under severe penalty for default, the day *before* the last day of the year. The Locke family had been exercising rights to mine gravel on federal land since the 1950s. Knowing they were required to file papers in order to retain these rights, they sent their daughter to the nearest BLM office, which told her that claims had to be filed by December 31. The Lockes filed on that date, and the BLM rejected the papers on the ground that they were too late.

Justice Marshall, for the Court, agreed with the BLM that the Lockes were out of luck: "While we will not allow a literal reading of a statute to produce a result 'demonstrably at odds with the intentions of its drafters,' with respect to filing deadlines a literal reading of Congress' words is generally the only proper reading of those words. To attempt to decide whether some date other than the one set out in the statute is the date actually 'intended' by Congress is to set sail on an aimless journey, for the purpose of a filing deadline would be just as well served by nearly any date a court might choose as by the date Congress has in fact set out in the statute. * * * [N]othing in the legislative history suggests why Congress chose December 30 over December 31, [b]ut '[d]eadlines are inherently arbitrary,' while fixed dates 'are often essential to accomplish necessary results.' " * * *

Justice Marshall continued: "[W]e are not insensitive to the problems posed by congressional reliance on the words 'prior to December 31.' But the fact that Congress might have acted with greater clarity or foresight does not give courts a *carte blanche* to redraft statutes in an effort to achieve that which Congress is perceived to have failed to do. 'There is a basic difference between filling a gap left by Congress' silence and rewriting rules that Congress has affirmatively and specifically enacted.' *Mobil Oil Corp. v. Higginbotham*, 436 U.S. 618, 625 (1978) [Chapter 6, Problem 6–3]. * * * [D]eference to the supremacy of the legislature, as well as recognition that congressmen typically vote on the language of a bill, generally requires us to assume that 'the legislative purpose is expressed by the ordinary meaning of the words used.' * * * The phrase 'prior to' may be clumsy, but its meaning is clear."

Justice Stevens, joined by **Justice Brennan**, dissented. In part, he argued: (1) FLPMA contained obvious drafting errors, which "should cause us to pause before concluding that Congress commanded blind allegiance to the remainder of the literal text" of the statute; (2) the BLM's implementing regulations do not repeat the statutory language, but rather state that filing must be accomplished "on or before December 30 of each year," suggesting that the BLM itself recognized that the statutory language was unclear; (3) indeed, the BLM once made the same mistake as the claimholders in *Locke*, for the agency had issued an information pamphlet that stated that documents must be filed "on or before December 31 of each [year]," demonstrating again that the statutory language is not "plain." Had the BLM issued regulations allowing filings on December 31, the Court surely would have upheld them, which suggests the anomaly that the agency "has more power to interpret an awkwardly drafted statute in an enlightened manner consistent with Congress' intent than does this Court." Justice Stevens continued: "The statutory scheme requires periodic filings on a calendar-year basis. The end of the calendar year is, of course, correctly described either as 'prior to the close of business on December 31,' or 'on or before December 31,' but it is surely understandable that the author of [this statute] might inadvertently use the words 'prior to December 31' when he meant to refer to the end of the calendar year. * * * That it was in fact an error seems rather clear to me because no one has suggested any rational basis for omitting just one day from the period in which an annual filing may be made, and I would not presume that Congress deliberately created a trap for the unwary by such an omission." The dissent concluded: "I have no doubt that Congress would have chosen to adopt a construction of the statute that filing take place by the end of the calendar year if its attention had been focused on this precise issue." Do you agree?

Query: How would Hart and Sacks have decided *Locke*? Can you think of a policy reason for requiring filing before December 31? Think hard, for this is not an impossible task. Suppose that the Lockes had shown up at the BLM at 11:00 p.m. on December 30, "before December 31," but after the BLM had closed for the day. Would they have satisfied the statute as interpreted by the Court? Is this example at all similar to the facts of *Locke*? To the example of the ordinance governing pharmacy closing mentioned at the outset of this chapter?

2. *Statutory Evolution in Light of Changed Circumstances*

WILLIAM ESKRIDGE, JR., DYNAMIC STATUTORY INTERPRETATION 125–28 (1994).[*] Interpretation can be viewed as an honest effort by

---

*   Reprinted by permission of the publisher from DYNAMIC STATUTORY INTERPRETATION by William N. Eskridge, Jr., pp. 125-128, Cambridge, Mass.: Harvard University Press, Copyright © 1994 by the President and Fellows of Harvard College.

an "agent" to apply the "principal's" directive to unforeseen circumstances. (When circumstances were foreseen and provided for by the principal, it might be said that there is no "interpretive" effort needed.) The dynamic nature of interpretation arises, in large part, out of the agent's need for practical accommodation of the directive to new circumstances. Consider the following homely example, adapted from Francis Lieber's famous "fetch me the soup meat" hypothetical.[d]

"* * * Williams, the head of the household, retains Diamond as a relational agent to run the household while Williams is away on business. The contract is detailed, setting forth Diamond's duties to care for Williams' two children, maintain the house, prepare the meals, and do the shopping on a weekly basis. One of the more specific directives is that Diamond fetch five pounds of soup meat every Monday (the regular shopping day), so that he can prepare enough soup for the entire week. Diamond knows from talking to Williams that by 'soup meat' she means a certain type of nutritious beef that is sold at several local stores. When Williams leaves, Diamond has no doubt as to what he is supposed to do. But over time his interpretation of the directive will change if the social, legal, and constitutional context changes so as to affect important assumptions made in Williams' original directive.

"Changes in Social Context. There are a number of changes in the world that would justify Diamond's deviation from the directive that he fetch five pounds of soup meat each Monday. For example, suppose Diamond goes to town one Monday and discovers that none of the stores has the precise kind of soup meat he knows Williams had in mind when she gave the order. Should he drive miles to other towns in search of the proper soup meat? Not necessarily. It might be reasonable for him to purchase a suitable alternative in town, especially if it appears in his judgment to be just as good for the children. One can imagine many practical reasons why, in a given week, Diamond should not follow the apparent command. The reasons for deviating are akin to the interpretive creation of 'exceptions' to a statute's broad mandate based on the interpreter's judgment about the statute's goals and the extent to which other goals should be sacrificed. [Recall Justice Brewer's opinion in *Holy Trinity Church* and Justice Brennan's opinion in *Weber.*]

"As the reasons multiply over time, one can imagine changed circumstances that effectively nullify Williams' directive altogether[.] Suppose Diamond discovers that one of the children has an allergy to soup meat. That child can continue to eat soup, but not with meat in it. Because Diamond realizes that one of the reasons Williams directed him to fetch soup meat every Monday was to ensure the good health and nourishment of the children, and because he believes that Williams would not want him to waste money on uneaten soup

---

d. See also Stephen Breyer, *Active Liberty: Interpreting Our Democratic Constitution* (2005); Richard Posner, *The Problems of Jurisprudence* ch. 7 (1990); Daniel Farber, *Legislative Deals and Statutory Bequests*, 75 Minn. L. Rev. 667 (1991); Philip Frickey, *Congressional Intent, Practical Reasoning, and the Dynamic Nature of Federal Indian Law*, 78 Calif. L. Rev. 1137 (1990); Lawrence Lessig, *Fidelity in Translation*, 71 Tex. L. Rev. 1165 (1993).

meat, he henceforth purchases only three pounds of soup meat per week. If both children are allergic to the soup meat, and Diamond does not care for the soup meat himself, he might be justified in entirely forgoing his directive to fetch it. Although he would be violating the original specific intent as well as the plain meaning of Williams's orders, Diamond could argue that his actions are consistent with her general intent that he act to protect the children's health and with her meta-intent that Diamond adapt specific directives to that end.

"New Legal Rules and Policies. The agent might receive inconsistent directives over time. Suppose that two months after Williams embarks on her trip, she reads in a 'Wellness Letter' that if children do not eat healthy foods, they will have cholesterol problems later in life. She sends Diamond a letter instructing him to place the children on a low-cholesterol diet, which should include Wendy's Bran Muffins and fresh apples. As a faithful relational agent, Diamond complies. He also reads up on the cholesterol literature, including the 'Wellness Letter,' and discovers that soup meat is high in cholesterol. He discontinues the weekly fetching of soup meat and fetches chicken instead because it is lower in cholesterol. Diamond's action is akin to a court's reconciliation of conflicting statutory mandates, in which one of the statutes often is given a narrowing interpretation to accommodate the policies of a later statute. * * *

"Changed circumstances might further alter Diamond's interpretation of Williams's inconsistent directives. Weeks after he has substituted chicken for soup meat, Diamond learns from the 'Wellness Letter' that Wendy's Bran Muffins actually do not help lower cholesterol, and that they have been found to cause cancer in rats. Furthermore, Diamond discovers that 50 percent of the apples sold in his region have a dangerous chemical on them. Diamond thereupon switches from Wendy's Bran Muffins to Richard's Bran Muffins, recommended by the 'Wellness Letter,' and from fresh apples to fresh oranges. Thus, not only has Diamond overthrown Williams' earlier directive on soup meat because of the new policy in her latter directive, but he has also altered her specific choice of low-cholesterol foods in the latter directive!

"New Meta-Policies. The relational agent's interpretation of his orders may well be influenced over time by changing meta-policies. The new meta-policies may be endogenous or exogenous. Endogenous meta-policies are those generated from the principal herself and are just a more dramatic form of inconsistent directives. Suppose that, after several months, Williams writes to Diamond that financial reversals impel her to cut back on household expenses. Food costs must thereafter be limited to $100 per week. Although he has long been directed to fetch soup meat every Monday, and there are other ways to economize, Diamond cuts back on soup meat, in part because it is the most expensive item on the shopping list. This is akin to a court's modifying an original statutory policy to take account of supervening statutory policies.

"Exogenous meta-policies are those generated from an authority greater than the principal. Suppose that Diamond has an unlimited food budget and no health concerns about soup meat, yet he stops fetching it on a weekly basis because the town is in a crisis period and meat of all sorts is being rationed; hence, Diamond could not lawfully fetch five pounds of soup meat per week.

This is akin to a court construing a statute narrowly to avoid constitutional problems based on the legislature's meta-intent not to pass statutes of questionable constitutionality.

"In all of these hypotheticals Diamond, our relational agent, has interpreted Williams's soup meat directive dynamically. Quite dynamically, in fact, because in most of the variations Diamond created substantial exceptions to or even negated the original specific meaning of the directive. Notwithstanding his dynamic interpretation of the directive, I believe that Diamond has been nothing but an honest agent."

Query: Consider how Eskridge's theory of changed circumstances could explain (and defend) the result in *Weber* (Chapter 1, § 3). Does it have any bearing on *Holy Trinity*, where the Court was construing a more recent statute? Is it a persuasive justification for dynamic readings of laws in the following state cases? If so, what "circumstances" have "changed," and why do any such changes support interpretations that seem to bend statutory language, perhaps beyond its breaking point?

IN THE MATTER OF JACOB
New York Court of Appeals, 1995
86 N.Y.2d 651, 636 N.Y.S.2d 716, 660 N.E.2d 397

KAYE, C.J. [delivered the opinion for the Court.]

[The appeal involved two petitions for adoption. In the *Jacob* case, the cohabiting boyfriend, Stephen T.K., of the child's biological mother, Roseanne M.A., moved to adopt Jacob. In the *Dana* case, the cohabiting female partner, G.M., of the child's biological mother, P.I., petitioned to adopt Dana. In both cases, the family courts denied the petitions as not falling within New York's adoption statute. The Court of Appeals, by a 4–3 vote, reversed.]

[S]ince adoption in this State is "solely the creature of . . . statute," the adoption statute must be strictly construed. What is to be construed strictly and applied rigorously in this sensitive area of the law, however, is legislative purpose as well as legislative language. Thus, the adoption statute must be applied in harmony with the humanitarian principle that adoption is a means of securing the best possible home for a child. * * *

This policy would certainly be advanced in situations like those presented here by allowing the two adults who actually function as a child's parents to become the child's legal parents. The advantages which would result from such an adoption include Social Security and life insurance benefits in the event of a parent's death or disability, the right to sue for the wrongful death of a parent, the right to inherit under rules of intestacy and eligibility for coverage under both parents' health insurance policies. In addition, granting a second parent adoption further ensures that two adults are legally entitled to make medical decisions for the child in case of emergency and are under a legal obligation for the child's economic support *(see,* Domestic Relations Law § 32).

Even more important, however, is the emotional security of knowing that in the event of the biological parent's death or disability, the other parent will have presumptive custody, and the children's relationship with their parents, siblings and other relatives will continue should the coparents separate. Indeed, viewed from the children's perspective, permitting the adoptions allows the children to achieve a measure of permanency with both parent figures * * * .

A second, related point of overriding significance is that the various sections comprising New York's adoption statute today represent a complex and not entirely reconcilable patchwork. Amended innumerable times since its passage in 1873, the adoption statute was last consolidated nearly 60 years ago, in 1938 (L 1938, ch 606). Thus, after decades of piecemeal amendment upon amendment, the statute today contains language from the 1870's alongside language from the 1990's. * * *

Despite ambiguity in other sections, one thing is clear: section 110 allows appellants to become adoptive parents. Domestic Relations Law § 110, entitled "Who May Adopt," provides that an "adult unmarried person or an adult husband and his adult wife together may adopt another person" (Domestic Relations Law § 110). Under this language, both appellant G. M. in *Matter of Dana* and appellant Stephen T. K. in *Matter of Jacob,* as adult unmarried persons, have standing to adopt and appellants are correct that the Court's analysis of section 110 could appropriately end here. [Although Jacob's adoption was a joint petition, his mother already enjoyed parental rights, and so only Stephen T.K.'s rights were really at stake in the petition. She faulted the dissenting opinion for reading too much into the word "together."]

The conclusion that appellants have standing to adopt is also supported by the history of section 110. The pattern of amendments since the end of World War II evidences a successive expansion of the categories of persons entitled to adopt regardless of their marital status or sexual orientation. [Section 110 was expanded in 1951 to allow adoptions by minors and in 1984 to allow adoptions by adults not yet divorced but living apart from their spouses pursuant to separation agreements.] Supporting [the 1984] amendment was New York's "strong policy of assuring that as many children as possible are adopted into suitable family situations" (Bill Jacket, L 1984, ch 218, Mem of Dept of Social Services, at 2 [June 19, 1984]). * * *

These amendments reflect some of the fundamental changes that have taken place in the makeup of the family. Today, for example, at least 1.2 of the 3.5 million American households which consist of an unmarried adult couple have children under 15 years old, more than a six-fold increase from 1970 *(see,* Current Population Reports, Population Characteristics, US Bur of Census, Marital Status & Living Arrangements, P20-478, at IX [1993]). Yet further recognition of this transformation is evidenced by the fact that unlike the States of New Hampshire and Florida (NH Rev Stat Annot § 170–B:4; Fla Stat Ann § 63.042 [3]), New York does not prohibit adoption by homosexuals. Indeed, as noted earlier, an administrative regulation is in place in this State forbidding the denial of an agency adoption based solely on the petitioner's sexual orientation *(18 NYCRR 421.*16 [h] [2]). * * *

Appellants having standing to adopt pursuant to Domestic Relations Law § 110, the other statutory obstacle relied upon by the lower courts in denying the petitions is the provision that "[a]fter the making of an order of adoption the natural parents of the adoptive child shall be relieved of all parental duties toward and of all responsibilities for and shall have no rights over such adoptive child or to his property by descent or succession" (Domestic Relations Law § 117[1][a]). Literal application of this language would effectively prevent these adoptions since it would require the termination of the biological mothers' rights upon adoption thereby placing appellants in the "Catch-22" of having to choose one of two coparents as the child's only legal parent. * * *

Both the title of section 117 ("Effect of adoption") and its opening phrase ("After the making of an order of adoption") suggest that the section has nothing to do with the standing of an individual to adopt, an issue treated exclusively in section 110. Rather, section 117 addresses the legal effect of an adoption on the parties and their property. [This reading of section 117 is directed by the Court's precedents and commentary on the section, as well as the section's textual focus on estate law.]

[E]ven though the language of section 117 still has the effect of terminating a biological parent's rights in the majority of adoptions between strangers — where there is a need to prevent unwanted intrusion by the child's former biological relatives to promote the stability of the new adoptive family — the cases before us are entirely different. As we recognized in *Matter of Seaman* (78 NY2d 451, 461), "complete severance of the natural relationship is not necessary when the adopted person remains within the natural family unit as a result of an intrafamily adoption." [The legislature has recognized this principle by amending section 117 to allow adoptions by stepparents and to allow adoptive parents in some circumstances to agree to a continuing relationship between the child and her or his biological parents. The latter amendment, allowing "open adoptions," overrode a Court of Appeals decision construing the adoption law too narrowly.]

Given the above, it is plain that an interpretation of section 117 that would limit the number of beneficial intrafamily adoptions cannot be reconciled with the legislative intent to authorize open adoptions and adoptions by minors. The coexistence of the statute's seemingly automatic termination language along with these more recent enactments creates a statutory puzzle not susceptible of ready resolution. * * *

"Where the language of a statute is susceptible of two constructions, the courts will adopt that which avoids injustice, hardship, constitutional doubts or other objectionable results" (*Kauffman & Sons Saddlery Co. v Miller,* 298 NY 38, 44 [Fuld, J.]; *see also,* McKinney's Cons Laws of NY, Book 1, Statutes § 150). Given that section 117 is open to two differing interpretations as to whether it automatically terminates parental rights in all cases, a construction of the section that would deny children like Jacob and Dana the opportunity of having their two de facto parents become their legal parents, based solely on their biological mother's sexual orientation or marital status, would not only be unjust under the circumstances, but also might raise constitutional concerns in light of the adoption statute's historically consistent purpose — the best interests of the child. *(See, e.g., Gomez v Perez,* 409 US 535, 538 [Equal Protection Clause prevents unequal treatment of children whose parents are unmarried]; *Plyler v Doe,* 457 US 202, 220 [State may not direct the onus of parent's perceived "misconduct against his (or her) children"]; *Matter of Burns v Miller Constr.,* 55 NY2d 501, 507–510 [New York statute requiring child born out of wedlock to prove "acknowledgment" by deceased parent did not further legitimate State interest].

These concerns are particularly weighty in *Matter of Dana.* Even if the Court were to rule against him on this appeal, the male petitioner in *Matter of Jacob* could still adopt by marrying Jacob's mother. Dana, however, would be irrevocably deprived of the benefits and entitlements of having as her legal parents the two individuals who have already assumed that role in her life, simply as a consequence of her mother's sexual orientation.

Any proffered justification for rejecting these petitions based on a governmental policy disapproving of homosexuality or encouraging marriage would not apply. * * * New York has not adopted a policy disfavoring adoption by either single persons or homosexuals. In fact, the most recent legislative document relating to the subject urges courts to construe section 117 in precisely the manner we have as it cautions against discrimination against "nonmarital children" and "unwed parents". An interpretation of the statute that avoids such discrimination or hardship is all the more appropriate here where a contrary ruling could jeopardize the legal status of the many New York children whose adoptions by second parents have already taken place *(e.g., Matter of Camilla,* 163 Misc 2d 272; *Matter of Evan,* 153 Misc 2d 844; *Matter of A. J. J.,* 108 Misc 2d 657). * * *

BELLACOSA, .J., dissenting. Judges Simons, Titone and I respectfully dissent and vote to affirm in each case. * * *

Although adoption has been practiced since ancient times, the authorization for this unique relationship derives solely from legislation. It has no common-law roots or evolution. Therefore, our Court has approved the proposition that the statutory adoption charter exclusively controls. [Judge Bellacosa also emphasized that the "transcendent societal goal in the field of domestic relations is to stabilize family relationships, particularly parent-child bonds. That State interest promotes permanency planning and provides protection for an adopted child's legally secure familial placement." The state has chosen not to recognize common-law marriages or "lesbian marriages."]

Domestic Relations Law § 110, entitled "Who May Adopt," provides at its outset that *"an adult unmarried person or an adult husband and his adult wife together* may adopt another person" (emphasis added). Married aspirants are directed to apply "together", i.e., jointly, as spouses, except under circumstances not applicable in these cases. [Appellant G.M., the lesbian co-parent in *Dana,* meets this requirement, but appellants Stephen T.K. and Roseanne M.A., the unmarried cohabitants in *Jacob,* do not.]

The legislative history of adoption laws over the last century also reveals a dynamic process with an evolving set of limitations. The original version enacted in 1873 provided: "Any minor child may be adopted *by any adult*" (L

1873, ch 830 [emphasis added]). In 1896, the Legislature cut back by stating that "[a]n adult unmarried person, or an adult husband or wife, or an adult husband and his adult wife together, may adopt a minor" (L 1896, ch 272, § 60; *see also,* L 1915, ch 352; L 1917, ch 149). This language was further restricted, in 1920, when the Legislature omitted from the statute the language "or an adult husband or wife" *(see,* L 1920, ch 433). Since enactment of the 1920 amendment, the statute has provided that "[a]n adult unmarried person or an adult husband and his adult wife *together* may adopt" (Domestic Relations Law § 110 [emphasis added]). The words chosen by the Legislature demonstrate its conclusion that a stable familial entity is provided by either a one-parent family or a two-parent family when the concentric interrelationships enjoy a legal bond. The statute demonstrates that the Legislature, by express will and words, concluded that households that lack legally recognized bonds suffer a relatively greater risk to the stability needed for adopted children and families, because individuals can walk out of these relationships with impunity and unknown legal consequences. * * *

Domestic Relations Law § 117 provides: "After the making of an order of adoption the natural parents of the adoptive child *shall be relieved of all parental duties toward and of all responsibilities for and* shall have no rights over such adoptive child *or* to his [or her] property by descent or succession" (emphasis added). The plain and overarching language and punctuation of section 117 cannot be judicially blinked, repealed or rendered obsolete by interpretation. [Judge Bellacosa cited precedent where the Court of Appeals had refused to read equitable exceptions into the plain language of section 117 to ameliorate its harsh application.]

A careful examination of the Legislature's unaltered intent based on the entire history of the statute reveals the original purpose of section 117 was to enfold adoptees within the exclusive embrace of their new families and to sever all relational aspects with the former family. That goal still applies and especially to the lifetime and lifelong relationships of the affected individuals, not just to the effect of dying intestate.

[Judge Bellacosa faulted the majority's concern that the statute be construed to avoid constitutional problems because (1) that concern had not been briefed or even mentioned by appellants, nor did the Attorney General have an opportunity to present the state's views, (2) the presumption of constitutionality augurs against vague and speculative doubts about a statute's constitutionality, and (3) such a concern could not override the plain meaning of the statute.] Ambiguity cannot directly or indirectly create or substitute for the lack of statutory authorization to adopt. These adoption statutes are luminously clear on one unassailable feature: no express legislative authorization is discernible for what is, nevertheless, permitted by the holdings today. Nor do the statutes anywhere speak of de facto, functional or second parent adoptions. Frankly, if the Legislature had intended to alter the definitions and interplay of its plenary, detailed adoption blueprint to cover the circumstances as presented here, it has had ample and repeated opportunities, means and words to effectuate such purpose plainly and definitively as a matter of notice, guidance, stability and reliability. It has done so before *(see, e.g.,* L 1984, ch 218 [permitting adoption by adults not yet divorced]; L 1951, ch 211 [permitting adoption by a minor]).

Because the Legislature did not do so here, neither should this Court in this manner. Cobbling law together out of interpretative ambiguity that transforms fundamental, societally recognized relationships and substantive principles is neither sound statutory construction nor justifiable lawmaking. * * *

LI v. YELLOW CAB OF CALIFORNIA, 13 Cal. 3d 804, 119 Cal. Rptr. 858, 532 P.2d 1226 (Cal. 1975). Although the doctrine of contributory negligence (barring all recovery to a tort plaintiff whose own negligence contributes in any way to her or his injury) is of judicial origin, see *Butterfield v. Forrester* (K.B. 1809) 103 Eng. Rep. 926, the California Supreme Court had long construed section 1714 of the Civil Code (1872) to have codified the doctrine as it stood at that date. Section 1714 provided: "Everyone is responsible, not only for the result of his willful acts, but also for an injury occasioned to another by his want of ordinary care or skill in the management of his property or person, *except so far as the latter has, willfully or by want of ordinary care, brought the injury upon himself.* The extent of liability in such cases is defined by the Title on Compensatory Relief." (Italics added.) Although the statutory language might easily be read to adopt a rule of comparative negligence (where the plaintiff's recovery is reduced according to her or his negligence but not eliminated entirely), the Supreme Court, in an opinion by **Justice Sullivan**, reaffirmed that the 1872 code had originally codified the rule of contributory negligence.[e] Nonetheless, the Court ruled that section 1714 should be reinterpreted to codify a rule of comparative negligence — the modern trend in other states (where it had mostly been adopted by statute rather than by judicial decision) and a practice that was apparently being informally followed by many juries in California and elsewhere.

The Court justified this updating, first, by reference to the flexible rules of construction the court has traditionally applied to the code. "The Civil Code was not designed to embody the whole law of private and civil relations, rights and duties; it is incomplete and partial; and except in those instances where its language clearly and unequivocally discloses an intention to depart from, alter,

----

e. Justice Sullivan noted that comparative negligence was virtually unheard of in American law in 1872 and relied on the Code Commissioners' Note that appeared immediately following section 1714 in the 1872 code. That note provided in full as follows: "Code La., § 2295; Code Napoleon, § 1383; Austin vs. Hudson River R.R. Co., 25 N.Y., p. 334; Jones vs. Bird, 5 B. & Ald., p. 837; Dodd vs. Holmes, 1 Ad. & El., p. 493. *This section modifies the law heretofore existing.* — See 20 N.Y., p. 67; 10 M. & W., p. 546; 5 C.B. (N.S.), p. 573. This class of obligations imposed by law seems to be laid down in the case of Baxter vs. Roberts, July Term, 1872, Sup.Ct. Cal. Roberts employed Baxter to perform a service which he (Roberts) knew to be perilous, without giving Baxter any notice of its perilous character; Baxter was injured. Held: that Roberts was responsible in damages for the injury which Baxter sustained. (See facts of case.)" (1 Annot. Civ. Code (Haymond & Burch 1874 Ed.) p. 519; italics added.) The Court unanimously construed this reference to be a legislative recognition of contributory negligence, as modified to incorporate the common-law exception of "last clear chance" (which explains the statute's "except so far as" clause).

or abrogate the common-law rule concerning a particular subject matter, a section of the Code purporting to embody such doctrine or rule will be construed in light of common-law decisions on the same subject." (*Estate of Elizalde* (1920) 188 P. 560, 562) Indeed, the Code itself said, "The rule of the common law, that statutes in derogation thereof are to be strictly construed, has no application to this Code. The Code establishes the law of this State respecting the subjects to which it relates, and its provisions are to be liberally construed with a view to effect its objects and to promote justice." (Civ. Code [1872] § 4.) Also, "[t]he provisions of this Code, so far as they are substantially the same as existing statutes or the common law, must be construed as *continuations* thereof, and not as new enactments." (*Id.* § 5; italics added.)

The Court further explained that its precedents had developed section 1714 in a common-law way. "For example, the statute by its express language speaks of causation only in terms of actual cause or cause in fact ('Every one is responsible * * * for an injury occasioned to another by his want of ordinary care.'), but this has not prevented active judicial development of the twin concepts of proximate causation and duty of care. Conversely, the presence of this statutory language has not hindered the development of rules which, in certain limited circumstances, permit a finding of liability *in the absence* of direct evidence establishing the defendant's negligence as the actual cause of damage. (See *Summers v. Tice* (1948) 199 P.2d 1, 5; *Ybarra v. Spangard* (1944) 154 P.2d 687.) By the same token we do not believe that the general language of section 1714 dealing with defensive considerations should be construed so as to stifle the orderly evolution of such considerations in light of emerging techniques and concepts. On the contrary we conclude that the rule of liberal construction made applicable to the code by its own terms (Civ. Code, § 4, discussed [above]) together with the Code's peculiar character as a continuation of the common law (see Civ. Code, § 5, also discussed [above]) permit if not require that section 1714 be interpreted so as to give dynamic expression to the fundamental precepts which it summarizes.

"The aforementioned precepts are basically two. The first is that one whose negligence has caused damage to another should be liable therefor. The second is that one whose negligence has contributed to his own injury should not be permitted to cast the burden of liability upon another." The legislature used what common law resources that existed in 1872 (namely, contributory negligence, with a last clear chance defense) to balance these precepts. By 1975, the common law had developed a more equitable way to balance them, namely, comparative negligence. Now that such a doctrine has been developed, and adopted in most other states, the court ruled that it should be read into section 1714.

Justice Clark dissented. "First, the majority's decision deviates from settled rules of statutory construction. A cardinal rule of construction is to effect the intent of the Legislature," which the court concededly violated. "The majority decision also departs significantly from the recognized limitation upon judicial action — encroaching on the powers constitutionally entrusted to the Legislature. . . . The majority's altering the meaning of section 1714, notwithstanding the original intent of the framers and the century-old judicial interpretation of the statute, represents no less than amendment by judicial fiat." Although society has changed, the proper process to update the statute is through legislative, not judicial, amendment.

NOTES ON *JACOB, LI*, AND DYNAMIC READINGS OF STATE CODES

1. *Common Law Judges Interpreting Civil Codes.* Statutory interpretation of a provision (like § 1714) in a comprehensive civil (or other) code is in some ways different from interpretation of a provision in a less integrated statutory scheme.[f] Recall our mention in Chapter 6, § 1 of civil law versus common law approaches to statutes — especially the code concept of the "equity of a statute," which encourages reasoning from one statute to another. The *Li* case points out another peculiarly code concept — that the statute itself will set forth rules of interpretation. The Italian Civil Code, for example, provides:[g]

> In interpreting the statute, no other meaning can be attributed to it than that made clear by the actual significance of the words * * * and by the intention of the legislature.

> If a controversy cannot be decided by a precise provision, consideration is given to provisions that regulate similar cases or analogous matters; if the case still remains in doubt, it is decided according to the general principles of the legal order of the state.

Note the similarities between this formulation and that of Hart and Sacks' general theory of statutory interpretation — and of the approach followed by Chief Judge Kaye in *Jacob.*

Likewise, the California Civil Code provisions quoted by the *Li* Court arguably mandate a "liberal" construction of the Code. Section 3510 of the California Civil Code also enacted in 1872 (not cited by the Court) is perhaps most pertinent to the Court's reworking of § 1714: "When the reason of a rule ceases, so should the rule itself." The leading commentator on the California Code, John Norton Pomeroy, argued that the Code provisions should be treated like common law precedents, to be expanded or modified as times changed. Pomeroy, *The True Method of Interpreting the Civil Code*, 4 West Coast Rptr. 109–10 (1884). *Li* seems to follow the Pomeroy precept.

Another way of understanding the dynamic interpretations in *Li* and *Jacob* is through the lens of common law judging. In contrast to federal courts, which are courts of strictly limited jurisdiction having little if any lawmaking authority, see Thomas Merrill, *The Common Law Powers of Federal Courts*, 52 U. Chi. L. Rev. 1, 32-35 (1985), state judiciaries are common law courts, with inherent lawmaking authority. Their common law authority to make law

---

f. On statutory interpretation of civil law codes, see John Henry Merryman, *The Civil Law Tradition* 40–49 (1969); *Interpreting Statutes: A Comparative Study* (Neil MacCormick & Robert Summers eds. 1991); Konrad Zweigert & Hans-Jurgen Puttfarken, *Statutory Interpretation — Civilian Style in Civilian Methodology*, 44 Tul. L. Rev. 673 (1970).

g. See generally Mauro Cappelleti, John Henry Merryman & Joseph Perillo, *The Italian Style — Interpretation in the Italian Legal System, an Introduction* (1967).

vests state judges with greater legitimacy as well as competence to update statutes to reflect new circumstances. See Chief Judge Judith Kaye, *State Courts at the Dawn of a New Century: Common Law Courts Reading Statutes and Constitutions*, 70 NYU L. Rev. 1 (1995). Additionally, most state court judges do not serve for life, and many are either initially elected by the voters or subject to retention elections. As a result, such judges are also more democratically accountable, and their accountability might give them greater freedom (a freedom which we should expect such judges to exercise cautiously). Do these rationales justify Chief Judge Kaye's significant recasting of the adoption statute in *Jacob*? Would her rationales be a better justification for *Li*, which involved a common law area (torts), an open-textured statute, and judges subject to retention elections?

2. *Reversing the Burden of Legislative Inertia as a Justification for Judicial Recognition of Second-Parent Adoptions.* The changed circumstance in *Jacob* is somewhat different from the one in *Li*. When New York passed its adoption law, the idea of two women raising a child in a "lesbian" household would have been inconceivable; the legislators in 1872 would have had the women arrested for violating the state sodomy law. By 1995, New York had judicially invalidated its sodomy law, and lesbian unions with children were not unusual. Like most other states, New York had amended its adoption law to accommodate "second-parent adoptions," but those did not include female couples whose unions were not recognized as "marriages" by the state.[h] (Section 117 allowed adoption only if the biological mother gave up her rights; the legislature had relaxed this rule for stepparent adoptions, but not second parents of the same sex.)

This legislative failure may have been due to ambivalence about lesbian and gay families — and so the New York Court of Appeals' willingness to update the statute may have been a move to *reverse the burden of legislative inertia* in these cases: second parents presumptively can adopt, until the legislature overrides that interpretation. Most state supreme courts in gay-tolerant states have followed Chief Judge Kaye's dynamic reading of state adoption statutes,[i] but some have gone the other way,[j] and some states have allowed joint lesbian or gay parenting through legislation recognizing their civil unions (Connecticut, New Jersey, Vermont) or domestic partnerships (California, Oregon, and

---

h. See Nancy Polikoff, *This Child Does Have Two Mothers: Redefining Parenthood To Meet the Needs of Children in Lesbian-Mother and Other Nontraditional Families*, 78 Geo. L.J. 459 (1990).

i. See *Sharon S. v. Superior Court*, 31 Cal.4th 417 (2003); *In re Hart*, 806 A.2d 1179 (Del. Fam. Ct. 2001); *In re M.M.D. and B.H.M.*, 662 A.2d 837 (D.C. 1995); *Petition of K.M. and D.M.*, 653 N.E.2d 888 (Ill. App. 1995); *Adoption of K.S.P.*, 804 N.E.2d 1253 (Ind. App. 2004); *Adoption of Tammy*, 619 N.E.2d 315 (Mass. 1993); *Adoptions of B.L.V.B. and E.L.V.B.*, 628 A.2d 1271 (Vt. 1993).

j. See *Adoption of Baby Z*, 724 A.2d 1035 (Conn. 1999); *Adoption of Luke*, 640 N.W.2d 374 (Neb. 2002); *Adoption of Jane Doe*, 719 N.E.2d 1071 (Ohio App. 1998); *In re Angel Lace M.*, 516 N.W.2d 678 (Wis. 1994). Wisconsin recognized de facto parentage, which is functionally similar to second-parent adoptions. See *In re Custody of H.S.H.-K.*, 533 N.W.2d 419 (1995).

Washington). In states that are not gay-tolerant, the matter is rarely litigated at the appellate level, and of course second parent adoption legislation is not possible.

Is this kind of political burden-shifting justifiable — or is it yet another example of hated "judicial activism"? Drawing from representation-reinforcing theories of judicial review, Eskridge, *Dynamic Statutory Interpretation* ch. 5, argues that reversing the burden of inertia is particularly justified when the political process has traditionally been hostile to a minority group. Not only does this kind of judicial updating level the playing field a little, but it places the burden on political groups that are actually able to attract the legislature's attention. If the will of the people is to deny lesbian and gay parents these rights, a decision granting relief in *Jacob* will probably be overridden in short order. (The converse case will not be: minorities traditionally disadvantaged in the political process find it doubly hard to persuade the legislature to do anything for them, because legislators fear backlash.)

3. *The Female Juror Cases, a Classic Example of Judicial Updating.* State statutes have often provided that juries are to be selected from a list of the qualified "electors" (i.e., voters) of the jurisdiction. Both the legislatures of Pennsylvania and Illinois adopted such statutes at a time when women were not allowed to vote in either state. After the ratification of the Nineteenth Amendment to the United States Constitution, which guaranteed women the right to vote, were women eligible to serve as jurors in these states by virtue of these statutes?

In *Commonwealth v. Maxwell*, 114 A. 825, 829 (Pa. 1921), the Supreme Court of Pennsylvania held that women were qualified to serve on juries:

> We then have the act of 1867, constitutionally providing that the jury commissioners are required to select "from the whole qualified electors of the respective county * * * persons, to serve as jurors in the several courts of such county," and the Nineteenth Amendment to the federal Constitution, putting women in the body of electors. * * *

> "Statutes framed in general terms apply to new cases that arise, and to new subjects that are created from time to time, and which come within their general scope and policy. It is a rule of statutory construction that legislative enactments in general and comprehensive terms, prospective in operation, apply alike to all persons, subjects, and business within their general purview and scope coming into existence subsequent to their passage." 25 Ruling Case Law, 778.

But in *People ex rel. Fyfe v. Barnett*, 150 N.E. 290, 292 (Ill. 1925), the Supreme Court of Illinois reached the opposite result:

> At the time of the passage by the Legislature of the act above mentioned, providing for the appointment of a jury commission and the making of jury lists, the words "voters" and "electors" were not ambiguous terms. They had a well-defined and settled meaning. [The Illinois Constitution of 1870 limited the franchise to "male citizen[s] of the United States, above the age of twenty-one."]

> The legislative intent that controls in the construction of a statute has reference to the Legislature which passed the given act. 25 R.C.L. 1029. Applying the rules of

construction herein mentioned, it is evident that when the Legislature enacted the law in question, which provided for the appointment of jury commissioners in counties having more than 250,000 inhabitants and imposing upon them the duty of making a jury list, using the words "shall prepare a list of all electors between the ages of twenty-one and sixty years, possessing the necessary legal qualifications for jury duty, to be known as the jury list," it was intended to use the words "electors" and "elector" as the same were then defined by the Constitution and laws of the state of Illinois. At that time the Legislature did not intend that the name of any women should be placed on the jury list, and must be held to have intended that the list should be composed of the names of male persons, only. In interpreting a statute, the question is what the words used therein meant to those using them. 25 R.C.L. 1029. The word "electors," in the statute here in question, meant male persons, only, to the legislators who used it. We must therefore hold that the word "electors," as used in the statute, means male persons, only, and that the petitioner was not entitled to have her name replaced upon the jury list of Cook County.

Accord, People v. Welosky, 177 N.E. 656 (Mass. 1931).

Hart and Sacks' *The Legal Process* 1172–85 (1994 ed.) discussed these cases. Their critical questions suggest several reasons why a court might interpret a statute beyond or against the original legislative intent (as the courts did in *Jacob* and in *Li*).

(a) Consider how these courts addressed the issue of legislative intent. Is the question whether the legislature that enacted the jury-selection statute had a specific intent concerning women as jurors? What is the likelihood that there was such a specific intent? Or is the issue whether the legislature intended the term "elector" to be frozen in the meaning given it by voter-qualification statutes in effect when the jury selection statutes were first enacted, or to vary as voter qualifications changed over time?

(b) What was the purpose of the juror-qualification statutes? Would that purpose be better served by interpreting "elector" as frozen to the factual setting prior to the ratification of the Nineteenth Amendment, or alternatively as embodying later developments? If the legislature had known that the Nineteenth Amendment was going to be adopted, wouldn't its members have wanted its juror statutes to conform to the expanded concept of citizenship represented by that Amendment?

(c) Shouldn't the court avoid an "irrational pattern of particular applications" of the statute? Hart and Sacks, *The Legal Process*, at 1125. Doesn't a court have an obligation to enhance law's overall "coherence," rather than recognizing inconsistent rules? Shouldn't the court be reluctant to interpret the juror-selection statutes in a way that runs against a fundamental legal principle or policy? Would the exclusion of women from juries have been unconstitutional when Hart and Sacks were writing? See *Hoyt v. Florida*, 368 U.S. 57 (1961) (no). If so, or even if the issue just raised difficult constitutional questions, wouldn't that provide a justification for construing the open-textured statute to include women? Consider these points as you read the cases in the next section.

3. *Coherence with Public Norms*

PUBLIC CITIZEN v. UNITED STATES DEPARTMENT OF JUSTICE, 491 U.S. 440 (1989). The question was whether the Standing Committee on the Federal Judiciary of the American Bar Association (ABA) was subject to the Federal Advisory Committee Act (FACA), 5 U.S.C. § 1 et seq., which imposes disclosure and open meeting requirements on a federal "advisory committee." The statute defines "advisory committee" as, among other things, any committee "established or utilized by the President [or] by one or more agencies, in the interest of obtaining advice or recommendations for the President." The President, through the Justice Department, routinely seeks the advice of the ABA committee concerning the qualifications of potential federal judicial nominees. **Justice Brennan's** majority opinion declined to hold that the ABA committee was within the statute's scope. He invoked *Holy Trinity Church* to escape the apparent meaning of "utilize," and after a lengthy evaluation of the legislative history concluded that "utilize" had been added late in the legislative process "simply to clarify that FACA applies to advisory committees established by the Federal Government in a generous sense of that term" — that is, in addition to groups formally established by the federal government, to groups formed indirectly by quasi-public organizations, such as the National Academy of Sciences, that are used and officially recognized as advisory to the executive branch.

Justice Kennedy, joined by **Chief Justice Rehnquist** and **Justice O'Connor**, concurred only in the judgment. (**Justice Scalia** did not participate in this case.) "Where the language of a statute is clear in its application, the normal rule is that we are bound by it. There is, of course, a legitimate exception to this rule, which the Court invokes, citing *Holy Trinity Church*, and with which I have no quarrel. Where the plain language of the statute would lead to 'patently absurd consequences' that 'Congress could not *possibly* have intended,' we need not apply the language in such a fashion. When used in a proper manner, this narrow exception to our normal rule of statutory construction does not intrude upon the lawmaking powers of Congress, but rather demonstrates a respect for the coequal Legislative Branch, which we assume would not act in an absurd way.

"This exception remains a legitimate tool of the judiciary, however, only as long as the Court acts with self-discipline by limiting the exception to situations where the result of applying the plain language would be, in a genuine sense, absurd, *i.e.*, where it is quite impossible that Congress could have intended the result, and where the alleged absurdity is so clear as to be obvious to most anyone. * * * In today's opinion, however, the Court disregards the plain language of the statute not because its application would be patently absurd, but rather because, on the basis of its view of the legislative history, the Court is 'fairly confident' that 'FACA should [not] be construed to apply to the ABA Committee.' I believe the Court's loose invocation of the 'absurd result' canon of statutory construction creates too great a risk that the Court is exercising its own 'WILL instead of JUDGMENT,' with the consequence of 'substituti[ng] [its own] pleasure to that of the legislative body.' The Federalist No. 78 (A. Hamilton)." Kennedy argued that it would not at all be "absurd" to apply the FACA to ABA committees and then concluded:

"Unable to show that an application of FACA according to the plain meaning of its terms would be absurd, the Court turns instead to the task of demonstrating that a straightforward reading of the statute would be inconsistent with the congressional purposes that lay behind its passage. To the student of statutory construction, this move is a familiar one. It is, as the Court identifies it, the classic *Holy Trinity* argument. '[A] thing may be within the letter of the statute and yet not within the statute, because not within its spirit, nor within the intention of its makers.' *Holy Trinity*. I cannot embrace this principle. Where it is clear that the unambiguous language of a statute embraces certain conduct, and it would not be patently absurd to apply the statute to such conduct, it does not foster a democratic exegesis for this Court to rummage through unauthoritative materials to consult the spirit of the legislation in order to discover an alternative interpretation of the statute with which the Court is more comfortable. It comes as a surprise to no one that the result of the Court's lengthy journey through the legislative history is the discovery of a congressional intent not to include the activities of the ABA Committee within the coverage of FACA. The problem with spirits is that they tend to reflect less the views of the world whence they come than the views of those who seek their advice.

"Lest anyone think that my objection to the use of the *Holy Trinity* doctrine is a mere point of interpretive purity divorced from more practical considerations, I should pause for a moment to recall the unhappy genesis of that doctrine and its unwelcome potential. * * * The central support for the Court's ultimate conclusion [in *Holy Trinity*] that Congress did not intend the law to cover Christian ministers is its lengthy review of the 'mass of organic utterances' establishing that 'this is a Christian nation,' and which were taken to prove that it could not 'be believed that a Congress of the United States intended to make it a misdemeanor for a church of this country to contract for the services of a Christian minister residing in another nation.' I should think the potential of this doctrine to allow judges to substitute their personal predilections for the will of the Congress is so self-evident from the case which spawned it as to require no further discussion of its susceptibility to abuse."

STATE OF NEW JERSEY v. 1979 PONTIAC TRANS AM etc.
New Jersey Supreme Court, 1985
487 A.2d 722, 98 N.J. 474

Opinion of POLLOCK, J. * * *

[On July 25, 1982, Orlando Figueroa and a companion were driving home from the shore in his father's Pontiac. Inebriated, the young men confiscated the "T-roof" of a Corvette and drove off with it. The police tracked down the youths and reclaimed the T-roof. Pursuant to N.J.S.A. 2C:64–3, the county moved to confiscate the father's Pontiac, and the courts granted the motion.]

[F]orfeiture refers to the divestiture without compensation of title to property used to further criminal activity. Statutes authorizing forfeiture stem from ancient religious beliefs that religious expiation was required of a chattel that caused a person's death. *Calero-Toledo v. Pearson Yacht Leasing Co.*, 416 U.S. 663, 680–81 (1974) (*Calero-Toledo*). * * *

Modern forfeiture statutes are supported by more contemporary considerations than those that originally gave rise to forfeiture. At present, forfeiture proceedings are often viewed as the only adequate means to protect against a particular offense, *e.g.*, the forfeiture of a still may be the only way to prevent the continued illegal distillation of alcohol. Consistent with that viewpoint, the New Jersey Organized Crime Task Force proposed the use of forfeiture as a civil remedy to combat organized crime. In addition, forfeiture is regarded as a means of encouraging owners to be more responsible in lending their personal property. Ultimately, forfeiture statutes are justifiable to the extent that they are a legitimate exercise of the police power.

Despite their utility to law enforcement officials, forfeitures remain disfavored in the law. One problem is that forfeitures result in the taking of private property for public use without compensation to the owner. The United States Supreme Court has recognized this problem under the fifth amendment of the United States Constitution, *U.S. v. U.S. Coin & Currency*, 401 U.S. [715,] 720–21; similar concerns arise under article 1, paragraph 20 of the New Jersey Constitution. Accordingly, New Jersey courts have required that forfeiture statutes be strictly construed "and in a manner as favorable to the person whose property is to be seized as is consistent with the fair principles of interpretation." *State v. One (1) Ford Van Econoline*, 154 N.J. Super. at 331–32.

In defining property subject to forfeiture, N.J.S.A. 2C:64–1 establishes two broad categories: (1) prima facie contraband, such as unlawfully possessed controlled dangerous substances and firearms, and (2) other kinds of property, such as conveyances "utilized in furtherance of an unlawful activity * * *." As originally enacted, N.J.S.A. 2C:64–1 applied only to "the defendant's interest" in the forfeited property. In 1981, however, the statute was broadened to apply to "any interest" that falls within the statutory definition of property subject to forfeiture. * * *

As a result of the 1981 amendment, that statute now provides:

No forfeiture under this chapter shall affect the rights of any lessor or any person holding a perfected security interest in property subject to seizure unless it shall appear that such person had knowledge of or consented to any act or omission upon which the right of forfeiture is based. Such rights are only to the extent of interest in the seized property and at the option of the entity funding the prosecuting agency involved may be extinguished by appropriate payment. * * *

Because forfeitures are not generally favored in the law, provisions relieving owners from the application of forfeiture statutes are liberally construed. Consistent with that perspective, we construe N.J.S.A. 2C:64–5 to exempt not only lessors and lienholders but also innocent owners who can prove that they were "uninvolved in and unaware of the wrongful activity, [and] that [they] had done all that reasonably could be expected to prevent the proscribed use of [their] property." *Calero-Toledo*, 416 U.S. at 689. As to these owners, it "would be difficult to conclude that forfeiture served legitimate purposes and was not unduly oppressive." *Id*. at 690. A stricter interpretation of the statute would run afoul of constitutional prohibitions against taking property without due process. *Id.*

In *Calero-Toledo*, the Court upheld the constitutionality of Puerto Rico's forfeiture statute as applied to an innocent lessor whose yacht was seized by the Puerto Rican government after the lessee was arrested for possession of marijuana. [The Court found that the lessor had not done all it reasonably could have done to prevent the illegal use of its vessel. In dicta, the Court said a forfeiture law would be unduly oppressive if applied to those owners who had not consented to and were unaware of the unlawful use of their property, provided they had done all that reasonably could be expected to prevent that use.]

Following the lead of the United States Supreme Court, we construe N.J.S.A. 2C:64–1 and –5 to exclude innocent owners who did not consent to or know of the illegal use of their property and who did all that reasonably could be expected to prevent that use. Thus construed, the statute survives the constitutional attack that it constitutes an unlawful taking of property without just compensation. See *Town Tobacconist v. Kimmelman*, 94 N.J. 85, 104 (1983) ("judicial surgery" used to save from constitutional attack the statutory definition of drug paraphernalia).

Reading into the statute an exemption for innocent owners who use due care to prevent unlawful use of their property is consistent with the legislative intent as expressed elsewhere in the statute. For example, N.J.S.A. 2C:64–2 provides that the forfeiture of *prima facie* contraband, such as controlled dangerous substances, is subject to the rights of owners. Because the Legislature acknowledged that the forfeiture of an item such as drugs was subject to rights of owners, it is reasonable to assume that the Legislature intended to provide a similar exemption for property that is not *prima facie* contraband. Furthermore, N.J.S.A. 2C:64–8 gives innocent owners up to three years to file a claim, if with due diligence they could not have discovered the seizure of the contraband. By restricting relief under N.J.S.A. 2C:64–8 to owners unaware of the unlawful use of the property, the Legislature apparently recognized that knowledge was relevant to forfeiture. * * *

Postscript. The U.S. Supreme Court (5–4) subsequently upheld the application of a state forfeiture law to an automobile half-owned by an innocent third party. *Bennis v. Michigan*, 516 U.S. 442 (1996). The Court characterized the quoted *Calero-Toledo* language as "obiter dictum" and abrogated it. The Court held that the innocence of the co-owner made no constitutional difference. Should the New Jersey Supreme Court now revisit its statutory interpretation in the *Trans Am* case?

NOTES ON *PUBLIC CITIZEN, TRANS AM,* AND COHERENCE-BASED JUSTIFICATIONS FOR "JUDICIAL SURGERY"

1. *Legal Process Theory and Judicial Surgery.* Neither *Public Citizen* nor *Trans Am* is easily justified by the purpose of the statute, the usual legal process move when judges are reading exceptions into a statutory text (recall

Weber (Chapter 1) or the first part of *Holy Trinity*). Although the author of the New Jersey opinion has analogized this kind of "judicial surgery" to the limited discretion afforded a musician interpreting a piece of music, Stewart Pollock, *The Art of Judging*, 71 NYU L. Rev. 591, 601–02 (1996), the strong arm given the statutory language makes the case look more like an exercise in "spurious interpretation," to use Roscoe Pound's terminology. Both Courts ultimately justify their exceedingly narrow readings by reference to larger public norms, like the second part of *Holy Trinity*. But the concurring Justices in *Public Citizen* excoriate the Court for this move, and the Christian Nation portions of *Holy Trinity* are surely controversial today even under a normativist approach. Can this methodology be defended under legal process assumptions?

One way to defend this approach is to say that it is properly respectful of the legislature: courts and agencies should assume that the legislature intends to adopt constitutional laws, and if new constitutional norms raise troubles for statutes, courts should trim the statutes back a little — so long as the "judicial surgery" is not too radical and does not undermine the statutory goal. Can that be said of the surgery performed in *Public Citizen* and *Trans Am*? Another way to defend this approach is by charging judges with a duty to make the law coherent. This is the basis for Hart and Sacks' maxim that "forbids a court to understand a legislature as directing a departure from a generally prevailing principle or policy of the law unless it does so clearly. This policy has special force when the departure is so great as to raise a serious question of constitutional power." *The Legal Process* 1377 (1994 ed.). Public norms, especially constitutional ones, have a "gravitational" pull on statutes.[k]

A final way to view these cases is to understand the role of judges as openly critical and normative. This does not sound like a legal process mode of thinking, but two leading process writers have developed precisely that idea. As you read the following notes, consider the separation of powers and majoritarian difficulties with each theory.

2. *Lon Fuller's Theory of the Repeatedly Retold Anecdote.* In his book, *Law in Quest of Itself* 8–9 (1940), Lon Fuller contested the positivist claim that fact is wholly independent of value — and interpretation independent of norms:

> If I attempt to retell a funny story which I have heard, the story as I tell it will be the product of two forces: (1) the story as I heard it . . . [and] (2) my conception of the point of the story, in other words, my notion of the story *as it ought to be*. . . If the story as I heard it was, in my opinion, badly told, I am guided largely by my conception of the story as it ought to be . . . On the other hand, if I had the story from a master raconteur, I may exert myself to reproduce his exact words . . . These two forces, then, supplement one another in shaping the story as I tell it. It is the product of the *is* and the *ought* working together. . . The two are inextricably interwoven, to the point where we can say that "the story" as an entity really embraces both of them. Indeed, if we look at the story across time, its reality becomes even more complex. The "point" of the story, which furnishes its essential unity, may in the course of

---

k. See William Eskridge, Jr., *Public Values in Statutory Interpretation*, 137 U. Pa. L. Rev. 1007 (1989).

retelling be changed. As it is brought out more clearly through the skill of successive tellers it becomes a new point; at some indefinable juncture the story has been so improved that it has become a new story. In a sense, then, the thing we call "the story" is not something that is, but something that becomes; it is not a hard chunk of reality, but a fluid process, which is as much directed by men's creative impulses, by their conception of the story as it ought to be, as it is by the original even which unlocked those impulses. The *ought* here is just as real, as a part of human experience, as the *is*, and the line between the two melts away in the common stream of telling and retelling into which they both flow.

"Exactly the same thing may be said of a statute or a decision," Fuller continues. "The statute or decision is not a segment of being, but, like the anecdote, a process of becoming." (*Id.* at 9–10.)

Fuller's justification for this way of approaching law is not its inevitability, however. Rather, he maintains that the interconnection between law and morality is a good thing. The main argument is one of coherence. Because the "bulk of human relations find their regulation outside the field of positive law," a continuous interpenetration of law and social morality creates a more seamless web of interconnected rights and duties (*id.* at 11–12). Fuller emphasized that such interconnection was necessary to the efficacy of law; without a link with changing social mores, law would not be able to achieve its goals or, worse, would lose the respect of the citizenry.[l]

Does Fuller's theory provide a good justification for the textual strong-arming in the *Trans Am* and *Public Citizen* cases? Consider a later version of his theory, discussed in the next note.

3. *"Chain Novels" and Dworkin's Theory of Law as Integrity.* Many legal scholars have followed Fuller's lead and have explored his idea that law is interpretive in some of the same ways that stories are.[m] Among the most distinctive of the post-Fuller theories is Ronald Dworkin's idea that law is an interpretive enterprise that seeks to "show it as the best work of art it can be." *Law as Interpretation*, 60 Tex. L. Rev. 527 (1982). Dworkin explains his vision of interpretation by reference to the idea of a "chain novel," id at 541–43:

> * * * Suppose that a group of novelists is engaged for a particular project and that they draw lots to determine the order of play. The lowest number writes the opening chapter of a novel, which he or she then sends to the next number, with the understand-

---

l. See Lon Fuller, *Human Interaction and the Law*, in *The Principles of Social Order: The Selected Essays of Lon L. Fuller* 211–46 (Kenneth Winston ed. 1981).

m. For uses of hermeneutics in statutory interpretation, see William Eskridge, Jr., *Gadamer/Statutory Interpretation*, 90 Colum. L. Rev. 609 (1990); Francis Mootz, III, *The Ontological Basis of Legal Hermeneutics: A Proposed Model of Inquiry Based on the Work of Gadamer, Habermas, and Ricoeur*, 68 B.U. L. Rev. 523 (1988); Dennis Patterson, *Wittgenstein and the Code: A Theory of Good Faith Performance and Enforcement under Article Nine*, 137 U. Pa. L. Rev. 335 (1988). On the connection between theories of statutory interpretation and philosophical postmodernism, see Peter Schanck, *Understanding Postmodern Thought and Its Implications for Statutory Interpretation*, 65 S. Cal. L. Rev. 2505 (1992).

ing that he is adding a chapter to that novel rather than beginning a new one, and then sends the two chapters to the next number, and so on. Now every novelist but the first has the dual responsibilities of interpreting and creating because each must read all that has gone before in order to establish, in the interpretivist sense, what the novel so far created is. He or she must decide what the characters are "really" like; what motives in fact guide them; what the point or theme of the developing novel is; how far some literary device or figure, consciously, or unconsciously used, contributes to these, and whether it should be extended or refined or trimmed or dropped in order to send the novel further in one direction rather than another. This must be interpretation in a non-intention-bound style because, at least for all novelists after the second, there is no single author whose intentions any interpreter can, by the rules of the project, regard as decisive. * * *

> Deciding hard cases at law is rather like this strange literary exercise. The similarity is most evident when judges consider and decide common-law cases; that is, when no statute figures centrally in the legal issue, and the argument turns on which rules or principles of law "underlie" the related decisions of other judges in the past. Each judge is then like a novelist in the chain. He or she must read through what other judges in the past have written not simply to discover what these judges have said, or their state of mind when they said it, but to reach an opinion about what these judges have collectively *done*, in the way that each of our novelists formed an opinion about the collective novel so far written.

In *Law's Empire* 313 (1986), Dworkin describes how the chain novel tells judges to interpret statutes:

> He will treat Congress as an author earlier than himself in the chain of law, though an author with special powers and responsibilities different from his own [as a judge], and he will see his own role as fundamentally the creative one of a partner continuing to develop, in what he believes is the best way, the statutory scheme Congress began. He will ask himself which reading of the act * * * shows the political history including and surrounding that statute in the better light. His view of how the statute should be read will in part depend on what certain congressmen said when debating it. But it will also depend on the best answer to political questions: how far Congress should defer to public opinion in matters of this sort, for example * * *.

How would Dworkin's theory apply to the *Trans Am* and *Public Citizen* cases?[n]

C. CONCERNS ABOUT LEGAL PROCESS THEORY, 1970s–80s

Legal process theory came into focus around the time of World War II. This was a period of relative consensus in America, sustained economic growth, and burgeoning optimism about government's ability to foster economic growth by solving market failures and creating opportunities. After the mid-1960s, America was a different society, as consensus collapsed on fundamental issues of war, family, and citizenship; economic growth faltered and oil price shocks introduced stagflation; and government came to be

---

n. On the application of his theory to *Weber*, see Dworkin, *How to Read the Civil Rights Act*, in Dworkin, *A Matter of Principle* (1985).

perceived as problematic, often even as a drain on society's productivity. These developments raised inevitable questions about statutory methodology. Some of them follow.

1. *The Need for a More Realistic View of the Legislative Process?* Recall our discussion of theories of legislatures in Chapter 1, § 2. One lesson of "public choice" theories is that legislators are not entirely "reasonable," as Hart and Sacks assume, and are often acting to extract "rents" for their constituents and supportive interest groups. Moreover, even reasonable legislators will disagree, and the resulting statutes may be compromises more than easily understood purposive enactments. Some law and economics scholars have argued from such theories that Hart and Sacks' purposive approach should therefore be reined back toward something like Pound's imaginative reconstruction. See Richard Posner, *The Federal Courts: Crisis and Reform* 286–93 (1985).

On the other hand, Hart and Sacks never claimed their "reasonable legislator" approach describes the legislature; they only said that courts should "attribute" purposes to the legislature, suggesting that theirs is a normative-based rather than a descriptive-based theory of interpretation. Why should ambiguous interest-group deals be enforced by courts if they do not serve a larger public purpose? See Jonathan Macey, *Promoting Public-Regarding Legislation Through Statutory Interpretation: An Interest Group Model*, 86 Colum. L. Rev. 223 (1986), who argues that rent-seeking legislators should be held to their stated public-regarding justifications.

2. *Does the Hart and Sacks Approach Submerge Substantive Issues Too Much?* Both pragmatic and critical scholars criticize legal process theory for suppressing useful substantive discussion. Judge Posner, for example, openly inquires about the practical consequences of different interpretations. See, e.g., Richard Posner, *How Judges Think* ch. 5 (draft 2007), and *The Problems of Jurisprudence* pt. 3 (1990). His practice is to figure out what is the most reasonable statutory interpretation, as applied to the facts before him, and then see if statutory text, history, and precedent foreclose the best option. This sounds a lot like Hart and Sacks, but Posner would say that he adds empirical data and systematic economic thinking that Hart and Sacks did not emphasize. Why not introduce rigorous, empirically based economic analysis into decisionmaking?

Critical scholars argue that legal process judges are making unarticulated value choices under the auspices of neutral craft. Allan Hutchinson and Derek Morgan, in *The Semiology of Statutes*, 21 Harv. J. Legis. 583, 593–94 (1984) (book review), state:

> While there has been a judicial capitulation to the supremacy of Parliament, that surrender is to a command to be obeyed begrudgingly according to its letter. Otherwise, it is of little consequence. For the courts, the triumph of statute over common law is a pyrrhic victory. But this betrays the ideological superstructure of adjudication. Words do not interpret themselves. A sentence will never mean exactly the same thing to any two different people or even the same thing to one person on different occasions. Meaning is shaped by the apperceptive mass of understanding and

background that an individual brings to bear on the external fact of a sound or series of marks. As words lack "self-evident reference," purpose and context are ultimately major determinants of meaning. However, as the expression of legislative intent is always more or less incomplete, it is doubtful whether any impartial method of adjudication can be fashioned in a liberal society. * * *

The necessity of engaging in such invention requires the courts to make substantive political decisions, the very decisions that semantic, historical or counter-factual approaches *claim* to avoid. No one single "construction" is inevitable or natural. Construction means choice. And choice confers power. Of course, this is not to suggest that judicial creativity breeds constitutional anarchy. Communities of interpretation have their own bonding mechanisms, a mixture of moral values and social customs. Interpretation is inextricably bound up with values and it is nowhere seriously suggested the values do not carry ideological underpinnings. The lesson to be gathered from this realization is quite simple. Courts that shield themselves behind descriptions of law as clear, predetermined and objective norms against which they pitch their neutral decisions are worthy of suspicion. * * *

On this understanding, a virtue of Justice Brewer's opinion in *Holy Trinity Church* is that it was candid about the values it was implementing (the Christian nation idea). Hart and Sacks' approach would likely generate the same result in the hands of a Justice Brewer, but perhaps a less candid discussion. Recall, too, Judge Handy's opinion in the Case of the Speluncean Explorers.

3. *The Appeal of Formalism.* Among judges, the most telling criticism of the legal process approach to statutory interpretation is that it neglects the virtues of a more formalist approach. Even contextualists might concede the attractions of the plain meaning rule, very ably defended by Judge Keen in Speluncean Explorers. First, it is arguably more consistent with the structure of the U.S. Constitution (and most state constitutions), which vests political power with the legislative and executive branches and only the judicial power with the courts, and which creates formal barriers to lawmaking that are disregarded when courts make new law. See John Manning, *Textualism as a Nondelegation Doctrine*, 97 Colum. L. Rev. 673 (1997). Second, and entirely within the legal process tradition, it can be argued that applying statutory plain meanings is more within the "judicial competence" than making policy or even scanning through legislative history to figure out whether the legislature "really meant" the apparent meaning of its statutory words. See Adrian Vermeule, *Legislative History and the Limits of Judicial Competence: The Untold Story of* Holy Trinity Church, 50 Stan. L. Rev. 1833 (1998).

Third, and in our view most powerfully, the ordinary meaning of statutory language is the common understanding of what the "rule of law" is. See Antonin Scalia, *The Rule of Law as a Law of Rules*, 56 U. Chi. L. Rev. 1175 (1989). Citizens ought to be able to open up the statute books and find out what the law requires of them. Once law is understood by the cognoscenti as purposes, spirits, and collective intents, the citizenry might lose faith in the externality of law — the objectivity of legal reasoning which provides us with some assurance that our problems are susceptible of the same rules as those of our neighbor (even if she is a rich and influential neighbor). The changes in

American society since the 1960s make an external vision of the rule of law even more important than before. In a society where so many values are open to contest, language may be the main thing we share in common. In a society where "the pie" is not expanding (the economy is stagnant), dividing the pie by an objective criterion becomes ever more critical.

A less complicated approach may also be more democracy-enhancing, because it places responsibility for updating statutes on the shoulders of the people and their legislators, rather than their unelected (federal and some state) or not-often-elected (most state) judges. Recall Judge Keen's argument that hard cases generating inequitable results should trigger a popular outrage that changes statutes more usefully and more democratically than judicial updating through a Hart-and-Sacks purpose approach. As potential examples of this phenomenon, consider the following cases.

TVA v. HILL
United States Supreme Court, 1978
437 U.S. 153, 98 S.Ct. 2279, 57 L.Ed.2d 117

CHIEF JUSTICE BURGER delivered the opinion of the Court.

[The Endangered Species Act of 1973, 87 Stat. 884, codified as amended at 16 U.S.C. § 1531 *et seq.*, authorized the Secretary of the Interior to declare species of animal life "endangered" and, upon such designation, triggered various protections for such species. Section 7 of the Act specified that all "Federal departments and agencies shall, * * * with the assistance of the Secretary, utilize their authorities in furtherance of the purposes of [the] Act by carrying out programs for the conservation of endangered species * * * and by taking such action necessary to insure that actions authorized, funded, or carried out by them do not jeopardize the continued existence of such endangered species and threatened species or result in the destruction or modification of habitat of such species which is determined by the Secretary * * * to be critical." 16 U.S.C. § 1536 (1976).

[Pursuant to the statute, the Secretary declared the snail darter (*Percina tanasi*) an endangered species and designated a portion of the Little Tennessee River as the only remaining natural habitat of the snail darter. That part of the river, however, would be flooded by operation of the Tellico Dam, a $100 million Tennessee Valley Authority (TVA) project that was under way in 1973 and was almost completed by 1976, when environmentalists sought an injunction against the dam's operation. The district court denied relief. It found that the dam would destroy the snail darter's critical habitat, but it noted that Congress, though fully aware of the snail darter problem, had continued to fund the Tellico Dam after 1973. The court concluded that the Act did not justify an injunction against a project initiated before enactment. The court of appeals reversed and ordered the lower court to enjoin completion of the dam.]

One would be hard pressed to find a statutory provision whose terms were any plainer than those in § 7 of the Endangered Species Act. Its very words affirmatively command all federal agencies "to *insure* that actions *authorized, funded, or carried out* by them do not *jeopardize* the continued existence" of an endangered species or "*result* in the destruction or modification of habitat of such species . . . ." 16 U.S.C. § 1536 (1976 ed.). (Emphasis added.) This language admits of no exception. Nonetheless, petitioner urges, as do the dissenters, that the Act cannot reasonably be interpreted as applying to a federal project which was well under way when Congress passed the Endangered Species Act of 1973. To sustain that position, however, we would be forced to ignore the ordinary meaning of plain language. It has not been shown, for example, how TVA can close the gates of the Tellico Dam without "carrying out" an action that has been "authorized" and "funded" by a federal agency. Nor can we understand how such action will "*insure*" that the snail darter's habitat is not disrupted. * * *

Concededly, this view of the Act will produce results requiring the sacrifice of the anticipated benefits of the project and of many millions of dollars in public funds. But examination of the language, history, and structure of the legislation under review here indicates beyond doubt that Congress intended endangered species to be afforded the highest of priorities.

[Chief Justice Burger examined statutes enacted in 1966 and 1969, which sought to discourage the taking of endangered species. Congressional hearings in 1973 revealed that strategies of encouragement had not abated the "pace of disappearance of species," which appeared to be "accelerating." H.R. Rep. No. 93–412, p. 4 (1973). The dominant theme of the hearings and debates on the 1973 Act was "the overriding need to devote whatever effort and resources were necessary to avoid further diminution of national and worldwide wildlife resources." Coggins, *Conserving Wildlife Resources: An Overview of the Endangered Species Act of 1973*, 51 N.D. L. Rev. 315, 321 (1975). Congressional committees expressed the "incalculable" value of lost species.]

Section 7 of the Act * * * provides a particularly good gauge of congressional intent. As we have seen, this provision had its genesis in the Endangered Species Act of 1966, but that legislation qualified the obligation of federal agencies by stating that they should seek to preserve endangered species only "*insofar as is practicable and consistent with their primary purposes . . . .*" Likewise, every bill introduced in 1973 contained a qualification similar to that found in the earlier statutes. * * * This type of language did not go unnoticed by those advocating strong endangered species legislation. A representative of the Sierra Club, for example, attacked the use of the phrase "consistent with the primary purpose" in proposed H.R. 4758, cautioning that the qualification "could be construed to be a declaration of congressional policy that other agency purposes are necessarily more important than protection of endangered species and would always prevail if conflict were to occur."

What is very significant in this sequence is that the final version of the 1973 Act carefully omitted all of the reservations described above. [The Senate bill contained a practicability reservation; the House bill had no qualifications. The Conference Committee rejected the Senate version of § 7 and adopted the House language. Explaining the Conference action, Representative Dingell pointed out that under existing law the Secretary of Defense has discretion to ignore dangers its bombing missions posed to the near-extinct whooping crane. "[O]nce the bill is enacted, [the Secretary of Defense] *would be required to take the proper steps*." Another example was the declining population of grizzly bears, whose habitats would have to be protected by the Department of Agriculture. "The purposes of the bill included the conservation of the species and of the ecosystems upon which they depend, and every agency of government is committed to see that those purposes are carried out. The agencies of Government can no longer plead that they can do nothing about it. *They can and they must. The law is clear.*" 119 Cong. Rec. 42913 (emphasis added by the Chief Justice).]

It is against this legislative background that we must measure TVA's claim that the Act was not intended to stop operation of a project which, like Tellico Dam, was near completion when an endangered species was discovered in its path. While there is no discussion of precisely this problem, the totality of congressional action makes it abundantly clear that the result we reach today is wholly in accord with both the words of the statute and the intent of Congress. The plain intent of Congress in enacting this statute was to halt and. reverse the trend toward species extinction, whatever the cost. This is reflected not only in the stated provisions of the Act, but in literally every section of the statute. All persons, including federal agencies, are specifically instructed not to "take" endangered species, meaning that no one is "to harass, harm, pursue, hunt, shoot, wound, kill, trap, capture, or collect" such life forms. 16 U.S.C. §§ 1532(14), 1538(a)(1)(B) (1976 ed.). * * *

[TVA also argued that Congress' continued funding of the Dam reflected a congressional judgment, embodied in appropriations statutes, that the Dam not be shut down. Appropriations committees were aware of the effect of the Dam on the snail darter.] There is nothing in the appropriations measures, as passed, which states that the Tellico Project was to be completed irrespective of the requirements of the Endangered Species Act. * * * To find a repeal of the Endangered Species Act under these circumstances would surely do violence to the " 'cardinal rule . . . that repeals by implication are not favored.' " *Morton v. Mancari*, 417 U.S. 535, 549 (1974), quoting *Posadas v. National City Bank*, 296 U.S. 497, 503 (1936). * * *

The doctrine disfavoring repeals by implication "applies with full vigor when . . . the subsequent legislation is an *appropriations* measure." *Committee for Nuclear Responsibility v. Seaborg*, 463 F.2d 783, 785 (D.C. Cir. 1971). This is perhaps an understatement since it would be more accurate to say that the policy applies with even *greater* force when the claimed repeal rests solely with an Appropriations Act. * * * When voting on appropriations measures, legislators are entitled to operate under the assumption that the funds will be devoted to purposes which are lawful and not for any purpose forbidden. [The Chief Justice also pointed to House Rule XX(2), which forbids amendments to appropriations bills which seeks to "chang[e] existing law." See also Senate Rule 16.4.] Thus, to sustain petitioner's position, we would be obliged to assume that Congress meant to repeal *pro tanto* § 7 of the Act by means of a procedure expressly prohibited under the rules of Congress.

[Chief Justice Burger rejected TVA's urging the Court to balance the harms of shutting down the dam against the dangers to the snail darter. Not only did the Court not consider itself competent to calibrate such a balance, but Congress had already made the judgment that no cost was too high to allow the federal government to imperil a species.] [I]n our constitutional system the commitment to the separation of powers is too fundamental for us to pre-empt congressional action by judicially decreeing what accords with "common sense and the public weal." Our Constitution vests such responsibilities in the political branches.

[JUSTICE POWELL's dissenting opinion, joined by Justice Blackmun, argued that the Court's opinion "disregards 12 years of consistently expressed congressional intent to complete the Tellico Project" and is "an extreme example of a literalist construction, not required by the language of the Act and adopted without regard to its manifest purpose." Citing *Holy Trinity Church*, Justice Powell contended that the Court ought not read the broad language of § 7 so sweepingly and, instead, ought to narrow the language so as to avoid "absurd results." He would have construed the "actions" governed by § 7 to be only those taken *after* 1973, when the statute was enacted.]

[JUSTICE REHNQUIST dissented on the ground that the legitimate debate over the statute's meaning properly informed the district court's decision not to enjoin work on the dam.]

GRIFFIN v. OCEANIC CONTRACTORS, INC.
Supreme Court of the United States, 1982
458 U.S. 564, 102 S.Ct. 3245, 73 L.Ed.2d 973

JUSTICE REHNQUIST delivered the opinion of the Court.

[In February 1976, Danny Griffin contracted to work as a senior pipeline welder on board vessels operated by respondent in the North Sea. The contract specified that petitioner's employment would extend "until December 15, 1976 or until Oceanic's 1976 pipeline committal in the North Sea is fulfilled, whichever shall occur first." The contract also provided that if Griffin quit the job prior to its termination date, or if his services were terminated for cause, he would be charged with the cost of transportation back to the United States. Oceanic reserved the right to withhold $137.50 from each of petitioner's first four paychecks "as a cash deposit for the payment of your return transportation in the event you should become obligated for its payment." On April 1, 1976, Griffin suffered an injury while working on the deck of the vessel readying it for sea. Oceanic refused to take responsibility for the injury or to furnish transportation back to the United States, and continued to retain $412.50 in earned wages that had been deducted from Griffin's first three paychecks for that purpose. He returned to the United States and on May 5, began working as a welder for another company operating in the North Sea.

[In 1978 Griffin brought suit against respondent under the Jones Act, § 20, 38 Stat. 1185, as amended, 46 U.S.C. § 688, and under general maritime law, seeking damages for respondent's failure to pay maintenance, cure, unearned wages, repatriation expenses, and the value of certain personal effects lost on board respondent's vessel. He also sought penalty wages under Rev.Stat. § 4529, as amended, 46 U.S.C. § 596, for respondent's failure to pay over the $412.50 in earned wages allegedly due upon discharge. The District Court found for Griffin and awarded damages totalling $23,670.40.]

In assessing penalty wages under 46 U.S.C. § 596, the court held that "[t]he period during which the penalty runs is to be determined by the sound discretion of the district court and depends on the equities of the case." It determined that the appropriate period for imposition of the penalty was from the date of discharge, April 1, 1976, through the date of petitioner's reemployment, May 5, 1976, a period of 34 days. Applying the statute, it computed a penalty of $6,881.60. Petitioner appealed the award of damages as inadequate. [The Fifth Circuit affirmed the district court judgment. The Supreme Court reversed and ruled that Oceanic owed Griffin more than $302,000 in penalty wages.]

[II.A] The language of the statute first obligates the master or owner of any vessel making coasting or foreign voyages to pay every seaman the balance of his unpaid wages within specified periods after his discharge.[6] It then provides:

> "Every master or owner who refuses or neglects to make payments in the manner hereinbefore mentioned without sufficient cause shall pay to the seaman a sum equal to two days' pay for each and every day during which payment is delayed beyond the respective periods * * *."

The statute in straightforward terms provides for the payment of double wages, depending upon the satisfaction of two conditions. First, the master or owner must have refused or failed to pay the seaman his wages within the periods specified. Second, this failure or refusal must be "without sufficient cause." Once these conditions are satisfied, however, the unadorned language of the statute dictates that the master or owner "*shall pay* to the seaman" the sums specified "*for each and every day* during which payment is delayed." The words chosen by Congress, given their plain meaning, leave no room for the exercise of discretion either in deciding whether to exact payment or in choosing the period of days by which the payment is to be calculated. As this Court described the statute many years ago, it "affords a definite and reasonable procedure by which the seaman may establish his right to recover double pay where his wages are unreasonably withheld." Our task is to give effect to the will of Congress, and where its will has been expressed in reasonably plain

---

6. The statute reads in full:

"The master or owner of any vessel making coasting voyages shall pay to every seaman his wages within two days after the termination of the agreement under which he was shipped, or at the time such seaman is discharged, whichever first happens; and in case of vessels making foreign voyages, or from a port on the Atlantic to a port on the Pacific, or vice versa, within twenty-four hours after the cargo has been discharged, or within four days after the seaman has been discharged, whichever first happens; and in all cases the seaman shall be entitled to be paid at the time of his discharge on account of wages a sum equal to one-third part of the balance due him. Every master or owner who refuses or neglects to make payment in the manner hereinbefore mentioned without sufficient cause shall pay to the seaman a sum equal to two days' pay for each and every day during which payment is delayed beyond the respective periods, which sum shall be recoverable as wages in any claim made before the court; but this section shall not apply to masters or owners of any vessel the seamen of which are entitled to share in the profits of the cruise or voyage. This section shall not apply to fishing or whaling vessels or yachts."

terms, "that language must ordinarily be regarded as conclusive." *Consumer Product Safety Comm'n v. GTE Sylvania, Inc.*, 447 U.S. 102, 108 (1980).

The District Court found that respondent had refused to pay petitioner the balance of his earned wages promptly after discharge, and that its refusal was "without sufficient cause." Respondent challenges neither of these findings. Although the two statutory conditions were satisfied, however, the District Court obviously did not assess double wages "for each and every day" during which payment was delayed, but instead limited the assessment to the period of petitioner's unemployment. Nothing in the language of the statute vests the courts with the discretion to set such a limitation.

[B] Nevertheless, respondent urges that the legislative purpose of the statute is best served by construing it to permit some choice in determining the length of the penalty period. In respondent's view, the purpose of the statute is essentially remedial and compensatory, and thus it should not be interpreted literally to produce a monetary award that is so far in excess of any equitable remedy as to be punitive.

Respondent, however, is unable to support this view of legislative purpose by reference to the terms of the statute. "There is, of course, no more persuasive evidence of the purpose of a statute than the words by which the legislature undertook to give expression to its wishes." *United States v. American Trucking Assns., Inc.*, 310 U.S. 534, 543 (1940). Nevertheless, in rare cases the literal application of a statute will produce a result demonstrably at odds with the intentions of its drafters, and those intentions must be controlling. We have reserved "some 'scope for adopting a restricted rather than a literal or usual meaning of its words where acceptance of that meaning * * * would thwart the obvious purpose of the statute.' " *Commissioner v. Brown*, 380 U.S. 563, 571 (1965) (quoting *Helvering v. Hammel*, 311 U.S. 504, 510–511 (1941)). This, however, is not the exceptional case.

As the Court recognized in *Collie v. Fergusson*, 281 U.S. 52 (1930), the "evident purpose" of the statute is "to secure prompt payment of seamen's wages * * * and thus to protect them from the harsh consequences of arbitrary and unscrupulous action of their employers, to which, as a class, they are peculiarly exposed." This was to be accomplished "by the imposition of a liability which is not exclusively compensatory, but designed to prevent, by its coercive effect, arbitrary refusals to pay wages, and to induce prompt payment when payment is possible." Thus, although the sure purpose of the statute is remedial, Congress has chosen to secure that purpose through the use of potentially punitive sanctions designed to deter negligent or arbitrary delays in payment.

The legislative history of the statute leaves little if any doubt that this understanding is correct. The law owes its origins to the Act of July 20, 1790, ch. 29, § 6, 1 Stat. 133, passed by the First Congress. Although the statute as originally enacted gave every seaman the right to collect the wages due under his contract "as soon as the voyage is ended," it did not provide for the recovery of additional sums to encourage compliance. Such a provision was added by the Shipping Commissioners Act of 1872, ch. 322, § 35, 17 Stat. 269, which provided for the payment of "a sum not exceeding the amount of two days' pay for each of the days, not exceeding ten days, during which payment is delayed." The Act of 1872 obviously established a ceiling of 10 days on the period during which the penalty could be assessed and, by use of the words "not exceeding," left the courts with discretion to choose an appropriate penalty within that period.

Congress amended the law again in 1898. As amended, it read in relevant part:

> "Every master or owner who refuses or neglects to make payment in manner hereinbefore mentioned without sufficient cause shall pay to the seaman a sum equal to one day's pay for each and every day during which payment is delayed beyond the respective periods." Act of Dec. 21, 1898, ch. 28, § 4, 30 Stat. 756.

The amending legislation thus effected two changes: first, it removed the discretion theretofore existing by which courts might award less than an amount calculated on the basis of each day during which payment was delayed, and, second, it removed the 10-day ceiling which theretofore limited the number of days upon which an award might be calculated. The accompanying Committee Reports identify the purpose of the legislation as "the amelioration of the condition of the American seamen," and characterize the amended wage penalty in particular as "designed to secure the promptest possible payment of wages." H.R.Rep. No. 1657, 55th Cong., 2d Sess., 2, 3 (1898). See also S.Rep. No. 832, 54th Cong., 1st Sess., 2 (1896). Nothing in the legislative history of the 1898 Act suggests that Congress intended to do anything other than what the Act's enacted language plainly demonstrates: to strengthen the deterrent effect of the statute by removing the courts' latitude in assessing the wage penalty.

The statute was amended for the last time in 1915 to increase further the severity of the penalty by doubling the wages due for each day during which payment of earned wages was delayed. Seamen's Act of 1915, ch. 153, § 3, 38 Stat. 1164. There is no suggestion in the Committee Reports or in the floor debates that, in so doing, Congress intended to reinvest the courts with the discretion it had removed in the Act of 1898. Resort to the legislative history, therefore, merely confirms that Congress intended the statute to mean exactly what its plain language says.

[III] Respondent argues, however, that a literal construction of the statute in this case would produce an absurd and unjust result which Congress could not have intended. The District Court found that the daily wage to be used in computing the penalty was $101.20. If the statute is applied literally, petitioner would receive twice this amount for each day after his discharge until September 17, 1980, when respondent satisfied the District Court's judgment.[9]

---

9. Respondent assumes that the penalty would run until September 17, 1980, since that was the date on which it finally paid petitioner the $412.50. Brief for Respondent 17. Petitioner, on the other hand, apparently assumes that the penalty period expired on May 6, 1980, the date of the District Court's judgment. Brief for Petitioner 19. Under our construction of the statute, the District Court's entry of judgment will not toll the running of the penalty period unless

Petitioner would receive over $300,000 simply because respondent improperly withheld $412.50 in wages. In respondent's view, Congress could not have intended seamen to receive windfalls of this nature without regard to the equities of the case.

It is true that interpretations of a statute which would produce absurd results are to be avoided if alternative interpretations consistent with the legislative purpose are available. See *United States v. American Trucking Assns., Inc.*, 310 U.S., at 542–543; *Haggar Co. v. Helvering*, 308 U.S. 389, 394 (1940). In refusing to nullify statutes, however hard or unexpected the particular effect, this Court has said:

> "Laws enacted with good intention, when put to the test, frequently, and to the surprise of the law maker himself, turn out to be mischievous, absurd or otherwise objectionable. But in such case the remedy lies with the law making authority, and not with the courts." *Crooks v. Harrelson*, 282 U.S. 55, 60 (1930).

It is highly probable that respondent is correct in its contention that a recovery in excess of $300,000 in this case greatly exceeds any actual injury suffered by petitioner as a result of respondent's delay in paying his wages. But this Court has previously recognized that awards made under this statute were not intended to be merely compensatory:

> "We think the use of this language indicates a purpose to protect seamen from delayed payments of wages by the imposition of a liability which is not exclusively compensatory, but designed to prevent, by its coercive effect, arbitrary refusals to pay wages, and to induce prompt payment when payment is possible." *Collie v. Fergusson*, 281 U.S., at 55–56.

It is in the nature of punitive remedies to authorize awards that may be out of proportion to actual injury; such remedies typically are established to deter particular conduct, and the legislature not infrequently finds that harsh consequences must be visited upon those whose conduct it would deter. It is probably true that Congress did not precisely envision the grossness of the difference in this case between the actual wages withheld and the amount of the award required by the statute. But it might equally well be said that Congress did not precisely envision the trebled amount of some damages awards in private antitrust actions, see *Reiter v. Sonotone Corp.*, 442 U.S. 330, 344–345 (1979), or that, because it enacted the Endangered Species Act, "the survival of a relatively small number of three-inch fish * * * would require the permanent halting of a virtually completed dam for which Congress ha[d] expended more than $1 million," *TVA v. Hill*, 437 U.S. 153, 172 (1978). It is enough that Congress intended that the language it enacted would be applied as we have applied it. The remedy for any dissatisfaction with the results in particular cases lies with Congress and not with this Court. Congress may amend the statute; we may not. * * *

---

delays beyond that date are explained by sufficient cause. * * *

JUSTICE STEVENS, with whom JUSTICE BLACKMUN joins, dissenting.

In final analysis, any question of statutory construction requires the judge to decide how the legislature intended its enactment to apply to the case at hand. The language of the statute is usually sufficient to answer that question, but "the reports are full of cases" in which the will of the legislature is not reflected in a literal reading of the words it has chosen.[1] In my opinion this is such a case. * * *

[II.A] In fixing the amount of the award of double wages, the District Court in this case may have reasoned that respondent had sufficient cause for its delay in paying the earned wages after petitioner obtained employment with another shipmaster, but that there was not sufficient cause for its failure to make payment before that time. Although this reasoning conflicts with a literal reading of § 596, it is perfectly consistent with this Court's contemporary construction of the statute in *Pacific Mail S.S. Co. v. Schmidt*, 241 U.S. 245 (1916). The teaching of Justice Holmes' opinion for the Court in that case is that the wrongful character of the initial refusal to pay does not mean that all subsequent delay in payment is also "without sufficient cause" within the meaning of the statute.

The controversy in *Pacific Mail* arose in 1913, when the statute provided that the sum recoverable as wages was measured by one day's pay, rather than double that amount, for each day that the wages were withheld without sufficient cause; the statute was otherwise exactly as it is today. The seaman was discharged on October 1, 1913, but $30.33 was withheld from his wages because he was believed responsible for the loss of some silverware. He filed an action on October 20, 1913, and on November 5, 1913, obtained a judgment for his wages and an additional sum of $151.59, representing the sum recoverable as wages for the period between October 1 and November 5, 1913. The District Court's decree established the proposition that the vessel owner's defenses did not constitute sufficient cause for refusing to pay the wages and requiring the seaman to sue to recover them.

The vessel owner prosecuted an unsuccessful appeal. The Court of Appeals not only affirmed the decision of the District Court, but also added an additional recovery of daily wages for the period between the entry of the original judgment on November 5 and the actual payment of the disputed wages. The Court of Appeals thus read the statute literally and ordered the result that the District Court's finding seemed to dictate. This Court, however, set aside the additional recovery, reaching a conclusion that cannot be reconciled with a wooden, literal reading of the statute. Concurrent findings of the District Court and the Court of Appeals established that the refusal to make the wage payment when due was without sufficient cause. Justice Holmes and his Brethren accepted that finding for purposes of decision, but

---

1. "It is a familiar rule, that a thing may be within the letter of the statute and yet not within the statute, because not within its spirit, nor within the intention of its makers. This has been often asserted, and the reports are full of cases illustrating its application. * * * " *Holy Trinity Church.*

reasoned that there was sufficient cause for the owner's decision to appeal and his refusal to pay while the appeal was pending.

The curious character of this Court's conclusion that reasons insufficient to justify the refusal to pay before the trial court's decision somehow became sufficient to justify a subsequent refusal to pay is not the most significant point to Justice Holmes' opinion. The case is primarily significant because its holding cannot be squared with a literal reading of the statute. Even though the initial refusal is without sufficient cause, statutory wages are not necessarily recoverable for the entire period until payment is made either to the seaman or to a stakeholder. A subsequent event — even though not expressly mentioned in the statute itself — may foreshorten the recovery period.

In *Pacific Mail* the subsequent event was the vessel owner's decision to appeal. The finding that that event provided sufficient cause for the delay after November 5, 1913, was made *sua sponte* by this Court. In this case the subsequent event was the reemployment of petitioner in a comparable job on May 5, 1976. The finding that that event — coupled with the failure to make any additional demand for almost two years thereafter — was sufficient cause for the delay after May 5, 1976, was made by the District Court. It is true that the judge did not expressly frame his decision in these terms, but his actual decision fits precisely the mold established by *Pacific Mail*. Both cases give a flexible reading to the "sufficient cause" language in the statute. They differ with respect to the nature of the subsequent event but not with respect to their departure from the statutory text. [Justice Stevens also cited *Collie v. Fergusson*, 281 U.S. 52 (1930), in which the Court refused to read the statute to penalize an employer for failing to pay wages because of its financial difficulties. The conclusions reached by Justice Stevens' analysis "dispel any notion that the statute means exactly what it says." Indeed, the same flexibility shown by the Supreme Court in *Collie* also characterized the lower federal courts' treatment of the statute from 1896 to 1966.]

[III] The construction permitting the district court to exercise some discretion in tailoring the double-wage award to the particular equities of the case is just as consistent with the legislative history of § 596 as the Court's new literal approach to this statute. In 1872, when Congress authorized the recovery of additional wages by seamen who were not paid within five days of their discharge, it used the word "shall" to make it clear that such a recovery must be awarded, but it allowed the district courts a limited discretion in setting the amount of such recovery.[17] The judge's discretion as to amount was limited in two ways: (1) the statutory wage rate could not be more than double

---

17. The 1872 version of § 596 provided in pertinent part:

"[E]very master or owner who neglects or refuses to make payment [of a seaman's earned wages within five days after the seaman's discharge] without sufficient cause shall pay to the seaman a sum not exceeding the amount of two days' pay for each of the days, not exceeding ten days, during which payment is delayed beyond the [five-day period]; and such sum shall be recoverable as wages in any claim made before the court * * *." Act of June 7, 1872, ch. 322, § 35, 17 Stat. 269.

the amount of the seaman's daily wage; and (2) the period for which the statutory wage could be awarded could not exceed 10 days.

Subsequent amendments to the statute did not remove the requirement that some recovery "shall" be awarded, but did modify both of the limits on the judge's discretion. With respect to the wage rate, Congress first specified that it should equal the daily rate — rather than double the daily rate — and later specified that the rate should be the double rate.[18] With respect to the period for which the statutory wage was payable, the 1898 amendment simply removed the 10-day limit. This amendment is subject to two different interpretations, one that would represent a rather unremarkable change and the other that would be both drastic and dramatic.

The unremarkable change would amount to nothing more than a removal of the narrow 10-day limit on the scope of the judge's discretion. The word "shall" would continue to do nothing more than require some recovery in an amount to be fixed by the judge, but in recognition of the reality that seamen might be stranded for more than 10 days, the recovery period could extend beyond 10 days. This sort of unremarkable change is consistent with the purpose of the statute, as well as with a legislative history that fails to make any comment on its significance. As Justice Rehnquist has perceptively observed in another context, the fact that the dog did not bark can itself be significant.[20]

The Court's construction of the amendment is, however, both drastic and dramatic. Instead of effecting a modest enlargement of the judge's discretion to do justice in these cases, the Court's construction effects a complete prohibition of judicial discretion. Instead of permitting recoveries for a period somewhat longer than 10 days, the amendment is construed as a command that even when the unresolved dispute persists for two or three years without any special hardship to the seaman, an automatic recovery must be ordered for the entire period regardless of the equitable considerations that may arise after the shipmaster's initial mistake has been made. Such a major change in both the potential amount of the statutory recovery and the character of the judge's authority would normally be explained in the committee reports or the debates if it had been intended. * * *

---

18. The 1898 version of § 596 provided in pertinent part:

"Every master or owner who refuses or neglects to make payment [of a seaman's earned wages within four days of the seaman's discharge] without sufficient cause shall pay to the seaman a sum equal to one day's pay for each and every day during which payment is delayed beyond the [four-day period], which sum shall be recoverable as wages in any claim made before the court * * *." Act of Dec. 21, 1898, § 4, 30 Stat. 756.

The 1915 amendment substituted "two days' pay" for "one day's pay." See Act of Mar. 4, 1915, § 3, 38 Stat. 1164–1165.

20. *Harrison v. PPG Industries, Inc.,* 446 U.S. 578, 602 (1980) (dissenting opinion); cf. A. Conan Doyle, Silver Blaze, in The Complete Sherlock Holmes 383 (1938).

NOTES ON *HILL*, *GRIFFIN*, AND THE
REVIVAL OF THE PLAIN MEANING RULE

1. *The Legislative Response in* Griffin *and in* TVA v. Hill. Chief Justice Burger's opinion in *TVA v. Hill* had an immediate legislative response. The Endangered Species Act Amendments of 1978, Pub. L. No. 95–632, § 7, 92 Stat. 3751, 3752–60 (1978), established an administrative mechanism for granting exemptions to the Act, and the Tellico Dam was specifically exempted by Congress in 1979. Pub. L. No. 96–69, tit. IV, 93 Stat. 437, 449 (1979).

Justice Rehnquist's argument for deferring to Congress to change the statute in *Griffin* had a very different legislative response. In 1983, Congress revised much of 46 U.S.C. through Pub. L. No. 98–89. Section 596 was repealed and replaced in part by 46 U.S.C. § 10313(g). The new provision says: "When payment is not made as provided [by the statute] without sufficient cause, the master or owner shall pay to the seaman 2 days' wages for each day payment is delayed." See also *id.* § 10504(c). Obviously, Congress did not change the language important to the Court's result in *Griffin*. Can you speculate why not?

2. *The Revival of the Plain Meaning Rule, 1976–86.* Although most commentators of the Burger Court's statutory opinions assumed that the Court was no more interested in the plain meaning rule than the Warren Court had been, e.g., Judge Patricia Wald, *Some Observations on the Use of Legislative History in the 1981 Supreme Court Term*, 68 Iowa L. Rev. 195, 195, 199 (1983), one commentator argued that *Griffin*'s literalism was more characteristic of the Burger Court's statutory interpretation than the legal process purpose approach was. See Richard Pildes, Note, *Intent, Clear Statements and the Common Law: Statutory Interpretation in the Supreme Court*, 95 Harv. L. Rev. 892 (1982).

On the one hand, *Hill* and similar cases suggest that the Burger Court would sometimes find the bare language of a statute determinative and would apply it stringently, even if it yielded unreasonable results. See, e.g., *Board of Governors of the Federal Reserve System v. Dimension Financial Corp.*, 474 U.S. 361 (1986); *United Air Lines v. McMann*, 434 U.S. 192 (1977). On the other hand, the Burger Court followed a rather "soft" version of the plain meaning rule, for it typically (as it did in *Hill* and *Griffin*) attempted to justify harsh results in light of the legislative history and purposes of the statute. See *CPSC v. GTE Sylvania*, 447 U.S. 102 (1980). Indeed, passages in *Griffin* can be read for the proposition that legislative intent controls interpretation, and that the primacy of statutory text is simply because it provides the best evidence of legislative intent. Moreover, sometimes the Burger Court went beyond even this understanding and interpreted statutes contrary to their apparent plain meaning, but consistent with their purposes and policies. See, e.g., *FDIC v. Philadelphia Gear Corp.*, 476 U.S. 426 (1986); *Midlantic Nat'l Bank v. New Jersey Dept. of Environmental Protection*, 474 U.S. 494 (1986).

3. *Shifting Fortunes of the Plain Meaning Rule (State Level).* In general, the plain meaning rule had greater staying power at the state level. That is, state courts were more likely to resolve issues of statutory interpretation merely

by construing the apparent meaning of the statutory language — without *any* examination of the statute's purpose or legislative history. See, e.g., *Bishop v. Linkway Stores, Inc.*, 655 S.W.2d 426 (Ark. 1983). We don't know why this is so, but the two most frequently mentioned reasons are the dearth of legislative history materials available for state statutes and a more restrained methodology practiced by many state judges.

This changed during the post-World War II era in some states. For example, California courts often eschewed a plain meaning approach. See, e.g., *People v. Hallner*, 277 P.2d 393 (Cal. 1954); *McKeag v. Board of Pension Comm'rs of Los Angeles*, 132 P.2d 198 (Cal. 1942). The California Supreme Court has often used a contextual approach to interpret legislation broadly to promote liberal social policy and fairness. For instance, *County of San Diego v. Muniz*, 583 P.2d 109 (Cal. 1978), involved a statute requiring former or present welfare recipients to reimburse the state if the person "acquires property." The Supreme Court construed "property" *not* to include wages, because deprivation of wages would undermine the overall goal of the welfare law to assist recipients in becoming self-supporting and would be unfair and oppressive.

Other states have looked beyond the plain language of state statutes more and more. Written or published legislative histories of state statutes are now more readily available, and this has given rise to a growing body of scholarship analyzing state court use of state legislative history.[o]

---

o. For scholarship tracing the decline of the plain meaning rule — and concomitant rise of the use of legislative history by state courts — as well as other state trends, see Shirley Abrahamson & Robert Hughes, *Shall We Dance? Steps for Legislators and Judges in Statutory Interpretation*, 75 Minn. L. Rev. 1045 (1991); Melinda Allison & James Hambleton, *Research in Texas Legislative History*, 47 Tex. B.J. 314 (1984); D.A. Divilbiss, *The Need for Comprehensive Legislative History in Missouri*, 36 J. Mo. B. 520 (1980); Kenneth Dortzbach, *Legislative History: The Philosophies of Justices Scalia and Breyer and the Use of Legislative History by the Wisconsin State Courts*, 80 Marq. L. Rev. 161 (1996); Walter Hurst, *The Use of Extrinsic Aids in Determining Legislative Intent in California: The Need for Standardized Criteria*, 12 Pac. L.J. 189 (1981) (student comment); Judith Kaye, *Things Judges Do: State Statutory Interpretation*, 13 Touro L. Rev. 595 (1997); Jack Landau, *Some Observations About Statutory Construction in Oregon*, 32 Willamette L. Rev. 1 (1996); Eric Lane, *How To Read a Statute in New York: A Response to Judge Kaye and Some More*, 28 Hofstra L. Rev. 85 (1999); Jean McKnight, *Compiling an Illinois Legislative History*, 85 Ill. B.J. 335 (1997); Maureen Bonace McMahon, *Legislative History in Ohio: Myths and Realities*, 46 Clev. St. L. Rev. 49 (1998); Michael Mullane, *Statutory Interpretation in Arkansas: How Arkansas Courts Interpret Statutes. A Rational Approach*, 2005 Ark. L. Notes 73; William Nast, *The Use of Legislative History in Construing Pennsylvania Statutes Part II*, Pa. L.J. Rep., May 25, 1981, at 18, col. 1; Donald O'Connor, *The Use of Connecticut Legislative History in Statutory Construction*, 58 Conn. B.J. 422 (1984); William Popkin, *Statutory Interpretation in State Courts — A Study of Indiana Opinions*, 24 Ind. L. Rev. 1155 (1991); Roy Pulvers & Wendy Willis, *Revolution and Evolution: What Is Going on with Statutory Interpretation in the Oregon Courts*, 56 Or. St. B. Bull. 13 (Jan. 1996); Robert Rhodes & Susan Seereiter, *The Search for Intent: Aids to Statutory Construction in Florida — An Update*, 13 Fla. St. U. L. Rev. 485 (1985); Fritz Snyder, *Researching Legislative Intent*, 51 Kan. B.A.J. 93 (1982); Karen Uno & Mark Stapke, *Evaluating Oregon Legislative History: Tailoring an Approach to the Legislative Process*, 61 Or. L. Rev. 421 (1982) (student comment); Laurel Wendt, *Researching Illinois Legislative Histories — A Practical Guide*, 1982 S. Ill. U. L.J. 601 (1982); Matthew Hertko, Note *Statutory*

SECTION 3. CURRENT DEBATES
IN STATUTORY INTERPRETATION

In this final section we survey the debates over appropriate method concerning statutory interpretation that began in the 1980s. The primary debate has involved the challenge of the "new textualism" against more traditional approaches relying on legislative purpose and intent. We introduce the new textualism in Part A. Part B considers the ramifications of economic approaches to statutory interpretation, and Part C does the same for pragmatic and critical approaches.

A. THE NEW TEXTUALISM

In the 1980s, a group of judges and executive officials (many of whom were former academics) developed a more constrained version of the plain meaning rule than that followed in cases like *Griffin* and *TVA v. Hill*. For example, Judge Frank Easterbrook's *Statutes' Domains*, 50 U. Chi. L. Rev. 533 (1983), insisted that courts have no authority even to apply a statute to a problem unless the statute's language clearly targets that problem. Easterbrook's *Legal Interpretation and the Power of the Judiciary*, 7 Harv. J.L. & Pub. Pol'y 87 (1984), argued that courts interpreting statutes have no business figuring out legislative intent, which is an incoherent concept (largely for the reasons suggested in 1930 by Professor Radin, but updated to reflect modern public choice theory (see Chapter 1, § 2)). Judge Antonin Scalia delivered a series of speeches in 1985–86, urging courts to abandon virtually any reference to legislative history, especially the committee reports referred to in *Griffin* and *TVA v. Hill*. The Department of Justice's Office of Legal Policy endorsed and developed these views in *Using and Misusing Legislative History: A Re-Evaluation of the Status of Legislative History in Statutory Interpretation* (Jan. 1989).

What we call "the new textualism"[a] is an approach to statutory interpretation developed by these and related thinkers. Although its proponents draw from legal process theory for their own purposes, their approach to statutory interpretation is very different from that supported by Professors Hart, Sacks, and Fuller. Also, new textualist construction is different from the plain

---

Interpretation in Illinois: Abandoning the Plain Meaning Rule for an Extratextual Approach, 2005 U. Ill. L. Rev. 377; Comment, *Legislative History in Washington*, 7 U. Puget Sound L. Rev. 571 (1984).

a. See William Eskridge, Jr., *The New Textualism*, 37 UCLA L. Rev. 621 (1990); Jonathan Molot, *The Rise and Fall of Textualism*, 106 Colum. L. Rev. 1 (2006); Judge Patricia Wald, *The Sizzling Sleeper: The Use of Legislative History in Construing Statutes in the 1988–89 Term of the United States Supreme Court*, 39 Am. U. L. Rev. 277 (1990); Nicholas Zeppos, *Justice Scalia's Textualism and the "New" New Legal Process*, 12 Cardozo L. Rev. 1597 (1991). For a short overview placing textualism in context with prior theories, see Philip Frickey, *From the Big Sleep to the Big Heat: The Revival of Theory in Statutory Interpretation*, 77 Minn. L. Rev. 241 (1992).

meaning rule of *TVA v. Hill* and *Griffin*,[b] as suggested by the exchanges in the cases that follow.

GREEN v. BOCK LAUNDRY MACHINE COMPANY
Supreme Court of the United States, 1989
490 U.S. 504, 109 S.Ct. 1981, 104 L.Ed.2d 557

JUSTICE STEVENS delivered the opinion of the Court.

[Green, a county prisoner on work-release at a car wash, reached inside a large dryer to stop it and had his arm torn off. At trial in his product liability action against the machine's manufacturer, he testified that he had been inadequately instructed about the machine's operation and dangerousness. Green admitted that he had been convicted of burglary and of conspiracy to commit burglary, both felonies, and those convictions were used by defendant to impeach his credibility. The jury returned a verdict for Bock Laundry. The Court of Appeals affirmed, rejecting Green's argument that the district court erred by denying his pretrial motion to exclude the impeaching evidence.]

[The Court's opinion noted that criticism of automatic admissibility of prior felony convictions to impeach civil witnesses, particularly civil plaintiffs, has been "longstanding and widespread."] Our task in deciding this case, however, is not to fashion the rule we deem desirable but to identify the rule that Congress fashioned. * * *

[I] Federal Rule of Evidence 609(a) provides:

"General Rule. For the purpose of attacking the credibility of a witness, evidence that the witness has been convicted of a crime shall be admitted if elicited from the witness or established by public record during cross-examination but only if the crime (1) was punishable by death or imprisonment in excess of one year under the law under which the witness was convicted, and the court determines that the probative value of admitting this evidence outweighs its prejudicial effect to the defendant, or (2) involved dishonesty or false statement, regardless of the punishment."

By its terms the Rule requires a judge to allow impeachment of any witness with prior convictions for felonies not involving dishonesty "only if" the probativeness of the evidence is greater than its prejudice "to the defendant." It follows that impeaching evidence detrimental to the prosecution in a criminal case "shall be admitted" without any such balancing.

The Rule's plain language commands weighing of prejudice to a defendant in a civil trial as well as in a criminal trial. But that literal reading would compel an odd result in a case like this. Assuming that all impeaching evidence has at least minimal probative value, and given that the evidence of plaintiff Green's convictions had some prejudicial effect on his case — but surely none on defendant Bock's — balancing according to the strict language

---

b. For commentary proposing a "textualist originalism" similar to the *TVA* and *Griffin* approach in place of the new textualism, see Martin Redish & Theodore Chung, *Democratic Theory and the Legislative Process: Mourning the Death of Originalism in Statutory Interpretation*, 68 Tul. L. Rev. 803 (1994).

of Rule 609(a)(1) inevitably leads to the conclusion that the evidence was admissible. In fact, under this construction of the Rule, impeachment detrimental to a civil plaintiff always would have to be admitted.

No matter how plain the text of the Rule may be, we cannot accept an interpretation that would deny a civil plaintiff the same right to impeach an adversary's testimony that it grants to a civil defendant. The Sixth Amendment to the Constitution guarantees a criminal defendant certain fair trial rights not enjoyed by the prosecution, while the Fifth Amendment lets the accused choose not to testify at trial. In contrast, civil litigants in federal court share equally the protections of the Fifth Amendment's Due Process Clause. Given liberal federal discovery rules, the inapplicability of the Fifth Amendment's protection against self-incrimination, and the need to prove their case, civil litigants almost always must testify in depositions or at trial. Denomination as a civil defendant or plaintiff, moreover, is often happenstance based on which party filed first or on the nature of the suit. Evidence that a litigant or his witness is a convicted felon tends to shift a jury's focus from the worthiness of the litigant's position to the moral worth of the litigant himself. It is unfathomable why a civil plaintiff — but not a civil defendant — should be subjected to this risk. Thus we agree with the Seventh Circuit that as far as civil trials are concerned, Rule 609(a)(1) "can't mean what it says." *Campbell v. Greer*, 831 F.2d 700, 703 (1987) [Posner, J.].

Out of this agreement flow divergent courses, each turning on the meaning of "defendant." The word might be interpreted to encompass all witnesses, civil and criminal, parties or not. It might be read to connote any party offering a witness, in which event Rule 609(a)(1)'s balance would apply to civil, as well as criminal, cases. Finally, "defendant" may refer only to the defendant in a criminal case. These choices spawn a corollary question: must a judge allow prior felony impeachment of all civil witnesses as well as all criminal prosecution witnesses, or is Rule 609(a)(1) inapplicable to civil cases, in which event Rule 403 would authorize a judge to balance in such cases?[*] Because the plain text does not resolve these issues, we must examine the history leading to enactment of Rule 609 as law.

[II] At common law a person who had been convicted of a felony was not competent to testify as a witness. "[T]he disqualification arose as part of the punishment for the crime, only later being rationalized on the basis that such a person was unworthy of belief." 3 J. Weinstein & M. Berger, Weinstein's Evidence paragraph 609[02], p. 609–58 (1988)[.] As the law evolved, this absolute bar gradually was replaced by a rule that allowed such witnesses to testify in both civil and criminal cases, but also to be impeached by evidence of a prior felony conviction or a *crimen falsi* misdemeanor conviction. In the

---

[*] *Editors' note*: Rule 403 provides that relevant evidence may be excluded "if its probative value is substantially outweighed by the danger of unfair prejudice, confusion of the issues, or misleading the jury, or by considerations of undue delay, waste of time, or needless presentation of cumulative evidence."

face of scholarly criticism of automatic admission of such impeaching evidence, some courts moved toward a more flexible approach.[11]

[The American Law Institute's Model Code of Evidence and the ABA's proposed Uniform Rules of Evidence recommended that trial judges be given discretion to exclude evidence of prior convictions in appropriate circumstances. In 1969, however, the Advisory Committee's proposed Rules of Evidence included Rule 6–09, which allowed all *crimen falsi* and felony convictions evidence without mention of judicial discretion. But the Committee's second draft Rule 609(a)] authorized the judge to exclude either felony or *crimen falsi* evidence upon determination that its probative value was "substantially outweighed by the danger of unfair prejudice." The Committee specified that its primary concern was prejudice to the witness-accused; the "risk of unfair prejudice to a party in the use of [convictions] to impeach the ordinary witness is so minimal as scarcely to be a subject of comment." Yet the text of the proposal was broad enough to allow a judge to protect not only criminal defendants, but also civil litigants and nonparty witnesses, from unfair prejudice.

[T]he Advisory Committee's revision of Rule 609(a) met resistance. The Department of Justice urged that the Committee supplant its proposal with the strict, amended version of the District Code. Senator McClellan objected to the adoption of the *Luck* doctrine and urged reinstatement of the earlier draft.

The Advisory Committee backed off. As Senator McClellan had requested, it submitted as its third and final draft the same strict version it had proposed in March 1969. * * * This Court forwarded the Advisory Committee's final draft to Congress on November 20, 1972.

The House of Representatives did not accept the Advisory Committee's final proposal. A Subcommittee of the Judiciary Committee recommended an amended version similar to the text of the present Rule 609(a), except that it avoided the current rule's ambiguous reference to prejudice to "the defendant." Rather, in prescribing weighing of admissibility of prior felony convictions, it used the same open-ended reference to "unfair prejudice" found in the Advisory Committee's second draft.

The House Judiciary Committee departed even further from the Advisory Committee's final recommendation, preparing a draft that did not allow impeachment by evidence of prior conviction unless the crime involved dishonesty or false statement. Motivating the change were concerns about the deterrent effect upon an accused who might wish to testify and the danger of unfair prejudice, "even upon a witness who was not the accused," from allowing impeachment by prior felony convictions regardless of their relation to the witness' veracity. H.R.Rep. No. 93–650, p. 11 (1973). Although the

---

11. In a seminal article, Dean Ladd questioned the traditional rule's "premise, that the doing of an act designated by organized society as a crime is itself an indication of testimonial unreliability," and advocated barring impeachment by evidence of convictions bearing no relation to a witness' truthfulness. Ladd, Credibility Tests — Current Trends, 89 U. Pa. L. Rev. 166, 176, 190 (1940). * * *

Committee Report focused on criminal defendants and did not mention civil litigants, its express concerns encompassed all nonaccused witnesses.

Representatives who advocated the automatic admissibility approach of the Advisory Committee's draft and those who favored the intermediate approach proposed by the Subcommittee both opposed the Committee's bill on the House floor. Four Members pointed out that the Rule applied in civil as well as criminal cases. The House voted to adopt the Rule as proposed by its Judiciary Committee.

The Senate Judiciary Committee proposed an intermediate path. For criminal defendants, it would have allowed impeachment only by *crimen falsi* evidence; for other witnesses, it also would have permitted prior felony evidence only if the trial judge found that probative value outweighed "prejudicial effect against the party offering that witness." This language thus required the exercise of discretion before prior felony convictions could be admitted in civil litigation. But the full Senate, prodded by Senator McClellan, reverted to the version that the Advisory Committee had submitted. See 120 Cong. Rec. 37076, 37083 (1974).

Conflict between the House bill, allowing impeachment only by *crimen falsi* evidence, and the Senate bill, embodying the Advisory Committee's automatic admissibility approach, was resolved by a Conference Committee. The conferees' compromise — enacted as Federal Rule of Evidence 609(a)(1) — authorizes impeachment by felony convictions, "but only if" the court determines that probative value outweighs "prejudicial effect to the defendant." The Conference Committee's Report makes it perfectly clear that the balance set forth in this draft, unlike the second Advisory Committee and the Senate Judiciary Committee versions, does not protect all nonparty witnesses:

> "The danger of prejudice to a witness other than the defendant (such as injury to the witness' reputation in his community) was considered and rejected by the Conference as an element to be weighed in determining admissibility. It was the judgment of the Conference that the danger of prejudice to a nondefendant witness is outweighed by the need for the trier of fact to have as much relevant evidence on the issue of credibility as possible." H.R.Conf.Rep. No. 93–1597, pp. 9–10 (1974).

Equally clear is the conferees' intention that the rule shield the accused, but not the prosecution, in a criminal case. Impeachment by convictions, the Committee Report stated, "should only be excluded where it presents a danger of improperly influencing the outcome of the trial by persuading the trier of fact to convict the defendant on the basis of his prior criminal record."

But this emphasis on the criminal context, in the Report's use of terms such as "defendant" and "to convict" and in individual conferees' explanations of the compromise,[26] raises some doubt over the Rule's pertinence to civil

---

26. Representative Dennis, who had stressed in earlier debates that the Rule would apply to both civil and criminal cases, see 120 Cong. Rec. 2377 (1974), explained the benefits of the Rule for criminal defendants and made no reference to benefits for civil litigants when he said: "[Y]ou can ask about all . . . felonies on cross examination, only if you can convince the

litigants.   The discussions suggest that only two kinds of witnesses risk prejudice — the defendant who elects to testify in a criminal case and witnesses other than the defendant in the same kind of case.   Nowhere is it acknowledged that undue prejudice to a civil litigant also may improperly influence a trial's outcome.   Although this omission lends support to [an] opinion that "legislative oversight" caused exclusion of civil parties from Rule 609(a)(1)'s balance, a number of considerations persuade us that the Rule was meant to authorize a judge to weigh prejudice against no one other than a criminal defendant.

A party contending that legislative action changed settled law has the burden of showing that the legislature intended such a change.   Cf. *Midlantic National Bank v. New Jersey Department of Environmental Protection*, 474 U.S. 494, 502 (1986).   The weight of authority before Rule 609's adoption accorded with the Advisory Committee's final draft, admitting all felonies without exercise of judicial discretion in either civil or criminal cases. Departures from this general rule had occurred overtly by judicial interpretation, as in *Luck*, or in evidence codes, such as the Model Code and the Uniform Rules.   Rule 609 itself explicitly adds safeguards circumscribing the common-law rule.   The unsubstantiated assumption that legislative oversight produced Rule 609(a)(1)'s ambiguity respecting civil trials hardly demonstrates that Congress intended silently to overhaul the law of impeachment in the civil context.

To the extent various drafts of Rule 609 distinguished civil and criminal cases, moreover, they did so only to mitigate prejudice to criminal defendants. Any prejudice that convictions impeachment might cause witnesses other than the accused was deemed "so minimal as scarcely to be a subject of comment." Advisory Committee's Note, 51 F.R.D., at 392.   Far from voicing concern lest such impeachment unjustly diminish a civil witness in the eyes of the jury, Representative Hogan declared that this evidence ought to be used to measure a witness' moral value.[27]   Furthermore, Representative Dennis — who in

---

court, and the burden is on the *government*, which is an important change in the law, that the probative value of the question is greater than the damage to the *defendant*; and that is damage or prejudice *to the defendant alone*." *Id.*, at 40894 (emphases supplied).

In the same debate Representative Hogan manifested awareness of the Rule's broad application. While supporting the compromise, he reiterated his preference for a rule

"that, for the purpose of attacking the credibility of a witness, *even if the witness happens to be the defendant in a criminal case*, evidence that he has been convicted of a crime is admissible and may be used to challenge that witness' credibility if the crime is a felony or is a misdemeanor involving dishonesty of [sic] false statement." *Id.*, at 40895 (emphasis added).

27.   "Suppose some governmental body instituted a civil action for damages, and the defendant called a witness who had been previously convicted of malicious destruction of public property.   Under the committee's formulation, the convictions could not be used to impeach the witness' credibility since the crimes did not involve dishonesty or false statement.   Yet, in the hypothetical case, as in any case in which the government was a party, justice would seem to me to require that the jury know that the witness had been carrying on some private war against society.   Should a witness with an anti-social background be allowed to stand on the same basis of believability before juries as law-abiding citizens with unblemished records?   I think not . . . .

advocating a Rule limiting impeachment to *crimen falsi* convictions had recognized the impeachment Rule's applicability to civil trials — not only debated the issue on the House floor, but also took part in the conference out of which Rule 609 emerged. See 120 Cong.Rec. 2377–2380, 39942, 40894–40895 (1974). These factors indicate that Rule 609(a)(1)'s textual limitation of the prejudice balance to criminal defendants resulted from deliberation, not oversight.

Had the conferees desired to protect other parties or witnesses, they could have done so easily. Presumably they had access to all of Rule 609's precursors, particularly the drafts prepared by the House Subcommittee and the Senate Judiciary Committee, both of which protected the civil litigant as well as the criminal defendant. Alternatively, the conferees could have amended their own draft to include other parties. They did not for the simple reason that they intended that only the accused in a criminal case should be protected from unfair prejudice by the balance set out in Rule 609(a)(1).

[Finally, the Court concluded that Rule 609, as the specific provision governing the facts of the case, controlled over the general balancing provisions of Rule 403. The Court affirmed the judgment for defendant.]

JUSTICE SCALIA, concurring in the judgment.

We are confronted here with a statute which, if interpreted literally, produces an absurd, and perhaps unconstitutional, result. Our task is to give some alternate meaning to the word "defendant" in Federal Rule of Evidence 609(a)(1) that avoids this consequence; and then to determine whether Rule 609(a)(1) excludes the operation of Federal Rule of Evidence 403.

I think it entirely appropriate to consult all public materials, including the background of Rule 609(a)(1) and the legislative history of its adoption, to verify that what seems to us an unthinkable disposition (civil defendants but not civil plaintiffs receive the benefit of weighing prejudice) was indeed unthought of, and thus to justify a departure from the ordinary meaning of the word "defendant" in the Rule. For that purpose, however, it would suffice to observe that counsel have not provided, nor have we discovered, a shred of evidence that anyone has ever proposed or assumed such a bizarre disposition. The Court's opinion, however, goes well beyond this. Approximately four-fifths of its substantive analysis is devoted to examining the evolution of Federal Rule of Evidence 609 * * * all with the evident purpose, not merely of confirming that the word "defendant" cannot have been meant literally, but of determining what, precisely, the Rule does mean.

I find no reason to believe that any more than a handful of the Members of Congress who enacted Rule 609 were aware of its interesting evolution from the 1942 Model Code; or that any more than a handful of them (if any) voted, with respect to their understanding of the word "defendant" and the relation-

Personally I am more concerned about the moral worth of individuals capable of engaging in such outrageous acts as adversely reflecting on a witness' character than I am of thieves . . . ." *Id.*, at 2376.

ship between Rule 609 and Rule 403, on the basis of the referenced statements in the Subcommittee, Committee, or Conference Committee Reports, or floor debates — statements so marginally relevant, to such minute details, in such relatively inconsequential legislation. The meaning of terms on the statute books ought to be determined, not on the basis of which meaning can be shown to have been understood by a larger handful of the Members of Congress; but rather on the basis of which meaning is (1) most in accord with context and ordinary usage, and thus most likely to have been understood by the *whole* Congress which voted on the words of the statute (not to mention the citizens subject to it), and (2) most compatible with the surrounding body of law into which the provision must be integrated — a compatibility which, by a benign fiction, we assume Congress always has in mind. I would not permit any of the historical and legislative material discussed by the Court, or all of it combined, to lead me to a result different from the one that these factors suggest.

I would analyze this case, in brief, as follows:

(1) The word "defendant" in Rule 609(a)(1) cannot rationally (or perhaps even constitutionally) mean to provide the benefit of prejudice-weighing to civil defendants and not civil plaintiffs. Since petitioner has not produced, and we have not ourselves discovered, even a snippet of support for this absurd result, we may confidently assume that the word was not used (as it normally would be) to refer to all defendants and only all defendants.

(2) The available alternatives are to interpret "defendant" to mean (a) "civil plaintiff, civil defendant, prosecutor, and criminal defendant," (b) "civil plaintiff and defendant and criminal defendant," or (c) "criminal defendant." Quite obviously, the last does least violence to the text. It adds a qualification that the word "defendant" does not contain but, unlike the others, does not give the word a meaning ("plaintiff" or "prosecutor") it simply will not bear. The qualification it adds, moreover, is one that could understandably have been omitted by inadvertence — and sometimes is omitted in normal conversation ("I believe strongly in defendants' rights"). Finally, this last interpretation is consistent with the policy of the law in general and the Rules of Evidence in particular of providing special protection to defendants in criminal cases.[*]

(3) As well described by the Court, the "structure of the Rules" makes it clear that Rule 403 is not to be applied in addition to Rule 609(a)(1).

I am frankly not sure that, despite its lengthy discussion of ideological evolution and legislative history, the Court's reasons for both aspects of its decision are much different from mine. I respectfully decline to join that

---

[*] Acknowledging the statutory ambiguity, the dissent would read "defendant" to mean "any party" because, it says, this interpretation "extend[s] the protection of judicial supervision to a larger class of litigants" than the interpretation the majority and I favor, which "takes protection *away* from litigants." But neither side in this dispute can lay claim to generosity without begging the policy question whether judicial supervision is better than the automatic power to impeach. We could as well say — and with much more support in both prior law and this Court's own recommendation — that our reading "extend[s] the protection of [the right to impeach with prior felony convictions] to a larger class of litigants" than the dissent's interpretation, which "takes protection *away* from litigants."

discussion, however, because it is natural for the bar to believe that the juridical importance of such material matches its prominence in our opinions — thus producing a legal culture in which, when counsel arguing before us assert that "Congress has said" something, they now frequently mean, by "Congress," a committee report; and in which it was not beyond the pale for a recent brief to say the following: "Unfortunately, the legislative debates are not helpful. Thus, we turn to the other guidepost in this difficult area, statutory language." * * *

JUSTICE BLACKMUN, with whom JUSTICE BRENNAN and JUSTICE MARSHALL join, dissenting.

* * * The majority concludes that Rule 609(a)(1) cannot mean what it says on its face. I fully agree.

I fail to see, however, why we are required to solve this riddle of statutory interpretation by reading the inadvertent word "defendant" to mean "criminal defendant." I am persuaded that a better interpretation of the Rule would allow the trial court to consider the risk of prejudice faced by any party, not just a criminal defendant. Applying the balancing provisions of Rule 609(a)(1) to all parties would have prevented the admission of unnecessary and inflammatory evidence in this case and will prevent other similar unjust results until Rule 609(a) is repaired, as it must be. The result the Court reaches today, in contrast, endorses "the irrationality and unfairness" of denying the trial court the ability to weigh the risk of prejudice to any party before admitting evidence of a prior felony for purposes of impeachment.

The majority's lengthy recounting of the legislative history of Rule 609 demonstrates why almost all that history is entitled to very little weight. Because the proposed rule changed so often — and finally was enacted as a compromise between the House and the Senate — much of the commentary cited by the majority concerns versions different from the Rule Congress finally enacted.

The only item of legislative history that focuses on the Rule as enacted is the Report of the Conference Committee. Admittedly, language in the Report supports the majority's position: the Report mirrors the Rule in emphasizing the prejudicial effect on the defendant, and also uses the word "convict" to describe the potential outcome. But the Report's draftsmanship is no better than the Rule's, and the Report's plain language is no more reliable an indicator of Congress' intent than is the plain language of the Rule itself.

Because the slipshod drafting of Rule 609(a)(1) demonstrates that clarity of language was not the Conference's forte, I prefer to rely on the underlying reasoning of the Report, rather than on its unfortunate choice of words, in ascertaining the Rule's proper scope. The Report's treatment of the Rule's discretionary standard consists of a single paragraph. After noting that the Conference was concerned with prejudice to a defendant, the Report states:

"The danger of prejudice to a witness other than the defendant (such as injury to the witness' reputation in the community) was considered and rejected by the Conference as an element to be weighed in determining admissibility. It was the judgment of the

Conference that the danger of prejudice to a nondefendant witness is outweighed by the need for the trier of fact to have as much relevant evidence on the issue of credibility as possible. Such evidence should only be excluded where it presents a danger of improperly influencing the outcome of the trial by persuading the trier of fact to convict the defendant on the basis of his prior criminal record."

The Report indicates that the Conference determined that any felony conviction has sufficient relevance to a witness' credibility to be admitted, even if the felony had nothing directly to do with truthfulness or honesty. In dealing with the question of undue prejudice, however, the Conference drew a line: it distinguished between two types of prejudice, only one of which it permitted the trial court to consider.

As the Conference observed, admitting a prior conviction will always "prejudice" a witness, who, of course, would prefer that the conviction not be revealed to the public. The Report makes clear, however, that this kind of prejudice to the witness' life outside the courtroom is not to be considered in the judicial balancing required by Rule 609(a)(1). Rather, the kind of prejudice the court is instructed to be concerned with is prejudice which "presents a danger of improperly influencing the outcome of the trial." Congress' solution to that kind of prejudice was to require judicial supervision: the conviction may be admitted only if "the court determines that the probative value of admitting this evidence outweighs its prejudicial effect to the defendant." Rule 609(a)(1).

Although the Conference expressed its concern in terms of the effect on a criminal defendant, the potential for prejudice to the outcome at trial exists in any type of litigation, whether criminal or civil, and threatens all parties to the litigation. The Report and the Rule are best read as expressing Congress' preference for judicial balancing whenever there is a chance that justice shall be denied a party because of the unduly prejudicial nature of a witness' past conviction for a crime that has no direct bearing on the witness' truthfulness. In short, the reasoning of the Report suggests that by "prejudice to the defendant," Congress meant "prejudice to a party," as opposed to the prejudicial effect of the revelation of a prior conviction to the witness' own reputation.

It may be correct, as Justice Scalia notes in his opinion concurring in the judgment, that interpreting "prejudicial effect to the defendant" to include only "prejudicial effect to [a] *criminal* defendant," and not prejudicial effect to other categories of litigants as well, does the "least violence to the text," if what we mean by "violence" is the interpolation of excess words or the deletion of existing words. But the reading endorsed by Justice Scalia and the majority does violence to the logic of the only rationale Members of Congress offered for the Rule they adopted.

Certainly the possibility that admission of a witness' past conviction will improperly determine the outcome at trial is troubling when the witness' testimony is in support of a criminal defendant. The potential, however, is no less real for other litigants. Unlike Justice Scalia, I do not approach the Rules of Evidence, which by their terms govern both civil and criminal proceedings, with the presumption that their general provisions should be read to "provid[e] special protection to defendants in criminal cases." Rather, the Rules themselves specify that they "shall be construed to secure fairness in administration . . . to the end that the truth may be ascertained and proceedings justly determined" in *all* cases. Rule 102. The majority's result does not achieve that end. * * *

As I see it, therefore, our choice is between two interpretations of Rule 609(a)(1), neither of which is completely consistent with the Rule's plain language. The majority's interpretation takes protection *away* from litigants — *i.e.*, civil defendants — who would have every reason to believe themselves entitled to the judicial balancing offered by the Rule. The alternative interpretation — which I favor — also departs somewhat from plain language, but does so by *extending* the protection of judicial supervision to a larger class of litigants — *i.e.*, to all parties. Neither result is compelled by the statutory language or the legislative history, but for me the choice between them is an easy one. I find it proper, as a general matter and under the dictates of Rule 102, to construe the Rule so as to avoid "unnecessary hardship," see *Burnet v. Guggenheim*, 288 U.S. 280, 285 (1933), and to produce a sensible result. * * *

NOTES ON *BOCK LAUNDRY* AND DIFFERENT FOUNDATIONALIST THEORIES IN ACTION

1. *Does Textualism Work in* Bock Laundry? Note that, like the other eight Justices, textualist Justice Scalia *also* rewrote the statute, which has a perfectly "plain meaning" in this case: The felony convictions of civil plaintiffs can always be introduced to impeach them, but those of civil defendants are subject to a balancing test. Of course, such a plain meaning surely is unconstitutional, but in that event why doesn't the textualist simply invalidate Rule 609(a)(1) (at least as far as civil cases) and apply the Rule 403 default rule, which would probably exclude Green's conviction from evidence?

Justice Scalia disregarded plain meaning in this case because he believed that Rule 609(a)(1) was absurd as written, that the absurdity was unintended, and that an unintended absurdity justifies departure from plain meaning. This is itself significant. By creating an exception to textualism when a statute requires unintended "absurd" consequences, is Justice Scalia not conceding that following statutory text is not all that is going on in statutory interpretation, and that current interpretive values have a role to play in statutory interpretation? While Justice Scalia surely believes that plain meaning can only be sacrificed in the rare absurd-result case, why not sacrifice plain meaning when it directs an "unreasonable" result that was probably unintended by Congress?

Although Justice Scalia agreed to rewrite the statute in *Bock Laundry*, his opinion dismissed the dissenting opinion's rewrite in favor of the majority's rewrite:

> The available alternatives [for rewriting the rule] are to interpret "defendant" to mean (a) "civil plaintiff, civil defendant, prosecutor and criminal defendant," (b) "civil

plaintiff and defendant and criminal defendant," or (c) "criminal defendant." Quite obviously, the last does least violence to the text.

Is that so obvious? In essence, Justice Blackmun's dissent rewrote Rule 609(a)(1) to permit impeaching convictions only when "the court determines that the probative value of admitting this evidence outweighs its prejudicial effect to *a party*" (new language italicized). Does this do more "violence" to the text than Justice Scalia's rewrite to permit impeaching convictions only when "the court determines that the probative value of admitting this evidence outweighs its prejudicial effect to the *criminal* defendant"?

Indeed, from a purely textualist perspective, Justice Blackmun's rewrite may be a better version, because Justice Scalia's rewrite leaves the statute as chaotic as it was originally. Rewritten Rule 609(a)(1) still applies in a civil case like *Bock Laundry*, and Justice Scalia's version tells the judge to follow a strange rule: Allow the witness to be impeached by his prior felony convictions, but only if its probative value outweighs its prejudice to the "criminal defendant." What criminal defendant? This is a civil case, after all. While the original Rule 609(a)(1) favored civil defendants over civil plaintiffs without apparent justification, it at least set forth a rule that could be applied by the district judge in a civil case. Under the pretense of doing "least violence" to the text, does Justice Scalia's rewrite deprive the judge of an intelligible rule?

In our view, the shortest way to rewrite Rule 609(a)(1) to reflect the understanding of the majority and of Justice Scalia *and* to have it make sense as a rule applicable to civil as well as criminal cases is something like the following: Allow a witness to be impeached by his prior criminal conviction "if the crime (1) was punishable by death or imprisonment in excess of one year under the law under which the witness was convicted, and, *in a criminal case*, the court determines that the probative value of admitting this evidence outweighs its prejudicial effect to the defendant" (new language italicized). Would this flunk Justice Scalia's test of doing "least violence" to the text?

2. *Does Imaginative Reconstruction Work Any Better?* Imaginative reconstruction also may be problematic in *Bock Laundry*, for the reasons suggested by Professor Radin and revived by the new textualists. Who can really tell what the median Member of Congress thought about this issue?

Recall that the House voted for a version of Rule 609(a) that would have given Green the benefit of a balancing test, and a similar version was voted out of the Senate Judiciary Committee. On the floor of the Senate, Senator McClellan proposed an amendment making all felony convictions admissible; his amendment failed by a 35–35 vote. 120 Cong. Rec. 37080 (1974). But on immediate motion for reconsideration, his amendment was adopted, 38–34, because a couple of new Senators showed up and a couple changed their votes. *Id.* at 37083. The median Senator was apparently (and ironically) Senator Stevens (R-Alaska): He voted against the McClellan amendment, for reconsideration, for the McClellan amendment, and then for the final conference bill, which adopted the ambiguous compromise. Why did he vote this way? What was his "intent"?

In 2006, we posed these very questions to Senator Stevens, who is still representing Alaska in the Senate (he is now the senior Senate Republican). Senator Stevens told us that the voting pattern for him and several other senators was "confused" as a matter of logic, but not as a matter of political collegiality. "As a former U.S. Attorney I favored the House and Senate Judiciary Committees' version — but McClellan was a friend. He had traveled to Alaska with me — and Jackson and Stennis were sort of mentors. This was my sixth year in the Senate — I voted with McClellan to take his 'compromise' to conference."[c]

In any event, the Senate did vote for a much more limited version of Rule 609(a) than the House, and so the key question for imaginative reconstruction is: What was the conference committee "deal" that was struck on Rule 609(a)? And of course that's completely unclear as well, since the conference report doesn't even mention civil cases, and Senator Stevens does not recall any consensus on the matter when he and other senators passed the conference bill by voice vote. Justice Stevens finds great significance in the conference action, but only because of a judicially created canon of statutory construction: If the dog (here, Congress) doesn't bark, assume that "nothing happened" — no radical change was made in the fabric of the law (recall the dog-doesn't-bark canon). Thus, Justice Stevens' imaginative reconstruction boils down to the application of a judicial presumption! And one that seems flimsy at best, because the common law rule was in the process of collapsing — and did collapse within the federal system the year after *Bock Laundry*. See the next note.

3. *Why Did the Court Go Through This Exercise?* As Justice Stevens' opinion noted, there was a proposed change to Rule 609(a) pending when the Supreme Court interpreted the Rule in *Bock Laundry*.[d] In January 1990 (soon after the decision in *Bock Laundry*), the Supreme Court notified Congress that it had adopted an amendment to Federal Rule of Evidence 609 to take effect on December 1, 1990, unless Congress by statute disapproved it. As explained in the report of the advisory committee, the amendment "does not disturb the special balancing test for the criminal defendant who chooses to testify, but applies the general balancing test of Rule 403 to protect all other litigants against unfair impeachment of witnesses." (Rule 403 is quoted in the editors' footnote in the majority opinion in *Bock Laundry*.) The report noted that the advisory committee had approved the proposed amendment prior to *Bock Laundry*, but had held it pending the outcome of the case. Congress never disapproved the revised Rule 609(a), and it went into effect on December 1, 1990.

---

c. Email from Lily Stevens (Senator Stevens's daughter) to Philip Frickey, April 5, 2006 (incorporating an email that Senator Stevens authorized his daughter to forward to Professor Frickey).

d. Pursuant to the Federal Rules Enabling Act, amendments to the Federal Rules of Evidence are proposed to the Supreme Court by an advisory committee established by the Judicial Conference of the United States. The Court then notifies Congress of the amendment, including any modifications made by the Court. After a waiting period, the amendment takes effect unless, in the interim, Congress has nullified it by statute.

After this amendment, Rule 609 provided:

a. General rule .— For purposes of attacking the credibility of a witness,

> (1) evidence that a witness other than an accused has been convicted of a crime shall be admitted, subject to Rule 403, if the crime was punishable by death or imprisonment in excess of one year under the law under which the witness was convicted, and evidence that an accused has been convicted of such a crime shall be admitted if the court determines that the probative value of admitting this evidence outweighs its prejudicial effect to the accused; and

> (2) evidence that any witness has been convicted of a crime shall be admitted if it involved dishonesty or false statement, regardless of the punishment.

ANTONIN SCALIA, *A MATTER OF INTERPRETATION* (1997).[*] In this published version of his Tanner Lectures delivered at Princeton University, Justice Antonin Scalia presents his *textualist* philosophy of legal interpretation. He contends that law students (brainwashed by the first-year indoctrination in common-law methodology) and law professors (who do the brainwashing) tend to approach statutory interpretation as an exercise in applying legal authorities to new factual settings in a manner which yields both a fair result in the case and works toward a just and efficient general rule. Such an equitable common-law approach is not appropriate for construing statutes in a democracy, Justice Scalia argues, because it is fundamentally anti-democratic (pp. 9–14). A theme of the Tanner Lectures is that the common law has its place, but in a democracy it is more important that judges be constrained by, and held to, the legislatively enacted statutory law, than that they do "justice" in the individual case.

Should the lodestar for statutory interpretation, then, be legislative *intent*? Most assuredly not! "It is the *law* that governs, not the intent of the lawgiver. That seems to me the essence of the famous American ideal set forth in the Massachusetts constitution: A government of laws, not of men. Men may intend what they will; but it is only the laws that they enact which bind us" (p. 17). Indeed, Justice Scalia argues that judges following a legislative-intent approach usually end up finding their own preferences in the statute, because "your best shot at figuring out what the legislature meant is to ask yourself what a wise and intelligent person *should* have meant; and that will surely bring you to the conclusion that the law means what you think it *ought* to mean — which is precisely how judges decide things under the common law" (p. 18). Note the implicit criticism of Hart and Sacks' theory, *supra*.

Justice Scalia then applies this critique to *Holy Trinity Church*. The Court interpreted the alien contract law contrary to its plain meaning because the Justices believed it inconsistent with legislative intent and purpose. Justice Scalia finds such an approach no more than invalid judicial lawmaking, although he would allow courts to correct scrivener's errors. "Well of course I think that the act was within the letter of the statute, and was therefore within

---

the statute: end of case" (p. 20). "The text is the law, and it is the text which must be observed" (p. 22), says the author, citing Justice Holmes (quoted *supra*, pp. 709-10).

The apparent plain meaning of a statutory text must be the alpha and the omega in a judge's interpretation of a statute. The apparent plain meaning is that which an ordinary speaker of the English language — twin sibling to the common law's reasonable person — would draw from the statutory text. That is what textualism *is*. What it is *not*, according to Justice Scalia, is either "strict constructionism" (p. 23), which gives statutory words their stingiest ambit, nor "nihilism" (p. 24), which reads words to mean anything and everything. "A text should not be construed strictly, and it should not be construed leniently; it should be construed reasonably, to contain all that it fairly means" (p. 23).

Nor is textualism canonical, maintains Justice Scalia. The Tanner Lectures are skeptical of "presumptions and rules of construction that load the dice for or against a particular result" (p. 27), because they "increase the unpredictability, if not the arbitrariness of judicial decisions" (p. 28). "To the honest textualist, all of these preferential rules and presumptions are a lot of trouble," says Scalia (p. 28). On the other hand, canons such as the rule of lenity (ambiguous penal statutes should be construed in favor of the defendant) might have been "validated by sheer antiquity," and other canons (such as the requirement of a clear statement for congressional abrogation of state immunity) might be defensible as rule-of-thumb presumptions about normal meaning (p. 29).[e]

Doctrinally, the most distinctive feature of Justice Scalia's legisprudence is an insistence that judges should almost never consult, and never rely on, the legislative history of a statute (pp. 29–37). Consistent with his concurring opinion in *Bock Laundry*, the Tanner Lectures identify several kinds of reasons for rejecting the relevance of legislative history. First, to the extent that legislative history is mined to determine legislative "intent," it must be rejected as a matter of constitutional principle. Legislative intent is not the proper goal for the statutory interpreter. This is a corollary of the rule of law: law must be objective and impersonal (the "government of laws"), not subjective and intentional ("and not of men").[f] This reason is related to Professor Radin's critique of legislative intent — and Justice Scalia's second objection to legislative history is very much an elaboration of Professor Radin's criticism two generations earlier.

Even if intent were a proper criterion and it were constitutional to consider the views of legislative subgroups, the debating history preceding statutory

---

e. For examples of Scalia's use of canons in judicial opinions, see his separate opinions in *Chisom* and *Casey* in this chapter, and in *Sweet Home* and *BFP* in chapter 8.

f. "Imagine how we would react to a bill that said, 'From today forward, the result in any opinion poll among members of Congress shall have the effect of law.' We would think the law a joke at best, unconstitutional at worst. This silly 'law' comes uncomfortably close, however, to the method by which courts deduce the content of legislation when they look to the subjective intent." Frank Easterbrook, *The Role of Original Intent in Statutory Construction*, 11 Harv. J.L. & Pub. Pol'y 59, 65 (1988).

enactment would not be reliable evidence of such intent. For most issues, there was no collective understanding; if there were such an understanding, public statements would often point in different directions, as some representatives would find it in their interest to plant misleading evidence. Indeed, the more courts have relied on legislative history, the less reliable it has become! "In earlier days, it was at least genuine and not contrived — a real part of the legislation's *history*, in the sense that it was part of the *development* of the bill, part of the attempt to inform and persuade those who voted. Nowadays, however, when it is universally known and expected that judges will resort to floor debates and (especially) committee reports as authoritative expressions of 'legislative intent,' affecting the courts rather than informing the Congress has become the primary purpose of the exercise" (p. 34).[g]

Justice Scalia also claims that legislators themselves do not read the committee reports (pp. 32–33). Critics respond that legislators do not read the statutes they enact, either. Justice Scalia replies that the claim to authority of the two sources is different: a committee report's (supposed) authority is bottomed on its being evidence of intent about the law, and so knowledge about its contents would seem critical; the statutory text, on the other hand, is law itself, whether or not anyone read or understood it before enactment (pp. 34–35).

In response to this reply, critics say that committee reports are authoritative evidence because of conventions by which Congress has delegated most of the detail work to committees, with the implication being that the committee product is presumptively the work of Congress. Unconstitutional! says Justice Scalia.[h] "The legislative power is the power to make laws, not the power to make legislators. It is nondelegable. Congress can no more authorize one committee to 'fill in the details' of a particular law in a binding fashion than it can authorize a committee to enact minor laws. * * * That is the very essence of the separation of powers [and Article I, Section 7, requiring bicameral approval and presentment to the President]. The only conceivable basis for considering committee reports authoritative, therefore, is that they are a genuine indication of the will of the entire house — which, as I have been at pains to explain, they assuredly are not" (p. 35).

Earlier thinkers — like Dean Pound and Professor Landis — had called for courts to consider legislative history, so that judges might be constrained by the legislators' preferences. This was a laudable impulse, Justice Scalia concedes, but it has not worked. Legislative history has augmented rather than amelio-

---

g. For a similar point, see William Eskridge, Jr. & John Ferejohn, *Politics, Interpretation, and the Rule of Law*, in *The Rule of Law* 265, 275 (NOMOS XXXVI, Ian Shapiro ed., 1994).

h. The following argument is supported and elaborated in detail by John Manning, *Textualism as a Nondelegation Doctrine*, 97 Colum. L. Rev. 673 (1997). But see Peter Strauss, *The Courts and the Congress: Should Judges Disdain Political History?*, 98 Colum. L. Rev. 242 (1998) (disagreeing with Manning and arguing in favor of the use of legislative history, particularly to discern statutory purpose). More broadly, Professor Strauss has contended that our common-law system legitimates judicial interpretive methods that range beyond textualism. See Peter Strauss, *The Common Law and Statutes*, 70 U. Colo. L. Rev. 225 (1999).

rated the discretion of the willful judge, and this is Justice Scalia's third major quarrel with the use of legislative history. "In any major piece of legislation, the legislative history is extensive, and there is something for everybody. As Judge Harold Leventhal used to say, the trick is to look over the heads of the crowd and pick out your friends" (p. 36).

Problem Applying the New Textualism

Problem 7–5. Justice Scalia would surely have voted with the majority in *TVA* and *Griffin*. How would he have written the opinions differently? Recall the different approaches to Title VII in the dissenting opinions in *Weber* by Justice Rehnquist and *Johnson* by Justice Scalia (Chapter 1, § 3). How would Justice Scalia have voted in *Shine* and *Li, supra*?

CHISOM v. ROEMER
Supreme Court of the United States, 1991
501 U.S. 380, 111 S.Ct. 2354, 115 L.Ed.2d 348

JUSTICE STEVENS delivered the opinion of the Court.

[Five of the seven members of the Louisiana Supreme Court are elected from single-member districts, each of which consists of a number of parishes (counties). The other two are elected from one multimember district. In three of the four parishes in this multimember district, more than three-fourths of the registered voters are white. In the fourth parish in the multimember district, Orleans Parish, which contains about half of the population of the multimember district and has about half the registered voters in the district, more than one-half of the registered voters are African American. A class of African American registered voters in Orleans Parish brought this action, contending that the use of the multimember district diluted the voting strength of the minority community in violation of section 2 of the Voting Rights Act, as amended in 1982. (For discussion of what minority vote dilution is and how section 5 and section 2 of the Voting Rights Act forbid minority vote dilution in some circumstances, see Chapter 2, § 1.) Under the controlling precedent in the Fifth Circuit, *League of United Latin American Citizens Council No. 4434 v. Clements*, 914 F.2d 620 (5th Cir. 1990) (en banc) ("*LULAC*"), section 2 was inapplicable to judicial elections.]

The text of § 2 * * * as originally enacted [in 1965] read as follows:

"SEC. 2. No voting qualification or prerequisite to voting, or standard, practice, or procedure shall be imposed or applied by any State or political subdivision to deny or abridge the right of any citizen of the United States to vote on account of race or color." * * *

At the time of the passage of the Voting Rights Act of 1965, § 2, unlike other provisions of the Act, did not provoke significant debate in Congress because it was viewed largely as a restatement of the Fifteenth Amendment. This Court took a similar view of § 2 in *Mobile v. Bolden*, 446 U.S. 55, 60–61 (1980). * * * Section 2 protected the right to vote, and it did so without making any distinctions or imposing any limitations as to which elections would fall within its purview. * * *

Justice Stewart's opinion for the plurality in *Mobile v. Bolden*, which held that there was no violation of either the Fifteenth Amendment or § 2 of the Voting Rights Act absent proof of intentional discrimination, served as the impetus for the 1982 amendment [to § 2]. * * *

Under the amended statute, proof of intent is no longer required to prove a § 2 violation. * * * The full text of § 2 as amended in 1982 reads as follows:

"SEC. 2. (a) No voting qualification or prerequisite to voting or standard, practice, or procedure shall be imposed or applied by any State or political subdivision in a manner which results in a denial or abridgement of the right of any citizen of the United States to vote on account of race or color, or in contravention of the guarantees set forth in section 4(f)(2), as provided in subsection (b).

"(b) A violation of subsection (a) is established if, based on the totality of circumstances, it is shown that the political processes leading to nomination or election in the State or political subdivision are not equally open to participation by members of a class of citizens protected by subsection (a) in that its members have less opportunity than other members of the electorate to participate in the political process and to elect representatives of their choice. The extent to which members of a protected class have been elected to office in the State or political subdivision is one circumstance which may be considered: *Provided*, That nothing in this section establishes a right to have members of a protected class elected in numbers equal to their proportion in the population."

The two purposes of the amendment are apparent from its text. Section 2(a) adopts a results test, thus providing that proof of discriminatory intent is no longer necessary to establish *any* violation of the section. Section 2(b) provides guidance about how the results test is to be applied.

Respondents contend, and the *LULAC* majority agreed, that Congress' choice of the word "representatives" in the phrase "have less opportunity than other members of the electorate to participate in the political process and to elect representatives of their choice" in section 2(b) is evidence of congressional intent to exclude vote dilution claims involving judicial elections from the coverage of § 2. We reject that construction because we are convinced that if Congress had such an intent, Congress would have made it explicit in the statute, or at least some of the Members would have identified or mentioned it at some point in the unusually extensive legislative history of the 1982 amendment.[23] * * *

The *LULAC* majority assumed that § 2 provides two distinct types of protection for minority voters — it protects their opportunity "to participate in the political process" and their opportunity "to elect representatives of their choice." Although the majority interpreted "representatives" as a word of

---

23. Congress' silence in this regard can be likened to the dog that did not bark. See A. Doyle, Silver Blaze, in The Complete Sherlock Holmes 335 (1927). Cf. *Harrison v. PPG Industries, Inc.*, 446 U.S. 578, 602 (1980) (Rehnquist, J., dissenting) ("In a case where the construction of legislative language such as this makes so sweeping and so relatively unorthodox a change as that made here, I think judges as well as detectives may take into consideration the fact that a watchdog did not bark in the night.").

limitation, it assumed that the word eliminated judicial elections only from the latter protection, without affecting the former. In other words, a standard, practice, or procedure in a judicial election, such as a limit on the times that polls are open, which has a disparate impact on black voters' opportunity to cast their ballots under § 2, may be challenged even if a different practice that merely affects their opportunity to elect representatives of their choice to a judicial office may not. This reading of § 2, however, is foreclosed by the statutory text and by our prior cases.

Any abridgement of the opportunity of members of a protected class to participate in the political process inevitably impairs their ability to influence the outcome of an election. As the statute is written, however, the inability to elect representatives of their choice is not sufficient to establish a violation unless, under the totality of the circumstances, it can also be said that the members of the protected class have less opportunity to participate in the political process. The statute does not create two separate and distinct rights. Subsection (a) covers every application of a qualification, standard, practice, or procedure that results in a denial or abridgement of "*the right*" to vote. The singular form is also used in subsection (b) when referring to an injury to members of the protected class who have less "opportunity" than others "to participate in the political process *and* to elect representatives of their choice." 42 U.S.C. § 1973 (emphasis added). It would distort the plain meaning of the sentence to substitute the word "or" for the word "and." Such radical surgery would be required to separate the opportunity to participate from the opportunity to elect.

The statutory language is patterned after the language used by Justice White in his opinions for the Court in *White v. Regester*, 412 U.S. 755 (1973) and *Whitcomb v. Chavis*, 403 U.S. 124 (1971).[*] In both opinions, the Court identified the opportunity to participate and the opportunity to elect as inextricably linked. In *White v. Regester*, the Court described the connection as follows: "The plaintiffs' burden is to produce evidence . . . that its members had less opportunity than did other residents in the district to participate in the political processes *and* to elect legislators of their choice." (emphasis added). And earlier, in *Whitcomb v. Chavis*, the Court described the plaintiffs' burden as entailing a showing that they "had less opportunity than did other . . . residents to participate in the political processes *and* to elect legislators of their choice." (emphasis added).

The results test mandated by the 1982 amendment is applicable to all claims arising under § 2. If the word "representatives" did place a limit on the coverage of the Act for judicial elections, it would exclude all claims involving such elections from the protection of § 2. For all such claims must allege an abridgement of the opportunity to participate in the political process *and* to elect representatives of one's choice. * * *

---

[*] *Editors' note: White* and *Whitcomb* were pre-*Bolden* cases in which the Court had suggested that the Constitution prohibited electoral structures or rules that had racially discriminatory effects, even without a showing that the government action in question was rooted in intentional discrimination. For further background, see Chapter 2, § 1.

Both respondents and the *LULAC* majority place their principal reliance on Congress' use [in § 2] of the word "representatives" instead of "legislators" in the phrase "to participate in the political process and to elect representatives of their choice." When Congress borrowed the phrase from *White v. Regester*, it replaced "legislators" with "representatives."[26] This substitution indicates, at the very least, that Congress intended the amendment to cover more than legislative elections. Respondents argue, and the majority agreed, that the term "representatives" was used to extend § 2 coverage to executive officials, but not to judges. We think, however, that the better reading of the word "representatives" describes the winners of representative, popular elections. If executive officers, such as prosecutors, sheriffs, state attorneys general, and state treasurers, can be considered "representatives" simply because they are chosen by popular election, then the same reasoning should apply to elected judges.

Respondents suggest that if Congress had intended to have the statute's prohibition against vote dilution apply to the election of judges, it would have used the word "candidates" instead of "representatives." But that confuses the ordinary meaning of the words. The word "representative" refers to someone who has prevailed in a popular election, whereas the word "candidate" refers to someone who is seeking an office. Thus, a candidate is nominated, not elected. When Congress used "candidate" in other parts of the statute, it did so precisely because it was referring to people who were aspirants for an office. See, e.g., 42 U.S.C. § 1971(b) ("any candidate for the office of President"), § 1971(e) ("candidates for public office"), § 1973i(c) ("any candidate for the office of President"), § 1973i(e)(2) ("any candidate for the office of President"), § 1973l(c) ("candidates for public or party office"), § 1973ff–2 ("In the case of the offices of President and Vice President, a vote for a named candidate"), § 1974 ("candidates for the office of President"), § 1974e ("candidates for the office of President").

The *LULAC* majority was, of course, entirely correct in observing that "judges need not be elected at all," and that ideally public opinion should be irrelevant to the judge's role because the judge is often called upon to disregard, or even to defy, popular sentiment. The Framers of the Constitution had a similar understanding of the judicial role, and as a consequence, they established that Article III judges would be appointed, rather than elected, and

---

26. The word "representatives" rather than "legislators" was included in Senator Robert Dole's compromise, which was designed to assuage the fears of those Senators who viewed the House's version, H.R. 3112, as an invitation for proportional representation and electoral quotas. Senator Dole explained that the compromise was intended both to embody the belief "that a voting practice or procedure which is discriminatory in result should not be allowed to stand, regardless of whether there exists a discriminatory purpose or intent" and to "delineat[e] what legal standard should apply under the results test and clarif[y] that it is not a mandate for proportional representation." Hearings on S. 53 et al. before the Subcommittee on the Constitution of the Senate Committee on the Judiciary, 97th Cong., 2d Sess., 60 (1982). Thus, the compromise was not intended to exclude any elections from the coverage of subsection (a), but simply to make clear that the results test does not require the proportional election of minority candidates in *any* election.

would be sheltered from public opinion by receiving life tenure and salary protection. Indeed, these views were generally shared by the States during the early years of the Republic. Louisiana, however, has chosen a different course. It has decided to elect its judges and to compel judicial candidates to vie for popular support just as other political candidates do.

The fundamental tension between the ideal character of the judicial office and the real world of electoral politics cannot be resolved by crediting judges with total indifference to the popular will while simultaneously requiring them to run for elected office. When each of several members of a court must be a resident of a separate district, and must be elected by the voters of that district, it seems both reasonable and realistic to characterize the winners as representatives of that district. * * * Louisiana could, of course, exclude its judiciary from the coverage of the Voting Rights Act by changing to a system in which judges are appointed, and in that way, it could enable its judges to be indifferent to popular opinion. The reasons why Louisiana has chosen otherwise are precisely the reasons why it is appropriate for § 2, as well as § 5, of the Voting Rights Act to continue to apply to its judicial elections.

The close connection between § 2 and § 5 further undermines respondents' view that judicial elections should not be covered under § 2. Section 5 requires certain States to submit changes in their voting procedures to the District Court of the District of Columbia or to the Attorney General for preclearance. Section 5 uses language similar to that of § 2 in defining prohibited practices: "any voting qualification or prerequisite to voting, or standard, practice, or procedure with respect to voting." This Court has already held that § 5 applies to judicial elections. *Clark v. Roemer*, 500 U.S. 646 (1991). If § 2 did not apply to judicial elections, a State covered by § 5 would be precluded from implementing a new voting procedure having discriminatory effects with respect to judicial elections, whereas a similarly discriminatory system already in place could not be challenged under § 2. It is unlikely that Congress intended such an anomalous result. * * *

Congress enacted the Voting Rights Act of 1965 for the broad remedial purpose of "rid[ding] the country of racial discrimination in voting." *South Carolina v. Katzenbach*, 383 U.S. 301, 315 (1966). In *Allen v. State Board of Elections*, 393 U.S. 544, 567 (1969), we said that the Act should be interpreted in a manner that provides "the broadest possible scope" in combatting racial discrimination. Congress amended the Act in 1982 in order to relieve plaintiffs of the burden of proving discriminatory intent, after a plurality of this Court had concluded that the original Act, like the Fifteenth Amendment, contained such a requirement. See *Mobile v. Bolden*. Thus, Congress made clear that a violation of § 2 could be established by proof of discriminatory results alone. It is difficult to believe that Congress, in an express effort to broaden the protection afforded by the Voting Rights Act, withdrew, without comment, an important category of elections from that protection. Today we reject such an anomalous view and hold that state judicial elections are included within the ambit of § 2 as amended.

The judgment of the Court of Appeals is reversed and the case is remanded for further proceedings consistent with this opinion.

JUSTICE SCALIA, with whom THE CHIEF JUSTICE and JUSTICE KENNEDY join, dissenting.

Section 2 of the Voting Rights Act is not some all-purpose weapon for well-intentioned judges to wield as they please in the battle against discrimination. It is a statute. I thought we had adopted a regular method for interpreting the meaning of language in a statute: first, find the ordinary meaning of the language in its textual context; and second, using established canons of construction, ask whether there is any clear indication that some permissible meaning other than the ordinary one applies. If not — and especially if a good reason for the ordinary meaning appears plain — we apply that ordinary meaning.

Today, however, the Court adopts a method quite out of accord with that usual practice. It begins not with what the statute says, but with an expectation about what the statute must mean absent particular phenomena ("*we are convinced* that if Congress had . . . an intent [to exclude judges] Congress would have made it explicit in the statute, or at least some of the Members would have identified or mentioned it at some point in the unusually extensive legislative history"); and the Court then interprets the words of the statute to fulfill its expectation. Finding nothing in the legislative history affirming that judges were excluded from the coverage of § 2, the Court gives the phrase "to elect representatives" the quite extraordinary meaning that covers the election of judges.

As method, this is just backwards, and however much we may be attracted by the result it produces in a particular case, we should in every case resist it. Our job begins with a text that Congress has passed and the President has signed. We are to read the words of that text as any ordinary Member of Congress would have read them, see Holmes, The Theory of Legal Interpretation, 12 Harv. L. Rev. 417 (1899), and apply the meaning so determined. In my view, that reading reveals that § 2 extends to vote dilution claims for the elections of representatives only, and judges are not representatives.

* * * I agree with the Court that [original § 2], directed towards intentional discrimination, applied to all elections, for it clearly said so:

> "No voting qualification or prerequisite to voting, or standard, practice, or procedure shall be imposed or applied by any State or political subdivision to deny or abridge the right of any citizen of the United States to vote on account of race or color."

The 1982 amendments, however, radically transformed the Act. As currently written, the statute proscribes intentional discrimination only if it has a discriminatory effect, but proscribes practices with discriminatory effect whether or not intentional. This new "results" criterion provides a powerful, albeit sometimes blunt, weapon with which to attack even the most subtle forms of discrimination. The question we confront here is how broadly the new remedy applies. The foundation of the Court's analysis, the itinerary for its journey in the wrong direction, is the following statement: "It is difficult to believe that Congress, in an express effort to broaden the protection afforded by the Voting Rights Act, withdrew, without comment, an important category of elections from that protection." There are two things wrong with this. First is the notion that Congress cannot be credited with having achieved anything of major importance by simply saying it, in ordinary language, in the text of a statute, "without comment" in the legislative history. As the Court colorfully puts it, if the dog of legislative history has not barked nothing of great significance can have transpired. Apart from the questionable wisdom of assuming that dogs will bark when something important is happening, see 1 T. Livius, The History of Rome 411–413 (1892) (D. Spillan translation), we have forcefully and explicitly rejected the Conan Doyle approach to statutory construction in the past. See *Harrison v. PPG Industries, Inc.*, 446 U.S. 578, 592 (1980) ("In ascertaining the meaning of a statute, a court cannot, in the manner of Sherlock Holmes, pursue the theory of the dog that did not bark"). We are here to apply the statute, not legislative history, and certainly not the absence of legislative history. Statutes are the law though sleeping dogs lie.

The more important error in the Court's starting-point, however, is the assumption that the effect of excluding judges from the revised § 2 would be to "withdr[aw] . . . an important category of elections from [the] protection [of the Voting Rights Act]." There is absolutely no question here of *withdrawing* protection. Since the pre-1982 content of § 2 was coextensive with the Fifteenth Amendment, the entirety of that protection subsisted in the Constitution, and could be enforced through the other provisions of the Voting Rights Act. Nothing was lost from the prior coverage; *all* of the new "results" protection was an add-on. The issue is not, therefore, as the Court would have it, whether Congress has cut back on the coverage of the Voting Rights Act; the issue is how far it has extended it. Thus, even if a court's expectations were a proper basis for interpreting the text of a statute, while there would be reason to expect that Congress was not "withdrawing" protection, there is no particular reason to expect that the supplemental protection it provided was any more extensive than the text of the statute said.

[Justice Scalia agreed with the *LULAC* majority that section 2 created two separate rights for protected classes: (1) "to participate in the political process" and (2) "to elect representatives of their choice." On this reading, judicial elections are subject to the first right, but not the second because judges are not "representatives."] The Court, petitioners, and petitioners' *amici* have labored mightily to establish that there is *a* meaning of "representatives" that would include judges, and no doubt there is. But our job is not to scavenge the world of English usage to discover whether there is any possible meaning of "representatives" which suits our preconception that the statute includes judges; our job is to determine whether the *ordinary* meaning includes them, and if it does not, to ask whether there is any solid indication in the text or structure of the statute that something other than ordinary meaning was intended.

There is little doubt that the ordinary meaning of "representatives" does not include judges, see Webster's Second New International Dictionary 2114 (1950). The Court's feeble argument to the contrary is that "representatives" means those who "are chosen by popular election." On that hypothesis, the fan-elected members of the baseball All-Star teams are "representatives" — hardly a common, if even a permissible, usage. Surely the word "representative" connotes one who is not only *elected by* the people, but who also, at a minimum, *acts on behalf of* the people. Judges do that in a sense — but not in the ordinary sense. As the captions of the pleadings in some States still display, it is the prosecutor who represents "the People"; the judge represents the Law — which often requires him to rule against the People. It is precisely because we do not *ordinarily* conceive of judges as representatives that we held judges not within the Fourteenth Amendment's requirement of "one person, one vote." *Wells v. Edwards*, 347 F.Supp. 453 (MD La.1972), aff'd, 409 U.S. 1095 (1973). The point is not that a State could not make judges in some senses representative, or that all judges must be conceived of in the Article III mold, but rather, that giving "representatives" its ordinary meaning, the ordinary speaker in 1982 would not have applied the word to judges, see Holmes, The Theory of Legal Interpretation, 12 Harv. L. Rev. 417 (1899). It remains only to ask whether there is good indication that ordinary meaning does not apply. * * *

While the "plain statement" rule may not be applicable, there is assuredly nothing whatever that points in the opposite direction, indicating that the ordinary meaning here should *not* be applied. Far from that, in my view the ordinary meaning of "representatives" gives clear purpose to congressional action that otherwise would seem pointless. As an initial matter, it is evident that Congress paid particular attention to the scope of elections covered by the "to elect" language. As the Court suggests, that language for the most part tracked this Court's opinions in *White v. Regester* and *Whitcomb v. Chavis*, but the word "legislators" was not copied. Significantly, it was replaced not with the more general term "candidates" used repeatedly elsewhere in the Act, see, *e.g.*, 42 U.S.C. §§ 1971(b), (e); 1973i(c), 1973l(c); 1973ff–2; 1974; 1974e, but with the term "representatives," which appears nowhere else in the Act (except as a proper noun referring to Members of the federal lower House, or designees of the Attorney General). The normal meaning of this term is broader than "legislators" (it includes, for example, school boards and city councils as well as senators and representatives) but narrower than "candidates."

The Court says that the seemingly significant refusal to use the term "candidate" and selection of the distinctive term "representative" are really inconsequential, because "candidate" could not have been used. According to the Court, since "candidate" refers to one who has been nominated but *not yet* elected, the phrase "to elect candidates" would be a contradiction in terms. The only flaw in this argument is that it is not true, as repeated usage of the formulation "to elect candidates" by this Court itself amply demonstrates. [Citing cases.] * * * In other words, far from being an impermissible choice, "candidates" would have been the natural choice, even if it had not been used repeatedly elsewhere in the statute. It is quite absurd to think that Congress went out of its way to replace that term with "representatives," in order to convey what "candidates" naturally suggests (*viz.*, coverage of *all* elections) and what "representatives" naturally does not.

A second consideration confirms that "representatives" in § 2 was meant in its ordinary sense. When given its ordinary meaning, it causes the statute to reproduce an established, eminently logical and perhaps practically indispensable limitation upon the availability of vote dilution claims. Whatever other requirements may be applicable to elections for "representatives" (in the sense of those who are not only elected by but act on behalf of the electorate), those elections, unlike elections for *all* office-holders, must be conducted in accordance with the equal-protection principle of "one person, one vote." And it so happens — more than coincidentally, I think — that in every case in which, prior to the amendment of § 2, we recognized the possibility of a vote dilution claim, the principle of "one person, one vote" was applicable. Indeed, it is the principle of "one person, one vote" that gives meaning to the concept of "dilution." One's vote is diluted if it is not, *as it should be*, of the same practical effect as everyone else's. Of course the mere fact that an election practice satisfies the constitutional requirement of "one person, one vote" does not establish that there has been no vote dilution for Voting Rights Act purposes, since that looks not merely to equality of individual votes but also to equality of minority blocs of votes. * * * But "one person, one vote" has been the premise and the necessary condition of a vote dilution claim, since it establishes the baseline for computing the voting strength that the minority bloc *ought* to have. As we have suggested, the first question in a dilution case is whether the "one person, one vote" standard is met, and if it is, the second is whether voting structures nonetheless operate to " 'minimize or cancel out the voting strength of racial or political elements of the voting population.' "

Well before Congress amended § 2, we had held that the principle of "one person, one vote" does not apply to the election of judges, *Wells v. Edwards*, 347 F.Supp. 453 (MD La.1972), aff'd, 409 U.S. 1095 (1973). If Congress was (through use of the extremely inapt word "representatives") making vote dilution claims available with respect to the election of judges, it was, for the first time, extending that remedy to a context in which "one person, one vote" did not apply. *That* would have been a significant change in the law, and given the need to identify some other baseline for computing "dilution," *that* is a matter which those who believe in barking dogs should be astounded to find unmentioned in the legislative history. If "representatives" is given its normal meaning, on the other hand, there is no change in the law (except elimination of the intent requirement) and the silence is entirely understandable. * * *

Finally, the Court suggests that there is something "anomalous" about extending coverage under § 5 of the Voting Rights Act to the election of judges, while not extending coverage under § 2 to the same elections. This simply misconceives the different roles of § 2 and § 5. The latter requires certain jurisdictions to preclear changes in election methods before those changes are implemented; it is a means of assuring in advance the absence of all electoral illegality, not only that which violates the Voting Rights Act but that which violates the Constitution as well. In my view, judges *are* within the scope of § 2 for nondilution claims, and thus for those claims, § 5 preclearance would enforce the Voting Rights Act with respect to judges. Moreover, intentional discrimination in the election of judges, whatever its form, is constitutionally prohibited, and the preclearance provision of § 5 gives the government a method by which to prevent that. The scheme makes entire sense without the need to bring judges within the "to elect" provision. * * *

As I said at the outset, this case is about method. The Court transforms the meaning of § 2, not because the ordinary meaning is irrational, or inconsistent with other parts of the statute, see, *e.g.*, *Green v. Bock Laundry*; *Public Citizen v. Department of Justice* (Kennedy, J., concurring in the judgment), but because it does not fit the Court's conception of what Congress must have had in mind. When we adopt a method that psychoanalyzes Congress rather than reads its laws, when we employ a tinkerer's toolbox, we do great harm. Not only do we reach the wrong result with respect to the statute at hand, but we poison the well of future legislation, depriving legislators of the assurance that ordinary terms, used in an ordinary context, will be given a predictable meaning. Our highest responsibility in the field of statutory construction is to read the laws in a consistent way, giving Congress a sure means by which it may work the people's will. We have ignored that responsibility today. I respectfully dissent.

[The dissenting opinion of JUSTICE KENNEDY is omitted.]

WEST VIRGINIA UNIVERSITY HOSPITALS v. CASEY, 499 U.S. 83 (1991). In a majority opinion by **Justice Scalia**, the Court held that 42 U.S.C. § 1988, which permits the award of "a reasonable attorney's fee" to prevailing plaintiffs in civil rights cases, does not authorize the award to prevailing plaintiffs of fees for services rendered to their attorneys by experts. Justice Scalia presented a straightforward textualist path to this result: "The record of statutory usage demonstrates convincingly that attorney's fees and expert fees are regarded as separate elements of litigation costs. While some fee-shifting provisions, like § 1988, refer only to 'attorney's fees,' many others explicitly shift expert witness fees *as well as* attorney's fees." Justice Scalia cited a variety of federal statutes, such as the Toxic Substances Control Act, 15 U.S.C. §§ 2618(d), 2619(c)(2), which provides that a prevailing party may recover "the costs of suit and reasonable fees for attorneys and expert witnesses." Justice Scalia explained that, if attorney's fees includes expert fees, "dozens of statutes referring to the two separately become an inexplicable exercise in redundancy."

In response to the argument that attorney's fees under § 1988 should include expert fees because had Congress thought about the issue it surely would have included them as recoverable (the imaginative reconstruction approach), Justice Scalia stated: "This argument profoundly mistakes our role. Where a statutory term presented to us for the first time is ambiguous, we construe it to contain that permissible meaning which fits most logically and comfortably into the body of both previously and subsequently enacted law. We do so not because that precise accommodative meaning is what the lawmakers must have had in mind (how could an earlier Congress know what a later Congress would enact?) but because it is our role to make sense rather than nonsense out of the *corpus juris*. But where, as here, the meaning of the term prevents such accommodation, it is not our function to eliminate clearly expressed inconsistency of policy, and to treat alike subjects that different Congresses have chosen to treat differently. The facile attribution of congressional 'forgetfulness' cannot justify such a usurpation. Where what is at issue is not a contradictory disposition within the same enactment, but merely a difference between more parsimonious policy of an earlier enactment and the more generous policy of a later one, there is no more basis for saying that the earlier Congress forgot than for saying that the earlier Congress felt differently. In such circumstances, the attribution of forgetfulness rests in reality upon the judge's assessment that the later statute contains the *better* disposition. But that is not for judges to prescribe."

Justice Stevens, joined by **Justices Marshall** and **Blackmun**, dissented. He contended that the primary source of meaning for § 1988 should not be the text of other statutes, but how the Court has interpreted § 1988's own text and legislative history. He would have provided a broad reading to "costs" and "a reasonable attorney's fee," either term being expansive enough to cover the expenses associated with "specialized litigation support that a trial lawyer needs and that the client customarily pays for." He also noted that the legislative history of § 1988 indicated that Congress intended to make prevailing plaintiffs whole.

Justice Stevens argued that the majority's textualism disserves democratic norms. He cited examples in which Congress has let stand statutory interpretation decisions rooted in "historical context, legislative history, and prior cases identifying the purpose that motivated the legislation." In contrast, "when the Court has put on its thick grammarian's spectacles and ignored the available evidence of congressional purpose and the teaching of prior cases construing a statute, the congressional response has been dramatically different."[i] He concluded: "In the domain of statutory interpretation, Congress is the master. It obviously has the power to correct our mistakes, but we do the country a disservice when we needlessly ignore persuasive evidence of Congress' actual purpose and require it 'to take the time to revisit the matter' and to restate its purpose in more precise English whenever its work product suffers from an omission or inadvertent error."

NOTES ON *CASEY, CHISOM,* AND THE NEW TEXTUALISM ON THE COURT

1. *The Rise of the New Textualism,1987–95, and Its Relationship to the Plain Meaning Rule.* The Court's practice changed after Justice Scalia's

---

i. Justice Stevens cited legislation effectively overruling the literalist decisions in *General Electric Co. v. Gilbert*, 429 U.S. 125 (1976) (discrimination on basis of pregnancy not gender discrimination violative of Title VII); *INS v. Phinpathya*, 464 U.S. 183 (1984) (requirement of "continuous physical presence" of aliens did not permit even temporary or inadvertent absences from United States); *Grove City College v. Bell*, 465 U.S. 555 (1984) (narrow reading of Title IX of Civil Rights Act, which prohibits gender discrimination in programs that receive federal financial assistance); *Wards Cove Packing Co. v. Atonio*, 490 U.S. 642 (1989) (reallocating burden of proof in Title VII cases); *Patterson v. McLean Credit Union*, 491 U.S. 164 (1989) (42 U.S.C. § 1981 does not forbid racial harassment in employment setting); *McNally v. United States*, 483 U.S. 350 (1987) (limiting mail fraud statute to the protection of property interests). For support of Justice Stevens' point, see William Eskridge, Jr., *Overriding Supreme Court Statutory Interpretation Decisions*, 101 Yale L.J. 331 (1991). For support for Stevens' more context-specific approach rather than Scalia's "whole code" methodology, see William Buzbee, *The One-Congress Fiction in Statutory Interpretation*, 149 U. Pa. L. Rev. 171 (2000).

appointment in 1986. Since then, the Court's statutory opinions have more often found a "plain meaning," less often examined legislative history to confirm the existence of a plain meaning, and in only a handful of instances relied on legislative history to interpret a statute against what the Court felt was its plain meaning. The Court's opinions also have tended to be more dogmatic about whether there is any ambiguity in statutes; it was much more likely to find a plain meaning in the 1990s than it was before 1986.[j] As in *Casey*, Justice Scalia's own opinions especially espouse the precepts of the new textualism, often with Justice Stevens in dissent (also as in *Casey*).[k]

The relationship between the new textualism and the old plain meaning rule is evident, but they are not the same thing. Justice Scalia's formulation of textualism at the beginning of his *Chisom* dissent, as well as his discussion in *A Matter of Interpretation*, stresses the "ordinary meaning" or "reasonable meaning" of statutory text. In his view, legislative history should never trump such ordinary meaning. In contrast, the old plain meaning rule, as exemplified by *Caminetti* (§ 1 of this chapter), operated as an exclusionary rule concerning the use of legislative history: if the statutory text was "plain," one could not consult legislative history; if the statutory text was ambiguous, legislative history was fair game. The softer approach to plain meaning in *TVA v. Hill* and *Griffin* was even less confining, stating merely that a statutory plain meaning was presumptively the interpretation to be given to the statute, but legislative history could be consulted to confirm that understanding (and in a rare case in which the legislative history conclusively demonstrated that the textual plain meaning was not the appropriate interpretation, the plain meaning could be jettisoned).

Today, "plain meaning" is, ironically, a deeply ambiguous term. Our sense is that courts that speak of "plain meaning" (though do not stop to define the term) are usually positing that the statute is quite clear in a literal sense — much more than "ordinary meaning" connotes. What we understand Justice Scalia to mean by "ordinary meaning" is the best (most coherent) textual understanding that emerges after close textual analysis, which then makes the result in the case plain on his terms — not merely the relatively rare "plain meaning" that leaps off the page to the experienced judge. It is regrettable that in some cases — both federal and state — judges have used the term "plain meaning" loosely, sometimes to mean a textual interpretation that is pretty obvious on the face of the statute (say, 90/10 clear) and sometimes to mean something similar to Justice Scalia's expression of the best textual understand-

---

j. See William Eskridge, Jr., *Dynamic Statutory Interpretation* ch. 7 (1994); Lawrence Solan, *The Language of Judges* (1993); Thomas Merrill, *Textualism and the Future of the* Chevron *Doctrine*, 72 Wash. U.L.Q. 351 (1994).

k. In this era, Justice Scalia applied the new textualism in opinions for the Court in *MCI Telecommunications Corp. v. American Tel. & Tel. Co.*, 512 U.S. 218 (1994) (Stevens in dissent); *BFP v. Resolution Trust Corp.*, 511 U.S. 531 (1994) (Stevens joining Souter dissent); *United States v. Nordic Village*, 503 U.S. 30 (1992) (Stevens in dissent); *Sullivan v. Everhart*, 494 U.S. 83 (1990) (Stevens in dissent); *Finley v. United States*, 490 U.S. 545 (1989) (Stevens in dissent); *Chan v. Korean AirLines, Ltd.*, 490 U.S. 122 (1989) (Stevens joining Brennan dissent); *Pierce v. Underwood*, 487 U.S. 552 (1988) (unanimous Court).

ing that emerges from close analysis of statutory provisions that, at the outset, may have seemed ambiguous, confusing, or at least complicated. The former approach to plain meaning is akin to a pretty literal approach to the face of the statute; the latter approach of Justice Scalia sees statutory interpretation to be something like a word puzzle, capable of being solved in almost all cases with a best answer emerging.

Although the Court's practice was influenced by the new textualism in the first few years of Justice Scalia's membership, the Court never completely accepted its tenets. In *Wisconsin Public Intervenor v. Mortier*, 501 U.S. 597, 610 n.4 (1991), all of the other Justices joined a footnote explicitly rejecting Justice Scalia's insistence that legislative history is irrelevant to proper statutory interpretation. And, as in *Chisom* and *Bock Laundry*, the Court still considered legislative background to statutes and is open to understanding a statute from the perspective of the legislators who enacted it. Often such decisions are written by Justices Stevens or Souter, with Justice Scalia dissenting, as in *Chisom*, or concurring only in the judgment, as in *Bock Laundry*.[l]

2. *1995 Onward.* According to Charles Tiefer, *The Reconceptualization of Legislative History in the Supreme Court*, 2000 Wis. L. Rev. 205, the new textualism is not only past its peak, but its strong claims have substantially been rejected by the Court.[m] Since 1995, the Court has often followed the approach pressed by Justice Breyer in *The Uses of Legislative History*, 65 S. Cal. L. Rev. 845 (1992) and by Justice Stevens in his various opinions — what Professor Tiefer calls "institutional legislative history." That is, the Court treats the legislative process as a group engaged in coordinated purposive action, in which the group relies on the guidance and judgment of subgroups (committees) and ratifies their publicly presented understandings when the group takes action (i.e., enacts statutes). Hence, statutory interpretation is neither an effort to imaginatively reconstruct a collective intent nor to divine the objective meaning the statutory text would have had when adopted, but instead is an effort to carry out the ongoing institutional project along the lines laid out in the public presentations of those institutional actors charged with developing the original statute. The discussion in Chapter 1 (p. 29) of "information theory" as an account of the operation of the legislative process supports the deployment of institutional legislative history.

---

l. For cases in this era, see *Landgraf v. USI Film Products*, 511 U.S. 244 (1994) (Stevens opinion, Scalia concurring in the judgment); *American Red Cross v. S.G.*, 505 U.S. 247 (1992) (Souter opinion, Scalia dissent); *United States v. R.L.C.*, 503 U.S. 291 (1992) (Souter plurality opinion, Scalia concurring in the judgment); *Taylor v. United States*, 495 U.S. 575 (1990) (Blackmun opinion, Scalia concurring in the judgment); *Crandon v. United States*, 494 U.S. 152 (1990) (Stevens opinion, Scalia concurring only in the judgment); *Blanchard v. Bergeron*, 489 U.S. 87 (1989) (White opinion, Scalia concurring only in the judgment).

m. In addition, see James Brudney & Corey Ditslear, *The Decline and Fall of Legislative History? Patterns of Supreme Court Reliance in the Burger and Rehnquist Eras,* 89 Judicature 220 (2006); Jonathan Molot, *The Rise and Fall of Textualism*, 106 Colum. L. Rev. 1 (2006); Lawrence Solan, *Learning Our Limits: The Decline of Textualism in Statutory Cases*, 1997 Wis. L. Rev. 235.

3. *So Where Is the Court's Methodology Now?* The Supreme Court has not entirely returned to the pre-Scalia days. Consider the following observations about where it is today. First, the text is now, more than it was 20 or 30 years ago, the central inquiry at the Supreme Court level and in other courts that are now following the Supreme Court's lead. A brief that starts off with, "The statute means thus-and-so because it says so in the committee report," is asking for trouble. Both advice and advocacy should start with the statutory text.

Because the Court frequently uses the dictionary to provide meaning to key statutory terms,[n] the advocate should incorporate this methodology as well. The effective advocate will note there are many theoretical problems with relying upon dictionaries to support textualism — e.g., they are not part of the text of a statute and might seem even further removed from it than legislative history; they are not necessarily "objective"; they are necessarily conservative, in the sense of reflecting past English usage rather than emerging usage; although judges may consult them in the hope of avoiding contextual, purposive inquiries, dictionaries usually present several definitions of a term and suggest (frequently quite explicitly, in a preface) that only through considering the context of usage can the term be properly defined. Although this is chaotic theoretically, as a practical matter this opens the door for advocates to engage in "dictionary shopping," as well as "definition shopping" within any particular dictionary.[o] In this respect, consider Justice Scalia's conclusion in *Chisom*, based on a dictionary, that the customary usage of "representative" excludes elected judges. Consult your own dictionary, or several: can you find a definition of "representative" that supports the majority's holding in *Chisom*?[p]

Second, the "contextual" evidence the Court is interested in is now statutory more than just historical context. Arguments that your position is more consistent with other parts of the same statute are typically winning arguments. Similarly, as *Casey* indicates, the Court today goes beyond the "whole act" rule to something like a "whole code" rule, searching the United States Code for

---

n. See Ellen Aprill, *The Law of the Word: Dictionary Shopping in the Supreme Court*, 30 Ariz. St. L.J. 275 (1998); Lawrence Solan, *Finding Ordinary Meaning in the Dictionary,* in *Language and the Law* 255 (Marlyn Robinson ed. 2003); Samuel Thumma & Jeffrey Kirchmeier, *The Lexicon Has Become a Fortress: The United States Supreme Court's Use of Dictionaries*, 47 Buff. L. Rev. 227 (1999); Note, *Looking It Up: Dictionaries and Statutory Interpretation*, 107 Harv. L. Rev. 1437, 1438 (1994) (first noting this trend).

o. See Note, *Looking It Up, supra*, at 1447 (describing the wide range of dictionaries the Court has consulted). Justice Scalia has suggested that it might follow the weight of dictionary definitions. See *MCI Telecommunications Corp. v. American Tel. & Tel. Co.*, 514 U.S. 218, 226–27, 228 n.3 (1994) (following "[v]irtually every dictionary" while rejecting the definition found in *Webster's Third*, which was published after the statute in question was enacted and in any event was less worthy of reliance because of "its portrayal of common error as proper usage"). In dissent, Justice Stevens disputed the weight of dictionary authority and concluded that, in any event, "[d]ictionaries can be useful aids in statutory interpretation, but they are no substitute for close analysis of what words mean as used in a particular statutory context." *Id.* at 240 (Stevens, J., dissenting).

p. See Note, *Looking It Up, supra*, at 1442 & n.37.

guidance on the usage of key statutory terms and phrases. For a recent example, consult *Arlington Central School District v. Murphy*, 126 S.Ct. 2455 (2006), where the Court narrowly construed the fee-shifting provision of a 1986 education-rights statute following the same methodology as *Casey*, over strong contrary legislative history and a powerful argument based on the statutory structure (both developed by Justice Breyer's dissenting opinion).

Third, the Court will still look at contextual evidence and is very interested in the public law background of the statute. If a statute seems to require an odd result (as in *Bock Laundry*), the Court will interrogate the background materials to find out why. If a statute overrides judicial or agency decisions (as in *Chisom*), the Court will usually be responsive to Congress' concerns. When the Justices are themselves divided as to what the statute's "plain meaning" is, as in *Weber* (which the Rehnquist Court reaffirmed in *Johnson v. Transportation Agency*, both excerpted in Chapter 1, § 3), at least some of them will examine the statute's background to figure out how the typical legislator would have read the statute. For all of these reasons, it remains important to research and brief the legislative history thoroughly. The effective advocate will appreciate that the presence of such materials in the briefs may influence the outcome more than the opinion in the case will indicate.[q]

With these factors in mind, can you find a sensible way in which three Justices (White, O'Connor, Souter) were in the majority in *both Chisom* and *Casey*? Some hints: Are the textual arguments equally strong in both cases? From the excerpts you have read, weigh the strength of the legislative history and the statutory purposes present in both cases as well, and in addition consider the subject matter and the current "stakes" involved in each case. Recall that in *Holy Trinity Church* the Court engaged in eclectic interpretation that was informed by every plausible theory of interpretation extant in the law except a rigid plain meaning rule. Were White, O'Connor, and Souter doing much the same thing?

ZUNI PUBLIC SCHOOL DISTRICT No. 89 v. DEPARTMENT OF EDUCATION, 127 S.Ct. 1534 (2007). The federal Impact Aid Act, 108 Stat. 3749, provides financial assistance to local school districts whose ability to finance public school education is adversely affected by a federal presence.

---

q. Consider the comments of Judge A. Raymond Randolph of the United States Court of Appeals for the District of Columbia Circuit, in *Dictionaries, Plain Meaning, and Context in Statutory Interpretation*, 17 Harv. J.L. & Pub. Pol'y 71, 76 (1994):

* * * Nearly every brief I see in cases involving issues of statutory construction contains a discourse on legislative history. This is a wise precaution on the part of appellate advocates. Counsel can never be sure that the court will find the words plain, and stop there. To be safe, in the event the court takes two steps instead of one, counsel must include a backup argument addressing the meaning of the statute in light of the legislative history. Judges read those briefs from cover to cover, or at least they are supposed to. I do. Somewhere during the reading, preliminary views begin to form. When the reading is done and the case has been analyzed and argued, how can it be said that the judge turned to the legislative history only after finding the statutory language ambiguous? The judge himself often cannot identify exactly when his perception of the words actually jelled. * * *

The statute prohibits a State from offsetting this federal aid by reducing state aid to a local district. So as not to interfere with a state program that seeks to equalize per-pupil expenditures, the statute contains an exception permitting a State to reduce its own local funding on account of the federal aid where the Secretary of Education finds that the state program "equalizes expenditures" among local school districts. 20 U.S.C. § 7709(b)(1). The Secretary is required to use a formula that compares the local school district with the greatest per-pupil expenditures in a State to the school district with the smallest per-pupil expenditures. If the former does not exceed the latter by more than 25 percent, the state program qualifies as one that "equalizes expenditures." In making this determination, the Secretary must "disregard [school districts] with per-pupil expenditures * * * above the 95th percentile or below the 5th percentile of such expenditures in the State." Id. § 7709(b)(2)(B)(i).

Department of Education regulations first promulgated more than 30 years ago provide that the Secretary will (1) create a list of school districts ranked in order of per-pupil expenditure; then (2) identify the relevant percentile cutoff point on that list based on a specific (95th or 5th) percentile of student population (essentially identifying those districts whose students account for the 5% of the State's total student population that lies at both the high and low ends of the spending distribution); and finally (3) compare the highest spending and lowest spending of the remaining school districts to see whether they satisfy the statute's requirement that the disparity between them not exceed 25%. Two New Mexico school districts challenged this method of calculation on the ground that it was inconsistent with the plain language of the "disregard" clause. According to the districts, the clause required the Department to disregard the bottom and top 5% of school districts by number (i.e., the top 5 and the bottom 5 if there were 100 districts) — and not to consider the districts' populations, as the Department was doing.

Justice Breyer's opinion for the Court ruled that the Department's method was permissible. First, it was consistent with the evolution of the statute. Congress first enacted an equalization law in 1974, which explicitly delegated to the Department authority to define the conditions under which equalization funds would be allowed. The Department issued regulations in 1976, essentially the same as those challenged. No one in Congress objected to those regulations, which the Department has administered them consistently. "The present statutory language originated in draft legislation that the Secretary himself sent to Congress in 1994. With one minor change (irrelevant to the present calculation controversy), Congress adopted that language without comment or clarification. No one at the time — no Member of Congress, no Department of Education official, no school district or State — expressed the view that this statutory language (which, after all, was supplied by the Secretary) was intended to require, or did require, the Secretary to change the Department's system of calculation, a system that the Department and school districts across the Nation had followed for nearly 20 years, without (as far as we are told) any adverse effect."

Second, the Department's approach was consistent with the purpose of the disregard clause, to exclude "outlier" districts from the calculation. The

Department originally explained why it did not follow a number-of-school-districts approach: "In States with a small number of large districts, an exclusion based on percentage of school districts might exclude from the measure of disparity a substantial percentage of the pupil population in those States. Conversely, in States with large numbers of small districts, such an approach might exclude only an insignificant fraction of the pupil population and would not exclude anomalous characteristics." 41 Fed. Reg. 26,324 (1976).

Third, the Department's approach was not inconsistent with the statutory language, which Justice Breyer thought ambiguous in light of his survey of technical and general dictionaries. The statutory language ("percentile") signifies only that the Department must divide districts into a population with a top 5% and a bottom 5%, but does not tell the Department how those "5%" figures must be calculated. "No dictionary definition we have found suggests that there is any *single* logical, mathematical, or statistical link between, on the one hand, the characterizing data (used for ranking purposes) and, on the other hand, the nature of the relevant population or how that population might be weighted for purposes of determining a percentile cutoff." When Congress has wanted to limit agency discretion in making such percentile rankings, it has phrased statutory language more precisely. For example, in another education-related law, Congress referred to "the school at the 20th percentile in the State, *based on enrollment,* among all schools *ranked by the percentage of students at the proficient level.*" 20 U.S.C. § 6311(b)(2)(E)(ii) (emphasis supplied by Justice Breyer).

Justice Breyer drew further "reassurance from the fact that no group of statisticians, nor any individual statistician, has told us directly in briefs, or indirectly through citation, that the language before us cannot be read as we have read it. This circumstance is significant, for the statutory language is technical, and we are not statisticians. And the views of experts (or their absence) might help us understand (though not control our determination of) what Congress had in mind."

Justice Scalia's dissenting opinion (joined by **Chief Justice Roberts** and **Justices Souter** and **Thomas**) faulted the majority for starting its analysis with the history and evolution of the statute, rather than its text. In his view, this "cart-before-the-horse approach" was inconsistent with the primary lesson of "Statutory Interpretation 101." (Writing also for **Justice Alito**, **Justice Kennedy** wrote a concurring opinion stating that he would be alarmed if Justice Breyer's order of treatment became "systemic." Justice Scalia responded that such deviant practices should be nipped in the bud, lest they become "systemic.")

Justice Scalia castigated the majority for finding ambiguity in a statute having a plain meaning. "This is not a scary math problem," and judges "do not need the cadre of the Court's number-crunching *amici* to guide our way." "The question is: Whose per-pupil expenditures or revenues? Or, in the Court's terminology, what 'population' is assigned the 'characteristic' 'per-pupil expenditure or revenue'? At first blush, second blush, or twenty-second blush, the answer is abundantly clear: local educational agencies. The statute requires the Secretary to 'disregard local educational agencies with' certain per-pupil figures above or below specified percentiles of those per-pupil figures. § 7709(b)(2)(B)(i). The attribute 'per-pupil expenditur[e] or revenu[e]' is assigned to LEAs [local educational agencies] — there is no mention of student population whatsoever. And thus under the statute, 'per-pupil expenditures or revenues' are to be arrayed using a population consisting of LEAs, so that percentiles are determined from a list of (in New Mexico) 89 per-pupil expenditures or revenues representing the 89 LEAs in the State. It is just that simple."

Concurring in the Court's opinion, **Justice Stevens** further opined that he would agree with the majority's interpretation in this case even if were inconsistent with statutory plain meaning. "There is no reason why we must confine ourselves to, or begin our analysis with, the statutory text if other tools of statutory construction provide better evidence of congressional intent with respect to the precise point at issue. As the Court's opinion demonstrates, this is a quintessential example of a case in which the statutory text was obviously enacted to adopt the rule that the Secretary administered both before and after the enactment of the rather confusing language found in 20 U.S.C. § 7709(b)(2)(B)(i). That text is sufficiently ambiguous to justify the Court's exegesis, but my own vote is the product of a more direct route to the Court's patently correct conclusion. This happens to be a case in which the legislative history is pellucidly clear and the statutory text is difficult to fathom." Justice Stevens justified his approach by reference to *Griffin*, where the Court followed statutory plain meaning consistent with its reading of the legislative history, and *Holy Trinity*, where it did not.

The latter reference sparked a further response from **Justice Scalia** (in a portion of his dissent joined by Chief Justice Roberts and Justice Thomas but not Justice Souter). *Holy Trinity*, "that miraculous redeemer of lost causes," is a dangerous precedent. "Thus, what judges believe Congress 'meant' (apart from the text) has a disturbing but entirely unsurprising tendency to be whatever judges think Congress *must* have meant, *i.e., should* have meant. In *Church of the Holy Trinity,* every Justice on this Court disregarded the plain language of a statute that forbade the hiring of a clergyman from abroad because, after all (they thought), 'this is a Christian nation,' so Congress could not have meant what it said. Is there any reason to believe that those Justices were lacking that 'intellectua[l] honest[y]' that Justice Stevens 'presume[s]' all our judges possess? Intellectual honesty does not exclude a blinding intellectual bias. And even if it did, the system of judicial amendatory veto over texts duly adopted by Congress bears no resemblance to the system of lawmaking set forth in our Constitution."

Query: What does this recent dust-up among the Justices tell you about the Court's current practice? Specifically, what is the current status of legislative history? Statutory purpose? The plain meaning rule? *Holy Trinity*?

B. ECONOMIC THEORIES OF STATUTORY INTERPRETATION

Economic theory assumes that individuals are rational actors who seek to maximize their utilities through actions reasonably designed to do so.

Institutions, too, may be rational actors, with their preferences usually determined by the views of the median senator, representative, or judge. Most purely economic theorizing is descriptive, helping us predict the behavior of groups of real people. Consider a simple example of how purely descriptive economic theorizing can enrich your thinking about statutory interpretation.

For most of us, law is prediction of the rules that interacting government institutions will apply to your facts. We ask the IRS, read the newspaper, call a government clerk, note the posted speed limit, or just absorb it by osmosis. Law as prediction also entails evolution through sequential institutional interaction.[r] Congress enacts statutes, agencies interpret and apply those statutes, the judiciary reviews agency actions and interpretations, and Congress periodically considers legislation updating the law or overriding errant interpretations. A consequence of this sequence is that each institution has trumping power. The agency can undo some legislative bargains by stingy enforcement, the Supreme Court can overturn the agency's application, and Congress can override the Court or the agency. Groups press for changes in the law by working the institution most favorable to their interests and then seeking to protect it against trumping by the next institution down the line.

Most of the time, law is in a *stable equilibrium*: none of the institutions wants to change the rule, in part because if any makes that effort it may be overridden by the next institution in the chain. As a weak political actor ("the least dangerous branch"), the Supreme Court usually locates and applies that political equilibrium, as it did in the affirmative action cases (*Weber* and *Johnson*) in Chapter 1, § 3. On the other hand, the equilibrium is often potentially unstable: one actor may be able to change the rule without being overridden. This is what happened in *Griffin*, where the Supreme Court imposed its rule-of-law values on a statute that apparently was understood for decades to embody a less generous compensation rule — and the issue was too conflictual (seafaring unions liking the Court's result, companies not) for Congress to override.

Political scientists and many law professors maintain that judges, especially Supreme Court Justices, also harbor substantive values that they read into statutes when they can.[s] *Casey* can be read as such an effort, for perhaps the

---

r. The model that follows was developed in William Eskridge, Jr. & John Ferejohn, *Politics, Interpretation, and the Rule of Law*, in *The Rule of Law* 265 (Nomos XXXVI, Ian Shapiro ed. 1993); William Eskridge, Jr. & Philip Frickey, *The Supreme Court, 1993 Term — Foreword: Law as Equilibrium*, 108 Harv. L. Rev. 26 (1994). For a different interactive model attempting to explain why interpretive methodology changes over time, see Adrian Vermeule, *The Cycles of Statutory Interpretation*, 68 U. Chi. L. Rev. 149 (2001). Vermeule suggests that legislators and judges develop inconsistent expectations of each other and engage in sequential interaction to affect the other's behavior — for example, judges consult legislative history; legislators notice and abuse the process by skewing the legislative history to affect interpretation; judges notice and stop using legislative history; legislators notice and stop abusing it; judges then start consulting the legislative history because it seems uncontaminated.

s. Lee Epstein & Jack Knight, *The Choices Justices Make* (1998); James Brudney & Corey Ditslear, *Canons of Construction and the Elusive Quest for Neutral Reasoning*, 58 Vand. L. Rev. 1, 6 (2005) (excerpted in Chapter 8, § 1C); Richard Revesz, *Environmental Regulation,*

majority of Justices strongly favor the "American rule" (providing that prevailing plaintiffs does not recover their attorney fees from losing defendants). Although Congress overrode *Casey* and other anti-fee-shifting decisions, the Court still relies on those precedents when the Justices can reasonably expect no override. See *Arlington Central School Board of Education v. Murphy*, 126 S.Ct. 2455 (2006) (narrow interpretation of fee-shifting law benefitting parents of disabled schoolchildren).

Some of these descriptive points, such as the political science view that judges mainly vote their substantive preferences, are controversial (but stubbornly resistant to refutation, we might add). You might maintain a healthy skepticism about the predictive claims of economics-based theories.[t] In the hands of legal scholars and judges, economics-based thinking is more typically harnessed for some kind of normative point. In this part of the chapter, we shall explore three different kinds of normative contributions law and economics might make to statutory interpretation. They draw from economists' *ex ante* approach to rules, from public choice theory, and from cost-benefit analysis.

1. *Ex Ante Approaches to the Debate between Textualists and Contextualists*

Most students, and many professors and judges, respond to "hard cases" from an *ex post* point of view: this result is unfair to or visits needless hardship upon a sympathetic claimant. From an economics point of view, hard cases make bad law because they invite *ex post* decisionmaking, where the judge creates rules and standards that are fair in the particular case — but often have excessive social costs. In law generally, and statutory interpretation particularly, economic theory would valorize an *ex ante* perspective: evaluate a decision or rule based on whether it sets up a rule that will be good for the average case and provides proper incentives for the citizenry — and not because you like its result in a particular case. The same kind of thinking can apply to general theories. What could be more reasonable than Hart and Sacks's notion that interpreters should apply statutes to carry out admirable public-regarding purposes? Some law and economics scholars agree with that.[u] Two prominent econo-judges have staked out dissenting positions.

Ideology, and the D.C. Circuit, 83 Va. L. Rev. 1717 (1997); Jeffrey Segal & Albert Cover, *Ideological Values and the Votes of U.S. Supreme Court Justices*, 83 Am. Pol. Sci. Rev. 557 (1989); Jeffrey Segal, *Separation-of-Powers Games in the Positive Theory of Congress and Courts,* 91 Am. Pol. Sci. Rev. 28-43 (1997).

t. For example, the sharpest predictions of economics-based theories tend to rest upon "strong" (not realistic) assumptions, such as the notion that judges seek to maximize the imposition of their policy views upon the law. If the assumptions are way off base, the predictions will usually be wrong. Economists rejoin: come up with a better theory!

u. Defending the Hart and Sacks approach from an *ex ante* perspective is Jonathan Macey, *Promoting Public-Regarding Legislation Through Statutory Interpretation: An Interest Group Model*, 86 Colum. L. Rev. 223 (1986). Macey argues that interpreting statutes to carry out their *announced* public-regarding purposes will raise the costs of rent-seeking and therefore reduce the costs of government.

William Landes and Richard Posner made an *ex ante* argument for applying original legislative intent in statutory cases, even when such application leads to harsh results. *The Independent Judiciary in an Interest-Group Perspective,* 18 J.L. & Econ. 875 (1976). They argued that judges must be faithful agents reconstructing original deals, not because that is required by the Constitution or the rule of law, but because any other rule would undermine the conditions under which statutes are enacted. *Ex ante*, such an originalist approach gives members of Congress and interest groups sufficient assurance that their deals will be enforced. To the extent that the enforcement of statutory deals is a good thing for our pluralist democracy, this is what judges ought to do. The Landes and Posner approach would consider legislative materials for whatever light they might shed on those deals.

Judge Frank Easterbrook (Posner's former academic and current court of appeals colleague) and Justice Scalia agree with Landes and Posner's *ex ante* way of thinking: the best approach to statutory interpretation is one that reassures citizens, interest groups, and legislators that statutory deals will be respected and enforced; this makes the operation of a pluralist representative government possible. They strenuously reject Landes and Posner's application of this method and maintain that the best evidence of statutory deals is the statutory text, with legislative history likely to mislead.

Treating statutes as contract-like deals is controversial,[v] but assume that this is an apt analogy. Consider how the different dealist theories play out in the following case.[w] Note how the approach Posner takes here is somewhat different than the theory he developed with Landes and reiterated just five years before this case, in Posner, *The Federal Courts: Crisis and Reform* 286-93 (1985).

UNITED STATES v. MARSHALL
United States Court of Appeals for the Seventh Circuit (en banc), 1990
908 F.2d 1312, *aff'd sub nom. Chapman v. United States*, 500 U.S. 453 (1991)

EASTERBROOK, CIRCUIT JUDGE. ~ Scalia would accept.

* * * Stanley J. Marshall was convicted after a bench trial and sentenced to 20 years' imprisonment for conspiring to distribute, and distributing, more than ten grams of LSD, enough for 11,751 doses. Patrick Brumm, Richard L. Chapman, and John M. Schoenecker were convicted by a jury of selling ten sheets (1,000 doses) of paper containing LSD. Because the total weight of the paper and LSD was 5.7 grams, a five-year mandatory minimum applied. The district court sentenced Brumm to 60 months (the minimum), Schoenecker to

---

v. E.g., Mark Movsesian, *Are Statutes Really "Legislative Bargains"? The Failure of the Contract Analogy in Statutory Interpretation,* 76 N.C. L. Rev. 1145 (1998).

w. Consistent with descriptive economic theory, Posner and Easterbrook, both law and economics "conservatives" appointed by President Reagan, vote the same way in the large majority of statutory cases, even if for different reasons. See Daniel Farber, *Do Theories of Statutory Interpretation Matter?*, 94 Nw. U.L. Rev. 1409 (2000). For a more general comparative examination of judicial practice with interpretive theories, see Frank Cross, *The Significance of Statutory Interpretive Methodologies,* 82 Notre Dame L. Rev. 1971 (2007).

63 months, and Chapman to 96 months' imprisonment. All four defendants confine their arguments on appeal to questions concerning their sentences.

The three questions we must resolve are these: (1) Whether 21 U.S.C. § 841(b)(1)(A)(v) and (B)(v), which set mandatory minimum terms of imprisonment — five years for selling more than one gram of a "mixture or substance containing a detectable amount" of LSD, ten years for more than ten grams — exclude the weight of the carrier medium. (2) Whether the weight tables in the sentencing guidelines likewise exclude the weight of any carrier. (3) Whether the statute and the guidelines are unconstitutional to the extent their computations are based on anything other than the weight of the pure drug. * * *

According to the Sentencing Commission, the LSD in an average dose weighs 0.05 milligrams. Twenty thousand pure doses are a gram. But 0.05 mg is almost invisible, so LSD is distributed to retail customers in a carrier. Pure LSD is dissolved in a solvent such as alcohol and sprayed on paper or gelatin; alternatively the paper may be dipped in the solution. After the solvent evaporates, the paper or gel is cut into one-dose squares and sold by the square. Users swallow the squares or may drop them into a beverage, releasing the drug. Although the gelatin and paper are light, they weigh much more than the drug. Marshall's 11,751 doses weighed 113.32 grams; the LSD accounted for only 670.72 mg of this, not enough to activate the five-year mandatory minimum sentence, let alone the ten-year minimum. The ten sheets of blotter paper carrying the 1,000 doses Chapman and confederates sold weighed 5.7 grams; the LSD in the paper did not approach the one-gram threshold for a mandatory minimum sentence. This disparity between the weight of the pure LSD and the weight of LSD-plus-carrier underlies the defendants' arguments.

If the carrier counts in the weight of the "mixture or substance containing a detectable amount" of LSD, some odd things may happen. Weight in the hands of distributors may exceed that of manufacturers and wholesalers. Big fish then could receive paltry sentences or small fish draconian ones. Someone who sold 19,999 doses of pure LSD (at 0.05 mg per dose) would escape the five-year mandatory minimum of § 841(b)(1)(B)(v) and be covered by § 841(b)(1)(C), which lacks a minimum term and has a maximum of "only" 20 years. Someone who sold a single hit of LSD dissolved in a tumbler of orange juice could be exposed to a ten-year mandatory minimum. Retailers could fall in or out of the mandatory terms depending not on the number of doses but on the medium: sugar cubes weigh more than paper, which weighs more than gelatin. One way to eliminate the possibility of such consequences is to say that the carrier is not a "mixture or substance containing a detectable amount" of the drug. Defendants ask us to do this.

Defendants' submission starts from the premise that the interaction of the statutory phrase "mixture or substance" with the distribution of LSD by the dose in a carrier creates a unique probability of surprise results. The premise may be unwarranted. The paper used to distribute LSD is light stuff, not the kind used to absorb ink. Chapman's 1,000 doses weighed about 0.16 ounces. More than 6,000 doses, even in blotter paper, weigh less than an ounce. Because the LSD in one dose weighs about 0.05 milligrams, the combination of LSD-plus-paper is about 110 times the weight of the LSD. The impregnated paper could be described as "0.9% LSD". * * *

This is by no means an unusual dilution rate for illegal drugs. Heroin sold on the street is 2% to 3% opiate and the rest filler. Sometimes the mixture is even more dilute, approaching the dilution rate for LSD in blotter paper. Heroin and crack cocaine, like LSD, are sold on the streets by the dose, although they are sold by weight higher in the distributional chain. * * *

It is not possible to construe the words of § 841 to make the penalty turn on the net weight of the drug rather than the gross weight of carrier and drug. The statute speaks of "mixture or substance containing a detectable amount" of a drug. "Detectable amount" is the opposite of "pure"; the point of the statute is that the "mixture" is not to be converted to an equivalent amount of pure drug.

The structure of the statute reinforces this conclusion. The 10-year minimum applies to any person who possesses, with intent to distribute, "100 grams or more of phencyclidine (PCP) or 1 kilogram or more of a mixture or substance containing a detectable amount of phencyclidine (PCP)", § 841(b)(1)(A)(iv). Congress distinguished the pure drug from a "mixture or substance containing a detectable amount of" it. All drugs other than PCP are governed exclusively by the "mixture or substance" language. Even brute force cannot turn that language into a reference to pure LSD. Congress used the same "mixture or substance" language to describe heroin, cocaine, amphetamines, and many other drugs that are sold after being cut — sometimes as much as LSD. There is no sound basis on which to treat the words "substance or mixture containing a detectable amount of", repeated verbatim for every drug mentioned in § 841 except PCP, as *different* things for LSD and cocaine although the language is identical, while treating the "mixture or substance" language as meaning the *same* as the reference to pure PCP in 21 U.S.C. § 841(b)(1)(A)(iv) and (B)(iv).

Although the "mixture or substance" language shows that the statute cannot be limited to pure LSD, it does not necessarily follow that blotter paper *is* a "mixture or substance containing" LSD. That phrase cannot include all "carriers". One gram of crystalline LSD in a heavy glass bottle is still only one gram of "statutory LSD". So is a gram of LSD being "carried" in a Boeing 747. How much mingling of the drug with something else is essential to form a "mixture or substance"? The legislative history is silent, but ordinary usage is indicative.

"Substance" may well refer to a chemical compound, or perhaps to a drug in a solvent. LSD does not react chemically with sugar, blotter paper, or gelatin, and none of these is a solvent. "Mixture" is more inclusive. Cocaine often is mixed with mannitol, quinine, or lactose. These white powders do not react, but it is common ground that a cocaine-mannitol mixture is a statutory "mixture".

LSD and blotter paper are not commingled in the same way as cocaine and lactose. What is the nature of their association? The possibility most favorable to defendants is that LSD sits on blotter paper as oil floats on water. Immiscible substances may fall outside the statutory definition of "mixture". The possibility does not assist defendants — not on this record, anyway. LSD is applied to paper in a solvent; after the solvent evaporates, a tiny quantity of LSD remains. Because the fibers absorb the alcohol, the LSD solidifies inside the paper rather than on it. You cannot pick a grain of LSD off the surface of the paper. Ordinary parlance calls the paper containing tiny crystals of LSD a mixture.

United States v. Rose, 881 F.2d 386 (7th Cir. 1989), like every other appellate decision that has addressed the question, concludes that the carrier medium for LSD, like the "cut" for heroin and cocaine, is a "mixture or substance containing a detectable amount" of the drug. Although a chemist might be able to offer evidence bearing on the question whether LSD and blotter paper "mix" any more fully than do oil and water, the record contains no such evidence. Without knowing more of the chemistry than this record reveals, we adhere to the unanimous conclusion of the other courts of appeals that blotter paper treated with LSD is a "mixture or substance containing a detectable quantity of" LSD.

Two reasons have been advanced to support a contrary conclusion: that statutes should be construed to avoid constitutional problems, and that some members of the sitting Congress are dissatisfied with basing penalties on the combined weight of LSD and carrier. Neither is persuasive.

A preference for giving statutes a constitutional meaning is a reason to construe, not to rewrite or "improve". * * * "[S]ubstance or mixture containing a detectable quantity" is not ambiguous. * * * Neither the rule of lenity nor the preference for avoiding constitutional adjudication justifies disregarding unambiguous language.

The canon about avoiding constitutional decisions, in particular, must be used with care, for it is a closer cousin to invalidation than to interpretation. It is a way to enforce the constitutional penumbra, and therefore an aspect of constitutional law proper. Constitutional decisions breed penumbras, which multiply questions. Treating each as justification to construe laws out of existence too greatly enlarges the judicial power. And heroic "construction" is unnecessary, given our conclusion [in discussion omitted here] that Congress possesses the constitutional power to set penalties on the basis of gross weight.

As for the pending legislation: subsequent debates are not a ground for avoiding the import of enactments. Although the views of a subsequent Congress are entitled to respect, ongoing debates do not represent the views of Congress. * * *

CUMMINGS, CIRCUIT JUDGE, with whom BAUER, CHIEF JUDGE, and WOOD, JR., CUDAHY, and POSNER, CIRCUIT JUDGES, join, dissenting.

[T]he United States District Court for the District of Columbia held that blotter paper was not a mixture or substance within the meaning of the statute. *United States v Healy*, 729 F.Supp. 140 (D.D.C. 1990). The court relied not only on ordinary dictionary definitions of the words mixture and substance but also on a November 30, 1988, Sentencing Commission publication, entitled

"Questions Most Frequently Asked About the Sentencing Guidelines," which states that the Commission has not taken a position on whether the blotter paper should be weighed. The conclusion that the Commission has not yet resolved this question is further supported by a Sentencing Commission Notice issued on March 3, 1989, which requested public comments on whether the Commission should exclude the weight of the carrier for sentencing purposes in LSD cases.[3]

The *Healy* court also stated that Congress could have intended the words "mixture or substance" to refer to the liquid in which the pure LSD is dissolved. Finally, the *Healy* court relied on a Guidelines table designed to provide a sentencing court with an equivalent weight for sentencing purposes in cases in which the number of doses distributed is known but the actual weight is unknown. The table provides that a dose of LSD weighs .05 milligrams. Guidelines § 2D1.1, Commentary, Drug Equivalency Tables. This weight closely approximates the weight of one dose of LSD without blotter paper, but is not an accurate reflection of one dose with blotter paper. * * *

Two subsequent pieces of legislative history * * * shed some light on this question. In a letter to Senator Joseph R. Biden, Jr., dated April 26, 1989, the Chairman of the Sentencing Commission, William W. Wilkens, Jr., noted the ambiguity in the statute as it is currently written:

> With respect to LSD, it is unclear whether Congress intended the carrier to be considered as a packaging material, or, since it is commonly consumed along with the illicit drug, as a dilutant ingredient in the drug mixture . . . . The Commission suggests that Congress may wish to further consider the LSD carrier issue in order to clarify legislative intent as to whether the weight of the carrier should or should not be considered in determining the quantity of LSD mixture for punishment purposes.

Presumably acting in response to this query, Senator Biden added to the Congressional Record for October 5, 1989, an analysis of one of a series of technical corrections to 21 U.S.C. § 841 that were under consideration by the Senate that day. This analysis states that the purpose of the particular correction at issue was to remove an unintended "inequity" from Section 841 caused by the decisions of some courts to include the weight of the blotter paper for sentencing purposes in LSD cases. According to Senator Biden, the correction "remedie[d] this inequity by removing the weight of the carrier from the calculation of the weight of the mixture or substance." This correction was adopted as part of Amendment No. 976 to S. 1711. 135 Cong.Rec. S12749 (daily ed. Oct. 5, 1989). The amended bill was passed by a unanimous vote of the Senate (*id.* at S12765) and is currently pending before the House.

Comments in more recent issues of the Congressional Record indicate that S. 1711 is not expected to pass the House of Representatives. See 136

---

3. The Commission has recently adopted several amendments and sent them to Congress for approval. Among these is an amendment to Application Note 11 to Guidelines Section 2D1.1. This amendment specifically states that the typical weight per dose of LSD that is given in the Weight Per Dose Table as .05 milligrams is the weight of the LSD alone and not of the LSD combined with any carrier. 55 Fed.Reg. 19197 (May 8, 1990). * * *

Cong.Rec. S943 (daily ed. Feb. 7, 1990). In the meantime, however, a second attempt to clarify Congress' intent in amending 21 U.S.C. § 841 to include the words mixture or substance has now been introduced in the Senate. On April 18, 1990, Senator Kennedy introduced an amendment to S. 1970 (a bill establishing constitutional procedures for the imposition of the death penalty) seeking to clarify the language of 21 U.S.C. § 841. That amendment, Amendment No. 1716, states:

> Section 841(b)(1) of title 21, United States Code, is amended by inserting the following new subsection at the end thereof: "(E) In determining the weight of a 'mixture or substance' under this section, the court shall not include the weight of the carrier upon which the controlled substance is placed, or by which it is transported."

136 Cong.Rec. S7069 (daily ed. May 24, 1990).

[Judge Cummings argued from this evidence that the draconian penalty scheme for LSD was simply a mistake never intended by Congress and that the Seventh Circuit should follow *Healy*.]

POSNER, CIRCUIT JUDGE, joined by BAUER, CHIEF JUDGE, and CUMMINGS, WOOD, JR., and CUDAHY, CIRCUIT JUDGES, dissenting.

* * * Based as it is on weight, [the § 841 sentencing scheme] works well for drugs that are sold by weight; and ordinarily the weight quoted to the buyer is the weight of the dilute form, although of course price will vary with purity. The dilute form is the product, and it is as natural to punish its purveyors according to the weight of the product as it is to punish moonshiners by the weight or volume of the moonshine they sell rather than by the weight of the alcohol contained in it. So, for example, under Florida law it is a felony to possess one or more gallons of moonshine, and a misdemeanor to possess less than one gallon, regardless of the alcoholic content. Fla.Stat. §§ 561.01, 562.451.

LSD, however, is sold to the consumer by the dose; it is not cut, diluted, or mixed with something else. Moreover, it is incredibly light. An average dose of LSD weighs .05 milligrams, which is less than two millionths of an ounce. To ingest something that small requires swallowing something much larger. Pure LSD in granular form is first diluted by being dissolved, usually in alcohol, and then a quantity of the solution containing one dose of LSD is sprayed or eyedropped on a sugar cube, or on a cube of gelatin, or, as in the cases before us, on an inch-square section of "blotter" paper. * * * After the solution is applied to the carrier medium, the alcohol or other solvent evaporates, leaving an invisible (and undiluted) spot of pure LSD on the cube or blotter paper. The consumer drops the cube or the piece of paper into a glass of water, or orange juice, or some other beverage, causing the LSD to dissolve in the beverage, which is then drunk. * * * [A] quart of orange juice containing one dose of LSD is not more, in any relevant sense, than a pint of juice containing the same one dose, and it would be loony to punish the purveyor of the quart more heavily than the purveyor of the pint. It would be like basing the punishment for selling cocaine on the combined weight of the cocaine and of the vehicle (plane, boat, automobile, or whatever) used to transport it or the syringe used to inject it or the pipe used to smoke it. The blotter paper, sugar cubes, etc. are the vehicles for conveying LSD to the consumer.

The weight of the carrier is vastly greater than that of the LSD, as well as irrelevant to its potency. There is no comparable disparity between the pure and the mixed form (if that is how we should regard LSD on blotter paper or other carrier medium) with respect to the other drugs in section 841, with the illuminating exception of PCP. There Congress specified alternative weights, for the drug itself and for the substance or mixture containing the drug. For example, the five-year minimum sentence for a seller of PCP requires the sale of either ten grams of the drug itself or one hundred grams of a substance or mixture containing the drug. 21 U.S.C. § 841(b)(1)(B)(iv).

Ten sheets of blotter paper, containing a thousand doses of LSD, weigh almost six grams. The LSD itself weighs less than a hundredth as much. If the thousand doses are on gelatin cubes instead of sheets of blotter paper, the total weight is less, but it is still more than two grams, which is forty times the weight of the LSD. In both cases, if the carrier plus the LSD constitutes the relevant "substance or mixture" (the crucial "if" in this case), the dealer is subject to the minimum mandatory sentence of five years. One of the defendants before us (Marshall) sold almost 12,000 doses of LSD on blotter paper. This subjected him to the ten-year minimum, and the Guidelines then took over and pushed him up to twenty years. Since it takes 20,000 doses of LSD to equal a gram, Marshall would not have been subject to even the five-year mandatory minimum had he sold the LSD in its pure form. And a dealer who sold fifteen times the number of doses as Marshall — 180,000 — would not be subject to the ten-year mandatory minimum sentence if he sold the drug in its pure form, because 180,000 doses is only nine grams.

At the other extreme, if Marshall were not a dealer at all but dropped a square of blotter paper containing a single dose of LSD into a glass of orange juice and sold it to a friend at cost (perhaps 35 cents), he would be subject to the ten-year minimum. The juice with LSD dissolved in it would be the statutory mixture or substance containing a detectable amount of the illegal drug and it would weigh more than ten grams (one ounce is about 35 grams, and the orange juice in a glass of orange juice weighs several ounces). So a person who sold one dose of LSD might be subject to the ten-year mandatory minimum sentence while a dealer who sold 199,999 doses in pure form would be subject only to the five-year minimum. Defendant Dean sold 198 doses, crowded onto one sheet of blotter paper: this subjected him to the five-year mandatory minimum, too, since the ensemble weighed slightly more than a gram. * * *

All this seems crazy but we must consider whether Congress might have had a reason for wanting to key the severity of punishment for selling LSD to the weight of the carrier rather than to the number of doses or to some reasonable proxy for dosage (as weight is, for many drugs). The only one suggested is that it might be costly to determine the weight of the LSD in the blotter paper, sugar cube, etc., because it is so light! That merely underscores the irrationality of basing the punishment for selling this drug on weight rather than on dosage. But in fact the weight is reported in every case I have seen, so apparently it can

Similarly situated people to be treated Similarly

be determined readily enough; it *has* to be determined in any event, to permit a purity adjustment under the Guidelines. If the weight of the LSD is difficult to determine, the difficulty is easily overcome by basing punishment on the number of doses, which makes much more sense in any event. To base punishment on the weight of the carrier medium makes about as much sense as basing punishment on the weight of the defendant. * * *

This is a quilt the pattern whereof no one has been able to discern. The legislative history is silent, and since even the Justice Department cannot explain the why of the punishment scheme that it is defending, the most plausible inference is that Congress simply did not realize how LSD is sold. The inference is reinforced by the statutory treatment of PCP. * * *

[The] irrationality is magnified when we compare the sentences for people who sell other drugs prohibited by 21 U.S.C. § 841. Marshall, remember, sold fewer than 12,000 doses and was sentenced to twenty years. Twelve thousand doses sounds like a lot, but to receive a comparable sentence for selling heroin Marshall would have had to sell ten kilograms, which would yield between one and two million doses. To receive a comparable sentence for selling cocaine he would have had to sell fifty kilograms, which would yield anywhere from 325,000 to five million doses. While the corresponding weight is lower for crack — half a kilogram — this still translates into 50,000 doses. * * *

Course in 3 Paragraphs

Well, what if anything can we judges do about this mess? The answer lies in the shadow of a jurisprudential disagreement that is not less important by virtue of being unavowed by most judges. It is the disagreement between the severely positivistic view that the content of law is exhausted in clear, explicit, and definite enactments by or under express delegation from legislatures, and the natural lawyer's or legal pragmatist's view that the practice of interpretation and the general terms of the Constitution (such as "equal protection of the laws") authorize judges to enrich positive law with the moral values and practical concerns of civilized society. Judges who in other respects have seemed quite similar, such as Holmes and Cardozo, have taken opposite sides of this issue. Neither approach is entirely satisfactory. The first buys political neutrality and a type of objectivity at the price of substantive injustice, while the second buys justice in the individual case at the price of considerable uncertainty and, not infrequently, judicial willfulness. It is no wonder that our legal system oscillates between the approaches. The positivist view, applied unflinchingly to this case, commands the affirmance of prison sentences that are exceptionally harsh by the standards of the modern Western world, dictated by an accidental, unintended scheme of punishment nevertheless implied by the words (taken one by one) of the relevant enactments. The natural law or pragmatist view leads to a freer interpretation, one influenced by norms of equal treatment; and let us explore the interpretive possibilities here. One is to interpret "mixture or substance containing a detectable amount of [LSD]" to exclude the carrier medium — the blotter paper, sugar or gelatin cubes, and orange juice or other beverage. That is the course we rejected in *United States v Rose, supra*, as have the other circuits. I wrote *Rose*, but I am no longer confident that its literal interpretation of the statute, under which the blotter paper, cubes, etc. are "substances" that "contain" LSD, is inevitable. The blotter paper, etc. are better viewed, I now think, as carriers, like the package in which a kilo of cocaine comes wrapped or the bottle in which a fifth of liquor is sold.

Interpreted to exclude the carrier, the punishment schedule for LSD would make perfectly good sense; it would not warp the statutory design. The comparison with heroin and cocaine is again illuminating. The statute imposes the five-year mandatory minimum sentence on anyone who sells a substance or mixture containing a hundred grams of heroin, equal to 10,000 to 20,000 doses. One gram of pure LSD, which also would trigger the five-year minimum, yields 20,000 doses. The comparable figures for cocaine are 3250 to 50,000 doses, placing LSD in about the middle. So Congress may have wanted to base punishment for the sale of LSD on the weight of the pure drug after all, using one and ten grams of the pure drug to trigger the five-year and ten-year minima (and corresponding maxima — twenty years and forty years). This interpretation leaves "substance or mixture containing" without a referent, so far as LSD is concerned. But we must remember that Congress used the identical term in each subsection that specifies the quantity of a drug that subjects the seller to the designated minimum and maximum punishments. In thus automatically including the same term in each subsection, Congress did not necessarily affirm that, for each and every drug covered by the statute, a substance or mixture containing the drug *must* be found.

The flexible interpretation that I am proposing is decisively strengthened by the constitutional objection to basing punishment of LSD offenders on the weight of the carrier medium rather than on the weight of the LSD. Courts often do interpretive handsprings to avoid having even to *decide* a constitutional question. In doing so they expand, very questionably in my view, the effective scope of the Constitution, creating a constitutional penumbra in which statutes wither, shrink, are deformed. A better case for flexible interpretation is presented when the alternative is to nullify Congress's action: when in other words there is not merely a constitutional question about, but a constitutional barrier to, the statute when interpreted literally. This is such a case.

[Judge Posner then argued that the sentencing scheme for LSD upheld by the majority violates the equal protection guarantee of the Fifth Amendment's due process clause, because of the "unequal treatment of people equally situated." That even the Justice Department cannot formulate a rational basis for the distinctions it has drawn from § 841 in LSD cases is persuasive evidence that Congress has to be sent back to the drawing board.]

The literal interpretation adopted by the majority is not inevitable. All interpretation is contextual. The words of the statute — interpreted against a background that includes a constitutional norm of equal treatment, a (closely related) constitutional commitment to rationality, an evident failure by both Congress and the Sentencing Commission to consider how LSD is actually produced, distributed, and sold, and an equally evident failure by the same two bodies to consider the interaction between heavy mandatory minimum sentences and the Sentencing Guidelines — will bear an interpretation that distinguishes between the carrier vehicle of the illegal drug and the substance or mixture containing a detectable amount of the drug. The punishment of the crack dealer is not determined by the weight of the glass tube in which he sells the crack; we should not lightly attribute to Congress a purpose of punishing the dealer in LSD according to the weight of the LSD carrier. We should not make Congress's handiwork an embarrassment to the members of Congress and to us.

NOTES ON THE LSD CASE AND *EX ANTE* THINKING

1. *Review: The New Textualism in Action.* Judge Easterbrook's opinion in the LSD case is an excellent example of the distinctive features of the new textualism: (a) focus on the text of the statute, including not just the plain meaning of the provision at issue, but also how that provision fits into the "whole statute"; (b) a rejection of, and some contempt for, legislative history as a context for interpreting the statute; and (c) a relatively black-and-white vision of what words mean. Note that judges on the Seventh Circuit were in sharp disagreement about whether LSD on blotter paper is a "mixture." Should the very fact of good-faith disagreement about the law's plain meaning be evidence that the statute has no plain meaning (as Professor Stephen Ross has suggested to us)?

In affirming *Marshall*, the Justices of the Supreme Court were also divided as to what "mixture" meant in the LSD sentencing law. See *Chapman v. United States*, 500 U.S. 453 (1991). While Judge Easterbrook relied on "ordinary usage" to define "mixture," Chief Justice Rehnquist's opinion for the Supreme Court relied on a dictionary definition of mixture as "two substances blended together so that the particles of one are diffused among the particles of the other." Because the LSD "is diffused among the fibers of the paper," the Chief Justice found a statutory plain meaning. This might be called a denotative approach to plain meaning: Apply the dictionary definition and see if it fits.

Professional linguists don't approach meaning in this way. They are willing to expand and contract meaning beyond its dictionary denotations. Words reflect categories which are fuzzy at the margins; the necessary and sufficient conditions for membership in the category are not completely accessible to us before the fact. Lawrence Solan, a Ph.D. linguist, in *When Judges Use the Dictionary*, 68 Am. Speech 50, 54–55 (1993), analyzes the *Marshall* case in this way:

> Calling the blotter paper impregnated with LSD a mixture seems odd for the same reason that it seems odd to call a pancake soaked with syrup *a pancake-syrup mixture*; or to call a wet towel *a water-cotton mixture*; or to call a towel that one has used to dry one's face during a tennis game *a cotton-sweat mixture*, or later, after the sweat has dried, *a cotton-salt mixture*. The last two I would call *a wet towel* and *a dirty towel*, respectively. In all of these examples, both substances have kept their character in a chemical sense, but one of the substances seems to have kept too much of its character for us to feel natural using the term *mixture*. * * *

> As an analytical matter, the Supreme Court in *Chapman* has erred by taking a concept that is fuzzy at the margins and substituting for it a definition that is subject to more refined application than the concept itself. * * *

If the new textualists cannot satisfy professional linguists with their insistence that a statute has a "plain meaning," what legitimacy does their approach offer? Recall that people's personal liberty (the terms of their incarceration) depended upon this semantic debate. On the other hand, is there some necessary reason why judicial and linguistic interpreters must agree on methodology?[x]

2. *Liberty versus* Ex Ante *Thinking?* Judge Easterbrook's first major article on interpretation urged that statutes not be construed beyond the "domain" clearly demarcated by their texts. He defended this approach on the basis of a libertarian presumption akin to the standard Chicago School idea that most things should not be regulated by the state and should be left to the free operation of the market:

> Those who wrote and approved the Constitution thought that most social relations would be governed by private agreements, customs, and understandings, not resolved in the halls of government. There is still at least a presumption that people's arrangements prevail unless expressly displaced by legal doctrine. All things are permitted unless there is some contrary rule. It is easier for an agency to justify the revocation of rules (or simple nonregulation) than the creation of new rules.

Easterbrook, *Statutes' Domains*, 50 U. Chi. L. Rev. 533, 549–50 (1983). Note that the libertarian position in *Marshall* is the one taken by Judges Cummings and Posner, not that of Judge Easterbrook, who sends the defendants into confinement for a long period of time. (The same is true for a new textualist approach to *Holy Trinity*; as it involves an issue of procedure.)

Consider an *ex ante* counterargument: a textualism that yields harsh results, as in the LSD case, sends a signal to judges that they should be careful not to make policy — and to Congress that its statutes will be interpreted "as written," and that any updating or fixing will have to be done by the legislators themselves. If they adopt the "tough love" of the new textualism, as Judge Keen argued in Speluncean Explorers, courts will actually enhance democracy and legislative accountability. Everyone will know that Congress, alone, is responsible for statutory applications, and voters can act accordingly. (Justice Scalia suggests such an argument in his Tanner Lectures, *supra*, and in some judicial opinions.) A problem is that there is no evidence that such tough love will have any effect on Congress, and knowledgeable commentators are skeptical. Professor James Brudney argues from the nature and structure of the politics of legislation that Congress cannot enact statutes with the degree of specification Justice Scalia would require.[y] An implication of Brudney's idea is that the new textualism has a likely libertarian effect (by reducing Congress' practical capacity to regulate), bringing us back to Judge Easterbrook's point in *Statute's Domain*.

3. Ex Ante *Arguments for an Approach that Considers Fairness.* Judge Posner is not considered a bleeding-heart liberal — the classic *ex post* position

---

x. For more on the use of dictionaries, see the notes following *Casey* and *Chisom, supra.*

y. James Brudney, *Congressional Commentary on Judicial Interpretations of Statutes: Idle Chatter or Telling Response?*, 93 Mich. L. Rev. 1 (1994).

— yet he voted to overturn the conviction. And he did so for reasons that go well beyond the original legislative intent approach he championed in the 1985 edition of *The Federal Courts*. Since 1990, Judge Posner has come completely out of the closet as a flexible pragmatic interpreter of statutes.[z]

There are some economic arguments for a more flexible approach than the one followed by the en banc majority. One is that a relentless textualism will undermine rather than cultivate the conditions for legislation: because deals will not be reasonably enforced, legislators will be more reluctant to make them; legislators might even lose confidence that the judiciary can be trusted to carry out statutes in a fair way. Another *ex ante* argument is that an unreasonable construction of the LSD law also undermines the overall legitimacy of our system of criminal justice (the small fry like Mr. Marshall are being treated really unfairly; many of those arrested are people of color), without any discernible offsetting benefit to criminal justice (such as increased deterrence). Congress has not shown enormous wisdom in this area, and if any institution is going to act responsibly it must be the judiciary.

A New LSD Problem

Problem 7–6. In 1993, the Sentencing Commission revised the method for calculating the weight of LSD for Sentencing Guideline purposes. Abandoning its former approach of weighing the entire blotter paper containing LSD, the amended Guideline told courts to give each dose of LSD on a carrier medium a presumed weight of 0.4 mg. U.S. Sentencing Comm'n, U.S. Sentencing Guidelines Manual § 2D1.1(c), n.* (H). The new method was retroactive.

Meirl Neal was sentenced to 192 months in prison for selling 11,456 doses of LSD on blotter paper. He moved to have his sentence reduced to between 70 and 87 months, the Guideline period for sale of 4.58 grams of LSD (11,456 times 0.4 mg). The Government argued that Neal should serve at least 120 months, because of the mandatory minimum sentence required by 21 U.S.C. § 841(b)(1)(A)(v), as interpreted in *Marshall/Chapman*. Neal argued that the blotter paper should now not be counted for purposes of the mandatory minimum, just as it is now not counted for purposes of setting the ordinary sentence. Should the courts have accepted Neal's argument and reduced his sentence? See *Neal v. United States*, 516 U.S. 284 (1996).

2. Advancing Public-Regarding Goals and Minimizing Rent-Seeking

Public choice theory is the application of economic principles to actions by the state. One conclusion reached by some public choice theorists, developed in Chapter 1, § 2, is that an interest-group-driven legislative process produces too few public-regarding statutes (i.e., those broadly distributing benefits as well as costs) and too many rent-seeking statutes (i.e., those distributing

---

z. Richard Posner, *The Problems of Jurisprudence* (1990); *Overcoming Law* (1995); and *How Judges Think* (2008). See also John Manning, *Statutory Pragmatism and Constitutional Structure*, 120 Harv. L. Rev. 1161 (2007) (evaluating Posner's approach from textualist perspective).

benefits to a small group, at the expense of the general public, and without an efficiency justification).

Frank Easterbrook, *The Supreme Court, 1983 Term — Foreword: The Court and the Economic System*, 98 Harv. L. Rev. 4, 14–15 (1984), suggested a general interpretive strategy for the judiciary to respond to this asymmetry:

> * * * There are two basic styles of statutory construction. In one the judge starts with the statute, attributes to it certain purposes (evils to be redressed), and then brings within the statute the class of activities that produce the same or similar objectionable results. The statute's reach goes on expanding so long as there are unredressed objectionable results. The judge interprets omissions and vague terms in the statute as evidence of want of time or foresight and fills in these gaps with more in the same vein. The maxim "Remedial statutes are to be liberally construed" sums up this approach.
>
> In the other approach the judge treats the statute as a contract. He first identifies the contracting parties and then seeks to discover what they resolved and what they left unresolved. For example, he may conclude that a statute regulating the price of fluid milk is a pact between milk producers and milk handlers designed to cut back output and raise price, to the benefit of both at the expense of consumers. A judge then implements the bargain as a faithful agent but without enthusiasm; asked to extend the scope of a back-room deal, he refuses unless the proof of the deal's scope is compelling. Omissions are evidence that no bargain was struck: some issues were left for the future, or perhaps one party was unwilling to pay the price of a resolution in its favor. Sometimes the compromise may be to toss an issue to the courts for resolution, but this too is a term of the bargain, to be demonstrated rather than presumed. What the parties did not resolve, the court should not resolve either. The maxim "Statutes in derogation of the common law are to be strictly construed" sums up this approach.
>
> These maxims are useless as guides to construction; every remedial statute is in derogation of the common law. Yet this hopeless conflict of maxims does not justify despair. The appropriate treatment of statutes depends on how they come to be and what they are for. A judge cannot set about rearranging economic relations on the basis of an ambiguous statute without first resolving a question about the nature of legislation. If statutes generally are designed to overcome "failures" in markets and to replace the calamities produced by unguided private conduct with the ordered rationality of the public sector, then it makes sense to use the remedial approach to the construction of statutes — or at least most of them. If, on the other hand, statutes often are designed to replace the outcomes of private transactions with monopolistic ones, to transfer the profits ("rents") of productive activity to a privileged few, then judges should take the beady-eyed contractual approach. The warehouseman does not deliver the grain without seeing the receipt, and so too with goodies dispensed by judges.

See also Jonathan Macey, *Promoting Public-Regarding Legislation Through Statutory Interpretation: An Interest Group Model*, 86 Colum. L. Rev. 223 (1986), who argues that public-interest statutes ought to be liberally interpreted by reference to their announced purposes. By raising the costs of rent-seeking, judges can contribute to the public welfare.

The Table below suggests the risks entailed in various kinds of statutes, together with counter-strategies courts could follow in applying those statutes.

Consider the application of this kind of thinking to cases like *Weber*, the affirmative action case in Chapter 1, § 3, and to the cases in this chapter. For example, into which quadrant would the alien contract labor law of *Holy Trinity* fit? If quadrant one, the Court's stingy construction becomes less defensible — but there is good reason to think the law was purely rent-seeking: unions were seeking to restrict the supply of labor so as to bid up wages in certain occupations. Congress has the power to enact such laws, but the Court ought not apply them beyond the original statutory target.

Table of Interpretive Strategies for Different Kinds of Laws

[1] Distributed Benefit/Distributed Cost Laws (General Interest)

Danger: These laws are usually in the public interest, but the legislature will often fail to update them as society and the underlying problem change.

Response: Courts can expand the law to new situations and develop it in common law fashion, subject to the limits imposed by the statutory text.

[2] Distributed Benefit/Concentrated Cost Laws

Danger: Regulated groups will tend to evade their statutory duties and press to "capture" the agency created to administer the law.

Response: Courts can monitor agency enforcement and private compliance, and open up procedures to assure excluded groups are heard. Courts can press the agency to be faithful to the stated public-regarding goal of the law.

[3] Concentrated Benefit/Distributed Cost Laws (Rent-Seeking)

Danger: Rent-seeking by special interest groups at the expense of the general public.

Response: Courts ought to construe the law narrowly to minimize the unwarranted benefits. Hold the statute to its public-regarding justifications.

[4] Concentrated Benefit/Concentrated Cost Laws

Danger: The statutory deal may grow unexpectedly lopsided over time.

Response: Do not attempt much judicial updating, unless affected groups are not able to get the legislature's attention.

Source: William Eskridge, Jr., *Politics Without Romance: Implications of Public Choice Theory for Statutory Interpretation*, 74 Va. L. Rev. 275, 325 (1988).

Consider how this kind of thinking applies to the following case.

PEREZ v. WYETH LABORATORIES, INC.
New Jersey Supreme Court, 1999
734 A.2d 1245

O'HERN, J., writing for a majority of the Court.

[Norplant is an FDA-approved, reversible contraceptive that prevents pregnancy for up to five years. Wyeth began a massive advertising campaign for Norplant in 1991, which it directed at women rather than at their doctors. Wyeth advertised on television and in women's magazines. None of the advertisements warned of any dangers or side effects associated with Norplant, but rather praised its convenience and simplicity. In 1995, several women filed lawsuits in various New Jersey counties claiming injuries that resulted from their use of Norplant. Their principal claim was that Wyeth failed to warn adequately about the side effects associated with the contraceptive, including weight gain, headaches, dizziness, nausea, diarrhea, acne, vomiting, fatigue, facial hair growth, numbness in the arms and legs, irregular menstruation, hair loss, leg cramps, anxiety and nervousness, vision problems, anemia, mood swings and depression, high blood pressure, and removal complications that resulted in scarring.

[Perez sought a determination of whether the "learned intermediary" doctrine applied. This doctrine generally relieves a pharmaceutical manufacturer of an independent duty to warn the ultimate user of prescription drugs, so long as it has supplied the physician with information about a drug's dangerous propensities and risks. The assumption of the doctrine is that the doctor will play the key role in informing and counseling the patient about the risks. Holding the doctrine applicable by reason of the New Jersey Products Liability Act, NJSA 2A:58C–1 to –11, the trial court dismissed those plaintiffs' complaints, concluding that even when a manufacturer advertises directly to the public, and a woman is influenced by the advertising campaign, a physician nevertheless retains the duty to weigh the benefits and risks associated with a drug before deciding whether the drug is appropriate for the patient.]

Our medical-legal jurisprudence is based on images of health care that no longer exist. At an earlier time, medical advice was received in the doctor's office from a physician who most likely made house calls if needed. The patient usually paid a small sum of money to the doctor. Neighborhood pharmacists compounded prescribed medicines. Without being pejorative, it is safe to say that the prevailing attitude of law and medicine was that the "doctor knows best."

Pharmaceutical manufacturers never advertised their products to patients, but rather directed all sales efforts at physicians. In this comforting setting, the law created an exception to the traditional duty of manufacturers to warn consumers directly of risks associated with the product as long as they warned health-care providers of those risks.

For good or ill, that has all changed. Medical services are in large measure provided by managed care organizations. Medicines are purchased in the pharmacy department of supermarkets and often paid for by third-party providers. Drug manufacturers now directly advertise products to consumers on the radio, television, the Internet, billboards on public transportation, and in magazines.

[New Jersey has accepted the learned intermediary doctrine as a defense in tort suits against drug companies, e.g., *Niemiera v. Schneider*, 114 N.J. 550, 559, 555 A.2d 1112 (1989). In light of the recent trend of mass-marketing drugs directly to consumers, see Jon D. Hanson & Douglas A. Kysar, *Taking Behavioralism Seriously: Some Evidence of Market Manipulation*, 112 Harv. L. Rev. 1420, 1456 (1999), the court was faced with the question whether the learned intermediary doctrine should still apply to such drugs, like Norplant.]

[T]he New Jersey Products Liability Act provides:

An adequate product warning or instruction is one that a reasonably prudent person in the same or similar circumstances would have provided with respect to the danger and that communicates adequate information on the dangers and safe use of the product, taking into account the characteristics of, and the ordinary knowledge common to, the persons by whom the product is intended to be used, or in the case of prescription drugs, taking into account the characteristics of, and the ordinary knowledge common to, the prescribing physician. If the warning or instruction given in connection with a drug or device or food or food additive has been approved or prescribed by the federal Food and Drug Administration under the "Federal Food, Drug, and Cosmetic Act," 52 Stat. 1040, 21 U.S.C. § 301 et seq., . . . a rebuttable presumption shall arise that the warning or instruction is adequate . . . .

N.J.S.A. 2A:58C–4.

The Senate Judiciary Committee Statement that accompanied L. 1987, c. 197 recites: "The subsection contains a general definition of an adequate warning and a special definition for warnings that accompany prescription drugs, since, in the case of prescription drugs, the warning is owed to the physician." See N.J.S.A. 2A:58C–1 (providing the Committee Statement). At oral argument, counsel for Wyeth was candid to acknowledge that he could not "point to a sentence in the statute" that would make the learned intermediary doctrine applicable to the manufacturers' direct marketing of drugs, but rather relied on the Committee Statement. Although the statute provides a physician-based standard for determining the adequacy of the warning due to a physician, the statute does not legislate the boundaries of the doctrine. For example, the Act does not purport to repeal a holding such as *Davis v. Wyeth Labs*, [399 F.2d 121 (9th Cir. 1968)], which required that manufacturers directly warn patients in mass inoculation cases. Rather, the statute governs the content of an "adequate product warning," when required. As noted [above], in 1987, direct-to-consumer marketing of prescription drugs was in its beginning stages. The Committee Statement observes that "the warning is owed to the physician" because drugs were then marketed to the physician. We believe that the part of the provision establishing "a presumption that a warning or instruction is adequate on drug or food products if the warning has been approved or prescribed by the Food and Drug Administration," Committee Statement, *supra*, will provide the benchmark for this decision.

[The court ruled that the rationales for the learned intermediary doctrine — deference to physicians and the integrity of the doctor-patient relationship — did not apply when the drug company marketed directly to patients. Hence, the doctrine was not legally available as a defense in this case.]

POLLOCK, J., dissenting.

* * * The majority opinion sustains itself only by ignoring the plain language of an unambiguous statute, the New Jersey Products Liability Act, N.J.S.A. 2A:58C–1 to –7 (NJPLA), and by substituting its own policy preference for that of the Legislature. * * * I respectfully dissent. * * *

The majority finds ambiguity in the NJPLA, stating that "although the statute provides a physician-based standard for determining the adequacy of the warning due to a physician, the statute does not legislate the boundaries of the

affected by other Acts, particularly where Congress has spoken subsequently and more specifically to the topic at hand. See *United States v. Estate of Romani*, 523 U.S. 517, 530-31 (1998); *United States v. Fausto*, 484 U.S. 439, 453 (1988). In addition, we must be guided to a degree by common sense as to the manner in which Congress is likely to delegate a policy decision of such economic and political magnitude to an administrative agency. * * *

[In Part IIA, Justice O'Connor concluded that the FDCA assumes that the FDA will refuse to approve unsafe drugs or devices and will remove them from the market as soon as it determines they are unsafe. E.g., 21 U.S.C. § 355(e)(1)-(3). Congress has enacted six statutes that require disclosure of information regarding tobacco products but do not ban their sale. E.g., 15 U.S.C. § 1331. Given the assumption of the FDCA, these statutes disallow the agency from finding that tobacco products fall within its health and safety regime. "A fundamental precept of the FDCA is that any product regulated by the FDA — but not banned — must be safe for its intended use. * * * Consequently, if tobacco products were within the FDA's jurisdiction, the Act would require the FDA to remove them from the market entirely. But a ban would contradict Congress' clear intent as expressed in its more recent, tobacco-specific legislation. The inescapable conclusion is that there is no room for tobacco products within the FDCA's regulatory scheme."]

[B] In determining whether Congress has spoken directly to the FDA's authority to regulate tobacco, we must also consider in greater detail the tobacco-specific legislation that Congress has enacted over the past 35 years. At the time a statute is enacted, it may have a range of plausible meanings. Over time, however, subsequent acts can shape or focus those meanings. The "classic judicial task of reconciling many laws enacted over time, and getting them to 'make sense' in combination, necessarily assumes that the implications of a statute may be altered by the implications of a later statute." *Fausto*. This is particularly so where the scope of the earlier statute is broad but the subsequent statutes more specifically address the topic at hand. As we recognized recently in *United States v. Estate of Romani*, "a specific policy embodied in a later federal statute should control our construction of the earlier statute, even though it has not been expressly amended."

Congress has enacted six separate pieces of legislation since 1965 addressing the problem of tobacco use and human health. Those statutes, among other things, require that health warnings appear on all packaging and in all print and outdoor advertisements, see 15 U.S.C. §§ 1331, 1333, 4402; prohibit the advertisement of tobacco products through "any medium of electronic communication" subject to regulation by the Federal Communications Commission (FCC), see §§ 1335, 4402(f); require the Secretary of Health and Human Services (HHS) to report every three years to Congress on research findings concerning "the addictive property of tobacco," 42 U.S.C. § 290aa–2(b)(2); and make States' receipt of certain federal block grants contingent on their making it unlawful "for any manufacturer, retailer, or distributor of tobacco products to sell or distribute any such product to any individual under the age of 18," § 300x–26(a)(1).

In adopting each statute, Congress has acted against the backdrop of the FDA's consistent and repeated statements that it lacked authority under the FDCA to regulate tobacco absent claims of therapeutic benefit by the manufacturer. In fact, on several occasions over this period, and after the health consequences of tobacco use and nicotine's pharmacological effects had become well known, Congress considered and rejected bills that would have granted the FDA such jurisdiction. Under these circumstances, it is evident that Congress' tobacco-specific statutes have effectively ratified the FDA's long-held position that it lacks jurisdiction under the FDCA to regulate tobacco products. Congress has created a distinct regulatory scheme to address the problem of tobacco and health, and that scheme, as presently constructed, precludes any role for the FDA.

[In 1964 congressional hearings responding to the Surgeon General's opinion that cigarette smoking is hazardous to one's health, FDA representatives testified that the agency did not have authority to regulate cigarettes or smoking under the FDCA. This was consistent with the position taken by the FDA's predecessor agency, the Bureau of Chemistry under the Pure Food & Drug Act of 1906.] And, as the FDA admits, there is no evidence in the text of the FDCA or its legislative history that Congress in 1938 even considered the applicability of the Act to tobacco products. Given the economic and political significance of the tobacco industry at the time, it is extremely unlikely that Congress could have intended to place tobacco within the ambit of the FDCA absent any discussion of the matter. * * *

Moreover, before enacting the FCLAA [Federal Cigarette Labeling and Advertising Act] in 1965, Congress considered and rejected several proposals to give the FDA the authority to regulate tobacco. In April 1963, Representative Udall introduced a bill "to amend the Federal Food, Drug, and Cosmetic Act so as to make that Act applicable to smoking products." H. R. 5973, 88th Cong., 1st Sess., 1. Two months later, Senator Moss introduced an identical bill in the Senate. S. 1682, 88th Cong., 1st Sess. (1963). In discussing his proposal on the Senate floor, Senator Moss explained that "this amendment simply places smoking products under FDA jurisdiction, along with foods, drugs, and cosmetics." 109 Cong. Rec. 10322 (1963). In December 1963, Representative Rhodes introduced another bill that would have amended the FDCA "by striking out 'food, drug, device, or cosmetic,' each place where it appears therein and inserting in lieu thereof 'food, drug, device, cosmetic, or smoking product.' " H. R. 9512, 88th Cong., 1st Sess., § 3 (1963). And in January 1965, five months before passage of the FCLAA, Representative Udall again introduced a bill to amend the FDCA "to make that Act applicable to smoking products." H. R. 2248, 89th Cong., 1st Sess., 1. None of these proposals became law.

Congress ultimately decided in 1965 to subject tobacco products to the less extensive regulatory scheme of the FCLAA, which created a "comprehensive Federal program to deal with cigarette labeling and advertising with respect to any relationship between smoking and health." Pub. L. 89–92, § 2, 79 Stat. 282. The FCLAA rejected any regulation of advertising, but it required the warning, "Caution: Cigarette Smoking May Be Hazardous to Your Health," to appear on all cigarette packages. *Id.*, § 4, 79 Stat. 283. In the Act's "Declaration of Policy," Congress stated that its objective was to balance the goals of ensuring that "the public may be adequately informed that cigarette smoking may be hazardous to health" and protecting "commerce and the national economy . . . to the maximum extent." *Id.*, § 2, 79 Stat. 282 (codified at 15 U.S.C. § 1331).

Not only did Congress reject the proposals to grant the FDA jurisdiction, but it explicitly preempted any other regulation of cigarette labeling: "No statement relating to smoking and health, other than the statement required by . . . this Act, shall be required on any cigarette package." *Id.*, § 5(a), 79 Stat. 283. The regulation of product labeling, however, is an integral aspect of the FDCA, both as it existed in 1965 and today. The labeling requirements currently imposed by the FDCA, which are essentially identical to those in force in 1965, require the FDA to regulate the labeling of drugs and devices to protect the safety of consumers. See 21 U.S.C. § 352; 21 U.S.C. § 352 (1964 ed. and Supp. IV). As discussed earlier, the Act requires that all products bear "adequate directions for use . . . as are necessary for the protection of users," 21 U.S.C. § 352(f)(1); 21 U.S.C. § 352(f)(1) (1964 ed.); requires that all products provide "adequate warnings against use in those pathological conditions or by children where its use may be dangerous to health," 21 U.S.C. § 352(f)(2); 21 U.S.C. § 352(f)(2) (1964 ed.); and deems a product misbranded "if it is dangerous to health when used in the dosage or manner, or with the frequency or duration prescribed, recommended, or suggested in the labeling thereof," 21 U.S.C. § 352(j); 21 U.S.C. § 352(j) (1964 ed.). In this sense, the FCLAA was — and remains — incompatible with FDA regulation of tobacco products. This is not to say that the FCLAA's preemption provision by itself necessarily foreclosed FDA jurisdiction. But it is an important factor in assessing whether Congress ratified the agency's position — that is, whether Congress adopted a regulatory approach to the problem of tobacco and health that contemplated no role for the FDA. * * *

Four years later, after Congress had transferred the authority to regulate substances covered by the Hazardous Substances Act (HSA) from the FDA to the Consumer Products Safety Commission (CPSC), the American Public Health Association, joined by Senator Moss, petitioned the CPSC to regulate cigarettes yielding more than 21 milligrams of tar. After the CPSC determined that it lacked authority under the HSA to regulate cigarettes, a District Court held that the Act did, in fact, grant the CPSC such jurisdiction and ordered it to reexamine the petition. Before the CPSC could take any action, however, Congress mooted the issue by adopting legislation that eliminated the agency's authority to regulate "tobacco and tobacco products." Consumer Product Safety Commission Improvements Act of 1976, Pub. L. 94–284, § 3(c), 90 Stat. 503 (codified at 15 U.S.C. § 1261(f)(2)). Senator Moss acknowledged that the "legislation, in effect, reversed" the District Court's decision, 121 Cong. Rec. 23563 (1975), and the FDA later observed that the episode was "particularly indicative of the policy of Congress to limit the regulatory authority over cigarettes by Federal Agencies," Letter to Action on Smoking and Health (ASH) Executive Director Banzhaf from FDA Commissioner Goyan (Nov. 25, 1980), App. 59. A separate statement in the Senate Report underscored that the legislation's purpose was to "unmistakably reaffirm the clear mandate of the Congress that the basic regulation of tobacco and tobacco products is governed by the legislation dealing with the subject, . . . and that any further regulation in this sensitive and complex area must be reserved for specific Congressional action." S. Rep. No. 94–251, p. 43 (1975) (additional views of Sens. Hartke, Hollings, Ford, Stevens, and Beall).

[Justice O'Connor assembled a boatload of subsequent statutes regulating smoking and drew extensively from their legislative history the proposition that Congress was consistently following a disclosure strategy and rejecting broader regulations of cigarettes and smoking. At various points, the FDA or other observers reminded congressional committees holding hearings on the tobacco problem that the FDA could not regulate the drug. The FDA also, in 1977, denied a citizen petition asking it to regulate cigarettes, on the ground that "[t]he interpretation of the Act by FDA consistently has been that cigarettes are not a drug unless health claims are made by the vendors." When the citizen group challenged the agency, the government argued that Congress had "acquiesced" in the FDA's no-jurisdiction stance, and the D.C. Circuit affirmed on that ground. The HHS Assistant Secretary told a congressional committee in 1983 that smoking had horrible health effects but that Congress's early legislation deprived HHS of any authority to regulate those ill effects. Congress incrementally expanded its regulation of tobacco with statutes authorizing and funding anti-smoking educational campaigns in the 1980s.]

In 1988, the Surgeon General released a report summarizing the abundant scientific literature demonstrating that "cigarettes and other forms of tobacco are addicting," and that "nicotine is psychoactive" and "causes physical dependence characterized by a withdrawal syndrome that usually accompanies nicotine abstinence." 1988 Surgeon General's Report 14. The report further concluded that the "pharmacologic and behavioral processes that determine tobacco addiction are similar to those that determine addiction to drugs such as heroin and cocaine." Id., at 15. In the same year, FDA Commissioner Young stated before Congress that "it doesn't look like it is possible to regulate tobacco under the Food, Drug and Cosmetic Act even though smoking, I think, has been widely recognized as being harmful to human health." [House Appropriations Subcomm. Hearing.] At the same hearing, the FDA's General Counsel testified that "what is fairly important in FDA law is whether a product has a therapeutic purpose," and "cigarettes themselves are not used for a therapeutic purpose as that concept is ordinarily understood." Between 1987 and 1989, Congress considered three more bills that would have amended the FDCA to grant the FDA jurisdiction to regulate tobacco products. See H. R. 3294, 100th Cong., 1st Sess. (1987); H. R. 1494, 101st Cong., 1st Sess. (1989); S. 769, 101st Cong., 1st Sess. (1989). As before, Congress rejected the proposals. In 1992, Congress instead adopted the Alcohol, Drug Abuse, and Mental Health Administration Reorganization Act, Pub. L. 102–321, § 202, 106 Stat. 394 (codified at 42 U.S.C. § 300x et seq.), which creates incentives for States to regulate the retail sale of tobacco products by making States' receipt of certain block grants contingent on their prohibiting the sale of tobacco products to minors.

Taken together, these actions by Congress over the past 35 years preclude an interpretation of the FDCA that grants the FDA jurisdiction to regulate tobacco products. We do not rely on Congress' failure to act — its consideration and rejection of bills that would have given the FDA this authority — in reaching this conclusion. Indeed, this is not a case of simple inaction by Congress that purportedly represents its acquiescence in an agency's position. To the contrary, Congress has enacted several statutes addressing the particular subject of tobacco and health, creating a distinct regulatory scheme for cigarettes and smokeless tobacco. In doing so, Congress has been aware of tobacco's health hazards and its pharmacological effects. It has also enacted this legislation against the background of the FDA repeatedly and consistently asserting that it lacks jurisdiction under the FDCA to regulate tobacco products as customarily marketed. Further, Congress has persistently acted to preclude a meaningful role for *any* administrative agency in making policy on the subject of tobacco and health. Moreover, the substance of Congress' regulatory scheme is, in an important respect, incompatible with FDA jurisdiction. Although the supervision of product labeling to protect consumer health is a substantial component of the FDA's regulation of drugs and devices, see 21 U.S.C. § 352 (1994 ed. and Supp. III), the FCLAA and the CSTHEA [Comprehensive Smokeless Tobacco Health Education Act] explicitly prohibit any federal agency from imposing any health-related labeling requirements on cigarettes or smokeless tobacco products, see 15 U. S C. §§ 1334(a), 4406(a).
* * *

JUSTICE BREYER, joined by JUSTICE STEVENS, JUSTICE SOUTER, and JUSTICE GINSBURG, dissenting.

The Food and Drug Administration (FDA) has the authority to regulate "articles (other than food) intended to affect the structure or any function of the body . . . ." Federal Food, Drug and Cosmetic Act (FDCA), 21 U.S.C. § 321(g)(1)(C). Unlike the majority, I believe that tobacco products fit within this statutory language.

In its own interpretation, the majority nowhere denies the following two salient points. First, tobacco products (including cigarettes) fall within the scope of this statutory definition, read literally. Cigarettes achieve their mood-stabilizing effects through the interaction of the chemical nicotine and the cells of the central nervous system. Both cigarette manufacturers and smokers alike know of, and desire, that chemically induced result. Hence, cigarettes are "intended to affect" the body's "structure" and "function," in the literal sense of these words.

Second, the statute's basic purpose — the protection of public health — supports the inclusion of cigarettes within its scope. See *United States* v. *Article of Drug . . . Bacto-Unidisk,* 394 U.S. 784, 798 (1969) (FDCA "is to be given *a liberal construction consistent with [its] overriding purpose to protect the public health*" (emphasis added)). Unregulated tobacco use causes "more than 400,000 people [to] die each year from tobacco-related illnesses, such as cancer, respiratory illnesses, and heart disease." 61 Fed. Reg. 44398 (1996). Indeed, tobacco products kill more people in this country every year "than . . . AIDS, car accidents, alcohol, homicides, illegal drugs, suicides, and fires, *combined*." *Ibid*. (emphasis added).

Despite the FDCA's literal language and general purpose (both of which support the FDA's finding that cigarettes come within its statutory authority), the majority nonetheless reads the statute as *excluding* tobacco products for two basic reasons:

(1) the FDCA does not "fit" the case of tobacco because the statute requires the FDA to prohibit dangerous drugs or devices (like cigarettes) outright, and the agency concedes that simply banning the sale of cigarettes is not a proper remedy; and

(2) Congress has enacted other statutes, which, when viewed in light of the FDA's long history of denying tobacco-related jurisdiction and considered together with Congress' failure explicitly to grant the agency tobacco-specific authority, demonstrate that Congress did not intend for the FDA to exercise jurisdiction over tobacco.

In my view, neither of these propositions is valid. Rather, the FDCA does not significantly limit the FDA's remedial alternatives. And the later statutes do not tell the FDA it cannot exercise jurisdiction, but simply leave FDA jurisdictional law where Congress found it. [C]f. Food and Drug Administration Modernization Act of 1997, 111 Stat. 2380 (codified at note following 21 U.S.C. § 321 (1994 ed., Supp. III)) (statute "shall" *not* "be construed to affect the question of whether" the FDA "has any authority to regulate any tobacco product").

The bulk of the opinion that follows will explain the basis for these latter conclusions. In short, I believe that the most important indicia of statutory meaning—language and purpose—along with the FDCA's legislative history (described briefly in Part I) are sufficient to establish that the FDA has authority to regulate tobacco. The statute-specific arguments against jurisdiction that the tobacco companies and the majority rely upon (discussed in Part II) are based on erroneous assumptions and, thus, do not defeat the jurisdiction-supporting thrust of the FDCA's language and purpose. The inferences that the majority draws from later legislative history are not persuasive, since (as I point out in Part III) one can just as easily infer from the later laws that Congress did not intend to affect the FDA's tobacco-related authority at all. And the fact that the FDA changed its mind about the scope of its own jurisdiction is legally insignificant because (as Part IV establishes) the agency's reasons for changing course are fully justified. [The FDA's stated reasons for not regulating were that it did not have evidence that the cigarette manufacturers "intended" for their product to have a medical effect; by the 1990s, there was ample evidence of such intent.]

In the majority's view, laws enacted since 1965 require us to deny jurisdiction, whatever the FDCA might mean in their absence. But why? Do those laws contain language barring FDA jurisdiction? The majority must concede that they do not. Do they contain provisions that are inconsistent with the FDA's exercise of jurisdiction? With one exception, the majority points to no such provision. Do they somehow repeal the principles of law * * * that otherwise would lead to the conclusion that the FDA has jurisdiction in this area? The companies themselves deny making any such claim. See Tr. of Oral Arg. 27 (denying reliance on doctrine of "partial repeal"). Perhaps the later laws "shape" and "focus" what the 1938 Congress meant a generation earlier. But this Court has warned against using the views of a later Congress to construe a statute enacted many years before. See *Pension Benefit Guaranty Corporation v. LTV Corp.,* 496 U.S. 633, 650 (1990) (later history is " 'a hazardous basis for inferring the intent of an earlier' Congress" (quoting *United States v. Price,* 361 U.S. 304, 313 (1960)). And, while the majority suggests that the subsequent history "controls our construction" of the FDCA, this Court expressly has held that such subsequent views are not "controlling." *Haynes v. United States,* 390 U.S. 85, 87–88 n.4 (1968). Regardless, the later statutes do not support the majority's conclusion. That is because, whatever individual Members of Congress after 1964 may have assumed about the FDA's jurisdiction, the laws they enacted did not embody any such "no jurisdiction" assumption. And one cannot automatically *infer* an antijurisdiction intent, as the majority does, for the later statutes are both (and similarly) consistent with quite a different congressional desire, namely, the intent to proceed without interfering with whatever authority the FDA otherwise may have possessed. As I demonstrate below, the subsequent legislative history is critically ambivalent, for it can be read *either* as (a) "ratifying" a no-jurisdiction assumption, *or* as (b) leaving the jurisdictional question just where Congress found it. And the fact that both inferences are "equally tenable," *Pension Benefit Guaranty Corp.*, prevents the majority from drawing from the later statutes the firm, antijurisdiction implication that it needs.

Consider, for example, Congress' failure to provide the FDA with express authority to regulate tobacco — a circumstance that the majority finds significant. In fact, Congress *both* failed to grant express authority to the FDA when the FDA denied it had jurisdiction over tobacco *and* failed to take that authority expressly away when the agency later asserted jurisdiction. See, *e.g.*, S. 1262, 104th Cong., 1st Sess., § 906 (1995) (failed bill seeking to amend FDCA to say that "nothing in this Act or any other Act shall provide the [FDA] with any authority to regulate in any manner tobacco or tobacco products"); see also H. R. 516, 105th Cong., 1st Sess., § 2 (1997) (similar); H. R. Res. 980, reprinted in 142 Cong. Rec. 5018 (1996) (Georgia legislators unsuccessfully requested that Congress "rescind any action giving the FDA authority" over tobacco); H. R. 2283, 104th Cong., 1st Sess. (1995) (failed bill "to prohibit the [FDA] regulation of the sale or use of tobacco"); H. R. 2414, 104th Cong., 1st Sess., § 2(a) (1995) (similar). Consequently, the defeat of various different proposed jurisdictional changes proves nothing. This history shows only that Congress could not muster the votes necessary either to grant or to deny the FDA the relevant authority. It neither favors nor disfavors the majority's position.

[We omit the remainder of Justice Breyer's lengthy opinion, but like Justice O'Connor's opinion it is worth reading in its entirety.]

NOTE ON THE FDA TOBACCO CASE AND THE SUPREME COURT AS A STRATEGIC ACTOR IN OUR POLITY

1. *Lawmaking as a Sequential Game.* This case might be an example of strategic behavior among legal institutions.[d] For years the FDA had known that tobacco was a deadly drug; one reason it did not move earlier was that it knew that any regulation would be overridden by Congress, where the tobacco companies were powerfully represented. President Clinton was a relatively anti-tobacco chief executive, who appointed Dr. David Kessler to head the FDA and would probably have backed up the FDA with a presidential veto of override legislation. (This would not have been possible under Presidents Reagan and Bush.) Armed with that political knowledge — as well as the medical and "intent" knowledge emphasized in Justice Breyer's dissent — the agency moved to regulate.

The FDA's problem was that the tobacco industry might be able to mobilize the judiciary to override the agency even if Congress-with-the-President would not. Affirming the Fourth Circuit (filled with tobacco farms in North Carolina and Virginia), the Supreme Court trumped the agency's initiative. Under the assumptions of rational choice theory, the Court might have been reluctant to act if it were likely to be overridden by Congress — but the Justices knew that would not happen, because relatively pro-tobacco Republicans controlled both houses of Congress in 2000. By reversing the default rule — from the FDA's regulation to the industry's nonregulation — the Court reversed the political outcome, and its resolution has thus far stuck.

2. *The Judiciary as a Part of the Rent-Seeking Process?* The FDA Tobacco Case can be viewed as one kind of caution about economic theories of statutory interpretation, such as ours and Judge Easterbrook's, that urge the courts to press statutes away from rent-seeking. The courts can be part of the interest-group process. Groups press for the appointment of friendly lawyers or ideologically compatible law professors as judges and then use the judiciary to overturn at least some of their defeats in the political process. This is easier to accomplish by "have" groups, because judges tend to be libertarian, either as a matter of philosophy or practicality (it is much easier for the courts to slow things down than to require the state to act), and "have" groups are usually trying to protect their freedom of action against government regulation.[e]

So the FDA Tobacco Case can be viewed, in part, as an expression of the majority Justices' personal aversion to aggressive state regulation of private industry. The five Justices in the majority are the most conservative Republican Justices; the four dissenters include the only two Democrats on the Court,

---

d. The model that follows was developed in William Eskridge, Jr. & John Ferejohn, *Politics, Interpretation, and the Rule of Law,* in *The Rule of Law* 265 (Nomos XXXVI, Ian Shapiro ed. 1993); William Eskridge, Jr. & Philip Frickey, *The Supreme Court, 1993 Term — Foreword: Law as Equilibrium,* 108 Harv. L. Rev. 26 (1994).

e. See also Mark Galanter, *Why the "Haves" Come Out Ahead: Speculations on the Limits of Legal Change,* 9 L. & Soc'y Rev. 95 (1974), which shows how Repeat-Player "Have" groups can deploy the litigation process to advance their goals even if judges are neutral or even hostile to their aims.

an Independent appointed by a Republican (Stevens), and a Republican who turned out to be more liberal than expected (Souter). The case can be viewed as a signal to the Clinton Administration that the Court will slap down new regulatory initiatives that are too ambitious. (Congress has shown itself unwilling to enact them; now the President and agencies cannot adopt them under prior authorizing statutes.) Is this assessment too harsh?

Opponents of the outcome in FDA Tobacco Case may view it as rent-seeking. For them, if ever the Court were to follow the Easterbrook idea of liberal construction of public-regarding statutes, it is this case, for there is little doubt that tobacco products represent rent-seeking of the worst sort: a special interest not only makes money at the expense of the public good, but at the expense of untold suffering and death. Moreover, the FDA's interpretation is consistent with, if not compelled by, the statutory text and purpose. How should supporters of the decision respond to these arguments? For an excellent analysis, see Richard Merrill, *The FDA May Not Regulate Tobacco Products as "Drugs" or "Medical Devices,"* 47 Duke L.J. 1071 (1998).

3. *The Rule of Law as a Judicial Preference.* There is another way of looking at the FDA Tobacco Case from an economic perspective. Whatever their political preferences, almost all federal judges carry or develop strong preferences for rule-of-law values, including predictability in the law, following orderly procedures, and acting only within authorized jurisdictional boundaries. From Justice O'Connor's point of view, the FDA Tobacco Case is a dramatic example of the power of the rule of law: these companies may be morally squalid, but regulation of moral squalor must still follow the proper procedures under the appropriate congressional authorization. As Professor Merrill puts it, the 1965 statute confirmed a longstanding political *deal*, that the FDCA did not regulate tobacco products, which would be subject to warning and disclosure regimes instead (the FCLAA and subsequent laws). Everything Congress did after 1965 reflected and reaffirmed that deal — until the FDA unilaterally abrogated it in 1996. Merrill, *FDA May Not Regulate Tobacco Products, supra*, at 1074-82.

In response, Justice Breyer's dissent argues that the statute's plain meaning (the rule of law's primary tool) and the Court's precedents (next-best tool) supported the agency. Thus, a "liberal" construction in this case was also a "literal" construction, for the statutory language includes tobacco and cigarettes. Justice O'Connor could respond that the FDA's assertion of jurisdiction to regulate tobacco products is inconsistent with the statutory structure, whereby dangerous drugs must be banned entirely. See Merrill, *FDA May Not Regulate Tobacco, supra*, at 1082-86.

Justice O'Connor also, apparently, rests her opinion upon an equilibrium-based idea: the longstanding agreement that the FDA could not regulate smoking without fresh congressional authorization, and the reliance interests it generated, have created a stable "rule of law" not perfectly reflected in the statutory text. This kind of response would be inconsistent with the philosophy of two of the Justices in the majority, Scalia and Thomas. But they swallowed, without a textualist whimper, Justice O'Connor's lengthy recitation of evidence from legislative hearings, reports, and debates to show that even though no tobacco statute limited the FDA's jurisdiction, many of them were enacted under the assumption that the FDA did not have such jurisdiction. A further irony: Justice O'Connor (with Justices Scalia and Thomas going along) deploys the kind of "institutional legislative history" that Justices Breyer and Stevens have championed — with Breyer and Stevens themselves in dissent based in part on the plain meaning rule.

C. PRAGMATIC AND CRITICAL THEORIES OF STATUTORY INTERPRETATION

1. *Pragmatic Theories*

In *How Judges Think* (2008), Judge Posner broadly distinguishes between "legalistic" and "pragmatic" theories of statutory interpretation. Legalistic theories claim that law is an autonomous discipline that can reach neutral interpretations through application of plain meanings (assisted perhaps with dictionaries and linguists), following precedent, reasoning by analogy, and the like. Pragmatic theories, in contrast, openly admit that law is not (entirely) separate from politics and that interpretation carries with it discretion and policy choice. Hart and Sacks's purpose-based interpretation is, by this reading, pragmatic, and Posner's current approach, well-illustrated in the LSD Case above, is an updated or more sophisticated version of legal process theory. Similarly pragmatic is Justice Stephen Breyer, as illustrated in his opinion for the Court in *Zuni*. See also Breyer, *Active Liberty: Interpreting Our Democratic Constitution* (2005).[f]

Another kind of *pragmatic* thinking focuses less on realistic consequences. Inspired by American pragmatic philosophers who rejected "foundationalist" thinking and urged multi-focal thinking, the following article reflects a practical approach to statutory interpretation that the authors believe best reflects what the Supreme Court (and most state courts) are actually doing in statutory cases.

WILLIAM ESKRIDGE, JR. AND PHILIP FRICKEY, *STATUTORY INTERPRETATION AS PRACTICAL REASONING*, 42 Stan. L. Rev. 321, 345–53 (1990). Professors Eskridge and Frickey criticize each of the leading "foundationalist" theories of interpretation — textualism, original intent, purpose — and find each wanting in the same ways. "[T]he leading foundationalist theories cannot redeem their claim to follow from the very nature of majoritarian democracy, that they do not yield objective and determinate answers, and that they cannot convincingly exclude other values, including current values. *Weber* [Chapter 1, § 3][and] *Griffin* illustrate our theoretical critique and suggest that the Supreme Court does not follow any one of the foundationalist theories. We now suggest that these observations form the basis for a positive theory which refuses to privilege intention, purpose or text as the sole touchstone of interpretation, but which both explains the

---

f. Although Breyer is a New Deal liberal who views state interventions as needed to *assure* ("active") liberty and Posner is a libertarian who views state interventions much more skeptically, their methodologies bear striking similarities.

Supreme Court's practice in statutory interpretation and, at the same time, reflects the insights of modern theories of interpretation.

"First, statutory interpretation involves creative policymaking by judges and is not just the Court's figuring out the answer that was put 'in' the statute by the enacting legislature. An essential insight of hermeneutics is that interpretation is a dynamic process, and that the interpreter is inescapably situated historically. 'Every age has to understand a transmitted text in its own way,' says Gadamer [in *Truth and Method* 263 (1965):]

> The real meaning of a text, as it speaks to the interpreter, does not depend on the contingencies of the author and whom he originally wrote for. It certainly is not identical with them, for it is always partly determined also by the historical situation of the interpreter and hence by the totality of the objective course of history. * * *

"Hermeneutics suggests that the text lacks meaning *until* it is interpreted. Given the importance of the interpretive horizon, which itself changes over time, interpretation must not 'chase the phantom of an historical object.' A text, then, is not meaningful 'in itself,' apart from possible interpreters and their historical contexts. Nor is it meaningful apart from the task of the interpreter. Gadamer argues, following Aristotle, that one does not 'understand' a text in the abstract, without an 'application' of the text to a specific problem. American pragmatism, also influenced by Aristotle, complements this hermeneutic insight. Reasoning in human affairs does not seek abstract answers, but concretely useful results. Theories of reasoning, for [William James, in *Pragmatism* (1907)] are simply 'mental modes of *adaptation* to reality, rather than revelations or gnostic answers.'

"Consider *Weber* in this light. The interpretive process is creative, not mechanical. Viewed in the context of the complex goals of the Civil Rights Act and subsequent difficulties in implementation, making sense of the statute's command not to 'discriminate' requires much more than finding a meaning for the term. Even if the interpretive process were viewed as retrieving the answer Congress would have reached in 1964 (had it deliberated on the issue), the inquiry involves 'imaginative' work by the judge. These lessons of *Weber* are consistent with the insights of modern literary theory, historiography, and philosophy: There is no interpretation without an interpreter, and the interpreter will interact with the text or historical event. Just as the interpreter learns from the text and history, so too does she speak to it. What was decisive in *Weber,* surely to Justice Blackmun and probably to other Justices in the majority as well, was what the interpreters learned about the statute from considering the facts of the case: More than a decade after the statute was enacted there were only 2 percent blacks in the craft workforce, contrasted with 39 percent blacks in the overall workforce.

"Second, because this creation of statutory meaning is not a mechanical operation, it often involves the interpreter's choice among several competing answers. Although the interpreter's range of choices is somewhat constrained by the text, the statute's history, and the circumstances of its application, the actual choice will not be 'objectively' determinable; interpretation will often depend upon political and other assumptions held by judges. Under Gadamer's [analysis], interpretation seeks 'to make the law concrete in each specific case,' and '[t]he creative supplementing of the law that is involved is a task that is reserved to the judge.' As a practical matter, how could it be otherwise? Many statutes leave key terms ambiguous, often intentionally, and thereby delegate rulemaking authority to courts or agencies. Over time, these ambiguities and unanswered questions multiply, as society changes and background legal assumptions change with it. Hermeneutics suggests that as the interpreter's own background context — her 'tradition' — changes, so too will her interpretive choices. * * *

"Third, when statutory interpreters make these choices, they are normally not driven by any single value — adhering to majoritarian commands *or* encouraging private reliance on statutory texts *or* finding the best answer according to modern policy — but are instead driven by multiple values. Both hermeneutics and pragmatism emphasize the complex nature of human reasoning. When solving a problem, we tend to test different solutions, evaluating each against a range of values and beliefs we hold as important. The pragmatic idea that captures this concept is the 'web of beliefs' metaphor. We all accept a number of different values and propositions that, taken together, constitute a web of intertwined beliefs about, for example, the role of statutes in our public law. Each of us may accord different weight to the specific values, but almost no one excludes any of the important values altogether. Decisionmaking is, therefore, polycentric, and thus cannot be linear and purely deductive. Instead, it is spiral and inductive: We consider the consistency of the evidence for each value before reaching a final decision, and even then check our decision against the values we esteem the most. Given this web of beliefs and the spiral form of decisionmaking, an individual's reasoning will depend very much on the context of the case at hand, and specifically on the relative strength of each consideration.

"Consider *Griffin* from the perspective of the web metaphor. A Justice who is a thoroughgoing textualist would surely agree with the *Griffin* result, given the relative clarity of the statutory language. But so could an intentionalist Justice: Although there is no smoking gun in the legislative history, the legislative context and the strong statutory language suggest that Congress would probably have favored substantial punitive sanctions had it addressed the issue. And so could a purposivist Justice, because surely one major purpose of the statute was to deter employer misconduct, which the $302,000 award in *Griffin* would seem to do. Even a Justice concerned only with fair results might applaud the *Griffin* result. In fact, seven Justices of differing jurisprudential stripes formed the majority in *Griffin,* and Justice Rehnquist's opinion justified the result by arguing from the relatively clear statutory language, the original legislative intent, the overall statutory purpose, and (to some extent) the reasonableness of the interpretation. Whether ultimately correct, the opinion in *Griffin,* by its strategy of cumulative assessment and weighing of factors potentially relevant to interpretation, seems more persuasive than would any foundationalist avenue to the same result. * * *

"In addition to the web of beliefs idea, two other metaphors, one drawn from the pragmatist tradition and one drawn from the hermeneutical tradition, suggest more precisely how a practical reasoning approach would work. First, consider Peirce's contrast of the chain and the cable. A chain is no stronger than its weakest link, because if any of the singly connected links should break, so too will the chain. In contrast, a cable's strength relies not on that of individual threads, but upon their cumulative strength as they are woven together. Legal arguments are often constructed as chains, but they tend to be more successful when they are cable-like. The Court's opinion in *Griffin* draws its strength from this phenomenon: The text, one probable purpose, some legislative history, and current policy each lend some — even if not unequivocal — support to the result. Each thread standing alone is subject to quarrel and objection; woven together, the threads persuaded both Justice Rehnquist *and* Justice Brennan, a not unimpressive achievement.

"In many cases of statutory interpretation, of course, the threads will not all run in the same direction. The cable metaphor suggests that in these cases the result will depend upon the strongest overall combination of threads. That, in turn, depends on which values the decisionmakers find most important, and on the strength of the arguments invoking each value. For most of the Supreme Court Justices, a persuasive textual argument is a stronger thread than an otherwise equally persuasive current policy or fairness argument, because of the reliance and legislative supremacy values implicated in following the clear statutory text. And a clear and convincing textual argument obviously counts more than one beclouded with doubts and ambiguities.

"Our model of practical reasoning in statutory interpretation is still not complete, for it lacks a dynamic element that is intrinsic to human reasoning in general, and interpretation in particular. The various arguments (the threads of our cable) do not exist in isolation; they interact with one another. A final metaphor that captures this interaction is the 'hermeneutical circle': A part can only be understood in the context of the whole, and the whole cannot be understood without analyzing its various parts. To interpret the statute in *Griffin,* for example, the interpreter will look at the text and the legislative history and the purpose and current values. But to evaluate the text, the interpreter will consider it in light of the whole enterprise, including the history, purpose, and current values. In other words, none of the interpretive threads can be viewed in isolation, and each will be evaluated in its relation to the other threads.

"Following Heidegger, Gadamer deploys the hermeneutical circle in a particularly interesting way, which roughly captures the dynamics of legal interpretation. Because we always approach texts from the perspective of our own historically situated horizon, we tend to project our 'preunderstandings' onto the text, viewed as a whole. That is essential to interpretation, because the preunderstandings are conditioned by tradition and, hence, help us link our horizon with that of the text. But the hermeneutical circle suggests that a true dialogue with the text requires the interpreter to reconsider her preunderstandings as she considers the specific evidence in the case, and then to formulate a new understanding, which in turn is subject to reconsideration. For Gadamer, the essential lesson of the circle metaphor is the hermeneutical attitude: 'A person trying to understand a text is prepared for it to tell him something.' The 'to and fro movement' involved in the hermeneutical circle is not just the interpreter's movement from a general view of the statute to the specific evidence and back again; rather, it requires her to test different understandings of the text in an ongoing effort to determine its proper interpretation.

"The positive metaphors of our analysis — the web of beliefs idea, the cable-versus-chain contrast, and the hermeneutical circle — suggest the contours of a practical reasoning model of statutory interpretation that roughly captures the Court's practice. Our model holds that an interpreter will look at a broad range of evidence — text, historical evidence, and the text's evolution — and thus form a preliminary view of the statute. The interpreter then develops that preliminary view by testing various possible interpretations against the multiple criteria of fidelity to the text, historical accuracy, and conformity to contemporary circumstances and values. Each criterion is relevant, yet none necessarily trumps the others. Thus while an apparently clear text, for example, will create insuperable doubts for a contrary interpretation if the other evidence reinforces it *(Griffin),* an apparently clear text may yield if other considerations cut against it (* * * *Weber).* As the interpreter comes to accept an interpretation (perhaps a confirmation of her preliminary view), she considers a congeries of supporting arguments, which may buttress her view much 'like the legs of a chair and unlike the links of a chain.'

"This dialectical method of statutory interpretation, which is familiar to us all, can be schematized as follows:

A PRACTICAL REASONING MODEL OF STATUTORY INTERPRETATION

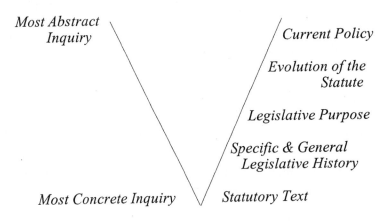

Most Abstract Inquiry

Current Policy

Evolution of the Statute

Legislative Purpose

Specific & General Legislative History

Most Concrete Inquiry   *Statutory Text*

"* * * [T]his model identifies the primary evidentiary inquiries in which the Court will engage. The model is, in crude imagery, a 'funnel of abstraction.' It is funnel-shaped for three reasons. First, the model suggests the hierarchy of sources that the Court has in fact assumed. For example, in formulating her preunderstanding of the statute *and* in testing it, the interpreter will value more highly a good argument based on the statutory text than a conflicting and equally strong argument based upon the statutory purpose. Second, the model suggests the degree of abstraction at each source. The sources at the bottom of the diagram involve more focused, concrete inquiries, typically with a more limited range of arguments. As the interpreter moves up the diagram, a broader range of arguments is available, partly because the inquiry is less concrete. Third, the model illustrates the pragmatistic and hermeneutical insights explained above: In formulating and testing her understanding of the statute, the interpreter will move up and down the diagram, evaluating and comparing the different considerations represented by each source of argumentation. * * *"

NOTE ON THE FUNNEL OF ABSTRACTION

On the whole, the funnel of abstraction is a descriptive theory of statutory interpretation: this is how the judicial (or administrative) mind goes about deciding statutory cases.[g] Think about how the funnel helps explain the decisions in this chapter, especially *Holy Trinity*, *Bock Laundry*, *Jacob*, *Li*, and *Chisom*, which openly follow the method, but also cases that don't seem to follow the method, like *Casey* and *Marshall*. Although Judge Easterbrook is not a "funnel judge," the judges who went along with his decision in *Marshall* might well have been — what might have been persuasive to them? Consider the debate among the Justices in *Brown & Williamson* as a debate about how to apply the funnel. How would the funnel apply to the issue raised by the Case of the Speluncean Explorers? Map out your analysis and then rethink it after you read the material that immediately follows. Next, take the reasoning and see if you can devise a more complicated model for understanding the courts' decisions. Finally, rethink the funnel from a normative perspective. What values should courts be pressing in statutory cases? The funnel assumes that the rule- of-law values (text, original intent, precedent) are the weightiest and that process and substantive values are relevant but less weighty. Should the text be as privileged as we assume it to be? Should it be as flexible as hermeneutics suggests? And so on. See how your normative deliberation edits or changes the funnel or your variation of it.

2. *Critical Theories*

Critical theory has not often found its way into the statutory interpretation literature, and critical scholars are unlikely to end up with judicial positions, but it is not hard to imagine what critical theories of statutory interpretation would look like.[h] Critical theory is typically deconstructive but can be reconstructive as well.

---

g. For evidence suggesting that this diagram accurately displays the factors routinely taken into account in judicial opinions interpreting statutes, see Nicholas Zeppos, *The Use of Authority in Statutory Interpretation: An Empirical Analysis*, 70 Tex. L. Rev. 1073 (1992).

h. By critical theory, we mean work that deconstructs statutory texts, typically in order to show how reactionary readings are ideologically rather than objectively grounded. See, e.g., J.M. Balkin, *Deconstructive Practice and Legal Theory*, 96 Yale L.J. 743 (1987); William Eskridge, Jr. & Gary Peller, *The New Public Law Movement: Moderation as a Postmodern Cultural Form*, 89 Mich. L. Rev. 707 (1991); Peter Schank, *Understanding Postmodern Thought and Its Implications for Statutory Interpretation*, 65 S. Cal. L. Rev. 2505 (1992).

Deconstruction, loosely put, opens up interpretive possibilities in statutory texts, the opposite agenda of textualist theories. In the famous *Weber* case (Chapter 1, § 3), Justice Brennan's deployment of section 703(j), which says the government cannot *require* race-based preferences to offset workforce imbalances, was playfully ironic, as it showed how the gaps in an anti-preference provision could support affirmative action under Title VII. The playfulness was exercised with a serious undertone of critique, however: Why should a provision put in to satisfy objectives of white conservatives not be *read* from the perspective of people of color? Brennan could, even more effectively, have made the same move with *discriminate*: What does the word mean to the Gramercy blacks who had been trying for a generation to break into the craft jobs? Indeed, white opponents could be seen as making a deconstructive move themselves, showing how the subjects arguably benefitting from centuries of slavery and apartheid could now claim to be objects of *reverse discrimination* when remediation for continuing segregation was adopted; this was particularly ironic in Weber's case, for he would not even have been eligible for a craft position if it were not for the affirmative action training program, which bypassed the older requirement of prior craft experience. The potentially playful seriousness of Brennan's arguments and the irony of Weber's position were lost on Justice Rehnquist, who cast Weber as a victim and accused Brennan of Orwellian doublethink. Like Rehnquist in *Weber*, Brewer in *Holy Trinity* (§ 1 of this chapter) was incapable of irony or deconstruction (he can be said to have trumped the law with God, a premodernist move), but his opinion can be defended by showing how chaotic the statutory text was and, more deeply, how language could not (or at least did not) capture what the sponsors of the bill were concerned with regulating.

By revealing multiple possibilities, this method deconstructs the *rule of law* itself. The common idea that "the rule of law is a law of rules" assumes a hierarchy whereby the subject (interpreter) retrieves the answer from the object (text) to which she pays homage. But if interpretation depends critically on the perspective of the interpreter, even more than what the text says, then the hierarchy is flipped: the seemingly subordinate subject actually controls the meaning of the supposedly superior object. All the foregoing theories of statutory interpretation — textualist, intentionalist, purposivist, and even pragmatic — deny or suppress this way the rule of law flips in cases like *Weber* and *Holy Trinity*. From the critical perspective, everybody knows this goes on, and they all stonewall it. Do not expect Scalia, Rehnquist, Brennan, or even Blackmun to confess, as Cardozo did several generations ago, that the hard work of judging is creative, for it happens when the conventional sources fail to provide interpretive closure. The strategy of the people in power whose work can be deconstructed is to ignore the critique or, if it cannot be ignored, to denounce it in eschatological terms as nihilist, or fascist, or even illiberal.[i]

---

i. The response in text can, naturally, be deconstructed. People in power dichotomize the issue as, If you don't accept our deterministic theory, the alternative is chaos. But their theory is not deterministic, except in a self-serving way; accepting a fair amount of honest indeterminacy can lead to less chaos than a great deal of hypocritical determinacy; public chaos might be better than state-legitimated injustice, which is a privatized form of chaos. And so on. See Gary

Critical theory can also be reconstructive, suggesting positive moves that interpreters could take in the face of pervasive indeterminacy. The statutory interpreter, especially judges given some degree of academic luxury by their life tenure, might become, perhaps episodically, a *counterhegemonic* force in our polity, insisting that unspoken voices be considered. A critical approach to *Weber* would, with Blackmun, candidly admit the play within the text of Title VII and the assumption of the enacting Congress that colorblind employment decisions would lead to workforce integration. But rather than looking at the *Weber* dilemma only from the perspective of the displaced white employees (Rehnquist) or of the politically powerful unions and employers (Blackmun), the critic might have thought about the issue from the perspective of the people of color who, rather than Weber, got the opportunity to train for craft positions because of the Steelworkers/Kaiser program. Was it discrimination to help them? Was their lack of qualification (they had less seniority than Weber) a function of prior race-based policies? What doors did the training program open up for them? Was there disabling resentment against them by people who felt the Webers were cheated out of their rightful spots?

Holy Trinity looks even more different when viewed critically. Brewer's soliloquy about the United States as a Christian Nation was obviously very important to his resolution of the case, yet that norm seems more exclusionary than visionary today. The statute itself has more than a whiff of xenophobia and racism about it, patterned as it was on earlier Chinese exclusionary laws. Brewer's opinion can be defended as a narrowing construction of a broadly sweeping, somewhat hysterical piece of legislation. Curtailing such laws is traditionally something judges have done, often to their great credit, in this country. But Brewer's resolution also created a new injustice in the statute: the upper class, professional, brain-toiling imported "alien" can enter the country, and only the working-class manual laborers and servants (unless they were domestic servants, exempted by § 5) were found to be excluded by the law. By carving out a theoretically large exception for professionals, *Holy Trinity* made a morally questionable statute more squalid (by adding a new class-based discrimination) and more palatable to the political culture (by exempting acceptable aliens from the prohibition). A counterhegemonic approach to the case would have given less emphasis to the Christian Nation, and more to the Equal Nation.

Such an aggressively counterhegemonic judiciary can readily be criticized, not only for undermining the rule of law and disrespecting the democratic process, but also for kamikaze normative arrogance. Unhappily, judges are neither well-trained in moral philosophy nor necessarily especially virtuous people themselves, and Alexander Hamilton was right to call their office the "least dangerous branch." How can we expect such state functionaries, first, to transcend their own prejudices and empathize with the poor or the outcast; second, to translate that empathy into concrete statutory interpretations that have real-world bite; and, third, to pursue truly other-regarding moral theory in the face of political criticism and threats to the judicial office? On the other

Peller, *The Metaphysics of American Law*, 73 Calif. L. Rev. 1151 (1985).

hand, pragmatists and even more formal theorists might be inspired by critical thinkers to shake up the status quo and kick some sacred cows more often, and to take a few calculated risks to do the right thing for the dispossessed of our society.

Consider the following excerpts from a symposium on the Case of the Speluncean Explorers, in which critical theorists added their own opinions to those of Judges Foster, Keen, and the others in Professor Fuller's leading article.

THE CASE OF THE SPELUNCEAN EXPLORERS: CONTEMPORARY PROCEEDINGS
61 Geo. Wash. U. L. Rev. 1754, 1755–63 (1993)[*]

NAOMI R. CAHN, J. * * * Although there can be no one feminist approach to statutory interpretation, the differing perspectives within feminism provide a basis for showing the dilemmas in a finding that the explorers violated, or did not violate, N.C.S.A. (N.S.) § 12–A. * * *

* * * The meaning of the language of the statute depends on who is reading the statute and where she places emphasis as to what different "plain meaning(s)" will emerge. Our statute requires that one "willfully take the life of another." This could mean that the explorers must have acted "willfully" in killing Roger Whetmore. * * * But perhaps they were "willfully" seeking to prolong their own lives rather than to take the life of Whetmore. * * * Is it a crime to seek to prolong life, regardless of the means? As liberal feminism suggests, the issue of individual choice is an important consideration. How were Whetmore's choices constructed? The record * * * does not give enough information about Roger Whetmore's "participation" in the decisionmaking process. The stories of the four defendants are not available to us and may not have been available to the jury. * * * What is presented in the trial court as the "facts," and then what we, as judges, do with those "facts," is critical to our application of the law. The plain meaning of the statute cannot exist apart from the context in which the statute is applied. * * *

* * * We are all familiar with the work of Carol Gilligan, [*In a Different Voice* (1982),] who identified two different methods of moral reasoning: one based on an ethic of care, and one based on an ethic of justice. Within the ethic of care, reasoning draws on interconnections between people and seeks to minimize harms to others; for example, statutes should be interpreted in the light of their effect on people's interactions and mutual interdependence. Within the ethic of justice, reasoning is based on hierarchies of values, seeking to do what is morally (or legally) right; for example, people's interactions should be interpreted in the light of whether they comply with the law as written. Within an ethic of justice statutory *interpretation* becomes more of an exercise in statutory *application*. * * * Our judgments should integrate insights from the two different ethics, seeking to do justice yet respecting connections between people and recognizing that our own (sometimes shifting) perspectives construct this decision.

Reasoning constructed solely under an ethic of care might find none of the defendants guilty. They examined all the different options, talked amongst themselves, and agreed to a solution initially suggested by Roger Whetmore. Rather than all five people dying, only one person died: The collective good was served at the expense of one individual. * * * Power was exercised responsibly and compassionately, in consideration of the rights and interests of the community of explorers. The explorers willfully considered the lives of each other and the impacts of different solutions on their survival before Whetmore died.

[Justice Cahn suggests that the ethic of care might also support conviction, because Whetmore withdrew from the compact before the lots were cast; the other explorers' decision to enforce the compact destroyed their community and disregarded Whetmore's objections. Similarly, the ethic of justice might support either conviction (the defendants violated the letter of the law) or acquittal (the self-defense rationale).]

Thus, I would remand this case with directions to the jury and trial judge to consider the context in which this case arose and to encourage them to use their own emotions as a guide to interpreting the statute and to deciding the meaning of "willfully." While this call for context is not a call for unrestrained emotions and standardless discretion, it is an invitation to integrate emotions with the application of standards and to use our power responsibly, morally, and generously.

MARY I. COOMBS, J. * * * Feminist method requires us to consider the effect of various possible, technically plausible interpretations of § 12–A on homicides that do not take place in caves. For example, there are numerous cases in which women who have been subjected to domestic violence kill their abusers. Lower courts have struggled with these cases, examining both the appropriate interpretation of the self-defense exception to the statute and such evidentiary questions as the admissibility of expert testimony on battered women's syndrome. Our decision here is likely to affect those cases. For example, if the self-defense exception were inapplicable to the Spelunceans because they deliberated before they killed Whetmore rather than acting impulsively, as Justice Tatting suggests, it might also be inapplicable to a woman who has endured a long and escalating pattern of abuse, because her action is not sudden.

On the other hand, women are more frequently victims than perpetrators of violence. What if we were to interpret § 12–A, as Justice Foster proposes, to include an implicit exception whenever the defendant is undeterrable? Would we open the door to exculpation of men who kill their wives and lovers in uncontrollable jealous rages? * * * I feel obliged to interpret the statute in the light of justice. Yet, I lack sufficient information to know what justice requires and sufficient perspicacity to draft an exception certain to have no unforeseen and undesirable broader consequences. * * *

Am I, then, left to join my brother Tatting in utter ambivalence and failure of nerve? Perhaps, but I at least see a more judicious way to avoid a task we ought not to have been given. This case reaches us in this form only because the jury (led by a foreman both male and a lawyer) evaded its assigned task. * * * Under the Newgarth Constitution, however, every defendant is entitled to a trial by jury. Nothing in the record indicates that the defendants personally waived that right, which is too fundamental to be waivable by counsel alone. I would therefore find this case, in the form presented to us, procedurally defective and remand for a new trial. * * *

[DWIGHT L.] GREENE, J. * * * I vote to affirm the convictions of the defendants but reverse their death sentences and remand for further proceedings consistent with this opinion. In doing so, I expressly rely on some of my perspectives as a Melanoderm.[2] As such, I generally favor expansive and contextual criminal adjudicatory processes by diverse juries, trial courts, and appellate courts. I believe that the Constitution of Newgarth requires some of this contextualization at sentencing. As developed below, however, there is no such contextual constraint on the predicate substantive, fact-finding process. As construed, many criminal laws are little more than automatic legal traps set for the less privileged. The privileged defendants in this case have been ensnared in one of these traps.

* * * Being Caucasoid confers many structural privileges in Newgarth. For example, Caucasoids can assume that the excess labor pool, three-quarters of which is Melanoderm, is available to them whenever they need it. Although the racial composition of the rescuers is not of record, we can assume that in this case, as in other similar rescue efforts, many of the rescuers were Melanoderms. Ten lives were lost rescuing these Caucasoids from their recreational follies.

[Justice Greene analyzes the structure of the Newgarth murder statute. It was enacted to reduce jury discretion: If the jurors found the predicate facts, "willfully" taking someone's life, then death is the required penalty. He also noted that the Court heard few cases under this sort of statute. It was usually enforced against Melanoderms, especially those accused of killing Caucasoids; such defendants did not have the resources to appeal their convictions, and Newgarth was no longer willing to fund criminal appeals as a matter of individual right.]

* * * There can be no argument but that the killing of Whetmore was knowing, deliberate, and intentional. Thus, the question before this Court is whether a knowing, deliberate, and intentional killing to enhance the probabilities of the defendants' survival can be deemed not willful. * * *

If I were starting on a clean interpretive slate * * * I would allow a jury composed of diverse participants to consider whether the defendants' actions were directly influenced by exogenous social circumstances. The finders of fact could consider whether circumstances beyond the killers' control, a kind

---

2. My use of the term Melanoderm incorporates the term Xanthoderm and the old terms Blacks, Yellows, and Coloreds, as well as the ancient terms African Americans and Latinos of color. Some of the perspectives upon which I rely have intellectual roots in the ancient schools of thought associated with what was called in the latter part of the twentieth century critical race theory.

of social duress, mitigated the killing. * * * Based on precedent, however, I am precluded from adopting such an open-ended fact-finding process in this case. This Court has construed the word "willfully" in a manner that precludes fact-finders from considering the influence of social circumstances.

The precedent to which I refer is obviously *Commonwealth v. Valjean.* In that case, a starving man was indicted for stealing a loaf of bread and offered his starving condition as a defense. * * * This Court affirmed that the social circumstances under which property is taken cannot be considered as negating a defendant's willfulness, even if the stolen property is the bread literally necessary to sustain life. This niggardly construction of willfulness controls the case now before the Court. * * *

[Justice Greene considers Justice Foster's argument that defendants had relapsed into a "state of nature," thereby enabling them to negotiate a new "social contract." Justice Greene questions whether Whetmore actually "consented" to this arrangement and whether consent is a defense to murder.]

Justice Foster's approach also reinforces an elitist perspective of contractarian social theory in our jurisprudence, which I reject. This approach provides options selectively under the criminal laws for the privileged while denying the same prerogatives to the unprivileged. Although the myth of an open society with transactions between and among freely contracting individuals is popular, it does not now reflect and never has reflected the reality of most people in Newgarth and certainly not that of Melanoderms. All contracts depend not only on the free will of the participants but also on their power within a real, not hypothetical social context. * * * [M]any Melanoderms and abandoned women and children live with inadequate education and in abject poverty, conditions they did not choose. These conditions, against which there is constant struggle, severely limit their power in social contracts. They are bound, nevertheless, by the laws of Newgarth.

Indeed, one could argue that in many of our ghettos conditions have deteriorated to a virtual state of nature "removed morally from the force of the legal order." Surely, this Court would be unwilling to excuse a group of Melanoderms from such a ghetto who formed their own social contract and imposed its outcomes on others within the community who dissented from that contract. Stated differently, assume Whetmore had been trapped in a ghetto during a riot with four nonrioting Melanoderms and food supplies were cut off. If these Melanoderms had used the same procedure used here to kill and eat Whetmore and then argued that their actions were in accord with their own social contract, such a specious argument would have been summarily rejected.

* * * In real life, as opposed to mythical states of nature, we are all limited in our ability to choose, and to contract, by social externalities [over which we have little or no control]. If the law is too constraining, then it must be changed for everyone. * * *

* * * [I]f the poor cannot be excused their poverty as sometimes necessitating the theft of the bread of life, then the privileged cannot be excused their killings to sustain their lives. The constraint imposed on the word "willfully" by *Valjean* limits the privileged just as it does the unprivileged. If social

circumstances are irrelevant in deciding whether the actions of the poor are willful, then social circumstances are irrelevant in deciding whether the actions of the privileged are willful. These defendants have been trapped by laws designed to deny the unprivileged contextual review in efficient criminal justice machines. This is the legislative will in which this Court concurred in *Valjean*. So be it. * * *

NOTE ON CRITICAL RACE AND FEMINIST THEORIES AND STATUTORY INTERPRETATION

Critical feminist and race theories can have at least three different kinds of insights about statutory interpretation. One kind of insight asks about the possible effect of a law or of an interpretation on women or racial minorities. Critical theory would insist that the law take into account these perspectives and cannot be considered "neutral" and surely not "universal" if it is not responsive to a variety of perspectives. This is reflected most strongly in Mary Coombs' opinion.

Another kind of insight wonders whether legal premises are neutral, whether assumptions that are foundational to law might not reflect a partial viewpoint. This is reflected most strongly in Dwight Greene's opinion. When you originally read our excerpts from Lon Fuller's article, did you feel "empathy" for the explorers? Did you feel less empathy for the explorers after reading the Coombs and Greene opinions?

A third (but surely not final) kind of insight might be about legal reasoning itself. All three of the critical opinions urge that law be more "contextualized," focusing more on the particular facts and less on universal principles. Naomi Cahn's opinion draws upon "cultural feminism," which contrasts an ethic of care with an ethic of justice. Although the latter is associated with traditional legal discourse, cultural feminism posits that there is no reason for law not to follow the ethic of care. Among the insights suggested by an ethic of care is a "resistance to the question." The original Speluncean Justices all answer the question as though they had a binary choice: Either affirm the convictions, or reverse them. All of our three new Speluncean Justices resist this binariness, and all three reconceptualize their alternatives (thereby avoiding the fate of Justice Tatting).

How would our critical panel (Justices Cahn, Coombs, and Greene) analyze the issue in *Holy Trinity Church*? *Locke*? *Weber*?

3. *Review of Various Theories of Statutory Interpretation*

The foregoing historical and theoretical introduction to statutory interpretation can, we admit, be a bit overwhelming. Between the various theories and the strong critiques that can be lodged against each of them, keeping track of everything can be difficult, and finding one's own moorings about which approach to prefer can be daunting indeed. We offer this discussion to review what we have seen and to provide a transition to Chapter 8.

When we think of a legal theory, we often suppose a rule or method that one follows to deduce the answer to a question. In this chapter, we examined three such deductive theories. Textualism, or plain meaning, posits that the court's role is to give the statutory text its plain or best meaning. Intentionalism posits that the court's role is to give the statute the meaning most consistent with the intentions of the enacting legislature. Purposivism (admittedly, an awkward term) posits that the court's role is to attribute to the statute the meaning most consistent with the general reasons why the enacting legislature believed the statute should be adopted. Another way to articulate purposivism is to recall the "mischief approach" of *Heydon's Case*, *supra*, under which the court first identifies the mischief in the prior law that the legislature wished to remedy and then interprets the statute to promote that remedial purpose. Much of the history of American statutory interpretation has involved the elaboration of the fine points of these theories (e.g., the old "plain meaning" approach versus the new textualism) and the competition among them for the hearts and opinions of judges.

Recently, several commentators have proposed less deductive methods of attributing meaning to statutes. These approaches, sometimes labeled "dynamic interpretation" or "practical reasoning," are inspired by hermeneutics, the study of interpretation in general. They all see statutory interpretation as essentially a practical, rather than primarily a theoretical or deductive, inquiry. On this understanding, the interpreter's task is to mediate the important factors in a statutory case — statutory text, the original context in which the statute was adopted, and the context in which the interpreters currently find themselves — rather than privilege one or more of these factors to the exclusion of the remainder. As this chapter indicates, your casebook authors fall into this last camp. Nonetheless, we do not agree among ourselves on all matters of statutory interpretation, and we hope that you will feel free to disagree with us in any or all respects.

In assessing the utility of the theories introduced in this chapter, we suggest three approaches.

1. Begin by engaging in empirical analysis. Which theory best describes the way American judges actually interpret statutes? We realize that this is an impossible question to answer completely, in part because you have not seen anything approaching the whole universe of American case law interpreting statutes. It may be possible at this point, however, to answer a subsidiary question: Based on the cases in this chapter, does any one theory capture the universal judicial practice? If, based on the cases we have read, it seems doubtful that a working majority on the current Supreme Court follows any one theory religiously, does that suggest that attorneys will find it impossible to advise clients about the probabilities in a hard statutory case (that is, one where the theories would produce different answers)? Or will the attorney skilled in statutory analysis (that is, you, once you complete this course and eventually graduate from law school) have the capacity to provide appropriate advice and to write strong briefs on either side of a hard statutory case? Recall, again, the revealing comparisons that can be made between *Chisom* and *Casey* (review note 3 following those cases).

As our joint article indicates, although we are not deductive theorists about statutory interpretation, we do believe theoretical inquiry is important in a statutory case. In our judgment, the hard cases are those in which the plausible competing theories conflict, and one role of theory (whether solely deductive or otherwise) is to develop a defensible, replicable model for resolving these conflicts. In this respect, some would say that even we are too theoretical. Some scholars, from the legal realists onward, have argued that judicial *decisionmaking*, as opposed to opinion writing, is barely theoretical at all.[j] We concede that judges reach decisions for a variety of reasons, and that pristine legal theory is not a high priority for many of them. We do reject the view, however, that theory makes no difference. Our view, expressed in the manner in which we have organized these materials, is that learning the craft of lawyering requires, among other things, the capacity to construct theoretical arguments persuasively within a given context.[k]

---

j. Consider Robert Martineau, *Craft and Technique, Not Canons and Grand Theories: A Neo-Realist View of Statutory Interpretation*, 62 Geo. Wash. L. Rev. 1, 26 (1993):

There are several key elements to the appellate process that the statutory interpretation scholar should keep in mind. First, the positions that the parties take in their arguments to a court are purely result-oriented. Their lawyers make the arguments, textual or contextual, that support their position. Second, the judges' primary concern prior to the decision conference is understanding the facts and contentions of the parties. Third, the decision conference is devoted primarily to result, not to the approach to be taken in the opinion. Fourth, the law clerk, often the person with the principal responsibility for drafting an opinion to support the decision, is not present at the decision conference. The judge assigned the opinion-writing responsibility directs the law clerk concerning the result and may instruct the clerk about the approach to be taken in the draft opinion. Finally, the other judges on the panel play some part, but not a major role, in the opinion's development.

* * * [An appellate] opinion would justify the development of canons and grand theories of statutory construction if it either reflected the thought processes by which the judges reached the decision or was argued in the document submitted to the judges that persuaded them to decide the case in the way they did. In fact, the opinion is neither. It is, rather, a reasoned justification of the decision prepared after the decision is made. The principal purpose of the opinion is to make the decision appear consistent with the facts and the relevant statutory and judicial authority.

On whether theories and scholarship concerning statutory interpretation have affected judicial practice, see Gregory Crespi, *The Influence of a Decade of Statutory Interpretation Scholarship on Judicial Rulings: An Empirical Analysis*, 53 SMU L. Rev. 9 (2000) (identifying an explosion in such scholarship over the past decade and increasing citation of several of these articles by judges, but speculating that the citations are included more to add academic pizzaz than to reflect influence upon actual decisionmaking); Daniel Farber, *Do Theories of Statutory Interpretation Matter? A Case Study*, 94 Nw. U. L. Rev. 1409 (2000) (finding only rare differences in outcome between Judges Posner and Easterbrook despite their differences in interpretive approach).

k. See Richard Posner, *The Problems of Jurisprudence* 100 (1990):

The most important thing that law school imparts to its students is a feel for the outer bounds of permissible legal argumentation at the time when the education is being imparted. (Later those bounds will change, of course.) What "thinking like a lawyer" means is not the use of special analytic powers but an awareness of approximately how plastic law is at the frontiers — neither infinitely plastic, * * * nor rigid and predetermined, as many laypersons think — and of the permissible "moves" in arguing for, or against, a change in the law. It is neither method nor doctrine, but a repertoire of acceptable arguments and a feel for the degree and character of doctrinal stability, or, more generally, for the contours of a professional culture — a professional culture lovable to some, hateful to others.

In concluding your empirical inquiry, consider whether context may affect the utility of a theory. For example, although none of us is a textualist, as appellate judges we might well give especially strong primacy to statutory text in some cases. Illustratively, the bankruptcy code is mammoth and complex, and none of us is much familiar with its complicated subject matter of secured financing, commercial transactions, and the like. To be sure, we might engage in flexible approaches to interpretation in uncomplicated bankruptcy cases involving obvious issues of justice, such as *Shine v. Shine*. In the complicated corporate bankruptcy case, however, we might pretty much stick with the statutory text, especially where no drafting error is apparent and policy arguments do not cut conclusively in either direction. We also might tend to defer to an interpreter with more expertise than ourselves, such as the specialized federal bankruptcy judges. Only after gaining greater familiarity and confidence with the bankruptcy code and the policy issues associated with it might we become more venturesome interpreters.[1]

2. Next, engage in normative analysis. What approach to statutory interpretation strikes you as the most attractive for the American legal system? Work hard to identify those values that lead you to this conclusion. What values ought to be important: Rule of law? Regularized decisionmaking by the institutions most competent to make each kind of decision? The best rule? If the last, what is the criterion for "best"? Efficiency? A conception of justice? (Whose — Rawls? Nozick?) Are all these values relevant? If so, how do you balance them?

In making your normative assessment, note that you do not escape empirical claims. For example, if textualism strikes you as the best approach because it is good to limit judicial discretion (a normative conclusion), you must assess criticisms of your conclusion from both empirical perspectives (e.g., textualism will not, in fact, operate to limit judicial discretion) and normative ones (e.g., handcuffing judges from reaching obviously just and right results in individual cases is wrong).

3. Finally, engage in doctrinal analysis. There is really no way to assess the utility of any approach to statutory interpretation without knowing the details of American legal doctrine. For example, textualism posits that legislative history should hardly ever be examined in the interpretive process. Is that consistent with the case law? Textualism — at least as articulated by Justice Scalia in his *Chisom* dissent — also posits that "established canons of statutory interpretation" should have a strong role in guiding the meaning of statutory text. What are these canons, and, in particular, how does one distinguish an

---

1. See generally Daniel Bussel, *Textualism's Failures: A Study of Overruled Bankruptcy Decisions*, 53 Vand. L. Rev. 887 (2000); Robert Rasmussen, *A Study of the Costs and Benefits of Textualism: The Supreme Court's Bankruptcy Cases*, 71 Wash. U. L.Q. 535 (1993). For the argument that statutes generally involve at least three interpretive communities (the policy community of specialists in government bureaucracies, the political community of elected officials, and the public) and that pragmatic interpreters should design their interpretive methodology in light of which community is the primary audience for the decision at hand, see William Blatt, *Interpretive Communities: The Missing Element in Statutory Interpretation*, 95 Nw. U. L. Rev. 629 (2001).

"established" one from a mere pretender? Are the legal rules or presumptions found in the canons empirically supportable? Normatively attractive? Similar "micro-level" inquiries will enrich your perspectives on the other theories as well. Last, but hardly least important, it will be your knowledge of and capacity to use these doctrinal details that will determine much about your success as an attorney, at least if you (as do most attorneys) end up practicing in an area in which statutes and administrative regulations provide much of the law. It is to these doctrines that we turn in the next chapter.

Chapter 8

DOCTRINES OF STATUTORY INTERPRETATION

The previous chapter introduced you to the history of statutory interpretation in the United States and to the major theories that have been debated (textualism old and new, intentionalism and imaginative reconstruction, purposivism and dynamic theories). This chapter turns to the doctrines that underlie these theories.

Section 1 considers the accepted *canons of statutory construction*. The canons have been the bedrock of Anglo-American interpretation for centuries. Although they were de-emphasized in federal courts after the New Deal, the canons remained critically important at the state level and have made a federal comeback since the mid-1980s. Section 1 introduces you to most of the canons traditionally used as *intrinsic aids* to statutory construction, as well as to canons based upon substantive values.

Next, Section 2 deals with sources *extrinsic* to the statutory text. Extrinsic evidence includes the common law, related statutes, and legislative history. Legislative history was not much used before 1892, when the Supreme Court decided *Holy Trinity Church* (Chapter 7, § 1). In the twentieth century, the Court has often used legislative history, and most state courts will consider it as well. The new textualism discussed in Chapter 7, § 3 questions reliance on legislative history, and we shall examine this and other critiques in this chapter.

Finally, Section 3 turns to the problem of interpreting laws enacted by the voters, not by the legislature. As discussed in Chapter 5, lawmaking by initiative is common in many states. Courts struggle in attempting to apply the traditional tools of statutory interpretation in this context, where the lawmaking body (the voters) is unlikely to have a discernable "intent" and lacks knowledge of the basic canons of interpretation.

SECTION 1. RULES, PRESUMPTIONS, AND CANONS OF STATUTORY INTERPRETATION

There are a good many rules of thumb for interpreting statutes. Called "maxims," "canons," or "principles" of construction, these rules are said to enable interpreters to draw inferences from the language, format, and subject matter of the statute. Most of the nineteenth century English and American treatises on statutory interpretation were organized around the canons, and the leading doctrinal compilation today (a descendant of an 1891 treatise) is an exhaustive canon-by-canon tour. Sutherland, *Statutes and Statutory Construction* (5th ed., Norman Singer ed.) (hereinafter referred to as Sutherland).[a] Many states have codified the traditional canons in their state codes. E.g., Minn. Stat. ch. 645; Pennsylvania Statutory Construction Act, 1 Pa. Consol. Stat. §§ 1921–1928 (hereinafter "Pa. Stat. Constr. Act"). See also 1 U.S.C. §§ 1–7 (codification of word-meaning canons).

There are basically three kinds of canons. First are the *textual canons*, which set forth inferences that are usually drawn from the drafter's choice of words, their grammatical placement in sentences, and their relationship to other parts of the statute. These are sometimes called *intrinsic aids*, for they assist the statutory interpreter in deriving probable meaning from the four corners of the statutory text. Part A of this Section sets forth many of these textual canons, with illustrations from state and federal cases.

A second genre consists of the *substantive canons*. These are presumptions about statutory meaning based upon substantive principles or policies drawn from the common law, other statutes, or the Constitution. An example is the "rule of lenity," which, based in part upon principles of fair notice, presumes that criminal statutes do not outlaw behavior unless the activity clearly comes within the sweep of the statutes. The substantive canons are explored in Part B. Part C then examines the rather intense theoretical debates over the textual and substantive canons and provides several practical problems on their usage.

Section 2 of this chapter will focus on the third group of maxims, the *reference canons*. These are sometimes called *extrinsic aids*. They are presumptive rules telling the interpreter what other materials — the common law, other statutes, legislative history (all explored in Section 2), as well as agency interpretations (Chapter 9) — might be consulted to figure out what the statute means. Canons such as the plain meaning rule, which severely limits the use of extrinsic evidence, and the rule of deference to agency decisions have made a big comeback since the mid-1980s and have generated an unusually rich debate. For a collection of canons used by the United States Supreme Court in recent years, see Appendix B of this casebook.

---

    a. Sutherland is the leading American treatise. Also valuable reference works are leading treatises in the United Kingdom, see P. St.J. Langan, *Maxwell on the Interpretation of Statutes* (12th ed. 1969), and F.A.R. Bennion, *Statutory Interpretation* (1997); Canada, see Ruth Sullivan, *Driedger on the Construction of Statutes* (4th ed. 2002); Ruth Sullivan, *Statutory Interpretation* (1997); Australia, see Donald Gifford, *Statutory Interpretation* (1990), and D.C. Pearce & R.S. Geddes, *Statutory Interpretation in Australia* (6th ed. 2006); New Zealand, see Jim Evans, *Statutory Interpretation: Problems of Communication* (1988); and South Africa, see G.E. Devenish, *Interpretation of Statutes* (1992). For a compendium surveying the practice in civil law countries as well, see *Interpreting Statutes: A Comparative Study* (D. Neil MacCormick & Robert Summers eds., 1991).

A. TEXTUAL CANONS

The starting point of statutory interpretation is to *read* the statute carefully. A number of rules — based either on general notions of English composition or syntax or the structure of a statute — have been stated as guides for finding meaning from the words of the statute and nothing else. These are called "intrinsic aids" or "textual canons" of interpretation. They are normally invoked by courts as conventional benchmarks for discerning the most appropriate use of language. Some judicial rhetoric to the contrary, text-based canons are decidedly not hard-and-fast rules; they are at best presumptions and might be considered most like adages. See Lawrence Solan, *The Language of Judges* ch. 2 (1993) (linguistic analysis of several textual canons), as well as Neil MacCormick, *Argumentation and Interpretation in Law*, 6 Ratio Juris 16 (1993) (discussing linguistic arguments as a category of interpretive argument). Consider the following problem as an introduction to the canons.

Introductory Problem: The No Vehicles in the Park Statute

Problem 8–1. In the wake of an accident in which a motorcycle speeding through Pierre Trudeau Park ran over and killed an elderly gentleman, the City Council enacted the following statute in 1980:

Sec. 1. The Council finds that vehicles create safety problems when they are operated in parks and further finds that the best solution is to ban any and all vehicles from all municipal parks.

Sec. 2. No vehicles of any kind shall be allowed in any municipal park. Any person who brings or drives a vehicle into one of these parks shall be guilty of a misdemeanor, which may be punished by a fine not exceeding $500 or by a two-day incarceration in the municipal jail, or both.

Sec. 3. "Vehicle" for purposes of this law means any mechanism for conveying a person from one place to another, including automobiles, trucks, motorcycles, and motor scooters. *Provided that*, bicycles shall be allowed in the park, so long as they are being pushed or carried and not ridden.

After a decade of spotty enforcement, a new constable, Barney Fife, adopts a strict, no-tolerance enforcement policy. In 1996, he arrests (a) a 13-year-old boy riding a skateboard through the park; (b) a mother pushing a baby carriage in the park; and (c) a 6-year-old girl riding her tricycle in the park. All three "perps" (and the parents of the child perps) challenge their arrests, on the ground that the statute does not apply to their conduct. How should the City Magistrate rule? Consider the following canons.

1. *Maxims of Word Meaning and Association*

(a) *Ordinary (and Technical) Meaning of Words.* Typically, courts will assume that the legislature uses words in their ordinary sense: What would these words convey to the "ordinary" or "reasonable" reader? To figure this out, judges may consult dictionaries,[b] but they will often just rely on their own linguistic experience or intuition to decide the most reasonable meaning of the words, given the context in which they are being used and applied. Ordinary meaning should be distinguished from literal meaning or strict construction; the latter connotes a narrow understanding of words used, while the former connotes the everyday understanding.

Linguists suggest that the interpreter start with the *prototypical* meaning of statutory words.[c] What is the core idea associated with a word or phrase? For example, this was the approach implicitly followed by Justice Brennan in *Weber*, the affirmative action case (Chapter 1, § 3): although some dictionaries define "discriminate" broadly enough to include any kind of differentiation, the core or prototypical use of the word requires some invidious intent. Thus, we do not say we "discriminate" against pears if we prefer peaches, nor (according to Brennan) do we say we "discriminate" against a minority if we give him a helping hand to counterbalance what we believe is an inferior starting point because of preexisting prejudice or stereotyping. Ordinary meaning, therefore, might be associated with prototypical meaning. This idea usually supports cautious, or restrictive, readings of statutes. See, e.g., *Holy Trinity Church* (Chapter 7, § 1) (confining "labor or service of any kind" to manual work); *Canada (Attorney General) v. Mossop*, [1991] 1 F.C. 18, 34 (Fed. Ct.), aff'd, [1993] 1 S.C.R. 554 (Can. Sup. Ct.) (applying the "core meaning" of "family" to exclude same-sex partnerships).

What if the statute is an old one? In that event, judges sometimes consult dictionaries and other evidence from the era in which the statute was enacted. For example, the Supreme Court in *St. Francis College v. Al-Khazraji*, 481 U.S. 604 (1987), interpreted the Civil Rights Act of 1866 to apply to discrimination against a person of Arab ancestry. Defendant had argued that any discrimination against an ethnic Arab was not actionable, because the statute only required the same protections as are "enjoyed by white citizens" and Arabs are ethnographically Caucasian. The Court invoked nineteenth-century dictionaries and encyclopedias to demonstrate that defendant's conception of race was not the one held in the nineteenth century, which viewed different ethnic "stock" and family "lineage" as different "races." Thus, these sources referred to Finns, Greeks, Basques, Arabs, Norwegians, Jews, and Hungarians as identifiable "races." For another example, see *Cook County v. United States*, 538 U.S. 119, 132 (2003), interpreting the False Claims Act of 1863.

In addition to special meanings that words may have had historically, words often have meanings limited to parlance in a trade, academic discipline, or

---

b. See Ellen Aprill, *The Law of the Word: Dictionary Shopping in the Supreme Court*, 30 Ariz. St. L.J. 275 (1998); Lawrence Solan, *When Judges Use the Dictionary*, 68 Am. Speech 50 (1993); Samuel Thumma & Jeffrey Kirchmeier, *The Lexicon Has Become a Fortress: The United States Supreme Court's Use of Dictionaries*, 47 Buff. L. Rev. 227 (1999); Note, *Looking It Up: Dictionaries and Statutory Interpretation*, 107 Harv. L. Rev. 1437 (1994).

c. See Lawrence Solan, *Learning Our Limits: The Decline of Textualism in Statutory Cases*, 1997 Wis. L. Rev. 235, 270–75 (explaining linguists' "prototype" theory and applying it to several statutory interpretation cases).

technical area. Where the statute itself deals with a technical, specialized subject, courts tend to adopt the specialized meaning of words used in the statute, unless that leads to an absurd result. For a hoary, and perhaps amusing, example of this maxim, see *Nix v. Hedden*, 149 U.S. 304, 305–07 (1893):

> This was an action, brought February 4, 1887, against the collector of the port of New York, to recover back duties, paid under protest, on tomatoes imported by the plaintiff from the West Indies in the spring of 1886, which the collector assessed under "Schedule G. — Provisions," of the Tariff Act of March 3, 1883, chap. 121, imposing a duty on "Vegetables in their natural state, or in salt or brine, not specially enumerated or provided for in this Act, ten per centum *ad valorem*"; and which the plaintiffs contended came within the clause in the free list of the same act. "Fruits, green, ripe or dried, not specially enumerated or provided for in this act." 22 Stat. 504, 519.

> At the trial, the plaintiff's counsel, after reading in evidence definitions of the words "fruit" and "vegetables" from Webster's Dictionary, Worchester's Dictionary and the Imperial Dictionary, called two witnesses, who had been for thirty years in the business of selling fruit and vegetables, and asked them, after hearing these definitions, to say whether these words had "any special meaning in trade or commerce, different from those read."

> One of the witnesses answered as follows: "Well, it does not classify all things there, but they are correct as far as they go. It does not take all kinds of fruit or vegetables; it takes a portion of them. I think the words 'fruit' and 'vegetable' have the same meaning in trade today that they had on March 1, 1883. I understand that the term 'fruit' is applied in trade only to such plants or parts of plants as contain the seeds. There are more vegetables than those in the enumeration given in Webster's Dictionary under the term 'vegetable,' as 'cabbage, cauliflower, turnips, potatoes, peas, beans, and the like,' probably covered by the words 'and the like.' "

> The other witnesses testified: "I don't think the term 'fruit' or the term 'vegetables' had in March 1883, and prior thereto, any special meaning in trade and commerce in this country, different from that which I have read here from the dictionaries."

> The plaintiff's counsel then read in evidence from the same dictionaries the definitions of the word "tomato."

> The defendant's counsel then read in evidence from Webster's dictionary the definitions of the words "pea," "egg plant," "cucumber," "squash," and "pepper."

> The plaintiff then read in evidence from Webster's and Worcester's dictionaries the definitions of "potato," "turnip," "parsnip," "cauliflower," "cabbage," "carrot," and "bean."

> No other evidence was offered by either party. The court, upon the defendant's motion, directed a verdict for him, which was returned, and judgment rendered therein. The plaintiffs duly excepted to the instruction, and sued out this writ of error. * * *

> There being no evidence that the words "fruit" and "vegetables" have acquired any special meaning in trade or commerce, they must receive their ordinary meaning. Of that meaning the court is bound to take judicial notice, as it does in regard to all words in our own tongue; and upon such a question dictionaries are admitted, not as evidence, but only as aids to the memory and understanding of the court.

Botanically speaking, tomatoes are the fruit of a vine, just as are cucumbers, squashes, beans and peas. But in the common language of the people, whether sellers or consumers of provisions, all these are vegetables, which are grown in kitchen gardens, and which, whether eaten cooked or raw, are, like potatoes, carrots, parsnips, turnips, beets, cauliflower, cabbage, celery and lettuce, usually served at dinner in, with, or after the soup, fish or meats which constitute the principal part of the repast, and not, like fruits generally, as dessert.

The attempt to class tomatoes as fruit is not unlike a recent attempt to class beans as seeds, of which Mr. Justice Bradley, speaking for this court, said: "We do not see why they should be classified as seeds, any more than walnuts should be so classified. Both are seeds in the language of botany or natural history, but not in commerce nor in common parlance. On the other hand, in speaking generally of provisions, beans may well be included under the term 'vegetables.' As an article of food on our tables, whether baked or boiled, or forming the basis of soup, they are used as a vegetable, as well as when ripe as when green. This is the principal use to which they are put. Beyond the common knowledge which we have on this subject, very little evidence is necessary, or can be produced." *Robertson v. Salomon*, 130 U.S. 412, 414 (1889).

See also *Zuni Pub. Sch. Dist. v. Department of Education,* 127 S.Ct. 1534, 1540 (2007), deferring to the experts when construing technical statutory language for determining whether a state aid program "equalizes expenditures."

A related maxim is this: "Where Congress uses terms that have accumulated settled meaning under either equity or the common law, a court must infer, unless the statute otherwise dictates, that Congress means to incorporate the established meaning of these terms." *NLRB v. Amax Coal Co.*, 453 U.S. 322, 329 (1981); accord, *Scheidler v. NOW*, 537 U.S. 393, 402 (2003); *United States v. Wells*, 519 U.S. 482, 491 (1997); *Community for Creative Non-Violence v. Reid*, 490 U.S. 730, 739 (1989); § 2A of this chapter. Compare *Jodrey Estate v. Nova Scotia,* [1980] 2 S.C.R. 774 (Can. Sup. Ct.) (reflecting the Canadian preference for following ordinary rather than technical meanings).

(b) *Noscitur a Sociis and Ejusdem Generis.* Words are social creatures: they travel in packs. Several canons suggest permissible inferences from the company that words keep. "Noscitur a sociis" translates as "[i]t is known from its associates." Light may be shed on the meaning of an ambiguous word by reference to words associated with it. "Thus, when two or more words are grouped together, and ordinarily have a similar meaning, but are not equally comprehensive, the general word will be limited and qualified by the special word." 2A Sutherland § 47.16, at 183; see *Maxwell, supra* note a, at 289–93 (hereinafter *Maxwell*); *Driedger, supra* note a, at 173–75 (hereinafter *Driedger*). For example, in *Jarecki v. G. D. Searle & Co.*, 367 U.S. 303 (1961), a federal income tax statute allowed allocation to other years of income "resulting from exploration, discovery, or prospecting." A drug manufacturer and a camera manufacturer argued that they should be allowed to take advantage of the allocation statute with respect to income from the sale of patented products because by definition such a product resulted from a "discovery." The Court disagreed. When interpreted in light of the associated words "exploration" and "prospecting," the term "discovery" meant only the discovery of mineral resources. See also *Gutierrez v. Ada*, 528 U.S. 250 (2000) (repeated statutory iteration of "any election" with Governor and Lieutenant Governor suggests that the context is limited to those two elections only).

"Ejusdem generis," a sibling of noscitur a sociis, translates as "[o]f the same kind, class, or nature." "Where general words follow specific words in a statutory enumeration, the general words are construed to embrace only objects similar in nature to those objects enumerated by the preceding specific words. Where the opposite sequence is found, i.e., specific words following general ones, the doctrine is equally applicable, and restricts application of the general term to things that are similar to those enumerated." 2A Sutherland § 47.17, at 188; see *Maxwell* 297–303; *Driedger* 175–86. The purpose of this rule is to give effect to all the words — the particular words indicate the class and the general words extend the provisions of the statute to everything else in the class (even though not enumerated by the specific words). See also *AT&T v. Iowa Utilities Bd.*, 525 U.S. 366, 408 (1999) (Thomas, J., dissenting in part); *Norfolk & Western Ry. Co. v. American Train Dispatchers Ass'n*, 499 U.S. 117, 129 (1991).

An example of the application of this canon is *Heathman v. Giles*, 374 P.2d 839 (Utah 1962). In that case, plaintiff brought an action for false arrest, malicious prosecution, and other torts against a prosecutor and deputy prosecutors. The trial court had dismissed the action because the plaintiff had failed to file a bond for the payment of any costs and attorneys' fees that might be awarded to defendants. The trial court relied upon a statute that required such a bond in actions brought against "any sheriff, constable, peace officer, state road officer, or any other person charged with the duty of enforcement of the criminal laws of this state * * * when such action arises out of, or in the course of the performance of his duty." The Supreme Court of Utah reversed, holding that the defendants were not "other persons charged with the duty of enforcement of the criminal laws" for purposes of this statute. The "other persons * * *" language, the court concluded, must be limited to persons of the "same class as those expressly mentioned." The court noted that the specified officers identified (*id.* at 840):

> are all badge-carrying officers * * * in the front line of law enforcement * * * who are charged with the duty of seeking out persons suspected of crime; and of making arrests and taking them into custody. In the nature of their duties they often must accost persons who are unknown to them; and sometimes those who may be dangerous characters. They are therefore required to take various risks, including that of being mistaken. It seems so plain that it is unnecessary to dwell on the matter that defendants as prosecuting attorneys, although "charged with the duty of enforcement of criminal laws," are officers of such a significantly different character that they are not within the class for whom the protections of this statute was intended. * * *

See also *Hodgerney v. Baker*, 88 N.E.2d 625 (Mass. 1949) (automobile not covered by ordinance forbidding the placing of "dirt, rubbish, wood, timber, or other material of any kind" tending to obstruct the streets).

Section 1 of the Federal Arbitration Act of 1926 excludes from coverage "contracts of employment of seamen, railroad employees, or any other class of workers engaged in foreign or interstate commerce." 9 U.S.C. § 1. The issue in *Circuit City Stores, Inc. v. Adams*, 532 U.S. 105 (2001), was whether the exclusion was limited to contracts involving *transportation* but not other kinds of employment contracts. Workers suing their employers generally want a court, not an arbitrator, especially for discrimination claims such as those in *Circuit City.* So the plaintiff argued that his job at a retail store, obviously engaged in "interstate commerce," fell within the exclusion: Congress, he argued, meant to exclude employment contracts generally, and used language tied to the jurisdictional basis of the FAA, the Commerce Clause. The Supreme Court rejected that reading, on the ground that *ejusdem generis* suggested that Congress meant the exclusion to be limited to contracts "like" those involving seamen and railroad workers — namely, transportation contracts.

Noscitur a sociis and ejusdem generis, like the other canons, are just aids to meaning, not ironclad rules. Thus, they have no value if the statute evidences a meaning contrary to their presumptions. See *United States v. Turkette*, 452 U.S. 576, 581 (1981). Dissenting in *Circuit City*, Justice Souter argued that the legislative purpose and specific history rebutted any presumption created by ejusdem generis. Both labor unions petitioning Congress for an exemption and Secretary of Commerce Herbert Hoover, the primary architect of the law, endorsed the broader view of the exclusion. (The Court found the statute sufficiently clear and rejected this evidence.)

Deployment of ejusdem generis involves a judgment — often a debatable one — about what it is that makes the items in the series "similar." The *Circuit City* Court found that the common denominator was "transportation contracts," while the dissenters found it to be "employment contracts within Congress's Commerce Clause power." For another example of such a debatable judgment, compare Justice Alito's opinion for the Court in *James v. United States*, 127 S.Ct. 1586, 1592 (2007) (holding that "attempted burglary" is a crime that "otherwise involves conduct that presents a serious risk of physical injury to another"), with Justice Scalia's dissenting characterization, id. at 1601–02. See generally 2A Sutherland § 47.17–.22 (discussing ejusdem generis and qualifications to its use); *Maxwell* 303–06.

(c) *Expressio unius.* Words omitted may be just as significant as words set forth. The maxim "expressio [or inclusio] unius est exclusio alterius" means "expression (or inclusion) of one thing indicates exclusion of the other." The notion is one of negative implication: the enumeration of certain things in a statute suggests that the legislature had no intent of including things not listed or embraced. "When a statute limits a thing to be done in a particular mode, it includes a negative of any other mode." *Raleigh & Galston R. Co. v. Reid,* 13 Wall. 269, 270 (1872). See *Tate v. Ogg*, 195 S.E. 496 (Va. 1938) (statute covering "any horse, mule, cattle, hog, sheep or goat" did not cover turkeys); Sutherland § 47.25 (discussing the limitations of the canon); *Maxwell* 293–97; *Driedger* 168–76.

As *Holy Trinity Church* (Chapter 7, § 1) exemplifies, courts feel free to refuse to apply the maxim when they believe it would lead to a result Congress did not intend.[d] One basic problem is that this canon, like many of the others, assumes that the legislature thinks through statutory language carefully, considering every possible variation. This is clearly not true, for the legislature often omits things because no one thinks about them or everyone assumes that courts will fill in gaps. See Richard Posner, *The Federal Courts: Crisis and Reform* 282 (1985). Some judges have suggested that the maxim is unreliable and should be invoked with caution because "it stands on the faulty premise that all possible alternative or supplemental provisions were necessarily considered and rejected by the [legislature]." *National Petroleum Refiners Ass'n v. FTC*, 482 F.2d 672, 676 (D.C. Cir. 1973). See also *Herman & MacLean v. Huddleston*, 459 U.S. 375, 388 (1983); *Director, Etc. v. Bethlehem Mines Corp.*, 669 F.2d 187 (4th Cir. 1982); *Gattis v. Chavez*, 413 F.Supp. 33 (D.S.C. 1976).

Another way of looking at this issue is to consider context, including normative context. If Mother tells Sally, "Don't hit, kick, or bite your sister Anne," Sally is *not* authorized by expressio unius to "pinch" her little sister. The reason is that the normative baseline (discerned from prior practice or just family culture) is "no harming sister," and the directive was an expression of that baseline that ought not be narrowly limited. Contrariwise, where the directive in question is a departure from the normative baseline, the canon ought to apply. For example, if Mother tells Sally, "You may have a cookie and a scoop of ice cream," Sally has implicitly been forbidden to snap up that candy bar lying on the kitchen table. For cases where normative statutory baselines augured against application of expressio unius, see, e.g., *Marrama v. Citizens Bank of Mass.*, 127 S.Ct. 1105, 1111–12 (2007) (Stevens, J.); *Christensen v. Harris County*, 529 U.S. 576, 583–84 (2000) (Thomas, J.).

But consider *Chan v. Korean Air Lines*, 490 U.S. 122 (1989), where the Supreme Court held that international air carriers do not lose their Warsaw Convention limitation on damages arising out of passenger injury or death when they fail to provide the passenger with the requisite notice of limitation on her ticket. Article 3(1) of the Convention requires such notice, and article 3(2) provides that if the carrier fails to deliver a ticket to the passenger it cannot avail itself of the Convention's liability limits. Although many lower courts had interpreted article 3(2) to include situations where the passenger received a ticket, but without the requisite notice, the Court, in an opinion by Justice Scalia, held to the contrary. Justice Scalia's key argument was that other sections of the Convention provide parallel rules for limiting carrier liability and providing notice thereof, for baggage checks (article 4) and cargo waybills (article 9). The various sections are identical in their notice requirements, but not in their remedies. Article 3 (passenger injury) provides

---

d. In that case, the statute that prohibited bringing into the United States an alien for employment exempted certain persons such as lecturers and domestic servants. Had the Court followed expressio unius, it would have held that the listed exceptions were the only ones not covered by the prohibition, and therefore that the church had violated the statute.

no remedy explicitly covering insufficient notice, while articles 4 and 9 explicitly waive liability limits for the carrier's failure to include the required notice in the documents given to the consumer. By negative implication, Scalia construed article 3 not to have the remedy that had been clearly provided in the other articles.

The dissenting opinion argued from the Convention's negotiating history that the lack of a similar remedy in article 3(2) was probably inadvertent. Justice Scalia considered such evidence inadmissible. If such evidence were admissible, would it persuade you that Justice Scalia's invocation of expressio unius was too hasty? Note that fellow textualist Judge Easterbrook considers expressio unius arguments question-begging and unreliable. See *In re American Reserve Corp.*, 840 F.2d 487, 492 (7th Cir. 1988). But at the Supreme Court level, arguments drawn from the expressio unius concept have had an enduring appeal.[e]

2. *Grammar Canons*

Although "justice should not be the hand maiden of grammar," *Value Oil Co. v. Irvington*, 377 A.2d 1225, 1231 (N.J. Super. 1977), the legislature is presumed to know and follow basic conventions of grammar and syntax. *Maxwell* 28. Like the canons discussed above, the following are more rules of thumb than commands.

(a) *Punctuation Rules.* "The punctuation canon in America * * * has assumed at least three forms: (1) adhering to the strict English rule that punctuation forms no part of the statute; (2) allowing punctuation as an aid in statutory construction; and (3) looking on punctuation as a less-than-desirable, last-ditch alternative aid in statutory construction. The last approach * * * seems to have prevailed as the majority rule." Ray Marcin, *Punctuation and the Interpretation of Statutes*, 9 Conn. L. Rev. 227, 240 (1977). The English rule noted by Marcin was adopted because "[a]t one time * * * punctuation [was] inserted by a clerk after the statute had been enacted by Parliament." U.S. legislatures (at both state and federal levels) generally consider and pass bills whose punctuation is not changed after enactment. 2A Sutherland § 47.15, at 179, argues that "an act should be read as punctuated unless there is some reason to do otherwise," such as an indication that such a reading would defeat the apparent intent of the legislature. "This is especially true where a statute has been repeatedly reenacted with the same punctuation, or has been the subject of numerous amendments without alteration of punctuation." See also *Driedger* 312–14; Pa. Stat. Constr. Act § 1923(b): "In no case shall

---

e. See, e.g., *Hinck v. United States,* 127 S.Ct. 2011, 2015 (2007) (Roberts, C.J.); *TRW, Inc. v. Andrews*, 534 U.S. 19 (2001) (Ginsburg, J.); *Solid Waste Agency v. Army Corps of Eng'rs*, 531 U.S. 159 (2001) (Rehnquist, C.J.); *City of Chicago v. Environmental Defense Fund*, 511 U.S. 328 (1994) (Scalia, J.,); *Key Tronic Corp. v. United States*, 511 U.S. 809, 818–19 (1994) (Stevens, J.); *United States v. Smith*, 499 U.S. 160 (1991) (Marshall, J.); *Mississippi Band of Choctaw Indians v. Holyfield*, 490 U.S. 30, 46–47 & n.22 (1989) (Brennan, J., who wrote the dissenting opinion in *Chan*); *Pittston Coal Group v. Sebben*, 488 U.S. 105, 115 (1989) (Scalia, J.); *Mackey v. Lanier Collections Agency & Serv.*, 486 U.S. 825, 836–37 (1988) (White, J.).

the punctuation of a statute control or affect the intention of the General Assembly in the enactment thereof but punctuation may be used in aid in the construction thereof * * *."

Consider *Tyrrell v. New York*, 53 N.E. 1111 (N.Y. 1899). A state statute provided that the salaries for persons employed as street cleaners "shall not exceed the following: * * * of the section foremen, one thousand dollars each; * * * of the hostlers, seven hundred and twenty dollars each, and extra pay for work on Sundays." (A "hostler" is someone who tends the horses in the stables.) The court ruled that a foreman was not entitled to extra pay for work on Sundays (*id.* at 1112):

> The punctuation of this statute is of material aid in learning the intention of the legislature. While an act of parliament is enacted as read, and the original rolls contain no marks of punctuation, a statute of this state is enacted as read and printed, so that the punctuation is a part of the act as passed, and appears in the roll when filed with the secretary of state.

The punctuation canon has *not* played a major role in the legisprudence of the U.S. Supreme Court. The Court found the punctuation rule decisive in *United States v. Ron Pair Enterprises, Inc.*, 489 U.S. 235 (1989), but otherwise this canon is rarely controlling. In *United States National Bank v. Independent Insurance Agents*, 508 U.S. 439 (1993), the Court in effect repunctuated a statute after concluding that a scrivener's error had occurred.

(b) *Referential and Qualifying Words: The Last Antecedent Rule.* Referential and qualifying words or phrases refer only to the last antecedent, unless contrary to the apparent legislative intent derived from the sense of the entire enactment. E.g., *Jama v. Immigration & Customs Enforcement*, 543 U.S. 345 (2005). For example, in a statute providing that "the limitation of an action will not be extended beyond six years of the act or omission of alleged malpractice by a nondiscovery thereof," the "thereof" refers to the "act or omission of alleged malpractice." *Anderson v. Shook*, 333 N.W.2d 708 (N.D. 1983). Similarly, a proviso applies only to the provision, clause, or word immediately preceding it.

Consider this recent example. The Social Security Act's disability benefits program is available to a worker whose "physical or mental impairment or impairments are of such severity that he is not only unable to do his previous work but cannot, considering his age, education, and work experience, engage in any other kind of substantial gainful work which exists in the national economy." 42 U.S.C. § 423(d)(2)(A). Pauline Thomas was an elevator operator until that job was eliminated from the economy; she claimed to be disabled from other jobs in the economy. The Third Circuit ruled that she was disabled, rejecting the agency's argument that she could still do "[her] previous work." Then-Judge Alito reasoned that "previous work" (like "any other kind of substantial gainful work") had to exist "in the national economy," but the Supreme Court unanimously reversed, based upon the rule of the last antecedent. Only the "other kind" of work — and *not* the "previous work" —

had to exist in the national economy. *Barnhart v. Thomas,* 540 U.S. 20, 26 (2003).[f]

The last antecedent rule can be trumped by the punctuation rule. "Evidence that a qualifying phrase is supposed to apply to all antecedents instead of only to the immediately preceding one may be found in the fact that it is separated from the antecedents by a comma." 2A Sutherland § 47.33, at 270. Thus, if the statutory definition in *Thomas* had included a comma before "exists in the national economy," Pauline Thomas would have had a better chance of success at a textually oriented Supreme Court. See also *In re Associated Commercial Protectors Ltd. v. Mason,* [1970] 13 D.L.R.3d 643 (Manitoba Q.B.), aff'd, 16 D.L.R.3d 478 (C.A.) (reading intent requirement in criminal statute to all antecedent acts, because of comma).

The last antecedent rule can also be negated by other statutory context. In *City of Corsicana v. Willman,* 216 S.W.2d 175 (Tex. 1948), the court declined to follow this rule to interpret the following statute:

> The said limits of the City of Corsicana may be extended so as to take in other territory, by ordinance duly passed by the Commission, in the manner and form as prescribed by the general laws of the State of Texas.

The court held that "in the manner * * * " modified "limits * * * may be extended," rather than "by ordinance passed * * *," because the general laws of the state had nothing to say about the manner or form by which municipalities adopt ordinances. Some courts have developed an "across the board rule" which is a special exception to the last antecedent rule: "[W]hen a clause follows several words in a statute and is applicable as much to the first word as to the others in the list, the clause should be applied to all of the words which preceded it." *Board of Trustees v. Judge,* 123 Cal. Rptr. 830, 834 (Cal. App. 1975).

(c) *Conjunctive versus Disjunctive Connectors: The "And" versus "Or" Rule.* The nature of the conjunctions connecting different words or phrases may be significant. Terms connected by the disjunctive "or" are often read to have separate meanings and significance.[g] For instance, 18 U.S.C. § 2114 (1988), prohibits assault with intent to rob "any person having lawful charge, control, or custody of any mail matter or of any money or other property of the United States." The issue in *Garcia v. United States,* 469 U.S. 70 (1984), was

---

f. Judge Alito did not dispute that "which exists in the national economy" modified "any other kind of substantial gainful work," the last antecedent point. Alito's argument was that by using "*any other* kind of work," Congress was demanding a parallelism between these other jobs which exist in the national economy and the applicant's "previous work." The Supreme Court responded: "Consider, for example, the case of parents who, before leaving their teenage son alone in the house for the weekend, warn him, 'You will be punished if you throw a party or engage in any other activity that damages the house.' If the son nevertheless throws a party and is caught, he should hardly be able to avoid punishment by arguing that the house was not damaged. The parents proscribed (1) a party, and (2) any other activity that damages the house." Is this a persuasive answer to Judge Alito?

g. Similarly, as *Chisom v. Roemer* (Chapter 7, § 3) indicates, the use of "and" usually is held to create a conjunctive rather than disjunctive meaning.

whether § 2114 applies to robbery of a Secret Service agent of his "flash money" (to be used to buy counterfeit currency from perpetrators). Petitioners argued that § 2114 only covered robbery of mail carriers, and that may have been the original focus of the statute. But the Court found the plain meaning clear: by separating "mail matter," "money," and "other property" with "or" (rather than "and"), Congress meant to include each of the three as an object of the statute and *not* to limit the statute to robbery of money and property in the custody of postal carriers. Why doesn't the ejusdem generis rule dictate the opposite result in *Garcia*? See *Schreiber v. Burlington Northern, Inc.*, 472 U.S. 1, 7–8 (1985) (interpreting "fraudulent, deceptive, or manipulative" language of Securities Act § 14(e) as all aimed at same thing: failures to disclose).

Linguists complicate the matter with these further observations: (1) The word "or" technically means "and/or" (a locution gaining in popularity). When I say "I want this or that," I might be saying I want either one item or the other, but I might also be saying I want both items. (2) In ordinary usage, people often use the two conjunctions interchangeably. "I want this and that" might signify that I want both items, or that I want only one. (3) De Morgan's Rules state that when preceded by a negative the logic is as follows:

Not (A *and* B) means Not A *or* Not B.

Not (A *or* B) means Not A *and* Not B.

See Solan, *Language of Judges,* 45–49. Professor Solan observes that courts do not always follow this logic, and typically for good reason.

The Comprehensive Crime Control Act of 1984 permits the United States to seize property used to commit crimes related to drug dealing. Under § 881(a)(7) such "real property" cannot be seized if the owner can establish (as an affirmative defense) that the criminal activity was "committed or omitted without the knowledge *or* consent of that owner." Can an owner prevail if he can only show lack of consent? Or does the owner also have to show lack of knowledge? If "without" has a negative connotation (which Solan and we think it does), De Morgan's Rules suggest that the defense requires both lack of knowledge (Not A) *and* lack of consent (Not B). But the Second Circuit held that the property owner could defend if he or she could show lack of consent, but only if the owner had taken reasonable steps to prevent illicit use of the property once the owner knew of such use. *United States v. 141st Street Corp.*, 911 F.2d 870, 878 (2d Cir. 1990). Solan says that this is an appropriate interpretation, notwithstanding De Morgan's Rules. Do you agree?

(d) *Mandatory versus Discretionary Language: The "May" versus "Shall" Rule.* When a statute uses mandatory language ("shall" rather than "may"), courts often interpret the statute to exclude discretion to take account of equitable or policy factors. See *Escondido Mut. Water Co. v. LaJolla Indians*, 466 U.S. 765 (1984); *Dunlop v. Bachowski*, 421 U.S. 560 (1975). On the other hand, ordinary usage does sometimes consider "may" and "shall" interchangeable. "You may help Mother" may be either permissive or directive, depending upon the circumstances.

The statute in *In re Cartmell's Estate*, 138 A.2d 588 (Vt. 1958), provided that probate matters of law are to be tried by a court, and "if a question of fact is to be decided, issue *may* be joined thereon under the direction of the court and a trial had by jury unless waived * * *." The trial court had denied a jury trial, over objections. The appeals court reversed: "The word 'may' can be construed as 'shall' or 'must' when such was the legislative intention." The court, correctly, assumed that "may" applied both to the phrase "be joined * * * court" and to "trial had by jury." Solan, *Language of Judges, supra*, at 46–48. Compare *Lopez v. Davis*, 531 U.S. 230 (2001) (a law providing that the sentence of a nonviolent offender "may be reduced" by the Bureau of Prisons vested discretion with the Bureau not only to deny or grant this benefit to specific nonviolent offenders, but also to create a new category of nonviolent offenders (those whose crime involved a firearm) who could not receive the benefit of its discretion).

(e) *Singular and Plural Numbers, Male and Female Pronouns.* One grammar rule that is *not* often followed by statutory interpreters is the difference between singular and plural nouns. "In determining the meaning of any act or resolution of Congress, unless the context otherwise indicates, words importing the singular include and apply to several persons, parties, or things; words importing the plural include the singular * * *." 1 U.S.C. § 1; accord, Interpretation Act of 1889, § 1(1)(b) (U.K.). Many states have analogous provisions. For example, the N.Y. Gen. Constr. Law § 35 (McKinney) provides: "Words in the singular number include the plural, and in the plural number include the singular." Like other rules of construction, however, New York courts will not consider this one decisive where it seems contrary to the apparent legislative purpose or intent. See, e.g., *Moynahan v. New York*, 98 N.E. 482 (N.Y. 1912).

A grammar rule even less often followed is the pronoun gender rule: He means a male referent, she a female referent. Because most statutes were drafted in eras when the main legal actors who counted were men, the male pronoun includes the female, and vice-versa. 1 U.S.C. § 2; Interpretation Act § 1(1)(a). Most states and the District of Columbia have a similar rule.

(f) *The Golden Rule (Against Absurdity) — and the Nietzsche Rule.* English-speaking jurisdictions have a few catch-all rules providing a mental check for the technical process of word-parsing and grammar-crunching. The *golden rule* is that interpreters should "adhere to the ordinary meaning of the words used, and to the grammatical construction, unless that * * * leads to any manifest absurdity or repugnance, in which case the language may be varied or modified, so as to avoid such inconvenience, but no further." *Becke v. Smith*, 150 Eng. Rep. 724, 726 (U.K. Exch. 1836). (See also Hart & Sack's excerpts from old British cases in Chapter 7, § 1). For example, an early admiralty statute required purchasers of a vessel to register it immediately and barred them from receiving favorable duty treatment until they did so. In *Willing v. United States*, 8 U.S. 48 (1807), Chief Justice Marshall allowed favorable duty treatment for purchasers who had bought the vessel at sea and therefore could not have registered the purchase until their return. A strict application of the statute under those circumstances would have been manifestly unreasonable, the Chief Justice reasoned.

The golden rule is, in short, an *absurd results* exception to the plain meaning rule. In *Thomas*, Judge Alito thought it absurd for the government to consider the applicant not disabled from working her previous job when it no longer existed. Writing for the Supreme Court, Justice Scalia disagreed. A claimant who is concededly able to do her previous job is *probably* able to perform a job *somewhere* in the national economy. Hence, the agency's position was at most stingy, but by no means an absurd proof rule for a program with limited resources.

Relatedly, courts should be willing to revise *scrivener's errors* — obvious mistakes in the transcription of statutes into the law books. See, e.g., *Lamie v. U.S. Trustee,* 540 U.S. 526, 530–31 (2004) (Court rewrites Bankruptcy Act to fix drafting error); *Green v. Bock Laundry* (Chapter 7, § 3) (all Justices agreeing to rewrite statute to correct an absurd provision that must have been the result of a scrivener's error); *Schooner Paulina's Cargo v. United States,* 11 U.S. 52, 67–68 (1812) (Marshall, C.J., revising statute to clean up scrivener's error).

The golden rule and its corollaries are now subject to academic debate. Although Justice Scalia recognized an absurd results exception to the plain meaning rule in *Bock Laundry* (concurring opinion), scholars of various persuasions maintain that an absurd results exception to plain meaning is inconsistent with the premises of the new textualism.[h] In *Zuni Pub. Sch. Dist. v. Department of Educ.,* 127 S.Ct. 1534, 1549–50 (2007), Justice Stevens's concurring opinion rests the absurd result exception upon notions of probable legislative intent: if a plain meaning interpretation is truly absurd, that is prima facie reason to think Congress did not intend it (absent evidence to the contrary, of course). Justice Scalia roundly denounced that approach, in absolute language suggesting that he now agrees with his critics that there should be no absurd result exception to the plain meaning rule. Id. at 1555–59 (Scalia, J., dissenting).

Friedrich Nietzsche admonished in *Mixed Opinions and Maxims* No. 137 (1879): "The worst readers are those who proceed like plundering soldiers: they pick up a few things they can use, soil and confuse the rest, and blaspheme the whole."[i] All the Justices would agree with this sentiment; indeed, both Stevens and Scalia invoke it in their *Zuni* debate. We read Nietzsche's lesson for the statutory interpreter to include the following: Be humble. Consider how other people use language. Be helpful to the project rather than hypertechnical.

---

h. E.g., William Eskridge, Jr., *Textualism, The Unknown Ideal?*, 96 Mich. L. Rev. 1509 (1998) (criticizing the new textualism for this inconsistency); John Manning, *The Absurdity Doctrine*, 116 Harv. L. Rev. 2387 (2003) (agreeing with Eskridge and urging textualists to abandon the absurd results canon); John Nagle, *Textualism's Exceptions*, Issues in Legal Scholarship (Nov. 2002), www.bepress.com/ils/iss3/art5 (same).

i. Friedrich Nietzsche, *On the Genealogy of Morals (and Other Works)* 175 (Walter Kaufman trans. and ed. 1967). David Krentel, Georgetown University Law Center, Class of 1995, brought this maxim to our attention.

3. *The Whole Act Rule*

Other rules or maxims of statutory interpretation are based upon the context within the statute of the relevant language. The Sutherland treatise identifies different approaches that have been used: interpretation of each section in isolation from the others; interpretation of all the sections of each part of a statute together; resolution of ambiguities based upon the purposes and goals set forth in the preamble to the statute; and interpretation of each section in the context of the whole enactment. The treatise endorses the "whole act rule" as "the most realistic in view of the fact that a legislature passes judgment upon the act as an entity, not giving one portion of the act any greater authority than another. Thus any attempt to segregate any portion or exclude any other portion from consideration is almost certain to distort the legislative intent." 2A Sutherland § 47.02, at 139; accord, *Bishop v. Linkway Stores, Inc.*, 655 S.W.2d 426 (Ark. 1983); *Maxwell* 47–64 (English background and current application of the whole act rule)*; Driedger* 259–321 (Canadian cases).

From its earliest cases, the U.S. Supreme Court has followed the whole act rule in construing statutes. E.g., *United States v. Fisher*, 6 U.S. (2 Cranch) 358 (1805); *United States v. Priestman*, 4 U.S. (Dall.) 29 (1800) (per curiam). "Statutory interpretation * * * is a holistic endeavor. A provision that may seem ambiguous in isolation is often clarified by the remainder of the statutory scheme — because the same terminology is used elsewhere in a context that makes its meaning clear, or because only one of the permissible meanings produces a substantive effect that is compatible with the rest of the law." *United Savings Ass'n of Texas v. Timbers of Inwood Forest Assocs.*, 484 U.S. 365, 371 (1988). "When 'interpreting a statute, the court will not look merely to a particular clause in which general words may be used, but will take in connection with it the whole statute * * * and the objects and policy of the law, as indicated by its various provisions, and give to it such a construction as will carry into execution the will of the legislature.' " *Kokoszka v. Belford*, 417 U.S. 642, 650 (1974); see also *Doe v. Chao*, 540 U.S. 614 (2004) (considering uncodified parts of the "whole act"). A critical assumption of the whole act approach is *coherence*: the interpreter presumes that the legislature drafted the statute as a document that is internally consistent in its use of language and in the way its provisions work together.[j] Note similarities to interpretation of contracts and sacred texts like the Bible.

The presumption of coherence is an unrealistic one: the legislature does not always approach statute-drafting the way God is thought to have dictated the Bible. Instead, statutes are often assembled the way Christmas trees are

---

j. See, e.g., *Ledbetter v. Goodyear Tire & Rubber Co.*, 127 S.Ct. 2162 (2007); *Gonzales v. Oregon*, 546 U.S. 243 (2006)*; Conroy v. Aniskoff*, 507 U.S. 511 (1993); *King v. St. Vincent's Hosp.*, 502 U.S. 215 (1991). See also *Canada Sugar Refining Co. v. Regina*, [1898] A.C. 735, 741 (U.K. House of Lords) (Davey, J.) (every clause of a law should be "construed with reference to the context and other clauses of the Act, so as, so far as possible, to make a consistent enactment of the whole statute"); *Greenshields v. Regina*, [1958] S.C.R. 216, 225 (Can. Sup. Ct.) ("a section or enactment must be construed as a whole, each portion throwing light, if need be, on the rest").

decorated, with ornaments being added or subtracted willy nilly, and at the last minute, just to satisfy enough interest groups and legislators to gain the majorities needed to get through various legislative vetogates (recall Chapter 1, § 2). Staff and drafting offices are supposed to clean up legislation to make it appropriate for inclusion in the code, but even the best drafters cannot always meld all the deals into a coherent whole. Nonetheless, courts all over the world operate under the coherence assumption. Can you think of a normative defense of it?

Consider some corollaries to the whole act rule. (Section 2C of this chapter takes you further to a "whole code rule": interpreters must consider the provision in light of the whole code as well as the whole statute.)

(a) *Titles.* Because Parliament's clerks, rather than Parliament, provided the titles of acts, the traditional English rule has been that the title could not be used for interpretive purposes. Thus, if the statute in Problem 8–1 had the title, "An Act to Prohibit Motorized Vehicles from the Park," English courts would have ignored this evidence of the statute's ambit. (The foregoing, by the way, is the *long title* of the statute; a *short title* would be something like the "The Motor Vehicles in the Park Act.") This is no longer the practice in most English-speaking jurisdictions, for the long title, and often a short title as well, are part of the legislative bill from the very beginning. In the United States, most state constitutions require the legislated enactment to have a title that gives accurate notice of the contents of the law.

As legislative practice has changed, so has the interpretive rule. According to 2A Sutherland 140, the "title cannot control the plain words of the statute" but "[i]n case of ambiguity the court may consider the title to resolve uncertainty in the purview [the body] of the act or for the correction of obvious errors." See also *Maxwell* 3–6 (long title but probably not short title may be used to resolve ambiguities); *Driedger* 290–96.

The U.S. Supreme Court in *Holy Trinity Church* (Chapter 7, § 1) considered the statute's long title as cogent evidence of its purpose and indeed reworked the statutory provision to be consistent with it. See also *Committee for the Commonwealth of Canada v. Canada*, [1991] 1 S.C.R. 139, 162–63 (Can. Sup. Ct.) (considering both long and short titles to determine that the ambit of a law prohibiting advertising and soliciting in airports did not extend to political advertising or soliciting). Generally, today's Supreme Court does not rely on statutory titles as important evidence of statutory meaning, though Justices will sometimes quote the title as marginally relevant context. E.g., *Porter v. Nussle*, 534 U.S. 516, 524 (2002).

(b) *Preambles and Purpose Clauses.*[k] The traditional English rule gave great weight to statutory preambles, because they were considered the best source for determining statutory purpose. The modern rule is more modest. American courts following the whole act approach have declined to give the

---

k. A *preamble* sets out the important facts or considerations that gave rise to the legislation. A *purpose clause* sets out the objectives the legislation seeks to achieve or the problems it tries to solve. In text, we shall refer to both as preambles.

preamble any greater weight than other parts of the statute (the title, purview, individual sections). "Thus the settled principle of law is that the preamble cannot control the enacting part of the statute in cases where the enacting part is expressed in clear, unambiguous terms" but "may be resorted to help discover the intention of the law maker." 2A Sutherland § 47.04, at 146; accord, *Attorney General v. Prince Ernest Augustus of Hanover*, [1957] A.C. 436, 467 (U.K. House of Lords) (preamble may be of some aid in discerning statutory purpose but tells the interpreter little about precisely how far the legislature has directed people to conform their activities to that goal); *Maxwell* 6–9 (examples of judicial use of preambles).

On the other hand, to the extent that the interpreter is able to find ambiguity and follows the Hart and Sacks purpose/context approach to statutory interpretation (Chapter 7, § 2), the preamble will be a particularly valuable contribution to the interpretive task. The Canadian Supreme Court, for example, vigorously relies on statutory preambles for this reason. In *Rawluk v. Rawluk*, [1990] 1 S.C.R. 70 (Can. Sup. Ct.), the issue was whether Ontario's Family Law Act precluded divorcing spouses from invoking the common law remedy of constructive trust, to assure equitable distribution of the marital property. Justice Cory's opinion for the Court looked to the preamble, which recognized that marriage is a "form of partnership" and sought an "orderly and equitable settlement of the affairs of the spouses" upon their decision to divorce. "These fundamental objectives are furthered by the use of the constructive trust remedy in appropriate circumstances. It provides a measure of individualized justice and fairness which is essential for the protection of marriage as a partnership of equals. Thus the preamble itself is sufficient to warrant the retention and application of this remedy." *Id.* at 90.[1]

A preamble played a key interpretive role in *Sutton v. United Airlines, Inc.*, 527 U.S. 471 (1999). The Americans with Disabilities Act (ADA) prohibits job discrimination against people with disabilities. The airline had refused to consider hiring Karen Sutton and Kimberly Hinton as pilots because of their eyesight, which was severely myopic. The airline argued that the two women (twins) were not persons with a disability under the statute. Because poor eyesight could be completely corrected by eyeglasses, Sutton, Hinton, and other myopics did not have a "physical or mental impairment that substantially limits one or more . . . major life activities." 42 U.S.C. § 12102(2)(C). This was an ironic construction of the ADA, for it would allow the airline to refuse to hire the sisters because of an impairment that the airline conceded was correctable. Yet the Supreme Court agreed, in part because the ADA's preamble found that 43 million people in the U.S. had disabilities, 42 U.S.C. § 12101(a)(1) — a far smaller number than people with poor enough vision to

---

1. See also *LeBlanc v. LeBlanc*, [1988] 1 S.C.R. 217, 221–22 (Can. Sup. Ct.) (statute should be construed in light of general principles set out in preamble); *Regina v. V.T.*, [1992] 1 S.C.R. 749, 765, 770 (Can. Sup. Ct.) (L'Heureux-Dubé, J.) (although preambles carry the same force as other provisions of the statute, generalized preamble statements will not trump longstanding principles of criminal procedure).

justify eyeglasses. *Id.* at 484–86; see *id.* at 494–95 (Ginsburg, J., concurring especially for this reason).

(c) *Provisos.* Provisos restrict the effect of statutory provisions or create exceptions to general statutory rules. They typically follow the provision being restricted or excepted, and start with: " * * *. *Provided that * * *.*" If there is doubt about the interpretation of a proviso, it is supposed to be strictly (narrowly) construed. "The reason for this is that the legislative purpose set forth in the purview of an enactment is assumed to express the legislative policy, and only those subjects expressly exempted by the proviso should be freed from the operation of the statute." 2A Sutherland § 47.08, at 156. We do not detect much interest in the proviso rule among recent Supreme Court Justices.

(d) *The Rule to Avoid Redundancy.* Under the whole act rule, the presumption is that every word and phrase adds something to the statutory command. Accordingly, it is a "cardinal rule of statutory interpretation that no provision should be construed to be entirely redundant." *Kungys v. United States*, 485 U.S. 759, 778 (1988) (plurality opinion by Scalia, J.); see, e.g., *Circuit City Stores, Inc. v. Adams,* 532 U.S. 105 (2001); *United States v. Alaska*, 521 U.S. 1 (1997); *Walters v. Metropolitan Educ. Ents., Inc.*, 519 U.S. 202 (1997); *Rake v. Wade*, 508 U.S. 464 (1993); *Colautti v. Franklin*, 439 U.S. 379, 392 (1979). "A construction which would leave without effect any part of the language of a statute will normally be rejected." *Maxwell* 36.

For example, the issue in *Western Union Telegraph Co. v. Lenroot*, 323 U.S. 490 (1945), was whether the Fair Labor Standards Act prohibition against child labor applied to telegraph messengers. The prohibition reached any shipment of "goods" in interstate commerce, and "goods" were defined as "wares, products, commodities, merchandise, and articles or subjects of commerce of any character." The telegraph company argued that its service was intangible and therefore not a "good." Both Judge Learned Hand for the Court of Appeals and Justice Jackson for the Supreme Court held that telegraph services were "subjects of commerce." Hand suggested that if the definition were read to include only tangible things, the term "subjects," which had been added by a special Senate amendment to "articles of commerce of any character," would add nothing to the statute.

The rule against redundancy is more at odds with the legislative drafting process than most of the other whole act rules, as words and phrases are added to important legislation right up to the last minute. Thus, the Court in *Gutierrez v. Ada*, 528 U.S. 250 (2000), declined to follow the rule against redundancy when other textual canons and common sense cut the other way. "But as one rule of construction among many, albeit an important one, the rule against redundancy does not necessarily have the strength to turn a tide of good cause to come out the other way."

Nonetheless, the rule against redundancy plays a more important role in Supreme Court opinions in the new millennium than it did in the old. *Circuit City* is but one example. Responding to Justice Souter's textual argument that "seamen, railroad employees, or any other class of workers engaged in foreign or interstate commerce" included all contract employees, Justice Kennedy's *Circuit City* opinion fell back on the rule against surplusage: "there would be no need for Congress to use the phrases 'seamen' and 'railroad employees' if these same classes of workers were subsumed within the meaning of the 'engaged in . . . commerce' residual clause."

　　(e) *Presumption of Consistent Usage — and of Meaningful Variation.* Under the holistic assumptions of the whole act rule, it is "reasonable to presume that the same meaning is implied by the use of the same expression in every part of the Act." *Maxwell* 278. Similarly, where a statutory word has been used in other statutes dealing with the same subject matter and has a settled meaning in those statutes, interpreters will presumptively follow the settled meaning. See § 2C1 of this chapter. Although this is viewed as a weak presumption in most English-speaking countries, it has emerged as a stronger one in the United States, where it is presumed that "identical words used in different parts of the same act are intended to have the same meaning." *Sullivan v. Stroop*, 496 U.S. 478, 484 (1990), followed in, e.g., *Powerex Corp. v. Reliant Energy Servs., Inc.,* 127 S.Ct. 2411 (2007); *Commissioner v. Lundy,* 516 U.S. 235, 249–50 (1996); *Gustafson v. Alloyd Co.,* 513 U.S. 561, 570 (1995). But see *Dewsnup v. Timm*, 502 U.S. 410, 417 & n.3 (1992) (finding such argument unilluminating).

　　The Equal Access to Justice Act, 28 U.S.C. § 2412(d)(1)(A), provides that a party prevailing in a lawsuit against the United States should be awarded attorney's fees, "unless the court finds that the position of the United States was substantially justified or that special circumstances make an award unjust." The prevailing private party argued that the government had to pay unless its position was "justified to a high degree." The Supreme Court in *Pierce v. Underwood*, 487 U.S. 552 (1988), found this a plausible construction of the words but accepted the government's interpretation, that it could avoid counsel fees if its position were reasonable, or "justified in the main." Justice Scalia's opinion found a plain meaning, because the term "substantially justified" is used elsewhere in the U.S. Code and in the Federal Rules of Civil Procedure, especially Rule 37. Courts had never interpreted the term to require a higher degree of justification, and Justice Scalia accepted that as dispositive.

　　"From the general presumption that the same expression is presumed to be used in the same sense throughout an Act or a series of cognate Acts, there follows the further presumption that a change of wording denotes a change in meaning." *Maxwell* 282; cf. *id.* at 286 (but this is a weak presumption). The leading American case for this presumption of meaningful variation is Chief Justice Marshall's opinion in *United States v. Fisher*, 6 U.S. 358, 388–97 (1805). A statute whose first four sections regulated the relationship between the United States and "receivers of public monies" had a fifth section which said that "where any revenue officer, or other person[,] hereafter becoming indebted to the United States . . . shall become insolvent, . . . the debt due to the United States shall be first satisfied." A competing creditor argued that § 5 should have been limited to receivers of public moneys, like §§ 1–4 and the title of the law, but Marshall found no reason to think that Congress intended a narrower ambit for § 5 and so read it without the limitation. Accord,

Lawrence v. Florida, 127 S.Ct. 1079, 1083–84 (2007); *Hamdan v. Rumsfeld,* 126 S.Ct. 2749, 2765–66 (2006).

Variation in terminology ought to have less force when one statute is adopted at a different time than another. E.g., *Gutierrez v. Ada,* 528 U.S. 250 (2000) (declining to apply a rule of meaningful variation when a later amendment used different terminology from the provision at issue). But when Congress changes a statute when reenacting it, the rule has renewed bite, as in *Osborn v. Bank of the United States,* 22 U.S. (9 Wheat.) 738, 817–18 (1824). The statute creating the first Bank of the United States contained a provision allowing the Bank to "sue and be sued * * * in Courts of record." The Supreme Court in 1810 construed that provision to afford no basis for federal jurisdiction in lawsuits involving the Bank. When the second Bank was established in 1816, the "sue and be sued" provision was changed to allow suits "in all State Courts having competent jurisdiction, and in any Circuit Court of the United States." Chief Justice Marshall construed the new language — pointedly expanding the language which was the focus of the earlier case — to be a congressional vesting of jurisdiction in circuit courts to hear lawsuits where the bank was a party. See also *Chisom v. Roemer* (Chapter 7, § 3) (1982 amendments to the Voting Rights Act abandoned the general language defining the ambit of § 2 and added a more specific term ["representatives"], which the dissenting opinion maintained was a deliberate narrowing of the provision's coverage).

A wedding of expressio unius and consistent usage is the rule that "[w]here Congress includes particular language in one section of a statute but omits it in another . . . , it is generally presumed that Congress acts intentionally and purposely in the disparate inclusion or exclusion." *Keene Corp. v. United States,* 508 U.S. 200, 208 (1993); accord, *Arlington Cent. Sch. Dist. Bd. of Educ. v. Murphy,* 126 S.Ct. 2455, 2461–63 (2006); *Gozlon-Peretz v. United States,* 498 U.S. 395, 404–05 (1991). The Court refined this canon in *Field v. Mans,* 516 U.S. 59, 67–76 (1995), where it held this negative implication rule was inapplicable when there was a reasonable explanation for the variation. "The more apparently deliberate the contrast, the stronger the inference, as applied, for example, to contrasting statutory sections originally enacted simultaneously in relevant respects. * * * The rule is weakest when it suggests results strangely at odds with other textual pointers, like the common-law language at work in the [bankruptcy] statute here." *Id.* at 75–76.

The Court vigorously debated use of this canon in *Lindh v. Murphy,* 521 U.S. 320 (1997). Chapter 154 of the Antiterrorism and Effective Death Penalty Act created new rules restricting prisoner access to the courts to challenge their sentences in death penalty cases; chapter 154 was by its terms applicable to pending cases. Chapter 153 applied to noncapital cases and had no provision one way or the other. Justice Souter's opinion for the Court reasoned by negative implication that Congress meant the new rules not be applicable to pending noncapital cases. Chief Justice Rehnquist's dissenting opinion objected that this was not sensible, because it treated capital defendants more harshly than noncapital defendants. He argued that the Act should be construed to apply to all pending cases.

(f) *Rule Against Interpreting a Provision in Derogation of Other Provisions.* An important corollary of the whole act rule is that one provision of a statute should not be interpreted in such a way as to derogate from other provisions of the statute (to the extent this is possible). An interpretation of provision 1 might derogate from other parts of the statute in one or more of the following ways:

- *operational conflict.* As interpreted, provision 1's operation conflicts with that of provision 2. For example, a citizen cannot obey provision 1 without violating provision 2.

- *philosophical tension.* As interpreted, provision 1 is in tension with an assumption of provision 2. For example, provision 2 might reflect a legislative compromise inconsistent with a broad reading of provision 1.

- *structural derogation.* Sharing elements of both operational conflict and philosophical tension, provision 1's interpretation might be at odds with the overall structure of the statute. Thus, provisions 2 and 3 might reflect a legislative policy that certain kinds of violations be handled administratively rather than judicially, which a broad view of judicially enforceable provision 1 might undermine.

For an example of cross-cutting derogations, see *Robinson v. Shell Oil Co.*, 519 U.S. 337, 345–46 (1997). To see these ideas in action, consider the following case, where both the majority and dissenting opinions relied on the anti-derogation canon, as well as other textualist maxims.

BABBITT v. SWEET HOME CHAPTER OF COMMUNITIES FOR A GREAT OREGON
Supreme Court of the United States, 1995
515 U.S. 687, 115 S.Ct. 2407, 132 L.Ed.2d 597

JUSTICE STEVENS delivered the opinion of the Court.

The Endangered Species Act of 1973 (ESA or Act), 87 Stat. 884, 16 U.S.C. § 1531 (1988 ed. and Supp. V), contains a variety of protections designed to save from extinction species that the Secretary of the Interior designates as endangered or threatened. Section 9 of the Act makes it unlawful for any person to "take" any endangered or threatened species. The Secretary has promulgated a regulation that defines the statute's prohibition on takings to include "significant habitat modification or degradation where it actually kills or injures wildlife." This case presents the question whether the Secretary exceeded his authority under the Act by promulgating that regulation.

Section 9(a)(1) of the Act provides the following protection for endangered species:

> Except as provided in sections 1535(g)(2) and 1539 of this title, with respect to any endangered species of fish or wildlife listed pursuant to section 1533 of this title it is unlawful for any person subject to the jurisdiction of the United States to—

> . . .

(B) take any such species within the United States or the territorial sea of the United States. [16 U.S.C. § 1538(a)(1).]

Section 3(19) of the Act defines the statutory term "take":

> The term "take" means to harass, harm, pursue, hunt, shoot, wound, kill, trap, capture, or collect, or to attempt to engage in any such conduct. [16 U.S.C. § 1532(19).]

The Act does not further define the terms it uses to define "take." The Interior Department regulations that implement the statute, however, define the statutory term "harm":

> *Harm* in the definition of "take" in the Act means an act which actually kills or injures wildlife. Such act may include significant habitat modification or degradation where it actually kills or injures wildlife by significantly impairing essential behavioral patterns, including breeding, feeding, or sheltering. [50 CFR § 17.3 (1994).]

This regulation has been in place since 1975.

A limitation on the § 9 "take" prohibition appears in § 10(a)(1)(B) of the Act, which Congress added by amendment in 1982. That section authorizes the Secretary to grant a permit for any taking otherwise prohibited by § 9(a)(1)(B) "if such taking is incidental to, and not the purpose of, the carrying out of an otherwise lawful activity." 16 U.S.C. § 1539(a)(1)(B).

In addition to the prohibition on takings, the Act provides several other protections for endangered species. Section 4, 16 U.S.C. § 1533, commands the Secretary to identify species of fish or wildlife that are in danger of extinction and to publish from time to time lists of all species he determines to be endangered or threatened. Section 5, 16 U.S.C. § 1534, authorizes the Secretary, in cooperation with the States, see § 1535, to acquire land to aid in preserving such species. Section 7 requires federal agencies to ensure that none of their activities, including the granting of licenses and permits, will jeopardize the continued existence of endangered species "or result in the destruction or adverse modification of habitat of such species which is determined by the Secretary . . . to be critical." 16 U.S.C. § 1536(a)(2).

[A group of small landowners, logging companies, and families dependent on the forest products industries and organizations that represent their interests brought this action to challenge the Secretary's definition of *harm* to include habitat modification and degradation. They specifically objected to the application of the regulation to protect the red-cockaded woodpecker and the spotted owl by prohibiting changes in their natural habitat that would have the effect of injuring or killing those animals. The court of appeals agreed with respondents' challenge, but the Supreme Court reversed.]

The text of the Act provides three reasons for concluding that the Secretary's interpretation is reasonable. First, an ordinary understanding of the word "harm" supports it. The dictionary definition of the verb form of "harm" is "to cause hurt or damage to: injure." Webster's Third New International Dictionary 1034 (1966). In the context of the ESA, that definition naturally encompasses habitat modification that results in actual injury or death to members of an endangered or threatened species.

Respondents argue that the Secretary should have limited the purview of "harm" to direct applications of force against protected species, but the dictionary definition does not include the word "directly" or suggest in any way that only direct or willful action that leads to injury constitutes "harm." Moreover, unless the statutory term "harm" encompasses indirect as well as direct injuries, the word has no meaning that does not duplicate the meaning of other words that § 3 uses to define "take." A reluctance to treat statutory terms as surplusage supports the reasonableness of the Secretary's interpretation.

Second, the broad purpose of the ESA supports the Secretary's decision to extend protection against activities that cause the precise harms Congress enacted the statute to avoid. In *TVA v. Hill*, 437 U.S. 153 (1978) [Chapter 7, § 2C], we described the Act as "the most comprehensive legislation for the preservation of endangered species ever enacted by any nation." Whereas predecessor statutes enacted in 1966 and 1969 had not contained any sweeping prohibition against the taking of endangered species except on federal lands, the 1973 Act applied to all land in the United States and to the Nation's territorial seas. As stated in § 2 of the Act, among its central purposes is "to provide a means whereby the ecosystems upon which endangered species and threatened species depend may be conserved . . . ."

In *Hill*, we construed § 7 as precluding the completion of the Tellico Dam because of its predicted impact on the survival of the snail darter. Both our holding and the language in our opinion stressed the importance of the statutory policy. "The plain intent of Congress in enacting this statute," we recognized, "was to halt and reverse the trend toward species extinction, whatever the cost. This is reflected not only in the stated policies of the Act, but in literally every section of the statute." Although the § 9 "take" prohibition was not at issue in *Hill*, we took note of that prohibition, placing particular emphasis on the Secretary's inclusion of habitat modification in his definition of "harm." In light of that provision for habitat protection, we could "not understand how TVA intends to operate Tellico Dam without 'harming' the snail darter." Congress' intent to provide comprehensive protection for endangered and threatened species supports the permissibility of the Secretary's "harm" regulation. * * *

Third, the fact that Congress in 1982 authorized the Secretary to issue permits for takings that § 9(a)(1)(B) would otherwise prohibit, "if such taking is incidental to, and not the purpose of, the carrying out of an otherwise lawful activity," 16 U.S.C. § 1539(a)(1)(B), strongly suggests that Congress understood § 9(a)(1)(B) to prohibit indirect as well as deliberate takings. The permit process requires the applicant to prepare a "conservation plan" that specifies how he intends to "minimize and mitigate" the "impact" of his activity on endangered and threatened species, 16 U.S.C. § 1539(a)(2)(A), making clear that Congress had in mind foreseeable rather than merely accidental effects on listed species. No one could seriously request an "incidental" take permit to avert § 9 liability for direct, deliberate action against a member of an endangered or threatened species, but respondents would read "harm" so narrowly that the permit procedure would have little more than that absurd purpose. "When Congress acts to amend a statute, we presume it intends its amendment to have real and substantial effect." Congress' addition of the § 10 permit provision supports the Secretary's conclusion that activities not intended to harm an endangered species, such as habitat modification, may constitute unlawful takings under the ESA unless the Secretary permits them.

[The court of appeals had come to a contrary conclusion on the basis of the *noscitur a sociis* canon: the surrounding words — such as pursue, hunt, shoot — connoted application of force directed at a particular animal. But other words, such as harass, do not so connote, and the lower court's construction would effectively write *harm* out of the statute entirely.]

We need not decide whether the statutory definition of "take" compels the Secretary's interpretation of "harm," because our conclusions that Congress did not unambiguously manifest its intent to adopt respondents' view and that the Secretary's interpretation is reasonable suffice to decide this case. See generally *Chevron, U.S.A., Inc. v. Natural Resources Defense Council* [Chapter 9, § 3]. The latitude the ESA gives the Secretary in enforcing the statute, together with the degree of regulatory expertise necessary to its enforcement, establishes that we owe some degree of deference to the Secretary's reasonable interpretation. See Breyer, Judicial Review of Questions of Law and Policy, 38 Admin. L. Rev. 363, 373 (1986). [Justice Stevens also rejected application of the rule of lenity, see § 2B1 below. Although there is a separate criminal sanction for "knowing" violations of the ESA, the Court has never applied the rule of lenity to review agency rules implementing a civil statute that has parallel criminal sanctions.]

Our conclusion that the Secretary's definition of "harm" rests on a permissible construction of the ESA gains further support from the legislative history of the statute. The Committee Reports accompanying the bills that became the ESA do not specifically discuss the meaning of "harm," but they make clear that Congress intended "take" to apply broadly to cover indirect as well as purposeful actions. The Senate Report stressed that " '[t]ake' is defined . . . in the broadest possible manner to include every conceivable way in which a person can 'take' or attempt to 'take' any fish or wildlife." S. Rep. No. 93–307, p. 7 (1973). The House Report stated that "the broadest possible terms" were used to define restrictions on takings. H.R. Rep. No. 93–412, p. 15 (1973). The House Report underscored the breadth of the "take" definition by noting that it included "harassment, *whether intentional or not.*" *Id.*, at 11 (emphasis added). The Report explained that the definition "would allow, for example, the Secretary to regulate or prohibit the activities of birdwatchers where the effect of those activities might disturb the birds and make it difficult for them to hatch or raise their young." *Ibid.* * * *

The definition of "take" that originally appeared in S. 1983 differed from the definition as ultimately enacted in [this] significant respect: It included "the destruction, modification, or curtailment of [the] habitat or range" of fish and wildlife. Respondents make much of the fact that the Commerce Committee removed this phrase from the "take" definition before S. 1983 went to the floor. See 119 Cong. Rec. 25663 (1973). We do not find that fact especially significant. The legislative materials contain no indication why the habitat protection provision was deleted. That provision differed greatly from the regulation at issue today. Most notably, the habitat protection in S. 1983 would have applied far more broadly than the regulation does because it made adverse habitat modification a categorical violation of the "take" prohibition, unbounded by the regulation's limitation to habitat modifications that actually kill or injure wildlife. The S. 1983 language also failed to qualify "modification" with the regulation's limiting adjective "significant." We do not believe the Senate's unelaborated disavowal of the provision in S. 1983 undermines the reasonableness of the more moderate habitat protection in the Secretary's "harm" regulation. [In footnote 19, Justice Stevens rejected the argument that statements by Senate and House sponsors supported the idea that the § 5 land acquisition provision and not § 9 was expected to be the ESA's remedy for habitat modification.]

The history of the 1982 amendment that gave the Secretary authority to grant permits for "incidental" takings provides further support for his reading of the Act. The House Report expressly states that "[b]y use of the word 'incidental' the Committee intends to cover situations in which it is known that a taking will occur if the other activity is engaged in but such taking is incidental to, and not the purpose of, the activity." H.R. Rep. No. 97–567, p. 31 (1982). This reference to the foreseeability of incidental takings undermines respondents' argument that the 1982 amendment covered only accidental killings of endangered and threatened animals that might occur in the course of hunting or trapping other animals. Indeed, Congress had habitat modification directly in mind: Both the Senate Report and the House Conference Report identified as the model for the permit process a cooperative state-federal response to a case in California where a development project threatened incidental harm to a species of endangered butterfly by modification of its habitat. See S. Rep. No. 97–418, p. 10 (1982); H.R. Conf. Rep. No. 97–835, pp. 30–32 (1982). Thus, Congress in 1982 focused squarely on the aspect of the "harm" regulation at issue in this litigation. Congress' implementation of a permit program is consistent with the Secretary's interpretation of the term "harm." * * *

JUSTICE SCALIA, with whom THE CHIEF JUSTICE [REHNQUIST] and JUSTICE THOMAS join, dissenting.

I think it unmistakably clear that the legislation at issue here (1) forbade the hunting and killing of endangered animals, and (2) provided federal lands and federal funds for the acquisition of private lands, to preserve the habitat of endangered animals. The Court's holding that the hunting and killing prohibition incidentally preserves habitat on private lands imposes unfairness to the point of financial ruin — not just upon the rich, but upon the simplest farmer who finds his land conscripted to national zoological use. I respectfully dissent.

[Justice Scalia objected to three features of the regulation, which, as he saw it, (1) failed to consider whether death or injury to wildlife is an intentional or even foreseeable effect of a habitat modification; (2) covered omissions as well as acts; and (3) considered injuries to future as well as present animal populations, and not just specific animals.] *None* of these three features of the regulation can be found in the statutory provisions supposed to authorize it. The term "harm" in § 1532(19) has no legal force of its own. An indictment or civil complaint that charged the defendant with "harming" an animal protected under the Act would be dismissed as defective, for the only *operative* term in the statute is to "take." If "take" were not elsewhere defined in the Act, none could dispute what it means, for the term is as old as the law itself. To "take," when applied to wild animals, means to reduce those animals, by killing or capturing, to human control. [Citing dictionaries, cases, and Blackstone.] This is just the sense in which "take" is used elsewhere in federal legislation and treaty. See, e.g., Migratory Bird Treaty Act, 16 U.S.C. § 703 (1988 ed., Supp. V) (no person may "pursue, hunt, take, capture, kill, [or] attempt to take, capture, or kill" any migratory bird); Agreement on the Conservation of Polar Bears, Nov. 15, 1973, Art. I, 27 U.S.T. 3918, 3921, T.I.A.S. No. 8409 (defining "taking" as "hunting, killing and capturing"). And that meaning fits neatly with the rest of § 1538(a)(1), which makes it unlawful not only to take protected species, but also to import or export them (§ 1538(a)(1)(A)); to possess, sell, deliver, carry, transport, or ship any taken species (§ 1538(a)(1)(D)); and to transport, sell, or offer to sell them in interstate or foreign commerce (§§ 1538(a)(1)(E), (F)). The taking prohibition, in other words, is only part of the regulatory plan of § 1538(a)(1), which covers all the stages of the process by which protected wildlife is reduced to man's dominion and made the object of profit. It is obvious that "take" in this sense — a term of art deeply embedded in the statutory and common law concerning wildlife — describes a class of acts (not omissions) done directly and intentionally (not indirectly and by accident) to particular animals (not populations of animals).

[Although "harm" has a range of meaning, the most likely in this statutory context is one that focuses on specific and intentional harming.] "Harm" is merely one of 10 prohibitory words in § 1532(19), and the other 9 fit the ordinary meaning of "take" perfectly. To "harass, pursue, hunt, shoot, wound, kill, trap, capture, or collect" are all affirmative acts (the provision itself describes them as "conduct," see § 1532(19)) which are directed immediately and intentionally against a particular animal — not acts or omissions that indirectly and accidentally cause injury to a population of animals. * * * What the nine other words in § 1532(19) have in common — and share with the narrower meaning of "harm" described above, but not with the Secretary's ruthless dilation of the word — is the sense of affirmative conduct intentionally directed against a particular animal or animals.

I am not the first to notice this fact, or to draw the conclusion that it compels. In 1981 the Solicitor of the Fish and Wildlife Service delivered a legal opinion on § 1532(19) that is in complete agreement with my reading:

> The Act's definition of "take" contains a list of actions that illustrate the intended scope of the term. . . . With the possible exception of "harm," these terms all represent forms of conduct that are directed against and likely to injure or kill *individual* wildlife. Under the principle of statutory construction, *ejusdem generis*, . . . the term "harm" should be interpreted to include only those actions that are directed against,

and likely to injure or kill, individual wildlife. [Memorandum of April 17, 1981 (emphasis in original).]

I would call it *noscitur a sociis*, but the principle is much the same: The fact that "several items in a list share an attribute counsels in favor of interpreting the other items as possessing that attribute as well." * * * [Moreover,] the Court's contention that "harm" in the narrow sense adds nothing to the other words underestimates the ingenuity of our own species in a way that Congress did not. To feed an animal poison, to spray it with mace, to chop down the very tree in which it is nesting, or even to destroy its entire habitat in order to take it (as by draining a pond to get at a turtle), might neither wound nor kill, but would directly and intentionally harm.

The penalty provisions of the Act counsel this interpretation as well. Any person who "knowingly" violates § 1538(a)(1)(B) is subject to criminal penalties under § 1540(b)(1) and civil penalties under § 1540(a)(1); moreover, under the latter section, any person "who otherwise violates" the taking prohibition (i.e., violates it unknowingly) may be assessed a civil penalty of $500 for each violation, with the stricture that "[e]ach such violation shall be a separate offense." This last provision should be clear warning that the regulation is in error, for when combined with the regulation it produces a result that no legislature could reasonably be thought to have intended: A large number of routine private activities — for example, farming, ranching, roadbuilding, construction and logging — are subjected to strict-liability penalties when they fortuitously injure protected wildlife, no matter how remote the chain of causation and no matter how difficult to foresee (or to disprove) the "injury" may be (e.g., an "impairment" of breeding). * * *

So far I have discussed only the immediate statutory text bearing on the regulation. But the definition of "take" in § 1532(19) applies "[f]or the purposes of this chapter," that is, it governs the meaning of the word *as used everywhere in the Act*. Thus, the Secretary's interpretation of "harm" is wrong if it does not fit with the use of "take" throughout the Act. And it does not. In § 1540(e)(4)(B), for example, Congress provided for the forfeiture of "[a]ll guns, traps, nets, and other equipment . . . used to aid the taking, possessing, selling, [etc.]" of protected animals. This listing plainly relates to "taking" in the ordinary sense. If environmental modification were part (and necessarily a major part) of taking, as the Secretary maintains, one would have expected the list to include "plows, bulldozers, and backhoes." * * * The Act is full of like examples. See, e.g., § 1538(a)(1)(D) (prohibiting possession, sale, and transport of "species taken in violation" of the Act). "[I]f the Act is to be interpreted as a symmetrical and coherent regulatory scheme, one in which the operative words have a consistent meaning throughout," *Gustafson v. Alloyd Co.*, 513 U.S. 561, 569 (1995), the regulation must fall.

The broader structure of the Act confirms the unreasonableness of the regulation. Section 1536 provides:

> Each Federal agency shall . . . insure that any action authorized, funded, or carried out by such agency . . . is not likely to jeopardize the continued existence of any endangered species or threatened species or *result in the destruction or adverse*

modification of habitat of such species which is determined by the Secretary . . . to be critical. [16 U.S.C. § 1536(a)(2) (emphasis added).]

The Act defines "critical habitat" as habitat that is "essential to the conservation of the species," §§ 1532(5)(A)(i), (A)(ii), with "conservation" in turn defined as the use of methods necessary to bring listed species "to the point at which the measures provided pursuant to this chapter are no longer necessary." § 1532(3).

These provisions have a double significance. Even if §§ 1536(a)(2) and 1538(a)(1)(B) were totally independent prohibitions — the former applying only to federal agencies and their licensees, the latter only to private parties — Congress's explicit prohibition of habitat modification in the one section would bar the inference of an implicit prohibition of habitat modification in the other section. "[W]here Congress includes particular language in one section of a statute but omits it in another . . . , it is generally presumed that Congress acts intentionally and purposely in the disparate inclusion or exclusion." *Keene Corp. v. United States*, 508 U.S. 200, 208 (1993). And that presumption against implicit prohibition would be even stronger where the one section which uses the language carefully defines and limits its application. That is to say, it would be passing strange for Congress carefully to define "critical habitat" as used in § 1536(a)(2), but leave it to the Secretary to evaluate, willy-nilly, impermissible "habitat modification" (under the guise of "harm") in § 1538(a)(1)(B).

In fact, however, §§ 1536(a)(2) and 1538(a)(1)(B) do *not* operate in separate realms; federal agencies are subject to *both*, because the "person[s]" forbidden to take protected species under § 1538 include agencies and departments of the Federal Government. See § 1532(13). This means that the "harm" regulation also contradicts another principle of interpretation: that statutes should be read so far as possible to give independent effect to all their provisions. See *Ratzlaf v. United States*, 510 U.S. 135, 140–41 (1994). By defining "harm" in the definition of "take" in § 1538(a)(1)(B) to include significant habitat modification that injures populations of wildlife, the regulation makes the habitat-modification restriction in § 1536(a)(2) almost wholly superfluous. As "critical habitat" is habitat "essential to the conservation of the species," adverse modification of "critical" habitat by a federal agency would also constitute habitat modification that injures a population of wildlife.

The Court makes * * * other arguments. First, "the broad purpose of the [Act] supports the Secretary's decision to extend protection against activities that cause the precise harms Congress enacted the statute to avoid." I thought we had renounced the vice of "simplistically . . . assum[ing] that *whatever furthers the statute's primary objective must be the law." Rodriguez v. United States*, 480 U.S. 522, 526 (1987) (*per curiam*) (emphasis in original). Deduction from the "broad purpose" of a statute begs the question if it is used to decide by what *means* (and hence to what *length*) Congress pursued that purpose; to get the right answer to that question there is no substitute for the hard job (or in this case, the quite simple one) of reading the whole text. "The

Act must do everything necessary to achieve its broad purpose" is the slogan of the enthusiast, not the analytical tool of the arbiter.

Second, the Court maintains that the legislative history of the 1973 Act supports the Secretary's definition. Even if legislative history were a legitimate and reliable tool of interpretation (which I shall assume in order to rebut the Court's claim); and even if it could appropriately be resorted to when the enacted text is as clear as this, but see *Chicago v. Environmental Defense Fund*, 511 U.S. 328, 337 (1994); here it shows quite the opposite of what the Court says. I shall not pause to discuss the Court's reliance on such statements in the Committee Reports as " '[t]ake' is defined . . . in the broadest possible manner to include every conceivable way in which a person can 'take' or attempt to 'take' any fish or wildlife." [S. Rep. No. 93–307, p. 7 (1973)]. This sort of empty flourish — to the effect that "this statute means what it means all the way" — counts for little even when enacted into the law itself. See *Reves v. Ernst & Young*, 507 U.S. 170, 183–84 (1993).

Much of the Court's discussion of legislative history is devoted to two items: first, the Senate floor manager's introduction of an amendment that added the word "harm" to the definition of "take," with the observation that (along with other amendments) it would " 'help to achieve the purposes of the bill' "; second, the relevant Committee's removal from the definition of a provision stating that "take" includes " 'the destruction, modification or curtailment of [the] habitat or range' " of fish and wildlife. The Court inflates the first and belittles the second, even though the second is on its face far more pertinent. But this elaborate inference from various pre-enactment actions and inactions is quite unnecessary, since we have direct evidence of what those who brought the legislation to the floor thought it meant — evidence as solid as any ever to be found in legislative history, but which the Court banishes to a footnote.

Both the Senate and House floor managers of the bill explained it in terms which leave no doubt that the problem of habitat destruction on private lands was to be solved principally by the land acquisition program of § 1534, while § 1538 solved a different problem altogether — the problem of takings. Senator Tunney stated:

> *Through [the] land acquisition provisions, we will be able to conserve habitats necessary to protect fish and wildlife from further destruction.*
>
> Although most endangered species are threatened primarily by the destruction of their natural habitats, a significant portion of these animals are subject to *predation by man for commercial, sport, consumption, or other purposes.* The provisions of [the bill] would prohibit the commerce in or the importation, exportation, or taking of endangered species . . . . [119 Cong. Rec. 25669 (1973) (emphasis added).]

The House floor manager, Representative Sullivan, put the same thought in this way:

> [T]he principal threat to animals stems from destruction of their habitat. . . . *[The bill] will meet this problem by providing funds for acquisition of critical habitat.* . . . It will also enable the Department of Agriculture to cooperate with willing landowners

who desire to assist in the protection of endangered species, *but who are understandably unwilling to do so at excessive cost to themselves.* Another hazard to endangered species arises from those who would *capture or kill them for pleasure or profit.* There is no way that the Congress can make it less pleasurable for a person to take an animal, but we can certainly make it less profitable for them to do so. [*Id.*, at 30162 (emphasis added).]

Habitat modification and takings, in other words, were viewed as different problems, addressed by different provisions of the Act. [Justice Scalia argued that these statements destroy the Court's legislative history case and that the Court has no response.]

Third, the Court seeks support from a provision that was added to the Act in 1982, the year after the Secretary promulgated the current regulation. The provision states:

> [T]he Secretary may permit, under such terms and conditions as he shall prescribe—
>
> . . .
>
> any taking otherwise prohibited by section 1538(a)(1)(B) . . . if such taking is incidental to, and not the purpose of, the carrying out of an otherwise lawful activity. [16 U.S.C. § 1539(a)(1)(B).]

This provision does not, of course, implicate our doctrine that reenactment of a statutory provision ratifies an extant judicial or administrative interpretation, for neither the taking prohibition in § 1538(a)(1)(B) nor the definition in § 1532(19) was reenacted. The Court claims, however, that the provision "strongly suggests that Congress understood [§ 1538(a)(1)(B)] to prohibit indirect as well as deliberate takings." That would be a valid inference if habitat modification were the only substantial "otherwise lawful activity" that might incidentally and nonpurposefully cause a prohibited "taking." Of course it is not. This provision applies to the many otherwise lawful takings that incidentally take a protected species — as when fishing for unprotected salmon also takes an endangered species of salmon. * * *

This is enough to show, in my view, that the 1982 permit provision does not support the regulation. I must acknowledge that the Senate Committee Report on this provision, and the House Conference Committee Report, clearly contemplate that it will enable the Secretary to permit environmental modification. But the *text* of the amendment cannot possibly bear that asserted meaning, when placed within the context of an Act that must be interpreted (as we have seen) not to prohibit private environmental modification. The neutral language of the amendment cannot possibly alter that interpretation, nor can its legislative history be summoned forth to contradict, rather than clarify, what is in its totality an unambiguous statutory text. There is little fear, of course, that giving no effect to the relevant portions of the Committee Reports will frustrate the real-life expectations of a majority of the Members of Congress. If they read and relied on such tedious detail on such an obscure point (it was not, after all, presented as a revision of the statute's prohibitory scope, but as a discretionary-waiver provision) the Republic would be in grave peril. * * *

[JUSTICE O'CONNOR wrote a separate concurring opinion, responding to some of Justice Scalia's concerns. "[T]he regulation's application is limited by ordinary principles of proximate causation, which introduce notions of foreseeability." For example, she disapproved of an application of the statute where the grazing of sheep was found to be a "taking" of palila birds, as the sheep destroyed seedlings which would have grown into trees needed by the bird for nesting. The chain of causation is simply too attenuated, Justice O'Connor concluded. Justice Scalia responded that this was Justice O'Connor's gloss on the statute, not the agency's. He chided his colleague for trying to have it both ways — deferring to the agency under *Chevron* (see Chapter 9, § 3) but then rewriting the regulation to suit her fancy. Justice Scalia concluded: "We defer to reasonable agency interpretations of ambiguous statutes precisely in order that agencies, rather than courts, may exercise policymaking discretion in the interstices of statutes. See *Chevron*, 467 U.S. at 843–45. Just as courts may not exercise an agency's power to adjudicate, and so may not affirm an agency order on discretionary grounds the agency has not advanced, so also this Court may not exercise the Secretary's power to regulate, and so may not uphold a regulation by adding to it even the most reasonable of elements it does not contain."]

NOTES ON *SWEET HOME* AND THE WHOLE ACT RULE

1. *The Debate in* Sweet Home. Notice, first, how many of the canons are relevant to the Justices' deliberations about the plain meaning of the text in this case: the ordinary meaning rule, and its corollaries regarding dictionaries and technical meaning; noscitur a sociis and (possibly) ejusdem generis; expressio (or inclusio) unius and other rules of negative implication; the rule against redundancy; the rule of consistent usage and of significant variation; and the anti-derogation rule. Notice also how the anti-derogation rule figures centrally in both majority and dissenting opinions. Justice Scalia emphasizes the structural conflict between Congress' asserted allocation of responsibilities in §§ 5 and 7 and the majority's broad interpretation of § 9; Justice Stevens emphasizes the philosophical and structural conflict between a narrow reading of § 9 and the statutory scheme established in § 10.

A problem immediately apparent from this case is that different canons cut in different directions. How can one resolve conflicting canonical signals? One way to resolve the conflict is resort to the statutory purpose, but that may only generalize the disagreement. The dissenters' sarcasm suggests the possibility that they were not sympathetic to the statutory goals of biodiversity: note their alarm that the "simplest farmer" finds his land "conscripted to national zoological use." Does this reflect a neutral interpretation of the law? Is the Nietzsche rule possibly applicable here?

Another kind of tiebreaker could be this: Qualitatively speaking, which side has more canons in support of its position? Which side is able to create a more complete — or more elegant — case for its interpretation? We are particularly impressed with the dissenters' ability to weave together a wide array of canons to support their position. Should this assure their triumph? If so, why did their usual ally, Justice O'Connor, jump ship? She might have been influenced by a third tiebreaker: the *political equilibrium* favored the agency (remember that she authored the Court's opinion in the FDA Tobacco Case, Chapter 7, § 3B). Indeed, the agency itself reflected the prevailing political consensus in this case, perhaps justifying the Court's deferring to its rule. See Chapter 9, § 3.

2. *Criticism of the Whole Act Rule.* Both the majority and the dissent in *Sweet Home* applied the whole act rule, reflecting its acceptance by most judges. Yet Richard Posner, *The Federal Courts: Crisis and Reform* 281 (1985), criticizes the whole act rule, first, because it imputes "omniscience" to the legislature and, second, because it assumes that a statute is written as a whole, internally coherent document (like a short story). These are faulty assumptions. "The conditions under which legislators work are not conducive to careful, farsighted, and parsimonious drafting. Nor does great care guarantee economy of language; a statute that is the product of compromise may contain redundant language as a by-product of the strains of the negotiating process."

Although the U.S. Supreme Court regularly invokes the whole act rule, several of its Justices have recognized that the arrangement and phraseology of different statutory provisions is often "the consequence of a legislative *accident*, perhaps caused by nothing more than the unfortunate fact that Congress is too busy to do all of its work as carefully as it should." *Delaware Tribal Business Comm. v. Weeks*, 430 U.S. 73, 97 (1977) (Stevens, J., dissenting) (emphasis in original), quoted in *Mountain States Tel. & Tel. v. Pueblo of Santa Ana*, 472 U.S. 237, 255 (1985) (Brennan, J., dissenting). Note that this latter point is a critique of the canons generally. Even if Judge Posner and Justice Stevens are correct descriptively, the whole act rule might be prescriptively correct. Think about both descriptive and prescriptive issues in connection with the case described in the next paragraph.

3. *A Case of Haphazard Drafting. Sorenson v. Secretary of the Treasury*, 475 U.S. 851 (1986), involved interpretation of the Omnibus Budget Reconciliation Act of 1981 (OBRA), Pub. L. No. 97–35, § 2331, 95 Stat. 860. The Act added provisions to the Social Security Act and the Internal Revenue Code to provide for "interception" of tax refunds for the benefit of state agencies which had been assigned child-support rights. Thus when a taxpayer is in arrears for his or her child support payments, and when the former spouse assigns them to a state (welfare) agency as a condition of receiving public assistance, the state can notify the IRS. The IRS will then give the state's recoupment claim priority over the taxpayer's claim for refunds of overpayment of federal income taxes. The issue in *Sorenson* was whether the "overpayment" which is subject to the recoupment claim includes refunds resulting from an earned-income credit. The Supreme Court held that it was. Section 6402(c), added by OBRA, provides that "*any* overpayment to be refunded * * * shall be reduced by the amount of any past-due support" (emphasis added). Section 6402(b), which was already in the Code, provides that if an earned-income credit exceeds taxpayer's tax liability, the excess amount is "considered an overpayment." Given the whole act rule that terms used in different parts of the statute should presumptively have the same meaning, the result follows.

But Justice Stevens' dissenting opinion pointed out the policy anomalies of the Court's result. The Earned Income Credit Program was created by Congress in 1975 to help keep low-income families off welfare: (1) social security taxes were assessed against earned income but not against welfare payments; (2) as a result, $500 a month in welfare meant more money in the pocket than $500 a month in earned income; (3) to redress this disincentive to work, Congress created a fully refundable credit for low income workers. Applying the OBRA recoupment scheme (one of the obscure goodies given to states in the 1981 reconciliation bill) to penalize low-income families is an accidental consequence of the statute's drafting; nothing in the legislative history supports any legislative desire to curtail the Earned Income Credit Program.

The Court's response to Justice Stevens was that "it defies belief that Congress was unaware" of the impact of the Intercept Program on the Earned Income Credit Program. Justice Stevens riposted: "With all due respect to the Court and to our hard working neighbors in the Congress, I think it 'defies belief' to assume that a substantial number of legislators were sufficiently familiar with OBRA to realize that somewhere in that vast piece of hurriedly enacted legislation there was a provision that changed the 6-year-old Earned Income Credit Program.[2]" In footnote 2, Justice Stevens quoted the following passage from N.Y. Times, July 1, 1981, p. A16, col. 1:

> Smoking a big cigar, the Speaker [of the House of Representatives] got angry again over the slap-dash quality of the bill [that became OBRA], with parts of it photocopied from memorandums, other parts handwritten at the last minute, and some final sections hastily crossed out in whorls of pencil marks. * * *

> But then he smiled, too, noting such cryptic and accidental entries in the bill as a name and phone number — "Ruth Seymour, 225-4844" — standing alone as if it were a special appropriation item.

There is a larger point to be drawn from Justice Stevens' criticisms. In the last generation, Congress has done an increasing amount of its work through gigantic and complex omnibus proposals, a process described in Chapter 4, § 2. Doesn't the majority's approach in *Sorenson* ignore the realities of drafting and enacting a budget reconciliation bill — often in the days or even hours before congressional recess, with provisions added and dropped at the last minute in the conference room? In light of this new operation of the legislative process, should federal courts rethink at least some of the canons of construction? Should there be special canons, or at least practices, for construing omnibus reconciliation legislation like that in *Sorenson*? For a proposal that such omnibus bills be approached cautiously, see Seth Grossman, *Tricameral Legislating: Statutory Interpretation in an Era of Conference Committee Ascendancy*, 9 NYU J. Leg. & Pub. Pol'y (2006).

B. SUBSTANTIVE CANONS

Most of the canons discussed in the previous part are linguistic or syntactic guidelines that are policy-neutral. Other canons represent substantive decisions, and hence their application is not policy-neutral. Traditionally, the main canons were directives to interpret different types of statutes "liberally" or "strictly." The old Anglo-American rule was that "remedial" statutes were to be liberally interpreted, while statutes in derogation of the common law were to be strictly interpreted. (But what remedial statute is not in derogation of the common law?)

More modern typologies of the liberal-versus-strict construction canons have emerged. Certain statutes (such as civil rights, securities, and antitrust statutes) are supposed to be liberally construed — in other words, applied expansively to new situations.[m] As Appendix B, reporting the Court's deployment of canons from the 1986 through the 2006 Terms, demonstrates, these liberal construction canons have not been often invoked by the Rehnquist and Roberts Courts. Other statutes are to be strictly construed — in other words, applied stingily. The rule of lenity, requiring strict construction of penal statutes, is the best example and is explored in some detail below. Strict construction of statutes, especially for quasi-constitutional reasons, has been highly popular in the Rehnquist and Roberts Courts.

One way to understand the remedial/strict construction distinction is suggested by linguists' theory of prototypes: words in a statute construed strictly should presumptively not be read beyond their prototypical meanings, while words in other statutes can be read beyond such meanings if consistent with the statutory purpose. In *Sweet Home*, Justice Stevens read the statutory term *take* beyond its prototypical meaning, because he understood the statute as a remedial one that Congress wanted read broadly, while Justice Scalia refused to read the term beyond its prototypical meaning, perhaps because this was a statute invading vested property rights. Thus, even cases seeming to be nothing but word-crunching exercises can be understood as reflecting profoundly substantive policy determinations by judges.

Consider other canons reflecting substantive judgments about how broadly to read the statute's text:

• *Strict Construction of Statutes in Derogation of Sovereignty.* If a statute is written in general language, it is presumed that it only applies to private parties; governments and their agencies are presumptively not included unless the statute clearly says so. See *Nevada Dep't Human Resources v. Hibbs*, 538 U.S. 721 (2003) (finding such clarity). This canon is based

---

m. The Supreme Court has invoked the liberal-construction maxim when interpreting civil rights legislation such as § 1983, see *Dennis v. Higgins*, 498 U.S. 439 (1991); *Gomez v. Toledo*, 446 U.S. 635 (1980); statutes providing benefits to seamen, *Cox v. Roth*, 348 U.S. 207 (1955), and to veterans, *King v. St. Vincent's Hosp.*, 502 U.S. 215, 221 n.9 (1991); and safety legislation such as the Occupational Safety and Health Act, *Whirlpool Corp. v. Marshall*, 445 U.S. 1 (1980). See generally William Eskridge, Jr. & John Ferejohn, *Super-Statutes*, 2001 Duke L.J. (super-statutes whose policy or principle comes to be entrenched in the public culture over time will be interpreted liberally to advance their policies or principles, and expansively vis-a-vis more ordinary statutes; examples include the Sherman Act of 1890, the Civil Rights Act of 1964, the Endangered Species Act of 1973 (the law at issue in *Sweet Home*)).

upon the old idea of sovereign immunity: the state cannot be sued or otherwise regulated without its consent. See 3 Sutherland § 62.01.[n]

• *Strict Construction of Public Grants.* Similarly, public grants by the government to private parties are to be construed narrowly, that is, in favor of the government. Sometimes, this precept has been justified on the grounds that such grants were gratuitous or solicited by the grantee, but the canon has been invoked in the whole range of cases — from leases and contracts with the government, to statutes allowing compromise settlements with the government, to pension and compensation laws for public officials.[o]

• *Strict Construction of (Some) Revenue Provisions.* 3 Sutherland § 66.01, announces that "it is a settled rule that tax laws are to be strictly construed against the state and in favor of the taxpayer. Where there is reasonable doubt as to the meaning of a revenue statute, the doubt is resolved in favor of those taxed." See *Gould v. Gould,* 245 U.S. 151 (1917). Generations of taxpayers who have lost lawsuits against the Internal Revenue Service over fine points of statutory interpretation would dispute that generalization. See *United States v. Fior D'Italia,* 536 U.S. 238, 242–43 (2002) (presuming that IRS-generated tax assessments are correct). Courts are turning to more liberal construction because of the necessary public purpose implicated in the system of taxation, "and it is the duty of the courts to see that no one, by mere technicalities which do not affect his substantial rights, shall escape his fair proportion of the public expenses." *Atlantic City Transp. Co. v. Walsh,* 25 N.J.Misc. 483, 55 A.2d 652 (1947); see 3 Sutherland § 66.02. Under this new thinking, the *tax-imposing* provisions would not be strictly construed — but the *tax-exempting* provisions ought to be.[p]

---

n. Since the absolute immunity of the state has eroded substantially in the last thirty years, this presumption has lost much of its original justification. A better rationale for the rule may be that the sovereign needs few constraints upon its freedom of activity as it decides how best to serve the public interest (though this explanation may be a naive view of the way government works). In the United States this rule has quasi-constitutional dimensions, since the states retained their basic immunities when they joined the union, see U.S. Const. amends. X–XI, and the federal government enjoys supremacy over states and their regulation. *Id.* art. VI. In any event, many states have statutes rejecting this rule of strict construction. 3 Sutherland § 62.04. For example: "The term 'person' may be construed to include the United States, this state, or any state or territory or any public or private corporation, as well as an individual." West's Rev. Code Wash. Ann. 1.16.080 (1961). These state rules, of course, are subject to the Supremacy Clause and may be invalid as regards the United States. E.g., *McCulloch v. Maryland,* 17 U.S. (4 Wheat.) 316 (1819).

o. 3 Sutherland § 63.04, posits that the main reason for this canon is a general tendency "to regard all such grants with extreme distrust, so that in all its dealings the government will not suffer loss." Yet the rule has not generally been applied when the grant is for a great public purpose, such as the land grants to railroads in return for their building the transcontinental railroad in the 1860s. E.g., *Leo Sheep v. United States,* 440 U.S. 668, 682 (1979); *Platt v. Union Pac. R.,* 99 U.S. (9 Otto) 48 (1878).

p. Public choice theory (Chapter 1, § 2) lends support to this suggestion. Rent-seeking interest groups can be expected to extract from the legislature special exemptions from the broad taxing provisions. Not only do these exemptions undermine the public fisc, but they tend to do

A second way of formulating substantive canons is as presumptions or rules of thumb that cut across different types of statutes and statutory schemes. These represent policies that the Court will "presume" Congress intends to incorporate into statutes, but such presumptions are rebuttable ones. Presumptions will generally not trump a contrary statutory text, legislative history, or purpose. See *Astoria Federal Savings & Loan Association v. Solimino*, 501 U.S. 104, 108 (1991). A presumption or rule of thumb can be treated as a starting point for discussion, a tiebreaker at the end of discussion, or just a balancing factor. The policies underlying interpretive presumptions are derived by courts from the Constitution, federal statutes, and the common law. Some examples of substantive presumptions:

- Presumption against congressional diminishment of American Indian rights. See *Hagen v. Utah*, 510 U.S. 399 (1994); *Montana v. Blackfeet Tribe*, 471 U.S. 759 (1985).

- Presumption of Indian tribal immunity from state regulation. See *Bryan v. Itasca County*, 426 U.S. 373 (1976).

- Presumption that Congress does not intend to pass statutes which violate international law. See *Sosa v. Alvarez-Machain*, 542 U.S. 692 (2004); *Weinberger v. Rossi*, 456 U.S. 25, 32 (1982); *Murray v. The Charming Betsy*, 2 Cranch 64, 118 (1804).

- Presumption that Congress does not intend to pass statutes which violate treaty obligations. See *Hamdan v. Rumsfeld*, 126 S.Ct. 2749 (2006).

- Presumption that Congress does not intend that statutes have extraterritorial application. See *Foley Brothers v. Filardo*, 336 U.S. 281 (1949).

- Presumption that Congress does not intend that substantive statutes be applied retroactively. See *Landgraf* (Chapter 6, § 3C).

- Presumption that Congress does not intend that federal regulation unnecessarily intrude into traditional state responsibilities (any more than is necessary to subserve national objectives). See *Rush Prudential HMO v. Moran*, 536 U.S. 355 (2002); *Cipollone v. Liggett Group, Inc.*, 505 U.S. 504 (1992); *Ray v. Atlantic Richfield Co.*, 435 U.S. 151, 157 (1978).

- Presumption that Congress will not withdraw the courts' traditional equitable discretion. See *Weinberger v. Romero-Barcelo*, 456 U.S. 305, 320 (1982); *Hecht Co. v. Bowles*, 321 U.S. 321, 330 (1944).

- Presumption that Congress will not withdraw all remedies or judicial avenues of relief when it recognizes a statutory right. See *South Carolina v. Regan*, 465 U.S. 367 (1984).

- Presumption of judicial review. See *Demore v. Kim*, 538 U.S. 510 (2003); *Dunlop v. Bachowski*, 421 U.S. 560 (1975); *Abbott Laboratories v. Gardner*, 387 U.S. 136 (1967).

---

so for already-advantaged groups, thereby making the income tax system much less progressive than it is advertised as being.

- Presumption against derogation of the President's traditional powers. See *Department of Navy v. Egan*, 484 U.S. 518, 527 (1988); *Haig v. Agee*, 453 U.S. 280 (1981).

A third way of formulating substantive canons is as *clear statement rules*, which are presumptions that can only be rebutted only by clear language in the text of the statute. See *Solimino*, 501 U.S. at 108–09 (contrasting presumptions and clear statement rules). Clear statement rules have been developed by the Supreme Court as expressions of quasi-constitutional values. For example, Congress cannot impose liability and process directly against the states unless the statutory text clearly says so (Section 1B2 below).

There is some mobility in the Court's articulation of these substantive canons. For example, in *EEOC v. Arabian American Oil Co.*, 499 U.S. 244, 258–59 (1991), a majority of the Court transformed the old *Foley Brothers* presumption against extraterritorial application (of Title VII in that case) into a clear statement rule, requiring explicit statutory language in order for a law to apply outside the United States. Justice Marshall's dissenting opinion objected to the Court's transformation. *Id.* at 263. Note here how the general rule that civil rights laws, like Title VII, should be liberally construed was itself trumped by the more specific canon against extraterritorial regulation.

As suggested above, substantive canons may vary in their impact upon interpretation, and it is critical to identify how a court is using a canon. By way of review, consider three possibilities alluded to above. First, sometimes courts will treat a substantive canon as merely a *tiebreaker* that affects the outcome only if, at the end of the basic interpretive process, the court is left unable to choose between the two competing interpretations put forward by the parties. Second, courts might treat substantive canons as *presumptions* that, at the beginning of the interpretive process, set up a presumptive outcome, which can be overcome by persuasive support for the contrary interpretation. Typically, the party attempting to overcome the presumption may use any potential evidence of statutory meaning (e.g., statutory text, legislative history, statutory purposes, policy arguments, and so on) to rebut the presumption. On this understanding, a presumption simply adds weight to one side of the balancing process captured by eclectic statutory interpretation. Third, courts may treat substantive canons as *clear statement rules*, which purport to compel a particular interpretive outcome unless there is a clear statement to the contrary. We shall call those canons "clear statement rules" when they may be overcome by clear statutory language and those canons "super-strong clear statement rules" when they may be overcome only by extremely clear statutory text (where the "clear statement" is, in effect, a targeted statement of textual meaning). Keep a sharp eye on which of these approaches is used to implement the canons that are discussed in the remainder of this part.

1. *The Rule of Lenity in Criminal Cases*

One of the hoariest canons of statutory interpretation states that laws whose purpose is to punish (usually by fine or imprisonment) must be construed strictly. This is called the "rule of lenity" in construing penal statutes: If the punitive statute does not clearly outlaw private conduct, the private actor cannot be penalized. While criminal statutes are the most obvious and common type of penal law, many civil statutes have been so classified by at least some jurisdictions; recall Justice Scalia's invocation of this idea in *Sweet Home.*[q]

What is the purpose of the rule of lenity?[r] In England, courts have long used this canon vigorously for humanitarian reasons "when the number of capital offences was still very large, when it was still punishable with death to cut down a cherry-tree." *Maxwell* 238.[s] Early practice in this country was ambivalent about the rule of lenity: state and federal courts sometimes invoked it, but in early prosecutions for public insurrections and seditious libel, federal judges in particular showed no lenity; the Marshall Court, however, firmly established the rule of lenity in American legisprudence.[t] Especially as penalties have been ameliorated, other kinds of reasons have been invoked to justify the rule of lenity.

For years, the leading justification has been *fair notice*. The state may not impose penalties upon people without clearly warning them about unlawful conduct and its consequences. A classic reference for this rationalization is *McBoyle v. United States*, 283 U.S. 25 (1931). A 1919 federal statute prohibited the transportation of stolen *motor vehicles* in interstate commerce. The law defined motor vehicle to "include an automobile, automobile truck, automobile wagon, motor cycle, or any other self-propelled vehicle not designed for running on rails." The issue in the case was whether defendant's transportation of a stolen airplane fell within the statute. Because *airplane* was not within the popular (or what linguists today call the prototypical) meaning of *motor vehicle*, Justice Holmes' opinion for the Court held that it did not. He justified lenity on grounds of notice:

> Although it is not likely that a criminal will carefully consider the text of the law before he murders or steals, it is reasonable that a fair warning should be given to the world in language that the common world will understand, of what the law intends to do if a certain line is passed. To make the warning fair, so far as possible the line should be clear. When a rule of conduct is laid down in words that evoke in the common mind only the picture of the vehicles moving on land, the statute should not be extended to aircraft, simply because it may seem to us that a similar policy applies,

---

q. Among the statutes to which this canon has been applied are (i) statutes whose penalties include forfeiture; (ii) statutes providing for "extra" damages beyond those needed to make the complainant whole, including punitive damages, treble damages, attorneys' fees, penalty interest (often part of the remedy under usury laws); (iii) statutes permitting revocation of a professional license or disbarment of lawyers; (iv) statutes against extortion or discrimination; (v) statutes declaring certain acts to be per se negligence; and (vi) others. See 3 Sutherland § 59.02.

r. For a comprehensive treatment, see Lawrence Solan, *Law, Language, and Lenity*, 40 Wm. & Mary L. Rev. 57 (1998).

s. The main line of cases are those construing Parliament's attempted narrowing of the "benefit of clergy" in ways that preserved it as a defense to the death penalty. See J.M. Beattie, *Crime and the Courts in England, 1600–1800* (1986); Livingston Hall, *Strict or Liberal Construction of Penal Statutes*, 48 Harv. L. Rev. 748 (1935).

t. See William Eskridge, Jr., *All About Words: Early Understandings of the "Judicial Power" in Statutory Interpretation, 1776–1806*, 101 Colum. L. Rev. 990 (2001). .

or upon the speculation that if the legislature had thought of it, very likely broader words would have been used.

Accord, *United States v. Lanier*, 520 U.S. 259, 265–66 (1997) (excellent elaboration of *McBoyle* and the various fair warning doctrines).

Under a fair warning rationalization, the rule of lenity is most appropriately applied to criminal statutes that create offenses that are *malum prohibitum* (bad only because they are prohibited) rather than *malum in se* (bad by their very nature).[u] Thus, a law criminalizing homicide doesn't have to be as clear in all respects as a law criminalizing hunting and fishing without a license from the state. But can this precept explain *McBoyle*? Or *Regina v. Harris*, 173 Eng. Rep. 198 (Cent. Crim. Ct. 1836), in which an English court held that one who bit off the end of the nose of another was not guilty of violating a statute punishing anyone "who shall unlawfully and maliciously stab, cut, or wound any person" because the statute reached only wounds inflicted by an instrument. In both those cases — and many others — defendants engaging in unquestionably squalid behavior got the benefit of the rule.

A justification related to fair notice might be the Anglo-American emphasis on mens rea as a presumptive requirement for criminal penalties. Although ignorance of the law is no defense to a crime, the inability of the reasonable defendant to know that his actions are criminal undermines the justice of inferring a criminal intent in some cases. It also suggests a corollary of the rule of lenity, namely, the presumption that criminal statutes carry with them a mens rea, or intentionality, requirement.

A dramatic illustration of the rule of lenity and its corollary is *Ratzlaf v. United States*, 510 U.S. 135 (1994), which construed the Money Laundering Control Act of 1986. Prior law required banks to report cash transactions in excess of $10,000; to prevent people from "structuring" their transactions to avoid the reports, the 1986 law made it illegal to make lower deposits for the purpose of evading the reporting requirements. The Court interpreted the statute to require *double scienter*: not only must the government prove that defendants Waldemar and Loretta Ratzlaf intended to evade the bank reporting law, but also that they knew about and intended to evade the anti-structuring law as well.[v] Justice Ginsburg's opinion for the Court emphasized that there were many benign reasons people would want to structure their transactions to avoid bank reporting requirements, including fear of burglary and a desire to

---

u. Oliver Wendell Holmes, Jr., *The Common Law* 50 (1881) (positing the malum in se/prohibitum distinction). See also J. Willard Hurst, *Dealing with Statutes* 64–65 (1982); John Calvin Jeffries, Jr., *Legality, Vagueness, and the Construction of Penal Statutes*, 71 Va. L. Rev. 189 (1985).

v. The Supreme Court similarly read special scienter requirements into a statute making it a crime to possess a "machine gun," *Staples v. United States*, 511 U.S. 600 (1994) (government must prove defendant knew the gun was a machine gun), or to distribute images of minors engaged in sexually explicit conduct, *United States v. X-Citement Video, Inc.*, 513 U.S. 64 (1994) (government must prove defendant knew the performer was actually a minor). See also *Cheek v. United States*, 498 U.S. 192 (1991) (taxpayer's honest but unreasonable belief that he did not have to pay taxes was a valid defense to a charge of wilful failure to pay taxes).

secrete assets from a spouse or tax inspectors. According to Justice Ginsburg, "structuring is not inevitably nefarious." *Id.* at 144. Four dissenting Justices argued that a double scienter requirement was not justified by the statutory language, would render the statute a nullity, and focused on unduly extreme cases.

A third justification for the rule of lenity was originally suggested by Chief Justice Marshall in *United States v. Wiltberger*, 18 U.S. 76, 92 (1820): separation of powers. After much debate, the Marshall Court adopted the proposition that Congress cannot delegate to judges and prosecutors power to make common law crimes, because the moral condemnation inherent in crimes ought only to be delivered by the popularly elected legislature. If the legislature alone has the authority to define crimes, it is inappropriate for judges to elaborate on criminal statutes so as to expand them beyond the clear import of their directive words adopted by the legislature. There is also a separation of powers concern that judicial expansion of criminal statutes, common law style, risks expanding prosecutorial discretion beyond that contemplated by the legislature. See Herbert Packer, *The Limits of the Criminal Sanction* 79–96 (1968).

Notwithstanding the antiquity and multiple rationales for the rule of lenity, it has fallen into decline since the New Deal. See generally Francis Allen, *The Erosion of Legality in American Criminal Justice: Some Latter-Day Adventures of the* Nulla Poena *Principle*, 29 Ariz. L. Rev. 385 (1987). As of 2006, twenty-eight states have abolished or even reversed the rule of lenity by statute.[w] Typical is Arizona Penal Code § 13-104, added in 1977: "The general rule that a penal statute is to be strictly construed does not apply to this title, but the provisions herein must be construed according to the fair meaning of their terms to promote justice and effect the objects of the law." The primary explanation for these anti-lenity statutes is that state legislatures in the late twentieth century were prone to invoke the criminal sanction liberally, and did not want judges obstructing such an expansion. If this rationale holds up, does that provide a reason *favoring* the rule of lenity? Do the rule's constitutional overtones trump such statutes under some circumstances? Cf. See *State v. Pena*, 683 P.2d 744, 748–49 (Ariz. App.), aff'd, 683 P.2d 743 (Ariz. 1984) (applying rule of lenity notwithstanding the legislative abrogation).

Criticism of the rule of lenity has not been limited to legislators, however. Professor Dan Kahan, *Lenity and Federal Common Law Crimes*, 1994 Sup. Ct. Rev. 345, maintains that the nondelegation reason is the only coherent justification for the rule of lenity, at least for federal criminal statutes, but further argues that the rule of lenity should be abolished as a canon of construction. The polity would be better off without the rule of lenity. Accord, John Calvin Jeffries, Jr., *Legality, Vagueness, and the Construction of Penal Statutes*, 71 Va. L. Rev. 189, 189 (1985) ("I believe that the rule of strict construction — at least as it is conventionally understood — is, and probably should be, defunct."). Normal interpretation of criminal statutes, without a

---

w. See Robert Yablon, "Lenity Without Strict Construction: Matching the Rule to Its Purposes" (Yale Law School SAW 2006) (collecting state statutes).

judicial thumb on either side of the scale, would promote a more orderly and less costly development of criminal law (common law style, the way commercial law has developed, for example), without much in the way of unfairness, especially if the Department of Justice cleared up ambiguities by authoritative interpretations of federal criminal statutes. Consider this thesis in light of the following cases. Is there a coherent rationale for the rule of lenity? Does it serve useful purposes? Or does it impose needless costs on the system?

MUSCARELLO v. UNITED STATES
Supreme Court of the United States, 1998
524 U.S. 125, 118 S.Ct. 1911, 141 L.Ed.2d 111

JUSTICE BREYER delivered the opinion of the Court.

[Section 924(c)(1) of 18 U.S.C. provides that "[w]hoever, during and in relation to any crime of violence or drug trafficking crime * * * uses or carries a firearm, shall, in addition to the punishment provided for such crime of violence or drug trafficking crime, be sentenced to imprisonment for five years[.]" The practical consequence of this provision is that someone who possessed a gun at the time of a drug offense gets a mandatory additional five-year sentence if § 924(c)(1) was violated; if that provision was not violated, the possession of the gun would be taken into account under the federal sentencing guidelines and would add some time to the sentence (perhaps a 30–40% enhancement) unless the gun was clearly not involved in the drug offense. Apparently it is almost always in the interest of the defendant to be subjected to the sentencing guidelines in this way rather than receive the mandatory additional sentence provided by § 924(c)(1). Accordingly, there has been much litigation concerning what the government must show beyond the mere possession of a gun during a drug offense to satisfy § 924(c)(1).

[In *Smith v. United States*, 508 U.S. 223 (1993), the Court held that, when a person traded a gun for drugs, he "used" the gun in violation of § 924(c)(1). Justice Scalia's dissenting opinion contended that the ordinary meaning of § 924(c)(1), read in context, is that "uses a firearm" means "uses the firearm as a weapon," and that in any event the issue was sufficiently doubtful for the rule of lenity to control the outcome in favor of the defendant. In *Bailey v. United States*, 516 U.S. 137 (1995), a unanimous Court held that the "use" element requires active employment of the firearm by the defendant, such that it did not apply to a defendant who had a gun in the trunk of his car in which illegal drugs were found or to a defendant who had a gun locked in a trunk in a closet in a bedroom where illegal drugs were stored.

[Muscarello unlawfully sold marijuana from his truck and confessed that he "carried" a gun in the truck's locked glove compartment " 'for protection in relation' to the drug offense." In a companion case, Donald Cleveland and Enrique Gray-Santana were arrested for stealing and dealing drugs; they had bags of guns in the locked trunk of their car at the scene. The issue was whether these defendants had "carrie[d]" a firearm within the meaning of § 924(c)(1).]

We begin with the statute's language. The parties vigorously contest the ordinary English meaning of the phrase "carries a firearm." Because they essentially agree that Congress intended the phrase to convey its ordinary, and not some special legal, meaning, and because they argue the linguistic point at length, we too have looked into the matter in more than usual depth. Although the word "carry" has many different meanings, only two are relevant here. When one uses the word in the first, or primary, meaning, one can, as a matter of ordinary English, "carry firearms" in a wagon, car, truck, or other vehicle that one accompanies. When one uses the word in a different, rather special, way, to mean, for example, "bearing" or (in slang) "packing" (as in "packing a gun"), the matter is less clear. But, for reasons we shall set out below, we believe Congress intended to use the word in its primary sense and not in this latter, special way.

Consider first the word's primary meaning. The Oxford English Dictionary gives as its *first* definition "convey, originally by cart or wagon, hence in any vehicle, by ship, on horseback, etc." 2 Oxford English Dictionary 919 (2d ed. 1989); see also Webster's Third New International Dictionary 343 (1986) (*first* definition: "move while supporting (*as in a vehicle* or in one's hands or arms)"); The Random House Dictionary of the English Language Unabridged 319 (2d ed. 1987) (*first* definition: "to take or support from one place to another; convey; transport").

The origin of the word "carries" explains why the first, or basic, meaning of the word "carry" includes conveyance in a vehicle. See The Barnhart Dictionary of Etymology 146 (1988) (tracing the word from Latin "carum," which means "car" or "cart"); 2 Oxford English Dictionary, *supra*, at 919 (tracing the word from Old French "carier" and the late Latin "carricare," which meant to "convey in a car") * * * .

The greatest of writers have used the word with this meaning. See, e.g., the King James Bible, 2 Kings 9:28 ("[H]is servants carried him in a chariot to Jerusalem"); *id.*, Isaiah 30:6 ("[T]hey will carry their riches upon the shoulders of young asses"). Robinson Crusoe says, "[w]ith my boat, I carry'd away every Thing." D. Defoe, Robinson Crusoe 174 (J. Crowley ed. 1972). And the owners of Queequeg's ship, Melville writes, "had lent him a [wheelbarrow], in which to carry his heavy chest to his boardinghouse." H. Melville, Moby Dick 43 (U. Chicago 1952). This Court, too, has spoken of the "carrying" of drugs in a car or in its "trunk." [Citations omitted.]

These examples do not speak directly about carrying guns. But there is nothing linguistically special about the fact that weapons, rather than drugs, are being carried. * * * And, to make certain that there is no special ordinary English restriction (unmentioned in dictionaries) upon the use of "carry" in respect to guns, we have surveyed modern press usage, albeit crudely, by searching computerized newspaper databases — both the New York Times data base in Lexis/Nexis, and the "US News" data base in Westlaw. We looked for sentences in which the words "carry," "vehicle," and "weapon" (or variations thereof) all appear. We found thousands of such sentences, and random sampling suggests that many, perhaps more than one third, are sentences used to convey the meaning at issue here, *i.e.*, the carrying of guns in a car. [Justice Breyer gave several examples of such newspaper stories.]

Now consider a different, somewhat special meaning of the word "carry" — a meaning upon which the linguistic arguments of petitioners and the dissent must rest. The Oxford English Dictionary's *twenty-sixth* definition of "carry" is "bear, wear, hold up, or sustain, as one moves about; habitually to bear about with one." Webster's [Third New International Dictionary] defines "carry" as "to move while supporting," not just in a vehicle, but also "in one's hands or arms." And Black's Law Dictionary defines the entire phrase "carry arms or weapons" as "[t]o wear, bear or carry them upon the person or in the clothing or in a pocket, for the purpose of use, or for the purpose of being armed and ready for offensive or defensive action in case of a conflict with another person."

These special definitions, however, do not purport to *limit* the "carrying of arms" to the circumstances they describe. No one doubts that one who bears arms on his person "carries a weapon." But to say that is not to deny that one may also "carry a weapon" tied to the saddle of a horse or placed in a bag in a car.

Nor is there any linguistic reason to think that Congress intended to limit the word "carries" in the statute to any of these special definitions. To the contrary, all these special definitions embody a form of an important, but secondary, meaning of "carry," a meaning that suggests support rather than movement or transportation, as when, for example, a column "carries" the weight of an arch. 2 Oxford English Dictionary, *supra*, at 919, 921. In this sense a gangster might "carry" a gun (in colloquial language, he might "pack a gun") even though he does not move from his chair. It is difficult to believe, however, that Congress intended to limit the statutory word to this definition — imposing special punishment upon the comatose gangster while ignoring drug lords who drive to a sale carrying an arsenal of weapons in their van.

We recognize, as the dissent emphasizes, that the word "carry" has other meanings as well. But those other meanings, (e.g., "carry all he knew," "carries no colours") are not relevant here. And the fact that speakers often do *not* add to the phrase "carry a gun" the words "in a car" is of no greater relevance here than the fact that millions of Americans did *not* see Muscarello carry a gun in his car. The relevant linguistic facts are that the word "carry" in its ordinary sense includes carrying in a car and that the word, used in its ordinary sense, keeps the same meaning whether one carries a gun, a suitcase, or a banana. * * *

We now explore more deeply the purely legal question of whether Congress intended to use the word "carry" in its ordinary sense, or whether it intended to limit the scope of the phrase to instances in which a gun is carried "on the person." We conclude that neither the statute's basic purpose nor its legislative history support circumscribing the scope of the word "carry" by applying an "on the person" limitation.

This Court has described the statute's basic purpose broadly, as an effort to combat the "dangerous combination" of "drugs and guns." *Smith v. United States*, 508 U.S. 223, 240 (1993). And the provision's chief legislative sponsor has said that the provision seeks "to persuade the man who is tempted to commit a Federal felony to leave his gun at home." 114 Cong. Rec. 22231 (1968) (Rep. Poff); see *Busic v. United States*, 446 U.S. 398, 405 (1980) (describing Poff's comments as "crucial material" in interpreting the purpose of § 924(c)); *Simpson v. United States*, 435 U.S. 6, 13–14 (1978) (concluding that Poff's comments are "clearly probative" and "certainly entitled to weight"); see also 114 Cong. Rec. 22243–22244 (statutes would apply to "the man who goes out taking a gun to commit a crime") (Rep. Hunt); *id.*, at 22244 ("Of course, what we are trying to do by these penalties is to persuade the criminal to leave his gun at home") (Rep. Randall); *id.*, at 22236 ("We are concerned . . . with having the criminal leave his gun at home") (Rep. Meskill).

From the perspective of any such purpose (persuading a criminal "to leave his gun at home") what sense would it make for this statute to penalize one who walks with a gun in a bag to the site of a drug sale, but to ignore a similar individual who, like defendant Gray-Santana, travels to a similar site with a similar gun in a similar bag, but instead of walking, drives there with the gun in his car? How persuasive is a punishment that is without effect until a drug dealer who has brought his gun to a sale (indeed has it available for use) actually takes it from the trunk (or unlocks the glove compartment) of his car? It is difficult to say that, considered as a class, those who prepare, say, to sell drugs by placing guns in their cars are less dangerous, or less deserving of punishment, than those who carry handguns on their person.

We have found no significant indication elsewhere in the legislative history of any more narrowly focused relevant purpose. * * * One legislator indicates that the statute responds in part to the concerns of law enforcement personnel, who had urged that "carrying short firearms in motor vehicles be classified as carrying such weapons concealed." *Id.*, at 22242 (Rep. May). Another criticizes a version of the proposed statute by suggesting it might apply to drunken driving, and gives as an example a drunken driver who has a "gun in his car." *Id.*, at 21792 (Rep. Yates). Others describe the statute as criminalizing gun "possession" — a term that could stretch beyond both the "use" of a gun and the carrying of a gun on the person. See *id.*, at 21793 (Rep. Casey); *id.*, at 22236 (Rep. Meskill); *id.*, at 30584 (Rep. Collier); *id.*, at 30585 (Rep. Skubitz).

We are not convinced by petitioners' remaining arguments[.] First, they say that our definition of "carry" makes it the equivalent of "transport." Yet, Congress elsewhere in related statutes used the word "transport" deliberately to signify a different, and broader, statutory coverage. The immediately preceding statutory subsection, for example, imposes a different set of penalties on one who, with an intent to commit a crime, "ships, transports, or receives a firearm" in interstate commerce. 18 U.S.C. § 924(b). Moreover, § 926A specifically "entitle[s]" a person "not otherwise prohibited . . . from transporting, shipping, or receiving a firearm" to "transport a firearm . . . from any place where he may lawfully possess and carry" it to "any other place" where he may do so. Why, petitioners ask, would Congress have used the word "transport," or used both "carry" and "transport" in the same provision, if it had intended to obliterate the distinction between the two?

The short answer is that our definition does not equate "carry" and "transport." "Carry" implies personal agency and some degree of possession, whereas "transport" does not have such a limited connotation and, in addition, implies the movement of goods in bulk over great distances. See Webster's Third New International Dictionary 343 (noting that "carry" means "moving to a location some distance away while supporting or maintaining off the ground" and "is a natural word to use in ref. to cargoes and loads on trucks, wagons, planes, ships, or even beasts of burden," while "transport refers to carriage in bulk or number over an appreciable distance and, typically, by a customary or usual carrier agency"); see also Webster's Dictionary of Synonyms 141 (1942). If Smith, for example, calls a parcel delivery service, which sends a truck to Smith's house to pick up Smith's package and take it to Los Angeles, one might say that Smith has shipped the package and the parcel delivery service has transported the package. But only the truck driver has "carried" the package in the sense of "carry" that we believe Congress intended. Therefore, "transport" is a broader category that includes "carry" but also encompasses other activity.

The dissent refers to § 926A and to another statute where Congress used the word "transport" rather than "carry" to describe the movement of firearms. 18 U.S.C. § 925(a)(2)(B). According to the dissent, had Congress intended "carry" to have the meaning we give it, Congress would not have needed to use a different word in these provisions. But as we have discussed above, we believe the word "transport" is broader than the word "carry."

And, if Congress intended "carry" to have the limited definition the dissent contends, it would have been quite unnecessary to add the proviso in § 926A requiring a person, to be exempt from penalties, to store her firearm in a locked container not immediately accessible. See § 926A (exempting from criminal penalties one who transports a firearm from a place where "he may lawfully possess and carry such firearm" but not exempting the "transportation" of a firearm if it is "readily accessible or is directly accessible from the passenger compartment of transporting vehicle"). The statute simply could have said that such a person may not "carry" a firearm. But, of course, Congress did not say this because that is not what "carry" means.

As we interpret the statutory scheme, it makes sense. Congress has imposed a variable penalty with no mandatory minimum sentence upon a person who "transports" (or "ships" or "receives") a firearm knowing it will be used to commit any "offense punishable by imprisonment for [more than] . . . one year," § 924(b), and it has imposed a 5-year mandatory minimum sentence upon one who "carries" a firearm "during and in relation to" a "drug trafficking crime," § 924(c). The first subsection imposes a less strict sentencing regime upon one who, say, ships firearms by mail for use in a crime elsewhere; the latter subsection imposes a mandatory sentence upon one who, say, brings a weapon with him (on his person or in his car) to the site of a drug sale.

Second, petitioners point out that, in *Bailey v. United States*, we considered the related phrase "uses . . . a firearm" found in the same statutory provision now before us. We construed the term "use" narrowly, limiting its application to the "active employment" of a firearm. Petitioners argue that it would be anomalous to construe broadly the word "carries," its statutory next-door neighbor.

In *Bailey*, however, we limited "use" of a firearm to "active employment" in part because we assumed "that Congress . . . intended each term to have a particular, non-superfluous meaning." A broader interpretation of "use," we said, would have swallowed up the term "carry." But "carry" as we interpret that word does not swallow up the term "use." "Use" retains the same independent meaning we found for it in *Bailey*, where we provided examples involving the displaying or the bartering of a gun. "Carry" also retains an independent meaning, for, under *Bailey*, carrying a gun in a car does not necessarily involve the gun's "active employment." More importantly, having construed "use" narrowly in *Bailey*, we cannot also construe "carry" narrowly without undercutting the statute's basic objective. For the narrow interpretation would remove the act of carrying a gun in a car entirely from the statute's reach, leaving a gap in coverage that we do not believe Congress intended.

Third, petitioners say that our reading of the statute would extend its coverage to passengers on buses, trains, or ships, who have placed a firearm, say, in checked luggage. To extend this statute so far, they argue, is unfair, going well beyond what Congress likely would have thought possible. They add that some lower courts, thinking approximately the same, have limited the scope of "carries" to instances where a gun in a car is immediately accessible, thereby most likely excluding from coverage a gun carried in a car's trunk or locked glove compartment. * * *

In our view, this argument does not take adequate account of other limiting words in the statute — words that make the statute applicable only where a defendant "carries" a gun *both* "during *and* in relation to" a drug crime. § 924(c)(1) (emphasis added). Congress added these words in part to prevent prosecution where guns "played" no part in the crime. See S. Rep. No. 98–225, at 314, n. 10.

Once one takes account of the words "during" and "in relation to," it no longer seems beyond Congress' likely intent, or otherwise unfair, to interpret the statute as we have done. If one carries a gun in a car "during" and "in relation to" a drug sale, for example, the fact that the gun is carried in the car's trunk or locked glove compartment seems not only logically difficult to distinguish from the immediately accessible gun, but also beside the point.

At the same time, the narrow interpretation creates its own anomalies. The statute, for example, defines "firearm" to include a "bomb," "grenade," "rocket having a propellant charge of more than four ounces," or "missile having an explosive or incendiary charge of more than one-quarter ounce," where such device is "explosive," "incendiary," or delivers "poison gas." 18 U.S.C. § 921(a)(4)(A). On petitioners' reading, the "carry" provision would not apply to instances where drug lords, engaged in a major transaction, took with them "firearms" such as these, which most likely could not be carried on the person.

Fourth, petitioners argue that we should construe the word "carry" to mean "immediately accessible." * * * That interpretation, however, is difficult to square with the statute's language, for one "carries" a gun in the glove compartment whether or not that glove compartment is locked. Nothing in the statute's history suggests that Congress intended that limitation. And, for reasons pointed out above, we believe that the words "during" and "in relation to" will limit the statute's application to the harms that Congress foresaw.

Finally, petitioners and the dissent invoke the "rule of lenity." The simple existence of some statutory ambiguity, however, is not sufficient to warrant application of that rule, for most statutes are ambiguous to some degree. " 'The rule of lenity applies only if, "after seizing everything from which aid can be derived," . . . we can make "no more than a guess as to what Congress intended." ' " *United States v. Wells*, 519 U.S. 482,499 (1997) [quoting earlier cases]. To invoke the rule, we must conclude that there is a " 'grievous ambiguity or uncertainty' in the statute." *Staples v. United States*, 511 U.S. 600, 619 n.17 (1994) (quoting *Chapman v. United States* [Chapter 7, § 3B]. Certainly, our decision today is based on much more than a "guess as to what Congress intended," and there is no "grievous ambiguity" here. The problem of statutory interpretation [in this case] is indeed no different from that in many of the criminal cases that confront us. Yet, this Court has never held that the rule of lenity automatically permits a defendant to win. [Affirmed.]

JUSTICE GINSBURG, with whom THE CHIEF JUSTICE [REHNQUIST], JUSTICE SCALIA, and JUSTICE SOUTER join, dissenting.

[Justice Ginsburg explained that defendants' gun possession would have adverse consequences even if § 924(c)(1) were held to be inapplicable. For example, the federal sentencing guidelines provided Muscarello a 6–12 month presumptive sentence for his involvement in the distribution of 3.6 kilograms of marijuana. The "two-level enhancement" under the guidelines for possession of a gun would increase the sentencing range to 10–16 months. If, instead, as the majority held, Muscarello violated § 924(c)(1), his sentence would reflect the underlying drug offense (6–12 months) *plus* the five-year mandatory additional sentence provided by § 924(c)(1).]

* * * Unlike the Court, I do not think dictionaries, surveys of press reports,[3] or the Bible[4] tell us, dispositively, what "carries" means embedded in § 924(c)(1). On definitions, "carry" in legal formulations could mean, *inter alia*, transport, possess, have in stock, prolong (carry over), be infectious, or

---

3. Many newspapers, the New York Times among them, have published stories using "transport," rather than "carry," to describe gun placements resembling petitioners'. [Quoting stories.]

4. The translator of the Good Book, it appears, bore responsibility for determining whether the servants of Ahaziah "carried" his corpse to Jerusalem. Compare [majority opinion] with, e.g., The New English Bible, 2 Kings 9:28 ("His servants *conveyed* his body to Jerusalem."); Saint Joseph Edition of the New American Bible ("His servants *brought* him in a chariot to Jerusalem."); Tanakh: The Holy Scriptures ("His servants *conveyed* him in a chariot to Jerusalem."); see also *id.*, Isaiah 30:6 ("They *convey* their wealth on the backs of asses."); The New Jerusalem Bible ("[T]hey *bear* their riches on donkeys' backs.") (emphasis added in all quotations).

wear or bear on one's person.[5] At issue here is not "carries" at large but "carries a firearm." The Court's computer search of newspapers is revealing in this light. Carrying guns in a car showed up as the meaning "perhaps more than one third" of the time. One is left to wonder what meaning showed up some two thirds of the time. Surely a most familiar meaning is, as the Constitution's Second Amendment ("keep and *bear* Arms") (emphasis added) and Black's Law Dictionary, at 214, indicate: "wear, bear, or carry . . . upon the person or in the clothing or in a pocket, for the purpose . . . of being armed and ready for offensive or defensive action in a case of conflict with another person."

On lessons from literature, a scan of Bartlett's and other quotation collections shows how highly selective the Court's choices are. If "[t]he greatest of writers" have used "carry" to mean convey or transport in a vehicle, so have they used the hydra-headed word to mean, *inter alia*, carry in one's hand, arms, head, heart, or soul, sans vehicle. [Justice Ginsburg quoted Isaiah 40:11, poems by Oliver Goldsmith and Rudyard Kipling, and Theodore Roosevelt's famous advice to "[s]peak softly and carry a big stick."][6]

These and the Court's lexicological sources demonstrate vividly that "carry" is a word commonly used to convey various messages. Such references, given their variety, are not reliable indicators of what Congress meant, in § 924(c)(1), by "carries a firearm."

Noting the paradoxical statement, " 'I *use* a gun to protect my house, but I've never had to *use* it,' " the Court in *Bailey* emphasized the importance of context — the statutory context. Just as "uses" was read to mean not simply "possession," but "active employment," so "carries," correspondingly, is properly read to signal the most dangerous cases — the gun at hand, ready for use as a weapon. It is reasonable to comprehend Congress as having provided mandatory minimums for the most life-jeopardizing gun-connection cases (guns in or at the defendant's hand when committing an offense), leaving other, less imminently threatening, situations for the more flexible guidelines regime. As the Ninth Circuit suggested, it is not apparent why possession of a gun in a drug dealer's moving vehicle would be thought more dangerous than gun possession on premises where drugs are sold: "A drug dealer who packs heat is more likely to hurt someone or provoke someone else to violence. A gun in a bag under a tarp in a truck bed [or in a bedroom closet] poses substantially less risk." *United States v. Foster*, 133 F.3d 704, 707 (1998) (en banc).

---

5. The dictionary to which this Court referred in *Bailey v. United States* contains 32 discrete definitions of "carry," including "[t]o make good or valid," "to bear the aspect of," and even "[t]o bear (a hawk) on the fist." See Webster's New International Dictionary of English Language 412 (2d ed. 1949).

6. Popular films and television productions provide corroborative illustrations. * * * [I]n the television series "M*A*S*H," Hawkeye Pierce (played by Alan Alda) presciently proclaims: "I will not carry a gun. . . . I'll carry your books, I'll carry a torch, I'll carry a tune, I'll carry on, carry over, carry forward, Cary Grant, cash and carry, carry me back to Old Virginia, I'll even 'hari-kari' if you show me how, but I will not carry a gun!" See http://www.geocities.com/Hollywood/8915/mashquotes.html.

For indicators from Congress itself, it is appropriate to consider word usage in other provisions of Title 18's chapter on "Firearms." The Court, however, does not derive from the statutory complex at issue its thesis that " '[c]arry' implies personal agency and some degree of possession, whereas 'transport' does not have such a limited connotation and, in addition, implies the movement of goods in bulk over great distances." [Quoting majority opinion.] Looking to provisions Congress enacted, one finds that the Legislature did not acknowledge or routinely adhere to the distinction the Court advances today; instead, Congress sometimes employed "transports" when, according to the Court, "carries" was the right word to use.

Section 925(a)(2)(B), for example, provides that no criminal sanction shall attend "the transportation of [a] firearm or ammunition carried out to enable a person, who lawfully received such firearm or ammunition from the Secretary of the Army, to engage in military training or in competitions." The full text of § 926A, rather than the truncated version the Court presents, is also telling:

> Notwithstanding any other provision of any law or any rule or regulation of a State or any political subdivision thereof, any person who is not otherwise prohibited by this chapter from transporting, shipping, or receiving a firearm shall be entitled to transport a firearm for any lawful purpose from any place where he may lawfully possess and carry such firearm to any other place where he may lawfully possess and carry such firearm if, during such transportation the firearm is unloaded, and neither the firearm nor any ammunition being transported is readily accessible or is directly accessible from the passenger compartment of such transporting vehicle: *Provided*, That in the case of a vehicle without a compartment separate from the driver's compartment the firearm or ammunition shall be contained in a locked container other than the glove compartment or console.

In describing when and how a person may travel in a vehicle that contains his firearm without violating the law, §§ 925(a)(2)(B) and 926A use "transport," not "carry," to "impl[y] personal agency and some degree of possession." [Again quoting majority opinion.][10]

Reading "carries" in § 924(c)(1) to mean "on or about [one's] person" is fully compatible with these and other "Firearms" statutes.[11]   For example,

---

10. The Court asserts that " 'transport' is a broader category that includes 'carry' but encompasses other activity." "Carry," however, is not merely a subset of "transport." A person seated at a desk with a gun in hand or pocket is carrying the gun, but is not transporting it. Yes, the words "carry" and "transport" often can be employed interchangeably, as can the words "carry" and "use." But in *Bailey*, this Court settled on constructions that gave "carry" and "use" independent meanings. Without doubt, Congress is alert to the discrete meanings of "transport" and "carry" in the context of vehicles, as the Legislature's placement of each word in § 926A illustrates. The narrower reading of "carry" preserves discrete meanings for the two words, while in the context of vehicles the Court's interpretation of "carry" is altogether synonymous with "transport." Tellingly, when referring to firearms traveling in vehicles, the "Firearms" statutes routinely use a form of "transport"; they never use a form of "carry."

11. The Government points to numerous federal statutes that authorize law enforcement officers to "carry firearms" and notes that, in those authorizing provisions, "carry" of course means "both on the person and in a vehicle." Brief for United States 31–32, and n. 18. Quite under § 925(a)(2)(B), one could carry his gun to a car, transport it to the shooting competition, and use it to shoot targets. Under the conditions of § 926A, one could transport her gun in a car, but under no circumstances could the gun be readily accessible while she travels in the car. "[C]ourts normally try to read language in different, but related, statutes, so as best to reconcile those statutes, in light of their purposes and of common sense." [*United States v. McFadden*, 13 F.3d 463, 467 (1st Cir. 1994) (Breyer, C.J., dissenting).] So reading the "Firearms" statutes, I would not extend the word "carries" in § 924(c)(1) to mean transports out of hand's reach in a vehicle.[12]

Section 924(c)(1), as the foregoing discussion details, is not decisively clear one way or another. The sharp division in the Court on the proper reading of the measure confirms, "[a]t the very least, . . . that the issue is subject to some doubt. Under these circumstances, we adhere to the familiar rule that, 'where there is ambiguity in a criminal statute, doubts are resolved in favor of the defendant.' " *Adamo Wrecking Co. v. United States*, 434 U.S. 275, 284–285 (1978); see *United States v. Granderson*, 511 U.S. 39, 54 (1994) ("[W]here text, structure, and history fail to establish that the Government's position is unambiguously correct — we apply the rule of lenity and resolve the ambiguity in [the defendant's] favor."). "Carry" bears many meanings, as the Court and the "Firearms" statutes demonstrate.[13] The narrower "on or about [one's]

---

right. But as viewers of "Sesame Street" will quickly recognize, "one of these things [a statute *authorizing* conduct] is not like the other [a statute *criminalizing* conduct]." The authorizing statutes in question are properly accorded a construction compatible with the clear purpose of the legislation to aid federal law enforcers in the performance of their official duties. It is fundamental, however, that a penal statute is not to be construed generously in the Government's favor. See, *e.g.*, *United States v. Bass*, 404 U.S. 336, 348 (1971).

12. The Court places undue reliance on Representative Poff's statement that § 924(c)(1) seeks " 'to persuade the man who is tempted to commit a Federal felony to leave his gun at home.' " See [majority opinion] (quoting 114 Cong. Rec. 22231 (1968)). As the Government argued in its brief to this Court in *Bailey*:

In making that statement, Representative Poff was not referring to the "carries" prong of the original Section 924(c). As originally enacted, the "carries" prong of the statute prohibited only the "unlawful" carrying of a firearm while committing an offense. The statute would thus not have applied to an individual who, for instance, had a permit for carrying a gun and carried it with him when committing an offense, and it would have had no force in "persuading" such an individual "to leave his gun at home." Instead, Representative Poff was referring to the "uses" prong of the original Section 924(c). [Quoting U.S. Brief in *Bailey*.]

Representative Poff's next sentence confirms that he was speaking of "uses," not "carries": "Any person should understand that if he *uses* his gun and is caught and convicted, he is going to jail." 114 Cong. Rec., at 22231 (emphasis added).

13. Any doubt on that score is dispelled by examining the provisions in the "Firearms" chapter, in addition to § 924(c)(1), that include a form of the word "carry": 18 U.S.C. § 922(a)(5) ("*carry out* a bequest"); §§ 922(s)(6)(B)(ii), (iii) ("*carry out* this subsection"); § 922(u) ("*carry away* [a firearm]"); 18 U.S.C.A. § 924(a)(6)(B)(ii) (Supp.1998) ("*carry* or otherwise possess or discharge or otherwise use [a] handgun"); 18 U.S.C. § 924(e)(2)(B) ("*carrying* of a firearm"); § 925(a)(2) ("*carried out* to enable a person"); § 926(a) ("*carry out* the provisions of this chapter"); § 926A ("lawfully possess and *carry* such firearm to any other place where he may lawfully possess and *carry* such firearm"); § 929(a)(1) ("uses or *carries* a firearm and is in possession of armor piercing ammunition"); § 930(d)(3) ("lawful *carrying* of

person" interpretation is hardly implausible nor at odds with an accepted meaning of "carries a firearm."

Overlooking that there will be an enhanced sentence for the gun-possessing drug dealer in any event, the Court asks rhetorically: "How persuasive is a punishment that is without effect until a drug dealer who has brought his gun to a sale (indeed has it available for use) actually takes it from the trunk (or unlocks the glove compartment) of his car?" Correspondingly, the Court defines "carries a firearm" to cover "a person who knowingly possesses and conveys firearms [anyplace] in a vehicle . . . which the person accompanies." Congress, however, hardly lacks competence to select the words "possesses" or "conveys" when that is what the Legislature means.[14] Notably in view of the Legislature's capacity to speak plainly, and of overriding concern, the Court's inquiry pays scant attention to a core reason for the rule of lenity: "[B]ecause of the seriousness of criminal penalties, and because criminal punishment usually represents the moral condemnation of the community, legislatures and not courts should define criminal activity. This policy embodies 'the instinctive distaste against men languishing in prison unless the lawmaker has clearly said they should.' " *United States v. Bass* (quoting H. Friendly, Mr. Justice Frankfurter and the Reading of Statutes, in Benchmarks 196, 209 (1967)). * * *

Postscript: Soon after the Court's opinion in *Muscarello*, Congress overrode *Bailey* in Pub. L. No. 105–386, 112 Stat. 3469 (1998). The new law amended 18 U.S.C. § 924(c)(1), to trigger the sentence-enhancement provisions where the defendant possesses a firearm "in furtherance of" one of the predicate offenses. An additional enhancement is triggered if the firearm is "brandished," and a yet-higher one if it is "discharged." Brandish is defined in new § 924(c)(4): "to display all or part of the firearm, or otherwise to make the presence of the firearm known to another person, regardless of whether the firearm is directly visible to that person." Does this new statute lend support to the majority's approach in *Muscarello*?

McNALLY v. UNITED STATES, 483 U.S. 350 (1987). The federal mail fraud statute, 18 U.S.C. § 1341, provides that "[w]hoever, having devised or intending to devise any scheme or artifice to defraud, or for obtaining money or property by means of false or fraudulent pretenses, representations, or promises, * * * for the purpose of executing such scheme or artifice or attempting to do so [uses the mails or causes them to be used,] shall be fined

---

firearms . . . in a Federal facility incident to hunting or other lawful purposes") (emphasis added in all quotations).

14. See, e.g., 18 U.S.C.A. § 924(a)(6)(B)(ii) (Supp.1998) ("if the person sold . . . a handgun . . . to a juvenile knowing . . . that the juvenile intended to *carry or otherwise possess* . . . the handgun . . . in the commission of a crime of violence"); 18 U.S.C. § 926A ("may lawfully *possess and carry* such firearm to any other place where he may lawfully *possess and carry* such firearm"); § 929(a)(1) ("uses or *carries a firearm and is in possession* of armor piercing ammunition"); § 2277 ("brings, *carries, or possesses* any dangerous weapon") (emphasis added in all quotations).

not more than $1,000 or imprisoned not more than five years, or both." The lower courts upheld the convictions of several public officials and one private party activist who made a deal with an insurance company, whereby the state would send business to the company, which in turn would send some of the commissions to other companies designated by the conspirators, including one company they owned. The record apparently did not demonstrate that the state had lost any money by virtue of this kickback scheme. The Court, in an opinion by **Justice White**, reversed the lower courts' interpretation of § 1341, concluding that the statute outlawed only those "frauds on the public" that result in a tangible loss to the public.

"As first enacted in 1872, as part of a recodification of the postal laws, the statute contained a general proscription against using the mails to initiate correspondence in furtherance of 'any scheme or artifice to defraud.' The sponsor of the recodification stated, in apparent reference to the antifraud provision, that measures were needed 'to prevent the frauds which are mostly gotten up in the large cities . . . by thieves, forgers, and rapscallions generally, for the purpose of deceiving and fleecing the innocent people in the country.' Insofar as the sparse legislative history reveals anything, it indicates that the original impetus behind the mail fraud statute was to protect the people from schemes to deprive them of their money or property. * * *

"As the Court long ago stated, * * * the words 'to defraud' commonly refer 'to wronging one in his property rights by dishonest methods or schemes,' and 'usually signify the deprivation of something of value by trick, deceit, chicane or overreaching.' *Hammerschmidt v. United States*, 265 U.S. 182, 188 (1924). [Congress' adding the phrase "or for obtaining money or property" in] 1909 does not indicate that Congress was departing from this common understanding. As we see it, adding the second phrase simply made it unmistakable that the statute reached false promises and misrepresentations as to the future as well as other frauds involving money or property.

"We believe that Congress' intent in passing the mail fraud statute was to prevent the use of the mails in furtherance of such schemes. The Court has often stated that when there are two rational readings of a criminal statute, one harsher than the other, we are to choose the harsher only when Congress has spoken in clear and definite language. * * * Rather than construe the statute in a manner that leaves its outer boundaries ambiguous and involves the Federal Government in setting standards of disclosure and good government for local and state officials, we read § 1341 as limited in scope to the protection of property rights. If Congress desires to go further, it must speak more clearly than it has."

Justice Stevens, in dissent, relied on the plain meaning of the statute, which prohibits the use of the United States mails for the purpose of executing "[1] *any* scheme or artifice to defraud, [2] *or* for obtaining money or property by means of false or fraudulent pretenses, representations, or promises, [3] *or* to sell, dispose of, loan, exchange, alter, give away, distribute, supply, or furnish or procure for unlawful use any counterfeit or spurious coin, obligation, security, or other article, or anything represented to be or intimated or held out to be such counterfeit or spurious article . . ." 18 U.S.C. § 1341 (emphasis and brackets added).

"As the language makes clear, each of these restrictions is independent. One can violate the second clause — obtaining money or property by false pretenses — even though one does not violate the third clause — counterfeiting. Similarly, one can violate the first clause — devising a scheme or artifice to defraud — without violating the counterfeiting provision. Until today it was also obvious that one could violate the first clause by devising a scheme or artifice to defraud, even though one did not violate the second clause by seeking to obtain money or property from his victim through false pretenses. Every court to consider the matter had so held. Yet, today, the Court, for all practical purposes, rejects this longstanding construction of the statute by imposing a requirement that a scheme or artifice to defraud does not violate the statute unless its purpose is to defraud someone of money or property. I am at a loss to understand the source or justification for this holding. Certainly no canon of statutory construction requires us to ignore the plain language of the provision.

"In considering the scope of the mail fraud statute it is essential to remember Congress's purpose in enacting it. Congress sought to protect the integrity of the United States mails by not allowing them to be used as 'instruments of crime.' *United States v. Brewer*, 528 F.2d 492, 498 (CA4 1975). 'The focus of the statute is upon the misuse of the Postal Service, not the regulation of state affairs, and Congress clearly has the authority to regulate such misuse of the mails.' *United States v. States*, 488 F.2d 761, 767 (CA8 1973), cert. denied, 417 U.S. 909 (1974). Once this purpose is considered, it becomes clear that the construction the Court adopts today is senseless. Can it be that Congress sought to purge the mails of schemes to defraud citizens of money but was willing to tolerate schemes to defraud citizens of their right to an honest government, or to unbiased public officials? Is it at all rational to assume that Congress wanted to ensure that the mails not be used for petty crimes, but did not prohibit election fraud accomplished through mailing fictitious ballots? Given Congress' 'broad purpose,' I 'find it difficult to believe, absent some indication in the statute itself or the legislative history, that Congress would have undercut sharply that purpose by hobbling federal prosecutors in their effort to combat' use of the mails for fraudulent schemes."

Postscript: Justice White's memorandum to the Conference, in which he circulated his opinion, expressed reservations about the broad holding but concluded: "But it is not rare that Opinions of the Court are no more persuasive than an opinion on the other side would have been. Of course, the saving grace in Statutory Construction cases is that Congress may have its way if it does not like the product of our work."[x] In 1988, Congress adopted 18

---

x. The Thurgood Marshall Papers, Library of Congress (Madison Building), Box 423, Folder 3 (Court memoranda regarding *McNally*, Nos. 86–234 & 86–286). Indeed, Congress does often override the Court's statutory decisions, and when the Court applies the rule of lenity to protect federal criminal defendants, the Department of Justice has the best record in the land for obtaining overrides. William Eskridge, Jr., *Overriding Supreme Court Statutory*

U.S.C. § 1346, which provides that for purposes of the mail fraud statute " 'scheme or artifice to defraud' includes a scheme or artifice to deprive another of the intangible right of honest services." The statute's legislative history indicates that it was meant to override *McNally* and reinstate the "intangible rights" theory.

NOTES ON *MUSCARELLO, McNALLY,* AND THE SUPREME COURT'S APPROACH TO CRIMINAL STATUTES

1. *The Rule of Lenity Cuts Across Political Lines.* Note the peculiar — perhaps unprecedented — lineup of Justices on both sides of the issue in *Muscarello*. The lineup in *McNally* is almost as odd, with Justices Scalia and Brennan in the majority and Stevens and O'Connor in dissent. The reason for the odd lineups is that the rule of lenity appeals to both civil libertarians (like Brennan, Marshall, Ginsburg) and high formalists who are fans of the nondelegation argument (like Scalia and perhaps Ginsburg), while a more expansive application of criminal statutes appeals to both pragmatists who are willing to apply common-law reasoning to statutory cases (like Stevens, O'Connor, Breyer) and hard-liners against criminals (Thomas perhaps). This heterogeneity also makes the rule of lenity cases hard to predict. We were surprised to find Scalia with the nontextualist majority in *McNally* and Rehnquist (usually a hard-liner in criminal cases) with the lenient *Muscarello* dissent.[y]

2. *The Supreme Court's Inconsistency in Applying the Rule of Lenity?* Can *McNally*, where the Court invoked lenity, and *Muscarello*, where it did not, be reconciled? The cases are similar: each involved broadly phrased federal statutes being applied to antisocial conduct. Some possible bases for distinction: (a) the statute was clearer in the firearms case; (b) Supreme Court precedent supported lenity in the mail fraud case but not the firearm case, where *Smith* had already construed "carry" in a broad way; or (c) the mail fraud case involved federal prosecution of state officials and so trenched on federalism values more deeply if broadly construed (as lower courts had been doing).[z] Even if those distinctions work to distinguish *Muscarello* from *McNally*, they do not distinguish it from *Ratzlaf*, where a clear statute that had not been construed by the Court and was not being applied to state officials was nonetheless applied leniently — indeed, in a way that rendered the statute

---

Interpretation Decisions, 101 Yale L.J. 331 (1991). Is this a good justification for writing a weak opinion, though?

y. The lineup in *Ratzlaf* was also substantially explicable along lines noted in text. The majority opinion, invoking lenity, was written by Ginsburg, a civil libertarian, and joined by libertarians Souter and Kennedy and by the formalist Scalia, while the dissent was written by the pragmatic Blackmun and joined by Rehnquist and Thomas, both tough on criminals, and by the highly pragmatic O'Connor. An oddity was that the pragmatic Stevens (no fan of the rule of lenity and surely not sympathetic to the Ratzlafs) provided the critical fifth vote for the majority.

z. In *McCormick v. United States*, 500 U.S. 257 (1991), the Court overturned a Hobbs Act prosecution of a state official who allegedly "extorted" campaign contributions from private parties.

unenforceable.[a] However one resolves the distinction between *Muscarello* and *McNally*, there are plenty of Supreme Court cases going one way or the other.

For example, the Court in *Chiarella v. United States*, 445 U.S. 222, 232, 233 (1980), held that an employee of the printer for paperwork involved in corporate takeover bids, who read the materials he was printing and used that knowledge to purchase stock before the takeover announcement, did not commit securities fraud. While the anti-fraud rule[b] had long applied to corporate officers, their agents, and their "tipees," the Supreme Court refused to expand its application to the printer's employee, because "he was not their agent, he was not a fiduciary, he was not a person in whom the sellers had placed their trust and confidence." The Supreme Court said that affirming such a conviction would have to "recogniz[e] a general duty between all participants in market transactions to forego actions based on material, nonpublic information. * * * This should not be undertaken absent some explicit evidence of Congressional intent."

Although the Supreme Court in *Chiarella* and *McNally* invoked the rule of lenity, *Muscarello* better reflects Supreme Court practice. Since 1984, the Court has cited the rule of lenity in just over one-fourth of its cases interpreting criminal statutes. In more than 60% of the cases, the Court has agreed with the government's interpretation.[c] Although there are still cases where the Court applies the rule of lenity, e.g., *Arthur Andersen LLP v. United States*, 544 U.S. 696 (2005); *Cleveland v. United States,* 531 U.S. 12 (2000), it remains unclear whether the rule has a systematic effect.

3. *Recent Rule of Lenity Developments: Sentencing, Legislative History, Civil Statutes.* For most of American history, the rule of lenity was applied only in the context of substantive criminal law, because sentencing was largely a matter of judicial discretion within well-defined statutory confines. *McNally* is an example. In the last 20 years, the law of sentencing has become more complex and less discretionary with judges— and the Supreme Court applied the rule of lenity to criminal sentencing in *United States v. R.L.C.*, 503 U.S. 291 (1992). See Phillip Spector, *The Sentencing Rule of Lenity,* 33 U. Toledo L. Rev. 511 (2002), who argues against application of the rule to sentencing statutes, on the ground that the notice, prosecutorial discretion, and nondele-

---

a. For students tough on crime, don't worry about the lenity in cases like *Ratzlaf,* for it was immediately overridden by Congress. See Pub. L. No. 103–325, § 411, 108 Stat. 2253 (1994). The most frequent legislative overrides come where the government loses criminal law cases. See Eskridge, *supra* note x (about 17% of the congressional overrides of Supreme Court statutory opinions, 1967–89, came in criminal law, all but two of the overrides being to expand liability where the Court had applied lenity).

b. Section 10(b) of the Securities Exchange Act of 1934, 15 U.S.C. § 78j(b) (1988), proscribes the use of "any manipulative or deceptive device or contrivance" in violation of SEC rules and "in connection with the purchase or sale of any security." Rule 10b–5 prohibits use of "any device, scheme or artifice to defraud" or any act or practice which would "operate as a fraud or deceit upon any person, in connection with the purchase or sale of any security." 17 C.F.R. § 240.10b–5 (1993).

c. See William Eskridge, Jr. & Lauren Baer, *The Supreme Court's Deference Continuum, An Empirical Study (from* Chevron *to* Hamdan), 86 Geo. L.J. (2008).

gation rationales do not apply nearly as strongly to sentencing laws as to those defining substantive crimes.

As in substantive criminal law cases, the Court will not invoke the rule of lenity in sentencing cases where the statutory directive is clear. See *Chapman v. United States*, 500 U.S. 453 (1991) (affirming the Easterbrook decision in *Marshall*, Chapter 7, § 3); *Gozlon-Peretz v. United States*, 498 U.S. 395 (1991). To the extent § 924, an enhancement statute, is viewed as a sentencing law, *Muscarello* illustrates the difficulty of figuring out when sentencing statutes are clear. (*Muscarello* and *Chapman* are also consistent with Spector's argument that the rule of lenity ought not be applied to sentencing statutes.)

As to this point, there is debate within the Court whether legislative history can be considered. In *R.L.C.*, a plurality of Justices stated that the application of the rule of lenity is reserved "for those situations in which a reasonable doubt persists about the statute's intended scope even *after* resort to the language and structure, legislative history, and motivating policies of the statute." See also *Smith v. United States*, 508 U.S. 223 (1993). Justice Scalia, joined by Justices Kennedy and Thomas, objected in *R.L.C.* to the presence of legislative history and statutory policies in this inquiry. Note that Kennedy and Thomas joined the Court's opinion in *Muscarello*, which relied on legislative history.

The Court has sometimes ruled that the rule of lenity also applies when a civil-type remedy is applied to a defendant for conduct violating a criminal-type statute. Thus, in *Hughey v. United States*, 495 U.S. 411 (1990), the Court applied the rule of lenity to a statute requiring a criminal defendant to provide restitution. And in *Crandon v. United States*, 494 U.S. 152 (1990), the Court invoked the rule of lenity to protect a civil defendant, where the applicable standard of conduct was found in a criminal statute.

———

PEOPLE v. DAVIS, 15 Cal.4th 1096, 938 P.2d 938, 64 Cal. Rptr.2d 879 (1997). Defendant Robert Vonroski Davis was charged with one count of murder and one count of attempted murder. In addition, three prior convictions were alleged under a "three-strikes law," § 667(b)–(i) of the Penal Code: a 1990 juvenile adjudication of felony assault; a 1991 juvenile adjudication of residential burglary; and a 1993 adult robbery conviction. The trial court granted Davis' motion that the two juvenile adjudications did not count as strikes. Davis was convicted of murder and attempted murder, and the judge sentenced him to thirty-five years to life, with a consecutive term of life plus five years. The court of appeal affirmed the conviction and reversed the trial court's order striking the prior juvenile adjudication for felony assault.

In general, the three-strikes legislation provides longer sentences for certain prior serious or violent felonies popularly denoted "strikes." A "two strike" case involves one prior qualifying felony; a "three strike" case involves two or more prior qualifying felonies. The statute's purpose is to provide greater punishment for recidivists (§ 667(b)). Section 667(d)(3) lists the requirements for a prior juvenile adjudication to qualify as a "strike":

(3) A prior juvenile adjudication shall constitute a prior felony conviction for purposes of sentence enhancement if:

(A) The juvenile was 16 years of age or older at the time he or she committed the prior offense.

(B) The prior offense is listed in Section 707(b) of the Welfare and Institutions Code or described in paragraph (1) [California prior serious or violent felony convictions] or (2) [other jurisdiction prior serious or violent felony convictions] as a felony.

(C) The juvenile was found to be a fit and proper subject to be dealt with under the juvenile court law.

(D) The juvenile was adjudged a ward of the juvenile court within the meaning of Section 602 of the Welfare and Institutions Code because the person committed an offense listed in Section 707(b) of the Welfare and Institutions Code. * * *

Defendant contended that § 667(d)(3)(C) required an express finding of fitness is required; the court majority, in an opinion by **Justice Brown**, disagreed and affirmed the trail judge's determination to count the juvenile convictions as strikes.

Under Welfare and Institutions Code § 602, "Any person who is under the age of 18 years when he violates any law of this state or of the United States or any ordinance of any city or county of this state defining crime other than an ordinance establishing a curfew based solely on age, is within the jurisdiction of the juvenile court, which may adjudge such person to be a ward of the court." A petition under this section "is the equivalent of a complaint in the adult court." The prosecutor may, however, also file a petition under Welfare and Institutions Code § 707 seeking a determination that the minor is unfit for treatment in the juvenile court system. When the juvenile is charged with a serious crime, and a § 707 petition is filed, the minor is "presumed to be not a fit and proper subject to be dealt with under the juvenile court law unless the juvenile court concludes . . . that the minor would be amenable to the care, treatment, and training program available through the facilities of the juvenile court based upon an evaluation of" various criteria. If the juvenile court makes a finding of fitness, it makes "[a] determination that the minor is a fit and proper subject to be dealt with under the juvenile court law . . . ." (§ 707(c))

"As the Court of Appeal recognized, '[p]roceedings under section 602 with the resulting adjudication of wardship and treatment of the minor under the jurisdiction of the juvenile court constitute[] an implied finding that the minor is a "fit and proper subject to be dealt with under the juvenile court law." ' " By its terms, subdivision (d)(3)(C) requires a finding, not an express finding, of fitness. * * * Indeed, if subdivision (d)(3)(C) were construed to require an express finding of fitness, this would so severely limit those juvenile adjudications that would qualify as 'strikes,' that such a result would seem to be at odds with the intent of section 667(b)–(i).

"Finally, a conclusion that subdivision (d)(3)(C) requires an express finding of fitness would evoke questions regarding the statute's constitutional validity. The difference in punishment that two otherwise similarly situated defendants would receive would depend solely on an *unsuccessful* motion for a determination that the minor is unfit for treatment in the juvenile court system. An express finding requirement would be analogous to a statute that set the punishment for a manslaughter conviction at five years if the prosecution originally charged the case as manslaughter, but ten years if the prosecution originally charged the case as murder and the defendant was convicted of the lesser charge of manslaughter. Such a statute would arguably be open to a variety of constitutional challenges such as equal protection, due process, and separation of powers. We see no basis for concluding that the Legislature made such an arguably irrational distinction here.

"Defendant asserts that concluding an implied finding satisfies subdivision (d)(3)(C) renders that subdivision superfluous. He essentially argues that subdivision (d)(3)(C) would then apply to anyone tried in juvenile, as opposed to adult court, and subdivision (d)(3) already expressly applies to prior juvenile adjudications. However, the presence of some duplication in a multiprong statutory test does not automatically render it meaningless. * * * For the reasons set forth above, we conclude the more reasonable interpretation is that an implied finding of fitness satisfies subdivision (d)(3)(C). The trial court therefore erred in striking defendant's prior juvenile adjudications for felony assault and residential burglary on this ground. * * *

Justice Mosk (joined by **Justice Werdegar**) dissented, on the ground that § 667(d)(3)(C) clearly required a finding of fitness, end of analysis. "[T]he majority's argument comes close to passing on the wisdom of the requirement of a finding of fitness contained in section 667(d)(3)(C). That would be impermissible. But, contrary to the majority, we can surely conclude that it is not 'irrational.' For we may deem it a kind of screening device, separating classes of juveniles — those as to whom a doubt about fitness had been raised (albeit subsequently resolved), and those as to whom such a doubt had not."

Moreover, the majority's interpretation makes the statute too harsh. "The substantive scope of possible strikes for prior juvenile adjudications is broader than that for prior felony convictions properly so called. The latter comprises 'violent' and 'serious' California felonies and certain out-of-state felonies. The former, by contrast, embraces those same felonies and also reaches beyond to Welfare and Institutions Code section 707(b) offenses, which cover such otherwise uncovered crimes as bribery of a witness [Welf. & Inst. Code, § 707(b)(19)]. Consequently, some offenses committed by a juvenile are possible strikes, but the same ones committed by an adult are not. Such a result is harsh and hard to justify. A limitation like that referred to might have a mitigating effect."

Justice Kennard also dissented. In response to the majority's concern that Davis' interpretation would render the statutory scheme irrational as to juveniles, she offered the following explanation: "Some 16-year-old delinquents are already dangerous, violent criminals. But there may be others whose acts reflect youthful immaturity rather than a commitment to crime. Perhaps it was a concern not to subject juvenile offenders in the latter category to the harsh penalties of the new Three Strikes law that led the Legislature, which had never before permitted juvenile adjudications to be used in adult court for purposes of enhancement, to include within the class of 'strikes' only those crimes that, in the prosecutor's view, were so serious as to require trying the minor as an adult."

Like Justice Mosk, Justice Kennard invoked the plain meaning of § 667 and, further, rebuked the court for adopting an interpretation that rendered § 667(d)(3)(C) surplusage. Because the statute has a plain meaning, the rule to avoid constitutional difficulties cannot be invoked, as the majority sought to do, see *People v. Anderson*, 43 Cal.3d 1104, 1146, 240 Cal.Rptr. 585, 742 P.2d 1306 (1987), and any general equal protection or due process problems with the literal interpretation are premature. She concluded her dissent with this:

"We are all concerned about the epidemic of violent crime in our society. The Three Strikes law that the Legislature enacted in March 1994 and that we construe today (§ 667[b]–[i]) reflects a toughening public attitude towards repeat offenders. That attitude is also reflected in the nearly identical Three Strikes initiative that was overwhelmingly passed by the voters just eight months later. (§ 1170.12.)

"A court construing a statute, however, can never be guided by public sentiment alone. Here, in construing the Three Strikes law, it is not enough to say that because the Legislature and the electorate wished to impose tougher penalties on repeat violent offenders, we should therefore give that enactment the harshest possible construction. Judges are constrained by the law. For the sake of the predictability and stability of the law, our guideposts in interpreting the Three Strikes law must be the usual principles of statutory construction that apply in every case, not our projections of the hopes and fears that led to the statute's enactment. In the words of United States Supreme Court Justice Felix Frankfurter: 'For judicial construction to stick close to what the legislation says and not draw prodigally upon unformulated purposes or directions makes for careful draftsmanship and for legislative responsibility. . . . Judicial expansion of meaning beyond the limits indicated is reprehensible because it encourages slipshodness in draftsmanship and irresponsibility in legislation. It also enlists too heavily the private . . . views of judges.' (Frankfurter, *Foreword, Symposium on Statutory Construction* [1950] 3 Vand. L. Rev. 365, 367–368.)"

NOTE ON *DAVIS* AND STATE CRIMINAL CODE CONSTRUCTIONS

What is most "striking" about *Davis* is that the court contravened clear statutory wording to extend a highly punitive statute to a defendant — an inversion of the rule of lenity. Yet the California Supreme Court has ruled that it will "construe a penal statute as favorably to the defendant as its language and the circumstances of its application may reasonably permit." *People v. Garcia*, 87 Cal. Rptr. 2d 114, 120 (Cal. 1999). What is going on? Consider some possible theories for the Court's sacrifice of the lenity principle.

First, California Penal Code § 4 revokes the rule of lenity and provides that penal statutes are to be construed according to "the fair import of their terms, with a view to effect its objects and to promote justice." How can § 4 be squared with *Garcia*? The most obvious answer is that the California courts consider the rule of lenity constitutionally required (and § 4 is therefore unconstitutional), but then *Davis* becomes even more of a mystery. Perhaps the rule of lenity, per *Garcia*, does not apply to sentencing laws, as Spector argues in *Sentencing Rule of Lenity*. Or perhaps the rule of lenity is dead as a rule of strict construction, but its underlying quasi-constitutional concerns survive. Robert Yablon suggests that state and federal judges in fact interpret vague criminal statutes in ways that avoid criminalizing ordinary, day-to-day conduct, that prevent prosecutors from exercising excessive discretion, and that help rationalize statutory schemes — but without recognizing a general rule of strict construction in *all* criminal cases.[d]

Second, Yablon's emphasis on having an overall rational scheme of crimes and punishments might help explain *Davis*, where the rationality principle might support the prosecutor. The majority wonders what conceivable reason the legislature would have had to count as strikes only those juvenile convictions where a prosecutor had sought adult treatment and the judge had ruled against it. This puzzle mobilizes not only the golden rule against absurd results, but also Hart and Sacks' notion that every statutory distinction must rest on an articulable reason or principle.

Third, the majority felt there were constitutional problems raised by a literal reading of § 667(d)(3)(C). As to that last problem, consider the following discussion.

2. *Interpretation to Avoid Constitutional Problems*

One justification for the rule of lenity arises from the constitutional notion that a legislature cannot penalize people who are wholly passive and unaware of any wrongdoing, based upon a vague criminal prohibition. See *Lambert v. California*, 355 U.S. 225 (1957); *Papachristou v. Jacksonville*, 405 U.S. 156 (1972). Assuming that the legislature is loathe to come close to enacting unconstitutional criminal statutes, courts will construe criminal penalties narrowly enough so that there is no question of the statute's constitutionality, as construed. Penal statutes, of course, are not the only ones that may venture close to the precipice beyond which a statute will fall athwart the Constitution, and the Supreme Court from time to time interprets non-penal statutes restrictively to avoid constitutional problems. Like the rule of lenity, this canon of construction has both defenders and detractors. Consider the following cases and the notes that follow.

UNITED STATES v. WITKOVICH, 353 U.S. 194 (1957). Witkovich was indicted under § 242(d) of the Immigration and Nationality Act of 1952, 66 Stat. 163, 208, on the charge that, as an alien against whom a final order of deportation had been outstanding for more than six months, he had willfully failed to give information to the Immigration and Naturalization Service (INS)

---

d. Robert Yablon, "Lenity Without Strict Construction: Matching the Rule to Its Purpose" (Yale Law School SAW, 2006). Yablon reconceptualized the rule of lenity through a brilliant examination of cases in Ohio, one of three states that have codified the rule of lenity rather than revoking it.

as required by that section. Appellee moved to dismiss the indictment on the grounds that it failed to state an offense within the statute and in the alternative, if it did so, that the statute was unconstitutional.

Section 242(d) provided for criminal penalties under the following circumstances:

> Any alien, against whom a final order of deportation * * * has been outstanding for more than six months, shall, pending eventual deportation, be subject to supervision under regulations prescribed by the Attorney General. Such regulations shall include provisions which will require any alien subject to supervision (1) to appear from time to time before an immigration officer for identification; (2) to submit, if necessary, to medical and psychiatric examination at the expense of the United States; (3) to give information under oath as to his nationality, circumstances, habits, associations, and activities, and such other information, whether or not related to the foregoing, as the Attorney General may deem fit and proper; and (4) to conform to such reasonable written restrictions on his conduct or activities as are prescribed by the Attorney General in his case. * * *

The Department of Justice used this statutory authority as the basis for asking Witkovich dozens of questions about his political activities, his association with the Slovene National Benefit Society and other groups, and even his social activities.[e] He was held criminally liable when he refused to answer. In an opinion by **Justice Frankfurter**, the Supreme Court ruled that the Department's questions were not authorized by § 242(d).

"The language of § 242(d)(3), if read in isolation and literally, appears to confer upon the Attorney General unbounded authority to require whatever information he deems desirable of aliens whose deportation has not been effected within six months after it has been commanded. The Government itself shrinks from standing on the breadth of these words. But once the tyranny of literalness is rejected, all relevant considerations for giving a rational content to the words become operative. A restrictive meaning for what appear to be plain words may be indicated by the Act as a whole, by the persuasive gloss of legislative history or by the rule of constitutional adjudica-

---

e. Some of the questions included the following:

"Q. Since the order of supervision was entered on March 4, 1954 have you attended any meeting of any organization other than the singing club?

"Q. Have you addressed any lodges of the Slovene National Benefit Society requesting their aid in your case, since the order of deportation was entered June 25, 1953?"

"Q. Have you attended any movies since your order of supervision was entered at the Cinema Annex, 3210 West Madison Street, Chicago?"

"Q. Are you acquainted with an individual named Irving Franklin?"

"Q. Are you now a member of the Communist Party of U.S.A.?"

"Q. Are you now or have you ever been a member of the United Committee of South Slavic Americans?"

tion, relied on by the District Court, that such a restrictive meaning must be given if a broader meaning would generate constitutional doubts.

"The preoccupation of the entire subsection of which clause (3) is a part is certainly with availability for deportation. Clause (1) requires the alien's periodic appearance for the purpose of identification, and clause (2) dealing with medical and psychiatric examination, when necessary, clearly is directed to the same end; and the 'reasonable written restrictions on [the alien's] conduct or activities' authorized by clause (4) have an implied scope to be gathered from the subject matter, *i. e.*, the object of the statute as a whole. Moreover, this limitation of 'reasonableness' imposed by clause (4) upon the Attorney General's power to restrict suggests that, if we are to harmonize the various provisions of the section, the same limitation must also be read into the Attorney General's seemingly limitless power to question under clause (3). For, assuredly, Congress did not authorize that official to elicit information that could not serve as a basis for confining an alien's activities. Nowhere in § 242(d) is there any suggestion of a power of broad supervision like unto that over a probationer. When Congress did want to deal with the far-flung interest of national security or the general undesirable conduct of aliens, it gave clear indication of this purpose, as in § 242(e). In providing for the release of aliens convicted of wilful failure to depart, that subsection specifically requires courts to inquire into both the effect of the alien's release upon national security and the likelihood of his continued undesirable conduct."

Justice Frankfurter also relied on the explanation for § 242(d)'s interrogation provisions by the Senate Judiciary Committee, where they originated. Contrasting its own approach with that of the House, which would have allowed detention, the Senate Committee said: " 'This provision in the bill as it passed the House of Representatives appears to present a constitutional question.' This history, although suggesting a desire to exercise continuing control over the activities as well as the availability of aliens whose deportation had been ordered but not effected, shows a strong congressional unwillingness to enact legislation that may subject the Attorney General's supervisory powers to constitutional challenge."

"Acceptance of the interpretation of § 242(d) urged by the Government would raise doubts as to the statute's validity. By construing the Act to confer power on the Attorney General and his agents to inquire into matters that go beyond assuring an alien's availability for deportation we would, at the very least, open up the question of the extent to which an administrative officer may inhibit deportable aliens from renewing activities that subjected them to deportation. This is not *Carlson v. Landon,* [342 U.S. 524 (1952),] where the question was whether an alien could be detained during the customarily brief period pending determination of deportability. Contrariwise, and as the Senate and House Committees recognized in passing on § 242(d), supervision of the undeportable alien may be a lifetime problem. In these circumstances, issues touching liberties that the Constitution safeguards, even for an alien 'person,' would fairly be raised on the Government's view of the statute.

"The path of constitutional concern in this situation is clear.

'When the validity of an act of the Congress is drawn in question, and even if a serious doubt of constitutionality is raised, it is a cardinal principle that this Court will first ascertain whether a construction of the statute is fairly possible by which the question may be avoided.' *Crowell v. Benson,* 285 U.S. 22, 62.

See also cases cited in the concurring opinion of Mr. Justice Brandeis in *Ashwander v. Tennessee Valley Authority,* 297 U.S. 288, 348 note 8. * * *

"Section 242(d) is part of a legislative scheme designed to govern and to expedite the deportation of undesirable aliens, and clause (3) must be placed in the context of that scheme. As the District Court held and as our own examination of the Act confirms, it is a permissible and therefore an appropriate construction to limit the statute to authorizing all questions reasonably calculated to keep the Attorney General advised regarding the continued availability for departure of aliens whose deportation is overdue."

In dissent, **Justice Clark** (joined only by **Justice Burton**) argued that the Court's interpretation was completely inconsistent with the statute's clear language, as well as the national security reasons Congress gave the Attorney General such broad authority. Under the INA, *all* aliens are under the supervision of the Department of Justice, with duties to register, be fingerprinted, and to report regularly to the Department. Section 242(d) was added because Congress felt that deportable aliens were more likely to engage in subversive activities and therefore required more particularized supervision.

"We believe that the purpose of the Act was to prevent a deportable alien from using the period of his further residence for the continuation of subversive, criminal, immoral, or other undesirable activities which formed the basis of his ordered deportation. * * * Several thousand alien Communists who have been finally ordered deported will from now on, due to the Court's decision today, be under virtually no statutory supervision. Still they will, in all probability, remain among us for neither they nor the countries of which they are nationals wish them to leave. To their countries they are potential agents. The House Committee on the Judiciary recognized this danger in its report on facilitating the deportation of aliens. Case histories set out in this report indicate that aliens ordered deported were refused visas by their native countries so that they might remain in the United States and carry on the very activities for which they were ordered deported."

Justice Clark found the Court's "constitutional problems" completely baffling. Congress has plenary authority over aliens, which the Court in *Carlson v. Landon* invoked as a basis for detaining deportable aliens. Thus, it was hard to see how the Attorney General's reading of the statute raised constitutional problems; if anything, the Court's reading of the statute was problematic. "In this respect the construction places an alien who has been under a final order of deportation for more than six months in a more favorable position than one who is under no order at all. Other aliens are obliged to report to the Attorney General when called upon to do so. Indeed, they must testify or claim their privilege. No privilege was claimed here. The Congress could not have intended the anomalous result reached today, one which is entirely foreign to its over-all plan of control over resident aliens."

NATIONAL LABOR RELATIONS BOARD v.
CATHOLIC BISHOP OF CHICAGO
Supreme Court of the United States, 1979
440 U.S. 490, 99 S.Ct. 1313, 59 L.Ed.2d 533

THE CHIEF JUSTICE [BURGER] delivered the opinion for the Court.

[The National Labor Relations Board (NLRB) exercised jurisdiction over lay faculty members at two groups of Roman Catholic high schools, certified unions as bargaining agents for the teachers, and ordered the schools to cease and desist their refusals to bargain with these unions. The NLRB asserted jurisdiction based on its policy of declining jurisdiction only when schools are "completely religious," not "religiously associated." The NLRB found that the schools in the instant case were in the latter category, since secular as well as religious topics were taught in the schools.

[The Court of Appeals denied enforcement of the NLRB order, and the Supreme Court affirmed. The Court first held that the NLRB distinction between schools that were "completely religious" and those that were "religiously associated" was not a workable guide for the exercise of the NLRB's discretionary jurisdiction. Recognizing that rejection of this distinction meant that the Board could extend its jurisdiction to all church-operated schools, the Court stated that the Free Exercise and Establishment Clauses of the First Amendment might preclude such an exercise of jurisdiction.]

Although the respondents press their claims under the Religion Clauses, the question we consider first is whether Congress intended the Board to have jurisdiction over teachers in church-operated schools. In a number of cases the Court has heeded the essence of Mr. Chief Justice Marshall's admonition in *Murray v. The Charming Betsy*, 2 Cranch 64, 118 (1804), by holding that an Act of Congress ought not be construed to violate the Constitution if any other possible construction remains available. Moreover, the Court has followed this policy in the interpretation of the Act now before us and related statutes.

In *Machinists v. Street*, 367 U.S. 740 (1961), for example, the Court considered claims that serious First Amendment questions would arise if the Railway Labor Act were construed to allow compulsory union dues to be used to support political candidates or causes not approved by some members. The Court looked to the language of the Act and the legislative history and concluded that they did not permit union dues to be used for such political purposes, thus avoiding "serious doubt of [the Act's] constitutionality." * * *

The values enshrined in the First Amendment plainly rank high "in the scale of our national values." In keeping with the Court's prudential policy it is incumbent on us to determine whether the Board's exercise of its jurisdiction here would give rise to serious constitutional questions. If so, we must first identify "the affirmative intention of the Congress clearly expressed" before concluding that the Act grants jurisdiction. [Quoting *McCulloch v. Sociedad Nacional de Marineros de Honduras*, 372 U.S. 10 (1963).]

In recent decisions involving aid to parochial schools we have recognized the critical and unique role of the teacher in fulfilling the mission of a church-operated school. What was said of the schools in *Lemon v. Kurtzman*, 403 U.S. 602, 617 (1971), is true of the schools in this case: "Religious authority necessarily pervades the school system." The key role played by teachers in such a school system has been the predicate for our conclusions that governmental aid channeled through teachers creates an impermissible risk of excessive governmental entanglement in the affairs of the church-operated schools. * * *

Only recently we again noted the importance of the teacher's function in a church school: "Whether the subject is 'remedial reading,' 'advanced reading,' or simply 'reading,' a teacher remains a teacher, and the danger that religious doctrine will become intertwined with secular instruction persists." *Meek v. Pittenger*, 421 U.S. 349, 370 (1975). Good intentions by government — or third parties — can surely no more avoid entanglement with the religious mission of the school in the setting of mandatory collective bargaining than in the well-motivated legislative efforts consented to by the church-operated schools which we found unacceptable in *Lemon* [and *Meek*.]

The Board argues that it can avoid excessive entanglement since it will resolve only factual issues such as whether an anti-union animus motivated an employer's action. But at this stage of our consideration we are not compelled to determine whether the entanglement is excessive as we would were we considering the constitutional issue. Rather, we make a narrow inquiry whether the exercise of the Board's jurisdiction presents a significant risk that the First Amendment will be infringed.

Moreover, it is already clear that the Board's actions will go beyond resolving factual issues. The Court of Appeals' opinion refers to charges of unfair labor practices filed against religious schools. The court observed that in those cases the schools had responded that their challenged actions were mandated by their religious creeds. The resolution of such charges by the Board, in many instances, will necessarily involve inquiry into the good faith of the position asserted by the clergy-administrators and its relationship to the school's religious mission. It is not only the conclusions that may be reached by the Board which may impinge on rights guaranteed by the Religion Clauses, but also the very process of inquiry leading to findings and conclusions.

The Board's exercise of jurisdiction will have at least one other impact on church-operated schools. The Board will be called upon to decide what are "terms and conditions of employment" and therefore mandatory subjects of bargaining. See 29 U.S.C. § 158(d). Although the Board has not interpreted that phrase as it relates to educational institutions, similar state provisions provide insight into the effect of mandatory bargaining. The Oregon Court of Appeals noted that "nearly everything that goes on in the schools affects teachers and is therefore arguably a 'condition of employment.' " *Springfield Education Assn. v. Springfield School Dist. No. 19*, 547 P.2d 647, 650 (Or. App. 1976). [The introduction of the mandatory bargaining process itself represents an encroachment by the government into the autonomy of the school's management, which in these cases is pursuing religious purposes that will be compromised.]

The church-teacher relationship in a church-operated school differs from the employment relationship in a public or other nonreligious school. We see no escape from conflicts flowing from the Board's exercise of jurisdiction over teachers in church-operated schools and the consequent serious First Amendment questions that would follow. We therefore turn to an examination of the National Labor Relations Act to decide whether it must be read to confer jurisdiction that would in turn require a decision on the constitutional claims raised by respondents.

There is no clear expression of an affirmative intention of Congress that teachers in church-operated schools should be covered by the Act. Admittedly, Congress defined the Board's jurisdiction in very broad terms; we must therefore examine the legislative history of the Act to determine whether Congress contemplated that the grant of jurisdiction would include teachers in such schools.

In enacting the National Labor Relations Act in 1935, Congress sought to protect the right of American workers to bargain collectively. The concern that was repeated throughout the debates was the need to assure workers the right to organize to counterbalance the collective activities of employers which had been authorized by the National Industrial Recovery Act. But congressional attention focused on employment in private industry and on industrial recovery. See, *e.g.*, 79 Cong.Rec. 7573 (1935) (remarks of Sen. Wagner).

Our examination of the statute and its legislative history indicates that Congress simply gave no consideration to church-operated schools. It is not without significance, however, that the Senate Committee on Education and Labor chose a college professor's dispute with the college as an example of employer-employee relations *not* covered by the Act. S.Rep. No. 573, 74th Cong., 1st Sess., 7 (1935).

Congress' next major consideration of the jurisdiction of the Board came during the passage of the Labor Management Relations Act of 1947 — the Taft-Hartley Act. In that Act Congress amended the definition of "employer" in § 2 of the original Act to exclude nonprofit hospitals. 61 Stat. 137, 29 U.S.C. § 152(2) (1970 ed.). There was some discussion of the scope of the Board's jurisdiction but the consensus was that nonprofit institutions in general did not fall within the Board's jurisdiction because they did not affect commerce. [Citing various portions of legislative history.]

The most recent significant amendment to the Act was passed in 1974, removing the exemption of nonprofit hospitals. Pub.L. 93–360, 88 Stat. 395. The Board relies upon that amendment as showing that Congress approved the Board's exercise of jurisdiction over church-operated schools. A close examination of that legislative history, however, reveals nothing to indicate an affirmative intention that such schools be within the Board's jurisdiction. Since the Board did not assert jurisdiction over teachers in a church-operated school until after the 1974 amendment, nothing in the history of the amendment can be read as reflecting Congress' tacit approval of the Board's action.

During the debate there were expressions of concern about the effect of the bill on employees of religious hospitals whose religious beliefs would not permit them to join a union. 120 Cong.Rec. 12946, 16914 (1974). The result of those concerns was an amendment which reflects congressional sensitivity to First Amendment guarantees:

> "Any employee of a health care institution who is a member of and adheres to established and traditional tenets or teachings of a bona fide religion, body, or sect which has historically held conscientious objections to joining or financially supporting labor organizations shall not be required to join or financially support any labor organization as a condition of employment; except that such employee may be required, in lieu of periodic dues and initiation fees, to pay sums equal to such dues and initiation fees to a nonreligious charitable fund exempt from taxation under section 501(c)(3) of title 26, chosen by such employee from a list of at least three such funds, designated in a contract between such institution and a labor organization, or if the contract fails to designate such funds, then to any such fund chosen by the employee." 29 U.S.C. § 169.

The absence of an "affirmative intention of the Congress clearly expressed" fortifies our conclusion that Congress did not contemplate that the Board would require church-operated schools to grant recognition to unions as bargaining agents for their teachers.

The Board relies heavily upon *Associated Press v. NLRB*, 301 U.S. 103 (1937). There the Court held that the First Amendment was no bar to the application of the Act to the Associated Press, an organization engaged in collecting information and news throughout the world and distributing it to its members. Perceiving nothing to suggest that application of the Act would infringe First Amendment guarantees of press freedoms, the Court sustained Board jurisdiction. Here, on the contrary, the record affords abundant evidence that the Board's exercise of jurisdiction over teachers in church-operated schools would implicate the guarantees of the Religion Clauses.

Accordingly, in the absence of a clear expression of Congress' intent to bring teachers in church-operated schools within the jurisdiction of the Board, we decline to construe the Act in a manner that could in turn call upon the Court to resolve difficult and sensitive questions arising out of the guarantees of the First Amendment Religion Clauses. [*Affirmed.*]

MR. JUSTICE BRENNAN, with whom MR. JUSTICE WHITE, MR. JUSTICE MARSHALL, and MR. JUSTICE BLACKMUN join, dissenting.

* * * The general principle of construing statutes to avoid unnecessary constitutional decisions is a well-settled and salutary one. The governing canon, however, is *not* that expressed by the Court today. The Court requires that there be a "clear expression of an affirmative intention of Congress" before it will bring within the coverage of a broadly worded regulatory statute certain persons whose coverage might raise constitutional questions. But those familiar with the legislative process know that explicit expressions of congressional intent in such broadly inclusive statutes are not commonplace. Thus, by strictly or loosely applying its requirement, the Court can virtually remake congressional enactments. * * *

The settled canon for construing statutes wherein constitutional questions may lurk was stated in *Machinists v. Street*, 367 U.S. 740 (1961), cited by the Court, *ante*:

> " 'When the validity of an act of the Congress is drawn in question, and even if a serious doubt of constitutionality is raised, it is a cardinal principle that this Court will first ascertain whether a construction of the statute is *fairly possible* by which the question may be avoided.' *Crowell v. Benson*, 285 U.S. 22, 62." *Id.*, at 749–750 (emphasis added).

This limitation to constructions that are "fairly possible" and "reasonable" acts as a brake against wholesale judicial dismemberment of congressional enactments. It confines the judiciary to its proper role in construing statutes, which is to interpret them so as to give effect to congressional intention. The Court's new "affirmative expression" rule releases that brake.

The interpretation of the National Labor Relations Act announced by the Court today is not "fairly possible." The Act's wording, its legislative history, and the Court's own precedents leave "the intention of the Congress * * * revealed too distinctly to permit us to ignore it because of mere misgivings as to power." Section 2(2) of the Act, 29 U.S.C. § 152(2), defines "employer" as:

> " * * * any person acting as an agent of an employer, directly or indirectly, *but shall not include* the United States or any wholly owned Government corporation, or any Federal Reserve Bank, or any State or political subdivision thereof, or any person subject to the Railway Labor Act, as amended from time to time, or any labor organization (other than when acting as an employer), or anyone acting in the capacity of officer or agent of such labor organization." (Emphasis added.)

Thus, the Act covers all employers not within the eight express exceptions. The Court today substitutes amendment for construction to insert one more exception — for church-operated schools. This is a particularly transparent violation of the judicial role: The legislative history reveals that Congress itself considered and rejected a very similar amendment.

[The 1935 Act could not have been written more broadly, and the NLRB rejected efforts to except nonprofit employers from its reach.] The Hartley bill, which passed the House of Representatives in 1947, would have provided the exception the Court today writes into the statute:

> "The term 'employer' * * * shall not include * * * any corporation, community chest, fund, or foundation organized and operated exclusively for *religious*, charitable, scientific, literary, or *educational* purposes, * * * no part of the net earnings of which inures to the benefit of any private shareholder or individual * * *." (Emphasis added.) H.R. 3020, 80th Cong., 1st Sess., § 2(2) (Apr. 18, 1947).

But the proposed exception was not enacted. The bill reported by the Senate Committee on Labor and Public Welfare did not contain the Hartley exception. Instead, the Senate proposed an exception limited to nonprofit hospitals, and passed the bill in that form. The Senate version was accepted by the House in conference, thus limiting the exception for nonprofit employers to nonprofit hospitals.

Even that limited exemption was ultimately repealed in 1974. In doing so, Congress confirmed the view of the Act expressed here: that it was intended to cover all employers — including nonprofit employers — unless expressly excluded, and that the 1947 amendment excluded only nonprofit hospitals. See H.R.Rep. No. 93–1051, p. 4 (1974); 120 Cong.Rec. 12938 (1974) (Senator Williams); 120 Cong.Rec. 16900 (1974) (Rep. Ashbrook). Moreover, it is significant that in considering the 1974 amendments, the Senate expressly rejected an amendment proposed by Senator Ervin that was analogous to the one the Court today creates — an amendment to exempt nonprofit hospitals operated by religious groups. Senator Cranston, floor manager of the Senate Committee bill and primary opponent of the proposed religious exception, explained:

> "[S]uch an exception for religiously affiliated hospitals would seriously erode *the existing national policy which holds religiously affiliated institutions generally such as* proprietary nursing homes, residential communities, and *educational facilities to the same standards as their nonsectarian counterparts*." 120 Cong.Rec. 12957 (1974) (emphasis added).

See also *ibid.* (Sen. Javits); 120 Cong.Rec. 12957 (1974) (Sen. Williams).

In construing the Board's jurisdiction to exclude church-operated schools, therefore, the Court today is faithful to neither the statute's language nor its history. Moreover, it is also untrue to its own precedents. "This Court has consistently declared that in passing the National Labor Relations Act, Congress intended to and did vest in the Board the fullest *jurisdictional* breadth constitutionally permissible under the Commerce Clause." *NLRB v. Reliance Fuel Oil Corp.*, 371 U.S. 224, 226 (1963) (emphasis in original). As long as an employer is within the reach of Congress' power under the Commerce Clause — and no one doubts that respondents are — the Court has held him to be covered by the Act regardless of the nature of his activity. Indeed, *Associated Press v. NLRB*, 301 U.S. 103 (1937), construed the Act to cover editorial employees of a nonprofit news-gathering organization despite a claim — precisely parallel to that made here — that their inclusion rendered the Act in violation of the First Amendment. Today's opinion is simply unable to explain the grounds that distinguish that case from this one.

Thus, the available authority indicates that Congress intended to include — not exclude — lay teachers of church-operated schools. The Court does not counter this with evidence that Congress *did* intend an exception it never stated. Instead, despite the legislative history to the contrary, it construes the Act as excluding lay teachers only because Congress did not state explicitly that they were covered. In Mr. Justice Cardozo's words, this presses "avoidance of a difficulty * * * to the point of disingenuous evasion." *Moore Ice Cream Co. v. Rose*, 289 U.S., at 379.[11]

---

11. Not even the Court's redrafting of the statute causes all First Amendment problems to disappear. The Court's opinion implies limitation of its exception to church-operated schools. That limitation is doubtless necessary since this Court has already rejected a more general exception for nonprofit organizations. See *Polish National Alliance v. NLRB*, 322 U.S. 643

NOTES ON THE "AVOIDANCE CANON"

1. *Different Ways of Framing the Avoidance Canon.* As the debate in *Catholic Bishop* indicates, there are several ways to express this canon:[f] When one interpretation of an ambiguous statute would be unconstitutional, choose another one that would pass constitutional muster. *Murray v. The Schooner Charming Betsy*, 6 U.S. 64 (1804). When one interpretation would raise serious constitutional problems, choose the one that would not. *United States ex rel. Attorney General v. Delaware & Hudson Co.*, 213 U.S. 366 (1909); cf. *Ex parte Bollman*, 8 U.S. 75 (1807). When one interpretation presents constitutional difficulties, do not impose it unless there has been an affirmative indication from Congress that it is required. *McCulloch v. Sociedad Nacional de Marineros de Honduras*, 372 U.S. 10 (1963).

The most aggressive way of framing the avoidance canon is *McCulloch*, which Chief Justice Burger invokes in *Catholic Bishop*. The dissenters assail the Chief Justice for this, and the *McCulloch* language is rarely applied today. But neither is the *Charming Betsy* language. Generally, the avoidance canon today follows the *Delaware & Hudson* language. Much of *Catholic Bishop* applies that language, and Justice Frankfurter's opinion in *Witkovich* clearly follows it and cites *Crowell v. Benson*, a leading case for that language.

There are many differences between *Witkovich* and *Catholic Bishop* (such as the ideology of the Court splits: "liberals" win in the earlier case, "conservatives" in the later one), but one similarity is striking: standard rule of law sources seem to cut *against* use of the avoidance canon, even suggesting that there was not really any statutory "ambiguity" to be resolved, yet the Court in both cases invoked the canon and effectively trumped the statutory plain meaning. Dissenting Justices in both cases made persuasive arguments that the statutes in question clearly supported the government's broad interpretations, as did key congressional committees (*Witkovich*) and sponsors (*Catholic Bishop*), and that the government's interpretation in both cases was clearly constitutional. Do you disagree with this characterization? If not, you have a mystery on your hands. Neither Chief Justice Burger nor Justice Frankfurter was known as a wild judicial activist in his era — yet each wrote opinions that

---

(1944). But such an exemption, available only to church-operated schools, generates a possible Establishment Clause *question* of its own. *Walz v. Tax Comm'n*, 397 U.S. 664 (1970), does not put that question to rest, for in upholding the property tax exemption for churches there at issue, we emphasized that New York had "not singled out * * * churches as such; rather, it has granted exemption to all houses of religious worship within a broad class of property owned by nonprofit, quasi-public corporations * * *." Like the Court, "at this stage of [my] consideration [I am] not compelled to determine whether the [Establishment Clause problem] is [as significant] as [I] would were [I] considering the constitutional issue." It is enough to observe that no matter which way the Court turns in interpreting the Act, it cannot avoid constitutional questions.

    f. For useful introductions, see Trevor Morrison, *Constitutional Avoidance in the Executive Branch*, 106 Colum. L. Rev. 1189 (2006); John Copeland Nagle, Delaware & Hudson *Revisited*, 72 Notre Dame L. Rev. 1495 (1997); Adrian Vermeule, *Saving Constructions*, 85 Geo. L.J. 1945 (1997).

are hard to justify as a matter of standard rule of law sources. What is going on?

2. *Values Underlying the Avoidance Canon.* There are a number of values the avoidance doctrine might serve, such as avoiding unnecessary constitutional holdings or advisory opinions by the Court. Consider three potentially important values. First, it may be a rule of thumb for ascertaining legislative intent. The avoidance interpreter assumes that the legislature would *not* have wanted to press constitutional limits. Fred Schauer, Ashwander *Revisited*, 1995 Sup, Ct. Rev. 71, finds such an implicit legislative intent theory most implausible. The assumption rests upon no evidence of actual legislative intent. In the average case, why shouldn't the enacting legislature prefer that its work product be given full force — and if it's unconstitutional the Court should say so openly so that there can be a full-blown constitutional controversy? See Jerry Mashaw, *Greed, Chaos, and Governance: Using Public Choice Theory to Improve Public Law* 105 (1997). Consider *Witkovich*: Is it plausible that Congress would have wanted the Court to trim back the statute in the way that it did? How about *Catholic Bishop*?

A second value of the avoidance canon is that it might provide a low-salience mechanism for giving effect to what Larry Sager calls "underenforced constitutional norms."[g] *Witkovich* exemplifies this idea. Judges are loathe to strike down immigration statutes, because of either the plenary powers idea or institutional competence concerns. But decisions like *Witkovich* are quite common, for reasons Hiroshi Motomura has identified: unwilling to close off congressional options through constitutional review, judges will give effect to due process and free speech norms through narrowing constructions.[h] And so the norm is vindicated — but Congress can (re)assert a broader result after deliberation and debate over a statutory amendment that clearly overrides the norm-adhering interpretation.

Consider ways in which this idea might apply to *Catholic Bishop*. Labor law has been another area where the avoidance canon has been especially active in the Supreme Court's jurisprudence. See the cases discussed in *Catholic Bishop*, as well as more recent cases such as *Edward J. DeBartolo Corp. v. Florida Gulf Coast Building & Constr. Trades Council*, 485 U.S. 568, 575 (1988) (now a leading citation for the *Witkovich/Crowell* expression of the canon).

---

g. William Eskridge, Jr. & Philip Frickey, *Quasi-Constitutional Law: Clear Statement Rules as Constitutional Lawmaking*, 45 Vand. L. Rev. 593 (1992), drawing from Lawrence Sager, *Fair Measure: The Legal Status of Underenforced Constitutional Norms*, 91 Harv. L. Rev. 1212 (1978). See also Neal Katyal, *Judges as Advicegivers*, 50 Stan. L. Rev. 1709 (1998); Ronald Krotoszynski, Jr., *Constitutional Flares: On Judges, Legislatures, And Dialogue*, 83 Minn. L. Rev. 1 (1998); Ernest Young, *Constitutional Avoidance, Resistance Norms, and the Preservation of Judicial Review*, 78 Tex. L. Rev. 1549, 1585–87 (2000).

h. Hiroshi Motomura, *Immigration Law After a Century of Plenary Power: Phantom Constitutional Norms and Statutory Interpretation*, 100 Yale L.J. 545, 561–75 (1990). There are good recent examples of Professor Motomura's thesis, such as *Zadvydas v. Davis*, 533 U.S. 678, 696-99 (2001); *INS v. St. Cyr*, 533 U.S. 289 (2001).

A third value for the avoidance canon is suggested by Professor Bickel's theory of the passive virtues.[i] One way that courts conserve their institutional capital is by techniques of avoidance. Standard techniques are for the Court to divest itself of constitutional cases whose resolution is premature by dismissing the complaint on procedural grounds such as standing, ripeness, etc. The avoidance canon represents a middle ground between pure passive virtues and constitutional invalidation. That middle ground allows the Court to slow down a political process that is moving too hastily and overriding human rights, but without incurring the full wrath of a political process that doesn't like to be thwarted. As one of us has argued, this theory best explains *Witkovich* and several other cases where the Warren Court impeded McCarthy-era initiatives, but without creating a full-blown constitutional crisis.[j] How might this theory apply to *Catholic Bishop*, which was handed down a generation later, and by a more conservative majority?

3. *Criticisms of the Avoidance Canon.* Perhaps the leading critique of the avoidance canon remains Judge Henry Friendly, *Mr. Justice Frankfurter and the Reading of Statutes*, in *Benchmarks* 211–12 (1967):

> Although questioning the doctrine of construction to avoid constitutional doubts is rather like challenging Holy Writ, the rule has always seemed to me to have almost as many dangers as advantages. For one thing, it is one of those rules that courts apply when they want and conveniently forget when they don't — some, perhaps, would consider that to be a virtue. * * * Some considerations advanced in its favor, such as the awesome consequences of "a decree of unconstitutionality," overlook that if the Court finds the more likely construction to be unconstitutional, another means of rescue — the principle of construing to avoid unconstitutionality — will be at hand. The strongest basis for the rule is thus that the Supreme Court ought not to indulge in what, if adverse, is likely to be only a constitutional advisory opinion. While there is force in this, the rule of "construing" to avoid constitutional doubts should, in my view, be confined to cases where the doubt is exceedingly real. Otherwise this rule, whether it be denominated one of statutory interpretation or, more accurately, of constitutional adjudication — still more accurately, of constitutional nonadjudication — is likely to become one of evisceration and tergiversation.

Judge Friendly's charge is that the avoidance canon will be an occasion for *stealth judicial activism*, which is both anti-democratic and unhealthy for the judiciary. Accord, Judge Richard Posner, *The Federal Courts: Crisis and Reform* 285 (1985); Lisa Kloppenberg, *Avoiding Constitutional Questions*, 35 B.C. L. Rev. 1003 (1994); John Manning, *The Nondelegation Doctrine as a Canon of Avoidance*, 2000 Sup. Ct. Rev. 223; John Nagle, *Delaware & Hudson Revisited*, 72 Notre Dame L. Rev. 1495 (1997).

---

i. Alexander Bickel, *The Least Dangerous Branch: The Supreme Court at the Bar of Politics* 156-69 (1962). Bickel's ideas about statutory interpretation are set forth in Alexander Bickel & Harry Wellington, *Legislative Purpose and the Judicial Process: The Lincoln Mills Case*, 71 Harv. L. Rev. 1 (1957).

j. Philip Frickey, *Getting from Joe to Gene (McCarthy): The Avoidance Canon, Legal Process Theory, and Narrowing Statutory Interpretation in the Early Warren Court*, 93 Cal. L. Rev. 397 (2005).

A corollary to Judge Friendly's charge is that the avoidance canon will be applied unpredictably. Even in the immigration area, where it has made regular appearances in Supreme Court opinions, this charge has much weight. For an example of a case where there were stronger constitutional doubts and less clear statutory language than in *Witkovich*, yet the Court refused to apply this canon (or the rule of lenity, which was also applicable), see *Almendarez-Torres v. United States*, 523 U.S. 224 (1998).[k] See also *Rust v. Sullivan*, 500 U.S. 173 (1991).

In evaluating the canon, get beyond *Witkovich*, where the Court was standing up to McCarthyism, and *Catholic Bishop,* where the Court was protecting religious freedom. Those might be constitutional values you find admirable. But consider application of the canon to constitutional values you find normatively unappealing, or just plain boring. For example, do you lose some enthusiasm for the canon after reading the following case?

DEPARTMENT OF COMMERCE v. U.S. HOUSE OF REPRESEN-TATIVES, 525 U.S. 316 (1999). Article I, § 2, cl. 3 of the Constitution apportions Representatives among the states "according to their respective Numbers" and requires that there be an "Enumeration" of the "Numbers" of people in the various states every ten years, "in such Manner as they [Congress] shall by Law direct." The Census Act, 13 U.S.C. § 1 et seq., delegates the responsibility for this endeavor to the Commerce Department, which for the 2000 census proposed to supplement its survey with statistical sampling techniques to cure what has been documented as an "undercount" of the population, especially of racial minorities and poor people. As revised in 1976, the statute says: "Except for the determination of population for purposes of apportionment of Representatives in Congress among the several States, the Secretary shall, if he considers it feasible, authorize the use of the statistical method known as 'sampling' in carrying out the provisions of this title." 13 U.S.C. § 195.

---

k. 8 U.S.C. § 1326(a) makes it a crime, "[s]ubject to subsection (b) of this section," for an alien who once was deported to return to the United States without special permission and authorizes a prison term up to two years. Section 1326(b)(2) says: "Notwithstanding subsection (a) of this section, in the case of any alien described in such subsection — * * * whose removal was subsequent to a conviction for commission of an aggravated felony, such alien shall be fined under such title, imprisoned not more than 20 years, or both." Hugo Almendarez-Torres admitted to a violation of § 1326(a), and admitted at his guilty plea hearing that he had been deported for three aggravated felonies. He argued that he could only be sentenced to two years imprisonment, and not 20 years, because the indictment had not charged him with a separate violation of § 1326(b). The Court rejected this claim, construing § 1326(b)(2) to be a sentence-enhancing provision for § 1326(a) and therefore not requiring a separate indictment. In dissent, Justice Scalia argued that this reading was constitutionally problematic (denying the defendant a jury trial, a rationale adopted in *Apprendi v. New Jersey*, 530 U.S. 466 (2000), and subsequent cases), and the statute was genuinely unclear. At common law, statutes providing higher maximum sentences for crimes committed by convicted felons were treated as separate crimes and not as mere enhancements, and the jury had to decide this element beyond a reasonable doubt. Given that common law background, § 1326(b)(2) would appear to be a separate crime.

Section 195 is ambiguous. It might mean that the Secretary has no discretion regarding sampling (if feasible) for use in various federal programs relying on census data, but does have discretion regarding sampling for use in the apportionment of Representatives. It might also mean that the Secretary may use sampling (if feasible) for program purposes but not for apportionment purposes. **Justice O'Connor**'s opinion resolved the ambiguity by reference to a principle of continuity (Part IIIA of her opinion). Joined by a majority of Justices on this point, Justice O'Connor reasoned that, because the Census Bureau's practice, required by statute before 1976, was never to use sampling techniques for apportionment purposes, "there is only one plausible reading of the amended § 195: It prohibits the use of sampling in calculating the population for purposes of apportionment."

The principle of continuity, moreover, was supported by the legislative history of the 1976 revision. Speaking for herself and only two other Justices, Justice O'Connor reasoned (Part IIIB): "At no point during the debates over these amendments did a single Member of Congress suggest that the amendments would so fundamentally change the manner in which the Bureau could calculate the population for purposes of apportionment. * * * [I]t tests the limits of reason to suggest that despite such silence, Members of Congress voting for those amendments intended to enact what would arguably be the single most significant change in the method of conducting the decennial census since its inception." Speaking again for five Justices (Part IV), Justice O'Connor invoked the avoidance canon and interpreted the statute to avoid the question whether adjusting the apportionment of Representatives based on sampling would violate Article I, § 2, cl. 3.

Justice Scalia, speaking also for **Chief Justice Rehnquist** and **Justices Kennedy** and **Thomas**, concurred in the Court's judgment and in part of the O'Connor opinion. These Justices found it "unquestionably doubtful whether the constitutional requirement of an 'actual Enumeration' is satisfied by statistical sampling" and so urged that the Census Act be construed so "as to avoid serious constitutional doubt." Hence, they resolved the ambiguity in the statute the same way Justice O'Connor did.

Justice Breyer dissented, on the ground that § 195 was not implicated in the case at all: it only regulated instances where the Secretary could use sampling as a *substitute* for actual counting, while the current proposal was to use sampling as a *supplement* for actual counting. **Justice Stevens**, joined by **Justices Souter** and **Ginsburg**, also dissented, on the ground that the 1976 revision was an explicit authorization for the Secretary to use sampling techniques for apportionment purposes. Section 141(a), as rewritten in 1976, says: "The Secretary shall * * * take a decennial census of the population * * * in such form and content as he may determine, including the use of sampling procedures and special surveys." Because nothing in § 195 countermands the broad authorization in § 141(a), the statute cannot be read the way the Court majority insisted it be read. (Justice Stevens also defended the constitutionality of his reading, joined by all three of the other dissenting Justices.)

Is Justice Stevens right as to the plain meaning of the statute's text? If so, how can the new textualists not follow the approach laid out by Justice

Kennedy in *Public Citizen* (Chapter 7, § 2B3): construe the law as written, and then strike it down if it contravenes the Constitution as written?

NOTE ON SEVERABILITY

When a provision in a statute is unconstitutional, should the court treat the remainder of the statute as good law, or declare the entire statute invalid? This is a question of *severability*. When the statute contains an express severability clause (instructing courts to save the remainder of the statute) or an express nonseverability clause, the issue would appear to be easy. Nonetheless, because such clauses are sometimes inserted as boilerplate in bills without much thought given to their effects, courts sometimes struggle with whether the clause should be given its full textual meaning if that seems inconsistent with the probable legislative intent concerning the particular severability issue.[1]

Often the statute is silent on the question. In that circumstance, "[u]nless it is evident that the Legislature would not have enacted those provisions which are within its power, independently of that which is not, the invalid part may be dropped if what is left is fully operative as a law." *Alaska Airlines v. Brock*, 480 U.S. 678, 684 (1987).

3. *The New Federalism Canons*

The Supreme Court in the 1980s and early 1990s created or clarified "clear statement rules" that reflect constitutional norms of federalism.[m] See *Pennhurst State School & Hospital v. Halderman*, 451 U.S. 1 (1981) (conditions attached to federal funding for state programs must be clear); *Atascadero State Hospital v. Scanlon*, 473 U.S. 234 (1985) (super-strong clear statement rule against congressional abrogation of state Eleventh Amendment immunity from suit in federal courts).[n] The following case is the most dramatic example to date of the Court's activity in protecting state sovereignty through the use of canons.

As background, note that in *Maryland v. Wirtz*, 392 U.S. 183 (1968), the Court upheld the application of the Fair Labor Standards Act's minimum wage provisions to state hospital and school employees, rejecting the claim that the Constitution forbids such direct federal regulation of important state functions. Then, in *National League of Cities v. Usery*, 426 U.S. 833 (1976), by a 5–4 vote, the Court overruled *Wirtz* and refused to apply the FLSA's minimum

---

l. For excellent critical analyses of the Court's severability jurisprudence, see Michael Shumsky, *Severability, Inseverability, and the Rule of Law*, 41 Harv. J. Leg. 227 (2004); Israel Friedman, *Inseverability Clauses in Statutes*, 64 U. Chi. L. Rev. 903 (1997) (student comment).

m. Recall our terminology: a "clear statement rule" requires that a statute be interpreted a certain way unless the contrary interpretation is clearly required by statutory text; a "super-strong clear statement rule" requires that the statutory text targets the issue unmistakably, especially through specific language.

n. See generally William Eskridge, Jr. & Philip Frickey, *Quasi-Constitutional Law: Clear Statement Rules as Constitutional Lawmaking*, 45 Vand. L. Rev. 593 (1992), surveying and analyzing the Court's aggressive deployment of these federalism-inspired super-strong clear statement rules.

wage and maximum hours provisions to many state and municipal employees. *National League of Cities* then met its own apparent demise in *Garcia v. San Antonio Metropolitan Transit Authority*, 469 U.S. 528 (1985), another 5–4 case, which explicitly overruled the nine-year-old precedent. As the next case demonstrates, what the Court taketh away as constitutional protection it can revive as canonical interpretive protection.

GREGORY v. ASHCROFT
Supreme Court of the United States, 1991
501 U.S. 452, 111 S.Ct. 2395, 115 L.Ed.2d 410

JUSTICE O'CONNOR delivered the opinion of the Court.

[It is a prima facie violation of the federal Age Discrimination in Employment Act (ADEA), 29 U.S.C. §§ 621–34, for an "employer" covered by the Act to specify a mandatory retirement age for "employees" over forty years of age who are covered by the Act. State and local governments are "employers" covered by the ADEA. In this case, the Missouri Constitution provided a mandatory retirement age of seventy for most state judges. Petitioners were state judges seeking to obtain a declaration that the mandatory retirement age violates the ADEA. The district court dismissed the action, concluding that the judges were "appointees on the policymaking level," a category of state officials excluded from the definition of "employees" covered by the Act. The Court of Appeals affirmed. What follows is Part II of Justice O'Connor's opinion.]

[IIA] As every schoolchild learns, our Constitution establishes a system of dual sovereignty between the States and the Federal Government. This Court also has recognized this fundamental principle. In *Tafflin v. Levitt*, 493 U.S. 455, 458 (1990), "[w]e beg[a]n with the axiom that, under our federal system, the States possess sovereignty concurrent with that of the Federal Government, subject only to limitations imposed by the Supremacy Clause." Over 120 years ago, the Court described the constitutional scheme of dual sovereigns:

" '[T]he people of each State compose a State, having its own government, and endowed with all the functions essential to separate and independent existence,' . . . '[W]ithout the States in union, there could be no such political body as the United States.' Not only, therefore, can there be no loss of separate and independent autonomy to the States, through their union under the Constitution, but it may be not unreasonably said that the preservation of the States, and the maintenance of their governments, are as much within the design and care of the Constitution as the preservation of the Union and the maintenance of the National government. The Constitution, in all its provisions, looks to an indestructible Union, composed of indestructible States." *Texas v. White*, 7 Wall. 700, 725 (1869), quoting *Lane County v. Oregon*, 7 Wall. 71, 76 (1869).

The Constitution created a Federal Government of limited powers. "The powers not delegated to the United States by the Constitution, nor prohibited by it to the States, are reserved to the States respectively, or to the people." U.S. Const., Amdt. 10. The States thus retain substantial sovereign authority under our constitutional system. As James Madison put it:

"The powers delegated by the proposed Constitution to the federal government are few and defined. Those which are to remain in the State governments are numerous and indefinite. . . . The powers reserved to the several States will extend to all the objects which, in the ordinary course of affairs, concern the lives, liberties, and properties of the people, and the internal order, improvement, and prosperity of the State." The Federalist No. 45, pp. 292–293 (C. Rossiter ed. 1961).

This federalist structure of joint sovereigns preserves to the people numerous advantages. It assures a decentralized government that will be more sensitive to the diverse needs of a heterogenous society; it increases opportunity for citizen involvement in democratic processes; it allows for more innovation and experimentation in government; and it makes government more responsive by putting the States in competition for a mobile citizenry.

Perhaps the principal benefit of the federalist system is a check on abuses of government power. "The 'constitutionally mandated balance of power' between the States and the Federal Government was adopted by the Framers to ensure the protection of 'our fundamental liberties.' " *Atascadero State Hospital v. Scanlon*, 473 U.S. 234, 242 (1985), quoting *Garcia v. San Antonio Metropolitan Transit Authority*, 469 U.S. 528, 572 (1985) (Powell, J., dissenting). Just as the separation and independence of the coordinate Branches of the Federal Government serves to prevent the accumulation of excessive power in any one Branch, a healthy balance of power between the States and the Federal Government will reduce the risk of tyranny and abuse from either front. Alexander Hamilton explained to the people of New York, perhaps optimistically, that the new federalist system would suppress completely "the attempts of the government to establish a tyranny":

"[I]n a confederacy the people, without exaggeration, may be said to be entirely the masters of their own fate. Power being almost always the rival of power, the general government will at all times stand ready to check usurpations of the state governments, and these will have the same disposition towards the general government. The people, by throwing themselves into either scale, will infallibly make it preponderate. If their rights are invaded by either, they can make use of the other as the instrument of redress." The Federalist No. 28, pp. 180–181 (C. Rossiter ed. 1961).

James Madison made much the same point:

"In a single republic, all the power surrendered by the people is submitted to the administration of a single government; and the usurpations are guarded against by a division of the government into distinct and separate departments. In the compound republic of America, the power surrendered by the people is first divided between two distinct governments, and then the portion allotted to each subdivided among distinct and separate departments. Hence a double security arises to the rights of the people. The different governments will control each other, at the same time that each will be controlled by itself." The Federalist No. 51, p. 323.

One fairly can dispute whether our federalist system has been quite as successful in checking government abuse as Hamilton promised, but there is no doubt about the design. If this "double security" is to be effective, there must be a proper balance between the States and the Federal Government.

These twin powers will act as mutual restraints only if both are credible. In the tension between federal and state power lies the promise of liberty.

The Federal Government holds a decided advantage in this delicate balance: the Supremacy Clause. U.S. Const., Art. VI, cl. 2. As long as it is acting within the powers granted it under the Constitution, Congress may impose its will on the States. Congress may legislate in areas traditionally regulated by the States. This is an extraordinary power in a federalist system. It is a power that we must assume Congress does not exercise lightly.

The present case concerns a state constitutional provision through which the people of Missouri establish a qualification for those who sit as their judges. This provision goes beyond an area traditionally regulated by the States; it is a decision of the most fundamental sort for a sovereign entity. Through the structure of its government, and the character of those who exercise government authority, a State defines itself as a sovereign. * * *

Congressional interference with this decision of the people of Missouri, defining their constitutional officers, would upset the usual constitutional balance of federal and state powers. For this reason, "it is incumbent upon the federal courts to be certain of Congress' intent before finding that federal law overrides" this balance. *Atascadero*. We explained recently:

> "[I]f Congress intends to alter the 'usual constitutional balance between the States and the Federal Government,' it must make its intention to do so 'unmistakably clear in the language of the statute.' *Atascadero*; see also *Pennhurst State School and Hospital v. Halderman*, 465 U.S. 89, 99 (1984). *Atascadero* was an Eleventh Amendment case, but a similar approach is applied in other contexts. Congress should make its intention 'clear and manifest' if it intends to pre-empt the historic powers of the States. . . . 'In traditionally sensitive areas, such as legislation affecting the federal balance, the requirement of clear statement assures that the legislature has in fact faced, and intended to bring into issue, the critical matters involved in the judicial decision.' "
> *Will v. Michigan Dept. of State Police*, 491 U.S. 58, 65 (1989).

This plain statement rule is nothing more than an acknowledgment that the States retain substantial sovereign powers under our constitutional scheme, powers with which Congress does not readily interfere.

In a recent line of authority, we have acknowledged the unique nature of state decisions that "go to the heart of representative government." [Here Justice O'Connor referred to cases holding that, although state exclusion of aliens from public employment generally raises serious equal protection questions, the Court has created a "political function" exception and upheld state programs limiting to citizens employment in positions that are "intimately related to the process of democratic self-government."]

These cases stand in recognition of the authority of the people of the States to determine the qualifications of their most important government officials. It is an authority that lies at " 'the heart of representative government.' " It is a power reserved to the States under the Tenth Amendment and guaranteed them by that provision of the Constitution under which the United States "guarantee[s] to every State in this Union a Republican Form of Government." U.S. Const., Art. IV, § 4.

The authority of the people of the States to determine the qualifications of their government officials is, of course, not without limit. Other constitutional provisions, most notably the Fourteenth Amendment, proscribe certain qualifications; our review of citizenship requirements under the political-function exception is less exacting, but it is not absent. Here, we must decide what Congress did in extending the ADEA to the States, pursuant to its powers under the Commerce Clause. See *EEOC v. Wyoming*, 460 U.S. 226 (1983) (the extension of the ADEA to employment by state and local governments was a valid exercise of Congress' powers under the Commerce Clause). As against Congress' powers "[t]o regulate Commerce . . . among the several States," U.S. Const., Art. I, § 8, cl. 3, the authority of the people of the States to determine the qualifications of their government officials may be inviolate.

We are constrained in our ability to consider the limits that the state-federal balance places on Congress' powers under the Commerce Clause. See *Garcia v. San Antonio Metropolitan Transit Authority* (declining to review limitations placed on Congress' Commerce Clause powers by our federal system). But there is no need to do so if we hold that the ADEA does not apply to state judges. Application of the plain statement rule thus may avoid a potential constitutional problem. Indeed, inasmuch as this Court in *Garcia* has left primarily to the political process the protection of the States against intrusive exercises of Congress' Commerce Clause powers, we must be absolutely certain that Congress intended such an exercise. "[T]o give the state-displacing weight of federal law to mere congressional *ambiguity* would evade the very procedure for lawmaking on which *Garcia* relied to protect states' interests." Lawrence Tribe, American Constitutional Law § 6–25, p. 480 (2d ed. 1988).

[IIB] In 1974, Congress extended the substantive provisions of the ADEA to include the States as employers. At the same time, Congress amended the definition of "employee" to exclude all elected and most high-ranking government officials. Under the Act, as amended:

> "The term 'employee' means an individual employed by any employer except that the term 'employee' shall not include any person elected to public office in any State or political subdivision of any State by the qualified voters thereof, or any person chosen by such officer to be on such officer's personal staff, or an appointee on the policymaking level or an immediate adviser with respect to the exercise of the constitutional or legal powers of the office." 29 U.S.C. § 630(f).

Governor Ashcroft contends that the § 630(f) exclusion of certain public officials also excludes judges, like petitioners, who are appointed to office by the Governor and are then subject to retention election. The Governor points to two passages in § 630(f). First, he argues, these judges are selected by an elected official and, because they make policy, are "appointee[s] on the policymaking level."

Petitioners counter that judges merely resolve factual disputes and decide questions of law; they do not make policy. Moreover, petitioners point out that the policymaking-level exception is part of a trilogy, tied closely to the elected-official exception. Thus, the Act excepts elected officials and: (1) "any person chosen by such officer to be on such officer's personal staff"; (2) "an appointee on the policymaking level"; and (3) "an immediate advisor with respect to the constitutional or legal powers of the office." Applying the maxim of statutory construction *noscitur a sociis* — that a word is known by the company it keeps — petitioners argue that since (1) and (3) refer only to those in close working relationships with elected officials, so too must (2). Even if it can be said that judges may make policy, petitioners contend, they do not do so at the behest of an elected official.

Governor Ashcroft relies on the plain language of the statute: It exempts persons appointed "at the policymaking level." [The Governor argued that state judges make policy in making common law decisions and exercising supervisory authority over the state bar. Moreover, state appellate judges have additional policymaking responsibilities: supervising inferior courts, establishing rules of procedure for the state courts, and developing disciplinary rules for the bar.]

The Governor stresses judges' policymaking responsibilities, but it is far from plain that the statutory exception requires that judges actually make policy. The statute refers to appointees "on the policymaking level," not to appointees "who make policy." It may be sufficient that the appointee is in a position requiring the exercise of discretion concerning issues of public importance. This certainly describes the bench, regardless of whether judges might be considered policymakers in the same sense as the executive or legislature.

Nonetheless, "appointee at the policymaking level," particularly in the context of the other exceptions that surround it, is an odd way for Congress to exclude judges; a plain statement that judges are not "employees" would seem the most efficient phrasing. But in this case we are not looking for a plain statement that judges are excluded. We will not read the ADEA to cover state judges unless Congress has made it clear that judges are *included*. This does not mean that the Act must mention judges explicitly, though it does not. Rather, it must be plain to anyone reading the Act that it covers judges. In the context of a statute that plainly excludes most important state public officials, "appointee on the policymaking level" is sufficiently broad that we cannot conclude that the statute plainly covers appointed state judges. Therefore, it does not.

The ADEA plainly covers all state employees except those excluded by one of the exceptions. Where it is unambiguous that an employee does not fall within one of the exceptions, the Act states plainly and unequivocally that the employee is included. It is at least ambiguous whether a state judge is an "appointee on the policymaking level." * * *

[IIC] The extension of the ADEA to employment by state and local governments was a valid exercise of Congress' powers under the Commerce Clause. *EEOC v. Wyoming.* In *Wyoming*, we reserved the questions whether Congress might also have passed the ADEA extension pursuant to its powers under § 5 of the Fourteenth Amendment, and whether the extension would have been a valid exercise of that power. We noted, however, that the principles of federalism that constrain Congress' exercise of its Commerce Clause powers are attenuated when Congress acts pursuant to its powers to enforce the Civil War Amendments. This is because those "Amendments were specifically designed as an expansion of federal power and an intrusion on state sovereignty." One might argue, therefore, that if Congress passed the ADEA extension under its § 5 powers, the concerns about federal intrusion into state government that compel the result in this case might carry less weight.

By its terms, the Fourteenth Amendment contemplates interference with state authority: "No State shall . . . deny to any person within its jurisdiction the equal protection of the laws." But this Court has never held that the Amendment may be applied in complete disregard for a State's constitutional powers. Rather, the Court has recognized that the States' power to define the qualifications of their officeholders has force even as against the proscriptions of the Fourteenth Amendment.

We return to the political-function cases. In *Sugarman* [*v. Dougall*, 413 U.S. 634 (1973)], the Court noted that "aliens as a class 'are a prime example of a "discrete and insular" minority * * * and that classifications based on alienage are 'subject to close judicial scrutiny.'" The *Sugarman* Court held that New York City had insufficient interest in preventing aliens from holding a broad category of public jobs to justify the blanket prohibition. At the same time, the Court established the rule that scrutiny under the Equal Protection Clause "will not be so demanding where we deal with matters resting firmly within a State's constitutional prerogatives." Later cases have reaffirmed this practice. See [cases concerning the "political-function" exception from strict scrutiny of state classifications disadvantaging aliens]. These cases demonstrate that the Fourteenth Amendment does not override all principles of federalism.

Of particular relevance here is *Pennhurst State School and Hospital v. Halderman*, 451 U.S. 1 (1981). The question in that case was whether Congress, in passing a section of the Developmentally Disabled Assistance and Bill of Rights Act, 42 U.S.C. § 6010 (1982 ed.), intended to place an obligation on the States to provide certain kinds of treatment to the disabled. Respondent Halderman argued that Congress passed § 6010 pursuant to § 5 of the Fourteenth Amendment, and therefore that it was mandatory on the States, regardless of whether they received federal funds. Petitioner and the United States, as respondent, argued that, in passing § 6010, Congress acted pursuant to its spending power alone. Consequently, § 6010 applied only to States accepting federal funds under the Act.

The Court was required to consider the "appropriate test for determining when Congress intends to enforce" the guarantees of the Fourteenth Amendment. We adopted a rule fully cognizant of the traditional power of the States: "Because such legislation imposes congressional policy on a State involuntarily, and because it often intrudes on traditional state authority, we should not quickly attribute to Congress an unstated intent to act under its authority to enforce the Fourteenth Amendment." Because Congress nowhere stated its intent to impose mandatory obligations on the States under its § 5 powers, we concluded that Congress did not do so.

The *Pennhurst* rule looks much like the plain statement rule we apply today. In *EEOC v. Wyoming*, the Court explained that *Pennhurst* established a rule of statutory construction to be applied where statutory intent is ambiguous. In light of the ADEA's clear exclusion of most important public officials, it is at least ambiguous whether Congress intended that appointed judges nonetheless be included. In the face of such ambiguity, we will not attribute to Congress an intent to intrude on state governmental functions regardless of whether Congress acted pursuant to its Commerce Clause powers or § 5 of the Fourteenth Amendment.

[The Court also held that the mandatory retirement requirement for judges did not violate the Equal Protection Clause of the Fourteenth Amendment, rejecting arguments that it was irrational to distinguish between judges who have reached age 70 and younger judges, and between judges 70 and over and other state employees of the same age who are not subject to mandatory retirement.]

JUSTICE WHITE, with whom JUSTICE STEVENS joins, concurring in part, dissenting in part, and concurring in the judgment.

[I] While acknowledging [the] principle of federal legislative supremacy, the majority nevertheless imposes upon Congress a "plain statement" requirement. The majority claims to derive this requirement from the plain statement approach developed in our Eleventh Amendment cases, see, *e.g.*, *Atascadero*, and applied two Terms ago in *Will*. The issue in those cases, however, was whether Congress intended a particular statute to extend to the States *at all*. In *Atascadero*, for example, the issue was whether States could be sued under § 504 of the Rehabilitation Act of 1973, 29 U.S.C. § 794. Similarly, the issue in *Will* was whether States could be sued under 42 U.S.C. § 1983. In the present case, by contrast, Congress has expressly extended the coverage of the ADEA to the States and their employees. Its intention to regulate age discrimination by States is thus "unmistakably clear in the language of the statute." *Atascadero*. The only dispute is over the precise details of the statute's application. We have never extended the plain statement approach that far, and the majority offers no compelling reason for doing so.

The majority also relies heavily on our cases addressing the constitutionality of state exclusion of aliens from public employment. In those cases, we held that although restrictions based on alienage ordinarily are subject to strict scrutiny under the Equal Protection Clause, the scrutiny will be less demanding for exclusion of aliens "from positions intimately related to the process of democratic self-government." This narrow "political function" exception to the strict scrutiny standard is based on the "State's historical power to exclude aliens from participation in its democratic political institutions." *Sugarman*.

It is difficult to see how the "political function" exception supports the majority's plain statement rule. First, the exception merely reflects a determination of the scope of the rights of aliens under the Equal Protection Clause. Reduced scrutiny is appropriate for certain political functions because "the right to govern is reserved to citizens." This conclusion in no way establishes a method for interpreting rights that are statutorily created by Congress, such as the protection from age discrimination in the ADEA. Second, it is one thing to limit *judicially-created* scrutiny, and it is quite another to fashion a restraint on *Congress'* legislative authority, as does the majority; the latter is both counter-majoritarian and an intrusion on a co-equal branch of the Federal Government. Finally, the majority does not explicitly restrict its rule to "functions that go to the heart of representative government," and may in fact be extending it much further to all "state governmental functions."

The majority's plain statement rule is not only unprecedented, it directly contravenes our decisions in *Garcia v. San Antonio Metropolitan Transit Authority* and *South Carolina v. Baker*, 485 U.S. 505 (1988). In those cases we made it clear "that States must find their protection from congressional regulation through the national political process, not through judicially defined spheres of unregulable state activity." We also rejected as "unsound in principle and unworkable in practice" any test for state immunity that requires a judicial determination of which state activities are "traditional," "integral," or "necessary." The majority disregards those decisions in its attempt to carve out areas of state activity that will receive special protection from federal legislation.

The majority's approach is also unsound because it will serve only to confuse the law. First, the majority fails to explain the scope of its rule. Is the rule limited to federal regulation of the qualifications of state officials? Or does it apply more broadly to the regulation of any "state governmental functions"? [Quoting majority opinion.] Second, the majority does not explain its requirement that Congress' intent to regulate a particular state activity be "plain to anyone reading [the federal statute]." Does that mean that it is now improper to look to the purpose or history of a federal statute in determining the scope of the statute's limitations on state activities? If so, the majority's rule is completely inconsistent with our pre-emption jurisprudence. See, *e.g.*, *Hillsborough County v. Automated Medical Laboratories, Inc.*, 471 U.S. 707, 715 (1985) (pre-emption will be found where there is a "clear and manifest *purpose*" to displace state law) (emphasis added). The vagueness of the majority's rule undoubtedly will lead States to assert that various federal statutes no longer apply to a wide variety of State activities if Congress has not expressly referred to those activities in the statute. Congress, in turn, will be forced to draft long and detailed lists of which particular state functions it meant to regulate.

The imposition of such a burden on Congress is particularly out of place in the context of the ADEA. Congress already has stated that all "individual[s] employed by any employer" are protected by the ADEA unless they are expressly excluded by one of the exceptions in the definition of "employee." See 29 U.S.C. § 630(f). The majority, however, turns the statute on its head, holding that state judges are not protected by the ADEA because "Congress has [not] made it clear that judges are *included*." * * *

The majority asserts that its plain statement rule is helpful in avoiding a "potential constitutional problem." It is far from clear, however, why there would be a constitutional problem if the ADEA applied to state judges, in light of our decisions in *Garcia* and *Baker*, discussed above. As long as "the national political *process* did not operate in a defective manner, the Tenth Amendment is not implicated." *Baker*. There is no claim in this case that the political process by which the ADEA was extended to state employees was inadequate to protect the States from being "unduly burden[ed]" by the Federal Government. In any event, as discussed below, a straightforward analysis of the ADEA's definition of "employee" reveals that the ADEA does not apply here. Thus, even if there were potential constitutional problems in extending the ADEA to state judges, the majority's proposed plain statement rule would not be necessary to avoid them in this case. Indeed, because this case can be decided purely on the basis of statutory interpretation, the majority's announcement of its plain statement rule, which purportedly is derived from constitutional principles, *violates* our general practice of avoiding the unnecessary resolution of constitutional issues.

My disagreement with the majority does not end with its unwarranted announcement of the plain statement rule. Even more disturbing is its treatment of Congress' power under § 5 of the Fourteenth Amendment. Section 5 provides that "[t]he Congress shall have power to enforce, by appropriate legislation, the provisions of this article." Despite that sweeping constitutional delegation of authority to Congress, the majority holds that its plain statement rule will apply with full force to legislation enacted to enforce the Fourteenth Amendment. The majority states: "In the face of . . . ambiguity, we will not attribute to Congress an intent to intrude on state governmental functions *regardless of whether Congress acted pursuant to its Commerce Clause powers or § 5 of the Fourteenth Amendment*." (Emphasis added).

The majority's failure to recognize the special status of legislation enacted pursuant to § 5 ignores that, unlike Congress' Commerce Clause power, "[w]hen Congress acts pursuant to § 5, not only is it exercising legislative authority that is plenary within the terms of the constitutional grant, it is exercising that authority under one section of a constitutional Amendment whose other sections by their own terms embody limitations on state authority." *Fitzpatrick v. Bitzer*, 427 U.S. 445, 456 (1976). Indeed, we have held that "principles of federalism that might otherwise be an obstacle to congressional authority are necessarily overridden by the power to enforce the Civil War Amendments 'by appropriate legislation.' Those Amendments were specifically designed as an expansion of federal power and an intrusion on state sovereignty."

The majority relies upon *Pennhurst State School and Hospital v. Halderman*, but that case does not support its approach. There, the Court merely stated that "we should not quickly attribute to Congress an unstated intent to act under its authority to enforce the Fourteenth Amendment." In other words, the *Pennhurst* presumption was designed only to answer the question whether a particular piece of legislation was enacted pursuant to § 5. That is very different from the majority's apparent holding that even when Congress *is* acting pursuant to § 5, it nevertheless must specify the precise details of its enactment.

The majority's departures from established precedent are even more disturbing when it is realized, as discussed below, that this case can be affirmed based on simple statutory construction.

[II] The statute at issue in this case is the ADEA's definition of "employee," which provides:

> "The term 'employee' means an individual employed by any employer except that the term 'employee' shall not include any person elected to public office in any State or political subdivision of any State by the qualified voters thereof, or any person chosen by such officer to be on such officer's personal staff, or an appointee on the policymaking level or an immediate adviser with respect to the exercise of the constitutional or legal powers of the office. The exemption set forth in the preceding sentence shall not include employees subject to the civil service laws of a State government, governmental agency, or political subdivision." 29 U.S.C. § 630(f).

A parsing of that definition reveals that it excludes from the definition of "employee" (and thus the coverage of the ADEA) four types of (non-civil service) state and local employees: (1) persons elected to public office; (2) the personal staff of elected officials; (3) persons appointed by elected officials to be on the policymaking level; and (4) the immediate advisers of elected officials with respect to the constitutional or legal powers of the officials' offices.

The question before us is whether petitioners fall within the third exception. * * * [I] conclude that petitioners are "on the policymaking level."

"Policy" is defined as "a definite course or method of action selected (as by a government, institution, group, or individual) from among alternatives and in the light of given conditions to guide and usu[ally] determine present and future decisions." Webster's Third New International Dictionary 1754 (1976). Applying that definition, it is clear that the decisionmaking engaged in by common-law judges, such as petitioners, places them "on the policymaking level." In resolving disputes, although judges do not operate with unconstrained discretion, they do choose "from among alternatives" and elaborate their choices in order "to guide and . . . determine present and future decisions." * * *

Moreover, it should be remembered that the statutory exception refers to appointees "on the policymaking level," not "policymaking employees." Thus, whether or not judges actually *make* policy, they certainly are on the same *level* as policymaking officials in other branches of government and therefore are covered by the exception. * * *

Petitioners argue that the "appointee[s] on the policymaking level" exception should be construed to apply "only to persons who advise or work closely with the elected official that chose the appointee." In support of that claim, petitioners point out that the exception is "sandwiched" between the "personal staff" and "immediate adviser" exceptions in § 630(f), and thus should be read as covering only similar employees.

Petitioners' premise, however, does not prove their conclusion. It is true that the placement of the "appointee" exception between the "personal staff" and "immediate adviser" exceptions suggests a similarity among the three. But the most obvious similarity is simply that each of the three sets of employees are connected in some way with elected officials: the first and third sets have a certain working relationship with elected officials, while the second is *appointed* by elected officials. There is no textual support for concluding that the second set must *also* have a close working relationship with elected officials. Indeed, such a reading would tend to make the "appointee" exception superfluous since the "personal staff" and "immediate adviser" exceptions would seem to cover most appointees who are in a close working relationship with elected officials.

Petitioners seek to rely on legislative history, but it does not help their position. There is little legislative history discussing the definition of "employee" in the ADEA, so petitioners point to the legislative history of the identical definition in Title VII, 42 U.S.C. § 2000e(f). If anything, that history tends to confirm that the "appointee[s] on the policymaking level" exception was designed to exclude from the coverage of the ADEA all high-level appointments throughout state government structures, including judicial appointments. * * *

[The dissenting opinion of JUSTICE BLACKMUN, joined by JUSTICE MARSHALL, is omitted.]

NOTES ON *GREGORY* AND CLEAR STATEMENT RULES

1. *Contrasting Approaches.* As Justice O'Connor noted, there is a respectable textual argument that the ADEA exceptions do not apply to appointed judges, in part because of the *noscitur a sociis* canon. But note that every other potential source of statutory meaning points in the other direction. See Philip Frickey, *Lawnet: The Case of the Missing (Tenth) Amendment*, 75 Minn. L. Rev. 755 (1991).

Consider first the absurd-result exception to the plain meaning approach, which even textualists will sometimes apply.[o] On the face of it, the exceptions provision to the ADEA seems to take elected judges completely out of the statute (and thus they can be required to step down at age 70), but protects appointed judges against any retirement requirement. This seems absolutely backwards from any public-policy perspective: if superannuated judges are to remain in authority, presumably that judgment should be made by the voters on a judge-by-judge basis, not as a categorical decision made by Congress. Why would Congress want to hogtie states in this manner? On the other hand, does the "absurdity" here rise to the level called for by Justice Kennedy in his separate opinion in *Public Citizen* (Chapter 7, § 2)? Is the apparent distinction between elected and appointed judges so irrational as to raise a serious

---

o. See Justice Kennedy's separate opinion in *Public Citizen* (Chapter 7, § 2) and Justice Scalia's separate opinion in *Bock Laundry* (Chapter 7, § 3).

constitutional question that should be avoided through statutory interpretation (cf. *Catholic Bishop of Chicago*)?

Sources of statutory meaning available to nontextualists strongly cut against the apparent plain meaning of the ADEA exceptions provision as well. The legislative history, irrelevant to Justice O'Connor because of her application of a super-strong clear statement rule, supports excepting these judges from the statute, as explained in a portion of Justice White's separate opinion that we have deleted. The statutory purpose, again irrelevant to Justice O'Connor's approach, seems narrower than the plain meaning of the exception; at least as originally conceived, the ADEA was designed to protect workers from being replaced by younger employees who would accept lower pay, and had little to do with persons who possess guaranteed tenure and who would be replaced by persons receiving the same salary. From the standpoint of public values, as Justice O'Connor suggests, the people of the state ought to be able to choose how to structure important governmental positions. But this need not lead to the creation of a super-strong clear statement rule: any kind of canon (a presumption at the outset, a tiebreaker at the end, a factor to be weighed in the interpretive process) based on federalism would surely be sufficient to tip the case to the conclusion Justice O'Connor desired. Why create the canonical equivalent of a nuclear weapon when a fly swatter would have been sufficient?

For a more recent debate among the Justices as to the application of the federalism canons in the context of the ADEA, compare *Kimel v. Florida Bd. of Regents*, 528 U.S. 62 (2000) (O'Connor, J., for the Court, finding that the ADEA does make it "unmistakably clear" that its remedial provision abrogates the states' Eleventh Amendment immunity from suit, but finding the abrogation unconstitutional), with *id.* at 654–59 (Thomas, J., dissenting in part) (arguing that the ADEA is not sufficiently clear in abrogating state Eleventh Amendment immunity). Does it matter which approach is taken? (Four dissenting Justices found statutory abrogation and believed it constitutional.)

2. *When Does the Canon Apply? What Does It Require?* As Justice White stressed, it is by no means clear what Congress must do to comply with the *Gregory* canon. Must Congress rely upon its legislative authority under section 5 of the Fourteenth Amendment, or may it rely upon its commerce power as well? To what kinds of state governmental operations does the canon apply? Note that in *Garcia* one justification for overruling *National League of Cities* was that the standard identified there for state immunity from federal regulation — the federal government could not "directly displace the States' freedom to structure integral operations in areas of traditional government functions" — proved too vague for any consistent application in the lower courts. Is the *Gregory* canon any clearer?

One would think that, at a minimum, the canon applies with full force to federal regulation of state judges. One would be wrong. In *Chisom v. Roemer* (Chapter 7, § 3), the majority of the Court applied section 2 of the Voting Rights Act to the election of state judges without any mention of the *Gregory* canon. *Chisom* and *Gregory* were decided *the same day*, and Justice O'Connor was in the majority in *Chisom* (and, of course, the author of *Gregory*)! Justice Scalia, dissenting in *Chisom*, began with his textualist approach, concluded that the key statutory term "representatives" did not include judges, and then asked whether any canon suggested a deviation from the textualist answer. He then had this to say:

> If the [*Gregory*] principle were applied here, we would have double reason to give "representatives" its ordinary meaning. It is true, however, that in *Gregory* interpreting the statute to include judges would have made them the only high-level state officials affected, whereas here the question is whether judges were excluded from a general imposition upon state elections that unquestionably exists; and in *Gregory* it was questionable whether Congress was invoking its powers under the Fourteenth Amendment (rather than merely the Commerce Clause), whereas here it is obvious. Perhaps those factors suffice to distinguish the two cases. Moreover, we tacitly rejected a "plain statement" rule as applied to unamended § 2 in *City of Rome v. United States*, 446 U.S. 156 (1980), though arguably that was before the rule had developed the significance it currently has. I am content to dispense with the "plain statement" rule in the present case[,] but it says something about the Court's approach to today's decision that the possibility of applying that rule never crossed its mind.

Fairly read, is *Gregory* susceptible to the potential distinctions between it and *Chisom* that Justice Scalia suggests? If not, are the two cases simply irreconcilable?

3. *The Relationship of Textualism and Super-Strong Clear Statement Rules*. Under Justice Scalia's formula for textualism set forth in his dissenting opinion in *Chisom*, it is critical to know what the "established canons" are and how they operate. How can the *Gregory* canon be an "established" one, when in fact the case took what was at most a presumption in prior cases and transformed it into a super-strong clear statement rule? What is Justice Scalia doing in the *Gregory* majority? Why didn't he join Justice White's more textualist concurring opinion?

Critics could suggest that cases like *Gregory* demonstrate that textualism fails to live up to its promise of providing objective interpretive methods in the face of outcomes judges cannot tolerate. In other words, every human interpretive technique, including textualism, needs a "safety valve" of some sort. For liberals, the *Holy Trinity Church* "purpose trumps plain meaning" approach sometimes serves this purpose, as in *Weber*. For conservative textualists who care about federalism, the safety valve when textualism gets them boxed in, as in *Gregory*, is the creation of a super-strong clear statement rule that trumps the result suggested by ordinary meaning. Is it fair to say that *Gregory* undercuts the textualist principle of constraining judicial discretion in interpretation? Is it fair to go even further and suggest that *Gregory* and *Chisom*, when read together, undermine the very notion of predictability and coherence in interpretation?

Another concern about *Gregory* is whether the notion of deference to ultimate congressional determination is more illusion than reality. The congressional agenda is limited, access to it is skewed in a variety of ways (toward more powerful interests, toward the interests of the federal, state, and local governments, and so on), and it is far easier to kill a bill than to pass a bill. Thus, in many circumstances at least, the use of a super-strong clear statement rule may be as "countermajoritarian" as invalidating the statute outright.

Yet another concern is whether the use of such rules may actually encourage judicial activism because it seems far easier to use them than to do constitutional decisionmaking. Because a decision like *Gregory* is made at the interpretive rather than the constitutional level, the visibility of the decision is lower and the attention paid to it even inside the Court may be less. Contrast the reaction to *Gregory* (except in limited academic and states' rights circles, virtually nothing) to the reaction to a hypothetical overruling of *Garcia* and a return to *National League of Cities* (where the Court's disrespect for stare decisis and return to a regime already arguably demonstrated to be unworkable would surely cause considerable controversy).

Ultimately, probably the most important question about the new superstrong clear statement rules is normative. In *Gregory*, for example, should the Court be promoting the value of federalism so strongly, or should it defer more to the political process (Congress and the President) to protect the states? Should the Court take into account congressional structures designed to protect federalism interests, such as the Unfunded Mandates Reform Act discussed in Chapter 4, § 3? Can textualists provide any objective grounding for the values promoted by their super-strong clear statement rules? Consider these quandaries in light of the next case.

BFP v. RESOLUTION TRUST CORP., 511 U.S. 531 (1994). Section 548 of the Bankruptcy Code, 11 U.S.C. § 548, sets forth the powers of a trustee in bankruptcy to avoid "fraudulent transfers" made within a year of the debtor's bankruptcy. Section 548(a)(2)(A) permits avoidance if the trustee can establish (1) that the debtor had an interest in property; (2) that a transfer of that interest occurred within one year of the filing of the bankruptcy petition; (3) that the debtor was insolvent at the time of the transfer or became insolvent as a result thereof; and (4) that the debtor received "less than a reasonably equivalent value in exchange for such transfer." The debtor in this case (BFP) was a company formed to buy a house; the lender subsequently foreclosed on the mortgage to the house and sold it at a foreclosure sale for $433,000; BFP filed for federal bankruptcy and moved to set aside the sale on the ground that $433,000 did not represent the home's "reasonably equivalent value," which BFP estimated at $725,000.

Justice Scalia, for the majority of the Court, held that "reasonably equivalent value," in the context of a foreclosure sale in compliance with state law, meant whatever price the property fetched, however low. Justice Scalia reasoned that tests invoking "fair market value" have no applicability in the forced-sale context. " 'The market value of . . . a piece of property is the price which it might be expected to bring if offered for sale in a fair market; not the price which might be obtained on a sale at public auction or a sale forced by the necessities of the owner, but such a price as would be fixed by negotiation and mutual agreement, after ample time to find a purchaser, as between a vendor who is willing (but not compelled) to sell and a purchaser who desires to buy but is not compelled to take the particular . . . piece of property.' Black's Law

Dictionary 971 (6th ed. 1990). In short, 'fair market value' presumes market conditions that, by definition, simply do not obtain in the context of a forced sale. An appraiser's reconstruction of 'fair market value' could show what similar property would be worth if it did not have to be sold within the time and manner strictures of state-prescribed foreclosure. But property that must be sold within those strictures is simply worth less."

Justice Souter, in dissent, objected that Justice Scalia's reading is at war with the "plain meaning" of the statutory text, which requires the trustee to evaluate the reasonableness of the transfer price, and the judicial inquiry is similar to other common law "reasonableness" ones. Moreover, Justice Souter observed, Justice Scalia's interpretation was considered and rejected by Congress in 1984, when it specifically extended § 548 to cover foreclosure sales.

Justice Scalia responded that the dissenters overlooked the extent to which a "reasonableness" inquiry would upset state foreclosure law. The purpose of foreclosure law is to establish procedures that will effect conveyance of property fairly and finally; any post hoc federal "reasonableness" inquiry would unsettle the finality of titles. "Absent an explicit statutory requirement to the contrary, we must assume the validity of this state-law regulatory background and take due account of its effect. 'The existence and force and function of established institutions of local government are always in the consciousness of lawmakers and, while their weight may vary, they may never be completely overlooked in the task of interpretation.' *Davies Warehouse Co. v. Bowles*, 321 U.S. 144, 154 (1944). Cf. *Gregory v. Ashcroft*."

Justice Scalia continued: "Federal statutes impinging upon important state interests 'cannot . . . be construed without regard to the implications of our dual system of government. . . . [W]hen the Federal Government takes over . . . local radiations in the vast network of our national economic enterprise and thereby radically readjusts the balance of state and national authority, those charged with the duty of legislating [must be] reasonably explicit.' F. Frankfurter, Some Reflections on the Reading of Statutes, 47 Colum. L. Rev. 527, 539–540 (1947). It is beyond question that an essential state interest is at issue here: we have said that 'the general welfare of society is involved in the security of the titles to real estate' and the power to ensure that security 'inheres in the very nature of [state] government.' *American Land Co. v. Zeiss*, 219 U.S. 47, 60 (1911). Nor is there any doubt that the interpretation urged by petitioner would have a profound effect upon that interest: the title of every piece of realty purchased at foreclosure would be under a federally created cloud. * * * To displace traditional State regulation in such a manner, the federal statutory purpose must be 'clear and manifest,' *English v. General Electric Co.*, 496 U.S. 72, 79 (1990). Cf. *Gregory v. Ashcroft*. Otherwise, the Bankruptcy Code will be construed to adopt, rather than to displace, pre-existing state law."

Justice Souter sharply criticized Justice Scalia's reliance on *Gregory*, which involved direct federal regulation of state employment rather than federal preemption of state regulatory power over the private sector. Justice Souter argued that *Gregory* concerns were not implicated, since *Gregory* had limited its rule to federal intrusions on matters "essential to their [the states'] independence." Au contraire, insisted Justice Scalia, "[t]his ignores the fact that it is not state authority over debtor-creditor law in general that is at stake in this case, but the essential sovereign interest in the security and stability of title to land."

NOTES ON THE *GREGORY-BFP* RULE IN ACTION AND CRITICISMS OF THE NEW FEDERALISM CANONS

1. BFP *in Action: the Predictability Problem.* Was *BFP* a predictable application of *Gregory*? If the outcome is mostly supportable by the policies of avoiding undue judicial interference with real estate markets and promoting efficiency in bankruptcy proceedings, should the majority have explicitly relied upon these policies rather than used the *Gregory* canon? No party in *BFP* had even cited *Gregory*, nor did the Ninth Circuit, whose interpretation was affirmed in *BFP*.

Nor is it clear how broadly *BFP* should be read. It might simply be an example of the presumption against federal preemption of traditional state regulatory regimes such as property, tort, *Cipollone v. Liggett Group, Inc.,* 505 U.S. 504 (1992); and family law. See *Rose v. Rose,* 481 U.S. 619, 635–36 (1987) (O'Connor, J., concurring). Or it might be a tougher clear statement rule when federal regulation threatens not only to preempt but also disrupt an area of traditional state regulation. Such arguments have been frequently made in recent years. Over Justice Scalia's objection, the Court was sympathetic to this argument in *Gonzales v. Oregon,* 546 U.S. 243 (2006), where the Department of Justice sought to preempt a state aid in dying law. Justice Scalia's plurality opinion in *Rapanos v. United States,* 126 S.Ct. 2208, 2224–25 (2006), followed *BFP* to overrule agency wetlands regulations that displaced large swaths of state property law. (*BFP* and *Rapanos,* read together, suggest that state property law regimes get more Supreme Court protection than tort regimes.)

2. *The Need for Super-Strong Rules Once the Court Gives Teeth to Previously Underenforced Constitutional Norms?* Does the *Gregory* rule add anything to the rule to avoid constitutional questions? Perhaps as a special application of the avoidance canon, *Gregory* might be defended on the ground that the Tenth Amendment was underenforced by the Supreme Court, which had rarely invalidated federal laws because they intruded into core state functions.[p] (The Court in *National League of Cities* in 1976 had invalidated such a law, but *Garcia* overruled it.) After *Gregory,* the Court has invalidated several federal statutory provisions on the ground that they commandeered state officials in violation of the Tenth Amendment. See *Printz v. United States,* 521 U.S. 898 (1997); *New York v. United States,* 505 U.S. 144 (1992). If these cases augur an overruling or narrowing of *Garcia,* should the Court trim back its use of the *Gregory* rule? See also *Kimel v. Florida Bd. of Regents,* 528 U.S. 62 (2000) (Court finds clear statement in ADEA abrogating

---

p. This was the defense provided *Gregory* in William Eskridge, Jr. & Philip Frickey, *Quasi-Constitutional Law: Clear Statement Rules as Constitutional Lawmaking,* 45 Vand. L. Rev. 593 (1992).

states' Eleventh Amendment immunity and then rules the abrogation unconstitutional).

The parallel to the avoidance canon suggests a further criticism of the *Gregory-BFP* rule: it is a kind of stealth constitutionalism.[q] If the Supreme Court had struck down the ADEA or Bankruptcy Act provisions as violations of the Tenth Amendment in these two cases, you can be sure that the *New York Times* would have given the cases front-page treatment; probably, a certain amount of controversy would have ensued. By announcing these results in statutory, rather than constitutional decisions, the Court avoided any serious public scrutiny or controversy (even Linda Greenhouse missed *BFP*). Was the Rehnquist Court in the 1990s behaving much like the Warren Court in the 1950s — so if you approve *Witkovich*, you might have to swallow *BFP*?

3. *The Problem of Congressional Reliance. Bait and Switch?* In Chapter 7, § 3C, we suggested that one important factor in assessing any theory of statutory interpretation is whether it is compatible with the assumptions about law held by other legal actors (the Congress, the President, attorneys, citizens). One way of criticizing the Court's creation of new super-strong clear statement rules is, then, to focus on the ways in which our political system has relied upon understandings that the Court is now unraveling through the use of these rules. The use of reliance arguments in statutory interpretation appeals not just to the traditional conservative idea of legislative supremacy, but also answers the Court's frequent riposte that legislative supremacy is not implicated unless something is clear on the face of the statute. Consider the following example.

The Education of the Handicapped Act (EHA) is a comprehensive statutory scheme to assure that disabled children may receive a free public education appropriate to their needs. The Act guarantees parental rights to participate in state planning of their children's educational needs and to challenge state plans they don't like. The statute imposes pervasive obligations on state and local governments, and it provides that "[a]ny party aggrieved by the findings and decision [made in the state or local administrative process] shall have the right to bring a civil action . . . in any State court of competent jurisdiction or in a district court of the United States without regard to the amount in controversy." 20 U.S.C. § 1415(e)(2). EHA's sponsor made it clear "that a parent or guardian may present a complaint alleging that a State or local educational agency has refused to provide services to which a child may be entitled" and may sue state and local governments in state or federal court. 121 Cong. Rec. 37415 (1975).

When the EHA was enacted in 1975, the above-noted evidence would probably have sufficed to abrogate the states' Eleventh Amendment immunity from suit in federal court, pursuant to *Employees v. Missouri Dep't of Public Health & Welfare*, 411 U.S. 279 (1973) (general jurisdictional grant plus explicit legislative history would be sufficient to abrogate Eleventh Amend-

---

q. William Eskridge, Jr. & Philip Frickey, *The Supreme Court, 1993 Term—Foreword: Law as Equilibrium*, 108 Harv. L. Rev. 4 (1994), criticizing *BFP* and related decisions as examples of stealth constitutionalism.

ment immunity). In *Atascadero State Hospital v. Scanlon*, 473 U.S. 234 (1985), however, the Court changed the rule for congressional abrogation of Eleventh Amendment immunity: "Congress may abrogate the States' constitutionally secured immunity from suit in federal court only by making its intention unmistakably clear in the language of the statute." The Court held that the Rehabilitation Act of 1973, another statute protecting the disabled, did not abrogate states' immunity, because there was no clear textual indication of such abrogation.

Sensing that the rules had changed, and reacting to the Court's restrictive interpretation of the Rehabilitation Act, Congress in 1986 enacted the following: "A State shall not be immune under the Eleventh Amendment * * * from suit in Federal Court for a violation of [enumerated provisions of the Rehabilitation Act], or the provisions of any other Federal statute prohibiting discrimination by recipients of Federal financial assistance." The latter clause clearly covers the EHA. Then, in *Dellmuth v. Muth*, 491 U.S. 223 (1989), a case that arose before the 1986 amendment, the Court held that the EHA did not abrogate state immunity. The Court pointed to the 1986 statute as a good example of the drafting clarity needed to abrogate immunity, and held that there was no abrogation before 1986.

Poor Congress. It thought it had abrogated state immunity in 1975, and given precedent in 1975 it probably had done so. Then it reiterated its intent in 1986, but the new statute was used by the Court to confirm Congress' failure to abrogate in 1975. This might be amusing if important rights were not involved.[r] The matter might become even worse for Congress. Following *Kimel*, the Supreme Court in *Board of Trustees, Univ. of Ala. v. Garrett*, 531 U.S. 356 (2001), ruled that Congress had no power under the Fourteenth Amendment to abrogate the states' Eleventh Amendment immunity in the Americans with Disabilities Act. The Court reasoned that Congress had not found enough of a "history and pattern" of intentional discrimination against people with disabilities by the states themselves to justify the exercise of its enforcement power under the Fourteenth Amendment. Under *Garrett*, Congress' repeated efforts to render the states liable for violations of the EHA might ultimately fail on constitutional grounds.

In assessing the statutory interpretation developments, be certain first that you understand the force of the *Atascadero* clear statement rule: Not only does it require abrogation of state immunity in the statute's text, without regard to legislative history, but the abrogation must be explicit and really clear. E.g., *Hoffman v. Connecticut Dep't of Income Maintenance*, 492 U.S. 96 (1989); *Will v. Michigan Dep't of State Police*, 491 U.S. 58 (1989). Thus *Atascadero*, like *Gregory*, fits our definition of a "super-strong clear statement rule." Others that the Court has created include the toughened rule against waivers of federal sovereign immunity, *United States v. Nordic Village*, 503 U.S. 30

---

r. Congress immediately overrode *Dellmuth* in the Education of the Handicapped Act of 1990, Pub. L. No. 101–476, § 103, 104 Stat. 1103, 1106, again with complaints that its expectations had been thwarted. It took Congress three statutes to effectuate a policy it thought had been effectuated in 1975.

(1992); the toughened rule against extraterritorial application of federal statutes, *EEOC v. Arabian American Oil Co.*, 499 U.S. 244 (1991); the rule against congressional derogation of traditional presidential powers, *Japan Whaling Ass'n v. American Cetacean Society*, 478 U.S. 221 (1986); and the rule created in 1981 that congressional conditions of grants to the states be explicit and clear, *Pennhurst State School and Hospital v. Halderman*, 451 U.S. 1 (1981).

A recent bait-and-switch debate occurred under the *Pennhurst* rule. Congress in a 1986 statute provided for "reasonable attorneys' fees as part of the costs" to prevailing litigants (usually parents) in cases arising under the Individuals with Disabilities Education Act. In *Arlington Central School District Board of Education v. Murphy*, 126 S.Ct. 2455 (2006), the Court invoked *Pennhurst* to require a more targeted statement in order to justify recovery of expert fees as part of an attorney's fees award. Dissenting Justices accused the Court of bait-and-switch: when Congress added the fees provision in 1986, it had every reason to believe — and the relevant committees expressed a belief — that the enacted language was sufficient to justify the award of expert witness fees. Such belief was undone by Supreme Court decisions handed down in 1987 and 1991 (*Casey*, digested in Chapter 7, § 3A) — decisions which Congress immediately overrode in the Civil Rights Act of 1991. The *Murphy* Court not only ignored the 1991 override, but cited the earlier decisions as confirming evidence that there was a plain meaning that trumped Congress's expectations. (Congress's override only extended to job discrimination cases, and not IDEA cases.)

The *Murphy* dissenters had another argument the *Dellmuth* dissenters did not have. It was not disputed that the 1986 statute not only added a provision giving attorneys' fees and other costs to prevailing parents, but also charged the GAO with collecting fee data and analyzing "the range of such *fees, costs and expenses* awarded in the actions and proceedings under such section, * * *and * * * *the number of hours spent by personnel, including attorneys and consultants.*" (Emphasis added.) The legislative history confirmed that this section was written under Congress's assumption that the 1986 authorization included expert witness fees. Thus, the parents had an argument grounded in the whole act, as well as the legislative history. The Court found this whole act evidence insufficient to refute the conventional text-based evidence. The dissenters expressed astonishment that the majority did not concede there was at least ambiguity in the statute, given this dramatic evidence.

C. DEBUNKING AND DEFENDING THE CANONS OF STATUTORY INTERPRETATION

KARL LLEWELLYN, *REMARKS ON THE THEORY OF APPELLATE DECISION AND THE RULES OR CANONS ABOUT HOW STATUTES ARE TO BE CONSTRUED*
3 Vand. L. Rev. 395, 401–06 (1950). Reprinted by permission.

When it comes to presenting a proposed construction in court, there is an accepted conventional vocabulary. As in argument over points of case-law, the accepted convention still, unhappily, requires discussion as if only one single correct meaning could exist. Hence there are two opposing canons on almost every point. An arranged selection is appended. Every lawyer must be familiar with them all: they are still needed tools of argument. At least as early as Fortescue the general picture was clear, on this, to any eye which would see.

Plainly, to make any canon take hold in a particular instance, the construction contended for must be sold, essentially, by means other than the use of the canon: The good sense of the situation and a *simple* construction of the available language to achieve that sense, *by tenable means, out of the statutory language.*

Canons of Construction

Statutory interpretation still speaks a diplomatic tongue. Here is some of the technical framework for maneuver.

Thrust	**But**	**Parry**
1. A statute cannot go beyond its text.		1. To effect its purpose a statute may be implemented beyond its text.
2. Statutes in derogation of the common law will not be extended by construction.		2. Such acts will be liberally construed if their nature is remedial.
3. Statutes are to be read in the light of the common law and a statute affirming a common law rule is to be construed in accordance with the common law.		3. The common law gives way to a statute which is inconsistent with it and when a statute is designed as a revision of a whole body of law applicable to a given subject it supersedes the common law.
4. Where a foreign statute which has received construction has been adopted, previous construction is adopted too.		4. It may be rejected where there is conflict with the obvious meaning of the statute or where the foreign decisions are unsatisfactory in reasoning or where the foreign interpretation is not in harmony with the spirit or policy of the laws of the adopting state.
5. Where various states have already adopted the statute, the parent state is followed.		5. Where interpretations of other states are inharmonious, there is no such restraint.

6. Statutes in pari materia must be construed together.

6. A statute is not in pari materia if its scope and aim are distinct or where a legislative design to depart from the general purpose or policy of previous enactments may be apparent.

7. A statute imposing a new penalty or forfeiture, or a new liability or disability, or creating a new right of action will not be construed as having a retroactive effect.

7. Remedial statutes are to be liberally construed and if a retroactive interpretation will promote the ends of justice, they should receive such construction.

8. Where design has been distinctly stated no place is left for construction.

8. Courts have the power to inquire into real — as distinct from ostensible — purpose.

9. Definitions and rules of construction contained in an interpretation clause are part of the law and binding.

9. Definitions and rules of construction in a statute will not be extended beyond their necessary import nor allowed to defeat intention otherwise manifested.

10. A statutory provision requiring liberal construction does not mean disregard of unequivocal requirements of the statute.

10. Where a rule of construction is provided within the statute itself the rule should be applied.

11. Titles do not control meaning; preambles do not expand scope; section headings do not change language.

11. The title may be consulted as a guide when there is doubt or obscurity in the body; preambles may be consulted to determine rationale, and thus the true construction of terms; section headings may be looked upon as part of the statute itself.

12. If language is plain and unambiguous it must be given effect.

12. Not when literal interpretation would lead to absurd or mischievous consequences or thwart manifest purpose.

13. Words and phrases which have received judicial construction before enactment are to be understood according to that construction.

13. Not if the statute clearly requires them to have a different meaning.

14. After enactment, judicial decision upon interpretation of particular terms and phrases controls.

14. Practical construction by executive officers is strong evidence of true meaning.

15. Words are to be taken in their ordinary meaning unless they are technical terms or words of art.

15. Popular words may bear a technical meaning and technical words may have a popular signification and they should be so construed as to agree with evident intention or to make the statute operative.

16. Every word and clause must be given effect.

16. If inadvertently inserted or if repugnant to the rest of the statute, they may be rejected as surplusage.

17. The same language used repeatedly in the same connection is presumed to bear the same meaning throughout the statute.

17. This presumption will be disregarded where it is necessary to assign different meanings to make the statute consistent.

18. Words are to be interpreted according to the proper grammatical effect of their arrangement within the statute.

18. Rules of grammar will be disregarded where strict adherence would defeat purpose.

19. Exceptions not made cannot be read.

19. The letter is only the "bark." Whatever is within the reason of the law is within the law itself.

20. Expression of one thing excludes another.

20. The language may fairly comprehend many different cases where some only are expressly mentioned by way of example.

21. General terms are to receive a general construction.

21. They may be limited by specific terms with which they are associated or by the scope and purpose of the statute.

22. It is a general rule of construction that where general words follow an enumeration they are to be held as applying only to persons and things of the same general kind or class specifically mentioned (*ejusdem generis*).

22. General words must operate on something. Further, ejusdem generis is only an aid in getting the meaning and does not warrant confining the operations of a statute within narrower limits than were intended.

23. Qualifying or limiting words or clauses are to be referred to the next preceding antecedent.

23. Not when evident sense and meaning require a different construction.

24. Punctuation will govern when a statute is open to two constructions.

24. Punctuation marks will not control the plain and evident meaning of language.

25. It must be assumed that language has been chosen with due regard to grammatical propriety and is not interchangeable on mere conjecture.

25. "And" and "or" may be read interchangeably whenever the change is necessary to give the statute sense and effect.

26. There is a distinction between words of permission and mandatory words.

26. Words imparting permission may be read as mandatory and words imparting command may be read as permissive when such construction is made necessary by evident intention or by the rights of the public.

27. A proviso qualifies the provision immediately preceding.

27. It may clearly be intended to have a wider scope.

28. When the enacting clause is general, a proviso is construed strictly.

28. Not when it is necessary to extend the proviso to persons or cases which come within its equity.

NOTES ON THE INTELLECTUAL WARFARE OVER CANONS OF STATUTORY INTERPRETATION

1. *Assault on the Citadel by Legal Realists and Critical Scholars.* Llewellyn's wonderful *tour de farce* is a justly celebrated exposure of the many faces of the canons of statutory construction, and it is representative of the legal realists' tendency to debunk legal formalisms. Their view was that nothing turned on them. Canons of construction, for example, "are useful only as facades, which for an occasional judge may add luster to an argument persuasive for other reasons." Frank Newman & Stanley Surrey, *Legislation — Cases and Materials* 654 (1955). Critical scholars of the 1970s and 1980s did not focus on the canons, but the perspective of many of them (intellectual heirs to the most skeptical realists) would go one step further. The canons are just part of the mystifying game that is played with legal logic, which is ultimately indeterminate. Critical scholars argue that legal reasoning can be oppressive by denying its own contingency, i.e., denying that there are other ways of looking at the situation. Perhaps the canons of construction might be deemed similarly oppressive, for they are part of the linguistic and logical pretense that the legislature goes about its work in a methodical, rational way

and that judicial interpreters can scientifically discern the proper meaning through simple rules.

2. *Legal Process Defense of the Canons.* Conventional legal process thinkers have tended to defend at least some of the canons against the mockery of the realists. For example, Henry Hart, Jr. & Albert Sacks, *The Legal Process* 1191 (Eskridge & Frickey eds. 1994) (tent. ed. 1958), responded to Llewellyn as follows:

> All this [skepticism], it is ventured, involves a misunderstanding of the function of the canons, and at bottom of the problem of interpretation itself. Of course, there are pairs of maxims susceptible of being invoked for opposing conclusions. Once it is understood that meaning depends upon context and that contexts vary, how could it be otherwise? Maxims should not be treated, any more than a dictionary, as saying what meaning a word or group of words *must* have in a given context. They simply answer the question whether a particular meaning is linguistically permissible, if the context warrants it. Is this not a useful function?

Professor Dickerson suggests that some of the canons "reflect the probabilities generated by normal usage or legislative behavior. These represent either (1) lexicographical judgments of how legislatures tend to use language and its syntactical patterns, or (2) descriptions of how legislatures tend to behave. They serve as useful presumptions of supposed actual legislative intent and are, therefore, modestly useful in carrying [out] legislative meaning." Reed Dickerson, *The Interpretation and Application of Statutes* 228 (1975).

3. *The Law & Economics Debate over the Canons.* The canons were subjected to sharp criticism by Judge Richard Posner in *Statutory Interpretation — In the Classroom and in the Courtroom*, 50 U. Chi. L. Rev. 800, 806–07 (1983). Judge Posner complains that "most of the canons are just wrong" in that (1) they do not reflect a code by which legislatures draft statutes, (2) they are not even common-sense guides to interpretation, (3) they do not operate to constrain the discretion of judges, and (4) they do not force legislatures to draft statutes with care. Judge Posner blasts one canon after another — from the plain meaning rule to expressio unius to the whole act rule — by showing that the canons rest on wholly unrealistic conceptions of the legislative process. For example, many of the canons erroneously assume legislative omniscience (*id.* at 811):

> Most canons of statutory construction go wrong not because they misconceive the nature of judicial interpretation or of the legislative or political process but because they impute omniscience to Congress. Omniscience is always an unrealistic assumption, and particularly so when one is dealing with the legislative process. The basic reason why statutes are so frequently ambiguous in application is not that they are poorly drafted — though many are — and not that the legislators failed to agree on just what they wanted to accomplish in the statute — though often they do fail — but that a statute necessarily is drafted in advance of, and with imperfect appreciation for the problems that will be encountered in, its application.

For a contrary position, Einer Elhauge, *Preference-Estimating Statutory Default Rules*, 102 Colum. L. Rev. 2027 (2002), argues that many of the canons actually "minimize political dissatisfaction with statutory results."

Congress, Elhauge suggests, is perfectly happy that the Court smooths over statutory potholes, integrates statutes with the larger legal terrain, and even sends some sensitive issues back for more work. Which is the more credible understanding of Congress? Can both be right?

From an economic point of view, it may be better to view the canons ex ante rather than ex post. Under an ex ante perspective, it may not matter whether a canon reflects legislative realities. Instead, the question is this: Does the legal process, including the lawmaking process, work *better* with this set of rules than with another set or with no rules at all? The canons might also be defended from an economic point of view as an *interpretive regime* that affords greater predictability for statutory interpreters. See William Eskridge, Jr. & John Ferejohn, *Politics, Interpretation, and the Rule of Law*, in *The Rule of Law* 265, 282–85 (Ian Shapiro ed. 1994), as well as Appendix B to this Casebook (a complex array of more than two hundred canons followed by the Rehnquist-Roberts Court), and Adrian Vermeule, *Interpretive Choice*, 75 NYU L. Rev. 74, 140–43 (2000), who argues that the Court should just pick a set of canons and stick with them. The problem with the canons as an interpretive regime is that the canons are not deployed in a completely predictable manner. (See the Brudney and Ditslear article, excerpted below, for some recent evidence along these lines.)

Also from an ex ante point of view, some of the canons can be understood as institutional default rules. The best example is the rule of lenity: when the Court interprets criminal statutes narrowly, Congress typically returns to the issue and often overrides the Court with a better-specified statutory crime. See William Eskridge, Jr., *Overriding Supreme Court Statutory Interpretation Decisions*, 101 Yale L.J. 331 (1991), as well as our notes after *Muscarello* and *McNally*. This dovetails perfectly with the best justification for the rule of lenity, the nondelegation idea. Eskridge and Frickey, *Quasi-Constitutional Law*, *supra*, argue that the avoidance canon, the federalism canons, and separation of powers canons can also be understood as requiring Congress — and not agencies or judges — to deliberate and decide to press constitutional envelopes. Accord, Einer Elhauge, *Preference-Eliciting Statutory Default Rules*, 102 Colum. L. Rev. 2162 (2002).

4. *Pragmatic Defenses of the Canons.* Geoffrey Miller, *Pragmatics and the Maxims of Interpretation*, 1990 Wis. L. Rev. 1179, presents a defense of many of the linguistic canons, showing them to be consistent with the teachings of (Gricean) philosophical linguistics. Gricean theory understands communication as a purposive, cooperative endeavor, and communicative precepts are means by which cooperation is facilitated. Thus, the canons might be understood as essential to the communicative process and therefore inevitable.

Perhaps the least ambitious defense of the canons is to posit that they are just a checklist of things to think about when approaching a statute. If context will guide interpretation of statutes whose language is ambiguous (and some whose language is not), then the canons may at least be a catalogue of contextual factors which might be investigated. Expressio unius, in this way, will stimulate an investigation into why the legislators did include only one thing and not the other. The rule of lenity will remind interpreters that penal laws require greater clarity and justification in their prohibitions, and that one should be aware of fairness problems in particular. The whole act maxim will suggest that other parts of the statute, including definitional provisions, be read for clues about how the drafters used certain words, phrases, and concepts. And so on.

Professor Mermin says that the canons of construction are similar to folksayings. Samuel Mermin, *Law and the Legal System: An Introduction* 264 (2d ed. 1982). Does "haste make waste" have any validity as a suggestion on how to live? What about "the early bird catches the worm," one obvious "parry" to this "thrust"? Or "nothing ventured, nothing gained" versus "discretion is the better part of valor"? Don't all of those sayings have some truth in them, depending upon the context? Do any of these sayings provide guidance in decisionmaking, or do they simply provide a *post hoc* explanation of why we made a certain decision? Judge Posner believes that the canons never contribute to judicial decisionmaking. Is this a decisive objection to them?

5. *Openly Normative Visions of the Canons.* Some scholars argue that the substantive canons represent a way for "public values" drawn from the Constitution, federal statutes, and the common law to play an important role in statutory interpretation. William Eskridge, Jr., *Public Values in Statutory Interpretation*, 137 U. Pa. L. Rev. 1007 (1989). Cass Sunstein, *Interpreting Statutes in the Regulatory State*, 103 Harv. L. Rev. 405, 507–08 (1989), argues that the canons ought to be central to statutory interpretation and proposes the following "principles for the regulatory state":

Constitutional Principles
1.   Avoiding constitutional invalidity/doubts
2.   Federalism
3.   Political accountability (nondelegation principle)
4.   Political deliberation,* checks and balances,* antipathy to naked interest-group transfers**
5.   Disadvantaged groups**
6.   Hearing rights
7.   Property and contract rights
8.   Welfare rights**
9.   Rule of law

Institutional Concerns
1.   Narrow construction of appropriations statutes
2.   Presumption in favor of judicial review
3.   Presumption against implied exemptions from taxation
4.   Presumption against implied repeals
5.   Question of administrative discretion*
6.   Cautious approach to legislative history
7.   Ratification, acquiescence,* stare decisis, and post-enactment history*

Counteracting Statutory Failure
1.   Presumption in favor of political accountability

2. Presumption against subversion of statute through collective action problems*
3. Presumption in favor of coordination and consistency
4. Presumption against obsolescence*
5. Narrow construction of procedural qualifications of substantive rights*
6. Understanding systemic effects of regulatory controls*
7. Presumption against irrationality and injustice*
8. Proportionality (against overzealous implementation)*
9. De minimis exceptions
10. Narrow construction of statutes embodying interest-group transfers (to counteract "deals")*
11. Broad construction of statutes protecting disadvantaged groups*
12. Broad construction of statutes protecting nonmarket values**
13. Avoiding private law principles**

Compare these with the canons the Rehnquist and Roberts Courts have actually deployed (Appendix B to this Casebook). We have placed an asterisk (*) by those of Sunstein's principles which enjoy little support in the current Court's assembly of canons. A double asterisk (**) means that we discern no explicit support, and implicit rejection in recent cases. Note that most of Sunstein's canons fall into one of these categories. He would respond that the canons not already in the Court's lexicon *should* be, for normative reasons regarding their usefulness for the modern regulatory state.

David Shapiro, in *Continuity and Change in Statutory Interpretation*, 67 N.Y.U. L. Rev. 921, 925 (1992), has provided a different justification for the canons: they promote legal stability, in that they assume "that close questions of statutory interpretation should be resolved in favor of continuity and against change."[s] A difficulty in assessing this claim is figuring out the relevant status quo: Does it consist of longstanding general assumptions in the legal community (embodied in many canons, particularly the substantive ones), or the specific legislative assumptions surrounding a particular statute, which may be undone if a canon controls statutory meaning? As the next note indicates, these competing definitions may create widely divergent conclusions about the dynamic or static impact of canons in interpretation. Shapiro concludes that promoting continuity rather than change is more often than not consistent with legislative purposes. This is also the position taken by Justice O'Connor's opinion in the Census Case, excerpted in the previous Section.

Justice Scalia says, in *A Matter of Interpretation* 28–29 (1997), that "all of these preferential rules and presumptions are a lot of trouble," for "it is virtually impossible to expect uniformity and objectivity [in statutory interpretation] when there is added, on one or the other side of the balance, a thumb of indeterminate weight" like the rule of lenity or the canon to avoid constitutional difficulties. In light of his own reliance on all the canons he denigrates, this is a remarkable statement, which the Justice immediately qualifies:

---

s. For an extended elaboration of this thesis, see Amanda Tyler, *Continuity, Coherence, and the Canons*, 99 Nw. U. L. Rev. 1389 (2005).

The rule of lenity is almost as old as the common law itself, so I suppose that is validated by sheer antiquity. * * * Some of the rules, perhaps, can be considered merely an exaggerated statement of what normal, no-thumb-on-the-scales interpretation would produce anyway. For example, since congressional elimination of state sovereign immunity is such an extraordinary act, one would normally expect it to be explicitly decreed rather than offhandedly implied — so something like a "clear statement" rule is merely normal interpretation. And the same, perhaps, with waiver of [federal] sovereign immunity.

Note how the Justice's defense is a broader version of Shapiro's rule of continuity. But it brings out a disturbing normative edge. For example, Congress has often legislated to exclude lesbians and gay men from ordinary legal entitlements, like marriage, military service, and immigration, and has never adopted a law that protects lesbians and gay men from the pervasive violence or discrimination directed at them. Does that mean Justice Scalia would recognize a clear statement rule, "Unless Congress clearly expresses a sentiment that lesbians and gay men are included in statutory protections, the Court should presume that they are excluded"?

6. *Dynamic Canons and the Problem of Legislative Supremacy. Catholic Bishop* illustrates the way in which the canons can contribute to the dynamic evolution of statutes. The dissenters may have more accurately discerned the expectations of Congress, but the Court majority found that evidence insufficient to require the result that they found constitutionally questionable. The Court's creation of a series of new or strengthened clear statement rules in the last few decades has generated results in case after case that would have surprised the enacting Congresses. Recall *Dellmuth* and *Gregory*. Also compare *EEOC v. Arabian Am. Oil Co. (Aramco)*, 499 U.S. 244 (1991) (Court invokes a clear statement rule as basis for holding that Title VII does not apply extraterritorially, to U.S. company allegedly discriminating against U.S. employees in its foreign offices), with *id.* at 263–64 (Marshall, J., dissenting) (arguing that the Court's clear statement rule was much tougher than the traditional presumption against extraterritoriality).

James Brudney and Corey Ditslear, *Canons of Construction and the Elusive Quest for Neutral Reasoning*, 58 Vand. L. Rev. 1 (2005). This article is a more systematic approach to the canons than any previous work of scholarship. The authors (a labor law professor and a political scientist) collected 630 Supreme Court workplace-law decisions between 1969 and 2003 and coded them by result (pro-labor liberal and pro-business conservative) and mode of reasoning. Using multiple regression analyses that control for other variables, Brudney and Ditslear found that the Rehnquist Court relied on linguistic canons (such as ejusdem generis) much more, and legislative history much less, than the Burger Court had done. *Circuit City, Inc. v. Adams*, 532 U.S. 105 (2001) (analyzed in § 1A1 of this chapter), exemplifies the Rehnquist Court's (and now the Roberts Court's) approach to labor cases.

More troubling is their finding that this methodological development is serving ideological purposes (pp. 53–69). As the authors summarize these findings at the beginning of their lengthy article (p. 6), "canon usage by justices identified as liberals tends to be linked to liberal outcomes, and canon reliance by conservative justices to be associated with conservative outcomes. We also found that canons are often invoked to justify conservative results in close cases — *i.e.*, those decided by a one-vote or two-vote margin. Indeed, closely divided cases in which the majority relies on substantive canons are more likely to reach conservative results than close cases where those canons are not invoked.

"In addition, we identified a subset of cases in which the majority relies on canons while the dissent invokes legislative history: these cases, almost all decided since 1988, have yielded overwhelmingly conservative results. Doctrinal analysis of illustrative decisions indicates that conservative members of the Rehnquist Court are using the canons in such contested cases to ignore — and thereby undermine — the demonstrable legislative preferences of Congress. Taken together, the association between canon reliance and outcomes among both conservative and liberal justices, the distinctly conservative influence associated with substantive canon reliance in close cases, and the recent tensions in contested cases between conservative majority opinions that rely on canons and liberal dissents that invoke legislative history, suggest that the canons are regularly used in an instrumental if not ideologically conscious manner."

Brudney and Ditslear apply their empirical findings to the theoretical debate over the utility of the canons. Their conclusions are as follows. First, the authors (pp. 95–102) are skeptical that the canons form an interpretive regime which can provide an ordering mechanism for legislators and lawyers to make statutory interpretation more predictable. Aside from the fact that legislators do not rely on the canons when drafting statutes, see Victoria Nourse & Jane Schacter, *The Politics of Legislative Drafting: A Congressional Case Study*, 77 NYU L. Rev. 575 (2002), legislators and lawyers cannot rely on the canons in predicting how statutes will be applied, because the canons are deployed in such an ideological way by both liberal and conservative judges. A neutral observer who just read the statute and the legislative history in *Circuit City*, for example, would have expected the Court to read the labor exemption to the Arbitration Act much more expansively than the five-Justice majority in fact did. Brudney and Ditslear offer almost two dozen equally dramatic canon-surprises from their dataset.

Second, and relatedly, Brudney and Ditslear's study (pp. 77–95) lends empirical support to relatively cynical accounts of the canons. Stephen Ross, *Where Have You Gone Karl Llewellyn? Should Congress Turn Its Lonely Eyes to You?*, 45 Vand. L. Rev. (1992), and Edward Rubin, *Modern Canons, Loose Canons, and the Limits of Practical Reason*, 45 Vand. L. Rev. 579 (1992), maintain that Supreme Court Justices, and perhaps other judges, use the canons strategically, to justify judicial policy preferences or to frustrate legislative intent. The malleability noted by Professor Llewellyn not only undermines canonical predictability, but allows the canons to be manipulated by result-oriented jurists. Brudney and Ditslear say their evidence is consistent with, though does not conclusively prove, this claim.

Third, Brudney and Ditslear (pp. 70–77) found some support for the hypothesis, first advanced by Jonathan Macey and Geoffrey Miller, *The Canons of Construction and Judicial Preferences*, 45 Vand. L. Rev. 647 (1992), that the canons are substitutes for judicial expertise and can reduce error costs in areas (such as ERISA and the procedural complexities of Title VII) where judicial knowledge and preferences are low. E.g., *Adams Fruit Co. v. Barrett*, 494 U.S. 638 (1990) (expressio unius provides the ground for a conservative Court to allow, without dissent, a private right of action under a technical migrant workers' law). Brudney and Ditslear add that such cases may be more strongly influenced by legislative purpose analysis and, most important, agency views than by canon reliance. In short, there is a correlation between canon invocation and technical issues but not necessarily any causal link.

These conclusions suggest that in the most technical areas of law — such as bankruptcy, civil procedure, energy regulation, intellectual property, taxation, telecommunications — canon usage would be more important and less ideologically slanted than in labor law. In less technical and more normatively charged areas — such as civil rights, criminal law and procedure, freedom of information, perhaps federal land law — canon usage would be less frequent and more ideologically slanted.

Problem for Applying the Textual and Substantive Canons

Problem 8–2. In 1972, the District of Columbia Metro Authority contracted with Pullman to purchase 745 subway cars. Frankly Unctuous, a D.C. superintendent of quality control, was specifically responsible for ensuring Pullman's compliance with contract specifications. Thus, if a component of one of the cars were defective upon Unctuous' inspection, he could force Pullman to replace or modify the part at its own expense. During the contract period (1972–78), Unctuous went on several excursions — to The Greenbrier in White Sulphur Springs, The Homestead in Hot Springs, and other resorts. The trips were paid for by Pullman, to the tune of an estimated $30,000. Unctuous was indicted for extortion under the Hobbs Act, 18 U.S.C. § 1951. At trial, Pullman project supervisor Ewell B. Surrey, who made the arrangements for the trips, testifies that Unctuous never demanded or solicited the excursions and that Pullman paid for them voluntarily, as a means of providing access to an official. "It was our normal course of business," he testifies. There is no testimony to the contrary. Both Unctuous and Surrey testify that Unctuous was a strict inspector and declared numerous components defective. Only once during the contract period was Pullman able to persuade Unctuous to change his mind.

The issue is whether this set of facts justifies prosecution of Unctuous under the Hobbs Act. The Hobbs Act reads as follows:

(a) Whoever in any way or degree obstructs, delays, or affects commerce or the movement of any article or commodity in commerce, by robbery or extortion or attempts or conspires so to do, or commits or threatens physical violence to any person or property in furtherance of a plan or purpose to do anything in violation of this section shall be fined not more than $10,000 or imprisoned not more than twenty years, or both.

(b) As used in this section —

(1) The term "robbery" means the unlawful taking or obtaining of personal property from the person or in the presence of another, against his will, by means of actual or threatened force, or violence, or fear of injury, immediate or future, to his person or property, or property in his custody or possession, or the person or property of a relative or member of his family or of anyone in his company at the time of the taking or obtaining.

(2) The term "extortion" means the obtaining of property from another, with his consent, induced by wrongful use of actual or threatened force, violence, or fear, or under color of official right.

Unctuous argues that he cannot be convicted under the Act, as he committed neither robbery or extortion. Although he may have received things from Pullman, he did not "induce" Pullman to give him these things, as § 1951(b)(2) requires. The Government responds: All the statute requires the prosecution to show for extortion is that (1) defendant obtained property of another with his consent (2) because of his official position, and (3) defendant knew the property was given him as a result of his official position. There is no requirement of inducement when a public official is accused of extortion, says the Government. Is such a reading grammatically plausible? (Hint: Consider the punctuation of § 1951(b)(2).) E.g., *United States v. Jannotti*, 673 F.2d 578 (3d Cir. 1982) (en banc), cert. denied, 457 U.S. 1106 (1982). The defendant argues that the statute does require a showing of "inducement." What is the grammatical basis for this argument?

Another interpretation of the Hobbs Act which the Government might suggest is that inducement is an element of the crime, but in the case of most public officials their acceptance of money from private parties who are under their authority is conclusively presumed to be induced by the officials if they knew the reason for the property transfer. Is this a sensible reading of the statute? Compare *United States v. Hedman*, 630 F.2d 1184, 1192, 1193 (7th Cir. 1980), cert. denied, 450 U.S. 965 (1981), with *United States v. O'Grady*, 742 F.2d 682 (2d Cir. 1984) (en banc). In the alternative, the Government argues that inducement (if a statutory requirement for conviction) can be established by demonstrating a pattern of repeated acceptances of substantial benefits by an official with discretionary power over the giver of those benefits. How should Unctuous respond to these alternative arguments? What canons might support his position?

NOTE ON INTERPRETIVE DIRECTIONS IN STATUTES

Sometimes the legislature attempts to direct the court in how to approach interpreting a particular statute. For example, a provision of the federal Racketeer Influenced and Corrupt Organizations Act (RICO), 18 U.S.C. § 1961, which contains criminal sanctions, provides that "[t]he provisions of this title shall be liberally construed to effectuate its remedial purposes." There could conceivably be some constitutional objections to such a provision — the most straightforward would be that it violates the separation of powers because it invades the court's power to say what the law is — but leaving that problem aside, what should a court do with it? In *Russello v. United States*, 464 U.S. 16, 26–27 (1983), the Court cited the RICO provision as well as legislative history to support a broad construction of the statute. In contrast, in *Reves v. Ernst & Young*, 507 U.S. 170, 183–84 (1993), the Court said the following about the RICO clause:

> * * * This clause obviously seeks to ensure that Congress' intent is not frustrated by an overly narrow reading of the statute, but it is not an invitation to apply RICO to new purposes that Congress never intended. Nor does the clause help us to determine what purposes Congress had in mind. Those must be gleaned from the statute through the normal means of interpretation. The clause " 'only serves as an aid for resolving an ambiguity; it is not to be used to beget one.' "

Does this leave any role for the interpretive clause at all?

Some states have adopted model interpretation acts that purport to guide judicial interpretation for all statutes. Chapter 645 of the Minnesota Statutes, for example, contains the following intriguing provisions:

645.16. LEGISLATIVE INTENT CONTROLS

The object of all interpretation and construction of laws is to ascertain and effectuate the intention of the legislature. Every law shall be construed, if possible, to give effect to all its provisions.

When the words of a law in their application to an existing situation are clear and free from all ambiguity, the letter of the law shall not be disregarded under the pretext of pursuing the spirit.

When the words of a law are not explicit, the intention of the legislature may be ascertained by considering, among other matters:

(1) The occasion and necessity for the law;

(2) The circumstances under which it was enacted;

(3) The mischief to be remedied;

(4) The object to be attained;

(5) The former law, if any, including other laws upon the same or similar subjects;

(6) The consequences of a particular interpretation;

(7) The contemporaneous legislative history; and

(8) Legislative and administrative interpretations of the statute.

645.17. PRESUMPTIONS IN ASCERTAINING LEGISLATIVE INTENT

In ascertaining the intention of the legislature the courts may be guided by the following presumptions:

(1) The legislature does not intend a result that is absurd, impossible of execution, or unreasonable;

(2) The legislature intends the entire statute to be effective and certain;

(3) The legislature does not intend to violate the constitution of the United States or of this state;

(4) When a court of last resort has construed the language of a law, the legislature in subsequent laws on the same subject matter intends the same construction to be placed upon such language; and

(5) The legislature intends to favor the public interest as against any private interest.

If a follower of Justice Scalia's textualism were appointed to the Minnesota Supreme Court, what should the new Justice do with these directives? Consider this question again after you have finished reading the next Section, which reveals more clearly the textualist aversion to the use of legislative intent arguments in statutory interpretation. If the statutory text tells the judge to follow legislative intent, what is the textualist to do?

For a thorough argument contending that Congress both has the authority to enact federal rules of statutory interpretation and should exercise that authority, see Nicholas Quinn Rosenkranz, *Federal Rules of Statutory Interpretation*, 115 Harv. L. Rev. 2085 (2002). For a critique and modification of this approach, see Adam Kiracofe, Note, *The Codified Canons of Statutory Construction: A Response And Proposal to Nicholas Rosenkranz's* Federal Rules of Statutory Interpretation, 84 B.U. L. Rev. 571 (2004). For a critique and counter-proposal suggesting that an organization like the American Law Institute formulate a restatement of statutory interpretation, see Gary O'Connor, *Restatement (First) of Statutory Interpretation*, 7 N.Y.U. J. Legis. & Pub. Pol'y 333 (2003-04). (Incidentally, Mr. O'Connor created the first website devoted entirely to issues of federal statutory construction. See http://www.statconblog.blogspot.com.)

SECTION 2. EXTRINSIC SOURCES FOR STATUTORY INTERPRETATION

Extrinsic aids for statutory interpretation are sources outside the text of the statute being interpreted. Such sources include the common law (examined in Part A of this Section), the legislative background of the statute (Part B), and other statutes and their interpretation (Part C). The traditional rule was that extrinsic aids should not be considered if the statute had a "plain meaning." But how can we be sure that the statute really has a plain meaning, without considering context? For example, if the legislature uses a term such as "fraud," which had an established common law meaning at the time, we should have to consult extrinsic evidence just to figure out what the plain meaning might be. Or if legislative discussions reveal a specialized use of the term "fraud," shouldn't they be relevant?

The new textualists introduced in Chapter 7, § 3A believe that the common law and other statutes are usually admissible extrinsic evidence, but legislative background or history is not. This position is examined more closely in Parts B(1) and (2). It has had some influence on the Supreme Court and the lower federal courts. Ironically, state courts have in the last several decades become more likely to consider legislative history, because documentary legislative materials are more readily available.[a]

A. THE COMMON LAW

The traditional rule in Anglo-American law was that statutes in derogation of the common law should be narrowly construed. This was the philosophy of Blackstone's *Commentaries*, which were pervasively influential at the founding of our constitutional republic, and in the early Supreme Court, especially in admiralty cases.[b] As the Supreme Court later articulated the principle, "[n]o statute is to be construed as altering the common law, farther than its words import." *Shaw v. Railroad Co.*, 101 U.S. (11 Otto) 557, 565 (1879). This canon reflected the foundational character of the common law as a regulatory regime. Any deviation from common-law rules needed special justification.

Such a rule has eroded in the modern regulatory statute, where statutes are the rule and common law the exception. For example, in *Isbrandtsen Co. v. Johnson*, 343 U.S. 779, 783 (1952), the Supreme Court held, in an admiralty proceeding by a seaman for wages earned, that the employer's common-law right to set off damages resulting from the seaman's dereliction of duty had been preempted by federal statute. The Court stated:

> Statutes which invade the common law or the general maritime law are to be read with a presumption favoring the retention of long-established and familiar principles, except when a statutory purpose to the contrary is evident. No rule of construction precludes giving a natural meaning to legislation like this that obviously is of a remedial, beneficial and amendatory character. It should be interpreted so as to effect its purpose. Marine legislation, at least since the Shipping Commissioners Act of June 7, 1872, 17 Stat. 262, should be construed to make effective its design to change the general maritime law so as to improve the lot of seamen.

Isbrandtsen noted, further, that federal statutes regulated virtually every aspect of a seaman's rights and duties, hence negating the force of the common law argument. This suggests another reason for the demise of the common law canon: statutes substantially occupy the field to regulate many areas of human activity, whereas in the nineteenth century (the heyday of the common law canon) statutory regulation was the exception.[c]

---

a. For a comprehensive overview, see Jos Torres & Steve Windsor, *State Legislative Histories: A Select, Annotated Bibliography*, 85 Law Libr. J. 545 (1993).

b. For our early history, see William Eskridge, Jr., *All About Words: The Original Understandings of the "Judicial Power" in Statutory Interpretation, 1776–1806*, 101 Colum. L. Rev. 990 (2001). The best historical source for eighteenth century English thinking is David Lieberman, *The Province of Legislation Determined* 16–20, 28, 52–72 (1989) (discussing the proliferation of mangled statutes in eighteenth-century England and Blackstone's disdainful attitude toward them, with judges being the main salvation by protecting the common law against bad statutes).

c. Compare *United States v. Texas*, 507 U.S. 529 (1993) (applying *Isbrandsten* standard but concluding that federal common law principle was not abrogated by federal statute).

Nonetheless, the common law remains an important extrinsic source for interpreting many statutes. As noted above, when the legislature deploys words with established common law meanings, courts will presume that those meanings are adopted by Congress. E.g., *Wallace v. Kato*, 127 S.Ct. 1091, 1095 (2007) (§ 1983); *Community for Creative Non-Violence v. Reid*, 490 U.S. 730, 739 (1989). Especially for older, more generally phrased statutes, the common law serves a broader "gap-filling" role: For issues entirely unaddressed by the statute, the interpreter might presume that the legislature intended to adopt the established common law rule. Consider the following problems and then a case excerpt to see how important the common law still is for filling in gaps.

Introductory Problem on the Common Law as Extrinsic Evidence

Problem 8–3. The Civil Rights Act of 1871, 17 Stat. 13, codified as amended at 42 U.S.C. § 1983, provides as follows:

> Every person who, under color of any statute, ordinance, regulation, custom, or usage, of any State or Territory or the District of Columbia, subjects, or causes to be subjected, any citizen of the United States or other person within the jurisdiction thereof to the deprivation of any rights, privileges, or immunities secured by the Constitution and laws, shall be liable to the party injured in an action at law, suit in equity, or other proper proceeding for redress.

This statute was passed in 1871, as part of the Reconstruction effort to ensure newly freed slaves their rights as citizens.

Carl Doe, an official of the NAACP, organizes a boycott of stores in Tylertown, Mississippi, because the stores follow segregated practices. He also organizes a sit-in. The sheriff arrests Doe for breach of the peace, and state Judge Joyce Judicious orders Doe to cease any and all activity meant to disrupt Tylertown businesses. Doe points out that a long line of Supreme Court First Amendment precedents render such an order "lawless," and Judge Judicious holds Doe in contempt and sentences him to a day in jail. When Judge Judicious' order is overturned, Doe sues the sheriff and the judge under § 1983 for violating his First Amendment rights. The sheriff settles the case with Doe, but Judge Judicious argues judicial immunity.

Judge Judicious demonstrates that at common law judges were immune from lawsuits arising out of their judicial duties. The Supreme Court in *Bradley v. Fisher*, 80 U.S. (13 Wall.) 335 (1871), endorsed absolute judicial immunity in order to protect the integrity of judicial decisionmaking, which would be compromised if the judge were worried about being sued by the losers of lawsuits. Because Congress may be assumed not to disturb such a long-established rule of immunity, § 1983 should be interpreted to include this immunity, argues Judicious.

Doe disagrees and cites to the legislative background of § 1983. During Reconstruction, the South was marked by disorder and violence, especially against the newly emancipated black citizens. Often this violence was accomplished under color of state law — through lynchings, rigged trials, and official harassment of freed slaves. The Reconstruction Congress enacted the

Civil Rights Act of 1866, 14 Stat. 27, to abate the violence. Section 2 of the 1866 Act provided criminal liability for any person who, under color of any law, deprived another of federal rights by reason of race. Most of the discussion of § 2 recognized that it would apply to state judges, for much of the oppression was conducted through state tribunals. A proposed amendment to exempt state judges from criminal liability failed. President Johnson vetoed the 1866 bill, in part because it would allow prosecution of state court judges. Members of Congress objected to President Johnson's reason. "I answer it is better to invade the judicial power of the State than permit it to invade, strike down, and destroy the civil rights of citizens. A judicial power perverted to such uses should be speedily invaded," argued Representative Lawrence. Congress passed the bill over the President's veto.

Another amendment not adopted in 1866 was Representative Bingham's proposal to substitute a civil action for the criminal penalties of § 2. (The bill's sponsor said the law's beneficiaries could not afford civil suits.) Violence against African Americans continued in the South, and this proposal was renewed in 1871. After President Grant informed Congress of the urgency of attacking the violence of Southern racists against blacks, Congress passed the Civil Rights Act of 1871, § 1 of which is the predecessor of § 1983. Representative Shellabarger, the main House sponsor of the 1871 bill, said on the floor of the House that § 2 of the 1866 Act was "the model" for § 1 of the 1871 bill. "[Section 2] provides a criminal proceeding in identically the same case as [§ 1] provides a civil remedy for, except that the deprivation under color of State law must, under the [1866 Act], have been on account of race, color, or former slavery." The Senate sponsor, Senator Edmunds, stated that § 1 was intended to carry out the principles of the 1866 Act. No one in Congress disputed the analogy.

There was little discussion of § 1 in Congress (most of the discussion focused on the criminal conspiracy provision of the 1871 bill). Opponents of § 1 stressed its invasion of judicial independence and cited to criminal prosecutions of judges under the 1866 Act. "By the first section, in certain cases, the judge of a State court, though acting under oath of office, is made liable to a suit in Federal court and subject to damages for his decision against a suitor," exclaimed Representative Lewis (an opponent of the 1871 bill). Although Representative Shellabarger often corrected opponents' mis-characterizations of his bill, he never disputed opponents' allegations that § 1 would render judges civilly liable. Supporters of the 1871 bill argued that in the South "courts are in many instances under the control of those who are wholly inimical to the impartial administration of law and equity" and that the criminal liability of the 1866 Act was not enough to stop those abuses of justice. The 1871 bill was passed overwhelmingly. This legislative back-ground, argues Doe, shows that the 1871 Congress did *not* expect that § 1 would include the common law's judicial immunity doctrine.

Would the Supreme Court accept Judicious' argument that she is immune from § 1983 in this case? Compare *Pierson v. Ray*, 386 U.S. 547 (1967).

If the Court interprets § 1983 to include a rule of absolute judicial immunity against damages liability, based upon the common law doctrine of judicial immunity existing in 1871, should it extend similar immunity to prosecutors? Although prosecutorial immunity is grounded on the same integrity-of-the-judicial-process basis as judicial immunity, there was no American case granting prosecutors common law immunity until *Griffith v. Slinkard*, 44 N.E. 1001 (Ind. 1896) and was not widely accepted by American courts until the 1930s. How would the Supreme Court decide this case? Compare *Imbler v. Pachtman*, 424 U.S. 409 (1976).

Now that you know something about § 1983, evaluate a different kind of issue: For officials who can be sued for damages, what damages might be allowed? Under what circumstances can punitive damages be awarded, for example? Consider the following case.

SMITH v. WADE
Supreme Court of the United States, 1983
461 U.S. 30, 103 S.Ct. 1625, 75 L.Ed.2d 632

JUSTICE BRENNAN delivered the opinion of the Court.

[Wade, an inmate of a Missouri state prison, brought a § 1983 suit against Smith and four guards and correction officials. Wade alleged that he was assaulted by cellmates and that defendants did nothing even though they knew or ought to have known that such an assault was likely to occur. The trial judge instructed the jury that Wade could obtain punitive damages if defendants' conduct were in reckless disregard of, or indifferent to, Wade's safety. The jury found Smith liable for both compensatory and punitive damages, and the circuit court affirmed. The issue before the Court was whether punitive damages may be awarded in a § 1983 action based upon a finding of reckless or callous disregard of, or indifference to, plaintiff's rights, or, as Smith contended, only upon a finding that the defendant acted with "actual malicious intent."]

Section 1983 is derived from § 1 of the Civil Rights Act of 1871, 17 Stat. 13. It was intended to create "a species of tort liability" in favor of persons deprived of federally secured rights. *Carey v. Piphus*, 435 U.S. 247, 253 (1978); *Imbler v. Pachtman*, 424 U.S. 409, 417 (1976). We noted in *Carey* that there was little in the section's legislative history concerning the damages recoverable for this tort liability. In the absence of more specific guidance, we looked first to the common law of torts (both modern and as of 1871), with such modification or adaptation as might be necessary to carry out the purpose and policy of the statute. We have done the same in other contexts arising under § 1983, especially the recurring problem of common-law immunities.[2]

---

2. [Citing cases, including *Imbler* and *Pierson* (Problem 8–3).]

Justice Rehnquist's dissent faults us for referring to modern tort decisions in construing § 1983. Its argument rests on the unstated and unsupported premise that Congress necessarily intended to freeze into permanent law whatever principles were current in 1871, rather than to incorporate applicable general legal principles as they evolve. The dissents are correct, of course, that when the language of the section and its legislative history provide no clear answer, we have found useful guidance in the law prevailing at the time when § 1983 was enacted; but it does not follow that that law is absolutely controlling or that current law is irrelevant. On the

[Smith conceded that punitive damages are available in a "proper" § 1983 action.] Smith argues, nonetheless, that this was not a "proper" case in which to award punitive damages. More particularly, he attacks the instruction that punitive damages could be awarded on a finding of reckless or callous disregard of or indifference to Wade's rights or safety. Instead, he contends that the proper test is one of actual malicious intent — "ill will, spite, or intent to injure." He offers two arguments for this position: first, that actual intent is the proper standard for punitive damages in all cases under § 1983; and second, that even if intent is not always required, it should be required here because the threshold for punitive damages should always be higher than that for liability in the first instance. We address these in turn.

[III] Smith does not argue that the common law, either in 1871 or now, required or requires a showing of actual malicious intent for recovery of punitive damages.

Perhaps not surprisingly, there was significant variation (both terminological and substantive) among American jurisdictions in the latter nineteenth century on the precise standard to be applied in awarding punitive damages — variation that was exacerbated by the ambiguity and slipperiness of such common terms as "malice" and "gross negligence."[8] Most of the confusion, however, seems to have been over the degree of negligence, recklessness, carelessness, or culpable indifference that should be required — not over whether actual intent was essential. On the contrary, the rule in a large majority of jurisdictions was that punitive damages (also called exemplary damages, vindictive damages, or smart money) could be awarded without a showing of actual ill will, spite, or intent to injure.

This Court so stated on several occasions, before and shortly after 1871. In *Philadelphia, W. & B.R. Co. v. Quigley*, 21 How. 202 (1859), a diversity libel suit, the Court held erroneous an instruction that authorized the jury to return a punitive award but gave the jury virtually no substantive guidance as to the proper threshold. We described the standard thus:

> "Whenever the injury complained of has been inflicted maliciously or wantonly, and with circumstances of contumely or indignity, the jury are not limited to the ascertainment of a simple compensation for the wrong committed against the aggrieved

---

contrary, if the prevailing view on some point of general tort law had changed substantially in the intervening century (which is not the case here), we might be highly reluctant to assume that Congress intended to perpetuate a now-obsolete doctrine. See *Carey v. Piphus* ("[O]ver the centuries the common law of torts has developed a set of rules to implement the principle that a person should be compensated fairly for injuries caused by the violation of his legal rights. These rules, defining the elements of damages and the prerequisites for their recovery, provide the appropriate starting point for the inquiry under § 1983 as well.") (footnote omitted). Indeed, in *Imbler* we recognized a common-law immunity that first came into existence 25 years after § 1983 was enacted. Under the dissents' view, *Imbler* was wrongly decided.

8. [Footnote 8 is 76 lines of the U.S. Reports, attacking Justice Rehnquist's assumption that in 1871 "malice," "wantonness," and "willfulness" all denoted ill will. Justice Brennan asserted that "[w]ith regard to 'malice' the assumption is dubious at best; with regard to 'wantonness' and 'willfulness,' it is just plain wrong."]

person. But the malice spoken of in this rule is not merely the doing of an unlawful or injurious act. The word implies that the act complained of was conceived in the spirit of mischief, *or of criminal indifference to civil obligations*." *Id.* at 214. * * *

The large majority of state and lower federal courts were in agreement that punitive damages awards did not require a showing of actual malicious intent; they permitted punitive awards on variously stated standards of negligence, recklessness, or other culpable conduct short of actual malicious intent.[12]

The same rule applies today. The Restatement (Second) of Torts (1977), for example, states: "Punitive damages may be awarded for conduct that is outrageous, because of the defendant's evil motive *or his reckless indifference to the rights of others*." *Id.*, § 908(2) (emphasis added); see also *id.*, Comment *b*. Most cases under state common law, although varying in their precise terminology, have adopted more or less the same rule, recognizing that punitive damages in tort cases may be awarded not only for actual intent to injure or evil motive, but also for recklessness, serious indifference to or disregard for the rights of others, or even gross negligence.[13]

The remaining question is whether the policies and purposes of § 1983 itself require a departure from the rules of tort common law. As a general matter, we discern no reason why a person whose federally guaranteed rights have been violated should be granted a more restrictive remedy than a person asserting an ordinary tort cause of action. Smith offers us no persuasive reason to the contrary.

Smith's argument, which he offers in several forms, is that an actual-intent standard is preferable to a recklessness standard because it is less vague. He points out that punitive damages, by their very nature, are not awarded to compensate the injured party. He concedes, of course, that deterrence of future egregious conduct is a primary purpose of both § 1983 and of punitive damages, see * * * Restatement (Second) of Torts § 908(1) (1979). But

---

12. * * * *Maysville & L.R. Co. v. Herrick*, 76 Ky. 122 (1877), held that the trial court correctly refused to instruct the jury that "willful or intentional wrong" was required to award punitive damages in a railroad accident case, remarking: "The absence of slight care in the management of a railroad station, or in keeping a railroad track in repair, is gross negligence; and to enable a passenger to recover punitive damages, in a case like this, it is not necessary to show the absence of all care, or 'reckless indifference to the safety of * * * passengers,' or 'intentional misconduct' on the part of the agents and officers of the company." *Id.*, at 127 (ellipsis in original). [Justice Brennan cited 30 cases in accord with this proposition.]

Justice Rehnquist's assertion that a "solid majority of jurisdictions" required actual malicious intent is simply untrue. In fact, there were fairly few jurisdictions that imposed such a requirement, and fewer yet that adhered to it consistently. Justice Rehnquist's attempt to establish this proposition with case citations does not offer him substantial support. Because the point is not of controlling significance, we will not tarry here to analyze his citations case-by-case or state-by-state, but will only summarize the main themes. [According to Justice Brennan, some of the dissenters' cases support the availability of punitive damages for recklessness, others are too equivocal to categorize, and others support the dissenters' interpretation only if one assumes that terms like "malice," "wantonness," and "criminal" always meant actual intent to injure.]

13. [Justice Brennan cited 33 recent state cases to support the proposition in text.]

deterrence, he contends, cannot be achieved unless the standard of conduct sought to be deterred is stated with sufficient clarity to enable potential defendants to conform to the law and to avoid the proposed sanction. Recklessness or callous indifference, he argues, is too uncertain a standard to achieve deterrence rationally and fairly. A prison guard, for example, can be expected to know whether he is acting with actual ill will or intent to injure, but not whether he is being reckless or callously indifferent.

Smith's argument, if valid, would apply to ordinary tort cases as easily as to § 1983 suits; hence, it hardly presents an argument for adopting a different rule under § 1983. In any event, the argument is unpersuasive. While, *arguendo*, an intent standard may be easier to understand and apply to particular situations than a recklessness standard, we are not persuaded that a recklessness standard is too vague to be fair or useful. In [*Milwaukee & St. Paul R. Co. v. Arms*, 91 U.S. (1 Otto) 489 (1876),] we adopted a recklessness standard rather than a gross negligence standard precisely because recklessness would better serve the need for adequate clarity and fair application. Almost a century later, in the First Amendment context, we held that punitive damages cannot be assessed for defamation in the absence of proof of "knowledge of falsity or reckless disregard for the truth." [*Gertz v. Robert Welch, Inc.*, 418 U.S. 323, 349 (1974).] Our concern in *Gertz* was that the threat of punitive damages, if not limited to especially egregious cases, might "inhibit the vigorous exercise of First Amendment freedoms" — a concern at least as pressing as any urged by Smith in this case. Yet we did not find it necessary to impose an actual-intent standard there. Just as Smith has not shown why § 1983 should give higher protection from punitive damages than ordinary tort law, he has not explained why it gives higher protection than we have demanded under the First Amendment.

More fundamentally, Smith's argument for certainty in the interest of deterrence overlooks the distinction between a standard for punitive damages and a standard of liability in the first instance. Smith seems to assume that prison guards and other state officials look mainly to the standard for punitive damages in shaping their conduct. We question the premise; we assume, and hope, that most officials are guided primarily by the underlying standards of federal substantive law — both out of devotion to duty, and in the interest of avoiding liability for compensatory damages. At any rate, the conscientious officer who desires clear guidance on how to do his job and avoid lawsuits can and should look to the standard for actionability in the first instance. The need for exceptional clarity in the standard for punitive damages arises only if one assumes that there are substantial numbers of officers who will not be deterred by compensatory damages; only such officers will seek to guide their conduct by the punitive damages standard. The presence of such officers constitutes a powerful argument *against* raising the threshold for punitive damages.

In this case, the jury was instructed to apply a high standard of constitutional right ("physical abuse of such base, inhumane and barbaric proportions as to shock the sensibilities"). It was also instructed, under the principle of qualified immunity, that Smith could not be held liable at all unless he was guilty of "a callous indifference or a thoughtless disregard for the consequences of [his] act or failure to act," or of "a flagrant or remarkably bad failure to protect" Wade. These instructions are not challenged in this Court, nor were they challenged on grounds of vagueness in the lower courts. Smith's contention that this recklessness standard is too vague to provide clear guidance and reasonable deterrence might more properly be reserved for a challenge seeking different standards of liability in the first instance. As for punitive damages, however, in the absence of any persuasive argument to the contrary based on the policies of § 1983, we are content to adopt the policy judgment of the common law — that reckless or callous disregard for the plaintiff's rights, as well as intentional violations of federal law, should be sufficient to trigger a jury's consideration of the appropriateness of punitive damages.

[Justice Brennan, finally, rejected Smith's last argument, that it was error for the court to describe the standard of punitive damages in terms similar to those of the basic liability under § 1983 (indifference to Wade's rights). Primary reliance was placed on the Restatement (Second) of Torts and the modern common law, which generally provide that where the standard for compensatory liability is as high or higher than the usual threshold for punitive damages, such damages may be given without requiring any extra showing.]

JUSTICE REHNQUIST, with whom THE CHIEF JUSTICE [BURGER] and JUSTICE POWELL join, dissenting.

The Court rejects a "wrongful intent" standard, instead requiring a plaintiff to show merely "reckless * * * indifference to the federally protected rights of others." The following justifications are offered by the Court for this result: first, the rule in "[m]ost cases [decided in the last 15 years] under state common law" is "more or less" equivalent to a recklessness standard; second, the Court asserts that a similar rule "prevail[ed] at the time when § 1983 was enacted"; and finally, there is an "absence of any persuasive argument" for not applying existing state tort rules to the federal statutory remedies available against state and local officials under § 1983. In my opinion none of these justifications, taken singly or together, supports the Court's result. First, the decisions of state courts in the last decade or so are all but irrelevant in determining the intent of the 42d Congress, and thus, the meaning of § 1983. Second, the Court's characterization of the common law rules prevailing when § 1983 was enacted is both oversimplified and misleading; in fact, the majority rule in 1871 seems to have been that some sort of "evil intent" — and not mere recklessness — was necessary to justify an award of punitive damages. Third, the Court's inability to distinguish a *state* court's award of punitive damages against a state officer from a *federal* court's analogous action under §§ 1983 and 1988 precludes it from adequately assessing the public policies implicated by its decision. Finally, the Court fails utterly to grapple with the cogent and persuasive criticisms that have been offered of punitive damages generally.

[Part I of Justice Rehnquist's dissenting opinion is a brief consideration of criticism of punitive damages. In light of this criticism, some states do not allow punitive damage awards, and others have required some sort of evil motive to justify punitive awards. This latter proposition is supported by footnote 3, which spends more than 120 lines analyzing nineteenth-century use of the terms "malice," "willfulness," and "wantonness." His overall point is that nineteenth-century thinkers reserved punitive awards for those who "subjectively" visited evil on their fellows, not those whose conduct was deemed to have failed an "objective" or recklessness standard.]

[II] At bottom, this case requires the Court to decide when a particular remedy is available under § 1983. Until today, the Court has adhered, with some fidelity, to the scarcely controversial principle that its proper role in interpreting § 1983 is determining what the 42d Congress intended. That § 1983 is to be interpreted according to this basic principle of statutory construction is clearly demonstrated by our many decisions relying upon the plain language of the section. The Court's opinion purports to pursue an inquiry into legislative intent, yet relies heavily upon state court decisions decided well after the 42d Congress adjourned. I find these cases unilluminating, at least in part because I am unprepared to attribute to the 42d Congress the truly extraordinary foresight that the Court seems to think it had. The reason our earlier decisions interpreting § 1983 have relied upon common law decisions is simple: members of the 42d Congress were lawyers, familiar with the law of their time. In resolving ambiguities in the enactments of that Congress, as with other Congresses, it is useful to consider the legal principles and rules that shaped the thinking of its Members. The decisions of state courts decided well after 1871, while of some academic interest, are largely irrelevant to what Members of the 42d Congress intended by way of a standard for punitive damages.

In an apparent attempt to justify its novel approach to discerning the intent of a body that deliberated more than a century ago, the Court makes passing reference to our decisions relating to common law immunities under § 1983. These decisions provide no support for the Court's analysis, since they all plainly evidence an attempt to discern the intent of the 42d Congress, albeit indirectly, by reference to the common law principles known to members of that body. * * * More recently, in *City of Newport v. Fact Concerts, Inc.*, 453 U.S. 247, 258 (1981), we said:

> It is by now well settled that the tort liability created by § 1983 cannot be understood in a historical vacuum * * *. One important assumption underlying the Court's decisions in this area is that members of the 42d Congress were familiar with common-law principles, including defenses previously recognized in ordinary tort litigation, and that they likely intended these common-law principles to obtain, absent specific provisions to the contrary.

Likewise, our other decisions with respect to common law immunities under § 1983 clearly reveal that our consideration of state common law rules is only a device to facilitate determination of Congressional intent. Decisions from the 1970s, relied on by the Court, are almost completely irrelevant to this inquiry into legislative intent.

[III] The Court also purports to rely on decisions, handed down in the second half of the last century by this Court, in drawing up its rule that mere recklessness will support an award of punitive damages. In fact, these decisions unambiguously support an actual malice standard. The Court rests primarily on *Philadelphia, W. & B.R. Co. v. Quigley*, 21 How. 202 (1859), a diversity tort action against a railroad. There, we initially observed that in "certain actions of tort," punitive damages might be awarded, and then described those actions as "[w]henever the injury complained of has been inflicted maliciously or wantonly, and with circumstances of contumely or indignity." *Id.* at 214. * * * [I]t was relatively clear at the time that "malice" required a showing of actual ill will or intent to injure. Perhaps foreseeing future efforts to expand the rule, however, we hastened to specify the type of malice that would warrant punitive damages: "the malice spoken of in this rule is not merely the doing of an unlawful or injurious act. The word implies that the act complained of *was conceived in the spirit of mischief, or of criminal indifference to civil obligations.*" It would have been difficult to have more clearly expressed the "actual malice" standard. We explicitly rejected an "implied malice" formulation, and then mandated inquiry into the "spirit" in which a defendant's act was "conceived."

[Justice Rehnquist analyzed other nineteenth century Supreme Court decisions consistent with his reading of *Quigley*.] In *Lake Shore & Michigan Southern Railway Co. v. Prentice*, 147 U.S. 101 (1893), the Court considered whether punitive damages were properly awarded against a railroad in a diversity action. The Court noted that the law on the subject was "well-settled," and paraphrased the *Quigley* standard: The jury may award punitive damages "if the defendant has acted wantonly, or oppressively, or with such malice as implies a spirit of mischief or criminal indifference to civil obligations." Then, * * * the Court explained this formulation, observing that a "*guilty intention* on the part of the defendant is *required* in order to charge him with exemplary or punitive damages." *Ibid.* (emphasis added). * * *

In addition, the decisions rendered by state courts in the years preceding and immediately following the enactment of § 1983 attest to the fact that a solid majority of jurisdictions took the view that the standard for an award of punitive damages included a requirement of ill will. To be sure, a few jurisdictions followed a broader standard; a careful review of the decisions at the time uncovers a number of decisions that contain some reference to "recklessness." And equally clearly, in more recent years many courts have adopted a standard including "recklessness" as the minimal degree of culpability warranting punitive damages.

Most clear of all, however, is the fact that at about the time § 1983 was enacted a considerable number of the 37 States then belonging to the Union required some showing of wrongful intent before punitive damages could be awarded.[12] As the cases set out in the margin reveal, it is but a statement of the

---

12. See, *e.g., Roberts v. Hiem*, 27 Ala. 678, 683 (1855) ("the law allows [punitive damages] whenever the trespass is committed in a rude, aggravating, or insulting manner, as malice may be inferred from these circumstances"); [citation of 76 state cases followed, most with quotations to illustrate Justice Rehnquist's position].

The Court's treatment of the law prevailing in 1871 relies principally upon state-court decisions from the 1880's and 1890's. These cases are admittedly somewhat more relevant to what the 42d Congress intended than the 20th-century cases cited by the Court; particularly if

obvious that "evil motive" was the general standard for punitive damages in many states at the time of the 42d Congress. * * *

[IV] Even apart from this historical background, I am persuaded by a variety of additional factors that the 42d Congress intended a "wrongful intent" requirement. As mentioned above, punitive damages are not, and never have been, a favored remedy. In determining whether Congress, not bound by *stare decisis*, would have embraced this often-condemned doctrine, it is worth considering the judgment of one of the most respected commentators in the field regarding the desirability of a legislatively enacted punitive damages remedy: "It is probable that, in the framing of a model code of damages today for use in a country unhampered by legal tradition, the doctrine of exemplary damages would find no place." C. McCormick, Damages 276 (1935).

In deciding whether Congress heeded such advice, it is useful to consider the language of § 1983 itself — which should, of course, be the starting point for any inquiry into legislative intent. Section 1983 provides:

> "Every person who, under color of any statute, ordinance, regulation, custom, or usage of any State * * * subjects, or causes to be subjected, any citizen of the United States or other person within the jurisdiction thereof to the deprivation of any rights, privileges, or immunities secured by the Constitution and laws, shall be liable to the party *injured* in an action at law, suit in equity, or other proper proceeding *for redress*." (emphasis added).

Plainly, the statutory language itself provides absolutely no support for the cause of action for punitive damages that the Court reads into the provision. Indeed, it merely creates "liab[ility] to the party injured * * * for redress." "Redress" means "[r]eparation of, satisfaction or compensation for, a wrong sustained or the loss resulting from this." 8 Oxford English Dictionary 310 (1933). And, as the Court concedes, punitive damages are not "reparation" or "compensation"; their very purpose is to punish, not to compensate. If Congress meant to create a right to recover punitive damages, then it chose singularly inappropriate words: both the reference to injured parties and to redress suggests compensation, and not punishment.

Other statutes roughly contemporaneous with § 1983 illustrate that if Congress wanted to subject persons to a punitive damages remedy, it did so explicitly. For example, in § 59, 16 Stat. 207, Congress created express

---

they explain prior decisions, these cases may reflect a well-settled understanding in a particular jurisdiction of the law regarding punitive damages. Yet, decisions handed down well after 1871 are considerably *less* probative of legislative intent than decisions rendered before or shortly subsequent to the enactment of § 1983: it requires no detailed discussion to demonstrate that a member of the 42d Congress would have been more influenced by a decision from 1870 than by one from the 1890's. Accordingly, the bulk of the cases cited by the Court must be ignored; they simply illustrate the historical shift in legal doctrine, pointed out in text, from an actual-intent standard to a recklessness standard. If the Court is serious in its attention to 19th-century law, analysis must focus on the common law as it stood at the time of the 42d Congress. Here, notwithstanding the Court's numerous attempts to explain why decisions do not mean what they plainly say, it remains clear that in a majority of jurisdictions, actual malice was required in order to recover punitive damages.

punitive damage remedies for various types of commercial misconduct. Likewise, the False Claims Act, § 15, 12 Stat. 698, provided a civil remedy of double damages and a $2,000 civil forfeiture penalty for certain misstatements to the Government. As one Court of Appeals has remarked, "Where Congress has intended [to create a right to punitive damages] it has found no difficulty in using language appropriate to that end." *United Mine Workers v. Patton*, 211 F.2d 742, 749 (CA4 1954). And yet, in § 1983 one searches in vain for some hint of such a remedy.

In the light of the foregoing indications, it is accurate to say that the foundation upon which the right to punitive damages under § 1983 rests is precarious, at the best. * * *

JUSTICE O'CONNOR, dissenting.

Although I agree with the result reached in Justice Rehnquist's dissent, I write separately because I cannot agree with the approach taken by either the Court or Justice Rehnquist. Both opinions engage in exhaustive, but ultimately unilluminating, exegesis of the common law of the availability of punitive damages in 1871. Although both the Court and Justice Rehnquist display admirable skills in legal research and analysis of great numbers of musty cases, the results do not significantly further the goal of the inquiry: to establish the intent of the 42d Congress. In interpreting § 1983, we have often looked to the common law as it existed in 1871, in the belief that, when Congress was silent on a point, it intended to adopt the principles of the common law with which it was familiar. This approach makes sense when there was a generally prevailing rule of common law, for then it is reasonable to assume that congressmen were familiar with that rule and imagined that it would cover the cause of action that they were creating. But when a significant split in authority existed, it strains credulity to argue that Congress simply assumed that one view rather than the other would govern. Particularly in a case like this one, in which those interpreting the common law of 1871 must resort to dictionaries in an attempt to translate the language of the late nineteenth century into terms that judges of the late twentieth century can understand, and in an area in which the courts of the earlier period frequently used inexact and contradictory language, we cannot safely infer anything about congressional intent from the divided contemporaneous judicial opinions. The battle of the string citations can have no winner.

Once it is established that the common law of 1871 provides us with no real guidance on this question, we should turn to the policies underlying § 1983 to determine which rule best accords with those policies. In *Fact Concerts*, we identified the purposes of § 1983 as preeminently to compensate victims of constitutional violations and to deter further violations. The conceded availability of compensatory damages, particularly when coupled with the availability of attorney's fees under § 1988, completely fulfills the goal of compensation, leaving only deterrence to be served by awards of punitive damages. We must then confront the close question whether a standard permitting an award of unlimited punitive damages on the basis of recklessness will chill public officials in the performance of their duties more than it will deter violations of the Constitution, and whether the availability of punitive damages for reckless violations of the Constitution in addition to attorney's fees will create an incentive to bring an ever-increasing flood of § 1983 claims, threatening the ability of the federal courts to handle those that are meritorious. Although I cannot concur in Justice Rehnquist's wholesale condemnation of awards of punitive damages in any context or with the suggestion that punitive damages should not be available even for intentional or malicious violations of constitutional rights, I do agree with the discussion in * * * his opinion of the special problems of permitting awards of punitive damages for the recklessness of public officials. Since awards of compensatory damages and attorney's fees already provide significant deterrence, I am persuaded that the policies counseling against awarding punitive damages for the recklessness of public officials outweigh the desirability of any incremental deterrent effect that such awards may have. Consequently, I dissent.

NOTES ON THE EVOLVING COMMON LAW
AS A SOURCE FOR CONSTRUING STATUTES

1. *Interpretation and the Common Law.* Justice Brennan's opinion for the Court argues that the common law in 1871 supports punitive damages for reckless misconduct. Perhaps, but would the common law have permitted a prisoner to obtain such damages from his or her jailer in the circumstances of *Smith v. Wade*? Certainly not! See, e.g., *Moxley v. Roberts*, 43 S.W. 482 (Ky. 1897) (jailer not liable for beating of one prisoner by another unless he actually knew of the beating and failed to stop it); *Williams v. Adams*, 85 Mass. (3 Allen) 171 (1861). Why didn't Justice Brennan just rely on the modern common law, which does support his position?

Contrary to Justice Rehnquist's dissent, the Supreme Court sometimes looks to modern common law to fill in the gaps of § 1983. See *Imbler v. Pachtman*, 424 U.S. 409, 421–22 (1976) (rule of prosecutorial immunity, which was first recognized 25 years after § 1983 was enacted); *Carey v. Piphus*, 435 U.S. 247, 257–58 (1978) (modern law is the starting point for determining which injuries are to be compensated under § 1983). Do you suppose the Congress that adopted § 1983 in 1871 intended that the common law of that era was to supply binding answers to questions left open by the statute? Do you think that the Congress intended courts to develop § 1983 law over time by reference to contemporary developments, and thus that § 1983 might mean one thing in 1871 and quite another thing today?

Note this puzzle: Justices Brennan and Rehnquist looked at the same historical evidence yet came up with diametrically opposed conclusions about what the "common law" was in 1871. The initial, and cynical, impulse is to think that they were just manipulating the evidence to support the result each wanted. A less cynical view is that, in this case, each Justice was an amateur historian, but like professional historians the Justices had to figure out which evidence was important, what to make of conflicting signals, and how to assimilate the evidence into an account. In this complicated task, isn't the perspective of the interpreter going to make a difference? Professional historians recognize this. Shouldn't the Justices? Indeed, this is a point suggested by Justice O'Connor's dissent.

2. *Common Law Statutes.* Going one step beyond Justice Brennan's approach, Judge Richard Posner has argued in *The Federal Courts: Crisis and Reform* (1985) that some statutes, such as § 1983 and the Sherman Act, are essentially "common law statutes." That is, briefly phrased statutes addressing an important societal problem may be the occasion for judicial evolution in the common law tradition, especially if the legislature does not amend the statutes. In legal process argot, courts are institutionally competent to fill in the gaps to a statutory scheme when Congress essentially leaves the statute to judicial elaboration. Does this suggest a defense of Justice Brennan's majority opinion?

Classic instances in which the Supreme Court has interpreted a simple and vague federal statute as evidencing a congressional intent that the federal courts are to resolve open questions by use of an essentially common law method include the antitrust prohibitions of the Sherman Act and § 301 of the Taft-Hartley Act, which gives federal district courts jurisdiction to hear suits for violation of collective bargaining agreements. See, e.g., *Textile Workers Union v. Lincoln Mills*, 353 U.S. 448 (1957) ("federal common law" under § 301). More recently, the Foreign Sovereign Immunities Act of 1976 (FSIA), 28 U.S.C. §§ 1331, 1602–1611 et al., sets forth guidelines for federal and state court treatment of the sovereign immunity defense by foreign states. The main exception to immunity is the "commercial activity" exception, *id.* § 1605(a)(2), but the Act gives no precise definition of commercial activity. "The courts would have a great deal of latitude in determining what is a 'commercial activity' for purposes of this bill," said the House Report, and courts have taken that as a charter to apply the most current common law approaches to the issue. For a recent example applying common law property concepts to fill out the details of the FSIA, see *Permanent Mission of India to the United Nations v. City of New York*, 127 S.Ct. 2352 (2007).

One corollary of the common law statute idea is that Supreme Court precedents interpreting them ought to have the normal stare decisis effect of common law precedents — and not the super-strong presumption of correctness that accompanies other statutory precedents (Chapter 6, Section 2B). See *Leegin Creative Leather Prods., Inc. v. PSKS, Inc.*, 127 S.Ct. 2705 (2007) (precisely this justification for overruling a Sherman Act precedent); *State Oil Co. v. Khan*, 522 U.S. 3 (1997) (same); William Eskridge, Jr., *Overruling Statutory Precedents*, 76 Geo. L.J. 1361 (1988). A number of Supreme Court decisions have overruled previous constructions of Section 1983, essentially for common law reasons. E.g., *Monell v. Department of Social Servs.*, 436 U.S. 658 (1978). It is very likely that a Roberts Court majority disagrees with the *Smith v. Wade* approach to punitive damages. Should the Court feel free to overrule *Smith*? Are there reasons to exercise caution? Jot down your thoughts and read the next note.

3. *Recent Statutory Treatment of Punitive Damages in Civil Rights Cases.* The Civil Rights Act of 1991 amended Title VII to permit awards of punitive damages in cases of intentional discrimination. New 42 U.S.C. § 1981a(b)(1) allows such an award if the complainant can show that defendant engaged in such discrimination "with malice or with reckless indifference to the federally

protected rights of an aggrieved individual." Carole Kolstad sues her employer for allegedly passing over her for promotion on the basis of her sex. She seeks punitive damages because the decisionmaker not only manipulated the rules to deny her the promotion, but also made repeated derogatory references to women. The lower courts refuse Kolstad a charge to the jury for punitive damages; they rule that, to satisfy § 1981a(b)(1), the complainant must show "egregious" misconduct beyond that which would justify a finding of intentional discrimination.

Following *Smith v. Wade*, the Supreme Court reversed the lower courts and interpreted the 1991 Act to allow punitive damages for reckless as well as egregious conduct. See *Kolstad v. American Dental Ass'n*, 527 U.S. 526 (1999). Should *Kolstad* augur against overruling *Smith v. Wade* in section 1983 cases — or does it now provide an *additional reason* to overrule? Under the whole code rule of meaningful variation (*Casey*, Chapter 7, § 3A), when Congress wants liberal punitive damage awards in civil rights statutes, it explicitly provides for such damages (the 1991 Act). Because § 1983 says nothing about punitive damages, should they be available at all?

How should the Court approach the separate issue of when an employer should be liable in punitive damages for unauthorized conduct on the part of its supervisors? What relevance should the common law of agency have in this inquiry? See *Burlington Indus., Inc. v. Ellerth*, 524 U.S. 642 (1998) (standards for employer liability for hostile work environment and quid pro quo sexual harassment by supervisors).

Another Problem on the Common Law and Statutes

Problem 8–4. Reconsider Problem 8–2, the application of the Hobbs Act to Frankly Unctuous, in light of the common law background uncovered by James Lindgren, *The Elusive Distinction Between Bribery and Extortion: From the Common Law to the Hobbs Act*, 35 UCLA L. Rev. 815 (1988). According to Lindgren, at common law extortion was committed by a public official who took "by colour of his office" money that was not due him for the performance of his official duties. 1 Hawkins, *Pleas of the Crown* 316 (6th ed. 1787). Hence, a demand for the money (an "inducement") was not an element of the offense at common law. By including private efforts to extort, the Hobbs Act expanded the definition of "extortion" beyond that of the common law, but there is no indication in its legislative history that the Act sought to narrow the common law definition. There is reference in the legislative history that the terms "robbery and extortion" were "based on the New York law." The New York extortion statute applied to a public officer "who asks, or receives, or agrees to receive" unauthorized compensation. N.Y. Penal Code § 557 (1881). With this evidence in mind, how would you interpret the Hobbs Act now? See *Evans v. United States*, 504 U.S. 255 (1992).

What if Unctuous raises this further common law argument: The "under color of office" language itself imposes a requirement not found in the Government's case against Unctuous. "At common law it was essential that the money or property be obtained under color of office, *that is, under the pretense that the officer was entitled thereto by virtue of his office. The money* or thing received must have been claimed or accepted by right of office, and the person paying must have yielded to official authority." 3 Ronald A. Anderson, *Wharton's Criminal Law and Procedure* § 1393, at 790–91 (1957) (emphasis added). Assume this is a correct characterization of the common law. Should the Court interpret the Hobbs Act to overturn Unctuous' conviction? See *Evans* (Thomas, J., dissenting).

Problem 8–5. A federal statute prohibits the knowing transportation of "falsely made, forged, altered or counterfeited securities" in interstate commerce. Brook and Crook purchased used cars in Pennsylvania, rolled back the cars' odometers, and fraudulently altered the Pennsylvania titles to reflect the reduced mileage. They then sent the titles to Frook, a Virginia resident. Frook took the titles to Virginia authorities, represented that he owned the cars, and was issued Virginia titles to the cars with the false mileage figures. Frook then sent the Virginia titles to Hook, a Maryland resident, where they were used to sell the cars to unsuspecting buyers. Has Hook violated the statute? Hook says "no," arguing that the Virginia titles he received were not "falsely made" by the Virginia authorities, who had no reason to suspect the accuracy of the information contained in the titles they issued. Hook also argues that, at common law, "falsely made" meant "forgery," and that a document genuinely issued by an appropriate official is therefore not "falsely made." Do you agree? What if a sizable minority of the common law decisions existing at the time the statute was enacted treated such a document as "forged" or "falsely made"? Should the rule of lenity provide an easy way out of this problem? See *Moskal v. United States*, 498 U.S. 103 (1990).

B. LEGISLATIVE BACKGROUND (HISTORY)

Statutory history is, in a broad sense, the entire circumstances of a statute's creation and evolution, a point illustrated by the materials in the first subpart that follows. The formal history of a statute's evolution is widely considered relevant to statutory interpretation, even in jurisdictions whose courts will not examine legislative debates. See, e.g., Donald Gifford, *Statutory Interpretation* 91–95 (1990) (Australia). The same is true for the United States, whose courts do generally examine legislative documents and debates. Thus, the Court in *United States v. Wells*, 519 U.S. 482 (1997), interpreted 18 U.S.C. § 1014, criminalizing false statements to federally insured banks, not to have a materiality requirement. Justice Souter's opinion for the Court relied on the formal history of federal criminal provisions regarding such statements. Section 1014 was a synthesis of thirteen different provisions, at least ten of which had no materiality requirements at the time. This background suggested that Congress did not expect § 1014 to have a materiality requirement.

In this country, the term *legislative history* is mostly used in a narrower sense, to refer to the internal legislative pre-history of a statute — the internal institutional progress of a bill to enactment and the deliberation accompanying that progress.[d] The record of that journey may be quite voluminous and often contains statements by all sorts of people — legislators, bureaucrats, citizens, experts — which support one or another interpretation of the statute. A preliminary issue is how to carry out legal research that will reveal all the components of a statute's legislative history.[e] Once the material is identified, the question turns to what stuff in this internal legislative history "counts" toward interpreting the statute, and how much weight each relevant component should receive. Four subparts (2–5) will explore judicial use (or misuse) of statements made in committee reports, statements in hearings and floor debates, statements by sponsors, and post-enactment statements by legislators and committees. The last subpart (6) will ask whether interpretive meaning can be derived from things that are *not* said or done in the legislature.

As you read the following materials, consider the suggestion of Judge Patricia Wald, in *Some Observations on the Use of Legislative History in the 1981 Supreme Court Term*, 68 Iowa L. Rev. 195, 214 (1983), that "consistent and uniform rules for statutory construction and use of legislative materials are not being followed today. It sometimes seems that citing legislative history is

---

d. Otto Hetzel, Michael Libonati & Robert Williams, *Legislative Law and Process* 589 (3d ed. 2001), gives an excellent checklist of the materials that will constitute the "legislative history" of a law:

    1. Floor debate.

    2. Planned colloquy.

    3. Prepared statements on submission of a bill, in committee hearings and at the time of floor debates.

    4. Revised and amended statements.

    5. Statements in committees by the relevant executive branch administrators.

    6. Committee reports.

    7. Transcripts of discussions at committee hearings.

    8. Statements and submissions by interested persons, both local or state government and private parties.

    9. Committee debates on "mark-up" of bills.

    10. Conference committee reports.

    11. Analysis of bills by legislative counsel.

    12. Analysis of bills by relevant executive departments.

    13. Amendments accepted or rejected.

    14. Actions on and discussions about separate bills on the same topic, offered by each house, or in contrast to a similar composite bill.

    15. Executive branch messages and proposals whether from the President, cabinet secretaries or from independent agencies.

    16. Prior relevant administrative action or judicial decisions, with or without congressional acknowledgment.

    17. Other subsequent or prior legislation, especially conflicting acts.

    18. Recorded votes.

    19. The status of the person speaking, *i.e.*, a sponsor, committee chairman, floor leader, etc.

    20. Actions taken and reports, hearings and debates on prior related legislation.

e. Many law schools offer courses in advanced legal research that deal with legislative history and have developed excellent reference materials. E.g., on federal legislative history research, see http://www.law.berkeley.edu/library/dynamic/guide.php?guide=alr/fedleg; http://www.law.berkeley.edu/library/dynamic/guide.php?guide=general/caLegis concerns California legislative history.

still, as my late colleague Harold Leventhal once observed, akin to 'looking over a crowd and picking out your friends.' "[f]

1. *The Circumstances Surrounding the Introduction and Consideration of Legislation*

LEO SHEEP CO. v. UNITED STATES
Supreme Court of the United States, 1979
440 U.S. 668, 99 S.Ct. 1403, 59 L.Ed.2d 677

MR. JUSTICE REHNQUIST delivered the opinion of the Court.

This is one of those rare cases evoking episodes in this country's history that, if not forgotten, are remembered as dry facts and not as adventure. Admittedly the issue is mundane: Whether the Government has an implied easement to build a road across land that was originally granted to the Union Pacific Railroad under the Union Pacific Act of 1862 — a grant that was part of a governmental scheme to subsidize the construction of the transcontinental railroad. But that issue is posed against the backdrop of a fascinating chapter in our history. As this Court noted in another case involving the Union Pacific Railroad, "courts, in construing a statute, may with propriety recur to the history of the times when it was passed; and this is frequently necessary, in order to ascertain the reason as well as the meaning of particular provisions in it." *United States v. Union Pacific R. Co.*, 91 U.S. 72, 79 (1875). In this spirit we relate the events underlying passage of the Union Pacific Act of 1862.

[I] The early 19th century — from the Louisiana Purchase in 1803 to the Gadsden Purchase in 1853 — saw the acquisition of the territory we now regard as the American West. During those years, however, the area remained a largely untapped resource, for the settlers on the eastern seaboard of the United States did not keep pace with the rapidly expanding western frontier. A vaguely delineated area forbiddingly referred to as the "Great American Desert" can be found on more than one map published before 1850, embracing much of the United States' territory west of the Missouri River. As late as 1860, for example, the entire population of the State of Nebraska was less than 30,000 persons, which represented one person for every five square miles of land area within the State.

With the discovery of gold at Sutter's Mill in California in 1848, the California gold rush began and with it a sharp increase in settlement of the West. Those in the East with visions of instant wealth, however, confronted the unenviable choice among an arduous 4-month overland trek, risking yellow fever on a 35-day voyage via the Isthmus of Panama, and a better than 4-month voyage around Cape Horn. They obviously yearned for another alternative, and interest focused on the transcontinental railroad.

---

f. Judge Leventhal's quip, in somewhat different form, has now made its way into the Supreme Court reports. Justice Scalia has offered it as a justification for his new textualism: "Judge Harold Leventhal used to describe the use of legislative history as the equivalent of entering a crowded cocktail party and looking over the heads of the guests for one's friends." *Conroy v. Aniskoff*, 507 U.S. 511, 519 (1993) (Scalia, J., concurring in the judgment).

The idea of a transcontinental railroad predated the California gold rush. From the time that Asa Whitney had proposed a relatively practical plan for its construction in 1844, it had, in the words of one of this century's leading historians of the era, "engaged the eager attention of promoters and politicians until dozens of schemes were in the air." The building of the railroad was not to be the unalloyed product of the free-enterprise system. There was indeed the inspiration of men like Thomas Durant and Leland Stanford and the perspiration of a generation of immigrants, but animating it all was the desire of the Federal Government that the West be settled. This desire was intensified by the need to provide a logistical link with California in the heat of the Civil War. That the venture was much too risky and much too expensive for private capital alone was evident in the years of fruitless exhortation; private investors would not move without tangible governmental inducement.

In the mid-19th century there was serious disagreement as to the forms that inducement could take. Mr. Justice Story, in his Commentaries on the Constitution, described one extant school of thought which argued that "internal improvements," such as railroads, were not within the enumerated constitutional powers of Congress. Under such a theory, the direct subsidy of a transcontinental railroad was constitutionally suspect — an uneasiness aggravated by President Andrew Jackson's 1830 veto of a bill appropriating funds to construct a road from Maysville to Lexington within the State of Kentucky.

The response to this constitutional "gray" area, and source of political controversy, was the "checkerboard" land-grant scheme. The Union Pacific Act of 1862 granted public land to the Union Pacific Railroad for each mile of track that it laid. Land surrounding the railway right-of-way was divided into "checkerboard" blocks. Odd-numbered lots were granted to the Union Pacific; even-numbered lots were reserved by the Government. As a result, Union Pacific land in the area of the right-of-way was usually surrounded by public land, and vice versa. The historical explanation for this peculiar disposition is that it was apparently an attempt to disarm the "internal improvement" opponents by establishing a grant scheme with "demonstrable" benefits. As one historian notes in describing an 1827 federal land grant intended to facilitate private construction of a road between Columbus and Sandusky, Ohio:

> "Though awkwardly stated, and not fully developed in the Act of 1827, this was the beginning of a practice to be followed in most future instances of granting land for the construction of specific internal improvements: donating alternate sections or one half of the land within a strip along the line of the project and reserving the other half for sale. . . . In later donations the price of the reserved sections was doubled so that it could be argued, as the *Congressional Globe* shows *ad infinitum*, that by giving half the land away and thereby making possible construction of the road, canal, or railroad, the government would recover from the reserved sections as much as it would have received from the whole." P. Gates, History of Public Land Law Development 345–346 (1968).

In 1850 this technique was first explicitly employed for the subsidization of a railroad when the Illinois delegation in Congress, which included Stephen

A. Douglas, secured the enactment of a bill that granted public lands to aid the construction of the Illinois Central Railroad. The Illinois Central and proposed connecting lines to the south were granted nearly three million acres along rights of way through Illinois, Mississippi, and Alabama, and by the end of 1854 the main line of the Illinois Central from Chicago to Cairo, Ill., had been put into operation. Before this line was constructed, public lands had gone begging at the Government's minimum price; within a few years after its completion, the railroad had disposed of more than one million acres and was rapidly selling more at prices far above those at which land had been originally offered by the Government.

The "internal improvements" theory was not the only obstacle to a transcontinental railroad. In 1853 Congress had appropriated moneys and authorized Secretary of War Jefferson Davis to undertake surveys of various proposed routes for a transcontinental railroad. Congress was badly split along sectional lines on the appropriate location of the route — so badly split that Stephen A. Douglas, now a Senator from Illinois, in 1854 suggested the construction of a northern, central, and southern route, each with connecting branches in the East. That proposal, however, did not break the impasse.

The necessary impetus was provided by the Civil War. Senators and Representatives from those States which seceded from the Union were no longer present in Congress, and therefore the sectional overtones of the dispute as to routes largely disappeared. Although there were no major engagements during the Civil War in the area between the Missouri River and the west coast which would be covered by any transcontinental railroad, there were two minor engagements which doubtless made some impression upon Congress of the necessity for being able to transport readily men and materials into that area for military purposes. * * *

These engagements gave some immediacy to the comments of Congressman Edwards of New Hampshire during the debate on the Pacific Railroad bill:

> "If this Union is to be preserved, if we are successfully to combat the difficulties around us, if we are to crush out this rebellion against the lawful authority of the Government, and are to have an entire restoration, it becomes us, with statesmanlike prudence and sagacity, to look carefully into the future, and to guard in advance against all possible considerations which may threaten the dismemberment of the country hereafter." Cong. Globe, 37th Cong., 2d Sess., 1703 (1862).

As is often the case, war spurs technological development, and Congress enacted the Union Pacific Act in May 1862. Perhaps not coincidentally, the Homestead Act was passed the same month.

The Union Pacific Act specified a route west from the 100th meridian, between a site in the Platte River Valley near the cities of Kearney and North Platte, Neb., to California. The original plan was for five eastern terminals located at various points on or near the Missouri River; but in fact Omaha was the only terminal built according to the plan.

The land grants made by the Union Pacific Act included all the odd-numbered lots within 10 miles on either side of the track. When the Union

Pacific's original subscription drive for private investment proved a failure, the land grant was doubled by extending the checkerboard grants to 20 miles on either side of the track. Private investment was still sluggish, and construction did not begin until July 1865, three months after the cessation of Civil War hostilities.[13] Thus began a race with the Central Pacific Railroad, which was laying track eastward from Sacramento, for the Government land grants which went with each mile of track laid. The race culminated in the driving of the golden spike at Promontory, Utah, on May 10, 1869.

[II] This case is the modern legacy of these early grants. Petitioners, the Leo Sheep Co. and the Palm Livestock Co., are the Union Pacific Railroad's successors in fee to specific odd-numbered sections of land in Carbon County, Wyo. These sections lie to the east and south of the Seminoe Reservoir, an area that is used by the public for fishing and hunting. Because of the checkerboard configuration, it is physically impossible to enter the Seminoe Reservoir sector from this direction without some minimum physical intrusion upon private land. In the years immediately preceding this litigation, the Government had received complaints that private owners were denying access over their lands to the reservoir area or requiring the payment of access fees. After negotiation with these owners failed, the Government cleared a dirt road extending from a local county road to the reservoir across both public domain lands and fee lands of the Leo Sheep Co. It also erected signs inviting the public to use the road as a route to the reservoir.

Petitioners initiated this action pursuant to 28 U.S.C. § 2409a to quiet title against the United States. The District Court granted petitioners' motion for summary judgment, but was reversed on appeal by the Court of Appeals for the Tenth Circuit. The latter court concluded that when Congress granted land to the Union Pacific Railroad, it implicitly reserved an easement to pass over the odd-numbered sections in order to reach the even-numbered sections that were held by the Government. Because this holding affects property rights in 150 million acres of land in the Western United States, we granted certiorari, and now reverse.

---

13. Construction would not have begun then without the Crédit Mobilier, a limited-liability company that was essentially owned by the promoters and investors of the Union Pacific. One of these investors, Oakes Ames, a wealthy New England shovel maker, was a substantial investor in Crédit Mobilier and also a Member of Congress. Crédit Mobilier contracted with the Union Pacific to build portions of the road, and by 1866 several individuals were large investors in both corporations. Allegations of improper use of funds and bribery of Members of the House of Representatives led to the appointment of a special congressional investigatory committee that during 1872 and 1873 looked into the affairs of Crédit Mobilier. These investigations revealed improprieties on the part of more than one Member of Congress, and the committee recommended that Ames be expelled from Congress. The investigation also touched on the career of a future President. See M. Leech & H. Brown, The Garfield Orbit (1978).

In 1872 the House of Representatives enacted a resolution condemning the policy of granting subsidies of public lands to railroads. Cong. Globe, 42d Cong., 2d Sess., 1585 (1872); see *Great Northern R. Co. v. United States*, 315 U.S. 262, 273–274 (1942). Of course, the reaction of the public or of Congress a decade after the enactment of the Union Pacific Act to the conduct of those associated with the Union Pacific cannot influence our interpretation of that Act today.

The Government does not claim that there is any express reservation of an easement in the Union Pacific Act that would authorize the construction of a public road on the Leo Sheep Co.'s property. Section 3 of the 1862 Act sets out a few specific reservations to the "checkerboard" grant. The grant was not to include land "sold, reserved, or otherwise disposed of by the United States," such as land to which there were homestead claims. Mineral lands were also excepted from the operation of the Act. Given the existence of such explicit exceptions, this Court has in the past refused to add to this list by divining some "implicit" congressional intent. In *Missouri, K. & T.R. Co. v. Kansas Pacific R. Co.*, 97 U.S. 491, 497 (1878), for example, this Court in an opinion by Mr. Justice Field noted that the intent of Congress in making the Union Pacific grants was clear: "It was to aid in the construction of the road by a gift of lands along its route, without reservation of rights, except such as were specifically mentioned * * *." The Court held that, although a railroad right-of-way under the grant may not have been located until years after 1862, by the clear terms of the Act only claims established prior to 1862 overrode the railroad grant; conflicting claims arising after that time could not be given effect. To overcome the lack of support in the Act itself, the Government here argues that the implicit reservation of the asserted easement is established by "settled rules of property law" and by the Unlawful Inclosures of Public Lands Act of 1885.

Where a private landowner conveys to another individual a portion of his lands in a certain area and retains the rest, it is presumed at common law that the grantor has reserved an easement to pass over the granted property if such passage is necessary to reach the retained property. These rights-of-way are referred to as "easements by necessity." There are two problems with the Government's reliance on that notion in this case. First of all, whatever right of passage a private landowner might have, it is not at all clear that it would include the right to construct a road for public access to a recreational area.[15] More importantly, the easement is not actually a matter of necessity in this case because the Government has the power of eminent domain. Jurisdictions have generally seen eminent domain and easements by necessity as alternative ways to effect the same result. For example, the State of Wyoming no longer recognizes the common-law easement by necessity in cases involving landlocked estates. It provides instead for a procedure whereby the landlocked owner can have an access route condemned on his behalf upon payment of the

---

15. It is very unlikely that Congress in 1862 contemplated this type of intrusion, and it could not reasonably be maintained that failure to provide access to the public at large would render the Seminoe Reservoir land useless. Yet these are precisely the considerations that define the scope of easements by necessity. As one commentator relied on by the Government notes: "As the name implies, these easements are the product of situations where the usefulness of land is at stake. The scope of the resultant easement embodies the best judgment of the court as to what is reasonably essential to the land's use. * * * Changes in the dominant parcel's use exert some, but not a great influence, in determining the scope of such easements." 3 [R. Powell, Real Property ¶ 416 (1978).] See, *e.g., Higbee Fishing Club v. Atlantic City Electric Co.*, 78 N.J.Eq. 434, 79 A. 326 (1911) (footpath, not roadway, proper scope of easement where use of dominant estate as clubhouse could not have been contemplated by parties to original grant).

necessary compensation to the owner of the servient estate. For similar reasons other state courts have held that the "easement by necessity" doctrine is not available to the sovereign.

The applicability of the doctrine of easement by necessity in this case is, therefore, somewhat strained, and ultimately of little significance. The pertinent inquiry in this case is the intent of Congress when it granted land to the Union Pacific in 1862. The 1862 Act specifically listed reservations to the grant, and we do not find the tenuous relevance of the common-law doctrine of ways of necessity sufficient to overcome the inference prompted by the omission of any reference to the reserved right asserted by the Government in this case. It is possible that Congress gave the problem of access little thought; but it is at least as likely that the thought which was given focused on negotiation, reciprocity considerations, and the power of eminent domain as obvious devices for ameliorating disputes.[18] So both as matter of common-law doctrine and as a matter of construing congressional intent, we are unwilling to imply rights-of-way, with the substantial impact that such implication would have on property rights granted over 100 years ago, in the absence of a stronger case for their implication than the Government makes here.

The Government would have us decide this case on the basis of the familiar canon of construction that, when grants to federal lands are at issue, any doubts "are resolved for the Government not against it." *Andrus v. Charlestone Stone Products Co.*, 436 U.S. 604, 617 (1978). But this Court long ago declined to apply this canon in its full vigor to grants under the railroad Acts. In 1885 this Court observed:

---

18. The intimations that can be found in the Congressional Globe are that there was no commonly understood reservation by the Government of the right to enter upon granted lands and construct a public road. Representative Cradlebaugh of Nevada offered an amendment to what became the Union Pacific Act of 1862 that would have reserved the right to the public to enter granted land and prospect for valuable minerals upon the payment of adequate compensation to the owner. The proposed amendment was defeated. The only Representative other than Cradlebaugh who spoke to it, Representative Sargent of California, stated:

"The amendment of the gentleman proposes to allow the public to enter upon the lands of any man, whether they be mineral lands or not, and prospect for gold and silver, and as compensation proposes some loose method of payment for the injuries inflicted. Now, sir, it may turn out that the man who thus commits the injuries may be utterly insolvent, not able to pay a dollar, and how is the owner of the property to be compensated for tearing down his dwellings, rooting up his orchards, and destroying his crops?" Cong. Globe, 37th Cong., 2d Sess., 1910 (1862).

In debates on an earlier Pacific Railroad bill it was explicitly suggested that there be "a reservation in every grant of land that [the Government] shall have a right to go through it, and take it at proper prices to be paid hereafter." The author of this proposal, Senator Simmons of Rhode Island, lamented the lack of such a reservation in the bill under consideration. Cong. Globe, 35th Cong., 2d Sess., 579 (1859). Apparently the intended purpose of this proposed reservation was to permit railroads to obtain rights-of-way through granted property at the Government's behest. Senator Simmons' comments are somewhat confused, but they certainly do not evince any prevailing assumption that the Government implicitly reserved a right-of-way through granted lands.

"The solution of [ownership] questions [involving the railroad grants] depends, of course, upon the construction given to the acts making the grants; and they are to receive such a construction as will carry out the intent of Congress, however difficult it might be to give full effect to the language used if the grants were by instruments of private conveyance. To ascertain that intent we must look to the condition of the country when the acts were passed, as well as to the purpose declared on their face, and read all parts of them together." *Winona & St. Peter R. Co. v. Barney*, 113 U.S. 618, 625 (1885).

[Justice Rehnquist then discussed the Unlawful Inclosures of Public Lands Act of 1885 and concluded that it was aimed at a different sort of problem: the use of fencing arrangements by cattlemen to deprive sheepherders of access to grazing lands. The Court's opinion concluded with the observation that Congress in 1862 did not anticipate these problems:] The order of the day was the open range — barbed wire had not made its presence felt — and the type of incursions on private property necessary to reach public land was not such an interference that litigation would serve any motive other than spite. Congress obviously believed that when development came, it would occur in a parallel fashion on adjoining public and private lands and that the process of subdivision, organization of a polity, and the ordinary pressures of commercial and social intercourse would work itself into a pattern of access roads. * * * It is some testament to common sense that the present case is virtually unprecedented, and that in the 117 years since the grants were made, litigation over access questions generally has been rare.

Nonetheless, the present times are litigious ones and the 37th Congress did not anticipate our plight. Generations of land patents have issued without any express reservation of the right now claimed by the Government. Nor has a similar right been asserted before. When the Secretary of the Interior has discussed access rights, his discussion has been colored by the assumption that those rights had to be purchased. This Court has traditionally recognized the special need for certainty and predictability where land titles are concerned, and we are unwilling to upset settled expectations to accommodate some ill-defined power to construct public thoroughfares without compensation. The judgment of the Court of Appeals for the Tenth Circuit is accordingly

Reversed.

MR. JUSTICE WHITE took no part in the consideration or decision of this case.

NOTES ON *LEO SHEEP* AND LEGISLATIVE CONTEXT

1. *The Sweep versus the Reality of History.* Reading Justice Rehnquist's opinion, you can almost feel the wagon train moving you West. The first part of the opinion, the historical saga of the railroad project, strikes us as cogent and useful. The next part, the legal reasoning, strikes us as less so. The unanimous Court is obviously following the "imaginative reconstruction" approach of Judge Hand and Dean Pound — putting oneself in the mindset of the 1862 Congress (see Chapter 7, § 1). But the Court's assertion that "[i]t is possible that Congress gave the problem of access little thought" strikes us as

an understatement. Is there any evidence adduced by the Court that the 1862 Congress gave *any* thought to the access issue? And if Congress had given some thought, surely it would have wanted the government to have a reasonable right of access. Is the Court's assumption credible that "the thought which was given focused on negotiation, reciprocity considerations, and the power of eminent domain" as ways of obtaining access? Congress in 1866, for example, enacted a statute giving any person free and unrestricted access over the public domain. Right of Way Act, 14 Stat. 251 (1866). If the 1862 Congress had "assumed" that it could negotiate a trade of railroad access through public lands in return for state access through the railroad's lands, why would Congress have given away that bargaining chip in 1866? Why would Congress in 1862 want to use eminent domain — paying money — for access rights that it could retain by simple statutory fiat? Would the venture capitalists (or robber barons, if you prefer) not have built the transcontinental railroad otherwise?

2. *The Flip Side of* Leo Sheep. Does the private grantee or its successor have an easement by necessity through the government's checkerboard squares? The leading discussion on this question argued that it does. Comment, *Easements by Way of Necessity Across Federal Lands*, 35 Wash. L. Rev. 105, 113–17 (1960). This remarkable student comment correctly anticipated the *Leo Sheep* result and reasoning but argued that the same result (no easement by necessity) should not occur for the converse situation. The common law objections in *Leo Sheep* — that easements by necessity are not created for recreational uses or for government entities which may obtain access through eminent domain — have no force when a private developer demands an easement through the government lands. Nor does the legislative policy argument work against the private grantee's easement, since private access would subserve the Congressional goal of developing the granted land as quickly as possible. Cf. *Utah v. Andrus*, 486 F.Supp. 995, 1002 (D. Utah 1979), *appeal dismissed per stip.*, Nos. 79–2307 & 79–2308 (10th Cir. Jan. 28 & Mar. 28, 1980) (Congress conveyed permanent rights of access to Utah when it granted school trust lands to the State as a means of generating revenue). A contrary position was taken in an Opinion by Attorney General Civiletti. 43 Op. Att'y Gen. 26 (1980). The opinion determined that easements by necessity did not run against the government, unless that was an implied term of the granting statute. "[L]and grants generally are to be strictly construed. This rule must be balanced against the conflicting rule that in some situations certain types of land grants may deserve a more liberal construction because of the circumstances surrounding passage of the statutes in question. [*Leo Sheep.*] Absent express language to the contrary, however, a grant should not be construed to include broad rights to use retained Government property, particularly in the case of gratuitous grants."

Consider this policy argument: not to infer an easement by necessity in the original grant would impel the United States and private grantees holding alternate checkerboard squares to cooperate. That is, if neither holder has an easement, each has an incentive to work out a reasonable deal with the other, or neither will be able to have meaningful access to its land. On the other hand, if the United States has no easement but the grantee does, the grantee has little incentive to reach a "fair" bargain with the United States, forcing the United States to pay a high price or go to the trouble and expense of condemning the easement through eminent domain. Once the Supreme Court has decided that the government does not have an easement, doesn't it make sense then to deny the easement for the private holders as well? (One might argue that the rule which would minimize transactions costs would be to give *both* the government and the private holders an easement, or give them both eminent domain power.)

3. *Subsequent Developments.* In any event, the context in which the *Leo Sheep* problem arose was vastly different from that in which the law was passed. A shift in statutory policy came in the late nineteenth century, to protect the nation's natural resources from the results of what was then perceived as excessively generous land grants earlier. See Roy Marvin Robbins, *Our Landed Heritage: The Public Domain, 1776–1970*, at 301–24 (1976). Thus after giving away more than 125 million acres of public land to the railroads, Congress discontinued the land grant policy in the 1890s. See Paul Wallace Gates, *History of Public Land Law Development* (1968). And in 1891, Congress passed a law authorizing the President to reserve forest lands from the public domain (thus taking them out of the coverage of the 1866 access law), Act of March 3, 1891, ch. 561, § 24, 26 Stat. 1103 (the Forest Reserve Act), and 20 million acres were thereby reserved by Presidential proclamation in 1897. Further reservations were made throughout the twentieth century, as federal policy decisively turned toward conserving what was becoming perceived as a scarce resource. The Wilderness Act of 1964, 78 Stat. 890, codified at 16 U.S.C. §§ 1131–1136 (1988), placed even greater restrictions on certain federal lands, and this leading Act was followed in the 1970s and 1980s by more wilderness designations by Congress. In 1976, Congress repealed the access law of 1866 and replaced it with Title V of the Federal Land Policy & Management Act of 1976, 90 Stat. 2744, 2776, codified at 43 U.S.C. §§ 1761–1770 (1988), which authorizes the Department of the Interior to grant rights of access through a discretionary system. Are these subsequent statutes and federal policies relevant to the issue whether private grantees have an absolute right of access across federal checkerboard lands?

2. *Committee Reports (and an Introduction to the Great Legislative History Debate)*

Most judges and scholars agree that committee reports should be considered as authoritative legislative history and should be given great weight (i.e., a statement in a committee report will usually count more than a statement by a single legislator). Justice Jackson, concurring in *Schwegmann Bros. v. Calvert Distillers Corp.*, 341 U.S. 384, 395 (1951), objected to the use of legislative materials to interpret statutes, but excepted committee reports from his quarrel. Jorge Carro & Andrew Brann, *The U.S. Supreme Court and the Use of Legislative Histories: A Statistical Analysis*, 22 Jurimeterics J. 294, 304 (1982), report that over a 40-year period, over 60% of the Supreme Court's citations to legislative history were references to committee reports. Our casual examination of Supreme Court opinions since 1982 suggests that the qualitative dominance of committee reports continues.

Committee reports appear particularly well-suited for the authoritative role they have played. Most legislation is essentially written in committee or subcommittee, and any collective statement by the members of that subgroup will represent the best-informed thought about what the proposed legislation is doing. Committee reports are also accessible documents, both in the sense of being easily located through legal research and of being easy to comprehend once found. They usually set forth the problem(s) calling forth the proposed legislation, the general solution(s) posited by the bill, and a section-by-section summary of the provisions of the bill. The report of a conference committee (where the two legislative chambers have passed different forms of the same bill and must resolve their differences in conference) typically sets forth, for each provision, the version passed by each chamber and what the conference committee did with the provision (and sometimes also an explanation why it took the action it did).

There are, on the other hand, limitations on the usefulness of committee reports in giving meaning to ambiguous statutes. First, there is sometimes *no* committee report for a particular bill or an important provision in the bill, because it has been added as part of the floor debate. This is especially true of many of the civil rights bills. Recall from Chapter 1, § 1, that the sex discrimination provision in Title VII was added as a floor amendment in the House (and as something of a surprise to the bill's sponsors); hence, there is no discussion of that critical amendment in the House Judiciary Committee report. There was no committee report for the Act in the Senate, because the sponsors avoided sending the House bill to committee, which was Senator Eastland's preserve. Compare *Hishon v. King & Spalding*, 467 U.S. 69, 75 & n.7 (1984) (relying on Senate report for civil rights bill that was similar but never enacted). And there was no conference committee report, because the House rapidly acceded to the Senate's revisions, the sponsors knowing that further delays in the bill's enactment might prove fatal. See also *Local 82, Furniture & Piano Moving Union v. Crowley*, 467 U.S. 526 (1984) (interpreting Landrum-Griffin Act, much of which was written on the House and Senate floor).

Second, the committee report is often as ambiguous as the statute. As a shorter, more compressed form of the statute, the committee report may even be misleading, as it leaves out important qualifications in its discussion of the proposed legislation or particular provisions. (The committee report is probably most useful as a statement of the goals and their relative importance in the statutory scheme, since most statutes do not carry with them statements of purpose.) Indeed, a striking feature of the committee report is that it is the end-product of the committee's consideration, and therefore comes at a stage of consensus. In many instances, the key point in the process is "mark-up" of the bill in committee or subcommittee, for it is there that the legislators make the critical choices and compromises and specifically reject proposed alternatives. See John Kernochan, *The Legislative Process* 25 (1981). Traditionally, there was no official record of mark-up sessions, a practice that has been opened up to the public somewhat in the last two decades. As a consequence, what is often the most revealing collection of statements was often not available, or admissible, in the process of statutory interpretation. See

Wald, *supra*, at 202. In the last twenty years, however, committee mark-ups, especially of tax bills, have increasingly been made available, either through quasi-official transcripts or unofficial reports in tax journals or online. One might therefore expect to see more references to these sources by judges willing to consider legislative history. E.g., *Regan v. Wald*, 468 U.S. 222 (1984) (both majority and dissenting opinions relying on explanation accompanying House committee mark-up).

Third, when there is a committee report and the report contains relevant statements, one might be suspicious of the usefulness of those statements under some circumstances. Lobbyists and lawyers maneuver endlessly to persuade staff members (who write the committee reports) or their legislative bosses to throw in helpful language in the reports when insertion of similar language would be inappropriate or infeasible for the statute itself. "Smuggling in" helpful language through the legislative history is a time-tested practice.

In state legislatures, committee reports can take a variety of forms, not all of which are published or are readily available to the public: (1) regular reports of standing committees or conference committees, like those produced in the U.S. Congress; (2) staff analysis of a pending bill, which is in many states the main document which is actually distributed to legislators; and (3) reports of special committees created to investigate and to resolve important problems expeditiously or to investigate problems, as well as reports of collections of experts (often "law revision commissions") who have drafted legislation adopted in the state. As *Li v. Yellow Cab Co.* (Chapter 7, § 2B) suggests, committee reports and similar documents are often used to interpret ambiguous statutes at the state level.

BLANCHARD v. BERGERON
Supreme Court of the United States, 1989
489 U.S. 87, 109 S.Ct. 939, 105 L.Ed.2d 181

JUSTICE WHITE delivered the opinion of the Court.

[A jury awarded Blanchard $5,000 in compensatory damages and $5,000 in punitive damages on his civil rights claim, under 42 U.S.C. § 1983, that he had been beaten by a sheriff's deputy. He sought attorney's fees under the 1976 Civil Rights Attorney's Fee Award Act, codified at 42 U.S.C. § 1988. The district court awarded $7,500 in fees. The Fifth Circuit, however, held that under its decision in *Johnson v. Georgia Highway Express, Inc.*, 488 F.2d 714 (5th Cir. 1974), the 40% contingency fee agreement Blanchard had entered into with his attorney set a ceiling on recoverable fees. Thus, the Fifth Circuit limited the fee award to $4,000 (40% of the $10,000 damages awarded).]

Section 1988 provides that the court, "in its discretion, may allow . . . a reasonable attorney's fee . . . ." The section does not provide a specific definition of "reasonable" fee, and the question is whether the award must be limited to the amount provided in a contingent fee agreement. The legislative history of the Act is instructive insofar as it tells us: "In computing the fee, counsel for prevailing parties should be paid, as is traditional with attorneys compensated by a fee-paying client, 'for all time reasonably expended on a matter.' " S.Rep. No. 94–1011, p. 6 (1976) (citing *Davis v. County of Los*

Angeles, 8 EPD ¶ 9444 (CD Cal. 1974); and *Stanford Daily v. Zurcher*, 64 F.R.D. 680, 684 (ND Cal. 1974)).

In many past cases considering the award of attorney's fees under § 1988, we have turned our attention to *Johnson v. Georgia Highway Express, Inc.*, a case decided before the enactment of the Civil Rights Attorney's Fee Award Act of 1976. As we stated in *Hensley v. Eckerhart*, 461 U.S. 424, 429–431 (1983), *Johnson* provides guidance to Congress' intent because both the House and Senate Reports refer to the 12 factors set forth in *Johnson* for assessing the reasonableness of an attorney's fee award. The Senate Report, in particular, refers to three District Court decisions that "correctly applied" the 12 factors laid out in *Johnson*.

In the course of its discussion of the factors to be considered by a court in awarding attorney's fees, the *Johnson* court dealt with fee arrangements:

> " 'Whether or not [a litigant] agreed to pay a fee and in what amount is not decisive. Conceivably, a litigant might agree to pay his counsel a fixed dollar fee. This might be even more than the fee eventually allowed by the court. Or he might agree to pay his lawyer a percentage contingent fee that would be greater than the fee the court might ultimately set. Such arrangements should not determine the court's decision. The criterion for the court is not what the parties agree but what is reasonable.' "

Yet in the next sentence, *Johnson* says "In no event, however, should the litigant be awarded a fee greater than he is contractually bound to pay, if indeed the attorneys have contracted as to amount." This latter statement, never disowned in the Circuit, was the basis for the decision below. But we doubt that Congress embraced this aspect of *Johnson*, for it pointed to the three District Court cases in which the factors are "correctly applied." Those cases clarify that the fee arrangement is but a single factor and not determinative. In *Stanford Daily v. Zurcher*, [*supra,*] for example, the District Court considered a contingent-fee arrangement to be a factor, but not dispositive, in the calculation of a fee award. In *Davis v. County of Los Angeles, supra*, the court permitted a fee award to counsel in a public interest firm which otherwise would have been entitled to no fee. Finally, in *Swann v. Charlotte-Mecklenburg Board of Education*, 66 F.R.D. 483 (WDNC 1975), the court stated that reasonable fees should be granted regardless of the individual plaintiff's fee obligations. *Johnson*'s "List of 12" thus provides a useful catalog of the many factors to be considered in assessing the reasonableness of an award of attorney's fees; but the one factor at issue here, the attorney's private fee arrangement, standing alone, is not dispositive.

The *Johnson* contingency-fee factor is simply that, a factor. The presence of a pre-existing fee agreement may aid in determining reasonableness. " 'The fee quoted to the client or the percentage of the recovery agreed to is helpful in demonstrating that attorney's fee expectations when he accepted the case.' " *Pennsylvania v. Delaware Valley Citizens' Council for Clean Air*, 483 U.S. 711 (1987), quoting *Johnson*. But as we see it, a contingent-fee contract does not impose an automatic ceiling on an award of attorney's fees and to hold otherwise would be inconsistent with the statute and its policy and purpose.

As we understand § 1988's provision for allowing a "reasonable attorney's fee," it contemplates reasonable compensation, in light of all of the circumstances, for the time and effort expended by the attorney for the prevailing plaintiff, no more and no less. Should a fee agreement provide less than a reasonable fee calculated in this manner, the defendant should nevertheless be required to pay the higher amount. The defendant is not, however, required to pay the amount called for in a contingent-fee contract if it is more than a reasonable fee calculated in the usual way. It is true that the purpose of § 1988 was to make sure that competent counsel was available to civil rights plaintiffs, and it is of course arguable that if a plaintiff is able to secure an attorney on the basis of a contingent or other fee agreement, the purpose of the statute is served if the plaintiff is bound by his contract. On that basis, however, the plaintiff should recover nothing from the defendant, which would be plainly contrary to the statute. And Congress implemented its purpose by broadly requiring all defendants to pay a reasonable fee to all prevailing plaintiffs, if ordered to do so by the court. Thus it is that a plaintiff's recovery will not be reduced by what he must pay his counsel. Plaintiffs who can afford to hire their own lawyers, as well as impecunious litigants, may take advantage of this provision. And where there are lawyers or organizations that will take a plaintiff's case without compensation, that fact does not bar the award of a reasonable fee. All of this is consistent with and reflects our decisions in cases involving court-awarded attorney's fees.

Hensley v. Eckerhart, [*supra*,] directed lower courts to make an initial estimate of reasonable attorney's fees by applying prevailing billing rates to the hours reasonably expended on successful claims. And we have said repeatedly that "[t]he initial estimate of a reasonable attorney's fee is properly calculated by multiplying the number of hours reasonably expended on the litigation times a reasonable hourly rate." The courts may then adjust this lodestar calculation by other factors. We have never suggested that a different approach is to be followed in cases where the prevailing party and his (or her) attorney have executed a contingent-fee agreement. To the contrary, * * * we have adopted the lodestar approach as the centerpiece of attorney's fee awards. The *Johnson* factors may be relevant in adjusting the lodestar amount but no one factor is a substitute for multiplying reasonable billing rates by a reasonable estimation of the number of hours expended on the litigation. * * *

If a contingent-fee agreement were to govern as a strict limitation on the award of attorney's fees, an undesirable emphasis might be placed on the importance of the recovery of damages in civil rights litigation. The intention of Congress was to encourage successful civil rights litigation, not to create a special incentive to prove damages and shortchange efforts to seek effective injunctive or declaratory relief. Affirming the decision below would create an artificial disincentive for an attorney who enters into a contingent fee agreement, unsure of whether his client's claim sounded in state tort law or in federal civil rights, from fully exploring all possible avenues of relief. Section 1988 makes no distinction between actions for damages and suits for equitable relief. Congress has elected to encourage meritorious civil rights claims because of the benefits of such litigation for the named plaintiff and for society at large, irrespective of whether the action seeks monetary damages.

It should also be noted that we have not accepted the contention that fee awards in § 1983 damages cases should be modeled upon the contingent-fee arrangements used in personal injury litigation. "[W]e reject the notion that a civil rights action for damages constitutes nothing more than a private tort suit benefiting only the individual plaintiffs whose rights were violated. Unlike most private tort litigants, a civil rights plaintiff seeks to vindicate important civil and constitutional rights that cannot be valued solely in monetary terms."

Respondent cautions us that refusing to limit recovery to the amount of the contingency agreement will result in a "windfall" to attorneys who accept § 1983 actions. Yet the very nature of recovery under § 1988 is designed to prevent any such "windfall." Fee awards are to be reasonable, reasonable as to billing rates and reasonable as to the number of hours spent in advancing the successful claims. Accordingly, fee awards, properly calculated, by definition will represent the reasonable worth of the services rendered in vindication of a plaintiff's civil rights claim. It is central to the awarding of attorney's fees under § 1988 that the district court judge, in his or her good judgment, make the assessment of what is a reasonable fee under the circumstances of the case. The trial judge should not be limited by the contractual fee agreement between plaintiff and counsel. * * *

JUSTICE SCALIA, concurring in part and concurring in the judgment.

I * * * join the opinion of the Court except that portion which rests upon detailed analysis of the Fifth Circuit's opinion in *Johnson* and the District Court decisions in *Swann*, *Stanford Daily*, and *Davis*. The Court carefully examines those opinions, separating holding from dictum, much as a lower court would study our opinions in order to be faithful to our guidance. The justification for this role reversal is that the Senate and House Committee Reports on the Civil Rights Attorney's Fees Awards Act of 1976 referred approvingly to *Johnson*, and the Senate Report alone referred to the three District Court opinions as having "correctly applied" *Johnson*. The Court resolves the difficulty that *Johnson* contradicts the three District Court opinions on the precise point at issue here by concluding in effect that the analysis in *Johnson* was dictum, whereas in the three District Court opinions it was a holding. Despite the fact that the House Report referred *only* to *Johnson*, and made no mention of the District Court cases, the Court "doubt[s] that Congress embraced this aspect of *Johnson*, for it pointed to the three District Court cases in which the factors are 'correctly applied.' "

In my view Congress did no such thing. Congress is elected to enact statutes rather than point to cases, and its Members have better uses for their time than poring over District Court opinions. That the Court should refer to the citation of three District Court cases in a document issued by a single committee of a single house as the action *of Congress* displays the level of unreality that our unrestrained use of legislative history has attained. I am confident that only a small proportion of the Members of Congress read either one of the Committee Reports in question, even if (as is not always the case) the Reports happened to have been published before the vote; that very few of those who did read them set off for the nearest law library to check out what was actually said in the four cases at issue (or in the more than 50 other cases cited by the House and Senate Reports); and that *no* Member of Congress came to the judgment that the District Court cases would trump *Johnson* on the point at issue here because the latter was dictum. As anyone familiar with modern-day drafting of congressional committee reports is well aware, the references to the cases were inserted, at best by a committee staff member on his or her own initiative, and at worst by a committee staff member at the suggestion of a lawyer-lobbyist; and the purpose of those references was not primarily to inform the Members of Congress what the bill meant (for that end *Johnson* would not merely have been cited, but its 12 factors would have been described, which they were not), but rather to influence judicial construction. What a heady feeling it must be for a young staffer, to know that his or her citation of obscure district court cases can transform them into the law of the land, thereafter dutifully to be observed by the Supreme Court itself.

I decline to participate in this process. It is neither compatible with our judicial responsibility of assuring reasoned, consistent, and effective applica-tion of the statutes of the United States, nor conducive to a genuine effectuation of congressional intent, to give legislative force to each snippet of analysis, and even every case citation, in committee reports that are increasingly unreliable evidence of what the voting Members of Congress actually had in mind. By treating *Johnson* and the District Court trilogy as fully authoritative, the Court today expands what I regard as our cases' excessive preoccupation with them — and with the 12-factor *Johnson* analysis in particular. * * * Except for the few passages to which I object, today's opinion admirably follows our more recent approach of seeking to develop an interpretation of the statute that is reasonable, consistent, and faithful to its apparent purpose, rather than to achieve obedient adherence to cases cited in the committee reports. I therefore join the balance of the opinion.

NOTE ON THE NEW TEXTUALIST
CRITIQUE OF COMMITTEE REPORTS

1. *Judge Scalia's Attack on Committee Reports.* Justice Scalia believes that committee reports, in particular, are untrustworthy legislative history. His first effort to explain his position systematically, an unpublished speech delivered at various law schools while he was a judge on the D.C. Circuit, is summarized, quoted, and criticized in Daniel Farber & Philip Frickey, *Legislative Intent and Public Choice*, 74 Va. L. Rev. 423 (1988). Judge Scalia also set forth his doubts in a concurring opinion in *Hirschey v. FERC*, 777 F.2d 1, 7–8 (D.C. Cir. 1985):

> I frankly doubt that it is ever reasonable to assume that the details, as opposed to the broad outlines of purpose, set forth in a committee report come to the attention of, much less are approved by, the house which enacts the committee's bill. And I think it time for courts to become concerned about the fact that routine deference to the detail of committee reports, and the predictable expansion in that detail which routine deference has produced, are converting a system of judicial construction into a system of committee-staff prescription.

Note the similarity to his reason for not joining the Court's opinion in *Bergeron*. In a footnote at the end of the first sentence of the above quotation,

Judge Scalia reported the following "illuminating exchange" in the Senate (*id.* at 7–8 n.1):

Mr. ARMSTRONG. * * * My question, which may take [the Chairman of the Committee on Finance] by surprise, is this: Is it the intention of the chairman that the Internal Revenue Service and the Tax Court and other courts take guidance as to the intention of Congress from the committee report which accompanies this bill?

Mr. DOLE. I would certainly hope so. * * *

Mr. ARMSTRONG. Mr. President, will the Senator tell me whether or not he wrote the committee report?

Mr. DOLE. Did I write the committee report?

Mr. ARMSTRONG. Yes.

Mr. DOLE. No; the Senator from Kansas did not write the committee report.

Mr. ARMSTRONG. Did any Senator write the committee report?

Mr. DOLE. I have to check.

Mr. ARMSTRONG. Does the Senator know of any Senator who wrote the committee report?

Mr. DOLE. I might be able to identify one, but I would have to search. I was here all during the time it was written, I might say, and worked carefully with the staff as they worked. * * *

Mr. ARMSTRONG. Mr. President, has the Senator from Kansas, the chairman of the Finance Committee, read the committee report in its entirety?

Mr. DOLE. I am working on it. It is not a bestseller, but I am working on it.

Mr. ARMSTRONG. Mr. President, did members of the Finance Committee vote on the committee report?

Mr. DOLE. No.

Mr. ARMSTRONG. Mr. President, the reason I raise the issue is not perhaps apparent on the surface, and let me just state it: * * * The report itself is not considered by the Committee on Finance. It was not subject to amendment by the Committee on Finance. It is not subject to amendment now by the Senate. * * *

* * * If there were matter within this report which was disagreed to by the Senator from Colorado or even by a majority of all Senators, there would be no way for us to change the report. I could not offer an amendment tonight to amend the committee report.

* * * [F]or any jurist, administrator, bureaucrat, tax practitioner, or others who might chance upon the written record of this proceeding, let me just make the point that this is not the law, it was not voted on, it is not subject to amendment, and we should discipline ourselves to the task of expressing congressional intent in the statute.

The co-parent of the new textualism has been Judge Frank Easterbrook of the Seventh Circuit, the author of the textualist en banc opinion in *Marshall*

(Chapter 7, § 3B1). Another of his opinions, *In re Sinclair*, is the next case in this chapter.

2. *Justice Scalia Updates His Critique of Committee Reports.* Since he has been elevated to the Supreme Court, Justice Scalia has developed a more systematic critique of the Court's traditional use of legislative history. See Antonin Scalia, *A Matter of Interpretation* (1997); *Bock Laundry* (Scalia, J., concurring in the judgment) (both excerpted in Chapter 7, § 3A).[g] Justice Scalia's more systematic critique goes well beyond the cynicism of *Bergeron* and rests upon a constitutional interpretation of Article I, § 7. Statutory text is the alpha and the omega of statutory interpretation because it is the only matter that is enacted as authoritative *law* under our constitutional rule of recognition (Article I, § 7).[h] Even if there were a coherent legislative "intent" (a matter Scalia disputes), it would have no authority as law under the Constitution. Like Judge Easterbrook, who developed the structural constitutional features of the new textualism at an earlier stage, Justice Scalia would be willing to examine legislative materials in the same manner he uses dictionaries — as evidence of how statutory language was used at the time.

3. *The Impact of the New Textualism in the Supreme Court.* Justice Scalia's critique has had an impact upon the Court's practice, which is now more cautious in its use of legislative history. It has had even more of an impact upon the arguments made by the Supreme Court Bar (especially the Solicitor General and others regularly arguing before the Court), who now emphasize and usually lead with their textual arguments and use legislative history to back up these contentions rather than as the touchstone of statutory meaning. And the new textualism has had an impact among the Justices (and perhaps beyond). The Rehnquist and Roberts Courts (1986 onward) have been less likely to rely heavily upon legislative history today than did the Burger Court (1969-1986). There are more decisions like *Circuit City* (where the majority refused to examine legislative materials) than *Sweet Home* (where even Justice

---

g. Some of Justice Scalia's classic criticisms are found in *Zuni Pub. Sch. Dist. No. 89 v. Department of Educ.*, 127 S.Ct. 1534, 1555–59 (2007) (Scalia, J., dissenting); *Hamdan v. Rumsfeld*, 126 S.Ct. 2749, 2815–17 (2006) (Scalia, J., dissenting); *Koons Buick Pontiac GMC, Inc. v. Nigh*, 543 U.S. 50, 70–76 (2004) (Scalia, J., dissenting); *Crosby v. National Foreign Trade Council*, 530 U.S. 363 (2000) (Scalia, J., concurring in the judgment); *Thunder Basin Coal Co. v. Reich*, 510 U.S. 200, 219 (1994) (Scalia, J., concurring in part and in the judgment); *Conroy v. Aniskoff*, 507 U.S. 511, 519 (1993) (Scalia, J., concurring in the judgment); *United States v. Thompson/Center Arms Co.*, 504 U.S. 505, 521 (1992) (Scalia, J., concurring in the judgment); *Union Bank v. Wolas*, 502 U.S. 151, 163 (1991) (Scalia, J., concurring); *Wisconsin Public Intervenor v. Mortier*, 501 U.S. 597, 617–23 (1991) (Scalia, J., concurring in the judgment); *Sullivan v. Finkelstein*, 496 U.S. 617, 631–32 (1990) (Scalia, J., concurring in all of the Court's opinion except footnote 8); *Begier v. IRS*, 496 U.S. 53, 67–71 (1990) (Scalia, J., concurring in the judgment).

h. William Eskridge, Jr., *The New Textualism*, 37 UCLA L. Rev. 621 (1990); John Manning, *Textualism as a Nondelegation Doctrine*, 97 Colum. L. Rev. 673 (1997); Jonathan Molot, *The Rise and Fall of Textualism*, 106 Colum. L. Rev. 1, 23–29 (2006).

Scalia relied on legislative materials) than there have been since the pre-New Deal era.[i]

Nonetheless, the new textualism has not swept the field. Although Justice Scalia has picked up a great deal of academic support, the majority of the commentators are unpersuaded.[j] The Supreme Court still relies on committee reports (even if less than before). Moreover, in *Wisconsin Public Intervenor v. Mortier*, 501 U.S. 597, 610 n.4 (1991), all of the other Justices joined in a footnote explicitly rejecting Justice Scalia's general position that legislative history is irrelevant to proper statutory interpretation. Especially after the appointment of Justice Breyer (a big fan of legislative history), the Supreme Court has relied on legislative materials more often in the late 1990s and first

---

i. E.g., James Brudney & Corey Ditslear, *The Decline and Fall of Legislative History? Patterns of Supreme Court Reliance in the Burger and Rehnquist Eras*, 89 Judicature 220 (2006); Michael Koby, *The Supreme Court's Declining Reliance on Legislative History: The Impact of Justice Scalia's Critique*, 36 Harv. J. Legis. 369 (1999). Because Justices Scalia and Thomas routinely refuse to join any majority opinion that relies upon legislative history, in any case in which their votes might be necessary to form a majority the Justice drafting the opinion may strategically avoid reliance upon legislative history. Thomas Merrill, *Textualism and the Future of the* Chevron *Doctrine*, 72 Wash. U. L.Q. 351 (1994).

j. Skeptical treatments include Stephen Breyer, *On the Uses of Legislative History in Interpreting Statutes*, 65 S. Cal. L. Rev. 845 (1992); George Costello, *Average Voting Members and Other "Benign Fictions": The Relative Reliability of Committee Reports, Floor Debates, and Other Sources of Legislative History*, 1990 Duke L.J. 39; William Eskridge, Jr., *Textualism, The Unknown Ideal?*, 96 Mich. L. Rev. 1509 (1998); Daniel Farber & Philip Frickey, *Legislative Intent and Public Choice*, 74 Va. L. Rev. 423 (1988); Philip Frickey, *Revisiting the Revival of Theory in Statutory Interpretation: A Lecture in Honor of Irving Younger*, 84 Minn. L. Rev. 199 (1999); Paul McGreal, *A Constitutional Defense of Legislative History*, 13 Wm. & Mary Bill Rts. J. 1267 (2005); Abner Mikva & Eric Lane, *The Muzak of Justice Scalia's Revolutionary Call To Read Unclear Statutes Narrowly*, 53 SMU L. Rev. 121 (2000); Stephen Ross & Daniel Tranen, *The Modern Parol Evidence Rule and Its Implications for New Textualist Statutory Interpretation*, 87 Geo. L.J. 195 (1998); Peter Strauss, *The Common Law and Statutes*, 70 U. Colo. L. Rev. 225 (1999); Patricia Wald, *The Sizzling Sleeper: The Use of Legislative History in Construing Statutes in the 1988–89 Term of the United States Supreme Court*, 39 Am. U.L. Rev. 277 (1990); Nicholas Zeppos, *Justice Scalia's Textualism: The "New" New Legal Process*, 12 Cardozo L. Rev. 1597 (1991).

Treatments sympathetic to Justice Scalia's approach include Frank Easterbrook, *Textualism and the Dead Hand*, 66 Geo. Wash. L. Rev. 1119 (1998); Alex Kozinski, *Should Reading Legislative History Be an Impeachable Offense?*, 31 Suffolk U.L. Rev. 807 (1998); John Manning, *Textualism as a Nondelegation Doctrine*, 97 Colum. L. Rev. 673 (1997); Jonathan Molot, *The Rise and Fall of Textualism*, 106 Colum. L. Rev. 1, 23-29 (2006); Frederick Schauer, *Statutory Construction and the Coordinating Function of Plain Meaning*, 1990 Sup. Ct. Rev. 231; Kenneth Starr, *Observations About the Use of Legislative History*, 1987 Duke L.J. 371; Adrian Vermeule, *Legislative History and the Limits of Judicial Competence: The Untold Story of* Holy Trinity Church, 50 Stan. L. Rev. 1833 (1998). Going beyond Justice Scalia (by excluding whole act evidence as well as legislative history), is Adrian Vermeule, *Judging Under Uncertainty: An Institutional Theory of Legal Interpretation* (2006).

With respect to the concern that difficulties in accessing legislative history should count against its usage, see Richard Danner, *Justice Jackson's Lament: Historical and Comparative Perspectives on the Availability of Legislative History*, 13 Duke J. Comp. & Int'l L. 151 (2003).

part of the new century.[k] It is too early to tell whether the Roberts Court will continue or reverse this trend.

In re SINCLAIR
United States Court of Appeals for the Seventh Circuit, 1989
870 F.2d 1340

EASTERBROOK, CIRCUIT JUDGE.

This case presents a conflict between a statute and its legislative history. The Sinclairs, who have a family farm, filed a bankruptcy petition in April 1985 under Chapter 11 of the Bankruptcy Act of 1978. In October 1986 Congress added Chapter 12, providing benefits for farmers, and the Sinclairs asked the bankruptcy court to convert their case from Chapter 11 to Chapter 12. The bankruptcy judge declined, and the district court affirmed. Each relied on § 302(c)(1) of the Bankruptcy Judges, United States Trustees, and Family Farmer Bankruptcy Act of 1986, Pub.L. 99–554, 100 Stat. 3088:

> The amendments made by subtitle B of title II shall not apply with respect to cases commenced under title 11 of the United States Code before the effective date of this Act.

The Sinclairs rely on the report of the Conference Committee, which inserted § 302(c)(1) into the bill:

> It is not intended that there be routine conversion of Chapter 11 and 13 cases, pending at the time of enactment, to Chapter 12. Instead, it is expected that courts will exercise their sound discretion in each case, in allowing conversions only where it is equitable to do so.
>
> Chief among the factors the court should consider is whether there is a substantial likelihood of successful reorganization under Chapter 12.
>
> Courts should also carefully scrutinize the actions already taken in pending cases in deciding whether, in their equitable discretion, to allow conversion. For example, the court may consider whether the petition was recently filed in another chapter with no further action taken. Such a case may warrant conversion to the new chapter. On the other hand, there may be cases where a reorganization plan has already been filed or confirmed. In cases where the parties have substantially relied on current law, availability [sic] to convert to the new chapter should be limited.

The statute says conversion is impossible; the report says that conversion is possible and describes the circumstances under which it should occur.

Which prevails in the event of conflict, the statute or its legislative history? The statute was enacted, the report just the staff's explanation. Congress votes

---

k. See Jane Schacter, *The Confounding Common Law Originalism in Recent Supreme Court Statutory Interpretation: Implications for the Legislative History Debate and Beyond*, 51 Stan. L. Rev. 1 (1998); Charles Tiefer, *The Reconceptualization of Legislative History in the Supreme Court*, 2000 Wis. L. Rev. 205. For a fairly recent example, and indeed the most lavish recent deployment of legislative history by a majority opinion (written by O'Connor but joined without cavil by Scalia and Thomas), see *FDA v. Brown & Williamson Tobacco Co.* (Chapter 7, § 3B3).

on the text of the bill, and the President signed that text. Committee reports help courts understand the law, but this report contradicts rather than explains the text. So the statute must prevail. * * *

Yet the advice from the Supreme Court about how to deal with our situation seems scarcely more harmonious than the advice from the legislature. The reports teem with statements such as: "When we find the terms of a statute unambiguous, judicial inquiry is complete," *Rubin v. United States*, 449 U.S. 424, 430 (1981). See also, e.g., *United States v. Ron Pair Enterprises, Inc.*, 489 U.S. 235 (1989) ("where, as here, the statute's language is plain, 'the sole function of the courts is to enforce it according to its terms.' "); [Judge Easterbrook cited several other cases, including *Locke* (Chapter 7, § 2B) and *TVA v. Hill* (Chapter 7, § 2C)]. Less frequently, yet with equal conviction, the Court writes: "When aid to the construction of the meaning of words, as used in the statute, is available, there certainly can be no 'rule of law' which forbids its use, however clear the words may appear on 'superficial examination.' " *United States v. American Trucking Assoc., Inc.*, 310 U.S. 534, 543–44 (1940) (footnotes omitted), repeated in *Train v. Colorado Public Interest Research Group, Inc.*, 426 U.S. 1, 10 (1976). See also, e.g., * * * *Holy Trinity Church* [Chapter 7, § 1]. Some cases boldly stake out a middle ground, saying, for example: "only the most extraordinary showing of contrary intentions from [the legislative history] would justify a limitation on the 'plain meaning' of the statutory language." *Garcia v. United States*, 469 U.S. 70, 75 (1984). See also, e.g., *Griffin* [Chapter 7, § 2C] * * * . This implies that once in a blue moon the legislative history trumps the statute (as opposed to affording a basis for its interpretation) but does not help locate such strange astronomical phenomena. These lines of cases have coexisted for a century, and many cases contain statements associated with two or even all three of them, not recognizing the tension.

What's a court to do? The answer lies in distinguishing among uses of legislative history. An unadorned "plain meaning" approach to interpretation supposes that words have meanings divorced from their contexts — linguistic, structural, functional, social, historical. Language is a process of communication that works only when authors and readers share a set of rules and meanings. What "clearly" means one thing to a reader unacquainted with the circumstances of the utterance — including social conventions prevailing at the time of drafting — may mean something else to a reader with a different background. Legislation speaks across the decades, during which legal institutions and linguistic conventions change. To decode words one must frequently reconstruct the legal and political culture of the drafters. Legislative history may be invaluable in revealing the setting of the enactment and the assumptions its authors entertained about how their words would be understood. It may show, too, that words with a denotation "clear" to an outsider are terms of art, with an equally "clear" but different meaning to an insider. It may show too that the words leave gaps, for short phrases cannot address all human experience; understood in context, the words may leave to the executive and judicial branches the task of adding flesh to bones. These we take to be the points of cases such as *American Trucking* holding that judges may learn from the legislative history even when the text is "clear". Clarity depends on context, which legislative history may illuminate. The process is objective; the search is not for the contents of the authors' heads but for the rules of language they used.

Quite different is the claim that legislative intent is *the* basis of interpretation, that the text of the law is simply evidence of the real rule. In such a regimen legislative history is not a way to understand the text but is a more authentic, because more proximate, expression of legislators' will. One may say in reply that legislative history is a poor guide to legislators' intent because it is written by the staff rather than by members of Congress, because it is often losers' history ("If you can't get your proposal into the bill, at least write the legislative history to make it look as if you'd prevailed"), because it becomes a crutch ("There's no need for us to vote on the amendment if we can write a little legislative history"), because it complicates the task of execution and obedience (neither judges nor those whose conduct is supposed to be influenced by the law can know what to do without delving into legislative recesses, a costly and uncertain process). Often there is so much legislative history that a court can manipulate the meaning of a law by choosing which snippets to emphasize and by putting hypothetical questions — questions to be answered by inferences from speeches rather than by reference to the text, so that great discretion devolves on the (judicial) questioner. Sponsors of opinion polls know that a small change in the text of a question can lead to large differences in the answer. Legislative history offers willful judges an opportunity to pose questions and devise answers, with predictable divergence in results. These and related concerns have lead to skepticism about using legislative history to find legislative intent. E.g., *Blanchard v. Bergeron* (Scalia, J., concurring); [Judge Easterbrook cited several lower court opinions, including Judge Scalia's separate opinion in *Hirschey*]. These cautionary notes are well taken, but even if none were salient there would still be a hurdle to the sort of argument pressed in our case.

Statutes are law, not evidence of law. References to "intent" in judicial opinions do not imply that legislators' motives and beliefs, as opposed to their public acts, establish the norms to which all others must conform. "Original meaning" rather than "intent" frequently captures the interpretive task more precisely, reminding us that it is the work of the political branches (the "meaning") rather than of the courts that matters, and that their work acquires its meaning when enacted ("originally"). Revisionist history may be revelatory; revisionist judging is simply unfaithful to the enterprise. Justice Holmes made the point when denouncing a claim that judges should give weight to the intent of a document's authors:

> [A statute] does not disclose one meaning conclusively according to the laws of language. Thereupon we ask, not what this man meant, but what those words would mean in the mouth of a normal speaker of English, using them in the circumstances in which they were used . . . . But the normal speaker of English is merely a special variety, a literary form, so to speak, of our old friend the prudent man. He is external to the particular writer, and a reference to him as the criterion is simply another instance of the externality of the law . . . . We do not inquire what the legislature meant; we ask only what the statute means.

Oliver Wendell Holmes, *The Theory of Legal Interpretation*, 12 Harv. L. Rev. 417, 417–19 (1899), reprinted in Collected Legal Papers 204, 207 (1920). Or as Judge Friendly put things in a variation on Holmes's theme, a court must search for "what Congress meant by what it said, rather than for what it meant *simpliciter*." Henry J. Friendly, *Mr. Justice Frankfurter and the Reading of Statutes*, in Benchmarks 218–19 (1967).

An opinion poll revealing the wishes of Congress would not translate to legal rules. Desires become rules only after clearing procedural hurdles, designed to encourage deliberation and expose proposals (and arguments) to public view and recorded vote. Resort to "intent" as a device to short-circuit these has no more force than the opinion poll — less, because the legislative history is written by the staff of a single committee and not subject to a vote or veto. The Constitution establishes a complex of procedures, including presidential approval (or support by two-thirds of each house). It would demean the constitutionally prescribed method of legislating to suppose that its elaborate apparatus for deliberation on, amending, and approving a text is just a way to create some *evidence* about the law, while the *real* source of legal rules is the mental processes of legislators. We know from *INS v. Chadha*, 462 U.S. 919 (1983) [Chapter 9,§ 2C], that the express disapproval of one house of Congress cannot change the law, largely because it removes the President from the process; it would therefore be surprising if "intents" subject to neither vote nor veto could be sources of law.

* * * If Congress were to reduce the rate of taxation on capital gains, "intending" that this stimulate economic growth and so yield more in tax revenue, the meaning of the law would be only that rates go down, not that revenue go up — a judge could not later rearrange rates to achieve the "intent" with respect to federal coffers. On the other hand, doubt about the meaning of a term found in the statute could well be resolved by harmonizing that provision with the structure of the rest of the law, understood in light of a contemporaneous explanation. In this sense legislative intent is a vital source of meaning even though it does not trump the text.

Concern about the source of law — is the statute law, or is it just evidence of the law? — lies behind statements such as: "[T]he language being plain, and not leading to absurd or wholly impracticable consequences, it is the sole evidence of the ultimate legislative intent." *Caminetti*. To treat the text as conclusive evidence of law is to treat it *as* law — which under the constitutional structure it is. Legislative history then may help a court discover but may not change the original meaning. *Pierce v. Underwood*, 487 U.S. 552 (1988). The "plain meaning" rule of *Caminetti* [Chapter 7, § 1] rests not on a silly belief that texts have timeless meanings divorced from their many contexts, not on the assumption that what is plain to one reader must be clear to any other (and identical to the plan of the writer), but on the constitutional allocation of powers. The political branches adopt texts through prescribed procedures; what ensues is the law. Legislative history may show the meaning of the texts — may show, indeed, that a text "plain" at first reading has a strikingly different meaning — but may not be used to show an "intent" at variance with the meaning of the text. *Caminetti* and *American Trucking* can comfortably coexist when so understood. This approach also supplies the underpinning for the belief that legislative history is "only admissible to solve doubt and not to create it", which punctuates the U.S. Reports. Legislative history helps us learn what Congress meant by what it said, but it is not a source of legal rules competing with those found in the U.S. Code.

Ours is now an easy case. Section 302(c)(1) of the statute has an ascertainable meaning, a meaning not absurd or inconsistent with the structure of the remaining provisions. It says that Chapter 11 cases pending on the date the law went into force may not be converted to Chapter 12. No legislative history suggests any other meaning. The committee report suggests, at best, a different intent. Perhaps a reader could infer that the committee planned to allow conversion but mistakenly voted for a different text. So two members of the committee have said since, calling § 302(c)(1) an oversight. See 133 Cong.Rec. S2273–76 (daily ed. Feb. 19, 1987) (Sen. Grassley), E544 (daily ed. Feb. 19, 1987) (Rep. Coelho). Not only the committee's remarks on conversion but also the omission of § 302(c)(1) from the section-by-section description of the bill suggest that whoever wrote the report (a staffer, not a Member of Congress) wanted § 302(c)(1) deleted and may have thought that had been accomplished. Still another possibility is that the Conference Committee meant to distinguish Chapter 11 from Chapter 13: to ban conversions from Chapter 11 (covered by § 302(c)(1)) but allow them from Chapter 13. On this reading the gaffe is the failure to delete the reference to Chapter 11 from the report, which could still stand as a treatment of conversions from Chapter 13.

Congress has done nothing to change § 302(c)(1), implying that the statement in the committee report may have been the error. It is easy to imagine opposing forces arriving at the conference armed with their own texts and legislative histories, and in the scramble at the end of session one version slipping into the bill and the other into the report. Whichever was the blunder, we know which one was enacted. What came out of conference, what was voted for by House and Senate, what was signed by the President, says that pending Chapter 11 cases may not be converted. Accordingly, pending Chapter 11 cases may not be converted.

NOTES ON *SINCLAIR* AND THE SEARCH FOR OBJECTIVITY IN STATUTORY INTERPRETATION

1. *Textual Evidence Judge Easterbrook Missed.* Judge Easterbrook cites § 302 of the 1986 statute, which seems to prevent conversion of the *Sinclair* proceeding. But the legislative history he cites is the Conference Committee language not of § 302, but of § 256(1), which amended 11 U.S.C. § 1112(d). Section 1112 is the provision of Chapter 11 that deals with conversions. As amended, it now reads:

(d) The Court may convert a case under this chapter to a case under chapter 12 or 13 of this title only if —

(1) the debtor requests such conversion;

(2) the debtor has not been discharged under section 1141(d) of this title; and

(3) if the debtor requests conversion to chapter 12 of this title, such conversion is equitable.

Is the statutory text 100% clear against conversion? It is only if § 256(1) is interpreted not to apply to pending proceedings (see Chapter 6, § 3C).

In light of this evidence, construct an argument that *In re Sinclair* is wrongly decided.[1] We have brought this evidence to Judge Easterbrook's attention, and he responded that it would not change his thinking about this case, because the new textual evidence was not briefed by the parties and in any event he was not persuaded that this new evidence created any statutory ambiguity. Does this additional information demonstrate ambiguity?

2. *Judicial Fears of the Mischievous Staffer.* An enduring image from Justice Scalia's *Bergeron* concurring opinion (and a standard trope in Scalia's speeches deriding legislative history) is the possibility that mischievous staffers will smuggle stuff into committee reports and thereby "trick" judges into bad interpretations that Congress did not "intend." Notice how staffers bent on mischief can do the same thing to statutory text. In *Sinclair,* Judge Easterbrook notes that several Members of Congress later said that a mistake somehow arose with respect to § 302(c)(1), the effective date provision, and that the Congress intended to allow conversion of pending farmer bankruptcy proceedings. There are at least three reasons to believe that this is accurate.

First, it is fishy that the Conference Report has no mention of § 302(c)(1). That the "dog didn't bark" in the Conference Report is odd in light of a second factor, the emergency nature of this law. The 1986 act creating Chapter 12 was adopted during the most serious farm economic depression since the 1930's. Farmers had been going under left and right, and Congress decided to ameliorate their debt situation somewhat by adopting Chapter 12, which is more favorable to farmers than is the bankruptcy scheme of Chapter 11, which is available to all debtors. This "help the farmers during this emergency" purpose of the 1986 statute seems in stark conflict with the notion that only future cases could be converted to new Chapter 12. Moreover, § 1112(d) as amended allows conversion only in cases in which it would be equitable, thereby providing some measure of protection to creditors in pending proceedings. Finally, according to prevalent rumors in one segment of the bankruptcy bar, at the behest of lending interests a Senate staff member put § 302 into the bill, contrary to the apparent wishes of the sponsors and supporters of the 1986 statute. It appears that sponsors and supporters of the statute did not even notice § 302 until well after the statute had been adopted. This may shed new light on why § 302 was not discussed in the section-by-section description of the bill in the conference committee report. This rumor

---

1. For an extraordinary discussion concerning broader jurisprudential issues lingering in the *Sinclair* case, see Paul Campos, *The Chaotic Pseudotext*, 94 Mich. L. Rev. 2178 (1996).

seems to turn on its head the complaint by new textualists that *legislative history* is unreliable stuff because of potential shenanigans by legislative staff.[m]

3. *Objectivity in Statutory Interpretation: Empirical Evidence from the Supreme Court's Labor Cases.* Complementing the image of the mischievous staffer in Justice Scalia's pitch for the new textualism is the result-oriented judge who will look out over the legislative history crowd and pick out his friends. You might review the *big cases* in this Casebook, such as *Weber*, the affirmative action case in Chapter 1; *Holy Trinity* and the FDA Tobacco Case in Chapter 7; and *Sweet Home* in this chapter. In all these cases, Justices (including Scalia, in *Sweet Home*) invoke legislative history to support results that match those Justices' apparent ideologies — but in all the cases except *Holy Trinity* the Justices also invoke textual plain meaning in the same way.

Properly phrased, the inquiry demanded by the new textualism's appeal to objectivity in judging is that a judge who looks at legislative history as well as text is *more likely* to read his or her ideological presuppositions into a statute than a judge who just looks at the text alone. There is no empirical evidence that this is the case — and now some evidence to the contrary. James Brudney and Corey Ditslear, *Liberal Justices' Reliance on Legislative History: Principle, Strategy, and the Scalia Effect* (draft 2007), did a deeper empirical analysis of the authors' dataset of 578 Supreme Court labor cases (1969-2003). Analyzing the voting records of the eight Justices conventionally considered "liberal," the authors reached the following conclusions:

> [F]or the eight liberals, the relationship between pro-employee outcomes and legislative history usage is not significant. If anything, legislative history reliance is associated with a somewhat neutralizing set of results. When liberal Justices use legislative history as part of their majority reasoning, they do so to help justify more than half of their *pro-employer* opinions for the Court but just under one-half of their *pro-employee* outcomes. Further evidence of this moderating association is that majority opinions authored by liberal Justices reach liberal outcomes 30 percent more often than conservative results when *not* relying on legislative history, but the liberal-conservative outcome differential declines to 21 percent when the majority opinion's reasoning includes legislative history.

For the Justices considered "conservative," Brudney and Ditslear found that reliance on legislative history was correlated with slightly more conservative voting. In short, legislative history of labor statutes, most of which were enacted by liberal Congresses, supported employer-oriented deals reached in the legislative process — and sometimes persuaded liberals to sacrifice their pro-employee biases. (An example of this phenomenon is *Muscarello* in § 1B1 of this chapter, where liberal Justice Breyer relied on legislative history to interpret ambiguous statutory language and impose a harsh sentence on gun-"carrying" defendants.) This is preliminary evidence *against* the judicial objectivity argument for textualism.

---

m. On end-of-the-game strategic moves in the legislative process, see William Rodgers, Jr., *The Lesson of the Red Squirrel: Consensus and Betrayal in the Environmental Statutes*, 5 J. Contemp. Health L. & Pol. 161 (1989).

On the other hand, Brudney and Ditslear also found that this moderating association has waned among the cohort of liberal Justices since Justice Scalia's appointment to the Court. The suggestion is that Justice Scalia's hard-hitting style has polarized the Court, pitting text-wielding conservatives against liberals clinging to legislative history. An example of this phenomenon is *Circuit City* (this chapter, § 1A), where conservatives rejected legislative history and liberals relied on it. Has Judge Leventhal's quip become a self-fulfilling prophesy?

PEREZ v. WYETH LABORATORIES, INC.
New Jersey Supreme Court, 1999
734 A.2d 1245

[Excerpted in Chapter 7, § 3B2]

NOTE ON THE NORPLANT CASE AND STATE COURT RELIANCE ON COMMITTEE AND BILL REPORTS[n]

The Norplant Case may be an unusually apt one for consideration of legislative history, as the statute itself contained a reference to the committee report.[o] In any event, **New Jersey** courts are among the most willing to rely on legislative history to construe statutes; judges in that state are willing to consider committee reports whether or not the statute's text is ambiguous. See *Miah v. Ahmed*, 846 A.2d 1233 (N.J. 2004); State *v. Hoffman*, 695 A.2d 236 (N.J. 1997); *Wingate v. Estate of Ryan*, 693 A.2d 457 (N.J. 1997). But see *New Jersey Civ. Serv. Ass'n v. State*, 443 A.2d 1070 (N.J. 1982) (committee reports may not trump clear words of statute).

Most states with large populations have relatively accessible committee and commission reports, and judges in those states will consider them, especially if statutes are ambiguous. Among these states are **California**, see, e.g., *People v. Allegheny Casualty Co.*, 41 Cal. 4th 704 (2007); *People v. Mendoza*, 4 P.3d 265 (Cal. 2000); *Conley v. Roman Catholic Archbishop of San Francisco*, 102 Cal. Rptr. 2d 679 (App. 2000); **Florida**, see, e.g., *White v. State*, 714 So. 2d 440 (Fla. 1998) (bill report, described in next paragraph); *State v. Pinder*, 678 So. 2d 410 (Fla. App. 1996); **Michigan**, see, e.g., *Kern v. Blethen-Coluni*, 612

---

n. Maame Ewusi-Mensah (Yale, Class of 2001) provided the research background and first draft of this Note, and David Snyder (Boalt, Class of 2008) updated it.

o. Compare *Landgraf* (Chapter 6, § 3), where the statute contained a provision limiting judicial reference to legislative history. Would a federal statute's explicit reference to committee reports satisfy Justice Scalia's concern that judicial reference to committee reports violates Article I, § 7 (bicameralism and presentment) and federal separation of powers? For example, had such a statutory provision been present in the Civil Rights Attorneys' Fees Act of 1976, construed in *Bergeron*, above, should Justice Scalia have gone along with the majority's invocation of the committee report, including its footnotes? Would that make you more willing to consider the footnotes as authoritative? Compare Jonathan Siegel, *The Use of Legislative History in a System of Separated Powers*, 53 Vand. L. Rev. 1457 (2000) (statutory incorporation by reference of legislative history removes separation-of-powers objection) with John Manning, *Putting Legislative History to a Vote: A Response to Professor Siegel*, 53 Vand. L. Rev. 1529 (2000) (taking contrary position).

N.W.2d 838 (Mich. App. 2000) (bill report); **Minnesota**, see, e.g., *First Nat'l Bank of Deerwood v. Gregg*, 556 N.W.2d 214 (Minn. 1996) (tape-recorded committee deliberations); **New York**, see, e.g., *Majewski v. Broadalbin-Perth Cent. School Dist.*, 91 N.Y.2d 577 (N.Y. Ct. App. 1998) (floor debates, changes to proposed bill, and post-enactment statements of governor); **Ohio**, see *Cuyahoga Met. Hous. Auth. v. City of Cleveland*, 578 N.E.2d 871 (Ohio App. 1989) (legislative reports and debates admissible but not to change clear statutory texts); **Pennsylvania**, see, e.g., *Commonwealth v. Ahlborn*, 626 A.2d 1265 (Pa. 1993) (explanation by committee chair); *Young v. Kaye*, 279 A.2d 759 (Pa. 1971) (drafting commission report); **Tennessee**, see, e.g., *City of Oak Ridge v. Roane County*, 563 S.W.2d 895 (Tenn. 1978); *Wachovia Bank of N.C. v. Johnson*, 26 S.W.3d 621 (Tenn. App. 2000); **Texas**, see, e.g., *Lee v. Mitchell*, 23 S.W.3d 209 (Tex. App. 2000) (committee reports entitled to some respect but are not controlling); Tex. Gov't Code § 311.023 (2007) ("In construing a statute, whether or not the statute is considered ambiguous on its face, a court may consider among other matters the . . . legislative history"); **Washington**, see, e.g., *Biggs v. Vail*, 830 P.2d 350 (Wash. 1992) (committee reports are admissible if statutory text not clear).

In some states a "bill report" is prepared by the committee staff after a bill is voted out of committee, but it is not necessarily reviewed by the committee or even its chair. The report typically contains a background statement, a summary of the bill's provisions, changes made by the committee, a list of the proponents and opponents who testified before the committee, and the pro and con arguments. Courts will sometimes discount these sources. In *Gates v. Jensen*, 595 P.2d 919 (Wash. 1979), the court failed to mention a bill report which explained the ambit of a statutory override of the Court's prior decisions imposing a rather strict standard of care in medical malpractice actions. Dissenting Justices argued from the bill report that the override went further than the majority was willing to take it. See also *Construction Indus. Force Account Coun. v. Amador Water Agency*, 71 Cal. Rptr. 4th 810 (Cal. App. 1999). The current trend among the states is to consider bill reports as weak but admissible evidence of legislative intent. Florida's Supreme Court has deemed bill reports "one touchstone of the legislative will." *White, supra*, 714 So. 2d at 441 n.2.

Consideration of committee reports and other legislative history is hardly a monopoly of large-population states. Practices similar to those in the previous paragraphs can be found in **Alaska**, see, e.g., *Gossman v. Greatland Directional Drilling, Inc.*, 973 P.2d 93 (Alaska 1999); **Arizona**, see, e.g., *O'Malley Lumber Co. v. Riley*, 613 P.2d 629 (Ariz. App. 1980); **Connecticut**, see, e.g., *Burke v. Fleet Nat'l Bank*, 742 A.2d 293 (Conn. 1999); *State v. Ledbetter*, 692 A.2d 713 (Conn. 1997); **Oregon**, see, e.g., *State v. Laemoa*, 533 P.2d 370 (Or. App. 1975); and other states. Some smaller states have no readily available legislative history, however, and there are too few reported decisions to discern a hard-and-fast rule for lawyer use of legislative history.

Finally, and not least important for the student, legislative history at the state level is generally more accessible than it was a generation ago — and judges are sometimes even encouraging counsel to research it. In *Dilleley v.*

State, 815 S.W.2d 623 (Tex. Crim. App. 1991), the appeals court not only relied on legislative history but, in an appendix to the court's opinion, provided counsel in future cases with a roadmap for researching legislative history in Texas. Increasingly, state legislative history is online. Some state supreme courts provide guides to researching legislative history on their websites. See, e.g., www.courts.wa.gov/library/?fa=library.display&fileID=legis (Supreme Court of Washington).

3. *Statements by Sponsors or Drafters of Legislation*

Next to committee reports, the most persuasive legislative materials are explanations of statutory meanings, and compromises reached to achieve enactment, by the sponsors and floor managers of the legislation. Recall that Senator Humphrey and the other primary sponsors of the Civil Rights Act of 1964 were primary sources of legislative history on both sides of the affirmative action debate in *United Steelworkers v. Weber* (Chapter 1, § 3). Because there was no Senate Report for that legislation, the sponsors' statements were most reliable. Recall, in this chapter, that even Justice Scalia relied on a sponsor's explanation as key evidence for his dissent in *Sweet Home*.

As the availability of legislative history for state statutes has dramatically increased, state courts, too, are relying on statements of sponsors to interpret statutes. See, e.g., *Commonwealth v. Ahlborn*, 626 A.2d 1265 (Pa. 1993) (relying on explanation of clarifying amendment, acquiesced in by the committee chair, as useful evidence of legislative intent); *Dillehey v. State*, 815 S.W.2d 623 (Tex. Crim. App. 1991) (relying on colloquy and providing counsel with roadmap for researching legislative history in Texas). On the other hand, statements by ordinary legislators are rarely given much, if any, weight. See *Murphy v. Kenneth Cole Productions, Inc.*, 40 Cal. 4th 1094 (2007) ("we do not consider the motives or understandings of individual legislators, including the bill's author"); *Quelimane Co. v. Stewart Title Guar. Co.*, 960 P.2d 513 (Cal. 1998).

The statements by sponsors are given such deference in part because the sponsors are the most knowledgeable legislators about the proposed bill and in part because their representations about the purposes and effects of the proposal are relied upon by other legislators. This approach is not without its detractors, however. Sponsors or their friends might have incentives to distort the legislative history through "planned colloquies." Congressman William Moorhead, in *A Congressman Looks at the Planned Colloquy and Its Effect in the Interpretation of Statutes*, 45 A.B.A.J. 1314, 1314 (1959), observed that Members of Congress are aware that courts will look to the record of floor debates, especially statements by sponsors of legislation, and that "by the use of the 'friendly colloquy', two [legislators] may be able to legislate more effectively than all of Congress." He continued:

> Many if not most bills are controversial to some degree, and often it may be desirable when drafting a bill to couch provisions in innocuous language in order to minimize possible objections during committee consideration. Naturally, however, the proponents of a particular viewpoint would like to insure that their interpretation be the accepted one. The friendly colloquy on the floor during debate can serve well in

this situation. Acquiescence by the committee [chair] in a stated intent will very likely be relied upon by the courts in the absence of objection or other reliable evidence of an opposite intent.

Note the similarity between this bit of realism about colloquies and the Armstrong-Dole exchange about committee reports (Note 1 after *Bergeron*).

Political scientists tend to discount this kind of evidence, because sponsors who distort the deals reached to achieve statutory enactments will not be trusted in future legislative deals. Moreover, judges have shown themselves increasingly sophisticated in handling such evidence. For a recent example, Justice Stevens interpreted the Detainee Treatment Act of 2005 to be not retroactive in *Hamdan v. Rumsfeld*, 126 S.Ct. 2749 (2006) (excerpted in Chapter 9, § 3B6). He relied on the statement of Senator Levin, one of the sponsors, and discounted statements by two other sponsors (Senators Kyl and Graham) whose remarks were apparently inserted into the Congressional Record *after the fact*. *Id.* at 2766–67 n.10. Characteristically, Justice Scalia objected that the majority's editing of the legislative history was not only selective, but illustrated the general unreliability of such materials. *Id.* at 2825–27 (Scalia, J., dissenting). See also *Landgraf v. USI Film Prods.* (Chapter 6, § 3).

Speaking of Justice Scalia, when he was a judge on the D.C. Circuit, one of his arguments against judicial use of legislative history was that the United Kingdom's House of Lords had long excluded its use.[p] He lost that argument in the case that follows — where the House of Lords found the statutory explication by the parliamentary floor manager not only decisive evidence, but evidence that flipped everyone's reading of the statute's "plain meaning."

PEPPER v. HART
House of Lords for the United Kingdom, 1992
[1993] 1 All E.R. 42, [1992] 3 W.L.R. 1032

[Malvern College allowed employees to send their children to the school for 20% of the fees paid by other parents. The employees and the tax collector agreed that this kind of fringe benefit was subject to income taxation, but disagreed on how to measure the benefit. The statute in question, § 63 of the Finance Act of 1976, defined "cash equivalent of the benefit," which was the measure of taxable benefit, as follows:

(1) The cash equivalent of any benefit chargeable to tax under section 61 above is an amount equal to the cost of the benefit, less so much (if any) of it as is made good by the employee to those providing the benefit.

(2) Subject to the following subsections, the cost of a benefit is the amount of any expense incurred in or in connection with its provision, and (here and in those

---

p. This argument was made in then-Judge Scalia's standard speech against legislative history, a copy of which was obtained and distributed by the *Virginia Law Review* and is analyzed in Daniel Farber & Philip Frickey, *Legislative Intent and Public Choice*, 74 Va. L. Rev. 423, 440–43 (1988).

subsections) includes a proper proportion of any expense relating partly to the benefit and partly to other matters.

Because the school in question had not been able to fill all its seats, its marginal costs in providing education to these children were minimal (involving a few items of equipment and food) and amounted to less than the fees paid by the employees. Accordingly, the employees argued that they had received no actual income at all, because the fringe benefit they received, measured as the (marginal) expense incurred by their employer, was less than the fees they had paid. The tax collector disagreed, arguing that the "expense incurred" should be average cost per pupil incurred by the school. When this case made its way to the Law Lords on appeal, they initially voted 4–1 in favor of the tax collector. On rehearing, when they were urged to consider the legislative history, the Law Lords expanded the appellate panel, which then reached the opposite result. In a landmark ruling under English law, the expanded panel abandoned the rule that British courts may not consult legislative history.]

LORD MACKAY OF CLASHFERN [LORD CHANCELLOR].

* * * The benefit which the taxpayers in this case received was the placing of their children in surplus places at the college, if as a matter of discretion the college agreed to do so. * * * They were in a similar position to the person coming along on a standby basis for an airline seat as against the passenger paying a full fare, and without the full rights of a standby passenger, in the sense that the decision whether or not to accommodate them in the college was entirely discretionary. If one regards the benefit in this light I cannot see that the cost incurred in, or in connection with, the provision of the benefit, can properly be held to include the cost incurred, in any event, in providing education to fee-paying pupils at the school who were there as a right in return for the fees paid in respect of them. * * * Although the later words of section 63(2) * * * provide that the expense incurred in, or in connection with, the provision of a benefit includes a proper proportion of any expense relating partly to the benefit and partly to other matters, I consider that the expenses incurred in provision of places for fee-paying pupils were wholly incurred in order to provide those places. * * * I conclude that looking at the matter from the point of view of expense incurred and not from the point of view of loss to the employer no expense could be regarded as having been incurred as a result of the decision of the authorities of the college to provide this particular benefit to the taxpayer.

Notwithstanding the views that have found favour with others I consider this to be a reasonable construction of the statutory provisions and I am comforted in the fact that, apart from an attempt to tax airline employees, which was taken to the Special Commissioners who decided in favour of the taxpayer, this has been the practice of the Inland Revenue in applying the relevant words where they have occurred in the Income Tax Acts for so long as they have been in force, until they initiated the present cases.

At the very least it appears to me that the manner in which I have construed the relevant provisions in their application to the facts in this appeal is a possible construction and that any ambiguity there should be resolved in favour of the taxpayer.

For these reasons I would allow these appeals. I should perhaps add that I was not a member of the committee who heard these appeals in the first hearing * * * .

But much wider issues than the construction of the Finance Act 1976 have been raised in these appeals and for the first time this House has been asked to consider a detailed argument on the extent to which reference can properly be made before a court of law in the United Kingdom to proceedings in Parliament recorded in Hansard.

For the appellant [taxpayers] Mr. Lester submits that it should now be appropriate for the courts to look at Hansard in order to ascertain the intention of the legislators as expressed in the proceedings on the Bill which has then been enacted in the statutory words requiring to be construed. This submission appears to me to suggest a way of making more effective proceedings in Parliament by allowing the court to consider what has been said in Parliament as an aid to resolving an ambiguity which may well have become apparent only as a result of the attempt to apply the enacted words to a particular case. * * *

The principal difficulty I have on this aspect of the case is that in Mr. Lester's submission reference to Parliamentary material as an aid to interpretation of a statutory provision should be allowed only with leave of the court and where the court is satisfied that such a reference is justifiable:

(a) to confirm the meaning of a provision as conveyed by the text, its object and purpose;

(b) to determine a meaning where the provision is ambiguous or obscure; or

(c) to determine the meaning where the ordinary meaning is manifestly absurd or unreasonable.

I believe that practically every question of *statutory* construction that comes before the courts will involve an argument that the case falls under one or more of these three heads. It follows that the parties' legal advisors will require to study Hansard [the official collection of parliamentary debates] in practically every such case to see whether or not there is any help to be gained from it. I believe this is an objection of real substance. It is a practical objection not one of principle * * *. Such an approach appears to me to involve the possibility at least of an immense increase in the cost of litigation in which statutory construction is involved. * * * [T]he Law Commission and the Scottish Law Commission, in their joint report on *The Interpretation of Statutes* (1969) (Law Com. no. 21) (Scot. Law Com. no. 11) and the Renton Committee Report on *The Preparation of Legislation* ((1975) Cmnd. 6053), advised against a relaxation on the practical grounds to which I have referred. * * *

[We omit the separate opinions of LORD BRIDGE OF HARWICH, LORD GRIFFITHS, LORD OLIVER OF AYLMERTON, LORD KEITH OF KINKEL, and LORD ACKNER. With varying degrees of enthusiasm, all five agreed with the following opinion by LORD BROWNE-WILKINSON. Lords Bridge and Oliver had voted in the first hearing to dismiss the appeal, but the Hansard materials impelled them to change their votes. Finding the statute ambiguous, Lord Griffiths had voted with the taxpayer in the first hearing.]

LORD BROWNE-WILKINSON. * * *

* * * [I]t is necessary first to refer to the legislation affecting the taxation of benefits in kind before 1975. Under the Finance Act 1948, section 39(1), directors and employees of bodies corporate earning more than £2,000 per annum were taxed under Schedule E on certain benefits in kind. The amount charged was the expense incurred by the body corporate "in or in connection with the provision" of the benefit in kind. By section 39(6) it was provided that references to expenses "incurred in or in connection with any matter includes a reference to a proper proportion of any expense incurred partly in or in connection with that matter." Employment by a school or charitable organisation was expressly excluded from the charge: sections 41(5) and 44. These provisions were re-enacted in the Income and Corporation Taxes Act 1970.

Those provisions covered in-house benefits as well as external benefits. We were told that after 1948 the Revenue sought to tax at least two categories of employees in receipt of in-house benefits. Higher-paid employees of the railways enjoy free or concessionary travel on the railways. The Revenue reached an agreement that such employees should be taxed on 20% (later 25%) of the full fare. Airline employees also enjoy concessionary travel. We were told that in the 1960s the Revenue sought to tax such employees on that benefit on the basis of the average cost to the airline of providing a seat, not merely on the marginal cost. The tax commissioners rejected such claim: the Revenue did not appeal. Therefore in practice from 1948 to 1975 the Revenue did not seek to extract tax on the basis of the average cost to the employer of providing in-house benefits.

In 1975 the government proposed a new tax on vouchers provided by an employer to his employees which could be exchanged for goods or services. Clause 33(1) of the Finance (No. 2) Bill 1975 provided that the employee was to be treated, on receipt of a voucher, as having received an emolument from his employment of an amount "equal to the expense incurred by the person providing the voucher in or in connection with the provision of the voucher and the money, goods or services for which it is capable of being exchanged." The statutory wording of the Bill was therefore similar to that in the Act of 1948 and in section 63(2) of the Finance Act 1976. On 1 July 1975 in the Standing Committee on the Bill (Standing Committee H), the Financial Secretary was asked about the impact of the clause on railwaymen. He gave the following answer:

> "Similarly, the railwayman travelling on his normal voucher will not be taxable either. The clause deals with the situation where a number of firms produce incentives of various kinds. In one or two instances, there is likely to be some liability concerning rail vouchers of a special kind, but in general, the position is as I have said and they will not be taxable."

He was then asked to explain why they would not be taxable and replied:

"Perhaps I can make clear why there is no taxable benefit in kind, because the provision of the service that he provides falls upon the employer. Clearly, the railways will run in precisely the same way whether the railwaymen use this facility or not, so there is no extra charge to the Railways Board itself therefore there would be no taxable benefits." * * *

The Finance Bill 1976 sought to make a general revision of the taxation of benefits in kind. The existing legislation on fringe benefits was to be repealed. Clause 52 of the Bill as introduced eventually became section 61 of the Act of 1976 and imposed a charge to tax on benefits in kind for higher-paid employees, i.e., those paid more than £5,000 per annum. Clause 54 of the Bill eventually became section 63 of the Act of 1976. As introduced, clause 54(1) provided that the cash equivalent of any benefit was to be an amount equal to "the cost of the benefit." Clause 54(2) provided that, except as provided in later subsections "the cost of a benefit is the amount of any expense incurred in or in connection with its provision." Crucially, clause 54(4) of the Bill sought to tax in-house benefits on a different basis from that applicable to external benefits. It provided that the cost of a benefit consisting of the provision of any service or facility which was also provided to the public (i.e., in-house benefits) should be the price which the public paid for such facility or service. Employees of schools were not excluded from the new charge.

Thus if the 1976 Bill had gone through as introduced, railway and airline employees would have been treated as receiving benefits in kind from concessionary travel equal to the open market cost of tickets and schoolmasters would have been taxed for concessionary education on the amount of the normal school fees.

After second reading, clause 52 of the Bill was committed to a committee of the whole House and clause 54 to Standing Committee E. On 17 May 1976, the House considered clause 52 and strong representations were made about the impact of clause 52 on airline and railway employees. At the start of the meeting of Standing Committee E on 17 June 1976 (before clause 54 was being discussed) the Financial Secretary to the Treasury, Mr. Robert Sheldon, made an announcement (Hansard, columns 893–895) in the following terms:

"The next point I wish to make concerns services and deals with the position of employees of organisations, bodies, or firms which provide services, where the employee is in receipt of those services free or at a reduced rate. Under Clause 54(4) the taxable benefit is to be based on the arm's length price of the benefit received. At present the benefit is valued on the cost to the employer. Representations have been made concerning airline travel and railway employees. . . . It was never intended that the benefit received by the airline employee would be the fare paid by the ordinary passenger. The benefit to him would never be as high as that, because of certain disadvantages that the employee has. Similar considerations, although of a different kind, apply to railway employees. I have had many interviews, discussions and meetings on this matter and I have decided to withdraw Clause 54(4). I thought I would mention this at the outset because so many details, which would normally be left until we reached that particular stage, will be discussed with earlier parts of the legislation. I shall give some reasons which weigh heavily in favour of the withdrawal of this provision. The first is the large difference between the cost of providing some services and the amount of benefit which under the Bill would be held to be received. There are a number of cases of this kind, and I would point out that air and rail journeys are only two of a number of service benefits which have a number of problems attached to them. But there is a large difference between the cost of the benefit to the employer and the value of that benefit as assessed. It could lead to unjustifiable situations resulting in a great number of injustices and I do not think we should continue with it. . . .

"The second reason for withdrawing Clause 54(4) is that these services would tend to be much less used. The problem would then arise for those who had advocated the continuation of this legislation that neither the employer nor the employee nor the Revenue would benefit from the lesser use of these services. This factor also weighed with me. The third reason is the difficulty of enforcement and administration which both give rise to certain problems. Finally, it was possible to withdraw this part of the legislation as the services cover not only a more difficult area, but a quite distinct area of these provisions, without having repercussions on some of the other areas. . . .

"A member: I, too, have talked to many airline employees about this matter, and I am not completely clear as to the purport of my Hon. Friend's remarks. Is he saying that these benefits will remain taxable but that the equivalent cost of the benefit will be calculated on some different basis? Or is he saying that these benefits will not be taxable at all?

"Financial Secretary: The existing law which applies to the taxation of some of these benefits will be retained. The position will subsequently be unchanged from what it is now before the introduction of this legislation."

[His Lordship quoted several further references where the Financial Secretary insisted that the government's intent was not to change the tax treatment previously afforded to railway and airline employees; they would and should be allowed to receive free travel and be assessed only for the extra cost to the employer.]

Simultaneously with the announcement to the standing committee, a press release was issued announcing the withdrawal of clause 54(4). It referred to the same matters as the Financial Secretary had stated to the Committee and concluded:

"The effect of deleting this subclause will be to continue the present basis of taxation of services, namely the cost to the employer of providing the service."

The point was further debated in committee on 22 June 1976. A member is reported as saying, at column 1013, that

"Like many others, I welcome the concession that has been made to leave out the airline staff and the railway employees and all the others that are left out by the dropping of clause 54(4)."

Another member, after referring to the particular reference in the Financial Secretary's statement to airline and railway employees, asked (at col 1023) whether the same distinction applied to services provided by hotel companies to their employees — that is, to rooms which are freely available for the general public in hotels being offered at a concessionary rate to employees of the hotel group. In response, the Financial Secretary said (at col 1024) of the position of such employees:

> "The position is, as he probably expected, the same as that which, following my announcement last week about the withdrawal of Clause 54(4), applies to other employees in service industries; the benefit is the cost to the employer. It is a good illustration of one of the reasons why I withdrew this subsection, in that the cost to the employer in this instance could be much less than the arm's length cost to the outside person taking advantage of such a service." (Column 1024.) * * *

The very question which is the subject matter of the present appeal was also raised. A member said, at columns 1091–1092:

> "I should be grateful for the Financial Secretary's guidance on these two points. . . . The second matter applies particularly to private sector, fee-paying schools where, as the Financial Secretary knows, there is often an arrangement for the children of staff in these schools to be taught at less than the commercial fee in other schools. I take it that because of the deletion of Clause 54(4) that is not now caught. Perhaps these examples will help to clarify the extent to which the Government amendment goes."

The Financial Secretary responded to this question as follows:

> "He mentioned the children of teachers. The removal of clause 54(4) will affect the position of a child of one of the teachers at the child's school, because now the benefit will be assessed on the cost to the employer, which would be very small indeed in this case." (Column 1098.)

Thereafter, clause 54 was not the subject of further debate and passed into law as it now stands as section 63 of the Act. * * *

Under present law, there is a general rule that reference to Parliamentary material as an aid to statutory construction is not permissible ("the exclusionary rule") * * *. The exclusionary rule was probably first stated by Willes J. in *Millar v. Taylor* (1769) 4 Burr. 2303, 2332. [Lord Browne-Wilkinson provided a brief history of the exclusionary rule and possible loopholes as well as criticisms that developed over time.]

My Lords, I have come to the conclusion that, as a matter of law, there are sound reasons for making a limited modification to the existing rule (subject to strict safeguards) unless there are constitutional or practical reasons which outweigh them. In my judgment, subject to the questions of the privileges of the House of Commons, reference to Parliamentary material should be permitted as an aid to the construction of legislation which is ambiguous or obscure or the literal meaning of which leads to an absurdity. Even in such cases references in court to Parliamentary material should only be permitted where such material clearly discloses the mischief aimed at or the legislative intention lying behind the ambiguous or obscure words. In the case of statements made in Parliament, as at present advised I cannot foresee that any statement other than the statement of the minister or other promoter of the Bill is likely to meet these criteria.

I accept Mr. Lester's submissions [for the taxpayers], but my main reason for reaching this conclusion is based on principle. Statute law consists of the words that Parliament has enacted. It is for the courts to construe those words and it is the court's duty in so doing to give effect to the intention of Parliament in using those words. It is an inescapable fact that, despite all the care taken in passing legislation, some statutory provisions when applied to the circumstances under consideration in any specific case are found to be ambiguous. One of the reasons for such ambiguity is that the members of the legislature in enacting the statutory provision may have been told what result those words are intended to achieve. Faced with a given set of words which are capable of conveying that meaning it is not surprising if the words are accepted as having that meaning. Parliament never intends to enact an ambiguity. Contrast with that the position of the courts. The courts are faced simply with a set of words which are in fact capable of bearing two meanings. The courts are ignorant of the underlying Parliamentary purpose. Unless something in other parts of the legislation discloses such purpose, the courts are forced to adopt one of the two possible meanings using highly technical rules of construction. In many, I suspect most, cases references to Parliamentary materials will not throw any light on the matter. But in a few cases it may emerge that the very question was considered by Parliament in passing the legislation. Why in such a case should the courts blind themselves to a clear indication of what Parliament intended in using those words? The court cannot attach a meaning to words which they cannot bear, but if the words are capable of bearing more than one meaning why should not Parliament's true intention be enforced rather than thwarted?

A number of other factors support this view. As I have said, the courts can now look at white papers and official reports for the purpose of finding the "mischief" sought to be corrected, although not at draft clauses or proposals for the remedying of such mischief. A ministerial statement made in Parliament is an equally authoritative source of such information: why should the courts be cut off from this source of information as to the mischief aimed at? In any event, the distinction between looking at reports to identify the mischief aimed at but not to find the intention of Parliament in enacting the legislation is highly artificial. Take the normal Law Commission Report which analyses the problem and then annexes a draft Bill to remedy it. It is now permissible to look at the report to find the mischief and at the draft Bill to see that a provision in the draft was *not* included in the legislation enacted. There can be no logical distinction between that case and looking at the draft Bill to see that the statute as enacted reproduced, often in the same words, the provision in the Law Commission's draft. Given the purposive approach to construction now adopted by the courts in order to give effect to the true intentions of the legislature, the fine distinctions between looking for the mischief and looking for the intention in using words to provide the remedy are technical and inappropriate. Clear and unambiguous statements made by ministers in Parliament are as much the background to the enactment of legislation as white papers and Parliamentary reports.

The decision in *Pickstone v. Freemans Plc.* [1989] A.C. 66 which authorises the court to look at ministerial statements made in introducing regulations which could not be amended by Parliament is logically indistinguishable from such statements made in introducing a statutory provision which, though capable of amendment, was not in fact amended. * * *

Text books often include reference to explanations of legislation given by a minister in Parliament, as a result of which lawyers advise their clients taking account of such statements and judges when construing the legislation come to know of them. In addition, a number of distinguished judges have admitted to breaching the exclusionary rule and looking at Hansard in order to seek the intention of Parliament. When this happens, the parties do not know and have no opportunity to address the judge on the matter. A vivid example of this occurred in the *Hadmor* case [1983] 1 A.C. 191 where Lord Denning in the Court of Appeal relied on his own researches into Hansard in reaching his conclusions: in the House of Lords, counsel protested that there were other passages to which he would have wished to draw the court's attention had he known that Lord Denning was looking at Hansard: see the *Hadmor* case at p. 233. It cannot be right for such information to be available, by a sidewind, for the court but the parties be prevented from presenting their arguments on such material. * * *

It is said that Parliamentary materials are not readily available to, and understandable by, the citizen and his lawyers who should be entitled to rely on the words of Parliament alone to discover his position. It is undoubtedly true that Hansard and particularly records of Committee debates are not widely held by libraries outside London and that the lack of satisfactory indexing of Committee stages makes it difficult to trace the passage of a clause after it is redrafted or renumbered. But such practical difficulties can easily be overstated. It is possible to obtain Parliamentary materials and it is possible to trace the history. The problem is one of expense and effort in doing so, not the availability of the material. In considering the right of the individual to know the law by simply looking at legislation, it is a fallacy to start from the position that all legislation is available in a readily understandable form in any event: the very large number of statutory instruments made every year are not available in an indexed form for well over a year after they have been passed. Yet, the practitioner manages to deal with the problem albeit at considerable expense. Moreover, experience in New Zealand and Australia (where the strict rule has been relaxed for some years) has not shown that the non-availability of materials has raised these practical problems.

Next, it is said that lawyers and judges are not familiar with Parliamentary procedures and will therefore have difficulty in giving proper weight to the Parliamentary materials. Although, of course, lawyers do not have the same experience of these matters as members of the legislature, they are not wholly ignorant of them. If, as I think, significance should only be attached to the clear statements made by a minister or other promoter of the Bill, the difficulty of knowing what weight to attach to such statements is not overwhelming. In the present case, there were numerous statements of view by members in the course of the debate which plainly do not throw any light on the true construction of section 63. What is persuasive in this case is a consistent series of answers given by the minister, after opportunities for taking advice from his officials, all of which point the same way and which were not withdrawn or varied prior to the enactment of the Bill.

Then it is said that court time will be taken up by considering a mass of Parliamentary material and long arguments about its significance, thereby increasing the expense of litigation. In my judgment, though the introduction of further admissible material will inevitably involve some increase in the use of time, this will not be significant as long as courts insist that Parliamentary material should only be introduced in the limited cases I have mentioned and where such material contains a clear indication from the minister of the mischief aimed at, or the nature of the cure intended, by the legislation. Attempts to introduce material which does not satisfy those tests should be met by orders for costs made against those who have improperly introduced the material. Experience in the United States of America, where legislative history has for many years been much more generally admissible than I am now suggesting, shows how important it is to maintain strict control over the use of such material. That position is to be contrasted with what has happened in New Zealand and Australia (which have relaxed the rule to approximately the extent that I favour): there is no evidence of any complaints of this nature coming from those countries.

There is one further practical objection which, in my view, has real substance. If the rule is relaxed legal advisers faced with an ambiguous statutory provision may feel that they have to research the materials to see whether they yield the crock of gold, i.e., a clear indication of Parliament's intentions. In very many cases the crock of gold will not be discovered and the expenditure on the research wasted. This is a real objection to changing the rule. However, again it is easy to overestimate the cost of such research: if a reading of Hansard shows that there is nothing of significance said by the minister in relation to the clause in question, further research will become pointless.

In sum, I do not think that the practical difficulties arising from a limited relaxation of the rule are sufficient to outweigh the basic need for the courts to give effect to the words enacted by Parliament in the sense that they were intended by Parliament to bear. Courts are frequently criticised for their failure to do that. This failure is due not to cussedness but to ignorance of what Parliament intended by the obscure words of the legislation. The courts should not deny themselves the light which Parliamentary materials may shed on the meaning of the words Parliament has used and thereby risk subjecting the individual to a law which Parliament never intended to enact.

[The last section of his Lordship's opinion discussed the "constitutional" issue whether adverting to Hansard is a "questioning" of the freedom of parliamentary speech and debate that is prohibited by article 9 of the Bill of Rights of 1688. His Lordship interpreted article 9 much like the U.S. Constitution's Speech and Debate Clause (see Chapter 3, § 2) and found it inapplicable.]

The Attorney General raised a further constitutional point, namely, that for the court to use Parliamentary material in construing legislation would be to confuse the respective roles of Parliament as the maker of law and the courts as the interpreter. I am not impressed by this argument. The law, as I have said, is to be found in the words in which Parliament has enacted. It is for the courts to interpret those words so as to give effect to that purpose. The question is whether, in addition to other aids to the construction of statutory words, the courts should have regard to a further source. Recourse is already had to white papers and official reports not because they determine the meaning of the statutory words but because they assist the court to make its own determination. I can see no constitutional impropriety in this. * * *

I therefore reach the conclusion, subject to any question of Parliamentary privilege, that the exclusionary rule should be relaxed so as to permit reference to Parliamentary materials where:

(a) legislation is ambiguous or obscure, or leads to an absurdity;

(b) the material relied on consists of one or more statements by a minister or other promoter of the Bill together if necessary with such other Parliamentary material as is necessary to understand such statements and their effect;

(c) the statements relied on are clear.

[In the present case, the statute was ambiguous and the Hansard materials clearly resolved the ambiguity in favor of the taxpayers.]

The question then arises whether it is right to attribute to Parliament as a whole the same intention as that repeatedly voiced by the Financial Secretary. In my judgment it is. It is clear from reading Hansard that the committee was repeatedly asking for guidance as to the effect of the legislation once subclause (4) of clause 54 was abandoned. That Parliament relied on the ministerial statements is shown by the fact that the matter was never raised again after the discussions in committee, that amendments were consequentially withdrawn and that no relevant amendment was made which could affect the correctness of the minister's statement. * * *

Having once looked at what was said in Parliament, it is difficult to put it out of mind. I have the advantage that, after the first hearing and before seeing the Parliamentary materials, I had reached the conclusion, in agreement with Vinelott J. and the Court of Appeal, that the Revenue's submissions were correct. If it is not permissible to take into account what was said by the Financial Secretary, I remain of the same view. * * *

NOTES ON *PEPPER* AND THE
DEMISE OF THE EXCLUSIONARY RULE

1. *The Abandonment of the Exclusionary Rule in English-Speaking Countries.* In the United Kingdom, *Pepper v. Hart* created quite a stir, and unleashed a fair amount of interest in legislative history by lower courts and, to a lesser extent, the House of Lords. An excellent survey by James Brudney, *Below the Surface: Comparative Legislative History Usage by the House of Lords and the Supreme Court*, 85 Wash. U.L. Rev. 1 (2007), demonstrates that much of the Hansard reliance is to minister (floor manager) explanations and

not to committee reports, which are not routinely generated in Parliament. On the other hand, Brudney found that during the post-*Pepper* period, the Lords have greatly increased their references to government white papers and commission reports, background documents with some similarity to our committee reports. In short, the Lords are explicitly considering a lot more background materials than they did twenty years ago.

Although the Law Lords remain divided over the wisdom of *Pepper*, a majority of them are committed to this new course of action, within limits that have yet to be determined once and for all.[q] In *Regina (Jackson) v. Attorney General*, [2005] All Eng. Law Rep. 1253, for example, the Lords unanimously upheld the famous Hunting Act, which deployed a 1911 statute to override House of Lords opposition to a popular measure. Lord Bingham's lead opinion rejected the relevance of Hansard as authoritative evidence of parliamentary "intent" but relied on the debates (including eight rejected proposals) to confirm the meaning of words Parliament used in the 1911 statute. Lord Nicholls's speech relied even more extensively on Hansard, as confirmation of what he and the other Lords considered the apparent meaning of the text. Lord Steyn objected to any use of Hansard in these circumstances.

The House of Lords' decision has had echoes throughout the Commonwealth countries. The leading Canadian treatise states: "Since the 1980s the [exclusionary] rule has been eroding at a rapid rate. Some courts have ignored it while other courts have carved out significant exceptions and qualifications. * * * The exclusionary rule in its traditional form is clearly dead." *Driedger* 486. See also David Duff, *Interpreting the Income Tax Act*, 47 Can. Tax. J. 471 & 741 (1999) (two-part article on use of legislative history in tax cases). The exclusionary rule had previously been abandoned in the United States, see *Holy Trinity* (Chapter 7, § 1); Australia, see Commonwealth Acts Interpretation Act § 15ab, discussed in Gifford, *supra*, at 126–29; and other Commonwealth countries. Many civil-law countries still follow such a rule or practice, however.

2. *When Should Legislative Materials Be Admissible? The Potato Chip Problem.* The key opinion is that of Lord Browne-Wilkinson, who admits legislative materials, but only in limited circumstances. But how should we characterize the holding of the case? This is more difficult than appears on first glance.

(a) *Sponsor Statements May Be Consulted When the Statute Is Ambiguous.* This appears to be the holding as articulated by Lord Browne-Wilkinson, and

---

q. For example, Lord Millett, *Construing Statutes*, 20 Stat. L. Rev. 107 (1999), maintained that *Pepper* was a mistake and that the Lords should return to their previous practice of relying exclusively on statutory text. Lord Hoffman praised *Pepper* for opening up probative evidence of legislative intent (and for discouraging government ministers from making promises to Parliament that they might later renounce) but was skeptical that the costs of extra research were worth these benefits. *The Intolerable Wrestle With Words and Meanings*, 114 S. A. L. J. 656, 669 (1997); see also *Robinson v. Secretary of State for Northern Ireland*, [2002] N. Ir. L. Rep. 390, 405 (Lord Hoffman, repeating his lament that *Pepper* generated large research costs, with scant benefit).

the U.S. Supreme Court sometimes says it follows a like rule. See, e.g., *Director, OWCP v. Greenwich Collieries*, 512 U.S. 267 (1994). But does this precept explain the decision in this case? The first committee of Law Lords found the statute unambiguous against the taxpayer; on the original panel, only Lord Griffith found ambiguity. Lord Chancellor Mackay found ambiguity on rehearing and voted for the taxpayer on that ground, but only Lord Griffith agreed with him. Other Lords, including Browne-Wilkinson, *found ambiguity only after they consulted the Hansard materials.*

(b) *Hansard Materials May Be Consulted to Confirm Statutory Plain Meaning.* The narrowest interpretation of *Pepper*, embraced by Lord Steyn and others, is that Hansard materials can only be introduced for textualist reasons, namely, to suggest or confirm standard usage of statutory terms and the plain meaning they have to reasonable speakers of the English language.

(c) *Hansard May Be Invoked to Clear Up Any Statutory Matters.* In the aftermath of *Pepper*, some Law Lords used the decision as a Magna Carta for browsing parliamentary debates for what they were worth, essentially ignoring Lord Browne-Wilkinson's suggested limits. See David Miers, *Taxing Perks and Interpreting Statutes:* Pepper v. Hart, 56 Mod. L. Rev. 695, 705–06 (1993). Few Lords in the new millennium openly endorse this position, and there are procedural hurdles in place,[r] but there is some indication that some lower court judges are running wild with legislative materials. Should this have been expected?

Aside from the precise limits suggested in this case, consider a *potato chip theory*, suggested by the U.S. history after *Holy Trinity*: once a court starts looking at the "best" legislative history, like committee reports and sponsor statements, other kinds of history will get smuggled in, on the ground that they provide "context" for understanding the committee reports (which of course provide "context" for understanding the text). Before long, everything becomes relevant and might be considered "for what it is worth" (the trend in modern evidence law, by the way). Just as you can never eat just one potato chip, you can never admit just one bit of legislative history. It might take decades for the potato chip process to develop, but the theory is that Hansard reliance will grow by fits and starts until there is some kind of crisis that pushes in the other direction.

3. *Relevance for the U.S. Debate?* Should *Pepper* suggest to the new textualists that they should adopt a more moderate skepticism about legislative materials?[s] If you were Justice Scalia, how would you have voted in *Pepper*?

---

r. The Lords directed that financial sanctions would be visited upon a party who relied on Hansard in a case that did not meet the three requirements of Lord Browne-Wilkinson's opinion. Also, the Lords issued a Practice Directive in 1994 (reaffirmed in 1999 and 2002) which required parties intending to invoke Hansard to give prior notice, including copies of the pages in Hansard and the argument to be made from it. Brudney, *Below the Surface.*

s. See, e.g., John Manning, *Textualism as a Nondelegation Doctrine*, 97 Colum. L. Rev. 673 (1997), which presents a constitutional justification for refusing to consider committee reports "authoritative" (in the way the statute is) but admitting them as evidence of what the statutory words might mean. On *Pepper* and American practice, see Michael Healy, *Legislative*

(Hint: Consider the *evolution* of the treatment of in-house benefits, from 1948 to 1993, nicely laid out in Lord Browne-Wilkinson's opinion. You can be a textualist and consider the formal evolution of the statutory scheme, as the U.S. Supreme Court did in *Leo Sheep*. What argument might a textualist draw from that?)

Brudney, *Below the Surface*, argues that the U.S. Supreme Court should conclude from the Mother Country's post-*Pepper* practice that the most fruitful debates focus not on the tired admissibility debate, but rather on the circumstances under which legislative history would be useful. "[S]hould legislative history be regarded as presumptively more valuable to help resolve textual ambiguities that stem from lack of foresight rather than lack of political consensus? Is legislative history accompanying omnibus bills generally less suitable for judicial use because congressional deals on such a grand scale are simply indecipherable? Should legislative history in certain subject areas be presumed to have less weight where the law is administered primarily by a federal agency rather than private parties, or where the statutory text tends to be detailed and technical rather than open-ended and of more general public interest?" Apply these questions to the next case.

KOSAK v. UNITED STATES
Supreme Court of the United States, 1984
465 U.S. 848, 104 S.Ct. 1519, 79 L.Ed.2d 860

JUSTICE MARSHALL delivered the opinion of the Court.

[While a serviceman stationed in Guam, Kosak assembled a large collection of art. When he was transferred from Guam to Philadelphia, he brought his art collection with him. He was subsequently charged with smuggling the collection into this country, but he was acquitted by a jury. The Customs Service then notified Kosak that the seized objects were subject to civil forfeiture under 19 U.S.C. § 1592 (1976), which at the time permitted confiscation of goods brought into the United States "by means of any false statement." Although the Customs Service returned the art, Kosak claimed that some of the objects were damaged and filed suit for $12,000 pursuant to the Federal Tort Claims Act, 28 U.S.C. §§ 1346(b), 2671–2680.]

The Federal Tort Claims Act, enacted in 1946, provides generally that the United States shall be liable, to the same extent as a private party, "for injury or loss of property, or personal injury or death caused by the negligent or wrongful act or omission of any employee of the Government while acting within the scope of his office or employment." 28 U.S.C. § 1346(b); see also 28 U.S.C. § 2674. The Act's broad waiver of sovereign immunity is, however, subject to 13 enumerated exceptions. 28 U.S.C. §§ 2680(a)–(f), (h)–(n). One of those exceptions, § 2680(c), exempts from the coverage of the statute "[a]ny claim arising in respect of * * * the detention of any goods or merchandise by

---

any officer of customs * * * ."[6] Petitioner asks us to construe the foregoing language to cover only claims "for damage caused by the detention itself and not for the negligent * * * destruction of property while it is in the possession of the customs service." By "damage caused by the detention itself," petitioner appears to mean harms attributable to an illegal detention, such as a decline in the economic value of detained goods (either because of depreciation or because of a drop in the price the goods will fetch), injury resulting from deprivation of the ability to make use of the goods during the period of detention, or consequential damages resulting from lack of access to the goods. The Government asks us to read the exception to cover all injuries to property sustained during its detention by customs officials.

The starting point of our analysis of these competing interpretations must, of course, be the language of § 2680(c). * * * At first blush, the statutory language certainly appears expansive enough to support the Government's construction; the encompassing phrase, "arising in respect of," seems to sweep within the exception all injuries associated in any way with the "detention" of goods. It must be admitted that this initial reading is not ineluctable; as Judge Weis, dissenting in the Court of Appeals, pointed out, it is possible (with some effort) to read the phrase "in respect of" as the equivalent of "as regards" and thereby to infer that "the statutory exception is directed to the fact of detention itself, and that alone." But we think that the fairest interpretation of the crucial portion of the provision is the one that first springs to mind: "any claim arising in respect of" the detention of goods means any claim "arising out of" the detention of goods, and includes a claim resulting from negligent handling or storage of detained property. * * *

The legislative history of § 2680(c), though meager, supports the interpretation of the provision that we have derived from its language and context. Two specific aspects of the evolution of the provision are telling. First, the person who almost certainly drafted the language under consideration clearly thought that it covered injury to detained property caused by the negligence of customs officials. It appears that the portion of § 2680(c) pertaining to the detention of goods was first written by Judge Alexander Holtzoff, one of the major figures in the development of the Tort Claims Act. In his Report explicating his proposals, Judge Holtzoff explained:

> "[The proposed provision would exempt from the coverage of the Act] [c]laims arising in respect of the assessment or collection of any tax or customs duty. This exception appears in all previous drafts. It is expanded, however, so as to include immunity from liability in respect of *loss in connection with the detention of goods or merchandise*

---

6. The full text of § 2680(c) provides:
     "The provisions of [28 U.S.C. §§ 2671–2679] and § 1346(b) of this title shall not apply to — * * *
     (c) Any claim arising in respect of the assessment or collection of any tax or customs duty, or the detention of any goods or merchandise by any officer of customs or excise or any other law-enforcement officer."
We have no occasion in this case to decide what kinds of "law-enforcement officer[s]," other than customs officials, are covered by the exception.

by any officer of customs or excise. The additional proviso has special reference to the detention of imported goods in appraisers' warehouses or customs houses, as well as seizures by law enforcement officials, internal revenue officers, and the like." A. Holtzoff, Report on Proposed Federal Tort Claims Bill 16 (1931) (Holtzoff Report) (emphasis added).[12]

Though it cannot be definitively established that Congress relied upon Judge Holtzoff's report, it is significant that the apparent draftsman of the crucial portion of § 2680(c) believed that it would bar a suit of the sort brought by petitioner.[13]

Second, the Congressional committees that submitted Reports on the various bills that ultimately became the Tort Claims Act suggested that the provision that was to become § 2680(c), like the other exceptions from the waiver of sovereign immunity, covered claims "arising out of" the designated conduct. Thus, for example, the House Judiciary Committee described the proposed exceptions as follows:

> "These exemptions cover claims arising out of the loss or miscarriage of postal matter; the assessment or collection of taxes or assessments; the detention of goods by customs officers; admiralty and maritime torts; deliberate torts such as assault and battery; and others." H.R. Rep. No. 1287, 79th Cong., 1st Sess., 6 (1945).

The Committees' casual use of the words, "arising out of," with reference to the exemption of claims pertaining to the detention of goods substantially undermines petitioner's contention that the phrase, "in respect of," was designed to limit the sorts of suits covered by the provision.

---

12. Judge Holtzoff went on to explain that "[t]his provision is suggested in the proposed draft of the bill submitted by the Crown Proceedings Committee in England in 1927 * * * ." Holtzoff Report at 16. The relevant portion of the bill to which Holtzoff referred was even more explicit:

"No proceedings shall lie under this section — * * *

(c) for or in respect of the loss of or any deterioration or damage occasioned to, or any delay in the release of, any goods or merchandise by reason of anything done or omitted to be done by any officer of customs and excise acting as such * * * ."

Report of Crown Proceedings Committee § 11(5)(c), pp. 17–18 (Apr. 1927). (It appears that this bill was never enacted into law in England.)

13. Mr. Holtzoff wrote his report while serving as Special Assistant to the Attorney General. He had been "assigned by Attorney General Mitchell to the special task of co-ordinating the views of the Government departments" regarding the proper scope of a tort claims statute. See Borchard, *The Federal Tort Claims Bill*, 1 U.Chi.L.Rev. 1, n. 2 (1933). Holtzoff submitted his report, in which his draft bill was contained, to Assistant Attorney General Rugg, who in turn transmitted it to the General Accounting Office of the Comptroller General. Insofar as Holtzoff's report embodied the views of the Executive Department at that stage of the debates over the tort claims bill, it is likely that, at some point, the report was brought to the attention of the Congressmen considering the bill. We agree with the dissent that, because the report was never introduced into the public record, the ideas expressed therein should not be given great weight in determining the intent of the legislature. But, in the absence of any direct evidence regarding how members of Congress understood the provision that became § 2680(c), it seems to us senseless to ignore entirely the views of its draftsman.

[Justice Marshall further concluded that this interpretation accords with the purposes of the statute: ensuring that certain governmental activities not be disrupted by the threat of damage suits; avoiding exposure for fraudulent or excessive claims; and not extending the coverage of the Act to suits for which adequate remedies were already available. Allowing suits against the government in cases such as this one might impair the efficiency of Customs' operations, reasoned Justice Marshall. Additionally, even at common law property owners had (and retain) a right to sue individual customs officers who damage their goods.]

Petitioner and some commentators argue that § 2680(c) should not be construed in a fashion that denies an effectual remedy to many persons whose property is damaged through the tortious conduct of customs officials. That contention has force, but it is properly addressed to Congress, not to this Court. The language of the statute as it was written leaves us no choice but to affirm the judgment of the Court of Appeals that the Tort Claims Act does not cover suits alleging that customs officials injured property that had been detained by the Customs Service.

JUSTICE STEVENS, dissenting.

The Government's construction of 28 U.S.C. § 2680(c) is not the one that "first springs" to my mind. Rather, I read the exception for claims arising "in respect of * * * the detention of any goods" as expressing Congress' intent to preclude liability attributable to the temporary interference with the owner's possession of his goods, as opposed to liability for physical damage to his goods. That seems to me to be the normal reading of the statutory language that Congress employed, and the one that most Members of Congress voting on the proposal would have given it. Moreover, my reading, unlike the Court's, is supported by an examination of the language used in other exceptions. Congress did not use the words "arising out of" in § 2680(c) but did use those words in three other subsections of the same section of the Act. See §§ 2680(b), (e) and (h). Absent persuasive evidence to the contrary, we should assume that when Congress uses different language in a series of similar provisions, it intends to express a different intention. * * *

In the entire 15 year history preceding the enactment of the Tort Claims Act in 1946, the Court finds only two "clues" that it believes shed any light on the meaning of § 2680(c). The first — the so-called "Holtzoff Report" — is nothing but an internal Justice Department working paper prepared in 1931 and never even mentioned in the legislative history of the 1946 Act. There is no indication that any Congressman ever heard of the document or knew that it even existed. The position of the majority — that it is "significant" that the "apparent draftsman" of the relevant language himself "believed that it would bar a suit of the sort brought by petitioner" — is manifestly ill-advised. The intent of a lobbyist — no matter how public spirited he may have been — should not be attributed to the Congress without positive evidence that elected legislators were aware of and shared the lobbyist's intent.

Unless we know more about the collective legislative purpose than can be gleaned from an internal document prepared by a person who was seeking legislative action, we should be guided by the sensible statement that "in construing a statute * * * the worst person to construe it is the person who is responsible for its drafting. He is very much disposed to confuse what he intended to do with the effect of the language which in fact has been employed." *Hilder v. Dexter*, [1902] A.C. 474, 477 (Halsbury, L.C., abstaining).[2] If the draftsman of the language in question intended it to cover such cases as this one, he failed.

The second "clue" relied upon by the majority consists of a brief summary in the House Committee Report which casually uses the prepositional phrase "arising out of" to introduce a truncated list of the exceptions. But the "casual" use of the latter phrase in the Committee Report is as understandable as it is insignificant. It is nothing more than an introduction. In such an introduction, precision of meaning is naturally and knowingly sacrificed in the interest of brevity. * * *

NOTES ON *KOSAK* AND THE VIEWS OF NONLEGISLATOR DRAFTERS

1. *Statements of Nonlegislative Drafters.* The majority opinion in *Kosak* realistically recognizes that much legislation is drafted by nonlegislators — executive officials and interest groups, mainly. But why should the views of a nonlegislator count — especially if the Court deems its inquiry as a search for the "intent" of *Congress*? Moreover, Holtzoff's memorandum was not "public." Distinguish between the testimony at congressional hearings by Holtzoff, in which Members of Congress could disagree with him (either then

---

2. The majority's analysis, it should be observed, puts the cart before the horse.

"The essence of bill drafting is placing a legislative proposal in the proper legal phraseology and form to achieve congressional intent. It is primarily a task of legal analysis and research rather than of composition * * *. Framing the legal language to embody congressional purpose is not as difficult as ascertaining what that purpose is in its entirety. While a committee (or an individual member of Congress, as the case may be) is in the process of working out what it wants to do, the legislative counsel assist it by explaining the effect of alternative proposals. Even after the committee (or Congressman) has settled upon the major outlines of a measure, subsidiary policy questions seem to unfold endlessly. The legislative counsel must point up all of those for the committee (or Congressman) to decide. To accomplish that, the legislative counsel must envisage the broad application of the proposed law in all of its ramifications." K. Kofmehl, Professional Staffs of Congress 189 (3d ed. 1977) (footnote omitted).

Many bills are of course initially drafted in the Executive Branch. After today's decision, we can anticipate executive agencies searching long dormant files for documents similar to the Holtzoff Report. We can also anticipate that private parties will attempt to capitalize on this new reservoir of "legislative" history as well, through discovery and perhaps the Freedom of Information Act. In light of the Government's reliance on the Holtzoff Report, presumably it will not assert that this kind of material is privileged when private parties are in search of "legislative" intent.

Finally, the language in some bills is initially drafted by private lobbyists. One doubts that the majority would find "significant" the intention of such a draftsman when that intention was not shared with the Congress.

or during subsequent floor debate),[t] and his Department of Justice memorandum, which was written before the bill was acted upon even by a committee and which may have represented only his (and not even the Department's) point of view. Why should the latter be entitled to any consideration at all? Are there other ways of thinking about statutory interpretation which make Judge Holtzoff's statement relevant? (Hint: maybe, like a good commentary in a treatise or a law review article, it makes the most sense of the legislation.) See generally Alison Giles, *The Value of Nonlegislators' Contributions to Legislative History*, 79 Geo. L.J. 359 (1991) (student note).

Notwithstanding these objections, the Supreme Court or individual Justices have occasionally relied on statements by public, nonlegislative officials who draft or promote statutes. See, e.g., *Circuit City Stores, Inc. v. Adams*, 532 U.S. 105, 128–29 (2001) (Stevens, J., dissenting) (dissenters relying on defense of statute by Secretary of Commerce; majority does not address this argument because of plain meaning rule); *Negonsott v. Samuels*, 507 U.S. 99, 106–09 (1993); *Gollust v. Mendell*, 501 U.S. 115, 125 & n.7 (1991); *Howe v. Smith*, 452 U.S. 473, 485 (1981); *Monroe v. Standard Oil Co.*, 452 U.S. 549, 558–59 (1981). Note, however, that (as in *Kosak*) the Court will not rely on these statements as the most probative — and certainly not the *only* — evidence of statutory meaning. There are very few state cases; almost all of them either reject or denigrate such evidence. E.g., *Hayes v. Continental Ins. Co.*, 872 P.2d 668 (Ariz. 1994).

2. *Statements of Private Drafters*. At least Holtzoff was a public servant. Should the Court consider authoritative the statements of interest groups which draft and press for legislation? In some instances the Court or some Justices have considered testimony about legislation by private groups or individuals who drafted or commented on the legislation. See, e.g., *Circuit City Stores*, 532 U.S. at 127 (Stevens, J., dissenting) (relying on explanation by ABA committee that originated the statute); *Gustafson v. Alloyd Co.*, 513 U.S. 561 (1995) (relying on statement by Professor Landis, submitted as part of legislative deliberations, as support for Court's text-based interpretation); *Jefferson County Pharmaceutical Assoc. v. Abbott Labs*, 460 U.S. 150, 159–62 (1983) (relying upon explanation of lobbyist who was principal drafter of the statute in question); *NLRB v. Robbins Tire & Rubber Co.*, 437 U.S. 214, 230–32 (1978) (relying on explanation of ABA Administrative Law Division, which had originally proposed the statutory amendment in question during Senate hearings). See also *Group Life & Health Inc. Co. v. Royal Drug Co.*, 440 U.S. 205 (1979); *Southland Corp. v. Keating*, 465 U.S. 1, 26–29 (1984) (O'Connor, J., dissenting).

3. *The New Textualist Approach to* Kosak. Justice Stevens' dissent reflects a textualist approach to *Kosak*. Would Justice Scalia (not on the Court in 1984) agree with Stevens' interpretation? You might think so, except that Scalia recognizes a new super-strong clear statement rule presuming against

---

t. Ironically, when Holtzoff's public testimony was relevant to an issue of interpretation, the Court ignored it. Compare *Sheridan v. United States*, 487 U.S. 392 (1988) (opinion of the Court), with *id.* at 410 (O'Connor, J., dissenting).

waivers of federal sovereign immunity. See *United States v. Nordic Village, Inc.*, 503 U.S. 30 (1992) (opinion for the Court by Scalia, Stevens in dissent). A corollary of that rule would be to construe waivers (such as the Federal Tort Claims Act) very narrowly or, correlatively, to construe reservations to such waivers (such as the § 2680 exceptions to the waiver) broadly. In that event, a new textualist could agree with the result reached by Justice Marshall.

Nordic Village reflects one of the criticisms of the new textualism: by removing or de-emphasizing legislative history (created by and reflecting the norms of legislators), textualist judges put more emphasis on the famously malleable substantive canons of statutory construction (created by and reflecting the norms of judges). In *Matter of Interpretation* (1997), Justice Scalia defends the *Nordic Village* super-strong clear statement rule as reflecting the likely "intent" of most legislators. Yet the Justice cites no evidence for this belief, nor for the further proposition that legislators "intend" to make federal sovereign immunity (a common law concept perpetuated by judges like Scalia) as hard to rebut as the Court treated it in *Nordic Village*.

4. *Legislative Deliberation: Hearings, Floor Debate, Rejected Proposals, and Dogs That Didn't Bark*

Compared to statements in committee reports, statements made during committee hearings and floor debates have traditionally received less weight in evaluating legislative intent. If the statement was made by a sponsor or informed supporter of the bill, courts might credit it as a reliable indication of legislative intent — as did the Supreme Court majority and dissenting opinions in *Weber* or as the House of Lords did in *Pepper v. Hart*. The conventional wisdom is that what is said in hearings and floor debates is usually of little value, except for confirmatory purposes. Reed Dickerson, *Statutory Interpretation: Dipping into Legislative History*, 11 Hofstra L. Rev. 1125, 1131–32 (1983).

Reflecting on the Burger Court's practice, Judge Patricia Wald, *Legislative History in the 1981 Term, supra*, at 202, opined that "[t]he hornbook rule that hearings are relevant only as background to show the purpose of the statute no longer holds. In many cases, the best explanation of what the legislation is about comes from the executive department or outside witnesses at the hearings." Indeed, since proposed legislation is frequently drafted by the executive department or by private interest groups, their statements and explanations at hearings might be the only truly informed explanation of the structure and operation of the statute. E.g., *Gustafson v. Alloyd Co.*, 513 U.S. 561 (1995) (testimony of academic expert commenting on interest group arguments made during congressional deliberations); *Lowe v. SEC*, 472 U.S. 181, 195–99 (1985) (testimony of industry witnesses at hearings); *Trbovich v. United Mine Workers of America*, 404 U.S. 528 (1972) (Senate hearing testimony by Senator John Kennedy, the sponsor, and Professor Archibald Cox, primary drafter of the proposed legislation). Now that many states record committee hearings, and still others provide staff summaries of statements made in them, state courts are coming to rely on statements made in those hearings."

Potentially relevant for similar reasons are presidential statements initiating or issued during congressional deliberations, especially when the President has been a prime mover behind a piece of legislation, as he was with the Civil Rights Act of 1964 and the Voting Rights Act of 1965. Thus, presidential transmittal letters or speeches advocating legislation have sometimes been considered useful legislative history, e.g., *NLRB v. Local 103, Int'l Ass'n of Bridge Workers*, 434 U.S. 335, 347 n.9 (1978); *Connell Construction Co. v. Plumbers & Steamfitters Local 100*, 421 U.S. 616, 629 n.8 (1975); *Western Union Telegraph Co. v. Lenroot*, 323 U.S. 490, 492 (1945). See generally Note, *The First Word: The President's Place in "Legislative History,"* 89 Mich. L. Rev. 399 (1990).

In a like spirit, Justices sometimes rely on floor debates, including exchanges between supporters and opponents. Although statements by legislators about bills they oppose are not reliable, see *NLRB v. Fruit & Vegetable Packers*, 377 U.S. 58, 66 (1964), exchanges with supporters may sharpen the precise deals that have been reached. An interesting illustration is *BankAmerica v. United States*, 462 U.S. 122 (1983), where the Court interpreted the Clayton Act's general bar to interlocking corporate directorates to be inapplicable to bank-nonbank interlocks.ᵛ Chief Justice Burger's opinion for the Court relied on the plain meaning of the statutory provision, the structure of the statute, the longstanding interpretation by the relevant regulatory agencies and subcommittees, and the legislative history. The theme of the legislative history was that many progressives wanted to prohibit bank-nonbank interlocks, and at various points in the process criticized the general provision in the proposed legislation for not barring them.

---

u. For state cases relying on statements in hearings, see, e.g., *Pacific Bell v. California State and Consumer Services Agency*, 275 Cal. Rptr. 62, 67–68 (Cal. App. 1990) (testimony in committee hearings); *People v. Luciano*, 662 P.2d 480, 482 n.4 (Colo. 1983) (recordings of Senate and House committee hearings); *In re Sheldon G.*, 583 A.2d 112, 116 & n.6 (Conn. 1990) (testimony in committee hearings); *Jackson v. Kansas City*, 235 Kan. 278 (Kan. 1984) (statements in committee hearings); *First Nat'l Bank of Deerwood v. Gregg*, 556 N.W.2d 214 (Minn. 1996) (tape-recorded hearings); *Wiseman v. Keller*, 358 N.W.2d 768 (Neb. 1984) (judiciary committee hearing); *Linlee Enters., Inc. v. State*, 445 A.2d 1130, 1131 (N.H. 1982) (House committee hearing and subcommittee report); *Dickinson v. Fund for Support of Free Public Schools*, 469 A.2d 1 (N.J. 1983) (statements made in subcommittee and committee hearings); *Golden v. Koch*, 415 N.Y.S.2d 330 (Sup. Ct. 1979) (committee hearings and report); *Sager v. McClenden*, 672 P.2d 697 (Ore. 1983) (minutes of committee hearings). A number of states have ruled that legislator statements during committee hearings cannot be the basis for the court's finding of legislative intent. See *State v. Miranda*, 715 A.2d 680 (Conn. 1998).

v. The fourth paragraph of Clayton Act § 8, 15 U.S.C. § 19, reads: "No person at the same time shall be a director in *any two or more corporations*, any one of which has capital, surplus, and undivided profits aggregating more than $1,000,000, engaged in whole or in part in commerce, *other than banks, banking associations, trust companies, and common carriers* subject to the Act to regulate commerce * * *." The second paragraph prohibits bank-bank interlocks.

The clinching evidence in *BankAmerica* was a colloquy among two supporters and an opponent at the close of the House debate. The opponent, Representative Mann, raised a point of order, that the House conferees had improperly agreed to a conference bill that cut back both Senate and House bills, which he construed as having regulated *all* bank interlocks. The supporters, Representatives Sherley and Webb, admonished Mann and asserted that the general catch-all bar never applied to banks, and the final version of the bill only regulated bank-bank interlocks in a special provision. The Chief Justice believed that these representations by supporters of the legislation were persuasive — and their cogency was confirmed when the Speaker overruled Mann's point of order, apparently on the ground that the House conferees had not betrayed the earlier deal.

BankAmerica is perhaps an unusual case, because the key colloquy occurred at the very end of the legislative debate and spoke directly, and dramatically, to the issue before the Court. In *Weber*, by way of contrast, Justice Brennan's majority opinion responded that all of Justice Rehnquist's parade of quotes critical of racial quotas were uttered before Title VII achieved its final form, laden with compromises, including § 703(j) (which Brennan found critical to his judgment that Congress was tolerant of *voluntary* affirmative action). "To permit what we regard as clear statutory language to be materially altered by such colloquies, which often take place before the bill has achieved its final form, would open the door to the inadvertent, or perhaps even planned, undermining of the language actually voted on by Congress * * *." *Regan v. Wald*, 468 U.S. 222, 237–42 (1984).

Because legislative history has become much more controversial, among federal judges at least, one might expect that references to congressional hearings and floor debates would dry up at the Supreme Court level. This has *not* been the case, as the following opinions and notes will reflect. The first two cases present a recurring issue: what to make of the *rejection* of legislative proposals in committee, on the floor of either chamber, in conference committee, and so forth. The third case brings together a host of legislative sources and the famous "dog that doesn't bark" canon.

FDA v. BROWN & WILLIAMSON TOBACCO CORP.
U.S. Supreme Court, 2000
529 U.S. 120, 120 S.Ct. 1291, 146 L.Ed.2d 121

[Excerpted in Chapter 7, § 3B3]

RAPANOS v. UNITED STATES, 126 S.Ct. 2208 (2006). The Federal Water Pollution Control Act Amendments of 1972 prohibit the discharge of pollutants into the nation's waters, excepting only discharges allowed in the Act. Section 404, administered by the Army Corps of Engineers, allows only administratively permitted discharge of dredge or fill into "navigable waters," which the statute defines as "waters of the United States, including the territorial seas." 33 U.S.C. § 1362(7). This statutory language reflected the *rejection* in Conference Committee of including the term "navigable" in

§ 1362(7)'s definition. "The Conferees fully intend that the term 'navigable waters' be given the broadest possible constitutional interpretation."

Under pressure from the EPA, the House, and the judiciary, the Army Corps adopted regulations in 1975 (finalized in 1977) defining "navigable waters" to include "wetlands" that are "adjacent" to (1) navigable waters as traditionally defined, (2) tributaries (including channels that are only episodically conduits of water) of navigable waters, and (3) interstate waters, whether or not navigable, and their tributaries. In addition, isolated wetlands are included if their degradation could affect interstate commerce.

The 1975 regulations were the subject of extensive committee hearings in both the House and Senate. Critics of the Corps's permit program attempted to insert limitations on the Corps's § 404 jurisdiction into the proposed 1977 clean water legislation. The House bill as reported out of committee proposed a redefinition of "navigable waters" that would have limited the Corps's authority under § 404 to waters navigable in fact and their adjacent wetlands (defined as wetlands periodically inundated by contiguous navigable waters). H.R. 3199, 95th Cong., 1st Sess., § 16 (1977). The bill reported by the Senate Committee on Environment and Public Works, by contrast, contained no redefinition of the scope of the "navigable waters" covered by § 404, and dealt with the perceived problem of over-regulation by exempting certain activities (primarily agricultural) from the permit requirement and by providing for assumption of some of the Corps's regulatory duties by federally approved state programs. S.1952, 95th Cong., 1st Sess., §49(b) (1977).

On the floor of the Senate, Senator Bentsen (D–TX) proposed an amendment to limit the scope of "navigable waters" along the lines set forth in the House bill. 123 Cong. Rec. 26710–26711 (1977). Reflecting the majority viewpoint, Senator Baker (R–TN) endorsed the Corps's regulations, because "comprehensive coverage of this program is essential for the protection of the aquatic environment." Id. at 26718. Other Senators (and Representatives) made similar comments. After extensive debate, the Senate rejected that amendment, 123 Cong. Rec. 26728 (1977), as did the Conference Committee reconciling the two versions of the Clean Water Act of 1977, 91 Stat. 1566.

The Supreme Court ruled in *United States v. Riverside Bayview Homes, Inc.*, 474 U.S. 121 (1985), that the Corps's regulation of a wetland that was adjacent to a navigable creek was a permissible construction of the statute. A unanimous Court ruled that "navigable waters of the United States" could include "wetlands that are not the result of flooding or permeation by water having its source in adjacent bodies of open water. The Corps has concluded that wetlands may affect the water quality of adjacent lakes, rivers, and streams even when the waters of those bodies do not actually inundate the wetlands. For example, wetlands that are not flooded by adjacent waters may still tend to drain into those waters. In such circumstances, the Corps has concluded that wetlands may serve to filter and purify water draining into adjacent bodies of water, and to slow the flow of surface runoff into lakes, rivers, and streams and thus prevent flooding and erosion. In addition, adjacent wetlands may 'serve significant natural biological functions, including food chain production, general habitat, and nesting, spawning, rearing and resting sites for aquatic . . .

species.' " The key evidence supporting the Corps's very broad definition was Congress's rejection of proposals to limit the Corps's jurisdiction in 1977 and the congressional discussions supporting the Corps' 1977 regulations (described above).

After *Bayview*, the Corps expanded its regulation to create a "Migratory Bird Rule," extending its wetlands jurisdiction to waters "[w]hich are or would be used as habitat" by migratory birds. The Supreme Court in *Solid Waste Agency v. Army Corps of Engineers*, 531 U.S. 159 (2001), invalidated this rule as inconsistent with the statutory definition. Chief Justice Rehnquist's opinion for the Court also invoked the avoidance doctrine, because the rule pressed against, and perhaps beyond, Congress's Commerce Clause authority.

Over the objection of four dissenting Justices (Stevens, Souter, Ginsburg, and Breyer), the *Solid Waste* Court rejected the Corps's argument that Congress in 1977 had "acquiesced" in its broad understanding of wetlands jurisdiction. Because the Migratory Bird Rule did not appear in the Corps' regulations until 1986, Chief Justice Rehnquist felt that Congress's actions in 1977 could not have ratified that interpretation. Justice Stevens's dissenting opinion took a broader view of Congress's 1977 action. When the Senate voted down the Bentsen Amendment and the Conference Committee rejected the House bill in 1977, Congress was not just rejecting a technical adjustment to the Corps' jurisdiction, but it was rejecting the understanding of the Corps's jurisdiction as founded on protecting *navigability* and embracing the new conception of jurisdiction as founded on protecting hydrological ecosystems. The majority declined to read Congress's actions so broadly.

In 1989, John Rapanos backfilled wetlands on a parcel of land in Michigan; the nearest body of traditionally navigable waters was 11 to 20 miles away. The Corps asserted jurisdiction over the land and prosecuted civil and criminal charges against Rapanos, who essentially ignored the government's warnings. The Corps's justification was that Rapanos's wetland was adjacent to a "tributary" of a navigable waterway. At trial, expert witnesses testified that Rapanos's wetlands were connected by drains to various navigable rivers and were critical to flood prevention in the aquatic ecosystem of the region. The Corps relied on *Bayview* and the 1977 Clean Water Act described above.

Writing for Chief Justice Roberts and Justices Thomas and Alito, **Justice Scalia**'s plurality opinion distinguished *Bayview*, where the wetlands were adjacent to a navigable creek, rather than the non-navigable drainage in Rapanos's case. Because *navigable waters* is defined very broadly in the CWA, Justice Scalia reasoned that the term could *not* be limited to the traditional (and narrow) understanding. But there must be *some* limit, and a survey of dictionaries suggested that *waters* must be limited to "continuously present, fixed bodies of water, as opposed to ordinarily dry channels through which water occasionally or intermittently flows." Justice Scalia's definition excluded "transitory puddles or ephemeral flows of water." This somewhat narrower understanding is reinforced by the fact that the statute's separate category of *point sources* clearly includes intermittent water flows.

Moreover, a narrower definition is consistent with the "policy of Congress to recognize, preserve, and protect the primary responsibilities and rights of the States to prevent, reduce, and eliminate pollution, [and] to plan the development and use * * * of land and water resources." § 1251(b). The Corps's expansive definition would eliminate "virtually all" state and local planning by bringing all decisions under a national authority, what Justice Scalia refers to as an "enlightened despot." The *BFP* canon closed the matter for the plurality: "We ordinarily expect a 'clear and manifest' statement from Congress to authorize an unprecedented intrusion into traditional state authority. *BFP*. The phrase 'the waters of the United States' hardly qualifies." Likewise, the Corps' definition stretches the statute potentially beyond Congress's Commerce Clause authority and so mobilizes the avoidance canon.

Justice Scalia dismissed the Corps's argument (adopted by the dissenting opinion filed by **Justice Stevens**) that the rejected proposals in 1977 constituted legislative adoption of the Corps' broad definition. "Congress takes no governmental action except by legislation. What the dissent refers to as 'Congress' deliberate acquiescence' should more appropriately be called Congress' failure to express any opinion. We have no idea whether the Members' failure to act in 1977 was attributable to their belief that the Corps' regulations were correct, or rather to their belief that the courts would eliminate any excesses, or indeed simply to their unwillingness to confront the environmental lobby. * * * '[Absent] such *overwhelming evidence* of acquiescence, we are loath to replace the plain text and original understanding of a statute with an amended agency interpretation.' *Solid Waste* (emphasis added).

"* * * [T]he dissent claims nothing more than that Congress 'conducted extensive debates about the Corps' regulatory jurisdiction over wetlands [and] rejected efforts to limit that jurisdiction . . . .' In fact, even that vague description goes too far. As recounted in *Riverside Bayview*, the 1977 debates concerned a proposal to 'limi[t] the Corps' authority under [§ 1344] to waters navigable in fact and their adjacent wetlands (defined as wetlands periodically inundated by contiguous navigable waters).' In rejecting this proposal, Congress merely failed to enact a limitation of 'waters' to include only navigable-in-fact waters — an interpretation we affirmatively reject today — and a definition of wetlands based on 'periodi[c] inundat[ion]' that appears almost nowhere in the briefs or opinions of those cases. No plausible interpretation of this legislative inaction can construe it as an implied endorsement of every jot and tittle of the Corps' 1977 regulations."

Concurring only in the result, but providing the needed fifth vote, **Justice Kennedy** followed the test announced in *Solid Waste*: to constitute *navigable waters* under the CWA, a wetland must possess a "significant nexus" to waters that are or were navigable in fact or that could reasonably be made navigable. *Solid Waste*, 531 U.S. at 167, 172. Because the lower court also did not follow this approach, Justice Kennedy voted to reverse and remand, and presumably the lower court on remand would have to apply the *Solid Waste* nexus standard, and not the more restrictive approach developed by Justice Scalia.

Justice Kennedy found the *Solid Waste* standard supportable by reference to the same dictionaries, statutory text and structure, balanced purpose, and common sense that Justice Scalia claimed for his approach — and with an additional bonus that the *Solid Waste* standard was supported by stare decisis, which is supposed to be super-strong in statutory cases. Justice Kennedy did not address the rejected proposal argument, probably because (unlike the dissenters) he joined the Court's discussion of it in *Solid Waste*.

NOTE ON REJECTED PROPOSALS

Justice O'Connor's opinion in the FDA Tobacco Case is the most lavish deployment in the Court's history of what might be called the *rejected proposal rule*, that interpreters should be reluctant to read statutes broadly when a committee, a chamber, or a conference committee rejected language explicitly encoding that broad policy. *Bayview* reflects this presumption as well. See also, e.g., *Hamdan v. Rumsfeld*, 126 S.Ct. 2749, 2765–66 (2006); *United States v. Yermian*, 468 U.S. 63 (1984) (relying on congressional adoption of broadening language of false swearing statute, 18 U.S.C. § 1001, after earlier bill was vetoed by President). Yet similar rejected proposal arguments were not persuasive to Court majorities in *Rapanos* and *Solid Waste*. How would you distinguish those cases? Or should they be signals that the Supreme Court should no longer follow a rejected proposal rule?

Commentators have been wary, because the range of reasons for rejecting a proposed amendment varies so widely. "It may be rejected by some legislators because they disagree with its substance (but not necessarily the same substance). On the other hand, those who agree with the substance may nevertheless vote against it as a spurious or unnecessary attempt to clarify. Simple non-action, being consistent with many explanations in circumstances not calling for consensus, has no probative value for any purpose." Dickerson, *supra*, at 1133; accord, *Solid Waste* (majority opinion's response to the dissenters); *Pattern Makers' League of North Am. v. NLRB*, 473 U.S. 95 (1985); William Eskridge, Jr., *Interpreting Legislative Inaction*, 87 Mich. L. Rev. 67 (1988) (collecting cases using and declining to use the rejected proposal rule); Wald, *supra*, at 202.

A broader point links Justice O'Connor's opinion for the Court in FDA Tobacco and Justice Stevens's dissenting opinions in *Solid Waste* and *Rapanos*. Both Justices find in the legislative deliberations evidence that Congress has both accepted and relied upon well-grounded agency policy stances as regards their regulatory mandate. In FDA Tobacco, there seems to have been a political consensus that the FDA did not have jurisdiction over tobacco products, and in the Wetlands Cases there seems to have been a similar consensus that the Corps has broad jurisdiction to protect hydrological ecosystems. Why did one consensus fail to move the Court while the other did move the Court? Consider not only the political preferences of the Justices, but also the Court's traditional role as braking or slowing down political actors.

MONTANA WILDERNESS ASSOCIATION v.
UNITED STATES FOREST SERVICE
United States Court of Appeals for the Ninth Circuit, May 14, 1981
Docket No. 80–3374

NORRIS, CIRCUIT JUDGE:

This appeal raises fundamental questions concerning the conflict between the ability of the executive branch of the federal government to manage public lands and the access rights of persons whose property is surrounded by those lands. Environmentalists and a neighboring property owner seek to block construction by Burlington Northern of roads over parts of the Gallatin National Forest. They appeal from a partial summary judgment in the district court granting Burlington Northern a right of access to its totally enclosed timber lands. The district court held that Burlington Northern has an easement by necessity or, alternatively, an implied easement under the Northern Pacific Land Grant of 1864. The defendants argue that the Alaska National Interest Lands Act of 1980, passed subsequent to the district court's decision, also grants Burlington Northern assured access to its land. The appellants contend that the doctrine of easement by necessity does not apply to the sovereign, that there was no implied easement conveyed by the 1864 land grant, and that the access provisions of the Alaska Lands Act do not apply to land outside the state of Alaska. We conclude that the appellants are correct on all three issues. We therefore reverse the partial summary judgment and remand the case for further proceedings.

Defendant-appellee Burlington Northern, Inc. owns timber land located within the Gallatin National Forest southwest of Bozeman, Montana. This land was originally acquired by its predecessor, the Northern Pacific Railroad, under the Northern Pacific Land Grant Act of 1864, 13 Stat. 365. The Act granted odd-numbered square sections of land to the railroad, which, with the even-numbered sections retained by the United States, formed a checkerboard pattern.

To harvest its timber, Burlington Northern in 1979 acquired a permit from defendant-appellee United States Forest Service, allowing it to construct an access road across national forest land. The proposed roads would cross the Buck Creek and Yellow Mules drainages, which are protected by the Montana Wilderness Study Act of 1977, Pub. L. 95–150, 91 Stat. 1243, as potential wilderness areas. The proposed logging and road-building will arguably disqualify the areas as wilderness under the Act. * * *

Appellees contend that the recently enacted Alaska National Interest Lands Conservation Act (Alaska Lands Act), Pub. L. No. 96–487, 94 Stat. 2371 (1980), establishes an independent basis for affirming the judgment of the district court. They argue that § 1323(a) of the Act requires that the Secretary of Agriculture provide access to Burlington Northern for its enclosed land. Upon examination of the statute and the legislative history, we do not find this interpretation of the Alaska Lands Act convincing.

Section 1323 is a part of the administrative provisions, Title XIII, of the Alaska Lands Act. Appellees argue that it is the only section of the Act which applies to the entire country; appellants argue that, like the rest of the Act, it applies only to Alaska. Section 1323 reads as follows:

> Sec. 1323. (a) Notwithstanding any other provision of law, and subject to such terms and conditions as the Secretary of Agriculture may prescribe, the Secretary shall provide such access to nonfederally owned land within the boundaries of the National Forest System as the Secretary deems adequate to secure to the owner the reasonable use and enjoyment thereof: *Provided*, That such owner comply with rules and regulations applicable to ingress and egress to or from the National Forest System.
>
> (b) Notwithstanding any other provision of law, and subject to such terms and conditions as the Secretary of the Interior may prescribe, the Secretary shall provide such access to nonfederally owned land surrounded by public lands managed by the Secretary under the Federal Land Policy and Management Act of 1976 (43 U.S.C. 1701–82) as the Secretary deems adequate to secure to the owner the responsible use and enjoyment thereof: *Provided*, That such owner comply with rules and regulations applicable to access across public lands.

This section provides for access to nonfederally-owned lands surrounded by certain kinds of federal lands. Subsection (b) deals with access to nonfederal lands "surrounded by public lands managed by the Secretary [of the Interior]." Section 102(3) of the Act defines "public lands" as certain lands "situated in Alaska." Subsection (b) is therefore limited by its terms to Alaska.

Subsection (a) deals with access to nonfederally-owned lands "within the boundaries of the National Forest System." The term "National Forest System" as used in § 1323(a) is to be interpreted as being limited to national forests in Alaska or as including the entire United States.

The parties have not directed us to, nor has our research disclosed, an established or generally accepted meaning for the term "National Forest System." The United States Code contains no statutory definitions for it. We find no record of Congressional use of the term prior to the enactment of the Federal Land Policy and Management Act of 1976. The term "National Forest System" appears in that Act but is nowhere defined; from the context, however, it is apparent that it is used there to refer to national forests anywhere in the United States. See 43 U.S.C. §§ 1701, *et seq*. The same Act also uses the term "public lands" and defines it as meaning lands "owned by the United States within the several States," clearly a definition different from that given the same term in the Alaska Lands Act.

We therefore perceive no basis for assuming that Congress necessarily used the term "National Forest System" in the Alaska Lands Act to refer to national forests in the United States generally. We think that in this context the meaning of the term is ambiguous and therefore look to other indicia.

The Act itself provides some help. Title V of the Act is entitled "National Forest System." Section 501(a) states: "The following units of the National Forest System are hereby expanded * * *." This language shows that Congress used the term "National Forest System" in this Act in a context which refers to and deals with national forests in Alaska. It is not unreasonable to read Section 1323(a) as referring to the "National Forest System" in the context in which it is used in Title V of the Act, rather than to all national forests in the United States.

As the parties agreed at oral argument, moreover, § 1323(b) is *in pari materia* with § 1323(a). The two subsections are placed together in the same section, and use not only a parallel structure but many of the same words and phrases. The natural interpretation is that they were meant to have the same effect, one on lands controlled by the Secretary of Agriculture, the other on lands controlled by the Secretary of the Interior. Since § 1323(b), by the definition of public lands in § 102(3), applies only to Alaskan land, a strong presumption arises that § 1323(a) was meant to apply only to Alaska as well.

That interpretation is confirmed by a review of the entire Act which discloses no other provision having nation-wide application.[4] To attach such a sweeping effect to this obscure and seemingly minor provision of the Act would seem incongruous under the circumstances. We therefore conclude that the language of the Act supports the interpretation that § 1323(a) applies only to national forests in Alaska. Bearing in mind that "[a]bsent a clearly expressed legislative intent to the contrary, [the statutory] language must ordinarily be regarded as conclusive," *Consumer Product Safety Commission v. GTE Sylvania*, 447 U.S. 102, 108 (1980), we turn to the legislative history.

Section 1323 was added to the Alaska Lands Bill by the Senate Committee on Energy and Natural Resources in its amendment to H.R. 39, originally passed by the House. S. Rep. No. 96–413, 96th Cong. 1st Sess. (1979). It was incorporated in the Tsongas substitute bill which replaced by amendment the Energy Committee's proposed bill, 126 Cong. Rec. S11099, S11140 (daily ed. Aug. 18, 1980). The Tsongas substitute bill was passed by the Senate, 126 Cong. Rec. S11193 (daily ed. Aug. 19, 1980), and House, 126 Cong. Rec. H10552 (daily ed. Nov. 12, 1980), and became law on December 1, 1980, 94 Stat. 2371.

Section 1323 is mentioned only twice in the Senate materials. The Energy Committee report discussed it in its section-by-section analysis, S. Rep. No. 96–413 at 310, and Senator Melcher, the author of the section, discussed it on the floor of the Senate, 126 Cong. Rec. S14770–71 (daily ed. Nov. 20, 1980).

---

4. The appellees concede that no other section of the Act applies nationwide. They argue, however, that because another provision of the Act, § 1110(b), gives access rights to all Alaskan inholders, § 1323(a) is superfluous unless it is interpreted to apply to the entire country. Section 1110(b), they argue, like § 1323(b), applies only to Alaska because it uses terms, "public lands" and "conservation system unit," which are defined to include only Alaskan land.

The flaw in appellee's argument is that however § 1323(a) is interpreted, § 1110(b) essentially duplicates the protection given Alaskan lands by § 1323 as a whole. Section 1110(b) overlaps § 1323(b) just as much as it overlaps § 1323(a). If, as appellees claim, § 1110(b) gives access to all Alaskan inholders and § 1323(a) gives access to holders of land surrounded by land administered by the Secretary of Agriculture, the inclusion of § 1323(b) in the Act makes no sense at all. Section 1323(b), after all, gives access to holders of Alaskan land surrounded by land administered by the Secretary of the Interior. Under this view, not only is § 1323(b) superfluous in light of § 1110(b), it is paired with a provision, § 1323(a), of parallel structure but widely different scope. We do not see how the existence of § 1110(b) gives much support to the appellees' position.

The remarks of Senator Melcher, however, were made on November 20th, eight days after Congress passed H.R. 39. His remarks clearly demonstrate that his personal understanding of the section is that it applies nationwide, but because they are the remarks of but one senator made subsequent to the passage of the bill they do not provide a reliable indication of the understanding of the Senate as a whole.

Although the appellees contend that the language of the Energy Committee report makes perfectly clear the Committee's intent that § 1323 apply nationwide, we do not find their interpretation of the report's language persuasive:

> This section is designed to remove the uncertainties surrounding the status of the rights of the owners of non-Federal lands to gain access to such lands across Federal lands. It has been the Committee's understanding that such owners had the right of access to their lands subject to reasonable regulation by either, the Secretary of Agriculture in the case of national forests, or by the Secretary of the Interior in the case of public lands managed by the Bureau of Land Management under the Federal Land Policy and Management Act of 1976. However, a recent District Court decision in Utah (*Utah v. Andrus et al.*, C79–0037, October 1, 1979, D.C. Utah) has cast some doubt over the status of these rights. Furthermore, the Attorney General is currently reviewing the issue because of differing interpretations of the law by the Departments of Agriculture and the Interior. * * *

> The Committee amendment is designed to resolve any lingering legal questions by making it clear that non-Federal landowners have a right of access [across] National Forests and public land, subject, of course, to reasonable rules and regulations.

S. Rep. No. 96–413 at 310.

While the Committee's intent to guarantee access is clear, it is less than clear whether this provision was meant to guarantee access outside of Alaska. The problem raised in the first paragraph — the differing interpretations of the law of access — is not confined to Alaska, but the scope of the remedy as set forth in the last paragraph could be so confined. As with § 1323 itself, the report uses indiscriminately terms defined in the Act as applying only to Alaskan land ("public land") and terms not so defined ("National Forests").

The absence of any reference to Alaska is not of much import. The report's discussion of other access provisions such as § 1110 and § 1111, which all parties agree apply only to Alaska, fails to mention Alaska and is as ambiguous about whether § 1110 and § 1111 apply nationwide as is the discussion of § 1323. S. Rep. No. 96–413 at 299–300.

What we find most significant in the legislative history in the Senate is the same thing that Sherlock Holmes found to be crucial in solving the case of the Hound of the Baskervilles — the failure of the dog to bark. The Alaska Lands bill was discussed endlessly on the Senate floor. There are numerous occasions when one would expect a change in current laws of access of the magnitude of the appellees' proposed interpretation of § 1323 to be discussed, mentioned or at least alluded to. Yet we have not found in the Senate debates, and appellees have not called to our attention, one single suggestion that anything in the Alaska Land Bill would affect access rights in the rest of the country. In Senator Tsongas' long, detailed comparison of his substitute bill with the Energy Committee bill, § 1323 is not mentioned. 126 Cong. Rec. S11193 (daily ed. Aug. 19, 1980).[6] In discussion about the adequacy of the substitute bill's access provisions (which include § 1323) no mention is made of a change in the law of access for the rest of the country. 126 Cong. Rec. S11061–62 (daily ed. Aug. 18, 1980). We find it difficult to believe that the Senate would have contemplated and effected a profound change in the law of access across government land for the entire country without ever mentioning it.

The legislative history in the House, which considered and passed the Tsongas substitute bill after it was passed by the Senate, also presents an ambiguous picture of § 1323. On October 2, 1980, Representative Udall, chairman of the Committee on Interior and Insular Affairs which had joint responsibility for the bill, introduced an amendment one section of which was to "make clear that [the bill] applies only to Alaska." 127 Cong. Rec. 10376 (daily ed. October 2, 1980). This amendment was never adopted. Representative Udall subsequently declared in prepared remarks inserted into the Congressional Record that although the final version of the bill was "ambiguously drafted and not expressly limited to Alaskan lands, the House believes that, as with all the other provisions of the bill, the language of the section applies only to lands within the State of Alaska." 126 Cong. Rec. H10549 (daily ed. Nov. 12, 1980). Representative Weaver stated that the section granting access rights to inholders on national forest and BLM lands "apparently applies not only to Alaska but also to the entire United States." 126 Cong. Rec. H8638 (daily ed. September 9, 1980). Representative Sieberling inserted into the record a summary of proposed amendments, which refers to Section 1323 as the "nationwide access amendment." 126 Cong.Rec. H10350 (daily ed. October 2, 1980). Representative AuCoin stated that one of the flaws of the final bill is that it "grants private inholders carte blanche access across national forest and public lands nationwide." 126 Cong. Rec. H10529–30 (daily ed. Nov. 12, 1980).

Appellees rely heavily upon an exchange of letters between Representatives Sieberling and Weaver, chairmen of the subcommittees responsible for the bill (Public Lands of the Committee on Interior and Insular Affairs and Forest of the Committee on Agriculture), and the Attorney General's office. In their letter, the representatives express concern over § 1323, which they state applies nationwide, and ask for a clarification of how different the § 1323 access language is from existing access provisions. It is indeed clear from their letter that they believed that § 1323 applies nationwide.

---

6. Neither did Senator Tsongas remark on § 1323 when it was first proposed in the Energy Committee bill, even though in his statement in the Committee report he spends several pages criticizing the bill's overbroad provisions on access. [Citing Senate Report, additional views of Senators Metzenbaum and Tsongas.] Yet the extension of § 1323(a) to the entire country would certainly have a greater impact than the other measures he discusses.

Appellees argue, on the basis of the September 5, 1980 return letter from Assistant Attorney General Alan Parker, that the Department of Justice confirmed this interpretation of § 1323. We interpret the letter differently. As we read the letter, the Assistant Attorney General assumed without analysis that the representatives' interpretation of § 1323 was correct, and proceeded to discuss in detail the effect of such a change in the law.

The exchanged letters are entitled to little weight. In general, off-the-record views of congressmen are not attributed to Congress as a whole. *See T.V.A. v. Hill*, 437 U.S. 153, 190–91 (1978). This is particularly true where, as here, there is no indication that the House as a whole was aware of the correspondence. *Id.* at 191–92.

In summary, the legislative history concerning § 1323 is surprisingly sparse. The report of the Senate committee which drafted the section is ambiguous. At times when the Senate could have been expected to comment on its intention to make a major change in current law, it did not. The only expression of intent that § 1323 apply nationwide came from a single senator eight days after the Alaska Lands Act was passed by Congress. In the House debates, three representatives suggested that § 1323 did apply nationwide, but the chairman of one of the responsible committees said it did not. Two chairmen of House subcommittees responsible for the bill did state in a letter to the Attorney General that they believed that § 1323 applied nationwide, but there is no indication that the contents of this letter were generally known by members of the House, and so the letter carries little weight in our analysis. We conclude that the ambiguous legislative history gives only slight support at best to the appellees' interpretation that § 1323 applies nationwide. It is not nearly sufficient to overcome the actual language of the statute, which we believe is more naturally read as applying only to Alaska.

Moreover, § 1323 as interpreted by the appellees would repeal by implication a portion of § 5(a) of the Wilderness Act, 16 U.S.C. § 1134(a).[7] "It is, of course, a cardinal principle of statutory construction that repeals by implication are not favored," *Radzanower v. Touche Ross & Co.*, 426 U.S. 148, 154 (1976), and that "the intention of the legislature to repeal must be clear and manifest." *Posadas v. National City Bank*, 296 U.S. 497, 503 (1936). Here it is far from clear that the legislature intended that § 1323 apply nationwide. We hold that § 1323 of the Alaska National Interest Lands Conservation Act is limited in its application to the state of Alaska, and so has no relevance to this case. * * *

---

7. 16 U.S.C. § 1134(a) gives the Secretary of Agriculture the choice between granting access to state or privately-owned land surrounded by wilderness land and permitting the exchange of the in-held land for federally-owned land of equal value. Section 1323(a), by making access mandatory, renders nugatory the land exchange provision. *See generally* Op. Att'y Gen. slip at 1, 23–30 (June 23, 1980).

NOTES ON THE "CHECKERBOARD CASE" AND STATEMENTS DURING LEGISLATIVE DELIBERATION

1. *The Ninth Circuit's Use of Legislative History.* A textualist would likely agree with Judge Norris' analysis of the statutory text, and then would stop. Why should the judge proceed any further? When Judge Norris does, he causes himself some trouble. Note his strategy: Even though the opinion adduces no affirmative support in the legislative history for its view that § 1323(a) only applies to Alaska, Judge Norris isolates all the evidence to the contrary and seeks to neuter each piece of evidence in isolation, either by demonstrating ambiguity or by denigrating the authority of the evidence. This technique — the "piecemeal critique" — is effective advocacy in response to a showing of a variety of evidence to the contrary, but shouldn't that evidence be allowed to have cumulative weight in assessing overall legislative intent? As you evaluate the following, consider whether an "intentionalist" interpreter would disagree with Judge Norris' outcome.

(a) *Committee Reports.* On first reading, the Senate Report in the Checkerboard Case is ambiguous. But reread the quoted language of the Report. The Senate wants to avoid the problems raised by a federal district court decision in Utah and the Attorney General's consideration (described in Note 2 after *Leo Sheep*). The Utah case (in the Tenth Circuit) is not controlling law in Alaska (in the Ninth Circuit). The Senate Report wants "to resolve *any* lingering legal questions by *making it clear* that non-Federal landowners have a right of access [across] National Forests" (emphasis added). While this Report is not 100% clear that § 1323(a) was meant to apply nationwide, isn't the more probable reading of the Report that it was?

(b) *Statements of Sponsors and Committee Chairs.* Senator Melcher, the sponsor of the amendment adding § 1323(a), explicitly said that it applied nationwide. Judge Norris denigrates this clear evidence by saying that it was uttered after the bill was passed by Congress (but before it had been signed by the President). But he doesn't say that Representative Udall's statements, upon which he relies, were inserted into the Congressional Record *after* the bill was passed. (Udall's remarks are reported in the *Record* for the day the bill was passed, but they are proceeded by a "bullet" [●], which signifies that they were not spoken on the floor of the House but were inserted later.) Indeed, look at the dates of the Udall and Melcher statements. Why might Udall have abandoned any attempt to amend the statute to make it clearly apply only to Alaska and instead simply uttered a comment that the unamended version had the same impact? Why might Melcher have made his comment? Which is the more reliable?

Leaving strategic considerations aside, consider the roles of the key players. Melcher, the sponsor of § 1323(a), and Representatives Seiberling and Weaver, chairs of the relevant House subcommittees, interpreted § 1323(a) to apply nationwide, in statements made to their respective chambers. Udall, chair of the House Committee, interpreted it otherwise, in a statement inserted after the fact. Yet Judge Norris treats Udall's statements as roughly equal to those of Melcher, Seiberling, and Weaver in combination. Isn't this wrong, especially in light of the common view that greater weight should be accorded statements of *supporters* of a provision over statements of *opponents*? See also *Ernst & Ernst v. Hochfelder*, 425 U.S. 185, 204 n.24 (1976).

(c) *Dialogue with Bureaucrats.* The exchange of letters between Seiberling/Weaver and the Justice Department concerning the effect of the Melcher amendment is not unusual in Congress. It is quite common in state legislatures, where assistants to state attorneys general typically advise legislative committees about the probable legal effects of bills. Since Seiberling and Weaver were key House negotiators, and the House accepted the Melcher amendment in negotiations, isn't this exchange of letters more significant than Judge Norris was willing to admit? Compare *Lindahl v. Office of Personnel Management*, 470 U.S. 768, 785 n.17 (1985), where the Supreme Court relied heavily on letters from the OPM Director to the Chairs of the Senate and House Committees to interpret amendments to the Civil Service Retirement Act. Judge Wald, *supra*, at 202–03, noted in the early 1980s an increasing tendency of lawyers to use, and judges to cite, unpublished portions of the legislative history to support their interpretations of statutes. See *Borrell v. United States Int'l Communication Agency*, 682 F.2d 981, 988 (D.C. Cir. 1982).

2. *Evidence Judge Norris (and Everybody Else) Missed.* Judge Norris makes much of the fact that Senator Melcher's statement that § 1323 applies nationwide was made on the floor of the Senate after the bill was passed. But on July 29, 1980 (well before the bill passed the Senate), Senator Melcher sent a letter to every Senator, explaining that he was opposed to a portion of one of the amendments that would be offered when the Alaska Lands bill came before the Senate. The letter explained that Melcher's amendment was in response to the recent Department of Justice opinion (described in Note 2 following *Leo Sheep, supra*) indicating that private checkerboard landowners did not have an automatic right of access across government land; Melcher considered the Department of Justice view an innovation that disrupted prior understandings among property owners and federal lands administrators. The letter then said:

> In the Alaskan Lands Bill, for Alaska only, specific access to state or private lands was explicitly guaranteed. In order to avoid any change in federal policy on this question, last October [1979] I introduced an amendment to that bill for continuing the historic policy of granting access to property inholders in all the rest of the Bureau of Land Management and National Forest lands. My amendment was accepted by the committee without objection and *it applies to landowners within federal lands (either in national forests or in public lands administered by the Bureau of Land Management) in all the rest of the states where such lands are located.* * * *

The letter warned that Amendment No. 1783, offered by Senators Tsongas and McGovern, would strike this committee amendment, and Melcher urged the other Senators to support his effort to preserve this national right of access provision.[w] Was Judge Norris wrong about the "deal" in Congress?

---

w. The letter is reproduced in *Oversight on The Montana Wilderness Study Act: Hearing Before the Subcomm. on Public Lands and Reserved Water of the Senate Comm. on Energy and Natural Resources*, 97th Cong., 1st Sess. 53 (May 28, 1981). Senator Melcher represents that the letter was sent to every Senator. *Id.* at 12. One of our students in the Georgetown

3. *The Dog That Didn't Bark Canon.* Although Judge Norris cited the wrong Sherlock Holmes story,[x] he is correct to say that the Supreme Court sometimes follows the *dog didn't bark* canon. That is, it may be significant that an intense congressional debate does not even mention an issue — suggesting that the statute contained no unusual departure from the status quo against which Congress was legislating. Thus, in a bill whose title and subject matter are all about Alaska, one would expect some special mention of a provision that adjusted important legal rights in the lower 49 states as well.

We have seen examples of it in *Zuni Public School District No. 89 v. Department of Education*, *Bock Laundry*, and *Chisom v. Roemer* (all in Chapter 7, § 3A). In *Chisom*, recall that Justice Scalia lustily assailed this canon on the grounds that it is highly subjective and unreliable (how one characterizes the "status quo" drives the operation of the canon, and that is quite subjective), as well as contrary to Justice Scalia's view (e.g., *Rapanos*) that Congress can proceed *only* through positive legislation adopted under Article I, § 7, and *never* through inaction, etc.

5. *Post-Enactment Legislative History ("Subsequent Legislative History")*

Statutes are often enacted and forgotten by the legislature. Sometimes, though, the legislature — or at least its members and committees — will continue to talk about the statute after enactment. Circumstances for post-enactment discussion include (1) proposals to amend the statute or to enact a new and related statute, including debate and hearings and committee reports on such proposals; (2) oversight hearings in response to agency and/or judicial implementation of the statute; and (3) efforts to "bend" interpretation of the statute. The statutory interpreter is torn between considering relevant evidence and avoiding strategic trickery. One way to set this balance would be to consider only "subsequent legislative history" that is tied to a subsequent statute enacted by the legislature. (The Supreme Court has not always limited itself in this way, as you will see in the notes after the following case.)

In the immediately preceding case, Judge Norris dismissed Senator Melcher's comment as mere subsequent legislative history. The following case is a later opinion on rehearing in the Checkerboard Case. Notice how Judge Norris' interpretation changed when he was confronted with different subsequent legislative history. Should he have changed his mind?

University Law Center, Class of 1990 came up with this "smoking gun" during class discussion. (Imagine our embarrassment that we didn't find this smoking gun when we worked on the case in private practice. This is one of the cases we have plundered from our experience as attorneys at the old Washington, D.C. law firm of Shea & Gardner (now absorbed into another law firm). Apparently, it did not occur to us that anything relevant to the Alaska Act would be found in the legislative history of another act, the Montana Wilderness Study Act. *Should* that have occurred to us? Keep this question in mind when you read the next case.)

x. In *Silver Blaze*, Sherlock Holmes solves the case of a missing racehorse by observing that the dog guarding the barn had not barked the night before when an intruder entered to get the horse; the deduction (elementary!) was that the culprit was someone the dog knew well. In *The Hound of the Baskervilles*, which Judge Norris cites, the dog barked quite a lot and did not contribute to Holmes's solution of the mystery.

MONTANA WILDERNESS ASSOCIATION v.
UNITED STATES FOREST SERVICE
United States Court of Appeals for the Ninth Circuit, 1981
655 F.2d 951, cert. denied, 455 U.S. 989

[After the May 1981 opinion, *supra*, which held that there was no easement created by the railroad land grant act of 1864 or the Alaska Lands Act of 1980, an intervening party defendant moved for reconsideration based upon yet another new statute, shedding light on the Alaska lands statute construed in the earlier opinion. In light of the new statute, the panel withdrew the May opinion and issued the instant opinion. Judge Norris, the author of the original panel opinion, also wrote the new one.]

The sole issue on appeal is whether Burlington Northern has a right of access across federal land to its inholdings of timberland. Appellees contend that the recently enacted Alaska National Interest Lands Conservation Act (Alaska Lands Act), Pub. L. No. 96–487, 94 Stat. 2371 (1980), establishes an independent basis for affirming the judgment of the district court. They argue that § 1323(a) of the Act requires that the Secretary of Agriculture provide access to Burlington Northern for its enclosed land.

Section 1323 is a part of the administrative provisions, Title XIII, of the Alaska Lands Act. Appellees argue that it is the only section of the Act which applies to the entire country; appellants argue that, like the rest of the Act, it applies only to Alaska. Section 1323 reads as follows:

> Sec. 1323. (a) Notwithstanding any other provision of law, and subject to such terms and conditions as the Secretary of Agriculture may prescribe, the Secretary shall provide such access to nonfederally owned land within the boundaries of the National Forest System as the Secretary deems adequate to secure to the owner the reasonable use and enjoyment thereof: *Provided*, That such owner comply with rules and regulations applicable to ingress and egress to or from the National Forest System.

> (b) Notwithstanding any other provision of law, and subject to such terms and conditions as the Secretary of the Interior may prescribe, the Secretary shall provide such access to nonfederally owned land surrounded by public lands managed by the Secretary under the Federal Land Policy and Management Act of 1976 (43 U.S.C. 1701–82) as the Secretary deems adequate to secure to the owner the responsible use and enjoyment thereof: *Provided*, That such owner comply with rules and regulations applicable to access across public lands.

This section provides for access to nonfederally-owned lands surrounded by certain kinds of federal lands. Subsection (b) deals with access to nonfederal lands "surrounded by public lands managed by the Secretary [of the Interior]." Section 102(3) of the Act defines "public lands" as certain lands "situated in Alaska." Subsection (b), therefore, is arguably limited by its terms to Alaska, though we do not find it necessary to settle that issue here. Our consideration of the scope of § 1323(a) proceeds under the assumption that § 1323(b) is limited to Alaska.

Subsection (a) deals with access to nonfederally-owned lands "within the boundaries of the National Forest System." The term "National Forest System" is not specifically defined in the Act.

The question before the court is whether the term "National Forest System" as used in § 1323(a) is to be interpreted as being limited to national forests in Alaska or as including the entire United States. We note at the outset that the bare language of § 1323(a) does not, when considered by itself, limit the provision of access to Alaskan land. We must look, however, to the context of the section to determine its meaning.

Elsewhere in the Act, Congress used the term "National Forest System" in a context which refers to and deals with national forests in Alaska. Title V of the Act is entitled "National Forest System." Section 501(a) states: "The following units of the National Forest System are hereby expanded * * *." It is not unreasonable to read Section 1323(a) as referring to the "National Forest System" in the context in which it is used in Title V of the Act, rather than to all national forests in the United States.

Congress did, however, supply us with a general definition of the term in another statute. Pub. Law 93–378, 88 Stat. 480 (1974). 16 U.S.C. § 1609(a) states *inter alia* that:

> Congress declares that the National Forest System consists of units of federally owned forest, range, and related lands throughout the United States and its territories, united into a nationally significant system dedicated to the long-term benefit for present and future generations, and that it is the purpose of their section to include all such areas into one integral system. The 'National Forest System' shall include all national forest lands reserved or withdrawn from the public domain of the United States * * *.

Application of this definition to § 1323(a) would necessarily yield the conclusion that the section was intended to have nation-wide effect. This seems especially so when Congress uses the term "National Forest System" in § 1323(a) without limitation or qualification.

As the parties agreed at oral argument, however, § 1323(b) is *in pari materia* with § 1323(a). The two subsections are placed together in the same section, and use not only a parallel structure but many of the same words and phrases. The natural interpretation is that they were meant to have the same effect, one on lands controlled by the Secretary of Agriculture, the other on lands controlled by the Secretary of the Interior. Since we assume that § 1323(b), by definition of public lands in § 102(3), applies only to Alaskan land, we face a presumption that § 1323(a) was meant to apply to Alaska as well.

That interpretation is supported by a review of the entire Act which discloses no other provision having nation-wide application. We therefore conclude that the language of the Act provides tentative support for the view that § 1323(a) applies only to national forests in Alaska. Bearing in mind that "[a]bsent a clearly expressed legislative intent to the contrary, [the statutory] language must ordinarily be regarded as conclusive," *Consumer Product Safety Commission v. GTE Sylvania*, 447 U.S. 102, 108 (1980), we turn to the legislative history.

The legislative history concerning § 1323 is surprisingly sparse. The report of the Senate committee which drafted the section is ambiguous.[7] At times when the Senate could have been expected to comment on its intention to make a major change in current law, it did not. The only expression of intent that § 1323 apply nation-wide came from a single senator eight days after the Alaska Lands Act was passed by Congress.[8] In the House debates, three representatives suggested that § 1323 did apply nation-wide, but the chairman of one of the responsible committees said it did not.[9] Two chairmen of House

---

7. The Energy Committee report discussed it in its section-by-section analysis, S.Rep. No. 96–413 at 310. (The Committee analysis mixes up §§ 1323 and 1324. Thus, the analysis entitled § 1324 is really concerned with § 1323 and vice versa.) Although the appellees contend that the language of the Energy Committee report makes perfectly clear the Committee's intent that § 1323 apply nationwide, we do not find their interpretation of the report's language persuasive:

This section is designed to remove the uncertainties surrounding the status of the rights of the owners of non-Federal lands to gain access to such lands across Federal lands. It has been the Committee's understanding that such owners had the right of access to their lands subject to reasonable regulation by either, the Secretary of Agriculture in the case of national forests, or by the Secretary of the Interior in the case of public lands managed by the Bureau of Land Management under the Federal Land Policy and Management Act of 1976. However, a recent District Court decision in Utah (*Utah v. Andrus et al.*, C79–0037, October 1, 1979, D.C. Utah) has cast some doubt over the status of these rights. Furthermore, the Attorney General is currently reviewing the issue because of differing interpretations of the law by the Departments of Agriculture and the Interior. * * *

The Committee amendment is designed to resolve any lingering legal questions by making it clear that non-Federal landowners have a right of access [across] National Forests and public land, subject, of course, to reasonable rules and regulations.

S.Rep. No. 96–413 at 310.

While the Committee's intent to guarantee access is clear, it is less than clear whether this provision was meant to guarantee access outside of Alaska. The problem raised in the first paragraph — the differing interpretations of the law of access — is not confined to Alaska, but the scope of the remedy as set forth in the last paragraph could be so confined. As with § 1323 itself, the report uses indiscriminately terms defined in the Act as applying only to Alaskan land ("public land") and terms not so defined ("National Forests").

8. Senator Melcher, the author of the section, discussed it on the floor of the Senate, 126 Cong.Rec. S14770–71 (daily ed. Nov. 20, 1980). The remarks of Senator Melcher, however, were made on November 20th, eight days after Congress passed H.R. 39. His remarks clearly demonstrate that his personal understanding of the section is that it applies nation-wide, but because they are the remarks of but one senator made subsequent to the passage of the bill they do not provide a reliable indication of the understanding of the Senate as a whole.

9. On October 2, 1980, Representative Udall, chairman of the Committee on Interior and Insular Affairs which had joint responsibility for the bill, introduced an amendment one section of which was to "make clear that [the bill] applies only to Alaska." 127 Cong. Rec. 10376 (daily ed. October 2, 1980). This amendment was never adopted. Representative Udall subsequently declared in prepared remarks inserted into the Congressional Record that although the final version of the bill was "ambiguously drafted and not expressly limited to Alaskan lands, the House believes that, as with all the other provisions of the bill, the language of the section applies only to lands within the State of Alaska." 126 Cong. Rec. H10549 (daily ed. Nov. 12, 1980). Representative Weaver stated that the section granting access rights to inholders on national forest and BLM lands "apparently applies not only to Alaska but also to the entire United States." 126 Cong. Rec. H8638 (daily ed. September 9, 1980). Representative Sieberling inserted into the record a summary of proposed amendments, which refers to Section

subcommittees responsible for the bill did state in a letter to the Attorney General that they believed that § 1323 applied nation-wide, but there is no indication that the contents of this letter were generally known by members of the House, and so the letter carries little weight in our analysis. All this gives only slight support at best to the appellees' interpretation that § 1323 applies nation-wide.

The appellees, however, have uncovered subsequent legislative history that, given the closeness of the issue, is decisive. Three weeks after Congress passed the Alaska Lands Act, a House-Senate Conference Committee considering the Colorado Wilderness Act interpreted § 1323 of the Alaska Lands Act as applying nation-wide:

> Section 7 of the Senate amendment contains a provision pertaining to access to non-Federally owned lands within national forest wilderness areas in Colorado. The House bill has no such provision.
>
> *The conferees agreed to delete the section because similar language has already passed Congress in Section 1323 of the Alaska National Interest Lands Conservation Act.*

H.R. Rep. No. 1521, 96th Cong., 2d Sess., 126 Cong. Rec. H11687 (daily ed. Dec. 3, 1980) (emphasis supplied).

This action was explained to both Houses during discussion of the Conference Report. *See* 126 Cong. Rec. S15571 (daily ed. Dec. 4, 1980) (remarks of Sen. Hart); *id.* at S15573 (remarks of Sen. Armstrong); *id.* at H11705 (daily ed. Dec. 3, 1980) (remarks of Rep. Johnson). Both houses then passed the Colorado Wilderness bill as it was reported by the Conference Committee.

Although a subsequent conference report is not entitled to the great weight given subsequent legislation, *Consumer Product Safety Commission v. GTE Sylvania*, 477 U.S. 102, 118 n.13 (1980), it is still entitled to significant weight, *Seatrain Shipbuilding Corp. v. Shell Oil Co.*, 444 U.S. 572 (1980), particularly where it is clear that the conferees had carefully considered the issue. The conferees, including Representatives Udall and Sieberling and Senator Melcher, had an intimate knowledge of the Alaska Lands Act.[11] Moreover, the Conference Committee's interpretation of § 1323 was the basis for their decision to leave out an access provision passed by one house. In these circumstances, the Conference Committee's interpretation is very persuasive. We conclude that it tips the balance decidedly in favor of the

---

1323 as the "nationwide access amendment." 126 Cong. Rec. H10350 (daily ed. October 2, 1980). Representative AuCoin stated that one of the flaws of the final bill is that it "grants private inholders carte blanche access across national forest and public lands nationwide." 126 Cong. Rec. H10529–30 (daily ed. Nov. 12, 1980).

11. The participation of Representative Udall is particularly noteworthy since he was the one congressman to proclaim in the legislative history of the Alaska Lands Act that § 1323 applied only to Alaska.

broader interpretation of § 1323.[12] We therefore hold that Burlington Northern has an assured right of access to its land pursuant to the nation-wide grant of access in § 1323. * * *

NOTES ON THE SECOND CHECKERBOARD OPINION AND THE USE OF POST-ENACTMENT STATEMENTS

1. *The Burger Court's Use of Subsequent Legislative History.* Is Judge Norris' reliance on subsequent legislative history persuasive? While the Supreme Court has said that subsequent statutes should inform interpretation of an earlier one, the Court has professed some skepticism about reliance on subsequent legislative statements. For example, in *Consumer Product Safety Comm'n v. GTE Sylvania*, 447 U.S. 102, 117–18 (1980), petitioners relied upon statements in a conference committee report concerning the 1976 amendments to the Consumer Product Safety Act that purported to interpret a section of the Act enacted in 1972 and not amended in 1976. The Court noted "the oft-repeated warning that 'the views of a subsequent Congress form a hazardous basis for inferring the intent of an earlier one.' " In a footnote, the Court further explained:

> Petitioners invoke the maxim that states: "Subsequent legislation declaring the intent of an earlier statute is entitled to great weight in statutory construction." With respect to subsequent *legislation*, however, Congress has proceeded formally through the legislative process. A mere statement in a conference report of such legislation as to what the Committee believes an earlier statute meant is obviously less weighty.

> The less formal types of subsequent legislative history provide an extremely hazardous basis for inferring the meaning of a congressional enactment.

In *Andrus v. Shell Oil Co.*, 446 U.S. 657 (1980), a case decided the same Term as *GTE Sylvania*, the Court stated: "While arguments predicated upon subsequent congressional actions may be weighed with extreme care, they should not be rejected out of hand as a source that a court may consider in the search for legislative intent." *Id.* at 666 n.8. In a third case decided the same Term, the Court adopted the interpretation of a 1936 statute set forth in a 1971 House committee report based on the theory that, "while the views of subsequent Congresses cannot override the unmistakable intent of the enacting

---

12. We recognize a facial problem or tension between § 1323(a) and a portion of § 5(a) of the Wilderness Act, 16 U.S.C. § 1134(a). We need not decide in this case whether there is repeal by implication. In passing, we note only that it is arguable that the two can stand together. § 1134(a) deals specifically with right of access "[i]n any case where State-owned or privately-owned land is completely surrounded by national forest lands *within areas designated by this chapter as wilderness* * * * ." (emphasis added). § 1323(a), on the other hand, deals with " * * * access to non-federally owned land within the boundaries of the National Forest System * * * ." § 1134(a) is addressed specifically to an area designated as "wilderness," while § 1323(a) is addressed to National Forest System lands in general. In cases involving wilderness areas, the Secretary has the option of exchanging land of equal value so that the wilderness area may be preserved. Thus, § 1134(a) could be construed to apply in the specific case of a wilderness area, and § 1323(a) could be construed to apply in all other cases.

Whether or not they are in fact irreconcilable we leave to another case when the issue is squarely presented for review.

one, * * * such views are entitled to significant weight, * * * and particularly so when the precise intent of the enacting Congress is obscure." *Seatrain Shipbuilding Corp. v. Shell Oil Co.*, 444 U.S. 572, 596 (1980). Later, in *South Carolina v. Regan*, 465 U.S. 367, 378 n.17 (1984), the Court once again "rejected" any suggestion that statutory interpretation can be informed by "the committee reports that accompany subsequent legislation."

2. *The Checkerboard Problem, Subsequent Legislative History, and the New Textualism.* The policy consequences of Judge Norris' new opinion seem quite malign. The fairest rule for checkerboard cases would be to give a right of reasonable access to both the government and the private holder, but this is precluded by *Leo Sheep, supra.* The second best rule, then, might be to deny rights of access to both parties, for their mutual dependence would probably lead to a deal approximating the best rule (but with more transactions costs). The worst rule is one in which one party has a right of access (*Montana Wilderness*) and the other does not (*Leo Sheep*). This does not create incentives to bargain and may force the government to pay extra money and high transactions costs to take the right of access through eminent domain.

Is this seemingly dysfunctional result compelled by § 1323(a)? Has Judge Norris persuaded you that Congress "intended" to deprive the public fisc of this money, and impair wilderness lands as well? Has Judge Norris even persuaded himself that his first opinion was wrong? Perhaps Judge Norris lost heart when Representative Udall — his bulwark in the first opinion — abandoned his earlier view of § 1323(a). So what? Wasn't Udall posturing in the first place? If Congress is going to create such a dysfunctional rule, shouldn't courts require explicit *statutory* language? If your instinct is "yes," then you need to bring a canon of interpretation into play. Could any established substantive canon apply here?

Subsequent legislative history is surely of no use to the new textualists. If ordinary legislative history is, as Justice Scalia argues, often cooked up by congressional staff and lobbyists to try to slant interpretation after the fact, the possibility for abuse is worse with subsequent legislative history, because there is less congressional monitoring and correction of misleading statements after the statute has been passed. One effect of the new textualism has been to push the current Court toward greater skepticism about the value of subsequent legislative history than the Court had shown in the 1970s and early 1980s. *Rapanos* and *Solid Waste* illustrate this reluctance, as the Court in both cases was extremely reluctant to read the 1972 Water Act in light of proposals rejected by Congress in 1977.[y] But even the skeptical decisions say that the

---

y. See *Massachusetts v. EPA*, 127 S.Ct. 1438, 1460 (2007); *Doe v. Chao,* 540 U.S. 614 (2004) (rejecting Privacy Act plaintiff's reliance on statutes in pari materia, when such statutes were enacted after the Privacy Act); *Central Bank of Denver N.A. v. First Interstate Bank of Denver N.A.*, 511 U.S. 164, 185–86 (1994) (ignoring congressional interpretations in 1983 and 1988 committee reports in interpreting 1934 statute); *Chapman v. United States*, 500 U.S. 453, 464 n.4 (1991), *aff'g Marshall v. United States* (Chapter 7, § 3B1) (refusing even to consider subsequent legislative discussion as evidence of statutory ambiguity in criminal sentencing case); *Sullivan v. Finkelstein*, 496 U.S. 617, 628 n.8 (1990) (rejecting arguments based upon

Court will consider subsequent legislative history if it is very persuasive and/or accompanied by an amendment to the statute. See *Solid Waste*; *Mackey v. Lanier Collections Agency & Service*, 486 U.S. 825, 839–40 (1988).

The Court in *Gozlon-Peretz v. United States*, 498 U.S. 395 (1991), accepted a "public reliance" type of argument similar to the one accepted by Judge Norris in the Second Checkerboard opinion: When a subsequent Congress assumes one interpretation of an earlier statute and acts upon that assumption in enacting a new statute, the Court will consider that as evidence in favor of the assumed interpretation. See also Justice Scalia's opinion concurring in the judgment in *Franklin v. Gwinnett County Public Schools* (Chapter 9, § 1B), arguing that the Court should generally be reluctant to imply causes of action to enforce federal statutes, but not when Congress has relied on that understanding in subsequent legislation. Compare *Public Employees Retirement System of Ohio v. Betts*, 492 U.S. 158, 167–68 (1989) (refusing to credit subsequent conference report's understanding of statutory meaning when Congress amended statute). See also the extensive use of such history, including references to discussions pertaining to bills never enacted into law, in *FDA v. Brown & Williamson Tobacco Corp.*

3. *Post-Enactment Testimony and Amicus Briefs by Legislators.* The second Checkerboard Opinion is just one example of how the battle to create legislative meaning can continue after the statute is enacted. Two other techniques have been used. One is the use of affidavits and depositions by legislators, especially at the state level (where legislative history is not always readily available or elaborate enough to provide much guidance). Some states consider such testimony "inadmissible evidence" of "legislative intent" but are, nonetheless, sometimes moved by it. For example, the Washington Supreme Court in *City of Spokane v. State*, 89 P.2d 826 (Wash. 1939), refused to admit affidavits or depositions of the Governor, Speaker of the House, chairs of the relevant committees, 33 Senators and 68 Representatives in one legislature and 33 Senators and 70 Representatives in the next legislature. Nonetheless, the Court overruled its prior interpretation of the statute, effectively conforming to the views pressed in the affidavits and depositions. Compare *Western Air Lines v. Board of Equalization*, 480 U.S. 123, 130 n.* (1987) (refusing to consider affidavit from lobbyist involved in the enactment of the law in question).

Another method is a legislator *amicus* brief. The Supreme Court in *Blanchette v. Connecticut General Ins. Corp.*, 419 U.S. 102 (1974), relied on the statements made at oral argument by Representative Brock Adams (D–Wash.), representing 36 Members of Congress, as evidence that the Act did not withdraw a Tucker Act remedy for just compensation. The *Gingles* case, discussed in Chapter 2, § 1B2, reached a result consistent with, and perhaps influenced by, an *amicus* brief filed by a dozen key Members of Congress,

---

subsequent committee print and report; in this case, Scalia, J., concurred but refused to join note 8, because he thought it inappropriate even to discuss subsequent legislative history); *United States v. Monsanto*, 491 U.S. 600, 609–10 (1989) (disregarding postenactment statements of several legislators).

opposing the Administration's interpretation of the Voting Rights Act Amendments of 1982.

Nine key legislators (six Democrats, then the majority party in Congress, and three key Republicans) involved in the controlling legislation filed an *amicus* brief in *Rapanos*.[z] Their brief provided a comprehensive examination of the evolution of wetlands regulation, from the Federal Water Pollution Control Act of 1948, through the transformational amendments in 1972 and concluding with the Clean Water Act of 1977. The theme of their brief was that the 1972 law "articulated one of the broadest ecosystem restoration and protection aspirations in all of environmental law." The mandate of the statute was for the EPA and the Army Corps to view the country as a collection of integrated hydrological ecosystems whose integrity was threatened, a threat that had dire consequences for flood control, safe drinking water, and damage to animal populations. The aggressive and comprehensive Corps regulations were affirmatively ratified by the 1977 statute. Although the *Rapanos* plurality rejected this analysis, it was adopted by the four dissenters and may have had an impact on Justice Kennedy, who followed its key points.

NOTES ON PRESIDENTIAL SIGNING OR VETO STATEMENTS

1. *Presidents' Use of Signing Statements.* Throughout history, Presidents have made statements about the bills they sign into law, and sometimes those statements have addressed important policy-related issues of statutory meaning, along one of at least three dimensions: (1) discussions highlighting important features of legislation; (2) objections to the constitutionality of some part of a law, usually with an indication that the administration would apply the law more narrowly than it was written; or (3) an intention to apply a law in a particular way, based upon the executive department's interpretation of that statute. See Curtis Bradley & Eric Posner, *Presidential Signing Statements and Executive Power*, 23 Const. Comm. 307 (2006).

The Reagan Administration used the presidential signing statement more aggressively for reasons (2) and (3) than prior administrations had done. In some statements, President Reagan took positions that were apparently inconsistent with congressional deals made in the enactment process. For example, Congress rebuffed Administration attempts to dilute the Safe Drinking Water Act of 1986 by giving the EPA discretion whether to compel local governments to maintain safe water. The bill said EPA "shall" (not "may") issue the safe-water orders. Yet in his signing statement, President Reagan declared that the new law did not "require" EPA to take any enforcement action. Also, the Administration gained wider publication for its signing statements. Such statements ordinarily appear in the Weekly Compilation of Presidential Documents, but beginning in 1986 the West Publishing Company has regularly included signing statements in its *United States Code Congressio-*

---

z. Brief of the Honorable John D. Dingell, John Conyers, Jr., Robert F. Drinan, Gary W. Hart, Kenneth Hechler, Charles McCarthy Mathias, Jr., Paul N. McCloskey, Jr., Charles B. Rangel, and Richard Schultz Schweiker, as *Amici Curiae* in Support of the Respondent, *Rapanos v. United States* (Nos. 04-1034 & 04-1384).

nal and Administrative News (USCCAN), which is the most readily accessible reference work for legislative history. Legal advisers to the President took the position that the President's statements are authoritative on issues of "legislative intent," perhaps trumping contrary statements of Senators and Representatives themselves.[a]

The Bush 41 Administration was similarly aggressive in its use of signing statements, with the Clinton Administration being moderately aggressive. Most aggressive of all has been the Bush 43 Administration. In his first five years, President George W. Bush challenged or sought to alter more than 800 statutory provisions, apparently more than the total number of provisions reinterpreted by all three of his immediate predecessors in their 20 years of combined service as Presidents. Bradley & Posner, *Presidential Signing Statements,* 324–25.

The Bush 43 signing statements have received more publicity, in part because they often rested upon a controversial understanding of the President's Article II powers. For example, the Detainee Treatment Act of 2005 banned cruel, inhuman, or degrading treatment of detainees, such as those at Guantanamo Bay, Cuba. When signing this bill (which his allies had resisted) into law, President Bush 43 stated that the executive branch would construe the ban "in a manner consistent with the constitutional authority of the President to supervise the unitary executive branch and as Commander in Chief and consistent with the constitutional limitations on the judicial power." This language was reminiscent of the language in the controversial memorandum of Bush 43 Administration Justice Department official John Yoo that argued that presidential agents are immune from prosecution for torture of suspects.

2. *Should Presidential Signing Statements Be Considered Persuasive of Statutory Meaning?* Reagan Administration Attorney General Edward Meese and some subsequent commentators maintain that presidential signing statements should "count" as evidence of statutory meaning, for the same reasons a committee report or a congressional sponsor's explanation might count. Academic commentators and the ABA have been reluctant to accept the argument that signing statements are authoritative, for the same reasons they are dubious about "subsequent legislative history" — it is unreliable evidence of the expectations of the enacting coalition, and there is too much opportunity for manipulation.[b] If an interpreter is a textualist, she would be suspicious of

---

a. *The New Republic,* 3 Nov. 1986, at 13–14. See also Memorandum from Samuel A. Alito, Jr., Deputy Assistant Attorney Gen., Office of Legal Counsel, to the Litigation Strategy Working Group (Feb. 5, 1986), available at http://www.archives.gov/news/samuel-alito/accession-060-89-269/Acc060-89-269-box6-SG-LSWG-AlitotoLSWG- Feb1986.pdf.

b. American Bar Association, Task Force on Presidential Signing Statements and the Separation of Powers Doctrine, Report with Recommendations (2006) (rejecting the Bush 43 Administration's aggressive use of signing statements); Marc Garber & Kurt Wimmer, *Presidential Signing Statements as Interpretations of Legislative Intent: An Executive Aggrandizement of Power,* 24 Harv. J. Legis. 363 (1987); William Popkin, *Judicial Use of Presidential Legislative History: A Critique,* 66 Ind. L.J. 699 (1991). See also Trevor Morrison, *Constitutional Avoidance in the Executive Branch,* 106 Colum. L. Rev. 1189 (2006), who argues against executive department reliance on the avoidance canon, which has been a

or uninterested in any such background material, whether originating in the Capitol or the White House. For more contextualist interpreters, problems of reliability are troubling: Congress cannot respond officially to the President's signing statement, whereas a misleading statement by a legislative sponsor can trigger all sorts of counterattacks (amendments to the bill, contrary statements by other Members, and so on). It is probably for these kinds of reasons that federal judges rarely mention presidential signing statements and almost never give them dispositive weight.[c]

On the other hand, for the same reasons that interpreters are usually interested in the views of the congressional sponsors, they might be interested in the views of the President, who effectively sponsors much major legislation and whose veto power (not to mention his status as chief of one of the two major political parties) gives him an important bargaining role in virtually all major legislation.[d] Such views provide useful policy or even linguistic context for understanding the statute, and they can be good evidence of where the political equilibrium lies. While the President might be tempted to negate deals made in Congress, the fact remains that Members can publicly denounce any such interpretation, as they have been doing, with increasing vigor, from the Reagan Administration through the Bush 43 Administration. Because the President is a repeat player on Capitol Hill, he or she has some incentive not to lie about what deals were made.

Finally, from a more formal perspective, in assessing presidential signing statements it may be useful to retreat to a fundamental issue, whether the bill is ambiguous. If it is, and if the congressional history does not clear up the problem, there may be good reason for the President to state that he or she is signing it based on a certain interpretation of it, at least so long as that interpretation is reasonable. In this circumstance, the President is not violating the text or legislative intent, and the President's good-faith interpretation may be a useful guide to courts and administrative agencies.[e] On the other hand, if the bill, as supplemented by the legislative history, is pretty clear on a point, our constitutional system seems to give the President only two options — to acquiesce (by signing it or by allowing it to go into law without presidential signature) or to veto it — and not the option of attempting to skew it in some

---

mainstay of controversial presidential signing statements since the Reagan Administration.

c. Among the few court of appeals decisions giving weight to signing statements, consider *United States v. Perlaza*, 439 F.3d 1149, 1163 (9th Cir. 2006) (Clinton signing statement confirms suggestion in conference report); *United States v. Gonzales*, 311 F.3d 440, 443 & n.2 (1st Cir. 2002) (similar); *United States v. Story*, 891 F.2d 988, 994 (2d Cir. 1989) (relying on a Reagan signing statement, among other factors, to resolve conflicting interpretations in the House and Senate legislative history).

d. Charles Cameron, *Veto Bargaining: Presidents and the Politics of Negative Power* (2000); William Eskridge, Jr. & John Ferejohn, *The Article I, Section 7 Game*, 80 Geo. L.J. 523 (1992).

e. For a vigorous defense of presidential signing statements as improving the transparency of law enforcement and interpretational debates, see Bradley & Posner, *Presidential Signing Statements*.

other direction. Although Congress may formally override a veto, it has no authoritative way to reject a signing statement (if the statute is already clear).

3. *Veto Statements.* Courts will sometimes rely on the President's veto statement. If Congress overrides the President's veto, then an interpreter might infer that Congress rejected the President's preferences. See *McDonald v. Santa Fe Trail Transportation Co.*, 427 U.S. 273, 295 & n.26 (1976); *Kennedy v. Mendoza-Martinez*, 372 U.S. 144, 178 & n.33 (1963); *United States v. CIO*, 335 U.S. 106, 138–39 (1948) (Rutledge, J., concurring in the result). If, instead, the bill is modified and enacted with the President's signature, the veto statement may provide a good understanding of the nature of the new bill. See *United States v. Yermian*, 468 U.S. 63, 72–75 (1984). In assessing whether the 1991 Civil Rights Act was retroactive, the Court in *Landgraf* (Chapter 6, § 3) considered President Bush's veto of the 1990 version of that legislation as relevant background.

Problem on Presidential Signing Statements

Problem 8–6. Congressional outrage at media accounts of torture of non-American prisoners by American guards and interrogators led to the enactment, by large margins, of the Detainee Treatment Act of 2005, Pub. L. No. 109–148, Div. A, tit. X (2005). As noted above, the Act sets limits on torture that President Bush resisted on grounds that they interfered with his executive authority to conduct the war on terror. For war-on-terror prisoners held at Guantanamo Bay, the Act also substitutes for habeas corpus a special summary appeals process to the D.C. Circuit. When the Act was passed, in 2005, numerous Guantanamo detainees were already pursuing habeas relief in the federal courts. The question arose whether the Act applied to (and therefore required dismissal of) habeas cases filed by those detainees and pending on the date of enactment.

Section 1005(e) of the DTA amended 28 U.S.C. § 2241 (the federal habeas law) by adding at the end the following:

> (e) Except as provided in section 1005 of the Detainee Treatment Act of 2005, no court, justice, or judge shall have jurisdiction to hear or consider —

> (1) an application for a writ of habeas corpus filed by or on behalf of an alien detained by the Department of Defense at Guantanamo Bay, Cuba; or

> (2) any other action against the United States or its agents relating to any aspect of the detention by the Department of Defense of an alien at Guantanamo Bay, Cuba, who—

> (A) is currently in military custody; or

> (B) has been determined by the United States Court of Appeals for the District of Columbia Circuit in accordance with the procedures set forth in section 1005(e) of the Detainee Treatment Act of 2005 to have been properly detained as an enemy combatant.

Section 1005(h)(1) provides that "this section shall take effect upon the date of the enactment of this Act." Section 1005(h)(2) says: "Paragraphs (2) and

(3) of subsection (e) shall apply with respect to any claim whose review is governed by one of such paragraphs and that is pending on or after the date of the enactment of this Act."

The government invoked the canon in favor of applying statutes conferring or ousting jurisdiction immediately, *Landgraf v. USI Film Prods.*, 511 U.S. 244, 274 (1994) (Chapter 6, § 3), while the habeas claimants relied on the presumption against retroactive application of new statutes. Id. at 280. The claimants relied on statements by Senator Levin, a sponsor, that the DTA would not apply to pending cases and objected to a proposal by Senator Graham, another sponsor, that would have made § 1005(e)(1) applicable to pending cases. The government responded with statements by Senators Graham and Kyl, a third sponsor, that the Act as passed applied to pending Guantanamo cases.

The government also invoked President Bush's signing statement, which said this: "[T]he executive branch shall construe section 1005 to preclude the Federal courts from exercising subject matter jurisdiction over any existing or future action, including applications for writs of habeas corpus, described in section 1005." See Statement on Signing the Department of Defense, Emergency Supplemental Appropriations to Address Hurricanes in the Gulf of Mexico, and Pandemic Influenza Act, 2006, 41 Weekly Comp. Pres. Doc. 1918 (Dec. 30, 2005).

This issue reached the Supreme Court, where the government argued that federal judges no longer had jurisdiction to adjudicate the Guantanamo habeas claims. What role, if any, should the President's signing statement have played in the Court's interpretation? (How should textualist Justices Scalia and Thomas treat the signing statement? Justices Breyer and Stevens?) In your view, what is the right interpretation? Compare *Hamdan v. Rumsfeld*, 126 S.Ct. 2764–69 (2006), with id. at 2810–17 (dissenting opinion).

6. *Legislative Inaction*

What the legislature doesn't do may be as significant as what it does. Recall the dog didn't bark canon: When no one in the legislative discussions says that an important policy is being changed, a court should presume that no big changes are intended. This canon is related to the *canon of continuity* defended by David Shapiro, *Continuity and Change in Statutory Interpretation*, 67 NYU L. Rev. 921 (1992). Shapiro maintains that the structure of American government suggests a constitutional bias against discontinuity in legal obligations and rights. Thus, in the absence of clear indications to the contrary, statutes should be construed to maintain established rules and practices.

You have already seen plenty of examples of judicial inferences (or not) from legislative inaction, especially in Chapter 7 and this chapter. There are three specific doctrines that relate to Congress's failure to do something, and it is useful to separate them out.[f]

(a) *The Acquiescence Rule.* If Congress is aware of an authoritative agency or judicial interpretation of a statute and doesn't amend the statute, the Court has sometimes presumed that Congress has "acquiesced" in the interpretation's correctness. The acquiescence rule was followed by the Court to reaffirm its own prior interpretations of statutes in *Johnson v. Transportation Agency* (Chapter 1, § 3B) and in *Flood v. Kuhn* (Chapter 6, § 2B). But the acquiescence rule can also support implicit congressional ratification of a uniform line of federal appellate interpretations or in a longstanding agency interpretation. E.g., *Zuni Pub. Sch. Dist. No. 89 v. Department of Educ.* (excerpted in Chapter 7, § 3A).

This rule is one that the new textualists find particularly abhorrent. E.g., *Johnson* (Scalia, J., dissenting). Absent "overwhelming evidence of acquiescence," the *Solid Waste* Court announced it is "loathe to replace the plain text and original understanding of a statute" with a new construction. Nonetheless, this doctrine is still invoked if there is concrete evidence Congress was aware of the longstanding interpretation and paid attention to the issue, as in the FDA Tobacco Case, where Justice Scalia himself signed onto dozens of pages of legislative history discussion. See also *Zuni Pub. Sch. District.*[g]

(b) *The Reenactment Rule.* If Congress reenacts a statute without making any material changes in its wording, the Court will often presume that Congress intends to incorporate authoritative agency and judicial interpretations of that language into the reenacted statute. The leading Supreme Court statement of this rule is found in *Lorillard v. Pons* (Part C1 of this section), which stated: "Congress is presumed to be aware of an administrative or judicial interpretation of a statute and to adopt that interpretation when it reenacts a statute without change." Like the acquiescence rule, the reenactment rule is much more likely to be invoked if the interpretation is a foundational one — that is, the interpretation is authoritative (namely, a leading Supreme Court case or the decision of the chief agency enforcing the law), settled, and likely to have yielded private and public reliance. See *Jama v. Immigration & Customs Enforcement*, 543 U.S. 345 (2005) (application of reenactment rule inappropriate because prior state of the law not well settled); *Fogerty v. Fantasy, Inc.*, 510 U.S. 517, 527–33 (1994) (same, and contrasting the well-

---

f. This account is drawn from James Brudney, *Congressional Commentary on Judicial Interpretations of Statutes: Idle Chatter or Telling Response?*, 93 Mich. L. Rev. 1 (1994); and William Eskridge, Jr., *Interpreting Legislative Inaction*, 87 Mich. L. Rev. 67 (1988), which also contains appendices listing cases following or declining to follow these doctrines.

g. See also *Evans v. United States*, 504 U.S. 255, 269 (1992) (assuming Congress had acquiesced in longstanding and highly visible interpretation of statute in lower courts); *Riverside Bayview* (Conference Committee killed House effort to overrule Corps of Engineers' jurisdiction over "wetlands"); *Heckler v. Day*, 467 U.S. 104 (1984) (congressional hearings on disability benefit delays did not produce legislation to hurry agency along); *Guardians Ass'n v. Civil Serv. Comm'n*, 463 U.S. 582, 593 & n.14 (1983) (opinion of White, J.) (acquiescence in Title VI regulations).

settled stature of Creedence Clearwater Revival "as one of the greatest American rock and roll bands of all time").

A dramatic invocation of the reenactment rule came in *Farragher v. City of Boca Raton*, 524 U.S. 775 (1998). The Court ruled that employers can be vicariously liable under Title VII for hostile work environments created or tolerated by supervisors, subject to a reasonableness defense. Justice Souter's opinion for the Court relied on the holding and reasoning in *Meritor Sav. Bank FSB v. Vinson*, 477 U.S. 57 (1986), which had greatly elaborated upon the spare language in Title VII that employers cannot "discriminate" because of sex by holding that "hostile environment sexual harassment" was prohibited. Dissenting Justices Thomas and Scalia objected that the Court's opinions were no more than "willful policymaking" in violation of the statute. Justice Souter responded that the holding and reasoning of *Meritor* was binding on the Court not only as a matter of stare decisis, but also because it had been ratified by Congress when it amended Title VII in 1991. See 524 U.S. at 792. Although the 1991 Act overrode a number of Supreme Court interpretations of Title VII, it left *Meritor* intact, which Justice Souter deemed "conspicuous. We thus have to assume that in expanding employers' potential liability under Title VII, Congress relied on our statements in *Meritor* about the limits of employer liability. To disregard those statements now * * * would be not only to disregard *stare decisis* in statutory interpretation, but to substitute our revised judgment about the proper allocation of the costs of harassment for Congress's considered decision on the subject." *Id.* at 804 n.4.

(c) *The Rejected Proposal Rule.* If Congress (in conference committee) or one chamber (on the floor) considers and rejects specific statutory language, the Court has often been reluctant to interpret the statute along lines of the rejected language. The leading case is *Runyon v. McCrary*, 427 U.S. 160 (1976), where the Court reaffirmed a debatable precedent interpreting the Civil Rights Act of 1866, based in large part upon its perception that the Senate in 1971 had rejected attempts to override that interpretation. See also the FDA Tobacco Case.

The *Solid Waste* Court expressed a more skeptical view of this kind of evidence. " '[F]ailed legislative proposals are "a particularly dangerous ground on which to rest an interpretation of a prior statute." ' *Central Bank of Denver N.A. v. First Interstate Bank of Denver N.A.*, 511 U.S. 164, 187 (1994). A bill can be proposed for any number of reasons, and it can be rejected for just as many others. The relationship between the actions and inactions of the 95th Congress and the intent of the 92d Congress in passing § 404(a) is also considerably attenuated. Because 'subsequent history is less illuminating than the contemporaneous evidence,' *Hagen v. Utah,* 510 U.S. 399, 420 (1994), respondents face a difficult task in overcoming the plain text and import of § 404(a)."

Consider these various doctrines in connection with the following case, which the FDA Tobacco Court relied on for its acquiescence argument.

BOB JONES UNIVERSITY v. UNITED STATES
Supreme Court of the United States, 1983
461 U.S. 574, 103 S.Ct. 2017, 76 L.Ed.2d 157

CHIEF JUSTICE BURGER delivered the opinion of the Court.

We granted certiorari to decide whether petitioners, nonprofit private schools that prescribe and enforce racially discriminatory admissions standards on the basis of religious doctrine, qualify as tax-exempt organizations under § 501(c)(3) of the Internal Revenue Code of 1954.

[I] Until 1970, the Internal Revenue Service granted tax-exempt status to private schools, without regard to their racial admissions policies, under § 501(c)(3) of the Internal Revenue Code, 26 U.S.C. § 501(c)(3),[6] and granted charitable deductions for contributions to such schools under § 170 of the Code, 26 U.S.C. § 170.[7]

On January 12, 1970, a three-judge District Court for the District of Columbia issued a preliminary injunction prohibiting the IRS from according tax-exempt status to private schools in Mississippi that discriminated as to admissions on the basis of race. *Green v. Kennedy*, 309 F. Supp. 1127, appeal dism'd *sub nom. Cannon v. Green*, 398 U.S. 956 (1970). Thereafter, in July 1970, the IRS concluded that it could "no longer legally justify allowing tax-exempt status [under § 501(c)(3)] to private schools which practice racial discrimination." IRS News Release July 7, 1970. At the same time, the IRS announced that it could not "treat gifts to such schools as charitable deductions for income tax purposes [under § 170]." By letter dated November 30, 1970, the IRS formally notified private schools, including those involved in this litigation, of this change in policy, "applicable to all private schools in the United States at all levels of education."

On June 30, 1971, the three-judge District Court issued its opinion on the merits of the Mississippi challenge. *Green v. Connally*, 330 F.Supp. 1150, summarily aff'd *sub nom. Coit v. Green*, 404 U.S. 997 (1971). That court approved the IRS's amended construction of the Tax Code. The court also held that racially discriminatory private schools were not entitled to exemption

---

6. Section 501(c)(3) lists the following organizations, which, pursuant to § 501(a), are exempt from taxation unless denied tax exemptions under other specified sections of the Code: "Corporations, and any community chest, fund, or foundation, *organized and operated exclusively for religious, charitable*, scientific, testing for public safety, literary, *or educational purposes*, or to foster national or international amateur sports competition (but only if no part of its activities involves the provision of athletic facilities or equipment), or for the prevention of cruelty to children or animals, no part of the net earnings of which inures to the benefit of any private shareholder or individual, no substantial part of the activities of which is carrying on propaganda, or otherwise attempting, to influence legislation * * *, and which does not participate in, or intervene in (including the publishing or distributing of statements), any political campaign on behalf of any candidate for public office." (Emphasis added.)

7. Section 170(a) allows deductions for certain "charitable contributions." Section 170(c)(2)(B) includes within the definition of "charitable contribution" a contribution or gift to or for the use of a corporation "organized and operated exclusively for religious, charitable, scientific, literary, or educational purposes * * *."

under § 501(c)(3) and that donors were not entitled to deductions for contributions to such schools under § 170. The court permanently enjoined the Commissioner of Internal Revenue from approving tax-exempt status for any school in Mississippi that did not publicly maintain a policy of nondiscrimination.

The revised policy on discrimination was formalized in Revenue Ruling 71–447, 1971–2 Cum. Bull. 230:

> "Both the courts and the Internal Revenue Service have long recognized that the statutory requirement of being 'organized and operated exclusively for religious, charitable, * * * or educational purposes' was intended to express the basic common law concept [of 'charity']. * * * All charitable trusts, educational or otherwise, are subject to the requirement that the purpose of the trust may not be illegal or contrary to public policy."

Based on the "national policy to discourage racial discrimination in education," the IRS ruled that "a [private] school not having a racially nondiscriminatory policy as to students is not 'charitable' within the common law concepts reflected in sections 170 and 501(c)(3) of the Code." * * *

[IIA] In Revenue Ruling 71–447, the IRS formalized the policy, first announced in 1970, that § 170 and § 501(c)(3) embrace the common-law "charity" concept. Under that view, to qualify for a tax exemption pursuant to § 501(c)(3), an institution must show, first, that it falls within one of the eight categories expressly set forth in that section, and second, that its activity is not contrary to settled public policy.

Section 501(c)(3) provides that "[c]orporations * * * organized and operated exclusively for religious, charitable * * * or educational purposes" are entitled to tax exemption. Petitioners argue that the plain language of the statute guarantees them tax-exempt status. They emphasize the absence of any language in the statute expressly requiring all exempt organizations to be "charitable" in the common-law sense, and they contend that the disjunctive "or" separating the categories in § 501(c)(3) precludes such a reading. Instead, they argue that if an institution falls within one or more of the specified categories it is automatically entitled to exemption, without regard to whether it also qualifies as "charitable." The Court of Appeals rejected that contention and concluded that petitioners' interpretation of the statute "tears section 501(c)(3) from its roots."

It is a well-established canon of statutory construction that a court should go beyond the literal language of a statute if reliance on that language would defeat the plain purpose of the statute. * * *

Section 501(c)(3) therefore must be analyzed and construed within the framework of the Internal Revenue Code and against the background of the congressional purposes. Such an examination reveals unmistakable evidence that, underlying all relevant parts of the Code, is the intent that entitlement to tax exemption depends on meeting certain common-law standards of charity — namely, that an institution seeking tax-exempt status must serve a public purpose and not be contrary to established public policy.

This "charitable" concept appears explicitly in § 170 of the Code. That section contains a list of organizations virtually identical to that contained in § 501(c)(3). It is apparent that Congress intended that list to have the same meaning in both sections.[10] In § 170, Congress used the list of organizations in defining the term "charitable contributions." On its face, therefore, § 170 reveals that Congress' intention was to provide tax benefits to organizations serving charitable purposes. The form of § 170 simply makes plain what common sense and history tell us: in enacting both § 170 and § 501(c)(3), Congress sought to provide tax benefits to charitable organizations, to encourage the development of private institutions that serve a useful public purpose or supplement or take the place of public institutions of the same kind.

Tax exemptions for certain institutions thought beneficial to the social order of the country as a whole, or to a particular community, are deeply rooted in our history, as in that of England. The origins of such exemptions lie in the special privileges that have long been extended to charitable trusts.[12]

More than a century ago, this Court announced the caveat that is critical in this case:

> "[I]t has now become an established principle of American law, that courts of chancery will sustain and protect * * * a gift * * * to public charitable uses, *provided the same is consistent with local laws and public policy* * * *." *Perin v. Carey*, 24 How. 465, 501 (1861) (emphasis added).

Soon after that, in 1877, the Court commented:

> "A charitable use, *where neither law nor public policy forbids*, may be applied to almost any thing *that tends to promote the well-doing and well-being of social man*." *Ould v. Washington Hospital for Foundlings*, 95 U.S. 303, 311 (emphasis added). * * *

---

10. The predecessor of § 170 originally was enacted in 1917, as part of the War Revenue Act of 1917, ch. 63, § 1201(2), 40 Stat. 330, whereas the predecessor of § 501(c)(3) dates back to the income tax law of 1894, Act of Aug. 27, 1894, ch. 349, 28 Stat. 509. There are minor differences between the lists of organizations in the two sections. Nevertheless, the two sections are closely related; both seek to achieve the same basic goal of encouraging the development of certain organizations through the grant of tax benefits. The language of the two sections is in most respects identical, and the Commissioner and the courts consistently have applied many of the same standards in interpreting those sections. To the extent that § 170 "aids in ascertaining the meaning" of § 501(c)(3), therefore, it is "entitled to great weight," *United States v. Stewart*, 311 U.S. 60, 64–65 (1940).

12. The form and history of the charitable exemption and deduction sections of the various income tax Acts reveal that Congress was guided by the common law of charitable trusts. See Simon, *The Tax-Exempt Status of Racially Discriminatory Religious Schools*, 36 Tax L.Rev. 477, 485–489 (1981). Congress acknowledged as much in 1969. The House Report on the Tax Reform Act of 1969, Pub.L. 91–172, 83 Stat. 487, stated that the § 501(c)(3) exemption was available only to institutions that served "the specified charitable purposes," H.R.Rep. No. 91–413, pt. 1, p. 35 (1969), and described "charitable" as "a term that has been used in the law of trusts for hundreds of years." *Id.*, at 43. We need not consider whether Congress intended to incorporate into the Internal Revenue Code any aspects of charitable trust law other than the requirements of public benefit and a valid public purpose.

When the Government grants exemptions or allows deductions all taxpayers are affected; the very fact of the exemption or deduction for the donor means that other taxpayers can be said to be indirect and vicarious "donors." Charitable exemptions are justified on the basis that the exempt entity confers a public benefit — a benefit which the society or the community may not itself choose or be able to provide, or which supplements and advances the work of public institutions already supported by tax revenues. History buttresses logic to make clear that, to warrant exemption under § 501(c)(3), an institution must fall within a category specified in that section and must demonstrably serve and be in harmony with the public interest. The institution's purpose must not be so at odds with the common community conscience as to undermine any public benefit that might otherwise be conferred.

[IIB] We are bound to approach these questions with full awareness that determinations of public benefit and public policy are sensitive matters with serious implications for the institutions affected; a declaration that a given institution is not "charitable" should be made only where there can be no doubt that the activity involved is contrary to a fundamental public policy. But there can no longer be any doubt that racial discrimination in education violates deeply and widely accepted views of elementary justice. Prior to 1954, public education in many places still was conducted under the pall of *Plessy v. Ferguson*, 163 U.S. 537 (1896); racial segregation in primary and secondary education prevailed in many parts of the country.[20] This Court's decision in *Brown v. Board of Education*, 347 U.S. 483 (1954), signalled an end to that era. Over the past quarter of a century, every pronouncement of this Court and myriad Acts of Congress and Executive Orders attest a firm national policy to prohibit racial segregation and discrimination in public education.

An unbroken line of cases following *Brown v. Board of Education* establishes beyond doubt this Court's view that racial discrimination in education violates a most fundamental national public policy, as well as rights of individuals.

> "The right of a student not to be segregated on racial grounds in schools * * * is indeed so fundamental and pervasive that it is embraced in the concept of due process of law." *Cooper v. Aaron*, 358 U.S. 1, 19 (1958).

In *Norwood v. Harrison*, 413 U.S. 455, 468–469 (1973), we dealt with a nonpublic institution:

> "[A] private school — even one that discriminates — fulfills an important educational function; *however, * * * [that] legitimate educational function cannot be isolated*

---

20. In 1894, when the first charitable exemption provision was enacted, racially segregated educational institutions would not have been regarded as against public policy. Yet contemporary standards must be considered in determining whether given activities provide a public benefit and are entitled to the charitable tax exemption. In *Walz v. Tax Comm'n*, 397 U.S. 664, 673 (1970), we observed: "Qualification for tax exemption is not perpetual or immutable; some tax-exempt groups lose that status when their activities take them outside the classification and new entities can come into being and qualify for exemption." Charitable trust law also makes clear that the definition of "charity" depends upon contemporary standards. *See, e.g.*, Restatement (Second) of Trusts § 374, Comment *a* (1959).

*from discriminatory practices * * *. [D]iscriminatory treatment exerts a pervasive influence on the entire educational process.*" (Emphasis added.)

Congress, in Titles IV and VI of the Civil Rights Act of 1964, Pub.L. 88–352, 78 Stat. 241, 42 U.S.C. §§ 2000c et seq., 2000c–6, 2000d et seq., clearly expressed its agreement that racial discrimination in education violates a fundamental public policy. Other sections of that Act, and numerous enactments since then, testify to the public policy against racial discrimination. See, *e.g.*, [the Voting Rights Act of 1965, Title VIII of the Civil Rights Act of 1968, the Emergency School Aid Acts of 1972 and 1978].

The Executive Branch has consistently placed its support behind eradication of racial discrimination. Several years before this Court's decision in *Brown v. Board of Education*, President Truman issued Executive Orders prohibiting racial discrimination in federal employment decisions, Exec. Order No. 9980, 3 CFR 720 (1943–1948 Comp.), and in classifications for the Selective Service, Exec. Order No. 9988, 3 CFR 726, 729 (1943–1948 Comp.). In 1957, President Eisenhower employed military forces to ensure compliance with federal standards in school desegregation programs. Exec. Order No. 10730, 3 CFR 389 (1954–1958 Comp.). And in 1962, President Kennedy announced:

> "[T]he granting of Federal assistance for * * * housing and related facilities from which Americans are excluded because of their race, color, creed, or national origin is unfair, unjust, and inconsistent with the public policy of the United States as manifested in its Constitution and laws." Exec. Order No. 11063, 3 CFR 652 (1959–1963 Comp.).

These are but a few of numerous Executive Orders over the past three decades demonstrating the commitment of the Executive Branch to the fundamental policy of eliminating racial discrimination.

Few social or political issues in our history have been more vigorously debated and more extensively ventilated than the issue of racial discrimination, particularly in education. Given the stress and anguish of the history of efforts to escape from the shackles of the "separate but equal" doctrine of *Plessy v. Ferguson*, it cannot be said that educational institutions that, for whatever reasons, practice racial discrimination, are institutions exercising "beneficial and stabilizing influences in community life," *Walz v. Tax Comm'n*, 397 U.S. 664, 673 (1970), or should be encouraged by having all taxpayers share in their support by way of special tax status.

There can thus be no question that the interpretation of § 170 and § 501(c)(3) announced by the IRS in 1970 was correct. That it may be seen as belated does not undermine its soundness. It would be wholly incompatible with the concepts underlying tax exemption to grant the benefit of tax-exempt status to racially discriminatory educational entities, which "exer[t] a pervasive influence on the entire educational process." *Norwood v. Harrison, supra.* Whatever may be the rationale for such private schools' policies, and however sincere the rationale may be, racial discrimination in education is contrary to public policy. Racially discriminatory educational institutions cannot be viewed as conferring a public benefit within the "charitable" concept discussed earlier, or within the congressional intent underlying § 170 and § 501(c)(3).

[IIC] [Chief Justice Burger rejected the argument that the IRS did not have the authority to issue the 1970 rule and that its longstanding prior policy could only be overturned by legislative amendment of the Code. He reasoned that the IRS had been given broad rulemaking power by Congress and, moreover, that the policy adopted by the IRS was fully consistent with national policy since *Brown* and the Civil Rights Act of 1964.]

[IID] The actions of Congress since 1970 leave no doubt that the IRS reached the correct conclusion in exercising its authority. It is, of course, not unknown for independent agencies or the Executive Branch to misconstrue the intent of a statute; Congress can and often does correct such misconceptions, if the courts have not done so. Yet for a dozen years Congress has been made aware — acutely aware — of the IRS rulings of 1970 and 1971. As we noted earlier, few issues have been the subject of more vigorous and widespread debate and discussion in and out of Congress than those related to racial segregation in education. Sincere adherents advocating contrary views have ventilated the subject for well over three decades. Failure of Congress to modify the IRS rulings of 1970 and 1971, of which Congress was, by its own studies and by public discourse, constantly reminded, and Congress' awareness of the denial of tax-exempt status for racially discriminatory schools when enacting other and related legislation make out an unusually strong case of legislative acquiescence in and ratification by implication of the 1970 and 1971 rulings.

Ordinarily, and quite appropriately, courts are slow to attribute significance to the failure of Congress to act on particular legislation. We have observed that "unsuccessful attempts at legislation are not the best of guides to legislative intent." Here, however, we do not have an ordinary claim of legislative acquiescence. Only one month after the IRS announced its position in 1970, Congress held its first hearings on this precise issue. Equal Educational Opportunity: Hearings before the Senate Select Committee on Equal Educational Opportunity, 91st Cong., 2d Sess. 1991 (1970). Exhaustive hearings have been held on the issue at various times since then. These include hearings in February 1982, after we granted review in this case. Administration's Change in Federal Policy Regarding the Tax Status of Racially Discriminatory Private Schools: Hearing before the House Committee on Ways and Means, 97th Cong., 2d Sess. (1982).

Nonaction by Congress is not often a useful guide, but the nonaction here is significant. During the past 12 years there have been no fewer than 13 bills introduced to overturn the IRS interpretation of § 501(c)(3). Not one of these bills has emerged from any committee, although Congress has enacted numerous other amendments to § 501 during this same period, including an amendment to § 501(c)(3) itself. Tax Reform Act of 1976, Pub.L. 94–455, § 1313(a), 90 Stat. 1730. It is hardly conceivable that Congress — and in this setting, any Member of Congress — was not abundantly aware of what was going on. In view of its prolonged and acute awareness of so important an issue, Congress' failure to act on the bills proposed on this subject provides added support for concluding that Congress acquiesced in the IRS rulings of 1970 and 1971.

The evidence of congressional approval of the policy embodied in Revenue Ruling 71–447 goes well beyond the failure of Congress to act on legislative proposals. Congress affirmatively manifested its acquiescence in the IRS policy when it enacted the present § 501(i) of the Code, Act of Oct. 20, 1976, Pub.L. 94–568, 90 Stat. 2697. That provision denies tax-exempt status to social clubs whose charters or policy statements provide for "discrimination against any person on the basis of race, color, or religion." Both the House and Senate Committee Reports on that bill articulated the national policy against granting tax exemptions to racially discriminatory private clubs. S. Rep. No. 94–1318, p. 8 (1976); H.R. Rep. No. 94–1353, p. 8 (1976).

Even more significant is the fact that both Reports focus on this Court's affirmance of *Green v. Connally*, 330 F.Supp. 1150 (DC 1971), as having established that "discrimination on account of race is inconsistent with an *educational institution's* tax-exempt status." S. Rep. No. 94–1318 at 7–8, and n. 5; H.R. Rep. No. 94–1353 at 8, and n. 5 (emphasis added). These references in congressional Committee Reports on an enactment denying tax exemptions to racially discriminatory private social clubs cannot be read other than as indicating approval of the standards applied to racially discriminatory private schools by the IRS subsequent to 1970, and specifically of Revenue Ruling 71–447.[27]

[In Part III, Chief Justice Burger rejected the argument that the IRS ruling violated the Free Exercise Clause of the First Amendment, and in Part IV he rejected the argument that the IRS ruling was not properly applied to the petitioners.]

[The concurring opinion of JUSTICE POWELL is omitted.]

---

27. Reliance is placed on scattered statements in floor debate by Congressmen critical of the IRS's adoption of Revenue Ruling 71–447. Those views did not prevail. That several Congressmen, expressing their individual views, argued that the IRS had no authority to take the action in question, is hardly a balance for the overwhelming evidence of congressional awareness of and acquiescence in the IRS rulings of 1970 and 1971. Petitioners also argue that the Ashbrook and Dornan Amendments to the Treasury, Postal Service, and General Government Appropriations Act of 1980, Pub.L. 96–74, §§ 103, 614, 615, 93 Stat. 559, 562, 576–577, reflect congressional opposition to the IRS policy formalized in Revenue Ruling 71–447. Those amendments, however, are directly concerned only with limiting more aggressive enforcement procedures proposed by the IRS in 1978 and 1979 and preventing the adoption of more stringent substantive standards. The Ashbrook Amendment, § 103 of the Act, applies only to procedures, guidelines, or measures adopted after August 22, 1978, and thus in no way affects the status of Revenue Ruling 71–447. In fact, both Congressman Dornan and Congressman Ashbrook explicitly stated that their amendments would have no effect on prior IRS policy, including Revenue Ruling 71–447, see 125 Cong.Rec. 18815 (1979) (Cong. Dornan: "[M]y amendment will not affect existing IRS rules which IRS has used to revoke tax exemptions of white segregated academies under Revenue Ruling 71–447 * * *."); *id.*, at 18446 (Cong. Ashbrook: "My amendment very clearly indicates on its face that all the regulations in existence as of August 22, 1978, would not be touched"). These amendments therefore do not indicate Congressional rejection of Revenue Ruling 71–447 and the standards contained therein.

JUSTICE REHNQUIST, dissenting.

The Court points out that there is a strong national policy in this country against racial discrimination. To the extent that the Court states that Congress in furtherance of this policy could deny tax-exempt status to educational institutions that promote racial discrimination, I readily agree. But, unlike the Court, I am convinced that Congress simply has failed to take this action and, as this Court has said over and over again, regardless of our view on the propriety of Congress' failure to legislate we are not constitutionally empowered to act for it.

In approaching this statutory construction question the Court quite adeptly avoids the statute it is construing. This I am sure is no accident, for there is nothing in the language of § 501(c)(3) that supports the result obtained by the Court. Section 501(c)(3) provides tax-exempt status for:

> "Corporations, and any community chest, fund, or foundation, organized and operated exclusively for religious, charitable, scientific, testing for public safety, literary, or educational purposes, or to foster national or international amateur sports competition (but only if no part of its activities involve the provision of athletic facilities or equipment), or for the prevention of cruelty to children or animals, no part of the net earnings of which inures to the benefit of any private shareholder or individual, no substantial part of the activities of which is carrying on propaganda, or otherwise attempting, to influence legislation (except as otherwise provided in subsection (h)), and which does not participate in, or intervene in (including the publishing or distributing of statements), any political campaign on behalf of any candidate for public office." 26 U.S.C. § 501(c)(3).

With undeniable clarity, Congress has explicitly defined the requirements for § 501(c)(3) status. An entity must be (1) a corporation, or community chest, fund, or foundation, (2) organized for one of the eight enumerated purposes, (3) operated on a nonprofit basis, and (4) free from involvement in lobbying activities and political campaigns. Nowhere is there to be found some additional, undefined public policy requirement.

The Court first seeks refuge from the obvious reading of § 501(c)(3) by turning to § 170 of the Internal Revenue Code, which provides a tax deduction for contributions made to § 501(c)(3) organizations. In setting forth the general rule, § 170 states:

> "There shall be allowed as a deduction any charitable contribution (as defined in subsection (c)) payment of which is made within the taxable year. A charitable contribution shall be allowable as a deduction only if verified under regulations prescribed by the Secretary." 26 U.S.C. § 170(a)(1).

The Court seizes the words "charitable contribution" and with little discussion concludes that "[o]n its face, therefore, § 170 reveals that Congress' intention was to provide tax benefits to organizations serving charitable purposes," intimating that this implies some unspecified common-law charitable trust requirement.

The Court would have been well advised to look to subsection (c) where, as § 170(a)(1) indicates, Congress has defined a "charitable contribution":

"For purposes of this section, the term 'charitable contribution' means a contribution or gift to or for the use of * * * [a] corporation, trust, or community chest, fund, or foundation * * * organized and operated exclusively for religious, charitable, scientific, literary, or educational purposes, or to foster national or international amateur sports competition (but only if no part of its activities involve the provision of athletic facilities or equipment), or for the prevention of cruelty to children or animals; * * * no part of the net earnings of which inures to the benefit of any private shareholder or individual; and * * * which is not disqualified for tax exemption under section 501(c)(3) by reason of attempting to influence legislation, and which does not participate in, or intervene in (including the publishing or distributing of statements), any political campaign on behalf of any candidate for public office." 26 U.S.C. § 170(c).

Plainly, § 170(c) simply tracks the requirements set forth in § 501(c)(3). Since § 170 is no more than a mirror of § 501(c)(3) and, as the Court points out, § 170 followed § 501(c)(3) by more than two decades, it is at best of little usefulness in finding the meaning of § 501(c)(3).

Making a more fruitful inquiry, the Court next turns to the legislative history of § 501(c)(3) and finds that Congress intended in that statute to offer a tax benefit to organizations that Congress believed were providing a public benefit. I certainly agree. But then the Court leaps to the conclusion that this history is proof Congress intended that an organization seeking § 501(c)(3) status "must fall within a category specified in that section *and must demonstrably serve and be in harmony with the public interest.*" (Emphasis added). To the contrary, I think that the legislative history of § 501(c)(3) unmistakably makes clear that *Congress has decided* what organizations are serving a public purpose and providing a public benefit within the meaning of § 501(c)(3) and has clearly set forth in § 501(c)(3) the characteristics of such organizations. In fact, there are few examples which better illustrate Congress' effort to define and redefine the requirements of a legislative Act.

The first general income tax law was passed by Congress in the form of the Tariff Act of 1894. A provision of that Act provided an exemption for "corporations, companies, or associations organized and conducted solely for charitable, religious, or educational purposes." The income tax portion of the 1894 Act was held unconstitutional by this Court, see *Pollock v. Farmers' Loan & Trust Co.*, 158 U.S. 601 (1895), but a similar exemption appeared in the Tariff Act of 1909 which imposed a tax on corporate income. The 1909 Act provided an exemption for "any corporation or association organized and operated exclusively for religious, charitable, or educational purposes, no part of the net income of which inures to the benefit of any private stockholder or individual."

With the ratification of the Sixteenth Amendment, Congress again turned its attention to an individual income tax with the Tariff Act of 1913. And again, in the direct predecessor of § 501(c)(3), a tax exemption was provided for "any corporation or association organized and operated exclusively for religious, charitable, scientific, or educational purposes, no part of the net income of which inures to the benefit of any private stockholder or individual." In subsequent Acts Congress continued to broaden the list of exempt purposes.

The Revenue Act of 1918 added an exemption for corporations or associations organized "for the prevention of cruelty to children or animals." The Revenue Act of 1921 expanded the groups to which the exemption applied to include "any community chest, fund, or foundation" and added "literary" endeavors to the list of exempt purposes. The exemption remained unchanged in the Revenue Acts of 1924, 1926, 1928, and 1932. In the Revenue Act of 1934 Congress added the requirement that no substantial part of the activities of any exempt organization can involve the carrying on of "propaganda" or "attempting to influence legislation." Again, the exemption was left unchanged by the Revenue Acts of 1936 and 1938.

The tax laws were overhauled by the Internal Revenue Code of 1939, but this exemption was left unchanged. When the 1939 Code was replaced with the Internal Revenue Code of 1954, the exemption was adopted in full in the present § 501(c)(3) with the addition of "testing for public safety" as an exempt purpose and an additional restriction that tax-exempt organizations could not "participate in, or intervene in (including the publishing or distributing of statements), any political campaign on behalf of any candidate for public office." Ch. 1, § 501(c)(3), 68A Stat. 163 (1954). Then in 1976 the statute was again amended adding to the purposes for which an exemption would be authorized, "to foster national or international amateur sports competition," provided the activities did not involve the provision of athletic facilities or equipment. Tax Reform Act of 1976, Pub. L. 94–455, § 1313(a), 90 Stat. 1730 (1976).

One way to read the opinion handed down by the Court today leads to the conclusion that this long and arduous refining process of § 501(c)(3) was certainly a waste of time, for when enacting the original 1894 statute Congress intended to adopt a common-law term of art, and intended that this term of art carry with it all of the common-law baggage which defines it. Such a view, however, leads also to the insupportable idea that Congress has spent almost a century adding illustrations simply to clarify an already defined common-law term. * * *

Perhaps recognizing the lack of support in the statute itself, or in its history, for the 1970 IRS change in interpretation, the Court finds that "[t]he actions of Congress since 1970 leave no doubt that the IRS reached the correct conclusion in exercising its authority," concluding that there is "an unusually strong case of legislative acquiescence in and ratification by implication of the 1970 and 1971 rulings." The Court relies first on several bills introduced to overturn the IRS interpretation of § 501(c)(3). But we have said before, and it is equally applicable here, that this type of congressional inaction is of virtually no weight in determining legislative intent. See *United States v. Wise*, 370 U.S. 405, 411 (1962); *Waterman S.S. Corp. v. United States*, 381 U.S. 252, 269 (1965). These bills and related hearings indicate little more than that a vigorous debate has existed in Congress concerning the new IRS position.

The Court next asserts that "Congress affirmatively manifested its acquiescence in the IRS policy when it enacted the present § 501(i) of the Code," a provision that "denies tax-exempt status to social clubs whose charters or policy statements provide for" racial discrimination. Quite to the contrary, it seems to me that in § 501(i) Congress showed that when it wants to add a requirement prohibiting racial discrimination to one of the tax-benefit provisions, it is fully aware of how to do it.

The Court intimates that the Ashbrook and Dornan Amendments also reflect an intent by Congress to acquiesce in the new IRS position. The amendments were passed to limit certain enforcement procedures proposed by the IRS in 1978 and 1979 for determining whether a school operated in a racially nondiscriminatory fashion. The Court points out that in proposing his amendment, Congressman Ashbrook stated: " 'My amendment very clearly indicates on its face that all the regulations in existence as of August 22, 1978, would not be touched.' " The Court fails to note that Congressman Ashbrook also said:

> "The IRS has no authority to create public policy * * *. So long as the Congress has not acted to set forth a national policy respecting denial of tax exemptions to private schools, it is improper for the IRS or any other branch of the Federal Government to seek denial of tax-exempt status * * *. There exists but a single responsibility which is proper for the Internal Revenue Service: To serve as tax collector." 125 Cong. Rec. 18444 (1979).

In the same debate, Congressman Grassley asserted: "Nobody argues that racial discrimination should receive preferred tax status in the United States. However, the IRS should not be making these decisions on the agency's own discretion. Congress should make these decisions." *Id.*, at 18448. The same debates are filled with other similar statements. While on the whole these debates do not show conclusively that Congress believed the IRS had exceeded its authority with the 1970 change in position, they likewise are far less than a showing of acquiescence in and ratification of the new position.

This Court continuously has been hesitant to find ratification through inaction. This is especially true where such a finding "would result in a construction of the statute which not only is at odds with the language of the section in question and the pattern of the statute taken as a whole, but also is extremely far reaching in terms of the virtually untrammeled and unreviewable power it would vest in a regulatory agency." *SEC v. Sloan*, 436 U.S. 103, 121 (1978). Few cases would call for more caution in finding ratification by acquiescence than the present ones. The new IRS interpretation is not only far less than a long-standing administrative policy, it is at odds with a position maintained by the IRS, and unquestioned by Congress, for several decades prior to 1970. The interpretation is unsupported by the statutory language, it is unsupported by legislative history, the interpretation has led to considerable controversy in and out of Congress, and the interpretation gives to the IRS a broad power which until now Congress had kept for itself. Where in addition to these circumstances Congress has shown time and time again that it is ready to enact positive legislation to change the Tax Code when it desires, this Court has no business finding that Congress has adopted the new IRS position by failing to enact legislation to reverse it.

I have no disagreement with the Court's finding that there is a strong national policy in this country opposed to racial discrimination. I agree with the Court that Congress has the power to further this policy by denying § 501(c)(3) status to organizations that practice racial discrimination. But as of yet Congress has failed to do so. Whatever the reasons for the failure, this Court should not legislate for Congress. * * *

NOTES ON *BOB JONES* AND THE "MEANING" OF LEGISLATIVE INACTION

1. *Criticisms of the Acquiescence Doctrine, Generally and in* Bob Jones. *Bob Jones* is now a leading citation for the acquiescence rule. That rule has, however, long been subject to criticism, see, e.g., Henry Hart, Jr. & Albert Sacks, *The Legal Process* 1313–70 (Eskridge & Frickey eds. 1994) (tent. ed. 1958); John Grabow, *Congressional Silence and the Search for Legislative Intent: A Venture into "Speculative Unrealities,"* 64 B.U.L. Rev. 737 (1984), and several current Justices strongly object to it. Dissenting from the Court's reaffirmation of *Weber* in *Johnson* (see Chapter 1, § 3B), Justice Scalia rejected the majority's invocation of legislative acquiescence. For him, "vindication by congressional inaction is a canard," because congressional inaction has no formal significance under Article I as interpreted in *INS v. Chadha* (see Chapter 9, § 2C), and no functional significance given difficulties in figuring out why Congress did nothing. More recently, the Supreme Court has become much more reluctant to accept legislative acquiescence arguments. See, e.g., *Patterson v. McLean Credit Union* (Chapter 6, § 2B), which rejected the dissenting opinion's reliance on legislative inaction (not only the acquiescence rule but also the reenactment and rejected proposal rules) as reason to reaffirm and expand the Court's decision in *Runyon v. McCrary.* Is there any special reason for a skeptic such as Justice Scalia to apply the acquiescence rule in a case like *Bob Jones*, or is this just another "canard"?

Note *Bob Jones'* inconsistent use of congressional inaction. The Court relies on the failure of Congress to overrule the 1971 revenue ruling: Congress, by doing nothing, acquiesced in the agency's action. The Court ignores the failure of Congress to overrule the IRS policy before 1971: that doesn't count, the Court seems to be saying. The Court ignores the repeated failure of Congress to enact statutes penalizing private education discrimination: Congress, by passing statutes which did not cover private schools, nonetheless disapproved of the private action. Is there any good reason to interpret congressional inaction as the Court does?

Justice Rehnquist is critical of the Court's reliance on legislative inaction in *Bob Jones* and, later when he was Chief Justice, in *Solid Waste.* Yet Justice Rehnquist has himself relied upon congressional inaction. See, e.g., *Weinberger v. Rossi*, 456 U.S. 25, 33 (1982) (Rehnquist, J.) (unless Congress says otherwise, Court will presume that it acquiesces in executive agreements). See also *Haig v. Agee*, 453 U.S. 280 (1981) (Burger, C.J.) (absent intent to repudiate executive interpretation of the Passport Act, Congress is presumed to acquiesce in it). Are these foreign-affairs cases more appropriate occasions for relying on legislative inaction than *Bob Jones* is?

2. *Reading Public Values into Statutes.* Mayer Freed and Daniel Polsby, in *Race, Religion & Public Policy*: Bob Jones University v. United States,

1983 Sup. Ct. Rev. 1, 5, object to Chief Justice Burger's reliance on general "public policy" — the Constitution, Title VI and other provisions of the Civil Rights Act — to rewrite § 501. None of the sources cited by Chief Justice Burger actually prohibited Bob Jones University's private race discrimination.[h] Isn't there something anomalous about "expanding" these constitutional and statutory authorities beyond their well-defined ambit? Moreover, Freed and Polsby argue that Chief Justice Burger's informal idea of "quasi-law" is inconsistent with the Chief Justice's strict, formalistic view of "law" in *INS v. Chadha* (Chapter 9, § 2C). Freed and Polsby believe that the world envisioned by the Chief Justice is "a manifold chock-full of law, either the law that was made by the actions of lawmakers or the law that was made by the lawmakers' nonaction. If there is any room at all in such a picture for private whim or liberty, it is not apparent where." Is this a fair statement of Chief Justice Burger's position? How can the Chief Justice justify his use of public policy?

Note that the Supreme Court sometimes refers to subsequent statutory developments in deciding cases — as it did in *Moragne* (Chapter 6, § 1). For other examples of the Court's willingness to extrapolate general public policy from a series of legislative enactments, see *Midlantic Nat'l Bank v. New Jersey Dep't of Envir. Prot.*, 474 U.S. 494 (1986) (reading policies of recent environmental laws into Bankruptcy Act); *Toll v. Moreno*, 458 U.S. 1 (1982) (creating general federal policy from a series of international agreements).

3. *Public Values or Public Hypocrisy?* Freed and Polsby accuse Chief Justice Burger of not being sufficiently "positivist" (i.e., following the rules written by Congress). Another kind of criticism would accuse Chief Justice Burger of being insufficiently "normativist" (i.e., making the law the "best" one can).

Bob Jones reads like a very high-minded opinion: How can we as a society subsidize segregated schools? We cannot! That sounds great, a ringing reaffirmation of *Brown v. Board of Education* in a somewhat different setting. But the reality is more complicated, and a great deal less inspiring. The Carter Administration's IRS issued regulations in 1978–79 placing burdens on schools with low minority percentages to "prove" their nondiscrimination. Congress reacted with the Ashbrook Amendment to a 1980 appropriations statute, which effectively barred the IRS from implementing the new regulations. When *Bob Jones* was decided, IRS enforcement depended heavily on "self-reporting": Institutions which admitted to race discrimination were the only ones to lose their tax exemptions. In short, only those institutions that discriminated as a matter of principle — like Bob Jones — lost their tax

---

h. Two anomalies should be noted here. First, some forms of race discrimination by private educational institutions were and are illegal under 42 U.S.C. § 1981. It is odd that Chief Justice Burger did not mention that in his survey of federal antidiscrimination laws and regulations. Second, the discrimination practiced by Bob Jones University changed in the 1970s. Before 1971, Bob Jones excluded African Americans from admission. Between 1971 and 1975 it admitted married African-American students and unmarried African Americans who had been staff members for four years or more. After 1975 it admitted unmarried African American students, but prohibited interracial marriages or dating. See Philip Heymann & Lance Leibman, *The Social Responsibilities of Lawyers: Case Studies* 139 (1988).

exemption. Institutions that deceived the IRS (or themselves) did not. Is this a "public value"?

At the same time Bob Jones was suing to recover its tax-exempt status, African-American parents were suing the IRS to enforce the nondiscrimination rule. Judge Ruth Bader Ginsburg of the D.C. Circuit wrote an opinion favorable to the parents, but the Supreme Court reversed. A year after the Court decided *Bob Jones*, it held (by a slender 5–4 majority) that these parents lacked "standing" to sue the IRS, thereby failing to satisfy the Court's "case or controversy" requirement. *Allen v. Wright*, 468 U.S. 737 (1984). The grudging approach to standing taken in *Allen* is an ironic contrast to the expansive approach to the antidiscrimination principle taken in *Bob Jones*. The contrast is all the more striking when it is noted that there were significant justiciability problems in *Bob Jones* itself. While *Bob Jones* was pending on appeal to the Supreme Court, the Reagan Administration switched sides and announced that it agreed with Bob Jones and wanted to change the regulation back to its pre-1970 status. Since the two parties in *Bob Jones University v. United States* both agreed that Bob Jones should be exempt, there was under most conventional readings of the Court's precedents no "case or controversy": the case was moot. But the Court kept it alive by appointing William Coleman, a prominent Washington attorney and former Secretary of Transportation in the Ford Administration, "to brief and argue this case, as *amicus curiae*, in support of the judgments below." See 456 U.S. 922 (1982) (order of Court). And Coleman, who represented neither party, won the case!

After 1984, the IRS was left with few incentives to enforce *Bob Jones*: Congress in the Ashbrook Amendment had signaled that it didn't want vigorous enforcement, President Reagan had formally abandoned the policy until it was forced back upon him by the Supreme Court, and private citizens who might object to the virtual abandonment of the policy (such as African-American parents) were not easily able to get into court (while any segregated school that loses its exemption of course has standing to sue the IRS). Is this a scenario likely to promote "public values"?

NOTE ON POST-ENACTMENT ACQUIESCENCE AND "LAW AS EQUILIBRIUM"

In Chapter 7, § 3B3, we suggested that one way to think about law is that it is the result of the equilibrium of institutional forces, rather than the result of formal deduction from first premises. From this perspective, an important issue in *Bob Jones* was how clear the practical equilibrium was in the early 1980s on the question whether the federal government should indirectly support racially segregated schools through tax preferences. Even if the IRS had taken a bold step a decade earlier, the lower courts had ratified it; if by 1980 the Congress and the executive branch were also settled in their support of that policy as well, then that policy is "law" in a very practical way (none of the three federal branches of government would change it) that should be apparent to such schools. When the Reagan Administration switched positions from that taken by the Nixon, Ford, and Carter Administrations, it was, under this perspective, changing the law, not returning the law to its "true" state, and therefore should have been allowed to do that only with the approval of Congress. The Court in *Bob Jones* recognized this practical reality and stabilized the law around its equilibrium point, leaving the Reagan Administration the option of seeking congressional authorization for reviving tax preferences for segregated schools. Is this a persuasive way to justify *Bob Jones*? You might want to apply a similar idea to the FDA Tobacco Case and the Court's recent cutbacks on the Army Corps' wetlands regulations in *Solid Waste* and *Rapanos*.[i]

Even if this explains *Bob Jones*, and even if you find it a good justification for the decision, this perspective leaves the Court a lot of room in which to affect the political balance, especially during periods of divided government when it is particularly hard for Congress to override the Court. An example is *Central Bank of Denver N.A. v. First Interstate Bank of Denver N.A.*, 511 U.S. 164 (1994). Justice Kennedy's majority opinion held that an action could not be brought alleging that defendant aided and abetted a violation of § 10(b) of the Securities Exchange Act of 1934, which prohibits securities fraud. In our judgment, this outcome upset a longstanding equilibrium to the contrary. *All* eleven federal courts of appeals that had considered the question had recognized a cause of action against aiders and abettors. Petitioner had asked the Court to address questions, such as the *mens rea* standard for aider and abettor liability, that also assumed that such a private right of action existed.

The Court *sua sponte* requested the parties to address the question whether the aiding and abetting action existed at all. Justice Kennedy's opinion stressed the plain meaning of § 10(b), which does not mention aiding and abetting liability. In dissent, Justice Stevens argued (1) that the majority had, in effect, engaged in "bait and switch" tactics (our term, not his) by applying the textualist interpretative approach to an old statute adopted by Congress in an era in which courts routinely elaborated upon rights of action, (2) that the majority had rejected a settled interpretation of law in terms of both judicial and administrative construction, which should be the province of Congress, not the Court, and (3) that actions of Congress since 1934 indicated congressional knowledge and approval of the implied right of action. One might add that, in light of this consensus, had a lawyer in the mid- to late-1980s informed Central Bank that it could *not* have been sued as an aider and abettor under § 10(b), that lawyer would have committed malpractice. (Recall that the certiorari petition filed by the lawyers for Central Bank did not even raise the question Justice Kennedy ultimately decided in Central Bank's favor.)

Problems on the Use of Legislative History

Problem 8–7. In 1975, Clive Michael Boutilier, a citizen of Canada, is excluded from the United States by the Immigration and Naturalization Service (INS), based upon a report by the Public Health Service (PHS) that Boutilier

---

i. *Solid Waste* (2001) and *Rapanos* (2006) were both handed down when the Republican Party controlled the Presidency, the House, and the Senate. After *Rapanos*, the Army Corps, under strong pressure from farmers, ranchers, mining companies, and the like, issued new wetlands regulations that cut back on the prior protections.

has had sex with other men. The PHS and INS believe that Boutilier's homosexual activities require them to exclude him, based upon the immigration law's requirement excluding from admission into this country "[a]liens afflicted with psychopathic personality, epilepsy, or a mental defect." 8 U.S.C. § 1182(a)(4) (repealed in 1990). Boutilier takes his case to the Supreme Court, challenging his exclusion on the ground that medical affidavits submitted to the PHS indicated he was mentally healthy and not afflicted with "psychopathic personality" or the other listed disabilities. The PHS and INS admit that the exclusion was based solely on Boutilier's homosexual activities.

The government argues that Congress' intent when it enacted the immigration law in 1952 was to exclude "homosexuals" generally. The PHS observes that the American Psychiatric Association's *Diagnostic and Statistical Manual: Mental Disorders* 38–39 (1952), then characterized "homosexuality" as a "sociopathic personality disturbance." Based upon this medical understanding, the PHS drafted the "psychopathic personality" exclusion in 1952, which it represented to House and Senate committees as including "homosexuality." Committee reports for both chambers relied on the PHS' representations to say that "psychopathic personality" was "sufficiently broad to provide for the exclusion of homosexuals and sex perverts." S. Rep. No. 1137, 82d Cong., 2d Sess. 9 (1952); accord, H.R. Rep. No. 1365, 82d Cong., 2d Sess. 42–48 (1952). No one in Congress disputed this characterization.

Boutilier argues, in response, that the APA has abandoned its prior characterization of homosexuality and deleted it as a pathology in the 1973 edition of its manual. Especially in light of an emerging medical consensus that homosexuality is not a mental illness, Boutilier argues that the vague statutory term "psychopathic personality" is not precise enough to justify his exclusion. As to the legislative history, Boutilier observes that the original Senate bill excluded "homosexuals or sex perverts"; that language was dropped in favor of the PHS' term "psychopathic personality." Because Congress declined to exclude all "homosexuals," the Court should not bend the vague statute in that direction. And, besides, Boutilier himself is not "homosexual," but "bisexual" in orientation and conduct.

How would the Supreme Court rule on Boutilier's appeal? See *Boutilier v. INS*, 363 F.2d 488 (2d Cir. 1966), *aff'd*, 387 U.S. 118 (1967). How would a "new textualist" vote? See William Eskridge, Jr., *Gadamer/Statutory Interpretation*, 90 Colum. L. Rev. 609 (1990).

Problem 8–8. Same facts as Problem 8–7, but assume further: In the early 1960s, a circuit court had accepted "the statute is too vague to cover 'homosexuals'" argument that we attributed to Boutilier. Congress immediately amended the exclusion to reach "[a]liens afflicted with psychopathic personality, *or sexual deviation*, or a mental defect" (new language emphasized). The committee reports establish that this amendment was intended to override the circuit court decision, on the ground that the decision had misconstrued the 1952 Congress' intent (relying on the PHS' representations) that the statutory exclusion "would encompass homosexuals and sex perverts." S. Rep. No. 748, 89th Cong., 1st Sess. 18 (1965). "To remove any doubt the Committee has specifically included the term 'sexual deviation' as a ground of exclusion in this bill." *Id.* at 19. If Boutilier had been excluded under this amended statute, is there any way the Court can avoid his exclusion? Compare *In re Longstaff*, 716 F.2d 1439 (5th Cir. 1983), with *Hill v. INS*, 714 F.2d 1470 (9th Cir. 1983).

C. INTERPRETATION IN LIGHT OF OTHER STATUTES

"Statutory interpretation is a holistic endeavor," so that a provision "that may seem ambiguous in isolation is often clarified by" the greater consistency of one interpretation with "the rest of the law." *United Savings Ass'n of Texas v. Timbers of Inwood Forest Assocs.*, 484 U.S. 365, 371 (1988). See *West Virginia Univ. Hosp. v. Casey* (Chapter 7, § 3A), which interpreted one statute authorizing prevailing parties to recover attorney's fees by examining the text of many other such statutes. There are several reasons an interpreter might consider other statutes, and each is associated with a statutory interpretation canon or doctrine:

- *the in pari materia rule:* other statutes might use the same terminology or address the same issue as the statute being interpreted (Subpart 1);

- *modeled or borrowed statute rule*: another statute might have been the template from which the statute in issue was designed (Subpart 2),

- *presumption against implied repeals*: there might be a later statute possibly changing the implications of the statute being interpreted (Subpart 3).

Note that the first two precepts are weaker versions of the rule that a word used several times in a statute is strongly presumed to have the same meaning every time it is used. See § 1A of this chapter and the debate in *Sweet Home*. The third precept is more complex, for it raises the possibility that statutes enacted at different times will be inconsistent with one another. How should interpreters figure out what law to apply when different statutes press in different directions? This conundrum vexed Judge Norris's two opinions in *Montana Wilderness, supra*. Subpart 3 will explore several different ways to reconcile apparently clashing statutes.

1. *Similar Statutes (the In Pari Materia Rule)*

CARTLEDGE v. MILLER
United States District Court, Southern District of New York, 1978
457 F.Supp. 1146

WEINFELD, DISTRICT JUDGE.

This case involves the construction of the provisions of the Employee Retirement Income Security Act of 1974 ("ERISA") which prohibit the assignment or alienation of employees' pension benefits and thereby exempt such benefits from attachment or garnishment by creditors. The issue presented is whether there exists an implied exception to these "anti-assignment or alienation" provisions with respect to orders for the support of a wife and dependent children issued by a state court pursuant to statutory authority. Defendants Rockland County (New York) and the Rockland County Support Collection Unit have obtained a state court order garnishing the pension of George Allen Cozart in order to fulfill support obligations and arrears owed to his wife, defendant Vivian Cozart. Also named as a defendant is the Family Court Judge who issued the order. Plaintiffs, members of the Pension Plan Committee created under the Pension Agreement between Clevepak Corporation and the United Paperworkers International Union (the "Pension Committee"), bring this action to enjoin the enforcement of the state court order on the ground that such enforcement would violate ERISA. Finding that ERISA's anti-assignment or alienation provisions do not preclude the execution of validly issued court orders enforcing family support rights, this Court denies the injunction and dismisses the action upon the merits.

[George Cozart was ordered in 1958 to make support payments to his estranged wife, Vivian. By 1965, however, his chronic failure to make support payments led to his incarceration for contempt of court. In 1967, still in arrears, his wages were attached in part to pay $35 per week to support Vivian and the dependent children. Still, the arrearage increased (to over $5,000 by the time he retired in 1977). In 1977 the assignee of Vivian's support rights sued George for the debt and sought attachment of his pension, regulated by ERISA — but the garnishee argued that the attachment would violate ERISA's mandate that "benefits provided under the [pension] plan may not be assigned or alienated." I.R.C. § 401(a)(13), 26 U.S.C. § 401(a)(13) (1976); ERISA § 206(d)(1), 29 U.S.C. § 1056(d)(1) (1976).]

Finding and exercising jurisdiction, the Court considers the merits of plaintiff's complaint, which asserts that the attachment of George Cozart's pension to fulfill his support obligations is an invalid "assignment or alienation" under ERISA. Plaintiff's contention is based upon a literal and strict reading of that section to exempt pension benefits from any and every levy, garnishment, or attachment. So read, plaintiff may be correct, but, "[o]n the other hand, it is a commonplace that a literal interpretation of the words of a statute is not always a safe guide to its meaning" and should be "disregarded when it defeats the manifest purpose of the statute as a whole." Thus defendants argue that an exception to the exemption embodied in ERISA's anti-assignment or alienation provisions must be implied in order to secure enforcement of Cozart's obligations to support his dependents.

The anti-assignment or alienation sections of ERISA have been authoritatively interpreted to preclude "[a]ny direct or indirect arrangement (whether revocable or irrevocable) whereby a party acquires from a participant or beneficiary a right or interest enforceable against the plan in, or to, all or any part of a plan benefit payment which is, or may become, payable to the participant or beneficiary."[39] And Congress intended that ERISA's provisions would "supersede any and all State laws insofar as they may * * * relate to any employee benefit plan."[40] These generalized proscriptions, however, are not

---

39.   Treas.Reg. § 1.401(a)–13(c)(1)(ii), *reported in* 43 Fed.Reg. 6942 (1978). The Internal Revenue Service's interpretation, always entitled to deference, finds support in the legislative history of ERISA. H.R.Conf.Rep. No. 93–1280, 93d Cong., 2d Sess. (1974) (for purposes of ERISA's anti-assignment or alienation provisions, "a garnishment or levy is not to be considered a voluntary assignment").

40.   ERISA § 514(a), 29 U.S.C. § 1144(a).

sufficient to infer that Congress meant to preclude the ancient family law right of maintenance and support and the issuance of process to enforce that right.

As a fundamental principle of statutory interpretation, courts have presumed that the basic police powers of the States, particularly the regulation of domestic relations, are not superseded by federal legislation unless that was the clear and manifest purpose of Congress. An important and pervasive state law policy is to enforce the support rights of dependent spouses and children, even when they require the attachment of assets or earnings normally inalienable or unassignable under state law.[42] Consequently, the Supreme Court has held that "[u]nless positively required by direct enactment the courts should not presume a design upon the part of Congress in relieving the unfortunate debtor to make the law a means of avoiding enforcement of the obligation, moral and legal, devolved upon the husband to support his wife and to maintain and educate his children."[43]

The debates and reports on ERISA furnish little or no direction toward the precise issue: nothing contained therein suggests that the proscription against assignment or alienation was intended to include family support payments. Indeed, an overall congressional purpose not to interfere with the States' power to enforce family support obligations may be gleaned from judicial interpretation of exemption provisions in other federal statutes. Though not exactly in *pari passu*, they indicate a general congressional intent not to preclude enforcement of family support obligations. Provisions so interpreted include the exemption sections of the Social Security Act,[45] the Veterans Benefits Act,[46] and the Railway Retirement Act,[47] as well as the Bankruptcy Act's

---

42. Substantial consensus exists among the state court systems in favor of excepting support rights from such exemptions. Indeed, the New York state courts have "uniformly rejected the argument that the pension statute protects a father against his obligation to support his family." *Cogollos v. Cogollos*, 402 N.Y.S.2d 929, 930 (Sup.Ct.1978) (citing cases). The California courts have been alone in criticizing this exception [citations omitted.]

43. *Wetmore v. Markoe*, 196 U.S. 68, 77 (1904).

45. Act of Aug. 14, 1935, § 207, 49 Stat. 624, *codified at* 42 U.S.C. § 407:
The right of any person to any future payment under this subchapter shall not be transferable or assignable, at law or in equity, and none of the moneys paid or payable or rights existing under this subchapter shall be subject to execution, levy, attachment, garnishment, or other legal process, or to the operation of any bankruptcy or insolvency law.
[Citations to cases interpreting § 207 to except support payments omitted.]

46. Pub.L. No. 85–857, § 3101(a), 72 Stat. 1229 (1958), *codified at* 38 U.S.C. § 3101(a):
Payments of benefits due or to become due under any law administered by the Veterans' Administration shall not be assignable except to the extent specifically authorized by law, and such payments made to, or on account of, a beneficiary shall be exempt from taxation, shall be exempt from the claim of creditors, and shall not be liable to attachment, levy, or seizure by or under any legal or equitable process whatever, either before or after receipt by the beneficiary.
[Citations to cases interpreting § 3101 to except support payments omitted.]

47. Act of Aug. 29, 1935, § 12, 49 Stat. 973, *codified at* 45 U.S.C. § 231m:
Notwithstanding any other law of the United States, or of any State, territory, or the District of Columbia, no annuity or supplemental annuity shall be assignable or be subject to any tax or to garnishment, attachment, or other legal process under any circumstances

provision for discharge of prior obligations.[48] The rationale behind such * * * interpretations of the will of Congress was aptly summarized by Judge, later Justice, Rutledge in *Schlaefer v. Schlaefer*:[49] "[T]he usual purpose of exemptions is to relieve the person exempted from the pressure of claims hostile to his dependents' essential needs as well as his own personal ones, not to relieve him of familial obligations and destroy what may be the family's last and only security, short of public relief."

Moreover, the goals underlying ERISA support the reasoning of this common law presumption. Originally introduced in 1967, ERISA was meant "to prescribe legislative remedies for the various deficiencies existing in the private pension plan systems," primarily relating to prior abuses in plan vesting, funding, termination, and fiduciary conduct.[51] In particular, Congress was solicitous of the "continued well-being and security of millions of employees *and their dependents* [who] are directly affected by these plans."[52] Rather than intending to undermine the family law rights of dependent spouses and children, the legislature was concerned that "employees and their beneficiaries" — the entire family — be protected by ERISA.[53]

Thus the conclusion is warranted that, like the previous congressional exemptions, ERISA's anti-assignment or alienation sections were included only "to protect a person and those dependent upon him from the claim of creditors," not to insulate a breadwinner from the valid support claims of spouse and offspring. This conclusion is buttressed by the *amicus* brief submitted on behalf of the Departments of Labor and the Treasury, which are charged with enforcement and interpretation of ERISA and whose interpretation of the Act, though not controlling, is entitled to great weight. The Government takes the position, which appears reasonable and correct, that

---

whatsoever, nor shall the payment thereof be anticipated * * *.
This section has been interpreted to except support payments [citations omitted], and courts have frequently "anticipated" such payments when applicable against support obligations [citations omitted].

48. Act of July 1, 1898, ch. 541, § 17(a), 30 Stat. 550: "A discharge in bankruptcy shall release a bankrupt from all of his provable debts, whether allowable in full or in part * * *." This exemption was interpreted in *Wetmore v. Markoe*, 196 U.S. 68 (1904), to except family support payments. Congress amended the Act in 1903 to provide for such exception explicitly. * * *

49. 71 U.S.App.D.C. 350, [358], 112 F.2d 177, [185] (1940).

51. S.Rep. No. 93–127, 93d Cong., 1st Sess. (1973).

52. ERISA § 2(a), 29 U.S.C. § 1001(a) (emphasis added).

53. ERISA § 2(c), 29 U.S.C. § 1001(c) (emphasis added):
It is hereby further declared to be the policy of this Act to protect interstate commerce, the Federal taxing power, and the interests of participants in private pension plans *and their beneficiaries* by improving the equitable character and the soundness of such plans * * *.
See also ERISA § 2(b), 29 U.S.C. § 1001(b) (similar language). Although ERISA § 3(8), 29 U.S.C. § 1002(8), defines "beneficiary" more narrowly, I take the term in its broader sense when it is used in the preamble, which was a general statement of the goals of the statute, not a technical recitation.

"family support decrees were not intended to be within the scope of the anti-alienation provisions of ERISA." * * *

Postscript: In 1984, Congress amended § 256(d) to add an explicit statutory exception for (3) "qualified domestic relations orders." Pub. L. No. 98-397, 98 Stat. 1426 (1984), codified at 29 U.S.C. § 1056(d)(3). A qualified domestic relations order is "any judgment, decree, or order (including approval of a property settlement agreement) which relates to the provision of child support, alimony payments, or marital property rights to a spouse, former spouse, child, or other dependent of a participant, and is made pursuant to a State domestic relations law (including a community property law)," new § 256(d)(3)(B)(ii), and meets various procedural and drafting requirements.

LORILLARD v. PONS
Supreme Court of the United States, 1978
434 U.S. 575, 98 S.Ct. 868, 55 L.Ed.2d 40

MR. JUSTICE MARSHALL delivered the opinion of the Court.

This case presents the question whether there is a right to a jury trial in private civil actions for lost wages under the Age Discrimination in Employment Act of 1967 (ADEA or Act), 81 Stat. 602, as amended, 88 Stat. 74, 29 U.S.C. § 621 *et seq.* (1970 ed. and Supp. V). * * *

[I] The ADEA broadly prohibits arbitrary discrimination in the workplace based on age. Although the ADEA contains no provision expressly granting a right to jury trial, respondent nonetheless contends that the structure of the Act demonstrates a congressional intent to grant such a right. Alternatively, she argues that the Seventh Amendment requires that in a private action for lost wages under the ADEA, the parties must be given the option of having the case heard by a jury. We turn first to the statutory question since " 'it is a cardinal principle that this Court will first ascertain whether a construction of the statute is fairly possible by which the [constitutional] question may be avoided.' " Because we find the statutory issue dispositive, we need not address the constitutional issue.

The enforcement scheme for the statute is complex — the product of considerable attention during the legislative debates preceding passage of the Act. Several alternative proposals were considered by Congress. The Administration submitted a bill, modeled after §§ 10(c), (e) of the National Labor Relations Act, 29 U.S.C. §§ 160(c), (e), which would have granted power to the Secretary of Labor to issue cease-and-desist orders enforceable in the courts of appeals, but would not have granted a private right of action to aggrieved individuals, S. 830, H.R. 4221, 90th Cong., 1st Sess. (1967). Senator Javits introduced an alternative proposal to make discrimination based on age unlawful under the Fair Labor Standards Act (FLSA), 29 U.S.C. § 201 *et seq.*; the normal enforcement provisions of the FLSA, 29 U.S.C. § 216 *et seq.*, (1970 ed. and Supp. V), then would have been applicable, permitting suits by either the Secretary of Labor or the injured individual, S. 788, 90th Cong., 1st Sess. (1967). A third alternative that was considered would have adopted the statutory pattern of Title VII of the Civil Rights Act of 1964 and utilized the Equal Employment Opportunity Commission.

The bill that was ultimately enacted is something of a hybrid, reflecting, on the one hand, Congress' desire to use an existing statutory scheme and a bureaucracy with which employers and employees would be familiar and, on the other hand, its dissatisfaction with some elements of each of the pre-existing schemes. Pursuant to § 7(b) of the Act, 29 U.S.C. § 626(b), violations of the ADEA generally are to be treated as violations of the FLSA. "Amounts owing * * * as a result of a violation" of the ADEA are to be treated as "unpaid minimum wages or unpaid overtime compensation" under the FLSA and the rights created by the ADEA are to be "enforced in accordance with the powers, remedies and procedures" of specified sections of the FLSA.

Following the model of the FLSA, the ADEA establishes two primary enforcement mechanisms. Under the FLSA provisions incorporated in § 7(b) of the ADEA, 29 U.S.C. § 626(b), the Secretary of Labor may bring suit on behalf of an aggrieved individual for injunctive and monetary relief. 29 U.S.C. §§ 216(c), 217 (1970 ed. and Supp. V). The incorporated FLSA provisions together with § 7(c) of the ADEA, 29 U.S.C. § 626(c), in addition, authorize private civil actions for "such legal or equitable relief as will effectuate the purposes of" the ADEA. Although not required by the FLSA, prior to the initiation of any ADEA action, an individual must give notice to the Secretary of Labor of his intention to sue in order that the Secretary can attempt to eliminate the alleged unlawful practice through informal methods. § 7(d), 29 U.S.C. § 626(d). After allowing the Secretary 60 days to conciliate the alleged unlawful practice, the individual may file suit. The right of the individual to sue on his own terminates, however, if the Secretary commences an action on his behalf. § 7(c), 29 U.S.C. § 626(c).

[II] Looking first to the procedural provisions of the statute, we find a significant indication of Congress' intent in its directive that the ADEA be enforced in accordance with the "powers, remedies, and *procedures*" of the FLSA. § 7(b), 29 U.S.C. § 626(b) (emphasis added). Long before Congress enacted the ADEA, it was well established that there was a right to a jury trial in private actions pursuant to the FLSA. Indeed, every court to consider the issue had so held. Congress is presumed to be aware of an administrative or judicial interpretation of a statute and to adopt that interpretation when it re-enacts a statute without change. So too, where, as here, Congress adopts a new law incorporating sections of a prior law, Congress normally can be presumed to have had knowledge of the interpretation given to the incorporated law, at least insofar as it affects the new statute.

That presumption is particularly appropriate here since, in enacting the ADEA, Congress exhibited both a detailed knowledge of the FLSA provisions and their judicial interpretation and a willingness to depart from those provisions regarded as undesirable or inappropriate for incorporation. For example, in construing the enforcement sections of the FLSA, the courts had consistently declared that injunctive relief was not available in suits by private individuals but only in suits by the Secretary. Congress made plain its decision to follow a different course in the ADEA by expressly permitting "such * * * equitable relief as may be appropriate to effectuate the purposes of [the ADEA] including without limitation judgments compelling employment, reinstatement or promotion" "in *any* action brought to enforce" the Act. § 7(b), 29 U.S.C. § 626(b) (emphasis added). Similarly, while incorporating into the ADEA the FLSA provisions authorizing awards of liquidated damages, Congress altered the circumstances under which such awards would be available in ADEA actions by mandating that such damages be awarded only where the violation of the ADEA is willful.[8] Finally, Congress expressly declined to incorporate into the ADEA the criminal penalties established for violations of the FLSA.

This selectivity that Congress exhibited in incorporating provisions and in modifying certain FLSA practices strongly suggests that but for those changes Congress expressly made, it intended to incorporate fully the remedies and procedures of the FLSA. Senator Javits, one of the floor managers of the bill, so indicated in describing the enforcement section which became part of the Act: "The enforcement techniques provided by [the ADEA] are directly analogous to those available under the Fair Labor Standards Act; in fact [the ADEA] incorporates by reference, to the greatest extent possible, the provisions of the [FLSA]." 113 Cong. Rec. 31254 (1967).[10] And by directing that actions for lost wages under the ADEA be treated as actions for unpaid minimum wages or overtime compensation under the FLSA, § 7(b), 29 U.S.C. § 626(b), Congress dictated that the jury trial right then available to enforce that FLSA liability would also be available in private actions under the ADEA.

This inference is buttressed by an examination of the language Congress chose to describe the available remedies under the ADEA. Section 7(b), 29 U.S.C. § 626(b), empowers a court to grant "*legal* or equitable relief" and § 7(c), 29 U.S.C. § 626(c), authorizes individuals to bring actions for "*legal* or equitable relief" (emphases added). The word "legal" is a term of art: In cases in which legal relief is available and legal rights are determined, the Seventh Amendment provides a right to jury trial. "[W]here words are employed in a statute which had at the time a well-known meaning at common law or in the law of this country they are presumed to have been used in that sense unless the

---

8. By its terms, 29 U.S.C. § 216(b) requires that liquidated damages be awarded as a matter of right for violations of the FLSA. However, in response to its dissatisfaction with that judicial interpretation of the provision, Congress enacted the Portal-to-Portal Pay Act of 1947, 61 Stat. 84, which, *inter alia*, grants courts authority to deny or limit liquidated damages where the "employer shows to the satisfaction of the court that the act or omission giving rise to such action was in good faith and that he had reasonable grounds for believing that his act or omission was not a violation of" the FLSA, § 11, 29 U.S.C. § 260 (1970 ed., Supp. V). Although § 7(e) of the ADEA, 29 U.S.C. § 626(e), expressly incorporates §§ 6 and 10 of the Portal-to-Portal Pay Act, 29 U.S.C. §§ 255 and 259 (1970 ed. and Supp. V), the ADEA does not make any reference to § 11, 29 U.S.C. § 260 (1970 ed., Supp. V).

10. Senator Javits made the only specific reference in the legislative history to a jury trial. He said:

"The whole test is somewhat like the test in an accident case — did the person use reasonable care. A jury will answer yes or no. The question here is: Was the individual discriminated against solely because of his age? The alleged discrimination must be proved and the burden of proof is upon the one who would assert that that was actually the case." 113 Cong.Rec. 31255 (1967).

It is difficult to tell whether Senator Javits was referring to the issue in ADEA cases or in accident cases when he said the jury will say yes or no.

context compels to the contrary." We can infer, therefore, that by providing specifically for "legal" relief, Congress knew the significance of the term "legal," and intended that there would be a jury trial on demand to "enforc[e] * * * liability for amounts deemed to be unpaid minimum wages or unpaid overtime compensation." § 7(b), 29 U.S.C. § 626(b).

Petitioner strives to find a contrary congressional intent by comparing the ADEA with Title VII of the Civil Rights Act of 1964, 42 U.S.C. § 2000e *et seq.* (1970 ed. and Supp. V), which petitioner maintains does not provide for jury trials. We, of course, intimate no view as to whether a jury trial is available under Title VII as a matter of either statutory or constitutional right. However, after examining the provisions of Title VII, we find petitioner's argument by analogy to Title VII unavailing. There are important similarities between the two statutes, to be sure, both in their aims — the elimination of discrimination from the workplace — and in their substantive prohibitions. In fact, the prohibitions of the ADEA were derived *in haec verba* from Title VII.[12] But in deciding whether a statutory right to jury trial exists, it is the remedial and procedural provisions of the two laws that are crucial and there we find significant differences.

Looking first to the statutory language defining the relief available, we note that Congress specifically provided for both "legal or equitable relief" in the ADEA, but did not authorize "legal" relief in so many words under Title VII. Compare § 7(b), 29 U.S.C. § 626(b), with 42 U.S.C. § 2000e–5(g) (1970 ed., Supp. V). Similarly, the ADEA incorporates the FLSA provision that employers "shall be liable" for amounts deemed unpaid minimum wages or overtime compensation, while under Title VII, the availability of backpay is a matter of equitable discretion. Finally, rather than adopting the procedures of Title VII for ADEA actions, Congress rejected that course in favor of incorporating the FLSA procedures even while adopting Title VII's substantive prohibitions. Thus, even if petitioner is correct that Congress did not intend there to be jury trials under Title VII, that fact sheds no light on congressional intent under the ADEA. Petitioner's reliance on Title VII, therefore, is misplaced. * * * [*Affirmed.*]

NOTES ON *CARTLEDGE, LORILLARD,* AND
REASONING FROM STATUTES IN PARI MATERIA

1. *Reasoning from One Statute to Another: What If There Are Several Statutory Analogies?* Both Judge Weinfeld in *Cartledge* and Justice Marshall in *Lorillard* rely on the interpretational history of similar statutes to justify their interpretations. Why do they consider this persuasive? Because Congress really and truly "intended" to incorporate all prior interpretations of similar statutes into a new statute? Because the other interpretations somehow

---

12. Title VII with respect to race, color, religion, sex, or national origin, and the ADEA with respect to age make it unlawful for an employer "to fail or refuse to hire or to discharge any individual," or otherwise to "discriminate against any individual with respect to his compensation, terms, conditions, or privileges of employment," on any of those bases. [Citing provisions of each statute.]

represent "wise" public policy? Because the interpretational history of these other statutes represents a reasoned policy context which ought to affect the evolution of a related statute, so as to give greater coherence to the law? See *Moragne v. States Marine Lines* (Chapter 6, § 1).

Even if justified in general, this approach has its limitations. One is that there may be more than one statute in pari materia, and the statutes may have been interpreted differently. E.g., *Ledbetter v. Goodyear Tire & Rubber Corp.*, 127 S.Ct. 2162 (2007), discussed in Note 2. Or there may be several "similar" statutes, but none quite the same as the statute being interpreted. Thus, in *Lorillard*, the Supreme Court rejected the proposed analogy with Title VII. Are the Court's reasons persuasive? Why should an alleged victim of age discrimination get a jury trial (ADEA), when an alleged victim of sex discrimination (Title VII) apparently does not get one?[j]

In 1974, Congress amended the ADEA to permit age discrimination lawsuits against the federal government. The enforcement provision says: "Any person aggrieved may bring a civil action in any Federal district court of competent jurisdiction for such legal or equitable relief as will effectuate the purposes of this Act." ADEA § 15(c), 29 U.S.C. § 633a(c). The Supreme Court held that § 15(c), unlike § 7, affords no jury trial right, finding the analogy to Title VII closer than the analogy to the FLSA. *Lehman v. Nakshian*, 453 U.S. 156 (1981). Is this consistent with *Lorillard*, upon which the four dissenting Justices relied? The majority responded that *Lorillard* is distinguishable (how?), the federal government is subject to jury trials only if it explicitly permits them (why?), and Congress in 1978 amended § 7(c) explicitly to allow ADEA jury trials but made no comparable amendment to § 15(c) (so what?).

2. *Different Statutes, Different Policies.* A second limitation on reasoning from one statute to another is that the new statute may embody policies or compromises subtly different from those in the similar statutes — if for no other reason than the different political context of the later statute. For example, the Supreme Court has interpreted Title VI of the Civil Rights Act of 1964 (prohibiting discrimination "under any program or activity receiving Federal financial assistance") to reach only instances of intentional discrimination. See *Guardians Ass'n v. Civil Serv. Comm'n of New York City*, 463 U.S. 582 (1983). Yet the Court in *Alexander v. Choate*, 469 U.S. 287, 294–99 (1985), was unwilling to limit § 504 of the Rehabilitation Act of 1973 (prohibiting discrimination or exclusion of any "qualified handicapped individual" "under any program or activity receiving Federal financial assistance") to instances of intentional discrimination. In dictum, the Court suggested that by 1973 national policy was more concerned with "disparate impact" discrimination than with the "intentional" discrimination that had been a focal point in 1964. *Id.* at 294–95 n.11. Ergo, the Court's interpretation of Title VI was not a helpful guide in its interpretation of § 504. Does this temporal dimension (evolving policy) help explain the result in *Lorillard*? See

---

j. Congress eliminated this disparity when it provided for jury trials in Title VII cases in the Civil Rights Act of 1991. See *Landgraf v. USI Film* (Chapter 6, § 3).

also *Webb v. Board of Ed. of Dyer County*, 471 U.S. 234 (1985) (rejecting analogy of Title VII attorney's fees provision as guide for interpreting 42 U.S.C. § 1988, because of different statutory schemes).

In *Ledbetter v. Goodyear Tire & Rubber Co.*, 127 S.Ct. 2162 (2007), the Supreme Court strictly enforced the limitations period imposed by Title VII on plaintiffs bringing pay discrimination complaints to the EEOC. Under the Court's approach, an employee subjected to intentional race or sex discrimination in pay has to file a complaint with the EEOC soon after the illegal pay differential first shows up (and before many plaintiffs are even aware of the discrimination, because they do not know how much everyone else is paid). Ledbetter argued that the Court has allowed equitable tolling of Equal Pay Act claims, a statutory analogy the Court rejected because EPA claims do not have to be brought before the EEOC first. The different statutory schemes required different interpretations of the limitations provisions. Indeed, the Court found a better analogy in the NLRA, also enforced by an agency. The Court had previously enforced that policy with similar strictness as it applied in *Ledbetter*.

3. *The Possibility of Compromise.* A third limitation on reasoning from one statute to another is that it may undermine deliberative legislative compromises. Recall Judge Weinfeld's analysis of judge-created exceptions to anti-assignment and alienation provisions in four different federal statutes (see footnotes 45–48). Note that Congress at least once responded to the judicially created exceptions by codifying them in the statute, as Judge Weinfeld pointed out in footnote 48. If Congress in the past has been willing to put such an exception in the statute, why did it not do the same in ERISA? Why should courts continue to do Congress' drafting work? In 1974, moreover, Congress made provision for a limited exception for alimony and support payments, 42 U.S.C. § 659(a) (1988):

> Notwithstanding any other provision of law, * * * moneys (the entitlement to which is based upon remuneration for employment) due from, or payable by, the United States * * * to any individual * * * shall be subject * * * to legal process brought for the enforcement * * * of his legal obligations to provide child support or make alimony payments.

Does this codification support or undermine Judge Weinfeld's position? As our postscript to *Cartledge* indicates, Congress subsequently codified Judge Weinfeld's result through an explicit ERISA amendment. How does Congress's ability to revisit ERISA cut as to the interpretive issue before Judge Weinfeld? If such an issue arose again today, might today's more textualist Court reason that judges should simply apply § 256(d)(1) as written, and leave it to Congress to create exceptions?

Consider also *Ridgway v. Ridgway*, 454 U.S. 46 (1981). Richard Ridgway, a career sergeant in the U.S. Army, was granted a divorce from his wife April in 1977. The state divorce decree required Richard to keep in force then-existing life insurance policies for the benefit of the three children. Richard remarried and changed the beneficiary to his second wife, Donna, contrary to the divorce decree. When he died, both April and Donna claimed the proceeds to the life insurance — April relying on state law and Donna relying on the Servicemen's Group Life Insurance Act of 1965, 79 Stat. 880, codified as amended at 38 U.S.C. § 765 *et seq.* (1982). The Act provides comprehensive life insurance for members of the armed services, including Richard, and stipulates that the service person can designate the beneficiary, *id.* § 770(a), and that payment of insurance proceeds is not subject to attachment or "any legal or equitable process whatever." *Id.* § 770(g). The Supreme Court held that § 770(a) & (g) preempts state property decrees for support and alimony pursuant to a divorce. The Act's policy that the statutory benefits actually reach the designated beneficiary and that the insurance be operated on a national level clashes with state family law and supersedes it. See also *Hisquierdo v. Hisquierdo*, 439 U.S. 572, 584 (1979).

Three Justices dissented. Justice Stevens' dissenting opinion relied heavily on *Schlaefer v. Schlaefer*, the same case which Judge Weinfeld considered persuasive in *Cartledge*, and on the equitable argument that Richard's designation of Donna as his beneficiary violated his moral duty to support his children. Surely Congress would not have intended such a scandalous result, argued the dissenters. (What canine metaphor is apt here?) The majority in *Ridgway* responded that "[a] result of this kind, of course, may be avoided if Congress chooses to avoid it," but Congress has not so chosen. Does the *Ridgway* case undermine the cogency of Judge Weinfeld's opinion in *Cartledge*? Compare *Rose v. Rose,* 481 U.S. 619 (1987).

2. *The Modeled or Borrowed Statute Rule*

Reasoning from statutes in pari materia (similar statutes) generally has greater force when the statutes are all in the same jurisdiction. Indeed, sometimes, as *Lorillard* indicates, such statutes have a familial relationship because the drafting of a newer statute (e.g., the ADEA) was modeled on existing statutes in the same jurisdiction (e.g., the FLSA, Title VII). As *Lorillard* exemplifies, courts routinely assume that, unless there are strong indications to the contrary, the newer statute should be interpreted consistently with the older statutes upon which it was modeled.

Borrowed statutes are those adapted by one jurisdiction from another jurisdiction. For example, if West Virginia were to enact a pension regulation statute, it might "borrow" the language used in ERISA's anti-alienation and assignment provision or that used in a similar statute of another state. See Frank Horack, Jr., *The Common Law of Legislation*, 23 Iowa L. Rev. 41 (1937) (one legislature will copy a successful prior statute from another jurisdiction, following a process Horack calls "stare de statute"). The issues of interpretation for borrowed statutes are subtly different from those concerning modeled statutes, in large part because the policies followed in one jurisdiction may be different from those followed in the original jurisdiction.

ZERBE v. STATE
Supreme Court of Alaska, 1978
578 P.2d 597

CONNOR, JUSTICE.

This appeal requires us to interpret those provisions of Alaska's government claims statute[1] which deal with claims which arise out of false imprisonment. Appellant's claim for damages against the state was dismissed by the trial court on the ground that it was barred by statute.

Stephen Zerbe's difficulties began when he was cited for driving an overweight truck. Zerbe's employer succeeded in having the complaint against Zerbe dismissed by informing the district attorney that the street on which Zerbe was driving was not a public street. Relying on the dismissal, Zerbe did not appear at the arraignment. An acting district judge who apparently had no knowledge that the complaint had been dismissed, issued a bench warrant for Zerbe's arrest. The bench warrant was served on Zerbe approximately five months later when Zerbe went to the police department to apply for a chauffeur's license.

Zerbe was taken to jail, and the guards apparently did not allow him to make any phone calls. As a result, Zerbe remained in custody for nine hours before he was able to post bail. Zerbe hired a lawyer and was successful in having the bench warrant quashed on grounds of the earlier dismissal. He then filed suit against the state, alleging that state employees were negligent in failing to properly inform the judge of the dismissal, and that jail personnel were negligent in failing to allow Zerbe to make a phone call to obtain bail.

Although the complaint was couched in terms of negligence, the state argued that plaintiff's cause of action arose out of false arrest and false imprisonment, and was, therefore, barred by AS 09.50.250.

The superior court, relying principally on federal cases interpreting similar language in the Federal Tort Claims Act (28 U.S.C. § 2680(h)), ruled that the gravamen of plaintiff's claim was "an improper arrest or imprisonment," and that Zerbe's claim was barred by the statute. This appeal followed.

Zerbe contends that the trial court erred in construing the complaint as alleging false arrest and false imprisonment, rather than common law negligence. Zerbe also challenges the constitutionality of Alaska's government claims statute. Because of our disposition of the first of appellant's points on appeal, we need not reach the constitutional question.

---

1. AS 09.50.250 provides in pertinent part as follows:

"*Actionable claims against the state.* A person or corporation having a contract, quasi-contract, or tort claim against the state may bring an action against the state in the superior court. * * * However, no action may be brought under this section if the claim * * *

(3) arises out of assault, battery, false imprisonment, false arrest, malicious prosecution, abuse of process, libel, slander, misrepresentation, deceit, or interference with contract rights."

As there is no Alaska case law interpreting the statute here in question, we turn for guidance to federal cases construing the similar federal provisions.[2] There are numerous federal cases which have interpreted 28 U.S.C. § 2680(h), the provision which exempts the federal government from any liability for

"[a]ny claim arising out of assault, battery, false imprisonment, false arrest, malicious prosecution, abuse of process, libel, slander, misrepresentation, deceit, or interference with contract rights. * * * "

Three federal cases squarely support the state's contention that although the complaint is drafted in terms of negligence, it actually is a claim *arising out of* false imprisonment and false arrest. * * *

The state's strongest authority comes from *Duenges v. United States*, 114 F.Supp. 751 (S.D.N.Y. 1953), in which the plaintiff had been arrested and imprisoned for desertion from the army when, in fact, he had been honorably discharged. Plaintiff's complaint, like Zerbe's, alleged that the government had negligently maintained its records, resulting in injuries to the plaintiff including loss of freedom, humiliation, fear, embarrassment, mental anguish, and loss of earnings. In granting the government's motion to dismiss, the court stated that

"* * * the Government's negligence could become an actionable wrong only upon the event of resulting injury. The injuries alleged derive from a false arrest and imprisonment. In an action of negligence 'damage is of the very gist and essence of the plaintiff's cause.' Here, false arrest and imprisonment are of the very gist and essence of the plaintiff's cause. Section 2680(h) of 28 U.S.C. specifically excludes from the provisions of the Federal Tort Claims Act claims 'arising out of * * * false imprisonment [and] false arrest * * *.' This suit arises out of false imprisonment and false arrest within the meaning of that section, and consequently, it does not come within the scope of the Act."

It should be noted that all three of these cases were disposed of in short opinions without any detailed analysis or discussion of policy considerations. Some of the other federal cases cited in support of the state's position are reasoned in greater depth, yet they appear to be distinguishable on their facts from the case at bar.

Although the federal cases barring recovery under § 2680(h) are in the numerical majority, a number of federal courts have held for the plaintiff in situations similar to Zerbe's. We find this line of cases to be the better reasoned. * * *

---

2. *See State v. Abbott*, 498 P.2d 712, 717 (Alaska 1972). Appellant correctly notes that the federal tort claims statute has been amended so that claims arising out of false arrest or false imprisonment are not barred if the claim arises from acts or omissions of investigative or law enforcement officers of the United States government. Appellant infers that under the statute as amended, claims such as his would be allowed. The state disputes this point. In any event, Alaska's statute has not been amended in accordance with the changed federal statute, and none of the federal cases cited by the parties to this appeal deals with the statute as amended. Therefore, the federal statute is quoted as it read before amendment. That Congress chose to amend this statute recently does not shed much light on the case at bar.

The most persuasive authority in support of plaintiff's position comes from *Quinones v. United States*, 492 F.2d 1269 (3d Cir. 1974). Quinones alleged that the government's failure to use due care in maintaining his personnel records had resulted in damage to his reputation. The district court dismissed the complaint because defamation was excluded from the Federal Tort Claims Act by § 2680(h). The Third Circuit reversed, finding that although the resulting harm was defamation, the plaintiff's cause of action sounded in negligence. The court distinguished the two torts by showing that defamation requires malice, whereas negligence merely requires duty, breach, proximate and actual cause, and damage. The court stated that one civil remedy does not preempt another, and added that "[i]t is not the publication of the incorrect employment history and record that serves as the foundation of plaintiff's complaint; it is the method in which the defendant maintained the record of his employment that is being criticized."

We adopt the reasoning of the Third Circuit in the *Quinones* case, and hold that it was negligent record keeping, rather than false imprisonment, which caused Zerbe's injuries. Zerbe's suit is therefore not barred by the false imprisonment exception to Alaska's government claims statute, but instead ought to have been treated in the same manner as any other negligence case against the state.[6]

Today, when various branches of government collect and keep copious records concerning numerous aspects of the lives of ordinary citizens, we are unwilling to deny recourse to those hapless people whose lives are disrupted because of careless record keeping or poorly programmed computers. We see no justification for immunizing the government from the damaging consequences of its clerical employees' failure to exercise due care.

Reversed and Remanded.

Opinion On Petition for Rehearing [583 P.2d 845]

CONNOR, JUSTICE.

The State of Alaska petitions for rehearing on the ground that we have overlooked, failed to consider, or misconceived a controlling principle or proposition of law. It asserts that in the opinion which we handed down in this case we did not consider the principle that when a statute is adopted from another jurisdiction it is presumed that interpretations of that statute by courts of that jurisdiction are also adopted with it.

---

6. This holding is consistent with previous decisions in which we have narrowly construed other exceptions to Alaska's government claims statute; *e.g., State v. Abbott*, 498 P.2d 712 (Alaska 1972) (narrowly construing AS 09.50.250(1), the discretionary state function exception); *State v. Stanley*, 506 P.2d 1284, 1291 (Alaska 1973) (negligence on the part of government employees "does not rise to the 'level of governmental policy decisions' to which the discretionary function immunity from suit applies.") *See also* Professor Van Alstyne's commentary in *California Government Tort Liability Supplement* § 5.63, at 24–25 (C.E.B.1967), quoted in *Sullivan v. County of Los Angeles*, 527 P.2d 865, 872 (Cal. 1974).

The state asserts that such cases as *Duenges v. United States*, 114 F.Supp. 751 (S.D.N.Y.1953), *Klein v. United States*, 167 F.Supp. 410 (E.D.N.Y.1958), *aff'd per curiam*, 268 F.2d 63 (2d Cir. 1959), and *United States v. Neustadt*, 366 U.S. 696 (1961), which interpret the federal act from which our own law was drawn, reach a result contrary to that which we reached in the case at bar. Therefore, it is urged, the case at bar was wrongly decided.

The state seeks to support its position by reference to our recent opinion in *Menard v. State*, 578 P.2d 966 (Alaska 1978), in which we resorted for guidance to the interpretations of our criminal assault statute by the Oregon Supreme Court prior to the statute's adoption as the law of Alaska. The state's petition then asserts that our failure to follow the doctrine concerning prior interpretations of adopted statutes results in "legal chaos," and that in determining Alaska law "predictions must be based on a 'result analysis' of decisions in this jurisdiction alone, presumably by ascertaining the trend of those decisions."

Thus, if the argument presented in the petition for rehearing is correct, this court has indulged in an indefensible interpretation of the Alaska tort claims act, and has issued two irreconcilable opinions on the same day.

The state's entire argument is built upon an erroneous major premise.

When a statute is adopted from another jurisdiction, it is not the interpretative decisions of all courts of that jurisdiction which are presumed to be adopted with the statute. As we have taken such pains to say in our earlier opinions, it is only the settled interpretations of the highest court of the other jurisdiction which are presumptively intended by the lawmaker to be adopted with the statute.

The cases of *Duenges v. United States, supra*, and *Klein v. United States, supra*, most certainly were not decisions of the sort which come within the presumption. It would be a curious, indeed irrational, doctrine under which we would somehow be hobbled indefinitely by the decisions of federal trial courts, rendered some years ago, in another part of the country. To our knowledge, no court has ever deemed itself so bound. The case of *United States v. Neustadt, supra*, to which the state alludes, concerns a different question than that presented in the case at bar. Because it is distinguishable it cannot come within the principle of adoptive construction.

It should be noted that the presumption is, in any event, not conclusive but merely a rule based on convenience and principles of *stare decisis*, whereby things once decided need not constantly be redetermined.

The rule is not invariably followed. It is conceivable, indeed likely, that if a precedent underlying an adopted statute were no longer vital or were poorly reasoned, we would decline to follow it. To do otherwise would represent mechanical jurisprudence of the worst kind.

Based as it is upon an untenable thesis, the petition for rehearing is devoid of merit, and it must be denied.

NOTE ON *ZERBE* AND
INTERPRETATION OF BORROWED STATUTES

Four Justices of the U.S. Supreme Court rejected the *Zerbe* reading of § 2680(h) in *United States v. Shearer*, 473 U.S. 52 (1985). Vernon Shearer was kidnapped and murdered by a serviceman who had been previously convicted of manslaughter. Shearer's administratrix sued the government for negligent supervision of the murderer. Chief Justice Burger's opinion found two reasons why the lawsuit could not be maintained. The first was that § 2680(h) barred suit: any injury flowing from intentional torts committed by federal employees is excluded, even if a claim against the government can be framed in terms of negligence. "Section 2680(h) does not merely bar claims *for* assault or battery; in sweeping language it excludes any claim *arising out of* assault or battery." Four Justices joined this part of the opinion; four Justices joined only the second part, involving a judge-created exception to the FTCA for military activity; one Justice did not participate. Assume that Chief Justice Burger's interpretation had been accepted by the Court. Should the Alaska Supreme Court reconsider *Zerbe*?

3. *Statutory Clashes — The Rule Against Implied Repeals*

Not only similar statutes in the same jurisdiction and statutes copied from other jurisdictions, but also subsequent statutes in the same jurisdiction may be sources of guidance concerning the appropriate interpretation of a statute. The second opinion in *Montana Wilderness* (§ 2B5 of this chapter) is an example of how a similar, subsequently enacted statute may sometimes shed light on a prior statutory provision. In *Babbitt v. Sweet Home* (§ 1A of this chapter), the Court was persuaded to read a provision of the Endangered Species Act of 1973 broadly, in part to assure its consistency with a 1982 amendment to the law.

Both opinions in *Montana Wilderness* point to a clash between the Alaska Lands Act (as applied nationwide in the second opinion) and the Wilderness Act. How do judges resolve apparently conflicting statutes? Obviously, if the more recent statute expressly provides that it controls, the issue is easy. Similarly, if the newer statute contains a savings clause, which states that it does not alter existing law, the older statute controls. Unfortunately, most of the time the more recent statute says nothing on this question. Typically, courts do their best to reconcile the statutes, based on the presumption of whole-code coherence. As the next case demonstrates, there is a longstanding canon in this area, which disfavors *implied repeals*.[k]

---

k. For an excellent analysis of this canon, see Karen Petroski, *Retheorizing the Presumption Against Implied Repeals*, 92 Cal. L. Rev. 487 (2004) (student comment).

MORTON v. MANCARI
Supreme Court of the United States, 1974
417 U.S. 535, 94 S.Ct. 2474, 41 L.Ed.2d 290

MR. JUSTICE BLACKMUN delivered the opinion of the Court.

The Indian Reorganization Act of 1934, also known as the Wheeler-Howard Act, 48 Stat. 984, 25 U.S.C. § 461 *et seq.*, accords an employment preference for qualified Indians in the Bureau of Indian Affairs (BIA or Bureau). Appellees, non-Indian BIA employees, challenged this preference as contrary to the anti-discrimination provisions of the Equal Employment Opportunity Act of 1972, 86 Stat. 103, 42 U.S.C. § 2000e et seq. (1970 ed., Supp. II), and as violative of the Due Process Clause of the Fifth Amendment. * * *

[I] Section 12 of the Indian Reorganization Act, 48 Stat. 986, 25 U.S.C. § 472, provides:

> "The Secretary of the Interior is directed to establish standards of health, age, character, experience, knowledge, and ability for Indians who may be appointed, without regard to civil-service laws, to the various positions maintained, now or hereafter, by the Indian Office, in the administration of functions or services affecting any Indian tribe. Such qualified Indians shall hereafter have the preference to appointment to vacancies in any such positions."

In June 1972, pursuant to this provision, the Commissioner of Indian Affairs, with the approval of the Secretary of the Interior, issued a directive (Personnel Management Letter No. 72–12) stating that the BIA's policy would be to grant a preference to qualified Indians not only, as before, in the initial hiring stage, but also in the situation where an Indian and a non-Indian, both already employed by the BIA, were competing for a promotion within the Bureau. The record indicates that this policy was implemented immediately.

Shortly thereafter, appellees, who are non-Indian employees of the BIA at Albuquerque, instituted this class action, on behalf of themselves and other non-Indian employees similarly situated, in the United States District Court for the District of New Mexico, claiming that the "so-called 'Indian Preference Statutes' " were repealed by the 1972 Equal Employment Opportunity Act and deprived them of rights to property without due process of law, in violation of the Fifth Amendment. * * *

After a short trial focusing primarily on how the new policy, in fact, has been implemented, the District Court concluded that the Indian preference was implicitly repealed by § 11 of the Equal Employment Opportunity Act of 1972, Pub. L. 92–261, 86 Stat. 111, 42 U.S.C. § 2000e–16(a) (1970 ed., Supp. II), proscribing discrimination in most federal employment on the basis of race.[6]

---

6. Section 2000e–16(a) reads:

"All personnel actions affecting employees or applicants for employment (except with regard to aliens employed outside the limits of the United States) in military departments as defined in section 102 of Title 5, in executive agencies (other than the General Accounting Office) as defined in section 105 of Title 5 (including employees and applicants for employment who are paid from nonappropriated funds), in the United States Postal Service and the Postal Rate Commission, in those units of the Government of the District of

Having found that Congress repealed the preference, it was unnecessary for the District Court to pass on its constitutionality. The court permanently enjoined appellants "from implementing any policy in the Bureau of Indian Affairs which would hire, promote, or reassign any person in preference to another solely for the reason that such person is an Indian." * * *

[II] The federal policy of according some hiring preference to Indians in the Indian service dates at least as far back as 1834. Since that time, Congress repeatedly has enacted various preferences of the general type here at issue.[8] The purpose of these preferences, as variously expressed in the legislative history, has been to give Indians a greater participation in their own self-government; to further the Government's trust obligation toward the Indian tribes[9]; and to reduce the negative effect of having non-Indians administer matters that affect Indian tribal life.

The preference directly at issue here was enacted as an important part of the sweeping Indian Reorganization Act of 1934. The overriding purpose of that particular Act was to establish machinery whereby Indian tribes would be able to assume a greater degree of self-government, both politically and economically. Congress was seeking to modify the then-existing situation whereby the primarily non-Indian-staffed BIA had plenary control, for all practical purposes, over the lives and destinies of the federally recognized Indian tribes. Initial congressional proposals would have diminished substantially the role of the BIA by turning over to federally chartered self-governing Indian communities many of the functions normally performed by the Bureau.[13] Committee sentiment, however, ran against such a radical change in the role of the BIA. The solution ultimately adopted was to strengthen tribal government while continuing the active role of the BIA, with the understanding that the Bureau would be more responsive to the interests of the people it was created to serve.

Columbia having positions in the competitive service, and in those units of the legislative and judicial branches of the Federal Government having positions in the competitive service, and in the Library of Congress shall be made free from any discrimination based on race, color, religion, sex, or national origin."

8. Act of May 17, 1882, § 6, 22 Stat. 88, and Act of July 4, 1884, § 6, 23 Stat. 97, 25 U.S.C. § 46 (employment of clerical, mechanical, and other help on reservations and about agencies); Act of Aug. 15, 1894, § 10, 28 Stat. 313, 25 U.S.C. § 44 (employment of herders, teamsters, and laborers, "and where practicable in all other employments" in the Indian service); Act of June 7, 1897, § 1, 30 Stat. 83, 25 U.S.C. § 274 (employment as matrons, farmers, and industrial teachers in Indian schools); Act of June 25, 1910, § 23, 36 Stat. 861, 25 U.S.C. § 47 (general preference as to Indian labor and products of Indian industry).

9. A letter, contained in the House Report to the 1934 Act, from President F. D. Roosevelt to Congressman Howard states:

"We can and should, without further delay, extend to the Indian the fundamental rights of political liberty and local self-government and the opportunities of education and economic assistance that they require in order to attain a wholesome American life. This is but the obligation of honor of a powerful nation toward a people living among us and dependent upon our protection." H.R.Rep. No. 1804, 73d Cong., 2d Sess., 8 (1934).

13. Hearings on H.R. 7902, Readjustment of Indian Affairs, 73d Cong., 2d Sess., 1–7 (1934) (hereafter House Hearings).

One of the primary means by which self-government would be fostered and the Bureau made more responsive was to increase the participation of tribal Indians in the BIA operations. In order to achieve this end, it was recognized that some kind of preference and exemption from otherwise prevailing civil service requirements was necessary.[16] Congressman Howard, the House sponsor, expressed the need for the preference:

> "The Indians have not only been thus deprived of civic rights and powers, but they have been largely deprived of the opportunity to enter the more important positions in the service of the very bureau which manages their affairs. Theoretically, the Indians have the right to qualify for the Federal civil service. In actual practice there has been no adequate program of training to qualify Indians to compete in these examinations, especially for technical and higher positions; and even if there were such training, the Indians would have to compete under existing law, on equal terms with multitudes of white applicants. * * * The various services on the Indian reservations are actually local rather than Federal services and are comparable to local municipal and county services, since they are dealing with purely local Indian problems. It should be possible for Indians with the requisite vocational and professional training to enter the service of their own people without the necessity of competing with white applicants for these positions. This bill permits them to do so." 78 Cong. Rec. 11729 (1934).

Congress was well aware that the proposed preference would result in employment disadvantages within the BIA for non-Indians.[17] Not only was this displacement unavoidable if room were to be made for Indians, but it was explicitly determined that gradual replacement of non-Indians with Indians within the Bureau was a desirable feature of the entire program for self-government.[18] Since 1934, the BIA has implemented the preference with a fair degree of success. The percentage of Indians employed in the Bureau rose from 34% in 1934 to 57% in 1972. This reversed the former downward trend, see n. 16, *supra*, and was due, clearly, to the presence of the 1934 Act. The Commissioner's extension of the preference in 1972 to promotions within the

---

16. "The bill admits qualified Indians to the position [*sic*] in their own service.

"Thirty-four years ago, in 1900, the number of Indians holding regular positions in the Indian Service, in proportion to the total of positions, was greater than it is today.

"The reason primarily is found in the application of the generalized civil service to the Indian Service, and the consequent exclusion of Indians from their own jobs." House Hearings 19 (memorandum dated Feb. 19, 1934, submitted by Commissioner Collier to the Senate and House Committees on Indian Affairs).

17. Congressman Carter, an opponent of the bill, placed in the Congressional Record the following observation by Commissioner Collier at the Committee hearings:

"[W]e must not blind ourselves to the fact that the effect of this bill if worked out would unquestionably be to replace white employees by Indian employees. I do not know how fast, but ultimately it ought to go very far indeed." 78 Cong. Rec. 11737 (1934).

18. "It should be possible for Indians to enter the service of their own people without running the gauntlet of competition with whites for these positions. Indian progress and ambition will be enormously strengthened as soon as we adopt the principle that the Indian Service shall gradually become, in fact as well as in name, an Indian service predominantly in the hands of educated and competent Indians." *Id.*, at 11731 (remarks of Cong. Howard).

BIA was designed to bring more Indians into positions of responsibility and, in that regard, appears to be a logical extension of the congressional intent.

[III] It is against this background that we encounter the first issue in the present case: whether the Indian preference was repealed by the Equal Employment Opportunity Act of 1972. Title VII of the Civil Rights Act of 1964 was the first major piece of federal legislation prohibiting discrimination in *private* employment on the basis of "race, color, religion, sex, or national origin." 42 U.S.C. § 2000e–2(a). Significantly, §§ 701(b) and 703(i) of that Act explicitly exempted from its coverage the preferential employment of Indians by Indian tribes or by industries located on or near Indian reservations. 42 U.S.C. §§ 2000e(b) and 2000e–2(i).[19] This exemption reveals a clear congressional recognition, within the framework of Title VII, of the unique legal status of tribal and reservation-based activities. The Senate sponsor, Senator Humphrey, stated on the floor by way of explanation:

> "This exemption is consistent with the Federal Government's policy of encouraging Indian employment and with the special legal position of Indians." 110 Cong. Rec. 12723 (1964).[20]

The 1964 Act did not specifically outlaw employment discrimination by the Federal Government. Yet the mechanism for enforcing longstanding Executive Orders forbidding Government discrimination had proved ineffective for the most part. In order to remedy this, Congress, by the 1972 Act, amended the 1964 Act and proscribed discrimination in most areas of federal employment. See n. 6, *supra*. In general, it may be said that the substantive anti-discrimination law embraced in Title VII was carried over and applied to the Federal Government. As stated in the House Report:

> "To correct this entrenched discrimination in the Federal service, it is necessary to insure the effective application of uniform, fair and strongly enforced policies. The present law and the proposed statute do not permit industry and labor organizations to be the judges of their own conduct in the area of employment discrimination. There is no reason why government agencies should not be treated similarly. * * *" H.R.Rep. No. 92–238, on H.R. 1746, pp. 24–25 (1971).

Nowhere in the legislative history of the 1972 Act, however, is there any mention of Indian preference.

Appellees assert * * * that since the 1972 Act proscribed racial discrimination in Government employment, the Act necessarily, albeit *sub silentio,*

---

19. Section 701(b) excludes "an Indian Tribe" from the Act's definition of "employer." Section 703(i) states:

> "Nothing contained in this subchapter shall apply to any business or enterprise on or near an Indian reservation with respect to any publicly announced employment practice of such business or enterprise under which a preferential treatment is given to any individual because he is an Indian living on or near a reservation."

20. Senator Mundt supported these exemptions on the Senate floor by claiming that they would allow Indians "to benefit from Indian preference programs now in operation or later to be instituted." 110 Cong.Rec. 13702 (1964).

repealed the provision of the 1934 Act that called for the preference in the BIA of one racial group, Indians, over non-Indians:

> "When a conflict such as in this case, is present, the most recent law or Act should apply and the conflicting Preferences passed some 39 years earlier should be impliedly repealed." Brief for Appellees 7.

We disagree. For several reasons we conclude that Congress did not intend to repeal the Indian preference and that the District Court erred in holding that it was repealed.

First: There are the above-mentioned affirmative provisions in the 1964 Act excluding coverage of tribal employment and of preferential treatment by a business or enterprise on or near a reservation. These 1964 exemptions as to private employment indicate Congress' recognition of the longstanding federal policy of providing a unique legal status to Indians in matters concerning tribal or "on or near" reservation employment. The exemptions reveal a clear congressional sentiment that an Indian preference in the narrow context of tribal or reservation-related employment did not constitute racial discrimination of the type otherwise proscribed. In extending the general anti-discrimination machinery to federal employment in 1972, Congress in no way modified these private employment preferences built into the 1964 Act, and they are still in effect. It would be anomalous to conclude that Congress intended to eliminate the longstanding statutory preferences in BIA employment, as being racially discriminatory, at the very same time it was reaffirming the right of tribal and reservation-related private employers to provide Indian preference. Appellees' assertion that Congress implicitly repealed the preference as racially discriminatory, while retaining the 1964 preferences, attributes to Congress irrationality and arbitrariness, an attribution we do not share.

Second: Three months after Congress passed the 1972 amendments, it enacted two *new* Indian preference laws. These were part of the Education Amendments of 1972, 86 Stat. 235, 20 U.S.C. §§ 887c(a) and (d), and § 1119a (1970 ed., Supp. II). The new laws explicitly require that Indians be given preference in Government programs for training teachers of Indian children. It is improbable, to say the least, that the same Congress which affirmatively approved and enacted these additional and similar Indian preferences was, at the same time, condemning the BIA preference as racially discriminatory. In the total absence of any manifestation of supportive intent, we are loathe to imply this improbable result.

Third: Indian preferences, for many years, have been treated as exceptions to Executive Orders forbidding Government employment discrimination. The 1972 extension of the Civil Rights Act to Government employment is in large part merely a codification of prior anti-discrimination Executive Orders that had proved ineffective because of inadequate enforcement machinery. There certainly was no indication that the substantive proscription against discrimination was intended to be any broader than that which previously existed. By codifying the existing anti-discrimination provisions, and by providing enforcement machinery for them, there is no reason to presume that Congress affirmatively intended to erase the preferences that previously had co-existed with broad anti-discrimination provisions in Executive Orders.

Fourth: Appellees encounter head-on the "cardinal rule * * * that repeals by implication are not favored." *Posadas v. National City Bank*, 296 U.S. 497, 503 (1936). They and the District Court read the congressional silence as effectuating a repeal by implication. There is nothing in the legislative history, however, that indicates affirmatively any congressional intent to repeal the 1934 preference. Indeed, as explained above, there is ample independent evidence that the legislative intent was to the contrary.

This is a prototypical case where an adjudication of repeal by implication is not appropriate. The preference is a longstanding, important component of the Government's Indian program. The anti-discrimination provision, aimed at alleviating minority discrimination in employment, obviously is designed to deal with an entirely different and, indeed, opposite problem. Any perceived conflict is thus more apparent than real.

In the absence of some affirmative showing of an intention to repeal, the only permissible justification for a repeal by implication is when the earlier and later statutes are irreconcilable. *Georgia v. Pennsylvania R. Co.*, 324 U.S. 439, 456–457 (1945). Clearly, this is not the case here. A provision aimed at furthering Indian self-government by according an employment preference within the BIA for qualified members of the governed group can readily co-exist with a general rule prohibiting employment discrimination on the basis of race. Any other conclusion can be reached only by formalistic reasoning that ignores both the history and purposes of the preference and the unique legal relationship between the Federal Government and tribal Indians.

Furthermore, the Indian preference statute is a specific provision applying to a very specific situation. The 1972 Act, on the other hand, is of general application. Where there is no clear intention otherwise, a specific statute will not be controlled or nullified by a general one, regardless of the priority of enactment. See, *e.g., Bulova Watch Co. v. United States*, 365 U.S. 753, 758 (1961); *Rodgers v. United States*, 185 U.S. 83, 87–89 (1902).

The courts are not at liberty to pick and choose among congressional enactments, and when two statutes are capable of co-existence, it is the duty of the courts, absent a clearly expressed congressional intention to the contrary, to regard each as effective. "When there are two acts upon the same subject, the rule is to give effect to both if possible * * *. The intention of the legislature to repeal 'must be clear and manifest.' " *United States v. Borden Co.*, 308 U.S. 188, 198 (1939). In light of the factors indicating no repeal, we simply cannot conclude that Congress consciously abandoned its policy of furthering Indian self-government when it passed the 1972 amendments.

We therefore hold that the District Court erred in ruling that the Indian preference was repealed by the 1972 Act. * * *

NOTES ON *MANCARI* AND INTERPRETATION
IN LIGHT OF SUBSEQUENT STATUTES

1. *Repeals by Implication. Mancari* introduces you to a canon of statutory interpretation not mentioned in § 1 of this chapter: repeals by implication are not favored.[1] This canon is subject to the criticism that it naively assumes legislative omniscience — legislators and their staff members do not search the statute books to ensure that new legislation will interfere minimally with established legislation. And why should they? Shouldn't new legislative policy be applied to full effect, liberally supplanting outdated prior statutes? On the other hand, the canon against implied repeals might be defended, "not only to avoid misconstruction of the law effecting the putative repeal, but also to preserve the intent of later Congresses that have already enacted laws that are dependent on the continued applicability of the law whose implicit repeal is in question." *Smith v. Robinson*, 468 U.S. 992, 1026 (1984) (Brennan, J., dissenting).

As Judge Norris recognized, *Mancari* is in tension with the Ninth Circuit's ultimate position in the Checkerboard Case: the Alaska Lands Act's access provision was found to repeal huge chunks of wilderness protection acts passed by Congress in the 1960s and 1970s. Why isn't the Checkerboard Case a much better case for *refusing* to allow repeals by implication?

2. *Applying the Canon in* Mancari. Figure out the best arguments against Justice Blackmun's reasons why no repeal by implication occurred in *Mancari*. (Hint: As to the first, Congress showed itself able to exempt Indians from the operation of antidiscrimination laws in 1964; the absence of any express exemption in the 1972 Act, then, gives a strong *expressio unius* argument to plaintiffs. In addition, sticking to the first argument made by Justice Blackmun, isn't it quite different to exempt an Indian tribe or a private employer from the coverage of an employment discrimination statute, on the one hand, and to exempt the federal government, on the other?) We think that the best arguments against Justice Blackmun's first three points are strong ones. If we are right, then the "repeal by implication" canon is crucial to the outcome of the case. As note 1 above suggests, that canon has some theoretical problems when it is stated broadly, as saying that repeals of *statutes* by implication are disfavored. Can the Blackmun result be saved by narrowing the canon to "repeals of *longstanding policies* are disfavored, especially where there is no collateral evidence (in other statutes, regulations, executive orders, authoritative committee reports, and the like) supporting the notion that the longstanding policy has been repudiated"? Does narrowing the canon in this way alleviate the general objections to it suggested in note 1 as well?

---

1. See also *Hamdan v. Rumsfeld,* 126 S.Ct. 2749, 2775 (2006); *Granholm v. Heald,* 544 U.S. 460 (2005); *County of Yakima v. Confederated Tribes & Bands of Yakima Indian Nation,* 502 U.S. 251 (1992); *St. Martin Evangelical Lutheran Church v. South Dakota,* 451 U.S. 772, 788 (1981); *Watt v. Alaska,* 451 U.S. 259 (1981); *Radzanower v. Touche Ross & Co.,* 426 U.S. 148, 154 (1976).

3. *Repeal of Treaties by Implication.* Treaties, like statutes, are the law of the land under the Supremacy Clause, U.S. Const., art. VI, and the Supreme Court has stated that "[a] treaty," like a statute, "will not be deemed to have been abrogated or modified by a later statute unless such purpose on the part of Congress has been clearly expressed." *Cook v. United States*, 288 U.S. 102, 120 (1933); see *Weinberger v. Rossi*, 456 U.S. 25 (1982). Consider the following problem. The United States in 1934 ratified the Warsaw Convention, which sets forth uniform rules governing air transportation. Article 22 sets a limit on carrier liability for lost cargo; the liability is expressed in terms of gold, a uniform international standard of value when the Convention was drafted in the 1920s. The United States suspended convertibility of the dollar for gold in 1971 and in 1978 passed a statute implementing an international agreement creating a new regime for international monetary cooperation. The CAB, charged with implementing the Warsaw Convention in the U.S., set the liability limits in 1978 at $9.07 per pound of lost cargo — the last figure it had used under the gold conversion approach before the 1978 statute. The Supreme Court in *TWA v. Franklin Mint Corp.*, 466 U.S. 243 (1984), rejected the Second Circuit's determination that the Warsaw Convention's liability limits were unenforceable as implicitly nullified by the 1978 statute, based upon the presumption against implied repeals. The Court noted that the presumption is potentially stronger in the case of treaties, because they usually have provisions requiring the U.S. to notify the other country (or countries) party to the treaty if the U.S. is withdrawing from it.

BRANCH v. SMITH
Supreme Court of the United States, 2003
538 U.S. 254, 123 S.Ct. 1429, 155 L.Ed.2d 407

JUSTICE SCALIA announced the judgment of the Court and delivered the opinion of the Court with respect to Parts I, II, and III-A, and an opinion with respect to Parts III-B and IV, in which THE CHIEF JUSTICE [REHNQUIST], JUSTICE KENNEDY, and JUSTICE GINSBURG join.

[The 2000 census caused Mississippi to lose one congressional seat. The state legislature failed to pass a new redistricting plan after the decennial census results were published in 2001. Beatrice Branch and others (state plaintiffs) filed suit in Mississippi state court, seeking a redistricting plan for the 2002 congressional elections. In November 2001, John Smith and others (federal plaintiffs) filed a similar action in federal court. The federal plaintiffs asked the court to order at-large elections pursuant to 2 U.S.C. § 2a(c)(5), or, alternatively, to devise its own redistricting plan. In December 2001, the state court adopted a redistricting plan, but the Department of Justice demanded more information before it would preclear the plan as required by the Voting Rights Act. Fearing that the state court plan would not be in place by March 1, 2002, the candidate qualification deadline, the federal court on February 26, 2002, enjoined use of the state court plan and directed that its own redistricting plan be used for the 2002 election. The state plaintiffs appealed this order. The Supreme Court ruled that the federal district court had properly enjoined enforcement of the state court redistricting plan. The main issue on appeal was whether the district court was also correct in drawing single-member, rather than at-large districts.]

[IIIA] Article I, § 4, cl. 1, of the Constitution provides that the "Times, Places and Manner of holding Elections for Senators and Representatives, shall be prescribed in each State by the Legislature thereof . . . ." It reserves to Congress, however, the power "at any time by Law [to] make or alter such Regulations, except as to the Places of chusing Senators." Pursuant to this authority, Congress in 1929 enacted the current statutory scheme governing apportionment of the House of Representatives. 2 U.S.C. §§ 2a(a), (b). In 1941, Congress added to those provisions a subsection addressing what is to be done pending redistricting:

> "Until a State is redistricted in the manner provided by the law thereof after any apportionment, the Representatives to which such State is entitled under such apportionment shall be elected in the following manner: (1) If there is no change in the number of Representatives, they shall be elected from the districts then prescribed by the law of such State, and if any of them are elected from the State at large they shall continue to be so elected; (2) if there is an increase in the number of Representatives, such additional Representative or Representatives shall be elected from the State at large and the other Representatives from the districts then prescribed by the law of such State; (3) if there is a decrease in the number of Representatives but the number of districts in such State is equal to such decreased number of Representatives, they shall be elected from the districts then prescribed by the law of such State; (4) if there is a decrease in the number of Representatives but the number of districts in such State is less than such number of Representatives, the number of Representatives by which such number of districts is exceeded shall be elected from the State at large and the other Representatives from the districts then prescribed by the law of such State; or (5) if there is a decrease in the number of Representatives and the number of districts in such State exceeds such decreased number of Representatives, they shall be elected from the State at large." § 2a(c).

In 1967, 26 years after § 2a(c) was enacted, Congress adopted § 2c, which provides, as relevant here:

> "In each State entitled in the Ninety-first Congress or in any subsequent Congress thereafter to more than one Representative under an apportionment made pursuant to the provisions of section 2a(a) of this title, there shall be established by law a number of districts equal to the number of Representatives to which such State is so entitled, and Representatives shall be elected only from districts so established, no district to elect more than one Representative . . . ."

The tension between these two provisions is apparent: Section 2c requires States entitled to more than one Representative to elect their Representatives from single-member districts, rather than from multimember districts or the State at large. Section 2a(c), however, requires multimember districts or at-large elections in certain situations; and with particular relevance to the present cases, in which Mississippi, by reason of the 2000 census, lost a congressional seat, § 2a(c)(5) requires at-large elections. Cross-appellants would reconcile the two provisions by interpreting the introductory phrase of § 2a(c) ("Until a State is redistricted in the manner provided by the law thereof after any apportionment") and the phrase "established by law" in § 2c to refer exclusively to *legislative* redistricting — so that § 2c tells the legislatures what to do (single-member districting) and § 2a(c) provides what will happen *absent* legislative action — in the present cases, the mandating of at-large elections.

The problem with this reconciliation of the provisions is that the limited role it assigns to § 2c (governing legislative apportionment but not judicial apportionment) is contradicted both by the historical context of § 2c's enactment and by the consistent understanding of all courts in the almost 40 years since that enactment. When Congress adopted § 2c in 1967, the immediate issue was precisely the involvement of the courts in fashioning electoral plans. The Voting Rights Act of 1965 had recently been enacted, assigning to the federal courts jurisdiction to involve themselves in elections. Even more significant, our decisions in [the one-person, one-vote cases] had ushered in a new era in which federal courts were overseeing efforts by badly malapportioned States to conform their congressional electoral districts to the constitutionally required one-person, one-vote standards. In a world in which the role of federal courts in redistricting disputes had been transformed from spectating to directing, the risk arose that judges forced to fashion remedies would simply order at-large elections.

At the time Congress enacted § 2c, at least six District Courts, two of them specifically invoking 2 U.S.C. § 2a(c)(5), had suggested that if the state legislature was unable to redistrict to correct malapportioned congressional districts, they would order the State's entire congressional delegation to be elected at large. * * * With all this threat of judicially imposed at-large elections, and (as far as we are aware) no threat of a legislatively imposed change to at-large elections, it is most unlikely that § 2c was directed solely at legislative reapportionment. [Indeed, lower courts have held as much.]

Of course the implausibility (given the circumstances of its enactment) that § 2c was meant to apply only to legislative reapportionment, and the unbroken unanimity of state and federal courts in opposition to that interpretation, would be of no consequence if the text of § 2c (and of § 2a(c)) unmistakably demanded that interpretation. But it does not. Indeed, it is more readily susceptible of the opposite interpretation.

The clause "there shall be established by law a number of districts equal to the number of Representatives to which such State is so entitled" could, to be sure, be so interpreted that the phrase "by law" refers only to legislative action. Its more common meaning, however, encompasses judicial decisions as well. * * *

In sum, § 2c is as readily enforced by courts as it is by state legislatures, and is just as binding on courts — federal or state — as it is on legislatures.

[IIIB] Having determined that in enacting 2 U.S.C. § 2c, Congress mandated that States are to provide for the election of their Representatives from single-member districts, and that this mandate applies equally to courts remedying a state legislature's failure to redistrict constitutionally, we confront the remaining question: what to make of § 2a(c)? As observed earlier, the texts of § 2c and § 2a(c)(5) are in tension. Representatives cannot be "elected only from districts," § 2c, while being elected "at large," § 2a(c). Some of the courts confronted with this conflict have concluded that § 2c repeals § 2a(c) by implication. There is something to be said for that position — especially since paragraphs (1) through (4) of § 2a(c) have become (because of postenactment decisions of this Court) in virtually all situations plainly unconstitutional. (The unlikely exception is the situation in which the decennial census makes no districting change constitutionally necessary.) Eighty percent of the section being a dead letter, why would Congress adhere to the flotsam of paragraph (5)?

We have repeatedly stated, however, that absent "a clearly expressed congressional intention," *Morton v. Mancari*, "repeals by implication are not favored." An implied repeal will only be found where provisions in two statutes are in "irreconcilable conflict," or where the latter act covers the whole subject of the earlier one and "is clearly intended as a substitute." So while there is a strong argument that § 2c was a substitute for § 2a(c), we think the better answer is that § 2a(c) — where what it prescribes is constitutional (as it is with regard to paragraph (5)) — continues to apply.

Section 2a(c) is, of course, only *provisionally* applicable. It governs the manner of election for Representatives in any election held "[u]ntil a State is redistricted in the manner provided by the law thereof after any apportionment." That language clashes with § 2c only if it is interpreted to forbid judicial redistricting unless the state legislature has first acted. On that interpretation, whereas § 2c categorically instructs courts to redistrict, § 2a(c)(5) forbids them to do anything but order at-large elections unless the state legislature has acted. But there is of course no need for such an interpretation. "Until a State is redistricted" can certainly refer to redistricting by courts as well as by legislatures. Indeed, that interpretation would seem the preferable one even if it were not a necessary means of reconciling the two sections. Under prior versions of § 2a(c), its default or stopgap provisions were to be invoked for a State "until the *legislature* of such State . . . [had] redistrict[ed] such State." Act of Jan. 16, 1901, ch. 93, § 4, 31 Stat. 734 (emphasis added); see Act of Feb. 7, 1891, ch. 116, § 4, 26 Stat. 736 ("until such State be redistricted as herein prescribed by the *legislature* of said State" (emphasis added)); Act of Feb. 25, 1882, ch. 20, § 3, 22 Stat. 6 ("shall be elected at large, unless the *Legislatures* of said States have provided or shall otherwise provide" (emphasis added)). These provisions are in stark contrast to the text of the current § 2a(c): "[u]ntil a State is redistricted in the manner provided by the law thereof."

If the more expansive (and more natural) interpretation of § 2a(c) is adopted, its condition can be met — and its demand for at-large elections suspended — by the very court that follows the command of § 2c. For when a court, state or federal, redistricts pursuant to § 2c, it necessarily does so "in the manner provided by [state] law." It must follow the "policies and preferences of the State, as expressed in statutory and constitutional provisions or in the reapportionment plans proposed by the state legislature," except, of course, when "adherence to state policy . . . detract[s] from the requirements of the Federal Constitution." Federal constitutional prescriptions, and federal statutory commands such as that of § 2c, are appropriately regarded, for purposes of § 2a(c), as a part of the state election law.

Thus, § 2a(c) is inapplicable *unless* the state legislature, and state and federal courts, have all failed to redistrict pursuant to § 2c. How long is a court to await that redistricting before determining that § 2a(c) governs a forthcoming election? Until, we think, the election is so imminent that no entity competent to complete redistricting pursuant to state law (including the mandate of § 2c) is able to do so without disrupting the election process. Only then may § 2a(c)'s stopgap provisions be invoked. Thus, § 2a(c) cannot be properly applied — neither by a legislature nor a court — as long as it is feasible for federal courts to effect the redistricting mandated by § 2c. So interpreted, § 2a(c) continues to function as it always has, as a last-resort remedy to be applied when, on the eve of a congressional election, no constitutional redistricting plan exists and there is no time for either the State's legislature or the courts to develop one. * * *

[The concurring opinion of JUSTICE KENNEDY has been omitted.]

JUSTICE STEVENS, with whom JUSTICE SOUTER and JUSTICE BREYER join, concurring in part and concurring in the judgment.

[Justice Stevens agreed with Parts I-III.A of Justice Scalia's opinion and with his result. But Justice Stevens believed that the portion of that statute that is codified at 2 U.S.C. § 2c impliedly repealed § 2a(c).]

The question whether an Act of Congress has repealed an earlier federal statute is similar to the question whether it has pre-empted a state statute. When Congress clearly expresses its intent to repeal or to pre-empt, we must respect that expression. When it fails to do so expressly, the presumption against implied repeals, like the presumption against pre-emption, can be overcome in two situations: (1) if there is an irreconcilable conflict between the provisions in the two Acts; or (2) if the later Act was clearly intended to "cove[r] the whole subject of the earlier one."

As I read the 1967 statute it entirely prohibits States that have more than one congressional district from adopting either a multimember district or electing their Representatives in at-large elections, with one narrow exception that applied to the 1968 election in two States. After a rather long and contentious legislative process, Congress enacted this brief provision:

"AN ACT

"For the relief of Doctor Ricardo Vallejo Samala and to provide for congressional redistricting.

"*Be it enacted by the Senate and House of Representatives of the United States of America in Congress assembled,* That, for the purposes of the Immigration and Nationality Act, Doctor Ricardo Vallejo Samala shall be held and considered to have been lawfully admitted to the United States for permanent residence as of August 30, 1959.

"In each State entitled in the Ninety-first Congress or in any subsequent Congress thereafter to more than one Representative under an apportionment made pursuant to the provisions of subsection (a) of section 22 of the Act of June 18, 1929, entitled 'An Act to provide for apportionment of Representatives' (46 Stat. 26), as amended, there shall be established by law a number of districts equal to the number of Representatives to which such State is so entitled, *and Representatives shall be elected only from districts so established*, no district to elect more than one Representative (except that a State which is entitled to more than one Representative and which has in all previous elections elected its Representatives at Large may elect its Representatives at Large to the Ninety-first Congress)." Pub. L. 90-196, 81 Stat. 581 (emphasis added).

The second paragraph of this statute enacts a general rule prohibiting States with more than one congressional Representative from electing their Representatives to Congress in at-large elections. That the single exception to this congressional command applied only to Hawaii and New Mexico, and only to the 1968 election, emphasizes the fact that the Act applies to every other State and every other election. Thus, it unambiguously forbids elections that would otherwise have been authorized by § 2a(c)(5). It both creates an "irreconcilable conflict" with the 1941 law and it "covers the whole subject" of at-large congressional elections. Under either of the accepted standards for identifying implied repeals, it repealed the earlier federal statute. In addition, this statute pre-empts the Mississippi statute setting the default rule as at-large elections.

The first paragraph of the 1967 statute suggests an answer to the question of why Congress failed to enact an express repeal of the 1941 law when its intent seems so obvious. The statute that became law in December 1967 was the final gasp in a protracted legislative process that began on January 17, 1967, when Chairman Celler of the House Judiciary Committee introduced H.R. 2508, renewing efforts made in the preceding Congress to provide legislative standards responsive to this Court's holding in *Wesberry v. Sanders* that the one-person, one-vote principle applies to congressional elections. The bill introduced by Representative Celler in 1967 contained express language replacing § 2a(c) in its entirety. H.R. 2508, as introduced, had three principal components that are relevant to the implied repeal analysis. First, the bill required single-member district elections: "[T]here shall be established by law a number of districts equal to the number of Representatives to which such State is so entitled; and Representatives shall be elected only from districts so established, no district to elect more than one Representative." H.R. 2508, 90th Cong., 1st Sess., p. 2 (1967). Second, the bill limited gerrymandering, requiring each district to "at all times be composed of contiguous territory, in as compact form as practicable." Third, the bill required proportional representation: "[N]o district established in any State for the Ninetieth or any subsequent Congress shall contain a number of persons, excluding Indians not taxed, more than 15 per centum greater or less than the average obtained" by dividing the population by the number of Representatives.

This bill generated great controversy and discussion. Importantly for present purposes, however, only two of the three components were discussed in depth at all. At no point, either in any of the numerous Conference Reports or lengthy floor debates, does any disagreement regarding the language expressly repealing § 2a(c) or the single-member district requirement appear. Rather, the debate was confined to the gerrymandering requirement, the proportionality rule, and the scope and duration of the temporary exceptions to the broad prohibition against at-large elections.

The House Judiciary Committee amended the bill, limiting the proportional differences between districts in all States to not exceed 10 percent and creating an exception to the general rule for the 91st and 92d Congresses (1968 and 1970 elections) that allowed for "the States of Hawaii and New Mexico [to] continue to elect their Representatives at large" and for the proportional differences to be as large as 30 percent. The House then passed this amended bill. The Senate Judiciary Committee then amended this bill, striking Hawaii from the exception and allowing for 35 percent, rather than 30 percent, variation between districts during the 91st and 92d Congresses. The bill went to conference twice, and the conference recommended two sets of amendments. The first Conference Report, issued June 27, 1967, recommended striking any exception to the general rule and limiting proportional variation to 10 percent or less. After this compromise failed to pass either the House or the Senate, the conference then recommended a measure that was very similar to the second paragraph of the private bill eventually passed — a general rule requiring single-member districts with an exception, of unlimited duration, for Hawaii and New Mexico. Importantly, every version of the bill discussed in the House Report, the Senate Report, and both Conference Reports contained a provision expressly repealing § 2a(c). In spite of these several modifications, the bill, as recommended by the last conference, failed to pass either chamber.

The decision to attach what is now § 2c to the private bill reflected this deadlock. Indeed, proponents of this attachment remarked that they sought to take the uncontroversial components of the prior legislation to ensure that Congress would pass some legislation in response to *Wesberry v. Sanders* [one-person, one-vote requirement for the House of Representatives]. The absence of any discussion, debate, or reference to the provision expressly repealing § 2a(c) in the private bill prevents its omission from the final bill as being seen as a deliberate choice by Congress. Any fair reading of the history leading up to the passage of this bill demonstrates that all parties involved were operating under the belief that the changes they were debating would completely replace § 2a(c). * * *

The history of the 1967 statute, coupled with the plain language of its text, leads to only one conclusion — Congress impliedly repealed § 2a(c). It is far wiser to give effect to the manifest intent of Congress than, as the plurality attempts, to engage in tortured judicial legislation to preserve a remnant of an obsolete federal statute and an equally obsolete state statute. * * *

JUSTICE O'CONNOR, with whom JUSTICE THOMAS joins, concurring in part and dissenting in part.

[Justice O'Connor agreed with the plurality's somewhat reluctant conclusion that § 2c does not impliedly repeal § 2a(c)(5).] Here, it is quite easy to read §§ 2c and 2a(c) together. A natural statutory reading of § 2a(c) gives force to both §§ 2c and 2a(c): Section 2a(c) applies "[u]ntil a State is redistricted in the manner provided by the law thereof." Section 2c applies *after* a State has "redistricted in the manner provided by the law thereof."

As both the plurality and Justice Stevens recognize, an implied repeal can exist only if the "provisions in the two acts are in irreconcilable conflict" or if "the later act covers the whole subject of the earlier one and is clearly intended as a substitute." Indeed, " 'when two statutes are capable of co-existence, it is the duty of the courts . . . to regard each as effective.' " We have not found *any* implied repeal of a statute since 1975. And outside the antitrust context, we appear not to have found an implied repeal of a statute since 1917. Because it is not difficult to read §§ 2a(c) and 2c in a manner that gives force to both statutes, § 2c cannot impliedly repeal § 2a(c).

The previous versions of §§ 2c and 2a(c) confirm that an implied repeal does not exist here. Since 1882, versions of §§ 2c and 2a(c) have coexisted. Indeed, the 1882, 1891, 1901, and 1911 apportionment statutes all contained the single-member district requirement as well as the at-large default requirement. Compare Act of Feb. 25, 1882, ch. 20, § 3, 22 Stat. 6 ("[T]he number to which such State may be entitled . . . *shall be elected by Districts* . . . , no one District electing more than one Representative" (emphasis added)) with *ibid*. (" . . . *shall be elected at large*, unless the Legislatures of said States have provided or shall otherwise provide before the time fixed by law for the next election of Representatives therein" (emphasis added)); Act of Feb. 7, 1891, ch. 116, § 3, 26 Stat. 735 ("[T]he number to which such State may be entitled . . . *shall be elected by districts*" and "[t]he *said districts shall be equal* to the number of Representatives to which such State may be entitled in Congress, no one district electing more than one Representative" (emphasis added)) with § 4, 26 Stat. 736 ("[S]uch additional Representative or Representatives *shall be elected by the State at large*" (emphasis added)); Act of Jan. 16, 1901, ch. 93, § 3, 31 Stat. 734 ("[T]he number to which such State may be entitled . . . *shall be elected by districts*" and "[t]he *said districts shall be equal* to the number of Representatives to which such State may be entitled in Congress, no one district electing more than one Representative" (emphasis added)) with § 4, 31 Stat. 734 ("[I]f the number hereby provided for shall in any State be less than it was before the change hereby made, then the whole number to such State hereby provided for *shall be elected at large*, unless the legislatures of said States have provided or shall otherwise provide before the time fixed by law for the next election of Representatives therein" (emphasis added)); Act of Aug. 8, 1911, ch. 5, § 3, 37 Stat. 14 ("[T]he Representatives . . . *shall be elected by districts*" and "[t]he *said districts shall be equal* to the number of Representatives to which such State may be entitled in Congress, no one district electing more than one Representative" (emphasis added)) with § 4, 37 Stat. 14 ("[S]uch additional Representative or Representatives *shall be elected by the State at large* . . . until such State shall be redistricted in the manner provided by the laws thereof"). * * *

Given this history of the two provisions coexisting in the same statute, I would not hold that § 2c impliedly repeals § 2a(c). The two statutes are "capable of co-existence" because each covers a different subject matter. *Morton v. Mancari*. Section 2c was not intended to cover the whole subject of § 2a(c) and was not "clearly intended as a substitute" for § 2a(c). Section 2a(c) (requiring at-large elections) applies unless or until the State redistricts, and

§ 2c (requiring single-member districts) applies once the State has completed the redistricting process. * * *

Justice Stevens argues that Congress intended to "'cove[r] the whole subject' " of at-large redistricting when it enacted § 2c in 1967. But the 1967 enactment of § 2c simply restored the prior balance between the at-large mandate and the single-member district mandate that had existed since 1882. To hold that an implied repeal exists, one would have to conclude that Congress repeatedly enacted two completely conflicting provisions in the same statute. The better reading is to give each provision a separate sphere of influence, with § 2a(c) applying until a "State is redistricted in the manner provided by the law thereof," and § 2c applying after the State is redistricted. Because the 1967 version of § 2c parallels the prior versions of § 2c, and because of the longstanding coexistence between the prior versions of §§ 2a(c) and 2c, Justice Stevens' argument that Congress "'clearly intended'" § 2c "'as a substitute' " for § 2a(c) is untenable.

Justice Stevens' strongest argument is that the legislative history indicates that "all parties involved were operating under the belief that the changes they were debating would completely replace § 2a(c)." Yet Justice Stevens acknowledges that Congress *could have* expressly repealed § 2a(c). Justice Stevens thinks the evidence that Congress tried to expressly repeal § 2a(c) four times cuts strongly in favor of an implied repeal here. But these four attempts to repeal § 2a(c) were unsuccessful. It is difficult to conclude that Congress can impliedly repeal a statute when it deliberately chose not to expressly repeal that statute. In this case, where the two provisions have co-existed historically, and where Congress explicitly rejected an express repeal of § 2a(c), I would not find an implied repeal of § 2a(c). * * *

[IIA] Although the plurality acknowledges that § 2a(c) remains in full force, it inexplicably adopts a reading of § 2a(c) that has no textual basis. Under § 2a(c)(5), the State must conduct at-large elections "[u]ntil a State is redistricted in the manner provided by the law thereof." Instead of simply reading the plain text of the statute, however, the plurality invents its own version of the text of § 2a(c). The plurality holds that "[u]ntil a State is redistricted . . . " means "[u]ntil . . . the election is so imminent that no entity competent to complete redistricting pursuant . . . to the mandate of § 2c [ ] is able to do so without disrupting the election process." But such a reading is not faithful to the text of the statute. Like Justice Stevens, I believe that the Court's interpretation of § 2a(c) is nothing more than "tortured judicial legislation." See also Scalia, *The Rule of Law as a Law of Rules*, 56 U. Chi. L. Rev. 1175, 1185 (1989) ("[W]hen one does not have a solid textual anchor or an established social norm from which to derive the general rule, its pronouncement appears uncomfortably like legislation"). * * *

Section 2a(c) contains *no* imminence requirement. It is not credible to say that "until a State is redistricted in the manner provided by the law thereof after any apportionment" means: "[u]ntil . . . the election is so imminent that no entity competent to complete redistricting pursuant to . . . the mandate of § 2c [ ] is able to do so without disrupting the election process." The plurality characterizes § 2a(c) as a "stopgap provisio[n]," but the text of § 2a(c) is not so limited. The plurality asks "[h]ow long is a court to await that redistricting before determining that § 2a(c) governs a forthcoming election?" Yet the text provides *no basis* for why the plurality would ask such a question. Indeed, the text tells us "how long" § 2a(c) should govern: "*until* a State is redistricted in the manner provided by the law thereof." (Emphasis added.) Under the plurality's reading, however, § 2a(c) would not apply even though § 2a(c) by its terms *should* apply, as the State has not yet "redistricted in the manner provided by the law thereof." The language of the statute cannot bear such a reading.

The dispositive question is what the text says it is: Has a State "redistricted in the manner provided by the law thereof"? 2 U.S.C. § 2a(c). "*Until* a State is redistricted in the manner provided by the law thereof after any apportionment," a court cannot draw single-member districts. (Emphasis added). The court must apply the terms of § 2a(c) and order at-large elections. If, however, the State is redistricted "in the manner provided by the law thereof," § 2c applies. Thus, *after* a State has been redistricted, if a court determines that the redistricting violates the Constitution or the Voting Rights Act, the correct remedy for such a violation is the § 2c procedure of drawing single-member districts that comport with federal statutory law and the Constitution. But "[u]ntil a State is redistricted in the manner provided by the law thereof," § 2a(c)(5) mandates that a court order at-large elections. In short, a court should enforce § 2a(c) *before* a "State is redistricted in the manner provided by the law thereof," and a court should enforce § 2c *after* a State has been "redistricted in the manner provided by the law thereof." * * *

NOTES ON *BRANCH*

1. *Holistic Textualism: When Has a Statute Been Implicitly Repealed? Implicitly Changed or Narrowed?* However you resolve this difficult case, there is much common ground among the Justices. To begin with, an implied repeal can exist only if the "provisions in the two acts are in irreconcilable conflict" or if "the later act covers the whole subject of the earlier one and is clearly intended as a substitute." Note the parallel to the approach the Court uses to determine whether a federal statute preempts state law. Like the *Mancari* presumption, the Court starts with a presumption against federal preemption of state law, especially in such core areas as contract and property law. (Recall Justice Scalia's opinion for the Court in *BFP*, which can be read as an example of the Court's reluctance to read federal statutes so broadly that they preempt fundamental portions of state property law.)

Second, unlike the presumption against federal preemption of state law, the *Mancari* presumption against implied repeals is one that is rarely overcome. As Justice O'Connor suggests, the presumption has usually been litigated, and occasionally, rebutted in antitrust cases. Antitrust defendants often argue that post-1890 regulatory statutes create implicit exceptions to the Sherman Act. They usually lose with such arguments but have occasionally prevailed, e.g., *United States v. National Ass'n of Securities Dealers*, 422 U.S. 694 (1975). Outside of the antitrust context, it is almost unheard of for federal judges to declare that a recent federal law has implicitly repealed a previous one.

One reason for the former phenomenon is a third point: " 'when two statutes are capable of co-existence, it is the duty of the courts . . . to regard each as effective.' " Judges will usually strain to reconcile federal statutes seemingly at odds. What norms underlie that level of conciliatory commitment? Sometimes judges will go to great lengths and show considerable imagination in such efforts, as Justice Scalia does in *Branch*. Is his reconciliation a success? Does it amount to "judicial legislation," as Justice O'Connor charged? Compare Judge Norris's effort to reconcile his interpretation of the Alaska Lands Act with the Wilderness Act in the published opinion in the Checkerboard Case.

Perhaps a better way to understand Justice Scalia's plurality opinion is through the lens of holistic interpretation, illustrated by the majority and dissenting opinions in *Sweet Home*. While judges may strain against finding an implicit *repeal*, they more willingly find that a subsequent statute has had effects on earlier statutes. Section 2a(c)(5) had a wider ambit for application before 1967. When Congress added § 2c to the U.S. Code, its new textual material had the effect (whatever Congress's actual intent) of narrowing the application of § 2a(c)(5). This is normal textualism, Justice Scalia is saying in *Branch*, and he probably considers Justice O'Connor's "judicial legislation" charge galling for that reason.

So the plurality opinion in *Branch* might be understood as a lesson in holistic textualism. Read the whole code as coherently as you can. Later-added provisions can change the scope of pre-existing text, but the faithful textualist should try to understand the entire text in a way that best preserves its integrity. Unless simply impossible, every sentence and every provision should be read as doing some work and providing some guidance to the citizenry and its judges.

2. *The Relevance of Legislative History?* Notice that Justice Scalia invokes the history of § 2c — the problem that apparently gave rise to the 1967 statute and its subsequent interpretation by lower courts. But, characteristically, he has no interest in the internal congressional history of § 2c, which is discussed in the concurring opinion. Can you read these legislative materials without coming to the conclusion that, yes, Congress understood that § 2c did repeal § 2a(c)(5)? Do the materials provide support for the textual proposition, also stressed by Justice Stevens, that §§ 2a(c)(5) and 2c are irreconcilable? Recall *Pepper v. Hart*. One way to read the House of Lords reversal in that case is that the extrinsic materials provided their Lordships with important context that helped them see the cogency of the pro-taxpayer reading of the statutory text. Could the legislative context surveyed by Justice Stevens serve this kind of textualist role? The plurality thinks not. Note that Justice Ginsburg joins the Scalia plurality rather than the Stevens concurring opinion.

As her opinion in the FDA Tobacco Case illustrates, Justice O'Connor is willing to look at cartloads of legislative history in appropriate circumstances. She objects to the Stevens reading of legislative history on the ground that Congress dropped the explicit preemption provision when it actually enacted the private bill containing § 2c. By negative implication, this supports the plurality's conclusion that § 2a(c)(5) was not repealed, she argues. "It is difficult to conclude that Congress can impliedly repeal a statute when it deliberately chose not to expressly repeal that statute." The adverb "deliberately" is a stretch. The point of Justice Stevens' legislative history discussion is that Congress, after repeated efforts, could not come to agreement on the other issues involved in the proposal and hastily passed the only part of it that was agreed upon (§ 2c). In the hurried and chaotic atmosphere of such last-minute maneuverings, the explicit repeal provision just got lost in the shuffle. Because § 2c was wholly uncontroversial, and no one objected to its entirely displacing § 2a(c), as earlier versions would have done, the likely inference is that the repealer provision was dropped without thought as to interpretive consequences. This is precisely the occasion where arguments from negative implication ought to have the least weight.

Reconsider the Great Legislative History debate discussed throughout Section 2B of this chapter. Does his refusal to consider legislative history lead Justice Scalia to a tortured and undemocratic interpretation of the statutes in play? Does the legislative history discussed by Justice Stevens really illuminate the debate, or does it allow the Justices to pick out their friends?

3. *Underlying Norms?* Another angle for viewing *Branch* is constitutional and statutory voting rights. Southern states like Mississippi had traditionally denied people of color the right to vote across the board. Once federal judges and executive officials started enforcing the rights of African Americans to vote, southern states adopted other mechanisms to marginalize such voters, including race-based gerrymanders and at-large voting. In states that have a majority-white population and racially polarized voting, at-large districts will assure a whites-only congressional delegation. At-large districts are not per se unconstitutional, but they have been found invalid all over the south under the Constitution or (more typically) the Voting Rights Act, because they are either intended or have the effect (Voting Rights Act) of perpetuating minority under-representation. See Chapter 2, § 1B.

The line of thought reflected in the previous paragraph was not the assumption of the Court or Congress in 1967, but was advanced in the 1980s. You can understand the alignment of Justices better in light of the norm against at-large districting in the south. The Justices most supportive of that norm (Stevens, Souter, Breyer) would displace § 2a(c)(5) entirely and let § 2c rule the field. The Justices less committed to that norm (Scalia, Rehnquist, Thomas, Kennedy, O'Connor) are willing to leave § 2a(c)(5) in place and allow at-large districts in some circumstances. Justice Ginsburg is the wild card, as she supports the norm but joins the Scalia plurality.

As noted above, § 2a(c)(5) is not unconstitutional, and applying it in *Branch* would probably not raise serious constitutional objections. But the at-large formula would not be acceptable to the Department of Justice under § 5 of the Voting Rights Act and would not likely be acceptable to a court under § 2 of that Act. So under a holistic understanding of the voting rights regime Congress has created since the 1960s, is there any appropriate room for § 2a(c)(5)?

SECTION 3. INTERPRETATION OF STATUTES CREATED BY POPULAR INITIATIVES

Now that we have completed our examination of the interpretation of legislatively created law, consider what different issues and difficulties might arise when interpreting laws that originate and are adopted outside the normal legislative process. About half the states allow voters to enact state statutes and constitutional amendments through initiatives (see Chapter 5). This Section will focus on popular lawmaking. Should interpretive techniques for ballot measures parallel those for legislative enactments, or should the fundamental differences in the two enactment procedures result in differing approaches to interpretation?

In a comprehensive treatment of these issues, Jane Schacter, in *The Pursuit of "Popular Intent": Interpretive Dilemmas in Direct Democracy*, 105 Yale L.J. 107 (1995), demonstrates that state courts routinely purport to use the same interpretive techniques regardless of statutory enactment process, usually stating that the linchpin of statutory meaning is the "intent" of the enacting authority. Professor Schacter criticizes this approach on empirical grounds. How can the people, at the polls, have some determinate intent about non-obvious issues arising under the measure? She suggests that any serious effort to understand voter intent would require an examination of the media coverage and advertising surrounding a ballot campaign, which social science research demonstrates affect the voters much more than formal sources such as the text of the ballot proposition and the official voter pamphlet distributed by the state. Yet state courts routinely refuse to consider the informal materials and counterfactually assume that voter intent coheres with the text of the ballot and pamphlet.

A recent example of this phenomenon is the Michigan marriage initiative, which added new Article 25, § 11 to the Michigan Constitution in 2004: "To secure and preserve the benefits of marriage for our society and for future generations of children, the union of one man and one woman in marriage shall be the only agreement recognized as a marriage or similar union for any purpose." The Michigan Attorney General and its Court of Appeals have interpreted that language to bar public employers from giving health care benefits to the "domestic partners" of lesbian and gay employees. *National Pride at Work, Inc. v. Governor*, 274 Mich.App. 147 (2007), appeal granted by the Michigan Supreme Court. The court ruled that the statutory language plainly applied to even the most limited domestic partnership benefits and refused to consider background materials — which demonstrated that the sponsors repeatedly assured voters that their marriage initiative would *not* affect domestic partnership benefits. See Glen Straszewski, *The Bait-and-Switch in Direct Democracy*, 2006 Wis. L. Rev. 17–74. Professor Straszewski argues that initiative proponents should be treated as sponsors accountable for their representations to the electorate, especially ones that appeal to popular prejudices (for purposes of judicial review) or that claim a narrow effect of their proposals if enacted (for purposes of statutory interpretation). Straszewski, *Rejecting the Myth of Popular Sovereignty and Applying an Agency Model to Direct Democracy*, 56 Vand. L. Rev. 395 (2003). See also Glenn

Smith, *Solving the "Initiatory Construction" Puzzle (and Improving Direct Democracy) by Appropriate Refocusing on Sponsor Intent*, 78 U. Colo. L. Rev. 257 (2007).

Sensitive to the problem Professor Straszewski identifies, Professor Schacter rejects a more capacious judicial consideration of informal materials on the grounds that they are unlikely to assist judges in choosing among the plausible interpretations surrounding ambiguous ballot measures and that judicial receptivity to arguments based on such materials will only encourage interest groups to manipulate media accounts and advertising for post-enactment judicial consumption. Schacter argues that, in place of an illusory search for voter intent, courts should craft principles of statutory interpretation specifically for the context of direct democracy. For example, she proposes that ballot propositions disadvantaging groups subject to the hostility of the majority — such as antigay measures like the Michigan marriage initiative — should be interpreted narrowly. On the other hand, initiatives that break through self-interested legislative gridlocks and seek to enhance the legitimacy of government processes — such as campaign finance restrictions or perhaps term limits — might be interpreted more liberally. See also Note, *Judicial Approaches to Direct Democracy*, 118 Harv. L. Rev. 2748 (2005).

One of us has attempted to develop a coherent interpretive regime for ballot measures. See Philip Frickey, *Interpretation on the Borderline: Constitution, Canons, Direct Democracy*, 1996 Ann. Surv. Am. L. 477.[a] His argument is premised on the notion that direct democracy is in tension with the federal constitutional principle of republican government. Because the Supreme Court has refused to invalidate state ballot measures on this ground, the voters must be given their due — ballot measures should be interpreted consistent with the plain meaning of their text and the obvious understandings of the voters concerning the core purposes of the measure. As to ambiguities, however, such measures should be interpreted narrowly, to limit their effects in displacing prior law enacted in republican fashion (i.e., by the legislature).

Professor Frickey's argument is premised on the notion that republican lawmaking is an underenforced constitutional norm worthy of protection through canons of statutory interpretation, as the Supreme Court has done with another less underenforced constitutional norm, federalism (in *Gregory v. Ashcroft* and related cases, see § 1B3 of this chapter). In addition to privileging republican enactments, this approach suggests that longstanding substantive canons should be more strongly applied in the context of ballot propositions. For example, because the voters are less capable than a legislature in evaluating whether a proposal satisfies constitutional norms, ballot propositions should be subjected to a more aggressive canon concerning the avoidance of serious

---

a. Another one of us has also written on lawmaking by voters and expressed the view that, when possible, ballot propositions should be understood as creating statutory law (which is subject to amendment by the legislature) rather than state constitutional amendments (which are entrenched against legislative modification). See Elizabeth Garrett, *Who Directs Direct Democracy?*, 4 U. Chi. L. Sch. Roundtable 17 (1997).

constitutional issues than would be applied to legislatively adopted laws. Consider this argument in light of the following case.[b]

EVANGELATOS v. SUPERIOR COURT, 44 Cal.3d 1188, 246 Cal.Rptr. 629, 753 P.2d 585 (1988). The voters of California approved Proposition 51, the "Fair Responsibility Act of 1986," which "modified the traditional, common law 'joint and several liability' doctrine [by] limiting an individual tortfeasor's liability for noneconomic damages to a proportion of such damages equal to the tortfeasor's own percentage of fault." Under the California Constitution, the measure took effect the day after the election. The proposition was silent on whether it applied to pending cases. A sharply divided California Supreme Court held that the measure did not apply to causes of action that accrued prior to the effective date.

Justice Arguelles, for the majority, noted that it would have been simple enough for the proponents of the measure to have drafted it expressly to apply to pending cases and that they should have been on notice that, in the absence of a retroactivity provision, courts were likely to apply it only prospectively. (See Chapter 6, § 3C.) The majority embraced a strong nonretroactivity principle, concluding that "in the absence of an express retroactivity provision, a statute will not be applied retroactively unless it is very clear from extrinsic sources that the Legislature or the voters must have intended a retroactive application." The majority stressed that nothing in the proposition's "findings and declaration of purpose" or in the ballot pamphlet distributed to the voters indicated that the retroactivity question "was actually consciously considered during the enactment process." The majority contended that a retroactive application could interfere with the reasonable expectations of plaintiffs in pending cases (who might have decided whom to sue and not to sue based on the law existing at the time suit was filed) and could result in a windfall to insurance companies.

In dissent, **Justice Kaufman,** joined by two colleagues, disputed whether California precedents required such a strong canon against retroactivity and whether retroactivity would produce unfairness in pending cases or an insurance windfall. He argued that the presumption of prospectivity should apply " 'only after, considering *all pertinent factors*, it is determined that it is impossible to ascertain the legislative intent.' " Two pertinent factors, the history of the times and the perceived evils to be remedied by the measure, strongly supported retroactive application. Proposition 51, a "tort reform" measure, was a response to the widely perceived "liability crisis" facing government agencies and private businesses. Section 3 of Proposition 51 stated:

---

b. For the argument that Schacter and Frickey are wrong in proposing different interpretive regimes for legislatively created laws and ballot measures because each of the flaws in lawmaking process that occurs in the latter also occurs in the former, see Jack Landau, *Interpreting Statutes Enacted by Initiative: An Assessment of Proposals To Apply Specialized Interpretive Rules,* 34 Willamette L. Rev. 487 (1998).

Findings and Declaration of Purpose

The People of the State of California find and declare as follows:

(a) The legal doctrine of joint and several liability, also known as "the deep pocket rule", has resulted in a system of inequity and injustice that has threatened financial bankruptcy of local governments, other public agencies, private individuals and businesses and has resulted in higher prices for goods and services to the public and in higher taxes to the taxpayers.

(b) Some governmental and private defendants are perceived to have substantial financial resources or insurance coverage and have thus been included in lawsuits even though there was little or no basis for finding them at fault. Under joint and several liability, if they are found to share even a fraction of the fault, they often are held financially liable for all the damage. The People — taxpayers and consumers alike — ultimately pay for these lawsuits in the form of higher taxes, higher prices and higher insurance premiums.

(c) Local governments have been forced to curtail some essential police, fire and other protections because of the soaring costs of lawsuits and insurance premiums.

Therefore, the People of the State of California declare that to remedy these inequities, defendants in tort actions shall be held financially liable in closer proportion to their degree of fault. To treat them differently is unfair and inequitable.

The People of the State of California further declare that reforms in the liability laws in tort actions are necessary and proper to avoid catastrophic economic consequences for state and local governmental bodies as well as private individuals and businesses.

Justice Kaufman concluded that, in light of both the text of § 3 and the spirit of the overall provision, "the inference is virtually inescapable that the electorate intended Proposition 51 to apply as soon and as broadly as possible. When the electorate voted to reform a system perceived as 'inequitable and unjust,' they obviously voted to change that system *now*, not in five or ten years when causes of action that accrued prior to Proposition 51 finally come to trial. * * * A crisis does not call for *future* action. It calls for action *now*, action across the board, action as broad and as comprehensive as the Constitution will allow. It is clear that the purposes of Proposition 51 will be fully served only if it is applied to all cases not tried prior to its effective date."

Query: Which approach to Proposition 51 makes the most sense: the canonical approach of the majority — which privileges legal continuity, perhaps especially in the context of ballot propositions — or the purposive approach of the dissent, which extends to ballot measures the "mischief rule" in *Heydon's Case* (§ 1 of Chapter 7), an approach originally embraced in the context of legislative enactments? How would Professors Schacter, Straszewski, and Frickey decide this case, based upon their different theories?

Problem Involving Popular Lawmaking

Problem 8–9. In 1990, California voters adopted Proposition 140, "The Political Reform Act of 1990," which imposed term limits on state elected officials and limited expenditures funding the state legislature. You have been asked to provide advice to several former state legislators who fear that this measure imposes a lifetime ban on their ever seeking election to the legislature again. They are hoping that you will figure out a persuasive argument for construing the Proposition as allowing them to seek office again. In addition, they have asked you to investigate whether the Proposition might be invalidated as inconsistent with either the federal or state constitution.

Familiarize yourself with the materials concerning direct democracy (Chapter 5), the single-subject rule (Chapter 3, § 3A),[c] "due process of lawmaking" (Chapter 4), and severability (§ 1B2 of this chapter). Then, after examining the following material concerning Proposition 140, provide the advice sought by your clients.

Each registered voter in California is mailed an official voter pamphlet. The pamphlet contains the text of each ballot measure, an official summary of it, and arguments for and against it prepared by proponents and opponents. The California pamphlet for the November 1990 election contained the following:[d]

PROPOSITION 140: TEXT OF PROPOSED LAW

This initiative measure is submitted to the people in accordance with the provisions of Article II, Section 8 of the Constitution.

This initiative measure expressly amends the Constitution by amending and combining sections thereof; therefore, new provisions proposed to be inserted or added are printed in *italic type* to indicate they are new.

PROPOSED LAW

Section 1. This measure shall be known and may be cited as "The Political Reform Act of 1990."

Section 2. Section 1.5 is added to Article IV of the California Constitution, to read:

SEC 1.5. The people find and declare that the Founding Fathers established system of representative government based upon free, fair and competitive elections. The increased concentration of political power in the hands of incumbent representatives has made our electoral system less free, less competitive and less representative.

The ability of legislators to serve unlimited number of terms, to establish their own retirement system, and to pay for staff and support services at state expense contribute heavily to the extremely high number of incumbents who are elected. These unfair incumbent advantages discourage qualified

---

c. The California Constitution establishes a single-subject requirement for initiatives: "An initiative measure embracing more than one subject may not be submitted to the electors or have any effect." Cal. Const. art. II, § 8, subd. (d).

d. We thank Professor Einer Elhauge, who served as counsel for the Secretary of State of California, and Thomas Gede, then Special Assistant Attorney General of California, for providing us with these materials.

candidates from seeking public office and create a class of career politicians, instead of the citizen representatives envisioned by the Founding Fathers. these career politicians become representatives of the bureaucracy, rather than of the people whom they are elected to represent.

To restore a free and democratic system of fair elections, and to encourage qualified candidates to seek public office, the people find and declare that the powers of incumbency must be limited. Retirement benefits must be restricted, state-financed incumbent staff and support services limited, and limitations placed upon the number of terms which may be served.

SEC. 3. Section 2 of Article IV of the California Constitution is amended to read:

SEC. 2. (a) The Senate has a membership of 40 Senators elected for 4-year terms, 20 to begin every 2 years. *No Senator may serve more than 2 terms.* The Assembly has a membership of 80 members elected for 2-year terms. *No member of the Assembly may serve more than 3 terms.* Their terms shall commence on the first Monday in December next following their election.

(b) Election of members of the Assembly shall be on the first Tuesday after the first Monday in November of even-numbered years unless otherwise prescribed by the Legislature. Senators shall be elected at the same time and place as members of the Assembly.

(c) A person is ineligible to be a member of the Legislature unless the person is an elector and has been a resident of the legislative district for one year, and a citizen of the United States and a resident of California for 3 years, immediately preceding the election.

(d) When a vacancy occurs in the Legislature, the Governor immediately shall hold an election to fill the vacancy.

SEC. 4. Section 4.5 is added to Article IV of the California Constitution, to read:

SEC. 4.5. Notwithstanding any other provision of this Constitution or existing law, a person elected to or serving in the Legislature on or after November 1, 1990, shall participate in the Federal Social Security (Retirement, Disability, Health Insurance) Program and the State shall pay only the employer's share of the contribution necessary to such participation. No other pension or retirement benefit shall accrue as a result of service in the Legislature, such service not being intended as a career occupation. This Section shall not be construed to abrogate or diminish any vested pension or retirement benefit which may have accrued under an existing law to a person holding or having held office in the Legislature, but upon adoption of this Act no further entitlement to nor vesting in any existing program shall accrue to any such person, other than Social Security to the extent herein provided.

SEC. 5. Section 7.5 is added to Article IV of the California Constitution to read:

SEC. 7.5. In the fiscal year immediately following the adoption of this Act, the total aggregate expenditures of the Legislature for the compensation of members and employees of, and the operating expenses and equipment for, the

Legislature may not exceed an amount equal to nine hundred fifty thousand dollars ($950,000) per member for that fiscal year or 80 percent of the amount of money expended for those purposes in the preceding fiscal year, whichever is less. For each fiscal year thereafter, the total aggregate expenditures may not exceed an amount equal to that expended for those purposes in the preceding fiscal year, adjusted and compounded by an amount equal to the percentage increase in the appropriations limit for the state established pursuant to Article XIII B.

SEC. 6. Section 2 of Article V of the California Constitution is amended to read:

SEC. 2. The Governor shall be elected every fourth year at the same time and places as members of the Assembly and hold office from the Monday after January 1 following the election until a successor qualifies. The Governor shall be an elector who has been a citizen of the United States and a resident of this State for 5 years immediately preceding the Governor's election. The Governor may hot hold other public office. *No Governor may serve more than 2 terms.*

SEC. 7. Section 11 of Article V of the California Constitution is amended to read:

SEC. 11. The Lieutenant Governor, Attorney General, Controller, Secretary of State, and Treasurer shall be elected at the same time and places and for the same term as the Governor. *No Lieutenant Governor, Attorney General, Controller, Secretary of State, or Treasurer may serve in the same office for more than 2 terms.*

SEC. 8. Section 2 of Article IX of the California Constitution is amended to read:

SEC. 2. A Superintendent of Public Instruction shall be elected by the qualified electors of the State at each gubernatorial election. The Superintendent of Public Instruction shall enter upon the duties of the office on the first Monday after the first day of January next succeeding each gubernatorial election. *No Superintendent of Public Instruction may serve more than 2 terms.*

SEC. 9. Section 17 of Article XIII of the California Constitution is amended to read:

SEC. 17. The Board of Equalization consists of 5 voting members: the Controller and 4 members elected for 4-year terms at gubernatorial elections. The state shall be divided into four Board of Equalization districts with the voters of each district electing one member. *No member may serve more than 2 terms.*

SEC. 10. Section 7 is added to Article XX of the California Constitution to read:

SEC. 7. The limitations on the number of terms prescribed by Section 2 of Article IV, Sections 2 and 11 of Article V, Section 2 of Article IX, and Section 17 of Article XIII apply only to terms to which persons are elected or appointed on or after November 6, 1990, except that an incumbent Senator whose office is not on the ballot for general election on that date may serve only one additional term. Those limitations shall not apply to any unexpired term to which a person is elected or appointed if the remainder of the term is less than half of the full term.

SEC. 11. Section 11 (d) is added to Article VII of the California Constitution to read:

SEC. 11. (a) The Legislators' Retirement System shall not pay any unmodified retirement allowance or its actuarial equivalent to any person who on or after January 1, 1987, entered for the first time any state office for which membership in the Legislators' Retirement System was elective or to any beneficiary or survivor of such a person, which exceeds the higher of (1) the salary receivable by the person currently serving in the office in which the retired person served, or (2) the highest salary that was received by the retired person while serving in that office.

(b) The Judges' Retirement System shall not pay any unmodified retirement allowance or its actuarial equivalent to any person who on or after January 1, entered for the first time any judicial office subject to the Judges' Retirement System or to any beneficiary or survivor of such a person, which exceeds the higher of (1) the salary receivable by the person currently serving in the judicial office in which the retired person served or (2) the highest salary that was received by the retired person while serving in that judicial office.

(c) The Legislature may define the terms used in this section.

(d) If any part of this measure or the application to any person or circumstance is held invalid, the invalidity shall not affect other provisions or applications which reasonably can be given effect without the invalid provision or application.

Official Title and Summary:

LIMITS ON TERMS OF OFFICE, LEGISLATORS' RETIREMENT, LEGISLATIVE OPERATING COSTS. INITIATIVE CONSTITUTIONAL AMENDMENT

- Persons elected or appointed after November 5, 1990, holding offices of Governor, Lieutenant Governor, Attorney General, Controller, Secretary of State, Treasurer, Superintendent of Public Instruction, Board of Equalization members, and State Senators, limited to two terms; members of the Assembly limited to three terms.

- Requires legislators elected or serving after November 1, 1990, to participate in federal Social Security program; precludes accrual of other pension and retirement benefits resulting from legislative service, except vested rights.

- Limits expenditures of Legislature for compensation and operating costs and equipment, to specified amount.

Summary of Legislative Analyst's Estimate of Net State and Local Government Fiscal Impact:

- The limitation on terms will have no fiscal effect.

- The restrictions on the legislative retirement benefits would reduce state costs by approximately $750,000 a year.

- To the extent that future legislators do not participate in the federal Social Security system, there would be unknown future savings to the state.

- Legislative expenditures in 1991-92 would be reduced by about 38 percent, or $70 million.

- In subsequent years, the measure would limit growth in these expenditures to the changes in the state's appropriations limit.

Analysis by the Legislative Analyst

Background

There are 132 elected state officials in California. This includes 120 legislators and 12 other state officials, including the Governor, Lieutenant Governor, and Attorney General. Currently, there is no limit on the number of terms that these officials can serve. Proposition 112, passed by the voters in June 1990, requires the annual salaries and benefits (excluding retirement) of these state officials to be set by a commission. Most of these officials participate in the federal Social Security system, and all have the option of participating in the Legislators' Retirement System. The vast majority of the 132 elected state officials participate in this retirement system. The system is supported by contributions from participating officials and the state.

Funding for the Legislature and its employees is included in the annual state budget. Before it becomes law, the budget must be approved by a two-thirds vote of the membership of both houses of the Legislature and must be signed by the Governor.

Proposal

This initiative makes three major changes to the California Constitution. First, it limits the number of terms that an elected state official can serve in the *same office* (the new office of Insurance Commissioner is not affected by this measure). Second, it prohibits legislators from earning state retirement benefits from their future service in the Legislature. Third, it limits the total amount of expenditures by the Legislature for salaries and operating expenses.

The specific provisions of this measure are:

Limits on the Terms of Elected State Officials

- The following state elected officials would be limited to no more than two four-year terms in the same office: Governor, Lieutenant Governor, Attorney General, Controller, Secretary of State, Superintendent of Public Instruction, Treasurer, members of the Board of Equalization, and State Senators.

- Members of the State Assembly would be limited to no more than three two-year terms in the same office.

- These limits apply to a state official who is elected on or after November 6, 1990. However, State Senators whose offices are *not* on the November 6, 1990 ballot may serve only one additional term.

Restrictions on Legislative Retirement Benefits

- This measure prohibits current and future legislators from earning state retirement benefits from their service in the Legislature on or after November 7, 1990. This restriction would not eliminate retirement benefits earned prior to that time.

- This measure requires a legislator serving in the Legislature on or after November 7, 1990 to participate in the federal Social Security system. (However, federal law may permit only current legislators who are presently participating in the federal Social Security system to continue to participate in the system. It may also prohibit future legislators from participating in the federal Society Security system.)

- This measure does not change the Social Security coverage or the state retirement benefits of other state elected officials such as the Governor, Lieutenant Governor, and Attorney General.

Limits on Expenditures by the Legislature

- This measure limits the amount of expenditures by the Legislature for salaries and operating expenses, beginning in the 1991-92 fiscal year.

- In 1991-92, these expenditures are limited to the *lower* of two amounts: (1) a total of $950,000 per Member or (2) 80 percent of the total amount of money expended in the previous year for these purposes. In future years, the measure limits expenditure growth to an amount equal to the percentage change in the state's appropriations limit.

Fiscal Effect

Limits on the Terms of Elected State Officials. This provision would not have any fiscal effect.

Restrictions on Legislative Retirement Benefits. The provision which prohibits current and future Members of the Legislature from earning state retirement benefits from legislative service on or after November 7, 1990 would reduce state costs by about $750,000 a year.

To the extent that future legislators do not participate in the federal Social Security system, the measure would result in unknown future savings to the state.

Limits on Expenditures by the Legislature. In 1991-92, expenditures by the Legislature would be reduced by about 38 percent, or $70 million. In subsequent years, this measure would limit growth in these expenditures to the changes in the state's appropriations limit.

Argument in Favor of Proposition 140

Proposition 140 will for the first time ever place a limit on the number of times a State official may serve in office.

A Yes Vote on Proposition 140 will reform a political system that has created a legislature of career politicians in California. It is a system that has given a tiny elite (only 120 people out of 30 million) almost limitless power over the lives of California's taxpayers and consumers.

Proposition 140, will limit State Senators to two terms (8 years); will limit Assembly members to three terms (6 years); and limit the Governor and other elected constitutional officers to two terms (8 years).

By reducing the amount they can spend on their personal office expenses, Proposition 140, will cut back on the 3,000 political staffers who serve the legislature in Sacramento. In the first year alone, according to the legislative analyst, it will save taxpayers $60 million.

Proposition 140, will end extravagant pensions for legislators. While most Californians have to depend on Social Security and their own savings, the legislative pension system often pays more than the legislator received while in office. In fact, 50 former officials receive $2,000.00 per month or more from the Legislative retirement fund.

Limiting Terms, will create more competitive elections, so good legislators will always have the opportunity to move up the ladder. Term limitation will end the ingrown, political nature of both houses — to the benefit of every man, woman and child in California.

Proposition 140, will remove the grip that vested interests have over the legislature and remove the huge political slush funds at the disposal of Senate and Assembly leaders.

Proposition 140 will put an end to the life-time legislators, who have developed cozy relationships with special interests. We all remember the saying, "Power corrupts and absolute power corrupts absolutely." But limit the terms of Legislative members, remove the Speaker's cronies, and we will also put an end to the Sacramento web of special favors and patronage.

Proposition 140 will end the reign of the Legislature's powerful officers — the Assembly Speaker (first elected a quarter of a century ago) and the Senate Leader (now into his third decade in the Legislature). Lobbyists and power brokers pay homage to these legislative dictators, for they control the fate of bills, parcel out money to the camp followers and hangers-on, and pull strings behind the scenes to decide election outcomes.

Incumbent legislators seldom lose. In the 1988 election, 100% of incumbent state senators and 96% of incumbent members of the assembly were re-elected. The British House of Lords — even the Soviet Legislature — has a higher turnover rate. Enough is Enough! It's time to put an end to a system that makes incumbents a special class of citizen and pays them a guaranteed annual wage from first election to the grave. Let's restore that form of government of citizens representing their fellow citizens.

VOTE YES ON PROPOSITION 140 TO *LIMIT STATE OFFICIALS TERM OF OFFICE!*

> PETER E. SCHABARUM
> *Chairman, Los Angeles County Board of Supervisors*
>
> LEWIS K. UHLER
> *President, National Tax-Limitation Committee*
>
> J.G. FORD, JR.
> *President, Marin United Taxpayers Association*

Rebuttal to Argument in Favor of Proposition 140

Proposition 140 is a proposal by a downtown Los Angeles politician to take away your right to choose your legislators. He has a history of taking away voting rights. He and two political cronies voted to spend $500,000.00 in tax dollars to hire a personal lawyer to defend him against Voting Rights Act violations in Federal Court. Newspapers call it an "outrageous back room deal."

His "Big Bucks" friends, including high-priced lobbyists, have lined his pockets with campaign contributions to help control who *you* can vote for.

- IF 140 PASSES, LOBBYISTS COULD SUBSTITUTE THEIR OWN PAID EMPLOYEES FOR THE INDEPENDENT STAFF RESEARCHERS OF THE LEGISLATURE ELIMINATED BY THIS MEASURE.

- 140 MISLEADS YOU ABOUT THE SO-CALLED "HIGH" COST OF THE LEGISLATURE — THE COST IS LESS THAN ½ PENNY PER TAX DOLLAR.

- THE BIGGEST LIE IS THE FACT THAT THEY DON'T TELL YOU THAT 140 IS A *LIFETIME BAN*.

This is a blatant power grab by Los Angeles contributors and lobbyists who have been wining and dining "Mr. Downtown Los Angeles" in government for SEVEN TERMS — OVER TWENTY YEARS.

Practice what you preach, "Mr. Downtown Los Angeles," Peter Schabarum. Cut *your own* budget and limit *your own* terms. Don't be a piggy and take away the people's rights after you have fully eaten at the table.

There is no need for 140. The vast majority of the Legislature *already* serves less than 10 years.

That's *your* choice.

Keep it.

Stop Downtown Los Angeles' power grab.

Vote no on 140!

> ED FOGLIA
> *President, California Teachers Association*

DAN TERRY
President, California Professional Firefighters

LINDA M. TANGREN
State Chair, California National Women's Political Caucus

Argument Against Proposition 140

Proposition 140 claims to mandate term limits. But in fact, it limits our voting rights.

This measure takes away the cherished constitutional right to freely cast a ballot for candidates of our choice.

We are asked to forfeit *our* right to decide *who our* individual representatives will be.

PROPOSITION 140'S LIFETIME BAN

140 does *not* limit *consecutive* terms of office. Instead 140 says:

- After serving six years in the Assembly, individuals will be constitutionally *banned for life* from ever serving in the Assembly.

- After serving eight years in the Senate, individuals will be constitutionally *banned for life* from ever serving in the Senate.

- Similar lifetime bans will be imposed on the Superintendent of Public Instruction and other statewide offices.

  There are no exceptions — not for merit, not for statewide emergencies, not for the overwhelming will of the people.

  Once banned, always banned.

PROPOSITION 140 IS UNFAIR

It treats everyone — good and bad, competent and incompetent — the same.

No matter how good a job someone does in office, they will be *banned for life.*

You won't even be able to write-in their names on your ballot. If you do, your vote won't count.

That's just not fair.

LIMITS OUR RIGHT TO CHOOSE

The backers of 140 don't trust us, the people, to choose our elected officials. So instead of promoting thoughtful reforms that help us weed out bad legislators, they impose a lifetime ban that eliminates good legislators and bad ones alike at the expense of our constitutional rights.

No eligible citizen should be *permanently banned* for life from seeking any office in a free society. And we should not be *permanently banned* from voting freely for the candidate of our choice.

Resist the rhetoric. Proposition 140 is not about restricting the powers of incumbency. It's about taking away our powers to choose.

PHONY PENSION REFORM

Proposition 140's retirement provisions are also misdirected and counterproductive.

140 does not eliminate the real abuses: double and triple dipping — the practice of taking multiple pensions.

Instead it raises new barriers to public office by banning our future representatives from earning *any* retirement except their current social security.

140's retirement ban won't hurt rich candidates. It will hurt qualified, ordinary citizens who are not rich and have to work hard to prove economic security for themselves and their families.

PROPOSITION 140 GOES TOO FAR

It upsets our system of constitutional checks and balances, forcing our representatives to become even more dependent on entrenched bureaucrats and shrewd lobbyists.

If its proponents were sincere about political reform, they wouldn't have cluttered it with so many unworkable provisions.

VOTE NO ON PROPOSITION 140

STOP THIS RADICAL AND DANGEROUS SCHEME! PROTECT OUR CONSTITUTIONAL RIGHTS. VOTE NO ON PROPOSITION 140'S LIFETIME BAN.

> DR. REGENE L. MITCHELL
> *President, Consumer Federation of California*
>
> LUCY BLAKE
> *Executive Director, California League of Conservation Voters*
>
> DAN TERRY
> *President, California Professional Firefighters*

Rebuttal to Argument Against Proposition 140

Proposition 140 restores *true* democracy, gives you *real* choices of candidates, protects *your* rights to be represented by someone who knows and cares about *your* wishes. It opens up the political system so *everyone* — not just the entrenched career politicians — can participate.

Proposition 140 will bring new ideas, workable policies and fresh cleansing air to Sacramento. All are needed badly. A stench of greed, and vote-selling hangs over Sacramento because lifetime-in-office incumbents think it's *their* government, not yours.

Californians polled by the state's largest newspaper say "most politicians are for sale," and "taking bribes is a relatively common practice" among lawmakers. Proposition 140 cuts the ties between corrupting special interest money and long-term legislators.

Why don't more people vote? Because incumbents have rigged the system in their favor so much, elections are meaningless. Even the worst of legislators get reelected 98% of the time. Honest, ethical, *truly* representative people who want to run for office don't stand a chance.

Do career legislators *really* earn their guaranteed salaries, extravagant pensions, limousines, air travel and other luxury benefits? No. They use *your* money and *your* government to buy themselves power and guaranteed reelections.

Who really opposes Proposition 140? It isn't ordinary people who have to work for a living. It's incumbent legislators and their camp followers. Beware of movie stars and celebrities in million-dollar TV ads, attacking Proposition 140. They're doing the dirty work for career politicians.

VOTE "YES!" ON PROPOSITION 140. ENOUGH, IS ENOUGH!

W. BRUCE LEE, II
Executive Director, California Business League

LEE A. PHELPS
Chairman, Alliance of California Taxpayers

ART PAGDAN, M.D.
National 1st V.P., Filipino-American Political Association

———

A final note from your casebook editors: As is customary in California, the November 1990 ballot did not reprint the text of Proposition 140 or any of the pro and con arguments. Instead, the voters were given this question:

TERMS OF OFFICE. LEGISLATURE. INITIATIVE CONSTITUTIONAL AMENDMENT. Limits: terms of specified state elected officials, legislators' retirement, pensions. Legislature's operating costs [continued to describe the predicted financial impact of the proposal, as required by state law].

Yes ____　　No ____

The measure passed by a margin of 52.17% to 47.83%.[e]

---

e. When you have finished your analysis, compare your conclusions with the published judicial opinions. See *Bates v. Jones*, 131 F.3d 843 (9th Cir. 1997) (en banc), *cert. denied*, 523 U.S. 1021 (1998), reversing the panel opinion of *Jones v. Bates*, 127 F.3d 839 (9th Cir. 1997); *Legislature v. Eu*, 54 Cal.3d 492, 286 Cal.Rptr. 283, 816 P.2d 1309 (1991), *cert. denied*, 503 U.S. 919 (1992).

Chapter 9

IMPLEMENTATION AND INTERPRETATION OF STATUTES IN THE ADMINISTRATIVE STATE

Under the system of mutually encroaching government powers described in *Federalist* #51 (Madison), the legislature shares lawmaking power with the executive and the judiciary. In Chapter 6, we suggested that statutes are not the end of lawmaking, but are often only the beginning; like judicial precedents and administrative decisions, they may be expanded beyond their terms, applied retroactively, and updated by courts and agencies in appropriate circumstances. We explore this theme — and the related theme of formalist versus realist reasoning in separation of powers problems — more systematically in this chapter.

There are a number of implementation choices available to the legislature. First, the legislature can authorize public enforcers to prosecute violators of the statute and exact some penalty from them (e.g., criminal laws). Second, the legislature can authorize victims of conduct violating the statute to sue the violators for damages and/or injunctive relief (e.g., the Uniform Commercial Code, most tort statutes). In these first two implementation choices, the legislature is authorizing courts to adjudicate the enforcement lawsuits and to develop the standards and rules of the statute. Third, the legislature can delegate the development of standards and/or the adjudication of violations to a public administrative agency or a private group (e.g., the federal securities laws, state licensing regulations). This last choice has been characteristic of the modern administrative state, whose history we trace in Section 1.

Section 1 not only examines the implementation choices — private enforcement, public enforcement, agency enforcement, or a combination of the three — available to the legislature, but also important legal issues related to these implementation choices. Is it legitimate for the legislature to delegate so much of its authority to agencies? At what point does delegation of *law implementing* power essentially become abdication of *lawmaking* power? If Congress has vested enforcement of the statute in an agency or a prosecutor, do courts have the authority to *imply* a cause of action from the statute for private parties as well?

It would be irrational for Congress to delegate substantial lawmaking power to other officials, without retaining some (and perhaps a great deal of) control over the exercise of that power. Not surprisingly, Congress has sought to exercise that sort of control, and Section 2 briefly explores these mechanisms under the lenses of both political and constitutional theory. Among the mechanisms explored will be (1) legislative oversight and investigations of agency enforcement; (2) the legislative veto; (3) control over agency personnel; (4) judicial review; (5) the appropriations power; and (6) the original structuring of the agency. Constitutional problems limit the usefulness of the first three mechanisms; the last three mechanisms are perfectly constitutional but somewhat indirect (and therefore inefficacious) means of congressional control.

Building upon the previous two chapters and the automobile safety case study in this chapter, Section 3 lays out a theory of how agency approaches to statutory interpretation will systematically tend to be different from court approaches to statutory interpretation (the focus of Chapters 7 and 8). Compared to courts, agencies will emphasize statutory purpose more than plain meaning, current legislative and even presidential preferences more than historic preferences (i.e., "original meaning" of statutes), and flexible adaptation of the statute to new circumstances more than following precedent. In short, agencies will be more *dynamic* statutory interpreters than courts will be.

What does this insight mean for judicial review of agency statutory interpretations? Reflecting the traditional role of courts to "declare the law," many judges and commentators maintain that courts should overrule dynamic agency applications that are inconsistent with judges's reading of statutes, following the criteria laid out in Chapter 8. The Administrative Procedure Act, discussed in Section 1, might be read this way. Reflecting the needs of the administrative state and the limited ability of judges to administer a vast legal interpretive regime, many judges and commentators have concluded that courts need to give agencies a lot of breathing room as they apply statutes. The U.S. Supreme Court's *Chevron* decision in 1984 might be read this way. Most of Section 3 will involve the Court's elaboration of *Chevron*, which has generated a complicated "jurisprudence of deference" at the Supreme Court level.

SECTION 1. LAW IMPLEMENTATION IN THE ADMINISTRATIVE STATE

State and federal criminal laws are typically enforced exclusively by official prosecution of offenders. Many other statutes provide for both civil and criminal penalties that may be enforced by official actions filed in court. For example, the Justice Department may bring a civil lawsuit for an injunction under the Sherman Act to prevent or terminate violations of the Act, or it may refer discovered violations to a U.S. Attorney's Office for criminal prosecution, or both.

Since 1875, however, public enforcement has gradually been transformed from such a *prosecutorial model*, in which a government agency or department brings lawsuits against statutory violators and the adjudication and development of rules is accomplished by courts, to a *bureaucratic model*. Under the bureaucratic model, the government agency or department itself adjudicates the individual prosecutions or makes the rules, and the only role for courts is limited judicial review of what the administrators have done. In this section, we present a short history of the modern administrative state, the main constitutional problems that it presents, and its relationship to the primary common law enforcement device — the private cause of action.

A. A BRIEF HISTORY OF THE MODERN ADMINISTRATIVE STATE[a]

1. *Origins: Regulatory Police.* Wherever there is government there is bureaucracy, but through most of the nineteenth century very little policy creation was done through bureaucracy in the United States. Most administrative activity was on the state level, in the form of rate regulation of natural monopolies, such as grain elevators, utilities, and railroads. There were 25 state railroad commissions in 1886, for example. The Supreme Court invalidated state railroad regulation under the Commerce Clause in *Wabash, St. Louis and Pac. Ry. v. Illinois*, 118 U.S. 557 (1886), which stimulated Congress to create the first major federal regulatory agency, the Interstate Commerce Commission (ICC), in 1887. 24 Stat. 379.[b] Congress established the Federal Trade Commission (FTC) in 1914 to enforce some of the antitrust laws and regulate unfair competition, the United States Shipping Board in 1916, the Federal Power Commission in 1920, and the Federal Radio Commission (predecessor to the Federal Communications Commission) in 1929. These commissions and the ICC were the first modern *independent federal agencies*, bureaucracies set up outside of the formal departments of the Executive Branch and with their own adjudicatory and rulemaking responsibilities.[c] See generally Geoffrey Miller, *Independent Agencies*, 1986 Sup. Ct. Rev. 41.

The philosophy behind the establishment of these agencies and bureaus by Populist reformers in the 1880s and 1890s and Progressives in the 1900s and 1910s was to "police" the excesses of businesses. Many laws were responses to scandals exposed during the Progressive Era. For example, the Pure Food

---

a. This history is drawn, in large part, from Robert Rabin, *Federal Regulation in Historical Perspective*, 38 Stan. L. Rev. 1189 (1986). See also Joseph Kearney & Thomas Merrill, *The Great Transformation of Regulated Industries Law*, 98 Colum. L. Rev. 1323 (1998)

b. Ironically, or perhaps appropriately, the ICC was also one of the first major regulatory agencies to be abolished by the Republican Congresses in the late 1990s who sought to reduce the federal bureaucracy.

c. At the same time Congress was creating independent agencies, it gave bureaus or divisions within the existing executive departments similar duties. The Patent Office had existed within the executive department since 1790, and what we now call the Immigration and Naturalization Service was established within the Justice Department in 1882 to adjudicate immigration claims. The Secretary of Agriculture accumulated a great amount of adjudicatory responsibility as a result of the Pure Food and Drug Act of 1906, 34 Stat. 768; the Meat Inspection Act of 1906–07, 34 Stat. 674, 1260; the Cotton Futures Act and the Warehouse Act of 1916, 39 Stat. 453 & 486; and later statutes. *E.g.*, 42 Stat. 159.

and Drug Act of 1906 and the Meat Inspection Act of 1906–07 were triggered by the publication of Upton Sinclair's *The Jungle*, which exposed horrid meat processing practices. Both the Populists, who favored draconian measures against the enemies of the farmer (especially railroads), and the Progressives, who favored marginal change, generally accepted the existing market mechanisms as the norm. They envisioned the work of the ICC and FTC and the Bureau of Chemistry (which administered the Pure Food and Drug Act) as merely facilitating the "natural" operation of the competitive market by preventing the intrusion of "unnatural" practices — fraud, price-fixing, and discrimination.[d]

The reformist approach in this early policing period was, therefore, ambivalent. The attitude of the judiciary was often openly hostile, as judges treated determinations by the ICC and FTC with little deference and refused to enforce well-justified agency requests. On the other hand, the ICC managed to increase its statutory power in 1906 and 1910, when Congress granted the agency authority to regulate rates. Courts gradually came to defer to the agency, though they also required it to follow essential procedural safeguards (a trial-type hearing) in order to develop an administrative record that could be the basis for meaningful judicial review. See, e.g., *ICC v. Louisville and Nashville Ry. Co.*, 227 U.S. 88, 93 (1913).

The evolution of the ICC brought to light a problem with viewing agencies merely as policing institutions. World War I was to underscore the problem, as lawmakers and the public began to perceive government boards as necessary to compel the private sector to meet the needs of the war effort. An immediate result of the war effort was the Transportation Act of 1920, 41 Stat. 456, which greatly expanded the powers of the ICC beyond the policing of price discrimination against shippers. During the war, the government ran the railroads, and the Act gave the ICC authority to do the same — by regulating rates, mergers and consolidations, and service schedules comprehensively (and, presumably, efficiently).

2. *The New Deal: Regulatory Planning and Market Management.* The Great Depression suggested to many that the "natural" operation of the market was not necessarily a good thing at all, and that much more government direction was needed. FDR's New Deal was a cluster of experiments proceeding in many different directions — from the aspirations of comprehensive industrial planning in the National Industrial Recovery Act to the ambitious subsidy program of the Agricultural Adjustment Act. Most of these regulatory initiatives rejected the policing approach of the Populists and Progressives. The New Deal measures were more comprehensive and affirmative (and sometimes managerial) approaches to a market that was seen to be structurally unfair and unreliable. The distinction between public and private spheres of American life became more blurred.

---

d. See 3 Robert Himmelberg, *Growth of the Regulatory State, 1900–1917: State and Federal Regulation of Railroads and Other Enterprises* (1994). For an argument that most of these early statutes represented rent-seeking by regulated interests, see Gabriel Kolko, *The Triumph of Conservatism: A Reinterpretation of American History* (1963).

The New Deal created an unprecedented array of new independent agencies and departmental bureaus. Some of them had brief lives. The National Industrial Recovery Act (NIRA), representing the New Deal's most ambitious effort at economic planning, did little to help the economy and was declared unconstitutional by the Supreme Court in *A.L.A. Schechter Poultry Corp. v. United States*, 295 U.S. 495 (1935). Other New Deal agencies have become part of our federal governance. The National Labor Relations Board (NLRB) was established as an independent agency outside the Labor Department to alleviate inequality in the labor market and to head off labor strife by adjudicating the existence of "unfair labor practices" by labor unions and management. It had the authority to enforce its determinations through "cease-and-desist" orders. The Securities and Exchange Commission (SEC) was established to prevent unstable capital markets by registering and regulating securities offerings according to the commands provided in the applicable statutes and SEC rules. The Federal Deposit Insurance Corporation (FDIC) was a response to the disastrous bank runs of the Great Depression and sought to improve confidence in the system by insuring small depositors. By 1941 there were, by one count, 19 separate lawmaking bureaus within the executive departments and 22 independent agencies. *Final Report of the Attorney General's Committee on Administrative Procedure* (1941).

As administrative agencies and bureaus proliferated, so did criticisms of them. But given the New Deal's transformation of attitudes about across-the-board federal structural intervention in the market, most criticisms did not focus on the appropriate field of administrative activity. Instead, critics targeted the inadequacies of agency procedure and judicial review: important property rights were being stripped away without proper procedural safeguards, such as trial-type hearing procedures and/or meaningful judicial review of the bureaucratic decision.[e] In 1945, the Attorney General endorsed legislation standardizing administrative procedure, and the Administrative Procedure Act (APA), 60 Stat. 237, codified as amended at 5 U.S.C. §§ 551–559, 701–706 *et al.*, was enacted in 1946.

On its face, the APA divides administrative decisions according to a *bipolar model*, to use Dean Ronald Cass's term. Administrative decisions are treated as either *rules* or *orders*. Rules are like statutes, for they are "designed to implement, interpret, or prescribe law or policy." 5 U.S.C. § 551(4). Most rules are *informal*, but the procedure generating most informal rules is the more

---

e. In 1938, the ABA Special Committee on Administrative Law, chaired by former Dean Roscoe Pound of the Harvard Law School, issued a report scathingly denouncing the new bureaucracy for malign "tendencies" to decide without a hearing, to consider matters not in the record, to disregard jurisdictional limits, and to conflate the legislative, prosecutorial, and adjudicative functions — all to the detriment of hapless regulated interests. In light of such criticisms, President Roosevelt appointed the Attorney General's Committee on Administrative Procedure, which concluded that the agencies and bureaus were generally doing a good job but that procedures needed to be regularized. A minority on the Committee believed that there were systematic problems with administrative procedures and strongly urged the adoption of a "Code of Standards of Fair Procedure." Between 1938 and 1945, the ABA had such legislation introduced in every session of Congress and lobbied hard for its adoption.

formal-sounding *notice-and-comment rulemaking*. In this process, the agency must publish notice of proposed rules in the Federal Register, followed by the opportunity for interested persons to submit comments, usually written, on the proposed rules. *Id.* § 553. See Cornelius Kerwin, *Rulemaking: How Government Agencies Write Law and Policy* (2d ed. 1999) (comprehensive description and analysis of notice-and-comment rulemaking); Peter Strauss, *The Rulemaking Continuum*, 41 Duke L.J. 1463 (1992) (the variety of rulemaking options).

Orders are like judicial decisions, for they constitute the "final disposition" of a controversy involving the statutory or agency rules. 5 U.S.C. § 551(6). Thus, the typical procedure for formal adjudicative orders is similar to trial in a court. If the enabling statute calls for decision "on the record after opportunity for agency hearing," *id.* §§ 554(a) & 556(a), the agency must not only provide particularized notice to the affected person, but it must also allow him or her "to present his [or her] case or defense by oral or documentary evidence, to submit rebuttal evidence, and to conduct such cross-examination as may be required for a full and true disclosure of facts." *Id.* § 556(d). The agency's decision must be based on the trial-type record and supported by reliable, probative, and substantial evidence. *Id.* § 557.[f] Sections 554 and 556–557 mandate at least a partial separation of functions between the prosecutorial staff and agency decisionmakers, particularly in formal adjudications. For example, formal adjudications are usually handled by *administrative law judges*, who have their own staff and are monitored and rewarded by the Civil Service Commission and not by the agency itself.

Sections 701–706 provide for judicial review of agency rules and orders. "Any person suffering legal wrong because of agency action, or adversely affected or aggrieved by agency action within the meaning of a relevant statute, is entitled to judicial review thereof," *id.* § 702, unless "(1) statutes preclude judicial review; or (2) agency action is committed to agency discretion by law." *Id.* § 701(a). In an action for judicial review, the court "shall" under § 706:

> (1) compel agency action unlawfully withheld or unreasonably delayed; and

> (2) hold unlawful and set aside agency action, findings, and conclusions found to be —

> (A) arbitrary, capricious, an abuse of discretion, or otherwise not in accordance with law;

> (B) contrary to constitutional right, power, privilege, or immunity;

---

f. The text sets forth the typical rulemaking and adjudication procedures. The APA has alternate procedures in each instance. Where the statute requires rulemaking decisions "on the record," §§ 556–557 set forth more detailed trial-like procedures. See *United States v. Florida East Coast Railway*, 410 U.S. 224 (1973) (essentially requiring these magic words to trigger the more burdensome formal rulemaking proceedings). The vast amount of agency work is done through informal adjudications, which is the term applied to any action that does not fall into one of the other three categories.

(C) in excess of statutory jurisdiction, authority, or limitations, or short of statutory right;

(D) without observance of procedure required by law;

(E) unsupported by substantial evidence in a case subject to sections 556 and 557 of this title or otherwise reviewed on the record of an agency hearing provided by statute; or

(F) unwarranted by the facts to the extent that the facts are subject to trial de novo by the reviewing court.

The APA compromise was essentially designed to recognize the legislative and adjudicative roles of independent agencies and departmental bureaus (both of which are included in the APA definition of "agency," *id.* § 551(1)), but also to "rein in" the bureaucratic state with procedural safeguards and judicial review to prevent arbitrary or unlawful action. The APA's enactment broadly validated the bureaucratic revolution of the New Deal and ushered in a period of relative consensus in favor of agency lawmaking in the 1950s.

3. *The Public Interest Era: Deregulation and New Kinds of Regulation.* Some scholars as early as the 1950s raised concerns that bureaucratic regulation of the economy is subject to bias and debilitation over time. Marver Bernstein, *Regulating Business by Independent Commission* (1955), for example, argued that agencies, like human beings, typically go through a "life cycle." The agency's *youth* is characterized by a crusading spirit engendered by its statutory mandate, but also by the agency's struggle to devise a regulatory strategy to deal with the better organized and often savvy industry to be regulated. The agency's *maturity* comes after it has lost much of the political support and enthusiasm that spawned its enabling statute, but in this period the agency "understands" the industry better and takes a less aggressive approach to regulating it, often becoming a "captive" of the regulated industry and even a pawn in the industry's own plans. *Senescence* comes when the agency grows not only less vital but also inflexible, a condition that may lead to some form of euthanasia. Later public choice scholars have been even less charitable in thinking about the typical agency biography than Bernstein was, characterizing agencies as captured from childhood by rent-seeking special interests.[g] The 1950s also saw the true beginnings of noneconomic regulatory activities stimulated first by the civil rights revolution, followed in the 1960s by the environmental movement.

These two developments inspired a new period of administrative law development in the 1960s and the 1970s. Bureaucracy became both more distrusted and better integrated into the great public interest movements of those decades. The regulatory emphasis has shifted from comprehensive

---

g. See, e.g., Anthony Downs, *Inside Bureaucracy* (1967); William Niskanen, *Bureaucracy and Representative Government* (1971); Sam Peltzman, *Toward a More General Theory of Regulation*, 19 J.L. & Econ. 211 (1976); George Stigler, *The Theory of Economic Regulation*, 2 Bell J. Econ. & Mgmt. Sci. 3 (1971).

direction of the economy to *command-and-control* statutes aimed at specific problems not traditionally thought of in market terms.

The Great Society was the linchpin of this shift. The Civil Rights Act of 1964, 78 Stat. 241, established an impressive range of bureaucratic sanctions for civil rights violations. For example, Titles III and IV of the Act authorized the Attorney General to file public lawsuits to desegregate public facilities and public education. Title VI provided for nondiscrimination in federally assisted programs. It was to be implemented by rules making federal grants, loans, or other financial assistance contingent upon the recipient's following nondiscriminatory policies.

Chapter 1 describes Title VII of the 1964 Act, which established the Equal Employment Opportunity Commission (EEOC) and charged it with rulemaking and adjudication of the very broad prohibition of employment discrimination. Though troubled with administrative problems over time, the EEOC served as a model for a new bureaucracy of conscience. Its intrusion into the affairs of corporations and state and local institutions helped broaden the concept of regulation. Government's agenda extended beyond the economic marketplace and toward concern for the creation of a "great society" in which racial, sexual, and ethnic equality would be recognized. Even many of the economic initiatives of the 1960s — the War on Poverty, Medicare, the Food Stamp Program — were aimed at different targets from traditional New Deal regulation. These programs, like Title VII, sought to help the poor and the disadvantaged, often without any attempted justification based upon systemic or isolated market failure.

The 1970s saw the societal transformation approach to regulation expand to include consumer rights, public health and safety, and environmental purity as important agenda items. Just as the regulatory *agenda* was changing, so was the regulatory *mechanism*. Both authorized and encouraged by the new generation of regulatory statutes, United States agencies in the 1970s showed unprecedented interest in *rulemaking* rather than adjudication and less formal mechanisms.

The National Traffic and Motor Vehicle Safety Act of 1966 exemplified the new approach. The NTMVSA and other regulatory statutes of this period tended to have more specific mandates, to focus authority in a single administrator (rather than a multi-member commission), to open up agencies to public input, and to focus agency action on the establishment of mandatory policy through general rules.[h] The agency rules themselves were different from what came before: rather than command-and-control models, agencies emphasized goals and limits, and left regulated institutions with choices about how to reach those goals and limits.

---

h. Jerry Mashaw, *The Story of* Motor Vehicle Manufacturers Association etc: *Law, Science, and Politics in the Administrative State*, in *Administrative Law Stories* 334, 339–42 (Peter Strauss ed., 2006); David Shapiro, *The Choice of Rulemaking or Adjudication in the Development of Administrative Policy*, 78 Harv. L. Rev. 921 (1965).

Closely following this new model was a wave of pollution control legislation, mainly the Clean Air Act Amendments of 1970 (CAA), 84 Stat. 1676, and the Federal Water Pollution Control Act Amendments of 1972 (FWPCA), 86 Stat. 816. Congress established ambitious mandates to clean up our environment. Most of the directives were very general, with the details filled in by the Environmental Protection Agency (EPA). The National Environmental Policy Act of 1969 (NEPA), 83 Stat. 852, and other statutes directed all federal departments and agencies to consider environmental effects when decisions are made. The Occupational Health and Safety Act of 1970, 84 Stat. 1590, created the Occupational Health and Safety Administration and directed it to enforce more stringent standards of safety in the workplace. Several pieces of landmark legislation worked to redistribute resources to the less well-off in society; Congress enacted the Food Stamp Act, 1 U.S.C. § 2011 et seq., Head Start programs, Medicare, and Medicaid, and it expanded welfare programs substantially.

These statutes marked a significant change in economic regulation as well. First, they redefined market imperfection. The New Deal approach defined costs rather mechanically, in terms of lost output and distorted flows of resources. Things like pollution and injuries were treated as *externalities* borne for the most part by those receiving them. Regulation in the 1970s compelled businesses to consider these social costs and to do something about them. Second, the public interest legislation of the 1970s at least implicitly recognized and built upon perceived biases in the federal bureaucracy. Many reformers argued that even the few agencies and bureaus that were not essentially captured by their regulated interests were limited by their statutory mandate to consider only a few policy concerns, usually of a material and tangible nature. The regulatory structures created in the 1970s insisted that quality of life concerns be factored into the bureaucratic calculus (NEPA) and often provided very specific substantive guidelines and time deadlines for agencies to accomplish their regulatory goals (CAA).

Other developments have sought to open up agency decisionmaking. For example, the Freedom of Information Act, 5 U.S.C. § 552, was passed in 1966, 80 Stat. 250, and significantly amended in 1974, 88 Stat. 1561, to require federal agencies and departments to disclose documents and information to persons requesting them, subject to specific exemptions in the Act. The purpose of the Act was to encourage citizens to monitor government performance and publicize problems. See also the Privacy Act of 1974, 88 Stat. 1896, codified at 5 U.S.C. § 552a (protecting personal information from disclosure). The Government in the Sunshine Act of 1976, 90 Stat. 1241, codified at *id.* § 552b, requires agencies headed by collegial bodies (e.g., FTC, SEC) to conduct their official business in public meetings, again subject to specific exemptions. Like the APA, these statutes were enacted to assure structures of agency decisionmaking that are responsive to the reasoned public interest. Indeed, this statutory liberalization in the 1970s was accompanied by more aggressive APA judicial review of agency decisions and procedures in the 1970s and 1980s, a phenomenon explored in Section 3.[i]

A CASE STUDY: THE NATIONAL TRAFFIC AND MOTOR VEHICLE SAFETY ACT OF 1966

As a result of charges by Ralph Nader and other policy entrepreneurs that automobiles were "unsafe at any speed," the issue of motor vehicle safety became a salient one on the national agenda. In a 1966 address to Congress, President Johnson declared that auto safety was a high priority issue for his administration. "The toll of Americans killed [on highways] since the introduction of the automobile is truly unbelievable. It is 1.5 million — more than all the combat deaths suffered in all wars." After numerous hearings, Congress enacted the National Traffic and Motor Vehicle Safety Act of 1966, Pub. L. No. 89–563, 80 Stat. 718, codified at 15 U.S.C. §§ 1381, 1391–1409, 1421–1425, which (together with the Highway Safety Act of 1966) created the National Traffic Safety Agency, later renamed the National Highway Traffic Safety Administration (NHTSA) within the new Department of Transportation.

Congress vested the agency with the authority to promulgate rules to establish "motor vehicle safety standards" that were "reasonable, practicable, and appropriate, * * * meet the need for motor vehicle safety, and * * * [were] stated in objective terms" (§ 1392). No one could sell or import into the United States motor vehicles or equipment not in conformity with these standards (15 U.S.C. § 1397). The penalty for selling or importing motor vehicles in violation of the § 1392 standards was $1,000 for each violation, to be assessed and possibly compromised by the Secretary of Transportation (§ 1398), as well as preliminary or final injunctive relief issued by a federal court at the behest of the United States (§ 1399). Additionally, a distributor or dealer in automobiles had a federal cause of action against a manufacturer or distributor, respectively, which sold it a vehicle or equipment not conforming to the standards and which failed to cure the problem through repurchase or replacement (§ 1400).

There was an exciting big idea underlying the Act. Prior efforts to effect auto safety, such as speed limits and drunk-driving sanctions, sought to *avoid accidents*. Epidemiologists noted that injuries and deaths were more proximately caused by the passenger's collision with parts of his own car, and not just the collisions of two cars. Hence, they proposed a second strategy for reducing death and injury: *redesign the automobile*. Mechanisms that hold the passenger in place (today's seatbelts and shoulder harnesses) or cushion the passenger from the chassis (today's airbags) could prevent injuries from the "second collision."

The Act, passed without a single negative vote in Congress, had a phenomenal beginning but has not lived up to its potential since then.

---

i. See also Peter Strauss, *From Expertise to Politics: The Transformation of American Rulemaking*, 31 Wake Forest L. Rev. 745 (1996) (tracing developments in rulemaking and regulations over the past decades).

According to Jerry Mashaw and David Harfst, *The Struggle for Auto Safety* (1990), the big problem has been the ability of the "Big Three" automakers (General Motors, Ford, Chrysler) to defeat or delay NHTSA's proposed regulations in judicial proceedings, executive department deliberations, and congressional oversight hearings. The upshot of these efforts has been that the agency has been unable to impose design changes that would save lives. According to Kevin McDonald, *Shifting Out of Park: Moving Auto Safety from Recalls to Reason* (2006), in contrast, the big problem has been neglect of human errors as the overwhelming cause of accidents and failure to attack accident-causing activities: tailgating, speeding, driving while drunk, and cell-phone use by drivers. Both McDonald and Mashaw-Harfst conclude that the NHTSA relies far too much on recalls as a method of regulation.

The auto industry was able to win cases which required NHTSA to prove that its regulations were practicable, *Paccar, Inc. v. NHTSA*, 573 F.2d 632 (9th Cir. 1978), but then made it hard for NHTSA to collect the data it needed to prove practicability. The auto industry also won favorable judicial decisions which required endless rounds of notice and discussion on even the most minute amendments to regulations. *Wagner Electric Corp. v. Volpe*, 466 F.2d 1013 (3d Cir. 1972). The courts were "inattentive to the opportunity costs of repeated cycles of notice and comment. With no apparent recognition of the potential for disruption it was creating, [*Wagner*] greatly complicated an increasingly unwieldy rulemaking process, legitimized opponents' dilatory tactics, and made information gathering much more difficult for the resource-strapped agency. * * * [N]ew rounds of notice and comment could go on for decades. All this in the name of procedural fairness to state agencies and consumer advocacy groups, who were about as common in agency rulemaking proceedings as Quakers at prize fights." Mashaw & Harfst, *Auto Safety*, 100.

The structure of American government arguably impeded the agency's ability to adopt strongly directive regulations. Since safety regulation had traditionally been accomplished at the state rather than federal level, NHTSA was often required to postpone action until states had their opportunities to address problems. Separation of powers also made NHTSA's assignment burdensome, because it gave the agency too many bosses; it was accountable to both the President and the Congress, which in the 1970s had very different regulatory philosophies. Congress with hundreds of members not only gave direction contrary to the President, but its members could not even agree with one another.

In the Motor Vehicle and Schoolbus Safety Amendments of 1974, Pub. L. No. 93–492, 88 Stat. 1477, Congress responded to some of the agency's concerns but also responded to concerns raised by the auto industry. Overall, the amendments made effective regulation more difficult, because the legislative coalition favoring strong highway safety measures (the coalition that had prevailed in 1966) was no longer able to control the legislative agenda or prevent raids on the agency's freedom. Thus, the 1974 Amendments imposed a legislative veto requirement on rules involving future passive restraints; under this provision, a vote of both houses of Congress could nullify any such regulation, without the President's signature. See § 2C of this chapter (discussing legislative vetoes which were later held to be unconstitutional). The 1974 Amendments also eliminated the agency's authority to adopt rules requiring an *interlock* between seat belts and a car's ignition, which prevented the car from starting unless belts were buckled. (See Mashaw & Harfst, *Auto Safety,* ch. 7, for the history of the 1974 Amendments.)

The disabilities recounted above eventually discouraged NHTSA from regulating auto safety though the adoption of motor vehicle safety rules, as the Act originally contemplated. This reality is particularly unfortunate because many of NHTSA's early standards, dealing with the interior of cars and manual safety belts, made significant contributions to safety, saved many lives, and cost relatively little money. Adapting to a legal and political culture that killed bold initiatives, NHTSA set its sights lower, focusing on the recall of cars with traditionally defined defects. The 1974 Amendments, in fact, expanded NHTSA's powers in this regard: upon notification of defects (§ 1413), the manufacturer had to provide an expeditious remedy (§ 1414), with federal courts available for enforcement of agency orders and with civil fines for violating the orders (§ 1415). The agency busied itself with the task of finding defects and requiring quick remedies. Recalls, which were originally not the primary purpose of the agency, statistically do little to contribute to auto safety, according to both McDonald and Mashaw-Harfst. We shall return to this agency and its problems throughout this chapter.

B. PRIVATE CAUSES OF ACTION IN THE BUREAUCRATIC STATE

The English common law considered private lawsuits the primary mode of enforcing both common law and statutes (even criminal statutes). The common law tradition of private enforcement, of course, is hardly moribund, and many statutes explicitly provide for enforcement by private lawsuits, unmediated by public enforcers. Examples include the Uniform Commercial Code, Title VII of the Civil Rights Act, and the Sherman Act and other antitrust statutes.

Several interesting conceptual questions are raised in connection with private law enforcement in the administrative state. One is whether the existence of agency enforcement may sometimes delay or preclude otherwise existing private lawsuits. Anomalously, the answer is that they can. The doctrine of "primary jurisdiction" applies to claims originally brought as court actions but in fact requiring "resolution of issues which, under a regulatory scheme, have been placed within the special competence of an administrative body; in such a case the judicial process is suspended pending referral of such issues to the administrative body for its views." *United States v. Western Pac. R. Co.,* 352 U.S. 59, 64 (1956). The policy reasons for referring such issues to an agency include preserving the uniformity and consistency of regulation and obtaining the insights of the agency, which has more experience and special insights into the market or issues being litigated. *Far East Conf. v.*

United States, 342 U.S. 570, 574–75 (1952). Is this traditional doctrine based upon concepts that retain current vitality?[j]

In some instances, the federal statutory scheme will be interpreted to strip individuals of their otherwise existing rights to sue. For example, in *Keogh v. Chicago and N.W. Ry.*, 260 U.S. 156 (1922), the Supreme Court held that plaintiff shippers could not sue for damages under the Sherman Act based upon claims that the published railroad rates filed and accepted by the ICC would have been lower but for an illegal conspiracy in restraint of trade. Still, relatively comprehensive regulatory schemes do not necessarily represent an implicit desire by Congress to eliminate other causes of action under federal statutes or state law. In *Nader v. Allegheny Airlines, Inc.*, 426 U.S. 290 (1976), the Supreme Court held that the Federal Aviation Act did not preempt Ralph Nader's common law action for fraud and misrepresentation when the defendant airline "bumped" him from a flight to which he had a ticket. How is this case different from *Keogh*? Should the Safety Act of 1966 (the case study concluding Part A) close off state tort remedies for car owners injured because of safety defects in their vehicles? See 15 U.S.C. § 1420 (explicit provision preserving state consumer remedies, but added to Safety Act only in 1974).

The second question is the converse of the first (almost): Does a private party have a cause of action to enforce a statute even though the statute does not explicitly set forth such a private cause of action? Again, the answer is sometimes yes, and again this answer has changed in response to the Court's evolving understanding of the implications of the modern administrative state.

The Court's early cases simply followed the common law approach: interests Congress sought to protect or benefit through a statute presumptively had a cause of action to enforce the statute by seeking injunctive relief or damages. See *Texas and Pacific Railroad Co. v. Rigsby*, 241 U.S. 33 (1916). After the New Deal, the Court was pressed to justify implied causes of action in light of the primary responsibility given to agencies for enforcement of many of the new regulatory statutes. If Congress had established an agency and vested it with enforcement authority, and had not explicitly authorized private enforcement, shouldn't the *Rigsby* presumption be reversed? The Warren Court seemingly thought not. In its leading decision, *J.I. Case Co. v. Borak*, 377 U.S. 426 (1964), the Court held that § 14(a) of the Securities Exchange

---

j. For example, in *Ricci v. Chicago Mercantile Exchange*, 409 U.S. 289 (1973), plaintiff brought an antitrust complaint alleging a conspiracy to strip him of his membership in the mercantile exchange. The Supreme Court affirmed a stay of the antitrust action pending proceedings before the Commodity Exchange Commission to determine whether the procedural rules of the local exchange had been followed in depriving plaintiff of his membership. After the Commission's decision, the trial court would be able to rule on defendant's claim of statutory antitrust immunity, which assumed full compliance with the procedural rules of the local exchange. The Supreme Court set out three "related premises" on which its decision was based: (1) the trial court was faced with a "substantial" claim of antitrust immunity (2) which depended on facts and findings which were within the statutory jurisdiction and expertise of the agency, and (3) adjudication of those facts by the agency promised to be of material aid in resolving the immunity question.

Act of 1934, 48 Stat. 895, codified at 15 U.S.C. § 78n(a) (1988), created an implied cause of action for private parties. As interpreted by the SEC, § 14(a) prohibits proponents of suggested corporate actions (in *Borak*, a merger) from promulgating false or misleading materials in connection with solicitation of shareholder proxies. The Court held that the Act's general authorization of federal court jurisdiction, in § 27, carried with it the creation of a cause of action for private parties. The Court explained that its interpretation was necessary to carry out the statute's purpose, "the protection of investors."

This rationale seems pretty simplistic, for it assumes that more enforcement is always better. What if Congress omitted a private cause of action from § 14 because it wanted a medium level of enforcement, carefully monitored by the SEC, which presumably could screen complaints and only pursue those that are most important and best supported by evidence? *Borak* responded to this argument (377 U.S. at 432):

> Private enforcement of the proxy rules provides a necessary supplement to Commission action. As in antitrust treble damage litigation, the possibility of civil damages or injunctive relief serves as a most effective weapon in the enforcement of the proxy requirements. The Commission advises that it examines over 2,000 proxy statements annually and each of them must necessarily be expedited. Time does not permit an independent examination of the facts set out in the proxy material and this results in the Commission's acceptance of the representations contained therein at their face value, unless contrary to other material on file with it. Indeed, on the allegations of respondent's complaint, the proxy material failed to disclose alleged unlawful market manipulation of the stock of ATC, and this unlawful manipulation would not have been apparent to the Commission until after the merger.

Borak was decided in 1964.

Implied Right of Action Problem

Problem 9–1. In 1971, Jane Doe sues General Motors in federal court, alleging that her Buick was in violation of a NHTSA standard and that the defect caused an accident, for which she seeks damages. Although the Act has no express cause of action for consumers like Doe, she relies on *Borak* and the Act's stated purpose, "to reduce traffic accidents" by establishing "motor vehicle safety standards." 15 U.S.C. § 1381. GM responds that the statutory scheme permits citizens to petition the agency to initiate investigations into alleged defects, with the implicit premise that citizen complaints should be channeled into the agency and not into courts.

Would a federal judge in 1971 find such an implied cause of action? See *Handy v. General Motors Corp.*, 518 F.2d 786 (9th Cir. 1975). Would it make a difference to you that Representative Eckhardt (D–Tex.) in 1974 urged Congress to recognize a private cause of action to challenge any NHTSA failure to proceed against an automotive defect? See 120 Cong. Rec. 27,807-08 (1974).

NOTE ON THE COURT'S POST-*BORAK* PRACTICE: SHIFT FROM LEGISLATIVE PURPOSE TO LEGISLATIVE INTENT

Reconsider your answer to Problem 9–1 after the Supreme Court rethought the notion of implied causes of action in *Cort v. Ash*, 422 U.S. 66 (1975). As in *Borak*, the plaintiff was a shareholder suing corporate directors for violating federal law. Unlike the earlier case, the federal statute in *Cort* was a criminal one, prohibiting corporations from contributing to presidential elections. 18 U.S.C. § 610 (1972). And unlike *Borak*, the Court did not find a private cause of action in order to effectuate the purpose of the statute. Justice Brennan's opinion in *Cort* announced the following approach (422 U.S. at 78):

> In determining whether a private remedy is implicit in a statute not expressly providing one, several factors are relevant. First, is the plaintiff "one of the class for whose *especial* benefit the statute was enacted," *Rigsby* (emphasis supplied [by the Court]) — that is, does the statute create a federal right in favor of the plaintiff? Second, is there any indication of legislative intent, explicit or implicit, either to create such a remedy or to deny one? Third, is it consistent with the underlying purposes of the legislative scheme to imply such a remedy for the plaintiff? And finally, is the cause of action one traditionally relegated to state law, in an area basically the concern of the States, so that it would be inappropriate to infer a cause of action based solely on federal law?

Cort declined to imply a private cause of action, because criminal statutes are usually enacted for the benefit of the public generally and because the legislative history of § 610 suggested that protecting shareholders was, at best, a secondary concern of Congress. Does *Cort* change your answer in *Doe v. General Motors*?

Although *Cort* cited and relied on *Borak* and is easily distinguishable because it involved a criminal statute, it marks a watershed in the legisprudence of implied causes of action. Before *Cort*, private causes of action were usually implied; after *Cort*, usually not. For an exception, see *Cannon v. University of Chicago*, 441 U.S. 677 (1979), where the Court implied a private cause of action for violation of Title IX of the Education Amendments of 1972, 20 U.S.C. § 1681, which prohibits sex discrimination in educational programs receiving federal money.

Dissenting in *Cannon*, Justice Powell mounted a powerful attack on the Court's practice. "Under Art. III, Congress alone has the responsibility for determining the jurisdiction of the lower federal courts. As the Legislative Branch, Congress also should determine when private parties are to be given causes of action under legislation it adopts. * * * When Congress chooses not to provide a private civil remedy, federal courts should not assume the legislative role of creating such a remedy and thereby enlarge their jurisdiction."

Justice Powell's critique had immediate bite. Writing for the Court in *Touche Ross & Co. v. Redington*, 442 U.S. 560 (1979), Justice Rehnquist opined that *Borak* and *Cort* were both obsolete and that the only test was whether Congress intended to create a cause of action; for this proposition, he cited the Stevens opinion in *Cannon*! See also *Merrell Dow Pharmaceuticals v. Thompson*, 478 U.S. 804, 811 (1986); *Merrill Lynch, Pierce, Fenner & Smith v. Curran*, 456 U.S. 353 (1982); *Transamerica Mortgage Advisors, Inc. (TAMA) v. Lewis*, 444 U.S. 11 (1979).

In *Thompson v. Thompson*, 484 U.S. 174 (1988), the Court held that the Parental Kidnapping Prevention Act did not create an implied cause of action in federal court to determine which of two conflicting state custody decrees is valid. Seven Justices joined Justice Marshall's opinion for the Court, which followed the *Cort/Cannon* analysis. The Court found persuasive the structure of the Act, which only worked to extend the Full Faith and Credit Clause to child custody determinations. Also, some specific legislative history suggested that the key legislative players assumed the statute would not create independent federal jurisdiction and would instead have its effect through state court proceedings following its dictates.

Justice Scalia concurred only in the Court's judgment and sharply criticized any reference to *Cort* or *Cannon*. In his view *Touche Ross* and *TAMA* "effectively" overruled the four-factor test of *Cort* and established that the only relevant consideration in such cases is whether Congress intended to create a private cause of action. (Justice O'Connor joined this part of Justice Scalia's discussion.) Justice Scalia then took up the position articulated by Justice Powell in *Cannon*, arguing that the Court has no authority to "imply" a cause of action not intended by Congress and that the Court should probably refuse to infer causes of action not explicitly created by Congress (*id.* at 191–92):

> It is, to be sure, not beyond imagination that in a particular case Congress may intend to create a private right of action, but chooses to do so by implication. One must wonder, however, whether the good produced by a judicial rule that accommodates this remote possibility is outweighed by its adverse effects. An enactment by implication cannot realistically be regarded as the product of the difficult lawmaking process our Constitution has prescribed. Committee reports, floor speeches, and even colloquies between Congressmen are frail substitutes for bicameral vote upon the text of a law and its presentment to the President. It is at best dangerous to assume that all the necessary participants in the law-enactment process are acting upon the same unexpressed assumptions. And likewise dangerous to assume that, even with the utmost self-discipline, judges can prevent the implications they see from mirroring the policies they favor. * * *
>
> If we were to announce a flat rule that private rights of action will not be implied in statutes hereafter enacted, the risk that that course would occasionally frustrate genuine legislative intent would decrease from its current level of minimal to virtually zero. * * * I believe, moreover, that Congress would welcome the certainty that such a rule would produce. Surely conscientious legislators cannot relish the current situation, in which the existence or nonexistence of a private right of action depends upon which of the opposing legislative forces may have guessed right as to the implications the statute will be found to contain.

Nonetheless, the opinion for the *Thompson* Court followed the *Cort v. Ash* approach, as it did also in *Suter v. Artist M*, 503 U.S. 347 (1992) (Rehnquist, C.J.). On the other hand, consistent with Justice Scalia's critique, the Court has followed the *Touche Ross/TAMA* skeptical approach (requiring positive evidence of congressional intent to create a private right of action) in *Gonzaga University v. Doe,* 536 U.S. 273 (2002) (no private right under the Family Education Rights and Privacy Act), and *Alexander v. Sandoval,* 532 U.S. 275 (2001) (no private right under Title VI's disparate impact regulations).

———

FRANKLIN v. GWINNETT COUNTY PUBLIC SCHOOLS, 503 U.S. 60 (1992). The issue was whether the implied right of action created in *Cannon* permits claims for damages in Title IX cases. **Justice White** wrote the opinion for the Court upholding such a claim. The opinion reasoned that once a cause of action has been inferred by the Court, the Court presumes "the availability of all appropriate remedies unless Congress has expressly indicated otherwise." Significantly, the opinion relied on *Bell v. Hood,* 327 U.S. 678 (1946), and *Borak,* which some observers thought were no longer relevant in light of the Court's recent focus on legislative intent. See also *Virginia Bankshares, Inc. v. Sandberg,* 501 U.S. 1083 (1991), where the Court reaffirmed the *Borak* cause of action and defined its remedies more precisely.

Gwinnett County urged the Court to find no damages remedy, based upon separation of powers precepts similar to those argued by Justice Powell in *Cannon* and Justice Scalia in *Thompson.* Justice White not only rejected this argument, but countered that separation of powers supported damages relief:

> In making this argument, respondents misconceive the difference between a cause of action and a remedy. Unlike the finding of a cause of action, which authorizes a court to hear a case or controversy, the discretion to award appropriate relief involves no such increase in judicial power. Federal courts cannot reach out to award remedies when the Constitution or laws of the United States do not support a cause of action. Indeed, properly understood respondents' position invites us to abdicate our historic judicial authority to award appropriate relief in cases brought in our court system. It is well to recall that such authority historically has been thought necessary to provide an important safeguard against abuses of legislative and executive power, as well as to insure an independent judiciary. Moreover, selective abdication of the sort advocated here would harm separation of powers principles in another way, by giving judges the power to render inutile causes of action authorized by Congress through a decision that *no* remedy is available.

Justice Scalia, joined by **Chief Justice Rehnquist** and **Justice Thomas,** disputed the Court's analysis. He argued that the *Bell v. Hood* presumption might be relevant

> when the legislature says nothing about remedy in expressly creating a private right of action; perhaps even when it says nothing about remedy in creating a private right of action by clear textual implication; but not, I think, when it says nothing about remedy in a statute in which the courts divine a private right of action on the basis of "contextual" evidence such as that in *Cannon,* which charged Congress with knowledge of a court of appeals' creation of a cause of action under a similarly worded statute. Whatever one thinks of the validity of the last approach, it surely rests on attributed rather than actual congressional knowledge. It does not demonstrate an explicit legislative decision to create a cause of action, and so could not be expected to be accompanied by a legislative decision to alter the application of *Bell v. Hood.*

Given the nature of *Cannon* and some of our earlier "implied right of action" cases, what the Court's analytical construct comes down to is this: Unless Congress expressly legislates a more limited remedial policy with respect to rights of action it does not know it is creating, it intends the full gamut of remedies to be applied. * * *

* * * In my view, when rights of action are judicially "implied," categorical limitations upon their remedial scope may be judicially implied as well. Although we have abandoned the expansive rights-creating approach exemplified by *Cannon* — and perhaps ought to abandon the notion of implied causes of action entirely, see *Thompson v. Thompson* (Scalia, J., concurring in judgment) — causes of action that came into existence under the *ancien regime* should be limited by the same logic that gave them birth. To require, with respect to a right that is not consciously and intentionally created, that any limitation of remedies must be express, is to provide, in effect, that the most questionable of private rights will also be the most expansively remediable.

Justice Scalia nonetheless concurred in the Court's judgment, on the ground that subsequent civil rights statutes enacted in 1986 and 1987 obviously relied and built upon *Cannon*'s cause of action and the assumption that it included the traditional damages remedy.

Title IX Postscript: The debate among the Justices in *Franklin* continued in subsequent Title IX cases. In *Gebser v. Lago Vista*, 524 U.S. 274 (1998), the Court ruled that Title IX's implied cause of action for damages includes cases of teacher-student sexual harassment, but only when a school district official who has authority to institute corrective measures has actual notice of and is deliberately indifferent to the teacher's misconduct. Justice O'Connor's opinion for the Court rejected claimants' argument that the standards for Title IX relief ought to be the same as that for relief under Title VII for workplace sexual harassment. (Title VII, of course, provides an explicit cause of action for workplace sex discrimination; Title IX's cause of action has been implied.) Justice Stevens' dissenting opinion viewed this limitation as a retreat from *Franklin*, where the entire Court had viewed the implied cause of action as having been ratified by Congress.

The analysis changed in *Davis v. Monroe County Bd. of Educ.*, 526 U.S. 629 (1999), where the Court expanded the Title IX cause of action to include sexual harassment by other students under the supervision of the school system. Justice O'Connor's opinion for the Court deployed *Gebser* as a basis for limiting principles: the school board would only be liable when its official (such as a principal) had actual notice of and was deliberately indifferent to the peer harassment. In dissent, Justice Kennedy (joined by the Chief Justice and Justices Scalia and Thomas) vigorously attacked the judicial lawmaking involved in this case. His words are worth quoting:

The Court has encountered great difficulty in establishing standards for deciding when to imply a private cause of action under a federal statute which is silent on the subject. We try to conform the judicial judgment to the bounds of likely congressional purpose but, as we observed in *Gebser*, defining the scope of the private cause of action in general, and the damages remedy in particular, "inherently entails a degree of speculation, since it addresses an issue on which Congress has not specifically spoken."

When the statute at issue is a Spending Clause statute [as Title IX is, but not the securities laws], this element of speculation is particularly troubling because it is in significant tension with the requirement that Spending Clause legislation give the States clear notice of the consequences of their acceptance of federal funds. Without doubt, the scope of potential damages liability is one of the most significant factors a school would consider in deciding whether to receive federal funds. Accordingly, the Court must not imply a private cause of action for damages unless it can demonstrate that the congressional purpose to create the implied cause of action is so manifest that the State, when accepting federal funds, had clear notice of the terms and conditions of its monetary liability.

Under this analysis, was *Cannon* not wrongly decided? How about *Franklin*, where the *Davis* dissenters went along with an extension of *Cannon*? Have they changed their minds? Are these decisions so wrong that they would have to be overruled?

More Problems on Private Rights of Action

Problem 9–2. Recall *Doe v. General Motors*, in which a consumer injured in an accident allegedly caused by a defect violating one of the NHTSA's motor vehicle standards asserted a private right of action in damages against the manufacturer. Jane Doe retains her state law tort claims, pursuant to 15 U.S.C. § 1420. Based upon the Supreme Court's precedents described or excerpted above, how would a federal court rule on Doe's assertion of an implied cause of action? See *George Byers Sons, Inc. v. East Europe Import Export, Inc.*, 488 F. Supp. 574 (D. Md. 1980).

Problem 9–3. The Air Carriers Access Act of 1986 (ACAA), 49 U.S.C. App. § 1374(c), stated: "No air carrier may discriminate against any otherwise qualified handicapped individual, by reason of such handicap, in the provision of air transportation." (The current codification, with minor changes, is at 49 U.S.C. § 41705.) The Department of Transportation is charged with enforcing this Act through fines. The Department has rarely fined a carrier for violating the statute, and scholars believe the Department does little or nothing to enforce the law. See Nancy Eisenhauer, *Implied Causes of Action Under Federal Statutes: The Air Carriers Access Act of 1986*, 59 U. Chi. L. Rev. 1183 (1992) (student comment).

Donna Roe is a quadriplegic who is scheduled to participate at an important conference on obstacles people with disabilities confront in the workplace. She purchased a ticket on an American Airlines flight, but the airline declined to let her travel, because of her disability. She missed the conference and sues for damages under the ACAA. Does she have an implied cause of action? See *Shinault v. American Airlines, Inc.*, 936 F.2d 796 (5th Cir. 1991); see also *Tallarico v. Trans World Airlines, Inc.*, 881 F.2d 566 (8th Cir. 1989); *Americans Disabled Accessible Public Transp. (ADAPT) v. Skywest Airlines, Inc.*, 762 F. Supp. 320 (D. Utah 1991).

C. THE NONDELEGATION DOCTRINE IN THE ADMINISTRATIVE STATE

The nondelegation doctrine posits that the legislature cannot delegate its inherent lawmaking powers to agencies without providing specific standards the bureaucracy shall apply in administering the delegation or, as Chief Justice Taft put it, laying down "an intelligible principle" to which the administrators must conform. *J.W. Hampton, Jr. & Co. v. United States*, 276 U.S. 394, 409 (1928). The doctrine reached the apex of its fame — or notoriety — when it was used by the Supreme Court to strike down most of the New Deal's National Industrial Recovery Act. *A.L.A. Schechter Poultry Corp. v. United States*, 295 U.S. 495 (1935). It has suffered a roller-coaster fate since the 1930s, however.

After President Franklin Roosevelt reconstituted the Supreme Court and the administrative state became an accepted part of our democracy, the nondelegation doctrine fell into constitutional disuse. In *Yakus v. United States*, 321 U.S. 414 (1944), the New Deal Court upheld a broad delegation of price control authority to the Office of Price Administration during World War II. The only "intelligible principle" in the statute was that prices be "fair and equitable" — and yet the court sustained the delegation. "Only if we could say that there is an absence of standards for the guidance of the Administrator's action, so that it would be impossible in a proper proceeding to ascertain whether the will of Congress has been obeyed, would we be justified in overriding its choice of means for effecting its declared purpose." Recently, the Supreme Court upheld provisions of the Clean Air Act that a lower appellate court had struck down on delegation grounds; the Court found sufficient intelligible principles in the Act to guide the agency. *Whitman v. American Trucking Ass'ns, Inc.*, 531 U.S. 457 (2001) (noting how rarely the Court has struck a federal statute down on nondelegation grounds).

The Economic Stabilization Act of 1970, 84 Stat. 799, codified at 12 U.S.C. § 1904 note, did not even have a "fair and equitable" standard when it authorized the President "to issue such orders and regulations as he may deem appropriate to stabilize prices, rents, wages, and salaries at levels not less than those prevailing on May 25, 1970." Nonetheless, when President Nixon exercised that power to freeze prices and wages in Executive Order 11615, 36 Fed. Reg. 15727 (1971), a special three-judge court rejected a nondelegation doctrine challenge. See *Amalgamated Meat Cutters and Butcher Workmen of North America v. Connolly*, 337 F. Supp. 737 (D.D.C. 1971) (three-judge court). Judge Leventhal constructed standards to guide presidential implementation of the Act from (1) its legislative history, which revealed the purposes of the law; (2) prior price control statutes, such as the one upheld in *Yakus*; and (3) judicial power to elaborate on implicit statutory terms, such as a "fairness and equitable" standard, enforceable through judicial review of the executive implementation decisions. In addition, the Court found that the agency's ability to act arbitrarily was blunted by a requirement that it promulgate additional standards to guide its actions taken under the statute. "This requirement, inherent in the Rule of Law and implicit in the Act, means that however broad the discretion of the Executive at the outset, the standard once developed limits the latitude of subsequent Executive action." *Id.* at 759. This period was the nadir of the nondelegation doctrine. Cf. *Mistretta v. United States*, 488 U.S. 361 (1989) (Court unanimously rejects nondelegation challenge to Sentencing Commission; majority opinion suggests that doctrine might be limited to "giving narrow constructions to statutory delegations that might otherwise be thought to be unconstitutional").

Although no federal statute has been invalidated by the Supreme Court pursuant to the nondelegation doctrine since the 1930s, individual Justices have occasionally invoked the doctrine. See, e.g., *Zemel v. Rusk*, 381 U.S. 1, 20 (1965) (Black, J., dissenting); *Industrial Union Dep't, AFL–CIO v. American Petroleum Institute*, 448 U.S. 607, 685–86 (1980) (Rehnquist, J., dissenting); *American Textile Mfrs. Inst., Inc. v. Donovan*, 452 U.S. 490, 543 (1981) (Rehnquist, J., dissenting). Moreover, some state courts still enforce a nondelegation doctrine.[k]

Notwithstanding the apparent demise of the nondelegation doctrine after *Schechter Poultry*, some scholars find the doctrine to be a useful concept and argue for its resurrection. Political scientist Theodore Lowi, in *The End of Liberalism: The Second Republic of the United States* (2d ed. 1979), argues that legislatures tend to avoid hard political choices by delegating virtually blanket authority to bureaucrats. Public choice theory, discussed in Chapter 1, § 2, reinforces Lowi's point. Public choice theorists posit that legislators' chief motivation is to achieve reelection. One effective method for achieving reelection is for legislators to spend most of their time doing things which their constituents find uncontroversial, such as casework helping constituents wind their way through the bureaucracy and pork barrel projects benefitting their districts. As to substantive legislation, the best strategy is usually to avoid positions that offend important electoral groups in the legislator's district. This can be done through ducking the issue entirely or, if that is impossible, delegating resolution of the most divisive issues to agencies. With Lowi, one can argue from a public choice perspective that the temptation to pass the substantive buck to agencies is as tempting as it is undemocratic (bureaucrats rather than legislators are making important policy choices) and counterproductive (the choices may be biased if the agency is captured and timid if the agency is not). See David Schoenbrod, *Power without Responsibility: How Congress Abuses the People Through Delegation* (1993).

Jerry Mashaw disputes the pessimistic public choice perspective on the nondelegation doctrine, and he argues instead that broad delegations to administrative agencies can sometimes ensure better policymaking. *Greed, Chaos, and Governance: Using Public Choice to Improve Public Law* 140-157 (1997). He demonstrates that broad delegations may actually reduce rent-seeking by interests groups because they inhibit vote-trading and deal-making. Once power has been delegated to an agency, lawmakers find it more difficult to offer bargains in that issue arena, and administrators cannot make tradeoffs

---

k. See Hans Linde, George Bunn, Fredericka Paff & W. Lawrence Church, *Legislative and Administrative Processes* 478 (2d ed. 1981); *Thygesen v. Callahan*, 385 N.E.2d 699, 700 (Ill. 1979) (a leading state case).

on issues outside their jurisdiction. In fact, some laws that result from the most questionable interest group activity are often very specifically worded to guarantee that bargainers get the deals they struck. Mashaw also argues that voters can often hold members of Congress accountable for broad delegations more easily than they can learn of specific deals found in the details of omnibus legislation. "No one has been able to demonstrate any systematic relationship between improving accountability, or enhancing the public welfare, or respecting the rule of law, and the specificity of legislation." Mashaw goes on to make the affirmative case for broad delegations, arguing that they take advantage of administrative expertise and flexibility. Furthermore, agencies may be more responsive to public desires, because they can often act more quickly than Congress can enact legislation, and they benefit from the President's accountability to a national electorate.[l]

In recent years, the nondelegation doctrine has also enjoyed an indirect revival at the Supreme Court level. As two of us noted in 1992, although "the Court has not invalidated a statute on [nondelegation] grounds since the 1930s," the Court now "refers to the nondelegation idea as a canon of statutory interpretation rather than as an enforceable constitutional doctrine."[m] We proposed that when agencies aggressively assert a broad jurisdiction not supported by a congressional authorization, clearly expressed in the statute, the Court ought to overrule the agency and insist on a more targeted statutory authorization.[n] Our thesis is confirmed by the Court's subsequent decisions in *Whitman*, which rejected a constitutional nondelegation challenge to the Clean Air Act but construed the Act narrowly in light of the apparent limiting principle, and in *MCI v. AT&T* (Section 3 of this chapter), which narrowly construed a telecommunications law on the ground that the broad revisionary authority claimed by the FCC had to be more clearly stated on the face of the statute for the Court to give it effect. See also *FDA v. Brown & Williamson Tobacco Co.* (Chapter 7, § 3B3). If a court is faced with an extremely broad delegation that might implicate constitutional concerns, it uses the canon to adopt a narrow interpretation that would restrain agency discretion. This approach is similar to the one used in *Yakus* or *Amalgamated Meat Cutters*,

---

l. See also Edward Rubin, *Law and Legislation in the Administrative State*, 89 Colum. L. Rev. 369 (1989) (offering a pragmatic justification for broad delegations); David Spence & Frank Cross, *A Public Choice Case for the Administrative State*, 89 Geo. L.J. 97 (2000) (using public choice theory to defend broad delegations). See generally *Symposium: The Phoenix Rises Again: The Nondelegation Doctrine from Constitutional and Policy Perspectives*, 20 Cardozo L. Rev. 731–1018 (1999) (providing various scholarly perspectives on the nondelegation doctrine).

m. William Eskridge, Jr. & Philip Frickey, *Quasi-Constitutional Law: Clear Statement Rules as Constitutional Lawmaking*, 45 Vand. L. Rev. 593, 607 (1992). See also Lisa Schultz Bressman, Schechter Poultry *at the Millennium: A Delegation Doctrine for the Administrative State*, 109 Yale L.J. 1399 (2000) (making a similar argument that the doctrine survives in the judicial requirement that agencies adopt rules to limit its discretion). For support in the cases, see, e.g., *Mistretta*, 488 U.S. at 373 n.7; *Industrial Union Dep't, AFL-CIO v. American Petroleum Inst.*, 448 U.S. 607 (1980).

n. See William Eskridge, Jr. & John Ferejohn, *The Article I, Section 7 Game*, 80 Geo. L.J. 523, 561–62 (1992).

discussed above, where the courts poured meaning into general statutory language to find intelligible guidelines and procedural requirements to limit agency discretion.

SECTION 2. CONGRESSIONAL INFLUENCE OVER STATUTORY IMPLEMENTATION

As we have seen, Congress delegates a great deal of rulemaking and adjudicatory authority to administrative agencies, subject to the very lenient limits set by the nondelegation doctrine and other more specific limitations explored in this section. Why would Congress hand off so many policy decision to strangers (agencies)? Here is the logic. If legislators decide to enact very specific laws through normal congressional procedures, they face the following costs: information costs as they gather and analyze the data necessary to make wise policy in a detailed way; procedural costs as the laws meet constitutional requirements like bicameralism and presentment; and bargaining costs as they assemble majority support through logrolling. See David Epstein & Sharyn O'Halloran, *Delegating Powers: A Transaction-Cost Approach to Policymaking Under Separate Powers* (1999).

The foregoing logic does not obviate the main problem with delegation, however. If legislators choose to delegate broadly, they face monitoring costs because bureaucrats may have their own policy objectives that diverge from Congress's. Economists would call this an *agency problem* (an agent may shirk or cheat on duties delegated her by a principal); some political scientists call it *bureaucratic drift*.[a] The interactive structure of law implementation in our constitutional system entrenches the problem of bureaucratic drift.

Consider the creation and implementation of statutes as a political "game," a notion introduced in Chapter 1, § 2. See William Eskridge, Jr. & John Ferejohn, *The Article I, Section 7 Game*, 80 Geo. L.J. 523 (1992). Each player in the game wants to impose its own policy preferences upon federal statutory policy, but no player will act in a way that subjects it to an immediate override; hence, the game is played backwards, each player anticipating the moves that would be made by the next (much as an attorney anticipates agency and judicial interpretations when she renders advice to a self-interested client). The following notations describe the important points in the game:

SQ	Existing policy (status quo)
H and S	Preferences of the median legislator in the two chambers of the legislature
P	Preferences of the President
h and s	Pivotal voter in veto override in the two chambers of the bicameral legislature

---

a. See Matthew McCubbins, Roger Noll, & Barry Weingast, *Structures and Process, Politics and Policy: Administrative Arrangements and the Political Control of Agencies*, 75 Va. L. Rev. 431, 439 (1989).

x   Statutory policy resulting from game

Under the circumstances of the Legislation Game, a statute will usually be enacted, for one example, when the status quo is objectionable from the perspectives of both Congress and the President, and their preferences for changing the status quo run in the same direction:

		x		
P	H	S	SQ	

Figure 1.   Statutory policy $H < x < S$ when
$P < H$, $S < SQ$

The ultimate statutory policy will fall somewhere between the preferences of the two legislative chambers (H and S). Figure 1 describes the political alignments (left being more liberal) during the New Deal and the Great Society, when many modern regulatory statutes were enacted. Indeed, Figure 1 reflects the political landscape when Congress enacted the Civil Rights Act of 1964 (the Senate filibuster, however, pushed "x" further to the right than we have it in Figure 1, however).

If Congress delegates authority to an executive agency, it is taking something of a political risk, however. As Figure 2 reveals, there is a chance that executive implementation of the statute (x) will press it toward a much more leftward departure from the status quo than Congress wanted or expected.

	x'		x		
h	P	H	S	SQ	
	A				

Figure 2.   Statutory policy may shift to x' = P = A when
implementation is delegated to an executive agency

As you see, the agency can set policy virtually anywhere it wants, unless Congress would be stimulated to override the agency's choice. Thus, in Figure 2 situations the agency with policy preferences near those of the President can propose any policy, x', at or to the right of the veto median of the more pro-presidential chamber, and Congress cannot successfully challenge this interpretation. Any attempt to do so would be successfully vetoed. Thus, instead of x — the policy that would have been adopted under Article I procedures — the administrative state (after a respectable delay) produces x'. (This is the argument Justice Rehnquist made in *Weber*, the affirmative action case in Chapter 1: the Civil Rights Act adopted a moderate race-blind policy, which the EEOC pressed leftward and the Court ultimately ratified.)

The game continues, of course, and changes policy yet again if a new President or agency is differently aligned from that of the original statute. This indeed happened after 1964. Since 1980, Presidents have been much more conservative than President Johnson, the leader who helped create the Civil Rights Act. Figure 3 maps the new preferences:

	x'	x		x"
h	P	H	S	P"
	A			A"

Figure 3.   Statutory policy shifts from x' to x" = A" when presidential preferences shift rightward (assuming congressional preferences are stable)

So in addition to the problem of bureaucratic drift, Figure 3 reveals a further problem of a *bureaucratic yo-yo*, where statutory policy bounces around, depending on who is elected President.[b] (Thus, the Reagan Administration cut back on diversity and affirmative action policies in the 1980s, while the Clinton Administration sought to revive them in the 1990s). The yo-yo problem would trouble Congress because statutory policy would not only deviate from its aggregated preferences, but also because the stable rule of law itself would be threatened.

Neither the drift nor the yo-yo problem is, in practice, as dramatic as Figures 1–3 suggest. The reason is that Congress has responded with various mechanisms to protect against problems of drift and yo-yo'ing. As in the rest of politics and government, nothing works perfectly well (or perfectly badly), but everything has some effect, often unanticipated of course.

Some of the mechanisms — notably oversight (Part A of this section), budgetary pressures (Part B), and legislative vetoes (Part C) — are ways that post-enacting Congresses try to influence, control, or check agency implementation of earlier-adopted statutes. Over time, these mechanisms do little to protect the original deal, but they do help the agency update the deal to account for new political circumstances and they may help prevent the agency from straying too far from the statutory purposes. On the other hand, because congressional subgroups are disproportionately influential in these mechanisms, they offer opportunities for rent-seeking and partiality that might cut against the public interest as well as the original deal.

Other mechanisms — tenure protections (Part D), agency design (Part E), and judicial review (Part F) — offer potentially greater protection for the original legislative policy choices and, perhaps, the public interest as well. This chapter's case study of the Motor Vehicle Safety Act, however, counsels against undue optimism on this front as well. Tenure protections might keep incompetents in place, design features will have unintended consequences over time, and judicial review is not the cure-all that law professors have traditionally maintained.

---

b. The scenario depicted in Figures 1–3 is not unusual in American politics. Consider the big shifts in the ideology of the presidency in 1952, 1960, 1968, 1976, 1980, 1992, and 2000.

A. LEGISLATIVE OVERSIGHT AND INVESTIGATION

A Congress that has delegated much of its lawmaking authority to agencies would rationally seek to monitor those agencies to assure their continued adherence to the original legislative delegation. Before 1933, there were few agencies to oversee, and Congress devoted little effort to monitoring. Agencies proliferated during the New Deal. Congress responded with the Legislative Reorganization Act of 1946, 60 Stat. 812, codified at 2 U.S.C. § 31 *et al.*, which signaled a new commitment to oversight and started a process by which Congress and its committees added legislative staff to accomplish this goal. The conventional wisdom of the 1950s was that oversight could effectively assure majoritarian control of policy.

Some political scientists suggest that the conventional wisdom was too optimistic because structural problems impede effective legislative oversight.[c] Thus, legislative oversight committees may become captured by the same forces that capture agencies — interested persons and firms, who provide information, ideas, and encouragement. Also, motivations of legislators are more important in determining oversight activity than is the availability of resources. "Unless [oversight] reveals a scandalous situation with possibilities for favorable publicity for the legislators, the work is considered dull and potentially troublesome."[d] There are opportunity costs for oversight; time spent monitoring agencies is time away from fundraising, casework, and enacting new programs to benefit constituents. The latter are activities that often mean more to a legislator's reelection chances than tedious oversight. Finally, and most important, partisan politics can eviscerate oversight: in periods where Congress is controlled by the same political party as the President (1993–95, 2003–07), one would expect little critical oversight. On the other hand, when at least one branch of Congress and the President are controlled by different parties, as has been the norm (1981–93, 1995–2001, May 2001–03, 2007–??), one would expect to see more aggressive oversight.

Whatever the partisan make-up of the federal government, positive political theorists argue that Congress can be expected to protect its institutional interests relatively vigorously. It is helpful to distinguish among the various forms of oversight because some actions that occur steadily are less public and thus may be overlooked. Although we tend to think first of formal committee hearings as the main mechanism to monitor agencies, in fact, much of the oversight done by legislators is informal. Lawmakers jawbone agency officials as policy is formulated, or they intervene on behalf of constituents to present arguments and perspectives. Although rules prohibit some forms of *ex parte*

---

c. For leading surveys of congressional oversight, and its problems, see, e.g., Martin James, *Congressional Oversight* (2002); Kathleen Bawn, *Choosing Strategies to Control the Bureaucracy: Statutory Constraints, Oversight, and the Committee System,* 13 J.L. Econ. & Org. 101 (1997); Morris Ogul, *Congressional Oversight: Structures and Incentives,* in *Congress Reconsidered* 317 (Lawrence Dodd & Bruce Oppenheimer eds. 2d ed. 1981); Charles Shipan, *Regulatory Regimes, Agency Actions, and the Conditional Nature of Congressional Influence,* 98 Am. Pol. Sci. Rev. 467 (2004).

d. Bernard Rosen, *Holding Government Bureaucracies Accountable* 21 (1982).

communications, particularly during formal adjudication, there are numerous ways for members of Congress to communicate with bureaucrats as rules as being considered. Mark Moran and Barry Weingast, for example, argue that the FTC is strongly influenced by subtle messages sent outside the formal oversight process and that this influence is statistically significant for both enforcement and policymaking initiatives by the FTC.[e] See also Joel Auerbach, *Keeping A Watchful Eye: The Politics of Congressional Oversight* (1990), arguing that vigorous congressional oversight is responsive to public demands for greater government accountability.

Various mechanisms exist to provide members of Congress with information that alerts them to the need for aggressive oversight or that supports them as they engage in monitoring. Mathew McCubbins and Thomas Schwartz describe two kinds of monitoring strategies. *Congressional Oversight Overlooked: Police Patrols Versus Fire Alarms*, 28 Am. J. Pol. Sci. 165 (1984). A *police patrol* strategy is time-consuming as legislators and their staffs regularly monitor to discover bureaucratic drift. In contrast, employing a *fire alarm* strategy saves congressional resources as members wait to hear the alarm raised by interest parties upset about agency policy. Once the alarm has been sounded, members can begin aggressive oversight, and they can ignore areas where no discontent is evident. In this way, lawmakers externalize some of the costs of oversight, perhaps engaging in police patrols only in arenas without much interest group activity and thus with less possibility of alarms. After they sound the alarm, lobbyists and interest groups continue to provide supporters with information and expertise to further reduce legislative monitoring costs.

Congress engages in a lot more oversight than it once did. Unfortunately, there is strong evidence that oversight has many problems.

1. *The Problem of Regulatory Priorities and Efficacy.* Oversight hearings, controlled by a congressional subgroup, may push agencies away from their public-regarding agendas. With their scarce resources, committed agencies have their hands full devising workable strategies and fighting off industry attacks. If an oversight committee is controlled or even influenced by the regulated industry, it can thwart agency regulation by pressuring the agency toward less intrusive (and often less efficacious) modes of regulation. Even well-intended oversight might undermine agency efficacy if it adds more to the agency' plate, as illustrated in the auto safety area.[f]

---

e. Barry Weingast & Mark Moran, *Bureaucratic Discretion or Congressional Control? Regulatory Policymaking at the Federal Trade Commission*, 91 J. Pol. Econ. 765 (1983); Weingast & Moran, *The Myth of the Runaway Bureaucracy: The Case of the FTC*, Regulation, May/June 1982, at 33. To the same effect is John Ferejohn's study of communications policy. See John Ferejohn & Charles Shipan, *Congressional Influence on Bureaucracy*, 6 J.L. Econ. & Org. 1 (1990) (special issue).

f. See Jerry Mashaw, *The Story of* Motor Vehicle Manufacturers Association etc: *Law, Science, and Politics in the Administrative State*, in *Administrative Law Stories* 334, 357–67 (Peter Strauss ed., 2006). See also Steven Balla & John Wright, *Interest Groups, Advisory Committees, and Congressional Control of the Bureaucracy*, 45 Am. J. Pol. Sci. 799 (2001).

Recall that the NHTSA's biggest regulatory initiative was Standard 208, which required automakers to produce cars that would protect passengers against injury under specified performance criteria. Manufacturers could meet the standard with airbags, automatic seatbelts, and other mechanisms. For various institutional reasons, after 1971, the only way to comply with the standard was an "ignition interlock" system, whereby the car would not start until all passengers engaged their seatbelts. The public was not pleased. Drivers disengaged their interlocks (which were mandatory for the 1974 auto market) and wrote their members of Congress against this intrusion into their "freedom to drive."

Responding to public outrage, Congress held several oversight hearings, and the result was a massive disruption in the agency's regulatory program. On the one hand, the auto industry and elected representatives alike had a field day deriding the interlock system. Senator Norris Cotton joked, to great laughter, that his car would not start when he placed groceries in the passenger's seat. Instead of placing them on the floor (duh!), the New Hampshire legislator belted "a pound of cheese and a loaf of bread" to satisfy the system. Although the experts maintained that ignition interlocks saved lives, popular resentment about inconveniences and infringements on their freedom to drive over-whelmed the theoretical safety gains.

On the other hand, oversight focused on a decidedly minor problem: schoolbus design. Of the 54,000+ annual death toll as a result of auto accidents, the agency found only a few dozen where an expensive schoolbus redesign might have saved the lives of schoolchildren. (As many as 80% of child deaths from schoolbus accidents occur *outside* of the bus.) Even sympathetic Members of Congress were appalled by agency's failure to focus on *children's deaths* because of schoolbus accidents. Representative Les Aspin, a liberal, berated the agency for "misusing the concept of cost-benefit analysis" (Mashaw, *Law, Science, and Politics*, 363–65).

The upshot of all this oversight was the Motor Vehicle and Schoolbus Safety Amendments of 1974, described earlier. These amendments forbade imposition of the ignition interlock (which saved hundreds and probably thousands of lives each year) and required the agency to impose stringent new design requirements on schoolbuses (which might save a life or three each year, at much greater expense). As Professor Mashaw wearily concludes, "[i]f Congress had wanted to protect the lives of children, it would have done better to re-energize NHTSA's lagging standard-setting enterprise as it applied to the passenger car" (*id.* at 367).

2. *Congressional Oversight and Individual Rights.* When Congress or its committees exercise vigorous oversight power, there may be problems involving overreaching or violation of individual rights. In the 1950s, several congressional committees engaged in what many regard as a "witch hunt" for Communists and "homosexuals" in American government and society. The legislative investigations often seemed bent on ruining peoples' reputations rather than on serving valid legislative goals, and courts through the 1950s and

1960s sometimes overturned contempt citations against uncooperative witnesses.[g]

The leading case was *Watkins v. United States*, 354 U.S. 178 (1957), in which the Supreme Court overturned a contempt conviction based upon its finding that the House Un-American Activities Committee had ventured far beyond its House-authorized arena of investigation. See also Judge Weinfeld's earlier decision in *United States v. Lamont*, 18 F.R.D. 27 (S.D.N.Y. 1955), *aff'd*, 236 F.2d 312 (2d Cir. 1956), which made similar findings for the Senate's Permanent Subcommittee on Investigations (chaired by Joseph McCarthy (R–Wis.)). Chief Justice Warren's opinion in *Watkins* suggested, moreover, that legislative investigations are limited to building a factual record for proposed legislation and providing information for the exercise of legislative insight. "We have no doubt that there is no congressional power to expose for the sake of exposure," concluded Warren. 354 U.S. at 200.

Although *Watkins'* holding was based on lack of "pertinency" of the questions asked to the mission delegated to the committee by Congress, see *Barenblatt v. United States*, 360 U.S. 109 (1959) (upholding contempt and distinguishing *Watkins*), Chief Justice Warren's concerns included the process's threat to First Amendment freedoms (354 U.S. at 197):

> Abuses of the investigative process may imperceptibly lead to abridgment of protected freedoms. The mere summoning of a witness and compelling him to testify, against his will, about his beliefs, expressions or associations is a measure of governmental interference. And when those forced revelations concern matters that are unorthodox, unpopular, or even hateful to the general public, the reaction in the life of the witness may be disastrous. This effect is even more harsh when it is past beliefs, expressions or associations that are disclosed and judged by current standards rather than those contemporary with the matters exposed. * * *

3. *The Problem of Agency Defiance and Executive Privilege.* A final problem with legislative oversight is that even when it is vigorous and public-seeking — and respectful of individual rights — it may face frustrating obstacles to obtaining information from the agency, particularly one located in the executive branch. Some of the recent oversight hearings during the Clinton and Bush 43 Administrations demonstrate that difficulty, as well as the political aspects of oversight. Perhaps one of the best examples of an oversight proceeding stymied by the need to obtain data from the executive branch arose out of the 1982 skirmishing between two House subcommittees and EPA Administrator Anne Burford Gorsuch over the EPA's allegedly lax enforcement of the Superfund Act's program for cleaning up existing hazardous waste-dumping sites.[h]

---

g. Witnesses refusing to answer questions posed by these committees or to produce documents requested by the committees were subject to criminal prosecution under 2 U.S.C. § 192.

h. Our description is a synopsis of the detailed account in Harold Bruff & Peter Shane, *The Law of Presidential Powers: Cases and Materials* (1988); Peter Shane, *Legal Disagreement and Negotiation in a Government of Laws: The Case of Executive Privilege Claims Against*

In the Gorsuch dispute, the EPA refused to turn over many documents which the subcommittees demanded. The General Counsel to the House Clerk opined that the subcommittees were entitled to those documents under their *Watkins* authority to investigate reported abuses in enforcement. In a memorandum analyzing the House position, the Office of Legal Counsel countered that the most relevant Supreme Court decision is *United States v. Nixon*, 418 U.S. 683 (1974), which found a constitutional basis for claims of executive privilege and held such claims superseded only in unusual circumstances, such as to provide evidence to be used in the criminal trials of former White House officials involved in the Watergate Scandal.

Ultimately, the Public Works Committee recommended that the House hold Gorsuch in contempt, which it did on December 16, 1982. See *United States v. House of Representatives of the United States*, 556 F. Supp. 150 (D.D.C. 1983) (dismissing Department of Justice lawsuit trying to head off contempt citation). In February and March 1983, the Administration reached compromises with the relevant subcommittees; in each case the Administration agreed to let the subcommittee examine enforcement documents, with protections to assure confidentiality. Gorsuch resigned as EPA Administrator on March 9, 1983.

Consider the lessons this case study might have for renewed oversight struggles between the Democratic Congress elected in 2006 and the (Republican) Bush 43 Administration over the Administration's hesitant response to global warming and other environmental concerns. The same *Watkins* and *Nixon* issues have been joined. What strategies should the committees be following?

B. CONGRESS' BUDGETARY AND APPROPRIATIONS POWER

Under Article I, § 8, clauses 1 and 18 and § 9, clause 7, Congress has virtually plenary power to determine how the United States' money will be spent. This power of the purse gives Congress an ongoing substantive power as well. For example, the power of the purse and oversight activities that we discussed previously are related. Much oversight occurs when programs are reauthorized or receive appropriations, not only in primary-purpose oversight hearings. Auerbach, *Keeping a Watchful Eye*, 130–33. The use of spending control to influence executive branch actions works in several different ways.

As you remember from Chapter 4, the statute establishing a program or agency does not also appropriate money to fund its activities. With regard to discretionary spending programs, the authorization process is separate from the appropriations process. What one Congress establishes as a statutory scheme can be negated entirely by a subsequent Congress' failure to fund that scheme or the agency administering it. More commonly, Congress will fund a statutory scheme and the agency, but the level of funding will depend upon Congress' attitude toward the scheme and the agency. An agency might have a strong incentive to move statutory policy close to the House or Senate position even though the agency's preferred policy would be protected by a presidential veto, if the agency fears that Congress will fail to fund it adequately in retaliation for the agency's policy position. This reveals the great advantage the appropriations power gives Congress: because the agency needs each Congress to act affirmatively to give it money, Congress has something of a backdoor "legislative veto" if it chooses to exercise it through the appropriations process. Moreover, because most appropriations of discretionary money must be renewed annually, the process provides Congress continuing influence.

It is impossible to tell how important the appropriations power is in this respect. The main limitation involves a coordination problem: the oversight (sub)committee cannot routinely pressure the agency to adopt new substantive policies by threatening to cut off funds, because separate appropriations subcommittees control funding. Unless the two different congressional entities share the same political preferences *and* can coordinate their activities, the funding weapon will be hard to deploy. Moreover, the preferences of the two (sub)committees can be expected to diverge most of the time. Because of the requirements of the congressional budget process, the appropriations committees are usually required to operate under a zero-sum mentality more often than the corresponding substantive committees: the primary goal of the former is to meet certain budget needs, while the primary goal of the latter is to solve social or economic problems. The NHTSA was caught in this bind. It received ample funding in the 1960s but suffered budget cuts as a consequence of general tightening-the-belt during the Nixon Administration and beyond. Even though the substantive committees were still quite keen on auto safety, the President and the appropriations committees were much more concerned with other budgetary priorities. Moreover, when Congress did bestir itself to focus on auto safety concerns, as during the interlock controversy in 1973–74, it is more likely to make the agency's job more difficult (with diminishing funds) by curtailing unpopular regulatory options and adding low priority issues (school-bus safety) to the already-crowded agency agenda.

Congress' spending power can be used as a mechanism of control in less direct ways than not funding or underfunding a particular agency. For example, committee reports accompanying appropriations bills include directives to agencies about how the money should be spent. Reports contain line items with specific instructions to fund particular projects, usually in the districts of key congressional players. Although language in committee reports is not legally binding, agencies usually follow the mandates in order to retain the good will of the appropriators whom they will face again next year. Not infrequently, Congress will include substantive restrictions in appropriations measures, which are legally binding because they meet the constitutional requirements for laws. This occurs even though congressional rules often forbid riders or other substantive legislation on an appropriations bill. Although such provisions obviously subject the appropriations bill to a possible veto, the President will sometimes swallow them because of the need to fund the government.

The Supreme Court has taken a balanced approach to substantive provisions into appropriations measures. On the one hand, repeals by implication are especially disfavored in the appropriations context. E.g., *TVA v. Hill*, 437 U.S. 153, 190 (1978), where the Court refused to credit continued congressional funding of the Tellico Dam as an amendment to the Endangered Species Act (ESA). On the other hand, Congress may amend substantive law in an appropriations statute, as long as it does so clearly. E.g., *Robertson v. Seattle Audubon Society*, 503 U.S. 429 (1992), where the Court applied an appropriations rider to allow timber-cutting that threatened the habitat of an endangered species (the spotted owl), which would otherwise have been a violation of the ESA.

C. THE LEGISLATIVE VETO OF AGENCY RULES

Another response to the tension between administrative lawmaking and majoritarian government has been the development of the *legislative veto*. The legislative veto is generally any statutory mechanism that renders the implementation or the continuing implementation of agency decisions or actions subject to some further form of legislative review or control, usually for a specified time period. The purpose of the legislative veto is to provide a quick mechanism to slow down or overturn administrative actions that are unresponsive to the legislature's aims in the original authorizing statute, without going through the obstacle course of the full legislative process. Hence, the power to nullify an administrative decision has been vested in joint action of both chambers of the legislature, action by only one house, or action by a legislative committee. (At the state level, there have been mechanisms for suspension, rather than veto, of agency decisions by joint legislative committees.) Any of these procedures is more streamlined than the normal legislative process; even a two-house legislative veto avoids the presentment clause. Getting around the President is important because he would presumably veto most legislative nullifications of regulations passed by agencies in his government, thereby requiring a supermajority in each house to implement congressional preferences.

The form of the veto can be either negative or positive. A *negative veto provision* (the typical one) stipulates that administrative decisions will be effective, unless the legislature or its designated subgroup actually disapproves the decisions. A *positive veto provision* requires legislative approval of the administrative decision before it becomes effective. A related concept is *laying over*: the executive is required to submit proposed decisions to the legislature or a designated subgroup, and the decisions do not go into effect for a specified period of time so that the full legislature can have an opportunity to study and take action on the proposed decisions. The Congressional Review Act, discussed in Chapter 4, § 3, passed in 1996 establishes such a procedure. Congress has 60 days after the promulgation of any regulation to disapprove, or overturn, it through enactment of a joint resolution signed by the President or passed over his veto.

The legislative veto idea was used sporadically in the early part of this century and was an important part of the Reorganization Act of 1932, 47 Stat. 382. Although President Hoover objected to the legislative veto in the 1932 Act as violating separation of powers, he accepted the provision in order to get the power to make changes in the executive branch. It was not until the 1970s that the legislative veto became a popular mechanism for greater legislative oversight of the administrative process. A Library of Congress study for the period 1932 to 1975 found 295 congressional review provisions in 196 federal statutes; for the year 1975 alone, there were 58 provisions in 21 statutes.[i] The trend accelerated in the late 1970s, as the following figures suggest:[j]

Form of Legislative Veto	1932–78	1979–82
One-House	71	24
Two-House	65	23
Committee	69	26
Other	0	5
Totals	205	78

Legislative veto provisions were attached to important legislation involving defense and foreign policy (e.g., the War Powers Resolution, 87 Stat. 555); energy and environmental policy (e.g., the Energy Policy and Conservation Act, 89 Stat. 871); consumer welfare policy (e.g., the Employee Retirement Income Security Act of 1974, 88 Stat. 829); and transportation policy (e.g., the Regional Rail Reorganization Act of 1973, 87 Stat. 985).[k] When Congress revisited the Motor Vehicle Safety Act in 1974, it required that any future regulation of passive restraints be subject to a two-house legislative veto.

State legislatures in the 1970s adopted a variety of legislative veto devices as well. The tendency at the state level was to create a committee, consisting either of legislators or bureaucrats or experts, to advise the legislature and, in some cases, to suspend operation of agency rules until the legislature could study them. Professor Levinson's survey of state legislative vetoes in the early 1980s revealed the following approaches:[l]

- No system of legislative supervision of agencies, relying on legislature to pass statutes (11 states);

---

i. Clark Norton, *Congressional Review, Deferral and Disapproval of Executive Actions: A Summary and Inventory of Statutory Authority* 8–12 (1976).

j. This table is taken from Joseph Cooper, *The Legislative Veto in the 1980s*, in *Congress Reconsidered* 364, 367 (Lawrence Dodd & Bruce Oppenheimer eds. 3d ed. 1985).

k. See Louis Fisher, *Constitutional Conflicts Between Congress and the President* 134–143 (3d, rev. ed. 1991).

l. See L. Harold Levinson, *Legislative and Executive Veto of Rules of Administrative Agencies: Models and Alternatives*, 24 Wm. & Mary L. Rev. 79, 81–83 (1982).

- Advisory committee to the state legislature, reviewing agency regulations and making recommendations for legislative action (15 states);

- Advisory committee to the state legislature, reviewing agency regulations and publicly commenting on them, with the committee's negative comments shifting the burden of the regulation's validity in the event of a legal challenge (3 states and the Model State Administrative Procedure Act);

- Legislative committee authorized to suspend the effectiveness of an agency rule pending legislative consideration of a statutory repeal (9 states);

- Two-house veto of agency rules (11 states);

- One-house veto of agency rules (1 state).

The concept of the legislative veto also drew criticisms from political scientists, who argued that they created as many problems for popular government as they solved, and from legal scholars, who argued that they were hard to reconcile with the concept of separation of powers. These constitutional concerns, and the political objections, generated a series of challenges to legislative vetoes at both the state and federal level.

IMMIGRATION & NATURALIZATION SERVICE v. CHADHA, 462 U.S. 919 (1983). Section 244(c)(2) of the Immigration and Nationality Act (8 U.S.C. § 1254(c)(2)) authorized one chamber of Congress, by resolution, to invalidate a decision by the executive to allow a deportable alien to remain in the United States. Chadha was an East Indian born in Kenya and holding a British passport. Pursuant to the Act, Chadha was able to obtain a suspension of his deportation. He had been deportable because he remained in the United States after the expiration of his nonimmigrant student visa. At the behest of Representative Eilberg, Chair of the Judiciary Committee Subcommittee on Immigration, the House overrode the suspension of Chadha's deportation. After the House action, the immigration judge reopened Chadha's case and ordered him deported. Chadha appealed the order through the Department of Justice, and then to the federal courts. The Ninth Circuit declared § 244(c)(2) unconstitutional. The Supreme Court affirmed.

Chief Justice Burger's opinion for the Court relied on Article I, § 7, the bicameralism and presentment requirements for congressional statutes and resolutions having the force of law. "These provisions of Art. I are integral parts of the constitutional design for the separation of powers." Thus, the presentment clauses of Article I, § 7 were carefully debated at the Philadelphia Convention. "The decision to provide the President with a limited and qualified power to nullify proposed legislation by veto was based on the profound conviction of the Framers that the powers conferred on Congress were the powers to be most carefully circumscribed. It is beyond doubt that lawmaking was a power to be shared by both Houses and the President. In The Federalist No. 73 (H. Lodge ed. 1888), Hamilton focused on the President's role in making laws:

'If even no propensity had ever discovered itself in the legislative body to invade the rights of the Executive, the rules of just reasoning and theoretic propriety would of themselves teach us that the one ought not to be left to the mercy of the other, but ought to possess a constitutional and effectual power of self-defense.' *Id.*, at 457–458.

See also The Federalist No. 51. In his Commentaries on the Constitution, Joseph Story makes the same point. 1 J. Story, Commentaries on the Constitution of the United States 614–615 (3d ed. 1858).

"The President's role in the lawmaking process also reflects the Framers' careful efforts to check whatever propensity a particular Congress might have to enact oppressive, improvident, or ill-considered measures. The President's veto role in the legislative process was described later during public debate on ratification:

'It establishes a salutary check upon the legislative body, calculated to guard the community against the effects of faction, precipitancy, or of any impulse unfriendly to the public good which may happen to influence a majority of that body * * *. The primary inducement to conferring the power in question upon the Executive is to enable him to defend himself; the secondary one is to increase the chances in favor of the community against the passing of bad laws through haste, inadvertence, or design.' The Federalist No. 73, *supra*, at 458 (A. Hamilton).

See also *The Pocket Veto Case*, 279 U.S. 655, 678 (1929); *Myers v. United States*, 272 U.S. 52, 123 (1926). The Court also has observed that the Presentment Clauses serve the important purpose of assuring that a 'national' perspective is grafted on the legislative process:

'The President is a representative of the people just as the members of the Senate and of the House are, and it may be, at some times, on some subjects, that the President elected by all the people is rather more representative of them all than are the members of either body of the Legislature whose constituencies are local and not countrywide . . . ." *Myers v. United States, supra*, 272 U.S., at 123.

"The bicameral requirement of Art. I, §§ 1, 7 was of scarcely less concern to the Framers than was the Presidential veto and indeed the two concepts are interdependent. By providing that no law could take effect without the concurrence of the prescribed majority of the Members of both Houses, the Framers reemphasized their belief, already remarked upon in connection with the Presentment Clauses, that legislation should not be enacted unless it has been carefully and fully considered by the Nation's elected officials. In the Constitutional Convention debates on the need for a bicameral legislature, James Wilson, later to become a Justice of this Court, commented:

'Despotism comes on mankind in different shapes. Sometimes in an Executive, sometimes in a military, one. Is there danger of a Legislative despotism? Theory & practice both proclaim it. If the Legislative authority be not restrained, there can be neither liberty nor stability; and it can only be restrained by dividing it within itself, into distinct and independent branches. In a single house there is no check, but the inadequate one, of the virtue & good sense of those who compose it.' 1 M. Farrand, *supra*, at 254. * * *

These observations are consistent with what many of the Framers expressed, none more cogently than Madison in pointing up the need to divide and disperse power in order to protect liberty:

> 'In republican government, the legislative authority necessarily predominates. The remedy for this inconveniency is to divide the legislature into different branches; and to render them, by different modes of election and different principles of action, as little connected with each other as the nature of their common functions and their common dependence on the society will admit.' The Federalist No. 51, *supra*, at 324.

See also The Federalist No. 62."

For those reasons, Chief Justice Burger concluded that the Court must strictly enforce both the presentment and the bicameralism requirements whenever Congress was seeking to exercise its *legislative* power. "Not every action taken by either House is subject to the bicameralism and presentment requirements of Art. I. Whether actions taken by either House are, in law and fact, an exercise of legislative power depends not on their form but upon 'whether they contain matter which is properly to be regarded as legislative in its character and effect.' S.Rep. No. 1335, 54th Cong., 2d Sess., 8 (1897)."

The House resolution abrogating the suspension of Chadha's deportation was such an action, because it "had the purpose and effect of altering the legal rights, duties and relations of persons, including the Attorney General, Executive Branch officials and Chadha, all outside the legislative branch. Section 244(c)(2) purports to authorize one House of Congress to require the Attorney General to deport an individual alien whose deportation otherwise would be cancelled under § 244. The one-House veto operated in this case to overrule the Attorney General and mandate Chadha's deportation; absent the House action, Chadha would remain in the United States. Congress has *acted* and its action has altered Chadha's status."

"The veto authorized by § 244(c)(2) doubtless has been in many respects a convenient shortcut; the 'sharing' with the Executive by Congress of its authority over aliens in this manner is, on its face, an appealing compromise. In purely practical terms, it is obviously easier for action to be taken by one House without submission to the President; but it is crystal clear from the records of the Convention, contemporaneous writings and debates, that the Framers ranked other values higher than efficiency. The records of the Convention and debates in the states preceding ratification underscore the common desire to define and limit the exercise of the newly created federal powers affecting the states and the people. There is unmistakable expression of a determination that legislation by the national Congress be a step-by-step, deliberate and deliberative process."

Justice Powell concurred only in the Court's judgment. He was unwilling to strike down the hundreds of legislative veto provisions that Congress had included in laws since the New Deal. "One reasonably may disagree with Congress' assessment of the veto's utility, but the respect due its judgment as a coordinate branch of Government cautions that our holding should be no more extensive than necessary to decide those cases. In my view, the case may be decided on a narrower ground. When Congress finds that a particular person does not satisfy the statutory criteria for permanent residence in this country it has assumed a judicial function in violation of the principle of separation of powers.

The argument of Justice Powell's opinion proceeded in three steps: First, the policy underlying constitutional separation of powers is that "[t]he accumulation of all powers legislative, executive and judiciary in the same hands * * * may justly be pronounced the very definition of tyranny." The Federalist No. 47. Second, the greatest separation of powers concern at the time the Constitution was adopted was that the legislature would arrogate too much power in its own hands. Some of the state legislatures had offended justice by deciding essentially judicial controversies involving individual rather than group rights. See The Federalist No. 48. Third, this is exactly what happened in *Chadha*: By applying a general rule to the six specific immigration cases, part of the legislature was doing something that appeared, to Justice Powell, to be "clearly adjudicatory." This situation, therefore, "raises the very danger the Framers sought to avoid — the exercise of unchecked power." Justice Powell also warned that because Congress does not operate in a judicial tradition, with regularized due process and other procedural safeguards, its adventitious intervention is most likely to deprive persons of their rights arbitrarily.

Justice White was the only dissenter. He characterized the legislative veto as "an important if not indispensable political invention that allows the President and Congress to resolve major constitutional and policy differences, assures the accountability of independent regulatory agencies, and preserves Congress' control over lawmaking. Perhaps there are other means of accommodation and accountability, but the increasing reliance of Congress upon the legislative veto suggests that the alternatives to which Congress must now turn are not entirely satisfactory.

"The history of the legislative veto also makes clear that it has not been a sword with which Congress has struck out to aggrandize itself at the expense of the other branches — the concerns of Madison and Hamilton. Rather, the veto has been a means of defense, a reservation of ultimate authority necessary if Congress is to fulfill its designated role under Article I as the Nation's lawmaker. While the President has often objected to particular legislative vetoes, generally those left in the hands of congressional committees, the Executive has more often agreed to legislative review as the price for a broad delegation of authority. To be sure, the President may have preferred unrestricted power, but that could be precisely why Congress thought it essential to retain a check on the exercise of delegated authority."

Justice White expressed concern that the Court should leap to invalidate all legislative vetoes on constitutional grounds when (1) the Constitution seems to offer no specific objection to the legislative veto; (2) Congress in the last 50 years has enacted hundreds of legislative vetoes without apparent constitutional qualms; (3) commentators are, at best, divided over the usefulness or invalidity of the device. Given the deep ambiguity of the constitutional or policy issues, the Court is unwise to sweep so broadly with its reasoning.

"The Court's holding today that all legislative-type action must be enacted through the lawmaking process ignores that legislative authority is routinely delegated to the Executive Branch, to the independent regulatory agencies, and to private individuals and groups. * * * There is no question but that agency rulemaking is lawmaking in any functional or realistic sense of the term. The Administrative Procedure Act, 5 U.S.C. § 551(4) provides that a 'rule' is an agency statement 'designed to implement, interpret, or prescribe law or policy.' When agencies are authorized to prescribe law through substantive rulemaking, the administrator's regulation is not only due deference, but is accorded 'legislative effect.' See, *e.g. Schweiker v. Gray Panthers*, 453 U.S. 34, 43–44 (1981); *Batterton v. Francis*, 432 U.S. 416 (1977). These regulations bind courts and officers of the federal government, may pre-empt state law, see, *e.g., Fidelity Federal Savings & Loan Assoc. v. De la Cuesta*, 458 U.S. 141 (1982), and grant rights to and impose obligations on the public. In sum, they have the force of law.

"If Congress may delegate lawmaking power to independent and executive agencies, it is most difficult to understand Article I as prohibiting Congress from also reserving a check on legislative power for itself. Absent the veto, the agencies receiving delegations of legislative or quasi-legislative power may issue regulations having the force of law without bicameral approval and without the President's signature. It is thus not apparent why the reservation of a veto over the exercise of that legislative power must be subject to a more exacting test. In both cases, it is enough that the initial statutory authorizations comply with the Article I requirements."

NOTES ON STRUCTURAL SEPARATION OF POWERS

1. *Different Visions of the Structure of the Constitution*. The three *Chadha* opinions offer strikingly different visions of the structures of constitutional law. The opinions of Justices Powell and White (who would allow legislative vetoes in many instances) take a functional approach to the separation of powers concept. Their main concern is that Congress should not usurp duties given to the executive (Justice White) or judicial (Justice Powell) powers. See Articles I–III of the Constitution.[m]

The Chief Justice's opinion seems to focus on a distinct but related issue of the circumstances under which Congress can legislate, under Article I, § 7. Because the Framers considered the lawmaking branch the most dangerous arm of government, they limited the instances in which Congress could act decisively by erecting anti-majoritarian barriers within the legislative process — bicameralism and presentment to the President. If Congress can make "law" without going through both Houses of Congress and the President, then there is a greater danger of abuse of legislative power, Chief Justice Burger contends. Is the Chief Justice right in focusing on this feature of the Constitu-

---

m. See Martin Redish, *The Constitution as Political Structure* 113–125 (1995) (arguing in favor of a pragmatic formalism in this area); E. Donald Elliott, INS v. Chadha: *The Administrative Constitution, the Constitution, and the Legislative Veto*, 1983 Sup. Ct. Rev. 125 (distinguishing between formalist and functionalist approaches to separation of powers issues).

tion, and treating it so strictly? His approach has been termed a formalist one, in contrast to the more functional approach reflected in the other opinions. How do Justices Powell and White justify their different focus?

2. *Policy Arguments.* Underlying the different constitutional visions of the various opinions in *Chadha* are probably different attitudes about the necessity or usefulness of the legislative veto. See generally Stanley Brubaker, *Slouching Toward Constitutional Duty: The Legislative Veto and the Delegation of Authority*, 1 Const. Comm. 81 (1984).

The chief argument for the legislative veto is that once the Court has allowed Congress to delegate enormous lawmaking power to agencies, with virtually no enforceable guidelines, Congress ought to be allowed to attach "strings" to that delegation, especially strings that allow the democratic process (Congress) to provide agencies with feedback having greater bite than oversight hearings. Moreover, the legislative veto provides flexibility in the conduct of public affairs in situations that could not have been foreseen by the Framers. Congress does not have the capacity to oversee the complicated regulatory state, and if it attempted to do so, the machinery of government would grind to a halt. "By delegating a qualified authority, Congress can maintain the system's energy, while by reserving authority to review proposed rules and acts, it can restore balance and accountability." *Id.* at 85.

Brubaker surveys several policy arguments against the legislative veto. First, the legislative veto distorts the legislative process. Legislation that would otherwise fail will pass if key legislators know that later they will have the opportunity to block offending provisions through the use of the legislative veto. This allows Congress to appear to be addressing hard questions, when in fact the legislative veto will thwart any substantial action by an administrative agency to address those questions.

Second, the legislative veto makes agencies vitally concerned with the views of entities other than the enacting Congress, which may be problematic. For example, because interest in the legislation will be lower when, months or years after its passage, the agency proposes implementing regulations, the task of reviewing those regulations will fall upon the congressional committees and subcommittees. "Thus a likely and apparently common occurrence is a significant skewing of the original legislative intent towards the interest of the congressmen on the overseeing committee or subcommittee and the groups and people most responsible for their re-election." *Id.* at 92. If committees are comprised of members with preferences more extreme than that of the body, a one-committee legislative veto may produce regulations far away from the preferences of the median legislator. In addition, the legislative veto allows subsequent Congresses a great deal of influence over the implementation of statutes passed in the past. Although this may allow for useful updating of policy without going through the procedural hurdles to enact new legislation, it may also allow for substantial shifts from the original intent of the enactors. Consider how a committee in a conservative Republican Congress might influence policies enacted by more liberal Democratic Congresses with very different ideological commitments. Is that legitimate?[n]

Third, the legislative veto may have encouraged very broad delegations because Congress could exert continuing and effective control over the agencies as they exercised their delegated authority. In other words, the incentive to constrain agency discretion *ex ante* by enacting detailed and precise statutes is less compelling if Congress has *ex post* tools to constrain agencies. For those who object to broad delegations, perhaps on the ground that they reduce political accountability, this possibility is disturbing. An excellent empirical study of the legislative veto suggests that it had some effect on the breadth of congressional delegations. See Jessica Korn, *The Power of Separation: American Constitutionalism and the Myth of the Legislative Veto* (1996). For example, after *Chadha* invalidated the legislative veto, members of Congress rescinded broad authority given the Secretary of Education with respect to Pell Grants and enacted their policy preferences more precisely. But other forces, practical and political, continue to discourage legislators from using specific and detailed statutory directive to reduce agency discretion, so the effect of *Chadha* in this area has not been substantial.

3. *Constitutionality of State Legislative Vetoes.* As an interpretation of Article I of the U.S. Constitution, *Chadha* does not control the validity of state legislative vetoes. Most states have followed *Chadha*, e.g., *Blank v. Department of Corrections,* 564 N.W.2d 130 (Mich. 1997), but there are some interesting variations.

In *Opinion of the Justices*, 431 A.2d 783 (N.H. 1981), the Court noted that New Hampshire's Constitution divides government into separate legislative, executive, and judicial powers; does not contemplate a "complete separation of powers" where a governmental power properly belongs to one branch of government; permits broad but not unlimited delegation of rulemaking powers to state agencies; and requires affirmative votes of both chambers of the legislature for a bill to become a law. The Court advised the legislature that a legislative committee veto is not valid under the New Hampshire Constitution but that other legislative veto arrangements were valid. "The objectives of the proposed legislation could be met and the constitutional objections minimized, if the statute were to provide for approval or rejection of the rules to be determined by a majority of a quorum of both houses, possibly acting pursuant to the recommendations of significantly representative committees, and then presented to the Governor for his approval. In such an instance, if any rule was rejected by either house or the Governor, its resubmission as a law would have to await enactment by the General Court and would be subject to a veto as with bills." Is this approach consistent with *Chadha*? Would it be much of a solution to the explosion of virtually unchecked agency lawmaking? See generally Philip Frickey, *The Constitutionality of Legislative Committee*

---

n. See Michael Herz, *The Legislative Veto in Times of Political Reversal:* Chadha *and the 104th Congress*, 14 Const. Comm. 319 (1997) (using game theory to demonstrate how legislative vetoes could radically shift regulatory outcomes when the partisan makeup of Congress changes). See also Eskridge & Ferejohn, *The Article I, Section 7 Game, supra.*

Suspension of Administrative Rules: The Case of Minnesota, 70 Minn. L. Rev. 1237 (1986).

The Idaho Supreme Court in *Mead v. Arnell*, 791 P.2d 410 (Ida. 1990), upheld a statute allowing the legislature to override agency rules by a concurrent resolution passed by both chambers but not submitted to the governor for veto. The court explicitly relied on Justice White's dissenting opinion in *Chadha*. Iowa's voters added a new article III, § 40 to that state's constitution in 1984:

> The general assembly may nullify an adopted administrative rule of a state agency by the passage of a resolution by a majority of all the members of each house of the general assembly.

New Jersey similarly amended its constitution in 1992.

Would these state developments violate the U.S. Constitution's requirement, art. IV, § 4, that states have a "Republican form of Government"? See *Van Sickle v. Shanahan*, 511 P.2d 223 (Kan. 1973) (provision in state constitution authorizing governor to reorganize state legislature, subject to one-house veto, does not violate Article IV, § 4).

4. *Severability of Unconstitutional Legislative Veto Provisions*. In *Alaska Airlines v. Brock*, 480 U.S. 678 (1987), the Supreme Court held that a legislative veto provision contained in the Airlines Deregulation Act of 1978, 92 Stat. 1705, was severable from the remainder of the statute. The Court suggested the following approach (*id.* at 685):

> * * * In considering this question [of severability] in the context of a legislative veto, it is necessary to recognize that the absence of the veto necessarily alters the balance of powers between the Legislative and Executive Branches of the Federal Government. Thus, it is not only appropriate to evaluate the importance of the veto in the original legislative bargain, but also to consider the nature of the delegated authority that Congress made subject to a veto. Some delegations of power to the Executive or to an independent agency may have been so controversial or so broad that Congress would have been unwilling to make the delegation without a strong oversight mechanism. The final test, for legislative vetoes as well as for other provisions, is the traditional one: the unconstitutional provisions must be severed unless the statute created in its absence is legislation that Congress would not have enacted.

This makes sense, but under this articulated approach the provision would seem nonseverable: the employee protections title was the only one in which Congress inserted a legislative veto, and that title was controversial. One concern about the title was that it would be administered by the Secretary of Labor, and therefore not under the normal oversight of the transportation committees. A House sponsor specifically spoke of the importance of the legislative veto to the employee protection title, and no one said anything to the contrary.

The Court starts with a presumption of severability. See *Heckler v. Mathews*, 465 U.S. 728, 738 & n.5 (1984). By assuming that Congress would have given away lawmaking power to an agency anyway, even if the strings attached to the original grant were invalidated, isn't the Court assuming that

Congress is irrational? Shouldn't the whole title be nullified, so that Congress itself could readjust the statutory scheme? See *Califano v. Westcott*, 443 U.S. 76 (1979) (Powell, J., dissenting). What would motivate the Court to cut legal corners in *Alaska Airlines*?[o]

5. *The Impact of* Chadha. Law professors tend to read great import into constitutional decisions; political scientists tend to see them gobbled up by larger structural features of American governance. So it has been with *Chadha*. Several scholars maintain that this decision had relatively little effect on congressional practice or on Congress-agency relations. On the one hand, congressional scholar Louis Fisher reports that many statutes enacted after *Chadha* continue to include legislative vetoes, and administrative agencies regularly attend to them as though they were the "law," seeking committee permission for certain decisions. See Louis Fisher, *The Legislative Veto: Invalidated, It Survives*, 56 Law & Contemp. Probs. 273 (1993).

On the other hand, Jessica Korn argues that other mechanisms, constitutional under *Chadha,* can and do work just as well as the legislative veto. She examines the subsequent history of the legislative veto in the Jackson-Vanik Amendment to the Trade Act of 1974, which terminated most-favored nation (MFN) trade status upon the vote of one house of Congress. Korn, *Power of Separation*, 91–115. She says the main value of the veto was as a fast-track vehicle for Congress to express frustration with presidential trade actions and to put pressure on the President to press congressional human rights concerns in negotiations with specific countries. Because Members wanted their views considered but did not want to be seen as upsetting foreign policy, Congress did not actually "veto" any MFN status until after *Chadha*. In any event, Korn argues, joint resolutions "conditioning" MFN status upon meeting human rights conditions have been a more effective vehicle for expression of Congress' concerns. Since such resolutions can be and usually are vetoed by the President, Congress can and does express concern without hurting foreign policy.

Korn's comprehensive study leads her to conclude that the practice was never a particularly important weapon in the arsenal of congressional oversight. "Members did not need the legislative shortcut to force executive branch officials to attend to congressional concerns, because the most useful sources of congressional oversight power — the power to make laws, and the power to require the executive branch and independent agency officials report [to committees] proposed actions before implementation — are well nestled in the authorities granted to members by Article I of the Constitution." *Id.* at 116. Of fourteen potential oversight mechanisms, some of which we discuss in this section, the legislative veto ranked last in terms of frequency of use and ninth in terms of effectiveness, according to Joel Auerbach, *Keeping a Watchful Eye: The Politics of Congressional Oversight* 132 (Table 6–1), 135 (Table 6–2) (1990).

---

o. Hint: The Court may be trying to ameliorate the disruptive impact of *Chadha*. Why would it want to do that?

Does it make sense to think that *Chadha* has had *no* effect, as these scholars seem to maintain? Are they not making the same error the Supreme Court made in *Alaska Airlines*, that is, thinking that legislative vetoes were just symbolic "add-ons"? Doesn't the *threat* of a one-House veto change the bargaining game between Congress and the President or an agency?

6. *The Line Item Veto Case.* In 1995, Congress enacted the Line Item Veto Act, 110 Stat. 1200, which authorized the President to "cancel" statutory items relating to discretionary spending or tax benefits if the President determined that cancellation would help reduce the budgetary deficit, not impair essential government functions, and not harm the national interest. In *Clinton v. City of New York*, 524 U.S. 417 (1997) (Chapter 3, § 3B), the Supreme Court invalidated the line item veto as inconsistent with Article I, § 7, as interpreted in *Chadha*. Justice Stevens's opinion for the Court contrasted the President's constitutional role *before* statutory enactment (the President can "return" an unacceptable bill with his "veto") with this *un*constitutional role of cancellation *after* statutory enactment. Does the reasoning of *Chadha* support this result? Is the line item veto as problematic as the legislative veto? You might recall the Eskridge and Ferejohn "Article I, Section 7 Game" as a way of thinking about this matter.

In dissent, Justice Breyer argued that the President was not creating a statute — he was simply exercising authority (routinely given him in prior statutes) not to spend all the money appropriated by Congress.[p] Justice Stevens's answer was that the Item Veto Act authorized the President to cancel statutory provisions and thereby prevent them from "having legal force or effect," 2 U.S.C. § 691e(4)(B)-(C), which is *legislative* in nature and not *implementational*. If the Act had not contained the "legal force or effect" language, the Court may have been more lenient. Justice Breyer responded, however, that Congress had previously given the Court and the President similar "force and effect" powers, e.g., 28 U.S.C. § 2072, without perceived constitutional difficulty.

Justice Breyer and Justice Scalia (in a separate dissenting opinion) believed that Congress's ability to give the President cancellation authority is limited by the nondelegation doctrine, but the statute easily revealed an "intelligible principle" to guide the President's exercise of discretion. Justice Breyer also asked: "Has the Congress given the President the 'wrong' kind of power, i.e., 'non-Executive' power?" To answer that question, he analyzed the item veto under the criteria in *Bowsher v. Synar*, excerpted in the next part of this section.

Query: If Congress really wants the President to have something like a line item veto authority, as a way of restraining Congress's tendency to undertax and over-spend, is there a way to do that after *Clinton*?

---

p. Congress has allowed the President discretion in the spending arena, e.g., *Train v. City of New York*, 420 U.S. 35 (1975), but not in the tax arena. Thus, the cancellation power might be more constitutionally problematic as to tax benefits than for discretionary spending.

D. LEGISLATIVE CONTROL THROUGH POWER OVER AGENCY OFFICIALS AND THEIR TENURE

As a matter of formal constitutional law, Congress can directly influence agency officials through the appointment and removal process.[q] (1) It may legislate a means by which "inferior Officers" are appointed. U.S. Const. Art. II, § 2, cl. 2; see *Morrison v. Olson*, 487 U.S. 654 (1988) (Congress can vest appointment of Independent Counsel "in Courts of Law"). (2) Although the President must name "other Officers of the United States," the President can only do so "with the Advice and Consent of the Senate." *Id.*; cf. *id.* Art. II, § 2, cl. 3 (President may make recess appointments without advice and consent). (3) The House may impeach and the Senate may remove any "civil Officer[]" of the United States." *Id.* Art. I, § 2, cl.5; Art. I, § 3, cls. 6–7; Art. II, § 4.

Jonathan Macey, *Organizational Design and Political Control of Administrative Agencies*, 8 J.L., Econ. & Org. 93, 100-08 (1992), argues that Congress has used this kind of authority in an innovative way for most of the last century — by insulating appointees from political pressure and removal. Thus, Congress's desire to establish a central banking authority that would keep inflation in check was a key reason why it ensured that the Federal Reserve Board would be an "independent" agency. Had the Fed been part of the executive branch, debtor groups (who benefit from inflation) would have more influence with the agency, through pressure from the President and congressional committees. The Federal Reserve Bank Act of 1914 has been very successful in this regard, but one might wonder whether its insulation of the agency from *presidential* control (the President cannot remove Fed officials as he can those in the executive branch) is a violation of Article II. Federal Reserve Board members are not "inferior Officers" under the Appointments Clause, and Article II might be read to deny Congress the right to design agencies in ways that denigrate from the "executive" authority to direct statutory implementation.[r]

The New Deal created several "independent" agencies having this feature. In *Humphrey's Executor v. United States*, 295 U.S. 602 (1935), the Supreme Court upheld a statute preventing the President from removing an FTC Commissioner unless for cause. Characterizing the independent agency as performing both adjudicative and "quasi-legislative" duties, the Court reasoned that Congress could restrict presidential power over such officers in ways it could not do for officials in purely executive agencies, under *Myers v. United States*, 272 U.S. 52 (1926). *Humphrey's Executor* suggested that Congress might have some room within the constitutional scheme to exercise direct

---

q. See generally Michael Gerhardt, *The Federal Appointments Process* (2000) (critiquing the modern appointments process and suggesting reforms).

r. The argument in text is especially compelling if it is true that Article II establishes a *unitary executive*, which must constitutionally be under the exclusive authority of the President. See Steven Calabresi & Saikrishna Prakash, *The President's Power to Execute the Laws*, 104 Yale L.J. 541 (1994) (explaining the "unitary executive"). But arguments against the constitutionality of independent agencies go beyond the unitary executive theory. E.g., Gary Lawson, *Delegation and Original Meaning*, 88 Va. L. Rev. 327 (2002).

control over officials implementing "quasi-legislative" duties. This hypothesis was tested in the litigation arising out of the famous Gramm-Rudman-Hollings balanced budget law.

BOWSHER v. SYNAR, 478 U.S. 714 (1986). Review the discussion of the Gramm-Rudman-Hollings (GRH) Act in Chapter 4, § 2A. As you remember, GRH was designed to eliminate the budget deficit through adherence to a set of deficit targets. If Congress failed to make spending and taxing changes in any year sufficient to meet the target, then a sequester would take place that would implement pro rata spending reductions in all eligible programs.

These automatic reductions were to be accomplished in three steps each year: (1) The executive Office of Management and Budget (OMB) and the legislative Congressional Budget Office (CBO) each estimated the federal deficit for the forthcoming fiscal year. If the projected deficit exceeded the targeted deficit, each calculated the program-by-program reductions needed to meet the target. The Directors of each independently reported all this information to the Comptroller General of the General Accounting Office (GAO), who is an agent of Congress (appointed by the President but removable by Congress). (2) The Comptroller General reviewed these reports and made his own report to the President. The Act required the President to issue a "sequestration order" to implement the spending reductions specified by the Comptroller General. (3) Congress had an opportunity to alter or implement the reductions by legislation. If nothing were done, the sequestration order automatically became effective.

The Supreme Court invalidated the enforcement provision of GRH. Having just read *Chadha*, you might think that GRH has the same structural problem as the legislative veto: It delegated important law-creating authority to an agent of the legislature, without requiring bicameral approval and presentment. **Justice Stevens** believed that the Act's enforcement provisions were invalid for this reason. He was convinced that Congress cannot delegate to one of its subgroups *or* agents the power "to make policy determinations that bind the Nation." But Justice Stevens spoke only for himself and for Justice Marshall. The Court followed another path to the same result.

Chief Justice Burger's opinion for the Court accepted Congress' characterization of sequestration as executive in nature; in other words, the Comptroller General was merely implementing a congressional policy decision. Executive actions can be delegated to executive branch entities and independent agencies without raising constitutional concerns. As you think back to some of the broad delegations sustained by the Court, this description of the sequester authority may not surprise you. The sequestration provisions included a number of specific guidelines to constrain the discretion of the implementing institution, particularly compared to other federal statutes. GRH specified which programs were eligible for cuts and which were exempt; it required uniformity; and it required pro rata cuts at the program, project and activity level.

Rather than applying his own opinion in *Chadha*, the Chief Justice picked up on the theme sounded by Justice Powell's *Chadha* concurring opinion: Separation of powers concerns are greatest when the legislature (the most powerful branch to begin with) invades the judicial (*Chadha*) or the executive (*Bowsher*) power. The Burger opinion argued that the GRH "usurped" executive power by giving an officer of Congress the authority to execute the laws. Such power can be unproblematically delegated to an executive branch entity; it cannot be retained by a direct agent of Congress. Burger's analysis is subject to several objections.

Justices **White** and **Blackmun** (dissenting) and Justices Marshall and Stevens (concurring in the judgment) found unrealistic the Court's suggestion that the Comptroller General would be "subservient" to Congress. The Comptroller General enjoys a 15-year term and may only be removed by Congress for (i) permanent disability; (ii) inefficiency; (iii) neglect of duty; (iv) malfeasance; or (iv) felony or conduct involving moral turpitude. 31 U.S.C. § 703(e)(1)(B). A Comptroller General has never been removed for policy reasons. Is there *any* reason to think that official might kowtow to Congress under the Gramm-Rudman Act? Aren't the Comptroller General's duties under the Act substantially limited by the OMB and CBO projections anyway?

Justices Marshall and Stevens argued that if the Court's opinion were taken literally — Congress may not "control" an official who performs "executive" rather than "legislative" powers — it would be an absurdity. The Capitol Police who arrest lawbreakers, the Sergeant-at-Arms who manages the congressional payroll, and the Capitol Architect who maintains the grounds are all agents of Congress who "execute" laws. Do those positions violate the Constitution?

NOTES ON THE GRAMM-RUDMAN CASE

1. *The Constitutionality of Independent Agencies?* Perhaps one reason *Bowsher* did not pursue the *Chadha* analysis is that the Court wanted to be careful not to question the constitutionality of independent agencies. In footnote 4 of its opinion, the Court made quite a point of the ease by which independent agencies, whose members are removable only by the President (if at all), pass muster under a test focusing on whether an executive official is controlled by Congress. This returns us to *Chadha*: If you *really* believe the Court's analysis there, how can you accept all the lawmaking that goes on in independent agencies? This was a focus of Justice White's *Chadha* dissent. The *Chadha* Court never faced up to this dilemma, and the *Bowsher* Court seemed embarrassed by the *Chadha* reasoning and so avoided the problem.

One of us has suggested a legal process answer to Justice White's concern:

> The nub of the problem * * * is whether the conception of the separation of powers that courts find themselves institutionally capable of enforcing is endangered more by legislative interference with agency rule making than by legislative delegation of limitless rule-making authority to agencies. * * * [A]lthough standardless delegation of rule-making authority implicates fundamental concerns involving the separation of powers, courts have considered themselves unable to referee in this arena. Moreover,

the delegation of legislative authority to a rival branch does not create any suspicions of self-interested institutional abuse, because the legislature is, at most, asking another branch to do the legislature's job rather than attempting to aggrandize to itself any roles that properly belong to another branch. * * * When a few legislators attempt to act as "super-administrators" performing functions similar to those of highly placed executive officials, the line between the executive and legislative branches becomes so blurred that basic principles of separation of powers are violated. Judicial suspicion of the functions of these legislators is heightened because here, unlike in the case of unqualified delegation of rule-making authority, the legislature appears to be intruding into the affairs of a coequal branch and conferring executive powers upon some of its members.

Frickey, *supra*, 70 Minn. L. Rev. at 1274. Do you agree?

2. *Does* Bowsher *Caution Against Congressional Micromanagement?* One might read *Bowsher* as suggesting a broad principle against *excessive* congressional control of statutory implementation. The vice in *Bowsher* was handing over statutory implementation to a congressional agent, but what if Congress hands over statutory implementation to an "independent" agency that Congress bullies into policy shifts because of *ex parte* pressure by Members of Congress, threats of funding cutoffs, or publicity and brutal accusations during oversight hearings? Surely, none of these mechanisms of congressional control is per se unconstitutional under *Bowsher*, but is there a *Bowsher* line that Congress would cross if it went "too far"? How might you define such a line?

3. *Implications of* Bowsher *and* Chadha *for Statutory Interpretation.* Recall the new textualist philosophy of statutory interpretation developed by Judge Easterbrook and Justice Scalia (Chapter 7, § 3A); one of the main themes of this philosophy is its disinclination to consider the legislative history of a statute to illuminate plain or clear statutory text (Chapter 8, § 2B). Construct an argument from *Chadha* and *Bowsher*, to the effect that the new textualist position enjoys support of constitutional dimensions. Compare John Manning, *Textualism as a Nondelegation Doctrine*, 97 Colum. L. Rev. 673 (1997), with Jonathan Siegel, *The Use of Legislative History in a System of Shared Powers*, 53 Vand. L. Rev. 1457 (2000). Is there a response to this argument from the perspective of these two decisions?

NOTE ON PRESIDENTIAL REVIEW OF AGENCY RULES

The President has many mechanisms available to control even the independent agencies:[s] (1) The President appoints the agency heads. Although the appointment is subject to Senate rejection, the President as the "first mover" has a lot of discretion to choose someone whose regulatory philosophy is compatible with his or her own. (2) The President's Office of Management

---

s. Much of the literature on this phenomenon has been contentious, because it arose out of the "deregulation wars" of the 1980s. Compare Congressman Edward Markey, Remarks at Program Presented by the Section of Administrative Law and Regulatory Practice, ABA (Oct. 14, 1988), in 41 Admin. L. Rev. 493–502 (1989), with Jonathan Macey, *Separated Powers and Positive Political Theory: The Tug of War Over Administrative Agencies*, 80 Geo. L.J. 671, 698–702 (1992).

and Budget (OMB) prepares the budget, which the President sends to Congress, which Congress of course changes, which the President can veto, and which the President then spends. Thus, the President has control at three points in the process. The President can use that power to punish agencies in disfavor and reward agencies in favor. (3) The White House has assumed a power to override some agency rules. This important authority requires a bit of explanation.[t]

The process of White House regulatory review began almost as soon as the "new" public interest agencies (NHTSA, EPA) were created; the Nixon, Ford, and Carter OMBs asked some agencies for cost-benefit justifications for their legislative rules. President Ronald Reagan's Executive Order 12,291, 3 C.F.R. 127 (1982), required agencies to submit proposed rules and a cost-benefit analysis to the OMB's Office of Information and Regulatory Affairs (OIRA). OIRA not only reviewed the rules with a vengeance, but also delayed rules that did not meet its cost-benefit specifications. OSHA and EPA were the main victims of OIRA's cutting analyses. Spurred by fire alarms from environmentalists, Congress howled, but did virtually nothing to curtail OIRA's transformation of "independent" agencies into arms of the executive.

President Clinton in 1993 revoked Executive Order 12,291 but imposed a similar structure to serve his own purposes in Executive Order 12,866, which returned review functions to OIRA and which ensured better access to the cost-benefit process to environmentalists and the like. 58 Fed. Reg. 51,735 (1993). The second Bush Administration seems inclined to continue cost-benefit review, presumably with a more business-friendly slant. Regulatory review seems here to stay, as we write in 2007. In light of *Humphrey's Executor* and the separation of powers embedded in Articles I–III of the Constitution, how can this presidential lawmaking power be defended?

One line of defense posed by political theorists is that the President, and only the President, can impose rationality upon the nation's regulatory policy. See Terry Moe & Scott Wilson, *Presidents and the Politics of Structure*, 57 L. & Contemp. Probs. 1 (1994). The President may have several institutional advantages in this respect. The main one is that there is a single President, usually with a mandate from a national electorate. Another is the Constitution's failure to shackle the Presidency with the procedural limitations like those visited upon Congress. Compare Article I, § 7 with Article II, § 2. The President therefore has both electoral (reelection) or personal (place in history) incentive and constitutional freedom to create institutions which tend toward policy coherence and rationality, rather than the cobbled together compromises and disorganization characteristic of congressional policymaking (at least according to critics of Congress). See also Elena Kagan, *Presidential Administration,* 114 Harv. L. Rev. 2245 (2001).

---

t. See Thomas McGarity, *Reinventing Rationality: The Role of Regulatory Analysis in the Federal Bureaucracy* (1991); Elizabeth Sanders, *The Presidency and the Bureaucratic State,* in *The Presidency and the Political System* (Michael Nelson ed. 1990); Robert Percival, *Checks Without Balance: Executive Office Oversight of the Environmental Protection Agency,* 54 Law & Contemp. Probs. 127 (Autumn 1991).

The reality of presidential power does not always correspond to this theory, however. Jide Nzelibe, for example, argues in *The Fable of the Nationalist President and the Parochial Congress*, 53 UCLA L. Rev. 1217 (2006), that the majoritarian-mandate argument for presidential primacy has been greatly overstated. On any given issue, the President is not as likely as Congress to reflect the preferences of the median voter. Moreover, the President is hardly immune from rent-seeking pressures and, on some issues, may be more corrupt than Congress in this regard.

Recall the history of the NHTSA's airbag rule. In 1971 NHTSA had proposed Standard 208, requiring that passive restraints be adopted in all cars. The auto industry objected to the cost of airbags and other restraints, but they were willing to put "interlocks" on their cars. Interlocks would prevent the car from being started unless the passengers fastened their seatbelts; an interlock would only add $40 to the cost of a car. NHTSA was uninterested, however. According to Mashaw & Harfst (*Auto Safety,* 132–33), Henry Ford II and Lee Iacocca met with President Nixon on April 27, 1971, sharing feelings about the cost-pinch that NHTSA was putting on the Big Three. Apparently, John Ehrlichman, the President's Domestic Adviser, directed the Department of Transportation to drop or delay airbags and adopt interlocks as the preferred technology. Transportation Secretary Volpe strenuously objected but was overridden in October 1971. NHTSA announced that passive protections would not be required until August 15, 1975 and that until then compliance with Standard 208 could be accomplished through an interlock. When the Sixth Circuit in *Chrysler* enjoined most of the alternatives required by Standard 208, the interlock (which was fine under the court's decision) became the only way to comply with the standard. Its introduction into cars during 1974 triggered a public outcry that fueled the congressional revolt against the NHTSA-safety coalition later that year.

The next stage in the airbag story is more interesting still (see Mashaw & Harfst, *Auto Safety,* 205–10). President Carter's Secretary of Transportation, Brock Adams, revived passive restraints in a 1977 order. The stage seemed set for delivery on the decade-long process, but implementation of the order by the industry was not due until President Carter's second term — an event derailed by the voters in 1980. President Reagan had run on a platform of getting the government out of people's lives, and one of the most intrusive agencies was NHTSA. On February 12, 1981, the agency proposed a one-year delay in the imposition of passive restraint requirements. Automakers supported the proposed delay, on the ground that it was unclear whether passive restraints would yield any increase in safety. The argument was that airbags are too expensive, so the industry would comply through passive seatbelts. But the public insisted that seatbelts be detachable. If, however, they were detachable, people would detach them, and they would have the same effect as manual belts. And cars already had manual belts. NHTSA accepted this argument, and on October 1981 the agency rescinded its passive restraints rule entirely. The Inside-the-Beltway belief is that the White House called the shot that killed Standard 208.

Evaluate the efficacy of presidential involvement in Standard 208's evolution. NHTSA's decision is appealed to the courts by insurance companies favoring the old standard. Should the courts overturn the executive action? Keep this in mind when you read Section 2F.

E. CONGRESS' POLICY CONTROL THROUGH DESIGN OF THE AGENCY'S STRUCTURE AND PROCEDURES

Oversight, *ex parte* contacts, the legislative veto, and appropriations pressure are all *ex post* methods for Congress to control the agencies to which it has delegated power. That is, these methods are after-the-fact: the agency does something Congress doesn't like, and Congress responds. Another way to control agency policy is *ex ante*: by careful design of the agency's procedure, jurisdiction, and composition, the enacting coalition can press agency policy in desired directions. McNollgast[u] have called this "hardwiring" the agency.

By the design of the agency's procedures and jurisdiction, the enacting Congress can create a very powerful or a very weak agency. We saw an example of the latter in Chapter 1. When Congress created the EEOC in the Civil Rights Act of 1964, it created procedural complexities and denied substantive rulemaking authority to the agency as part of the deal with conservative Senator Dirksen, who wanted to protect small businesses against too much federal meddling in their affairs.[v] (Dirksen correctly believed that the agency would be captive of pro-civil rights super-regulatory activists.) Although the EEOC has been a more successful policy entrepreneur than Dirksen probably would have wanted, his deal has ensured that the more conservative Supreme Court is a more constant check on EEOC interpretations than has been the case for other agencies (Section 3A of this chapter).

Another important design question is this: How many different interests is the agency going to represent and if the agency will have to fight for regulatory turf? For instance, the SEC is much more influenced by the New York Stock Exchange than the EEOC is influenced by employers or the EPA is influenced by chemical companies, because the SEC works only with a handful of stock exchanges across the country and must compete with Commodities Future Trading Commission (CFTC) and the Comptroller of the Currency for regulatory "turf" in the financial world. The EEOC and EPA, in contrast, must deal with hundreds of different companies in a wide range of businesses, and they are the primary federal agencies dealing with job discrimination and pollution, respectively. See also Edward Zelinsky, *James Madison and Public*

---

u. Matthew McCubbins, Roger Noll, and Barry Weingast have combined their names and efforts to create McNollgast. The hardwiring concept is developed in McNollgast, *Administrative Procedures as Instruments of Political Control*, 3 J.L. Econ. & Org. 243 (1987). See also Jonathan Macey, *Separated Powers and Positive Political Theory: The Tug of War Over Administrative Agencies*, 80 Geo. L.J. 671 (1992).

v. For an excellent exegesis of the complex "deal" with Dirksen, see Daniel Rodriguez & Barry Weingast, *The Positive Political Theory of Legislative History: New Perspectives on the 1964 Civil Rights Act and Its Interpretation,* 151 U. Pa. L. Rev. 1417 (2003).

Choice at Gucci Gulch: A Procedural Defense of Tax Expenditures and Tax Institutions, 102 Yale L.J. 1165 (1993) (making this point about the scope of interest group conflict in the tax arena).

Thus, if the enacting congressional coalition wants an agency's policy to be pro-industry, it will give the agency a small clientele and make it battle with other agencies for regulatory responsibilities. If the enacting coalition wants the agency to deal with industry in a more adversarial way, the enacting Congress will give the agency a wide ranging clientele with competing interests and give the agency a monopoly on that type of regulation. Moreover, Congress might insulate the agency from political pressure, as it has done with the Federal Reserve Board, by ensuring long terms for agency heads, forbidding *ex parte* communications, and the like.

Perhaps most important are the procedural rules established for the agency. The Supreme Court has discouraged the federal judiciary from adding procedural requirements to those in the APA and in the agency's particular enabling act. Hence, there is great room for congressional differentiation among agencies. By requiring more extensive notice and comment for rules than required by the APA, Congress can hamper the agency's ability to move decisively. There are numerous examples of Congress' enacting into the substantive legislation a requirement that agencies follow the sort of hybrid rulemaking that the D.C. Circuit had tried to impose through judicial doctrine.

One particularly good example of this occurred in the 1970s with the Federal Trade Commission. See Korn, *Separation of Powers*, chap. 4. During this time, the FTC was harshly criticized as the worst example of an agency "running amok" (a description by Rep. Risenhoover (D–Okla.)). It had very broad authority over the economy to prohibit unfair or deceptive trade practices. It was promulgating regulations that affected doctors, lawyers, funeral home directors, auto manufacturers, used car dealers, advertisers, oil companies, and cereal producers. Congress responded to concerns about the "rogue" agency by requiring that the FTC go through significantly more burdensome procedures before any rules could be promulgated. The agency had to hold actual hearings on proposed rules and allow cross-examination. The hybrid rulemaking procedure "made it impossible for the FTC to develop industry-wide rules away from public scrutiny." *Id.* at 55. Korn concludes that the procedures did not meet the objectives of the enactors because they were not accompanied by the enactment of more specific substantive guidelines for the FTC and because the agency could affect industry through investigations and other actions besides rulemaking.

The enabling statute can require consultation with advisory groups, or with designated types of experts, and can insist that a diversity of perspectives be heard. The statute can provide counsel fees for certain groups appearing before an agency. These requirements serve two functions, according to Matthew McCubbins, Roger Noll & Barry R. Weingast ("McNollgast"), *Structure and Process, Politics and Policy: Administrative Arrangements and the Political Control of Agencies*, 75 Va. L. Rev. 431, 472–73 (1989). First, they enfranchise particular groups of people who now have an enhanced right to have their views heard and considered. Second, the structure improves the fire alarm system of congressional monitoring because it more widely disseminates relevant information. Another increasingly popular method of control through institutional design is to require the agency to conduct extensive cost-benefit analysis before regulating. See Pablo Spiller & Emerson Tiller, *Decisions Costs and the Strategic Design of Administrative Process and Judicial Review*, 26 J. Legal Stud. 347 (1997). Not only may this analysis change the substance of the regulation by making costs and benefits more salient, but requiring agencies to expend limited resources on these studies also means they will have fewer funds for other activities. Spiller and Tiller conclude that Congress can control agencies by requiring certain allocations of decision costs and resources and that this is often accomplished through structure and institutional design.

McNollgast's hardwiring hypothesis remains to be tested, but consider some provisional caveats. The main one is that it is very hard to predict (for very long) the consequences of a certain institutional arrangement. The creators of the NHTSA sincerely wanted the agency to be a success, gave it great independence and full control over its regulatory turf, sought to assure broad participation in the agency's rulemaking proceedings, and insisted upon scientific and objective bases for the agency's standards. Yet very early on the agency ran into more troubles than its creators expected: the retirement of President Johnson and election of Richard Nixon undermined the agency and drained its budget, the requirement that the first agency rules be tied to existing standards started the agency off on a conservative footing from which it never fully escaped, the notice and comment rulemaking procedures and accompanying judicial review became crippling once the Big Three automakers organized themselves and decided to take an aggressive stance in court challenges — challenges that were being initiated at exactly the time when the judicial and academic culture was becoming enamored of hard look judicial review.

Also, it is not always accurate to speak of an "enacting coalition" that "designs" the agency. Most agencies are designed over a period of years, reflecting the inputs of several "coalitions," sometimes even in the same year. For example, the NHTSA's design — which was none too coherent in 1966 — became laughably incoherent in 1974, when three different coalitions effected statutory changes: (1) The original, safety at almost any cost, coalition was able to add rulemaking authority and recall authority to buttress the agency. (2) A coalition reflecting the consumer revolt against "interlocks" inserted substantive and procedural restrictions into the statute at the same time. (3) Yet another coalition forced the NHTSA to regulate schoolbuses, which the agency had decided were not cost-effective to regulate before 1974.

F. JUDICIAL REVIEW OF AGENCY RULES AND ORDERS

Another way that Congress can regulate agencies is by assuring judicial review of agency action under the Administrative Procedure Act (APA), analyzed in Section 1. If the federal courts were able to enforce Congress' original directives upon the agency, then Congress could feel more comfortable about delegating lawmaking authority to those agencies. Consistent with this idea and with the further idea that judicial review can counteract "capture" of the agency by "special interests," administrative law in the 1960s and 1970s grew more aggressive, especially in the Court of Appeals for the District of Columbia Circuit. The main developments were (1) the establishment of a strong presumption in favor of judicial review of agency action or inaction, and the enlargement of the class of interests which can invoke judicial review; (2) more searching judicial review based upon a detailed agency justification for its decision, including an indication that reasonable alternatives were considered; and (3) judicial policing of informal lobbying of agency officials by special interests. See Richard Stewart, *The Reformation of American Administrative Law*, 88 Harv. L. Rev. 1669, 1716 (1975). As you examine these developments, consider the drawbacks of expanded judicial review.

1. *Expanding Judicial Review of Discretionary Administrative Action.* As noted above, the APA explicitly provides for judicial review of agency actions. Formal adjudication and rulemaking must be supported by "substantial evidence"; informal action, including notice and comment rulemaking, must not be "arbitrary and capricious." In *Citizens to Preserve Overton Park, Inc. v. Volpe*, 401 U.S. 402 (1971), the Supreme Court applied the arbitrary and capricious standard in the context of an informal adjudication, where there was a written record and only a few public hearings, none of which rose to the level of a judicial proceeding. The Department of Transportation Act of 1966, 80 Stat. 931, codified at 49 U.S.C. § 1653(f) (1964, Supp. V, 1969), and the Federal-Aid Highway Act of 1966, 80 Stat. 771, codified at 23 U.S.C. § 138 (1964, Supp. V, 1969), prohibited the Secretary of Transportation from authorizing the use of federal funds to finance construction of highways through public parks if a "feasible and prudent" alternative route existed. Proposed Interstate 40 would have cut across Overton Park, a 342-acre park in Memphis, Tennessee. Pursuant to the above statutes, the Secretary approved the highway project in 1968; concerned citizens and a national environmental group sued the Secretary, on the ground that it would be "feasible and prudent" to route I–40 around Overton Park.

The lower courts dismissed the lawsuit because of the Secretary's broad discretion to approve highway routes. The Supreme Court, in an opinion by Justice Marshall, reversed. The Court made short shrift of the Government's argument that informal, discretionary decisions are not reviewable. The Court saw nothing to meet the Court's standard of "'clear and convincing evidence' of a * * * legislative intent" to restrict access to judicial review. *Abbott Laboratories v. Gardner*, 387 U.S. 136, 141 (1967). "Similarly, the Secretary's decision here does not fall within the exception for action 'committed to agency discretion.' This is a very narrow exception. * * * The legislative history of the Administrative Procedure Act indicates that it is applicable in those rare instances where 'statutes are drawn in such broad terms that in a given case there is no law to apply.' S. Rep. No. 752, 79th Cong., 1st Sess., 26 (1945)." Both relevant statutes provided that the Secretary "shall not approve any program or project" that requires the use of any public parkland "unless (1) there is no feasible and prudent alternative to the use of such land, and (2) such program includes all possible planning to minimize harm to such park * * *." Such language was sufficiently directive to foreclose a finding that these determinations were committed to agency discretion.

The Court determined that review should be limited, however, to whether the Secretary's action was "arbitrary or capricious" under APA § 706(2)(A). The reviewing court should conduct a review that is "thorough, probing, in-depth" and "must consider whether the [agency] decision was based on a consideration of the relevant factors and whether there has been a clear error of judgment. * * * Although this inquiry into the facts is to be searching and careful, the ultimate standard of review is a narrow one. The court is not empowered to substitute its judgment for that of the agency." In *Overton Park*, the Court remanded the case to the district court to obtain from the Secretary a statement of reasons that might be reviewed. The Secretary on remand was ultimately unable to justify his decision and so declined to approve the parkland route. See *Citizens to Preserve Overton Park, Inc. v. Brinegar*, 494 F.2d 1212 (6th Cir. 1974), cert. denied, 421 U.S. 991 (1975). After more back-and-forth between local authorities and the Nixon, Ford, and Carter Adminis-trations, the whole idea of an east-west expressway through Memphis was abandoned. The park and its protectors won. Had the public?

Peter Strauss has reassessed *Overton Park*.[w] Strauss found the statutory directive much less clear than Justice Marshall did and credited legislative history which assumed that the Secretary would consider the importance of the parkland, along with cost, community disruption, and other factors. The Secretary did consider park values, and plans were changed several times in response to park concerns. By requiring that parklands be given paramount rather than ordinary consideration, the Court was imposing values by judicial dictate on the Secretary that were not clearly those Congress had put into the statute. Strauss maintains that the political balance between park values and efficient roadbuilding values was disrupted by the Court's hurried, blunderbuss decision.

The Supreme Court struck a different balance in *Heckler v. Chaney*, 470 U.S. 821 (1985), which upheld the refusal by the Food and Drug Administra-tion (FDA) to investigate the applicability of the federal food and drug standards to the use of lethal injections in some states as their means of imposing the death penalty. Justice Rehnquist's opinion for the Court stated that an agency's decision not to prosecute or enforce, whether through civil or criminal process, is a decision generally committed to an agency's absolute discretion. "[A]n agency decision not to enforce often involves a complicated balancing of a number of factors which are peculiarly within its expertise. Thus, the agency must not only assess whether a violation has occurred, but whether agency resources are best spent on this violation or another, whether the agency is likely to succeed if it acts, whether the particular enforcement action requested best fits the agency's overall policies, and indeed, whether the agency has enough resources to undertake the action at all." Additionally, when an agency refuses to prosecute, "it generally does not exercise its

---

w. See Peter Strauss, *Revisiting* Overton Park: *Political and Judicial Controls over Administrative Actions Affecting the Community*, 39 U.C.L.A. L. Rev. 1251 (1992), deepened in Strauss, *Citizens to Preserve Overton Park v. Volpe — Of Politics and Law, Young Lawyers and the Highway Goliath*, in *Administrative Law Stories* 258–332 (Peter Strauss ed., 2006).

coercive power over an individual's liberty or property rights, and thus does not infringe upon areas that courts often are called upon to protect."

2. *How Scrutinizing Should Judicial Review Be? The "Hard Look Doctrine."* The *Overton Park* litigation was a signal not just that a presumption of reviewability under the APA was to be enthusiastically applied, but also that judicial scrutiny should have teeth. Such review has become known as the *hard look doctrine*, because courts scrutinize agency rationales and justifications so closely. See Harold Leventhal, *Environmental Decisionmaking and the Role of the Courts*, 122 U. Pa. L. Rev. 509 (1973); *Ethyl Corp. v. EPA*, 541 F.2d 1, 68–69 (D.C. Cir. 1976) (Leventhal, J., concurring). Hard-look review requires that the agency examine all relevant evidence, to explain its decisions in detail, to justify departures from past practices, and to consider all reasonable alternatives before reading a final policy decision." Hard look requires a well-reasoned explanation of agency policy; courts in most cases do not pass on the merits of the decision, merely the support the agency provides. Thus, in some cases, a rule that is remanded to the agency for further consideration is adopted again in similar form, but the agency provides a better explanation.

Critics of the hard look approach of aggressive review of agency policy (*Overton Park*) worry that it has led to agency *ossification* because second-guessing by nonexpert courts has undermined agencies' ability to act decisively on important national policies.[x] Mashaw and Harfst provide a specific example. NHTSA's Standard 208 proposed in 1969 that automakers be required by 1973 to adopt "passive" restraints (ones that consumers had no choice but to use, like airbags and automatic seatbelts) that would meet the agency's performance criteria. The criteria were phrased in terms of the effects produced on an anthropomorphic "dummy" in frontal barrier crashes at 30 miles per hour. Standard 208, expected to save thousands of lives at relatively low cost, was delayed substantially by judicial hard looks. The Sixth Circuit enjoined implementation of Standard 208 in *Chrysler Corp. v. Department of Transportation*, 472 F.2d 659 (6th Cir. 1972), on the ground that the test dummy approach specified in the regulation did not provide a sufficiently "objective" standard in light of the Safety Act legislative history. But the history only suggested that standards be phrased in "objective terms," and the parties had all but ignored the issue until the judicial hard look made it central. Just as *Overton Park* threw road planning into turmoil for the rest of the 1970s,

---

x. See, e.g., Shep Melnick, *Administrative Law and Bureaucratic Reality*, 44 Admin. L. Rev. 245, 246 (1992) ("Judicial review has subjected agencies to debilitating delay and uncertainty. Courts have heaped new tasks on agencies while decreasing their ability to perform any of them. They have forced agencies to substitute trivial pursuits for important ones."). But see William Jordan, III, *Ossification Revisited: Does Arbitrary and Capricious Review Significantly Interfere with Agency Ability to Achieve Regulatory Goals Through Informal Rulemaking?*, 94 Nw. U. L. Rev. 393 (2000) (arguing that arbitrary and capricious review has not significantly impeded agencies in pursuit of policy goals). See also Mark Seidenfeld, *Demystifying Deossification: Rethinking Recent Proposals to Modify Judicial Review of Notice and Comment Rulemaking*, 75 Tex. L. Rev. 483 (1997) (surveying and analyzing arguments and reform proposals).

so *Chrysler* and other hard look decisions criticizing Standard 208 threw the NHTSA into turmoil for the remainder of the decade (Harfst & Mashaw, *Auto Safety*, ch. 5).

Kevin McDonald disputes the ossification theory in general and Mashaw and Harfst's view that judicial review undermined the NHTSA. McDonald, *Shifting Out of Park*, 96–97.[y] From the industry's point of view, the NHTSA has had a winning record in court and has been able to impose most of the design changes it believes will improve highway safety. As McDonald sees it, the NHTSA's (and the nation's) big problem is democracy: since 1974, Congress has not shared the agency's priorities. (McDonald thinks that Congress has been misguided in focusing on minor defects that are the objects of recalls and in failing to focus on driver errors, which cause the overwhelming majority of accidents.)

In any event, judges have backed away from the hard-look doctrine. In *Syracuse Peace Council v. FCC*, 867 F.2d 654 (D.C. Cir. 1989), Judge Stephen Williams accepted the FCC's decision to reject the "fairness doctrine" that it had applied in the past to require broadcast media licensees to provide coverage of issues of public interest and to provide opportunities for the airing of contrasting viewpoints. The FCC claimed, *inter alia*, that the requirements of the fairness doctrine actually discouraged broadcasters from covering controversial issues. The study that "proved" a chilling effect on speech was based primarily on the representations of broadcasters in a survey. At its height, the hard look doctrine would have been applied to call into question this sort of evidence from arguably self-interested parties. Judge Williams' opinion seems more willing to give the benefit of the doubt to the expert regulatory commission, however. Furthermore, although Williams explicitly found that the FCC rule was based on a misunderstanding of the law, he did not remand it to the agency for a reconsideration. Rather, the correct understanding "appear[s] so obvious and compelling that a remand to extract the magic words from the Commission would be pure waste."

In a similar use of a soft-glance rather than a hard-look analysis, Judge Posner upheld regulations adopted by OSHA regulating occupational exposure to blood-borne pathogens, a rule designed to protect health care workers from hepatitis and AIDS. *American Dental Ass'n v. Martin*, 984 F.2d 823 (7th Cir. 1993), cert. denied, 510 U.S. 859 (1993). The opinion has a much more deferential tone than *Overton Park* and its progeny. Much regulation occurs under conditions of uncertainty, Posner argues, and in such cases, the conclusions of experts on technical issues "are entitled to respect by the nonspecialist, biomedically unsophisticated Article III judiciary, at least in the absence of a more systematic showing of harms" by the challengers. Whether these cases represent a trend away from hard look review, at least in the context of notice-and-comment rulemaking and other informal decisions, remains to be seen.

---

y. The discussion in text also draws from comments Mr. McDonald emailed to Professor Philip Frickey regarding Chapter 9 of this casebook, June 27, 2007.

3. *Procedural Requirements in Rulemaking Proceedings.* When an agency engages in informal rulemaking, it is acting like a legislature (APA § 553) and so does not have to follow the formal procedures of adjudication (APA § 554), where the agency is acting like a court. Under a benign view of agency decisionmaking, this makes perfect sense. But if one fears that the agency has been captured by special interests, one fears that the informal rulemaking process might easily be "corrupted." A few decades ago, the D.C. Circuit considered procedural ways to open up such rulemaking, a process ostensibly halted by the Supreme Court. See Gillian Metzger, *The Story of Vermont Yankee: A Cautionary Tale of Judicial Review and Nuclear Waste,* in *Administrative Law Stories* 124–67 (Peter Strauss ed., 2006).

The D.C. Circuit in *Home Box Office, Inc. v. FCC,* 567 F.2d 9 (D.C. Cir. 1977), overturned rules easing limitations on cable and pay television programming in part because of evidence that the public docket for the proposed rules was "a sham" and the "real" deliberations had been conducted privately between the Commissioners and industry representatives. The Court read *Overton Park* to require that agency decisions be rendered upon a record that discloses all relevant evidence and argumentation that the agency considered. Hence, a decision in which there were undisclosed *ex parte* communications was invalid.

Home Box Office generated great criticism. The introduction of this feature into informal rulemaking threatened a valuable flow of information. Not only do members of the industry have detailed, first-hand information that is intrinsically useful, but it could be a check on the information developed by agency staffs. The dialogue between administrators and the private sector is a necessary part of regulation. Retreating from *Home Box Office,* the D.C. Circuit in *Sierra Club v. Costle,* 657 F.2d 298, 402–04 (D.C. Cir. 1981), only required the EPA to docket descriptions of oral communications which are of "central relevance" to the rulemaking proceedings. The Court in *Sierra Club* also faced objections that the EPA's rule was invalid because of undisclosed contacts between agency decisionmakers and the White House and one Member of Congress, Senator Byrd (D–W.Va.). Judge Wald's opinion exempted most such contacts from the rule that *ex parte* communications be docketed, based upon principles of separation of powers.

Home Box Office was something of a judicial disaster, but its core idea — that agencies should observe judicial norms of openness when they affect private parties and the public interest — did not die. In the 1970s, The D.C. Circuit in some instances required some form of oral hearings, with cross-examination, in § 553 informal rulemaking. For example, in *Mobil Oil Corp. v. Federal Power Comm'n,* 483 F.2d 1238 (D.C. Cir. 1973), a suit to review the FPC's order setting minimum rates charged by natural gas pipelines for transporting liquid hydrocarbons, Judge Wilkey agreed that even when an agency is not statutorily required to engage in formal rulemaking, it must in some circumstances afford interested persons an opportunity to test the evidence upon which the agency intends to rely. The Court held that "the rule that the 'whole record' be considered — both evidence for and against — means that procedures must provide some mechanism for interested parties to introduce adverse evidence and criticize evidence introduced by others" (*id.* at 1258). See also *International Harvester Co. v. Ruckelshaus*, 478 F.2d 615 (D.C. Cir. 1973) (Leventhal, J.), analyzed in Stephen Williams, *"Hybrid Rulemaking" Under the Administrative Procedure Act: A Legal and Empirical Analysis*, 42 U. Chi. L. Rev. 401 (1975).

The Supreme Court, however, was hostile to "judicializing" rulemaking proceedings. For example, in *United States v. Florida East Coast Ry. Co.*, 410 U.S. 224 (1973), the Court held that language in the Interstate Commerce Act requiring the ICC to act "after hearing" did not require very formal procedures in ICC rulemaking, because this language was not the equivalent of "on the record after opportunity for an agency hearing" used in § 553(c) to trigger formal rulemaking procedures. By limiting the circumstances in which formal rulemaking was required to those in which the organic statute used the magic words, this case helped to usher in the Era of Rulemaking. Unless the statute required more, agencies could use notice-and-comment proceedings to promulgate regulations. Under the explicit terms of the APA, few specific procedures are required for such rulemaking. Only if hybrid rulemaking was codified or imposed judicially would the agencies be directly required to do more than provide notice, compile and consider written comments, and issue the rule with a "concise general statement" of its basis and purpose. The hard look review might require substantially more than a "concise" statement to satisfy the courts, but the agencies would have flexibility in their choice of procedures through which to develop a sufficient record.

Thus, the Court's decision in *Vermont Yankee Nuclear Power Co. v. Natural Resources Defense Council, Inc.*, 435 U.S. 519 (1978), is a milestone for the administrative state because the Court passed on the legitimacy of judicially imposed hybrid procedures. See Metzger, *The Story of Vermont Yankee*, for a comprehensive analysis. In 1971, Vermont Yankee applied to the Atomic Energy Commission for a license to operate a nuclear plant in Vernon, Vermont. NRDC opposed the application, in part because of alleged environmental effects of operations to reprocess fuel or to dispose of wastes resulting from the reprocessing operations. The environmental issue was excluded from consideration by the Licensing Board which conducted the adjudicatory hearing, but in 1972 the Commission itself began rulemaking proceedings on the issue of what consideration should be given by the Licensing Board to the environmental effects of the uranium fuel cycle. The Commission's notice set forth two possible rules. In 1973, the Commission scheduled a hearing on the alternative rules and made available to the public an Environmental Survey prepared by its staff. Both written and oral comments were received, and the Commission in 1974 issued a rule requiring consideration of such environmental impact. Although that rule was inconsistent with the practice of the Licensing Board in the Vermont Yankee proceeding, the Commission affirmed the grant of an operating license to Vermont Yankee. On appeal, the D.C. Circuit found that although the Commission had followed all the § 553 procedures for informal rulemaking, and more, the Court found the procedures inadequate overall and remanded for the agency to follow procedures permitting greater public scrutiny of information upon which the Commission relied.

The Supreme Court, in an opinion by Justice Rehnquist, pointedly criticized the D.C. Circuit's "Monday morning quarterbacking" of the agency's procedures. Rehnquist cited *Florida East Coast Railway* for the proposition that § 553 of the APA "established the maximum procedural requirements which Congress was willing to have the courts impose upon agencies in conducting rulemaking procedures." While "[t]his is not to say necessarily that there are no circumstances which would ever justify a court in overturning agency action because of a failure to employ procedures beyond those required by statute * * * such circumstances, if they exist, are extremely rare." Moreover, apart from the APA, "this Court has for more than four decades emphasized that the formulation of procedures was basically to be left within the discretion of the agencies to which Congress had confided the responsibility for substantive judgments." The Court reversed the D.C. Circuit's invalidation of the procedures used in the agency's informal rulemaking and remanded to the D.C. Circuit to review the rule on the merits.

Does *Vermont Yankee* implicitly overrule *Home Box Office*? *Mobil Oil*? Is there any way to distinguish those cases?[z] Notwithstanding *Vermont Yankee*, federal courts of appeals have continued to impose procedural requirements on "informal" rulemaking — but under cover of liberally "interpreting" the notice-and-comment requirements of § 553, rather than imposing them as a matter of administrative common law. See Gary Lawson, *Federal Administrative Law* 240-83 (4th ed. 2007) (disapproving); Metzger, *Story of Vermont Yankee* (acquiescent).

Problem on Judicial Review of Agency Action

Problem 9–4. The NHTSA in 1970 proposed to amend Standard 108's provisions governing turn signals and warning flashers. Later, the agency indicated that it would abandon the "sampling" methodology it had allowed in the past (a random sample of flashers were tested) and would require testing of all automobiles. Since the agency did not propose to relax performance criteria, the proposal would upgrade the standard significantly. Wagner Electric Company objected that this sampling change was not indicated in the earlier notice of proposed rulemaking, and NHTSA issued a new notice which proposed to eliminate sampling.

Among the comments, Wagner and other companies urged relaxation of the performance criteria if sampling were adopted and urged, further, that yet another round of notice-and-comment should be commenced, so that the issues could be considered together. NHTSA's final rule, issued in 1971, eliminated sampling but also downgraded the performance criteria. Wagner sued to overturn the rule, on the ground that there was no single notice that the agency

---

z. For a fascinating discussion of *Vermont Yankee*, particularly given his prominence as a textualist, see Antonin Scalia, Vermont Yankee: *The APA, The D.C. Circuit, and the Supreme Court*, 1978 Sup. Ct. Rev. 345. For an illuminating debate about the case, see Clark Byse, Vermont Yankee *and the Evolution of Administrative Procedure: A Somewhat Different View*, 91 Harv. L. Rev. 1823 (1978); Richard Stewart, Vermont Yankee *and the Evolution of Administrative Procedure*, 91 Harv. L. Rev. 1805 (1978).

was considering both elimination of sampling and downgrading performance criteria. NHTSA responded that its sampling notice contained the usual reservation that its rule might encompass related matters and that several commenters had, like Wagner, fully commented on the matter.

Will the court overturn the rule? See *Wagner Electric Corp. v. Volpe*, 466 F.2d 1013 (3d Cir. 1972). Would a judicial invalidation be inconsistent with *Vermont Yankee*? Reconsider your answer after reading the next case.

MOTOR VEHICLE MANUFACTURERS ASS'N v. STATE FARM MUTUAL AUTOMOBILE INS. CO.
Supreme Court of the United States, 1983
463 U.S. 29, 103 S.Ct. 2856, 77 L. Ed. 2d 443

JUSTICE WHITE delivered the opinion of the Court.

The development of the automobile gave Americans unprecedented freedom to travel, but exacted a high price for enhanced mobility. Since 1929, motor vehicles have been the leading cause of accidental deaths and injuries in the United States. * * * Congress responded by enacting the National Traffic and Motor Vehicle Safety Act of 1966. The Act, created for the purpose of "reduc[ing] traffic accidents and deaths and injuries to persons resulting from traffic accidents," 15 U.S.C. § 1381, directs the Secretary of Transportation or his delegate to issue motor vehicle safety standards that "shall be practicable, shall meet the need for motor vehicle safety, and shall be stated in objective terms." 15 U.S.C. § 1392(a). In issuing these standards, the Secretary is directed to consider "relevant available motor vehicle safety data," whether the proposed standard "is reasonable, practicable and appropriate" for the particular type of motor vehicle, and the "extent to which such standards will contribute to carrying out the purposes" of the Act. 15 U.S.C. § 1392(f)(1), (3), (4).

The Act also authorizes judicial review under the provisions of the Administrative Procedure Act (APA), 5 U.S.C. § 706, of all "orders establishing, amending, or revoking a Federal motor vehicle safety standard," 15 U.S.C. § 1392(b). Under this authority, we review today whether NHTSA acted arbitrarily and capriciously in revoking the requirement in Motor Vehicle Safety Standard 208 that new motor vehicles produced after September 1982 be equipped with passive restraints to protect the safety of the occupants of the vehicle in the event of a collision. Briefly summarized, we hold that the agency failed to present an adequate basis and explanation for rescinding the passive restraint requirement and that the agency must either consider the matter further or adhere to or amend Standard 208 along lines which its analysis supports.

[I] As originally issued by the Department of Transportation in 1967, Standard 208 simply required the installation of seatbelts in all automobiles. 32 Fed.Reg. 2408, 2415 (Feb. 3, 1967). It soon became apparent that the level of seatbelt use was too low to reduce traffic injuries to an acceptable level. The Department therefore began consideration of "passive occupant restraint systems" — devices that do not depend for their effectiveness upon any action taken by the occupant except that necessary to operate the vehicle. Two types of automatic crash protection emerged: automatic seatbelts and airbags. The automatic seatbelt is a traditional safety belt, which when fastened to the interior of the door remains attached without impeding entry or exit from the vehicle, and deploys automatically without any action on the part of the passenger. The airbag is an inflatable device concealed in the dashboard and steering column. It automatically inflates when a sensor indicates that deceleration forces from an accident have exceeded a preset minimum, then rapidly deflates to dissipate those forces. The life-saving potential of these devices was immediately recognized, and in 1977, after substantial on-the-road experience with both devices, it was estimated by NHTSA that passive restraints could prevent approximately 12,000 deaths and over 100,000 serious injuries annually. 42 Fed.Reg. 34,298.

In 1969, the Department formally proposed a standard requiring the installation of passive restraints, 34 Fed.Reg. 11,148 (July 2, 1969), thereby commencing a lengthy series of proceedings. In 1970, the agency revised Standard 208 to include passive protection requirements, 35 Fed.Reg. 16,927 (Nov. 3, 1970), and in 1972, the agency amended the standard to require full passive protection for all front seat occupants of vehicles manufactured after August 15, 1975. 37 Fed.Reg. 3911 (Feb. 24, 1972). In the interim, vehicles built between August 1973 and August 1975 were to carry either passive restraints or lap and shoulder belts coupled with an "ignition interlock" that would prevent starting the vehicle if the belts were not connected. On review, the agency's decision to require passive restraints was found to be supported by "substantial evidence" and upheld. *Chrysler Corp. v. Dep't of Transportation*, 472 F.2d 659 (CA6 1972).

In preparing for the upcoming model year, most car makers chose the "ignition interlock" option, a decision which was highly unpopular, and led Congress to amend the Act to prohibit a motor vehicle safety standard from requiring or permitting compliance by means of an ignition interlock or a continuous buzzer designed to indicate that safety belts were not in use. Motor Vehicle and Schoolbus Safety Amendments of 1974, Pub.L. 93–492, § 109, 88 Stat. 1482, 15 U.S.C. § 1410b(b). The 1974 Amendments also provided that any safety standard that could be satisfied by a system other than seatbelts would have to be submitted to Congress where it could be vetoed by concurrent resolution of both houses. 15 U.S.C. § 1410b(b)(2).

The effective date for mandatory passive restraint systems was extended for a year until August 31, 1976. 40 Fed.Reg. 16,217 (April 10, 1975); *id.*, at 33,977 (Aug. 13, 1975). But in June 1976, Secretary of Transportation William T. Coleman, Jr., initiated a new rulemaking on the issue, 41 Fed.Reg. 24,070 (June 9, 1976). After hearing testimony and reviewing written comments, Coleman extended the optional alternatives indefinitely and suspended the passive restraint requirement. Although he found passive restraints technologically and economically feasible, the Secretary based his decision on the expectation that there would be widespread public resistance to the new systems. He instead proposed a demonstration project involving up to 500,000 cars installed with passive restraints, in order to smooth the way for public acceptance of mandatory passive restraints at a later date. Department of Transportation, The Secretary's Decision Concerning Motor Vehicle Occupant Crash Protection (December 6, 1976).

Coleman's successor as Secretary of Transportation disagreed. Within months of assuming office, Secretary Brock Adams decided that the demonstration project was unnecessary. He issued a new mandatory passive restraint regulation, known as Modified Standard 208. 42 Fed.Reg. 34,289 (July 5, 1977); 42 CFR § 571.208 (1978). The Modified Standard mandated the phasing in of passive restraints beginning with large cars in model year 1982 and extending to all cars by model year 1984. The two principal systems that would satisfy the Standard were airbags and passive belts; the choice of which system to install was left to the manufacturers. In *Pacific Legal Foundation v. Dep't of Transportation*, 593 F.2d 1338 (CADC), cert. denied, 444 U.S. 830 (1979), the Court of Appeals upheld Modified Standard 208 as a rational, nonarbitrary regulation consistent with the agency's mandate under the Act. The standard also survived scrutiny by Congress, which did not exercise its authority under the legislative veto provision of the 1974 Amendments.

Over the next several years, the automobile industry geared up to comply with Modified Standard 208. As late as July, 1980, NHTSA reported:

> "On the road experience in thousands of vehicles equipped with airbags and automatic safety belts has confirmed agency estimates of the life-saving and injury-preventing benefits of such systems. When all cars are equipped with automatic crash protection systems, each year an estimated 9,000 more lives will be saved and tens of thousands of serious injuries will be prevented."

NHTSA, Automobile Occupant Crash Protection, Progress Report No. 3, p. 4. In February 1981, however, Secretary of Transportation Andrew Lewis reopened the rulemaking due to changed economic circumstances and, in particular, the difficulties of the automobile industry. 46 Fed.Reg. 12,033 (Feb. 12, 1981). Two months later, the agency ordered a one-year delay in the application of the standard to large cars, extending the deadline to September 1982, 46 Fed.Reg. 21,172 (April 9, 1981) and at the same time, proposed the possible rescission of the entire standard. 46 Fed.Reg. 21,205 (April 9, 1981). After receiving written comments and holding public hearings, NHTSA issued a final rule (Notice 25) that rescinded the passive restraint requirement contained in Modified Standard 208.

[II] In a statement explaining the rescission, NHTSA maintained that it was no longer able to find, as it had in 1977, that the automatic restraint requirement would produce significant safety benefits. Notice 25, 46 Fed.Reg. 53,419 (Oct. 29, 1981). This judgment reflected not a change of opinion on the effectiveness of the technology, but a change in plans by the automobile industry. In 1977, the agency had assumed that airbags would be installed in 60% of all new cars and automatic seatbelts in 40%. By 1981 it became apparent that automobile manufacturers planned to install the automatic seatbelts in approximately 99% of the new cars. For this reason, the life-saving potential of airbags would not be realized. Moreover, it now appeared that the overwhelming majority of passive belts planned to be installed by manufacturers could be detached easily and left that way permanently. Passive belts, once detached, then required "the same type of affirmative action that is the stumbling block to obtaining high usage levels of manual belts." 46 Fed.Reg., at 53421. For this reason, the agency concluded that there was no longer a basis for reliably predicting that the standard would lead to any significant increased usage of restraints at all.

In view of the possibly minimal safety benefits, the automatic restraint requirement no longer was reasonable or practicable in the agency's view. The requirement would require approximately $1 billion to implement and the agency did not believe it would be reasonable to impose such substantial costs on manufacturers and consumers without more adequate assurance that sufficient safety benefits would accrue. In addition, NHTSA concluded that automatic restraints might have an adverse effect on the public's attitude toward safety. Given the high expense and limited benefits of detachable belts, NHTSA feared that many consumers would regard the standard as an instance of ineffective regulation, adversely affecting the public's view of safety regulation and, in particular, "poisoning . . . popular sentiment toward efforts to improve occupant restraint systems in the future." 46 Fed.Reg., at 53424.

[The United States Court of Appeals for the District of Columbia Circuit invalidated the agency's rule rescinding the passive restraint requirement, on the ground that it was arbitrary and capricious and therefore in violation of the APA. 680 F.2d 206 (1982).]

[III. The Court held that the APA fully applied to NHTSA's rulemaking proceeding, and that a reviewing court has an obligation to set aside any rule found to be "arbitrary, capricious, an abuse of discretion, or otherwise not in accordance with law." 5 U.S.C. § 706(2)(A); see *Overton Park*. The Court rejected Motor Vehicle's argument that an agency's rescission of a rule should be governed by the same narrow standard as the agency's refusal to issue a rule in the first place.]

[Justice White explained the "arbitrary and capricious" standard of review.] [T]he agency must examine the relevant data and articulate a satisfactory explanation for its action including a "rational connection between the facts found and the choice made." *Burlington Truck Lines Inc. v. United States*, 371 U.S. 156, 168 (1962). In reviewing that explanation, we must "consider whether the decision was based on a consideration of the relevant factors and whether there has been a clear error of judgment." *Bowman Transp. Inc. v. Arkansas-Best Freight System*, [419 U.S. 281, 285 (1974)]. Normally, an agency rule would be arbitrary and capricious if the agency has relied on factors which Congress has not intended it to consider, entirely failed to consider an important aspect of the problem, offered an explanation for its decision that runs counter to the evidence before the agency, or is so implausible that it could not be ascribed to a difference in view or the product of agency expertise. The reviewing court should not attempt itself to make up for such deficiencies; we may not supply a reasoned basis for the agency's action that the agency itself has not given. * * * For purposes of these cases, it is also relevant that Congress required a record of the rulemaking proceedings to be compiled and submitted to a reviewing court, 15 U.S.C. § 1394, and intended that agency findings under the Motor Vehicle Safety Act would be supported by "substantial evidence on the record considered as a whole." S.Rep. No. 1301, 89th Cong., 2d Sess. 8 (1966); H.R.Rep. No. 1776, 89th Cong., 2d Sess. 21 (1966).

[In Part IV, Justice White rejected the lower court's requirement that NHTSA was obligated to provide "increasingly clear and convincing reasons" for its action. The Court of Appeals relied on post-1974 congressional signals (such as Congress's failure to override the Carter-era NHTSA initiatives) to infer a "congressional commitment to the concept of automatic crash protection devices for vehicle occupants." Justice White found the lower court's reading of the materials misguided. Also, "this Court has never suggested that the *standard* of review is enlarged or diminished by subsequent congressional action. While an agency's interpretation of a statute may be confirmed or ratified by subsequent congressional failure to change that interpretation, *Bob Jones University* [Chapter 8, § 2B6], in the cases before us, even an unequivocal ratification — short of statutory incorporation — of the passive restraint standard would not connote approval or disapproval of an agency's later decision to rescind the regulation. That decision remains subject to the arbitrary and capricious standard."]

[V] The ultimate question before us is whether NHTSA's rescission of the passive restraint requirement of Standard 208 was arbitrary and capricious. We conclude, as did the Court of Appeals, that it was. We also conclude, but for somewhat different reasons, that further consideration of the issue by the agency is therefore required. * * *

[A] The first and most obvious reason for finding the rescission arbitrary and capricious is that NHTSA apparently gave no consideration whatever to modifying the Standard to require that airbag technology be utilized. Standard 208 sought to achieve automatic crash protection by requiring automobile manufacturers to install either of two passive restraint devices: airbags or automatic seatbelts. There was no suggestion in the long rulemaking process that led to Standard 208 that if only one of these options were feasible, no passive restraint standard should be promulgated. Indeed, the agency's original proposed Standard contemplated the installation of inflatable restraints in all cars. Automatic belts were added as a means of complying with the standard because they were believed to be as effective as airbags in achieving the goal of occupant crash protection. 36 Fed.Reg. 12,858, 12,859 (July 8, 1971). At that time, the passive belt approved by the agency could not be detached. Only later, at a manufacturer's behest, did the agency approve of the detachability feature — and only after assurances that the feature would not compromise the safety benefits of the restraint. Although it was then foreseen that 60% of the new cars would contain airbags and 40% would have automatic seatbelts, the ratio between the two was not significant as long as the passive belt would also assure greater passenger safety.

The agency has now determined that the detachable automatic belts will not attain anticipated safety benefits because so many individuals will detach the mechanism. Even if this conclusion were acceptable in its entirety, standing alone it would not justify any more than an amendment of Standard 208 to disallow compliance by means of the one technology which will not provide effective passenger protection. It does not cast doubt on the need for a passive restraint standard or upon the efficacy of airbag technology. In its most recent rulemaking, the agency again acknowledged the lifesaving potential of the airbag:

> "The agency has no basis at this time for changing its earlier conclusions in 1976 and 1977 that basic airbag technology is sound and has been sufficiently demonstrated to be effective in those vehicles in current use . . . ."

NHTSA Final Regulatory Impact Analysis (RIA) at XI-4 (Oct. 1981). Given the effectiveness ascribed to airbag technology by the agency, the mandate of the Act to achieve traffic safety would suggest that the logical response to the faults of detachable seatbelts would be to require the installation of airbags. At the very least this alternative way of achieving the objectives of the Act should have been addressed and adequate reasons given for its abandonment. But the agency not only did not require compliance through airbags, it also did not even consider the possibility in its 1981 rulemaking. Not one sentence of its rulemaking statement discusses the airbags-only option. * * * [W]hat we said in *Burlington Truck Lines v. United States* is apropos here:

> "There are no findings and no analysis here to justify the choice made, no indication of the basis on which the [agency] exercised its expert discretion. We are not prepared to and the Administrative Procedure Act will not permit us to accept such . . . practice . . . . Expert discretion is the lifeblood of the administrative process, but 'unless we make the requirements for administrative action strict and demanding, *expertise*, the strength of modern government, can become a monster which rules with no practical limits on its discretion.' "

We have frequently reiterated that an agency must cogently explain why it has exercised its discretion in a given manner, and we reaffirm this principle again today.

The automobile industry has opted for the passive belt over the airbag, but surely it is not enough that the regulated industry has eschewed a given safety device. For nearly a decade, the automobile industry waged the regulatory equivalent of war against the airbag and lost — the inflatable restraint was proved sufficiently effective. Now the automobile industry has decided to employ a seatbelt system which will not meet the safety objectives of Standard 208. This hardly constitutes cause to revoke the Standard itself. Indeed, the Motor Vehicle Safety Act was necessary because the industry was not sufficiently responsive to safety concerns. The Act intended that safety standards not depend on current technology and could be "technology-forcing" in the sense of inducing the development of superior safety design. If, under the statute, the agency should not defer to the industry's failure to develop safer cars, which it surely should not do, *a fortiori* it may not revoke a safety standard which can be satisfied by current technology simply because the industry has opted for an ineffective seatbelt design. * * *

[In Part VB, Justice White ruled that NHTSA was "too quick to dismiss the safety benefits of automatic seatbelts." Although an agency may decline to issue and may revoke a safety standard "on the basis of serious uncertainties about its efficacy, those uncertainties must be supported in the administrative record and reasonably explained. In this case, there was no direct evidence in the record supporting NHTSA's finding that detachable automatic belts cannot be predicted to yield a substantial increase in usage. Evidence in the record revealed more than a doubling of seat belt use under those circumstances. For one example, Volkswagen between 1975 and 1980 sold 350,000 Rabbits equipped with passive seatbelts guarded by an ignition interlock. NHTSA found that seatbelt use in Rabbits averaged 34% where the cars had regular manual belts, and 84% for the detachable passive belts. Although Justice White maintained that the agency had discretion to refuse to generalize from studies of Rabbit drivers to the general population of drivers, the agency was required to consider a fact that it neglected but that critically distinguishes detachable automatic belts and ordinary manual ones: A detachable passive belt requires an affirmative act to detach it, while a manual belt can be safely ignored. "Thus, inertia — a factor which the agency's own studies have found significant in explaining the current low usage rates for seatbelts — works in *favor* of, not *against*, use of the protective device." This would suggest that seatbelt use by occasional users would be substantially increased by detachable passive belts. "Whether this is in fact the case is a matter for the agency to decide, but it must bring its expertise to bear on the question."]

The agency is correct to look at the costs as well as the benefits of Standard 208. The agency's conclusion that the incremental costs of the requirements were no longer reasonable was predicated on its prediction that the safety benefits of the regulation might be minimal. Specifically, the agency's fears that the public may resent paying more for the automatic belt systems is expressly dependent on the assumption that detachable automatic belts will not produce more than "negligible safety benefits." 46 Fed.Reg., at 53,424. When the agency reexamines its findings as to the likely increase in seatbelt usage, it must also reconsider its judgment of the reasonableness of the monetary and other costs associated with the Standard. In reaching its judgment, NHTSA should bear in mind that Congress intended safety to be the preeminent factor under the Motor Vehicle Safety Act. [Quoting committee reports for the Safety Act.] * * *

JUSTICE REHNQUIST, with whom THE CHIEF JUSTICE [BURGER], JUSTICE POWELL, and JUSTICE O'CONNOR join, concurring in part and dissenting in part.

I join Parts I, II, III, IV, and V-A of the Court's opinion. In particular, I agree that, since the airbag and continuous spool automatic seatbelt were explicitly approved in the standard the agency was rescinding, the agency should explain why it declined to leave those requirements intact. In this case, the agency gave no explanation at all. Of course, if the agency can provide a rational explanation, it may adhere to its decision to rescind the entire standard.

I do not believe, however, that NHTSA's view of detachable automatic seatbelts was arbitrary and capricious. The agency adequately explained its decision to rescind the standard insofar as it was satisfied by detachable belts.

The statute that requires the Secretary of Transportation to issue motor vehicle safety standards also requires that "[e]ach such . . . standard shall be practicable [and] shall meet the need for motor vehicle safety." 15 U.S.C. § 1392(a). The Court rejects the agency's explanation for its conclusion that there is substantial uncertainty whether requiring installation of detachable automatic belts would substantially increase seatbelt usage. The agency chose not to rely on a study showing a substantial increase in seatbelt usage in cars equipped with automatic seatbelts and an ignition interlock to prevent the car from being operated when the belts were not in place *and* which were voluntarily purchased with this equipment by consumers. It is reasonable for the agency to decide that this study does not support any conclusion concerning the effect of automatic seatbelts that are installed in all cars whether the consumer wants them or not and are not linked to an ignition interlock system.

The Court rejects this explanation because "there would seem to be grounds to believe that seatbelt use by occasional users will be substantially increased by the detachable passive belts," and the agency did not adequately explain its rejection of these grounds. It seems to me that the agency's explanation, while by no means a model, is adequate. The agency acknowledged that there would probably be some increase in belt usage, but concluded that the increase would be small and not worth the cost of mandatory detachable automatic belts. 46 F.R. 53421–54323 (1981). The agency's obligation is to articulate a " 'rational connection between the facts found and the choice made.' " I believe it has met this standard. * * *

The agency's changed view of the standard seems to be related to the election of a new President of a different political party. It is readily apparent that the responsible members of one administration may consider public resistance and uncertainties to be more important than do their counterparts in a previous administration. A change in administration brought about by the people casting their votes is a perfectly reasonable basis for an executive agency's reappraisal of the costs and benefits of its programs and regulations. As long as the agency remains within the bounds established by Congress, it is entitled to assess administrative records and evaluate priorities in light of the philosophy of the administration.

NOTES ON *STATE FARM*

1. *Right or Wrong?* Did the Court do the right thing in this case — either from the Court's point of view, or the nation's? Write down your answer in the margin, and read on.

2. *The Proper Role of the Judiciary in the Implementation of Public Policy?* In light of your experience with the implementation of the Safety Act, what do you think the role of the Court should be: (1) Agent of Congress? If so, which Congress — the enacting one, the amending one, or the current one? (2) Independent principal, imposing the Court's own values, thwarting agencies implementing bad policies, and rewarding agencies that protect the Court's conception of the public interest? (3) Independent principal, imposing rule of law values? If so, what does the rule of law require in *State Farm*?

Chapter 11 of Mashaw and Harfst's book asks this question: Does the participation of the judiciary in the statutory implementation game advance the public interest? Their analysis suggests some doubt that the Court performs a useful role. The judiciary is the forum of choice whenever the government tries to upset traditional ways of doing things (ways easily translated into "rights"). Thus, the courts were a forum for the auto industry to harass the agency and delay implementation of its rules. The proceduralization of the rulemaking process rendered it less decisive and more vulnerable to shifts in public opinion and presidential leadership. Recall the wild shifts in Standard 208 from the Johnson Administration to the Nixon-Ford Administration to the Carter Administration to the Reagan Administration.

Adverse judicial decisions in the 1970s (the hard look decade) directly contributed to the interlock debacle and contributed less directly to an increasingly cautious attitude toward regulation. For example, *Chrysler* required "objective" testing standards that the agency's "dummy" regulations did not meet. This requirement discouraged the agency from imposing rules before it had "objective" scientific evidence well in hand, and thereby prevented the sort of experimentation and technology-forcing rules that the early experts thought were necessary to make genuine advances to reduce auto injuries and fatalities. More generally, the adverse judicial decisions discouraged NHTSA from proceeding by rulemaking, which had been the agency's original mandate and was probably its only hope for regulatory success. Favorable judicial decisions in response to NHTSA's recall campaigns, on the other hand, encouraged the agency to rely more and more heavily on that less effective regulatory mechanism. Like a pavlovian dog, NHTSA was trained by the judiciary to quail at the thought of rules and salivate at the prospect of recalls.

Mashaw and Harfst are pessimistic about the role of the "legal culture" and of multiple principals in our administrative state of separated powers. "[T]he combination of congressional oversight and appropriations, Executive Office intervention and monitoring, and judicial review, has sharply limited the degree to which NHTSA could translate [its regulatory] aspirations into concrete technological requirements." (Mashaw & Harfst 228.) Do you find this level of pessimism persuasive? Jot down your initial thoughts in the margin, and then read the next note.

3. *The Aftermath of* State Farm. Transportation Secretary Elizabeth Dole initiated rulemaking to answer the Court's inquiries, and 7,800 comments were filed. On July 17, 1984, Dole issued the final rule, which (1) dropped mandatory airbags like a lead balloon and (2) required phasing in "automatic occupant restraints" (including airbags as a option for the manufacturer) between 1986 and 1989, unless (3) before April 1, 1989, two-thirds of the U.S. population are covered by state mandatory seat belt use laws meeting NHTSA's conditions. 49 Fed. Reg. 28,962–63 (1984).

By endorsing state mandatory seat belt laws as the preferred form of regulation, the agency seemed to revert to the old command-and-control regime that had been ineffective and to retreat from the proven-to-be-effective mandatory-redesign regime. State Farm challenged this rule, but the D.C. Circuit held the lawsuit premature. *State Farm Mutual Automobile Ins. Co. v. Dole*, 802 F.2d 474 (D.C. Cir. 1986).

With the support of the auto industry as well as new groups such as Mothers Against Drunk Driving (MADD), almost all the states adopted mandatory seatbelt laws — but most were careful *not* to satisfy the requirements of the Dole rule. "As a consequence, the American public got both airbags and mandatory use laws." Mashaw, *Law, Science, and Politics*, 385. Most surprisingly, *both* kinds of regulations captured the imagination of Americans. We the People started buckling up in record numbers *and* demanded more airbags from manufacturers than the law required. Although Professor Mashaw reports these results with no dimming of his customary pessimism, do they suggest that the judiciary might play a productive role in the evolution of statutory policy?

Contrast McDonald's more recent account. Looking back on more than a generation of expensive federal regulation of auto safety, he argues that the NHTSA's focus on passive standards has reduced occupant fatality risk by only 15-20%, not an impressive amount given the tens of billions of dollars in cost and the much greater traffic safety achieved in Canada, Europe, and Australia, which focus on seat belts and driver error. McDonald, *Shifting Out of Park*, 18–19; Leonard Evans, *Traffic Safety* 117 (2004). Indeed, in the United States, reducing the speed limit has had greater safety effects than all the design changes posed by the NHTSA. McDonald, 42 n.65.

SECTION 3. JUDICIAL DEFERENCE TO AGENCY INTERPRETATIONS

Return to basic issues of statutory interpretation covered in Chapter 8. The assumption of that chapter was the rules and guidelines followed by courts, especially the U.S. Supreme Court. Jerry Mashaw, *Agency Statutory Interpretation*, Issues in Legal Scholarship, Issue 3: Dynamic Statutory Interpretation (2002): Article 9, available at www.bepress.com/ils/iss3/art9, argues that agencies and courts will and *ought to* follow different approaches to statutory interpretation, because of their different institutional competences and responsibilities. The table below is reproduced from his article and encapsulates his normative suggestions.

Mashaw Table of Canons for Institutionally Responsible Statutory Interpretation

Canon for Statutory Interpretation	Appropriate for Agencies?	Appropriate for Courts?
1. *Follow presidential directives unless clearly outside your authority*	Yes	No
2. *Interpret to avoid raising constitutional questions*	No	Yes
3. *Use legislative history as a primary interpretive guide*	Yes	No

4. *Interpret to give energy and breadth to all legislative programs within your jurisdiction*	Yes	No
5. *Engage in activist lawmaking*	Yes	No
6. *Respect all judicial precedent*	No	Yes
7. *Interpret to lend coherence to the overall legal order*	No	Yes
8. *Pay particular to the strategic parameters of interpretive efficiency*	Yes	No
9. *Interpret to secure hierarchical control over subordinates*	Yes	No
10. *Pay constant attention to your contemporary political milieu*	Yes	No

Source: Mashaw, *Agency Statutory Interpretation*

Many items in Mashaw's table might be questioned. For example, item 5 strikes us as meaningless without a careful definition of "activist" (which for most lawyers = any interpretation they strongly disagree with). And Trevor Morrison, *Constitutional Avoidance in the Executive Branch,* 106 Colum. L. Rev. 1189 (2006), vigorously argues, contra Mashaw, that agencies should consider the avoidance canon when they interpret statutes. Consider a dramatic example of statutory interpretation "outside the courts," in the following Problem.

Problem on Executive Interpretation

Problem 9–5. In the wake of the al Qaeda-organized attacks on the World Trade Center and the Pentagon on 9/11/01, President Bush authorized the National Security Agency (NSA) to intercept international communications into and out of the United States of persons linked to al Qaeda or related terrorist organizations. The President subsequently explained that his purpose was to "establish an early warning system to detect and prevent another catastrophic terrorist attack on the United States." Presidential Press Conference, December 19, 2005. "[A] two-minute phone conversation between somebody linked to al Qaeda here and an operative overseas could lead directly to the loss of thousands of lives." Id. (Since 9/11, al Qaeda leaders have repeatedly promised to deliver another attack on American soil. The group has done so successfully in Spain, Indonesia, and England since 9/11.)

Because terrorists pose such a huge threat and move quickly from place to place, the President maintains that protocols Congress set in place (1978) for long-term electronic communications monitoring are no longer appropriate and must be supplemented with emergency shorter-term measures. NSA activities are "carefully reviewed every 45 days to ensure that [they are] being used properly." Id. The Attorney General monitors for legality, and NSA officials themselves monitor to assure protection of civil liberties.

Civil libertarians assailed the NSA wiretapping program, and Members of Congress expressed concern. You are the General Counsel to the Senate Judiciary Committee, chaired in 2006 by Senator Arlen Specter (R–Pa.). Senator Specter wonders whether the NSA program is legal. It might violate the Fourth Amendment, which the Supreme Court has construed to require warrants and probable cause for wiretaps, e.g., *Katz v. United States*, 389 U.S. 347 (1967), but the Court has never definitively ruled on the Fourth Amendment validity of surveillance to investigate foreign-sponsored terrorist activities. See *United States v. United States District Court*, 407 U.S. 297 (1972) (reserving this issue).

Set the Fourth Amendment questions aside. Instead, Senator Specter asks you to tell him whether the NSA program is a legitimate exercise of the President's authority, especially in light of prior legislation. The following materials will help you frame an answer to Senator Specter.[a]

January 9, 2006 Letter from Scholars and Former Government Officials [Curtis A. Bradley et al.] to Congressional Leadership in Response to Justice Department Letter of December 22, 2005.[b] In 1978, Congress enacted the Foreign Intelligence Surveillance Act (FISA). "With minor exceptions, FISA authorizes electronic surveillance only upon certain specified showings, and only if approved by a court. The statute specifically allows for warrantless *wartime* domestic electronic surveillance — but only for the first fifteen days of a war. 50 USC § 1811. It makes criminal any electronic surveillance not authorized by statute, id. § 1809; and it expressly establishes FISA and specified provisions of the federal criminal code (which govern wiretaps for criminal investigation) as the "*exclusive* means by which electronic surveillance . . . may be conducted." 18 USC § 2511(2)(f) (emphasis added)."

The Department of Justice conceded that FISA did not authorize the NSA program, but argued that the AUMF [Authorization for the Use of Military Force] did. Signed on September 18, 2001, the AUMF empowers the President to use "all necessary and appropriate force against" al Qaeda. According to the DOJ, collecting "signals intelligence" on the enemy, including U.S. phone tapping, is a "fundamental incident of war" authorized by the AUMF.

The scholars advanced several reasons they thought the President was wrong about that: (1) The statute specifically addressing the matter of wiretaps (FISA) governs the more generally phrased law (AUMF), under accepted principles of statutory interpretation. Also, (2) repeals by implication, the

---

a. These materials are taken from the appendices to David Cole & Martin Lederman, *The National Security Agency's Domestic Spying Program: Framing the Debate,* 81 Ind. L.J. 1363-1424 (May 2006).

b. This Letter, 81 Ind. L.J. at 1364–72, was a response to the December 22, 2005 Letter from Department of Justice to the Leadership of the Senate Select Committee on Intelligence and House Permanent Select Committee on Intelligence," id. at 1359–62.

effect of the DOJ's broad AUMF interpretation, are disfavored in the law. Finally, (3) Members of Congress advised the Attorney General that legislation amending the FISA to allow this program would not be feasible. "It is one thing, however, to say that foreign battlefield capture of enemy combatants is an incident of waging war that Congress intended to authorize. It is another matter entirely to treat unchecked warrantless *domestic* spying as included in that authorization, especially where an existing statute specifies that other laws are the 'exclusive means' by which electronic surveillance may be conducted and provides that even a declaration of war authorizes such spying only for a fifteen-day emergency period.

"* * * [T]he [old] federal law involving wiretapping specifically provided that '[n]othing contained in this chapter or in section 605 of the Communications Act of 1934 shall limit the constitutional power of the President . . . to obtain foreign intelligence information deemed essential to the security of the United States.' 18 USC § 2511(3) (1976).

"But FISA specifically repealed that provision, FISA § 201(c), 92 Stat. 1797, and replaced it with language dictating that FISA and the criminal code are the 'exclusive means' of conducting electronic surveillance. In doing so, Congress did not deny that the President has constitutional power to conduct electronic surveillance for national security purposes; rather, Congress properly concluded that 'even if the President has the inherent authority in the absence of legislation to authorize warrantless electronic surveillance for foreign intelligence purposes, Congress has the power to regulate the conduct of such surveillance by legislating a reasonable procedure, which then becomes the exclusive means by which such surveillance can be conducted.' HR Rep. No. 95–1282 (1978). * * *

"Congress plainly has authority to regulate domestic wiretapping by federal agencies under its Article I powers, and the DOJ does not suggest otherwise. Indeed, when FISA was enacted, the Justice Department agreed that Congress had power to regulate such conduct, and could require judicial approval of foreign intelligence surveillance. [S. Rep. No. 95–604, pt. 1, at 16 (1977), et al.] * * *"

U.S. Department of Justice, "Legal Authorities Supporting the Activities of the National Security Agency Described by the President," January 19, 2006.[c] "As Congress expressly recognized in the AUMF, 'the President has authority under the Constitution to take action to deter and prevent acts of international terrorism against the United States,' AUMF pmbl., especially in the context of the current conflict. Article II of the Constitution vests in the President all executive powers of the United States, including the power to act as Commander in Chief of the Armed Forces, *see* U.S. Const. Art. II, § 2, and authority over the conduct of the Nation's foreign affairs. As the Supreme Court has explained, '[t]he President is the sole organ of the nation in its external relations, and its sole representative with foreign nations.'

---

c. This Letter, 81 Ind. L.J. at 1373–1413, was a response to the Scholars' Letter of January 9 and a detailed elaboration of arguments suggested in the Department's Letter of December 22.

United States v. Curtiss-Wright Export Corp., 299 U.S. 304 (1936). In this way, the Constitution gives the President inherent power to protect the Nation from foreign attack, *see, e.g., The Prize Cases,* 67 U.S. 635, 668 (1863), and to protect national security information, *see, e.g., Department of the Navy v. Egan,* 484 U.S. 518, 527 (1988).

"To carry out these responsibilities, the President must have authority to gather information necessary for the execution of his office. The Founders, after all, intended the federal Government to be clothed with all authority necessary to protect the Nation. *See, e.g., The Federalist* * * * No. 41 (James Madison) ('Security against foreign danger is one of the primitive objects of civil society . . .. The powers requisite for attaining it must be effectually confided to the federal councils.'). Because of the structural advantages of the Executive Branch, the Founders also intended that the President would have the primary responsibility and necessary authority as Commander in Chief and Chief Executive to protect the Nation and to conduct the Nation's foreign affairs. See, e.g., *The Federalist* No.70, at 471–72 (Hamilton); *see also Johnson v. Eisentrager,* 339 U.S. 763, 788 (1950) ('this [constitutional] grant of war power includes all that is necessary and proper for carrying these powers into execution'). Thus, it has long been recognized that the President has the authority to use secretive means to collect intelligence necessary for the conduct of foreign affairs and military campaigns. [*Curtiss-Wright* et al.]

"In reliance on these principles, a consistent understanding has developed that the President has inherent constitutional authority to conduct warrantless searches and surveillance within the United States for foreign intelligence purposes. Wiretaps for such purposes thus have been authorized by Presidents at least since the administration of Franklin Roosevelt in 1940. *See, e.g., United States v. United States District Court,* 444 F.2d 651, 669–71 (6th Cir. 1971) (reproducing as an appendix memoranda from Presidents Roosevelt, Truman, and Johnson). In a Memorandum to Attorney General Jackson, President Roosevelt wrote on May 21, 1940:

> You are, therefore, authorized and directed in such cases as you may approve, after investigation of the need in each case, to authorize the necessary investigation agents that they are at liberty to secure information by listening devices directed to the conversation or other communications of persons suspected of subversive activities against the Government of the United States, including suspected spies. You are requested furthermore to limit these investigations so conducted to a minimum and limit them insofar as possible to aliens. *Id.* at 670 (appendix A).

President Truman approved a memorandum drafted by Attorney General Tom Clark in which the Attorney General advised that 'it is as necessary as it was in 1940 to take the investigative measures' authorized by President Roosevelt to conduct electronic surveillance 'in cases vitally affecting the domestic security.' *Id.* Indeed, while the FISA was being debated during the Carter Administration, Attorney General Griffin Bell testified that 'the current bill recognizes no inherent power of the President to conduct electronic surveillance, and I want to interpolate here to say that *this does not take away the power [of] the President under the Constitution.*' Foreign Intelligence

Electronic Surveillance Act of 1978: Hearings on H.R. 5764 [et al.] Before the Subcomm. on Legislation of the House Comm. on Intelligence, 95th Cong., 2d Sess. 15 (1978) (emphasis added) * * *.

"On September 14, 2001, in its first legislative response to the attacks of September 11th, Congress gave its express approval to the President's military campaign against al Qaeda and, in the process, confirmed the well-accepted understanding of the President's Article II powers. *See* AUMF § 2(a). In the preamble to the AUMF, Congress stated that 'the President has authority under the Constitution to take action to deter and prevent acts of international terrorism against the United States,' AUMF pmbl., and thereby acknowledged the President's inherent constitutional authority to defend the United States. This clause 'constitutes an extraordinarily sweeping recognition of independent presidential *constitutional* power to employ the war power to combat terrorism.' Michael Stokes Paulsen, Youngstown *Goes to War*, 19 Const. Comment. 215, 252 (2002). This striking recognition of presidential authority cannot be discounted as the product of excitement in the immediate aftermath of September 11th, for the same terms were repeated by Congress more than a year later in the Authorization for the Use of Military Force Against Iraq Resolution of 2002. Pub. L. No. 107–243, pmbl., 116 Stat. 1498, 1500 (Oct. 16, 2002) ('The President has authority under the Constitution to take action in order to deter and prevent acts of international terrorism against the United States . . . .'). In the context of the conflict with al Qaeda and related terrorist organizations, therefore, Congress has acknowledged a broad executive authority to 'deter and prevent' further attacks against the United States.

"The AUMF passed by Congress on September 14, 2001, does not lend itself to a narrow reading. Its expansive language authorizes the President 'to use all *necessary and appropriate force* against those nations, organizations, or persons *he determines* planned, authorized, committed, or aided the terrorist attacks that occurred on September 11, 2001.' AUMF § 2(a) (emphasis added). In the field of foreign affairs, and particularly that of war powers and national security, congressional enactments are to be broadly construed where they indicate support for authority long asserted and exercised by the Executive Branch. * * * This authorization transforms the struggle against al Qaeda and related terrorist organizations from what Justice Jackson called 'a zone of twilight,' in which the President and Congress may have concurrent powers whose 'distribution is uncertain,' *Youngstown* (Jackson, J., concurring), into a situation in which the President's authority it at its maximum because 'it includes all that he possesses in his own right plus all that Congress can delegate,' *id.* With regard to these fundamental tools of warfare — and, as demonstrated below, warrantless electronic surveillance against the declared enemy is one such tool — the AUMF places the President's authority at its zenith under *Youngstown.* * * *

"The Supreme Court's interpretation of the scope of the AUMF in *Hamdi v. Rumsfeld*, 542 U.S. 507 (2004), strongly supports this reading of the AUMF. In *Hamdi*, five members of the Court [the O'Connor plurality plus the Thomas dissent] found that the AUMF authorized the detention of an American within the United States, notwithstanding a statute that prevents the detention of U.S.

citizens 'except pursuant to an Act of Congress.' 18 USC § 4001(a). Drawing on historical materials and 'longstanding law-of-war principles,' a plurality of the Court concluded that detention of combatants who fought against the United States as part of an organization 'known to have supported' al Qaeda 'is so fundamental and accepted an incident to war as to be an exercise of the "necessary and appropriate force" Congress has authorized the President to use.' *Id.* at 518; *see also id.* at 587 (Thomas, J., dissenting) 9agreeing with the plurality that the joint resolution authorized the President to 'detain those arrayed against our troops'); *accord, Quirin*, 317 U.S. at 26–29, 38 (recognizing the President's authority to capture and try agents of the enemy in the United States even if they had never 'entered the theatre or zone of active military operations'). Thus, even though the AUMF does not say anything expressly about detention, the Court nevertheless found that it satisfied section 4001(a)'s requirement that detention be congressionally authorized. * * *

"The history of warfare — including the consistent practice of Presidents since the earliest days of the Republic — demonstrates that warrantless intelligence surveillance against the enemy is a fundamental incident of the use of military force, and this history confirms the statutory authority provided by the AUMF. Electronic surveillance is a fundamental tool of war that must be included in any natural reading of the AUMF's authorization to use 'all necessary and appropriate force.' "

The Department argued that, from General Washington onward, American leaders have "intercepted communications for wartime intelligence purposes and, if necessary, has done so within its own borders." This practice continued during World War II and, according to one historian, "helped shorten the war by perhaps two years."

"* * * [S]ection 109 of FISA prohibits any person from intentionally 'engag[ing] . . . in electronic surveillance under color of law *except as authorized by statute.*' 50 USC § 1809(a)(1) (emphasis added). * * *

"The AUMF qualifies as a 'statute' authorizing electronic surveillance within the meaning of section 109 of FISA. * * * As explained above, it is not necessary to demarcate the outer limits of the AUMF to conclude that it encompasses electronic surveillance targeted at the enemy. Just as a majority of the Court concluded in *Hamdi* that the AUMF authorizes detention of U.S. citizens who are enemy combatants without expressly mentioning the President's long-recognized power to detain, so too does it authorize the use of electronic surveillance without specifically mentioning the President's equally long-recognized power to engage in communications intelligence targeted at the enemy. And just as the AUMF satisfies the requirement in 18 USC § 4001(a) that no U.S. citizen be detained 'except pursuant to an Act of Congress,' so too does it satisfy section 109's requirement for statutory authorization of electronic surveillance. * * *"

Section 111 of FISA, 50 USC § 1811, which capped presidential surveillance even in time of war without court authorization at fifteen days, "cannot reasonably be read as Congress's final word on electronic surveillance during wartime. * * * Rather, section 111 represents Congress's recognition that it would likely have to return to the subject and provide additional authorization to conduct warrantless electronic surveillance outside FISA during time of war. * * *

"Nothing in the terms of section 111 disables Congress from authorizing such electronic surveillance as a traditional incident of war through a broad, conflict-specific authorization for the use of military force, such as the AUMF. * * *

"* * * Nevertheless, some might argue that sections 109 and 111 of the FISA, along with section 2511(2)(f)'s 'exclusivity' provision and section 2511(2)(e)'s liability exception for officers engaged in FISA-authorized surveillance, are best read to suggest that FISA requires that subsequent authorizing legislation specifically amend FISA in order to free the Executive from FISA's enumerated procedures. As detailed above, this is not the better reading of FISA. But even if these provisions were ambiguous, any doubt as to whether the AUMF and FISA should be understood to allow the President to make tactical military decisions to authorize surveillance outside the parameters of FISA must be resolved to avoid the serious constitutional questions that a contrary interpretation would raise.

"It is well established that the first task of any interpreter faced with a statute that may present an unconstitutional infringement on the powers of the President is to determine whether the statute may be construed to avoid the constitutional difficulty. '[I]f an otherwise acceptable construction of a statute would raise serious constitutional problems, and where an alternative interpretation of the statute is "fairly possible," then we are obligated to construe the statute to avoid such problems.' *INS v. St. Cyr*, 533 U.S. 289, 299–300 (2001); *Ashwander v. TVA*, 297 U.S. 288, 345–48 (1936) (Brandeis, J., concurring). Moreover, the canon of constitutional avoidance has particular importance in the realm of national security, where the President's constitutional authority is at its highest. See *Department of the Navy v. Egan*, 484 U.S. 518, 530 (1988); William N. Eskridge, Jr., *Dynamic Statutory Interpretation* 325 (1994) (describing '[s]uper-strong rule against congressional interference with the President's authority over foreign affairs and national security')." The AUMF should be interpreted broadly, and FISA narrowly, to avoid constructions where FISA would unconstitutionally obstruct the President's Commander-in-Chief powers.

The concluding portion of the Letter argued that the NSA program did not violate the Fourth Amendment.

February 2, 2006 Letter from Scholars and Former Government Officials to Congressional Leadership in Response to Justice Department Whitepaper of January 19, 2006. The Scholars found no authorization for illegal wiretapping in the AUMF, especially in light of section 111. "An amendment to FISA of the sort that would presumably be required to authorize the NSA program here would be a momentous statutory development, undoubtedly subject to serious legislative debate. It is decidedly *not* the sort of thing that Congress would enact *inadvertently*. As the Supreme Court recently noted, "'Congress does not alter the fundamental details of a regulatory scheme in vague terms or ancillary provisions — it does not, one might say, hide elephants in mouseholes.'" *Gonzales v. Oregon*, 126 S.Ct. 904, 921 (2006) (quoting *Whitman v. American Trucking Ass'ns*, 531 U.S. 457, 468 (2001))."

Section 111 also distinguishes this situation from that in *Hamdi*. The detention statute in *Hamdi* did not mention detention of citizens in wartime. "Had there been a statute on the books providing that when Congress declares war, the President may detain Americans as 'enemy combatants' *only* for the first fifteen days of the conflict, the Court could not reasonably have read the AUMF to authorize silently what Congress had specifically sought to limit. Yet that is what the DOJ's argument would require here. [See also 18 USC § 2511(2)(f), which specifies that FISA and the criminal code are the 'exclusive means' by which electronic surveillance can be conducted. DOJ concedes that its interpretation requires an implicit repeal of § 2511, which is strongly disfavored in the law.]

"The argument that conduct undertaken by the Commander in Chief that has some relevance to 'engaging the enemy' is immune from congressional regulation finds no support in, and is directly contradicted by, both case law and historical precedent. *Every* time the Supreme Court has confronted a statute limiting the Commander-in-Chief's authority, it has upheld the statute. No precedent holds that the President, when acting as Commander in Chief, is free to disregard an Act of Congress, much less a *criminal statute* enacted by Congress, that was designed specifically to restrain the President as such. [See, e.g., *Little v. Barreme*, 6 U.S. 170 (1804), holding unlawful a presidential seizure of a ship coming *from* France during the Quasi-War with France, when Congress authorized seizure only of ships going *to* France.]

"In fact, as cases such as *Hamdi* and *Rasul* demonstrate, Congress has routinely enacted statutes regulating the Commander-in-Chief's 'means and methods of engaging the enemy.' It has subjected the Armed Forces ti the Uniform Code of Military Justice, which expressly restricts the means they use in 'engaging the enemy.' It has enacted statutes setting forth the rules for governing occupied territory. And, most recently, it has enacted statutes prohibiting torture under all circumstances, 18 USC §§ 2340–2340A, and prohibiting the use of cruel, inhuman, and degrading treatment. Pub. L. No. 109–148, Div. A, tit X, § 1003, 119 Stat. 2739–40 (2005). These limitations make ample sense in light of the overall constitutional structure. Congress has the explicit power 'To make Rules for the Government and Regulation of the land and naval Forces.' US Const., art. I, § 8, cl. 14. The President has the explicit constitutional obligation to 'take Care that the Laws be faithfully executed,' U.S. Const., art. II, § 3 — including FISA. And Congress has the explicit power to 'make all Laws which shall be necessary and proper for carrying into Execution . . . all . . . Powers vested by this Constitution in the Government of the United States, or in any Department or Officer thereof.' US Const., art. I, [§ 8, cl. 18].

"If the DOJ were correct that Congress cannot interfere with the Commander in Chief's discretion in 'engaging the enemy,' all of these statutes would be unconstitutional. Yet the President recently conceded that Congress may constitutionally bar him from engaging in torture. Torturing a suspect, no less than wiretapping an American, might provide information about the enemy that could conceivably help prevent a terrorist attack, yet the President has now conceded that Congress can prohibit that conduct. * * *"

The Letter also argued that FISA does not unduly interfere with the President's ability to gather intel. FISA only applies if the target is a US person in the US, or where the surveillance "acquisition" occurs in the US. 50 USC § 1801(f)(1)-(2). FISA does not prohibit wiretapping; it only requires approval, including after-the-fact approval so long as the petition is filed within 72 hours. 50 USC § 1805(f). "As such, the statute cannot reasonably be said to intrude impermissibly upon the President's ability to 'engage the enemy,' and certainly does not come anywhere close to 'prohibit[ing] the President from undertaking actions necessary to fulfill his constitutional obligation to protect the Nation from foreign attack.' DOJ Memo."

Queries: This exchange illustrates most of Mashaw's *proposed* canons for agencies and the executive to interpret statutes. Is this a model that seems attractive to you? If not, can you come up with one that would work better? Relevant to the Mashaw-Morrison debate, do you think the executive branch handled the constitutional arguments productively?

Final question: Assume that one of the Americans subject to the President's wiretapping brought a justiciable claim in federal court, challenging the President's authority under FISA. How would the Supreme Court handle this case? More to the point: How much, if at all, would the Court "defer" to the executive interpretation of FISA and AUMF? How much deference *should* the Court give? What considerations should influence the deference equation?

A. THE BASIC FRAMEWORK: *SKIDMORE* and *CHEVRON*

The New Deal approach to deference was founded on the comparative expertise of courts and agencies: the former should defer to the experts who worked with the statute day-in and day-out and developed wisdom about what worked and what did not. The leading case was *Skidmore v. Swift & Co.*, 323 U.S. 134 (1944). Employees sued their employer to recover overtime pay unlawfully withheld under the Fair Labor Standards Act. The employer argued that the "extra" time they alleged was inactive time and not "hours worked" for purposes of the Act.

The Administrator (the Department of Labor official charged with implementing the Act) filed an *amicus* brief with the Supreme Court which described the flexible approach he had taken to the "inactive duty" issue. In his view, the on-call duty time spent sleeping and eating should not be included in "hours worked," but the remainder of the on-call time should be.

Justice Jackson's opinion for the *Skidmore* Court observed that the Administrator's practices and his recommendation in this case did not constitute a "binding" interpretation of the statute, but they were entitled to "respect," because they "constituted a body of experience and informed judgment" regarding workplace practices. "The weight of such a judgment in a particular case will depend upon the thoroughness evident in its consideration, the validity of its reasoning, its consistency with earlier and later pronouncements, and all those factors which give it power to persuade, if lacking power to control." The Court followed the Administrator's judgment and reversed the court below upon this point of law.

Soon after the APA's adoption, in 1946, Louis Jaffe explained how the modern administrative state fit into the traditional statutory interpretation framework, while at the same time altering it subtly. Jaffe, *Judicial Review: Question of Law*, 69 Harv. L. Rev. 239 (1955). Consistent with *Marbury* and APA § 706, the Supreme Court remained the expositor of what the law is, but when interpreting vague or ambiguous regulatory statutes the Court was naturally open to agency inputs. Sometimes the Court found that the statute was relatively clear, but other times statutory vagueness suggested a range of possible meanings and the Court was willing to accept the agency's interpretation if it were within that range, as in *Skidmore* and later decisions such as *Udall v. Tallman*, 380 U.S. 1, 16 (1965).

Jaffe also believed that the New Deal had regularized a different kind of agency role. In many statutes, Congress had (consistent with the APA) delegated to agencies the authority to create binding "law," usually through formal adjudications and legislative rules. Under *those* circumstances, Jaffe suggested that the role of the Court was more like deferential judicial review that the Court then applied to social and economic legislation. Likewise, when reviewing agency *lawmaking*, the Court should give the agency's rule the benefit of the doubt and overturn it only if it was *unreasonable*, in light of the statutory text and purposes. Jaffe, *Judicial Review, supra*, 243–44. This idea was the germ for what would become *Chevron*. Consider the leading cases.

GENERAL ELECTRIC CO. v. GILBERT, 429 U.S. 125 (1976). General Electric Co. provided for all of its employees a disability plan which paid weekly nonoccupational sickness and accident benefits. Excluded from the plan's coverage were disabilities arising from pregnancy. Female employees challenged this plan as sex discrimination in violation of Title VII. The Supreme Court, in an opinion by **Justice Rehnquist**, held that the exclusion of pregnancy was not sex discrimination, relying on *Geduldig v. Aiello*, 417 U.S. 484 (1974), where the Court stated that state discrimination in employee plans on the basis of pregnancy did not violate the Fourteenth Amendment. The reasoning for both decisions was that failure to provide pregnancy benefits is not "discrimination based upon gender as such." Justice Rehnquist conceded that Title VII, as interpreted by the Court, prohibited discriminatory effects as well as intended discrimination. But he concluded that query with the assertion that there was insufficient evidence that the plan in question selected risks that had discriminatory effects. "As there is no proof that the package is in fact worth more to men than to women, it is impossible to find any gender-based discrimination in the scheme simply because women disabled as a result of pregnancy do not receive benefits * * *."

The employees relied on a 1972 regulation issued by the EEOC and urged the Court to defer to it. The Court ruled that the EEOC regulation was not entitled to deference. To begin with, Title VII did not confer upon the EEOC authority to promulgate substantive rules. The proper level of deference for such informal agency views was set forth in *Skidmore v. Swift & Co.*, 323 U.S. 134, 140 (1944). [The Court quoted the language from the beginning of this part.]

The 1972 guideline fared badly under this standard, first, because it was not a "contemporaneous interpretation of Title VII, since it was first promulgated eight years after the enactment of that Title. More important, the 1972 guideline flatly contradicted the position which the agency had enunciated at an earlier date, closer to the enactment of the governing statute," specifically, an opinion letter by the General Counsel of the EEOC, dated October 17, 1966, which opined that an employer policy excluding pregnancy from its disability policy did not violate Title VII. Most important, the EEOC interpretation was inconsistent with the interpretation of the Wage and Hour Administrator of § 6(d) of the Equal Pay Act to permit employers to offer different levels of disability benefits to male and female employees. Section 703(h) of Title VII explicitly permits practices allowed under § 6 of the Equal Pay Act.

Justice Brennan (joined by **Justice Marshall**) dissented, disputing the majority's concept of what is "sex discrimination" and urging deference to the EEOC, as the Court did in *Albemarle Paper Co. v. Moody*, 422 U.S. 405, 431 (1975); *Griggs v. Duke Power Co.,* 401 U.S. 424, 433–34 (1971). Justice Brennan argued that the EEOC moved slowly and deliberatively toward a policy on pregnancy and maternity, because the agency needed more information and study of this difficult issue:

> Therefore, while some eight years had elapsed prior to the issuance of the 1972 guideline, and earlier opinion letters had refused to impose liability on employers during this period of deliberation, no one can or does deny that the final EEOC determination followed thorough and well-informed consideration. Indeed, realistically viewed, this extended evaluation of an admittedly complex problem and an unwillingness to impose additional, potentially premature costs on employers during the decisionmaking stages ought to be perceived as a practice to be commended. It is bitter irony that the care that preceded promulgation of the 1972 guideline is today condemned by the Court as tardy indecisiveness, its unwillingness irresponsibly to challenge employers' practices during the formative period is labeled as evidence of inconsistency, and this indecisiveness and inconsistency are bootstrapped into reasons for denying the Commission's interpretation its due deference.

Justice Brennan maintained that the 1972 EEOC rule was consistent with congressional actions also occurring in the 1970s (a series of statutes extending various employment protections to pregnant women), and with studies showing that "pregnancy exclusions built into disability programs both financially burden women workers and act to break down the continuity of the employment relationship, thereby exacerbating women's comparatively transient role in the labor force. In dictating pregnancy coverage under Title VII, the EEOC's guideline merely settled upon a solution now accepted by every other Western industrial country."

Postscript: Congress responded to *Gilbert* with the Pregnancy Discrimination Act of 1978, Pub. L. No. 95–555, 92 Stat. 2076, codified at 42 U.S.C. § 2000e(k), which establishes that "discrimination on the basis of * * * sex" in Title VII includes denial of pregnancy benefits. The Supreme Court in *Newport News Shipbuilding & Dry Dock Co. v. EEOC*, 462 U.S. 669 (1983), held that the 1978 amendment not only overruled the *Gilbert* result, but also invalidated the *Gilbert* Court's narrow approach to discrimination.

CHEVRON, U.S.A., INC. v.
NATURAL RESOURCES DEFENSE COUNCIL
Supreme Court of the United States, 1984
467 U.S. 837, 104 S.Ct. 2778, 81 L.Ed.2d 694

JUSTICE STEVENS delivered the opinion of the Court.

In the Clean Air Act Amendments of 1977, Pub. L. 95–95, 91 Stat. 685, Congress enacted certain requirements applicable to States that had not achieved the national air quality standards established by the Environmental Protection Agency (EPA) pursuant to earlier legislation. The amended Clean Air Act required these "nonattainment" States to establish a permit program regulating "new or modified major stationary sources" of air pollution. Generally, a permit may not be issued for a new or modified major stationary source unless several stringent conditions are met.[1] The EPA regulation promulgated to implement this permit requirement allows a State to adopt a plantwide definition of the term "stationary source."[2] Under this definition, an existing plant that contains several pollution-emitting devices may install or modify one piece of equipment without meeting the permit conditions if the alteration will not increase the total emissions from the plant. The question presented by these cases is whether EPA's decision to allow States to treat all of the pollution-emitting devices within the same industrial grouping as though they were encased within a single "bubble" is based on a reasonable construction of the statutory term "stationary source." * * *

[II] When a court reviews an agency's construction of the statute which it administers, it is confronted with two questions. First, always, is the question whether Congress has directly spoken to the precise question at issue. If the intent of Congress is clear, that is the end of the matter, for the court, as well as the agency, must give effect to the unambiguously expressed intent of

---

1. Section 172(b)(6), 42 U.S.C. § 7502(b)(6), provides:

"The plan provisions required by subsection (a) shall — * * *

"(6) require permits for the construction and operation of new or modified major stationary sources in accordance with section 173 (relating to permit requirements)." 91 Stat. 747.

2. "(i) 'Stationary source' means any building, structure, facility, or installation which emits or may emit any air pollutant subject to regulation under the Act.

"(ii) 'Building, structure, facility, or installation' means all of the pollutant-emitting activities which belong to the same industrial grouping, are located on one or more contiguous or adjacent properties, and are under the control of the same person (or persons under common control) except the activities of any vessel." 40 CFR §§ 51.18(j)(1)(i) and (ii) (1983).

Congress.[9] If, however, the court determines Congress has not directly addressed the precise question at issue, the court does not simply impose its own construction on the statute, as would be necessary in the absence of an administrative interpretation. Rather, if the statute is silent or ambiguous with respect to the specific issue, the question for the court is whether the agency's answer is based on a permissible construction of the statute.[11]

"The power of an administrative agency to administer a congressionally created . . . program necessarily requires the formulation of policy and the making of rules to fill any gap left, implicitly or explicitly, by Congress." If Congress has explicitly left a gap for the agency to fill, there is an express delegation of authority to the agency to elucidate a specific provision of the statute by regulation. Such legislative regulations are given controlling weight unless they are arbitrary, capricious, or manifestly contrary to the statute. Sometimes the legislative delegation to an agency on a particular question is implicit rather than explicit. In such a case, a court may not substitute its own construction of a statutory provision for a reasonable interpretation made by the administrator of an agency.

We have long recognized that considerable weight should be accorded to an executive department's construction of a statutory scheme it is entrusted to administer, and the principle of deference to administrative interpretations

> "has been consistently followed by this Court whenever decision as to the meaning or reach of a statute has involved reconciling conflicting policies, and a full understanding of the force of the statutory policy in the given situation has depended upon more than ordinary knowledge respecting the matters subjected to agency regulations.

> ". . . If this choice represents a reasonable accommodation of conflicting policies that were committed to the agency's care by the statute, we should not disturb it unless it appears from the statute or its legislative history that the accommodation is not one that Congress would have sanctioned." *United States v. Shimer*, 367 U.S. 374, 382, 383 (1961).

In light of these well-settled principles it is clear that the Court of Appeals misconceived the nature of its role in reviewing the regulations at issue. Once it determined, after its own examination of the legislation, that Congress did not actually have an intent regarding the applicability of the bubble concept to the permit program, the question before it was not whether in its view the concept is "inappropriate" in the general context of a program designed to improve air quality, but whether the Administrator's view that it is appropriate in the context of this particular program is a reasonable one. Based on the examination of the legislation and its history which follows, we agree with the

---

9. The judiciary is the final authority on issues of statutory construction and must reject administrative constructions which are contrary to clear congressional intent. If a court, employing traditional tools of statutory construction, ascertains that Congress had an intention on the precise question at issue, that intention is the law and must be given effect.

11. The court need not conclude that the agency construction was the only one it permissibly could have adopted to uphold the construction, or even the reading the court would have reached if the question initially had arisen in a judicial proceeding.

Court of Appeals that Congress did not have a specific intention on the applicability of the bubble concept in these cases, and conclude that the EPA's use of that concept here is a reasonable policy choice for the agency to make.

[The 1977 Amendments added a definition of "major stationary source," as "any stationary facility or source of air pollutants which directly emits, or has the potential to emit, one hundred tons per year or more of any air pollutant." Justice Stevens found this definition ambiguous. Examining the legislative history, he found only that Congress sought to accommodate both the "economic interest in permitting capital improvements to continue and the environmental interest in improving air quality." There was no clear evidence as to how Congress expected this balance to be carried out with regard to stationary sources.]

In these cases the Administrator's interpretation represents a reasonable accommodation of manifestly competing interests and is entitled to deference: the regulatory scheme is technical and complex, the agency considered the matter in a detailed and reasoned fashion, and the decision involves reconciling conflicting policies. Congress intended to accommodate both interests, but did not do so itself on the level of specificity presented by these cases. Perhaps that body consciously desired the Administrator to strike the balance at this level, thinking that those with great expertise and charged with responsibility for administering the provision would be in a better position to do so; perhaps it simply did not consider the question at this level; and perhaps Congress was unable to forge a coalition on either side of the question, and those on each side decided to take their chances with the scheme devised by the agency. For judicial purposes, it matters not which of these things occurred.

Judges are not experts in the field, and are not part of either political branch of the Government. Courts must, in some cases, reconcile competing political interests, but not on the basis of the judges' personal policy preferences. In contrast, an agency to which Congress has delegated policymaking responsibilities may, within the limits of that delegation, properly rely upon the incumbent administration's views of wise policy to inform its judgments. While agencies are not directly accountable to the people, the Chief Executive is, and it is entirely appropriate for this political branch of the Government to make such policy choices — resolving the competing interests which Congress itself either inadvertently did not resolve, or intentionally left to be resolved by the agency charged with the administration of the statute in light of everyday realities.

When a challenge to an agency construction of a statutory provision, fairly conceptualized, really centers on the wisdom of the agency's policy, rather than whether it is a reasonable choice within a gap left open by Congress, the challenge must fail. In such a case, federal judges — who have no constituency — have a duty to respect legitimate policy choices made by those who do. The responsibilities for assessing the wisdom of such policy choices and resolving the struggle between competing views of the public interest are not judicial ones: "Our Constitution vests such responsibilities in the political branches." *TVA v. Hill*, 437 U.S. 153, 195 (1978). * * *

The judgment of the Court of Appeals is reversed.

JUSTICE MARSHALL and JUSTICE REHNQUIST did not participate in the consideration or decision of these cases.

JUSTICE O'CONNOR did not participate in the decision of these cases.

NOTES ON *CHEVRON* AND DEFERENCE
TO ADMINISTRATIVE INTERPRETATIONS

1. *Traditional Doctrine of Deference to Agency Interpretations. Gilbert* reflects the *Skidmore* approach to deference. The Court majority saw the EEOC as an agency that could not make up its mind as to exactly how the sex discrimination bar should apply to pregnancy-based employer exclusions. One might even find some suggestion in the opinion that the Court thought the EEOC was a captive of civil rights groups.

The Court's *Skidmore* jurisprudence had become quite complicated by the time *Gilbert* was decided. Colin Diver, *Statutory Interpretation in the Administrative State,* 133 U. Pa. L. Rev. 349, 562 n.95 (1985), set forth a "partial list"(!) of circumstances which the Court had considered in deciding whether to defer to administrative interpretations:

> A partial list of the factors cited by the Court would include: (1) whether the agency construction was rendered contemporaneously with the statute's passage, *see, e.g.,* Norwegian Nitrogen Prods. Co. v. United States, 288 U.S. 294, 315 (1933); (2) whether the agency's construction is of longstanding application, *see, e.g.,* NLRB v. Bell Aerospace Co., 416 U.S. 267, 275 (1974); (3) whether the agency has maintained its position consistently (even if infrequently), *see, e.g.,* Haig v. Agee, 453 U.S. 280, 293 (1981); (4) whether the public has relied on the agency's interpretation, *see, e.g.,* Udall v. Tallman, 380 U.S. 1, 18 (1965); (5) whether the interpretation involves a matter of "public controversy," *see, e.g.,* United States v. Rutherford, 442 U.S. 544, 545 (1979); (6) whether the interpretation is based on "expertise" or involves a "technical and complex" subject, *see, e.g.,* Aluminum Co. of Am. v. Central Lincoln People's Util. Dist., [467 U.S. 380 (1984)]; (7) whether the agency has rulemaking authority, *see, e.g.,* FCC v. National Citizens Comm. for Broadcasting, 436 U.S. 75, 793 (1978); (8) whether agency action is necessary to set the statute in motion, *see, e.g.,* Ford Motor Credit Co. v. Milhollin, 444 U.S. 555, 565–66 (1980); (9) whether Congress was aware of the agency interpretation and failed to repudiate it, *see, e.g.,* Zemel v. Rusk, 381 U.S. 1, 11 (1965); and (10) whether the agency has expressly addressed the application of the statute to its proposed action, *see, e.g.,* Investment Co. Inst. v. Camp, 401 U.S. 617, 627–28 (1971).

Does Diver's list support the Court's application of *Skidmore* in *Gilbert*? How would this list apply to the issue in *Chevron*?

2. *The Accidental Birth of a New Regime.* The "bubble concept" adopted by the EPA was twice rebuffed in the D.C. Circuit, but the Reagan Administration pressed it before the Supreme Court in an effort to reduce judicial interference with its deregulatory agency initiatives. Representing the EPA, Deputy Solicitor General Paul Bator came up with a brilliant legal argument to counter the D.C. Circuit's conclusion that the bubble concept went beyond the statute. Bator argued that Congress's purpose was complex — to clean up the nation's air (the lower court's focus), but at a reasonable cost to industry (the

EPA's focus). Because the statute was fairly open-ended, the EPA had considerable discretion in setting this policy balance, and federal judges should not upset that balance unless the EPA's view was clearly contrary to the statute.[d]

Penned by the first "political" deputy within the SG's Office, Bator's brief was a roadmap for relief from excessive regulatory burdens that was a hallmark of the Reagan Administration. Liberal Justice William Brennan was suspicious of Bator's framework, but the Administration caught some lucky breaks as Justices dropped out of the case like flies in a hailstorm.[e] Their biggest break, though, was that the legality of the bubble concept was impossibly complicated for the Court. Apparently the shakiest voice in the original 4–3 conference vote to reverse the D.C. Circuit, Justice Stevens explained his tentative willingness to side with the EPA: "When I am so confused, I go with the agency." (Conference Notes by Justice Blackmun.) Encouraged by Justice White, the assigning Justice in the case, Justice Stevens not only accepted Bator's argument from complex statutory purpose, but went further to write an opinion that was analytically quite innovative.

3. *The Different Approach of* Chevron. *Chevron* seems to reflect a different analytical approach to deference issues than *Gilbert* does. To begin with, the new approach is more formal and much simplified: Step One asks whether Congress specifically addressed the interpretive question. Justice Stevens' opinion, refreshingly, says this is an issue Congress fudged. In that event, the Court moved to Step Two, which asks whether the agency's interpretation is "reasonable." If so, the Court has an obligation to defer. "Where an agency acts pursuant to delegated legislative authority, the task of interpretation is merely to define the boundaries" of what Peter Strauss calls the "zone of indeterminacy" within which Congress has authorized the agency to act.[f]

Chevron is also an important recognition of dynamic statutory interpretation in the modern administrative state, because it recognizes that first-order statutory interpretation will usually be accomplished by politically accountable — and therefore politically protean — agencies; because it further recognizes

---

d. On the Bator brief and its background, see Thomas Merrill, *The Story of* Chevron: *The Making of an Accidental Landmark*, in *Administrative Law Stories* 398, 412–14 (Peter Strauss ed., 2006).

e. Although liberal Justice Brennan voted to affirm the D.C. Circuit, his liberal colleague Thurgood Marshall was absent due to illness. After voting with Brennan to affirm, Justice O'Connor also dropped out of the case because of a potential conflict of interest after her father died. See Memorandum from O'Connor to the Conference, June 14, 1984, in the Papers of Harry A. Blackmun, Library of Congress, Madison Building, Box 397, Folder 7. Also out of the case was Justice Rehnquist, who would probably have been a voice for deference. (As O'Connor mentioned during Conference, the bubble concept was helpful to smelters and other ailing industries in Arizona, her and Rehnquist's home state. See Blackmun's Conference Notes for *Chevron*, id.)

f. Michael Herz, *Deference Running Riot: Separating Interpretation and Lawmaking Under* Chevron, 6 Admin. L.J. Am. U. 187, 199 (1992), quoting Peter Strauss, *One Hundred Fifty Cases Per Year: Some Implications of the Supreme Court's Limited Resources for Judicial Review of Agency Action*, 87 Colum. L. Rev. 1093, 1124 (1987).

that under general statutory language that does not target the interpretive issue (step one) there may be several "reasonable" agency interpretations, any of which must be upheld (step two); and because it recognizes that agency interpretations may themselves change over time. "An initial agency interpretation is not carved in stone. On the contrary, the agency, to engage in informal rulemaking, must consider varying interpretations and the wisdom of its policy on a continuing basis." 467 U.S. at 863–64.

Finally, *Chevron* rests the idea of deference on the greater democratic legitimacy that agencies enjoy over courts in making policy choices that have been left open by Congress. This is both more and less formalist than the approach followed in *Gilbert*. It is less formalist, because deference ought not depend on whether Congress has officially delegated rulemaking responsibilities to the agency, or on whether the agency's opinion was contemporaneous with the enactment of the statute. It is more formalist, because *Chevron* seems to require deference even when the agency is responding to pressure from the President to move statutory policy in ways that Congress would not have adopted. This may have been the case with *Chevron* itself. The liberal Democratic House of Representatives would probably not have favored the bubble concept, but the Reagan Administration very much did.

4. *Hostile Critical Reception. Chevron* had more than its share of critics. Then-Judge Breyer objected that a broad reading of *Chevron* is inconsistent with the judicial role articulated in both *Marbury* and in the Administrative Procedure Act (APA). Both require courts to exercise independent judgment to declare what the law of the land is. See Stephen Breyer, *Judicial Review of Questions of Law and Policy*, 38 Ad. L. Rev. 363, 370 (1986); see also Cynthia Farina, *Statutory Interpretation and the Balance of Power in the Administrative State*, 89 Colum. L. Rev. 452 (1989) (developing this objection in detail). "[T]he present law of judicial review of administrative decisionmaking, the heart of administrative law, contains an important anomaly," Breyer continued. "The law (1) requires courts to defer to agency judgments about *matters of law*, but (2) it also suggests that courts conduct independent, 'in-depth' reviews of agency judgments about *matters of policy*. [E.g., *State Farm,* Section 2F of this chapter.] Is this not the exact opposite of a rational system? Would one not expect courts to conduct a stricter review of matters of law, where courts are more expert, but more lenient review of matters of policy, where agencies are more expert?" 38 Ad. L.Rev. at 397.

John Duffy, *Administrative Common Law in Judicial Review*, 77 Tex. L. Rev. 113, 199–302 (1998), maintained that the APA and *Chevron* can be reconciled only by understanding that regulatory statutes delegate to agencies the power to interpret ambiguous statutory commands, so long as the agencies' decisions do not conflict with other provisions of law. "Thus, *Chevron* is primarily a case about delegation, not deference." *Id.* at 202. Should Duffy's argument, however, require the kind of statute-specific inquiry that Breyer suggests?

5. *Was There a* Chevron *Revolution? Preliminary Soundings.* The conventional wisdom in administrative law is, or at least until recently was, that *Chevron* was a revolutionary decision which ushered in a new period of greater

deference to agency interpretations of statutes they are charged with enforcing.[g] This might be questioned or qualified.

On the one hand, deference to agencies was a trend long preceding *Chevron*. Peter Schuck & E. Donald Elliott, *To the* Chevron *Station: An Empirical Study of Federal Administrative Law*, 1990 Duke L.J. 984, conclude from a lengthy historical study of federal appellate review of agency determinations that long before *Chevron* agency affirmance rates were on the rise in the federal courts — especially during the 1970s, even though that was the heyday of "hard look" review in the D.C. Circuit (which supposedly subjected administrative decisions to a greater degree of review).

On the other hand, it is not clear how much *Chevron* changed the prevailing Supreme Court practice. Since the New Deal, the Court had been deferential to agency decisions, sometimes with language presaging *Chevron*. In *Batterton v. Francis*, 432 U.S. 416 (1979), the Court held that when Congress delegates lawmaking authority to an agency (HEW), "Congress entrusts the Secretary, rather than to the courts, the primary responsibility for interpreting the statutory term." Once the agency has authoritatively construed the statute through legislative rules, the reviewing court "is not free to set aside the agency regulations simply because it would have interpreted the statute in a different manner."

Just as the Court was often highly deferential before *Chevron*, it was often pretty scrutinizing after *Chevron*. For example, in *INS v. Cardoza-Fonseca*, 480 U.S. 421 (1987), the Court not only rejected the INS' interpretation of its obligations not to deport noncitizens who have a "well-founded fear" of political persecution, 8 U.S.C. § 1158(a), but laid out a detailed legal regime for the INS to follow. Justice Stevens (the author of *Chevron*) wrote the majority opinion, which dissenting Justice Powell felt was not very deferential to the INS.

Moreover, the Supreme Court reaffirmed the approach it took in *Gilbert*. Not only has the Court reiterated that it will not defer to the EEOC (absent a special reason to do so), see *EEOC v. Aramco*, 499 U.S. 244 (1991), but the Court in *Christensen v. Harris County*, 529 U.S. 576, 586–88 (2000), *id.* at 596–97 (Breyer, J., dissenting on other grounds), reaffirmed the *Skidmore* standard for weighing the views of an agency when expressed through informal opinions and letters. In both cases, Justice Scalia objected that the *Chevron* theory for deference (the superior legitimacy agencies had in filling in genuine statutory gaps) should apply to the EEOC and to informal but public rulings by

---

g. This is the assumption of many of the earlier articles analyzing and criticizing *Chevron* and its progeny. See, e.g., Farina, *supra*; Richard Pierce, *Political Control Versus Impermissible Bias in Agency Decisionmaking: Lessons from* Chevron *to Mistretta*, 57 U. Chi. L. Rev. 481 (1990); Sidney Shapiro & Robert Glicksman, *Congress, the Supreme Court, and the Quiet Revolution in Administrative Law*, 1988 Duke L.J. 819; Peter Strauss, *One Hundred Fifty Cases Per Year: Some Implications of the Supreme Court's Limited Resources for Judicial Review of Agency Action*, 87 Colum. L. Rev. 1093 (1987); Cass Sunstein, *Law and Administration After* Chevron, 90 Colum. L. Rev. 2071 (1990).

the agency, but agreed that the EEOC's interpretations should be set aside because they were inconsistent with the statute.

6. *Think Critically about What "Deference" Means.* In *Cardoza-Fonseca, Aramco,* and *Christensen,* Justice Scalia found plain meanings inconsistent with the agency views and so ruled against the agencies even under the *Chevron*-deference standard. Can a judge be "deferential" to agency constructions of ambiguous laws yet still overturn many agency constructions, on the ground that the laws are unambiguous? Should a "deferential" approach extend to an agency's practical understanding of statutory language in cases such as *Aramco*?

For institutional, selection-of-case reasons, a highly deferential Supreme Court need not actually *agree* with agencies in most cases.[h] If agencies are winning most of the cases at the lower court level, because those judges are *Chevron*-deferring, then the cases actually making it to the Supreme Court might reflect even more agency goose eggs (bad interpretations) than would otherwise be the case.[i] Consider the following case: agency goose egg? Or raw deal for an energetic agency trying to ease regulatory burdens?

MCI TELECOMMUNICATIONS CORP. v. AT&T
Supreme Court of the United States, 1994
512 U.S. 218, 114 S.Ct. 2223, 129 L.Ed.2d 182

JUSTICE SCALIA delivered the opinion for the Court.

Section 203(a) of Title 47 of the United States Code requires communications common carriers to file tariffs with the Federal Communications Commission, and § 203(b) authorizes the Commission to "modify" any requirement of § 203. These cases present the question whether the Commission's decision to make tariff filing optional for all nondominant long-distance carriers is a valid exercise of its modification authority.

---

h. Indeed, the post-*Chevron Supreme* Court was often not particularly deferential. Thomas Merrill, *Judicial Deference to Executive Precedent,* 101 Yale L.J. 969 (1992), found that the Supreme Court before 1984 deferred to agencies in 75% of the surveyed cases (consistent with the Schuck and Elliott findings for lower court deference), that the Court after 1984 usually didn't cite *Chevron* or follow its framework in deciding whether to defer to agencies (consistent with *Cardoza-Fonseca*), and that when the Court did apply the *Chevron* framework it only deferred to agencies in 59% of the cases, well below the pre-*Chevron* figure of 75%, and below the overall deference rate after 1984 of 70% (a most surprising finding). These findings should be read cautiously, however, because Merrill's study could not evaluate the possibility that parties would fail to appeal agency decisions that before *Chevron* might have looked more vulnerable.

i. Schuck & Elliott, Chevron *Station,* found that the D.C. Circuit's agency agreement rates went up significantly in the years immediately after *Chevron.* Other scholars have found an ongoing *Chevron* effect at the lower court level, e.g., Thomas Miles & Cass Sunstein, *Do Judges Make Regulatory Policy? An Empirical Examination of* Chevron, 73 U. Chi. L. Rev. 823 (2006) (examining court of appeals decisions reviewing EPA and NLRB decisions). Kristin Hickman & Mathew Krueger, *In Search of the Modern* Skidmore *Standard,* 108 Colum. L. Rev. (forthcoming 2008), found a statistically significant amount of *Skidmore* deference among the courts of appeals.

[The Communications Act of 1934, 48 Stat. 1064, as amended, authorized the FCC to regulate the rates charged for communication services to ensure that they were reasonable and nondiscriminatory. The requirements of § 203 that common carriers file their rates with the Commission and charge only the filed rate were the centerpiece of the Act's regulatory scheme. For the next 40 years, AT&T had a virtual monopoly over the nation's telephone service, but in the 1970s new competitors emerged. During the 1980s, the Commission allowed, and briefly required, nondominant carriers an exemption from the tariff requirements. The Supreme Court accepted AT&T's challenge to the agency rule.]

The dispute between the parties turns on the meaning of the phrase "modify any requirement" in § 203(b)(2). Petitioners [MCI and the FCC] argue that it gives the Commission authority to make even basic and fundamental changes in the scheme created by that section. We disagree. The word "modify" — like a number of other English words employing the root "mod-" (deriving from the Latin word for "measure"), such as "moderate," "modulate," "modest," and "modicum" — has a connotation of increment or limitation. Virtually every dictionary we are aware of says that "to modify" means to change moderately or in minor fashion. See, e.g., Random House Dictionary of the English Language 1236 (2d ed. 1987) ("to change somewhat the form or qualities of; alter partially; amend"); [similar references from Webster's Third New International Dictionary, Oxford English Dictionary, and Black's Law Dictionary].

In support of their position, petitioners cite dictionary definitions contained in, or derived from, a single source, Webster's Third New International Dictionary 1452 (1981) (Webster's Third), which includes among the meanings of "modify," "to make a basic or important change in." Petitioners contend that this establishes sufficient ambiguity to entitle the Commission to deference in its acceptance of the broader meaning, which in turn requires approval of its permissive detariffing policy. See *Chevron*. In short, they contend that the courts must defer to the agency's choice among available dictionary definitions. * * *

Most cases of verbal ambiguity in statutes involve * * * a selection between accepted alternative meanings shown as such by many dictionaries. One can envision (though a court case does not immediately come to mind) having to choose between accepted alternative meanings, one of which is so newly accepted that it has only been recorded by a single lexicographer. (Some dictionary must have been the very first to record the widespread use of "projection," for example, to mean "forecast.") But what petitioners demand that we accept as creating an ambiguity here is a rarity even rarer than that: a meaning set forth in a single dictionary (and, as we say, its progeny) which not only *supplements* the meaning contained in all other dictionaries, but *contradicts* one of the meanings contained in virtually all other dictionaries. Indeed, contradicts one of the alternative meanings contained in the out-of-step dictionary itself — for * * * Webster's Third itself defines "modify" to connote *both* (specifically) major change *and* (specifically) minor change. It is hard to see how that can be. When the word "modify" has come to mean *both* "to change in some respects" *and* "to change fundamentally" it will in fact mean *neither* of those things. It will simply mean "to change," and some adverb will have to be called into service to indicate the great or small degree of the change.

If that is what the peculiar Webster's Third definition means to suggest has happened — and what petitioners suggest by appealing to Webster's Third — we simply disagree. "Modify," in our view, connotes moderate change. It might be good English to say that the French Revolution "modified" the status of the French nobility — but only because there is a figure of speech called understatement and a literary device known as sarcasm. And it might be unsurprising to discover a 1972 White House press release saying that "the Administration is modifying its position with regard to prosecution of the war in Vietnam" — but only because press agents tend to impart what is nowadays called "spin." Such intentional distortions, or simply careless or ignorant misuse, must have formed the basis for the usage that Webster's Third, and Webster's Third alone, reported.[3] It is perhaps gilding the lily to add this: In 1934, when the Communications Act became law — the most relevant time for determining a statutory term's meaning, see *Perrin v. United States*, 444 U.S. 37, 42–45 (1979) — Webster's Third was not yet even contemplated. To our knowledge *all* English dictionaries provided the narrow definition of "modify," including those published by G. & C. Merriam Company. We have not the slightest doubt that is the meaning the statute intended. * * *

Since an agency's interpretation of a statute is not entitled to deference when it goes beyond the meaning that the statute can bear, *Chevron*, the Commission's permissive detariffing policy can be justified only if it makes a less than radical or fundamental change in the Act's tariff-filing requirement. The Commission's attempt to establish that no more than that is involved greatly understates the extent to which its policy deviates from the filing requirement, and greatly undervalues the importance of the filing requirement itself. [Tariff-filing is at the heart of the regulatory scheme, because it provides the data by which the FCC can police rate-discrimination and unreasonableness in charges.]

Bearing in mind, then, the enormous importance to the statutory scheme of the tariff-filing provision, we turn to whether what has occurred here can be considered a mere "modification." The Commission stresses that its detariffing policy applies only to nondominant carriers, so that the rates charged to over half of all consumers in the long-distance market are on file with the Commission. It is not clear to us that the proportion of customers affected, rather than

---

3. That is not an unlikely hypothesis. Upon its long-awaited appearance in 1961, Webster's Third was widely criticized for its portrayal of common error as proper usage. See, e.g., Follett, Sabotage in Springfield, 209 Atlantic 73 (Jan. 1962); Barzun, What is a Dictionary? 32 The American Scholar 176, 181 (spring 1963); Macdonald, The String Unwound, 38 The New Yorker 130, 156–157 (Mar. 1962). An example is its approval (without qualification) of the use of "infer" to mean "imply": "infer" "5: to give reason to draw an inference concerning: HINT (did not take part in the debate except to ask a question inferring that the constitution must be changed — Manchester Guardian Weekly)." Webster's Third New International Dictionary 1158 (1961).

the proportion of carriers affected, is the proper measure of the extent of the exemption (of course *all* carriers in the long-distance market are exempted, except AT&T). But even assuming it is, we think an elimination of the crucial provision of the statute for 40% of a major sector of the industry is much too extensive to be considered a "modification." What we have here, in reality, is a fundamental revision of the statute, changing it from a scheme of rate regulation in long-distance common-carrier communications to a scheme of rate regulation only where effective competition does not exist. That may be a good idea, but it was not the idea Congress enacted into law in 1934. * * *

[JUSTICE O'CONNOR took no part in the consideration or decision of these cases.]

JUSTICE STEVENS, with whom JUSTICE BLACKMUN and JUSTICE SOUTER join, dissenting. * * *

Although the majority observes that further relaxation of tariff-filing requirements might more effectively enhance competition, it does not take issue with the Commission's conclusions that mandatory filing of tariff schedules serves no useful purpose and is actually counterproductive in the case of carriers who lack market power. As the Commission had noted in its prior detariffing orders, if a nondominant carrier sought to charge inflated rates, "customers would simply move to other carriers." Moreover, an absence of market power will ordinarily preclude firms of any kind from engaging in price discrimination. The Commission plausibly concluded that any slight enforcement benefits a tariff-filing requirement might offer were outweighed by the burdens it would put on new entrants and consumers. Thus, the sole question for us is whether the FCC's policy, however sensible, is nonetheless inconsistent with the Act.

In my view, each of the Commission's detariffing orders was squarely within its power to "modify any requirement" of § 203. Section 203(b)(2) plainly confers at least some discretion to modify the general rule that carriers file tariffs, for it speaks of "*any* requirement." Section 203(c) of the Act, ignored by the Court, squarely supports the FCC's position; it prohibits carriers from providing service without a tariff "*unless otherwise provided by or under authority of this Act.*" Section 203(b)(2) is plainly one provision that "otherwise provides," and thereby authorizes, service without a filed schedule. The FCC's authority to modify § 203's requirements in "particular instances" or by "general order applicable to special circumstances or conditions" emphasizes the expansive character of the Commission's authority: modifications may be narrow or broad, depending upon the Commission's appraisal of current conditions. From the vantage of a Congress seeking to regulate an almost completely monopolized industry, the advent of competition is surely a "special circumstance or condition" that might legitimately call for different regulatory treatment. * * *

According to the Court, the term "modify," as explicated in all but the most unreliable dictionaries, rules out the Commission's claimed authority to relieve nondominant carriers of the basic obligation to file tariffs. Dictionaries can be useful aids in statutory interpretation, but they are no substitute for close analysis of what words mean as used in a particular statutory context. Even if the sole possible meaning of "modify" were to make "minor" changes,[3] further elaboration is needed to show why the detariffing policy should fail. The Commission came to its present policy through a series of rulings that gradually relaxed the filing requirements for nondominant carriers. Whether the current policy should count as a cataclysmic or merely an incremental departure from the § 203(a) baseline depends on whether one focuses on particular carriers' obligations to file (in which case the Commission's policy arguably works a major shift) or on the statutory policies behind the tariff-filing requirement (which remain satisfied because market constraints on nondominant carriers obviate the need for rate filing). When § 203 is viewed as part of a statute whose aim is to constrain monopoly power, the Commission's decision to exempt nondominant carriers is a rational and "measured" adjustment to novel circumstances — one that remains faithful to the core purpose of the tariff-filing section. See Black's Law Dictionary 1198 (3d ed. 1933) (defining "modification" as "A change; an alteration which introduces new elements into the details, or cancels some of them, but leaves *the general purpose and effect of the subject-matter* intact").

The Court seizes upon a particular sense of the word "modify" at the expense of another, long-established meaning that fully supports the Commission's position. That word is first defined in Webster's Collegiate Dictionary 628 (4th ed. 1934) as meaning "to limit or reduce in extent or degree." The Commission's permissive detariffing policy fits comfortably within this common understanding of the term. The FCC has in effect adopted a general rule stating that "if you are dominant you must file, but if you are nondominant you need not." The Commission's partial detariffing policy — which excuses nondominant carriers from filing *on condition that* they remain nondominant — is simply a relaxation of a costly regulatory requirement that recent developments had rendered pointless and counterproductive in a certain class of cases.

A modification pursuant to § 203(b)(1), like any other order issued under the Act, must of course be consistent with the purposes of the statute. On this point, the Court asserts that the Act's prohibition against unreasonable and discriminatory rates "would not be susceptible of effective enforcement if rates were not publicly filed." That determination, of course, is for the Commission to make in the first instance. But the Commission has repeatedly explained that (1) a carrier that lacks market power is entirely unlikely to charge unreasonable or discriminatory rates, (2) the statutory bans on unreasonable charges and price discrimination apply with full force regardless of whether carriers have to file tariffs, (3) any suspected violations by nondominant carriers can be addressed on the Commission's own motion or on a damages complaint filed pursuant to § 206, and (4) the FCC can reimpose a tariff requirement should

---

3. As petitioner MCI points out, the revolutionary consent decree providing for the breakup of the Bell System was, per AT&T's own proposal, entitled "Modification of Final Judgment." See *United States v. American Telephone & Telegraph Co.*, 552 F.Supp. 131 (D.C. 1982), aff'd, 460 U.S. 1001 (1983).

violations occur. The Court does not adequately respond to the FCC's explanations, and gives no reason whatsoever to doubt the Commission's considered judgment that tariff filing is altogether unnecessary in the case of competitive carriers; the majority's ineffective enforcement argument lacks any evidentiary or historical support. * * *

The filed tariff provisions of the Communications Act are not ends in themselves, but are merely one of several procedural *means* for the Commission to ensure that carriers do not charge unreasonable or discriminatory rates. The Commission has reasonably concluded that this particular means of enforcing the statute's substantive mandates will prove counterproductive in the case of nondominant long-distance carriers. Even if the 1934 Congress did not define the scope of the Commission's modification authority with perfect scholarly precision, this is surely a paradigm case for judicial deference to the agency's interpretation, particularly in a statutory regime so obviously meant to maximize administrative flexibility. Whatever the best reading of § 203(b)(2), the Commission's reading cannot in my view be termed unreasonable. It is informed (as ours is not) by a practical understanding of the role (or lack thereof) that filed tariffs play in the modern regulatory climate and in the telecommunications industry. Since 1979, the FCC has sought to adapt measures originally designed to control monopoly power to new market conditions. It has carefully and consistently explained that mandatory tariff-filing rules frustrate the core statutory interest in rate reasonableness. The Commission's use of the "discretion" expressly conferred by § 203(b)(2) reflects "a reasonable accommodation of manifestly competing interests and is entitled to deference: the regulatory scheme is technical and complex, the agency considered the matter in a detailed and reasoned fashion, and the decision involves reconciling conflicting policies." *Chevron*. The FCC has permissibly interpreted its § 203(b)(2) authority in service of the goals Congress set forth in the Act. We should sustain its eminently sound, experience-tested, and uncommonly well-explained judgment.

NOTES ON *MCI*, THE NEW TEXTUALISM, AND EXCESSIVE LEGISLATIVE DELEGATIONS TO AGENCIES

1. *The New Textualism and* Chevron: *Should the Court Consider Legislative History?* In *Cardoza-Fonseca* (1987), only Justice Scalia adhered to the view that *Chevron* permits overturning agency action only when the agency view clashes with a clear statutory text. All other Justices consulted the legislative history to determine the validity of the agency view under *Chevron*. Justice Scalia has continued to press his view that statutory text and structure are the only relevant inquiries in the first step in the *Chevron* analysis (has Congress specifically addressed the issue?). Justice Stevens' approach, that other traditional tools such as legislative history and purpose are also relevant in step one, seemed to lose ground on the Court after *Cardoza-Fonseca*.

In *K Mart Corp. v. Cartier, Inc.*, 486 U.S. 281 (1988) (upholding two Customs rules and invalidating a third), a majority of Justices refused to examine legislative history. After *K Mart*, the status of legislative history in *Chevron* analysis seemed unclear. Like *MCI*, many of the Court's post-*K Mart* cases have focused only on textual arguments and have refused to give serious consideration to legislative history.[j]

An interesting example is *City of Chicago v. Environmental Defense Fund*, 511 U.S. 328 (1994).[k] The issue in the case was whether waste combustion ash generated by a municipal resource recovery incinerator was exempt from hazardous waste regulation under Subtitle C of the Resource Conservation and Recovery Act (RCRA). Without explicit statutory support, the EPA had supported a RCRA exemption for municipal waste incineration in the early 1980s, and in 1984 Congress added § 3001(i) to provide that "[a] resource recovery facility recovering energy from the mass burning of municipal solid waste" would not be "deemed to be treating, storing, disposing of, or otherwise managing hazardous wastes for the purposes of [Subtitle C],"42 U.S.C. § 6921(i). Municipalities assumed that § 3001(i) also allowed them to dispose of the ash created in such process without the expensive protections required by Subtitle C. The EPA sent mixed signals on the ash issue, before siding with the municipalities in a 1992 memorandum developed in connection with the *City of Chicago* case. The EPA memorandum argued that the statutory balance of environmental protection and reasonable costs could best be achieved through a broad exemption, for cities faced enormous costs if they had to dispose of ash under Subtitle C. Moreover, the legislative history of § 3001(i) supported this balance. The Senate report accompanying § 3001(i) said that "[a]ll waste management activities of such a facility, including the *generation*, transportation, treatment, storage and disposal of waste shall be covered by the exclusion."[l] All this background persuaded Justice Stevens, but he found himself in dissent. Justice Scalia's opinion for the Court ruled § 3001(i) unambiguous: the *facility* is exempt from Subtitle C, but there is no mention and therefore no exemption for the *ash* produced in the facility and subsequently disposed of by the city. Scalia not only refused to credit the Senate report with any value, but deployed it to prove his point: the report included *generation* of waste as one of the activities exempted by section 3001(i), a term notably absent from the statute itself. *Inclusio unius est exclusio alterius* (§ 1A of Chapter 8).

On the other hand, there have also been many post-*K Mart* decisions in which the Court considered legislative history and other nontextual arguments when doing a *Chevron* analysis. E.g., *FDA v. Brown & Williamson Tobacco Corp.* (Chapter 7, § 3B3); *Babbitt v. Sweet Home* (Chapter 8, § 1A). In *Wisconsin Public Intervenor v. Mortier*, 501 U.S. 597, 610 n.4 (1991), the

---

j. See, e.g., *Rapanos v. United States*, 126 S.Ct. 2208 (2006) (plurality opinion of Scalia, J.); *Solid Waste Agency v. Army Corps of Eng'rs*, 531 U.S. 159 (2001); *Sutton v. United Airlines. Inc.*, 527 U.S. 471, 482 (1999); *AT&T v. Iowa Utilities Bd.*, 525 U.S. 366 (1999); *National Railroad Passenger Corporation v. Boston & Maine Corp.*, 503 U.S. 407, 417 (1992) (all Justices join in majority opinion by Kennedy, J., which says that only statutory text is relevant for *Chevron* analysis).

k. Our discussion of *City of Chicago* draws from Richard Lazarus & Claudia Newman, City of Chicago v. Environmental Defense Fund: *Searching for Plain Meaning in Unambiguous Ambiguity*, 4 N.Y.U. Env. L.J. 1 (1995).

l. S. Rep. No. 284, 98th Cong., 1st Sess. 61 (1983) (emphasis added).

Court *Chevron*-deferred to an agency interpretation that the federal pesticide law did not preempt state law. In determining whether Congress had directly addressed this question (*Chevron* Step 1), the Court examined the legislative history as well as the statutory text. Justice White's opinion marshaling legislative history won over the votes of Chief Justice Rehnquist and Justice O'Connor, who had originally thought that the statutory scheme "occupied the field" and therefore preempted state law (according to Justice Blackmun's conference notes). In dissent, Justice Scalia mounted a full-scale assault on the Court's reliance on legislative history — an assault that drew no support from any other Justice. See also William Eskridge, Jr. & Lauren Baer, *The Supreme Court's Deference Continuum, An Empirical Analysis (*Chevron *to* Hamdan*)*, 96 Geo. L.J. (forthcoming April 2008) (finding that the Court relies on legislative history *more* often in *Chevron* cases than in other statutory interpretation cases).

Consider a suggestion made by the Seventh Circuit in *Bankers Life & Cas. Co. v. United States*, 142 F.3d 973 (1998). "While this circuit has examined legislative history during the first step of *Chevron*, we now seem to lean toward reserving consideration of legislative history and other appropriate factors until the second *Chevron* step." This suggested approach would focus on statutory text and structure to determine whether the law is ambiguous (step one) and, if so, would consider legislative history and the statutory purpose evaluating the reasonableness of the agency's construction (step two). One might evaluate *Sweet Home* (the spotted owl case) along these lines. The statutory text was ambiguous as to whether destruction of habitat constituted a taking of endangered animals, and so the Justices should have evaluated the agency's position under step two of *Chevron*. The various legislative discussions surrounding the 1973 statute (relied on by dissenting Justice Scalia) and its 1982 amendment (relied on by Justice Stevens' opinion for the Court) would then have been relevant to the reasonableness of the agency's choice.

2. *The Implications of the New Textualism for Deference, More Generally.* If Justice Scalia's position on *Chevron* were adopted by the Court, agency rules might be *more* prone to reversal than under Justice Stevens' position. Justice Scalia explains why this might be so in his article, *Judicial Deference to Administrative Interpretation of Law*, 1989 Duke L.J. 511, 521:

> * * * One who finds *more* often (as I do) that the meaning of a statute is apparent from its text and from its relationship with other laws, thereby finds *less* often that the triggering requirement for *Chevron* deference exists. It is thus relatively rare that *Chevron* will require me to accept an interpretation which, though reasonable, I would not personally adopt. Contrariwise, one who abhors a "plain meaning" rule, and is willing to permit the apparent meaning of a statute to be impeached by legislative history, will more frequently find agency-liberating ambiguity. * * *

In *K Mart*, for example, the Justices willing to consider legislative background were much more sympathetic to what the agency was trying to do than were the Justices who just considered the statutory text.

That a textualist approach to *Chevron* might be less deferential to agency interpretations is supported by Professor Merrill's empirical study, which found that in 1988–90 (the period of new textualist ascendancy) *Chevron*'s framework was applied in more cases than it had been in 1985–86 (51% to 32%) but that the agency view had prevailed much less often overall (59% to 72%). 101 Yale L.J. at 992 (Table 3). Merrill speculates that textualism may lead to a "permanent subordination of the *Chevron* doctrine."[m]

A milder conclusion suggested by Justice Scalia's law review article would be that the new textualism is more likely to resolve cases at step one of *Chevron* (the agency is either right or wrong) and is less likely to get to step two, which is where deference really kicks in (the law is unclear, so the agency can make a choice the judges would not have otherwise made). Others are skeptical that methodology per se is decisive. See Eskridge & Baer, *Deference Continuum* (reporting relatively low agency agreement rates for textualist Justices Scalia and Thomas, but even lower rates for Justice Stevens, who relies on legislative history). Indeed, there are plenty of cases where Justice Scalia's textualism is more lenient toward agency interpretations than it was in *MCI* or *Sweet Home*.[n]

3. MCI, *Dictionaries, and Excessive Delegations. MCI* is a leading case for the Court's well-honed deployment of dictionaries. The Court faults *Webster's Third* for too readily incorporating ordinary usage — which would seem to be most desirable for enterprises like discerning the meaning an ordinary reader would draw from the statute. One might argue, however, that legislative drafters use language more formally, and thus more consistently with the

---

m. Thomas Merrill, *Textualism and the* Chevron *Doctrine*, 72 Wash. U.L.Q. 351, 372 (1994). He suggests (*id.*, footnotes, citing case examples, omitted):

This has to do with the style of judging associated with textualism. Intentionalism mandates an "archeological" excavation of the past, producing opinions written in the style of the dry archivist sifting through countless documents in search of the tell-tale smoking gun of congressional intent. Textualism, in contrast, seems to transform statutory interpretation into a kind of exercise in judicial ingenuity. The textualist judge treats questions of interpretation like a puzzle to which it is assumed there is one right answer. The task is to assemble the various pieces of linguistic data, dictionary definitions, and canons into the best (most coherent, most explanatory) account of the meaning of the statute. This exercise places a great premium on cleverness. In one case the outcome turns on the place of a comma, in another on the inconsistency between a comma and rules of grammar, in a third on the conflict between quotation marks and the language of the text. One day arguments must be advanced in support of broad dictionary definitions; the next day in support of narrow dictionary definitions. New canons of construction and clear statement rules must be invented and old ones reinterpreted.

This active, creative approach to interpretation is subtly incompatible with an attitude of deference toward other institutions — whether the other institution is Congress or an administrative agency. In effect, the textualist interpreter does not *find* the meaning of the statute so much as *construct* the meaning. Such a person will very likely experience some difficulty in deferring to the meanings that other institutions have developed.

n. E.g., *Massachusetts v. EPA*, 127 S.Ct. 1438, 1473–74 (2007) (Scalia, J., dissenting) (deferring to EPA interpretation narrowly construing its broad statutory authority over greenhouse gases allegedly contributing to global warming); *Gonzales v. Oregon*, 543 U.S. 243 (2006) (Scalia, J., dissenting) (deferring to Department of Justice interpretation preempting state death-with-dignity law).

prescriptive approach of *Webster's Second. MCI* also involves a methodological debate over the extent to which policy context matters.

One reading of *MCI* is that it supports a rule or presumption against excessive delegations. Recall from Section 1, the Supreme Court will not enforce the nondelegation doctrine anymore — it will not strike down, as a constitutional violation, even extremely broad legislative delegations of lawmaking authority to administrative agencies. The Court can still give this "underenforced constitutional norm" some teeth, however, by "canonizing" it: Thus, the Court will be reluctant to read statutory delegations broadly, for fear that this will encourage the legislature to make excessive delegations. Does this reading make *MCI* a more persuasive opinion? How can this be reconciled with *Chevron*?

This reading of *MCI* reappeared in *FDA v. Brown & Williamson*, (Chapter 7, § 3B3), where the Court said:

> Deference under *Chevron* to an agency's construction of a statute that it administers is premised on the theory that a statute's ambiguity constitutes an implicit delegation from Congress to the agency to fill in the statutory gaps. In extraordinary cases, however, there may be reason to hesitate before concluding that Congress has intended such an implicit delegation.

> * * * Owing to its unique place in American history and society, tobacco has its own unique political history. Congress, for better or for worse, has created a distinct regulatory scheme for tobacco products, squarely rejected proposals to give the FDA jurisdiction over tobacco, and repeatedly acted to preclude any agency from exercising significant policymaking authority in the area. Given this history and the breadth of the authority that the FDA has asserted, we are obliged to defer not to the agency's expansive construction of the statute, but to Congress' consistent judgment to deny the FDA this power. [The Court then discussed *MCI*.]

> As in *MCI*, we are confident that Congress could not have intended to delegate a decision of such economic and political significance to an agency in so cryptic a fashion.

529 U.S. at 159–60. Is this a persuasive deployment of *MCI*? Should this precept have counseled a different result in some of the other cases where the Court has deferred to agencies, such as *Sweet Home*? *Bob Jones*?

UNITED STATES v. MEAD CORP.
Supreme Court of the United States, 2001
533 U.S. 218, 121 S.Ct. 2164, 150 L.Ed.2d 292

JUSTICE SOUTER delivered the opinion of the Court.

The question is whether a tariff classification ruling by the United States Customs Service deserves judicial deference. The Federal Circuit rejected Customs's invocation of *Chevron* in support of such a ruling, to which it gave no deference. We agree that a tariff classification has no claim to judicial deference under *Chevron,* there being no indication that Congress intended such a ruling to carry the force of law, but we hold that under *Skidmore*, the ruling is eligible to claim respect according to its persuasiveness. * * *

[II.A] When Congress has "explicitly left a gap for an agency to fill, there is an express delegation of authority to the agency to elucidate a specific provision of the statute by regulation," *Chevron*, and any ensuing regulation is binding in the courts unless procedurally defective, arbitrary or capricious in substance, or manifestly contrary to the statute. See APA, 5 U.S.C. § 706(2)(A), (D). But whether or not they enjoy any express delegation of authority on a particular question, agencies charged with applying a statute necessarily make all sorts of interpretive choices, and while not all of those choices bind judges to follow them, they certainly may influence courts facing questions the agencies have already answered. "[T]he well-reasoned views of the agencies implementing a statute 'constitute a body of experience and informed judgment to which courts and litigants may properly resort for guidance,'" *Bragdon* v. *Abbott,* 524 U.S. 624, 642 (1998) (quoting *Skidmore*), and "[w]e have long recognized that considerable weight should be accorded to an executive department's construction of a statutory scheme it is entrusted to administer ... ." *Chevron* (footnote omitted).

The fair measure of deference to an agency administering its own statute has been understood to vary with circumstances, and courts have looked to the degree of the agency's care, its consistency, formality, and relative expertness, and to the persuasiveness of the agency's position, see *Skidmore*. * * * Justice Jackson summed things up in *Skidmore:*

> "The weight [accorded to an administrative] judgment in a particular case will depend upon the thoroughness evident in its consideration, the validity of its reasoning, its consistency with earlier and later pronouncements, and all those factors which give it power to persuade, if lacking power to control."

Since 1984, we have identified a category of interpretive choices distinguished by an additional reason for judicial deference. This Court in *Chevron* recognized that Congress not only engages in express delegation of specific interpretive authority, but that "[s]ometimes the legislative delegation to an agency on a particular question is implicit." Congress, that is, may not have expressly delegated authority or responsibility to implement a particular provision or fill a particular gap. Yet it can still be apparent from the agency's generally conferred authority and other statutory circumstances that Congress would expect the agency to be able to speak with the force of law when it addresses ambiguity in the statute or fills a space in the enacted law, even one about which "Congress did not actually have an intent" as to a particular result. When circumstances implying such an expectation exist, a reviewing court has no business rejecting an agency's exercise of its generally conferred authority to resolve a particular statutory ambiguity simply because the agency's chosen resolution seems unwise, but is obliged to accept the agency's position if Congress has not previously spoken to the point at issue and the agency's interpretation is reasonable; *cf.* 5 U.S.C. §§706(2) (a reviewing court shall set aside agency action, findings, and conclusions found to be "arbitrary, capricious, an abuse of discretion, or otherwise not in accordance with law").

We have recognized a very good indicator of delegation meriting *Chevron* treatment in express congressional authorizations to engage in the process of rulemaking or adjudication that produces regulations or rulings for which deference is claimed. [Citing cases, including *Gilbert*, that apply only *Skidmore* deference to EEOC interpretations.] It is fair to assume generally that Congress contemplates administrative action with the effect of law when it provides for a relatively formal administrative procedure tending to foster the fairness and deliberation that should underlie a pronouncement of such force. Thus, the overwhelming number of our cases applying *Chevron* deference have reviewed the fruits of notice-and-comment rulemaking or formal adjudication. That said, and as significant as notice-and-comment is in pointing to *Chevron* authority, the want of that procedure here does not decide the case, for we have sometimes found reasons for *Chevron* deference even when no such administrative formality was required and none was afforded, see, *e.g., NationsBank of N. C., N. A.* v. *Variable Annuity Life Ins. Co.,* 513 U.S. 251, 256–257, 263 (1995). The fact that the tariff classification here was not a product of such formal process does not alone, therefore, bar the application of *Chevron*.

There are, nonetheless, ample reasons to deny *Chevron* deference here. The authorization for classification rulings, and Customs's practice in making them, present a case far removed not only from notice-and-comment process, but from any other circumstances reasonably suggesting that Congress ever thought of classification rulings as deserving the deference claimed for them here.

[II.B] No matter which angle we choose for viewing the Customs ruling letter in this case, it fails to qualify under *Chevron*. On the face of the statute, to begin with, the terms of the congressional delegation give no indication that Congress meant to delegate authority to Customs to issue classification rulings with the force of law. We are not, of course, here making any global statement about Customs's authority, for it is true that the general rulemaking power conferred on Customs authorizes some regulation with the force of law, or "legal norms" * * *. It is true as well that Congress had classification rulings in mind when it explicitly authorized, in a parenthetical, the issuance of "regulations establishing procedures for the issuance of binding rulings prior to the entry of the merchandise concerned," 19 U.S.C. § 1502(a). The reference to binding classifications does not, however, bespeak the legislative type of activity that would naturally bind more than the parties to the ruling, once the goods classified are admitted into this country. And though the statute's direction to disseminate "information" necessary to "secure" uniformity, *ibid.*, seems to assume that a ruling may be precedent in later transactions, precedential value alone does not add up to *Chevron* entitlement; interpretive rules may sometimes function as precedents, see Strauss, *The Rulemaking Continuum*, 41 Duke L.J. 1463, 1472–1473 (1992), and they enjoy no *Chevron* status as a class. In any event, any precedential claim of a classification ruling is counterbalanced by the provision for independent review of Customs classifications by the CIT [Court of International Trade]; the scheme for CIT review includes a provision that treats classification rulings on par with the Secretary's rulings on "valuation, rate of duty, marking, restricted merchandise, entry requirements, drawbacks, vessel repairs, or similar matters," § 1581(h). It is hard to imagine a congressional understanding more at odds with the *Chevron* regime.

It is difficult, in fact, to see in the agency practice itself any indication that Customs ever set out with a lawmaking pretense in mind when it undertook to make classifications like these. Customs does not generally engage in notice-and-comment practice when issuing them, and their treatment by the agency makes it clear that a letter's binding character as a ruling stops short of third parties; Customs has regarded a classification as conclusive only as between itself and the importer to whom it was issued, and even then only until Customs has given advance notice of intended change. Other importers are in fact warned against assuming any right of detrimental reliance.

Indeed, to claim that classifications have legal force is to ignore the reality that 46 different Customs offices issue 10,000 to 15,000 of them each year. Any suggestion that rulings intended to have the force of law are being churned out at a rate of 10,000 a year at an agency's 46 scattered offices is simply self-refuting. Although the circumstances are less startling here, with a Headquarters letter in issue, none of the relevant statutes recognizes this category of rulings as separate or different from others; there is thus no indication that a more potent delegation might have been understood as going to Headquarters even when Headquarters provides developed reasoning, as it did in this instance.

Nor do the amendments to the statute made effective after this case arose disturb our conclusion. The new law requires Customs to provide notice-and-comment procedures only when modifying or revoking a prior classification ruling or modifying the treatment accorded to substantially identical transactions; and under its regulations, Customs sees itself obliged to provide notice-and-comment procedures only when "changing a practice" so as to produce a tariff increase, or in the imposition of a restriction or prohibition, or when Customs Headquarters determines that "the matter is of sufficient importance to involve the interests of domestic industry." 19 C.F.R. §§ 177.10(c)(1), (2). The statutory changes reveal no new congressional objective of treating classification decisions generally as rulemaking with force of law, nor do they suggest any intent to create a *Chevron* patchwork of classification rulings, some with force of law, some without.

In sum, classification rulings are best treated like "interpretations contained in policy statements, agency manuals, and enforcement guidelines." *Christensen*. They are beyond the *Chevron* pale.

[II.C] To agree with the Court of Appeals that Customs ruling letters do not fall within *Chevron* is not, however, to place them outside the pale of any deference whatever. *Chevron* did nothing to eliminate *Skidmore*'s holding that an agency's interpretation may merit some deference whatever its form, given the "specialized experience and broader investigations and information" available to the agency, and given the value of uniformity in its administrative and judicial understandings of what a national law requires.

There is room at least to raise a *Skidmore* claim here, where the regulatory scheme is highly detailed, and Customs can bring the benefit of specialized experience to bear on the subtle questions in this case: whether the daily planner with room for brief daily entries falls under "diaries," when diaries are grouped with "notebooks and address books, bound; memorandum pads, letter pads and similar articles"; and whether a planner with a ring binding should qualify as "bound," when a binding may be typified by a book, but also may have "reinforcements or fittings of metal, plastics, etc." A classification ruling in this situation may therefore at least seek a respect proportional to its "power to persuade," *Skidmore*. Such a ruling may surely claim the merit of its writer's thoroughness, logic and expertness, its fit with prior interpretations, and any other sources of weight.

[II.D] Underlying the position we take here, like the position expressed by Justice Scalia in dissent, is a choice about the best way to deal with an inescapable feature of the body of congressional legislation authorizing administrative action. That feature is the great variety of ways in which the laws invest the Government's administrative arms with discretion, and with procedures for exercising it, in giving meaning to Acts of Congress. Implementation of a statute may occur in formal adjudication or the choice to defend against judicial challenge; it may occur in a central board or office or in dozens of enforcement agencies dotted across the country; its institutional lawmaking may be confined to the resolution of minute detail or extend to legislative rulemaking on matters intentionally left by Congress to be worked out at the agency level.

Although we all accept the position that the Judiciary should defer to at least some of this multifarious administrative action, we have to decide how to take account of the great range of its variety. If the primary objective is to simplify the judicial process of giving or withholding deference, then the diversity of statutes authorizing discretionary administrative action must be declared irrelevant or minimized. If, on the other hand, it is simply implausible that Congress intended such a broad range of statutory authority to produce only two varieties of administrative action, demanding either *Chevron* deference or none at all, then the breadth of the spectrum of possible agency action must be taken into account. Justice Scalia's first priority over the years has been to limit and simplify. The Court's choice has been to tailor deference to variety. This acceptance of the range of statutory variation has led the Court to recognize more than one variety of judicial deference, just as the Court has recognized a variety of indicators that Congress would expect *Chevron* deference.

Our respective choices are repeated today. Justice Scalia would pose the question of deference as an either-or choice. On his view that *Chevron* rendered *Skidmore* anachronistic, when courts owe any deference it is *Chevron* deference that they owe. Whether courts do owe deference in a given case turns, for him, on whether the agency action (if reasonable) is "authoritative." The character of the authoritative derives, in turn, not from breadth of delegation or the agency's procedure in implementing it, but is defined as the "official" position of an agency, and may ultimately be a function of administrative persistence alone.

The Court, on the other hand, said nothing in *Chevron* to eliminate *Skidmore's* recognition of various justifications for deference depending on statutory circumstances and agency action; *Chevron* was simply a case recognizing that even without express authority to fill a specific statutory gap, circumstances pointing to implicit congressional delegation present a particularly insistent call for deference. Indeed, in holding here that *Chevron* left *Skidmore* intact and applicable where statutory circumstances indicate no intent to delegate general authority to make rules with force of law, or where such authority was not invoked, we hold nothing more than we said last Term in response to the particular statutory circumstances in *Christensen*, to which Justice Scalia then took exception, see 529 U.S., at 589, just as he does again today.

We think, in sum, that Justice Scalia's efforts to simplify ultimately run afoul of Congress's indications that different statutes present different reasons for considering respect for the exercise of administrative authority or deference to it. Without being at odds with congressional intent much of the time, we believe that judicial responses to administrative action must continue to differentiate between *Chevron* and *Skidmore,* and that continued recognition of *Skidmore* is necessary for just the reasons Justice Jackson gave when that case was decided.

Since the *Skidmore* assessment called for here ought to be made in the first instance by the Court of Appeals for the Federal Circuit or the CIT, we go no further than to vacate the judgment and remand the case for further proceedings consistent with this opinion.

JUSTICE SCALIA, dissenting.

Today's opinion makes an avulsive change in judicial review of federal administrative action. Whereas previously a reasonable agency application of an ambiguous statutory provision had to be sustained so long as it represented the agency's authoritative interpretation, henceforth such an application can be set aside unless "it appears that Congress delegated authority to the agency generally to make rules carrying the force of law," as by giving an agency "power to engage in adjudication or notice-and-comment rulemaking, or . . . some other [procedure] indicati[ng] comparable congressional intent," and "the agency interpretation claiming deference was promulgated in the exercise of that authority." What was previously a general presumption of authority in agencies to resolve ambiguity in the statutes they have been authorized to enforce has been changed to a presumption of no such authority, which must be overcome by affirmative legislative intent to the contrary. And whereas previously, when agency authority to resolve ambiguity did not exist the court was free to give the statute what it considered the best interpretation, henceforth the court must supposedly give the agency view some indeterminate amount of so-called *Skidmore* deference. We will be sorting out the consequences of the *Mead* doctrine, which has today replaced the *Chevron* doctrine, for years to come. I would adhere to our established jurisprudence, defer to the reasonable interpretation the Customs Service has given to the statute it is charged with enforcing, and reverse the judgment of the Court of Appeals.

[I.A] As to principle: The doctrine of *Chevron* — that all *authoritative* agency interpretations of statutes they are charged with administering deserve deference — was rooted in a legal presumption of congressional intent, important to the division of powers between the Second and Third Branches.

When, *Chevron* said, Congress leaves an ambiguity in a statute that is to be administered by an executive agency, it is presumed that Congress meant to give the agency discretion, within the limits of reasonable interpretation, as to how the ambiguity is to be resolved. By committing enforcement of the statute to an agency rather than the courts, Congress committed its initial and primary interpretation to that branch as well.

There is some question whether *Chevron* was faithful to the text of the Administrative Procedure Act (APA), which it did not even bother to cite. But it was in accord with the origins of federal-court judicial review. Judicial control of federal executive officers was principally exercised through the prerogative writ of mandamus. That writ generally would not issue unless the executive officer was acting plainly beyond the scope of his authority.

> "The questions mooted before the Secretary and decided by him were whether the fund is a tribal fund, whether the tribe is still existing and whether the distribution of the annuities is to be confined to members of the tribe . . . . These are all questions of law the solution of which requires a construction of the act of 1889 and other related acts. A reading of these acts shows that they fall short of plainly requiring that any of the questions be answered in the negative and that in some aspects they give color to the affirmative answers of the Secretary. That the construction of the acts insofar as they have a bearing on the first and third questions is sufficiently uncertain to involve the exercise of judgment and discretion is rather plain . . . .
>
> "From what has been said it follows that the case is not one in which mandamus will lie." *Wilbur* v. *United States ex rel. Kadrie*, 281 U.S. 206, 221–222 (1930).

Statutory ambiguities, in other words, were left to reasonable resolution by the Executive.

The basis in principle for today's new doctrine can be described as follows: The background rule is that ambiguity in legislative instructions to agencies is to be resolved not by the agencies but by the judges. Specific congressional intent to depart from this rule must be found — and while there is no single touchstone for such intent it can generally be found when Congress has authorized the agency to act through (what the Court says is) relatively formal procedures such as informal rulemaking and formal (and informal?) adjudication, and when the agency in fact employs such procedures. The Court's background rule is contradicted by the origins of judicial review of administrative action. But in addition, the Court's principal criterion of congressional intent to supplant its background rule seems to me quite implausible. There is no necessary connection between the formality of procedure and the power of the entity administering the procedure to resolve authoritatively questions of law. The most formal of the procedures the Court refers to — formal adjudication — is modeled after the process used in trial courts, which of course are not generally accorded deference on questions of law. The purpose of such a procedure is to produce a closed record for determination and review of the facts — which implies nothing about the power of the agency subjected to the procedure to resolve authoritatively questions of law.

As for informal rulemaking: While formal adjudication procedures are *prescribed* (either by statute or by the Constitution), informal rulemaking is more typically *authorized* but not required. Agencies with such authority are free to give guidance through rulemaking, but they may proceed to administer their statute case-by-case, "making law" as they implement their program (not necessarily through formal adjudication). Is it likely — or indeed even plausible — that Congress meant, when such an agency chooses rulemaking, to accord the administrators of that agency, *and their successors*, the flexibility of interpreting the ambiguous statute now one way, and later another; but, when such an agency chooses case-by-case administration, to eliminate all future agency discretion by having that same ambiguity resolved authoritatively (and forever) by the courts? Surely that makes no sense. It is also the case that certain significant categories of rules — those involving grant and benefit programs, for example, are exempt from the requirements of informal rulemaking. See 5 U.S.C. §553(a)(2). Under the Court's novel theory, when an agency takes advantage of that exemption its rules will be deprived of *Chevron* deference, *i.e.*, authoritative effect. Was this either the plausible intent of the APA rulemaking exemption, or the plausible intent of the Congress that established the grant or benefit program? * * *

[In Part II.B, Justice Scalia lamented the terrible "practical effects" of the Court's new rule.] (1) The principal effect will be protracted confusion. As noted above, the one test for *Chevron* deference that the Court enunciates is wonderfully imprecise: whether "Congress delegated authority to the agency generally to make rules carrying the force of law, ... as by ... adjudication[,] notice-and-comment rulemaking, or ... some other [procedure] indicati[ng] comparable congressional intent." But even this description does not do justice to the utter flabbiness of the Court's criterion, since, in order to maintain the fiction that the new test is really just the old one, applied consistently throughout our case law, the Court must make a virtually open-ended exception to its already imprecise guidance: In the present case, it tells us, the absence of notice-and-comment rulemaking (and "[who knows?] [of] some other [procedure] indicati[ng] comparable congressional intent") is not enough to decide the question of *Chevron* deference, "for we have sometimes found reasons for *Chevron* deference even when no such administrative formality was required and none was afforded." The opinion then goes on to consider a grab bag of other factors — including the factor that used to be the sole criterion for *Chevron* deference: whether the interpretation represented the *authoritative* position of the agency. It is hard to know what the lower courts are to make of today's guidance.

(2) Another practical effect of today's opinion will be an artificially induced increase in informal rulemaking. Buy stock in the GPO. Since informal rulemaking and formal adjudication are the only more-or-less safe harbors from the storm that the Court has unleashed; and since formal adjudication is not an option but must be mandated by statute or constitutional command; informal rulemaking — which the Court was once careful to make voluntary unless required by statute — will now become a virtual necessity. As I have described, the Court's safe harbor requires not merely that the agency have been given rulemaking authority, but also that the agency have *employed*

rulemaking as the means of resolving the statutory ambiguity. (It is hard to understand why that should be so. Surely the mere *conferral* of rulemaking authority demonstrates — if one accepts the Court's logic — a congressional intent to allow the agency to resolve ambiguities. And given that intent, what difference does it make that the agency chooses instead to use another perfectly permissible means for that purpose?) Moreover, the majority's approach will have a perverse effect on the rules that do emerge, given the principle (which the Court leaves untouched today) that judges must defer to reasonable agency interpretations of their own regulations. Agencies will now have high incentive to rush out barebones, ambiguous rules construing statutory ambiguities, which they can then in turn further clarify through informal rulings entitled to judicial respect.

(3) Worst of all, the majority's approach will lead to the ossification of large portions of our statutory law. Where *Chevron* applies, statutory ambiguities remain ambiguities subject to the agency's ongoing clarification. They create a space, so to speak, for the exercise of continuing agency discretion. As *Chevron* itself held, the Environmental Protection Agency can interpret "stationary source" to mean a single smokestack, can later replace that interpretation with the "bubble concept" embracing an entire plant, and if that proves undesirable can return again to the original interpretation. For the indeterminately large number of statutes taken out of *Chevron* by today's decision, however, ambiguity (and hence flexibility) will cease with the first judicial resolution. *Skidmore* deference gives the agency's current position some vague and uncertain amount of respect, but it does not, like *Chevron*, *leave* the matter within the control of the Executive Branch for the future. Once the court has spoken, it becomes *unlawful* for the agency to take a contradictory position; the statute now *says* what the court has prescribed. It will be bad enough when this ossification occurs as a result of judicial determination (under today's new principles) that there is no affirmative indication of congressional intent to "delegate"; but it will be positively bizarre when it occurs simply because of an agency's failure to act by rulemaking (rather than informal adjudication) before the issue is presented to the courts.

One might respond that such ossification would not result if the agency were simply to readopt its interpretation, after a court reviewing it under *Skidmore* had rejected it, by repromulgating it through one of the *Chevron*-eligible procedural formats approved by the Court today. Approving this procedure would be a landmark abdication of judicial power. It is worlds apart from *Chevron* proper, where the court does not *purport* to give the statute a judicial interpretation — except in identifying the scope of the statutory ambiguity, as to which the court's judgment is final and irreversible. (Under *Chevron* proper, when the agency's authoritative interpretation comes within the scope of that ambiguity — and the court therefore approves it — the agency will not be "overruling" the court's decision when it later decides that a different interpretation (still within the scope of the ambiguity) is preferable.) By contrast, under this view, the reviewing court will not be holding the agency's authoritative interpretation within the scope of the ambiguity; but will be holding that the agency has not used the "delegation-conferring" procedures, and that the court must therefore *interpret the statute on its own*–but subject to reversal if and when the agency uses the proper procedures.

* * * I know of no case, in the entire history of the federal courts, in which we have allowed a judicial interpretation of a statute to be set aside by an agency — or have allowed a lower court to render an interpretation of a statute subject to correction by an agency. As recently as 1996, we rejected an attempt to do *precisely* that. In *Chapman* v. *United States*, 500 U.S. 453 (1991) [affirming *Marshall v. United States*, excerpted and discussed in Chapter 7, § 3B, we had held that the weight of the blotter paper bearing the lysergic acid diethylamide (LSD) must be counted for purposes of determining whether the quantity crossed the 10-gram threshold of 21 U.S.C. § 841(b)(1)(A)(v) imposing a minimum sentence of 10 years. At that time the United States Sentencing Commission applied a similar approach under the Sentencing Guidelines, but had taken no position regarding the meaning of the statutory provision. The Commission later changed its Guidelines approach, and, according to the petitioner in *Neal* v. *United States*, 516 U.S. 284 (1996), made clear its view that the statute bore that meaning as well. The petitioner argued that we should defer to that new approach. We would have none of it.

> "Were we, for argument's sake, to adopt petitioner's view that the Commission intended the commentary as an interpretation of §§841(b)(1), and that the last sentence of the commentary states the Commission's view that the dose-based method is consistent with the term 'mixture or substance' in the statute, he still would not prevail. The Commission's dose-based method cannot be squared with *Chapman* . . . . In these circumstances, we need not decide what, if any, deference is owed the Commission in order to reject its alleged contrary interpretation. Once we have determined a statute's meaning, we adhere to our ruling under the doctrine of *stare decisis*, and we assess an agency's later interpretation of the statute against that settled law."

There is, in short, no way to avoid the ossification of federal law that today's opinion sets in motion. What a court says is the law after according *Skidmore* deference will be the law forever, beyond the power of the agency to change even through rulemaking.

(4) And finally, the majority's approach compounds the confusion it creates by breathing new life into the anachronism of *Skidmore*, which sets forth a sliding scale of deference owed an agency's interpretation of a statute that is dependent "upon the thoroughness evident in [the agency's] consideration, the validity of its reasoning, its consistency with earlier and later pronouncements, and all those factors which give it power to persuade, if lacking power to control"; in this way, the appropriate measure of deference will be accorded the "body of experience and informed judgment" that such interpretations often embody. Justice Jackson's eloquence notwithstanding, the rule of *Skidmore* deference is an empty truism and a trifling statement of the obvious: A judge should take into account the well-considered views of expert observers.

It was possible to live with the indeterminacy of *Skidmore* deference in earlier times. But in an era when federal statutory law administered by federal agencies is pervasive, and when the ambiguities (intended or unintended) that those statutes contain are innumerable, totality-of-the-circumstances *Skidmore* deference is a recipe for uncertainty, unpredictability, and endless litigation. To condemn a vast body of agency action to that regime (all except rulemaking, formal (and informal?) adjudication, and whatever else might now and then be included within today's intentionally vague formulation of affirmative congressional intent to "delegate") is irresponsible.

[In Part II of his dissenting opinion, Justice Scalia criticized the majority's approach as an important departure from the Court's post-*Chevron* precedents as well as *Chevron* itself. In Part III, Justice Scalia explained why *Chevron*, properly understood, required deference to the Customs Service. "*Chevron* sets forth an across-the-board presumption, which operates as a background rule of law against which Congress legislates: Ambiguity means Congress intended agency discretion. Any resolution of the ambiguity by the administering agency that is authoritative — that represents the official position of the agency — must be accepted by the courts if it is reasonable." Given that precept as his starting point, Justice found nothing in the customs statute to rebut the presumptive discretion Congress gave the Service to draw lines as to tariff categories. In Part IV, Justice Scalia maintained that deference was required by *NationsBank of N. C., N. A.* v. *Variable Annuity Life Ins. Co.,* 513 U. S. 251 (1995), which the Court acknowledged as an instance in which *Chevron* deference is warranted notwithstanding the absence of formal adjudication, notice-and-comment rulemaking, or comparable administrative formality.]

[Justice Scalia ended his opinion with a flourish, first dissenting from the Court's holding, that the case be remanded for the lower court to apply *Skidmore* deference, instead of reversing and remanding for the lower court to affirm the agency's interpretation.] I dissent even more vigorously from the reasoning that produces the Court's judgment, and that makes today's decision one of the most significant opinions ever rendered by the Court dealing with the judicial review of administrative action. Its consequences will be enormous, and almost uniformly bad.

NOTES ON *MEAD* AND RECENT
REPORTS ON THE *"CHEVRON* REVOLUTION"

1. *The Grounding of* Chevron *on the Notion of Delegated Authority to Issue Orders or Rules Having the Force of Law: The Court's Uneven Application.* The Court's decision in *Mead* makes clear that the normative basis for *Chevron*'s deference-plus regime is congressional intent to delegate *lawmaking* authority to agencies. See Thomas Merrill & Kristin Hickman, Chevron's *Domain,* 89 Geo. L.J. 833 (2001).[o] Again over the dissents of Justice Scalia, the Court reaffirmed this understanding in *National Cable & Telecommunications Ass'n v. Brand X Internet Services,* 545 U.S. 967 (2005), and *Gonzales v. Oregon,* 546 U.S. 243 (2006) (excerpted below).

---

o. See also Thomas Merrill, *Rethinking Article I, Section I: From Nondelegation to Exclusive Delegation,* 104 Colum. L. Rev. 2097 (2004).

Although this is the Court's official test, it is one that the post-*Chevron* Court has applied unevenly, at best. On the one hand, the Court does not seem to have a clear idea of when Congress has vested agencies with authority to create rules or orders having the "force of law." Thus, the Court often treats NLRB orders as having the force of law, even though that is clearly incorrect as a technical or historical matter: the NLRA says that the agency's orders would *not* have legal effect unless the agency or a party went to court and obtained an order to that effect. See Thomas Merrill & Kathryn Tongue Watts, *Agency Rules with the Force of Law: The Original Convention*, 116 Harv. L. Rev. 467 (2002). Indeed, the EPA rule in *Chevron* was not, in 1984, a rule having the force of law. *Id.* at 587.

The Court's approach is further complicated in *Mead*, where the Court says that Congress might implicitly delegate lawmaking authority to an agency. See also *Barnhart v. Walton,* 535 U.S. 212 (2002) (providing an even more functional *Skidmore*-like approach to *Chevron* than *Mead*). It is far from clear what kinds of statutory schemes would amount to an "implicit" delegation, and the lower courts have shown evidence of increased confusion since *Mead*.[p]

On the other hand, the Court's deployment of *Chevron* has been underwhelming even in those cases where there has been an explicit grant of lawmaking authority, liberally defined to include statutes that grant formal adjudication authority (e.g., NLRA) or substantive rulemaking authority (e.g., Clean Air Act). The Eskridge and Baer study surveyed 1,104 post-*Chevron* Supreme Court decisions between 1984 and 2006 where an agency statutory interpretation was presented to the Court. In 8.3% of those cases, the Court majority applied the *Chevron* framework, even though almost 27% of those cases involved agency decisions pursuant to explicit grants of formal adjudicatory or legislative (substantive) rulemaking authority. About 10% of the *Chevron* cases involved very informal agency action clearly not derived from lawmaking grants — agency letters, interpretive guidances, and even opinions voiced in *amicus* briefs. Eskridge & Baer, *Deference Continuum*.

The Eskridge and Baer study also found that the Court followed pre-*Chevron* deference-plus (i.e., non-*Skidmore*) regimes in 4.8% of their 1,104 case database. Most of these involved deference to NLRB, IRS, HHS, and FDA interpretations. The conceptual basis for these cases fell somewhere between *Chevron* and *Skidmore*: Congress has vested such-and-such agency with authority to carry out the statutory purpose; to carry out the congressional purpose, the agency needs interpretational breathing room; hence, courts ought to defer to reasonable agency readings of the statute. E.g., *Beth Israel Hospital v. NLRB*, 437 U.S. 483 (1978), applied in *Auciello Iron Works v. NLRB*, 517 U.S. 781 (1996) (NLRB); *National Muffler Dealers v. United States*, 440 U.S.

---

p. E.g., Lisa Schultz Bressman, *How* Mead *Muddled Judicial Review of Agency Action?,* 58 Vand. L. Rev. 1443 (2005); Adrian Vermeule, Mead *in the Trenches*, 71 Geo. Wash. L. Rev. 347 (2003) (*Mead* has created very muddy trenches). See also Eskridge & Baer, *Deference Continuum* (even the Supreme Court seems to have become more inconsistent in its application of the *Mead* approach after *Mead*).

472 (1979), applied in *Cottage Savs. Ass'n v. Commissioner*, 499 U.S. 554 (1991) (IRS).

2. *The Survival — Indeed, Flourishing — of* Skidmore. *Mead* confirmed the survival of *Skidmore* as the default deference regime. The Eskridge and Baer study identified 6.7% of the cases in their database as ones where the Court explicitly applied *Skidmore* deference, almost as many cases where the Court applied *Chevron* during their time period (1984–2006). Moreover, in 17.8% of the cases Eskridge and Baer collected, the Court explicitly relied on or was clearly influenced by an agency rule or *amicus* brief (the format followed by the agency in *Skidmore*), albeit without citation of *Skidmore* or an announcement that the Court was "deferring." Eskridge & Baer, *Deference Continuum*. The authors call this last group of cases *Skidmore*-Lite. Not only has *Skidmore* not been overruled, but it has perhaps been the dominant deference regime within the Supreme Court.

The Eskridge and Baer study confirmed the importance of the *Skidmore* norm, based upon the agency's comparative competence, by analyzing agency win-rates by subject area. The chart below is a small but representative sampling of their findings:

Statutory Subject Matter	Primary Deference Regime/ Secondary Regime	Agency Win Rate
Pensions	No deference/*Skidmore*-Lite	82.5%
Foreign Affairs and National Security	No deference/*Skidmore*	78.5%
Tax	No deference/*Skidmore*	75.7%
Bankruptcy	No deference/*Skidmore*-Lite	75.0%
Entitlements	No deference/*Chevron*	71.9%
Environmental Law	No deference/*Chevron*	68.4%
Civil Rights	No deference/*Skidmore*	61.0%
Indian Law	No deference/*Skidmore*	51.6%

Source: Eskridge & Baer, *Deference Continuum*.

Note that the dominant deference regime for all categories is "no deference."

Even this summary illustrates the authors' argument that the primary mechanism for agency success at the Supreme Court level is neither formal lawmaking delegation nor *Chevron* deference, but statutory subject matter. For statutes that are technical and instrumental to some routine economic or foreign affairs goal, the Court is unlikely to be nearly as knowledgeable as the agency and is likely to find its submissions persuasive. For statutes that involve meaty allocational issues, whether of federal-state relations or group rights or employer-employee relations, the Court will tend to be less agreeable.

A final way that *Skidmore* has persevered is that its contextual factors have proven to be influential even in cases where the agency decision was pursuant to a congressional delegation of lawmaking authority (liberally defined), precisely the cases where *Chevron* is supposed to be the governing approach. Yet in those cases, agency success rates were significantly higher when the agency interpretation had been consistent over time, did not raise thorny constitutional issues, and had generated discernible public or private reliance.

3. *Evidence of Ideological Voting by the Justices in Agency Deference Cases.* In the wake of *Mead*, a number of academic studies found evidence of ideological voting in agency deference cases. For example, consider the Eskridge and Baer study of 1,104 cases in which agency interpretations were in play found the following pattern of voting:

Agreement with Agency Interpretations, by Justice (*Chevron* to *Hamdan*)

Supreme Court Justice (Tenure)	Agreement with Agency Overall	Agreement with Liberal Agency Interpretations	Agreement with Conservative Agency Interpretations
Warren Burger (1969–86)	82.3%	75.9%	87.0%
Byron White (1962–93)	74.0%	71.9%	76.3%
Lewis Powell (1971–87)	72.7%	73.9%	73.0%
Stephen Breyer (1994–)	72.0%	79.5%	64.9%
William Rehnquist (1971–2006)	70.6%	59.4%	79.1%
Ruth Bader Ginsburg (1993–)	69.5%	77.1%	61.9%
Anthony Kennedy (1986–)	69.3%	61.8%	74.0%
David Souter (1990–)	68.7%	75.6%	62.5%
Sandra Day O'Connor (1981–2007)	68.6%	61.5%	73.7%
Harry Blackmun (1970–1993)	65.1%	80.6%	55.3%
Antonin Scalia (1986–)	64.5%	53.8%	71.6%
Clarence Thomas (1991–)	63.1%	46.8%	75.8%
John Paul Stevens (1975–)	60.9%	79.2%	49.6%
Thurgood Marshall (1967–91)	55.6%	84.8%	38.8%
William Brennan (1956–90)	52.6%	81.6%	36.7%

Source: Eskridge & Baer, *Deference Continuum*.

These data reveal a wide variance of judicial willingness to go along with agency interpretations: Warren Burger, Byron White, and Lewis Powell were quite deferential, while William Brennan and Thurgood Marshall went against agency views most of the time. Surprisingly, John Paul Stevens, the author of *Chevron*, is one of the least deferential.

Eskridge and Baer found pretty much the same pattern when they limited their analysis to the *Chevron* cases in their database or to the 267 cases involving agency interpretations pursuant to delegated lawmaking authority. (The Justices had slightly higher deference rates, but the ideological pattern remained the same.) Analyzing only cases following *Chevron* for a shorter time period, Cass Sunstein and Thomas Miles found somewhat more pronounced ideological voting and report that Justice Scalia is far less deferential (59%) than Justices Breyer (89.5%), Ginsburg (86%), Souter (81%), and Stevens (73%). See Thomas J. Miles & Cass R. Sunstein, *Do Judges Make Regulatory Policy? An Empirical Investigation of* Chevron, 73 U. Chi. L. Rev. 823 (2006).

Eskridge and Baer also caution that there may be a selection bias at work, especially during the Clinton Administration, which was a primary focus of the Miles and Sunstein study. Between 1993 and 2001, a Democratic Administration may have had more success getting its liberal positions before the Court than in persuading the Justices that its positions were correct. If the liberal agency decisions were relatively "weaker" on the merits, that would explain the lower deference rates for conservative Justices like Scalia.

B. IMPORTANT *CHEVRON* ISSUES

So long as the Supreme Court sticks with the *Mead* understanding of *Chevron*, the linchpin is whether the agency interpretation is pursuant to a congressional delegation of authority to issue orders or rules having the force of law. The implications of this conceptual basis for *Chevron* are spelled out in Thomas Merrill & Kristin Hickman, Chevron's *Domain*, 89 Geo. L.J. 833 (2001). Consider some of these issues as the Supreme Court has wrestled with them.

1. *Is the Agency Acting Within Its Delegated Authority?*

If the *Chevron* deference-boost rests upon congressional delegation of lawmaking authority, then the Court should make sure that Congress has delegated such authority to the agency in general *and* as applied to the issue in suit. Merrill & Hickman, Chevron's *Domain*, call this Step 0 of *Chevron*. Although written as a Step 1 opinion, *MCI v. AT&T* may be read as an early example of Step 0. Consider the following case, which is clearly Step 0 and illustrates the complexity that Step 0 inquiries might have.

GONZALES v. OREGON
United States Supreme Court, 2006
546 U.S. 243, 126 S.Ct. 904, 163 L.Ed.2d 748

JUSTICE KENNEDY delivered the opinion of the Court.

In 1994, Oregon became the first State to legalize assisted suicide when voters approved a ballot measure enacting the Oregon Death With Dignity Act (ODWDA). ODWDA, which survived a 1997 ballot measure seeking its repeal, exempts from civil or criminal liability state-licensed physicians who, in compliance with the specific safeguards in ODWDA, dispense or prescribe a lethal dose of drugs upon the request of a terminally ill patient.

The drugs Oregon physicians prescribe under ODWDA are regulated under a federal statute, the Controlled Substances Act (CSA or Act). 84 Stat. 1242, as amended, 21 U.S.C. § 801 et seq. The CSA allows these particular drugs to be available only by a written prescription from a registered physician. In the ordinary course the same drugs are prescribed in smaller doses for pain alleviation.

A November 9, 2001 Interpretive Rule issued by the Attorney General addresses the implementation and enforcement of the CSA with respect to ODWDA. It determines that using controlled substances to assist suicide is not a legitimate medical practice and that dispensing or prescribing them for this purpose is unlawful under the CSA. The Interpretive Rule's validity under the CSA is the issue before us.

[I.] We turn first to the text and structure of the CSA. Enacted in 1970 with the main objectives of combating drug abuse and controlling the legitimate and illegitimate traffic in controlled substances, the CSA creates a comprehensive, closed regulatory regime criminalizing the unauthorized manufacture, distribution, dispensing, and possession of substances classified in any of the Act's five schedules. 21 U.S.C. § 841; 21 U.S.C. § 844. The Act places substances in one of five schedules based on their potential for abuse or dependence, their accepted medical use, and their accepted safety for use under medical supervision. Schedule I contains the most severe restrictions on access and use, and Schedule V the least. 21 U.S.C. § 812. Congress classified a host of substances when it enacted the CSA, but the statute permits the Attorney General to add, remove, or reschedule substances. He may do so, however, only after making particular findings, and on scientific and medical matters he is required to accept the findings of the Secretary of Health and Human Services (Secretary). These proceedings must be on the record after an opportunity for comment. See 21 U.S.C. § 811.

The present dispute involves controlled substances listed in Schedule II, substances generally available only pursuant to a written, nonrefillable prescription by a physician. 21 U.S.C. § 829(a). A 1971 regulation promulgated by the Attorney General requires that every prescription for a controlled substance "be issued for a legitimate medical purpose by an individual practitioner acting in the usual course of his professional practice." 21 CFR § 1306.04(a) (2005).

To prevent diversion of controlled substances with medical uses, the CSA regulates the activity of physicians. To issue lawful prescriptions of Schedule II drugs, physicians must "obtain from the Attorney General a registration issued in accordance with the rules and regulations promulgated by him." 21 U.S.C. § 822(a)(2). The Attorney General may deny, suspend, or revoke this registration if, as relevant here, the physician's registration would be "inconsistent with the public interest." § 824(a)(4); § 822(a)(2). When deciding whether a practitioner's registration is in the public interest, the Attorney General "shall" consider:

"(1) The recommendation of the appropriate State licensing board or professional disciplinary authority.

"(2) The applicant's experience in dispensing, or conducting research with respect to controlled substances.

"(3) The applicant's conviction record under Federal or State laws relating to the manufacture, distribution, or dispensing of controlled substances.

"(4) Compliance with applicable State, Federal, or local laws relating to controlled substances.

"(5) Such other conduct which may threaten the public health and safety." § 823(f).

The CSA explicitly contemplates a role for the States in regulating controlled substances, as evidenced by its pre-emption provision.

"No provision of this subchapter shall be construed as indicating an intent on the part of the Congress to occupy the field in which that provision operates . . . to the exclusion of any State law on the same subject matter which would otherwise be within the authority of the State, unless there is a positive conflict between that provision . . . and that State law so that the two cannot consistently stand together." § 903.

[After Oregon voters adopted that state's DWDCA in 1994 and reaffirmed it in a 1997 referendum, several Senators, including John Ashcroft of Missouri, petitioned Attorney General Janet Reno to override the Oregon law through an interpretation of the CSA declaring that use of controlled substances for "assisted suicide" was a federal crime. Reno declined, but when Ashcroft himself became Attorney General, he issued the Directive. The Ninth Circuit rejected his interpretation, and Ashcroft appealed. He argued that his Interpretive Rule was entitled to *Chevron* deference. Because Congress had not directly addressed the issue of "assisted suicide," the Court should defer to his interpretation. (Ashcroft also argued that he was entitled to super-deference because he was interpreting the 1971 regulation.)]

[II. After rejecting Ashcroft's argument for super-deference because he was construing a Department rule, the Court considered his *Chevron* deference argument and posed the *Mead* question: Has Congress delegated lawmaking authority to the Attorney General to preempt this kind of state law?] The Attorney General has rulemaking power to fulfill his duties under the CSA. The specific respects in which he is authorized to make rules, however, instruct us that he is not authorized to make a rule declaring illegitimate a medical standard for care and treatment of patients that is specifically authorized under state law. * * *

The CSA gives the Attorney General limited powers, to be exercised in specific ways. His rulemaking authority under the CSA is described in two provisions: (1) "The Attorney General is authorized to promulgate rules and regulations and to charge reasonable fees relating to the registration and control of the manufacture, distribution, and dispensing of controlled substances and to listed chemicals," 21 U.S.C. § 821; and (2) "The Attorney General may promulgate and enforce any rules, regulations, and procedures which he may deem necessary and appropriate for the efficient execution of his functions under this subchapter," 21 U.S.C. § 871(b). As is evident from these sections, Congress did not delegate to the Attorney General authority to carry out or effect all provisions of the CSA. Rather, he can promulgate rules relating only to "registration" and "control," and "for the efficient execution of his functions" under the statute.

Turning first to the Attorney General's authority to make regulations for the "control" of drugs, this delegation cannot sustain the Interpretive Rule's attempt to define standards of medical practice. Control is a term of art in the CSA. "As used in this subchapter," § 802 — the subchapter that includes § 821 —

> "The term 'control' means to add a drug or other substance, or immediate precursor, to a schedule under part B of this subchapter, whether by transfer from another schedule or otherwise." § 802(5).

To exercise his scheduling power, the Attorney General must follow a detailed set of procedures, including requesting a scientific and medical evaluation from the Secretary. See 21 U.S.C. §§ 811, 812. The statute is also specific as to the manner in which the Attorney General must exercise this authority: "Rules of the Attorney General under this subsection [regarding scheduling] shall be made on the record after opportunity for a hearing pursuant to the rulemaking procedures prescribed by [the Administrative Procedure Act, 5 U.S.C. § 553]." 21 U.S.C. § 811(a). The Interpretive Rule now under consideration does not concern the scheduling of substances and was not issued after the required procedures for rules regarding scheduling, so it cannot fall under the Attorney General's "control" authority. * * *

We turn, next, to the registration provisions of the CSA. Before 1984, the Attorney General was required to register any physician who was authorized by his State. The Attorney General could only deregister a physician who falsified his application, was convicted of a felony relating to controlled substances, or had his state license or registration revoked. The CSA was amended in 1984 to allow the Attorney General to deny registration to an applicant "if he determines that the issuance of such registration would be inconsistent with the public interest." 21 U.S.C. § 823(f). Registration may also be revoked or suspended by the Attorney General on the same grounds. § 824(a)(4). In determining consistency with the public interest, the Attorney General must * * * consider five factors, including: the State's recommendation; compliance with state, federal, and local laws regarding controlled substances; and public health and safety. § 823(f).

The Interpretive Rule cannot be justified under this part of the statute. It does not undertake the five-factor analysis and concerns much more than registration. Nor does the Interpretive Rule on its face purport to be an application of the registration provision in § 823(f). It is, instead, an interpretation of the substantive federal law requirements (under 21 CFR § 1306.04 (2005)) for a valid prescription. It begins by announcing that assisting suicide is not a "legitimate medical purpose" under § 1306.04, and that dispensing controlled substances to assist a suicide violates the CSA. 66 Fed. Reg. 56608 (2001). Violation is a criminal offense, and often a felony, under 21 U.S.C. § 841. The Interpretive Rule thus purports to declare that using controlled substances for physician-assisted suicide is a crime, an authority that goes well beyond the Attorney General's statutory power to register or deregister.

The Attorney General's deregistration power, of course, may carry implications for criminal enforcement because if a physician dispenses a controlled substance after he is deregistered, he violates § 841. The Interpretive Rule works in the opposite direction, however: it declares certain conduct criminal, placing in jeopardy the registration of any physician who engages in that conduct. To the extent the Interpretive Rule concerns registration, it simply states the obvious because one of the five factors the Attorney General must consider in deciding the "public interest" is "[c]ompliance with applicable State, Federal, or local laws relating to controlled substances." 21 U.S.C. § 823(f)(4). The problem with the design of the Interpretive Rule is that it cannot, and does not, explain why the Attorney General has the authority to decide what constitutes an underlying violation of the CSA in the first place. The explanation the Government seems to advance is that the Attorney General's authority to decide whether a physician's actions are inconsistent with the "public interest" provides the basis for the Interpretive Rule.

By this logic, however, the Attorney General claims extraordinary authority. If the Attorney General's argument were correct, his power to deregister necessarily would include the greater power to criminalize even the actions of registered physicians, whenever they engage in conduct he deems illegitimate. This power to criminalize — unlike his power over registration, which must be exercised only after considering five express statutory factors — would be unrestrained. It would be anomalous for Congress to have so painstakingly described the Attorney General's limited authority to deregister a single physician or schedule a single drug, but to have given him, just by implication, authority to declare an entire class of activity outside "the course of professional practice," and therefore a criminal violation of the CSA. * * * See also *Adams Fruit Co. v. Barrett,* 494 U.S. 638, 649–50 (1990) (holding that a delegation of authority to promulgate motor vehicle safety "*standards*" did not include the authority to decide the pre-emptive scope of the federal statute because "[n]o such delegation regarding [the statute's] enforcement provisions is evident in the statute").

The same principle controls here. It is not enough that the terms "public interest," "public health and safety," and "Federal law" are used in the part of the statute over which the Attorney General has authority. The statutory terms "public interest" and "public health" do not call on the Attorney General, or any other Executive official, to make an independent assessment of the meaning of federal law. The Attorney General did not base the Interpretive Rule on an application of the five-factor test generally, or the "public health and safety" factor specifically. Even if he had, it is doubtful the Attorney General could cite the "public interest" or "public health" to deregister a physician simply because he deemed a controversial practice permitted by state law to have an illegitimate medical purpose. * * *

The authority desired by the Government is inconsistent with the design of the statute in other fundamental respects. The Attorney General does not have the sole delegated authority under the CSA. He must instead share it with, and in some respects defer to, the Secretary [of the Department of Health and Human Services], whose functions are likewise delineated and confined by the statute. The CSA allocates decisionmaking powers among statutory actors so that medical judgments, if they are to be decided at the federal level and for the limited objects of the statute, are placed in the hands of the Secretary. In the scheduling context, for example, the Secretary's recommendations on scientific and medical matters bind the Attorney General. The Attorney General cannot control a substance if the Secretary disagrees. 21 U.S.C. § 811(b). See H.R. Rep. No. 91–1444, pt. 1, p. 33 (1970) (the section "is not intended to authorize the Attorney General to undertake or support medical and scientific research [for the purpose of scheduling], which is within the competence of the Department of Health, Education, and Welfare").

In a similar vein the 1970 Act's regulation of medical practice with respect to drug rehabilitation gives the Attorney General a limited role; for it is the Secretary who, after consultation with the Attorney General and national medical groups, "determine[s] the appropriate methods of professional practice in the medical treatment of . . . narcotic addiction." 42 U.S.C. § 290bb-2a; see 21 U.S.C. § 823(g) (2000 ed. and Supp. II) (stating that the Attorney General shall register practitioners who dispense drugs for narcotics treatment when the Secretary has determined the applicant is qualified to treat addicts and the Attorney General has concluded the applicant will comply with record keeping and security regulations); H.R. Rep. No. 93–884, p 6 (1974) ("This section preserves the distinctions found in the [CSA] between the functions of the Attorney General and the Secretary . . . . All decisions of a medical nature are to be made by the Secretary . . . . Law enforcement decisions respecting the security of stocks of narcotics drugs and the maintenance of records on such drugs are to be made by the Attorney General").

Post enactment congressional commentary on the CSA's regulation of medical practice is also at odds with the Attorney General's claimed authority to determine appropriate medical standards. In 1978, in preparation for ratification of the Convention on Psychotropic Substances, Feb. 21, 1971, [1979–1980] 32 U. S. T. 543, T. I. A. S. No. 9725, Congress decided it would implement the United States' compliance through "the framework of the procedures and criteria for classification of substances provided in the" CSA. 21 U.S.C. § 801a (3). It did so to ensure that "nothing in the Convention will interfere with ethical medical practice in this country as determined by [the Secretary] on the basis of a consensus of the views of the American medical and scientific community." *Ibid.*

The structure of the CSA, then, conveys unwillingness to cede medical judgments to an Executive official who lacks medical expertise. In interpreting statutes that divide authority, the Court has recognized: "Because historical familiarity and policymaking expertise account in the first instance for the presumption that Congress delegates interpretive lawmaking power to the agency rather than to the reviewing court, we presume here that Congress intended to invest interpretive power in the administrative actor in the best position to develop these attributes." *Martin v. OSHRC,* 499 U.S. 144, 153 (1991). This presumption works against a conclusion that the Attorney General has authority to make quintessentially medical judgments. * * *

The idea that Congress gave the Attorney General such broad and unusual authority through an implicit delegation in the CSA's registration provision is not sustainable. "Congress, we have held, does not alter the fundamental details of a regulatory scheme in vague terms or ancillary provisions — it does not, one might say, hide elephants in mouseholes." *Whitman v. American Trucking Assns., Inc.,* 531 U.S. 457, 468 (2001); see *FDA v. Brown & Williamson* ("[W]e are confident that Congress could not have intended to delegate a decision of such economic and political significance to an agency in so cryptic a fashion").

The importance of the issue of physician-assisted suicide, which has been the subject of an "earnest and profound debate" across the country, [*Washington v. Glucksberg,* 521 U.S., 702, 735 (1997), which upheld a state prohibition on physician-assisted suicide, in part on the argument that the states should have discretion to decide such issues for themselves], makes the oblique form of the claimed delegation all the more suspect. Under the Government's theory, moreover, the medical judgments the Attorney General could make are not limited to physician-assisted suicide. Were this argument accepted, he could decide whether any particular drug may be used for any particular purpose, or indeed whether a physician who administers any controversial treatment could be deregistered. This would occur, under the Government's view, despite the statute's express limitation of the Attorney General's authority to registration and control, with attendant restrictions on each of those functions, and despite the statutory purposes to combat drug abuse and prevent illicit drug trafficking.

[III. Finding no delegation, and therefore no *Chevron* deference, the Court considered the Attorney General's facts and arguments a la *Skidmore* as it interpreted the CSA to determine whether Congress meant to preempt laws like the ODWDA.] The statute and our case law amply support the conclusion that Congress regulates medical practice insofar as it bars doctors from using their prescription-writing powers as a means to engage in illicit drug dealing and trafficking as conventionally understood. Beyond this, however, the statute manifests no intent to regulate the practice of medicine generally. The silence is understandable given the structure and limitations of federalism, which allow the States " 'great latitude under their police powers to legislate as to the protection of the lives, limbs, health, comfort, and quiet of all persons.' " *Medtronic, Inc. v. Lohr*, 518 U.S. 470, 475 (1996).

* * * [W]e find only one area in which Congress set general, uniform standards of medical practice. Title I of the Comprehensive Drug Abuse Prevention and Control Act of 1970, of which the CSA was Title II, provides that

> "[The Secretary], after consultation with the Attorney General and with national organizations representative of persons with knowledge and experience in the treatment of narcotic addicts, shall determine the appropriate methods of professional practice in the medical treatment of the narcotic addiction of various classes of narcotic addicts, and shall report thereon from time to time to the Congress." § 4, 84 Stat. 1241, codified at 42 U.S.C. § 290bb-2a.

This provision strengthens the understanding of the CSA as a statute combating recreational drug abuse, and also indicates that when Congress wants to regulate medical practice in the given scheme, it does so by explicit language in the statute [and with consultation involving the medical experts in HHS]. * * *

JUSTICE SCALIA, joined by CHIEF JUSTICE ROBERTS and JUSTICE THOMAS, dissenting.

* * * Setting aside the implicit delegation inherent in Congress's use of the undefined term "prescription" in § 829, the Court's reading of "control" in § 821 is manifestly erroneous. The Court urges that "control" is a term defined in part A of the subchapter (entitled "Introductory Provisions") to mean "to add a drug or other substance . . . to a schedule *under part B of this subchapter*," 21 U.S.C. § 802(5) (emphasis added). But § 821 is not included in "part B of this subchapter," which is entitled "Authority to Control; Standards and Schedules," and consists of the sections related to *scheduling*, 21 U.S.C.A. §§ 811–814 (main ed. and Supp. 2005), where the statutory definition is uniquely appropriate. Rather, § 821 is found in *part C* of the subchapter, §§ 821–830, entitled "Registration of Manufacturers, Distributors, and Dispensers of Controlled Substances," which includes all and only the provisions relating to the "manufacture, distribution, and dispensing of controlled substances," § 821. The artificial definition of "control" in § 802(5) has no conceivable application to the use of that word in § 821. Under that definition, "control" must take a *substance* as its direct object, see 21 U.S.C. § 802(5) ("to add a drug or other substance . . . to a schedule") — and that is how "control" is consistently used throughout *part B*. See, *e.g.*, §§ 811(b) ("proceedings . . . to *control* a drug or other substance"), 811(c) ("each drug or other substance proposed to be *controlled* or removed from the schedules"), 811(d)(1) ("If *control* is required . . . the Attorney General shall issue an order *controlling* such drug . . ."), 812(b) ("Except where *control* is required . . . a drug or other substance may not be placed in any schedule . . ."). In § 821, by contrast, the term "control" has as its object, not "a drug or other substance," but rather the *processes* of "manufacture, distribution, and dispensing of

controlled substances." It could not be clearer that the artificial definition of "control" in § 802(5) is inapplicable. It makes no sense to speak of "adding the manufacturing, distribution, and dispensing of substances to a schedule." We do not force term-of-art definitions into contexts where they plainly do not fit and produce nonsense. What is obviously intended in § 821 is the ordinary meaning of "control" — namely, "[t]o exercise restraining or directing influence over; to dominate; regulate; hence, to hold from action; to curb," Webster's Second 580. "Control" is regularly used in this ordinary sense elsewhere in *part C* of the subchapter.

When the word is given its ordinary meaning, the Attorney General's interpretation of the prescription requirement of § 829 plainly "relat[es] to the . . . *control* of the . . . dispensing of controlled substances," 21 U.S.C. § 821 (emphasis added), since a prescription is the chief requirement for "dispensing" such drugs, see § 829. The same meaning is compelled by the fact that § 821 is the first section not of part B of the subchapter, which deals entirely with "control" in the artificial sense, but of part C, every section of which relates to the "registration and control of the manufacture, distribution, and dispensing of controlled substances," § 821. It would be peculiar for the first section of this part to authorize rulemaking for matters covered by the *previous* part. The only sensible interpretation of § 821 is that it gives the Attorney General interpretive authority over the provisions of part C, all of which "relat[e] to the registration and control of the manufacture, distribution, and dispensing of controlled substances." These provisions include *both* the prescription requirement of § 829 and the criteria for registration and deregistration of §§ 823 and 824.

Even if the Directive were entitled to no deference whatever, the most reasonable interpretation of the Regulation and of the statute would produce the same result. Virtually every relevant source of authoritative meaning confirms that the phrase "legitimate medical purpose" does not include intentionally assisting suicide. "Medicine" refers to "[t]he science and art dealing with the prevention, cure, or alleviation of disease." Webster's Second 1527. The use of the word "legitimate" connotes an *objective* standard of "medicine," and our presumption that the CSA creates a uniform federal law regulating the dispensation of controlled substances means that this objective standard must be a federal one. As recounted in detail in the memorandum for the Attorney General that is attached as an appendix to the Directive (OLC Memo), virtually every medical authority from Hippocrates to the current American Medical Association (AMA) confirms that assisting suicide has seldom or never been viewed as a form of "prevention, cure, or alleviation of disease," and (even more so) that assisting suicide is not a "legitimate" branch of that "science and art." Indeed, the AMA has determined that " '[p]hysician-assisted suicide is fundamentally incompatible with the physician's role as a healer.' " *Glucksberg*. "[T]he overwhelming weight of authority in judicial decisions, the past and present policies of nearly all of the States and of the Federal Government, and the clear, firm and unequivocal views of the leading associations within the American medical and nursing professions, establish that assisting in suicide . . . is not a legitimate medical purpose." OLC Memo. See also *Glucksberg* (prohibitions or condemnations of assisted suicide in 50

jurisdictions, including 47 States, the District of Columbia, and 2 Territories).
* * *

Even if the Regulation did not exist and "prescription" in § 829 could not be interpreted to require a "legitimate medical purpose," the Directive's conclusion that "prescribing, dispensing, or administering federally controlled substances . . . by a physician . . . may 'render his registration . . . inconsistent with the public interest' and therefore subject to possible suspension or revocation under 21 U.S.C. [§] 824(a)(4)," 66 Fed. Reg. 56608, would nevertheless be unassailable in this Court.

Sections 823(f) and 824(a) explicitly grant the Attorney General the authority to register and deregister physicians, and his discretion in exercising that authority is spelled out in very broad terms. He may refuse to register or deregister if he determines that registration is "inconsistent with the public interest," 21 U.S.C. § 823(f), after considering five factors, the fifth of which is "[s]uch other conduct which may threaten the public health and safety," § 823(f)(5). As the Court points out, these broad standards were enacted in the 1984 amendments for the specific purpose of *freeing* the Attorney General's discretion over registration from the decisions of state authorities.

The fact that assisted-suicide prescriptions are issued in violation of § 829 is of course sufficient to support the Directive's conclusion that issuing them may be cause for deregistration: such prescriptions would violate the fourth factor of § 823(f), namely "[c]ompliance with applicable . . . Federal . . . laws relating to controlled substances," 21 U.S.C. § 823(f)(4). But the Attorney General did not rely solely on subsection (f)(4) in reaching his conclusion that registration would be "inconsistent with the public interest"; nothing in the text of the Directive indicates that. Subsection (f)(5) ("[s]uch other conduct which may threaten the public health and safety") provides an independent, alternative basis for the Directive's conclusion regarding deregistration — provided that the Attorney General has authority to interpret "public interest" and "public health and safety" in § 823(f) to exclude assisted suicide.

Three considerations make it perfectly clear that the statute confers authority to interpret these phrases upon the Attorney General. First, the Attorney General is solely and explicitly charged with administering the registration and deregistration provisions. See §§ 823(f), 824(a). By making the criteria for such registration and deregistration such obviously ambiguous factors as "public interest" and "public health and safety," Congress implicitly (but clearly) gave the Attorney General authority to interpret those criteria — *whether or not* there is any explicit delegation provision in the statute. "Sometimes the legislative delegation to an agency on a particular question is implicit rather than explicit. In such a case, a court may not substitute its own construction of a statutory provision for a reasonable interpretation made by the administrator of an agency." *Chevron*. The Court's exclusive focus on the *explicit* delegation provisions is, at best, a fossil of our pre-*Chevron* era; at least since *Chevron*, we have not conditioned our deferral to agency interpretations upon the existence of explicit delegation provisions. *Mead* left this principle of implicit delegation intact.

Second, even if explicit delegation were required, Congress provided it in § 821, which authorizes the Attorney General to "promulgate rules and regulations . . . relating to the *registration and control* of the manufacture, distribution, and dispensing of controlled substances . . . ." (Emphasis added.) Because "dispensing" refers to the delivery of a controlled substance "pursuant to the lawful order of a practitioner," 21 U.S.C. § 802(10), the deregistration of such practitioners for writing impermissible orders "relat[es] to the registration . . . of the . . . dispensing" of controlled substances, 21 U.S.C.A. § 821 (Supp. 2005).

Third, § 821 also gives the Attorney General authority to promulgate rules and regulations "relating to the . . . control of the . . . dispensing of controlled substances." As discussed earlier, it is plain that the *ordinary* meaning of "control" must apply to § 821, so that the plain import of the provision is to grant the Attorney General rulemaking authority over all the provisions of part C of the CSA, 21 U.S.C. §§ 821–830. Registering and deregistering the practitioners who issue the prescriptions necessary for lawful dispensation of controlled substances plainly "relat[es] to the . . . control of the . . . dispensing of controlled substances." § 821.

The Attorney General is thus authorized to promulgate regulations interpreting §§ 823(f) and 824(a), both by implicit delegation in § 823(f) and by two grounds of explicit delegation in § 821. The Court nevertheless holds that this triply unambiguous delegation cannot be given full effect because "the design of the statute" evinces the intent to grant the Secretary of Health and Human Services exclusive authority over scientific and medical determinations. This proposition is not remotely plausible. The Court cites as authority for the Secretary's exclusive authority two specific areas in which his medical determinations are said to be binding on the Attorney General — with regard to the "scientific and medical evaluation" of a drug's effects that precedes its scheduling, § 811(b), and with regard to "the appropriate methods of professional practice in the medical treatment of the narcotic addiction of various classes of narcotic addicts," 42 U.S.C. § 290bb-2a. Far from establishing a general principle of Secretary supremacy with regard to all scientific and medical determinations, the fact that Congress granted the Secretary specifically defined authority in the areas of scheduling and addiction treatment, *without otherwise mentioning him* in the registration provisions, suggests, to the contrary, that Congress envisioned *no* role for the Secretary in that area — where, as we have said, interpretive authority was both implicitly and explicitly conferred upon the Attorney General.

Even if we could rewrite statutes to accord with sensible "design," it is far from a certainty that the Secretary, rather than the Attorney General, ought to control the registration of physicians. Though registration decisions sometimes require judgments about the legitimacy of medical practices, the Department of Justice has seemingly had no difficulty making them. But unlike decisions about whether a substance should be scheduled or whether a narcotics addiction treatment is legitimate, registration decisions are not exclusively, or even primarily, concerned with "medical [and] scientific" factors. See 21 U.S.C. § 823(f). Rather, the decision to register, or to bring an action to deregister, an individual *physician* implicates all the policy goals and competing enforcement priorities that attend any exercise of prosecutorial discretion. It is entirely reasonable to think (as Congress evidently did) that it would be easier for the Attorney General occasionally to make judgments about the legitimacy of medical practices than it would be for the Secretary to get into the business of law enforcement. It is, in other words, perfectly consistent with an intelligent "design of the statute" to give the Nation's chief law enforcement official, not its chief health official, broad discretion over the substantive standards that govern registration and deregistration. That is *especially* true where the contested "scientific and medical" judgment at issue has to do with the legitimacy of physician-assisted suicide, which ultimately rests, not on "science" or "medicine," but on a naked value judgment. It no more depends upon a "quintessentially medical judgmen[t]" than does the legitimacy of polygamy or eugenic infanticide. And it requires no particular *medical* training to undertake the objective inquiry into how the continuing traditions of Western medicine have consistently treated this subject. The Secretary's supposedly superior "medical expertise" to make "medical judgments" is strikingly irrelevant to the case at hand.

The Court also reasons that, even if the CSA grants the Attorney General authority to interpret § 823(f), the Directive does not purport to exercise that authority, because it "does not undertake the five-factor analysis" of § 823(f) and does not "on its face purport to be an *application* of the registration provision in § 823(f)." This reasoning is sophistic. It would be improper — indeed, *impossible* — for the Attorney General to "undertake the five-factor analysis" of § 823(f) and to "appl[y] the registration provision" outside the context of an actual enforcement proceeding. But of course the Attorney General may issue regulations to clarify his interpretation of the five factors, and to signal how he will apply them in future enforcement proceedings. That is what the Directive plainly purports to do by citing § 824(a)(4), and that is why the Directive's conclusion on deregistration is couched in conditional terms: "Such conduct by a physician . . . *may* 'render his registration . . . inconsistent with the public interest' and therefore subject to *possible* suspension or revocation under 21 U.S.C. [§]824(a)(4)." 66 Fed. Reg. 56608 (emphasis added).

It follows from what we have said that the Attorney General's authoritative interpretations of "public interest" and "public health and safety" in § 823(f) are subject to *Chevron* deference. As noted earlier, the Court does not contest that the absence of notice-and-comment procedures for the Directive renders *Chevron* inapplicable. And there is no serious argument that "Congress has directly spoken to the precise question at issue," or that the Directive's interpretations of "public health and safety" and "inconsistent with the public interest" are not "permissible." *Chevron.* On the latter point, in fact, the condemnation of assisted suicide by 50 American jurisdictions supports the Attorney General's view. The Attorney General may therefore weigh a physician's participation in assisted suicide as a factor counseling against his registration, or in favor of deregistration, under § 823(f).

In concluding to the contrary, the Court merely presents the conclusory assertion that "it is doubtful the Attorney General could cite the 'public interest' or 'public health' to deregister a physician simply because he deemed a controversial practice permitted by state law to have an illegitimate medical purpose." But why on earth not? — especially when he has interpreted the relevant statutory factors in advance to give fair warning that such a practice is "inconsistent with the public interest." The Attorney General's discretion to determine the public interest in this area is admittedly broad — but certainly no broader than other congressionally conferred Executive powers that we have upheld in the past.

NOTES ON THE OREGON AID-IN-DYING CASE AND DEFERENCE FOR ISSUES OF AGENCY AUTHORITY

1. *The Debate over Textual Authorization for the Attorney General.* The take-no-prisoners debate between Justices Kennedy and Scalia provides an occasion for the student of legislation to practice her or his skills with the statutory interpretation rules and practices covered in Chapter 8. Note especially the skillful combination of dictionary meanings, grammatical analyses, and structural points made in the dissent. Justice Scalia has excellent arguments for the proposition that the Ashcroft Directive is literally within at least one of the CSA delegations, maybe several of them. Such a reading may also fit with the CSA's purpose, which was to create a federal regulatory regime for the dispensation of drugs by doctors. Yet this deft wedding of Reagan Era textualism and New Deal purposivism is not persuasive to Justices Kennedy and O'Connor, Reagan conservatives who are probably not great friends to the death-with-dignity movement. Why are they not persuaded?

Here's one way of understanding why some pretty conservative jurists rejected Justice Scalia's legal arguments. Consider this: Parents A and B retain babysitter C to look after their beloved child while they attend the opera. Their instructions to C: "You are in charge; we delegate you all decisions regarding his care while we are gone." In a tragic twist of fate, the baby has a terrible accident, and C rushes him to the hospital. The hospital asks C who has authority to make decisions about treatment options, risk assessment, and even possible termination of life support. Can C legitimately respond that she is "authorized" to make those decisions? A strict reading of the instructions might suggest "yes," but common sense makes us sure the answer is "no."

This is probably the point of the Court's invocation of the idea that Congress does not hide elephants in mouseholes. Assuming this point, however, why would Justices O'Connor and Kennedy consider the "assisted suicide" rule an "elephant" and not a "mouse"? If the CSA represented a federalization of drug regulation, why isn't the Ashcroft Directive simply the routine agency decision suggested by the dissenters? Does a negative answer to that question rest upon a reservation of a special judicial role for aid-in-dying issues?

2. *Deference to the Agency's View of Its Own Jurisdiction or Delegated Authority?* Justice Scalia has long argued that the Court should defer to agency interpretations of its own authority or jurisdiction. His reason is that there is

"no discernible line between an agency's exceeding its own authority and an agency's exceeding authorized application of its authority." *Mississippi Power & Light v. Mississippi ex rel. Moore*, 487 U.S. 354, 381–82 (1988) (Scalia, J., concurring in the judgment). He does not press this point in *Oregon*, presumably because he believes his plain meaning arguments are unanswerable. Is there a cogent response to this concern?

Although the Supreme Court has not settled the broad question whether *Chevron* applies to expansive agency interpretations of its own authority, the logic of the Court's *Chevron's* jurisprudence suggests the non-deferential approach taken by the *Oregon* majority. Because *Mead* held that *Chevron* rests upon Congress's delegation of lawmaking authority to the agency, courts ought to take care that there actually *has been such a delegation.*[q] Reflecting this logic, there are in fact a number of precedents where the Court has taken a non-deferential approach to agency interpretations of their own jurisdiction; the FDA Tobacco Case is one of them.

By the way, if *Chevron* deference does not apply to the agency's interpretation of its own delegated authority, shouldn't *Skidmore* deference apply to that issue? Would *Skidmore* have made a difference to the *Oregon* Court on the delegation issue?

3. *Deference When Congress Has Delegated Responsibilities to More than One Agency.* The Oregon Aid-in-Dying Case is an example of a growing range of controversies involving several possibly relevant agencies. Recall that one reason the *Gilbert* Court rejected the EEOC's understanding of pregnancy exclusions as being sex discrimination was that another body had reached a different interpretation. In addition to inter-agency *conflict* is the problem of *primacy* among agencies. As Justice Kennedy was in *Oregon*, the Court is usually pretty particular about matching the most apparently authorized agency with an award of deference. E.g., *Martin v. OSHRC*, 499 U.S. 144 (1991), where the Court ruled that in OSHA cases deference was owed to the Department of Labor, which issues substantive rules, rather than the Commission which adjudicates controversies by applying rules to facts.

Sometimes, the Court has been very picky about this matching game. For example, in *Sutton v. United Air Lines, Inc.*, 527 U.S. 471 (1999), the Court interpreted the ADA's definition of "disability" to exclude conditions easily corrected for. (The plaintiffs lost their jobs as airline pilots because they had poor vision; the Court held that this was not a disability, because it could be corrected by eyeglasses. The employer's policy was that corrected vision was still disqualifying. Catch 22.) Although the EEOC had been given rulemaking authority for implementing the jobs title of the Act, which was the basis for

---

q. E.g., Ernest Gellhorn & Paul Verkuil, *Controlling* Chevron-*Based Delegations,* 20 Cardozo L. Rev. 989, 1006–17 (1999); Merrill & Hickman, Chevron's *Domain*; Bressman, *How* Mead *Has Muddled,* 1469–74 (after *Mead,* lower courts have tended to avoid applying *Chevron* deference to issues of agency jurisdiction or authority); Eskridge & Baer, *Deference Continuum,* which found relatively unimpressive agency win rates for issues where the agency was interpreting its own jurisdiction or authority. But see Kevin M. Stack, *The Statutory President,* 90 Iowa L. Rev. 539, 594–95 (2005) (agreeing with the Scalia position).

Sutton's claims, the Court ruled that the EEOC was *not* delegated authority to determine the scope of the ADA's coverage of "disability," which was defined in a different title to the Act (as to which there was no agency with delegated lawmaking authority).

4. *Deference in Matters of Criminal Law.* The *Oregon* majority was troubled that Ashcroft was expansively interpreting a statute imposing serious criminal liability. Recall from Chapter 8 that the rule of lenity theoretically requires anti-deference — presumptive rejection of the agency's interpretation — when a criminal statute is ambiguous. Indeed, Justice Scalia is one of the few Justices who seems to apply the rule of lenity with rigor and even enthusiasm — but not in *Oregon.* Why not? Apparently, Justice Scalia views the notice and nondelegation policies underlying the rule of lenity to be satisfied by an open rule promulgated by the Attorney General pursuant to congressional authorization. Accord, Dan Kahan, *Is* Chevron *Relevant to Federal Criminal Law?*, 110 Harv. L. Rev. 469 (1996) (arguing that criminal law should move in precisely this direction).

Note that *Chevron* might apply in federal criminal sentencing law. Congress has vested the Sentencing Commission with substantive rulemaking authority as regards sentencing, and the Court sometimes gave *Chevron* deference to the Sentencing Guidelines before they were partially nullified. See *Stinson v. United States*, 508 U.S. 36 (1993). Should *Stinson* make us more willing to defer in cases like *Oregon*?

5. *Ideological Voting in* Chevron *Cases.* Recall that commentators are finding that ideology is a better predictor of the Justices' voting patterns in agency deference cases than doctrine. The Oregon Aid-in-Dying Case helps us see how this works. Notice the completely different linguistic as well as normative attitudes in the majority and chief dissenting opinions. Note the majority's repeated citations to *Glucksberg* (the constitutional "right to die" case) and its treatment of aid-in-dying as a matter for serious national debate. These and other bits of textual evidence suggest that the majority understands the matter as a possible privacy right of persons to choose "death with dignity." It is for this *normative* reason that the majority thinks that aid-in-dying is an "elephant" that cannot hide in a normative "mousehole"? Consider, in addition, the federalism argument that Oregon ought to have authority to decide the question of aid in dying without federal intervention.

The dissenters, in contrast, rhetorically agree with Ashcroft that this is "assisted suicide," a half step away from murder. Because the matter has long been settled by religious doctrine, state law, and national policy, this is no "elephant," but is instead a mouse hiding in the mousehole. It is for this *normative* reason that the dissenters believe it outrageous for the majority to treat Oregon's law as a great matter for state experimentation and deviance from settled national policy.

The process by which the Justices are voting their norms more than their dictionaries is, by the way, probably unconscious. In our view, the process by which one's own normative horizon influences one's interpretation of canonical texts is not only unconscious, but inevitable. Social scientists would explain this phenomenon as an example of framing effects and cognitive dissonance: the way an interpreter frames the issue (Can the Attorney General head off murder?) drives her thinking, and indeed she will filter evidence through the lens of this frame. Philosophers would cite this as an example of how interpretation is an activity by which we come to be who we are.

2. *Does the Agency Have Broader Freedom to Interpret Its Own Rules?*

Since the New Deal, the Supreme Court has sometimes given special super-deference to agency interpretations of their own regulations. Such interpretations are "controlling unless plainly erroneous or inconsistent with the regulation." *Bowles v. Seminole Rock & Sand Co.*, 325 U.S. 410, 414 (1945). The *Seminole Rock* rule apparently survives *Chevron*, as illustrated by *Auer v. Robbins*, 519 U.S. 452 (1997). This very issue was the first claim by the Attorney General in the Oregon Aid-in-Dying Case.

GONZALES v. OREGON, 546 U.S. 243 (2006). Under the Controlled Substances Act (CSA), Schedule II substances are generally available only pursuant to a written, nonrefillable prescription by a physician. 21 U.S.C. § 829(a). A 1971 regulation promulgated by the Department of Justice requires that every prescription for a controlled substance "be issued for a legitimate medical purpose by an individual practitioner acting in the usual course of his professional practice." 21 CFR § 1306.04(a). Attorney General Ashcroft presented his Directive preempting the Oregon Death With Dignity Act, as an interpretation of the Department's 1971 regulation and therefore entitled to *Seminole Rock* super-deference.

Justice Kennedy's opinion for the Court rejected this assertion of deference. "*Auer* involved a disputed interpretation of the Fair Labor Standards Act of 1938 as applied to a class of law enforcement officers. Under regulations promulgated by the Secretary of Labor, an exemption from overtime pay depended, in part, on whether the employees met the 'salary basis' test. In this Court the Secretary of Labor filed an *amicus* brief explaining why, in his view, the regulations gave exempt status to the officers. We gave weight to that interpretation, holding that because the applicable test was 'a creature of the Secretary's own regulations, his interpretation of it is, under our jurisprudence, controlling unless plainly erroneous or inconsistent with the regulation.'

"In *Auer*, the underlying regulations gave specificity to a statutory scheme the Secretary was charged with enforcing and reflected the considerable experience and expertise the Department of Labor had acquired over time with respect to the complexities of the Fair Labor Standards Act. Here, on the other hand, the underlying regulation does little more than restate the terms of the statute itself. The language the Interpretive Rule addresses comes from Congress, not the Attorney General, and the near-equivalence of the statute and regulation belies the Government's argument for *Auer* deference. [21 U.S.C. §§ 812(b), 830(b)(3)(A)(ii).]

"* * * Simply put, the existence of a parroting regulation does not change the fact that the question here is not the meaning of the regulation but the meaning of the statute. An agency does not acquire special authority to interpret its own words when, instead of using its expertise and experience to formulate a regulation, it has elected merely to paraphrase the statutory language.

"Furthermore, * * * if there is statutory authority to issue the Interpretive Rule it comes from the 1984 amendments to the CSA that gave the Attorney General authority to register and deregister physicians based on the public interest. The regulation was enacted before those amendments, so the Interpretive Rule cannot be justified as indicative of some intent the Attorney General had in 1971. That the current interpretation runs counter to the 'intent at the time of the regulation's promulgation,' is an additional reason why *Auer* deference is unwarranted. *Thomas Jefferson Univ. v. Shalala*, 512 U.S. 504, 512 (1994)."

In dissent, **Justice Scalia** questioned whether there was any authority creating a "parroting" exception to *Auer*. "Even if there were an antiparroting canon, however, it would have no application here. The Court's description of 21 CFR § 1306.04 as a regulation that merely 'paraphrase[s] the statutory language' is demonstrably false. In relevant part, the Regulation interprets the word 'prescription' as it appears in 21 U.S.C. § 829, which governs the dispensation of controlled substances other than those on Schedule I (which may not be dispensed at all). Entitled '[p]rescriptions,' § 829 requires, with certain exceptions not relevant here, 'the written prescription of a practitioner' (usually a medical doctor) for the dispensation of Schedule II substances (§ 829(a)), 'a written or oral prescription' for substances on Schedules III and IV (§ 829(b)), and no prescription but merely a 'medical purpose' for the dispensation of Schedule V substances (§ 829(c)).

"As used in this section, 'prescription' is susceptible of at least three reasonable interpretations. First, it might mean any oral or written direction of a practitioner for the dispensation of drugs. Second, in light of the requirement of a 'medical purpose' for the dispensation of Schedule V substances, see § 829(c), it might mean a practitioner's oral or written direction for the dispensation of drugs that the practitioner believes to be for a legitimate medical purpose. See Webster's New International Dictionary 1954 (2d ed. 1950) (defining 'prescription' as '[a] written direction for the preparation and use of a *medicine*'); *id.*, at 1527 (defining 'medicine' as '[a]ny substance or preparation used in *treating disease*') (emphases added). Finally, 'prescription' might refer to a practitioner's direction for the dispensation of drugs that serves an *objectively* legitimate medical purpose, regardless of the practitioner's *subjective* judgment about the legitimacy of the anticipated use. See *ibid.*

"The Regulation at issue constricts or clarifies the statute by adopting the last and narrowest of these three possible interpretations of the undefined statutory term: 'A prescription for a controlled substance to be effective must be issued for a legitimate medical purpose . . . .' 21 CFR § 1306.04(a) (2005). * * *

"The Court points out that the Regulation adopts some of the phrasing employed in unrelated sections of the statute. This is irrelevant. A regulation that significantly clarifies the meaning of an otherwise ambiguous statutory provision is not a 'parroting' regulation, *regardless* of the sources that the agency draws upon for the clarification. Moreover, most of the statutory phrases that the Court cites as appearing in the Regulation, see *ibid.* (citing 21 U.S.C. §§ 812(b) ('currently accepted medical use'), 829(c) ('medical purpose'), 802(21) ('in the course of professional practice')), are inapposite because they do *not* 'parrot' the *only* phrase in the Regulation that the Directive purported to construe. None of them includes the key word "legitimate," which gives the most direct support to the Directive's theory that § 829(c) presupposes a uniform federal standard of medical practice.

"Since the Regulation does not run afowl (so to speak) of the Court's newly invented prohibition of 'parroting'; and since the Directive represents the agency's own interpretation of that concededly valid regulation; the only question remaining is whether that interpretation is 'plainly erroneous or inconsistent with the regulation'; otherwise, it is 'controlling.' *Auer*. This is not a difficult question. The Directive is assuredly valid insofar as it interprets 'prescription' to require a medical purpose that is 'legitimate' as a matter of *federal* law — since that is an interpretation of 'prescription' that we ourselves have adopted. *Webb v. United States*, 249 U.S. 96 (1919), was a prosecution under the Harrison Act of a doctor who wrote prescriptions of morphine 'for the purpose of providing the user with morphine sufficient to keep him comfortable by maintaining his customary use.' The dispositive issue in the case was whether such authorizations were 'prescriptions' within the meaning of § 2(b) of the Harrison Act, predecessor to the CSA. We held that 'to call such an order for the use of morphine a physician's prescription would be so plain a perversion of meaning that no discussion of the subject is required.' Like the Directive, this interprets 'prescription' to require medical purpose that is legitimate as a matter of federal law. And the Directive is also assuredly valid insofar as it interprets 'legitimate medical purpose' as a matter of federal law to exclude physician-assisted suicide, because that is not only a permissible but indeed the most natural interpretation of that phrase.' "

NOTE ON AGENCY INTERPRETATIONS OF THEIR OWN REGULATIONS

Although he does not answer the Court's chronology point (the incongruity of the Department's using new 1984 rulemaking authority to "interpret" a 1971 administrative rule), Justice Scalia presents a typically powerful legal analysis in defense of the Attorney General's *Seminole-Auer* argument for deference. Technically speaking, the Attorney General's Directive does seem like an "interpretation" of the 1971 Rule. One might wonder why this legal point was not more persuasive to more Justices. Consider a few observations.

Agency interpretations of its own rules can come in a variety of formats — *amicus* briefs (as in *Auer*), directives or interpretive rules/guidances (as in *Oregon*), opinion letters (SEC and IRS especially), and so forth. Generally, agency interpretations in these formats are entitled to *Skidmore* deference, as in the Oregon Aid-in-Dying Case — but if the agency can relate them somehow to an existing *Chevron*-eligible rule, then it can not only jump

Skidmore, but also jump *Chevron*, all the way to *Seminole-Auer*. This concern with "agency bootstrapping" is probably what worried Justice Kennedy, and it has certainly worried other Justices, e.g., *Thomas Jefferson Univ. Hospital*, 512 U.S. at 525 (Thomas, J., dissenting), and commentators, e.g., John Manning, *Constitutional Structure and Judicial Deference to Agency Interpretations of Agency Rules*, 96 Colum. L. Rev. 612 (1996).

The Eskridge and Baer survey of 1,104 Supreme Court cases between *Chevron* and *Hamdan* identified 155 cases where an agency said it was interpreting its own prior rules — yet the Court applied *Seminole-Auer* super-deference in only 12 of those cases, a surprisingly low number unless the bootstrapping concern is at work. See Eskridge & Baer, *Deference Continuum*. Perhaps *Seminole* is most relevant under the circumstances identified in *Auer*: the regulatory concept in play is one that the agency itself created (pursuant to a valid congressional delegation) and is now interpreting. Otherwise, the Justices are cautious.

3. *Should Courts Defer When the Agency Interpretation Presents Serious Constitutional Difficulties?*

Yet another way to read the Oregon Aid-in-Dying Case is through a constitutional lens. Five Justices (O'Connor, Stevens, Souter, Ginsburg, Breyer), all in the *Oregon* majority, had opined in *Washington v. Glucksberg* that they were open to recognizing a "constitutionally cognizable interest in controlling the circumstances of his or her imminent death," in at least some instances. Without any constitutional nuance or case-by-case reservation, the Ashcroft Directive made aid-in-dying a crime under any and all circumstances. Justice Kennedy's opinion mentioned the "earnest and profound debate" over the constitutionality of state efforts to ban all forms of euthanasia as one reason the Court was reluctant to find a congressional delegation to the Attorney General on this issue. Most and perhaps all of the majority Justices found the Ashcroft Directive constitutionally problematic in the breadth of its intrusion into private decisionmaking and state policymaking. It seems very likely that none of the dissenting Justices had these constitutional problems.

Does the existence of potential constitutional problems make a difference in the Court's overall willingness to defer? What would be the theoretical basis for that? One might presume that Congress does not normally delegate to agencies the authority to press constitutional limits, and so constitutional concerns would show up at Step 0, as in the *Oregon* case. Or one might invoke the avoidance canon in Step 1: when there are two possible meanings of statutory language, the Court should for institutional process reasons follow the one that does not raise constitutional problems. (In that event, the avoidance canon would trump *Chevron*. The Court has in fact gone that route in some *Chevron*-eligible cases. E.g., *Department of Commerce v. U.S. House of Representatives* (Chapter 8, § 1B2).) One can even imagine the constitutional analysis coming in Step 2: an agency interpretation is not "reasonable" if it raises constitutional concerns when a more cautious interpretation would just as easily subserve congressional goals.

Do these arguments lose their cogency when fewer than five Justices flag constitutional problems? Perhaps surprisingly, the Eskridge and Baer study suggests not. They identified 75 cases where at least one Justice flagged a constitutional concern with the agency's interpretation, the agency view prevailed only 45.3 percent of the time, while the agency view won in 70.7 percent of the cases where no Justice raised constitutional concerns. This is the most dramatic differential in their study and strongly suggests that agencies do *not* get nearly as much deference when there are constitutional concerns with their interpretations.

A Problem of Deference When There Are Constitutional Issues

Problem 9–6. In 1970, Congress enacted Title X of the Public Health Service Act, 84 Stat. 1499, 1504, which provides federal funding for family-planning services. The purposes of the Act expressed in section 2 are:

> (1) to assist in making comprehensive voluntary family planning services readily available to all persons desiring such services; * * *

> (5) to develop and make readily available information (including educational materials) on family planning and population growth to all persons desiring such information.

The Act authorizes the provision of federal funds to support the establishment and operation of voluntary family planning projects and empowers the Secretary of Health and Human Services to promulgate regulations imposing conditions on grant recipients to ensure that "grants will be effectively utilized for the purposes for which made."

Section 1 of the Act authorizes the Secretary to "make grants to and enter into contracts with public or nonprofit private entities to assist in the establishment and operation of voluntary family planning projects which shall offer a broad range of acceptable and effective family planning methods and services." Section 1008 provides: "None of the funds appropriated under this Act shall be used in programs where abortion is a method of family planning." According to the conference report for the Act, the section 1008 restriction was to ensure that Title X funds would "be used only to support preventive family planning services, population research, infertility services, and other related medical, informational, and educational opportunities."

The Secretary's 1971 regulations implementing the Act described the kind of services that grant recipients had to provide in order to be eligible for federal funding. Pursuant to section 1008, the regulations stipulated that "the project will not provide abortions as a method of family planning." The 1971 regulations, even as revised in 1986, did not regulate the form of counseling or the distribution of information at federally funded projects.

In 1988, the Secretary promulgated new regulations to clarify the "family planning" services that Title X funds may be used to assist. Section 59.2 of the new regulations limits Title X services to "preconceptual counseling, education, and general reproductive health care (including obstetric or prenatal care)." Section 59.8(a)(1) specifies that henceforth a "Title X project may not provide counseling concerning the use of abortion as a method of family planning or provide referral for abortion as a method of family planning." Section 59.8(a)(2)–(3) makes clear that Title X programs have to refer pregnant women to other services, but doctors in the program cannot "steer" expectant mothers to health care providers who perform abortions. Even if the client specifically requests referral to an abortion provider, the Title X program cannot do so, nor can doctors associated with the program. According to section 59.8(b)(5), the appropriate response is that "the project does not consider abortion an appropriate method of family planning and therefore does not counsel or refer for abortion."

Grantees and doctors immediately challenge the new regulations. What arguments can they invoke against the Secretary's interpretation of section 1008? What arguments should the Secretary make in response? How would the Supreme Court analyze and decide this issue? Compare *Rust v. Sullivan*, 500 U.S. 173 (1991).

PALM BEACH COUNTY CANVASSING BOARD v. HARRIS
Florida Supreme Court, 2000, 772 So.2d 1220
vacated and remanded sub nom. Bush v. Palm Beach Canvassing Bd., 531 U.S. 70 (2000).

[On November 8, 2000, the Florida Division of Elections reported that George W. Bush had received 2,909,135 votes for President in that state, narrowly winning Florida over Albert Gore, Jr., who received 2,907,351 votes. An automatic recount narrowed the gap between the candidates, with Bush still in the lead. On November 9, the Florida Democratic Party Executive Committee requested that manual recounts be conducted in Broward, Palm Beach, and Volusia Counties. The Florida Division of Elections determined, however, in Advisory Opinion DE 00–10, that absent unforeseen circumstances returns from all counties must be received by 5:00 p.m., November 14, 2000, in order to comply with Fla. Stat. § 101.111(1). Based on this advisory opinion, the Florida Secretary of State announced that she would ignore returns submitted after that cut-off time.

[Volusia, joined by Palm Beach, went to court for an injunction barring the Secretary from ignoring returns after that time. The trial court ruled on November 14 that the deadline was mandatory but that the Secretary had discretion to accept amended returns filed after that date. The Secretary announced on November 15 that she would not exercise her discretion to accept amended returns from Volusia and Palm Beach Counties; Gore and the Democratic Party filed suit to compel the Secretary to accept the amended returns. The trial court denied relief, and the Florida Supreme Court accepted an expedited appeal to consider, first, the circumstances authorizing an elections board to require a county-wide manual recount under § 102.166(5) and, second, whether the Secretary could accept the recounts submitted after the passing of the § 101.111(1) deadline.]

[II] Twenty-five years ago, this Court commented that the will of the people, not a hyper-technical reliance upon statutory provisions, should be our guiding principle in election cases:

[T]he real parties in interest here, not in the legal sense but in realistic terms, are the voters. They are possessed of the ultimate interest and it is they whom we must give primary consideration. The contestants have direct interests certainly, but the office they seek is one of high public service and of upmost importance to the people, thus subordinating their interest to that of the people. Ours is a government of, by and for the people. Our federal and state constitutions guarantee the right of the people to take an active part in the process of that government, which for most of our citizens means participation via the election process. *The right to vote is the right to participate; it is also the right to speak, but more importantly the right to be heard.* We must tread carefully on that right or we risk the unnecessary and unjustified muting of the public voice. By refusing to recognize an otherwise valid exercise of the right of a citizen to vote for the sake of sacred, unyielding adherence to statutory scripture, we would in effect nullify that right. *aggressive*

Boardman v. Esteva, 323 So. 2d 259, 263 (Fla. 1975) (emphasis added). We consistently have adhered to the principle that the will of the people is the paramount consideration. Our goal today remains the same as it was a quarter of a century ago, i.e., to reach the result that reflects the will of the voters, whatever that might be. This fundamental principle, and our traditional rules of statutory construction, guide our decision today. * * *

[IV] The first issue this Court must resolve is whether a County Board may conduct a countywide manual recount where it determines there is an error in vote tabulation that could affect the outcome of the election. Here, the Division issued opinion DE 00–13, which construed the language "error in vote tabulation" to exclude the situation where a discrepancy between the original machine return and sample manual recount is due to the manner in which a ballot has been marked or punched.

Florida courts generally will defer to an agency's interpretation of statutes and rules the agency is charged with implementing and enforcing. Florida courts, however, will not defer to an agency's opinion that is contrary to law. We conclude that the Division's advisory opinion regarding vote tabulation is contrary to law because it contravenes the plain meaning of section 102.166(5).

Pursuant to section 102.166(4)(a), a candidate who appears on a ballot, a political committee that supports or opposes an issue that appears on a ballot, or a political party whose candidate's name appeared on the ballot may file a written request with the County Board for a manual recount. This request must be filed with the Board before the Board certifies the election results or within seventy-two hours after the election, whichever occurs later. Upon filing the written request for a manual recount, the canvassing board may authorize a manual recount. The decision whether to conduct a manual recount is vested in the sound discretion of the Board. If the canvassing board decides to authorize the manual recount, the recount must include at least three precincts and at least one percent of the total votes cast for each candidate or issue, with the person who requested the recount choosing the precincts to be recounted. If the manual recount indicates an "error in the vote tabulation which could affect the outcome of the election," the county canvassing board "shall":

(a) Correct the error and recount the remaining precincts with the vote tabulation system;

(b) Request the Department of State to verify the tabulation software; *or*

(c) Manually recount all ballots. § 102.166(5)(a)–(c), Fla. Stat. (2000) (emphasis added).

The issue in dispute here is the meaning of the phrase "error in the vote tabulation" found in section 102.166(5). The Division opines that an "error in the vote tabulation" only means a counting error resulting from incorrect election parameters or an error in the vote tabulating software. We disagree.

The plain language of section 102.166(5) refers to an error in the vote tabulation rather than [in] the vote tabulation system. On its face, the statute does not include any words of limitation; rather, it provides a remedy for any type of mistake made in tabulating ballots. The Legislature has utilized the phrase "vote tabulation system" and "automatic tabulating equipment" in section 102.166 when it intended to refer to the voting system rather than the vote count. Equating "vote tabulation" with "vote tabulation system" obliterates the distinction created in section 102.166 by the Legislature.

Sections 101.5614(5) and (6) also support the proposition that the "error in vote tabulation" encompasses more than a mere determination of whether the vote tabulation system is functioning. Section 101.5614(5) provides that "[n]o vote shall be declared invalid or void if there is a clear indication of the intent of the voter as determined by the canvassing board." Conversely, section 101.5614(6) provides that any vote in which the board cannot discern the intent of the voter must be discarded. Taken together, these sections suggest that "error in the vote tabulation" includes errors in the failure of the voting machinery to read a ballot and not simply errors resulting from the voting machinery.

Moreover, section 102.141(4), which outlines the board's responsibility in the event of a recount, states that the Board "shall examine the counters on the machines or the tabulation of the ballots cast in each precinct in which the office or issue appeared on the ballot and determine whether the returns correctly reflect the votes cast." § 102.141, Fla. Stat. (2000). Therefore, an "error in the vote tabulation" includes a discrepancy between the number of votes determined by a voter tabulation system and the number of voters determined by a manual count of a sampling of precincts pursuant to section 102.166(4).

Although error cannot be completely eliminated in any tabulation of the ballots, our society has not yet gone so far as to place blind faith in machines. In almost all endeavors, including elections, humans routinely correct the errors of machines. For this very reason, Florida law provides a human check on both the malfunction of tabulation equipment and error in failing to accurately count the ballots. Thus, we find that the Division's opinion DE 00-13 regarding the ability of county canvassing boards to authorize a manual recount is contrary to the plain language of the statute.

Having concluded that the county canvassing boards have the authority to order countywide manual recounts, we must now determine whether the Commission [i.e., the Secretary of State, the Director of the Division of Elections, and the Governor] must accept a return after the seven-day deadline set forth in sections 102.111 and 102.112 under the circumstances presented. * * *

[VI] The provisions of the Code are ambiguous in two significant areas. First, the time frame for conducting a manual recount under section 102.166(4) is in conflict with the time frame for submitting county returns under sections 102.111 and 102.112. Second, the mandatory language in section 102.111 conflicts with the permissive language in 102.112.

[A. *The Recount Conflict*] Section 102.166(1) states that "[a]ny candidate for nomination or election, or any elector qualified to vote in the election related to such candidacy, shall have the right to protest the returns of the election as being erroneous by filing with the appropriate canvassing board a sworn written protest." The time period for filing a protest is "prior to the time the canvassing board certifies the results for the office being protested or within 5 days after midnight of the date the election is held, whichever occurs later."

Section 102.166(4)(a), the operative subsection in this case, further provides that, in addition to any protest, "any candidate whose name appeared on the ballot . . . or any political party whose candidates' names appeared on the ballot may file a written request with the county canvassing board for a manual recount" accompanied by the "reason that the manual recount is being requested." Section 102.166(4)(b) further provides that the written request may be made prior to the time the Board certifies the returns or within seventy-two hours after the election, whichever occurs later:

> (4)(a) Any candidate whose name appeared on the ballot, any political committee that supports or opposes an issue which appeared on the ballot, or any political party whose candidates' names appeared on the ballot may file a written request with the county canvassing board for a manual recount. The written request shall contain a statement of the reason the manual recount is being requested.
>
> (b) *Such request must be filed with the canvassing board prior to the time the canvassing board certifies the results for the office being protested or within 72 hours after midnight of the date the election was held, whichever occurs later.* § 102.166, Fla. Stat. (2000) (emphasis added).

[The Board "may" then authorize a recount, including at least three precincts and 1% of the total votes for the protesting candidate. If the manual recount then indicates an error in the vote tabulation which could affect the election, the Board "shall" either "(a) [c]orrect the error and recount the remaining precincts * * * ; (b) [r]equest the Secretary of State to verify the tabulation software; or (c) [m]anually recount all ballots." § 102.166(5).]

Under this scheme, a candidate can request a manual recount at any point prior to certification by the Board and such action can lead to a full recount of all the votes in the county. Although the Code sets no specific deadline by which a manual recount must be completed, logic dictates that the period of time required to complete a full manual recount may be substantial, particularly in a populous county, and may require several days. The protest provision thus conflicts with section 102.111 and 102.112, which state that the Boards "must" submit their returns to the Elections Canvassing Commission by 5:00 p.m. of the seventh day following the election or face penalties. For instance, if a party files a pre-certification protest on the sixth day following the election and requests a manual recount and the initial manual recount indicates that a full countywide recount is necessary, the recount procedure in most cases could not be completed by the deadline in sections 102.111 and 102.112, i.e., by 5:00 p.m. of the seventh day following the election.

[B. *The "Shall" and "May" Conflict*] In addition to the conflict in the above statutes, sections 102.111 and 102.112 contain a dichotomy. Section 102.111, which sets forth general criteria governing the State Canvassing Commission, was enacted in 1951 as part of the Code and provides as follows:

> (1) * * * The Elections Canvassing Commission shall, as soon as the official results are compiled from all counties, certify the returns of the election and determine and declare who has been elected for each office. * * * *If the county returns are not received by the Department of State by 5 p.m. of the seventh day following an election, all missing counties shall be ignored*, and the results shown by the returns on file shall be certified. § 102.111, Fla. Stat. (2000) (emphasis added).

The Legislature in 1989 revised chapter 102 to include section 102.112, which provides that returns not received after a certain date "may" be ignored and that members of the County Board "shall" be fined:

> (1) The county canvassing board or a majority thereof shall file the county returns for the election of a federal or state officer with the Department of State immediately after the certification of the election returns. Returns must be filed by 5 p.m. on the 7th day following the first primary and general election and by 3 p.m. on the 3rd day following the second primary. *If the returns are not received by the department by the time specified, such returns may be ignored* and the results on file at that time may be certified by the department. * * *

> [Subsection (2) sets forth fines against board members "for each day such returns are late," and (3) establishes a procedure for board members to appeal such fines.] § 102.112, Fla. Stat. (2000) (emphasis added).

The above statutes conflict. Whereas section 102.111 is mandatory, section 102.112 is permissive. While it is clear that the Boards must submit returns by 5 p.m. of the seventh day following the election or face penalties, the circumstances under which penalties may be assessed are unclear.

[VII] Legislative intent — as always — is the polestar that guides a court's inquiry into the provisions of the Florida Election Code. Where the language of the code is clear and amenable to a reasonable and logical interpretation, courts are without power to diverge from the intent of the Legislature as expressed in the plain language of the Code. As noted above, however, chapter 102 is unclear concerning both the time limits for submitting the results of a manual recount and the penalties that may be assessed by the Secretary. In light of this ambiguity, the Court must resort to traditional rules of statutory construction in an effort to determine legislative intent.

First, it is well-settled that where two statutory provisions are in conflict, the specific statute controls the general statute. In the present case, whereas section 102.111 in its title and text addresses the general makeup and duties of the Elections Canvassing Commission, the statute only tangentially addresses the penalty for returns filed after the statutory date, noting that such returns "shall" be ignored by the Department. Section 102.112, on the other hand, directly addresses in its title and text both the "deadline" for submitting returns and the "penalties" for submitting returns after a certain date; the statute expressly states that such returns "may" be ignored and that dilatory Board members "shall" be fined. Based on the precision of the title and text, section 102.112 constitutes a specific penalty statute that defines both the deadline for filing returns and the penalties for filing returns thereafter and section 102.111 constitutes a non-specific statute in this regard. The specific statute controls the non-specific statute.

Second, it also is well-settled that when two statutes are in conflict, the more recently enacted statute controls the older statute. In the present case, the provision in section 102.111 stating that the Department "shall" ignore returns was enacted in 1951 as part of the Code. On the other hand, the penalty provision in section 102.112 stating that the Department "may" ignore returns was enacted in 1989 as a revision to chapter 102. The more recently enacted provision may be viewed as the clearest and most recent expression of legislative intent.

Third, a statutory provision will not be construed in such a way that it renders meaningless or absurd any other statutory provision. In the present case, section 102.112 contains a detailed provision authorizing the assessment of fines against members of a dilatory County Canvassing Board. The fines are personal and substantial, i.e., $200 for each day the returns are not received. If, as the Secretary asserts, the Department were required to ignore all returns received after the statutory date, the fine provision would be meaningless. For example, if a Board simply completed its count late and if the returns were going to be ignored in any event, what would be the point in submitting the returns? The Board would simply file no returns and avoid the fines. But, on the other hand, if the returns submitted after the statutory date would not be ignored, the Board would have good reason to submit the returns and accept the fines. The fines thus serve as an alternative penalty and are applicable only if the Department may count the returns.

Fourth, related statutory provisions must be read as a cohesive whole. As stated in *Forsythe v. Longboat Key Beach Erosion Control Dist.*, 604 So. 2d 452, 455 (Fla. 1992), "all parts of a statute must be read together in order to achieve a consistent whole. Where possible, courts must give effect to all statutory provisions and construe related statutory provisions in harmony with another." In this regard we consider the provisions of section 102.166 and 102.168.

Section 102.166 states that a candidate, political committee, or political party may request a manual recount any time before the County Canvassing Board certifies the results to the Department and, if the initial manual recount indicates a significant error, the Board "shall" conduct a countywide manual recount in certain cases. Thus, if a protest is filed on the sixth day following an election and a full manual recount is required, the Board, through no fault of its own, will be unable to submit its returns to the Department by 5:00 p.m. on the seventh day following the election. In such a case, if the mandatory provision in section 102.111 were given effect, the votes of the county would be ignored for the simple reason that the Board was following the dictates of a different section of the Code. The Legislature could not have intended to penalize County Canvassing Boards for following the dictates of the Code.

And finally, when the Legislature enacted the Code in 1951, it envisioned that all votes cast during a particular election, including absentee ballots, would be submitted to the Department at one time and would be treated in a uniform fashion. Section 97.012(1) states that it is the Secretary's responsibility to "[o]btain and maintain uniformity in the application, operation, and interpretation of the election laws." Chapter 101 provides that all votes, including absentee ballots, must be received by the Supervisor no later than 7 p.m. on the day of the election. Section 101.68(2)(d) expressly states that "[t]he votes on absentee ballots shall be included in the total vote of the county." Chapter 102 requires that the Board submit the returns by 5 p.m. on the seventh day following the election.

The Legislature thus envisioned that when returns are submitted to the Department, the returns "shall" embrace all the votes in the county, including absentee ballots. This, of course, is not possible because our state statutory scheme has been superseded by federal law governing overseas voters; overseas ballots must be counted if received no later than ten days following the election (i.e., the ballots do *not* have to be received by 7 p.m. of the day of the election, as provided by state law). In light of the fact that overseas ballots cannot be counted after until the seven day deadline has expired, the mandatory language in section 102.111 has been supplanted by the permissive language of section 102.112.

Further, although county returns must be received by 5 p.m. on the seventh day following an election, the "official results" that are to be compiled in order to certify the returns and declare who has been elected must be construed in pari materia with section 101.5614(8), which specifies that "write-in, absentee *and manually counted results* shall constitute the official return of the election." (Emphasis added).

Under this statutory scheme, the County Canvassing Boards are required to submit their returns to the Department by 5 p.m. of the seventh day following the election. The statutes make no provision for exceptions following a manual recount. If a Board fails to meet the deadline, the Secretary is not required to ignore the county's returns but rather is permitted to ignore the returns within the parameters of this statutory scheme. To determine the circumstances under which the Secretary may lawfully ignore returns filed pursuant to the provisions of section 102.166 for a manual recount, it is necessary to examine the interplay between our statutory and constitutional law at both the state and federal levels.

[VIII] * * * To the extent that the Legislature may enact laws regulating the electoral process, those laws are valid only if they impose no "unreasonable or unnecessary" restraints on the right of suffrage:

> The declaration of rights expressly states that "all political power is inherent in the people." Article I, Section 1, Florida Constitution. The right of the people to select their own officers is their sovereign right, and the rule is against imposing unnecessary and unreasonable [restraints on that right]. . . . *Unreasonable or unnecessary* restraints on the elective process are prohibited.

Treiman v. Malmquist, 342 So. 2d 972, 975 (Fla. 1977) (emphasis added).

Because election laws are intended to facilitate the right of suffrage, such laws must be liberally construed in favor of the citizens' right to vote:

> Generally, the courts, in construing statutes relating to elections, hold that the same should receive a liberal construction in favor of the citizen whose right to vote they tend to restrict and in so doing to prevent disfranchisement of legal voters and the intention of the voters should prevail when counting ballots . . . . It is the intention of the law to obtain an honest expression of the will or desire of the voter.

State ex rel. Carpenter v. Barber, 198 So. 49, 51 (Fla. 1940). Courts must not lose sight of the fundamental purpose of election laws: The laws are intended to facilitate and safeguard the right of each voter to express his or her will in the context of our representative democracy. Technical statutory requirements must not be exalted over the substance of this right.

Based on the foregoing, we conclude that the authority of the Florida Secretary of State to ignore amended returns submitted by a County Canvassing Board may be lawfully exercised only under limited circumstances as we set forth in this opinion. The clear import of the penalty provision of section 102.112 is to deter Boards from engaging in dilatory conduct contrary to statutory authority that results in the late certification of a county's returns. This deterrent purpose is achieved by the fines in section 102.112, which are substantial and personal and are levied on each member of a Board. The alternative penalty, i.e., ignoring the county's returns, punishes not the Board members themselves but rather the county's electors, for it in effect disenfranchises them.

Ignoring the county's returns is a drastic measure and is appropriate only if the returns are submitted to the Department so late that their inclusion will compromise the integrity of the electoral process in either of two ways: (1) by precluding a candidate, elector, or taxpayer from contesting the certification of an election pursuant to section 102.168; or (2) by precluding Florida voters from participating fully in the federal electoral process. In either case, the Secretary must explain to the Board her reason for ignoring the returns and her action must be adequately supported by the law. To disenfranchise electors in an effort to deter Board members, as the Secretary in the present case proposes, is unreasonable, unnecessary, and violates longstanding law. [The Secretary made no such claim in this case.] * * *

Because of the unique circumstances and extraordinary importance of the present case, wherein the Florida Attorney General and the Florida Secretary of State have issued conflicting advisory opinions concerning the propriety of conducting manual recounts, and because of our reluctance to rewrite the Florida Election Code, we conclude that we must invoke the equitable powers of this Court to fashion a remedy that will allow a fair and expeditious resolution of the questions presented here.

Accordingly, in order to allow maximum time for contests pursuant to section 102.168, amended certifications must be filed with the Elections Canvassing Commission by 5 p.m. on Sunday, November 26, 2000 and the Secretary of State and the Elections Canvassing Commission shall accept any such amended certifications received by 5 p.m. on Sunday, November 26, 2000, provided that the office of the Secretary of State, Division of Elections is open in order to allow receipt thereof. If the office is not open for this special purpose on Sunday, November 26, 2000, then any amended certifications shall be accepted until 9 a.m. on Monday, November 27, 2000. The stay order entered on November 17, 2000, by this Court shall remain in effect until the expiration of the time for accepting amended certifications set forth in this opinion. The certificates made and signed by the Elections Canvassing Commission pursuant to section 102.121 shall include the amended returns accepted through the dates set forth in this opinion.

NOTES ON *PALM BEACH CANVASSING BOARD* AND THE ROLE OF CANONS IN JUDICIAL EVALUATION OF AGENCY INTERPRETATIONS

1. *The Subsequent History of* Palm Beach Canvassing Bd. v. Harris. The U.S. Supreme Court unanimously vacated the foregoing opinion, on the ground that the Florida court's interpretation of the statutes may have been influenced by their view of the state constitution. *Bush v. Palm Beach County Canvassing Bd.*, 541 U.S. 1046 (2000) (per curiam). The Court's reasoning was as follows: In normal cases, the Supreme Court would not second-guess a state court in this way. Article II of the U.S. Constitution,[r] however, as well as a federal statute, 3 U.S.C. § 5,[s] vest the state "Legislature," alone, with the

---

r. "Each state shall appoint, in such Manner as the Legislature thereof may direct, a Number of Electors, equal to the whole Number of Senators and Representatives to which the State may be entitled in the Congress * * *." U.S. Const., Art. I, § 1, cl. 2.

s. "If any State shall have provided, by laws enacted prior to the day fixed for the appointment of the electors, for its final determination of any controversy or contest concerning the appointment of all or any of the electors of such State, by judicial or other methods or procedures, and such determination shall have been made at least six days before the time fixed for the meeting of the electors, such determination made pursuant to such law so existing on said day, and made at least six days prior to said time of meeting of the electors, shall be conclusive, and shall govern in the counting of the electoral votes as provided in the Constitution, and as hereinafter regulated, so far as the ascertainment of the electors appointed by such State is concerned." 3 U.S.C. § 5.

authority to determine the procedures by which the state chooses its electors for President. Thus, the Constitution has delegated an important federal role to the state legislature, not to the legislature-cum-court. The state court's only role is to determine what procedures the Legislature has *actually* chosen, not what procedures the state constitution — superseded on this point by federal law — would require the Legislature to choose in state elections. The Supreme Court remanded the case to the state courts. (On remand, the Florida Supreme Court reaffirmed its prior interpretation.) For a discussion of the Article II issue, see Samuel Issacharoff, Pamela Karlan & Richard Pildes, *When Elections Go Bad* (2001).

On November 26, the Florida Elections Canvassing Commission certified the Bush electors for that state. Vice President Gore immediately challenged the certification under the state contest law, Fla. Stat. § 102.168, which allows a contest if there is "[r]eceipt of a number of illegal votes or rejection of a number of legal votes sufficient to change or place in doubt the result of the election." Reversing the trial court in several respects, a divided Florida Supreme Court in *Gore v. Harris*, 772 So.2d 1243 (Dec. 8, 2000), ruled that Miami-Dade and other counties must conduct manual recounts of "under-votes," those ballots the machines did not count but where the intent of the voter might be discerned through examination of "chads" created by a partial punch-through in the ballot and even of "dimples," or indentations not amounting to punch-throughs. The court ruled that the "intent of the voter" was the standard each county must follow. The recounts were to be completed by December 12, the federal safe-harbor date under 3 U.S.C. § 5 (if a state has chosen electors by that date, they cannot be challenged). (A second date, December 18, was also important, because that's when the electors would cast their votes for President.) The recounts began but were stayed by the U.S. Supreme Court on December 9. *Bush v. Gore*, 531 U.S. 1046 (2000). The Supreme Court reversed the second Florida Supreme Court decision on December 12, on the ground that the state recount procedures violated the Equal Protection Clause. *Bush v. Gore*, 531 U.S. 98 (2000) (per curiam). Florida certified its Bush electors, and the next day candidate Gore conceded the election to Governor Bush.

2. *Was the Florida Supreme Court's Statutory Interpretation Beyond the Pale? Should the Court Have Deferred?* A concurring opinion in *Bush v. Gore* maintained that the state court constructions of the state statutes violated Article II on the ground that they rewrote the Legislature's directives. 541 U.S. at 113 (Rehnquist, C.J., joined by Scalia and Thomas, JJ., concurring). The Chief Justice maintained that the state court's interpretation misread the legislature's election-contest law, in its view that a fraction of "undervote" ballots were "legal votes" that needed to be counted and in its remedy of new manual recounts, which threatened Florida's compliance with the safe-harbor December 12 deadline. These were criticisms of the Florida court's December 8 opinion, not its November 21 opinion, but other criticisms applied to the earlier opinion as well. The Chief Justice would have ruled that "[n]o reasonable person would call it [i.e., an undervote, where the voter did not completely punch through] 'an error in the vote tabulation,' " within the meaning of § 102.166(5). (Hint: look up *tabulate* in the dictionary.) The

Chief Justice also criticized the Florida court for failing to defer to the "reasonable interpretation" offered by the administrative official (Secretary of State Katharine Harris, the Bush campaign chief in the state) and insisting instead on its "peculiar one." *Id.* at 537.

The dissenting opinions essentially took the position that the Florida court made a reasonable interpretation of its own state law and, therefore, should receive the deference the Chief reserved for the administrators. *Id.* at 542 (Stevens, J., dissenting); *id.* at 544 (Souter, J., dissenting); *id.* at 546–52 (Ginsburg, J., dissenting). In short, while the Florida justices would have appreciated more deference to their efforts to make sense of the statutory scheme and construct a fair but expeditious recount procedure, the Florida election administrators would have appreciated more deference to their efforts to bring the factious election to a close. Even under the Florida Supreme Court's opinion, the Secretary of State had discretion in receiving late vote tallies because of manual recounts. Why was it that the Secretary was found to have abused her discretion? Was there no room for deference — at least as to that?

The answer in *Palm Beach Canvassing Board* seems to have been, in part, that the Secretary was not giving proper weight to the state constitutional right to vote. The U.S. Supreme Court's first opinion rejected reliance on the state constitution — but the state court could then have relied on the federal constitutional right to vote (Chapter 2). But under federal precedents, it appears doubtful that a decision by a state election board to call a halt to manual recounts in order to meet a statutory deadline would violate anyone's federal right to vote. (It's hard to imagine a different result under the Florida Constitution, but there are fewer precedents to guide prediction.) If that's right, then the interpretive principle seems to have no traction. This recalls the quandary we raised in connection with *Catholic Bishop* in Chapter 8: Should a court go out of its way to avoid a constitutional difficulty if it's clear that both statutory approaches actually are constitutional? So should the state court have deferred to the Secretary in the exercise of her discretion? Recall Justice Breyer's 1986 article, *supra*, which argued for a statute-specific approach to deference. Is there good reason for a court not to defer in matters of voting law?

Another angle, unexamined in the various opinions, is that agency *litigating positions* are not entitled to *Chevron* deference under federal law. See *Bowen v. Georgetown Univ. Hosp.*, 488 U.S. 204 (1988); *United States v. Western Elec. Co.*, 900 F.2d 283, 297 (D.C. Cir. 1990). For example, in the rule of lenity cases, courts do not defer to Department of Justice guidelines for implementing criminal laws, in part because they are developed for purposes of litigation. To the extent that the administrative interpretations in *Palm Beach Canvassing Board* were "litigating positions," they are probably not entitled to deference. But were they litigating positions?

3. *Deference and Canons of Construction.* Deference to administrative interpretations is, among other things, one of the canons of statutory construction. But under the *Chevron* framework, that canon has no application if the statute is otherwise clear. One way to determine whether the statute is clear is

to examine it through the lens of the various canons — precisely as the Florida Supreme Court did (and it found the statute clear, so deference was unwarranted). The debate rehearsed in our note about legislative history after *Chevron* can be understood in this light.

All judges agree that determination of statutory clarity under *Chevron* step one requires consideration of the textual canons or the principles embedded in them. Thus, U.S. Supreme Court Justices have refused to defer to agency interpretations when their Step 1 inquiry has found a statutory plain meaning based on such canonical chestnuts as the rule against surplusage, e.g., *National Credit Union Admin. v. First Nat'l Bank & Trust Co.*, 522 U.S. 479, 500, 502 (1998); noscitur a sociis, e.g., *Sweet Home*, *supra* (Scalia, J., dissenting); inclusio unius, e.g., *City of Chicago*, *supra*; the dictionary rule, e.g., *MCI*, *supra*; and so forth.

The role of substantive canons in the *Chevron* analysis is even murkier. Like the Florida Supreme Court, the U.S. Supreme Court seems to consider such canons highly relevant in determining whether there is a statutory plain meaning that terminates the inquiry with step one. See Elizabeth Garrett, *Legal Scholarship in the Age of Legislation*, 34 Tulsa L.J. 679, 695–96 (1999) (discussing the relationship between substantive canons and textualism). Note the irony, therefore, in the U.S. Supreme Court's first and second decisions reviewing the Florida court. The kind of substantive canon the Florida court invoked in *Palm Beach Canvassing Board* is, according to the U.S. Supreme Court in other cases, a part of the plain meaning inquiry. The message of the earlier U.S. Supreme Court cases is that the interpretive process itself requires a court to consider substantive canons — a message in some tension with the first opinion in the Bush and Gore election mess. Moreover, the concurring Justices in the second Supreme Court opinion (Rehnquist, Scalia, Thomas) are aggressive users of constitutional clear statement rules — yet they faulted the Florida court for a milder invocation of the kinds of rules that they regularly deploy.

NOTE ON DEFERENCE TO AGENCIES IN THE STATE COURTS[t]

Chevron has received a mixed reception in the state courts. The dominant view is probably a posture of weak deference, in which courts give complete deference (akin to *Chevron* step two) to agency interpretations only in limited circumstances, such as where the interpretation is long-standing or the product of the agency's particular expertise. Otherwise, these courts cling to their traditional prerogative to review questions of law de novo, which allows them to substitute their judgment for that of the agency where they believe the agency has incorrectly construed the statute. *See* Eric Lane, *How to Read a Statute*, 28 Hofstra L. Rev. 85, 123–24 (1999). A smaller, but nonetheless significant, number of states have adopted full *Chevron* deference (or something akin to it), while another group goes to the opposite extreme, affording agencies little or no respect on question of statutory construction.

---

t. Brian Willen (Yale Law, Class of 2001) provided the research and first draft for this Note. David Snyder (Boalt Law, Class of 2008) updated it.

See Michael Asimow et al., *State and Federal Administrative Law* § 9.2 (1998).

The majority position is well illustrated by *Connecticut State Medical Society v. Connecticut Board of Examiners in Podiatry*, 546 A.2d 830 (Conn. 1988). There, the state's podiatry board had interpreted the statutory term "foot" to include the ankle. The **Connecticut** Supreme Court overturned this construction, holding that the dictionary definition of the word, rather than the agency's understanding of the legislature's intent, provided the proper resolution of the interpretation question. The court's approach to the *Chevron* issue is interesting and instructive. First, the court describes statutory interpretation as "purely a question of law," which requires less deference to the agency than would normally be shown in judicial review of administrative action. The court then suggests that only when the statute has previously been subjected to judicial scrutiny or to "time-tested agency interpretations" should a court afford the agency's interpretation any "special deference." Here, the court held that because "neither the board nor the courts have previously ruled on the issue presented . . . such deference is not due."

Also representative of this relaxed deference approach are **Michigan**, see *West Bloomfield Hospital. v. Certificate of Need Bd.*, 550 N.W.2d 223, 227 (Mich. 1996) ("The appellate courts, on judicial review, will give the agency's construction such weight as it concludes is appropriate on full consideration of the statutory criteria and the record of the case on review."); **New Jersey**, see *In re Petition For Authorization To Conduct A Referendum On Withdrawal Of North Haledon School Dist. From Passaic County Manchester Regional High School*, 854 A.2d 327 (N.J. 2004) (courts are "in no way bound by the agency's interpretation of a statute or its determination of a strictly legal issue. * * * The judiciary may intervene in those rare circumstances in which an agency action is clearly inconsistent with [the agency's] statutory mission or with other State policy"); *In re Distribution of Liquid Assets*, 168 N.J. 1, 773 A.2d 6 (2001) (citing *Chevron*, but nonetheless concluding that courts are "in no way bound" by agency interpretations and do not sit simply to "rubber stamp" agency determinations); *James v. Board of Trustees of Public Employees' Retirement System*, 753 A.2d 1061, 1066 (N.J. 2000) (suggesting that where an administrative interpretation is not "longstanding and consistent," the courts are within their power to construe the statute on their own by trying to ascertain the intent of the legislature); **New York**, see *Lorillard Tobacco Co. v. Roth*, 786 N.E.2d 7, 10 (2003) ("[A]n agency's interpretation of the statutes it administers must be upheld absent demonstrated irrationality or unreasonableness," but where "the question is one of pure statutory reading and analysis, dependent only on accurate apprehension of legislative intent, there is little basis to rely on any special competence or expertise of the administrative agency"); *Seittelman v. Sabol*, 697 N.E.2d 154, 157 (N.Y. 1998) (holding that though deference is the norm, where "the question is one of pure statutory reading and analysis, dependent only on accurate apprehension of legislative intent," courts need not rely on the agency, and remain "free to ascertain the proper interpretation from the statutory language and legislative intent"); and **Ohio**, see *State ex rel. Celebrezze v. Natl. Lime & Stone Co.*, 627 N.E.2d 538 (Ohio 1994) (substituting a *Chevron*-style rule with a different interpretive canon, a substantive one holding that any uncertainty about the scope of an environmental law should be resolved "in favor of the person or entity (manufacturer or otherwise) affected by the law," regardless of how the agency has construed the statute).

States that have adopted a *Chevron*-like posture include **Colorado**, see *Coffman v. Colorado Common Cause*, 102 P.3d 999 (Colo. 2004) (noting that while agency review "is not binding on this court," agency decisions "will be sustained unless arbitrary or capricious"); *North Colorado Medical Center, Inc. v. Committee on Anticompetitive Conduct*, 914 P.2d 902, 907 (Colo. 1996) (citing *Chevron* for the proposition that the "interpretation of a statute by the agency charged with enforcement of that statute is generally entitled to deference"); *El Paso County Bd. of Equalization v. Craddock*, 850 P.2d 702, 704–05 (Colo. 1993) (observing that while agency constructions of statutes are not binding, courts nonetheless "afford deference to the interpretation given the statute by the officer or agency charged with its administration"); **Florida**, see *Donato v. AT&T*, 767 So.2d 1146, 1153 (Fla. 2000) (adopting a two-step, *Chevron*-style analysis in which courts show great deference to agency construction of statutes of "doubtful meaning," but are not bound by such interpretations where the text is not ambiguous); **Massachusetts**, see *Protective Life Ins. Co. v. Sullivan*, 682 N.E.2d 624, 627–28 (Mass. 1997) (granting "substantial deference" to agency interpretations, so long as not contrary to the "plain language of the statute and its underlying purpose"); and **Pennsylvania**, see *Tool Sales & Service Co. v. Commonwealth*, 637 A.2d 607, 613 (Pa. 1993) (holding that an agency's interpretation is to be afforded deference when it does not clearly contradict the statutory language and that the state courts are not to disregard administrative interpretations unless they are "clearly erroneous"). **West Virginia** has explicitly adopted *Chevron* itself for reviewing interpretations offered by the state's administrative agencies. See *Shroyer v. Harrison County Bd. of Educ.*, 564 S.E.2d 425 (W.Va. 2002) (citing *Chevron* for the proposition that "the court first must ask whether the Legislature has directly spoken to the precise question at issue. If the intention of the Legislature is clear, that is the end of the matter, and the agency's position only can be upheld if it conforms to the Legislature's intent. No deference is due the agency's interpretation at this stage."); *Maikotter v. University of West Virginia Bd. of Trustees*, 527 S.E.2d 802 (W.Va. 1999).

Other states, such as **Washington**, have articulated a formal *Chevron* approach, but have, in practice, departed from a posture of deference. Compare *Waste Management of Seattle, Inc. v. Utilities and Transp. Comm'n*, 869 P.2d 1034, 1038 (Wash. 1994) ("Where an agency is charged with the administration and enforcement of a statute, the agency's interpretation of an ambiguous statute is accorded great weight in determining legislative intent.") and *Sebastian v. Department of Labor and Industries*, 12 P.3d 594 (Wash. 2000) (finding that the text of the statute at issue was ambiguous, but refusing to show deference to the relevant agency construction and instead applying, over a vigorous dissent a different interpretive canon: the rule that coverage provisions of remedial statutes are to be construed broadly, and the limitations on coverage narrowly).

Such backsliding also characterizes the situation in **California**. The state's basic approach is to show substantial deference to administrative agencies. See *People ex rel. Lungren v. Superior Court*, 926 P.2d 1042, 1051 (Cal. 1996) ("Although not necessarily controlling, as where made without the authority of or repugnant to the provisions of a statute, the contemporaneous administrative construction of [an] enactment by those charged with its enforcement is entitled to great weight, and courts generally will not depart from such construction unless it is clearly erroneous or unauthorized."). However, in certain circumstances, the courts have has departed significantly from the *Chevron* principle. E.g., *Henning v. Industrial Welfare Comm'n*, 762 P.2d. 442, 451 (Cal. 1988) (holding that while "in the abstract, a current administrative interpretation would ordinarily be entitled to great weight," a non-contemporaneous interpretation that "flatly contradicts the position which the agency had enunciated at an earlier date, closer to the enactment of the statute" cannot command significant deference). In *Henning*, Justice Broussard, concurring, went even further, arguing that because statutory interpretation is an act of judicial power, once the court has endorsed "a particular interpretation of a statute, an administrative agency lacks authority to interpret the statute differently." *Id.* at 455. In a more recent case, *City of Long Beach v. Department of Industrial Relations*, 102 P.3d 904, 910 (Cal. 2004), the California Supreme Court reaffirmed the court's role as the ultimate arbiter of statutory interpretation, despite the court's commitment in *Lungren* to agency deference: "[A]lthough we give the Department's interpretation great weight * * * this court bears the ultimate responsibility for construing the statute."

An example of a no-deference state is **Delaware**, which has explicitly declined to adopt *Chevron*. See *Public Water Supply Co. v. DiPasquale*, 735 A.2d 378, 382–83 (Del. 1999) ("A reviewing court may accord due weight, but not defer, to an agency interpretation of a statute administered by it. A reviewing court will not defer to such an interpretation as correct merely because it is rational or not clearly erroneous.")

4. *Does Agency Deference Apply to Issues of Preemption?*

The Supremacy Clause of Article VI requires that federal statutes be the supreme law of the land and that state courts enforce them rather than state law when they are inconsistent, or "preempted." There are three different circumstances when state law, such as the Oregon Death With Dignity Act, is preempted by federal law. First, a valid federal statute can stipulate that it preempts state law, and the Court will follow that statutory directive (unless there is a constitutional problem). E.g., *Shaw v. Delta Airlines*, 463 U.S. 85 (1983). Of course, Congress can also write a "non-preemption," *saving clause* into legislation, which will direct courts not to find preemptive force to the legislation.

Second, a federal statute will preempt state law whose operation is inconsistent with that of the federal statutory scheme. This applies not only "where compliance with both federal and state regulations is a physical impossibility," *Florida Lime & Avocado Growers, Inc. v. Paul*, 373 U.S. 132, 142–43 (1963), but also where the state law "stands as an obstacle to the accomplishment and execution of the full purposes and objectives of Congress." *Hines v. Davidowitz*, 312 U.S. 52, 67 (1967).

Third is "field" preemption. "The scheme of federal regulations may be so pervasive as to make reasonable the inference that Congress left no room for the States to supplement it. Or the Act of Congress may touch a field in which the federal interest is so dominant that the federal system will be assumed to preclude enforcement of state laws of the same subject." *Rice v. Santa Fe Elevator Corp.*, 331 U.S. 218, 230 (1947). Areas such as immigration, naturalization, and regulation of noncitizens are examples of fields where federal legislation is likely to be preemptive. E.g., *Toll v. Moreno*, 458 U.S. 1 (1982).

Assume you have a federal statute, such as the Motor Vehicle Safety Act explored in this chapter, which delegates lawmaking and other authority to an agency such as the NHTSA. The agency might have important input in a court's determination of the scope of federal preemption. First, Congress might give the agency direct authority to preempt state law through notice-and-comment rulemaking. Such rules would clearly be subject to *Chevron* deference. Second, Congress might delegate to the agency the authority to adopt substantive rules which could then be the basis for federal preemption the same as explicit statutory rules would. The validity of such rules would be evaluated under *Chevron*, but the agency's understanding of their preemptive force would probably entail only *Skidmore* deference. Third, the agency might, on its own, present its views, usually through interpretive guidances or an *amicus* briefs. What level of deference should that entail?

As you ponder that question, recall that the Supreme Court has recognized a substantive canon that is relevant: "The historic police powers of the States [are] not to be superseded by . . . Federal Act unless that [is] the clear and manifest purpose of Congress." *Cipollone v. Liggett Group, Inc.*, 505 U.S. 504, 516 (1992) (Stevens, J.). How does this canon relate to the three different kinds of preemption *and* to the three kinds of agency inputs? Consider the following case.

GEIER v. HONDA MOTOR CO.
United States Supreme Court, 2000
529 U.S. 861, 120 S.Ct. 1913, 146 L.Ed.2d 914

JUSTICE BREYER delivered the opinion of the Court.

[In 1992, petitioner Alexis Geier, driving a 1987 Honda Accord, collided with a tree and was seriously injured. The car was equipped with manual shoulder and lap belts which Geier had buckled up at the time. The car was not equipped with airbags or other passive restraint devices. Geier and her parents, also petitioners, sued the car's manufacturer, American Honda under District of Columbia tort law. They claimed that American Honda had designed its car negligently and defectively because it lacked a driver's side airbag. The District Court dismissed the lawsuit on grounds of preemption: Because Geier's lawsuit sought to establish a stricter safety standard (an airbag requirement) than FMVSS 208 (which permits choice between airbags and passive restraints), the asserted tort claim was pre-empted by a provision of the

Safety Act of 1966 which pre-empts "any safety standard" that is not identical to a federal safety standard applicable to the same aspect of performance, 15 U.S.C. § 1392(d). Disagreeing, the Supreme Court held that the pre-emption provision was inapplicable because of a saving provision, which says that "compliance with" a federal safety standard "does not exempt any person from any liability under common law." 15 U.S.C. § 1397(k). The saving clause assumes that there are some significant number of common-law liability cases to save.]

[III] We have just said that the saving clause *at least* removes tort actions from the scope of the express pre-emption clause. Does it do more? In particular, does it foreclose or limit the operation of ordinary pre-emption principles insofar as those principles instruct us to read statutes as pre-empting state laws (including common-law rules) that "actually conflict" with the statute or federal standards promulgated thereunder? Petitioners concede, as they must in light of *Freightliner Corp. v. Myrick,* 514 U.S. 280 (1995), that the pre-emption provision, by itself, does not foreclose (through negative implication) "any possibility of implied [conflict] pre-emption." But they argue that the saving clause has that very effect. * * *

Nothing in the language of the saving clause suggests an intent to save state-law tort actions that conflict with federal regulations. The words "compliance" and "does not exempt" sound as if they simply bar a special kind of defense, namely, a defense that compliance with a federal standard automatically exempts a defendant from state law, whether the Federal Government meant that standard to be an absolute requirement or only a minimum one. See Restatement (Third) of Torts: Products Liability § 4(b), Comment *e* (1997) (distinguishing between state-law compliance defense and a federal claim of pre-emption). It is difficult to understand why Congress would have insisted on a compliance-with-federal-regulation precondition to the provision's applicability had it wished the Act to "save" all state-law tort actions, regardless of their potential threat to the objectives of federal safety standards promulgated under that Act. Nor does our interpretation conflict with the purpose of the saving provision, say by rendering it ineffectual. As we have previously explained, the saving provision still makes clear that the express pre-emption provision does not of its own force pre-empt common-law tort actions. And it thereby preserves those actions that seek to establish greater safety than the minimum safety achieved by a federal regulation intended to provide a floor.

Moreover, this Court has repeatedly "declined to give broad effect to saving clauses where doing so would upset the careful regulatory scheme established by federal law." *United States* v. *Locke,* 529 U.S. 89 (2000). We find this concern applicable in the present case. And we conclude that the saving clause foresees — it does not foreclose — the possibility that a federal safety standard will pre-empt a state common-law tort action with which it conflicts. We do not understand the dissent to disagree, for it acknowledges that ordinary pre-emption principles apply, at least sometimes. * * *

Why, in any event, would Congress not have wanted ordinary pre-emption principles to apply where an actual conflict with a federal objective is at stake?

Some such principle is needed. In its absence, state law could impose legal duties that would conflict directly with federal regulatory mandates, say, by premising liability upon the presence of the very windshield retention requirements that federal law requires. Insofar as petitioners' argument would permit common-law actions that "actually conflict" with federal regulations, it would take from those who would enforce a federal law the very ability to achieve the law's congressionally mandated objectives that the Constitution, through the operation of ordinary pre-emption principles, seeks to protect. To the extent that such an interpretation of the saving provision reads into a particular federal law toleration of a conflict that those principles would otherwise forbid, it permits that law to defeat its own objectives, or potentially, as the Court has put it before, to " 'destroy itself.' " We do not claim that Congress lacks the constitutional power to write a statute that mandates such a complex type of state/federal relationship. But there is no reason to believe Congress has done so here. * * *

[IV] The basic question, then, is whether a common-law "no airbag" action like the one before us actually conflicts with FMVSS 208. We hold that it does.

In petitioners' and the dissent's view, FMVSS 208 sets a minimum airbag standard. As far as FMVSS 208 is concerned, the more airbags, and the sooner, the better. But that was not the Secretary's view. DOT's comments, which accompanied the promulgation of FMVSS 208, make clear that the standard deliberately provided the manufacturer with a range of choices among different passive restraint devices. Those choices would bring about a mix of different devices introduced gradually over time; and FMVSS 208 would thereby lower costs, overcome technical safety problems, encourage technological development, and win widespread consumer acceptance — all of which would promote FMVSS 208's safety objectives. See generally 49 Fed. Reg. 28962 (1984).

[Justice Breyer surveyed the history of rule 208, already explicated in this chapter.] Read in light of this history, DOT's own contemporaneous explanation of FMVSS 208 makes clear that the 1984 version of FMVSS 208 reflected the following significant considerations. First, buckled up seatbelts are a vital ingredient of automobile safety. Second, despite the enormous and unnecessary risks that a passenger runs by not buckling up manual lap and shoulder belts, more than 80% of front seat passengers would leave their manual seatbelts unbuckled. Third, airbags could make up for the dangers caused by unbuckled manual belts, but they could not make up for them entirely.

Fourth, passive restraint systems had their own disadvantages, for example, the dangers associated with, intrusiveness of, and corresponding public dislike for, nondetachable automatic belts. Fifth, airbags brought with them their own special risks to safety, such as the risk of danger to out-of-position occupants (usually children) in small cars.

Sixth, airbags were expected to be significantly more expensive than other passive restraint devices, raising the average cost of a vehicle price $320 for full frontal airbags over the cost of a car with manual lap and shoulder seatbelts (and potentially much more if production volumes were low). And the agency worried that the high replacement cost — estimated to be $800 — could lead car owners to refuse to replace them after deployment. Seventh, the public, for reasons of cost, fear, or physical intrusiveness, might resist installation or use of any of the then-available passive restraint devices — a particular concern with respect to airbags.

FMVSS 208 reflected these considerations in several ways. Most importantly, that standard deliberately sought variety — a mix of several different passive restraint systems. It did so by setting a performance requirement for passive restraint devices and allowing manufacturers to choose among different passive restraint mechanisms, such as airbags, automatic belts, or other passive restraint technologies to satisfy that requirement. And DOT explained why FMVSS 208 sought the mix of devices that it expected its performance standard to produce. DOT wrote that it had *rejected* a proposed FMVSS 208 "all airbag" standard because of safety concerns (perceived or real) associated with airbags, which concerns threatened a "backlash" more easily overcome "if airbags" were "not the only way of complying." It added that a mix of devices would help develop data on comparative effectiveness, would allow the industry time to overcome the safety problems and the high production costs associated with airbags, and would facilitate the development of alternative, cheaper, and safer passive restraint systems. And it would thereby build public confidence necessary to avoid another interlock-type fiasco.

The 1984 FMVSS 208 standard also deliberately sought a *gradual* phase-in of passive restraints. It required the manufacturers to equip only 10% of their car fleet manufactured after September 1, 1986, with passive restraints. It then increased the percentage in three annual stages, up to 100% of the new car fleet for cars manufactured after September 1, 1989. And it explained that the phased-in requirement would allow more time for manufacturers to develop airbags or other, better, safer passive restraint systems. It would help develop information about the comparative effectiveness of different systems, would lead to a mix in which airbags and other nonseatbelt passive restraint systems played a more prominent role than would otherwise result, and would promote public acceptance. * * *

In effect, petitioners' tort action depends upon its claim that manufacturers had a duty to install an airbag when they manufactured the 1987 Honda Accord. Such a state law — *i.e.*, a rule of state tort law imposing such a duty — by its terms would have required manufacturers of all similar cars to install airbags rather than other passive restraint systems, such as automatic belts or passive interiors. It thereby would have presented an obstacle to the variety and mix of devices that the federal regulation sought. It would have required all manufacturers to have installed airbags in respect to the entire District-of-Columbia-related portion of their 1987 new car fleet, even though FMVSS 208 at that time required only that 10% of a manufacturer's nationwide fleet be equipped with any passive restraint device at all. It thereby also would have stood as an obstacle to the gradual passive restraint phase-in that the federal regulation deliberately imposed. In addition, it could have made less likely the adoption of a state mandatory buckle-up law. Because the rule of law for which petitioners contend would have stood "as an obstacle to the accomplishment and execution of" the important means-related federal objectives that we have just discussed, it is pre-empted. * * *

One final point: We place some weight upon DOT's interpretation of FMVSS 208's objectives and its conclusion, as set forth in the Government's brief, that a tort suit such as this one would " 'stand as an obstacle to the accomplishment and execution' " of those objectives. Brief for United States as *Amicus Curiae* 25–26 (quoting *Hines v. Davidowitz*, 312 U.S. 52, 67 (1941)). Congress has delegated to DOT authority to implement the statute; the subject matter is technical; and the relevant history and background are complex and extensive. The agency is likely to have a thorough understanding of its own regulation and its objectives and is "uniquely qualified" to comprehend the likely impact of state requirements. And DOT has explained FMVSS 208's objectives, and the interference that "no airbag" suits pose thereto, consistently over time. In these circumstances, the agency's own views should make a difference. * * *

[We omit the dissenting opinion of JUSTICE STEVENS, joined by JUSTICES SOUTER, THOMAS, and GINSBURG. Most of the dissenters' arguments are mentioned in the notes following the decision.]

NOTES ON *GEIER* AND FEDERAL PREEMPTION OF STATE LAW

1. *The Debate Among the Justices.* Key to Justice Breyer's opinion is the Court's belief that allowing state courts to find that airbags are sometimes required to satisfy the manufacturer's duty of care would undermine the federal statute's compromise, whereby manufacturers would have choices. Justice Stevens's dissent objected that case-by-case adjudications would not establish a hard-and-fast rule that airbags were required; not only could different juries reach different results, but manufacturers could win all the cases if they showed airbags to be ineffective or other methods just as effective.

The dissenters also argued that the Court ignored the *Cipollone* presumption and was too willing to preempt the state tort suit. Was it clear that preemption was required by the "clear and manifest purpose of Congress"? Justice Stevens also insisted that the majority's holding was in tension with the saving clause: "The saving clause in the Safety Act unambiguously expresses a decision by Congress that compliance with a federal safety standard does not exempt a manufacturer from *any* common-law liability. In light of this reference to common-law liability in the saving clause, Congress surely would have included a similar reference in § 1392(d) if it had intended to pre-empt such liability. Cf.. *Chicago v. Environmental Defense Fund,* 511 U.S. 328, 338 (1994) (noting presumption that Congress acts intentionally when it includes particular language in one section of a statute but omits it in another)." Should the Court be especially chary of preempting state common law under "inconsistent application" preemption when there is a saving clause?

Note, finally, that state law is essentially preempted by an agency rule and not by a statutory provision. Although the agency had authority to issue the rule, see *State Farm*, the Court ought to think twice before giving the rule preemptive authority to displace state law, especially in light of the federalism presumption of *Cipollone*. Note, too, the possible relevance of Justice Stevens' opinion in *Mow Sun Wong* (Chapter 4, § 1): The Court should not allow agency opinions to venture too far into constitutionally murky territory and should, essentially, remand the issue for Congress, not just the agency, to make such constitutionally sensitive policy choices. Should this argument have had some weight in *Geier*?

2. *Titanic Concerns: Under-enforcement versus Over-enforcement of Safety Norms?* Addressing this issue, Ralph Nader and Joe Page had argued in *Automobile-Design Liability and Compliance with Federal Standards*, 64 Geo. Wash. L. Rev. 415, 419 (1996), that the statutory minimum should not preclude state regulation that raised the floor. Apart from the saving clause, which seemed to embody this philosophy, Nader and Page invoked the *Titanic* precedent. That famous vessel had fully "complied with British governmental regulations setting minimum requirements for lifeboats when it left port on its final, fateful voyage with boats capable of carrying only about [half] of the people on board," W. Wade, The *Titanic*: End of a Dream 68 (1986), yet one might reasonably conclude that the *Titanic* had not satisfied its duty of care to the other half of the passengers who lost their lives when the ship sunk in ice-cold waters. Because people's lives are at stake just as much in auto safety regulation, Nader and Page maintained that states ought to be able to raise the floor. The dissenting Justices agreed and cited their article and its *Titanic* analogy. Their position was that the majority was standing in the way of permissible enforcement of the safety norm. The Court may have even been seen as pandering to the auto industry's determination to *underenforce* safety norms.

The majority did not respond but might have said that the regulatory scheme sought a balance of safety and cost. To be blunt, NHTSA was willing to trade off human lives (more people would die in accidents each year) for cost savings by manufacturers. This may seem terrible, but don't forget that the nation's decision to allow automobiles on the road and to travel 65 miles per hour has predictable costs in human lives each year — lives that could be saved if all of us suffered the inconvenience of not being able to drive (or drive so fast) on the open road. The majority's view was that Congress had authorized the agency to make these kinds of trade-offs (recall Justice White's opinion in *State Farm*, not to mention Justice Stevens's opinion in *Chevron*). Hence, the dissenters' position would have *overenforced* safety norms.

3. *Should the Court Defer to the Agency in Preemption Cases?* How should *Chevron/Skidmore* interact with *Cipollone* in these cases? Justice Thomas has reconciled the different authorities with the suggestion that the Court should be *less* deferential if the federal agency is pushing for preemption and *more* deferential when the agency is arguing against preemption, especially in conflict or field preemption cases. *Pharmacological Res. & Mfrs. v. Walsh*, 538 U.S. 644, 675–83 (2003) (Thomas, J., concurring in the judgment). This

is consistent with his dissenting vote in *Geier*, but not his dissenting vote in the Oregon Aid-in-Dying Case. And, of course, the *Geier* majority gives significant credit to the Department's views.

Nina Mendelson, Chevron *and Preemption*, 102 Mich. L. Rev. 737 (2004), argues against *Chevron* deference for agency views regarding preemption. Although she demonstrates that agencies are more accountable to state interests than the Court or (surprisingly) Congress, she cautions against *Chevron* deference because courts continue to have some comparative advantages in evaluating preemption claims and because agencies will often tend to expand their own authority at the expense of the states. Mendelson believes that agencies often have useful contributions and so favors *Skidmore* deference as appropriate — the same accommodation reached by Justice Breyer in *Geier* and Justice Kennedy in *Oregon*.

5. *Deference and* Stare Decisis

In *National Cable & Telecommunications Ass'n v. Brand X Internet Servs.*, 545 U.S. 967 (2005), the Supreme Court *Chevron*-deferred to FCC interpretations even though they went against lower court constructions of the statute. *Brand X* confirmed the longstanding view that agencies can refuse to acquiesce in lower court interpretations and can continue to litigate statutory issues. But what if the Supreme Court has construed the statute? Under what circumstances should the Court *Chevron*-defer in the face of contrary Supreme Court precedent?

NEAL v. UNITED STATES, 516 U.S. 284 (1996). In *Chapman v. United States*, 500 U.S. 493 (1991), the Court had interpreted 18 U.S.C. § 841(b)(1)(A)(v)'s mandatory minimum sentence for LSD to include blotter paper in determining weight of the substance possessed by the defendant. (*Chapman* affirmed the Seventh Circuit's judgment in *Marshall*, Chapter 7.) In 1991, the Sentencing Commission also considered the blotter paper in determining the base sentence for defendants convicted of LSD possession. The Commission reversed that position in 1993, retroactively amending its Guidelines to assign a smaller weight for each LSD dose.

Having been convicted for selling 11,456 doses of LSD on blotter paper, Meirl Neal moved to reduce his sentence, not only under the Guidelines, but also beneath the ten-year mandatory minimum of § 841. He argued that the Court should reconsider *Chapman* in light of the Commission's revision of the Guidelines. Writing for a unanimous Court, **Justice Kennedy** rejected Neal's argument.

To begin with, Justice Kennedy found that the Commission's Guideline was only intended to affect the base sentence level, and not the 1986 statute fixing mandatory minimum sentences for drug offenses. (Indeed, the Guidelines recognize the distinct regulatory goals, as well as the tensions, of the two sentencing regimes.) This was a tacit acknowledgment by the Commission that it has no authority to override the 1986 statute, as authoritatively construed by the Supreme Court.

"Once we have determined a statute's meaning, we adhere to our ruling under the doctrine of *stare decisis*, and we assess an agency's later interpretation of the statute against that settled law." The Court will overrule precedents when (1) there is "compelling evidence bearing on Congress's original intent"; (2) new legal developments have weakened the "conceptual underpinnings" of the prior decisions; or (3) the prior decisions are irreconcilable with "competing legal doctrines or policies." E.g., *Patterson v. McLean Credit Union*, 491 U.S. 164, 173 (1989). But the new Guideline did not create such a compelling case, and the Court held firm to *stare decisis*. "Congress, not this Court, has the responsibility for revising its statutes. Were we to alter our statutory interpretations from case to case, Congress would have less reason to exercise its responsibility to correct statutes that are thought to be unwise or unfair."

Justice Kennedy concluded with a reservation. Hypothetical situations involving very heavy carriers and very little LSD (such as one dose in a glass of juice) could present due process problems that the routine case would not. In light of the earlier materials, how should the Court handle such cases? Should it strike down the statute as applied, or construe it narrowly?

NOTE ON *CHEVRON* AND *STARE DECISIS*:
THE CASE OF THE OVER-REGULATED WETLANDS

An issue not settled in *Neal* is whether a Supreme Court decision, such as *Chevron* itself, deferring to an agency interpretation within the zone of reasonableness left by the statute, then bars the agency from changing its interpretation. The reasoning of *Chevron* suggests not: "An initial agency interpretation is not carved in stone. On the contrary, the agency, to engage in informal rulemaking, must consider varying interpretations and the wisdom of its policy on a continuing basis." 467 U.S. at 863–64.

Periodically, the Court or individual Justices will signal this flexibility to agencies. In *Rapanos v. United States*, 126 S.Ct. 2208 (2006), the Court evaluated the broad understanding held by the Army Corps of Engineers of its jurisdiction protecting "waters of the United States," 33 U.S.C. § 1362(7). The Corps took the position that private backfilling of wetlands adjacent to a non-navigable tributary could not be pursued without a permit. A plurality of the Court rejected the Corps' broad assertion of jurisdiction, mainly because it went beyond the statute's plain meaning, id. at 2220–24 (plurality opinion of Scalia, J.), but also because the Corps' sweeping definition would be an "unprecedented intrusion into traditional state authority" over wetlands, id. at 2224 (citing *BFP*, Chapter 8, § 1B3), and "stretches the outer limits of Congress's commerce power and raises difficult questions about the ultimate scope of that power." Id. Concurring only in the judgment, Justice Kennedy read into the statute a requirement that the Corps' jurisdiction depends on a "significant nexus between the wetlands in question and the navigable waters in the traditional sense." Id. at 2248.

All five majority Justices were bothered by the Corps' disinclination to admit any significant limiting principle to its jurisdiction over wet places in the United States. In a separate concurring opinion, Chief Justice Roberts urged the Corps or the EPA to clarify the reach of their jurisdiction through legislative notice-and-comment rulemaking, as they had started to do in 2003 (after an earlier Supreme Court defeat). "Given the broad, somewhat ambiguous, but nonetheless clearly limiting terms Congress employed in the Clean Water Act, the Corps and the EPA would have enjoyed plenty of room to operate in developing *some* notion of an outer bound to the reach of their authority." Id. at 2236. Justice Kennedy agreed, id. at 2247, and Justice Breyer (in dissent) urged the Corps to develop regulations addressing Justice Kennedy's nexus approach, id. at 2266.

Although a particularly dramatic example, the Case of the Backfilled Wetlands illustrates the reach and limits of *stare decisis* in *Chevron* cases. (All nine Justices agreed that the Corps' interpretation was governed by *Chevron*.) On the one hand, the Corps is probably bound by the Kennedy "nexus" requirement, as it reflected the outer bound of jurisdiction adopted by a Court majority. On the other hand, the Corps has considerable discretion to develop particular rules and/or standards for different scenarios. Justice Kennedy's test is so general that the agency surely has a lot of room for discretionary but reasoned judgment. Note that the *Chevron* room for discretionary judgment depends in large part on how broadly (Kennedy) or narrowly (Scalia) the Court writes its opinion about what the statute *requires* of the agency.

For other cases where concurring Justices have made similar pitches, see *Norfolk Southern Ry. v. Shankin*, 529 U.S. 344 (2000) (Breyer, J., concurring); *Christensen v. Harris County*, 529 U.S. 576 (2000) (Souter, J., concurring).

6. *Deference in National Security and Foreign Affairs*

In *United States v. Curtiss-Wright Export Co.*, 299 U.S. 304 (1936), the Court opined that "congressional legislation . . . within the international field must often accord to the President a degree of discretion and freedom from statutory restriction which would not be admissible were domestic affairs alone involved." The source of this discretion in statutory enforcement was grounded in Article II — in the inherent powers of the President to represent the nation in foreign matters and to protect America's security interests.

Curtiss-Wright deference is theoretically distinguishable from *Chevron* deference. Because it rests upon the President's Article II powers, rather than Congress's Article I authority, *Curtiss-Wright* deference does not necessarily depend upon a statutory delegation of lawmaking responsibilities, although the power of its presumption might be augmented by such delegation. Moreover, the *Curtiss-Wright* rule is a more deferential standard than *Chevron*: the executive department interpretation prevails not only in cases of statutory ambiguity, but also in cases where Congress has not clearly trumped the agency or presidential construction.

For example, the Court in *Department of the Navy v. Egan*, 484 U.S. 518 (1988), ruled against judicial review of presidential revocation of security clearances. Given the President's broad powers to protect national security and conduct foreign policy, the Court reasoned that, "unless Congress specifically has provided otherwise, courts traditionally [should be] . . . reluctant to intrude upon the authority of the Executive in military and national security affairs."

Egan is a strong post-*Chevron* statement of *Curtiss-Wright* deference, but is a rare instance where the Court invokes such deference. See Eskridge & Baer, *Deference Continuum* (reporting that the Court invoked *Curtiss-Wright* deference in fewer than 10% of its foreign affairs and national security docket). For a recent debate over this doctrine, consider the following case.

HAMDAN v. RUMSFELD, 126 S.Ct. 2749 (2006). The Supreme Court ruled that presidential military commissions dispensing summary justice could not legally try Salim Ahmed Hamdan, a Yemeni national apprehended by American allies in Afghanistan and turned over to American authorities; since 2002, he has been detained at our naval base in Guantanamo. The government claimed that Hamdan was the chauffeur of terrorist Osama bin Laden and had engaged in various activities supporting al Qaeda. In 2003, President Bush deemed Hamdan triable by a military commission as defined in the Military Order of November 13, 2001. In 2004, the United States charged him with "conspiracy to commit crimes triable by military commission" and ruled that the commissions would not follow the procedures provided for court martials in the Uniform Code of Military Justice (UCMJ) or for prisoners of war stipulated in the Geneva Conventions.

In a petition for habeas corpus, Hamdan challenged the legality of such a trial. Reversing the D.C. Circuit, the Supreme Court, in an opinion by **Justice Stevens**, agreed with Hamdan. **Justice Kennedy** concurred in most of the Stevens opinion and wrote a lengthy separate statement. Three Justices (Scalia, Thomas, Alito) dissented; Chief Justice Roberts did not participate (as he had joined the lower court opinion the Court was reviewing, and reversing).

Justice Stevens' opinion provided the following background which was not disputed among the Justices: "The common law governing military commissions may be gleaned from past practice and what sparse legal precedent exists. Commissions historically have been used in three situations. First, they have substituted for civilian courts at times and in places where martial law has been declared. Their use in these circumstances has raised constitutional questions, see *Duncan v. Kahanamoku*, 327 U. S. 304 (1946); [*Ex parte*] *Milligan*, 4 Wall. 2, 121–122 [1866], but is well recognized. Second, commissions have been established to try civilians 'as part of a temporary military government over occupied enemy territory or territory regained from an enemy where civilian government cannot and does not function.' *Duncan*, 327 U. S., at 314 see *Milligan,* 4 Wall., at 141–142 (Chase, C.J., concurring in judgment) (distinguishing '*martial law proper*' from '*military government*' in occupied territory). Illustrative of this second kind of commission is the one that was established, with jurisdiction to apply the German Criminal Code, in occupied Germany following the end of World War II. See *Madsen v. Kinsella*, 343 U.S. 341, 356 (1952).

"The third type of commission, convened as an 'incident to the conduct of war' when there is a need 'to seize and subject to disciplinary measures those enemies who in their attempt to thwart or impede our military effort have violated the law of war,' *Quirin*, 317 U.S., at 28–29, has been described as 'utterly different' from the other two. Not only is its jurisdiction limited to offenses cognizable during time of war, but its role is primarily a factfinding one — to determine, typically on the battlefield itself, whether the defendant has violated the law of war. The last time the U.S. Armed Forces used the law-of-war military commission was during World War II. In *Quirin*, this Court sanctioned President Roosevelt's use of such a tribunal to try Nazi saboteurs captured on American soil during the War. And in *Yamashita*, we held that a military commission had jurisdiction to try a Japanese commander for failing to prevent troops under his command from committing atrocities in the Philippines. 327 U.S. 1 [1946]."

The Administration's military commissions were of the third type. Most of the debate within the Court involved three fascinating matters of statutory interpretation and military law.

1. *Justiciability.* **Justice Stevens'** opinion for the Court ruled that neither the Detainees Treatment Act of 2005 (which sharply curtailed judicial review in many respects) nor principles of abstention supported the United States' position that the Court should dismiss Hamdan's habeas petition on justiciability grounds. The Court worried that a broad interpretation of the DTA would "rais[e] grave questions about Congress' authority to impinge upon this Court's appellate jurisdiction, particularly in habeas cases." Speaking for the three dissenters, **Justice Scalia** argued that the case should have been dismissed on these grounds. Justice Scalia summarily dismissed Hamdan's argument that curtailment of judicial review raised constitutional concerns. The DTA provides a narrow mechanism for Hamdan to present his constitutional arguments, and the Exceptions Clause of Article III allows Congress wide latitude to regulate the Court's appellate jurisdiction.

2. *Authorization: The Framework.* The main issue was whether the President had the authority to deploy these military commissions to impose sanctions (including death) on suspected enemy combatants. **Justice Stevens** emphasized the primary of Congress in setting rules for military engagement. "Exigency alone, of course, will not justify the establishment and use of penal tribunals not contemplated by Article I, §8 and Article III, §1 of the Constitution unless some other part of that document authorizes a response to the felt need. See *Ex parte Milligan* ('Certainly no part of the judicial power of the country was conferred on [military commissions]'). And that authority, if it exists, can derive only from the powers granted jointly to the President and Congress in time of war. *Yamashita*.

"The Constitution makes the President the 'Commander in Chief' of the Armed Forces, Art. II, §2, cl. 1, but vests in Congress the powers to 'declare War . . . and make Rules concerning Captures on Land and Water,' Art. I, §8, cl. 11, to 'raise and support Armies,' id., cl. 12, to 'define and punish . . . Offences against the Law of Nations,' id., cl. 10, and 'To make Rules for the Government and Regulation of the land and naval Forces,' id., cl. 14.

"The interplay between these powers was described by Chief Justice Chase in the seminal case of *Ex parte Milligan*:

'The power to make the necessary laws is in Congress; the power to execute in the President. Both powers imply many subordinate and auxiliary powers. Each includes all authorities essential to its due exercise. But neither can the President, in war more than in peace, intrude upon the proper authority of Congress, nor Congress upon the proper authority of the President . . . . Congress cannot direct the conduct of campaigns, nor can the President, or any commander under him, without the sanction of Congress, institute tribunals for the trial and punishment of offences, either of soldiers or civilians, unless in cases of a controlling necessity, which justifies what it compels, or at least insures acts of indemnity from the justice of the legislature.' 4 Wall., at 139–140.

Whether Chief Justice Chase was correct in suggesting that the President may constitutionally convene military commissions 'without the sanction of Congress' in cases of 'controlling necessity' is a question this Court has not answered definitively, and need not answer today."

Writing for the three dissenters, **Justice Thomas** emphasized that "the structural advantages attendant to the Executive Branch — namely, the decisiveness, 'activity, secrecy, and dispatch' that flow from the Executive's 'unity' (quoting The Federalist No. 70, p. 472 (J. Cooke ed. 1961) (A. Hamilton)) — led the Founders to conclude that the 'President ha[s] primary responsibility — along with the necessary power — to protect the national security and to conduct the Nation's foreign relations.' Consistent with this conclusion, the Constitution vests in the President '[t]he executive Power,' Art. II, §1, provides that he 'shall be Commander in Chief' of the Armed Forces, §2, and places in him the power to recognize foreign governments[.] This Court has observed that these provisions confer upon the President broad constitutional authority to protect the Nation's security in the manner he deems fit. See, e.g., *Prize Cases*, 2 Black 635, 668 (1863) ('If a war be made by invasion of a foreign nation, the President is not only authorized but bound to resist force by force . . . without waiting for any special legislative authority'); *Fleming v. Page*, 9 How. 603, 615 (1850) (acknowledging that the President has the authority to 'employ [the Nation's Armed Forces] in the manner he may deem most effectual to harass and conquer and subdue the enemy').

"Congress, to be sure, has a substantial and essential role in both foreign affairs and national security. But 'Congress cannot anticipate and legislate with regard to every possible action the President may find it necessary to take or every possible situation in which he might act,' and '[s]uch failure of Congress . . . does not, "especially . . . in the areas of foreign policy and national security," imply "congressional disapproval" of action taken by the Executive.' *Dames & Moore v. Regan*, 453 U.S. 654, 678 (1981). Rather, in these domains, the fact that Congress has provided the President with broad authorities does not imply — and the Judicial Branch should not infer — that Congress intended to deprive him of particular powers not specifically enumerated. See *Dames & Moore*) ('[T]he enactment of legislation closely related to the question of the President's authority in a particular case which evinces legislative intent to accord the President broad discretion may be considered to invite measures on independent presidential responsibility.')." Following a *Curtiss-Wright* approach strongly deferential to presidential authority, Justice Thomas argued that application of that framework in military matters required *expansive* interpretation of congressional authorizations to meet the unpredictable demands of war.

3. *Authorization: Statutory Analysis.* The Court ruled that the Administration's deployment of a military commission in Hamdan's case was "incompatible with the expressed or implied will of Congress." The dissenters, in contrast, found the matter to fall within the President's "authority is at its maximum, for it includes all that he possesses in his own right plus all that Congress can delegate."

The Court ruled that UCMJ Article 21, adopted in 1950, did *not* authorize the Bush Administration military commissions. **Justice Stevens** offered three reasons: (1) Article 21 authorizes military commissions to try "offenders or offenses" that "by statute or by the law of war may be tried by" such commissions. The government could point to no statute, and conspiracy to commit war crimes is not a recognized violation of the law of war. In contrast, the sabotage in *Quirin* was an accepted violation of the law of war. This reason commanded only a plurality of the eight-Justice Court (Stevens, Souter, Ginsburg, Breyer), but the other two commanded a majority. (2) The military commissions did not comport with UCMJ Article 36(b), which requires uniformity in procedural rules under the UCMJ unless "impracticable." The Court ruled that Article 36(b) creates a baseline whereby the court-martial procedures presumptively apply to military commissions; the Bush Administration's commission's relaxed evidentiary rules and its failure to give the defendant access to all the evidence against him were important departures from the court-martial rules that the Administration could not justify. (3) Until Hamdan is judged to be an enemy combatant, the 1949 Geneva Conventions require that he be subject to punishment only by a "regularly constituted court affording all the judicial guarantees which are recognized as indispensable by civilized peoples."

Justice Kennedy's concurring opinion emphasized the following procedural differences between the Bush Administration military commissions and court-martials that were not justified: (a) quasi-independent military judges preside over court-martials, while any military lawyer can preside over a military commission; (b) the Appointing Authority controls the number of judges and various procedural appeals for military commissions, but not for court-martials; (c) military commissions follow relaxed evidentiary rules and consider evidence without the accused even being present.

Writing for the three dissenters, **Justice Thomas** sharply disagreed. He argued that (a) UCMJ Article 21 constituted an explicit congressional authorization for the military commission in Hamdan's case, and Article 36 constituted virtually a blank check for the President to devise special procedures for those tribunals; (b) the Iraq War Authorization for Military Force was a separate congressional authorization; and (c) the Geneva Conventions create no judicially enforceable rights for unlawful combatants in Hamdan's position. Also speaking for the three dissenters, **Justice Alito** argued that the military commissions satisfy the Geneva Conventions and the requirements of UCMJ Articles 21 and 36.

In his extensive analysis, Justice Thomas approached the same statutory materials that the Court analyzed, but did so with a more expansive eye. Specifically, he deferred to the President's judgment about what was needed to fight terrorism effectively and his interpretation of the relevant statutes and treaties, considered past practice relevant and read it expansively, and stressed the process that the President's Military Order and the DTA afforded accused terrorists like Hamdan.

As to the last point, consider the Government's Brief, page 4: "Petitioner is entitled to appointed military legal counsel, 32 C.F.R. 9.4(c)(2), and may retain a civilian attorney (which he has done), 32 C.F.R. 9.4(c)(2)(iii)(B). Petitioner is entitled to the presumption of innocence, 32 C.F.R. 9.5(b), proof beyond a reasonable doubt, 32 C.F.R. 9.5(c), and the right to remain silent, 32 C.F.R. 9.5(f). He may confront witnesses against him, 32 C.F.R. 9.5(i), and may subpoena his own witnesses, if reasonably available, 32 C.F.R. 9.5(h). Petitioner may personally be present at every stage of the trial unless he engages in disruptive conduct or the prosecution introduces classified or otherwise protected information for which no adequate substitute is available and whose admission will not deprive him of a full and fair trial, 32 C.F.R. 9.5(k); Military Commission Order No. 1 (Dep't of Defense Aug. 31, 2005) §6(B)(3) and (D)(5)(b). If petitioner is found guilty, the judgment will be reviewed by a review panel, the Secretary of Defense, and the President, if he does not designate the Secretary as the final decisionmaker. 32 C.F.R. 9.6(h). The final judgment is subject to review in the Court of Appeals for the District of Columbia Circuit and ultimately in this Court. See DTA §1005(e)(3), 119 Stat. 2743; 28 U. S. C. 1254(1)."

NOTE ON *CURTISS-WRIGHT* DEFERENCE

In considering the cogency of Justice Thomas's dissenting opinion, consider the President's "inherent powers" under Article II. (This was the conceptual basis for *Curtiss-Wright* itself.) If there were no statute, the President as Commander-in-Chief would have inherent authority to deal with prisoners of war and enemy combatants. This would include the authority to establish tribunals for the summary trial of enemy agents, prisoners, etc. The UCMJ (1950) channels and perhaps cabins that authority, but the issue in *Hamdan* was what limits the UCMJ actually placed on the President. Article II might require, as *Curtiss-Wright* suggests, that the UCMJ be read to displace the President's inherent authority only when it has clearly done so. See *Egan*. Is there any flaw in this argument?

The issues of military justice and the conduct of the war on terror would seem even more centrally implicated by *Curtiss-Wright* than those adjudicated in *Egan*, yet the *Hamdan* Court applied neither *Curtiss-Wright* nor *Chevron* deference. Is there a sufficient distinction between the two cases? Why were the majority Justices so undeferential in *Hamdan*?

C. QUO VADIS THE *"CHEVRON* REVOLUTION"?

Commentators and judges agree there has been a *"Chevron* Revolution" of some sort, but its contours remain unclear, especially after *Mead.* Among the courts of appeals, Schuck & Elliott, Chevron *Station,* demonstrates that *Chevron* had an immediate and significant impact. Subsequent scholars report that *Chevron* is now the most cited Supreme Court decision in our history, and the evidence is strong that lower courts are applying *Chevron* extensively. E.g., Orin Kerr, *Shedding Light on* Chevron: *An Empirical Study of the* Chevron *Doctrine in the U.S. Courts of Appeals,* 15 Yale J. on Reg. 1 (1998). Moreover, lower court judges have not only applied *Skidmore* deference in many non-*Chevron* cases, but have applied it with serious attention to agency inputs. See Kristin Hickman & Mathew Krueger, *In Search of the Modern* Skidmore *Standard,* 108 Colum. L. Rev. (forthcoming 2008).

There is also anecdotal but cogent evidence that agencies themselves have internalized the new *Chevron* regime as freeing them up to make more decisions on policy or political rather than legal lines. See E. Donald Elliot, Chevron *Matters: How the* Chevron *Doctrine Redefined the Roles of Congress, Courts, and Agencies in Environmental Law,* 16 Vill. Envtl. L.J. 1, 11–12 (2005). There is even more systematic evidence that the lower courts are not only applying *Skidmore,* but have agreed with agency interpretations in more than 60% of the *Skidmore* cases decided in the last five years. See Hickman & Krueger, *Modern* Skidmore *Standard..*

The evidence is most equivocal at the Supreme Court itself, however. The Court was highly deferential to agency rules and interpretations before *Chevron* and has continued to be deferential after *Chevron.* It remains unclear whether *Chevron* has had any influence at the Supreme Court level — beyond creating the increasingly complicated legisprudence that we have presented in this section. Consider matters concretely. Is there any reason to believe that the Court would have decided the leading cases in this chapter any differently in the pre-*Chevron* era — the Oregon Aid-in-Dying Case? The Airbags Tort Case? The Navy Security Clearance Case? The Military Commissions Case? Except for Justice Breyer's opinion in *Geier,* the opinions for the Court were *reasoned* differently under the *Chevron* criteria, but the fundamental role of agency views, the key precepts, and the results in the cases are not affected at all in our view.

Moreover, as this Section has demonstrated, the Supreme Court follows a much more elaborate *deference continuum* than is captured by the simple *Chevron-Skidmore* dichotomy. The Eskridge and Baer study gives us a complete lay of the land in the 1,104 Supreme Court cases between *Chevron* and *Hamdan* where an agency interpretation was in play.

Supreme Court Deference Regimes, *Chevron* to *Hamdan*

Deference Regime (% Cases)	Deference Accorded	Basis for Deference	Subject Areas
Curtiss-Wright (0.9%)	Super-strong deference in national security cases	Article II + Congressional Delegation	Foreign Affairs; Immigration; National Security
Seminole Rock (1.1%)	Strong deference for agency interpretations of own regulations	Congressional Delegation + Agency Expertise	Entitlements; Tax; Telecommunications
Chevron (8.3%)	Defer to reasonable interpretations unless Congress has directly addressed the issue	Congressional Delegation	Energy; Envir'l; Entitlements; Immigration; Labor; Securities; Transportation
Beth Israel (4.8%)	Defer to reasonable interpretations if consistent with statute	Congressional Purposes	Health; Immigration; Labor; Taxation
Skidmore (6.7%)	Consider agency views for persuasive value (e.g., policy goals and reliance interests)	Agency Expertise and Experience	Civil Rights; Education; Energy; Environmental; Transportation
Skidmore-Lite (17.8%)	Consider agency-generated factual materials + background rules	Agency Expertise and Experience	Antitrust; Bankruptcy; Civil Rights; Energy; Intellectual Property; Indian Law; Pensions
No Deference (53.6%)	Court follows ordinary, ad hoc judicial reasoning	No basis for deference	All areas of Supreme Court practice are dominated by this category
Anti-Deference (6.8%)	Presumption *against* agency interpretation	Constitutional Values	Criminal Law; Immigration

Source: Eskridge & Baer, *Deference Continuum.*

Assume that this chart accurately reflects the Court's practice since *Chevron*. Eskridge and Baer also report that when the Court applies the *Chevron* framework the agency wins 76.2% of the time, a very high agreement rate. But the agency win rate is also very high when the Court invokes other deference regimes: 80.6% when the Court follows a *Skidmore*-Lite approach; 73.5% when the Court invokes *Skidmore*; 73.5% when it invokes *Beth Israel*; 90.9% when it invokes *Seminole Rock*; and 100.0% when it invokes *Curtiss-Wright* deference. All these figures are inflated by the fact that the Court probably cites these deference regimes primarily when it is inclined to decide in favor of the agency. Recall Eskridge and Baer's finding that the Court follows *Chevron* in only one-third of the cases where it is potentially applicable (and in some cases where it is not, under *Mead*). The same is even more true for the other regimes: they are rarely applied even when theoretically applicable.

What a mess.

Surely this elaborate continuum can be simplified, and if simplified maybe the Justices would follow it more faithfully. But how should the continuum be simplified? Different Justices and academic commentators have come up with a dizzying array of proposed simplifications — which cut in all sorts of different directions. In concluding this chapter, we offer you several clusters of theories, and you are responsible for developing the approach that makes the best legal sense. You might want to apply these theories to some of the harder cases presented in this and the previous chapters, namely, *Weber,* where the Court followed the EEOC; *Brown & Williamson*, where the Court rejected an FDA rule; *Sweet Home*, where the Court followed a Department of Interior rule; *Oregon*, where the Court rejected a Department of Justice Directive; and the FISA debate between President Bush 43 and Congress (the Problem opening this Section).

1. *Sharpen* Chevron *and* Skidmore *Within the* Mead *Framework*

The dominant impulse among judges and law professors has been to work within the assumptions of *Mead* and to sharpen *Chevron* and *Skidmore* accordingly. Most of these commentators would be happy to absorb *Beth Israel* and *Seminole Rock* into *Chevron*, and to jettison or deemphasize *Curtiss-Wright* deference. Most of them would reject *Mead's* notion that Congress can delegate lawmaking authority *implicitly*; this notion has created endless confusion among lower courts. E.g., Lisa Schultz Bressman, *How* Mead *Has Muddled Judicial Review of Agency Action*, 58 Vand. L. Rev. 1443 (2005).

Different authors, of course, have come up with somewhat different prescriptions. More important, different authors have emphasized different normative underpinnings of *Mead.*.

(a) *Legislative supremacy.* Probably the most important normative assumption of *Mead* is legislative supremacy: both judges and administrators are faithful agents of congressional directives embodied in statutes. Congress's intent as to who decides is just as important as its intent as to what the decision ought to be. For an excellent constitutional analysis of Congress's power to delegate lawmaking authority to agencies, see Thomas Merrill, *Rethinking Article I, Section 1: From Nondelegation to Exclusive Delegation,* 104 Colum. L. Rev. 2097 (2004).

In Chevron's *Domain,* Professors Thomas Merrill and Kristen Hickman anticipated *Mead's* holding that an agency interpretation is entitled to *Chevron* deference *only* when it is pursuant to congressional delegation of lawmaking authority to the agency. They lay out the doctrinal consequences for this foundation, including the notion that courts should *not Chevron*-defer to an agency's interpretation of its own jurisdiction or authority. Thus, for them,

Chevron Step 0 is critical, and the Oregon Aid-in-Dying Case exemplifies the kind of inquiry the Court should be engaging.

Professors Thomas Merrill and Kathryn Tongue Watts complicate the implications of *Mead* in *Agency Rules with the Force of Law: The Original Convention,* 116 Harv. L. Rev. 467 (2002). They demonstrate that the longstanding legislative tradition for delegating "lawmaking" authority required an expression of direct sanctions for violation of an agency rule or order. Many of the cases where the Court has applied *Chevron* deference — including *Chevron* itself — did not meet this conventional test. Because they require a court order to be enforceable, NLRB orders are not properly considered "lawmaking" delegations for this reason. The authors discuss various ways their discoveries could push the *Chevron* line of cases but come to no firm conclusions.

(b) *Democratic legitimacy.* In our democracy, the legitimacy of legislation (the moral reason we accept and obey its commands) rests in part on popular participation or, at least, the accountability of elected representatives to We the People for the laws they adopt. In the modern administrative state, most of the actual rules are developed by unelected agencies, and so there is a potential democracy deficit.

Henry Richardson, *Democratic Autonomy: Public Reasoning About the Ends of Policy* (2003), argues that agencies can contribute to rather than derogate from democratic decisionmaking when they engage in notice-and-comment rulemaking which replicates the legislative process (proposal, popular feedback, deliberated decision, with opportunity for people to object). Richardson's focus, therefore, would not be the fact of legislative *delegation,* but instead the manner in which delegated *lawmaking* is accomplished. Thus, the agency decisions in *Mead, Oregon,* and *Hamdan* (administrative or presidential fiat) do not deserve *Chevron* deference — while the decision in *Chevron* (notice-and-comment rulemaking) does.

Complementing Richardson's analysis, Lisa Schultz Bressman, *Beyond Accountability: Arbitrariness and Legitimacy in the Administrative State*, 78 NYU L. Rev. 461 (2003), argues that we ought to be even more concerned about administrative arbitrariness than political accountability. Her prescription is that notice-and-comment rulemaking is most likely to produce decisions that reflect reasoned judgment and not arbitrary fiat. Accord, Mark Seidenfeld, *A Syncopated* Chevron: *Emphasizing Reasoned Decisionmaking in Reviewing Agency Interpretations of Statutes*, 73 Tex. L. Rev. 83 (1994).

(c) *Institutional competence.* Few scholars have focused on *Skidmore,* which is not only the default regime under the *Chevron* jurisprudence, but is a default regime that both dominates *Chevron* and generates high agency win rates. In recent empirical articles, one focusing on the Supreme Court and the other on lower courts, two sets of scholars have sought to clarify *Skidmore* with a focus on *institutional competence.* Competence is the old New Deal theme: agencies are better qualified than judges to make certain kinds of policies. In *Deference Continuum,* Eskridge and Baer found that the Justices' inability to handle technical issues in the fields of intellectual property, telecommunications, taxation, pensions, and bankruptcy generated high levels of deference to agency interpretations, whatever the deference regime the Court invoked. In contrast, more normative arenas such as criminal, Indian affairs, civil rights, and labor law found the Justices agreeing less often, again regardless of the deference regime invoked or applicable. (An implication of their empirical study, which Eskridge and Baer endorse normatively, is that *Skidmore* factors like institutional competence show up in *Chevron* cases as well.)

Focusing on *Skidmore* as the critical regime even before *Mead,* Eskridge and Baer urge the Court to focus on three factors: (1) the rule of law, including agency consistency and public reliance on agency interpretations; (2) comparative institutional competence, with technical issues, matters of regulatory tradeoffs, and uncertainty better handled by agencies and bigger normative issues as those where courts should be more scrutinizing; and (3) legitimacy, with open processes and public participation being pluses for the agency. For a *Skidmore* sliding scale that emphasizes dangers of agency capture, see Hickman & Krueger.

2. *Reject* Mead *in Favor of Greater Deference to Agency Interpretations*

A number of other commentators reject or would go beyond *Mead* and would read *Chevron* much more expansively than the Supreme Court has thus far been willing to do. These scholars are broadly critical of judicial "interference" in the ongoing administration of statutory schemes and urge that agency monitoring is better left to the political than the judicial process. Most of these scholars favor an expanded reading of *Chevron*, a vigorous revival of *Curtiss-Wright*, and a diminished role for *Skidmore* (which they tend to reject as exemplifying what is wrong with the Court's deference jurisprudence).

As before, there are many theoretical ways to reach this conclusion.

(a) *Agencies rather than courts as the preferred congressional agents.* A respected administrative law scholar before his appointment as a judge, Justice Scalia finds no inconsistency between congressional supremacy and a broad reading of *Chevron* that defers to any interpretation adopted by the head of an agency that is not a litigating position. His argument is that any ambiguity or gap that Congress leaves in a statute is an implicit delegation of lawmaking authority to the agency Congress has charged with enforcing the statute. *Mead,* 533 U.S. at 256–57; Antonin Scalia, *Judicial Deference to Administrative Interpretations of Law,* 1989 Duke L.J. 511, 516.

Professor John Duffy, *Administrative Common Law in Judicial Review,* 77 Tex. L. Rev. 113, 193–99 (1998), responds that such a broad reading of *Chevron* is inconsistent with the text, structure, and original meaning of the Administrative Procedure Act, especially 5 U.S.C. §§ 558(b) (limits on agency sanctions) and 706(2) (judicial review of agency action), which Duffy believes codify a *Marbury* model of judicial review for agency decisions (under which it is the responsibility of the judiciary to say what the law is). Justice Scalia does not read the APA so restrictively, and scholars are now thinking about deeper responses he might have to Professor Duffy's critique.

Jack Goldsmith and John Manning, *The President's Completion Power*, 115 Yale L.J. 2280 (2006), argue for a "completion power" in Article II, namely "the President's authority to prescribe incidental details needed to carry into execution a legislative scheme, even in the absence of any congressional authorization to complete that scheme." The authors rely on historical practice, where the President has exercised such a "completion power" with the acquiescence of both Congress and the Court. E.g., *Dames & Moore v. Regan*, 453 U.S. 654 (1981); Proposed Executive Order Entitled "Federal Regulation," 5 Op. Off. Legal Counsel 59 (1981) (defending presidential cost-benefit review of proposed agency rules).

Goldsmith and Manning justify a broad reading of *Chevron* in light of the completion power: "while Congress can legitimately give either courts or agencies ultimate authority to resolve statutory ambiguities or fill up statutory interstices, it is more consistent with the background premises of our constitutional democracy to embrace a default rule that Congress prefers to leave such completion power in the hands of the more accountable executive." 115 Yale L.J. at 2299. This constitutional default rule would inform one's reading of the APA as well as *Chevron* and would provide Justice Scalia with an argument for his notion that statutory ambiguities represent an implicit delegation of lawmaking authority to agencies, not courts. Interestingly, Professors Goldsmith and Manning do not maintain that *Mead* is wrongly decided, but do argue for a narrow reading of *Mead* that leaves plenty of room for a broad reading of *Chevron*.

(b) *Democratic legitimacy.* Recall that *Chevron* emphasized the relatively greater accountability of agencies (responsible to the nationally elected President) compared with federal courts (responsible to the unelected Supreme Court). Dean Elena Kagan, *Presidential Administration,* 114 Harv. L. Rev. 2245 (2001), takes this normative point one step further to support something like the Scalia position. When the President has taken a role in an agency interpretation *or* it has been adopted by the President's appointee (the agency head), see David Barron & Elena Kagan, Chevron's *Nondelegation Doctrine*, 2001 Sup. Ct. Rev. 201, 234–57 (amending the suggestions of her earlier article), then federal judges ought to *Chevron*-defer. According to Dean Kagan, the main advantage of this approach would be *national transparency.* The buck stops with the President, and any policy option he or she chooses will be subject to national examination and critique — much more legitimate checks than those offered by judicial review. 114 Harv. L. Rev. at 2332–33.

Professor Bressman, *Beyond Accountability,* 503–13, wonders how Dean Kagan's proposal would work as a practical matter. Pointing to numerous examples, Bressman questions whether presidential interventions are either transparent or public-regarding. A lot of presidential interventions are either behind-the-scenes or below the media radar, but can easily be trumpeted by the Solicitor General if needed to give an agency interpretation a boost. Moreover, many presidential interventions represent the worst sort of rent-seeking politics. It is not clear that the balance of rent-seeking and public-regarding presidential interventions weighs in favor of the latter. See also Jide Nzelibe, *The Fable of the Nationalist President and the Parochial Congress*, 53 UCLA

L. Rev. 1217 (2006), arguing that the President does not necessarily represent a national majoritarian constituency any better than Congress does.

A more modest proposal is that made in Kevin Stack, *The Statutory President*, 90 Iowa L. Rev. 539 (2005). Professor Stack argues that *Chevron* deference ought to apply to congressionally authorized lawmaking by the President. Other scholars would go much further in situations where the President is acting to protect national security or engage in matters touching foreign affairs. For example, Curtis Bradley & Jack Goldsmith, *Congressional Authorization and the War on Terrorism*, 118 Harv. L. Rev. 2047, 2100–06 (2005), argue that congressional authorizations for the President's use of force against foreign enemies should be interpreted to include previous presidential practices *and* should be interpreted not to interfere with the President's inherent powers to respond to international emergencies and threats.

(c) *Institutional competence.* Professor Neil Komesar argues in *Imperfect Alternatives: Choosing Institutions in Law, Economics, and Public Policy* (1994), that lawmakers and commentators must consider the institutional costs as well as the benefits of having judges involved in public policy decisions. His book points out that the structural limitations of the judiciary create significant costs for statutory as well as constitutional judicial review. Although he does not address *Chevron,* Professor Komesar's analytical framework is playing an important role in the *Chevron* debate, with some of the most judge-critical voices explicitly invoking his framework. Professor Frank Cross, *Pragmatic Pathologies of Judicial Review of Administrative Rule-making*, 78 N.C.L. Rev. 1013 (2000), for example, argues that judges should play little if any role in second-guessing agency rules, for they are ignorant and easy prey for rent-seeking special interests. See also David Spence & Frank Cross, *A Public Choice Case for the Administrative State*, 89 Geo. L.J. 97 (2000).

Also following Professor Komesar's framework, Professor Adrian Vermeule argues in *Judging Under Uncertainty* (2006) that judges should always defer to agencies (even their litigating positions) and indeed should defer to agency choices about what substantive canons of statutory interpretation should govern their own positions. Professor Vermeule would not only overturn *Mead*, but would go further than Justice Scalia. Under his approach, a federal judge could only overrule an agency interpretation if it were inconsistent with the plain text of the statute, without *any* reference to contextual considerations such as statutory structure, the whole act, other parts of the U.S. Code, or legislative history.

Less ambitious institutional criticisms have been made by other commentators. They maintain that judicial review of agency rulemaking has been counterproductive because judges are not sufficiently knowledgeable, because judicial interventions tend to be legalistic and thereby derogate from the agency's purposive activities, and because even well-considered judicial interventions may have counterproductive side effects. These problems are illustrated by Jerry Mashaw and Harfst's *The Struggle for Auto Safety* (1990), which we have summarized at various points in this chapter. Professor Mashaw, in particular, has urged courts to be more deferential in the sense that judges need to leave agencies alone so that they can do the jobs Congress has given them. For this reason, he supports a broad reading of *Chevron*. See Jerry Mashaw, *Prodelegation: Why Administrators Should Make Political Decisions,* 1 J.L. Econ. & Org. 81, 91–99 (1985). Professor Mashaw would probably be even more deferential in practice than Justice Scalia has been, because he would allow agencies a wide berth in construing statutory language that Justice Scalia would often consider clear and therefore confining.

3. *Synthesize* Chevron *and* Skidmore

Justice Stephen Breyer has long been a critic of *Chevron* deference as inconsistent with the judicial role. E.g., Breyer, *Judicial Review of Law and Policy*, 38 Ad. L.J. 363 (1986); accord, Cynthia Farina, *Statutory Interpretation and the Balance of Power in the Administrative State,* 89 Colum. L. Rev. 452 (1989). Yet he has not urged the overruling of *Chevron* or the abandonment of its two-step framework. Instead, Justice Breyer seems to apply *Chevron* as a special case of general *Skidmore* (Article III) deference, and the *Mead* notion of congressionally delegated lawmaking authority as a big "plus" in the *Skidmore* scale.

For example, in *Barnhart v. Walton*, 535 U.S. 212 (2002), decided soon after *Mead*, Justice Breyer wrote for the Court in affirming a recent rule adopted by the Social Security Administration. His opinion cheerfully announced that *Chevron* was applicable, because Congress had delegated lawmaking authority to the agency. But the opinion continued the threshold analysis with the further observations that *Chevron*'s applicability was confirmed by the agency's expertise and its longstanding adherence to that interpretation for years before the rule was adopted — classic *Skidmore* considerations. Id. at 219–22.

The upshot of Breyer's point of view would be that *Skidmore* is the rule, with pluses being awarded for congressional delegation (as in *Chevron*) or agency expertise (as in *Chevron* or perhaps *Egan*, the security clearance case) or foreign affairs subject matter (as in *Curtiss-Wright*). And minuses subtracted for agency wishi-washiness, secret processes, or lack of obvious expertise (all exemplified in *Gonzales v. Oregon*). Although this sounds kind of radical after almost a quarter century of *Chevron*, Justice Breyer's approach is not so dissimilar from what the Supreme Court has actually been doing. According to Eskridge & Baer, *Deference Continuum*, agency success rates have no correlation with announced deference regime and strong correlation with perceived agency expertise and consistency of the agency's position over time (the same *Skidmore* factors Justice Breyer emphasized in *Barnhart*).

Notice, finally, that Justice Breyer is the most deferential Justice on the current Court, according to the Eskridge and Baer study.

Appendix A

THE CONSTITUTION OF
THE UNITED STATES

We the People of the United States, in Order to form a more perfect Union, establish Justice, insure domestic Tranquility, provide for the common defence, promote the general Welfare, and secure the Blessings of Liberty to ourselves and our Posterity, do ordain and establish this Constitution for the United States of America.

ARTICLE I

Section 1. All legislative Powers herein granted shall be vested in a Congress of the United States, which shall consist of a Senate and House of Representatives.

Section 2. [1] The House of Representatives shall be composed of Members chosen every second Year by the People of the several States, and the Electors in each State shall have the Qualifications requisite for Electors of the most numerous Branch of the State Legislature.

[2] No Person shall be a Representative who shall not have attained to the Age of twenty five Years, and been seven Years a Citizen of the United States, and who shall not, when elected, be an Inhabitant of that State in which he shall be chosen.

[3] Representatives and direct Taxes shall be apportioned among the several States which may be included within this Union, according to their respective Numbers, which shall be determined by adding to the whole Number of free Persons, including those bound to Service for a Term of Years, and excluding Indians not taxed, three fifths of all other Persons. The actual Enumeration shall be made within three Years after the first Meeting of the Congress of the United States, and within every subsequent Term of ten Years, in such Manner as they shall by Law direct. The Number of Representatives shall not exceed one for every thirty Thousand, but each State shall have at Least one Representative; and until such enumeration shall be made, the State of New Hampshire shall be entitled to chuse three, Massachusetts eight, Rhode Island and Providence Plantations one, Connecticut five, New York six, New

Jersey four, Pennsylvania eight, Delaware one, Maryland six, Virginia ten, North Carolina five, South Carolina five, and Georgia three.

[4] When vacancies happen in the Representation from any State, the Executive Authority thereof shall issue Writs of Election to fill such Vacancies.

[5] The House of Representatives shall chuse their Speaker and other Officers; and shall have the sole Power of Impeachment.

Section 3. [1] The Senate of the United States shall be composed of two Senators from each State, chosen by the Legislature thereof, for six Years; and each Senator shall have one Vote.

[2] Immediately after they shall be assembled in Consequence of the first Election, they shall be divided as equally as may be into three Classes. The Seats of the Senators of the first Class shall be vacated at the Expiration of the second Year, of the second Class at the Expiration of the fourth Year, and of the third Class at the Expiration of the sixth Year, so that one third may be chosen every second Year; and if Vacancies happen by Resignation, or otherwise, during the Recess of the Legislature of any State, the Executive thereof may make temporary Appointments until the next Meeting of the Legislature, which shall then fill such Vacancies.

[3] No Person shall be a Senator who shall not have attained to the Age of thirty Years, and been nine Years a Citizen of the United States, and who shall not, when elected, be an Inhabitant of that State for which he shall be chosen.

[4] The Vice President of the United States shall be President of the Senate, but shall have no Vote, unless they be equally divided.

[5] The Senate shall chuse their other Officers, and also a President pro tempore, in the Absence of the Vice President, or when he shall exercise the Office of President of the United States.

[6] The Senate shall have the sole Power to try all Impeachments. When sitting for that Purpose, they shall be on Oath or Affirmation. When the President of the United States is tried, the Chief Justice shall preside: And no Person shall be convicted without the Concurrence of two thirds of the Members present.

[7] Judgment in Cases of Impeachment shall not extend further than to removal from Office, and disqualification to hold and enjoy any Office of honor, Trust, or Profit under the United States: but the Party convicted shall nevertheless be liable and subject to Indictment, Trial, Judgment, and Punishment, according to Law.

Section 4. [1] The Times, Places and Manner of holding Elections for Senators and Representatives, shall be prescribed in each State by the Legislature thereof; but the Congress may at any time by Law make or alter such Regulations, except as to the Places of chusing Senators.

[2] The Congress shall assemble at least once in every Year, and such Meeting shall be on the first Monday in December, unless they shall by Law appoint a different Day.

Section 5. [1] Each House shall be the Judge of the Elections, Returns, and Qualifications of its own Members, and a Majority of each shall constitute a Quorum to do Business; but a smaller Number may adjourn from day to day, and may be authorized to compel the Attendance of absent Members, in such Manner, and under such Penalties as each House may provide.

[2] Each House may determine the Rules of its Proceedings, punish its Members for disorderly Behaviour, and, with the Concurrence of two thirds, expel a Member.

[3] Each House shall keep a Journal of its Proceedings, and from time to time publish the same, excepting such Parts as may in their Judgment require Secrecy; and the Yeas and Nays of the Members of either House on any question shall, at the Desire of one fifth of those Present, be entered on the Journal.

[4] Neither House, during the Session of Congress, shall without the Consent of the other, adjourn for more than three days, nor to any other Place than that in which the two Houses shall be sitting.

Section 6. [1] The Senators and Representatives shall receive a Compensation for their Services, to be ascertained by Law, and paid out of the Treasury of the United States. They shall in all Cases, except Treason, Felony, and Breach of the Peace, be privileged from Arrest during their Attendance at the Session of their respective Houses, and in going to and returning from the same; and for any Speech or Debate in either House, they shall not be questioned in any other Place.

[2] No Senator or Representative shall, during the Time for which he was elected, be appointed to any civil Office under the Authority of the United States, which shall have been created, or the Emoluments whereof shall have been encreased during such time; and no Person holding any Office under the United States, shall be a Member of either House during his Continuance in Office.

Section 7. [1] All Bills for raising Revenue shall originate in the House of Representatives; but the Senate may propose or concur with Amendments as on other Bills.

[2] Every Bill which shall have passed the House of Representatives and the Senate, shall, before it become a Law, be presented to the President of the United States; If he approve he shall sign it, but if not he shall return it, with his Objections to that House in which it shall have originated, who shall enter the Objections at large on their Journal, and proceed to reconsider it. If after such Reconsideration two thirds of that House shall agree to pass the Bill, it shall be sent, together with the Objections, to the other House, by which it shall likewise be reconsidered, and if approved by two thirds of that House, it shall become a Law. But in all such Cases the Votes of both Houses shall be determined by Yeas and Nays, and the Names of the Persons voting for and against the Bill shall be entered on the Journal of each House respectively. If any Bill shall not be returned by the President within ten Days (Sundays excepted) after it shall have been presented to him, the Same shall be a Law,

in like Manner as if he had signed it, unless the Congress by their Adjournment prevent its Return, in which Case it shall not be a Law.

[3] Every Order, Resolution, or Vote to which the Concurrence of the Senate and House of Representatives may be necessary (except on a question of Adjournment) shall be presented to the President of the United States; and before the Same shall take Effect, shall be approved by him, or being disapproved by him, shall be repassed by two thirds of the Senate and House of Representatives, according to the Rules and Limitations prescribed in the Case of a Bill.

Section 8. [1] The Congress shall have Power To lay and collect Taxes, Duties, Imposts and Excises, to pay the Debts and provide for the common Defence and general Welfare of the United States; but all Duties, Imposts and Excises shall be uniform throughout the United States;

[2] To borrow Money on the credit of the United States;

[3] To regulate Commerce with foreign Nations, and among the several States, and with the Indian Tribes;

[4] To establish an uniform Rule of Naturalization, and uniform Laws on the subject of Bankruptcies throughout the United States;

[5] To coin Money, regulate the Value thereof, and of foreign Coin, and fix the Standard of Weights and Measures;

[6] To provide for the Punishment of counterfeiting the Securities and current Coin of the United States;

[7] To establish Post Offices and Post Roads;

[8] To promote the Progress of Science and useful Arts, by securing for limited Times to Authors and Inventors the exclusive Right to their respective Writings and Discoveries;

[9] To constitute Tribunals inferior to the supreme Court;

[10] To define and punish Piracies and Felonies committed on the high Seas, and Offences against the Law of Nations;

[11] To declare War, grant Letters of Marque and Reprisal, and make Rules concerning Captures on Land and Water;

[12] To raise and support Armies, but no Appropriation of Money to that Use shall be for a longer Term than two Years;

[13] To provide and maintain a Navy;

[14] To make Rules for the Government and Regulation of the land and naval Forces;

[15] To provide for calling forth the Militia to execute the Laws of the Union, suppress Insurrections and repel Invasions;

[16] To provide for organizing, arming, and disciplining, the Militia, and for governing such Part of them as may be employed in the Service of the

United States, reserving to the States respectively, the Appointment of the Officers, and the Authority of training the Militia according to the discipline prescribed by Congress;

[17]   To exercise exclusive Legislation in all Cases whatsoever, over such District (not exceeding ten Miles square) as may, by Cession of particular States and the Acceptance of Congress, become the Seat of the Government of the United States, and to exercise like Authority over all Places purchased by the Consent of the Legislature of the State in which the Same shall be, for the Erection of Forts, Magazines, Arsenals, dock-Yards, and other needful Buildings;—And

[18]   To make all Laws which shall be necessary and proper for carrying into Execution the foregoing Powers, and all other Powers vested by this Constitution in the Government of the United States, or in any Department or Officer thereof.

Section 9. [1] The Migration or Importation of such Persons as any of the States now existing shall think proper to admit, shall not be prohibited by the Congress prior to the Year one thousand eight hundred and eight, but a Tax or duty may be imposed on such Importation, not exceeding ten dollars for each Person.

[2]   The Privilege of the Writ of Habeas Corpus shall not be suspended, unless when in Cases of Rebellion or Invasion the public Safety may require it.

[3]   No Bill of Attainder or ex post facto Law shall be passed.

[4]   No Capitation, or other direct, Tax shall be laid, unless in Proportion to the Census or Enumeration herein before directed to be taken.

[5]   No Tax or Duty shall be laid on Articles exported from any State.

[6]   No Preference shall be given by any Regulation of Commerce or Revenue to the Ports of one State over those of another: nor shall Vessels bound to, or from, one State, be obliged to enter, clear, or pay Duties in another.

[7]   No Money shall be drawn from the Treasury, but in Consequence of Appropriations made by Law; and a regular Statement and Account of the Receipts and Expenditures of all public Money shall be published from time to time.

[8]   No Title of Nobility shall be granted by the United States: And no Person holding any Office of Profit or Trust under them, shall, without the Consent of the Congress, accept of any present, Emolument, Office, or Title, of any kind whatever, from any King, Prince, or foreign State.

Section 10.   [1]   No State shall enter into any Treaty, Alliance, or Confederation; grant Letters of Marque and Reprisal; coin Money; emit Bills of Credit; make any Thing but gold and silver Coin a Tender in Payment of Debts; pass any Bill of Attainder, ex post facto Law, or Law impairing the Obligation of Contracts, or grant any Title of Nobility.

[2] No State shall, without the Consent of the Congress, lay any Imposts or Duties on Imports or Exports, except what may be absolutely necessary for executing its inspection Laws: and the net Produce of all Duties and Imposts, laid by any State on Imports or Exports, shall be for the Use of the Treasury of the United States; and all such Laws shall be subject to the Revision and Controul of the Congress.

[3] No State shall, without the Consent of Congress, lay any Duty of Tonnage, keep Troops, or Ships of War in time of Peace, enter into any Agreement or Compact with another State, or with a foreign Power, or engage in War, unless actually invaded, or in such imminent Danger as will not admit of delay.

ARTICLE II

Section 1. [1] The executive Power shall be vested in a President of the United States of America. He shall hold his Office during the Term of four Years, and, together with the Vice President, chosen for the same Term, be elected, as follows:

[2] Each State shall appoint, in such Manner as the Legislature thereof may direct, a Number of Electors, equal to the whole Number of Senators and Representatives to which the State may be entitled in the Congress: but no Senator or Representative, or Person holding an Office of Trust or Profit under the United States, shall be appointed an Elector.

[3] The electors shall meet in their respective States, and vote by ballot for two Persons, of whom one at least shall not be an Inhabitant of the same State with themselves. And they shall make a List of all the Persons voted for, and of the Number of Votes for each; which List they shall sign and certify, and transmit sealed to the Seat of the Government of the United States, directed to the President of the Senate. The President of the Senate shall, in the Presence of the Senate and House of Representatives, open all the Certificates, and the Votes shall then be counted. The Person having the greatest Number of Votes shall be the President, if such Number be a Majority of the whole Number of Electors appointed; and if there be more than one who have such Majority, and have an equal Number of Votes, then the House of Representatives shall immediately chuse by Ballot one of them for President; and if no Person have a Majority, then from the five highest on the List the said House shall in like Manner chuse the President. But in chusing the President, the Votes shall be taken by States, the Representation from each State having one Vote; A quorum for this Purpose shall consist of a Member or Members from two thirds of the States, and a Majority of all the States shall be necessary to a Choice. In every Case, after the Choice of the President, the Person having the greatest Number of Votes of the Electors shall be the Vice President. But if there should remain two or more who have equal Votes, the Senate shall chuse from them by Ballot the Vice-President.

[4] The Congress may determine the Time of chusing the Electors, and the Day on which they shall give their Votes; which Day shall be the same throughout the United States.

[5] No Person except a natural born Citizen, or a Citizen of the United States, at the time of the Adoption of this Constitution, shall be eligible to the Office of President; neither shall any Person be eligible to that Office who shall not have attained to the Age of thirty five Years, and been fourteen Years a Resident within the United States.

[6] In Case of the Removal of the President from Office, or of his Death, Resignation, or Inability to discharge the Powers and Duties of the said Office, the Same shall devolve on the Vice President, and the Congress may by Law provide for the Case of Removal, Death, Resignation or Inability, both of the President and Vice President, declaring what Officer shall then act as President, and such Officer shall act accordingly, until the Disability be removed, or a President shall be elected.

[7] The President shall, at stated Times, receive for his Services, a Compensation, which shall neither be encreased nor diminished during the Period for which he shall have been elected, and he shall not receive within that Period any other Emolument from the United States, or any of them.

[8] Before he enter on the Execution of his Office, he shall take the following Oath or Affirmation: "I do solemnly swear (or affirm) that I will faithfully execute the Office of President of the United States, and will to the best of my Ability, preserve, protect and defend the Constitution of the United States."

Section 2. [1] The President shall be Commander in Chief of the Army and Navy of the United States, and of the Militia of the several States, when called into the actual Service of the United States; he may require the Opinion, in writing, of the principal Officer in each of the executive Departments, upon any Subject relating to the Duties of their respective Offices, and he shall have Power to grant Reprieves and Pardons for Offenses against the United States, except in Cases of Impeachment.

[2] He shall have Power, by and with the Advice and Consent of the Senate, to make Treaties, provided two thirds of the Senators present concur; and he shall nominate, and by and with the Advice and Consent of the Senate, shall appoint Ambassadors, other public Ministers and Consuls, Judges of the supreme Court, and all other Officers of the United States, whose Appointments are not herein otherwise provided for, and which shall be established by Law: but the Congress may by Law vest the Appointment of such inferior Officers, as they think proper, in the President alone, in the Courts of Law, or in the Heads of Departments.

[3] The President shall have Power to fill up all Vacancies that may happen during the Recess of the Senate, by granting Commissions which shall expire at the End of their next Session.

Section 3. He shall from time to time give to the Congress Information of the State of the Union, and recommend to their Consideration such Measures as he shall judge necessary and expedient; he may, on extraordinary Occasions, convene both Houses, or either of them, and in Case of Disagreement between them, with Respect to the Time of Adjournment, he may adjourn them

[3] The Senators and Representatives before mentioned, and the Members of the several State Legislatures, and all executive and judicial Officers, both of the United States and of the several States, shall be bound by Oath or Affirmation, to support this Constitution; but no religious Test shall ever be required as a Qualification to any Office or public Trust under the United States.

ARTICLE VII

The Ratification of the Conventions of nine States, shall be sufficient for the Establishment of this Constitution between the States so ratifying the Same.

ARTICLES IN ADDITION TO, AND AMENDMENT OF, THE CONSTITUTION OF THE UNITED STATES OF AMERICA, PROPOSED BY CONGRESS, AND RATIFIED BY THE LEGISLATURES OF THE SEVERAL STATES, PURSUANT TO THE FIFTH ARTICLE OF THE ORIGINAL CONSTITUTION.

AMENDMENT I [1791]

Congress shall make no law respecting an establishment of religion, or prohibiting the free exercise thereof; or abridging the freedom of speech, or of the press; or the right of the people peaceably to assemble, and to petition the Government for a redress of grievances.

AMENDMENT II [1791]

A well regulated Militia, being necessary to the security of a free State, the right of the people to keep and bear Arms, shall not be infringed.

AMENDMENT III [1791]

No Soldier shall, in time of peace be quartered in any house, without the consent of the Owner, nor in time of war, but in a manner to be prescribed by law.

AMENDMENT IV [1791]

The right of the people to be secure in their persons, houses, papers, and effects, against unreasonable searches and seizures, shall not be violated, and no Warrants shall issue, but upon probable cause, supported by Oath or affirmation, and particularly describing the place to be searched, and the persons or things to be seized.

AMENDMENT V [1791]

No person shall be held to answer for a capital, or otherwise infamous crime, unless on a presentment or indictment of a Grand Jury, except in cases arising in the land or naval forces, or in the Militia, when in actual service in time of War or public danger; nor shall any person be subject for the same offence to be twice put in jeopardy of life or limb; nor shall be compelled in any criminal case to be a witness against himself, nor be deprived of life, liberty, or property, without due process of law; nor shall private property be taken for public use, without just compensation.

AMENDMENT VI [1791]

In all criminal prosecutions, the accused shall enjoy the right to a speedy and public trial, by an impartial jury of the State and district wherein the crime shall have been committed, which district shall have been previously ascertained by law, and to be informed of the nature and cause of the accusation; to be confronted with the witnesses against him; to have compulsory process for obtaining witnesses in his favor, and to have the Assistance of Counsel for his defence.

AMENDMENT VII [1791]

In Suits at common law, where the value in controversy shall exceed twenty dollars, the right of trial by jury shall be preserved, and no fact tried by a jury, shall be otherwise re-examined in any Court of the United States, than according to the rules of the common law.

AMENDMENT VIII [1791]

Excessive bail shall not be required, nor excessive fines imposed, nor cruel and unusual punishments inflicted.

AMENDMENT IX [1791]

The enumeration in the Constitution, of certain rights, shall not be construed to deny or disparage others retained by the people.

AMENDMENT X [1791]

The powers not delegated to the United States by the Constitution, nor prohibited by it to the States, are reserved to the States respectively, or to the people.

AMENDMENT XI [1798]

The Judicial power of the United States shall not be construed to extend to any suit in law or equity, commenced or prosecuted against one of the United States by Citizens of another State, or by Citizens or Subjects of any Foreign State.

AMENDMENT XII [1804]

The Electors shall meet in their respective states and vote by ballot for President and Vice-President, one of whom, at least, shall not be an inhabitant of the same state with themselves; they shall name in their ballots the person voted for as President, and in distinct ballots the person voted for as Vice-President, and they shall make distinct lists of all persons voted for as President, and of all persons voted for as Vice-President, and of the number of votes for each, which lists they shall sign and certify, and transmit sealed to the seat of the government of the United States, directed to the President of the Senate;—The President of the Senate shall, in the presence of the Senate and House of Representatives, open all the certificates and the votes shall then be counted;—The person having the greatest number of votes for President, shall be the President, if such number be a majority of the whole number of Electors appointed; and if no person have such majority, then from the persons having the highest numbers not exceeding three on the list of those voted for as President, the House of Representatives shall choose immediately, by ballot, the President. But in choosing the President, the votes shall be taken by states, the representation from each state having one vote; a quorum for this purpose shall consist of a member or members from two-thirds of the states, and a majority of all the states shall be necessary to a choice. And if the House of Representatives shall not choose a President whenever the right of choice shall devolve upon them, before the fourth day of March next following, then the Vice-President shall act as President, as in the case of the death or other constitutional disability of the President. The person having the greatest number of votes as Vice-President, shall be the Vice-President, if such number be a majority of the whole number of Electors appointed, and if no person have a majority, then from the two highest numbers on the list, the Senate shall choose the Vice-President; a quorum for the purpose shall consist of two-thirds of the whole number of Senators, and a majority of the whole number shall be necessary to a choice. But no person constitutionally ineligible to the office of President shall be eligible to that of Vice-President of the United States.

AMENDMENT XIII [1865]

Section 1. Neither slavery nor involuntary servitude, except as a punishment for crime whereof the party shall have been duly convicted, shall exist within the United States, or any place subject to their jurisdiction.

Section 2. Congress shall have power to enforce this article by appropriate legislation.

AMENDMENT XIV [1868]

Section 1. All persons born or naturalized in the United States, and subject to the jurisdiction thereof, are citizens of the United States and of the State wherein they reside. No State shall make or enforce any law which shall abridge the privileges or immunities of citizens of the United States; nor shall any State deprive any person of life, liberty, or property, without due process of law; nor deny to any person within its jurisdiction the equal protection of the laws.

Section 2. Representatives shall be apportioned among the several States according to their respective numbers, counting the whole number of persons in each State, excluding Indians not taxed. But when the right to vote at any election for the choice of electors for President and Vice President of the United States, Representatives in Congress, the Executive and Judicial officers of a State, or the members of the Legislature thereof, is denied to any of the male inhabitants of such State, being twenty-one years of age, and citizens of the United States, or in any way abridged, except for participation in rebellion, or other crime, the basis of representation therein shall be reduced in the proportion which the number of such male citizens shall bear to the whole number of male citizens twenty-one years of age in such State.

Section 3. No person shall be a Senator or Representative in Congress, or elector of President and Vice President, or hold any office, civil or military, under the United States, or under any State, who, having previously taken an oath, as a member of Congress, or as an officer of the United States, or as a member of any State legislature, or as an executive or judicial officer of any State, to support the Constitution of the United States, shall have engaged in insurrection or rebellion against the same, or given aid or comfort to the enemies thereof. But Congress may by a vote of two-thirds of each House, remove such disability.

Section 4. The validity of the public debt of the United States, authorized by law, including debts incurred for payment of pensions and bounties for services in suppressing insurrection or rebellion, shall not be questioned. But neither the United States nor any State shall assume or pay any debt or obligation incurred in aid of insurrection or rebellion against the United States, or any claim for the loss or emancipation of any slave; but all such debts, obligations and claims shall be held illegal and void.

Section 5. The Congress shall have power to enforce, by appropriate legislation, the provisions of this article.

AMENDMENT XV [1870]

Section 1. The right of citizens of the United States to vote shall not be denied or abridged by the United States or by any State on account of race, color, or previous condition of servitude.

Section 2. The Congress shall have power to enforce this article by appropriate legislation.

AMENDMENT XVI [1913]

The Congress shall have power to lay and collect taxes on incomes, from whatever source derived, without apportionment among the several States, and without regard to any census or enumeration.

AMENDMENT XVII [1913]

[1] The Senate of the United States shall be composed of two Senators from each State, elected by the people thereof, for six years; and each Senator shall have one vote. The electors in each State shall have the qualifications requisite for electors of the most numerous branch of the State legislatures.

[2] When vacancies happen in the representation of any State in the Senate, the executive authority of such State shall issue writs of election to fill such vacancies: *Provided*, That the legislature of any State may empower the executive thereof to make temporary appointments until the people fill the vacancies by election as the legislature may direct.

[3] This amendment shall not be so construed as to affect the election or term of any Senator chosen before it becomes valid as part of the Constitution.

AMENDMENT XVIII [1919]

Section 1. After one year from the ratification of this article the manufacture, sale, or transportation of intoxicating liquors within, the importation thereof into, or the exportation thereof from the United States and all territory subject to the jurisdiction thereof for beverage purposes is hereby prohibited.

Section 2. The Congress and the several States shall have concurrent power to enforce this article by appropriate legislation.

Section 3. This article shall be inoperative unless it shall have been ratified as an amendment to the Constitution by the legislatures of the several States, as provided in the Constitution, within seven years from the date of the submission hereof to the States by the Congress.

AMENDMENT XIX [1920]

[1] The right of citizens of the United States to vote shall not be denied or abridged by the United States or by any State on account of sex.

[2] Congress shall have power to enforce this article by appropriate legislation.

AMENDMENT XX [1933]

Section 1. The terms of the President and Vice President shall end at noon on the 20th day of January, and the terms of Senators and Representatives at noon on the 3d day of January, of the years in which such terms would have ended if this article had not been ratified; and the terms of their successors shall then begin.

Section 2. The Congress shall assemble at least once in every year, and such meeting shall begin at noon on the 3d day of January, unless they shall by law appoint a different day.

Section 3. If, at the time fixed for the beginning of the term of the President, the President elect shall have died, the Vice President elect shall become President. If a President shall not have been chosen before the time fixed for the beginning of his term, or if the President elect shall have failed to qualify, then the Vice President elect shall act as President until a President shall have qualified; and the Congress may by law provide for the case wherein neither a President elect nor a Vice President elect shall have qualified, declaring who shall then act as President, or the manner in which one who is to act shall be selected, and such person shall act accordingly until a President or Vice President shall have qualified.

Section 4. The Congress may by law provide for the case of the death of any of the persons from whom the House of Representatives may choose a President whenever the right of choice shall have devolved upon them, and for the case of the death of any of the persons from whom the Senate may choose a Vice President whenever the right of choice shall have devolved upon them.

Section 5. Sections 1 and 2 shall take effect on the 15th day of October following the ratification of this article.

Section 6. This article shall be inoperative unless it shall have been ratified as an amendment to the Constitution by the legislatures of three-fourths of the several States within seven years from the date of its submission.

AMENDMENT XXI [1933]

Section 1. The eighteenth article of amendment to the Constitution of the United States is hereby repealed.

Section 2. The transportation or importation into any State, Territory, or possession of the United States for delivery or use therein of intoxicating liquors, in violation of the laws thereof, is hereby prohibited.

Section 3. This article shall be inoperative unless it shall have been ratified as an amendment to the Constitution by conventions in the several States, as provided in the Constitution, within seven years from the date of the submission hereof to the States by the Congress.

AMENDMENT XXII [1951]

Section 1. No person shall be elected to the office of the President more than twice, and no person who has held the office of President, or acted as President, for more than two years of a term to which some other person was elected President shall be elected to the office of the President more than once. But this Article shall not apply to any person holding the office of President when this Article was proposed by the Congress, and shall not prevent any person who may be holding the office of President, or acting as President, during the term within which this Article becomes operative from holding the office of President or acting as President during the remainder of such term.

Section 2. This article shall be inoperative unless it shall have been ratified as an amendment to the Constitution by the legislatures of three-fourths of the several States within seven years from the date of its submission to the States by the Congress.

AMENDMENT XXIII [1961]

Section 1. The District constituting the seat of Government of the United States shall appoint in such manner as the Congress may direct:

A number of electors of President and Vice President equal to the whole number of Senators and Representatives in Congress to which the District would be entitled if it were a State, but in no event more than the least populous State; they shall be in addition to those appointed by the States, but they shall be considered, for the purposes of the election of President and Vice President, to be electors appointed by a State; and they shall meet in the District and perform such duties as provided by the twelfth article of amendment.

Section 2. The Congress shall have power to enforce this article by appropriate legislation.

AMENDMENT XXIV [1964]

Section 1. The right of citizens of the United States to vote in any primary or other election for President or Vice President, for electors for President or Vice President, or for Senator or Representative in Congress, shall not be denied or abridged by the United States or any State by reason of failure to pay any poll tax or other tax.

Section 2. The Congress shall have power to enforce this article by appropriate legislation.

AMENDMENT XXV [1967]

Section 1. In case of the removal of the President from office or of his death or resignation, the Vice President shall become President.

Section 2. Whenever there is a vacancy in the office of the Vice President, the President shall nominate a Vice President who shall take office upon confirmation by a majority vote of both Houses of Congress.

Section 3. Whenever the President transmits to the President pro tempore of the Senate and the Speaker of the House of Representatives his written declaration that he is unable to discharge the powers and duties of his office, and until he transmits to them a written declaration to the contrary, such powers and duties shall be discharged by the Vice President as Acting President.

Section 4. Whenever the Vice President and a majority of either the principal officers of the executive departments or of such other body as Congress may by law provide, transmit to the President pro tempore of the Senate and the Speaker of the House of Representatives their written declaration that the President is unable to discharge the powers and duties of his office, the Vice President shall immediately assume the powers and duties of the office as Acting President.

Thereafter, when the President transmits to the President pro tempore of the Senate and the Speaker of the House of Representatives his written declaration that no inability exists, he shall resume the powers and duties of his office unless the Vice President and a majority of either the principal officers of the executive department or of such other body as Congress may by law provide, transmit within four days to the President pro tempore of the Senate and the Speaker of the House of Representatives their written declaration that the President is unable to discharge the powers and duties of his office. Thereupon Congress shall decide the issue, assembling within forty-eight hours for that purpose if not in session. If the Congress, within twenty-one days after receipt of the latter written declaration, or, if Congress is not in session, within twenty-one days after Congress is required to assemble, determines by two-thirds vote of both Houses that the President is unable to discharge the powers and duties of his office, the Vice President shall continue to discharge the same as Acting President; otherwise, the President shall resume the powers and duties of his office.

AMENDMENT XXVI [1971]

Section 1. The right of citizens of the United States, who are eighteen years of age or older, to vote shall not be denied or abridged by the United States or by any State on account of age.

Section 2. The Congress shall have power to enforce this article by appropriate legislation.

Amendment XXVII [1992]

No law, varying the compensation for the services of the Senators and Representatives, shall take effect, until an election of Representatives shall have intervened.

Appendix B

THE SUPREME COURT'S CANONS OF STATUTORY INTERPRETATION

This is a collection of canons invoked by the Supreme Court from the 1986 through the 2006 Terms and divided into categories that parallel the typology provided in Chapter 8.[*]

TEXTUAL CANONS

- Plain meaning rule: follow the plain meaning of the statutory text,[1] except when textual plain meaning requires an absurd result[2] or suggests a scrivener's error.[3]

LINGUISTIC INFERENCES

- *Expressio* (or *inclusio*) *unius*: expression of one thing suggests the exclusion of others.[4] Inapplicable if context suggests listing is not comprehensive.[5]

---

*. Diana Rusk, Yale Law School Class of 2009, provided invaluable assistance in the preparation of this appendix.

1. Massachusetts v. EPA, 127 S.Ct. 1438, 1459–63 (2007); Arlington Cent. Sch. Dist. Bd. of Educ. v. Murphy, 126 S.Ct. 2455, 2459 (2006); Barnhart v. Thomas, 540 U.S. 20, 26–29 (2003); West Virginia Univ. Hosps. v. Casey, 499 U.S. 83 (1991); United States v. Providence Journal Co., 485 U.S. 693, 700–01 (1988).

2. Zuni Pub. Sch. Dist. No. 89 v. Department of Educ., 127 S.Ct. 1534, 1549–50 (2007) (Stevens, J., concurring); United States v. Wilson, 503 U.S. 329, 334 (1992); Green v. Bock Laundry Mach. Co., 490 U.S. 504, 509–11 (1989). This exception is controversial within the Court, e.g., *Zuni*, 127 S.Ct. at 1555–59 (Scalia, J., dissenting).

3. Lamie v. United States Trustee, 540 U.S. 526, 530–31 (2004); United States Nat'l Bank v. Independent Ins. Agents, 508 U.S. 439, 462 (1993).

4. Hinck v. United States, 127 S.Ct. 2011, 2015 (2007); TRW, Inc. v. Andrews, 534 U.S. 19 (2001); City of Chicago v. Environmental Def. Fund, 511 U.S. 328 (1994); United States v. Smith, 499 U.S. 160 (1991); Mississippi Band of Choctaw Indians v. Holyfield, 490 U.S. 30, 46–47 & n.22 (1989); Chan v. Korean Air Lines, Ltd., 490 U.S. 122, 133–34 (1989).

5. Marrama v. Citizens Bank of Mass., 127 S.Ct. 1105, 1111–12 (2007); Christensen v. Harris County, 529 U.S. 576, 583–84 (2000); Burns v. United States, 501 U.S. 129, 136 (1991); Sullivan v. Hudson, 490 U.S. 877, 891–92 (1989).

- *Noscitur a sociis*: interpret a general term to be similar to more specific terms in a series.[6] *Noscitur* is often not helpful when applied to a technical statute whose details were hammered out through a complex process.[7]

- *Ejusdem generis*: interpret a general term to reflect the class of objects reflected in more specific terms accompanying it.[8] *Ejusdem* might be trumped by other canons, such as the rule against redundancy.[9]

- Follow ordinary usage of terms, unless Congress gives them a specified or technical meaning.[10]

- Where Congress uses terms that have settled meaning, either by common usage or through the common law, interpreters should apply that settled meaning.[11]

- Defer to experts, including agencies, regarding the meaning of technical terminology.[12]

- Follow dictionary definitions of terms,[13] unless Congress has provided a specific definition.[14] Consider dictionaries of the era in which the statute was enacted.[15] For technical terms, consult specialized dictionaries.[16] Do not credit nonstandard, "idiosyncratic" dictionary definitions.[17]

---

6. Gustafson v. Alloyd Co., 513 U.S. 561, 575 (1995); Beecham v. United States, 511 U.S. 368, 371 (1994); Dole v. United Steelworkers of Am., 494 U.S. 26, 36 (1990); Massachusetts v. Morash, 490 U.S. 107, 114–15 (1989).

7. S.D. Warren Co. v. Maine Bd. of Envtl. Prot., 126 S.Ct. 1843, 1849–50 (2006).

8. James v. United States, 127 S.Ct. 1586, 1592 (2007); Circuit City Stores, Inc. v. Adams, 532 U.S. 105 (2001); Hughey v. United States, 495 U.S. 411, 419 (1990); Norfolk & Western Ry. Co. v. American Train Dispatchers' Ass'n, 499 U.S. 117, 129 (1991).

9. Babbitt v. Sweet Home Chapter of Communities for a Great Oregon, 515 U.S. 687 (1995).

10. Lopez v. Gonzales, 127 S.Ct. 625, 630 (2006); Pasquantino v. United States, 544 U.S. 349, 355 (2005); Will v. Michigan Dep't of State Police, 491 U.S. 58, 64 (1989).

11. Stewart v. Dutra Constr. Co., 543 U.S. 481, 487 (2005); Scheidler v. NOW, Inc., 537 U.S. 393, 402 (2003); United States v. Wells, 519 U.S. 482, 491 (1997); Community for Creative Non-Violence v. Reid, 490 U.S. 730, 739 (1989).

12. Zuni Pub. Sch. Dist. No. 89 v. Department of Educ., 127 S.Ct. 1534, 1540 (2007).

13. Limtiaco v. Comacho, 127 S.Ct. 1413, 1416 (2007) (Black's); Rapanos v. United States, 126 S.Ct. 2208, 2221 (2006) (plurality opinion of Scalia, J.) (Webster's Second); Muscarello v. United States, 524 U.S. 125 (1998) (Oxford English); Pittston Coal Group v. Sebben, 488 U.S. 105, 113 (1988) (Webster's Third).

14. Babbitt v. Sweet Home Chapter of Communities for a Great Oregon, 515 U.S. 687 (1995).

15. Permanent Mission of India to the United Nations v. City of New York, 127 S.Ct. (2007); Cook County v. United States *ex rel.* Chandler, 538 U.S. 119, 125–27 (2003); St. Francis College v. Al-Khazraji, 481 U.S. 604 (1987).

16. Zuni Pub. Sch. Dist. No. 89 v. Department of Educ., 127 S.Ct. 1534, 1544, 1546 (2007).

17. MCI v. AT&T, 512 U.S. 218 (1994) (disrespecting *Webster's Third* for including colloquial as well as standard definitions).

- Rules of Construction Act, 1 U.S.C. § 1 et seq., contains default definitions that apply if Congress fails to define a particular term.[18]

- A statute has a plain meaning if you'd use its terminology at a cocktail party, and "no one would look at you funny."[19]

GRAMMAR AND SYNTAX

- Punctuation rule: Congress is presumed to follow accepted punctuation standards, so that placements of commas and other punctuation are assumed to be meaningful.[20]

- Grammar rule: Congress is presumed to follow accepted standards of grammar.[21]

- Rule of the last antecedent: referential and qualifying words or phrases refer only to the last antecedent, unless contrary to the apparent legislative intent derived from the sense of the entire enactment.[22] Do not have to apply this rule if not practical.[23]

- "May" is usually precatory and connotes decisionmaking discretion,[24] while "shall" is usually mandatory and suggests less discretion.[25]

- "Or" means in the alternative.[26]

TEXTUAL INTEGRITY (WHOLE ACT RULE)

- Each statutory provision should be read by reference to the whole act.[27] Statutory interpretation is a "holistic" endeavor.[28]

---

18. Stewart v. Dutra Constr. Co., 543 U.S. 481 (2005).

19. Johnson v. United States, 529 U.S. 694, 718 (2000) (Scalia, J., dissenting).

20. Jama v. Immigration & Customs Enforcement, 543 U.S. 335, 344 (2005) (significance of periods); United States v. Ron Pair Enters., 489 U.S. 235, 241–42 (1989) (comma placement); San Francisco Arts & Athletics, Inc. v. United States Olympic Comm'n, 483 U.S. 522, 528–29 (1987).

21. Limtiaco v. Camacho, 127 S.Ct. 1413, 1419 (2007); Rapanos v. United States, 126 S.Ct. 2208, 2220–21 (2006) (plurality opinion of Scalia, J.); Jama v. Immigration & Customs Enforcement, 543 U.S. 335 (2005).

22. Jama v. Immigration & Customs Enforcement, 543 U.S. 335 (2005); Barnhart v. Thomas, 540 U.S. 20, 26 (2003); Nobelman v. American Savs. Bank, 508 U.S. 324, 330 (1993).

23. Nobelman v. American Sav. Bank, 508 U.S. 324, 330–31 (1993).

24. Jama v. Immigration & Customs Enforcement, 543 U.S. 335 (2005); Lopez v. Davis, 531 U.S. 230 (2001) ("may" vests wide discretion in agency).

25. Mallard v. United States Dist. Ct., 490 U.S. 296, 302 (1989).

26. Hawaiian Airlines v. Norris, 512 U.S. 246, 253–54 (1994).

27. Ledbetter v. Goodyear Tire & Rubber Co., 127 S.Ct. 2162 (2007); Gonzales v. Oregon, 546 U.S. 243, 273–74 (2006); Doe v. Chao, 540 U.S. 614 (2004) (considering uncodified parts of the "whole act"); Clark v. Martinez, 543 U.S. 371 (2005); Babbitt v. Sweet Home Chapter of Communities for a Great Oregon, 515 U.S. 687 (1995); Pavelic & Leflore v. Marvel Entm't Group, 493 U.S. 120, 123–24 (1989); Massachusetts v. Morash, 490 U.S. 107, 114–15 (1989).

28. United Sav. Ass'n v. Timbers of Inwood Forest Assocs., Ltd., 484 U.S. 365, 371 (1988).

- The statute's preamble may provide clues to statutory meaning,[29] as may the title.[30]

- Presumption against redundancy: avoid interpreting a provision in a way that would render other provisions of the statute superfluous or unnecessary.[31] This presumption must give way when offset by other evidence of statutory meaning, however.[32]

- Presumption of statutory consistency: interpret the same or similar terms in a statute the same way.[33] Presumption rebutted when other evidence suggests Congress was using the same term in different ways.[34]

- Presumption of meaningful variation: different statutory wording suggests different statutory meaning,[35] especially when Congress considered and rejected the alternate wording.[36] Presumption inapplicable when there is a reasonable explanation for variation (e.g., different provisions are enacted at different times).[37]

- Avoid interpreting a provision in a way that is inconsistent with the overall structure of the statute[38] *or* with another provision[39] *or* with a subsequent

---

29. Sutton v. United Airlines, Inc., 527 U.S. 471 (1999); id. (Ginsburg, J., concurring).

30. Porter v. Nussle, 534 U.S. 516, 524 (2002). This is an exceedingly weak canon and has not been a key reason in any Rehnquist-Roberts Court case.

31. Circuit City Stores, Inc. v. Adams, 532 U.S. 105 (2001); United States v. Alaska, 521 U.S. 1 (1997); Walters v. Metropolitan Educ. Enters., Inc., 519 U.S. 202 (1997); Rake v. Wade, 508 U.S. 464 (1993); Kungys v. United States, 485 U.S. 759, 778 (1988) (plurality opinion by Scalia, J.).

32. Gutierrez v. Ada, 528 U.S. 250 (2000); Landgraf v. USI Film Prods., 511 U.S. 240, 259–60 (1994).

33. Powerex Corp. v. Reliant Energy Servs., Inc., 127 S.Ct. 2411 (2007); IBP, Inc. v. Alvarez, 546 U.S. 21, 34 (2005); Commissioner v. Lundy, 516 U.S. 235, 249–50 (1996); Gustafson v. Alloyd Co., 513 U.S. 561, 570 (1995); Sullivan v. Stroop, 496 U.S. 478, 484 (1990); United Sav. Ass'n v. Timbers of Inwood Forest Assocs., Ltd., 484 U.S. 365, 371 (1988).

34. Environmental Defense v. Duke Energy Corp., 127 S.Ct. 1423, 1432 (2007); Robinson v. Shell Oil Co., 519 U.S. 337, 343–44 (1997); Dewsnup v. Timm, 502 U.S. 410, 417 & n.3 (1992)

35. Lawrence v. Florida, 127 S.Ct. 1079, 1083–84 (2007); Lopez v. Gonzales, 127 S.Ct. 625, 630–31 (2006); Lindh v. Murphy, 521 U.S. 320 (1997); Keene Corp. v. United States, 508 U.S. 200, 208 (1993); Gozlon-Peretz v. United States, 498 U.S. 395, 404–05 (1991). The leading case is Russello v. United States, 464 U.S. 16, 23 (1983).

36. Hamdan v. Rumsfeld, 126 S.Ct. 2749, 2765–66 (2006).

37. Gutierrez v. Ada, 528 U.S. 250 (2000); Field v. Mans, 516 U.S. 59, 67–69 (1995).

38. Ledbetter v. Goodyear Tire & Rubber Co., 127 S.Ct. 2162 (2007); Beck v. PACE Int'l Union, 127 S.Ct. 2310 (2007).

39. Babbitt v. Sweet Home Chapter of Communities for a Great Oregon, 515 U.S. 687 (1995); Gade v. National Solid Waste Management Ass'n, 505 U.S. 88, 100–01 (1992); United Sav. Ass'n v. Timbers of Inwood Forest Assocs., Ltd., 484 U.S. 365, 371 (1988).

amendment to the statute[40] *or* with another statute enacted by a Congress relying on a particular interpretation.[41]

- Presumption of purposive amendment: statutory amendments are meant to have real and substantial effect.[42]

- Avoid the implication of broad congressional delegation of agency authority when statute carefully limits agency authority in particular matters.[43]

- Avoid broad readings of statutory provisions if Congress has specifically provided for the broader policy in more specific language elsewhere.[44]

- Broad term is presumptively ambiguous if Congress has elsewhere used more targeted terminology.[45]

- Specific provisions targeting a particular issue apply instead of provisions more generally covering the issue.[46]

- Provisos and statutory exceptions should be read narrowly.[47]

- Do not create exceptions in addition to those specified by Congress.[48]

EXTRINSIC SOURCE CANONS

AGENCY INTERPRETATIONS

- *Skidmore* deference. Agency interpretations are entitled to respect to the extent that they have "power to persuade" based upon consistency, factual basis, and expertise.[49] Contrariwise, agency views that are shifting or insufficiently developed have little or no persuasive value.[50]

---

40. Gonzales v. Oregon, 546 U.S. 243, 257–58 (2006).

41. FDA v. Brown & Williamson Tobacco Corp., 529 U.S. 120, 144 (2000).

42. Rumsfeld v. Forum for Academic & Institutional Rights, Inc., 547 U.S. 47 (2006); Babbitt v. Sweet Home Chapter of Communities for a Great Oregon, 515 U.S. 687 (1995).

43. Gonzales v. Oregon, 547 U.S. 243, 262–63 (2006).

44. Arlington Cent. Sch. Dist. Bd. of Educ. v. Murphy, 126 S.Ct. 2455, 2461–63 (2006); Jama v. Immigration & Customs Enforcement, 543 U.S. 335 (2005); Custis v. United States, 511 U.S. 485, 491 (1994); West Virginia Univ. Hosps. v. Casey, 499 U.S. 83, 99 (1991).

45. Zuni Pub. Sch. Dist. No. 89 v. Department of Educ., 127 S.Ct. 1534, 1545 (2007).

46. Green v. Bock Laundry Mach. Co., 490 U.S. 504, 524–26 (1989); Crawford Fitting Co. v. J.T. Gibbons, Inc., 482 U.S. 437, 444–45 (1987).

47. Cherokee Nation of Oklahoma v. Leavitt, 543 U.S. 631 (2005); Commissioner v. Clark, 489 U.S. 726, 739 (1989).

48. United States v. Smith, 499 U.S. 160, 166–67 (1991).

49. Beck v. PACE Int'l Union, 127 S.Ct. 2310 (2007); Gonzales v. Oregon, 546 U.S. 243, 255–56 (2006); United States v. Mead Corp., 533 U.S. 218, 226–27 (2001); EEOC v. Arabian Am. Oil Co., 499 U.S. 244 (1991). The leading case is Skidmore v. Swift & Co., 323 U.S. 134, 140 (1944).

50. Burlington Northern & Santa Fe Ry. v. White, 126 S.Ct. 2405, 2413–14 (2006).

- Even informal and unsettled agency interpretations (such as those embodied in handbooks or litigation briefs) may be useful confirmations for the interpreter's interpretation of statutory language.[51]

- *Chevron* deference. "Reasonable" agency interpretations pursuant to congressional delegation of lawmaking authority are binding on courts unless Congress has directly addressed the issue.[52] *Chevron* might also apply to notice-and-comment rules filling statutory gaps that the agency reasonably treats as binding on itself and the public.[53] The agency's discretion is at its height when the agency decides not to enforce a statute.[54]

- For *Chevron* purposes, whether Congress has delegated the agency lawmaking authority is itself a matter of statutory interpretation.[55] Presumption against congressional delegation of authority for agency to make fundamental changes in the statute.[56] The Court demands a clear statement authorizing agency constructions that press the envelope of constitutional validity.[57]

- *Seminole Rock* deference. Agency interpretation of its own regulations is controlling unless "plainly erroneous or inconsistent with the regulation."[58] Rule does not apply when agency rule merely "parrots" the statute,[59] or where agency interpretation has been unstable over time.[60]

- *Curtiss-Wright* deference. In matters of foreign affairs and national security, presidential or executive statutory interpretations enjoy a super-strong

---

51. S.D. Warren Co. v. Maine Bd. of Envtl. Prot., 126 S.Ct. 1843, 1848–49 (2006).

52. Zuni Pub. Sch. Dist. No. 89 v. Department of Educ., 127 S.Ct. 1534, 1540–46 (2007); id. at 1550–51 (Kennedy, J., concurring); National Cable & Telecommunications Ass'n v. Brand X Internet Servs., 545 U.S. 967 (2005); ABF Freight Sys., Inc. v. NLRB, 510 U.S. 317, 324 (1994); Sullivan v. Everhart, 494 U.S. 83, 88–89 (1990); K Mart Corp. v. Cartier, Inc., 486 U.S. 281, 291–92 (1988). The leading case is Chevron U.S.A., Inc. v. Natural Resources Defense Council, 467 U.S. 837 (1984).

53. Long Island Care at Home, Ltd. v. Coke, 127 S.Ct. 2339 (2007).

54. Massachusetts v. EPA, 127 S.Ct. 1438, 1459 (2007).

55. Gonzales v. Oregon, 546 U.S. 243 (2006).

56. Gonzales v. Oregon, 546 U.S. 243 (2006); FDA v. Brown & Williamson Tobacco Corp., 529 U.S. 120 (2000); MCI v. AT&T, 512 U.S. 218 (1994).

57. Rapanos v. United States, 126 S.Ct. 2208, 2224–25 (2006) (plurality opinion of Scalia, J.); Edward J. Debartolo Corp. v. Florida Gulf Coast Building & Constr. Trades Council, 485 U.S. 568, 575 (1988).

58. Auer v. Robbins, 519 U.S. 452, 461–63 (1997); Thomas Jefferson Univ. v. Shalala, 512 U.S. 504, 512 (1994); Mullins Coal Co. v. Director, Office of Workers' Compensation Programs, 484 U.S. 135, 159 (1987). The leading case is Bowles v. Seminole Rock & Sand Co., 325 U.S. 410, 414 (1945).

59. Gonzales v. Oregon, 546 U.S. 243, 257 (2006).

60. Commissioner v. Schleier, 515 U.S. 323 (1995); Bowen v. Georgetown Univ. Hosp., 488 U.S. 204 (1988).

presumption of correctness.[61] (The executive is still bound by statutory and treaty directives.[62]) Similar deference for executive branch views of federal jurisdiction over foreign states.[63]

- Courts accord great weight to executive department interpretation of treaties.[64]

CONTINUITY IN LAW

- Super-strong presumption of correctness for statutory precedents,[65] sometimes including statutory precedents whose narrow holding has been overridden by Congress.[66] The super-strong rule against overruling statutory precedents is inapplicable to the Sherman Act, which is a common law statute.[67]

- Wrongly decided precedents that are also inconsistent with recent legal developments can be overruled.[68]

- Where Supreme Court decision follows an agency interpretation filling a gap in the law left by Congress (*Chevron*), a revised agency interpretation through rulemaking is not barred by *stare decisis*.[69]

- Presumption of continuity: Congress does not create discontinuities in legal rights and obligations without some clear statement.[70]

---

61. Hamdi v. Rumsfeld, 542 U.S. 507, 518 (2004) (plurality opinion of O'Connor, J.); id. at 580–81 (Thomas, J., concurring in part, with a stronger statement); Cheney v. U.S. Dist. Court, 542 U.S. 367 (2004); Crosby v. National Foreign Trade Council, 530 U.S. 363 (2000); Department of Navy v. Egan, 484 U.S. 518 (1988). The leading case is United States v. Curtiss–Wright Export Corp., 299 U.S. 304 (1936).

62. Hamdan v. Rumsfeld, 126 S.Ct. 2749 (2006).

63. Republic of Austria v. Altmann, 541 U.S. 677, 689–90 (2004).

64. Sanchez–Llamas v. Oregon, 126 S.Ct. 2669 (2006); El Al Israel Airlines v. Tsui Yuan Tseng, 525 U.S. 155 (1999).

65. Rita v. United States, 168 L.Ed.2d 203, 220–24 (2007) (Stevens, J., concurring); id. at 224 (Scalia, J., concurring in the judgment); Hohn v. United States, 524 U.S. 236, 251 (1998); Neal v. United States, 516 U.S. 284 (1996); California v. FERC, 495 U.S. 490, 498–99 (1990); Patterson v. McLean Credit Union, 491 U.S. 164 (1989).

66. Ledbetter v. Goodyear Tire & Rubber Co., 127 S.Ct. 2162 (2007); Arlington Cent. Sch. Dist. Bd. of Educ. v. Murphy, 126 S.Ct. 2455 (2006). This canon is controversial within the Court. See *Ledbetter*, 127 S.Ct. at 2182–84 (Ginsburg, J., dissenting).

67. Leegin Creative Leather Prods. v. PSKS, Inc., 127 S.Ct. 2705 (2007); State Oil Co. v. Khan, 522 U.S. 3 (1997).

68. Leegin Creative Leather Prods. v. PSKS, Inc., 127 S.Ct. 2705 (2007); Bowles v. Russell, 127 S.Ct. 2360 (2007); Rodriguez de Quijas v. Shearson/American Express, Inc., 490 U.S. 477, 480–81 (1989).

69. Central Laborers' Pension Fund v. Heinz, 541 U.S. 739, 751 (2004) (Breyer, J., concurring); Norfolk Southern Ry. v. Shankin, 529 U.S. 344 (2000) (Breyer, J., concurring); Christensen v. Harris County, 529 U.S. 576, 589 (2000) (Souter, J., concurring); United States v. Watts, 519 U.S. 148 (1997) (Breyer, J., concurring).

70. Green v. Bock Laundry Mach. Co., 490 U.S. 504, 521–22 (1989); Finley v. United States, 490 U.S. 545, 554 (1989).

- Presumption against repeals by implication.[71] But where there is a clear repugnancy between a more recent statutory scheme and an earlier one, partial repeal will be inferred.[72]

- Presumption against hiding elephants in mouseholes: Congress usually does not alter the fundamental details of a regulatory scheme in vague or ancillary provisions.[73]

- Presumption that Congress uses same term consistently in different statutes.[74]

- Presumption that statutes be interpreted consistent with international law and treaties.[75] But international agreements do not trump the plain meaning of federal statutes.[76]

- Borrowed statute rule: when Congress borrows a statute, it adopts by implication interpretations placed on that statute,[77] absent indication to the contrary.[78]

- In pari materia rule: when similar statutory provisions are found in comparable statutory schemes, interpreters should presumptively apply them the same way.[79]

- Re-enactment rule: when Congress re-enacts a statute, it incorporates settled interpretations of the re-enacted statute.[80] The rule is inapplicable when there is no settled standard Congress could have known.[81]

---

71. Hamdan v. Rumsfeld, 126 S.Ct. 2749, 2775 (2006); Granholm v. Heald, 544 U.S. 460 (2005); Branch v. Smith, 538 U.S. 254, 273 (2003); Pittsburgh & Lake Erie R.R. v. Railway Labor Executives' Ass'n, 491 U.S. 490, 509 (1989); Traynor v. Turnage, 485 U.S. 535, 547–48 (1988). The leading case is Morton v. Mancari, 417 U.S. 535 (1974).

72. Credit Suisse Securities (USA) LLC v. Billing, 127 S.Ct. 2383 (2007).

73. Gonzales v. Oregon, 546 U.S. 243, 267 (2006); Whitman v. American Trucking Ass'ns, Inc., 531 U.S. 457, 468 (2001); FDA v. Brown & Williamson Tobacco Corp., 529 U.S. 120, 160 (2000).

74. Hawaiian Airlines v. Norris, 512 U.S. 246, 254 (1994); Smith v. United States, 508 U.S. 223, 234–35 (1993); Pierce v. Underwood, 487 U.S. 552 (1988).

75. Spector v. Norwegian Cruise Line Ltd., 545 U.S. 119 (2005); id. at 142 (Ginsburg, J., concurring in part and in the judgment); Hamdi v. Rumsfeld, 542 U.S. 507 (2004) (plurality opinion of O'Connor, J.); INS v. Cardoza-Fonseca, 480 U.S. 421 (1987) (strong presumption when statute is implementing an international agreement).

76. Societe Nationale Industrielle Aerospatialle v. U.S. Dist. Ct., 482 U.S. 522, 538–39 (1987).

77. Molzof v. United States, 502 U.S. 301, 307 (1992); Metropolitan Life Ins. Co. v. Taylor, 481 U.S. 58, 65–66 (1987).

78. Shannon v. United States, 512 U.S. 573, 581 (1994).

79. Ledbetter v. Goodyear Tire & Rubber Co., 127 S.Ct. 2162, 2176–78 (2007) (finding NLRA but not EPA analogous to Title VII for limitations purposes).

80. Davis v. United States, 495 U.S. 472, 482 (1990); Pierce v. Underwood, 487 U.S. 552 (1988).

81. Jama v. Immigration & Customs Enforcement, 543 U.S. 335 (2005).

- Acquiescence rules: consistent agency or Supreme Court interpretation known to Congress is presumed correct.[82] Also, consider unbroken line of lower court decisions interpreting statute, but do not give them decisive weight.[83]

EXTRINSIC LEGISLATIVE SOURCES

- Statutory history (the formal evolution of a statute, as Congress amends it over the years) is always potentially relevant.[84]

- Consider legislative history (the internal evolution of a statute before enactment) if the statute is ambiguous.[85] But legislative history of an obsolete provision is unlikely to be probative.[86]

- Committee reports (especially conference committee reports reflecting the understanding of both House and Senate) are the most authoritative legislative history,[87] but cannot trump a textual plain meaning,[88] and should not be relied on if they are themselves ambiguous or imprecise.[89]

- Committee report language that cannot be tied to a specific statutory provision cannot be credited.[90] House and Senate reports inconsistent with one another should be discounted.[91]

---

82. Zuni Pub. Sch. Dist. No. 89 v. Department of Educ., 127 S.Ct. 1534 (2007) (agency interpretation); FDA v. Brown & Williamson Tobacco Corp., 529 U.S. 120 (2000) (agency).

83. Gonzalez v. Crosby, 545 U.S. 524 (2005); General Dynamics Land Sys., Inc. v. Cline, 540 U.S. 581 (2004); National Archives & Records Admin. v. Favish, 541 U.S. 157 (2004); Monessen Sw. Ry. Co. v. Morgan, 486 U.S. 330, 338–39 (1988).

84. Powerex Corp. v. Reliant Energy Servs., Inc., 127 S.Ct. 2411 (2007) (Scalia, J.); Ballard v. Commissioner, 544 U.S. 40 (2005). Unlike reference to internal legislative materials, this canon is *not* controversial within the Court.

85. Safeco Ins. Co. of Am. v. Burr, 127 S.Ct. 2201 (2007); Zuni Pub. Sch. Dist. No. 89 v. Department of Educ., 127 S.Ct. 1534 (2007); Gonzales v. Oregon, 546 U.S. 243, 257–58 (2006); Rumsfeld v. Forum for Academic & Institutional Rights, 547 U.S. 47 (2006); Koons Buick Pontiac GMC, Inc. v. Nigh, 543 U.S. 50, 62–64 (2004); id. at 65–66 (Stevens, J., concurring); FDA v. Brown & Williamson Tobacco Corp., 529 U.S. 120 (2000); Babbitt v. Sweet Home Chapter of Communities for a Great Oregon, 515 U.S. 687 (1995); Wisconsin Pub. Intervenor v. Mortier, 501 U.S. 597, 610 n.4 (1991). This canon is controversial within the Court. See id. at 616–17 (Scalia, J., concurring in the judgment).

86. James v. United States, 127 S.Ct. 1586, 1593 (2007).

87. Tellabs, Inc. v. Makor Issues & Rights, Ltd., 127 S.Ct. 2499 (2007); Rumsfeld v. Forum for Academic & Institutional Rights, 547 U.S. 47 (2006); Cherokee Nation of Oklahoma v. Leavitt, 543 U.S. 631 (2005); Intel Corp. v. Advanced Micro Devices, Inc., 542 U.S. 241 (2004); Jones v. R.R. Donnelley & Sons Co., 541 U.S. 369 (2004); Boeing Co. v. United States, 537 U.S. 437 (2003); Johnson v. DeGrandy, 512 U.S. 997, 1010–11 & n.9 (1994).

88. Arlington Cent. Sch. Dist. Bd. of Educ. v. Murphy, 126 S.Ct. 2455, 2463 (2006); id. at 2464–65 (Ginsburg, J., concurring in part); City of Chicago v. Environmental Def. Fund, 511 U.S. 328, 337 (1994); American Hosp. Ass'n v. NLRB, 499 U.S. 606, 613 (1991). This canon is controversial within the Court. See *Murphy*, 126 S.Ct. at 2466–68 (Breyer, J., dissenting).

89. Marrama v. Citizens Bank of Mass., 127 S.Ct. 1105, 1110 (2007); Small v. United States, 544 U.S. 385 (2005).

90. Shannon v. United States, 512 U.S. 573, 583 (1994).

91. Moreau v. Klevenhagen, 508 U.S. 22, 26 (1993).

- Caution against interpretation considered and rejected by floor vote of a chamber of Congress or committee.[92] Cautionary principle inapplicable when it is not clear why Congress rejected the proposal.[93]

- Floor statements, especially by statutory sponsors, can be used to confirm apparent meaning.[94]

- Public give-and-take between Members of Congress and executive department drafters or sponsors during committee hearings are relevant if they illuminate a shared meaning of statutory language by the participants closest to the process.[95]

- The "dog didn't bark" canon: presumption that prior legal rule should be retained if no one in legislative deliberations even mentioned the rule or discussed any changes in the rule.[96]

- Views of a subsequent Congress are a hazardous basis for inferring the intent of an earlier one,[97] but are sometimes relevant.[98] Subsequent legislation clearly incorporating these views is relevant and persuasive.[99]

---

92. Hamdan v. Rumsfeld, 126 S.Ct. 2749, 2765–66 (2006); Doe v. Chao, 540 U.S. 614 (2004); F. Hoffman-LaRoche, Ltd. v. Empangran S.A., 540 U.S. 1088 (2004); FDA v. Brown & Williamson Tobacco Corp., 529 U.S. 120, 144 (2000); Department of Revenue v. ACF Indus., 510 U.S. 332, 345–36 (1994).

93. Safeco Ins. Co. of Am. v. Burr, 127 S.Ct. 2201 (2007); Rapanos v. United States, 126 S.Ct. 2208 (2006) (plurality opinion of Scalia, J.); Solid Waste Agency v. Army Corps of Eng'rs, 531 U.S. 159, 169 (2001).

94. Hamdan v. Rumsfeld, 126 S.Ct. 2749, 2767 n.10, 2769 (2006); Department of Revenue v. ACF Indus., Inc., 510 U.S. 332, 345–46 (1994).

95. General Dynamics Land Sys., Inc. v. Cline, 540 U.S. 581 (2004); FDA v. Brown & Williamson Tobacco Corp., U.S. (2000); Hagen v. Utah, 510 U.S. 399, 418 (1994); Darby v.Cisneros, 509 U.S. 137, 147–51 (1993).

96. Zuni Pub. Sch. Dist. No. 89 v. Department of Educ., 127 S.Ct. 1534, 1541 (2007); Chisom v. Roemer, 501 U.S. 380, 396 & n.23 (1991).

97. Massachusetts v. EPA, 127 S.Ct. 1438, 1460 (2007); Doe v. Chao, 540 U.S. 614 (2004); Solid Waste Agency v. Army Corps of Eng'rs, 531 U.S. 159, 170 (2001); Sullivan v. Finkelstein, 496 U.S. 617, 628 n.8 (1990).

98. Musick, Peeler & Garrett v. Employers Ins. of Wassau, 508 U.S. 286, 293 (1993). This canon is controversial within the Court. Sullivan v. Finkelstein, 496 U.S. 617, 631–32 (1990) (Scalia, J., concurring in part).

99. FDA v. Brown & Williamson Tobacco Corp., 529 U.S. 120, 144 (2000); Babbitt v. Sweet Home Chapter of Communities for a Great Oregon, 515 U.S. 687 (1995); Franklin v. Gwinnett County Pub. Sch., 503 U.S. 60 (1990); id. at 77–78 (Scalia, J., concurring in the judgment); Bowen v. Yuckert, 482 U.S. 137, 149–51 (1987).

SUBSTANTIVE POLICY CANONS

CONSTITUTION-BASED CANONS

- Avoidance canon: avoid interpretations that would render a statute unconstitutional *or* that would raise serious constitutional difficulties.[100] Inapplicable if statute would clearly survive constitutional attack, or if statutory text is clear.[101]

1. *Separation of Powers*

- Super-strong rule against congressional interference with President's inherent powers, his executive authority.[102] Avoid interpretations whereby judges would interfere with foreign affairs.[103]

- Rule against review of President's core executive actions for "abuse of discretion."[104]

- Where Congress appropriates money without specific textual restrictions, the executive has leeway as to its expenditure, unlimited by more informal signals.[105]

- Rule of special treatment of President and Vice-President as litigants, affording them special privileges so as not to interfere with their official duties.[106]

- Rule against congressional curtailment of the judiciary's "inherent powers" or its "equity" powers.[107]

- Rule against congressional expansion of Article III injury in fact to include intangible and procedural injuries.[108]

---

100. Rapanos v. United States, 126 S.Ct. 2208, 2224–25 (2006) (plurality opinion of Scalia, J.); Cherokee Nation of Oklahoma v. Leavitt, 543 U.S. 631 (2005); Zadvydas v. Davis, 533 U.S. 678, 696–99 (2001); Public Citizen v. United States Dep't of Justice, 491 U.S. 440, 465–66 (1989); Edward J. Debartolo Corp. v. Florida Gulf Coast Building & Constr. Trades Council, 485 U.S. 568, 575 (1988).

101. Peretz v. United States, 501 U.S. 923, 932 (1991); Rust v. Sullivan, 500 U.S. 173, 182 (1991).

102. Department of Navy v. Egan, 484 U.S. 518, 527 (1988); Morrison v. Olson, 487 U.S. 654, 682–83 (1988); Carlucci v. Doe, 488 U.S. 93, 99 (1988; United States v. Johnson, 481 U.S. 681, 690–91 (1987).

103. Sosa v. Alvarez-Machain, 542 U.S. 692 (2004).

104. Franklin v. Massachusetts, 505 U.S. 788, 800–01 (1991).

105. Cherokee Nation of Oklahoma v. Leavitt, 543 U.S. 631 (2005); Lincoln v. Vigil, 508 U.S. 182, 191 (1993).

106. Cheney v. U.S. Dist. Court, 542 U.S. 367 (2004).

107. Chambers v. Nasco, Inc., 501 U.S. 32, 43–44 (1991).

108. Lujan v. Defenders of Wildlife, 504 U.S. 555, 557–61 (1992); id. at 579–80 (Kennedy, J., concurring in part).

- Presumption that Congress does not delegate authority without sufficient guidelines.[109]

- Presumption against "implying" causes of action into federal statutes.[110]

- Presumption that U.S. law conforms to U.S. international obligations.[111] Presumption that Congress takes account of the legitimate sovereign interests of other nations when it writes American laws.[112]

- Rule against congressional abrogation of Indian treaty rights.[113]

- Presumption favoring severability of unconstitutional provisions.[114]

2. *Federalism*

- Super-strong rule against federal invasion of "core state functions."[115] Strong presumption against statutory interpretations that would alter the federal-state balance.[116]

- Super-strong rule against federal abrogation of states' Eleventh Amendment immunity from lawsuits in federal courts.[117] Eleventh Amendment rules does not apply to municipalities and counties.[118]

- Super-strong rule against inferring conditions on federal grants to the states under the Spending Clause; conditions must be expressed clearly and

---

109. Mistretta v. United States, 488 U.S. 361, 373 n.7 (1989).

110. Virginia Bancshares, Inc. v. Sandberg, 501 U.S. 1083, 1102–05 (1991); Thompson v. Thompson, 484 U.S. 174, 179 (1988).

111. Hamdan v. Rumsfeld, 126 S.Ct. 2749, 2793–98 (2006); id. at 2802–04 (Kennedy, J., concurring in part and in the judgment); Sale v. Haitian Centers Council, 509 U.S. 155, 173–74 (1993).

112. Microsoft Corp. v. AT&T, 127 S.Ct. 1746, 1758 (2007); F. Hoffmann-LaRoche Ltd. v. Empagran S.A., 542 U.S. 155, 164 (2004).

113. South Dakota v. Bourland, 508 U.S. 679, 687 (1993).

114. Alaska Airlines, Inc. v. Brock, 480 U.S. 678, 684 (1987).

115. Rapanos v. United States, 126 S.Ct. 2208, 2224–25 (2006) (plurality opinion of Scalia, J.); Nixon v. Missouri Municipal League, 541 U.S. 125 (2004); BFP v. Resolution Trust Corp., 511 U.S. 531, 544 (1994); Gregory v. Ashcroft, 501 U.S. 452, 461–64 (1991).

116. Gonzales v. Oregon, 546 U.S. 243 (2006); Owasso Indep. Sch. Dist. v. Falvo, 534 U.S. 426 (2002); Raygor v. Regents of the Univ. of Minn., 534 U.S. 533 (2002); BFP v. Resolution Trust Corp., 511 U.S. 531, 544 (1994); Gregory v. Ashcroft, 501 U.S. 452, 461–64 (1991); Will v. Michigan Dep't of State Police, 491 U.S. 58, 65 (1989).

117. Nevada Dep't of Human Resources v. Hibbs, 538 U.S. 721 (2003) (finding abrogation); Raygor v. Regents of the Univ. of Minn., 534 U.S. 533 (2001); Blatchford v. Native Village of Noatak, 501 U.S. 775, 779 (1991); Dellmuth v. Muth, 491 U.S. 223, 227–28 (1989); Pennsylvania v. Union Gas, 491 U.S. 1, 7 (1989) (finding abrogation). The leading case is Atascadero State Hosp. v. Scanlon, 473 U.S. 234, 241 (1985).

118. Jinks v. Richland County, 538 U.S. 456 (2003).

unambiguously.[119] Sometimes the Court will require less than targeted statutory language, so long as states are reasonably on notice of conditions, as through agency guidances to that effect.[120]

- Presumption against federal preemption of traditional state regulation.[121] Presumption trumped if clear statutory language or the statutory purpose requires preemption.[122]

- Presumption against federal regulation of intergovernmental taxation by the states.[123]

- Presumption against application of federal statutes to state and local political processes,[124] except when statutory plain meaning or other factors counsel in favor of such application.[125]

- Presumption against congressional derogation from state's land claims based upon its entry into Union on an "equal footing" with all other states.[126] Presumption that upon statehood, the new state acquires title to the land under navigable rivers.[127]

- Rule against federal habeas review of state criminal convictions unless prisoner has properly exhausted state remedies.[128] Rule against federal habeas review of state criminal convictions supported by independent state ground.[129]

- Presumption of finality of state convictions for purposes of habeas review.[130]

---

119. Arlington Cent. Sch. Dist. Bd. of Educ. v. Murphy, 126 S.Ct. 2455, 2458–59 (2006); Barnes v. Gorman, 536 U.S. 181 (2002); Gonzaga Univ. v. Doe, 536 U.S. 273 (2002); Blessing v. Freestone, 520 U.S. 329 (1997); Suter v. Artist M., 503 U.S. 347 (1991). The leading case is Pennhurst State Sch. & Hosp. v. Halderman, 451 U.S. 1 (1981).

120. Davis v. Monroe County Bd. of Educ., 526 U.S. 629 (1999); Franklin v. Gwinnett County Pub. Sch., 503 U.S. 60 (1992).

121. Bates v. Dow Agrosciences LLC, 544 U.S. 431 (2005); Rush Prudential HMO v. Moran, 536 U.S. 355 (2002); Medtronic, Inc. v. Lohr, 518 U.S. 470 (1996); Hawaiian Airlines v. Norris, 512 U.S. 246, 252 (1994); BFP v. Resolution Trust Corp., 511 U.S. 531, 544 (1994); Cipollone v. Liggett Group, Inc., 505 U.S. 504 (1992); California v. ARC Am. Corp., 490 U.S. 93, 100–01 (1989); Rose v. Rose, 481 U.S. 619, 635–36 (1987) (O'Connor, J., concurring in part).

122. Geier v. Honda Motor Co., 529 U.S. 861 (2000).

123. Davis v. Michigan Dep't of Treasury, 489 U.S. 803, 810 (1989).

124. City of Columbia v. Omni Outdoor Advertising, Inc., 499 U.S. 365, 373 (1991); McCormick v. United States, 500 U.S. 257, 269 n.6 (1988); McNally v. United States, 483 U.S. 350, 361 n.9 (1987).

125. Evans v. United States, 504 U.S. 255, 270–71 (1992).

126. Utah Div'n of State Lands v. United States, 482 U.S. 193, 196 (1987).

127. Idaho v. United States, 533 U.S. 262 (2001).

128. O'Sullivan v. Boerckel, 526 U.S. 838, 845 (1999).

129. Sanchez-Llamas v. Oregon, 126 S.Ct. 2669, 2682 (2006); Massaro v. United States, 538 U.S. 500, 504 (2003); Wright v. West, 505 U.S. 277, 289 (1992); Coleman v. Thompson, 501 U.S. 722, 729 (1991).

130. Brecht v. Abrahamson, 507 U.S. 619, 635–38 (1993).

- Narrow construction of federal court jurisdictional grants that would siphon cases away from state courts.[131]

- Rule against reading an ambiguous federal statute to authorize states to engage in activities that would violate the dormant commerce clause.[132]

- Rule favoring concurrent state and federal court jurisdiction over federal claims.[133]

- Rule that Indian sovereignty is limited to Indian Tribe members and designated tribal territories.[134]

- Presumption that states can tax activities within their borders, including Indian tribal activities,[135] but also presumption that states cannot tax on Indian lands.[136]

- Principle that federal equitable remedies must consider interests of state and local authorities.[137]

- Presumption that Congress borrows state statutes of limitations for federal statutory schemes.[138]

3. *Due Process*

- Rule of lenity: rule against applying punitive sanctions if there is ambiguity as to underlying criminal liability or criminal penalty.[139] Rule is trumped when Congress clearly intended to criminalize the conduct in question.[140]

---

131. Kokkonen v. Guardian Life Ins. Co. of Am., 511 U.S. 375, 377 (1994); Finely v. United States, 490 U.S. 545, 552–54 (1989).

132. Granholm v. Heald, 544 U.S. 460 (2005); Wyoming v. Oklahoma, 502 U.S. 437, 458 (1992).

133. Tafflin v. Levitt, 493 U.S. 455, 458 (1990); Yellow Freight Sys., Inc. v. Donnelly, 494 U.S. 820, 823 (1990).

134. Atkinson Trading Co. v. Shirley, 532 U.S. 645 (2001).

135. Cotton Petroleum Corp. v. New Mexico, 490 U.S. 163, 174 (1989).

136. Oklahoma Tax Comm'n v. Sac and Fox Nation, 508 U.S. 114 (1993); County of Yakima v. Confederates Tribes & Bands of the Yakima Indian Nation, 502 U.S. 251, 268 (1992).

137. Raygor v. Regents of the Univ. of Minn., 534 U.S. 533 (2002); Spallone v. United States, 493 U.S. 265, 276 (1990).

138. Wallace v. Kato, 127 S.Ct. 1091 (2007); Lampf, Pleva, Lipkind, Prupis & Petigrow v. Gilbertson, 501 U.S. 350, 355–56 (1991).

139. Arthur Andersen LLP v. United States, 544 U.S. 696 (2005); Cleveland v. United States, 531 U.S. 12 (2000) (explaining both notice and nondelegation rationales); United States v. Aguilar, 515 U.S. 593 (1995); United States v. Granderson, 511 U.S. 39 (1994); United States v. Kozminski, 487 U.S. 931, 939 (1988).

140. Muscarello v. United States, 524 U.S. 125 (1998); Chapman v. United States, 500 U.S. 453, 463–64 (1991).

- Rule of lenity may apply to civil sanction that is punitive or when underlying liability is criminal.[141]

- Rule against criminal penalties imposed without showing of specific intent.[142] But willfulness requirement in civil sanction cases typically includes to reckless conduct as well.[143]

- Super-strong rule against implied congressional abrogation or repeal of habeas corpus.[144]

- Rule against interpreting statutes to be retroactive,[145] even if statute is curative or restorative.[146]

- Rule against interpreting statutes to deny a right to jury trial.[147]

- Presumption in favor of judicial review,[148] especially for constitutional questions, but not for agency decisions not to prosecute.

- Presumption against pre-enforcement challenges to implementation.[149]

- Presumption against exhaustion of remedies requirement for lawsuit to enforce constitutional rights.[150]

- Presumption that judgments will not be binding upon persons not party to adjudication.[151]

- Presumption against national service of process unless authorized by Congress.[152]

- Presumption against foreclosure of private enforcement of important federal rights.[153]

---

141. Crandon v. United States, 494 U.S. 152, 158 (1990). The Court applies this canon very unevenly. E.g., Babbitt v. Sweet Home Chapter of Communities for a Great Oregon, 515 U.S. 687 (1995).

142. Arthur Andersen LLP v. United States, 544 U.S. 696 (2005); Bryan v. United States, 524 U.S. 184, 191–92 (1998); Ratzlaf v. United States, 510 U.S. 135, 137 (1994); Cheek v. United States, 498 U.S. 192, 200–01 (1991).

143. Safeco Ins. Co. of Am. v. Burr, 127 S.Ct. 2201 (2007); McLaughlin v. Richland Shoe Co., 486 U.S. 128, 132–33 (1988).

144. Demore v. Kim, 538 U.S. 510 (2003); INS v. St. Cyr, 533 U.S. 289 (2001).

145. Fernandez-Vargas v. Gonzales, 126 S.Ct. 2422 (2006); Landgraf v. USI Film Prods., 511 U.S. 244 (1994).

146. Rivers v. Raodway Express, 511 U.S. 298 (1994).

147. Gomez v. United States, 490 U.S. 858, 863 (1989).

148. Demore v. Kim, 538 U.S. 510 (2003); Webster v. Doe, 486 U.S. 592 (1988).

149. Thunder Basin Coal Co. v. Reich, 510 U.S. 200, 208–10 (1994).

150. McCarthy v. Madigan, 503 U.S. 140, 146–49 (1992).

151. Martin v. Wilks, 490 U.S. 755, 761–62 (1989).

152. Omni Capital Int'l v. Rudolf Wolff & Co., 484 U.S. 97, 107–08 (1987).

153. Wilder v. Virginia Hosp. Ass'n, 496 U.S. 498, 520–21 (1990). This presumption is probably no longer viable. See Gonzaga Univ. v. Doe, 536 U.S. 273 (2002).

- Presumption that preponderance of the evidence standard applies in civil cases.[154]

COMMON LAW-BASED CANONS

- Presumption in favor of following common law usage and rules where Congress has employed words or concepts with well-settled common law traditions.[155] Presumption inapplicable when Congress has directly addressed the issue[156] or when common law usage is inconsistent with statutory purpose.[157]

- Rule against extraterritorial application of U.S. law.[158] Presumption that Congress legislates with domestic concerns in mind.[159]

- American laws apply to foreign-flag ships in U.S. territory and affecting Americans, but will not apply to the "internal affairs" of a foreign-flag ship unless there is a clear statutory statement to that effect.[160]

- Super-strong rule against waivers of United States sovereign immunity.[161] Once sovereign immunity has been waived, equitable doctrines might be applied.[162]

---

154. Grogan v. Garner, 498 U.S. 279, 286 (1991).

155. Permanent Mission of India to the United Nations v. City of New York, 127 S.Ct. 2352 (2007) (FSIA); Wallace v. Kato, 127 S.Ct. 1091, 1095 (2007) (§ 1983); Norfolk Southern Ry. v. Sorrell, 127 S.Ct. 799 (2007) (FELA); Hamdan v. Rumsfeld, 126 S.Ct. 2749, 2775–86 (2006) (UCMJ); Dixon v. United States, 126 S.Ct. 2437 (2006) (defense to federal crimes); Dura Pharmaceuticals, Inc. v. Broudo, 544 U.S. 336 (2005) (§ 10(b)); Stewart v. Dutra Constr. Co., 543 U.S. 481, 487 (2005) (LWHCA); United States v. Texas, 507 U.S. 529, 534 (1993) (Debt Collection Act); Nationwide Mut. Ins. Co. v. Darden, 503 U.S. 318 (1992) (ERISA); Kamen v. Kemper Fin. Servs., Inc., 500 U.S. 90, 98–99 (1991) (Investment Company Act); Community for Creative Nonviolence v. Reid, 490 U.S. 730, 739–40 (1989) (Copyright Act).

156. Pasquantino v. United States, 544 U.S. 349, 356 (2005).

157. Taylor v. United States, 495 U.S. 575, 593–95 (1990).

158. Microsoft Corp. v. AT&T, 127 S.Ct. 1746, 1758 (2007); F. Hoffman-LaRoche, Ltd. v. Empangran S.A., 540 U.S. 1088 (2004); Sale v. Haitian Centers Council, 509 U.S. 155 (1993); EEOC v. Arabian Am. Oil Co., 499 U.S. 244, 248 (1991); Argentine Republic v. Amerada Hess Shipping Corp., 488 U.S. 428, 440 (1989).

159. Small v. United States, 544 U.S. 385 (2005); Smith v. United States, 507 U.S. 197, 204 n.5 (1993).

160. Spector v. Norwegian Cruise Line Ltd., 545 U.S. 119 (2005).

161. United States v. White Mt. Apache Tribe, 537 U.S. 465, 472–73 (2003); United States v. Nordic Village, Inc., 503 U.S. 30 (1992); Ardestani v. INS, 502 U.S. 129 (1991); United States v. Dalm, 494 U.S. 596, 608 (1990).

162. Irwin v. Department of Veterans Affairs, 498 U.S. 89, 94–96 (1990).

- Super-strong rule against congressional abrogation of state immunity from suit.[163] Common law rule does not apply to counties and other subdivisions created by the states.[164]

- Rule that debts to the United States shall bear interest[165]

- Presumption against conveyance of U.S. public lands to private parties.[166]

- Rule presuming against attorney fee-shifting in federal courts and federal statutes,[167] and narrow construction of fee-shifting statutes to exclude costs that are not explicitly identified.[168]

- Presumption that jury finds facts, judge declares law.[169]

- Rule presuming that law takes effect on date of enactment.[170]

- Presumption that public (government) interest not be prejudiced by negligence of federal officials.[171]

- Presumption that federal agencies launched into commercial world with power to "sue and be sued" are not entitled to sovereign immunity.[172]

- Presumption favoring enforcement of forum selection clauses.[173]

- Presumption that federal judgment has preclusive effect in state administrative proceedings.[174]

- Presumption importing common law immunities into federal civil rights statutes.[175]

---

163. Alden v. Maine, 527 U.S. 706, 713 (1999) (announcing that state immunity from suit was based on common law, not just Eleventh Amendment). This canon is controversial within the Court. See id. at 760 (Souter, J., dissenting).

164. Northern Ins. Co. of N.Y. v. Chatham County, 126 S.Ct. 1689, 1693 (2006).

165. United States v. Texas, 507 U.S. 529 (1993).

166. Utah Div. of State Lands v. United States, 482 U.S. 193, 197–98 (1987).

167. Key Tronic Corp. v. United States, 511 U.S. 809 (1994). The leading case is Alyeska Pipeline Serv. Co. v. Wilderness Society, 421 U.S. 240 (1975).

168. Arlington Cent. Sch. Dist. Bd. of Educ. v. Murphy, 126 S.Ct. 2455, 2461–63 (2006); West Virginia Univ. Hosps., Inc. v. Casey, 499 U.S. 83 (1991).

169. Shannon v. United States, 512 U.S. 573 (1994).

170. Gozlon-Peretz v. United States, 498 U.S. 395 (1991).

171. United States v. Montalvo-Murillo, 495 U.S. 711, 717–18 (1990).

172. Loeffler v. Frank, 486 U.S. 549, 554–55 (1988).

173. Carnival Cruise Lines v. Shute, 499 U.S. 585, 589 (1991); Stewart Org. v. Ricoh Corp., 487 U.S. 22, 33 (1988) (Kennedy, J., concurring).

174. Astoria Fed. Sav. & Loan Ass'n v. Solimino, 501 U.S. 104, 108 (1991).

175. Burns v. Reed, 500 U.S. 478, 484–85 (1991); Forrester v. White, 484 U.S. 219, 225–26 (1988).

STATUTE-BASED CANONS

- Purposive construction: interpret ambiguous statutes so as best to carry out their statutory purposes.[176] Avoid "incongruous results."[177] Caution: no law pursues its purpose at all costs, and text-based limits on a law's scope are part of its "purpose."[178]

1. *General canons*

- Presumption against repeals by implication.[179] But where there is a clear repugnancy between a more recent statutory scheme and an earlier one, partial repeal will be inferred.[180]

- *In pari materia*: similar statutes should be interpreted similarly,[181] unless legislative history or purpose suggests material differences.[182]

- Presumption *against* private right of action unless statute expressly provides one,[183] but once recognized a private right of action carries with it all traditional remedies.[184] Regulations cannot create a private cause of action not authorized by the statute.[185]

- A precisely drawn, detailed statute preempts or governs a more general statute or remedies.[186]

---

176. Zuni Pub. Sch. Dist. No. 89 v. Department of Educ., 127 S.Ct. 1534 (2007); Massachusetts v. EPA, 127 S.Ct. 1438, 1462–63 (2007); Burlington Northern & Santa Fe Ry. v. White, 126 S.Ct. 2405, 2412–14 (2006); Jones v. R.R. Donnelley & Sons Co., 541 U.S. 369 (2004); PGA Tour, Inc. v. Martin, 532 U.S. 661 (2001); Reves v. Ernst & Young, 494 U.S. 56, 60–61 (1990).

177. Winkelman v. Parma City Sch. Dist., 127 S.Ct. 1994, 2004–05 (2007); Nixon v. Missouri Municipal League, 541 U.S. 125 (2004).

178. Rapanos v. United States, 126 S.Ct. 2208, 2232 (2006) (plurality opinion of Scalia, J.).

179. See sources in note 71, *supra*.

180. Credit Suisse Securities (USA) LLC v. Billing, 127 S.Ct. 2383 (2007).

181. Powerex Corp. v. Reliant Energy Servs., Inc., 127 S.Ct. 2411 (2007); Ledbetter v. Goodyear Tire & Rubber Co., 127 S.Ct. 2162 (2007); John Hancock Mut. Life Ins. Co. v. Harris Trust & Sav. Bank, 510 U.S. 86, 101–06 (1993); Morales v. TWA, Inc., 504 U.S. 374 (1992); Communications Workers v. Beck, 487 U.S. 735, 750–52 (1988); Wimberly v. Labor & Indus. Relations Comm'n, 479 U.S. 511, 517 (1987).

182. Ledbetter v. Goodyear Tire & Rubber Co., 127 S.Ct. 2162 (2007); Fogerty v. Fantasy, Inc., 510 U.S. 517 (1994).

183. Gonzaga Univ. v. Doe, 536 U.S. 273 (2002); Blessing v. Freestone, 520 U.S. 329 (1997); Suter v. Artist M., 503 U.S. 347 (1992).

184. Franklin v. Gwinnett County Pub. Sch., 503 U.S. 60 (1992).

185. Alexander v. Sandoval, 532 U.S. 275 (2001).

186. Credit Suisse Securities (USA) LLC v. Billing, 127 S.Ct. 2383 (2007); EC Term of Years Trust v. United States, 127 S.Ct. 1763, 1767 (2007). The leading case is Brown v. General Serv. Admin., 425 U.S. 820, 834 (1976).

- When Congress enacts a specific remedy when no remedy was clearly recognized previously, the new remedy is regarded as exclusive.[187]

- Presumption against creating exemptions in a statute that has none.[188] Narrow interpretation of explicit exemptions.[189]

- Allow *de minimis* exceptions to statutory rules, so long as they do not undermine statutory policy.[190]

2. *Process canons*

- Presumption that adjudicative bodies are vested with inherent authority to sanction abusive litigation practices.[191] Judges presumptively have discretion to raise procedural errors sua sponte.[192]

- Presumption that statutory exhaustion requirements entail implicit requirements that the petitioner follow the proper procedures; failing that, the petitioner has not met statutory exhaustion requirements.[193]

- Strict construction of statutes authorizing appeals.[194] Rule that Court of Claims is proper forum for Tucker Act claims against federal government.[195]

- Rule that "sue and be sued" clauses waive sovereign immunity and should be liberally construed.[196] Presumption that statute creating agency and authorizing it to "sue and be sued" also creates federal subject matter jurisdiction for lawsuits by and against the agency.[197]

- American rule: strong presumption that each side bears its own costs in adjudications.[198] Super-strong rule against finding statutory authorization of witness fees as costs unless the statute refers explicitly to witness fees.[199]

---

187. Hinck v. United States, 127 S.Ct. 2011 (2007).

188. City of Chicago v. Environmental Def. Fund, 511 U.S. 328, 337 (1994).

189. John Hancock Mut. Life Ins. Co. v. Harris Trust & Sav. Bank, 510 U.S. 86, 96–97 (1994); United States Dep't of Justice v. Landano, 508 U.S. 165 (1993); Citicorp Indus. Credit, Inc. v. Brock, 483 U.S. 27, 33–35 (1987).

190. Wisconsin Dep't of Revenue v. William Wrigley, Jr., Co., 505 U.S. 214 (1992).

191. Marrama v. Citizens Bank of Mass., 127 S.Ct. 1105, 1112 (2007).

192. Day v. McDonough, 547 U.S. 198 (2006).

193. Woodford v. Ngo, 126 S.Ct. 2378, 2384–86 (2006); see also O'Sullivan v. Boerckel, 526 U.S. 838, 845 (1999) (similar rule in habeas corpus law).

194. Bowles v. Russell, 127 S.Ct. 2360 (2007); Hohn v. United States, 524 U.S. 236, 247 (1998); California Coastal Comm'n v. Granite Rock Co., 480 U.S. 572, 579 (1987).

195. Preseault v. ICC, 494 U.S. 1, 11–12 (1990).

196. FDIC v. Meyer, 510 U.S. 471 (1994).

197. American Nat'l Red Cross v. S.G., 505 U.S. 247 (1992).

198. Buckhannon Bd. & Care Home, Inc. v. West Virginia Dep't Health & Human Resources, 532 U.S. 598 (2001). The leading case is Alyeska Pipeline Serv. Co. v. Wilderness Soc'y, 421 U.S. 240 (1975).

199. Arlington Cent. Sch. Dist. Bd. of Educ. v. Murphy, 126 S.Ct. 2455, 2462 (2006); Crawford Fitting Co. v. J.T. Gibbons, Inc., 482 U.S. 437, 445 (1987).

- Rule that the burden of proof is on the party requesting benefits or entitlements from the state.[200]

- Rule that nonjurisdictional process objections (e.g., exhaustion of remedies, venue) are waived if not timely raised.[201]

3. *Specific statutory subject areas*

- **Antitrust.** Sherman Act should be applied in light of its overall purpose of benefitting consumers.[202]

- Presumption against application of Sherman Act to activities authorized by states.[203]

- Exemption from antitrust liability should not be lightly inferred.[204] Principle that statutes should not be interpreted to create anti-competitive effects.[205]

- **Arbitration.** Federal court deference to arbitral awards, even where the Federal Arbitration Act is not by its terms applicable.[206]

- Strong presumption in favor of arbitration and of enforcing labor arbitration agreements.[207]

- Rule favoring arbitration of federal statutory claims.[208]

- **Banking.** National Bank Act policy shielding national banks from "burdensome" state regulation.[209] But national banks are subject to state laws not conflicting with the NBA's purposes.[210].

- **Bankruptcy.** Bankruptcy Act should be construed in light of its overall purpose, to give a fresh start to the class of "honest but unfortunate debtors."[211]

---

200. NLRB v. Kentucky River Community Care, Inc., 532 U.S. 706 (2001).

201. Kontrick v. Ryan, 540 U.S. 443 (2004).

202. Weyerhauser v. Ross-Simmons Hardwood Lumber, 127 S.Ct. 1069 (2007).

203. City of Columbia v. Omni Outdoor Advertising, Inc., 499 U.S. 365, 370 (1991).

204. Credit Suisse Securities (USA) LLC v. Billing, 127 S.Ct. 2383 (2007).

205. Two Pesos, Inc. v. Taco Cabana, Inc., 505 U.S. 763 (1992).

206. United Paperworkers Int'l Union v. Misco, Inc., 484 U.S. 29, 36–37 (1987).

207. Howsam v. Dean Witter Reynolds, Inc., 537 U.S. 79, 83 (2002); Groves v. Ring Screw Works, Ferndale Fastener Div'n, 498 U.S. 168, 173 (1990).

208. Circuit City Stores, Inc. v. Adams, 532 U.S. 105 (2001); Gilmer v. Interstate/Johnson Lane Corp., 500 U.S. 20, 26 (1991); Shearson/American Express, Inc. v. McMahon, 482 U.S. 220, 226–27 (1987).

209. Watters v. Wachovia Bank, 127 S.Ct. 1559, 1566–67 (2007); Beneficial Nat'l Bank v. Anderson, 539 U.S. 1, 10 (2003); Barnett Bank of Marion County, N.A. v. Nelson, 517 U.S. 25, 32–34 (1996).

210. Atherton v. FDIC, 519 U.S. 213, 221–22 (1997).

211. Marrama v. Citizens Bank of Mass., 127 S.Ct. 1105, 1111 (2007).

- Presumption that the Bankruptcy Act of 1978 preserved prior bankruptcy doctrines.[212]

- Where statute is ambiguous, courts should create gapfilling rules that are familiar, objective, and less expensive to administer.[213]

- **Civil Procedure & Jurisdiction.** Subject-matter jurisdictional rules will be strictly enforced and applied.[214] Court-created "exceptions" to statutory jurisdictional grounds are strongly disfavored[215] and, even if recognized, will be narrowly construed.[216]

- Federal Rules of Civil Procedure apply in habeas cases, except to the extent they are inconsistent with the Habeas Corpus Rules.[217]

- Presumption that time-limitation periods, venue, and other nonjurisdictional requirements are waivable.[218]

- **Civil Rights.** Aspects of section 1983 not governed by state law are governed by federal rules conforming to common law tort principles.[219]

- Title VII of the Civil Rights Act should be interpreted to effectuate its goal of a workplace where individuals are not discriminated against because of their racial, ethnic, religious, or gender-based status.[220] But Title VII does not set forth a general code of workplace civility.[221]

- Voting Rights Act should be interpreted in light of its core purpose of preventing race discrimination in voting and fostering a transformation of America into a society no longer fixated on race.[222]

- **Criminal Law and Sentencing.** Rule of lenity: ambiguities in criminal statutes shall be decided in favor of the accused.[223] Likewise, ambiguous sentencing provisions should be interpreted against the government.[224]

---

212. Dewsnup v. Timm, 502 U.S. 410 (1992).

213. Till v. CSC Credit Corp., 541 U.S. 465 (2004) (plurality opinion of Stevens, J.).

214. Bowles v. Russell, 127 S.Ct. 2360 (2007);

215. Bowles v. Russell, 127 S.Ct. 2360 (2007).

216. Marshall v. Marshall, 547 U.S. 293 (2006) (narrow interpretation of "probate exception"); Ankenbrandt v. Richards, 504 U.S. 689 (1992) (narrow interpretation of "domestic relations exception").

217. Woofard v. Garceau, 538 U.S. 202, 208 (2003).

218. Eberhart v. United States, 546 U.S. 12, 17–18 (2006) (per curiam).

219. Wallace v. Kato, 127 S.Ct. 1091, 1095 (2007).

220. Burlington Northern & Santa Fe Ry. v. White, 126 S.Ct. 2405, 2412 (2006).

221. Oncale v. Sundowner Offshore Servs., Inc., 523 U.S. 75, 80 (1998); Faragher v. Boca Raton, 524 U.S. 775, 788 (1998).

222. League of United Latin Am. Citizens v. Perry, 126 S.Ct. 2594, 2618 (2006); Georgia v. Ashcroft, 539 U.S. 461, 490 (2003).

223. See sources in note 138, *supra*.

224. United States v. R.L.C., 503 U.S. 291 (1992).

- Failure of U.S. Attorneys to initiate criminal prosecutions in the past is evidence that the Attorney General's current reading of the statute is too broad.[225]

- Even when courts are not bound by Sentencing Commission interpretations, such interpretations may be considered.[226]

- **Environmental Law.** Environmental laws should be applied in light of their overall purpose of cleaning up the environment at a reasonable cost.[227]

- NEPA contains an implicit "rule of reason," relieving agencies of filing environmental impact statements that would serve no statutory purpose.[228]

- **Immigration.** Construe ambiguities in deportation statutes in favor of aliens.[229]

- **Indian Law.** Rule against state taxation of Indian tribes and reservation activities.[230]

- Presumption against national "diminishment" of Indian lands.[231]

- Longstanding assertion of state jurisdiction over Indian lands creates justifiable expectations of sovereign authority.[232]

- Presumption against criminal jurisdiction by an Indian tribe over a nonmember.[233]

- Presumption that party cannot invoke federal jurisdiction until she has exhausted her remedies in Indian tribal courts.[234]

- **Labor Law.** Rule against statutory interference in labor-management discipline disputes.[235]

---

225. Lopez v. Gonzales, 127 S.Ct. 625, 632 (2006).

226. James v. United States, 127 S.Ct. 1586, 1595–96 (2007).

227. Massachusetts v. EPA, 127 S.Ct. 1438 (2007).

228. Department of Transportation v. Public Citizen, 541 U.S. 752 (2004); Marsh v. Oregon Natural Resources Council, 490 U.S. 360, 373–74 (1989).

229. INS v. St. Cyr, 533 U.S. 289, 320 (2001); INS v. Cardoza-Fonseca, 480 U.S. 421, 449 (1987). This canon is applied with an unusual level of unpredictability. Compare, e.g., INS v. Elias-Zacarias, 502 U.S. 478 (1992).

230. California v. Cabazon Band of Mission Indians, 480 U.S. 202, 208 (1987).

231. Hagen v. Utah, 510 U.S. 399 (1994).

232. City of Sherrill v. Oneida Indian Nation of N.Y., 544 U.S. 197 (2005); Hagen v. Utah, 510 U.S. 399, 421 (1994).

233. Duro v. Reina, 495 U.S. 676, 693–94 (1990).

234. Iowa Mut. Ins. Co. v. LaPlante, 480 U.S. 9, 15–17 (1987).

235. Eastern Associated Coal Corp. v. UMW Dist. 17, 531 U.S. 57 (2000).

- **Patent Law.** Practice and precedent of Patent Office are particularly persuasive evidence of statutory meaning in this area, given the much greater competence of that Office.[236]

- Especially strong presumption against extraterritorial application of federal patent law.[237]

- **Taxation.** Presumption that IRS tax assessments are correct.[238]

- Narrow interpretation of exemptions from federal taxation.[239] Presumption against taxpayer claiming income tax deduction.[240]

- Presumption that tax valuation statutes follow majority approach, and that departures from the majority approach would be signaled with clear statutory language.[241]

- **Veterans Benefits.** Principle that veterans' benefits statutes be construed liberally for their beneficiaries.[242]

---

236. Festo Corp. v. Shoketsu Kinzoku Kogyo Kabushiki Co., 535 U.S. 722 (2002).

237. Microsoft Corp. v. AT&T, 127 S.Ct. 1746, 1758–59 (2007).

238. United States v. Fior D'Italia, 536 U.S. 238, 242–43 (2002).

239. United States v. Burke, 504 U.S. 229 (1992) (Souter, J., concurring in the judgment); United States v. Wells Fargo Bank, 485 U.S. 351, 357 (1988).

240. INDOPCO, Inc. v. Commissioner, 503 U.S. 79 (1992).

241. Limitiaco v. Camacho, 127 S.Ct. 1413, 1420 (2007).

242. King v. St. Vincent's Hosp., 502 U.S. 215 (1991).

Index

References are to Pages

Administrative agencies:
  administrative state, overview: 1119-1126
  agency interpretation: 1185-1283
  congressional control over agency officers: 1160-1163
  congressional control over agency structure: 1166-1168
  congressional control over appropriations: 1146-1148
  congressional control over implementation: 1139-1185
  judicial review of agency action: 1168-1185
  nondelegation doctrine: 1136-1139
  President of U.S. and: 1163-1166
  See also Statutes; Statutory interpretation

Ballot access regulation: 227-235

Campaign finance regulation: 235-297

Civil Rights Act of 1964:
  story of: 2-23
  Title VII:
    affirmative action and: 87-115
    disparate impact and: 41-47, 81-87, 115-120
    generally: 38-42

Common law:
  Background for statutory interpretation: 956-971
  Retroactivity or prospectivity of judicial decisions and: 649-663
  Statutes as sources of principles: 588-629
  See also Legisprudence; Statutes

Congress of United States:
  awareness of judicial decisions: 436-437
  budget/appropriations power over agencies: 1146-1148
  budget process: 446-508
  concurrent budget resolution: 460, 491-492
  constitutional structures of: 24, 66, 125, 411-413
  control over agency officials: 1160-1163
  control over agency structure: 1166-1168
  control over statutory implementation: 1139-1185
  Federalism Act and: 518-522
  legislative veto: 1148-1159
  line item veto: 365-387, 455
  Senate, particular characteristics of: 129, 412-414
  supermajority voting rules: 469-470, 472-474, 504

Unfunded Mandates Reform Act
   and: 31, 511-518
See also Civil Rights Act of 1964;
   Legislatures

Critical legal studies: see Statutes;
   Statutory interpretation

Direct democracy:
   due process and: 559-574
   equal protection and: 535-559
   interpretation of ballot measures:
      558-559, 1101-1115
   overview of legal issues concern-
      ing: 535-543
   overview of process: 523-535
   recall: 574-586
   single-subject rule and: 536-544
   See also Due process of lawmaking

Drafting of legislation: See Statutory
   drafting

Due process of lawmaking: Chapter
   4, *passim*

Ethical requirements of law-
   yer/lobbyist: 348-356

Executive branch of government:
   line item veto: 365-387
   See also Administrative agencies;
      President of the United States;
      Statutory implementation

First Amendment: 206-207, 232-
   297, 318-319, 327-333, 528-529

Gerrymandering: See Vote

Law and economics: see Statutes;
   Statutory interpretation

Legal process theory: see Statutes;
   Statutory interpretation

Legislation:
   barriers to passage: 5-6, 68
   drafting: See Statutory drafting
   process of passage of bill: 24-38
   theories of:
      institutional: 75-82, 84-86,
      pluralist (interest group): 29-30,
         48-65, 123, 236-237
      proceduralist: 65-74
   See also Civil Rights Act of 1964;
      Congress of United States; Direct
      democracy; Legislatures; Public
      choice theory; Representation;
      Republicanism; Statutes; Statu-
      tory interpretation

Legislatures:
   agenda and: 26-27, 64
   bicameral approval and present-
      ment to executive: 24, 411-414
   bribery of members: 302-310, 397-
      405
   calendar: 10-12, 31-33
   campaign finance regulation: See
      Campaign finance regulation
   cloture: 6, 15-33, 471-474
   committees:
      conference committees: 35-37,
         470, 484-485
      generally: 24-38, 125-127, 433
      jurisdiction: 27-28
      mark-up: 8
      reports: 30-31, 67.   See also
         Statutory interpretation: legis-
         lative history
      Rules Committee: 10-12, 31-32,
         498
   common law immunities of mem-
      bers: 404-408
   conflicts of interest: 311-318
   "conscientious legislator": 428-435
   discharge petitions: 11, 28, 258
   eligibility, exclusion, and expulsion
      of members: 196-235
   enrolled bill rule: 414-420

equitable limits on injunctive relief against members: 405-408
extortion by members: 310-311
filibuster: 6, 17-21, 32, 33, 258, 461, 471-472, 517
floor consideration: 12-15, 16-22, 33-35
honoraria: 311-316
immunities of members: 387-408
legislative veto: 1148-1159
line item veto and: 365-387
lobbying, regulation of: See Lobbying, regulation of
member standing to sue: 474-477
norms and folkways: 24
omnibus legislation: 25, 36, 376-365, 461, 464, 470, 471, 477, 498, 500, 510, 514
process of passing a bill, generally: 24-38
public purpose requirement: 357-360
response to judicial decision: 420-436
revenue bills, special procedures for: 415-417
rules protecting against special interest legislation: 357-387
single-subject rule for legislation: 357-365
size: 126
special legislation: 357-365
speech or debate clause protections of members: 387-404
summits and: 36-37, 463-464
term limits for committee chairs: 28-29, 225
term limits for legislators: 124, 126-127, 208-226
time limit for legislative session: 126, 419-420
uniformity requirements: 357-358
voting in: 34-35
See also Civil Rights Act of 1964; Congress of United States; Direct democracy; Due process of law-making; Legislation; Representation; Statutes; Statutory interpretation; Vote

Legisprudence: Chapter 6, *passim.* See also Statutes; Statutory interpretation

Line item veto: See Legislatures; President of the United States

Lobbying, regulation of: 318-356

Local government: 127, 134-137

Political Contributions and expenditures: See Campaign finance regulation

Political parties:
ballots and: 227-235
campaign finance regulation and: 235-297
fusion candidacies: 229-230
in the legislature: 63
theories of: 230

Positive political theory: 73-75, 84-87, 1139-1141. See also Public choice theory; Statutory interpretation: institutional strategic interaction and equilibrium and

President of the United States:
budget process and: 452-461, 466-467
Civil Rights Act of 1964 and: 5, 7-8, 11, 23, 26
involvement in legislative process: 26-27, 63-69
Line Item Veto Act and: 365-387, 454
presentment of legislation for approval or veto: 24, 37-38, 411-412, 1148-1159

role in statutory implementation: 1163-1166
strategic interaction with Congress: 1139-1141
See also Statutory implementation; Statutory interpretation

Public choice theory: 50-65, 71-74, 750, 812-818. See also Positive political theory; Statutory interpretation: institutional strategic interaction and equilibrium and.

Representation:
theories of: 123-124, 299-309
See also Legislatures; Vote

Republicanism: 68-72, 123-125, 237, 246-247

Severability: 443-444, 922

Statutes:
as principled law: 588-629
critical legal studies and: 625-628
law and economics and: 623-625
legal process theory and: 598-622
"new legal process" and: 628-629
private causes of action: 1128-1135
prospectivity or retroactivity of: 663-688
stare decisis in statutory cases: 631-649
See also Congress of the United States; Legislation; Legislatures; Legisprudence; Statutory interpretation

Statutory drafting: 435-446

Statutory implementation:
capture theory of agencies: 58
generally: Chapter 9, *passim*
institutional theory and: 80-82

Statutory interpretation:
administrative interpretation: 1185-1283
avoiding constitutional questions: 907-922
ballot propositions: 558-559, 1101-1115
canons of statutory interpretation: 435-438, 847-955
clear statement rules: 435-437, 884, 922-941
coherence with public norms: 743-749, 907-922
coherence with other statutes: 1066-1100
common law background: 956-971
critical legal scholarship and: 835-842
dynamic: 86-104, 729-742
eclecticism and: 691-712, 830-835, 842-846
federalism canons: 922-941
formalism and: 749-798
"funnel of abstraction": 830-835
implied repeals: 1081-1100
institutional strategic interaction and equilibrium and: 818-830, 1063-1064, 1140-1141
intentionalism: 86-104, 704-712. See also Statutory interpretation: legislative history
law and economics and: 800-812
legal process theory and: 712-749
legislative history: 765-798, 971-1066. See also Statutory interpretation: intentionalism; textualism
legislative inaction and: 104-115, 1047-1066
modeled or borrowed statutes: 1073-1081
plain meaning rule: 694, 703-704, 749-764, 848, 861, 933, 955. See also Statutory interpretation: textualism
pragmatic theory: 830-835

public choice theory and: 749-750, 812-818

purposivism: 86-104, 693-703, 712-749

reference canons: 848, 955-1100, 1185-1283

rule of lenity: 884-907

scrivener's error: 723-729

statutes in pari materia: 1066-1100

substantive canons: 848, 880-941

textual canons: 849-880

textualism: 765-768, 847, 861, 935-941, 955, 988-990, 997, 1013, 1020, 1041, 1098-1099, 1163, 1209-1213

theories of, critical review: 842-846

See also Statutes

Vote:

alternatives to simple majority vote: 193-195, 469-474

gerrymandering techniques: 128

one person, one vote: 128-135, 192-193, 206

political gerrymandering: 174-195

racial vote dilution: 135-155

redistricting to promote minority representation: 155-174

right to, conceptions of: 127-128

Voting Rights Act: 148-155, 194

Voting Rights Act: See Vote